Encyclopedia of
Abortion in
the United States

Second Edition

Encyclopedia of Abortion in the United States

Second Edition

LOUIS J. PALMER, JR., *and*
XUEYAN Z. PALMER

McFarland & Company, Inc., Publishers
Jefferson, North Carolina, and London

Louis J. Palmer, Jr., has also written these works for McFarland: *Encyclopedia of Capital Punishment in the United States*, 2d ed. (2008); *Encyclopedia of DNA and the United States Criminal Justice System* (2004); *Organ Transplants from Executed Prisoners: An Argument for the Creation of Death Sentence Organ Removal Statutes* (1999); *The Death Penalty: An American Citizen's Guide to Understanding Federal and State Laws* (1998).

LIBRARY OF CONGRESS CATALOGUING-IN-PUBLICATION DATA

Palmer, Louis J.
Encyclopedia of abortion in the United States. — 2nd ed. /
Louis J. Palmer, Jr., and Xueyan Z. Palmer.
p. cm.
Includes bibliographical references and index.

ISBN 978-0-7864-3838-9
illustrated case binding : 50# alkaline paper ∞

1. Abortion — United States — Encyclopedias.
I. Palmer, Xueyan Z., 1964– II. Palmer, Louis J. Encyclopedia of abortion in the United States. III. Title.
HQ767.5.U5P35 2009 363.460973'03 — dc22 2008031047

British Library cataloguing data are available

Manufactured in the United States of America

McFarland & Company, Inc., Publishers
Box 611, Jefferson, North Carolina 28640
www.mcfarlandpub.com

To the memory of Xueyan's mother,
Zhang Zhaorong (1935–1992),
and to her father, Zhang Fuchen

Contents

Preface

The second edition of this encyclopedia encompasses numerous changes that have occurred in state and federal laws since publication of the first edition. The amended state and federal laws reflect legislative expansion over the control of many aspects of abortion. Further, subsequent to the first edition the United States Supreme Court issued a few important abortion opinions, such as the approval of a federal ban on partial-birth abortion in *Gonzales v. Carhart*. The second edition of the encyclopedia has attempted to keep pace with, and outline in a meaningful way, the rapid changes that have occurred. In addition, the second edition has been enhanced by the use of more than forty photographs and more than three hundred charts and graphs.

As was pointed out in the first edition, before the 1973 decision by the United States Supreme Court in *Roe v. Wade*, which legalized abortion in the nation, the issue of abortion was not a headline news item. The decision in *Roe* dramatically altered this situation and made the issue of abortion one of the most explosive and controversial issues confronting the United States. The second edition attempts to capture the growing history of abortion from the founding of the nation to its present status.

The history of abortion embraces political, legal, social, religious, and medical issues. The entries provided in this work address each of the broad categories that make up the history of abortion in the nation. Included are entries that summarize every opinion rendered by the United States Supreme Court on the issue of abortion through the year 2007. There are also entries showing the "voting" position taken on abortion by every Supreme Court Justice who has participated in an abortion decision. An entry for each state includes the actual abortion laws of the state. A summary for each statute has been provided to assist the nonspecialist reader with understanding the laws.

There are entries in the encyclopedia devoted to many of the leading abortion organizations in the nation, both "pro-life" and "pro-choice." Entries are also included which summarize lawful and unlawful activities of those who oppose and those who advocate for abortion. Many entries are devoted to the issue of abortion violence and demonstrations and the laws designed to combat such protests.

Other entries are devoted to such topics as the different methods of abortion, contraceptive devices, male and female reproductive systems, and the gestational development of the fetus. The issues of embryonic cloning, embryo/fetal stem cell research, assisted reproductive technology, and surrogacy are covered in the encyclopedia. There are entries that explain many of the major birth defects and sexual diseases that impact on the abortion decision.

The authors hope that this encyclopedia will provide readers and researchers with useful information on the broadest possible range of abortion-related topics.

Louis J. Palmer, Jr. • Xueyan Z. Palmer • *Charleston, West Virginia*

THE ENCYCLOPEDIA

A

Abdominal Circumference *see* **Gestational Age**

Abdominal Pregnancy *see* **Ectopic Pregnancy**

Abortifacient

Abortifacient is a chemical agent or drug that causes a pregnancy to terminate prematurely and induce an abortion. The most common abortifacients are mifepristone and methotrexate/misoprostol. In addition, there are several herbal abortifacients that are believed to cause abortion. *See also* **Herbal Abortifacients; Instillation Methods; Methotrexate Induced Abortion; Mifepristone Induced Abortion**

Abortion

Abortion refers to the premature expulsion from a woman's uterus of an embryo or fetus before it is adequately developed to survive. An abortion may be generally classified as natural or induced. Both types of abortion may involve the termination of an embryo or fetus. A natural abortion occurs because of some health problem with the embryo or fetus, or a health problem with the mother that negatively impacts the embryo or fetus. An induced abortion occurs through the intentional intervention of a health care provider. Far more natural abortions occur annually than do induced abortions.

A natural abortion is broadly subdivided as a miscarriage or stillbirth. If an embryo or fetus dies in the uterus and is expelled by the body before 20 weeks of gestation, it is called a spontaneous abortion or miscarriage. Stillbirth refers to an infant delivered 20 weeks or more after gestation without signs of life. An induced abortion is broadly subdivided as elective, eugenic or therapeutic. When a woman decides to end her pregnancy voluntarily, not due to health reasons, the abortion is called elective. An induced abortion is called eugenic when it is done to prevent the birth of a child with severe birth defects. When an abortion is done to prevent serious harm or injury to the pregnant woman it is called therapeutic.

Legal status of a fetus in England under the common law. Prior to 1600 the fetus was largely neglected by the common law courts of England. At least two cases involving the death of fetuses are known to have been brought in the courts. In the decision of *Twinslayer's Case*, 1 Edw. 3 (1327) a defendant was charged with beating a pregnant woman. The woman was carrying twins; one child was stillborn and the other died a few days after birth. The case was never brought to conclusion because of other charges against the defendant. In the second decision, *Abortionist's Case*, 22 Edw. 3 (1348), a defendant was charged with causing the death of a fetus; but the case was dismissed because of insufficient evidence.

Although the royal courts neglected providing protection for a fetus, the ecclesiastical courts of England prohibited aborting a fetus that had reached the stage of "quickening." The stage of quickening occurred when the pregnant woman first discerned movements by the fetus.

The indifference of common law courts to a fetus changed in the 1600s, as a result of dicta in the decision of *Sim's Case*, 75 Eng. Rep. 1075 (1601). The decision in *Sim's Case* was a "trespass" action brought against a defendant who had tried to induce an abortion by physically assaulting a woman. The woman's child was born alive but died shortly after birth. Two of the judges in the case went on record as stating that the death of the child was a homicide. This nonbinding dicta would eventually be the basis for English legal commentators, such as the eminent jurist Blackstone, to write that under the common law an abortion after a fetus had "quickened" was manslaughter.

Legal status of a fetus in America prior to 1960. The American colonies accepted the English commentators' interpretation of the common law as criminalizing abortion induced after a fetus had quickened. After the colonies became states, the common law rule against abortions remained in force. This fact was echoed in a footnote of an opinion in one of the earliest reported American abortion cases, *Commonwealth v. Bangs*, 9 Mass. 387 (1812).

The decision in *Bangs* involved the prosecution of the defendant for administering a drug with the intent to procure an abortion. The defendant was convicted of the charge. On appeal the defendant argued that the indictment failed to correctly set out the offense of criminal abortion. It was said in the opinion that "[a]n attempt to procure abortion, even when the pregnant woman is not quick with child, is a misdemeanor at the common law." After examining the facts of the case, the appellate court agreed with the defendant that the indictment failed to sufficiently allege criminal abortion. It was said in the opinion that the indictment failed to assert that an abortion had actually occurred, and failed to allege that the pregnant women was "quick" with child.

It was not until the 1800s that the status of a fetus began to be find its way in state statutes. The impetus for legislative enactments came from England. In 1803 an English law was passed which prohibited all abortions by drugs or poisons and provided for the death penalty for an abortion that was committed after a fetus had quickened. The first state to follow England's lead was Connecticut. In 1821 Connecticut enacted the first statute in the nation prohibiting abortion. By the early 1900's all states and the District of Columbia had enacted criminal abortion statutes.

Abortion reform 1950 to 1972. It has been estimated that during the period abortion was illegal throughout the nation, over 1 million illegal abortions a year were performed. More than 5,000 women died annually from illegal abortions. Although no reliable data has ever been collected, researchers are in agreement that self-induced abortion was a huge problem during the period that abortion was outlawed.

A movement for abortion reform began in the 1950s that was led by physicians and culminated in 1959, when the American Law Institute proposed a model penal code for state abortion laws. The Institute advocated legalizing abortion for reasons that included the mental or physical health of the mother, pregnancy due to rape or incest, and fetal deformity. The push for reform was due to increased demands for abortion and health risks posed to women seeking out "back alley" abortions. As a result of the movement for reform, by 1972 the majority of states reformed their abortion laws, in varying degrees, to conform with the Institute's proposal. A few states permitted abortion only to protect the woman's physical and mental health: Arkansas, California, Colorado, Delaware, Florida, Georgia, Kansas, Maryland, New Mexico, North Carolina, Oregon, South Carolina, and Virginia. Mississippi permitted abortion to preserve the woman's life and for pregnancies resulting from rape. The majority of states permitted abortion only to preserve the life of the woman: Alabama, Arizona, Connecticut, District of Columbia, Idaho, Illinois, Indiana, Iowa, Kentucky, Maine, Massachusetts, Michigan, Minnesota, Missouri, Montana, Nebraska, Nevada, New Jersey, North Dakota, Ohio, Oklahoma, Rhode Island, South Dakota, Tennessee, Texas, Utah, Vermont, West Virginia, Wisconsin, and Wyoming. Three states continued to prohibit all abortions: Louisiana, New Hampshire, and Pennsylvania. Four states went further than the Institute's proposal and repealed criminal penalties for abortions performed in early pregnancy, subject to procedural and health requirements: Alaska, Hawaii, New York, and Washington. New York had the most liberal statute which allowed abortion on demand, up to 24 weeks gestation.

Legal status of fetus in the United States after 1972. In a decisive decision rendered in 1973 by the United State Supreme Court, *Roe v. Wade*, the legal status of a fetus was dramatically altered throughout the nation. The decision in *Roe* held that during the first trimester of pregnancy, a woman has a constitutionally protected right to privacy in making a determination of whether to have an abortion. The right of privacy was grounded in the liberty component of the Due Process Clause of the Fourteenth Amendment. In decisions subsequent to *Roe* the Supreme Court clarified the constitutional contours of a woman's right to an abortion. In *Planned Parenthood of Southeastern Pennsylvania v. Casey* the Supreme Court abandoned *Roe's* trimester standard, and held that states may not prohibit abortions performed before fetal viability. Fetal viability arises when, in the determination of a physician, there is a reasonable likelihood that a fetus is capable of survival outside the woman's body with or without artificial aid. However, even when a fetus has been determined to be viable, an abortion may occur if it is necessary to preserve the woman's health or life. States may ban abortion when a fetus is determined to be viable, except when a woman's health or life is at risk. It has been held that states may regulate abortion generally, so long as they do not impose an undue burden or substantial obstacle in the path of a woman seeking an abortion before the fetus attains viability.

First trimester abortion. The gestation period for the first trimester abortions ranges between four and twelve weeks. The most frequent abortions performed are first trimester abortions. It has been estimated that out of the total number of abortions performed each year, 90 percent are first trimester abortions. First trimester abortions are the safest, least expensive, and easiest to perform. Two states, New York and Kentucky, specifically provide by statute that women may perform self-abortion during the first trimester (under physician guidance).

Second trimester abortion. Second trimester abortions account for less than 10 percent of terminated pregnancies in the United States per year. The stage of gestation in the second trimester is between thirteen to twenty-four weeks of pregnancy. The abortion procedures used in second trimester abortions are more painful, costly, and unsafe.

Third trimester abortion. The gestation period for third trimester abortions is between twenty-five and twenty-eight weeks. Third trimester abortions only occur about 1 out of every 10,000 or roughly .5 percent of all abortions performed each year. Third trimester abortions are the most controversial because they can involve the partial-birth abortion procedure. Abortions of this type are usually therapeutic or eugenic. Women seeking third trimester abortions do so because of a catastrophic fetal anomaly or genetic disorder that guar-

ABORTIONS PERFORMED IN THE UNITED STATES 1973-2004

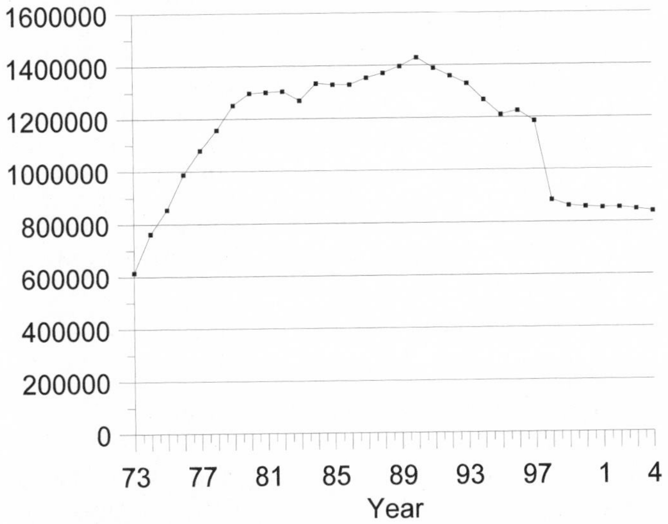

Source: **National Center for Health Statistics. For certain years the data does not include statistics from Alaska, California, New Hampshire, Oklahoma and West Virginia.**

ABORTIONS BY RACE IN THE UNITED STATES 2000-2004

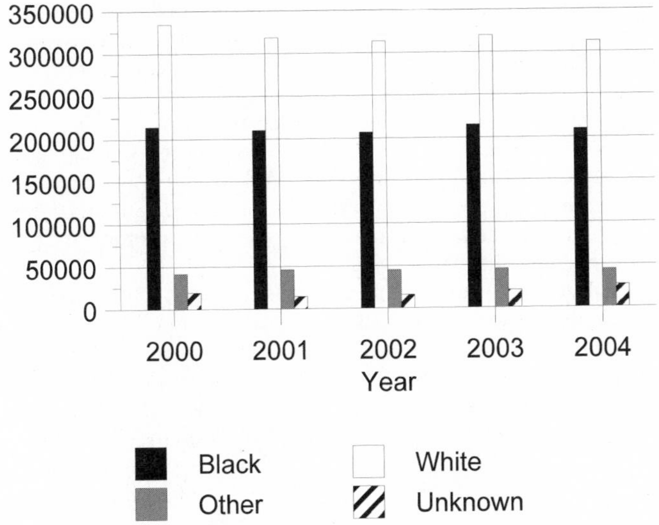

Source: National Center for Health Statistics.

ABORTIONS BY MARITAL STATUS IN THE UNITED STATES 2000-2004

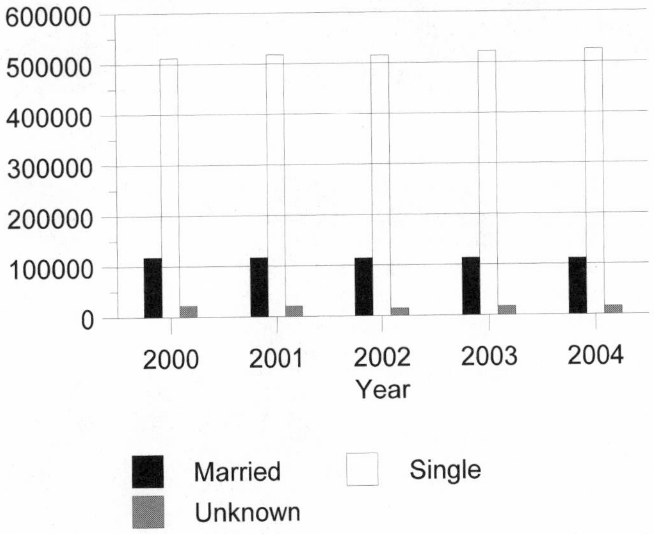

Source: National Center for Health Statistics.

Abortion by Weeks of Gestation in the United States 2000–2004

	Weeks of Gestation						
Year	*≤8*	*9–10*	*11–12*	*13–15*	*16–20*	*>21*	*Unknown*
2000	368,690	125,373	64,380	39,289	27,407	9,108	7,923
2001	357,517	115,164	60,241	37,509	25,929	8,654	5,228
2002	400,637	121,598	63,575	39,880	27,219	9,312	12,962
2003	401,259	119,125	64,327	41,269	27,575	9,383	12,225
2004	400,197	112,936	60,323	41,517	24,837	8,365	12,701
Total	1,928,300	594,196	312,846	199,464	132,967	44,822	51,039

Source: National Center for Health Statistics.

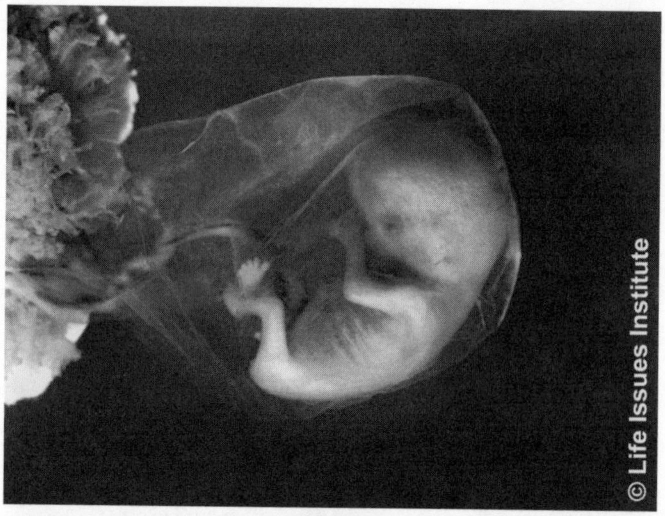

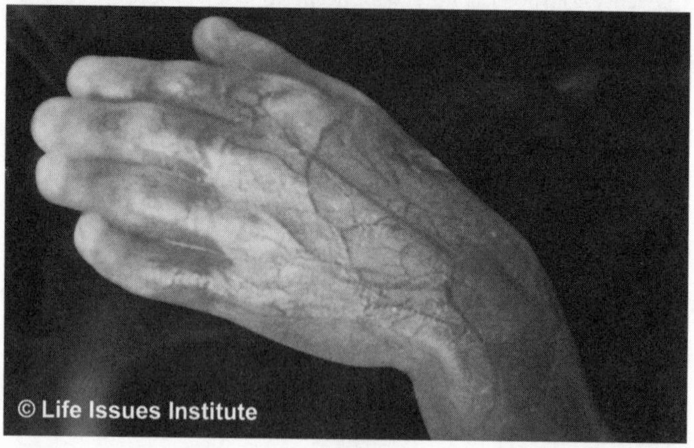

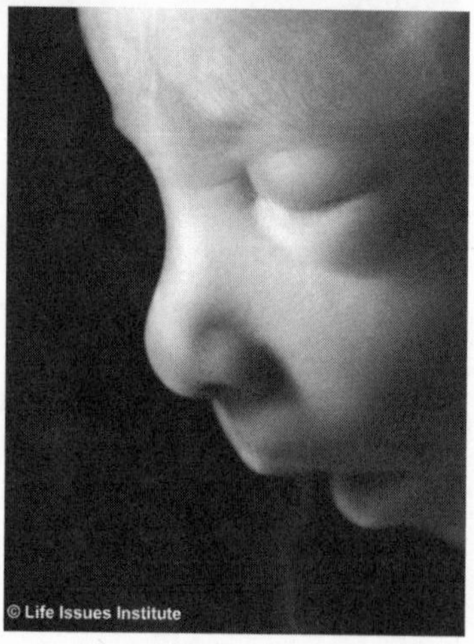

Top: **This is an image of an eight-week-old fetus. *Above:* This is an image of the left hand of a twelve-week-old fetus. *Right:* This is an image of the face of a sixteen-week-old fetus (Life Issues Institute, all rights reserved).**

antees death, suffering, or serious disability for the baby if the pregnancy was to continue to term; or because a woman's life would be in danger if the fetus was carried to term. Third trimester abortions are the most painful, expensive and dangerous to perform. *See also* **Complications During and After Abortion; Criminal Abortions; Eugenic Abortion; Failed Abortion; Methods of Abortion; Miscarriage; Planned Parenthood of Southeastern Pennsylvania v. Casey; Roe v. Wade; Septic Abortion; Stillbirth; Therapeutic Abortion**

Abortion Access Project

Abortion Access Project (AAP) was founded in 1992 by physicians and social justice activists. The organization is headquartered in Cambridge, Massachusetts. The executive director of AAP is Melanie Zurek. AAP believes that (1) all people should be able to obtain needed health care including abortion; (2) all people have the right to make free and informed decisions about their bodies, in particular regarding sexuality, pregnancy and birth; and (2) all people have the right to accurate and clear information and education about achieving and preventing pregnancy, pregnancy, and all of its possible outcomes. The work of AAP involves (1) looking for gaps in abortion access that no one else is addressing and seeking to create and support innovative responses to these gaps; (2) working to effect changes within health care and reproductive health activism that increase the participation of a wide range of health care providers in providing and connecting women to abortion care and that result in the increased accessibility of abortion; (3) working with local partners to achieve locally-driven, locally-relevant goals, and coordinate and connect this work to national organizations also interested in expanding access; and (4) working to create and support initiatives that can impact not only the local situation but also inform and inspire broader, systemic improvements in the way abortion is delivered and accessed. *See also* **Pro-Choice Organizations**

Abortion Clinics OnLine

Abortion Clinics OnLine (ACOL) is an internet website created in 1995, by Ann Rose. ACOL is a directory service comprised of providers of abortion and other reproductive health care. The directory is comprised of websites of over 400 providers of abortion services and other reproductive healthcare. The providers are private physicians, state licensed abortion clinics, private abortion clinics, and hospital abortion services. The abortion clinics listed in the directory are in 40 states, as well as international countries. ACOL does not prescreen clinics. *See also* **Pro-Choice Organizations**

Abortion Complications *see* **Complications During and After Abortion**

Abortion Violence, Property Destruction and Demonstrations

The 1973 decision of the United States Supreme Court in *Roe v. Wade*, legalizing abortion throughout the nation, became the catalyst for a persistent wave of violence, property destruction and demonstrations by organizations and individuals who oppose abortion. The terrorist-like tactics of militant anti-abortionists have intimidated the individuals who make up the abortion profession. For example, between the period 1980 and 1992, there was a 15 percent reduction in the number of doctors performing abortions in the nation. Particularly hardest hit were rural areas, which saw a decline of 55 percent in the number of abortion providers during the latter period. It has been estimated that there are no abortion providers in more than 84 percent of the counties in the nation.

The majority of militant anti-abortionist terrorist activities have occurred in California. Other states with significant intimidating activities include Florida, Texas and New York. In addition to actual violence, property destruction and demonstrations, anti-abortionist tactics also include vandalism, burglary, stalking, death threats, hate mail, and harassing phone calls.

In an attempt to help law enforcement officials gain control over militant anti-abortion activities, the National Abortion Federation and the Planned Parenthood Federation of America established a reward of up to $100,000 per incident, for information leading to the arrest and conviction of persons responsible for arson fires, bombings, and serious acts of violence at abortion and family planning clinics. In addition, two states (California and Oregon) have created specific statutes that make it a criminal offense to bomb a health care facility.

(1) Violence. There were nearly 3,000 acts of violence carried out against abortion providers between 1977 and 2000. The violence in-

cluded over 100 assault and battery incidents, 2 kidnappings, more than 15 attempted murders, and 6 murders.

(i) August 1982. Don Benny Anderson, with the help of two associates, kidnapped an Illinois abortionist, Dr. Hector Zevallos and his wife Rosalie Jean. The couple was released unharmed after eight days. Anderson received a 42 year sentence for the kidnapping.

(ii) March 10, 1993 — Michael Griffin shot and killed Dr. David Gunn in Pensacola, Florida. This was the first known murder of a physician by a militant anti-abortionist. Griffin was prosecuted and sentenced to life in prison.

(iii) August 19, 1993 — Rachelle R. Shannon shot Dr. George Tiller in both arms outside his clinic in Wichita, Kansas. Shannon was convicted and sentenced to 11 years in prison.

(iv) July 29, 1994 — Militant abortionist Paul Hill shot down Dr. John Bayard Britton and his volunteer escort, James H. Barrett, outside a Pensacola, Florida abortion clinic. Hill also wounded Barrett's wife, June, in the attack. Hill was prosecuted and became the first militant anti-abortionist to receive a sentence of death. Hill was executed in 2003.

(v) December 30, 1994 — Militant abortionist John C. Salvi opened fire with a rifle inside two different abortion clinics in Brookline, Massachusetts, killing two receptionists, Shannon Lowney and Leanne Nichols, and wounding five others. Salvi was sentenced to life in prison without parole. However, he committed suicide in prison in 1996.

(vi) December 18, 1996 — Dr. Calvin Jackson was stabbed and wounded outside a clinic in New Orleans. A suspect was apprehended, but later released.

(vii) January 16, 1997 — Two bombs explode in a building in Atlanta that contains an abortion clinic. Seven people were injured. Authorities charged militant anti-abortionist Eric Robert Rudolph with the crime. In 2005 Rudolph pled guilty to numerous charges and was given a total of five life imprisonment sentences.

(viii) January 29, 1998 — A bomb exploded at a Birmingham, Alabama abortion clinic that killed a security guard, Robert Sanderson, and severely injured nurse Emily Lyons. This was the first bombing attack to cause a fatality. Authorities charged militant anti-abortionist Eric Robert Rudolph with the crime. Rudolph evaded capture and a $1 million dollar reward was made for his apprehension. In 2003 Rudolph was arrested in North Carolina. In 2005 Rudolph pled guilty to numerous charges and was given a total of five life imprisonment sentences.

(ix) October 23, 1998 — A sniper killed Dr. Barnett Slepian at his residence in Amherst, New York. Authorities charged militant anti-abortionist James Charles Kopp with the murder. Kopp fled to France but was later returned to the United States. Kopp was eventually convicted of state and federal crimes and sentenced to life in prison.

(x) Butyric acid attacks. Butyric acid is a chemical found in perfumes and disinfectants. It is a colorless liquid that has an extremely unpleasant and long-lasting odor. Militant anti-abortionists began using butyric acid as a weapon against abortion facilities in the 1990s. The chemical is sprayed into clinics. Its pungent odor causes headaches, nausea and vomiting. There have been over 100 butyric acid attacks.

(xi) Anthrax Threats. Beginning in 1998, militant anti-abortionists began sending letters to abortion clinics and family planning organizations threatening exposure to anthrax. Anthrax is an acute infectious disease caused by the spore-forming bacterium Bacillus anthracis. The spores can be produced in a dry form (for biological warfare) which may be stored and ground into particles. If anthrax is inhaled it can cause respiratory failure and death within a week. Antibiotics exist but are only effective early during the infection. There has been one anthrax prosecution of an anti-abortionist, Clayton Waagner, by the federal government. Waagner was sentenced to 19 years in prison.

(2) Property destruction. There have been almost 300 bomb and arson incidents at abortion clinics since 1977. Persons responsible for the vast majority of the incidents have not been identified and, in many instances, statutes of limitation for prosecution have run. The structural costs of the arson and bombing campaign have been estimated to be between $10 and $20 million. Some of the resolved arson and bombing cases appear below with the year each incident occurred.

BOMBING AT ABORTION CLINICS 1982-2007

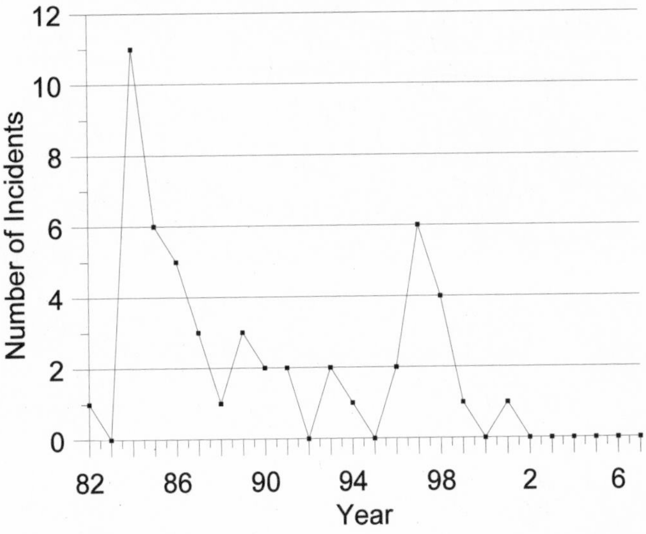

Source: **Bureau of Alcohol, Tobacco and Firearms; National Abortion Federation.**

ARSON AT ABORTION CLINICS IN THE UNITED STATES 1982-2007

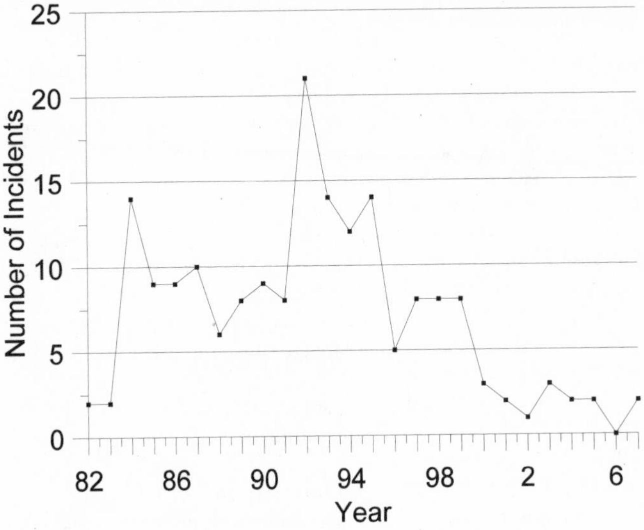

Source: **Bureau of Alcohol, Tobacco and Firearms; National Abortion Federation.**

Arson

(i) 1976 — Joseph C. Stockett was convicted of arson in causing $19,000 worth of damage to an Oregon abortion facility. Stockett served two years in prison.

(ii) 1979 — Peter Burkin was found not guilty by reason of insanity in causing over $100,000 in arson damage to a New York abortion facility.

(iii) 1983— Jospeh Grace was sentenced by a Virginia court to 10–20

States with Statutes That Prohibit Impeding Access to and from Abortion Facilities

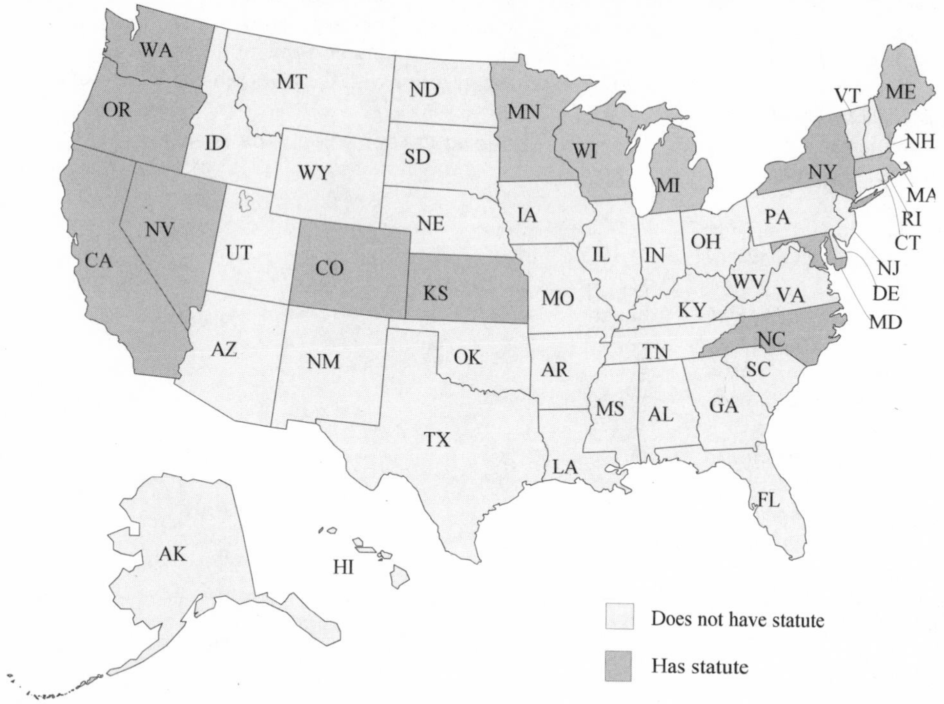

***District of Columbia has statute.**

years imprisonment for clinic arson that caused over $250,000 in damages.

(iv) 1983–84— Curtis Beseda was sentenced by a federal court in Washington to two consecutive 10 year prison terms for several clinic arsons that caused $180,000 in damages.

(v) 1984— Kenneth Shields, Thomas Spinks and Michael Bray were convicted of clinic arson in Delaware, Maryland and Virginia. Shields and Spinks received 15 year prison sentences; and Bray received a six year sentence. The damage caused by their conduct was over $200,000.

(vi) 1985— Brent Paul Braud, Derrick James Jarreau, John David Newchurch, and Charles Albert Cheshire Jr. were convicted of several clinic arsons in Louisiana. Braud and Jarreau received 2 year prison sentences; Newchurch was sentenced to 5 years; and Cheshire was sentenced to 5 years. The damage caused by their conduct was over $300,000.

(vii) 1985— John Brockhoeft was convicted of clinic arson in Ohio and was sentenced to 7 years imprisonment. He caused over $100,000 in damages.

(viii) 1985–87— Majorie Reed was convicted of several arsons in Ohio and sentenced to 5 years imprisonment. She caused over $200,000 in damages.

(ix) 1986–87— David Holman was sentenced by an Illinois court to 18 months imprisonment for several clinic arsons that resulted in minor damage.

(x) 1988— Shannon Taylor was convicted of several clinic arson attacks in California and sentenced to 8 years in prison. Taylor's conduct caused $50,000 in damages.

(xi) 1990— Daniel J. Carver was sentenced to three years in prison for a clinic arson attack in Oregon. About $15,000 in damages was caused.

(xii) 1992— Michael Andrew Fix was sentenced to 2 years in prison for several clinic arsons in Nevada. Fix caused damage at $5,000.

(xiii) 1993— Joshua Graff was sentenced to 39 months in prison for committing clinic arson in Texas. The damage caused totaled $20,000.

(xiv) 1997— James Anthony Mitchell was sentenced to 10 years in prison for clinic arson in Virginia. Property damage was $25,000.

(xv) 1997— Peter Howard was sentenced in California to 15 years in prison after being caught driving a truck with incendiary devices through an abortion clinic door.

(xvi) 1999— Martin Uphoff received a sentence of 60 months in prison for clinic arson in South Dakota. Property damage was minimal.

Bomb

(i) 1984— Kenneth Shields, Thomas Spinks and Michael Bray were convicted of clinic bomb attacks in Washington, D.C. and Maryland. Shields and Spinks received 15 year sentences; and Bray received a 6 year sentence. The damage caused to property was over $500,000.

(ii) 1984— Matthew Goldsby, James Simmons, Kathren Simmons and Kaye Wiggins were convicted of participating in a clinic bomb attack in Florida. Matthew and James were sentenced to 10 years in prison. Kathren and Kaye received probation sentences. The damage caused by their conduct was in excess of $225,000.

(iii) 1985–86— Dennis John Malvasi, Carl Cenera, Frank Wright, Jr., and Donald C. Pryor, Jr. were convicted of clinic bombing attacks in New York. Malvasi was sentenced to 5 years in prison; Cenera received a 3 year sentence; Wright received a 2 year sentence; and Pryor died while awaiting sentencing. The damage caused by their attacks was minor.

(iv) 1987— Dorman Owens, Joanne Kreipel, Cheryl Sullinger, Randy Sullinger, Chris Harmon, Robin Harmon and Erick Svelmoe were convicted of participating in a clinic bomb attack in California. Their sentences ranged from 149 days in jail to five years in prison. The damage caused by their attack was minimal.

(v) 1997— John Yankowski was convicted of a clinic bomb attack in Montana. He was sentenced to 5 years in prison. The damage caused by the attack was about $2,000.

(vi) 2006— Robert Francis Weiler, Jr. pleaded guilty to federal charges of possessing a pipe bomb, being a felon in possession of a firearm and attempting to destroy or damage an abortion clinic. He was sentenced to five years in prison.

(vii) 2007— Paul Ross Evans pled guilty to attempting to use a weapon of mass to blow up a clinic. Evans was sentenced to 40 years in prison.

(3) Demonstrations. Anti-abortionist demonstrations have involved picketing, blockades, sit-ins, marches, and mass rallies. Since 1977 there have been more than 30,000 demonstrations throughout the country and more than 15,000 arrests.

The use of demonstrations to protest against abortion became popular in the late 1980s, as a result of the activities of one anti-abortion group called Operation Rescue. This organization shocked the abortion world with its blockades of clinic entrances and the willingness of its members to be arrested. The tactics of Operation Rescue were adopted by groups all across the nation. There were thousands of arrests nationwide as clinics increasingly became political battlefields.

In response to the disruption and intimidation caused by anti-abortion demonstrations, the federal government passed the 1994 Freedom of Access to Clinic Entrances Act (FACE). FACE created criminal penalties for certain types of anti-abortion demonstration activity. Several states have enacted statutes similar to FACE.

In *Hill v. Colorado* the United States Supreme Court upheld a Colorado statute that made it unlawful for any person within 100 feet of an abortion facility's entrance to knowingly approach within 8 feet of another person, without that person's consent, in order to pass a leaflet, handbill, display a sign, engage in oral protest, education, or counseling with that person. In *Schenck v. Pro Choice Network of Western New York* the Supreme Court upheld certain federal trial court injunction provisions that imposed fixed buffer zone limitations at abortion clinics, while finding the First Amendment was violated by certain provisions that imposed floating buffer zone limitations. In *Frisby v. Schultz* the Supreme Court upheld the constitutional validity of a town ordinance that was created to prevent pro-life picketing at the residence of an abortion doctor. In *Madsen v. Women's Health Clinic, Inc.* the Supreme Court upheld parts of an injunction that restricted noise by anti-abortionists at a clinic and imposed a 36 foot buffer zone around the clinic entrances and driveway. However, *Madsen* invalidated parts of the injunction which imposed a 36 foot buffer zone around private property to the north and west of the clinic, a restriction on the use of images observable by clinic patients, a 300 foot no approach zone around the clinic, and a 300 foot buffer zone around the residences. *See also* **Army of God; Buffer Zones at Abortion Facilities; Evans, Paul Ross; Freedom of Access to Clinic Entrances Act; Frisby v. Schultz; Hill, Paul; Hill v. Colorado; Kopp, James Charles; Griffin, Michael Frederick; Madsen v. Women's Health Clinic, Inc.; Nuremberg Files; Operation Rescue; Pro-Life Action League; Rudolph, Eric Robert; Salvi, John C. III; Schenck v. Pro Choice Network of Western New York; Shannon, Rachelle Ranae; Waagner, Clayton; Weiler, Robert Francis, Jr.**

Abruptio *see* **Placenta Abruptio**

Acardiac Twins *see* **Twin Reversed Arterial Perfusion**

ACCESS

ACCESS is a California based pro-choice organization that was started in 1993. The executive director of ACCESS is Destiny Lopez. The organization was created to make reproductive health and choice a concrete reality for all women. ACCESS uses a combination of direct services, community education and policy advocacy to promote reproductive options and access to quality health care for low-income and uninsured women, young women, immigrant women and women in rural or isolated areas of California. The organization operates a telephone Hotline that provides free and confidential information, referrals, peer counseling and advocacy on the full range of reproductive health services including abortion, birth control, pregnancy, prenatal care, pap smears and gyn care, infertility, and STD testing and treatment. *See also* **Pro-Choice Organizations**

Achondroplasia

Achondroplasia is a genetic bone disorder that causes the most common type of dwarfism. It affects about one in every 20,000 births. The disorder can be inherited or result from a spontaneous gene mutation. A child has a 50 percent chance of inheriting the disorder if one parent has achondroplasia. Should both parents have the disorder, the child's chance of having achondroplasia increases to 75 percent. Infants who inherit achondroplasia from both parents seldom live beyond a few months. In over 80 percent of achondroplasia births the disorder is not inherited, but results from a spontaneous new gene mutation that occurs in the egg or sperm. There is no specific treatment to correct achondroplasia, but associated abnormalities such as club feet may be corrected. Prenatal tests can be performed to diagnose or rule out achondroplasia. *See also* **Birth Defects and Abortion**

Adrenoleukodystrophy

Adrenoleukodystrophy is a congenital disorder involving long chain fatty acid metabolism that affects the adrenal glands, nervous system and testes. There are several different forms of the disease. Some symptoms include seizures and delayed neurological development, abnormal adrenal function, changes in muscle tone, and coma. The disorder can kill. Some complications from the disorder are treated with supplemental steroids (such as cortisone and cortisol). The disorder occurs in about 1 out of 20,000 births. *See also* **Birth Defects and Abortion**

Advertisement

States have attempted to prohibit various commercial advertising activity involving the distribution of abortion information. Statutes have been enacted which attempted to prohibit selling or circulating any publication that encouraged or promoted abortions; banned mailing unsolicited advertisements for contraceptives; prohibited the sale or distribution of contraceptive of any kind to a minor; prohibited anyone other than a licensed pharmacist to distribute contraceptives to adults; prohibited anyone to advertise or display contraceptives; and prohibited anyone from giving away a drug, medicine, instrument, or article for the prevention of conception. All of these restrictions have been found unconstitutional by the United States Supreme Court. *See also* **Bigelow v. Virginia; Bolger v. Youngs Drug Products Corp.; Carey v. Population Services International; Comstock Act; Eisenstadt v. Baird; Griswold v. Connecticut**

Advocates for Life Ministries

Advocates for Life Ministries (AFLM) was a pro-life organization that was founded in Portland, Oregon, in 1985 by its director Andrew Burnett. Burnett was subjected to numerous arrests for setting up abortion clinic blockades in Portland and around the nation. He founded AFLM primarily as a clearinghouse for those who promote the use of force against abortion providers. AFLM published a magazine called *Life Advocate*. The magazine regularly featured reports on clinic bombings and arson attacks, as well as providing a platform for those advocating force against abortion providers. One of AFLM's most prominent members was Rachelle R. Shannon, who was sentenced to 11 years imprisonment for the attempted murder of Dr. George Tiller. As a result of numerous civil lawsuits brought against AFLM and its leaders, the organization disbanded in 1999. *See also* **Pro-Life Organizations**

Afterbirth *see* **Placenta**

Age and Abortion

The majority of abortions take place for women aged 20 to 29. This age group made up 55.6 percent of all abortions that occurred between the period 2000 to 2004. During this same period teenage girls 15 to 19 years of age had a higher number of abortions (17.1 percent) than women in the age group of 30 to 34 (14.6 percent), 35–39 (8.4 percent) and women 40 and over (3 percent). *See also* **Abortion**

See charts at top of page 10.

Agenesis of the Corpus Callosum

Agenesis of the corpus callosum is a rare congenital disorder involving a partial or complete absence of the corpus callosum (the area

Abortion by Age Group in the United States 2000-2004
Age Group (yrs)

Year	<15	15–19	20–24	25–29	30–34	35–39	≥40	Unknown
2000	4,973	138,313	249,403	174,174	107,873	63,926	21,639	5,839
2001	4,764	133,236	253,616	171,199	111,053	63,688	22,532	5,405
2002	4,584	127,793	252,500	171,181	112,584	63,651	23,734	6,770
2003	4,581	126,151	251,800	170,743	111,996	63,130	23,703	4,358
2004	4,339	122,590	244,716	170,146	109,022	62,416	23,663	4,024
Total	23,241	648,083	1,252,035	857,443	552,528	316,811	115,271	26,396

Source: National Center for Health Statistics.

PERCENTAGE DISTRIBUTION OF ABORTION BY AGE IN THE U.S. 2000-2004

33.0% 17.1% 0.6% 0.7% 3.0% 8.4% 14.6% 22.6%

Age Group

- ■ <15
- ▤ 15-19
- ■ 20-24
- ▥ 25-29
- ■ 30-34
- ■ 35-39
- □ >40
- □ Unknown

Source: National Center for Health Statistics.

of the brain connecting the two cerebral hemispheres). Symptoms of the disorder include seizures, feeding problems, impairments in mental and physical development, hand-eye coordination, and visual and auditory problems. The disorder can cause death, but in most cases it does not. Many of the problems associated with the disorder are treatable. *See also* **Birth Defects and Abortion**

Aicardi Syndrome

Aicardi syndrome is a congenital disorder that is characterized by the partial or complete absence of the corpus callosum (the area of the brain connecting the two cerebral hemispheres). Symptoms of the disorder include infantile spasms, mental retardation, and eye abnormalities. This disorder affects only females. There is no cure for the disease. Treatment involves management of seizures and intervention programs for mental retardation. *See also* **Birth Defects and Abortion**

AIDS *see* HIV/AIDS

Alabama

(1) OVERVIEW

The state of Alabama enacted its first criminal abortion statute on January 9, 1841. The statute underwent several amendments prior to the 1973 decision by the United States Supreme Court in *Roe v. Wade*, which legalized abortion in the nation. In spite of the decision in *Roe*, Alabama has not repealed its pre–*Roe* criminal abortion statute. However, the statute is constitutionally infirm.

Alabama has taken affirmative steps to respond to *Roe* and its progeny. The state has addressed several abortion issues by statute that in-

clude post-viability abortion, partial-birth abortion, abortion by minors, informed consent, fetal death report, and injury to pregnant woman.

(2) PRE-ROE ABORTION BAN

As previously indicated, Alabama has not repealed its pre–*Roe* criminal abortion statute. Under the now unconstitutional statute, abortion was criminalized if it was not performed to preserve the life or health of the woman. The pre–Roe abortion ban statute is set out below.

Alabama Code § 13A-13-7. Inducing or attempting to induce abortion, miscarriage, or premature delivery of woman

Any person who willfully administers to any pregnant woman any drug or substance or uses or employs any instrument or other means to induce an abortion, miscarriage or premature delivery or aids, abets or prescribes for the same, unless the same is necessary to preserve her life or health

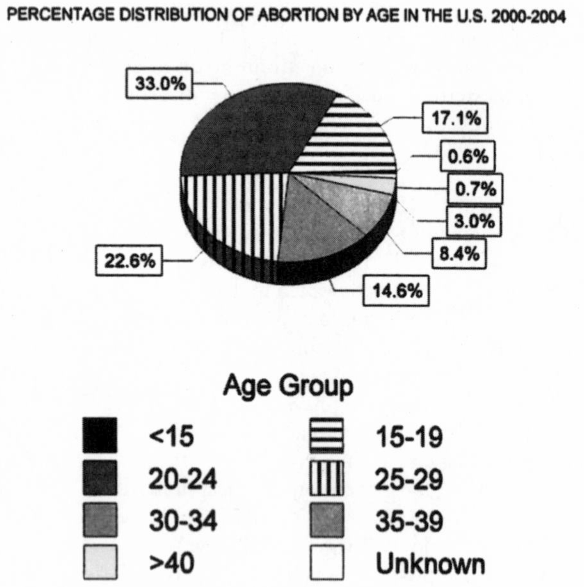

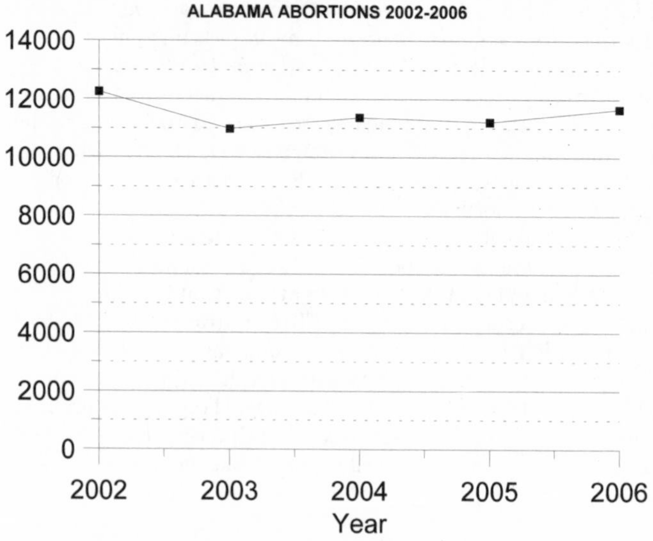

ALABAMA ABORTIONS 2002-2006

Source: Alabama Center for Health Statistics.

ALABAMA ABORTIONS BY RACE 2002-2006

■ White □ Black ■ Other

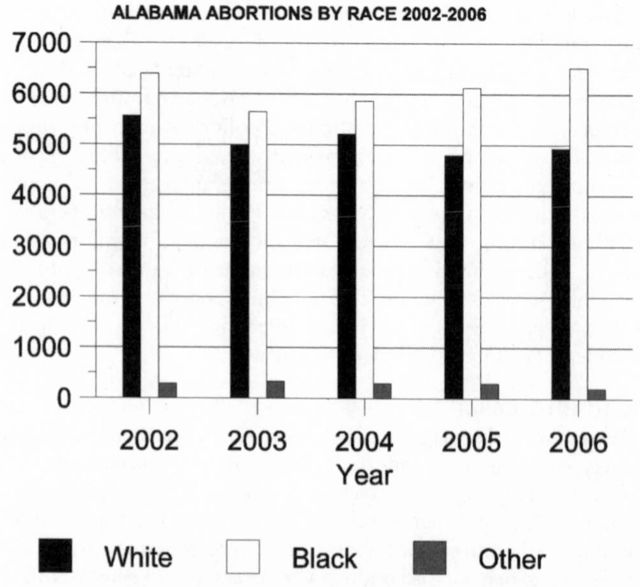

Source: Alabama Center for Health Statistics.

Alabama Abortion By Age Group 2002–2006

Year	<15	15–19	20–24	25–29	30–34	35–39	≥40	Unknown
	Age Group (yrs)							
2002	115	2,131	4,433	2,872	1,585	797	311	5
2003	106	1,886	3,988	2,473	1,531	737	253	5
2004	113	1,994	4,072	2,670	1,521	738	250	12
2005	97	1,992	3,917	2,575	1,577	788	260	5
2006	98	2,082	4,078	2,799	1,511	819	267	0
Total	529	10,085	20,488	13,389	7,725	3,879	1,341	27

Source: **Alabama Center for Health Statistics.**

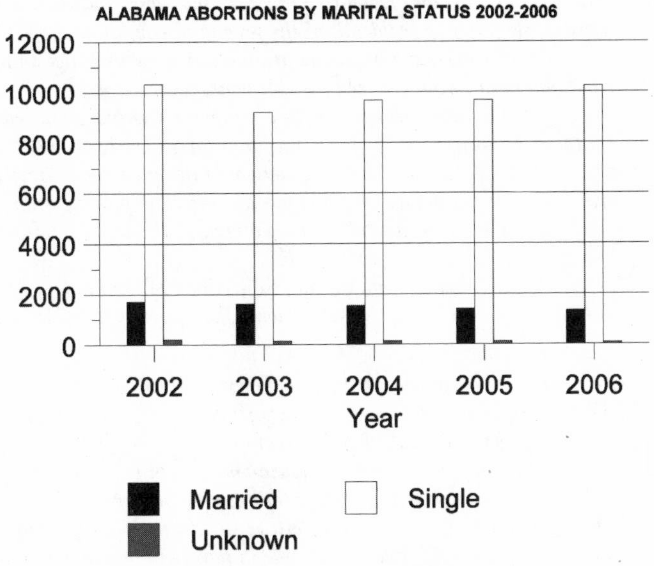

Source: **Alabama Center for Health Statistics.**

Alabama Abortion by Education Level of Female 2002–2006

Year	<7	7–9	10–11	12	≥13	Unknown
	Education Level Completed					
2002	68	387	1,204	4,722	5,249	619
2003	35	358	962	3,509	4,857	1,258
2004	40	367	1,050	3,571	5,042	1,300
2005	52	372	1,074	3,385	5,096	1,232
2006	58	459	1,185	3,678	5,656	618
Total	253	1,943	5,475	18,865	25,900	5,027

Source: **Alabama Center for Health Statistics.**

Alabama Prior Abortion by Female 2002–2006

Year	None	1	2	3	4	5	6	7	8	≥9	Not known
	Prior Abortion										
2002	7,895	2,999	946	259	77	31	4	5	1	2	30
2003	7,061	2,638	861	245	77	27	10	6	4	3	47
2004	7,239	2,834	856	271	91	32	10	4	2	2	29
2005	7,413	2,642	806	236	64	18	8	0	0	8	16
2006	7,606	2,796	898	229	70	18	9	3	1	4	20
Total	37,214	13,909	4,367	1,240	379	126	41	18	8	19	142

Source: **Alabama Center for Health Statistics.**

and done for that purpose, shall on conviction be fined not less than $100.00 nor more than $1,000.00 and may also be imprisoned in the county jail or sentenced to hard labor for the county for not more than 12 months.

(3) POST-VIABILITY ABORTION

Alabama has enacted a penal statute that prohibits post-viability abortions, except to save the life of the woman or to prevent the woman from having a severe health problem if the child was carried to term. A post-viability abortion must be found necessary by two physicians, the abortion has to take place in a hospital, and two physicians are required to be present during the abortion. It is required by Alabama that a woman who is more than 19 weeks pregnant must, before obtaining an abortion, undergo testing for fetal viability. The post-viability statutes have been discussed in *Summit Medical Associates v. James*, 984 F.Supp. 1404 (M.D.Ala. 1998), affirmed in part, reversed in part 180 F.3d 1326 (11th Cir. 1999). The post-viability statutes are set out below.

Alabama Code § 26-22-1. Legislative findings and intent

(a) The public policy of the State of Alabama is to protect life, born and unborn. This is particularly true concerning unborn life that is capable of living outside the womb. The Legislature of the State of Alabama finds there are abortions being done in Alabama after the time of viability and in violation of its public policy.

(b) The Legislature specifically finds the following:

(1) Medical evidence shows there is a survival rate of babies born between ages 23 weeks to 29 weeks gestational age of 64 percent to 94 percent.

(2) In Webster v. Reproductive Health Services, 492 U.S. 499 (1989), the United States Supreme Court determined that viability may occur as early as 23 to 24 weeks gestational age. Also, the United States Supreme Court determined that requiring fetal viability testing at 20 weeks gestational age is constitutional, because there is up to a four week margin of error in determining gestational age.

(3) In the latest year of Alabama statistical reporting, 1994, there were reported to be 182 abortions performed at 20 or more weeks gestational age. There were also 70 abortions performed where no gestational age was stated.

(c) Subject to life and health exceptions to the mother, it is the intent of the Legislature to ban abortions of any unborn child that is capable of living outside the womb. To permit otherwise is a wanton disregard of human life.

Alabama Code § 26-22-2. Definitions

The following words shall have the following meanings:

(1) ABORTION. The use of any means to terminate the clinically diagnosable pregnancy of a woman with knowledge that the termination by those means will, with reasonable likelihood, cause the death of the unborn child.

(2) FERTILIZATION. The fusion of a human spermatozoon with a human ovum.

(3) GESTATIONAL AGE. The age of the unborn child as calculated from the first day of the last menstrual period of the pregnant woman.

(4) HOSPITAL. An institution licensed pursuant to the provisions of the law of this state.

(5) LIVE BIRTH. When used with regard to a human being, means that the human being was completely expelled or extracted from his or her mother and after such separation, breathed or showed evidence of any of the following: Beating of the heart, pulsation of the umbilical cord, definite movement of voluntary muscles, or any brain-wave activity.

(6) MEDICAL EMERGENCY. The condition, which, on the basis of the physician's good-faith clinical judgment, so complicates a pregnancy as to necessitate the immediate abortion of her pregnancy to avert her death or for which a delay will create serious risk of substantial and irreversible impairment of a major bodily function.

(7) PREGNANT. The female reproductive condition of having a developing fetus in the body and commences with fertilization.

Alabama Abortion by Weeks of Gestation 2002–2006

Weeks of Gestation	2002	2003	2004	2005	2006	Total
	Year					
≤6	3,160	2,907	3,502	3,473	3,198	16,240
7	2,665	2,090	2,129	1,902	2,187	10,973
8	1,807	1,623	1,426	1,515	1,529	7,900
9	1,285	1,169	1,015	1,028	1,192	5,689
10	768	725	738	747	824	3,802
11	622	604	604	609	658	3,097
12	489	440	468	479	550	2,426
13	371	339	369	366	455	1,900
14	285	291	279	274	257	1,386
15	178	194	216	229	225	1,042
16	179	152	153	154	167	805
17	127	112	114	127	117	597
18	93	111	115	118	114	551
19	80	73	81	87	78	399
20	55	54	65	49	49	272
21	47	36	42	22	23	170
22	30	22	18	10	3	83
23	2	3	1	2	0	8
24	0	0	1	0	0	1
25	0	0	0	0	0	0
≥26	1	0	0	0	0	1
Not known	5	34	34	20	28	121

Source: **Alabama Center for Health Statistics.**

(8) UNBORN CHILD and FETUS. An individual organism of the species Homo sapiens from fertilization until live birth.

(9) VIABLE and VIABILITY. The stage of fetal development when, in the judgment of the physician based upon the particular facts of the case before him or her and in light of the most advanced medical technology and information available to him or her, there is a reasonable likelihood of sustained survival of the unborn child outside the body of his or her mother, with or without artificial support.

Alabama Code § 26-22-3.
Prohibition, exceptions, and regulations

(a) Prohibition. Except as provided in subsection (b), no person shall intentionally, knowingly, or recklessly perform or induce an abortion when the unborn child is viable.

(b) Exceptions.

(1) It shall not be a violation of subsection (a) if an abortion is performed by a physician and that physician reasonably believes that it is necessary to prevent either the death of the pregnant woman or the substantial and irreversible impairment of a major bodily function of the woman. No abortion shall be deemed authorized under this paragraph if performed on the basis of a claim or a diagnosis that the woman will engage in conduct which would result in her death or in substantial and irreversible impairment of a major bodily function.

(2) It shall not be a violation of subsection (a) if the abortion is performed by a physician and that physician reasonably believes, after making a determination of the viability of the unborn child in compliance with Section 26-22-4 relating to the determination of viability, that the unborn child is not viable.

(c) Abortion regulated. Except in the case of a medical emergency which, in the reasonable medical judgment of the physician performing the abortion, prevents compliance with a particular requirement of this subsection, no abortion which is authorized under subsection (b)(1) shall be performed unless each of the following conditions are met:

(1) The physician performing the abortion certifies in writing that, based upon his or her medical examination of the pregnant woman and his or her medical judgment, the abortion is necessary to prevent either the death of the pregnant woman or serious risk of substantial and irreversible impairment of a major bodily function.

(2) The physician's judgment with respect to the necessity for the abortion has been concurred in by one other licensed physician who certifies in writing that, based upon his or her separate personal medical examination of the pregnant woman and his or her medical judgment, the abortion is necessary to prevent either the death of the pregnant woman or the substantial and irreversible impairment of a major bodily function of the woman.

(3) The abortion is performed in a hospital.

(4) The physician terminates the pregnancy in a manner which provides the best opportunity for the unborn child to survive, unless the physician determines, in his or her good faith medical judgment, that termination of the pregnancy in that manner poses a significantly greater risk either of the death of the pregnant woman or the substantial and irreversible impairment of a major bodily function of the woman than would other available methods.

(5) The physician performing the abortion arranges for the attendance, in the same room in which the abortion is to be completed, of a second physician who shall take control of the child immediately after complete extraction from the mother and shall provide immediate medical care for the child, taking all reasonable steps necessary to preserve the child's life and health.

(d) Penalty. Any person who violates subsection (a) commits a Class A felony. Any person who violates subsection (c) commits a Class C felony.

Alabama Code § 26-22-4. Viability testing

Except in the case of a medical emergency, prior to performing an abortion upon a woman subsequent to her first 19 weeks of pregnancy, the physician shall determine whether, in his or her good faith medical judgment, the child is viable. When the physician has determined that a child is viable, he or she shall report the basis for his or her determination that the abortion is necessary to prevent either the death of the pregnant woman or the substantial and irreversible impairment of a major bodily function of the woman. When the physician has determined that a child is not viable after the first 19 weeks of pregnancy, he or she shall report the basis for such determination.

Alabama Code § 26-22-5. Interpretation

Nothing in this chapter shall be construed to recognize a right to abortion or to make legal an abortion that is otherwise unlawful.

(4) PARTIAL-BIRTH ABORTION

Alabama criminalizes partial-birth abortions. Under state's statutes any physician who performs a partial-birth abortion is guilty of a felony offense. In addition to the ban on partial-birth abortions, Alabama has provided a civil cause of action for a married man whose spouse obtains a partial-birth abortion. In the case of a minor, the maternal grandparents of the fetus may file a civil lawsuit. The state does not permit a woman to be prosecuted for allowing a partial-birth abortion to be performed on her.

Alabama's partial-birth abortion statutes are invalid under the United States Supreme Court decision in *Stenberg v. Carhart*, which invalidated Nebraska's ban on partial-birth abortion. In fact, Alabama's ban on partial-birth abortion was found unconstitutional in *Summit Medical Associates v. Siegelman*, 130 F.Supp.2d 1307 (M.D.Ala. 2001). The statutes were also addressed in *Summit Medical Associates v. James*, 984 F.Supp. 1404 (M.D.Ala. 1998), affirmed in part, reversed in part 180 F.3d 1326 (11th Cir. 1999). Although Alabama's partial-birth abortion statutes, as currently written, are invalid, the United States Supreme Court approved of a federal statute that bans partial-birth abortion, in the case of *Gonzales v. Carhart*. The text of Alabama's partial-birth abortion statutes are set out below.

Alabama Code § 26-23-1. Short title

This chapter may be cited as the "Alabama Partial-Birth Abortion Ban Act of 1997."

Alabama Code § 26-23-2. Definitions

As used in this chapter, the following terms shall have the following meanings:

(1) FATHER. The biological father of the human fetus.

(2) MOTHER. The female who is pregnant with a live human fetus which may be subject to a partial-birth abortion under this chapter.

(3) PARTIAL-BIRTH ABORTION. An abortion in which the person performing the abortion partially vaginally delivers a living fetus before killing the fetus and completing the delivery.

(4) PHYSICIAN. A doctor of medicine or osteopathy legally authorized to practice medicine and surgery by the state or any other individual legally authorized by the state to perform abortions. This definition shall also include any individual who is not a physician or is not otherwise legally authorized by the state to perform abortions, but who nevertheless performs a partial-birth abortion.

Alabama Code § 26-23-3. Felony conviction

Any physician who knowingly performs a partial-birth abortion within this state and thereby kills a human fetus shall be guilty of a Class C felony and upon conviction thereof shall be punished as prescribed by law.

Alabama Code § 26-23-4. Life of mother exception

Section 26-23-3 shall not apply to a partial-birth abortion that is necessary to save the life of a mother.

Alabama Code § 26-23-5. Civil action

The father, if married to the mother at the time she receives a partial-birth abortion procedure, and if the mother has not attained the age of 18 years at the time of the abortion, the maternal grandparents of the fetus, may in a civil action obtain appropriate relief, unless the pregnancy resulted from the plaintiff's criminal conduct or the plaintiff consented to the abortion. The relief shall be limited to monetary compensation for all injuries, psychological and physical, occasioned by a violation under this chapter and monetary punitive compensation as allowed by law.

Alabama Code § 26-23-6. Conspiracy

A woman upon whom a partial-birth abortion is performed may not be prosecuted under this chapter for a conspiracy to violate this chapter or for any other offense which is unlawful under this chapter.

(5) ABORTION BY MINORS

Under the laws of Alabama no physician may perform an abortion upon an unemancipated minor unless he/she first obtains the written consent of either parent or the legal guardian of the minor. If a minor's pregnancy was caused by sexual intercourse with her natural father, adoptive father, stepfather or legal guardian, then written notice of the abortion to the minor's mother is sufficient.

In compliance with federal constitutional law, Alabama has provided a judicial waiver procedure for an unemancipated minor to obtain an abortion without parental or guardian consent. If an unemancipated minor elects not to seek, or cannot for any reason obtain consent from either of her parents or legal guardian, the minor may petition a trial court for a waiver of the consent requirement. A minor has a right to an attorney at the proceeding and if she cannot afford one, the court must appoint her an attorney. If a minor chooses, she may represent herself. The required parental or guardian consent may be waived if the court finds either (1) that the minor is mature and well-informed enough to make the abortion decision on her own, or (2) that performance of the abortion would be in the best interest of the minor. An expedited appeal is available to any minor to whom the court denies a waiver of consent. The Alabama supreme court upheld the validity of the abortion statutes for minors in *Ex Parte Anonymous*, 531 So.2d 901 (Ala. 1988). Issues involving the abortion statutes for minors have been litigated in the following cases: *In re Anonymous*, 2007 WL 987479 (Ala.App.2007); *In re Anonymous*, 956 So.2d 427 (Ala.App. 2006); *In re Anonymous*, 905 So.2d 845 (Ala.App. 2005); *Moragne v. Moragne*, 888 So.2d 1280 (Ala.App. 2004); *In re Anonymous*, 888 So.2d 1265 (Ala.App. 2004); *Ex Parte Anonymous*, 889 So.2d 525 (Ala.2003); *Ex Parte Anonymous*, 889 So.2d 518 (Ala. 2003), on remand 889 So.2d 524; *In re Anonymous*, 869 So.2d 498 (Ala.App. 2003); *In re Anonymous*, 833 So.2d 75 (Ala.App. 2002); *In re Anonymous*, 812 So.2d 1221 (Ala.App. 2001); *In re Anonymous*, 812 So.2d 1218 (Ala.App. 2001); *Ex Parte Anonymous*, 810 So.2d 786 (Ala. 2001); *Ex Parte Anonymous*, 808 So.2d 1030 (Ala. 2001); *Ex Parte Anonymous*, 806 So.2d 1269 (Ala. 2001); *In re Anonymous*, 805 So.2d 726 (Ala.App. 2001); *Ex Parte Anonymous*, 803 So.2d 542 (Ala. 2001); *In re Anonymous*, 782 So.2d 791 (Ala.App. 2000); *In re Anonymous*, 771 So.2d 1043 (Ala.App. 2000); *In re Anonymous*, 770 So.2d 1107 (Ala.App. 2000). The abortion statutes for minors are set out below.

Alabama Code § 26-21-1. Legislative purpose and findings

(a) It is the intent of the legislature in enacting this parental consent provision to further the important and compelling state interests of: (1) protecting minors against their own immaturity, (2) fostering the family structure and preserving it as a viable social unit, and (3) protecting the rights of parents to rear children who are members of their household.

(b) The legislature finds as fact that: (1) immature minors often lack the ability to make fully informed choices that take account of both immediate and long-range consequences, (2) the medical, emotional and psychological consequences of abortion are serious and can be lasting, particularly when the patient is immature, (3) the capacity to become pregnant and the capacity for mature judgment concerning the wisdom of an abortion are not necessarily related, (4) parents ordinarily possess information essential to a physician's exercise of his best medical judgment concerning the child, and (5) parents who are aware that their minor daughter has had an abortion may better insure that she receives adequate medical attention after her abortion. The legislature further finds that parental consultation is usually desirable and in the best interests of the minor.

Alabama Code § 26-21-2. Definitions

For purposes of this chapter, the following definitions shall apply:

(1) MINOR. Any person under the age of 18 years;

(2) EMANCIPATED MINOR. Any minor who is or has been married or has by court order otherwise been legally freed from the care, custody and control of her parents;

(3) ABORTION. The use of any instrument, medicine, drug or any other substance or device with intent to terminate the pregnancy of a woman known to be pregnant, with intent other than to increase the probability of a live birth, to preserve the life or health of the child after live birth, or to remove a dead or dying unborn child.

Alabama Code § 26-21-3. Written consent for minor

(a) Except as otherwise provided in subsections (b) and (e) of this section and Sections 26-21-4 and 26-21-5 hereof, no person shall perform an abortion upon an unemancipated minor unless he or his agent first obtains the written consent of either parent or the legal guardian of the minor.

(b) If the minor's pregnancy was caused by sexual intercourse with the minor's natural father, adoptive father or stepfather or legal guardian, then written notice to the minor's mother by certified mail shall be sufficient.

(c) The person who shall perform the abortion or his agent shall obtain or be provided with the written consent from either parent or legal guardian stating the names of the minor, parent or legal guardian, that he or she is informed that the minor desires an abortion and does consent

to the abortion, the date, and shall be signed by either parent or legal guardian. The unemancipated minor shall verify on the same form, by her signature and in the presence of such person who shall perform the abortion or his agent, that said signature of the parents, parent or legal guardian is authentic. The consent shall be kept as a part of the minor's patient file for four years.

(d) If the minor is emancipated, the person who shall perform the abortion or his agent shall obtain a written statement stating the name of the emancipated minor, that the minor is emancipated, the type of emancipation, the date and shall be signed by the minor. The written statement shall be signed in the presence of the person who shall perform the abortion or his agent and witnessed by him or the agent. The emancipated minor shall also provide a license or certificate of marriage, judgment or decree of divorce, order of emancipation or relieving her of the disabilities of nonage, or other court document evidencing her marriage, divorce, or emancipation. A copy of any such document shall be attached to the written statement and kept as a part of the minor's patient file for four years.

(e) A minor who elects not to seek or does not or cannot for any reason, including unavailability or refusal by either or both parents or legal guardian, obtain consent from either of her parents or legal guardian under this section, may petition, on her own behalf, the juvenile court, or court of equal standing, in the county in which the minor resides or in the county in which the abortion is to be performed for a waiver of the consent requirement of this section pursuant to the procedure of Section 26-21-4.

Alabama Code § 26-21-4. Judicial bypass

(a) A minor who elects not to seek or does not or cannot for any reason, obtain consent from either of her parents or legal guardian, may petition, on her own behalf, the juvenile court, or the court of equal standing, in the county in which the minor resides or in the county in which the abortion is to be performed for a waiver of the consent requirement of this chapter. Notice by the court to the minor's parents, parent or legal guardian shall not be required or permitted. The requirements and procedures under this chapter shall apply and are available to minors whether or not they are residents of this state.

(b) The minor may participate in proceedings in the court on her own behalf. The court shall advise her that she has a right to be represented by an attorney and that if she is unable to pay for the services of an attorney one will be appointed for her. If the court appoints an attorney to represent her such attorney shall be compensated as provided in Section 15-12-21. If the minor petitioner chooses to represent herself, such pleadings, documents or evidence that she may file with the court shall be liberally construed by the court so as to do substantial justice. Hearsay evidence shall be admissible.

(c) The court shall insure that the minor is given assistance in preparing and filing the petition and shall insure that the minor's identity is kept confidential. Such assistance may be provided by court personnel including intake personnel of juvenile probation services.

(d) The petition required in Section 26-21-3(e) shall be made under oath and shall include all of the following:

(1) A statement that the petitioner is pregnant;

(2) A statement that the petitioner is unmarried, under 18 years of age, and unemancipated;

(3) A statement that the petitioner wishes to have an abortion without the consent of either parent or legal guardian.

(4) An allegation of either or both of the following:

a. That the petitioner is sufficiently mature and well enough informed to intelligently decide whether to have an abortion without the consent of either of her parents or legal guardian.

b. That one or both of her parents or her guardian has engaged in a pattern of physical, sexual, or emotional abuse against her, or that the consent of her parents, parent or legal guardian otherwise is not in her best interest.

(5) A statement as to whether the petitioner has retained an attorney and the name, address and telephone number of her attorney.

(e) Court proceedings shall be given such precedence over other pending matters as is necessary to insure that the court may reach a decision promptly, but in no case, except as provided herein, shall the court fail to rule within 72 hours of the time the petition is filed, Saturdays, Sundays, and legal holidays excluded. Provided, however, this time requirement may be extended on the request of the minor. If a juvenile court judge is not available for the hearing provided herein, the clerk of the court in which the petition was filed shall forthwith notify the presiding circuit court judge and the presiding circuit court judge of the circuit shall immediately appoint a district or circuit court level judge to hear the petition.

(f) The required consent shall be waived if the court finds either:

(1) That the minor is mature and well-informed enough to make the abortion decision on her own; or

(2) That performance of the abortion would be in the best interest of the minor.

(g) A court that conducts proceedings under this section shall issue written and specific factual findings and legal conclusions supporting its decision and shall order that a confidential record of the evidence be maintained for at least four years. A transcript of the proceedings shall be recorded and if there is an appeal as provided in subsection (h), a transcript of the proceedings shall be prepared forthwith.

(h) An expedited confidential and anonymous appeal shall be available to any minor to whom the court denies a waiver of consent. If notice of appeal is given, the record of appeal shall be completed and the appeal shall be perfected within five days from the filing of the notice of appeal. Briefs shall not be required but may be permitted. Because time may be of the essence regarding the performance of the abortion, the Alabama Supreme Court shall issue promptly such additional rules as it deems are necessary to insure that appeals under this section are handled in an expeditious, confidential and anonymous manner.

(i) All proceedings under this chapter shall be confidential and anonymous. In all pleadings or court documents, the minor shall be identified by initials only.

(j) No fees or costs shall be required of any minor who avails herself of the procedures provided by this section.

Alabama Code § 26-21-5. Medical emergencies

This chapter shall not apply when, in the best clinical judgment of the attending physician on the facts of the case before him, a medical emergency exists that so compromises the health, safety or well-being of the mother as to require an immediate abortion. A physician who does not comply with Sections 26-21-3 and 26-21-4 by reason of this exception shall state in the medical record of the abortion, the medical indications on which his judgment was based.

Alabama Code § 26-21-6. Penalties for violation of chapter

Any person who intentionally performs or causes to be performed an abortion in violation of the provisions of this chapter or intentionally fails to conform to any requirement of this chapter, shall be guilty of a Class A misdemeanor. Any person found guilty under this section shall immediately forfeit any professional license they may hold.

Alabama Code § 26-21-7. Nonliability of physician

No physician who complies with the parental consent requirement(s) of this chapter shall be liable in any manner to the minor upon whom the abortion was performed for any claim whatsoever arising out of or based on the disclosure of any information concerning the medical condition of such minor to her parent(s) or legal guardian(s); provided that a physician who performs an abortion pursuant to a court order obtained under the provisions of this chapter, shall not disclose any information regarding same to the parent(s) or legal guardian(s) of the minor unless such disclosure is made pursuant to a court order. In no event shall the physician be under any duty to initiate proceedings in any court to secure a waiver of the parental consent requirement on behalf of any minor who has requested that an abortion be performed.

Alabama Code § 26-21-8. Confidentiality of records

(a) Records and information involving court proceedings conducted pursuant to Section 26-21-4 shall be confidential and shall not be disclosed other than to the minor, her attorney and necessary court personnel. Nothing in this subsection shall prohibit the keeping of statistical records and information as long as the anonymity of the minor is in no way compromised.

(b) Any person who shall disclose any records or information made confidential pursuant to subsection (a) of this section shall be guilty of a Class C misdemeanor.

(c) Provided, however, any person who performs abortions, or his agent, shall furnish to the Bureau of Vital Statistics, on confidential forms furnished by the bureau, the following: (1) the number of abortions performed on each unemancipated and emancipated minor with written consent; (2) the number of abortions performed on each unemancipated and emancipated minor pursuant to juvenile or other court proceedings pursuant to Section 26-21-3(e); and (3) the number of abortions performed pursuant to Section 26-21-5 on each unemancipated and emancipated minor. Such reporting shall be provided annually as prescribed by the Bureau of Vital Statistics which shall be retained by the bureau for at least seven years. Such information prescribed shall include nonconfidential statistics, including but not limited to: age, race and education level of minor.

(6) INFORMED CONSENT

Alabama has enacted informed consent legislation. Under the statutes a physician must inform and give to a woman, at least 24 hours before performing an abortion, a copy of printed materials which list agencies that offer assistance, adoption agencies, development of the unborn child, methods and risks of abortion and childbirth, father's obligations, and alternatives to abortion. The statutes also impose other requirements concerning information that a woman must be given prior to an abortion. One provision in the statutes, requiring payment of a fee for printed materials, was found invalid in *Summit Medical Center of Alabama, Inc. v. Riley*, 284 F.Supp.2d 1350 (M.D.Ala. 2003). The statutes have also been reviewed in *Summit Medical Center of Alabama, Inc. v. Riley*, 318 F.Supp.2d 1109 (M.D. Ala.2003) and *Summit Medical Center of Alabama, Inc. v. Siegelman*, 227 F.Supp.2d 1194 (M.D.Ala. 2002). The informed consent statutes are set out below.

Alabama Code § 26-23A-1. Short title

This chapter shall be known and cited as "The Woman's Right to Know Act."

Alabama Code § 26-23A-2. Legislative findings; purpose

(a) The Legislature of the State of Alabama finds that:

(1) It is essential to the psychological and physical well-being of a woman considering an abortion that she receive complete and accurate information on her alternatives.

(2) Most abortions are performed in clinics devoted solely to providing abortions and family planning services. Most women who seek abortions at these facilities do not have any relationship with the physician who performs the abortion, before or after the procedure. Most women do not return to the facility for post-surgical care. In most instances, the woman's only actual contact with the physician occurs simultaneously with the abortion procedure, with little opportunity to receive counseling concerning her decision.

(3) The decision to abort is an important, and often a stressful one, and it is desirable and imperative that it be made with full knowledge of its nature and consequences. The medical, emotional, and psychological consequences of an abortion are serious and can be lasting or life threatening.

(b) Based on the findings in subsection (a), it is the purpose of this chapter to ensure that every woman considering an abortion receives complete information on the procedure, risks, and her alternatives and to ensure that every woman who submits to an abortion procedure does so only after giving her voluntary and informed consent to the abortion procedure.

Alabama Code § 26-23A-3. Definitions

For the purposes of this chapter, the following terms have the following meanings:

(1) ABORTION. The use or prescription of any instrument, medicine, drug, or any other substance or device with the intent to terminate the pregnancy of a woman known to be pregnant. Such use or prescription is not an abortion if done with the intent to save the life or preserve the health of an unborn child, remove a dead unborn child, or to deliver an unborn child prematurely in order to preserve the health of both the mother (pregnant woman) and her unborn child.

(2) CONCEPTION. The fusion of a human spermatozoon with a human ovum.

(3) EMANCIPATED MINOR. Any minor who is or has been married or has by court order otherwise been legally freed from the care, custody, and control of her parents.

(4) GESTATIONAL AGE. The time that has elapsed since the first day of the woman's last menstrual period.

(5) MEDICAL EMERGENCY. That condition which, on the basis of the physician's good faith clinical judgment, so complicates the medical condition of a pregnant woman as to necessitate the immediate abortion of her pregnancy to avert her death or in which a delay will create serious risk of substantial and irreversible impairment of a major bodily function.

(6) MINOR. Any person under the age of 18 years.

(7) PHYSICIAN. Any person licensed to practice medicine in this state. The term includes medical doctors and doctors of osteopathy.

(8) PREGNANT or PREGNANCY. The female reproductive condition of having an unborn child in the mother's (woman's) body.

(9) QUALIFIED PERSON. An agent of the physician who is a psychologist, licensed social worker, licensed professional counselor, registered nurse, or physician.

(10) UNBORN CHILD. The offspring of any human person from conception until birth.

(11) VIABLE. That stage of fetal development when the life of the unborn child may be continued indefinitely outside the womb by natural or artificial life-supportive systems.

(12) WOMAN. Any female person.

Alabama Code § 26-23A-4.
Voluntary and informed consent required for abortion

Except in the case of a medical emergency, no abortion shall be performed or induced without the voluntary and informed consent of the woman upon whom the abortion is to be performed or induced. Except in the case of a medical emergency, consent to an abortion is voluntary and informed if and only if:

(a) At least 24 hours before the abortion, the physician who is to perform the abortion, the referring physician, or a qualified person has informed and provided the woman in person, or by return receipt certified mail restricted delivery, and if by mail, again in person prior to the abortion, a copy of the printed materials in Section 26-23A-5 which list agencies that offer assistance, adoption agencies, development of the unborn child, methods and risks of abortion and child-

birth, father's obligations, and alternatives to abortion. Mailing of the materials in Section 26-23A-5 may be arranged by telephone.

(b) Prior to an abortion, the physician who is to perform the abortion, the referring physician, or a qualified person has informed the woman in person:

(1) The name of the physician who will perform the abortion in writing or a business card.

(2) The nature of the proposed abortion method and associated risks and alternatives that a reasonable patient would consider material to the decision of whether or not to undergo the abortion.

(3) The probable gestational age of the unborn child at the time the abortion is to be performed, and the probable anatomical and physiological characteristics of the unborn child at the time the abortion is to be performed. If the unborn child is viable or has reached a gestational age of more than 19 weeks, that:

a. The unborn child may be able to survive outside the womb.

b. The woman has the right to request the physician to use the method of abortion that is most likely to preserve the life of the unborn child, provided such abortion is not otherwise prohibited by law.

c. If the unborn child is born alive, the attending physician has the legal obligation to take all reasonable steps necessary to maintain the life and health of the child.

(4) The physician who is to perform the abortion or the referring physician is required to perform an ultrasound on the unborn child before the abortion. The woman has a right to view the ultrasound before an abortion. The woman shall complete a required form to acknowledge that she either saw the ultrasound image of her unborn child or that she was offered the opportunity and rejected it.

(5) She has the right to view the videotape and ultrasound of her unborn child as described in Section 26-23A-6.

(6) Any need for anti–Rh immune globulin therapy, and if she is Rh negative, the likely consequences of refusing such therapy and the cost of the therapy.

(7) She cannot be forced or required by anyone to have an abortion. She is free to withhold or withdraw her consent for an abortion without affecting her right to future care or treatment and without the loss of any state or federally funded benefits to which she might otherwise be entitled.

(c) The woman shall complete and sign a form that she has received the information of subsections (a) and (b), and does provide her informed consent for an abortion on her unborn child.

(d) Prior to the performance of an abortion, the physician who is to perform the abortion or his or her agent shall receive the signed receipt of the certified mail dated 24 hours before the abortion, if mailed, and the signed forms that she has received the information of subsections (a) and (b) before the abortion, had the opportunity to view the video and the ultrasound of her unborn child, and provided her informed consent for an abortion. The abortion facility shall retain the signed receipt, signed forms, and the ultrasound in the woman's medical file for the time required by law, but not less than four years.

Alabama Code § 26-23A-5. Publication of required materials

(a) The Department of Public Health shall publish within 180 days after October 14, 2002, and shall update on an annual basis, the following easily comprehensible printed materials:

(1) Geographically indexed printed materials designed to inform the woman of public and private agencies and services available to provide medical and financial assistance to a woman through pregnancy, prenatal care, upon childbirth, and while her child is dependent. The materials shall include a comprehensive list of the agencies, a description of the services offered, and the telephone numbers and addresses of the agencies.

(2) The printed materials shall include a list of adoption agencies geographically indexed and that the law permits adoptive parents to pay the cost of prenatal care, childbirth and neonatal care.

(3) Printed materials that inform the pregnant woman of the probable anatomical and physiological characteristics of the unborn child at two-week gestational increments from fertilization to full term. It shall include color photographs of the developing child at each of the two-week gestational increments, a clear description of the unborn child's development, any relevant information on the possibility of the unborn child's survival, and dimensions of the unborn child. The materials shall be realistic, clear, objective, non-judgmental, and designed to convey only accurate scientific information about the unborn child at the various gestational ages.

(4) The materials shall contain objective information describing the methods of abortion procedures commonly employed and the medical risks of each, and the medical risks associated with carrying a child to term.

(5) The printed materials shall list the support obligations of the father of a child who is born alive.

(6) The printed materials shall state that it is unlawful for any individual to coerce a woman to undergo an abortion, that any physician who performs an abortion upon a woman without her informed consent may be liable to her for damages in a civil action at law.

(7) The material shall include the following statement: "There are many public and private agencies willing and able to help you to carry your child to term, and to assist you and your child after your child is born, whether you choose to keep your child or place him or her for adoption. The State of Alabama strongly urges you to contact those agencies before making a final decision about abortion. The law requires that your physician or his or her agent give you the opportunity to call agencies like these before you undergo an abortion."

(b) The materials in subsection (a) shall be in a bound booklet, shall contain large clear photographs, and shall be printed in a typeface large enough to be clearly legible.

(c) The materials required under this section and the videotape described in Section 26-23A-6 shall be available to the general public, from the Department of Public Health upon request, and appropriate number to any person, facility, or hospital. The department may charge a reasonable fee based on the cost of producing the materials and videotape.

Alabama Code § 26-23A-6.
Availability of information in video format

(a) All facilities where abortions are performed and all facilities of physicians who refer for abortion shall have video viewing equipment. The video that may be shown to those who want to see it shall be identified by title, updated from time to time by the Department of Public Health, and shall be objective, non-judgmental, and designed to convey accurate scientific and medical information, and shall contain at a minimum, the information required in subdivisions (3), (4), (5), (6), and (7) of subsection (a) of Section 26-23A-5.

(b) All facilities where abortions are performed and all facilities of physicians who refer for abortion shall have ultrasound equipment. An ultrasound shall be performed on each unborn child before an abortion is performed.

(c) The Department of Public Health shall develop a signature form for verifying that she has received the complete information as described in Section 26-23A-4, was offered the opportunity of viewing the video and ultrasound image of her unborn child, and provides her informed consent for an abortion on her unborn child.

(d) Facilities as used in this section shall not include hospitals that do

not regularly or routinely perform abortions or are otherwise not defined by any statute or regulation as an abortion or reproductive health center. This shall not, however, relieve any facility or physician to whom this section is applicable from the obligations stated herein.

Alabama Code § 26-23A-7.
Abortions to be performed by physician

Only a physician may perform an abortion.

Alabama Code § 26-23A-8. Medical emergency abortions

(a) Where a medical emergency compels the performance of an abortion, the physician shall inform the woman, before the abortion if possible, of the medical indications supporting his or her judgment that an abortion is necessary to avert her death or to avert substantial and irreversible impairment of a major bodily function.

(b) The Department of Public Health shall develop a signature form for recording the medical conditions associated with a medical emergency abortion. A signed copy of the abortion, and the original copy retained in the woman's medical file for the time required by law, but not less than four years.

Alabama Code § 26-23A-9. Violations

(a) Any person who intentionally, knowingly, or recklessly violates this chapter is guilty on a first offense of a Class B misdemeanor, on a second offense of a Class A misdemeanor, and on a third or subsequent offense of a Class C felony.

(b) After two convictions within a 12-month period of any person or persons at a specific abortion or reproductive health center, the license of such center shall be suspended for a period of 24 months and may be reinstated after that time only on conditions as the Department of Public Health requires to assure compliance with this chapter.

Alabama Code § 26-23A-10. Remedies

In addition to whatever remedies are available under the common or statutory law of this state, failure to comply with the requirements of this chapter shall:

(1) Provide a basis for a civil action for compensatory and punitive damages. Any conviction under this chapter shall be admissible in a civil suit as prima facie evidence of a failure to obtain an informed consent or parental or judicial consent. The civil action may be based on a claim that the act was a result of simple negligence, gross negligence, wantonness, willfulness, intention, or other legal standard of care.

(2) Provide a basis for professional disciplinary action under any applicable statutory or regulatory procedure for the suspension or revocation of any license for physicians, psychologists, licensed social workers, licensed professional counselors, registered nurses, or other licensed or regulated persons. Any conviction of any person for any failure to comply with the requirements of this chapter shall result in the automatic suspension of his or her license for a period of at least one year and shall be reinstated after that time only on such conditions as the appropriate regulatory or licensing body shall require to insure compliance with this chapter.

(3) Provide a basis for recovery for the woman for the wrongful death of the child, whether or not the unborn child was viable at the time the abortion was performed or was born alive.

Alabama Code § 26-23A-11. Anonymity in court proceedings

In every civil or criminal proceeding or action brought under this chapter, the court shall rule whether the anonymity of any woman upon whom an abortion has been performed or attempted, shall be preserved from public disclosure if she does not give her consent to such disclosure. The court, upon motion or sua sponte, shall issue written orders to the parties, witnesses, and counsel and shall direct the sealing of the record and exclusion of individuals from courtrooms or hearing rooms to the extent necessary to safeguard her identity from public disclosure. In the absence of written consent of the woman upon whom an abortion has been performed or attempted, anyone, other than a public official, who brings an action under Section 26-23A-10 shall do so under a pseudonym. This section may not be construed to conceal the identity of the plaintiff or of witnesses from the defendant.

Alabama Code § 26-23A-12. Construction of chapter

Nothing in this chapter shall be construed as creating or recognizing a right to abortion. It is not the intention of this chapter to make lawful an abortion that is currently unlawful nor to deny a woman an abortion that is lawful. Following abortion counseling, the withdrawal of consent to an abortion must be followed with appropriate referrals to ensure adequate care for a child that is to be delivered.

Alabama Code § 26-23A-13. Severability

If any one or more provision, section, subsection, sentence, clause, phrase, or word of this chapter or the application thereof to any person or circumstance is found to be invalid or unconstitutional, the same is hereby declared to be severable and the balance of this chapter shall remain effective. The Legislature hereby declares that it would have passed this chapter, and each provision, section, subsection, sentence, clause, phrase, or word thereof, irrespective of the fact that any one or more provision, section, subsection, sentence, clause, phrase, or word be declared invalid or unconstitutional.

(7) FETAL DEATH REPORT

Alabama requires a report of every fetal death, including induced abortion, be made to a state agency. The statute addressing the issue is set out below.

Alabama Code § 22-9A-13. Reports of fetal death

(a) A report of fetal death shall be filed with the Office of Vital Statistics, or as otherwise directed by the State Registrar, within five days after the occurrence is known if the fetus has advanced to, or beyond, the twentieth week of uterogestation.

(1) When a fetal death occurs in an institution, the person in charge of the institution or his or her designated representative shall prepare and file the report.

(2) When a fetal death occurs outside an institution, the physician in attendance shall prepare and file the report.

(3) When a fetal death occurs without medical attendance, the county medical examiner, the state medical examiner, or the coroner shall determine the cause of fetal death and shall prepare and file the report.

(4) When a fetal death occurs in a moving conveyance and the fetus is first removed from the conveyance in this state or when a dead fetus is found in this state and the place of fetal death is unknown, the fetal death shall be reported in this state. The county where the fetus was first removed from the conveyance or the dead fetus was found shall be considered the county of fetal death.

(b) A report of induced termination of pregnancy for each induced termination of pregnancy which occurs in this state shall be filed with the Office of Vital Statistics, or as otherwise directed by the State Registrar, no later than 10 days after the last day of the month during which the procedure was performed.

(1) When the induced termination of pregnancy is performed in an institution, the person in charge of the institution or his or her designated representative shall prepare and file the report.

(2) When the induced termination of pregnancy is performed outside an institution, the physician in attendance shall prepare and file the report.

(3) Reports of induced termination of pregnancy shall not contain the name or the address of the patient whose pregnancy was termi-

nated, nor shall the report contain any other information identifying the patient.

(4) Individual induced termination of pregnancy reports shall be maintained in strict confidence by the Office of Vital Statistics, shall not be available for public inspection, shall not be available in court for any purpose, and shall not be subject to discovery in any civil action except as provided in subdivision (b)(5) of this section.

(5) The Office of Vital Statistics shall periodically make available aggregate data about the induced terminations of pregnancy performed in this state, but the Office of Vital Statistics shall not release the names of individual physicians or other staff members employed by institutions performing induced terminations of pregnancy. The Office of Vital Statistics shall not release the number of procedures performed by any particular institution or physician, except at the request of the board or its attorney pursuant to an investigation of civil or criminal legal action related to licensure or the need for licensure of health facilities or similar investigation or legal action for failure to file reports required by this section.

(6) The State Registrar may authorize the use of other aggregate statistical data for official government use.

(c) The reports required under this section are statistical reports only and are not to be incorporated into the official records of the Office of Vital Statistics. Certified copies of these records shall not be issued by the Office of Vital Statistics. Except when copies of reports must be maintained pursuant to subdivision (b)(5) of this section, the State Registrar shall dispose of all individual reports received as soon as practicable after data from the forms is transferred to the database of the Center for Health Statistics, or after the board or its attorney declares there is no further need for the forms pursuant to subdivision (b)(5) of this section. Such disposal shall follow procedures of the State Records Commission.

(d) Subsection (c) shall also apply to all records of fetal death and induced termination of pregnancy filed in the Office of Vital Statistics prior to adoption of this chapter.

(8) INJURY TO PREGNANT WOMAN

Alabama has made it a criminal offense to cause the death of a fetus through injury to a pregnant woman. The statute addressing the issue is set out below.

Alabama Code § 13A-6-1. Definitions

(a) As used in Article 1 and Article 2, the following terms shall have the meanings ascribed to them by this section:

(1) CRIMINAL HOMICIDE. Murder, manslaughter, or criminally negligent homicide.

(2) HOMICIDE. A person commits criminal homicide if he intentionally, knowingly, recklessly or with criminal negligence causes the death of another person.

(3) PERSON. The term, when referring to the victim of a criminal homicide or assault, means a human being, including an unborn child in utero at any stage of development, regardless of viability.

(b) Article 1 or Article 2 shall not apply to the death or injury to an unborn child alleged to be caused by medication or medical care or treatment provided to a pregnant woman when performed by a physician or other licensed health care provider.

Mistake, or unintentional error on the part of a licensed physician or other licensed health care provider or his or her employee or agent or any person acting on behalf of the patient shall not subject the licensed physician or other licensed health care provider or person acting on behalf of the patient to any criminal liability under this section.

Medical care or treatment includes, but is not limited to, ordering, dispensation or administration of prescribed medications and medical procedures.

(c) A victim of domestic violence or sexual assault may not be charged under Article 1 or Article 2 for the injury or death of an unborn child caused by a crime of domestic violence or rape perpetrated upon her.

(d) Nothing in Article 1 or Article 2 shall permit the prosecution of (1) any person for conduct relating to an abortion for which the consent of the pregnant woman or a person authorized by law to act on her behalf has been obtained or for which consent is implied by law or (2) any woman with respect to her unborn child.

(e) Nothing in this section shall make it a crime to perform or obtain an abortion that is otherwise legal. Nothing in this section shall be construed to make an abortion legal which is not otherwise authorized by law.

Alan Guttmacher Institute *see* **Guttmacher Institute**

Alaska

(1) OVERVIEW

The state of Alaska enacted its first criminal abortion statute on March 3, 1899. Shortly before the 1973 decision by the United States Supreme Court in *Roe v. Wade*, which legalized abortion in the nation, Alaska had repealed its criminal abortion statute. Alaska has taken affirmative steps to respond to *Roe* and its progeny. The state has addressed numerous abortion issues by statute that include general abortion limitations, abortion by minors, partial-birth abortion, informed consent, fetal death report, and injury to pregnant woman.

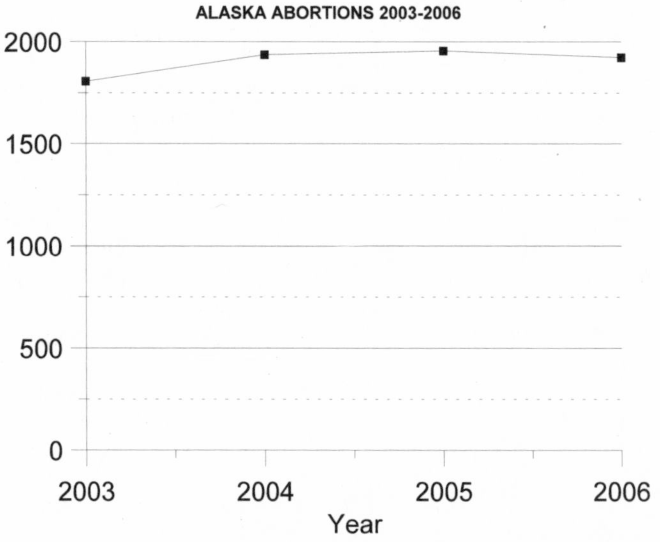

Source: **Alaska Bureau of Vital Statistics.**

Alaska Abortion by Age Group 2003–2006
Age Group (yrs)

Year	*<15*	*15–19*	*20–24*	*25–29*	*30–34*	*35–39*	*≥40*	*Unknown*
2003	12	373	600	364	232	152	67	6
2004	10	417	677	389	236	139	68	1
2005	12	374	679	421	242	146	77	5
2006	7	362	667	447	224	147	54	15
Total	41	1,526	2,623	1,621	934	584	266	27

Source: **Alaska Bureau of Vital Statistics.**

(2) GENERAL ABORTION LIMITATIONS

Alaska's general abortion limitations statute restricts the performance of abortions to physicians. The statute requires a woman be in the state at least thirty days before having an abortion. It also provides a civil cause action for an abortion performed on a minor that was not done in compliance with statutory requirements. Under the

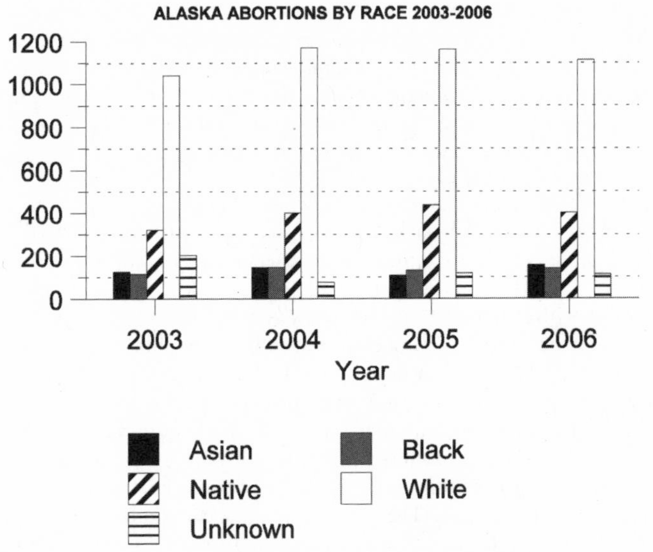

Source: Alaska Bureau of Vital Statistics.

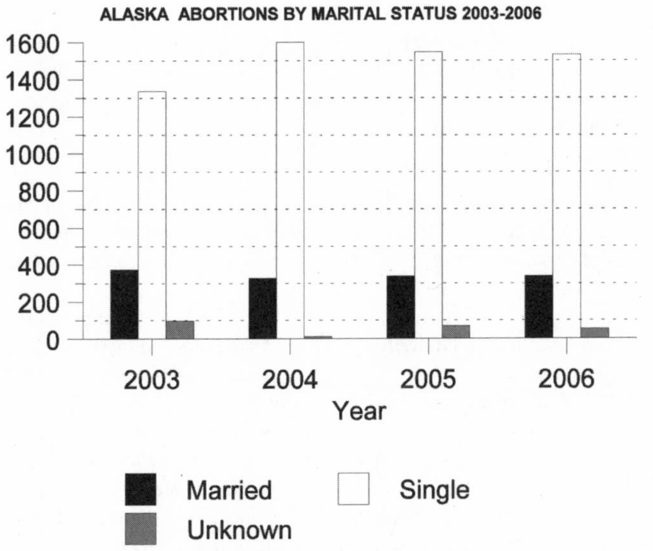

Source: Alaska Bureau of Vital Statistics.

Alaska Abortion by Education Level of Female 2003–2006

	Education Level Completed			
Year	*<12*	*12*	*≥13*	*Unknown*
2003	197	628	439	542
2004	271	873	574	219
2005	282	826	684	164
2006	264	996	454	209
Total	1,014	3,323	2,151	1,134

Source: Alaska Bureau of Vital Statistics.

statute hospitals and employees are not obligated to participate in performing abortions. However, in *Valley Hosp. Ass'n v. Mat-Su Coalition for Choice*, 948 P.2d 963 (Alaska 1997) the Alaska supreme court held that the statutory provision declaring that hospitals are not required to participate in abortions was unconstitutional to extent that it applied to quasi-public institutions. The general abortion limitations statute was also addressed in *State v. Planned Parenthood of*

Alaska Prior Abortion by Female 2003–2006

	Prior Abortion						
Year	*None*	*1*	*2*	*3*	*4*	*≥5*	*Not known*
2003	1,111	409	170	57	23	15	21
2004	1,223	442	187	41	20	11	13
2005	1,281	431	126	50	23	9	36
2006	1,146	466	184	64	20	16	27
Total	4,761	1,748	667	212	86	51	97

Source: Alaska Bureau of Vital Statistics.

Alaska Abortion by Weeks of Gestation 2003–2006

	Year				
Weeks of Gestation	*2003*	*2004*	*2005*	*2006*	***Total***
1–4	25	42	23	26	116
5–8	991	1,081	1,101	1,127	4,300
9–12	687	723	733	655	2,798
13–16	64	72	76	87	29
17–20	11	11	5	0	27
21–24	1	1	1	0	3
Not known	27	7	17	28	79

Source: Alaska Bureau of Vital Statistics.

Alaska, Inc., 35 P.3d 30 (Alaska 2001); *State v. Planned Parenthood of Alaska, Inc.*, 28 P.3d 904 (Alaska 2001); *Bird v. Municipality of Anchorage*, 787 P.2d 119 (Alaska 1990); and *Cleveland v. Municipality of Anchorage*, 631 P.2d 1073 (Alaska 1981). The text of the statute, two other relevant statutes, are set out below.

Alaska Code § 18.16.090. Definitions

In this chapter,

(1) "abortion" means the use or prescription of an instrument, medicine, drug, or other substance or device to terminate the pregnancy of a woman known to be pregnant, except that "abortion" does not include the termination of a pregnancy if done with the intent to

(A) save the life or preserve the health of the unborn child;

(B) deliver the unborn child prematurely to preserve the health of both the pregnant woman and the woman's child; or

(C) remove a dead unborn child;

(2) "unemancipated" means that a woman who is unmarried and under 17 years of age has not done any of the following:

(A) entered the armed services of the United States;

(B) become employed and self-subsisting;

(C) been emancipated under AS 09.55.590; or

(D) otherwise become independent from the care and control of the woman's parent, guardian, or custodian.

Alaska Code § 08.64.105. Regulation of abortion procedures

The [state medical] board shall adopt regulations necessary to carry into effect the provisions of AS 18.16.010 and shall define ethical, unprofessional, or dishonorable conduct as related to abortions, set standards of professional competency in the performance of abortions, and establish procedures and set standards for facilities, equipment, and care of patients in the performance of an abortion.

Alaska Code § 18.16.010. General abortion limitations

(a) An abortion may not be performed in this state unless

(1) the abortion is performed by a physician licensed by the State Medical Board under AS 08.64.200;

(2) the abortion is performed in a hospital or other facility approved for the purpose by the Department of Health and Social Services or a hospital operated by the federal government or an agency of the federal government;

(3) before an abortion is knowingly performed or induced on an unmarried, unemancipated woman under 17 years of age, consent has been given as required under AS 18.16.020 or a court has author-

ized the minor to consent to the abortion under AS 18.16.030 and the minor consents; for purposes of enforcing this paragraph, there is a rebuttable presumption that a woman who is unmarried and under 17 years of age is unemancipated;

(4) the woman is domiciled or physically present in the state for 30 days before the abortion; and

(5) the applicable requirements of AS 18.16.060 have been satisfied.

(b) Nothing in this section requires a hospital or person to participate in an abortion, nor is a hospital or person liable for refusing to participate in an abortion under this section.

(c) A person who knowingly violates a provision of this section, upon conviction, is punishable by a fine of not more than $1,000, or by imprisonment for not more than five years, or by both.

(d) Repealed by SLA 1997, ch. 14, § 6, eff. July 31, 1997.

(e) A person who performs or induces an abortion in violation of (a)(3) of this section is civilly liable to the pregnant minor and the minor's parents, guardian, or custodian for compensatory and punitive damages.

(f) It is an affirmative defense to a prosecution or claim for a violation of (a)(3) of this section that the pregnant minor provided the person who performed or induced the abortion with false, misleading, or incorrect information about the minor's age, marital status, or emancipation, and the person who performed or induced the abortion did not otherwise have reasonable cause to believe that the pregnant minor was under 17 years of age, unmarried, or unemancipated.

(g) It is an affirmative defense to a prosecution or claim for violation of (a)(3) of this section that compliance with the requirements of (a)(3) of this section was not possible because an immediate threat of serious risk to the life or physical health of the pregnant minor from the continuation of the pregnancy created a medical emergency necessitating the immediate performance or inducement of an abortion. In this subsection, "medical emergency" means a condition that, on the basis of the physician's or surgeon's good faith clinical judgment, so complicates the medical condition of a pregnant minor that

(1) an immediate abortion of the minor's pregnancy is necessary to avert the minor's death; or

(2) a delay in providing an abortion will create serious risk of substantial and irreversible impairment of a major bodily function of the pregnant minor.

(h) A physician or other health care provider is liable for failure to obtain the informed consent of a person as required under AS 18.16.060 if the claimant establishes by a preponderance of the evidence that the provider has failed to inform the person of the common risks and reasonable alternatives to the proposed abortion procedure and that, but for that failure, the person would not have consented to the abortion procedure.

(i) It is a defense to any action for the alleged failure to obtain the informed consent of a person under (h) of this section that

(1) the risk not disclosed is too commonly known or is too remote to require disclosure; or

(2) the person who is the subject of the alleged failure to obtain the informed consent stated to the physician or other health care provider that the person would or would not undergo the abortion procedure regardless of the risk involved or that the person did not want to be informed of the matters to which the person would be entitled to be informed.

(j) In an action under (h) of this section, there is a rebuttable presumption that an abortion was performed with the pregnant woman's informed consent if the person who performed the abortion submits into evidence a copy of the woman's written certification required under AS 18.16. 060(b).

Alaska Code § 13.52.050. Decisions for exceptional procedures

Unless there is a durable power of attorney for health care or another writing clearly expressing an individual's intent to the contrary, an agent or surrogate may not consent on behalf of a patient to an abortion ... except when the abortion ... is necessary to preserve the life of the patient or to prevent serious impairment of the health of the patient.

(3) ABORTION BY MINORS

Under the laws of Alaska no physician may perform an abortion upon an unemancipated minor unless he/she first obtains the written consent of either parent or the legal guardian of the minor. In compliance with federal constitutional law, Alaska has provided a judicial waiver procedure for an unemancipated minor to obtain an abortion without parental or guardian consent. If an unemancipated minor elects not to seek, or cannot for any reason obtain consent from either of her parents or legal guardian, the minor may petition a trial court for a waiver of the consent requirement. A minor has a right to an attorney at the proceeding and if she cannot afford one, the court must appoint her an attorney. The required parental consent may be waived if the court finds (1) that the minor is mature and well-informed enough to make the abortion decision on her own, (2) evidence of physical abuse, sexual abuse, or a pattern of emotional abuse of the minor by one or both of her parents or guardian, or (2) that performance of the abortion would be in the best interest of the minor. An expedited appeal is available to any minor to whom the court denies a waiver of consent. The abortion statutes for minors were addressed in *State v. Planned Parenthood of Alaska, Inc.*, 35 P.3d 30 (Alaska 2001). The statutes are set out below.

Alaska Code § 18.16.020. Consent required for minor

A person may not knowingly perform or induce an abortion upon a minor who is known to the person to be pregnant, unmarried, under 17 years of age, and unemancipated unless, before the abortion, at least one of the following applies:

(1) one of the minor's parents or the minor's guardian or custodian has consented in writing to the performance or inducement of the abortion;

(2) a court issues an order under § 18.16.030 authorizing the minor to consent to the abortion without consent of a parent, guardian, or custodian, and the minor consents to the abortion; or

(3) a court, by its inaction under § 18.16.030, constructively has authorized the minor to consent to the abortion without consent of a parent, guardian, or custodian, and the minor consents to the abortion.

Alaska Code § 18.16.030. Judicial bypass

(a) A woman who is pregnant, unmarried, under 17 years of age, and unemancipated who wishes to have an abortion without the consent of a parent, guardian, or custodian may file a complaint in the superior court requesting the issuance of an order authorizing the minor to consent to the performance or inducement of an abortion without the consent of a parent, guardian, or custodian.

(b) The complaint shall be made under oath and must include all of the following:

(1) a statement that the complainant is pregnant;

(2) a statement that the complainant is unmarried, under 17 years of age, and unemancipated;

(3) a statement that the complainant wishes to have an abortion without the consent of a parent, guardian, or custodian;

(4) an allegation of either or both of the following:

(A) that the complainant is sufficiently mature and well enough informed to decide intelligently whether to have an abortion without the consent of a parent, guardian, or custodian; or

(B) that one or both of the minor's parents or the minor's

guardian or custodian was engaged in physical abuse, sexual abuse, or a pattern of emotional abuse against the minor, or that the consent of a parent, guardian, or custodian otherwise is not in the minor's best interest;

(5) a statement as to whether the complainant has retained an attorney and, if an attorney has been retained, the name, address, and telephone number of the attorney.

(c) The court shall fix a time for a hearing on any complaint filed under (a) of this section and shall keep a record of all testimony and other oral proceedings in the action. The hearing shall be held at the earliest possible time, but not later than the fifth business day after the day that the complaint is filed. The court shall enter judgment on the complaint immediately after the hearing is concluded. If the hearing required by this subsection is not held by the fifth business day after the complaint is filed, the failure to hold the hearing shall be considered to be a constructive order of the court authorizing the complainant to consent to the performance or inducement of an abortion without the consent of a parent, guardian, or custodian, and the complainant and any other person may rely on the constructive order to the same extent as if the court actually had issued an order under this section authorizing the complainant to consent to the performance or inducement of an abortion without such consent.

(d) If the complainant has not retained an attorney, the court shall appoint an attorney to represent the complainant.

(e) If the complainant makes only the allegation set out in (b)(4)(A) of this section and if the court finds by clear and convincing evidence that the complainant is sufficiently mature and well enough informed to decide intelligently whether to have an abortion, the court shall issue an order authorizing the complainant to consent to the performance or inducement of an abortion without the consent of a parent, guardian, or custodian. If the court does not make the finding specified in this subsection, it shall dismiss the complaint.

(f) If the complainant makes only the allegation set out in (b)(4)(B) of this section and the court finds that there is clear and convincing evidence of physical abuse, sexual abuse, or a pattern of emotional abuse of the complainant by one or both of the minor's parents or the minor's guardian or custodian, or by clear and convincing evidence the consent of the parents, guardian, or custodian of the complainant otherwise is not in the best interest of the complainant, the court shall issue an order authorizing the complainant to consent to the performance or inducement of an abortion without the consent of a parent, guardian, or custodian. If the court does not make the finding specified in this subsection, it shall dismiss the complaint.

(g) If the complainant makes both of the allegations set out in (b)(4) of this section, the court shall proceed as follows:

(1) the court first shall determine whether it can make the finding specified in (e) of this section and, if so, shall issue an order under that subsection; if the court issues an order under this paragraph, it may not proceed under (f) of this section; if the court does not make the finding specified in (e) of this section, it shall proceed under (2) of this subsection;

(2) if the court under (1) of this subsection does not make the finding specified in (e) of this section, it shall proceed to determine whether it can make the finding specified in (f) of this section and, if so, shall issue an order under that subsection; if the court does not make the finding specified in (f) of this section, it shall dismiss the complaint.

(h) The court may not notify the parents, guardian, or custodian of the complainant that the complainant is pregnant or wants to have an abortion.

(i) If the court dismisses the complaint, the complainant has the right to appeal the decision to the supreme court, and the superior court immediately shall notify the complainant that there is a right to appeal.

(j) If the complainant files a notice of appeal authorized under this section, the superior court shall deliver a copy of the notice of appeal and the record on appeal to the supreme court within four days after the notice of appeal is filed. Upon receipt of the notice and record, the clerk of the supreme court shall place the appeal on the docket. The appellant shall file a brief within four days after the appeal is docketed. Unless the appellant waives the right to oral argument, the supreme court shall hear oral argument within five days after the appeal is docketed. The supreme court shall enter judgment in the appeal immediately after the oral argument or, if oral argument has been waived, within five days after the appeal is docketed. Upon motion of the appellant and for good cause shown, the supreme court may shorten or extend the maximum times set out in this subsection. However, in any case, if judgment is not entered within five days after the appeal is docketed, the failure to enter the judgment shall be considered to be a constructive order of the court authorizing the appellant to consent to the performance or inducement of an abortion without the consent of a parent, guardian, or custodian, and the appellant and any other person may rely on the constructive order to the same extent as if the court actually had entered a judgment under this subsection authorizing the appellant to consent to the performance or inducement of an abortion without consent of another person. In the interest of justice, the supreme court, in an appeal under this subsection, shall liberally modify or dispense with the formal requirements that normally apply as to the contents and form of an appellant's brief.

(k) Each hearing under this section, and all proceedings under (j) of this section, shall be conducted in a manner that will preserve the anonymity of the complainant. The complaint and all other papers and records that pertain to an action commenced under this section, including papers and records that pertain to an appeal under this section, shall be kept confidential and are not public records under § 40.25.110—40.25.120.

(l) The supreme court shall prescribe complaint and notice of appeal forms that shall be used by a complainant filing a complaint or appeal under this section. The clerk of each superior court shall furnish blank copies of the forms, without charge, to any person who requests them.

(m) A filing fee may not be required of, and court costs may not be assessed against, a complainant filing a complaint under this section or an appellant filing an appeal under this section.

(n) Blank copies of the forms prescribed under (l) of this section and information on the proper procedures for filing a complaint or appeal shall be made available by the court system at the official location of each superior court, district court, and magistrate in the state. The information required under this subsection must also include notification to the minor that

(1) there is no filing fee required for either form;

(2) no court costs will be assessed against the minor for procedures under this section;

(3) an attorney will be appointed to represent the minor if the minor does not retain an attorney;

(4) the minor may request that the superior court with appropriate jurisdiction hold a telephonic hearing on the complaint so that the minor need not personally be present.

(4) PARTIAL-BIRTH ABORTION

Alaska criminalizes partial-birth abortions, except under limited conditions. Until it is definitively determined by a court, Alaska's partial-birth abortion statute may be invalid under the United States Supreme Court decision in *Stenberg v. Carhart*, which invalidated Nebraska's ban on partial-birth abortion. On the other hand, Alaska's partial-birth abortion statute, as currently written, may be valid under the United States Supreme Court decision in *Gonzales v. Carhart*, which approved of a federal statute that bans partial-birth abortion. The text of Alaska's partial-birth abortion statute is set out below.

Alaska Code § 18.16.050. Partial-birth abortions

(a) Notwithstanding compliance with AS 18.16.010, a person may not knowingly perform a partial-birth abortion unless a partial-birth abortion is necessary to save the life of a mother whose life is endangered by a physical disorder, illness, or injury and no other medical procedure would suffice for that purpose. Violation of this subsection is a class C felony.

(b) A woman upon whom a partial-birth abortion is performed may not be prosecuted under this section or under any other law if the prosecution is based on this section.

(c) In this section, "partial-birth abortion" means an abortion in which the person performing the abortion partially vaginally delivers a living fetus before killing the fetus and completing the delivery.

(5) INFORMED CONSENT

Alaska has an informed consent statute. Under the statute an abortion cannot be performed, except for a health emergency, until the person is given specific information and thereafter consents. The state also requires that an internet website be maintained to provide an alternative source for a person to view the information required prior to an abortion. The statutes are set out below.

Alaska Code § 18.16.060. Informed consent requirements

(a) Except as provided in (d) of this section, a person may not knowingly perform or induce an abortion without the voluntary and informed consent of

(1) a woman on whom an abortion is to be performed or induced;

(2) the parent, guardian, or custodian of a pregnant, unemancipated minor if required under AS 18.16.020; or

(3) a pregnant, unemancipated minor if authorized by a court under AS 18.16.030.

(b) Consent to an abortion is informed and voluntary when the woman or another person whose consent is required certifies in writing that the physician who is to perform the abortion, a member of the physician's staff who is a licensed health care provider, or the referring physician has verbally informed the woman or another person whose consent is required of the name of the physician who will perform the procedure and the gestational estimation of the pregnancy at the time the abortion is to be performed and has provided either

(1) the Internet information required to be maintained under AS 18.05.032; the physician or a member of the physician's staff who is a licensed health care provider shall provide a copy of the Internet information if a person requests a written copy; if a member of the physician's staff provides the information required under this paragraph, the member of the physician's staff shall offer the opportunity to consult with the physician; or

(2) information about the nature and risks of undergoing or not undergoing the proposed procedure that a reasonable patient would consider material to making a voluntary and informed decision of whether to undergo the procedure.

(c) The information required in (b) of this section shall be provided before the procedure in a private setting to protect privacy, maintain the confidentiality of the decision, ensure that the information focuses on the individual circumstances, and ensure an adequate opportunity to ask questions. Provision of the information telephonically or by electronic mail, regular mail, or facsimile transmittal before the person's appointment satisfies the requirements of this subsection as long as the person whose consent is required under (a) of this section has an opportunity to ask questions of the physician after receiving the information.

(d) Notwithstanding (a) of this section, informed consent that meets the requirements of (a)—(c) of this section is not required in the case of a medical emergency or if the pregnancy is the result of sexual assault under AS 11.41.410—11.41.427, sexual abuse of a minor under AS 11.41.434—11.41.440, incest under AS 11.41.450, or an offense under a law of another jurisdiction with elements similar to one of these offences. In this subsection, "medical emergency" means a condition that, on the basis of a physician's good faith clinical judgment, so complicates the medical condition of a pregnant woman that

(1) the immediate termination of the woman's pregnancy is necessary to avert the woman's death; or

(2) a delay in providing an abortion will create serious risk of substantial and irreversible impairment of a major bodily function of the woman.

Alaska Code § 18.05.032.
Information relating to pregnancy and pregnancy alternatives

(a) The department shall maintain on the Internet, in printable form, standard information that

(1) contains geographically indexed material designed to inform a person of public and private agencies, services, clinics, and facilities that are available to assist a woman with the woman's reproductive choices; the department shall include information about at least the following types of agencies, services, clinics, and facilities:

(A) agencies, services, clinics, and facilities designed to assist a woman through pregnancy, including adoption agencies, and counseling services;

(B) agencies, services, clinics, and facilities that provide abortion options and counseling and post-abortion counseling and services; and

(C) agencies, services, clinics, and facilities designed to assist with or provide contraceptive options and counseling for appropriate family planning;

(2) includes a comprehensive regional directory of the agencies, services, clinics, and facilities that request to be identified by the department under (1) of this subsection, a description of the services they offer, and the manner in which the agencies, services, clinics, and facilities may be contacted, including telephone numbers;

(3) provides information concerning the eligibility for medical assistance benefits for prenatal care, childbirth, neonatal care, abortion services, women's health care, and contraception;

(4) states that informed and voluntary consent is required under AS 18.16.060 for an abortion;

(5) provides information concerning the process by which a mother of a child may establish a child support order to assist in the support of a child;

(6) describes the fetal development of a typical unborn child at two-week gestational increments from fertilization to full-term, including links to photographs of a typical unborn child at four-week gestational increments, and relevant information about the possibility of an unborn child's survival at the various gestational ages; the information must be objective, nonjudgmental information that is reviewed and approved for medical accuracy by recognized obstetrical and gynecological specialists designated by the State Medical Board and designed to convey only accurate scientific information about unborn children at various gestational ages;

(7) contains objective, unbiased information that is reviewed and approved for medical accuracy by recognized obstetrical and gynecological specialists designated by the State Medical Board and that describes the methods of abortion procedures and treatments commonly employed and the medical risks and possible complications commonly associated with each procedure and treatment, as well as the possible physical and psychological effects that have been associated with having an abortion;

(8) contains objective, unbiased information that is reviewed and approved for medical accuracy by recognized obstetrical and gynecological specialists designated by the State Medical Board and that describes the possible medical risks and complications commonly as-

sociated with pregnancy and childbirth, as well as the possible physical and psychological effects that have been associated with carrying a child to term;

(9) contains objective, unbiased information that is reviewed and approved for medical accuracy by recognized obstetrical and gynecological specialists designated by the State Medical Board and that concerns the harmful effects on an unborn child when a woman consumes alcohol, tobacco, or illegal drugs during pregnancy;

(10) contains objective, unbiased, and comprehensive information that is reviewed and approved for medical accuracy by recognized obstetrical and gynecological specialists designated by the State Medical Board and that describes the different types of available contraceptive choices, including abstinence and natural family planning, that describes the methods of contraception that are intended to prevent fertilization and the methods that are intended to prevent implantation of a fertilized egg, and that describes the reliability, psychological effects, medical risks, and complications commonly associated with each method;

(11) contains a disclaimer on the website home page concerning the graphic or sensitive nature of the information contained on the website;

(12) contains a signature form by which a person may indicate the person has reviewed the information.

(b) The department shall adopt regulations establishing procedures for establishing and maintaining the information under this section.

(c) In this section,

(1) "abortion" has the meaning given in AS 18.16.090;

(2) "fertilization" means the fusion of a human spermatozoon with a human ovum;

(3) "gestational age" means the age of the unborn child as calculated from the first day of the last menstrual period of a pregnant woman;

(4) "unborn child" means the offspring of a human being in utero at various stages of biological development.

(6) FETAL DEATH REPORT

Alaska requires a report of every induced abortion be made to a state agency. The statute addressing the issue is set out below.

Alaska Code § 18.50.245. Report of induced abortion

(a) A hospital, clinic, or other institution where an induced termination of pregnancy is performed in the state shall submit a report directly to the state registrar within 30 days after the induced termination is completed. The report may not contain the name of the patient whose pregnancy was terminated but must contain the information required by the state registrar in regulations adopted under this section.

(b) When an induced termination of pregnancy is performed by a physician outside of a hospital, clinic, or other institution, the physician shall submit the report required under this section within 30 days after the induced termination of pregnancy is completed.

(c) For purposes of this section,

(1) an induced termination of pregnancy is considered to be performed where the act interrupting the pregnancy is performed even if the resultant expulsion of the product of conception occurs elsewhere;

(2) prescription of a medicine by a physician who knows that the medicine will be taken with the intention of inducing termination of a pregnancy is considered to be the act that interrupts the pregnancy even if the medicine is taken outside of the physician's presence; and

(3) an induced termination of pregnancy is considered to be completed when the product of conception is extracted or expulsed.

(d) The state registrar shall annually prepare a statistical report based on the reports received under this section. The report must include the types of information required under (e) of this section, except that the statistical report may not identify or give information that can be used to identify the name of any physician who performed an induced termination of pregnancy, the name of any facility in which an induced termination of pregnancy occurred, or the name of the municipality or community in which the induced termination of pregnancy occurred. The data gathered from the reports received under this section may only be presented in aggregate statistics, not individually, so that specific individuals may not be identified. After preparation of the annual report, the state registrar shall destroy the reports received under this section.

(e) The state registrar shall adopt regulations to implement this section. The regulations that establish the information that will be required in a report of an induced termination of pregnancy

(1) must require information substantially similar to the information required under the United States Standard Report of Induced Termination of Pregnancy, as published by the National Center for Health Statistics, Centers for Disease Control and Prevention, United States Department of Health and Human Services, in April 1998, as part of DHHS Publication No. (PHS) 98-1117;

(2) must require, if known, whether the unidentified patient requested and received a written copy of the information required to be maintained on the Internet under AS 18.05.032; and

(3) may not include provisions that would violate a woman's privacy by requiring the woman's name or any identifying information in the report.

(7) INJURY TO PREGNANT WOMAN

Alaska has made it a criminal offense to cause the death of a fetus through injury to a pregnant woman. The statutes addressing the issue are set out below.

Alaska Code § 11.41.150. Murder of an unborn child

(a) A person commits the crime of murder of an unborn child if the person

(1) with intent to cause the death of an unborn child or of another person, causes the death of an unborn child;

(2) with intent to cause serious physical injury to an unborn child or to another person or knowing that the conduct is substantially certain to cause death or serious physical injury to an unborn child or to another person, causes the death of an unborn child;

(3) while acting alone or with one or more persons, commits or attempts to commit arson in the first degree, kidnapping, sexual assault in the first degree, sexual assault in the second degree, sexual abuse of a minor in the first degree, sexual abuse of a minor in the second degree, burglary in the first degree, escape in the first or second degree, robbery in any degree, or misconduct involving a controlled substance under AS 11.71.010(a), 11.71.020(a), 11.71.030(a)(1) or (2), or 11.71.040(a)(1) or (2), and, in the course of or in furtherance of that crime or in immediate flight from that crime, any person causes the death of an unborn child;

(4) knowingly engages in conduct that results in the death of an unborn child under circumstances manifesting an extreme indifference to the value of human life; for purposes of this paragraph, a pregnant woman's decision to remain in a relationship in which domestic violence, as defined in AS 18.66.990, has occurred does not constitute conduct manifesting an extreme indifference to the value of human life.

(b) A person may not be convicted under (a)(3) of this section if the only underlying crime is burglary, the sole purpose of the burglary is a criminal homicide, and the unborn child killed is the intended victim of the defendant. However, if the defendant causes the death of another unborn child, the defendant may be convicted under (a)(3) of this section. Nothing in this subsection precludes a prosecution for or conviction of murder in the first degree or murder in the second degree, murder of an unborn child under AS 11.41.150 (a)(1), (2), or (4), or any other crime.

(c) Murder of an unborn child is an unclassified felony.

Alaska Code § 11.41.160. Manslaughter of an unborn child

(a) A person commits the crime of manslaughter of an unborn child if, under circumstances not amounting to murder of an unborn child, the person intentionally, knowingly, or recklessly causes the death of an unborn child.

(b) Manslaughter of an unborn child is a class A felony.

Alaska Code § 11.41.170.
Criminally negligent homicide of an unborn child

(a) A person commits the crime of criminally negligent homicide of an unborn child if, with criminal negligence, the person causes the death of an unborn child.

(b) Criminally negligent homicide of an unborn child is a class B felony.

Alaska Code § 11.41.180. Applicability of fetal homicide statutes

[Alaska Code §§] 11.41.150—11.41.170 do not apply to acts that

(1) cause the death of an unborn child if those acts were committed during a legal abortion to which the pregnant woman consented or a person authorized by law to act on her behalf consented, or for which such consent is implied by law;

(2) are committed under usual and customary standards of medical practice during diagnostic testing, therapeutic treatment, or to assist a pregnancy; or

(3) are committed by a pregnant woman against herself and her own unborn child.

Alcohol and Pregnancy *see* **Fetal Alcohol Syndrome**

Alexander Disease

Alexander disease is congenital disorder of the nervous system. The disease affects males mostly. Symptoms of the disorder include mental retardation, abnormal growth, dementia, enlargement of the brain and head and seizures. There is no cure for the disease. Most children with the disease do not survive past the age of 6. *See also* **Birth Defects and Abortion**

Alito, Samuel Anthony, Jr.

Samuel Anthony Alito, Jr. was nominated by President George W. Bush to fill an associate justice vacancy on the United States Supreme Court. The nomination was confirmed by the Senate and Justice Alito took his seat on the Supreme Court on January 31, 2006. Justice Alito came to the Supreme Court with a reputation of having a conservative judicial philosophy.

Justice Altio was born in Trenton, New Jersey on April 1, 1950. He received an undergraduate from Princeton University in 1972, and a law degree from Yale Law School in 1975. Justice Alito served as a law clerk for the United States Court of Appeals for the Third Circuit the first year after graduating from law school. He was subsequently employed as a federal attorney with several agencies from 1977–1990. In 1990 Justice Alito was appointed to the United States Court of Appeals for the Third Circuit.

During Justice Alito's tenure on the Supreme Court he has voted in a few abortion related cases. Thus far his voting pattern indicates that he is not in favor of using the constitution to expand abortion rights for women.

(1) Concurring opinions written. Justice Alito wrote a concurring opinion in *Federal Election Commission v. Wisconsin Right to Life, Inc.*, which held that the electioneering communications provisions of a federal statute violated a pro-life organization's First Amendment right to broadcast political issue oriented advertisements shortly before primary and general elections.

(2) Majority opinions voted with only. Justice Alito voted with the majority opinion in *Gonzales v. Carhart*, which held that the Partial-Birth Abortion Ban Act of 2003 was not facially unconstitutional, because it outlined the abortion procedure that was banned, and the Act did not have to provide an exception for the health of a woman.

Justice Alito came to the Supreme Court with a reputation of supporting the views of pro-life abortion advocates (collection, Supreme Court Historical Society, photograph by Steve Petteway, Supreme Court).

Alliance for Reproductive Justice

Alliance for Reproductive Justice (ARL) is pro-choice organization that is based in Anchorage, Alaska. ARL was created to protect and promote reproductive rights and services through education, advocacy and referrals. The organization promotes policies and practices that protect women's access to comprehensive sexual and reproductive health care through education and grassroots organizing strategies. ARL seeks to empower women, girls and men to improve reproductive health care services, including abortion care, and related policies in Alaska. *See also* **Pro-Choice Organizations**

Alloimmune Factors

Alloimmune factors refers to possible causes for early spontaneous abortion. These factors are believed to cause the rejection of embryonic or fetal tissue by a woman's immune system. Normally a woman's immune system forms "blocking antibodies" in response to pregnancy. The blocking antibodies prevent a woman's immune system's efforts to reject the pregnancy. When the blocking antibodies fail to respond or respond to slowly, the pregnancy is left unprotected and a spontaneous abortion would result from the normal process of the immune system's attack or rejection of foreign tissue. This attack is made by what are called "natural killer cells" (cells that normally function as a defense against malignant cells and cells infected with viruses, bacteria, and protozoa). *See also* **Miscarriage**

Alpers' Disease

Alpers' disease is a congenital disorder involving progressive degeneration of the brain. Symptoms include seizures, developmental delay, progressive mental retardation, blindness, liver failure and dementia. There is no cure for the disease. Treatment may involve anticonvulsants for the seizures and physical therapy. The disease is usually fatal within the first 10 years of life. *See also* **Birth Defects and Abortion**

Alpha-Fetoprotein Screening *see* **Obstetric Triple Screen**

Amenorrhea

Amenorrhea refers to the absence of a menstrual period and is one of the first indicators of pregnancy. A woman will also experience amenorrhea for anywhere from 6 weeks to 3 months after giving birth (longer if she breast-feeds). *See also* **Anovulation; Chadwick's Sign; Hegar's Sign; Lactational Amenorrhea Method; Pregnancy Test**

American Association of University Women

The American Association of University Women (AAUW) is a national organization created to promote education and equity for women and girls. The national headquarters of AAUW is located in Washington, D.C. AAUW The president of AAUW is Ruth Sweetser. For more than a century, AAUW has influenced legislative debate on critical issues such as education, sex discrimination, civil rights, welfare reform, vocational education, pay equity, family and medical leave, and health care reform. The organization has over 150,000 members, with more than 1,500 branches nationwide. AAUW supports the right of every woman to safe and comprehensive reproductive health care. The organization believes that decisions concerning reproductive health care are personal ones, and that the right to make informed decisions should be available to all women. *See also* **Pro-Choice Organizations**

American Civil Liberties Union

The American Civil Liberties Union (ACLU) was founded by Roger Baldwin in 1920. The national headquarters of ACLU is located in New York City. The executive director of ACLU is Anthony D. Romero. ACLU was the first nonprofit public interest law firm of its kind in the nation. The stated mission of ACLU is to assure that the federal constitutional Bill of Rights are preserved, protected and enforced. National projects that ACLU has been involved with include: AIDS, arts censorship, capital punishment, children's rights, education reform, lesbian and gay rights, immigrants' rights, national security, privacy and technology, prisoners' rights, reproductive freedom, voting rights, women's rights and workplace rights

ACLU has a long history in defending reproductive rights. In 1929 ACLU provided legal counsel to defend Margaret Sanger's (founder of Planned Parenthood Federation of America) right to inform the public about birth control. ACLU filed an amicus brief in the 1965 United States Supreme Court decision in *Griswold v. Connecticut* (striking down state prohibition against the sale or use of contraceptives). In 1971 ACLU argued before the Supreme Court in the case of *United States v. Vuitch* (the first abortion case to be heard by the Supreme Court). ACLU participated in the 1973 Supreme Court decision in *Roe v. Wade* (legalizing abortion), and argued *Roe*'s companion case, *Doe v. Bolton*.

Since 1974 ACLU has litigated abortion and other reproductive issues through a program it created, called the Reproductive Freedom Project (RFP). RFP is New York based and is under the leadership of a director, Louise Melling.

From 1981 to 1996, RFP has successfully challenged state restrictions on Medicaid funding for abortion in California, Massachusetts, New Jersey, Oregon, Connecticut, Vermont, Alaska, Idaho, Illinois, and New Mexico. In 1990 RFP successfully litigated *Hodgson v. Minnesota* before the Supreme Court (securing pregnant teens the option of getting court approval for an abortion). In 1992 RFP litigated *Planned Parenthood v. Casey* before the Supreme Court and persuaded the Court to reaffirm the core right to privacy first established in *Roe*. RFP was instrumental in 1994 in advising members of Congress in drafting the federal Freedom of Access to Clinic Entrances Act (providing legal redress for abortion clinic violence). *See also* **Pro-Choice Organizations**

American Coalition of Life Activists

American Coalition of Life Activists (ACLA) was a pro-life organization that was founded in 1994, in Portland, Oregon. ACLA was headed by David Crane. A primary activity of ACLA was that of using the Internet to attack abortion providers and disseminate personal information on them. This activity became the subject of a federal law suit in California in the late 1990s. The law suit named ACLA as one of the defendants. The plaintiffs in the case sought to stop use of the Internet as a method for provoking violence against abortion providers. The case was tried before a jury and a verdict was returned against ACLA and the other defendants in the amount of $107 million dollars. Although the verdict was subsequently overturned by a federal appeals court on March 28, 2001, the verdict was later reinstated by the same appellate court in *Planned Parenthood of Columbia/Willamette, Inc. v. American Coalition of Life Activists*, 290 F.3d 1058 (9th Cir. 2002). ACLA appeared to have stopped functioning after the civil suit. *See also* **Pro-Life Organizations**

American Life League

American Life League (ALL) is a Virginia based pro-life organization that was founded in 1979, by Judie Brown. ALL coordinates with churches and other local groups to maximize support for positive pro-life work. The organization seeks to establish social policies that promote traditional family values, which means recognizing: (1) the destructive effects of the contraceptive mentality on the traditional family and on society as a whole; (2) the relationship between the practice of contraception and promiscuity, abortion, escalating rates of divorce, increased incidence of venereal diseases, physiological and psychological damage (to both women and men) and the rapid spread of AIDS; and (3) the true nature of the birth control pill, IUD, RU-486, Depo-Provera, Norplant, morning after pill and other chemicals and devices that control birth in several ways, including the aborting of preborn children. The ultimate goal of ALL is the ratification of an amendment to the federal constitution that prohibits abortion. ALL is involved with such projects as Celebrate Life magazine, Rock for Life, STOPP International, and the Crusade for the Defense of Our Catholic Church. The organization also coordinates a network of more than 60 local and regional pro-life groups across the nation. *See also* **Pro-Life Organizations**

American Medical Association's Opposition to Abortion *see* **Storer, Horatio R.**

American Medical Women's Association

The American Medical Women's Association (AMWA) was founded in 1915, by Dr. Bertha VanHoosen, for the purpose of advancing women in the medical profession and improving women's health. AMWA has its national headquarters in Philadelphia, Pennsylvania. The president of AMWA is Dr. Claudia S. Morrissey. The organization's membership includes 10,000 women physicians and medical students.

AMWA is active in providing and developing leadership, advocacy, education, expertise, mentoring, and strategic alliances. The organization is also committed to reproductive and sexual health as integral components of women's overall health. AMWA has taken the position that it is the responsibility of the medical profession to reduce the incidence of situations that lead to a woman's diminished control of her sexual life. It believes that contraception information and devices should be available to all sexually active persons, and that the decision to continue or interrupt a pregnancy should belong to the pregnant woman, in consultation with her physician. *See also* **Pro-Choice Organizations**

Americans United for Life

Americans United for Life (AUL) is a Chicago based pro-life organization. Clarke D. Forsythe is the president of the organization. AUL is considered the first national pro-life organization in America. The organization has been committed to defending human life through judicial, legislative, and educational efforts at both the federal and state levels since 1971. AUL has a 50-state network of pro-life legislators and other pro-life leaders. It has worked with over 30 states concerning woman's-right-to-know legislation. AUL devised and promoted the legal strategy against increased Medicaid funding of abortion in the states. The organization is involved with helping states pass laws which require women to be informed about the link between abortion and breast cancer. *See also* **Pro-Life Organizations**

Amniocentesis

Amniocentesis is a diagnostic procedure that involves insertion of a hollow needle through the abdominal wall into the uterus, and withdrawing a small amount of fluid from the sac surrounding the fetus. This test is usually performed when a problem with the fetus is suspected. The test can detect chromosomal disorders, structural defects, as well as many rare inherited metabolic disorders. The procedure may also be used to identify suspected problems such as Rh incompatibility or infection. This procedure presents a slight chance of infection or injury to the fetus, including causing a miscarriage. There were 112,776 amniocentesis procedures performed in 1998. *See also* **Chorionic Villus Sampling; Obstetric Triple Screen**

Amniotic Fluid Embolism

Amniotic fluid embolism is a condition involving amniotic fluid filtering into uterine veins, following a tear in the placental membranes, and obstructing the functioning of the woman's lungs. This condition is fatal to the woman and the fetus. Research indicates 25 percent of women affected die within one hour of onset. *See also* **Stillbirth**

Amniotic Sac

The amniotic sac is the membrane within the uterus that contains the fetus. It forms a protective layer for the fetus. The amniotic sac protects the fetus from bacteria in the vagina. If the amniotic sac is ruptured the fetus would be susceptible to infection. A fetus must be delivered within 18 hours after a rupture. Labor usually begins shortly after or before rupture of the amniotic sac.

In addition to containing the fetus, the amniotic sac also contains the placenta and amniotic fluid. The amniotic sac is composed of a cavity and two membranes: amnion and chorion.

Amniotic fluid. Amniotic fluid is a yellowish-like liquid contained in the amniotic sac. Most of the fluid is contributed to by the urine of the fetus. It increases in volume as the fetus grows. The fluid is circulated by the fetus about every 3 hours. Several functions are provided by the fluid for the fetus, including: providing a cushion to prevent injury; allows for fetal movement and musculoskeletal growth; maintains a proper temperature; and prevents heat loss. An excessive amount of fluid (polyhydramnios) could cause congenital defects. An inadequate amount of fluid (oligohydramnios) could cause fetal deformities.

The amniotic fluid can be tested, using amniocentesis, to determine whether the fetus has a significant risk of a chromosome abnormality. In addition, the level of fluid maintained provides a good indicator as to whether the fetus' kidneys are functioning normally, as well as other organs. The level of fluid may also be used as an indicator of whether or not the fetus should be delivered by induction or C-section.

Amnion. The amnion is the inner membrane of the amniotic sac. It is the membrane that immediately surrounds the fetus.

Chorion. The chorion is the outer membrane that surrounds the fetus. The embryonic tissue that forms the placenta is developed from the chorion.

A test, called chorion villus sampling, is frequently used to make specific determinations about the fetus. The test involves inserting a needle into the chorion and drawing a tissue sample into a syringe. The tissue sample provides cells containing the chromosome and genetic make-up of the fetus. These cells can be used to reveal whether the fetus has normal chromosomes or diseases such as cystic fibrosis, muscular dystrophies, Huntington's disease and hemophilia.

Amniotic cavity. The amniotic cavity is the space within the amniotic sac, in which the fetus is contained along with amniotic fluid. *See also* **Fetal Development**

Amniotomy

Amniotomy is a procedure that requires rupturing the amniotic sac for the purpose of hastening or inducing labor. It may also be done to determine whether meconium (fetal feces) has impaired the fetus. This procedure carries a risk of causing umbilical cord compression and exposure of the fetus to bacteria in the birth canal.

Anders v. Floyd

Forum: United States Supreme Court.
Case Citation: Anders v. Floyd, 440 U.S. 445 (1979).
Date Argued: Did not argue.
Date of Decision: March 5, 1979.
Opinion of Court: Per Curiam.
Concurring opinion: None.
Dissenting Opinion: Stewart, J.
Counsel for Appellant: Not reported.
Counsel for Appellee: Not reported.
Amicus Brief for Appellant: Not reported.
Amicus Brief for Appellee: Not reported.
Issue Presented: Whether federal district court erred in enjoining enforcement of a South Carolina statute that imposed criminal punishment for performing an abortion on a viable fetus?

Case Holding: Federal district court erred in enjoining enforcement of a South Carolina statute that imposed criminal punishment for performing an abortion on a viable fetus.

Background facts of case: A physician was indicted by the state of South Carolina for performing an abortion on a fetus that was 25 weeks old. The physician filed a petition in a federal district court to prevent enforcement of the criminal abortion statute. A special three-judge district court panel found the statute unconstitutional because of the manner in which it defined the prohibition of performing an abortion on a viable fetus. The United States Supreme Court granted certiorari to address the issue.

Majority opinion delivered Per Curiam: It was determined in the per curiam opinion that the district committed error. The opinion stated tersely:

The District Court enjoined the prosecution, concluding that under *Roe v. Wade,* 410 U.S. 113, 98 S.Ct. 705, 35 L.Ed.2d 147, (1973), there was no possibility of obtaining a constitutionally binding conviction of appellee. Because the District Court may have reached this conclusion on the basis of an erroneous concept of "viability," which refers to potential, rather than actual, survival of the fetus outside the womb, *Colautti v. Franklin,* 439 U.S. 379, 389, 99 S.Ct. 675, 682, 58 L.Ed.2d 596 (1979) the judgment is vacated and the case is remanded to the United States District Court for the District of South Carolina for further consideration in light of *Colautti.*

Disposition of case: The judgment of the district court was vacated and the case remanded.

Dissenting without opinion by Justice Stewart: Justice Stewart dissented without rendering a separate opinion or statement.

Anembryonic Pregnancy *see* **Blighted Ovum**

Anencephaly

Anencephaly is a congenital neural tube defect that involves the absence of both the skull and cerebral portions of the brain. This disorder occurs when the upper portion of the neural tube fails to close. The specific reason for this is not known. Research has shown, however, that low levels of folic acid may contribute to the condition. Symptoms of the defect include absence of the skull, absence of the brain, abnormalities of facial features and heart defects. This condition affects approximately 4 out of 10,000 births. This condition is terminal and no treatment has been found to alter this outcome. *See also* **Birth Defects and Abortion; Encephaloceles; Folic Acid and Pregnancy; Spina Bifida**

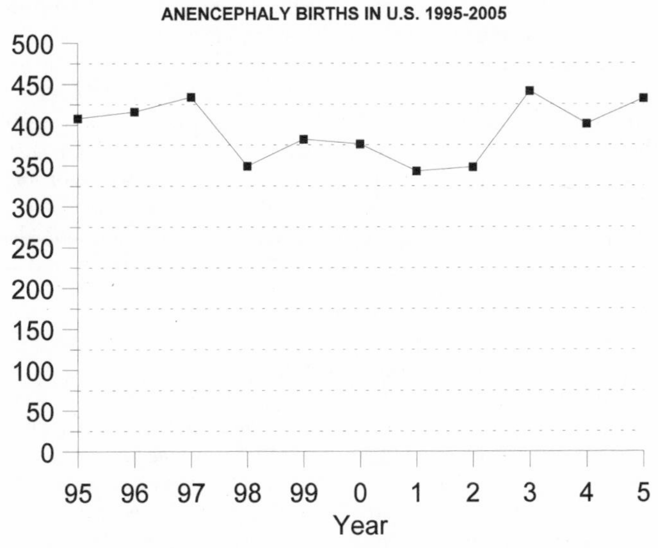

Source: **Centers for Disease Control and Prevention.**

Angelman Syndrome

Angelman syndrome is a disorder involving severe congenital mental retardation, unusual facial appearance, and muscular abnormalities. Symptoms of the disease include balance problems, hand flapping, developmental delay, and speech problems. Treatments for symptoms of the disease include physical therapy and anticonvulsant medications. *See also* **Birth Defects and Abortion**

Anovulation

Anovulation refers to the non-pregnancy related failure of an ovary to release an egg every month. Without ovulation, a woman cannot become pregnant. Anovulation may occur because of infertility, erratic menstrual cycles, low or excessive body weight, emotional and physical stress, or medications. Another common cause of anovulation is the polycystic ovarian syndrome. Women with this syndrome fail to regularly release eggs and therefore have irregular menstrual cycles. A common treatment for anovulation involves medications with progesterone and estrogen. *See also* **Amenorrhea; Polycystic Ovarian Syndrome and Pregnancy**

Antepartum Hemorrhage *see* **Placenta Previa**

Anthrax Threats *see* **Abortion Violence, Property Destruction and Demonstrations**

Antiphospholipid Antibody Syndrome

Antiphospholipid antibody syndrome is a disorder involving the formation of blood clots in the veins or arteries. Symptoms of the disorder include loss of vision; numbness, tingling, or weakness in the face or limbs; stroke; and seizures. Women who are pregnant and have the disorder are at a high risk for complications. The disorder has been associated with poor fetal growth, spontaneous abortion and stillbirth. It is believed that the pregnancy complications are due to blood clots in the blood vessels of the placenta. Medications are available for treatment of the disorder during pregnancy. *See also* **Blood Clotting and Pregnancy; Miscarriage; Stillbirth**

Appendicitis and Pregnancy

Appendicitis involves inflammation of the appendix. The condition produces general cramping pain. Appendicitis in a pregnant women can elude diagnosis because the appendix rises in the abdomen as pregnancy progresses, causing the cramping pain it produces to appear as normal pregnancy pains. Failure to diagnose the condition could lead to the appendix rupturing. A high fatality rate is associated with a ruptured appendix in pregnant women. *See* **Stillbirth**

Arizona

(1) OVERVIEW

The state of Arizona enacted its first criminal abortion statute in 1865. The statute underwent a few amendments prior to the 1973 decision by the United States Supreme Court in *Roe v. Wade*, which legalized abortion in the nation. In spite of the decision in *Roe*, Arizona has not repealed its pre–*Roe* criminal abortion statute. However, under *Roe* the statute is constitutionally infirm.

Arizona has taken affirmative steps to respond to *Roe* and its progeny. The state has addressed numerous abortion issues by statute that include partial-birth abortion, post-viability abortion, viability testing, a ban on fetal or embryo experiments, use of facilities and people, abortion by minors, public funds for abortion, abortion clinic and physician requirements, fetal remains, foster care providers, human cloning, injury to pregnant woman.

(2) PRE-ROE ABORTION BAN

As previously indicated, Arizona has not repealed its pre–*Roe* criminal abortion statutes. The statutes remain on the books even though they were expressly found to violate the constitution of Arizona in *Nelson v. Planned Parenthood of Tucson*, 505 P.2d 580 (Ariz.Ct.App. 1973). Under the now unconstitutional statutes, abortion was criminalized if it was not performed to preserve the life of the woman. Arizona punished both the abortion provider and the woman. The state also criminalized abortion advertising. The pre–*Roe* abortion statutes are set out below.

Arizona Code § 13-3603. Providing abortion

A person who provides, supplies or administers to a pregnant woman,

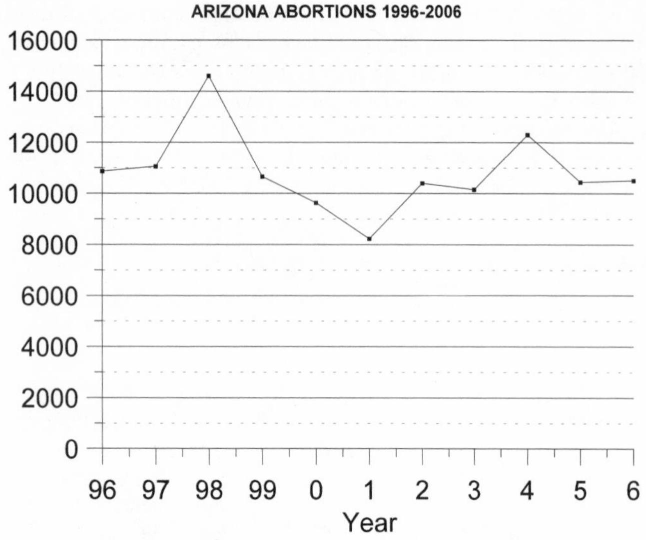

Source: **Arizona Department of Health Services.**

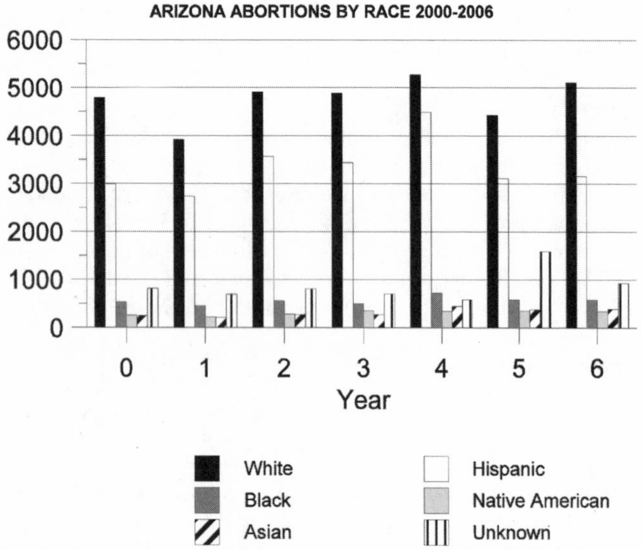

Source: **Arizona Department of Health Services.**

Arizona Abortion by Age Group 2000–2006
Age Group (yrs)

Year	*<15*	*15–17*	*18–19*	*20–24*	*25–29*	*30–34*	*35–39*	*≥40*	*Unknown*
2000	57	684	1,247	3,041	1,988	1,260	728	258	368
2001	46	540	942	2,624	1,689	1,100	601	225	459
2002	44	705	1,246	3,365	2,041	1,380	789	306	521
2003	60	614	1,193	3,465	2,066	1,360	737	325	325
2004	44	703	1,473	4,202	2,598	1,614	969	355	343
2005	54	582	1,256	3,489	2,195	1,329	797	310	434
2006	69	624	1,226	3,527	2,243	1,380	876	446	115
Total	374	4,452	8,583	23,713	14,820	9,423	5,497	2,225	2,565

Source: **Arizona Department of Health Services.**

or procures such woman to take any medicine, drugs or substance, or uses or employs any instrument or other means whatever, with intent thereby to procure the miscarriage of such woman, unless it is necessary to save her life, shall be punished by imprisonment in the state prison for not less than two years nor more than five years.

Arizona Abortion by Education Level of Female 2000–2006
Education Level Completed

Year	*≤12*	*≥13*	*Unknown*
2000	3,257	2,537	3,837
2001	2,604	1,777	3,845
2002	3,029	2,156	5,212
2003	2,444	1,889	5,821
2004	3,321	2,726	6,254
2005	1,435	1,330	7,681
2006	6,226	1,415	2,865
Total	22,316	13,830	35,515

Source: **Arizona Department of Health Services.**

Arizona Code § 13-3604. Soliciting abortion

A woman who solicits from any person any medicine, drug or substance whatever, and takes it, or who submits to an operation, or to the use of any means whatever, with intent thereby to procure a miscarriage, unless it is necessary to preserve her life, shall be punished by imprisonment in the state prison for not less than one nor more than five years.

Arizona Code § 13-3605. Advertising abortion services

A person who wilfully writes, composes or publishes a notice or advertisement of any medicine or means for producing or facilitating a miscarriage or abortion, or for prevention of conception, or who offers his services by a notice, advertisement or otherwise, to assist in the accomplishment of any such purposes, is guilty of a misdemeanor.

(3) PARTIAL-BIRTH ABORTION

Arizona criminalizes partial-birth abortions. However, the ban may be invalid as a result of the United States Supreme Court decision in *Stenberg v. Carhart*, which invalidated a Nebraska statute that prohibited partial-birth abortions. Additionally, a federal district court issued an order enjoining enforcement of the statute in *Planned Parenthood of Southern Arizona v. Wood*, 982 F.Supp. 1369 (D.Ariz. 1997). However, Arizona's partial-birth abortion statute may be valid under the United States Supreme Court decision in *Gonzales v. Carhart*, which approved of a federal statute that bans partial-birth abortion. Arizona has provided a civil cause of action for a married man whose spouse obtains a partial-birth abortion. In the case of a minor, the maternal grandparents of the fetus may file a civil lawsuit. The text of Arizona' s partial-birth abortion statute is set out below.

§ 13-3603.01. Partial-birth abortion offense

A. A person who knowingly performs a partial-birth abortion and who kills a human fetus is guilty of a class 6 felony.

B. This section does not apply to a partial-birth abortion that is necessary to save the life of a mother whose life is endangered by a physical disorder, illness or injury if no other medical procedure would save the mother's life.

C. The father of the fetus if married to the mother at the time she receives a partial-birth abortion and the maternal grandparents of the fetus if the mother is not at least eighteen years of age at the time of the partial-birth abortion may bring a civil action to obtain appropriate relief unless the pregnancy resulted from the plaintiff's criminal conduct or the plaintiff consented to the partial-birth abortion. Relief pursuant to this subsection includes the following:

1. Monetary damages for all injuries resulting from the partial-birth abortion, including psychological and physical damages.

2. Damages in an amount equal to three times the cost of the partial-birth abortion.

D. This section does not subject a woman upon whom a partial-birth

Arizona Abortion by Weeksof Gestation 2000–2006

	Year							
Weeks of Gestation	*2000*	*2001*	*2002*	*2003*	*2004*	*2005*	*2006*	*Total*
≤6	1,280	1,306	2,597	3,178	3,811	2,474	2,877	14,345
7	1,852	1,207	1,910	1,738	2,389	2,057	2,277	13,430
8	1,817	1,235	1,499	1,323	1,968	1,643	1,649	11,134
9	1,082	944	931	825	1,036	993	1,143	6,954
10	852	655	726	626	810	688	752	5,109
11	461	396	483	512	616	511	513	3,492
12	293	335	325	282	419	343	342	2,339
13	270	249	275	200	263	276	245	1,778
14	231	179	199	166	194	175	149	1,293
15	178	156	167	153	234	140	111	1,139
16	103	100	118	94	117	85	80	697
17	119	86	96	96	84	72	84	637
18	138	97	131	99	110	65	70	710
19	104	74	89	84	88	77	62	578
20	22	13	34	34	37	43	49	232
≥21	6	42	38	74	99	129	100	488
Unknown	823	1,152	779	670	26	675	3	4,128

Source: **Arizona Department of Health Services.**

Arizona Prior Abortion by Female 2000–2006

	Prior Abortion	
Year	*None*	*≥1*
2000	6,160	3,471
2001	5,271	2,955
2002	6,561	3,846
2003	6,606	3,548
2004	7,778	4,523
2005	6,453	3,993
2006	6,390	4,116
Total	45,219	26,452

Source: **Arizona Department of Health Services.**

abortion is performed to criminal prosecution or civil liability under this section.

E. For the purposes of this section:

1. "Partial-birth abortion" means an abortion in which the person performing the abortion partially vaginally delivers a living fetus before killing the fetus and completing the delivery.

2. "Person" includes a physician who is licensed pursuant to title 32, chapter 13 or 17, a person who is legally authorized by this state to perform abortions or a person who is not legally authorized by this state to perform abortions but who directly performs a partial-birth abortion.

(4) POST-VIABILITY ABORTION

Arizona has enacted statutes that prohibit post-viability abortions, except to preserve the life or health of the woman. Two physicians are required to be present during a post-viability abortion. The post-viability statutes are set out below.

Arizona Code § 36-2301.
Duty to promote life of fetus or embryo delivered alive

If an abortion is performed and a human fetus or embryo is delivered alive, it is the duty of any physician performing such abortion and any additional physician in attendance as required by § 36-2301.01 to see that all available means and medical skills are used to promote, preserve and maintain the life of such fetus or embryo.

Arizona Code § 36-2301.01. Abortion of viable fetus

A. A physician shall not knowingly perform an abortion of a viable fetus unless:

1. The physician states in writing before the abortion is performed that the abortion is necessary to preserve the life or health of the woman, specifying the medical indications for and the probable health consequences of the abortion. The physician shall attach a copy of this statement to any fetal death report filed pursuant to § 11-593 or fetal death registration filed pursuant to § 36-329, subsection C.

2. The physician uses the available method or technique of abortion most likely to preserve the life and health of the fetus, unless the use of such method or technique would present a greater risk to the life or health of the woman than the use of another available method or technique.

3. The physician states in writing the available methods or techniques considered, the method or technique used and the reasons for choosing that method or technique. The physician shall attach a copy of this statement to any fetal death report filed pursuant to § 11-593 or fetal death registration filed pursuant to § 36-329, subsection C.

4. In addition to the physician performing the abortion, there is another physician in attendance who shall take control of and provide immediate medical care for a living child born as a result of the abortion.

5. The physician takes all reasonable steps during the performance of the abortion, consistent with the procedure used and in keeping with good medical practice, to preserve the life and health of the fetus, if these steps do not pose an increased risk to the life or health of the woman on whom the abortion is performed.

B. This section does not apply if there is a medical emergency.

C. As used in this section and § 36-2301.02:

1. "Abortion" means the use of an instrument, medicine or drug or other substance or device with the intent to terminate a pregnancy for reasons other than to increase the probability of a live birth, to preserve the life or health of the child after live birth, to terminate an ectopic pregnancy or to remove a dead fetus. Abortion does not include birth control devices or oral contraceptives.

2. "Medical emergency" means a condition that, on the basis of the physician's good faith clinical judgment, so complicates a pregnancy as to necessitate the immediate abortion of the pregnancy to avoid the woman's death or for which a delay will create serious risk of substantial and irreversible impairment of a major bodily function.

3. "Viable fetus" means the unborn offspring of human beings that has reached a stage of fetal development so that, in the judgment of the attending physician on the particular facts of the case, there is a reasonable probability of the fetus' sustained survival outside the uterus, with or without artificial support.

4. "Physician" means any person licensed under title 32, chapter 13 or 17.

(5) VIABILITY TESTING

It is required by Arizona that a woman who is more than 12 weeks pregnant must, before obtaining an abortion, undergo ultrasound testing for fetal viability. Part of the viability testing statute was found invalid in *Tucson Woman's Clinic v. Eden*, 379 F.3d 531(9th Cir. 2004), because it required abortion clinics release unredacted medical records, ultrasound pictures and incident reports. The statute is set out below.

Arizona Code § 36-2301.02. Viability testing

A. Beginning on January 1, 2001, a person shall not knowingly perform an abortion after twelve weeks' gestation unless the person estimates the gestational age of the fetus based on biparietal diameter and femur length according to the Hadlok measurement system or other equivalent measurement systems using ultrasound examination as provided in rule.

B. Beginning on January 1, 2001, a person shall not knowingly perform an abortion after twelve weeks' gestation unless the person ensures that a copy of each ultrasound result taken of a fetus of a woman as a result of a second or third trimester abortion is sent to persons or corporations contracted pursuant to this section. The person performing the abortion shall ensure that the ultrasound result or results from the woman is sent in a manner that is distinguishable from, and not mixed with, any other set of ultrasound results and is accompanied with a copy of any report that notes the estimate of the fetus' gestational age that was made before the abortion.

C. The department of health services shall contract with qualified public or private persons or corporations for review of ultrasound results to determine compliance with this section. The department shall issue requests for proposals for the purpose of establishing contracts pursuant to this section. At a minimum, the contracts shall require the contractor to review ultrasound results to verify the accuracy of the fetus' estimated gestational age made before the abortion and to verify that the estimate was made in reasonable compliance with the Hadlok measurement system or another equivalent measurement system as provided in rule.

D. The contractor shall use a statistically valid method of sampling to conduct the review of ultrasound results from a woman as a result of a second trimester abortion of a fetus of up to eighteen weeks' gestation. The contractor shall conduct a review of all ultrasound results from a woman as a result of an abortion of a fetus of eighteen or more weeks' gestation.

E. Beginning on January 1, 2001, on a monthly basis, persons or corporations providing ultrasound review services to the department pursuant to this section shall file a report with the director regarding ultrasound results, noting:

1. Any instances in which the contractor believes there was a significant inaccuracy in the estimated gestational age of the fetus made before the abortion.

2. Any circumstances that, based on the contractor's professional judgment, might explain a significant inaccuracy reported pursuant to paragraph 1 of this subsection.

3. Whether there was reasonable compliance pursuant to subsection C of this section.

4. Whether, based on the results of the review of each ultrasound, the physician should have filed a fetal death certificate with the department of health services as required by § 36-329, subsection C.

F. The department of health services shall forward the report or portions of the report within thirty working days to the appropriate professional regulatory boards for their review and appropriate action.

G. Except as provided by subsection F of this section, the reports required by this section are confidential and disclosable by the department or its contractor only in aggregate form for statistical or research purposes. Except as provided by subsection F of this section, information relating to any physician, hospital, clinic or other institution shall not be released. Personally identifiable patient information shall not be released by the department or its contractor.

(6) BAN ON FETAL OR EMBRYO EXPERIMENTS

Arizona has banned fetal and embryo experiments, except where necessary to diagnose a disease or condition in the mother of the fetus or embryo. The statute banning such experiments was held unconstitutional in *Forbes v. Woods*, 71 F.Supp.2d 1015 (D.Ariz. 1999), affirmed 236 F.3d 1009 (9th Cir. 2000). The text of the statute is set out below.

Arizona Code § 36-2302.
Experimentation on human fetus or embryo prohibited

A. A person shall not knowingly use any human fetus or embryo, living or dead, or any parts, organs or fluids of any such fetus or embryo resulting from an induced abortion in any manner for any medical experimentation or scientific or medical investigation purposes except as is strictly necessary to diagnose a disease or condition in the mother of the fetus or embryo and only if the abortion was performed because of such disease or condition.

B. The physician-patient privilege as provided in § 13-4062, paragraph 4 shall not prevent the production of documents or records relevant to an investigation arising under this section. All documents or records produced in an action brought pursuant to this section shall be inspected by the court in camera, and before the documents or records are released to the requesting party, the court shall remove the names and other identifying information, if any, of the patients and substitute pseudonyms.

C. This section shall not prohibit routine pathological examinations conducted by a medical examiner or hospital laboratory provided such pathological examination is not a part of or in any way related to any medical or scientific experimentation.

(7) USE OF FACILITIES AND PEOPLE

Under the laws of Arizona hospitals are not required to allow abortions at their facilities. The employees and physicians at hospitals that do allow abortions are permitted to refuse to take part in abortions. The statute permitting such refusal was upheld in *Roe v. Arizona Bd. of Regents*, 549 P.2d 150 (Ariz. 1976). Further, Arizona has a statute which prohibits abortions from being performed at state educational facilities. The text of the statutes are set out below.

Arizona Code § 36-2151.
Right to refuse to participate in abortion

No hospital is required to admit any patient for the purpose of performing an abortion. A physician, or any other person who is a member of or associated with the staff of a hospital, or any employee of a hospital, doctor, clinic, or other medical or surgical facility in which an abortion has been authorized, who shall state in writing an objection to such abortion on moral or religious grounds shall not be required to participate in the medical or surgical procedures which will result in the abortion.

Arizona Code § 15-1630.
Abortion at educational facility prohibited

No abortion shall be performed at any facility under the jurisdiction of the Arizona board of regents unless such abortion is necessary to save the life of the woman having the abortion.

(8) ABORTION BY MINORS

Under the laws of Arizona no physician may perform an abortion upon an unemancipated minor unless he/she first obtains the written consent of either parent or the legal guardian of the minor. In compliance with federal constitutional law, Arizona has provided a judicial waiver procedure for an unemancipated minor to obtain an abortion without parental or guardian consent. If an unemancipated minor elects not to seek, or cannot for any reason obtain consent from either of her parents or legal guardian, the minor may petition a trial court for a waiver of the consent requirement. A minor has a right to an attorney at the proceeding and if she cannot afford one, the court must appoint her an attorney. If a minor chooses, she may represent herself. The required parental or guardian consent may be waived if the court finds either (1) that the minor is mature and well-informed enough to make the abortion decision on her own, or (2) that performance of the abortion would be in the best interest of the minor. An expedited appeal is available to any minor to whom the court denies a waiver of consent.

Parental consent or judicial authorization is not required when a minor's pregnancy was caused by sexual intercourse with her father, step-father, uncle, grandparent, sibling, adoptive parent, legal guardian or foster parent or by a person who lives in the same household with the minor and the minor's mother. The statute has been addressed in *In re B.S.*, 74 P.3d 285 (Ariz.App. 2003); *Planned Parenthood of Southern Arizona v. Lawall (II)*, 307 F.3d 783 (9th Cir. 2002); *Planned Parenthood of Southern Arizona v. Lawall (I)*, 180 F.3d 1022 (9th Cir. 1999); and *Planned Parenthood of Southern Arizona v. Neely*, 130 F.3d 400 (9th Cir. 1997). The text of the statute is set out below.

Arizona Code § 36-2152.
Parental consent and judicial bypass

A. A person shall not knowingly perform an abortion on a pregnant unemancipated minor unless the attending physician has secured the written consent from one of the minor's parents or the minor's guardian or conservator or unless a judge of the superior court authorizes the physician to perform the abortion pursuant to subsection B.

B. A judge of the superior court shall, on petition or motion, and after an appropriate hearing, authorize a physician to perform the abortion if the judge determines that the pregnant minor is mature and capable of giving informed consent to the proposed abortion. If the judge determines that the pregnant minor is not mature or if the pregnant minor does not claim to be mature, the judge shall determine whether the performance of an abortion on her without the consent from one of her parents or her guardian or conservator would be in her best interests and shall authorize a physician to perform the abortion without consent if the judge concludes that the pregnant minor's best interests would be served.

C. The pregnant minor may participate in the court proceedings on her own behalf. The court may appoint a guardian ad litem for her. The court shall advise her that she has the right to court appointed counsel and shall, on her request, provide her with counsel unless she appears through private counsel or she knowingly and intelligently waives her right to counsel.

D. Proceedings in the court under this section are confidential and have precedence over other pending matters. Members of the public shall not inspect, obtain copies of or otherwise have access to records of court proceedings under this section unless authorized by law. A judge who conducts proceedings under this section shall make in writing specific factual findings and legal conclusions supporting the decision and shall order a confidential record of the evidence to be maintained including the judge's own findings and conclusions. The minor may file the petition using a fictitious name. For purposes of this subsection, public does not include judges, clerks, administrators, professionals or other persons employed by or working under the supervision of the court or employees of other public agencies who are authorized by state or federal rule or law to inspect and copy closed court records.

E. The court shall hold the hearing and shall issue a ruling within forty-eight hours, excluding weekends and holidays, after the petition is filed. If the court fails to issue a ruling within this time period the petition is deemed to have been granted and the consent requirement is waived.

F. An expedited confidential appeal is available to a pregnant minor for whom the court denies an order authorizing an abortion without parental consent. The appellate court shall hold the hearing and issue a ruling within forty-eight hours, excluding weekends and holidays, after the petition for appellate review is filed. Filing fees are not required of the pregnant minor at either the trial or the appellate level.

G. Parental consent or judicial authorization is not required under this section if either:

1. The pregnant minor certifies to the attending physician that the pregnancy resulted from sexual conduct with a minor by the minor's parent, stepparent, uncle, grandparent, sibling, adoptive parent, legal guardian or foster parent or by a person who lives in the same household with the minor and the minor's mother. The physician performing the abortion shall report the sexual conduct with a minor to the proper law enforcement officials pursuant to § 13-3620 and shall preserve and forward a sample of the fetal tissue to these officials for use in a criminal investigation.

2. The attending physician certifies in the pregnant minor's medical record that, on the basis of the physician's good faith clinical judgment, the pregnant minor has a condition that so complicates her medical condition as to necessitate the immediate abortion of her pregnancy to avert her death or for which a delay will create serious risk of substantial and irreversible impairment of major bodily function.

H. A person who performs an abortion in violation of this section is guilty of a class 1 misdemeanor. A person is not subject to any liability under this section if the person establishes by written evidence that the person relied on evidence sufficient to convince a careful and prudent person that the representations of the pregnant minor regarding information necessary to comply with this section are true.

I. For purposes of this section:

1. "Abortion" means the use of an instrument, medicine or drug or other substance or device with the intent to terminate a pregnancy for reasons other than to increase the probability of a live birth, to preserve the life or health of the child after a live birth, to terminate an ectopic pregnancy or to remove a dead fetus. Abortion does not include birth control devices or oral contraceptives that inhibit or prevent ovulation, fertilization or the implantation of a fertilized ovum within the uterus.

2. "Fetus" means any individual human organism from fertilization until birth.

(9) PUBLIC FUNDS FOR ABORTION

Arizona prohibits the use of state and local public funds to pay for abortions, except to save the life of the woman. The statute was found in *Doe v. Arpaio*, 150 P.3d 1258 (Ariz. App. 2007) and *Simat Corp. v. Arizona Health Care Cost Containment System*, 56 P.3d 28 (Ariz. 2002). The text of the statute is set out below.

Arizona Code § 35-196.02. Use of public funds for abortion

Notwithstanding any provisions of law to the contrary, no public funds nor tax monies of this state or any political subdivision of this state nor any federal funds passing through the state treasury or the treasury of any political subdivision of this state may be expended for payment to any person or entity for the performance of any abortion unless an abortion is necessary to save the life of the woman having the abortion.

(10) ABORTION CLINIC AND PHYSICIAN REQUIREMENTS

Arizona has provided by statute for specific minimum requirements that abortion clinics and physicians must have. The statutory requirements are set out below.

Arizona Code § 36-449.01. Definitions

In this article, unless the context otherwise requires:

1. "Abortion" means the use of a surgical instrument or a machine with the intent to terminate a woman's pregnancy for reasons other than to increase the probability of a live birth, to preserve the life or health of the child after live birth, to terminate an ectopic pregnancy or to remove a dead fetus. Abortion does not include birth control devices or oral contraceptives.

2. "Abortion clinic" means a facility, other than an accredited hospital, in which five or more first trimester abortions in any month or any second or third trimester abortions are performed.

3. "Director" means the director of the department of health services.

4. "Viable fetus" has the same meaning prescribed in § 36-2301.01.

Arizona Code § 36-449.02.
Abortion clinics; licensure requirements

A. Beginning on April 1, 2000, an abortion clinic shall meet the same licensure requirements as prescribed in article 2 of this chapter for health care institutions.

B. An abortion clinic that holds an unclassified health care facility license issued before the effective date of this article may retain that classification until April 1, 2000 subject to compliance with all laws that relate to unclassified health care facilities.

C. Beginning on April 1, 2000, abortion clinics shall comply with department requirements for abortion clinics and department rules that govern abortion clinics.

Arizona Code § 36-449.03. Abortion clinics; rules

A. The director shall adopt rules for an abortion clinic's physical facilities. At a minimum these rules shall prescribe standards for:

1. Adequate private space that is specifically designated for interviewing, counseling and medical evaluations.

2. Dressing rooms for staff and patients.

3. Appropriate lavatory areas.

4. Areas for preprocedure hand washing.

5. Private procedure rooms.

6. Adequate lighting and ventilation for abortion procedures.

7. Surgical or gynecologic examination tables and other fixed equipment.

8. Postprocedure recovery rooms that are supervised, staffed and equipped to meet the patients' needs.

9. Emergency exits to accommodate a stretcher or gurney.

10. Areas for cleaning and sterilizing instruments.

11. Adequate areas for the secure storage of medical records and necessary equipment and supplies.

12. The display in the abortion clinic, in a place that is conspicuous to all patients, of the clinic's current license issued by the department.

B. The director shall adopt rules to prescribe abortion clinic supplies and equipment standards, including supplies and equipment that are required to be immediately available for use or in an emergency. At a minimum these rules shall:

1. Prescribe required equipment and supplies, including medications, required for the conduct, in an appropriate fashion, of any abortion procedure that the medical staff of the clinic anticipates performing and for monitoring the progress of each patient throughout the procedure and recovery period.

2. Require that the number or amount of equipment and supplies at the clinic is adequate at all times to assure sufficient quantities of clean and sterilized durable equipment and supplies to meet the needs of each patient.

3. Prescribe required equipment, supplies and medications that shall be available and ready for immediate use in an emergency and requirements for written protocols and procedures to be followed by staff in an emergency, such as the loss of electrical power.

4. Prescribe required equipment and supplies for required laboratory tests and requirements for protocols to calibrate and maintain laboratory equipment at the abortion clinic or operated by clinic staff.

5. Require ultrasound equipment in those facilities that provide abortions after twelve weeks' gestation.

6. Require that all equipment is safe for the patient and the staff, meets applicable federal standards and is checked annually to ensure safety and appropriate calibration.

C. The director shall adopt rules relating to abortion clinic personnel. At a minimum these rules shall require that:

1. The abortion clinic designate a medical director of the abortion clinic who is licensed pursuant to title 32, chapter 13, 17 or 29.

2. Physicians performing surgery are licensed pursuant to title 32, chapter 13 or 17, demonstrate competence in the procedure involved and are acceptable to the medical director of the abortion clinic.

3. A physician with admitting privileges at an accredited hospital in this state is available.

4. If a physician is not present, a registered nurse, nurse practitioner, licensed practical nurse or physician's assistant is present and remains at the clinic when abortions are performed to provide postoperative monitoring and care until each patient who had an abortion that day is discharged.

5. Surgical assistants receive training in counseling, patient advocacy and the specific responsibilities of the services the surgical assistants provide.

6. Volunteers receive training in the specific responsibilities of the services the volunteers provide, including counseling and patient advocacy as provided in the rules adopted by the director for different types of volunteers based on their responsibilities.

D. The director shall adopt rules relating to the medical screening and evaluation of each abortion clinic patient. At a minimum these rules shall require:

1. A medical history including the following:

(a) Reported allergies to medications, antiseptic solutions or latex.

(b) Obstetric and gynecologic history.

(c) Past surgeries.

2. A physical examination including a bimanual examination estimating uterine size and palpation of the adnexa.

3. The appropriate laboratory tests including:

(a) For an abortion in which an ultrasound examination is not performed before the abortion procedure, urine or blood tests for pregnancy performed before the abortion procedure.

(b) A test for anemia.

(c) Rh typing, unless reliable written documentation of blood type is available.

(d) Other tests as indicated from the physical examination.

4. An ultrasound evaluation for all patients who elect to have an abortion after twelve weeks' gestation. The rules shall require that if a person who is not a physician performs an ultrasound examination, that person shall have documented evidence that the person completed a course in the operation of ultrasound equipment as prescribed in rule. The physician or other health care professional shall review, at the request of the patient, the ultrasound evaluation results with the patient before the abortion procedure is performed, including the probable gestational age of the fetus.

5. That the physician is responsible for estimating the gestational age of the fetus based on the ultrasound examination and obstetric standards in keeping with established standards of care regarding the estimation of fetal age as defined in rule and shall write the estimate in the patient's medical history. The physician shall keep original prints of each ultrasound examination of a patient in the patient's medical history file.

E. The director shall adopt rules relating to the abortion procedure. At a minimum these rules shall require:

1. That medical personnel is available to all patients throughout the abortion procedure.

2. Standards for the safe conduct of abortion procedures that conform to obstetric standards in keeping with established standards of care regarding the estimation of fetal age as defined in rule.

3. Appropriate use of local anesthesia, analgesia and sedation if ordered by the physician.

4. The use of appropriate precautions, such as the establishment of intravenous access at least for patients undergoing second or third trimester abortions.

5. The use of appropriate monitoring of the vital signs and other defined signs and markers of the patient's status throughout the abortion procedure and during the recovery period until the patient's condition is deemed to be stable in the recovery room.

F. The director shall adopt rules that prescribe minimum recovery room standards. At a minimum these rules shall require that:

1. Immediate postprocedure care consists of observation in a supervised recovery room for as long as the patient's condition warrants.

2. The clinic arrange hospitalization if any complication beyond the management capability of the staff occurs or is suspected.

3. A licensed health professional who is trained in the management of the recovery area and is capable of providing basic cardiopulmonary resuscitation and related emergency procedures remains on the premises of the abortion clinic until all patients are discharged.

4. A physician with admitting privileges at an accredited hospital in this state remains on the premises of the abortion clinic until all patients are stable and are ready to leave the recovery room and to facilitate the transfer of emergency cases if hospitalization of the patient or viable fetus is necessary. A physician shall sign the discharge order and be readily accessible and available until the last patient is discharged.

5. A physician discusses RhO(d) immune globulin with each patient for whom it is indicated and assures it is offered to the patient in the immediate postoperative period or that it will be available to her within seventy-two hours after completion of the abortion procedure. If the patient refuses, a refusal form approved by the department shall be signed by the patient and a witness and included in the medical record.

6. Written instructions with regard to postabortion coitus, signs of possible problems and general aftercare are given to each patient. Each patient shall have specific instructions regarding access to medical care for complications, including a telephone number to call for medical emergencies.

7. There is a specified minimum length of time that a patient remains in the recovery room by type of abortion procedure and duration of gestation.

8. The physician assures that a licensed health professional from the abortion clinic makes a good faith effort to contact the patient by telephone, with the patient's consent, within twenty-four hours after surgery to assess the patient's recovery.

9. Equipment and services are located in the recovery room to provide appropriate emergency resuscitative and life support procedures pending the transfer of the patient or viable fetus to the hospital.

G. The director shall adopt rules that prescribe standards for follow-up visits. At a minimum these rules shall require that:

1. A postabortion medical visit is offered and, if requested, scheduled for three weeks after the abortion, including a medical examination and a review of the results of all laboratory tests.

2. A urine pregnancy test is obtained at the time of the follow-up visit to rule out continuing pregnancy. If a continuing pregnancy is suspected, the patient shall be evaluated and a physician who performs abortions shall be consulted.

H. The director shall adopt rules to prescribe minimum abortion clinic incident reporting. At a minimum these rules shall require that:

1. The abortion clinic records each incident resulting in a patient's or viable fetus' serious injury occurring at an abortion clinic and shall report them in writing to the department within ten days after the incident. For the purposes of this paragraph, "serious injury" means an injury that occurs at an abortion clinic and that creates a serious risk of substantial impairment of a major body organ.

2. If a patient's death occurs, other than a fetal death properly reported pursuant to law, the abortion clinic reports it to the department not later than the next department work day.

3. Incident reports are filed with the department and appropriate professional regulatory boards.

I. The department shall not release personally identifiable patient or physician information.

J. The rules adopted by the director pursuant to this section do not limit the ability of a physician or other health professional to advise a patient on any health issue.

(11) FETAL REMAINS

Arizona provides by statute for issues involving aborted fetal remains. Under the laws a death certificate is required for an aborted fetus that had a gestational period of 20 weeks or had a specific weight. In addition, the state does not require a transportation permit be obtained for movement of an aborted fetus under specific circumstances. The statutes are set out below.

Arizona Code § 36-329. Fetal death certificate registration

A. A hospital, abortion clinic, physician or midwife shall submit a completed fetal death certificate to the state registrar for registration within seven days after the fetal death for each fetal death occurring in this state after a gestational period of twenty completed weeks or if the product of human conception weighs more than three hundred fifty grams.

B. The requirements for registering a fetal death certificate are the same as the requirements for registering a death certificate prescribed in § 36-325.

Arizona Code § 36-326(F). Disposition transit permit

F. A hospital or abortion clinic is not required to obtain a disposition-transit permit if a product of human conception is expelled or extracted at the hospital or abortion clinic and all the following apply:

1. The gestation period of the product of human conception is less than twenty weeks or, if the gestation period is unknown, the weight of the product of human conception is less than three hundred fifty grams.

2. A county medical examiner's investigation is not required.

3. The woman on whom the abortion was performed has authorized the hospital or abortion clinic to dispose of the product of human conception.

(12) FOSTER CARE PROVIDERS

Arizona provides by statute that foster care providers cannot consent to a ward having an abortion. The statute addressing the issue is set out below.

Arizona Code § 8-514.05(C). Foster care provider

C. The foster parent, group home staff, foster home staff, relative or other person or agency in whose care the child is currently placed pursuant to this article or article 4 of this chapter:

1. May give consent for the following:

(a) Evaluation and treatment for emergency conditions that are not life threatening.

(b) Routine medical and dental treatment and procedures, including early periodic screening diagnosis and treatment services, and services by health care providers to relieve pain or treat symptoms of common childhood illnesses or conditions.

2. Shall not consent to:

(a) General anesthesia.

(b) Surgery.

(c) Testing for the presence of the human immunodeficiency virus.

(d) Blood transfusions.

(e) Abortions.

(13) HUMAN CLONING

Arizona has enacted a statute that prohibits the expenditure of public funds for human cloning. The statute is set out below.

Arizona Code § 35-196.04.
Use of public monies for human cloning

A. Notwithstanding any other law, tax monies of this state or any political subdivision of this state, federal monies passing through the state treasury or the treasury of any political subdivision of this state or any other public monies shall not be used by any person or entity, including any state funded institution or facility, for human somatic cell nuclear transfer, commonly known as human cloning.

B. This section does not restrict areas of scientific research that are not specifically prohibited by this section, including research in the use of nuclear transfer or other cloning techniques to produce molecules, deoxyribonucleic acid, cells other than human embryos, tissues, organs, plants or animals other than humans.

C. For the purposes of this section, "human somatic cell nuclear transfer" means human asexual reproduction that is accomplished by introducing the genetic material from one or more human somatic cells into a fertilized or unfertilized oocyte whose nuclear material has been removed or inactivated so as to produce an organism, at any stage of development, that is genetically virtually identical to an existing or previously existing human organism.

(14) INJURY TO PREGNANT WOMAN

Arizona has made it a criminal offense to cause the death of a fetus through injury to a pregnant woman. The statutes addressing the issue are set out below.

Arizona Code § 13-1102. Negligent homicide

A. A person commits negligent homicide if with criminal negligence the person causes the death of another person, including an unborn child.

B. An offense under this section applies to an unborn child in the womb at any stage of its development. A person may not be prosecuted under this section if any of the following applies:

1. The person was performing an abortion for which the consent of the pregnant woman, or a person authorized by law to act on the pregnant woman's behalf, has been obtained or for which the consent was implied or authorized by law.

2. The person was performing medical treatment on the pregnant woman or the pregnant woman's unborn child.

3. The person was the unborn child's mother.

C. Negligent homicide is a class 4 felony.

Arizona Code § 13-1103. Manslaughter

A. A person commits manslaughter by:

***

5. Knowingly or recklessly causing the death of an unborn child by any physical injury to the mother.

B. An offense under subsection A, paragraph 5 of this section applies to an unborn child in the womb at any stage of its development. A person shall not be prosecuted under subsection A, paragraph 5 of this section if any of the following applies:

1. The person was performing an abortion for which the consent of the pregnant woman, or a person authorized by law to act on the pregnant woman's behalf, has been obtained or for which the consent was implied or authorized by law.

2. The person was performing medical treatment on the pregnant woman or the pregnant woman's unborn child.

3. The person was the unborn child's mother.

C. Manslaughter is a class 2 felony.

Arizona Code § 13-1104. Second degree murder

A. A person commits second degree murder if without premeditation:

1. The person intentionally causes the death of another person, including an unborn child or, as a result of intentionally causing the death of another person, causes the death of an unborn child; or

2. Knowing that the person's conduct will cause death or serious physical injury, the person causes the death of another person, including an unborn child or, as a result of knowingly causing the death of another person, causes the death of an unborn child; or

3. Under circumstances manifesting extreme indifference to human life, the person recklessly engages in conduct that creates a grave risk of death and thereby causes the death of another person, including an unborn child or, as a result of recklessly causing the death of another person, causes the death of an unborn child.

B. An offense under this section applies to an unborn child in the womb at any stage of its development. A person may not be prosecuted under this section if any of the following applies:

1. The person was performing an abortion for which the consent of the pregnant woman, or a person authorized by law to act on the pregnant woman's behalf, has been obtained or for which the consent was implied or authorized by law.

2. The person was performing medical treatment on the pregnant woman or the pregnant woman's unborn child.

3. The person was the unborn child's mother.

C. Second degree murder is a class 1 felony and is punishable as provided by § 13-604, subsection S, § 13-604.01 if the victim is under fifteen years of age or is an unborn child or § 13-710.

Arizona Code § 13-1105. First degree murder

A. A person commits first degree murder if:

1. Intending or knowing that the person's conduct will cause death, the person causes the death of another person, including an unborn child, with premeditation or, as a result of causing the death of another person with premeditation, causes the death of an unborn child.

2. Acting either alone or with one or more other persons the person commits or attempts to commit sexual conduct with a minor under § 13-1405, sexual assault under § 13-1406, molestation of a child under § 13-1410, terrorism under § 13-2308.01, marijuana offenses under § 13-3405, subsection A, paragraph 4, dangerous drug offenses under § 13-3407, subsection A, paragraphs 4 and 7, narcotics offenses under § 13-3408, subsection A, paragraph 7 that equal or exceed the statutory threshold amount for each offense or combination of offenses, involving or using minors in drug offenses under § 13-3409, kidnapping under § 13-1304, burglary under § 13-1506, 13-1507 or 13-1508, arson under § 13-1703 or 13-1704, robbery under § 13-1902, 13-1903 or 13-1904, escape under § 13-2503 or 13-2504, child abuse under § 13-3623, subsection A, paragraph 1, or unlawful flight from a pursuing law enforcement vehicle under § 28-622.01 and in the course of and in furtherance of the offense or immediate flight from the offense, the person or another person causes the death of any person.

3. Intending or knowing that the person's conduct will cause death to a law enforcement officer, the person causes the death of a law enforcement officer who is in the line of duty.

B. Homicide, as prescribed in subsection A, paragraph 2 of this section, requires no specific mental state other than what is required for the commission of any of the enumerated felonies.

C. An offense under subsection A, paragraph 1 of this section applies to an unborn child in the womb at any stage of its development. A person shall not be prosecuted under subsection A, paragraph 1 of this section if any of the following applies:

1. The person was performing an abortion for which the consent of the pregnant woman, or a person authorized by law to act on the pregnant woman's behalf, has been obtained or for which the consent was implied or authorized by law.

2. The person was performing medical treatment on the pregnant woman or the pregnant woman's unborn child.

3. The person was the unborn child's mother.

D. First degree murder is a class 1 felony and is punishable by death or life imprisonment as provided by §§ 13-703 and 13-703.01.

Arkansas

(1) OVERVIEW

The state of Arkansas enacted its first criminal abortion statute on February 16, 1838. The statute underwent a few amendments prior to the 1973 decision by the United States Supreme Court in *Roe v. Wade*, which legalized abortion in the nation. In spite of the decision in *Roe*, Arkansas has not repealed its pre–*Roe* criminal abortion statute. However, under *Roe* the statute is constitutionally infirm.

Arkansas has taken affirmative steps to respond to *Roe* and its progeny. The state has addressed numerous abortion issues by statute that include post-viability abortion, partial-birth abortion, abortion by minors, abortion by physician only, public funds for abortion, use of facilities and people, injury to a pregnant woman, ultrasound images, informed consent, fetal pain awareness, abortion facilities, fetal death report, disposal of fetal remains, human cloning, and pro-life license plate. In addition, an amendment was made to Arkansas' constitution that reflected the general pro-life position of the state. Amendment 68, section 2 of the state's constitution provides that "[t]he policy of Arkansas is to protect the life of every unborn child from conception until birth, to the extent permitted by the Federal Constitution."

(2) PRE-ROE ABORTION BAN

As previously indicated, Arkansas has not repealed its pre–*Roe* criminal abortion statutes. The statutes remain on the books even after being expressly found to violate the constitution of Arkansas in *Smith v. Bentley*, 493 F.Supp. 916 (E.D. Ark. 1980). The statutes are set out below.

Arkansas Code § 5-61-101. Inducing person to have abortion

(a) It is unlawful for any person to induce another person to have an abortion or to willfully terminate the pregnancy of a woman known to be pregnant with the intent to cause fetal death unless the person is licensed to practice medicine in the State of Arkansas.

(b) Violation of subsection (a) of this section is a Class D felony.

(c) Nothing in this section shall be construed to allow the charging or conviction of a woman with any criminal offense in the death of her own unborn child in utero.

Arkansas Code § 5-61-102. Unlawful abortion

(a) It shall be unlawful for anyone to administer or prescribe any medicine or drugs to any woman with child, with the intent to produce an abortion or premature delivery of any fetus before or after the period of quickening or to produce or attempt to produce such abortion by any other means.

(b) Any person violating a provision of this section is guilty of a Class D felony.

(c) Nothing in this section shall be construed to allow the charging or conviction of a woman with any criminal offense in the death of her own unborn child in utero.

(3) POST-VIABILITY ABORTION

Arkansas has enacted penal statutes that prohibit post-viability abortions, except to preserve the life or health of the woman; or when pregnancy to a minor resulted from rape or incest. Two physicians are required to be present during a post-viability abortion. The statutes are set out below.

Arkansas Code § 20-16-701. General Assembly; intention

(a) It is the intention of the General Assembly to regulate abortions in a manner consistent with the decisions of the United States Supreme Court.

(b) All provisions and all terms shall be construed so as to be consistent with those decisions.

Arkansas Code § 20-16-702. Definitions

As used in this subchapter:

(1) "Abortion" means the intentional termination of the pregnancy of a mother with an intention other than to increase the probability of a live birth or to remove a dead or dying fetus;

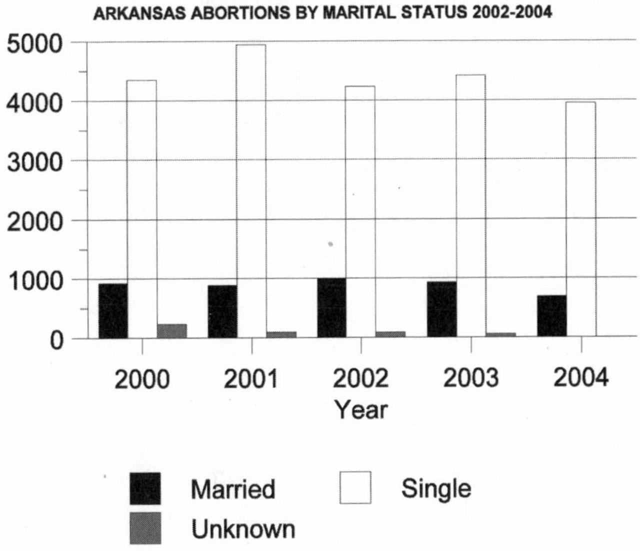

Source: **Arkansas Department of Health and Human Services.**

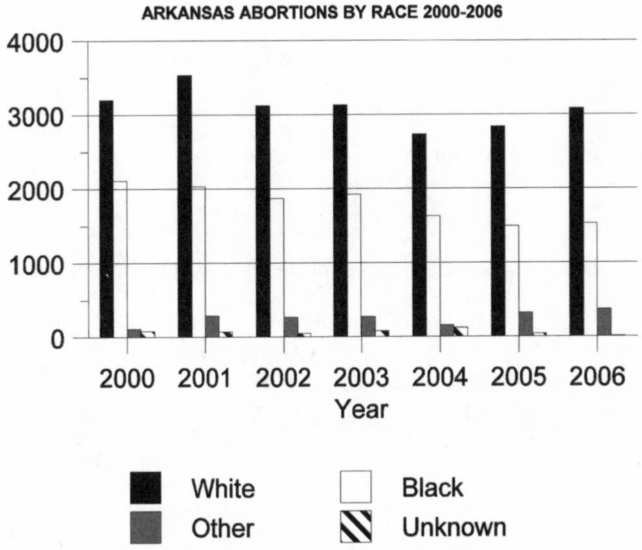

Source: **Arkansas Department of Health and Human Services.**

(2) "Physician" means any person licensed to practice medicine in this state; and

(3) "Viable fetus" means a fetus which can live outside the womb.

Arkansas Code § 20-16-703. Viability of fetus

For the purpose of this subchapter, a fetus shall be presumed not to be viable prior to the end of the twenty-fifth week of the pregnancy.

Arkansas Code § 20-16-704. Penalty

(a) A violation of this subchapter shall be a Class A misdemeanor.

(b) Nothing in this subchapter shall be construed to allow the charging or conviction of a woman with any criminal offense in the death of her own unborn child in utero.

Arkansas Code § 20-16-705. Post-viability ban

(a) No abortion of a viable fetus shall be performed unless necessary to preserve the life or health of the woman.

(b) Before a physician may perform an abortion upon a pregnant woman after such time as her fetus has become viable, the physician shall

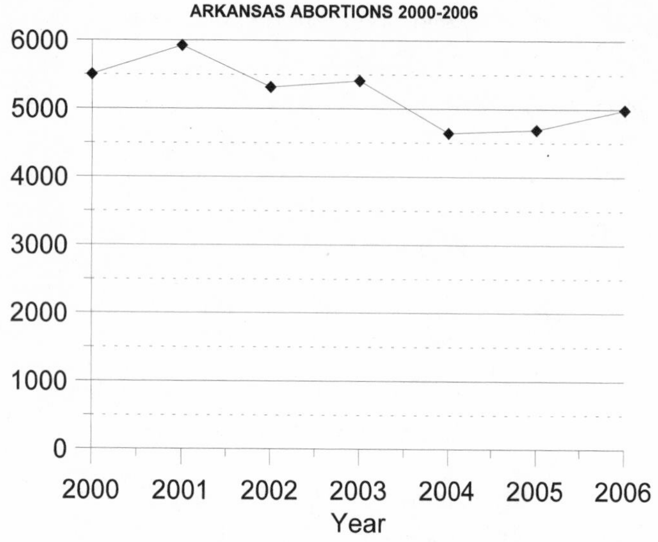

Source: **Arkansas Department of Health and Human Services.**

Arkansas Prior Abortion by Female 2000–2006

Prior Abortion

Year	*None*	*1*	*2*	*≥3*	*Not known*
2000	2,409	1,408	397	169	1,118
2001	3,848	1,477	431	165	3
2002	3,266	1,400	437	194	19
2003	3,353	1,372	470	208	5
2004	not reported	n/r	n/r	n/r	n/r
2005	2,775	969	448	281	2
2006	3,115	1,140	459	272	2
Total	18,766	7,766	2,642	1,289	1,149

Source: **Arkansas Department of Health and Human Services.**

Arkansas Abortion by Age Group 2000–2006

Age Group (yrs)

Year	*<15*	*15–19*	*20–24*	*25–29*	*30–34*	*35–39*	*≥40*	*Unknown*
2000	56	1,102	1,905	1,239	640	390	117	52
2001	54	1,130	2,046	1,301	781	440	147	25
2002	54	942	1,833	1,244	681	388	136	28
2003	52	963	1,837	1,269	718	377	183	9
2004	49	835	1,461	1,084	667	393	151	4
2005	45	740	1,588	1,070	727	395	129	1
2006	46	910	1,592	1,182	665	442	148	3
Total	356	6,622	12,262	8,389	4,879	2,825	1,011	122

Source: **Arkansas Department of Health and Human Services.**

first certify in writing that the abortion is necessary to preserve the life or health of the woman and shall further certify in writing the medical indications for the abortion and the probable health consequences.

(c) This subchapter shall not prohibit the abortion of a viable fetus if the pregnancy is the result of rape or incest perpetrated on a minor.

Arkansas Code § 20-16-706. Performance of abortion generally

(a) Any physician who performs an abortion upon a woman carrying a viable fetus shall utilize the available method or technique of abortion most likely to preserve the life and health of the viable fetus.

(b) In cases in which the method or technique of abortion which would most likely preserve the life and health of the viable fetus would present a greater risk to the life and health of the woman than another available method or technique, the physician may utilize the other method or technique.

(c) In all cases in which the physician performs an abortion upon a viable fetus, the physician shall certify in writing the available method or techniques considered and the reasons for choosing the method or technique employed.

Arkansas Code § 20-16-707. Physicians required

(a) An abortion of a viable fetus shall be performed or induced only when there is in attendance a physician other than the physician performing or inducing the abortion who shall take control of and provide immediate medical care for a child born as a result of the abortion.

(b) During the performance of the abortion, the physician performing it and, subsequent to the abortion, the physician required by this section to be in attendance shall take all reasonable steps in keeping with good medical practice, consistent with the procedure used, to preserve the life and health of the viable fetus; provided that it does not pose an increased risk to the life or health of the woman.

(4) PARTIAL-BIRTH ABORTION

Arkansas criminalizes performance of partial-birth abortions, unless it is done to preserve the life of the woman. The ban is probably infirm as a result of the United States Supreme Court decision in *Stenberg v. Carhart*, which invalidated a Nebraska statute that prohibited partial-birth abortions. Additionally, a federal court issued an order enjoining enforcement of the statute in *Little Rock Family Planning Services v. Jegley*, 192 F.3d 794 (8th Cir. 1999). However, in the later decision of *Gonzales v. Carhart* the United States Supreme Court approved of a federal statute banning partial-birth abortion. Arkansas' partial-birth abortion statutes are set out below.

Arkansas Code § 5-61-201. Short title

This subchapter may be cited as the "Partial-Birth Abortion Ban Act of 1997."

Arkansas Code § 5-61-202. Definition of partial-birth abortion

As used in this subchapter, "partial-birth abortion" means an abortion in which the person performing the abortion partially vaginally delivers a living fetus before taking the life of the fetus and completing the delivery or as defined by the United States Supreme Court.

Arkansas Code § 5-61-203. Partial-birth abortion offense

(a) Any person who knowingly performs a partial-birth abortion and thereby takes the life of a human fetus shall be guilty of a Class D felony.

(b) A woman upon whom a partial-birth abortion is performed may not be prosecuted under this section for conspiracy, solicitation, attempt, or complicity to violate this section.

(c) It is an affirmative defense to a prosecution under this section, which must be proved by a preponderance of the evidence, that the partial-birth abortion was performed by a physician who reasonably believed:

(1) The partial-birth abortion was necessary to save the life of the woman upon whom it was performed; and

(2) No other form of abortion would suffice for that purpose.

(d)(1) Prior to charging a person under this section, a prosecutor shall refer the investigation to the State Medical Board, which shall determine whether the procedure at issue in the investigation is a partial-birth abortion as defined by this subchapter.

(2) If the board determines that the procedure being investigated is not a partial-birth abortion as defined by this subchapter, the prosecutor shall not proceed with the case.

(e) This subchapter is operative and shall be enforced to the extent permitted by the United States Constitution and laws.

Arkansas Code § 5-61-204. Professional sanction

(a) Any person who knowingly performs a partial-birth abortion is subject to disciplinary action by the State Medical Board.

Arkansas Abortion by Weeks of Gestation 2000–2006

Weeks of Gestation	2000	2001	2002	2003	2004	2005	2006	Total
	Year							
≤6	1,425	1,787	1,500	1,584	1,389	1,473	1,576	10,734
7	835	780	802	797	655	645	675	5,189
8	667	711	680	683	486	580	634	4,441
9	565	538	521	511	430	433	544	3,542
10	389	455	394	400	375	334	371	2,718
11	289	333	293	286	237	257	277	1,972
12	200	258	228	228	193	186	187	1,480
13	170	203	171	171	154	151	172	1,192
14	175	166	156	133	116	125	120	991
15	149	162	118	135	116	114	105	899
16	166	127	107	100	119	86	71	776
17	114	139	97	106	111	89	72	728
18	115	101	83	101	103	94	73	670
19	87	111	64	69	72	77	74	554
20	94	43	62	62	60	49	35	405
≥21	28	6	37	42	26	2	1	142
Not known	33	4	3	0	2	0	1	43

Source: **Arkansas Department of Health and Human Services.**

(b) Disciplinary action taken by the board against a physician who violates this subchapter shall include, as determined by the board:

(1) A fine not greater than ten thousand dollars ($10,000);

(2) Suspension of the physician's license for a period not greater than one (1) year; or

(3) Revocation of the physician's license.

(5) ABORTION BY MINORS

Under the laws of Arkansas no physician may perform an abortion upon an unemancipated minor without the written consent of a parent or guardian. In compliance with federal constitutional law, Arkansas has provided a judicial waiver procedure for an unemancipated minor to obtain an abortion without parental consent. If an unemancipated minor elects not to obtain consent from either of her parents, the minor may petition a trial court for a waiver of the consent requirement. A minor has a right to an attorney at the proceeding and if she cannot afford one, the court must appoint her an attorney. If a minor chooses, she may represent herself. The abortion statutes for minors are set out below.

Arkansas Code § 20-16-801. Consent required

Except as otherwise provided in §§ 20-16-804 and 20-16-805, no person may perform an abortion upon an unemancipated minor or upon a woman for whom a guardian or custodian has been appointed because of a finding of incompetency unless the person or the person's agent first obtains the written consent of either parent or the legal guardian or custodian.

Arkansas Code § 20-16-802. Definitions

As used in this subchapter:

(1) "Abortion" means the intentional termination of the pregnancy of a woman known to be pregnant with an intention other than to increase the probability of a live birth or to remove a dead or dying fetus;

(2) "Medical emergency" means a condition that, on the basis of the physician's good faith clinical judgment, so complicates the medical condition of a pregnant woman as to necessitate the immediate abortion of her pregnancy to avert her death or for which a delay will create serious risk of substantial and irreversible impairment of a major bodily function;

(3) "Minor" means an individual under eighteen (18) years of age;

(4) "Parent" means:

(A) Either parent of the pregnant woman if they are both living;

(B) One (1) parent of the pregnant woman if only one (1) is living or if the second one cannot be located through reasonably diligent effort; or

(C) The court-appointed guardian or custodian if the pregnant woman has one; and

(5) "Unemancipated minor" means a minor who is under the care, custody, and control of her parent or parents.

Arkansas Code § 20-16-803. Manner of consent

(a) The person who performs the abortion or his or her agent shall obtain or be provided with the written consent from either parent or legal guardian.

(b) The written consent shall include, but not be limited to, the following information:

(1) The name and birthdate of the minor or incompetent woman;

(2) The name of the parent or legal guardian;

(3) A statement from the parent or legal guardian that he or she is aware that the minor desires an abortion and that he or she does consent to the abortion;

(4) The date; and

(5) The notarized signature of the parent or legal guardian.

(c) A notarized signature is not required if the person who performs the abortion or his or her agent witnesses the signature of the parent or legal guardian and signs the written consent as a witness.

(d) Prior to signing the written consent as a witness, the person who performs the abortion or his or her agent shall obtain from the parent or legal guardian positive proof of identification in the form of a valid photo identification card.

(e) A photocopy of the proof of identification and the written consent statement shall be maintained in the minor's or incompetent woman's medical records for a period of five (5) years from the date of the abortion.

Arkansas Code § 20-16-804. Judicial bypass

Notwithstanding the provisions of §§ 20-16-801 and 20-16-803, if a pregnant minor or incompetent woman elects not to obtain the consent of one (1) or both parents or guardian or custodian, then:

(1)(A) Any judge of a circuit court, upon petition or motion and after an appropriate hearing, shall authorize a physician to perform the abortion if the judge determines that the pregnant minor or incompetent woman is mature and capable of giving informed consent to the proposed abortion.

(B) If the judge determines that the pregnant minor or incompetent woman is not mature or if the pregnant woman does not claim to be mature, the judge shall determine whether the performance of an abortion upon her without consent of her parents, guardian, or custodian would be in her best interests and shall authorize a physician to perform the abortion without the consent if the judge concludes that the pregnant minor or incompetent woman's best interests would be served by such an action;

(2)(A) Such a pregnant minor or incompetent woman may participate in proceedings in the court on her own behalf. However, the court shall advise her that she has a right to court-appointed counsel and upon her request shall provide her with such counsel.

(B) The minor or incompetent person shall have the right to file her petition in the circuit court using a pseudonym or using solely her initials;

(3) Court proceedings under this section shall be confidential and shall ensure the anonymity of the minor or incompetent person. All court proceedings under this section shall be sealed, and all docu-

ments related to this petition shall be confidential and shall not be available to the public;

(4) These proceedings shall be given precedence over other pending matters to the extent necessary to ensure that the court reaches a decision promptly and without delay so as to serve the best interests of the pregnant minor or incompetent woman;

(5) The judge shall make in writing specific factual findings and legal conclusions supporting the decision and shall order a record of the evidence to be maintained, including the judge's own findings and conclusions;

(6)(A) An expedited confidential appeal shall be available to any such pregnant minor or incompetent woman for whom the court denies an order authorizing an abortion without consent.

(B) An order authorizing an abortion without consent shall not be subject to appeal; and

(7) No filing fees shall be required of any such pregnant minor or incompetent woman at either the trial or the appellate level.

Arkansas Code § 20-16-805. Limitations on requirement

Consent shall not be required under this subchapter if:

(1) The attending physician certifies in the pregnant minor or incompetent woman's medical record that there is a medical emergency and there is insufficient time to obtain the required consent; or

(2) A judicial bypass is obtained under § 20-16-804.

Arkansas Code § 20-16-806. Penalty

(a) The performance of an abortion in violation of this subchapter shall be a Class A misdemeanor and shall be grounds for a civil action by a person whose consent is required.

(b) Nothing in this subchapter shall be construed to allow the charging or conviction of a woman with any criminal offense in the death of her own unborn child in utero.

Arkansas Code § 20-16-807. Construction of provisions

This subchapter is not intended to create and shall not be construed to create an affirmative right to legal abortion.

Arkansas Code § 20-16-808.
When consent of parent not required

Consent under this subchapter shall not be required to be obtained from a parent if:

(1) Both of the parents' whereabouts are unknown; or

(2)(A) If the minor has only one (1) living parent and the minor states by affidavit that the parent has committed incest with the minor, has raped the minor, or has otherwise sexually abused the minor.

(B) The attending physician shall report the abuse as provided under § 12-12-504 and § 12-12-507.

Arkansas Code § 20-16-809.
When consent of guardian not required

A minor shall not be required to obtain consent under this subchapter if the guardianship or custody order has expired or is otherwise no longer in effect.

Arkansas Code § 20-16-810.
Information reported by abortion providers

(a) In addition to other information reported by an abortion provider to the Division of Health of the Department of Health and Human Services, the following information shall be reported for each induced termination of pregnancy:

(1) Whether parental consent was required;

(2) Whether parental consent was obtained; and

(3) Whether a judicial bypass was obtained.

(b) The division shall revise its forms utilized by abortion providers to report an induced termination of pregnancy by including the reporting of information required by this section.

(6) ABORTION BY PHYSICIAN ONLY

Arkansas has made it a felony offense for anyone to perform an abortion who is not a physician. The criminal statute is set out below.

Arkansas Code § 5-61-101.
Abortion licensed medical practitioner

(a) It shall be unlawful for any person to induce another person to have an abortion or to willfully terminate the pregnancy of a woman known to be pregnant with the intent to cause fetal death unless such person shall be licensed to practice medicine in the State of Arkansas.

(b) Violation of this provision shall be a Class D felony.

(c) Nothing in this section shall be construed to allow the charging or conviction of a woman with any criminal offense in the death of her own unborn child in utero.

(7) PUBLIC FUNDS FOR ABORTION

Arkansas has sought to restrict the use of public funds for abortion through an amendment to the state's constitution. Amendment 68, section 1 of the state's constitution provides that "[n]o public funds will be used to pay for any abortion, except to save the mother's life." In *Dalton v. Little Rock Family Planning Services*, the United States Supreme Court held that this amendment was invalid to the extent that federal Medicaid funds given to Arkansas had to be made available for abortions involving incest or rape pregnancies. *Dalton* found that the amendment was valid for any purely state funded program. Subsequent to *Dalton*, the state supreme court also found in *Hodges v. Huckabee*, 995 S.W.2d 341 (Ark. 1999), that the amendment was unenforceable to the extent that it was in conflict with federal law.

(8) USE OF FACILITIES AND PEOPLE

Under the laws of Arkansas hospitals are not required to allow abortions at their facilities. The employees and physicians at hospitals that do allow abortions are permitted to refuse to take part in abortions. The statute is set out below.

Arkansas Code § 20-16-601. Refusal to participate in abortions

(a) No person shall be required to perform or participate in medical procedures which result in the termination of pregnancy. The refusal of any person to perform or participate in these medical procedures shall not be a basis for civil liability to any person nor a basis for any disciplinary or any other recriminatory action against him.

(b) No hospital, hospital director, or governing board shall be required to permit the termination of human pregnancies within its institution, and the refusal to permit the procedures shall not be grounds for civil liability to any person nor a basis for any disciplinary or other recriminatory action against it by the state or any person.

(c) The refusal of any person to submit to an abortion or to give consent for an abortion shall not be grounds for loss of any privileges or immunities to which the person would otherwise be entitled, nor shall submission to an abortion or the granting of consent for an abortion be a condition precedent to the receipt of any public benefits.

(9) INJURY TO PREGNANT WOMAN

The state of Arkansas has made it a criminal offense to cause the death of a fetus through injury to a pregnant woman. The statutes addressing the issue are set out below.

Arkansas Code § 5-1-102. Definitions

***

(13)(A) "Person," "actor," "defendant," "he," "she," "her," or "him" includes:

(i) Any natural person; and

(ii) When appropriate, an "organization" as defined in § 5-2-501.

(B)(i)(a) As used in §§ 5-10-101— 5-10-105 [capital murder, first and second degree murder, manslaughter, negligent homicide], "person" also includes an unborn child in utero at any stage of development.

(b) "Unborn child" means a living fetus of twelve (12) weeks or greater gestation.

(ii) This subdivision (13)(B) does not apply to:

(a) An act that causes the death of an unborn child in utero if the act was committed during a legal abortion to which the woman consented;

(b) An act that is committed pursuant to a usual and customary standard of medical practice during diagnostic testing or therapeutic treatment; or

(c) An act that is committed in the course of medical research, experimental medicine, or an act deemed necessary to save the life or preserve the health of the woman.

(iii) Nothing in this subdivision (13)(B) shall be construed to allow the charging or conviction of a woman with any criminal offense in the death of her own unborn child in utero.

Arkansas Code § 5-13-201 Battery in the first degree

(a) A person commits battery in the first degree if:

(A) He causes physical injury to a pregnant woman in the commission of a felony or a Class A misdemeanor causing her to suffer a miscarriage or stillbirth as a result of that injury; or

(B) He recklessly causes physical injury to a pregnant woman or causes physical injury to a pregnant woman under circumstances manifesting extreme indifference to the value of human life causing her to suffer a miscarriage or stillbirth as a result of that injury.

(c) Battery in the first degree is a Class B felony.

(10) ULTRASOUND IMAGES

Arkansas requires by statute that if an abortion physician uses ultrasound imaging, he/she must allow the woman to view the ultrasound before performing the abortion. The statute is set out below.

Arkansas Code § 20-16-602. Viewing of ultrasound images

(a) All physicians who use ultrasound equipment in the performance of an abortion shall inform the woman that she has the right to view the ultrasound image of her unborn child before an abortion is performed.

(b)(1) The physician shall certify in writing that the woman was offered an opportunity to view the ultrasound image and shall obtain the woman's acceptance or rejection to view the image in writing.

(2) If the woman accepts the offer and requests to view the ultrasound image, she shall be allowed to view it.

(c) The physician's certification together with the woman's signed acceptance or rejection shall be placed in the woman's medical file in the physician's office and kept for three (3) years.

(d) Any physician who fails to inform the woman that she has the right to view the ultrasound image of her unborn child before an abortion is performed or fails to allow her to view the ultrasound image upon her request may be subject to disciplinary action by the Arkansas State Medical Board.

(11) INFORMED CONSENT

Arkansas prohibits an abortion, except for medical emergencies, taking place until after a woman has been provided with statutorily required informed consent information. Some of the information required to be disclosed include: the name of the physician performing the abortion, the medical risks associated with the abortion procedure, the gestational age of the fetus at the time the abortion is to be performed and the medical risks associated with carrying the fetus to term. The statutes are set out below.

Arkansas Code § 20-16-901. Title

This subchapter shall be known and may be cited as the "Woman's Right to Know Act of 2001."

Arkansas Code § 20-16-902. Definitions

As used in this subchapter:

(1) "Abortion" means the use or prescription of any instrument, medicine, drug, or any other substance or device intentionally to terminate the pregnancy of a woman known to be pregnant, for a purpose other than to increase the probability of a live birth, to preserve the life or health of the child after a live birth, or to remove a dead fetus;

(2) "Attempt to perform an abortion" means an act or an omission of a statutorily required act that under the circumstances as the actor believes them to be constitutes a substantial step in a course of conduct planned to culminate in the termination of a pregnancy in Arkansas;

(3) "Board" means the Arkansas State Medical Board or the appropriate health care professional licensing board;

(4) "Division" means the Division of Health of the Department of Health and Human Services;

(5) "Director" means the Director of the Division of Health of the Department of Health and Human Services;

(6) "Gestational age" means the age of the fetus as calculated from the first day of the last menstrual period of the pregnant woman;

(7) "Medical emergency" means any condition which, on the basis of the physician's good faith clinical judgment, so complicates the medical condition of a pregnant woman as to necessitate the immediate termination of her pregnancy to avert her death or for which a delay will create serious risk of impairment of a major bodily function which is substantial and deemed to be irreversible;

(8) "Physician" means any person licensed to practice medicine in this state; and

(9) "Probable gestational age of the fetus' means what in the judgment of the physician will with reasonable probability be the gestational age of the fetus at the time the abortion is planned to be performed.

Arkansas Code § 20-16-903. Informed consent

(a) No abortion shall be performed in this state except with the voluntary and informed consent of the woman upon whom the abortion is to be performed.

(b) Except in the case of a medical emergency, consent to an abortion is voluntary and informed only if:

(1) Prior to and in no event on the same day as the abortion, the woman is told the following, by telephone or in person, by the physician who is to perform the abortion, by a referring physician, or by an agent of either physician:

(A) The name of the physician who will perform the abortion;

(B) The medical risks associated with the particular abortion procedure to be employed;

(C) The probable gestational age of the fetus at the time the abortion is to be performed;

(D) The medical risks associated with carrying the fetus to term; and

(E) That a spouse, boyfriend, parent, friend or other person can not force her to have an abortion.

(2)(A)(i) The information required by subdivision (b)(1) of this section may be provided by telephone without conducting a physical examination or tests of the woman.

(ii) If the information is supplied by telephone, the information may be based both on facts supplied to the physician or his or her agent by the woman and on whatever other relevant information is reasonably available to the physician or his or her agent.

(B) The information required by subdivision (b)(1) of this section may not be provided by a tape recording but shall be provided during a consultation in which the physician or his or her

agent is able to ask questions of the woman and the woman is able to ask questions of the physician.

(C) If a physical examination, tests, or other new information subsequently indicates the need in the medical judgment of the physician for a revision of the information previously supplied to the woman, that revised information may be communicated to the woman at any time prior to the performance of the abortion.

(D) Nothing in this section may be construed to preclude provision of required information through a translator in a language understood by the woman;

(3) Prior to and in no event on the same day as the abortion, the woman is informed, by telephone or in person, by the physician who is to perform the abortion, by a referring physician, or by an agent of either physician:

(A) That medical assistance benefits may be available for prenatal care, childbirth, and neonatal care;

(B) That the father is liable to assist in the support of her child, even in instances in which the father has offered to pay for the abortion;

(C) That she has the option to review the printed or electronic materials described in § 20-16-904 and that those materials:

(i) Have been provided by the State of Arkansas; and

(ii) Describe the fetus and list agencies that offer alternatives to abortion; and

(D) That if the woman chooses to exercise her option to view the materials:

(i) In a printed form, the materials shall be mailed to her by a method chosen by her; or

(ii) Via the internet, she shall be informed prior to and in no event on the same day as the abortion of the specific address of the website where the materials can be accessed;

(4) The information required by subdivision (b)(3) of this section may be provided by a tape recording if provision is made to record or otherwise register specifically whether the woman does or does not choose to review the printed materials;

(5) Prior to the termination of the pregnancy, the woman certifies in writing that the information described in subdivision (b)(1) of this section and her options described in subdivision (b)(3) of this section have been furnished to her and that she has been informed of her option to review the information referred to in subdivision (b)(3)(C) of this section;

(6) Prior to the abortion, the physician who is to perform the procedure or the physician's agent receives a copy of the written certification prescribed by subdivision (b)(5) of this section;

(7) Before the abortion procedure is performed, the physician shall confirm with the patient that she has received information regarding:

(A) The medical risks associated with the particular abortion procedure to be employed;

(B) The probable gestational age of the unborn child at the time the abortion is to be performed; and

(C) The medical risks associated with carrying the fetus to term; and

(D) That a spouse, boyfriend, parent, friend, or other person can not force her to have an abortion.

(c) The Arkansas State Medical Board shall promulgate regulations to ensure that physicians who perform abortions, referring physicians, or agents of either physician comply with all the requirements of this section.

Arkansas Code § 20-16-904. Printed materials

(a) The Division of Health of the Department of Health and Human Services shall cause to be published in English and in each language which is the primary language of two percent (2%) or more of the state's population and shall update on an annual basis the following printed materials in such a way as to ensure that the information is easily comprehensible:

(1) At the option of the division:

(A) Geographically indexed materials designed to inform the woman of public and private agencies, including adoption agencies, and services available to assist a woman through pregnancy, upon childbirth, and while the child is dependent, including:

(i) A comprehensive list of the agencies available;

(ii) A description of the services they offer; and

(iii) A description of the manner, including telephone numbers, in which they might be contacted; or

(B) Printed materials, including a toll-free telephone number which may be called twenty-four (24) hours per day to obtain orally a list and description of agencies in the locality of the caller and of the services they offer; and

(2)(A) Materials designed to inform the woman of the probable anatomical and physiological characteristics of the fetus at two-week gestational increments from the time when a woman can be known to be pregnant to full term, including:

(i) Any relevant information on the possibility of the fetus' survival; and

(ii) Pictures or drawings representing the development of fetuses at two-week gestational increments, provided that the pictures or drawings shall describe the dimensions of the fetus and shall be realistic and appropriate for the stage of pregnancy depicted.

(B) The materials shall be objective, nonjudgmental, and designed to convey only accurate scientific information about the fetus at the various gestational ages.

(C) The material shall also contain objective information describing:

(i) The methods of termination of pregnancy procedures commonly employed;

(ii) The medical risks commonly associated with each of those procedures;

(iii) The possible detrimental psychological effects of termination of pregnancy; and

(iv) The medical risks commonly associated with carrying a child to term.

(b) The materials referred to in subsection (a) of this section shall be printed in a typeface large enough to be clearly legible.

(c) The materials required under this section shall be available at no cost from the division and shall be distributed upon request in appropriate numbers to any person, facility, or hospital.

(d)(1) The division shall develop and maintain a secure website to provide the information described under subsection (a) of this section.

(2) The website shall be maintained at a minimum resolution of 72 pixels per inch.

Arkansas Code § 20-16-905. Medical emergency

When a medical emergency compels the performance of an abortion, the physician shall inform the woman, prior to the abortion if possible, of the medical indications supporting the physician's judgment that:

(1) An abortion is necessary to avert her death; or

(2) A delay will create a serious risk of impairment of a major bodily function which is substantial and deemed to be irreversible.

Arkansas Code § 20-16-906. Regulations

(a) The Division of Health of the Department of Health and Human Services shall develop and promulgate regulations regarding reporting requirements.

(b) The Center for Health Statistics of the Division of Health of the

Department of Health and Human Services shall ensure that all information collected by the center regarding abortions performed in this state shall be available to the public in printed form and on a twenty-four-hour basis on the center's website, provided that in no case shall the privacy of a patient or doctor be compromised.

(c) The information collected by the center regarding abortions performed in this state shall be continually updated.

(d)(1)(A) By June 3 of each year, the division shall issue a public report providing statistics on the number of women provided information and materials pursuant to this subchapter during the previous calendar year.

(B) Each report shall also provide the statistics for all previous calendar years, adjusted to reflect any additional information received after the deadline.

(2) The division shall take care to ensure that none of the information included in the public reports could reasonably lead to the identification of any individual who received information in accordance with § 20-16-903(1) or 20-16-903(3).

Arkansas Code § 20-16-907. Penalties

(a) A person who knowingly or recklessly performs or attempts to perform a termination of a pregnancy in violation of this subchapter shall be subject to disciplinary action by the Arkansas State Medical Board.

(b) No penalty may be assessed against the woman upon whom the abortion is performed or attempted to be performed.

(c) No penalty or civil liability may be assessed for failure to comply with any provision of § 20-16-903 unless the Division of Health of the Department of Health and Human Services has made the printed materials available at the time that the physician or the physician's agent is required to inform the woman of her right to review them.

Arkansas Code § 20-16-908.
Identity preserved from public disclosure

(a) In every proceeding or action brought under this subchapter, the court or board shall rule, upon motion or sua sponte, whether the identity of any woman upon whom a termination of pregnancy has been performed or attempted shall be preserved from public disclosure if she does not give her consent to disclosure.

(b) If the court or board rules that the woman's anonymity should be preserved, the court or board shall order the parties, witnesses, and counsel to preserve her anonymity and shall direct the sealing of the record and the exclusion of individuals from courtrooms or hearing rooms to the extent necessary to safeguard her identity from public disclosure.

(c) Each order to preserve the woman's anonymity shall be accompanied by specific written findings explaining:

(1) Why the anonymity of the woman should be preserved from public disclosure;

(2) Why the order is essential to that end;

(3) How the order is narrowly tailored to serve that interest; and

(4) Why no reasonable less restrictive alternative exists.

(d) This section shall not be construed to conceal the identity of the plaintiff or of witnesses from the defendant.

(12) FETAL PAIN AWARENESS

Arizona has enacted statutes that require a physician inform a woman about fetal pain. Under the statutes a woman must be told whether an anesthetic would eliminate organic pain to the fetus. The statutes are set out below.

Arkansas Code § 20-16-1101. Title

This subchapter shall be known and may be cited as the "Unborn Child Pain Awareness and Prevention Act."

Arkansas Code § 20-16-1102. Definitions

As used in this subchapter:

(1)(A) "Abortion" means the use or prescription of any instrument, medicine, drug, or other substance or device intentionally to terminate the pregnancy of a female known to be pregnant.

(B) However, "abortion" does not include the termination of a pregnancy if the termination is intended to:

(i) Increase the probability of a live birth;

(ii) Preserve the life or health of the child after live birth; or

(iii) Remove a dead fetus who died as the result of a spontaneous miscarriage;

(2) "Attempt to perform an abortion" means an act or an omission of a statutorily required act that under the circumstances as the actor believes them to be constitutes a substantial step in a course of conduct planned to culminate in the termination of a pregnancy in this state;

(3) "Gestational age" means the age of the unborn child as calculated from the first day of the last menstrual period of the pregnant woman;

(4) "Medical emergency" means any condition that on the basis of the physician's good-faith clinical judgment so complicates the medical condition of a pregnant female that:

(A) The immediate abortion of her pregnancy is necessary to prevent her death; or

(B) A delay will create a serious risk of substantial and irreversible impairment of a major bodily function of the pregnant female;

(5) "Physician" means a person authorized or licensed to practice medicine under the Arkansas Medical Practices Act, §§ 17-95-201 et seq., 17-95-301 et seq., and 17-95-401 et seq., and a person authorized to practice osteopathy under § 17-91-101 et seq.;

(6) "Probable gestational age" means the age that with reasonable probability in the judgment of a physician will be the gestational age of the unborn child at the time the abortion is planned to be performed; and

(7) "Unborn child" means a member of the species Homo sapiens from fertilization until birth.

Arkansas Code § 20-16-1103.
Unborn-child pain awareness information

Except in the case of a medical emergency:

(1) At least twenty-four (24) hours before an abortion is performed on an unborn child whose probable gestational age is twenty (20) weeks or more, the physician performing the abortion or the physician's agent shall inform the pregnant female by telephone or in person:

(A) She has the right to review the printed materials described in § 20-16-1105;

(B) These materials are available on a state-sponsored website; and

(C) What the website address is;

(2) The physician or the physician's agent shall orally inform the pregnant female that:

(A) The materials have been provided by the State of Arkansas; and

(B) They contain information on pain in relation to the unborn child;

(3) If the pregnant female chooses to view the materials other than on the website, the materials shall either:

(A) Be given to her at least twenty-four (24) hours before the abortion; or

(B) Mailed to her at least seventy-two (72) hours before the abortion by certified mail, restricted delivery to addressee, so that the postal employee may deliver the mail only to the pregnant female;

(4) If provisions are made to record or otherwise register specifically whether the female does or does not choose to have the printed materials given or mailed to her, the information required by this section may be provided by a tape recording;

(5) The pregnant female shall certify in writing before the abortion that:

(A) The information described in subdivision (1) of this section has been furnished her; and

(B) She has been informed of her opportunity to review the printed materials described in § 20-16-1105; and

(6) Before the abortion is performed, the physician who is to perform the abortion or the physician's agent shall:

(A) Obtain a copy of the written certification required under subdivision (5) of this section; and

(B) Retain it on file with the female's medical record for at least three (3) years following the date of receipt.

Arkansas Code § 20-16-1104. Unborn-child pain prevention

(a) Except in the case of a medical emergency, before an abortion is performed on an unborn child whose gestational age is twenty (20) weeks or more, the physician performing the abortion or the physician's agent shall inform the pregnant female:

(1) Whether an anesthetic or analgesic would eliminate or alleviate organic pain to the unborn child that could be caused by the particular method of abortion to be employed; and

(2) Of the particular medical risks associated with the particular anesthetic or analgesic.

(b) After presenting the information required in subsection (a) of this section and with the consent of the pregnant female, the physician shall administer the anesthetic or analgesic.

Arkansas Code § 20-16-1105. Printed information

(a)(1)(A) The Division of Health of the Department of Health and Human Services shall publish in English and in each language that is the primary language of two percent (2%) or more of the state's population printed materials with the following statement concerning unborn children of twenty (20) weeks gestational age or more:

"By twenty (20) weeks gestation, the unborn child has the physical structures necessary to experience pain. There is evidence that by twenty (20) weeks gestation unborn children seek to evade certain stimuli in a manner that in an infant or an adult would be interpreted to be a response to pain. Anesthesia is routinely administered to unborn children who are twenty (20) weeks gestational age or more who undergo prenatal surgery."

(B) The materials shall be objective, nonjudgmental, and designed to convey only accurate scientific information about the human fetus at the various gestational ages.

(2) The Department of Health and Human Services shall make the materials available on the department's website.

(3) The materials referred to in subdivision (a)(1) of this section shall be printed in a typeface large enough to be clearly legible.

(b)(1) The department's website shall be maintained at a minimum resolution of seventy-two (72) dots per inch.

(2) All pictures appearing on the website shall be a minimum of two hundred by three hundred (200 X 300) pixels.

(3) All letters on the website shall be presented in a minimum of 11-point type.

(4) All information and pictures shall be accessible with an industry-standard browser that requires no additional plug-ins.

(c) Upon request, the division shall make available to any person, facility, or hospital at no cost and in appropriate numbers the materials required under this section.

Arkansas Code § 20-16-1106. Internet website

(a) The Department of Health and Human Services shall include on its website the information described in § 20-16-1105.

(b) No information regarding persons who use the website shall be collected or maintained.

(c) The department shall monitor the website on a daily basis to prevent and correct tampering.

Arkansas Code § 20-16-1107. Medical emergency

If a medical emergency compels a physician to perform an abortion, the physician shall inform the pregnant female before the abortion is performed, if possible, of the medical indications supporting the physician's judgment that:

(1) An abortion is necessary to prevent her death; or

(2) A twenty-four-hour delay will create a serious risk of substantial and irreversible impairment of a major bodily function of the pregnant female.

Arkansas Code § 20-16-1108. Reporting

(a) The Division of Health of the Department of Health and Human Services shall prepare a reporting form for physicians containing a reprint of this subchapter and listing:

(1)(A) The number of females to whom the physician or an agent of the physician provided the information described in § 20-16-1103(1).

(B) Of that number, the number provided by telephone and the number provided in person.

(C) Of each of the numbers described in this subdivision (a)(1) and subdivision (a)(2) of this section, the number provided in the capacity of:

(i) A physician who is to perform the abortion; or

(ii) An agent of the physician;

(2) The number of females who did not avail themselves of the opportunity to obtain a copy other than on the website of the printed information described in § 20-16-1105;

(3) The number who, to the best of the reporting physician's information and belief, went on to obtain the abortion;

(4) The number of abortions performed by the physician for which information otherwise required to be provided at least twenty-four (24) hours before the abortion was not so provided because an immediate abortion was necessary to prevent the female's death; and

(5) The number of abortions for which information otherwise required to be provided at least twenty-four (24) hours before the abortion information was not so provided because a delay would create serious risk of substantial and irreversible impairment of a major bodily function of the pregnant female.

(b) The division shall ensure that copies of the reporting forms described in subsection (a) of this section are provided:

(1) Within one hundred twenty (120) days after August 12, 2005, to all physicians licensed to practice in this state;

(2) To each physician who subsequently becomes newly licensed to practice in this state, at the same time as official notification to that physician that the physician is so licensed; and

(3) By December 1 of each year after the calendar year in which this subchapter becomes effective, to all physicians licensed to practice in this state.

(c) By February 28 of each year following a calendar year in any part of which this subchapter was in effect, each physician who provided or whose agent provided information to one (1) or more females in accordance with § 20-16-1103 during the previous calendar year shall submit to the division a copy of the form described in subsection (a) of this section with the requested data entered accurately and completely.

(d)(1) For each of the items listed in subsection (a) of this section, the division shall issue by June 30 of each year a public report providing sta-

tistics compiled by the division on the basis of reports for the previous calendar year submitted in accordance with this section.

(2) Each report shall also provide the statistics for all previous calendar years, adjusted to reflect any additional information from late or corrected reports.

(3) The division shall ensure that none of the information included in the public reports could reasonably lead to the identification of any individual providing or provided information in accordance with § 20-16-1103(1) or § 20-16-1103(2).

(e) So long as reporting forms are sent to all licensed physicians in the state at least one (1) time every year and the report described in this section is issued at least one (1) time every year, the division, in order to achieve administrative convenience or fiscal savings, or to reduce the burden of reporting requirements, may:

(1) Alter any of the dates established in this section; or

(2) Consolidate the forms or reports described in this section with other forms or reports issued by the division.

(f)(1) The division shall assess against a physician who fails to submit a report required under this section within thirty (30) days after the due date a fee of five hundred dollars ($500) for each additional thirty-day period or portion of a thirty-day period during which the report is overdue.

(2)(A) If a physician who is required to report under this section has not submitted a report or has submitted an incomplete report more than one (1) year following the due date of the report, the division may bring an action in a court of competent jurisdiction to seek an order requiring the physician to submit a complete report within a period established by the court.

(B) Failure of the physician to file the complete report within the court-ordered period is punishable as civil contempt.

Arkansas Code § 20-16-1109. Penalties

(a) A person who knowingly or recklessly performs or attempts to perform a termination of a pregnancy in violation of this subchapter shall be subject to disciplinary action by the Arkansas State Medical Board.

(b) No penalty may be assessed against the woman upon whom the abortion is performed or attempted to be performed.

(c) No penalty or civil liability may be assessed for failure to comply with any provision of this subchapter unless the Division of Health of the Department of Health and Human Services has made the printed materials available at the time that the physician or the physician's agent is required to inform the woman of her right to review them.

Arkansas Code § 20-16-1110. Civil remedies

(a) An action seeking actual and punitive damages may be brought against a person who performed an abortion in knowing or reckless violation of this subchapter by:

(1) Any person upon whom the abortion was performed;

(2) The father of the unborn child who was the subject of the abortion; or

(3) A grandparent of the unborn child who was the subject of the abortion.

(b) Any female upon whom an abortion has been attempted in violation of this subchapter may bring an action for actual and punitive damages against a person who attempted to perform the abortion in knowing or reckless violation of this subchapter.

(c)(1) If the Division of Health of the Department of Health and Human Services fails to issue the public report required under § 20-16-1108, any group of ten (10) or more citizens of this state may seek an injunction in a court of competent jurisdiction against the Director of the Division of Health of the Department of Health and Human Services requiring that a complete report be issued within a period established by the court.

(2) Failure of the director to obey an injunction issued under subdivision (c)(1) of this section is punishable as civil contempt.

(d)(1) If judgment is rendered in favor of the plaintiff in any action described in this section, the court shall assess a reasonable attorney's fee in favor of the plaintiff against the defendant.

(2) If judgment is rendered in favor of the defendant and if the court finds that the plaintiff's suit was frivolous and brought in bad faith, the court shall assess a reasonable attorney's fee in favor of the defendant against the plaintiff.

Arkansas Code § 20-16-1111. Privacy in court proceedings

(a) In every civil or criminal action brought under this subchapter in which any female upon whom an abortion has been performed or attempted has not given her consent to disclosure of her identity, the court shall determine whether the anonymity of the female shall be preserved from public disclosure.

(b)(1) The court, upon motion or sua sponte, shall make a ruling on preserving the anonymity of the female.

(2) If the court determines that the female's anonymity should be preserved, that court shall:

(A) Issue appropriate orders to the parties, witnesses, and counsel;

(B) Direct the sealing of the record; and

(C) Order the exclusion of individuals from courtrooms or hearing rooms to the extent necessary to safeguard the anonymity of the female.

(3) Each order issued under subdivisions (b)(1) and (2) of this section shall be accompanied by specific written findings explaining:

(A) Why the anonymity of the female should be preserved from public disclosure;

(B) Why the order is essential to that end;

(C) Why no reasonable less restrictive alternative exists; and

(D) How the order is narrowly tailored to preserve the anonymity of the female.

(c) In the absence of written consent of the female upon whom an abortion has been performed or attempted, anyone other than a public official who brings an action under § 20-16-1110(a) shall do so under a pseudonym.

(d) This section may not be construed to conceal the identity of the plaintiff or witnesses from the defendant.

(13) ABORTION FACILITIES

Arkansas has provided by statute for the regulation of facilities that perform abortion. Such facilities are required to pay an annual licensing fee. The statute addressing the matter is set out below.

Arkansas Code § 20-9-302. Abortion facilities

(a) Any clinic, health center, or other facility in which the pregnancies of women known to be pregnant are willfully terminated or aborted, which activity is a primary function of the clinic, health center, or facility, shall be licensed by the Division of Health of the Department of Health and Human Services. The facilities, equipment, procedures, techniques, and conditions of those clinics or similar facilities shall be subject to periodic inspection by the division.

(b) The division may adopt appropriate rules and regulations regarding the facilities, equipment, procedures, techniques, and conditions of clinics and other facilities subject to the provisions of this section to assure that the facilities, equipment, procedures, techniques, and conditions are aseptic and do not constitute a health hazard.

(c) The division may levy and collect an annual fee of five hundred dollars ($500) per facility for issuance of a permanent license to an abortion facility.

(d) Applicants for a license shall file applications upon such forms as are prescribed by the division. A license shall be issued only for the premises and persons in the application and shall not be transferable.

(e) A license shall be effective on a calendar-year basis and shall ex-

pire on December 31 of each calendar year. Applications for annual license renewal shall be postmarked no later than January 2 of the succeeding calendar year. License applications for existing institutions received after that date shall be subject to a penalty of two dollars ($2.00) per day for each day after January 2.

(f) Subject to such rules and regulations as may be implemented by the Chief Fiscal Officer of the State, the disbursing officer for the division may transfer all unexpended funds relative to the abortion clinics that pertain to fees collected, as certified by the Chief Fiscal Officer of the State, to be carried forward and made available for expenditures for the same purpose for any following fiscal year.

(g) All fees levied and collected under this section are special revenues and shall be deposited into the State Treasury, there to be credited to the Public Health Fund.

(14) FETAL DEATH REPORT

Arkansas provides by statute for reporting abortions and issuing fetal death certificates. The matters are addressed in the statute set out below.

Arkansas Code § 20-18-603. Reporting of certain fetal deaths

(a)(1)(A) Each fetal death when the fetus weighs three hundred fifty grams (350 g) or more, or if weight is unknown, the fetus completed twenty (20) weeks' gestation or more, calculated from the date the last normal menstrual period began to the date of delivery, that occurs in this state shall be reported within five (5) days after delivery to the Division of Vital Records of the Division of Health of the Department of Health and Human Services or as otherwise directed by the State Registrar of Vital Records. All induced terminations of pregnancy shall be reported in the manner prescribed in subsection (b) of this section and shall not be reported as fetal deaths.

(B) When a dead fetus is delivered in an institution, the person in charge of the institution or his or her designated representative shall prepare and file the fetal death certificate.

(C) When a dead fetus is delivered outside an institution, the physician in attendance at or immediately after delivery shall prepare and file the fetal death certificate.

(D) When a fetal death required to be reported by this section occurs without medical attendance at or immediately after the delivery, or when inquiry is required by § 12-12-301 et seq. or § 14-15-301 et seq. or otherwise provided by law, the State Medical Examiner or coroner shall investigate the cause of fetal death and shall prepare and file the report within five (5) days.

(E) When a fetal death occurs in a moving conveyance and the fetus is first removed from the conveyance in this state or when a fetus is found in this state and the place of fetal death is unknown, the fetal death shall be reported in this state. The place where the fetus was first removed from the conveyance or the fetus was found shall be considered the place of fetal death.

(2) Spontaneous fetal deaths when the fetus has completed less than twenty (20) weeks of gestation and when the fetus weighs less than three hundred fifty grams (350 g) shall be reported as prescribed in subsection (b) of this section.

(b) Each induced termination of pregnancy which occurs in this state regardless of the length of gestation shall be reported to the Division of Vital Records within five (5) days by the person in charge of the institution in which the induced termination of pregnancy was performed. If the induced termination of pregnancy was performed outside an institution, the attending physician shall prepare and file the report.

(c)(1) The reports required under this subsection are statistical reports to be used only for medical and health purposes and shall not be incorporated into the permanent official records of the system of vital statistics. A schedule for the disposition of these reports shall be provided for by regulation.

(2) Reports required under this section shall not include the name or other personal identification of the individual having an induced or spontaneous termination of pregnancy.

(15) DISPOSAL OF FETAL REMAINS

With limited exceptions, Arkansas has criminalized fetal experiments and the sale of fetal parts. The statute addressing the matter is set out below.

Arkansas Code § 20-17-802. Remains from abortion

(a) Any physician who performs an abortion shall ensure that the fetal remains and all parts thereof are disposed of in a fashion similar to that in which other tissue is disposed.

(b)(1) No person shall perform any biomedical or behavioral research on a fetus born alive as the result of a legal abortion unless the research is for the exclusive benefit of the fetus so born.

(2) No person shall perform any biomedical or behavioral research on any fetus born dead as the result of a legal abortion, or on any fetal tissue produced by the abortion, without permission of the mother.

(c) No person shall buy, sell, give, exchange, or barter or offer to buy, sell, give, exchange, or barter any fetus born dead as a result of a legal abortion or any organ, member, or tissue of fetal material resulting from a legal abortion.

(d) No person shall possess either a fetus born dead as a result of a legal abortion or any organ, member, or tissue of fetal material resulting from a legal abortion.

(e) This section shall not apply to:

(1) A physician performing a legal abortion or a pathologist performing a pathological examination as the result of a legal abortion and shall not apply to an employee, agent, or servant of such a physician or pathologist;

(2) The staff, faculty, students, or governing body of any institution of higher learning or institution of secondary education to the extent of courses of instruction taught and research conducted at the institutions;

(3) Licensed physicians or their employees, agents, and servants while in the conduct of medical research; or

(4) Any licensed physician when performing a standard autopsy examination.

(f) Any person violating this provision shall be guilty of a Class A misdemeanor.

(16) HUMAN CLONING

Arkansas has enacted statutes that prohibit human cloning by any person or entity, public or private. The statutes permit certain types of scientific research that does not involve cloning of human life. The statutes are set out below.

Arkansas Code § 20-16-1001. Definitions

As used in this subchapter:

(1) "Asexual reproduction" means reproduction not initiated by the union of oocyte and sperm;

(2) "Embryo" means an organism of the species homo sapiens from the single cell stage to eight (8) weeks of development;

(3) "Fetus" means an organism of the species homo sapiens from eight (8) weeks of development until complete expulsion or extraction from a woman's body or removal from an artificial womb or other similar environment designed to nurture the development of the organism;

(4) "Human cloning" means human asexual reproduction, accomplished by introducing the genetic material from one (1) or more human somatic cells into a fertilized or unfertilized oocyte whose nuclear material has been removed or inactivated so as to produce a living organism, at any stage of development, that is genetically

virtually identical to an existing or previously existing human organism;

(5) "Oocyte" means the human female germ cell, the egg; and

(6) "Somatic cell" means a diploid cell, having a complete cell of chromosomes, obtained or derived from a living or deceased human body at any stage of development.

§ 20-16-1002. Prohibited acts

(a) It is unlawful for any person or entity, public or private, to intentionally or knowingly:

(1) Perform or attempt to perform human cloning;

(2) Participate in an attempt to perform human cloning;

(3) Ship, transfer, or receive for any purpose an embryo produced by human cloning; or

(4) Ship, transfer, or receive, in whole or in part, any oocyte, embryo, fetus, or human somatic cell for the purpose of human cloning.

(b) A violation of subdivision (a)(1) of this section or a violation of subdivision (a)(2) of this section, or both, is a Class C felony.

(c) A violation of subdivision (a)(3) of this section or a violation of subdivision (a)(4) of this section, or both, is a Class A misdemeanor.

(d)(1) In addition to any criminal penalty that may be levied, any person or entity that violates any provision of this section shall be subject to a fine of not less than two hundred fifty thousand dollars ($250,000) or two (2) times the amount of any pecuniary gain that is received by the person or entity, whichever is greater.

(2) All fines collected shall be placed into the general revenues of the State of Arkansas.

Arkansas Code § 20-16-1003. Scientific research

(a) This subchapter does not restrict areas of scientific research not specifically prohibited by this subchapter, including research into the use of nuclear transfer or other cloning techniques to produce molecules, deoxyribonucleic acid, cells other than human embryos, tissues, organs, plants, or animals other than humans.

(b) This subchapter does not apply to in vitro fertilization, the administration of fertility-enhancing drugs, or other medical procedures used to assist a woman in becoming or remaining pregnant so long as that procedure is not specifically intended to result in the gestation or birth of a child who is genetically identical to another conceptus, embryo, fetus, or human being, living or dead.

(17) PRO-LIFE LICENSE PLATE

In 2003 the Arkansas legislature enacted statutes authorizing the issuance of "Choose Life" license plates for motor vehicles. The statutes were repealed in 2005. However, in 2005 the state also enacted another statute permitting the continued issuance of such license plates. The statute is set out below.

Arkansas Code § 27-24-1402. Existing special license plates

(a) The following special license plates that represent various special interests and that were in existence or authorized by law on or before April 13, 2005, shall continue to be issued by the Director of the Department of Finance and Administration to a motor vehicle owner who is otherwise eligible to license a motor vehicle in this state and who pays the additional fees for the special license plate unless other eligibility requirements are specifically stated in this subchapter:

(1) Ducks Unlimited;

(2) Committed to Education;

(3) Choose Life;

(4) Susan G. Komen Breast Cancer Education, Research, and Awareness;

(5) Boy Scouts of America;

(6) Arkansas Cattlemen's Foundation;

(7) Organ Donor Awareness; and

(8) Arkansas Realtors(r) Association.

(b) The Department of Finance and Administration shall continue to collect the fee for the design-use contribution or for fund-raising purposes, and the following organizations shall continue to receive funds and be authorized to use the funds from the fee for the design-use contribution for special license plates that were in effect before April 13, 2005, and that are continued under this subchapter:

(1) Ducks Unlimited, Inc., for the Ducks Unlimited special license plate;

(2) Arkansas Committed to Education Foundation for the Committed to Education special license plate;

(3) Arkansas Right to Life for the Choose Life special license plate;

(4) Arkansas Affiliate of the Susan G. Komen Foundation for the Susan G. Komen Breast Cancer Education, Research, and Awareness special license plate;

(5) Boy Scouts of America, Quapaw Area Council of Arkansas, for the Boy Scouts of America special license plate;

(6) Arkansas Cattlemen's Foundation for the Arkansas Cattlemen's Foundation special license plate; and

(7) Regional Organ Recovery Agency for the Organ Donor Awareness special license plate.

(c)(1) Within thirty (30) days after April 13, 2005, the director shall notify the organizations listed in subsection (b) of this section that received the funds or were authorized to use the funds from a design-use contribution fee for a special license plate that is continued under this chapter and that was in effect before April 13, 2005, and the State Highway Commission of a change in the law regarding special license plates.

(2)(A) The organization shall submit to the director an application that includes the following:

(i) The organization's financial plan for the use of the proceeds from the special license plate; and

(ii) An affidavit signed by an official of the organization that states that the proceeds from the special license plate will be used according to the financial plan submitted with the application.

(B)(i) The organization shall submit the information required under this subsection within one hundred twenty (120) days after April 13, 2005.

(ii) If the organization fails to comply with this subdivision (c)(2)(B) within one hundred twenty (120) days after April 13, 2005, then the director shall notify the organization that proceeds from the special license plate design-use contribution fee will no longer be remitted to the organization or the organization will no longer be able to use the proceeds until the organization complies with this subdivision.

(C) The department shall not remit funds to the organization or allow the organization to use the proceeds from the special license plate unless the organization complies with the provisions of this section.

(d) Every special license plate continued under this subchapter shall be discontinued on April 7, 2007, unless an application is submitted to and approved by the director ninety (90) days prior to April 1, 2007, that establishes the organization's compliance with the following conditions:

(1) The organization is a state agency or a nonprofit organization that has been approved for tax exempt status under Section 501(c)(3) of the Internal Revenue Code as in effect on January 1, 2005;

(2) The organization is based, headquartered, or has a chapter in Arkansas;

(3) The purpose of the organization is for social, civic, entertainment, or other purposes;

(4)(A) Except as provided under subdivision (d)(4)(B) of this section, the name of the organization is not the name of a special product, a trademark, or a brand name.

(B) This condition shall not apply to a trademark if the or-

ganization or entity with control of the trademark has provided a written authorization for its use;

(5)(A) Except as provided under subdivision (d)(5)(B) of this section, the name of the organization is not interpreted by the department as promoting a special product, a trademark, or a brand name.

(B) This condition shall not apply to a trademark if the organization or entity with control of the trademark has provided a written authorization for its use;

(6) The organization is not a political party;

(7) The organization was not created primarily to promote a specific political belief; and

(8) The organization shall not have as its primary purpose the promotion of any specific religion, faith, or anti-religion.

Army of God

Army of God (AOG) is the term used by some militant anti-abortionists who believe that a spiritual authority directs their campaign to end abortion in the United States. AOG is considered a leaderless network of people who subscribe to tactics that are contained in a small manual entitled *When Life Hurts, We Can Help... THE ARMY OF GOD.* The author of the manual is not known. The manual sets out 99 ways to stop abortion, including arson, bombing, use of butyric acid and other toxic chemicals, as well as numerous methods of vandalism. Also described in the manual are instructions for making explosives. AOG adherents are known to be responsible for at least a dozen acts of violence.

Authorities have only been able to identify adherents to AOG through the arrest of certain people who have claimed allegiance to AOG. The first known adherent to AOG was militant anti-abortionist Don Benny Anderson. Anderson was imprisoned after he kidnapped an Illinois abortion doctor and his wife in 1982. At that time Anderson claimed to be the leader of AOG. Anderson is now serving a 42 year federal prison sentence. Other militant anti-abortionists who were prosecuted for violent acts and claimed affiliation with the AOG include Joseph Grace (arson), John Brockhoeft (bombing), Michael Bray (bombing), and Rachelle R. Shannon (attempted murder). An internet website is maintained for AOG by the Rev. Donald Spitz at http://www.armyofgod.com. *See also* **Abortion Violence, Property Destruction and Demonstrations; Bray, Michael; Shannon, Rachelle Ranae**

Arteriovenous Malformation

Arteriovenous malformation is a congenital disorder that involves an abnormal development of blood vessels, which leads to a tangled web of arteries and veins. The disorder may occur in the brain, brainstem, or spinal cord. The most common symptoms include bleeding, seizures, headaches, and paralysis or loss of speech, memory, or vision. The disorder can cause death. Some of the problems associated with the disorder may be treated with surgery, embolization (closing off vessels by injecting glue into them), and radiation. *See also* **Birth Defects and Abortion**

Artificial Insemination *see* **Assisted Reproductive Technology**

Ascending Infection

Ascending infection refers to bacterial infections in pregnant women that arise from the vagina and cross the cervix. These infections may cause spontaneous abortion or stillbirth. *See also* **Miscarriage; Stillbirth**

Asherman's Syndrome

Asherman's syndrome is a disorder involving the formation of fibrous bands of scar tissue in the uterus. This condition may come about naturally or as a result of having an abortion using the surgical technique of dilation and curettage. Regardless of how the disorder originates, it poses a high risk for pregnancy complications. The disorder is known to cause ectopic pregnancies, spontaneous abortions and infertility. Effective pre-pregnancy treatment is available for the disorder. *See also* **Dilation and Curettage**

Assisted Reproductive Technology

Assisted reproductive technology (ART) is the phrase used to describe procedures that involve human reproduction without engaging in sexual intercourse. ART has been called a medical miracle because it allows couples to have children when, for one reason or another, they cannot do so naturally. Globally, ART is responsible for the birth of more than 500,000 healthy children. Statistics have shown that pregnancies associated with ART are more likely to result in multiple births than naturally conceived pregnancies.

The first ART procedure was created in England in 1977, by Drs. Patrick Steptoe and Robert Edwards. The two doctors were confronted with a patient, Lesley Brown, who suffered from closed fallopian tubes and therefore could not bear children. Steptoe and Edwards discovered a procedure to help Mrs. Brown. The procedure required removing an egg from Mrs. Brown, placing it inside of a laboratory dish and adding sperm from her husband, John Brown. After the egg was fertilized outside the womb, it was inserted into Mrs. Brown's uterus. As a result of the implantation, Mrs. Brown gave birth to a daughter, Louise Joy Brown, on July 25, 1978 (the so called first test tube baby). The birth occurred at England's Oldham General Hospital. (The first birth in the United States using the ART procedure occurred in 1981, when Elizabeth Carr was born at Eastern Virginia Medical School, Norfolk, Virginia.)

The ART procedure used by Steptoe and Edwards is called in vitro fertilization. Several variations of this procedure have developed and include: gamete intrafallopian transfer, zygote intrafallopian transfer, artificial insemination, and intracytoplasmic sperm injection.

In vitro fertilization. The in vitro fertilization (IVF) procedure is primarily used for women who have problems with their fallopian tubes. The initial step in the IVF procedure requires giving a woman specific medication to stimulate her ovaries to produce a number of eggs. The eggs are then harvested by a technique which involves the introduction of a needle through the vaginal wall guided by an ultrasonic probe (this technique is called transvaginal ultrasound-guided oocyte aspiration). The harvested eggs are then placed in a "baby incubator," where sperm from the woman's partner is then introduced. After several days the resulting embryos are transferred, using a tubular instrument, through the cervix and into the uterus. Within 12

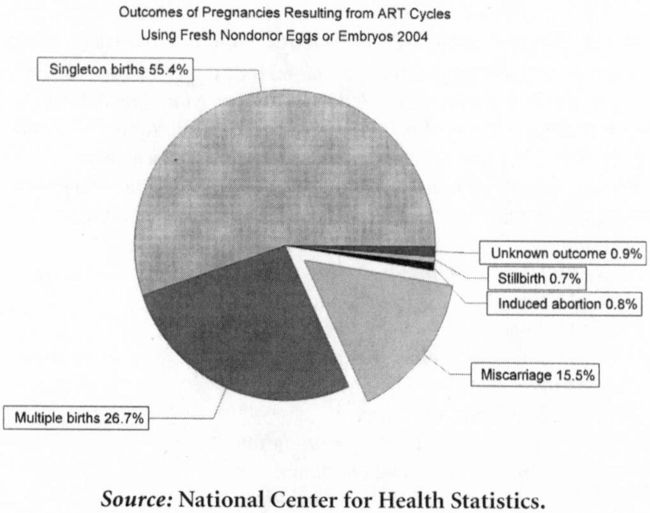

Source: **National Center for Health Statistics.**

days a pregnancy test is performed to determine whether the implantation was successful.

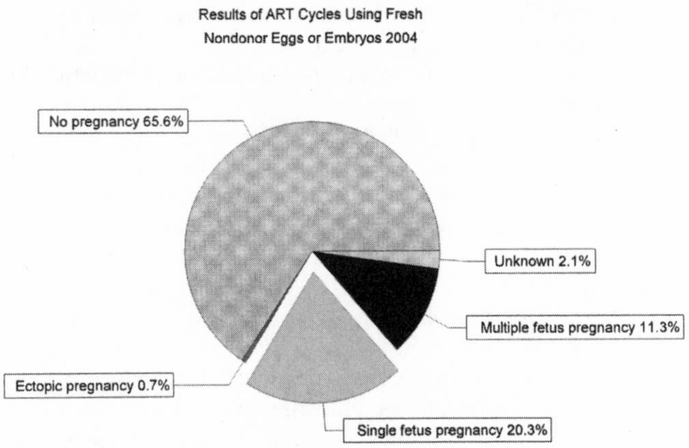

Source: **National Center for Health Statistics.**

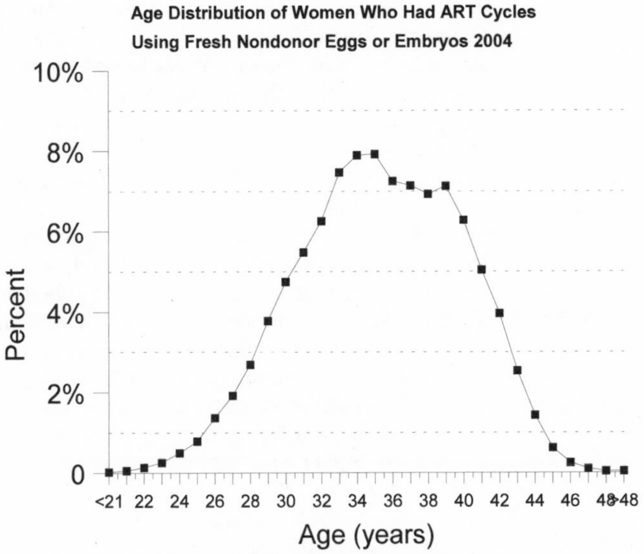

Source: **National Center for Health Statistics.**

Gamete intrafallopian transfer. The gamete intrafallopian transfer (GIFT) (unfertilized egg and sperm are gametes) technique was introduced in 1984 by Dr. Ricardo Asch. GIFT was developed to help couples who had unexplained infertility problems, provided that the woman has at least one open fallopian tube. This procedure involves placing eggs and sperm in the fallopian tubes and allowing fertilization to take place there (in IVF fertilization occurs outside the woman). The initial step involves using fertility drugs to stimulate the production of eggs. Once this is successful, the eggs are removed and placed inside a catheter (tube). Sperm is taken from the woman's partner and washed (removal of the seminal plasma) inside a centrifuge. After washing, the sperm is placed inside a separate catheter. The eggs and sperm are mixed in a syringe together and then inserted via laparoscopy into the woman's fallopian tubes. If fertilization occurs, the developing embryos will then move to and implant in the uterus.

Zygote intrafallopian transfer. The zygote intrafallopian transfer (ZIFT) technique was developed in 1986, and is a combination of GIFT and IVF. ZIFT involves allowing eggs and sperm to fertilize, but not cultured into embryos (this is the zygote stage). The fertilized

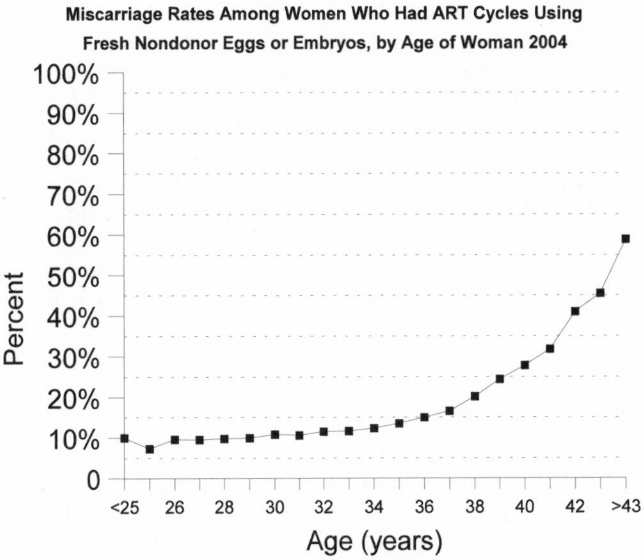

Source: **National Center for Health Statistics.**

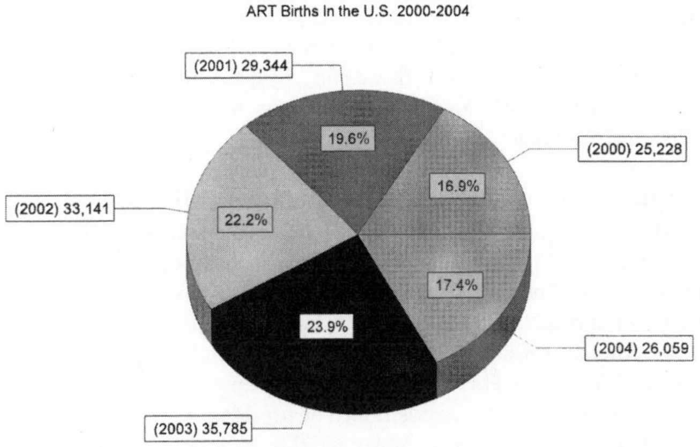

Source: **National Center for Health Statistics.**

eggs and sperm are then transferred to the fallopian tubes using either a laparoscopy (GIFT method) or an ultrasonic probe (IVF method).

Artificial insemination. Artificial insemination (AI) was first used as a method of stimulating reproduction in cattle and horses. AI technology eventually was transferred to helping humans reproduce. The procedure is an option usually when a male has a low sperm count, sperm are unable to get through the woman's cervical mucus, or psychological problems that affect sexual performance (such as impotence).

AI may be used with the sperm of a woman's partner or a donor's sperm. Donor's sperm are used when the male partner has an untreatable infertility problem. The use of donor sperm has become viable because of technology that permits freezing and unthawing sperm (so called "sperm banks" collect sperm for this purpose). The use of frozen sperm leads to pregnancy about 60 percent of the time, whereas freshly collected sperm has a success rate of about 90 percent.

The AI procedure requires injecting sperm with a syringe either into the vagina or directly into the uterus. There are three AI techniques: homologous insemination, intracervical insemination, and intrauterine insemination.

Homologous insemination (also called cup insemination) requires placement of washed sperm in a diaphragm-like cup and inserting it at the cervix. Intracervical insemination involves placing sperm in a centrifuge and spinning it to obtain the best sperm. The sperm is then collected and placed in a catheter, that is inserted directly into the cervical canal. Intrauterine insemination requires washing sperm and placing it in a centrifuge with a sample of the male's blood. After spinning the sperm and blood, the best sperm are removed and placed in a catheter, which is inserted directly into the uterus.

Intracytoplasmic sperm injection. Intracytoplasmic sperm injection (ICSI) is a technique perfected by Dr. Andre Van Steirteghem of Belgium, for use during an in vitro fertilization procedure. ICSI is used for men who have very low sperm count, few good-quality sperm, have missing vas deferens (the pair of tubes that carries seminal fluid from the testes to the penis) or men who are unable to reverse a vasectomy. The technique involves using micromanipulators to inject a single sperm into a mature egg.

Under the ICSI procedure the woman will be given fertility drugs to stimulate her ovaries to develop several mature eggs. The eggs will then be removed. Next, a needle is used to retrieve sperm from the man's testicle. Individual sperm is then isolated and injected into individual eggs. Several days after fertilization, two or three embryos are then inserted into the woman's uterus through her cervix using a catheter. After about two weeks, the woman can take a pregnancy test.

Critics of this procedure worry about long-term health and development problems for children conceived using "bad" sperm. One study has suggested that children conceived through ICSI may develop slower mentally than those conceived through the traditional in vitro fertilization procedure. *See also* **Cryopreservation; Embryo Cloning; Surrogacy**

Association of Reproductive Health Professionals

The Association of Reproductive Health Professionals (ARHP) was founded in 1963. Initially ARHP was primarily an educational vehicle for physicians specializing in obstetrics and gynecology. In time, however, it broadened its scope to include family practitioners, internal medicine, pediatrics, physician assistants and pharmacists. The national headquarters of ARHP is in Washington, D.C. ARHP has taken a strong pro-choice position. The president of ARHP is Wayne C. Shields. ARHP believes that women should not be denied the right to choose abortion, and that abortion services should be covered by private and government health insurance programs in order to increase its safety and availability. ARHP also believes that the risks and benefits of all abortion methods should be included in a comprehensive reproductive health education curriculum; abortion training should be available in all medical schools, residency, and other post graduate medical education; and that physicians who do not perform abortions because of religious/moral beliefs, have an obligation to provide their patients with a timely referral to another medical professional known to provide abortions, and to inform their patients that they are being referred for personal, not professional, reasons. *See also* **Pro-Choice Organizations**

Atomic Dog *see* **Kopp, James Charles**

Autoimmune Diseases

Autoimmune diseases involves a breakdown in the body's immune system that causes the system to attack body organs. The list of autoimmune diseases is composed of more than 80 disorders that adversely affect such body organs as the liver, kidneys, adrenal glands, ovaries, pancreas and muscles. Types of autoimmune diseases include: multiple sclerosis, Crohn's disease, Grave's disease, Hashimoto's thyroiditis, psoriasis, and rheumatoid arthritis. Out of an estimated eight and a half million people with autoimmune diseases in the United States, nearly 80 percent are women. Researchers believe that during pregnancy, the mother or the fetus may produce an autoimmune reaction in the other. *See also* **Birth Defects and Abortion**

Automobile Workers v. Johnson Controls, Inc.

Forum: United States Supreme Court.

Case Citation: Automobile Workers v. Johnson Controls, Inc., 499 U.S. 187 (1991).

Date Argued: October 10, 1990.

Date of Decision: March 20, 1991.

Opinion of Court: Blackmun, J., in which Marshall, Stevens, O'Connor, and Souter, JJ., joined.

Concurring Opinion: White, J., in which Rehnquist, C.J., and Kennedy, J., joined.

Concurring Opinion: Scalia, J.

Dissenting Opinion: None.

Counsel for Appellants: Marsha S. Berzon argued; on the brief were Jordan Rossen, Ralph O. Jones, and Laurence Gold.

Counsel for Appellee: Stanley S. Jaspan argued; on the brief were Susan R. Maisa, Anita M. Sorensen, Charles G. Curtis, Jr., and John P. Kennedy.

Amicus Brief for Appellants: United States et al. by Solicitor General Starr, Assistant Attorney General Dunne, Deputy Solicitor General Roberts, Deputy Assistant Attorney General Clegg, Clifford M. Sloan, David K. Flynn, Charles A. Shanor, Gwendolyn Young Reams, Lorraine C. Davis, and Carolyn L. Wheeler; for the State of California et al. by John K. Van de Kamp, Attorney General, Andrea Sheridan Ordin, Chief Assistant Attorney General, Marian M. Johnston, Supervising Deputy Attorney General, and Manuel M. Medeiros, Deputy Attorney General; for the Commonwealth of Massachusetts et al. by James M. Shannon, Attorney General of Massachusetts, Jennifer Wriggins, Marjorie Heins, and Judith E. Beals, Assistant Attorneys General, and by the Attorneys General for their respective States as follows: Robert K. Corbin of Arizona, Clarine Nardi Riddle of Connecticut, Charles M. Oberly III of Delaware, Robert A. Butterworth of Florida, William J. Guste, Jr., of Louisiana, James E. Tierney of Maine, Frank J. Kelley of Michigan, Hubert H. Humphrey III of Minnesota, Robert M. Spire of Nebraska, Robert J. Del Tufo of New Jersey, Robert Abrams of New York, Anthony J. Celebrezze, Jr., of Ohio, Robert H. Henry of Oklahoma, Hector Rivera-Cruz of Puerto Rico, Jim Mattox of Texas, Jeffrey L. Amestoy of Vermont, Godfrey R. de Castro of the Virgin Islands, and Kenneth O. Eikenberry of Washington; for the American Civil Liberties Union et al. by Joan E. Bertin, Elisabeth A. Werby, and Isabelle Katz Pinzler; for the American Public Health Association et al. by Nadine Taub and Suzanne L. Mager; for Equal Rights Advocates et al. by Susan Deller Ross and Naomi R. Cahn; for the NAACP Legal Defense and Educational Fund, Inc., et al., by Julius LeVonne Chambers, Charles Stephen Ralston, and Ronald L. Ellis; and for Trial Lawyers for Public Justice by Arthur H. Bryant.

Amicus Brief for Appellee: Chamber of Commerce of the United States of America by Timothy B. Dyk, Willis J. Goldsmith, Stephen A. Bokat, and Robin S. Conrad; for Concerned Women for America by Jordan W. Lorence, Cimron Campbell, and Wendell R. Bird; for the Equal Employment Advisory Council et al. by Robert E. Williams, Douglas S. McDowell, Garen E. Dodge, Jan S. Amundson, and Quentin Riedel; for the Industrial Hygiene Law Project by Jack Levy and Ilise Levy Feitshans; for the National Safe Workplace Institute by James D. Holzhauer; for the United States Catholic Conference by Mark E. Chopko and John A. Liekweg; and for the Washington Legal Foundation by Daniel J. Popeo, Paul D. Kamenar, and John C. Scully.

Issue Presented: Whether an employer may exclude a fertile female employee from certain jobs because of its concern for the health of the fetus the woman might conceive?

Case Holding: Title VII of the Civil Rights Act forbids sex-specific fetal-protection policies by employers.

Background facts of case: The appellee, Johnson Controls, Inc., manufactured batteries. In the manufacturing process, the element lead is a primary ingredient. Occupational exposure to lead entails health risks, including the risk of harm to any fetus carried by a female employee. In 1982 the appellee instituted a policy that excluded women from jobs that exposed them to lead. The policy stated: "...[W]omen who are pregnant or who are capable of bearing children will not be placed into jobs involving lead exposure or which could expose them to lead through the exercise of job bidding, bumping, transfer or promotion rights." In 1984 the appellants, female employees, filed a class action lawsuit in a federal district court in Wisconsin challenging the appellee's fetal-protection policy as sex discrimination that violated Title VII of the Civil Rights Act of 1964 (42 U.S.C. 2000e et seq). The district court granted summary judgment dismissal for the appellee. The Seventh Circuit court of appeals affirmed. The Supreme Court granted certiorari to consider the matter.

Majority opinion by Justice Blackmun: Justice Blackmun held that the appellee's fetal-protection policy was unlawfully discriminatory. He addressed the issue as follows:

> The bias in Johnson Controls' policy is obvious. Fertile men, but not fertile women, are given a choice as to whether they wish to risk their reproductive health for a particular job. [Title VII] of the Civil Rights Act of 1964 prohibits sex-based classifications in terms and conditions of employment, in hiring and discharging decisions, and in other employment decisions that adversely affect an employee's status. [Appellee's] fetal-protection policy explicitly discriminates against women on the basis of their sex. The policy excludes women with childbearing capacity from lead-exposed jobs, and so creates a facial classification based on gender....
>
> ... Johnson Controls' policy classifies on the basis of gender and childbearing capacity, rather than fertility alone. [Appellee] does not seek to protect the unconceived children of all its employees. Despite evidence in the record about the debilitating effect of lead exposure on the male reproductive system, Johnson Controls is concerned only with the harms that may befall the unborn offspring of its female employees.... Johnson Controls' policy is facially discriminatory, because it requires only a female employee to produce proof that she is not capable of reproducing.
>
> Our conclusion is bolstered by the Pregnancy Discrimination Act of 1978 (PDA), 42 U.S.C. 2000e(k), in which Congress explicitly provided that, for purposes of Title VII, discrimination on the basis of sex includes discrimination because of or on the basis of pregnancy, childbirth, or related medical conditions. The Pregnancy Discrimination Act has now made clear that, for all Title VII purposes, discrimination based on a woman's pregnancy is, on its face, discrimination because of her sex. In its use of the words "capable of bearing children" in the 1982 policy statement as the criterion for exclusion, Johnson Controls explicitly classifies on the basis of potential for pregnancy. Under the PDA, such a classification must be regarded, for Title VII purposes, in the same light as explicit sex discrimination. [Appellee] has chosen to treat all its female employees as potentially pregnant; that choice evinces discrimination on the basis of sex....
>
> Under Title VII an employer may discriminate on the basis of religion, sex, or national origin in those certain instances where religion, sex, or national origin is a bona fide occupational qualification reasonably necessary to the normal operation of that particular business or enterprise (BFOQ). We therefore turn to the question whether Johnson Controls' fetal-protection policy is one of those "certain instances" that come within the BFOQ exception....
>
> We have no difficulty concluding that Johnson Controls cannot establish a BFOQ. Fertile women, as far as appears in the record, participate in the manufacture of batteries as efficiently as anyone else. Johnson Controls' professed moral and ethical concerns about the welfare of the next generation do not suffice to establish a BFOQ of female sterility. Decisions about the welfare of future children must be left to the parents who conceive, bear, support, and raise them, rather than to the employers who hire those parents. Congress has mandated this choice through Title VII, as amended by the PDA. Johnson Controls has attempted to exclude women because of their reproductive capacity. Title VII and the PDA simply do not allow a woman's dismissal because of her failure to submit to sterilization.

Disposition of case: The judgment of the court of appeals was reversed, and the case was remanded for further proceedings.

Concurring opinion by Justice White: Justice White concurred in the judgment by the majority opinion. He wrote separately to point out that he did not believe that in no circumstances could the BFOQ employer defense ever be used. Justice White stated:

> The Court properly holds that Johnson Controls' fetal protection policy overtly discriminates against women, and thus is prohibited by Title VII unless it falls within the bona fide occupational qualification (BFOQ) exception. The Court erroneously holds, however, that the BFOQ defense is so narrow that it could never justify a sex-specific fetal protection policy. I nevertheless concur in the judgment of reversal because, on the record before us, summary judgment in favor of Johnson Controls was improperly entered by the District Court and affirmed by the Court of Appeals.

Concurring opinion by Justice Scalia: Justice Scalia agreed with the disposition of the case. He wrote separately to make the following points:

> First, I think it irrelevant that there was evidence in the record about the debilitating effect of lead exposure on the male reproductive system. Even without such evidence, treating women differently on the basis of pregnancy constitutes discrimination on the basis of sex, because Congress has unequivocally said so.
>
> Second, the Court points out that Johnson Controls has shown no factual basis for believing that all or substantially all women would be unable to perform safely the duties of the job involved. In my view, this is not only somewhat academic in light of our conclusion that the company may not exclude fertile women at all, it is entirely irrelevant. By reason of the Pregnancy Discrimination Act, it would not matter if all pregnant women placed their children at risk in taking these jobs, just as it does not matter if no men do so. As Judge Easterbrook put it in his dissent [in the court of appeals], "Title VII gives parents the power to make occupational decisions affecting their families. A legislative forum is available to those who believe that such decisions should be made elsewhere."

Ayotte v. Planned Parenthood of Northern New England

Forum: United States Supreme Court.

Case Citation: Ayotte v. Planned Parenthood of Northern New England, 546 U.S. 320 (2006).

Date Argued: November 30, 2005.

Date of Decision: January 18, 2006.

Opinion of Court: O'Connor, J., unanimous.

Concurring Opinion: None.

Dissenting Opinion: None.

Counsel for Appellant: Kelly A. Ayotte argued; on the brief were Michael A. Delaney, Daniel J. Mullen, Laura E.B. Lombardi, and Anthony I. Blenkinsop.

Counsel for Appellees: Jennifer Dalven argued; on the brief were Dara Klassel, Martin P. Honigberg, Steven R. Shapiro, Louise Melling, Talcott Camp, Corinne Schiff, Brigitte Amiri, Diana Kasdan, and Lawrence A. Vogelman.

Amicus Brief for Appellant: Minnesota Governor Tim Pawlenty and North Dakota Governor John Hoeven; United States; American Center for Law and Justice; Harlon Reeves; James P. Weiers, Ken Bennett, Mark Anderson, Laura Knaperek, Linda Gray, Center for Arizona Policy; New Hampshire Legislators; Association of American Physicians & Surgeons, John M. Thorp, Jr.; Maureen L. Curley; Family Research Council, Inc., Focus on the Family; University Faculty for Life; Loren Leman, Alaska Legislators; American Association of Pro Life Obstetricians and Gynecologists, Christian Medical Association, Catholic Medical Association, Alliance Defense Fund, National Association of Evangelicals, Concerned Women for America, Christian Legal Society; National Legal Foundation; Texas, Alabama, Arkansas, Colorado, Delaware, Florida, Idaho, Kansas, Michigan, Mississippi, North Dakota, Ohio, Pennsylvania, South Dakota, Tennessee, Utah, Virginia, Wyoming; Horatio R. Storer Foundation, Inc.; Eagle Forum Education & Legal Defense Fund; Liberty Counsel; Margie Riley, Laurette Elsberry; United States Conference of Catholic Bishops, Roman Catholic Bishop of Manchester; Thomas More Society; Kathleen Souza, John S. Barnes, Jr., Robert K. Boyce, Robert J. Letourneau, Sheila Roberge, Michael A. Balboni, Peter Batula, David J. Bettencourt, David L. Buhlman, Harriet E. Cady, Paul C. Ingbretson, Daniel C. Itse, Rogers J. Johnson, Phyllis M. Katsakiores, Thomas J. Langlais, Robert J. L'heureux, Paul Mirski, Richard W. Morris, Sandra J. Reeves, Robert H. Ro; and Rutherford Institute.

Amicus Brief for Appellees: NARAL Pro-Choice America Foundation; National Coalition Against Domestic Violence; American College of Obstetricians and Gynecologists, American Medical Association, New Hampshire Medical Society, American Academy of Pediatrics, New Hampshire Pediatric Society, Society for Adolescent Medicine, American Psychiatric Association, North American Society of Adolescent and Pediatric Gynecology, National Medical Association, and American Public Health Association; Organizations Committed to Women's Equality; Center for Reproductive Rights and 30 Organizations Committed to Preserving the Constitutional Right to Abortion; Religious Coalition for Reproductive Choice and Forty-One Other Religious and Religiously Affiliated Organizations; John H. Lynch Governor of the State of New Hampshire; State Rep. Terie Norelli and Over One Hundred Other State Legislators; Center for Adolescent Health & the Law, National Association of Social Workers, National Association of Social Workers New Hampshire Chapter; and Thomas Sharpe.

Issue Presented: Whether the absence of a health exception in New Hampshire's parental notification abortion statute required the entire statute be invalidated?

Case Holding: The absence of a health exception in New Hampshire's parental notification abortion statute did not require the entire statute be invalidated.

Background facts of case: The appellees filed a civil rights lawsuit under 42 U.S.C. § 1983, in a federal district court seeking to prohibit enforcement of New Hampshire's Parental Notification Prior to Abortion Act of 2003 (the Act). The appellees alleged that the Act was unconstitutional because, among other things, it failed to permit a physician to promptly provide an abortion to a minor whose health may be at risk by a delay in complying with the notification requirement. The district court agreed with the appellees and declared the Act unconstitutional in its entirety. An appellate court affirmed the decision. The United States Supreme Court granted certiorari to consider the issue.

Unanimous opinion by Justice O'Connor: Justice O'Connor held that while the Act was invalid because it failed to provide a health exception, it may be possible to fashion a remedy that would not strike down the Act in its entirety. The opinion addressed the issue as follows:

> New Hampshire does not dispute, and our precedents hold, that a State may not restrict access to abortions that are necessary, in appropriate medical judgment, for preservation of the life or health of the mother....
>
> And New Hampshire has conceded that, under our cases, it would be unconstitutional to apply the Act in a manner that subjects minors to significant health risks.
>
> We turn to the question of remedy: When a statute restricting access to abortion may be applied in a manner that harms women's health, what is the appropriate relief? Generally speaking, when confronting a constitutional flaw in a statute, we try to limit the solution to the problem. We prefer, for example, to enjoin only the unconstitutional applications of a statute while leaving other applications in force, or to sever its problematic portions while leaving the remainder intact....
>
> In this case, the courts below chose the most blunt remedy-permanently enjoining the enforcement of New Hampshire's parental notification law and thereby invalidating it entirely....
>
> In the case that is before us, however, we agree with New Hampshire that the lower courts need not have invalidated the law wholesale. [Appellees], too, recognize the possibility of a modest remedy: They pleaded for any relief "just and proper," and conceded at oral argument that carefully crafted injunctive relief may resolve this case. Only a few applications of New Hampshire's parental notification statute would present a constitutional problem. So long as they are faithful to legislative intent, then, in this case the lower courts can issue a declaratory judgment and an injunction prohibiting the statute's unconstitutional application.

Disposition of case: The judgment of the appellate court was vacated and the case was remanded for the imposition of a less harsh remedy.

Note: A year after the decision in the case the New Hampshire legislature repealed the Act. *See also* **Minors and Abortion; Section 1983**

B

Bacterial Vaginosis *see* **Vaginitis**

Baird, Bill

Bill Baird began a campaign in New York during the 1960s to promote the use of birth control and abortion. He opened what is believed to be the first abortion referral clinic in 1964, in Hempstead, New York. Baird's personal crusade reportedly caused him to be arrested and jailed eight times in five states for conducting lectures on birth control and abortion. His activities resulted in three decisions by the United States Supreme Court that involved him: *Bellotti v. Baird I*, *Bellotti v. Baird II*, and *Eisenstadt v. Baird.* Baird founded and operates the Pro Choice League. *See also* **Bellotti v. Baird I, Bellotti v. Baird II, Eisenstadt v. Baird**

Banquet of the White Rose

On January 21, 1996, militant anti-abortionists Michael Bray of Maryland and Donald Spitz of Virginia sponsored the first annual Banquet of the White Rose. The banquet is a ceremony to praise the accomplishments of militant anti-abortionists. The event is scheduled every 21st of January, the eve of the United States Supreme Court's decision of *Roe v. Wade* in 1973.

The name "banquet of the white rose" was taken from a secret society that was started in Munich, Germany, in July of 1942, by a group of German students and educators who opposed Adolph Hitler. *See also* **Abortion Violence, Property Destruction and Demonstrations**

Baptists for Life

Baptists for Life is a pro-life organization that was established in 1984 in Grand Rapids, Michigan by Mark B. Blocher. The executive director of the organization is M. Thomas Lothamer. The organization serves fundamental Baptist and bible churches throughout the country. It provides religious based pro-life education, training and research for member churches. The organization has established of a pregnancy care center in Grand Rapids, now known as the Alpha Women's Center. *See also* **Pro-Life Organizations**

Barrier Methods

Barrier methods refers to any contraceptive device that involves the use of a physical barrier to prevent sperm from reaching an egg. A diaphragm used in conjunction with spermicide is an example of a barrier method. Barrier methods have popularity because they do not cause systemic side effects or alter a female's hormone pattern. In general, however, female barrier methods are not as effective in preventing pregnancy as other non-barrier methods. *See also* **Contraception**

Basal Body Temperature Method *see* **Natural Family Planning Methods**

Basal Cell Nevus Syndrome

Basal cell nevus syndrome is a congenital disorder affecting the skin, nervous system, eyes, endocrine glands, and bones. The disorder causes an unusual facial appearance, a predisposition for skin cancer, seizures, mental retardation, blindness, deafness, bone abnormalities and brain tumors. Treatment for this disorder varies with the problems presented. *See also* **Birth Defects and Abortion**

Batten Disease

Batten disease is a congenital disorder of the nervous system. Symptoms of the disease include mental impairment, seizures, and progressive loss of sight and motor skills. The disease eventually renders children blind, bedridden, and demented. There is no treatment that can stop or reverse the course of the disease. Death may result by the late teens. *See* **Birth Defects and Abortion**

Beal v. Doe

Forum: United States Supreme Court.

Case Citation: Beal v. Doe, 432 U.S. 438 (1977).

Date Argued: January 11, 1977.

Date of Decision: June 20, 1977.

Opinion of Court: Powell, J., in which Burger, C. J., and Stewart, White, Rehnquist, and Stevens, JJ., joined.

Concurring Opinion: None.

Dissenting Opinion: Brennan, J., in which Marshall and Blackmun, JJ., joined.

Dissenting Opinion: Marshall, J.

Dissenting Opinion: Blackmun, J., in which Brennan and Marshall, JJ., joined.

Counsel for Appellants: Norman J. Watkins, Deputy Attorney General of Pennsylvania, argued; on the brief were Robert P. Kane, Attorney General, and J. Justin Blewitt, Jr., Deputy Attorney General.

Counsel for Appellees: Judd F. Crosby argued and filed a brief.

Amicus Brief for Appellants: William F. Hyland, Attorney General, Stephen Skillman, Assistant Attorney General, and Erminie L. Conley, Deputy Attorney General, for the State of New Jersey.

Amicus Brief for Appellees: David S. Dolowitz, Melvin L. Wulf, and Judith M. Mears for the American Public Health Assn. et al.

Issue Presented: Whether Title XIX of the Social Security Act requires Pennsylvania to fund under its Medicaid program the cost of all abortions that are permissible under state law?

Case Holding: Pennsylvania's refusal to extend medicaid coverage to nontherapeutic abortions was not invalid nor inconsistent with Title XIX of the Social Security Act.

Background facts of case: Title XIX of the Social Security Act, 42 U.S.C. 1396 et seq., established the medicaid program under which participating states may provide federally funded medical assistance to needy persons. The appellees, women who were eligible for medical assistance under Pennsylvania's medicaid plan, were denied financial assistance for abortions pursuant to the state's regulations limiting such assistance to abortions that were certified by physicians as medically necessary. The appellees filed a lawsuit in a federal district court in Pennsylvania, challenging the validity of the regulations. The appellants, state officials, were named as defendants. The district court found that the medical necessity restriction was valid under Title XIX, but that regulations violated the Equal Protection Clause. The Third Circuit court of appeals reversed on the statutory issue, holding that Title XIX prohibits participating states from requiring a physician's certificate of medical necessity as a condition for funding abortions. The court of appeals therefore did not reach the constitutional issue. The Supreme Court granted certiorari to consider the issue.

Majority opinion by Justice Powell: Justice Powell found that Pennsylvania's medicaid regulations limiting funding for abortions complied with Title XIX. He wrote as follows:

> Pennsylvania's regulation comports fully with Title XIX's broadly stated primary objective to enable each State, as far as practicable, to furnish medical assistance to individuals whose income and resources are insufficient to meet the costs of necessary medical services. Although serious statutory questions might be presented if a state Medicaid plan excluded necessary medical treatment from its coverage, it is hardly inconsistent with the objectives of the Act for a State to refuse to fund unnecessaryperhaps desirable — medical services....
>
> ... [W]e do not [believe] that the exclusion of nontherapeutic abortions from Medicaid coverage is unreasonable under Title XIX. As we acknowledged in Roe v. Wade, the State has a valid and important interest in encouraging childbirth. We expressly recognized in Roe the important and legitimate interest of the State in protecting the potentiality of human life. That interest alone does not, at least until approximately the third trimester, become sufficiently compelling to justify unduly burdensome state interference with the woman's constitutionally protected privacy interest. But it is a significant state interest existing throughout the course of the woman's pregnancy. [Appellees] point to nothing in either the language or the legislative history of Title XIX that suggests that it is unreasonable for a participating State to further this unquestionably strong and legitimate interest in encouraging normal childbirth. Absent such a showing, we will not presume that Congress intended to condition a State's participation in the Medicaid program on its willingness to undercut this important interest by subsidizing the costs of nontherapeutic abortions....
>
> We therefore hold that Pennsylvania's refusal to extend Medicaid coverage to nontherapeutic abortions is not inconsistent with Title XIX. We make clear, however, that the federal statute leaves a State free to provide such coverage if it so desires.

Disposition of case: The judgment of the court of appeals was reversed.

Dissenting opinion by Justice Brennan: Justice Brennan disagreed with the majority decision. He wrote in dissent as follows:

> Though the question presented by this case is one of statutory interpretation, a difficult constitutional question would be raised where Title XIX of the Social Security Act, is read not to require funding of elective abortions. Since the Court should first ascertain whether a construction of the statute is fairly possible by which the constitutional question may be avoided, Title XIX, in my view, read fairly in light of the principle of avoidance of unnecessary constitutional decisions, requires agreement with the Court of Appeals that the legislative history of Title XIX and our abortion cases compel the conclusion that elective abortions constitute medically necessary treatment for the condition of pregnancy. I would therefore find that Title XIX requires that Pennsylvania pay the costs of elective abortions for women who are eligible participants in the Medicaid program.

Dissenting opinion by Justice Marshall: Justice Marshall dissented from the majority decision. He wrote as follows:

> It is all too obvious that the governmental actions in these cases, ostensibly taken to encourage women to carry pregnancies to term, are in reality intended to impose a moral viewpoint that no State may constitutionally enforce. Since efforts to overturn [Roe v. Wade and Doe v. Bolton] have been unsuccessful, the opponents of abortion have attempted every imaginable means to circumvent the commands of the Constitution and impose their moral choices upon the rest of society. The present cases involve the most vicious attacks yet devised. The impact of the regulations here falls tragically upon those among us least able to help or defend themselves. As the Court well knows, these regulations inevitably will have the practical effect of preventing nearly all poor women from obtaining safe and legal abortions.
>
> The enactments challenged here brutally coerce poor women to bear children whom society will scorn for every day of their lives. Many thousands of unwanted minority and mixed-race children now spend blighted lives in foster homes, orphanages, and reform schools. Many children of the poor, sadly, will attend second-rate segregated schools. And opposition remains strong against increasing Aid to Families With Dependent Children benefits for impoverished mothers and children, so that there is little chance for the children to grow up in a decent environment. I am appalled at the ethical bankruptcy of those who preach a "right to life" that means, under present social policies, a bare existence in utter misery for so many poor women and their children.

Dissenting opinion by Justice Blackmun: Justice Blackmun disagreed with the majority decision. He wrote the following:

> The Court today ... allows the States, and such municipalities as choose to do so, to accomplish indirectly what the Court in Roe v. Wade and Doe v. Bolton ... said they could not do directly. The Court concedes the existence of a constitutional right but denies the realization and enjoyment of that right on the ground that existence and realization are separate and distinct. For the individual woman concerned, indigent and financially helpless ... the result is punitive and tragic. Implicit in the Court's holdings is the condescension that she may go elsewhere for her abortion. I find that disingenuous and alarming....
>
> There is another world out there, the existence of which the Court, I suspect, either chooses to ignore or fears to recognize. And so the cancer of poverty will continue to grow. This is a sad day for those who regard the Constitution as a force that would serve justice to all evenhandedly and, in so doing, would better the lot of the poorest among us.

See also **Hyde Amendment**

Bellotti v. Baird I

Forum: United States Supreme Court.
Case Citation: Bellotti v. Baird, 428 U.S. 132 (1976).
Date Argued: March 23, 1976.
Date of Decision: July 1, 1976.
Opinion of Court: Blackmun, J.
Concurring Opinion: None.
Dissenting Opinion: None.
Counsel for Appellants: S. Stephen Rosenfeld, Assistant Attorney General of Massachusetts, argued; on the brief were Francis X. Bellotti, Attorney General, Michael Eby and Garrick F. Cole, Assistant Attorneys General. Brian A. Riley argued; on the brief were Thomas P. McMahon and Thomas P. Russell.
Counsel for Appellees: Roy Lucas argued and filed a brief.
Amicus Brief for Appellants: None.
Amicus Brief for Appellees: None.
Issue Presented: Whether the constitution was violated by Massachusetts' parental consent abortion statute for minors?
Case Holding: The federal district court had to certify appropriate questions to the supreme judicial court of Massachusetts, concerning the interpretation of that state's parental consent abortion statute for minors, before ruling on the statute's constitutionality.
Background facts of case: Under Massachusetts' abortion statute parental consent was required before an abortion could be performed on a pregnant minor. If one or both parents refused such consent, however, judicial bypass was provided so that the abortion could be obtained by order of a judge. The appellees, abortion providers and a minor, filed a class action lawsuit in a federal district court in Massachusetts challenging the constitutionality of the statute. The appellants, state officials, were named as defendants. A third party citizen was also allowed to intervene as a defendant. The district court found the statute unconstitutional in creating a parental veto over abortions for minors, in that the statute applied even to those minors capable of giving informed consent. The Supreme Court granted certiorari to consider the matter.
Unanimous opinion by Justice Blackmun: Justice Blackmun determined that the Court would not address the merits of the case. Instead, it was held that the district court had to ask the state's highest court to provide guidance as to the interpretation to give the statute. Justice Blackmun wrote as follows:

> In deciding this case, we need go no further than the claim that the District Court should have abstained pending construction of the statute by the Massachusetts courts. As we have held on numerous occasions, abstention is appropriate where an unconstrued state statute is susceptible of a construction by the state judiciary which might avoid in whole or in part the necessity for federal constitutional adjudication, or at least materially change the nature of the problem.
>
> We do not accept appellees' assertion that the Supreme Judicial Court of Massachusetts inevitably will interpret the statute so as to create a parental veto, require the superior court to act other than in the best interests of the minor, or impose undue burdens upon a minor capable of giving an informed consent....
>
> Whether the Supreme Judicial Court will so interpret the statute, or whether it will interpret the statute to require consideration of factors not mentioned above, impose burdens more serious than those suggested, or create some unanticipated interference with the doctor-patient relationship, we cannot now determine. Nor need we determine what factors are impermissible or at what point review of consent and good cause in the case of a minor becomes unduly burdensome.... Indeed, in the absence of an authoritative construction, it is impossible to define precisely the constitutional question presented....
>
> The importance of speed in resolution of the instant litigation is manifest. Each day the statute is in effect, irretrievable events, with substantial personal consequences, occur. Although we do not mean to intimate that abstention would be improper in this

case were certification not possible, the availability of certification greatly simplifies the analysis.

Disposition of case: The judgment of the district court was vacated and the case remanded for further proceedings.

Bellotti v. Baird II

Forum: United States Supreme Court.

Case Citation: Bellotti v. Baird, 443 U.S. 622 (1979).

Date Argued: February 27, 1979.

Date of Decision: July 2, 1979.

Opinion of Court: Powell, J., in which Burger, C. J., and Stewart and Rehnquist, JJ., joined.

Concurring Opinion: Rehnquist, J.

Concurring Opinion: Stevens, J., in which Brennan, Marshall, and Blackmun, JJ., joined.

Dissenting Opinion: White, J.

Counsel for Appellants: Garrick F. Cole, Assistant Attorney General of Massachusetts, argued; on the brief were Francis X. Bellotti, Attorney General, Michael B. Meyer and Thomas R. Kiley, Assistant Attorneys General. Brian A. Riley argued; on the brief was Thomas P. Russell.

Counsel for Appellees: Joseph J. Balliro argued; on the brief was Joan C. Schmidt. John H. Henn argued; on the brief were Scott C. Moriearty, Sandra L. Lynch, Loyd M. Starrett, and John Reinstein.

Amicus Brief for Appellants: Stuart D. Hubbell and Robert A. Destro filed a brief for the Catholic League for Religious and Civil Rights et al.

Amicus Brief for Appellees: Eve W. Paul, Harriet F. Pilpel, and Sylvia A. Law for the Planned Parenthood Federation of America, Inc., et al.

Issue Presented: Whether the constitution was violated by an interpretation given to Massachusetts' abortion statute, by its highest court, that required parental notice of a judicial bypass proceeding invoked by a minor; and that permitted a judge to deny an abortion even though the minor proved she had enough maturity to make an independent decision?

Case Holding: Massachusetts' abortion statute for minors violated the constitution in light of the interpretation given by the state's highest court, that required parental notice of a judicial bypass proceeding invoked by a minor, and permitted a judge to deny an abortion even though the minor proved she had enough maturity to make an independent decision.

Background facts of case: Under Massachusetts' abortion statute parental consent was required before an abortion could be performed on a pregnant minor. If one or both parents refused such consent, however, judicial bypass was provided so that the abortion could be obtained by order of a judge. The appellees, abortion providers and a minor, filed a class action lawsuit in a federal district court in Massachusetts challenging the constitutionality of the statute. The appellants, state officials, were named as defendants. A third party citizen was also allowed to intervene as a defendant. The district court found the statute unconstitutional. The case was appealed to the United States Supreme Court. The Supreme Court vacated the judgment in *Bellotti v. Baird I* and remanded the case for the district court to submit certified questions about the statute to the Massachusetts supreme judicial court.

On remand, the district court certified several questions to the state's highest court. Supreme Judicial Court. Among the questions certified was whether the statute permitted a minor to obtain judicial consent to an abortion without any parental consultation whatsoever; and whether a trial court could refuse to allow an abortion even though a minor proved she was mature enough to make such a decision. The state's highest court responded by answering that parental notice of the judicial bypass proceeding had to be given; and that a judge could deny the abortion even though the minor proved she had enough maturity to make the decision. Following the response by the supreme judicial court, the district court again declared the statute unconstitutional and enjoined its enforcement. Both the state officials and the intervening citizen appealed to the United States Supreme Court. The Supreme Court granted certiorari and consolidated the appeals.

Plurality opinion by Justice Powell: Justice Powell announced the judgment of the Court affirming the district court decision and wrote a plurality opinion. The plurality opinion provided the following rationale for the judgment:

> ... [T]he Court has held that the States validly may limit the freedom of children to choose for themselves in the making of important, affirmative choices with potentially serious consequences. These rulings have been grounded in the recognition that, during the formative years of childhood and adolescence, minors often lack the experience, perspective, and judgment to recognize and avoid choices that could be detrimental to them....
>
> But we are concerned here with a constitutional right to seek an abortion. The abortion decision differs in important ways from other decisions that may be made during minority. The need to preserve the constitutional right and the unique nature of the abortion decision, especially when made by a minor, require a State to act with particular sensitivity when it legislates to foster parental involvement in this matter....
>
> We conclude, therefore, that under state regulation such as that undertaken by Massachusetts, every minor must have the opportunity—if she so desires—to go directly to a court without first consulting or notifying her parents. If she satisfies the court that she is mature and well enough informed to make intelligently the abortion decision on her own, the court must authorize her to act without parental consultation or consent. If she fails to satisfy the court that she is competent to make this decision independently, she must be permitted to show that an abortion nevertheless would be in her best interests. If the court is persuaded that it is, the court must authorize the abortion. If, however, the court is not persuaded by the minor that she is mature or that the abortion would be in her best interests, it may decline to sanction the operation.
>
> ... For the reasons stated above, the constitutional right to seek an abortion may not be unduly burdened by state-imposed conditions upon initial access to court....
>
> ... We [also] agree with the District Court that [the state's laws] cannot constitutionally permit judicial disregard of the abortion decision of a minor who has been determined to be mature and fully competent to assess the implications of the choice she has made.

Disposition of case: The judgment of the district court was affirmed.

Concurring opinion by Justice Rehnquist: Justice Rehnquist wrote a terse concurring opinion in which he commented on the division in the Court that resulted in a plurality opinion. He remarked that "literally thousands of judges cannot be left with nothing more than the guidance offered by a truly fragmented holding of this Court."

Concurring opinion by Justice Stevens: Justice Stevens concurred in the judgment of the Court. He wrote the following:

> In Roe v. Wade the Court held that a woman's right to decide whether to terminate a pregnancy is entitled to constitutional protection. In Planned Parenthood of Central Missouri v. Danforth, the Court held that a pregnant minor's right to make the abortion decision may not be conditioned on the consent of one parent. I am persuaded that these decisions require affirmance of the District Court's holding that the Massachusetts statute is unconstitutional....
>
> In short, it seems to me that this litigation is governed by Danforth; to the extent this statute differs from that in Danforth, it

> is potentially even more restrictive of the constitutional right to decide whether or not to terminate a pregnancy. Because the statute has been once authoritatively construed by the Massachusetts Supreme Judicial Court, and because it is clear that the statute as written and construed is not constitutional, I agree ... that the District Court's judgment should be affirmed. Because [plurality] opinion goes further, however, and addresses the constitutionality of an abortion statute that Massachusetts has not enacted, I decline to join [the plurality] opinion.

Dissenting opinion by Justice White: Justice White disagreed with the judgment of the majority. He believed the statute passed constitutional muster. Justice White wrote as follows:

> I was in dissent in Planned Parenthood of Central Missouri v. Danforth, on the issue of the validity of requiring the consent of a parent when an unmarried woman under 18 years of age seeks an abortion. I continue to have the views I expressed there.... I would not, therefore, strike down this Massachusetts law.
>
> ... [E]ven if a parental consent requirement of the kind involved in Danforth must be deemed invalid, that does not condemn the Massachusetts law, which, when the parents object, authorizes a judge to permit an abortion if he concludes that an abortion is in the best interests of the child. Going beyond Danforth, the Court now holds it unconstitutional for a State to require that in all cases parents receive notice that their daughter seeks an abortion and, if they object to the abortion, an opportunity to participate in a hearing that will determine whether it is in the "best interests" of the child to undergo the surgery. Until now, I would have thought inconceivable a holding that the United States Constitution forbids even notice to parents when their minor child who seeks surgery objects to such notice and is able to convince a judge that the parents should be denied participation in the decision.

Bendectin

Bendectin is the brand name of a drug that is used for the treatment of nausea and vomiting during pregnancy (morning sickness). The drug was marketed and widely used in the United States until 1983. The demise of the drug in the United States began in 1979, with the publication of an article in the National Enquirer that suggested the drug caused birth defects. The article was the purported findings of two researchers, Alan Done and William McBride. Although both researchers were eventually discredited, a flood of law suits (more than 2000 by the mid–1980s) by mothers who took the drug and their children caused its manufacturer to stop selling the drug in the United States (it is sold in Canada under a different name). Credible research studies that followed the article by McBride and Done have not conclusively shown that the drug causes birth defects. The Food and Drug Administration has retained its approval of the drug for morning sickness. *See also* **Daubert v. Merrell Dow Pharmaceuticals, Inc; Morning Sickness**

Benjamin, David

Dr. David Benjamin was a physician who worked at a clinic called Metro Women's Center in Queens, New York. On July 9, 1993, a 33 year old woman named Guadalupe Negron went to the facility to have an abortion. Dr. Benjamin performed the abortion on the morning of July 9. After the abortion Guadalupe moved to the recovery room and was left unattended. After a short period of time Guadalupe was discovered bleeding profusely. Paramedics were brought in and found that Dr. Benjamin had accidentally inserted a breathing tube into Guadalupe's stomach, instead of her trachea, and thereby caused stomach fluids to be lodged in her lungs. Guadalupe died as a result of the abortion. An autopsy report found that in trying to extract a 20-week fetus, Dr. Benjamin had lacerated Guadalupe's cervix and punctured her uterus.

On August 10, 1993, a New York grand jury returned a four count indictment against Dr. Benjamin as a result of Guadalupe's death. The indictment charged him with second degree murder and other offenses. On August 3, 1995, a jury returned a verdict convicting Dr. Benjamin of second degree murder. He was sentenced to 25 years to life in prison. The case was reported in *People v. Benjamin*, 705 N.Y.S.2d 386 (2000). *See also* **Complications During and After Abortion**

Benten, Leona

Leona Benten is credited with making the first open attempt to defy a United States importation ban on the abortion pill RU-486 (Mifepristone). In 1992 Ms. Benten traveled to France to obtain RU-486. She was pregnant at the time. Ms. Benten returned to the United States with the pill in July of 1992. The pill was seized by federal customs officials. A federal district court judge entered a preliminary injunction ordering the RU-486 to be turned over to Ms. Benten for use as an abortifacient. However, the Court of Appeals for the Second Circuit stayed the injunction pending the appeal by federal authorities. Ms. Benten challenged the Second Circuit's stay in the United States Supreme Court. The Supreme Court refused to vacate the stay. The Second Circuit eventually ruled that Ms. Benten could not possess the pill in the United States. *See also* **Mifepristone Induced Abortion**

Berkeley Students for Life

Berkeley Students for Life is a pro-life student-run organization on the campus of Berkeley. The organization works to provide pro-life educational services to the university community. Its members engage in dialogues that challenge the arguments for permitting abortion. Other activities engaged in include hosting lectures, installing baby-changing tables in women's bathrooms on campus, placing ads on the campus to challenge pro-choice assumptions and promote a positive image of motherhood, putting together a brochure of resources in Berkeley for student-parents, and working with a local pregnancy help center. *See also* **Pro-Life Organizations**

Bicornuate Uterus

There are several of ways that a uterus can be shaped differently from normal. The most common abnormal type of uterus is the bicornuate uterus, which means a uterus has two horns. This condition is caused by something that goes wrong in the development of the uterine cavity. It can pose a high risk for spontaneous abortion because of insufficient blood flow to the fetus. Some reports have shown the condition to have a spontaneous abortion rate of about 30 percent. The condition also may cause preterm birth, breech presentation, and necessitate caesarean section birth. *See also* **Retroverted Uterus**

Bigelow v. Virginia

Forum: United States Supreme Court.

Case Citation: Bigelow v. Virginia, 421 U.S. 809 (1975).

Date Argued: December 18, 1974.

Date of Decision: June 16, 1975.

Opinion of Court: Blackmun, J., in which Burger, C. J., and Douglas, Brennan, Stewart, Marshall, and Powell, JJ., joined.

Concurring Opinion: None.

Dissenting Opinion: Rehnquist, J., in which White, J., joined.

Counsel for Appellant: Melvin L. Wulf and John C. Lowe argued; on the brief were Joel M. Gora, Judith Mears, and F. Guthrie Gordon III.

Counsel for Appellee: D. Patrick Lacy, Jr., Assistant Attorney General of Virginia, argued; on the brief were Andrew P. Miller, Attorney General, Anthony F. Troy, Deputy Attorney General, and Paul L. Gergoudis, Assistant Attorney General.

Amicus Brief for Appellant: Raymond T. Bonner and Alan B. Morrison for Public Citizen et al.

Amicus Brief for Appellee: Michael M. Kearney for Virginia Right to Life, Inc.

Issue Presented: Whether the First Amendment was violated by a Virginia penal statute that prohibited selling or circulating any publication that encouraged or promoted abortions?

Case Holding: The Free Speech and Free Press Clauses of the First Amendment were violated by a Virginia penal statute that prohibited selling or circulating any publication that encouraged or promoted abortions.

Background facts of case: On February 8, 1971 the appellant, the editor of a Virginia newspaper, published a New York City organization's advertisement announcing that it would arrange low-cost abortions for women in accredited hospitals and clinics in New York (where abortions were legal). The appellant was subsequently prosecuted for violating a Virginia statute which made it crime to sell or circulate any publication that encouraged or promoted abortions. The trial court found the appellant guilty and sentenced him to pay a fine of $500. The Virginia supreme court affirmed the judgment. The appellant filed an appeal with the United States Supreme Court. The Supreme Court summarily vacated the judgment and remanded the case for Virginia's highest court to reconsider the matter, in light of the intervening decision of *Roe v. Wade*, which legalized abortion in the nation. On remand, the Virginia supreme court again affirmed the judgment. The state's highest court held that the decision in *Roe* did not address the issue of abortion advertising. The state appellate court also rejected the appellant's First Amendment claim of free speech and press. The Supreme Court granted certiorari to consider the issue.

Majority opinion by Justice Blackmun: Justice Blackmun found that Virginia's statute violated the First Amendment. He wrote as follows:

> The central assumption made by the Supreme Court of Virginia was that the First Amendment guarantees of speech and press are inapplicable to paid commercial advertisements. Our cases, however, clearly establish that speech is not stripped of First Amendment protection merely because it appears in that form.
>
> The fact that the particular advertisement in appellant's newspaper had commercial aspects or reflected the advertiser's commercial interests did not negate all First Amendment guarantees. The State was not free of constitutional restraint merely because the advertisement involved sales or solicitations, or because appellant was paid for printing it, or because appellant's motive or the motive of the advertiser may have involved financial gain. The existence of commercial activity, in itself, is no justification for narrowing the protection of expression secured by the First Amendment....
>
> ... The advertisement published in appellant's newspaper did more than simply propose a commercial transaction. It contained factual material of clear public interest. Portions of its message, most prominently the lines, "Abortions are now legal in New York. There are no residency requirements," involve the exercise of the freedom of communicating information and disseminating opinion.
>
> Viewed in its entirety, the advertisement conveyed information of potential interest and value to a diverse audience — not only to readers possibly in need of the services offered, but also to those with a general curiosity about, or genuine interest in, the subject matter or the law of another State and its development, and to readers seeking reform in Virginia.... Also, the activity advertised pertained to constitutional interests. Thus, in this case, appellant's First Amendment interests coincided with the constitutional interests of the general public....
>
> A State does not acquire power or supervision over the internal affairs of another State merely because the welfare and health of its own citizens may be affected when they travel to that State. It may seek to disseminate information so as to enable its citizens to make better informed decisions when they leave. But it may not, under the guise of exercising internal police powers, bar a citizen of another State from disseminating information about an activity that is legal in that State.
>
> We conclude, therefore, that the Virginia courts erred in their assumptions that advertising, as such, was entitled to no First Amendment protection and that appellant Bigelow had no legitimate First Amendment interest. We need not decide in this case the precise extent to which the First Amendment permits regulation of advertising that is related to activities the State may legitimately regulate or even prohibit....
>
> If application of this statute were upheld under these circumstances, Virginia might exert the power sought here over a wide variety of national publications or interstate newspapers carrying advertisements similar to the one that appeared in Bigelow's newspaper or containing articles on the general subject matter to which the advertisement referred. Other States might do the same. The burdens thereby imposed on publications would impair, perhaps severely, their proper functioning. We know from experience that liberty of the press is in peril as soon as the government tries to compel what is to go into a newspaper. The policy of the First Amendment favors dissemination of information and opinion, and the guarantees of freedom of speech and press were not designed to prevent the censorship of the press merely, but any action of the government by means of which it might prevent such free and general discussion of public matters as seems absolutely essential.
>
> We conclude that Virginia could not apply [its statute] ... to appellant's publication of the advertisement in question without unconstitutionally infringing upon his First Amendment rights.

Disposition of case: The judgment of the Virginia supreme court was reversed.

Dissenting opinion by Justice Rehnquist: Justice Rehnquist disagreed with the majority opinion. He did not believe that the statute violated the First Amendment. He wrote as follows:

> Assuming arguendo that this advertisement is something more than a normal commercial proposal, I am unable to see why Virginia does not have a legitimate public interest in its regulation. The Court apparently concedes, and our cases have long held, that the States have a strong interest in the prevention of commercial advertising in the health field — both in order to maintain high ethical standards in the medical profession and to protect the public from unscrupulous practices. And the interest asserted by the Supreme Court of Virginia in the Virginia statute was the prevention of commercial exploitation of those women who elect to have an abortion....
>
> ... I think the Court today simply errs in assessing Virginia's interest in its statute because it does not focus on the impact of the practices in question on the State. Although the commercial referral agency, whose advertisement in Virginia was barred, was physically located outside the State, this physical contact says little about Virginia's concern for the touted practices. Virginia's interest in this statute lies in preventing commercial exploitation of the health needs of its citizens. So long as the statute bans commercial advertising by publications within the State, the extraterritorial location at which the services are actually provided does not diminish that interest.
>
> Since the statute in question is a reasonable regulation that serves a legitimate public interest, I would affirm the judgment of the Supreme Court of Virginia.

Biliary Atresia

Biliary atresia is a congenital disorder involving an abnormal development of the bile ducts inside or outside the liver. This condition causes blockage of bile flow from the liver to the gallbladder. This situation may cause liver damage and cirrhosis of the liver. Left untreated the condition is eventually fatal. The disorder occurs in approximately 1 out of 20,000 live births. There is no known way to prevent the disorder. Immediate surgery is required to correct the problem. In some instances a liver transplant may be required. *See also* **Birth Defects and Abortion**

Billings Method *see* **Natural Family Planning Methods**

Biophysical Profile

A biophysical profile involves the use of ultrasound or other devices to evaluate fetal well-being before birth. The evaluation consists of examining the fetus' breathing movements, gross body movements, muscle tone, and the amount of amniotic fluid present. Each of these areas have a predetermined scoring standard. In addition, the examination may involve performing a non-stress test. This involves monitoring the fetus' heart rate for a period of 20 or more minutes. *See also* **Fetal Monitoring**

Biopsy

Biopsy refers to the removal of a small piece of human tissue in order to perform tests to determine presence or absence of a disease, infection or other abnormality.

Biparietal Diameter *see* **Gestational Age**

Birth Canal

The birth canal is the passageway through which the fetus travels during birth and includes the cervix, vagina and vulva. *See also* **Female Reproductive System**

Birth Control *see* **Contraception**

Birth Control Patch *see* **Patch Contraceptive**

Birth Control Pill

The birth control pill (the Pill) is an oral contraceptive that was designed for use by women. The Pill was developed by Drs. Gregory Pincus, Min-Chueh Chang and John Rock. The first commercially produced birth control pill, Enovid-10, was first marketed in the United States in 1960. Approximately 10.7 million American women now use the Pill. It is the most widely used method of non-surgical contraception.

The Pill is composed of two hormones, an estrogen and a progestin. The estrogen is used to stop the development of the egg in the ovary. The progestin alters the mucus in the cervix and helps prevent sperm from reaching the egg. The Pill also prevents the lining of the uterus from becoming fully developed, so that there is little likelihood that a fertilized egg will become implanted in the uterus. Most pills used today contain 30 to 35 mcg of estrogen and 0.5 mg to 1 mg progestin.

To obtain the Pill requires a prescription, or they can be obtained from a health care professional. The Pill is distributed in a package, in units of 21 or 28 pills. It is taken every day for 21 days. In the package of 28, 7 sugar or dummy pills are taken for the remaining 7 days. In the package of 21, no pill is taken for 7 days after the last one is taken. If the Pill is taken consistently and correctly, less than one in 1,000 women using it will become pregnant every year.

Some of the side effects of the Pill include: irregular bleeding for the first few months after starting the Pill; increased appetite; depression or moodiness; headaches and dizziness; nausea and vomiting; weight change; high blood pressure; breast tenderness; and missed periods. Some widely reported studies suggest that in certain groups of women the risk of breast cancer increases with oral contraceptive use. However, other studies have found no significant increased risk. The Pill, on the other hand, has been found to help prevent cancer of the ovaries and cancer of the endometrium (the lining of the uterus).

Mini-Pill. The mini-pill was introduced in the early 1970s. This version of the Pill contains only progestin (the Pill contains estrogen and progestin). The mini-pill works primarily by suppressing ovulation. It creates changes in the cervix and uterus that make it difficult for sperm to unite with an egg. Mini-pills pose few of the risks associated with the Pill. However, mini-pills have two primary drawbacks: they may cause irregular bleeding and they have proven to be less effective in preventing pregnancy.

Multiphasic Pill. In 1982 a new version of the Pill, called the "biphasic" pill, was introduced on the market. In 1984 the "triphasic" pill was introduced. These multiphasic pills are low-dose pills in which the ratio of progestin to estrogen, changes during the 21 days the Pill is taken.

Extended-cycle Pill. Starting in 2003 a new contraceptive pill was placed on the market. This new pill is popularly known as extended-cycle birth control pill. Two brand names for this pill are Seasonique and Seasonale. This pill allows women to have four periods per year, instead one per month. The pill is said to be 99 percent effective in preventing pregnancy. Seasonique and Seasonale.

Continuous Period-skipping Pill. In 2007 the Food and Drug Administration approved the sale of a continuous period-skipping birth control pill. This birth control pill is designed to permanently suppress the menstrual cycle. The brand name for this pill is Lybrel. *See also* **Contraception**

Birth Defects and Abortion

Birth defects (also called congenital defects) are physical abnormalities that are present at birth. They take the form of syndromes, diseases, disorders and malformations. Birth defects are caused by events preceding birth. Some birth defects are inherited through abnormal genes from one or both parents. Other birth defects may be due to spontaneous and unexplained changes in genes, or the result of a chromosomal abnormality. Although the causes of most birth defects are unknown, there are factors which are known to increase the risk of birth defects. These factors include: nutritional deficiency, trauma, alcohol, radiation, environmental factors, certain drugs, infections and hereditary disorders. There are more than 4,000 known birth defects.

Birth defects may affect organs, senses, limbs, or mental development. The defects range from minor to serious. A major birth defect occurs in about 3 percent of all births. It is estimated that about

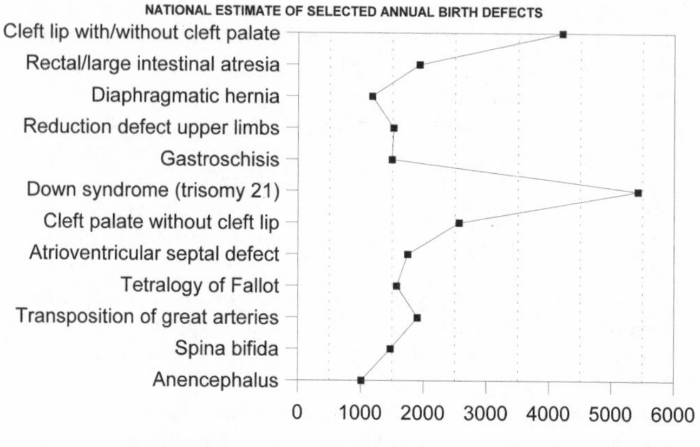

Source: **Centers for Disease Control and Prevention.**

120,000 babies are born each year in the United States with a birth defect. Birth defects are the leading cause of infant mortality in the United States. They account for more than 20 percent of all infant deaths. Annually, about 8,000 infants born with birth defects die during their first year of life.

Numerous advances in medical science now make it possible for approximately 250 birth defects to be detected while the fetus is still in the womb. While no reliable statistics exist, researchers do not dispute the fact that a significant number of abortions occur annually because of the detection of fetal birth defects. This type of abortion is called eugenic abortion. Such an abortion may not legally occur once a fetus has reached a stage of being able to survive outside the womb with or without artificial aid. *See also* **Achondroplasia; Adrenoleukodystrophy; Agenesis of the Corpus Callosum; Aicardi Syndrome; Alexander Disease; Alpers' Disease; Anencephaly; Angelman Syndrome; Arteriovenous Malformation; Basal Cell Nevus Syndrome; Batten Disease; Biliary Atresia; Cat Cry Syndrome; Cerebral Palsy; Chediak-Higashi Syndrome; Cleft Lip and Palate; Clubfoot; Coffin-Lowry Syndrome; Congenital Heart Defect; Congenital Hypothyroidism; Congenital Rubella Syndrome; Cystic Fibrosis; Cystic Hygromas; Dandy-Walker Syndrome; Diaphragmatic Hernia; Down Syndrome; Empty Sella Syndrome; Encephaloceles; Fanconi's Anemia; Fetal Alcohol Syndrome; Fetal Tumors; Fragile X Syndrome; Friedreich's Ataxia; Gaucher's Disease; Genital and Urinary Tract Birth Defects; Hallervorden-Spatz Disease; Hirschsprung's Disease; Holoprosencephaly; Huntington's Disease; Hutchinson-Gilford Syndrome; Hydrocephalus; Infantile Refsum; Joubert Syndrome; Krabbe Disease; Leigh's Disease; Lesch-Nyhan Syndrome; Lissencephaly; Marfan's Syndrome; Metachromatic Leukodystrophy; Microcephaly; Mobius Syndrome; Muscular Dystrophy; Neurofibromatoses; Niemann-Pick Disease; Noonan Syndrome; Osteogenesis Imperfecta; Pelizaeus-Merzbacher Disease; PKU; Respiratory Distress Syndrome; Porencephaly; Rh Incompatibility; Riley-Day Syndrome; Sickle Cell Anemia; Spina Bifida; Tay-Sachs Disease; Tetralogy of Fallot; Toxoplasmosis; Trisomy 13; Trisomy 18; Tuberous Sclerosis; Turner's Syndrome; Von Hippel-Lindau Disease; Werdnig-Hoffmann Disease; Wilson's Disease; Zellweger Syndrome**

Birth Trauma *see* **Trauma and Pregnancy**

Black, Hugo L.

Hugo L. Black (1886–1971) served as an associate justice of the United States Supreme Court from 1937 to 1971. While on the Supreme Court Justice Black was known as a moderate who maintained an intractable belief that the Bill of Rights were intended to curtail the authority of States over their citizens.

Justice Black was born in Harlan, Alabama. His higher education began at a medical college, but he soon lost interest and enrolled at the University of Alabama Law School, where he graduated in 1906. Justice Black's early legal career was spent in private practice and as a prosecutor. In 1917 he joined the Army and rose to the rank of captain before resigning his commission. After leaving the Army Black resumed a private law practice until his election to the United States Senate in 1926. Eleven years later, in 1937, President Franklin D. Roosevelt nominated Justice Black to the Supreme Court.

While on the Supreme Court Justice Black was involved in only a few abortion related decisions decided by the Court. He wrote the majority opinion in *United States v. Vuitch*, which held that the criminal abortion statute of the District of Columbia, which only permitted therapeutic abortions, was not constitutionally. In *Griswold v. Connecticut* Justice Black wrote an opinion dissenting from the majority decision, which held that the right of privacy found in the constitution prohibited enforcement of a Connecticut statute that made it a crime to give married persons contraceptive information and devices. He did not believe the statute violated the constitution. Justice Black issued a statement dissenting from the majority decision in *Poe v. Ullman*, which held that the appellants did not have standing to challenge the constitutionality of a Connecticut statute, that made it a crime to give married persons contraceptive information and devices. He believed the appellants had standing.

Blackmun, Harry A.

Harry A. Blackmun (1908–1999) served as an associate justice of the United States Supreme Court from 1970 to 1994. Justice Blackmun started out on the Supreme Court with a conservative philosophy that eventually was transformed into a liberal ideology and interpretation of the Constitution, with respect to individual liberties and rights.

Justice Blackmun was born in Nashville, Illinois. His family would eventually move to St. Paul, Minnesota, where he met his childhood friend Warren Earl Burger (former Supreme Court chief justice). Justice Blackmun attended Harvard University, where he obtained a degree in mathematics. In 1932 he graduated from Harvard Law School.

After leaving law school Justice Blackmun worked as a law clerk briefly for a Federal Court of Appeals judge, before going into private practice. During his years in private practice Justice Blackmun managed to find time to teach law courses at St. Paul College of Law and at the University of Minnesota Law School. In 1959 President Dwight D. Eisenhower nominated Justice Blackmun to the Federal Court of Appeals for the Eighth Circuit. As an appeals court judge he carved out a reputation as a conservative jurist. In 1970 President Richard M. Nixon nominated Justice Blackmun for a position on the Supreme Court.

Distribution of the Abortion Voting Pattern of Justice Blackmun Based Upon Opinions Filed by the Supreme Court

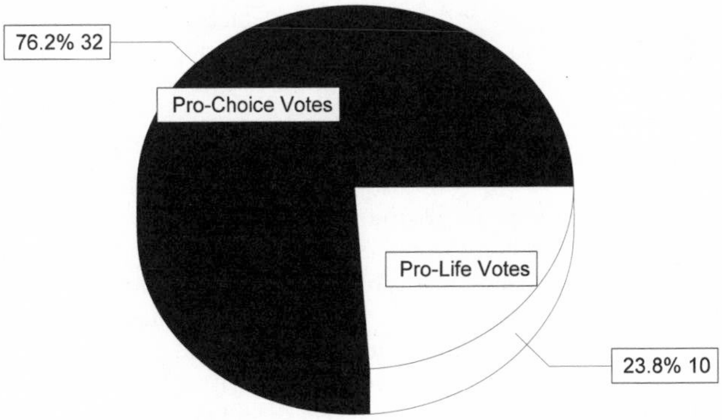

During Justice Blackmun's tenure on the Supreme Court he issued a significant number of abortion related opinions (the most famous being *Roe v. Wade*). The written opinions and opinions simply voted on by Justice Blackmun, indicate that he was in favor of using the constitution to expand abortion rights for women.

(1) Unanimous opinions written. In *Bellotti v. Baird I* Justice Blackmun wrote a unanimous opinion, which held that the federal district court had to certify appropriate questions to the supreme judicial court of Massachusetts, concerning the interpretation of that state's parental consent abortion statute for minors, before ruling on its constitutionality.

(2) Majority opinions written. In *Roe v. Wade* Justice Blackmun

wrote the majority opinion, which held that the liberty component of the Due Process Clause of the Fourteenth Amendment prohibited states from criminalizing or preventing elective first trimester abortions. Justice Blackmun wrote the majority opinion in *Doe v. Bolton*, which held that the Due Process Clause of the Fourteenth Amendment was violated by provisions in Georgia's abortion statutes that required (1) abortions take place in accredited hospitals, (2) that an abortion be approved by a hospital abortion committee, (3) that the need for an abortion be confirmed by two independent physicians, and (4) that a woman seeking an abortion be a resident of Georgia.

Justice Blackmun wrote the majority decision in *Thornburgh v. American College of Obstetricians and Gynecologists*, which invalidated provisions in Pennsylvania's abortion statute that provided for maternal informed consent, abortion alternative printed information, abortion reporting requirements, determination of fetal viability, degree of care required in post-viability abortions, and a second-physician requirement. In *Diamond v. Charles*, Justice Blackmun wrote the majority opinion, which held that a citizen did not have standing to appeal a decision invalidating parts of Illinois' abortion statute that (1) imposed criminal penalties for violating a prescribed standard of care that had to be exercised by a physician in performing an abortion of a viable fetus, and of a possibly viable fetus; and (2) imposed criminal penalties for physicians who failed to provide patients with information about the type of abortifacient used. In *Colautti v. Franklin* Justice Blackmun wrote the majority opinion, which held that the constitution was violated by a vague and ambiguous provision in Pennsylvania's abortion statute that subjected a physician who performed an abortion to potential criminal liability, if he/she failed to utilize a statutorily prescribed technique when the fetus was viable or when there was sufficient reason to believe that the fetus may be viable.

In *Automobile Workers v. Johnson Controls, Inc.* Justice Blackmun wrote the majority opinion, which held that Title VII of the Civil Rights Act forbids sex-specific fetal-protection policies by an employer, that exclude a fertile female employee from certain jobs because of the employer's concern for the health of the fetus the woman might conceive. In *Daubert v. Merrell Dow Pharmaceuticals, Inc.*, a case involving children born with severe birth defects, Justice Blackmun wrote the opinion for the Supreme Court, which held that the *Frye* rule on admissibility of expert testimony did not survive the enactment of the Federal Rules of Evidence.

Justice Blackmun wrote the majority opinion in *Planned Parenthood of Missouri v. Danforth*, which held that the constitution was not violated by provisions in Missouri's abortion statute involving the definition of fetal viability, woman's written consent, and record keeping and reporting requirements; but that the constitution prohibited the requirements concerning spousal consent, parental consent for minor, banning saline amniocentesis abortions, and physician's standard of care. Justice Blackmun wrote the majority opinion in *Bigelow v. Virginia*, which held that the Free Speech and Free Press Clauses of the First Amendment were violated by a Virginia penal statute that prohibited selling or circulating any publication that encouraged or promoted abortions.

(3) Majority opinions voted with only. In *Madsen v. Women's Health Clinic, Inc.*, Justice Blackmun voted with the majority opinion, which upheld parts of an injunction that restricted noise by anti-abortionists at a clinic and imposed a 36 foot buffer zone around the clinic entrances and driveway. However, *Madsen* ruled that the Free Speech Clause was violated by a 36 foot buffer zone as applied to the private property to the north and west of the clinic, a restriction on the use of images observable by clinic patients, a 300 foot no approach zone around the clinic, and a 300 foot buffer zone around the residences, because these restrictions swept more broadly than necessary to accomplish the permissible goals of the injunction. Justice Blackmun voted with a unanimous Supreme Court in *National Organization for Women, Inc. v. Scheidler*, which held that a group of pro-choice organizations could maintain a RICO civil lawsuit against several anti-abortion individuals and groups.

Justice Blackmun voted with the majority opinion in *United States Catholic Conference v. Abortion Rights Mobilization*, which allowed the appellants to challenge having to turn over documents in a lawsuit seeking to strip them of their tax exempt status because of their active political abortion work. Justice Blackmun voted with the majority opinion in *Bolger v. Youngs Drug Products Corp.*, which held that a provision of the Comstock Act, 39 U.S.C. § 3001(e)(2), that prohibited mailing unsolicited advertisements for contraceptives violated the Free Speech Clause of the First Amendment. Justice Blackmun voted with the majority opinion in *City of Akron v. Akron Center for Reproductive Health, Inc.*, which invalidated an abortion ordinance that provided requirements for parental consent, informed consent, waiting period, hospitalization and disposal of fetal remains.

Justice Blackmun joined the majority opinion in *Simopoulos v. Virginia*, which upheld a Virginia statute requiring second trimester abortions be performed at hospitals, because under the statute an adequately equipped clinic could, upon proper application, obtain an outpatient hospital license that permitted the performance of second-trimester abortions. In *Carey v. Population Services International* Justice Blackmun voted with the majority opinion, which held that the constitution prohibited enforcement of a New York statute that made it a crime (1) for any person to sell or distribute any contraceptive of any kind to a minor under the age of 16 years; (2) for anyone other than a licensed pharmacist to distribute contraceptives to persons 16 or over; and (3) for anyone, including licensed pharmacists, to advertise or display contraceptives. Justice Blackmun joined the majority opinion in *Anders v. Floyd*, which held that a federal district court erred in enjoining enforcement of a South Carolina statute that imposed criminal punishment for performing an abortion on a viable fetus.

In *Connecticut v. Menillo* Justice Blackmun joined the majority per curiam opinion, which held that the constitution was not violated by criminal abortion statutes that prohibit nonphysicians from attempting or performing abortions at any stage of a pregnancy. In *Withrow v. Larkin* Justice Blackmun joined a unanimous opinion, which held that constitutional due process was not violated by the mere fact that a Wisconsin medical examining board had the authority to both, investigate and adjudicate, allegations against a physician that included, among other things, permitting a nonphysician to perform an abortion. Justice Blackmun voted with the majority opinion in *Burns v. Alcala*, which held that states receiving federal financial aid under the program of Aid to Families with Dependent Children, were not required to offer welfare benefits to pregnant women for their unborn children.

Justice Blackmun voted with the majority opinion in *Geduldig v. Aiello*, which held that the Equal Protection Clause of the Fourteenth Amendment did not require a private sector employee disability insurance program, operated by the state of California, provide coverage for employee disabilities associated with normal pregnancies. In *Weinberger v. Hynson, Westcott & Dunning* Justice Blackmun joined the majority opinion, which held that the Food and Drug Administration could not deny a drug manufacturer a hearing to obtain marketing approval for a drug called Lutrexin, which provided treatment for premature labor and threatened and habitual abortion. In *Frisby v. Schultz* Justice Blackmun voted with the majority opinion, which upheld the constitutional validity of a town ordinance that was created to prevent pro-life picketing at the residence of an abortion doctor.

(4) Plurality opinions written. Justice Blackmun wrote a plurality

opinion and announced the judgment of the Supreme Court in *Singleton v. Wulff*, which held that the Eighth Circuit court of appeals had jurisdiction to determine whether abortion providers had standing to challenge a provision in Missouri's abortion statute that limited medicaid payment for abortions, but it did not have jurisdiction to rule that the provision violated the constitution because the district court did not address the issue.

(5) Concurring opinions written. Justice Blackmun concurred with the majority opinion in *Eisenstadt v. Baird*, which held that the Equal Protection Clause of the Fourteenth Amendment was violated by a Massachusetts statute that made it a crime to give away a drug, medicine, instrument, or article for the prevention of conception except in the case of (1) a physician prescribing it for a married person, or (2) a pharmacist furnishing it to a married person presenting a physician's prescription.

(6) Concurring opinions voted with only. Justice Blackmun concurred in the majority judgment in *Bellotti v. Baird II*, which held that Massachusetts' abortion statute for minors violated the constitution in light of an interpretation given by the state's highest court, that required parental notice of a judicial bypass proceeding invoked by a minor, and permitted a judge to deny an abortion even though the minor proved she had enough maturity to make an independent decision.

(7) Dissenting opinions written. Justice Blackmun wrote a dissenting opinion in *Rust v. Sullivan*, which upheld federal regulations that prohibited pro-abortion counseling, referral, and advocacy by health care providers. In *Ohio v. Akron Center for Reproductive Health* Justice Blackmun wrote an opinion dissenting from the majority decision, which upheld the constitutionality of Ohio's abortion statute notice and judicial bypass requirements for pregnant female minors. Justice Blackmun wrote an opinion dissenting from the majority decision in *Harris v. McRae*, which held that medicaid funding restrictions for abortion by the Hyde Amendment, did not violate the Due Process Clause nor the equal protection component of the Fifth Amendment. He believed the Hyde Amendment violated the constitution. Justice Blackmun wrote an opinion dissenting from the majority decision in *Beal v. Doe*, which held that Pennsylvania's refusal to extend medicaid coverage to nontherapeutic abortions was not invalid nor inconsistent with Title XIX of the Social Security Act. He believed Title XIX required funding for all abortions.

(8) Dissenting opinions voted with only. Justice Blackmun dissented from the opinion in *Bray v. Alexandria Clinic*, which held that the Civil Rights Act of 1871, 42 U.S.C. § 1985(3), did not provide a cause of action against persons obstructing access to abortion clinics. He believed that the statute could be used by abortionists. In *H. L. v. Matheson* Justice Blackmun dissented from the majority opinion, which held that the constitution was not violated by Utah's requirement that the parents of a minor be notified, if possible, prior to performing an abortion. He believed the parental notification requirement violated the constitution. In *Williams v. Zbaraz* Justice Blackmun dissented from the majority opinion, which held that in light of the requirements of the Hyde Amendment, the Equal Protection Clause of the Fourteenth Amendment was not violated by an Illinois statute that prohibited state medicaid payment for abortions, except when necessary to save the life of the pregnant woman. He believed the statute violated the constitution.

In *Maher v. Roe* Justice Blackmun dissented from the majority opinion, which held that the Equal Protection Clause of the Fourteenth Amendment did not prohibit Connecticut from excluding nontherapeutic abortions from its medicaid program. He believed the Equal Protection Clause required funding all abortions. Justice Blackmun dissented from the per curiam opinion in *Poelker v. Doe*, which held that the Equal Protection Clause of the Fourteenth Amendment was not violated by a policy of the city of St. Louis, Missouri that denied publicly funded abortions to indigent women at city hospitals, except when a woman's health or life was in danger. He believed the city's policy violated the constitution.

(9) Concurring and dissenting opinions written. In *Planned Parenthood of Southeastern Pennsylvania v. Casey*, Justice Blackmun wrote a concurring and dissenting opinion. He dissented from the majority's decision that the constitution was not violated by provisions in Pennsylvania's abortion statute that provided for: medical emergency abortion; 24 hour waiting period for abortion; parental notice and judicial bypass for abortion by a minor; and certain abortion facility reporting requirements. He concurred in the majority's decision that found two provisions in the abortion statute unconstitutional: spousal notification before obtaining an abortion, and a requirement that a woman inform the abortion provider the reason for not notifying her spouse.

Justice Blackmun wrote a concurring and dissenting opinion in *Webster v. Reproductive Health Services*, which upheld Missouri's prohibition on the use of public facilities or employees to perform abortions and a requirement that physicians conduct viability tests prior to performing abortions. He concurred only in the majority's decision that a prohibition on public funding of abortion counseling was rendered moot and would not be analyzed. In *Planned Parenthood Assn. v. Ashcroft* Justice Blackmun wrote an opinion concurring and dissenting from the majority/plurality opinion, which held that the constitution was violated by Missouri's requirement that second trimester abortions take place in a hospital; but that the constitution was not violated by the state's requirement that a pathology report for each abortion be performed, that a second physician be present during abortions performed after viability, and parental or judicial consent for abortion by minors. Justice Blackmun believed that all of the provisions of the statute violated the constitution.

Justice Blackmun wrote an opinion concurring and dissenting from the majority decision in *United States v. Vuitch*, which held that the criminal abortion statute of the District of Columbia, which only permitted therapeutic abortions, was not constitutionally vague insofar as there was no ambiguity in its use of the word health and it did not shift to the defendant the burden of proving innocence. He believed the statute was constitutionally valid, but that the Court did not have jurisdiction to hear the case.

(10) Concurring and dissenting opinions voted with only. Justice Blackmun voted to concur and dissent in *Hodgson v. Minnesota*, which upheld the constitutionality of Minnesota's requirement that a pregnant female minor could not obtain an abortion until at least 48 hours after both of her parents had been notified, except when (1) the attending physician certified that an immediate abortion was necessary to prevent the minor's death; (2) the minor declared that she was a victim of parental abuse or neglect; or (3) a court of competent jurisdiction ordered the abortion to proceed without notice upon proof that the minor was mature and capable of giving informed consent or that an abortion without notice to both parents would be in the minor's best interest. Justice Blackmun dissented from the Court's determination that, although the two-parent notification requirement was invalid, the judicial bypass option cured the defect.

In *Federal Election Commission v. Massachusetts Citizens for Life, Inc.* Justice Blackmun voted to concur and dissent from the majority decision, which held that federal law that prohibited the appellee from using its treasury funds to promote pro-life political candidates violated the Free Speech Clause of the First Amendment. Justice Blackmun agreed with the majority that the law applied to the appellee, but dissented from the decision to find the law unconstitutional.

Blackwell, Elizabeth

Elizabeth Blackwell (1821–1910) was the first female physician in the United States and a strong opponent of abortion. She was born in Bristol, England. Her family moved to New York in 1832. In 1847 Blackwell decided to attend medical school. After being denied entrance into 29 schools, she received an acceptance letter from Geneva Medical College in New York. When Blackwell graduated from the school in 1849, at the top of her class, she became the first female physician in the nation.

As a gynecologist, Blackwell possessed a passion for the well-being of women and children. This passion caused her to speak out against abortion and the physical dangers it presented to women. Her commitment in this regard led her to found the New York Infirmary for Indigent Women and Children in 1857 and the London School of Medicine for Women in 1875. Blackwell also wrote a number of books, which included *The Physical Education of Girls* (1852) and *Pioneer Work in Opening the Medical Profession to Women* (1895). *See also* **Early Feminist Opposition to Abortion**

Bladder Exstrophy *see* **Genital and Urinary Tract Birth Defects**

Blastocyte *see* **Fetal Development**

Blighted Ovum

A blighted ovum (also called anembryonic pregnancy) is considered to be a form of spontaneous abortion. It is characterized by a fertilized egg that develops into a gestational sac and attaches itself to the uterine wall, but the embryo fails to develop. Often, there is no bleeding or other signs of the failed pregnancy. A woman may not realize that a miscarriage occurred until a doctor makes the discovery during a prenatal examination. A blighted ovum may occur because of chromosomal defects or the poor quality of the egg or sperm. *See also* **Miscarriage**

Blood Clotting and Pregnancy

Blood clots form as a result of blood tissue transforming into a soft, semi-solid mass or clump (coagulation). When this occurs the clots can obstruct the flow of blood and thereby deprive tissues of normal blood flow and oxygen. Clotting may also be caused by fat, amniotic fluid, bone marrow, a tumor fragment, or an air bubble (common in air travel). There are various disorders associated with blood clotting, such as deep venous thrombosis, pulmonary embolism, protein C or S deficiency, fibrinolytic capacity, factor XII deficiency, and antithrombin III deficiency.

Studies have shown that blood clotting is especially dangerous to pregnant women. Pregnant women who have a blood clotting disorder are at an increased risk for having a spontaneous abortion or stillbirth. This risk is posed because a developing fetus depends on the blood vessels in the placenta and umbilical cord. A blood clot can cut off and reduce the blood supply to the fetus, thereby robbing the fetus of oxygen and nutrients that are needed. Potential treatment for blood clotting in pregnant women include anti-clotting drugs, such as heparin and aspirin. *See also* **Antiphospholipid Antibody Syndrome; Miscarriage; Stillbirth**

Bolger v. Youngs Drug Products Corp.

Forum: United States Supreme Court.

Case Citation: Bolger v. Youngs Drug Products Corp., 463 U.S. 60 (1983).

Date Argued: January 12, 1983.

Date of Decision: June 24, 1983.

Opinion of Court: Marshall, J., in which Burger, C. J., and White, Blackmun, and Powell, JJ., joined.

Concurring Opinion: Rehnquist, J., in which O'Connor, J., joined.

Concurring Opinion: Stevens, J.

Dissenting Opinion: None.

Justice Not Participating: Brennan, J.

Counsel for Appellants: David A. Strauss argued; on the brief were Solicitor General Lee and Deputy Solicitor General Geller.

Counsel for Appellee: Jerold S. Solovy argued; on the brief were Robert L. Graham and Laura A. Kaster.

Amicus Brief for Appellants: None.

Amicus Brief for Appellee: Robert D. Joffe, Eve W. Paul, and Dara Klassel filed a brief for the Planned Parenthood Federation of America, Inc., et al.; Michael L. Burack, Charles S. Sims, and Janet Benshoof filed a brief for the American Civil Liberties Union.

Issue Presented: Whether the Comstock Act, which prohibited mailing unsolicited advertisements for contraceptives, violated the First Amendment?

Case Holding: The Comstock Act's complete ban on mailing unsolicited advertisements for contraceptives violated the First Amendment.

Background facts of case: The appellee, Youngs Drug Products Corp., was engaged in the manufacture, sale, and distribution of contraceptives. The appellee marketed its products primarily through sales to chain warehouses and wholesale distributors, who in turn sold contraceptives to retail pharmacists, who then sold those products to individual customers. In 1979 the appellee decided to undertake a campaign of unsolicited mass mailings to members of the public. The mailings included three types of materials: (1) multi-page, multi-item flyers promoting a large variety of products available at a drugstore, including prophylactics; (2) flyers exclusively or substantially devoted to promoting prophylactics; and (3) informational pamphlets discussing the desirability and availability of prophylactics in general. The federal Postal Service contacted the appellee and issued a warning that the proposed mailing violated a provision of the Comstock Act, 39 U.S.C. § 3001(e)(2), which prohibited mailing unsolicited advertisements for contraceptives. A violation of the provision was subject to criminal and civil penalties. The appellee decided to challenge enforcement of the provision by suing the appellants, federal officials, in a federal district court in Washington, D.C. The appellee alleged that the statute, as applied its mailings, violated the First Amendment.

The district court determined that the statute by its plain language, prohibited all three types of proposed mailings. The court then addressed the constitutionality of the statute as applied to these mailings. After finding all three types of materials to be commercial solicitations, the court concluded that the statutory prohibition was more extensive than necessary to the interests asserted by the federal government, and it therefore held that the statute's absolute ban on the three types of mailings violated the First Amendment. The appellants brought a direct appeal to the Supreme Court.

Majority opinion by Justice Marshall: Justice Marshall determined that the challenged provision of the Comstock Act was unconstitutional. He wrote as follows:

> ...The State may deal effectively with false, deceptive, or misleading sales techniques. The State may also prohibit commercial speech related to illegal behavior. In this case, however, appellants have never claimed that Youngs' proposed mailings fall into any of these categories. To the contrary, advertising for contraceptives not only implicates substantial individual and societal interests in the free flow of commercial information, but also relates to activity which is protected from unwarranted state interference. Youngs' proposed commercial speech is therefore clearly protected by the First Amendment. Indeed, where — as in this case — a speaker desires to convey truthful information relevant to important social issues such as family planning and the

prevention of venereal disease, we have previously found the First Amendment interest served by such speech paramount.

... The prohibition in 3001(e)(2) originated in 1873 as part of the Comstock Act, a criminal statute designed "for the suppression of Trade in and Circulation of obscene Literature and Articles of immoral Use." Appellants do not purport to rely on justifications for the statute offered during the 19th century. Instead, they advance interests that concededly were not asserted when the prohibition was enacted into law. This reliance is permissible since the insufficiency of the original motivation does not diminish other interests that the restriction may now serve.

In particular, appellants assert that the statute (1) shields recipients of mail from materials that they are likely to find offensive and (2) aids parents' efforts to control the manner in which their children become informed about sensitive and important subjects such as birth control....

We have, of course, recognized the important interest in allowing addressees to give notice to a mailer that they wish no further mailings which, in their sole discretion, they believe to be erotically arousing or sexually provocative. But we have never held that the Government itself can shut off the flow of mailings to protect those recipients who might potentially be offended. The First Amendment does not permit the government to prohibit speech as intrusive unless the captive audience cannot avoid objectionable speech. Recipients of objectionable mailings, however, may effectively avoid further bombardment of their sensibilities simply by averting their eyes. Consequently, the short, though regular, journey from mail box to trash can is an acceptable burden, at least so far as the Constitution is concerned.

The second interest asserted by appellants— aiding parents' efforts to discuss birth control with their children — is undoubtedly substantial. Parents have an important guiding role to play in the upbringing of their children which presumptively includes counseling them on important decisions. As a means of effectuating this interest, however, 3001(e)(2) fails to withstand scrutiny.

To begin with, 3001(e)(2) provides only the most limited incremental support for the interest asserted. We can reasonably assume that parents already exercise substantial control over the disposition of mail once it enters their mailboxes.... Under these circumstances, a ban on unsolicited advertisements serves only to assist those parents who desire to keep their children from confronting such mailings, who are otherwise unable to do so, and whose children have remained relatively free from such stimuli.

This marginal degree of protection is achieved by purging all mailboxes of unsolicited material that is entirely suitable for adults. We have previously made clear that a restriction of this scope is more extensive than the Constitution permits, for the government may not reduce the adult population to reading only what is fit for children. The level of discourse reaching a mailbox simply cannot be limited to that which would be suitable for a sandbox....

Section 3001(e)(2) is also defective because it denies to parents truthful information bearing on their ability to discuss birth control and to make informed decisions in this area. Because the proscribed information may bear on one of the most important decisions parents have a right to make, the restriction of the free flow of truthful information constitutes a basic constitutional defect regardless of the strength of the government's interest.

Disposition of case: The judgment of the district court was affirmed.

Concurring opinion by Justice Rehnquist: Justice Rehnquist concurred in the Court's judgment, but believed that a different analysis was necessary to distinguish speech through the use of the mail, from other forms of protected speech.

Concurring opinion by Justice Stevens: Justice Stevens agreed with the judgment of the Court. He wrote separately to make the following point:

Even if it may not intend to do so, the Court's opinion creates the impression that commercial speech is a fairly definite category of communication that is protected by a fairly definite set of rules that differ from those protecting other categories of speech. That impression may not be wholly warranted. Moreover, as I have previously suggested, we must be wary of unnecessary insistence on rigid classifications, lest speech entitled to constitutional protection be inadvertently suppressed....

The statute at issue in this case censors ideas, not style. It prohibits appellee from mailing any unsolicited advertisement of contraceptives, no matter how unobtrusive and tactful; yet it permits anyone to mail unsolicited advertisements of devices intended to facilitate conception, no matter how coarse or grotesque. It thus excludes one advocate from a forum to which adversaries have unlimited access. I concur in the Court's judgment that the First Amendment prohibits the application of the statute to these materials.

Born Alive Infants Protection Act

The Born Alive Infants Protection Act of 2002 is a federal statute sponsored by pro-life members of Congress. The Act specifies that any member of the human race who is born alive at any stage of development, is considered a human being and subject to equal protection under the law, even if born as a result of an induced abortion. The text of the Act is set out below.

1 U.S.C.A. § 8. Born alive infant

(a) In determining the meaning of any Act of Congress, or of any ruling, regulation, or interpretation of the various administrative bureaus and agencies of the United States, the words "person," "human being," "child," and "individual," shall include every infant member of the species homo sapiens who is born alive at any stage of development.

(b) As used in this section, the term "born alive," with respect to a member of the species homo sapiens, means the complete expulsion or extraction from his or her mother of that member, at any stage of development, who after such expulsion or extraction breathes or has a beating heart, pulsation of the umbilical cord, or definite movement of voluntary muscles, regardless of whether the umbilical cord has been cut, and regardless of whether the expulsion or extraction occurs as a result of natural or induced labor, cesarean section, or induced abortion.

(c) Nothing in this section shall be construed to affirm, deny, expand, or contract any legal status or legal right applicable to any member of the species homo sapiens at any point prior to being "born alive" as defined in this section.

The impetus for passage of the Act involved the abortion procedure known as partial-birth abortion, and the United States Supreme Court's decision in *Stenberg v. Carhart*, which struck down a Nebraska statute that banned partial-birth abortion. The United States House of Representatives' report that accompanied the Act stated its purpose as follows:

HOUSE REPORT NO. 107-186

It has long been an accepted legal principle that infants who are born alive, at any stage of development, are persons who are entitled to the protections of the law. But recent changes in the legal and cultural landscape have brought this well-settled principle into question.

In Stenberg v. Carhart, for example, the United States Supreme Court struck down a Nebraska law banning partial-birth abortion, a procedure in which an abortionist delivers an unborn child's body until only the head remains inside of the womb, punctures the back of the child's skull with scissors, and sucks the child's brains out before completing the delivery. What was described in Roe v. Wade as a right to abort "unborn children" has thus been extended by the Court to include the violent destruction of partially-born children just inches from complete birth.

The Carhart Court considered the location of an infant's body at the moment of death during a partial-birth abortion-delivered partly outside the body of the mother-to be of no legal significance in ruling on the constitutionality of the Nebraska law. Instead, implicit in the Carhart decision was the pernicious notion that a partially-born infant's entitlement to the protections of the law is dependent upon whether or not the partially-born child's mother wants him or her.

Following Stenberg v. Carhart, on July 26, 2000, the United States Court of Appeals for the Third Circuit made that point explicit in Planned Parenthood of Central New Jersey v. Farmer, in the course of striking down New Jersey's partial-birth abortion ban. According to the Third Circuit, under Roe and Carhart, it is "nonsensical" and "based on semantic machinations" and "irrational line-drawing" for a legislature to conclude that an infant's location in relation to his or her mother's body has any relevance in determining whether that infant may be killed. Instead, the Farmer Court repudiated New Jersey's classification of the prohibited procedure as being a "partial birth," and concluded that a child's status under the law, regardless of the child's location, is dependent upon whether the mother intends to abort the child or to give birth. Thus, the Farmer Court stated that, in contrast to an infant whose mother intends to give birth, an infant who is killed during a partial-birth abortion is not entitled to the protections of the law because "[a] woman seeking an abortion is plainly not seeking to give birth."

The logical implications of Carhart and Farmer are both obvious and disturbing. Under the logic of these decisions, once a child is marked for abortion, it is wholly irrelevant whether that child emerges from the womb as a live baby. That child may still be treated as though he or she did not exist, and would not have any rights under the law-no right to receive medical care, to be sustained in life, or to receive any care at all. And if a child who survives an abortion and is born alive would have no claim to the protections of the law, there would, then, be no basis upon which the government may prohibit an abortionist from completely delivering an infant before killing it or allowing it to die. The "right to abortion," under this logic, means nothing less than the right to a dead baby, no matter where the killing takes place.

Credible public testimony received by the Subcommittee on the Constitution of the Committee on the Judiciary indicates that this is, in fact, already occurring. According to eyewitness accounts, "induced-labor" or "live-birth" abortions are indeed being performed, resulting in live-born premature infants who are simply allowed to die, sometimes without the provision of even basic comfort care such as warmth and nutrition.

The purposes of H.R. 2175, the "Born-Alive Infants Protection Act of 2001" are:

(1) 'to repudiate the flawed notion that a child's entitlement to the protections of the law is dependent upon whether that child's mother or others want him or her;

(2) 'to repudiate the flawed notion that the right to an abortion means the right to a dead baby, regardless of where the killing takes place;

(3) 'to affirm that every child who is born alive-whether as a result of induced abortion, natural labor, or caesarean section-bears an intrinsic dignity as a human being which is not dependent upon the desires, interests, or convenience of any other person, and is entitled to receive the full protections of the law; and

(4) 'to establish firmly that, for purposes of Federal law, the term "person" includes an infant who is completely expelled or extracted from his or her mother and who is alive, regardless of whether or not the baby's development is believed to be, or is in fact, sufficient to permit long-term survival, and regardless of whether the baby survived an abortion.

Subsequent to the passage of the Act, the Supreme Court decided the case of *Gonzales v. Carhart*, which approved of a federal statute that banned partial-birth abortion. *See also* **Gonzales v. Carhart; Partial-Birth Abortion Ban Act; Stenberg v. Carhart**

Bowel Obstruction and Pregnancy

Bowel obstruction occurs when something blocks the passage of waste from the body. This condition is treatable and typically involves abdominal pain, nausea, vomiting, and fever. Bowel obstruction can be devastating during pregnancy if not treated timely. If gangrene arises from the condition it can be fatal to the fetus. *See also* **Miscarriage; Stillbirth**

Bradley Method *see* **Natural Childbirth Methods**

Bradycardia

Bradycardia refers to an abnormally low fetal heart rate. Abnormally low fetal heart rates can signal problems with the fetus that require the fetus' immediate delivery. *See also* **Fetal Distress; Fetal Monitoring**

Brandeis, Louis D.

Louis D. Brandeis (1856–1941) served as an associate justice on the United States Supreme Court from 1916 to 1939. While on the Supreme Court Brandeis was known as a progressive jurist who interpreted the Constitution in a manner that gave the greatest protection to individual freedoms from government encroachment.

Justice Brandeis was born in Louisville, Kentucky. Although he did not obtain an undergraduate college degree, Justice Brandeis was considered a brilliant student of life. He enrolled in Harvard Law School and received a law degree in 1877. After law school Justice Brandeis embarked on a legal career that, while making him wealthy, brought him immense respect as an intellectual vanguard within the nation's legal community. He wrote articles and books along the way and became affectionately known as the "People's Lawyer."

In 1916 President Woodrow Wilson withstood political controversy to nominate Justice Brandeis as the first Jewish American member of the Supreme Court. While on the Supreme Court Justice Brandeis took part in only one Supreme Court decision involving abortion related issues. Justice Brandeis voted with a unanimous opinion in *State of Missouri ex rel. Hurwitz v. North*, which held that the constitution was not violated when a physician was prevented from issuing subpoenas to have witnesses attend a hearing to revoke his medical license for performing an unlawful abortion, because the applicable rules required taking depositions of witnesses who would not voluntarily attend the hearing.

Bray, Michael

Michael Bray is a co-founder of the Bowie Crofton Pregnancy Center (1982) and Reformation Lutheran Church (1984) in Bowie, Maryland, and a militant opponent of abortion. The Rev. Bray was imprisoned from 1985 to1989 after being convicted in connection of a series of abortion clinic bombings. He authored a book, *A Time to Kill* (1993), which examines the classical doctrine of defensive action and considers its application in the anti-abortion cause. The Rev. Bray is considered a hero and national leader for anti-abortionists who will not join the ranks of mainstream anti-abortionists who condemn violence. He presided over the White Rose Banquet, sponsored annually by Reformation Lutheran Church from 1996 until 2000. The Banquet honored anti-abortion prisoners who had been jailed for violent acts against abortionists and their facilities. *See also* **Abortion Violence, Property Destruction and Demonstrations; Banquet of the White Rose; Bray v. Alexandria Women's Health Clinic**

Bray v. Alexandria Women's Health Clinic

Forum: United States Supreme Court.

Case Citation: Bray v. Alexandria Women's Health Clinic, 506 U.S. 263 (1993).

Date Argued: October 16, 1991; Reargued October 6, 1992.

Date of Decision: January 13, 1993.

Opinion of Court: Scalia, J., in which Rehnquist, C.J., and White, Kennedy, and Thomas, JJ., joined.

Concurring Opinion: Kennedy, J.

Concurring and Dissenting Opinion: Souter, J.

Dissenting Opinion: Stevens, J., in which Blackmun, J., joined.

Dissenting Opinion: O'Connor, J., in which Blackmun, J., joined.

Counsel for Appellants: Jay Alan Sekulow argued; on the brief were James M. Henderson, Sr., Douglas W. Davis, Thomas Patrick Monaghan, Walter M. Weber, and James E. Murphy.

Counsel for Appellees: John H. Schafer argued; on the brief were William H. Allen, Mr. Eisenstein, Alison Wetherfield, and Helen Neuborne. Deborah A. Ellis reargued; on the brief were Martha F. Davis, Sally F. Goldfarb, John H. Schafer, and Laurence J. Eisenstein.

Amicus Brief for United States in Support of Appellees: Deputy Solicitor General Roberts argued; on the brief were Solicitor General Starr, Assistant Attorney General Gerson, Paul J. Larkin, Jr., Barbara L. Herwig, and Lowell V. Sturgill, Jr.

Amicus Brief for Appellants: American Victims of Abortion by James Bopp, Jr., and Richard E. Coleson; for Concerned Women for America by Andrew J. Ekonomou and Mark N. Troobnick; for Feminists for Life of America et al. by Christine Smith Torre and Edward R. Grant; for the Free Congress Foundation by Eric A. Daly and Jordan P. Secola, and George J. Mercer; for the Southern Center for Law & Ethics by Albert L. Jordan; for Woman Exploited by Abortion et al. by Samuel Brown Casey, Victor L. Smith, and David L. Llewellyn; for Daniel Berrigan et al. by Wendall R. Bird and David J. Myers; and for James Joseph Lynch, Jr., pro se.

Amicus Brief for Appellees: Robert Abrams, Attorney General of New York, pro se, O. Peter Sherwood, Solicitor General, Sanford M. Cohen and Shelley B. Mayer, Assistant Attorneys General, and Mary Sue Terry, Attorney General of Virginia, pro se; for the American Civil Liberties Union et al. by Judith Levin, Steven R. Shapiro, John A. Powell, Burt Neuborne, and Elliot M. Mincberg; for Falls Church, Virginia, by David R. Lasso; for the NAACP Legal Defense and Educational Fund, Inc., by Julius L. Chambers, Charles Stephen Ralston, and Eric Schnapper; for the National Abortion Federation et al. by Elaine Metlin, Roger K. Evans, and Eve W. Paul; and for 20 Organizations Committed to Women's Health and Women's Equality by Dawn Johnsen, Lois Eisner Murphy, and Marcy J. Wilder.

Issue Presented: Whether the Civil Rights Act of 1871, 42 U.S.C. § 1985(3), provides a federal cause of action against persons obstructing access to abortion clinics?

Case Holding: Section 1985(3) does not provide a federal cause of action against persons obstructing access to abortion clinics.

Background facts of case: The appellees were clinics that perform abortions and organizations that support abortion. The appellants were Operation Rescue, an unincorporated association whose members oppose abortion, and six individuals. The appellees filed a federal lawsuit, alleging federal civil rights violations and state causes of action, against the appellants for conducting demonstrations at abortion clinics in the Washington, D.C. area. Following trial, the district court ruled that appellees had violated § 1985(3) by conspiring to deprive women seeking abortions of their right to interstate travel. The district court also ruled for appellants on their pendent state law claims of trespass and public nuisance. The trial court enjoined the appellees from trespassing on, or obstructing access to, abortion clinics in specified Virginia counties and cities in the Washington, D.C., metropolitan area. The Fourth Circuit court of appeals affirmed. The Supreme Court granted certiorari to consider whether § 1985(3) could be used in the context of abortion protests.

Majority opinion by Justice Scalia: Justice Scalia found that § 1985(3) was not intended to be used for a cause of action involving abortion protests. It was held that the statute was intended to remedy discrimination. Justice Scalia wrote as follows:

> To begin with, we reject the apparent conclusion of the District Court that opposition to abortion constitutes discrimination against the class of women seeking abortion. Whatever may be the precise meaning of a "class" ... the term unquestionably connotes something more than a group of individuals who share a desire to engage in conduct that the 1985(3) defendant disfavors. Otherwise, innumerable tort plaintiffs would be able to assert causes of action under 1985(3) by simply defining the aggrieved class as those seeking to engage in the activity the defendant has interfered with.
>
> [Appellees'] contention, however, is that the alleged class-based discrimination is directed not at women seeking abortion, but at women in general. We find it unnecessary to decide whether that is a qualifying class under 1985(3), since the claim that [appellants'] opposition to abortion reflects an animus against women in general must be rejected. We do not think that the animus requirement can be met only by maliciously motivated, as opposed to assertedly benign, discrimination against women.... The record in this case does not indicate that [appellants'] demonstrations are motivated by a purpose directed specifically at women as a class; to the contrary, the District Court found that [appellants] define their "rescues" not with reference to women, but as physical intervention between abortionists and the innocent victims, and that all [appellants] share a deep commitment to the goals of stopping the practice of abortion and reversing its legalization....
>
> [Appellees'] federal claim fails for a second, independent reason: A 1985(3) private conspiracy "for the purpose of depriving ... any person or class of persons of the equal protection of the laws, or of equal privileges and immunities under the laws," requires an intent to deprive persons of a right guaranteed against private impairment. No intent to deprive of such a right was established here.

Disposition of case: The judgment of the Fourth Circuit was reversed in part and vacated in part, and the case was remanded for further proceedings.

Concurring opinion by Justice Kennedy: Justice Kennedy concurred in the majority decision. He wrote a few passing comments aimed at ridiculing the dissenting opinions.

Concurring and Dissenting opinion by Justice Souter: Justice Souter concurred in the majority decision to remand that case for further consideration. He dissented, however, from the majority's decision to find that no cause of action existed under § 1985(3). He wrote as follows:

> Accordingly, I conclude that the prevention clause [of § 1985(3)] may be applied to a conspiracy intended to hobble or overwhelm the capacity of duly constituted state police authorities to secure equal protection of the laws, even when the conspirators' animus is not based on race or a like class characteristic, and even when the ultimate object of the conspiracy is to violate a constitutional guarantee that applies solely against state action.
>
> These facts would support a conclusion that [appellants'] conspiracy had a purpose of preventing or hindering the constituted authorities of Virginia from giving or securing to all persons within Virginia the equal protection of the laws, and it might be fair to read such a finding between the lines of the District Court's express conclusions. But the finding was not express, and the better course is to err on the side of seeking express clarification. Certainly that is true here, when other Members of the Court

think it appropriate to remand for further proceedings. I conclude therefore that the decision of the Court of Appeals should be vacated and the case be remanded for consideration of purpose, and for a final determination whether implementation of this conspiracy was actionable under the prevention clause of 42 U.S.C. 1985(3).

Dissenting opinion by Justice Stevens: Justice Stevens dissented from the majority decision. He believed that § 1985(3) could be used by the appellees. Justice Stevens wrote:

> It is unfortunate that the Court has analyzed this case as though it presented an abstract question of logical deduction, rather than a question concerning the exercise and allocation of power in our federal system of government. The Court ignores the obvious (and entirely constitutional) congressional intent behind 1985(3) to protect this Nation's citizens from what amounts to the theft of their constitutional rights by organized and violent mobs across the country....
>
> Pursuant to their overall conspiracy, [appellants] have repeatedly engaged in "rescue" operations that violate local law and harm innocent women. [Appellants] trespass on clinic property and physically block access to the clinic, preventing patients, as well as physicians and medical staff, from entering the clinic to render or receive medical or counseling services. Uncontradicted trial testimony demonstrates that [appellants'] conduct created a substantial risk that existing or prospective patients may suffer physical or mental harm. [Appellants] make no claim that their conduct is a legitimate form of protected expression....
>
> In sum, it is irrelevant whether the Court is correct in its assumption that opposition to abortion does not necessarily evidence an intent to disfavor women. Many opponents of abortion respect both the law and the rights of others to make their own decisions on this important matter. [Appellants], however, are not mere opponents of abortion; they are defiant lawbreakers who have engaged in massive concerted conduct that is designed to prevent all women from making up their own minds about not only the issue of abortion in general, but also whether they should (or will) exercise a right that all women — and only women — possess.
>
> Indeed, the error that infects the Court's entire opinion is the unstated and mistaken assumption that this is a case about opposition to abortion. It is not. It is a case about the exercise of federal power to control an interstate conspiracy to commit illegal acts. I have no doubt that most opponents of abortion, like most members of the citizenry at large, understand why the existence of federal jurisdiction is appropriate in a case of this kind.

Dissenting opinion by Justice O'Connor: Justice O'Connor disagreed with the majority decision. She believed that § 1985(3) was a vehicle to fight abortion protestors with Justice O'Connor wrote the following:

> [Appellants] act in organized groups to overwhelm local police forces and physically blockade the entrances to [appellees'] clinics with the purpose of preventing women from exercising their legal rights. Title 42 U.S.C. 1985(3) provides a federal remedy against private conspiracies aimed at depriving any person or class of persons of the equal protection of the laws, or of equal privileges and immunities under the laws. In my view, [appellees'] injuries and [appellants'] activities fall squarely within the ambit of this statute....
>
> If women are a protected class under 1985(3), and I think they are, then the statute must reach conspiracies whose motivation is directly related to characteristics unique to that class. The victims of [appellants'] tortious actions are linked by their ability to become pregnant and by their ability to terminate their pregnancies, characteristics unique to the class of women. [Appellants'] activities are directly related to those class characteristics, and therefore, I believe, are appropriately described as class based within the meaning of our holding in [other decisions].
>
> [Appellants] assert that, even if their activities are class based, they are not motivated by any discriminatory animus, but only by their profound opposition to the practice of abortion. I do not doubt the sincerity of that opposition. But in assessing the motivation behind [appellants'] actions, the sincerity of their opposition cannot surmount the manner in which they have chosen to express it. [Appellants] are free to express their views in a variety of ways, including lobbying, counseling, and disseminating information. Instead, they have chosen to target women seeking abortions, and to prevent them from exercising their equal rights under law. Even without relying on the federally protected right to abortion, [appellants'] activities infringe on a number of state-protected interests, including the state laws that make abortion legal, and the state laws that protect against force, intimidation, and violence. It is undeniably [appellants'] purpose to target a protected class, on account of their class characteristics, and to prevent them from the equal enjoyment of these personal and property rights under law....
>
> The statute was intended to provide a federal means of redress to the targets of private conspiracies seeking to accomplish their political and social goals through unlawful means. Today the Court takes yet another step in restricting the scope of the statute, to the point where it now cannot be applied to a modern-day paradigm of the situation the statute was meant to address. I respectfully dissent.

Breast Cancer

Breast cancer is a malignant growth that starts in the tissues of the breast. Many factors have been associated with the onset of breast cancer, including the following: age (more than 80 percent of breast cancer cases occur in women over 50); genetic factors and family history of breast cancer; early menstruation and late menopause; birth control pills; excessive alcohol use; and radiation. Symptoms of breast cancer include breast lump, change in the size or shape of the breast, abnormal nipple discharge, and breast pain.

Breast cancer is by far the most common cancer in women who are pregnant, or women who have recently given birth. The disease occurs in about 1 out of every 3,000 pregnancies. Breast cancer has a high incident rate in women between the ages 32 and 38. Research suggests survival of pregnant women with breast cancer may be worse than in nonpregnant women at all stages. However, this finding may be due to delayed diagnosis in pregnant women.

Terminating a pregnancy does not appear to effect the outcome of breast cancer, and is therefore not usually considered as a treatment option. It some instances, depending on the gestational age of the fetus, termination of the fetus may be an option if the cancer treatment

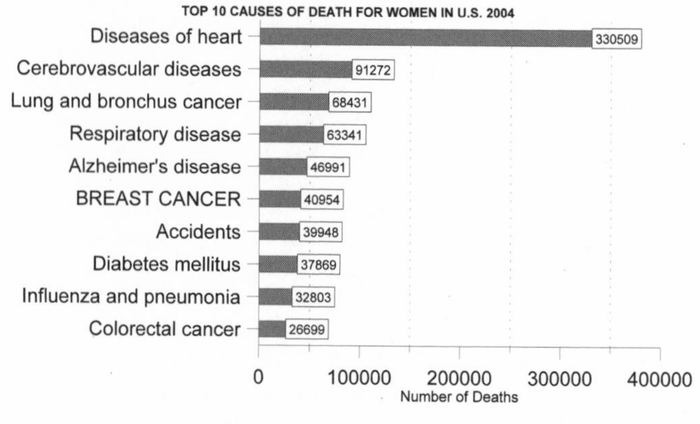

Source: **Centers for Disease Control and Prevention.**

options for the mother are severely limited by continuing the pregnancy. Breast cancer is not known to damage the fetus, since breast cancer cells apparently do not transfer to the fetus from the mother.

Surgery is usually recommended as the first method of treatment for breast cancer in pregnant women. Should chemotherapy be necessary after surgery, it will probably not be given during the first 3 months of the pregnancy. Although chemotherapy given after this time usually will not cause birth defects, it may cause early labor and low birthweight. Radiation therapy is usually not an option during pregnancy, due to the risk posed to the fetus.

The stage of breast cancer generally is the best indicator of the probable outcome. The five-year survival rate for women who receive appropriate treatment ranges from 95 percent to 7 percent. Even with appropriate treatments, breast cancer may spread to other parts of the body such as the lungs, liver, and bones. *See also* **Breast Cancer and Abortion; Cancer and Pregnancy; Therapeutic Abortion**

Breast Cancer and Abortion

Numerous national and international studies have been done which link abortion to breast cancer. These studies have associated abortion with breast cancer based upon a theory involving a pregnant woman's biological preparation for the production of milk. This theory holds that a pregnant woman's breasts start a natural process of developing a hormone that causes cells to multiply dramatically. If the pregnancy is not aborted, the cells are shaped into milk ducts and the body automatically stops the cell multiplication. However, if the fetus is aborted, the cells are not transformed into milk ducts; they remain as undifferentiated cells and carry the potential for becoming cancer cells.

As additional evidence of the link between breast cancer and abortion, researchers have drawn upon raw numbers. For example, in 1972 (the year before abortion was legalized in the nation) about 90,000 women developed breast cancer. In 1982 roughly 120,000 women developed breast cancer; and in 1992 about 180,000 women developed breast cancer. It has been argued that the dramatic increase in breast cancer is correlated with the legalization and use of abortion.

Other studies have refuted a link between breast cancer and abortion. These studies suggest that the increased incidents of breast cancer are due to better medical technology in diagnosing the disease, and greater participation by women in seeking out that technology. *See also* **Breast Cancer; Cancer and Pregnancy**

Breech Delivery *see* **Presentation and Position of the Fetus**

Brennan, William J., Jr.

William J. Brennan, Jr. (1906–1997) served as an associate justice on the United States Supreme Court from 1956 to 1990. While on the Supreme Court Justice Brennan was known as an expansive interpreter of the Constitution, with respect to individual liberties and rights.

Justice Brennan was born in Newark, New Jersey. He received a bachelor of science degree from the Wharton School of Finance and Commerce, at the University of Pennsylvania. After he receiving a scholarship to attend Harvard University Law School, Justice Brennan studied law under Felix Frankurter. Both the student of law and professor of law would eventually serve on the Supreme Court together.

After graduating near the top of his law school class in 1931, Justice Brennan spent a few years in private practice before World War II broke out. While in the Army he rose to the rank of colonel. Justice Brennan returned home after the war and picked up his legal practice. By 1949 he found himself appointed as a New Jersey trial court judge. His outstanding service as a trial judge earned Justice Brennan an appointment to the New Jersey Supreme Court in 1952.

Distribution of the Abortion Voting Pattern of Justice Brennan Based Upon Opinions Filed by the Supreme Court

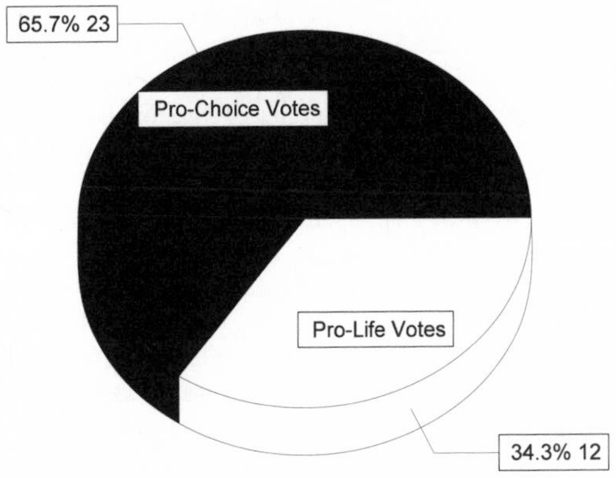

After four years of service on New Jersey's highest court, Justice Brennan was tapped by President Dwight D. Eisenhower in 1956 to serve on the United States Supreme Court. During Justice Brennan's tenure on the Supreme Court he issued a significant number of abortion related opinions. The written opinions and opinions simply voted on by Justice Brennan, indicate that he was in favor of using the constitution to expand abortion rights for women.

(1) Unanimous opinions voted with only. In *Bellotti v. Baird I* Justice Brennan voted with a unanimous opinion, which held that the federal district court had to certify appropriate questions to the supreme judicial court of Massachusetts, concerning the interpretation of that state's parental consent abortion statute for minors, before ruling on its constitutionality. In *Withrow v. Larkin* Justice Brennan joined a unanimous opinion, which held that constitutional due process was not violated by the mere fact that a Wisconsin medical examining board had the authority to both, investigate and adjudicate, allegations against a physician that included, among other things, permitting a nonphysician to perform an abortion.

(2) Majority opinions written. In *Federal Election Commission v. Massachusetts Citizens for Life, Inc.* Justice Brennan wrote the majority opinion, which held that federal law that prohibited the appellee from using its treasury funds to promote pro-life political candidates violated the Free Speech Clause of the First Amendment. In *Carey v. Population Services International* Justice Brennan wrote the majority opinion, which held that the constitution prohibited enforcement of a New York statute that made it a crime (1) for any person to sell or distribute any contraceptive of any kind to a minor under the age of 16 years; (2) for anyone other than a licensed pharmacist to distribute contraceptives to persons 16 or over; and (3) for anyone, including licensed pharmacists, to advertise or display contraceptives.

Justice Brennan wrote the majority opinion in *Eisenstadt v. Baird*, which held that the Equal Protection Clause of the Fourteenth Amendment was violated by a Massachusetts statute that made it a crime to give away a drug, medicine, instrument, or article for the prevention of conception except in the case of (1) a physician prescribing it for a married person, or (2) a pharmacist furnishing it to a married person presenting a physician's prescription.

(3) Majority opinions voted with only. Justice Brennan voted with the majority opinion in *United States Catholic Conference v. Abortion Rights Mobilization*, which allowed the appellants to challenge having to turn over documents in a lawsuit seeking to strip them of their tax exempt status because of their active political abortion work. Justice Brennan joined the majority decision in *Thornburgh v. American College of Obstetricians and Gynecologists*, which invalidated provisions in

Pennsylvania's abortion statute that provided for maternal informed consent, abortion alternative printed information, abortion reporting requirements, determination of fetal viability, degree of care required in post-viability abortions, and a second-physician requirement. In *Diamond v. Charles*, Justice Brennan joined the majority opinion, which held that a citizen did not have standing to appeal a decision invalidating parts of Illinois' abortion statute that (1) imposed criminal penalties for violating a prescribed standard of care that had to be exercised by a physician in performing an abortion of a viable fetus, and of a possibly viable fetus; and (2) imposed criminal penalties for physicians who failed to provide patients with information about the type of abortifacient used.

Justice Brennan voted with the majority opinion in *City of Akron v. Akron Center for Reproductive Health, Inc.*, which invalidated an abortion ordinance that provided requirements for parental consent, informed consent, waiting period, hospitalization and disposal of fetal remains. Justice Brennan joined the majority opinion in *Simopoulos v. Virginia*, which upheld a Virginia statute requiring second trimester abortions be performed at hospitals, because under the statute an adequately equipped clinic could, upon proper application, obtain an outpatient hospital license that permitted the performance of second-trimester abortions. In *Colautti v. Franklin* Justice Brennan joined the majority opinion, which held that the constitution was violated by a vague and ambiguous provision in Pennsylvania's abortion statute that subjected a physician who performed an abortion to potential criminal liability, if he/she failed to utilize a statutorily prescribed technique when the fetus was viable or when there was sufficient reason to believe that the fetus may be viable.

Justice Brennan voted the majority opinion in *Planned Parenthood of Missouri v. Danforth*, which held that the constitution was not violated by provisions in Missouri's abortion statute involving the definition of fetal viability, woman's written consent, and record keeping and reporting requirements; but that the constitution prohibited the requirements concerning spousal consent, parental consent for minor, banning saline amniocentesis abortions, and physician's standard of care. In *Connecticut v. Menillo* Justice Brennan joined the majority per curiam opinion, which held that the constitution was not violated by criminal abortion statutes that prohibit nonphysicians from attempting or performing abortions at any stage of a pregnancy. Justice Brennan joined the majority opinion in *Bigelow v. Virginia*, which held that the Free Speech and Free Press Clauses of the First Amendment were violated by a Virginia penal statute that prohibited selling or circulating any publication that encouraged or promoted abortions. Justice Brennan voted with the majority opinion in *Burns v. Alcala*, which held that states receiving federal financial aid under the program of Aid to Families with Dependent Children, were not required to offer welfare benefits to pregnant women for their unborn children.

In *Roe v. Wade* Justice Brennan joined the majority opinion, which held that the liberty component of the Due Process Clause of the Fourteenth Amendment prohibited states from criminalizing or preventing elective first trimester abortions. Justice Brennan voted with the majority opinion in *Doe v. Bolton*, which held that the Due Process Clause of the Fourteenth Amendment was violated by provisions in Georgia's abortion statutes that required (1) abortions take place in accredited hospitals, (2) that an abortion be approved by a hospital abortion committee, (3) that the need for an abortion be confirmed by two independent physicians, and (4) that a woman seeking an abortion be a resident of Georgia. Justice Brennan joined the majority opinion in *Anders v. Floyd*, which held that a federal district court erred in enjoining enforcement of a South Carolina statute that imposed criminal punishment for performing an abortion on a viable fetus.

(4) Plurality opinions voted with only. Justice Brennan joined the plurality opinion that announced the judgment of the Supreme Court in *Singleton v. Wulff*, which held that the Eighth Circuit court of appeals had jurisdiction to determine whether abortion providers had standing to challenge a provision in Missouri's abortion statute that limited medicaid payment for abortions, but it did not have jurisdiction to rule that the provision violated the constitution because the district court did not address the issue.

(5) Concurring opinions written. Justice Brennan wrote an opinion concurring in the majority decision in *Poe v. Ullman*, which held that the appellants did not have standing to challenge the constitutionality of a Connecticut statute, that made it a crime to give married persons contraceptive information and devices.

(6) Concurring opinions voted with only. Justice Brennan concurred in the majority judgment in *Bellotti v. Baird II*, which held that Massachusetts' abortion statute for minors violated the constitution in light of an interpretation given by the state's highest court, that required parental notice of a judicial bypass proceeding invoked by a minor, and permitted a judge to deny an abortion even though the minor proved she had enough maturity to make an independent decision. In *Griswold v. Connecticut* Justice Brennan concurred with the majority opinion, which held that the right of privacy found in the constitution prohibited enforcement of a Connecticut statute that made it a crime to give married persons contraceptive information and devices.

(7) Dissenting opinions written. In *Frisby v. Schultz* Justice Brennan wrote an opinion dissenting from the majority decision, which upheld the constitutional validity of a town ordinance that was created to prevent pro-life picketing at the residence of an abortion doctor. He believed the ordinance was too broad in scope. Justice Brennan wrote an opinion dissenting from the majority decision in *Harris v. McRae*, which held that medicaid funding restrictions for abortion by the Hyde Amendment, did not violate the Due Process Clause nor the equal protection component of the Fifth Amendment. He believed the Hyde Amendment violated the constitution.

Justice Brennan wrote an opinion dissenting from the majority opinion in *Beal v. Doe*, which held that Pennsylvania's refusal to extend medicaid coverage to nontherapeutic abortions was not invalid nor inconsistent with Title XIX of the Social Security Act. He believed Title XIX required funding for all abortions. In *Maher v. Roe* Justice Brennan wrote an opinion dissenting from the majority decision, which held that the Equal Protection Clause of the Fourteenth Amendment did not prohibit Connecticut from excluding nontherapeutic abortions from its medicaid program. He believed the Equal Protection Clause required funding all abortions. Justice Brennan wrote an opinion dissenting from the per curiam decision in *Poelker v. Doe*, which held that the Equal Protection Clause of the Fourteenth Amendment was not violated by a policy of the city of St. Louis, Missouri that denied publicly funded abortions to indigent women at city hospitals, except when a woman's health or life was in danger. He believed the city's policy violated the constitution.

Justice Brennan wrote an opinion dissenting from the majority decision in *Geduldig v. Aiello*, which held that the Equal Protection Clause of the Fourteenth Amendment did not require a private sector employee disability insurance program, operated by the state of California, provide coverage for employee disabilities associated with normal pregnancies. He believed the Equal Protection Clause was violated.

(8) Dissenting opinions voted with only. In *Ohio v. Akron Center for Reproductive Health* Justice Brennan voted to dissent from the majority decision, which upheld the constitutionality of Ohio's abortion statute notice and judicial bypass requirements for pregnant female minors. In *H. L. v. Matheson* Justice Brennan dissented from the majority opinion, which held that the constitution was not violated by Utah's requirement that the parents of a minor be notified, if possible, prior

to performing an abortion. He believed the parental notification requirement violated the constitution. In *Williams v. Zbaraz* Justice Brennan dissented from the majority opinion, which held that in light of the requirements of the Hyde Amendment, the Equal Protection Clause of the Fourteenth Amendment was not violated by an Illinois statute that prohibited state medicaid payment for abortions, except when necessary to save the life of the pregnant woman. He believed the statute violated the constitution.

(9) Concurring and dissenting opinions voted with only. Justice Brennan voted to concur and dissent in *Hodgson v. Minnesota*, which upheld the constitutionality of Minnesota's requirement that a pregnant female minor could not obtain an abortion until at least 48 hours after both of her parents had been notified, except when (1) the attending physician certified that an immediate abortion was necessary to prevent the minor's death; (2) the minor declared that she was a victim of parental abuse or neglect; or (3) a court of competent jurisdiction ordered the abortion to proceed without notice upon proof that the minor was mature and capable of giving informed consent or that an abortion without notice to both parents would be in the minor's best interest. Justice Brennan dissented from the Court's determination that, although the two-parent notification requirement was invalid, the judicial bypass option cured the defect.

Justice Brennan voted to concur and dissent in *Webster v. Reproductive Health Services*, which upheld Missouri's prohibition on the use of public facilities or employees to perform abortions and a requirement that physicians conduct viability tests prior to performing abortions. He concurred only in the majority's decision that a prohibition on public funding of abortion counseling was rendered moot and would not be analyzed. In *Planned Parenthood Assn. v. Ashcroft* Justice Brennan concurred and dissented from the majority/plurality opinion, which held that the constitution was violated by Missouri's requirement that second trimester abortions take place in a hospital; but that the constitution was not violated by the state's requirement that a pathology report for each abortion be performed, that a second physician be present during abortions performed after viability, and parental or judicial consent for abortion by minors. Justice Brennan believed that all of the provisions of the statute violated the constitution. Justice Brennan voted to concur and dissent from the majority decision in *United States v. Vuitch*, which held that the criminal abortion statute of the District of Columbia, which only permitted therapeutic abortions, was not constitutionally vague insofar as there was no ambiguity in its use of the word health and it did not shift to the defendant the burden of proving innocence. He believed the statute was constitutionally valid, but that the Court did not have jurisdiction to hear the case.

Breyer, Stephen G.

Stephen G. Breyer was appointed to the United States Supreme Court in 1994. The early opinions by Justice Breyer have shown a pragmatic and moderate judicial philosophy.

Justice Breyer was born in San Francisco on August 15, 1938. Prior to attending Harvard Law School, he obtained an A.B. degree from Stanford University and a B.A. degree from Oxford University. Justice Breyer received his law degree from Harvard in 1964.

Prior to his elevation to the Supreme Court, Justice Breyer engaged in a variety of legal work. He clerked for Supreme Court Justice Arthur J. Goldberg after leaving law school. Justice Breyer left his clerkship position after two years and became an assistant U.S. Attorney General. During his employment with the Attorney General's office, Justice Breyer managed to teach courses at Harvard Law School. He was also an aide to Senator Edward M. Kennedy during the 1970s, as well as chief counsel for the Senate Judiciary Committee. President Jimmy Carter nominated Justice Breyer to the U.S. Court of Appeals for the

Distribution of the Abortion Voting Pattern of Justice Breyer Based Upon Opinions Filed by the Supreme Court

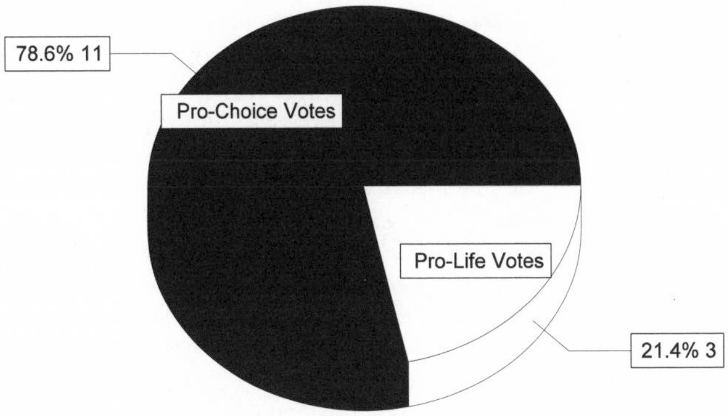

First Circuit, but he was confirmed by the Senate under the administration of President Ronald Reagan.

In 1994 President Clinton selected Justice Breyer to fill a vacancy on the Supreme Court. The Senate confirmed the nomination on July 29, 1994. Justice Breyer has issued several abortion opinions since coming to the Supreme Court. The written opinions and opinions simply voted on by Justice Breyer, indicate that he is in favor of using the constitution to expand abortion rights for women.

(1) Unanimous opinions written. Justice Breyer wrote a unanimous opinion in *Scheidler v. National Organization for Women, Inc. (II)*, which held that pro-choice advocates could not sue pro-life advocates under the Hobbs Act for allegations of physical violence that did not involve extortion.

(2) Unanimous opinions voted with only. In *Dalton v. Little Rock Family Planning Services*, Justice Breyer voted with a unanimous Court

Justice Breyer's voting pattern favors the views of pro-choice advocates (collection, Supreme Court Historical Society, photograph by Steve Petteway, Supreme Court).

in holding that an amendment to Arkansas' constitution which limited medicaid payment only to therapeutic abortions, was invalid to the extent that medicaid funds had to be made available for incest or rape pregnancies, but was valid for any purely state funded program. Justice Breyer joined the unanimous opinion in *Ayotte v. Planned Parenthood of Northern New England*, which held that the absence of a health exception in New Hampshire's parental notification abortion statute did not require the entire statute be invalidated.

(3) Majority opinions written. In *Stenberg v. Carhart*, Justice Breyer wrote the majority opinion which found Nebraska's statute banning partial-birth abortion unconstitutional.

(4) Majority opinions voted with only. Justice Breyer voted with the majority in *Ferguson v. City of Charleston*, in holding that patient consent or a search warrant was needed in order for a government hospital to turn over to the police drug test results that showed a woman used illegal drugs during her pregnancy. In *Hill v. Colorado* Justice Breyer voted with the majority in upholding a Colorado statute that made it unlawful for any person within 100 feet of an abortion facility's entrance, to knowingly approach within 8 feet of another person, without that person's consent, in order to pass a leaflet, handbill, display a sign, engage in oral protest, education, or counseling with that person. Justice Breyer voted with the majority opinion in *Federal Election Commission v. Beaumont*, which held that the Federal Election Campaign Act's prohibition on corporate expenditures and contributions directly to candidates in federal elections, applies to a nonprofit pro-life organization.

(5) Concurring opinions voted with only. In *Lambert v. Wicklund* Justice Breyer concurred with the majority in holding that the constitution was not violated by a provision in Montana's abortion statute that allowed a court to waive the parental notice requirement for minors, if notification was not in minor's best interest. Justice Breyer voted to concur in *Scheidler v. National Organization for Women, Inc. (I)*, which held that evidence did not support finding that pro-life advocates violated the Hobbs Act, Travel Act and state law extortion crimes, for the purpose of awarding damages and granting an injunction against them under RICO.

(6) Dissenting opinions voted with only. Justice Breyer joined the dissenting opinion in *Leavitt v. Jane L.*, which held that the invalidity of Utah's statute regulating pregnancies 20 weeks old or less, may be severed so as to preserve that portion of the abortion statute that regulated pregnancies of more than 20 weeks. Justice Breyer joined the dissent in *Federal Election Commission v. Wisconsin Right to Life, Inc.*, which held that the electioneering communications provisions of a federal statute violated a pro-life organization's First Amendment right to broadcast political issue oriented advertisements shortly before primary and general elections. Justice Breyer joined the dissenting opinion in *Gonzales v. Carhart*, which held that the Partial-Birth Abortion Ban Act of 2003 was not facially unconstitutional, because it outlined the abortion procedure that was banned, and the Act did not have to provide an exception for the health of a woman. Justice Breyer joined the dissenting opinion in *Mazurek v. Armstrong*, which held that Montana's requirement that abortions be performed only by physicians was constitutionally valid.

(7) Concurring and dissenting opinions written. Justice Breyer wrote a concurring and dissenting opinion in *Schenck v. Pro Choice Network of Western New York*, which held that a federal trial court's injunction provisions imposing fixed buffer zone limitations on abortion protesters were constitutional, but the provisions imposing floating buffer zone limitations violated the First Amendment. Justice Breyer believed that the floating buffer zone limitations were valid also.

Brooklyn Pro-Choice Network

Brooklyn Pro-Choice Network (BPCN) is a pro-choice organization headquartered in Brooklyn, New York. The organization supports the right of all women to protect and determine their mental and physical health, regardless of economic status. The mission of BPCN is to (1) advocate for the right of women to choose when and if to bear children; (2) maintain access to safe and legal abortion; (3) insure decent and affordable prenatal and child care; (4) promote sex education and family planning curricula in the schools, beginning in the early grades; and (5) distribute information on women's health issues. *See also* **Pro-Choice Organizations**

Brown, Sarah

Sarah Brown was born on July 15, 1993. She was a survivor of an attempted abortion by her mother. Sarah's mother was 15 years old and in late-term pregnancy when she visited a clinic in Wichita, Kansas to have the abortion. During the procedure the abortionist injected potassium chloride in two places in Sarah's fetal head. The mother was then told to leave and return the next day to have the fetus expelled. However, when the mother left she became ill and was taken to a hospital. While at the hospital the mother gave birth to Sarah. The potassium chloride did not kill her. It did, however, severely damage her brain and left her blind and unable to walk. Sarah was adopted as an infant by Bill and Mary Brown. The Browns cared for Sarah until she died of kidney failure, at age five, on September 28, 1998. *See also* **Survivors of Abortion**

Buffer Zones at Abortion Facilities

In response to abortion facility violence and intimidation by pro-life advocates, a number of states enacted buffer zone legislation to prevent pro-life advocates from getting too close to abortion facili-

States with Statutes That Allow Civil Lawsuits Against Those Who Impede Access to and from Abortion Facilities

**District of Columbia does not have statute.*

ties. In *Hill v. Colorado* the United States Supreme Court upheld a Colorado statute that made it unlawful for any person within 100 feet of an abortion facility's entrance, to knowingly approach within 8 feet of another person, without that person's consent, in order to pass a leaflet, handbill, display a sign, engage in oral protest, education, or counseling with that person. In *Schenck v. Pro Choice Network of Western New York* the Supreme Court upheld certain federal trial court injunction provisions that imposed fixed buffer zone limitations at abortion clinics, while finding unconstitutional certain provisions that imposed floating buffer zone limitations.

In *Madsen v. Women's Health Clinic, Inc.* the Supreme Court upheld parts of an injunction that imposed a 36 foot buffer zone around the clinic entrances and driveway. However, *Madsen* ruled that the Free Speech Clause of the federal constitution was violated by a 36 foot buffer zone as applied to the private property to the north and west of the clinic, a 300 foot no approach zone around the clinic, and a 300 foot buffer zone around the residences, because these restrictions swept more broadly than necessary to accomplish the permissible goals of the injunction. *See also* **Abortion Violence, Property Destruction and Demonstrations; Freedom of Access to Clinic Entrances Act; Madsen v. Women's Health Clinic, Inc.; Hill v. Colorado; Schenck v. Pro Choice Network of Western New York**

Burger, Warren Earl

Warren Earl Burger (1907–1995) served as Chief Justice of the United States Supreme Court from 1969 to 1986. While on the Supreme Court Chief Justice Burger was known as a centrist who never strayed to the left or right in his interpretation of the Constitution.

Chief Justice Burger was born in St. Paul, Minnesota. The humble background of his family caused him to resort to nontraditional means for obtaining an education. He worked as an insurance agent while taking undergraduate extension courses at the University of Minnesota. He eventually received a law degree from St. Paul College of Law in 1931, while taking night law school classes.

Chief Justice Burger's career as a private attorney was modest and uneventful. His path to the Supreme Court did not begin in earnest until his appointment in 1952 as an assistant United States Attorney General. That position landed him an appointment in 1956 as an appellate judge on the Court of Appeals for the District of Columbia. In 1969 President Richard M. Nixon appointed him as Chief Justice of the Supreme Court.

During Chief Justice Burger's tenure on the Supreme Court he issued several abortion related opinions. The written opinions and opinions simply voted on by Chief Justice Burger, indicate that he

Distribution of the Abortion Voting Pattern of Chief Justice Burger Based Upon Opinions Filed by the Supreme Court

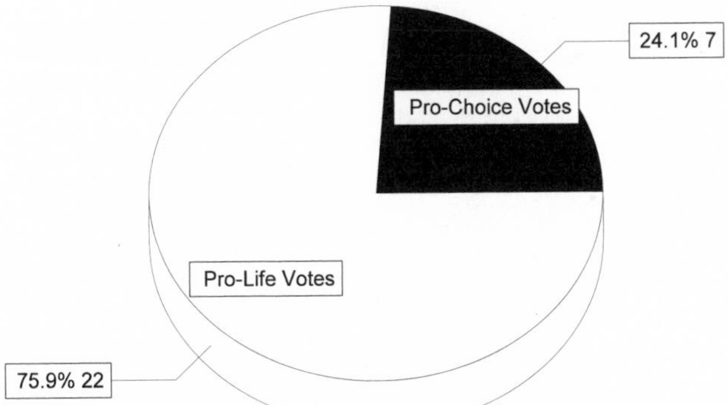

was not in favor of using the constitution to expand abortion rights for women.

(1) Unanimous opinions voted with only. In *Bellotti v. Baird I* Chief Justice Burger voted with a unanimous opinion, which held that the federal district court had to certify appropriate questions to the supreme judicial court of Massachusetts, concerning the interpretation of that state's parental consent abortion statute for minors, before ruling on its constitutionality. In *Withrow v. Larkin* Chief Justice Burger joined a unanimous opinion, which held that constitutional due process was not violated by the mere fact that a Wisconsin medical examining board had the authority to both, investigate and adjudicate, allegations against a physician that included, among other things, permitting a nonphysician to perform an abortion.

(2) Majority opinions written. In *H. L. v. Matheson* Chief Justice Burger wrote the majority opinion, which held that the constitution was not violated by Utah's requirement that the parents of a minor be notified, if possible, prior to performing an abortion.

(3) Majority opinions voted with only. Chief Justice Burger voted with the majority opinion in *Bolger v. Youngs Drug Products Corp.*, which held that a provision of the Comstock Act, 39 U.S.C. § 3001(e)(2), that prohibited mailing unsolicited advertisements for contraceptives violated the Free Speech Clause of the First Amendment. Chief Justice Burger voted with the majority opinion in *City of Akron v. Akron Center for Reproductive Health, Inc.*, which invalidated an abortion ordinance that provided requirements for parental consent, informed consent, waiting period, hospitalization and disposal of fetal remains. In *Planned Parenthood Assn. v. Ashcroft* Chief Justice Burger voted with the majority/plurality opinion, which held that the constitution was violated by Missouri's requirement that second trimester abortions take place in a hospital; but that the constitution was not violated by the state's requirement that a pathology report for each abortion be performed, that a second physician be present during abortions performed after viability, and parental or judicial consent for abortion by minors.

Chief Justice Burger joined the majority opinion in *Simopoulos v. Virginia*, which upheld a Virginia statute requiring second trimester abortions be performed at hospitals, because under the statute an adequately equipped clinic could, upon proper application, obtain an outpatient hospital license that permitted the performance of second-trimester abortions. Chief Justice Burger joined the majority opinion in *Harris v. McRae*, which held that medicaid funding restrictions for abortion by the Hyde Amendment, did not violate the Due Process Clause nor the equal protection component of the Fifth Amendment. In *Williams v. Zbaraz* Chief Justice Burger voted with the majority opinion, which held that in light of the requirements of the Hyde Amendment, the Equal Protection Clause of the Fourteenth Amendment was not violated by an Illinois statute that prohibited state medicaid payment for abortions, except when necessary to save the life of the pregnant woman. Chief Justice Burger joined the majority judgment in *Bellotti v. Baird II*, which held that Massachusetts' abortion statute for minors violated the constitution in light of an interpretation given by the state's highest court, that required parental notice of a judicial bypass proceeding invoked by a minor, and permitted a judge to deny an abortion even though the minor proved she had enough maturity to make an independent decision.

Chief Justice Burger joined the majority opinion in *Beal v. Doe*, which held that Pennsylvania's refusal to extend medicaid coverage to nontherapeutic abortions was not invalid nor inconsistent with Title XIX of the Social Security Act. Chief Justice Burger joined the majority per curiam opinion in *Poelker v. Doe*, which held that the Equal Protection Clause of the Fourteenth Amendment was not violated by a policy of the city of St. Louis, Missouri that denied publicly funded abortions to indigent women at city hospitals, except when a woman's health or life was in danger. In *Connecticut v. Menillo* Chief Justice Burger joined the majority per curiam opinion, which held that the constitution was not violated by criminal abortion statutes that prohibit nonphysicians from attempting or performing abortions at any stage of a pregnancy. Chief Justice Burger joined the majority opinion in *Bigelow v. Virginia*, which held that the Free Speech and Free Press Clauses of the First Amendment were violated by a Virginia penal statute that prohibited selling or circulating any publication that encouraged or promoted abortions.

Chief Justice Burger voted with the majority opinion in *Burns v. Alcala*, which held that states receiving federal financial aid under the program of Aid to Families with Dependent Children, were not required to offer welfare benefits to pregnant women for their unborn children. Chief Justice Burger voted with the majority opinion in *Geduldig v. Aiello*, which held that the Equal Protection Clause of the Fourteenth Amendment did not require a private sector employee disability insurance program, operated by the state of California, provide coverage for employee disabilities associated with normal pregnancies. In *Weinberger v. Hynson, Westcott & Dunning* Chief Justice Burger joined the majority opinion, which held that the Food and Drug Administration could not deny a drug manufacturer a hearing to obtain marketing approval for a drug called Lutrexin, which provided treatment for premature labor and threatened and habitual abortion. Chief Justice Burger voted with the majority opinion in *United States v. Vuitch*, which held that the criminal abortion statute of the District of Columbia, which only permitted therapeutic abortions, was not constitutionally vague insofar as there was no ambiguity in its use of the word health and it did not shift to the defendant the burden of proving innocence. Chief Justice Burger joined the majority opinion in *Anders v. Floyd*, which held that a federal district court erred in enjoining enforcement of a South Carolina statute that imposed criminal punishment for performing an abortion on a viable fetus.

(4) *Concurring opinions written.* In *Maher v. Roe* Chief Justice Burger wrote an opinion concurring in the majority decision, which held that the Equal Protection Clause of the Fourteenth Amendment did not prohibit Connecticut from excluding nontherapeutic abortions from its medicaid program. Chief Justice Burger wrote an opinion concurring with the majority decision in *Doe v. Bolton*, which held that the Due Process Clause of the Fourteenth Amendment was violated by provisions in Georgia's abortion statutes that required (1) abortions take place in accredited hospitals, (2) that an abortion be approved by a hospital abortion committee, (3) that the need for an abortion be confirmed by two independent physicians, and (4) that a woman seeking an abortion be a resident of Georgia.

(5) *Concurring opinions voted with only.* In *Diamond v. Charles*, Chief Justice Burger concurred in the majority opinion, which held that a citizen did not have standing to appeal a decision invalidating parts of Illinois' abortion statute that (1) imposed criminal penalties for violating a prescribed standard of care that had to be exercised by a physician in performing an abortion of a viable fetus, and of a possibly viable fetus; and (2) imposed criminal penalties for physicians who failed to provide patients with information about the type of abortifacient used. In *Roe v. Wade* Chief Justice Burger concurred in the majority opinion, which held that the liberty component of the Due Process Clause of the Fourteenth Amendment prohibited states from criminalizing or preventing elective first trimester abortions.

(6) *Dissenting opinions written.* Chief Justice Burger wrote a dissenting opinion in *Thornburgh v. American College of Obstetricians and Gynecologists*, which invalidated provisions in Pennsylvania's abortion statute that provided for maternal informed consent, abortion alternative printed information, abortion reporting requirements, determination of fetal viability, degree of care required in post-viability abortions, and a second-physician requirement. Chief Justice Burger wrote an opinion dissenting from the majority decision in *Eisenstadt v. Baird*, which held that the Equal Protection Clause of the Fourteenth Amendment was violated by a Massachusetts statute that made it a crime to give away a drug, medicine, instrument, or article for the prevention of conception except in the case of (1) a physician prescribing it for a married person, or (2) a pharmacist furnishing it to a married person presenting a physician's prescription. He believed the statute was constitutionally valid.

(7) *Dissenting opinions voted with only.* In *Colautti v. Franklin* Chief Justice Burger dissented from the majority decision, which held that the constitution was violated by a vague and ambiguous provision in Pennsylvania's abortion statute that subjected a physician who performed an abortion to potential criminal liability, if he/she failed to utilize a statutorily prescribed technique when the fetus was viable or when there was sufficient reason to believe that the fetus may be viable. He believed the provision was constitutionally valid. In *Carey v. Population Services International* Chief Justice Burger dissented from the majority decision, which held that the constitution prohibited enforcement of a New York statute that made it a crime (1) for any person to sell or distribute any contraceptive of any kind to a minor under the age of 16 years; (2) for anyone other than a licensed pharmacist to distribute contraceptives to persons 16 or over; and (3) for anyone, including licensed pharmacists, to advertise or display contraceptives. He believed the statute passed constitutional muster.

(8) *Concurring and dissenting opinions voted with only.* Chief Justice Burger voted to concur and dissent from the majority decision in *Planned Parenthood of Missouri v. Danforth*, which held that the constitution was not violated by provisions in Missouri's abortion statute involving the definition of fetal viability, woman's written consent, and record keeping and reporting requirements; but that the constitution prohibited the requirements concerning spousal consent, parental consent for minor, banning saline amniocentesis abortions, and physician's standard of care. Chief Justice Burger believed that all of the provisions of the statute were constitutionally valid.

Chief Justice Burger voted to concur and dissent in *Singleton v. Wulff*, which held that the Eighth Circuit court of appeals had jurisdiction to determine whether abortion providers had standing to challenge a provision in Missouri's abortion statute that limited medicaid payment for abortions, but it did not have jurisdiction to rule that the provision violated the constitution because the district court did not address the issue. He dissented from language in the plurality opinion that indicated the abortion providers could assert on remand, in addition to their own rights, the constitutional rights of their patients who would be eligible for medicaid assistance in obtaining elective abortions.

Burns v. Alcala

Forum: United States Supreme Court.

Case Citation: Burns v. Alcala, 420 U.S. 575 (1975).

Date Argued: January 22, 1975.

Date of Decision: March 18, 1975.

Opinion of Court: Powell, J., in which Burger, C. J., and Brennan, Stewart, White, Blackmun, and Rehnquist, JJ., joined.

Concurring Opinion: None.

Dissenting Opinion: Marshall, J.

Not Participating: Douglas, J.

Counsel for Appellants: Richard C. Turner, Attorney General of Iowa, argued; on the brief was Lorna Lawhead Williams, Special Assistant Attorney General.

Counsel for Appellees: Robert Bartels argued and filed a brief.

Amicus Brief for Appellants: Solicitor General Bork, Keith A. Jones, and John B. Rhinelander for the United States; by Robert L. Shevin,

Attorney General, Eva Dunkerley Peck, and Chester G. Senf for the State of Florida; by Andrew P. Miller, Attorney General of Virginia, and Stuart H. Dunn and Karen C. Kincannon, Assistant Attorneys General, for Lukhard, Director of the Department of Welfare, Commonwealth of Virginia; and by Ronald A. Zumbrun and John H. Findley for the Pacific Legal Foundation.

Amicus Brief for Appellees: George R. Moscone for the American Association for Maternal and Child Health et al.

Issue Presented: Whether states receiving federal financial aid under the program of Aid to Families with Dependent Children must offer welfare benefits to pregnant women for their unborn children?

Case Holding: States receiving federal financial aid under the program of Aid to Families with Dependent Children were not required to offer welfare benefits to pregnant women for their unborn children.

Background facts of case: The appellees, indigent pregnant women, filed a lawsuit in a federal district court in Iowa, after they applied for welfare assistance but were refused on the ground that they had no dependent children eligible for the Aid to Families with Dependent Children program. The appellants, state officials, were named as defendants. The appellees contended that an Iowa policy of denying benefits to unborn children conflicted with the federal standard of eligibility for such aid. The district court held that unborn children are dependent children and that by denying them benefits Iowa had departed impermissibly from the federal standard of eligibility. The Eighth Circuit court of appeals affirmed. The Supreme Court granted certiorari to consider the issue.

Majority opinion by Justice Powell: Justice Powell ruled that the applicable federal law did not require the payment of welfare benefits for unborn children. He addressed the matter as follows:

> The Court has held that under 402 (a) (10) of the Social Security Act, 42 U.S.C. 602 (a) (10), federal participation in state AFDC programs is conditioned on the State's offering benefits to all persons who are eligible under federal standards. The State must provide benefits to all individuals who meet the federal definition of dependent child and who are needy under state standards, unless they are excluded or aid is made optional by another provision of the Act....
>
> Our analysis of the Social Security Act does not support a conclusion that the legislative definition of dependent child includes unborn children. Following the axiom that words used in a statute are to be given their ordinary meaning in the absence of persuasive reasons to the contrary, and reading the definition of dependent child in its statutory context, we conclude that Congress used the word "child" to refer to an individual already born, with an existence separate from its mother....
>
> [Appellees] have ... relied on HEW's regulation allowing payment of AFDC benefits on behalf of unborn children. They ask us to defer to the agency's longstanding interpretation of the statute it administers. [Appellees] have provided the Court with copies of letters and interoffice memoranda that preceded adoption of this policy in 1941 by HEW's predecessor, the Bureau of Public Assistance. These papers suggest that the agency initially may have taken the position that the statutory phrase "dependent children" included unborn children.
>
> A brief filed by the Solicitor General on behalf of HEW in this case disavows [appellees'] interpretation of the Act. HEW contends that unborn children are not included in the federal eligibility standard and that the regulation authorizing federal participation in AFDC payments to pregnant women is based on the agency's general authority to make rules for efficient administration of the Act. The regulation is consistent with this explanation. It appears in a subsection with other rules authorizing temporary aid, at the option of the States, to individuals in the process of gaining or losing eligibility for the AFDC program. For example, one of the accompanying rules authorizes States to pay AFDC benefits to a relative 30 days before the eligible child comes to live in his home. HEW's current explanation of the regulation deprives [appellees'] argument of any significant support from the principle that accords persuasive weight to a consistent, longstanding interpretation of a statute by the agency charged with its administration....
>
> In this case [appellees] did not, and perhaps could not, challenge HEW's policy of allowing States the option of paying AFDC benefits to pregnant women. We therefore have no occasion to decide whether HEW has statutory authority to approve federal participation in state programs ancillary to those expressly provided in the Social Security Act, or whether [the statute] authorizes HEW to fund benefits for unborn children as a form of temporary aid to individuals who are in the process of qualifying under federal standards.

Disposition of case: The judgment of the court of appeals was reversed.

Dissenting opinion by Justice Marshall: Justice Marshall disagreed with the majority opinion. He argued as follows:

> The majority has parsed the language and touched on the legislative history of the Act in an effort to muster support for the view that unborn children were not meant to benefit from the Act. Even given its best face, however, this evidence provides only modest support for the majority's position. The lengthy course of administrative practice cuts quite the other way....
>
> The majority makes only passing reference to the administrative practice of 30 years' duration, under which unborn children were deemed eligible for federal AFDC payments where state programs provided funds for them. According to the majority, this longstanding administrative practice is deprived of any significant weight by HEW's present suggestion that it has always treated unborn children as being outside the statutory definition of dependent child. The agency's characterization of its former position, however, misrepresents the history of the administrative practice.
>
> As early as 1941 the Bureau of Public Assistance faced the problem of whether unborn children were covered by ... the Act. At that time, the Board determined that under the Act federal funds could be provided to the States for aid to unborn children. The agency's governing regulation in the HEW Handbook of Public Assistance Administration expressly included unborn children among those eligible for aid on the basis of the same eligibility conditions as apply to other children. The language of the regulation and the inclusion of unborn children among five other classes of children eligible for AFDC payments under the definition of dependent child make it evident that the agency deemed unborn children to come within the terms of ... the Act....
>
> Even if the agency's new position is not discounted as a reaction to the exigencies of the moment, the policies underlying the doctrine of administrative interpretation require more than simply placing a thumb on the side of the scale that the agency currently favors. The agency's determination that unborn children are eligible for matching federal aid was made early in the life of the program, and the administrators of the Act determined only a few years after the Act's passage that making AFDC payments available to unborn children was consistent with the statutory purposes. This contemporaneous and long-applied construction of the eligibility provision and purposes of the Act is entitled to great weight — particularly in the case of a statute that has been before the Congress repeatedly and has been amended numerous times. The majority contends that because of the details of the unsuccessful 1972 legislative effort to exclude unborn children from coverage, the [appellees] can claim little benefit from the natural inference that the statute still included them among those eligible for aid. This may be so, but in light of the history of the administrative interpretation ..., I cannot agree that the Act, in its present form, should be read to exclude the unborn from eligibility.

Butler, Pierce

Pierce Butler (1866–1939) served as an associate justice of the United States Supreme Court from 1923 to 1939. While on the Supreme Court Justice Butler was known as a conservative who was philosophically opposed to government regulation of the economy.

Justice Butler was born in Dakota County, Minnesota. He received two undergraduate degrees from Carleton College in 1887. Justice Butler did not receive a formal education in the law. He was a legal apprentice for a law firm in St. Paul. He would eventually be admitted to the Minnesota bar in 1888. As a private attorney Justice Butler established a national reputation representing railroad companies. In 1922 President Warren G. Harding nominated Justice Butler to the Supreme Court.

Justice Butler was involved in only one abortion related opinion while on the Supreme Court. Justice Butler voted with a unanimous opinion in *State of Missouri ex rel. Hurwitz v. North*, which held that the constitution was not violated when a physician was prevented from issuing subpoenas to have witnesses attend a hearing to revoke his medical license for performing an unlawful abortion, because the applicable rules required taking depositions of witnesses who would not voluntarily attend the hearing.

Butyric Acid Attacks *see* **Abortion Violence, Property Destruction and Demonstrations**

C

Caesarean Section

Delivery of a baby through an abdominal incision is called caesarean section (C-section). This procedure is performed when a vaginal birth is not possible or is not safe for the mother or child. About 20 percent of all births in the United States are performed using this procedure. Some of the reasons that C-sections are performed to protect the infant include: developmental abnormality of the fetus, problems with the uterus, problems with the cervix or birth canal, and problems with the placenta and umbilical cord. Some of the reasons the procedure is used to protect the mother include: infant's head is too large, prolonged labor, abnormal position of the baby, buttocks-first delivery, crosswise position, and pregnancy at older age (over 40). In most instances mothers and infants recover well after the procedure. However, studies have shown that women undergoing vaginal birth, after having a C-section, are likely to suffer a ruptured uterus, which can kill the mother, her baby or both.

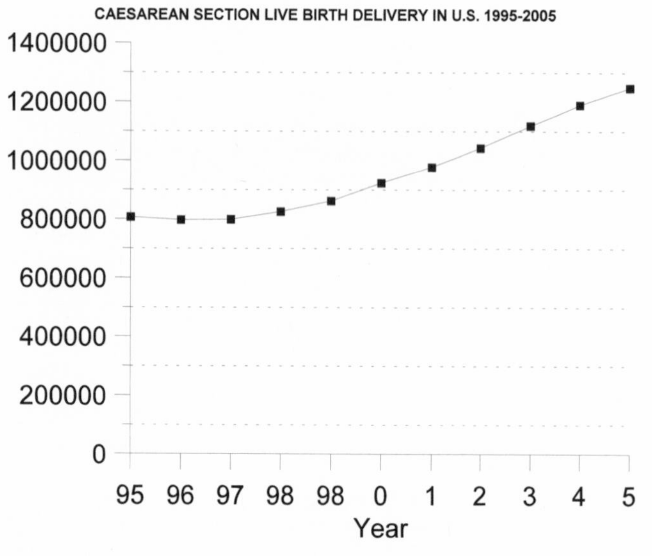

Source: **National Center for Health Statistics.**

Calendar Method *see* **Natural Family Planning Methods**

California

(1) OVERVIEW

The state of California enacted its first criminal abortion statute on April 16, 1850. The statute underwent several amendments prior to the 1973 decision by the United States Supreme Court in *Roe v. Wade*, which legalized abortion in the nation. California has taken affirmative steps to respond to *Roe* and its progeny. The state has addressed numerous abortion issues by statute that include reproductive privacy, civil lawsuit for blockading abortion facility, criminal/civil action for obstructing abortion facility or harming abortionists, prohibit child from suing parent for wrongful birth, confidential address for pro-choice advocates, prohibiting use of internet to post private information about pro-choice advocates, exempting disclosure of abortion provider information by public agency, requiring physician perform abortion, abortion clinic bombings, collecting anti-abortion crime data, abortion for prisoners, training in abortion services, abortion by minors, use of facilities and people, criminal ban on anti-abortion activities, fetal experimentation, human cloning, health care service plan abortion notification requirements, injury to pregnant woman.

(2) REPRODUCTIVE PRIVACY

California has taken the initiative to codify a woman's right to have an abortion when a fetus is not viable. Further, the state has permits an abortion when a fetus is viable, but the woman's life or health would be endangered if the fetus was carried to term. The statutes addressing the matters are setout below.

California Health & Safety Code § 123460. Short title

This article shall be known and may be cited as the Reproductive Privacy Act.

California Health & Safety Code § 123462. Legislative findings

The Legislature finds and declares that every individual possesses a fundamental right of privacy with respect to personal reproductive decisions. Accordingly, it is the public policy of the State of California that:

(a) Every individual has the fundamental right to choose or refuse birth control.

(b) Every woman has the fundamental right to choose to bear a child or to choose and to obtain an abortion, except as specifically limited by this article.

(c) The state shall not deny or interfere with a woman's fundamental right to choose to bear a child or to choose to obtain an abortion, except as specifically permitted by this article.

California Health & Safety Code § 123464. Definitions

The following definitions shall apply for purposes of this chapter:

(a) "Abortion" means any medical treatment intended to induce the termination of a pregnancy except for the purpose of producing a live birth.

(b) "Pregnancy" means the human reproductive process, beginning with the implantation of an embryo.

(c) "State" means the State of California, and every county, city,

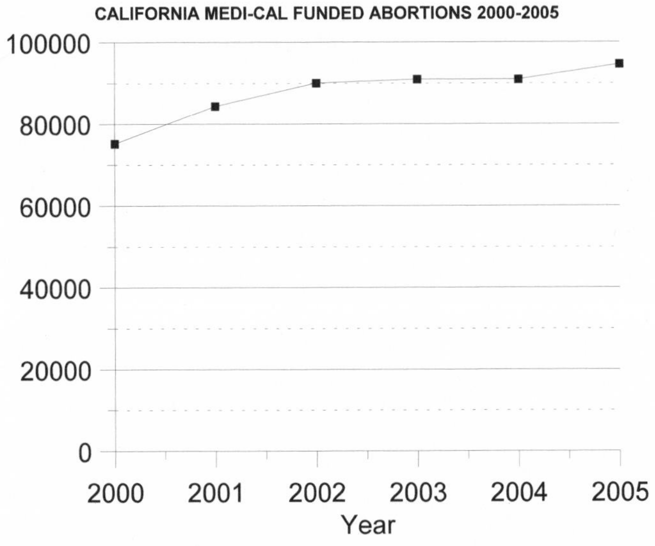

Source: California Department of Health Services.

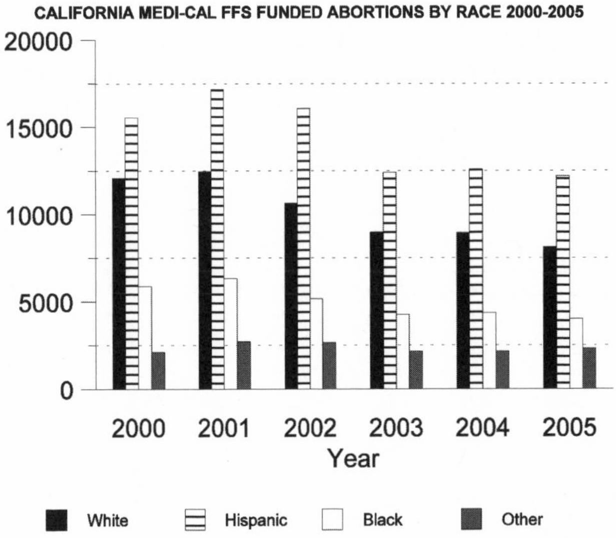

Source: California Department of Health Services.

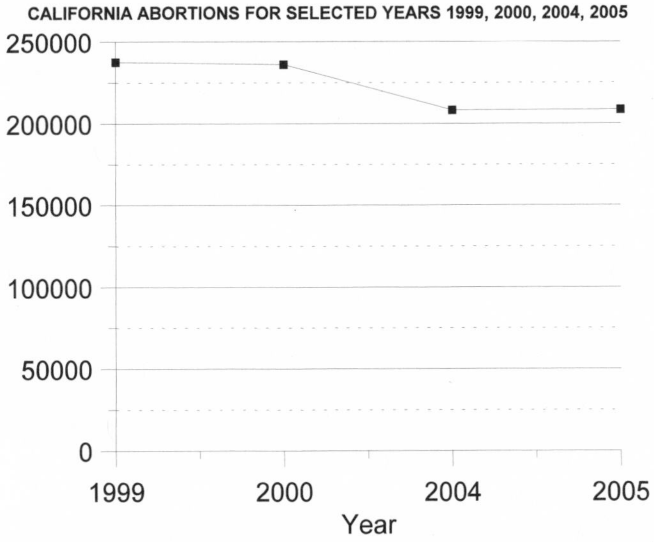

Source: Guttmacher Institute: Trends in Abortion in California (2008).

California Medi-Cal FFS Funded Abortion By Age Group 2000–2005

Age Group (yrs)

Year	*<15*	*15–17*	*18–19*	*20–24*	*25–29*	*30–34*	*≥35*	*Unknown*
2000	183	3,369	6,408	15,726	9,327	5,992	4,683	106
2001	174	3,341	6,493	16,996	10,534	6,687	5,189	157
2002	207	3,634	7,027	18,457	11,654	7,152	5,774	0
2003	298	4,483	7,132	17,188	10,223	6,379	4,505	32
2004	280	4,427	7,285	18,006	10,993	6,701	4,849	10
2005	264	4,057	7,315	18,510	11,222	6,535	4,858	22
Total	1,406	23,311	41,660	104,883	63,953	39,446	29,858	327

Source: California Department of Health Services.

town and municipal corporation, and quasi-municipal corporation in the state.

(d) "Viability" means the point in a pregnancy when, in the good faith medical judgment of a physician, on the particular facts of the case before that physician, there is a reasonable likelihood of the fetus' sustained survival outside the uterus without the application of extraordinary medical measures.

California Health & Safety Code § 123466.
Woman's right to have abortion

The state may not deny or interfere with a woman's right to choose or obtain an abortion prior to viability of the fetus, or when the abortion is necessary to protect the life or health of the woman.

California Health & Safety Code § 123468.
Unauthorized abortions

The performance of an abortion is unauthorized if either of the following is true:

(a) The person performing or assisting in performing the abortion is not a health care provider authorized to perform or assist in performing an abortion pursuant to Section 2253 of the Business and Professions Code.

(b) The abortion is performed on a viable fetus, and both of the following are established:

(1) In the good faith medical judgment of the physician, the fetus was viable.

(2) In the good faith medical judgment of the physician, continuation of the pregnancy posed no risk to life or health of the pregnant woman.

California Health & Safety Code § 123425.
Decisions on abortion

The refusal of any person to submit to an abortion ... or to give consent therefor shall not be grounds for loss of any privileges or immunities to which the person would otherwise be entitled, nor shall submission to an abortion ... or the granting of consent therefor be a condition precedent to the receipt of any public benefits. The decision of any person to submit to an abortion ... or to give consent therefor shall not be grounds for loss of any privileges or immunities to which the person would otherwise be entitled, nor shall the refusal to submit to an abortion ... or to give consent therefor be a condition precedent to the receipt of any public benefits.

California Health & Safety Code § 123435.
Infant born alive in course of abortion

The rights to medical treatment of an infant prematurely born alive in the course of an abortion shall be the same as the rights of an infant of similar medical status prematurely born spontaneously.

(3) CIVIL LAWSUIT FOR BLOCKADING ABORTION FACILITY

California has responded to blockading of abortion facilities by pro-life advocates, by permitting a civil lawsuit to be brought against those who engage in such conduct. The statutes addressing the issue are set out below.

California Civil Code § 3427. Definitions

As used in this title:

(a) "Aggrieved" means and refers to any of the following persons or entities:

(1) A person physically present at a health care facility when a commercial blockade occurs whose access is obstructed or impeded.

(2) A person physically present at a health care facility when a commercial blockade occurs whose health care is disrupted.

(3) A health care facility where a commercial blockade occurs, its employees, contractors, or volunteers.

(4) The owner of a health care facility where a commercial blockade occurs or of the building or property upon which the health care facility is located.

(b) "Commercial blockade" means acts constituting the tort of commercial blockade, as defined in Section 3427.1.

(c) "Disrupting the normal functioning of a health care facility" means intentionally rendering or attempting to render a health care facility temporarily or permanently unavailable or unusable by a licensed health practitioner, the facility's staff, or patients. "Disrupting the normal functioning of a health care facility" does not include acts of the owner of the facility, an agent acting on behalf of the owner, or officers or employees of a governmental entity acting to protect the public health or safety.

(d) "Health care facility" means a facility that provides health care services directly to patients, including, but not limited to, a hospital, clinic, licensed health practitioner's office, health maintenance organization, diagnostic or treatment center, neuropsychiatric or mental health facility, hospice, or nursing home.

California Civil Code § 3427.1. Commercial blockade

It is unlawful, and constitutes the tort of commercial blockade for a person, alone or in concert with others, to intentionally prevent an individual from entering or exiting a health care facility by physically obstructing the individual's passage or by disrupting the normal functioning of a health care facility.

California Civil Code § 3427.2. Civil damages

A person or health care facility aggrieved by the actions prohibited by this title may seek civil damages from those who committed the prohibited acts and those acting in concert with them.

California Civil Code § 3427.3.
Safeguarding individual privacy

The court having jurisdiction over a civil proceeding under this title shall take all steps reasonably necessary to safeguard the individual privacy and prevent harassment of a health care patient, licensed health practitioner, or employee, client, or customer of a health care facility who is a party or witness in the proceeding, including granting protective orders. Health care patients, licensed health practitioners, and employees, clients, and customers of the health care facility may use pseudonyms to protect their privacy.

California Civil Code § 3427.4. Construction

This title shall not be construed to impair any constitutionally protected activity or any activities protected by the labor laws of this state or the United States of America.

(4) CRIMINAL/CIVIL ACTION FOR OBSTRUCTING ABORTION FACILITY OR HARMING ABORTIONISTS

California has made it a criminal and civil offense to obstruct access to abortion facilities, or commit crimes against pro-choice advocates. The statutes addressing the matter are set out below.

California Penal Code § 423. Short title

This title shall be known and may be cited as the California Freedom of Access to Clinic ... Entrances Act, or the California FACE Act.

California Penal Code § 423.1. Definitions

The following definitions apply for the purposes of this title:

(a) "Crime of violence" means an offense that has as an element the use, attempted use, or threatened use of physical force against the person or property of another.

(b) "Interfere with" means to restrict a person's freedom of movement.

(c) "Intimidate" means to place a person in reasonable apprehension of bodily harm to herself or himself or to another.

(d) "Nonviolent" means conduct that would not constitute a crime of violence.

(e) "Physical obstruction" means rendering ingress to or egress from a reproductive health services facility ... impassable to another person, or rendering passage to or from a reproductive health services facility ... unreasonably difficult or hazardous to another person.

(f) "Reproductive health services" means reproductive health services provided in a hospital, clinic, physician's office, or other facility and includes medical, surgical, counseling, or referral services relating to the human reproductive system, including services relating to pregnancy or the termination of a pregnancy.

(g) "Reproductive health services client, provider, or assistant" means a person or entity that is or was involved in obtaining, seeking to obtain, providing, seeking to provide, or assisting or seeking to assist another person, at that other person's request, to obtain or provide any services in a reproductive health services facility, or a person or entity that is or was involved in owning or operating or seeking to own or operate, a reproductive health services facility.

(h) "Reproductive health services facility" includes a hospital, clinic, physician's office, or other facility that provides or seeks to provide reproductive health services and includes the building or structure in which the facility is located.

California Penal Code § 423.2. Elements of offense

Every person who, except a parent or guardian acting towards his or her minor child or ward, commits any of the following acts shall be subject to the punishment specified in Section 423.3.

(a) By force, threat of force, or physical obstruction that is a crime of violence, intentionally injures, intimidates, interferes with, or attempts to injure, intimidate, or interfere with, any person or entity because that person or entity is a reproductive health services client, provider, or assistant, or in order to intimidate any person or entity, or any class of persons or entities, from becoming or remaining a reproductive health services client, provider, or assistant.

***

(c) By nonviolent physical obstruction, intentionally injures, intimidates, or interferes with, or attempts to injure, intimidate, or interfere with, any person or entity because that person or entity is a reproductive health services client, provider, or assistant, or in order to intimidate any person or entity, or any class of persons or entities, from becoming or remaining a reproductive health services client, provider, or assistant.

***

(e) Intentionally damages or destroys the property of a person, entity, or facility, or attempts to do so, because the person, entity, or facility is a reproductive health services client, provider, assistant, or facility.

California Penal Code § 423.3. Punishment

(a) A first violation of subdivision (c) ... of Section 423.2 is a misdemeanor, punishable by imprisonment in a county jail for a period of not more than six months and a fine not to exceed two thousand dollars ($2,000).

(b) A second or subsequent violation of subdivision (c) ... of Section 423.2 is a misdemeanor, punishable by imprisonment in a county jail for a period of not more than six months and a fine not to exceed five thousand dollars ($5,000).

(c) A first violation of subdivision (a) [or] (e) of Section 423. 2 is a misdemeanor, punishable by imprisonment in a county jail for a period of not more than one year and a fine not to exceed twenty-five thousand dollars ($25,000).

(d) A second or subsequent violation of subdivision (a) [or] (e) of Section 423.2 is a misdemeanor, punishable by imprisonment in a county jail for a period of not more than one year and a fine not to exceed fifty thousand dollars ($50,000).

(e) In imposing fines pursuant to this section, the court shall consider applicable factors in aggravation and mitigation set out in Rules 4.421 and 4.423 of the California Rules of Court, and shall consider a prior violation of the federal Freedom of Access to Clinic Entrances Act of 1994 (18 U.S.C. Sec. 248), or a prior violation of a statute of another jurisdiction that would constitute a violation of Section 423.2 or of the federal Freedom of Access to Clinic Entrances Act of 1994, to be a prior violation of Section 423.2.

(f) This title establishes concurrent state jurisdiction over conduct that is also prohibited by the federal Freedom of Access to Clinic Entrances Act of 1994 (18 U.S.C. Sec. 248), which provides for more severe misdemeanor penalties for first violations and felony-misdemeanor penalties for second and subsequent violations. State law enforcement agencies and prosecutors shall cooperate with federal authorities in the prevention, apprehension, and prosecution of these crimes, and shall seek federal prosecutions when appropriate.

(g) No person shall be convicted under this article for conduct in violation of Section 423.2 that was done on a particular occasion where the identical conduct on that occasion was the basis for a conviction of that person under the federal Freedom of Access to Clinic Entrances Act of 1994 (18 U.S.C. Sec. 248).

California Penal Code 423.4. Civil actions

(a) A person aggrieved by a violation of Section 423.2 may bring a civil action to enjoin the violation, for compensatory and punitive damages, and for the costs of suit and reasonable fees for attorneys and expert witnesses.... With respect to compensatory damages, the plaintiff may elect, at any time prior to the rendering of a final judgment, to recover, in lieu of actual damages, an award of statutory damages in the amount of one thousand dollars ($1,000) per exclusively nonviolent violation, and five thousand dollars ($5,000) per any other violation, for each violation committed.

(b) The Attorney General, a district attorney, or a city attorney may bring a civil action to enjoin a violation of Section 423.2, for compensatory damages to persons aggrieved as described in subdivision (a) and for the assessment of a civil penalty against each respondent. The civil penalty shall not exceed two thousand dollars ($2,000) for an exclusively nonviolent first violation, and fifteen thousand dollars ($15,000) for any other first violation, and shall not exceed five thousand dollars ($5,000) for an exclusively nonviolent subsequent violation, and twenty-five thousand dollars ($25,000) for any other subsequent violation. In imposing civil penalties pursuant to this subdivision, the court shall consider a prior violation of the federal Freedom of Access to Clinic Entrances Act of 1994 (18 U.S.C. Sec. 248), or a prior violation of a statute of another jurisdiction that would constitute a violation of Section 423.2 or the federal Freedom of Access to Clinic Entrances Act of 1994, to be a prior violation of Section 423.2.

(c) No person shall be found liable under this section for conduct in violation of Section 423.2 done on a particular occasion where the identical conduct on that occasion was the basis for a finding of liability by that person under the federal Freedom of Access to Clinic Entrances Act of 1994 (18 U.S.C. Sec. 248).

California Penal Code § 423.5. Privacy by court

(a)(1) The court in which a criminal or civil proceeding is filed for a violation of subdivision (a), (c), or (e) of Section 423.2 shall take all action reasonably required, including granting restraining orders, to safeguard the health, safety, or privacy of either of the following:

(A) A reproductive health services client, provider, or assistant who is a party or witness in the proceeding.

(B) A person who is a victim of, or at risk of becoming a victim of, conduct prohibited by subdivision (a), (c), or (e) of Section 423.2.

***

(b) Restraining orders issued pursuant to paragraph (1) of subdivision (a) may include provisions prohibiting or restricting the photographing of persons described in subparagraphs (A) and (B) of paragraph (1) of subdivision (a) when reasonably required to safeguard the health, safety, or privacy of those persons....

(c) A court may, in its discretion, permit an individual described in subparagraph (A) or (B) of paragraph (1) of subdivision (a) to use a pseudonym in a civil proceeding described in paragraph (1) of subdivision (a) when reasonably required to safeguard the health, safety, or privacy of those persons....

California Penal Code § 423.6. Construction of title

This title shall not be construed for any of the following purposes:

(a) To impair any constitutionally protected activity, or any activity protected by the laws of California or of the United States of America.

(b) To provide exclusive civil or criminal remedies or to preempt or to preclude any county, city, or city and county from passing any law to provide a remedy for the commission of any of the acts prohibited by this title or to make any of those acts a crime.

(c) To interfere with the enforcement of any federal, state, or local laws regulating the performance of abortions or the provision of other reproductive health services.

(d) To negate, supercede, or otherwise interfere with the operation of any provision of Chapter 10 (commencing with Section 1138) of Part 3 of Division 2 of the Labor Code.

(e) To create additional civil or criminal remedies or to limit any existing civil or criminal remedies to redress an activity that interferes with the exercise of any other rights protected by the First Amendment to the United States Constitution or of Article I of the California Constitution.

(f) To preclude prosecution under both this title and any other provision of law, except as provided in subdivision (g) of Section 423.3.

California Penal Code § 602.11.
Obstructing passage to health care facilities

(a) Any person, alone or in concert with others, who intentionally prevents an individual from entering or exiting a health care facility, place of worship, or school by physically detaining the individual or physically obstructing the individual's passage shall be guilty of a misdemeanor punishable by imprisonment in the county jail, or a fine of not more than two hundred fifty dollars ($250), or both, for the first offense; imprisonment in the county jail for not less than five days and a fine of not more than five hundred dollars ($500) for the second offense; and imprisonment in the county jail for not less than 30

days and a fine of not more than two thousand dollars ($2,000) for a third or subsequent offense. However, the court may order the defendant to perform community service, in lieu of any fine or any imprisonment imposed under this section, if it determines that paying the fine would result in undue hardship to the defendant or his or her dependents.

(b) As used in subdivision (a), the following terms have the following meanings:

(1) "Physically" does not include speech.

(2) "Health care facility" means a facility licensed pursuant to Chapter 1 (commencing with Section 1200) of Division 2 of the Health and Safety Code, a health facility licensed pursuant to Chapter 2 (commencing with Section 1250) of Division 2 of the Health and Safety Code, or any facility where medical care is regularly provided to individuals by persons licensed under Division 2 (commencing with Section 500) of the Business and Professions Code, the Osteopathic Initiative Act, or the Chiropractic Initiative Act.

(3) "Person" does not include an officer, employee, or agent of the health care facility, or a law enforcement officer, acting in the course of his or her employment.

(c) This section shall not be interpreted to prohibit any lawful activities permitted under the laws of the State of California or by the National Labor Relations Act in connection with a labor dispute.

(5) PROHIBIT CHILD FROM SUING PARENT FOR WRONGFUL BIRTH

California has taken measures to prevent children from suing their parents on a theory of wrongful birth. The statutes addressing the issue are set out below.

California Civil Code § 43.6. Immunity from liability

(a) No cause of action arises against a parent of a child based upon the claim that the child should not have been conceived or, if conceived, should not have been allowed to have been born alive.

(b) The failure or refusal of a parent to prevent the live birth of his or her child shall not be a defense in any action against a third party, nor shall the failure or refusal be considered in awarding damages in any such action.

(c) As used in this section "conceived" means the fertilization of a human ovum by a human sperm.

(6) CONFIDENTIAL ADDRESS FOR PRO-CHOICE ADVOCATES

California has provided for the creation of a system that will allow pro-choice advocates to obtain confidential addresses from the state Secretary of State. To qualify for such an address, an applicant must show, as a minimum, that he/she is an abortion provider, employee, or volunteer who is fearful for his/her safety or that of a family member because of his/her affiliation with a reproductive health care services facility. The statutes addressing the matter are set out below.

California Government Code § 6215.
Legislative findings and declarations

The Legislature finds and declares the following:

(a) Persons working in the reproductive health care field, specifically the provision of terminating a pregnancy, are often subject to harassment, threats, and acts of violence by persons or groups.

(b) In 2000, 30 percent of respondents to a Senate Office of Research survey of 172 California reproductive health care providers reported they or their families had been targets of acts of violence by groups that oppose reproductive rights at locations away from their clinics or offices.

(c) Persons and groups that oppose reproductive rights attempt to stop the provision of legal reproductive health care services by threatening reproductive health care service providers, clinics, employees, volunteers, and patients. The names, photographs, spouses' names, and home addresses of these providers, employees, volunteers, and patients have been posted on Internet Web sites. From one Web site list that includes personal information of reproductive health care service providers, seven persons have been murdered and 14 have been injured. As of August 5, 2002, there are 78 Californians listed on this site. The threat of violence toward reproductive health care service providers and those who assist them has clearly extended beyond the clinic and into the home.

(d) Nationally, between 1992 and 1996, the number of reproductive health care service providers declined by 14 percent. Nearly one out of every four women must travel more than 50 miles to obtain reproductive health care services dealing with the termination of a pregnancy. There exists a fear on the part of physicians to enter the reproductive health care field and to provide reproductive health care services.

(e) Reproductive health care services are legal medical procedures. In order to prevent potential acts of violence from being committed against providers, employees, and volunteers who assist in the provision of reproductive health care services and the patients seeking those services, it is necessary for the Legislature to ensure that the home address information of these individuals is kept confidential.

(f) The purpose of this chapter is to enable state and local agencies to respond to requests for public records without disclosing the residential location of a reproductive health care services provider, employee, volunteer, or patient, to enable interagency cooperation with the Secretary of State in providing address confidentiality for reproductive health care services providers, employees, volunteers, and patients, and to enable state and local agencies to accept a program participant's use of an address designated by the Secretary of State as a substitute mailing address.

California Government Code § 6215.1. Definitions

Unless the context clearly requires otherwise, the definitions in this section apply throughout this chapter.

(a) "Address" means a residential street address, school address, or work address of an individual, as specified on the individual's application to be a program participant under this chapter.

(b) "Reproductive health care services" means health care services relating to the termination of a pregnancy in a reproductive health care services facility.

(c) "Reproductive health care services provider, employee, volunteer, or patient" means a person who obtains, provides, or assists, at the request of another person, in obtaining or providing reproductive health care services, or a person who owns or operates a reproductive health care services facility.

(d) "Reproductive health care services facility" includes a hospital, an office operated by a licensed physician and surgeon, a licensed clinic, or other licensed health care facility that provides reproductive health care services and includes only the building or structure in which the reproductive health care services are actually provided.

California Government Code § 6215.2.
Application for confidential address

(a) An adult person, a parent or guardian acting on behalf of a minor, or a guardian acting on behalf of an incapacitated person may apply to the Secretary of State to have an address designated by the Secretary of State to serve as the person's address or the address of the minor or incapacitated person. An application shall be completed in person at a community-based assistance program designated by the Secretary of State. The application process shall include a requirement that the applicant shall meet with a counselor and receive orientation information about the program. The Secretary of State shall approve an application if it is filed in the manner and on the form prescribed by the Secretary of State and if it contains all of the following:

(1) If the applicant alleges that the basis for the application is that the applicant, or the minor or incapacitated person on whose behalf the application is made, is a reproductive health care service provider, employee, or volunteer who is fearful for his or her safety or the safety of his or her family because of his or her affiliation with a reproductive health care services facility, the application shall be accompanied by all of the following:

(A) Documentation showing that the individual is to commence employment or is currently employed as a provider or employee at a reproductive health care services facility or is volunteering at a reproductive health care services facility.

(B) A certified statement signed by a person authorized by the reproductive health care services facility stating that the facility or any of its providers, employees, volunteers, or patients is or was the target of threats or acts of violence within one year of the date of the application. A person who willfully certifies as true any material matter pursuant to this section which he or she knows to be false is guilty of a misdemeanor.

(C) A sworn statement that the applicant fears for his or her safety or the safety of his or her family, or the safety of the minor or incapacitated person on whose behalf the application is made due to his or her affiliation with the reproductive health care services facility providing the declaration described in subparagraph (B).

(2) If the applicant alleges that the basis for the application is that the applicant is a reproductive health care services facility volunteer, the application shall, in addition to the documents specified in paragraph (1), be accompanied by reproductive health care services facility documentation showing the length of time the volunteer has committed to working at the facility.

(3) If the applicant alleges that the basis of the application is that the applicant, or the minor or incapacitated person on whose behalf the application is made, is a person who is or has been the target of threats or acts of violence because he or she is obtaining or seeking to obtain services at a reproductive health care services facility within one year of the date of the application, the application shall be accompanied by the following:

(A) A sworn statement that the applicant has good reason to fear for his or her safety or the safety of his or her family.

(B) Any police, court, or other government agency records or files that show any complaints of the alleged threats or acts of violence.

(4) A designation of the Secretary of State as agent for purposes of service of process and for the purpose of receipt of mail.

(A) Service on the Secretary of State of any summons, writ, notice, demand, or process shall be made by delivering to the address confidentiality program personnel of the office of the Secretary of State two copies of the summons, writ, notice, demand, or process.

(B) If a summons, writ, notice, demand, or process is served on the Secretary of State, the Secretary of State shall immediately cause a copy to be forwarded to the program participant at the address shown on the records of the address confidentiality program so that the summons, writ, notice, demand, or process is received by the program participant within three days of the Secretary of State's having received it.

(C) The Secretary of State shall keep a record of all summonses, writs, notices, demands, and processes served upon the Secretary of State under this section and shall record the time of that service and the Secretary of State's action.

(D) The office of the Secretary of State and any agent or person employed by the Secretary of State shall be held harmless from any liability in any action brought by any person injured or harmed as a result of the handling of first-class mail on behalf of program participants.

(5) The mailing address where the applicant can be contacted by the Secretary of State, and the telephone number or numbers where the applicant can be called by the Secretary of State.

(6) The address or addresses that the applicant requests not be disclosed for the reason that disclosure will increase the risk of acts of violence toward the applicant.

(7) The signature of the applicant and of any individual or representative of any office designated in writing who assisted in the preparation of the application, and the date on which the applicant signed the application.

(b) Applications shall be filed with the office of the Secretary of State.

(c) Applications submitted by a reproductive health care services facility, its providers, employees, or volunteers shall be accompanied by payment of a fee to be determined by the Secretary of State. This fee shall not exceed the actual costs of enrolling in the program. In addition, annual fees may also be assessed by the Secretary of State to defray the actual costs of maintaining this program. Annual fees assessed by the Secretary of State shall also be used to reimburse the General Fund for any amounts expended from that fund for the purposes of this chapter. No applicant who is a patient of a reproductive health care services facility shall be required to pay an application fee or the annual fee under this program.

(d) The Address Confidentiality for Reproductive Health Care Services Fund is hereby created in the General Fund. Upon appropriation by the Legislature, moneys in the fund are available for the administration of the program established pursuant to this chapter.

(e) Upon filing a properly completed application, the Secretary of State shall certify the applicant as a program participant. Applicants, with the exception of reproductive health care services facilities volunteers, shall be certified for four years following the date of filing unless the certification is withdrawn, or invalidated before that date. Reproductive health care services facility volunteers shall be certified until six months from the last date of volunteering with the facility. The Secretary of State shall by rule establish a renewal procedure.

(f) A person who falsely attests in an application that disclosure of the applicant's address would endanger the applicant's safety or the safety of the applicant's family or the minor or incapacitated person on whose behalf the application is made, or who knowingly provides false or incorrect information upon making an application, is guilty of a misdemeanor. A notice shall be printed in bold type and in a conspicuous location on the face of the application informing the applicant of the penalties under this subdivision.

California Government Code § 6215.3.
Cancellation of participation in program

(a) The Secretary of State may cancel a program participant's certification if there is a change in the residential address from the one listed on the application, unless the program participant provides the Secretary of State with at least seven days' prior notice of the change of address.

(b) The Secretary of State may cancel a program participant's certification if mail forwarded by the secretary to the program participant's address is returned as nondeliverable.

(c) The Secretary of State shall cancel certification of a program participant who applies using false information.

(d) The Secretary of State shall cancel certification of a program participant who fails to disclose a change in employment status, or termination as a provider or volunteer.

(e) Any records or documents pertaining to a program participant shall be retained and held confidential for a period of three years after termination of certification and then destroyed without further notice.

California Government Code § 6215.4.
Withdrawal from program

(a) A program participant may withdraw from program participation by submitting to the address confidentiality program manager written notification of withdrawal and his or her current identification card. Certification shall be terminated on the date of receipt of this notification.

(b) The address confidentiality program manager may terminate a program participant's certification and invalidate his or her authorization card for any of the following reasons:

(1) The program participant's certification term has expired and certification renewal has not been completed.

(2) The address confidentiality program manager has determined that false information was used in the application process or that participation in the program is being used as a subterfuge to avoid detection of illegal or criminal activity or apprehension by law enforcement.

(3) The program participant no longer resides at the residential address listed on the application, and has not provided at least seven days' prior notice in writing of a change in address.

(4) A service of process document or mail forwarded to the program participant by the address confidentiality program manager is returned as nondeliverable.

(5) The program participant who is a provider, employee, or volunteer fails to disclose a change in employment, or termination as volunteer or provider.

(c) If termination is a result of paragraph (1), (3), (4), or (5) of subdivision (b), the address confidentiality program manager shall send written notification of the intended termination to the program participant. The program participant shall have five business days in which to appeal the termination under procedures developed by the Secretary of State.

(d) The address confidentiality program manager shall notify in writing the county elections official and authorized personnel of the appropriate county clerk's office, and county recording office of the program participant's certification withdrawal, invalidation, expiration, or termination.

(e) Upon receipt of this termination notification, authorized personnel shall transmit to the address confidentiality program manager all appropriate administrative records pertaining to the program participant and the record transmitting agency is no longer responsible for maintaining the confidentiality of a terminated program participant's record.

(f) Following termination of program participant certification as a result of paragraph (2) of subdivision (b), the address confidentiality program manager may disclose information contained in the participant's application.

California Government Code § 6215.5.
Request state and local agencies use address

(a) A program participant may request that state and local agencies use the address designated by the Secretary of State as his or her address. When creating a public record, state and local agencies shall accept the address designated by the Secretary of State as a program participant's substitute address, unless the Secretary of State has determined both of the following:

(1) The agency has a bona fide statutory or administrative requirement for the use of the address that would otherwise be confidential under this chapter.

(2) This address will be used only for those statutory and administrative purposes and shall not be publicly disseminated.

(b) A program participant may request that state and local agencies use the address designated by the Secretary of State as his or her address. When modifying or maintaining a public record, excluding the record of any birth, fetal death, death, or marriage registered under Division 102 (commencing with Section 102100) of the Health and Safety Code, state and local agencies shall accept the address designated by the Secretary of State as a program participant's substitute address, unless the Secretary of State has determined both of the following:

(1) The agency has a bona fide statutory or administrative requirement for the use of the address that would otherwise be confidential under this chapter.

(2) This address will be used only for those statutory and administrative purposes and shall not be publicly disseminated.

(c) A program participant may use the address designated by the Secretary of State as his or her work address.

(d) The office of the Secretary of State shall forward all first-class mail and all mail sent by a governmental agency to the appropriate program participants. The office of the Secretary of State shall not handle or forward packages regardless of size or type of mailing.

(e) Notwithstanding subdivision (a), program participants shall comply with the provisions specified in subdivision (d) of Section 1808.21 of the Vehicle Code if requesting suppression of the records maintained by the Department of Motor Vehicles. Program participants shall also comply with all other provisions of the Vehicle Code relating to providing current address information to the department.

California Government Code § 6215.6.
Registering and voting in confidential manner

A program participant who is otherwise qualified to vote may seek to register and vote in a confidential manner pursuant to Section 2166.5 of the Elections Code.

California Government Code § 6215.7.
Viewing participant's address

The Secretary of State may not make a program participant's address, other than the address designated by the Secretary of State, available for inspection or copying, except under any of the following circumstances:

(a) If requested by a law enforcement agency, to the law enforcement agency.

(b) If directed by a court order, to a person identified in the order.

(c) If certification has been canceled.

California Government Code § 6215.8.
Agencies assisting applicants

The Secretary of State shall designate state and local agencies and nonprofit agencies that may assist persons applying to be program participants. Any assistance and counseling rendered by the office of the Secretary of State or its designees to applicants shall in no way be construed as legal advice.

California Government Code § 6215.9. Adoption of rules

The Secretary of State may adopt rules to facilitate the administration of this chapter by state and local agencies. The Secretary of State shall administer this chapter together with and in the same manner as the Address Confidentiality For Victims of Domestic Violence and Stalking (Safe at Home) program.

California Government Code § 6216. Report to legislature

(a) The Secretary of State shall submit to the Legislature, no later than January 10 of each year, a report that includes the total number of applications received for the program established by this chapter. The report shall disclose the number of program participants within

each county and shall also describe any allegations of misuse relating to election purposes.

(b) The Secretary of State shall commence accepting applications under this program on April 1, 2003.

(c) The Secretary of State shall submit to the Legislature by July 1, 2006, a report that includes the total number of pieces of mail forwarded to program participants, the number of program participants during the program's duration, the average length of time a participant remains in the program, and the targeted code changes needed to improve the program's efficiency and cost-effectiveness.

California Government Code § 6217. Duration of chapter

This chapter shall remain in effect only until January 1, 2013, and as of that date is repealed, unless a later enacted statute, that is enacted before January 1, 2013, deletes or extends that date.

(7) PROHIBITING USE OF INTERNET TO POST PRIVATE INFORMATION ABOUT PRO-CHOICE ADVOCATES

In an effort to protect pro-choice advocates from threats or harm, California has enacted laws that ban posting private information about them on the internet. Under the laws no one may post on the internet the home address, home telephone number, or image of any abortion provider, employee, volunteer, or patient of a reproductive health services facility with the intent to cause injury. Anyone violating statutory prohibition may be subject to a civil lawsuit. The statutes addressing the issue are set out below.

California Government Code § 6218.
Prohibiting posting on Internet private information

(a)(1) No person, business, or association shall knowingly publicly post or publicly display on the Internet the home address, home telephone number, or image of any provider, employee, volunteer, or patient of a reproductive health services facility or other individuals residing at the same home address with the intent to do either of the following:

(A) Incite a third person to cause imminent great bodily harm to the person identified in the posting or display, or to a coresident of that person, where the third person is likely to commit this harm.

(B) Threaten the person identified in the posting or display, or a coresident of that person, in a manner that places the person identified or the coresident in objectively reasonable fear for his or her personal safety.

(2) A provider, employee, volunteer, or patient of a reproductive health services facility whose home address, home telephone number, or image is made public as a result of a violation of paragraph (1) may do either or both of the following:

(A) Bring an action seeking injunctive or declarative relief in any court of competent jurisdiction. If a jury or court finds that a violation has occurred, it may grant injunctive or declarative relief and shall award the successful plaintiff court costs and reasonable attorney's fees.

(B) Bring an action for money damages in any court of competent jurisdiction. In addition to any other legal rights or remedies, if a jury or court finds that a violation has occurred, it shall award damages to that individual in an amount up to a maximum of three times the actual damages, but in no case less than four thousand dollars ($4,000).

(b)(1) No person, business, or association shall publicly post or publicly display on the Internet the home address or home telephone number of any provider, employee, volunteer, or patient of a reproductive health services facility if that individual has made a written demand of that person, business, or association to not disclose his or her home address or home telephone number. A demand made under this paragraph shall include a sworn statement declaring that the person is subject to the protection of this section and describing a reasonable fear for the safety of that individual or of any person residing at the individual's home address, based on a violation of subdivision (a). A written demand made under this paragraph shall be effective for four years, regardless of whether or not the individual's affiliation with a reproductive health services facility has expired prior to the end of the four-year period.

(2) A provider, employee, volunteer, or patient of a reproductive health services facility whose home address or home telephone number is made public as a result of a failure to honor a demand made pursuant to paragraph (1) may bring an action seeking injunctive or declarative relief in any court of competent jurisdiction. If a jury or court finds that a violation has occurred, it may grant injunctive or declarative relief and shall award the successful plaintiff court costs and reasonable attorney's fees.

(3) This subdivision shall not apply to a person or entity defined in Section 1070 of the Evidence Code.

(c)(1) No person, business, or association shall solicit, sell, or trade on the Internet the home address, home telephone number, or image of a provider, employee, volunteer, or patient of a reproductive health services facility with the intent to do either of the following:

(A) Incite a third person to cause imminent great bodily harm to the person identified in the posting or display, or to a coresident of that person, where the third person is likely to commit this harm.

(B) Threaten the person identified in the posting or display, or a coresident of that person, in a manner that places the person identified or the coresident in objectively reasonable fear for his or her personal safety.

(2) A provider, employee, volunteer, or patient of a reproductive health services facility whose home address, home telephone number, or image is solicited, sold, or traded in violation of paragraph (1) may bring an action in any court of competent jurisdiction. In addition to any other legal rights and remedies, if a jury or court finds that a violation has occurred, it shall award damages to that individual in an amount up to a maximum of three times the actual damages, but in no case less than four thousand dollars ($4,000).

(d) An interactive computer service or access software provider, as defined in Section 230(f) of Title 47 of the United States Code, shall not be liable under this section unless the service or provider intends to abet or cause bodily harm that is likely to occur or threatens to cause bodily harm to a provider, employee, volunteer, or patient of a reproductive health services facility or any person residing at the same home address.

(e) Nothing in this section is intended to preclude punishment under any other provision of law.

California Government Code § 6218.05. Definitions

For purposes of this chapter, the following terms have the following meanings:

(a) "Reproductive health care services" means health care services relating to the termination of a pregnancy in a reproductive health care services facility.

(b) "Reproductive health care services provider, employee, volunteer, or patient" means a person who obtains, provides, or assists, at the request of another person, in obtaining or providing reproductive health care services, or a person who owns or operates a reproductive health care services facility.

(c) "Reproductive health care services facility" includes a hospital, an office operated by a licensed physician and surgeon, a licensed clinic or a clinic exempt from licensure, or other licensed health care

facility that provides reproductive health care services and includes only the building or structure in which the reproductive health care services are actually provided.

(d) "Publicly post" or "publicly display" means to intentionally communicate or otherwise make available to the general public.

(e) "Image" includes, but is not limited to, any photograph, video footage, sketch, or computer-generated image that provides a means to visually identify the person depicted.

(8) EXEMPTING DISCLOSURE OF ABORTION PROVIDER INFORMATION BY PUBLIC AGENCY

California has provided for an exemption of the public's right to access information from public agencies. Under the exemption any personal information received by a public agency regarding the employees, volunteers, board members, owners, partners, officers, or contractors of a reproductive health services facility, may be prohibited from disclosure if requested by the affected person. The statute addressing the issue is set out below.

California Government Code § 6254.18.
Exemption from disclosure of personal information

(a) Nothing in this chapter shall be construed to require disclosure of any personal information received, collected, or compiled by a public agency regarding the employees, volunteers, board members, owners, partners, officers, or contractors of a reproductive health services facility who have notified the public agency pursuant to subdivision (d) if the personal information is contained in a document that relates to the facility.

(b) For purposes of this section, the following terms have the following meanings:

(1) "Contractor" means an individual or entity that contracts with a reproductive health services facility for services related to patient care.

(2) "Personal information" means the following information related to an individual that is maintained by a public agency: social security number, physical description, home address, home telephone number, statements of personal worth or personal financial data filed pursuant to subdivision (n) of Section 6254, personal medical history, employment history, electronic mail address, and information that reveals any electronic network location or identity.

(3) "Public agency" means all of the following:

(A) The State Department of Health Care Services.

(B) The Department of Consumer Affairs.

(C) The Department of Managed Health Care.

(D) The State Department of Public Health.

(4) "Reproductive health services facility" means the office of a licensed physician and surgeon whose specialty is family practice, obstetrics, or gynecology, or a licensed clinic, where at least 50 percent of the patients of the physician or the clinic are provided with family planning or abortion services.

(c) Any person may institute proceedings for injunctive or declarative relief or writ of mandate in any court of competent jurisdiction to obtain access to employment history information pursuant to Sections 6258 and 6259. If the court finds, based on the facts of a particular case, that the public interest served by disclosure of employment history information clearly outweighs the public interest served by not disclosing the information, the court shall order the officer or person charged with withholding the information to disclose employment history information or show cause why he or she should not do so pursuant to Section 6259.

(d) In order for this section to apply to an individual who is an employee, volunteer, board member, officer, or contractor of a reproductive health services facility, the individual shall notify the public agency to which his or her personal information is being submitted or has been submitted that he or she falls within the application of this section. The reproductive health services facility shall retain a copy of all notifications submitted pursuant to this section. This notification shall be valid if it complies with all of the following:

(1) Is on the official letterhead of the facility.

(2) Is clearly separate from any other language present on the same page and is executed by a signature that serves no other purpose than to execute the notification.

(3) Is signed and dated by both of the following:

(A) The individual whose information is being submitted.

(B) The executive officer or his or her designee of the reproductive health services facility.

(e) The privacy protections for personal information authorized pursuant to this section shall be effective from the time of notification pursuant to subdivision (d) until either one of the following occurs:

(1) Six months after the date of separation from a reproductive health services facility for an individual who has served for not more than one year as an employee, contractor, volunteer, board member, or officer of the reproductive health services facility.

(2) One year after the date of separation from a reproductive health services facility for an individual who has served for more than one year as an employee, contractor, volunteer, board member, or officer of the reproductive health services facility.

(f) Within 90 days of separation of an employee, contractor, volunteer, board member, or officer of the reproductive health services facility who has provided notice to a public agency pursuant to subdivision (c), the facility shall provide notice of the separation to the relevant agency or agencies.

(g) Nothing in this section shall prevent the disclosure by a government agency of data regarding age, race, ethnicity, national origin, or gender of individuals whose personal information is protected pursuant to this section, so long as the data contains no individually identifiable information.

(9) REQUIRING PHYSICIAN PERFORM ABORTION

California requires that an abortion be performed by a physician with a valid license. Criminal penalties may be imposed against anyone performing an abortion who does not have a valid physician's license. The statute addressing the issue is set out below.

California Business & Professions Code § 2253.
Physician perform abortion

(a) Failure to comply with the Reproductive Privacy Act (Article 2.5 (commencing with Section 123460) of Chapter 2 of Part 2 of Division 106 of the Health and Safety Code) in performing, assisting, procuring or aiding, abetting, attempting, agreeing, or offering to procure an illegal abortion constitutes unprofessional conduct.

(b)(1) A person is subject to Sections 2052 and 2053 if he or she performs or assists in performing a surgical abortion, and at the time of so doing, does not have a valid, unrevoked, and unsuspended license to practice as a physician and surgeon as provided in this chapter, or if he or she assists in performing a surgical abortion and does not have a valid, unrevoked, and unsuspended license or certificate obtained in accordance with some other provision of law that authorizes him or her to perform the functions necessary to assist in performing a surgical abortion.

(2) A person is subject to Sections 2052 and 2053 if he or she performs or assists in performing a nonsurgical abortion, and at the time of so doing, does not have a valid, unrevoked, and unsuspended license to practice as a physician and surgeon as provided in this chapter, or does not have a valid, unrevoked, and unsuspended license or certificate obtained in accordance with some other provision of law that authorizes him or her to perform or ass-

ist in performing the functions necessary for a nonsurgical abortion.

(c) For purposes of this section, "nonsurgical abortion" includes termination of pregnancy through the use of pharmacological agents.

(10) ABORTION CLINIC BOMBINGS

California has responded to violent and aggressive anti-abortion activities by enacted legislation that criminalizes the use of explosives to terrorize abortion advocates. The statute addressing the issue is set out below.

California Penal Code § 11413. Clinic bombing

(a) Any person who explodes, ignites, or attempts to explode or ignite any destructive device or any explosive, or who commits arson, in or about any of the places listed in subdivision (b), for the purpose of terrorizing another or in reckless disregard of terrorizing another is guilty of a felony, and shall be punished by imprisonment in the state prison for three, five, or seven years, and a fine not exceeding ten thousand dollars ($10,000).

(b) Subdivision (a) applies to the following places:

(1) Any health facility licensed under Chapter 2 (commencing with Section 1250) of Division 2 of the Health and Safety Code, or any place where medical care is provided by a licensed health care professional.

(2) Omitted.

(3) The buildings, offices, and meeting sites of organizations that counsel for or against abortion or among whose major activities are lobbying, publicizing, or organizing with respect to public or private issues relating to abortion.

(4–10) Omitted.

(d) As used in this section, "terrorizing" means to cause a person of ordinary emotions and sensibilities to fear for personal safety.

(e) Nothing in this section shall be construed to prohibit the prosecution of any person pursuant to Section 12303.3 or any other provision of law in lieu of prosecution pursuant to this section.

(11) COLLECTING ANTI-ABORTION CRIME DATA

California has enacted statutes requiring the collection of anti-abortion crime data. Under the statutes the State Attorney General is primarily responsible for implementing procedures to collect and analyze information relating to anti-abortion crimes, that include the threatened commission of these crimes and persons suspected of committing the crimes or making the threats. The statutes addressing the matter are set out below.

California Penal Code § 13775. Short title

This title shall be known and may be cited as the Reproductive Rights Law Enforcement Act.

California Penal Code § 13776. Definitions

The following definitions apply for the purposes of this title:

(a) "Anti-reproductive-rights crime" means a crime committed partly or wholly because the victim is a reproductive health services client, provider, or assistant, or a crime that is partly or wholly intended to intimidate the victim, any other person or entity, or any class of persons or entities from becoming or remaining a reproductive health services client, provider, or assistant. "Anti-reproductive-rights crime" includes, but is not limited to, a violation of subdivision (a) or (c) of Section 423.2.

(b) "Subject matter experts" includes, but is not limited to, the Commission on the Status of Women, law enforcement agencies experienced with anti-reproductive-rights crimes, including the Attorney General and the Department of Justice, and organizations such as the American Civil Liberties Union, the American College of Obstetricians and Gynecologists, the California Council of Churches, the California Medical Association, the Feminist Majority Foundation, NARAL Pro-Choice California, the National Abortion Federation, the California National Organization for Women, the Planned Parenthood Federation of America, Planned Parenthood Affiliates of California, and the Women's Health Specialists clinic that represent reproductive health services clients, providers, and assistants.

(c) "Crime of violence," "nonviolent," "reproductive health services;" "reproductive health services client, provider, or assistant;" and "reproductive health services facility" each has the same meaning as set forth in Section 423.1.

California Penal Code § 13777. Attorney General role

(a) Except as provided in subdivision (d), the Attorney General shall do each of the following:

(1) Collect and analyze information relating to anti-reproductive-rights crimes, including, but not limited to, the threatened commission of these crimes and persons suspected of committing these crimes or making these threats. The analysis shall distinguish between crimes of violence, including, but not limited to, violations of subdivisions (a) and (e) of Section 423.2, and nonviolent crimes, including, but not limited to, violations of subdivision (c) of Section 423.2. The Attorney General shall make this information available to federal, state, and local law enforcement agencies and prosecutors in California.

(2) Direct local law enforcement agencies to report to the Department of Justice, in a manner that the Attorney General prescribes, any information that may be required relative to anti-reproductive-rights crimes. The report of each crime that violates Section 423.2 shall note the subdivision that prohibits the crime. The report of each crime that violates any other law shall note the code, section, and subdivision that prohibits the crime. The report of any crime that violates both Section 423.2 and any other law shall note both the subdivision of Section 423.2 and the other code, section, and subdivision that prohibits the crime.

(3) On or before July 1, 2003, and every July 1 thereafter, submit a report to the Legislature analyzing the information it obtains pursuant to this section.

(4)(A) Develop a plan to prevent, apprehend, prosecute, and report anti-reproductive-rights crimes, and to carry out the legislative intent expressed in subdivisions (c), (d), (e), and (f) of Section 1 of the act that enacts this title in the 2001-02 Regular Session of the Legislature.

(B) Make a report on the plan to the Legislature by December 1, 2002. The report shall include recommendations for any legislation necessary to carry out the plan.

(b) In carrying out his or her responsibilities under this section, the Attorney General shall consult the Governor, the Commission on Peace Officer Standards and Training, and other subject matter experts.

(c) To avoid production and distribution costs, the Attorney General may submit the reports that this section requires electronically or as part of any other reports that he or she submits to the Legislature, and shall post the reports that this section requires on the Department of Justice Web site.

(d) The Attorney General shall implement this section to the extent the Legislature appropriates funds in the Budget Act or another statute for this purpose.

California Penal Code § 13777.2. Advisory committee

(a) The Commission on the Status of Women shall convene an advisory committee consisting of one person appointed by the Attorney General and one person appointed by each of the organizations named in subdivision (b) of Section 13776 that chooses to appoint a member, and any other subject matter experts the commission may appoint. The advisory committee shall elect its chair and any other

officers of its choice.

(b) The advisory committee shall make a report by December 31, 2007, to the Committees on Health, Judiciary, and Public Safety of the Senate and Assembly, to the Attorney General, the Commission on Peace Officer Standards and Training, and the Commission on the Status of Women. The report shall evaluate the implementation of Chapter 899, Statutes of 2001 and the effectiveness of the plan developed by the Attorney General pursuant to subparagraph (A) of paragraph (4) of Section 13777. The report shall also include recommendations concerning whether the Legislature should extend or repeal the sunset dates in Section 13779, recommendations regarding any other legislation, and recommendations for any other actions by the Attorney General, Commission on Peace Officer Standards and Training, or the Commission on the Status of Women.

(c) The Commission on the Status of Women shall transmit the report of the advisory committee to the appropriate committees of the Legislature, including, but not limited to, the Committees on Health, Judiciary, and Public Safety in the Senate and Assembly, and make the report available to the public, including by posting it on the Commission on the Status of Women's Web site. To avoid production and distribution costs, the Commission on the Status of Women may submit the report electronically or as part of any other report that the Commission on the Status of Women submits to the Legislature.

(d) The Commission on Peace Officer Standards and Training shall make the telecourse that it produced in 2002 pursuant to subdivision (a) of Section 13778 available to the advisory committee. However, before providing the telecourse to the advisory committee or otherwise making it public, the commission shall remove the name and face of any person who appears in the telecourse as originally produced who informs the commission in writing that he or she has a reasonable apprehension that making the telecourse public without the removal will endanger his or her life or physical safety.

(e) Nothing in this section requires any state agency to pay for compensation, travel, or other expenses of any advisory committee member.

California Penal Code § 13778. Law enforcement courses

(a) The Commission on Peace Officer Standards and Training, utilizing available resources, shall develop a two-hour telecourse on anti-reproductive-rights crimes and make the telecourse available to all California law enforcement agencies as soon as practicable after chaptering of the act that enacts this title in the 2001-2002 session of the Legislature.

(b) Persons and organizations, including, but not limited to, subject-matter experts, may make application to the commission, as outlined in Article 3 (commencing with Section 1051) of Division 2 of Title 11 of the California Code of Regulations, for certification of a course designed to train law enforcement officers to carry out the legislative intent expressed in paragraph (1) of subdivision (d) of Section 1 of the act that enacts this title in the 2001-02 Regular Session.

(c) In developing the telecourse required by subdivision (a), and in considering any applications pursuant to subdivision (b), the commission, utilizing available resources, shall consult the Attorney General and other subject matter experts, except where a subject matter expert has submitted, or has an interest in, an application pursuant to subdivision (b).

California Penal Code § 13779. Repealer

This title shall remain in effect until January 1, 2009, and as of that date is repealed unless a later enacted statute deletes or extends that date.

(12) ABORTION FOR PRISONERS

California provides by statute for females in prison, jail or a juvenile facility to have an abortion, consistent with that which is allowed by law. The statutes addressing the issue are set out below.

California Penal Code § 3405. Abortion by State prison inmates

No condition or restriction upon the obtaining of an abortion by a prisoner, pursuant to the [Reproductive Privacy Act], other than those contained in that act, shall be imposed. Prisoners found to be pregnant and desiring abortions, shall be permitted to determine their eligibility for an abortion pursuant to law, and if determined to be eligible, shall be permitted to obtain an abortion.

The rights provided for females by this section shall be posted in at least one conspicuous place to which all female prisoners have access.

California Penal Code § 3406.
Abortion physician for State prisoners

Any female prisoner shall have the right to summon and receive the services of any physician and surgeon of her choice in order to determine whether she is pregnant. The warden may adopt reasonable rules and regulations with regard to the conduct of examinations to effectuate this determination.

If the prisoner is found to be pregnant, she is entitled to a determination of the extent of the medical services needed by her and to the receipt of these services from the physician and surgeon of her choice. Any expenses occasioned by the services of a physician and surgeon whose services are not provided by the institution shall be borne by the prisoner.

Any physician providing services pursuant to this section shall possess a current, valid, and unrevoked certificate to engage in the practice of medicine issued pursuant to Chapter 5 (commencing with Section 2000) of Division 2 of the Business and Professions Code.

The rights provided for prisoners by this section shall be posted in at least one conspicuous place to which all female prisoners have access.

California Penal Code § 3409.
Family planning for State prisoners

(a) Any woman inmate shall upon her request be allowed to continue to use materials necessary for (1) personal hygiene with regard to her menstrual cycle and reproductive system and (2) birth control measures as prescribed by her physician.

(b) Each and every woman inmate shall be furnished by the department with information and education regarding the availability of family planning services.

(c) Family planning services shall be offered to each and every woman inmate at least 60 days prior to a scheduled release date. Upon request any woman inmate shall be furnished by the department with the services of a licensed physician or she shall be furnished by the department or by any other agency which contracts with the department with services necessary to meet her family planning needs at the time of her release.

California Penal Code § 4028. Abortion by local jail inmates

No condition or restriction upon the obtaining of an abortion by a female detained in any local detention facility, pursuant to the [Reproductive Privacy Act], other than those contained in that act, shall be imposed. Females found to be pregnant and desiring abortions shall be permitted to determine their eligibility for an abortion pursuant to law, and if determined to be eligible, shall be permitted to obtain an abortion.

For the purposes of this section, "local detention facility" means any city, county, or regional facility used for the confinement of any female person for more than 24 hours.

The rights provided for females by this section shall be posted in at least one conspicuous place to which all female prisoners have access.

California Welfare & Institutions Code § 220.
Abortion for female in local juvenile facility

No condition or restriction upon the obtaining of an abortion by a female detained in any local juvenile facility, pursuant to the [Reproductive Privacy Act], other than those contained in that act, shall be imposed. Females found to be pregnant and desiring abortions, shall be permitted to determine their eligibility for an abortion pursuant to law, and if determined to be eligible, shall be permitted to obtain an abortion.

For the purposes of this section, "local juvenile facility" means any city, county, or regional facility used for the confinement of female juveniles for more than 24 hours.

The rights provided for females by this section shall be posted in at least one conspicuous place to which all females have access.

California Welfare & Institutions Code § 221.
Family planning for juvenile

(a) Any female confined in a state or local juvenile facility shall upon her request be allowed to continue to use materials necessary for (1) personal hygiene with regard to her menstrual cycle and reproductive system and (2) birth control measures as prescribed by her physician.

(b) Any female confined in a state or local juvenile facility shall upon her request be furnished by the confining state or local agency with information and education regarding prescription birth control measures.

(c) Family planning services shall be offered to each and every woman inmate at least 60 days prior to a scheduled release date. Upon request any woman inmate shall be furnished by the confining state or local agency with the services of a licensed physician, or she shall be furnished by the confining state or local agency or by any other agency which contracts with the confining state or local agency, with services necessary to meet her family planning needs at the time of her release.

(d) For the purposes of this section, "local juvenile facility" means any city, county, or regional facility used for the confinement of juveniles for more than 24 hours.

California Welfare & Institutions Code § 222.
Abortion by physician for juvenile in local facility

(a) Any female in the custody of a local juvenile facility shall have the right to summon and receive the services of any physician and surgeon of her choice in order to determine whether she is pregnant. If she is found to be pregnant, she is entitled to a determination of the extent of the medical services needed by her and to the receipt of those services from the physician and surgeon of her choice. Any expenses occasioned by the services of a physician and surgeon whose services are not provided by the facility shall be borne by the female.

(b) A ward shall not be shackled by the wrists, ankles, or both during labor, including during transport to a hospital, during delivery, and while in recovery after giving birth, subject to the security needs described in this section. Pregnant wards temporarily taken to a hospital outside the facility for the purposes of childbirth shall be transported in the least restrictive way possible, consistent with the legitimate security needs of each ward. Upon arrival at the hospital, once the ward has been declared by the attending physician to be in active labor, the ward shall not be shackled by the wrists, ankles, or both, unless deemed necessary for the safety and security of the ward, the staff, and the public.

(c) For purposes of this section, "local juvenile facility" means any city, county, or regional facility used for the confinement of juveniles for more than 24 hours.

(d) The rights provided to females by this section shall be posted in at least one conspicuous place to which all female wards have access.

California Welfare & Institutions Code § 1773.
Abortion for juvenile in state facility

(a) No condition or restriction upon the obtaining of an abortion by a female committed to the Division of Juvenile Facilities, [Reproductive Privacy Act], other than those contained in that act, shall be imposed. Females found to be pregnant and desiring abortions shall be permitted to determine their eligibility for an abortion pursuant to law, and if determined to be eligible, shall be permitted to obtain an abortion.

(b) The rights provided for females by this section shall be posted in at least one conspicuous place to which all females have access.

California Welfare & Institutions Code § 1774.
Pregnancy services for juvenile in state facility

(a) Any female who has been committed to the authority shall have the right to summon and receive the services of any physician and surgeon of her choice in order to determine whether she is pregnant. The director may adopt reasonable rules and regulations with regard to the conduct of examinations to effectuate that determination.

(b) If she is found to be pregnant, she is entitled to a determination of the extent of the medical services needed by her and to the receipt of those services from the physician and surgeon of her choice. Any expenses occasioned by the services of a physician and surgeon whose services are not provided by the facility shall be borne by the female.

(c) A ward who gives birth while under the jurisdiction of the Department of Corrections and Rehabilitation, Division of Juvenile Facilities, or a community treatment program has the right to the following services:

(1) Prenatal care.

(2) Access to prenatal vitamins.

(3) Childbirth education.

(d) A ward shall not be shackled by the wrists, ankles, or both during labor, including during transport to a hospital, during delivery, and while in recovery after giving birth, subject to the security needs described in this section. Pregnant wards temporarily taken to a hospital outside the facility for the purposes of childbirth shall be transported in the least restrictive way possible, consistent with the legitimate security needs of each ward. Upon arrival at the hospital, once the ward has been declared by the attending physician to be in active labor, the ward shall not be shackled by the wrists, ankles, or both, unless deemed necessary for the safety and security of the ward, the staff, and the public.

(e) Any physician providing services pursuant to this section shall possess a current, valid, and unrevoked certificate to engage in the practice of medicine issued pursuant to Chapter 5 (commencing with Section 2000) of Division 2 of the Business and Professions Code.

(f) The rights provided to females by this section shall be posted in at least one conspicuous place to which all female wards have access.

(13) TRAINING IN ABORTION SERVICES

California provides by statute that residency programs in obstetrics and gynecology include training in abortion services. The statute is set out below.

California Health & Safety Code § 123418.
Residency programs in obstetrics and gynecology

Subject to all other provisions of this article, all residency programs in obstetrics and gynecology shall comply with the program requirements for residency education in obstetrics and gynecology of the Accreditation Council for Graduate Medical Education, which require that in addition to education and training in in-patient care, the program in obstetrics-gynecology be geared toward the development of competence in the pro-

vision of ambulatory primary health care for women, including, but not limited to, training in the performance of abortion services.

(14) ABORTION BY MINORS

Under the laws of California no physician may perform an abortion upon an unemancipated minor unless he/she first obtains the written consent of either parent or the legal guardian of the minor. In compliance with federal constitutional law, California has provided a judicial waiver procedure for an unemancipated minor to obtain an abortion without parental or legal guardian consent. If an unemancipated minor elects not to seek, or cannot for any reason obtain consent from either of her parents or legal guardian, the minor may petition a trial court for a waiver of the consent requirement. A minor has a right to an attorney at the proceeding and if she cannot afford one, the court must appoint her an attorney. If a minor chooses, she may represent herself. The required parental or legal guardian consent may be waived if the court finds either (1) that the minor is mature and well-informed enough to make the abortion decision on her own, or (2) that performance of the abortion would be in the best interest of the minor. An expedited appeal is available to any minor to whom the court denies a waiver of consent.

Although California's requirements for a minor to obtain an abortion are similar to requirements in other states that have been approved by the United States Supreme Court, the California supreme court found the requirements violated the state constitution in *American Academy of Pediatrics v. Lungren*, 940 P.2d 797 (Cal. 1997). In spite of the decision by the California supreme court the state legislature has not repealed the requirements for a minor to obtain an abortion. The statute is set out below.

California Health & Safety Code § 123450.
Parental consent and judicial bypass

(a) Except in a medical emergency requiring immediate medical action, no abortion shall be performed upon an unemancipated minor unless she first has given her written consent to the abortion and also has obtained the written consent of one of her parents or legal guardian.

(b) If one or both of an unemancipated, pregnant minor's parents or her guardian refuse to consent to the performance of an abortion, or if the minor elects not to seek the consent of one or both of her parents or her guardian, an unemancipated pregnant minor may file a petition with the juvenile court. If, pursuant to this subdivision, a minor seeks a petition, the court shall assist the minor or person designated by the minor in preparing the petition and notices required pursuant to this section. The petition shall set forth with specificity the minor's reasons for the request. The court shall ensure that the minor's identity is confidential. The minor may file the petition using only her initials or a pseudonym. An unemancipated pregnant minor may participate in the proceedings in juvenile court on her own behalf, and the court may appoint a guardian ad litem for her. The court shall, however, advise her that she has a right to court-appointed counsel upon request. The hearing shall be set within three days of the filing of the petition. A notice shall be given to the minor of the date, time, and place of the hearing on the petition.

(c) At the hearing on a minor's petition brought pursuant to subdivision (b) for the authorization of an abortion, the court shall consider all evidence duly presented, and order either of the following:

(1) If the court finds that the minor is sufficiently mature and sufficiently informed to make the decision on her own regarding an abortion, and that the minor has, on that basis, consented thereto, the court shall grant the petition.

(2) If the court finds that the minor is not sufficiently mature and sufficiently informed to make the decision on her own regarding an abortion, the court shall then consider whether performance of the abortion would be in the best interest of the minor. In the event that the court finds that the performance of the abortion would be in the minor's best interest, the court shall grant the petition ordering the performance of the abortion without consent of, or notice to, the parents or guardian. In the event that the court finds that the performance of the abortion is not in the best interest of the minor, the court shall deny the petition.

Judgment shall be entered within one court day of submission of the matter.

(d) The minor may appeal the judgment of the juvenile court by filing a written notice of appeal at any time after the entry of the judgment. The Judicial Council shall prescribe, by rule, the practice and procedure on appeal and the time and manner in which any record on appeal shall be prepared and filed. These procedures shall require that the notice of the date, time, and place of hearing, which shall be set within five court days of the filing of notice of appeal, shall be mailed to the parties by the clerk of the court. The appellate court shall ensure that the minor's identity is confidential. The minor may file the petition using only her initials or a pseudonym. Judgment on appeal shall be entered within one court day of submission of the matter.

(e) No fees or costs incurred in connection with the procedures required by this section shall be chargeable to the minor or her parents, or either of them, or to her legal guardian.

(f) It is a misdemeanor, punishable by a fine of not more than one thousand dollars ($1,000), or by imprisonment in the county jail of up to 30 days, or both, for any person to knowingly perform an abortion on an unmarried or unemancipated minor without complying with the requirements of this section.

(15) USE OF FACILITIES AND PEOPLE

California provides by statute that the employees and physicians at hospitals that permit abortions are permitted to refuse to take part in abortions. The statute also provides that nonprofit, religious-based hospitals or clinics are not required to allow abortions at their facilities. In the case of *Brownfield v. Daniel Freeman Marina Hospital*, 256 Cal.Rptr. 240 (1989) the statute was discussed and applied. The statute is set out below.

California Health & Safety Code § 123420.
Refusal to participate in abortions

(a) No employer or other person shall require a physician, a registered nurse, a licensed vocational nurse, or any other person employed or with staff privileges at a hospital, facility, or clinic to directly participate in the induction or performance of an abortion, if the employee or other person has filed a written statement with the employer or the hospital, facility, or clinic indicating a moral, ethical, or religious basis for refusal to participate in the abortion. No such employee or person with staff privileges in a hospital, facility, or clinic shall be subject to any penalty or discipline by reason of his or her refusal to participate in an abortion. No such employee of a hospital, facility, or clinic that does not permit the performance of abortions, or person with staff privileges therein, shall be subject to any penalty or discipline on account of the person's participation in the performance of an abortion in other than the hospital, facility, or clinic. No employer shall refuse to employ any person because of the person's refusal for moral, ethical, or religious reasons to participate in an abortion, unless the person would be assigned in the normal course of business of any hospital, facility, or clinic to work in those parts of the hospital, facility, or clinic where abortion patients are cared for. No provision of this article prohibits any hospital, facility, or clinic that permits the performance of abortions from inquiring whether an employee or prospective employee would advance a moral, ethical, or religious basis for refusal to participate in an abortion before hiring

or assigning that person to that part of a hospital, facility, or clinic where abortion patients are cared for. The refusal of a physician, nurse, or any other person to participate or aid in the induction or performance of an abortion pursuant to this subdivision shall not form the basis of any claim for damages.

(b) No medical school or other facility for the education or training of physicians, nurses, or other medical personnel shall refuse admission to a person or penalize the person in any way because of the person's unwillingness to participate in the performance of an abortion for moral, ethical, or religious reasons. No hospital, facility, or clinic shall refuse staff privileges to a physician because of the physician's refusal to participate in the performance of abortion for moral, ethical, or religious reasons.

(c) Nothing in this article shall require a nonprofit hospital or other facility or clinic that is organized or operated by a religious corporation or other religious organization and licensed pursuant to Chapter 1 (commencing with Section 1200) or Chapter 2 (commencing with Section 1250) of Division 2, or any administrative officer, employee, agent, or member of the governing board thereof, to perform or to permit the performance of an abortion in the facility or clinic or to provide abortion services. No such nonprofit facility or clinic organized or operated by a religious corporation or other religious organization, nor its administrative officers, employees, agents, or members of its governing board shall be liable, individually or collectively, for failure or refusal to participate in any such act. The failure or refusal of any such corporation, unincorporated association or individual person to perform or to permit the performance of such medical procedures shall not be the basis for any disciplinary or other recriminatory action against such corporations, unincorporated associations, or individuals. Any such facility or clinic that does not permit the performance of abortions on its premises shall post notice of that proscription in an area of the facility or clinic that is open to patients and prospective admittees.

(d) This section shall not apply to medical emergency situations and spontaneous abortions. Any violation of this section is a misdemeanor.

(16) FETAL EXPERIMENTATION

California has provided by statute for banning experimentation on any aborted product of human conception, except fetal remains. The statutes addressing the issue are set out below.

California Health & Safety Code § 123440.
Fetal experimentation

(a) It is unlawful for any person to use any aborted product of human conception, other than fetal remains, for any type of scientific or laboratory research or for any other kind of experimentation or study, except to protect or preserve the life and health of the fetus. "Fetal remains," as used in this section, means a lifeless product of conception regardless of the duration of pregnancy. A fetus shall not be deemed to be lifeless for the purposes of this section, unless there is an absence of a discernible heartbeat.

(b) In addition to any other criminal or civil liability that may be imposed by law, any violation of this section constitutes unprofessional conduct within the meaning of the Medical Practice Act, Chapter 5 (commencing with Section 2000) of Division 2 of the Business and Professions Code.

California Health & Safety Code § 123445.
Disposal of fetal remains

(a) Except as provided in subdivision (b), at the conclusion of any scientific or laboratory research or any other kind of experimentation or study upon fetal remains, the fetal remains shall be promptly interred or disposed of by incineration.

Storage of the fetal remains prior to the completion of the research, experimentation, or study shall be in a place not open to the public, and the method of storage shall prevent any deterioration of the fetal remains that would create a health hazard.

(b) Subdivision (a) shall not apply to public or private educational institutions. Any violation of this section is a misdemeanor.

(17) HUMAN CLONING

California prohibits human cloning and the sale of fetal material for the purpose cloning. The statutes addressing the issue are set out below.

California Health & Safety Code § 24185. Cloning ban

(a) No person shall clone a human being or engage in human reproductive cloning.

(b) No person shall purchase or sell an ovum, zygote, embryo, or fetus for the purpose of cloning a human being.

(c) For purposes of this chapter, the following definitions apply:

(1) "Clone" means the practice of creating or attempting to create a human being by transferring the nucleus from a human cell from whatever source into a human or nonhuman egg cell from which the nucleus has been removed for the purpose of, or to implant, the resulting product to initiate a pregnancy that could result in the birth of a human being.

(2) "Department" means the State Department of Health Services.

(3) "Human reproductive cloning" means the creation of a human fetus that is substantially genetically identical to a previously born human being. The department may adopt, interpret, and update regulations, as necessary, for purposes of more precisely defining the procedures that constitute human reproductive cloning.

California Health & Safety Code § 24186.
Advisory committee on human cloning

(a)(1) The department shall establish an advisory committee for purposes of advising the Legislature and the Governor on human cloning and other issues relating to human biotechnology. The committee shall be composed of at least nine members, appointed by the Director of Health Services, who shall serve without compensation.

(2) The committee shall include at least one representative from the areas of medicine, religion, biotechnology, genetics, law, and from the general public. The committee shall also include not less than three independent bioethicists who possess the qualifications described in paragraph (3).

(3) The independent bioethicists selected to serve on the committee shall reflect a representative range of religious and ethical perspectives in California regarding the issues of human cloning and human biotechnology. An independent bioethicist serving on the advisory committee shall not be employed by, consult with or have consulted with, or have any direct or indirect financial interest, in any corporation engaging in research relating to human cloning or human biotechnology. A person with any affiliation to the grant-funded cloning research programs operated by the University of California or the California State University is also prohibited from serving as a bioethicist on the advisory committee.

(b) On or before December 31, 2003, and annually thereafter, the department shall report to the Legislature and the Governor regarding the activities of the committee.

(c) The activities of the committee shall, to the extent that funds are available, be funded by the department out of existing resources.

California Health & Safety Code § 24187.
Administrative penalties

For violations of Section 24185, the State Director of Health Services may, after appropriate notice and opportunity for hearing, by order, levy administrative penalties as follows:

(a) If the violator is a corporation, firm, clinic, hospital, laboratory, or research facility, by a civil penalty of not more than one million dollars ($1,000,000) or the applicable amount under subdivision (c), whichever is greater.

(b) If the violator is an individual, by a civil penalty of not more than two hundred fifty thousand dollars ($250,000) or the applicable amount under subdivision (c), whichever is greater.

(c) If any violator derives pecuniary gain from a violation of this section, the violator may be assessed a civil penalty of not more than an amount equal to the amount of the gross gain multiplied by two.

(d) The administrative penalties shall be paid to the General Fund.

California Business and Professions Code § 16004.
City license revocation

Any license issued [by a city] to a business pursuant to this chapter shall be revoked for a violation of Section 24185 of the Health and Safety Code, relating to human cloning.

California Business and Professions Code § 16105.
County license revocation

Any license issued [by a county] to a business pursuant to this chapter shall be revoked for a violation of Section 24185 of the Health and Safety Code, relating to human cloning.

(18) HEALTH CARE SERVICE PLAN ABORTION NOTIFICATION REQUIREMENTS

California requires by statute that health care service plans inform potential participants that certain providers used by the plan may not offer abortion and other services. The statutes addressing the matter are set out below.

California Health & Safety Code § 1363.02.
Reproductive health services information

(a) The Legislature finds and declares that the right of every patient to receive basic information necessary to give full and informed consent is a fundamental tenet of good public health policy and has long been the established law of this state. Some hospitals and other providers do not provide a full range of reproductive health services and may prohibit or otherwise not provide sterilization, infertility treatments, abortion, or contraceptive services, including emergency contraception. It is the intent of the Legislature that every patient be given full and complete information about the health care services available to allow patients to make well informed health care decisions.

(b) On or before July 1, 2001, a health care service plan that covers hospital, medical, and surgical benefits shall do both of the following:

(1) Include the following statement, in at least 12-point boldface type, at the beginning of each provider directory:

"Some hospitals and other providers do not provide one or more of the following services that may be covered under your plan contract and that you or your family member might need: family planning; contraceptive services, including emergency contraception; sterilization, including tubal ligation at the time of labor and delivery; infertility treatments; or abortion. You should obtain more information before you enroll. Call your prospective doctor, medical group, independent practice association, or clinic, or call the health plan at (insert the health plan's membership services number or other appropriate number that individuals can call for assistance) to ensure that you can obtain the health care services that you need."

(2) Place the statement described in paragraph (1) in a prominent location on any provider directory posted on the health plan's website, if any, and include this statement in a conspicuous place in the plan's evidence of coverage and disclosure forms.

(c) A health care service plan shall not be required to provide the statement described in paragraph (1) of subdivision (b) in a service area in which none of the hospitals, health facilities, clinics, medical groups, or independent practice associations with which it contracts limit or restrict any of the reproductive services described in the statement.

(d) This section shall not apply to specialized health care service plans or Medicare supplement plans.

California Insurance Code § 10604.1.
Disability insurer health services information

(a) The Legislature finds and declares that the right of every patient to receive basic information necessary to give full and informed consent is a fundamental tenet of good public health policy and has long been the established law of this state. Some hospitals and other providers do not provide a full range of reproductive health services and may prohibit or otherwise not provide sterilization, infertility treatments, abortion, or contraceptive services, including emergency contraception. It is the intent of the Legislature that every patient be given full and complete information about the health care services available to allow patients to make well informed health care decisions.

(b) On or before July 1, 2001, every disability insurer that provides coverage for hospital, medical, or surgical benefits, and which provides a list of network providers to prospective insureds and insureds, shall do both of the following:

(1) Include the following statement, in at least 12-point boldface type, at the beginning of each provider directory:

"Some hospitals and other providers do not provide one or more of the following services that may be covered under your policy and that you or your family member might need: family planning; contraceptive services, including emergency contraception; sterilization, including tubal ligation at the time of labor and delivery; infertility treatments; or abortion. You should obtain more information before you become a policyholder or select a network provider. Call your prospective doctor or clinic, or call the insurer at (insert the insurer's membership services number or other appropriate number that individuals can call for assistance) to ensure that you can obtain the health care services that you need."

(2) Place the statement described in paragraph (1) in a prominent location on any provider directory posted on the insurer's website, if any, and include this statement in a conspicuous place in the insurer's evidence of coverage and disclosure forms.

(c) A disability insurer shall not be required to provide the statement described in paragraph (1) of subdivision (b) in a service area in which none of the hospitals, health facilities, clinics, medical groups, or independent practice associations with which it contracts limit or restrict any of the reproductive services described in the statement.

(d) This section shall not apply to vision-only, dental-only, accident-only, specified disease, hospital indemnity, Medicare supplement, long-term care, or disability income insurance.

(19) INJURY TO PREGNANT WOMAN

California has made it a criminal offense to cause the death of a fetus through injury to a pregnant woman. The statute addressing the issue is set out below.

California Penal Code § 187. Murder defined

(a) Murder is the unlawful killing of a human being, or a fetus, with malice aforethought.

(b) This section shall not apply to any person who commits an act that results in the death of a fetus if any of the following apply:

(1) The act complied with the Therapeutic Abortion Act, Article 2 (commencing with Section 123400) of Chapter 2 of Part 2 of Division 106 of the Health and Safety Code.

(2) The act was committed by a holder of a physician's and surgeon's certificate, as defined in the Business and Professions Code, in a case where, to a medical certainty, the result of childbirth would be death of the mother of the fetus or where her death from childbirth, although not medically certain, would be substantially certain or more likely than not.

(3) The act was solicited, aided, abetted, or consented to by the mother of the fetus.

(c) Subdivision (b) shall not be construed to prohibit the prosecution of any person under any other provision of law.

California Pro-Life Council

California Pro-Life Council (CPLC) is a California based pro-life organization that began in the 1970s as an affiliate of National Right

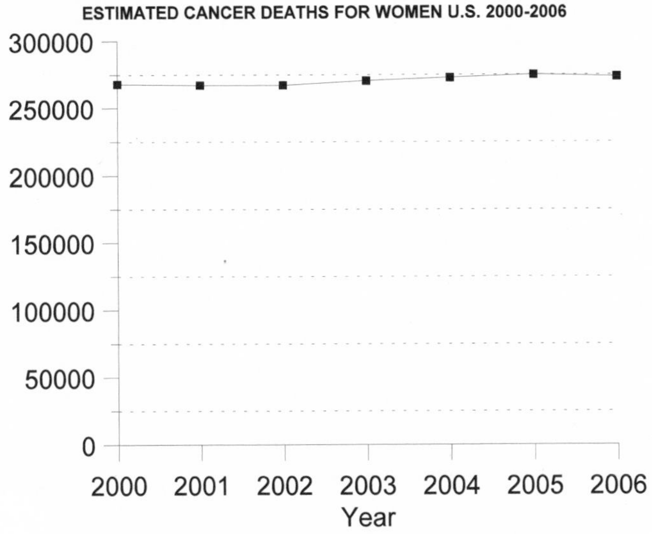

Source: **American Cancer Society.**

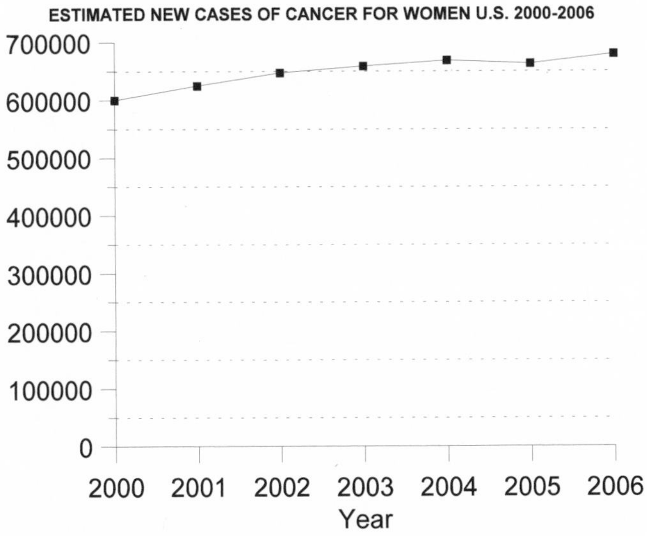

Source: **American Cancer Society.**

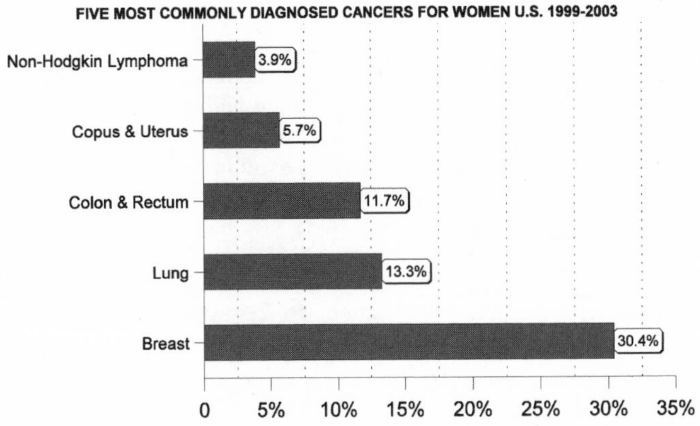

Source: **North American Association of Central Cancer Registries.**

to Life Committee. CPLC believes that abortion can be ended through working within the law to change the law, and by changing public opinion through education. To this end, CPLC provides educational forums for the public, and works with legislators to fashion laws aimed at the eventual elimination of abortion. *See also* **Pro-Life Organizations**

Cancer and Pregnancy

There are over 100 different cancer diseases that can affect different parts of the human body. More than 1 million Americans develop cancer each year. It is the second leading cause of death after heart disease in the United States. Cancer is the major cause of death in women between the ages of 35 and 74. Although cancer diseases generally are not known to transfer from a pregnant woman to her fetus, cancer during pregnancy carries the risk of requiring a therapeutic abortion in order to fully treat the woman, or exposing the fetus to birth defects. Generally, if a cancer is in its early stage during a pregnancy, treatment that may harm the fetus can be held off until the child is born.

A late stage cancer poses a risk to the fetus because of the aggressive methods of treatment that may be necessary to save the life of the mother. The primary methods of cancer treatment are: surgery, radiation therapy and chemotherapy. Utilization of radiation therapy or chemotherapy carries the risk of causing birth defects in a fetus. Surgically removing a cancer becomes problematic for the life of the fetus depending upon the location of the cancer, e.g., cancer in the uterus or cervix. *See also* **Breast Cancer; Breast Cancer and Abortion; Cervical Cancer; Endometrial Cancer; Fallopian Tube Cancer; Gestational Trophoblastic Tumors; Ovarian Cancer; Sarcoma of the Uterus; Vaginal Cancer; Vulva Cancer**

Candidiasis *see* **Vaginitis**

Cano, Sandra Besing

Sandra Besing-Cano (b. 1948) was the real name of the plaintiff in the 1973 United States Supreme Court decision in *Doe v. Bolton* which, together with *Roe v. Wade*, legalized abortion in the nation. In the mid–1990s Cano publicly repudiated the facts underlying the case. She alleged that while she was pregnant, she sought out legal advice to regain custody of her two children who had been taken away by a Georgia child welfare agency; and to also obtain legal help in divorcing her husband. Cano alleged that the attorney she consulted spoke with her about having an abortion. Cano refused to have an abortion and stated that she was opposed to abortion. According to Cano, the lawyer proceeded to file the lawsuit seeking to challenge Georgia's abortion laws, even though Cano did not want an abortion. Cano eventually gave birth and placed the child up for adoption. *See also* **Doe v. Bolton; McCorvey, Norma**

Care Net

Care Net is a pro-life organization that supports a network of over 600 pregnancy help centers the United States and Canada. These centers provide free pregnancy tests, counseling and other practical help to pregnant women. Care Net also trains 600 center leaders at an annual national conference, in addition to providing expert legal support. *See also* **Pregnancy Help Centers**

Carey v. Population Services International

Forum: United States Supreme Court.

Case Citation: Carey v. Population Services International, 431 U.S. 678 (1977).

Date Argued: January 10, 1977.

Date of Decision: June 9, 1977.

Opinion of Court: Brennan, J., in which Stewart, Marshall, Blackmun, White, Powell and Stevens, JJ., joined.

Concurring Opinion: White, J.

Concurring Opinion: Powell, J.

Concurring Opinion: Stevens, J.

Dissenting Without Comment: Burger, C. J.

Dissenting Opinion: Rehnquist, J.

Counsel for Appellants: Arlene R. Silverman, Assistant Attorney General of New York, argued; on the brief were Louis J. Lefkowitz, Attorney General, and Samuel A. Hirshowitz, First Assistant Attorney General.

Counsel for Appellees: Michael N. Pollet argued; on the brief was Steven Delibert.

Amicus Brief for Appellants: None.

Amicus Brief for Appellees: Melvin L. Wulf, Judith M. Mears, and Rena Uviller for the American Civil Liberties Union; and by Harriet F. Pilpel and Eve W. Paul for the Planned Parenthood Federation of America et al.

Issue Presented: Whether the constitution was violated by a New York statute that made it a crime (1) for any person to sell or distribute any contraceptive of any kind to a minor under the age of 16 years; (2) for anyone other than a licensed pharmacist to distribute contraceptives to persons 16 or over; and (3) for anyone, including licensed pharmacists, to advertise or display contraceptives?

Case Holding: The constitution prohibited enforcement of a New York statute that made it a crime (1) for any person to sell or distribute any contraceptive of any kind to a minor under the age of 16 years; (2) for anyone other than a licensed pharmacist to distribute contraceptives to persons 16 or over; and (3) for anyone, including licensed pharmacists, to advertise or display contraceptives.

Background facts of case: Under a New York statute, § 6811(8) it was made a crime (1) for any person to sell or distribute any contraceptive of any kind to a minor under the age of 16 years; (2) for anyone other than a licensed pharmacist to distribute contraceptives to persons 16 or over; and (3) for anyone, including licensed pharmacists, to advertise or display contraceptives. As a consequence of this statute the appellees, contraceptive providers, filed a lawsuit in a federal district court in New York challenging the constitutionality of the statute. The appellants, state officials, were named as defendants. The district court held that the statute violated the constitution. The Supreme Court granted certiorari to consider the issue.

Majority opinion by Justice Brennan: Justice Brennan found that New York's statute contravened the constitution and was therefore unenforceable. He addressed each aspect of the statute as follows:

> Limiting the distribution of nonprescription contraceptives to licensed pharmacists clearly imposes a significant burden on the right of the individuals to use contraceptives if they choose to do so. The burden is, of course, not as great as that under a total ban on distribution. Nevertheless, the restriction of distribution channels to a small fraction of the total number of possible retail outlets renders contraceptive devices considerably less accessible to the public, reduces the opportunity for privacy of selection and purchase, and lessens the possibility of price competition.... Just as in Griswold v. Connecticut, where the right of married persons to use contraceptives was diluted or adversely affected by permitting a conviction for giving advice as to its exercise, so here, to sanction a medical restriction upon distribution of a contraceptive not proved hazardous to health would impair the exercise of the constitutional right....
>
> Appellants ... suggest that 6811 (8) furthers other state interests. But none of them is comparable to those the Court has heretofore recognized as compelling. Appellants argue that the limitation of retail sales of nonmedical contraceptives to pharmacists (1) expresses a proper concern that young people not sell contraceptives; (2) allows purchasers to inquire as to the relative qualities of the varying products and prevents anyone from tampering with them; and (3) facilitates enforcement of the other provisions of the statute. The first hardly can justify the statute's incursion into constitutionally protected rights, and in any event the statute is obviously not substantially related to any goal of preventing young people from selling contraceptives. Nor is the statute designed to serve as a quality control device. Nothing in the record suggests that pharmacists are particularly qualified to give advice on the merits of different nonmedical contraceptives, or that such advice is more necessary to the purchaser of contraceptive products than to consumers of other nonprescription items. Why pharmacists are better able or more inclined than other retailers to prevent tampering with prepackaged products, or, if they are, why contraceptives are singled out for this special protection, is also unexplained. As to ease of enforcement, the prospect of additional administrative inconvenience has not been thought to justify invasion of fundamental constitutional rights.
>
> The District Court also held unconstitutional, as applied to nonprescription contraceptives, the provision of 6811 (8) prohibiting the distribution of contraceptives to those under 16 years of age. Appellants contend that this provision of the statute is constitutionally permissible as a regulation of the morality of minors, in furtherance of the State's policy against promiscuous sexual intercourse among the young....
>
> Since the State may not impose a blanket prohibition, or even a blanket requirement of parental consent, on the choice of a minor to terminate her pregnancy, the constitutionality of a blanket prohibition of the distribution of contraceptives to minors is a fortiori foreclosed. The State's interests in protection of the mental and physical health of the pregnant minor, and in protection of potential life are clearly more implicated by the abortion decision than by the decision to use a nonhazardous contraceptive.
>
> Appellants argue, however, that significant state interests are served by restricting minors' access to contraceptives, because free availability to minors of contraceptives would lead to increased sexual activity among the young, in violation of the policy of New York to discourage such behavior. The argument is that minors' sexual activity may be deterred by increasing the hazards attendant on it. The same argument, however, would support a ban on abortions for minors, or indeed support a prohibition on abortions, or access to contraceptives, for the unmarried, whose sexual activity is also against the public policy of many States. Yet, in each of these areas, the Court has rejected the argument, noting in Roe v. Wade, that no court or commentator has taken the argument seriously....
>
> The District Court's holding that the prohibition of any advertisement or display of contraceptives is unconstitutional was clearly correct. Only last Term Virginia Pharmacy Bd. v. Virginia Citizens Consumer Council held that a State may not completely suppress the dissemination of concededly truthful information

about entirely lawful activity, even when that information could be categorized as commercial speech. Just as in that case, the statute challenged here seeks to suppress completely any information about the availability and price of contraceptives.... [T]here can be no contention that the regulation is a mere time, place, and manner restriction, or that it prohibits only misleading or deceptive advertisements, or that the transactions proposed in the forbidden advertisements are themselves illegal in any way.

Disposition of case: The judgment of the district court was affirmed.

Concurring opinion by Justice White: Justice White concurred in the Courts judgment. He wrote separately to point out that he did "not regard the opinion ... as declaring unconstitutional any state law forbidding extramarital sexual relations." He also stated that "the State has not demonstrated that the prohibition against distribution of contraceptives to minors measurably contributes to the deterrent purposes which the State advances as justification for the restriction."

Concurring opinion by Justice Powell: Justice Powell concurred in the Court's judgment. He believed, however, that the Court may have gone too far in its reasoning. Justice Powell wrote as follows:

> The Court apparently would subject all state regulation affecting adult sexual relations to the strictest standard of judicial review. Under today's decision, such regulation may be justified only by compelling state interests, and must be narrowly drawn to express only those interests. Even regulation restricting only the sexual activity of the young must now be justified by a significant state interest, a standard that is apparently less rigorous than the standard the Court would otherwise apply. In my view, the extraordinary protection the Court would give to all personal decisions in matters of sex is neither required by the Constitution nor supported by our prior decisions....
>
> In sum, the Court quite unnecessarily extends the reach of cases like Griswold and Roe. Neither our precedents nor sound principles of constitutional analysis require state legislation to meet the exacting compelling state interest standard whenever it implicates sexual freedom. In my view, those cases make clear that that standard has been invoked only when the state regulation entirely frustrates or heavily burdens the exercise of constitutional rights in this area. This is not to say that other state regulation is free from judicial review. But a test so severe that legislation rarely can meet it should be imposed by courts with deliberate restraint in view of the respect that properly should be accorded legislative judgments.

Concurring opinion by Justice Stevens: Justice Stevens agreed with the judgment of the Court. He wrote separately to make the following points:

> Common sense indicates that many young people will engage in sexual activity regardless of what the New York Legislature does; and further, that the incidence of venereal disease and premarital pregnancy is affected by the availability or unavailability of contraceptives. Although young persons theoretically may avoid those harms by practicing total abstention, inevitably many will not. The statutory prohibition denies them and their parents a choice which, if available, would reduce their exposure to disease or unwanted pregnancy.
>
> The State's asserted justification is a desire to inhibit sexual conduct by minors under 16. Appellants do not seriously contend that if contraceptives are available, significant numbers of minors who now abstain from sex will cease abstaining because they will no longer fear pregnancy or disease. Rather appellants' central argument is that the statute has the important symbolic effect of communicating disapproval of sexual activity by minors. In essence, therefore, the statute is defended as a form of propaganda, rather than a regulation of behavior.
>
> Although the State may properly perform a teaching function, it seems to me that an attempt to persuade by inflicting harm on the listener is an unacceptable means of conveying a message that is otherwise legitimate. The propaganda technique used in this case significantly increases the risk of unwanted pregnancy and venereal disease. It is as though a State decided to dramatize its disapproval of motorcycles by forbidding the use of safety helmets. One need not posit a constitutional right to ride a motorcycle to characterize such a restriction as irrational and perverse.
>
> Even as a regulation of behavior, such a statute would be defective. Assuming that the State could impose a uniform sanction upon young persons who risk self-inflicted harm by operating motorcycles, or by engaging in sexual activity, surely that sanction could not take the form of deliberately injuring the cyclist or infecting the promiscuous child. If such punishment may not be administered deliberately, after trial and a finding of guilt, it manifestly cannot be imposed by a legislature, indiscriminately and at random. This kind of government-mandated harm, is, in my judgment, appropriately characterized as a deprivation of liberty without due process of law.

Dissenting without comment by Chief Justice Burger: The Chief Justice dissented from the Court's decision, but gave no statement as to why he disagreed with the Court.

Dissenting opinion by Justice Rehnquist: Justice Rehnquist disagreed with the Court's decision. He wrote as follows:

> ... There comes a point when endless and ill-considered extension of principles originally formulated in quite different cases produces such an indefensible result that no logic chopping can possibly make the fallacy of the result more obvious. The Court here in effect holds that the First and Fourteenth Amendments not only guarantee full and free debate before a legislative judgment as to the moral dangers to which minors within the jurisdiction of the State should not be subjected, but goes further and absolutely prevents the representatives of the majority from carrying out such a policy after the issues have been fully aired.
>
> No questions of religious belief, compelled allegiance to a secular creed, or decisions on the part of married couples as to procreation, are involved here. New York has simply decided that it wishes to discourage unmarried minors under 16 from having promiscuous sexual intercourse with one another. Even the Court would scarcely go so far as to say that this is not a subject with which the New York Legislature may properly concern itself.
>
> That legislature has not chosen to deny to a pregnant woman, after the fait accompli of pregnancy, the one remedy which would enable her to terminate an unwanted pregnancy. It has instead sought to deter the conduct which will produce such faits accomplis. The majority of New York's citizens are in effect told that however deeply they may be concerned about the problem of promiscuous sex and intercourse among unmarried teenagers, they may not adopt this means of dealing with it. The Court holds that New York may not use its police power to legislate in the interests of its concept of the public morality as it pertains to minors. The Court's denial of a power so fundamental to self-government must, in the long run, prove to be but a temporary departure from a wise and heretofore settled course of adjudication to the contrary. I would reverse the judgment of the District Court.

Cat Cry Syndrome

Cat cry syndrome is a genetic disorder involving the deletion of information on chromosome 5. The cause of this defect is not known. Infants with the disorder commonly have a distinctive cat-like cry — hence the name given to the syndrome. The disorder causes severe mental retardation, low birthweight, small head, and partial webbing of fingers or toes. No specific treatment is available for the disorder. *See also* **Birth Defects and Abortion**

Catholic Campaign for America

The Catholic Campaign for America (CCA) was created as a lay Catholic pro-life organization that is headquartered in Michigan. CCA has essentially adopted and promoted the official position of the Catholic Church on abortion. The organization takes the position that from the first moment of conception, human life must be recognized as having the rights of a person. It views abortion as morally wrong and a sin. CCA was formed for the purpose of energizing and mobilizing Catholics to renew their faith and help transform American public policy, culture and society. The organization utilizes educational resources and seminars to provide a forum in which Catholics may learn about Catholic social teaching on abortion. *See also* **Pro-Life Organizations; Religion and Abortion**

Catholics for a Free Choice

Catholics for a Free Choice (CFC) is an organization that was formed in 1973 by Joan Harriman, Patricia Fogarty McQuillan, and Meta Mulcahy. The national headquarters of CFC is in Washington, D.C. The organization is headed by its president, Jon O'Brien. CFC was created to engage in research, policy analysis, education, and advocacy on issues of gender equality and reproductive health. A guiding belief held by CFC is that Catholic bishops do not represent the views of Catholic people on reproductive rights issues, including abortion. CFC has worked to organize and educate Catholic women and men who support legal access to abortion. The organization conducts seminars and workshops, as well as providing technical assistance, publishing and collaboration with other organizations. CFC also publishes a quarterly newsjournal called *Conscience*. *See also* **Pro-Choice Organizations; Religion and Abortion**

Center for Reproductive Law and Policy *see* **Center for Reproductive Rights**

Center for Reproductive Rights

The Center for Reproductive Rights (CRR) (formerly the Center for Reproductive Law and Policy) was founded in 1992 by reproductive rights attorneys and activists. CRR is headquartered in New York City. The president of CRR is Nancy Northup. CRR was created to protect the right of women to abortion. The organization believes that laws and policies that protect and advance reproductive rights of women are essential. Such laws and policies should secure women's access to basic health services, including contraception, abortion, education, and safe pregnancy care. CRR is committed to promoting reproductive rights for every individual; securing universal, safe and affordable contraception; ensuring safe, accessible, and legal abortion; advancing the reproductive rights of adolescents; achieving equal access to reproductive health care for low-income and minority women; and protecting health care providers from violence and coercion.

Some of the accomplishments of CRR include (1) investigating the laws and policies governing women's reproductive lives in 50 countries around the globe through its publication of the Women of the World series; (2) securing and restoring Medicaid funds for low-income women who need abortions through state and federal lawsuits; (3) taking part in the case of *Ferguson v. City of Charleston*, in which the United States Supreme Court struck down a drug testing scheme that targeted pregnant women; (4) taking part in the case of *Stenberg v. Carhart*, in which the United States Supreme Court struck down Nebraska's ban on partial-birth abortion; and (5) gaining approval for emergency contraception by the Food and Drug Administration and petitioning for its availability over-the-counter. *See also* **Pro-Choice Organizations**

Cerebral Palsy

Cerebral palsy is a term used to describe a group of disorders caused by injury to the parts of the brain that control the ability to use muscles. In most instances, the cause of the brain abnormality is unknown. More than 80 percent of people with cerebral palsy developed it either before they were born or in infancy. Every year about 8,000 infants and approximately 1,500 pre-school age children are diagnosed with cerebral palsy. About 500,000 people in the United States have some form of the disease.

Some of the known causes of the disease include: infections during pregnancy; insufficient oxygen for the fetus; prematurity; complications of labor and delivery; incompatibility between the blood of the mother and the fetus. Roughly 10 percent of children with cerebral palsy acquire it after birth, as a result of brain injuries that occur during the first few years of life.

Symptoms of cerebral palsy differ from person to person, but some common symptoms include: difficulty with fine motor tasks, maintaining balance or walking, involuntary movements, seizures, and mental impairment. Cerebral palsy is a lifelong disorder. In most instances, the factor which caused the disorder may not be preventable. However, proper prenatal care can improve the odds of giving birth to a child without the disorder.

Treatment for cerebral palsy is determined by the symptoms exhibited by the child. Some common treatments include medications, physical therapy, special education, walkers, wheel chairs, braces, glasses, hearing aids, and institutionalization.

There are four primary types of cerebral palsy: spastic, athetoid, ataxic and mixed.

Spastic. Spastic cerebral palsy refers to disorders that cause stiff and difficult movement. This condition can manifest itself in just the legs, or one side of the body, or in the legs and arms. Roughly 70 percent of cerebral palsy victims have the spastic form.

Athetoid. Athetoid cerebral palsy refers to involuntary and uncontrolled movement. This form of the disease can make it difficult to sit or walk. It may also affect speech. About 20 percent of cerebral palsy victims have the athetoid form.

Ataxic. Ataxic cerebral palsy involves a faulty sense of balance and depth perception. Around 10 percent of cerebral palsy victims have the ataxic form.

Mixed. It is not rare for some people to have more than one type of cerebral palsy. The most common mixed cerebral palsy is spasticity and athetoid. *See also* **Birth Defects and Abortion**

Cervical Cancer

Cervical cancer is a disease in which malignant cancer cells are formed in the tissues of the cervix. The disease does not form suddenly. There is a gradual change from a normal cervix, to precancer cervix, to cancer cervix. This process usually takes several years but sometimes can happen in less than a year. For many women, precancerous changes may go away without any treatment. In others, if the precancers are treated, true cancers can be prevented.

Cervical cancer was once the most common cause of cancer death for women in the United States. However, between 1955 and 1992 the number of deaths from cervical cancer in the nation declined by 74 percent. The primary reason for this decline was the increased use of the Pap smear test (a screening procedure that permits diagnosis of precancer and early cancer). There were roughly 11,892 women diagnosed with cervical cancer in the United States in the year 2004. An estimated 3,850 deaths occurred from the disease in the same year.

Usually cervical cancer in its earliest stages will not display any symptoms. When symptoms do appear the most common are: persistent vaginal discharge; abnormal vaginal bleeding; loss of appetite and weight loss; fatigue; pelvic, back, or leg pain; and leaking of urine or

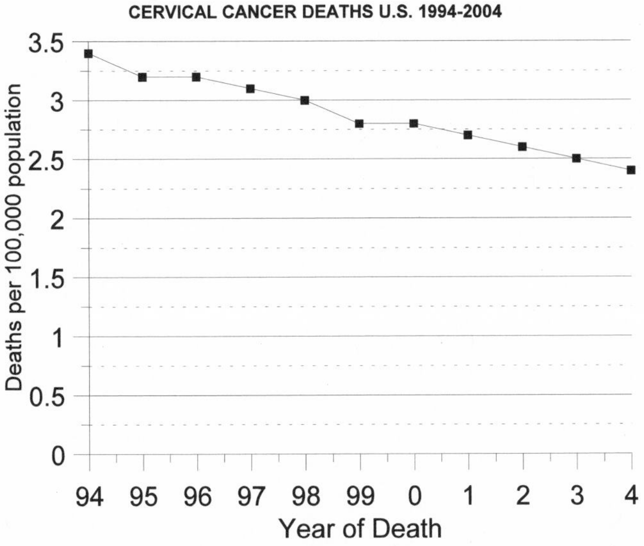

Source: **National Cancer Institute.**

feces. Risk factors associated with cervical cancer include: early age of first sexual intercourse; birth control pill; smoking; poor diet; multiple sexual partners; infections from genital herpes or chlamydia; and weakened immune systems.

Roughly 1 percent of all cervical cancers occur in pregnant women or women who recently gave birth. It is the most commonly diagnosed malignancy during pregnancy. The fact of pregnancy generally has no adverse effect on cervical cancer, and the cervical cancer has no effect on the pregnancy. However, there is a 20 percent risk of miscarriage during the first trimester, if the cervix is manipulated inappropriately in trying to obtain tissue for analysis. Also, certain treatment methods, if used, would require a therapeutic abortion or could cause birth defects.

The method of treatment for cervical cancer depends on the type of cancer; its stage, size and shape; the age and general health of the woman; and a woman's desire to bear children after treatment. In its earliest stages, cervical cancer may be cured by destroying the precancerous or cancerous tissue. This may be done in various ways without removing the uterus so that a woman is still capable of having children. In other cases, a removal of the uterus (hysterectomy) is performed, with or without removal of the ovaries.

In the more advanced stages of the disease, a hysterectomy may be performed which requires removal of the uterus and much of the surrounding tissues, including internal lymph nodes; or it may be necessary to remove all of the organs of the pelvis, including the bladder and rectum. Radiation and chemotherapy may be used before or after surgery.

Many factors determine the outcome of cervical cancer after treatment, including the type of cancer and its stage of development. The 5-year survival rate for women with cervical cancer, who had appropriate treatment, ranges from 85 percent to 14 percent. *See also* **Cancer and Pregnancy; Therapeutic Abortion**

Cervical Cap

A cervical cap is a contraceptive device. It is a thimble shaped device that fits snugly onto the cervix. It is used in conjunction with a spermicide cream or jelly. Cervical caps keep sperm from joining the egg by blocking the opening to the uterus and preventing sperm from entering. The spermicide cream or jelly that is applied to the cervical cap immobilizes sperm. Out of every 100 women who use a cervical cap, about 18 will become pregnant during the first year of use. Cervical caps are known to offer some protection against certain sexually transmitted diseases such as gonorrhea and chlamydia.

In order to use a cervical cap a pelvic examination by a health care provider is needed to determine the correct size. A cervical cap may be purchased at a drugstore or clinic. In order to use a cervical cap properly it must be inserted before sexual intercourse, and must remain in place about eight hours after intercourse. A cervical cap should not be left in place for more than 48 hours. Side effects from use of a cervical cap include: bladder infections; toxic shock syndrome (high fever, diarrhea, vomiting, sore throat, body aches, dizziness, and weakness); and abnormal cell growth. *See also* **Contraception**

Cervical Pregnancy *see* **Ectopic Pregnancy**

Cervix *see* **Cervical Cancer; Female Reproductive System**

Chadwick's Sign

Chadwick's sign is an indicator of pregnancy. It involves a bluish coloration of the vulva, vagina and cervix at about 6 to 8 weeks after conception. *See also* **Amenorrhea; Hegar's Sign; Pregnancy Test**

Chancroid

Chancroid is a sexually transmitted disease caused by a bacterium called *Haemophilus ducreyi.* The disease may be transmitted through oral, vaginal, or anal intercourse. Chancroid produces painful sores on the skin of the genitals. The symptoms in women include painful urination or defecation, painful intercourse, rectal bleeding, or vaginal discharge. Symptoms usually appear four to seven days after exposure. The disease is not common in the United States.

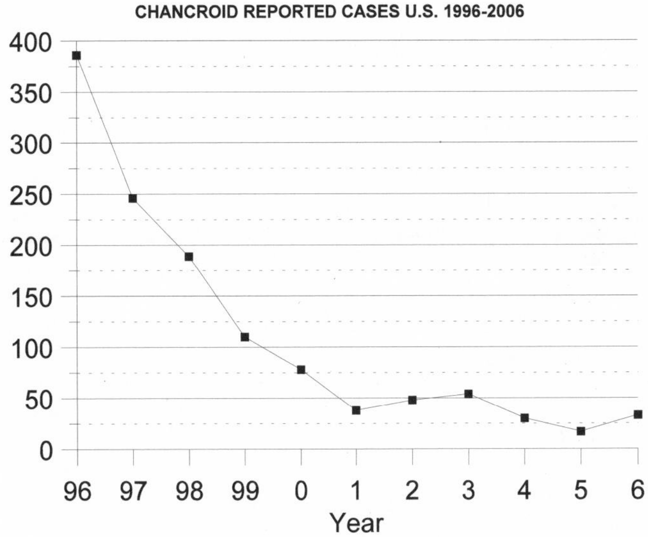

Source: **Centers for Disease Control and Prevention.**

If chancroid is untreated it can infect and swell the glands located in the groin. The disease is considered especially dangerous because the sores it causes increase the chances of getting HIV (the cause of AIDS). Chancroid can be treated effectively with one of several antibiotics (e.g., sulfonamides, tetracyclines, streptomycin, or chloramphenicol). Using latex condoms may prevent the spread of chancroid. *See also* **Sexually Transmitted Diseases**

Chediak-Higashi Syndrome

Chediak-Higashi syndrome is a congenital disorder of the immune system. The disorder causes chronic infection, neurological disease, and early death. Those that survive the disorder develop unsteady gaits and nerve abnormalities in the limbs. There is no specific treatment for the disorder. Types of treatments that are used include bone marrow transplants and antibiotics. The terminal phase of the disease is not treatable. *See also* **Birth Defects and Abortion**

Chemical Pregnancy

Chemical pregnancy refers to a spontaneous abortion. The word "chemical" is used because the only medical or clinical evidence that there was in fact a pregnancy, is through a lab test that indicates an implantation occurred, but it only developed long enough to raise the woman's blood level. Chemical pregnancies are usually caused by some genetic defect in the egg or sperm or both. *See also* **Blighted Ovum; Clinical Pregnancy; Luteal Phase Defect**

Child Custody Protection Act

The Child Custody Protection Act was a bill that was sponsored by pro-life members of Congress beginning in the late 1990s. This bill would prohibit anyone, except a parent, from taking a pregnant minor across state lines for an abortion if the minor did not meet her home state's parental involvement requirements. The bill makes no exceptions for other family members, such as grandparents, aunts, or siblings to escort minors across state lines. The bill has been criticized on the grounds that many teenaged girls from abusive or unsupportive families are afraid to inform their parents of their decision to have an abortion. Under the bill such teenagers would not have the option of turning to another trusted adult to help them access abortion services in another state.

Childbirth and Labor

Labor pains leading up to the delivery of the fetus usually begin about two weeks before the actual birth. This point in time may be viewed in three stages.

(1) First stage. The first stage is generally the longest part of labor. This stage is divided into three phases: early phase, active phase and transition phase.

(i) Early phase. The early phase of labor can take from 12 to 14 hours for a first pregnancy. The cervix will dilate (expand) to roughly three centimeters in the early phase. The membranes will rupture and the amniotic fluid that surrounds the fetus in the uterus will be discharged. Contractions in this period will be moderate and last about 45 seconds. They may occur every 5 to 20 minutes apart. The woman may experience nausea, leg cramps, backache and shakiness.

(ii) Active phase. The active phase of labor should last no more than three hours, though it can be as high as six hours. Contractions may be a minute apart and last three to four minutes. The cervix should dilate to 8 centimeters. The woman will experience increased back and leg pains, continued bleeding, anxiety and exhaustion. A woman should go to a hospital at this point.

(iii) Transition phase. During the transition phase of labor the cervix will dilate to 10 centimeters. Contractions will last anywhere from 60 to 90 minutes and be two to three minutes apart. Bleeding will continue as well as leg cramps, nausea and exhaustion.

(2) Second stage. The second stage of labor will bring the fetus into the world. This stage may last one to two hours. Contractions will last about 90 minutes and be two to five minutes apart. Various methods of pain relief may be given to the woman, which include: general anesthesia, spinal anesthesia, epidural anesthesia, narcotic pain killers and entonox. The baby will move down the birth canal, usually head first. Once the baby's head can be seen in the vaginal opening, he/she will be removed from the womb.

(3) Third stage. The third stage involves removal of the placenta. Contractions will continue to allow the placenta and other tissue to be expelled. The placenta can take from five to 30 minutes to be removed. The umbilical cord will be cut and the woman will be examined for any tear that requires repairing. The neonate will be given an APGAR test (appearance, pulse, grimace, activity and respiration) to assess his/her health; eyedrops to prevent infection. *See also* **Caesarean Section; Induced Labor; Natural Childbirth Methods; Presentation and Position of the Fetus**

Children of the Rosary

Children of the Rosary (COTR) is a pro-life prayer organization that was founded in 1990, by Katherine Sabelko. COTR is headquartered in Glendale, Arizona. The organization follows the teachings of the Roman Catholic Church. COTR's abortion activities include praying at abortion facilities and working to educate people about abortion and the rights of the pre-born child. The organization distributes newsletters, newsgrams and flyers. COTR works closely with pro-life coordinators from parishes, churches and church affiliated organizations. *See also* **Pro-Life Organizations**

Chlamydia

Chlamydia is a sexually transmitted disease that is caused by a bacterium called *chlamydia trachomatis.* The infection is one of the most widespread sexually transmitted diseases in the United States. It is estimated that more than 3 million people are infected each year. The disease can be contracted during oral, vaginal, or anal sexual contact with an infected partner. Chlamydia can cause serious problems in men and women, as well as in newborn babies of infected mothers.

Most people who contract chlamydia do not become sick and therefore are unaware that they have the disease. Those who do have symptoms may have an abnormal discharge from the vagina or penis, or pain while urinating. When symptoms appear it is usually within one to three weeks after being infected. The disease is curable using an antibiotic (azithromycin, doxycycline, erythromycin or ofloxacin). Penicillin will not cure chlamydia infections. The chances of contracting chlamydia or transmitting it to one's partner can be reduced by using male latex condoms during sexual intercourse.

Untreated chlamydia infections in men may lead to pain or swelling in the testicles pouch area (scrotal area). Eventually, severe damage to the male reproductive system can occur. In women, untreated chlamydia infections can lead to pelvic inflammatory disease. If a baby is exposed to the disease in the birth canal during delivery, the child may develop an eye infection or pneumonia. *See also* **Pelvic Inflammatory Disease; Sexually Transmitted Diseases**

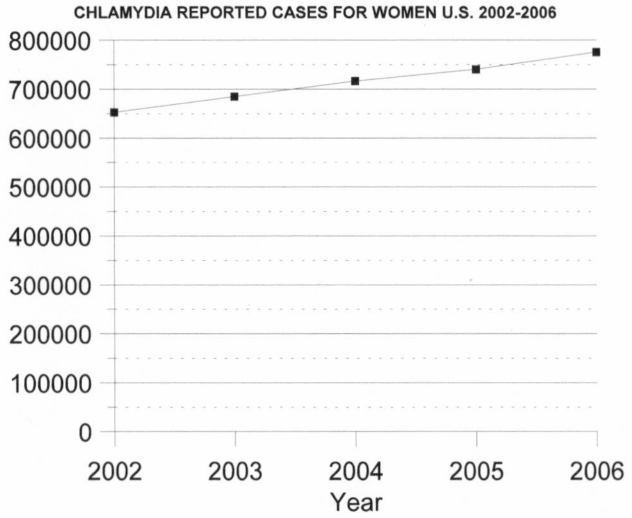

Source: **Centers for Disease Control and Prevention.**

Choice of Miscarriage or Induced Abortion

An ultrasound examination can determine the viability of a pregnancy as early as six weeks gestation. That is, an ultrasound can determine early on the presence or absence of a heartbeat, ectopic pregnancy, threatened miscarriage or molar pregnancy. The information has been used to give some pregnant women, who intended to have an abortion, the option of choosing a miscarriage over an abortion. In most instances a miscarriage will be less costly. *See also* **Miscarriage**

Choice USA

Choice USA is a Washington, D.C., based pro-choice organization that was founded in 1992. The executive director of Choice is Kierra Johnson. Choice is focused on mobilizing and providing ongoing support to the upcoming generation of leaders who promote and protect reproductive choice both now and in the future. The organization is dedicated to the right of each person to decide when and if they will have sex, when and if they will be pregnant, and when and if they will have a child. Choice believes that in order to make such personal decisions, accurate information and safe, legal reproductive health services must be available to everyone. Choice is engaged in several concrete works that include campaigns to (1) lower birth control costs on campuses; (2) support emergency contraception; and (3) repeal of the Hyde Amendment. The organization has also established the "Reproductive Justice Organizing Academy." The Academy is a program designed to provide training and support to emerging pro-choice leaders. *See also* **Pro-Choice Organizations**

Choose Life Automobile License Plate

In the mid–1990s pro-life advocates began to demand that states produce motor vehicle license plates that contained the slogan "Choose Life." The words denote support for adoption as an alternative choice to abortion. The license plate movement was successful in

This is an illustration of a Florida "Choose Life" license plate (Choose Life, Inc.).

Florida when Governor Jeb Bush signed into law, on June 10, 1999, the first government authorized "Choose Life" license plate. Several states have followed Florida and enacted legislation authorizing the use of "Choose Life" license plates. The states include Alabama, Arkansas, Connecticut, Georgia, Hawaii, Indiana, Kentucky, Louisiana, Maryland, Mississippi, Montana, Ohio, Oklahoma, Pennsylvania, South Carolina, South Dakota and Tennessee. Pro-choice advocates have waged legal battles to invalidate statutes that authorize the issuance of "Choose Life" license plates. One such battle was fought in the case of *Planned Parenthood of South Carolina Inc. v. Rose*, 361 F.3d 786 (4th Cir. 2004), where a federal court invalidated South Carolina's statute on the grounds that the statute violated the First Amendment because it regulated access to a speech forum on the basis of viewpoint. Subsequent to the decision in the case the South Carolina legislature enacted another "Choose Life" license plate statute.

Two states offer both "Choose Life" and "Pro-Choice" license plates. Those states are Hawaii and Montana.

States That Authorize the Issuance of "Choose Life" License Plates

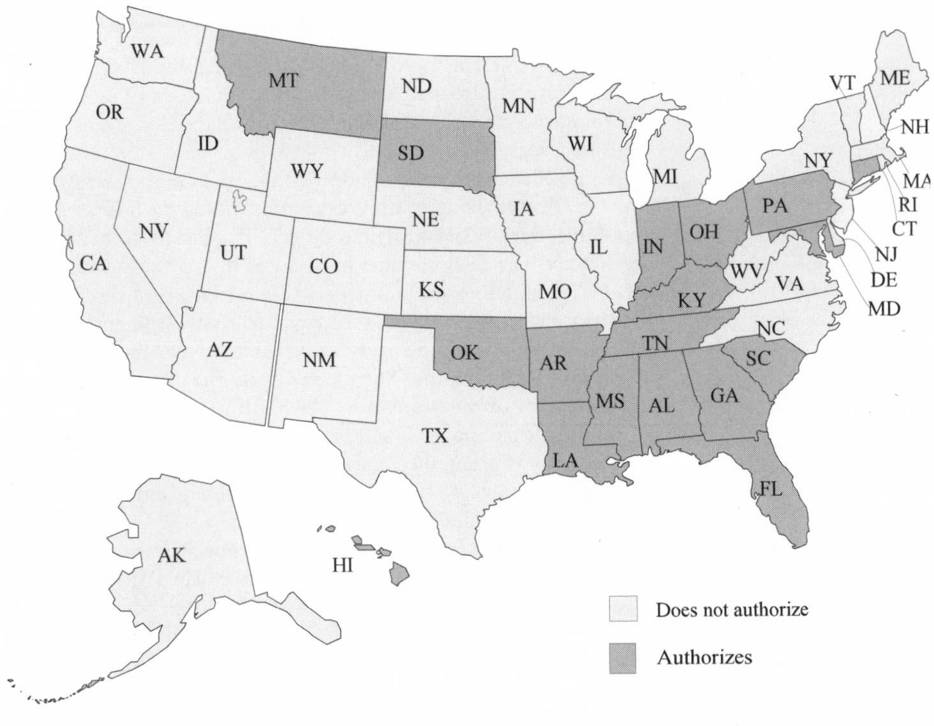

**District of Columbia does authorize.*

Choose Life, Inc.

Choose Life, Inc. (CLI) is a Florida based pro-life organization. CLI was founded in 1997 by Randy Harris, a Marion County Commissioner, and others for the purpose of galvanizing support and funds to have the Florida legislature enact a law authorizing the issuance of "Choose Life" license plates. After several setbacks, CLI was successful in getting legislation signed into law in 1999.

Subsequent to helping make Florida the first state to authorize "Choose Life" license plates, CLI continued to operate for the purpose of helping others obtain legislation in other states authorizing the use of license plates. CLI advocates the use of proceeds from the sale of such license plates be used to facilitate and encourage adoption as an alternative for women with unplanned pregnancies. *See also* **Pro-Life Organizations**

Chorion *see* **Amniotic Sac**

Chorionic Villus Sampling

Chorionic villus sampling (CVS) is a diagnostic prenatal test that was introduced in the United States in 1983. CVS involves taking a small tissue sample from outside the sac where the fetus develops. Once removed the tissue is examined to determine possible fetal birth defects. This test is not routinely administered to pregnant women because it has a risk of causing miscarriage or other complications. *See also* **Amniocentesis**

Christian Coalition of America

Christian Coalition of America (CCA) is a pro-life organization headquartered in Washington, D.C. The organization was founded in 1989 by Rev. Pat Robertson, who resigned as its president in December of 2001. CCA was formed for the purpose of giving Christians a voice in government. One aspect of this voice that CCA has articulated, is the desire that abortion be prohibited in the nation. CCA advocates strengthening the family, protecting preborn innocent human life and defending the institution of marriage. The organization actively represents the pro-life point of view before local councils, school boards, state legislatures and Congress. Its members train leaders for effective social and political action, and inform pro-family voters about timely relevant issues and legislation. *See also* **Pro-Life Organizations**

Christians and Jews for Life

Christians and Jews for Life (CJL) is a pro-life organization founded by Christian and Jewish leaders for the purpose of bringing the two religious communities together to affirm the sanctity of human life. The president of the organization is Virginia based Chris Gersten. CJL promotes legislative and non-legislative approaches to reducing abortion. The organization holds regional conferences to discuss how the two religious communities may work together on the issue of abortion. The specific policies which CJL supports include legislation to ban partial-birth abortion, informed consent, parental notification before an abortion can be performed on a minor, and child custody protection. It also supports the expansion of maternity group homes for unwed mothers, modification of adoption laws to facilitate adoption, and abstinence education. *See also* **Pro-Life Organizations**

City of Akron v. Akron Center for Reproductive Health, Inc.

Forum: United States Supreme Court.

Case Citation: City of Akron v. Akron Center for Reproductive Health, Inc., 462 U.S. 416 (1983).

Date Argued: November 30, 1982.

Date of Decision: June 15, 1983.

Opinion of Court: Powell, J., in which Burger, C. J., and Brennan, Marshall, Blackmun, and Stevens, JJ., joined.

Concurring Opinion: None.

Dissenting Opinion: O'Connor, J., in which White and Rehnquist, JJ., joined.

Counsel for Appellants: Alan G. Segedy argued; on the brief were Robert D. Pritt and Robert A. Destro.

Counsel for Appellees: Stephan Landsman argued; on the brief were Janet Benshoof, Suzanne M. Lynn, Nan D. Hunter, Lois J. Lipton, and Gordon Beggs.

Amicus Brief for United States in Support of Appellants: Solicitor General Lee argued; on the brief were Assistant Attorney General McGrath and Deputy Solicitor General Geller.

Amicus Brief for Appellants and Appellees: Delores V. Horan for Feminists for Life; and by Lynn D. Wardle for the United Families Foundation et al.; Bruce J. Ennis, Jr., and Donald N. Bersoff for the American Psychological Association; Sylvia A. Law, Nadine Taub, and Ellen J. Winner for the Committee for Abortion Rights and Against Sterilization Abuse et al.; M. Carolyn Cox and Lynn Bregman for the American College of Obstetricians and Gynecologists et al.; by David B. Hopkins for the American Public Health Association; by Dennis J. Horan, Victor G. Rosenblum, Patrick A. Trueman, and Thomas J. Marzen for Americans United for Life; for California Women Lawyers et al.; by Charles E. Rice for the Catholic League for Religious and Civil Rights; by Rhonda Copelon for Certain Religious Organizations; by Jack R. Bierig for the College of American Pathologists; by Ronald J. Suster for Lawyers for Life; by Alan Ernest for the Legal Defense Fund for Unborn Children; by Judith Levin for the National Abortion Federation; by Jack Greenberg, James M. Nabrit III, and Judith Reed for the NAACP Legal Defense and Educational Fund, Inc.; by Phyllis N. Segal, Judith I. Avner, and Jemera Rone for the National Organization for Women et al.; by Eve W. Paul and Dara Klassel for the Planned Parenthood Federation of America, Inc., et al.; by James Arthur Gleason for Womankind, Inc.; by Nancy Reardan for Women Lawyers of Sacramento et al; and by Susan Frelich Appleton and Paul Brest for Certain Law Professors.

Issue Presented: Whether the constitution was violated by an ordinance of the city of Akron that imposed abortion requirements involving parental consent, informed consent, waiting period, hospitalization and disposal of fetal remains?

Case Holding: The constitution was violated by each of the provisions of Akron's abortion ordinance.

Background facts of case: In February of 1978 the city of Akron, Ohio, passed an ordinance regulating abortions performed there. Among the provisions of the ordinance were the following: (1) requirement that all abortions performed after the first trimester of pregnancy to be performed in a hospital; (2) prohibiting a physician from performing an abortion on an unmarried minor under the age of 15 unless the consent of one of her parents was obtained or unless the minor obtained an order from a court having jurisdiction over her that the abortion be performed; (3) requirement that the attending physician inform an abortion patient of the status of her pregnancy, the development of her fetus, the date of possible viability, the physical and emotional complications that may result from an abortion, and the availability of agencies to provide her with assistance and information with respect to birth control, adoption, and childbirth, and also inform her of the particular risks associated with her pregnancy and the abortion technique to be employed; (4) prohibiting a physician from performing an abortion until 24 hours after the pregnant woman signs a consent form; and (5) requirement that physicians performing abortions ensure that fetal remains are disposed of in a humane and sanitary manner. A violation of the ordinance was punishable as a misdemeanor.

The appellees, abortion providers, filed a lawsuit in a federal district court in Ohio challenging the constitutionality of the ordinance. The appellants, the city of Akron and three of its officials, were named as defendants. The district court invalidated four provisions: requirement of parental notice and consent; requirement of disclosure of facts concerning the woman's pregnancy, fetal development, the complications of abortion, and agencies available to assist the woman; and disposal of fetal remains. The court upheld the constitutionality of the remainder of the ordinance. The Sixth Circuit court of appeals affirmed in part and reversed in part. Both parties appealed. The Supreme Court granted certiorari for both appeals. (Although both parties were technically designated as appellants and appellees, they are not given the dual designations here.)

Majority opinion by Justice Powell: Justice Powell reversed the judgment of the court of appeals that upheld appellants' hospitalization requirement, but affirmed the remainder of the decision invalidating the provisions on parental consent, informed consent, waiting period, and disposal of fetal remains. The opinion addressed the matters as follows:

> There can be no doubt that [the] second trimester hospitalization requirement places a significant obstacle in the path of women

seeking an abortion. A primary burden created by the requirement is additional cost to the woman. The Court of Appeals noted that there was testimony that a second trimester abortion costs more than twice as much in a hospital as in a clinic. Moreover, the court indicated that second trimester abortions were rarely performed in Akron hospitals. Thus, a second trimester hospitalization requirement may force women to travel to find available facilities, resulting in both financial expense and additional health risk. It therefore is apparent that a second trimester hospitalization requirement may significantly limit a woman's ability to obtain an abortion....

... By preventing the performance of ... abortions in an appropriate nonhospital setting, Akron has imposed a heavy, and unnecessary, burden on women's access to a relatively inexpensive, otherwise accessible, and safe abortion procedure. [The requirement] has the effect of inhibiting the vast majority of abortions after the first 12 weeks, and therefore unreasonably infringes upon a woman's constitutional right to obtain an abortion.

We turn next to the provision prohibiting a physician from performing an abortion on a minor pregnant woman under the age of 15 unless he obtains the informed written consent of one of her parents or her legal guardian or unless the minor obtains an order from a court having jurisdiction over her that the abortion be performed or induced. The District Court invalidated this provision.... The Court of Appeals affirmed....

... Akron may not make a blanket determination that all minors under the age of 15 are too immature to make this decision or that an abortion never may be in the minor's best interest without parental approval.

... It is reasonable to assume ... that a state court presented with a state statute specifically governing abortion consent procedures for pregnant minors will attempt to construe the statute consistently with constitutional requirements. This suit, however, concerns a municipal ordinance that creates no procedures for making the necessary determinations. Akron seeks to invoke the Ohio statute governing juvenile proceedings, but that statute neither mentions minors' abortions nor suggests that the Ohio Juvenile Court has authority to inquire into a minor's maturity or emancipation. In these circumstances, we do not think that the Akron ordinance, as applied in Ohio juvenile proceedings, is reasonably susceptible of being construed to create an opportunity for case-by-case evaluations of the maturity of pregnant minors. We therefore affirm the Court of Appeals' judgment that [the requirement] is unconstitutional....

... [W]e believe that [the informed consent requirement] attempts to extend the State's interest in ensuring informed consent beyond permissible limits. First, it is fair to say that much of the information required is designed not to inform the woman's consent but rather to persuade her to withhold it altogether. [The ordinance] requires the physician to inform his patient that the unborn child is a human life from the moment of conception, a requirement inconsistent with the Court's holding in Roe v. Wade that a State may not adopt one theory of when life begins to justify its regulation of abortions. Moreover, much of the detailed description of the anatomical and physiological characteristics of the particular unborn child required ... would involve at best speculation by the physician....

An additional, and equally decisive, objection to [the informed consent requirement] is its intrusion upon the discretion of the pregnant woman's physician. This provision specifies a litany of information that the physician must recite to each woman regardless of whether in his judgment the information is relevant to her personal decision. For example, even if the physician believes that some of the risks outlined in [the ordinance] are nonexistent for a particular patient, he remains obligated to describe them to her.... [A] State may require that a physician make certain that his patient understands the physical and emotional implications of having an abortion. But Akron has gone far beyond merely describing the general subject matter relevant to informed consent. By insisting upon recitation of a lengthy and inflexible list of information, Akron unreasonably has placed obstacles in the path of the doctor upon whom [the woman is] entitled to rely for advice in connection with her decision....

Requiring physicians personally to discuss the abortion decision, its health risks, and consequences with each patient may in some cases add to the cost of providing abortions, though the record here does not suggest that ethical physicians will charge more for adhering to this typical element of the physician-patient relationship. Yet in Roe and subsequent cases we have stressed repeatedly the central role of the physician, both in consulting with the woman about whether or not to have an abortion, and in determining how any abortion was to be carried out....

We are not convinced, however, that there is as vital a state need for insisting that the physician performing the abortion, or for that matter any physician, personally counsel the patient in the absence of a request. The State's interest is in ensuring that the woman's consent is informed and unpressured; the critical factor is whether she obtains the necessary information and counseling from a qualified person, not the identity of the person from whom she obtains it....

In so holding, we do not suggest that the State is powerless to vindicate its interest in making certain the important and stressful decision to abort is made with full knowledge of its nature and consequences. Nor do we imply that a physician may abdicate his essential role as the person ultimately responsible for the medical aspects of the decision to perform the abortion. A State may define the physician's responsibility to include verification that adequate counseling has been provided and that the woman's consent is informed. In addition, the State may establish reasonable minimum qualifications for those people who perform the primary counseling function. In light of these alternatives, we believe that it is unreasonable for a State to insist that only a physician is competent to provide the information and counseling relevant to informed consent. We affirm the judgment of the Court of Appeals that [the informed consent provision] is invalid.

The Akron ordinance prohibits a physician from performing an abortion until 24 hours after the pregnant woman signs a consent form. The District Court upheld this provision on the ground that it furthered Akron's interest in ensuring that a woman's abortion decision is made after careful consideration of all the facts applicable to her particular situation. The Court of Appeals reversed, finding that the inflexible waiting period had no medical basis, and that careful consideration of the abortion decision by the woman is beyond the state's power to require. We affirm the Court of Appeals' judgment....

We find that Akron has failed to demonstrate that any legitimate state interest is furthered by an arbitrary and inflexible waiting period. There is no evidence suggesting that the abortion procedure will be performed more safely. Nor are we convinced that the State's legitimate concern that the woman's decision be informed is reasonably served by requiring a 24-hour delay as a matter of course. The decision whether to proceed with an abortion is one as to which it is important to afford the physician adequate discretion in the exercise of his medical judgment. In accordance with the ethical standards of the profession, a physician will advise the patient to defer the abortion when he thinks this will be beneficial to her. But if a woman, after appropriate counseling, is prepared to give her written informed consent and proceed with the abortion, a State may not demand that she delay the effectuation of that decision.

[T]he Akron ordinance requires physicians performing abortions to insure that the remains of the unborn child are disposed of in a humane and sanitary manner. The Court of Appeals found that the word "humane" was impermissibly vague as a definition of conduct subject to criminal prosecution. The court invalidated the entire provision, declining to sever the word "humane" in order to uphold the requirement that disposal be sanitary. We affirm this judgment.

Akron contends that the purpose of [provision] is simply to preclude the mindless dumping of aborted fetuses onto garbage piles. It is far from clear, however, that this provision has such a limited intent. The phrase "humane and sanitary" does, as the Court of Appeals noted, suggest a possible intent to mandate some sort of decent burial of an embryo at the earliest stages of formation. This level of uncertainty is fatal where criminal liability is imposed. Because [the provision] fails to give a physician fair notice that his contemplated conduct is forbidden, we agree that it violates the Due Process Clause.

Disposition of case: The judgment of the court of appeals invalidating those sections of the ordinance that dealt with parental consent, informed consent, a 24-hour waiting period, and the disposal of fetal remains was affirmed. The remaining portion of the judgment, sustaining the requirement that all second trimester abortions be performed in a hospital, was reversed.

Dissenting opinion by Justice O'Connor: Justice O'Connor disagreed with the majority decision. She took the position that all of the requirements of the ordinance passed constitutional muster. Justice O'-Connor wrote:

> In Roe v. Wade the Court held that the "right of privacy ... founded in the Fourteenth Amendment's concept of personal liberty and restrictions upon state action ... is broad enough to encompass a woman's decision whether or not to terminate her pregnancy." The parties in these cases have not asked the Court to re-examine the validity of that holding and the court below did not address it. Accordingly, the Court does not re-examine its previous holding. Nonetheless, it is apparent from the Court's opinion that neither sound constitutional theory nor our need to decide cases based on the application of neutral principles can accommodate an analytical framework that varies according to the "stages" of pregnancy, where those stages, and their concomitant standards of review, differ according to the level of medical technology available when a particular challenge to state regulation occurs. The Court's analysis of the Akron regulations is inconsistent both with the methods of analysis employed in previous cases dealing with abortion, and with the Court's approach to fundamental rights in other areas.
>
> Our recent cases indicate that a regulation imposed on a lawful abortion is not unconstitutional unless it unduly burdens the right to seek an abortion. In my view, this "unduly burdensome" standard should be applied to the challenged regulations throughout the entire pregnancy without reference to the particular stage of pregnancy involved. If the particular regulation does not unduly burden the fundamental right, then our evaluation of that regulation is limited to our determination that the regulation rationally relates to a legitimate state purpose. Irrespective of what we may believe is wise or prudent policy in this difficult area, the Constitution does not constitute us as Platonic Guardians nor does it vest in this Court the authority to strike down laws because they do not meet our standards of desirable social policy, wisdom, or common sense.

Note: Most of the rulings in this case were eventually overruled in *Planned Parenthood of Southeastern Pennsylvania v. Casey*. *See also* **Planned Parenthood of Southeastern Pennsylvania v. Casey**

Civil Liberties and Public Policy Program

The Civil Liberties and Public Policy Program (CLPPP) is an organization located at Hampshire College in Amherst, Massachusetts. CLPPP acts as a resource to the academic community and the reproductive rights movement. The organization's goals include promoting leadership for young women; presenting policy statements on reproductive freedom; and developing strategies for advancing reproductive freedom. CLPPP offers educational courses and publishes materials and videos. One of the practical aspects of CLPPP's work is its coordination of the annual National Young Women's Day of Action on colleges throughout the country. This event has been designated to commemorate the death of Rosie Jimenez, the first young woman known to die from an illegal abortion after Congress passed the Hyde Amendment which denied federal Medicaid funding for abortions. In 1999, over 250 campuses and communities participated in the event by organizing speak-outs, rallies, voter registration, postcard signing, video screenings, panel discussions, and other activities. *See also* **Pro-Choice Organizations**

Clark, Tom C.

Tom C. Clark (1899–1977) served as an associate justice of the United States Supreme Court from 1949 to 1967. While on the Supreme Court Justice Clark was known as a conservative who shifted to the center during his last years on the Court.

Justice Clark was born in Dallas, Texas. In the early 1920s he attended the University of Texas, where he studied law and eventually received a degree. After college Justice Clark joined his father's law firm for a short period of time. His legal career shifted into full gear when he left private practice and began a long service as a State and Federal government attorney in various aspects of the law. From 1945 to 1949 Justice Clark served as United States Attorney General under President Harry S. Truman. In 1949 President Truman appointed him to the Supreme Court.

While on the Supreme Court Justice Clark was involved in two reproductive health opinions. In *Griswold v. Connecticut* Justice Clark voted with the majority opinion, which held that the right of privacy found in the constitution prohibited enforcement of a Connecticut statute that made it a crime to give married persons contraceptive information and devices. Justice Clark joined a plurality opinion in *Poe v. Ullman*, which held that the appellants did not have standing to challenge the constitutionality of a Connecticut statute, that made it a crime to give married persons contraceptive information and devices.

Cleft Lip and Palate

A cleft lip is an opening in the upper lip. A cleft palate is an opening in the roof of the mouth. These are congenital abnormalities that can occur alone or together. Clefts occur due to an incomplete development of the lip or palate of the fetus. The disorders occur in over 5,000 babies born each year in the United States. Cleft abnormalities can cause feeding difficulties and problems with the development of speech. While neither disorder can be prevented, extended surgery can correct the disorders. *See also* **Birth Defects and Abortion**

Clergy Consultation Service on Abortion

The Clergy Consultation Service on Abortion (CCSA) was founded in New York in 1967, by Rev. Howard Moody of the Judson Memorial Church. Rev. Moody enlisted the aid of about 25 religious leaders to help run CCSA. The organization was created in response to abortion being illegal throughout the nation, and the hazards posed to women seeking unlawful abortions from incompetent abortionists. CCSA obtained information on abortion providers who were competent, and thereafter acted as a referral service in sending women to abortion providers on its list. The organization became a model for the creation of similar organizations throughout the nation. It was estimated that CCSA referred several thousand women for abortions, before abortion was legalized in 1973. *See also* **Pro-Choice Organizations**

Clinic *see* **Hospital/Clinic Abortion Requirements**

Clinic Blockades and Demonstrations *see* **Abortion Violence, Property Destruction and Demonstrations**

Clinical Pregnancy

A clinical pregnancy refers to a pregnancy that has been documented by an ultrasound examination, which identifies an embryonic heartbeat or the presence of a gestational sac in a woman. *See also* **Chemical Pregnancy**

Cloning *see* **Embryo Cloning**

Clubfoot

Clubfoot (also called talipes equinovarus) is the most common lower body congenital disorder. It is believed that both genetic and environmental factors in a fetus' development play a role in causing clubfoot. The disorder forces the affected foot to point downward, with toes turned inward, while the bottom of the foot is twisted inward. The condition occurs in 1 out of 1,000 live births. One or both feet may suffer the disorder. Male infants are affected twice as often as female infants.

There is no way to prevent clubfoot. However, the deformities caused by clubfoot may be corrected with or without surgery. Left untreated, the affected foot cannot move up and down in a normal way. *See also* **Birth Defects and Abortion**

CMV

CMV (cytomegalovirus) is a sexually transmitted disease that can be easily spread by other means such as saliva, breast milk, transplanted organs, and blood transfusions. The disease is very common and infects between 50 percent and 85 percent of adults in the United States by 40 years of age. Once a person becomes infected, the virus remains alive, but usually dormant within that person's body for life. Serious problems rarely occur unless the person's immune system is suppressed due to therapeutic drugs or disease. Therefore, for the vast majority of people, CMV infection is not a serious problem. In otherwise healthy persons, the disease usually produces no symptoms. When symptoms do appear they include swollen lymph glands, fever, and fatigue. CMV is incurable.

A woman who has CMV while pregnant can transmit the disease to the fetus. Although most babies infected with CMV before birth do not develop any symptoms, the disease is the leading cause of congenital infection in the United States. CMV infection may cause abortion, stillbirth, or postnatal death from hemorrhage or anemia. It is estimated that 6,000 babies each year develop life-threatening complications from congenital CMV infection at birth, or may suffer serious problems later in life, including mental retardation, blindness, deafness, or epilepsy. Congenital CMV is the most common cause of progressive deafness in children.

CMV can be life-threatening for persons with suppressed immune systems. Persons with HIV infection or AIDS may develop severe CMV infections, including CMV retinitis, an eye disease that can lead to blindness, and ulcerative disease of the colon or esophagus. *See also* **Sexually Transmitted Diseases**

Coarctation of the Aorta *see* **Congenital Heart Defect**

Coerce Abortion

Under federal law it is a criminal offense for any government entity, employee or person receiving federal funds, to coerce a female into having an abortion. There is also a federal statute which prohibits entry into the United States of any foreigner who, in his or her country, compelled women to have abortions or forced sterilization on men or women. The ban does not apply to specific foreign dignitaries. The statutes addressing the matter are set out below.

42 U.S.C.A. § 300a-8. Penalty for coercing

Any—

(1) officer or employee of the United States,

(2) officer or employee of any State, political subdivision of a State, or any other entity, which administers or supervises the administration of any program receiving Federal financial assistance, or

(3) person who receives, under any program receiving Federal financial assistance, compensation for services,

who coerces or endeavors to coerce any person to undergo an abortion or sterilization procedure by threatening such person with the loss of, or disqualification for the receipt of, any benefit or service under a program receiving Federal financial assistance shall be fined not more than $1,000 or imprisoned for not more than one year, or both.

8 U.S.C.A. § 1182e. Denial of entry into United States

(a) Notwithstanding any other provision of law, the Secretary of State may not issue any visa to, and the Attorney General may not admit to the United States, any foreign national whom the Secretary finds, based on credible and specific information, to have been directly involved in the establishment or enforcement of population control policies forcing a woman to undergo an abortion against her free choice or forcing a man or woman to undergo sterilization against his or her free choice, unless the Secretary has substantial grounds for believing that the foreign national has discontinued his or her involvement with, and support for, such policies.

(b) The prohibitions in subsection (a) shall not apply in the case of a foreign national who is a head of state, head of government, or cabinet level minister.

(c) The Secretary of State may waive the prohibitions in subsection (a) with respect to a foreign national if the Secretary—

(1) determines that it is important to the national interest of the United States to do so; and

(2) provides written notification to the appropriate congressional committees containing a justification for the waiver.

Coffin-Lowry Syndrome

Coffin-Lowry syndrome is a congenital disorder involving a defective gene on the X chromosome. The disorder causes skeletal, head and facial abnormalities, mental retardation, respiratory problems, hearing impairment, and heart and kidney problems. There is no cure for the disorder. Some problems associated with the disorder may be treated with physical and speech therapy. *See also* **Birth Defects and Abortion**

Colautti v. Franklin

Forum: United States Supreme Court.

Case Citation: Colautti v. Franklin, 439 U.S. 379 (1979).

Date Argued: October 3, 1978.

Date of Decision: January 9, 1979.

Opinion of Court: Blackmun, J., in which Brennan, Stewart, Marshall, Powell, and Stevens, JJ., joined.

Concurring Opinion: None.

Dissenting Opinion: White, J., in which Burger, C. J., and Rehnquist, J., joined.

Counsel for Appellants: Carol Los Mansmann, Special Assistant Attorney General of Pennsylvania, argued; on the brief was J. Jerome Mansmann, Special Assistant Attorney General.

Counsel for Appellees: Roland Morris argued and filed a brief.

Amicus Brief for Appellants: Dennis J. Horan, John D. Gorby, Victor G. Rosenblum, and Dolores V. Horan for Americans United for Life, Inc.

Amicus Brief for Appellees: Burt Neuborne and Sylvia Law for the American Public Health Assn. et al.

Issue Presented: Whether the constitution was violated by a provision in Pennsylvania's abortion statute that subjected a physician who performed an abortion to potential criminal liability if he/she failed to utilize a statutorily prescribed technique when the fetus was viable or when there was sufficient reason to believe that the fetus may be viable?

Case Holding: The constitution was violated by a vague and ambiguous provision in Pennsylvania's abortion statute that subjected a physician who performed an abortion to potential criminal liability, if he/she failed to utilize a statutorily prescribed technique when the fetus was viable or when there was sufficient reason to believe that the fetus may be viable.

Background facts of case: In 1974 the appellees, abortion providers, filed a lawsuit in a federal district court in Pennsylvania challenging constitutionality of many provisions in the state's abortion statute. The appellants, state officials, were named as defendants. After several years of litigation, the case boiled down to a determination of the constitutionality of Section 5(a) of the abortion statute. This provision subjected a physician who performed an abortion to potential criminal liability if he/she failed to utilize a statutorily prescribed technique when the fetus was viable or when there was sufficient reason to believe that the fetus may be viable. The district court found the provision was unconstitutional. The Supreme Court granted certiorari to consider the issue.

Majority opinion by Justice Blackmun: Justice Blackmun found the provision unconstitutional. In doing so, he wrote as follows:

> Section 5 (a) requires every person who performs or induces an abortion to make a determination, based on his experience, judgment or professional competence, that the fetus is not viable. If such person determines that "the fetus is viable, or if there is sufficient reason to believe that the fetus may be viable," then he must adhere to the prescribed standard of care. This requirement contains a double ambiguity. First, it is unclear whether the statute imports a purely subjective standard, or whether it imposes a mixed subjective and objective standard. Second, it is uncertain whether the phrase "may be viable" simply refers to viability, as that term has been defined in [our cases], or whether it refers to an undefined penumbral or "gray" area prior to the stage of viability....
>
> ... The ... statute does not afford broad discretion to the physician. Instead, it conditions potential criminal liability on confusing and ambiguous criteria. It therefore presents serious problems of notice, discriminatory application, and chilling effect on the exercise of constitutional rights.
>
> The vagueness of the viability-determination requirement of 5 (a) is compounded by the fact that the Act subjects the physician to potential criminal liability without regard to fault.... [N]either the Pennsylvania law of criminal homicide, nor the Abortion Control Act, requires that the physician be culpable in failing to find sufficient reason to believe that the fetus may be viable.
>
> This Court has long recognized that the constitutionality of a vague statutory standard is closely related to whether that standard incorporates a requirement of mens rea. Because of the absence of a scienter requirement in the provision directing the physician to determine whether the fetus is or may be viable, the statute is little more than a trap for those who act in good faith....
>
> We also conclude that the standard-of-care provision of 5 (a) is impermissibly vague....
>
> The statute does not clearly specify, as appellants imply, that the woman's life and health must always prevail over the fetus' life and health when they conflict. The woman's life and health are not mentioned in the first part of the stated standard of care, which sets forth the general duty to the viable fetus; they are mentioned only in the second part which deals with the choice of abortion procedures. Moreover, the second part of the standard directs the physician to employ the abortion technique best suited to fetal survival so long as a different technique would not be necessary in order to preserve the life or health of the mother....
>
> Consequently, it is uncertain whether the statute permits the physician to consider his duty to the patient to be paramount to his duty to the fetus, or whether it requires the physician to make a trade-off between the woman's health and additional percentage points of fetal survival. Serious ethical and constitutional difficulties, that we do not address, lurk behind this ambiguity. We hold only that where conflicting duties of this magnitude are involved, the State, at the least, must proceed with greater precision before it may subject a physician to possible criminal sanctions.

Disposition of case: The judgment of the district court was affirmed.

Dissenting opinion by Justice White: Justice White dissented from the majority opinion. He argued that the statute was constitutional as follows:

> In affirming the District Court, the Court does not in so many words agree with the District Court but argues that it is too difficult to know whether the Pennsylvania Act simply intended, as the State urges, to go no further than Roe v. Wade permitted in protecting a fetus that is potentially able to survive or whether it intended to carve out a protected period prior to viability as defined in Roe. The District Court, although otherwise seriously in error, had no such trouble with the Act. It understood the "may be viable" provision as an attempt to protect a period of potential life, precisely the kind of interest that Roe protected but which the District Court erroneously thought the State was not entitled to protect.... Only those with unalterable determination to invalidate the Pennsylvania Act can draw any measurable difference insofar as vagueness is concerned between "viability" defined as the ability to survive and "viability" defined as that stage at which the fetus may have the ability to survive. It seems to me that, in affirming, the Court is tacitly disowning the ... "potential ability" component of viability as that concept was described in Roe. This is a further constitutionally unwarranted intrusion upon the police powers of the States....
>
> In any event, I cannot join the Court in its determined attack on the Pennsylvania statute. As in the case with a mistaken viability determination under 5 (a), there is no basis for asserting the lack of a scienter requirement in a prosecution for violating the standard-of-care provision. I agree with the State that there is not the remotest chance that any abortionist will be prosecuted on the basis of a goodfaith mistake regarding whether to abort, and if he does, with respect to which abortion technique is to be used. If there is substantial doubt about this, the Court should not complain of a lack of an authoritative state construction, as it does, but should direct abstention and permit the state courts to address the issues in the light of the Pennsylvania homicide laws with which those courts are so much more familiar than are we or any other federal court....
>
> What the Court has done is to issue a warning to the States, in the name of vagueness, that they should not attempt to forbid or regulate abortions when there is a chance for the survival of the fetus, but it is not sufficiently large that the abortionist considers the fetus to be viable. This edict has no constitutional warrant, and I cannot join it.

Colorado

(1) Overview

The state of Colorado enacted its first criminal abortion statute on November 5, 1861. The statute underwent several amendments prior to the 1973 decision by the United States Supreme Court in *Roe v.*

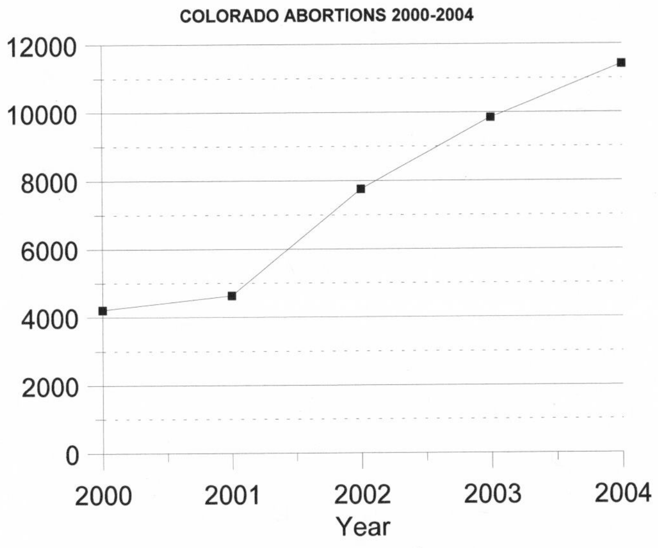

Source: National Center for Health Statistics.

Colorado Abortion By Age Group 2000–2004

Year	Age Group (yrs) <15	15-19	20-24	25-29	30-34	35-39	≥40	Unknown
2000	26	907	1,362	822	543	389	145	21
2001	30	976	1,511	891	587	443	183	12
2002	47	1,491	2,620	1,583	992	674	329	21
2003	52	1,692	3,287	2,084	1,399	886	414	38
2004	55	2,089	3,828	2,464	1,556	937	458	30
Total	210	7,155	12,608	7,844	5,077	3,329	1,529	122

Source: National Center for Health Statistics.

Colorado Abortion by Weeks of Gestation 2000–2004

Weeks of Gestation	Year 2000	2001	2002	2003	2004	Total
≤8	2,184	2,498	4,694	6,046	7,305	22,727
9–10	938	917	1,397	1,665	1,720	6,637
11–12	474	506	741	854	967	3,542
13–15	296	334	445	594	729	2,398
16–20	138	193	238	384	402	1,355
≥21	144	159	184	229	246	962
Not known	41	26	58	80	46	251

Source: National Center for Health Statistics.

Wade, which legalized abortion in the nation. In spite of the decision in *Roe*, Colorado has not repealed its pre-*Roe* criminal abortion statutes. However, the statutes, in large part, are constitutionally infirm.

Colorado has taken affirmative steps to respond to *Roe* and its progeny. Colorado has addressed several abortion issues by statute that include abortion by minors, public funds for abortion, a ban on abortion clinic violence, use of facilities and people, unlawful termination of pregnancy, ban sale of fetal tissue.

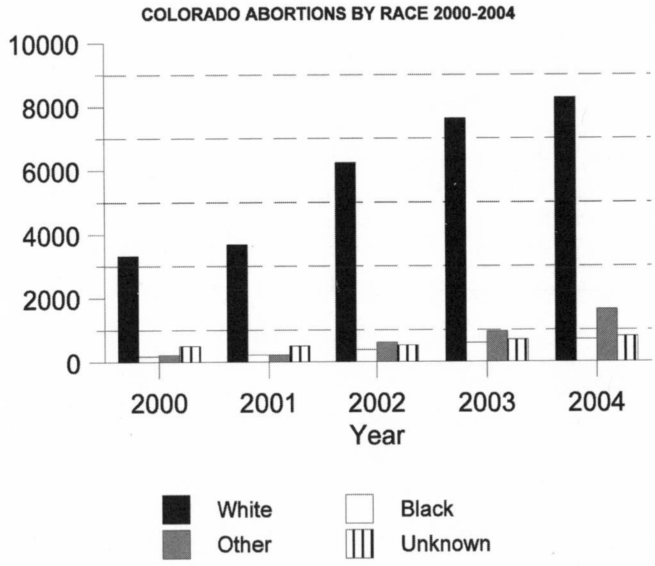

Source: National Center for Health Statistics.

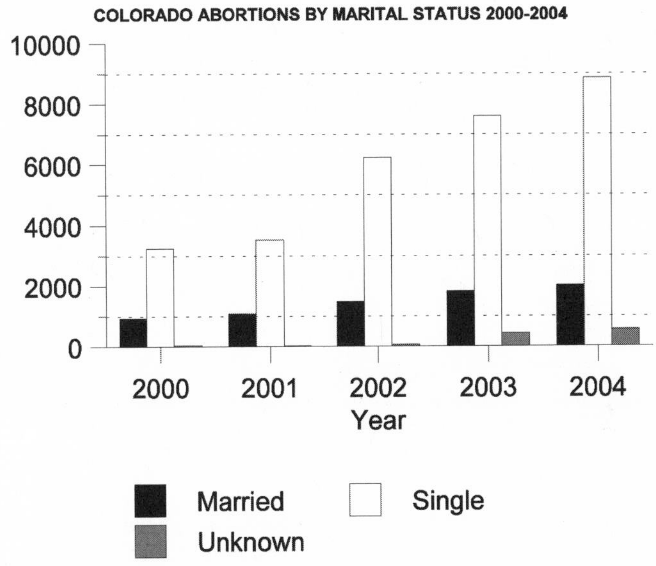

Source: National Center for Health Statistics.

Colorado Prior Abortion by Female 2000–2004

Year	Prior Abortion None	1	2	≥3	Not known
2000	2,483	1,121	292	94	225
2001	2,955	1,145	298	129	106
2002	5,043	1,879	563	203	69
2003	6,369	2,454	698	259	72
2004	6,685	3,105	875	404	346
Total	23,535	9,704	2,726	1,089	818

Source: National Center for Health Statistics.

(2) PRE-ROE ABORTION BAN

As previously indicated, Colorado has not repealed its pre-*Roe* criminal abortion statutes. The statutes remain on the books even though they were expressly found to violate the constitution of Colorado in *People v. Norton*, 507 P.2d 862 (Colo. 1973) and *Foe v. Vanderhoof*, 389 F.Supp. 947 (D.Colo. 1975). Under the now unconstitutional statutes, abortion was criminalized if it was not performed to preserve the woman's life or prevent serious physical or mental impairment; or to prevent the birth of child with serious fetal birth defects; or to prevent a birth resulting from rape or incest. Colorado also prohibited the sale or advertising of abortifacients. The statutes are set out below.

Colorado Code § 18-6-101. Definitions

As used in sections 18-6-101 to 18-6-104, unless the context otherwise requires:

(1) "Justified medical termination" means the intentional ending of the pregnancy of a woman at the request of said woman or, if said woman is under the age of eighteen years, then at the request of the woman and her then living parent or guardian, or, if the woman is married and living with her husband, at the request of said woman and her husband, by a licensed physician using accepted medical procedures in a licensed hospital upon written certification by all of the members of a special hospital board that:

(a) Continuation of the pregnancy, in their opinion, is likely to result in: The death of the woman; or the serious permanent impairment of the physical health of the woman; or the serious permanent impairment of the mental health of the woman as confirmed in writing under the signature of a licensed doctor of medicine specializing in psychiatry; or the birth of a child with grave and permanent physical deformity or mental retardation; or

(b) Less than sixteen weeks of gestation have passed and that the pregnancy resulted from conduct defined as criminal in sections 18-3-402 and 18-3-403, or if the female person is unmarried and has not reached her sixteenth birthday at the time of such conduct regardless of the age of the male, or incest, as defined in sections 18-6-301 and 18-6-302, and that the district attorney of the judicial district in which the alleged sexual assault or incest has occurred has informed the committee in writing over his signature that there is probable cause to believe that the alleged violation did occur.

(2) "Licensed hospital" means one licensed or certificated by the department of public health and environment.

(3) "Pregnancy" means the implantation of an embryo in the uterus.

(4) "Special hospital board" means a committee of three licensed physicians who are members of the staff of the hospital where the proposed termination would be performed if certified in accordance with subsection (1) of this section, and who meet regularly or on call for the purpose of determining the question of medical justification in each individual case, and which maintains a written record, signed by each member, of the proceedings and deliberations of the board.

Colorado Code § 18-6-102. Criminal abortion

(1) Any person who intentionally ends or causes to be ended the pregnancy of a woman by any means other than justified medical termination or birth commits criminal abortion.

(2) Criminal abortion is a class 4 felony, but if the woman dies as a result of the criminal abortion, it is a class 2 felony.

Colorado Code § 18-6-103. Pretended criminal abortion

(1) Any person who intentionally pretends to end the real or apparent pregnancy of a woman by any means other than justified medical termination or birth commits pretended criminal abortion.

(2) Pretended criminal abortion is a class 5 felony, but if the woman dies as a result of the pretended criminal abortion, it is a class 2 felony.

Colorado Code § 18-6-104. Failure to comply

Nothing in sections 18-6-101 to 18-6-104 requires a hospital to admit any patient under said sections for the purposes of performing an abortion, nor is any hospital required to appoint a special hospital board as defined in section 18-6-101(4). A person who is a member of or associated with the staff of a hospital or any employee of a hospital in which a justified medical termination has been authorized and who states in writing an objection to the termination on moral or religious grounds is not required to participate in the medical procedures which result in the termination of a pregnancy, and the refusal of any such person to participate does not form the basis for any disciplinary or other recriminatory action against the person.

Colorado Code § 18-6-105. Distributing abortifacients

(1) A person commits distributing abortifacients if he distributes or sells to or for any person other than a licensed medical doctor or osteopathic physician any drug, medicine, instrument, or other substance which is in fact an abortifacient and which he knows to be an abortifacient, and reasonably believes will be used as an abortifacient.

(2) Distributing abortifacients is a class 1 misdemeanor.

Colorado Code § 25-1-665. Advertising to procure abortion

No person, in any manner except as provided in section 25-1-666, shall advertise, publish, sell, or publicly expose for sale any pills, powders, drugs, or combination of drugs designed expressly for the use of females for the purpose of procuring an abortion.

Colorado Code § 25-1-666. Sale of drug producing abortion

Any drug or medicine known to be designed and expressly prepared for producing abortion shall be sold only upon the written prescription of an established practicing physician of the city, village, or county in which the sale is made, and the druggist or dealer selling the same, in a book provided for that purpose, shall register the name of the purchaser, the date of the sale, the kind and quantity of the medicine sold, and the name and residence of the physician prescribing the same.

Colorado Code § 25-1-667. Penalty

Any person violating any of the provisions of sections 25-1-665 and 25-1-666, upon conviction thereof, shall be punished by a fine of not less than twenty-five dollars nor more than one hundred dollars.

(3) ABORTION BY MINORS

Under the laws of Colorado no physician may perform an abortion upon an unemancipated minor unless he/she first notifies either parent of the minor 48 hours before the abortion. This requirement was held unconstitutional in *Planned Parenthood of the Rocky Mountains Services Corporation v. Owens*, 107 F.Supp.2d 1271 (D.Colo. 2000), because it failed to have an exception for emergency health reasons. Subsequent to in *Owens*, the Colorado legislature amended its statutes to permit an emergency health exception for minors. After the amendment, the statutes were found valid in *In re Doe*, 166 P.3d 293 (Colo.App. 2007). Parental notice is not required by Colorado when a minor states that she is the victim of child abuse or neglect by the acts or omissions of the person who would be entitled to notice. Colorado has also provided a judicial waiver procedure for an unemancipated minor to obtain an abortion without parental notice. Under this procedure an unemancipated minor may petition a trial court for a waiver of the notice requirement. A minor has a right to an attorney at the proceeding and if she cannot afford one, the court may appoint her an attorney. If a minor chooses, she may represent herself. The required parental notice may be waived if the court finds either (1) that the minor is mature and well-informed enough to make the abortion decision on her own, or (2) that performance of the abortion would be in the best interest of the minor. An expedited appeal is available to any minor to whom the court denies a waiver of notice. The statutes are set out below.

Colorado Code § 12-37.5-101. Short title

This article shall be known and may be cited as the "Colorado Parental Notification Act."

Colorado Code § 12-37.5-102. Legislative declaration

(1) The people of the state of Colorado, pursuant to the powers reserved to them in Article V of the Constitution of the state of Colorado, declare that family life and the preservation of the traditional family unit are of vital importance to the continuation of an orderly society;

that the rights of parents to rear and nurture their children during their formative years and to be involved in all decisions of importance affecting such minor children should be protected and encouraged, especially as such parental involvement relates to the pregnancy of an unemancipated minor, recognizing that the decision by any such minor to submit to an abortion may have adverse long-term consequences for her.

(2) The people of the state of Colorado, being mindful of the limitations imposed upon them at the present time by the federal judiciary in the preservation of the parent-child relationship, hereby enact into law the following provisions.

Colorado Code § 12-37.5-103. Definitions

As used in this article, unless the context otherwise requires:

(1) "Minor" means a person under eighteen years of age.

(2) "Parent" means the natural or adoptive mother and father of the minor who is pregnant, if they are both living; one parent of the minor if only one is living, or if the other parent cannot be served with notice, as hereinafter provided; or the court-appointed guardian of such minor if she has one or any foster parent to whom the care and custody of such minor shall have been assigned by any agency of the state or county making such placement.

(3) "Abortion" for purposes of this article means the use of any means to terminate the pregnancy of a minor with knowledge that the termination by those means will, with reasonable likelihood, cause the death of the minor's unborn offspring.

(4) "Clergy member" means a priest; a rabbi; a duly ordained, commissioned, or licensed minister of a church; a member of a religious order; or a recognized leader of any religious body.

(5) "Medical emergency" means a condition that, on the basis of the physician's good-faith clinical judgment, so complicates the medical condition of a pregnant minor as to necessitate a medical procedure necessary to prevent the pregnant minor's death or for which a delay will create a serious risk of substantial and irreversible impairment of a major bodily function.

(6) "Relative of the minor" means a minor's grandparent, adult aunt, or adult uncle, if the minor is not residing with a parent and resides with the grandparent, adult aunt, or adult uncle.

Colorado Code § 12-37.5-104. Parental notification

(1) No abortion shall be performed upon an unemancipated minor until at least 48 hours after written notice of the pending abortion has been delivered in the following manner:

(a) The notice shall be addressed to the parent at the dwelling house or usual place of abode of the parent. Such notice shall be delivered to the parent by:

(I) The attending physician or member of the physician's immediate staff who is over the age of eighteen; or

(II) The sheriff of the county where the service of notice is made, or by his deputy; or

(III) Any other person over the age of eighteen years who is not related to the minor; or

(IV) A clergy member who is over the age of eighteen.

(b) Notice delivered by any person other than the attending physician shall be furnished to and delivered by such person in a sealed envelope marked "Personal and Confidential" and its content shall not in any manner be revealed to the person making such delivery.

(c) Whenever the parent of the minor includes two persons to be notified as provided in this article and such persons reside at the same dwelling house or place of abode, delivery to one such person shall constitute delivery to both, and the 48-hour period shall commence when delivery is made. Should such persons not reside together and delivery of notice can be made to each of them, notice shall be delivered to both parents, unless the minor shall request that only one parent be notified, which request shall be honored and shall be noted by the physician in the minor's medical record. Whenever the parties are separately served with notice, the 48-hour period shall commence upon delivery of the first notice.

(d) The person delivering such notice, if other than the physician, shall provide to the physician a written return of service at the earliest practical time, as follows:

(I) If served by the sheriff or his deputy, by his certificate with a statement as to date, place, and manner of service and the time such delivery was made.

(II) If by any other person, by his affidavit thereof with the same statement.

(III) Return of service shall be maintained by the physician.

(e)(I) In lieu of personal delivery of the notice, the same may be sent by postpaid certified mail, addressed to the parent at the usual place of abode of the parent, with return receipt requested and delivery restricted to the addressee. Delivery shall be conclusively presumed to occur and the 48-hour time period as provided in this article shall commence to run at 12:00 o'clock noon on the next day on which regular mail delivery takes place.

(II) Whenever the parent of the minor includes two persons to be notified as provided in this article and such persons reside at the same dwelling house or place of abode, notice addressed to one parent and mailed as provided in the foregoing subparagraph shall be deemed to be delivery of notice to both such persons. Should such persons not reside together and notice can be mailed to each of them, such notice shall be separately mailed to both parents unless the minor shall request that only one parent shall be notified, which request shall be honored and shall be noted by the physician in the minor's medical record.

(III) Proof of mailing and the delivery or attempted delivery shall be maintained by the physician.

(2)(a) Notwithstanding the provisions of subsection (1) of this section, if the minor is residing with a relative of the minor and not a parent, the written notice of the pending abortion shall be provided to either the relative of the minor or a parent.

(b) If a minor elects to provide notice to a person specified in paragraph (a) of this subsection (2), the notice shall be provided in accordance with the provisions of subsection (1) of this section.

(3) At the time the physician, licensed health care professional, or staff of the physician or licensed health care professional informs the minor that notice must be provided to the minor's parents prior to performing an abortion, the physician, licensed health care professional, or the staff of the physician or licensed health care professional must inform the minor under what circumstances the minor has the right to have only one parent notified.

Colorado Code § 12-37.5-105. Notice exception

(1) No notice shall be required pursuant to this article if:

(a) The person or persons who may receive notice pursuant to section 12-37.5-104(1) certify in writing that they have been notified; or

(a.5) The person whom the minor elects to notify pursuant to section 12-37.5-104(2) certifies in writing that he or she has been notified; or

(b) The pregnant minor declares that she is a victim of child abuse or neglect by the acts or omissions of the person who would be entitled to notice, as such acts or omissions are defined in "The Child Protection Act of 1987," as set forth in title 19, article 3, of the Colorado Revised Statutes, and any amendments thereto, and the attending physician has reported such child abuse or neglect as required by the said act. When reporting such child abuse or neglect, the physician shall not reveal that he or she learned of the abuse or neglect as the result of the minor seeking an abortion.

(c) The attending physician certifies in the pregnant minor's med-

ical record that a medical emergency exists and there is insufficient time to provide notice pursuant to section 12-37.5-104; or

(d) A valid court order is issued pursuant to section 12-37.5-107.

Colorado Code § 12-37.5-106. Penalties

(1) Any person who performs or attempts to perform an abortion in willful violation of this article:

(a) Deleted by Laws 2003, Ch. 355, § 7, eff. June 3, 2003.

(b) Shall be liable for damages proximately caused thereby.

(2) It shall be an affirmative defense to any civil proceedings if the person establishes that:

(a) The person relied upon facts or information sufficient to convince a reasonable, careful and prudent person that the representations of the pregnant minor regarding information necessary to comply with this article were bona fide and true; or

(b) The abortion was performed to prevent the imminent death of the minor child and there was insufficient time to provide the required notice.

(3) Any person who counsels, advises, encourages or conspires to induce or persuade any pregnant minor to furnish any physician with false information, whether oral or written, concerning the minor's age, marital status, or any other fact or circumstance to induce or attempt to induce the physician to perform an abortion upon such minor without providing written notice as required by this article commits a class 5 felony and shall be punished as provided in section 18-1.3-401, C.R.S.

Colorado Code § 12-37.5-107. Judicial bypass

(1) Deleted by Laws 2003, Ch. 355, § 8, eff. June 3, 2003.

(2)(a) If any pregnant minor elects not to allow the notification required pursuant to section 12-37.5-104, any judge of a court of competent jurisdiction shall, upon petition filed by or on behalf of such minor, enter an order dispensing with the notice requirements of this article if the judge determines that the giving of such notice will not be in the best interest of the minor, or if the court finds, by clear and convincing evidence, that the minor is sufficiently mature to decide whether to have an abortion. Any such order shall include specific factual findings and legal conclusions in support thereof and a certified copy of such order shall be provided to the attending physician of said minor and the provisions of section 12-37.5-104(1) and section 12-37.5-106 shall not apply to the physician with respect to such minor.

(b) The court, in its discretion, may appoint a guardian ad litem for the minor and also an attorney if said minor is not represented by counsel.

(c) Court proceedings under this subsection (2) shall be confidential and shall be given precedence over other pending matters so that the court may reach a decision promptly without delay in order to serve the best interests of the minor. Court proceedings under this subsection (2) shall be heard and decided as soon as practicable but in no event later than four days after the petition is filed.

(d) Notwithstanding any other provision of law, an expedited confidential appeal to the court of appeals shall be available to a minor for whom the court denies an order dispensing with the notice requirements of this article. Any such appeal shall be heard and decided no later than five days after the appeal is filed. An order dispensing with the notice requirements of this article shall not be subject to appeal.

(e) Notwithstanding any provision of law to the contrary, the minor is not required to pay a filing fee related to an action or appeal filed pursuant to this subsection (2).

(f) If either the district court or the court of appeals fails to act within the time periods required by this subsection (2), the court in which the proceeding is pending shall immediately issue an order dispensing with the notice requirements of this article.

(g) The Colorado supreme court shall issue rules governing the judicial bypass procedure, including rules that ensure that the confidentiality of minors filing bypass petitions will be protected. The Colorado supreme court shall also promulgate a form petition that may be used to initiate a bypass proceeding. The Colorado supreme court shall promulgate the rules and form governing the judicial bypass procedure by August 1, 2003. Physicians shall not be required to comply with this article until forty-five days after the Colorado supreme court publishes final rules and a final form.

Colorado Code § 12-37.5-108. Limitations

(1) This article shall in no way be construed so as to:

(a) Require any minor to submit to an abortion; or

(b) Prevent any minor from withdrawing her consent previously given to have an abortion; or

(c) Permit anything less than fully informed consent before submitting to an abortion.

(2) This article shall in no way be construed as either ratifying, granting or otherwise establishing an abortion right for minors independently of any other regulation, statute or court decision which may now or hereafter limit or abridge access to abortion by minors.

(4) PUBLIC FUNDS FOR ABORTION

Colorado prohibited the use of public funds to pay for abortions under the state's constitution and by statutes. The ban on the use of public funds was found unconstitutional in *Hern v. Beye*, 57 F.3d 906 (10th Cir. 1995), because the state failed to provide for all the exceptions required by federal law. The unenforceable statutory and constitutional provisions are set out below (one statute, Colorado Code § 25.5-3-106, is not reproduced here).

Colorado Constitution Art. 5 § 50.
Public funding of abortion forbidden

No public funds shall be used by the State of Colorado, its agencies or political subdivisions to pay or otherwise reimburse, either directly or indirectly, any person, agency or facility for the performance of any induced abortion, PROVIDED HOWEVER, that the General Assembly, by specific bill, may authorize and appropriate funds to be used for those medical services necessary to prevent the death of either a pregnant woman or her unborn child under circumstances where every reasonable effort is made to preserve the life of each.

Colorado Code § 25.5-4-415. No public funds for abortion

(1) It is the purpose of this section to implement the provisions of section 50 of article V of the Colorado constitution, adopted by the registered electors of the state of Colorado at the general election November 6, 1984, which prohibits the use of public funds by the state of Colorado or its agencies or political subdivisions to pay or otherwise reimburse, directly or indirectly, any person, agency, or facility for any induced abortion.

(2) If every reasonable effort has been made to preserve the lives of a pregnant woman and her unborn child, then public funds may be used pursuant to this section to pay or reimburse for necessary medical services, not otherwise provided for by law.

(3)(a) Except as provided in paragraph (b) of this subsection (3), any necessary medical services performed pursuant to this section shall be performed only in a licensed health care facility by a provider who is a licensed physician.

(b) However, such services may be performed in other than a licensed health care facility if, in the medical judgment of the attending physician, the life of the pregnant woman or her unborn child is substantially threatened and a transfer to a licensed health care facility would further endanger the life of the pregnant woman or her unborn child. Such medical services may be performed in other than a licensed health care facility if the medical services are necessitated by a life-endangering circumstance described in subparagraph (II) of paragraph (b) of subsection (6) of this section and if there is no li-

censed health care facility within a thirty-mile radius of the place where such medical services are performed.

(4)(a) Any physician who renders necessary medical services pursuant to subsection (2) of this section shall report the following information to the state department:

(I) The age of the pregnant woman and the gestational age of the unborn child at the time the necessary medical services were performed;

(II) The necessary medical services which were performed;

(III) The medical condition which necessitated the performance of necessary medical services;

(IV) The date such necessary medical services were performed and the name of the facility in which such services were performed.

(b) The information required to be reported pursuant to paragraph (a) of this subsection (4) shall be compiled by the state department and such compilation shall be an ongoing public record; except that the privacy of the pregnant woman and the attending physician shall be preserved.

(5) For purposes of this section, pregnancy is a medically diagnosable condition.

(6) For the purposes of this section:

(a)(I) "Death" means:

(A) The irreversible cessation of circulatory and respiratory functions; or

(B) The irreversible cessation of all functions of the entire brain, including the brain stem.

(II) A determination of death under this section shall be in accordance with accepted medical standards.

(b) "Life-endangering circumstance" means:

(I) The presence of a medical condition, other than a psychiatric condition, as determined by the attending physician, which represents a serious and substantial threat to the life of the pregnant woman if the pregnancy continues to term;

(II) The presence of a lethal medical condition in the unborn child, as determined by the attending physician and one other physician, which would result in the impending death of the unborn child during the term of pregnancy or at birth; or

(III) The presence of a psychiatric condition which represents a serious and substantial threat to the life of the pregnant woman if the pregnancy continues to term. In such case, unless the pregnant woman has been receiving prolonged psychiatric care, the attending licensed physician shall obtain consultation from a licensed physician specializing in psychiatry confirming the presence of such a psychiatric condition. The attending physician shall report the findings of such consultation to the state department.

(c) "Necessary medical services" means any medical procedures deemed necessary to prevent the death of a pregnant woman or her unborn child due to life-endangering circumstances.

(7) If any provision of this section or application thereof is held invalid, such invalidity shall not affect other provisions or applications of this section which can be given effect without the invalid provision or application, and to this end the provisions of this section are declared severable.

(8) Use of the term "unborn child" in this section is solely for the purposes of facilitating the implementation of section 50 of article V of the state constitution, and its use shall not affect any other law or statute nor shall it create any presumptions relating to the legal status of an unborn child or create or affect any distinction between the legal status of an unborn child and the legal status of a fetus.

(9) This section shall be repealed if section 50 of article V of the Colorado constitution is repealed.

Colorado Code § 25.5-5-318. Health services by school districts

(1) As used in this section:

(a) "School district" means any board of cooperative services established pursuant to article 5 of title 22, C.R.S., any state educational institution that serves students in kindergarten through twelfth grade including, but not limited to, the Colorado school for the deaf and the blind, created in article 80 of title 22, C.R.S., and any public school district organized under the laws of Colorado, except a junior college district.

***

(10)(a) A school district that provides health services under contract pursuant to this section may provide the health services directly or through contractual relationships or agreements with public or private entities, as allowed by applicable federal regulations. However, no moneys shall be expended in any form for abortions, except as provided in section 25.5-4-415 or as required by federal law.

(5) BAN ON ABORTION CLINIC VIOLENCE

Colorado enacted a statute which makes it unlawful for any person within 100 feet of an abortion facility's entrance, to knowingly approach within 8 feet of another person, without that person's consent, in order to pass a leaflet, handbill, display a sign, engage in oral protest, education, or counseling with that person. In *Hill v. Colorado* the United States Supreme Court upheld this restriction. Colorado has also provided for a civil action against anyone who violates the ban on abortion clinic harassment. The statutes addressing the issues are set out below.

Colorado Code § 18-9-122. Prohibited activities near facilities

(1) The general assembly recognizes that access to health care facilities for the purpose of obtaining medical counseling and treatment is imperative for the citizens of this state; that the exercise of a person's right to protest or counsel against certain medical procedures must be balanced against another person's right to obtain medical counseling and treatment in an unobstructed manner; and that preventing the willful obstruction of a person's access to medical counseling and treatment at a health care facility is a matter of statewide concern. The general assembly therefore declares that it is appropriate to enact legislation that prohibits a person from knowingly obstructing another person's entry to or exit from a health care facility.

(2) A person commits a class 3 misdemeanor if such person knowingly obstructs, detains, hinders, impedes, or blocks another person's entry to or exit from a health care facility.

(3) No person shall knowingly approach another person within eight feet of such person, unless such other person consents, for the purpose of passing a leaflet or handbill to, displaying a sign to, or engaging in oral protest, education, or counseling with such other person in the public way or sidewalk area within a radius of one hundred feet from any entrance door to a health care facility. Any person who violates this subsection (3) commits a class 3 misdemeanor.

(4) For the purposes of this section, "health care facility" means any entity that is licensed, certified, or otherwise authorized or permitted by law to administer medical treatment in this state.

(5) Nothing in this section shall be construed to prohibit a statutory or home rule city or county or city and county from adopting a law for the control of access to health care facilities that is no less restrictive than the provisions of this section.

(6) In addition to, and not in lieu of, the penalties set forth in this section, a person who violates the provisions of this section shall be subject to civil liability, as provided in section 13-21-106.7, C.R.S.

Colorado Code § 13-21-106.7. Civil damages

(1) A person is entitled to recover damages and to obtain injunctive relief from any person who commits or incites others to commit the offense

of preventing passage to or from a health care facility or engaging in prohibited activity near a health care facility, as defined in section 18-9-122(2), C.R.S.

(2) A conviction for criminal obstruction of passage to or from a health care facility pursuant to section 18-9-122, C.R.S., shall not be a condition precedent to maintaining a civil action pursuant to the provisions of this section.

(6) USE OF FACILITIES AND PEOPLE

Colorado addressed the issue of using facilities and employees to perform abortions in a pre–*Roe v. Wade* statute that is still valid in part. Under the statute hospitals are not required to allow abortions at their facilities. The employees and physicians at hospitals that do allow abortions are permitted to refuse to take part in abortions. The statute addressing the issue is set out below.

Colorado Code § 18-6-104.
Right to refuse to participate in abortion

Nothing ... requires a hospital to admit any patient ... for the purposes of performing an abortion.... A person who is a member of or associated with the staff of a hospital or any employee of a hospital in which [an abortion] has been authorized and who states in writing an objection to the termination on moral or religious grounds is not required to participate in the medical procedures which result in the termination of a pregnancy, and the refusal of any such person to participate does not form the basis for any disciplinary or other recriminatory action against the person.

(7) UNLAWFUL TERMINATION OF PREGNANCY

Colorado has made it a criminal offense to terminate a pregnancy unlawfully. The statutes addressing the matter are set out below.

Colorado Code § 18-3.5-101. Unlawful termination of pregnancy

(1) A person commits the offense of unlawful termination of a pregnancy if, with intent to terminate unlawfully the pregnancy of another person, the person unlawfully terminates the other person's pregnancy.

(2) Unlawful termination of a pregnancy is a class 4 felony.

Colorado Code § 18-3.5-102. Exclusions

Nothing in this article shall permit the prosecution of a person for providing medical treatment, including but not limited to an abortion, in utero treatment, or treatment resulting in live birth, to a pregnant woman for which the consent of the pregnant woman, or a person authorized by law to act on her behalf, has been obtained or for which consent is implied by law.

(8) BAN SALE OF FETAL TISSUE

Colorado prohibits trafficking in fetal tissue for anything of value. The statute addressing the matter is set out below.

Colorado Code § 25-2-111.5. Transfer of fetal tissue

(1) The general assembly hereby finds, determines, and declares that the United States congress enacted 42 U.S.C. sec. 289g-2, prohibiting the acquisition, receipt, or other transfer of human fetal tissue for valuable consideration if the transfer affects interstate commerce. The general assembly determines and declares that the acquisition, receipt, or other transfer of human fetal tissue for valuable consideration affects intrastate commerce and is not in the public interest of the residents of Colorado. Therefore, the general assembly finds, determines, and declares that the exchange for valuable consideration of human fetal tissue should be prohibited.

(2)(a) No physician or institution that performs procedures for the induced termination of pregnancy shall transfer such tissue for valuable consideration to any organization or person that conducts research using fetal tissue or that transplants fetal tissue for therapeutic purposes. For the purposes of this section, "valuable consideration" includes, but is not limited to:

(I) Any lease-sharing agreement in excess of the current market value for commercial rental property for the area in which the physician's or institution's place of business is located;

(II) Any lease-sharing agreement that is based on the term or number of induced terminations of pregnancy performed by such physician or institution;

(III) Any moneys, gifts in lieu of money, barter arrangements, or exchange of services that do not constitute reasonable payment associated with the transportation, implantation, processing, preservation, quality control, or storage of human fetal tissue as defined in 42 U.S.C. sec. 289g-2; or

(IV) Any agreement to purchase fetal tissue for a profit.

(b) Nothing in this subsection (2) shall prevent the disposition of fetal tissue from an induced termination of pregnancy pursuant to part 4 of article 15 of this title.

(3) Any physician or institution that violates subsection (2) of this section shall be fined by the state registrar not more than ten thousand dollars, depending upon the severity of the violation.

(4) The department of public health and environment may promulgate rules related to enforcement activities necessary to implement subsections (2) and (3) of this section.

Colorado Right to Life

Colorado Right to Life (CRL) is a Denver based pro-life organization that was founded on December 21, 1970. CRLC was formed in response to the Colorado legislature's enactment of a statute on April 25, 1967, that allowed abortion under limited circumstances. Through its president, Joe Riccobono, CRL seeks to promote reverence and respect for human life, whether born or unborn. CRL works to educate the community to the dangers of abortion and to encourage a favorable spiritual, physical and cultural environment that would put an end to abortion. *See also* **Pro-Life Organizations**

Coma and Pregnancy

Women who are pregnant and fall into a coma, either from a severe injury or medication, are at an increased risk of spontaneous abortion, stillbirth, therapeutic abortion and premature birth. In extremely rare instances, a pregnant woman in a coma may give full-term birth. One such incident occurred at a hospital in Cincinnati, Ohio on July 23, 2001. On that date twenty-four-year-old Chastity Cooper gave birth to a daughter, Alexis Michelle Cooper. Chastity was two weeks pregnant when she had an automobile accident that placed her in a coma. The accident occurred in Kentucky on November 25, 2000. Hospital officials believed that Chastity's delivery may have been the longest comatose pregnancy in the nation that resulted in a live birth.

Commission on Civil Rights

The United States Commission on Civil Rights was created for the purpose of investigating allegations of deprivations of civil rights because of color, race, religion, sex, age, disability, or national origin; or as a result of any pattern or practice of fraud; of the right of citizens of the United States to vote and have votes counted. The Commission was authorized by Congress to study and collect information relating to discrimination or denials of equal protection of the laws under the Constitution of the United States because of color, race, religion, sex, age, disability, or national origin, or in the administration of justice. In an effort to curtail the authority of the Commission, Congress expressly prohibited the Commission from engaging an abortion studies. The statute addressing the issue is set out below.

42 U.S.C.A. § 1975a(f) Duties of Commission

(f) Limitation relating to abortion

Nothing in this chapter or any other Act shall be construed as authorizing the Commission, its advisory committees, or any other per-

son under its supervision or control to study and collect, make appraisals of, or serve as a clearinghouse for any information about laws and policies of the Federal Government or any other governmental authority in the United States, with respect to abortion.

Complete Abortion *see* **Miscarriage**

Complications During and After Abortion

Studies suggest that legalized abortion in the United States has dramatically reduced the risk of death to women having abortions. However, death has not stopped. During the period 1973 to 1987, there were 305 women who died while having an abortion. Death of a woman occurs in one out of every 160,000 abortions. The risk of death associated with abortion increases with the length of pregnancy. It has been estimated that this risk is one death out of every 530,000 abortions performed less than 9 weeks gestation; one death per 17,000 abortions between 16–20 weeks gestation; and one death per 6,000 abortions performed after 20 weeks of gestation. Overall, the rate of death from full term delivery is much higher than the death rate associated with an abortion.

Complications during abortion. There are many different types of complications that can occur during an abortion. Included on the list of the most common problems are: uterine injury, cervical injury, bladder or bowel perforations, inflammation of the reproductive organs, fevers, convulsions, shock, and coma.

Complications after abortion. A successful abortion does not end the potential consequences of an abortion. Some post-abortion complications include: retained tissue from aborted fetus, miscarriages, difficulties in subsequent labor and delivery, pre-term and post-term births, handicapped births, pelvic inflammatory disease, increased risk of tubal pregnancy, and sterility. In addition, studies have also been done which show strong evidence that abortion increases the risk of a woman getting breast cancer. Studies have also found that some woman experience post-abortion psychological problems.

Illustrative cases of deaths from abortion:

(1) Apodaca, Mickey

Mickey Apodaca was twenty-eight years old and pregnant when she decided to have an abortion. Apodaca had the abortion performed at a clinic in El Paso, Texas on April 11, 1984. During the abortion her

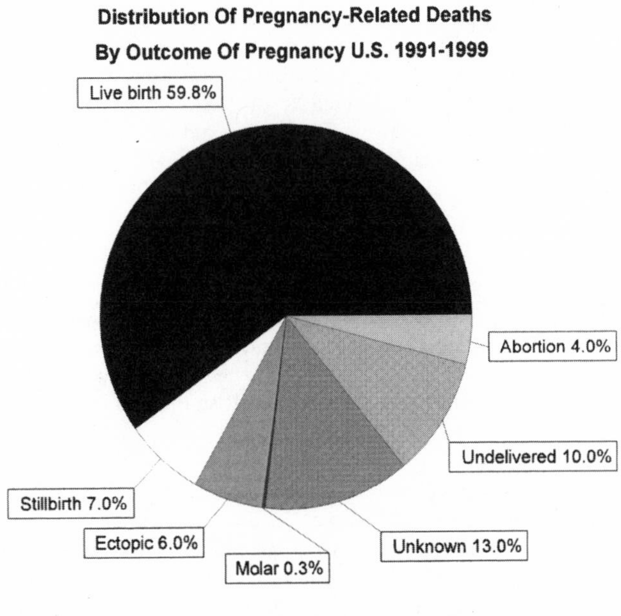

Source: National Center for Health Statistics.

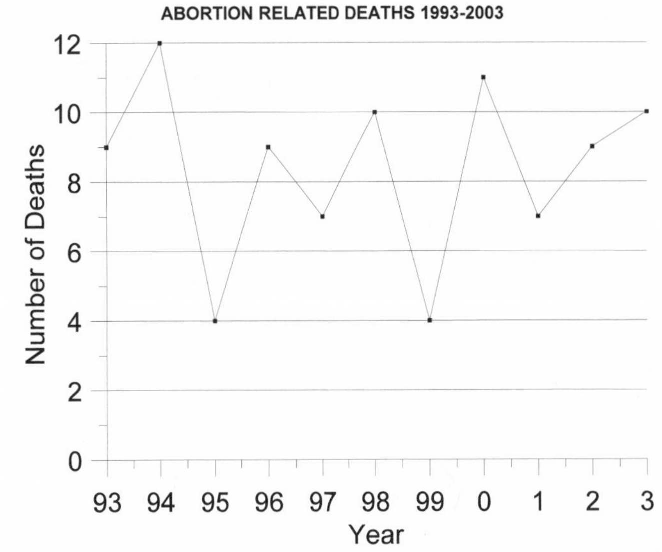

Source: National Center for Health Statistics.

uterus was perforated and she began bleeding uncontrollably. Apodaca was rushed from the clinic to a nearby hospital, where she died soon after from bleeding and complications during the abortion.

After Apodaca's death it was discovered that the person performing the abortion was actually out on bond, pending an appeal of a 1983 conviction for murder in another abortion case. Criminal charges were brought against the abortionist for Apodaca's death, but the charges were later dismissed.

(2) Bell, Deanna

Deanna Bell was only 13 years old when she became pregnant in 1992. Arrangements were made for her to have an abortion at a Chicago clinic on September 5 of that year. During the abortion procedure complications arose when amniotic fluid entered Bell's blood stream. She died as a result during the procedure.

(3) Bleavins, Cassandra K.

Cassandra K. Bleavins was 20 years old when she became pregnant in 1971. She sought and obtained a legal abortion at a Los Angeles County facility on September 2. About two weeks after the abortion, Bleavins returned to the abortion facility due to complications. She was treated with invasive surgery and returned home. Two days after returning home, Bleavins had to once again be taken to the abortion facility. While being treated she fell into a coma and had to be rushed to a hospital. Bleavins died a day after entering the hospital. It was later determined that she bled to death because of a torn uterine lining obtained during the abortion.

(4) Boom, Linda

Linda Boom learned in 1995 that she was pregnant and that the fetus had Down syndrome. She decided to have a eugenics abortion. Boom went to an abortion facility in Milwaukee, Wisconsin. During the abortion procedure chemicals that should have been injected into the fetus were instead injected into Boom's bloodstream. She subsequently died from the chemicals on September 22, 1995.

(5) Byrd, Belinda

Belinda Byrd was 37 years old and pregnant in 1987. She decided to obtain an abortion on January 24 of that year. The abortion was performed at a hospital in Los Angeles. After the procedure ended Byrd developed complications while still at the hospital. She sustained massive internal bleeding which sent her into a coma. Byrd was taken to another hospital for treatment, but died several days later.

(6) Cortez, Liliana

Liliana Cortez (1964–1986) went to a Los Angeles medical center on September 20, 1986, to have an abortion. During the abortion procedure complications arose with her heart, and she had to be rushed to a nearby hospital. Cortez died in the hospital five days later due to the complications from the abortion.

(7) Dowdy, Tamika

Tamika Dowdy was 22 years old and pregnant in 1998. She decided to have an abortion. In December of 1998 she went to a medical facility in Brooklyn, New York, to have the abortion. Complications arose during the procedure and Dowdy's heart stopped. She was rushed to a nearby hospital where she was pronounced dead.

(8) Garcia, Jammie

Jammie Garcia was 15 years old and pregnant in 1994. In February of that year she was taken to a Texas abortion clinic. The abortion was performed and she went home. Several days later Garcia she was rushed to a hospital due to a severe fever and vomiting. While at the hospital it was discovered that Garcia's uterus and cervix had been torn during the abortion. Garcia died several days after being admitted to the hospital.

(9) Gutierrez, Carolina

Carolina Gutierrez was 21 years old and pregnant with her third child in 1996. She decided to abort the child. Gutierrez went to an abortion clinic in Florida on December 19. During the abortion procedure complications arose and she had to be rushed to a nearby hospital. Gutierrez remained in the hospital in serious condition for seven weeks, before she died from infections caused by the abortion.

(10) Hamptlon, Sharon

Sharon Hamptlon (1969–1996) went to a California medical center on December 13, 1996 to have an abortion. During the abortion her uterus was punctured. Apparently this fact was not known to the abortionist, because Hamptlon was sent home after the abortion procedure was finished. She died en route to her home. The abortionist involved, Dr. Bruce Steir, eventually pled guilty to involuntary manslaughter in the death of Hamptlon, and was forced to relinquish his medical license.

(11) Heim, Donna

Donna Heim (1966–1986) was pregnant in 1986 and decided to have an abortion. On August 12 of that year, she went to a California medical center for the abortion. During the procedure complications arose and Heim went into a coma. She was rushed to a nearby hospital, but died the following day.

(12) Herron, Lou Ann

Lou Ann Herron was 33 years old and pregnant in 1998. She decided to have an abortion and went to a clinic in Phoenix, Arizona. During the abortion procedure complications arose after Herron's uterine lining was lacerated. She began bleeding profusely and had to be taken to a nearby hospital. She died shortly after arriving at the hospital. The abortionist, John Biskind, and a clinic administrator, Carol Schadoff, were charged with criminal homicide in the death of Herron. Both were eventually convicted in February of 2001.

(13) Madden, Michelle

Michelle Madden was 18 years old when she became pregnant in 1986. She was a college freshman and epileptic. Due to concerns stemming from her use of epilepsy medications, Madden decided to abort the fetus in November. She went to a medical center in Mobile, Alabama to have the abortion. After the procedure was over Madden went home. Within three days she had to be hospitalized. While at the hospital it was learned that fetal remains had been left inside Madden after the abortion. Several days after her hospitalization, Madden died from infections stemming from the negligently performed abortion.

(14) Moore, Sylvia

Sylvia Moore (1968–1986) was 18 years old and pregnant in 1986. In December of that year she went to a local Chicago clinic for an abortion. After the abortion was done, Moore was forced to leave the clinic even though she was experiencing complications from the procedure. She managed to find a nearby hospital. Shortly after she was admitted to the hospital, Moore died. It was subsequently determined that during the abortion procedure Moore's uterus, cervix and vagina had lacerations. A plastic object was also found inside her body.

(15) Pena, Mary

Mary Pena was 43 years old and pregnant in 1984. In December of that year she decided to have an abortion. Pena went to a Los Angeles health facility for the procedure. During the course of the abortion, Pena received severe cuts to her cervix and uterine lining. She bled profusely and eventually died as efforts were being made to stop the bleeding.

(16) Ravenell, Dawn

Dawn Ravenell (1971–1985) was a pregnant adolescent living in New York City in 1985. She managed to keep knowledge of her pregnancy from her parents, and secretly arranged to have an abortion on January 24. On that date Ravenell went to a medical center to have the abortion. During the course of the procedure complications arose and she suffered a cardiac arrest before going into a coma. Ravenell was rushed to a nearby hospital. She died three weeks after entering the hospital without ever regaining consciousness.

(17) Sanchez, Angela

Angela Sanchez (1967–1993) went to a Santa Ana, California clinic for an abortion in 1993. During the course of the abortion complications arose and Sanchez died. The abortionist attempted to dispose of the body, but was caught. After a police investigation into the matter, it was learned that the abortionist, Alicia Hanna, was not a physician. Felony charges were brought against Hanna and she was eventually convicted of second degree murder and sentenced to prison.

(18) Suddeth, Jennifer

Jennifer Suddeth (1965–1982) obtained an abortion from a Los Angeles County clinic in 1982. As she left the clinic and returned home she began bleeding from her vaginal area. The bleeding became profuse when she arrived home. An ambulance was summoned, but before paramedics arrived, she died. It was later learned that her uterine lining was lacerated during the abortion and resulted in her death. The abortionist was charged with criminal homicide, but a jury acquitted him of the charge.

(19) Tyke, Maureen Lynne

Maureen Lynne Tyke was 21 years old when she became pregnant in 1983. Although she lived in Pennsylvania, she traveled to Florida to abort the pregnancy. During the abortion procedure, which occurred in May of 1983, complications arose and Tyke had to be rushed to a hospital. She died several days later due to heart inflammation that was attributed to the abortion. *See also* **High-Risk Pregnancy**

Comstock Act

The United States Congress passed the Comstock Act in 1873, calling it an "Act of the Suppression of Trade in, and Circulation of, Obscene Literature and Articles of Immoral Use." The Act was named for Anthony Comstock, a nongovernmental official who undertook a personal crusade against matters he considered to be obscene. The Act criminalized publication, distribution, and possession of information, devices or medications for procuring abortions or contraception. A violation of the Act was punishable by up to five years imprisonment and a fine of up to $2,000.

Much of the provision in the Act dealing with contraception was repealed by Congress in 1971. It was held by the Supreme Court in *Bolger v. Youngs Drug Products Corp.* that a provision of the Comstock Act that prohibited mailing unsolicited advertisements for contraceptives violated the Free Speech Clause of the First Amendment.

The current version of the Act continues to prohibit mailing abortion matters. The abortion provisions have not been enforced since the 1973 United States Supreme Court decision legalizing abortion in *Roe v. Wade*. The Act has been expanded to include the distribution of abortion matter over the Internet. The current text of the Act is set out below.

18 U.S.C.A. § 1461. Mailing obscene or crime-inciting matter

Every obscene, lewd, lascivious, indecent, filthy or vile article, matter, thing, device, or substance; and—

Every article or thing designed, adapted, or intended for producing abortion, or for any indecent or immoral use; and

Every article, instrument, substance, drug, medicine, or thing which is advertised or described in a manner calculated to lead another to use or apply it for producing abortion, or for any indecent or immoral purpose; and

Every written or printed card, letter, circular, book, pamphlet, advertisement, or notice of any kind giving information, directly or indirectly, where, or how, or from whom, or by what means any of such mentioned matters, articles, or things may be obtained or made, or where or by whom any act or operation of any kind for the procuring or producing of abortion will be done or performed, or how or by what means abortion may be produced, whether sealed or unsealed; and

Every paper, writing, advertisement, or representation that any article, instrument, substance, drug, medicine, or thing may, or can, be used or applied for producing abortion, or for any indecent or immoral purpose; and

Every description calculated to induce or incite a person to so use or apply any such article, instrument, substance, drug, medicine, or thing—

Is declared to be nonmailable matter and shall not be conveyed in the mails or delivered from any post office or by any letter carrier.

Whoever knowingly uses the mails for the mailing, carriage in the mails, or delivery of anything declared by this section or section 3001(e) of title 39 to be nonmailable, or knowingly causes to be delivered by mail according to the direction thereon, or at the place at which it is directed to be delivered by the person to whom it is addressed, or knowingly takes any such thing from the mails for the purpose of circulating or disposing thereof, or of aiding in the circulation or disposition thereof, shall be fined under this title or imprisoned not more than five years, or both, for the first such offense, and shall be fined under this title or imprisoned not more than ten years, or both, for each such offense thereafter.

The term "indecent," as used in this section includes matter of a character tending to incite arson, murder, or assassination.

18 U.S.C.A. § 1462.
Importation or transportation of obscene matters

Whoever brings into the United States, or any place subject to the jurisdiction thereof, or knowingly uses any express company or other common carrier or interactive computer service (as defined in section 230(e)(2) of the Communications Act of 1934), for carriage in interstate or foreign commerce—

(a) any obscene, lewd, lascivious, or filthy book, pamphlet, picture, motion-picture film, paper, letter, writing, print, or other matter of indecent character; or

(b) any obscene, lewd, lascivious, or filthy phonograph recording, electrical transcription, or other article or thing capable of producing sound; or

(c) any drug, medicine, article, or thing designed, adapted, or intended for producing abortion, or for any indecent or immoral use; or any written or printed card, letter, circular, book, pamphlet, advertisement, or notice of any kind giving information, directly or indirectly, where, how, or of whom, or by what means any of such mentioned articles, matters, or things may be obtained or made; or

Whoever knowingly takes or receives, from such express company or other common carrier or interactive computer service (as defined in section 230(e)(2) of the Communications Act of 1934) any matter or thing the carriage or importation of which is herein made unlawful—

Shall be fined under this title or imprisoned not more than five years, or both, for the first such offense and shall be fined under this title or imprisoned not more than ten years, or both, for each such offense thereafter.

39 U.S.C.A. § 3001(e). Nonmailable matter

(e)(1) Any matter which is unsolicited by the addressee and which is designed, adapted, or intended for preventing conception (except unsolicited samples thereof mailed to a manufacturer thereof, a dealer therein, a licensed physician or surgeon, or a nurse, pharmacist, druggist, hospital, or clinic) is nonmailable matter, shall not be carried or delivered by mail, and shall be disposed of as the Postal Service directs.

(2) Any unsolicited advertisement of matter which is designed, adapted, or intended for preventing conception is nonmailable matter, shall not be carried or delivered by mail, and shall be disposed of as the Postal Service directs unless the advertisement—

(A) is mailed to a manufacturer of such matter, a dealer therein, a licensed physician or surgeon, or a nurse, pharmacist, druggist, hospital, or clinic; or

(B) accompanies in the same parcel any unsolicited sample excepted by paragraph (1) of this subsection.

An advertisement shall not be deemed to be unsolicited for the purposes of this paragraph if it is contained in a publication for which the addressee has paid or promised to pay a consideration or which he has otherwise indicated he desires to receive.

See also **Advertisement; Bigelow v. Virginia; Bolger v. Youngs Drug Products Corp.; Carey v. Population Services International; Contraception; Griswold v. Connecticut; Tariff Act**

Comstock, Anthony *see* **Comstock Act**

Conception

Conception is the point in time when a female egg is penetrated by a male sperm. The union of egg and sperm starts the fertilization process and the beginning of the potential birth of a baby. *See also* **Fetal Development; Gestational Age**

Conceptus

Conceptus refers to everything that is included in the gestational sac, e.g., fetus, placenta and fluids.

Concerned Women for America

Concerned Women for America (CWA) is a Washington, D.C., based pro-life organization. CWA was founded in 1979 by its chairperson Beverly LaHaye. The president of CWA is Wendy Wright. The organization has a membership that is estimated at more than 500,000 people. As part of its anti-abortion work, CWA engages in legislative lobbying and provides crisis pregnancy centers. The organization publishes a magazine called *Family Voice*. *See also* **Pro-Life Organizations**

Condoms

Condoms are prophylactic devices that are used during sexual intercourse to prevent pregnancy. The devices exist for both men and women.

Male condom. The male condom is an over-the-counter birth control device that can be bought without a prescription. The condom is composed of a thin sheet of latex or polyurethane. It is unfolded over the penis to allow a pocket at the end of the device to collect sperm. The condom prevents sperm from entering the vagina.

Female condom. The female condom (also called vaginal pouch) was introduced on the market in 1994. It is a pre-lubricated polyurethane loose-fitting sheath designed to prevent pregnancy. The condom is inserted much like a diaphragm. There is an inner ring positioned at each end of the condom. Insertion is done by squeezing and inserting the closed end of the condom so that it covers the opening of the cervix. The ring of the open end rests outside of the vagina after insertion. The condom should be removed immediately and thrown away after intercourse. *See also* **Contraception**

Congenital

Congenital refers to any abnormality or defect that occurs to the embryo or fetus during development in the womb. *See also* **Birth Defects and Abortion**

Congenital Heart Defect

A congenital heart defect occurs when the heart or blood vessels near the heart do not develop normally before birth. Heart defects range in severity from mild problems to very severe malformations. Infants born with simple heart defects usually survive into adulthood without any significant limitations. Children who survive with severe defects will usually have significant health limitations and may have learning difficulties.

In most cases the cause of congenital heart defects is not known. The disease may be the result of a viral infection or alcohol or drug use by the mother during pregnancy. There are approximately 35,000 babies born each year with a congenital heart defect. Infants born with congenital heart defects die more often in the first year of life than children with any other birth defect. Some of the most common defects include: hypoplastic left heart syndrome, pulmonary stenosis, coarctation of the aorta, tricuspid atresia, and patent ductus arteriosus.

Hypoplastic left heart syndrome. Hypoplastic left heart syndrome is a birth defect involving under-development of the left side of the heart. Infants born with this syndrome become pale, have breathing difficulties, and are unable to feed. Most infants with this defect die within the first month of being born. In some cases the syndrome can be successfully treated through surgery or a heart transplant.

Pulmonary stenosis. Pulmonary stenosis involves a defective pulmonary valve that does not open properly. The pulmonary valve must open to allow blood to flow from the right ventricle to the lungs. When this does not occur the right ventricle must pump harder than normal to overcome the obstruction. The obstruction can usually be corrected without surgery, though in some cases open heart surgery may be needed. This condition occurs in about 1 out of 8000 infants.

Coarctation of the aorta. Coarctation of the aorta is a condition where the aorta is pinched and obstructs blood flow to the lower part of the body. Symptoms of this defect may develop as early as the first week after birth. The condition may cause congestive heart failure or high blood pressure that requires early surgery.

Tricuspid atresia. Tricuspid atresia is a condition involving the absence of tricuspid valve, which means no blood can flow from the right atrium to the right ventricle. This condition causes the right ventricle to be small and not fully developed. An infant's blood is thereby deprived of all the oxygen needed, which causes the child to look blue. Usually surgery is needed to increase blood flow to the lungs. In some infants too much blood flows to the lungs and surgery is needed to reduce it.

Patent ductus arteriosus. Patent ductus arteriosus is a condition where the channel between the pulmonary artery and the aorta fails to close at birth. This condition causes some of the blood in the left side of the heart to go the lungs instead of to the general circulation. This defect occurs in 60 out of 100,000 infants. The condition can be treated without surgery, but in some cases surgery may be necessary. If the defect is not corrected the infant has a risk of developing heart failure or an infection of the lining of the heart chambers and heart valves by bacteria, fungi, viruses, or other microorganisms. *See also* **Birth Defects and Abortion**

Congenital Hypothyroidism

Congenital hypothyroidism is a disorder involving the absence of thyroid function in a newborn. The condition may result from the absence or lack of development of the thyroid gland or destruction of the thyroid gland. The disorder affects 1 out of every 7,000 births. Symptoms of the disorder include a puffy face, dull look, large tongue, dry brittle hair, decreased muscle tone, and jaundice. Most of the symptoms of the disorder can be treated if the disease is timely diagnosed. If untreated timely, the disorder can lead to severe mental retardation and growth retardation. *See* **Birth Defects and Abortion**

Congenital Rubella Syndrome

Congenital rubella syndrome is a group of physical abnormalities that develop in a fetus as a result of the mother being exposed to the rubella virus (German measles) during pregnancy. Some of the symptoms of the disease include low birthweight, feeding problems, diarrhea, pneumonia, meningitis, blood and liver abnormalities, skin rash, abnormally small head, lethargy, hearing loss, eye defects, seizures, heart defects, damaged central nervous system, increased risk of diabetes and mental retardation. The infection can cause miscarriage or stillbirth. There is no specific treatment for congenital rubella syndrome. Symptoms are treated as they appear. The disease can be completely prevented through vaccination prior to pregnancy. The success of vaccination is evident in that the disease dropped from 57,686 cases in 1969, to only 345 cases in 1998. *See also* **Birth Defects and Abortion**

Congenital Syphilis *see* **Syphilis**

Congenital Toxoplasmosis *see* **Toxoplasmosis**

Connecticut

(1) OVERVIEW

The state of Connecticut enacted its first criminal abortion statute in 1821. This statute became the first criminal abortion statute in the nation. The statute underwent several amendments prior to the 1973 decision by the United States Supreme Court in *Roe v. Wade*, which legalized abortion in the nation. Prior to and shortly after *Roe*, the Supreme Court issued several decisions involving Connecticut's reproductive health laws.

Connecticut has taken affirmative steps, through statutes and administrative regulations, to respond to *Roe* and its progeny. Through administrative regulations Connecticut permits health care professionals to refuse to participate in abortions for moral or religious reasons; require all women seeking abortions be fully informed of the possible health consequences and alternatives to abortion; and limited the performance of abortion to physicians. Connecticut has addressed a few abortion issues by statute that include pre-viability and post-viability abortion, abortion by minors, consent for mentally handicapped, abortion facility regulations, and human cloning.

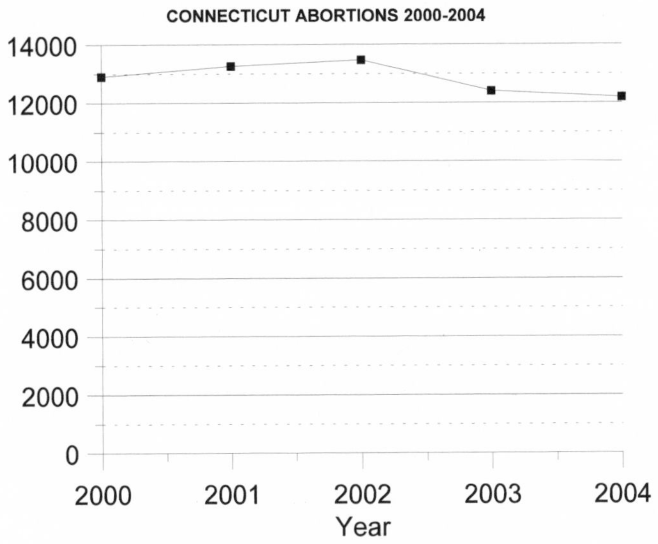

Source: National Center for Health Statistics.

Connecticut Abortion by Age Group 2000–2004

Year	<15	15–19	20–24	25–29	30–34	35–39	≥40	Unknown
2000	68	2,612	4,134	2,731	1,776	1,054	309	224
2001	67	2,739	4,322	2,717	1,839	1,090	386	110
2002	80	2,671	4,407	2,814	1,872	1,112	371	143
2003	74	2,401	4,116	2,559	1,722	1,049	354	129
2004	63	2,263	3,917	2,736	1,724	1,016	381	89
Total	352	12,686	20,896	13,557	8,933	5,321	1,801	695

Age Group (yrs)

Source: National Center for Health Statistics.

Connecticut Abortion by Weeks of Gestation 2000–2004

Weeks of Gestation	2000	2001	2002	2003	2004	Total
≤8	7,480	7,226	8,049	7,496	7,497	37,748
9–10	2,543	2,328	2,441	2,226	2,121	11,659
11–12	1,306	1,218	1,276	1,202	1,133	6,135
13–15	734	781	740	665	814	3,734
16–20	356	390	350	375	317	1,788
≥21	24	25	40	54	28	171
Not known	465	1,297	590	386	279	3,017

Source: National Center for Health Statistics.

(2) UNITED STATES SUPREME COURT DECISIONS

In 1965 the United States Supreme Court issued its first major reproductive health decision in *Griswold v. Connecticut*. *Griswold* held that the right of privacy found in the constitution, prohibited enforcement of a Connecticut statute that made it a crime to give married persons contraceptive information and devices. The Supreme Court issued an opinion in 1975, in the case of *Connecticut v. Menillo*, which held that the federal constitution was not violated by application of a provision in Connecticut's criminal abortion statute that punished "nonphysicians" who attempted or performed abortions at any stage of a pregnancy. In 1977 it was ruled in *Maher v. Roe* by the Supreme Court that the Equal Protection Clause of the Fourteenth Amendment did not prohibit Connecticut from excluding nontherapeutic abortions from its Medicaid program. However, in *Doe v. Maher*, 515 A.2d 134 (Conn.Super. 1986) a Connecticut trial court ruled that the state's policy of permitting state medical assistance only for therapeutic abortions violated the state constitution.

(3) PRE-VIABILITY AND POST-VIABILITY ABORTION

Connecticut expressly permits abortions by statute prior to fetal viability. The state has also affirmatively banned post-viability abortions, except to save the life or health of the woman. The statute addressing the issues is set out below.

Connecticut Code § 19a-602.
Pregnancy prior to and after viability

(a) The decision to terminate a pregnancy prior to the viability of the fetus shall be solely that of the pregnant woman in consultation with her physician.

(b) No abortion may be performed upon a pregnant woman after viability of the fetus except when necessary to preserve the life or health of the pregnant woman.

(4) ABORTION BY MINORS

Under the laws of Connecticut a pregnant minor is not required to notify or obtain consent of her parents or guardian before having an abortion. Connecticut grants a minor the exclusive right to decide whether her parents or guardian should be notified. Abortion providers are required to provide a minor with meaningful information about the risks of abortions and alternatives. The statute addressing the matter is set out below.

Connecticut Code § 19a-601. Information provided to minors

(a) Prior to the performance of an abortion upon a minor, a physician or counselor shall provide pregnancy information and counseling in accordance with this section in a manner and language that will be understood by the minor. The physician or counselor shall:

(1) Explain that the information being given to the minor is being given objectively and is not intended to coerce, persuade or induce the minor to choose to have an abortion or to carry the pregnancy to term;

(2) Explain that the minor may withdraw a decision to have an abortion at any time before the abortion is performed or may reconsider a decision not to have an abortion at any time within the time period during which an abortion may legally be performed;

(3) Explain to the minor the alternative choices available for managing the pregnancy, including: (A) Carrying the pregnancy to term and keeping the child, (B) carrying the pregnancy to term and placing the child for adoption, placing the child with a relative or obtaining voluntary foster care for the child, and (C) having an abortion, and explain that public and private agencies are available to assist the minor with whichever alternative she chooses and that a list of these agencies and the services available from each will be provided if the minor requests;

(4) Explain that public and private agencies are available to provide birth control information and that a list of these agencies and the services available from each will be provided if the minor requests;

(5) Discuss the possibility of involving the minor's parents, guardian or other adult family members in the minor's decision-making concerning the pregnancy and whether the minor believes that involvement would be in the minor's best interests; and

(6) Provide adequate opportunity for the minor to ask any questions concerning the pregnancy, abortion, child care and adoption, and provide information the minor seeks or, if the person cannot provide the information, indicate where the minor can receive the information.

(b) After the person provides the information and counseling to a minor as required by this section, such person shall have the minor sign and date a form stating that:

(1) The minor has received information on alternatives to abortion and that there are agencies that will provide assistance and that a list of these agencies and the services available from each will be provided if the minor requests;

(2) The minor has received an explanation that the minor may withdraw an abortion decision or reconsider a decision to carry a pregnancy to term;

(3) The alternatives available for managing the pregnancy have been explained to the minor;

(4) The minor has received an explanation about agencies available to provide birth control information and that a list of these agencies and the services available from each will be provided if the minor requests;

(5) The minor has discussed with the person providing the information and counseling the possibility of involving the minor's parents, guardian or other adult family members in the minor's decision-making about the pregnancy;

(6) If applicable, the minor has determined that not involving the minor's parents, guardian or other adult family members is in the minor's best interests; and

(7) The minor has been given an adequate opportunity to ask questions.

(c) The person providing the information and counseling shall also sign and date the form and shall include such person's business address and business telephone number. The person shall keep a copy for such minor's medical record and shall give the form to the minor or, if the minor requests and if such person is not the attending physician, transmit the form to the minor's attending physician. Such medical record shall be maintained as otherwise provided by law.

(d) The provision of pregnancy information and counseling by a physician or counselor which is evidenced in writing containing the information and statements provided in this section and which is signed by the minor shall be presumed to be evidence of compliance with the requirements of this section.

(e) The requirements of this section shall not apply when, in the best medical judgment of the physician based on the facts of the case before him, a medical emergency exists that so complicates the pregnancy or the health, safety or well-being of the minor as to require an immediate abortion. A physician who does not comply with the requirements of this section by reason of this exception shall state in the medical record of the abortion the medical indications on which his judgment was based.

(5) CONSENT FOR MENTALLY HANDICAPPED

Connecticut provides by statute that a guardian of a mentally handicapped person cannot consent to an abortion by the person, except for health reasons. The statute addressing the matter is set out below.

Connecticut Code § 45a-677(e). Guardian powers

(e) A plenary guardian or limited guardian of a person with mental retardation shall not have the power or authority:

(1–8) Omitted.

(9) to consent on behalf of the ward to an abortion or removal of a body organ, except in accordance with applicable statutory procedures when necessary to preserve the life or prevent serious impairment of the physical or mental health of the ward.

(6) ABORTION FACILITY REGULATIONS

Connecticut provides by statute for the creation of regulations to govern facilities that offer abortion services. The statute is set out below.

Connecticut Code § 19a-116. Regulation for abortion facilities

The Commissioner of Public Health shall adopt regulations, in accordance with chapter 54, establishing standards to control and ensure the quality of medical care provided to any pregnant woman undergoing an induced abortion at any outpatient clinic regulated under the Public Health Code. Such standards shall include, but are not limited to, provisions concerning: (1) The verification of pregnancy and a determination of the duration of such pregnancy; (2) preoperative instruction and counseling; (3) operative permission and informed consent; (4) postoperative counseling including family planning; and (5) minimum qualifications for counselors.

(7) ABORTION CLINICS, STAFF AND INFORMED CONSENT

Connecticut provides by administrative regulation for abortion clinic requirements. These requirements include matters pertaining to equipment, staffing qualifications and information that must be given to a patient. The regulation is reproduced in part below.

Connecticut Admin. Code § 19a-116-1.
Abortion clinics, staff and informed consent

Outpatient clinics which offer abortion services shall comply with sections 19-13-D45 through 19-13-D54 of the Regulations of Connecticut State Agencies and in addition thereto, shall comply with the following provisions:

(a) Facilities, equipment and care shall be consistent with the national standards of the American College of Obstetrics and Gynecology.

(b) Any women seeking an abortion shall be given:

(1) Verification of the diagnosis and duration of pregnancy, including preoperative history and physical examination;

(2) Information and an explanation of the procedure to be followed in accordance with subsection (c) of this section;

(3) Counseling about her decision;

(4) Laboratory tests, including blood grouping and Rh factor;

(5) Preventive therapy if at risk for Rh sensitization;

(6) Examination of tissue by a pathologist;

(7) Consultation as to the need for follow-up care;

(8) Information on family planning;

(9) A written discharge summary which indicates the patient's status and discharge plan, signed by both the patient and a licensed or certified health care provider, a copy of which shall be given to the patient and a copy shall be retained as part of the medical record; and

(10) Information regarding access to her medical record, which shall include a statement of patient confidentiality and the requirement for written consent for release of information to persons not otherwise authorized by law to access the record.

(c) Informed consent. Prior to performing an abortion, a counselor shall obtain informed consent from the woman seeking to have the abortion. Informed consent shall exist only when a consent form is completed voluntarily and in accordance with the following provisions:

(1) An individual who obtains informed consent from a woman for an abortion procedure shall:

(A) Offer to answer any questions the patient may have concerning the procedure;

(B) Provide a copy of the informed consent form to the patient as described in subdivision (2) of this subsection;

(C) Provide all of the following information orally to the patient:

(i) A thorough explanation of the procedures to be performed; and

(ii) A full description of the discomforts and risks that may accompany or follow the performance of the procedure; and

(D) Assure the patient that an interpreter is provided to assist the patient if she does not understand the language used on the consent form or the language used by the counselor obtaining consent.

(2) Consent form requirements

(A) A consent form shall clearly spell out in language the patient can understand the nature and consequences of the procedure which shall be used.

(B) The consent form shall be signed and dated by:

(i) the patient;

(ii) the interpreter, if one is provided;

(iii) the counselor who obtains the consent; and

(iv) the physician who will perform the procedure.

(d) Staff qualifications

(1) All counselors in an abortion clinic shall have background preparation in social work, psychology, counseling, nursing, or ministry. Such preparation shall have been obtained in formal course work or through in-service staff training.

(2) Those counselors who do not have a graduate degree in any of the above mentioned fields shall be supervised by a person with such a graduate degree. Such supervision shall consist of the direction, inspection, and on-site observation of the activities of the counselors in performance of their duties.

(8) GENERAL ABORTION REQUIREMENTS

Connecticut provides by administrative regulation that abortions must be performed by a physician, impose certain duties on physicians and clinics, and permits persons to refuse to participate in abortions. The regulation addressing the matters is set out below.

Connecticut Admin. Code § 19-13-D54.
General abortion requirements

(a) No abortion shall be performed at any stage of pregnancy except by a person licensed to practice medicine and surgery in the state of Connecticut.

(b) All induced abortions will be reported within seven days by the physician performing the procedure to the state commissioner of public health who will maintain such reports in a confidential file and use them only for statistical purposes except in cases involving licensure. Such reports will specify date of abortion, place where performed, age of woman and town and state of residence, approximate duration of pregnancy, method of abortion, and explanation of any complications. The name of the woman will not be given. These records will be destroyed within two years after date of receipt. In addition, a fetal death certificate shall be filed for each fetus born dead which is the result of gestation of not less than twenty weeks, or a live birth certificate shall be filed for each fetus born alive regardless of gestational age, as provided in sections 7-48 and 7-60 of the Connecticut General Statutes. If a live born fetus subsequently dies, a death certificate shall be filed as provided in section 7-62b of the Connecticut General Statutes.

(c) All induced abortions after the second trimester as verified by ultrasound, last menstrual period and pelvic exam, shall be done only in a licensed hospital with a department of obstetrics and gynecology and a department of anesthesiology.

(d) All outpatient clinics operated by corporations or municipalities where abortions are performed shall develop standards to control the quality of medical care provided to women having abortions. These standards shall include but not necessarily be limited to:

(1) verification of pregnancy and determination of duration of pregnancy;

(2) pre-operative instruction and counseling;

(3) operative permission and informed consent;

(4) pre-operative history and physical examination;

(5) pre-operative laboratory procedure for blood Rh factor;

(6) prevention of Rh sensitization;

(7) examination of the tissue by a pathologist;

(8) receiving and recovery room facilities;

(9) a standard operating room;

(10) post-operative counseling including family planning; and

(11) a permanent record.

(e) There shall be a mechanism for continuing review to evaluate the quality of records and the quality of clinical work. This review shall include all deaths, complications, infections and such other cases as shall be determined by the chief of the department of obstetrics and gynecology of the hospital or the clinic medical director.

(f) No person shall be required to participate in any phase of an abortion that violates his or her judgment, philosophical, moral or religious beliefs.

(g) If the newborn shows signs of life following an abortion, those measures used to support life in a premature infant shall be employed.

(h) During the third trimester of pregnancy, abortions may be performed only when necessary to preserve the life or health of the expectant mother.

(9) HUMAN CLONING

Connecticut has created a criminal statute that prohibits human cloning. The state does allow research involving embryonic stem cells under certain conditions. A special fund, advisory committee and peer review committee have been established for embryonic stem cell research. The statutes addressing the issues are set out below.

Connecticut Code § 19a-32d. Prohibition on human cloning

(a) As used in sections 19a-32d to 19a-32g, inclusive, and section 4-28e:

(1) "Institutional review committee" means the local institutional review committee specified in 21 USC 360j(g)(3)(A)(i), as amended from time to time, and, when applicable, an institutional review board established in accordance with the requirements of 45 CFR 46, Subpart A, as amended from time to time.

(2) "Cloning of a human being" means inducing or permitting a replicate of a living human being's complete set of genetic material to develop after gastrulation commences.

(3) "Gastrulation" means the process immediately following the blastula state when the hollow ball of cells representing the early embryo undergoes a complex and coordinated series of movements that results in the formation of the three primary germ layers, the ectoderm, mesoderm and endoderm.

(4) "Embryonic stem cells" means cells created through the joining of a human egg and sperm or through nuclear transfer that are sufficiently undifferentiated such that they cannot be identified as components of any specialized cell type.

(5) "Nuclear transfer" means the replacement of the nucleus of a human egg with a nucleus from another human cell.

(6) "Eligible institution" means (A) a nonprofit, tax-exempt academic institution of higher education, (B) a hospital that conducts biomedical research, or (C) any entity that conducts biomedical research or embryonic or human adult stem cell research.

(b) No person shall knowingly (1) engage or assist, directly or indirectly, in the cloning of a human being, (2) implant human embryos created by nuclear transfer into a uterus or a device similar to a uterus, or (3) facilitate human reproduction through clinical or other use of human embryos created by nuclear transfer. Any person who violates the provisions of this subsection shall be fined not more than one hundred thousand dollars or imprisoned not more than ten years, or both. Each violation of this subsection shall be a separate and distinct offense.

(c) (1) A physician or other health care provider who is treating a patient for infertility shall provide the patient with timely, relevant and appropriate information sufficient to allow that person to make an informed and voluntary choice regarding the disposition of any embryos or embryonic stem cells remaining following an infertility treatment.

(2) A patient to whom information is provided pursuant to subdivision (1) of this subsection shall be presented with the option of storing, donating to another person, donating for research purposes,

or otherwise disposing of any unused embryos or embryonic stem cells.

(3) A person who elects to donate for stem cell research purposes any human embryos or embryonic stem cells remaining after receiving infertility treatment, or unfertilized human eggs or human sperm shall provide written consent for that donation and shall not receive direct or indirect payment for such human embryos, embryonic stem cells, unfertilized human eggs or human sperm.

(4) Any person who violates the provisions of this subsection shall be fined not more than fifty thousand dollars or imprisoned not more than five years, or both. Each violation of this subsection shall be a separate and distinct offense.

(d) A person may conduct research involving embryonic stem cells, provided (1) the research is conducted with full consideration for the ethical and medical implications of such research, (2) the research is conducted before gastrulation occurs, (3) prior to conducting such research, the person provides to the Commissioner of Public Health documentation verifying that any human embryos, embryonic stem cells, unfertilized human eggs or human sperm used in such research have been donated voluntarily in accordance with the provisions of subsection (c) of this section, on a form and in the manner prescribed by the Commissioner of Public Health, (4) the general research program under which such research is conducted is reviewed and approved by an institutional review committee, as required under federal law, and (5) the specific protocol used to derive stem cells from an embryo is reviewed and approved by an institutional review committee.

(e) The Commissioner of Public Health shall enforce the provisions of this section and may adopt regulations, in accordance with the provisions of chapter 54, relating to the administration and enforcement of this section. The commissioner may request the Attorney General to petition the Superior Court for such order as may be appropriate to enforce the provisions of this section.

(f) Any person who conducts research involving embryonic stem cells in violation of the requirements of subdivision (2) of subsection (d) of this section shall be fined not more than fifty thousand dollars, or imprisoned not more than five years, or both.

Connecticut Code § 19a-32e. Stem Cell Research Fund

(a) There is established the "Stem Cell Research Fund" which shall be a separate, nonlapsing account within the General Fund. The fund may contain any moneys required or permitted by law to be deposited in the fund and any funds received from any public or private contributions, gifts, grants, donations, bequests or devises to the fund. The Commissioner of Public Health may make grants-in-aid from the fund in accordance with the provisions of subsection (b) of this section.

(b) Not later than June 30, 2006, the Stem Cell Research Advisory Committee established pursuant to section 19a-32f shall develop an application for grants-in-aid under this section for the purpose of conducting embryonic or human adult stem cell research and may receive applications from eligible institutions for such grants-in-aid on and after said date. The Stem Cell Research Advisory Committee shall require any applicant for a grant-in-aid under this section to conduct stem cell research to submit (1) a complete description of the applicant's organization, (2) the applicant's plans for stem cell research and proposed funding for such research from sources other than the state of Connecticut, and (3) proposed arrangements concerning financial benefits to the state of Connecticut as a result of any patent, royalty payment or similar rights developing from any stem cell research made possible by the awarding of such grant-in-aid. Said committee shall direct the Commissioner of Public Health with respect to the awarding of such grants-in-aid after considering recommendations from the Stem Cell Research Peer Review Committee established pursuant to section 19a-32g.

(c) Commencing with the fiscal year ending June 30, 2006, and for each of the nine consecutive fiscal years thereafter, until the fiscal year ending June 30, 2015, not less than ten million dollars shall be available from the Stem Cell Research Fund for grants-in-aid to eligible institutions for the purpose of conducting embryonic or human adult stem cell research, as directed by the Stem Cell Research Advisory Committee established pursuant to section 19a-32f. Any balance of such amount not used for such grants-in-aid during a fiscal year shall be carried forward for the fiscal year next succeeding for such grants-in-aid.

Connecticut Code § 19a-32f. Stem Cell Advisory Committee

(a) (1) There is established a Stem Cell Research Advisory Committee. The committee shall consist of the Commissioner of Public Health and eight members who shall be appointed as follows: Two by the Governor, one of whom shall be nationally recognized as an active investigator in the field of stem cell research and one of whom shall have background and experience in the field of bioethics; one each by the president pro tempore of the Senate and the speaker of the House of Representatives, who shall have background and experience in private sector stem cell research and development; one each by the majority leaders of the Senate and House of Representatives, who shall be academic researchers specializing in stem cell research; one by the minority leader of the Senate, who shall have background and experience in either private or public sector stem cell research and development or related research fields, including, but not limited to, embryology, genetics or cellular biology; and one by the minority leader of the House of Representatives, who shall have background and experience in business or financial investments. Members shall serve for a term of four years commencing on October first, except that members first appointed by the Governor and the majority leaders of the Senate and House of Representatives shall serve for a term of two years. No member may serve for more than two consecutive four-year terms and no member may serve concurrently on the Stem Cell Research Peer Review Committee established pursuant to section 19a-32g. All initial appointments to the committee shall be made by October 1, 2005. Any vacancy shall be filled by the appointing authority.

(2) On and after July 1, 2006, the advisory committee shall include eight additional members who shall be appointed as follows: Two by the Governor, one of whom shall be nationally recognized as an active investigator in the field of stem cell research and one of whom shall have background and experience in the field of ethics; one each by the president pro tempore of the Senate and the speaker of the House of Representatives, who shall have background and experience in private sector stem cell research and development; one each by the majority leaders of the Senate and House of Representatives, who shall be academic researchers specializing in stem cell research; one by the minority leader of the Senate, who shall have background and experience in either private or public sector stem cell research and development or related research fields, including, but not limited to, embryology, genetics or cellular biology; and one by the minority leader of the House of Representatives, who shall have background and experience in business or financial investments. Members shall serve for a term of four years, except that (A) members first appointed by the Governor and the majority leaders of the Senate and House of Representatives pursuant to this subdivision shall serve for a term of two years and three months, and (B) members first appointed by the remaining appointing authorities shall serve for a term of four years and three months. No member appointed pursuant to this subdivision may serve for more than two consecutive four-year terms and no such member may serve concurrently on the Stem Cell Research Peer Review Committee established pursuant to section 19a-32g. All initial appointments to the committee pursuant to this subdivision shall be made by July 1, 2006. Any vacancy shall be filled by the appointing authority.

(b) The Commissioner of Public Health shall serve as the chairperson

of the committee and shall schedule the first meeting of the committee, which shall be held no later than December 1, 2005.

(c) All members appointed to the committee shall work to advance embryonic and human adult stem cell research. Any member who fails to attend three consecutive meetings or who fails to attend fifty per cent of all meetings held during any calendar year shall be deemed to have resigned from the committee.

(d) Notwithstanding the provisions of any other law, it shall not constitute a conflict of interest for a trustee, director, partner, officer, stockholder, proprietor, counsel or employee of any eligible institution, or for any other individual with a financial interest in any eligible institution, to serve as a member of the committee. All members shall be deemed public officials and shall adhere to the code of ethics for public officials set forth in chapter 10. Members may participate in the affairs of the committee with respect to the review or consideration of grant-in-aid applications, including the approval or disapproval of such applications, except that no member shall participate in the affairs of the committee with respect to the review or consideration of any grant-in-aid application filed by such member or by any eligible institution in which such member has a financial interest, or with whom such member engages in any business, employment, transaction or professional activity.

(e) The Stem Cell Research Advisory Committee shall (1) develop, in consultation with the Commissioner of Public Health, a donated funds program to encourage the development of funds other than state appropriations for embryonic and human adult stem cell research in this state, (2) examine and identify specific ways to improve and promote for-profit and not-for-profit embryonic and human adult stem cell and related research in the state, including, but not limited to, identifying both public and private funding sources for such research, maintaining existing embryonic and human adult stem-cell-related businesses, recruiting new embryonic and human adult stem-cell-related businesses to the state and recruiting scientists and researchers in such field to the state, (3) establish and administer, in consultation with the Commissioner of Public Health, a stem cell research grant program which shall provide grants-in-aid to eligible institutions for the advancement of embryonic or human adult stem cell research in this state pursuant to section 19a-32e, and (4) monitor the stem cell research conducted by eligible institutions that receive such grants-in-aid.

(f) Connecticut Innovations, Incorporated shall serve as administrative staff of the committee and shall assist the committee in (1) developing the application for the grants-in-aid authorized under subsection (e) of this section, (2) reviewing such applications, (3) preparing and executing any assistance agreements or other agreements in connection with the awarding of such grants-in-aid, and (4) performing such other administrative duties as the committee deems necessary.

(g) Not later than June 30, 2007, and annually thereafter until June 30, 2015, the Stem Cell Research Advisory Committee shall report, in accordance with section 11-4a, to the Governor and the General Assembly on (1) the amount of grants-in-aid awarded to eligible institutions from the Stem Cell Research Fund pursuant to section 19a-32e, (2) the recipients of such grants-in-aid, and (3) the current status of stem cell research in the state.

Connecticut Code 19a-32g. Stem Cell Peer Review Committee

(a) (1) There is established a Stem Cell Research Peer Review Committee. The committee shall consist of five members appointed by the Commissioner of Public Health. All members appointed to the committee shall (A) have demonstrated knowledge and understanding of the ethical and medical implications of embryonic and human adult stem cell research or related research fields, including, but not limited to, embryology, genetics or cellular biology, (B) have practical research experience in human adult or embryonic stem cell research or related research fields, including, but not limited to, embryology, genetics or cellular biology, and (C) work to advance embryonic and human adult stem cell research. Members shall serve for a term of four years commencing on October first, except that three members first appointed by the Commissioner of Public Health shall serve for a term of two years. No member may serve for more than two consecutive four-year terms and no member may serve concurrently on the Stem Cell Research Advisory Committee established pursuant to section 19a-32f. All initial appointments to the committee shall be made by October 1, 2005. Any member who fails to attend three consecutive meetings or who fails to attend fifty per cent of all meetings held during any calendar year shall be deemed to have resigned from the committee.

(2) On and after July 1, 2007, the Commissioner of Public Health may appoint such additional members to the Stem Cell Research Peer Review Committee as the commissioner deems necessary for the review of applications for grants-in-aid, provided the total number of Stem Cell Research Peer Review Committee members does not exceed fifteen. Such additional members shall be appointed as provided in subdivision (1) of this subsection, except that such additional members shall serve for a term of two years from the date of appointment.

(b) All members shall be deemed public officials and shall adhere to the code of ethics for public officials set forth in chapter 10. No member shall participate in the affairs of the committee with respect to the review or consideration of any grant-in-aid application filed by such member or by any eligible institution in which such member has a financial interest, or with which such member engages in any business, employment, transaction or professional activity.

(c) Prior to the awarding of any grants-in-aid for embryonic or human adult stem cell research pursuant to section 19a-32e, the Stem Cell Research Peer Review Committee shall review all applications submitted by eligible institutions for such grants-in-aid and make recommendations to the Commissioner of Public Health and the Stem Cell Research Advisory Committee established pursuant to section 19a-32f with respect to the ethical and scientific merit of each application.

(d) The Peer Review Committee shall establish guidelines for the rating and scoring of such applications by the Stem Cell Research Peer Review Committee.

(e) All members of the committee shall become and remain fully cognizant of the National Academies Guidelines For Human Embryonic Stem Cell Research, as from time to time amended, and the committee may make recommendations to the Stem Cell Research Advisory Committee and the Commissioner of Public Health concerning the adoption of said guidelines, in whole or in part, in the form of regulations adopted pursuant to chapter 54.

Connecticut v. Menillo

Forum: United States Supreme Court.
Case Citation: Connecticut v. Menillo, 423 U.S. 9 (1975).
Date Argued: Not argued.
Date of Decision: November 11, 1975.
Opinion of Court: Per Curiam.
Concurring Without Opinion: White, J.
Dissenting Opinion: None.
Counsel for Appellant: Not reported.
Counsel for Appellee: Not reported.
Amicus Brief for Appellant: Not reported.
Amicus Brief for Appellee: Not reported.

Issue Presented: Whether the constitution was violated by application of Connecticut's criminal abortion statute to a nonphysician?

Case Holding: The constitution was not violated by criminal abortion statutes that prohibit nonphysicians from attempting or performing abortions at any stage of a pregnancy.

Background facts of case: The appellee, Patrick Menillo, was convicted in 1971 of attempting to procure an abortion in violation of

Connecticut's criminal abortion statute. The appellee was not a physician and did not have any medical training. The Connecticut supreme court overturned his conviction, after holding that under the United States Supreme Court decision in *Roe v. Wade*, the Connecticut statute was null and void. The United States Supreme Court summarily granted the state's petition for certiorari to consider the issue.

Majority opinion delivered Per Curiam: The per curiam opinion determined that *Roe v. Wade* did not invalidate criminal abortion statutes, insofar as abortions performed or attempted by nonphysicians. The opinion addressed the issue as follows:

> The statute under which Menillo was convicted makes criminal an attempted abortion by any person. The Connecticut Supreme Court felt compelled to hold this statute null and void, and thus incapable of constitutional application even to someone not medically qualified to perform an abortion, because it read Roe v. Wade to have done the same thing to the similar Texas statutes. But Roe did not go so far.
>
> In Roe we held that [the Texas statutes], which permitted termination of pregnancy at any stage only to save the life of the expectant mother, unconstitutionally restricted a woman's right to an abortion. We went on to state that as a result of the unconstitutionality of [the limitation] the Texas abortion statutes had to fall as a unit, and it is that statement which the Connecticut Supreme Court and courts in some other States have read to require the invalidation of their own statutes even as applied to abortions performed by nonphysicians. In context, however, our statement had no such effect. Jane Roe had sought to have an abortion performed by a competent, licensed physician, under safe, clinical conditions, and our opinion recognized only her right to an abortion under those circumstances. That the Texas statutes fell as a unit meant only that they could not be enforced ... in contravention of a woman's right to a clinical abortion by medically competent personnel. We did not hold the Texas statutes unenforceable against a nonphysician abortionist, for the case did not present the issue.
>
> Moreover, the rationale of our decision supports continued enforceability of criminal abortion statutes against nonphysicians. Roe teaches that a State cannot restrict a decision by a woman, with the advice of her physician, to terminate her pregnancy during the first trimester because neither its interest in maternal health nor its interest in the potential life of the fetus is sufficiently great at that stage. But the insufficiency of the State's interest in maternal health is predicated upon the first trimester abortion's being as safe for the woman as normal childbirth at term, and that predicate holds true only if the abortion is performed by medically competent personnel under conditions insuring maximum safety for the woman. Even during the first trimester of pregnancy, therefore, prosecutions for abortions conducted by nonphysicians infringe upon no realm of personal privacy secured by the Constitution against state interference. And after the first trimester the ever-increasing state interest in maternal health provides additional justification for such prosecutions.

Disposition of case: The judgment of the Connecticut supreme court was vacated.

Concurring without opinion Justice White: Justice White concurred in the judgment without rendering a separate opinion or statement.

Consent *see* **Informed Consent Before Abortion**

Contraception

The term contraception refers to the intentional prevention of fertilization of a female egg, so as to prevent pregnancy. The desire to control female reproduction dates back to ancient history. All societies utilized some method to attempt to prevent conception. Some of the documented ancient forms of birth control include: drinking mercury, a variety of plant and herbal concoctions, and diluted copper ore; using pessary suppositories that would form a coating over the cervix (grass, bamboo tissue, cloth, dung, or sponge); insertion of crude devices into the vagina over the cervix; douching; condoms; and varieties of rhythm methods.

Contraception use in the United States was an "underground" activity for over 70 years, as a result of the Comstock Act of 1873. (The Act got its popular name from a strong anti-obscenity crusader, Anthony Comstock.) Under the Act it was unlawful to publish, distribute, or possess information, devices or medication about contraception. Many states passed similar laws.

In 1961 *Poe v. Ullman* became the first case to reach the United States Supreme Court challenging a law prohibiting contraception information and devices. However, the Court held in *Poe* that the appellants did not have standing to challenge the constitutionality of a Connecticut statute, that made it a crime to give married persons contraceptive information and devices. The same statute was brought before the Supreme Court in 1965 in *Griswold v. Connecticut*. This time, however, the Court reached the merits of the dispute and held that the right of privacy found in the constitution, prohibited enforcement of a Connecticut statute that made it a crime to give married persons contraceptive information and devices.

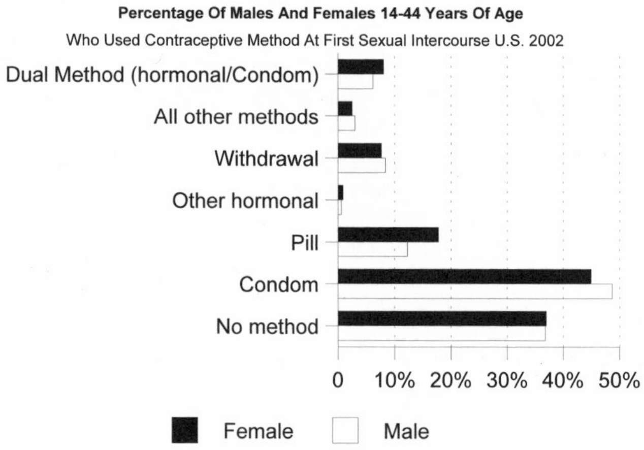

Source: **National Center for Health Statistics.**

The Supreme Court held in *Eisenstadt v. Baird* that the Equal Protection Clause of the Fourteenth Amendment was violated by a Massachusetts statute that made it a crime to give away a drug, medicine, instrument, or article for the prevention of conception except in the case of (1) a physician prescribing it for a married person, or (2) a pharmacist furnishing it to a married person presenting a physician's prescription. In *Carey v. Population Services International* the Supreme Court held that the constitution prohibited enforcement of a New York statute that made it a crime (1) for any person to sell or distribute any contraceptive of any kind to a minor under the age of 16 years; (2) for anyone other than a licensed pharmacist to distribute contraceptives to persons 16 or over; and (3) for anyone, including licensed pharmacists, to advertise or display contraceptives. *See also* **Advertisement; Birth Control Pill; Carey v. Population Services International; Cervical Cap; Bolger v. Youngs Drug Products Corp.; Comstock Act; Condoms; Depo-Provera Contraceptive Injection; Diaphragm; Eisenstadt v. Baird; Griswold v. Connecticut; Intrauterine Contraceptive Devices; Lactational Amenorrhea Method; Lunelle; Morning After Pill; Natural Family Planning Methods; Norplant; Patch Contraceptive; Poe v. Ullman; Spermicides**

Contraction

Contraction refers to the rhythmic-like squeezing of the uterine muscle to facilitate expulsion of a fetus. *See also* **Dilation; Effacement**

Copper-T *see* **Intrauterine Contraceptive Devices**

Cord Accident

A cord accident refers to a problem caused by a fetus' umbilical cord that resulted in stillbirth. The most frequent causes of cord failure are: amniotic fluid problems, abnormally functioning placenta, abnormal pulse pressure in the cord and improper placement of the cord. A cord accident could involve the cord being wrapped around the fetus' neck, a collapsed cord, or cord blood vessel rupture. Although cord accidents occur in the third trimester, they can occur in the second trimester. *See also* **Stillbirth**

Cordocentesis

Cordocentesis is a fetal blood test that involves the insertion of a thin hollow needle through a woman's abdominal wall, and into the uterus to withdraw a sample of blood from the umbilical cord. The blood test is used to determine the presence of Down syndrome or other fetal chromosomal abnormality, and to detect the presence of infectious disease. *See also* **Fetal Monitoring**

Cornual Pregnancy *see* **Ectopic Pregnancy**

Craniosynostosis

Craniosynostosis is a congenital disorder involving the improper fusion of skull fibrous joints and skull bones. This condition results in an abnormal shape of the infant skull, and occasionally the growth of the facial bones is affected as well. This disorder may cause headaches, visual loss, or developmental delays. Surgical procedures may correct the deformity caused by the disorder. *See also* **Birth Defects and Abortion**

Criminal Abortions

The United States Supreme Court's ruling in *Roe v. Wade* and its progeny, prohibit states from criminalizing or prohibiting abortions performed by licensed physicians prior to fetal viability or after fetal viability when a woman's life or health would be endangered in carrying a fetus to term. The majority of states impose criminal penalties against anyone who performs a post-viability abortion, if the woman's life or health was not in danger. Additionally, a minority of states still retain their pre–*Roe* criminal abortion statutes, although the statutes are unconstitutional.

Prosecuting a woman. Under the common law a woman could not be prosecuted for consenting to an unlawful abortion or causing any harm to a fetus. Prior the Supreme Court's decision to legalize abortion in *Roe v. Wade*, the majority of states followed the common law rule and did not allow prosecution of women who had illegal abortions. The common law rule continues to be reflected in the majority of post–*Roe* abortion statutes that ban abortion when a fetus is viable.

A few states impose criminal sanctions against a woman who consents to a post-viability abortion, when her life or health was not in danger. The pre–*Roe* criminal abortion statutes of Arizona, Delaware, Oklahoma, and Wisconsin which have not been repealed, punished a woman for having an unlawful abortion. While these statutes are unconstitutional with respect to pre-viability abortions, the statutes may still be valid as to post viability abortions that do not occur in compliance with the laws of each state. The post–*Roe* abortion statutes of the states of Idaho, Nevada, and New York provide criminal penalties for a woman who submits to an abortion in a manner inconsistent with legal prescriptions.

South Carolina permits criminal sanctions to be imposed on women who use illegal drugs during pregnancy. In *Whitner v. State*, 492 S.E.2d 777 (S.C. 1997) the South Carolina supreme court held that a pregnant woman could be criminally prosecuted for ingesting cocaine during her third trimester of pregnancy and causing the baby to be born with cocaine derivatives in its system.

States with Statutes That Ban Post-Viability Abortion

State	*Prohibits*	*Life exception*	*Health exception*	*Viability testing*
Ala.	X	X	X	after 18 wks
Alaska				
Ariz.	X	X	X	after 11wks
Ark.	X	X	X	
Cal.	X	X	X	
Colo.	X	X	X	
Conn.				
Del.				
D.C.				
Fla.	X	X	X	
Ga.	X	X	X	
Haw.	X	X	X	
Idaho	X	X		
Ill.	X	X	X	
Ind.	X	X	X	
Iowa	X	X	X	
Kan.	X	X	X	
Ky.	X	X	X	
La.	X	X	X	after 18 wks
Maine	X	X	X	
Md.	X	X	X	
Mass.	X	X	X	
Mich.				
Minn.	X	X	X	
Miss.				
Mo.	X	X	X	after 18 wks
Mont.	X	X	X	
Neb.	X	X	X	
Nev.	X	X	X	
N.H.				
N.J.				
N.M.				
N.Y.	X	X		
N.C.	X	X	X	
N.D.	X	X	X	
Ohio	X	X	X	after 21 wks
Okla.	X	X	X	
Ore.				
Penn.	X	X	X	
R.I.	X	X		
S.C.	X	X	X	
S.D.	X	X	X	
Tenn.	X	X	X	
Tex.	X	X	X	
Utah	X	X	X	
Vt.				
Va.	X	X		
Wash.	X	X	X	
W.Va.				
Wis.	X	X	X	
Wyo.	X	X	X	

United States Supreme Court decisions. In *Connecticut v. Menillo* the Supreme Court held that the constitution was not violated by criminal abortion statutes that prohibit nonphysicians from attempting or performing abortions at any stage of a pregnancy. The Supreme Court, in *Simopoulos v. Virginia*, upheld a Virginia penal statute requiring second trimester abortions be performed at hospitals. The defendant in *Simopoulos* was a doctor who had been convicted of performing an abortion in an unlicensed clinic.

In *Colautti v. Franklin* it was held by the Supreme Court that the constitution was violated by a vague and ambiguous provision in Pennsylvania's abortion statute that subjected a physician who performed an abortion to potential criminal liability, if he/she failed to utilize a

STATES THAT DID NOT REPEAL ALL OF THEIR PRE-ROE CRIMINAL ABORTION LAWS

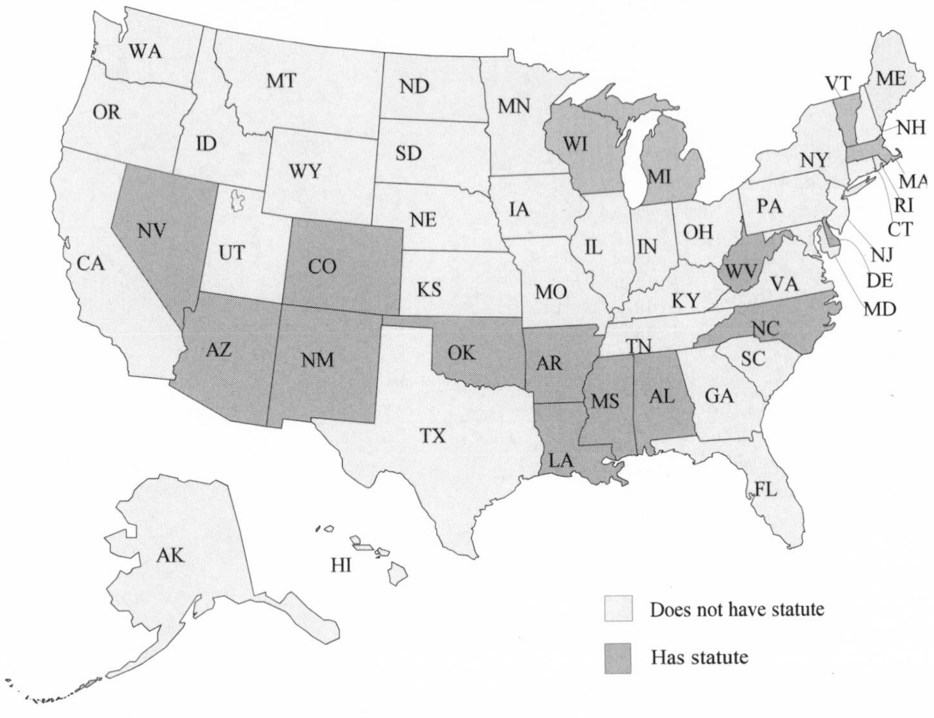

*District of Columbia does not have statute.

statutorily prescribed technique when the fetus was viable or when there was sufficient reason to believe that the fetus may be viable. The Supreme Court held in *Bigelow v. Virginia* that the Free Speech and Free Press Clauses of the First Amendment were violated by a Virginia penal statute that prohibited selling or circulating any publication that encouraged or promoted abortions.

In the 1971 decision of *United States v. Vuitch* the Supreme Court held that the criminal abortion statute of the District of Columbia, which only permitted therapeutic abortions, was not constitutionally vague insofar as there was no ambiguity in its use of the word health and it did not shift to the defendant the burden of proving innocence. *See also* **Bigelow v. Virginia; Connecticut v. Menillo; Roe v. Wade; Simopoulos v. Virginia; United States v. Vuitch**

Crown-Rump Length ***see*** **Gestational Age**

Cryobank ***see*** **Cryopreservation**

Cryopreservation

Cryopreservation is the process of freezing sperm, eggs, embryos, umbilical cord stem cells and other tissue for future use. The technique requires maintaining cells and tissue at extremely cold temperatures. The freezing process is done gradually so as not to damage cells and tissues. Frozen cells and tissues are maintained in tanks of liquid nitrogen. They can be stored in this manner for up to 10 years. Facilities that maintain the frozen cells and tissues are called cryobanks.

Technological development in assisted reproductive processes has been a primary factor in the development of cryopreservation. Infertile couples utilize cryobanks to obtain sperm, eggs or embryos for implantation in the woman. Couples who are not infertile can have their sperm, eggs or embryos stored at cryobanks, as security against future infertility. *See also* **Assisted Reproductive Technology; Embryo Cloning; Embryonic and Fetal Stem-Cell Research; Umbilical Cord Blood Transplantation**

C-Section *see* **Caesarean Section**

Culdocentesis

Culdocentesis is a procedure involving withdrawal of fluid from a pregnant woman's pelvic cavity. This procedure is done to ascertain any abnormalities such as blood or infectious agents. It is also used to diagnose ectopic pregnancy. The procedure requires insertion of a needle through the vagina and into an area near the uterus. Fluid is then removed and examined. If the fluid contains nonclotting blood, a ruptured ectopic pregnancy may be present. *See also* **Ectopic Pregnancy**

Cystic Fibrosis

Cystic fibrosis is an inherited disease that affects the respiratory and digestive systems. The disease adversely affects the mucus and sweat glands of the body by causing thick mucus to develop in the breathing passages of the lungs. This condition predisposes an affected person to chronic lung infections. Complications from the disease include pneumonia, respiratory failure, liver disease, diabetes, osteoporosis, arthritis, male infertility and death. Treatment for the disease includes antibiotics, pancreatic enzymes, vitamin supplements, bronchodilators and possible lung transplant. The disease is more prevalent in Caucasians than other racial groups. *See also* **Birth Defects and Abortion**

Cystic Hygromas

Cystic hygromas is a congenital condition involving malformations affecting the fetal neck in the form of multiple cysts. This condition results in the obstruction of blood flow. In most instances this condition will cause spontaneous abortion. *See also* **Birth Defects and Abortion**

D

D & C *see* **Dilation and Curettage**

D & E *see* **Dilation and Evacuation**

D & X *see* **Dilation and Extraction**

Dalkon Shield

The Dalkon Shield was an intrauterine contraceptive device that was marketed in the United States from 1971 until 1974. The Food and Drug Administration forced the device off the market because of side effects caused to women, such as pelvic inflammatory disease, infertility, miscarriages and loss of female organs. The company which marketed the device, A.H. Robins Co., was thrown into bankruptcy after mass litigation by adversely affected women. The company had sold over 3 million of the devices in the United States. By April of 2000, the company had paid out more than $3 billion in damages. *See also* **Contraception**

Dalton v. Little Rock Family Planning Services

Forum: United States Supreme Court.

Case Citation: Dalton v. Little Rock Family Planning Services, 516 U.S. 474 (1996).

Date Argued: Not Argued.

Date of Decision: March 18, 1996.

Opinion of Court: Per Curiam.

Concurring Opinion: None.

Dissenting Opinion: None.

Counsel for Appellants: Not Reported.

Counsel for Appellees: Not Reported.

Amicus Brief for Appellants: Not Reported.

Amicus Brief for Appellees: Not Reported.

Issue Presented: Whether Amendment 68 of the Arkansas constitution was totally invalid because it allowed Medicaid payment for an abortion only when a woman's life was in danger, even though federal law required such payment when a pregnancy resulted from rape or incest?

Case Holding: Amendment 68 of the Arkansas constitution was invalid only to the extent it conflicted with federal law, but it was valid as to any program funded exclusively with state money.

Background facts of case: The appellees, Medicaid providers and physicians who perform abortions, filed a lawsuit in a federal district court in Arkansas in November of 1993, against the appellants, Arkansas state officials, seeking injunctive and declaratory relief with respect to Amendment 68 of the Arkansas constitution. The Amendment prohibited the use of state funds to pay for any abortion except to save the mother's life. The appellees contended that the Amendment was inconsistent with federal law, which required states to fund medically necessary abortions where the pregnancy resulted from an act of rape or incest. The district court granted relief and enjoined enforcement of the Amendment. The Eighth Circuit appellate court affirmed. The Supreme Court granted certiorari to consider the matter.

Unanimous opinion delivered Per Curiam: The per curiam opinion noted that under the doctrine of pre-emption, state law is displaced to the extent that it actually conflicts with federal law. However, it was said that a federal court should not extend its invalidation of state law further than necessary to dispose of the case before it. The opinion pointed out that the Amendment was affected by federal law only in cases where a eligible-eligible woman seeks to abort a pregnancy resulting from an act of rape or incest and the abortion is not necessary to save the woman's life. The Amendment was valid, however, with respect to state programs that receive no federal funding. The opinion concluded that "[b]ecause Amendment 68 was challenged only insofar as it conflicted with [federal Medicaid law], it was improper to enjoin its application to funding that does not involve the Medicaid program."

Disposition of case: The decision of the Eighth Circuit was reversed insofar as it affirmed the scope of the injunction, and the case was remanded for entry of an order enjoining the enforcement of the Amendment only to the extent that it imposed obligations inconsistent with federal law.

Dandy-Walker Syndrome

Dandy-Walker syndrome is a congenital brain disorder involving the fourth ventricle and cerebellum. Symptoms of the disorder include vomiting, convulsions, abnormal breathing patterns, and malformations of the face, limbs, and heart. Treatment for the disorder focuses on specific treatable conditions. The disorder can cause death. *See also* **Birth Defects and Abortion**

Daubert v. Merrell Dow Pharmaceuticals, Inc.

Forum: United States Supreme Court.

Case Citation: Daubert v. Merrell Dow Pharmaceuticals, Inc., 509 U.S. 579 (1993).

Date Argued: March 30, 1993.

Date of Decision: June 28, 1993.

Opinion of Court: Blackmun, J., in which White, O'Connor, Scalia, Kennedy, Souter, and Thomas, JJ., joined.

Concurring and Dissenting Opinion: Rehnquist, C.J., in which Stevens, J., joined.

Counsel for Appellants: Michael H. Gottesman argued; on the brief were Kenneth J. Chesebro, Barry J. Nace, David L. Shapiro, and Mary G. Gillick.

Counsel for Appellee: Charles Fried argued; on the brief were Charles R. Nesson, Joel I. Klein, Richard G. Taranto, Hall R. Marston, George E. Berry, Edward H. Stratemeier, and W. Glenn Forrester.

Amicus Brief for Appellants: State of Texas et al. by Dan Morales, Attorney General of Texas, Mark Barnett, Attorney General of South Dakota, Marc Racicot, Attorney General of Montana, Larry Echo-Hawk, Attorney General of Idaho, and Brian Stuart Koukoutchos; for the American Society of Law, Medicine and Ethics et al. by Joan E. Bertin, Marsha S. Berzon, and Albert H. Meyerhoff; for the Association of Trial Lawyers of America by Jeffrey Robert White and Roxanne Barton Conlin; for Ronald Bayer et al. by Brain Stuart Koukoutchos, Priscilla Budeiri, Arthur Bryant, and George W. Conk; and for Daryl E. Chubin et al. by Ron Simon and Nicole Schultheis.

Amicus Brief for Appellee: United States by Acting Solicitor General Wallace, Assistant Attorney General Gerson, Miguel A. Estrada, Michael Jay Singer, and John P. Schnitker; for the American Insurance Association by William J. Kilberg, Paul Blankenstein, Bradford R. Clark, and Craig A. Berrington; for the American Medical Association et al. by Carter G.. Phillips, Mark D. Hopson, and Jack R. Bierig; for the American Tort Reform Association by John G. Kester and John W. Vardaman, Jr.; for the Chamber of Commerce of the United States by Timothy B. Dyk, Stephen A. Bokat, and Robin S. Conrad; for the Pharmaceutical Manufacturers Association by Louis R. Cohen and Daniel Marcus; for the Product Liability Advisory Council, Inc., et al. by Victor E. Schwartz, Robert P. Charrow, and Paul F. Rothstein; for the Washington Legal Foundation by Scott G. Campbell, Daniel J. Popeo, and Richard A. Samp; and for Nicolaas Bloembergen et al. by Martin S. Kaufman.

Issue Presented: Whether the admission of expert testimony under *Frye v. United States*, 293 F. 1013 (D.C Cir. 1923) remains good law after the enactment of the Federal Rules of Evidence?

Case Holding: The *Frye* rule on admissibility of expert testimony did not survive the enactment of the Federal Rules of Evidence.

Background facts of case: The appellants, Jason Daubert and Eric Schuller, were minor children who were born with serious birth defects. They sued the appellee, Merrell Dow Pharmaceuticals, Inc., in California state court, alleging that the birth defects had been caused by their respective mothers' ingestion of Bendectin, an anti-nausea drug marketed by the appellee. The case was removed to federal court on diversity of jurisdiction grounds. After extensive discovery, the appellee moved for summary judgment dismissal, contending that Bendectin did not cause birth defects in humans and that the appellants would be unable to produce any admissible evidence to the contrary. The appellants responded with the testimony of eight experts, who had concluded that Bendectin could cause birth defects.

The district court granted appellee's motion for summary judgment on the grounds that the appellants failed to present expert testimony that was sufficiently established to have general acceptance in the field to which it belongs. The Ninth Circuit court of appeals affirmed on the grounds that under *Frye v. United States*, 293 F. 1013 (D.C. Cir. 1923), expert opinion based on a scientific technique was inadmissible unless the technique was "generally accepted" as reliable in the relevant scientific community. The Supreme Court granted certiorari to consider the standard for admitting expert testimony.

Majority opinion by Justice Blackmun: Justice Blackmun noted that for 70 years the "general acceptance" test of *Frye* was the dominant standard for determining the admissibility of novel scientific evidence at trial. However, it was said that when the federal courts adopted Rule 702 of the Federal Rules of Evidence, the *Frye* test was no longer valid. Rule 702, governing expert testimony, provides:

> If scientific, technical, or other specialized knowledge will assist the trier of fact to understand the evidence or to determine a fact in issue, a witness qualified as an expert by knowledge, skill, experience, training, or education, may testify thereto in the form of an opinion or otherwise.

Justice Blackmun went on to reject the continued use of the *Frye* test and stated the Court's reasoning as follows:

> Nothing in the text of this Rule establishes "general acceptance" as an absolute prerequisite to admissibility. Nor does [appellee] present any clear indication that Rule 702 or the Rules as a whole were intended to incorporate a "general acceptance" standard. The drafting history makes no mention of Frye, and a rigid "general acceptance" requirement would be at odds with the "liberal thrust" of the Federal Rules and their general approach of relaxing the traditional barriers to opinion testimony....
>
> To summarize: "General acceptance" is not a necessary precondition to the admissibility of scientific evidence under the Federal Rules of Evidence, but the Rules of Evidence — especially Rule 702 — do assign to the trial judge the task of ensuring that an expert's testimony both rests on a reliable foundation and is relevant to the task at hand. Pertinent evidence based on scientifically valid principles will satisfy those demands.

Disposition of case: The judgment of the court of appeals was vacated, and the case was remanded for further proceedings.

Concurring and dissenting opinion by Chief Justice Rehnquist: The Chief Justice agreed with the Supreme Court that Rule 702 supplanted the *Frye* test. He dissented from discussion in the opinion that went beyond the narrow issue of the validity of the *Frye* test. He stated succinctly: "I think the Court would be far better advised in this case to decide only the questions presented, and to leave the further development of this important area of the law to future cases." *See also* **Bendectin**

Dead Fetus Syndrome

Dead fetus syndrome is the term used to describe a condition that affects a woman when a dead fetus has not been expelled from her womb. When a fetus dies spontaneously, but has not been discarded by the uterus, an abnormal activation of blood clotting systems can develop in response to the release of anti-clotting chemicals from the retained dead fetus. *See also* **Miscarriage**

Death of Women Consenting to Abortion *see* **Complications During and After Abortion**

Deep-Vein Thrombosis and Pregnancy

Deep-vein thrombosis (also called venous thromboembolism) occurs when blood clots form in the deep veins of the legs, lower-abdomen and inner-thigh area. This condition may cause a blockage in blood flow from the legs back to the heart, or a piece of the clot may be carried back through the heart and settle in a blood vessel, blocking its flow. For pregnant women this condition is the leading cause of maternal mortality due to medical complications. Even when the condition is timely treated, certain treatment therapies are known to be fatal to the fetus. *See also* **Stillbirth**

Delaware

(1) OVERVIEW

The state of Delaware enacted its first criminal abortion statute on February 13, 1883. The statute underwent several amendments prior to the 1973 decision by the United States Supreme Court in *Roe v. Wade*, which legalized abortion in the nation. In spite of the decision in *Roe*, Delaware has not repealed its pre-*Roe* criminal abortion statutes. However, the statutes are constitutionally infirm.

Delaware has taken affirmative steps, through statutes and administrative regulations, to respond to *Roe* and its progeny. Through administrative rules Delaware prohibits the use of state funds to pay for abortions, except for therapeutic abortions and pregnancies resulting from rape or incest. Delaware has addressed numerous abortion issues by statute that include informed consent and waiting period, use of facilities and people, injury to pregnant woman, abortion by minors, residency requirement, and reporting abortion.

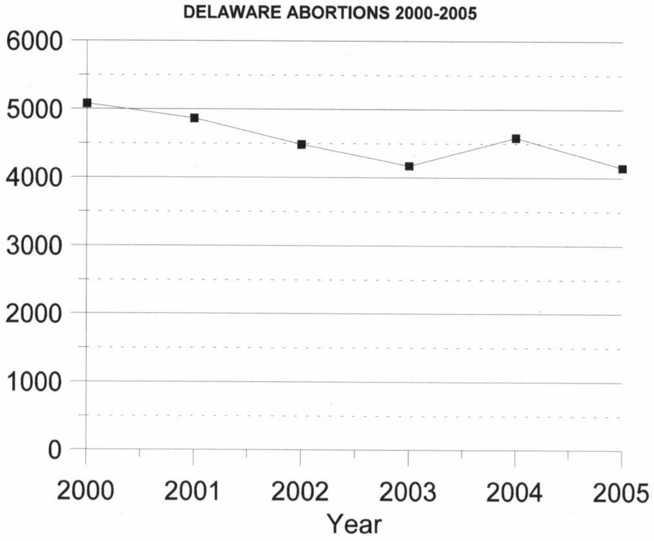

Source: **Delaware Health Statistics Center.**

Delaware Abortion by Age Group 2000–2005
Age Group (yrs)

Year	*<15*	*15–17*	*18–19*	*20–24*	*25–29*	*30–34*	*35–39*	*≥40*
2000	43	477	649	1,692	1,094	624	382	121
2001	48	467	559	1,660	1,012	632	369	122
2002	38	412	552	1,529	907	597	338	115
2003	29	357	508	1,410	902	530	318	122
2004	30	351	530	1,595	1,007	618	349	108
2005	22	318	458	1,441	950	515	344	100
Total	210	2,382	3,256	9,327	5,872	3,516	2,100	688

Source: **Delaware Health Statistics Center.**

(2) PRE-ROE ABORTION BAN

As previously indicated, Delaware has not repealed its pre-*Roe* criminal abortion statutes. Under the now unconstitutional statutes, abortion was criminalized if it was not performed to preserve the health or life of the woman, to prevent the birth of a child with severe deformity or mental retardation, or because the pregnancy resulted

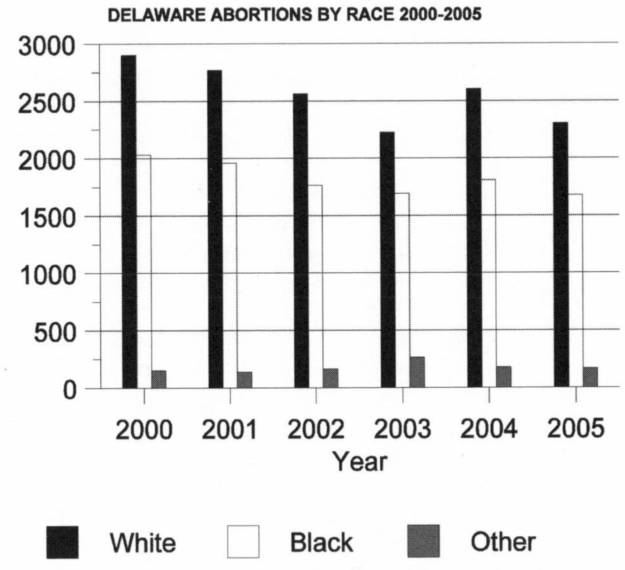

Source: Delaware Health Statistics Center.

Delaware Abortion by Education Level of Female 2000–2005

Education Level Completed

Year	*<9*	*9–11*	*12*	*1–3 College*	*4+ College*	*Unknown*
2000	91	780	2,274	1,090	599	248
2001	105	763	2,228	985	481	307
2002	105	657	2,131	908	401	286
2003	62	619	1,890	782	343	480
2004	111	751	2,113	754	475	384
2005	86	522	2,093	622	292	533
Total	560	4,092	12,729	5,141	2,591	2,238

Source: Delaware Health Statistics Center.

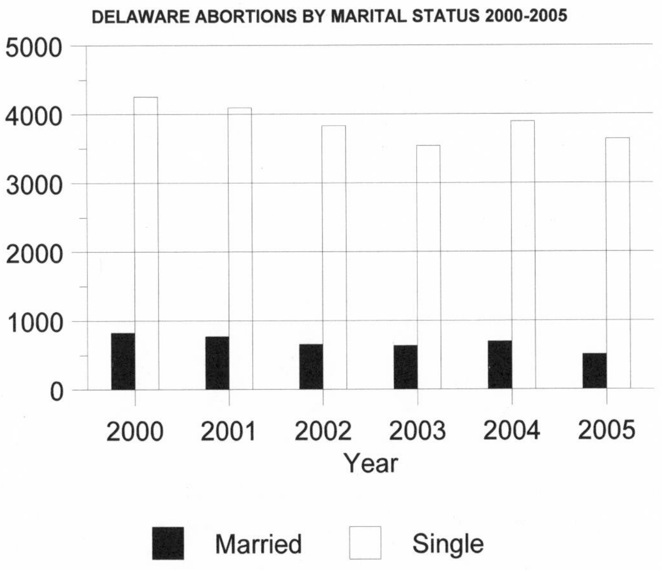

Source: Delaware Health Statistics Center.

from rape or incest. The state also made it a crime to provide or sell instruments or drugs that caused abortion, and imposed criminal penalties against a woman who consented to an abortion. Additionally, it was made a criminal offense if a woman died during an abortion. The pre–*Roe* abortion statutes are set out below.

Delaware Code Ti. 11, § 654. Abortion defined

Delaware Abortion by Weeks of Gestation 2000–2005

Weeks of Gestation	*2000*	*2001*	*2002*	*2003*	*2004*	*2005*	*Total*
<7	1,128	1,067	934	1,050	1,322	1,210	6,711
7	826	834	748	695	827	722	4,652
8	852	787	722	648	674	651	4,334
9–10	1,090	1,054	1,052	779	777	739	5,491
11–12	593	526	480	497	458	384	2,938
13–15	335	381	368	298	340	288	2,010
16–20	234	206	167	148	165	134	1,054
≥21	12	9	11	17	6	10	65
Not known	12	5	6	44	19	10	96

Source: Delaware Health Statistics Center.

Delaware Prior Abortion by Female 2000–2005

Prior Abortion

Year	*None*	*1*	*2*	*≥3*	*Not known*
2000	2,861	1,428	512	275	6
2001	2,785	1,232	524	327	1
2002	2,566	1,150	458	306	8
2003	2,366	1,081	389	237	103
2004	2,655	1,145	463	296	29
2005	2,644	886	396	215	7
Total	15,877	6,922	2,742	1,656	154

Source: Delaware Health Statistics Center.

"Abortion" means an act committed upon or with respect to a female, whether by another person or by the female herself, whether directly upon her body or by the administering, taking or prescription of drugs or in any other manner, with intent to cause a miscarriage of such female.

Delaware Code Ti. 24, § 1790.
Limitation on terminating pregnancy

(a) No person shall terminate or attempt to terminate or assist in the termination or attempt at termination of a human pregnancy otherwise than by birth, except that a physician licensed by this State may terminate a human pregnancy or aid or assist or attempt a termination of a human pregnancy if such procedure takes place in a hospital accredited by a nationally recognized medical or hospital accreditation authority, upon authorization by a hospital abortion review authority appointed by the hospital if 1 or more of the following conditions exist:

(1) Continuation of the pregnancy is likely to result in the death of the mother;

(2) There is substantial risk of the birth of the child with grave and permanent physical deformity or mental retardation;

(3) The pregnancy resulted from:

a. Incest, or

b. A rape or unlawful sexual intercourse in the first or second degree committed as a result of force or bodily harm or threat of force or bodily harm, and the Attorney General of this State has certified to the hospital abortion review authority in writing over the Attorney General's signature that there is probable cause to believe that the alleged rape or unlawful sexual intercourse in the first or second degree did occur, except that during the first 48 hours after the alleged rape or unlawful sexual intercourse in the first or second degree no certification by the Attorney General shall be required;

(4) Continuation of the pregnancy would involve substantial risk of permanent injury to the physical or mental health of the mother.

(b) In no event shall any physician terminate or attempt to terminate or assist in the termination or attempt at termination of a human pregnancy otherwise than by birth unless:

(1) Not more than 20 weeks of gestation have passed (except in the case of a termination pursuant to subsection (a)(1) of this section or where the fetus is dead); and

(2) Two physicians licensed by this State, 1 of whom may be the physician proposed to perform the abortion, certify to the abortion review authority of the hospital where the procedure is to be performed that they are of the opinion, formed in good faith, that 1 of the circumstances set forth in subsection (a) of this section exists (except that no such certification is necessary for the circumstances set forth in subsection (a)(3)b of this section); where the personal physician of an expectant mother claims that she has a mental or emotional condition, a psychiatrist licensed by this State shall, in addition to the personal physician, certify to the abortion review authority of the hospital where such procedure is to be performed that the physician is of the opinion, formed in good faith, that 1 of the circumstances set forth in subsection (a) of this section exists (except that no such certification is necessary for the circumstances set forth in subsection (a)(3)b of this section); and

(3) In the case of an unmarried female under the age of 18 or mentally ill or incompetent, there is filed with the hospital abortion review authority the written consent of the parents or guardians as are then residing in the same household with the consenting female, or, if such consenting female does not reside in the same household with either of her parents or guardians, then with the written consent of 1 of her parents or guardians.

(c) The hospital abortion review authority of each hospital in which a procedure or procedures are performed pursuant to this section shall, on or before the 1st day of March in each year, file with the Department of Health and Social Services a written report of each such procedure performed pursuant to the authorization of such authority during the preceding calendar year setting forth grounds for each such authorization but not including the names of patients aborted.

Delaware Code Ti. 24, § 1795. Live birth following abortion

(a) In the event an abortion or an attempted abortion results in the live birth of a child, the person performing or inducing such abortion or attempted abortion and all persons rendering medical care to the child after its birth must exercise that degree of medical skill, care and diligence which would be rendered to a child who is born alive as the result of a natural birth.

(b) Nothing found in this section shall be deemed to preclude prosecution under any other applicable section of the Delaware Code for knowing or reckless conduct which is detrimental to the life or health of an infant born as a result of a procedure designed to terminate pregnancy. Anyone who knowingly violates this section shall be guilty of a class A misdemeanor.

Delaware Code Ti. 11, § 651. Abortion class F felony

A person is guilty of abortion when the person commits upon a pregnant female an abortion which causes the miscarriage of the female, unless the abortion is a therapeutic abortion. Abortion is a class F felony.

Delaware Code Ti. 24, § 1766(b). Abortion penalty

A person who terminates or attempts to terminate or assists in the termination of a human pregnancy otherwise than by birth, except in accordance with subchapter IX of this chapter, is guilty of a class C felony and shall be fined not more than $5,000 and imprisoned not less than 2 nor more than 10 years.

Delaware Code Ti. 11, § 652. Penalty for woman

A female is guilty of self-abortion when she, being pregnant, commits or submits to an abortion upon herself which causes her abortion, unless the abortion is a therapeutic abortion. Selfabortion is a class A misdemeanor.

Delaware Code Ti. 24, § 1792. Providing abortion devices

No person shall, unless the termination of a human pregnancy has been authorized pursuant to § 1790 of this title:

(1) Sell or give, or cause to be sold or given, any drug, medicine, preparation, instrument or device for the purpose of causing, inducing or obtaining a termination of such pregnancy; or

(2) Give advice, counsel or information for the purpose of causing, inducing or obtaining a termination of such pregnancy; or

(3) Knowingly assist or cause by any means whatsoever the obtaining or performing of a termination of such pregnancy.

Delaware Code Ti. 11, § 653.
Abortion devices class B misdemeanor

A person is guilty of issuing abortional articles when the person manufactures, sells or delivers any instrument, article, medicine, drug or substance with intent that the same be used in committing an abortion upon a female in circumstances which would constitute a crime defined by this Criminal Code. Issuing abortional articles is a class B misdemeanor.

Delaware Code Ti. 11, § 632(4).
Death of woman during abortion

A person is guilty of manslaughter when:

The person commits upon a female an abortion which causes her death, unless such abortion is a therapeutic abortion and the death is not the result of reckless conduct....

(3) INFORMED CONSENT AND WAITING PERIOD

Prior to an abortion Delaware requires that a woman be fully informed of the procedure to be used, the risks involved and alternatives to abortion. An abortion may not take place until 24 hours after a woman has given her written consent to an abortion. The statute addressing these issues was held invalid in *Planned Parenthood of Delaware v. Brady*, 250 F.Supp.2d 405 (D.Del. 2003), because it failed to provide for a health exception. The statute addressing the matter is set out below.

Delaware Code Ti. 24, § 1794. Consent and waiting period

(a) No abortion may be performed unless the woman submitting to the abortion first gives her written consent to the abortion stating that she freely and voluntarily consents to the abortion and that she has received a full explanation of the abortion procedure and effects, including, but not limited to, the following:

(1) The abortion procedure to be utilized.

(2) The probable effects of the abortion procedure on the woman, including the effects on her child-bearing ability and effects on possible future pregnancies.

(3) The facts of fetal development as of the time the proposed abortion is to be performed.

(4) The risks attendant to the procedure.

(5) An explanation of the reasonable alternatives to abortion and of the reasonable alternative procedures or methods of abortion.

(b) No abortion may be performed on a woman within 24 hours after giving written consent pursuant to subsection (a) of this section unless, in the opinion of her treating physician, an emergency situation presenting substantial danger to the life of the woman exists.

In the event a woman's treating physician determines an abortion is necessary because an emergency situation presenting substantial danger to the life of the woman existed and such woman is unable to give her consent to an abortion, an abortion may be performed on such woman.

(4) USE OF FACILITIES AND PEOPLE

Under the laws of Delaware hospitals are not required to allow abortions at their facilities. The employees and physicians at hospitals that do allow abortions are permitted to refuse to take part in abortions. The statute addressing the issue is set out below.

Delaware Code Ti. 24, § 1791.
Right to refuse to participate in abortion

(a) No person shall be required to perform or participate in medical procedures which result in the termination of pregnancy; and the refusal

of any person to perform or participate in these medical procedures shall not be a basis for civil liability to any person, nor a basis for any disciplinary or other recriminatory action against the person.

(b) No hospital, hospital director or governing board shall be required to permit the termination of human pregnancies within its institution, and the refusal to permit such procedures shall not be grounds for civil liability to any person, nor a basis for any disciplinary or other recriminatory action against it by the State or any person.

(c) The refusal of any person to submit to an abortion or to give consent shall not be grounds for loss of any privileges or immunities to which such person would otherwise be entitled, nor shall submission to an abortion or the granting of consent be a condition precedent to the receipt of any public benefits.

(5) INJURY TO PREGNANT WOMAN

Delaware makes it a felony offense to assault a pregnant woman and cause the death of her fetus. The statute addressing the issue is set out below.

Delaware Code Ti. 11, § 606. Abuse of a pregnant female

(a) A person is guilty of abuse of a pregnant female in the first degree when in the course of or in furtherance of the commission or attempted commission of assault in the third degree any violent felony against or upon a pregnant female, or while in immediate flight therefrom, the person intentionally and without her consent causes the unlawful termination of her pregnancy.

(b) It is no defense to a prosecution under this section that the person was unaware that the victim was pregnant.

(c) Prosecution under this section does not preclude prosecution under any other section of the Delaware Code. Abuse of a pregnant female in the first degree is a class B felony.

(6) ABORTION BY MINORS

Under the laws of Delaware no physician may perform an abortion upon an unemancipated minor, until 24 hours after notice of the operation has been given to either parent of the minor, or other enumerated persons. In compliance with federal constitutional law, Delaware has provided a judicial waiver procedure for an unemancipated minor to obtain an abortion without parental notice. If an unemancipated minor elects not to provide notice to either of her parents, the minor may petition a trial court for a waiver of the notice requirement. The required parental notice may be waived if the court finds either (1) that the minor is mature and well-informed enough to make the abortion decision on her own, or (2) that performance of the abortion would be in the best interest of the minor. An expedited appeal is available to any minor to whom the court denies a waiver of notice. The statutes addressing the issues are set out below.

Delaware Code Ti. 24, § 1780. Short title

This subchapter shall be known and may be cited as the Parental Notice of Abortion Act.

Delaware Code Ti. 24, § 1781. Legislative purpose and findings

(a) The General Assembly of the State finds as fact that:

(1) Immature minors often lack the ability to make fully informed choices that take into account both immediate and long-range consequences;

(2) The physical, emotional, and psychological consequences of teen pregnancy are serious and can be lasting, particularly when the patient is immature;

(3) The capacity to become pregnant and the capacity for mature judgment concerning how to choose among the alternatives for managing that pregnancy are not necessarily related;

(4) Parents ordinarily possess information essential to enable a physician to exercise the physician's best medical judgment concerning the child;

(5) Parents who are aware that their minor daughter has had an abortion can ensure that she receives adequate medical attention after the abortion;

(6) Parental consultation is usually desirable and in the best interest of their minor children and parents ordinarily act in the best interest of their minor children; and

(7) Parental involvement legislation enacted in other states has been shown to have significant impact in reducing abortion, birth and pregnancy rates among minors.

(b) It is the intent of the General Assembly of the State in enacting this parental notice provision to further the important and compelling State interests of:

(1) Protecting minors against their own immaturity;

(2) Fostering the family structure and preserving it as a viable social unit;

(3) Protecting the rights of parents to rear children who are members of their household; and

(4) Protecting the health and safety of minor children.

Delaware Code Ti. 24, § 1782. Definitions

For purposes of this subchapter, the following definitions will apply.

(1) "Abortion" means the use of any instrument, medicine, drug or any other substance or device to terminate the pregnancy of a woman known to be pregnant, with an intention other than to increase the probability of a live birth, to preserve the life or health of the child after live birth, or to remove a dead fetus.

(2) "Coercion" means restraining or dominating the choice of a minor female by force, threat of force, or deprivation of food and shelter.

(3) "Emancipated minor" means any minor female who is or has been married or has, by court order or otherwise, been freed from the care, custody and control of her parents or any other legal guardian.

(4) "Licensed mental health professional" means a person licensed under the Division of Professional Regulation of the State as a:

(a) Psychiatrist;

(b) Psychologist; or

(c) Licensed professional counselor of mental health.

(5) "Medical emergency" means that condition which, on the basis of the physician or other medically authorized person's good faith clinical judgment, so complicates the medical condition of the pregnant minor as to necessitate the immediate abortion of her pregnancy to avert her death or for which delay will create serious risk of substantial and irreversible impairment of a major bodily function.

(6) "Minor" means a female person under the age of 16.

Delaware Code Ti. 24, § 1783. Parental notice

No physician or other medically authorized person shall perform an abortion upon an unemancipated minor until complying with the following notification provisions:

(a) No physician or other medically authorized person shall perform an abortion upon an unemancipated minor unless the physician, medically authorized person, or an agent of the physician or of the medically authorized person has given at least 24 hours actual notice to one or both parents (either custodial or non-custodial), a grandparent, a licensed mental health professional (who shall not be an employee or under contract to an abortion provider except employees or contractors of an acute care hospital) or to the legal guardian of the pregnant minor of the intention to perform the abortion, or unless the physician, medically authorized person, or an agent of the physician or of the medically authorized person has received a written statement or oral communication from another physician or medically authorized person, hereinafter called the "referring physician or medically authorized person," certifying that the referring physician or medically authorized person has given such notice. If the person con-

tacted pursuant to this subsection is not the parent or guardian, the person so contacted must explain to the minor the options available to her include adoption, abortion and full-term pregnancy, and must agree that it is in the best interest of the minor that a waiver of the parental notice requirement be granted. Any licensed mental health professional so contacted shall certify that the professional has performed an assessment of the specific factors and circumstances of the minor subject to the evaluation including but not limited to the age and family circumstances of the minor and the long-term and short-term consequences to the minor of termination or continuation of the pregnancy.

(i) No physician or other abortion provider shall charge a referral fee to a person authorized under this section to receive notice; nor shall a person authorized under this section to receive notice charge a referral fee to a physician or other abortion provider.

(ii) Nothing in this section shall affect the obligations of a person pursuant to other provisions of this Code to report instances of child abuse to the appropriate government agencies.

(b) A minor may petition the Family Court ("Court") of any county of this State for a waiver of the notice requirement of this section pursuant to the procedures of § 1784 of this title. A physician who has received a copy of a court order granting a waiver application under § 1784 of this title shall not, at any time, give notice of the minor's abortion to any person without the minor's written permission.

Delaware Code Ti. 24, § 1784. Judicial bypass

(a) The Court shall consider waiving the notice requirement of § 1783 of this title upon the proper application of a minor. The application shall be in writing, signed by the minor, and verified by her oath or affirmation before a person authorized to perform notarial acts. It shall designate:

(1) The minor's name and residence address;

(2) A mailing address where the Court's order may be sent and a telephone number where messages for the minor may be left;

(3) That the minor is pregnant;

(4) That the minor desires to obtain an abortion;

(5) Each person for whom the notice requirement is sought to be waived; and

(6) The particular facts and circumstances which indicate that the minor is mature and well-informed enough to make the abortion decision on her own and/or that it is in the best interest of the minor that notification pursuant to § 1783 of this title be waived.

(b) The Court, by a judge, shall grant the written application for a waiver if the facts recited in the application establish that the minor is mature and well-informed enough to make the abortion decision on her own or that it is in the best interest of the minor that notification pursuant to § 1783 of this title be waived. The Court shall presume that married parents not separated and grandparents are complete confidants, such that, on application to waive the notice requirement as to either, grounds to waive the notice requirement as to one parent or grandparent shall constitute grounds to waive the notice requirement as to the spouse thereof.

(c) If the Court fails to rule within 5 calendar days of the time of the filing of the written application, the application shall be deemed granted; in which case, on the 6th day, the Court shall issue an order stating that the application is deemed granted.

(d) The Court shall mail 3 copies of any order to the mailing address identified in the application on the day the order issues, shall attempt to notify the minor by telephone on the day the order issues, and if so requested, shall make copies of the order available at Court chambers for the minor.

(e) An expedited appeal to the Supreme Court shall be available to any minor whose petition is denied by a judge of the Family Court. Notice of intent to appeal shall be given within 2 days of the receipt of actual notice of the denial of the petition. The Supreme Court shall advise the minor that she has a right to court-appointed counsel and shall provide her with such counsel upon request, at no cost to the minor. The Supreme Court shall expedite proceedings to the extent necessary and appropriate under the circumstances. The Supreme Court shall notify the minor of its decision consistent with subsection (d) of this section.

(f) No court shall assess any fee or cost upon a minor for any proceeding under this section.

(g) Each court shall provide by rule for the confidentiality of proceedings under this subchapter, but shall continue to initiate investigations into any allegations of past abuse where otherwise appropriate, without disclosing that an application under this subchapter was the source of the information prompting the investigation.

Delaware Code Ti. 24, § 1786. Coercion prohibited.

No parent, guardian, or other person shall coerce a minor to undergo an abortion or to continue a pregnancy. Any minor who is threatened with such coercion may apply to a court of competent jurisdiction for relief. The court shall provide the minor with counsel, give the matter expedited consideration, and grant such relief as may be necessary to prevent such coercion. Should a minor be denied the financial support of her parents or legal guardian by reason of her refusal to undergo abortion or to continue a pregnancy, she shall be considered emancipated for purposes of eligibility for assistance benefits.

Delaware Code Ti. 24, § 1787. Medical emergency exception

The requirements of § 1783, § 1784 and § 1786 of this title shall not apply when, in the best medical judgment of the physician or other medically authorized person, based on the facts of the case, a medical emergency exists that so complicates the pregnancy as to require an immediate abortion.

Delaware Code Ti. 24, § 1788. Counseling to affected persons

The Division of Child Mental Health Services, Department of Services for Children, Youth and Their Families, shall offer counseling and support to any minor who is pregnant and is considering filing or has filed an application under this subchapter, if the minor requests such services. Notwithstanding any contrary statute, no notification of the request for or provision of such services to the minor shall be provided to any person, nor shall the consent of any person thereto be required.

Delaware Code Ti. 24, § 1789. Penalty and criminal jurisdiction

(a) Any person who intentionally performs an abortion with knowledge that, or with reckless disregard as to whether, the person upon whom the abortion has been performed is an unemancipated minor, and who intentionally or knowingly fails to conform to any requirement of this subchapter, shall be guilty of a class A misdemeanor.

(b) The Superior Court shall have exclusive jurisdiction of violations of this section.

Delaware Code Ti. 24, § 1789A. Notice and avoidance of liability

In any prosecution pursuant to § 1789 of this title, the State shall prove beyond a reasonable doubt that the physician (or other medically authorized person) who performed the abortion did not have a good faith belief on that physician's part that actual notice was given by such physician (or other medically authorized person), that physician's agent, or the referring physician or another medically authorized person to a person listed in § 1783(a) of this title as qualified to receive notice. In any civil case, the plaintiff must prove the absence of such a good faith belief by clear and convincing evidence.

Delaware Code Ti. 24, § 1789B. Civil damages available

Failure to give notice pursuant to the requirements of this subchapter is prima facie evidence of interference with family relations in appropriate civil actions. The law of this State shall not be construed to preclude the award of punitive damages in any civil action relevant to violations of this subchapter. Nothing in this subchapter shall be construed to limit the common law rights of parents.

(7) RESIDENCY REQUIREMENT

Delaware provides by statute that a woman must be in the state at least 120 days before an abortion may be performed. The statute addressing the issue is set out below.

Delaware Code Ti. 24, § 1793. Residency

(a) No person shall be authorized to perform a termination of a human pregnancy within the State upon a female who has not been a resident of this State for a period of at least 120 days next before the performance of an operative procedure for the termination of a human pregnancy.

(b) This section shall not apply to such female who is gainfully employed in this State at the time of conception, or whose spouse is gainfully employed in this State at the time of conception or to such female who has been a patient, prior to conception, of a physician licensed by this State, or to such female who is attempting to secure the termination of her pregnancy for the condition specified in § 1790(a)(1) of this title.

(8) REPORTING ABORTION

Delaware requires by statute that all induced abortions be reported to the proper state agency. The statute addressing the issue is set out below.

Delaware Code Ti. 16, § 3133. Reports of induced abortion

Each induced termination of pregnancy which occurs in this State, regardless of the length of gestation, shall be reported to the Delaware Health Statistics Center within the Bureau of Health Planning and Resources Management by the person in charge or a designated representative of the institution or abortion facility in which the induced termination of pregnancy was performed. If the induced termination of pregnancy was performed outside an institution or abortion facility, the attending physician shall prepare and file the report. Such reporting shall occur within 30 days after the end of the month in which the induced termination of pregnancy was performed. These reports are to be used only for purposes of statistical analysis and shall not be incorporated into the permanent official records of the system of vital statistics. The reporting form shall include only those items recommended by the federal agency responsible for national vital statistics except that it shall not include any item that allows identification of patients or physicians. Furthermore, no statistical analysis shall be released which identifies the reporting institution or abortion facility.

Demonstrations *see* **Abortion Violence, Property Destruction and Demonstrations**

Dennett, Mary Ware

Mary Ware Dennett (1872–1947) was born in Worcester, Massachusetts and educated at Miss Capen's School for Girls in Northampton, Massachusetts. She also studied at the Boston Museum of Fine Arts. Dennett was an outspoken advocate of women's rights. From 1908 to 1910, she served as field secretary of the Massachusetts Woman Suffrage Association, and from 1910 to 1914 she worked in New York City as the corresponding secretary of the National American Woman Suffrage Association. In 1915 Dennett became an advocate of birth control and the right of women to choose abortion. She founded the Voluntary Parenthood League in 1918. As director of the League, Dennett lobbied for the repeal of legislation that restricted abortion and the dissemination of contraceptives. In 1926 Dennett published a pamphlet, *Birth Control Laws*, that presented a frank discussion of laws that prohibited access to birth control information and arguments for the free dissemination of such information.

The most controversial writing by Dennett was her publication of an essay in 1918 entitled *The Sex Side of Life: An Explanation for Young People*. The essay was banned from the mails as obscene in 1922. In 1928 Dennett was indicted for violating federal laws after she continued to distribute the essay through the mail. She was convicted of the charges in 1929, but the conviction was later reversed on appeal in 1930.

Depo-Provera Contraceptive Injection

Depo-Provera (D-P) is the brand name of a prescription method of birth control. It is formally called depot-medroxyprogesterone acetate. D-P is a hormone like progesterone, one of the hormones that regulates the menstrual cycle. D-P is designed to prevent pregnancy by keeping the ovaries from releasing eggs and thickens cervical mucus to keep sperm from joining eggs. D-P is given as an intramuscular injection. It is administered in the buttocks or the upper arm, once every three months. D-P is considered 99 percent effective. Side effects from D-P include menstrual irregularities, depression, headaches, nervousness or weight changes. *See also* **Contraception**

DES

DES (diethylstilbestrol) is a synthetic estrogen drug that was believed to prevent pregnant women from having a miscarriage. The drug was used by an estimated 5 to 10 million pregnant women in the United States between the period 1938–1971. DES was banned for use by pregnant women after 1971, when scientists revealed that the drug did not work and was in fact harmful.

Research began to surface in the 1960s which suggested that when DES was given during the first 5 months of pregnancy, it adversely interfered with the development of the reproductive system of a fetus. By 1971 researchers learned that the drug was associated with the development of vaginal and cervical cancer in young women who were exposed to the drug while in their mothers' womb. Further studies have suggested that the daughters of women who used DES during pregnancy may suffer structural changes in the vagina, uterus, and cervix; may have irregular menstruation; and may have an increased risk of miscarriage, ectopic pregnancy, infertility, and premature delivery.

Other research has suggested that the sons of women who used DES during pregnancy may have testicular abnormalities, such as undescended testicles or abnormally small testicles. Research has not been decisive on the risk of testicular or prostate cancer due to fetal exposure to DES. *See also* **Birth Defects and Abortion**

Devanter, Willis Van

Willis Van Devanter (1859–1941) served as an associate justice of the United States Supreme Court from 1910 to 1937. While on the Supreme Court Justice Devanter was known as a conservative who favored big business.

Justice Devanter was born in Marion, Indiana. He was educated at Indiana Asbury University and the University of Cincinnati Law School, where he received a law degree in 1881. Justice Devanter's early legal career was spent in private practice in Indiana and Wyoming. In 1903 he was appointed by President Theodore Roosevelt to the Eighth Circuit Court of Appeals. Seven years later, in 19310, President William Howard Taft nominated Justice Devanter to the Supreme Court.

While on the Supreme Court Justice Devanter was involved in only one abortion related opinion. Justice Devanter voted with a unanimous opinion in *State of Missouri ex rel. Hurwitz v. North*, which held that the constitution was not violated when a physician was prevented from issuing subpoenas to have witnesses attend a hearing to revoke his medical license for performing an unlawful abortion, because the applicable rules required taking depositions of witnesses who would not voluntarily attend the hearing.

Devereux, George

George Devereux (1908–1985) was born in Hungarian Transylvania. He was educated in France and the United States. Devereux obtained a Ph.D. in anthropology at the University of California at Berkeley in 1935. He was also trained in psychoanalysis. In 1955 Devereux reported in a study, which was widely excepted, that abortion has been practiced in almost all human communities from the earliest times. Devereux reached his conclusion after a study of abortion in several hundred preindustrial societies.

Diabetes and Pregnancy

Diabetes is a common condition in which the body either fails to produce enough insulin or does not use insulin properly. Untreated diabetes may lead to an accumulation of high levels of sugar in the blood, which in turn can damage blood vessels, nerves, eyes and kidneys. Daily insulin injections are used by many people to prevent these complications.

Women who are pregnant and have diabetes pose some risks to their babies. If a woman has uncontrolled diabetes she is at a greater risk of having a baby with a serious birth defect. She is also at an increased risk of having a spontaneous abortion or stillbirth. With proper personal and prenatal care, a woman with diabetes may have no problems with her child because of the disease.

Gestational diabetes. Women who are pregnant and have never had diabetes before, but have high blood sugar levels during pregnancy are said to have gestational diabetes. There are 135,000 cases of gestational diabetes every year in the United States. The disorder usually begins in the fifth or sixth month of pregnancy and generally goes away after the baby is born. However, complications may arise during pregnancy if the diabetes is not treated. This situation could cause the baby to have a low blood sugar level or jaundice, or weigh much more than is normal. Untreated gestational diabetes can also cause a more difficult delivery or necessitate a caesarean section. *See also* **Heart Disease and Pregnancy; Kidney Disease and Pregnancy; Liver Disease and Pregnancy**

Diamond v. Charles

Forum: United States Supreme Court.

Case Citation: Diamond v. Charles, 476 U.S. 54 (1986).

Date Argued: November 5, 1985.

Date of Decision: April 30, 1986.

Opinion of Court: Blackmun, J., in which Burger, C. J., and Brennan, Marshall, Powell, Rehnquist and O'Connor, JJ., joined.

Concurring Opinion: O'Connor, J., in which Burger, C. J., and Rehnquist, J., joined.

Concurring Statement: White, J.

Dissenting Opinion: None.

Counsel for Appellant: Dennis J. Horan argued; on the briefs were Victor G. Rosenblum, Edward R. Grant, and Maura K. Quinlan.

Counsel for Appellees: R. Peter Carey argued; on the brief were Colleen K. Connell, Frank Susman, Janet Benshoof, and Nan D. Hunter.

Amicus Brief for Appellant: United States by Acting Solicitor General Fried, Acting Assistant Attorney General Willard, Deputy Assistant Attorney General Kuhl, John F. Cordes, and John M. Rogers; for the Catholic League for Religious and Civil Rights by Steven Frederick McDowell; and for Senator Gordon J. Humphrey et al. by Robert A. Destro and Basile J. Uddo.

Amicus Brief for Appellees: Attorney General of New York by Robert Abrams, pro se, Robert Hermann, Solicitor General, Rosemarie Rhodes, Assistant Attorney General, and Lawrence S. Kahn, Sanford M. Cohen, and Martha J. Olson, Assistant Attorneys General; for the American Medical Association et al. by Benjamin W. Heineman, Jr., Carter G. Phillips, Newton N. Minow, Jack R. Bierig, Stephan E. Lawton, Joel I. Klein, Joseph A. Keyes, Jr., and Ann E. Allen; for the Center for Constitutional Rights et al. by Anne E. Simon, Nadine Taub, Rhonda Copelon, and Judith Levin; for the National Abortion Rights Action League et al. by Lynn I. Miller; for the National Organization for Women et al. by Diane E. Thompson; and for Planned Parenthood Federation of America, Inc., et al. by Dara Klassel and Eve W. Paul.

Issue Presented: Whether an Illinois citizen had standing to appeal a decision finding certain aspects of Illinois' abortion statute invalid?

Case Holding: The Illinois citizen lacked standing to appeal the decision that found find certain aspects of Illinois' abortion statute invalid.

Background facts of case: The appellees, abortion providers, filed a class action lawsuit in a federal district court in Illinois, challenging the constitutionality of certain provision's of the state's abortion statute. The state was named as a defendant. The appellant, Diamond (a doctor opposed to abortion), was allowed to intervene as a defendant. The district court ultimately entered a permanent injunction barring enforcement of provisions in the statute which (1) imposed criminal penalties for violating a prescribed standard of care that had to be exercised by a physician in performing an abortion of a viable fetus, and of a possibly viable fetus; and (2) imposed criminal penalties for physicians who failed to provide patients with information about the type of abortifacient used. The Seventh Circuit court of appeals affirmed the judgment. The state of Illinois did not appeal the judgment to the United States Supreme Court. However, Dr. Diamond did file an appeal. The attorney general of Illinois subsequently submitted a letter indicating it was interested in the case, though no appeal was filed. The Supreme Court addressed the issue of whether Dr. Diamond could appeal without the state.

Majority opinion by Justice Blackmun: Justice Blackmun held that the appeal could not be allowed without the state as a party. He wrote the following:

> Article III of the Constitution limits the power of federal courts to deciding "cases" and "controversies." This requirement ensures the presence of the concrete adverseness which sharpens the presentation of issues upon which the court so largely depends for illumination of difficult constitutional questions. The presence of a disagreement, however sharp and acrimonious it may be, is insufficient by itself to meet Art. III's requirements. This Court consistently has required, in addition, that the party seeking judicial resolution of a dispute show that he personally has suffered some actual or threatened injury as a result of the putatively illegal conduct of the other party....
>
> Had the State of Illinois invoked this Court's appellate jurisdiction ... and sought review of the Court of Appeals' decision, the "case" or "controversy" requirement would have been met, for a State has standing to defend the constitutionality of its statute. Diamond argues that Illinois' "letter of interest" demonstrates the State's continued concern with the enforcement of its Abortion Law, and renders the State the functional equivalent of an appellant. Accordingly, Diamond asserts, there is no jurisdictional problem in the case. This claim must be rejected....
>
> Had the State sought review, this Court's Rule 10.4 makes clear that Diamond, as an intervening defendant below, also would be entitled to seek review, enabling him to file a brief on the merits, and to seek leave to argue orally. But this ability to ride "piggyback" on the State's undoubted standing exists only if the State is in fact an appellant before the Court; in the absence of the State in that capacity, there is no case for Diamond to join.
>
> Diamond's status as an intervenor below, whether permissive or as of right, does not confer standing sufficient to keep the case alive in the absence of the State on this appeal. Although intervenors are considered parties entitled, among other things, to seek review by this Court, an intervenor's right to continue a suit

in the absence of the party on whose side intervention was permitted is contingent upon a showing by the intervenor that he fulfills the requirements of Art. III.

Disposition of case: The appeal was dismissed for want of jurisdiction.

Concurring opinion by Justice O'Connor: Justice O'Connor concurred in the Court's judgment, but argued that Dr. Diamond lacked standing to appeal because "was not a proper intervenor in the Court of Appeals, and therefore Illinois [was] not before this Court in any capacity, because Diamond was not authorized to bring this appeal[.]"

Concurring statement by Justice White: Justice White issued a statement that he concurred in the judgment of the Court.

Diaphragm

The diaphragm is a contraceptive device. It is a dome shaped, shallow cup with a flexible rim that fits in the vagina and over the cervix. It is used in conjunction with a spermicide cream or jelly. Diaphragms keep sperm from joining the egg by blocking the opening to the uterus and preventing sperm from entering. The spermicide cream or jelly that is applied to the diaphragm immobilizes sperm. Out of every 100 women who use a diaphragm, about 18 will become pregnant during the first year of use. Diaphragms are known to offer some protection against certain sexually transmitted diseases such as gonorrhea and chlamydia.

In order to use a diaphragm a pelvic examination by a health care provider is needed to determine the correct size. A diaphragm may be purchased at a drugstore or clinic. In order to use a diaphragm properly it must be inserted up to six hours before sexual intercourse, and must remain in place six to eight hours after intercourse. A diaphragm should not be left in place for more than 24 hours. Side effects from use of a diaphragm include: bladder infections; toxic shock syndrome (high fever, diarrhea, vomiting, sore throat, body aches, dizziness, and weakness); and abnormal cell growth. *See also* **Contraception**

Diaphragmatic Hernia

Diaphragmatic hernia is a congenital disorder involving an abnormal opening in the diaphragm that causes part of the abdominal organs (stomach, small intestine, spleen, part of the liver, and the kidney) to move into the chest cavity. This condition is due to improper fusion of structures during fetal development. It usually leads to respiratory distress and collapse of the lungs. Symptoms of the disorder include severe breathing difficulty and bluish coloration of the skin. There is in no known prevention for this condition. The disorder requires immediate surgery to place the abdominal organs into the abdominal cavity and repair of the opening in the diaphragm. Prognosis after surgery depends upon the development of the lung tissue. Babies who survive may have some long-term lung disease. *See also* **Birth Defects and Abortion**

Dickinson, Robert Latou

Robert Latou Dickinson (1861–1950) was considered one of the most eminent gynecologists of his time, as well as a pioneer in the contraceptive movement in the United States. Dickinson, who was born in Jersey City, New Jersey, was educated at Brooklyn Polytechnic Institute, as well schools in Germany and Switzerland, and prior to receiving his medical degree from Long Island College Hospital in 1882.

After leaving medical school, Dickinson set up a medical practice in Brooklyn, New York, where he specialized in obstetrics and gynecology. Dickinson was credited with developing several new surgical techniques, including the use of electric cauterization for intrauterine sterilizations. In addition, he was one of the first physicians to use aseptic ligatures for tying the umbilical cord.

Dickinson's most noteworthy work involved his support for several feminist causes, the most significant being birth control. His devotion to this cause lead him to establish the National Committee on Maternal Health in 1923. This organization was created to study and address problems involving contraception, fertility, abortion, sterilization, and sexuality. In time Dickinson became one of the most important advocates in the medical community for the legalization of contraception. Dickinson authored and co-authored several books that included: *Human Sex Anatomy*; *The Single Woman: A Medical Study in Sex Education*; and *A Thousand Marriages: A Medical Study of Sex Adjustment.*

Dilatation *see* **Dilation**

Dilation

Dilation, also called dilatation, refers to the widening or opening of the cervix during labor in preparation for expelling a fetus or performing an abortion. *See also* **Contraction; Effacement**

Dilation and Curettage

Dilation and curettage (D & C) (also called sharp curettage) is a commonly used first trimester surgical abortion procedure. This pro-

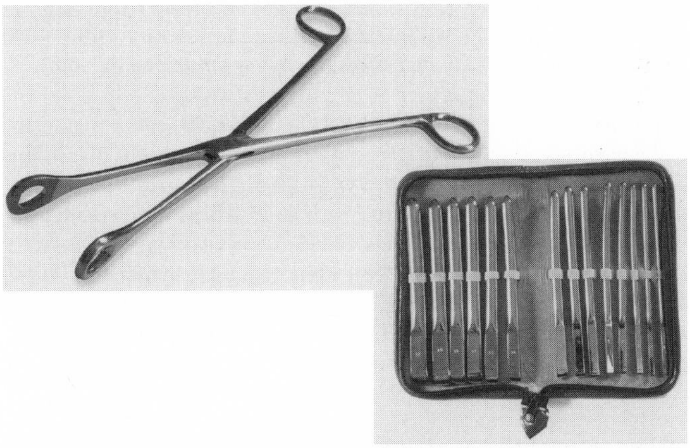

Left: **Forceps are used to tear apart a fetus during the dilation and evacuation abortion procedure.** ***Right:*** **Dilators are used to aid in opening the cervix for an abortion (both photographs: Grantham Collection, all rights reserved).**

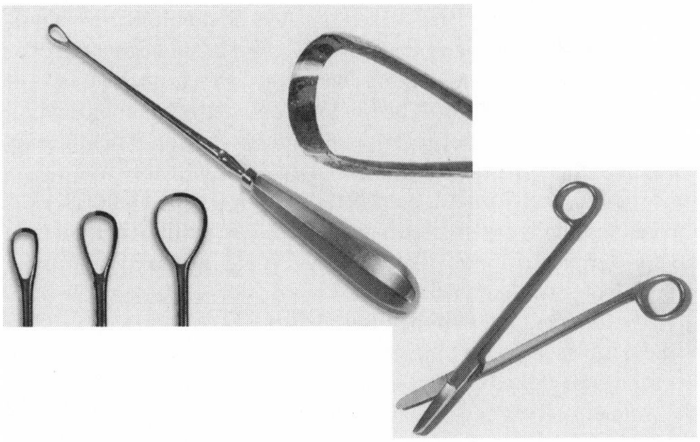

Above left: **A curette is used to tear apart and scrape away a fetus during the dilation and curettage abortion procedure.** ***Above right:*** **Embryotomy scissors are used during an abortion to cut off the head and limbs of a fetus (both photographs Grantham Collection, all rights reserved).**

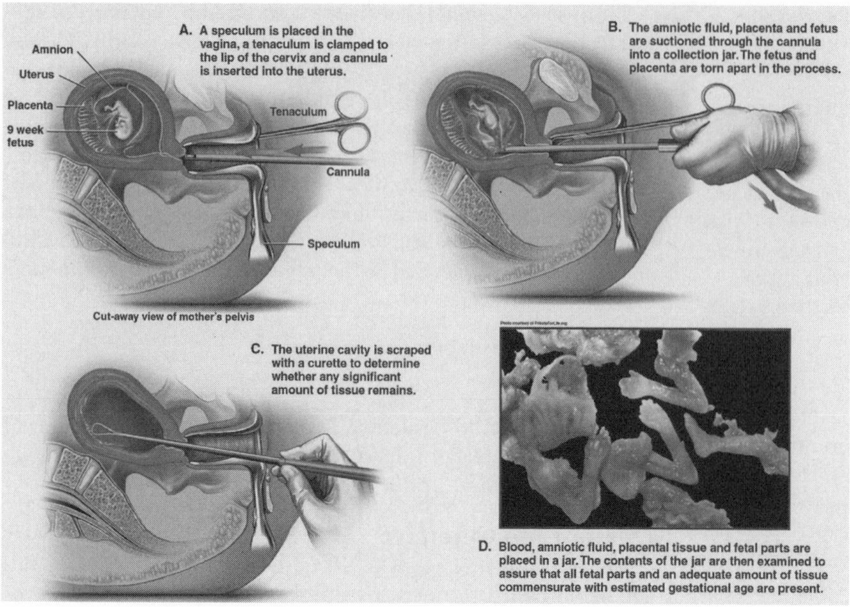

A. A speculum is placed in the vagina, a tenaculum is clamped to the lip of the cervix and a cannula is inserted into the uterus.
Amnion
Uterus
Placenta
9 week fetus
Tenaculum
Cannula
Speculum
Cut-away view of mother's pelvis
B. The amniotic fluid, placenta and fetus are suctioned through the cannula into a collection jar. The fetus and placenta are torn apart in the process.
C. The uterine cavity is scraped with a curette to determine whether any significant amount of tissue remains.
D. Blood, amniotic fluid, placental tissue and fetal parts are placed in a jar. The contents of the jar are then examined to assure that all fetal parts and an adequate amount of tissue commensurate with estimated gestational age are present.

***Below:* Vacuum aspiration (a.k.a. suction curettage) abortion of a 9-week-old fetus. Under this method a fetus is suctioned out of the womb (illustration copyright © 2008 Nucleus Medical Art, all rights reserved, www.nucleusinc.com).**

cedure may be performed under local anesthesia, IV sedation, or general anesthesia. During the D&C procedure a speculum is placed inside the vagina to keep the vaginal walls apart. The doctor will hold the cervix, the opening to the uterus, with an instrument called a tenaculum. Several narrow metal rods, called dilators, will be inserted into the cervix to open it slightly. The uterine contents are then torn apart and scraped away with a curette. The D & C procedure generally takes about ten minutes. Side effects from D & C may include cramping, excessive bleeding, high temperature or clotting. *See also* **Methods of Abortion**

Dilation and Evacuation

Dilation and evacuation (D & E) is a second trimester abortion procedure. The D & E procedure was described by the United States Supreme Court in *Gonzalez v. Carhart* as follows:

A doctor must first dilate the cervix at least to the extent needed to insert surgical instruments into the uterus and to maneuver them to evacuate the fetus. The steps taken to cause dilation differ by physician and gestational age of the fetus. A doctor often begins the dilation process by inserting osmotic dilators, such as laminaria (sticks of seaweed), into the cervix. The dilators can be used in combination with drugs, such as misoprostol, that increase dilation. The resulting amount of dilation is not uniform, and a doctor does not know in advance how an individual patient will respond. In general the longer dilators remain in the cervix, the more it will dilate. Yet the length of time doctors employ osmotic dilators varies. Some may keep dilators in the cervix for two days, while others use dilators for a day or less.

After sufficient dilation the surgical operation can commence. The woman is placed under general anesthesia or conscious sedation. The doctor, often guided by ultrasound, inserts grasping forceps through the woman's cervix and into the uterus to grab the fetus. The doctor grips a fetal part with the forceps and pulls it back through the cervix and vagina, continuing to pull even after meeting resistance from the cervix. The friction causes the fetus to tear apart. For example, a leg might be ripped off the fetus as it is pulled through the cervix and out of the woman. The process of evacuating the fetus piece by piece continues until it has been completely removed. A doctor may make 10 to 15 passes with the forceps to evacuate the fetus in its entirety, though sometimes removal is completed with fewer passes. Once the fetus has been evacuated, the placenta and any remaining fetal material are suctioned or scraped out of the uterus. The doctor examines the different parts to ensure the entire fetal body has been removed.

Some doctors, especially later in the second trimester, may kill the fetus a day or two before performing the surgical evacuation. They inject digoxin or potassium chloride into the fetus, the umbilical cord, or the amniotic fluid. Fetal demise may cause contractions and make greater dilation possible. Once dead, moreover, the fetus' body will soften, and its removal will be easier. Other doctors refrain from injecting chemical agents, believing it adds risk with little or no medical benefit.

The D & E procedure generally takes about ten to twenty minutes. Side effects from D & E may include cramping, excessive bleeding, high temperature or blood clotting. *See also* **Methods of Abortion**

Dilation and Extraction

Dilation and extraction (D & X) (also called "partial-birth abortion" and "intact D & E") is a late term abortion procedure that is typically performed when the life of the mother is at risk, or the fetus is determined to have severe abnormalities. The D & X procedure takes three days to complete. A woman's cervix is dilated the first two days with laminaria. On the third day, the fetus is extracted through the birth canal feet first, leaving only the head inside. A physician then punctures the base of the skull of the fetus with surgical scissors. A suction catheter is then inserted to remove all of the fetus' brain tissue, thereby rending it dead. The dead fetus is then completely removed from the woman's body.

In the case of *Stenberg v. Carhart* the Supreme Court invalidated a Nebraska statute which had banned the use of D & X. However, the subsequent case of *Gonzales v. Carhart* the Supreme Court upheld a federal statute which banned use of D & X. *See also* **Gonzales v. Carhart; Methods of Abortion; Partial-Birth Abortion; Partial-Birth Abortion Ban Act; Stenberg v. Carhart**

District of Columbia

(1) OVERVIEW

The District of Columbia enacted its first criminal abortion statute on January 19, 1872. The statute underwent several amendments prior to the 1973 decision by the United States Supreme Court in *Roe v. Wade*, which legalized abortion in the nation. In the 1971 decision of *United States v. Vuitch* the United States Supreme Court held that the criminal abortion statute of the District of Columbia was not constitutionally vague, insofar as there was no ambiguity in its use of the word "health" and it did not shift to the defendant the burden of proving innocence. In *Davis v. Columbia Hosp. for Women Med. Ctr., Inc.*, 125 WLR 205 (Super. Ct. 1997), a District of Columbia court held that the statute was valid only as to prohibiting post-viability abortions, except where necessary to protect the life or health of the mother. The District of Columbia repealed its criminal abortion statute in 2004. Even so, the District of Columbia has not taken any significant affirmative steps, through statutes or administrative regulations, to respond to *Roe* and its progeny. The only meaningful areas specifically addressed by statute concerns guardian of wards and impeding access to facilities.

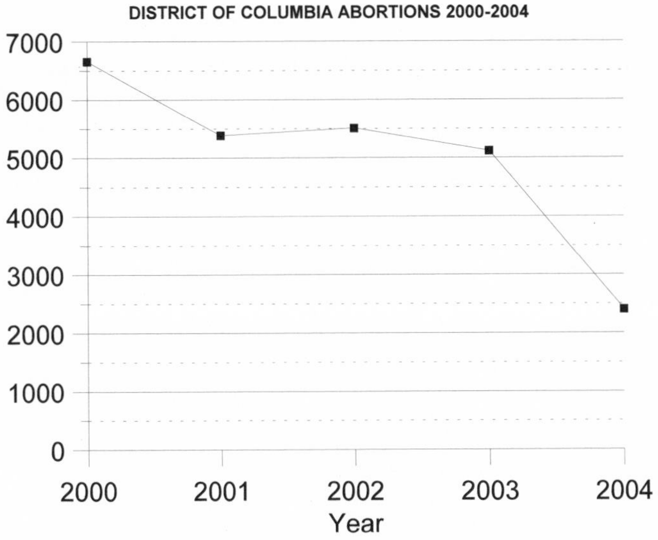

DISTRICT OF COLUMBIA ABORTIONS 2000-2004

Source: National Center for Health Statistics.

District of Columbia Abortion by Age Group 2000–2004

Year	<15	15–19	20–24	25–29	30–34	35–39	≥40	Unknown
2000	68	1,206	2,211	1,634	876	505	158	1
2001	46	1,107	1,892	1,187	669	363	120	1
2002	40	1,073	1,804	1,330	775	349	140	0
2003	27	968	1,702	1,322	650	342	120	0
2004	65	374	711	567	381	218	85	0
Total	246	4,728	8,320	6,040	3,351	1,777	623	2

Age Group (yrs)

Source: National Center for Health Statistics.

District of Columbia Abortion by Weeks Of Gestation 2000–2004

Weeks of Gestation	2000	2001	2002	2003	2004	Total
≤8	2,937	2,060	2,564	2,504	1,540	11,605
9–10	1,761	1,583	1,441	1,208	289	6,282
11–12	889	809	611	598	153	3,060
13–15	582	543	532	492	230	2,379
16–20	286	397	359	317	189	1,548
≥21	0	0	0	0	0	0
Not known	204	3	4	2	0	213

Year

Source: National Center for Health Statistics.

(2) GUARDIAN OF WARDS

The District of Columbia prohibits a guardian from consenting to an abortion for a minor or incapacitated female. The statutes addressing the issue is set out below.

D.C. Code § 21-2047(c). Guardian authority

(c) A guardian shall not have the power:

(1) To consent to an abortion ... except to preserve the life or prevent the immediate serious impairment of the physical health of the incapacitated individual, unless the power to consent is expressly set forth in the order of appointment or after subsequent hearing and order of the court.

D.C. Code § 21-2211. Guardian authority

No person authorized to act pursuant to § 21-2210 shall have the power:

(1) To consent to an abortion, sterilization or psycho-surgery, unless authorized by a court.

DISTRICT OF COLUMBIA ABORTIONS BY RACE 2000-2004

■ White ☐ Black ▨ Other ▨ Unknown

Source: National Center for Health Statistics.

DISTRICT OF COLUMBIA ABORTIONS BY MARITAL STATUS 2002-2004

■ Married ☐ Single ▨ Unknown

Source: National Center for Health Statistics.

(3) IMPEDING ACCESS TO FACILITIES

The District of Columbia prohibits anti-abortion conduct that impedes the flow of traffic into and out of health care facilities. The statute addressing the issue is set out below.

D.C. Code § 22-1314.02. Impeding access to facility

(a) It shall be unlawful for a person, except as otherwise authorized by District or federal law, alone or in concert with others, to willfully or recklessly interfere with access to or from a medical facility or to willfully or recklessly disrupt the normal functioning of such facility by:

(1) Physically obstructing, impeding, or hindering the free passage of an individual seeking to enter or depart the facility or from the common areas of the real property upon which the facility is located;

(2) Making noise that unreasonably disturbs the peace within the facility;

(3) Trespassing on the facility or the common areas of the real property upon which the facility is located;

(4) Telephoning the facility repeatedly to harass or threaten own-

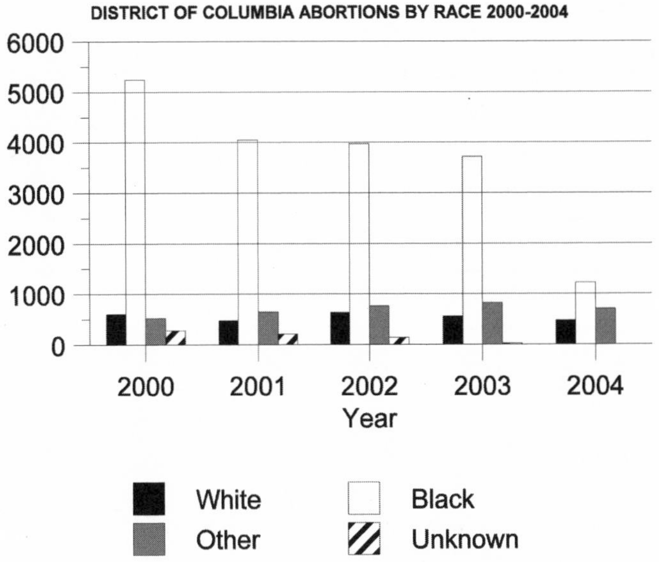

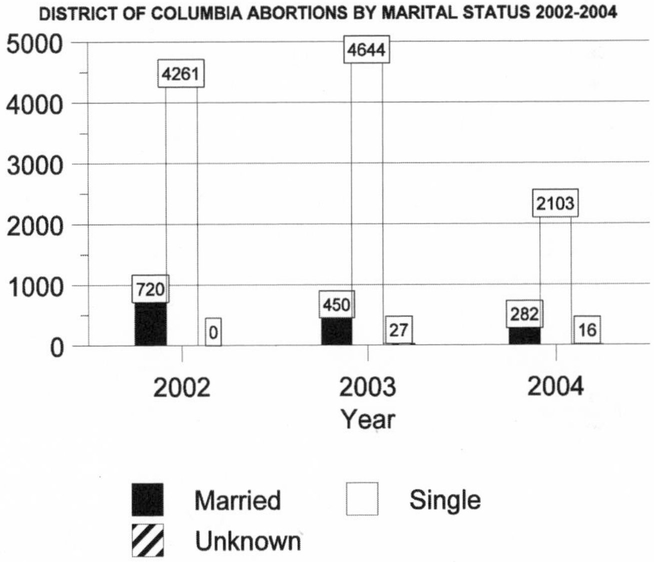

ers, agents, patients, and employees, or knowingly permitting any telephone under his or her control to be so used for the purpose of threatening owners, agents, patients, and employees; or

(5) Threatening to inflict injury on the owners, agents, patients, employees, or property of the medical facility or knowingly permitting any telephone under his or her control to be used for such purpose.

(b) A person shall not act alone or in concert with others with the intent to prevent a health professional or his or her family from entering or leaving the health professional's home.

(c) Subsections (a) and (b) of this section shall not be construed to prohibit any otherwise lawful picketing or assembly.

(d) Any person who violates subsections (a) or (b) of this section, upon conviction, shall be fined not more than $1,000, imprisoned for not more than 180 days, or both.

Doe v. Bolton

Forum: United States Supreme Court.

Case Citation: Doe v. Bolton, 410 U.S. 179 (1973).

Date Argued: December 13, 1971; reargued October 11, 1972.

Date of Decision: January 22, 1973.

Opinion of Court: Blackmun, J., in which Burger, C. J., and Douglas, Brennan, Stewart, Marshall, and Powell, JJ., joined.

Concurring Opinion: Burger, C. J.

Concurring Opinion: Douglas, J.

Dissenting Opinion: White, J., in which Rehnquist, J., joined.

Dissenting Opinion: Rehnquist, J.

Counsel for Appellants: Margie Pitts Hames argued; on the brief were Reber F. Boult, Jr., Charles Morgan, Jr., Elizabeth Roediger Rindskopf, and Tobiane Schwartz.

Counsel for Appellees: Dorothy T. Beasley argued; on the brief were Arthur K. Bolton, Attorney General of Georgia, Harold N. Hill, Jr., Executive Assistant Attorney General, Courtney Wilder Stanton, Assistant Attorney General, Joel Feldman, Henry L. Bowden, and Ralph H. Witt.

Amicus Brief for Appellants and Appellees: Roy Lucas for the American College of Obstetricians and Gynecologists et al.; by Dennis J. Horan, Jerome A. Frazel, Jr., Thomas M. Crisham, and Delores V. Horan for Certain Physicians, Professors and Fellows of the American College of Obstetrics and Gynecology; by Harriet F. Pilpel, Nancy F. Wechsler, and Frederic S. Nathan for Planned Parenthood Federation of America, Inc., et al.; by Alan F. Charles for the National Legal Program on Health Problems of the Poor et al.; by Marttie L. Thompson for State Communities Aid Assn.; by Alfred L. Scanlan, Martin J. Flynn, and Robert M. Byrn for the National Right to Life Committee; by Helen L. Buttenwieser for the American Ethical Union et al.; by Norma G. Zarky for the American Association of University Women et al.; by Nancy Stearns for New Women Lawyers et al.; by the California Committee to Legalize Abortion et al.; by Robert E. Dunne for Robert L. Sassone; and by Ferdinand Buckley pro se.

Issue Presented: Whether the constitution was violated by provisions in Georgia's abortion statutes that required (1) abortions take place in accredited hospitals, (2) that an abortion be approved by a hospital abortion committee, (3) that the need for an abortion be confirmed by two independent physicians, and (4) that a woman seeking an abortion be a resident of Georgia?

Case Holding: The Due Process Clause of the Fourteenth Amendment was violated by provisions in Georgia's abortion statutes that required (1) abortions take place in accredited hospitals, (2) that an abortion be approved by a hospital abortion committee, (3) that the need for an abortion be confirmed by two independent physicians, and (4) that a woman seeking an abortion be a resident of Georgia.

Background facts of case: In 1970 the abortion statutes of Georgia prohibited an abortion except when a pregnant woman's life or her health was in danger, the fetus would likely be born with a serious defect, or the pregnancy resulted from rape. In order for a statutorily authorized abortion to occur (1) the woman had to be a Georgia resident; (2) the abortion had to be performed in a hospital accredited by a Joint Commission on Accreditation of Hospitals (JCAH); (3) the abortion procedure had to be approved by the hospital staff abortion committee; and (4) the performing physician's decision that the abortion was statutorily authorized had to be confirmed by two other licensed physicians. In April of 1970 the appellants, Mary Doe and a group of abortion providers, filed a lawsuit in a federal district court in Georgia challenging the constitutionality of the state's abortion statutes. The district court ruled that the statutes which limited abortion to therapeutic, eugenic and rape circumstances, violated the constitution. However, the court upheld the validity of the remaining statutes. The appellants filed an appeal with the Supreme Court, regarding the statutes found to be valid. The Supreme Court granted certiorari to consider the issues.

Majority opinion by Justice Blackmun: Justice Blackmun held that the Due Process Clause of the Fourteenth Amendment was violated by the JCAH accredited hospital provision, approval by the hospital abortion committee, confirmation by two independent physicians, and residency requirement. He addressed each matter as follows:

> The Joint Commission on Accreditation of Hospitals is an organization without governmental sponsorship or overtones. No question whatever is raised concerning the integrity of the organization or the high purpose of the accreditation process. That process, however, has to do with hospital standards generally and has no present particularized concern with abortion as a medical or surgical procedure. In Georgia, there is no restriction on the performance of non-abortion surgery in a hospital not yet accredited by the JCAH so long as other requirements imposed by the State, such as licensing of the hospital and of the operating surgeon, are met. Furthermore, accreditation by the Commission is not granted until a hospital has been in operation at least one year....
>
> We hold that the JCAH-accreditation requirement does not withstand constitutional scrutiny in the present context. It is a requirement that simply is not based on differences that are reasonably related to the purposes of the Act in which it is found.
>
> This is not to say that Georgia may not or should not, from and after the end of the first trimester, adopt standards for licensing all facilities where abortions may be performed so long as those standards are legitimately related to the objective the State seeks to accomplish.... The State, on the other hand, has not presented persuasive data to show that only hospitals meet its acknowledged interest in insuring the quality of the operation and the full protection of the patient. We feel compelled to agree with appellants that the State must show more than it has in order to prove that only the full resources of a licensed hospital, rather than those of some other appropriately licensed institution, satisfy these health interests. We hold that the hospital requirement of the Georgia law, because it fails to exclude the first trimester of pregnancy, is also invalid. In so holding we naturally express no opinion on the medical judgment involved in any particular case, that is, whether the patient's situation is such that an abortion should be performed in a hospital, rather than in some other facility.
>
> The second aspect of the appellants' procedural attack relates to the hospital abortion committee....
>
> ... Viewing the Georgia statute as a whole, we see no constitutionally justifiable pertinence in the structure for the advance approval by the abortion committee. With regard to the protection of potential life, the medical judgment is already completed prior to the committee stage, and review by a committee once removed from diagnosis is basically redundant. We are not cited to any

other surgical procedure made subject to committee approval as a matter of state criminal law. The woman's right to receive medical care in accordance with her licensed physician's best judgment and the physician's right to administer it are substantially limited by this statutorily imposed overview....

We conclude that the interposition of the hospital abortion committee is unduly restrictive of the patient's rights and needs that, at this point, have already been medically delineated and substantiated by her personal physician. To ask more serves neither the hospital nor the State.

... There remains ... the required confirmation by two Georgia-licensed physicians in addition to the recommendation of the pregnant woman's own consultant (making under the statute, a total of six physicians involved, including the three on the hospital's abortion committee). We conclude that this provision, too, must fall.

... The reasons for the presence of the confirmation step in the statute are perhaps apparent, but they are insufficient to withstand constitutional challenge. Again, no other voluntary medical or surgical procedure for which Georgia requires confirmation by two other physicians has been cited to us. If a physician is licensed by the State, he is recognized by the State as capable of exercising acceptable clinical judgment. If he fails in this, professional censure and deprivation of his license are available remedies. Required acquiescence by co-practitioners has no rational connection with a patient's needs and unduly infringes on the physician's right to practice. The attending physician will know when a consultation is advisable — the doubtful situation, the need for assurance when the medical decision is a delicate one, and the like. Physicians have followed this routine historically and know its usefulness and benefit for all concerned....

The appellants attack the residency requirement of the Georgia law as violative of the right to travel.... A requirement of this kind, of course, could be deemed to have some relationship to the availability of post-procedure medical care for the aborted patient.

Nevertheless, we do not uphold the constitutionality of the residence requirement. It is not based on any policy of preserving state-supported facilities for Georgia residents, for the bar also applies to private hospitals and to privately retained physicians. There is no intimation, either, that Georgia facilities are utilized to capacity in caring for Georgia residents. Just as the Privileges and Immunities Clause protects persons who enter other States to ply their trade, so must it protect persons who enter Georgia seeking the medical services that are available there. A contrary holding would mean that a State could limit to its own residents the general medical care available within its borders. This we could not approve.

Disposition of case: The judgment of the district court was modified and, as so modified, was affirmed.

Concurring opinion by Chief Justice Burger: The Chief Justice wrote a concurring opinion that was also for another case decided in the same Term of Court, *Roe v. Wade* (involving the invalidation of the criminal abortion statutes of Texas). He wrote the following regarding both cases:

> I agree that, under the Fourteenth Amendment to the Constitution, the abortion statutes of Georgia and Texas impermissibly limit the performance of abortions necessary to protect the health of pregnant women, using the term health in its broadest medical context. I am somewhat troubled that the Court has taken notice of various scientific and medical data in reaching its conclusion; however, I do not believe that the Court has exceeded the scope of judicial notice accepted in other contexts.
>
> In oral argument, counsel for the State of Texas informed the Court that early abortion procedures were routinely permitted in certain exceptional cases, such as nonconsensual pregnancies resulting from rape and incest. In the face of a rigid and narrow statute, such as that of Texas, no one in these circumstances should be placed in a posture of dependence on a prosecutorial policy or prosecutorial discretion. Of course, States must have broad power, within the limits indicated in the opinions, to regulate the subject of abortions, but where the consequences of state intervention are so severe, uncertainty must be avoided as much as possible. For my part, I would be inclined to allow a State to require the certification of two physicians to support an abortion, but the Court holds otherwise. I do not believe that such a procedure is unduly burdensome, as are the complex steps of the Georgia statute, which require as many as six doctors and the use of a hospital certified by the JCAH.

Concurring opinion by Justice Douglas: Justice Douglas agreed with the majority opinion. He wrote a concurring opinion that was also intended for the Court's decision in *Roe v. Wade*. Justice Douglas made following points in his concurrence:

> The Georgia statute is at war with the clear message of these cases — that a woman is free to make the basic decision whether to bear an unwanted child. Elaborate argument is hardly necessary to demonstrate that childbirth may deprive a woman of her preferred lifestyle and force upon her a radically different and undesired future. For example, rejected applicants under the Georgia statute are required to endure the discomforts of pregnancy; to incur the pain, higher mortality rate, and aftereffects of childbirth; to abandon educational plans; to sustain loss of income; to forgo the satisfactions of careers; to tax further mental and physical health in providing child care; and, in some cases, to bear the lifelong stigma of unwed motherhood, a badge which may haunt, if not deter, later legitimate family relationships....
>
> There is no doubt that the State may require abortions to be performed by qualified medical personnel. The legitimate objective of preserving the mother's health clearly supports such laws. Their impact upon the woman's privacy is minimal. But the Georgia statute outlaws virtually all such operations — even in the earliest stages of pregnancy. In light of modern medical evidence suggesting that an early abortion is safer healthwise than childbirth itself, it cannot be seriously urged that so comprehensive a ban is aimed at protecting the woman's health. Rather, this expansive proscription of all abortions along the temporal spectrum can rest only on a public goal of preserving both embryonic and fetal life....
>
> In summary, the enactment is overbroad. It is not closely correlated to the aim of preserving prenatal life. In fact, it permits its destruction in several cases, including pregnancies resulting from sex acts in which unmarried females are below the statutory age of consent. At the same time, however, the measure broadly proscribes aborting other pregnancies which may cause severe mental disorders. Additionally, the statute is overbroad because it equates the value of embryonic life immediately after conception with the worth of life immediately before birth.

Dissenting opinion by Justice White: Justice White disagreed with the majority decision. His dissenting opinion was also intended to express his dissent from the Court's decision in *Roe v. Wade*. Justice White wrote as follows:

> At the heart of the controversy in these cases are those recurring pregnancies that pose no danger whatsoever to the life or health of the mother but are, nevertheless, unwanted for any one or more of a variety of reasons—convenience, family planning, economics, dislike of children, the embarrassment of illegitimacy, etc. The common claim before us is that for any one of such reasons, or for no reason at all, and without asserting or claiming any threat to life or health, any woman is entitled to an abortion at her request if she is able to find a medical advisor willing to undertake the procedure.

The Court for the most part sustains this position: During the period prior to the time the fetus becomes viable, the Constitution of the United States values the convenience, whim, or caprice of the putative mother more than the life or potential life of the fetus; the Constitution, therefore, guarantees the right to an abortion as against any state law or policy seeking to protect the fetus from an abortion not prompted by more compelling reasons of the mother.

With all due respect, I dissent. I find nothing in the language or history of the Constitution to support the Court's judgment. The Court simply fashions and announces a new constitutional right for pregnant mothers and, with scarcely any reason or authority for its action, invests that right with sufficient substance to override most existing state abortion statutes. The upshot is that the people and the legislatures of the 50 States are constitutionally disentitled to weigh the relative importance of the continued existence and development of the fetus, on the one hand, against a spectrum of possible impacts on the mother, on the other hand. As an exercise of raw judicial power, the Court perhaps has authority to do what it does today; but in my view its judgment is an improvident and extravagant exercise of the power of judicial review that the Constitution extends to this Court.

The Court apparently values the convenience of the pregnant mother more than the continued existence and development of the life or potential life that she carries. Whether or not I might agree with that marshaling of values, I can in no event join the Court's judgment because I find no constitutional warrant for imposing such an order of priorities on the people and legislatures of the States. In a sensitive area such as this, involving as it does issues over which reasonable men may easily and heatedly differ, I cannot accept the Court's exercise of its clear power of choice by interposing a constitutional barrier to state efforts to protect human life and by investing mothers and doctors with the constitutionally protected right to exterminate it. This issue, for the most part, should be left with the people and to the political processes the people have devised to govern their affairs.

It is my view, therefore, that the Texas statute is not constitutionally infirm because it denies abortions to those who seek to serve only their convenience rather than to protect their life or health....

Likewise, because Georgia may constitutionally forbid abortions to putative mothers who, like the plaintiff in this case, do not fall within the reach of its criminal code, I have no occasion, and the District Court had none, to consider the constitutionality of the procedural requirements of the Georgia statute as applied to those pregnancies posing substantial hazards to either life or health. I would reverse the judgment of the District Court in the Georgia case.

Dissenting opinion by Justice Rehnquist: Justice Rehnquist referenced to his dissenting opinion in *Roe v. Wade*, as the basis for his dissent. He wrote as follows:

> The holding in Roe v. Wade that state abortion laws can withstand constitutional scrutiny only if the State can demonstrate a compelling state interest, apparently compels the Court's close scrutiny of the various provisions in Georgia's abortion statute. Since, as indicated by my dissent in Wade, I view the compelling-state-interest standard as an inappropriate measure of the constitutionality of state abortion laws, I respectfully dissent from the majority's holding.

See also **Cano, Sandra Besing; Roe v. Wade**

Doppler Ultrasound Scanning

Doppler ultrasound scanning is a procedure used to measure the velocity of blood flow in a fetus and the fetus' heart rate. The device is placed on the woman's abdomen. It will print out data for interpretation. The device provides a view of the fetus' heart tones, in relationship to the woman's contractions. Normally the device is limited in use to high-risk pregnancies. *See also* **Fetal Monitoring**

Douglas, William O.

William O. Douglas (1898–1980) served as an associate justice of the United States Supreme Court from 1939 to 1975. While on the Supreme Court Justice Douglas was known as a progressive thinker who sought to expand the reach of the Constitution for the protection of individual freedoms from government control.

Justice Douglas was born in Maine, Minnesota. He graduated from Whitman College in 1920, and went on to attend Columbia Law School where he graduated in 1925. Justice Douglas' resume included teaching at the law schools of Columbia and Yale, as well as an appointment to the Securities and Exchange Commission. In 1939 President Franklin D. Roosevelt nominated Justice Douglas to the Supreme Court.

During Justice Douglas' tenure on the Supreme Court he issued a number of abortion related opinions. The written opinions and opinions simply voted on by Justice Douglas, indicate that he was in favor of using the constitution to expand abortion rights for women.

Distribution of the Abortion Voting Pattern of Justice Douglas Based Upon Opinions Filed by the Supreme Court

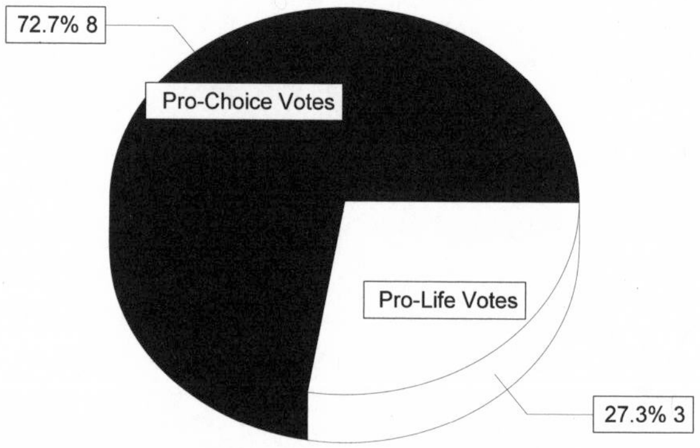

(1) Unanimous opinions voted with only. In *Withrow v. Larkin* Justice Douglas joined a unanimous opinion, which held that constitutional due process was not violated by the mere fact that a Wisconsin medical examining board had the authority to both, investigate and adjudicate, allegations against a physician that included, among other things, permitting a nonphysician to perform an abortion.

(2) Majority opinions written. In *Weinberger v. Hynson, Westcott & Dunning* Justice Douglas wrote the majority opinion, which held that the Food and Drug Administration could not deny a drug manufacturer a hearing to obtain marketing approval for a drug called Lutrexin, which provided treatment for premature labor and threatened and habitual abortion. In *Griswold v. Connecticut* Justice Douglas wrote the majority opinion, which held that the right of privacy found in the constitution prohibited enforcement of a Connecticut statute that made it a crime to give married persons contraceptive information and devices.

(3) Majority opinions voted with only. In *Connecticut v. Menillo* Justice Douglas joined the majority per curiam opinion, which held that the constitution was not violated by criminal abortion statutes that prohibit nonphysicians from attempting or performing abortions at any stage of a pregnancy. Justice Douglas joined the majority opinion in *Bigelow v. Virginia*, which held that the Free Speech and Free Press Clauses of the First Amendment were violated by a Virginia penal

statute that prohibited selling or circulating any publication that encouraged or promoted abortions.

(4) Concurring opinions written. Justice Douglas wrote an opinion concurring with the majority decision in *Doe v. Bolton*, which held that the Due Process Clause of the Fourteenth Amendment was violated by provisions in Georgia's abortion statutes that required (1) abortions take place in accredited hospitals, (2) that an abortion be approved by a hospital abortion committee, (3) that the need for an abortion be confirmed by two independent physicians, and (4) that a woman seeking an abortion be a resident of Georgia. Justice Douglas wrote an opinion concurring in the majority decision in *Eisenstadt v. Baird*, which held that the Equal Protection Clause of the Fourteenth Amendment was violated by a Massachusetts statute that made it a crime to give away a drug, medicine, instrument, or article for the prevention of conception except in the case of (1) a physician prescribing it for a married person, or (2) a pharmacist furnishing it to a married person presenting a physician's prescription.

(5) Concurring opinions voted with only. In *Roe v. Wade* Justice Douglas concurred in the majority opinion, which held that the liberty component of the Due Process Clause of the Fourteenth Amendment prohibited states from criminalizing or preventing elective first trimester abortions.

(6) Dissenting opinions written. Justice Douglas wrote an opinion dissenting from the majority decision in *Poe v. Ullman*, which held that the appellants did not have standing to challenge the constitutionality of a Connecticut statute, that made it a crime to give married persons contraceptive information and devices. He believed the appellants had standing and that the statute was unconstitutional.

(7) Dissenting opinions voted with only. Justice Douglas dissented from the majority decision in *Geduldig v. Aiello*, which held that the Equal Protection Clause of the Fourteenth Amendment did not require a private sector employee disability insurance program, operated by the state of California, provide coverage for employee disabilities associated with normal pregnancies. He believed the Equal Protection Clause was violated.

(8) Concurring and dissenting opinions written. Justice Douglas wrote an opinion concurring and dissenting from the majority decision in *United States v. Vuitch*, which held that the criminal abortion statute of the District of Columbia, which only permitted therapeutic abortions, was not constitutionally vague insofar as there was no ambiguity in its use of the word health and it did not shift to the defendant the burden of proving innocence. He believed the statute was constitutionally invalid.

Doula

The term doula is derived from the Greek and means "woman caregiver of another woman." Doulas have become an increasing part of childbirth in the United States. Doulas are trained individuals who help expectant couples draft birth plans, offer moral support during labor, and provide advice and assistance during the weeks following birth. They are not trained to give medical support (this distinguishes doulas from midwives). Doulas work in homes, hospitals and birth centers. Studies have shown that pregnant women who utilize the services of doulas tend to experience shorter labors, as a result of emotional support and guidance. *See also* **Midwife**

Down Syndrome

Down syndrome (also called trisomy 21 or Mongolism) is a genetic disorder that is caused by an extra chromosome 21. Characteristics of the disease include mental retardation, heart defects, intestinal malformations, visual and hearing impairment, a small and abnormally shaped head, a flattened nose, protruding tongue, upward slanting eyes and increased risk of thyroid problems and leukemia. The average mental age achieved by a Down syndrome victim is 8 years old. Down syndrome affects approximately one out of 1,000 babies. There are about 350,000 individuals with Down syndrome in the United States. There is no cure for Down syndrome. Prenatal testing can diagnose or rule out Down syndrome. *See also* **Birth Defects and Abortion**

Drug Use and Pregnancy

Research has shown that pregnant women who use unlawful drugs such as cocaine, marijuana, methamphetamines, PCP or heroin, expose fetuses to these drugs through their bloodstream. This situation can lead to problems such as miscarriage, premature labor, low birthweight, drug addiction and a higher risk of birth defects.

In addition to unlawful drugs, many commonly taken medications can endanger the health of newborns. Anti-epileptic medications such as dilantin and tegretol, have been associated with heart and facial defects, as well as mental retardation. Premature labor has been associated with antimigraine drugs. Certain prescribed acne medications like accutane are associated with mental retardation, heart defects, ear and eye abnormalities, facial abnormalities and miscarriage. Anti-inflammatory medications like aspirin and ibuprofen, may increase the risk of uncontrolled bleeding for both mother and baby, as well as interfere with the production of the hormones that stimulate labor. Certain anticoagulant drugs used to treat heart disease and stroke, have been associated with facial deformities and mental retardation.

The Food and Drug Administration utilizes 5 categories of labeling for drugs that may be used during pregnancy:

Label A: Studies in women fail to demonstrate a risk to the fetus.

Label B: Animal studies fail to show a risk to the fetus and no human studies were done; or animal studies show a negative effect on the fetus but studies in pregnant women failed to show a risk to the fetus.

Label C: Animal studies show toxicity, human studies inadequate but benefit of use may exceed risk.

Label D: Evidence of human fetal risk exists, but benefits may make use of the drug acceptable despite the risks.

Label X: Studies have demonstrated human fetal abnormalities, and the risk clearly outweighs any possible benefits.

In *Weinberger v. Hynson, Westcott & Dunning* the Supreme Court held that the Food and Drug Administration could not deny a drug manufacturer a hearing to obtain marketing approval for a drug called Lutrexin, which provided treatment for premature labor and threatened and habitual abortion.

Prosecution of women for illegal drug use during pregnancy. The vast majority of states adhere to the common law rule which precludes criminal prosecution of a pregnant woman for engaging in conduct that endangered the health of a fetus. South Carolina has rejected the common law rule with respect to illegal drug use during pregnancy. In *Whitner v. State*, 492 S.E.2d 777 (S.C. 1997) the South Carolina Supreme Court held that a viable fetus was a child within the meaning of the criminal child abuse laws of the state. Therefore, it was reasoned in *Whitner*, a pregnant woman could be criminally prosecuted for ingesting cocaine during her third trimester of pregnancy and causing the baby to be born with cocaine derivatives in its system.

Giving the police drug test results. The United States Supreme Court held in 2001, in the case of *Ferguson v. City of Charleston*, that federal constitutional restrictions applied to drug test results obtained from a pregnant woman by government hospitals that showed the woman used illegal drugs during pregnancy. *Ferguson* required such facilities obtain a search warrant to perform drug tests or the valid consent of the pregnant woman, before the results of the drug test could be disclosed to the police for criminal prosecution. *See also* **Birth Defects and Abortion; Epilepsy and Pregnancy; Ferguson v. City of Charleston; Fetal Alcohol Syndrome; Smoking and Pregnancy; Weinberger v. Hynson, Westcott & Dunning**

Duke Students for Life

Duke Students for Life (DSL) is a student-run pro-life organization that was created in late 1970s on the campus of Duke University. DSL is devoted to upholding the value of life through promoting awareness, education, support, and counseling. The organization takes the position that every human life is equally valuable from conception to natural death. DSL seeks to challenge the freedom of choice that it believes cripples women into thinking they cannot care for their children. *See also* **Pro-Life Organizations**

Dysmenorrhea

Dysmenorrhea (also called cramps) refers to painful menstruation caused by abnormal uterine contractions. Symptoms of the disorder include sharp cramps, headaches, nausea, vomiting, diarrhea and fatigue. Treatments for the disorder include analgesics, antiprostaglandins and hormones. *See also* **Menarche; Menopause; Menstrual Cycle; Premenstrual Syndrome**

Dystocia

Dystocia refers to a difficult and abnormally slow labor. There are generally four potential factors that may cause dystocia. First, uterine contractions may be either too weak or out of sync to open up the cervix. Second, the fetus may not be lined up correctly to easily pass through the birth canal. Third, the woman's pelvis may be too narrow to allow the fetus to pass through the birth canal. Fourth, there may be other abnormalities with the birth canal. Determination of the exact cause of dystocia dictates the treatment, e.g., surgical intervention or induced labor medications. *See also* **Caesarean Section; Induced Labor**

E

Eagle Forum

Eagle Forum is an Illinois based pro-life organization that was founded by its president Phyllis Schlafly, in 1972. The organization has an estimated membership of 80,000 people. The Eagle Forum engages in pro-life legislative lobbying and campus outreach work. It is also active in filing amicus curae briefs supporting pro-life issues through the Eagle Forum Education & Legal Defense Fund. The organization publishes a monthly newsletter called the *Phyllis Schlafly Report*. *See also* **Pro-Life Organizations**

Early Abortion and Late Abortion

A distinction is made between an early abortion (before 12th week of pregnancy) and a late abortion (between 12th and 20th week), because more difficulties are encountered in late abortions. After the 12th week of pregnancy, the placenta is more developed and has greater blood supply, which makes bleeding more likely during the abortion. Also, fetal bones will have begun to form and grow firmer, which makes for a greater possibility of perforating the uterus during evacuation. Additionally, dilating the cervix enough to pass the fetus is more difficult for a late abortion. *See also* **Abortion**

Early Feminist Opposition to Abortion

During the 19th century American feminist began a movement that demanded equality in all aspects of society, particularly the right to vote and hold political office. This movement was lead by such women as Elizabeth Cady Stanton, Susan B. Anthony, Elizabeth Blackwell, Alice Paul, Paulina Wright Davis, Eleanor Kirk and Matilda Joslyn Gage. Although feminist demanded the right to control their own destinies as full partners with men in the development of the nation, they did not view the right to decide whether or not to have an abortion as part of the freedom they fought to obtain. On the issue of abortion, early feminists were universal in condemning the practice. They viewed their position on abortion as being consistent with their struggle for equality. Early feminist denounced abortion on the grounds that it was a male tool for sexually exploiting women and avoiding the responsibility of supporting a family. *See also* **Blackwell, Elizabeth**

Eclampsia

Eclampsia is a condition affecting a pregnant woman that involves the occurrence of seizures usually during the third trimester. The reason for the condition is not known. The disorder occurs in about 1 out of 1,500 pregnancies. The condition may be treated with magnesium sulfate. Research has shown that prolonging pregnancies when eclampsia arises may result in complications for the mother, as well as infant death. If the pregnancy is over 28 weeks, delivery of the fetus is usually recommended. In severe situations where the pregnancy is less than 24 weeks, induction of labor is usually recommended, although the likelihood of the fetus surviving is minimal. The condition also increases the risk for placenta abruptio. *See also* **Placenta Abruptio; Preeclampsia**

Ectopic Pregnancy

Ectopic pregnancy is a potentially life-threatening pregnancy in which implantation of the fertilized egg occurs outside the uterus. This condition can cause a woman to have massive, rapid bleeding, and even die. Ectopic pregnancies are the second leading cause of pregnancy related deaths during the first trimester and represent 9 percent of all pregnancy related deaths in the nation. It is estimated that 100,000 ectopic pregnancies occur each year. The cause of ectopic pregnancies is not known, but there are some factors known to associate with the condition: sexually transmitted diseases, fertility drugs, prior operations on the fallopian tube, and cigarette smoking. Most ectopic pregnancies are diagnosed in the first eight weeks of pregnancy.

Although there have been a few reports of fetuses surviving up to full term, all ectopic pregnancies end in miscarriage, stillbirth or induced abortion. Roughly 25 percent of all ectopic pregnancies terminate before a pregnancy has been confirmed. When the diagnosis of an ectopic pregnancy is made, several treatment options are available. An early diagnosed pregnancy may be allowed to spontaneously absorb and discharge itself; or absorption can be done using a drug called methotrexate. In other instances surgery will be performed to abort the fetus.

There are several types of ectopic pregnancies. Most of which concern the location of the pregnancy:

Ruptured ectopic pregnancy. This is a pregnancy that has eroded or torn through the tissue in which it has implanted, causing bleeding in the woman from exposed vessels.

Persistent ectopic pregnancy. This is a condition involving continued growth of living tissue after conservative treatment of an ectopic pregnancy.

Heterotopic pregnancy. This is a multiple pregnancy in which one embryo implants normally in the uterine cavity and another embryo implants outside the uterus. This condition occurs in 1 out 30,000 pregnancies.

Cervical pregnancy. This is a pregnancy that is located in the wall of the cervix. A cervical pregnancy is considered an extremely dangerous condition because of the risk of uncontrollable bleeding. Less than 1 percent of all ectopic pregnancies occur in the cervix.

Tubal pregnancy. This pregnancy occurs in different locations of the fallopian tube. Roughly 95 percent of all ectopic pregnancies occur in the fallopian tube. When tubal pregnancy occurs on the interstitial part of the fallopian tube, the pregnancy is called interstitial pregnancy or cornual pregnancy. Termination of a tubal pregnancy is called tubal abortion.

Abdominal pregnancy. This is a pregnancy that originates in the fallopian tube, but is expelled and implants in the abdomen, where it continues to grow. Less than 2 percent of ectopic pregnancies occur in the abdomen.

Ovarian pregnancy. This is a pregnancy that is located in the ovary. There have been 5 reported cases of ovarian pregnancies coming to term. Less than 3 percent of ectopic pregnancies occur in the ovary. *See also* **Vaginal Douching and the Risk of Ectopic Pregnancy**

Edwards Syndrome *see* **Trisomy 18**

Effacement

Effacement is the process by which the cervix thins and merges with the uterine wall in preparation for expelling a fetus. *See also* **Contraction; Dilation**

Eisenstadt v. Baird

Forum: United States Supreme Court.

Case Citation: Eisenstadt v. Baird, 405 U.S. 438 (1972).

Date Argued: November 17–18, 1971.

Date of Decision: March 22, 1972.

Opinion of Court: Brennan, J., in which Douglas, Stewart, and Marshall, JJ., joined.

Concurring Opinion: Douglas, J.

Concurring Opinion: White, J., in which Blackmun, J., joined.

Dissenting Opinion: Burger, C. J.

Not Participating: Powell and Rehnquist, JJ.

Counsel for Appellant: Joseph R. Nolan, Special Assistant Attorney General of Massachusetts, argued; on the brief were Robert H. Quinn, Attorney General, John J. Irwin, Jr., and Ruth I. Abrams, Assistant Attorneys General, and Garrett H. Byrne.

Counsel for Appellee: Joseph D. Tydings argued; on the brief was Joseph J. Balliro.

Amicus Brief for Appellant: None.

Amicus Brief for Appellee: Harriet F. Pilpel and Nancy F. Wechsler for the Planned Parenthood Federation of America, Inc.; by Roger P. Stokey for the Planned Parenthood League of Massachusetts; by Melvin L. Wulf for the American Civil Liberties Union et al.; and by Sylvia S. Ellison for Human Rights for Women, Inc.

Issue Presented: Whether the constitution was violated by a Massachusetts statute that made it a crime to give away a drug, medicine, instrument, or article for the prevention of conception except in the case of (1) a physician prescribing it for a married person, or (2) a pharmacist furnishing it to a married person presenting a physician's prescription?

Case Holding: The Equal Protection Clause of the Fourteenth Amendment was violated by a Massachusetts statute that made it a crime to give away a drug, medicine, instrument, or article for the prevention of conception except in the case of (1) a physician prescribing it for a married person, or (2) a pharmacist furnishing it to a married person presenting a physician's prescription.

Background facts of case: The appellee, William Baird, was convicted by the state of Massachusetts for giving a young woman a package of Emko vaginal foam contraceptive at the close of a lecture he had given Under the state's laws it was a felony offense for anyone to give away a drug, medicine, instrument, or article for the prevention of conception except in the case of (1) a physician prescribing it for a married person, or (2) a pharmacist furnishing it to a married person presenting a physician's prescription. After the Massachusetts supreme judicial court affirmed the conviction, the appellee filed a writ of habeas corpus in a federal district court. The district court denied relief. However, the First Circuit court of appeals vacated the dismissal after finding the statute violated the Equal Protection Clause of the Fourteenth Amendment. The Supreme Court granted certiorari to consider the matter.

Majority opinion by Justice Brennan: Justice Brennan found that the statute under which the appellee was convicted violated the constitution. He wrote as follows:

> ... [T]he object of the legislation is to discourage premarital sexual intercourse. Conceding that the State could, consistently with the Equal Protection Clause, regard the problems of extramarital and premarital sexual relations as evils of different dimensions and proportions, requiring different remedies, we cannot agree that the deterrence of premarital sex may reasonably be regarded as the purpose of the Massachusetts law....
>
> ... The Supreme Judicial Court ... held that the purpose of the [statute] was to serve the health needs of the community by regulating the distribution of potentially harmful articles....
>
> ... If health were the rationale ..., the statute would be both discriminatory and overbroad.... If there is need to have a physician prescribe (and a pharmacist dispense) contraceptives, that need is as great for unmarried persons as for married persons.... Furthermore, we must join the Court of Appeals in noting that not all contraceptives are potentially dangerous. As a result, if the Massachusetts statute were a health measure, it would not only invidiously discriminate against the unmarried, but also be overbroad with respect to the married....
>
> ... We conclude, accordingly, that, despite the statute's superficial earmarks as a health measure, health, on the face of the statute, may no more reasonably be regarded as its purpose than the deterrence of premarital sexual relations.
>
> If the Massachusetts statute cannot be upheld as a deterrent to fornication or as a health measure, may it, nevertheless, be sustained simply as a prohibition on contraception? The Court of Appeals analysis led inevitably to the conclusion that, so far as morals are concerned, it is contraceptives per se that are considered immoral....
>
> If under *Griswold v. Connecticut* the distribution of contraceptives to married persons cannot be prohibited, a ban on distribution to unmarried persons would be equally impermissible.... If the right of privacy means anything, it is the right of the individual, married or single, to be free from unwarranted governmental intrusion into matters so fundamentally affecting a person as the decision whether to bear or beget a child.
>
> ... We hold that by providing dissimilar treatment for married and unmarried persons who are similarly situated, [the state's laws] violate the Equal Protection Clause.

Disposition of case: The judgment of the court of appeals was affirmed.

Concurring opinion by Justice Douglas: Justice Douglas agreed with the majority decision. However, he believed the case could have been disposed of on a different constitutional basis. He wrote as follows:

> While I join the opinion of the Court, there is for me a narrower ground for affirming the Court of Appeals. This to me is a simple First Amendment case, that amendment being applicable to the States by reason of the Fourteenth....
>
> Baird gave an hour's lecture on birth control and as an aid to understanding the ideas which he was propagating he handed out one sample of one of the devices whose use he was endorsing. A person giving a lecture on coyote-getters would certainly improve his teaching technique if he passed one out to the audience; and he would be protected in doing so unless of course the device was loaded and ready to explode, killing or injuring peo-

ple. The same holds true in my mind for mousetraps, spray guns, or any other article not dangerous per se on which speakers give educational lectures.

It is irrelevant to the application of these principles that Baird went beyond the giving of information about birth control and advocated the use of contraceptive articles. The First Amendment protects the opportunity to persuade to action whether that action be unwise or immoral, or whether the speech incites to action.

In this case there was not even incitement to action. There is no evidence or finding that Baird intended that the young lady take the foam home with her when he handed it to her or that she would not have examined the article and then returned it to Baird, had he not been placed under arrest immediately upon handing the article over.

First Amendment rights are not limited to verbal expression. The right to petition often involves the right to walk. The right of assembly may mean pushing or jostling. Picketing involves physical activity as well as a display of a sign. A sit-in can be a quiet, dignified protest that has First Amendment protection even though no speech is involved, as we held in Brown v. Louisiana. Putting contraceptives on display is certainly an aid to speech and discussion. Handing an article under discussion to a member of the audience is a technique known to all teachers and is commonly used. A handout may be on such a scale as to smack of a vendor's marketing scheme. But passing one article to an audience is merely a projection of the visual aid and should be a permissible adjunct of free speech. Baird was not making a prescription nor purporting to give medical advice. Handing out the article was not even a suggestion that the lady use it. At most it suggested that she become familiar with the product line.

Concurring opinion by Justice White: Justice White concurred in the Court's judgment. He wrote separately to make the following points:

> Baird ... was found guilty of giving away vaginal foam. Inquiry into the validity of this conviction does not come to an end merely because some contraceptives are harmful and their distribution may be restricted. Our general reluctance to question a State's judgment on matters of public health must give way where, as here, the restriction at issue burdens the constitutional rights of married persons to use contraceptives. In these circumstances we may not accept on faith the State's classification of a particular contraceptive as dangerous to health. Due regard for protecting constitutional rights requires that the record contain evidence that a restriction on distribution of vaginal foam is essential to achieve the statutory purpose, or the relevant facts concerning the product must be such as to fall within the range of judicial notice.
>
> Neither requirement is met here. Nothing in the record even suggests that the distribution of vaginal foam should be accompanied by medical advice in order to protect the user's health. Nor does the opinion of the Massachusetts court or the State's brief filed here marshal facts demonstrating that the hazards of using vaginal foam are common knowledge or so incontrovertible that they may be noticed judicially. On the contrary, the State acknowledges that Emko is a product widely available without prescription. Given Griswold v. Connecticut and absent proof of the probable hazards of using vaginal foam, we could not sustain appellee's conviction had it been for selling or giving away foam to a married person. Just as in Griswold, where the right of married persons to use contraceptives was diluted or adversely affected by permitting a conviction for giving advice as to its exercise, so here, to sanction a medical restriction upon distribution of a contraceptive not proved hazardous to health would impair the exercise of the constitutional right.
>
> That Baird could not be convicted for distributing Emko to a married person disposes of this case. Assuming, arguendo, that the result would be otherwise had the recipient been unmarried, nothing has been placed in the record to indicate her marital status. The State has maintained that marital status is irrelevant because an unlicensed person cannot legally dispense vaginal foam either to married or unmarried persons. This approach is plainly erroneous and requires the reversal of Baird's conviction; for on the facts of this case, it deprives us of knowing whether Baird was in fact convicted for making a constitutionally protected distribution of Emko to a married person.

Dissenting opinion by Chief Justice Burger: The Chief Justice dissented from the majority opinion. He believed the conviction was constitutionally valid. The Chief Justice wrote the following:

> The judgment of the Supreme Judicial Court of Massachusetts in sustaining appellee's conviction for dispensing medicinal material without a license seems eminently correct to me and I would not disturb it. It is undisputed that appellee is not a physician or pharmacist and was prohibited under Massachusetts law from dispensing contraceptives to anyone, regardless of marital status. To my mind the validity of this restriction on dispensing medicinal substances is the only issue before the Court, and appellee has no standing to challenge that part of the statute restricting the persons to whom contraceptives are available. There is no need to labor this point, however, for everyone seems to agree that if Massachusetts has validly required, as a health measure, that all contraceptives be dispensed by a physician or pursuant to a physician's prescription, then the statutory distinction based on marital status has no bearing on this case....
>
> The need for dissemination of information on birth control is not impinged in the slightest by limiting the distribution of medicinal substances to medical and pharmaceutical channels as Massachusetts has done by statute. The appellee has succeeded, it seems, in cloaking his activities in some new permutation of the First Amendment although his conviction rests in fact and law on dispensing a medicinal substance without a license. I am constrained to suggest that if the Constitution can be strained to invalidate the Massachusetts statute underlying appellee's conviction, we could quite as well employ it for the protection of a curbstone quack, reminiscent of the medicine man of times past, who attracted a crowd of the curious with a soapbox lecture and then plied them with free samples of some unproved remedy. Massachusetts presumably outlawed such activities long ago, but today's holding seems to invite their return.

Elective Abortion *see* **Abortion**

Elliot Institute

The Elliot Institute is an Illinois based organization that was founded in 1988 by David C. Reardon, its director. The Institute is primarily concerned with performing original research and education on the impact of abortion on women, men, siblings, and society. One of the key research findings by the Institute is that women who aborted their first pregnancies are five times more likely to engage in subsequent abuse of drugs or alcohol compared to women who carried to term. *See also* **Pro-Life Organizations**

Embryo *see* **Fetal Development**

Embryo Cloning

The term "clone" refers to an organism genetically identical to another organism. A British biologist, J.B.S. Haldane, is credited with coining the term in a speech he gave in 1963. Embryo cloning involves removing one or more cells from an embryo and cultivating the cell so that it develops into a separate embryo with the same DNA as the original. Clones must have DNA from only one source. Sexually reproduced offspring must have DNA from two sources. Two types of embryo cloning experiments have taken place: animal and human.

The 20th century ended with the development of a mature science for cloning animals. The 21st century holds out the promise of developing an exact science of human embryo cloning from the successes of animal embryo cloning.

Development of embryo cloning using non-human organisms. It was in 1902 that Hans Spemann, a German embryologist, performed the first successful crude embryo clone. Spemann split a two celled salamander embryo in two parts. After the division, each cell grew to be an adult salamander. In 1928 Spemann performed the first experiment that transferred the nucleus of a salamander embryo cell to a cell without a nucleus. A normal salamander embryo grew from this single cell. Spemann published the results of his nuclear transfer experiment in a book, "Embryonic Development and Induction." In that book, Spemann proposed the idea of cloning from adult cell nuclei. He was never able to achieve this feat.

It was not until 1952 that Spemann's vision of adult cell cloning was first realized. In that year two American scientists, Robert Briggs and Thomas J. King, cloned tadpoles. Briggs and King transplanted a nucleus from a frog embryo somatic cell into unfertilized eggs. The eggs developed into tadpoles and many metamorphosed into juvenile frogs. The technique used by Briggs and King, nuclear transfer, became the prototype experiment for cloning multicellular organisms.

Cloning went into hibernation after the breakthrough by Briggs and King. Activity picked up in the 1980s, however. In 1980 Louise Clarke and John Carbon cloned a gene involved in cell division in yeast cells. In 1981 a team of Chinese scientists successfully cloned a fish — a golden carp. In 1984 a Danish scientist, Steen Willadsen, successfully cloned a sheep from embryo cells. Willadsen's work was credited as the first cloning of a mammal using nuclear transfer method (the technique of transferring the nucleus of one cell to another). In 1985 Willadsen cloned cattle from differentiated one week old embryo cells. In 1986 a team of scientist from the University of Wisconsin, Neal First, Randal Prather, and Willard Eyestone, cloned a cow from early embryo cells.

In 1995 Scottish embryologist Ian Wilmut and English biologist Keith Campbell cloned two sheep, named Megan and Morag, from differentiated embryo cells. In 1996 Wilmut and Campbell cloned a sheep, named Dolly, from adult differentiated cells. In 1997 scientists at the Oregon Regional Primate Research Center reported that they had produced sibling rhesus monkeys from cloned embryos. 1998 a team of scientists at the University of Hawaii, Teruhiko Wakayama, Ryuzo Yanagimachi, Tony Perry, Maurizio Zuccotti and K.R. Johnson, reported the production of a large number of live mice from injecting nuclei taken from adult ovarian cells enucleated eggs. The scientists also reported that they successfully recloned the first clones. A Japanese team of researchers, led by Yoko Kato, announced in 1998 that they had produced eight calves from cells derived from one adult cow. It was reported in 2000 that pigs were cloned for the first time by Alan Coleman and his research team in Scotland.

As a result of research in animal cloning, three techniques for cloning have developed:

(1) Twinning technique. The twinning technique involves splitting off a cell from an embryo. When an egg is fertilized by sperm it begins dividing. If the division results in multiple embryo cells, the cells can be separated and implanted into the uteri of different separate mothers. This process will result in clones from the initial fertilized egg.

(2) Nuclear transfer technique. The nuclear transfer technique (also called the Roslin technique) requires the use of two cells (a donor cell and an egg cell). The nucleus of the unfertilized egg cell must be removed (enucleated). The donor cell is then forced into a dormant phase (called Gap Zero or G0 cell stage). This dormant phase causes the donor cell to shut down but not die. The donor cell's nucleus is then placed inside the egg cell, either through cell fusion or transplantation. The egg cell then begins forming an embryo. Once this happens, the embryo is then inserted into a surrogate mother. If the process is done correctly, a clone of donor animal will be born.

(3) Honolulu technique. The Honolulu technique uses a donor cell and egg cell. However, unlike the nuclear transfer technique, the Honolulu technique utilizes a donor cell that is in a natural state of dormancy (not forced). Once the nucleus of the unfertilized egg cell is removed, the donor nucleus is inserted. After several hours, the egg cell is then placed in a chemical culture to jumpstart the cell's growth (fertilization). After being jumpstarted, the egg cell develops into an embryo. The embryo can then be transplanted into the surrogate mother and carried to term. The Honolulu technique is the superior technique for cloning embryo.

Emergence of human embryo cloning. The protocol used in cloning human embryos is similar to the cloning of animal embryos. A major difference in the procedure is that unlike animal embryo cloning, the human embryo process requires removal of a protective membrane (zona pellucida) that covers the internal contents of the embryo. This membrane provides the necessary nutrients for the first several cell divisions that occur within the embryo.

For human embryo cloning, sperm cells and egg cells are gathered from donors at fertility clinics, and are joined using in vitro fertilization procedures to form an embryo. As an alternate method, researchers gather already produced embryos from fertility clinics. Once an embryo is produced, it is allowed to develop several cells. A chemical solution is then introduced to dissolve the membrane that covers the embryo. When the membrane is dissolved the cells within the embryo are freed. The cells are then coated with an artificially produced membrane. The resulting individual cells are then considered new embryos, all of which have the same exact genetic information. If allowed, these cells would divide and eventually form a human being.

In 1994 a research team from George Washington Medical Center,

STATES WITH STATUTES THAT BAN HUMAN CLONING

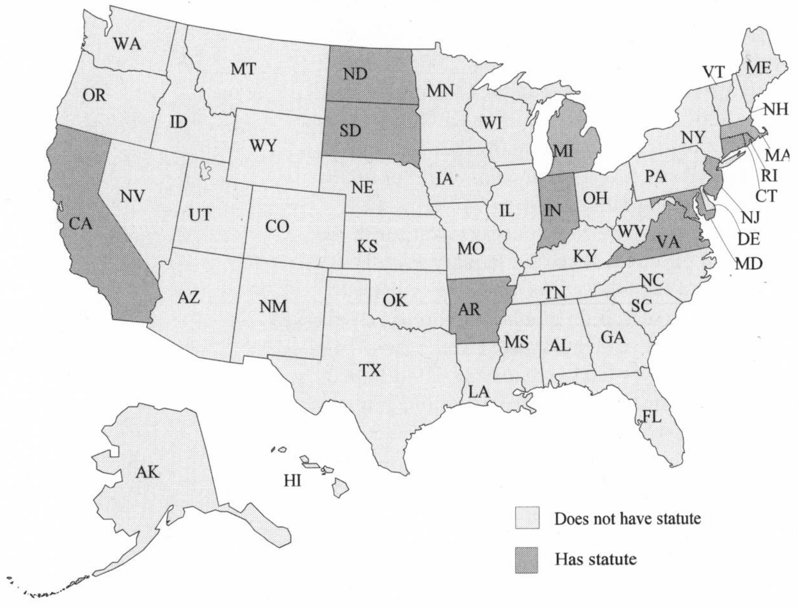

District of Columbia does not have statute.

led by Robert Stillman and Jerry Hall, made the first public announcement of an attempt to clone using human embryo. Stillman and Hall cloned 17 flawed human embryos. The embryos used by them were not able to produce human beings, because they were fertilized by more than one sperm cell. The embryos were destined to die during their development because of the extra set of chromosomes donated by the second sperm cell. The new embryos grew and divided as expected, but eventually died before reaching the 64-cell stage of development.

In 1998 an American biotechnology company in Worcester, Massachusetts, Advanced Cell Technology, announced that it took the nucleus from a human cell of Dr. Jose Cibelli and inserted it into a cow's egg. The human genes activated and the egg began to divide. It was destroyed at the 32-cell stage; long before it would have become Dr. Cibelli's clone. On November 25, 2001 Advanced Cell Technology announced that it had cloned a human embryo, in a groundbreaking experiment aimed not at creating a human being, but at using the embryo for stem cells used to treat diseases.

In a hotly disputed report, a South Korean medical research team headed by Dr. Kim Seung-bo of Kyunghee University Hospital, announced on December 16, 1998 that they successfully cultivated a human embryo using human cells. The report indicated that the research team took an adult cell from a woman in her 30s, fused the nucleus into another egg cell, and started the egg growing as if it had been fertilized. They stopped the process once the egg had divided into four cells.

Dr. Richard Seed, a physicist, announced in 1998 that he would head a project to clone human beings. Dr. Seed's announcement drew heated criticism from law makers around the country who oppose cloning human beings. A similar announcement was made in 2000 by an American fertility specialist, Panayiotis Zavos. Dr. Zavos reported that he would lead a team of international scientists in helping infertile couples bear clones as early as 2003.

Legal status of human embryo cloning. In 1997 President Bill Clinton announced a proposed 5 year ban on human embryo cloning. In 2001 President George Bush indicated he supported Congressional legislation that would criminalize all human cloning. Congress, as well as many state legislatures, has debated several bills that would limit or totally prevent human embryo cloning.

Britain became the first country to authorize the cloning of human embryos in January 2001. However, Britain has allowed such cloning only for the purpose of research on stem-cells found in embryos. The embryo clones created would have to be destroyed after 14 days. *See also* **Assisted Reproductive Technology; Cryopreservation; Embryonic and Fetal Stem-Cell Research**

Embryo Cryopreservation *see* **Cryopreservation**

Embryo Reabsorption *see* **Vanishing Twin Syndrome**

Embryonic and Fetal Stem-Cell Research

Embryonic and fetal stem-cell research involves biomedical research using cells from human embryos and fetuses. Stem-cells are pluripotent, which means that unlike more mature cells, they have the capacity to develop into any organ of the body. They can morph into any given type of body cell, including muscle cells, nerve cells and blood cells. Researchers believe that stem-cells provide an all-

States with Statutes That Ban Embryo or Fetal Experiments

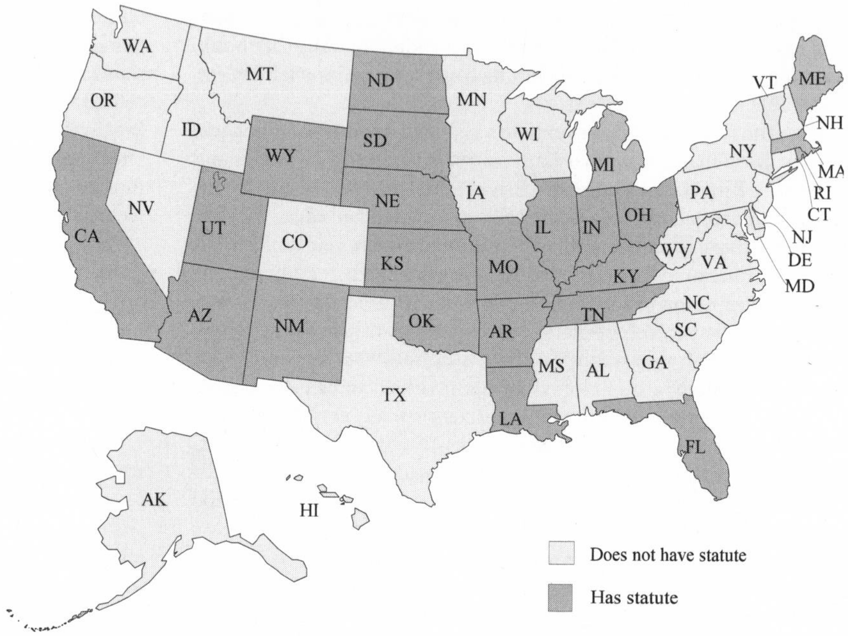

**District of Columbia does not have statute.*

States with Statutes That Ban the Sale of an Embryo or Fetus

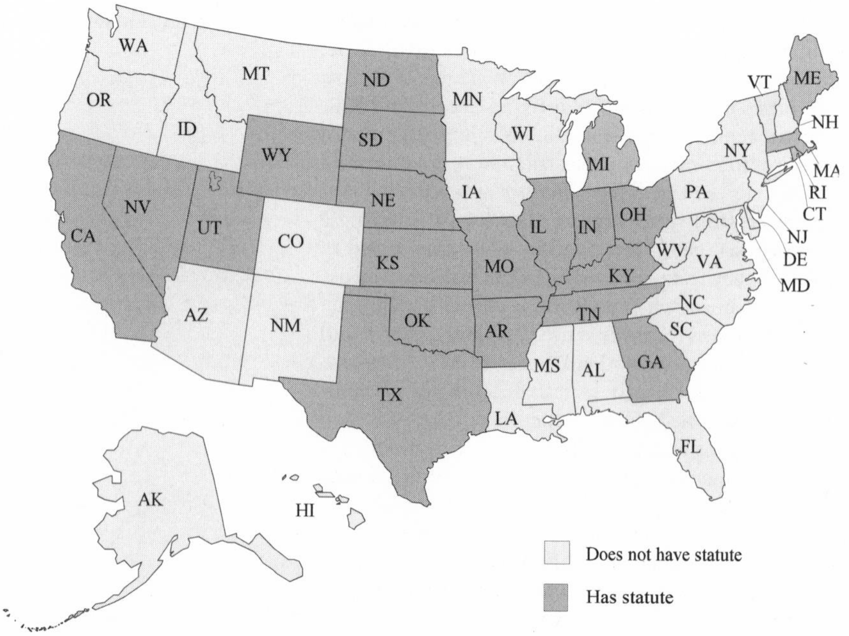

**District of Columbia does not have statute.*

purpose material for patching up the human body and replacing failing tissues and organs. It is believed that stem-cells may provide cures for a range of debilitating diseases and conditions, including spinal injuries, diabetes and Alzheimer's disease.

The first publicly known attempt to isolate and culture stem-cells from human embryos in vitro was published in 1994. That attempt failed. However, in November of 1998 James Thompson of the University of Wisconsin and John Gearheart of Johns Hopkins University School of Medicine, announced that they had succeeded in growing human embryonic stem-cells. Carrying out separate experiments, Thompson derived his stem-cells from early-stage embryos and Gearheart isolated stem-cells from non-living fetuses. Gearheart was able to grow one cell line. Thompson established five independent cell lines which generated tissue cells such as cartilage, bone, muscle, neural and gut cells.

Embryonic and fetal stem-cell research has brought about controversy in the abortion arena. The debate between those who oppose and those who support stem-cell research generated a compromise in federal funding for such research. On August 25, 2000 the National Institutes of Health (NIH) (a division of the Department of Health and Human Services) issued guidelines for funding stem-cell research. Under the guidelines studies utilizing stem-cells derived from human embryos may be conducted using NIH funds only if the cells were derived from human embryos that were created for the purposes of fertility treatment and were in excess of the clinical need of the individuals seeking such treatment. The guidelines provide that funds may be used to support research to derive stem-cells from fetal tissue. Areas of research that are ineligible for NIH funding include: (1) the derivation of stem-cells from human embryos; (2) research in which human stem-cells are utilized to create or contribute to a human embryo; (3) research utilizing stem-cells that were derived from human embryos created for research purposes, rather than for fertility treatment; (4) research in which human stem-cells are derived using somatic cell nuclear transfer, i.e., the transfer of a human somatic cell nucleus into a human or animal egg; (5) research in which human stem-cells are combined with an animal embryo; and (6) research in which human stem-cells are used in combination with somatic cell nuclear transfer for the purposes of reproductive cloning of a human. *See also* **Cryopreservation; Embryo Cloning; Fetal Research Act; Umbilical Cord Blood Transplantation**

Embryonic Period

The embryonic period is considered the first 10 weeks of gestation. *See also* **Fetal Development; Fetal Period**

Emergency Contraceptive

Emergency contraceptives are devises that may be used to prevent pregnancy after unprotected sexual intercourse has occurred. *See also* **Contraception; Intrauterine Contraceptive Devices; Morning After Pill**

EMILY's List

EMILY's (Early Money Is Like Yeast) List is a Washington, D.C., based pro-choice political organization that was founded in 1985. The president of the organization is Ellen R. Malcolm. The organization was created to promote and support pro-choice female Democratic candidates for public office. It has more than 68,000 members and has raised millions of dollars to help elect 69 pro-choice Democratic women members of Congress, 13 senators, 8 governors, and 364 women to state and local office. *See also* **Pro-Choice Organizations**

Employer Fetal-Protection Policies

There are many employment-settings where substances are produced that could be harmful to the fetus of pregnant female workers. Some employers have responded to this situation by issuing policies that prohibit pregnant, or childbearing capacity, female workers from taking on jobs that would expose them to substances that may be harmful to fetuses. However, in *Automobile Workers v. Johnson Controls, Inc.* the United States Supreme Court held that Title VII forbids sex-specific fetal-protection policies by an employer, that exclude a fertile female employee from certain jobs because of the employer's concern for the health of the fetus the woman might conceive. *See also* **Automobile Workers v. Johnson Controls, Inc.**

Empty Sella Syndrome

Empty sella syndrome is a congenital disorder involving fluid filling an empty space in the brain, as a result of a deformity in the brain. Symptoms of the disorder include abnormal facial features, short stature, headaches, and vision problems. The condition is not life-threatening and treatment is aimed at remedying specific problems that arise. *See also* **Birth Defects and Abortion**

Encephaloceles

Encephaloceles are congenital neural tube defects that are characterized by a sac-like protrusion of brain tissue and membranes through an abnormal opening in the skull. This condition is the result of the failure of the neural tube to close during the development of the fetus. Symptoms of this defect include paralysis of all 4 limbs, developmental delay, vision problems, mental and growth retardation, and seizures. Surgery may be performed to place the tissues back into the skull and remove the sac. The prognosis for infants with the disorder depends upon what brain tissue is involved, the location of the sac, and the accompanying brain malformations. *See also* **Anencephaly; Birth Defects and Abortion; Folic Acid and Pregnancy; Spina Bifida**

Encyclical Evangelium Vitae

The encyclical *Evangelium Vitae* (Gospel of Life) was a document published by Pope John Paul II (1920–2005) on March 30, 1995. The encyclical addressed a number of issues including abortion, euthanasia, the family, feminism, self-defense, population growth, birth control, and the death penalty. One of the most prominent and controversial issues addressed in the encyclical concerned the Pope's denunciation of all forms of abortion. The encyclical characterized abortion as government sanctioned murder. It was stated by the Pope that there was a fundamental right to life for all preborn human beings. The encyclical argued that abortion and contraception were tools of the wealthy designed to control the poor and weak. Ultimately the encyclical saw abortion as a symbol of humankind's divorce from God.

Although the encyclical has been used by pro-life advocates to bolster their position against abortion, the encyclical did not have a major impact in the United States on the issue of abortion. It did, however, contribute to some controversy as it related to capital punishment in the United States. *See also* **Religion and Abortion**

Encyclical Humanae Vitae

The encyclical *Humanae Vitae* (Human Life) was a document published by Pope Paul VI (1897–1978) on July 29, 1968. The encyclical presented a statement on the Catholic Church's opposition to artificial birth control. This statement came three years after the 1965 landmark decision by the United States Supreme Court in *Griswold v. Connecticut*, which had the effect of making possession and use of contraception devices legal throughout the nation. The encyclical became controversial for Catholics in the United States primarily because *Griswold* made it legal to use contraceptives. For Catholics in the nation the encyclical posed the dilemma of using that which the law permitted or abstaining from such use because it was considered a sin by their faith. Most Catholics did what the law permitted. While the vast majority of the Catholic leadership in the nation accepted the encyclical, some, like Father Charles Curran of the Catholic University of America, did not. Father Curran's opposition to the encyclical cost him his position as a university professor. *See also* **Religion and Abortion**

Endometrial Ablation

Endometrial ablation is a medical procedure that involves the removal or destruction of the endometrium (lining of the uterus). This procedure is an alternative to hysterectomy for women with heavy uterine bleeding who are wish to avoid hysterectomy. *See also* **Hysterectomy**

Endometrial Cancer

The endometrium is a layer of tissue that lines the walls of the uterus. Endometrial cancer is a disease in which malignant cancer cells are found on the endometrium. It is the most common gynecologic cancer in the United States. Deaths from endometrial cancer are relatively few, however, because the disease is usually found at its earliest stages. The disease occurs most often in women aged 55 to 69, and rarely occurs before a woman reaches menopause. Increased risk factors for the disease include: obesity, increased levels of natural oestrogen, and late menopause. Symptoms of endometrial cancer include: chronic pelvic pain, low resistance to infections, post-menopausal bleeding, in pre-menopausal women erratic periods or bleeding, and pain during sex.

In the rare instance that a woman with endometrial cancer is pregnant, problems could rise for the fetus. The fact of pregnancy generally has no adverse effect on endometrial cancer, and endometrial cancer has no effect on the pregnancy. However, if certain cancer treatment methods are used during pregnancy, it may become necessary to have a therapeutic abortion, or the fetus could be exposed to birth defects.

There are four basic types of treatments for endometrial cancer: surgery, radiation therapy, chemotherapy and hormone therapy. The five-year survival rate for women who receive appropriate treatment ranges from 95 percent to less than 5 percent. *See also* **Breast Cancer and Pregnancy; Cervical Cancer; Fallopian Tube Cancer; Gestational Trophoblastic Tumors; Ovarian Cancer; Sarcoma of the Uterus; Vaginal Cancer; Vulva Cancer**

Endometriosis

Endometriosis is a condition in which tissue that normally lines a woman's uterus grows in other areas of her body. The abnormal tissue growth can occur in the pelvic area, ovaries, bowel, rectum or bladder. About 10 to 15 percent of American women of childbearing age have the disorder.

Once the abnormal tissues implant outside of the uterus they become a problem. Each month the ovaries of a woman of childbearing age produces hormones that stimulate the uterus to prepare for a fertilized egg. The abnormal tissues that are outside of the uterus regularly attempt to respond to this signal. As a consequence, the responses of the abnormal tissue cause scarring and adhesions in the reproductive area. These adhesions can eventually make transfer of an egg to the fallopian tube difficult or impossible. The adhesions may also prevent passage of a fertilized egg down the fallopian tube to the uterus. It is estimated that about 40 percent of infertile women have the disorder. Additionally, pregnant women with the disorder have a higher risk of having an ectopic pregnancy, which will end in a spontaneous abortion. *See also* **Ectopic Pregnancy**

Endometrium *see* **Female Reproductive System**

Epilepsy and Pregnancy

Epilepsy is considered the most commonly encountered major neurologic complication of pregnancy. An epileptic woman who becomes pregnant is at an increased risk of having adverse pregnancy outcomes that include fetal death, severe birth defects and developmental delay. In addition, a pregnant epileptic women is likely to have seizures more frequently.

A central concern with a pregnant woman who is epileptic is the potential consequences of a seizure on the fetus. Falls from epileptic seizures could inflict abdominal trauma that cause preterm labor, fetal death or malformations.

Research has shown that pregnant women who take anti-epileptic medications have about an 8 percent chance of having a child with a birth defect, compared to about 3 percent for nonepileptic pregnant women. It has also been shown that the rate of fetal death is three times greater for women with epilepsy. Heath care professionals attempt to lessen the negative impact of such drugs on a fetus, by providing prenatal care that includes the use of folic acid, vitamin K and monotherapy with a single anti-epileptic drug. With proper care and monitoring more than 90 percent of pregnancies in women with epilepsy are uncomplicated.

The five most common anti-epileptic medications used by women with epilepsy are phenytoin, valproic acid (Depakene), carbamazepine (Tegretol), phenobarbital and primidone. It has been shown that all of these drugs are associated with fetal head and facial abnormalities, cardiac defects and neural tube defects. *See also* **Drug Use and Pregnancy**

Episiotomy

Episiotomy refers to an incision in the area of skin between the vagina and the anus. This procedure is done to facilitate delivery of a fetus and to prevent lacerations to the womb. It is used when a fetus is in distress during the delivery process. The medical community is at odds with the procedure because of a tendency to rely on it when it is not necessary. *See also* **Caesarean Section**

Epispadias *see* **Genital and Urinary Tract Birth Defects**

Estrogens

Estrogens are a group of female hormones (estradiol, estrone and estriol) that are essential for the reproductive process. They also have an effect on about 300 different tissues throughout a female's body. The high estrogen levels that are present during the reproductive years derive from the ovaries, which also produce progesterone. Estrogens can also be formed by other tissues, such as body fat, skin, and muscle. The total estrogen produced after menopause is far less than that produced during the reproductive years. *See also* **Progesterone**

Eugenic Abortion

Eugenic abortion is an elective abortion that is performed when it has been medically determined that a fetus, if born alive, would suffer from a severe debilitating physical or mental birth defect. Prior to the 1973 decision by United States Supreme Court in *Roe v. Wade*, which permitted first trimester abortions, eugenic abortions were illegal in the nation. Eugenic abortions are not legally permitted when a fetus is viable, i.e., capable of living outside the womb with or without artificial aid. *See also* **Abortion; Birth Defects and Abortion; Eugenics; Therapeutic Abortion**

Eugenics

The term eugenics is said to refer to the study of ways to improve the human condition through population control. The word is derived from the Greek and means "good birth." In 1883, an Englishman named Francis Galton is said to have coined the term eugenics.

Galton used the word for conceptualizing his belief that society would be better served by controlling human reproduction so that "unfit" people were not born.

Galton's notion of controlling human reproduction so that only "fit" people were born, is traced to the writings and ideas of Thomas Robert Malthus, an Englishman who published a book in 1789 entitled *Essay on the Principle of Population*. Malthus believed that the human population should be controlled because of the inability to feed everyone. Galton was also influenced in his eugenic thinking by the work of his cousin, Charles Darwin. In Darwin's publication of *The Origin of Species* in 1859 and *The Descent of Man* in 1871, he espoused the idea that only the "fittest" survived in nature and the weak fell by the wayside.

The seeds of Galton's eugenicist thinking took root in 1907 with the founding of the Eugenic Education Society of England. In 1910 eugenics crossed the Atlantic with the founding of the Eugenics Record Office (ERO) in the United States. The ERO promoted eugenics in the United States as a way of controlling the reproduction of poor people who would inevitably exact greater taxes from the wealthy in order to survive. The ideas of ERO were eventually taken over in 1922 with the founding of the American Eugenics Society (AEO).

It was through the AEO that eugenics was firmly placed into operation in the United States. AEO funded numerous birth control organizations whose mission was to promote birth control among the poor in the United States. The high point of AEO's work culminated with the United States Supreme Court decision in 1973, *Roe v. Wade*, legalizing limited abortion in the nation. Much of the opinion written by Justice Blackman in *Roe* is said to be attributed to the writings of a eugenicist, Professor Glanville Williams. *See also* **Birth Defects and Abortion; Eugenic Abortion; Roe v. Wade**

Evans, Paul Ross

In May of 2007, twenty-seven-year-old Paul Ross Evans was indicted by a federal grand jury in Austin, Texas on charges of attempting to use a weapon of mass destruction; malicious attempt to damage a building and property by means of explosive and fire; possession of a destructive device by a convicted felon; and use and carrying of a destructive device in relation to a crime of violence. The prosecution of Evans began on April 25, 2007, when federal and local law enforcement officials responded to a call by the manager of Austin Women's Health Center, a clinic where abortions are perform. The manager informed the officials that a suspicious looking package was outside of the clinic. Once the police arrived it was determined that the suspicious package was a cooler that contained a homemade bomb. Law enforcement officials ordered the clinic evacuated, and used a robot to detonate the bomb. The police were able to quickly trace the bomb to Evans, after learning that some of the materials used in the bomb were purchased from two nearby stores. Evans made the purchases with a credit card. After his arrest and indictment, Evans pled guilty in July of 2007 to attempting to use a weapon of mass destruction. In October of 2007, Evans was sentenced to 40 years in prison. *See also* **Abortion Violence, Property Destruction and Demonstrations**

F

Failed Abortion

A failed abortion refers to a continued intrauterine pregnancy after an attempt to abort the pregnancy. Failure to terminate pregnancy is relatively common with very early abortions. When this occurs the fetus may be allowed to go to full term or a subsequent attempt at an abortion may occur. *See also* **Abortion**

Fallopian Tube Cancer

Fallopian tube cancer is an extremely rare disease in which malignant cancer cells are found in the tissues of the fallopian tube. The disease primarily afflicts women over 50, but may occur in younger women.

In the rare instance that a woman with fallopian tube cancer is pregnant, problems could rise for the fetus. The fact of pregnancy generally has no adverse effect on fallopian tube cancer, and fallopian tube cancer has no effect on the pregnancy. However, if certain cancer treatment methods are used during pregnancy, it may become necessary to have a therapeutic abortion, or the fetus could be exposed to birth defects. Treatment for the disease includes surgery, chemotherapy and radiation therapy. *See also* **Cancer and Pregnancy; Therapeutic Abortion**

Fallopian Tubes *see* **Female Reproductive System**

False Labor *see* **Premature Labor**

Family Planning Advocates of New York State

Family Planning Advocates of New York State (FPA) was founded in 1977 and is headquartered in Albany, New York. FPA is dedicated to protecting and expanding access to a full range of reproductive health services. The organization actively engages in policy analysis, legislative work, coalition building and educational efforts. FPA conducts field activities throughout New York in an effort to build coalitions and stimulate pro-choice grassroots organizing. FPA communicates with the state governor's office and state agencies to promote reproductive health services. In 1987, FPA established the Education Fund of FPA. The Education Fund's activities are dedicated to informing individuals, organizations, communities and policymakers about the importance of ensuring universal access to a full range of reproductive health care services. Some of the work being carried on by the Education Fund include publishing fact sheets, newsletters, articles and guides; producing educational videos; conducting informational workshops and training sessions; providing speakers and panelists for regional, state and national conferences; and responding to requests for information from throughout the state and nation. *See also* **Pro-Choice Organizations**

Family Research Council

Family Research Council (FRC) is a Washington, D.C., based pro-life organization. FRC was founded in 1983 by Gary L. Bauer. The president of FRC is Tony Perkins. The organization has a membership that is estimated at more than 400,000 people. As part of its anti-abortion work, FRC engages in legislative lobbying and outreach programs for youth. The organization publishes a pamphlet called *Washington Watch*. *See also* **Pro-Life Organizations**

Tony Perkins is the president of Family Research Council (Tony Perkins).

Fanconi's Anemia

Fanconi's anemia is an inherited blood disorder involving failure of bone marrow to produce all types of blood cells. The disease can cause skin pigment changes, kidney malformations, deafness, male infertility, hip, leg, and toe abnormalities and mental retardation. Treatment for the disorder includes bone marrow transplant (when a suitable donor is found), blood transfusions and antibiotics. In spite of available treatments, the condition leaves its victims predisposed to leukemia, liver cancer and other cancers. *See also* **Birth Defects and Abortion**

Father's Rights

The United States Supreme Court has made clear that the decision to have an abortion belongs to the woman. The father of a fetus, regardless of whether he is the spouse of the woman, cannot interfere with a woman's decision to have an abortion. In *Planned Parenthood of Southeastern Pennsylvania v. Casey* the Supreme Court invalidated a provision in Pennsylvania's abortion statute that required a married woman inform her spouse of her decision to have an abortion, before she would be allowed to have one. The Supreme Court invalidated a provision in Missouri's statute, in *Planned Parenthood of Missouri v. Danforth*, that required a woman seek the consent of a spouse before having an abortion.

PERCENTAGE DISTRIBUTION OF ABORTIONS BY MARITAL STATUS
U.S. 1994-2004

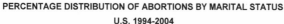

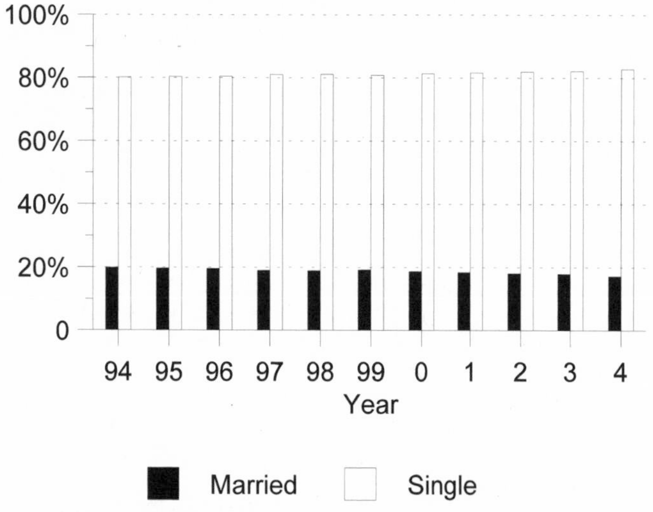

Source: **National Center for Health Statistics.**

Notwithstanding the decisions in *Casey* and *Danforth*, several states continue to provide by statute that a married woman must give her spouse pre-abortion notice — Kentucky, Louisiana (married minor must give notice), Pennsylvania, and Rhode Island. Three states, Illinois, North Dakota and South Carolina, require that a married woman obtain pre-abortion consent from her spouse. *See also* **Planned Parenthood of Missouri v. Danforth; Planned Parenthood of Southeastern Pennsylvania v. Casey**

Federal Abortion Statutes *see* **Born Alive Infants Protection Act; Coerce Abortion; Commission on Civil Rights; Comstock Act; Federal Employees and Abortion; Federal Female Prisoners and Abortion; Fetal Research Act; Foreign Abortionist Entering the United States; Freedom of Access to Clinic Entrances Act; Helms Amendment; Mexico City Policy; Hyde Amendment; Military and Abortion; Native American Women and Abortion Funding; Partial-Birth Abortion Ban Act; Pregnancy Discrimination Act; Refusal to Perform Abortion; Tariff Act; Title X of the Public Health Service Act; Unborn Victims of Violence Act**

Federal Election Commission v. Beaumont

Forum: United States Supreme Court.

Case Citation: Federal Election Commission v. Beaumont, 539 U.S. 146 (2003).

Date Argued: March 25, 2003.

Date of Decision: June 16, 2003.

Opinion of Court: Souter, J., in which Rehnquist, C.J., Stevens, O'-Connor, Ginsburg, and Breyer, JJ., joined.

Concurring Opinion: Kennedy, J.

Dissenting Opinion: Thomas, J., in which Scalia, J., joined.

Counsel for Appellant: Paul D. Clement argued; on the brief were Theodore B. Olson, Robert D. McCallum, Jr., Gregory G. Garre, Douglas N. Letter, Edward Himmelfarb, and Jonathan H. Levy.

Counsel for Appellees: James Bopp, Jr., argued; on the brief were Richard E. Coleson, Thomas J. Marzen, and James Madison.

Amicus Brief for Appellant: Association of Trial Lawyers of America; Brennan Center for Justice at New York University School of Law; Public Citizen, Inc., Common Cause, Democracy 21, Campaign and Media Legal Center, and Center For Responsive Politics.

Amicus Brief for Appellees: Pacific Legal Foundation; Realcampaignreform.Org, Inc., Conservative Legal Defense and Education Fund, Gun Owners of America, Inc., English First, and U.S. Justice Foundation.

Issue Presented: Whether the Federal Election Campaign Act's prohibition on corporate expenditures and contributions directly to candidates in federal elections applies to a nonprofit pro-life organization?

Case Holding: The Federal Election Campaign Act's prohibition on corporate expenditures and contributions directly to candidates in federal elections applies to a nonprofit pro-life organization.

Background facts of case: A pro-life organization, North Carolina Right to Life, Inc. (NCRL) and others, sued the Federal Election Commission, in order to stop enforcement of a provision in the Federal Election Campaign Act, which prohibited corporations from making expenditures and contributions directly to candidates in federal elections. A federal district found that the Act was unconstitutional as it applied to NCRL. A court of appeals affirmed. The United States Supreme Court granted certiorari to consider the issue.

Majority opinion by Justice Souter: Justice Souter held that the Act was not unconstitutional and could be applied to NCRL. The opinion addressed the issue as follows:

> Any attack on the federal prohibition of direct corporate political contributions goes against the current of a century of congressional efforts to curb corporations' potentially deleterious influences on federal elections....
>
> Since 1907, there has been continual congressional attention to corporate political activity, sometimes resulting in refinement of the law, sometimes in overhaul. One feature, however, has stayed intact throughout this careful legislative adjustment of the federal electoral laws, and much of the periodic amendment was meant to strengthen the original, core prohibition on direct corporate contributions. The Foreign Corrupt Practices Act of 1925, for example, broadened the ban on contributions to include "anything of value," and criminalized the act of receiving a contribution to match the criminality of making one. So, in another instance, the 1947 Labor Management Relations Act drew labor unions permanently within the law's reach and invigorated the earlier prohibition to include "expenditure[s]" as well.
>
> Today, as in 1907, the law focuses on the special characteristics

of the corporate structure that threaten the integrity of the political process....

In sum, our cases on campaign finance regulation represent respect for the legislative judgment that the special characteristics of the corporate structure require particularly careful regulation. And we have understood that such deference to legislative choice is warranted particularly when Congress regulates campaign contributions, carrying as they do a plain threat to political integrity and a plain warrant to counter the appearance and reality of corruption and the misuse of corporate advantages....

That historical prologue would discourage any broadside attack on corporate campaign finance regulation or regulation of corporate contributions, and NCRL accordingly questions [the Act] only to the extent the law places nonprofit advocacy corporations like itself under the general ban on direct contributions. But not even this more focused challenge can claim a blank slate....

The upshot is that, although we have never squarely held against NCRL's position here, we could not hold for it without recasting our understanding of the risks of harm posed by corporate political contributions, of the expressive significance of contributions, and of the consequent deference owed to legislative judgments on what to do about them. NCRL's efforts, however, fail to unsettle existing law on any of these points.

Disposition of case: The judgment of the appellate court was reversed.

Concurring opinion by Justice Kennedy: Justice Kennedy concurred in the judgment of the majority opinion. He wrote tersely that he would have cast a different vote, if the case had involved "the distinction between contributions and expenditures under the whole scheme of campaign finance regulation[.]"

Dissenting opinion by Justice Thomas: Justice Thomas dissenting from the majority opinion. He wrote tersely that he believed campaign finance law was unconstitutional.

See also **Federal Election Commission v. Massachusetts Citizens for Life, Inc.**

Federal Election Commission v. Massachusetts Citizens for Life, Inc.

Forum: United States Supreme Court.

Case Citation: Federal Election Commission v. Massachusetts Citizens for Life, Inc., 479 U.S. 238 (1986).

Date Argued: October 7, 1986.

Date of Decision: December 15, 1986.

Opinion of Court: Brennan, J., in which Marshall, Powell, O'Connor, and Scalia, JJ., joined.

Concurring Opinion: O'Connor, J.

Concurring and Dissenting Opinion: Rehnquist, C. J., in which White, Blackmun, and Stevens, JJ., joined.

Counsel for Appellant: Charles N. Steele argued; on the brief was Richard B. Bader.

Counsel for Appellee: Francis H. Fox argued; on the brief was E. Susan Garsh.

Amicus Brief for Appellant: Roger M. Witten, William T. Lake, Carol F. Lee, and Archibald Cox for Common Cause.

Amicus Brief for Appellee: American Civil Liberties Union et al. by Marjorie Heins, Burt Neuborne, and Jack Novik; for the Catholic League for Religious and Civil Rights by Steven Frederick McDowell; for the Chamber of Commerce of the United States by Judith K. Richmond, Stephen A. Bokat, Robin S. Conrad, and Jan W. Baran; for the Home Builders Association of Massachusetts by Wayne S. Henderson; for the National Rifle Association of America by James J. Featherstone and Richard E. Gardiner; and for Joseph M. Scheidler et al. by Edward R. Grant and Maura K. Quinlan. Jane E. Kirtley, David Barr, Nancy H. Hendry, J. Laurent Scharff, and Bruce W. Sanford filed a brief for the Reporters Committee for Freedom of the Press et al.

Issue Presented: Whether the Federal Election Campaign Act prohibited the appellee from using its treasury funds to promote pro-life political candidates and, if so, whether application of the Act was constitutional?

Case Holding: The Act prohibited the use of the appellee's treasury funds to promote political candidates, but it was unconstitutional.

Background facts of case: The appellee, Massachusetts Citizens for Life, Inc., was incorporated in 1973 as a nonprofit corporation under the laws of Massachusetts. The appellee was created to foster respect for human life and to defend the right to life of all human beings, born and unborn, through educational, political and other forms of activities. In September of 1978 the appellee published a "Special Edition" of its newsletter. The Special Edition exhorted readers to vote pro-life in upcoming primary elections in Massachusetts, listed the candidates for each state and federal office in every voting district in the state, and identified each one as either pro-life or pro-abortion. The Special Edition was financed by money taken from appellee's general treasury funds. A complaint was filed with appellant, Federal Election Commission, alleging that financing for the Special Edition violated the Federal Election Campaign Act, which prohibited corporations from using treasury funds to make an expenditure in connection with any federal election, and required that any expenditure for such purpose be financed by voluntary contributions to a separate segregated fund. After an investigation, the appellant filed a complaint in a federal district court, seeking a civil penalty and other relief. The district court granted appellee's motion for summary judgment dismissal, holding that the Act did not apply to appellee but that if it did it was unconstitutional as a violation of the First Amendment. The First Circuit court of appeals held that the statute was applicable to appellee, but that it was unconstitutional. The Supreme Court granted certiorari to consider the issue.

Majority opinion by Justice Brennan: Justice Brennan held that the Act applied to the appellee's financing of the Special Edition newsletter, but that application of the Act violated the constitution. The opinion addressed the matters as follows:

> We agree with the Court of Appeals that the "Special Edition" is not outside the reach of [the Act]. First, we find no merit in appellee's contention that preparation and distribution of the "Special Edition" does not fall within [the Act's] definition of expenditure.... [T]he general definitions section of the Act contains a broader definition of expenditure, including within that term the provision of anything of value made for the purpose of influencing any election for Federal office....
>
> We need not decide whether the regular [appellee] newsletter is exempt under this provision, because, even assuming that it is, the "Special Edition" cannot be considered comparable to any single issue of the newsletter. It was not published through the facilities of the regular newsletter, but by a staff which prepared no previous or subsequent newsletters. It was not distributed to the newsletter's regular audience, but to a group 20 times the size of that audience, most of whom were members of the public who had never received the newsletter....
>
> In sum, we hold that [appellee's] publication and distribution of the Special Edition is in violation of [the Act]. We therefore turn to the constitutionality of that provision as applied to appellee....
>
> The [appellant] minimizes the impact of the legislation upon [appellee's] First Amendment rights by emphasizing that the corporation remains free to establish a separate segregated fund, composed of contributions earmarked for that purpose by the donors, that may be used for unlimited campaign spending. However, the corporation is not free to use its general funds for campaign advocacy purposes. While that is not an absolute restriction

on speech, it is a substantial one. Moreover, even to speak through a segregated fund, [the appellee] must make very significant efforts....

Our conclusion is that [the Act's] restriction of independent spending is unconstitutional as applied to [appellee], for it infringes protected speech without a compelling justification for such infringement. We acknowledge the legitimacy of Congress' concern that organizations that amass great wealth in the economic marketplace not gain unfair advantage in the political marketplace.

Regardless of whether that concern is adequate to support application of [the Act] to commercial enterprises, a question not before us, that justification does not extend uniformly to all corporations. Some corporations have features more akin to voluntary political associations than business firms, and therefore should not have to bear burdens on independent spending solely because of their incorporated status.

In particular, [the appellee] has three features essential to our holding that it may not constitutionally be bound by [the Act's] restriction on independent spending. First, it was formed for the express purpose of promoting political ideas, and cannot engage in business activities. If political fundraising events are expressly denominated as requests for contributions that will be used for political purposes, including direct expenditures, these events cannot be considered business activities. This ensures that political resources reflect political support. Second, it has no shareholders or other persons affiliated so as to have a claim on its assets or earnings. This ensures that persons connected with the organization will have no economic disincentive for disassociating with it if they disagree with its political activity. Third, [the appellee] was not established by a business corporation or a labor union, and it is its policy not to accept contributions from such entities. This prevents such corporations from serving as conduits for the type of direct spending that creates a threat to the political marketplace.

... Where at all possible, government must curtail speech only to the degree necessary to meet the particular problem at hand, and must avoid infringing on speech that does not pose the danger that has prompted regulation. In enacting the provision at issue in this case, Congress has chosen too blunt an instrument for such a delicate task.

Disposition of case: The judgment of the court of appeals was affirmed.

Concurring opinion by Justice O'Connor: Justice O'Connor agreed with the majority decision, but wrote separately to make the following point:

> In my view, the significant burden on [appellee] this case comes not from the disclosure requirements that it must satisfy, but from the additional organizational restraints imposed upon it by the Act. As the Court has described, engaging in campaign speech requires [appellee] to assume a more formalized organizational form and significantly reduces or eliminates the sources of funding for groups such as [appellee] with few or no members. These additional requirements do not further the Government's informational interest in campaign disclosure, and, for the reasons given by the Court, cannot be justified by any of the other interests identified by the Federal Election Commission. Although the organizational and solicitation restrictions are not invariably an insurmountable burden on speech, in this case the Government has failed to show that groups such as [appellee] pose any danger that would justify infringement of its core political expression. On that basis, I join in the Court's judgment that [the Act] is unconstitutional as applied to [appellee].

Concurring and dissenting opinion by Chief Justice Rehnquist: The Chief Justice agreed with the majority that expenditures for the Special Edition newsletter violated the Act. However, he dissented from the majority's determination that the Act was unconstitutional. The Chief Justice wrote as follows:

> I do not dispute that the threat from corporate political activity will vary depending on the particular characteristics of a given corporation; it is obvious that large and successful corporations with resources to fund a political war chest constitute a more potent threat to the political process than less successful business corporations or nonprofit corporations. It may also be that those supporting some nonbusiness corporations will identify with the corporations' political views more frequently than the average shareholder of General Motors would support the political activities of that corporation. These distinctions among corporations, however, are distinctions in degree that do not amount to differences in kind. As such, they are more properly drawn by the Legislature than by the Judiciary. Congress expressed its judgment in [the Act] that the threat posed by corporate political activity warrants a prophylactic measure applicable to all groups that organize in the corporate form. Our previous cases have expressed a reluctance to fine-tune such judgments; I would adhere to that counsel here.

See also **Federal Election Commission v. Beaumont**

Federal Election Commission v. Wisconsin Right to Life, Inc.

Forum: United States Supreme Court.

Case Citation: Federal Election Commission v. Wisconsin Right to Life, Inc., 127 S.Ct. 2652 (2007).

Date Argued: April 25, 2007.

Date of Decision: June 25, 2007.

Opinion of Court: Roberts, C.J., in which Kennedy, Scalia, Thomas and Alito, JJ., joined.

Concurring Opinion: Alito, J.

Concurring Opinion: Scalia, J., in which Kennedy and Thomas, JJ., joined.

Dissenting Opinion: Souter, J., in which Stevens, Ginsburg and Breyer, JJ., joined.

Counsel for Appellants: Paul D. Clement and Seth P. Waxman; on the brief were Thomasenia P. Duncan, Richard B. Bader, David Kolker, Harry J. Summers, Kevin Deeley, Gregory G. Garre, Malcolm L. Stewart, Lawrence H. Norton, Roger M. Witten, Shane T. Stansbury, Pratik A. Shah, Randolph D. Moss, Danielle Spinelli, Brent Bickley, Kevin Whelan, Donald J. Simon, Scott L. Nelson, Trevor Potter, J. Gerald Hebert, Paul S. Ryan, Charles G. Curtis, Jr., David Anstaett, Alan B. Morrison, Bradley S. Phillips and Grant A. Davis-Denny.

Counsel for Appellee: James Bopp, Jr. argued; on the brief were M. Miller Baker, Michael S. Nadel, Richard E. Coleson, Jeffrey P. Gallant and Raeanna S. Moore.

Amicus Brief for Appellants: League of Women Voters of the United States, Common Cause, Inc., The Greenlining Institute, United States Public Interest Research Group, Richard Briffault, Richard L. Hasen Committee for Economic Development, Norman Ornstein, Thomas Mann, Anthony Corrado Norman Dorsen, Aryeh Neier, Burt Neuborne, and John Shattuck.

Amicus Brief for Appellee: Alliance for Justice, Mitch McConnell, Coalition of Public Charities, Citizens United, Citizens United Foundation, Gun Owners of America, Inc., Gun Owners Foundation, Joyce Meyer Ministries, Conservative Legal Defense and Education Fund, Free Speech Coalition, Inc., Free Speech Defense and Education Fund, Inc., Lincoln Institute, Public Advocate of the United States, DownsizeDC.org, Downsize DC Foundation, National Association of Realtors, National Rifle Association, American Federation of Labor and Congress of Industrial Organizations, Family Research Council, Free Market Foundation, Home School Legal Defense Association, Republican National Committee, American Center for Law and Justice, Focus on the Family, Center for Competitive Politics, Institute for Justice, Reason Foundation, Individual Rights Foundation, Cato Institute, Chamber of Commerce of the United States of America and American Civil Liberties Union.

Issue Presented: Whether electioneering communications provisions of a federal statute violated a pro-life organization's First Amendment right to broadcast political issue oriented advertisements shortly before primary and general elections?

Case Holding: The electioneering communications provisions of a federal statute violated a pro-life organization's First Amendment right to broadcast political issue oriented advertisements shortly before primary and general elections.

Background facts of case: The Appellee, Wisconsin Right to Life, Inc., wanted to run advertisements during a state primary election and general federal election that were critical of United States Senators who prevented Republican nominated federal judges from being confirmed. However, under the electioneering communications provisions of the Bipartisan Campaign Reform Act (BCRA) the advertisements were prohibited. Consequently, the Appellee filed a federal lawsuit against the Federal Election Commission (FEC) seeking a judicial determination that electioneering communications provisions of BCRA violated the Appellee's First Amendment right to free speech. The federal district court denied relief. The Appellee appealed to the Supreme Court. The nation's high court reversed the lower court and remanded the case for further consideration. After the case was remanded four members of Congress were allowed to intervene as defendants. The district court, on remand, found that the federal statute violated the Appellee's rights under the First Amendment. The Supreme Court thereafter granted certiorari to consider the issue.

Plurality opinion by Chief Justice Roberts: The Chief Justice rendered the judgment of the Court that the electioneering provisions of BCRA violated the Appellee's First Amendment rights. The plurality opinion rejected FEC's argument that the determination of whether BCRA violated the First Amendment should be done through use of an "intent" test. The Chief Justice rejected the "intent" test and decided that the issue should be viewed objectively. The Chief Justice reasoned as follows:

> [W]e decline to adopt a test for as-applied challenges turning on the speaker's intent to affect an election. The test to distinguish constitutionally protected political speech from speech that BCRA may proscribe should provide a safe harbor for those who wish to exercise First Amendment rights. The test should also reflect our profound national commitment to the principle that debate on public issues should be uninhibited, robust, and wide-open. A test turning on the intent of the speaker does not remotely fit the bill.
>
> Far from serving the values the First Amendment is meant to protect, an intent-based test would chill core political speech by opening the door to a trial on every ad within the terms of [the statute], on the theory that the speaker actually intended to affect an election, no matter how compelling the indications that the ad concerned a pending legislative or policy issue. No reasonable speaker would choose to run an ad covered by BCRA if its only defense to a criminal prosecution would be that its motives were pure. An intent-based standard blankets with uncertainty whatever may be said, and offers no security for free discussion....
>
> The freedom of speech ... guaranteed by the Constitution embraces at the least the liberty to discuss publicly and truthfully all matters of public concern without previous restraint or fear of subsequent punishment. To safeguard this liberty, the proper standard for an as-applied challenge to BCRA must be objective, focusing on the substance of the communication rather than amorphous considerations of intent and effect.... In short, it must give the benefit of any doubt to protecting rather than stifling speech.
>
> In light of these considerations, a court should find that an ad is the functional equivalent of express advocacy only if the ad is susceptible of no reasonable interpretation other than as an appeal to vote for or against a specific candidate. Under this test, WRTL's three ads are plainly not the functional equivalent of express advocacy. First, their content is consistent with that of a genuine issue ad: The ads focus on a legislative issue, take a position on the issue, exhort the public to adopt that position, and urge the public to contact public officials with respect to the matter. Second, their content lacks indicia of express advocacy: The ads do not mention an election, candidacy, political party, or challenger; and they do not take a position on a candidate's character, qualifications, or fitness for office.
>
> Despite these characteristics, appellants assert that the content of WRTL's ads alone betrays their electioneering nature. Indeed, the FEC suggests that *any* ad covered by [the statute] that includes "an appeal to citizens to contact their elected representative" is the "functional equivalent" of an ad saying defeat or elect that candidate. We do not agree....
>
> Freedom of discussion, if it would fulfill its historic function in this nation, must embrace all issues about which information is needed or appropriate to enable the members of society to cope with the exigencies of their period. Discussion of issues cannot be suppressed simply because the issues may also be pertinent in an election. Where the First Amendment is implicated, the tie goes to the speaker, not the censor....
>
> Because WRTL's ads are not express advocacy or its functional equivalent, and because appellants identify no interest sufficiently compelling to justify burdening WRTL's speech, we hold that BCRA is unconstitutional as applied to WRTL's ... ads.

Disposition of case: The judgment of the lower court was affirmed.

Concurring opinion by Justice Alito: In a terse concurring opinion Justice Alito joined the plurality opinion, in doing so he wrote:

> I join the principal opinion because I conclude (a) that [the statute], as applied, cannot constitutionally ban any advertisement that may reasonably be interpreted as anything other than an appeal to vote for or against a candidate, (b) that the ads at issue here may reasonably be interpreted as something other than such an appeal, and (c) that because [the statute] is unconstitutional as applied to the advertisements before us, it is unnecessary to go further and decide whether [the statute] is unconstitutional on its face.

Concurring opinion by Justice Scalia: Justice Scalia joined the judgment of the Court, but not its reasoning. He wrote in his concurring opinion that the Court should have found the electioneering communications provision of BCRA to be unconstitutional on its face.

Dissenting opinion by Justice Souter: Justice Souter dissented from the Court's judgment. He argued that BCRA was constitutionally sound and did not violate the First Amendment rights of the Appellant. Justice Souter made the following observations:

> Throughout the 2004 senatorial campaign, WRTL made no secret of its views about who should win the election and explicitly tied its position to the filibuster issue. Its PAC issued at least two press releases saying that its "Top Election Priorities" were to "Re-elect George W. Bush" and "Send Feingold Packing!" In one of these, the Chair of WRTL's PAC was quoted as saying, "'We do not want Russ Feingold to continue to have the ability to thwart President Bush's judicial nominees.'" The Spring 2004 issue of the WRTL PAC's quarterly magazine ran an article headlined "Radically Pro-Abortion Feingold Must Go!," which reported that "Feingold has been active in his opposition to Bush's judicial nominees" and said that "the defeat of Feingold must be uppermost in the minds of Wisconsin's pro-life community in the 2004 elections."...

WRTL's planned airing of the ads had no apparent relation to any Senate filibuster vote but was keyed to the timing of the senatorial election. WRTL began broadcasting the ads on July 26, 2004, four days after the Senate recessed for the summer, and although the filibuster controversy raged on through 2005, WRTL did not resume running the ads after the election. During the campaign period that the ads did cover, Senator Feingold's support of the filibusters was a prominent issue. His position was well known, and his Republican opponents, who vocally opposed the filibusters, made the issue a major talking point in their campaigns against him.

In sum, any Wisconsin voter who paid attention would have known that Democratic Senator Feingold supported filibusters against Republican presidential judicial nominees, that the propriety of the filibusters was a major issue in the senatorial campaign, and that WRTL along with the Senator's Republican challengers opposed his reelection because of his position on filibusters. Any alert voters who heard or saw WRTL's ads would have understood that WRTL was telling them that the Senator's position on the filibusters should be grounds to vote against him.

Given these facts, it is beyond all reasonable debate that the ads are constitutionally subject to regulation[.]

Federal Employees and Abortion

An appropriations amendment has been attached to funding for the Federal Employees Health Benefits (FEHB) program, beginning in fiscal year 1983, that prohibits coverage for abortions unless the woman's health is in danger or in cases of rape or incest. Since the amendment's inception, there have only been two years, 1993 and 1994, that it has not been passed. The abortion payment ban impacts about 1.2 million women of reproductive age who depend on FEHB coverage. *See also* **Insurance Coverage for Abortion; Public Resources for Abortions**

Federal Female Prisoners and Abortion

An appropriations amendment has been attached to funding for the Federal Bureau of Prisons (FBP), beginning in fiscal year 1987, that prohibits government payment for a prisoner's abortion unless the woman's health is in danger or in cases of rape. Since the amendment's inception there has only been one year, 1994, that it has not been passed. In 2005, there were approximately 12,422 women confined in facilities operated by FBP. The 1996 policy statement of FBP's abortion program is set out below.

P.S. 6070.05. Birth Control, Pregnancy, Child Placement and Abortion

1. Purpose and Scope. The Bureau of Prisons provides an inmate with medical and social services related to birth control, pregnancy, child placement, and abortion. The Warden shall ensure compliance with the applicable law regarding these matters.

2. Program Objectives. The expected results of this program are:

a. Interested inmates will receive appropriate information on birth control.

b. A pregnant inmate will be provided medical, case management, and counseling services.

c. A pregnant inmate will be offered medical, religious, and social counseling to aid her in making a decision whether to carry the pregnancy to full term or to have an elective abortion.

d. A pregnant inmate, who so chooses, will be provided an elective abortion at Bureau expense, only when the life of the mother would be endangered if the fetus is carried to term, or in the case of rape.

e. Inmates will receive assistance, including access to community child placement agencies, to place newborn children in appropriate homes.

f. A staff member who wishes not to be involved in arranging an elective abortion will not be required to do so.

See also **Public Resources for Abortions**

Female Condom *see* **Condoms**

Female Reproductive System

The female reproductive system is designed for carrying out the reproduction of life. The system is composed of several distinct organs. The primary organs may be grouped as internal and external.

(1) INTERNAL ORGANS

The primary internal female reproductive organs include the vagina, uterus, cervix, ovaries, and fallopian tubes.

Vagina. The vagina (also called the birth canal) is a passageway that connects the cervix with the external genitalia (vulva). It has muscular walls that are equipped with numerous blood vessels and is about two and one-half to four inches long. The walls of the vagina become erect when a woman is sexually aroused. This erection is caused by extra blood that is pumped into its vessels. The vagina serves three functions: it is a receptacle for the male penis during sexual intercourse; it is an outlet for blood and tissue during menstruation; and it is the passageway for a neonate to pass through at birth.

Uterus. The uterus (also called the womb), is a hollow, pear-shaped organ in which a fertilized egg becomes embedded and is nourished and allowed to develop until birth. It is located in the pelvic cavity behind the bladder and in front of the bowel. The uterus is lined with tissues that undergo changes during a woman's menstrual cycle. If an egg is unfertilized during the menstrual cycle, the uterus will expel blood and tissues. If an egg is fertilized and implanted, the uterus will progressively stretch from three to four inches in length, to a size that accommodates the growing fetus. During pregnancy, the walls of the uterus increase from two to three ounces, to roughly two pounds. The uterus will eventually shrink back to its normal size once the fetus is delivered.

The main parts of the uterus include myometrium, endometrium and perimetrium.

(i) Myometrium. The myometrium is the middle and thickest layer of the uterus. It is composed of four layers of smooth muscle. It will contract during menstruation to help expel blood and tissue. During fetal delivery it will contract to propel the fetus out of the uterus. The myometrium expands during pregnancy to hold the growing fetus.

(ii) Endometrium. The endometrium is the innermost layer of the uterus. It is composed of three layers: basal layer, spongy layer and compact layer (the spongy and compact layers constitute the decidual layer). The endometrium has a rich blood supply and is glandular in nature. Throughout the menstrual cycle, it grows progressively thicker to prepare the uterus for potential implantation of an embryo. When there is an implant it will act as the site of connection for the placenta, to allow nutrient exchange between the blood supply of the woman and fetus. In the absence of implantation, a portion of the endometrium is shed during menstruation.

(iii) Perimetrium. The perimetrium is the outer layer of the uterus. It consists essentially of simple squamous cells over a thin sheet of connective tissue. The perimetrium has extrauterine connective tissue structures, such as ligaments, that provide mechanical support to the uterus.

Cervix. The cervix is the tubular shaped neck of the uterus that protrudes into the upper portion of the vagina. It is about one inch long and is penetrated by the cervical canal. The canal allows for passage of sperm into the uterus, and passage out of the uterus of menstrual waste and the fetus.

Ovaries. There are two ovary, one on each side of the uterus and just below the opening to the fallopian tubes. Each ovary is about the size of a walnut, measuring less than two inches long and less than one inch wide. The ovaries have two main functions: egg (ovum) and hormone production.

The ovaries are composed of thousands of sacs called graafian follicles, each of which contains an immature egg. While in this condition the eggs are not capable of being fertilized by a sperm until they undergo a maturing process, which culminates in their release from the ovary at the time of ovulation. Usually only one egg is released per month. A released egg travels into the fallopian tube, where it may or may not be fertilized by a sperm, and it then travels to the uterus. A fertilized egg gets implanted into the lining of the uterus and develops into a fetus. An unfertilized egg is released out of the body during menstruation.

The ovaries also produce the hormones estrogen and progesterone. Estrogen and progesterone control and regulate the menstrual cycle, as well as pregnancy. They also help with the development of breasts and other features specific to a woman.

Fallopian tubes. The fallopian tubes (also called uterine tubes or oviducts) are hollow muscular tubes extending from the uterus to the ovary. It is about three inches in length. One end of the tube opens into the uterus, while the other end expands into a funnel shape near the ovary. When an egg is expelled from the ovary it is propelled into the opening of the tube. After sexual intercourse, sperm swim up from the uterus into the tube. The lining of the tube and its secretions sustain both the egg and the sperm for fertilization. If the egg is fertilized, the embryo will normally go into the endometrium and start to form a placenta. However, if the embryo implants in the tube, or another area outside the uterus, an ectopic pregnancy occurs. About 98 percent of ectopic pregnancies occur in the tube. Surgical removal of the embryo would be necessary to prevent complications to the woman resulting from ectopic pregnancy.

(2) External Organ

The external female organ performs two major functions. It allows entry of the penis for the purpose of ejaculating sperm to fertilize the egg, and it protects the more sensitive internal genital organs from pathogens that can produce infection. The primary external female reproductive organ is the vulva. The vulva is comprised of the mons pubis, the labia, clitoris, hymen, perineum and glands of Bartholin.

Mons pubis. The mons pubis is the pad-like fatty tissue that covers the pubic bone below the abdomen. It protects the pubic bone from the impact of sexual intercourse.

Labia majora. The labia majora are the outer lips of the vulva. They consist of pad-like fatty tissue that wrap around the vulva from the mons pubis to the perineum. Pubic hair usually cover these labia. They also contain numerous sweat and oil glands.

Labia minora. The labia minora are the inner lips of the vulva. They are thin stretches of tissue within the labia majora that fold and protect the vagina, urethra, and clitoris.

Clitoris. The clitoris is a small body of tissue that is sexually sensitive. It is protected by the prepuce (or clitoral hood), a covering of tissue. During sexual excitement, the clitoris may extend and cause the hood to retract to make it more accessible to stimulation.

Hymen. The hymen is a very thin membrane that partially covers the vaginal opening. It is the time honored symbol of virginity, although it may be torn by heavy exercising or the insertion of a tampon.

Perineum. The perineum is the short stretch of tissue starting at the lower end of the vulva and extending to the anus. It often tears during birth to accommodate passage of the child.

Glands of Bartholin. The glands of Bartholin are two tiny ducts that are located on each side of the mouth of the vagina. The mucus which serves as the lubrication for intercourse is produced by the glands. *See also* **Fetal Development; Male Reproductive System**

Feminist Majority Foundation

The Feminist Majority Foundation (FMF) was founded in 1987 by Peg Yorkin, Eleanor Smeal, Katherine Spillar, Toni Carabillo, and Judith Meuli. The president of FMF is Eleanor Smeal. FMF was established for the purpose of creating innovative educational programs and strategies to further women equality and empowerment, to reduce violence toward women, and to increase the health and economic well-being of women. The organization has taken a strong position in favor of abortion. FMF supports safe, legal and accessible abortions, including Medicaid funding and access for minors. *See also* **Pro-Choice Organizations**

Feminist Women's Health Center

Feminist Women's Health Center (FWHC) was established in 1980, in Yakima, Washington. FWHC was created to promote and protect the rights of women to choose and receive reproductive health care. The organization was particularly focused upon bringing reproductive choice to women in a large rural area of the state known as Central Washington. FWHC employs more than 70 women and men, serves over 7000 women annually, and operates three clinics (in Yakima, Renton and Tacoma). The organization is committed to: keeping abortion safe, legal, accessible, and acceptable; training physicians; assuring abortion coverage under insurance and Medicaid; helping women with limited financial resources; protecting against violence at clinics; standing up for women who seek abortions services; and expanding the availability of abortion information. *See also* **Pro-Choice Organizations**

Feminists for Life

Feminists for Life (FFL) is a pro-life organization based in Washington, D.C., that was established in 1972. Through its president, Serrin M. Foster, FFL has sought to limit the right to abortion by engaging in general educational, outreach and advocacy strategies. It has also established a College Outreach Program that challenges students to question abortion and asks college and university administrators to provide resources for pregnant and parenting students. FFL publishes a magazine called *The American Feminist*. *See also* **Pro-Life Organizations**

Femur Length *see* **Gestational Age**

Ferguson v. City of Charleston

Forum: United States Supreme Court.

Case Citation: Ferguson v. City of Charleston, 121 S.Ct. 1281 (2001).

Date Argued: October 4, 2000.

Date of Decision: March 21, 2001.

Opinion of the Court: Stevens, J., in which O'Connor, Souter, Ginsburg, and Breyer, JJ., joined.

Concurring Opinion: Kennedy, J.

Dissenting Opinion: Scalia, J., in which Rehnquist, C. J., and Thomas, J., joined.

Counsel for Appellants: Not Reported.

Counsel for Appellees: Not Reported.

Amicus Brief for Appellants: Not Reported.

Amicus Brief for Appellees: Not Reported.

Issue Presented: Whether the interest in using the threat of criminal sanctions to deter pregnant women from using cocaine can justify a departure from the general rule that an official nonconsensual search is unconstitutional if not authorized by a valid warrant?

Case Holding: A state hospital's performance of a diagnostic test to obtain evidence of a patient's criminal conduct for law enforcement purposes is an unreasonable search if the patient has not consented to the procedure.

Background facts of case: The appellants in the case were 10 pregnant women who received obstetrical care at the Medical University of South Carolina (MUSC) beginning in 1988. Each of the woman were arrested after medical tests revealed they used cocaine while pregnant, in violation of South Carolina law. The women filed a federal lawsuit against the appellees, the city of Charleston, South Carolina, law enforcement officials and representatives of MUSC. The lawsuit was based on a theory that the drug testing was an illegal search within the meaning of the Fourth Amendment of the federal constitution. A jury returned a verdict in favor of the appellees after finding the appellants consented to the testing. On appeal to the Fourth Circuit the jury verdict was upheld. However, the appellate court did not determine whether the evidence supported finding that the appellants consented to the testing. In stead, the appellate court found that the testing or search was reasonable as a matter of law under the doctrine of "special needs." Under this doctrine a search is lawful, in certain exceptional circumstances, when the search is conducted pursuant to a policy designed to serve non-law enforcement objectives. The Supreme Court granted certiorari, to review the appellate court's holding on the special needs issue.

Majority opinion by Justice Stevens: Justice Stevens found that because MUSC was a state hospital, the members of its staff were government actors, subject to the search requirements of the Fourth Amendment. He also determined that the urine tests conducted by MUSC staff members were searches within the meaning of the Fourth Amendment. It was also said that throughout the development and application of MUSC's drug testing policy, the Charleston prosecutors and police were extensively involved in the day-to-day administration of the policy. The opinion found that, although the drug testing policy was designed to force woman into drug treatment programs, it could not be justified under the special needs doctrine. The drug testing could only be carried out with a search warrant or the consent of the appellants. Justice Stevens summoned up the position of the Court as follows:

> While the ultimate goal of the program may well have been to get the women in question into substance abuse treatment and off of drugs, the immediate objective of the searches was to generate evidence for law enforcement purposes in order to reach that goal. The threat of law enforcement may ultimately have been intended as a means to an end, but the direct and primary purpose of MUSC's policy was to ensure the use of those means. In our opinion, this distinction is critical. Because law enforcement involvement always serves some broader social purpose or objective, under [appellees'] view, virtually any nonconsensual suspicionless search could be immunized under the special needs doctrine by defining the search solely in terms of its ultimate, rather than immediate, purpose. Such an approach is inconsistent with the Fourth Amendment. Given the primary purpose of the Charleston program, which was to use the threat of arrest and prosecution in order to force women into treatment, and given the extensive involvement of law enforcement officials at every stage of the policy, this case simply does not fit within the closely guarded category of "special needs."
>
> The fact that positive test results were turned over to the police does not merely provide a basis for distinguishing our prior cases applying the "special needs" balancing approach to the determination of drug use. It also provides an affirmative reason for enforcing the strictures of the Fourth Amendment. While state hospital employees, like other citizens, may have a duty to provide the police with evidence of criminal conduct that they inadvertently acquire in the course of routine treatment, when they undertake to obtain such evidence from their patients for the specific purpose of incriminating those patients, they have a special obligation to make sure that the patients are fully informed about their constitutional rights, as standards of knowing waiver require.

Disposition of case: The judgment of the Fourth Circuit was reversed, and the case was remanded for a determination as to whether the evidence supported finding that the appellants consented to the drug testing.

Concurring opinion by Justice Kennedy: Justice Kennedy agreed with the majority opinion that, absent consent, the search was illegal under the Fourth Amendment. The critical points that he wished to express in his concurrence are as follows:

> In my view, it is necessary and prudent to be explicit in explaining the limitations of today's decision. The beginning point ought to be to acknowledge the legitimacy of the State's interest in fetal life and of the grave risk to the life and health of the fetus, and later the child, caused by cocaine ingestion. Infants whose mothers abuse cocaine during pregnancy are born with a wide variety of physical and neurological abnormalities. Prenatal exposure to cocaine can also result in developmental problems which persist long after birth. There can be no doubt that a mother's ingesting this drug can cause tragic injury to a fetus and a child. There should be no doubt that South Carolina can impose punishment upon an expectant mother who has so little regard for her own unborn that she risks causing him or her lifelong damage and suffering. The State, by taking special measures to give rehabilitation and training to expectant mothers with this tragic addiction or weakness, acts well within its powers and its civic obligations.
>
> The holding of the Court, furthermore, does not call into question the validity of mandatory reporting laws such as child abuse laws which require teachers to report evidence of child abuse to the proper authorities, even if arrest and prosecution is the likely result. That in turn highlights the real difficulty. As this case comes to us, and as reputable sources confirm, we must accept the premise that the medical profession can adopt acceptable criteria for testing expectant mothers for cocaine use in order to provide prompt and effective counseling to the mother and to take proper medical steps to protect the child. If prosecuting authorities then adopt legitimate procedures to discover this information and prosecution follows, that ought not to invalidate the testing. One of the ironies of the case, then, may be that the program now under review, which gives the cocaine user a second and third chance, might be replaced by some more rigorous system. We must, however, take the case as it comes to us; and the use of handcuffs, arrests, prosecutions, and police assistance in designing and implementing the testing and rehabilitation policy cannot be sustained under our previous cases concerning mandatory testing.
>
> My discussion has endeavored to address the permissibility of a law enforcement purpose in this artificial context. The role played by consent might have affected our assessment of the issues.... Had we the prerogative to discuss the role played by consent, the case might have been quite a different one. All are in agreement, of course, that the Court of Appeals will address these issues in further proceedings on remand.

Dissenting opinion by Justice Scalia: Justice Scalia did not believe that the drug testing violated the Fourth Amendment. He took the position that the appellants consented to drug testing and that the Fourth Amendment did not prevent medical authorities from turning drug test results over to the police. The main points of Justice Scalia's position were stated as follows:

> Until today, we have *never* held — or even suggested — that material which a person voluntarily entrusts to someone else cannot be given by that person to the police, and used for whatever evidence it may contain. Without so much as discussing the point, the Court today opens a hole in our Fourth Amendment jurisprudence, the size and shape of which is entirely indeterminate....

I think it clear, therefore, that there is no basis for saying that obtaining of the urine sample was unconstitutional. The special-needs doctrine is thus quite irrelevant, since it operates only to validate searches and seizures that are otherwise unlawful....

The cocaine tests started in April 1989, neither at police suggestion nor with police involvement. Expectant mothers who tested positive were referred by hospital staff for substance-abuse treatment, an obvious health benefit to both mother and child. And, since "[i]nfants whose mothers abuse cocaine during pregnancy are born with a wide variety of physical and neurological abnormalities," which require medical attention, the tests were of additional medical benefit in predicting needed postnatal treatment for the child. Thus, in their origin — before the police were in any way involved — the tests had an immediate, not merely an "ultimate" purpose of improving maternal and infant health. Several months after the testing had been initiated, a nurse discovered that local police were arresting pregnant users of cocaine for child abuse, the hospital's general counsel wrote the county solicitor to ask "what, if anything, our Medical Center needs to do to assist you in this matter," the police suggested ways to avoid tainting evidence, and the hospital and police in conjunction used the testing program as a means of securing what the Court calls the "ultimate" health benefit of coercing drug-abusing mothers into drug treatment. Why would there be any reason to believe that, once this policy of using the drug tests for their "ultimate" health benefits had been adopted, use of them for their original, immediate, benefits somehow disappeared, and testing somehow became in its entirety nothing more than a "pretext" for obtaining grounds for arrest? On the face of it, this is incredible. The only evidence of the exclusively arrest-related purpose of the testing adduced by the Court is that the police-cooperation policy itself does not describe how to care for cocaine-exposed infants. But of course it does not, since that policy, adopted months after the cocaine testing was initiated, had as its only health object the "ultimate" goal of inducing drug treatment through threat of arrest. Does the Court really believe (or even hope) that, once invalidation of the program challenged here has been decreed, drug testing will cease?

As I indicated at the outset, it is not the function of this Court — at least not in Fourth Amendment cases — to weigh petitioners' privacy interest against the State's interest in meeting the crisis of "crack babies" that developed in the late 1980's. I cannot refrain from observing, however, that the outcome of a wise weighing of those interests is by no means clear. The initial goal of the doctors and nurses who conducted cocaine-testing in this case was to refer pregnant drug addicts to treatment centers, and to prepare for necessary treatment of their possibly affected children. When the doctors and nurses agreed to the program providing test results to the police, they did so because (in addition to the fact that child abuse was required by law to be reported) they wanted to use the sanction of arrest as a strong incentive for their addicted patients to undertake drug-addiction treatment. And the police themselves used it for that benign purpose, as is shown by the fact that only 30 of 253 women testing positive for cocaine were ever arrested, and only 2 of those prosecuted.

See also **Drug Use and Pregnancy**

Fertility Awareness *see* **Natural Family Planning Methods**

Fertilization *see* **Fetal Development**

Fetal Alcohol Syndrome

Fetal alcohol syndrome (FAS) is the term used to describe certain birth defects in babies that may occur when mothers drink alcohol while pregnant. Although the medical profession has an historically based understanding that consuming alcohol during pregnancy caused some problems to newborns, it was not until 1968 that a French doctor, Paul Lemoine, published the first scientific study of children born to alcoholic mothers who had similar features and behaviors. Dr. Lemoine's findings prompted a more sophisticated study that was published in 1973 by a team of clinicians from the University of Washington (Drs. Kenneth Jones, David Smith, Christy Ulleland, Ann Streissguth). The Washington team coined the name, FAS, for the disorder reported by Dr. Lemoine.

Alcohol consumed by a pregnant woman passes through the placental barrier to the fetus. The alcohol interferes with the ability of the fetus to obtain adequate oxygen and nourishment for normal cell development in the brain and other body organs. Consequently, the consumption of alcohol by a pregnant woman can adversely affect the development of the baby. Research has shown that alcohol use during the first trimester poses a greater threat than drinking during the second trimester; and drinking during the second trimester is more threatening than use in the third trimester. Although the deceptive nature of the symptoms of FAS make it hard for researchers to accurately determine the prevalence of the birth defect, it has been estimated that from 5,000 to 10,000 children are born with FAS each year in the United States. Although no cure exists for FAS, the birth defect is preventable if women abstain from alcohol use during pregnancy.

Children born with FAS require a lifetime of special care. Some of the classic FAS abnormalities include: growth deficiency in the fetus and newborn; delayed development with decreased mental functioning; facial abnormalities; heart defects; and limb abnormalities. FAS is recognized as the leading cause of mental retardation and the second most common birth defect. Some babies with alcohol-related birth defects do not have the classic FAS symptoms. This line of birth defects is sometimes referred to as fetal alcohol effects (FAE). *See also* **Birth Defects and Abortion; Drug Use and Pregnancy; Smoking and Pregnancy**

Fetal Chromosome Error

Humans have 46 chromosomes. In reproduction normally the egg cell and the sperm cell each start out with 46 chromosomes. The egg and sperm will undergo cell division and the 46 chromosomes will divide in half, leaving the egg and the sperm cells with 23 chromosomes each. After the egg and sperm fertilize, the embryo will end up with a complete set of 46 chromosomes, half from the father and half from the mother. Sometimes an error occurs when an egg or sperm cell form, or during fertilization. The error can be fatal or cause severe birth defects. The origin of a chromosome error may be either maternal, paternal or both.

Researchers have concluded that roughly half of all spontaneous abortions, occurring before 14 weeks of gestation, are due to fetal chromosome error. Approximately 11 percent of all stillbirths are due to chromosome error. In addition, because many chromosome errors can be determined during prenatal testing, woman can be informed of nonfatal severe birth defects and choose whether to have an induced abortion or give birth. *See also* **Birth Defects and Abortion; Eugenic Abortion; FISH Test**

Fetal Death Report

A majority of states require by statute that abortion providers complete a report of all induced abortions, and to forward the same to the proper authorities. Many of the abortion reporting statutes are relatively straightforward. However, a number of state statutes outline complicated and detailed requirements that, in essence, act as a deterrent to physicians who want to perform abortions. An example of an abortion reporting statute taken from Illinois is set out below.

Illinois Code Ch. 720, § 510/10.
Reports of abortion (abridged version)

A report of each abortion performed shall be made to the Department on forms prescribed by it. Such report forms shall not identify the pa-

STATES WITH STATUTES THAT REQUIRE PHYSICIANS TO SUBMIT FETAL DEATH REPORTS

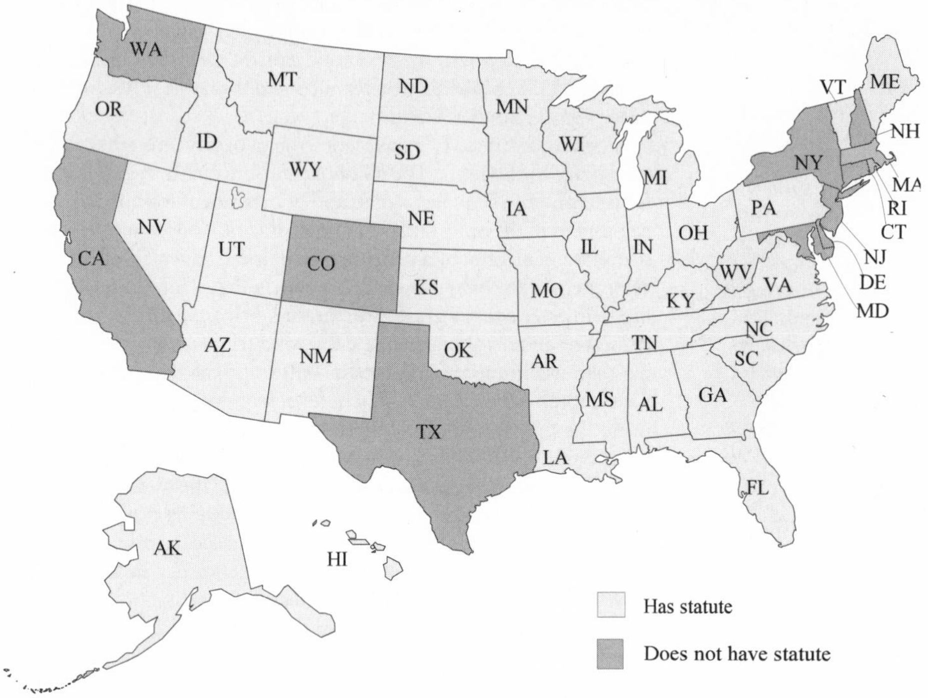

District of Columbia does not have statute.

tient by name, but by an individual number to be noted in the patient's permanent record in the possession of the physician, and shall include information concerning:

(1) Identification of the physician who performed the abortion and the facility where the abortion was performed and a patient identification number;

(2) State in which the patient resides;

(3) Patient's date of birth, race and marital status;

(4) Number of prior pregnancies;

(5) Date of last menstrual period;

(6) Type of abortion procedure performed;

(7) Complications and whether the abortion resulted in a live birth;

(8) The date the abortion was performed;

(9) Medical indications for any abortion performed when the fetus was viable;

(10) The information required by Sections 6(1)(b) and 6(4)(b) of this Act, if applicable;

(11) Basis for any medical judgment that a medical emergency existed when required under Sections 6(2)(a) and 6(6) and when required to be reported in accordance with this Section by any provision of this Law; and

(12) The pathologist's test results pursuant to Section 12 of this Act.

Such form shall be completed by the hospital or other licensed facility, signed by the physician who performed the abortion or pregnancy termination, and transmitted to the Department not later than 10 days following the end of the month in which the abortion was performed.

Fetal Development

Fetal development or conception begins in the fallopian tube, when a male sperm penetrates a female egg and begins the fertilization process. Joining of the egg and sperm produces a single cell called a zygote. Over the course of a few days the zygote will multiply the number of cells through division. This conglomerate of cells is called a morula. Additional cell division takes place and the morula becomes an outer shell with an attached group of cells. At this point in development the morula is called a blastocyte. The blastocyte will journey down the fallopian tube, between the 7th and 9th day after conception, and implant itself in the lining of the uterus (endometrium).

Around the 15th day after conception the embryonic phase begins. It will last until about the 8th week. During embryonic phase the cells of the embryo divide and take on specific functions. This process is called tissue differentiation. It is required for the different kinds of cell types that make up a human being (e.g., blood cells, kidney cells, nerve cells).

Weeks 3–8 of the embryonic phase. Rapid development of the embryo occurs from the 3rd week through the 8th week. In the 3rd week the embryo begins heart formation, brain and spinal cord formation, and the beginnings of the gastrointestinal tract.

Greater development follows during the 4th and 5th weeks, though the embryo is only about ⅛ inch long. In this period there will be formation of tissue that develops into the vertebra, the lower jaw, hyoid bone, and the cartilage of the larynx. There will also be formation of structures of the ears and eyes. Arms, legs, feet, and hands will show rudimentary development, along with rudimentary blood through the main vessels. The heart will develop further and present a regular rhythm. The brain develops into five areas and some cranial nerves will be visible.

The 6th week will bring formation of the nose, upper lip, trachea, two lung buds, and palate; and further development of the brain, upper and lower jaws, ears, arms, legs, hands, feet and blood circulation. The heart is nearly fully developed and the tail is receding.

During the 7th week all essential organs will have begun to form. The head is more rounded and eyes move forward on the face, as eyelids begin to form. The palate is nearing completion, the tongue begins to form, and the gastrointestinal tract separates.

By the 8th week the embryo is developed enough to be called a fetus. It now resembles a human being, though it is only a little over an inch long in length. All organs and structures are formed to some degree. Facial features continue to develop, the eyelids begin to fuse, the ears begin to take their final shape (though still set low on the head), external genitalia form, long bones begin to form, the anal passage opens, circulation through the umbilical cord is well developed, and muscles are able to contract.

Weeks 9–12 of the fetal phase. The fetus reaches a length of about 3.2 inches during this period. The head comprises almost half of the fetus' size, but the neck is present. The face is well formed, the ears are more pronounced, the eyelids close, tooth buds form, digits are well formed, the urogenital tract completes development, genitals appear well differentiated, red blood cells are produced in the liver, and fetal heart tones may be heard with electronic devices.

Weeks 13–16 of the fetal phase. The fetus reaches a length of about 6 inches during this period. A fine hair, called lanugo, develops on the

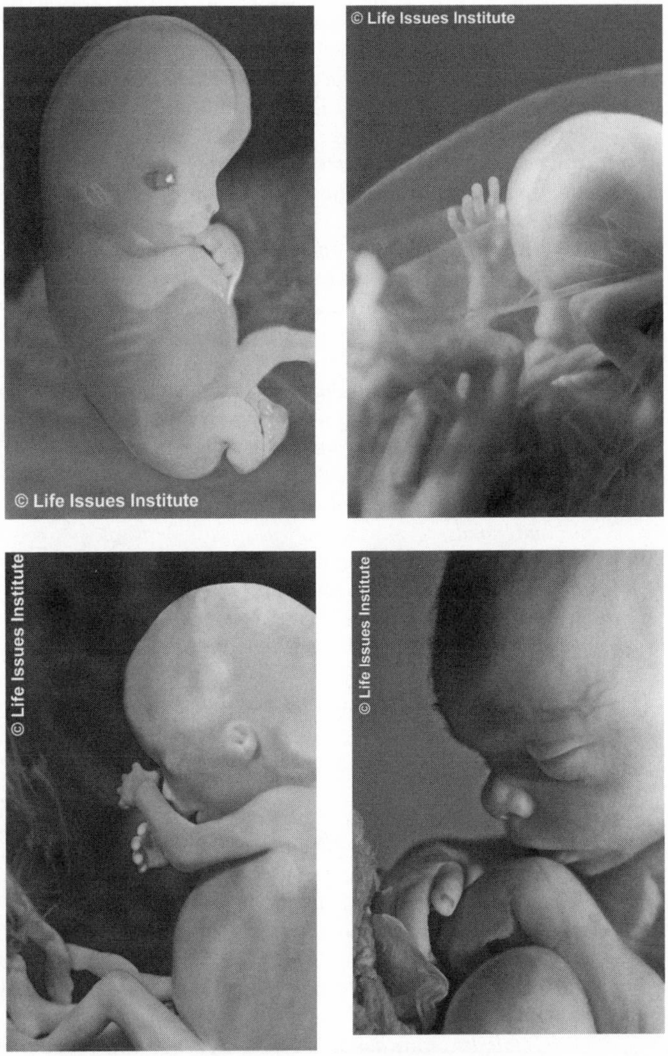

Top left: **This is an image of a seven-week-old fetus.** ***Top right:*** **This is an image of a fourteen-week-old fetus.** ***Bottom left:*** **This is an image of a sixteen-week-old fetus.** ***Bottom right:*** **This is an image of a twenty-week-old fetus (all photographs from Life Issues Institute, all rights reserved).**

head. The skin of the fetus is nearly transparent. Bones become harder as more muscle tissue and bones develop. The fetus is able to swallow amniotic fluid, as well as make active movements. Meconium is filtered in the intestinal tract. Lungs are further developed, sweat glands develop, and the liver and pancreas produce fluid secretions.

Weeks 17–20 of the fetal phase. During this period the fetus reaches a length of 8 inches. Lanugo hair covers the entire body, while the skin becomes less transparent as fat begins to deposit. Nipples begin to appear, along with eyebrows and lashes. Nails appear on the fingers and toes. The heartbeat of the fetus can be heard with a stethoscope. The fetus is more active as muscle development increases. Quickening is evident (the mother can feel the fetus moving).

Weeks 21–24 of the fetal phase. The fetus reaches a length of 11.2 inches during this period and weighs about 1 lb. 10 oz. The entire body of the fetus is covered in vernix caseosa (a protective substance secreted by the fetus). The hair on the head is longer and eyebrows and eyelashes are well formed. Thicker skin develops on the hands and feet, and footprints and fingerprints form.

Weeks 25–28 of the fetal phase. During this time the fetus reaches a length of 15 inches, and weighs about 2 lbs. 11 oz. Rapid brain development occurs, as the nervous system develops enough to control some body functions. Eyelids open and close, while testicles begin descent into the scrotum if the fetus is male.

Weeks 29–32 of the fetal phase. The fetus will reach a length of about 15–17 inches during this phase and weigh about 4 lbs. 6 oz. There is a rapid increase in the amount of body fat, increased control over body functions, full development of bones (though soft and pliable), and body temperature is partially self-controlled. The fetus also begins storing iron, calcium, and phosphorus. The respiratory system is still immature, but it develops to the point where gas exchange is possible. The fetus may be born alive and survive at this point, though the possibility of death is high.

Weeks 33–36 of the fetal phase. During this time the fetus reaches a length of about 16–19 inches and weighs about 5 lbs. 12 oz. to 6 lbs. 12 oz. The lanugo hair begins to disappear. There is an increase in body fat. The fingernails grow to the end of the fingertips. There is increased central nervous system control over body functions. A fetus delivered during this time has a high possibility of surviving, but may need artificial support.

Weeks 37–40 of the fetal phase. Full-term delivery is considered 38 weeks and any delivery over that time is post-term. The fetus will fill the entire uterus now. During this period the fetus may be 17 to 22 inches in length, and typically weigh 7½ lbs. (males tend to weigh slightly more than females). The lanugo hair is gone except on the upper arms and shoulders. Fingernails extend beyond the fingertips and there are small breast buds present on both sexes. Hair on the head is coarse and thicker. *See also* **Amniotic Sac; Female Reproductive System; Male Reproductive System; Placenta; Umbilical Cord**

Fetal Distress

Fetal distress is a medical term without precise meaning. It generally refers to a deteriorating fetal state brought on by the stress of labor. The condition is a factor in causing stillbirth and neonatal death. It is estimated that fetal distress causes over 1100 infant deaths each year in the United States. The deaths are usually attributed to a decrease in intrauterine oxygen and birth suffocation. Fetal distress has also been implicated as a factor in contributing to cerebral palsy and mental retardation.

Fetal Gasoline Syndrome *see* **Fetal Solvent Syndrome**

Fetal Monitoring

Fetal monitoring refers to the use of electronic devices to observe a fetus' heart rate for indications of stress during labor and birth. The monitoring is designed to permit interpretation of the fetus' ability to tolerate labor, and to ascertain whether the fetus has sufficient reserve oxygen. Fetal monitoring may be external or internal. That is, devices may be placed in the womb for direct contact with the fetus, or devices may be attached to the outside of the woman's body. *See also* **Biophysical Profile; Cordocentesis; Doppler Ultrasound Scanning; Fetal Scalp Electrode; Fetoscope; Telemetry Monitor**

Fetal Pain Awareness Consultation

A few states, Arkansas, Illinois, and Oklahoma, require abortion providers inform pregnant women of the possibility of their fetus enduring pain from the abortion procedure. This information is required to be given so that the woman can decide whether to allow the fetus to be given an anesthetic prior to the abortion. The text of Illinois' pain awareness statute is set out below.

Illinois Code Ch. 720, § 510/6(6). Fetal pain awareness

When the fetus is viable and when there exists reasonable medical certainty (a) that the particular method of abortion to be employed will cause organic pain to the fetus, and (b) that use of an anesthetic or analgesic would abolish or alleviate organic pain to the fetus caused by the particular method of abortion to be employed, then the physician who is to perform the abortion or his agent or the referring physician or his agent shall inform the woman upon whom the abortion is to be performed that such an anesthetic or analgesic is available, if he knows it to be available, for use to abolish or alleviate organic pain caused to the fetus by the particular method of abortion to be employed. Any person who performs an abortion with knowledge that any such reasonable medical certainty exists and that such an anesthetic or analgesic is available, and intentionally fails to so inform the woman or to ascertain that the woman has been so informed commits a Class B misdemeanor. The foregoing requirements of subsection (6) of Section 6 shall not apply (a) when in the medical judgment of the physician who is to perform the abortion or the referring physician based upon the particular facts of the case before him: (i) there exists a medical emergency, or (ii) the administration of such an anesthetic or analgesic would decrease a possibility of sustained survival of the fetus apart from the body of the mother, with or without artificial support, or (b) when the physician who is to perform the abortion administers an anesthetic or an analgesic to the woman or the fetus and he knows there exists reasonable medical certainty that such use will abolish organic pain caused to the fetus during the course of the abortion.

Fetal Period

The fetal period is considered to begin around the 11th week of gestation and continues until expulsion. *See also* **Embryonic Period; Fetal Development**

Fetal Reabsorption *see* **Vanishing Twin Syndrome**

Fetal Reduction *see* **Multifetal Pregnancy Reduction**

Fetal Research Act

Congress passed the Fetal Research Act in 1993. Under the Act federal authorities are prohibited from supporting or conducting research on a fetus, unless it is to enhance the well-being of the fetus or will pose no added risk of suffering, injury, or death to the fetus. The Act also prohibits interstate selling of fetal tissue. The statutes addressing the issues are set out below.

42 U.S.C.A. § 289g. Fetal research

(a) The Secretary may not conduct or support any research or experimentation, in the United States or in any other country, on a nonviable living human fetus ex utero or a living human fetus ex utero for whom viability has not been ascertained unless the research or experimentation —

(1) may enhance the well-being or meet the health needs of the fetus or enhance the probability of its survival to viability; or

(2) will pose no added risk of suffering, injury, or death to the fetus and the purpose of the research or experimentation is the development of important biomedical knowledge which cannot be obtained by other means.

(b) In administering the regulations for the protection of human research subjects which —

(1) apply to research conducted or supported by the Secretary;

(2) involve living human fetuses in utero; and

(3) are published in section 46.208 of part 46 of title 45 of the Code of Federal Regulations;

or any successor to such regulations, the Secretary shall require that the risk standard (published in section 46.102(g) of such part 46 or any successor to such regulations) be the same for fetuses which are intended to be aborted and fetuses which are intended to be carried to term.

42 U.S.C.A. § 289g-1. Research on transplantation of fetal tissue

(a) Establishment of program

(1) The Secretary may conduct or support research on the transplantation of human fetal tissue for therapeutic purposes.

(2) Human fetal tissue may be used in research carried out under paragraph (1) regardless of whether the tissue is obtained pursuant to a spontaneous or induced abortion or pursuant to a stillbirth.

(b) Informed consent of donor

(1) In research carried out under subsection (a) of this section, human fetal tissue may be used only if the woman providing the tissue makes a statement, made in writing and signed by the woman, declaring that —

(A) the woman donates the fetal tissue for use in research described in subsection (a) of this section;

(B) the donation is made without any restriction regarding the identity of individuals who may be the recipients of transplantations of the tissue; and

(C) the woman has not been informed of the identity of any such individuals.

(2) In research carried out under subsection (a) of this section, human fetal tissue may be used only if the attending physician with respect to obtaining the tissue from the woman involved makes a statement, made in writing and signed by the physician, declaring that —

(A) in the case of tissue obtained pursuant to an induced abortion —

(i) the consent of the woman for the abortion was obtained prior to requesting or obtaining consent for a donation of the tissue for use in such research;

(ii) no alteration of the timing, method, or procedures used to terminate the pregnancy was made solely for the purposes of obtaining the tissue; and

(iii) the abortion was performed in accordance with applicable State law;

(B) the tissue has been donated by the woman in accordance with paragraph (1); and

(C) full disclosure has been provided to the woman with regard to —

(i) such physician's interest, if any, in the research to be conducted with the tissue; and

(ii) any known medical risks to the woman or risks to her privacy that might be associated with the donation of the tissue and that are in addition to risks of such type that are associated with the woman's medical care.

(c) In research carried out under subsection (a) of this section, human fetal tissue may be used only if the individual with the principal responsibility for conducting the research involved makes a statement, made in writing and signed by the individual, declaring that the individual —

(1) is aware that —

(A) the tissue is human fetal tissue;

(B) the tissue may have been obtained pursuant to a spontaneous or induced abortion or pursuant to a stillbirth; and

(C) the tissue was donated for research purposes;

(2) has provided such information to other individuals with responsibilities regarding the research;

(3) will require, prior to obtaining the consent of an individual to be a recipient of a transplantation of the tissue, written acknowledgment of receipt of such information by such recipient; and

(4) has had no part in any decisions as to the timing, method, or procedures used to terminate the pregnancy made solely for the purposes of the research.

(d) Availability of statements for audit

(1) In research carried out under subsection (a) of this section,

human fetal tissue may be used only if the head of the agency or other entity conducting the research involved certifies to the Secretary that the statements required under subsections (b)(2) and (c) of this section will be available for audit by the Secretary.

(2) Any audit conducted by the Secretary pursuant to paragraph (1) shall be conducted in a confidential manner to protect the privacy rights of the individuals and entities involved in such research, including such individuals and entities involved in the donation, transfer, receipt, or transplantation of human fetal tissue. With respect to any material or information obtained pursuant to such audit, the Secretary shall—

(A) use such material or information only for the purposes of verifying compliance with the requirements of this section;

(B) not disclose or publish such material or information, except where required by Federal law, in which case such material or information shall be coded in a manner such that the identities of such individuals and entities are protected; and

(C) not maintain such material or information after completion of such audit, except where necessary for the purposes of such audit.

(e) Applicability of State and local law

(1) The Secretary may not provide support for research under subsection (a) of this section unless the applicant for the financial assistance involved agrees to conduct the research in accordance with applicable State law.

(2) The Secretary may conduct research under subsection (a) of this section only in accordance with applicable State and local law.

(f) The Secretary shall annually submit to the Committee on Energy and Commerce of the House of Representatives, and to the Committee on Labor and Human Resources of the Senate, a report describing the activities carried out under this section during the preceding fiscal year, including a description of whether and to what extent research under subsection (a) of this section has been conducted in accordance with this section.

(g) For purposes of this section, the term "human fetal tissue" means tissue or cells obtained from a dead human embryo or fetus after a spontaneous or induced abortion, or after a stillbirth.

42 U.S.C.A. § 289g-2. Prohibitions regarding human fetal tissue

(a) It shall be unlawful for any person to knowingly acquire, receive, or otherwise transfer any human fetal tissue for valuable consideration if the transfer affects interstate commerce.

(b) It shall be unlawful for any person to solicit or knowingly acquire, receive, or accept a donation of human fetal tissue for the purpose of transplantation of such tissue into another person if the donation affects interstate commerce, the tissue will be or is obtained pursuant to an induced abortion, and—

(1) the donation will be or is made pursuant to a promise to the donating individual that the donated tissue will be transplanted into a recipient specified by such individual;

(2) the donated tissue will be transplanted into a relative of the donating individual; or

(3) the person who solicits or knowingly acquires, receives, or accepts the donation has provided valuable consideration for the costs associated with such abortion.

(c) It shall be unlawful for any person or entity involved or engaged in interstate commerce to—

(1) solicit or knowingly acquire, receive, or accept a donation of human fetal tissue knowing that a human pregnancy was deliberately initiated to provide such tissue; or

(2) knowingly acquire, receive, or accept tissue or cells obtained from a human embryo or fetus that was gestated in the uterus of a nonhuman animal.

(d) Criminal penalties for violations

(1) Any person who violates subsection (a), (b), or (c) of this section shall be fined in accordance with Title 18, subject to paragraph (2), or imprisoned for not more than 10 years, or both.

(2) With respect to the imposition of a fine under paragraph (1), if the person involved violates subsection (a) or (b)(3) of this section, a fine shall be imposed in an amount not less than twice the amount of the valuable consideration received.

(e) For purposes of this section:

(1) The term "human fetal tissue" has the meaning given such term in section 289g-1(g) of this title.

(2) The term "interstate commerce" has the meaning given such term in section 321(b) of Title 21.

(3) The term "valuable consideration" does not include reasonable payments associated with the transportation, implantation, processing, preservation, quality control, or storage of human fetal tissue.

See also **Embryonic and Fetal Stem-Cell Research**

Fetal Scalp Electrode

A fetal scalp electrode is a device used to record the heart rate of a fetus during labor and delivery. The device is inserted through the vagina and attached to the fetus' scalp. It establishes electrical contact between fetal skin and an external monitoring device. The monitoring can only take place after the membranes of the amniotic sac have ruptured. The device is usually only used in high-risk situations where the fetus may be in danger of fetal distress. There is a slight risk of infection near the site where a small puncture is made to attach the device to the fetus' scalp. *See also* **Fetal Monitoring**

Fetal Solvent Syndrome

Fetal solvent syndrome (also called fetal gasoline syndrome) is a disorder associated with pregnant women seeking to get "high" by sniffing or inhaling organic solvents such as paint, lacquer, glue and gasoline. These solvents contain chemicals that can be fatal to a fetus or cause severe birth defects and brain damage. *See also* **Organic Solvents and Pregnancy**

Fetal Surgery

The majority of fetal congenital malformations are treated after birth. However, because of advancements in methods of prenatal diagnosis, some fetal anomalies may be treated through surgery while the fetus is still in the womb. Fetal surgery usually involves opening the uterus with a caesarean surgical incision, removing the fetus and surgically correcting the fetal abnormality. The fetus is then returned to the uterus and the incision is closed.

Fetal surgery jeopardizes the pregnancy and may place the woman at risk as well. Therefore, the procedure normally is only performed when a correctable problem exists that has the potential of severely harming the fetus or mother, if surgery is not done.

Fetal Transfusion Syndrome

Fetal transfusion syndrome is a condition that occurs only with twins. The condition involves the transfer of blood from one fetus (donor) directly to the other fetus (donee) while in the womb. In this situation the donor twin is usually smaller, anemic and dehydrated; while the donee twin is larger and has too much blood volume (polycythemic). Depending on the severity of the transfusion, both fetuses may be at risk. The risk to the donor is from an inadequate blood volume, and the risk to the donee is from too much blood. While this situation could result in the death of one or both twins, the prognosis for both maybe good when there is proper medical intervention. *See also* **Multifetal Pregnancy Reduction; Monoamnionic Twin Gestation; Monochorionic Twin Gestation; Multiple Gestation; Twin Reversed Arterial Perfusion; Vanishing Twin Syndrome**

Fetal Tumors

There are many types of tumors that can develop during fetal development. Many of them can cause serious illness or death to a fetus or neonate. Fetal tumors may affect any external part of a fetus' body and many internal places. Through the use of ultrasound fetal tumors can be detected and options given to a woman based upon the type of tumor found. The options may include intrauterine treatment, abortion or simply monitoring the fetus. Some of the more serious fetal tumors include: cervical teratoma, intracranial tumors, rhabdomyoma of heart, intrapericardial teratoma and sacrococcygeal teratoma.

Cervical teratoma. Cervical teratoma is a tumor found in the fetal neck that is composed of tissues foreign to cervical region. The exact cause of this tumor is not known. It is a deadly tumor that has a very high rate of stillbirth and neonatal death. The cause of death is usually upper airway obstruction. In some instances surgery has been successful in treating the tumor.

Intracranial tumors. There are several types of intracranial tumors that affect fetuses. They are all located inside the cranium and may appear cystic, solid or both. These tumors are almost always fatal. Some deaths are stillbirth and others are neonate.

Rhabdomyoma of heart. Rhabdomyoma of heart is a tumor that causes excessive growth of muscle elements within the cardiac walls. It is the most common primary cardiac tumor in fetuses. The tumor can cause stillbirth, neonate death, seizures and mental retardation.

Intrapericardial teratoma. Intrapericardial teratoma is a tumor that is usually located in the right side of the heart. It can grow 2–3 times the size of the heart. This tumor will usually cause stillbirth or neonate death.

Sacrococcygeal teratoma. Sacrococcygeal teratoma is tumor that develops in the buttocks region. The cause of this condition is not understood. It is the most common tumor in neonates, occurring in about 1 out of every 35,000 live births. The tumor has a high stillbirth rate because of cardiac complications it may cause. It may also be a threat to the woman. The condition may be treated with surgery. *See also* **Birth Defects and Abortion**

Feticide

A few states, Georgia, Indiana, Iowa and Louisiana, have enacted statutes that create a specific offense called feticide. Feticide refers to the unlawful killing of a fetus. This offense may generally be defined as the intentional injury to a pregnant woman that causes the death of a fetus, under circumstances that would constitute murder if the pregnant woman had died. One state, Missouri, refers to the offense of feticide as infanticide. Several other states, Kentucky, Minnesota, Nebraska, North Dakota, Pennsylvania, South Dakota, and Virginia, have feticide-like statutes, but they do not call the offense feticide. *See also* **Injury to Pregnant Woman; Unborn Victims of Violence Act**

Fetoscope

A fetoscope is a fetal stethoscope. The device is used for listening to fetal heart sounds. Its use is limited insofar as not allowing continuous monitoring as do electronic devices. *See also* **Fetal Monitoring**

Fetoscopy

A fetoscopy is a fibre optic, tubular telescope that is used to look at the fetus while it is still in the womb. To use the device requires a tiny incision in the women's abdominal wall so that the telescope can be passed into the uterus to directly view the fetus. *See also* **Fetal Monitoring**

Fetus *see* **Fetal Development**

Fifth Amendment

The Due Process Clause of the Fifth Amendment to the federal constitution provides as follows: "No person shall be ... deprived of life, liberty, or property, without due process of law." This Clause is applicable only against the federal government.

In *Rust v. Sullivan* the Supreme Court found that the liberty interest in the Due Process Clause was not violated by federal regulations that prohibited pro-abortion counseling, referral, and advocacy by health care providers. The Supreme Court ruled in *Harris v. McRae*, that the Medicaid funding restrictions for abortion by the Hyde Amendment, did not violate the Due Process Clause nor the equal protection component of the Fifth Amendment. *See also* **Fourteenth Amendment; Harris v. McRae; Rust v. Sullivan**

Finkbine, Sherri

Sherri Finkbine (b. 1932) was the host of a popular and leading national children's television show in the early 1960s called Romper Room. In 1962, while in Europe vacationing, Finkbine became ill and was inadvertently given a sedative drug called thalidomide. Upon returning from Europe to her home in Arizona, Finkbine became pregnant while still taking the drug. After becoming pregnant she learned that thalidomide caused severe birth defects. Finkbine decided to have a eugenic abortion.

Although local health care providers had agreed to perform the abortion, the national publicity that surrounded her abortion decision forced them to change their minds. Finkbine was compelled to go to Sweden to obtain the abortion. As a result of her actions, Finkbine lost her television show. However, because of the national division that was generated by her circumstances, Finkbine is credited with planting the seed for events that unfolded in 1973 when the United States Supreme Court legalized abortion in the nation. *See also* **Thalidomide**

First Amendment

The First Amendment of the federal constitution has been used to attack pro-life and pro-choice legislation and activities. The Amendment reads as follows: "Congress shall make no law respecting an establishment of religion, or prohibiting the free exercise thereof; or abridging the freedom of speech, or of the press, or the right of the people peaceably to assemble, and to petition the Government for a redress of grievances."

In *Hill v. Colorado* the United States Supreme Court held that the Free Speech Clause of the First Amendment was not violated by a Colorado statute that made it unlawful for any person within 100 feet of an abortion facility's entrance, to knowingly approach within 8 feet of another person, without that person's consent, in order to pass a leaflet, handbill, display a sign, engage in oral protest, education, or counseling with that person. In *Schenck v. Pro Choice Network of Western New York* the Supreme Court upheld certain federal trial court injunction provisions that imposed fixed buffer zone limitations at abortion clinics, while finding the First Amendment was violated by certain provisions that imposed floating buffer zone limitations.

In *Madsen v. Women's Health Clinic, Inc.* the Supreme Court upheld parts of an injunction that restricted noise by anti-abortionists at a clinic and imposed a 36 foot buffer zone around the clinic entrances and driveway. However, *Madsen* ruled that the Free Speech Clause was violated by a 36 foot buffer zone as applied to the private property to the north and west of the clinic, a restriction on the use of images observable by clinic patients, a 300 foot no approach zone around the clinic, and a 300 foot buffer zone around the residences, because these restrictions swept more broadly than necessary to accomplish the permissible goals of the injunction.

In *Rust v. Sullivan* the Supreme Court found that the Free Speech

Clause was not violated by federal regulations that prohibited pro-abortion counseling, referral, and advocacy by health care providers. In *Frisby v. Schultz* the United States Supreme Court held that the Free Speech Clause was not violated by a town ordinance that was created to prevent pro-life picketing at the residence of an abortion doctor. In *Federal Election Commission v. Massachusetts Citizens for Life, Inc.* the Supreme Court held that federal law that prohibited the appellee from using its treasury funds to promote pro-life political candidates violated the Free Speech Clause. It was held by the Supreme Court in *Bolger v. Youngs Drug Products Corp.*, that a provision of the Comstock Act, 39 U.S.C. § 3001(e)(2), that prohibited mailing unsolicited advertisements for contraceptives violated the Free Speech Clause of the First Amendment. The Supreme Court held in *Bigelow v. Virginia* that the Free Speech and Free Press Clauses of the First Amendment were violated by a Virginia penal statute that prohibited selling or circulating any publication that encouraged or promoted abortions. *See also* **Bigelow v. Virginia; Bolger v. Youngs Drug Products Corp.; Federal Election Commission v. Massachusetts Citizens for Life, Inc.; Hill v. Colorado; Madsen v. Women's Health Center, Inc.; Rust v. Sullivan; Schenck v. Pro Choice Network of Western New York**

First Trimester Abortion *see* **Abortion**

FISH Test

The FISH test (fluorescence in situ hybridization test) is a method of chromosome analysis that is performed with amniotic fluid. This test can provide evidence of congenital fetal disorders. *See also* **Fetal Chromosome Error**

Florida

(1) OVERVIEW

The state of Florida enacted its first criminal abortion statute on August 6, 1868. The statute underwent several amendments prior to the 1973 decision by the United States Supreme Court in *Roe v. Wade*, which legalized abortion in the nation. Although Florida has taken affirmative steps through statutes to respond to *Roe* and its progeny, it still retains a few pre-*Roe* abortion prohibitions. Post-*Roe* statutes have been enacted covering general abortion guidelines, partial-birth abortion, abortion by minors, injury to a pregnant woman, ban on selling embryos, fetal death report, facilities for abortion, abortion clinic rules, abortion referral agencies, abortion consent for incapacitated female, and pro-life license plate.

(2) PRE-ROE PROHIBITIONS

As previously indicated, Florida still retains some abortion prohibitions that are invalid under *Roe v. Wade* and its progeny. The prohibitions are set out below.

Florida Code § 797.02. Advertising drugs, etc., for abortion

Whoever knowingly advertises, prints, publishes, distributes or circulates, or knowingly causes to be advertised, printed, published, distributed or circulated, any pamphlet, printed paper, book, newspaper notice, advertisement, or reference containing words or language giving or conveying any notice, hint, or reference to any person, or the name of any person, real or fictitious, from whom, or to any place, house, shop, or office where any poison, drug, mixture, preparation, medicine, or noxious thing, or any instrument or means whatever, or any advice, direction, information, or knowledge may be obtained for the purpose of causing or procuring the miscarriage of any woman pregnant with child, shall be guilty of a misdemeanor of the first degree, punishable as provided in s. 775.082 or s. 775.083.

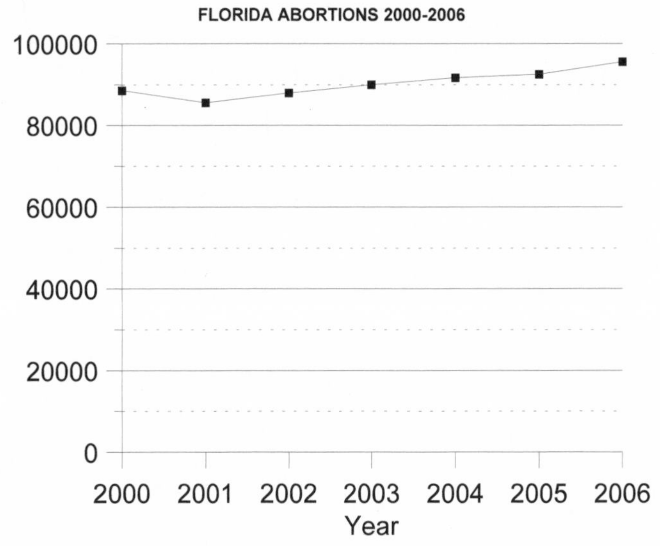

Source: **Florida Department of Health.**

Florida Abortion by Weeks of Gestation 2000–2006

	Year							
Weeks of Gestation	*2000*	*2001*	*2002*	*2003*	*2004*	*2005*	*2006*	*Total*
≤12	80,639	77,985	78,997	81,188	82,782	84,006	86,938	572,535
13–24	7,872	7,572	8,180	8,742	8,918	7,825	8,633	57,742
≥25	50	32	61	59	10	13	4	229
Not known	2	0	726	6	0	19	11	764

Source: **Florida Department of Health.**

Florida Abortion by Reason 2000–2006

	Year							
AbortionReason	*2000*	*2001*	*2002*	*2003*	*2004*	*2005*	*2006*	*Total*
Personal Choice	87,199	84,343	86,445	88,409	90,315	90,866	93,541	621,118
Physical Condition	453	350	439	514	460	514	649	3,379
Mental Condition	143	109	72	80	19	54	144	621
Abnormal Fetus	430	454	482	457	501	606	676	3,606
Other	330	314	521	535	411	473	574	3,158
Not known	8	19	5	0	4	0	2	38

Source: **Florida Department of Health.**

(3) GENERAL ABORTION GUIDELINES

Florida's general abortion statute sets out several restrictions on abortion. Under the statute a third trimester or post-viability abortion may only occur if the woman's life or health is in danger. All abortions must be performed by a physician. Women seeking abortions must provide written consent for the procedure and must be fully informed of the possible health consequences and alternatives to abortion, prior to the procedure. The informed consent provision of the statute was found unconstitutional by a state appellate court in *State v. Presidential Women's Center*, 707 So.2d 1145 (Fla.Ct.App. 1998).

A provision is contained in the general abortion statute that prohibits partial-birth abortion. This provision, however, was found unconstitutional in *A Choice for Women v. Butterworth*, 54 F.Supp.2d 1148 (S.D.Fla. 1998). Under the statute a woman's husband or, in the case of a minor, the maternal grandparents of fetus could bring a lawsuit over the occurrence of a partial-birth abortion. Although Florida did not repeal the partial-birth abortion provision after it was invalidated, the state did enact another separate statute (discussed below) banning partial-birth abortion.

Fetal experimentation has also been prohibited under the general abortion statute. Additionally, the statute permits medical facilities, their employees and physicians to refuse to participate in abortions. The general abortion provisions are set out below.

Florida Code § 390.011. Definitions

As used in this chapter, the term:

(1) "Abortion" means the termination of human pregnancy with an intention other than to produce a live birth or to remove a dead fetus.

(2) "Abortion clinic" or "clinic" means any facility in which abortions are performed. The term does not include:

(a) A hospital; or

(b) A physician's office, provided that the office is not used primarily for the performance of abortions.

(3) "Agency" means the Agency for Health Care Administration.

(4) "Department" means the Department of Health.

(5) "Hospital" means a facility as defined in s. 395.002(12) and licensed under chapter 395 and part II of chapter 408.

(6) "Partial-birth abortion" means a termination of pregnancy in which the physician performing the termination of pregnancy partially vaginally delivers a living fetus before killing the fetus and completing the delivery.

(7) "Physician" means a physician licensed under chapter 458 or chapter 459 or a physician practicing medicine or osteopathic medicine in the employment of the United States.

(8) "Third trimester" means the weeks of pregnancy after the 24th week of pregnancy.

Florida Code § 390.0111. Terminating a pregnancy

(1) Termination in third trimester; when allowed.— No termination of pregnancy shall be performed on any human being in the third trimester of pregnancy unless:

(a) Two physicians certify in writing to the fact that, to a reasonable degree of medical probability, the termination of pregnancy is necessary to save the life or preserve the health of the pregnant woman; or

(b) The physician certifies in writing to the medical necessity for legitimate emergency medical procedures for termination of pregnancy in the third trimester, and another physician is not available for consultation.

(2) Performance by physician required.— No termination of pregnancy shall be performed at any time except by a physician as defined in § 390.011.

(3) Consents required.— A termination of pregnancy may not be performed or induced except with the voluntary and informed written consent of the pregnant woman or, in the case of a mental incompetent, the voluntary and informed written consent of her court-appointed guardian.

(a) Except in the case of a medical emergency, consent to a termination of pregnancy is voluntary and informed only if:

1. The physician who is to perform the procedure, or the referring physician, has, at a minimum, orally, in person, informed the woman of:

a. The nature and risks of undergoing or not undergoing the proposed procedure that a reasonable patient would consider material to making a knowing and willful decision of whether to terminate a pregnancy.

b. The probable gestational age of the fetus at the time the termination of pregnancy is to be performed.

c. The medical risks to the woman and fetus of carrying the pregnancy to term.

2. Printed materials prepared and provided by the department have been provided to the pregnant woman, if she chooses to view these materials, including:

a. A description of the fetus.

b. A list of agencies that offer alternatives to terminating the pregnancy.

c. Detailed information on the availability of medical assistance benefits for prenatal care, childbirth, and neonatal care.

3. The woman acknowledges in writing, before the termination of pregnancy, that the information required to be provided under this subsection has been provided. Nothing in this paragraph is intended to prohibit a physician from providing any additional information which the physician deems material to the woman's informed decision to terminate her pregnancy.

(b) In the event a medical emergency exists and a physician cannot comply with the requirements for informed consent, a physician may terminate a pregnancy if he or she has obtained at least one corroborative medical opinion attesting to the medical necessity for emergency medical procedures and to the fact that to a reasonable degree of medical certainty the continuation of the pregnancy would threaten the life of the pregnant woman. In the event no second physician is available for a corroborating opinion, the physician may proceed but shall document reasons for the medical necessity in the patient's medical records.

(c) Violation of this subsection by a physician constitutes grounds for disciplinary action under § 458.331 or § 459.015. Substantial compliance or reasonable belief that complying with the requirements of informed consent would threaten the life or health of the patient is a defense to any action brought under this paragraph.

(4) Standard of medical care to be used during viability.— If a termination of pregnancy is performed during viability, no person who performs or induces the termination of pregnancy shall fail to use that degree of professional skill, care, and diligence to preserve the life and health of the fetus which such person would be required to exercise in order to preserve the life and health of any fetus intended to be born and not aborted. "Viability" means that stage of fetal development when the life of the unborn child may with a reasonable degree of medical probability be continued indefinitely outside the womb. Notwithstanding the provisions of this subsection, the woman's life and health shall constitute an overriding and superior consideration to the concern for the life and health of the fetus when such concerns are in conflict.

(5) Partial-birth abortion prohibited; exception.—

(a) No physician shall knowingly perform a partial-birth abortion.

(b) A woman upon whom a partial-birth abortion is performed may not be prosecuted under this section for a conspiracy to violate the provisions of this section.

(c) This subsection shall not apply to a partial-birth abortion that is necessary to save the life of a mother whose life is endangered by a physical disorder, illness, or injury, provided that no other medical procedure would suffice for that purpose.

(6) Experimentation on fetus prohibited; exception.— No person shall use any live fetus or live, premature infant for any type of scientific, research, laboratory, or other kind of experimentation either prior to or subsequent to any termination of pregnancy procedure except as necessary to protect or preserve the life and health of such fetus or premature infant.

(7) Fetal remains.— Fetal remains shall be disposed of in a sanitary and appropriate manner and in accordance with standard health practices, as provided by rule of the Department of Health. Failure to dispose of fetal remains in accordance with department rules is a misdemeanor of the second degree, punishable as provided in § 775.082 or § 775.083.

(8) Refusal to participate in termination procedure.— Nothing in this section shall require any hospital or any person to participate in the termination of a pregnancy, nor shall any hospital or any person be liable for such refusal. No person who is a member of, or associated with, the staff of a hospital, nor any employee of a hospital or physician in which

or by whom the termination of a pregnancy has been authorized or performed, who shall state an objection to such procedure on moral or religious grounds shall be required to participate in the procedure which will result in the termination of pregnancy. The refusal of any such person or employee to participate shall not form the basis for any disciplinary or other recriminatory action against such person.

(9) Exception.— The provisions of this section shall not apply to the performance of a procedure which terminates a pregnancy in order to deliver a live child.

(10) Penalties for violation.— Except as provided in subsections (3) and (7):

(a) Any person who willfully performs, or actively participates in, a termination of pregnancy procedure in violation of the requirements of this section commits a felony of the third degree, punishable as provided in § 775.082, § 775.083, or § 775.084.

(b) Any person who performs, or actively participates in, a termination of pregnancy procedure in violation of the provisions of this section which results in the death of the woman commits a felony of the second degree, punishable as provided in § 775.082, § 775.083, or § 775.084.

(11) Civil action pursuant to partial-birth abortion; relief.—

(a) The father, if married to the mother at the time she receives a partial-birth abortion, and, if the mother has not attained the age of 18 years at the time she receives a partial-birth abortion, the maternal grandparents of the fetus may, in a civil action, obtain appropriate relief, unless the pregnancy resulted from the plaintiff's criminal conduct or the plaintiff consented to the abortion.

(b) In a civil action under this section, appropriate relief includes:

1. Monetary damages for all injuries, psychological and physical, occasioned by the violation of subsection (5).

2. Damages equal to three times the cost of the partial-birth abortion.

(4) PARTIAL-BIRTH ABORTION

As previously indicated, Florida enacted a second criminal partial-birth abortion law after its first law on the issue was expressly found unconstitutional by a federal district court. The second law may also be invalid as a result of the United States Supreme Court decision in *Stenberg v. Carhart*, which invalidated a Nebraska statute that prohibited partial-birth abortions. On the other hand, if Florida's new law is found to come within the United States Supreme Court decision in *Gonzales v. Carhart*, which upheld a federal partial-birth abortion statute, then the new law is valid. Florida's partial-birth abortion ban statutes are set out below.

Florida Code § 782.30. Short title

Sections 782.30-782.36 may be cited as the "Partial-Birth Abortion Act."

Florida Code § 782.32. Definitions

As used in this act, the term:

(1) "Partially born" means the living fetus's intact body, with the entire head attached, is presented so that:

(a) There has been delivered past the mother's vaginal opening:

1. The fetus's entire head, in the case of a cephalic presentation, up until the point of complete separation from the mother whether or not the placenta has been delivered or the umbilical cord has been severed; or

2. Any portion of the fetus's torso above the navel, in the case of a breech presentation, up until the point of complete separation from the mother whether or not the placenta has been delivered or the umbilical cord has been severed.

(b) There has been delivered outside the mother's abdominal wall:

1. The fetus's entire head, in the case of a cephalic presentation, up until the point of complete separation from the mother whether or not the placenta has been delivered or the umbilical cord has been severed; or

2. Any portion of the child's torso above the navel, in the case of a breech presentation, up until the point of complete separation from the mother whether or not the placenta has been delivered or the umbilical cord has been severed.

(2) "Living fetus" means any unborn member of the human species who has a heartbeat or discernible spontaneous movement.

(3) "Suction or sharp curettage abortion" means an abortion, as defined in chapter 390, in which the developing fetus and the products of conception are evacuated from the uterus through a suction cannula with an attached vacuum apparatus or with a sharp curette.

Florida Code § 782.34. Partial-birth abortion offense

Except as provided in § 782.36, any person who intentionally kills a living fetus while that fetus is partially born commits the crime of partial-birth abortion, which is a felony of the second degree, punishable as provided in § 775.082, § 775.083, or § 775.084.

Florida Code § 782.36. Exceptions to partial-birth abortion ban

(1) A patient receiving a partial-birth-abortion procedure may not be prosecuted under this act.

(2) This act does not apply to a suction or sharp curettage abortion.

(3) This act does not constitute implicit approval of other types of abortion, which remain subject to all other applicable laws of this state.

(4) This act does not prohibit a physician from taking such measures as are necessary to save the life of a mother whose life is endangered by a physical disorder, physical illness, or physical injury, provided that every reasonable precaution is also taken, in such cases, to save the fetus' life.

(5) ABORTION BY MINORS

Florida has a constitutional provision which authorizes the legislature to implement laws requiring parental notice before a minor obtains an abortion. Under the laws of Florida no physician may perform an abortion upon an unemancipated minor, unless he/she first notifies either parent or the legal guardian of the minor. An abortion may not occur until 48 hours after such notice has been made. However, in compliance with federal constitutional law, Florida has provided a judicial waiver procedure for an unemancipated minor to obtain an abortion without parental or guardian notice. The minor may petition a trial court for a waiver of the notice requirement. A minor has a right to an attorney at the proceeding and if she cannot afford one, the court must appoint her an attorney. If a minor chooses, she may represent herself. The required parental or guardian notice may be waived if the court finds that (1) the minor is mature and well-informed enough to make the abortion decision on her own, (2) the minor is a victim of child abuse or sexual abuse by one or both of her parents or her guardian, or (3) the performance of the abortion would be in the best interest of the minor. An expedited appeal is available to any minor to whom the court denies a waiver of notification. The statute has been litigated in the following cases: *Womancare of Orlando, Inc. v. Agwunobi*, 448 F.Supp.2d 1309 (N.D.Fla. 2006); *In re Doe*, 948 So.2d 30 (Fla.App. 2006); *In re Doe*, 943 So.2d 806 (Fla.App. 2006); *In re Doe*, 924 So.2d 935 (Fla.App. 2006); *In re Doe*, 921 So.2d 753 (Fla.App. 2006); *Womancare of Orlando, Inc. v. Agwunobi*, 448 F.Supp. 2d 1293 (N.D.Fla. 2005); *In re Doe*, 932 So.2d 278 (Fla.App. 2005); *In re A.S.*, 909 So.2d 524 (Fla.App. 2005).The constitutional provision and statutes addressing issues involving minors are set out below.

Florida Const. Art. 10 § 22. Parental notice

The legislature shall not limit or deny the privacy right guaranteed to a minor under the United States Constitution as interpreted by the United

States Supreme Court. Notwithstanding a minor's right of privacy provided in Section 23 of Article I, the Legislature is authorized to require by general law for notification to a parent or guardian of a minor before the termination of the minor's pregnancy. The Legislature shall provide exceptions to such requirement for notification and shall create a process for judicial waiver of the notification.

Florida Code § 390.01114. Parental notice and judicial bypass

(1) Short title.— This section may be cited as the "Parental Notice of Abortion Act."

(2) Definitions.— As used in this section, the term:

(a) "Actual notice" means notice that is given directly, in person or by telephone, to a parent or legal guardian of a minor, by a physician, at least 48 hours before the inducement or performance of a termination of pregnancy, and documented in the minor's files.

(b) "Child abuse" has the same meaning as s. 39.0015(3).

(c) "Constructive notice" means notice that is given in writing, signed by the physician, and mailed at least 72 hours before the inducement or performance of the termination of pregnancy, to the last known address of the parent or legal guardian of the minor, by certified mail, return receipt requested, and delivery restricted to the parent or legal guardian. After the 72 hours have passed, delivery is deemed to have occurred.

(d) "Medical emergency" means a condition that, on the basis of a physician's good faith clinical judgment, so complicates the medical condition of a pregnant woman as to necessitate the immediate termination of her pregnancy to avert her death, or for which a delay in the termination of her pregnancy will create serious risk of substantial and irreversible impairment of a major bodily function.

(e) "Sexual abuse" has the meaning ascribed in s. 39.01.

(f) "Minor" means a person under the age of 18 years.

(3) Notification required.—

(a) Actual notice shall be provided by the physician performing or inducing the termination of pregnancy before the performance or inducement of the termination of the pregnancy of a minor. The notice may be given by a referring physician. The physician who performs or induces the termination of pregnancy must receive the written statement of the referring physician certifying that the referring physician has given notice. If actual notice is not possible after a reasonable effort has been made, the physician performing or inducing the termination of pregnancy or the referring physician must give constructive notice. Notice given under this subsection by the physician performing or inducing the termination of pregnancy must include the name and address of the facility providing the termination of pregnancy and the name of the physician providing notice. Notice given under this subsection by a referring physician must include the name and address of the facility where he or she is referring the minor and the name of the physician providing notice. If actual notice is provided by telephone, the physician must actually speak with the parent or guardian, and must record in the minor's medical file the name of the parent or guardian provided notice, the phone number dialed, and the date and time of the call. If constructive notice is given, the physician must document that notice by placing copies of any document related to the constructive notice, including, but not limited to, a copy of the letter and the return receipt, in the minor's medical file.

(b) Notice is not required if:

1. In the physician's good faith clinical judgment, a medical emergency exists and there is insufficient time for the attending physician to comply with the notification requirements. If a medical emergency exists, the physician may proceed but must document reasons for the medical necessity in the patient's medical records;

2. Notice is waived in writing by the person who is entitled to notice;

3. Notice is waived by the minor who is or has been married or has had the disability of nonage removed under s. 743.015 or a similar statute of another state;

4. Notice is waived by the patient because the patient has a minor child dependent on her; or

5. Notice is waived under subsection (4).

(c) Violation of this subsection by a physician constitutes grounds for disciplinary action under s. 458.331 or s. 459.015.

(4) Procedure for judicial waiver of notice.—

(a) A minor may petition any circuit court in a judicial circuit within the jurisdiction of the District Court of Appeal in which she resides for a waiver of the notice requirements of subsection (3) and may participate in proceedings on her own behalf. The petition may be filed under a pseudonym or through the use of initials, as provided by court rule. The petition must include a statement that the petitioner is pregnant and notice has not been waived. The court shall advise the minor that she has a right to court-appointed counsel and shall provide her with counsel upon her request at no cost to the minor.

(b) Court proceedings under this subsection must be given precedence over other pending matters to the extent necessary to ensure that the court reaches a decision promptly. The court shall rule, and issue written findings of fact and conclusions of law, within 48 hours after the petition is filed, except that the 48-hour limitation may be extended at the request of the minor. If the court fails to rule within the 48-hour period and an extension has not been requested, the petition is granted, and the notice requirement is waived.

(c) If the court finds, by clear and convincing evidence, that the minor is sufficiently mature to decide whether to terminate her pregnancy, the court shall issue an order authorizing the minor to consent to the performance or inducement of a termination of pregnancy without the notification of a parent or guardian. If the court does not make the finding specified in this paragraph or paragraph (d), it must dismiss the petition.

(d) If the court finds, by a preponderance of the evidence, that there is evidence of child abuse or sexual abuse of the petitioner by one or both of her parents or her guardian, or that the notification of a parent or guardian is not in the best interest of the petitioner, the court shall issue an order authorizing the minor to consent to the performance or inducement of a termination of pregnancy without the notification of a parent or guardian. If the court finds evidence of child abuse or sexual abuse of the minor petitioner by any person, the court shall report the evidence of child abuse or sexual abuse of the petitioner, as provided in s. 39.201. If the court does not make the finding specified in this paragraph or paragraph (c), it must dismiss the petition.

(e) A court that conducts proceedings under this section shall provide for a written transcript of all testimony and proceedings and issue written and specific factual findings and legal conclusions supporting its decision and shall order that a confidential record be maintained, as required under s. 390.01116. At the hearing, the court shall hear evidence relating to the emotional development, maturity, intellect, and understanding of the minor, and all other relevant evidence. All hearings under this section, including appeals, shall remain confidential and closed to the public, as provided by court rule.

(f) An expedited appeal shall be available, as the Supreme Court provides by rule, to any minor to whom the circuit court denies a waiver of notice. An order authorizing a termination of pregnancy without notice is not subject to appeal.

(g) No filing fees or court costs shall be required of any pregnant minor who petitions a court for a waiver of parental notification under this subsection at either the trial or the appellate level.

(h) No county shall be obligated to pay the salaries, costs, or expenses of any counsel appointed by the court under this subsection.

(5) Proceedings.— The Supreme Court is requested to adopt rules and forms for petitions to ensure that proceedings under subsection (4) are handled expeditiously and in a manner consistent with this act. The Supreme Court is also requested to adopt rules to ensure that the hearings protect the minor's confidentiality and the confidentiality of the proceedings.

(6) Report.— The Supreme Court, through the Office of the State Courts Administrator, shall report by February 1 of each year to the Governor, the President of the Senate, and the Speaker of the House of Representatives on the number of petitions filed under subsection (4) for the preceding year, and the timing and manner of disposal of such petitions by each circuit court.

Florida Code § 390.01116. Waiver of notice petition

When a minor petitions a circuit court for a waiver, as provided in s. 390.01114, of the notice requirements pertaining to a minor seeking to terminate her pregnancy, any information in a record held by the circuit court or an appellate court which could be used to identify the minor is confidential and exempt from s. 119.07(1) and s. 24(a), Art. I of the State Constitution.

(6) INJURY TO A PREGNANT WOMAN

Under specific circumstances, Florida makes it a criminal offense to cause the death of a viable fetus through the use of an automobile. The state also has a statute that criminalizes any willful conduct that causes injury to a pregnant woman and the death of her fetus. The statutes addressing the matters are set out below.

Florida Code § 782.071. Vehicular homicide

"Vehicular homicide" is the killing of a human being, or the killing of a viable fetus by any injury to the mother, caused by the operation of a motor vehicle by another in a reckless manner likely to cause the death of, or great bodily harm to, another.

(1) Vehicular homicide is:

(a) A felony of the second degree, punishable as provided in s. 775.082, s. 775.083, or s. 775.084.

(b) A felony of the first degree, punishable as provided in s. 775.082, s. 775.083, or s. 775.084, if:

1. At the time of the accident, the person knew, or should have known, that the accident occurred; and

2. The person failed to give information and render aid as required by s. 316.062.

This paragraph does not require that the person knew that the accident resulted in injury or death.

(2) For purposes of this section, a fetus is viable when it becomes capable of meaningful life outside the womb through standard medical measures.

(3) A right of action for civil damages shall exist under s. 768.19, under all circumstances, for all deaths described in this section.

(4) In addition to any other punishment, the court may order the person to serve 120 community service hours in a trauma center or hospital that regularly receives victims of vehicle accidents, under the supervision of a registered nurse, an emergency room physician, or an emergency medical technician pursuant to a voluntary community service program operated by the trauma center or hospital.

Florida Code § 782.09. Killing of fetus by injury to mother

(1) The unlawful killing of an unborn quick child, by any injury to the mother of such child which would be murder if it resulted in the death of such mother, shall be deemed murder in the same degree as that which would have been committed against the mother. Any person, other than the mother, who unlawfully kills an unborn quick child by any injury to the mother:

(a) Which would be murder in the first degree constituting a capital felony if it resulted in the mother's death commits murder in the first degree constituting a capital felony, punishable as provided in s. 775.082.

(b) Which would be murder in the second degree if it resulted in the mother's death commits murder in the second degree, a felony of the first degree, punishable as provided in s. 775.082, s. 775.083, or s. 775.084.

(c) Which would be murder in the third degree if it resulted in the mother's death commits murder in the third degree, a felony of the second degree, punishable as provided in s. 775.082, s. 775.083, or s. 775.084.

(2) The unlawful killing of an unborn quick child by any injury to the mother of such child which would be manslaughter if it resulted in the death of such mother shall be deemed manslaughter. A person who unlawfully kills an unborn quick child by any injury to the mother which would be manslaughter if it resulted in the mother's death commits manslaughter, a felony of the second degree, punishable as provided in s. 775.082, s. 775.083, or s. 775.084.

(3) The death of the mother resulting from the same act or criminal episode that caused the death of the unborn quick child does not bar prosecution under this section.

(4) This section does not authorize the prosecution of any person in connection with a termination of pregnancy pursuant to chapter 390.

(5) For purposes of this section, the definition of the term "unborn quick child" shall be determined in accordance with the definition of viable fetus as set forth in s. 782.071.

(7) BAN ON SELLING EMBRYOS

The state of Florida has attempted to address the market demand for embryos used in experiments by banning advertisement and the sale of human embryos. The statute addressing the matter is set out below.

Florida Code § 873.05. Advertising or selling embryos

(1) No person shall knowingly advertise or offer to purchase or sell, or purchase, sell, or otherwise transfer, any human embryo for valuable consideration.

(2) As used in this section, the term "valuable consideration" does not include the reasonable costs associated with the removal, storage, and transportation of a human embryo.

(3) A person who violates the provisions of this section is guilty of a felony of the second degree, punishable as provided in § 775.082, § 775.083, or § 775.084.

(8) FETAL DEATH REPORT

Florida requires that all induced abortions be reported to authorities. The statute addressing the issue is set out below.

Florida Code § 390.0112. Termination of pregnancies reporting

(1) The director of any medical facility in which any pregnancy is terminated shall submit a monthly report which contains the number of procedures performed, the reason for same, and the period of gestation at the time such procedures were performed to the agency. The agency shall be responsible for keeping such reports in a central place from which statistical data and analysis can be made.

(2) If the termination of pregnancy is not performed in a medical facility, the physician performing the procedure shall be responsible for reporting such information as required in subsection (1).

(3) Reports submitted pursuant to this section shall be confidential and exempt from the provisions of s. 119.07(1) and shall not be revealed except upon the order of a court of competent jurisdiction in a civil or criminal proceeding.

(4) Any person required under this section to file a report or keep any records who willfully fails to file such report or keep such records may be subject to a $200 fine for each violation. The agency shall be required to impose such fines when reports or records required under this section

have not been timely received. For purposes of this section, timely received is defined as 30 days following the preceding month.

(9) FACILITIES FOR ABORTION

Florida requires all abortions take place in facilities licensed to perform abortions or in the office of a physician. The state also requires that all third trimester abortions occur at a hospital. The statute addressing the matter is set out below.

Florida Code § 797.03. Licensed facility for abortion

(1) It is unlawful for any person to perform or assist in performing an abortion on a person, except in an emergency care situation, other than in a validly licensed hospital or abortion clinic or in a physician's office.

(2) It is unlawful for any person or public body to establish, conduct, manage, or operate an abortion clinic without a valid current license.

(3) It is unlawful for any person to perform or assist in performing an abortion on a person in the third trimester other than in a hospital.

(4) Any person who willfully violates any provision of this section is guilty of a misdemeanor of the second degree, punishable as provided in § 775.082 or § 775.083.

(10) ABORTION CLINIC RULES

Florida has provided by statute for the creation of rules that govern abortion facilities, procedures, patient care and disposal of aborted fetuses. The state has also provided by statute for licensure requirements of clinics. The statutes addressing the issues are set out below.

Florida Code § 390.012. Agency rules

(1) The agency may develop and enforce rules pursuant to ss. 390.001-390.018 and part II of chapter 408 for the health, care, and treatment of persons in abortion clinics and for the safe operation of such clinics.

(a) The rules shall be reasonably related to the preservation of maternal health of the clients.

(b) The rules shall be in accordance with s. 797.03 and may not impose an unconstitutional burden on a woman's freedom to decide whether to terminate her pregnancy.

(c) The rules shall provide for:

1. The performance of pregnancy termination procedures only by a licensed physician.

2. The making, protection, and preservation of patient records, which shall be treated as medical records under chapter 458.

(2) For clinics that perform abortions in the first trimester of pregnancy only, these rules shall be comparable to rules that apply to all surgical procedures requiring approximately the same degree of skill and care as the performance of first trimester abortions.

(3) For clinics that perform or claim to perform abortions after the first trimester of pregnancy, the agency shall adopt rules pursuant to ss. 120.536(1) and 120.54 to implement the provisions of this chapter, including the following:

(a) Rules for an abortion clinic's physical facilities. At a minimum, these rules shall prescribe standards for:

1. Adequate private space that is specifically designated for interviewing, counseling, and medical evaluations.

2. Dressing rooms for staff and patients.

3. Appropriate lavatory areas.

4. Areas for preprocedure hand washing.

5. Private procedure rooms.

6. Adequate lighting and ventilation for abortion procedures.

7. Surgical or gynecological examination tables and other fixed equipment.

8. Postprocedure recovery rooms that are equipped to meet the patients' needs.

9. Emergency exits to accommodate a stretcher or gurney.

10. Areas for cleaning and sterilizing instruments.

11. Adequate areas for the secure storage of medical records and necessary equipment and supplies.

12. The display in the abortion clinic, in a place that is conspicuous to all patients, of the clinic's current license issued by the agency.

(b) Rules to prescribe abortion clinic supplies and equipment standards, including supplies and equipment that are required to be immediately available for use or in an emergency. At a minimum, these rules shall:

1. Prescribe required clean and sterilized equipment and supplies, including medications, required for the conduct, in an appropriate fashion, of any abortion procedure that the medical staff of the clinic anticipates performing and for monitoring the progress of each patient throughout the procedure and recovery period.

2. Prescribe required equipment, supplies, and medications that shall be available and ready for immediate use in an emergency and requirements for written protocols and procedures to be followed by staff in an emergency, such as the loss of electrical power.

3. Prescribe equipment and supplies for required laboratory tests and requirements for protocols to calibrate and maintain laboratory equipment or equipment operated by clinic staff at the abortion clinic.

4. Require ultrasound equipment.

5. Require that all equipment is safe for the patient and the staff, meets applicable federal standards, and is checked annually to ensure safety and appropriate calibration.

(c) Rules relating to abortion clinic personnel. At a minimum, these rules shall require that:

1. The abortion clinic designate a medical director who is licensed to practice medicine in this state and who has admitting privileges at a licensed hospital in this state or has a transfer agreement with a licensed hospital within reasonable proximity of the clinic.

2. If a physician is not present after an abortion is performed, a registered nurse, licensed practical nurse, advanced registered nurse practitioner, or physician assistant shall be present and remain at the clinic to provide postoperative monitoring and care until the patient is discharged.

3. Surgical assistants receive training in counseling, patient advocacy, and the specific responsibilities associated with the services the surgical assistants provide.

4. Volunteers receive training in the specific responsibilities associated with the services the volunteers provide, including counseling and patient advocacy as provided in the rules adopted by the director for different types of volunteers based on their responsibilities.

(d) Rules relating to the medical screening and evaluation of each abortion clinic patient. At a minimum, these rules shall require:

1. A medical history including reported allergies to medications, antiseptic solutions, or latex; past surgeries; and an obstetric and gynecological history.

2. A physical examination, including a bimanual examination estimating uterine size and palpation of the adnexa.

3. The appropriate laboratory tests, including:

a. For an abortion in which an ultrasound examination is not performed before the abortion procedure, urine or blood tests for pregnancy performed before the abortion procedure.

b. A test for anemia.

c. Rh typing, unless reliable written documentation of blood type is available.

d. Other tests as indicated from the physical examination.

4. An ultrasound evaluation for all patients who elect to have an abortion after the first trimester. The rules shall require that if a person who is not a physician performs an ultrasound examination, that person shall have documented evidence that he or she has completed a course in the operation of ultrasound equipment as prescribed in rule. The physician, registered nurse, licensed practical nurse, advanced registered nurse practitioner, or physician assistant shall review, at the request of the patient, the ultrasound evaluation results, including an estimate of the probable gestational age of the fetus, with the patient before the abortion procedure is performed.

5. That the physician is responsible for estimating the gestational age of the fetus based on the ultrasound examination and obstetric standards in keeping with established standards of care regarding the estimation of fetal age as defined in rule and shall write the estimate in the patient's medical history. The physician shall keep original prints of each ultrasound examination of a patient in the patient's medical history file.

(e) Rules relating to the abortion procedure. At a minimum, these rules shall require:

1. That a physician, registered nurse, licensed practical nurse, advanced registered nurse practitioner, or physician assistant is available to all patients throughout the abortion procedure.

2. Standards for the safe conduct of abortion procedures that conform to obstetric standards in keeping with established standards of care regarding the estimation of fetal age as defined in rule.

3. Appropriate use of general and local anesthesia, analgesia, and sedation if ordered by the physician.

4. Appropriate precautions, such as the establishment of intravenous access at least for patients undergoing post-first trimester abortions.

5. Appropriate monitoring of the vital signs and other defined signs and markers of the patient's status throughout the abortion procedure and during the recovery period until the patient's condition is deemed to be stable in the recovery room.

(f) Rules that prescribe minimum recovery room standards. At a minimum, these rules shall require that:

1. Postprocedure recovery rooms are supervised and staffed to meet the patients' needs.

2. Immediate postprocedure care consists of observation in a supervised recovery room for as long as the patient's condition warrants.

3. The clinic arranges hospitalization if any complication beyond the medical capability of the staff occurs or is suspected.

4. A registered nurse, licensed practical nurse, advanced registered nurse practitioner, or physician assistant who is trained in the management of the recovery area and is capable of providing basic cardiopulmonary resuscitation and related emergency procedures remains on the premises of the abortion clinic until all patients are discharged.

5. A physician shall sign the discharge order and be readily accessible and available until the last patient is discharged to facilitate the transfer of emergency cases if hospitalization of the patient or viable fetus is necessary.

6. A physician discusses Rho(D) immune globulin with each patient for whom it is indicated and ensures that it is offered to the patient in the immediate postoperative period or that it will be available to her within 72 hours after completion of the abortion procedure. If the patient refuses the Rho(D) immune globulin, a refusal form approved by the agency shall be signed by the patient and a witness and included in the medical record.

7. Written instructions with regard to postabortion coitus, signs of possible problems, and general aftercare are given to each patient. Each patient shall have specific written instructions regarding access to medical care for complications, including a telephone number to call for medical emergencies.

8. There is a specified minimum length of time that a patient remains in the recovery room by type of abortion procedure and duration of gestation.

9. The physician ensures that a registered nurse, licensed practical nurse, advanced registered nurse practitioner, or physician assistant from the abortion clinic makes a good faith effort to contact the patient by telephone, with the patient's consent, within 24 hours after surgery to assess the patient's recovery.

10. Equipment and services are readily accessible to provide appropriate emergency resuscitative and life support procedures pending the transfer of the patient or viable fetus to the hospital.

(g) Rules that prescribe standards for followup care. At a minimum, these rules shall require that:

1. A postabortion medical visit that includes a medical examination and a review of the results of all laboratory tests is offered.

2. A urine pregnancy test is obtained at the time of the followup visit to rule out continuing pregnancy.

3. If a continuing pregnancy is suspected, the patient shall be evaluated and a physician who performs abortions shall be consulted.

(h) Rules to prescribe minimum abortion clinic incident reporting. At a minimum, these rules shall require that:

1. The abortion clinic records each incident that results in serious injury to a patient or a viable fetus at an abortion clinic and shall report an incident in writing to the agency within 10 days after the incident occurs. For the purposes of this paragraph, "serious injury" means an injury that occurs at an abortion clinic and that creates a serious risk of substantial impairment of a major bodily organ.

2. If a patient's death occurs, other than a fetal death properly reported pursuant to law, the abortion clinic reports it to the department not later than the next department workday.

(4) The rules adopted pursuant to this section shall not limit the ability of a physician to advise a patient on any health issue.

(5) The provisions of this section and the rules adopted pursuant hereto shall be in addition to any other laws, rules, and regulations which are applicable to facilities defined as abortion clinics under this section.

(6) The agency may adopt and enforce rules, in the interest of protecting the public health, to ensure the prompt and proper disposal of fetal remains and tissue resulting from pregnancy termination.

(7) If any owner, operator, or employee of an abortion clinic fails to dispose of fetal remains and tissue in a manner consistent with the disposal of other human tissue in a competent professional manner, the license of such clinic may be suspended or revoked, and such person is guilty of a misdemeanor of the first degree, punishable as provided in s. 775.082 or s. 775.083.

Florida Code § 390.014. Licenses

(1) The requirements of part II of chapter 408 shall apply to the provision of services that require licensure pursuant to ss. 390.011-390.018 and part II of chapter 408 and to entities licensed by or applying for such licensure from the Agency for Health Care Administration pursuant to ss. 390.011-390.018. A license issued by the agency is required in order to operate a clinic in this state.

(2) A separate license shall be required for each clinic maintained on separate premises, even though it is operated by the same management as another clinic; but a separate license shall not be required for separate buildings on the same premises.

(3) In accordance with s. 408.805, an applicant or licensee shall pay

a fee for each license application submitted under this part and part II of chapter 408. The amount of the fee shall be established by rule and may not be less than $70 or more than $500.

(4) Counties and municipalities applying for licenses under this act shall be exempt from the payment of the license fees.

Florida Code § 390.015. Application for license

In addition to the requirements of part II of chapter 408, an application for a license to operate an abortion clinic shall be made to the agency and must include the location of the clinic for which application is made and a statement that local zoning ordinances permit such location.

Florida Code § 390.018. Administrative fine

In addition to the requirements of part II of chapter 408, the agency may impose a fine upon the clinic in an amount not to exceed $1,000 for each violation of any provision of this part, part II of chapter 408, or applicable rules.

(11) ABORTION REFERRAL AGENCIES

Florida provides by statute that abortion referral agencies must provide certain information to a female seeking an abortion. Failure to provide such information is deemed a criminal offense. The statute addressing the issue is set out below.

Florida Code § 390.025. Abortion referral or counseling agencies

(1) As used in this section, an "abortion referral or counseling agency" is any person, group, or organization, whether funded publicly or privately, that provides advice or help to persons in obtaining abortions.

(2) An abortion referral or counseling agency, before making a referral or aiding a person in obtaining an abortion, shall furnish such person with a full and detailed explanation of abortion, including the effects of and alternatives to abortion. If the person advised is a minor, a good faith effort shall be made by the referral or counseling agency to furnish such information to the parents or guardian of the minor. No abortion referral or counseling agency shall charge or accept any fee, kickback, or compensation of any nature from a physician, hospital, clinic, or other medical facility for referring a person thereto for an abortion.

(3) Any person who violates the provisions of this section is guilty of a misdemeanor of the first degree, punishable as provided in s. 775.082 or s. 775.083.

(12) ABORTION CONSENT FOR INCAPACITATED FEMALE

Florida does not permit a guardian of any description to consent to an abortion for an incapacitated female, without first obtaining court approval. The statutes addressing the issue are set out below.

Florida Code § 765.113. Restrictions on providing consent

Unless the principal expressly delegates such authority to the surrogate in writing, or a surrogate or proxy has sought and received court approval pursuant to rule 5.900 of the Florida Probate Rules, a surrogate or proxy may not provide consent for:

(1) Abortion, sterilization, electroshock therapy, psychosurgery, experimental treatments that have not been approved by a federally approved institutional review board in accordance with 45 C.F.R. part 46 or 21 C.F.R. part 56, or voluntary admission to a mental health facility.

(2) Withholding or withdrawing life-prolonging procedures from a pregnant patient prior to viability as defined in s. 390.0111(4).

Florida Code § 744.3215(4). Rights of incapacitated person

(4) Without first obtaining specific authority from the court, as described in s. 744.3725, a guardian may not:

***

(e) Consent on behalf of the ward to the performance of a sterilization or abortion procedure on the ward.

(13) PRO-LIFE LICENSE PLATE

Florida authorizes the issuance of "Choose Life" license plates for motor vehicles. The statute addressing the issue is set out below.

Florida Code § 320.08058(29). Specialty license plates

(29) Choose Life license plates.—

(a) The department shall develop a Choose Life license plate as provided in this section. The word "Florida" must appear at the bottom of the plate, and the words " Choose Life " must appear at the top of the plate.

(b) The annual use fees shall be distributed annually to each county in the ratio that the annual use fees collected by each county bears to the total fees collected for the plates within the state. Each county shall distribute the funds to nongovernmental, not-for-profit agencies within the county, which agencies' services are limited to counseling and meeting the physical needs of pregnant women who are committed to placing their children for adoption. Funds may not be distributed to any agency that is involved or associated with abortion activities, including counseling for or referrals to abortion clinics, providing medical abortion-related procedures, or proabortion advertising, and funds may not be distributed to any agency that charges women for services received.

1. Agencies that receive the funds must use at least 70 percent of the funds to provide for the material needs of pregnant women who are committed to placing their children for adoption, including clothing, housing, medical care, food, utilities, and transportation. Such funds may also be expended on infants awaiting placement with adoptive parents.

2. The remaining funds may be used for adoption, counseling, training, or advertising, but may not be used for administrative expenses, legal expenses, or capital expenditures.

3. Each agency that receives such funds must submit an annual attestation to the county. Any unused funds that exceed 10 percent of the funds received by an agency during its fiscal year must be returned to the county, which shall distribute them to other qualified agencies.

Florida Right to Life

Florida Right to Life (FRL) was founded in 1971, and is the largest pro-life organization in the state of Florida. The president of FRL is Lynda Bell. FRL is dedicated to protecting innocent human life that is threatened by abortion. The organization takes the position that life begins at conception and ends at natural death. FRL advocates its pro-life views through education and lobbying for legislation. *See also* **Pro-Life Organizations**

Focus on the Family

Focus on the Family is a Colorado based pro-life organization that was founded in 1977 by Dr. James C. Dobson. The organization sponsors 74 different programs and employs nearly 1,300 people to operate the programs. Some of the pro-life activities done by the organization include working through local religious leaders to coordinate pro-family efforts; operating crisis pregnancy centers; legislative lobbying; putting on radio programs that are broadcast in more than 90 countries; and

Dr. James C. Dobson founded Focus on the Family as a pro-life organization in 1977 (James C. Dobson).

providing publications that have been translated into 26 languages. *See also* **Pro-Life Organizations**

Folic Acid and Pregnancy

Folic acid is a B vitamin. Foods that contain natural folic acid include: orange juice, other citrus fruits and juices, leafy green vegetables, beans and whole-grain products. Studies have shown that taking the B vitamin folic acid every day, before and during early pregnancy, may prevent up to 70 percent of neural tube defects (birth defects of the brain and spinal cord). *See also* **Anencephaly; Encephaloceles; Spina bifida**

Forceps Delivery

Forceps are used, when necessary, to aid in the delivery of a live birth. They are composed of two long metal blades that are shaped like spoons. To utilize forceps requires insertion in the vagina, with the metal blades pressed against both sides of the fetus' head. Once the forceps are locked together, the fetus is carefully and slowly extracted from the womb. Although forceps may bruise the fetus' head and face, they protect the fetus' head from pressure imposed in the birth canal. Any damage caused to the fetus by the forceps usually clears up rapidly after birth. The device is normally used when the fetus has an abnormal presentation or position in the womb, or is premature. *See also* **Presentation and Position of the Fetus; Vacuum Extractor**

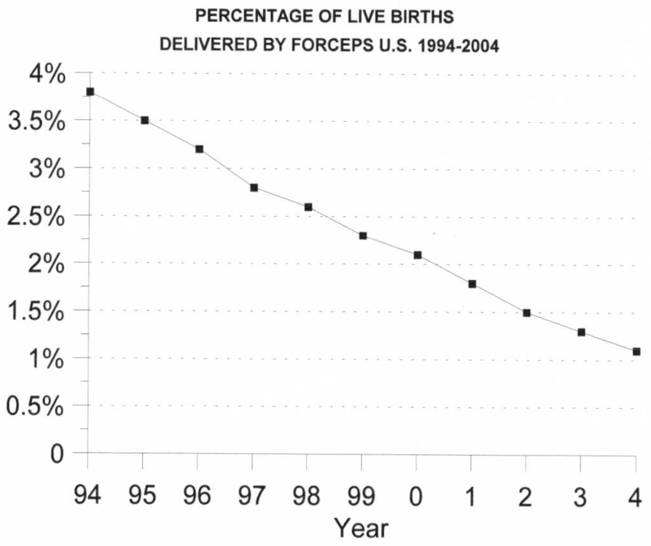

Source: **National Center for Health Statistics.**

Foreign Abortionist Entering the United States

The federal government prohibits entry into the United States of any foreigner who, in his or her country, compelled women to have abortions, or forced sterilization on men or women. The ban does not apply to specifically enumerated foreign dignitaries. The statute addressing the matter is set out below.

8 U.S.C.A. § 1182e. Denial of entry in the United States

(a) Notwithstanding any other provision of law, the Secretary of State may not issue any visa to, and the Attorney General may not admit to the United States, any foreign national whom the Secretary finds, based on credible and specific information, to have been directly involved in the establishment or enforcement of population control policies forcing a woman to undergo an abortion against her free choice or forcing a man or woman to undergo sterilization against his or her free choice, unless the Secretary has substantial grounds for believing that the foreign national has discontinued his or her involvement with, and support for, such policies.

(b) The prohibitions in subsection (a) of this section shall not apply in the case of a foreign national who is a head of state, head of government, or cabinet level minister.

(c) The Secretary of State may waive the prohibitions in subsection (a) with respect to a foreign national if the Secretary—

(1) determines that it is important to the national interest of the United States to do so; and

(2) provides written notification to the appropriate congressional committees containing a justification for the waiver.

40 Days for Life

40 Days for Life (40-DFL) is a pro-life organization that began in 2004 in College Station, Texas. The founder and director of 40-DFL is David Bereit. The idea for the organization is said to have occurred during a pro-life prayer service in College Station, when the worshipers prayed for an answer about how to reduce abortion in their area. It is said that God answered them by stating that they should promote the sanctity of life for 40 days. As a result of this revelation, 40-DFL was born with a mission to embark on campaigns that draw attention to the evils of abortion through the use of a three-point program: (1) prayer and fasting, (2) constant vigil, and (3) community outreach. In 2007 the first annual national 40-DFL campaign was conducted. This event took place from September 26 through November 4, 2007, simultaneously in more than 80 cities in 33 states. *See also* **Pro-Life Organizations**

Fourteenth Amendment

The Fourteenth Amendment of the federal constitution was adopted to impose restrictions on the power of state governments over their citizenry. The Amendment contains a Due Process Clause and Equal Protection Clause, both of which have been invoked in abortion litigation.

Due Process Clause. The Due Process Clause provides as follows: "No State shall ... deprive any person of life, liberty, or property, without due process of law." In *Roe v. Wade* the United States Supreme Court held that a right of privacy was founded in the "liberty" provision of the Due Process Clause of the Fourteenth Amendment. *Roe* held that the right of privacy was deemed broad enough to encompass a woman's decision whether or not to terminate her pregnancy in the first trimester, without state restrictions. The Supreme Court also held in *Planned Parenthood of Southeastern Pennsylvania v. Casey*, that the "liberty" provision of the Due Process Clause provided protection of a woman's decision to terminate her pregnancy prior to fetal viability. *Casey* held that the constitutional protection included a prohibition against imposing undue burdens on a woman's right to a pre-viability abortion and post-viability therapeutic abortion.

Equal Protection Clause. The Equal Protection Clause provides as follows: "No State shall ... deny to any person within its jurisdiction the equal protection of the laws." In *Williams v. Zbaraz* the Supreme Court held that in light of the requirements of the Hyde Amendment, the Equal Protection Clause was not violated by an Illinois statute that prohibited state Medicaid payment for abortions, except when necessary to save the life of the pregnant woman. In *Maher v. Roe* the Supreme Court held that the Equal Protection Clause did not prohibit Connecticut from excluding nontherapeutic abortions from its Medicaid program. It was held *Poelker v. Doe* by the Supreme Court that the Equal Protection Clause was not violated by a policy of the city of St. Louis, Missouri that denied publicly funded abortions to indigent women at city hospitals, except when a woman's health or life was in danger. In *Geduldig v. Aiello* the Supreme Court held that the Equal Protection Clause did not require a private sector employee disability insurance program, operated by the state of California, provide coverage for employee disabilities associated with normal pregnancies. The Supreme Court held in *Eisenstadt v. Baird* that the Equal Protection Clause was violated by a Massachusetts statute that made it a crime to give away a drug, medicine, instrument, or article for the prevention of conception except in the case of (1) a physician prescribing it for a married person, or (2) a pharmacist furnishing it to a married person presenting a physician's prescription. *See also* **Eisenstadt v. Baird; Fifth Amendment; Geduldig v. Aiello; Maher v. Roe; Planned Parenthood of Southeastern Pennsylvania v. Casey; Poelker v. Doe; Roe v. Wade; Williams v. Zbaraz**

Fourth Amendment

The Fourth Amendment to the federal constitution states: "The right of the people to be secure in their persons, houses, papers, and effects, against unreasonable searches and seizures, shall not be violated, and no Warrants shall issue, but upon probable cause, supported by Oath or affirmation, and particularly describing the place to be searched, and the persons or things to be seized." This Amendment was used by the United States Supreme Court in *Ferguson v. City of Charleston*, to hold that a search warrant or patient consent was needed in order for a government hospital to turn over to the police, drug test results that showed a woman used illegal drugs during her pregnancy. *Ferguson* found that taking drug testing, for the purpose of turning over the results to the police, was a search within the meaning of the Fourth Amendment. *See also* **Ferguson v. City of Charleston**

Fragile X Syndrome

Fragile X syndrome is a genetic disorder caused by a break in the long arm of the X chromosome. Symptoms of the disorder include mental retardation, large ears and oversized testes in the male. The disorder is the most common genetically inherited form of mental retardation. It occurs in about 1 out of 2,000 male births and 1 out of 1,000 females. There is no specific treatment for the disorder. *See also* **Birth Defects and Abortion**

Frankfurter, Felix

Felix Frankfurter (1882–1965) served as an associate justice of the United States Supreme Court from 1939 to 1962. While on the Supreme Court Justice Frankfurter was known as a liberal constructionist of the Constitution in his early years, but forged a significant shift to the conservative side in later years.

Justice Frankfurter was born in Vienna. His family immigrated to the United States when he was about twelve years old. He received an undergraduate degree from New York's City College and obtained a law degree from Harvard Law School. After graduating from law school Justice Frankfurter spent a number of years as an attorney for the Federal government. In 1914 he returned to Harvard Law School to teach. In 1939 President Franklin D. Roosevelt appointed Justice Frankfurter to the Supreme Court.

Justice Frankfurter wrote only one abortion related opinion. He wrote the plurality opinion in *Poe v. Ullman*, which held that the appellants did not have standing to challenge the constitutionality of a Connecticut statute, that made it a crime to give married persons contraceptive information and devices.

Freedom of Access to Clinic Entrances Act

In 1994, the Freedom of Access to Clinic Entrances Act (FACE), 18 U.S.C. § 248, was enacted by Congress and signed by President Bill Clinton, to protect both those providing and those receiving reproductive health care services. The legislation was in response to escalating violence at abortion clinics and violent attacks against abortionist and those seeking abortions. FACE prohibits the use of force, threats of force, or physical obstruction to injure, intimidate, or interfere with persons obtaining or providing reproductive health services. In addition, the law prohibits damage to or destruction of the property of a facility providing reproductive health services and provides criminal penalties and civil remedies for violations. FACE has had an impact on the decline in certain types of violence at abortion clinics. Although militant pro-life violence continues, clinic blockades have dwindled and some other types of violence against abortion providers and their patients have also decreased. The statute is set out below.

18 U.S.C.A. § 248. Freedom of Access to Clinic Entrances Act

(a) Whoever

(1) by force or threat of force or by physical obstruction, intentionally injures, intimidates or interferes with or attempts to injure, intimidate or interfere with any person because that person is or has been, or in order to intimidate such person or any other person or any class of persons from, obtaining or providing reproductive health services;

(2) by force or threat of force or by physical obstruction, intentionally injures, intimidates or interferes with or attempts to injure, intimidate or interfere with any person lawfully exercising or seeking to exercise the First Amendment right of religious freedom at a place of religious worship; or

(3) intentionally damages or destroys the property of a facility, or attempts to do so, because such facility provides reproductive health services, or intentionally damages or destroys the property of a place of religious worship, shall be subject to the penalties provided in subsection (b) and the civil remedies provided in subsection (c), except that a parent or legal guardian of a minor shall not be subject to any penalties or civil remedies under this section for such activities insofar as they are directed exclusively at that minor.

(b) Whoever violates this section shall

(1) in the case of a first offense, be fined in accordance with this title, or imprisoned not more than one year, or both; and

(2) in the case of a second or subsequent offense after a prior conviction under this section, be fined in accordance with this title, or imprisoned not more than 3 years, or both; except that for an offense involving exclusively a nonviolent physical obstruction, the fine shall be not more than $10,000 and the length of imprisonment shall be not more than six months, or both, for the first offense; and the fine shall, notwithstanding section 3571, be not more than $25,000 and the length of imprisonment shall be not more than 18 months, or both, for a subsequent offense; and except that if bodily injury results, the length of imprisonment shall be not more than 10 years, and if death results, it shall be for any term of years or for life.

(c) Civil Remedies.

(1) Right of action.

(A) Any person aggrieved by reason of the conduct prohibited by subsection (a) may commence a civil action for the relief set forth in subparagraph (B), except that such an action may be brought under subsection (a)(1) only by a person involved in providing or seeking to provide, or obtaining or seeking to obtain, services in a facility that provides reproductive health services, and such an action may be brought under subsection (a)(2) only by a person lawfully exercising or seeking to exercise the First Amendment right of religious freedom at a place of religious worship or by the entity that owns or operates such place of religious worship.

(B) In any action under subparagraph (A), the court may award appropriate relief, including temporary, preliminary or permanent injunctive relief and compensatory and punitive damages, as well as the costs of suit and reasonable fees for attorneys

and expert witnesses. With respect to compensatory damages, the plaintiff may elect, at any time prior to the rendering of final judgment, to recover, in lieu of actual damages, an award of statutory damages in the amount of $5,000 per violation.

(2) Action by attorney general of the United States.

(A) If the Attorney General of the United States has reasonable cause to believe that any person or group of persons is being, has been, or may be injured by conduct constituting a violation of this section, the Attorney General may commence a civil action in any appropriate United States District Court.

(B) In any action under subparagraph (A), the court may award appropriate relief, including temporary, preliminary or permanent injunctive relief, and compensatory damages to persons aggrieved as described in paragraph (1)(B). The court, to vindicate the public interest, may also assess a civil penalty against each respondent—

(i) in an amount not exceeding $10,000 for a nonviolent physical obstruction and $15,000 for other first violations; and

(ii) in an amount not exceeding $15,000 for a nonviolent physical obstruction and $25,000 for any other subsequent violation.

(3) Actions by state attorneys general.

(B) In any action under subparagraph (A), the court may award appropriate relief, including temporary, preliminary or permanent injunctive relief, compensatory damages, and civil penalties as described in paragraph (2)(B).

(d) Nothing in this section shall be construed—

(1) to prohibit any expressive conduct (including peaceful picketing or other peaceful demonstration) protected from legal prohibition by the First Amendment to the Constitution;

(2) to create new remedies for interference with activities protected by the free speech or free exercise clauses of the First Amendment to the Constitution, occurring outside a facility, regardless of the point of view expressed, or to limit any existing legal remedies for such interference;

(3) to provide exclusive criminal penalties or civil remedies with respect to the conduct prohibited by this section, or to preempt State or local laws that may provide such penalties or remedies; or

(4) to interfere with the enforcement of State or local laws regulating the performance of abortions or other reproductive health services.

(e) Definitions.— As used in this section:

(1) Facility.— The term "facility" includes a hospital, clinic, physician's office, or other facility that provides reproductive health services, and includes the building or structure in which the facility is located.

(2) Interfere with.— The term "interfere with" means to restrict a person's freedom of movement.

(3) Intimidate.— The term "intimidate" means to place a person in reasonable apprehension of bodily harm to him- or herself or to another.

(4) Physical obstruction.— The term "physical obstruction" means rendering impassable ingress to or egress from a facility that provides reproductive health services or to or from a place of religious worship, or rendering passage to or from such a facility or place of religious worship unreasonably difficult or hazardous.

(5) Reproductive health services.— The term "reproductive health services" means reproductive health services provided in a hospital, clinic, physician's office, or other facility, and includes medical, surgical, counselling or referral services relating to the human reproductive system, including services relating to pregnancy or the termination of a pregnancy.

(6) State.— The term "State" includes a State of the United States, the District of Columbia, and any commonwealth, territory, or possession of the United States.

See also **Abortion Violence, Property Destruction and Demonstrations; Buffer Zones at Abortion Facilities**

Freedom of Choice Act

The Freedom of Choice Act is a bill that has been sponsored by pro-choice members of Congress beginning in 1989. The bill is intended to codify the United States Supreme Court's decision in *Roe v. Wade*, which legalized abortion in the nation. No version of the bill has ever been passed by Congress. The 2007 version of the bill is set out below.

SEC. 1. SHORT TITLE.

This Act may be cited as the "Freedom of Choice Act."

SEC. 2. FINDINGS.

Congress finds the following:

(1) The United States was founded on core principles, such as liberty, personal privacy, and equality, which ensure that individuals are free to make their most intimate decisions without governmental interference and discrimination.

(2) One of the most private and difficult decisions an individual makes is whether to begin, prevent, continue, or terminate a pregnancy. Those reproductive health decisions are best made by women, in consultation with their loved ones and health care providers.

(3) In 1965, in Griswold v. Connecticut (381 U.S. 479), and in 1973, in Roe v. Wade (410 U.S. 113) and Doe v. Bolton (410 U.S. 179), the Supreme Court recognized that the right to privacy protected by the Constitution encompasses the right of every woman to weigh the personal, moral, and religious considerations involved in deciding whether to begin, prevent, continue, or terminate a pregnancy.

(4) The Roe v. Wade decision carefully balances the rights of women to make important reproductive decisions with the State's interest in potential life. Under Roe v. Wade and Doe v. Bolton, the right to privacy protects a woman's decision to choose to terminate her pregnancy prior to fetal viability, with the State permitted to ban abortion after fetal viability except when necessary to protect a woman's life or health.

(5) These decisions have protected the health and lives of women in the United States. Prior to the Roe v. Wade decision in 1973, an estimated 1,200,000 women each year were forced to resort to illegal abortions, despite the risk of unsanitary conditions, incompetent treatment, infection, hemorrhage, disfiguration, and death. Before Roe, it is estimated that thousands of women died annually in the United States as a result of illegal abortions.

(6) In countries in which abortion remains illegal, the risk of maternal mortality is high. According to the World Health Organization, of the approximately 600,000 pregnancy-related deaths occurring annually around the world, 80,000 are associated with unsafe abortions.

(7) The Roe v. Wade decision also expanded the opportunities for women to participate equally in society. In 1992, in Planned Parenthood v. Casey (505 U.S. 833), the Supreme Court observed that, "[t]he ability of women to participate equally in the economic and social life of the Nation has been facilitated by their ability to control their reproductive lives."

(8) Even though the Roe v. Wade decision has stood for more than 34 years, there are increasing threats to reproductive health and freedom emerging from all branches and levels of government. In 2006, South Dakota became the first State in more than 15 years to enact a ban on abortion in nearly all circumstances. Supporters of this ban have admitted it is an attempt to directly challenge Roe in the courts. Other States are considering similar bans.

(9) Further threatening Roe, the Supreme Court recently upheld the first-ever Federal ban on an abortion procedure, which has no ex-

ception to protect a woman's health. The majority decision in Gonzales v. Carhart (05-380, slip op. April 18, 2007) and Gonzales v. Planned Parenthood Federation of America fails to protect a woman's health, a core tenet of Roe v. Wade. Dissenting in that case, Justice Ginsburg called the majority's opinion "alarming," and stated that, "[f]or the first time since Roe, the Court blesses a prohibition with no exception safeguarding a woman's health." Further, she said, the Federal ban "and the Court's defense of it cannot be understood as anything other than an effort to chip away at a right declared again and again by this Court."

(10) Legal and practical barriers to the full range of reproductive services endanger women's health and lives. Incremental restrictions on the right to choose imposed by Congress and State legislatures have made access to reproductive care extremely difficult, if not impossible, for many women across the country. Currently, 87 percent of the counties in the United States have no abortion provider.

(11) While abortion should remain safe and legal, women should also have more meaningful access to family planning services that prevent unintended pregnancies, thereby reducing the need for abortion.

(12) To guarantee the protections of Roe v. Wade, Federal legislation is necessary.

(13) Although Congress may not create constitutional rights without amending the Constitution, Congress may, where authorized by its enumerated powers and not prohibited by the Constitution, enact legislation to create and secure statutory rights in areas of legitimate national concern.

(14) Congress has the affirmative power under section 8 of article I of the Constitution and section 5 of the 14th amendment to the Constitution to enact legislation to facilitate interstate commerce and to prevent State interference with interstate commerce, liberty, or equal protection of the laws.

(15) Federal protection of a woman's right to choose to prevent or terminate a pregnancy falls within this affirmative power of Congress, in part, because—

(A) many women cross State lines to obtain abortions and many more would be forced to do so absent a constitutional right or Federal protection;

(B) reproductive health clinics are commercial actors that regularly purchase medicine, medical equipment, and other necessary supplies from out-of-State suppliers; and

(C) reproductive health clinics employ doctors, nurses, and other personnel who travel across State lines in order to provide reproductive health services to patients.

SEC. 3. DEFINITIONS.

In this Act:

(1) GOVERNMENT— The term "government" includes a branch, department, agency, instrumentality, or official (or other individual acting under color of law) of the United States, a State, or a subdivision of a State.

(2) STATE— The term "State" means each of the States, the District of Columbia, the Commonwealth of Puerto Rico, and each territory or possession of the United States.

(3) VIABILITY— The term "viability" means that stage of pregnancy when, in the best medical judgment of the attending physician based on the particular medical facts of the case before the physician, there is a reasonable likelihood of the sustained survival of the fetus outside of the woman.

SEC. 4. INTERFERENCE WITH REPRODUCTIVE HEALTH PROHIBITED.

(a) Statement of Policy— It is the policy of the United States that every woman has the fundamental right to choose to bear a child, to terminate a pregnancy prior to fetal viability, or to terminate a pregnancy after fetal viability when necessary to protect the life or health of the woman.

(b) Prohibition of Interference— A government may not—

(1) deny or interfere with a woman's right to choose—

(A) to bear a child;

(B) to terminate a pregnancy prior to viability; or

(C) to terminate a pregnancy after viability where termination is necessary to protect the life or health of the woman; or

(2) discriminate against the exercise of the rights set forth in paragraph (1) in the regulation or provision of benefits, facilities, services, or information.

(c) Civil Action— An individual aggrieved by a violation of this section may obtain appropriate relief (including relief against a government) in a civil action.

SEC. 5. SEVERABILITY.

If any provision of this Act, or the application of such provision to any person or circumstance, is held to be unconstitutional, the remainder of this Act, or the application of such provision to persons or circumstances other than those as to which the provision is held to be unconstitutional, shall not be affected thereby.

SEC. 6. RETROACTIVE EFFECT.

This Act applies to every Federal, State, and local statute, ordinance, regulation, administrative order, decision, policy, practice, or other action enacted, adopted, or implemented before, on, or after the date of enactment of this Act.

Friedreich's Ataxia

Friedreich's ataxia is a congenital disorder involving progressive damage to nerve tissue in the spinal cord and nerves that control muscle movement in the arms and legs. Symptoms of the disorder include difficulty in walking, foot deformities, arm and leg problems, curvature of the spine, chest pain, shortness of breath, and heart problems. There is no effective treatment for the disorder. However, many of the complications associated with the disorder may be treated. Death in early childhood occurs for those with heart disorders caused by the disease. Those who survive childhood usually are confined to a wheelchair and become completely incapacitated. *See also* **Birth Defects and Abortion**

Frisby v. Schultz

Forum: United States Supreme Court.

Case Citation: Frisby v. Schultz, 487 U.S. 474 (1988).

Date Argued: April 20, 1988.

Date of Decision: June 27, 1988.

Opinion of Court: O'Connor, J., in which Rehnquist, C. J., and Blackmun, Scalia, and Kennedy, JJ., joined.

Concurring Opinion: White, J.,

Dissenting Opinion: Brennan, J., in which Marshall, J., joined.

Dissenting Opinion: Stevens, J.

Counsel for Appellants: Harold H. Fuhrman argued and filed brief.

Counsel for Appellees: Steven Frederick McDowell argued; on the brief was Walter M. Weber.

Amicus Brief for Appellants: National Institute of Municipal Law Officers by William I. Thornton, Jr., Roy D. Bates, William H. Taube, Roger F. Cutler, Robert J. Alfton, James K. Baker, Joseph N. deRaismes, Frank B. Gummey III, Robert J. Mangler, Neal E. McNeill, Analeslie Muncy, Dante R. Pellegrini, Clifford D. Pierce, Jr., Charles S. Rhyne, and Benjamin L. Brown; for the National League of Cities et al. by Benna Ruth Solomon and Mark B. Rotenberg; and for the Pacific Legal Foundation by Ronald A. Zumbrun and Robin L. Rivett.

Amicus Brief for Appellees: American Civil Liberties Union et al. by Harrey Grossman, Jane M. Whicher, Jonathan K. Baum, John A. Powell, Steven R. Shapiro, and William Lynch; for the American Federation of Labor and Congress of Industrial Organizations by Marsha S. Berzon and Laurence Gold; and for the Rutherford Institute et al. by Robert R. Melnick, William Bonner, John F. Southworth, Jr., W. Charles Bundren, Alfred J. Lindh, Ira W. Still III, William B. Hollberg, Randall A. Pentiuk, Thomas W. Strahan, John W. Whitehead, A. Eric Johnston, and David E. Morris.

Issue Presented: Whether an ordinance by the town of Brookfield, Wisconsin that completely banned picketing before or about any residence violated the First Amendment?

Case Holding: The ordinance did not violate the First Amendment.

Background facts of case: The town Brookfield, Wisconsin passed an ordinance in 1985 that made it unlawful for any person to engage in picketing before or about the residence or dwelling of any individual in the town. The ordinance was enacted in response to pro-life advocates who picketed regularly on a public street outside the Brookfield residence of a doctor who performed abortions at two clinics in neighboring towns. The ordinance was challenged by the appellees, Sandra C. Schultz and Robert C. Braun, who were opposed to abortion and wished to express their views on the subject by picketing in front of the doctor's residence. The appellees filed a lawsuit in a federal district court in Wisconsin, seeking a declaratory as well as preliminary and permanent injunctive relief, on the grounds that the ordinance violated the First Amendment. The appellants, town officials, were named as defendants.

The district court granted appellees' motion for a preliminary injunction. The court concluded that the ordinance was not narrowly tailored enough to restrict protected speech in a public forum. The Seventh Circuit court of appeals affirmed. The Supreme Court granted certiorari to consider the matter.

Majority opinion by Justice O'Connor: Justice O'Connor held that the ordinance did not violate the First Amendment. She wrote as follows:

> The First Amendment permits the government to prohibit offensive speech as intrusive when the "captive" audience cannot avoid the objectionable speech. The target of the focused picketing banned by the Brookfield ordinance is just such a "captive." The resident is figuratively, and perhaps literally, trapped within the home, and because of the unique and subtle impact of such picketing is left with no ready means of avoiding the unwanted speech.... Accordingly, the Brookfield ordinance's complete ban of that particular medium of expression is narrowly tailored.
>
> Of course, this case presents only a facial challenge to the ordinance. Particular hypothetical applications of the ordinance—to, for example, a particular resident's use of his or her home as a place of business or public meeting, or to picketers present at a particular home by invitation of the resident—may present somewhat different questions. Initially, the ordinance by its own terms may not apply in such circumstances, since the ordinance's goal is the protection of residential privacy, and since it speaks only of a "residence or dwelling," not a place of business. Moreover, since our First Amendment analysis is grounded in protection of the unwilling residential listener, the constitutionality of applying the ordinance to such hypotheticals remains open to question. These are, however, questions we need not address today in order to dispose of appellees' facial challenge.
>
> Because the picketing prohibited by the Brookfield ordinance is speech directed primarily at those who are presumptively unwilling to receive it, the State has a substantial and justifiable interest in banning it. The nature and scope of this interest make the ban narrowly tailored. The ordinance also leaves open ample alternative channels of communication and is content neutral. Thus, largely because of its narrow scope, the facial challenge to the ordinance must fail.

Disposition of case: The judgment of the court of appeals was reversed.

Concurring opinion by Justice White: Justice White concurred in the Court's judgment. He wrote separately to stress the following points:

> The Court endorses a narrow construction of the ordinance by relying on the town counsel's representations, made at oral argument, that the ordinance forbids only single-residence picketing. In light of the view taken by the lower federal courts and the apparent failure of counsel below to press on those courts the narrowing construction that has been suggested here, I have reservations about relying on counsel's statements as an authoritative statement of the law....
>
> There is nevertheless sufficient force in the town counsel's representations about the reach of the ordinance to avoid application of the overbreadth doctrine in this case, which as we have frequently emphasized is such "strong medicine" that it has been employed by the Court sparingly and only as a last resort. In my view, if the ordinance were construed to forbid all picketing in residential neighborhoods, the overbreadth doctrine would render it unconstitutional on its face and hence prohibit its enforcement against those, like appellees, who engage in single-residence picketing. At least this would be the case until the ordinance is limited in some authoritative manner. Because the representations made in this Court by the town's legal officer create sufficient doubts in my mind, however, as to how the ordinance will be enforced by the town or construed by the state courts, I would put aside the overbreadth approach here, sustain the ordinance as applied in this case, which the Court at least does, and await further developments.

Dissenting opinion by Justice Brennan: Justice Brennan disagreed with the majority opinion. He believed the ordinance was too broad and therefore unconstitutional. Justice Brennan wrote as follows:

> The Court today sets out the appropriate legal tests and standards governing the question presented, and proceeds to apply most of them correctly. Regrettably, though, the Court errs in the final step of its analysis, and approves an ordinance banning significantly more speech than is necessary to achieve the government's substantial and legitimate goal....
>
> ... First, the ordinance applies to all picketers, not just those engaged in the protest giving rise to this challenge. Yet the Court cites no evidence to support its assertion that picketers generally, or even appellees specifically, desire to communicate only with the "targeted resident." While picketers' signs might be seen from the resident's house, they are also visible to passersby. To be sure, the audience is limited to those within sight of the picket, but focusing speech does not strip it of constitutional protection. Even the site-specific aspect of the picket identifies to the public the object of the picketers' attention. Nor does the picketers' ultimate goal—to influence the resident's conduct—change the analysis; ... such a goal does not defeat First Amendment protection.
>
> A second flaw in the Court's reasoning is that it assumes that the intrusive elements of a residential picket are inherent.... Contrary to the Court's declaration in this regard, it seems far more likely that a picketer who truly desires only to harass those inside a particular residence will find that goal unachievable in the face of a narrowly tailored ordinance substantially limiting, for example, the size, time, and volume of the protest. If, on the other hand, the picketer intends to communicate generally, a carefully crafted ordinance will allow him or her to do so without intruding upon or unduly harassing the resident. Consequently, the discomfort to which the Court must refer is merely that of knowing there is a person outside who disagrees with someone inside. This may indeed be uncomfortable, but it does not implicate the town's interest in residential privacy and therefore does not warrant silencing speech.

A valid time, place, or manner law neutrally regulates speech only to the extent necessary to achieve a substantial governmental interest, and no further. Because the Court is unwilling to examine the Brookfield ordinance in light of the precise governmental interest at issue, it condones a law that suppresses substantially more speech than is necessary. I dissent.

Dissenting opinion by Justice Stevens: Justice Stevens dissented from the decision of the majority. He argued that the ordinance was unconstitutional because it was too broad in scope. Justice Stevens wrote the following:

> The picketing that gave rise to the ordinance enacted in this case was obviously intended to do more than convey a message of opposition to the character of the doctor's practice; it was intended to cause him and his family substantial psychological distress. As the record reveals, the picketers' message was repeatedly redelivered by a relatively large group — in essence, increasing the volume and intrusiveness of the same message with each repeated assertion. As is often the function of picketing, during the periods of protest the doctor's home was held under a virtual siege. I do not believe that picketing for the sole purpose of imposing psychological harm on a family in the shelter of their home is constitutionally protected. I do believe, however, that the picketers have a right to communicate their strong opposition to abortion to the doctor, but after they have had a fair opportunity to communicate that message, I see little justification for allowing them to remain in front of his home and repeat it over and over again simply to harm the doctor and his family. Thus, I agree that the ordinance may be constitutionally applied to the kind of picketing that gave rise to its enactment.
>
> On the other hand, the ordinance is unquestionably "overbroad" in that it prohibits some communication that is protected by the First Amendment...
>
> In this case the overbreadth is unquestionably real. Whether or not it is substantial in relation to the plainly legitimate sweep of the ordinance is a more difficult question. My hunch is that the town will probably not enforce its ban against friendly, innocuous, or even brief unfriendly picketing, and that the Court may be right in concluding that its legitimate sweep makes its overbreadth insubstantial. But there are two countervailing considerations that are persuasive to me. The scope of the ordinance gives the town officials far too much discretion in making enforcement decisions; while we sit by and await further developments, potential picketers must act at their peril. Second, it is a simple matter for the town to amend its ordinance and to limit the ban to conduct that unreasonably interferes with the privacy of the home and does not serve a reasonable communicative purpose. Accordingly, I respectfully dissent.

Full-Term Delivery

Full-term delivery refers to the birth of a child who is 37 or more weeks of gestation. See chart at the top of column 2. *See also* **Pre-Term Pregnancy**

Funding Abortions *see* **Public Resources for Abortions**

G

Gag Rule *see* **Mexico City Policy; Title X of the Public Health Service Act**

FULL-TERM DELIVERY BY LOW-INCOME WOMEN U.S. 1996-2006

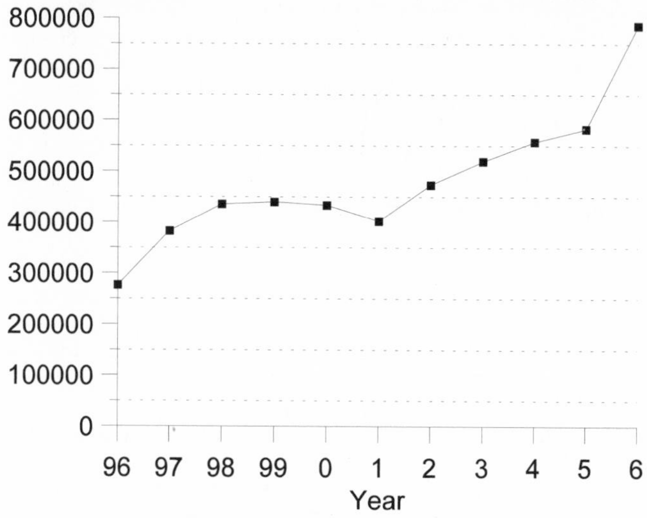

Source: **Pediatric and Pregnancy Nutrition Surveillance System.**

Gamble, Clarence

Clarence Gamble (1894–1966) was the grandson of James Gamble, one of the co-founders of the company called Proctor and Gamble. Clarence was educated at Princeton University, where he received an undergraduate degree in 1914, and Harvard Medical School, where he received a medical degree in 1920. Through his association with people like Dr. Robert Latou Dickinson, Margaret Sanger and Dr. Elizabeth Campbell, Clarence took a strong interest in providing women with information on birth control. As a result of this interest, Clarence is regarded as being one of the main forces behind the movement to gain acceptance for birth control methods in the United States.

With the financial assistance of Clarence, in 1929 Dr. Campbell was able to open the Cincinnati Maternal Health Clinic, which dispensed information on birth control to Cincinnati women. This clinic was one of only a few such clinics in the nation at the time. In 1937, Clarence began to provide funds for education and distribution of birth control supplies through the North Carolina State Board of Health. This event made North Carolina the first state to incorporate birth control in a public health program. By the end of the 1930s, Clarence had provided help in establishing birth control clinics in 40 cities, in 14 states. Clarence was also active directly with numerous organizations that included being president of the Pennsylvania Birth Control Federation, member of the Executive Committee of the American Birth Control League, medical field director of the Birth Control Clinical Research Bureau, and treasurer and board member of the National Committee on Maternal Health.

In 1957, Clarence founded the Pathfinder Fund (now called Pathfinder International). Through this organization Clarence was able to help fund the development and distribution of contraceptive devices and provide for the spread of contraception information world-wide. *See also* **Pathfinder International**

Gamete Intrafallopian Transfer *see* **Assisted Reproductive Technology**

Gaucher's Disease

Gaucher's disease is a congenital disorder involving the accumulation of a fatty substance (glucocerebroside) in the spleen, liver, lungs, bone marrow, and the brain. There are three forms of this disorder. The type 1 form of the disease displays symptoms of fatigue, low blood, enlarged liver and spleen, skeletal weakness, and lung and kidney impairment. In the type 2 form, symptoms include enlarged liver and spleen and extensive brain damage. In the type 3 form of the disorder, symptoms include enlarged liver and spleen, brain damage and seizures. Effective treatment exists for the type 1 form of the disease, such as enzyme replacement therapy. There is no effective treatment for type 2 and 3. Death usually occurs in infancy for type 2 and 3 victims. *See also* **Birth Defects and Abortion**

Geduldig v. Aiello

Forum: United States Supreme Court.

Case Citation: Geduldig v. Aiello, 417 U.S. 484 (1974).

Date Argued: March 26, 1974.

Date of Decision: June 17, 1974.

Opinion of Court: Stewart, J., in which Burger, C. J., and White, Blackmun, Powell, and Rehnquist, JJ., joined.

Concurring Opinion: None.

Dissenting Opinion: Brennan, J., in which Douglas and Marshall, JJ., joined.

Counsel for Appellant: Joanne Condas, Deputy Attorney General of California, argued; on the brief were Evelle J. Younger, Attorney General, and Elizabeth Palmer, Assistant Attorney General.

Counsel for Appellees: Wendy W. Williams argued; on the brief were Peter Hart Weiner, Roland C. Davis, and Victor J. Van Bourg.

Amicus Brief for Appellant: Milton A. Smith, Gerard C. Smetana, Lawrence D. Ehrlich, and Jerry Kronenberg for the Chamber of Commerce of the United States; by Ronald A. Zumbrun and Raymond M. Momboisse for the Pacific Legal Foundation; by Richard D. Godown and Myron G. Hill, Jr., for the National Association of Manufacturers of the United States; by Willard Z. Carr, Jr., for the Merchants and Manufacturers Assn.; by F. Mark Garlinghouse and James D. Hutchinson for the American Telephone and Telegraph Co.; and by Theophil C. Kammholz, Stanley R. Strauss, John S. Battle, Jr., and J. Robert Brame III for the General Electric Co.

Amicus Brief for Appellees: Joseph T. Eddins and Beatrice Rosenberg for the United States Equal Employment Opportunity Commission; by Ruth Bader Ginsburg and Melvin L. Wulf for the American Civil Liberties Union et al.; by J. Albert Woll, Laurence Gold, and Thomas E. Harris for the American Federation of Labor and Congress of Industrial Organization; by Winn Newman and Ruth Weyand for the International Union of Electrical, Radio and Machine Workers, AFL-CIO-CLC; by Joseph N. Onek for Women's Equity Action League et al.; and by Harry I. Rand for the Physicians Forum.

Issue Presented: Whether the Equal Protection Clause of the Fourteenth Amendment was violated by a California disability insurance program that paid disability benefits to employees in private employment, but did not provide coverage for employee disabilities associated with normal pregnancies?

Case Holding: The Equal Protection Clause of the Fourteenth Amendment did not require a private sector employee disability insurance program, operated by the state of California, provide coverage for employee disabilities associated with normal pregnancies.

Background facts of case: The state of California administered a disability insurance program that paid benefits to persons in private employment who were temporarily unable to work because of disability not covered by workmen's compensation. The program did not cover disabilities associated with pregnancy. The appellees, Carolyn Aiello, Augustina Armendariz, Elizabeth Johnson and Jacqueline Jaramillo, filed a lawsuit in a federal district court in California challenging the constitutionality of the program's exclusion of disabilities resulting from pregnancy. Aiello and Johnson had ectopic pregnancies that had to be aborted; Armendariz had a spontaneous abortion; and Jaramillo experienced a normal pregnancy. Their lawsuit named the appellant, a state official, as the defendant. The district court held that the disability insurance program violated the Equal Protection Clause of the Fourteenth Amendment. The Supreme Court granted certiorari to consider the issue.

Majority opinion by Justice Stewart: Justice Stewart held that the issue in the case was moot as to appellees Aiello, Johnson and Armendariz, because a subsequent decision by the California appellate court found that the program could not exclude disability coverage for pregnancies that were not normal. However, the case was still alive as to the issue of whether the program could exclude coverage for appellee Jaramillo's normal pregnancy. Justice Stewart held that the Equal Protection Clause was not violated because the program excluded disability coverage for normal pregnancies. The opinion addressed the matters as follows:

> Shortly before the District Court's decision in this case, the California Court of Appeal, in a suit brought by a woman who suffered an ectopic pregnancy, Rentzer v. Unemployment Insurance Appeals Board, 108 Cal. Rptr. 336 (1973), held that [the applicable statute] does not bar the payment of benefits on account of disability that results from medical complications arising during pregnancy....
>
> Because of the Rentzer decision and the revised administrative guidelines that resulted from it, the appellees Aiello, Armendariz, and Johnson, whose disabilities were attributable to causes other than normal pregnancy and delivery, became entitled to benefits under the disability insurance program, and their claims have since been paid. With respect to appellee Jaramillo, however, whose disability stemmed solely from normal pregnancy and childbirth, [the statute] continues to bar the payment of any benefits. It is evident that only Jaramillo continues to have a live controversy with the appellant as to the validity of [the statute]. The claims of the other appellees have been mooted by the change that Rentzer worked in the construction and application of that provision. Thus, the issue before the Court on this appeal is whether the California disability insurance program invidiously discriminates against Jaramillo and others similarly situated by not paying insurance benefits for disability that accompanies normal pregnancy and childbirth.
>
> We cannot agree that the exclusion of this disability from coverage amounts to invidious discrimination under the Equal Protection Clause. California does not discriminate with respect to the persons or groups which are eligible for disability insurance protection under the program. The classification challenged in this case relates to the asserted underinclusiveness of the set of risks that the State has selected to insure. Although California has created a program to insure most risks of employment disability, it has not chosen to insure all such risks, and this decision is reflected in the level of annual contributions exacted from participating employees. This Court has held that, consistently with the Equal Protection Clause, a State may take one step at a time, addressing itself to the phase of the problem which seems most acute to the legislative mind. The legislature may select one phase of one field and apply a remedy there, neglecting the others. Particularly with respect to social welfare programs, so long as the line drawn by the State is rationally supportable, the courts will not interpose their judgment as to the appropriate stopping point. The Equal Protection Clause does not require that a State must choose between attacking every aspect of a problem or not attacking the problem at all....
>
> It is evident that a totally comprehensive program would be substantially more costly than the present program and would inevitably require state subsidy, a higher rate of employee contribution, a lower scale of benefits for those suffering insured disabilities, or some combination of these measures. There is nothing in the Constitution, however, that requires the State to subordinate or compromise its legitimate interests solely to create a more comprehensive social insurance program than it already has.

The State has a legitimate interest in maintaining the self-supporting nature of its insurance program. Similarly, it has an interest in distributing the available resources in such a way as to keep benefit payments at an adequate level for disabilities that are covered, rather than to cover all disabilities inadequately. Finally, California has a legitimate concern in maintaining the contribution rate at a level that will not unduly burden participating employees, particularly low-income employees who may be most in need of the disability insurance.

These policies provide an objective and wholly non-invidious basis for the State's decision not to create a more comprehensive insurance program than it has. There is no evidence in the record that the selection of the risks insured by the program worked to discriminate against any definable group or class in terms of the aggregate risk protection derived by that group or class from the program. There is no risk from which men are protected and women are not. Likewise, there is no risk from which women are protected and men are not.

Disposition of case: The judgment of the district court was reversed.

Dissenting opinion by Justice Brennan: Justice Brennan disagreed with the majority decision. He believed the Equal Protection Clause was violated. He wrote as follows:

> ... [T]he Court today rejects appellees' equal protection claim and upholds the exclusion of normal-pregnancy-related disabilities from coverage under California's disability insurance program on the ground that the legislative classification rationally promotes the State's legitimate cost-saving interests....
>
> ... Disabilities caused by pregnancy, however, like other physically disabling conditions covered by the [California] Code, require medical care, often include hospitalization, anesthesia and surgical procedures, and may involve genuine risk to life. Moreover, the economic effects caused by pregnancy-related disabilities are functionally indistinguishable from the effects caused by any other disability: wages are lost due to a physical inability to work, and medical expenses are incurred for the delivery of the child and for postpartum care. In my view, by singling out for less favorable treatment a gender-linked disability peculiar to women, the State has created a double standard for disability compensation: a limitation is imposed upon the disabilities for which women workers may recover, while men receive full compensation for all disabilities suffered, including those that affect only or primarily their sex, such as prostatectomies, circumcision, hemophilia, and gout. In effect, one set of rules is applied to females and another to males. Such dissimilar treatment of men and women, on the basis of physical characteristics inextricably linked to one sex, inevitably constitutes sex discrimination.
>
> In the past, when a legislative classification has turned on gender, the Court has justifiably applied a standard of judicial scrutiny more strict than that generally accorded economic or social welfare programs. Yet, by its decision today, the Court appears willing to abandon that higher standard of review without satisfactorily explaining what differentiates the gender-based classification employed in this case from those found unconstitutional in [other cases]. The Court's decision threatens to return men and women to a time when traditional equal protection analysis sustained legislative classifications that treated differently members of a particular sex solely because of their sex.

Genetic Diseases *see* **Birth Defects and Abortion**

Genital and Urinary Tract Birth Defects

Genital and urinary tract birth defects occur in about 1 out of 10 babies. While some defects are known to be inherited, the cause of most conditions are unknown. Such defects can affect the urethra, bladder, kidneys, ureters, and the female and male genitals. Some the disorders are minor, while others can cause such problems as urinary tract infections, blockages, pain, and kidney damage. Some genital and urinary tract disorders can be diagnosed before or after birth.

There are numerous disorders associated the genital and urinary tract. Some of the most common disorders include: renal agenesis, polycystic kidney disease, bladder exstrophy, hydronephrosis, epispadias and hypospadias.

Renal agenesis. Renal agenesis is a disorder that involves one or both kidneys being missing. Roughly 1 out of 500 infants are born with a single kidney. Although such infants may lead a normal life, they may be prone to kidney failure, kidney infections, kidney stones, and high blood pressure.

Approximately 1 out of 4,000 infants are born with both kidneys missing. This condition leads to underdeveloped lungs. Consequently, about one-third of these infants will be stillborn, while the remainder die during the few first days of life. No treatment exists that can save such infants.

Polycystic kidney disease. Polycystic kidney disease is a condition that results in the growth of cysts in the kidneys and reduced kidney function. It may also cause kidney failure, urinary tract infections, pain, and high blood pressure. In most instances cysts cause few or no problems. Medications can be used to treat problems such as high blood pressure and urinary tract infections. Treatment for kidney failure may be done through dialysis or a kidney transplant.

A rare form of the polycystic kidney disease, called autosomal recessive, can cause death within the first few days of birth. This condition is caused when both parents pass along the gene for the disorder to the child.

Bladder exstrophy. Bladder exstrophy is a condition in which the bladder is turned inside out and located on the outside of the abdomen. This disorder occurs in about 1 out of 30,000 births. Male infants are affected nearly five times more often than female infants. The condition may be corrected through surgery.

Hydronephrosis. Hydronephrosis is a condition that involves swelling of one or both kidneys. The swelling produces a blockage that causes an accumulation of urine. This condition may cause urine to back up, damage or destroy the kidneys. The blockage may be corrected through surgery after birth. In some instances it may be necessary to remedy the condition through surgery before the infant is delivered.

Epispadias. Epispadias is a condition that affects the urethra and genitals. In female infants the clitoris may be split and the urinary opening may be abnormally placed. In male infants the condition causes the urethra to split and makes an opening on the upper surface of the penis. Nearly half of all infants with epispadias have bladder control problems. The condition may be corrected through surgery.

Hypospadias. Hypospadias is a disorder affecting the male urethra. With this defect the urethra fails to extend to the tip of the penis, causing the opening of the urethra to be positioned along the underside of the penis. Surgery can be performed to correct this condition. This condition affects nearly 1 percent of all male infants. *See also* **Birth Defects and Abortion**

Genital Herpes

Genital herpes is a sexually transmitted disease that is caused by the herpes simplex virus (HSV). There are two types of HSV: HSV-1 and HSV-2. The HSV-1 usually infects the lips and cause fever blisters or cold sores. HSV-2 is the usual cause of genital herpes. Both HSV-1 and HSV-2 can produce lesions in and around the vaginal area, on the penis, around the anal opening, and on the buttocks or thighs. Although the infection can stay in the body indefinitely, the number of outbreaks tends to go down over a period of years. Genital herpes infection is common in the United States. Nationwide, 45 million people are infected with HSV-2. HSV-2 infection is more common in women (one out of four women) than in men (one out of five).

REPORTED OCCURRENCE OF GENITAL HERPES U.S. 1996-2006

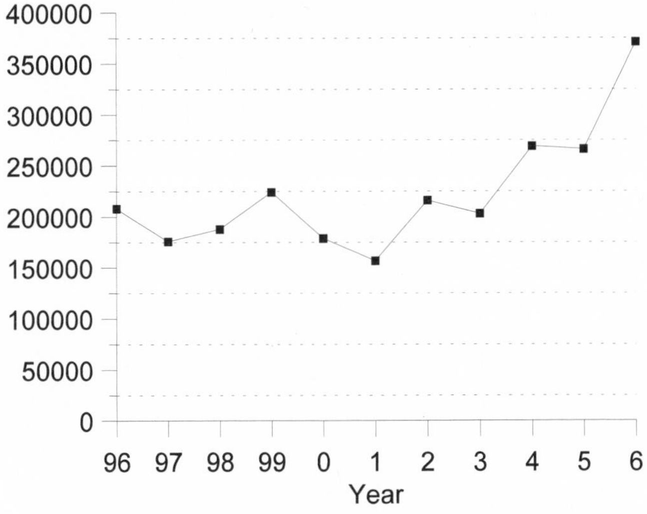

Source: National Disease and Therapeutic Index.

Most people contract genital herpes while having sex with someone who is having a herpes "outbreak." This outbreak means that HSV is active. When active, virus sores shed and infect the partner. A person with genital herpes also can infect a sexual partner during oral sex. Usually, when a person becomes infected with herpes for the first time, the symptoms will appear within two to ten days. The first symptom episodes usually last two to three weeks. Early symptoms of herpes outbreak include: itching or burning feeling in the genital or anal area; discharge of fluid from the vagina; pain in the legs, buttocks, or genital area; and feeling of pressure in the abdomen. Sores will appear within a few days near where the virus entered the body, such as on the mouth, penis, or vagina. After several days the sores become crusty and then heal. Other symptoms that may appear with the first episode include fever, headache, muscle aches, painful or difficult urination, and swollen glands in the groin area.

HSV-2 can cause potentially fatal infections in infants if the mother is shedding the virus at the time of delivery. If a woman has active genital herpes at delivery, a cesarean delivery is usually performed. Additionally, researchers believe HSV-2 may play a major role in the spread of HIV (the virus that causes AIDS). Herpes can make people more susceptible to HIV infection.

There is no cure for genital herpes. However, medicines that may be prescribed to treat disease include: acyclovir (treats the first and/or later episodes of genital herpes); famciclovir (treats later episodes of genital herpes); and valacyclovir (treats later episodes of genital herpes). The use of latex condoms can help protect against infection. However, condoms do not provide complete protection because the condom may not cover the herpes sores, and viral shedding may nevertheless occur. *See also* **Sexually Transmitted Diseases**

Genital HPV

Genital HPV (human papillomavirus) is the name of a group of viruses that consists of more than 100 different strains or types. Some of the viruses are considered high-risk types and may cause cancer of the cervix, anus, and penis. Genital HPV is transmitted during sexual intercourse. Over 5 million Americans get a genital HPV infection each year.

There is no cure for genital HPV. The infection usually goes away on its own. Cancer-related types are more likely to persist. Most genital HPV infections have no signs or symptoms, therefore most people who have the disease do not know they are infected. Some people will develop visible genital warts.

REPORTED OCCURRENCE OF GENITAL WARTS U.S. 1996-2006

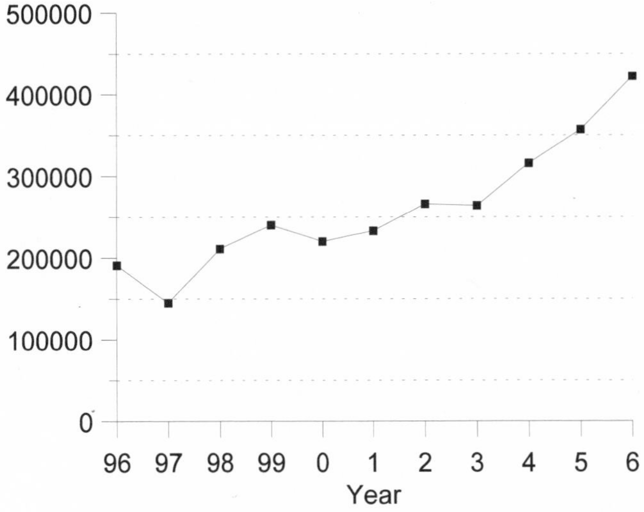

Source: National Disease and Therapeutic Index.

Genital warts. Genital warts (venereal warts) are the most easily recognized sign of genital HPV infection. The warts are soft, moist, pink or red swellings. In women the warts occur outside and inside of the vagina, the cervix, uterus, or around the anus. In men genital warts usually are seen on the tip of the penis, the scrotum, or around the anus. It is rare, but genital warts may also develop in the mouth or throat of a person who has had oral sex with an infected person. Genital warts can surface within several weeks after sexual contact with an infected person, or they can take months to appear.

Pregnant women who have genital warts may encounter a number of problems. The warts can get large enough to make it difficult to urinate. If the warts are in the vagina, they can cause obstruction during delivery. Although it is rare, pregnant women can pass genital warts to their baby during delivery. A newborn exposed to the infection can develop warts in the larynx (voice box). This is a potentially life-threatening condition for the child that may require laser surgery to prevent obstruction of the breathing passages.

Genital warts may disappear without treatment. If this does not occur, several treatment options are available. Different types of creams and solutions may be used. In some cases warts are removed by surgery, laser treatment, freezing (cryosurgery), or burning (electrocautery). In some instances an antiviral drug (alpha interferon) is injected directly into warts that returned after initial treatment. Although treatments can remove the warts, they do not get rid of the virus. Using male latex condoms during sexual activity can reduce the risk of getting genital HPV and genital warts. *See also* **Sexually Transmitted Diseases**

Genital Warts *see* **Genital HPV**

Georgetown University Right to Life

Georgetown University Right to Life is a pro-life student-run organization on the campus of Georgetown University. The organization's mission is to protect human life from conception to natural death. Activities engaged in by the group includes holding candlelight vigils, hosting speakers, attending pro-life conferences, and placing 4,000 pink and blue flags on campus grounds to commemorate the reported number of daily fetal deaths in the United States. *See also* **Pro-Life Organizations**

Georgia

(1) OVERVIEW

The state of Georgia enacted its first criminal abortion statute on February 25, 1876. The statute underwent several amendments prior to the 1973 decision by the United States Supreme Court in *Roe v. Wade*, which legalized abortion in the nation. Georgia has taken affirmative steps through statutes to respond to *Roe* and its progeny. The state's initial statutory responses to Roe were invalidated by the United States Supreme Court in *Doe v. Bolton*. In *Doe* the Supreme Court held that the Due Process Clause of the Fourteenth Amendment was violated by provisions in Georgia's abortion statutes that required (1) abortions take place in accredited hospitals, (2) that an abortion be approved by a hospital abortion committee, (3) that the need for an abortion be confirmed by two independent physicians, and (4) that a woman seeking an abortion be a resident of Georgia.

Georgia amended its abortion statutes after the decision in *Doe*. Abortion issues addressed by statute include general abortion guidelines, disposal of fetus and fetal death report for minor, partial-birth abortion, abortion by minors, use of facilities and people, injury to pregnant woman, prohibit sale of fetus, informed consent, ban on public school abortion services, and pro-life license plate.

(2) GENERAL ABORTION GUIDELINES

Georgia makes it a felony offense to perform an abortion outside the guidelines of its general abortion statute. The statute restricts the performance of abortions to physicians. Abortions after the first trimester must be performed at a licensed facility. The statute also purports to require all third trimester abortions be performed after three physicians certify that the abortion is necessary to preserve the life or health of the woman. However, this provision is invalid based upon decisions of the United States Supreme Court, to the extent the provision impedes a woman's right to pre-viability abortion. The statutes are set out below.

Georgia Code § 16-12-140. Criminal abortion

(a) Except as otherwise provided in Code Section 16-12-141, a person commits the offense of criminal abortion when he administers any medicine, drugs, or other substance whatever to any woman or when he uses any instrument or other means whatever upon any woman with intent to produce a miscarriage or abortion.

(b) A person convicted of the offense of criminal abortion shall be punished by imprisonment for not less than one nor more than ten years.

Georgia Code § 16-12-141. Performing abortion

(a) Nothing in this article shall be construed to prohibit an abortion performed by a physician duly licensed to practice medicine and surgery pursuant to Chapter 34 of Title 43, based upon his or her best clinical judgment that an abortion is necessary, except that Code Section 16-12-144 is a prohibition of a particular abortion method which shall apply to both duly licensed physicians and laypersons.

(b)(1) No abortion is authorized or shall be performed after the first trimester unless the abortion is performed in a licensed hospital, in a licensed ambulatory surgical center, or in a health facility licensed as an abortion facility by the Department of Human Resources.

(2) An abortion shall only be performed by a physician licensed under Article 2 of Chapter 34 of Title 43.

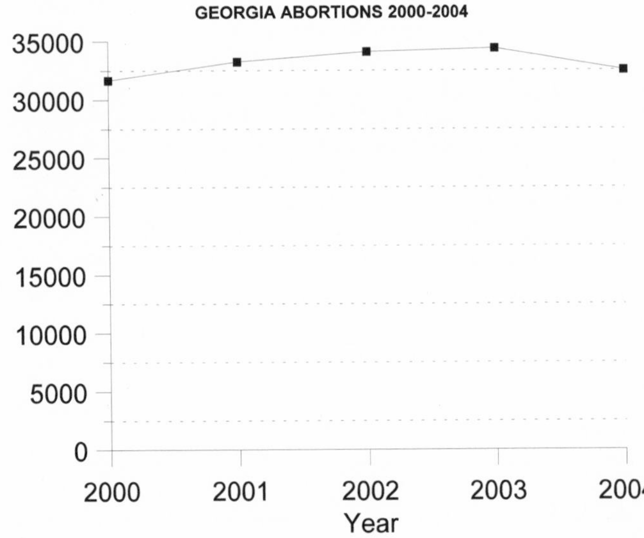

Source: National Center for Health Statistics.

Georgia Abortion by Age Group 2000–2004

Year	Age Group (yrs) <15	15–19	20–24	25–29	30–34	35–39	≥40
2000	268	5,176	10,550	7,737	4,648	2,556	743
2001	305	5,176	11,116	7,880	5,160	2,724	887
2002	270	5,042	11,437	8,241	5,441	2,819	841
2003	281	5,157	11,568	7,999	5,543	2,891	924
2004	252	4,994	10,552	7,718	5,284	2,768	945
Total	1,376	25,545	55,223	39,575	26,076	13,758	4,340

Source: National Center for Health Statistics.

Georgia Abortion by Weeks of Gestation 2000–2004

Weeks of Gestation	Year 2000	2001	2002	2003	2004	Total
≤8	15,783	17,792	18,788	19,074	18,020	89,457
9–10	7,377	7,224	6,947	6,909	6,484	34,941
11–12	3,966	3,773	3,597	3,569	3,416	18,321
13–15	2,093	2,093	2,188	2,177	1,968	10,519
16–20	1,647	1,588	1,696	1,653	1,572	8,156
≥21	812	778	875	981	1,053	4,499

Source: National Center for Health Statistics.

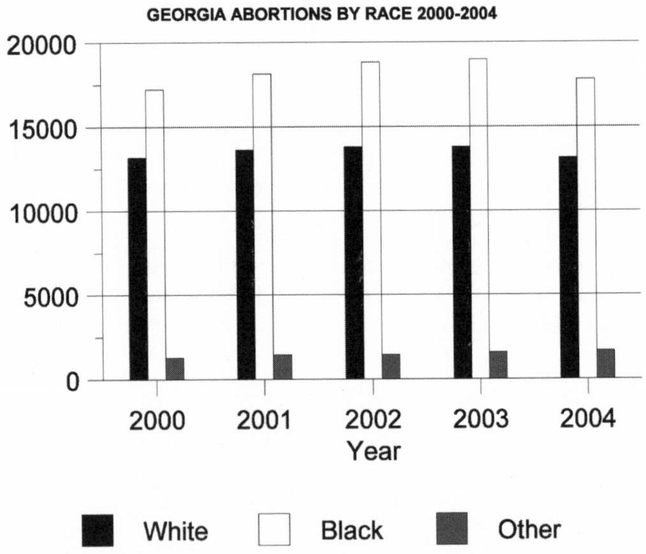

Source: National Center for Health Statistics.

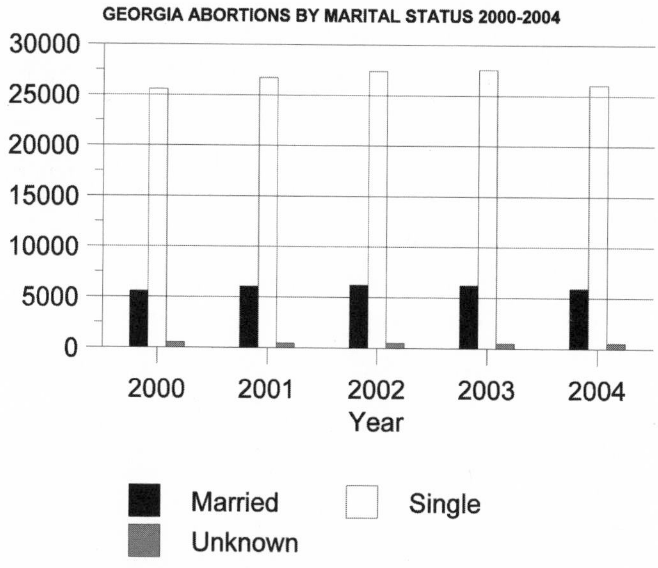

Source: National Center for Health Statistics.

Georgia Prior Abortion by Female 2000-2004

Prior Abortion

Year	*None*	*1*	*2*	*≥3*	*Not known*
2000	18,420	8,726	2,913	1,459	160
2001	19,795	8,686	3,069	1,549	140
2002	20,599	8,666	3,066	1,628	132
2003	20,788	8,033	3,065	1,577	0
2004	19,294	8,319	2,811	1,427	662
Total	98,896	42,430	14,924	7,640	1,094

Source: National Center for Health Statistics.

(c) No abortion is authorized or shall be performed after the second trimester unless the physician and two consulting physicians certify that the abortion is necessary in their best clinical judgment to preserve the life or health of the woman. If the product of the abortion is capable of meaningful or sustained life, medical aid then available must be rendered.

(d) The performing physician shall file with the commissioner of human resources within ten days after an abortion procedure is performed a certificate of abortion containing such statistical data as is determined by the Department of Human Resources consistent with preserving the privacy of the woman. Hospital or other licensed health facility records shall be available to the district attorney of the judicial circuit in which the hospital or health facility is located.

Georgia Code § 16-12-143. Failure to file report

A person who fails to file or maintain in complete form any of the written reports required in this article within the time set forth is guilty of a misdemeanor.

(3) PARTIAL-BIRTH ABORTION

Georgia criminalizes partial-birth abortions. However, law may be invalid as a result of the United States Supreme Court decision in *Stenberg v. Carhart*, which invalidated a Nebraska statute that prohibited partial-birth abortions. On the other hand, if Georgia's statute is found to come within the United States Supreme Court decision in *Gonzales v. Carhart*, which upheld a federal partial-birth abortion statute, then the law is valid. Georgia has provided a civil lawsuit remedy for the father of a fetus destroyed through partial-birth abortion. In the case of a minor, the maternal grandparents of the fetus may file a civil lawsuit. The statute is set out below.

Georgia Code § 16-12-144. Partial-birth abortion offense

(a) As used in this Code section, the term:

(1) "Fetus" means the biological offspring of human parents.

(2) "Partial-birth abortion" means an abortion in which the person performing the abortion partially vaginally delivers a living human fetus before ending the life of the fetus and completing the delivery.

(b) Any person who knowingly performs a partial-birth abortion and thereby ends the life of a human fetus shall, upon conviction thereof, be punished by a fine not to exceed $5,000.00, imprisonment for not more than five years, or both. This prohibition shall not apply to a partial-birth abortion that is necessary to save the life of the mother because her life is endangered by a physical disorder, physical illness, or physical injury, including a life-endangering condition caused by or arising from the pregnancy itself, provided that no other medical procedure will suffice to save the mother's life.

(c) (1) The father of the fetus, and the maternal grandparents of the fetus if the mother has not attained the age of 18 years of age at the time of the abortion, may obtain appropriate relief in a civil action, unless the pregnancy resulted from the plaintiff's criminal conduct or the plaintiff consented to the abortion.

(2) Such relief shall include:

(A) Money damages for all injuries, psychological and physical, occasioned by the violation of this Code section; and

(B) Statutory damages equal to three times the cost of the partial-birth abortion.

(d) A woman upon whom a partial-birth abortion is performed may not be prosecuted under this Code section for violating this Code section or any provision thereof, or for conspiracy or for an attempt to violate this Code section or any provision thereof.

(4) ABORTION BY MINORS

Under the laws of Georgia no physician may perform an abortion upon an unemancipated minor, unless the minor produces a written statement from her parent or legal guardian indicating the parent or the legal guardian was notified of the intended abortion. Notification may also be made directly by the treating physician. Further, notification must be made at least 24 hours before the abortion. In compliance with federal constitutional law, Georgia has provided a judicial waiver procedure for an unemancipated minor to obtain an abortion without parental or guardian notification. The minor may petition a trial court for a waiver of the notification requirement. A minor has a right to an attorney at the proceeding and if she cannot afford one, the court must appoint her an attorney. If a minor chooses, she may represent herself. The required parental notification may be waived if the court finds either (1) that the minor is mature and well-informed enough to make the abortion decision in consultation with her physician, or (2) that notification would not be in the best interest of the minor. An expedited appeal is available to any minor to whom the court denies a waiver of consent. The notification procedure was upheld in *Planned Parenthood Ass'n v. Miller*, 934 F.2d 1462 (11th Cir. 1991). The statutes addressing the issues are set out below.

Georgia Code § 15-11-110. Short title

This article shall be known and may be cited as the "Parental Notification Act."

Georgia Code § 15-11-111. Definitions

As used in this article, the term:

(1) "Abortion" means the use or prescription of any instrument, medicine, drug, or any other substance or device with the intent to terminate the pregnancy of a female known to be pregnant. The term "abortion" shall not include the use or prescription of any instrument, medicine, drug, or any other substance or device employed solely to

increase the probability of a live birth, to preserve the life or health of the child after live birth, or to remove a dead unborn child who died as a result of a spontaneous abortion. The term "abortion" also shall not include the prescription or use of contraceptives.

(2) "Proper identification" means any document issued by a governmental agency containing a description of the person, the person's photograph, or both, including, but not limited to, a driver's license, an identification card authorized under Code Sections 40-5-100 through 40-5-104 or similar identification card issued by another state, a military identification card, a passport, or an appropriate work authorization issued by the United States Immigration and Naturalization Service.

(3) "Unemancipated minor" means any person under the age of 18 who is not or has not been married or who is under the care, custody, and control of such person's parent or parents, guardian, or the juvenile court of competent jurisdiction.

Georgia Code § 15-11-112. Parental notice

(a) No physician or other person shall perform an abortion upon an unemancipated minor under the age of 18 years unless:

(1)(A) The minor seeking an abortion shall be accompanied by a parent or guardian who shall show proper identification and state that the parent or guardian is the lawful parent or guardian of the minor and that the parent or guardian has been notified that an abortion is to be performed on the minor;

(B) The physician or the physician's qualified agent gives at least 24 hours' actual notice, in person or by telephone, to a parent or guardian of the pending abortion and the name and address of the place where the abortion is to be performed; provided, however, that, if the person so notified indicates that he or she has been previously informed that the minor was seeking an abortion or if the person so notified has not been previously informed and he or she clearly expresses that he or she does not wish to consult with the minor, then in either event the abortion may proceed in accordance with Chapter 9A of Title 31; or

(C) The physician or a physician's qualified agent gives written notice of the pending abortion and the address of the place where the abortion is to be performed, sent by certified mail, return receipt requested with delivery confirmation, addressed to a parent or guardian at the usual place of abode of the parent or guardian. Unless proof of delivery is otherwise sooner established, such notice shall be deemed delivered 48 hours after mailing. The time of mailing shall be recorded by the physician or agent in the minor's file. The abortion may be performed 24 hours after the delivery of the notice; provided, however, that, if the person so notified certifies in writing that he or she has been previously informed that the minor was seeking an abortion or if the person so notified has not been previously informed and he or she certifies in writing that he or she does not wish to consult with the minor, then in either event the abortion may proceed in accordance with Chapter 9A of Title 31; and

(2) The minor signs a consent form stating that she consents, freely and without coercion, to the abortion.

(b) If the unemancipated minor or the physician or a physician's qualified agent, as the case may be, elects not to comply with any one of the requirements of subparagraph (a)(1)(A), (a)(1)(B), or (a)(1)(C) of this Code section, or if the parent or legal guardian of the minor cannot be located, the minor may petition, on the minor's own behalf or by next friend, any juvenile court in the state for a waiver of such requirement pursuant to the procedures provided for in Code Section 15-11-114. The juvenile court shall assist the minor or next friend in preparing the petition and notices required pursuant to this Code section. Venue shall be lawful in any county, notwithstanding Code Section 15-11-29.

(c) No abortion shall be performed unless the requirements of subparagraph (a)(1)(A), (a)(1)(B), or (a)(1)(C) of this Code section have been met or the minor has obtained a court order waiving such requirements.

Georgia Code § 15-11-113. Hearing

Notwithstanding Code Sections 15-11-38, 15-11-38.1, and 15-11-39, the unemancipated minor or next friend shall be notified of the date, time, and place of the hearing in such proceedings at the time of filing the petition. The hearing shall be held within three days of the date of filing, excluding Saturdays, Sundays, and holidays. The parents or guardian or person standing in loco parentis of the unemancipated minor shall not be served with the petition or with a summons or otherwise notified of the proceeding. If a hearing is not held within the time prescribed in this Code section, the petition shall be deemed granted.

Georgia Code § 15-11-114. Judicial bypass

(a) An unemancipated minor may participate in proceedings in the court on such minor's own behalf and the court shall advise such minor of the right to court appointed counsel and shall provide such minor with such counsel upon request or if such minor is not already adequately represented.

(b) All court proceedings under this Code section shall be conducted in a manner to preserve the complete anonymity of the parties and shall be given such precedence over other pending matters as is necessary to ensure that a decision is reached by the court as expeditiously as is possible under the circumstances of the case. In no event shall the name, address, birth date, or social security number of such minor be disclosed.

(c) The requirement of subparagraph (a)(1)(A), (a)(1)(B), or (a)(1)(C) of Code Section 15-11-112 shall be waived if the court finds either:

(1) That the unemancipated minor is mature enough and well enough informed to make the abortion decision in consultation with her physician, independently of the wishes of such minor's parent or guardian; or

(2) That the notice to a parent or, if the minor is subject to guardianship, the legal guardian pursuant to Code Section 15-11-112 would not be in the best interests of the minor.

(d) A court that conducts proceedings under this Code section shall issue written and specific factual findings and legal conclusions supporting its decision and shall order that a record of the evidence be maintained. The juvenile court shall render its decision within 24 hours of the conclusion of the hearing and a certified copy of same shall be furnished immediately to the minor. If the juvenile court fails to render its decision within 24 hours after the conclusion of the hearing, then the petition shall be deemed granted. All juvenile court records shall be sealed in a manner which will preserve anonymity.

(e) An expedited appeal completely preserving the anonymity of the parties shall be available to any unemancipated minor to whom the court denies a waiver of notice. The appellate courts are authorized and requested to issue promptly such rules as are necessary to preserve anonymity and to ensure the expeditious disposition of procedures provided by this Code section. In no event shall the name, address, birth date, or social security number of such minor be disclosed during the expedited appeal or thereafter.

(f) No filing fees shall be required of any unemancipated minor who uses the procedures provided by this Code section.

Georgia Code § 15-11-115. Applicability of law

The requirements and procedures of this article shall apply to all unemancipated minors within this state whether or not such persons are residents of this state.

Georgia Code § 15-11-116. Medical emergency

This article shall not apply when, in the best clinical judgment of the attending physician on the facts of the case before him, a medical emer-

gency exists that so complicates the condition of the minor as to require an immediate abortion. A person who performs an abortion as a medical emergency under the provisions of this Code section shall certify in writing the medical indications on which this judgment was based when filing such reports as are required by law.

Georgia Code § 15-11-117. Civil and criminal immunities

Any physician or any person employed or connected with a physician, hospital, or health care facility performing abortions who acts in good faith shall be justified in relying on the representations of the unemancipated minor or of any other person providing the information required under this article. No physician or other person who furnishes professional services related to an act authorized or required by this article and who relies upon the information furnished pursuant to this article shall be held to have violated any criminal law or to be civilly liable for such reliance, provided that the physician or other person acted in good faith.

Georgia Code § 15-11-118. Violations

Any person who violates the provisions of this article shall be guilty of a misdemeanor and any person who intentionally encourages another to provide false information pursuant to this article shall be guilty of a misdemeanor.

(5) DISPOSAL OF FETUS AND FETAL DEATH REPORT FOR MINOR

Georgia requires specific reports be filed by physicians performing abortions on minors. The reports seek information on whether proper consent was obtained. The state also provides that all aborted fetuses must be cremated or buried. In addition, Georgia requires all induced abortions be reported. The statutes addressing the issues are set out below.

Georgia Code § 16-12-141.1.
Aborted fetuses and reporting requirements

(a)(1) Every hospital and clinic in which abortions are performed or occur spontaneously, and any laboratory to which the aborted fetuses are delivered, shall provide for the disposal of the aborted fetuses by cremation, interment, or other manner approved of by the commissioner of human resources. The hospital, clinic, or laboratory may complete any laboratory tests necessary for the health of the woman or her future offspring prior to disposing of the aborted fetus.

(2) Each hospital, clinic, and laboratory shall report, on a form of the type and confidentiality provided for in subsection (d) of Code Section 16-12-141, and provided by the commissioner of human resources, the manner in which it disposes of the aborted fetus. Such reports shall be made annually by December 31 and whenever the method of disposal changes. The commissioner of human resources shall provide forms for reporting under this Code section.

(b) Any hospital, clinic, or laboratory violating the provisions of subsection (a) of this Code section shall be punished by a fine of not less than $1,000.00 nor more than $5,000.00.

(c) Within 90 days after May 10, 2005, the Department of Human Resources shall prepare a reporting form for physicians which shall include:

(1) The number of females whose parent or guardian was provided the notice required in paragraph (1) of subsection (a) of Code Section 15-11-112 by the physician or such physician's agent; of that number, the number of notices provided personally under subparagraphs (a)(1)(A) and (a)(1)(B) of Code Section 15-11-112 and the number of notices provided by mail under subparagraph (a)(1)(C) of Code Section 15-11-112; and, of each of those numbers, the number of females who, to the best of the reporting physician's information and belief, went on to obtain the abortion;

(2) The number of females upon whom the physician performed an abortion without providing to the parent or guardian of a minor the notice required by subsection (a) of Code Section 15-11-112; and of that number, the number of females for which subsection (b) of Code Section 15-11-112 and Code Section 15-11-116 were applicable;

(3) The number of abortions performed upon a female by the physician after receiving judicial authorization pursuant to subsection (b) of Code Section 15-11-112 and Code Section 15-11-114; and

(4) The same information described in paragraphs (1), (2), and (3) of this subsection with respect to females for whom a guardian or conservator has been appointed.

(d) The Department of Human Resources shall ensure that copies of the reporting forms described in subsection (c) of this Code section, together with a reprint of this Code section, are provided:

(1) Within 120 days after May 10, 2005, to all health facilities licensed as an abortion facility by the Department of Human Resources;

(2) To each physician licensed or who subsequently becomes licensed to practice medicine in this state at the same time as official notification to that physician that the physician is so licensed; and

(3) By December 1 of every year, other than the calendar year in which forms are distributed in accordance with paragraph (1) of this subsection, to all health facilities licensed as an abortion facility by the Department of Human Resources.

(e) By February 28 of each year following a calendar year in any part of which this subsection was in effect, each physician who provided, or whose agent provided, the notice described in subsection (a) of Code Section 15-11-112 and any physician who knowingly performed an abortion upon a female or upon a female for whom a guardian or conservator had been appointed because of a finding of incompetency during the previous calendar year shall submit to the Department of Human Resources a copy of the form described in subsection (c) of this Code section with the requested data entered accurately and completely.

(f) Reports that are submitted more than 30 days following the due date shall be subject to a late fee of $500.00 for that period and the same fee for each additional 30 day period or portion of a 30 day period in which they remain overdue. Any physician required to report in accordance with this Code section who submits an incomplete report or fails to submit a report for more than one year following the due date may, in an action brought by the Department of Human Resources, be directed by a court of competent jurisdiction to submit a complete report within a period stated by court order or be subject to sanctions for civil contempt.

(g) By June 30 of each year, the Department of Human Resources shall issue a public report providing statistics for the previous calendar year compiled from all the reports covering that year submitted in accordance with this Code section for each of the items listed in subsection (c) of this Code section. The report shall also include statistics which shall be obtained by the Administrative Office of the Courts giving the total number of petitions or motions filed under subsection (b) of Code Section 15-11-112 and, of that number, the number in which the court appointed a guardian ad litem, the number in which the court appointed counsel, the number in which the judge issued an order authorizing an abortion without notification, the number in which the judge denied such an order, and, of the last, the number of denials from which an appeal was filed, the number of such appeals that resulted in the denials being affirmed, and the number of such appeals that resulted in reversals of such denials. Each report shall also provide the statistics for all previous calendar years for which such a public statistical report was required to be issued, adjusted to reflect any additional information from late or corrected reports. The Department of Human Resources shall ensure that none of the information included in the public reports could reasonably lead to the identification of any individual female or of any female for whom a guardian or conservator has been appointed.

(h) The Department of Human Resources may by regulation alter the dates established by paragraph (3) of subsection (d) and subsections (e) and (g) of this Code section or consolidate the forms or reports to achieve administrative convenience or fiscal savings or to reduce the burden of re-

porting requirements so long as reporting forms are sent to all facilities licensed as an abortion facility by the Department of Human Resources at least once every year and the report described in subsection (g) of this Code section is issued at least once each year.

(i) The Department of Human Resources shall ensure that the names and identities of the physicians filing reports under this Code section shall remain confidential. The names and identities of such physicians shall not be subject to Article 4 of Chapter 18 of Title 50.

Georgia Code § 31-10-19. Reports of induced abortion

Each induced termination of pregnancy which occurs in this state, regardless of the length of gestation or weight, shall be reported directly to the department within ten days by the person in charge of the institution or clinic, or designated representative, in which the induced termination of pregnancy was performed. If the induced termination of pregnancy was performed outside an institution or clinic, the attending physician shall prepare and file the report within the time specified by this Code section.

(6) USE OF FACILITIES AND PEOPLE

Under the laws of Georgia hospitals or other medical facilities are not required to allow abortions at their facilities. The employees and physicians at hospitals or other medical facilities that do allow abortions are permitted to refuse to take part in abortions. Georgia also permits pharmacists to refuse to provide medications for abortions. The statute addressing the matter is set out below.

Georgia Code § 16-12-142.
Right to refuse to participate in abortion

(a) Nothing in this article shall require a hospital or other medical facility or physician to admit any patient under the provisions of this article for the purpose of performing an abortion. In addition, any person who states in writing an objection to any abortion or all abortions on moral or religious grounds shall not be required to participate in procedures which will result in such abortion; and the refusal of the person to participate therein shall not form the basis of any claim for damages on account of such refusal or for any disciplinary or recriminatory action against the person. The written objection shall remain in effect until the person revokes it or terminates his association with the facility with which it is filed.

(b) Any pharmacist who states in writing an objection to any abortion or all abortions on moral or religious grounds shall not be required to fill a prescription for a drug which purpose is to terminate a pregnancy; and the refusal of the person to fill such prescription shall not form the basis of any claim for damages on account of such refusal or for any disciplinary or recriminatory action against the person; provided, however, that the pharmacist shall make all reasonable efforts to locate another pharmacist who is willing to fill such prescription or shall immediately return the prescription to the prescription holder. The written objection shall remain in effect until the person revokes it or terminates his or her association with the facility with which it is filed. Nothing in this subsection shall be construed to authorize a pharmacist to refuse to fill a prescription for birth control medication, including any process, device, or method to prevent pregnancy and including any drug or device approved by the federal Food and Drug Administration for such purpose.

(7) INJURY TO PREGNANT WOMAN

Georgia has created several statutes that make it a criminal offense to injure a pregnant woman and her fetus. The state has created a specific crime called "feticide," for an injury to a pregnant woman that causes the death of a fetus. Convictions for feticide were obtained in *Kempson v. State*, 602 S.E.2d 587 (Ga. 2004) and *Ward v. State*, 417 S.E.2d 130 (Ga. 1992). The statutes addressing the issue are set out below.

Georgia Code § 16-5-80. Feticide offense

(a) For the purposes of this Code section, the term "unborn child" means a member of the species homo sapiens at any stage of development who is carried in the womb.

(b) A person commits the offense of feticide if he or she willfully and without legal justification causes the death of an unborn child by any injury to the mother of such child, which would be murder if it resulted in the death of such mother, or if he or she, when in the commission of a felony, causes the death of an unborn child.

(c) A person convicted of the offense of feticide shall be punished by imprisonment for life.

(d) A person commits the offense of voluntary manslaughter of an unborn child when such person causes the death of an unborn child under circumstances which would otherwise be feticide and if such person acts solely as the result of a sudden, violent, and irresistible passion resulting from serious provocation sufficient to excite such passion in a reasonable person; provided, however, that, if there should have been an interval between the provocation and the killing sufficient for the voice of reason and humanity to be heard, of which the jury in all cases shall be the judge, the killing shall be attributed to deliberate revenge and be punished as feticide.

(e) A person convicted of the offense of voluntary manslaughter of an unborn child shall be guilty of a felony and shall be punished by imprisonment for not less than one nor more than 20 years.

(f) Nothing in this Code section shall be construed to permit the prosecution of:

(1) Any person for conduct relating to an abortion for which the consent of the pregnant woman, or person authorized by law to act on her behalf, has been obtained or for which such consent is implied by law;

(2) Any person for any medical treatment of the pregnant woman or her unborn child; or

(3) Any woman with respect to her unborn child.

Georgia Code § 16-5-28. Assault of unborn child

(a) For the purposes of this Code section, the term "unborn child" means a member of the species homo sapiens at any stage of development who is carried in the womb.

(b) A person commits the offense of assault of an unborn child when such person, without legal justification, attempts to inflict violent injury to an unborn child.

(c) Any person convicted of the offense of assault of an unborn child shall be guilty of a misdemeanor.

(d) Nothing in this Code section shall be construed to permit the prosecution of:

(1) Any person for conduct relating to an abortion for which the consent of the pregnant woman, or person authorized by law to act on her behalf, has been obtained or for which such consent is implied by law;

(2) Any person for any medical treatment of the pregnant woman or her unborn child; or

(3) Any woman with respect to her unborn child.

Georgia Code § 16-5-29. Battery of an unborn child

(a) For the purposes of this Code section, the term "unborn child" means a member of the species homo sapiens at any stage of development who is carried in the womb.

(b) A person commits the offense of battery of an unborn child when such person, without legal justification, intentionally inflicts physical harm upon an unborn child.

(c) A person convicted of the offense of battery of an unborn child shall be guilty of a misdemeanor.

(d) Nothing in this Code section shall be construed to permit the prosecution of:

(1) Any person for conduct relating to an abortion for which the consent of the pregnant woman, or person authorized by law to act on her behalf, has been obtained or for which such consent is implied by law;

(2) Any person for any medical treatment of the pregnant woman or her unborn child; or

(3) Any woman with respect to her unborn child.

Georgia Code § 16-5-20. Simple assault

(a) A person commits the offense of simple assault when he or she either:

(1) Attempts to commit a violent injury to the person of another; or

(2) Commits an act which places another in reasonable apprehension of immediately receiving a violent injury.

(b–f) Omitted.

(g) Any person who commits the offense of simple assault against a female who is pregnant at the time of the offense shall, upon conviction thereof, be punished for a misdemeanor of a high and aggravated nature.

(h) Nothing in this Code section shall be construed to permit the prosecution of:

(1) Any person for conduct relating to an abortion for which the consent of the pregnant woman, or person authorized by law to act on her behalf, has been obtained or for which such consent is implied by law;

(2) Any person for any medical treatment of the pregnant woman or her unborn child; or

(3) Any woman with respect to her unborn child.

For the purposes of this subsection, the term "unborn child" means a member of the species homo sapiens at any stage of development who is carried in the womb.

Georgia Code § 16-5-23.1. Battery

(a) A person commits the offense of battery when he or she intentionally causes substantial physical harm or visible bodily harm to another.

(b) As used in this Code section, the term "visible bodily harm" means bodily harm capable of being perceived by a person other than the victim and may include, but is not limited to, substantially blackened eyes, substantially swollen lips or other facial or body parts, or substantial bruises to body parts.

(c–g) Omitted.

(h) Any person who commits the offense of battery against a female who is pregnant at the time of the offense shall, upon conviction thereof, be punished for a misdemeanor of a high and aggravated nature.

(8) PROHIBIT SALE OF FETUS

Georgia makes it a criminal offense for anyone to sell or buy a fetus. The statute addressing the issue is set out below.

Georgia Code § 16-12-160. Unlawful to buy or sell human body

(a) It shall be unlawful, except as provided in subsection (b) of this Code section, for any person, firm, or corporation to buy or sell, to offer to buy or sell, or to assist another in buying or selling or offering to buy or sell a human body or any part of a human body or buy or sell a human fetus or any part thereof.

(b) The prohibition contained in subsection (a) of this Code section shall not apply to:

(1) The purchase or sale of whole blood, blood plasma, blood products, blood derivatives, other self-replicating body fluids, or hair;

(2) A gift or donation of a human body or any part of a human body or any procedure connected therewith as provided in Article 6 of Chapter 5 of Title 44 or to the payment of a processing fee in connection with such gift or donation if such fee is paid to a bank or storage facility, as those terms are defined in Code Section 44-5-142;

(3) The reimbursement of actual expenses, including medical costs, lost income, and travel expenses, incurred by a living person in giving or donating a part of the person's body;

(4) The payment of financial assistance under a plan of insurance or other health care coverage;

(5) The purchase or sale of human tissue, organs, or other parts of the human body for health sciences education; or

(6) The payment of reasonable costs associated with the removal, storage, or transportation of a human body or any part of a human body given or donated for medical or scientific purposes.

(c) Any person, firm, or corporation convicted of violating subsection (a) of this Code section shall be guilty of a felony and, upon conviction thereof, shall be punished by a fine not exceeding $5,000.00 or by imprisonment for not less than one year nor more than five years, or both.

(9) INFORMED CONSENT

Georgia has enacted informed consent statutes. Under those statutes a woman must be given certain information 24 hours prior to an abortion. Some of the information required to be disclosed include informing the woman of the particular medical risks associated with the abortion procedure, the probable gestational age of the unborn child at the time the abortion would be performed, and the medical risks associated with carrying the unborn child to term. The statutes are set out below.

Georgia Code § 31-9A-1. Short title

This chapter shall be known and may be cited as the "Woman's Right to Know Act."

Georgia Code § 31-9A-2. Definitions

As used in this chapter, the term:

(1) "Abortion" means the use or prescription of any instrument, medicine, drug, or any other substance or device with the intent to terminate the pregnancy of a female known to be pregnant. The term "abortion" shall not include the use or prescription of any instrument, medicine, drug, or any other substance or device employed solely to increase the probability of a live birth, to preserve the life or health of the child after live birth, or to remove a dead unborn child who died as the result of a spontaneous abortion. The term "abortion" also shall not include the prescription or use of contraceptives.

(2) "Medical emergency" means any condition which, on the basis of the physician's good faith clinical judgment, so complicates the medical condition of a pregnant female as to necessitate the immediate abortion of her pregnancy to avert her death or for which a delay will create serious risk of substantial or irreversible impairment of a major bodily function.

(3) "Physician" means a person licensed to practice medicine under Article 2 of Chapter 34 of Title 43.

(4) "Probable gestational age of the unborn child" means the physician's best professional estimate of the probable gestational age of the unborn child at the time an abortion is to be performed.

(5) "Qualified agent" means the agent of the physician who is a patient educator, licensed psychologist, licensed social worker, licensed professional counselor, licensed physician's assistant, registered nurse, or physician.

(6) "Secure Internet website" means a website that is safeguarded from having its content altered other than by the commissioner of human resources.

(7) "Unborn child" or "fetus" means a member of the species homo sapiens from fertilization until birth.

Georgia Code § 31-9A-3. Voluntary and informed consent

No abortion shall be performed in this state except with the voluntary and informed consent of the female upon whom the abortion is to be performed. Notwithstanding any provision of law to the contrary, except in the case of a medical emergency, consent to an abortion is voluntary and informed if and only if:

(1) The female is told the following, by telephone or in person, by the physician who is to perform the abortion, by a qualified agent of the physician who is to perform the abortion, by a qualified agent of a referring physician, or by a referring physician, at least 24 hours before the abortion:

(A) The particular medical risks to the individual patient associated with the particular abortion procedure to be employed, when medically accurate;

(B) The probable gestational age of the unborn child at the time the abortion would be performed; and

(C) The medical risks associated with carrying the unborn child to term.

The information required by this paragraph may be provided by telephone without conducting a physical examination or tests of the patient, in which case the information required to be provided may be based on facts supplied to the physician by the female and whatever other relevant information is reasonably available to the physician. Such information may not be provided by a tape recording but must be provided during a consultation in which the physician or a qualified agent of the physician is able to ask questions of the female and the female is able to ask questions of the physician or the physician's qualified agent. If in the medical judgment of the physician any physical examination, tests, or other information subsequently provided to the physician requires a revision of the information previously supplied to the patient, that revised information shall be communicated to the patient prior to the performance of the abortion. Nothing in this Code section may be construed to preclude provision of required information in a language understood by the patient through a translator;

(2) The female is informed, by telephone or in person, by the physician who is to perform the abortion, by a referring physician, or by a qualified agent of the physician who is to perform the abortion at least 24 hours before the abortion:

(A) That medical assistance benefits may be available for prenatal care, childbirth, and neonatal care;

(B) That the father will be liable pursuant to subsection (a) of Code Section 19-7-49 to assist in the support of her child;

(C) How to obtain a list of health care providers, facilities, and clinics that offer to perform ultrasounds free of charge; such list shall be arranged geographically and shall include the name, address, hours of operation, and telephone number of each listed entity; and

(D) That she has the right to review the printed materials described in Code Section 31-9A-4 and that these materials are available on a state sponsored website at a stated website address. The physician or the physician's qualified agent shall orally inform the female that materials have been provided by the State of Georgia and that they describe the unborn child, list agencies that offer alternatives to abortion, and contain information on fetal pain. If the female chooses to view the materials other than on the website, they shall either be given to her at least 24 hours before the abortion or mailed to her at least 72 hours before the abortion by certified mail, restricted delivery to addressee.

The information required by this paragraph may be provided by a tape recording if provision is made to record or otherwise register specifically whether the female does or does not choose to review the printed materials other than on the website;

(3) The female certifies in writing, prior to the abortion, that the information described in paragraphs (1) and (2) of this Code section has been furnished her and that she has been informed of her opportunity to review the information referred to in subparagraph (D) of paragraph (2) of this Code section;

(4) For all cases in which an ultrasound is performed prior to conducting an abortion or a pre-abortion screen:

(A) The woman shall at the conclusion of the ultrasound be offered the opportunity to view the fetal image and hear the fetal heartbeat. The active ultrasound image shall be of a quality consistent with standard medical practice in the community, contain the dimensions of the unborn child, and accurately portray the presence of external members and internal organs, including but not limited to the heartbeat, if present or viewable, of the unborn child. The auscultation of fetal heart tone shall be of a quality consistent with standard medical practice in the community; and

(B) At the conclusion of these actions and prior to the abortion, the female certifies in writing that:

(i) She was provided the opportunity described in subparagraph (A) of this paragraph;

(ii) Whether or not she elected to view the sonogram; and

(iii) Whether or not she elected to listen to the fetal heartbeat, if present; and

(5) Prior to the performance of the abortion, the physician who is to perform the abortion or the physician's qualified agent receives a copy of the written certifications prescribed by paragraphs (3) and (4) of this Code section and retains them on file with the female's medical record for at least three years following the date of receipt.

Georgia Code § 31-9A-4. Materials made available by department

(a) The Department of Human Resources shall cause to be published in English and in each language which is the primary language of 2 percent or more of the state's population and shall cause to be available on the state website provided for in subsection (d) of this Code section the following printed materials in such a way as to ensure that the information is easily comprehensible:

(1) Geographically indexed materials designed to inform the female of public and private agencies and services available to assist a female through pregnancy, upon childbirth, and while the child is dependent, including adoption agencies, which shall include a comprehensive list of the agencies available, a description of the services they offer, and a description of the manner, including telephone numbers and website addresses, in which they might be contacted or, at the option of such department, printed materials including a toll-free, 24 hour telephone number which may be called to obtain, orally or by a tape recorded message tailored to the ZIP Code entered by the caller, such a list and description of agencies in the locality of the caller and of the services they offer;

(1.1) Geographically indexed materials designed to inform the female of public and private facilities and services available to assist a female with obtaining an ultrasound which shall include a comprehensive list of the facilities available, a description of the services they offer, and a description of the manner, including telephone numbers and website addresses, in which they might be contacted or, at the option of such department, printed materials including a toll-free, 24 hour telephone number which may be called to obtain, orally or by a tape recorded message tailored to the ZIP Code entered by the caller, such a list and description of facilities in the locality of the caller and of the services they offer;

(2) Materials designed to inform the female of the probable anatomical and physiological characteristics of the unborn child at two-week gestational increments from the time when a female can be known to be pregnant to full term, including any relevant information on the possibility of the unborn child's survival and pictures representing the development of unborn children at two-week gestational increments, provided that any such pictures must contain the dimensions of the fetus and must be factually accurate for the stage of pregnancy depicted. The materials shall be objective, nonjudgmen-

tal, and designed to convey only factually accurate scientific information about the unborn child at the various gestational ages. The material shall also contain objective information describing the methods of abortion procedures commonly employed, the medical risks commonly associated with each such procedure, the possible detrimental psychological effects of abortion, and the medical risks commonly associated with carrying a child to term; and

(3) Materials with the following statement concerning unborn children of 20 weeks' or more gestational age:

"By 20 weeks' gestation, the unborn child has the physical structures necessary to experience pain. There is evidence that by 20 weeks' gestation unborn children seek to evade certain stimuli in a manner which in an infant or an adult would be interpreted to be a response to pain. Anesthesia is routinely administered to unborn children who are 20 weeks' gestational age or older who undergo prenatal surgery."

The materials shall be objective, nonjudgmental, and designed to convey only accurate scientific information about the unborn child at the various gestational ages.

(b) The materials referred to in subsection (a) of this Code section shall be printed in a typeface large enough to be clearly legible. All pictures and print appearing on the website shall be clearly legible. All information and pictures shall be accessible with an industry standard browser, requiring no additional plug-ins.

(c) The materials required under this Code section shall be available at no cost from the Department of Human Resources upon request and in a reasonably appropriate number to any person, facility, or hospital.

(d) The Department of Human Resources shall develop and maintain a secure Internet website to provide the information described in this Code section. No information regarding who uses the website shall be collected or maintained. The Department of Human Resources shall monitor the website on a weekly basis to prevent and correct tampering.

Georgia Code § 31-9A-5. Medical emergency

(a) When a medical emergency compels the performance of an abortion, the physician shall inform the female prior to the abortion, if medically reasonable and prudent, of the medical indications supporting the physician's judgment that an abortion is medically necessary to avert her death or that a 24 hour delay will create serious risk of substantial or irreversible impairment of a major bodily function.

(b) Any physician who complies with subsection (a) of this Code section shall not be held civilly liable to a patient for failure to obtain informed consent to an abortion.

Georgia Code § 31-9A-6. Reporting form for physicians

(a) The Department of Human Resources shall prepare a reporting form for physicians performing abortions in a health facility licensed as an abortion facility by the Department of Human Resources containing a reprint of this chapter and listing:

(1) The number of females to whom the physician provided the information described in paragraph (1) of Code Section 31-9A-3; of that number, the number to whom the information was provided by telephone and the number to whom the information was provided in person; and of each of those numbers, the number to whom the information was provided by a referring physician and the number to whom the information was provided by a physician who is to perform the abortion;

(2) The number of females to whom the physician or a qualified agent of the physician provided the information described in paragraph (2) of Code Section 31-9A-3; of that number, the number to whom the information was provided by telephone and the number to whom the information was provided in person; of each of those numbers, the number to whom the information was provided by a referring physician and the number to whom the information was provided by a physician who is to perform the abortion; and of each of those numbers, the number to whom the information was provided by the physician and the number to whom the information was provided by a qualified agent of the physician;

(3) The number of females who availed themselves of the opportunity to obtain a copy of the printed information described in Code Section 31-9A-4, other than on the website, and the number who did not; and of each of those numbers, the number who, to the best of the reporting physician's information and belief, went on to obtain the abortion; and

(4) The number of females who were provided the opportunity to view the fetal image and hear the fetal heartbeat; of that number, the number who elected to view the sonogram and the number who elected to listen to the fetal heartbeat, if present.

(b) The Department of Human Resources shall ensure that copies of the reporting forms described in subsection (a) of this Code section are provided:

(1) Not later than September 7, 2005, to all health facilities licensed as an abortion facility by the Department of Human Resources;

(2) To each physician licensed or who subsequently becomes licensed to practice in this state, at the same time as official notification to that physician that the physician is so licensed; and

(3) By December 1 of each year, other than the calendar year in which forms are distributed in accordance with paragraph (1) of this subsection, to all health facilities licensed as an abortion facility by the Department of Human Resources.

(c) By February 28 of each year following a calendar year in any part of which this chapter was in effect, each physician who provided, or whose qualified agent provided, information to one or more females in accordance with Code Section 31-9A-3 during the previous calendar year shall submit to the Department of Human Resources a copy of the form described in subsection (a) of this Code section with the requested data entered accurately and completely.

(d) Nothing in this Code section shall be construed to preclude the voluntary or required submission of other reports or forms regarding abortions.

(e) Reports that are not submitted within a grace period of 30 days following the due date shall be subject to a late fee of $500.00 for that period and the same fee for each additional 30 day period or portion of a 30 day period the reports are overdue. Any physician required to submit a report in accordance with this Code section who submits an incomplete report or fails to submit a report for more than one year following the due date may, in an action brought by the Department of Human Resources, be directed by a court of competent jurisdiction to submit a complete report within a period stated by court order or may be subject to sanctions for civil contempt.

(f) By June 30 of each year, the Department of Human Resources shall issue a public report providing statistics for the previous calendar year compiled from all of the reports covering that year submitted in accordance with this Code section for each of the items listed in subsection (a) of this Code section. Each report shall also provide the statistics for all previous calendar years adjusted to reflect any additional information from late or corrected reports. The Department of Human Resources shall ensure that none of the information included in the public reports could reasonably lead to the identification of any individual who provided information in accordance with Code Section 31-9A-3 or 31-9A-4.

(g) The Department of Human Resources may, by regulation, alter the dates established by subsection (c) or (e) of this Code section or paragraph (3) of subsection (b) of this Code section or may consolidate the forms or reports described in this Code section with other forms or reports for reasons including, but not limited to, achieving administrative convenience or fiscal savings or reducing the burden of reporting requirements, so long as reporting forms are sent to all facilities licensed as an

abortion facility by the Department of Human Resources at least once every year and the report described in subsection (f) of this Code section is issued at least once every year.

(h) The Department of Human Resources shall ensure that the names and identities of the physicians filing reports under this chapter shall remain confidential. The names and identities of such physicians shall not be subject to Article 4 of Chapter 18 of Title 50.

Georgia Code § 31-9A-6.1. Failure to comply

In addition to whatever remedies are available under the common or statutory law of this state, failure to comply with the requirements of this chapter shall be reported to the Composite State Board of Medical Examiners for disciplinary action.

Georgia Code § 31-9A-7. Proceedings relating to chapter

In any civil proceeding or action relating to this chapter or a breach of duty under this chapter, the court shall rule whether the anonymity of any female upon whom an abortion has been performed shall be preserved from public disclosure if she does not give her consent to such disclosure. The court, upon motion or sua sponte, shall make such a ruling and, upon determining that her anonymity should be preserved, shall issue orders to the parties, witnesses, and counsel and shall direct the sealing of the record and exclusion of individuals from courtrooms or hearing rooms to the extent necessary to safeguard her identity from public disclosure. Each such order shall be accompanied by specific written findings explaining why the anonymity of the female should be preserved from public disclosure, why the order is essential to that end, how the order is narrowly tailored to serve that interest, and why no reasonable less restrictive alternative exists. This Code section may not be construed to conceal the identity of the plaintiff or of witnesses from the defendant.

Georgia Code § 31-9A-8. Severability

If any one or more provisions, Code sections, subsections, sentences, clauses, phrases, or words of this chapter or the application thereof to any person or circumstance is found to be unconstitutional, the same is declared to be severable, and the balance of this chapter shall remain effective notwithstanding such unconstitutionality. The General Assembly declares that it would have enacted this chapter and each Code section, subsection, sentence, clause, phrase, or word thereof irrespective of the fact that any one or more provisions, Code sections, subsections, sentences, clauses, phrases, or words would be declared unconstitutional.

(10) BAN ON PUBLIC SCHOOL ABORTION SERVICES

Georgia prohibits public schools from providing any services related to abortion or reproduction. The statute addressing the issue is set out below.

Georgia Code § 20-2-773. Banned health services by public school

(a) No facility operated on public school property or operated by a public school district and no employee of any such facility acting within the scope of such employee's employment shall provide any of the following health services to public school students:

(1) Distribution of contraceptives;

(2) Performance of abortions;

(3) Referrals for abortion; or

(4) Dispensing abortifacients.

(b) The Department of Education and local units of administration are prohibited from utilizing state funds for the distribution of contraceptives.

(11) PRO-LIFE LICENSE PLATE

Georgia authorizes the issuance of "Choose Life" license plates. The statute addressing the issue is set out below.

Georgia Code § 40-2-86.21. Special license plates

(a)(1) As used in this Code section, the term:

(A) "Manufacturing fee" means a $25.00 fee paid at the time a metal special license plate is issued.

(B) "Special tag renewal fee" means a $25.00 fee paid at the time a revalidation decal is issued for a special license plate.

(2) The General Assembly has determined that the issuance of special license plates to support an agency or fund or a program beneficial to the people of this state that is administered by a nonprofit corporation organized under Section 501(c)(3) of Title 26 of the Internal Revenue Code and dedicating a portion of the funds raised from the sale of these special license plates is in the best interests of the people of this state. Therefore, the special license plates listed in subsection(o) of this Code section shall be issued by the department beginning on July 1, 2007, if all of the requirements of subsections (b) through (k) of this Code section have been satisfied. The license plates listed in subsections (m) and (n) of this Code section shall continue to be issued so long as they meet the requirements of subsections (b), (c), (f), (g), (i), (j), and (k) of this Code section.

(b) The agency, fund, or nonprofit corporation sponsoring the special license plate, in cooperation with the commissioner, shall design special distinctive license plates appropriate to promote the program benefited by the sale of the special license plate. The special license plates must be of the same size as general issue motor vehicle license plates and shall include a unique design and identifying number, whereby the total number of characters does not exceed six. No two recipients shall receive identically numbered plates. The graphic on the special license plate shall be placed to the left of the alphanumeric characters and shall be no larger than three inches by three inches. The agency, fund, or nonprofit corporation sponsoring the license plate may request the assignment of the first of 100 in a series of license plates upon payment of an additional initial registration fee of $25.00 for each license plate requested.

(c) Notwithstanding the provisions of subsection (b) of this Code section, no special license plate shall be produced until such time as the State of Georgia has, through a licensing agreement or otherwise, received such licenses or other permissions as may be required to produce the special license plate. The design of the initial edition of any special license plate, as well as the design of subsequent editions and excepting only any part or parts of the designs owned by others and licensed to the state, shall be owned solely by the State of Georgia for its exclusive use and control, except as authorized by the commissioner. The commissioner may take such steps as may be necessary to give notice of and protect such right, including the copyright or copyrights. However, such steps shall be cumulative of the ownership and exclusive use and control established by this subsection as a matter of law, and no person shall reproduce or otherwise use such design or designs, except as authorized by the commissioner.

(d) Beginning on January 1, 2007, any Georgia resident who is the owner of a motor vehicle, except a vehicle registered under the International Registration Plan, upon complying with the motor vehicle laws relating to registration and licensing of motor vehicles and upon the payment of the manufacturing fee and the special tag renewal fee in addition to the regular motor vehicle registration fee shall be able to apply for a special license plate listed in subsection(o) of this Code section. Revalidation decals shall be issued for special license plates in the same manner as provided for general issue license plates.

(e) The manufacturing fee and the special tag renewal fee derived from the sale of special license plates listed in subsection(o) of this Code section shall be apportioned as follows: $1.00 to the county tag agent, $2.00 to the department, $12.00 to be deposited into the general fund, and $10.00 to be dedicated to the sponsoring agency, fund, or nonprofit corporation as permitted by Article III, Section IX, Paragraph VI(n) of the Constitution.

(f) Before the department disburses to the agency, fund, or nonprofit corporation funds from the sale of special license plates, the agency, fund, or nonprofit corporation must provide a written statement stating the manner in which such funds shall be utilized. In addition, a nonprofit cor-

poration must provide the department with documentation of its nonprofit status under Section 501(c)(3) of Title 26 of the Internal Revenue Code. The purposes for which the funds shall be utilized must be the same as those specified in subsections (m) and (n) of this Code section authorizing the dedication to the agency, fund, or nonprofit corporation of revenue from the sale of special license plates. The agency, fund, or nonprofit corporation shall periodically provide to the commissioner an audit of the use of the funds or other evidence of use of the funds satisfactory to the commissioner. If it is determined that the funds are not being used for the purposes set forth in the statement provided by the agency, fund, or nonprofit corporation, the department shall withhold payment of such funds until such noncompliance issues are resolved.

(g) An applicant may request a special license plate any time during the applicant's registration period. If such a license plate is to replace a current valid license plate, the special license plate if issued under subsection (m) of this Code section shall be issued with appropriate decals attached upon payment of the manufacturing fee but without payment of the special tag renewal fee. However, special license plates issued under subsections (n) and (o) of this Code section shall be issued with appropriate decals attached upon payment of the manufacturing fee and the special tag renewal fee.

(h) No special license plate authorized pursuant to subsection(o) of this Code section shall be issued except upon the receipt by the department of at least 1,000 applications. The special license plate shall have an application period of two years after the date on which the application period becomes effective for payment of the manufacturing fee. After such time if the minimum number of applications is not met, the department shall not continue to accept the manufacturing fee, and all fees shall be refunded to applicants.

(i) The department shall not be required to continue to manufacture the special license plate if the number of active registrations falls below 500 registrations at any time during the period provided for in subsection (b) of Code Section 40-2-31. A current registrant may continue to renew such special license plate during his or her annual registration period upon payment of the special tag renewal fee, if applicable, which shall be collected by the county tag agent at the time of collection of other registration fees and shall be remitted to the state as provided in Code Section 40-2-34. The department may continue to issue such special license plates that it has in its inventory to assist in achieving the minimum number of registrations. If the special license plate falls below 500 active registrations at any time during the period provided for in subsection (b) of Code Section 40-2-31, the sponsoring agency, fund, or nonprofit corporation shall be required again to obtain 1,000 applications accompanied by the manufacturing fee to continue to manufacture the special license plate.

(j) Special license plates shall be transferred from one vehicle to another vehicle in accordance with the provisions of Code Section 40-2-80.

(k) Special license plates shall be issued within 30 days of application once the requirements of this Code section have been met.

(1) The commissioner is authorized and directed to establish procedures and promulgate rules and regulations to effectuate the purposes of this Code section.

(m–n) Omitted.

(o)(1) The General Assembly has determined that license plates supporting the agencies, funds, or nonprofit corporations listed in this subsection shall be issued for the purposes indicated and with a portion of the revenue being disbursed to the agency, fund, or nonprofit corporation indicated in this subsection. The revenue disbursement for the special license plates in this subsection shall be as described in subsection (e) of this Code section.

(2–24) Omitted.

(25) A special license plate displaying the logo of Choose Life, Inc. The words " Choose Life " must appear at the bottom. The funds raised by the sale of this special license plate shall be disbursed to Choose Life of Georgia, Inc., to be distributed among nonprofit corporations in Georgia that counsel women to consider adoption.

Gestational Age

The duration of a pregnancy is determined by gestational age. Gestational age is generally calculated as the time from the first day of the last menstrual period, to the day of birth (menstrual age). However, conception actually occurs around the 14th day after the first day of the last menstrual period. The conception date is not usually known, therefore the beginning date for the pregnancy is usually set as the first day of the last menstrual period.

Abortion by Weeks of Gestation in the United States 2000–2004

Year	Weeks of Gestation ≤8	9–10	11–12	13–15	16–20	≥21	Unknown
2000	368,690	125,373	64,380	39,289	27,407	9,108	7,923
2001	357,517	115,164	60,241	37,509	25,929	8,654	5,228
2002	400,637	121,598	63,575	39,880	27,219	9,312	12,962
2003	401,259	119,125	64,327	41,269	27,575	9,383	12,225
2004	400,197	112,936	60,323	41,517	24,837	8,365	12,701
Total	1,928,300	594,196	312,846	199,464	132,967	44,822	51,039

Source: **National Center for Health Statistics, Abortion Surveillance.**

Gestation normally lasts 40 weeks or 280 days. A delivery that occurs before 37 weeks of gestation is considered premature. To improve the accuracy of gestational age estimates, several tests using ultrasound have been developed. These tests seek to determine gestational age through extrapolation from measurements of the size of the gestational sac, embryo and fetus. The most common tests include: mean sac diameter; crown-rump length; biparietal diameter; femur length; and abdominal circumference. *See also* **Abortion**

Gestational Diabetes *see* **Diabetes and Pregnancy**

Gestational Trophoblastic Tumors

Gestational trophoblastic tumors (GTT) are disorders involving the abnormal growth of the placenta. The disorders are always associated with a pregnancy. GTT may follow a spontaneous abortion, an ectopic pregnancy, or a full-term pregnancy. Risk factors for GTT include: blood type (blood types B or AB are at slightly higher risk than type A or O); lack of carotene or vitamin A in diet; birth control pills; and prior GTT. The only guaranteed way to avoid developing GTT is never to become pregnant. GTT disorders may be classified as follows: hydatidiform mole, invasive mole, choriocarcinoma, and placental-site trophoblastic tumor

Hydatidiform mole. Hydatidiform mole (also called molar pregnancy) involves the failure of an embryo to form or to malform. This is a condition where tissue around a fertilized egg, which would normally develop into the placenta, develops as an abnormal cluster of cells. There are two types of hydatidiform moles: complete and partial. A complete mole will normally have little or no fetal development. In contrast, a partial mole is associated with a developing fetus. The fetus will die usually within nine weeks, after the last menstrual period, although in rare instances it can survive to term.

The potential causes of this condition include defects in the egg, abnormalities within the uterus, or nutritional deficiencies. A complete or partial hydatidiform mole will trigger a positive pregnancy test and eventually they may become cancerous. (More than 80 percent of hydatidiform moles are benign.) Very often the mole will naturally expel from the uterus by the fourth month of pregnancy. The mole does not spread outside of the uterus to other parts of the body. Symptoms of the disease include vaginal bleeding, abdominal swelling, vomiting and anemia.

Approximately 1 out of 1,500 pregnancies are molar. Women under 20 or over 40 years of age, or who have had more than one miscarriage, are at a greater risk of having a molar pregnancy. The health risk posed to a woman by a molar pregnancy includes heavy bleeding and development of a rare pregnancy-related form of cancer (choriocarcinoma). It is recommended that a woman who has had a molar pregnancy refrain from becoming pregnant for one year.

Invasive mole. An invasive mole (chorioadenoma destruens) is actually a variant of hydatidiform mole that has invaded the uterine wall. It is said that an invasive mole is less aggressive than a true hydatidiform mole. An invasive mole develops in less than 20 percent of all molar pregnancies. Symptoms of the disease include bleeding, discharge from the vagina, pain in the pelvic region, abdominal swelling, dry cough, chest pain, and trouble breathing. Invasive moles are usually diagnosed about 6 months after a hydatidiform mole has been evacuated. They can cause hemorrhaging.

Choriocarcinoma. Choriocarcinoma is a malignant tumor that develops from the cells that cover the placenta. In about one-half of all cases of the disease it is preceded by a molar pregnancy. The disease also occurs following a full term pregnancy about one-fourth of the time. The remaining incidents follow an abortion, ectopic pregnancy, or genital tumor. The disease can spread from the uterus to other parts of the body. Symptoms of the disease include bleeding, discharge from the vagina, pain in the pelvic region, abdominal swelling, dry cough, chest pain, and trouble breathing. The disease occurs in about 1 out of every 40,000 pregnancies. Women over 40 are more susceptible to the disease.

Placental-site trophoblastic tumor. Placental-site trophoblastic tumor is an extremely rare tumor that arises at the placental implantation site after a hydatidiform mole has been evacuated. It is a variant of the choriocarcinoma. Symptoms of the disease includes bleeding, severe abdominal pain and swelling. Although it is curable, the condition is usually fatal when it has disseminated.

Treatment for GTT. There are two kinds of treatment for GTT: surgical removal or the use of chemotherapy drugs. If surgical removal is used the health care provider will perform a dilation and curettage operation or hysterectomy. In rare circumstances radiation therapy may be used to treat the cancer when it has spread to other parts of the body. *See also* **Cancer and Pregnancy**; **Therapeutic Abortion**

Ginsburg, Ruth Bader

Ruth Bader Ginsburg was appointed as an associate justice of the United States Supreme Court in 1993. Justice Ginsburg's early opinions have indicated a moderate approach to constitutional interpretation.

Justice Ginsburg was born in Brooklyn, New York, on March 15, 1933. She received an undergraduate degree from Cornell University in 1954. Subsequently she attended Harvard Law School and Columbia Law School, where she obtained a law degree. After law school Justice Ginsburg clerked for a Federal District Court judge before taking a teaching position at Rutgers University School of Law. Justice Ginsburg left teaching in 1972 in order to taking up a legal advocacy position with the Women's Rights Project of the American Civil Liberties Union. In 1993 President Bill Clinton appointed Justice Ginsburg to the Supreme Court.

During Justice Ginsburg's tenure on the Supreme Court she has issued a number of abortion related opinions. The written opinions and opinions simply voted on by Justice Ginsburg, indicate that she is in favor of using the constitution to expand abortion rights for women.

(1) Unanimous opinions voted with only. In *Dalton v. Little Rock Family Planning Services*, Justice Ginsburg voted with a unanimous Court in holding that an amendment to Arkansas' constitution which limited Medicaid payment only to therapeutic abortions, was invalid to the extent that Medicaid funds had to be made available for incest or rape pregnancies, but was valid for any purely state funded program. Justice Ginsburg voted with a unanimous Court in *National Organization for Women, Inc. v. Scheidler*, which held that a group of pro-choice organizations could maintain a RICO civil lawsuit against several anti-abortion individuals and groups. Justice Ginsburg voted with a unanimous Court in *Scheidler v. National Organization for Women, Inc. (II)*, which held pro-choice advocates could not sue pro-life advocates under the Hobbs Act for allegations of physical violence that did not involve extortion. Justice Ginsburg joined the unanimous opinion in *Ayotte v. Planned Parenthood of Northern New England*, which held that the absence of a health exception in New Hampshire's parental notification abortion statute did not require the entire statute be invalidated.

(2) Majority opinions voted with only. Justice Ginsburg voted with the majority in *Ferguson v. City of Charleston*, in holding that patient consent or a search warrant was needed in order for a government hospital to turn over to the police drug test results that showed a woman used illegal drugs during her pregnancy. In *Hill v. Colorado* Justice Ginsburg voted with the majority opinion in upholding a Colorado statute that made it unlawful for any person within 100 feet of an abor-

Justice Ginsburg's voting pattern favors the views of pro-choice advocates (collection, Supreme Court Historical Society, photograph by Steve Petteway, Supreme Court).

Distribution of the Abortion Voting Pattern of Justice Ginsburg Based Upon Opinions Filed by the Supreme Court

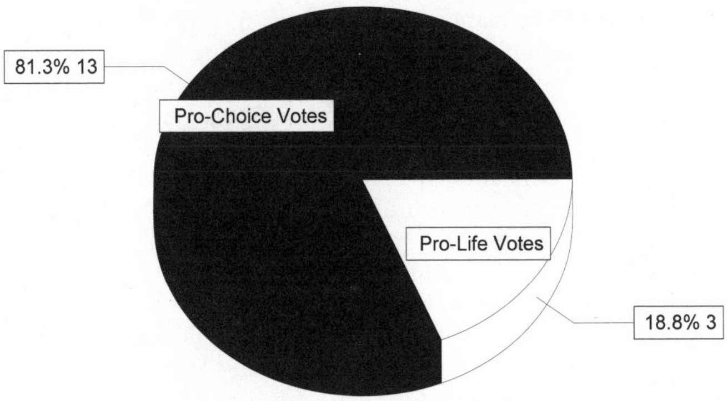

tion facility's entrance, to knowingly approach within 8 feet of another person, without that person's consent, in order to pass a leaflet, handbill, display a sign, engage in oral protest, education, or counseling with that person. Justice Ginsburg voted with the majority in *Schenck v. Pro Choice Network of Western New York*, which held that a federal trial court's injunction provisions imposing fixed buffer zone limitations on abortion protesters were constitutional, but the provisions imposing floating buffer zone limitations violated the First Amendment.

In *Madsen v. Women's Health Clinic, Inc.*, Justice Ginsburg voted with the majority opinion, which upheld parts of an injunction that restricted noise by anti-abortionists at a clinic and imposed a 36 foot buffer zone around the clinic entrances and driveway. However, *Madsen* ruled that the Free Speech Clause was violated by a 36 foot buffer zone as applied to the private property to the north and west of the clinic, a restriction on the use of images observable by clinic patients, a 300 foot no approach zone around the clinic, and a 300 foot buffer zone around the residences, because these restrictions swept more broadly than necessary to accomplish the permissible goals of the injunction. Justice Ginsburg voted with the majority in *Federal Election Commission v. Beaumont*, which held that the Federal Election Campaign Act's prohibition on corporate expenditures and contributions directly to candidates in federal elections, applies to a nonprofit pro-life organization.

(3) Concurring opinions written. In *Stenberg v. Carhart*, Justice Ginsburg wrote a concurring opinion that agreed with the majority's decision to find Nebraska's statute banning partial-birth abortion unconstitutional. Justice Ginsburg wrote a concurring opinion in *Scheidler v. National Organization for Women, Inc. (I)*, which held that evidence did not support finding that pro-life advocates violated the Hobbs Act, Travel Act and state law extortion crimes, for the purpose of awarding damages and granting an injunction against them under RICO.

(4) Concurring opinions voted with only. In *Lambert v. Wicklund* Justice Ginsburg concurred with the majority in holding that the constitution was not violated by a provision in Montana's abortion statute that allowed a court to waive the parental notice requirement for minors, if notification was not in minor's best interest.

(5) Dissenting opinions voted with only. Justice Ginsburg joined the dissenting opinion in *Leavitt v. Jane L.*, which held that the invalidity of Utah's statute regulating pregnancies 20 weeks old or less, may be severed so as to preserve that portion of the abortion statute that regulated pregnancies of more than 20 weeks. Justice Ginsburg joined the dissenting opinion in *Federal Election Commission v. Wisconsin Right to Life, Inc.*, which held that the electioneering communications provisions of a federal statute violated a pro-life organization's First Amendment right to broadcast political issue oriented advertisements shortly before primary and general elections. Justice Ginsburg joined the dissenting opinion in *Mazurek v. Armstrong*, which held that Montana's requirement that abortions be performed only by physicians was constitutionally valid.

(6) Dissenting opinions written. Justice Ginsburg wrote a dissenting opinion in *Gonzales v. Carhart*, which held that the Partial-Birth Abortion Ban Act of 2003 was not facially unconstitutional, because it outlined the abortion procedure that was banned, and the Act did not have to provide an exception for the health of a woman.

Goldberg, Arthur J.

Arthur J. Goldberg (1908–1990) served as an associate justice of the United States Supreme Court from 1962 to 1965. While on the Supreme Court Justice Goldberg was known as a liberal interpreter of the Constitution, particularly with respect to individual liberties and rights.

Justice Goldberg was born in Chicago, Illinois. He was a 1929 graduate of Northwestern University Law School. Much of Justice Goldberg's private law practice was spent representing labor organizations. He was able to gain national prominence as a result of his representation of labor groups. President John F. Kennedy appointed him as Secretary of Labor in 1961. In 1962 President Kennedy filled a vacancy of the Supreme Court by appointing Justice Goldberg to the position.

Justice Goldberg was involved in only one abortion related opinion while on the Supreme Court. In *Griswold v. Connecticut* Justice Goldberg wrote an opinion concurring with the majority decision, which held that the right of privacy found in the constitution prohibited enforcement of a Connecticut statute that made it a crime to give married persons contraceptive information and devices.

Gonorrhea

Gonorrhea is a sexually transmitted disease that is caused by a bacterium called *Neisseria gonorrhoeae.* The disease is spread during vaginal, oral, or anal sexual intercourse. Gonorrhea can infect the urethra (urinal canal), the mouth, throat, or the rectum in women and men. The infection can spread to other parts of the body (e.g., a person can get an eye infection after touching an infected area and then touching the eyes). In women specifically, the disease infects the cervix and

REPORTED OCCURRENCE OF GONORRHEA BY WOMEN U.S. 2002-2006

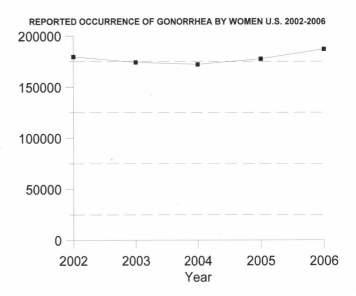

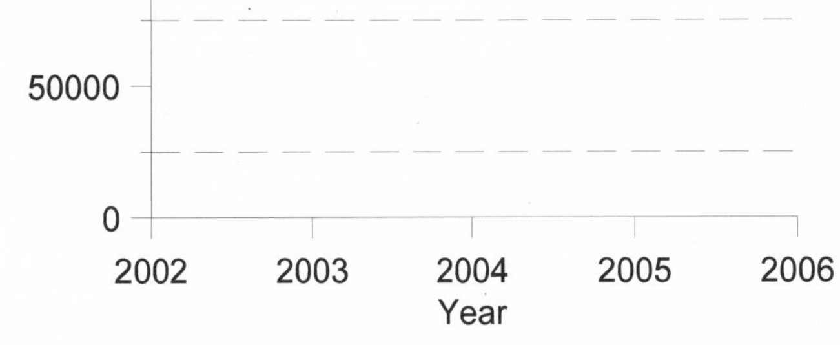

Source: **Centers for Disease Control and Prevention.**

can spread into the uterus and fallopian tubes, resulting in pelvic inflammatory disease. A pregnant woman infected with gonorrhea can pass the disease to the newborn infant during delivery, which may cause blindness, joint infection, or a life-threatening blood infection in the child. It is estimated that 650,000 cases of gonorrhea occur annually in the United States.

The early symptoms of gonorrhea usually appear within two to ten days after sexual contact with an infected partner. For women the first symptoms include a painful or burning sensation when urinating and abnormal vaginal discharge. Later symptoms for women include cramps and pain, bleeding between menstrual periods, fever and vomiting. Symptoms for men include a burning sensation when urinating, a yellowish white discharge from the penis, and painful or swollen testicles. Symptoms associated with rectal infection include anal itching and occasional painful bowel movements. Infections in the throat cause few symptoms.

Gonorrhea is curable. The disease is treated with antibiotics (ceftriaxone, cefixime, ciprofloxacin or ofloxacin). Left untreated, gonorrhea can have grave consequences. In men, gonorrhea can cause a painful condition of the testicles that may lead to infertility if left untreated. It can also affect the prostate and can lead to scarring inside the urethra, making urination difficult. For women the most common result of untreated gonorrhea is pelvic inflammatory disease (PID). PID can lead to internal abscesses, long-lasting pelvic pain, and infertility. Additionally, PID can cause infertility or damage the fallopian tubes enough to increase the risk of ectopic pregnancy (a life-threatening condition in which a fertilized egg grows outside the uterus, usually in a fallopian tube). For men and women, untreated gonorrhea can spread to the blood or joints. This condition can be life-threatening. Also, persons with the disease are more susceptible to contracting HIV (the virus that causes AIDS). The risk of contracting gonorrhea may be decreased through the use of latex condoms. *See also* **Pelvic Inflammatory Disease; Sexually Transmitted Diseases**

Gonzales v. Carhart

Forum: United States Supreme Court.

Case Citation: Gonzales v. Carhart, 127 S.Ct. 1610 (2007).

Date Argued: November 8, 2006.

Date of Decision: April 18, 2007.

Opinion of Court: Kennedy, J., in which Roberts, C. J., Scalia, Thomas, and Alito, JJ., joined.

Concurring Opinion: Thomas, J., in which Scalia, J., joined.

Dissenting Opinion: Ginsburg, J., in which Stevens, Souter, and Breyer, JJ., joined.

Counsel for Appellants: Paul D. Clement argued; on the briefs were Peter D. Keisler, Gregory G. Garre, Gregory G. Katsas, Kannon K. Shanmugam, Marleigh D. Dover, Catherine Y. Hancock, and Teal Luthy Miller.

Counsel for Appellees: Priscilla Smith and Eve C. Gartner argued; on the briefs were Jerry M. Hug, Janet Crepps, Nan E. Strauss, Sanford M. Cohen, Dennis J. Herrera, Therese M. Stewart, Aleeta Van Runkle, Kathleen S. Morris, Beth H. Parker, Roger K. Evans, and Helene T. Krasnoff.

Amicus Brief for Appellants: Ronald W. Meyer; Christian Medical and Dental Associations and the Catholic Medical Association; Professor Hadley Arkes and The Claremont Institute Center for Constitutional Jurisprudence; Matercare International, Jack A. Andonie, M.D., and Raymond F. Gasser, PH.D.; Jill Stanek and the Association of Pro-Life Physicians; Christian Legal Society, National Association of Evangelicals, Pro-Life Legal Defense Fund, Alliance Defense Fund and Concerned Women for America; National Legal Foundation; Brief of Faith and Action, Institute in Basic Life Principles, International Reapers Foundation, The National Clergy Council and Illinois State Senator David Syverson; American Center for Law and Justice; Thomas More Society, Inc.; John M. Thorp, Jr., M.D.; Jill Stanek; Sandra Cano and 180 Women Injured by Abortion; Gianna Jessen, Zachary Klopfenstein, Terry and Jill Klopfenstein, and the Center for Moral Clarity; Foundation for Moral Law, Inc.; Congressman Ron Paul and Association of American Physicians and Surgeons; United States Conference of Catholic Bishops and Other Religious Organizations; American Center for Law and Justice, 78 Members of Congress, and the Committee to Protect the Ban on Partial Birth Abortion; Horatio R. Storer Foundation, Inc.; National Legal Foundation; States of Texas, Alabama, Arkansas, Florida, Indiana, Missouri, North Dakota, Ohio, Pennsylvania, South Carolina, South Dakota, Utah, and Virginia; Thomas More Law Center, the National Pro-Life Alliance, and the Catholic League for Religious and Civil Rights; Judicial Watch, Inc.; United States Justice Foundation, Traditional Values Coalition, California Republican Assembly, and California State Assemblyman Raymond S. Haynes; Family Research Council and Focus on the Family; American Association of Pro Life Obstetricians and Gynecologists, Senator Tom Coburn, M.D., Congressman Charles Boustany, Jr., M.D., Congressman Michael Burgess, M.D., Congressman Phil Gingrey, M.D., Congressman Dave Weldon, M.D., C. Everett Koop, M.D., Edmund D. Pellegrino, M.D.; Eagle Forum Education & Legal Defense Fund; Pro-Life Legal Defense Fund, Alliance Defense Fund, Christian Legal Society, Christian Medical Association, Concerned Women for America, and National Association of Evangelicals; Right to Life Advocates, Inc.; Rutherford Institute; and Margie Riley and Laurette Elsberry.

Amicus Brief for Appellees: American Medical Women's Association, American Public Health Association; American Civil Liberties Union, New York Civil Liberties Union, National Abortion Federation; California Medical Association; Former Federal Prosecutors; Institute for Reproductive Health Access and Fifty-Two Clinics and Organizations; Religious Coalition for Reproductive Choice and Thirty-Four Other Religious and Religiously Affiliated Organizations and Individual Clergy and Theologians; 52 Members of Congress; National Women's Law Center and 31 Other Organizations Committed to the Safest Health Care for Women; American College of Obstetricians and Gynecologists; NARAL Pro-Choice America Foundation; David L. Faigman and Ashutosh A. Bhagwat; Professor George W. Cobb, Professor Mary W. Gray, Professor Norman Henderson, Professor John J. McArdle, Professor James Trussell, and Professor Jeffrey A. Witmer; and Cato Institute.

Issue Presented: Whether the Partial-Birth Abortion Ban Act of 2003 was facially unconstitutional?

Case Holding: The Partial-Birth Abortion Ban Act of 2003 was not facially unconstitutional, because it outlined the abortion procedure that was banned, and the Act did not have to provide an exception for the health of a woman.

Background facts of case: The case involved two separate law suits that were consolidated for purposes of appeal. In the first case several plaintiffs sued the United States Attorney General in a federal court in Nebraska, seeking to prevent enforcement of the Partial-Birth Abortion Ban Act of 2003 (the Act). A federal district judge found the Act unconstitutional based upon a prior decision by the United States Supreme in *Stenberg v. Carhart*, 530 U.S. 914 (2000). A court of appeals affirmed the ruling.

In the second case several plaintiffs sued the Attorney General in a federal court in California, seeking to prevent enforcement of the Act. A federal district judge found the Act unconstitutional based upon the decision *Stenberg*. A court of appeals affirmed the ruling. The Supreme Court granted certiorari in both cases and consolidated them.

Majority opinion by Justice Kennedy: Justice Kennedy distinguished the Act from the Nebraska partial-birth abortion ban statute that was found unconstitutional in *Stenberg*. He wrote that the Act was more specific than the Nebraska statute in outlining the particular procedure that was banned. Justice Kennedy also found that even though the Act and the invalidated statute in *Stenberg* both failed to provide an exception for a woman's health, the issue did not require the Act to be invalidated in a facial challenge to its constitutionality. The opinion addressed both issues as follows:

> [T]he Act departs in material ways from the statute in *Stenberg*. It adopts the phrase "delivers a living fetus," instead of " delivering ... a living unborn child, or a substantial portion thereof." The Act's language, unlike the statute in *Stenberg*, expresses the usual meaning of "deliver" when used in connection with "fetus," namely, extraction of an entire fetus rather than removal of fetal pieces. The Act thus displaces the interpretation of "delivering" dictated by the Nebraska statute's reference to a "substantial portion" of the fetus....
>
> The identification of specific anatomical landmarks to which the fetus must be partially delivered also differentiates the Act from the statute at issue in *Stenberg*. The Court in *Stenberg* interpreted "substantial portion" of the fetus to include an arm or a leg. The Act's anatomical landmarks, by contrast, clarify that the removal of a small portion of the fetus is not prohibited. The landmarks also require the fetus to be delivered so that it is partially "outside the body of the mother." To come within the ambit of the Nebraska statute, on the other hand, a substantial portion of the fetus only had to be delivered into the vagina; no part of the fetus had to be outside the body of the mother before a doctor could face criminal sanctions.
>
> By adding an overt-act requirement Congress sought further to meet the Court's objections to the state statute considered in *Stenberg*. The Act makes the distinction the Nebraska statute failed to draw by differentiating between the overall partial-birth abortion and the distinct overt act that kills the fetus. The fatal overt act must occur after delivery to an anatomical landmark, and it must be something other than [the] completion of delivery....
>
> The Act's furtherance of legitimate government interests bears upon, but does not resolve, the next question: whether the Act has the effect of imposing an unconstitutional burden on the abortion right because it does not allow use of the barred procedure where necessary, in appropriate medical judgment, for [the] preservation of the ... health of the mother. The prohibition in the Act would be unconstitutional, under precedents we here assume to be controlling, if it subject[ed] [women] to significant health risks....
>
> [R]elying on the Court's opinion in *Stenberg*, respondents contend that an abortion regulation must contain a health exception if substantial medical authority supports the proposition that banning a particular procedure could endanger women's health. As illustrated by respondents' arguments and the decisions of the Courts of Appeals, *Stenberg* has been interpreted to leave no margin of error for legislatures to act in the face of medical uncertainty.
>
> A zero tolerance policy would strike down legitimate abortion regulations, like the present one, if some part of the medical community were disinclined to follow the proscription. This is too exacting a standard to impose on the legislative power, exercised in this instance under the Commerce Clause, to regulate the medical profession. Considerations of marginal safety, including the balance of risks, are within the legislative competence when the regulation is rational and in pursuit of legitimate ends. When standard medical options are available, mere convenience does not suffice to displace them; and if some procedures have different risks than others, it does not follow that the State is altogether barred from imposing reasonable regulations. The Act is not invalid on its face where there is uncertainty over whether the barred procedure is ever necessary to preserve a woman's health, given the availability of other abortion procedures that are considered to be safe alternatives.

Disposition of case: The judgments of the appellate courts were reversed.

Concurring opinion by Justice Thomas: Justice Thomas joined the majority opinion. He wrote a terse concurring opinion simply "to reiterate my view that the Court's abortion jurisprudence, including *Casey* and *Roe v. Wade*, 410 U.S. 113, 93 S.Ct. 705, 35 L.Ed.2d 147 (1973), has no basis in the Constitution."

Dissenting opinion by Justice Ginsburg: Justice Ginsburg dissented from the majority opinion. She argued that the case could not be distinguished from *Stenberg* and that the Act was unconstitutional for failing to provide an exception for a woman's health. Justice Ginsburg wrote as follows:

> Seven years ago, in *Stenberg v. Carhart*, 530 U.S. 914, 120 S.Ct. 2597, 147 L.Ed.2d 743 (2000), the Court invalidated a Nebraska statute criminalizing the performance of a medical procedure that, in the political arena, has been dubbed "partial-birth abortion." With fidelity to the *Roe-Casey* line of precedent, the Court held the Nebraska statute unconstitutional in part because it lacked the requisite protection for the preservation of a woman's health.
>
> Today's decision is alarming. It refuses to take *Casey* and *Stenberg* seriously. It tolerates, indeed applauds, federal intervention to ban nationwide a procedure found necessary and proper in certain cases by the American College of Obstetricians and Gynecologists. It blurs the line, firmly drawn in *Casey*, between previability and postviability abortions. And, for the first time since *Roe*, the Court blesses a prohibition with no exception safeguarding a woman's health.
>
> I dissent from the Court's disposition. Retreating from prior rulings that abortion restrictions cannot be imposed absent an exception safeguarding a woman's health, the Court upholds an Act that surely would not survive under the close scrutiny that previously attended state-decreed limitations on a woman's reproductive choices.

Note: The decision in the case was very narrow, in that it only held that the Act was valid in the context of a facial challenge to its constitutionality. What this means is that it may be possible that under certain facts, the Act could be found unconstitutional when applied to a specific woman seeking to have a partial-birth abortion for health reasons. *See also* **Dilation and Extraction; Methods of Abortion; Partial-Birth Abortion; Partial-Birth Abortion Ban Act; Stenberg v. Carhart**

Griffin, Michael Frederick

Michael Frederick Griffin (b. 1961) was a militant anti-abortionist operating out of Pensacola, Florida. On the morning of March 10, 1993, Griffin and other militant anti-abortion demonstrators went to a Pensacola abortion clinic where obstetrician-gynecologist Dr. David Gunn worked. As Dr. Gunn exited his car in the parking lot of the clinic, Griffin shot him three times in the back. Dr. Gunn died several hours later. The death of Dr. Gunn was the first murder of a physician by an militant anti-abortionist in American history. Griffin was arrested and convicted of the murder. He was sentenced to life in prison on March 5, 1994. *See also* **Abortion Violence, Property Destruction and Demonstrations**

Griswold v. Connecticut

Forum: United States Supreme Court.
Case Citation: Griswold v. Connecticut, 381 U.S. 479 (1965).
Date Argued: March 29–30, 1965.
Date of Decision: June 7, 1965.

Opinion of Court: Douglas, J., in which Warren, C. J., and Brennan, Clark, and Goldberg, JJ., joined.

Concurring Opinion: Goldberg, J., in which Warren, C. J., and Brennan, J., joined.

Concurring Opinion: Harlan, J.

Concurring Opinion: White, J.

Dissenting Opinion: Black, J., in which Stewart, J., joined.

Dissenting Opinion: Stewart, J., in which Black, J., joined.

Counsel for Appellants: Thomas I. Emerson argued; on the brief was Catherine G. Roraback.

Counsel for Appellee: Joseph B. Clark argued; on the brief was Julius Maretz.

Amicus Brief for Appellants: Whitney North Seymour and Eleanor M. Fox for Dr. John M. Adams et al.; by Morris L. Ernst, Harriet F. Pilpel and Nancy F. Wechsler for the Planned Parenthood Federation of America, Inc.; by Alfred L. Scanlon for the Catholic Council on Civil Liberties, and by Rhoda H. Karpatkin, Melvin L. Wulf and Jerome E. Caplan for the American Civil Liberties Union et al.

Amicus Brief for Appellee: None.

Issue Presented: Whether the constitution was violated by a Connecticut statute that made it a crime to give married persons contraceptive information and devices?

Case Holding: The right of privacy found in the constitution prohibited enforcement of a Connecticut statute that made it a crime to give married persons contraceptive information and devices.

Background facts of case: A Connecticut statute made it a crime for any person to use any drug or article to prevent conception. The appellants, the director of the Planned Parenthood League of Connecticut, its medical director and a physician, were convicted of violating the statute by giving married persons information and medical advice on how to prevent conception and prescribing a contraceptive device. The state appellate courts affirmed the convictions. The Supreme Court granted certiorari to consider the constitutionality of the statute.

Majority opinion by Justice Douglas: Justice Douglas found the statute violated a right of privacy found in several provisions of the constitution. He wrote as follows:

> The present case ... concerns a relationship lying within the zone of privacy created by several fundamental constitutional guarantees. And it concerns a law which, in forbidding the use of contraceptives rather than regulating their manufacture or sale, seeks to achieve its goals by means having a maximum destructive impact upon that relationship. Such a law cannot stand in light of the familiar principle, so often applied by this Court, that a governmental purpose to control or prevent activities constitutionally subject to state regulation may not be achieved by means which sweep unnecessarily broadly and thereby invade the area of protected freedoms. The very idea is repulsive to the notions of privacy surrounding the marriage relationship.
>
> We deal with a right of privacy older than the Bill of Rights—older than our political parties, older than our school system. Marriage is a coming together for better or for worse, hopefully enduring, and intimate to the degree of being sacred. It is an association that promotes a way of life, not causes; a harmony in living, not political faiths; a bilateral loyalty, not commercial or social projects. Yet it is an association for as noble a purpose as any involved in our prior decisions.

Disposition of case: The judgment of the supreme court of Connecticut was reversed.

Concurring opinion by Justice Goldberg: Justice Goldberg agreed with the decision in the case. He wrote separately to make the following points:

> I agree with the Court that Connecticut's birth-control law unconstitutionally intrudes upon the right of marital privacy, and I join in its opinion and judgment. Although I have not accepted the view that due process as used in the Fourteenth Amendment incorporates all of the first eight Amendments, I do agree that the concept of liberty protects those personal rights that are fundamental, and is not confined to the specific terms of the Bill of Rights. My conclusion that the concept of liberty is not so restricted and that it embraces the right of marital privacy though that right is not mentioned explicitly in the Constitution is supported both by numerous decisions of this Court....
>
> Although the Connecticut birth-control law obviously encroaches upon a fundamental personal liberty, the State does not show that the law serves any subordinating state interest which is compelling or that it is necessary to the accomplishment of a permissible state policy. The State, at most, argues that there is some rational relation between this statute and what is admittedly a legitimate subject of state concern — the discouraging of extra-marital relations. It says that preventing the use of birth-control devices by married persons helps prevent the indulgence by some in such extramarital relations. The rationality of this justification is dubious, particularly in light of the admitted widespread availability to all persons in the State of Connecticut, unmarried as well as married, of birth-control devices for the prevention of disease, as distinguished from the prevention of conception. But, in any event, it is clear that the state interest in safeguarding marital fidelity can be served by a more discriminately tailored statute, which does not, like the present one, sweep unnecessarily broadly, reaching far beyond the evil sought to be dealt with and intruding upon the privacy of all married couples. Here, as elsewhere, where precision of regulation must be the touchstone in an area so closely touching our most precious freedoms. The State of Connecticut does have statutes, the constitutionality of which is beyond doubt, which prohibit adultery and fornication. These statutes demonstrate that means for achieving the same basic purpose of protecting marital fidelity are available to Connecticut without the need to invade the area of protected freedoms.

Concurring opinion by Justice Harlan: Justice Harlan concurred in the judgment of the Court, but not its reasoning. He wrote as follows:

> I fully agree with the judgment of reversal, but find myself unable to join the Court's opinion....
>
> In my view, the proper constitutional inquiry in this case is whether this Connecticut statute infringes the Due Process Clause of the Fourteenth Amendment because the enactment violates basic values implicit in the concept of ordered liberty.... I believe that it does. While the relevant inquiry may be aided by resort to one or more of the provisions of the Bill of Rights, it is not dependent on them or any of their radiations. The Due Process Clause of the Fourteenth Amendment stands, in my opinion, on its own bottom.

Concurring opinion by Justice White: Justice White agreed with the judgment of the Court, but did not concur in its reasoning. He wrote as follows:

> In my view this Connecticut law as applied to married couples deprives them of liberty without due process of law, as that concept is used in the Fourteenth Amendment. I therefore concur in the judgment of the Court reversing these convictions....
>
> The Connecticut anti-contraceptive statute deals rather substantially with [the marriage] relationship. For it forbids all married persons the right to use birth-control devices, regardless of whether their use is dictated by considerations of family planning. The anti-use statute, together with the general aiding and abetting statute, prohibits doctors from affording advice to married persons on proper and effective methods of birth control. And the clear effect of these statutes, as enforced, is to deny disadvantaged citizens of Connecticut, those without either ade-

quate knowledge or resources to obtain private counseling, access to medical assistance and up-to-date information in respect to proper methods of birth control. In my view, a statute with these effects bears a substantial burden of justification when attacked under the Fourteenth Amendment.

Dissenting opinion by Justice Black: Justice Black dissented from the Court's decision. He did not believe that the statute violated the constitution. Justice Black wrote the following:

> ... I do not to any extent whatever base my view that this Connecticut law is constitutional on a belief that the law is wise or that its policy is a good one. In order that there may be no room at all to doubt why I vote as I do, I feel constrained to add that the law is every bit as offensive to me as it is to ... the majority....
>
> Had the doctor defendant here, or even the nondoctor defendant, been convicted for doing nothing more than expressing opinions to persons coming to the clinic that certain contraceptive devices, medicines or practices would do them good and would be desirable, or for telling people how devices could be used, I can think of no reasons at this time why their expressions of views would not be protected by the First and Fourteenth Amendments, which guarantee freedom of speech. But speech is one thing; conduct and physical activities are quite another. The two defendants here were active participants in an organization which gave physical examinations to women, advised them what kind of contraceptive devices or medicines would most likely be satisfactory for them, and then supplied the devices themselves, all for a graduated scale of fees, based on the family income. Thus these defendants admittedly engaged with others in a planned course of conduct to help people violate the Connecticut law. Merely because some speech was used in carrying on that conduct — just as in ordinary life some speech accompanies most kinds of conduct — we are not in my view justified in holding that the First Amendment forbids the State to punish their conduct. Strongly as I desire to protect all First Amendment freedoms, I am unable to stretch the Amendment so as to afford protection to the conduct of these defendants in violating the Connecticut law....

Dissenting opinion by Justice Stewart: Justice Stewart did not believe that the statute violated the constitution. He wrote in dissent as follows:

> Since 1879 Connecticut has had on its books a law which forbids the use of contraceptives by anyone. I think this is an uncommonly silly law. As a practical matter, the law is obviously unenforceable, except in the oblique context of the present case. As a philosophical matter, I believe the use of contraceptives in the relationship of marriage should be left to personal and private choice, based upon each individual's moral, ethical, and religious beliefs. As a matter of social policy, I think professional counsel about methods of birth control should be available to all, so that each individual's choice can be meaningfully made. But we are not asked in this case to say whether we think this law is unwise, or even asinine. We are asked to hold that it violates the United States Constitution. And that I cannot do....
>
> At the oral argument in this case we were told that the Connecticut law does not conform to current community standards. But it is not the function of this Court to decide cases on the basis of community standards. We are here to decide cases agreeably to the Constitution and laws of the United States. It is the essence of judicial duty to subordinate our own personal views, our own ideas of what legislation is wise and what is not. If, as I should surely hope, the law before us does not reflect the standards of the people of Connecticut, the people of Connecticut can freely exercise their true Ninth and Tenth Amendment rights to persuade their elected representatives to repeal it. That is the constitutional way to take this law off the books.

Group B Strep

Group B strep (GBS) is an active germ that is found in men and women. It may exist in the bowel, vagina, bladder, or throat. Most people who carry GBS do not become ill. However, approximately 20 percent of men and nonpregnant women with GBS die of the disease.

GBS is found in the vaginal or rectal areas of 10 to 35 percent of all healthy adult women. It is in these women, if they are pregnant, that GBS may take its toll. GBS causes illness primarily in pregnant women and their babies. Approximately 17,000 pregnancy cases occur annually in the United States. In pregnant women, GBS can cause bladder infections, womb infections and stillbirth.

A fetus may come in contact with GBS before or during birth, if the mother carries GBS in the rectum or vagina. Approximately one out of every 200 babies whose mothers carry GBS, develop symptoms of the disease that include: pneumonia, sepsis (blood infection) and meningitis (infection of the fluid and lining surrounding the brain). About 6 percent of babies with GBS die. Of the babies who live, the vast majority go on to develop normally. Fifteen to 30 percent of GBS-infected babies who develop meningitis suffer neurologic damage in the form of cerebral palsy, sight and hearing loss, or mental retardation. There are two treatments that are in common use: oral antibiotics and IV antibiotics during labor. *See also* **Birth Defects and Abortion**

Guttmacher, Dr. Alan F.

Dr. Alan F. Guttmacher (1898–1974) was a distinguished obstetrician-gynecologist, author and a major leader in the birth control movement. Dr. Guttmacher embraced the birth control movement in the 1920s while an intern. He was motivated to join the movement after witnessing a woman die from a botched abortion. Dr. Guttmacher's dedication in the struggle to change laws that denied women the freedom to legally chose abortion, took him to the forefront of many projects. He organized family planning programs at Johns Hopkins Hospital and Mt. Sinai Hospital. After his 1952 appointment as director of Obstetrics and Gynecology at Mt. Sinai Hospital, Dr. Guttmacher assumed increasing responsibilities in directing the activities of Planned Parenthood Federation of America. His leadership role with the organization lead to his appointment as president of the organization in 1962. From that position Dr. Guttmacher lectured around the world. *See also* **Guttmacher Institute**

Guttmacher Institute

The Guttmacher Institute (Institute) is the leading think tank on sexual and reproductive health in the United States and worldwide, with offices in New York and Washington, D.C. The organization was established in 1968 under the name of Center for Family Planning Program Development. The Institute became an entirely independent 501(c)(3) organization and changed its name in 1977 to honor one of its leaders, Dr. Alan F. Guttmacher. The president of the Institute is Dr. Sharon L. Camp.

Dr. Sharon L. Camp is president of the Guttmacher Institute. The institute is the leading think tank on sexual and reproductive health in the United States and worldwide, with offices in New York and Washington, D.C. (Sharon L. Camp).

The Institute works to advance sexual and reproductive health through an interrelated program of social science research, policy analysis and public education designed to generate new ideas, encourage enlightened public debate, promote sound policy and program development and, ultimately, inform individual decision making. The Institute envisions a society in which men and women may freely exercise their rights and responsibilities regarding sexual behavior, reproduction and family formation. The organization believes that it is essential for society to respect and protect personal decision-making, with regard to unwanted pregnancies, abortion and births, as well as the establishment of public and private-sector policies that support individuals and couples in their efforts to become responsible and supportive parents. The Institute also takes the position that it is vital to eradicate gender inequality worldwide and the attainment of equal status, rights and responsibilities for women. The Institute publishes *Perspectives on Sexual and Reproductive Health, International Family Planning Perspectives, the Guttmacher Policy Review* and other special reports on sexual and reproductive health and rights. *See also* **Guttmacher, Dr. Alan F.; Pro-Choice Organizations**

Gynecologist

A gynecologist is a physician who specializes in diagnosing and treating diseases peculiar to the female reproductive tract, including disease conditions of the mammary glands and the urinary tract. *See also* **Obstetrician; Perinatologist; Physician Abortion Requirements**

H

Habitual Abortion *see* **Miscarriage**

Hallervorden-Spatz Disease

Hallervorden-Spatz disease is a congenital disease involving a progressive degeneration of the nervous system. Symptoms of this disorder include distorted muscle contractions of the limbs, muscle rigidity, seizures, dementia, difficulty speaking, mental retardation and visual impairment. There is no cure for the disease, although some treatment is provided for some symptoms. Death usually results within a decade after the onset of the disease. *See also* **Birth Defects and Abortion**

Harlan, John M. II

John M. Harlan II (1899–1971) served as an associate justice of the United States Supreme Court from 1955 to 1971. While on the Supreme Court Justice Harlan was known as a conservative interpreter of the Constitution.

Justice Harlan was born in Chicago, Illinois. He graduated from Princeton University in 1920, and subsequently studied abroad at Oxford University on a Rhodes Scholarship. Upon returning to the United States Harlan enrolled in New York Law School, where he graduated in 1924. Justice Harlan worked in private practice before taking a job as a Federal attorney. In 1954 President Dwight D. Eisenhower nominated Justice Harlan for the Supreme Court. The Senate confirmed the nomination in 1955.

Justice Harlan wrote three abortion related opinions while on the Supreme Court. He wrote an opinion concurring and dissenting from the majority decision in *United States v. Vuitch*, which held that the criminal abortion statute of the District of Columbia, which only permitted therapeutic abortions, was not constitutionally vague insofar as there was no ambiguity in its use of the word health and it did not shift to the defendant the burden of proving innocence. He believed the statute was constitutionally valid, but that the Court did not have jurisdiction to hear the case. In *Griswold v. Connecticut* Justice Harlan wrote an opinion concurring with the majority decision, which held that the right of privacy found in the constitution prohibited enforcement of a Connecticut statute that made it a crime to give married persons contraceptive information and devices. Justice Harlan wrote an opinion dissenting from the majority decision in *Poe v. Ullman*, which held that the appellants did not have standing to challenge the constitutionality of a Connecticut statute, that made it a crime to give married persons contraceptive information and devices. He believed the appellants had standing and that the statute was unconstitutional.

Harris v. McRae

Forum: United States Supreme Court.

Case Citation: Harris v. McRae, 448 U.S. 297 (1980).

Date Argued: April 21, 1980.

Date of Decision: June 30, 1980.

Opinion of Court: Stewart, J., in which Burger, C. J., and White, Powell, and Rehnquist, JJ., joined.

Concurring Opinion: White, J.

Dissenting Opinion: Brennan, J., in which Marshall and Blackmun, JJ., joined.

Dissenting Opinion: Marshall, J.

Dissenting Opinion: Blackmun, J.

Dissenting Opinion: Stevens, J.

Counsel for Appellant: Solicitor General McCree argued; on the brief were Assistant Attorney General Daniel and Eloise E. Davies.

Counsel for Appellees: Rhonda Copelon argued; on the brief were Nancy Stearns, Sylvia Law, Ellen K. Sawyer, Janet Benshoof, Judith Levin, Harriet Pilpel, and Eve Paul.

Amicus Brief for Appellant: John T. Noonan, Jr., and William B. Ball for Representative Jim Wright et al.; and by Wilfred R. Caron and Patrick F. Geary for the United States Catholic Conference.

Amicus Brief for Appellees: Robert Abrams, Attorney General, Shirley Adelson Siegel, Solicitor General, and Peter Bienstock, Arnold D. Fleischer, and Barbara E. Levy, Assistant Attorneys General, for the State of New York et al., joined by Rufus L. Edmisten, Attorney General of North Carolina, William F. O'Connell, Special Deputy Attorney General, and Steven Mansfield Shaber, Associate Attorney General, and James A. Redden, Attorney General of Oregon; by Leo Pfeffer for the American Ethical Union et al.; by Barbara Ellen Handschu for the Association of Legal Aid Attorneys of the City of New York — District 65 — U. A. W. et al.; and by Phyllis N. Segal and Judith I. Avner for the National Organization for Women et al.

Issue Presented: Whether the constitution was violated by a requirement of the Hyde Amendment, that states receiving federal Medicaid funds could not use such funds to pay for abortions, except in limited circumstances?

Case Holding: The Medicaid funding restrictions for abortion by the Hyde Amendment, did not violate the Due Process Clause nor the equal protection component of the Fifth Amendment.

Background facts of case: Under Title XIX of the Social Security Act Congress established a Medicaid program to provide federal financial assistance to states that choose to reimburse certain costs of medical treatment for needy persons. Beginning in 1976 an appropriations bill, called the Hyde Amendment, was used to limit the use of any federal Medicaid funds to reimburse the cost of abortions. On the day that Congress enacted the initial version of the Hyde Amendment the appellees, abortion providers and Medicaid recipients, filed a lawsuit in a federal district court in New York seeking to enjoin the enforcement of the funding restriction on abortions. The appellant, the Secretary of Health, Education, and Welfare, was named as the defendant. After lengthy proceedings, the district court invalidated all versions of the Hyde Amendment on constitutional grounds. The Supreme Court granted certiorari to consider whether the Hyde Amendment violated the Due Process Clause of the Fifth Amendment and its equal protection component.

Majority opinion by Justice Stewart: Justice Stewart rejected the constitutional challenges to the Hyde Amendment. He addressed each matter as follows:

> ... [R]egardless of whether the freedom of a woman to choose to terminate her pregnancy for health reasons lies at the core or the periphery of the due process liberty recognized in Roe v. Wade, it simply does not follow that a woman's freedom of choice carries with it a constitutional entitlement to the financial resources to avail herself of the full range of protected choices... [A]lthough government may not place obstacles in the path of a woman's exercise of her freedom of choice, it need not remove those not of its own creation. Indigency falls in the latter category. The financial constraints that restrict an indigent woman's ability to enjoy the full range of constitutionally protected freedom of choice are the product not of governmental restrictions on access to abortions, but rather of her indigency. Although Congress has opted to subsidize medically necessary services generally, but not certain medically necessary abortions, the fact remains that the Hyde Amendment leaves an indigent woman with at least the same range of choice in deciding whether to obtain a medically necessary abortion as she would have had if Congress had chosen to subsidize no health care costs at all. We are thus not persuaded that the Hyde Amendment impinges on the constitutionally protected freedom of choice recognized in Wade.
>
> Although the liberty protected by the Due Process Clause affords protection against unwarranted government interference with freedom of choice in the context of certain personal decisions, it does not confer an entitlement to such funds as may be necessary to realize all the advantages of that freedom. To hold otherwise would mark a drastic change in our understanding of the Constitution. It cannot be that because government may not prohibit the use of contraceptives, or prevent parents from sending their child to a private school, government, therefore, has an affirmative constitutional obligation to ensure that all persons have the financial resources to obtain contraceptives or send their children to private schools. To translate the limitation on governmental power implicit in the Due Process Clause into an affirmative funding obligation would require Congress to subsidize the medically necessary abortion of an indigent woman even if Congress had not enacted a Medicaid program to subsidize other medically necessary services. Nothing in the Due Process Clause supports such an extraordinary result. Whether freedom of choice that is constitutionally protected warrants federal subsidization is a question for Congress to answer, not a matter of constitutional entitlement. Accordingly, we conclude that the Hyde Amendment does not impinge on the due process liberty recognized in Wade....
>
> The guarantee of equal protection under the Fifth Amendment is not a source of substantive rights or liberties, but rather a right to be free from invidious discrimination in statutory classifications and other governmental activity. It is well settled that where a statutory classification does not itself impinge on a right or liberty protected by the Constitution, the validity of classification must be sustained unless the classification rests on grounds wholly irrelevant to the achievement of any legitimate governmental objective. This presumption of constitutional validity, however, disappears if a statutory classification is predicated on criteria that are, in a constitutional sense, "suspect," the principal example of which is a classification based on race.
>
> ... [T]he Hyde Amendment violates no constitutionally protected substantive rights ... [and] is not predicated on a constitutionally suspect classification....
>
> ... [T]he principal impact of the Hyde Amendment falls on the indigent. But that fact does not itself render the funding restriction constitutionally invalid, for this Court has held repeatedly that poverty, standing alone, is not a suspect classification....
>
> ... [T]he Hyde Amendment, by encouraging childbirth except in the most urgent circumstances, is rationally related to the legitimate governmental objective of protecting potential life. By subsidizing the medical expenses of indigent women who carry their pregnancies to term while not subsidizing the comparable expenses of women who undergo abortions (except those whose lives are threatened), Congress has established incentives that make childbirth a more attractive alternative than abortion for persons eligible for Medicaid. These incentives bear a direct relationship to the legitimate congressional interest in protecting potential life. Nor is it irrational that Congress has authorized federal reimbursement for medically necessary services generally, but not for certain medically necessary abortions. Abortion is inherently different from other medical procedures, because no other procedure involves the purposeful termination of a potential life....
>
> Where, as here, the Congress has neither invaded a substantive constitutional right or freedom, nor enacted legislation that purposefully operates to the detriment of a suspect class, the only requirement of equal protection is that congressional action be rationally related to a legitimate governmental interest. The Hyde Amendment satisfies that standard. It is not the mission of this Court or any other to decide whether the balance of competing interests reflected in the Hyde Amendment is wise social policy. If that were our mission, not every Justice who has subscribed to the judgment of the Court today could have done so. But we cannot, in the name of the Constitution, overturn duly enacted statutes simply because they may be unwise, improvident, or out of harmony with a particular school of thought. Rather, when an issue involves policy choices as sensitive as those implicated here, the appropriate forum for their resolution in a democracy is the legislature.

Disposition of case: The judgment of the district court was reversed.

Concurring opinion by Justice White: Justice White agreed with the majority opinion and wrote separately to make the following points:

> ... As the Court points out, Roe v. Wade did not purport to adjudicate a right to have abortions funded by the government, but only to be free from unreasonable official interference with private choice. At an appropriate stage in a pregnancy, for example, abortions could be prohibited to implement the governmental interest in potential life, but in no case to the damage of the health of the mother, whose choice to suffer an abortion rather than risk her health the government was forced to respect.
>
> Roe v. Wade thus dealt with the circumstances in which the governmental interest in potential life would justify official interference with the abortion choices of pregnant women. There is no such calculus involved here. The Government does not seek to interfere with or to impose any coercive restraint on the choice of any woman to have an abortion. The woman's choice remains unfettered, the Government is not attempting to use its interest in life to justify a coercive restraint, and hence in disbursing its Medicaid funds it is free to implement rationally what Roe v. Wade recognized to be its legitimate interest in a potential life by covering the medical costs of childbirth but denying funds for abortions. Neither Roe v. Wade nor any of the cases decided in its wake invalidates this legislative preference. We decided as much in Maher v. Roe, when we rejected the claims that refusing funds for nontherapeutic abortions while defraying the medical costs of childbirth, although not an outright prohibition, nevertheless

infringed the fundamental right to choose to terminate a pregnancy by abortion and also violated the equal protection component of the Fifth Amendment. I would not abandon Maher and extend Roe v. Wade to forbid the legislative policy expressed in the Hyde Amendment.

Dissenting opinion by Justice Brennan: Justice Brennan dissented from the Court's decision. In doing so, he wrote as follows:

> ... I write separately to express my continuing disagreement with the Court's mischaracterization of the nature of the fundamental right recognized in Roe v. Wade, and its misconception of the manner in which that right is infringed by federal and state legislation withdrawing all funding for medically necessary abortions.
>
> Roe v. Wade held that the constitutional right to personal privacy encompasses a woman's decision whether or not to terminate her pregnancy. Roe and its progeny established that the pregnant woman has a right to be free from state interference with her choice to have an abortion — a right which, at least prior to the end of the first trimester, absolutely prohibits any governmental regulation of that highly personal decision. The proposition for which these cases stand thus is not that the State is under an affirmative obligation to ensure access to abortions for all who may desire them; it is that the State must refrain from wielding its enormous power and influence in a manner that might burden the pregnant woman's freedom to choose whether to have an abortion. The Hyde Amendment's denial of public funds for medically necessary abortions plainly intrudes upon this constitutionally protected decision, for both by design and in effect it serves to coerce indigent pregnant women to bear children that they would otherwise elect not to have....
>
> Moreover, it is clear that the Hyde Amendment not only was designed to inhibit, but does in fact inhibit the woman's freedom to choose abortion over childbirth. Pregnancy is unquestionably a condition requiring medical services. Treatment for the condition may involve medical procedures for its termination, or medical procedures to bring the pregnancy to term, resulting in a live birth. Abortion and childbirth, when stripped of the sensitive moral arguments surrounding the abortion controversy, are simply two alternative medical methods of dealing with pregnancy. In every pregnancy, one of these two courses of treatment is medically necessary, and the poverty-stricken woman depends on the Medicaid Act to pay for the expenses associated with that procedure. But under the Hyde Amendment, the Government will fund only those procedures incidental to childbirth. By thus injecting coercive financial incentives favoring childbirth into a decision that is constitutionally guaranteed to be free from governmental intrusion, the Hyde Amendment deprives the indigent woman of her freedom to choose abortion over maternity, thereby impinging on the due process liberty right recognized in Roe v. Wade.

Dissenting opinion by Justice Marshall: Justice Marshall disagreed with the majority decision. He wrote in dissent as follows:

> ... Under the Hyde Amendment, federal funding is denied for abortions that are medically necessary and that are necessary to avert severe and permanent damage to the health of the mother. The Court's opinion studiously avoids recognizing the undeniable fact that for women eligible for Medicaid — poor women — denial of a Medicaid-funded abortion is equivalent to denial of legal abortion altogether. By definition, these women do not have the money to pay for an abortion themselves. If abortion is medically necessary and a funded abortion is unavailable, they must resort to back-alley butchers, attempt to induce an abortion themselves by crude and dangerous methods, or suffer the serious medical consequences of attempting to carry the fetus to term. Because legal abortion is not a realistic option for such women, the predictable result of the Hyde Amendment will be a significant increase in the number of poor women who will die or suffer significant health damage because of an inability to procure necessary medical services.
>
> The legislation before us is the product of an effort to deny to the poor the constitutional right recognized in Roe v. Wade, even though the cost may be serious and long-lasting health damage.... [T]he premise underlying the Hyde Amendment was repudiated in Roe v. Wade, where the Court made clear that the state interest in protecting fetal life cannot justify jeopardizing the life or health of the mother. The denial of Medicaid benefits to individuals who meet all the statutory criteria for eligibility, solely because the treatment that is medically necessary involves the exercise of the fundamental right to chose abortion, is a form of discrimination repugnant to the equal protection of the laws guaranteed by the Constitution. The Court's decision today marks a retreat from Roe v. Wade and represents a cruel blow to the most powerless members of our society. I dissent.

Dissenting opinion by Justice Blackmun: Justice Blackmun wrote a terse dissenting opinion indicating that he joined the dissent of Justice Brennan.

Dissenting opinion by Justice Stevens: Justice Stevens dissented from the majority opinion. He wrote the following:

> If a woman has a constitutional right to place a higher value on avoiding either serious harm to her own health or perhaps an abnormal childbirth than on protecting potential life, the exercise of that right cannot provide the basis for the denial of a benefit to which she would otherwise be entitled. The Court's sterile equal protection analysis evades this critical though simple point. The Court focuses exclusively on the "legitimate interest in protecting the potential life of the fetus." It concludes that since the Hyde Amendments further that interest, the exclusion they create is rational and therefore constitutional. But it is misleading to speak of the Government's legitimate interest in the fetus without reference to the context in which that interest was held to be legitimate. For Roe v. Wade squarely held that the States may not protect that interest when a conflict with the interest in a pregnant woman's health exists. It is thus perfectly clear that neither the Federal Government nor the States may exclude a woman from medical benefits to which she would otherwise be entitled solely to further an interest in potential life when a physician, in appropriate medical judgment, certifies that an abortion is necessary for the preservation of the life or health of the mother. The Court totally fails to explain why this reasoning is not dispositive here....
>
> Having decided to alleviate some of the hardships of poverty by providing necessary medical care, the government must use neutral criteria in distributing benefits. It may not deny benefits to a financially and medically needy person simply because he is a Republican, a Catholic, or an Oriental — or because he has spoken against a program the government has a legitimate interest in furthering. In sum, it may not create exceptions for the sole purpose of furthering a governmental interest that is constitutionally subordinate to the individual interest that the entire program was designed to protect. The Hyde Amendments not only exclude financially and medically needy persons from the pool of benefits for a constitutionally insufficient reason; they also require the expenditure of millions and millions of dollars in order to thwart the exercise of a constitutional right, thereby effectively inflicting serious and long-lasting harm on impoverished women who want and need abortions for valid medical reasons. In my judgment, these Amendments constitute an unjustifiable, and indeed blatant, violation of the sovereign's duty to govern impartially. *See also* **Hyde Amendment**

Hawaii

(1) Overview

The state of Hawaii enacted its first criminal abortion statute in 1850. Shortly before the 1973 decision by the United States Supreme Court in *Roe v. Wade*, which legalized abortion in the nation, Hawaii had repealed its criminal abortion statute. In the wake *Roe*, Hawaii has enacted only minimal legislation addressing abortion issues. The state has a general abortion statute and a fetal death report statute.

HAWAII ABORTIONS 2000-2006

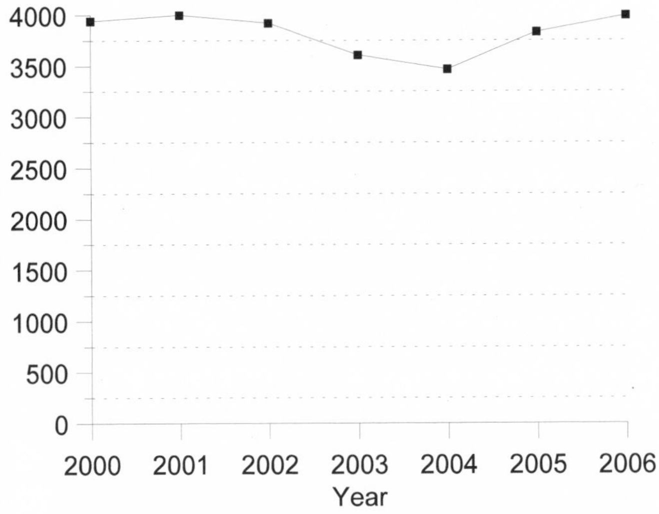

Source: **Hawaii Department of Health.**

Hawaii Abortion by Age Group 2000–2006

Year	Age Group (yrs) *<18*	*18–19*	*20–24*	*25–29*	*30–34*	*35–39*	*≥40*
2000	363	583	1,196	803	504	360	124
2001	378	529	1,266	764	548	358	156
2002	357	480	1,246	794	551	364*	125*
2003	354	447	1,178	708	464	332*	125*
2004	329	369	1,157	742	450	268	152
2005	353	412	1,261	838	503	320	144
2006	386	438	1,343	843	514	321	145
Total	2,520	3,258	8,647	5,492	3,534	2,323	971

Source: **Hawaii Department of Health.**
***Estimate.**

HAWAII ABORTIONS BY RACE 2000-2006

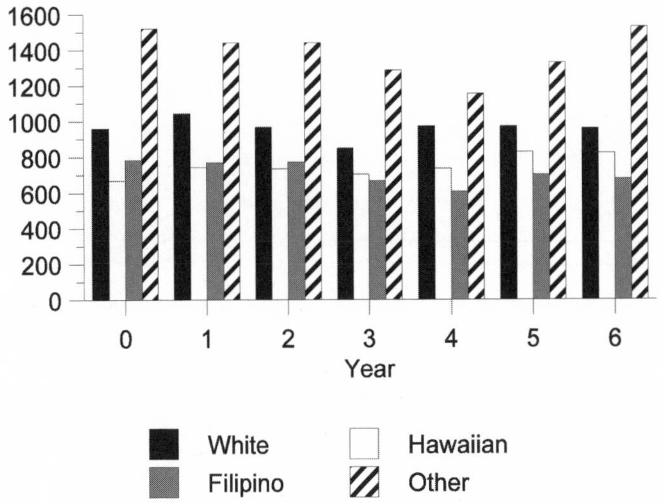

Source: **Hawaii Department of Health.**

HAWAII ABORTIONS BY MARITAL STATUS 2000-2006

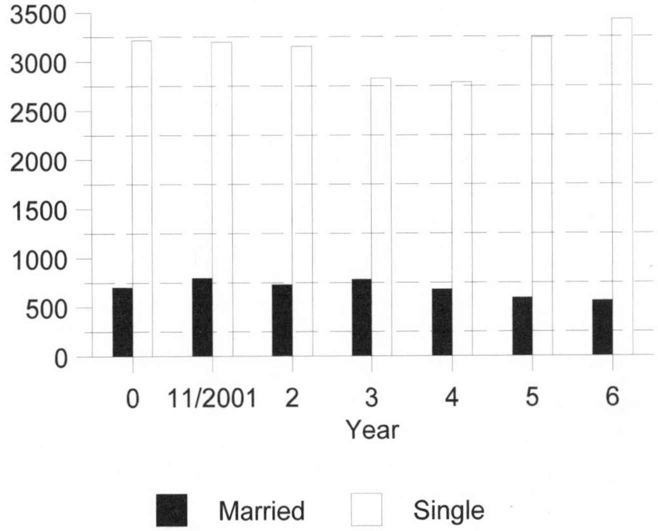

Source: **Hawaii Department of Health.**

Hawaii Abortion by Weeks of Gestation 2000–2004

Weeks of Gestation	Year *2000*	*2001*	*2002*	*2003*	*2004*	*Total*
≤8	1,845	1,773	1,983	1,713	1,735	9,049
9–10	1,018	977	811	834	740	4,380
11–12	545	551	464	490	477	2,527
13–15	226	305	327	277	245	1,380
16–20	237	300	269	237	231	1,274
≥21	40	64	37	27	24	192
Not known	30	29	29	30	15	133

Source: **National Center for Health Statistics.**

(2) General Abortion Limitations

Hawaii requires abortions be performed by physicians at licensed medical facilities or a physician's office. Hawaii permits post-viability abortions only for health reasons. The state permits medical facilities and health care personnel to refuse to participate in abortions. The statute addressing the issues is set out below.

Hawaii Code § 453-16. General abortion limitations

(a) No abortion shall be performed in this state unless:

(1) The abortion is performed by a licensed physician or surgeon, or by a licensed osteopathic physician and surgeon; and

(2) The abortion is performed in a hospital licensed by the department of health or operated by the federal government or an agency thereof, or in a clinic or physician's office.

(b) Abortion shall mean an operation to intentionally terminate the pregnancy of a nonviable fetus. The termination of a pregnancy of a viable fetus is not included in this section.

(c) The State shall not deny or interfere with a female's right to choose or obtain an abortion of a nonviable fetus or an abortion that is necessary to protect the life or health of the female.

(d) Any person who knowingly violates subsection (a) shall be fined not more than $1,000 or imprisoned not more than five years, or both.

(e) Nothing in this section shall require any hospital or any person to

Hawaii Prior Abortion by Female 2000–2004
Prior Abortion

Year	*None*	*1*	*2*	*≥3*	*Not known*
2000	2,077	1,041	438	316	69
2001	2,508	840	343	262	46
2002	2,195	963	399	307	56
2003	2,090	885	366	238	29
2004	1,986	891	336	224	30
Total	10,856	4,620	1,882	1,347	230

Source: **National Center for Health Statistics.**

participate in an abortion nor shall any hospital or any person be liable for a refusal.

(3) FETAL DEATH REPORT

Hawaii requires that all induced abortions be reported and that death certificates be issued. The statute addressing the issue is set out below.

Hawaii Code § 338-9 Fetal death certificates

(a) The person in charge of the disposition of the body shall file with the department of health in Honolulu or with the local agent of the department of health in the district in which the death or fetal death occurred, or a dead body was found, a certificate of death or fetal death within three days after the occurrence, except that reports of intentional terminations of pregnancy performed in accordance with section 453-16 may be deferred for up to one month.

(b) In preparing a certificate of death or fetal death the person in charge of the disposition of the body shall:

(1) Obtain and enter on the certificate the personal data and other information pertaining to the deceased person required by the department from the person best qualified to supply them;

(2) Present the certificate of death to the physician last in attendance upon the deceased, or to the coroner's physician, who shall thereupon certify the cause of death to the physician's best knowledge and belief, or present the certificate of fetal death to the physician, midwife, or other person in attendance at the fetal death, who shall certify the fetal death and such medical data pertaining thereto as can be furnished; provided that fetal deaths of less than twenty-four weeks or intentional terminations of pregnancy performed in accordance with section 453-16 may be certified by a nurse or other employee based upon the physician's records; and

(3) Notify immediately the appropriate local agent, if the death occurred without medical attendance, or if the physician last in attendance fails to sign the death certificate. In such event the local agent shall inform the local health officer, and refer the case to the local health officer for immediate investigation and certification of the cause of death prior to issuing a permit for burial, or other disposition of the body. When the local health officer is not a physician or when there is no such officer, the local agent may complete the certificate on the basis of information received from relatives of the deceased or others having knowledge of the facts.

If the circumstances of the case suggest that the death or fetal death was caused by other than natural causes, the local agent shall refer the case to the coroner for investigation and certification.

(c) A death certificate may be filed by the next of kin and accepted by the local agent without meeting the requirements set forth above when there has been a judicial finding and declaration by a court of record that a person is dead; provided that the certificate is in a form approved by the department and has been certified by the clerk of court.

Heart Disease and Pregnancy

Heart disease may be congenital or acquired (life style). Whatever its source, heart disease is the number one killer of women in the United States. Women who are pregnant and have a heart disease are faced with an additional risk imposed by the disease. Roughly 1 percent of women who have severe heart disease die as a result of the pregnancy. Should a woman suffer a heart failure during pregnancy, the fetus may die or be born prematurely. Studies have shown that women who have a congenital heart disease have a higher risk of having a baby with some type of heart defect. Women with certain disorders affecting the right side of the heart, such as Eisenmenger's syndrome, are at risk of dying during labor or shortly afterward. *See also* **Diabetes and Pregnancy; High Blood Pressure and Pregnancy; Kidney Disease and Pregnancy; Liver Disease and Pregnancy**

Hegar's Sign

Hegar's sign is a method of determining pregnancy. Under this test if there is a soft consistency of a compressible area between the cervix and the body of the uterus, a woman is pregnant. *See also* **Amenorrhea; Chadwick's Sign; Pregnancy Test**

HELLP Syndrome

HELLP (hemolysis, elevated liver, low platelet) syndrome is a condition that affects pregnant women who have an inadequate number of red blood cells (hemolytic anemia) and elevated liver enzymes. This condition causes nausea, vomiting, abdominal pain and headaches. The condition may start long before a pregnancy reaches term. However, when the condition arises delivery is imperative because the mother may suffer permanent liver damage if delivery is delayed. About 25 percent of the deliveries made under this circumstance results in neonatal death. The syndrome occurs in roughly 10 percent of pregnant women who experience preeclampsia or eclampsia. *See also* **Eclampsia, Preeclampsia**

Helms Amendment

In 1973 former Senator Jesse Helms (R. North Carolina) (b. 1921) successfully attached an amendment to the Foreign Assistance Act that limited federal spending under the Act. The amendment, called Helms Amendment, prohibits the use of federal funds allocated under the Act from being used for the performance, motivation, or coercion of abortion. The Helms Amendment is set out below:

22 U.S.C.A. § 2151b(f). Public funds and abortion

(1) None of the funds made available to carry out subchapter I of this chapter may be used to pay for the performance of abortions as a method of family planning or to motivate or coerce any person to practice abortions.

(2) None of the funds made available to carry out subchapter I of this chapter may be used to pay for the performance of involuntary sterilizations as a method of family planning or to coerce or provide any financial incentive to any person to undergo sterilizations.

(3) None of the funds made available to carry out subchapter I of this chapter may be used to pay for any biomedical research which relates, in whole or in part, to methods of, or the performance of, abortions or involuntary sterilization as a means of family planning.

A legal attack on the Helms Amendment was made in *Planned Parenthood Federation of America, Inc. v. Agency for Intern. Development*, 915 F.2d 59 (2d Cir. 1990) In that case it was held by the Second Circuit Court of Appeals that the federal constitutional rights to free speech, association and privacy were not violated because family planning grants to a foreign nongovernmental organization was conditioned upon the organization's certifying that it did not perform or actively promote abortion as a method of family planning. In another case, *Alan Guttmacher Institute v. McPherson*, 616 F.Supp. 195 (S.D.N.Y. 1985), a federal district court upheld the termination of funding for a journal which published articles and information in the field of international population control and family planning, including neutral articles on abortion. *See also* **Mexico City Policy; Public Resources for Abortions; United States Agency for International Development**

Helpers of God's Precious Infants

Helpers of God's Precious Infants (HGPI) is pro-life organization started in Brooklyn, New York, by Monsignor Philip J. Reilly of the Monastery of the Most Precious Blood. HGPI is active in providing prayers at abortion clinics and "sidewalk counseling." The offering of prayer is central to the work of HGPI. In its Mission statement, HGPI has said the following regarding prayer:

Monsignor Philip J. Reilly of the Monastery of the Most Precious Blood, founded Helpers of God's Precious Infants as a pro-life organization in Brooklyn, New York (Philip J. Reilly).

The *Prayers* come to the abortion mill to pray for an hour or more, on any morning that the babies are going to be killed. They carry on a most important spiritual battle, as they stand outside the mill. They pray in a spirit of reparation: for their own sins; the sin of abortion; and particularly for the deaths that will occur while they stand outside on that day. They pray for women going into the abortion mill: for the abortionist and his staff; for the neighboring community; for their legislators; for the religious leaders of the nation; and for all who, through indifference, do nothing to try to stop abortion.

The organization also provides post-abortion reconciliation counseling through a program called Rachel's Helpers. HGPI also puts out an online newsletter called Helpers Newsletter. *See also* **Pro-Life Organizations**

Hepatitis B Virus

Hepatitis B virus (HBV) is a sexually transmitted disease that may also be contracted through blood. The virus can be transmitted from mother to baby at birth. Infants born to mothers who have HBV receive a special immunization series to prevent viral transmission. Mild symptoms of HBV include loss of appetite, tiredness; body aches, diarrhea, vomiting; and yellow skin or eyes (jaundice). HBV can also cause liver damage (cirrhosis), liver cancer, and death. It is estimated that each year in the United States 200,000 people contract HBV. Overall, an estimated 1.25 million people in the nation have HBV. Anywhere from 4,000 to 5,000 people die each year from HBV related chronic liver disease or liver cancer.

There is no cure for HBV, but a vaccine exists which may prevent the disease. HBV vaccine has been recommended as a routine infant vaccination since 1991, and as a routine adolescent vaccination since 1995. Health officials also recommend the vaccination for adults who are at increased risk of HBV infection. The list of such people include: sexually active heterosexual adults with more than one sex partner in the prior 6 months or a history of a sexually transmitted disease; men who have sex with men; and illicit injection drug users. Use of latex condoms may help prevent contraction of HBV. *See also* **Sexually Transmitted Diseases**

Herbal Abortifacients

Herbal abortifacients generally raise the level of toxins (poisonous substances) in a woman's bloodstream so high that a fetus cannot develop or survive. It is not recommended that abortifacient herbs be used before the seventh week of pregnancy. It is believed that if an herbal abortifacient fails to cause an abortion, the fetus will be born with birth defects. Some of the commonly used herbal abortifacients include blue cohosh, cotton root bark, pennyroyal, and tansy.

(i) *Blue cohosh* is also known popularly as papoose root, squaw root, blueberry root, blue or yellow ginseng and beechdrops. Blue Cohosh is an herbal abortifacient that is composed of two substances, caulosaponin and caulophyllasaponin, that induce strong uterine contractions. This abortifacient is not recommended for women with heart or kidney problems, diabetes or glaucoma, or women who are not supposed to use the birth control pill.

(ii) *Cotton root bark*, also called levant cotton, is bark from the root of a cotton plant. As an herbal abortifacient cotton root bark prevents the corpus luteum from producing progesterone, which is needed to maintain a pregnancy. The primary concern with using cotton root bark lies in the many chemicals that farmers use to grow cotton.

This early 1900s bottle of cotton root bark was used to cause an abortion (Grantham Collection, all rights reserved).

(iii) *Pennyroyal* is also popularly known as squaw mint, mosquito plant, American pennyroyal, European pennyroyal, mock pennyroyal, squaw balm, tickweed, fleabane, and lurk-in-the-ditch. This herb causes the uterine muscles to contract to induce abortion. Pennyroyal is said to be most effective as hot tea. Pennyroyal is known to cause multi-organ failure if taken improperly that can cause death.

(iv) *Tansy* is also popularly known as bachelor's buttons, hindheel, common tansy, bitter buttons, parsley fern, ginger plant and, golden button. This herb works by causing irritation to the uterus that result in strong contractions. The oil from this herb is known to be fatal if ingested. Tansy should not be used by women with epileptic seizures, or liver or kidney problems. See also **Abortifacient**

Herpes Simplex Virus *see* **Genital Herpes**

Heterotopic Pregnancy *see* **Ectopic Pregnancy**

High Blood Pressure and Pregnancy

More than half of all women in the United States develop high blood pressure at some point in their lives. High blood pressure in pregnant women is a serious condition. A pregnant woman with severe high blood pressure requires special care. One reason for this, is that pregnancy can aggravate high blood pressure and may cause the woman to have brain swelling, a stroke, kidney or heart failure, or she could die. High blood pressure may also cause an early detachment of the placenta from the uterine wall. This condition could kill the fetus because the fetus' source of oxygen and nutrients would be cut off. In addition, the fetus is at risk even if the placenta does not detach, because high blood pressure may reduce the blood supply to the placenta, thereby impairing the fetus' development. In severe cases it may be necessary to induce abortion, if a woman does not wish to risk taking potent drugs to lower her blood pressure; and when such drugs do not improve the woman's condition, an induced abortion may be necessary to save her life. *See also* **Heart Disease and Pregnancy**

High-Risk Pregnancy

A high-risk pregnancy is a condition in which death or birth defect may occur to the fetus before or after delivery. Proper prenatal care may determine whether a pregnancy is high-risk, and allow for treatment that may prevent death or birth defect to the fetus. Fetal death occurs in about 17 out of every 1000 births in the nation. Nearly 120,000 babies are born each year in the United States with a birth defect. *See also* **Birth Defects and Abortion; Complications During and After Abortion; Miscarriage; Stillbirth**

SELECT CAUSES OF INFANT MORTALITY AND RATES U.S. 2002

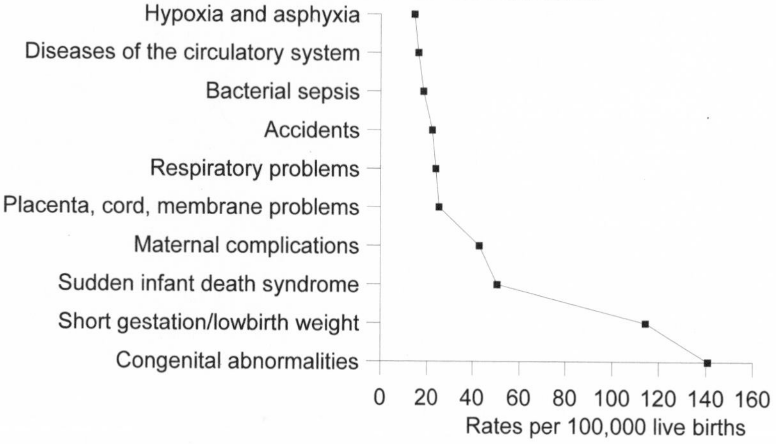

Source: **National Center for Health Statistics.**

Hill, Paul

Paul Hill (1954–2003) was a Presbyterian minister and militant anti-abortionist. He was living in Pensacola, Florida in 1994 when he began plotting the murder of 69-year-old Dr. John Bayard Britton. On the morning of July 29, 1994, Hill decided to carry out his plot. He drove to the clinic where Dr. Britton worked, the Ladies Center Clinic in Pensacola. Dr. Britton arrived at the clinic as a passenger in the truck of his usual escort, 74-year-old James Barrett, a retired Air Force lieutenant colonel. The two men were accompanied by Barrett's wife, 69-year-old June Barrett. Hill approached the three senior citizens with a pistol and opened fire. He killed Dr. Britton and Lt. Col. Barrett. Mrs. Barrett was seriously wounded.

Hill was captured and prosecuted by the federal government and the state of Florida. The federal trial was held first. Hill was convicted of violating the federal Freedom of Access to Clinic Entrances Act and given two life sentences. Although Hill had legal representation in the federal case, he refused legal assistance in his state prosecution. The jury in the state case found Hill guilty of two counts of murder and one count of attempted murder. On December 6, 1994 the trial judge handed down two death sentences and a term of imprisonment of 13 years. One of the arguments Hill made in his appeal to the state supreme court, was that the trial judge should not have allowed him to represent himself. The appellate court rejected the argument. The state of Florida executed Hill by lethal injection on September 3, 2003. Hill's death marked the first execution of a person for killing an abortion provider. *See also* **Abortion Violence, Property Destruction and Demonstrations**

Hill v. Colorado

Forum: United States Supreme Court.

Case Citation: Hill v. Colorado, 530 U.S. 703 (2000).

Date Argued: January 19, 2000.

Date of Decision: June 28, 2000.

Opinion of Court: Stevens, J., in which Rehnquist, C. J., and O'Connor, Souter, Ginsburg, and Breyer, JJ., joined.

Concurring Opinion: Souter, J., in which O'Connor, Ginsburg, and Breyer, JJ., joined.

Dissenting Opinion: Scalia, J., in which Thomas, J., joined.

Dissenting Opinion: Kennedy, J.

Counsel for Appellants: Not Reported.

Counsel for Appellee: Not Reported.

Amicus Brief for Appellants: Not Reported.

Amicus Brief for Appellee: Not Reported.

Issue Presented: Whether the First Amendment right of free speech was violated by a Colorado statute that made it unlawful for any person within 100 feet of an abortion facility's entrance, to knowingly approach within 8 feet of another person, without that person's consent, in order to pass a leaflet, handbill, display a sign, engage in oral protest, education, or counseling with that person?

Case Holding: Colorado's statute was content neutral and narrowly tailored, and therefore did not violate the First Amendment.

Background facts of case: In 1993 Colorado passed a statute which made it unlawful for any person within 100 feet of an abortion facility's entrance to knowingly approach within 8 feet of another person, without that person's consent, in order to pass a leaflet, handbill, display a sign, engage in oral protest, education, or counseling with that person. Several months after the statute was passed the appellants, Leila Jeanne Hill, Audrey Himmelmann, and Everitt W. Simpson, Jr., filed a complaint in a state court seeking to enjoin enforcement of the statute. The appellants alleged that prior to the enactment of the statute, they had engaged in sidewalk counseling on the public sidewalks within 100 feet of the entrances to abortion facilities. They further alleged that such activities frequently entailed being within eight feet of other persons and that the new statute prevented the exercise of their fundamental constitutional right to free speech. The state trial court dismissed the complaint after finding the statute imposed content-neutral time, place, and manner restrictions that were narrowly tailored to serve a significant government interest. The appellate court of Colorado affirmed the trial court's dismissal. The state supreme court refused to hear the appeal.

The case was taken to the United States Supreme Court. The Supreme Court vacated the judgment in light of its holding in *Schenck v. Pro-Choice Network of Western New York*, that an injunctive provision creating a speech-free floating buffer zone with a 15-foot radius violated the First Amendment. On remand, the state appellate court reinstated its previous judgment and the state supreme court affirmed. The Supreme Court granted certiorari to consider the matter.

Majority opinion by Justice Stevens: Justice Stevens found that the facts of Colorado's statute were distinguished from the decision in *Schenck*. It was said that although the statute prohibited speakers from approaching unwilling listeners, it did not require a speaker to move away from anyone passing by. Nor did it place any restriction on the content of any message that anyone may wish to communicate to anyone else, either inside or outside the regulated areas. It did, however, make it more difficult to give unwanted advice, particularly in the form of a handbill or leaflet, to persons entering or leaving an abortion facility. Justice Stevens went on to find that the statute was content neutral as follows:

> First, it is not a "regulation of speech." Rather, it is a regulation of the places where some speech may occur. Second, it was not adopted "because of disagreement with the message it conveys." This conclusion is supported not just by the Colorado courts' interpretation of legislative history, but more importantly by the State Supreme Court's unequivocal holding that the statute's "restrictions apply equally to all demonstrators, regardless of viewpoint, and the statutory language makes no reference to the content of the speech." Third, the State's interests in protecting access and privacy, and providing the police with clear guidelines, are unrelated to the content of the demonstrators' speech. As we have repeatedly explained, government regulation of expressive activity is "content neutral" if it is justified without reference to the content of regulated speech....
>
> We also agree with the state courts' conclusion that [the statute] is a valid time, place, and manner regulation ... because it is "narrowly tailored." We already have noted that the statute serves governmental interests that are significant and legitimate and that the restrictions are content neutral. We are likewise persuaded that the statute is "narrowly tailored" to serve those interests and that it leaves open ample alternative channels for communication. As we have emphasized on more than one occasion, when a content-neutral regulation does not entirely foreclose any means of communication, it may satisfy the tailoring requirement even though it is not the least restrictive or least intrusive means of serving the statutory goal.
>
> ... Under this statute, absolutely no channel of communication is foreclosed. No speaker is silenced. And no message is prohibited.... To the contrary, this statute ... allows every speaker to engage freely in any expressive activity communicating all messages and viewpoints subject only to the narrow place requirement imbedded within the "approach" restriction.

Disposition of case: The judgment of the Colorado supreme court was affirmed.

Concurring opinion by Justice Souter: Justice Souter concurred in the majority opinion. In doing so, he made the following observations:

> It is important to recognize that the validity of punishing some expressive conduct, and the permissibility of a time, place, or manner restriction, does not depend on showing that the particular behavior or mode of delivery has no association with a particular subject or opinion. Draft card burners disapprove of the draft, and abortion protesters believe abortion is morally wrong. There is always a correlation with subject and viewpoint when the law regulates conduct that has become the signature of one side of a controversy. But that does not mean that every regulation of such distinctive behavior is content based as First Amendment doctrine employs that term. The correct rule, rather, is captured in the formulation that a restriction is content based only if it is imposed because of the content of the speech, and not because of offensive behavior identified with its delivery.
>
> Since this point is as elementary as anything in traditional speech doctrine, it would only be natural to suppose that today's disagreement between the Court and the dissenting Justices must turn on unusual difficulty in evaluating the facts of this case. But it does not. The facts overwhelmingly demonstrate the validity of [the statute] as a content-neutral regulation imposed solely to regulate the manner in which speakers may conduct themselves within 100 feet of the entrance of a health care facility.
>
> No one disputes the substantiality of the government's interest in protecting people already tense or distressed in anticipation of medical attention (whether an abortion or some other procedure) from the unwanted intrusion of close personal importunity by strangers. The issues dividing the Court, then, go to the content neutrality of the regulation, its fit with the interest to be served by it, and the availability of other means of expressing the desired message (however offensive it may be even without physically close communication).

Dissenting opinion by Justice Scalia: Justice Scalia disagreed with the majority position that the statute was content neutral. He stated his position as follows:

> Colorado's statute makes it a criminal act knowingly to approach within 8 feet of another person on the public way or sidewalk area within 100 feet of the entrance door of a health care facility for the purpose of passing a leaflet to, displaying a sign to, or engaging in oral protest, education, or counseling with such person. Whatever may be said about the restrictions on the other types of expressive activity, the regulation as it applies to oral communications is obviously and undeniably content-based. A speaker wishing to approach another for the purpose of communicating any message except one of protest, education, or counseling may do so without first securing the other's consent. Whether a speaker must obtain permission before approaching within eight feet — and whether he will be sent to prison for failing to do so — depends entirely on what he intends to say when he gets there. I have no doubt that this regulation would be deemed content-based in an instant if the case before us involved antiwar protesters, or union members seeking to "educate" the public about the reasons for their strike.... But the jurisprudence of this Court has a way of changing when abortion is involved....
>
> Those whose concern is for the physical safety and security of clinic patients, workers, and doctors should take no comfort from today's decision. Individuals or groups intent on bullying or frightening women out of an abortion, or doctors out of performing that procedure, will not be deterred by Colorado's statute; bullhorns and screaming from eight feet away will serve their purposes well. But those who would accomplish their moral and religious objectives by peaceful and civil means, by trying to persuade individual women of the rightness of their cause, will be deterred; and that is not a good thing in a democracy. This Court once recognized, as the Framers surely did, that the freedom to speak and persuade is inseparable from, and antecedent to, the survival of self-government. The Court today rotates that essential safety valve on our democracy one-half turn to the right, and no one who seeks safe access to health care facilities in Colorado or elsewhere should feel that her security has by this decision been enhanced.

Dissenting opinion by Justice Kennedy: Justice Kennedy dissented from the majority opinion. He believed that the statute impermissibly restricted First Amendment free speech rights. Justice Kennedy wrote as follows:

> The Court's holding contradicts more than a half century of well-established First Amendment principles. For the first time, the Court approves a law which bars a private citizen from passing a message, in a peaceful manner and on a profound moral issue, to a fellow citizen on a public sidewalk. If from this time forward the Court repeats its grave errors of analysis, we shall have no longer the proud tradition of free and open discourse in a public forum....
>
> The statute makes it a criminal offense to "knowingly approach another person within eight feet of such person, unless such other person consents, for the purpose of passing a leaflet or handbill to, displaying a sign to, or engaging in oral protest, education, or counseling with such other person in the public way or side-

walk area within a radius of one hundred feet from any entrance door to a health care facility." The law imposes content-based restrictions on speech by reason of the terms it uses, the categories it employs, and the conditions for its enforcement. It is content based, too, by its predictable and intended operation. Whether particular messages violate the statute is determined by their substance. The law is a prime example of a statute inviting screening and censoring of individual speech; and it is serious error to hold otherwise....

The Colorado statute offends settled First Amendment principles in another fundamental respect. It violates the constitutional prohibitions against vague or overly broad criminal statutes regulating speech. The enactment's fatal ambiguities are multiple and interact to create further imprecisions. The result is a law more vague and overly broad than any criminal statute the Court has sustained as a permissible regulation of speech. The statute's imprecisions are so evident that this, too, ought to have ended the case without further discussion.

See also **Buffer Zones at Abortion Facilities; Schenck v. Pro-Choice Network of Western New York**

Hirschsprung's Disease

Hirschsprung's disease (also called congenital megacolon) is a congenital disorder involving an obstruction of the large intestine caused by inadequate muscular movement of the bowel. This condition allows an accumulation of intestinal contents behind the obstruction, resulting in distention of the bowel and abdomen, failure to pass meconium, failure to pass stool and vomiting. The disorder occurs about 5 times more often in males than in females. Surgery is usually required to correct the problem. *See also* **Birth Defects and Abortion**

HIV/AIDS

HIV (human immunodeficiency virus) is the virus that causes AIDS (acquired immune deficiency syndrome). AIDS was first reported in the United States in 1981. Since then more than 600,000 cases of AIDS have been reported in the nation, and as many as 900,000 Americans may be infected with HIV. Most people with HIV infection will develop AIDS. However, AIDS will not develop in someone who is not infected with HIV.

HIV is usually spread by sexual contact with an infected partner. The virus can enter the body through vaginal, oral or anal sex. It is also known that HIV may be spread among injection drug users by the sharing of needles or syringes contaminated with the blood of someone infected with the virus. Women can transmit HIV to their fetuses during pregnancy or delivery. The virus may also be spread to babies through the breast milk of mothers infected with the disease. In general, babies born to mothers who have HIV have a 25 percent to 30 percent chance of being infected with HIV. There may be less of a chance of passing HIV to a newborn if the mother has a cesarean delivery

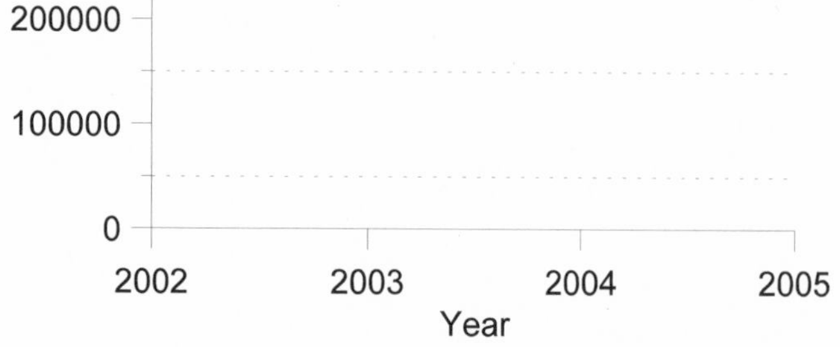

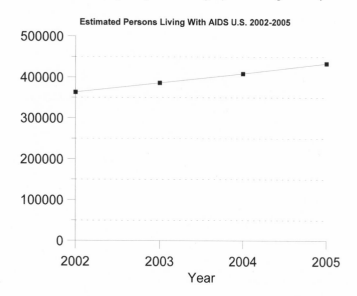

Source: **Centers for Disease Control and Prevention.**

Many people do not develop any symptoms when they first become infected with HIV. Some people, however, have a flu-like illness within several months after exposure to the virus. Severe symptoms may not surface for years after HIV first enters the body. During this relative dormant period, however, HIV is actively multiplying, infecting and killing cells of the immune system. As the immune system deteriorates, a variety of complications begins to surface. One of the first such symptoms experienced may be large lymph nodes (swollen glands) that may be enlarged for more than three months. Other symptoms that may arise before the onset of AIDS include a lack of energy, weight loss, fevers, yeast infections, skin rashes, pelvic inflammatory disease, or short-term memory loss.

AIDS. AIDS is the fifth leading cause of death among persons between ages 25 and 44 in the United States. More than 448,000 deaths have been attributed to AIDS. The term AIDS applies to the most advanced stages of HIV infection. The definition of AIDS includes 26 clinical conditions that affect people. Most of these conditions are "opportunistic infections," which rarely cause harm in healthy individuals. Opportunistic infections common in people with AIDS, cause such symptoms as coughing, shortness of breath, seizures, mental symptoms such as confusion and forgetfulness, severe and persistent diarrhea, fever, vision loss, severe headaches, weight loss, extreme fatigue, nausea, vomiting, lack of coordination, coma, abdominal cramps, or difficult or painful swallowing. People with AIDS are particularly prone to developing various cancers. These cancers are usually more aggressive and difficult to treat in people with AIDS.

There is no cure for AIDS, however, therapies have been developed to fight both HIV infection and its associated infections and cancers. The Food and Drug Administration has approved a number of drugs for the disease: NRTIs (nucleoside analog reverse transcriptase inhibitors); AZT (zidovudine), ddC (zalcitabine), ddI (didanosine), D4T (stavudine), and 3TC (lamivudine). These drugs may slow the spread of HIV in the body and delay the onset of opportunistic infections, but they do not prevent transmission of HIV to other individuals. The risk of HIV transmission from a pregnant woman to her fetus is significantly reduced if she takes AZT during pregnancy, labor and delivery, and her baby takes it for the first six weeks of life.

Since no vaccine for HIV is available, the only way to prevent infection by the virus is to avoid behaviors that put a person at risk of infection, such as sharing needles and having unprotected sex. *See also* **Sexually Transmitted Diseases**

H. L. v. Matheson

Forum: United States Supreme Court.

Case Citation: H. L. v. Matheson, 450 U.S. 398 (1981).

Date Argued: October 6, 1980.

Date of Decision: March 23, 1981.

Opinion of Court: Burger, C. J., in which Stewart, White, Powell, and Rehnquist, JJ., joined.

Concurring Opinion: Powell, J., in which Stewart, J., joined.

Concurring Opinion: Stevens, J.

Dissenting Opinion: Marshall, J., in which Brennan and Blackmun, JJ., joined.

Counsel for Appellant: David S. Dolowitz argued and filed a brief.

Counsel for Appellees: Paul M. Tinker, Assistant Attorney General of Utah, argued; on the brief was Robert B. Hansen, Attorney General.

Amicus Brief for Appellant: Abigail English and Pauline H. Tesler for the Coalition for the Medical Rights of Women et al.; and by Eve W. Paul and Harriet F. Pilpel for the Planned Parenthood Federation of America, Inc., et al.

Amicus Brief for Appellees: Dennis J. Horan, Victor G. Rosenblum, John D. Gorby, Patrick A. Trueman, and Dolores V. Horan for Americans United for Life.

Issue Presented: Whether the constitution was violated by a requirement in Utah's abortion statute that a physician must notify, if possible, the parents of an unemancipated pregnant minor prior to performing an abortion on the minor?

Case Holding: The constitution was not violated by Utah's requirement that the parents of a minor be notified, if possible, prior to performing an abortion.

Background facts of case: In the spring of 1978 the appellant, an unemancipated 15-year-old girl, discovered she was pregnant. She consulted with a social worker and a physician. The physician advised the appellant that an abortion would be in her best medical interest, but that under the abortion laws of Utah, her parents had to first be informed. The appellant did not want her parents notified. Consequently, a lawsuit was filed on behalf of the appellant in a Utah trial court, seeking to challenge the constitutionality of the abortion notification statute. The suit named the appellees, state officials, as defendants. The trial court upheld the constitutionality of the statute. The Utah supreme court affirmed. The United States Supreme Court granted certiorari to consider the matter.

Majority opinion by Chief Justice Burger: The Chief Justice found the statute did not violate the federal constitution. He wrote as follows:

> Although we have held that a state may not constitutionally legislate a blanket, unreviewable power of parents to veto their daughter's abortion, a statute setting out a mere requirement of parental notice does not violate the constitutional rights of an immature, dependent minor....
>
> The Utah statute gives neither parents nor judges a veto power over the minor's abortion decision.... As applied to immature and dependent minors, the statute plainly serves the important considerations of family integrity and protecting adolescents.... In addition, as applied to that class, the statute serves a significant state interest by providing an opportunity for parents to supply essential medical and other information to a physician. The medical, emotional, and psychological consequences of an abortion are serious and can be lasting; this is particularly so when the patient is immature. An adequate medical and psychological case history is important to the physician. Parents can provide medical and psychological data, refer the physician to other sources of medical history, such as family physicians, and authorize family physicians to give relevant data....
>
> That the requirement of notice to parents may inhibit some minors from seeking abortions is not a valid basis to void the statute as applied to appellant.... The Constitution does not compel a state to finetune its statutes so as to encourage or facilitate abortions. To the contrary, state action encouraging childbirth except in the most urgent circumstances is rationally related to the legitimate governmental objective of protecting potential life.

Disposition of case: The judgment of the Utah supreme court was affirmed.

Concurring opinion by Justice Powell: Justice Powell concurred in the Court's decision. He wrote separately to make the following points:

> ... I join the opinion of the Court on the understanding that it leaves open the question whether [the statute] unconstitutionally burdens the right of a mature minor or a minor whose best interests would not be served by parental notification.
>
> On the facts of this case, I agree with the Court that [the statute] is not an unconstitutional burden on appellant's right to an abortion. Numerous and significant interests compete when a minor decides whether or not to abort her pregnancy. The right to make that decision may not be unconstitutionally burdened. In addition, the minor has an interest in effectuating her decision to abort, if that is the decision she makes. The State, aside from the interest it has in encouraging childbirth rather than abortion, has an interest in fostering such consultation as will assist the minor in making her decision as wisely as possible. The State also may have an interest in the family itself, the institution through which we inculcate and pass down many of our most cherished values, moral and cultural. Parents have a traditional and substantial interest in, as well as a responsibility for, the rearing and welfare of their children, especially during immature years....
>
> In sum, a State may not validly require notice to parents in all cases, without providing an independent decisionmaker to whom a pregnant minor can have recourse if she believes that she is mature enough to make the abortion decision independently or that notification otherwise would not be in her best interests.... The circumstances relevant to the abortion decision by a minor can and do vary so substantially that absolute rules—requiring parental notice in all cases or in none—would create an inflexibility that often would allow for no consideration of the rights and interests identified above. Our cases have never gone to this extreme, and in my view should not.

Concurring opinion by Justice Stevens: Justice Stevens concurred in the judgment of the Court. He wrote separately to indicate that he believed the Court should have examined the "class action" status of the case. Justice Stevens expressed his views as follows:

> As the Court points out, this is a class action in which the appellant represents all unmarried minor women who are suffering unwanted pregnancies and desire to terminate the pregnancies but may not do so because of their physicians' insistence on complying with [the notification law] of the Utah Code. The Utah Supreme Court held that the statute may validly be applied to all members of that class. This appeal therefore squarely presents the question whether that holding is consistent with the Constitution of the United States. The Court, however, declines to reach this question and instead decides the narrower question presented by the appellant's particular factual situation. Because I believe we have a duty to answer the broader question decided by the Utah Supreme Court, I am unable to join the opinion of the Court....
>
> Because my view in this case ... is that the State's interest in protecting a young pregnant woman from the consequences of an incorrect abortion decision is sufficient to justify the parental-notice requirement, I agree that the decision of the Utah Supreme Court should be affirmed.

Dissenting opinion by Justice Marshall: Justice Marshall dissented from the Court's decision. He believed that the parental notification requirement violated the constitution. Justice Marshall wrote as follows:

> The ideal of a supportive family so pervades our culture that it may seem incongruous to examine burdens imposed by a statute requiring parental notice of a minor daughter's decision to terminate her pregnancy. This Court has long deferred to the bonds which join family members for mutual sustenance. Especially in times of adversity, the relationships within a family can offer the security of constant caring and aid. Ideally, a minor facing an important decision will naturally seek advice and support from her parents, and they in turn will respond with comfort and wisdom. If the pregnant minor herself confides in her family, she plainly relinquishes her right to avoid telling or involving them. For a minor in that circumstance, the statutory requirement of parental notice hardly imposes a burden.
>
> Realistically, however, many families do not conform to this

ideal. Many minors, like appellant, oppose parental notice and seek instead to preserve the fundamental, personal right to privacy. It is for these minors that the parental notification requirement creates a problem. In this context, involving the minor's parents against her wishes effectively cancels her right to avoid disclosure of her personal choice. Moreover, the absolute notice requirement publicizes her private consultation with her doctor and interjects additional parties in the very conference held confidential in Roe v. Wade. Besides revealing a confidential decision, the parental notice requirement may limit access to the means of effectuating that decision. Many minor women will encounter interference from their parents after the state-imposed notification. In addition to parental disappointment and disapproval, the minor may confront physical or emotional abuse, withdrawal of financial support, or actual obstruction of the abortion decision. Furthermore, the threat of parental notice may cause some minor women to delay past the first trimester of pregnancy, after which the health risks increase significantly. Other pregnant minors may attempt to self-abort or to obtain an illegal abortion rather than risk parental notification. Still others may forsake an abortion and bear an unwanted child, which, given the minor's probable education, employment skills, financial resources and emotional maturity may be exceptionally burdensome. The possibility that such problems may not occur in particular cases does not alter the hardship created by the notice requirement on its face. And that hardship is not a mere disincentive created by the State, but is instead an actual state-imposed obstacle to the exercise of the minor woman's free choice. For the class of pregnant minors represented by appellant, this obstacle is so onerous as to bar the desired abortions. Significantly, the interference sanctioned by the statute does not operate in a neutral fashion. No notice is required for other pregnancy-related medical care, so only the minor women who wish to abort encounter the burden imposed by the notification statute....

Ideally, facilitation of supportive conversation would assist the pregnant minor during an undoubtedly difficult experience. Again, however, when measured against the rationality of the means employed, the Utah statute simply fails to advance this asserted goal. The statute imposes no requirement that the notice be sufficiently timely to permit any discussion between the pregnant minor and the parents. Moreover, appellant's claims require us to examine the statute's purpose in relation to the parents who the minor believes are likely to respond with hostility or opposition. In this light, the statute is plainly overbroad. Parental consultation hardly seems a legitimate state purpose where the minor's pregnancy resulted from incest, where a hostile or abusive parental response is assured, or where the minor's fears of such a response deter her from the abortion she desires. The absolute nature of the statutory requirement, with exception permitted only if the parents are physically unavailable, violates the requirement that regulations in this fundamentally personal area be carefully tailored to serve a significant state interest. The need to preserve the constitutional right and the unique nature of the abortion decision, especially when made by a minor, require a State to act with particular sensitivity when it legislates to foster parental involvement in this matter. Because Utah's absolute notice requirement demonstrates no such sensitivity, I cannot approve its interference with the minor's private consultation with the physician during the first trimester of her pregnancy.

Hobbs Act

The Hobbs Act is a federal statute that was designed to prevent, among other things, the use of extortion to impede interstate commerce. Pro-choice advocates have attempted to use this statute to bring a civil lawsuit against pro-life advocates for their conduct in obstructing abortion providers. However, the United States Supreme Court has indicated that the statute cannot be used in such a manner. The Hobbs Act is set out below.

18 U.S.C.A. § 1951(a).

Interference with commerce by threats or violence

(a) Whoever in any way or degree obstructs, delays, or affects commerce or the movement of any article or commodity in commerce, by robbery or extortion or attempts or conspires so to do, or commits or threatens physical violence to any person or property in furtherance of a plan or purpose to do anything in violation of this section shall be fined under this title or imprisoned not more than twenty years, or both.

See also **National Organization for Women, Inc. v. Scheidler; Scheidler v. National Organization for Women, Inc. (I); Scheidler v. National Organization for Women, Inc. (II)**

Hodgson v. Minnesota

Forum: United States Supreme Court.

Case Citation: Hodgson v. Minnesota, 497 U.S. 417 (1990).

Date Argued: November 29, 1989.

Date of Decision: June 25, 1990.

Opinion of Court: Justice Stevens, J., in which Marshall, Brennan, Blackmun and O'Connor, JJ., joined in part.

Concurring Opinion: O'Connor, J.

Concurring and Dissenting Opinion: Marshall, J., in which Brennan and Blackmun, JJ., joined.

Concurring and Dissenting Opinion: Scalia, J.

Concurring and Dissenting Opinion: Kennedy, J., in which Rehnquist, C.J., and White and Scalia, JJ., joined.

Counsel for Appellants: Janet Benshoof argued; on the brief were Rachel N. Pine, Lynn M. Paltrow, Kathryn Kolbert, John A. Powell, William Z. Pentelovitch, and Rebecca A. Palmer.

Counsel for Appellee: John R. Tunheim, Chief Deputy Attorney General of Minnesota, argued; on the brief were Hubert H. Humphrey III, Attorney General, Catharine F. Haukedahl, Solicitor General, Kenneth E. Raschke, Jr., Assistant Attorney General, and John B. Galus, Special Assistant Attorney General.

Amicus Brief for Appellants and Appellee: United States by Solicitor General Starr, Acting Assistant Attorney General Schiffer, Deputy Solicitor General Merrill, Paul J. Larkin, Jr., Stephen J. Marzen, and Steven R. Valentine; for the State of Louisiana et al. by William J. Guste, Jr., Attorney General of Louisiana, Jenifer Schaye and Meredith H. Lieux, Assistant Attorneys General, Jo Ann P. Levert, Thomas A. Rayner, Robert K. Corbin, Attorney General of Arizona, William L. Webster, Attorney General of Missouri, and Ernest D. Preate, Jr., Attorney General of Pennsylvania; for 274 Organizations in Support of Roe v. Wade by Kathleen M. Sullivan, Susan R. Estrich, Barbara Jordan, and Estelle H. Rogers; for the American Academy of Medical Ethics by Joseph W. Dellapenna; for the American College of Obstetricians and Gynecologists et al. by Carter G. Phillips, Elizabeth H. Esty, Ann E. Allen, Stephan E. Lawton, Laurie R. Rockett, and Joel I. Klein; for American Family Association, Inc., by Peggy M. Coleman; for the Catholic League for Religious and Civil Rights et al. by Nancy J. Gannon and Thomas W. Strahan; for the Center for Population Options et al. by John H. Henn; for the Elliot Institute for Social Sciences Research et al. Stephen R. Kaufmann; for Focus on the Family et al. by H. Robert Showers; for the Knights of Columbus by Brendan V. Sullivan, Jr., Kevin J. Hasson, and Carl A. Anderson; for the Lutheran Church–Missouri Synod by Philip E. Draheim; for the National Right to Life Committee, Inc., by James Bopp, Jr.; for the United States Catholic Conference by Mark E. Chopko; for Representative Christopher H. Smith et al. by Mr. Bopp; for Members of the General Assembly of the Commonwealth of Pennsylvania by Maura K. Quinlin and Philip J. Murren; for 13 Individual Members of the Panel in Adolescent Pregnancy and Childbearing or the Committee on Child Development Research and Public Policy by Hannah E. M. Lieberman and Pamela H. Anderson; for James Joseph Lynch, Jr., pro se; Clarke D. Forsythe and Kent Masterson Brown filed a brief for the Association of American Physicians and Surgeons; for the American Psychological Association et al. by Donald N. Bersoff and Mark D. Schneider; and for the Anti-Defamation League of B'Nai B'rith et al. by Kenneth J. Bialkin, Peggy L. Kerr, Meyer Eisenberg, Justin J. Finger, Jeffrey P. Sinensky, Steven M. Freeman, Jill L. Kahn, and Livia D. Thompson.

Issue Presented: Whether the federal constitution was violated by a requirement in Minnesota's abortion statute that a pregnant female minor could not obtain an abortion until at least 48 hours after both of her parents had been notified?

Case Holding: The 48 hour waiting period was valid. The two-parent notification violated the constitution, but because the statute contained a judicial bypass option to parental notification, the statute was constitutionally valid in its entirety.

Background facts of case: In 1988 the state of Minnesota, appellee, enacted an abortion statute which provided that a female minor (under 18 years of age) could not obtain an abortion until at least 48 hours after both of her parents had been notified. The two-parent notice requirement could be waived if (1) the attending physician certified that an immediate abortion was necessary to prevent the minor's death; (2) the minor declared that she was a victim of parental abuse or neglect; or (3) a court of competent jurisdiction ordered the abortion to proceed without notice upon proof that the minor was mature and capable of giving informed consent or that an abortion without notice to both parents would be in the minor's best interest. A lawsuit challenging the statute was filed in a federal district court in Minnesota by the appellants, abortion providers and pregnant minors. The appellants sought to enjoin enforcement of the statute on the grounds that it violated the Due Process and Equal Protection Clauses of the Fourteenth Amendment. The district court declared the statute unconstitutional in its entirety, and enjoined its enforcement. The Eighth Circuit court of appeals reversed. The court of appeals found that the two-parent notice requirement was invalid, but because of the judicial bypass provision, the statute passed constitutional muster in its entirety. Both the appellants and appellee appealed to the Supreme Court. The Supreme Court granted certiorari for both appeals. (Although both parties were technically designated as appellants and appellee, they are not given the dual designations here.)

Majority/dissenting opinion by Justice Stevens: Justice Stevens announced the Court's judgment to affirm the decision by the court of appeals and the opinion of the Court with respect to approval of the waiting period of 48 hours and the disapproval of the two-parent notice requirement. However, he wrote in dissent to the Court's determination that because of the judicial bypass provision, the statute was constitutional in its entirety in spite of the objectionable two-parent notice requirement. The matters were addressed by Justice Stevens as follows:

> The 48-hour delay imposes only a minimal burden on the right of the minor to decide whether or not to terminate her pregnancy. Although the District Court found that scheduling factors, weather, and the minor's school and work commitments may combine, in many cases, to create a delay of a week or longer between the initiation of notification and the abortion, there is no evidence that the 48-hour period itself is unreasonable or longer than appropriate for adequate consultation between parent and child. The statute does not impose any period of delay once the parents or a court, acting in loco parentis, express their agreement that the minor is mature or that the procedure would be in her best interest....
>
> It is equally clear that the requirement that both parents be notified, whether or not both wish to be notified or have assumed responsibility for the upbringing of the child, does not reasonably further any legitimate state interest. The usual justification for a parental consent or notification provision is that it supports the authority of a parent who is presumed to act in the minor's best interest, and thereby assures that the minor's decision to terminate her pregnancy is knowing, intelligent, and deliberate. To the extent that such an interest is legitimate, it would be fully served by a requirement that the minor notify one parent, who can then seek the counsel of his or her mate or any other party when such advice and support is deemed necessary to help the child make a difficult decision. In the ideal family setting, of course, notice to either parent would normally constitute notice to both. A statute requiring two-parent notification would not further any state interest in those instances. In many families, however, the parent notified by the child would not notify the other parent. In those cases, the State has no legitimate interest in questioning one parent's judgment that notice to the other parent would not assist the minor or in presuming that the parent who has assumed parental duties is incompetent to make decisions regarding the health and welfare of the child....
>
> We therefore hold that this requirement violates the Constitution....
>
> The Court holds that the constitutional objection to the two-parent notice requirement is removed by the judicial bypass option provided in ... the Minnesota statute. I respectfully dissent from that holding....
>
> A judicial bypass that is designed to handle exceptions from a reasonable general rule, and thereby preserve the constitutionality of that rule, is quite different from a requirement that a minor — or a minor and one of her parents — must apply to a court for permission to avoid the application of a rule that is not reasonably related to legitimate state goals. A requirement that a minor acting with the consent of both parents apply to a court for permission to effectuate her decision clearly would constitute an unjustified official interference with the privacy of the minor and her family. The requirement that the bypass procedure must be invoked when the minor and one parent agree that the other parent should not be notified represents an equally unjustified governmental intrusion into the family's decisional process. When the parents are living together and have joint custody over the child, the State has no legitimate interest in the communication between father and mother about the child.

Disposition of case: The judgment of the court of appeals was affirmed.

Concurring opinion by Justice O'Connor: Justice O'Connor agreed with the majority that Minnesota's two-parent notification was invalid, but that the judicial bypass provision cured the defect. She wrote as follows:

> I agree with Justice Stevens that Minnesota has offered no sufficient justification for its interference with the family's decisionmaking processes created by [the] two-parent notification....
>
> Minnesota's two-parent notice requirement is all the more unreasonable when one considers that only half of the minors in the State of Minnesota reside with both biological parents. A third live with only one parent. Given its broad sweep and its failure to serve the purposes asserted by the State in too many cases, I join the Court's striking of [the provision]....
>
> In a series of cases, this Court has explicitly approved judicial bypass as a means of tailoring a parental consent provision so as to avoid unduly burdening the minor's limited right to obtain an abortion.... [The judicial bypass] passes constitutional muster because the interference with the internal operation of the family required by [the two-parent notification] simply does not exist where the minor can avoid notifying one or both parents by use of the bypass procedure.

Concurring and Dissenting opinion by Justice Marshall: Justice Marshall concurred in the decision to invalidate the two-parent notification requirement, but dissented from the decision to permit the requirement to stand because of the judicial bypass provision. He wrote as follows:

> ... For the reasons stated by the Court, Minnesota's two-parent notification requirement is not even reasonably related to a legitimate state interest. Therefore, that requirement surely would not pass the strict scrutiny applicable to restrictions on a woman's fundamental right to have an abortion.
>
> I dissent from the judgment of the Court, however, that the judicial bypass option renders the parental notification and 48-hour delay requirements constitutional. The bypass procedure cannot save those requirements because the bypass itself is unconstitutional, both on its face and as applied. At the very least, this scheme substantially burdens a woman's right to privacy without advancing a compelling state interest. More significantly, in some instances it usurps a young woman's control over her own body by giving either a parent or a court the power effectively to veto her decision to have an abortion.

Concurring and Dissenting opinion by Justice Scalia: Justice Scalia wrote a terse concurring and dissenting opinion in which he indicated that the Court did not have constitutional authority to determine state-based abortion issues. He wrote: "I continue to dissent from this enterprise of devising an Abortion Code, and from the illusion that we have authority to do so."

Concurring and Dissenting opinion by Justice Kennedy: Justice Kennedy dissented from the Court's decision that the two-parent notification was invalid. He concurred in the decision that the judicial bypass validated any objections to the two-parent notification requirement. Justice Kennedy wrote as follows:

> ...The Minnesota Legislature, like the legislatures of many States, has found it necessary to address the issue of parental notice in its statutory laws. In my view it has acted in a permissible manner.
>
> All must acknowledge that it was reasonable for the legislature to conclude that in most cases notice to both parents will work to the minor's benefit. This is true not only in what the Court calls the "ideal family setting," where both parents and the minor live under one roof, but also where the minor no longer lives with both parents. The Court does not deny that many absent parents maintain significant ties with their children, and seek to participate in their lives, to guide, to teach, and to care for them. It is beyond dispute that these attachments, in cases not involving mistreatment or abuse, are essential to the minor's wellbeing, and that parental notice is supportive of this kind of family tie. Although it may be true that notice to one parent will often result in notice to both, the State need not rely upon the decision of one parent to notify the other, particularly where both parents maintain ties with their daughter but not with each other, and when both parents share responsibilities and duties with respect to the child....
>
> Because a majority of the Court holds that the two-parent notice requirement ... is unconstitutional, it is necessary for the Court to consider whether the same notice requirement is constitutional if the minor has the option of obtaining a court order permitting the abortion to proceed in lieu of the required notice. Assuming, as I am bound to do for this part of the analysis, that the notice provisions standing alone are invalid, I conclude that the two-parent notice requirement with the judicial bypass alternative is constitutional....

Holmes, Oliver Wendell, Jr.

Oliver Wendell Holmes, Jr. (1841–1935) served as an associate justice of the United States Supreme Court from 1902 to 1932. While on the Supreme Court Justice Holmes was known as a moderate and pragmatic interpreter of the Constitution.

Justice Holmes was born in Boston, Massachusetts. He graduated from Harvard College in 1861. When the Civil War erupted, he enlisted in the Union Army as an officer. After the war he went on to graduate from Harvard Law School in 1866. In 1881 Justice Holmes published his famous and influential book, *The Common Law*. His legal career included teaching at Harvard Law School and serving on the Supreme Judicial Court of Massachusetts as chief justice. In 1902 President Theodore Roosevelt nominated Justice Holmes to the Supreme Court.

Justice Holmes was involved in only one abortion related decision while on the Supreme Court. Justice Holmes voted with a unanimous opinion in *State of Missouri ex rel. Hurwitz v. North*, which held that the constitution was not violated when a physician was prevented from issuing subpoenas to have witnesses attend a hearing to revoke his medical license for performing an unlawful abortion, because the applicable rules required taking depositions of witnesses who would not voluntarily attend the hearing.

Holoprosencephaly

Holoprosencephaly is a congenital disorder involving the failure of the forebrain of the embryo to divide and form bilateral cerebral hemispheres. In many cases this disorder causes spontaneous intrauterine death. Infants born alive have symptoms that include severe facial defects (a single eye or missing nose), seizures and mental retardation. There is no effective treatment for this disease. Death may result shortly after birth. *See also* **Birth Defects and Abortion**

Homebirth *see* **Natural Childbirth Methods**

Homologous Insemination *see* **Assisted Reproductive Technology**

Hospital/Clinic Abortion Requirements

Abortions are generally required to be performed at licensed facilities. Such facilities include hospitals and clinics. The United States Supreme Court has been called upon to address several issues concerning the location of abortions and reporting requirements.

Restricting abortions to hospitals. In *City of Akron v. Akron Center for Reproductive Health, Inc.*, *Planned Parenthood Assn. v. Ashcroft* and *Doe v. Bolton* the United States Supreme Court held that states could not restrict the performance of abortions exclusively to hospitals. This ruling was based upon the greater cost for an abortion at a hospital, rather than a clinic, and the relative safety of performing abortions at clinics. The Supreme Court, in *Simopoulos v. Virginia*, upheld a Virginia statute requiring second trimester abortions be performed at hospitals, because under the statute an adequately equipped clinic could, upon proper application, obtain an outpatient hospital license that permitted the performance of second trimester abortions.

Prohibiting abortions at government facilities. The Supreme Court held in *Webster v. Reproductive Health Services* that states could prohibit the performance of abortions at government owned hospitals. It was held *Poelker v. Doe* by the Supreme Court that the Equal Protection Clause of the Fourteenth Amendment was not violated by a policy of the city of St. Louis, Missouri that denied publicly funded abortions to indigent women at city hospitals, except when a woman's health or life was in danger.

Reporting requirements. The Supreme Court determined in *Planned Parenthood of Southeastern Pennsylvania v. Casey* that states may impose stringent record keeping requirements on facilities that perform abortions. The decision in *Casey* overruled the opinion in *Thornburgh v. American College of Obstetricians and Gynecologists*, which had held that states could not impose reporting requirements on abortion facilities. Some of the reporting requirements that have been approved subsequent to *Thornburgh* being overruled, include reporting: the name and address of the facility; identifying the physician; the woman's age; the number of prior pregnancies and prior abortions the woman has had; gestational age of fetus; the type of abortion procedure; the date of the abortion; whether there were any preexisting medical conditions which would complicate pregnancy; medical complications with the abortion; where applicable, the basis for the determination that the abortion was medically necessary; the weight of the aborted fetus; and quarterly reports showing the number of abortions performed broken down by trimester. States may not require disclosure of the name of a woman having an abortion.

Hospital abortion committees. In *Doe v. Bolton* the Supreme Court held that states could not require hospital abortion committees approve of an abortion, before it could be performed.

Restricting counseling. In *Rust v. Sullivan* the Supreme Court upheld federal regulations that prohibited pro-abortion counseling, referral, and advocacy by health care providers.

Performing abortion at unlicensed facility. In *Simopoulos v. Virginia* the Supreme Court upheld the conviction of a doctor who performed an abortion at an unlicensed facility, in violation of state law. *See also* **City of Akron v. Akron Center for Reproductive Health, Inc.; Doe v. Bolton; Physician Abortion Requirements; Planned Parenthood Assn. v. Ashcroft; Planned Parenthood of Missouri v. Danforth; Planned Parenthood of Southeastern Pennsylvania v. Casey; Poelker v. Doe; Rust v. Sullivan; Simopoulos v. Virginia; Thornburgh v. American College of Obstetricians and Gynecologists; Webster v. Reproductive Health Services**

Human Life Amendment

The proposed Human Life Amendment to the federal constitution was first introduced in Congress on March 10, 1975 by Senator James L. Buckley (Cons. N.Y.) and Senator Jesse Helms (R. N.C). As first proposed, the Amendment stated: "The paramount right to life is vested in each human being from the moment of fertilization without regard to age, health or condition of dependency." The Amendment has never received the required two-thirds affirmative vote from the Senate, in order to be put to the voters.

The Amendment has been opposed on the grounds that it would end abortion in the nation, because its meaning implies that every human being possesses the right to life, regardless of whether that life is an embryo, fetus, infant, or adult. With its adoption, the Amendment would extend to preborn human life constitutional equal protection to be born alive that could not be deprived without due process of law. It has also been argued that the Amendment would prohibit use of contraceptives to prevent fertilization, in addition to subjecting women to homicide investigations and prosecution if they had a miscarriage or gave birth to a stillborn child.

Human Life International

Human Life International (HLI) is a Virginia based pro-life organization that was founded in 1981 by Fr. Paul Marx. The president of HLI is Rev. Thomas J. Euteneuer. HLI has 53 branch offices in 39 countries. It is active in grassroots anti-abortion work. The organization sponsors boycotts, sidewalk counseling, clinic blockades, and outreach programs for youth. HLI publishes a monthly newsletter called *HLI Reports* and a Spanish quarterly newsletter called *Escoge la Vida*. *See also* **Pro-Life Organizations**

Human Life of Washington

Human Life of Washington (HLW) is a pro-life organization that was incorporated 1970, in response to efforts to modify the state of Washington's ban on abortion. The organization is headed by Dan Kennedy. The organization engages in such activities as voter identification programs, local advertising campaigns, coordinating speaking engagements, and setting up fair booths. The group publishes a newspaper, HUMAN LIFE News, six times a year. HLW also has an education program that teaches a consistent pro-life philosophy. The education program trains speakers to make pro-life presentations at schools, universities, churches, civic and professional groups all across the state. HLW lobbies state legislators and provides support to pro-life candidates for political office. *See also* **Pro-Life Organizations**

Human Papillomavirus *see* **Genital HPV**

Huntington's Disease

Huntington's disease is a congenital disorder involving degeneration of nerve cells in the brain due to a faulty gene. Symptoms of the disorder include progressive loss of mental functions, speech impairment, psychosis, paranoia, hallucinations, and abnormal facial and body movements. There is no cure for the disease. Treatment involves slowing the progression of the disease. Usually the symptoms do not appear until adulthood. The disorder is usually fatal within 15 to 20 years. *See also* **Birth Defects and Abortion**

Hutchinson-Gilford Syndrome

Hutchinson-Gilford syndrome (also called progeria) is a disease that produces rapid aging in children. It is believed that the disorder is hereditary, but the exact cause is not known. The disorder causes growth failure during the first year of a child's life. Symptoms of the disorder include a small and thin frame, large head, baldness, narrow face, and old looking skin. The disorder leads to the development of atherosclerosis (a form of arteriosclerosis). Children with the disorder usually die in their early teens. There is no known prevention or treatment for the disorder. *See also* **Birth Defects and Abortion**

Hyde Amendment

Title XIX of the Social Security Act, 42 U.S.C. 1396 et seq., established the Medicaid program under which participating states may provide federally funded medical assistance to needy persons. In 1976 former United States Representative Henry J. Hyde (R–Ill.) (1924–2007) sought to limit abortion funding for needy persons by initiating what became known as the Hyde Amendment. The amendment was an appropriation bill, not permanent law, that was included in the annual budget for the Department of Labor, Health and Human Services, Education and related agencies. The Hyde Amendment prohibited use of Title XIX funds by states for abortions, except under specified conditions. In 1980 the United States Supreme Court held in *Harris v. McRae* that the Hyde Amendment was constitutional.

Limiting use of Medicaid funds. The federal Medicaid program allows for the use of federal and state funds for health care coverage for low income individuals, including coverage for pregnancy. Approximately 9.3 million women of child-bearing age receive Medicaid benefits. As a result of the Hyde Amendment these women cannot use their federally funded Medicaid benefits for abortions, except in the case of therapeutic abortions or pregnancies resulting from rape or incest. The Hyde Amendment does not restrict states from using their own funds to pay for abortions. (The District of Columbia is prohibited from using its locally generated funds to pay for abortions.) A large minority of states have resorted to the use of their own funds to pay for abortions for low income women.

In *Dalton v. Little Rock Family Planning Services*, the United States Supreme Court held that an amendment to Arkansas' constitution which limited Medicaid payment only to therapeutic abortions, was invalid to the extent that Medicaid funds had to be made available for incest or rape pregnancies, but was valid for any purely state funded program. In *Williams v. Zbaraz* the Supreme Court held that in light of the requirements of the Hyde Amendment, the Equal Protection Clause of the Fourteenth Amendment was not violated by an Illinois statute that prohibited state Medicaid payment for abortions, except when necessary to save the life of the pregnant woman. The Supreme Court held in *Beal v. Doe* that Pennsylvania's refusal to extend Medicaid coverage to nontherapeutic abortions was not invalid nor inconsistent with Title XIX of the Social Security Act.

Limiting use of Medicare funds. Medicare health coverage is funded exclusively by the federal government for the elderly and certain disabled individuals. Over 600,000 disabled women under the age 45 depend on Medicare for their health coverage. Under the Hyde Amendment these women cannot use Medicare for payment of abortions, except in the case of therapeutic abortions or pregnancies resulting from rape or incest. *See also* **Beal v. Doe; Dalton v. Little Rock Family Planning Services; Harris v. McRae; Public Resources for Abortions**

Hydrocephalus

Hydrocephalus is a birth defect associated with excessive fluid in the brain. The disorder may be caused by tumors of the central nervous system, intrauterine infection, or trauma before or after birth. Treatment for the disorder is aimed at minimizing or preventing brain damage. If the disorder is not treated, a child has a 60 percent chance of dying; those who survive will have varying degrees of intellectual, physical, and neurologic disabilities. *See also* **Birth Defects and Abortion**

Hydronephrosis *see* **Genital and Urinary Tract Birth Defects**

Hyperemesis Gravidarum

Hyperemesis gravidarum (HG) is severe form of morning sickness that afflicts pregnant women. The disorder causes severe vomiting and nausea. HG, unlike morning sickness, may complicate pregnancies by causing physiological changes that may affect the fetus and woman. Researchers have reported maternal weight loss, dehydration, and renal injury resulting from HG. There is also a risk that a woman may develop brain damage due to persistent vomiting caused by HG. A fetus is at risk for premature birth, low birthweight, central nervous system impairment; and male fetuses are susceptible to testicular cancer. Medications are available to treat HG. *See also* **Morning Sickness**

Hyperthermia and Pregnancy

Hyperthermia involves an abnormally high body temperature. A normal body temperature averages about 98.6°F. If a pregnant woman reaches a body temperature of 102°F or higher, for an extended period of time, the fetus may be in danger. Hyperthermia is usually caused by a fever due to illness. Some studies have shown that if a woman has hyperthermia during early pregnancy the fetus is at an increased risk for birth defects called neural tube defects (e.g., spina bifida or anencephaly). There have also been reports that hyperthermia may cause fetal heart defects and spontaneous abortion. Appropriate prenatal care may prevent hyperthermia. *See also* **Birth Defects; Miscarriage**

Hyperthyroidism and Pregnancy

Hyperthyroidism is a disorder caused by the effects of the production of too much thyroid hormone on tissues of the body. This condition is present in 2 out of every 1000 pregnancies. Left untreated during pregnancy, the disorder may cause preterm delivery, fetal birth defects, spontaneous abortion or maternal heart failure. Treatments are available to reduce the risks caused by the disorder for pregnant women. However, a few of the treatment medications can have an adverse effect on the fetus, if given in the wrong quantities. *See also* **Hypothyroidism and Pregnancy**

Hypnobirthing *see* **Natural Childbirth Methods**

Hypoplastic Left Heart Syndrome *see* **Congenital Heart Defect**

Hypospadias *see* **Genital and Urinary Tract Birth Defects**

Hypothyroidism and Pregnancy

Hypothyroidism is a disorder in which the thyroid gland produces insufficient thyroid hormone, which causes symptoms associated with a slow metabolism. The disorder affects over five million Americans. Treatment for the disorder is usually successful and allows most people to live a fully normal life. However, the disorder can be problematic for women who have the disorder and are pregnant. The two most common complications in pregnant women with hypothyroidism are spontaneous abortions (miscarriages) and pregnancy-induced hypertension. It is estimated that the disorder causes a spontaneous abortion in 6 out of every 1000 pregnancies. The disorder also increases the risk of birth defects. Proper prenatal care, that includes anti-thyroid medications, may prevent miscarriages and birth defects. In rare cases a pregnant woman may have to undergo surgery to remove the thyroid gland during her pregnancy. *See also* **Hyperthyroidism and Pregnancy**

Hypoxia

Hypoxia refers to an insufficient supply of oxygen to the fetus. This condition may lead to fetal asphyxia, which may cause stillbirth or neonatal death. Hypoxia occurs in roughly 17 out of every 100,000 births. Studies have also suggested that hypoxia is associated with cerebral palsy. It is also known to increase the risk of caesarean delivery.

Hysterectomy

Hysterectomy is the surgical removal of the uterus. Should the ovaries be also removed, the procedure is called a "total" hysterectomy. A hysterectomy ends a woman's ability to become pregnant. Some of the common health reasons that may necessitate a hysterectomy include: fibroid tumors (non-cancerous uterine tumors), heavy abnormal vaginal bleeding, tissue from the lining of the uterus attaches itself to other pelvic structures (endometriosis), weakening of the supporting muscles and ligaments of the uterus (uterine prolapse), and cancer of the uterus and possibly of the ovaries.

The uterus may be removed by a surgeon making a vertical or horizontal incision in the abdomen, or using a technique called laparoscopically assisted vaginal hysterectomy (LAVH). The LAVH procedure involves making tiny incisions in the abdomen that serve as entry ports for a camera and operating tools. Once the uterus is severed, it is removed though the vagina.

Side effects associated with a hysterectomy include severe vaginal bleeding, bowel or bladder injury, infection, persistent pain, increased risk of heart attack, fatigue, weight gain, aching joints, urinary tract disorders, depression and lower sexual response. It has been estimated that more than 500 women die each year as a result of the operation. *See also* **Endometrial Ablation; Male Sterilization; Tubal Ligation**

Hysterectomy Abortion

A hysterectomy abortion is a second trimester procedure for terminating a pregnancy. The procedure is similar to a cesarean section, but its intent is to deliver an aborted fetus. During the procedure a doctor will usually cut the umbilical cord in-utero and wait several minutes for the fetus to expire. Thereafter, the woman's entire uterus and the dead fetus are removed. *See also* **Methods of Abortion**

Hysterotomy Abortion

Hysterotomy abortion is similar to a cesarean section. However, the intent of a hysterotomy is to abort the fetus. Hysterotomy is used during second trimester pregnancies. It may also be used when a saline or prostaglandin abortion has failed or when a tubal ligation is done. The procedure involves cutting the abdomen open and removing the contents of the womb. A hysterotomy is a major surgical procedure that has inherent difficulties, possible complications, and a potentially painful recovery. *See also* **Methods of Abortion**

Idaho Abortion by Age Group 2000–2006

Year	Age Group (yrs) *≤14*	*15–19*	*20–24*	*25–29*	*30–34*	*35–39*	*40–44*	*≥45*	*Unknown*
2000	7	159	270	160	92	78	33	2	0
2001	4	168	220	145	95	71	29	5	1
2002	4	176	259	171	110	73	35	1	0
2003	3	178	304	171	137	74	43	1	0
2004	2	189	302	191	151	95	32	1	0
2005	6	208	330	267	138	107	41	2	0
2006	8	257	398	268	162	112	42	1	1
Total	34	1,335	2,083	1,373	885	610	255	13	2

Source: **Idaho Department of Health and Welfare.**

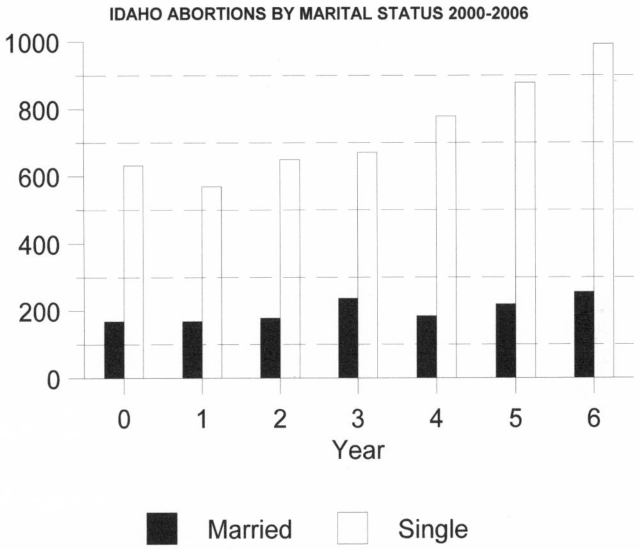

Source: **Idaho Department of Health and Welfare.**

I

Idaho

(1) OVERVIEW

The state of Idaho enacted its first criminal abortion statute on February 4, 1864. The statute underwent several amendments prior to the 1973 decision by the United States Supreme Court in *Roe v. Wade*, which legalized abortion in the nation. Idaho has taken affirmative steps to respond to *Roe* and its progeny. Through statutes Idaho has addressed numerous abortion issues that include general abortion guidelines, unlawful abortion, partial-birth abortion, abortion by minors, informed consent and waiting period, use of facilities and people, ban advertising and selling abortifacients, use of public funds, insurance policies for abortion, prohibit wrongful birth lawsuit, fetal death report, and injury to pregnant woman.

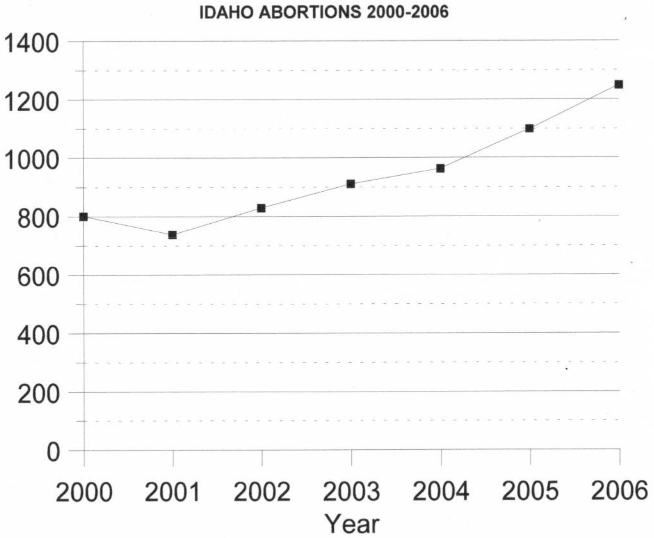

Source: **Idaho Department of Health and Welfare.**

Idaho Abortion by Weeks of Gestation 2000–2006

Weeks of Gestation	Year *2000*	*2001*	*2002*	*2003*	*2004*	*2005*	*2006*	*Total*
<9	476	488	501	540	585	645	804	4,039
9–10	217	153	211	236	238	303	258	1,616
11–12	74	74	87	103	111	118	135	702
13–15	14	12	18	13	18	15	37	127
16–20	12	6	8	12	6	13	8	65
21–24	4	1	2	3	5	4	3	22
≥25	1	2	1	1	0	1	2	8
Not known	3	2	1	3	0	0	2	11

Source: **Idaho Department of Health and Welfare.**

Idaho Prior Abortion by Female 2000–2006

Year	Prior Abortion *None*	*1*	*2*	*≥3*	*Not known*
2000	637	117	33	13	1
2001	597	96	29	14	2
2002	627	149	39	12	2
2003	691	159	38	16	7
2004	725	182	39	13	4
2005	856	177	46	15	5
2006	976	199	48	19	7
Total	5,109	1,079	272	102	28

Source: **Idaho Department of Health and Welfare.**

(2) GENERAL ABORTION GUIDELINES

Under the laws of Idaho only physicians are authorized to perform abortions. Idaho has set out guidelines for performing first and second trimester abortions that appear to give physicians more control over the abortion decision than *Roe* and its progeny allow. To the extent that this statutory provision infringes upon pre-viability abortion, it is invalid under the federal constitution. The state has also attempted to prohibit all third trimester abortions, except to save the life of the woman. The statutes addressing general abortion guidelines are set out below

IDAHO ABORTIONS BY RACE 2000-2006

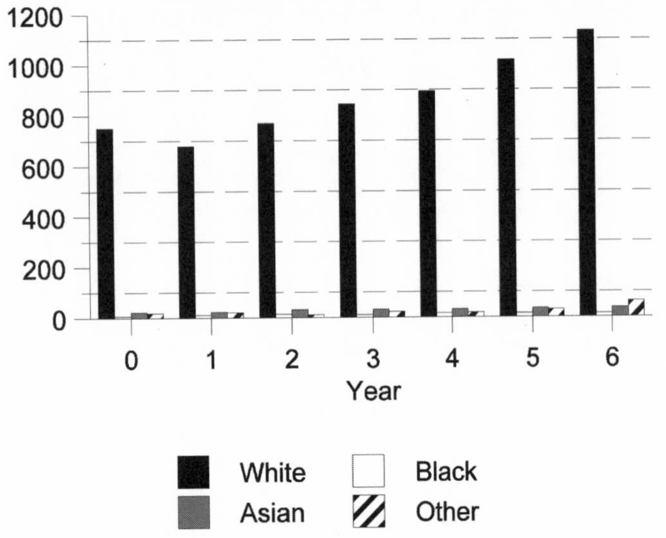

Source: **Idaho Department of Health and Welfare.**

Idaho Code § 18-601. Interpretation of statutes and constitution

The supreme court of the United States having held in the case of "Planned Parenthood v. Casey" that the states have a "profound interest" in preserving the life of preborn children, Idaho hereby expresses the fundamental importance of that "profound interest" and it is hereby declared to be the public policy of this state that all state statutes, rules and constitutional provisions shall be interpreted to prefer, by all legal means, live childbirth over abortion.

Idaho Code § 18-604. Definitions

As used in this act:

(1) "Abortion" means the use of any means to intentionally terminate the clinically diagnosable pregnancy of a woman with knowledge that the termination by those means will, with reasonable likelihood, cause the death of the unborn child except that, for the purposes of this chapter, abortion shall not mean the use of an intrauterine device or birth control pill to inhibit or prevent ovulations, fertilization or the implantation of a fertilized ovum within the uterus.

(2) "Department" means the Idaho department of health and welfare.

(3) "Emancipated" means any minor who has been married or is in active military service.

(4) "Fetus" and "unborn child." Each term means an individual organism of the species homo sapiens from fertilization until live birth.

(5) "First trimester of pregnancy" means the first thirteen (13) weeks of a pregnancy.

(6) "Hospital" means an acute care, general hospital in this state, licensed as provided in chapter 13, title 39, Idaho Code.

(7) "Informed consent" means a voluntary and knowing decision to undergo a specific procedure or treatment. To be voluntary, the decision must be made freely after sufficient time for contemplation and without coercion by any person. To be knowing, the decision must be based on the physician's accurate and substantially complete explanation of:

(a) A description of any proposed treatment or procedure;

(b) Any reasonably foreseeable complications and risks to the patient from such procedure, including those related to reproductive health; and

(c) The manner in which such procedure and its foreseeable complications and risks compare with those of each readily available alternative to such procedure, including childbirth and adoption.

The physician must provide the information in terms which can be understood by the person making the decision, with consideration of age, level of maturity and intellectual capability.

(8) "Medical emergency" means a condition which, on the basis of the physician's good faith clinical judgment, so complicates the medical condition of a pregnant woman as to necessitate the immediate abortion of her pregnancy to avert her death or for which a delay will create serious risk of substantial and irreversible impairment of a major bodily function.

(9) "Minor" means a woman less than eighteen (18) years of age.

(10) "Pregnant" and "pregnancy." Each term shall mean the reproductive condition of having a developing fetus in the body and commences with fertilization.

(11) "Physician" means a person licensed to practice medicine and surgery or osteopathic medicine and surgery in this state as provided in chapter 18, title 54, Idaho Code.

(12) "Second trimester of pregnancy" means that portion of a pregnancy following the thirteenth week and preceding the point in time when the fetus becomes viable, and there is hereby created a legal presumption that the second trimester does not end before the commencement of the twenty-fifth week of pregnancy, upon which presumption any licensed physician may proceed in lawfully aborting a patient pursuant to section 18-608, Idaho Code, in which case the same shall be conclusive and unrebuttable in all civil or criminal proceedings.

(13) "Third trimester of pregnancy" means that portion of a pregnancy from and after the point in time when the fetus becomes viable.

(14) Any reference to a viable fetus shall be construed to mean a fetus potentially able to live outside the mother's womb, albeit with artificial aid.

Idaho Code § 18-608. Abortion conditions

The provisions of sections 18-605 and 18-606 shall not apply to and neither this act, nor other controlling rule of Idaho law, shall be deemed to make unlawful an abortion performed by a physician if:

(1) When performed upon a woman who is in the first trimester of pregnancy, the same is performed following the attending physician's consultation with the pregnant patient and a determination by the physician that such abortion is appropriate in consideration of such factors as in his medical judgment he deems pertinent, including, but not limited to physical, emotional, psychological and/or familial factors, that the child would be born with some physical or mental defect, that the pregnancy resulted from rape, incest or other felonious intercourse, and a legal presumption is hereby created that all illicit intercourse with a girl below the age of sixteen (16) shall be deemed felonious for purposes of this section, the patient's age and any other consideration relevant to her well-being or directly or otherwise bearing on her health and, in addition to medically diagnosable matters, including but not limited to such factors as the potential stigma of unwed motherhood, the imminence of psychological harm or stress upon the mental and physical health of the patient, the potential stress upon all concerned of an unwanted child or a child brought into a family already unable, psychologically or otherwise, to care for it, and/or the opinion of the patient that maternity or additional offspring probably will force upon her a distressful life and future; the emotional or psychological consequences of not allowing the pregnancy to continue, and the aid and assistance available to the pregnant patient if the pregnancy is allowed to continue; provided, in consideration of all such factors, the physician may rely upon the statements of and the positions taken by the pregnant patient, and the physician shall not be deemed to have held himself out as possessing

special expertise in such matters nor shall he be held liable, civilly or otherwise, on account of his good faith exercise of his medical judgment, whether or not influenced by any such nonmedical factors. Abortions permitted by this subsection shall only be lawful if and when performed in a hospital or in a physician's regular office or a clinic which office or clinic is properly staffed and equipped for the performance of such procedures and respecting which the responsible physician or physicians have made satisfactory arrangements with one or more acute care hospitals within reasonable proximity thereof providing for the prompt availability of hospital care as may be required due to complications or emergencies that might arise.

(2) When performed upon a woman who is in the second trimester of pregnancy, the same is performed in a hospital and is, in the judgment of the attending physician, in the best medical interest of such pregnant woman, considering those factors enumerated in subsection (1) of this section and such other factors as the physician deems pertinent.

(3) When performed upon a woman who is in the third trimester of pregnancy the same is performed in a hospital and, in the judgment of the attending physician, corroborated by a like opinion of a consulting physician concurring therewith, either is necessary for the preservation of the life of such woman or, if not performed, such pregnancy would terminate in birth or delivery of a fetus unable to survive. Third trimester abortions undertaken for preservation of the life of a pregnant patient, as permitted by this subsection, shall, consistent with accepted medical practice and with the well-being and safety of such patient, be performed in a manner consistent with preservation of any reasonable potential for survival of a viable fetus.

Idaho Code § 18-608A. Persons authorized to perform abortions

It is unlawful for any person other than a physician to cause or perform an abortion.

(3) UNLAWFUL ABORTION

Idaho imposes criminal penalties on anyone who performs an abortion that is not in compliance with its statutory requirements. The state also provides criminal penalties for a woman who submits to an abortion in a manner inconsistent with legal requirements. The statutes addressing the matters are set out below.

Idaho Code § 18-605. Unlawful abortion

(1) Every person not licensed or certified to provide health care in Idaho who knowingly, except as permitted by this chapter, provides, supplies or administers any medicine, drug or substance to any woman or uses or employs any instrument or other means whatever upon any then-pregnant woman with intent thereby to cause or perform an abortion shall be guilty of a felony and shall be fined not to exceed five thousand dollars ($5,000) and/or imprisoned in the state prison for not less than two (2) and not more than five (5) years.

(2) Any person licensed or certified to provide health care pursuant to title 54, Idaho Code, and who knowingly, except as permitted by the provisions of this chapter, provides, supplies or administers any medicine, drug or substance to any woman or uses or employs any instrument or other means whatever upon any then-pregnant woman with intent to cause or perform an abortion shall:

(a) For the first violation, be subject to professional discipline and be assessed a civil penalty of not less than one thousand dollars ($1,000), payable to the board granting such person's license or certification;

(b) For the second violation, have their license or certification to practice suspended for a period of not less than six (6) months and be assessed a civil penalty of not less than two thousand five hundred dollars ($2,500), payable to the board granting such person's license or certification; and

(c) For each subsequent violation, have their license or certification to practice revoked and be assessed a civil penalty of not less than five thousand dollars ($5,000), payable to the board granting such person's license or certification.

(3) Any person who is licensed or certified to provide health care pursuant to title 54, Idaho Code, and who knowingly violates the provisions of this chapter is guilty of a felony punishable as set forth in subsection (1) of this section, separate from and in addition to the administrative penalties set forth in subsection (2) of this section.

Idaho Code § 18-606. Accomplice to unlawful abortion

Except as permitted by this act: (1) Every person who, as an accomplice or accessory to any violation of section 18-605, induces or knowingly aids in the production or performance of an abortion; and

(2) Every woman who knowingly submits to an abortion or solicits of another, for herself, the production of an abortion, or who purposely terminates her own pregnancy otherwise than by a live birth, shall be deemed guilty of a felony and shall be fined not to exceed five thousand dollars ($5,000) and/or imprisoned in the state prison for not less than one (1) and not more than five (5) years; provided, however, that no hospital, nurse, or other health care personnel shall be deemed in violation of this section if in good faith providing services in reliance upon the directions of a physician or upon the hospital admission of a patient for such purpose on the authority of a physician.

(4) PARTIAL-BIRTH ABORTION

Idaho criminalizes partial-birth abortions. However, until it is definitively determined by a court, Idaho's partial-birth abortion statute may be invalid under the United States Supreme Court decision in *Stenberg v. Carhart*, which invalidated Nebraska's ban on partial-birth abortion. On the other hand, Idaho's partial-birth abortion statute, as currently written, may be valid under the United States Supreme Court decision in *Gonzales v. Carhart*, which approved of a federal statute that bans partial-birth abortion. In addition to purporting to ban partial-birth abortions, Idaho has provided a civil cause of action for a married man whose spouse obtains a partial-birth abortion. In the case of a minor, the maternal grandparents of the fetus may file a civil lawsuit. The statute addressing the matters is set out below.

Idaho Code § 18-613. Partial-birth abortion

(1) Prohibited acts. Any physician who knowingly performs a partial-birth abortion and thereby kills a human fetus shall be subject to the penalties imposed in section 18-605, Idaho Code. This section shall not apply to partial-birth abortions necessary to save the life of the mother when her life is endangered by a physical disorder, illness or injury.

(2) Definitions. As used in this section:

(a) "Partial-birth abortion" means an abortion in which the person performing the abortion partially vaginally delivers a living fetus before killing the fetus and completing the delivery.

(b) The phrase "vaginally delivers a living fetus before killing the fetus" means deliberately and intentionally delivering into the vagina a living fetus, or a substantial portion of the fetus, for the purpose of performing a procedure the physician knows will kill the fetus, and which kills the fetus.

(c) "Physician" has the same meaning provided in section 18-604, Idaho Code. However, any individual who is not a physician or not otherwise legally authorized by this state to perform abortions, but who nevertheless directly performs a partial-birth abortion, shall be subject to the prohibitions described in this section.

(3)(a) Civil actions. The father of the aborted fetus, if married to the mother of the aborted fetus at the time of the abortion; or the maternal grandparents of the aborted fetus, if the mother is not at least eighteen (18) years of age at the time of the abortion, may bring a civil action against the defendant physician to obtain appropriate relief. Provided however,

that a civil action by the plaintiff father is barred if the pregnancy resulted from criminal conduct by the plaintiff father or he consented to the abortion. Further, a civil action by the plaintiff maternal grandparents is barred if the pregnancy is the result of criminal conduct by a maternal grandparent or a maternal grandparent consented to the abortion.

(b) As used in this section, "appropriate relief" shall include:

(i) Money damages for all mental and physical injuries suffered by the plaintiff as a result of the abortion performed in violation of this section;

(ii) Money damages equal to three (3) times the cost of performing the abortion procedure.

(4)(a) Hearing. A physician accused of violating this section may request a hearing before the state board of medicine to determine whether the mother's life was endangered by a physical disorder, illness or injury and therefor whether performing the abortion was necessary to save the mother's life.

(b) The findings of the board of medicine regarding the issues described in subsection (4)(a) of this section are admissible at the criminal and civil trials of the defendant physician. Upon a motion by the defendant physician, the court shall delay the beginning of the criminal and civil trials for not more than thirty (30) days to permit the hearing to take place.

(5) Immunity. A woman upon whom a partial-birth abortion is performed shall not be prosecuted for violations of this section, for conspiracy to violate this section, or for violations of section 18-603, 18-605 or 18-606, Idaho Code, in regard to the partial-birth abortion performed.

(5) ABORTION BY MINORS

Under the laws of Idaho no physician may perform an abortion upon an unemancipated minor unless he/she first obtains the written consent of either parent. In compliance with federal constitutional law, Idaho has provided a judicial waiver procedure for an unemancipated minor to obtain an abortion without parental consent. The minor may petition a trial court for a waiver of the consent requirement. A minor has a right to an attorney at the proceeding and if she cannot afford one, the court must appoint her an attorney. If a minor chooses, she may represent herself. The required parental consent may be waived if the court finds either (1) that the minor is mature and well-informed enough to make the abortion decision on her own, or (2) that performance of the abortion would be in the best interest of the minor. An expedited appeal is available to any minor to whom the court denies a waiver of consent. The state also requires statistical reporting of judicial proceedings involving minors and abortions performed on minors. The statutes addressing the issues are set out below.

Idaho Code § 18-602. Legislative findings and intent

(1) The legislature finds:

(a) That children have a special place in society that the law should reflect;

(b) That minors too often lack maturity and make choices that do not include consideration of both immediate and long-term consequences;

(c) That the medical, emotional and psychological consequences of abortion and childbirth are serious and can be lasting, particularly when the patient is immature;

(d) That the capacity to become pregnant and the capacity for mature judgment concerning the wisdom of bearing a child or of having an abortion are not necessarily related;

(e) That parents, when aware that their daughter is pregnant or has had an abortion are in the best position to ensure that she receives adequate medical attention during her pregnancy or after her abortion;

(f) That except in rare cases, parents possess knowledge regarding their child which is essential for a physician to exercise the best medical judgment for that child;

(g) That when a minor is faced with the difficulties of an unplanned pregnancy, the best interests of the minor are always served when there is careful consideration of the rights of parents in rearing their child and the unique counsel and nurturing environment that parents can provide;

(h) That informed consent is always necessary for making mature health care decisions.

(2) It is the intent of the legislature in enacting section 18-609A, Idaho Code, to further the following important and compelling state interests recognized by the United States supreme court in:

(a) Protecting minors against their own immaturity;

(b) Preserving the integrity of the family unit;

(c) Defending the authority of parents to direct the rearing of children who are members of their household;

(d) Providing a pregnant minor with the advice and support of a parent during a decisional period;

(e) Providing for proper medical treatment and aftercare when the life or physical health of the pregnant minor is at serious risk in the rare instance of a sudden and unexpected medical emergency.

Idaho Code § 18-609A. Parental consent and judicial bypass

(1) Except as otherwise provided in this section, a person shall not knowingly perform an abortion on a pregnant unemancipated minor unless the attending physician has secured the written consent from one (1) of the minor's parents or the minor's guardian or conservator.

(2) A judge of the district court shall, on petition or motion, and after an appropriate hearing, authorize a physician to perform the abortion if the judge determines, by clear and convincing evidence, that:

(a) The pregnant minor is mature and capable of giving informed consent to the proposed abortion; or

(b) The performance of an abortion would be in her best interests.

(3) The pregnant minor may participate in the court proceedings on her own behalf. The court may appoint a guardian ad litem for her. The court shall provide her with counsel unless she appears through private counsel.

(4) Proceedings in the court under this section shall be closed and have precedence over other pending matters. A judge who conducts proceedings under this section shall make in writing specific factual findings and legal conclusions supporting the decision and shall order a confidential record of the evidence to be maintained including the judge's own findings and conclusions. The minor may file the petition using a fictitious name. All records contained in court files of judicial proceedings arising under the provisions of this section shall be confidential and exempt from disclosure pursuant to section 9-340G, Idaho Code. Dockets and other court records shall be maintained and court proceedings undertaken so that the names and identities of the parties to actions brought pursuant to this section will not be disclosed to the public.

(5) The court shall hold the hearing within forty-eight (48) hours, excluding weekends and holidays, after the petition is filed, and shall issue its ruling at the conclusion of the hearing. If the court fails to issue its ruling at the conclusion of the hearing, the petition is deemed to have been granted and the consent requirement is waived.

(6) An expedited confidential appeal is available to a pregnant minor for whom the court denies an order authorizing an abortion without parental consent. A minor shall file her notice of appeal within five (5) days, excluding weekends and holidays, after her petition was denied by the district court. The appellate court shall hold the hearing within forty-eight (48) hours, excluding weekends and holidays, after the notice of appeal is filed and shall issue its ruling at the conclusion of the hearing. If the appellate court fails to issue its ruling at the conclusion of the hearing, the petition is deemed to have been granted and the consent require-

ment is waived. Filing fees are not required of the pregnant minor at either the district court or the appellate level.

(7) Parental consent or judicial authorization is not required under this section if either:

(a) The pregnant minor certifies to the attending physician that the pregnancy resulted from rape as defined in section 18-6101, Idaho Code, excepting subsection 1. thereof, or sexual conduct with the minor by the minor's parent, stepparent, uncle, grandparent, sibling, adoptive parent, legal guardian or foster parent.

(b) A medical emergency exists for the minor and the attending physician records the symptoms and diagnosis upon which such judgment was made in the minor's medical record.

Idaho Code § 18-609F. Reporting by courts

The administrative director of the courts shall compile statistics for each calendar year, accessible to the public, including:

(1) The total number of petitions filed pursuant to section 18-609A, Idaho Code; and

(2) The number of such petitions filed where a guardian ad litem was requested and the number where a guardian ad litem or other person acting in such capacity was appointed; and

(3) The number of petitions where counsel appeared for the minor without court appointment; and

(4) The number of petitions where counsel was requested by the minor and the number where counsel was appointed by the court; and

(5) The number of such petitions for which the right to self-consent was granted; and

(6) The number of such petitions for which the court granted its informed consent; and

(7) The number of such petitions which were denied; and

(8) The number of such petitions which were withdrawn by the minor; and

(9) For categories described in subsections (3), (4) and (7) of this section, the number of appeals taken from the court's order in each category; and

(10) For each of the categories set out in subsection (9) of this section, the number of cases for which the district court's order was affirmed and the number of cases for which the district court's order was reversed; and

(11) The age of the minor for each petition; and

(12) The time between the filing of the petition and the hearing of each petition; and

(13) The time between the hearing and the decision by the court for each petition; and

(14) The time between the decision and filing a notice of appeal for each case, if any; and

(15) The time of extension granted by the court in each case, if any.

Idaho Code § 18-609G. Statistical records

(1) The bureau of vital statistics of the department of health and welfare shall, in addition to other information required pursuant to section 39-261, Idaho Code, require the complete and accurate reporting of information relevant to each abortion performed upon a minor which shall include, at a minimum, the following:

(a) Whether the abortion was performed following the physician's receipt of:

(i) The written informed consent of a parent, guardian or conservator and the minor; or

(ii) The written informed consent of an emancipated minor for herself; or

(iii) The written informed consent of a minor for herself pursuant to a court order granting the minor the right to self-consent; or

(iv) The court order which includes a finding that the performance of the abortion, despite the absence of the consent of a parent, is in the best interests of the minor; or

(v) Certification from the pregnant minor to the attending physician pursuant to section 18-609A, Idaho Code, that parental consent is not required because the pregnancy resulted from rape as defined in section 18-6101, Idaho Code, excepting subsection 1. thereof, or sexual conduct with the minor by the minor's parent, stepparent, uncle, grandparent, sibling, adoptive parent, legal guardian or foster parent.

(b) If the abortion was performed due to a medical emergency and without consent from a parent, guardian or conservator or court order, the diagnosis upon which the attending physician determined that the abortion was immediately necessary due to a medical emergency.

(2) The knowing failure of the attending physician to perform any one (1) or more of the acts required under this section is grounds for discipline pursuant to section 54-1814(6), Idaho Code, and shall subject the physician to assessment of a civil penalty of one hundred dollars ($100) for each month or portion thereof that each such failure continues, payable to the bureau of vital statistics of the department of health and welfare, but such failure shall not constitute a criminal act.

Idaho Code § 18-614. Defenses to prosecution

(1) No physician shall be subject to criminal or administrative liability for causing or performing an abortion upon a minor in violation of subsection (1) of section 18-609A, Idaho Code, if prior to causing or performing the abortion the physician obtains either positive identification or other documentary evidence from which a reasonable person would have concluded that the woman seeking the abortion was either an emancipated minor or was not then a minor and if the physician retained, at the time of receiving the evidence, a legible photocopy of such evidence in the physician's office file for the woman.

(2) For purposes of this section, "positive identification" means a lawfully issued state, district, territorial, possession, provincial, national or other equivalent government driver's license, identification card or military card, bearing the person's photograph and date of birth, the person's valid passport or a certified copy of the person's birth certificate.

Idaho Code § 18-610. Refusal to consent

Notwithstanding any provision of law permitting valid consent for medical or surgical procedures to be given by a person or persons other than the patient, the refusal of any pregnant woman, irrespective of age or competence, to submit to an abortion shall be grounds for a physician or hospital otherwise authorized to proceed, to decline performance of an abortion and/or to submit the matter of consent to adjudication by a court of competent jurisdiction.

Idaho Code § 9-340G. Exemption from disclosure

In accordance with section 18-609A, Idaho Code, the following records are exempt from public disclosure: all records contained in court files of judicial proceedings arising under section 18-609A, Idaho Code, are exempt from disclosure.

(6) INFORMED CONSENT

Prior to an abortion, Idaho requires that a woman be fully informed of the procedure to be used, the risks involved, alternatives to abortion, and additional matters. An abortion may not take place until at least 24 hours after a woman has been given the required information. The statute addressing the matters is set out below.

Idaho Code § 18-609. Informed consent and waiting period

(1) Any physician may perform an abortion not prohibited by this act and any hospital or other facility described in section 18-608, Idaho Code, may provide facilities for such procedures without, in the absence of negligence, incurring civil liability therefor to any person including, but not

limited to, the pregnant patient and the prospective father of the fetus to have been born in the absence of abortion, if informed consent for such abortion has been duly given by the pregnant patient.

(2) In order to provide assistance in assuring that the consent to an abortion is truly informed consent, the director of the department of health and welfare shall publish easily comprehended, nonmisleading and medically accurate printed material to be made available at no expense to physicians, hospitals or other facilities providing abortion and abortion-related services, and which shall contain the following:

(a) Descriptions of the services available to assist a woman through a pregnancy, at childbirth and while the child is dependent, including adoption services, a comprehensive list of the names, addresses, and telephone numbers of public and private agencies that provide such services and financial aid available;

(b) Descriptions of the physical characteristics of a normal fetus, described at two (2) week intervals, beginning with the fourth week and ending with the twenty-fourth week of development, accompanied by scientifically verified photographs of a fetus during such stages of development. The description shall include information about physiological and anatomical characteristics; and

(c) Descriptions of the abortion procedures used in current medical practices at the various stages of growth of the fetus and any reasonable foreseeable complications and risks to the mother, including those related to subsequent child bearing.

(3) Except in the case of a medical emergency, no abortion shall be performed unless, prior to the abortion, the attending physician or the attending physician's agent certifies in writing that the materials provided by the director have been provided to the pregnant patient at least twenty-four (24) hours before the performance of the abortion. If the materials are not available from the director of the department of health and welfare, no certification shall be required. The attending physician, or the attending physician's agent, shall provide any other information required under this act. All physicians or their agents who use ultrasound equipment in the performance of an abortion shall inform the patient that she has the right to view the ultrasound image of her unborn child before an abortion is performed. If the patient requests to view the ultrasound image, she shall be allowed to view it before an abortion is performed. The physician or agent shall also offer to provide the patient with a physical picture of the ultrasound image of her unborn child prior to the performance of the abortion, and shall provide it if requested by the patient. In addition to providing the material, the attending physician may provide the pregnant patient with such other information which in the attending physician's judgment is relevant to the pregnant patient's decision as to whether to have the abortion or carry the pregnancy to term.

(4) Within thirty (30) days after performing any abortion without certification and delivery of the materials, the attending physician, or the attending physician's agent, shall cause to be delivered to the director of the department of health and welfare, a report signed by the attending physician, preserving the patient's anonymity, denoting the medical emergency that excused compliance with the duty to deliver the materials. The director of the department of health and welfare shall compile the information annually and report to the public the total number of abortions performed in the state where delivery of the materials was excused; provided that any information so reported shall not identify any physician or patient in any manner which would reveal their identities.

(5) If section 18-608(3), Idaho Code, applies to the abortion to be performed and the pregnant patient is an adult and for any reason unable to give a valid consent thereto, the requirement for that pregnant patient's consent shall be met as required by law for other medical or surgical procedures and shall be determined in consideration of the desires, interests and welfare of the pregnant patient.

(6) The knowing failure of the attending physician to perform any one (1) or more of the acts required under subsection (4) of this section or section 39-261, Idaho Code, is grounds for discipline pursuant to section 54-1814(6), Idaho Code, and shall subject the physician to assessment of a civil penalty of one hundred dollars ($100) for each month or portion thereof that each such failure continues, payable to the vital statistics unit of the department of health and welfare, but such failure shall not constitute a criminal act.

(7) USE OF FACILITIES AND PEOPLE

Under the laws of Idaho hospitals are not required to allow abortions at their facilities. The employees and physicians at hospitals that do allow abortions are permitted to refuse to take part in abortions. The statute addressing the issue is set out below.

Idaho § 18-612. Refusal to participate in abortion

Nothing in this act shall be deemed to require any hospital to furnish facilities or admit any patient for any abortion if, upon determination by its governing board, it elects not to do so. Neither shall any physician be required to perform or assist in any abortion, nor shall any nurse, technician or other employee of any physician or hospital be required by law or otherwise to assist or participate in the performance or provision of any abortion if he or she, for personal, moral or religious reasons, objects thereto. Any such person in the employ or under the control of a hospital shall be deemed to have sufficiently objected to participation in such procedures only if he or she has advised such hospital in writing that he or she generally or specifically objects to assisting or otherwise participating in such procedures. Such notice will suffice without specification of the reason therefor. No refusal to accept a patient for abortion or to perform, assist or participate in any such abortion as herein provided shall form the basis of any claim for damages or recriminatory action against the declining person, agency or institution.

(8) BAN ADVERTISING AND SELLING ABORTIFACIENTS

Idaho has prohibited advertising medicines for abortions and selling abortifacients. The laws setting out such prohibitions are in conflict with decisions by the United States Supreme Court. The statutes addressing the matters are set out below.

Idaho Code § 18-603. Advertising medicines

Every person, except licensed physicians of this state and those licensed or registered health care providers hereinafter referred to acting under their direct supervision or medical order, who wilfully publishes any notice or advertisement of any medicine or means for producing or facilitating a miscarriage or abortion, or for the prevention of conception, or who offers his services by any notice, advertisement, or otherwise to assist in the accomplishment of any such purpose, is guilty of a felony. A licensed physician or licensed or registered health care provider acting at his direction or medical order may lawfully provide examinations, prescriptions, devices and informational materials regarding prevention of conception to any person requesting the same who, in the good faith judgment of the physician or such provider, is sufficiently intelligent and mature to understand the nature and significance thereof.

Idaho Code § 18-607. Selling abortifacients

A person who sells, offers to sell, possesses with intent to sell, advertises, or displays for sale anything specially designed to terminate a pregnancy, or held out by the actor as useful for that purpose, commits a misdemeanor, unless:

(1) The sale, offer or display is to a physician or druggist or to an intermediary in a chain of distribution to physicians or druggists; or

(2) The same is made upon prescription or order of a physician; or

(3) The possession is with intent to sell as authorized in paragraphs (1) and (2) of this section; or

(4) The advertising is addressed to persons named in paragraph (1) of this section and confined to trade or professional channels not likely to reach the general public.

(9) USE OF PUBLIC FUNDS

Idaho prohibits the use of state public funds to pay for abortions, except to save the life of the woman, or the pregnancy resulted from rape or incest. The statute addressing the issue is set out below.

Idaho Code § 56-209c. Use of public funds for abortion

No funds available to the department of health and welfare, by appropriation or otherwise, shall be used to pay for abortions, unless it is the recommendation of two (2) consulting physicians that an abortion is necessary to save the life or health of the mother, or unless the pregnancy is a result of rape or incest as determined by the courts.

(10) INSURANCE POLICIES FOR ABORTION

Idaho requires health insurance policies exclude coverage for elective abortions, unless a premium is specifically charged for the coverage. The statutes addressing the issue are set out below.

Idaho Code § 41-2142. Insurance for elective abortions

All policies, contracts, plans or certificates of disability insurance delivered, issued for delivery or renewed in this state after the effective date of this section shall exclude coverage for elective abortions. Such exclusion may be waived by endorsement and the payment of a premium therefor. Availability of such coverage shall be at the option of the insurance carrier. For purposes of this section, an "elective abortion" means an abortion for any reason other than to preserve the life of the female upon whom the abortion is performed.

Idaho Code § 41-3924.
Limitation of benefits for elective abortions

All policies, contracts, plans or certificates delivered, issued for delivery or renewed in this state by an organization offering a managed care plan for which a certificate of authority is required shall exclude coverage for elective abortions. Such exclusion may be waived by endorsement and the payment of a premium therefor. Availability of such coverage shall be at the option of the contractor. For purposes of this section, an "elective abortion" means an abortion for any reason other than to preserve the life of the female upon whom the abortion is performed.

Idaho Code § 41-3439. Benefits for elective abortions

All individual nongroup or subscriber's policies, contracts, plans or certificates delivered, issued for delivery or renewed in this state after the effective date of this section shall exclude coverage for elective abortions except. Such exclusion may be waived by endorsement and the payment of a premium therefor. Availability of such coverage shall be at the option of the service corporation. For purposes of this section, an "elective abortion" means an abortion for any reason other than to preserve the life of the female upon whom the abortion is performed.

(11) PROHIBIT WRONGFUL BIRTH LAWSUIT

Idaho does not permit a civil lawsuit by any one alleging that a person would not have been born alive, if an abortion had been performed. The law prohibiting such a claim was upheld in *Vanvooren v. Astin*, 111 P.3d 125 (Idaho 2005). The statute addressing the matter is set out below.

Idaho Code § 5-334.
Act or omission preventing abortion not actionable

(1) A cause of action shall not arise, and damages shall not be awarded, on behalf of any person, based on the claim that but for the act or omission of another, a person would not have been permitted to have been born alive but would have been aborted.

(2) The provisions of this section shall not preclude causes of action based on claims that, but for a wrongful act or omission, fertilization would not have occurred, maternal death would not have occurred or handicap, disease, defect or deficiency of an individual prior to birth would have been prevented, cured or ameliorated in a manner that preserved the health and life of the affected individual.

(12) FETAL DEATH REPORT

Idaho requires that every induced abortion be reported to the proper authorities. The statute addressing the issue is set out below.

Idaho Code § 39-261. Induced abortion reporting

(a) The vital statistics unit shall establish an induced abortion reporting form, which shall be used for the reporting of every induced abortion performed in this state. However, no information shall be collected which would identify the woman who had the abortion. Such form shall be prescribed by the department and shall include as a minimum the items required by the standard reporting form as recommended by the national center for health statistics, of the United States department of health and human services.

The completed form shall be filed by the attending physician and sent to the vital statistics unit within fifteen (15) days after the end of each reporting month. The submitted form shall be an original, typed or written legibly in durable ink, and shall not be deemed complete until every item of information required shall have been provided or its omission satisfactorily accounted for. Carbon copies shall not be acceptable.

(b) The department of health and welfare shall prepare and keep on permanent file compilations of the information submitted on the induced abortion reporting forms pursuant to such rules and regulations as established by the department of health and welfare, which compilations shall be a matter of public record.

(13) INJURY TO PREGNANT WOMAN

Idaho makes it a criminal offense to injure a fetus through injury to a pregnant woman. The statutes addressing the matter are set out below.

Idaho Code § 18-4016. Definition of human embryo and fetus

(1) For purposes of this chapter "embryo" or "fetus" shall mean any human in utero.

(2) Nothing in this chapter, arising from the killing of an embryo or fetus, shall be construed to permit the prosecution:

(a) Of any person for conduct relating to an abortion for which the consent of the pregnant woman, or a person authorized by law to act on her behalf, has been obtained or for which such consent is implied by law;

(b) Of any person for any medical treatment of the pregnant woman or her embryo or fetus; or

(c) Of any woman with respect to her embryo or fetus.

Idaho Code § 18-4001. Murder

Murder is the unlawful killing of a human being including, but not limited to, a human embryo or fetus, with malice aforethought or the intentional application of torture to a human being, which results in the death of a human being. Torture is the intentional infliction of extreme and prolonged pain with the intent to cause suffering. It shall also be torture to inflict on a human being extreme and prolonged acts of brutality irrespective of proof of intent to cause suffering. The death of a human being caused by such torture is murder irrespective of proof of specific intent to kill; torture causing death shall be deemed the equivalent of intent to kill.

Idaho Code § 18-4006. Manslaughter

Manslaughter is the unlawful killing of a human being including, but not limited to, a human embryo or fetus, without malice. It is of three (3) kinds:

1. Voluntary — upon a sudden quarrel or heat of passion.

2. Involuntary — in the perpetration of or attempt to perpetrate any unlawful act, other than those acts specified in section 18-4003(d), Idaho Code; or in the commission of a lawful act which might produce death, in an unlawful manner, or without due caution and circumspection; or in the operation of any firearm or deadly weapon in a reckless, careless or negligent manner which produces death.

3. Vehicular— in which the operation of a motor vehicle is a significant cause contributing to the death because of:

(a) The commission of an unlawful act, not amounting to a felony, with gross negligence; or

(b) The commission of a violation of section 18-8004 or 18-8006, Idaho Code; or

(c) The commission of an unlawful act, not amounting to a felony, without gross negligence.

Notwithstanding any other provision of law, any evidence of conviction under subsection 3.(b) shall be admissible in any civil action for damages resulting from the occurrence. A conviction for the purposes of subsection 3.(b) means that the person has pled guilty or has been found guilty, notwithstanding the form of the judgment(s) or withheld judgment(s).

Idaho Code § 18-907. Aggravated battery

(1) A person commits aggravated battery who, in committing battery:

(a) Causes great bodily harm, permanent disability or permanent disfigurement; or

(b) Uses a deadly weapon or instrument; or

(c) Uses any vitriol, corrosive acid, or a caustic chemical of any nature; or

(d) Uses any poison or other noxious or destructive substance or liquid; or

(e) Upon the person of a pregnant female, causes great bodily harm, permanent disability or permanent disfigurement to an embryo or fetus.

(2) For purposes of this section the terms "embryo" or "fetus" shall mean any human in utero.

(3) There shall be no prosecution under subsection (1)(e) of this section:

(a) Of any person for conduct relating to an abortion for which the consent of the pregnant female, or person authorized by law to act on her behalf, has been obtained or for which such consent is implied by law.

(b) Of any person for any medical treatment of the pregnant female or her embryo or fetus; or

(c) Of any female with respect to her embryo or fetus.

Illinois

(1) OVERVIEW

The state of Illinois enacted its first criminal abortion statute on January 6, 1827. The statute underwent several amendments prior to

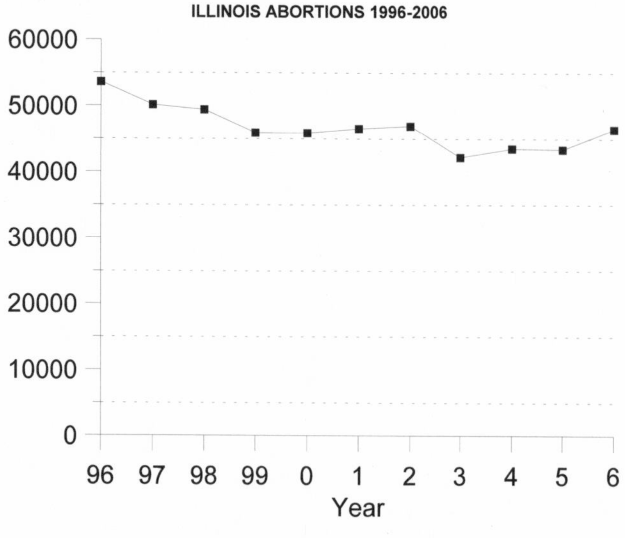

Source: **Illinois Department of Public Health.**

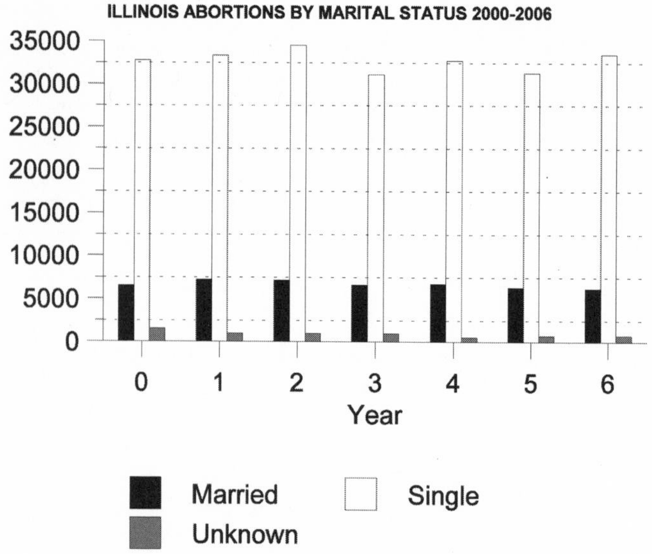

Source: **Illinois Department of Public Health.**

Illinois Abortion by Age Group 2000–2006

Age Group (yrs)

Year	*≤14*	*15–17*	*18–19*	*20–24*	*25–29*	*30–34*	*35–39*	*≥40*
2000	295	3,267	4,755	13,177	9,552	5,344	3,117	1,008
2001	298	3,063	4,523	13,314	9,388	6,040	3,393	1,167
2002	281	2,902	4,477	13,714	9,854	6,367	3,520	1,259
2003	287	2,820	4,042	12,063	8,968	5,931	3,173	1,167
2004	308	2,942	4,258	12,430	9,235	6,056	3,299	1,254
2005	237	2,798	3,874	11,753	9,103	5,810	3,400	1,178
2006	282	2,875	3,959	12,376	9,771	5,946	3,678	1,207
Total	1,988	20,667	29,888	88,827	65,871	41,494	23,580	8,240

Source: **Illinois Department of Public Health.**

the 1973 decision by the United States Supreme Court in *Roe v. Wade*, which legalized abortion in the nation. Illinois has taken affirmative steps to respond to *Roe* and its progeny. The state has addressed numerous abortion issues by statute that include the Abortion Act of 1975, partial-birth abortion, husband's rights, and abortion by minors, use of facilities and people, public funds for abortion, injury to a pregnant woman, and fetal wrongful death lawsuit.

(2) ABORTION ACT OF 1975

Illinois has addressed many abortion issues under its Abortion Act of 1975. The Act prohibits an abortion unless it is medically necessary. This provision was held unconstitutional in *Charles v. Carey*, 579 F.Supp. 464 (N.D.Ill. 1983), affirmed in part, reversed in part 749 F.2d 452 (7th Cir. 1984). The Act prohibits post-viability abortions, except to preserve the life or health of the woman. Under the Act a physician is required to use an abortion method to preserve the life of a fetus when there is a reasonable likelihood or possibility that the fetus could live with or without artificial aid. The Act makes it a criminal offense for anyone to sell or engage in experiments with a fetus. Pursuant to the Act an abortion is prohibited when it is requested by a woman who desired an abortion solely because of the sex of the fetus. The Act requires all abortions be reported to the proper authorities. The Act prohibits payment of a fee to anyone for referring another person for an abortion. Under the Act criminal penalties are imposed for selling abortifacients. The provisions of the Act are set out below.

Illinois Code Ch. 720, § 510/15. Short title

This Act shall be known and may be cited as the "Illinois Abortion Law of 1975."

Illinois Code Ch. 720, § 510/1. Legislative intention

It is the intention of the General Assembly of the State of Illinois to reasonably regulate abortion in conformance with the decisions of the United States Supreme Court of January 22, 1973. Without in any way restricting the right of privacy of a woman or the right of a woman to an abortion under those decisions, the General Assembly of the State of Illinois do solemnly declare and find in reaffirmation of the longstanding policy of this State, that the unborn child is a human being from the time of conception and is, therefore, a legal person for purposes of the unborn child's right to life and is entitled to the right to life from conception under the laws and Constitution of this State. Further, the General Assembly finds and declares that longstanding policy of this State to protect the right to life of the unborn child from conception by prohibiting abortion unless necessary to preserve the life of the mother is impermissible only because of the decisions of the United States Supreme Court and that, therefore, if those decisions of the United States Supreme Court are ever reversed or modified or the United States Constitution is amended to allow protection of the unborn then the former policy of this State to prohibit abortions unless necessary for the preservation of the mother's life shall be reinstated.

It is the further intention of the General Assembly to assure and protect the woman's health and the integrity of the woman's decision whether or not to continue to bear a child, to protect the valid and compelling state interest in the infant and unborn child, to assure the integrity of marital and familial relations and the rights and interests of persons who participate in such relations, and to gather data for establishing criteria for medical decisions. The General Assembly finds as fact, upon hearings and public disclosures, that these rights and interests are not secure in the economic and social context in which abortion is presently performed.

Illinois Code Ch. 720, § 510/2. Definitions

Unless the language or context clearly indicates a different meaning is intended, the following words or phrases for the purpose of this Law shall be given the meaning ascribed to them:

(1) "Viability" means that stage of fetal development when, in the medical judgment of the attending physician based on the particular facts of the case before him, there is a reasonable likelihood of sustained survival of the fetus outside the womb, with or without artificial support.

(2) "Physician" means any person licensed to practice medicine in all its branches under the Illinois Medical Practice Act of 1987, as amended.

(3) "Department" means the Department of Public Health, State of Illinois.

(4) "Abortion" means the use of any instrument, medicine, drug or any other substance or device to terminate the pregnancy of a woman known to be pregnant with an intention other than to increase the probability of a live birth, to preserve the life or health of the child after live birth, or to remove a dead fetus.

(5) "Fertilization" and "conception" each mean the fertilization of a human ovum by a human sperm, which shall be deemed to have occurred at the time when it is known a spermatozoon has penetrated the cell membrane of the ovum.

(6) "Fetus" and "unborn child" each mean an individual organism of the species homo sapiens from fertilization until live birth.

(7) "Abortifacient" means any instrument, medicine, drug, or any other substance or device which is known to cause fetal death when employed in the usual and customary use for which it is manufactured, whether or not the fetus is known to exist when such substance or device is employed.

(8) "Born alive," "live born," and "live birth," when applied to an individual organism of the species homo sapiens, each mean he or she was completely expelled or extracted from his or her mother and after such separation breathed or showed evidence of any of the following: beating of the heart, pulsation of the umbilical cord, or definite movement of voluntary muscles, irrespective of the duration of pregnancy and whether or not the umbilical cord has been cut or the placenta is attached.

Illinois Code Ch. 720, § 510/3.1. Medical Judgment

Medical Judgment. No abortion shall be performed except by a physician after either (a) he determines that, in his best clinical judgment, the abortion is necessary, or (b) he receives a written statement or oral communication by another physician, hereinafter called the "referring physician," certifying that in the referring physician's best clinical judgment the abortion is necessary. Any person who intentionally or knowingly performs an abortion contrary to the requirements of Section 3.1 commits a Class 2 felony.

Illinois Code Ch. 720, § 510/5.
Preservation of mother and viability of fetus

(1) When the fetus is viable no abortion shall be performed unless in the medical judgment of the attending or referring physician, based on the particular facts of the case before him, it is necessary to preserve the life or health of the mother. Intentional, knowing, or reckless failure to conform to the requirements of subsection (1) of Section 5 is a Class 2 felony.

(2) When the fetus is viable the physician shall certify in writing, on a form prescribed by the Department under Section 10 of this Law, the medical indications which, in his medical judgment based on the particular facts of the case before him, warrant performance of the abortion to preserve the life or health of the mother.

Illinois Code Ch. 720, § 510/6.
Preservation fetus and experimentation with fetus

(1)(a) Any physician who intentionally performs an abortion when, in his medical judgment based on the particular facts of the case before him, there is a reasonable likelihood of sustained survival of the fetus outside the womb, with or without artificial support, shall utilize that method of abortion which, of those he knows to be available, is in his medical judgment most likely to preserve the life and health of the fetus.

(b) The physician shall certify in writing, on a form prescribed by the Department under Section 10 of this Act, the available methods considered and the reasons for choosing the method employed.

(c) Any physician who intentionally, knowingly, or recklessly violates the provisions of Section 6(1)(a) commits a Class 3 felony.

(2)(a) No abortion shall be performed or induced when the fetus is viable unless there is in attendance a physician other than the physician performing or inducing the abortion who shall take control of and provide immediate medical care for any child born alive as a result of the abortion. This requirement shall not apply when, in the medical judgment of the physician performing or inducing the abortion based on the particular facts of the case before him, there exists a medical emergency; in such a case, the physician shall describe the basis of this judgment on the form prescribed by Section 10 of this Act. Any physician who intentionally performs or induces such an abortion and who intentionally, knowingly, or recklessly fails to arrange for the attendance of such a second physician in violation of Section 6(2)(a) commits a Class 3 felony.

(b) Subsequent to the abortion, if a child is born alive, the physician required by Section 6(2)(a) to be in attendance shall exercise the same degree of professional skill, care and diligence to preserve the life and health of the child as would be required of a physician providing immediate medical care to a child born alive in the course of a pregnancy termination which was not an abortion. Any such physician who intentionally, knowingly, or recklessly violates Section 6(2)(b) commits a Class 3 felony.

(3) The law of this State shall not be construed to imply that any living individual organism of the species homo sapiens who has been born alive is not an individual under the "Criminal Code of 1961," approved July 28, 1961, as amended.

(4)(a) Any physician who intentionally performs an abortion when, in his medical judgment based on the particular facts of the case before him, there is a reasonable possibility of sustained survival of the fetus outside the womb, with or without artificial support, shall utilize that method of abortion which, of those he knows to be available, is in his medical judgment most likely to preserve the life and health of the fetus.

(b) The physician shall certify in writing, on a form prescribed by the Department under Section 10 of this Act, the available methods considered and the reasons for choosing the method employed.

(c) Any physician who intentionally, knowingly, or recklessly violates the provisions of Section 6(4)(a) commits a Class 3 felony.

(5) Nothing in Section 6 requires a physician to employ a method of abortion which, in the medical judgment of the physician performing the abortion based on the particular facts of the case before him, would increase medical risk to the mother.

(6) When the fetus is viable and when there exists reasonable medical certainty (a) that the particular method of abortion to be employed will cause organic pain to the fetus, and (b) that use of an anesthetic or analgesic would abolish or alleviate organic pain to the fetus caused by the particular method of abortion to be employed, then the physician who is to perform the abortion or his agent or the referring physician or his agent shall inform the woman upon whom the abortion is to be performed that such an anesthetic or analgesic is available, if he knows it to be available, for use to abolish or alleviate organic pain caused to the fetus by the particular method of abortion to be employed. Any person who performs an abortion with knowledge that any such reasonable medical certainty exists and that such an anesthetic or analgesic is available, and intentionally fails to so inform the woman or to ascertain that the woman has been so informed commits a Class B misdemeanor. The foregoing requirements of subsection (6) of Section 6 shall not apply (a) when in the medical judgment of the physician who is to perform the abortion or the referring physician based upon the particular facts of the case before him: (i) there exists a medical emergency, or (ii) the administration of such an anesthetic or analgesic would decrease a possibility of sustained survival of the fetus apart from the body of the mother, with or without artificial support, or (b) when the physician who is to perform the abortion administers an anesthetic or an analgesic to the woman or the fetus and he knows there exists reasonable medical certainty that such use will abolish organic pain caused to the fetus during the course of the abortion.

(7) No person shall sell or experiment upon a fetus produced by the fertilization of a human ovum by a human sperm unless such experimentation is therapeutic to the fetus thereby produced. Intentional violation of this section is a Class A misdemeanor. Nothing in this subsection (7) is intended to prohibit the performance of in vitro fertilization.

(8) No person shall intentionally perform an abortion with knowledge that the pregnant woman is seeking the abortion solely on account of the sex of the fetus. Nothing in Section 6(8) shall be construed to proscribe the performance of an abortion on account of the sex of the fetus because of a genetic disorder linked to that sex. If the application of Section 6(8) to the period of pregnancy prior to viability is held invalid, then such invalidity shall not affect its application to the period of pregnancy subsequent to viability.

Illinois Code Ch. 720, § 510/10. Reports of abortion

A report of each abortion performed shall be made to the Department on forms prescribed by it. Such report forms shall not identify the patient by name, but by an individual number to be noted in the patient's permanent record in the possession of the physician, and shall include information concerning:

(1) Identification of the physician who performed the abortion and the facility where the abortion was performed and a patient identification number;

(2) State in which the patient resides;

(3) Patient's date of birth, race and marital status;

(4) Number of prior pregnancies;

(5) Date of last menstrual period;

(6) Type of abortion procedure performed;

(7) Complications and whether the abortion resulted in a live birth;

(8) The date the abortion was performed;

(9) Medical indications for any abortion performed when the fetus was viable;

(10) The information required by Sections 6(1)(b) and 6(4)(b) of this Act, if applicable;

(11) Basis for any medical judgment that a medical emergency existed when required under Sections 6(2)(a) and 6(6) and when required to be reported in accordance with this Section by any provision of this Law; and

(12) The pathologist's test results pursuant to Section 12 of this Act.

Such form shall be completed by the hospital or other licensed facility, signed by the physician who performed the abortion or pregnancy termination, and transmitted to the Department not later than 10 days following the end of the month in which the abortion was performed.

In the event that a complication of an abortion occurs or becomes known after submission of such form, a correction using the same patient identification number shall be submitted to the Department within 10 days of its becoming known.

The Department may prescribe rules and regulations regarding the administration of this Law and shall prescribe regulations to secure the confidentiality of the woman's identity in the information to be provided under the "Vital Records Act." All reports received by the Department shall be treated as confidential and the Department shall secure the woman's anonymity. Such reports shall be used only for statistical purposes.

Upon 30 days public notice, the Department is empowered to require reporting of any additional information which, in the sound discretion of the Department, is necessary to develop statistical data relating to the protection of maternal or fetal life or health, or is necessary to enforce the provisions of this Law, or is necessary to develop useful criteria for medical decisions. The Department shall annually report to the General Assembly all statistical data gathered under this Law and its recommendations to further the purpose of this Law.

The requirement for reporting to the General Assembly shall be satisfied by filing copies of the report with the Speaker, the Minority Leader and the Clerk of the House of Representatives and the President, the Minority Leader and the Secretary of the Senate and the Legislative Research Unit, as required by Section 3.1 of "An Act to revise the law in relation to the General Assembly," approved February 25, 1874, as amended, and filing such additional copies with the State Government Report Distribution Center for the General Assembly as is required under paragraph (t) of Section 7 of the State Library Act.

Illinois Code Ch. 720, § 510/10.1. Reports of abortion complications

Any physician who diagnoses a woman as having complications resulting from an abortion shall report, within a reasonable period of time, the diagnosis and a summary of her physical symptoms to the Illinois Department of Public Health in accordance with procedures and upon forms required by such Department. The Department of Public Health shall define the complications required to be reported by rule. The complications defined by rule shall be those which, according to contemporary medical standards, are manifested by symptoms with severity equal to or greater than hemorrhaging requiring transfusion, infection, incomplete abortion, or punctured organs. If the physician making the diagno-

sis of a complication knows the name or location of the facility where the abortion was performed, he shall report such information to the Department of Public Health.

Any physician who intentionally violates this Section shall be subject to revocation of his license pursuant to paragraph (22) of Section 22 of the Medical Practice Act of 1987.

Illinois Code Ch. 720, § 510/11. Violations of Act

(1) Any person who intentionally violates any provision of this Law commits a Class A misdemeanor unless a specific penalty is otherwise provided. Any person who intentionally falsifies any writing required by this Law commits a Class A misdemeanor.

Intentional, knowing, reckless, or negligent violations of this Law shall constitute unprofessional conduct which causes public harm under Section 22 of the Medical Practice Act of 1987, as amended; Sections 10-45 and 15-50 of the Nursing and Advanced Practice Nursing Act, and Section 21 of the Physician Assistant Practice Act of 1987, as amended.

Intentional, knowing, reckless or negligent violations of this Law will constitute grounds for refusal, denial, revocation, suspension, or withdrawal of license, certificate, or permit under Section 30 of the Pharmacy Practice Act of 1987, as amended; Section 7 of the Ambulatory Surgical Treatment Center Act, effective July 19, 1973, as amended; and Section 7 of the Hospital Licensing Act.

(2) Any hospital or licensed facility which, or any physician who intentionally, knowingly, or recklessly fails to submit a complete report to the Department in accordance with the provisions of Section 10 of this Law and any person who intentionally, knowingly, recklessly or negligently fails to maintain the confidentiality of any reports required under this Law or reports required by Sections 10.1 or 12 of this Law commits a Class B misdemeanor.

(3) Any person who sells any drug, medicine, instrument or other substance which he knows to be an abortifacient and which is in fact an abortifacient, unless upon prescription of a physician, is guilty of a Class B misdemeanor. Any person who prescribes or administers any instrument, medicine, drug or other substance or device, which he knows to be an abortifacient, and which is in fact an abortifacient, and intentionally, knowingly or recklessly fails to inform the person for whom it is prescribed or upon whom it is administered that it is an abortifacient commits a Class C misdemeanor.

(4) Any person who intentionally, knowingly or recklessly performs upon a woman what he represents to that woman to be an abortion when he knows or should know that she is not pregnant commits a Class 2 felony and shall be answerable in civil damages equal to 3 times the amount of proved damages.

Illinois Code Ch. 720, § 510/11.1. Abortion referral fee

(a) The payment or receipt of a referral fee in connection with the performance of an abortion is a Class 4 felony.

(b) For purposes of this Section, "referral fee" means the transfer of anything of value between a doctor who performs an abortion or an operator or employee of a clinic at which an abortion is performed and the person who advised the woman receiving the abortion to use the services of that doctor or clinic.

Illinois Code Ch. 720, § 510/12. Analysis of fetal tissue

The dead fetus and all tissue removed at the time of abortion shall be submitted for a gross and microscopic analysis and tissue report to a board eligible or certified pathologist as a matter of record in all cases. The results of the analysis and report shall be given to the physician who performed the abortion within 7 days of the abortion and such physician shall report any complications relevant to the woman's medical condition to his patient within 48 hours of receiving a report if possible. Any evidence of live birth or of viability shall be reported within 7 days, if possible, to the Department by the pathologist. Intentional failure of the pathologist to report any evidence of live birth or of viability to the Department is a Class B misdemeanor.

Illinois Code Ch. 720, § 510/12.1.
Fetal deaths not due to abortion

Nothing in this Act shall prohibit the use of any tissues or cells obtained from a dead fetus or dead premature infant whose death did not result from an induced abortion, for therapeutic purposes or scientific, research, or laboratory experimentation, provided that the written consent to such use is obtained from one of the parents of such fetus or infant.

Illinois Code Ch. 720, § 510/14. Severability

(1) If any provision, word, phrase or clause of this Act or the application thereof to any person or circumstance shall be held invalid, such invalidity shall not affect the provisions, words, phrases, clauses or application of this Act which can be given effect without the invalid provision, word, phrase, clause, or application, and to this end the provisions, words, phrases, and clauses of this Act are declared to be severable.

(2) Within 60 days from the time this Section becomes law, the Department shall issue regulations pursuant to Section 10. Insofar as Section 10 requires registration under the "Vital Records Act," it shall not take effect until such regulations are issued. The Department shall make available the forms required under Section 10 within 30 days of the time this Section becomes law. No requirement that any person report information to the Department shall become effective until the Department has made available the forms required under Section 10. All other provisions of this amended Law shall take effect immediately upon enactment.

(3) PARTIAL-BIRTH ABORTION

Illinois criminalizes partial-birth abortions. However, it was held in *Hope Clinic v. Ryan*, 995 F.Supp. 847 (N.D.Ill. 1998), reversed, 195 F.3d 857 (7th Cir. 1999), vacated, 120 S.Ct. 2738 (2000) that Illinois' partial-birth abortion statute was unconstitutional. The state has not repealed the statute.

Illinois also has a statute that, in the case of a minor having an abortion, permits a lawsuit to be filed by the maternal grandparents of a fetus that was destroyed by partial-birth abortion. In addition, the state expressly exempts a pregnant woman from criminal prosecution because of a partial-birth abortion. The statutes addressing the matters are set out below.

Illinois Code Ch. 720, § 513/1. Short title

Short title. This Act may be cited as the Partial-birth Abortion Ban Act.

Illinois Code Ch. 720, § 513/5. Definitions

In this Act:

"Partial-birth abortion" means an abortion in which the person performing the abortion partially vaginally delivers a living human fetus or infant before killing the fetus or infant and completing the delivery. The terms "fetus" and "infant" are used interchangeably to refer to the biological offspring of human parents.

Illinois Code Ch. 720, § 513/10. Partial-birth abortions offense

Any person who knowingly performs a partial-birth abortion and thereby kills a human fetus or infant is guilty of a Class 4 felony. This Section does not apply to a partial-birth abortion that is necessary to save the life of a mother because her life is endangered by a physical disorder, physical illness, or physical injury, including a life-endangering condition caused by or arising from the pregnancy itself, provided that no other medical procedure would suffice for that purpose.

Illinois Code Ch. 720, § 513/15. Civil lawsuit

The maternal grandparents of the fetus or infant, if the mother has not attained the age of 18 years at the time of the abortion, may in a civil action obtain appropriate relief unless the pregnancy resulted from the plaintiff's criminal conduct or the plaintiff consented to the abortion. The relief shall include money damages for all injuries, psychological and physical, occasioned by the violation of this Act and statutory damages equal to 3 times the cost of the partial-birth abortion.

Illinois Code Ch. 720, § 513/20. Prosecution of woman prohibited

A woman on whom a partial-birth abortion is performed may not be prosecuted under this Act, for a conspiracy to violate this Act, or for an offense under Article 31 of the Criminal Code of 1961 based on a violation of this Act, nor may she be held accountable under Article 5 of the Criminal Code of 1961 for an offense based on a violation of this Act.

(4) HUSBAND'S RIGHTS

Illinois has a statute which allows a husband to prevent his wife from having an abortion. This statute is unenforceable in view of two decisions by the United States Supreme Court. In *Planned Parenthood of Southeastern Pennsylvania v. Casey* the Supreme Court invalidated a provision in Pennsylvania's abortion statute that required a married woman inform her spouse of her decision to have an abortion, before she would be allowed to have one. The Supreme Court invalidated a provision in Missouri's abortion statute, in *Planned Parenthood of Missouri v. Danforth*, that required a woman seek the consent of a spouse before having an abortion. Illinois also has a statute which exempts a husband from liability for the cost of an abortion he did not consent to having. The Illinois statutes are set out below.

Illinois Code Ch. 735, § 5/11-107.1. Rights of the father

In any case when a married woman wishes to have an abortion performed upon her, and her spouse, who is the father of the unborn child, is opposed to the performance of that abortion, a court may hear testimony from both parties and balance the rights and interests of those parties.

When the interests of the husband in preventing the abortion outweigh those of the wife in having an abortion performed after the unborn child is viable, the court may issue an injunction against the performance of the abortion but only where the court makes a finding that the mother's life or physical health are not in danger.

Illinois Code Ch. 750, § 65/15(b). Family expenses

(b) No spouse shall be liable for any expense incurred by the other spouse when an abortion is performed on such spouse, without the consent of such other spouse, unless the physician who performed the abortion certifies that such abortion is necessary to preserve the life of the spouse who obtained such abortion.

(5) ABORTION BY MINORS

Under the laws of Illinois no physician may perform an abortion upon an unemancipated minor, until 48 hours after notice of the operation has been given to an adult family member of the minor. Notice is not required in a medical emergency situation, or if the minor was a victim of sexual abuse, neglect, or physical abuse by an adult family member. In compliance with federal constitutional law, Illinois has provided a judicial waiver procedure for an unemancipated minor to obtain an abortion without notice to an adult family member. The minor may petition a trial court for a waiver of the notice requirement. A minor has a right to an attorney at the proceeding and if she cannot afford one, the court must appoint her an attorney. If a minor chooses, she may represent herself. The required notice to an adult family member may be waived if the court finds either (1) that the minor is mature and well-informed enough to make the abortion decision on her own, or (2) that performance of the abortion would be in the best interest of the minor. An expedited appeal is available to any minor to whom the court denies a waiver of notice. Illinois also has a statute which exempts a nonconsenting parent from having to pay for a minor's abortion. The statutes addressing the matters are set out below.

Illinois Code Ch. 750, § 70/1. Short title

This Act may be cited as the Parental Notice of Abortion Act of 1995.

Illinois Code Ch. 750, § 70/5. Legislative findings and purpose

Legislative findings and purpose. The General Assembly finds that notification of a family member as defined in this Act is in the best interest of an unemancipated minor, and the General Assembly's purpose in enacting this parental notice law is to further and protect the best interests of an unemancipated minor.

The medical, emotional, and psychological consequences of abortion are sometimes serious and long-lasting, and immature minors often lack the ability to make fully informed choices that consider both the immediate and long-range consequences.

Parental consultation is usually in the best interest of the minor and is desirable since the capacity to become pregnant and the capacity for mature judgment concerning the wisdom of an abortion are not necessarily related.

Illinois Code Ch. 750, § 70/10. Definitions

As used in this Act:

"Abortion" means the use of any instrument, medicine, drug, or any other substance or device to terminate the pregnancy of a woman known to be pregnant with an intention other than to increase the probability of a live birth, to preserve the life or health of a child after live birth, or to remove a dead fetus.

"Actual notice" means the giving of notice directly, in person, or by telephone.

"Adult family member" means a person over 21 years of age who is the parent, grandparent, step-parent living in the household, or legal guardian.

"Constructive notice" means notice by certified mail to the last known address of the person entitled to notice with delivery deemed to have occurred 48 hours after the certified notice is mailed.

"Incompetent" means any person who has been adjudged as mentally ill or developmentally disabled and who, because of her mental illness or developmental disability, is not fully able to manage her person and for whom a guardian of the person has been appointed under Section 11a-3(a)(1) of the Probate Act of 1975.

"Medical emergency" means a condition that, on the basis of the physician's good faith clinical judgment, so complicates the medical condition of a pregnant woman as to necessitate the immediate abortion of her pregnancy to avert her death or for which a delay will create serious risk of substantial and irreversible impairment of major bodily function.

"Minor" means any person under 18 years of age who is not or has not been married or who has not been emancipated under the Emancipation of Mature Minors Act.

"Neglect" means the failure of an adult family member to supply a child with necessary food, clothing, shelter, or medical care when reasonably able to do so or the failure to protect a child from conditions or actions that imminently and seriously endanger the child's physical or mental health when reasonably able to do so.

"Physical abuse" means any physical injury intentionally inflicted by an adult family member on a child.

"Physician" means any person licensed to practice medicine in all its branches under the Illinois Medical Practice Act of 1987.

"Sexual abuse" means any sexual conduct or sexual penetration as defined in Section 12-12 of the Criminal Code of 1961 that is prohibited by the criminal laws of the State of Illinois and committed against a minor by an adult family member as defined in this Act.

Illinois Code Ch. 750, § 70/15. Notice and waiting period

No person shall knowingly perform an abortion upon a minor or upon an incompetent person unless the physician or his or her agent has given at least 48 hours actual notice to an adult family member of the pregnant minor or incompetent person of his or her intention to perform the abortion, unless that person or his or her agent has received a written statement by a referring physician certifying that the referring physician or his or her agent has given at least 48 hours notice to an adult family member of the pregnant minor or incompetent person. If actual notice is not possible after a reasonable effort, the physician or his or her agent must give 48 hours constructive notice.

Illinois Code Ch. 750, § 70/20. Exceptions to notice

Notice shall not be required under this Act if:

(1) the minor or incompetent person is accompanied by a person entitled to notice; or

(2) notice is waived in writing by a person who is entitled to notice; or

(3) the attending physician certifies in the patient's medical record that a medical emergency exists and there is insufficient time to provide the required notice; or

(4) the minor declares in writing that she is a victim of sexual abuse, neglect, or physical abuse by an adult family member as defined in this Act. The attending physician must certify in the patient's medical record that he or she has received the written declaration of abuse or neglect. Any notification of public authorities of abuse that may be required under other laws of this State need not be made by the person performing the abortion until after the minor receives an abortion that otherwise complies with the requirements of this Act; or

(5) notice is waived under Section 25.

Illinois Code Ch. 750, § 70/25. Judicial bypass

(a) The requirements and procedures under this Section are available to minors and incompetent persons whether or not they are residents of this State.

(b) The minor or incompetent person may petition any circuit court for a waiver of the notice requirement and may participate in proceedings on her own behalf. The court shall appoint a guardian ad litem for her. Any guardian ad litem appointed under this Act shall act to maintain the confidentiality of the proceedings. The circuit court shall advise her that she has a right to court-appointed counsel and shall provide her with counsel upon her request.

(c) Court proceedings under this Section shall be confidential and shall ensure the anonymity of the minor or incompetent person. All court proceedings under this Section shall be sealed. The minor or incompetent person shall have the right to file her petition in the circuit court using a pseudonym or using solely her initials. All documents related to this petition shall be confidential and shall not be made available to the public.

These proceedings shall be given precedence over other pending matters to the extent necessary to ensure that the court reaches a decision promptly. The court shall rule and issue written findings of fact and conclusions of law within 48 hours of the time that the petition is filed, except that the 48-hour limitation may be extended at the request of the minor or incompetent person. If the court fails to rule within the 48-hour period and an extension is not requested, then the petition shall be deemed to have been granted, and the notice requirement shall be waived.

(d) Notice shall be waived if the court finds by a preponderance of the evidence either:

(1) that the minor or incompetent person is sufficiently mature and well enough informed to decide intelligently whether to have an abortion, or

(2) that notification under Section 15 of this Act would not be in the best interests of the minor or incompetent person.

(e) A court that conducts proceedings under this Section shall issue written and specific factual findings and legal conclusions supporting its decision and shall order that a confidential record of the evidence and the judge's findings and conditions be maintained.

(f) An expedited confidential appeal shall be available, as the Supreme Court provides by rule, to any minor or incompetent person to whom the circuit court denies a waiver of notice. An order authorizing an abortion without notice shall not be subject to appeal.

(g) The Supreme Court is respectfully requested to promulgate any rules and regulations necessary to ensure that proceedings under this Act are handled in an expeditious and confidential manner.

(h) No fees shall be required of any minor or incompetent person who avails herself of the procedures provided by this Section.

Illinois Code Ch. 750, § 70/30. Minor's consent to abortion

A person may not perform an abortion on a minor without the minor's consent, except in a medical emergency.

Illinois Code Ch. 750, § 70/35. Reports

The Department of Public Health shall comply with the reporting requirements set forth in the consent decree in Herbst v. O'Malley, case no. 84-C-5602 in the U.S. District Court for the Northern District of Illinois, Eastern Division.

Illinois Code Ch. 750, § 70/40. Penalties

(a) Any physician who willfully fails to provide notice as required under this Act before performing an abortion on a minor or an incompetent person shall be referred to the Illinois State Medical Disciplinary Board for action in accordance with Section 22 of the Medical Practice Act of 1987.

(b) Any person, not authorized under this Act, who signs any waiver of notice for a minor or incompetent person seeking an abortion, is guilty of a Class C misdemeanor.

Illinois Code Ch. 750, § 70/45. Immunity

Any physician who, in good faith, provides notice in accordance with Section 15 or relies on an exception under Section 20 shall not be subject to any type of civil or criminal liability or discipline for unprofessional conduct for failure to give required notice.

Illinois Code Ch. 750, § 70/50.
Severability and inseverability

If any provision of this Act or its application to any person or circumstance is held invalid, the invalidity of that provision or application does not affect other provisions or applications of the Act that can be given effect without the invalid provision or application, except that Section 25 is inseverable to the extent that if all or any substantial and material part of Section 25 is held invalid, then the entire Act is invalid.

Illinois Code Ch. 750, § 65/15(c). Family expenses

(c) No parent shall be liable for any expense incurred by his or her minor child when an abortion is performed on such minor child without the consent of both parents of such child, if they both have custody, or the parent having custody, or legal guardian of such child, unless the physician who performed the abortion certifies that such abortion is necessary to preserve the life of the minor child who obtained such abortion.

(6) USE OF FACILITIES AND PEOPLE

Under the laws of Illinois hospitals are not required to allow abortions at their facilities. The employees and physicians at hospitals that do allow abortions are permitted to refuse to take part in abortions. The statutes addressing the matter are set out below.

Illinois Code Ch. 745, § 30/1.
Right to refuse to participate in abortion

(a) No physician, nurse or other person who refuses to recommend, perform or assist in the performance of an abortion, whether such abortion be a crime or not, shall be liable to any person for damages allegedly arising from such refusal.

(b) No hospital that refuses to permit the performance of an abortion upon its premises, whether such abortion be a crime or not, shall be li-

able to any person for damages allegedly arising from such refusal.

(c) Any person, association, partnership or corporation that discriminates against another person in any way, including, but not limited to, hiring, promotion, advancement, transfer, licensing, granting of hospital privileges, or staff appointments, because of that person's refusal to recommend, perform or assist in the performance of an abortion, whether such abortion be a crime or not, shall be answerable in civil damages equal to 3 times the amount of proved damages, but in no case less than $2,000.

(d) The license of any hospital, doctor, nurse or any other medical personnel shall not be revoked or suspended because of a refusal to permit, recommend, perform or assist in the performance of an abortion.

Illinois Code Ch. 720, § 510/13.
Conscientious objections to abortion

No physician, hospital, ambulatory surgical center, nor employee thereof, shall be required against his or its conscience declared in writing to perform, permit or participate in any abortion, and the failure or refusal to do so shall not be the basis for any civil, criminal, administrative or disciplinary action, proceeding, penalty or punishment. If any request for an abortion is denied, the patient shall be promptly notified.

(7) PUBLIC FUNDS FOR ABORTION

Illinois prohibits expenditure of state funds to pay for abortions, except when necessary to save the life of the woman. In *Williams v. Zbaraz* the United States Supreme Court held that in light of the requirements of the federal Hyde Amendment, the Equal Protection Clause of the Fourteenth Amendment was not violated by Illinois' prohibition on the use of state funds to pay for abortions, except when necessary to save the life of the pregnant woman. The statutes addressing the matter are set out below.

Illinois Code Ch. 305, § 5/5-5(17).
Limiting public funds for abortion

The Illinois Department, by rule, shall determine the quantity and quality of and the rate of reimbursement for the medical assistance for which payment will be authorized, and the medical services to be provided, which may include all or part of the following: ... (17) any other medical care, and any other type of remedial care recognized under the laws of this State, but not including abortions, or induced miscarriages or premature births, unless, in the opinion of a physician, such procedures are necessary for the preservation of the life of the woman seeking such treatment, or except an induced premature birth intended to produce a live viable child and such procedure is necessary for the health of the mother or her unborn child.

Illinois Code Ch. 305, § 5/6-1. Limiting financial aid

Financial aid in meeting basic maintenance requirements shall be given under this Article to or in behalf of persons who meet the eligibility conditions of Sections 6-1.1 through 6-1. 10. In addition, each unit of local government subject to this Article shall provide persons receiving financial aid in meeting basic maintenance requirements with financial aid for either (a) necessary treatment, care, and supplies required because of illness or disability, or (b) acute medical treatment, care, and supplies only. If a local governmental unit elects to provide financial aid for acute medical treatment, care, and supplies only, the general types of acute medical treatment, care, and supplies for which financial aid is provided shall be specified in the general assistance rules of the local governmental unit, which rules shall provide that financial aid is provided, at a minimum, for acute medical treatment, care, or supplies necessitated by a medical condition for which prior approval or authorization of medical treatment, care, or supplies is not required by the general assistance rules of the Illinois Department. Nothing in this Article shall be construed to permit the granting of financial aid where the purpose of such aid is to obtain an abortion, induced miscarriage or induced premature birth unless, in the opinion of a physician, such procedures are necessary for the preservation of the life of the woman seeking such treatment, or except an induced premature birth intended to produce a live viable child and such procedure is necessary for the health of the mother or her unborn child.

Illinois Code Ch. 5, § 375/6(a). State employee health program

(a) The program of health benefits shall provide for protection against the financial costs of health care expenses incurred in and out of hospital including basic hospital-surgical-medical coverages. The program may include, but shall not be limited to, such supplemental coverages as out-patient diagnostic X-ray and laboratory expenses, prescription drugs, dental services, hearing evaluations, hearing aids, the dispensing and fitting of hearing aids, and similar group benefits as are now or may become available. However, nothing in this Act shall be construed to permit, on or after July 1, 1980, the non-contributory portion of any such program to include the expenses of obtaining an abortion, induced miscarriage or induced premature birth unless, in the opinion of a physician, such procedures are necessary for the preservation of the life of the woman seeking such treatment, or except an induced premature birth intended to produce a live viable child and such procedure is necessary for the health of the mother or the unborn child.

(8) INJURY TO A PREGNANT WOMAN

Several criminal statutes have been enacted by Illinois that punishes unlawful injury or death to a fetus. The statutes addressing the matter are set out below.

Illinois Code Ch. 720, § 5/12-3.1. Battery of an unborn child

(a) A person commits battery of an unborn child if he intentionally or knowingly without legal justification and by any means causes bodily harm to an unborn child.

(b) For purposes of this Section, (1) "unborn child" shall mean any individual of the human species from fertilization until birth, and (2) "person" shall not include the pregnant woman whose unborn child is harmed.

(c) Battery of an unborn child is a Class A misdemeanor.

(d) This Section shall not apply to acts which cause bodily harm to an unborn child if those acts were committed during any abortion, as defined in Section 2 of the Illinois Abortion Law of 1975, as amended, to which the pregnant woman has consented. This Section shall not apply to acts which were committed pursuant to usual and customary standards of medical practice during diagnostic testing or therapeutic treatment.

Illinois Code Ch. 720, § 5/12-4.4.
Aggravated battery of an unborn child

(a) A person who, in committing battery of an unborn child, intentionally or knowingly causes great bodily harm, or permanent disability or disfigurement commits aggravated battery of an unborn child.

(b) Sentence. Aggravated battery of an unborn child is a Class 2 felony.

Illinois Code Ch. 720, § 5/9-3.2.
Involuntary manslaughter and reckless homicide

(a) A person who unintentionally kills an unborn child without lawful justification commits involuntary manslaughter of an unborn child if his acts whether lawful or unlawful which cause the death are such as are likely to cause death or great bodily harm to some individual, and he performs them recklessly, except in cases in which the cause of death consists of the driving of a motor vehicle, in which case the person commits reckless homicide of an unborn child.

(b) Sentence.

(1) Involuntary manslaughter of an unborn child is a Class 3 felony.

(2) Reckless homicide of an unborn child is a Class 3 felony.

(c) For purposes of this Section, (1) "unborn child" shall mean any

individual of the human species from fertilization until birth, and (2) "person" shall not include the pregnant woman whose unborn child is killed.

(d) This Section shall not apply to acts which cause the death of an unborn child if those acts were committed during any abortion, as defined in Section 2 of the Illinois Abortion Law of 1975, as amended, to which the pregnant woman has consented. This Section shall not apply to acts which were committed pursuant to usual and customary standards of medical practice during diagnostic testing or therapeutic treatment.

(e) The provisions of this Section shall not be construed to prohibit the prosecution of any person under any other provision of law, nor shall it be construed to preclude any civil cause of action.

Illinois Code Ch. 720, § 5/9-2.1 Voluntary manslaughter

(a) A person who kills an unborn child without lawful justification commits voluntary manslaughter of an unborn child if at the time of the killing he is acting under a sudden and intense passion resulting from serious provocation by another whom the offender endeavors to kill, but he negligently or accidentally causes the death of the unborn child. Serious provocation is conduct sufficient to excite an intense passion in a reasonable person.

(b) A person who intentionally or knowingly kills an unborn child commits voluntary manslaughter of an unborn child if at the time of the killing he believes the circumstances to be such that, if they existed, would justify or exonerate the killing under the principles stated in Article 7 of this Code, but his belief is unreasonable.

(c) Voluntary Manslaughter of an unborn child is a Class 1 felony.

(d) For purposes of this Section, (1) "unborn child" shall mean any individual of the human species from fertilization until birth, and (2) "person" shall not include the pregnant woman whose unborn child is killed.

(e) This Section shall not apply to acts which cause the death of an unborn child if those acts were committed during any abortion, as defined in Section 2 of the Illinois Abortion Law of 1975, as amended, to which the pregnant woman has consented. This Section shall not apply to acts which were committed pursuant to usual and customary standards of medical practice during diagnostic testing or therapeutic treatment.

Illinois Code Ch. 720, § 5/9-1.2 Intentional Homicide

(a) A person commits the offense of intentional homicide of an unborn child if, in performing acts which cause the death of an unborn child, he without lawful justification:

(1) either intended to cause the death of or do great bodily harm to the pregnant woman or her unborn child or knew that such acts would cause death or great bodily harm to the pregnant woman or her unborn child; or

(2) he knew that his acts created a strong probability of death or great bodily harm to the pregnant woman or her unborn child; and

(3) he knew that the woman was pregnant.

(b) For purposes of this Section, (1) "unborn child" shall mean any individual of the human species from fertilization until birth, and (2) "person" shall not include the pregnant woman whose unborn child is killed.

(c) This Section shall not apply to acts which cause the death of an unborn child if those acts were committed during any abortion, as defined in Section 2 of the Illinois Abortion Law of 1975, as amended, to which the pregnant woman has consented. This Section shall not apply to acts which were committed pursuant to usual and customary standards of medical practice during diagnostic testing or therapeutic treatment.

(d) The sentence for intentional homicide of an unborn child shall be the same as for first degree murder, except that:

(1) the death penalty may not be imposed;

(2) if the person committed the offense while armed with a firearm, 15 years shall be added to the term of imprisonment imposed by the court;

(3) if, during the commission of the offense, the person personally discharged a firearm, 20 years shall be added to the term of imprisonment imposed by the court;

(4) if, during the commission of the offense, the person personally discharged a firearm that proximately caused great bodily harm, permanent disability, permanent disfigurement, or death to another person, 25 years or up to a term of natural life shall be added to the term of imprisonment imposed by the court.

(e) The provisions of this Act shall not be construed to prohibit the prosecution of any person under any other provision of law.

(9) FETAL WRONGFUL DEATH LAWSUIT

Except in the case of a lawful abortion, Illinois permits a civil lawsuit to be filed for the death of a fetus. The statute addressing the issue is set out below.

Illinois Code Ch. 740, 180/2.2. Fetal death cause of action

The state of gestation or development of a human being when an injury is caused, when an injury takes effect, or at death, shall not foreclose maintenance of any cause of action under the law of this State arising from the death of a human being caused by wrongful act, neglect or default.

There shall be no cause of action against a physician or a medical institution for the wrongful death of a fetus caused by an abortion where the abortion was permitted by law and the requisite consent was lawfully given. Provided, however, that a cause of action is not prohibited where the fetus is live-born but subsequently dies.

There shall be no cause of action against a physician or a medical institution for the wrongful death of a fetus based on the alleged misconduct of the physician or medical institution where the defendant did not know and, under the applicable standard of good medical care, had no medical reason to know of the pregnancy of the mother of the fetus.

Illinois Federation for Right to Life

Illinois Federation for Right to Life (IFRL) is a pro-life organization that has been in existence since 1973. The president of IFRL is Linda Behnken. IFRL is the largest pro-life organization in Illinois. The organization works to present fully detailed and factual information upon which individuals and the general public may make an informed decision about the various topics of fetal development, abortion, and alternatives to abortion. IFRL publishes *IFRL News,* the only statewide pro-life newspaper in Illinois. The organization also sponsors educational seminars and conventions to train volunteers; as well as providing support to elect pro-life candidates to state and federal office. *See also* **Pro-Life Organizations**

Illinois State University Collegians for Life

Illinois State University Collegians for Life is a student-run pro-life organization in Normal, Illinois. The organization has set out three primary objectives: (1) to ensure that the truth about abortion is being disseminated at the university, (2) to provide assistance when possible to women in need, and (3) to participate in activism (trips to abortion clinics and prayer). The group intends to create a cemetery of the innocents on the university grounds, and sponsor pro-life debates. *See also* **Pro-Life Organizations**

Impaired Pregnancy

Impaired pregnancy refers to a fetus that is abnormal due to environmental, genetic, chromosomal, or unknown causes. *See also* **Birth Defects and Abortion**

Implantation

Implantation refers to the placement of a fertilized egg in the uterine lining (endometrium). This occurs about 7 days after conception. Occasionally implantation occurs outside the uterine and results in an ectopic pregnancy. *See also* **Ectopic Pregnancy; Fetal Development**

In Utero

In utero refers to a condition that occurs within the uterus during pregnancy.

In Vitro Fertilization *see* **Assisted Reproductive Technology**

Incarcerated Pregnant Women

Women who are incarcerated (jail or prison) have a right to necessary medical treatment that is paid for with public funds. A few issues have been raised in federal courts concerning the right of incarcerated pregnant women to have elective abortions. For example, in *Monmouth County Correctional Institutional Inmates v. Lanzaro*, 834 F.2d 326 (3d Cir. 1987) it was held that a New Jersey county regulation requiring female inmates to secure court-ordered releases to obtain abortion while in the county's custody was unconstitutional, and that its regulation requiring inmates to obtain their own financing for abortion was unconstitutional. In *Roe v. Crawford*, 2008 WL 187513 (8th Cir. 2008) it was held that a policy by the Missouri Department of Corrections which prohibited transporting female inmates for elective abortions was unconstitutional. In *Doe v. Barron*, 92 F.Supp.2d 694 (S.D.Ohio 1999) it was held that a regulation by an Ohio correctional facility that required pregnant inmates obtain a court order before obtaining an elective abortion was invalid. However, in *Victoria W. v. Larpenter*, 369 F.3d 475 (5th Cir. 2004) it was held that a policy by Louisiana prisons that required pregnant inmates obtain a court order before obtaining an elective abortion was not unconstitutional.

California is the only state that has statutes which expressly authorize elective abortion for incarcerated women and minors. The statutes are reproduced below.

California Penal Code § 3405. Abortion by State prison inmates

No condition or restriction upon the obtaining of an abortion by a prisoner, pursuant to the [Reproductive Privacy Act], other than those contained in that act, shall be imposed. Prisoners found to be pregnant and desiring abortions, shall be permitted to determine their eligibility for an abortion pursuant to law, and if determined to be eligible, shall be permitted to obtain an abortion.

The rights provided for females by this section shall be posted in at least one conspicuous place to which all female prisoners have access.

California Penal Code § 3406.
Abortion physician for State prisoners

Any female prisoner shall have the right to summon and receive the services of any physician and surgeon of her choice in order to determine whether she is pregnant. The warden may adopt reasonable rules and regulations with regard to the conduct of examinations to effectuate this determination.

If the prisoner is found to be pregnant, she is entitled to a determination of the extent of the medical services needed by her and to the receipt of these services from the physician and surgeon of her choice. Any expenses occasioned by the services of a physician and surgeon whose services are not provided by the institution shall be borne by the prisoner.

Any physician providing services pursuant to this section shall possess a current, valid, and unrevoked certificate to engage in the practice of medicine issued pursuant to Chapter 5 (commencing with Section 2000) of Division 2 of the Business and Professions Code.

The rights provided for prisoners by this section shall be posted in at least one conspicuous place to which all female prisoners have access.

California Penal Code § 4028. Abortion by local jail inmates

No condition or restriction upon the obtaining of an abortion by a female detained in any local detention facility, pursuant to the [Reproductive Privacy Act], other than those contained in that act, shall be imposed. Females found to be pregnant and desiring abortions shall be permitted to determine their eligibility for an abortion pursuant to law and if determined to be eligible, shall be permitted to obtain an abortion.

For the purposes of this section, "local detention facility" means any city, county, or regional facility used for the confinement of any female person for more than 24 hours.

The rights provided for females by this section shall be posted in at least one conspicuous place to which all female prisoners have access.

California Welfare & Institutions Code § 220.
Abortion for female in local juvenile facility

No condition or restriction upon the obtaining of an abortion by a female detained in any local juvenile facility, pursuant to the [Reproductive Privacy Act], other than those contained in that act, shall be imposed. Females found to be pregnant and desiring abortions, shall be permitted to determine their eligibility for an abortion pursuant to law, and if determined to be eligible, shall be permitted to obtain an abortion.

For the purposes of this section, "local juvenile facility" means any city, county, or regional facility used for the confinement of female juveniles for more than 24 hours.

The rights provided for females by this section shall be posted in at least one conspicuous place to which all females have access.

Incompetent Cervix

Incompetent cervix is a condition in which a woman's cervix is weakened. This is a condition that can be congenital, or arise because of a cervical injury during a prior pregnancy. The problem posed by the condition is that when a growing fetus presses on the cervix, it may open and lead to the expulsion and spontaneous abortion of the fetus. This usually occurs during the second trimester. Cervical incompetence is estimated to be the cause of about 25 percent of all second trimester losses. If an incompetent cervix condition is diagnosed during weeks 14–16, the cervix can be stitched closed (cerclage). *See also* **Miscarriage; Mucus Plug**

Incomplete Abortion *see* **Miscarriage**

Indiana

(1) OVERVIEW

The state of Indiana enacted its first criminal abortion statute on February 7, 1835. The statute underwent several amendments prior to the 1973 decision by the United States Supreme Court in *Roe v. Wade*, which legalized abortion in the nation. Indiana has taken affirmative steps to respond to *Roe* and its progeny. The state has addressed numerous abortion issues by statute that include general abortion guidelines, informed consent, post-viability abortion, abortion by minors, public funds and abortion, use of facilities and people, banning fetal experiments and sale, ban wrongful birth lawsuit, injury to pregnant woman, and ban human cloning.

(2) GENERAL ABORTION GUIDELINES

Under the general abortion statute of Indiana an abortion performed after fetal viability may only occur, when a physician certifies that such an abortion is necessary to save the life or health of the woman. The state also has a more specific post-viability statute that references to the general abortion statute. The general abortion statute also prohibits partial-birth abortion, except when necessary to save the life of the woman. However, the ban on partial-birth abortion is probably infirm as a result of the United States Supreme Court decision in

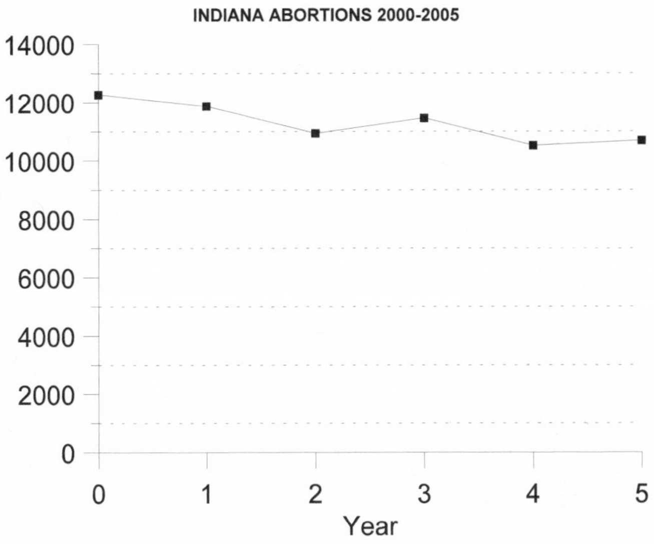

Source: Indiana Department of Health.

Indiana Abortion by Education Level of Female 2000–2005
Education Level Completed

Year	*<12*	*12*	*≥13*	*Unknown*
2000	1,723	5,879	2,666	2,004
2001	1,681	5,689	2,662	1,841
2002	1,520	5,233	2,109	2,075
2003	1,550	5,047	2,436	2,425
2004	1,475	4,656	2,574	1,809
2005	1,649	5,302	2,705	1,030
Total	9,598	31,806	15,152	11,184

Source: Indiana Department of Health.

Stenberg v. Carhart, which invalidated a Nebraska statute that prohibited partial-birth abortions. On the other hand, Indiana's partial-birth abortion statute may be valid under the United States Supreme Court decision in *Gonzales v. Carhart*, which approved of a federal statute that bans partial-birth abortion. The state's general abortion guidelines are set out below.

Indiana Code § 16-34-1-1. Childbirth preferred

Childbirth is preferred, encouraged, and supported over abortion.

Indiana Code § 16-18-2-1. Abortion defined

"Abortion" means the termination of human pregnancy with an intention other than to produce a live birth or to remove a dead fetus.

Indiana Code § 16-34-2-1. General abortion guidelines

(a) Abortion shall in all instances be a criminal act, except when performed under the following circumstances:

(1) During the first trimester of pregnancy for reasons based upon the professional, medical judgment of the pregnant woman's physician if:

(A) the abortion is performed by the physician;

(B) the woman submitting to the abortion has filed her consent with her physician. However, if in the judgment of the physician the abortion is necessary to preserve the life of the woman, her consent is not required; and

(C) the woman submitting to the abortion has filed with her physician the written consent of her parent or legal guardian if required under section 4 of this chapter.

(2) After the first trimester of pregnancy and before viability, for reasons based upon the professional, medical judgment of the pregnant woman's physician if:

(A) all the circumstances and provisions required for legal abortion during the first trimester are present and adhered to; and

(B) the abortion is performed in a hospital or ambulatory outpatient surgical center.

(3) Except as provided in subsection (b), after viability of the fetus

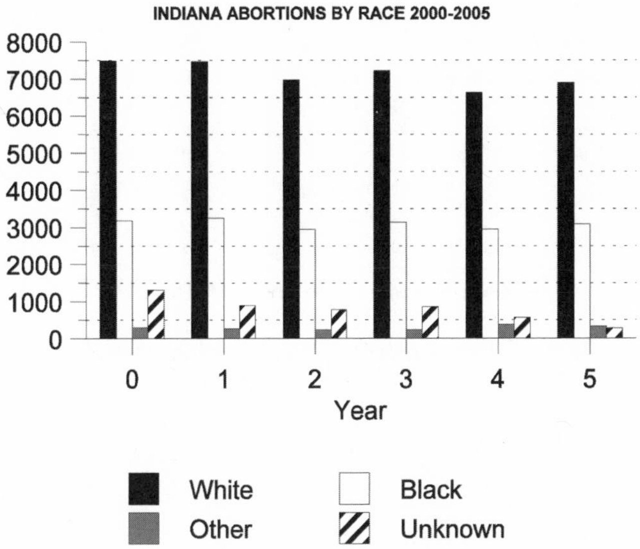

Source: Indiana Department of Health.

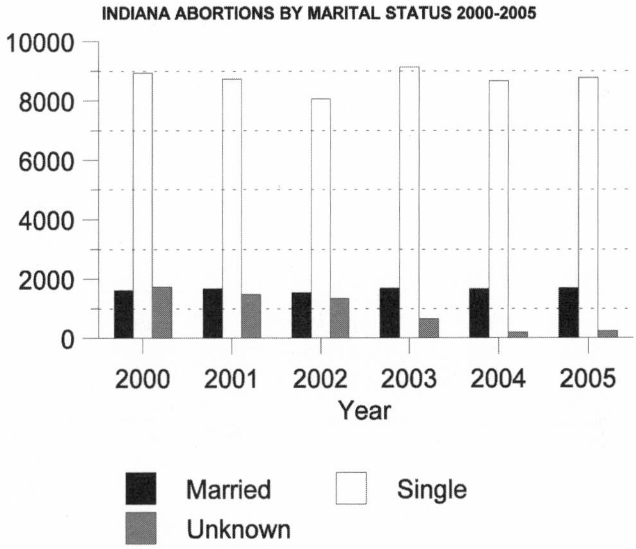

Source: Indiana Department of Health.

Indiana Abortion by Age Group 2000–2005
Age Group (yrs)

Year	*≤14*	*15–17*	*18–19*	*20–24*	*25–29*	*30–34*	*35–39*	*≥40*	*Unknown*
2000	92	728	1,453	4,228	2,824	1,500	909	307	231
2001	68	640	1,330	4,309	2,593	1,538	854	331	210
2002	65	641	1,189	3,881	2,487	1,478	793	284	119
2003	72	558	1,198	4,087	2,480	1,662	865	329	207
2004	48	514	1,112	3,685	2,375	1,460	806	320	184
2005	41	550	1,166	3,676	2,476	1,519	844	297	117
Total	386	3,631	7,448	23,866	15,235	9,157	5,071	1,868	1,068

Source: Indiana Department of Health.

Indiana Prior Abortion by Female 2000–2005

Prior Abortion

Year	*None*	*1*	*2*	*3*	*≥4*	*Not known*
2000	7,031	3,186	1,027	350	177	501
2001	7,112	3,083	922	272	150	334
2002	6,618	2,689	884	265	132	349
2003	6,576	2,781	888	278	138	797
2004	5,893	2,496	857	247	148	873
2005	5,732	2,654	925	265	142	968
Total	38,962	16,889	5,503	1,677	887	3,822

Source: **Indiana Department of Health.**

Indiana Abortion by Weeks of Gestation 2000–2005

Weeks of Gestation	*2000*	*2001*	*2002*	*2003*	*2004*	*2005*	*Total*
<9	7,753	7,705	7,262	7,619	6,342	6,499	43,180
9–12	3,998	3,579	3,237	3,078	3,132	3,353	20,377
13–15	204	229	169	194	208	238	1,242
16–20	163	140	129	100	119	118	769
Not known	154	220	140	467	713	478	2,172

Source: **Indiana Department of Health.**

for reasons based upon the professional, medical judgment of the pregnant woman's physician if:

(A) all the circumstances and provisions required for legal abortion before viability are present and adhered to;

(B) the abortion is performed in compliance with section 3 of this chapter; and

(C) before the abortion the attending physician shall certify in writing to the hospital in which the abortion is to be performed, that in the attending physician's professional, medical judgment, after proper examination and review of the woman's history, the abortion is necessary to prevent a substantial permanent impairment of the life or physical health of the pregnant woman. All facts and reasons supporting the certification shall be set forth by the physician in writing and attached to the certificate.

(b) A person may not knowingly or intentionally perform a partial birth abortion unless a physician reasonably believes that:

(1) performing the partial birth abortion is necessary to save the mother's life; and

(2) no other medical procedure is sufficient to save the mother's life.

Indiana Code § 16-18-2-267.5. Partial-birth abortion defined

"Partial birth abortion" means an abortion in which the person performing the abortion partially vaginally delivers a living fetus before killing the fetus and completing the delivery.

Indiana Code § 16-34-2-1.2.
Medical emergency of necessity for abortion

When a medical emergency compels the performance of an abortion, the physician who will perform the abortion shall inform the woman, before the abortion if possible, of the medical indications supporting the physician's judgment that an abortion is necessary to avert:

(1) the woman's death; or

(2) a substantial and irreversible impairment of a major bodily function.

Indiana Code § 16-18-2-223.5. Medical emergency defined

"Medical emergency," for purposes of IC 16-34, means a condition that, on the basis of the attending physician's good faith clinical judgment, complicates the medical condition of a pregnant woman so that it necessitates the immediate termination of her pregnancy to avert her death or for which a delay would create serious risk of substantial and irreversible impairment of a major bodily function.

Indiana Code § 16-34-2-2.
Responsibilities of attending physician

It shall be the responsibility of the attending physician to do the following:

(1) Determine in accordance with accepted medical standards which trimester the pregnant woman receiving the abortion is in.

(2) Determine whether the fetus is viable.

(3) Certify that determination as part of any written reports required of the attending physician by the state department or the facility in which the abortion is performed.

Indiana Code § 16-34-2-5. Forms to be completed by physician

(a) Every medical facility where abortions may be performed shall be supplied with forms drafted by the state department, the purpose and function of which shall be the improvement of maternal health and life through the compilation of relevant maternal life and health factors and data, and a further purpose and function shall be to monitor all abortions performed in Indiana to assure the abortions are done only under the authorized provisions of the law. Such forms shall include, among other things, the following:

(1) The age of the woman who is aborted.

(2) The place where the abortion is performed.

(3) The full name and address of the physicians performing the abortion.

(4) The name of the father if known.

(5) If after viability, the medical reason for the abortion.

(6) The medical procedure employed to administer the abortion.

(7) The mother's obstetrical history, including dates of other abortions, if any.

(8) The results of pathological examinations if performed.

(9) Information as to whether the fetus was delivered alive.

(10) Records of all maternal deaths occurring within the health facility where the abortion was performed.

(b) The form provided for in subsection (a) shall be completed by the physician performing the abortion and shall be transmitted to the state department not later than July 30 for each abortion performed in the first six (6) months of that year and not later than January 30 for each abortion performed for the last six (6) months of the preceding year. Each failure to file the form on time as required is a Class B misdemeanor.

Indiana Code § 16-34-2-7. Performance of unlawful abortion

(a) Except as provided in subsections (b) and (c), a person who knowingly or intentionally performs an abortion not expressly provided for in this chapter commits a Class C felony.

(b) A physician who performs an abortion intentionally or knowingly in violation of section 1(a)(1)(C) or 4 of this chapter commits a Class A misdemeanor.

(c) A person who knowingly or intentionally performs an abortion in violation of section 1.1 of this chapter commits a Class A infraction.

(d) A woman upon whom a partial birth abortion is performed may not be prosecuted for violating or conspiring to violate section 1(b) of this chapter.

(3) INFORMED CONSENT

Prior to an abortion Indiana requires that a woman be fully informed of the procedure to be used, the risks involved and alternatives to abortion. An abortion may not take place until 18 hours after a woman has given her written consent to an abortion. A federal district court ruled in *A Woman's Choice–East Side Women's Clinic v. Newman*, 980 F.Supp. 962 (S.D.Ind. 1997) that some of the matters required to be stated to a woman under the statute are constitutionally invalid. The statute is set out below.

Indiana Code § 16-34-2-1.1.
Informed consent and waiting period

(a) An abortion shall not be performed except with the voluntary and informed consent of the pregnant woman upon whom the abortion is to be performed. Except in the case of a medical emergency, consent to an abortion is voluntary and informed only if the following conditions are met:

(1) At least eighteen (18) hours before the abortion and in the presence of the pregnant woman, the physician who is to perform the abortion, the referring physician or a physician assistant (as defined in IC 25-27.5-2-10), an advanced practice nurse (as defined in IC 25-23-1-1(b)), or a midwife (as defined in IC 34-18-2-19) to whom the responsibility has been delegated by the physician who is to perform the abortion or the referring physician has orally informed the pregnant woman of the following:

(A) The name of the physician performing the abortion.

(B) The nature of the proposed procedure or treatment.

(C) The risks of and alternatives to the procedure or treatment.

(D) The probable gestational age of the fetus, including an offer to provide:

(i) a picture or drawing of a fetus;

(ii) the dimensions of a fetus; and

(iii) relevant information on the potential survival of an unborn fetus;

at this stage of development.

(E) The medical risks associated with carrying the fetus to term.

(F) The availability of fetal ultrasound imaging and auscultation of fetal heart tone services to enable the pregnant woman to view the image and hear the heartbeat of the fetus and how to obtain access to these services.

(2) At least eighteen (18) hours before the abortion, the pregnant woman will be orally informed of the following:

(A) That medical assistance benefits may be available for prenatal care, childbirth, and neonatal care from the county office of family and children.

(B) That the father of the unborn fetus is legally required to assist in the support of the child. In the case of rape, the information required under this clause may be omitted.

(C) That adoption alternatives are available and that adoptive parents may legally pay the costs of prenatal care, childbirth, and neonatal care.

(3) The pregnant woman certifies in writing, before the abortion is performed, that the information required by subdivisions (1) and (2) has been provided.

(b) Before an abortion is performed, the pregnant woman may, upon the pregnant woman's request, view the fetal ultrasound imaging and hear the auscultation of the fetal heart tone if the fetal heart tone is audible.

(4) POST-VIABILITY ABORTION

Under Indiana's general abortion statute, supra, a post-viability abortion may only occur when necessary to save the life or health of the woman. Under the state's specific post-viability abortion statute there is a requirement that the procedure take place in a hospital, and that two physicians be present. The statutes are set out below.

Indiana Code § 16-18-2-365. Viability defined

"Viability," for purposes of IC 16-34, means the ability of a fetus to live outside the mother's womb.

Indiana Code § 16-34-2-3. Post-viability abortion

(a) All abortions performed after a fetus is viable shall be:

(1) governed by section 1(a)(3) and 1(b) of this chapter;

(2) performed in a hospital having premature birth intensive care units, unless compliance with this requirement would result in an increased risk to the life or health of the mother; and

(3) performed in the presence of a second physician as provided in subsection (b).

(b) An abortion may be performed after a fetus is viable only if there is in attendance a physician, other than the physician performing the abortion, who shall take control of and provide immediate care for a child born alive as a result of the abortion. During the performance of the abortion, the physician performing the abortion, and after the abortion, the physician required by this subsection to be in attendance, shall take all reasonable steps in keeping with good medical practice, consistent with the procedure used, to preserve the life and health of the viable unborn child. However, this subsection does not apply if compliance would result in an increased risk to the life or health of the mother.

(c) Any fetus born alive shall be treated as a person under the law, and a birth certificate shall be issued certifying the child's birth even though the child may subsequently die, in which event a death certificate shall be issued. Failure to take all reasonable steps, in keeping with good medical practice, to preserve the life and health of the live born person shall subject the responsible persons to Indiana laws governing homicide, manslaughter, and civil liability for wrongful death and medical malpractice.

(d) If, before the abortion, the mother, and if married, her husband, has or have stated in writing that she does or they do not wish to keep the child in the event that the abortion results in a live birth, and this writing is not retracted before the abortion, the child, if born alive, shall immediately upon birth become a ward of the county office of family and children.

(5) ABORTION BY MINORS

Under the laws of Indiana no physician may perform an abortion upon an unemancipated minor unless he/she first obtains the written consent of either parent or the legal guardian of the minor. In compliance with federal constitutional law, Indiana has provided a judicial waiver procedure for an unemancipated minor to obtain an abortion without parental or guardian consent. If an unemancipated minor elects not to seek, or cannot for any reason obtain consent from either of her parents or legal guardian, the minor may petition a trial court for a waiver of the consent requirement. A minor has a right to an attorney at the proceeding and if she cannot afford one, the court must appoint her an attorney. If a minor chooses, she may represent herself. The required parental or guardian consent may be waived if the court finds either (1) that the minor is mature and well-informed enough to make the abortion decision on her own, or (2) that performance of the abortion would be in the best interest of the minor. An expedited appeal is available to any minor to whom the court denies a waiver of consent. The statute addressing the matters is set out below.

Indiana Code § 16-34-2-4. Consent and judicial bypass

(a) No physician shall perform an abortion on an unemancipated pregnant woman less than eighteen (18) years of age without first having obtained the written consent of one (1) of the parents or the legal guardian of the minor pregnant woman.

(b) A minor:

(1) who objects to having to obtain the written consent of her parent or legal guardian under this section; or

(2) whose parent or legal guardian refuses to consent to an abortion may petition, on her own behalf or by next friend, the juvenile court for a waiver of the parental consent requirement under subsection (a).

(c) A physician who feels that compliance with the parental consent requirement in subsection (a) would have an adverse effect on the welfare of the pregnant minor or on her pregnancy may petition the juvenile

court within twenty-four (24) hours of the abortion request for a waiver of the parental consent requirement under subsection (a).

(d) The juvenile court must rule on a petition filed by a pregnant minor under subsection (b) or by her physician under subsection (c) within forty-eight (48) hours of the filing of the petition. Before ruling on the petition, the court shall consider the concerns expressed by the pregnant minor and her physician. The requirement of parental consent under this section shall be waived by the juvenile court if the court finds that the minor is mature enough to make the abortion decision independently or that an abortion would be in the minor's best interests.

(e) Unless the juvenile court finds that the pregnant minor is already represented by an attorney, the juvenile court shall appoint an attorney to represent the pregnant minor in a waiver proceeding brought by the minor under subsection (b) and on any appeals. The cost of legal representation appointed for the minor under this section shall be paid by the county.

(f) A minor or her physician who desires to appeal an adverse judgment of the juvenile court in a waiver proceeding under subsection (b) or (c) is entitled to an expedited appeal, under rules to be adopted by the supreme court.

(g) All records of the juvenile court and of the supreme court or the court of appeals that are made as a result of proceedings conducted under this section are confidential.

(h) A minor who initiates legal proceedings under this section is exempt from the payment of filing fees.

(i) This section shall not apply where there is an emergency need for a medical procedure to be performed such that continuation of the pregnancy provides an immediate threat and grave risk to the life or health of the pregnant woman and the attending physician so certifies in writing.

(6) PUBLIC FUNDS AND ABORTION

Indiana restricts the use of public funds for abortions, except to save the life of the woman. However, the law providing such restrictions was held invalid in *Humphreys v. Clinic for Women, Inc.*, 796 N.E.2d 247 (Ind. 2003). The statute addressing the issue is set out below.

Indiana Code § 16-34-1-2. Public funds

Neither the state nor any political subdivision of the state may make a payment from any fund under its control for the performance of an abortion unless the abortion is necessary to preserve the life of the pregnant woman.

(7) USE OF FACILITIES AND PEOPLE

Under the laws of Indiana hospitals are not required to allow abortions at their facilities. The employees and physicians at hospitals that do allow abortions are permitted to refuse to take part in abortions. The statutes addressing the matter are set out below.

Indiana Code § 16-34-1-3. Hospitals may refuse abortion services

No private or denominational hospital shall be required to permit its facilities to be utilized for the performance of abortions.

Indiana Code § 16-34-1-4. Physicians and employees

No (1) physician; or

(2) employee or member of the staff of a hospital or other facility in which an abortion may be performed shall be required to perform an abortion or to assist or participate in the medical procedures resulting in or intended to result in an abortion, if that individual objects to such procedures on ethical, moral, or religious grounds.

Indiana Code § 16-34-1-5. Abortion participation

No person shall be required, as a condition of training, employment, pay, promotion, or privileges, to agree to perform or participate in the performing of abortions.

Indiana Code § 16-34-1-6.
Discrimination based upon moral beliefs

No hospital or other person shall discriminate against or discipline a person because of the person's moral beliefs concerning abortion.

Indiana Code § 16-34-1-7. Civil actions

A civil action for damages or reinstatement of employment, or both, may be brought for any violation of sections 4 through 6 of this chapter.

(8) BANNING FETAL EXPERIMENTS AND SALE

Indiana has banned sale and experimentation on fetuses in the state, and prohibits transporting fetuses out of the state for experiments. The statutes addressing the matter are set out below.

Indiana Code § 16-34-2-6. Fetal experiments prohibited

No experiments except pathological examinations may be conducted on any fetus aborted under this chapter, nor may any fetus so aborted be transported out of Indiana for experimental purposes. A person who conducts such an experiment or so transports such a fetus commits a Class A misdemeanor.

Indiana Code § 35-46-5-1. Fetal tissue trafficking

(a) As used in this section, "fetal tissue" means tissue from an infant or a fetus who is stillborn or aborted.

(b) As used in this section, "human organ" means the kidney, liver, heart, lung, cornea, eye, bone marrow, bone, pancreas, or skin of a human body.

(c) As used in this section, "item of value" means money, real estate, funeral related services, and personal property. "Item of value" does not include:

(1) the reasonable payments associated with the removal, transportation, implantation, processing, preservation, quality control, and storage of a human organ; or

(2) the reimbursement of travel, housing, lost wages, and other expenses incurred by the donor of a human organ related to the donation of the human organ.

(d) A person who intentionally acquires, receives, sells, or transfers in exchange for an item of value:

(1) a human organ for use in human organ transplantation; or

(2) fetal tissue;

commits unlawful transfer of human tissue, a Class C felony.

Indiana Code § 35-46-5-3.
Unlawful transfer of human organism

(a) A person who knowingly or intentionally purchases or sells a human ovum, zygote, embryo, or fetus commits unlawful transfer of a human organism, a Class C felony.

(b) This section does not apply to the following:

(1) The transfer to or receipt by a woman donor of an ovum of an amount for:

(A) earnings lost due to absence from employment;

(B) travel expenses;

(C) hospital expenses;

(D) medical expenses; and

(E) recovery time in an amount not to exceed three thousand dollars ($3, 000);

concerning a treatment or procedure to enhance human reproductive capability through in vitro fertilization, gamete intrafallopian transfer, or zygote intrafallopian transfer.

(2) The following types of stem cell research:

(A) Adult stem cell.

(B) Fetal stem cell, as long as the biological parent has given written consent for the use of the fetal stem cells.

(9) BAN WRONGFUL BIRTH LAWSUIT

Indiana has banned lawsuits claiming that a person would not have been born if an abortion had taken place. The statute addressing the issue is set out below.

Indiana Code § 34-12-1-1. Failure to abort

A person may not maintain a cause of action or receive an award of damages on the person's behalf based on the claim that but for the negligent conduct of another, the person would have been aborted.

(10) INJURY TO PREGNANT WOMAN

Under the laws of Indiana killing a viable fetus under certain circumstances may constitute murder, voluntary or involuntary manslaughter, or feticide. The statutes addressing the matter are set out below.

Indiana Code § 35-42-1-1(4). Murder

A person who knowingly or intentionally kills a fetus that has attained viability commits murder, a felony.

Indiana Code § 35-42-1-3. Voluntary manslaughter

(a) A person who knowingly or intentionally:

(1) kills another human being; or

(2) kills a fetus that has attained viability while acting under sudden heat commits voluntary manslaughter, a Class B felony. However, the offense is a Class A felony if it is committed by means of a deadly weapon.

(b) The existence of sudden heat is a mitigating factor that reduces what otherwise would be murder under section 1(1) of this chapter to voluntary manslaughter.

Indiana Code § 35-42-1-4(c). Involuntary manslaughter

A person who kills a [viable] fetus while committing or attempting to commit:

(1) a Class C or Class D felony that inherently poses a risk of serious bodily injury;

(2) a Class A misdemeanor that inherently poses a risk of serious bodily injury; or

(3) battery commits involuntary manslaughter, a Class C felony. However, if the killing results from the operation of a vehicle, the offense is a Class D felony.

Indiana Code § 35-42-1-6. Feticide

A person who knowingly or intentionally terminates a human pregnancy with an intention other than to produce a live birth or to remove a dead fetus commits feticide, a Class C felony. This section does not apply to an abortion performed in compliance with [state law].

(11) BAN HUMAN CLONING

Indiana has banned human cloning and prohibited the use of public funds for human cloning experiments. The statutes addressing the matter are set out below.

Indiana Code § 16-34.5-1-1. General assembly declaration

The general assembly declares that human cloning is against public policy.

Indiana Code § 16-34.5-1-2.
Use of public funds, facilities, or employees

The state, a state educational institution, or a political subdivision of the state may not use public funds, facilities, or employees to knowingly participate in cloning or attempted cloning.

Indiana Code § 16-18-2-56.5. Cloning defined

(a) "Cloning" means the use of asexual reproduction to create or grow a human embryo from a single cell or cells of a genetically identical human.

(b) The term does not include:

(1) a treatment or procedure to enhance human reproductive capability through the manipulation of human oocytes or embryos, including the following:

(A) In vitro fertilization.

(B) Gamete intrafallopian transfer.

(C) Zygote intrafallopian transfer; or

(2) the following types of stem cell research:

(A) Adult stem cell.

(B) Fetal stem cell, as long as the biological parent has given written consent for the use of the fetal stem cells.

(C) Embryonic stem cells from lines that are permissible for use under applicable federal law.

Indiana Code § 35-46-5-2.
Unlawful participation in human cloning

(a) This section does not apply to in vitro fertilization.

(b) As used in this section, "cloning" has the meaning set forth in IC 16-18-2-56.5.

(c) A person who knowingly or intentionally:

(1) participates in cloning;

(2) implants or attempts to implant a cloned human embryo into a uterine environment to initiate a pregnancy; or

(3) ships or receives a cloned human embryo;

commits unlawful participation in human cloning, a Class D felony.

Indiana Code § 16-21-3-4.
Revocation of hospital license for cloning

Notwithstanding section 1 of this chapter, the state department shall revoke the license of a hospital licensed under this article if, after appropriate notice and an opportunity for a hearing, the state health commissioner proves by a preponderance of the evidence that the hospital:

(1) knowingly allows the hospital's facilities to be used for cloning or attempted cloning; or

(2) knowingly allows the hospital's employees, in the course of the employee's employment, to participate in cloning or attempted cloning.

Indiana Code § 25-22.5-8-5.
Revocation of physician license for cloning

(a) As used in this section, "cloning" has the meaning set forth in IC 16-18-2-56.5.

(b) Notwithstanding IC 25-1-9, the board shall revoke the license of a physician if, after appropriate notice and an opportunity for a hearing, the attorney general proves by a preponderance of the evidence that the physician knowingly participated in cloning or attempted cloning.

Indiana Religious Coalition for Reproductive Choice

Indiana Religious Coalition for Reproductive Choice (IRC) is a prochoice organization headquartered in Lafayette, Indiana. IRC believes that reproductive freedom is an essential element of religious liberty and that reproductive decisions must remain with the woman, to be made in keeping with her religious principles and conscience. The organization does not advocate for abortion; it advocates for the right of women and men to make their own decisions about their reproductive life, in consultation with their faith tradition. IRC supports (1) efforts to strengthen family planning programs; (2) efforts to make birth control affordable and accessible; and (3) education for youth and adults to help them learn how to prevent unintended pregnancy and limit or space their children. The organization sponsors a program called the "All Options Clergy Counseling Program," which informs the woman and her spouse, partner or parents about each of her pregnancy options: parenting, adoption or abortion. *See also* **Pro-Choice Organizations**

Indiana Right to Life

Indiana Right to Life (IRL) is a pro-life organization. The organization believes that human life, at any and every stage of development, is sacred and deserving of respect and protection under the law. IRL engages in activity to educate the public on the subject of abortion and advocates for legislation and constitutional changes to protect the right to life of all innocent human beings. The organization's largest educational effort is its Media Project, which involves nationwide pro-life television commercials that provide women with information on pregnancy help centers. *See also* **Pro-Life Organizations**

Induced Abortion *see* **Abortion**

Induced Labor

Induced labor refers to the use of artificial methods (usually drugs) to start labor. Medications such as pitocin, dinoprostone, prostaglandin and cytotec are often used to induce labor (Cytotec has not been approved by the Food and Drug Administration for induced labor). Roughly one out of every three labors in the United States are induced. Many reasons may factor into the decision to induce labor. For example, labor may be induced because a problem developed that could affect the health of the mother or fetus (or both); it may be that a pregnancy has gone past term; or for the purpose of carrying out an abortion.

Complications are associated with induced labor. In some instances induced labor is the cause of a delivery having to be made with a caesarean section, forceps or vacuum extraction. The fetal and placental circulation may be impaired and fetal distress may result. In many instances induced labor simply does not work. Induced labors are likely to be more painful than naturally occurring labors. Induced labors can also be more stressful for the fetus that is to be delivered. *See also* **Childbirth and Labor**

Inevitable Abortion *see* **Miscarriage**

Infant Mortality *see* **High-Risk Pregnancy**

Infanticide *see* **Feticide**

Infantile Refsum

Infantile refsum is a congenital disorder involving the reduction or absence of certain cell structures (peroxisomes) in the body and the accumulation of acid (phytanic) in blood and tissue. The disorder causes visual impairment, hearing loss, decreased muscle tone, impaired muscle coordination, enlargement of the liver and facial abnormalities. There is no cure for the disease and death generally follows within a decade of its onset. *See also* **Birth Defects and Abortion**

Infected Abortion *see* **Septic Abortion**

Infertility

Infertility refers to the inability to conceive a child after trying for one year. This condition affects about 5.3 million Americans of reproductive age. The cause of infertility may be due to physical or health problems with a woman or man, or both. *See also* **Assisted Reproductive Technology; Surrogacy**

Informed Consent Before Abortion

In *City of Akron v. Akron Center for Reproductive Health, Inc.* and *Thornburgh v. American College of Obstetricians and Gynecologists*, the United States Supreme Court took the position that states could not create laws that provided detailed abortion information that a pregnant woman had to be given prior to having an abortion. However, the Supreme Court reversed its position in *Planned Parenthood of Southeastern Pennsylvania v. Casey*. Under *Casey*, states can impose requirements that a woman be informed thoroughly about abortion, prior to having one. Such requirements may include a physician informing the woman of the nature of the procedure, the health risks of the abortion and of childbirth, and the probable gestational age of the unborn child. States may also require a physician or a qualified nonphysician inform the woman of the availability of printed materials describing the fetus and providing information about medical assistance for childbirth, information about child support from the father, and a list of agencies which provide adoption and other services as alternatives to abortion. It is also acceptable to require a woman to certify in writing that she was informed of the availability of the printed materials and was provided with them if she wanted them. *See also* **City of Akron v. Akron Center for Reproductive Health, Inc.; Planned Parenthood of Missouri v. Danforth; Planned Parenthood of Southeastern Pennsylvania v. Casey; Thornburgh v. American College of Obstetricians and Gynecologists; Waiting Period for Abortion**

STATES WITH STATUTES REQUIRING INFORMED CONSENT PRIOR TO ABORTION

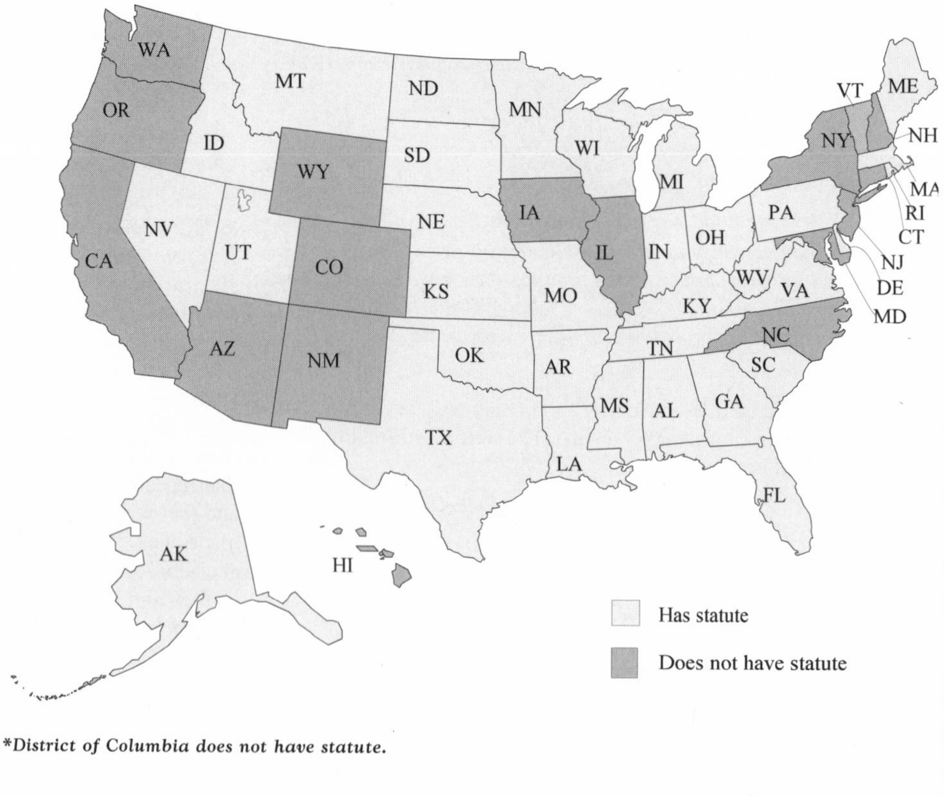

**District of Columbia does not have statute.*

Injury to Pregnant Woman

A majority of states impose criminal sanctions against anyone who unlawfully injures a pregnant woman and thereby injures or causes the

States That Impose Criminal Punishment for Injury to a Pregnant Woman That Harms Fetus

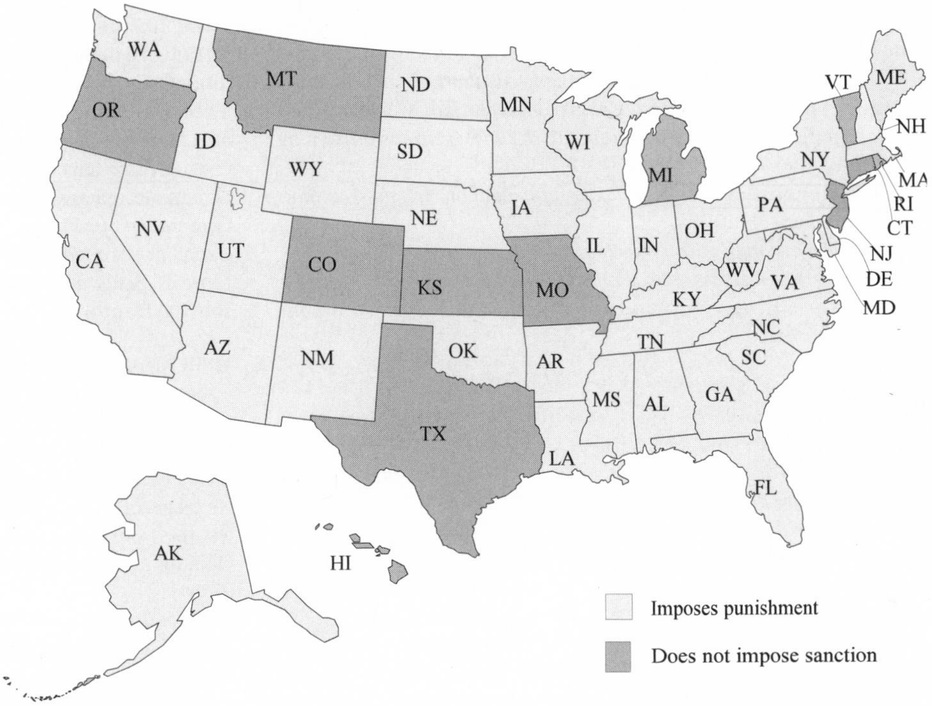

*District of Columbia does not have statute.

death of her fetus. The statutes below, taken from Georgia's penal code, illustrate the types of offenses that states have created to protect fetuses.

Georgia Code § 16-5-80. Feticide offense

(a) For the purposes of this Code section, the term "unborn child" means a member of the species homo sapiens at any stage of development who is carried in the womb.

(b) A person commits the offense of feticide if he or she willfully and without legal justification causes the death of an unborn child by any injury to the mother of such child, which would be murder if it resulted in the death of such mother, or if he or she, when in the commission of a felony, causes the death of an unborn child.

(c) A person convicted of the offense of feticide shall be punished by imprisonment for life.

(d) A person commits the offense of voluntary manslaughter of an unborn child when such person causes the death of an unborn child under circumstances which would otherwise be feticide and if such person acts solely as the result of a sudden, violent, and irresistible passion resulting from serious provocation sufficient to excite such passion in a reasonable person; provided, however, that, if there should have been an interval between the provocation and the killing sufficient for the voice of reason and humanity to be heard, of which the jury in all cases shall be the judge, the killing shall be attributed to deliberate revenge and be punished as feticide.

(e) A person convicted of the offense of voluntary manslaughter of an unborn child shall be guilty of a felony and shall be punished by imprisonment for not less than one nor more than 20 years.

(f) Nothing in this Code section shall be construed to permit the prosecution of:

(1) Any person for conduct relating to an abortion for which the consent of the pregnant woman, or person authorized by law to act on her behalf, has been obtained or for which such consent is implied by law;

(2) Any person for any medical treatment of the pregnant woman or her unborn child; or

(3) Any woman with respect to her unborn child.

Georgia Code § 16-5-28. Assault of unborn child

(a) For the purposes of this Code section, the term "unborn child" means a member of the species homo sapiens at any stage of development who is carried in the womb.

(b) A person commits the offense of assault of an unborn child when such person, without legal justification, attempts to inflict violent injury to an unborn child.

(c) Any person convicted of the offense of assault of an unborn child shall be guilty of a misdemeanor.

(d) Nothing in this Code section shall be construed to permit the prosecution of:

(1) Any person for conduct relating to an abortion for which the consent of the pregnant woman, or person authorized by law to act on her behalf, has been obtained or for which such consent is implied by law;

(2) Any person for any medical treatment of the pregnant woman or her unborn child; or

(3) Any woman with respect to her unborn child.

Georgia Code § 16-5-29. Battery of an unborn child

(a) For the purposes of this Code section, the term "unborn child" means a member of the species homo sapiens at any stage of development who is carried in the womb.

(b) A person commits the offense of battery of an unborn child when such person, without legal justification, intentionally inflicts physical harm upon an unborn child.

(c) A person convicted of the offense of battery of an unborn child shall be guilty of a misdemeanor.

(d) Nothing in this Code section shall be construed to permit the prosecution of:

(1) Any person for conduct relating to an abortion for which the consent of the pregnant woman, or person authorized by law to act on her behalf, has been obtained or for which such consent is implied by law;

(2) Any person for any medical treatment of the pregnant woman or her unborn child; or

(3) Any woman with respect to her unborn child.

Georgia Code § 16-5-20. Simple assault

(a) A person commits the offense of simple assault when he or she either:

(1) Attempts to commit a violent injury to the person of another; or

(2) Commits an act which places another in reasonable apprehension of immediately receiving a violent injury.

(b–f) Omitted.

(g) Any person who commits the offense of simple assault against a fe-

male who is pregnant at the time of the offense shall, upon conviction thereof, be punished for a misdemeanor of a high and aggravated nature.

(h) Nothing in this Code section shall be construed to permit the prosecution of:

(1) Any person for conduct relating to an abortion for which the consent of the pregnant woman, or person authorized by law to act on her behalf, has been obtained or for which such consent is implied by law;

(2) Any person for any medical treatment of the pregnant woman or her unborn child; or

(3) Any woman with respect to her unborn child.

For the purposes of this subsection, the term "unborn child" means a member of the species homo sapiens at any stage of development who is carried in the womb.

Georgia Code § 16-5-23.1. Battery

(a) A person commits the offense of battery when he or she intentionally causes substantial physical harm or visible bodily harm to another.

(b) As used in this Code section, the term "visible bodily harm" means bodily harm capable of being perceived by a person other than the victim and may include, but is not limited to, substantially blackened eyes, substantially swollen lips or other facial or body parts, or substantial bruises to body parts.

(c–g) Omitted.

(h) Any person who commits the offense of battery against a female who is pregnant at the time of the offense shall, upon conviction thereof, be punished for a misdemeanor of a high and aggravated nature.

See also **Feticide; Unborn Victims of Violence Act**

Instillation Methods

During the late second and third trimester pregnancies abortions may be performed using instillation techniques. Instillation techniques require injection of drugs or chemicals through the abdomen or cervix into the amniotic sac to cause the abortion. The most commonly used drugs or chemicals are prostaglandins, saline and urea.

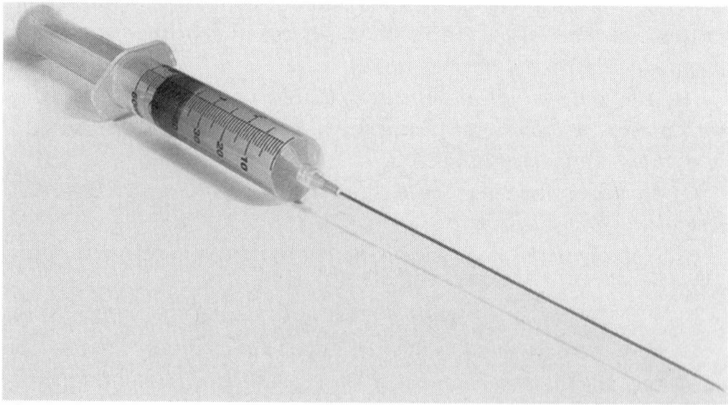

This syringe with spinal needle is used to inject chemicals into a fetus to cause death (Grantham Collection, all rights reserved).

Prostaglandins. Prostaglandins are naturally produced chemicals which normally aid in the birthing process. However, injection of concentrations of artificial prostaglandins into the amniotic sac induces labor and results in abortion. In some instances salt or another toxin is first injected to ensure a successful abortion. Side effects from this procedure include retained placenta, cervical trauma, infection, hemorrhage, cardiac arrest and rupture of the uterus.

Urea. Urea is a nitrogen-based solution which is injected into the amniotic sac. It can be used with oxytocin or prostaglandins to induce labor and cause the mother to deliver the dead baby. Side effects from this procedure include nausea, vomiting, cervical injuries and endometritis, an infection of the lining of the uterus.

Saline amniocentesis. Abortion by saline amniocentesis involves insertion of a needle through the woman's abdomen to extract amniotic fluid. Once this is done a solution of concentrated salt is injected with a needle into the amniotic sac. The solution causes the abortion. Side effects from this procedure include a condition called consumption coagulopathy (uncontrolled blood clotting the body) with severe hemorrhage as well as side effects on the central nervous system. In *Planned Parenthood of Missouri v. Danforth* the United States Supreme Court struck down a Missouri statute that banned the use of saline amniocentesis. *See also* **Methods of Abortion; Planned Parenthood of Missouri v. Danforth**

Insurance Coverage for Abortion

Based upon a study performed by the Guttmacher Institute, it was found that a minority of states impose restrictions on providing insurance coverage for abortion. The states of Idaho, Kentucky, Missouri, North Dakota, and Oklahoma allow a private insurer to offer coverage for an abortion only when the woman's life is endangered, unless the woman pays a specific premium for an abortion on demand. Oklahoma also permits coverage when the pregnancy is due to rape or incest.

Several states also impose restrictions on insurance coverage for abortions under insurance policies that cover public employees. The states of Illinois, Nebraska, and North Dakota allow coverage only when an abortion is necessary to save the life of the woman. Massachusetts allows coverage for an abortion to save the life or health of the woman; unless the woman pays a specific premium for an abortion on demand. The states of Mississippi, Ohio, Pennsylvania, Rhode Island and Virginia allow coverage only when an abortion is necessary to save the life of the woman, or the pregnancy resulted from rape or incest. Mississippi and Virginia also allow coverage for an abnormal fetus. Colorado and Kentucky prohibit insurance coverage under all circumstances. *See also* **Federal Employees and Abortion; Public Resources for Abortions**

Intact D & E *see* **Dilation and Extraction**

International Abortion Laws

In the majority of countries in the world abortion is permitted under certain conditions. Those conditions range from having to perform an abortion to save a woman's life, to pregnancies involving rape or incest. Only a minority of countries permit abortion on demand without any social or health justification.

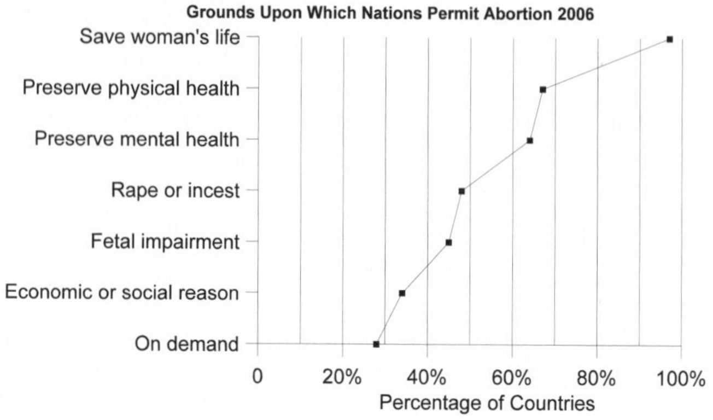

Source: **United Nations World Abortion Policies 2007.**

International Life Services

International Life Services (ILS) is a Los Angeles based pro-life organization that was founded in 1985, by Sister Paula Vandegaer. ILS was created to promote positive pro-life and pro-family values. It does this through education, counseling, and volunteers. ILS has an education division that produces a magazine, audio and visual training tapes, and sponsors an annual regional conference to develop leadership among pro-life service groups. The organization's counseling division provides training for the staff members of pro-life pregnancy help centers. ILS also provides a training manual for volunteers, provides insurance for them, and assists them with on-going consultation. *See also* **Pro-Life Organizations**

Interrupted Pregnancy

An interrupted pregnancy is a pregnancy in which labor is induced before the end of the nine-month term. *See also* **Abortion; Miscarriage; Pre-Term Pregnancy; Stillbirth**

Interstitial Pregnancy *see* **Ectopic Pregnancy**

Intracervical Insemination *see* **Assisted Reproductive Technology**

Intracytoplasmic Sperm Injection *see* **Assisted Reproductive Technology**

Intrauterine Contraceptive Devices

Intrauterine devices (IUDs) are small and flexible plastic contraceptive instruments that contain copper or a hormone. The hormone device, called progestasert, releases a continuous small amount of progestin. This device must be replaced every year. The copper device, called Copper-T, can be left in place for 10 years. The Copper-T device can be inserted up to five days after unprotected intercourse to prevent pregnancy. IUDs are obtained by prescription only and inserted by a health care provider.

About eight out of 1,000 women using Copper-T will become pregnant during the first year of use. Roughly less than three women in 100 using progestasert will become pregnant during the first year of use. Side effects from IUDs include: becoming embedded in the uterus and requiring surgery for removal; heavy menstrual bleeding; spotting between periods; menstrual cramps; expulsion of device; uterine puncture; infections; and infertility. *See also* **Contraception; Morning After Pill**

Intrauterine Growth Retardation *see* **Low Birthweight**

Intrauterine Insemination *see* **Assisted Reproductive Technology**

Intrauterine Pressure Catheter

An intrauterine pressure catheter is an instrument that is inserted into the uterus during labor to measure the pressure within the uterus. These measurements help in ascertaining the frequency and intensity of uterine contractions. This information is critical for assessing slowed or stopped labor contractions that could endanger the woman or the fetus. A diagnosis of slowed or stopped labor may necessitate the use of a labor inducing medication.

Iowa

(1) OVERVIEW

The state of Iowa enacted its first criminal abortion statute on January 25, 1839. The statute underwent several amendments prior to the 1973 decision by the United States Supreme Court in *Roe v. Wade*, which legalized abortion in the nation. Iowa has respond to *Roe* and its progeny through enactment of several statutes. The abortion issues addressed by statute include abortion crimes, partial-birth abortion, abortion by minors, use of facilities and people, fetal death report, sale of abortifacients, and employer health insurance.

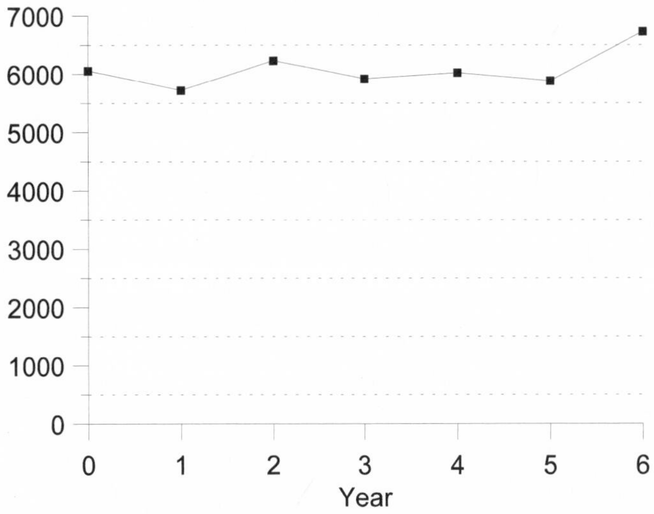

Source: **Iowa Department of Public Health.**

Iowa Abortion by Weeks of Gestation 2000–2006

	Year							
Weeks of Gestation	*2000*	*2001*	*2002*	*2003*	*2004*	*2005*	*2006*	*Total*
≤13	5,685	5,415	5,913	5,562	5,682	5,592	6,409	40,258
14-28	366	297	297	324	326	278	300	2,188
≥29	0	0	0	0	0	0	0	0
Not known	8	10	20	30	14	11	19	112

Source: **Iowa Department of Public Health.**

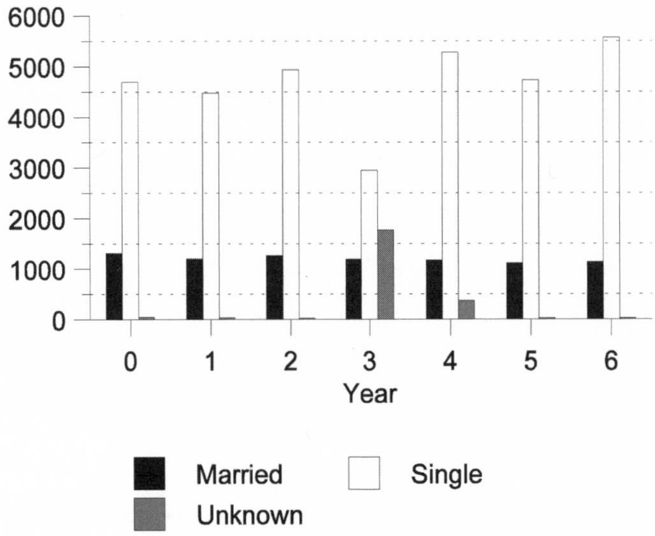

Source: **Iowa Department of Public Health.**

(2) ABORTION CRIMES

Iowa maintains a feticide statute that proscribes an abortion after the second trimester. The state also has a statute that creates various offenses for performing nonconsensual abortions. Additionally, a mur-

Iowa Abortion by Education Level of Female 2000–2006
Education Level Completed

Year	*<9*	*9–12*	*≥13*	*Unknown*
2000	119	5631	121	188
2001	101	5374	99	148
2002	128	5905	103	94
2003	111	5127	592	86
2004	124	2723	2906	269
2005	113	2268	2557	31
2006	143	3071	3423	91
Total	839	30,099	9,801	907

Source: **Iowa Department of Public Health.**

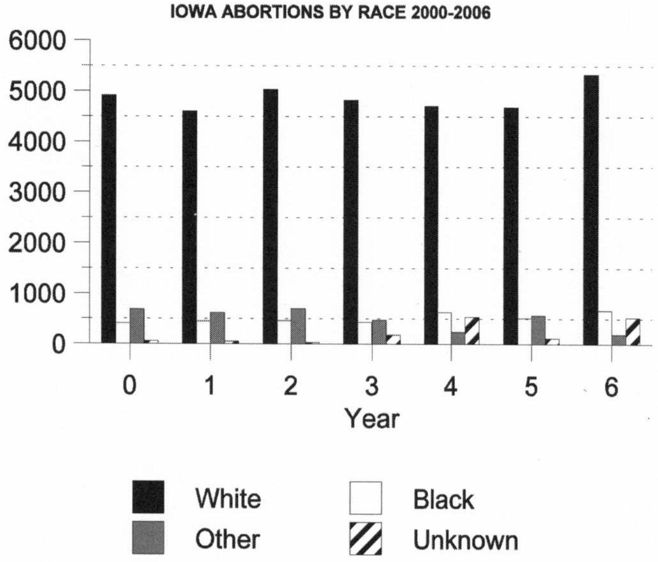

Source: **Iowa Department of Public Health.**

der statute has been created for killing a viable fetus aborted alive, as well as a statute imposing a duty to preserve alive a viable fetus. The statutes are set out below.

Iowa Code § 707.7. Feticide

Any person who intentionally terminates a human pregnancy, with the knowledge and voluntary consent of the pregnant person, after the end of the second trimester of the pregnancy where death of the fetus results commits feticide. Feticide is a class "C" felony.

Any person who attempts to intentionally terminate a human pregnancy, with the knowledge and voluntary consent of the pregnant person, after the end of the second trimester of the pregnancy where death of the fetus does not result commits attempted feticide. Attempted feticide is a class "D" felony.

This section shall not apply to the termination of a human pregnancy performed by a physician licensed in this state to practice medicine or surgery when in the best clinical judgment of the physician the termination is performed to preserve the life or health of the pregnant person or of the fetus and every reasonable medical effort not inconsistent with preserving the life of the pregnant person is made to preserve the life of a viable fetus.

Any person who terminates a human pregnancy, with the knowledge and voluntary consent of the pregnant person, who is not a person licensed to practice medicine and surgery under the provisions of chapter 148, or an osteopathic physician and surgeon licensed to practice osteopathic medicine and surgery under the provisions of chapter 150A, commits a class "C" felony.

Iowa Code § 707.8. Nonconsensual termination

1. A person who terminates a human pregnancy without the consent of the pregnant person during the commission of a forcible felony is guilty of a class "B" felony.

2. A person who terminates a human pregnancy without the consent of the pregnant person during the commission of a felony or felonious assault is guilty of a class "C" felony.

3. A person who intentionally terminates a human pregnancy without the knowledge and voluntary consent of the pregnant person is guilty of a class "C" felony.

4. A person who unintentionally terminates a human pregnancy by any of the means provided pursuant to section 707.6A, subsection 1, is guilty of a class "C" felony.

5. A person who by force or intimidation procures the consent of the pregnant person to a termination of a human pregnancy is guilty of a class "C" felony.

6. A person who unintentionally terminates a human pregnancy while drag racing in violation of section 321.278 is guilty of a class "D" felony.

7. A person who unintentionally terminates a human pregnancy without the knowledge and voluntary consent of the pregnant person by the commission of an act in a manner likely to cause the termination of or serious injury to a human pregnancy is guilty of an aggravated misdemeanor.

8. A person commits an aggravated misdemeanor when the person intentionally causes serious injury to a human pregnancy by the commission of an act in a manner likely to cause the termination of or serious injury to a human pregnancy.

9. A person commits an aggravated misdemeanor when the person unintentionally causes serious injury to a human pregnancy by any of the means described in section 707.6A, subsection 1.

10. A person commits a serious misdemeanor when the person unintentionally causes serious injury to a human pregnancy by the commission of an act in a manner likely to cause the termination of or serious injury to the human pregnancy.

11. For the purposes of this section "serious injury to a human pregnancy" means, relative to the human pregnancy, disabling mental illness, or bodily injury which creates a substantial risk of death or which causes serious permanent disfigurement, or protracted loss or impairment of the function of any bodily member or organ, and includes but is not limited to skull fractures, rib fractures, and metaphyseal fractures of the long bones.

12. As used in this section, actions which cause the termination of or serious injury to a pregnancy do not apply to any of the following:

a. An act or omission of the pregnant person.

b. A termination of or a serious injury to a pregnancy which is caused by the performance of an approved medical procedure performed by a person licensed in this state to practice medicine and surgery or osteopathic medicine and surgery, irrespective of the duration of the pregnancy and with or without the voluntary consent of the pregnant person when circumstances preclude the pregnant person from providing consent.

c. An act committed in self-defense or in defense of another person or any other act committed if legally justified or excused.

Iowa Code § 707.9. Murder of fetus

A person who intentionally kills a viable fetus aborted alive shall be guilty of a class "B" felony.

Iowa Code § 707.10. Duty to preserve the life of the fetus

A person who performs or induces a termination of a human pregnancy and who willfully fails to exercise that degree of professional skill, care, and diligence available to preserve the life and health of a viable fetus shall be guilty of a serious misdemeanor.

Iowa Code § 702.20. Viability defined

"Viability" is that stage of fetal development when the life of the unborn child may be continued indefinitely outside the womb by natural or artificial life support systems. The time when viability is achieved may vary with each pregnancy, and the determination of whether a particular fetus is viable is a matter of responsible medical judgment.

(3) PARTIAL-BIRTH ABORTION

Iowa criminalizes partial-birth abortions. Until it is definitively determined by a court, Iowa's partial-birth abortion statute may be invalid under the United States Supreme Court decision *in Stenberg v. Carhart*, which invalidated Nebraska's ban on partial-birth abortion. On the other hand, Iowa's partial-birth abortion statute, as currently written, may be valid under the United States Supreme Court decision in *Gonzales v. Carhart*, which approved of a federal statute that bans partial-birth abortion. Under the statute Iowa has provided a civil cause of action for the father of the fetus or a nonconsenting mother of the fetus. In the case of a minor, the maternal grandparents of the fetus may file a civil lawsuit. The text of Iowa's partial-birth abortion statute is set out below.

Iowa Code § 707.8A. Partial-birth abortion offense

1. As used in this section, unless the context otherwise requires:

a. "Abortion" means abortion as defined in section 146.1.

b. "Fetus" means a human fetus.

c. "Partial-birth abortion" means an abortion in which a person partially vaginally delivers a living fetus before killing the fetus and completing the delivery.

d. "Vaginally delivers a living fetus before killing the fetus" means deliberately and intentionally delivering into the vagina a living fetus or a substantial portion of a living fetus for the purpose of performing a procedure the person knows will kill the fetus, and then killing the fetus.

2. A person shall not knowingly perform or attempt to perform a partial-birth abortion. This prohibition shall not apply to a partial-birth abortion that is necessary to save the life of the mother whose life is endangered by a physical disorder, physical illness, or physical injury.

3. This section shall not be construed to create a right to an abortion.

4. a. The mother on whom a partial-birth abortion is performed, the father of the fetus, or if the mother is less than eighteen years of age or unmarried at the time of the partial-birth abortion, a maternal grandparent of the fetus, may bring an action against a person violating subsection 2 to obtain appropriate relief, unless the pregnancy resulted from the plaintiff's criminal conduct or the plaintiff consented to the partial-birth abortion.

b. In an action brought under this subsection, appropriate relief may include any of the following:

(1) Statutory damages which are equal to three times the cost of the partial-birth abortion.

(2) Compensatory damages for all injuries, psychological and physical, resulting from violation of subsection 2.

5. A person who violates subsection 2 is guilty of a class "C" felony.

6. A mother upon whom a partial-birth abortion is performed shall not be prosecuted for violation of subsection 2 or for conspiracy to violate subsection 2.

7. a. A licensed physician subject to the authority of the board of medicine who is accused of a violation of subsection 2 may seek a hearing before the board on whether the physician's conduct was necessary to save the life of the mother whose life was endangered by a physical disorder, physical illness, or physical injury.

b. The board's findings concerning the physician's conduct are admissible at the criminal trial of the physician. Upon a motion of the physician, the court shall delay the beginning of the trial for not more than thirty days to permit the hearing before the board of medicine to take place.

(4) ABORTION BY MINORS

Iowa's abortion laws for minors also require that a minor be given specific information regarding abortion and childcare prior to an abortion. Under the laws of Iowa no physician may perform an abortion upon an unemancipated minor, until 48 hours after notice of the operation has been given to either parent of the minor. In compliance with federal constitutional law, Iowa has provided a judicial waiver procedure for an unemancipated minor to obtain an abortion without parental notice. If an unemancipated minor elects not to provide notice to either of her parents, the minor may petition a trial court for a waiver of the notice requirement. A minor has a right to an attorney at the proceeding and if she cannot afford one, the court must appoint her an attorney. If a minor chooses, she may represent herself. The required parental notice may be waived if the court finds either (1) that the minor is mature and well-informed enough to make the abortion decision on her own, or (2) that performance of the abortion would be in the best interest of the minor. An expedited appeal is available to any minor to whom the court denies a waiver of notice. The statutes addressing the matters are set out below.

Iowa Code § 135L.1. Definitions

As used in this chapter unless the context otherwise requires:

1. "Abortion" means an abortion as defined in chapter 146.

2. "Adult" means a person eighteen years of age or older.

3. "Child-placing agency" means any agency, public, semipublic, or private, which represents itself as placing children, receiving children for placement, or actually engaging in placement of children and includes the department of human services.

4. "Court" means the juvenile court.

5. "Grandparent" means the parent of an individual who is the parent of the pregnant minor.

6. "Medical emergency" means a condition which, based upon a physician's judgment, necessitates an abortion to avert the pregnant minor's death, or for which a delay will create a risk of serious impairment of a major bodily function.

7. "Minor" means a person under eighteen years of age who has not been and is not married.

8. "Parent" means one parent or a legal guardian or custodian of a pregnant minor.

9. "Responsible adult" means an adult, who is not associated with an abortion provider, chosen by a pregnant minor to assist the minor in the decision-making process established in this chapter.

Iowa Code § 135L.2. Decision-making assistance program

1. A decision-making assistance program is created to provide assistance to minors in making informed decisions relating to pregnancy. The program shall offer and include all of the following:

a. (1) A video, to be developed by a person selected through a request for proposals process or other contractual agreement, which provides information regarding the various options available to a pregnant minor with regard to the pregnancy, including a decision to continue the pregnancy to term and retain parental rights following the child's birth, a decision to continue the pregnancy to term and place the child for adoption following the child's birth, and a decision to terminate the pregnancy through abortion. The video shall provide the information in a manner and language, including but not limited to the use of closed captioning for the hearing-impaired, which could be understood by a minor.

(2) The video shall explain that public and private agencies are available to assist a pregnant minor with any alternative chosen.

(3) The video shall explain that if the pregnant minor decides to continue the pregnancy to term, and to retain parental rights to the child, the father of the child is liable for the support of the child.

(4) The video shall explain that tendering false documents is a fraudulent practice in the fourth degree pursuant to section 135L.6.

b. Written decision-making materials which include all of the following:

(1) Information regarding the options described in the video including information regarding the agencies and programs available to provide assistance to the pregnant minor in parenting a child; information relating to adoption including but not limited to information regarding child-placing agencies; and information regarding abortion including but not limited to the legal requirements relative to the performance of an abortion on a pregnant minor. The information provided shall include information explaining that if a pregnant minor decides to continue the pregnancy to term and to retain parental rights, the father of the child is liable for the support of the child and that if the pregnant minor seeks public assistance on behalf of the child, the pregnant minor shall, and if the pregnant minor is not otherwise eligible as a public assistance recipient, the pregnant minor may, seek the assistance of the child support recovery unit in establishing the paternity of the child, and in seeking support payments for a reasonable amount of the costs associated with the pregnancy, medical support, and maintenance from the father of the child, or if the father is a minor, from the parents of the minor father. The information shall include a listing of the agencies and programs and the services available from each.

(2) A workbook which is to be used in viewing the video and which includes a questionnaire and exercises to assist a pregnant minor in viewing the video and in considering the options available regarding the minor's pregnancy.

(3) A detachable certification form to be signed by the pregnant minor certifying that the pregnant minor was offered a viewing of the video and the written decision-making materials.

2. a. The video shall be available through the state and local offices of the Iowa department of public health, the department of human services, and the judicial branch and through the office of each licensed physician who performs abortions.

b. The video may be available through the office of any licensed physician who does not perform abortions, upon the request of the physician; through any nonprofit agency serving minors, upon the request of the agency; and through any other person providing services to minors, upon the request of the person.

3. During the initial appointment between a licensed physician from whom a pregnant minor is seeking the performance of an abortion and a pregnant minor, the licensed physician shall offer the viewing of the video and the written decision-making materials to the pregnant minor, and shall obtain the signed and dated certification form from the pregnant minor. A licensed physician shall not perform an abortion on a pregnant minor prior to obtaining the completed certification form from a pregnant minor.

4. A pregnant minor shall be encouraged to select a responsible adult, preferably a parent of the pregnant minor, to accompany the pregnant minor in viewing the video and receiving the decision-making materials.

5. To the extent possible and at the discretion of the pregnant minor, the person responsible for impregnating the pregnant minor shall also be involved in the viewing of the video and in the receipt of written decision-making materials.

6. Following the offering of the viewing of the video and of the written decision-making materials, the pregnant minor shall sign and date the certification form attached to the materials, and shall submit the completed form to the licensed physician. The licensed physician shall also provide a copy of the completed certification form to the pregnant minor.

Iowa Code § 135L.3. Notice and judicial bypass

1. A licensed physician shall not perform an abortion on a pregnant minor until at least forty-eight hours' prior notification is provided to a parent of the pregnant minor.

2. The licensed physician who will perform the abortion shall provide notification in person or by mailing the notification by restricted certified mail to a parent of the pregnant minor at the usual place of abode of the parent. For the purpose of delivery by restricted certified mail, the time of delivery is deemed to occur at twelve o'clock noon on the next day on which regular mail delivery takes place, subsequent to the mailing.

3. If the pregnant minor objects to the notification of a parent prior to the performance of an abortion on the pregnant minor, the pregnant minor may petition the court to authorize waiver of the notification requirement pursuant to this section in accordance with the following procedures:

a. The court shall ensure that the pregnant minor is provided with assistance in preparing and filing the petition for waiver of notification and shall ensure that the pregnant minor's identity remains confidential.

b. The pregnant minor may participate in the court proceedings on the pregnant minor's own behalf. The court may appoint a guardian ad litem for the pregnant minor and the court shall appoint a guardian ad litem for the pregnant minor if the pregnant minor is not accompanied by a responsible adult or if the pregnant minor has not viewed the video as provided pursuant to section 135L.2. In appointing a guardian ad litem for the pregnant minor, the court shall consider a person licensed to practice psychology pursuant to chapter 154B, a licensed social worker pursuant to chapter 154C, a licensed marital and family therapist pursuant to chapter 154D, or a licensed mental health counselor pursuant to chapter 154D to serve in the capacity of guardian ad litem. The court shall advise the pregnant minor of the pregnant minor's right to court-appointed legal counsel, and shall, upon the pregnant minor's request, provide the pregnant minor with court-appointed legal counsel, at no cost to the pregnant minor.

c. The court proceedings shall be conducted in a manner which protects the confidentiality of the pregnant minor and notwithstanding section 232.147 or any other provision to the contrary, all court documents pertaining to the proceedings shall remain confidential and shall be sealed. Only the pregnant minor, the pregnant minor's guardian ad litem, the pregnant minor's legal counsel, and persons whose presence is specifically requested by the pregnant minor, by the pregnant minor's guardian ad litem, or by the pregnant minor's legal counsel may attend the hearing on the petition.

d. Notwithstanding any law or rule to the contrary, the court proceedings under this section shall be given precedence over other pending matters to ensure that the court reaches a decision expeditiously.

e. Upon petition and following an appropriate hearing, the court shall waive the notification requirements if the court determines either of the following:

(1) That the pregnant minor is mature and capable of providing informed consent for the performance of an abortion.

(2) That the pregnant minor is not mature, or does not claim to be mature, but that notification is not in the best interest of the pregnant minor.

f. The court shall issue specific factual findings and legal conclusions, in writing, to support the decision.

g. Upon conclusion of the hearing, the court shall immediately issue a written order which shall be provided immediately to the pregnant minor, the pregnant minor's guardian ad litem, the pregnant minor's legal counsel, or to any other person designated by the pregnant minor to receive the order.

h. An expedited, confidential appeal shall be available to a pregnant minor for whom the court denies a petition for waiver of notification. An order granting the pregnant minor's application for waiver of notification is not subject to appeal. Access to the appellate courts for the purpose of an appeal under this section shall be provided to a pregnant minor twenty-four hours a day, seven days a week.

i. A pregnant minor who chooses to utilize the waiver of notification procedures under this section shall not be required to pay a fee at any level of the proceedings. Fees charged and court costs taxed in connection with a proceeding under this section are waived.

j. If the court denies the petition for waiver of notification and if the decision is not appealed or all appeals are exhausted, the court shall advise the pregnant minor that, upon the request of the pregnant minor, the court will appoint a licensed marital and family therapist to assist the pregnant minor in addressing any intrafamilial problems. All costs of services provided by a court-appointed licensed marital and family therapist shall be paid by the court through the expenditure of funds appropriated to the judicial branch.

k. Venue for proceedings under this section is in any court in the state.

l. The supreme court shall prescribe rules to ensure that the proceedings under this section are performed in an expeditious and confidential manner. The rules shall require that the hearing on the petition shall be held and the court shall rule on the petition within forty-eight hours of the filing of the petition. If the court fails to hold the hearing and rule on the petition within forty-eight hours of the filing of the petition and an extension is not requested, the petition is deemed granted and waiver of the notification requirements is deemed authorized. The court shall immediately provide documentation to the pregnant minor and to the pregnant minor's legal counsel if the pregnant minor is represented by legal counsel, demonstrating that the petition is deemed granted and that waiver of the notification requirements is deemed authorized. Resolution of a petition for authorization of waiver of the notification requirement shall be completed within ten calendar days as calculated from the day after the filing of the petition to the day of issuance of any final decision on appeal.

m. The requirements of this section regarding notification of a parent of a pregnant minor prior to the performance of an abortion on a pregnant minor do not apply if any of the following applies:

(1) The abortion is authorized in writing by a parent entitled to notification.

(2)(a) The pregnant minor declares, in a written statement submitted to the attending physician, a reason for not notifying a parent and a reason for notifying a grandparent of the pregnant minor in lieu of the notification of a parent. Upon receipt of the written statement from the pregnant minor, the attending physician shall provide notification to a grandparent of the pregnant minor, specified by the pregnant minor, in the manner in which notification is provided to a parent.

(b) The notification form shall be in duplicate and shall include both of the following:

(i) A declaration which informs the grandparent of the pregnant minor that the grandparent of the pregnant minor may be subject to civil action if the grandparent accepts notification.

(ii) A provision that the grandparent of the pregnant minor may refuse acceptance of notification.

(3) The pregnant minor's attending physician certifies in writing that a medical emergency exists which necessitates the immediate performance of an abortion, and places the written certification in the medical file of the pregnant minor.

(4) The pregnant minor declares that the pregnant minor is a victim of child abuse pursuant to section 232.68, the person responsible for the care of the child is a parent of the child, and either the abuse has been reported pursuant to the procedures prescribed in chapter 232, division III, part 2, or a parent of the child is named in a report of founded child abuse. The department of human services shall maintain confidentiality under chapter 232 and shall not release any information in response to a request for public records, discovery procedures, subpoena, or any other means, unless the release of information is expressly authorized by the pregnant minor regarding the pregnant minor's pregnancy and abortion, if the abortion is obtained. A person who knowingly violates the confidentiality provisions of this subparagraph is guilty of a serious misdemeanor.

(5) The pregnant minor declares that the pregnant minor is a victim of sexual abuse as defined in chapter 709 and has reported the sexual abuse to law enforcement.

n. A licensed physician who knowingly performs an abortion in violation of this section is guilty of a serious misdemeanor.

o. All records and files of a court proceeding maintained under this section shall be destroyed by the clerk of court when one year has elapsed from any of the following, as applicable:

(1) The date that the court issues an order waiving the notification requirements.

(2) The date after which the court denies the petition for waiver of notification and the decision is not appealed.

(3) The date after which the court denies the petition for waiver of notification, the decision is appealed, and all appeals are exhausted.

p. A person who knowingly violates the confidentiality requirements of this section relating to court proceedings and documents is guilty of a serious misdemeanor.

Iowa Code § 135L.6. Fraudulent practice

A person who does any of the following is guilty of a fraudulent practice in the fourth degree pursuant to section 714.12:

1. Knowingly tenders a false original or copy of the signed and dated certification form described in section 135L.2, to be retained by the licensed physician.

2. Knowingly tenders a false original or copy of the notification document mailed to a parent or grandparent of the pregnant minor under this chapter, or a false original or copy of the order waiving notification relative to the performance of an abortion on a pregnant minor.

Iowa Code § 135L.7. Immunities

1. With the exception of the civil liability which may apply to a grandparent of a pregnant minor who accepts notification under this chapter, a person is immune from any liability, civil or criminal, for any act, omission, or decision made in connection with a good faith effort to comply with the provisions of this chapter.

2. This section shall not be construed to limit civil liability of a person for any act, omission, or decision made in relation to the performance of a medical procedure on a pregnant minor.

Iowa Code § 135L.8. Adoption of rules

The Iowa department of public health shall adopt rules to implement the notification procedures pursuant to this chapter including but not limited to rules regarding the documents necessary for notification of a parent or grandparent of a pregnant minor who is designated to receive notification under this chapter.

(5) USE OF FACILITIES AND PEOPLE

Under the laws of Iowa hospitals are not required to allow abortions at their facilities. The employees and physicians at hospitals that do allow abortions are permitted to refuse to take part in abortions.

Iowa Code § 146.1.
Persons refusing to participate in abortion

An individual who may lawfully perform, assist, or participate in medical procedures which will result in an abortion shall not be required against that individual's religious beliefs or moral convictions to perform, assist, or participate in such procedures. A person shall not discriminate against any individual in any way, including but not limited to employment, promotion, advancement, transfer, licensing, education, training or the granting of hospital privileges or staff appointments, because of the individual's participation in or refusal to participate in recommending, performing or assisting in an abortion procedure. For the purposes of this chapter, "abortion" means the termination of a human pregnancy with the intent other than to produce a live birth or to remove a dead fetus. Abortion does not include medical care which has as its primary purpose the treatment of a serious physical condition requiring emergency medical treatment necessary to save the life of a mother.

Iowa Code § 146.2. Hospitals refusing to perform abortions

A hospital, which is not controlled, maintained and supported by a public authority, shall not be required to permit the performance of an abortion. The refusal to permit such procedures shall not be grounds for civil liability to any person nor a basis for any disciplinary or other recriminatory action against the hospital.

(6) FETAL DEATH REPORT

Iowa requires that all abortions be reported to the proper authorities. The statute addressing the matter is set out below.

Iowa Code § 144.29A. Termination of pregnancy reporting

1. A health care provider who initially identifies and diagnoses a spontaneous termination of pregnancy or who induces a termination of pregnancy shall file with the department a report for each termination within thirty days of the occurrence. The health care provider shall make a good faith effort to obtain all of the following information that is available with respect to each termination:

a. The confidential health care provider code as assigned by the department.

b. The report tracking number.

c. The maternal health services region of the Iowa department of public health, as designated as of July 1, 1997, in which the patient resides.

d. The race of the patient.

e. The age of the patient.

f. The marital status of the patient.

g. The educational level of the patient.

h. The number of previous pregnancies, live births, and spontaneous or induced terminations of pregnancies.

i. The month and year in which the termination occurred.

j. The number of weeks since the patient's last menstrual period and a clinical estimate of gestation.

k. The method used for an induced termination, including whether mifepristone was used.

2. It is the intent of the general assembly that the information shall be collected, reproduced, released, and disclosed in a manner specified by rule of the department, adopted pursuant to chapter 17A, which ensures the anonymity of the patient who experiences a termination of pregnancy, the health care provider who identifies and diagnoses or induces a termination of pregnancy, and the hospital, clinic, or other health facility in which a termination of pregnancy is identified and diagnosed or induced. The department may share information with federal public health officials for the purposes of securing federal funding or conducting public health research. However, in sharing the information, the department shall not relinquish control of the information, and any agreement entered into by the department with federal public health officials to share information shall prohibit the use, reproduction, release, or disclosure of the information by federal public health officials in a manner which violates this section. The department shall publish, annually, a demographic summary of the information obtained pursuant to this section, except that the department shall not reproduce, release, or disclose any information obtained pursuant to this section which reveals the identity of any patient, health care provider, hospital, clinic, or other health facility, and shall ensure anonymity in the following ways:

a. The department may use information concerning the report tracking number or concerning the identity of a reporting health care provider, hospital, clinic, or other health facility only for purposes of information collection. The department shall not reproduce, release, or disclose this information for any purpose other than for use in annually publishing the demographic summary under this section.

b. The department shall enter the information, from any report of termination submitted, within thirty days of receipt of the report, and shall immediately destroy the report following entry of the information. However, entry of the information from a report shall not include any health care provider, hospital, clinic, or other health facility identification information including, but not limited to, the confidential health care provider code, as assigned by the department.

c. To protect confidentiality, the department shall limit release of information to release in an aggregate form which prevents identification of any individual patient, health care provider, hospital, clinic, or other health facility. For the purposes of this paragraph, "aggregate form" means a compilation of the information received by the department on termination of pregnancies for each information item listed, with the exceptions of the report tracking number, the health care provider code, and any set of information for which the amount is so small that the confidentiality of any person to whom the information relates may be compromised. The department shall establish a methodology to provide a statistically verifiable basis for any determination of the correct amount at which information may be released so that the confidentiality of any person is not compromised.

3. Except as specified in subsection 2, reports, information, and records submitted and maintained pursuant to this section are strictly confidential and shall not be released or made public upon subpoena, search warrant, discovery proceedings, or by any other means.

4. The department shall assign a code to any health care provider who may be required to report a termination under this section. An application procedure shall not be required for assignment of a code to a health care provider.

5. A health care provider shall assign a report tracking number which enables the health care provider to access the patient's medical information without identifying the patient.

6. To ensure proper performance of the reporting requirements under this section, it is preferred that a health care provider who practices within a hospital, clinic, or other health facility authorize one staff person to fulfill the reporting requirements.

7. For the purposes of this section, "health care provider" means an individual licensed under chapter 148, 148C, 148D, 150, 150A, or 152, or any individual who provides medical services under the authorization of the licensee.

8. For the purposes of this section, "inducing a termination of pregnancy" means the use of any means to terminate the pregnancy of a woman known to be pregnant with the intent other than to produce a live birth or to remove a dead fetus.

9. For the purposes of this section, "spontaneous termination of pregnancy" means the occurrence of an unintended termination of pregnancy at any time during the period from conception to twenty weeks gestation and which is not a spontaneous termination of pregnancy at any time during the period from twenty weeks or greater which is reported to the department as a fetal death under this chapter.

(7) SALE OF ABORTIFACIENTS

Iowa retains statutes from the early 1900s that banned the sale of certain drugs used to induce abortions. The statutes are set out below.

Iowa Code § 205.1. Sale of abortifacients

No person shall sell, offer or expose for sale, deliver, give away, or have in the person's possession with intent to sell, except upon the original written prescription of a licensed physician, dentist, or veterinarian, any cotton root, ergot, oil of tansy, oil of savin, or derivatives of any of said drugs.

Iowa Code § 205.2. Exception

The requirements of section 205.1 that certain drugs shall be furnished only upon written prescription, shall not apply to the sale of such drugs to persons who wholesale or retail the same, nor to any licensed physician, dentist, or veterinarian for use in the practice of that person's profession.

(8) EMPLOYER HEALTH INSURANCE

Iowa provides by statute that employers may exclude coverage for abortion from their health insurance plans. The statute addressing the issue is set out below.

Iowa Code § 216.13 (2). Abortion coverage

2. A health insurance program provided by an employer may exclude coverage of abortion, except where the life of the mother would be endangered if the fetus were carried to term or where medical complications have arisen from an abortion.

Iowa Right to Life Committee

Iowa Right to Life Committee (IRLC) is a pro-life organization that identifies, educates, and mobilizes the pro-life population of Iowa. IRLC is the largest pro-life organization in the state of Iowa. The organization, through education and other public awareness programs, strives to provide an effective voice for those who are threatened by abortion. Some of the work engaged in by IRLC includes a mail campaign aimed at sending educational letters to female college students to alert them of the consequences of abortion; a centurion outreach program designed to help abortionists leave the abortion industry by providing limited financial support while they look for other work; abstinence campaign that involves teaching students that they should abstain from sex until married; white cross campaign which involves placement of crosses in churchyards to show the number of fetuses destroyed; and recruitment of pro-life candidates to run for public office in city, county, state and federal elections. *See also* **Pro-Life Organizations**

IUD *see* **Intrauterine Contraceptive Devices**

Ivy League Coalition for Life

The Ivy League Coalition for Life is a pro-life student-run organization that consists of about 20 colleges, including schools in the Ivy League. The organization's mission is to provide a network of communication for pro-life groups on campuses. The members provide information on pro-life speakers and communicate about pro-life events that take place at member schools. They also organize two conferences each year to discuss contemporary pro-life issues in higher education. *See also* **Pro-Life Organizations**

J

Jail *see* **Incarcerated Pregnant Women**

Jane

Jane was a term used in Chicago from 1969 to 1973, by women seeking an illegal abortion. The term was an entrance passage to an organization founded in Chicago in 1969 by Amy Kesselman, Heather Booth, Vivian Rothstein and Naomi Weisstein. The organization founded by the four woman was called the Abortion Counseling Service of the Chicago Women's Liberation Union. The organization acted as a referral source for women seeking an inexpensive, but safe abortion. When the person who performed most of the abortions for the organization was arrested, members of the organization began performing abortions. Several members were ultimately arrested and prosecuted. It was estimated that over 10,000 abortions were performed through Jane's underground work.

Jessen, Gianna

Gianna Jessen's mother went to an abortion facility in California on April 6, 1977 to abort her. The pregnancy was 7½ months long when preparations were made by clinic staff to have a saline abortion. However, the physician who was supposed to perform the abortion was not present during the preparation period. While waiting on the doctor, Jessen was prematurely expelled from her mother's womb alive. Jessen was born with cerebral palsy. She was eventually adopted. On April 22, 1996, Jessen spoke to the Congressional Constitution Subcommittee of the House Judiciary Committee about her experiences and opposition to abortion. *See also* **Survivors of Abortion**

Jews for Life

Jews for Life (JFL) is a pro-life organization founded by Bonnie Chernin Rogoff of New York City. JFL was created to reflect the traditional Jewish pro-life perspective on abortion. The organization seeks to enlighten and inform the public about the consequences that have befallen women since the legalization of abortion. JFL takes the position that unborn life is sacred and worthy of protection. It also believes that the current pro-choice position of mainstream liberal Jewish organizations is antithetical to the traditional teachings. JFL's primary pro-life work is done on its website, where it provides a forum for articles, political commentaries, and analysis of government policy as it pertains to abortion. *See also* **Pro-Life Organizations**

Jiminez, Rosie

The abortion related death of Rosie Jiminez on October 3, 1977 became a symbol for the need to have governmental funds to help pay the cost of abortion for indigent women. Jiminez was pregnant but wanted an abortion. She was unable to afford the cost for a clinical abortion and could not obtain one through Medicaid, which she had twice previously done, because of Congressional passage of the Hyde Amendment. The Hyde Amendment cut off Medicaid funding for abortion starting in 1977. As a result of her indigency, Jiminez was forced to have an abortion in a setting that was considered illegal. She died from complications during the abortion. Jiminez is considered the first known victim of the Hyde Amendment. *See also* **Complications During and After Abortion; Hyde Amendment; Public Resources for Abortions**

Jordi, Stephen John

Stephen John Jordi (b. 1968) was arrested by the FBI in Miami, Florida on November 11, 2003, for allegedly plotting to bomb abortion clinics and commit acts of violence against abortion providers. The FBI became aware of Jordi's plan as a result of information supplied by his brother. Based upon the information given by Jordi's brother, the FBI sent an informant to meet with Jordi. The facts of the planned bombings were described in *United States v. Jordi*, 418 F.3d 1212 (11th Cir. 2005) as follows:

According to the government, sometime in August 2003, Jordi concocted a plan whereby he would destroy abortion clinics using explosive devices. During tape recorded meetings with a confidential source, Jordi explained that his actions would be justified to prevent the deaths of unborn children. At one of those meetings, Jordi said, "I do not have the means to kill abortion doctors, but I do have the means to bomb clinics. Maybe that way I can dissuade other doctors from performing abortions." Jordi explained to the confidential source that he had been learning how to live off the land so that he could sustain himself when he was on the run after the bombings had started. Between August and November of 2003, Jordi met numerous times with the confidential source to discuss plans for bombing abortion clinics. On a couple of occasions, they surveilled South Florida abortion clinics. Jordi later indicated to the confidential source that he would not bomb any clinics in South Florida but would go north to begin his bombing spree.

Jordi bought gas cans, gasoline, starter fluid, and flares in preparation for the proposed bombings. He also purchased a handgun and silencer from the confidential source. Shortly thereafter, Jordi arranged to have his family moved to Pensacola, Florida. This was a prerequisite to beginning the bombing spree according to Jordi's earlier conversations with the confidential source. Jordi, after being placed under oath, agreed with the facts as recited by the government.

After Jordi's arrest he was indicted for intent to commit a crime of violence, distributing explosives information, and possessing an unregistered silencer weapon. Jordi eventually pleaded guilty to one count of attempted firebombing of a reproductive health clinic. He was sentenced to five years in federal prison on July 8, 2004. *See also* **Abortion Violence, Property Destruction and Demonstrations**

Joubert Syndrome

Joubert syndrome is a congenital disorder that is characterized by absence or underdevelopment of a part of the brain that controls balance and coordination. The disorder causes lack of muscle control, abnormal breathing, sleep apnea, abnormal eye and tongue movements, malformations involving extra fingers and toes, seizures and mild mental retardation. Treatment for the disease is done based upon specific manifestations of the disorder, and may include physical and speech therapy. *See also* **Birth Defects and Abortion**

Judicial Bypass *see* **Minors and Abortion**

Juneau Pro-Choice Coalition

Juneau Pro-Choice Coalition (JPCC) is an organization founded in 1992, in Juneau, Alaska. The organization was created to promote public awareness through education and advocacy of the importance of preserving a woman's right to self-determination of her reproductive life. JPCC believes that all women should have access to safe and legal reproductive health services. The group engages in political activity that includes supporting pro-choice candidates for public office, informing pro-choice voters in about candidates for public office, and serving as a watchdog to mobilize people to act when reproductive health issues are at stake. *See also* **Pro-Choice Organizations**

K

Kansans for Life

Kansans for Life (KFL) is a nonprofit pro-life educational organization. The regional headquarters of KFL is in Overland Park, Kansas. The executive director of KFL is Mary Kay Culp. KFL dedicated to protecting and defending the right to life of all humans from the moment of conception to natural death. The organization offers, as a free service to the public, educational items and information, pregnancy help and referrals, access to its libraries, pro-life speakers, media representation, as well as sponsor educational forums and events on various aspects of the sanctity of human life issue. KFL has a legislative department that lobbies pro-life issues in the Kansas legislature, and a political action committee that endorses pro-life candidates during elections. *See also* **Pro-Life Organizations**

Kansas

(1) OVERVIEW

The state of Kansas enacted its first criminal abortion statute on March 3, 1868. The statute underwent several amendments prior to the 1973 decision by the United States Supreme Court in *Roe v. Wade*, which legalized abortion in the nation. Kansas has taken affirmative steps to respond to *Roe* and its progeny. Through statutes Kansas has addressed numerous abortion issues that include general abortion guidelines, informed consent, partial-birth abortion, abortion by minors, fetal tissue restrictions, use of facilities and people, fetal death report, and impeding access to facility.

(2) GENERAL ABORTION GUIDELINES

Kansas prohibits post-viability abortion, except to preserve the woman's life or health. Two physicians must concur in the necessity of a post-viability abortion. The state mandates fetal viability testing prior to the performance of an abortion. The general abortion guideline statutes are set out below.

Kansas Code § 65-6701. Definitions

As used in this act:

(a) "Abortion" means the use of any means to intentionally terminate a pregnancy except for the purpose of causing a live birth. Abortion does not include: (1) The use of any drug or device that inhibits or prevents ovulation, fertilization or the implantation of an embryo; or (2) disposition of the product of in vitro fertilization prior to implantation.

(b) "Counselor" means a person who is: (1) Licensed to practice medicine and surgery; (2) licensed to practice psychology; (3) licensed to practice professional or practical nursing; (4) registered to practice professional counseling; (5) licensed as a social worker; (6) the holder of a master's or doctor's degree from an accredited graduate school of social work; (7) registered to practice marriage and family therapy; (8) a licensed physician assistant; or (9) a currently ordained member of the clergy or religious authority of any religious denomination or society. Counselor does not include the physician who performs or induces the abortion or a physician or other person who assists in performing or inducing the abortion.

(c) "Department" means the department of health and environment.

(d) "Gestational age" means the time that has elapsed since the first day of the woman's last menstrual period.

(e) "Medical emergency" means that condition which, on the basis of the physician's good faith clinical judgment, so complicates the medical condition of a pregnant woman as to necessitate the imme-

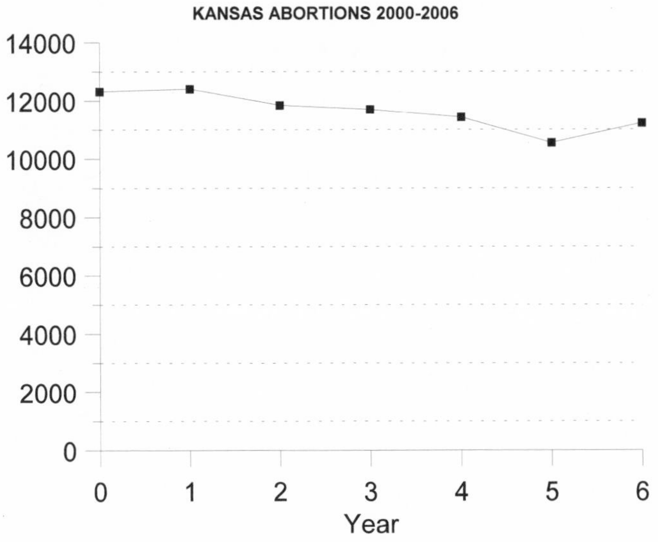

Source: Kansas Department of Health and Environment.

Kansas Abortion by Age Group 2000–2006

	Age Group (yrs)							
Year	*<15*	*15–19*	*20–24*	*25–29*	*30–34*	*35–39*	*40–44*	*≥45*
2000	102	2,412	4,204	2,681	1,605	980	321	18
2001	83	2,376	4,305	2,614	1,711	982	318	15
2002	88	2,243	4,110	2,541	1,637	893	308	24
2003	78	2,005	4,217	2,615	1,579	869	312	22
2004	79	1,943	3,941	2,630	1,621	873	321	20
2005	56	1,793	3,645	2,470	1,428	846	280	24
2006	67	1,888	3,774	2,706	1,543	963	256	24
Total	553	14,660	28,196	18,257	11,124	6,406	2,116	147

Source: Kansas Department of Health and Environment.

diate abortion of her pregnancy to avert her death or for which a delay will create serious risk of substantial and irreversible impairment of a major bodily function.

(f) "Minor" means a person less than 18 years of age.

(g) "Physician" means a person licensed to practice medicine and surgery in this state.

(h) "Pregnant" or "pregnancy" means that female reproductive condition of having a fetus in the mother's body.

(i) "Qualified person" means an agent of the physician who is a psychologist, licensed social worker, registered professional counselor, registered nurse or physician.

(j) "Unemancipated minor" means any minor who has never been: (1) Married; or (2) freed, by court order or otherwise, from the care, custody and control of the minor's parents.

(k) "Viable" means that stage of gestation when, in the best medical judgment of the attending physician, the fetus is capable of sustained survival outside the uterus without the application of extraordinary medical means.

Kansas Code § 65-6702. Drugs or devices for birth control

(a) The use of any drug or device that inhibits or prevents ovulation, fertilization or implantation of an embryo and disposition of the product of in vitro fertilization prior to implantation are lawful in this state and neither the state nor any political subdivision of the state shall prohibit the use of any such drug or device or the disposition of such product.

(b) No political subdivision of the state shall regulate or restrict abortion.

Kansas Code § 65-6703. Abortion prohibited when fetus viable

(a) No person shall perform or induce an abortion when the fetus is viable unless such person is a physician and has a documented referral from another physician not legally or financially affiliated with the physician performing or inducing the abortion and both physicians determine

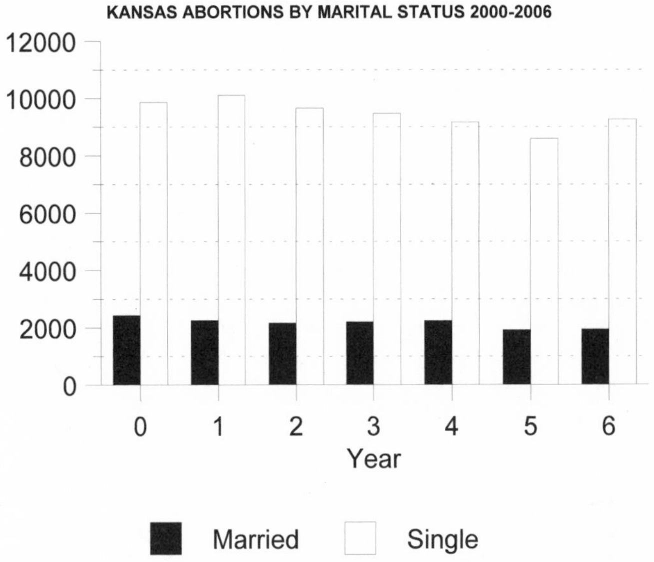

Source: Kansas Department of Health and Environment.
*Data for unknown marital status too small to reflect on graph.

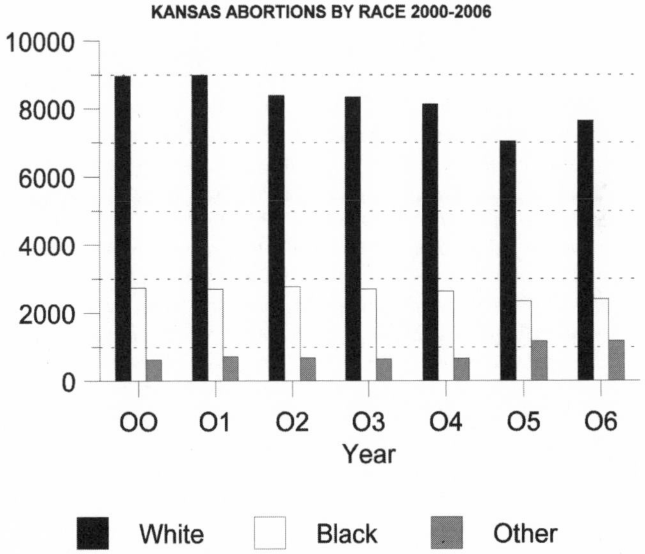

Source: Kansas Department of Health and Environment.

Kansas Abortion by Weeks of Gestation 2000–2006

	Year							
Weeks of Gestation	*2000*	*2001*	*2002*	*2003*	*2004*	*2005*	*2006*	*Total*
<8	7,226	7,301	7,027	7,077	6,910	6,580	7,078	49,199
9–12	3,059	3,152	2,927	2,806	2,638	2,403	2,533	19,518
13–16	854	819	863	854	850	762	820	5,822
17–21	525	477	447	455	511	372	393	3,180
≥22	639	635	564	491	518	414	380	3,641
Not known	20	20	16	14	0	11	17	98

Source: Kansas Department of Health and Environment.

that: (1) The abortion is necessary to preserve the life of the pregnant woman; or (2) a continuation of the pregnancy will cause a substantial and irreversible impairment of a major bodily function of the pregnant woman.

(b) (1) Except in the case of a medical emergency, prior to performing an abortion upon a woman, the physician shall determine the gestational age of the fetus according to accepted obstetrical and neonatal practice and standards applied by physicians in the same or similar circumstances. If the physician determines the gestational age is less than 22 weeks, the physician shall document as part of the medical records of the woman the basis for the determination.

(2) If the physician determines the gestational age of the fetus is 22 or more weeks, prior to performing an abortion upon the woman the physician shall determine if the fetus is viable by using and exercising that degree of care, skill and proficiency commonly exercised by the ordinary skillful, careful and prudent physician in the same or similar circumstances. In making this determination of viability, the physician shall perform or cause to be performed such medical examinations and tests as are necessary to make a finding of the gestational age of the fetus and shall enter such findings and determinations of viability in the medical record of the woman.

(3) If the physician determines the gestational age of a fetus is 22 or more weeks, and determines that the fetus is not viable and performs an abortion on the woman, the physician shall report such determinations and the reasons for such determinations in writing to the medical care facility in which the abortion is performed for inclusion in the report of the medical care facility to the secretary of health and environment under K.S.A. 65-445 and amendments thereto or if the abortion is not performed in a medical care facility, the physician shall report such determinations and the reasons for such determinations in writing to the secretary of health and environment as part of the written report made by the physician to the secretary of health and environment under K.S.A. 65-445 and amendments thereto.

(4) If the physician who is to perform the abortion determines the gestational age of a fetus is 22 or more weeks, and determines that the fetus is viable, both physicians under subsection (a) determine in accordance with the provisions of subsection (a) that an abortion is necessary to preserve the life of the pregnant woman or that a continuation of the pregnancy will cause a substantial and irreversible impairment of a major bodily function of the pregnant woman and the physician performs an abortion on the woman, the physician who performs the abortion shall report such determinations, the reasons for such determinations and the basis for the determination that an abortion is necessary to preserve the life of the pregnant woman or that a continuation of the pregnancy will cause a substantial and irreversible impairment of a major bodily function of the pregnant woman in writing to the medical care facility in which the abortion is performed for inclusion in the report of the medical care facility to the secretary of health and environment under K.S.A. 65-445 and amendments thereto or if the abortion is not performed in a medical care facility, the physician who performs the abortion shall report such determinations, the reasons for such determinations and the basis for the determination that an abortion is necessary to preserve the life of the pregnant woman or that a continuation of the pregnancy will cause a substantial and irreversible impairment of a major bodily function of the pregnant woman in writing to the secretary of health and environment as part of the written report made by the physician to the secretary of health and environment under K.S.A. 65-445 and amendments thereto.

(5) The physician shall retain the medical records required to be kept under paragraphs (1) and (2) of this subsection (b) for not less than five years and shall retain a copy of the written reports required under paragraphs (3) and (4) of this subsection (b) for not less than five years.

(c) A woman upon whom an abortion is performed shall not be prosecuted under this section for a conspiracy to violate this section pursuant to K.S.A. 21-3302, and amendments thereto.

(d) Nothing in this section shall be construed to create a right to an abortion. Notwithstanding any provision of this section, a person shall not perform an abortion that is prohibited by law.

(e) As used in this section, "viable" means that stage of fetal development when it is the physician's judgment according to accepted obstetrical or neonatal standards of care and practice applied by physicians in the same or similar circumstances that there is a reasonable probability that the life of the child can be continued indefinitely outside the mother's womb with natural or artificial life-supportive measures.

(f) If any provision of this section is held to be invalid or unconstitutional, it shall be conclusively presumed that the legislature would have enacted the remainder of this section without such invalid or unconstitutional provision.

(g) Upon a first conviction of a violation of this section, a person shall be guilty of a class A nonperson misdemeanor. Upon a second or subsequent conviction of a violation of this section, a person shall be guilty of a severity level 10, nonperson felony.

Kansas Code § 65-6707. Severability clause

If any provision of this act or its application to any person or circumstance is held invalid, the remainder of the act or the application of the provision to other persons or circumstances is not affected.

(3) INFORMED CONSENT

Prior to an abortion Kansas requires that a woman be fully informed of the procedure to be used, the risks involved and alternatives to abortion. An abortion may not take place until 24 hours after a woman has given her written consent to an abortion. The statutes addressing the matters are set out below.

Kansas Code § 65-6708. Woman's-right-to-know act

K.S.A. 65-6701 and K.S.A. 65-6708 to 65-6715, inclusive, and amendments thereto shall be known and may be cited as the woman's-right-to-know act.

Kansas Code § 65-6709. Consent and waiting period

No abortion shall be performed or induced without the voluntary and informed consent of the woman upon whom the abortion is to be performed or induced. Except in the case of a medical emergency, consent to an abortion is voluntary and informed only if:

(a) At least 24 hours before the abortion the physician who is to perform the abortion or the referring physician has informed the woman in writing of:

(1) The name of the physician who will perform the abortion;

(2) a description of the proposed abortion method;

(3) a description of risks related to the proposed abortion method, including risks to the woman's reproductive health and alternatives to the abortion that a reasonable patient would consider material to the decision of whether or not to undergo the abortion;

(4) the probable gestational age of the fetus at the time the abortion is to be performed and that Kansas law requires the following: "No person shall perform or induce an abortion when the fetus is viable unless such person is a physician and has a documented referral from another physician not financially associated with the physician performing or inducing the abortion and both physicians determine that: (1) The abortion is necessary to preserve the life of the pregnant woman; or (2) the fetus is affected by a severe or life-threatening deformity or abnormality." If the child is born alive, the attending physician has the legal obligation to take all reasonable steps necessary to maintain the life and health of the child;

(5) the probable anatomical and physiological characteristics of the fetus at the time the abortion is to be performed;

(6) the medical risks associated with carrying a fetus to term; and

(7) any need for anti–Rh immune globulin therapy, if she is Rh negative, the likely consequences of refusing such therapy and the cost of the therapy.

(b) At least 24 hours before the abortion, the physician who is to perform the abortion, the referring physician or a qualified person has informed the woman in writing that:

(1) Medical assistance benefits may be available for prenatal care, childbirth and neonatal care, and that more detailed information on the availability of such assistance is contained in the printed materials given to her and described in K.S.A. 65-6710 and amendments thereto;

(2) the printed materials in K.S.A. 65-6710 and amendments thereto describe the fetus and list agencies which offer alternatives to abortion with a special section listing adoption services;

(3) the father of the fetus is liable to assist in the support of her child, even in instances where he has offered to pay for the abortion except that in the case of rape this information may be omitted; and

(4) the woman is free to withhold or withdraw her consent to the abortion at any time prior to invasion of the uterus without affecting her right to future care or treatment and without the loss of any state or federally-funded benefits to which she might otherwise be entitled.

(c) Prior to the abortion procedure, prior to physical preparation for the abortion and prior to the administration of medication for the abortion, the woman shall meet privately with the physician who is to perform the abortion and such person's staff to ensure that she has an adequate opportunity to ask questions of and obtain information from the physician concerning the abortion.

(d) At least 24 hours before the abortion, the woman is given a copy of the printed materials described in K.S.A. 65-6710 and amendments thereto. If the woman asks questions concerning any of the information or materials, answers shall be provided to her in her own language.

(e) The woman certifies in writing on a form provided by the department, prior to the abortion, that the information required to be provided under subsections (a), (b) and (d) has been provided and that she has met with the physician who is to perform the abortion on an individual basis as provided under subsection (c). All physicians who perform abortions shall report the total number of certifications received monthly to the department. The department shall make the number of certifications received available on an annual basis.

(f) Prior to the performance of the abortion, the physician who is to perform the abortion or the physician's agent receives a copy of the written certification prescribed by subsection (e) of this section.

(g) The woman is not required to pay any amount for the abortion procedure until the 24-hour waiting period has expired.

Kansas Code § 65-6710. Informed consent materials

(a) The department shall cause to be published and distributed widely, within 30 days after the effective date of this act, and shall update on an annual basis, the following easily comprehensible printed materials:

(1) Geographically indexed materials designed to inform the woman of public and private agencies and services available to assist a woman through pregnancy, upon childbirth and while her child is dependent, including but not limited to, adoption agencies. The materials shall include a comprehensive list of the agencies, a description of the services they offer and the telephone numbers and addresses of the agencies; and inform the woman about available medical assistance benefits for prenatal care, childbirth and neonatal care and about the support obligations of the father of a child who is born alive. The department shall ensure that the materials described in this section are comprehensive and do not directly or indirectly promote, exclude or discourage the use of any agency or service described in this section. The materials shall also contain a toll-free 24-hour a day telephone number which may be called to obtain, orally, such a list and description of agencies in the locality of the caller and of the services they offer. The materials shall state that it is unlawful for any individual to coerce a woman to undergo an abortion, that any physician who performs an abortion upon a woman without her informed consent may be liable to her for damages. Kansas law permits adoptive parents to pay costs of prenatal care, childbirth and neonatal care. The materials shall include the following statement:

'Many public and private agencies exist to provide counseling and information on available services. You are strongly urged to seek their assistance to obtain guidance during your pregnancy. In addition, you are encouraged to seek information on abortion services, alternatives to abortion, including adoption, and resources available to postpartum mothers. The law requires that your physician or the physician's agent provide the enclosed information.'

(2) Materials that inform the pregnant woman of the probable anatomical and physiological characteristics of the fetus at two-week gestational increments from fertilization to full term, including pictures or drawings representing the development of a fetus at two-week gestational increments, and any relevant information on the possibility of the fetus' survival. Any such pictures or drawings shall contain the dimensions of the fetus and shall be realistic. The materials shall be objective, nonjudgmental and designed to convey only accurate scientific information about the fetus at the various gestational ages. The material shall also contain objective information describing the methods of abortion procedures commonly employed, the medical risks commonly associated with each such procedure and the medical risks associated with carrying a fetus to term.

(3) A certification form to be used by physicians or their agents under subsection (e) of K.S.A. 65-6709 and amendments thereto, which will list all the items of information which are to be given to women by physicians or their agents under the woman's-right-to-know act.

(b) The materials required under this section shall be printed in a typeface large enough to be clearly legible. The materials shall be made available in both English and Spanish language versions.

(c) The materials required under this section shall be available at no cost from the department upon request and in appropriate number to any person, facility or hospital.

Kansas Code § 65-6711. Medical emergency

Where a medical emergency compels the performance of an abortion, the physician shall inform the woman, before the abortion if possible, of the medical indications supporting the physician's judgment that an abortion is necessary to avert her death or to avert substantial and irreversible impairment of a major bodily function.

Kansas Code § 65-6712. Failure to provide informed consent

Any physician who intentionally, knowingly or recklessly fails to provide in accordance with K.S.A. 65-6709 and amendments thereto the printed materials described in K.S.A. 65-6710 and amendments thereto, whether or not an abortion is actually performed on the woman, is guilty of unprofessional conduct as defined in K.S.A. 65-2837 and amendments thereto.

Kansas Code § 65-6713. Civilly liable to patient

Any physician who complies with the provisions of this act shall not be held civilly liable to a patient for failure to obtain informed consent to the abortion.

Kansas Code § 65-6714. Severability clause

The provisions of this act are declared to be severable, and if any provision, word, phrase or clause of the act or the application thereof to any person shall be held invalid, such invalidity shall not affect the validity of the remaining portions of the woman's-right-to-know act.

Kansas Code § 65-6715. Limitations of act

(a) Nothing in the woman's-right-to-know act shall be construed as creating or recognizing a right to abortion.

(b) It is not the intention of the woman's-right-to-know act to make lawful an abortion that is currently unlawful.

(4) PARTIAL-BIRTH ABORTION

Kansas criminalizes partial-birth abortions, except when performed to preserve the live or health of the woman. Until it is definitively determined by a court, Kansas' partial-birth abortion statute may be invalid under the United States Supreme Court decision *in Stenberg v. Carhart*, which invalidated Nebraska's ban on partial-birth abortion. On the other hand, Kansas' partial-birth abortion statute, as currently written, may be valid under the United States Supreme Court decision in *Gonzales v. Carhart*, which approved of a federal statute that bans partial-birth abortion. The text of Kansas' partial-birth abortion statute is set out below.

Kansas Code § 65-6721. Partial-birth abortion offense

(a) No person shall perform or induce a partial birth abortion on a viable fetus unless such person is a physician and has a documented referral from another physician not legally or financially affiliated with the physician performing or inducing the abortion and both physicians determine: (1) The abortion is necessary to preserve the life of the pregnant woman; or (2) a continuation of the pregnancy will cause a substantial and irreversible impairment of a major physical or mental function of the pregnant woman.

(b) As used in this section:

(1) "Partial birth abortion" means an abortion procedure which includes the deliberate and intentional evacuation of all or a part of the intracranial contents of a viable fetus prior to removal of such otherwise intact fetus from the body of the pregnant woman.

(2) "Partial birth abortion" shall not include the: (A) Suction curettage abortion procedure; (B) suction aspiration abortion procedure; or (C) dilation and evacuation abortion procedure involving dismemberment of the fetus prior to removal from the body of the pregnant woman.

(c) If a physician determines in accordance with the provisions of subsection (a) that a partial birth abortion is necessary and performs a partial birth abortion on the woman, the physician shall report such determination and the reasons for such determination in writing to the medical care facility in which the abortion is performed for inclusion in the report of the medical care facility to the secretary of health and environment under K.S.A. 65-445 and amendments thereto or if the abortion is not performed in a medical care facility, the physician shall report the reasons for such determination in writing to the secretary of health and environment as part of the written report made by the physician to the secretary of health and environment under K.S.A. 65-445 and amendments thereto. The physician shall retain a copy of the written reports required under this subsection for not less than five years.

(d) A woman upon whom an abortion is performed shall not be prosecuted under this section for a conspiracy to violate this section pursuant to K.S.A. 21-3302, and amendments thereto.

(e) Nothing in this section shall be construed to create a right to an abortion. Notwithstanding any provision of this section, a person shall not perform an abortion that is prohibited by law.

(f) Upon conviction of a violation of this section, a person shall be guilty of a severity level 10 person felony.

(5) ABORTION BY MINORS

Kansas requires that a minor be given extensive counseling and information as an initial step in the abortion procedures for minors. Under the laws of the state no physician may perform an abortion upon an unemancipated minor unless he/she first provides notice of the abortion to a parent or the legal guardian of the minor. In compliance with federal constitutional law, Kansas has provided a judicial waiver procedure for an unemancipated minor to obtain an abortion without parental or guardian notice. The minor may petition a trial court for a waiver of the notice requirement. A minor has a right to an attorney at the proceeding and if she cannot afford one, the court must appoint her an attorney. If a minor chooses, she may represent herself. The required parental or guardian notice may be waived if the court finds either (1) that the minor is mature and well-informed enough to make the abortion decision on her own, or (2) that performance of the abortion would be in the best interest of the minor. An expedited appeal is available to any minor to whom the court denies a waiver of consent. The statutes addressing the issue of abortions for minors are set out below.

Kansas Code § 65-6704. Required information and counseling

(a) Before the performance of an abortion upon a minor, a counselor shall provide pregnancy information and counseling in a manner that can be understood by the minor and allows opportunity for the minor's questions to be addressed. A parent or guardian, or a person 21 or more years of age who is not associated with the abortion provider and who has a personal interest in the minor's well-being, shall accompany the minor and be involved in the minor's decision-making process regarding whether to have an abortion. Such information and counseling shall include:

(1) The alternatives available to the minor, including abortion, adoption and other alternatives to abortion;

(2) an explanation that the minor may change a decision to have an abortion at any time before the abortion is performed or may decide to have an abortion at any time while an abortion may be legally performed;

(3) make available to the minor information on agencies available to assist the minor and agencies from which birth control information is available;

(4) discussion of the possibility of involving the minor's parent or parents, other adult family members or guardian in the minor's decision-making; and

(5) information regarding the provisions of K.S.A. 65-6705 and the minor's rights under such provisions.

(b) After the performance of an abortion on a minor, a counselor shall provide counseling to assist the minor in adjusting to any post-abortion problems that the minor may have.

(c) After the counselor provides information and counseling to a minor as required by this section, the counselor shall have the minor sign and date a statement setting forth the requirements of subsections (a) and (b) and declaring that the minor has received information and counseling in accordance with those requirements.

(d) The counselor shall also sign and date the statement and shall include the counselor's business address and business telephone number. The counselor shall keep a copy for the minor's medical record and shall give the form to the minor or, if the minor requests and if the counselor is not the attending physician, transmit the statement to the minor's attending physician. Such medical record shall be maintained as otherwise provided by law.

(e) The provision by a counselor of written materials which contain information and counseling meeting the requirements of subsections (a) and (b) and which is signed by the minor shall be presumed to be evidence of compliance with the requirements of this section.

(f) The requirements of subsection (a) shall not apply when, in the

best medical judgment of the attending physician based on the facts of the case, an emergency exists that threatens the health, safety or well-being of the minor as to require an abortion. A physician who does not comply with the requirements of this section by reason of this exception shall state in the medical record of the abortion the medical indications on which the physician's judgment was based.

Kansas Code § 65-6705. Notice and judicial bypass

(a) Before a person performs an abortion upon an unemancipated minor, the person or the person's agent must give actual notice of the intent to perform such abortion to one of the minor's parents or the minor's legal guardian or must have written documentation that such notice has been given unless, after receiving counseling as provided by subsection (a) of K.S.A. 65-6704, the minor objects to such notice being given. If the minor so objects, the minor may petition, on her own behalf or by an adult of her choice, the district court of any county of this state for a waiver of the notice requirement of this subsection. If the minor so desires, the counselor who counseled the minor as required by K.S.A. 65-6704 shall notify the court and the court shall ensure that the minor or the adult petitioning on the minor's behalf is given assistance in preparing and filing the application.

(b) The minor may participate in proceedings in the court on the minor's own behalf or through the adult petitioning on the minor's behalf. The court shall provide a court-appointed counsel to represent the minor at no cost to the minor.

(c) Court proceedings under this section shall be anonymous and the court shall ensure that the minor's identity is kept confidential. The court shall order that a confidential record of the evidence in the proceeding be maintained. All persons shall be excluded from hearings under this section except the minor, her attorney and such other persons whose presence is specifically requested by the applicant or her attorney.

(d) Notice shall be waived if the court finds by a preponderance of the evidence that either: (1) The minor is mature and well-informed enough to make the abortion decision on her own; or (2) notification of a person specified in subsection (a) would not be in the best interest of the minor.

(e) A court that conducts proceedings under this section shall issue written and specific factual findings and legal conclusions supporting its decision as follows:

(1) Granting the minor's application for waiver of notice pursuant to this section, if the court finds that the minor is mature and well-enough informed to make the abortion decision without notice to a person specified in subsection (a);

(2) granting the minor's application for waiver if the court finds that the minor is immature but that notification of a person specified in subsection (a) would not be in the minor's best interest; or

(3) denying the application if the court finds that the minor is immature and that waiver of notification of a person specified in subsection (a) would not be in the minor's best interest.

(f) The court shall give proceedings under this section such precedence over other pending matters as necessary to ensure that the court may reach a decision promptly. The court shall issue a written order which shall be issued immediately to the minor, or her attorney or other individual designated by the minor to receive the order. If the court fails to rule within 48 hours, excluding Saturdays and Sundays, of the time of the filing of the minor's application, the application shall be deemed granted.

(g) An expedited anonymous appeal shall be available to any minor. The record on appeal shall be completed and the appeal shall be perfected within five days from the filing of the notice to appeal.

(h) The supreme court shall promulgate any rules it finds are necessary to ensure that proceedings under this act are handled in an expeditious and anonymous manner.

(i) No fees shall be required of any minor who avails herself of the procedures provided by this section.

(j) (1) No notice shall be required under this section if:

(A) The pregnant minor declares that the father of the fetus is one of the persons to whom notice may be given under this section;

(B) in the best medical judgment of the attending physician based on the facts of the case, an emergency exists that threatens the health, safety or well-being of the minor as to require an abortion; or

(C) the person or persons who are entitled to notice have signed a written, notarized waiver of notice which is placed in the minor's medical record.

(2) A physician who does not comply with the provisions of this section by reason of the exception of subsection (j)(1)(A) must inform the minor that the physician is required by law to report the sexual abuse to the department of social and rehabilitation services. A physician who does not comply with the requirements of this section by reason of the exception of subsection (j)(1)(B) shall state in the medical record of the abortion the medical indications on which the physician's judgment was based.

(k) Any person who intentionally performs an abortion with knowledge that, or with reckless disregard as to whether, the person upon whom the abortion is to be performed is an unemancipated minor, and who intentionally and knowingly fails to conform to any requirement of this section, is guilty of a class A person misdemeanor.

(1) Except as necessary for the conduct of a proceeding pursuant to this section, it is a class B person misdemeanor for any individual or entity to willfully or knowingly: (1) Disclose the identity of a minor petitioning the court pursuant to this section or to disclose any court record relating to such proceeding; or (2) permit or encourage disclosure of such minor's identity or such record.

Kansas Code § 65-67a09. Child rape protection act

(a) This section shall be known and may be cited as the child rape protection act.

(b) As used in this section:

(1) 'Abortion' has the meaning provided in K.S.A. 65-6701, and amendments thereto.

(2) 'Physician' means any person licensed to practice medicine and surgery.

(c) Any physician who performs an abortion on a minor who was less than 14 years of age at the time of the abortion procedure shall preserve, in accordance with rules and regulations adopted by the attorney general pursuant to this section, fetal tissue extracted during such abortion. The physician shall submit such tissue to the Kansas bureau of investigation or to a laboratory designated by the director of the Kansas bureau of investigation.

(d) The attorney general shall adopt rules and regulations prescribing:

(1) The amount and type of fetal tissue to be preserved and submitted by a physician pursuant to this section;

(2) procedures for the proper preservation of such tissue for the purpose of DNA testing and examination;

(3) procedures for documenting the chain of custody of such tissue for use as evidence;

(4) procedures for proper disposal of fetal tissue preserved pursuant to this section;

(5) a uniform reporting instrument mandated to be utilized by physicians when submitting fetal tissue under this section which shall include the name of the physician submitting the fetal tissue and the name, complete address of residence and name of the parent or legal guardian of the minor upon whom the abortion was performed; and

(6) procedures for communication with law enforcement agencies regarding evidence and information obtained pursuant to this section.

(e) Failure of a physician to comply with any provision of this section or any rule or regulation adopted hereunder:

(1) Shall constitute unprofessional conduct for the purposes of K.S.A. 65-2837, and amendments thereto; and

(2) is a class A, nonperson misdemeanor upon a first conviction and a severity level 10, nonperson felony upon a second or subsequent conviction.

(6) FETAL TISSUE RESTRICTIONS

Under the laws of Kansas trafficking in fetal tissue or organs is prohibited. The state criminalizes the sale of fetal tissue, as well as experimentation on fetal tissue. The statutes addressing the issues are set out below.

Kansas Code § 65-67a01. Definitions

As used in this act:

(a) "Abortion" means an abortion as defined by K.S.A. 65-6701, and amendments thereto.

(b) (1) "Consideration" means:

(A) Any payment made or debt incurred;

(B) any gift, honorarium or recognition of value bestowed;

(C) any price, charge or fee which is waived, forgiven, reduced or indefinitely delayed;

(D) any loan or debt which is canceled or otherwise forgiven; or

(E) the transfer of any item from one person to another or provision of any service or granting of any opportunity for which a charge is customarily made, without charge or for a reduced charge.

(2) "Consideration" shall not mean:

(A) A payment in an amount not to exceed $25 for the cost of transporting, processing, preserving and storing fetal tissue; or

(B) a payment in an amount not to exceed the actual cost, as documented by the delivery service, of transporting fetal tissue.

(c) "Delivery service" means a common carrier as defined by K.S.A. 66-105, and amendments thereto, or other person or entity used to transport fetal tissue.

(d) "Fetal tissue" means any tissue, cells or organs obtained from a dead human embryo or fetus after an abortion or after a stillbirth.

(e) "Person" means a person as defined by K.S.A. 65-425, and amendments thereto.

(f) "Stillbirth" means a stillbirth as defined by K.S.A. 65-2401, and amendments thereto.

Kansas Code § 65-67a02. Construction of act

Except as specifically provided by this act, nothing in this act shall be construed as either permitting or prohibiting the use of fetal tissue for any type of scientific, research, laboratory or other kind of experimentation either prior to or subsequent to any abortion or stillbirth.

Kansas Code § 65-67a03. When act not applicable

This act shall not apply to:

(a) The transfer of fetal tissue to a pathologist for testing or examination; or

(b) the transfer of fetal tissue for the purpose of immediate burial, cremation or final disposition.

Kansas Code § 65-67a04. Prohibit fetal tissue sale

(a) No person shall solicit, offer, knowingly acquire or accept or transfer any fetal tissue for consideration.

(b) No person shall solicit, offer or knowingly acquire or accept or transfer any fetal tissue for the purpose of transplantation of such tissue into another person if:

(1) The fetal tissue will be or is obtained pursuant to an abortion; and

(2) (A) the donation of such fetal tissue will be or is made pursuant to a promise to the donating individual that the donated tissue will be transplanted into a recipient specified by such donating individual;

(B) such fetal tissue will be transplanted into a relative of the donating individual; or

(C) the person who solicits or knowingly acquires or accepts the donation of such fetal tissue has provided consideration for the costs associated with such abortion.

(c) Any person who intentionally, knowingly or recklessly violates this section shall be guilty of a severity level 2, nonperson felony.

Kansas Code § 65-67a05. Transfers of tissue

(a) Every person who transfers fetal tissue to another person shall submit annually a written report to the secretary of the department of health and environment which contains the following:

(1) The date of transfer;

(2) a description of the fetal tissue;

(3) the name and address of the transferor and the transferee;

(4) the amount of consideration received by the transferor for making the transfer;

(5) the mode of transfer or shipment; and

(6) the name of the delivery service.

(b) The identity of the woman donating the fetal tissue shall be confidential and shall not be included in any report required by this section.

(c) No person shall ship fetal tissue without disclosing to the delivery service that human tissue is contained in such shipment.

(d) Except as provided herein, information obtained by the secretary of health and environment under this section shall be confidential and shall not be disclosed in a manner that would reveal the identity of any person who submits a report to the secretary under this section. Such information, including information identifying any person submitting a report hereunder, may be disclosed to the attorney general upon a showing that a reasonable cause exists to believe that a violation of this act has occurred. Any information disclosed to the attorney general pursuant to this subsection shall be used solely for the purposes of a criminal prosecution.

(e) For the purpose of maintaining confidentiality, reports required by this section shall identify the name and address of the person submitting such report only by confidential code number assigned by the secretary of health and environment to such person and the department of health and environment shall maintain such reports only by such number.

(f) Any person who intentionally, knowingly or recklessly violates this section shall be guilty of a class A nonperson misdemeanor.

Kansas Code § 65-67a06. Prohibit fetal experiments

(a) No person shall offer any monetary or other inducement to any other person for the purpose of procuring an abortion for the medical, scientific, experimental or therapeutic use of fetal organs or tissue.

(b) No person shall offer or accept any valuable consideration for the fetal organs or tissue resulting from an abortion. Nothing in this subsection shall prohibit payment for burial or other final disposition of the fetal remains or payment for a pathological examination, autopsy or postmortem examination of the fetal remains.

(c) Any person who intentionally, knowingly or recklessly violates this section shall be guilty of a severity level 2, nonperson felony.

Kansas Code § 65-67a07. Consent of donor

(a) No person shall use fetal organs or tissue for medical, scientific, experimental or therapeutic use without the voluntary and informed consent of the woman donating such tissue. Such consent shall not be discussed or obtained prior to obtaining the consent required under K.S.A. 65-6709, and amendments thereto.

(b) A person who intentionally, knowingly or recklessly violates this section shall be guilty of a severity level 2, nonperson felony.

Kansas Code § 65-67a08. Severability

If any provision of this section [act] is held to be invalid or unconstitutional, it shall be presumed conclusively that the legislature would have enacted the remainder of this section [act] without such invalid or unconstitutional provision.

(7) USE OF FACILITIES AND PEOPLE

Kansas prohibits abortions at facilities operated by its public university hospital, and permits any hospital to refuse to conduct abortions. The state also permits physicians and other medical professionals to refuse to participate in abortions. The statutes addressing the matters are set out below.

Kansas Code § 76-3308(i).
University of Kansas Hospital Authority

Notwithstanding any provision of law to the contrary, no abortion shall be performed, except in the event of a medical emergency, in any medical facility, hospital or clinic owned, leased or operated by the authority. The provisions of this subsection are not applicable to any member of the physician faculty of the university of Kansas school of medicine on property not owned, leased or operated by the authority. As used in this subsection, "medical emergency" means a pregnant woman's medical condition that, on the basis of a physician's good-faith clinical judgment, necessitates an immediate abortion to avert the woman's death or to avert a serious risk of substantial and irreversible impairment of a major bodily function.

Kansas Code § 65-443. Refusal to participate in abortion

No person shall be required to perform or participate in medical procedures which result in the termination of a pregnancy, and the refusal of any person to perform or participate in those medical procedures shall not be a basis for civil liability to any person. No hospital, hospital administrator or governing board of any hospital shall terminate the employment of, prevent or impair the practice or occupation of or impose any other sanction on any person because of such person's refusal to perform or participate in the termination of any human pregnancy.

Kansas Code § 65-444. Hospital refusal to permit

No hospital, hospital administrator or governing board shall be required to permit the termination of human pregnancies within its institution and the refusal to permit such procedures shall not be grounds for civil liability to any person. A hospital may establish criteria and procedures under which pregnancies may be terminated within its institution, in addition to those which may be prescribed by licensing, regulating or accrediting agencies: Provided, No pregnancy shall be purposely terminated until the opinions of three (3) duly licensed physicians attesting to the necessity of such termination have been recorded in writing in the permanent records of the hospital, except in an emergency as defined in section 21-3407 (2) (b) of the Kansas criminal code.

(8) FETAL DEATH REPORT

Kansas requires that all abortions be reported to the proper authorities. The statute addressing the matter is set out below.

Kansas Code § 65-445. Reporting abortions

(a) Every medical care facility shall keep written records of all pregnancies which are lawfully terminated within such medical care facility and shall annually submit a written report thereon to the secretary of health and environment in the manner and form prescribed by the secretary. Every person licensed to practice medicine and surgery shall keep a record of all pregnancies which are lawfully terminated by such person in a location other than a medical care facility and shall annually submit a written report thereon to the secretary of health and environment in the manner and form prescribed by the secretary.

(b) Each report required by this section shall include the number of pregnancies terminated during the period of time covered by the report, the type of medical facility in which the pregnancy was terminated, information required to be reported under K.S.A. 65-6703 and amendments thereto if applicable to the pregnancy terminated, and such other information as may be required by the secretary of health and environment, but the report shall not include the names of the persons whose pregnancies were so terminated.

(c) Information obtained by the secretary of health and environment under this section shall be confidential and shall not be disclosed in a manner that would reveal the identity of any person licensed to practice medicine and surgery who submits a report to the secretary under this section or the identity of any medical care facility which submits a report to the secretary under this section, except that such information, including information identifying such persons and facilities may be disclosed to the state board of healing arts upon request of the board for disciplinary action conducted by the board and may be disclosed to the attorney general upon a showing that a reasonable cause exists to believe that a violation of this act has occurred. Any information disclosed to the state board of healing arts or the attorney general pursuant to this subsection shall be used solely for the purposes of a disciplinary action or criminal proceeding. Except as otherwise provided in this subsection, information obtained by the secretary under this section may be used only for statistical purposes and such information shall not be released in a manner which would identify any county or other area of this state in which the termination of the pregnancy occurred. A violation of this subsection (c) is a class A nonperson misdemeanor.

(d) In addition to such criminal penalty under subsection (c), any person licensed to practice medicine and surgery or medical care facility whose identity is revealed in violation of this section may bring a civil action against the responsible person or persons for any damages to the person licensed to practice medicine and surgery or medical care facility caused by such violation.

(e) For the purpose of maintaining confidentiality as provided by subsections (c) and (d), reports of terminations of pregnancies required by this section shall identify the person or facility submitting such reports only by confidential code number assigned by the secretary of health and environment to such person or facility and the department of health and environment shall maintain such reports only by such number.

(9) IMPEDING ACCESS TO FACILITY

Kansas has responded to violent anti-abortion activities by creating a criminal trespass statute. The statute prohibits impeding access to or from health care facilities. The statute is set out below.

Kansas Code § 21-3721. Impeding facility

(a) Criminal trespass is:

(1) Omitted.

(2) entering or remaining upon or in any public or private land or structure in a manner that interferes with access to or from any health care facility by a person who knows such person is not authorized or privileged to do so and such person enters or remains thereon or therein in defiance of an order not to enter or to leave such land or structure personally communicated to such person by the owner of the health care facility or other authorized person.

(b) Omitted.

(c) (1) Criminal trespass is a class B nonperson misdemeanor.

(2) Upon a conviction of a violation of subsection (a)(1)(C), a person shall be sentenced to not less than 48 consecutive hours of imprisonment which must be served either before or as a condition of any grant of probation or suspension, reduction of sentence or parole.

(d) Omitted.

Kennedy, Anthony M.

Anthony M. Kennedy was appointed as an associate justice of the United States Supreme Court in 1988. While on the Supreme Court Justice Kennedy has been known as a conservative interpreter of the Constitution.

Justice Kennedy was born on July 28, 1936, in Sacramento, California. He received an undergraduate degree from Stanford University in 1958, and a law degree from Harvard University Law School in 1961. Justice Kennedy's legal career included a private practice, teaching at McGeorge School of Law, and thirteen years as an appellate judge on the Ninth Circuit Court of Appeals. In 1988 President Ronald Reagan appointed Justice Kennedy to the Supreme Court.

Distribution of the Abortion Voting Pattern of Justice Kennedy Based Upon Opinions Filed by the Supreme Court

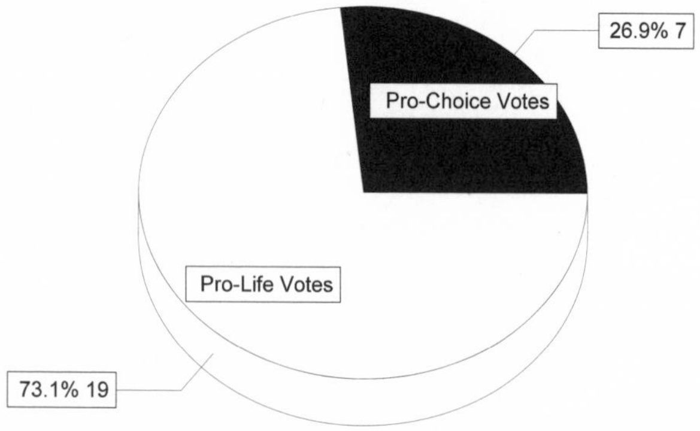

Justice Kennedy's voting pattern favors the view of pro-life advocates (collection, Supreme Court Historical Society, photograph by Robin Reid, Reid Photography).

During Justice Kennedy's tenure on the Supreme Court he has issued a number of abortion related opinions. The written opinions and opinions simply voted on by Justice Kennedy, indicate that he is not in favor of using the constitution to expand abortion rights for women.

(1) Unanimous opinions voted with only. In *Dalton v. Little Rock Family Planning Services*, Justice Kennedy voted with a unanimous Court in holding that an amendment to Arkansas' constitution which limited Medicaid payment only to therapeutic abortions, was invalid to the extent that Medicaid funds had to be made available for incest or rape pregnancies, but was valid for any purely state funded program. Justice Kennedy voted with a unanimous Court in *Scheidler v. National Organization for Women, Inc. (II)*, which held pro-choice advocates could not sue pro-life advocates under the Hobbs Act for allegations of physical violence that did not involve extortion. Justice Kennedy joined a unanimous opinion in *Ayotte v. Planned Parenthood of Northern New England*, which held that the absence of a health exception in New Hampshire's parental notification abortion statute did not require the entire statute be invalidated.

(2) Majority opinions written. In *Planned Parenthood of Southeastern Pennsylvania v. Casey*, Justice Kennedy wrote a joint majority/plurality opinion with Justices O'Connor and Souter. The opinion held that the constitution was not violated by provisions in Pennsylvania's abortion statute that provided for: medical emergency abortion; 24 hour waiting period for abortion; parental notice and judicial bypass for abortion by a minor; and certain abortion facility reporting requirements. The decision found two provisions in the abortion statute unconstitutional: spousal notification before obtaining an abortion, and a requirement that a woman inform the abortion provider the reason for not notifying her spouse. Justice Kennedy wrote the majority opinion in *Gonzales v. Carhart*, which held that the Partial-Birth Abortion Ban Act of 2003 was not facially unconstitutional, because it outlined the abortion procedure that was banned, and the Act did not have to provide an exception for the health of a woman.

In *Ohio v. Akron Center for Reproductive Health* Justice Kennedy wrote the majority opinion, which upheld the constitutionality of Ohio's abortion statute notice and judicial bypass requirements for pregnant female minors. Justice Kennedy wrote the majority opinion in *United States Catholic Conference v. Abortion Rights Mobilization*, which allowed the appellants to challenge having to turn over documents in a lawsuit seeking to strip them of their tax exempt status because of their active political abortion work.

(3) Majority opinions voted with only. In *Lambert v. Wicklund* Justice Kennedy voted with the majority in holding that the constitution was not violated by a provision in Montana's abortion statute that allowed a court to waive the parental notice requirement for minors, if notification was not in minor's best interest. Justice Kennedy joined the majority opinion in *Mazurek v. Armstrong*, which held that Montana's requirement that abortions be performed only by physicians was constitutionally valid. Justice Kennedy voted with the majority in *Leavitt v. Jane L.*, which held that the invalidity of Utah's statute regulating pregnancies 20 weeks old or less, may be severed so as to preserve that portion of the abortion statute that regulated pregnancies of more than 20 weeks.

Justice Kennedy voted with the majority in *Rust v. Sullivan*, which upheld federal regulations that prohibited pro-abortion counseling, referral, and advocacy by health care providers. In *Daubert v. Merrell*

Dow Pharmaceuticals, Inc., a case involving children born with severe birth defects, Justice Kennedy voted with the majority in holding that the *Frye* rule on admissibility of expert testimony did not survive the enactment of the Federal Rules of Evidence.

Justice Kennedy voted with the majority decision in *Webster v. Reproductive Health Services*, which upheld Missouri's prohibition on the use of public facilities or employees to perform abortions and a requirement that physicians conduct viability tests prior to performing abortions. In *Frisby v. Schultz* Justice Kennedy voted with the majority opinion, which upheld the constitutional validity of a town ordinance that was created to prevent pro-life picketing at the residence of an abortion doctor. Justice Kennedy joined the majority opinion in *Scheidler v. National Organization for Women, Inc. (I)*, which held that evidence did not support finding that pro-life advocates violated the Hobbs Act, Travel Act and state law extortion crimes, for the purpose of awarding damages and granting an injunction against them under RICO.

(4) Concurring opinions written. Justice Kennedy wrote a concurring opinion in *Ferguson v. City of Charleston* which held that patient consent or a search warrant was needed, in order for a government hospital to turn over to the police drug test results that showed a woman used illegal drugs during her pregnancy. Justice Kennedy wrote a concurring opinion in *Bray v. Alexandria Clinic*, which held that the Civil Rights Act of 1871, 42 U.S.C. § 1985(3), did not provide a cause of action against persons obstructing access to abortion clinics. Justice Kennedy wrote a concurring opinion in *Federal Election Commission v. Beaumont*, which held that the Federal Election Campaign Act's prohibition on corporate expenditures and contributions directly to candidates in federal elections, applies to a nonprofit pro-life organization.

(5) Concurring opinions voted with only. Justice Kennedy concurred in *National Organization for Women, Inc. v. Scheidler*, which held that a group of pro-choice organizations could maintain a RICO civil lawsuit against several anti-abortion individuals and groups. In *Automobile Workers v. Johnson Controls, Inc.*, Justice Kennedy voted to concur in the majority opinion, which held that Title VII of the Civil Rights Act forbids sex-specific fetal-protection policies by an employer, that exclude a fertile female employee from certain jobs because of the employer's concern for the health of the fetus the woman might conceive. Justice Kennedy joined the concurring opinion in *Federal Election Commission v. Wisconsin Right to Life, Inc.*, which held that the electioneering communications provisions of a federal statute violated a pro-life organization's First Amendment right to broadcast political issue oriented advertisements shortly before primary and general elections.

(6) Dissenting opinions written. In *Stenberg v. Carhart*, Justice Kennedy wrote a dissenting opinion opposing the majority's decision to find Nebraska's statute banning partial-birth abortion unconstitutional. In *Hill v. Colorado* Justice Kennedy wrote a dissenting opinion in which he disagreed with the majority decision to uphold a Colorado statute that made it unlawful for any person within 100 feet of an abortion facility's entrance, to knowingly approach within 8 feet of another person, without that person's consent, in order to pass a leaflet, handbill, display a sign, engage in oral protest, education, or counseling with that person.

(7) Concurring and dissenting opinions written. Justice Kennedy wrote a concurring and dissenting opinion in *Hodgson v. Minnesota*, which upheld the constitutionality of Minnesota's requirement that a pregnant female minor could not obtain an abortion until at least 48 hours after both of her parents had been notified, except when (1) the attending physician certified that an immediate abortion was necessary to prevent the minor's death; (2) the minor declared that she was a victim of parental abuse or neglect; or (3) a court of competent jurisdiction ordered the abortion to proceed without notice upon proof that the minor was mature and capable of giving informed consent or that an abortion without notice to both parents would be in the minor's best interest. Justice Kennedy dissented from the Court's determination that the two-parent notification requirement was invalid, but concurred in the determination that the judicial bypass option cured the defect.

(8) Concurring and dissenting opinions voted with only. Justice Kennedy voted to concur and dissent in *Schenck v. Pro Choice Network of Western New York*, which held that a federal trial court's injunction provisions imposing fixed buffer zone limitations on abortion protesters were constitutional, but the provisions imposing floating buffer zone limitations violated the First Amendment. Justice Kennedy believed that the fixed buffer zone limitations were invalid also. In *Madsen v. Women's Health Clinic, Inc.*, Justice Kennedy voted to concur in part and dissent in part. The decision in *Madsen* upheld parts of an injunction that restricted noise by anti-abortionists at a clinic and imposed a 36 foot buffer zone around the clinic entrances and driveway. Justice Kennedy voted to dissent from that part of the decision. However, *Madsen* ruled that the Free Speech Clause was violated by a 36 foot buffer zone as applied to the private property to the north and west of the clinic, a restriction on the use of images observable by clinic patients, a 300 foot no approach zone around the clinic, and a 300 foot buffer zone around the residences, because these restrictions swept more broadly than necessary to accomplish the permissible goals of the injunction. Justice Kennedy voted to concur with the majority's decision finding some provisions in the injunction violated the Free Speech Clause.

Kentucky

(1) OVERVIEW

The state of Kentucky enacted its first criminal abortion statute on March 22, 1910. The statute underwent several amendments prior to the 1973 decision by the United States Supreme Court in *Roe v. Wade*, which legalized abortion in the nation. Kentucky has taken affirmative steps to respond to *Roe* and its progeny. The state has addressed numerous abortion issues by statute that include abortion guidelines and standards, informed consent, spousal notice, restrictions on abortion methods, abortion by minors, use of facilities and people, public funds for abortion, fetal experimentation, insurance policy, abortion facilities, fetal death report, and injury to pregnant woman.

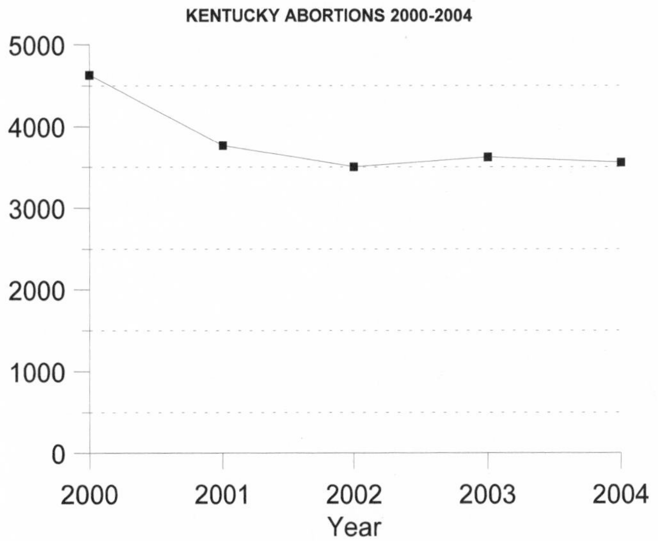

Source: **National Center for Health Statistics.**

Kentucky Abortion by Age Group 2000-2004

Age Group (yrs)

Year	<15	15–19	20–24	25–29	30–34	35–39	≥40	Unknown
2000	37	801	1,581	1,057	640	359	120	35
2001	28	613	1,296	862	500	323	116	27
2002	18	530	1,183	794	511	312	108	46
2003	35	573	1,145	795	566	345	124	38
2004	27	543	1,093	825	565	333	134	37
Total	145	3,060	6,298	4,333	2,782	1,672	602	183

Source: National Center for Health Statistics.

Kentucky Abortion by Weeks of Gestation 2000–2004

Year

Weeks of Gestation	2000	2001	2002	2003	2004	Total
≤8	2,281	1,985	1,965	2,126	2,036	10,393
9–10	989	757	595	548	573	3,462
11–12	586	492	363	367	396	2,204
13–15	361	263	282	266	273	1,445
16–20	330	201	215	227	212	1,185
≥21	74	62	64	50	54	304
Not known	9	4	18	28	13	72

Source: National Center for Health Statistics.

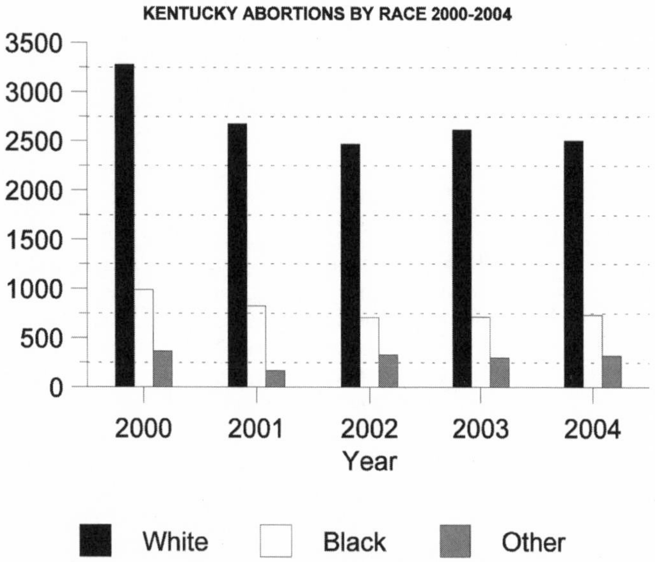

Source: National Center for Health Statistics.

(2) ABORTION GUIDELINES AND STANDARDS

Kentucky restricts an abortion to being performed by a physician, except during the first trimester. During the first trimester the state authorizes self-abortion (performed using medically prescribed abortifacients). The state also places limitations on the performance of an abortion, prior to fetal viability, that were found unconstitutional in *Eubanks v. Brown*, 604 F.Supp. 141 (W.D.Ky. 1984) and *Wolfe v. Schroering*, 388 F.Supp. 631 (W.D.Ky. 1974). Kentucky has enacted a statute that prohibits post-viability abortions, except to save the life of the woman or to prevent the woman from having a severe health problem if the child was carried to term. The state requires a birth certificate be issued for an aborted fetus that is born alive, but subsequently dies. The statutes addressing the matters are set out below.

Kentucky Code § 311.710. Legislative findings

The General Assembly of the Commonwealth of Kentucky hereby finds and declares:

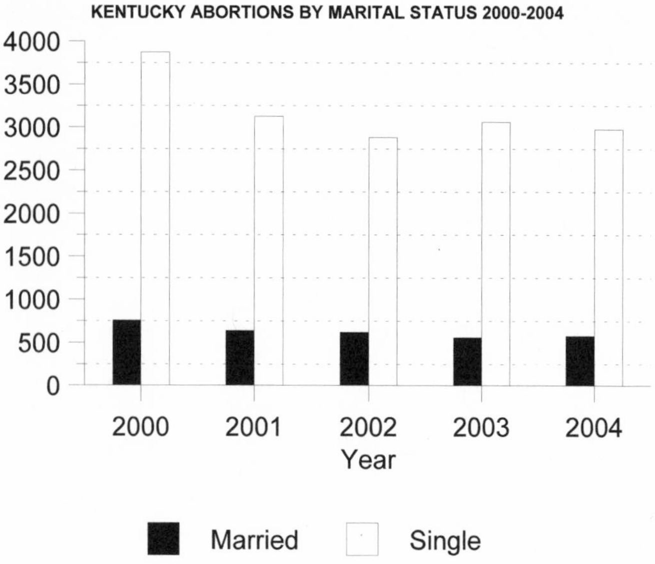

Source: National Center for Health Statistics.

Kentucky Prior Abortion by Female 2000–2004

Prior Abortion

Year	None	1	2	≥3	Not known
2000	2,636	1,193	482	319	0
2001	2,137	925	405	297	0
2002	1,916	898	403	285	0
2003	1,996	934	389	302	0
2004	1,958	897	405	296	1
Total	10,643	4,847	2,084	1,499	1

Source: National Center for Health Statistics.

(1) That it is in the interest of the people of the Commonwealth of Kentucky that every precaution be taken to insure the protection of every viable unborn child being aborted, and every precaution be taken to provide life-supportive procedures to insure the unborn child its continued life after its abortion; and

(2) That currently, in the Commonwealth, there is inadequate legislation to protect the life, health and welfare of pregnant women and unborn human life; and

(3) That it is in the interest of the people of the Commonwealth of Kentucky to maintain accurate statistical data to aid in providing proper maternal health regulations.

(4) It is the intention of the General Assembly of the Commonwealth of Kentucky to assure the integrity and autonomy of a woman's decision whether to submit to an abortion or to carry her child to term, to protect the rights and interests of a minor incompetent woman and her parents in the context of abortion, to further the Commonwealth's compelling interest in protecting the formal integrity of the marital relation and the procreative rights and interests of the husband, and to provide for the development of statistical data. The General Assembly finds as fact that the rights and interests furthered by this chapter are not secure in the context in which abortion is presently performed.

(5) It is the present intention of the General Assembly to protect the valid and compelling interests of the Commonwealth and its inhabitants without unduly burdening a woman's constitutional privacy rights as delineated by the courts. If, however, the United States Constitution is amended or relevant judicial decisions are reversed or modified, the declared policy of this Commonwealth to recognize and

to protect the lives of all human beings regardless of their degree of biological development shall be fully restored.

Kentucky Code § 311.720. Definitions

As used in KRS 311.710 to 311.820, and laws of the Commonwealth unless the context otherwise requires:

(1) "Abortion" shall mean the use of any means whatsoever to terminate the pregnancy of a woman known to be pregnant with intent to cause fetal death;

(2) "Hospital" shall mean those institutions licensed in the Commonwealth of Kentucky pursuant to the provisions of KRS Chapter 216;

(3) "Consent" as used in KRS 311.710 to 311.820 with reference to those who must give their consent shall mean an informed consent expressed by a written agreement to submit to an abortion on a written form of consent to be promulgated by the secretary for health and family services;

(4) "Cabinet" shall mean the Cabinet for Health and Family Services of the Commonwealth of Kentucky;

(5) "Fetus" shall mean a human being from fertilization until birth;

(6) "Human being" shall mean any member of the species homo sapiens from fertilization until death;

(7) "Partial-birth abortion" shall mean an abortion in which the physician performing the abortion partially vaginally delivers a living fetus before killing the fetus and completing the delivery;

(8) "Vaginally delivers a living fetus before killing the fetus" shall mean deliberately and intentionally delivers into the vagina a living fetus, or a substantial portion thereof, for the purpose of performing a procedure the physician knows will kill the fetus, and kills the fetus;

(9) "Physician" shall mean any person licensed to practice medicine in the Commonwealth or osteopathy pursuant to the provisions of this chapter;

(10) "Viability" shall mean that stage of human development when the life of the unborn child may be continued by natural or life-supportive systems outside the womb of the mother;

(11) "Accepted medical procedures" shall mean procedures of the type performed in the manner and in a facility with equipment sufficient to meet the standards of medical care which physicians engaged in the same or similar lines of work, would ordinarily exercise and devote to the benefit of their patients;

(12) "Medical emergency" means any condition which, on the basis of the physician's good faith clinical judgment, so complicates the medical condition of a pregnant female as to necessitate the immediate abortion of her pregnancy to avert her death or for which a delay will create serious risk of substantial and irreversible impairment of a major bodily function;

(13) "Medical necessity" means a medical condition of a pregnant woman that, in the reasonable judgment of the physician who is attending the woman, so complicates the pregnancy that it necessitates the immediate performance or inducement of an abortion; and

(14) "Probable gestational age of the embryo or fetus" means the gestational age that, in the judgment of a physician, is, with reasonable probability, the gestational age of the embryo or fetus at the time that the abortion is planned to be performed.

Kentucky Code § 311.723. Abortion guidelines

(1) No abortion shall be performed except by a physician after either:

(a) He determines that, in his best clinical judgment, the abortion is necessary; or

(b) He receives what he reasonably believes to be a written statement signed by another physician, hereinafter called the "referring physician," certifying that in the referring physician's best clinical judgment the abortion is necessary, and, in addition, he receives a copy of the report form required by KRS 213.055.

(2) No abortion shall be performed except in compliance with regulations which the cabinet shall issue to assure that:

(a) Before the abortion is performed, the pregnant woman shall have a private medical consultation either with the physician who is to perform the abortion or with the referring physician in a place, at a time and of a duration reasonably sufficient to enable the physician to determine whether, based upon his best clinical judgment, the abortion is necessary;

(b) The physician who is to perform the abortion or the referring physician will describe the basis for his best clinical judgment that the abortion is necessary on a form prescribed by the cabinet as required by KRS 213.055; and

(c) Paragraph (a) of this subsection shall not apply when, in the medical judgment of the attending physician based on the particular facts of the case before him, there exists a medical emergency. In such a case, the physician shall describe the basis of his medical judgment that an emergency exists on a form prescribed by the cabinet as required by KRS 213.055.

(3) Notwithstanding any statute to the contrary, nothing in this chapter shall be construed as prohibiting a physician from prescribing or a woman from using birth control methods or devices, including, but not limited to, intrauterine devices, oral contraceptives, or any other birth control method or device.

Kentucky Code § 311.750. Abortion by physician

Subject to the provisions of KRS 311.760(1), no person other than a licensed physician shall perform an abortion.

Kentucky Code § 311.760. Minimum standards

An abortion may be performed in this state only under the following circumstances:

(1) During the first trimester of pregnancy by a woman upon herself upon the advice of a licensed physician or by a licensed physician.

(2) After the first trimester of pregnancy, except in cases of emergency to protect the life or health of the pregnant woman, where an abortion is permitted under other provisions of KRS 311.710 to 311.820, by a duly licensed physician in a hospital duly licensed by the Kentucky Health Facilities and Health Services Certificate of Need and Licensure Board.

Kentucky Code § 311.780.
Prohibition of abortion after viability

No abortion shall be performed or prescribed knowingly after the unborn child may reasonably be expected to have reached viability, except when necessary to preserve the life or health of the woman. In those instances where an abortion is performed under this section, the person performing the abortion shall take all reasonable steps in keeping with reasonable medical practices to preserve the life and health of the child, including but not limited to KRS 311.760(2).

Kentucky Code § 311.790.
Birth and death certificates for attempted abortion

Any child which is live born after an induced termination of pregnancy shall be fully recognized as a human person under the law and a birth certificate shall be issued certifying the birth of the live-born person even though the person may die thereafter. In the event death does ensue, a death certificate shall be issued. Both the birth and death certificates shall be issued as required by KRS 213.046, 213.051, and 213.076.

Kentucky Code § 311.810. Refusal to submit to abortion

No woman may be denied governmental assistance or be otherwise discriminated against or otherwise subjected to coercion in any way for accepting or refusing to accept or submit to an abortion, which she may do or not do for any reason without explanation.

Kentucky Code § 311.820. Abortion referral agency

(1) As used in this section, an abortion referral or counseling agency is any person, group, or organization, whether funded publicly or privately, that provides advice or help to persons in obtaining abortions.

(2) No abortion referral or counseling agency shall charge or accept any fee, kickback, or compensation of any nature from a physician, hospital, clinic or other medical facility for referring a person thereto for an abortion.

Kentucky Code § 311.830. Severability

If any section of this chapter or any part of any section shall be invalid or unconstitutional, the declaration of such invalidity shall not affect the validity of the remaining portions thereof.

Kentucky Code § 311.990 (10). Abortion guidelines penalty

(a) Any person who intentionally or knowingly performs an abortion contrary to the requirements of KRS 311.723(1) shall be guilty of a Class D felony; and

(b) Any person who intentionally, knowingly, or recklessly violates the requirements of KRS 311.723(2) shall be guilty of a Class A misdemeanor.

Kentucky Code § 311.990 (16). Minimum standards penalty

Any person who violates KRS 311.760(2) shall be guilty of a Class D felony.

Kentucky Code § 311.990 (17). Post-viability penalty

Any person who violates KRS ... 311.780 shall be guilty of a Class D felony.

Kentucky Code § 311.990 (19). Refusal to submit penalty

Any person who violates KRS 311.810 shall be guilty of a Class A misdemeanor.

Kentucky Code § 311.990 (23). Abortion referral penalty

Any person who violates the provisions of KRS 311.820 shall be guilty of a Class A misdemeanor.

(3) INFORMED CONSENT

Prior to an abortion Kentucky requires that a woman be fully informed of the procedure to be used, the risks involved and alternatives to abortion. An abortion may not take place until 24 hours after a woman has given her written consent to an abortion, except in the case of a medical emergency. The statute addressing the matters is set out below.

Kentucky Code § 311.725. Consent and waiting period

(1) No abortion shall be performed or induced except with the voluntary and informed written consent of the woman upon whom the abortion is to be performed or induced. Except in the case of a medical emergency, consent to an abortion is voluntary and informed if and only if:

(a) At least twenty-four (24) hours prior to the abortion, a physician, licensed nurse, physician assistant, or social worker to whom the responsibility has been delegated by the physician has verbally informed the woman of all of the following:

1. The nature and purpose of the particular abortion procedure or treatment to be performed and of those medical risks and alternatives to the procedure or treatment that a reasonable patient would consider material to the decision of whether or not to undergo the abortion;

2. The probable gestational age of the embryo or fetus at the time the abortion is to be performed; and

3. The medical risks associated with the pregnant woman carrying her pregnancy to term;

(b) At least twenty-four (24) hours prior to the abortion, in an individual, private setting, a physician, licensed nurse, physician assistant, or social worker to whom the responsibility has been delegated by the physician has informed the pregnant woman that:

1. The cabinet publishes the printed materials described in paragraphs (a) and (b) of subsection (2) of this section and that she has a right to review the printed materials and that copies will be provided to her by the physician, licensed nurse, physician assistant, or social worker free of charge if she chooses to review the printed materials;

2. Medical assistance benefits may be available for prenatal care, childbirth, and neonatal care, and that more detailed information on the availability of such assistance is contained in the printed materials published by the cabinet; and

3. The father of the fetus is liable to assist in the support of her child, even in instances where he has offered to pay for the abortion;

(c) At least twenty-four (24) hours prior to the abortion, a copy of the printed materials has been provided to the pregnant woman if she chooses to view these materials;

(d) The pregnant woman certifies in writing, prior to the performance or inducement of the abortion:

1. That she has received the information required to be provided under paragraphs (a), (b), and (c) of this subsection; and

2. That she consents to the particular abortion voluntarily and knowingly, and she is not under the influence of any drug of abuse or alcohol; and

(e) Prior to the performance or inducement of the abortion, the physician who is scheduled to perform or induce the abortion or the physician's agent receives a copy of the pregnant woman's signed statement, on a form which may be provided by the physician, on which she consents to the abortion and that includes the certification required by paragraph (d) of this subsection.

(2) By January 1, 1999, the cabinet shall cause to be published in English in a typeface not less than 12 point type the following materials:

(a) Materials that inform the pregnant woman about public and private agencies and services that are available to assist her through her pregnancy, upon childbirth, and while her child is dependent, including, but not limited to, adoption agencies. The materials shall include a comprehensive list of the available agencies and a description of the services offered by the agencies and the telephone numbers and addresses of the agencies, and inform the pregnant woman about available medical assistance benefits for prenatal care, childbirth, and neonatal care and about the support obligations of the father of a child who is born alive. The cabinet shall ensure that the materials are comprehensive and do not directly or indirectly promote, exclude, or discourage the use of any agency or service described in this section; and

(b) Materials that inform the pregnant woman of the probable anatomical and physiological characteristics of the zygote, blastocyte, embryo, or fetus at two (2) week gestational increments for the first sixteen (16) weeks of her pregnancy and at four (4) week gestational increments from the seventeenth week of her pregnancy to full term, including any relevant information regarding the time at which the fetus possibly would be viable. The materials shall use language that is understandable by the average person who is not medically trained, shall be objective and nonjudgmental, and shall include only accurate scientific information about the zygote, blastocyte, embryo, or fetus at the various gestational increments. The materials shall include, for each of the two (2) of four (4) week increments specified in this paragraph, a pictorial or photographic depiction of the zygote, blastocyte, embryo, or fetus. The materials shall also include, in a conspicuous manner, a scale or other explanation that is understandable by the average person and that can be used to determine the actual size of the zygote, blastocyte, embryo, or fetus at a particular gestational increment as contrasted with the depicted size of the zygote, blastocyte, embryo, or fetus at that gestational increment.

(3) Upon submission of a request to the cabinet by any person, hospital, physician, or medical facility for one (1) or more copies of the materials published in accordance with subsection (2) of this section, the cabinet shall make the requested number of copies of the materials available to the person, hospital, physician, or medical facility that requested the copies.

(4) If a medical emergency or medical necessity compels the performance or inducement of an abortion, the physician who will perform or induce the abortion, prior to its performance or inducement if possible, shall inform the pregnant woman of the medical indications supporting the physician's judgment that an immediate abortion is necessary. Any physician who performs or induces an abortion without the prior satisfaction of the conditions specified in subsection (1) of this section because of a medical emergency or medical necessity shall enter the reasons for the conclusion that a medical emergency exists in the medical record of the pregnant woman.

(5) If the conditions specified in subsection (1) of this section are satisfied, consent to an abortion shall be presumed to be valid and effective.

(6) The failure of a physician to satisfy the conditions of subsection (1) of this section prior to performing or inducing an abortion upon a pregnant woman may be the basis of disciplinary action pursuant to KRS 311.595.

(7) The cabinet shall charge a fee for each copy of the materials distributed in accordance with subsections (1) and (3) of this section. The fee shall be sufficient to cover the cost of the administration of the materials published in accordance with subsection (2) of this section, including the cost of preparation and distribution of materials.

(4) SPOUSAL NOTICE

Kentucky requires, when applicable, that the spouse of a woman be notified by the physician prior to performing an abortion. This statute is invalid, however, under decisions by the United States Supreme Court. In *Planned Parenthood of Southeastern Pennsylvania v. Casey* the Supreme Court invalidated a provision in Pennsylvania's abortion statute that required a married woman inform her spouse of her decision to have an abortion, before she would be allowed to have one. The Supreme Court invalidated a provision in Missouri's statute, in *Planned Parenthood of Missouri v. Danforth*, that required a woman seek the consent of a spouse before having an abortion. In addition, a federal district court in *Eubanks v. Brown*, 604 F.Supp. 141 (W.D.Ky. 1984) expressly ruled that Kentucky's spousal notice statute was infirm. The statutes addressing the matter are set out below.

Kentucky Code § 311.735. Spousal notice

(1) Prior to performing an abortion, the physician who is to perform the abortion or his agent shall notify, if reasonably possible, the spouse of the woman upon whom the abortion is to be performed. If it is not reasonably possible to notify the spouse prior to the abortion, the physician or his agent shall do so, if reasonably possible, within thirty (30) days of the abortion.

(2)(a) The requirements of this section shall not apply if, before the abortion is performed, either party to a marriage has filed a petition for dissolution of marriage which has been served on the respondent;

(b) The requirements of this section shall not apply when, in the medical judgment of the attending physician based on the particular facts of the case before him, there exists a medical emergency. In such a case, the physician shall describe the basis of his medical judgment that such an emergency exists on a form prescribed by the cabinet as required by KRS 213.055, and the physician or his agent shall notify, if reasonably possible, the spouse of the woman upon whom the abortion was performed, within thirty (30) days of the abortion.

(3) Failure to notify a spouse as required by this section is prima facie evidence of interference with family relations in appropriate civil actions. The law of this Commonwealth shall not be construed to preclude the award of punitive damages or damages for emotional distress, even if unaccompanied by physical complications in any civil action brought pursuant to violations of this section. Nothing in this section shall be construed to limit the common law rights of a husband.

Kentucky Code § 311.990 (14). Penalty

Any person who performs an abortion upon a married woman either with knowledge or in reckless disregard of whether KRS 311.735 applies to her and who intentionally, knowingly, or recklessly fails to conform to the requirements of KRS 311.735 shall be guilty of a Class D felony.

(5) RESTRICTIONS ON ABORTION METHODS

Kentucky prohibits partial-birth abortion and abortions performed using the saline method. The ban on partial-birth abortion was held invalid in *Eubanks v. Stengel*, 224 F.3d 576 (6th Cir. 2000), and the saline ban was invalidated in *Wolfe v. Schroering*, 541 F.2d 523 (6th Cir. 1976). The statutes addressing the matters are set out below.

Kentucky Code § 311.765. Partial-birth abortion

No physician shall perform a partial-birth abortion.

Kentucky Code § 311.770. Saline method

After the first trimester no person shall perform the form of abortion known as the saline method of abortion.

Kentucky Code § 311.990 (11). Partial-birth abortion penalty

(a) 1. Any physician who performs a partial-birth abortion in violation of KRS 311.765 shall be guilty of a Class D felony. However, a physician shall not be guilty of the criminal offense if the partial-birth abortion was necessary to save the life of the mother whose life was endangered by a physical disorder, illness, or injury.

2. A physician may seek a hearing before the State Board of Medical Licensure on whether the physician's conduct was necessary to save the life of the mother whose life was endangered by a physical disorder, illness, or injury. The board's findings, decided by majority vote of a quorum, shall be admissible at the trial of the physician. The board shall promulgate administrative regulations to carry out the provisions of this subparagraph.

3. Upon a motion of the physician, the court shall delay the beginning of the trial for not more than thirty (30) days to permit the hearing, referred to in subparagraph 2. of this paragraph, to occur.

(b) Any person other than a physician who performs a partial-birth abortion shall not be prosecuted under this subsection but shall be prosecuted under provisions of law which prohibit any person other than a physician from performing any abortion.

(c) No penalty shall be assessed against the woman upon whom the partial-birth abortion is performed or attempted to be performed.

Kentucky Code § 311.990 (17). Saline abortion penalty

Any person who violates KRS 311.770 ... shall be guilty of a Class D felony.

(6) ABORTION BY MINORS

Under the laws of Kentucky no physician may perform an abortion upon an unemancipated minor unless he/she first obtains the written consent of either parent or the legal guardian of the minor. In compliance with federal constitutional law, Kentucky has provided a judicial waiver procedure for an unemancipated minor to obtain an abortion without parental or guardian consent. A minor may petition a trial court for a waiver of the consent requirement. A minor has a right to an attorney at the proceeding and if she cannot afford one, the court must appoint her an attorney. If a minor chooses, she may represent herself. The required parental or guardian consent may be waived if the court finds either (1) that the minor is mature and well-informed enough to make the abortion decision on her own, or (2) that performance of the abortion would be in the best interest of the minor.

An expedited appeal is available to any minor to whom the court denies a waiver of consent. The statutes addressing the matters are set out below.

Kentucky Code § 311.732. Consent and judicial bypass

(1) For purposes of this section the following definitions shall apply:

(a) "Minor" means any person under the age of eighteen (18);

(b) "Emancipated minor" means any minor who is or has been married or has by court order or otherwise been freed from the care, custody, and control of her parents; and

(c) "Abortion" means the use of any instrument, medicine, drug, or any other substance or device with intent to terminate the pregnancy of a woman known to be pregnant with intent other than to increase the probability of a live birth, to preserve the life or health of the child after live birth, or to remove a dead fetus.

(2) No person shall perform an abortion upon a minor unless:

(a) The attending physician or his agent secured the informed written consent of the minor and one (1) parent or legal guardian;

(b) The minor is emancipated and the attending physician or his agent has received the informed written consent of the minor; or

(c) The minor elects to petition any Circuit or District Court of the Commonwealth pursuant to subsection (3) of this section and obtain an order pursuant to subsection (4) of this section granting consent to the abortion and the attending physician or his agent has received the informed written consent of the minor.

(3) Every minor shall have the right to petition any Circuit or District Court of the Commonwealth for an order granting the right to self-consent to an abortion pursuant to the following procedures:

(a) The minor or her next friend may prepare and file a petition setting forth the request of the minor for an order of consent to an abortion;

(b) The court shall insure that the minor prepares or her next friend is given assistance in preparing and filing the petition and shall insure that the minor's identity is kept anonymous;

(c) The minor may participate in proceedings in the court on her own behalf or through her next friend and the court shall appoint a guardian ad litem for her. The court shall advise her that she has a right to court-appointed counsel and shall provide her with such counsel upon her request;

(d) All proceedings under this section shall be anonymous and shall be given preference over other matters to insure that the court may reach a decision promptly, but in no case shall the court fail to rule within seventy-two (72) hours of the time of application, provided that the seventy-two (72) hour limitation may be extended at the request of the minor; and

(e) The court shall hold a hearing on the merits of the petition before reaching a decision. The court shall hear evidence at the hearing relating to the emotional development, maturity, intellect, and understanding of the minor; the nature, possible consequences, and alternatives to the abortion; and any other evidence that the court may find useful in determining whether the minor should be granted majority rights for the purpose of consenting to the abortion or whether the abortion is in the best interest of the minor.

(4) The court shall enter a written order, making specific factual findings and legal conclusions supporting its decision as follows:

(a) Granting the petition for an abortion if the court finds that the minor is mature and well informed enough to make the abortion decision on her own;

(b) Granting consent to the abortion if the court finds that the performance of the abortion would be in the minor's best interest; or

(c) Deny the petition, if the court finds that the minor is immature and that performance of the abortion would not be in the minor's best interest.

(5) Any minor shall have the right of anonymous and expedited appeal to the Court of Appeals, and that court shall give precedence over other pending matters.

(6) No fees shall be required of any minor who declares she has no sufficient funds to pursue the procedures provided by this section.

(7) The Supreme Court is respectfully requested to promulgate any rules and regulations it feels are necessary to ensure that proceedings under this section are handled in an expeditious and anonymous manner.

(8) The requirements of subsections (2), (3), and (4) of this section shall not apply when, in the best medical judgment of the physician based on the facts of the case before him, a medical emergency exists that so complicates the pregnancy as to require an immediate abortion. A physician who does not comply with subsection (2), (3), or (4) of this section due to the utilization of this exception shall certify in writing the medical indications upon which his judgment was based.

(9) A report indicating the basis for any medical judgment that warrants failure to obtain consent pursuant to this section shall be filed with the Cabinet for Health and Family Services on a form supplied by the cabinet. This report shall be confidential.

(10) Failure to obtain consent pursuant to the requirements of this section is prima facie evidence of failure to obtain informed consent and of interference with family relations in appropriate civil actions. The law of this state shall not be construed to preclude the award of exemplary damages in any appropriate civil action relevant to violations of this section. Nothing in this section shall be construed to limit the common-law rights of parents.

Kentucky Code § 311.990 (12) & (13). Penalty

(12) Any person who intentionally performs an abortion with knowledge that, or with reckless disregard as to whether, the person upon whom the abortion is to be performed is an unemancipated minor, and who intentionally or knowingly fails to conform to any requirement of KRS 311.732 is guilty of a Class A misdemeanor.

(13) Any person who negligently releases information or documents which are confidential under KRS 311.732 is guilty of a Class B misdemeanor.

(7) USE OF FACILITIES AND PEOPLE

Kentucky prohibits public hospitals from performing abortions, except to save the life of a woman. Under the laws of Kentucky private hospitals are not required to allow abortions at their facilities. The employees and physicians at hospitals that do allow abortions are permitted to refuse to take part in abortions. It was held in *Wolfe v. Schroering*, 541 F.2d 523 (6th Cir. 1976) that public hospitals may not refuse to perform abortions for ethical, moral, religious, or professional reasons. The statutes addressing the matters are set out below.

Kentucky Code § 311.800. Right to refuse to participate in abortion

(1) No publicly owned hospital or other publicly owned health care facility shall perform or permit the performance of abortions, except to save the life of the pregnant woman.

(2) In the event that a publicly owned hospital or publicly owned health facility is performing or about to perform an abortion in violation of subsection (1) of this section, and law enforcement authorities in the county have failed or refused to take action to stop such a practice, any resident of the county in which the hospital or health facility is located, may apply to the Circuit Court of that county for an injunction or other court process to require compliance with subsection (1) of this section.

(3) No private hospital or private health care facility shall be required to, or held liable for refusal to, perform or permit the performance of abortion contrary to its stated ethical policy.

(4) No physician, nurse staff member or employee of a public or private hospital or employee of a public or private health care facility, who

shall state in writing to such hospital or health care facility his objection to performing, participating in, or cooperating in, abortion on moral, religious or professional grounds, be required to, or held liable for refusal to, perform, participate in, or cooperate in such abortion.

(5) It shall be an unlawful discriminatory practice for the following:

(a) Any person to impose penalties or take disciplinary action against, or to deny or limit public funds, licenses, certifications, degrees, or other approvals or documents of qualification to, any hospital or other health care facility due to the refusal of such hospital or health care facility to perform or permit to be performed, participate in, or cooperate in, abortion by reason of objection thereto on moral, religious or professional grounds, or because of any statement or other manifestation of attitude by such hospital or health care facility with respect to abortion; or,

(b) Any person to impose penalties or take disciplinary action against, or to deny or limit public funds, licenses, certifications, degrees, or other approvals or documents of qualification to any physician, nurse or staff member or employee of any hospital or health care facility, due to the willingness or refusal of such physician, nurse or staff member or employee to perform or participate in abortion by reason of objection thereto on moral, religious or professional grounds, or because of any statement or other manifestation of attitude by such physician, nurse or staff member or employee with respect to abortion; or,

(c) Any public or private agency, institution or person, including a medical, nursing or other school, to deny admission to, impose any burdens in terms of conditions of employment upon, or otherwise discriminate against any applicant for admission thereto or any physician, nurse, staff member, student or employee thereof, on account of the willingness or refusal of such applicant, physician, nurse, staff member, student or employee to perform or participate in abortion or sterilization by reason of objection thereto on moral, religious or professional grounds, or because of any statement or other manifestation of attitude by such person with respect to abortion or sterilization if that health care facility is not operated exclusively for the purposes of performing abortions or sterilizations.

Kentucky Code § 311.990 (21). Penalty

Any administrator, officer, or employee of a publicly owned hospital or publicly owned health care facility who performs or permits the performance of abortions in violation of KRS 311.800(1) shall be guilty of a Class A misdemeanor.

(8) PUBLIC FUNDS FOR ABORTION

Kentucky prohibits the use of public funds to pay for abortions, except to save the life of the woman. The statutes addressing the issue are set out below.

Kentucky Code § 311.715. Public funds

No public funds shall be used for the purpose of obtaining an abortion or paying for the performance of an abortion. Public medical facilities may be used for the purpose of conducting research into or the performance of in-vitro fertilization as long as such procedures do not result in the intentional destruction of a human embryo. For purposes of this section, "public funds" means any money of the Commonwealth of Kentucky, any department, agency or instrumentality thereof, or any money of any county, city, agency or instrumentality thereof or any money of any other political subdivision of the Commonwealth, agency or instrumentality thereof. Nothing in this section shall be deemed to deprive a woman of all appropriate medical care necessary to prevent her physical death. Nothing in this section shall be construed to allow public funds to pay for in-vitro fertilization procedures performed on any individual patient.

Kentucky Code § 205.010(3). Public assistance

"Public assistance" means money grants, assistance in kind, or services to or for the benefit of needy aged, needy blind, needy permanently and totally disabled persons, needy children, or persons with whom a needy child lives or a family containing a combination of these categories, except that the term shall not be construed to permit the granting of financial aid where the purpose of such aid is to obtain an abortion. For purposes of this section and KRS 205.560, "abortion" means an act, procedure, device, or prescription administered or prescribed for a pregnant woman by any person, including the pregnant woman herself, producing premature expulsion of the fetus. Abortion does not include an induced premature birth intended to produce a live viable child.

Kentucky Code § 205.560 (1). State Medicaid program

The scope of medical care for which the Cabinet for Health and Family Services undertakes to pay shall be designated and limited by regulations promulgated by the cabinet, pursuant to the provisions in this section. Within the limitations of any appropriation therefor, the provision of complete upper and lower dentures to recipients of Medical Assistance Program benefits who have their teeth removed by a dentist resulting in the total absence of teeth shall be a mandatory class in the scope of medical care. Payment to a dentist of any Medical Assistance Program benefits for complete upper and lower dentures shall only be provided on the condition of a preauthorized agreement between an authorized representative of the Medical Assistance Program and the dentist prior to the removal of the teeth. The selection of another class or other classes of medical care shall be recommended by the council to the secretary for health and family services after taking into consideration, among other things, the amount of federal and state funds available, the most essential needs of recipients, and the meeting of such need on a basis insuring the greatest amount of medical care as defined in KRS 205.510 consonant with the funds available, including but not limited to the following categories, except where the aid is for the purpose of obtaining an abortion.

(9) FETAL EXPERIMENTATION

Kentucky has provided a criminal ban on fetal experiments or trafficking in human fetuses. The statute addressing the matter is set out below.

Kentucky Code § 436.026. Fetal experimentation banned

Any person who shall sell, transfer, distribute, or give away any live or viable aborted child or permits such child to be used for any form of experimentation shall be guilty of a Class B felony. Nothing contained in this section shall be construed as prohibiting adoption or foster care proceedings pursuant to the provisions of the laws of the Commonwealth.

(10) INSURANCE POLICY

Kentucky prohibits issuance of insurance policies for elective abortions unless a specific premium is paid for such coverage. The statute addressing the matter is set out below.

Kentucky Code § 304.5-160.
Health insurance for elective abortions

(1) No health insurance contracts, plans or policies delivered or issued for delivery in the state shall provide coverage for elective abortions except by an optional rider for which there must be paid an additional premium. For purposes of this section, an "elective abortion" means an abortion for any reason other than to preserve the life of the female upon whom the abortion is performed.

(2) This section shall be applicable to all contracts, plans or policies of:

(a) All health insurers subject to Subtitle 17 of KRS Chapter 304; and

(b) All group and blanket health insurers subject to Subtitle 18 of KRS Chapter 304; and

(c) All nonprofit hospital, medical, surgical, dental and health service corporations subject to Subtitle 32 of KRS Chapter 304; and

(d) All health maintenance organizations subject to Subtitle 38 of KRS Chapter 304; and

(e) Any provision of medical, hospital, surgical and funeral benefits and of coverage against accidental death or injury, when such benefits or coverage are incidental to or part of other insurance described in KRS 304.5-070(1); and

(f) All employers who provide health insurance for employees on a self-insured basis.

(11) ABORTION FACILITIES

Kentucky has provided by statute for the creation of regulations for abortion facilities. The state requires abortion facilities make written agreements with other providers in case of a complication occurring with an abortion. The statutes addressing the matter are set out below.

Kentucky Code § 216B.0431. Procedures for abortion facilities

(1) The [Cabinet for Health and Family Services] shall, no later than September 1, 1998, and subject to the provisions of KRS Chapter 13A, promulgate administrative regulations providing licensure standards and procedures for abortion facilities. The cabinet shall begin enforcing the administrative regulations on March 1, 1999.

(2) Any person operating an abortion facility for which a license is required under this chapter may apply for the license prior to March 1, 1999.

(3) Each abortion facility shall report monthly to the cabinet the information required by the cabinet by administrative regulation for each abortion performed in the facility.

(4) Licensed acute-care hospitals shall be exempt from the provisions of this section, except for any reporting requirements issued by the cabinet.

Kentucky Code § 216B.0435.
Emergency agreements between facilities

(1) Each abortion facility shall enter into a written agreement with a licensed acute-care hospital capable of treating patients with unforeseen complications related to an abortion facility procedure by which agreement the hospital agrees to accept and treat these patients.

(2) If unforeseen complications arise prior to or during an abortion facility procedure, the patient shall be transferred to the licensed acute-care hospital with which the abortion facility has a written agreement as provided under subsection (1) of this section or to the hospital selected by the patient, if the patient so chooses.

(3) Each abortion facility shall enter into a written agreement with a licensed local ambulance service for the transport of any emergency patient within the scope of subsection (1) of this section to the licensed acute-care hospital.

(4) The written agreements of an abortion facility with an acute-care hospital and with a local ambulance service shall be filed by the abortion facility with the [Cabinet for Health and Family Services].

Kentucky Code § 216B.042.
Authority for administrative regulations

(1) The [Cabinet for Health and Family Services] shall:

(a) Establish by promulgation of administrative regulation under KRS Chapter 13A reasonable application fees for licenses and promulgate other administrative regulations necessary for the proper administration of the licensure function;

(b) Issue, deny, revoke, modify, or suspend licenses or provisional licenses in accordance with the provisions of this chapter;

(c) Establish licensure standards and procedures to ensure safe, adequate, and efficient abortion facilities, health facilities and health services. These regulations, under KRS Chapter 13A, shall include, but need not be limited to:

1. Patient care standards and safety standards, minimum operating standards, minimum standards for training, required licenses for medical staff personnel, and minimum standards for maintaining patient records;

2. Licensure application and renewal procedures; and

3. Classification of health facilities and health services according to type, size, range of services, and level of care; and

(d) Compile in a single document, maintain, and make available to abortion facilities and the public during regular business hours all licensure standards and procedures promulgated under KRS Chapter 13A related to abortion facilities.

(2) The cabinet may authorize its agents or representatives to enter upon the premises of any health care facility for the purpose of inspection and under the conditions set forth in administrative regulations promulgated under KRS Chapter 13A by the cabinet.

(3) The cabinet may revoke licenses or certificates of need for specific health facilities or health services or recommend the initiation of disciplinary proceedings for health care providers on the basis of the knowing violation of any provisions of this chapter.

Kentucky Code § 15.241. Violations by abortion facilities

The Attorney General, upon certification by the secretary of the Cabinet for Health and Family Services, shall seek injunctive relief in a court of proper jurisdiction to prevent violations of the provisions of KRS Chapter 216B regarding abortion facilities or the administrative regulations promulgated in furtherance thereof in cases where other administrative penalties and legal sanctions imposed have failed to prevent or cause a discontinuance of the violation.

Kentucky Code § 216B.990. Penalties

(1) Any person who, in willful violation of this chapter, operates a health facility or abortion facility without first obtaining a license or continues to operate a health facility or abortion facility after a final decision suspending or revoking a license shall be fined not less than five hundred dollars ($500) nor more than ten thousand dollars ($10,000) for each violation.

(2) Any person who, in willful violation of this chapter, acquires major medical equipment, establishes a health facility, or obligates a capital expenditure without first obtaining a certificate of need, or after the applicable certificate of need has been withdrawn, shall be fined one percent (1%) of the capital expenditure involved but not less than five hundred dollars ($500) for each violation.

(3) Any hospital acting by or through its agents or employees which violates any provision of KRS 216B.400 shall be punished by a fine of not less than one hundred dollars ($100) nor more than five hundred dollars ($500).

(4) Any hospital acting by or through its agents or employees which violates any provision of KRS 311.241 to 311.245 shall be punished by a fine of not less than one hundred dollars ($100) nor more than five hundred dollars ($500).

(5) Any hospital violating the provisions of KRS 311.241 may be denied a license to operate under the provisions of this chapter.

(6) Any health facility which willfully violates KRS 216B.250 shall be fined one hundred dollars ($100) per day for failure to post required notices and one hundred dollars ($100) per instance for willfully failing to provide an itemized statement within the required time frames.

(7) In addition to the civil penalties established under KRS 216B.306(1) and (4), any person who advertises, solicits boarders, or operates a boarding home without first obtaining a registration as required by KRS 216B.305 and any person who aids or abets the operation of a boarding home that is not registered shall be imprisoned for no more than twelve (12) months.

(8) Any person or entity establishing, managing, or operating an abortion facility or conducting the business of an abortion facility which otherwise violates any provision of this chapter or any administrative regulation promulgated thereunder regarding abortion facilities shall be subject to revocation or suspension of the license of the abortion facility. In addition, any violation of any provision of this chapter regarding abor-

tion facilities or any administrative regulation related thereto by intent, fraud, deceit, unlawful design, willful and deliberate misrepresentation, or by careless, negligent, or incautious disregard for the statute or administrative regulation, either by persons acting individually or in concert with others, shall constitute a violation and shall be punishable by a fine not to exceed one thousand dollars ($1,000) for each offense. Each day of continuing violation shall be considered a separate offense. The venue for prosecution of the violation shall be in any county of the state in which the violation, or any portion thereof, occurred.

(9) Any hospital acting by or through its agents or employees that violates any provision of KRS 216B.150 shall be punished by a fine of not less than one hundred dollars ($100) nor more than five hundred dollars ($500) for each violation.

(12) FETAL DEATH REPORT

Kentucky requires that all induced fetal deaths be reported to the appropriate authorities. The statutes addressing the matter are set out below.

Kentucky Code § 213.101. Induced abortion reported

Each induced termination of pregnancy which occurs in the Commonwealth, regardless of the length of gestation, shall be reported to the Vital Statistics Branch by the person in charge of the institution within fifteen (15) days after the end of the month in which the termination occurred. If the induced termination of pregnancy was performed outside an institution, the attending physician shall prepare and file the report within fifteen (15) days after the end of the month in which the termination occurred. The report shall collect no information which will identify the physician, woman, or man involved. The name of the person completing the report and the reporting institution shall not be subject to disclosure under KRS 61.870 to 61.884.

Kentucky Code § 213.106 Use of reports

The reports required under KRS 213.101 are statistical reports to be used only for medical and health purposes and shall not be incorporated into the permanent official records of the system of vital statistics.

(13) INJURY TO PREGNANT WOMAN

Kentucky has enacted fetal homicide statutes for injury to a pregnant woman that causes the death of a fetus. The statutes are set out below.

Kentucky Code § 507A.010. Definitions

(1) As used in this chapter:

(a) "Abortion" has the same meaning as in KRS 311.720;

(b) "Health care provider" has the same meaning as in KRS 304.17A-005; and

(c) "Unborn child" means a member of the species homo sapiens in utero from conception onward, without regard to age, health, or condition of dependency.

(2) In a prosecution for the death of an unborn child, nothing in this chapter shall apply to acts performed by or at the direction of a health care provider that cause the death of an unborn child if those acts were committed:

(a) During any abortion for which the consent of the pregnant woman has been obtained or for which the consent is implied by law in a medical emergency; or

(b) As part of or incident to diagnostic testing or therapeutic medical or fertility treatment, provided that the acts were performed with that degree of care and skill which an ordinarily careful, skilled, and prudent health care provider or a person acting under the provider's direction would exercise under the same or similar circumstances.

(3) Nothing in this chapter shall apply to any acts of a pregnant woman that caused the death of her unborn child.

Kentucky Code § 507A.020. Fetal homicide in the first degree

(1) A person is guilty of fetal homicide in the first degree when:

(a) With intent to cause the death of an unborn child or with the intent necessary to commit an offense under KRS 507.020(1)(a), he causes the death of an unborn child; except that in any prosecution, a person shall not be guilty under this subsection if he acted under the influence of extreme emotional disturbance for which there was a reasonable explanation or excuse, the reasonableness of which is to be determined from the viewpoint of a person in the defendant's situation under the circumstances as the defendant believed them to be. However, nothing contained in this section shall constitute a defense to a prosecution for or preclude a conviction of fetal homicide in the second degree or any other crime; or

(b) Including but not limited to the operation of a motor vehicle under circumstances manifesting extreme indifference to human life, he wantonly engages in conduct which creates a grave risk of death to an unborn child and thereby causes the death of an unborn child.

(2) Fetal homicide in the first degree is a capital offense.

Kentucky Code § 507A.030. Fetal homicide in the second degree

(1) A person is guilty of fetal homicide in the second degree when:

(a) With intent to cause serious physical injury to an unborn child or with the intent necessary to commit an offense under KRS 507.030(1)(a), he causes the death of an unborn child; or

(b) With intent to cause the death of an unborn child or with the intent necessary to commit an offense under KRS 507.030(1)(b), he causes the death of an unborn child under circumstances which do not constitute fetal homicide in the first degree because he acts under the influence of extreme emotional disturbance, as defined in KRS 507A.020(1)(a).

(2) Fetal homicide in the second degree is a Class B felony.

Kentucky Code § 507A.040. Fetal homicide in the third degree

(1) A person is guilty of fetal homicide in the third degree when he wantonly causes the death of an unborn child, including but not limited to situations where the death results from the person's operation of a motor vehicle.

(2) Fetal homicide in the third degree is a Class C felony.

Kentucky Code § 507A.050. Fetal homicide in the fourth degree

(1) A person is guilty of fetal homicide in the fourth degree when, with recklessness, he causes the death of an unborn child.

(2) Fetal homicide in the fourth degree is a Class D felony.

Kentucky Code § 507A.060. Death sentence prohibited

The death of an unborn child shall not result in the imposition of a sentence of death, either as a result of the violation of KRS 507A.020 or as a result of the aggravation of another capital offense under KRS 532.025(2).

Kentucky Religious Coalition for Reproductive Choice

Kentucky Religious Coalition for Reproductive Choice (KRC) is a pro-choice organization that was founded in 1973, by Doris Schneider. KRC is headquartered in Louisville, Kentucky. The organization engages in education and advocacy, to bring the moral power of religious communities to ensure reproductive choice and health throughout Kentucky. KRC members are involved in a variety of activities that include: legislative advocacy, publishing a quarterly newsletter and other printed material, hosting a Roe v. Wade Awards Banquet, counseling and training for clergy, facilitate the creation of local pro-choice groups throughout the state, putting on training sessions and workshops, providing problem pregnancy all-options counseling by clergy, sponsor booth at fairs, and working to ensure that local hospitals provide comprehensive reproductive healthcare services. *See also* **Pro-Choice Organizations**

Kentucky Right to Life Association

Kentucky Right to Life Association (KRLA) is a pro-life organization that was founded in 1973. The executive director of KRLA is Margie Montgomery. KRLA seeks to restore legal protection to preborn babies. The organization believes that every human being has an inalienable right to life that must be protected. Its members engage in educational programs, fund-raising, legislative action, voter surveys, and political action. *See also* **Pro-Life Organizations**

Kidney Disease and Pregnancy

Kidney disease is the fifth most common cause of death in the United States. Pregnant women with mild kidney disease usually have uncomplicated pregnancies. This not the case, however, for women with severe kidney failure. In many cases the disorder prevents women from becoming pregnant. In the event they do conceive, their pregnancies may be complicated, and usually result in a premature birth. Women who are pregnant and are receiving dialysis treatment will typically have a spontaneous abortion (miscarriage). Because of the problems posed by severe kidney conditions, women are generally discouraged from becoming pregnant. *See also* **Diabetes and Pregnancy; Heart Disease and Pregnancy; Liver Disease and Pregnancy**

Knowlton, Charles

Charles Knowlton (1800–1850) is credited with writing the most influential birth control publication of the 19th century. Born in Templeton, Massachusetts, Knowlton received a medical degree in 1824 from Dartmouth College. In 1832, while residing in Ashfield, Massachusetts, Knowlton anonymously published a book that gave advice on birth control methods and was entitled *The Fruits of Philosophy: or The Private Companion of Young Married People*. His book marked the first work of its kind to be published in the United States. Knowlton's book brought immediate controversy. He was prosecuted for publishing the work, shortly after it was released, and sentenced to three months hard labor. Knowlton was not fazed by the punishment. In 1833 he published another edition of the book using his name as author.

The Fruits of Philosophy presented a detailed and explicit account of the reproductive system of women and men, as well as commentary on contraceptive methods and the right of women to have abortions. Throughout the course of the numerous revised editions of his book, Knowlton was subject to criminal prosecutions. He wrote that he understood that the society for which he wrote was not ready for the frank discussion of sexuality that he presented, but that he was determined to move society to another level of understanding. The force of Knowlton's book was evident long after his death when, in 1877, Charles Bradlaug and Annie Besant republished the book in England. They were both prosecuted by English authorities for printing the book. Unlike Knowlton's fate in the United States, Bradlaug and Besant eventually were found innocent of the charges against them.

Kopp, James Charles

James Charles Kopp was known in anti-abortion circles as "Atomic Dog." Kopp was born in California in 1954. He graduated from the University of California at Santa Cruz in 1976, with a bachelor's degree in marine biology. In 1995 Kopp allegedly shot and wounded an abortion doctor in Canada. Kopp was able to escape Canadian authorities over the incident. On October 23, 1998, Kopp was alleged to have shot and killed Dr. Bernard Slepian. Dr. Slepian was a 52-year-old obstetrician who performed abortions. Dr. Slepian was shot by a rifle fired into his Amherst, New York, home. Kopp disappeared several days after the shooting and evaded arrest until his capture in France on March 29, 2001. France initially refused to extradite Kopp to face federal and state charges, because of the possibility of Kopp receiving the death penalty if found guilty. However, an agreement was reached between French and federal authorities which assured the French that Kopp would not be exposed to the death penalty, if extradited back to the United States. Kopp was finally returned to stand trial in the United States in June of 2002.

Subsequent to Kopp's return to the United States he was initially prosecuted by the state of New York for the murder of Dr. Slepian. Kopp's trial was conducted before a judge and not a jury (at his request). During the trial in 2003, the judge found Kopp guilty of second degree murder. Kopp was sentenced on May 9, 2003, to 25 years to life in prison.

At the conclusion of the state prosecution, Kopp was charged by the federal government with violating federal law in causing the death of Dr. Slepian. Kopp was convicted on the federal charge and on June 20, 2007, he was sentenced to life in prison. *See also* **Abortion Violence, Property Destruction and Demonstrations**

Krabbe Disease

Krabbe disease is an inherited disorder involving a deficiency of certain enzyme and a resulting destruction of the fatty material that surrounds many of the nerves. This condition leads to a progressive destruction of the nervous system. Symptoms of the disorder include feeding problems, failure to thrive, fevers, seizures, visual and hearing loss, and vomiting. There is no specific treatment for the disorder. Death usually occurs before the second year of life. *See also* **Birth Defects and Abortion**

K.U. Pro-Choice Coalition

The K.U. Pro-Choice Coalition is a student-run organization on the campus of the University of Kansas. The organization is active in promoting pro-choice candidates for political office, speaking out in the campus community on behalf of pro-choice issues, and informing legislators and politicians about their views on the right of women to have unrestricted reproductive choices. The group provides assistance in protecting clinics and their employees, and in escorting women to clinics. *See also* **Pro-Choice Organizations**

L

Laaoo

Laaoo refers to the process of expelling a fetus from the uterus.

Labor *see* **Childbirth and Labor; Induced Labor**

Laci and Conner's Law *see* **Unborn Victims of Violence Act**

Lactational Amenorrhea Method

The lactational amenorrhea method (LAM) is a natural birth control procedure. LAM is based on the postpartum infertility that occurs when a woman breast-feeds her newborn child. Breast-feeding tends to postpone the return of ovulation and menstruation after delivery. However, ovulation can and does eventually return. LAM may be used by women who breast-feed, have not had menses since giving birth, and are less than six months postpartum. The birth control properties of LAM last only for the duration of breast-feeding. *See also* **Contraception; Natural Family Planning Methods**

Lamaze Method *see* **Natural Childbirth Methods**

Lambert v. Wicklund

Forum: United States Supreme Court.

Case Citation: Lambert v. Wicklund, 520 U.S. 292 (1997).

Date Argued: Not Argued.

Date of Decision: March 31, 1997.

Opinion of Court: Per Curiam.

Concurring Opinion: Stevens, J., in which Ginsburg and Breyer, JJ., joined.

Dissenting Opinion: None.

Counsel for Appellants: Not Reported.

Counsel for Appellees: Not Reported.

Amicus Brief for Appellants: Not Reported.

Amicus Brief for Appellees: Not Reported.

Issue Presented: Whether the constitution was violated by a provision in Montana's abortion statute that allowed a court to waive the parental notice requirement for minors, if notification was not in minor's best interest?

Case Holding: The constitution was not violated by a provision in Montana's abortion statute that allowed a court to waive the parental notice requirement for minors, if notification was not in minor's best interest.

Background facts of case: The appellees, physicians and other medical personnel, filed a law suit in a federal district court in Montana, seeking a declaration that the state's abortion statute requiring parental notice for minors violated the constitution. The district court held that a provision in the statute allowing waiver of the notice requirement, if notification was not in minor's best interest, violated the constitution. The Ninth Circuit court of appeals affirmed. The Supreme Court granted certiorari to consider the matter.

Majority opinion delivered Per Curiam: The per curiam opinion found that the challenged provision in Montana's abortion statute passed constitutional muster. The opinion reasoned as follows:

> In 1995, Montana enacted the Parental Notice of Abortion Act. The Act prohibits a physician from performing an abortion on a minor unless the physician has notified one of the minor's parents or the minor's legal guardian 48 hours in advance. However, an unemancipated minor may petition the state youth court to waive the notification requirement, pursuant to the statute's judicial bypass provision. The provision gives the minor a right to court-appointed counsel, and guarantees expeditious handling of the minor's petition. The minor's identity remains anonymous, and the proceedings and related documents are kept confidential.
>
> If the court finds by clear and convincing evidence that any of the following three conditions are met, it must grant the petition and waive the notice requirement: (i) the minor is sufficiently mature to decide whether to have an abortion; (ii) "there is evidence of a pattern of physical, sexual, or emotional abuse of the minor by one of her parents, a guardian, or a custodian; or (iii) the notification of a parent or guardian is not in the best interests of the minor. It is this third condition which is at issue here.
>
> ... The District Court for the District of Montana ... held that the Act was unconstitutional because the third condition set out above was too narrow. According to the District Court, our precedents require that judicial bypass mechanisms authorize waiver of the notice requirement whenever the abortion would be in the minor's best interests, not just when notification would not be in the minor's best interests.....
>
> ... [A] judicial bypass procedure requiring a minor to show that parental notification is not in her best interests is equivalent to a judicial bypass procedure requiring a minor to show that abortion without notification is in her best interests....
>
> [Appellees] claim that there is a constitutionally significant distinction between requiring a minor to show that parental notification is not in her best interests, and requiring a minor to show that an abortion (without such notification) is in her best interests. But the Montana statute draws no such distinction, and respondents cite no Montana state-court decision suggesting that the statute permits a court to separate the question whether parental notification is not in a minor's best interest from an inquiry into whether abortion (without notification) is in the minor's best interest....

Disposition of case: The judgment of the court of appeals was reversed.

Concurring opinion by Justice Stevens: Justice Stevens concurred in the decision of the Court. He believed the disposition of the case was controlled by a prior decision of the Court. Justice Stevens wrote as follows:

> We assumed in Ohio v. Akron Center for Reproductive Health (Akron II), that a young woman's demonstration that an abortion would be in her best interest was sufficient to meet the requirements of the Ohio statute's judicial bypass provision. In my view, that case requires us to make the same assumption here. Whether that is a necessary showing is a question we need not reach.
>
> In Akron II, we upheld a statute authorizing a judicial bypass of a parental notice requirement on the understanding that Ohio required the juvenile court to authorize the procedure whenever it determined that the abortion is in the minor's best interest. Given the fact that the relevant text of the Montana statute at issue in this case is essentially identical to the Ohio provision, ... it is surely appropriate to assume that the Montana provision also requires the court to authorize the minor's consent whenever the abortion is in her best interests. So understood, the Montana statute is plainly constitutional under our ruling in Akron II. Because the Court of Appeals erroneously construed the statute in a manner that caused that court to hold the statute unconstitutional, I agree with the majority that the judgment below should be reversed.

Laminaria *see* **Dilation and Evacuation**

Late Abortion *see* **Early Abortion and Late Abortion**

Lead and Pregnancy

The primary sources of lead exposure are lead-based paints, contaminated soil, and occupational environments. High levels of lead exposure to a women during pregnancy can be a serious problem for the fetus. Lead crosses freely through the placenta as early as 12 weeks gestation. Exposure by women to high levels of lead during pregnancy can cause spontaneous abortions and stillbirth. Studies have shown that children who had prenatal lead exposure suffer neurological impairment and mental deficiencies. Women who are at risk for exposure to increased lead levels during pregnancy should have their blood levels monitored. Prenatal vitamins may help lower blood-lead levels. *See also* **Mercury and Pregnancy**

League of Women Voters of the United States

The League of Women Voters of the United States (League) was established in 1920 by Carrie Chapman Catt (six months before the 19th amendment to the federal constitution was ratified, giving women the right to vote). The national headquarters of the League is in Washington, D.C., and its president is Mary G. Wilson. The stated policy of the League is to encourage active participation of citizens in government, increase understanding of major public policy issues, and influence public policy through education and advocacy.

One area that the League has shown a strong commitment to is abortion. In 1983 the League announced its position that public policy of society must affirm the constitutional right of privacy of the individual to make reproductive choices. The League supports opposition to any restrictions on the right to abortion. It has filed numerous federal and state appellate court amicus briefs in support of abortion issues, in addition to lobbying federal and state legislators to prevent corrosion of abortion rights and to expand abortion rights. *See also* **Pro-Choice Organizations**

LEARN Northeast

LEARN Northeast (LN) is a pro-life organization headquartered in Montclair, New Jersey. LN is part of the Life Education and Resource Network, a national network of Christian pro-life/pro-family advocates. The director of LN is Pastor Clenard Howard Childress, Jr. One of the primary goals of LN is to facilitate a strong and viable network of African-American pro-life/pro-family advocates. Some of the work done by LN includes: sponsoring an annual "Say-So" March to highlight the impact of abortion on the African-American community; taking part in the Genocide Awareness Project, a traveling abortion photo-mural exhibition. *See also* **Pro-Life Organizations**

Pastor Clenard Howard Childress, Jr., is the director of LEARN Northeast, a pro-life organization headquartered in Montclair, New Jersey (Clenard Howard Childress, Jr.).

Leavitt v. Jane L.

Forum: United States Supreme Court.

Case Citation: Leavitt v. Jane L., 518 U.S. 137 (1996).

Date Argued: Not Argued.

Date of Decision: June 17, 1996. *Opinion of Court*: Per Curiam.

Concurring Opinion: None.

Dissenting Opinion: Justice Stevens, in which Souter, Ginsburg, and Breyer, JJ., joined.

Counsel for Appellant: Not Reported.

Counsel for Appellee: Not Reported.

Amicus Brief for Appellant: Not Reported.

Amicus Brief for Appellee: Not Reported.

Issue Presented: Whether an unconstitutional provision in Utah's abortion statute may be severed from the remainder of the statute?

Case Holding: The invalidity of Utah's statute regulating pregnancies 20 weeks old or less, may be severed so as to preserve that portion of the abortion statute that regulated pregnancies of more than 20 weeks.

Background facts of case: The appellee, Jane L., filed a lawsuit in a federal district court in Utah, seeking to have the state's abortion statute declared unconstitutional. The pertinent provisions of the statute established two regimes of regulation for abortion, based on the term of the pregnancy. With respect to pregnancies 20 weeks old or less, the statute permitted abortions only under five enumerated circumstances. As to pregnancies of more than 20 weeks, the statute permitted abortions under only three of the five enumerated circumstances. The district court found the provision of the statute regulating abortion prior to 20 weeks gestation to be unconstitutional, but found the provision regulating abortion after 20 weeks gestation to be both constitutional and severable. On appeal by the appellee with regard to finding the post-twenty weeks provision constitutional, the Tenth Circuit appeals court held that the provision could not be enforced, regardless of its constitutionality, because it was not severable from the invalidated portion of the law. The United States Supreme Court granted certiorari and summarily decided the issue.

Majority opinion delivered Per Curiam: It was said in the per curiam opinion that the issue of severability was a matter of state law. After reviewing Utah's pronouncement on severability, the Supreme Court held that the appellate court's decision could not stand. The per curiam opinion issued the following ruling:

> ... The court's severability ruling was based on its view that the Utah Legislature would not have wanted to regulate the later-term abortions unless it could regulate the earlier-term abortions as well. Whatever the validity of such speculation as a general matter, in the present case it is flatly contradicted by a provision in the very part of the Utah Code at issue, explicitly stating that each statutory provision was to be regarded as having been enacted independently of the others. Because we regard the Court of Appeals' determination as to the Utah Legislature's intent to be irreconcilable with that body's own statement on the subject, we grant the petition for certiorari as to this aspect of the judgment of the Court of Appeals, and summarily reverse.

Disposition of case: The opinion of the Tenth Circuit was summarily reversed and the case was remanded.

Concurring opinion: None.

Dissenting opinion by Justice Stevens: Justice Stevens dissented from the per curiam opinion based upon a procedural issue. He argued that the Supreme Court failed to follow its own internal rule, that prohibits the Court from deciding an issue involving purely state law. The dissent made the following observations:

> The severability issue discussed in the Court's per curiam opinion is purely a question of Utah law. It is contrary to our settled practice to grant a petition for certiorari for the sole purpose of deciding a state-law question ruled upon by a federal court of appeals. The justifications for that practice are well established: the courts of appeals are more familiar with and thus better qualified than we to interpret the laws of the States within their Circuits; the decision of a federal court (even this Court) on a question of state law is not binding on state tribunals; and a decision of a state-law issue by a court of appeals, whether right or wrong, does not have the kind of national significance that is the typical predicate for the exercise of our certiorari jurisdiction....
>
> However irregular such grants were in the past, they are now virtually unheard-of. Indeed, in 1980 we codified our already longstanding practice by eliminating as a consideration for deciding whether to review a case the fact that "a court of appeals has ... decided an important state or territorial question in a way in conflict with applicable state or territorial law." That deletion — the only deletion of an entire category of cases— was intended to communicate our view that errors in the application of state law are not a sound reason for granting certiorari, except in the most extraordinary cases. Tellingly, the majority does not cite a single example during the past 16 years in which we have departed from this reemphasized practice. This case should not be the first. Accordingly, I respectfully dissent from the decision to grant the petition.

Leboyer Method *see* **Natural Childbirth Methods**

Leigh's Disease

Leigh's disease is a congenital disorder involving rapid degeneration of the central nervous system. Symptoms of disease include loss of head control, seizures, lack of muscle tone, heart problems and impairment of respiratory and kidney function. While treatment is provided for some of the symptoms of the disorder, death usually occurs within a few years. *See also* **Birth Defects and Abortion**

Lesch-Nyhan Syndrome

Lesch-Nyhan syndrome is a congenital disorder involving an enzyme deficiency (HPRT). Symptoms of the disease include self-mutilating behavior, blood in the urine, pain and swelling of the joints, vomiting, impaired kidney function, uncontrolled muscle movements, and mental retardation. Some medications are provided to treat symptoms of the disease, but the disorder is fatal. *See also* **Birth Defects and Abortion**

Libertarians for Life

Libertarians for Life (LFL) is a Maryland based pro-life organization that was founded in 1976 by Doris Gordon. Ms. Gordon, who describes herself as a Jewish atheist and former abortion-choicer, founded LFL to show why abortion is a wrong, not a right under libertarianism's basic principle not to aggress against or violate the rights of innocent people. Using reasoning intended to be expressly scientific and philosophical, LFL takes the position that: (1) human zygotes, embryos, and fetuses are actual human beings, persons with the right not to be killed; (2) fathers as well as mothers owe their immature children the necessities of life; (3) the right to control one's own body is trumped by the parental obligation to protect one's prenatal children in the womb; (4) no government, nor any individual, has a just power to legally depersonify anyone, born or preborn; and (5) the proper purpose of the law is to side with the innocent, not against them. LFL explains its positions in articles on its website, www.L4L.org. *See also* **Pro-Life Organizations**

Doris Gordon, who describes herself as a Jewish atheist and former abortion-choicer, founded the Libertarians for Life in 1976 (Doris Gordon).

Peggy E. Loonan is the founder and executive director of Life and Liberty for Women (Peggy E. Loonan).

Life and Liberty for Women

Life and Liberty for Women (LLW) is a pro-choice organization that was founded by its executive director, Peggy E. Loonan. The organization is headquartered in Fort Collins, Colorado. Some of the activities carried on by LLW include: (1) utilizing graphic and emotional pictures that depict the horrific sights and sounds of illegal abortion in order to educate the generations who have grown up since *Roe v. Wade*; (2) engage in counter-demonstrations, displaying on street corners graphic sights of illegal abortion; and (3) educating post–*Roe* generations that the only way to protect the life of women determined to terminate their unintended pregnancies, is to combine accessible, safe, legal abortion services with abstinent-based age appropriate comprehensive sex education, greater birth control availability, and greater male responsibility in pregnancy prevention. *See also* **Pro-Choice Organizations**

Life and Liberty Ministries

Life and Liberty Ministries (LLM) is a Virginia based pro-life organization that was founded in 1994 by Dennis Green. LLM established a maternity facility for pregnant women called "Liberty Home." The organization does extensive "street outreach," in an attempt to persuade women not to have abortions. LLM has an annual "Face The Truth Tour," in which its members travel for a week counseling against abortion through the use of religious principles. *See also* **Pro-Life Organizations**

Life Dynamics

Life Dynamics is a pro-life organization that was founded in Denton, Texas in 1992, by Mark Crutcher. The organization has two primary functions. It promotes an abortion medical malpractice litigation campaign, which is designed to provide litigation support services for attorneys representing women who have been killed, injured, or sexually assaulted while having abortions. The organization also has a direct mail program, which is designed to educate members of the medical community about the realities of becoming involved in abortion. *See also* **Pro-Life Organizations**

Life Education Fund of Colorado

The Life Education Fund of Colorado is a pro-life organization that was founded in 1993. The purpose of the organization is to educate the public about abortion through the development and utilization of educational materials suitable for dissemination through the mass media. At its inception the organization produced two informative videos: Gifts of Life (portraying the approach and services of Colorado's pregnancy help centers) and Parents' Love Denied (focusing on the importance of parental involvement before a minor has an abortion). The organization has expanded its media outlet by entering the television advertising marketplace in 1996. Through this medium the organization has produced state-wide pro-life campaigns on major network and cable stations. *See also* **Pro-Life Organizations**

Life Enterprises Unlimited

Life Enterprises Unlimited is a pro-life organization founded in Mobile, Alabama during the 1990s by David C. Trosch, a Catholic priest. Trosch was prohibited from overseeing his parish after he took a public position that was interpreted as meaning abortion providers can be killed as a moral means of defense for the innocent unborn. He has spoken on many national talk shows defending his position on "justifiable homicide." *See also* **Pro-Life Organizations**

Lissencephaly

Lissencephaly is a congenital disorder characterized by the lack of normal folds (convolutions) in the brain, and an abnormally small head. Symptoms of the disorder may include unusual facial appearance, seizures, severe psychomotor retardation, and respiratory infections. The disease kills many during infancy, while leaving others severely retarded. In a few instances individuals have modest physical and mental development. Severe malformations of the brain caused by the disease do not respond to treatment. However, some complications, like seizures, may be treated. *See also* **Birth Defects and Abortion**

Live Birth

Live birth refers to any fetus delivered with signs of life after 20 or more weeks of gestation. If such a fetus was delivered during an attempt of an abortion, but is able to live with or without artificial support, the fetus may not legally be destroyed. *See also* **Abortion**

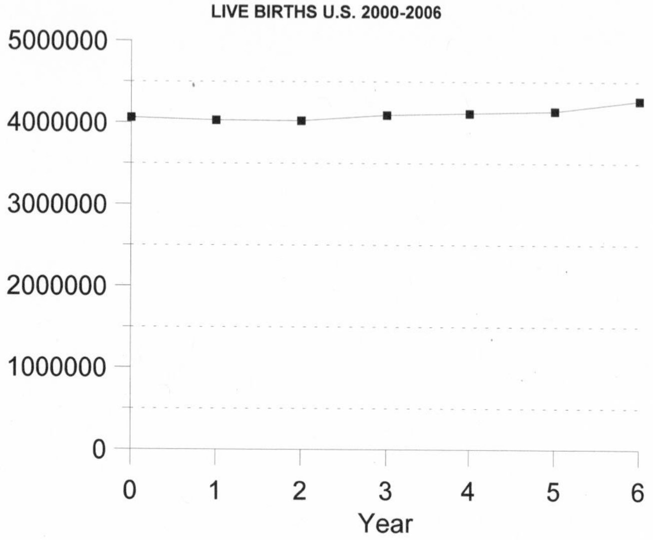

Source: **National Center for Health Statistics.**

Liver Disease and Pregnancy

Pregnant women with liver disease are generally not at a great risk of pregnancy complications. However, women who are pregnant and have severe liver problems, such as chronic active hepatitis or cirrhosis (liver damage with scarring) will have complications (often such women have difficulty becoming pregnant). Severe liver disease carries a high risk of spontaneous abortion or premature birth. Women with such a condition are also likely to have massive bleeding in varicose veins around the esophagus. *See also* **Diabetes and Pregnancy; Heart Disease and Pregnancy; Kidney Disease and Pregnancy**

Lofrumento, Barbara

In 1962 Barbara Lofrumento was a 19-year-old college student living in New York with her parents. Lofrumento became pregnant and sought the advice of her parents. A decision was made for her to have an unlawful abortion. Lofrumento's parents contacted a doctor in the borough of Queens, Dr. Harvey Norman Lothringer, who agreed to perform the abortion. On June 3, 1962, Lofrumento was taken to Dr. Lothringer's home for the abortion. She was never seen alive again.

While Dr. Lothringer was performing the abortion complications arose and Lofrumento died. Dr. Lothringer attempted to cover up the death by dismembering and crushing Lofrumento's body. After doing so he flushed the remains down his toilet. Dr. Lothringer left the country immediately afterwards. However, before doing so, he arranged for a plumber to unclog his drain pipes during his absence. While unclogging the drain pipes the plumber discovered what appeared to be human bones lodged in the pipes. The bones were turned over to the police and, after forensic analysis proved that the bones were human, an investigation was launched. The police discovered clothing that Lofrumento's parents identified as belonging to her. They also found the body of the five month old fetus that was aborted. Lofrumento's dentist was able to identify a section of her jaw that had teeth still in it.

A nationwide manhunt for Dr. Lothringer was set in motion. Authorities ultimately learned that he had fled the country and was in France. He was captured there and extradited back to the United States. In 1964 Dr. Lothringer pleaded guilty to second degree manslaughter and was sentenced to eight years in prison. He served four years before being paroled. Dr. Lothringer was able to eventually regain his medical license and resumed his career as a psychiatrist in 1978. *See also* **Complications During and After Abortion**

Louisiana

(1) OVERVIEW

The state of Louisiana enacted its first criminal abortion statute in 1856. The statute underwent a few amendments prior to the 1973 decision by the United States Supreme Court in *Roe v. Wade*, which legalized abortion in the nation. In spite of the decision in *Roe*, Louisiana has retained its pre–*Roe* criminal abortion statutes. However, under *Roe* the statutes are constitutionally infirm.

Louisiana has taken affirmative steps to respond to *Roe* and its progeny. The state has addressed numerous abortion issues by statute that include general abortion guidelines, informed consent, spousal consent for emancipated minor, partial-birth abortion, abortion by minors, public funds for abortion, use of facilities and people, fetal experiments, crimes against fetus, fetal death report, abortion facilities and pro-life license plates.

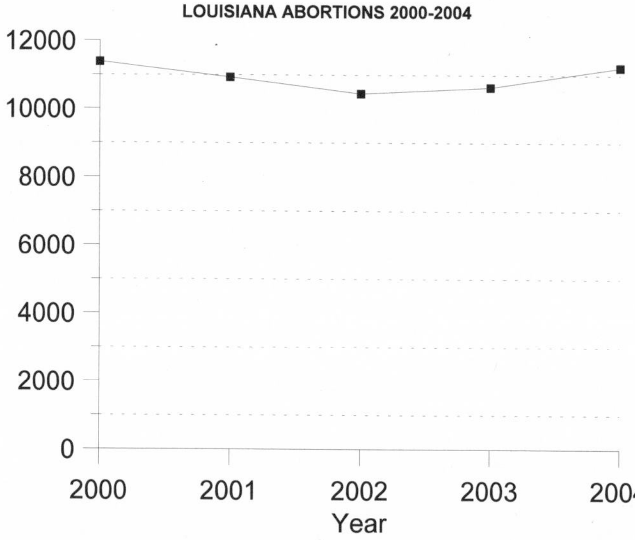

Source: **Louisiana Department of Health and Hospitals.**

(2) PRE-ROE ABORTION BAN

As previously indicated, Louisiana has retained its pre–*Roe* criminal abortion statutes. The statutes remain on the books even though they were expressly found to violate the constitution in *Sojourner T. v. Edwards*, 974 F.2d 27 (5th Cir. 1992) and *Weeks v. Connick*, 733 F.Supp. 1036 (E.D.La. 1990). Under the statutes, abortion was criminalized if it was not performed to preserve the life or health of the fetus, or to save the life or health of the woman. The state also provides criminal sanctions for anyone who unlawfully and intentionally kills an aborted viable fetus or a live child during delivery. In addition, the state criminalized abortion advertising and distribution of abortifacients. Louisiana also amended its abortion statutes in 2006, to add a statute which purports to reinstate its ban on abortion if the United States Supreme Court overturns the *Roe* decision. The statutes addressing the matters are set out below.

Louisiana Abortion by Age Group 2000–2004

Year	Age Group (yrs) <15	15-19	20-24	25-29	30-34	35-39	≥40	Unknown
2000	115	2,045	4,133	2,618	1,364	800	245	64
2001	85	1,868	4,001	2,611	1,378	700	251	38
2002	97	1,765	3,794	2,430	1,325	728	242	70
2003	103	1,767	3,899	2,475	1,356	692	278	72
2004	103	1,855	4,048	2,672	1,410	718	265	153
Total	503	9,300	19,875	12,806	6,833	3,638	1,281	397

Source: Louisiana Department of Health and Hospitals.

Louisiana Abortion by Weeks of Gestation 2000–2004

Weeks of Gestation	Year 2000	2001	2002	2003	2004	Total
≤8	5,165	4,971	5,026	5,358	5,703	26,223
9	1,496	1,375	1,229	1,172	1,179	6,451
10	1,120	1,076	965	944	886	4,991
11	815	764	631	670	639	3,519
12	581	494	437	465	443	2,420
13	581	617	621	488	597	2,904
14	302	288	280	280	271	1,421
15	264	233	234	228	274	1,233
16	178	211	183	165	203	940
17	139	149	109	118	106	621
18	102	92	82	97	130	503
19	138	137	119	125	137	656
20	85	109	97	99	145	535
≥21	311	340	292	275	358	1,576
Not known	106	76	146	158	153	639

Source: Louisiana Department of Health and Hospitals.

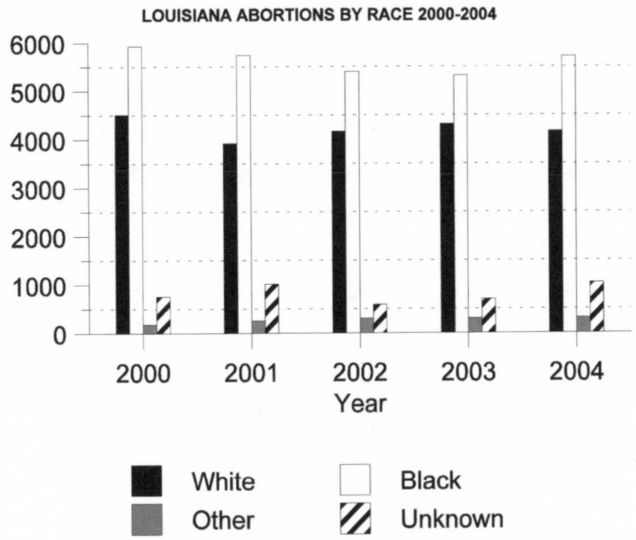

Source: National Center for Health Statistics.

Louisiana Code § 14:87. Abortion prohibitions

A. (1) Abortion is the performance of any of the following acts, with the specific intent of terminating a pregnancy:

(a) Administering or prescribing any drug, potion, medicine or any other substance to a female; or

(b) Using any instrument or external force whatsoever on a female.

(2) This Section shall not apply to the female who has an abortion.

B. It shall not be unlawful for a physician to perform any of the acts described in Subsection A of this Section if performed under the following circumstances:

(1) The physician terminates the pregnancy in order to preserve the life or health of the unborn child or to remove a stillborn child.

(2) The physician terminates a pregnancy for the express purpose of saving the life, preventing the permanent impairment of a life sustaining organ or organs, or to prevent a substantial risk of death of the mother.

(3) The physician terminates a pregnancy by performing a medical procedure necessary in reasonable medical judgment to prevent the death or substantial risk of death due to a physical condition, or to prevent the serious, permanent impairment of a life-sustaining organ of a pregnant woman.

C. As used in this Section, the following words and phrases are defined as follows:

(1) "Physician" means any person licensed to practice medicine in this state.

(2) "Unborn child" means the unborn offspring of human beings from the moment of fertilization until birth.

D. (1) Whoever commits the crime of abortion shall be imprisoned at hard labor for not less than one nor more than ten years and shall be fined not less than ten thousand dollars nor more than one hundred thousand dollars.

(2) This penalty shall not apply to the female who has an abortion.

Louisiana Code § 14:87.1. Killing a child during delivery

Killing a child during delivery is the intentional destruction, during parturition of the mother, of the vitality or life of a child in a state of being born and before actual birth, which child would otherwise have been born alive; provided, however, that the crime of killing a child during delivery shall not be construed to include any case in which the death of a child results from the use by a physician of a procedure during delivery which is necessary to save the life of the child or of the mother and is used for the express purpose of and with the specific intent of saving the life of the child or of the mother.

Whoever commits the crime of killing a child during delivery shall be imprisoned at hard labor in the penitentiary for life.

Louisiana Code § 14:87.4. Abortion advertising

Abortion advertising is the placing or carrying of any advertisement of abortion services by the publicizing of the availability of abortion services.

Whoever commits the crime of abortion advertising shall be imprisoned, with or without hard labor, for not more than one year or fined not more than five thousand dollars, or both.

Louisiana Code § 14:87.5. Killing a viable fetus

The intentional failure to sustain the life and health of an aborted viable infant shall be a crime. The intentional failure to sustain the life and health of an aborted viable infant is the intentional failure, by any physician or person performing or inducing an abortion, to exercise that degree of professional care and diligence, and to perform such measures as constitute good medical practice, necessary to sustain the life and health of an aborted viable infant, when the death of the infant results. For purposes of this Section, "viable" means that stage of fetal development when the life of the unborn child may be continued indefinitely outside the womb by natural or artificial life-supporting systems. Any person who commits the crime of intentional failure to sustain the life and health of an aborted viable infant shall be imprisoned at hard labor for not more than twenty-one years.

Louisiana Code §14:88. Distribution of abortifacients

Distribution of abortifacients is the intentional:

(1) Distribution or advertisement for distribution of any drug, potion, instrument, or article for the purpose of procuring an abortion; or

(2) Publication of any advertisement or account of any secret drug or nostrum purporting to be exclusively for the use of females, for preventing conception or producing abortion or miscarriage.

Whoever commits the crime of distribution of abortifacients shall be fined not more than five hundred dollars, or imprisoned for not more than six months, or both.

Louisiana Code § 40:1299.30. Human life protection act

A. The provisions of this Act shall become effective immediately upon, and to the extent permitted, by the occurrence of any of the following circumstances:

(1) Any decision of the United States Supreme Court which reverses, in whole or in part, Roe v. Wade, 410 U.S. 113, 93 S.Ct. 705, 35 L.Ed. 2d 147 (1973), thereby, restoring to the state of Louisiana the authority to prohibit abortion.

(2) Adoption of an amendment to the United States Constitution which, in whole or in part, restores to the state of Louisiana the authority to prohibit abortion.

B. The provisions of this Act shall be effective relative to the appropriation of Medicaid funds, to the extent consistent with any executive order by the President of the United States, federal statute, appropriation rider, or federal regulation that sets forth the limited circumstances in which states must fund abortion to remain eligible to receive federal Medicaid funds pursuant to 42 U.S.C. 1396, et. seq.

C. No person may knowingly administer to, prescribe for, or procure for, or sell to any pregnant woman any medicine, drug, or other substance with the specific intent of causing or abetting the termination of the life of an unborn human being. No person may knowingly use or employ any instrument or procedure upon a pregnant woman with the specific intent of causing or abetting the termination of the life of an unborn human being.

D. Any violation of this Section shall be prosecuted pursuant to R.S. 14:87.

E. Nothing in this Section may be construed to prohibit the sale, use, prescription, or administration of a contraceptive measure, drug or chemical, if it is administered prior to the time when a pregnancy could be determined through conventional medical testing and if the contraceptive measure is sold, used, prescribed, or administered in accordance with manufacturer instructions.

F. It shall not be a violation of Subsection C of this Section for a licensed physician to perform a medical procedure necessary in reasonable medical judgment to prevent the death or substantial risk of death due to a physical condition, or to prevent the serious, permanent impairment of a life-sustaining organ of a pregnant woman. However, the physician shall make reasonable medical efforts under the circumstances to preserve both the life of the mother and the life of her unborn child in a manner consistent with reasonable medical practice.

G. Medical treatment provided to the mother by a licensed physician which results in the accidental or unintentional injury or death to the unborn child is not a violation of Subsection C of this Section.

H. Nothing in this Section may be construed to subject the pregnant mother upon whom any abortion is performed or attempted to any criminal conviction and penalty.

I. The following terms as used in this Section shall have the following meanings:

(1) "Pregnant" means the human female reproductive condition, of having a living unborn human being within her body throughout the entire embryonic and fetal stages of the unborn child from fertilization to full gestation and childbirth.

(2) "Unborn human being" means an individual living member of the species, homo sapiens, throughout the entire embryonic and fetal stages of the unborn child from fertilization to full gestation and childbirth.

(3) "Fertilization" means that point in time when a male human sperm penetrates the zona pellucida of a female human ovum.

J. This Section shall be known, and may be cited, as the Human Life Protection Act.

(3) GENERAL ABORTION GUIDELINES

Louisiana requires that all abortions be performed by physicians. It is required by Louisiana that, after a fetus is believed to be viable, a woman must undergo testing for fetal viability before having an authorized abortion. Louisiana has enacted a statute that expressly prohibits post-viability abortions, except to preserve the life or health of the woman. The state also provides guidelines for an abortion for a rape or incest victim. In addition, the statute provides a civil cause of action to a woman for any injuries that result from having an abortion. The statutes addressing the matters are set out below.

Louisiana Code § 40:1299.35.0. Legislative intent

It is the intention of the Legislature of the State of Louisiana to regulate abortion to the extent permitted by the decisions of the United States Supreme Court. The Legislature does solemnly declare and find in reaffirmation of the longstanding policy of this State, that the unborn child is a human being from the time of conception and is, therefore, a legal person for purposes of the unborn child's right to life and is entitled to the right to life from conception under the laws and Constitution of this State. Further, the Legislature finds and declares that the longstanding policy of this State is to protect the right to life of the unborn child from conception by prohibiting abortion impermissible only because of the decisions of the United States Supreme Court and that, therefore, if those decisions of the United States Supreme Court are ever reversed or modified or the United States Constitution is amended to allow protection of the unborn then the former policy of this State to prohibit abortions shall be enforced.

Louisiana Code § 40:1299.35.1. Definitions

As used in R.S. 40:1299.35.0 through 1299.35.18, the following words have the following meanings:

(1) "Abortion" or "induced abortion" means the act of using or prescribing any instrument, medicine, drug, or any other substance, device, or means with the intent to terminate the clinically diagnosable pregnancy of a woman with knowledge that the termination by those means will, with reasonable likelihood, cause the death of the unborn child. Such use, prescription, or means is not an abortion if done with the intent to:

(a) Save the life or preserve the health of an unborn child.

(b) Remove a dead unborn child caused by spontaneous abortion, missed abortion, or inevitable abortion.

(c) Remove an ectopic pregnancy.

(2) "Conception" and "fertilization" each mean the fusion of a human spermatozoon with a human ovum.

(3) "Gestational age" means the age of the unborn child as measured by the time elapsed since the first day of the last menstrual period as determined by a physician and confirmed through the use of an ultrasound test of a quality generally used in existing medical practice.

(4) "Good faith medical judgment" means a physician's use of reasonable care and diligence, along with his best judgment, in the application of his skill. The standard of care required of every health care provider, except a hospital, in rendering professional services or health care to a patient, shall be to exercise that degree of skill ordinarily employed, under similar circumstances, by the members of his profession in good standing in the same community or locality, but if the physician was performing abortion procedures that are considered to be included in the areas of a medical specialty, then the standard shall be that of the degree of skill ordinarily employed, under

similar circumstances, by one practicing in good standing in that specialty.

(5) "Infant" means the offspring of human parents from the moment of live birth, regardless of the duration of gestation in the womb prior to live birth.

(6) "Live birth" or "born alive," with respect to a member of the species homo sapiens, means the complete expulsion or extraction from its mother of that member, at any stage of development, who after that expulsion or extraction breathes or shows signs of life such as beating of the heart, pulsation of the umbilical cord, or definite movement of voluntary muscles, whether or not the umbilical cord has been cut or the placenta is attached, and regardless of whether the expulsion or extraction occurs as a result of natural or induced labor, cesarean section, or induced abortion.

(7) "Physician" means a person licensed to practice medicine in the state of Louisiana.

(8) "Pregnant" means that female reproductive condition of having a developing embryo or fetus in the uterus which commences at fertilization and implantation.

(9) "Unborn child" or "fetus" means the unborn offspring of human beings from the moment of conception through pregnancy and until live birth.

(10) "Viable" and "viability" each mean that stage of fetal development when, in the judgment of the physician based upon the particular facts of the case before him, and in light of the most advanced medical technology and information available to him, there is a reasonable likelihood of sustained survival of the unborn child outside the body of his mother, with or without artificial support.

Louisiana Code § 40:1299.35.2. Viability testing

A. No person shall perform or induce an abortion unless that person is a physician licensed to practice medicine in the state of Louisiana.

B. Before a physician performs an abortion on a woman he has reason to believe is carrying an unborn child of twenty or more weeks gestational age, the physician, by use of his good faith medical judgment, shall first determine if the unborn child is viable.

C. In order to preserve the health of the woman, and in order to make a finding of the gestational age, weight, and lung maturity of the unborn child, the physician intending to terminate a pregnancy of twenty or more weeks gestational age shall first perform or cause to be performed an ultrasound examination of the unborn child of a quality commonly used by the ordinary skillful, careful, and prudent physician engaged in similar practice under the same or similar conditions. The physician shall provide the option of viewing the ultrasound images to the pregnant woman as the test is being performed. The physician shall enter such findings and determination of viability in the medical record of the pregnant woman, along with photographs or prints of the ultrasound evidencing the findings.

Louisiana Code § 40:1299.35.3. Born-alive infant

A. In determining the meaning of any statute or of any rule, regulation, or interpretation of the various administrative agencies of this state, the words "person," "human being," "child," and "individual" include every infant member of the species homo sapiens who is born alive at any stage of development.

B. An infant at any stage of development who has survived an abortion procedure resulting in his or her live birth shall be given reasonable and immediate medical care as provided in R.S. 40:1299.35.4(C).

Louisiana Code § 40:1299.35.4. Post-viability ban

A. Before a physician may perform an abortion upon a pregnant woman whose unborn child is viable, such physician shall first certify in writing that the abortion is necessary to preserve the life or health of the woman and shall further certify in writing the medical indications for such abortion and the probable health consequences.

B. Any physician who performs an abortion upon a woman carrying a viable unborn child shall utilize the available method or technique of abortion most likely to preserve the life and health of the unborn child. In cases where the method or technique of abortion which would most likely preserve the life and health of the unborn child would present a greater risk to the life and health of the woman than another available method or technique, the physician may utilize such other method or technique. In all cases where the physician performs an abortion upon a viable unborn child, the physician shall certify in writing the available method or techniques considered and the reasons for choosing the method or technique employed.

C. An abortion of a viable unborn child shall be performed or induced only when there is in attendance a physician other than the physician performing or inducing the abortion who shall take control of and provide immediate medical care for an infant born alive as a result of the abortion. During the performance of the abortion, the physician performing it, and subsequent to the abortion, the physician required by this Section to be in attendance, shall take all reasonable steps in keeping with good medical practice, consistent with the procedure used, to preserve the life and health of the viable unborn child and born-alive infant, respectively, provided that it does not pose an increased risk to the life or health of the woman.

Louisiana Code § 40:1299.35.7.
Abortion sought due to rape or incest

A. Whenever an abortion is being sought pursuant to R.S. 40:1299.34.5 to terminate a pregnancy resulting from an alleged act of rape, prior to the abortion all of the following requirements shall be met:

(1) The rape victim shall report the rape to a law enforcement official unless the treating physician certifies in writing that in the physician's professional opinion, the victim was too physically or psychologically incapacitated to report the rape.

(2) The victim certifies that the pregnancy is the result of rape, which certificate shall be witnessed by the treating physician.

B. Whenever an abortion is being sought pursuant to R.S. 40:1299.34.5 to terminate a pregnancy resulting from an alleged act of incest, prior to the abortion all of the following requirements shall be met:

(1) The victim of incest shall report the act of incest to a law enforcement official unless the treating physician certifies in writing that in the physician's professional opinion the victim was too physically or psychologically incapacitated to report the incest.

(2) The victim certifies that the pregnancy is the result of incest, which certificate shall be witnessed by the treating physician.

C. The failure of the victim to comply with Subsection A or B, as applicable, shall not subject the victim to the provisions of R.S. 40:1299.35.18.

D. Whenever an abortion is being sought pursuant to R.S. 40:1299.34.5 to terminate a pregnancy resulting from an alleged act of rape or incest, the victim may request spiritual counseling and shall be offered the same informed consent information, without the twenty-four-hour delay, contained in R.S. 40:1299.35.6(B), prior to the performance of the abortion.

Louisiana Code § 40:1299.35.12. Emergency

The provisions of R.S. 40:1299.35.2, 1299.35.4, 1299.35.5, and 1299.35.6 shall not apply when a medical emergency compels the immediate performance of an abortion because the continuation of the pregnancy poses an immediate threat and grave risk to the life or permanent physical health of the pregnant woman. Within twenty-four hours, the attending physician shall certify to the emergency need for the abortion and shall enter such certification in the medical record of the pregnant woman.

Louisiana Code § 40:1299.35.15. Instructions subsequent to abortion

Any physician who shall perform or induce an abortion, shall subsequent to the abortion being performed or induced, provide his patient with specific oral and written medical instructions to be followed by that patient in order to insure her safe recovery from the abortion.

Louisiana Code § 40:1299.35.18. Penalties

Whoever violates the provisions of this Part shall be fined not more than one thousand dollars, or imprisoned for not more than two years, or both.

Louisiana Code § 9:2800.12.
Liability for termination of a pregnancy

A. Any person who performs an abortion is liable to the mother of the unborn child for any damage occasioned or precipitated by the abortion, which action survives for a period of three years from the date of discovery of the damage with a peremptive period of ten years from the date of the abortion.

B. For purposes of this Section:

(1) "Abortion" means the deliberate termination of an intrauterine human pregnancy after fertilization of a female ovum, by any person, including the pregnant woman herself, with an intention other than to produce a live birth or to remove a dead unborn child.

(2) "Damage" includes all special and general damages which are recoverable in an intentional tort, negligence, survival, or wrongful death action for injuries suffered or damages occasioned by the unborn child or mother.

(3) "Unborn child" means the unborn offspring of human beings from the moment of conception through pregnancy and until termination of the pregnancy.

C. (1) The signing of a consent form by the mother prior to the abortion does not negate this cause of action, but rather reduces the recovery of damages to the extent that the content of the consent form informed the mother of the risk of the type of injuries or loss for which she is seeking to recover.

(2) The laws governing medical malpractice or limitations of liability thereof provided in Title 40 of the Louisiana Revised Statutes of 1950 are not applicable to this Section.

(4) INFORMED CONSENT

Prior to an abortion Louisiana requires that a woman be fully informed of the procedure to be used, the risks involved and alternatives to abortion. An abortion may not take place until 24 hours after a woman has been provided with all statutorily required information. Louisiana provides both criminal and civil penalties for a violation of its informed consent and waiting period statute. The statute is set out below.

Louisiana Code § 40:1299.35.6. Consent and waiting period

A. The Legislature of Louisiana finds that:

(1) Act No. 435 of the 1978 Regular Session of the Legislature required the obtaining of the informed consent of a pregnant woman to the performance of an abortion. This law was declared unconstitutional in the cases of Margaret S. v. Edwards, and in Margaret S. v. Treen.

(2) By Act No. 435 of the 1978 Regular Session of the Legislature (R.S. 40:1299.35.7) a twenty-four-hour waiting period was required between the signing of an informed consent and the performance of an abortion. This law was repealed by Act No. 418 of the 1980 Regular Session of the Legislature because of the decision of the federal court in Margaret S. v. Edwards.

(3) Subsequent to the above-referenced court decisions and legislative enactments, the United States Supreme Court has rendered a decision in the case of Planned Parenthood of Pennsylvania v. Casey, which upheld the constitutionality of the Pennsylvania law which required informed consent, parental consent, and a twenty-four-hour waiting period prior to an abortion, and which decision has therefore impliedly overruled the decisions in the Margaret S. cases.

(4) The judicial obstacles to such legislation now having been removed by virtue of the Casey decision, the legislature finds that it is in the public interest and in furtherance of the general health and welfare of the citizens of this state to reenact provisions of law similar to those heretofore either declared unconstitutional or repealed for the following reasons:

(a) It is essential to the psychological and physical well-being of a woman considering an abortion that she receive complete and accurate information on her alternatives.

(b) The knowledgeable exercise of a woman's decision to have an abortion depends on the extent to which the woman receives sufficient information to make an informed choice between two alternatives, giving birth or having an abortion.

(c) The vast majority of all abortions are performed in clinics devoted solely to providing abortions and family planning services. Most women who seek abortions at these facilities do not have any relationship with the physician who performs the abortion, before or after the procedure. They do not return to the facility for postsurgical care. In most instances, the woman's only actual contact with the physician occurs simultaneously with the abortion procedure, with little opportunity to receive counseling concerning her decision.

(d) The decision to abort "is an important, and often a stressful one, and it is desirable and imperative that it be made with full knowledge of its nature and consequences," Planned Parenthood v. Danforth.

(e) "The medical, emotional, and psychological consequences of an abortion are serious and can be lasting ...," H.L. v. Matheson.

(f) Abortion facilities or providers offer only limited and/or impersonal counseling opportunities.

(g) Many abortion facilities or providers hire untrained and unprofessional "counselors" whose primary goal is to sell abortion services.

(5) Based on the above findings, it is the purpose of this Act to:

(a) Ensure that every woman considering an abortion receive complete information on her alternatives and that every woman submitting to an abortion do so only after giving her voluntary and informed consent to the abortion procedure.

(b) Protect unborn children from a woman's uninformed decision to have an abortion.

(c) Reduce "the risk that a woman may elect an abortion only to discover later, with devastating psychological consequences, that her decision was not fully informed," Planned Parenthood v. Casey.

(d) Ensure that every woman considering an abortion receive complete information regarding the availability of anesthesia or analgesics that would eliminate or alleviate organic pain to the unborn child that could be caused by the particular method of abortion to be employed.

B. After a woman is determined to be pregnant, no abortion shall be performed or induced without the voluntary and informed consent of the woman upon whom the abortion is to be performed or induced. Except in the case of a medical emergency, consent to an abortion is voluntary and informed if and only if:

(1) At least twenty-four hours before the abortion, the physician who is to perform the abortion or the referring physician has informed the woman, orally and in person, of:

(a) The name of the physician who will perform the abortion.

(b) A description of the proposed abortion method and of those risks (including risks to the woman's reproductive health) and alternatives to the abortion that a reasonable patient would consider material to the decision of whether or not to undergo the abortion.

(c) The probable gestational age of the unborn child at the

time the abortion is to be performed; and, if the unborn child is viable or has reached the gestational age of twenty-four weeks and the abortion may be otherwise lawfully performed under existing law, that:

(i) The unborn child may be able to survive outside the womb.

(ii) The woman has the right to request the physician to use the method of abortion that is most likely to preserve the life of the unborn child.

(iii) If the unborn child is born alive, that attending physicians have the legal obligation to take all reasonable steps necessary to maintain the life and health of the child.

(d) The probable anatomical and physiological characteristics of the unborn child at the time the abortion is to be performed.

(e) The medical risks associated with carrying her child to term.

(f) Any need for anti–Rh immune globulin therapy, if she is Rh negative, the likely consequences of refusing such therapy, and a good faith estimate of the cost of the therapy.

(g) The availability of anesthesia or analgesics to alleviate or eliminate organic pain to the unborn child that could be caused by the method of abortion to be employed.

(h) The option of reviewing and receiving an explanation of an obstetric ultrasound image of the unborn child. Nothing contained in this Subparagraph shall require a woman to view or receive an explanation of the obstetric ultrasound images. Neither the physician or the woman shall be penalized should the woman choose not to view or receive an explanation of the obstetric ultrasound images.

(2)(a) At least twenty-four hours before the abortion, the physician who is to perform the abortion, the referring physician, or a qualified person has informed the woman, orally and in person, that:

(i) Medical assistance benefits may be available for prenatal care, childbirth, and neonatal care, and that more detailed information on the availability of such assistance is contained in the printed materials which shall be given to her and described in this Section.

(ii) The printed materials describe the unborn child and list agencies which offer alternatives to abortion.

(iii) The father of the unborn child is liable to assist in the support of her child, even in instances where he has offered to pay for the abortion. In the case of rape, this information may be omitted.

(iv) She is free to withhold or withdraw her consent to the abortion at any time before or during the abortion without affecting her right to future care or treatment and without the loss of any state or federally funded benefits to which she might otherwise be entitled.

(b) For purposes of this Paragraph, "qualified person" shall mean an agent of the physician who is a psychologist, licensed social worker, licensed professional counselor, registered nurse, or physician.

(3) The information required by this Section is provided to the woman individually and in a private room to protect her privacy and maintain the confidentiality of her decision, to ensure that the information focuses on her individual circumstances, and that she has an adequate opportunity to ask questions.

(4) At least twenty-four hours before the abortion, the woman is given a copy of the printed materials described in this Section by the physician who is to perform the abortion, the referring physician, or a qualified person as defined in Subparagraph (2)(b) of this Subsection. If the woman is unable to read the materials, they shall be read to her. If the woman asks questions concerning any of the information or materials, answers shall be provided to her in her own language. If an interpreter is necessary, the cost of such interpreter shall be borne by the state of Louisiana.

(5) The woman certifies in writing on a form provided by the Department of Health and Hospitals, prior to the abortion, that the information and materials required to be provided under this Section have been provided. All physicians who perform abortions shall report the total number of certifications received monthly to the department. The department shall make the number of certifications received available on an annual basis.

(6) Prior to the performance of the abortion, the physician who is to perform the abortion or his agent receives a copy of the written certification required by this Section.

(7) The woman is not required to pay any amount for the abortion procedures until the twenty-four-hour period has expired.

C. (1) The Department of Health and Hospitals shall cause to be published in English, within ninety days after June 20, 1995, and shall update on an annual basis, the following easily comprehensible printed materials:

(a) Geographically indexed materials designed to inform the woman of public and private agencies and services available to assist a woman through pregnancy, upon childbirth, and while her child is dependent, including but not limited to adoption agencies. The materials shall include a comprehensive list of the agencies, a description of the services they offer, and the telephone number and addresses of the agencies, and inform the woman about available medical assistance benefits for prenatal care, childbirth, and neonatal care, and about the support obligations of the father of a child who is born alive. The department shall ensure that the materials described in this Section are comprehensive and do not directly or indirectly promote, exclude, or discourage the use of any agency or service described in this Section. The materials shall also contain a toll-free, all-hours-a-day telephone number which may be called to obtain orally such a list and description of agencies in the locality of the caller and of the services they offer. Such toll-free telephone number shall be funded by the Department of Health and Hospitals. The materials shall state that it is unlawful for any individual to coerce a woman to undergo an abortion, that any physician who performs an abortion upon a woman without her informed consent may be liable to her for damages in a civil action at law, and that the law permits adoptive parents to pay costs of prenatal care, childbirth, and neonatal care. The materials shall include the following statements:

(i) "There are many public and private agencies willing and able to help you to carry your child to term, and to assist you and your child after your child is born, whether you choose to keep your child or to place her or him for adoption. The state of Louisiana strongly urges you to contact them before making a final decision about abortion. The law requires that your physician or his agent give you the opportunity to call agencies like these before you undergo an abortion."

(ii) "By twenty weeks gestation, the unborn child has the physical structures necessary to experience pain. There is evidence that by twenty weeks gestation unborn children seek to evade certain stimuli in a manner which in an infant or an adult would be interpreted to be a response to pain. Anesthesia is routinely administered to unborn children who are twenty weeks gestational age or older who undergo prenatal surgery."

(b) Materials that inform the pregnant woman of the probable anatomical and physiological characteristics of the unborn child at two-week gestational increments from fertilization to full term, including color pictures or drawings representing the devel-

opment of unborn children at two-week gestational increments, and any relevant information on the possibility of the unborn child's survival; provided that any such color pictures or drawings must contain the dimensions of the unborn child and must be realistic. The materials shall be objective, nonjudgmental, and designed to convey only accurate scientific information about the unborn child at the various gestational ages. The material shall also contain objective information describing the methods of abortion procedures commonly employed, the medical risks commonly associated with each such procedure, and the medical risks commonly associated with carrying a child to term.

(c) A certification form to be used by physicians or their agents as provided in Paragraph B(5) of this Section, which will list all the items of information which are to be given to women by physicians or their agents as required by this Section.

(2) The materials shall be printed in a typeface large enough to be clearly legible.

(3) The materials required under this Section shall be available at no cost from the department upon request and in appropriate number to any person, facility, or hospital.

(4) The department shall promulgate rules and regulations relative to the appropriate number and methods of reporting at no cost.

D. Medical emergency. Where a medical emergency compels the performance of an abortion, the physician shall orally inform the woman, before the abortion, if possible, of the medical indications supporting his judgment that an abortion is necessary to avert her death or to avert substantial and irreversible impairment of a major bodily function.

E. Reporting requirements. Any physician who has provided the information and materials to any woman in accordance with the requirements of this Section shall provide to the department:

(1) With respect to a woman upon whom an abortion is performed, all information as required by R.S. 40:1299.35.10 as well as the date upon which the information and materials required to be provided under this Section were provided, as well as an executed copy of the certification form required by Paragraph B(5) of this Section.

(2) With respect to any woman to whom the information and materials have been provided in accordance with this Section, but upon whom the physician has not performed an abortion, the name and address of the facility where the required information was provided and the information as required by R.S. 40:1299.35.10(A)(1) and (4) through (18) inclusive, and if executed by the woman, a copy of the certification form required by Paragraph B(5) of this Section.

F. (1) Any person who intentionally, knowingly, or recklessly fails to comply with all the requirements of this Section shall be subject to the penalties provided in R.S. 40:1299.35.18.

(2) No physician shall be guilty of violating this Section if he or she can demonstrate, by a preponderance of the evidence, that he or she reasonably believed that furnishing the required information would have resulted in a severely adverse effect on the physical or mental health of the pregnant woman.

G. In addition to whatever remedies are otherwise available under the law of this state, failure to comply with the requirements of this Section shall:

(1) Provide a basis for a civil malpractice action. Any intentional violation of this Section shall be admissible in a civil suit as prima facie evidence of a failure to obtain an informed consent. When requested, the court shall allow a woman to proceed using solely her initials or a pseudonym and may close any proceedings in the case and enter other protective orders to preserve the privacy of the woman upon whom the abortion was performed.

(2) Provide a basis for professional disciplinary action under R.S. 37:1261 et seq.

(3) Provide a basis for recovery for the woman for the death of her unborn child under Louisiana Civil Code Article 2315.2, whether or not the unborn child was viable at the time the abortion was performed, or was born alive.

H. Any physician who complies with the provisions of this Section may not be held civilly liable to his patient for failure to obtain informed consent to the abortion under this Section. Any and all other rights and remedies are preserved to the patient.

I. The provisions of the Act which originated as House Bill No. 2246 of the 1995 Regular Session of the Legislature are declared to be severable, and if any provision, word, phrase, or clause of the Act or the application thereof to any person shall be held invalid, such invalidity shall not affect the validity of the remaining portions of the Act.

J. Construction. (1) Nothing in this Section shall be construed as creating or recognizing a right to abortion.

(2) It is not the intention of this Section to make lawful an abortion that is unlawful on June 20, 1995 or which later becomes unlawful.

K. The author and coauthors who sponsored or cosponsored the Act which originated as House Bill No. 2246 of the 1995 Regular Session of the Legislature in his or her official standing and capacity shall intervene as a matter of right in any case in which the constitutionality of this Section is challenged.

(5) SPOUSAL CONSENT FOR EMANCIPATED MINOR

Louisiana has a statute that requires a minor emancipated by marriage obtain the consent of her spouse prior to having an abortion. This statute violates decisions of the United States Supreme Court. In *Planned Parenthood of Southeastern Pennsylvania v. Casey* the Supreme Court invalidated a provision in Pennsylvania's abortion statute that required a married woman inform her spouse of her decision to have an abortion, before she would be allowed to have one. The Supreme Court invalidated a provision in Missouri's statute, in *Planned Parenthood of Missouri v. Danforth*, that required a woman seek the consent of a spouse before having an abortion. Moreover, the Supreme Court issued a terse per curiam opinion in *Guste v. Jackson*, 429 U.S. 399 (1977), wherein it affirmed part of a federal district court's ruling invalidating Louisiana's requirement of spousal consent for an emancipated minor. The statute is set out below.

Louisiana Code § 40:1299.33.(D)
Spousal consent for emancipated minor

No abortion shall be performed on any woman unless prior to the abortion she shall have been advised, orally and in writing, that she is not required to submit to the abortion and that she may refuse any abortion for any reason and without explanation and that she shall not be deprived of any governmental assistance or any other kind of benefits for refusing to submit to an abortion. This provision shall be of full force and effect notwithstanding the fact that the woman in question is a minor, in which event said minor's parents, or if a minor emancipated by marriage, the minor's husband, shall also be fully advised of their right to refuse an abortion for the minor in the same manner as the minor is advised. Compliance with this provision shall be evidenced by the written consent of the woman that she submits to the abortion voluntarily and of her own free will, and by written consent of her parents, if she is an unmarried minor, and by consent of her husband if she is a minor emancipated by marriage, such written consent to set forth the written advice given and the written consent and acknowledgment that a full explanation of the abortion procedure to be performed has been given and is understood.

(6) PARTIAL-BIRTH ABORTION

Louisiana criminalizes partial-birth abortions through enactment of two statutes in 2007. The state had prior partial-birth abortion statute that was probably infirm as a result of the United States

Supreme Court decision in *Stenberg v. Carhart*, which invalidated a Nebraska statute that prohibited partial-birth abortions. Additionally, a federal appellate court issued an order enjoining enforcement of the penal statute in *Causeway Medical Suite v. Foster*, 221 F.3d 811 (5th Cir. 2000). The revised statutes mimic the definition of partial-birth abortion that is contained in a federal statute and was approved of by the United States Supreme Court in *Gonzales v. Carhart*. Louisiana also has a partial-birth abortion statutes that provide a civil cause of action for the biological father of a fetus destroyed through partial-birth abortion. In the case of a minor, the maternal grandparents of the fetus may file a civil lawsuit. The statutes are set out below.

Louisiana Code § 14:32.10. Physician or others criminal penalty

A. As used in this Section, the following definitions shall apply unless otherwise indicated:

(1) "Partial birth abortion" means an abortion in which:

(a) The person performing the abortion deliberately and intentionally vaginally delivers a living fetus until, in the case of a head-first presentation, the entire fetal head is outside the body of the mother, or, in the case of breech presentation, any part of the fetal trunk past the navel is outside the body of the mother, for the purpose of performing an overt act that the person knows will kill the partially delivered living fetus.

(b) The person performing the abortion performs the overt act, other than completion of delivery, that kills the partially delivered living fetus.

(2) "Physician" means a natural person who is the holder of an allopathic (M.D.) degree or an osteopathic (D.O.) degree from a medical college in good standing with the Louisiana State Board of Medical Examiners who holds a license, permit, certification, or registration issued by the Louisiana State Board of Medical Examiners to engage in the practice of medicine in this state. For the purposes of this Paragraph, "the practice of medicine" means the holding out of one's self to the public as being engaged in the business of, or the actual engagement in, the diagnosing, treating, curing, or relieving of any bodily or mental disease, condition, infirmity, deformity, defect, ailment, or injury in any human being, other than himself, whether by the use of any drug, instrument or force, whether physical or psychic, or of what other nature, or any other agency or means; or the examining, either gratuitously or for compensation, of any person or material from any person for such purpose whether such drug, instrument, force, or other agency or means is applied to or used by the patient or by another person; or the attending of a woman in childbirth without the aid of a licensed physician or midwife.

B. This Section does not apply to a partial birth abortion that is necessary to save the life of the mother whose life is endangered by a physical disorder, physical illness or physical injury, including a life-endangering physical condition caused by or arising from the pregnancy itself.

C. Notwithstanding any provision of law to the contrary, a woman upon whom the partial birth abortion is performed shall not be subject to prosecution for a violation of this Section as a principal, accessory, or coconspirator thereto.

D. Any person who is not a physician or not otherwise legally authorized by the state to perform abortions, but who nevertheless directly performs a partial birth abortion, shall be subject to the provisions of this Section.

E. Any physician or person who knowingly performs a partial birth abortion and thereby kills a human fetus shall be imprisoned at hard labor for not less than one nor more than ten years, fined not less than ten thousand nor more than one hundred thousand dollars, or both.

F. (1) A physician charged with an offense under this Section may seek a hearing before the Louisiana State Board of Medical Examiners on whether the physician's conduct was necessary to save the life of the mother whose life was endangered by a physical disorder, physical illness, or physical injury, including a life-endangering physical condition caused by or arising from the pregnancy itself.

(2) The findings on that issue are admissible on that issue at the trial of the physician. Upon motion of the physician, the court shall delay the beginning of the trial for not more than thirty days to permit such hearing to take place.

Louisiana Code § 14:32.11. Physician criminal penalty

A. Any physician who knowingly performs a partial birth abortion and thereby kills a human fetus shall be imprisoned at hard labor for not less than one nor more than ten years, fined not less than ten thousand nor more than one hundred thousand dollars, or both. This Section shall not apply to a partial birth abortion that is necessary to save the life of a mother whose life is endangered by a physical disorder, physical illness, or physical injury, including a life-endangering physical condition caused by or arising from the pregnancy itself.

B. For purposes of this Section, the following words have the following meanings:

(1) "Partial birth abortion" means an abortion in which:

(a) The person performing the abortion deliberately and intentionally vaginally delivers a living fetus until, in the case of a head-first presentation, the entire fetal head is outside the body of the mother, or, in the case of breech presentation, any part of the fetal trunk past the navel is outside the body of the mother for the purpose of performing an overt act that the person knows will kill the partially delivered living fetus; and

(b) Performs the overt act, other than completion of delivery, that kills the partially delivered living fetus.

(2) "Physician" means a doctor of medicine or osteopathy legally authorized to practice medicine and surgery by the state in which the doctor performs such activity, or any other individual legally authorized by this state to perform abortions, provided, however, that any individual who is not a physician or not otherwise legally authorized by this state to perform abortions, but who nevertheless directly performs a partial birth abortion, shall be subject to the provisions of this Section.

C. (1) A defendant charged with an offense under this Section may seek a hearing before the Louisiana State Board of Medical Examiners on whether the physician's conduct was necessary to save the life of the mother whose life was endangered by a physical disorder, physical illness, or physical injury, including a life-endangering physical condition caused by or arising from the pregnancy itself. The report of the board shall be discoverable.

(2) The findings on that issue are admissible on that issue at the trial of the defendant. Upon a motion of the defendant, the court shall delay the beginning of the trial for not more than thirty days to permit such a hearing to take place.

D. A woman upon whom a partial birth abortion is performed shall not be subject to prosecution for a violation of this Section as a principal, accessory, or coconspirator thereto.

Louisiana Code § 40:1299.35.16.
Partial-birth abortion civil remedy

A. There is hereby created a cause of action for civil damages for injuries and wrongful death, as more fully set forth in Louisiana Civil Code Articles 2315.1 and 2315.2, for a partial birth abortion procedure, except that such causes of action shall only be maintained by the following persons:

(1) The natural or biological father of the aborted infant or fetus, unless such father is a person of the full age of majority and consented to the abortion, or unless his criminal conduct caused the pregnancy.

(2) The mother of the aborted infant or fetus, unless the mother

is a person of the full age of majority and consented to the partial birth abortion.

(3) The parents or guardian on behalf of the mother of the aborted infant or fetus if the mother was a minor at the time of the abortion, unless the parents or guardian consented to the partial birth abortion.

B. For the purposes of this Section:

(1) "Partial birth abortion" means an abortion in which: (a) the person performing the abortion deliberately and intentionally vaginally delivers a living fetus until, in the case of a head-first presentation, the entire fetal head is outside the body of the mother, or, in the case of breech presentation, any part of the fetal trunk past the navel is outside the body of the mother for the purpose of performing an overt act that the person knows will kill the partially delivered living fetus; and (b) performs the overt act, other than completion of delivery, that kills the partially delivered living fetus.

(2) "Physician" means a doctor of medicine or osteopathy legally authorized to practice medicine and surgery by the state in which the doctor performs such activity, or any other individual legally authorized by this state to perform abortions, provided, however, that any individual who is not a physician or not otherwise legally authorized by this state to perform abortions, but who nevertheless directly performs a partial birth abortion, shall be subject to the provisions of this Section.

C. This Section shall not apply to a partial birth abortion that is necessary to save the life of a mother whose life is endangered by a physical disorder, physical illness, or physical injury, including a life-endangering physical condition caused by or arising from the pregnancy itself. .

Louisiana Code § 40:1299.35.17.
Civil action against abortionist

A. No licensed physician or any other person shall perform a partial birth abortion on a female unless the procedure performed is necessary to save the life of the female because her life is endangered by a physical disorder, physical illness or physical injury, including a life-endangering physical condition caused by or arising from the pregnancy itself.

B. As used in this Section, the following definitions shall apply unless otherwise indicated:

(1) "Partial birth abortion" means an abortion in which:

(a) The person performing the abortion deliberately and intentionally vaginally delivers a living fetus until, in the case of a head-first presentation, the entire fetal head is outside the body of the mother, or, in the case of breech presentation, any part of the fetal trunk past the navel is outside the body of the mother, for the purpose of performing an overt act that the person knows will kill the partially delivered living fetus.

(b) The person performing the abortion performs the overt act, other than completion of delivery, that kills the partially delivered living fetus.

(2) "Physician" means a natural person who is the holder of an allopathic (M.D.) degree or an osteopathic (D.O.) degree from a medical college in good standing with the Louisiana State Board of Medical Examiners who holds a license, permit, certification, or registration issued by the Louisiana State Board of Medical Examiners to engage in the practice of medicine in this state. For the purposes of this Paragraph, "the practice of medicine" means the holding out of one's self to the public as being engaged in the business of, or the actual engagement in, the diagnosing, treating, curing, or relieving of any bodily or mental disease, condition, infirmity, deformity, defect, ailment, or injury in any human being, other than himself, whether by the use of any drug, instrument or force, whether physical or psychic, or of what other nature, or any other agency or means; or the examining, either gratuitously or for compensation, of any person or material from any person for such purpose whether such drug, instrument, force, or other agency or means is applied to or used by the patient or by another person; or the attending of a woman in childbirth without the aid of a licensed physician or midwife.

C. Any person who is not a physician or not otherwise legally authorized by the state to perform abortions, but who nevertheless directly performs a partial birth abortion, shall be subject to the provisions of this Section.

D. There is hereby created a cause of action for civil damages for injuries and wrongful death as more fully set forth in Louisiana Civil Code Articles 2315.1 and 2315.2, except that such causes of action shall only be maintained by the following persons:

(1) The natural or biological father of the aborted infant or fetus, unless such father's criminal conduct caused the pregnancy.

(2) The mother of the aborted infant or fetus, unless the mother is a person of the full age of majority and consented to the partial birth abortion.

(3) The parents or guardian on behalf of the mother of the aborted infant or fetus if the mother was a minor at the time of the abortion, unless the parents or guardian consented to the partial birth abortion.

E. (1) A physician charged with an offense under this Section may seek a hearing before the Louisiana State Board of Medical Examiners on whether the physician's conduct was necessary to save the life of the mother whose life was endangered by a physical disorder, physical illness, or physical injury, including a life-endangering physical condition caused by or arising from the pregnancy itself.

(2) The findings on that issue are admissible on that issue at the trial of the physician. Upon motion of the physician, the court shall delay the beginning of the trial for not more than thirty days to permit such hearing to take place.

(7) ABORTION BY MINORS

Under the laws of Louisiana no physician may perform an abortion upon an unemancipated minor unless he/she first obtains the written consent of either parent or the legal guardian of the minor. In compliance with federal constitutional law, Louisiana has provided a judicial waiver procedure for an unemancipated minor to obtain an abortion without parental or guardian consent. The minor may petition a trial court for a waiver of the consent requirement. The required parental or guardian consent may be waived if the court finds either (1) that the minor is mature and well-informed enough to make the abortion decision on her own, or (2) that notification to a parent or legal guardian would not be in the best interest of the minor. An expedited appeal is available to any minor to whom the court denies a waiver of consent. The matters addressed by the statute are set out below.

Louisiana Code § 40:1299.35.5. Consent and judicial bypass

A. No physician shall perform or induce an abortion upon any pregnant woman who is under the age of eighteen years and who is not emancipated judicially or by marriage unless the physician has received one of the following documents:

(1) A notarized statement signed by the mother, father, legal guardian, or tutor of the minor declaring that the affiant has been informed that the minor intends to seek an abortion and that the affiant consents to the abortion.

(2) A court order as provided in Subsection B of this Section.

B. The following provisions shall apply to all applications for court orders by minors seeking abortions and appeals from denials of applications:

(1) Jurisdiction to hear applications shall be in the court having juvenile jurisdiction in the parish where the abortion is to be performed or the parish in which the minor is domiciled.

(2) Each clerk of each court which has jurisdiction to hear such ap-

plications shall prepare application forms in clear and concise language which shall provide step-by-step instructions for filling out and filing the application forms. All application forms shall be submitted to the attorney general for his approval. Each clerk shall assist each minor who requests assistance in filling out or filing the application forms.

(3)(a) Each application shall be heard in chambers, anonymously, in a summary manner, within four days, excluding legal holidays, of the filing thereof.

(b)(i) Prior to such ex parte hearing, the court may require the minor to participate in an evaluation and counseling session with a mental health professional from the Department of Health and Hospitals, office of mental health, or a staff member from the Department of Social Services, office of community services, or both. The court may refer the petitioner, if necessary, to the appropriate Department of Health and Hospitals, office of mental health regional office to arrange the evaluation and counseling session within the four-day period prior to the ex parte hearing, as provided in this Paragraph. This referral may be made by the clerk upon the minor's filing the application when the court has issued a standing order authorizing same and the circumstances fit the criteria of the standing order therefor.

(ii) Such evaluation and counseling session shall be for the purpose of developing trustworthy and reliable expert opinion concerning the minor's sufficiency of knowledge, insight, judgment, and maturity with regard to her abortion decision in order to aid the court in its decision and to make the state's resources available to the court for this purpose. Persons conducting such sessions may employ the information and printed materials referred to in R.S. 40:1299.35.6 in examining how well the minor interviewed is informed about pregnancy, fetal development, abortion risks and consequences, and abortion alternatives, and should also endeavor to verify that the minor is seeking an abortion of her own free will and is not acting under intimidation, threats, abuse, undue pressure, or extortion by any other persons.

(iii) The results of such evaluation and counseling shall be reported to the court by the most expeditious means, commensurate with security and confidentiality, to assure receipt by the court prior to or at the ex parte hearing.

(4) If the court, using reasoned judgment and evidentiary evaluation, finds, by clear and convincing evidence, that the minor is sufficiently mature and well enough informed to make the decision concerning the abortion on her own, the court shall issue an order authorizing the minor to act on the matter without parental consultation or consent.

(5) If the court finds that the minor is not sufficiently mature and well enough informed to make a decision intelligently among the alternatives, the court shall decide whether or not it would be in the best interest of the minor to notify her parents or guardian of the proceedings. If the court finds that it is in the minor's best interest to notify her parents or guardian, the court shall so notify and reconvene the proceedings within forty-eight hours with the parents or guardian present to advise and counsel the minor and aid the court in making its determination whether or not the abortion would be in the best interest of the minor.

(6) If the court finds that the minor is not sufficiently mature and well enough informed to make the decision concerning the abortion and further finds that it would not be in the minor's best interest to notify her parents or guardian, the court shall issue an order authorizing the abortion if the court finds, by clear and convincing evidence, that the abortion would be in the best interest of the minor. However, ... the court may deny the abortion request of an immature minor in the absence of parental consultation if it concludes that her best interests would be served thereby.

(7) In all cases, the court shall issue its final judgment and order immediately upon completion of the reconvened hearing, if there is one, or immediately upon completion of the original ex parte hearing, if there is no reconvened hearing, and in any case where unusual justification exists for taking the matter under advisement, the court shall report taking the matter under advisement to the Supreme Court of Louisiana and to the court of appeal for the circuit to which appeals lie from the court and shall issue its final judgment and order within forty-eight hours after taking the matter under advisement at the completion of such hearing. Appeals from decisions of the court hearing the application shall be by trial de novo in the court of appeal.

(8) Each clerk of each court of appeal shall prepare appeal forms in clear and concise language which shall provide step-by-step instructions for filling out and filing the appeal forms. All appeal forms shall be submitted to the attorney general for his approval. Each clerk shall assist each minor who requests assistance in filling out or filing the appeal forms.

(9) Each appeal shall be heard in chambers, anonymously, in a summary manner, and within forty-eight hours of the filing thereof.

(10) The decision of the court of appeal shall be based on the criteria provided in Paragraphs (4), (5), and (6) of this Subsection, and such court shall issue its final judgment and order within forty-eight hours of its hearing.

(11) Each minor who declares to the clerk of the court hearing the application or appeal that she does not have sufficient funds to pay for the costs of the application or the appeal shall be allowed to proceed in forma pauperis.

(12) Each minor who files an application or an appeal shall be entitled to an initial hearing and a determination by the court independently of any notice to or consultation with her parents, tutor, or guardian.

(13) Except as otherwise provided in this Section, or as otherwise provided by rule of court, hearings of applications and appeals shall be conducted in accordance with the provisions of the Louisiana Children's Code.

C. (1) Nothing in this Section shall be construed as creating or recognizing a right to abortion.

(2) It is not the intention of this Section to make lawful an abortion that is unlawful on July 10, 1997, or which later becomes unlawful.

D. Nothing in this Section shall be deemed or construed to affect or alter existing law on the confidentiality of proceedings and records related thereto, except to the extent specifically contained in this Section.

(8) PUBLIC FUNDS FOR ABORTION

Louisiana prohibits the use of state and local public funds to pay for abortions and for use of government facilities, except to save the life of the woman or when the pregnancy resulted from rape. A prior version of the statute was found unconstitutional in *Hope Medical Group for Women v. Edwards*, 860 F.Supp. 1149 (E.D.La. 1994). The statute is set out below.

Louisiana Code § 40:1299.34.5. Use of public funds

A. Notwithstanding any other provision of law to the contrary, no public funds, made available to any institution, board, commission, department, agency, official, or employee of the state of Louisiana, or of any local political subdivision thereof, whether such funds are made available by the government of the United States, the state of Louisiana, or of a local governmental subdivision, or from any other public source shall be used in any way for, to assist in, or to provide facilities for an abortion, except when the abortion is medically necessary to prevent the death of the mother.

B. Notwithstanding any other provision of law to the contrary, no public funds made available to any institution, board, commission, department, agency, official, or employee of the state of Louisiana, or of any local political subdivision thereof, whether such funds are made available by the government of the United States, the state of Louisiana, or a local governmental subdivision, or from any other public source, shall be used in any way for, to assist in, or to provide facilities for an abortion, except for any of the following:

(1) Whenever the abortion is necessary to save the life of the mother.

(2) Whenever the abortion is being sought to terminate a pregnancy resulting from an alleged act of rape and all of the requirements of R.S. 40:1299.35.7(A) are met.

(3) Whenever the abortion is being sought to terminate a pregnancy resulting from an alleged act of incest and all of the requirements of R.S. 40:1299.35.7(B) are met.

C. The secretary of the Department of Health and Hospitals shall promulgate rules to insure that no funding of any abortion shall be made based upon a claim of rape or incest until the applicable requirements of R.S. 40:1299.35.7 have been complied with and written verification has been obtained from the physician performing the abortion and from the law enforcement official to whom the report is made, if applicable.

D. Subsection A of this Section shall be superseded and Subsections B and C and R.S. 40:1299.35.7 shall become effective only when the circumstances in Subparagraph (1)(a) or in Subparagraph (2)(a) occur:

(1)(a) A decision or order of a court of competent jurisdiction is rendered declaring the provisions of Subsection A unconstitutional, inconsistent with federal law, or otherwise unenforceable based on inconsistency with the Hyde Amendment, or enjoins the state or any of its officials from enforcing Subsection A while at the same time accepting federal funds pursuant to Title XIX, as modified by the Hyde Amendment, and then only if, as, and when a stay pending all appeals of the decision or order is denied, or, if a stay is granted, such stay expires or is no longer effective.

(b) If such a decision or order is rendered, the state Department of Justice, on behalf of the state, shall vigorously and expeditiously pursue judicial remedies seeking to obtain a stay pending all appeals of the decision or order and its reversal.

(2)(a) An order or decision of a court of competent jurisdiction is rendered affirming a finding of the administrator of the Health Care Financing Administration of the United States Department of Health and Human Services that Subsection A fails to substantially comply with the Hyde Amendment or denying a stay of the finding of the administrator and then only if, as, and when the state receives formal notification from the administrator that Medicaid funds, including but not limited to the federal percentage of Medicaid assistance payments pursuant to 42 U.S.C. 1396 et seq. allocated to the state from the United States government, will be withheld or terminated on a specified date.

(b) If the administrator finds that the state is in noncompliance with the Hyde Amendment as it relates to funding certain abortions, the governor, the state Department of Justice, and the state Department of Health and Hospitals, on behalf of the state, shall vigorously and expeditiously pursue administrative and judicial remedies to obtain a stay of the finding and its reversal.

(c) If such a decision or order is rendered by a court, the state Department of Justice, on behalf of the state, shall vigorously and expeditiously pursue judicial remedies seeking to obtain a stay of the decision or order and to seek its reversal.

E. If Subsections B and C and R.S. 40:1299.35.7 become effective and subsequently the federal requirement for acceptance of Medicaid funds, that public funds be made available for abortions resulting from pregnancy due to rape or incest, is no longer applicable to the state of Louisiana, then on the same day, the provisions of Subsections B and C and R.S. 40:1299.35.7 shall be superseded and the provisions of Subsection A shall be effective to the fullest extent allowed by law.

(9) USE OF FACILITIES AND PEOPLE

Under the laws of Louisiana medical facilities are not required to allow abortions. The employees and physicians at medical facilities that do allow abortions are permitted to refuse to take part in abortions. The state also has a statute that prohibits the denial of government financial assistance to anyone, including a pregnant woman, who refuses to take part in an abortion. Louisiana prohibits government employees from providing abortion counseling. The statutes addressing the matters are set out below.

Louisiana Code § 40:1299.31.
Medical people may refuse to participate

A. No physician, nurse, student or other person or corporation shall be held civilly or criminally liable, discriminated against, dismissed, demoted, or in any way prejudiced or damaged because of his refusal for any reason to recommend, counsel, perform, assist with or accommodate an abortion.

B. No worker or employee in any social service agency, whether public or private, shall be held civilly or criminally liable, discriminated against, dismissed, demoted, in any way prejudiced or damaged, or pressured in any way for refusal to take part in, recommend or counsel an abortion for any woman.

Louisiana Code § 40:1299.32.
Medical facilities may refuse to participate

No hospital, clinic or other facility or institution of any kind shall be held civilly or criminally liable, discriminated against, or in any way prejudiced or damaged because of any refusal to permit or accommodate the performance of any abortion in said facility or under its auspices.

Louisiana Code § 40:1299.33.
Governmental assistance discrimination

A. The term governmental assistance as used in this section shall include federal, state and local grants, loans and all other forms of financial and other aid from any level of government or from any governmental agency.

B. No woman shall be denied governmental assistance or be otherwise discriminated against or pressured in any way for refusing to accept or submit to an abortion, which she may do for any reason and without explanation.

C. No hospital, clinic, or other medical or health facility, whether public or private, shall ever be denied governmental assistance or be otherwise discriminated against or otherwise be pressured in any way for refusing to permit its facilities, staff or employees to be used in any way for the purpose of performing any abortion.

D. No abortion shall be performed on any woman unless prior to the abortion she shall have been advised, orally and in writing, that she is not required to submit to the abortion and that she may refuse any abortion for any reason and without explanation and that she shall not be deprived of any governmental assistance or any other kind of benefits for refusing to submit to an abortion.... Compliance with this provision shall be evidenced by the written consent of the woman that she submits to the abortion voluntarily and of her own free will....

Louisiana Code § 40:1299.34.
Government employees counseling abortion

No person employed by the state of Louisiana, by contract or otherwise, or any subdivision or agency thereof, and no person employed in any public or private social service agency, by contract or otherwise, including workers therein, which is a recipient of any form of governmental assistance, shall require or recommend that any woman have an abor-

tion. Notwithstanding anything contained herein to the contrary, this Section shall not apply to a doctor of medicine, currently licensed by the Louisiana State Board of Medical Examiners pursuant to R.S. 37:1261 et seq., who is acting to save or preserve the life of the pregnant woman.

(10) FETAL EXPERIMENTS

Louisiana prohibits experimentation on an embryo, fetus or live birth. The state provides by statute for disposal of aborted fetuses. The statutes addressing the matters are set out below.

Louisiana Code § 40:1299.35.13. Fetal experimentation

No person shall experiment on an unborn child or on a child born as the result of an abortion, whether the unborn child or child is alive or dead, unless the experimentation is therapeutic to the unborn child or child.

Louisiana Code § 14:87.2. Human experimentation banned

Human experimentation is the use of any live born human being, without consent of that live born human being, as hereinafter defined, for any scientific or laboratory research or any other kind of experimentation or study except to protect or preserve the life and health of said live born human being, or the conduct, on a human embryo or fetus in utero, of any experimentation or study except to preserve the life or to improve the health of said human embryo or fetus.

A human being is live born, or there is a live birth, whenever there is the complete expulsion or extraction from its mother of a human embryo or fetus, irrespective of the duration of pregnancy, which after such separation, breathes or shows any other evidence of life such as beating of the heart, pulsation of the umbilical cord, or movement of voluntary muscles, whether or not the umbilical cord has been cut or the placenta is attached.

Whoever commits the crime of human experimentation shall be imprisoned at hard labor for not less than five nor more than twenty years, or fined not more than ten thousand dollars, or both.

Louisiana Code § 40:1299.35.14. Disposal of remains

A. Each physician who performs or induces an abortion which does not result in a live birth shall insure that the remains of the child are disposed of in accordance with rules and regulations which shall be adopted by the Department of Health and Human Resources.

B. The provisions of this Section shall not apply to, and shall not preclude, instances in which the remains of the child are provided for in accordance with the provisions of R.S. 8:651 et seq.

C. The attending physician shall inform each woman upon whom he performs or induces an abortion of the provisions of this Section within twenty-four hours after the abortion is performed or induced.

(11) CRIMES AGAINST FETUS

Louisiana has created the crime of feticide and divided the offense into three degrees. The statutes addressing the matters are set out below.

Louisiana Code § 14:32.5. Feticide defined

A. Feticide is the killing of an unborn child by the act, procurement, or culpable omission of a person other than the mother of the unborn child. The offense of feticide shall not include acts which cause the death of an unborn child if those acts were committed during any abortion to which the pregnant woman or her legal guardian has consented or which was performed in an emergency as defined in R.S. 40:1299.35.12. Nor shall the offense of feticide include acts which are committed pursuant to usual and customary standards of medical practice during diagnostic testing or therapeutic treatment.

B. Criminal feticide is of three grades:

(1) First degree feticide.

(2) Second degree feticide.

(3) Third degree feticide.

Louisiana Code §14:32.6. First degree feticide

A. First degree feticide is:

(1) The killing of an unborn child when the offender has a specific intent to kill or to inflict great bodily harm.

(2) The killing of an unborn child when the offender is engaged in the perpetration or attempted perpetration of aggravated rape, forcible rape, aggravated arson, aggravated burglary, aggravated kidnapping, second degree kidnapping, assault by drive-by shooting, aggravated escape, armed robbery, first degree robbery, second degree robbery, cruelty to juveniles, second degree cruelty to juveniles, terrorism, or simple robbery, even though he has no intent to kill or inflict great bodily harm.

B. Whoever commits the crime of first degree feticide shall be imprisoned at hard labor for not more than fifteen years.

Louisiana Code §14:32.7. Second degree feticide

A. Second degree feticide is:

(1) The killing of an unborn child which would be first degree feticide, but the offense is committed in sudden passion or heat of blood immediately caused by provocation of the mother of the unborn child sufficient to deprive an average person of his self control and cool reflection. Provocation shall not reduce a first degree feticide to second degree feticide if the jury finds that the offender's blood had actually cooled, or that an average person's blood would have cooled, at the time the offense was committed.

(2) A feticide committed without any intent to cause death or great bodily harm:

(a) When the offender is engaged in the perpetration or attempted perpetration of any felony not enumerated in Article 32.6 (first degree feticide), or of any intentional misdemeanor directly affecting the person; or

(b) When the offender is resisting lawful arrest by means, or in a manner, not inherently dangerous, and the circumstances are such that the killing would not be first degree feticide under Article 32.6.

B. Whoever commits the crime of second degree feticide shall be imprisoned at hard labor for not more than ten years.

Louisiana Code §14:32.8. Third degree feticide

A. Third degree feticide is:

(1) The killing of an unborn child by criminal negligence. The violation of a statute or ordinance shall be considered only as presumptive evidence of such negligence.

(2) The killing of an unborn child caused proximately or caused directly by an offender engaged in the operation of, or in actual physical control of, any motor vehicle, aircraft, vessel, or other means of conveyance whether or not the offender had the intent to cause death or great bodily harm whenever any of the following conditions exist:

(a) The offender is under the influence of alcoholic beverages as determined by chemical tests administered under the provisions of R.S. 32:662.

(b) The offender's blood alcohol concentration is 0.08 percent or more by weight based upon grams of alcohol per one hundred cubic centimeters of blood.

(c) The offender is under the influence of any controlled dangerous substance listed in Schedule I, II, III, IV, or V as set forth in R.S. 40:964 and such condition was a contributing factor to the killing.

B. Whoever commits the crime of third degree feticide shall be fined not less than two thousand dollars and shall be imprisoned with or without hard labor for not more than five years.

(12) FETAL DEATH REPORT

Louisiana requires that all induced abortions be reported to the appropriate authorities. The statutes addressing the matter are set out below.

Louisiana Code § 40:1299.35.8. Records

A. Each physician shall retain and make part of the medical record of each pregnant woman upon whom an abortion is performed or induced, copies of the following:

(1) The certificate required by R.S. 40:1299.35.4.

(2) The consent form or court order required by R.S. 40:1299.35.5, if applicable.

(3) The consent form required by R.S. 40:1299.35.6.

(4) The reports required by R.S. 40:1299.35.10.

(5) The certificate required by R.S. 40:1299.35.12, if applicable.

B. The physician shall retain the documents required in Subsection A of this Section for not less than seven years.

Louisiana Code § 40:1299.35.10. Reports

A. An individual abortion report for each abortion performed or induced shall be completed by the attending physician. The report shall be confidential and shall not contain the name or address of the woman. The report shall include:

(1) Patient number.

(2) Name and address of the facility at which the abortion was performed or induced.

(3) Date of abortion.

(4) The parish and municipality, if any, in which the pregnant woman resides.

(5) Age of pregnant woman.

(6) Race.

(7) Marital status.

(8) Number of previous pregnancies.

(9) Educational background.

(10) Number of living children.

(11) Number of previous induced abortions.

(12) Date of last induced abortion.

(13) Date of live birth.

(14) Method of contraception at time of conception, if any.

(15) Date of beginning of last menstrual period.

(16) Medical condition of woman at time of abortion.

(17) Rh type of pregnant woman.

(18) A photographic print or image produced as the result of the ultrasound test required to inform the woman of the probable gestational age of the unborn child in accordance with R.S. 40:1299.35.6 (B)(1)(c) and R.S. 40:1299.35.1(3) to determine viability of the unborn child in accordance with R.S. 40:1299.35.2(C).

(19) Type of abortion procedure.

(20) Reason for abortion.

(21) Complications by type.

(22) Type of procedure done after the abortion.

(23) Type of family planning recommended.

(24) Type of additional counseling given.

(25) Signature of attending physician.

(26) Copies, with the name and address obliterated, of the certificates and consent forms required by R.S. 40:1299.35.8.

B. An individual complication report for any post-abortion care performed upon a woman shall be completed by the physician providing such post-abortion care. The report shall include:

(1) The date of the abortion.

(2) The name and address of the facility where the abortion was performed or induced.

(3) The nature of the abortion complication diagnosed or treated.

(4) The name and address of the facility where the post-abortion care was performed.

C. All abortion reports shall be signed by the attending physician and submitted to the Department of Health and Hospitals within thirty days after the date of the abortion. All complication reports shall be signed by the physician providing the post-abortion care and submitted to the Department of Health and Hospitals within thirty days after the date of the completion of the post-abortion care.

D. The Department of Health and Hospitals shall be responsible for collecting all abortion reports and complication reports and collating and evaluating all data gathered therefrom, and shall annually publish a statistical report based on such data from abortions performed in the previous calendar year.

Louisiana Code § 40:1299.35.11. Forms

The Department of Health and Hospitals shall make available to physicians performing abortions in this state the forms for preparing the records and reports required by R.S. 40:1299.35.8 and R.S. 40:1299.35.10.

Louisiana Code § 40:63. Induced termination of pregnancy data

The purpose of this Part shall be the compilation of relevant maternal life and health factors and data concerning abortions which may be used in the improvement of maternal health and life. The further purpose and function of this Part shall be to serve as a monitor on all induced terminations of pregnancies performed in the state of Louisiana to assure that they are performed only in accordance with the provisions of law.

Louisiana Code § 40:64. Forms for collection of data

The state registrar shall prescribe forms for the collection of information and statistics with respect to abortions. Such forms shall require, but not be limited to, the following information:

(1) The age, marital status, and state and parish (county) of residence of the woman who is aborted.

(2) The place where the abortion is performed.

(3) The full name and address of the physician or physicians performing the abortion.

(4) The age, marital status, and state and parish (county) of residence of the father, if known.

(5) Medical reason for the abortion.

(6) Medical procedure employed to procure the abortion.

(7) The length of the aborted fetus.

(8) The weight of the aborted fetus.

(9) Other significant conditions of the fetus and mother; and

(10) The results of pathological examinations of all aborted fetuses, as required by R.S. 40:1299.35.4.

Louisiana Code § 40:65. Completion of forms

The information required by the form for which provision is made in R.S. 40:64 shall be completed by the physician or physicians performing the abortion in each case in which an abortion is performed. Such completed form shall be transmitted by the physician or physicians to the vital records registry within fifteen days of the performing of such abortion.

Louisiana Code § 40:66. Failure to complete form

Failure to complete such form as required in R.S. 40:65 shall be a misdemeanor punishable by imprisonment for ninety days in jail or by a five hundred dollar fine, or both. Such failure to complete such form and to timely transmit same shall be admissible as evidence that the unreported abortion was illegal.

Louisiana Code § 40:48. Birth and death certificates

A. Whenever an abortion procedure results in a live birth, a birth certificate shall be issued certifying the birth of said born human being even though said human being may thereafter die. For the purposes of this Section a human being is live born, or there is a live birth, whenever there is the complete expulsion or extraction from its mother of a human embryo or fetus, irrespective of the duration of pregnancy, which after such separation, breathes or shows any other evidence of life such as beating of the heart, pulsation of the umbilical cord, or movement of the voluntary muscles, whether or not the umbilical cord has been cut or the pla-

centa is attached. In the event death does ensue after a short time, a death certificate shall be issued. Both the birth and the death certificates shall be issued in accordance with the provisions of this Part and of rules and regulations of the Department of Health and Hospitals.

B. Each induced termination of pregnancy which occurs in this state shall be reported to the vital records registry within fifteen days by the person in charge of the institution in which the induced termination of pregnancy was performed. If the induced termination of pregnancy was performed outside an institution, the physician in attendance at or immediately after delivery shall prepare and file the report.

(13) ABORTION FACILITIES

Louisiana has statutory requirements for licensing facilities that perform abortions. The statutes addressing the matter are set out below.

Louisiana Code § 40:2175.1. Short title

This Part may be cited as the "Outpatient Abortion Facility Licensing Law."

Louisiana Code § 40:2175.2. Purpose

The purpose of this Part is to authorize the Department of Health and Hospitals to promulgate and publish rules and regulations to provide for the health, safety, and welfare of women in outpatient abortion facilities and for the safe operation of such facilities. The rules shall be reasonably related to the purpose expressed in this Section and shall not impose a legally significant burden on a woman's freedom to decide whether to terminate her pregnancy.

Louisiana Code § 40:2175.3. Definitions

For purposes of this Part, the following definitions apply:

(1) "Abortion" means any surgical procedure performed after pregnancy has been medically verified with the intent to cause the termination of the pregnancy other than for the purpose of producing a live birth, removing an ectopic pregnancy, or removing a dead fetus caused by a spontaneous abortion.

(2) "First trimester" means the time period from six to fourteen weeks after the first day of the last menstrual period.

(3) "Licensee" means the person, partnership, corporation, association, organization, or professional entity on whom rests the ultimate responsibility and authority for the conduct of the outpatient abortion facility.

(4) "Licensing agency" means the Louisiana Department of Health and Hospitals.

(5) "Outpatient abortion facility" means any outpatient facility, other than a hospital as defined in R.S. 40:2102 or an ambulatory surgical center as defined in R.S. 40:2133, in which any second trimester or five or more first trimester abortions per month are performed.

(6) "Second trimester" means the time period from fourteen to twenty-three weeks after the first day of the last menstrual period.

(7) "Secretary" means the secretary of the Louisiana Department of Health and Hospitals.

Louisiana Code § 40:2175.4. License required

A. An outpatient abortion facility may not be established or operated in this state without an appropriate license issued under this Part.

B. A license issued to an outpatient abortion facility is valid for only one location.

C. A license issued to an outpatient abortion facility shall be valid for one year from the date of issuance, unless revoked prior to that date.

D. A license issued to an outpatient abortion facility is not transferable or assignable.

E. A license issued to an outpatient abortion facility shall be posted in a conspicuous place on the licensed premises.

Louisiana Code § 40:2175.5. Licensing standards

The licensing agency shall promulgate and publish rules, regulations, and licensing standards to provide for the health, safety, and welfare of women in outpatient abortion facilities and for the safe operation of such facilities. The rules, regulations, and licensing standards shall become effective upon approval of the secretary of the Department of Health and Hospitals in accordance with the Administrative Procedure Act. The initial rules, regulations, and licensing standards shall not become effective until approved by the House Committee on Health and Welfare and the Senate Committee on Health and Welfare. No outpatient abortion facility shall be required to obtain a license under this Part until the initial rules, regulations, and licensing standards are adopted and promulgated in accordance with the Administrative Procedure Act.

Louisiana Code § 40:2175.6. License issuance

A. An applicant for an outpatient abortion facility license must submit an application to the licensing agency on a form prescribed by the agency.

B. Each application must be accompanied by a nonrefundable license fee in an amount set by the licensing agency in accordance with R.S. 40:2006. The fees herein levied and collected shall be paid into the general fund.

C. Following receipt of the application and licensing fee, the licensing agency shall issue a license if, after an on-site inspection, it finds that the outpatient abortion facility meets the requirements established under this Part and the licensing standards adopted in pursuance thereof. The licensing agency must perform an on-site inspection of the outpatient abortion facility prior to issuance of the initial license.

D. As a condition for renewal of a license, the licensee must submit to the licensing agency the annual renewal application along with the annual renewal licensing fee. Upon receipt of the annual renewal application and the annual renewal licensing fee, the licensing agency shall determine if the outpatient abortion facility continues to meet the requirements established under this Part and the licensing standards adopted in pursuance thereof. The licensing agency may perform an on-site inspection upon annual renewal. If the outpatient abortion facility continues to meet the requirements established under this Part and the licensing standards adopted in pursuance thereof, a license shall be issued which is valid for one year.

E. A provisional license may be issued in cases where additional time is needed for the outpatient abortion facility to comply fully with the requirements established under this Part and the licensing standards adopted in pursuance thereof. The licensing agency may issue a provisional license to an outpatient abortion facility for a period not to exceed six months only if the failure to comply is not detrimental to the health or safety of the women seeking treatment in the outpatient abortion facility. The deficiencies which preclude the outpatient abortion facility from being in full compliance must be cited at the time the provisional license is issued.

F. The licensing agency may perform an on-site inspection at reasonable times as necessary to ensure compliance with this Part.

G. The procedure of denial, suspension, or revocation of a license, and appeal therefrom, shall be the same as provided for the licensing of hospitals as contained in R.S. 40:2110.

(14) PRO-LIFE LICENSE PLATES

Louisiana has authorized the creation and distribution of official state license plates that carry the pro-life slogan "Choose Life." Funds generated from the sale of such license plates have been designated for distribution to qualified pro-life advocacy groups. The statute addressing the matter is set out below.

Louisiana Code § 47:463.61. Pro-life license plates

A. The secretary of the Department of Public Safety and Corrections shall establish a special prestige license plate to be known as the "Choose

Life" plate, provided there is a minimum of one hundred applicants for such plate. The license plate shall be restricted to passenger cars, pickup trucks, vans, motorcycles, and recreational vehicles. However, there must be a minimum of one thousand applicants for motorcycle license plates. The license plate shall be of a color and design selected by the Choose Life Advisory Council provided it is in compliance with R.S. 47:463(A)(3), and shall bear the legend "Choose Life."

B. The prestige license plate shall be issued, upon application, to any citizen of Louisiana in the same manner as any other motor vehicle license plate.

C. The annual fee for this special prestige license plate shall be twenty-five dollars, in addition to the regular motor vehicle license fee provided in R.S. 47:463, to be distributed in the manner set forth in Subsection F of this Section and a three dollar and fifty cent handling fee to be retained by the department to offset a portion of administrative costs.

D. The department shall collect the fee for the prestige license plate and forward the fee to the state treasurer for immediate deposit in the state treasury.

E. (1) A Choose Life Advisory Council, hereinafter referred to as the "Council," shall be established to design and review grant applications for qualifying organizations, and shall make recommendations regarding the awarding of grants to the state treasurer. Members of the Council shall serve one-year terms, on a voluntary basis, commencing on October 1, 1999, and shall receive no compensation or reimbursement of any type. Council members are hereby authorized to serve successive terms. The Council shall meet at least once annually, and shall be comprised of the following members:

(a) The president, or his designee, from the American Family Association.

(b) The president, or his designee, from the Louisiana Family Forum.

(c) The president, or his designee, from the Concerned Women for America organization.

(2) At the discretion of the Council, membership may be extended to add members representing the following:

(a) Physicians specializing in obstetrics.

(b) Physicians specializing in pediatrics.

(c) Women who have surrendered children for adoption.

(d) Couples who have adopted children.

(e) Adoption advocacy groups.

(f) Board-certified social workers.

(g) Certified counselors.

F. (1) After compliance with the requirements of Article VII, Section 9(B) of the Constitution of Louisiana relative to the Bond Security and Redemption Fund, an amount equal to the monies received by the state treasury pursuant to provisions of Subsection D of this Section shall be deposited into the Choose Life Fund, which is hereby created as a special fund in the state treasury and hereafter referred to as the "fund." All unexpended and unencumbered monies in the fund at the end of the fiscal year shall remain in the fund. Monies in the fund shall be invested by the state treasurer in the same manner as monies in the state general fund and interest earned on the investment of such monies shall be deposited into the fund. Monies in the fund shall only be withdrawn pursuant to an appropriation by the legislature solely for the purposes provided by this Section.

(2) An organization wishing to qualify for receipt of funds shall submit an affidavit affirming its qualifications, which shall include a pledge to spend the money in accordance with the provisions of this Section, to the Council and shall qualify as tax exempt under Section 501(c)(3) of the Internal Revenue Code of 1954, as amended. Furthermore, an organization wishing to qualify for receipt of funds shall demonstrate it provides counseling and other services intended to meet the needs of expectant mothers considering adoption for their unborn child. No monies deposited into the fund shall be distributed to any organization involved in, or associated with counseling for, or referrals to, abortion clinics, providing medical abortion-related procedures, or pro-abortion advertising.

(3) Organizations receiving monies under this Section shall use at least fifty percent of such funds to provide for the material needs of expectant mothers considering adoption for their unborn child, including clothing, housing, medical care, food, utilities, and transportation. Such monies may also be used to meet the needs of infants awaiting placement with adoptive parents. The remaining funds may be used for counseling, training, and providing pregnancy testing, but shall not be used for administrative, legal, or capital expenditures.

G. The state treasurer, based on the recommendations of the Council, shall annually disburse from the fund an equal amount to each of the qualifying organizations, and shall make available, upon request, the name and the amount of monies disbursed to each organization. An organization receiving monies from the fund may be required to submit an annual audit prepared by a certified public accountant, at the discretion of the state treasurer and the Council. The state treasurer and the Council shall review the distribution and expenditure of funds under this Section at least once every three years to ensure funds are disbursed and expended in accordance with the provisions of this Section.

H. The secretary may establish rules and regulations to implement the provisions of this Section, including but not limited to rules and regulations governing the collection and disbursement of fees, the transfer and disposition of such license plates, the colors available, and the design criteria.

Low Birthweight

Low birthweight (also called intrauterine growth retardation) involves the delayed growth of a fetus for its gestational age. Usually the organ systems are mature, even though the fetus is small. One out of every 14 babies born each year in the United States suffers from low birthweight. A baby is deemed to have low birthweight if he or she weighs less 2,500 grams (less than 6 pounds) at birth. Low birthweight babies are susceptible to serious health problems during infancy, and have a greater risk of long-term health problems. It is estimated that low birthweight is associated with 60 percent of infant deaths. A woman's health problems may impact birthweight (e.g., high blood pressure, diabetes, infections, organ problems). Complications that may result from low birthweight include breathing problems, heart problems, salt or water imbalances, low blood sugar, jaundice, anemia, bleeding in the brain, inflammation of the intestine, poor vision or blindness, and learning and behavioral problems. In addition, birth asphyxia (lack of oxygen) may occur during the birthing process. Many low birthweight problems are treatable and cause no long-term adverse consequences. Adequate prenatal care may reduce the risk of having a low birthweight baby. *See also* **Prior Abortion and Future Pregnancy**

Infants Born Low Birthweight U.S. 1998–2002

	Year					
Birth Weight	*1998*	*1999*	*2000*	*2001*	*2002*	*Total*
<500 grams	5,950	5,912	5,952	5,956	6,268	30,038
500–999 grams	22,471	22,815	22,797	22,648	22,845	113,576
1000–1499 grams	28,555	28,750	29,218	29,250	29,431	145,204
1500–1999 grams	58,921	59,531	60,793	60,804	61,652	301,701
2000–2499 grams	182,311	184,175	188,270	190,089	193,881	938,726

Source: **National Center for Health Statistics.**

Lunelle

Lunelle is a contraceptive medication that is injected by a clinician in a woman's arm, buttocks, or thigh every month to prevent pregnancy. Lunelle contains the hormones estrogen and progestin. It is effective against pregnancy for only one month. Possible side effects include blood clots, irregular bleeding, loss of monthly period, weight loss or gain, depression, nausea, heart attack, and stroke. *See also* **Contraception**

Lupus

Lupus (also called systemic lupus erythematosus) is an inflammatory autoimmune disorder. The exact cause of lupus is not known. The most common symptoms of the disorder include joint pain, mouth ulcers, skin rashes, fever, kidney problems, and high blood pressure. Lupus can be a life threatening disorder and may affect every organ in the body. Women are affected by the disorder far more frequently than men.

Pregnant women with the disorder are at a high risk for spontaneous abortion and other complications. The actual risk for a spontaneous abortion is as high as 40 percent. Babies that are born may be very small, have rashes throughout the body and suffer heart problems. Pregnant women with lupus are also more likely to develop high blood pressure, diabetes, hyperglycemia (high blood sugar), and kidney complications. Some drugs that are used to treat lupus should not be taken during pregnancy because they may harm the fetus. *See also* **Autoimmune Diseases**

Luteal Phase Defect

Luteal phase defect (LPD) is a hormone disorder that can cause a spontaneous abortion. LTD is believed to usually result from the inadequate effect of progesterone on the lining of the uterine wall. This comes about because of the mistiming of the menstrual and ovulatory cycles, which must work together for a pregnancy to be successful. When the timing is not correct, the uterine lining fails to become sufficient to sustain a fertilized egg.

Progesterone is produced by the ovary after ovulation (the process by which an egg escapes from the ovary). Usually, the ovary makes progesterone for two weeks. If a pregnancy does not occur, the ovary stops producing progesterone. (The drop in progesterone levels causes a woman to have her period). If pregnancy does occur, the ovary will continue to produce progesterone. This process generally occurs by eight weeks following conception. Should the ovary fail to make enough progesterone, or if the lining of the uterus does not respond properly to progesterone, implantation of a fertilized egg can be negatively affected and result in a spontaneous abortion. Many women with this disorder usually are never aware that conception has occurred. LTD can be treated with prescribed progesterone in the form of pills or suppositories. *See also* **Menstrual Cycle; Miscarriage**

Diana Schroeder is the president of Lutherans for Life, a pro-life organization started in 1979 (Diana Schroeder).

Lutherans for Life

Lutherans for Life (LFL) is a pro-life organization that was started in 1979. LFL is neither a church body, nor a denomination, but a voluntary organization. The organization has 15 state/regional federations across the United States. The president of LFL is Diana Schroeder of Nevada, Iowa. LFL believes that the Church is compelled by God's Word to speak and act on behalf of those who are vulnerable and defenseless. Therefore, LFL strives to give witness, from a biblical perspective, to the Church and society on these and other related issues such as chastity, post-abortion healing, and family living. Affiliates of LFL have established pregnancy centers, post-abortion ministries, and congregational programs that provide supportive services for those confronted with unplanned pregnancies. The organization publishes a quarterly journal called LifeDate, which provides news and commentary offering a Biblical Law/Gospel perspective on life issues such as abortion, post-abortion, end-of-life, bioethics and Creation, and family life. LFL holds an annual national conference. LFL joined two amicus curia briefs in abortion cases submitted to the United States Supreme Court. *See also* **Pro-Life Organizations**

M

McCorvey, Norma

Norma McCorvey (b. 1947) was the real name of the plaintiff in the 1973 United States Supreme Court decision *Roe v. Wade*, which legalized abortion in the nation. In 1995 McCorvey publicly stated that the case was based upon a lie, and that she was not raped as alleged in her lawsuit. She concocted the story in hopes that it would increase her chances of obtaining an abortion. McCorvey did not obtain the abortion. She gave birth and placed the child up for adoption. After going public with her recantation, McCorvey became a pro-life activist and has fought to have *Roe* overturned. *See also* **Cano, Sandra Besing; Roe v. Wade**

McReynolds, James C.

James C. McReynolds (1862–1946) served as an associate justice of the United States Supreme Court from 1914 to 1941. While on the Supreme Court Justice McReynolds was known as an ultra conservative interpreter of the Constitution.

Justice McReynolds was born in Elkton, Kentucky. He received an undergraduate degree from Vanderbilt University in 1882, and a law degree from the University of Virginia School of Law in 1884. Justice McReynolds' legal career included private practice, teaching at Vanderbilt and United States Attorney General. In 1914 President Woodrow Wilson appointed Justice McReynolds to the Supreme Court.

While on the Supreme Court Justice McReynolds was involved in only one abortion related decision. Justice McReynolds voted with a unanimous opinion in *State of Missouri ex rel. Hurwitz v. North*, which held that the constitution was not violated when a physician was prevented from issuing subpoenas to have witnesses attend a hearing to revoke his medical license for performing an unlawful abortion, because the applicable rules required taking depositions of witnesses who would not voluntarily attend the hearing.

Machine Vacuum Aspiration

Machine vacuum aspiration (MVA) (also called suction curettage) is an abortion procedure used to suction out fetal contents. This procedure is used during the first 6 to 12 weeks of pregnancy. Hours before or a day prior to an MVA procedure, a cervical dilator is placed in the woman's cervix to open it up. At the time of the procedure the woman may be placed under local anesthetic. The MVA procedure itself involves the insertion of a hollow tube (cannula), that is attached to a bottle and a pump, into the cervical canal. The pump provides the suctioning power to extract the fetus. MVA usually takes between

10 and 15 minutes. **See also Methods of Abortion; Mini Vac Aspiration**

Madame Restell

In her lifetime, Madame Restell was the most famous abortionist in the United States. Madame Restell was born in 1812, in Gloucestershire, England. The name given to her at birth was Ann Trow. She married at age sixteen and gave birth to a daughter. In 1931 she immigrated to New York City with her husband and daughter. Her husband died a few years after their arrival. In 1936 she married Charles R. Lohman, a man who made his living selling concoctions that allegedly prevented pregnancy and caused abortions. It was through the influence of Lohman that she reinvented herself and took on a name that became synonymous with abortion — Madame Restell.

By 1839 Madame Restell was running local newspaper advertisements proclaiming to be a physician and midwife, and offering contraception and abortion services. Opposition to her services quickly arose. Over the course of several years she was indicted at least six times for performing abortions. None of the charges led to a conviction. It was not until 1847 that the law was able to impose a modicum of punishment on her. She was arrested at that time for having performed an abortion on Maria Bodine, who was seven months pregnant. Her trial, the longest in pre–Civil War America, attracted tremendous attention, with supporters, adversaries and newspaper reporters lining the courtroom. She was ultimately convicted of a charge less serious than performing an abortion and was sentenced to one year in prison.

Upon her release from prison, Madame Restell resumed her work as a provider of contraception devices and abortions. Through the use of a mail-order service, her business became very lucrative and she amassed a fortune. For a long period of time she was able to keep law enforcement officials out of her affairs through bribery. Madame Restell's abortionist career came to an end in 1878. Her downfall came as a result of one of the nation's most infamous moral reformers, Anthony Comstock.

Comstock was one of the leaders of the New York Society for the Suppression of Vice, as well as the force behind Congressional legislation that, in 1873, made it unlawful to publish, distribute, or possess information, devices or medication about contraception or abortion. This legislation eventually bore the name Comstock Act.

On January 28, 1878 Comstock approached Madame Restell under the pretense of wanting to purchase contraceptives from her. Several days after she responded to Comstock's request, Madame Restell was arrested for illegally trafficking in contraception and abortion devices. She never made it to trial. On the morning that she was scheduled to appear in court, April 1, 1878, Madame Restell committed suicide by cutting her throat. *See also* **Comstock Act**

Madsen v. Women's Health Center, Inc.

Forum: United States Supreme Court.

Case Citation: Madsen v. Women's Health Clinic, Inc., 512 U.S. 753 (1994).

Date Argued: April 28, 1994.

Date of Decision: June 30, 1994.

Opinion of Court: Rehnquist, C. J., in which Blackmun, O'Connor, Souter, and Ginsburg, JJ., joined; and in which Stevens, Scalia, Kennedy, and Thomas JJ., joined in part.

Concurring Opinion: Souter, J.

Concurring and Dissenting Opinion: Stevens, J.

Concurring and Dissenting Opinion: Scalia, J., in which Kennedy and Thomas, JJ., joined.

Counsel for Appellants: Not Reported.

Counsel for Appellees: Not Reported.

Amicus Brief for Appellants: Not Reported.

Amicus Brief for Appellees: Not Reported.

Issue Presented: Whether the Free Speech Clause of the federal constitution was violated by an injunction against abortion protestors that imposed a noise restriction at an abortion clinic, a 36 foot buffer zone around the clinic entrances and driveway, a 36 foot buffer zone around private property to the north and west of the clinic, a restriction on the use of images observable by clinic patients, a 300 foot no approach zone around the clinic, and a 300 foot buffer zone around the residences in the area?

Case Holding: The noise restrictions and the 36 foot buffer zone around the clinic entrances and driveway were constitutionally valid, because they did not burden more speech than necessary to eliminate the unlawful conduct targeted by the injunction. The Free Speech Clause was violated by the 36 foot buffer zone as applied to the private property to the north and west of the clinic, the restriction on the use of images observable by clinic patients, the 300 foot no approach zone around the clinic, and the 300 foot buffer zone around the residences, because these restrictions swept more broadly than necessary to accomplish the permissible goals of the injunction.

Background facts of case: The appellants, abortion protestors, were engaged in disruptive anti-abortion activities near the site of an abortion clinic in Melbourne, Florida. The appellees, abortion providers, filed a lawsuit in a Florida state court to halt the protests. In September of 1992, the state court permanently enjoined the appellants from blocking or interfering with public access to the clinic, and from physically abusing persons entering or leaving the clinic. Six months after the injunction was issued, the trial court issued a broader injunction, that prohibited the conduct of appellants as follows:

(1) At all times on all days, from entering the premises and property of the Aware Woman Center for Choice....

(2) At all times on all days, from blocking, impeding, inhibiting, or in any other manner obstructing or interfering with access to, ingress into and egress from any building or parking lot of the Clinic.

(3) At all times on all days, from congregating, picketing, patrolling, demonstrating or entering that portion of public right of way or private property within [36] feet of the property line of the Clinic....

(4) During the hours of 7:30 A.M. through noon, on Mondays through Saturdays, during surgical procedures and recovery periods, from singing, chanting, whistling, shouting, yelling, use of bullhorns, auto horns, sound amplification equipment or other sounds or images observable to or within earshot of the patients inside the Clinic.

(5) At all times on all days, in an area within [300] feet of the Clinic, from physically approaching any person seeking the services of the Clinic unless such person indicates a desire to communicate....

(6) At all times on all days, from approaching, congregating, picketing, patrolling, demonstrating or using bullhorns or other sound amplification equipment within [300] feet of the residence of any of the [appellees'] employees, staff, owners or agents, or blocking or attempting to block, barricade, or in any other manner, temporarily or otherwise, obstruct the entrances, exits or driveways of the residences of any of the [appellees'] employees, staff, owners or agents. The [appellants] and those acting in concert with them are prohibited from inhibiting or impeding or attempting to impede, temporarily or otherwise, the free ingress or egress of persons to any street that provides the sole access to the street on which those residences are located.

(7) At all times on all days, from physically abusing, grabbing, intimidating, harassing, touching, pushing, shoving, crowding or assaulting persons entering or leaving, working at or using services at the [appellees'] Clinic or trying to gain access to, or leave, any of the homes of owners, staff or patients of the Clinic.

(8) At all times on all days, from harassing, intimidating or physically abusing, assaulting or threatening any present or former doctor,

health care professional, or other staff member, employee or volunteer who assists in providing services at the [appellees'] Clinic.

(9) At all times on all days, from encouraging, inciting, or securing other persons to commit any of the prohibited acts listed herein.

The Florida supreme court upheld the constitutionality of the trial court's injunction. However, shortly before the Florida supreme court's opinion was announced, the federal Eleventh Circuit court of appeals issued an opinion invalidating the injunction as unconstitutional. The United States Supreme Court granted certiorari to resolve the conflict between the Florida supreme court and the federal court of appeals.

Majority opinion by Chief Justice Rehnquist: The Chief Justice found that some of the restrictions imposed by the injunction passed constitutional muster, while others were in valid. The opinion addressed the issues as follows:

> We begin with the 36 foot buffer zone. The state court prohibited [appellants] from "congregating, picketing, patrolling, demonstrating or entering" any portion of the public right of way or private property within 36 feet of the property line of the clinic as a way of ensuring access to the clinic. This speech free buffer zone requires that [appellants] move to the other side of Dixie Way and away from the driveway of the clinic, where the state court found that they repeatedly had interfered with the free access of patients and staff....
>
> The 36 foot buffer zone protecting the entrances to the clinic and the parking lot is a means of protecting unfettered ingress to and egress from the clinic, and ensuring that [appellants] do not block traffic on Dixie Way....
>
> The need for a complete buffer zone near the clinic entrances and driveway may be debatable, but some deference must be given to the state court's familiarity with the facts and the background of the dispute between the parties even under our heightened review.... On balance, we hold that the 36 foot buffer zone around the clinic entrances and driveway burdens no more speech than necessary to accomplish the governmental interest at stake....
>
> The inclusion of private property on the back and side of the clinic in the 36 foot buffer zone raises different concerns. The accepted purpose of the buffer zone is to protect access to the clinic and to facilitate the orderly flow of traffic on Dixie Way. Patients and staff wishing to reach the clinic do not have to cross the private property abutting the clinic property on the north and west, and nothing in the record indicates that [appellants'] activities on the private property have obstructed access to the clinic. Nor was evidence presented that protestors located on the private property blocked vehicular traffic on Dixie Way. Absent evidence that [appellants] standing on the private property have obstructed access to the clinic, blocked vehicular traffic, or otherwise unlawfully interfered with the clinic's operation, this portion of the buffer zone fails to serve the significant government interests relied on by the Florida Supreme Court. We hold that on the record before us the 36 foot buffer zone as applied to the private property to the north and west of the clinic burdens more speech than necessary to protect access to the clinic....
>
> We hold that the limited noise restrictions imposed by the state court order burden no more speech than necessary to ensure the health and well being of the patients at the clinic. The First Amendment does not demand that patients at a medical facility undertake Herculean efforts to escape the cacophony of political protests. If overamplified loudspeakers assault the citizenry, government may turn then down. That is what the state court did here, and we hold that its action was proper.
>
> The same, however, cannot be said for the "images observable" provision of the state court's order. Clearly, threats to patients or their families, however communicated, are proscribable under the First Amendment. But rather than prohibiting the display of signs that could be interpreted as threats or veiled threats, the state court issued a blanket ban on all "images observable." This broad prohibition on all "images observable" burdens more speech than necessary to achieve the purpose of limiting threats to clinic patients or their families.... This provision of the injunction violates the First Amendment.
>
> The state court ordered that [appellants] refrain from physically approaching any person seeking services of the clinic "unless such person indicates a desire to communicate" in an area within 300 feet of the clinic. The state court was attempting to prevent clinic patients and staff from being "stalked" or "shadowed" by the [appellants] as they approached the clinic.
>
> But it is difficult, indeed, to justify a prohibition on all uninvited approaches of persons seeking the services of the clinic, regardless of how peaceful the contact may be, without burdening more speech than necessary to prevent intimidation and to ensure access to the clinic. Absent evidence that the protesters' speech is independently proscribable (i.e., fighting words or threats), or is so infused with violence as to be indistinguishable from a threat of physical harm, this provision cannot stand.... The "consent" requirement alone invalidates this provision; it burdens more speech than is necessary to prevent intimidation and to ensure access to the clinic.
>
> The final substantive regulation challenged by [appellants] relates to a prohibition against picketing, demonstrating, or using sound amplification equipment within 300 feet of the residences of clinic staff. The prohibition also covers impeding access to streets that provide the sole access to streets on which those residences are located....
>
> ... [T]he 300 foot zone would ban general marching through residential neighborhoods, or even walking a route in front of an entire block of houses. The record before us does not contain sufficient justification for this broad a ban on picketing; it appears that a limitation on the time, duration of picketing, and number of pickets outside a smaller zone could have accomplished the desired result.

Disposition of case: The judgment of the Florida supreme court was affirmed in part, and reversed in part.

Concurring opinion by Justice Souter: Justice Souter wrote a terse one paragraph concurring opinion wherein he stated the following:

> I join the Court's opinion and write separately only to clarify two matters in the record. First, the trial judge made reasonably clear that the issue of who was acting "in concert" with the named defendants was a matter to be taken up in individual cases, and not to be decided on the basis of protesters' viewpoints. Second, petitioners themselves acknowledge that the governmental interests in protection of public safety and order, of the free flow of traffic, and of property rights are reflected in Florida law.

Concurring and dissenting opinion by Justice Stevens: Justice Stevens concurred in the majority's decision to affirm part of the injunction order. He dissented, however, on the disposition of the injunction provision that prohibited anti-abortion protestors from approaching abortionists and their patients. Justice Stevens wrote as follows:

> The "physically approaching" prohibition entered by the trial court is no broader than the protection necessary to provide relief for the violations it found. The trial judge entered this portion of the injunction only after concluding that the injunction was necessary to protect the clinic's patients and staff from "uninvited contacts, shadowing and stalking" by [appellants]. The protection is especially appropriate for the clinic patients given that the trial judge found that [appellants'] prior conduct caused higher levels of "anxiety and hypertension" in the patients, increasing the risks associated with the procedures that the patients seek. Whatever the proper limits on a court's power to restrict a speaker's ability to physically approach or follow an unwilling listener, surely the First Amendment does not prevent a trial

court from imposing such a restriction given the unchallenged findings in this case....

I thus conclude that, under the circumstances of this case, the prohibition against "physically approaching" in the 300 foot zone around the clinic withstands [appellants'] First Amendment challenge. I therefore dissent from Part III-D [of the opinion].

Concurring and dissenting opinion by Justice Scalia: Justice Scalia concurred in the majority's decision to invalidate parts of the injunction. He dissented, however, from that part of the opinion that upheld some of the injunction provisions. Justice Scalia wrote as follows:

> The judgment in today's case has an appearance of moderation and Solomonic wisdom, upholding as it does some portions of the injunction while disallowing others. That appearance is deceptive. The entire injunction in this case departs so far from the established course of our jurisprudence that in any other context it would have been regarded as a candidate for summary reversal....
>
> Because I believe that the judicial creation of a 36 foot zone in which only a particular group, which had broken no law, cannot exercise its rights of speech, assembly, and association, and the judicial enactment of a noise prohibition, applicable to that group and that group alone, are profoundly at odds with our First Amendment precedents and traditions, I dissent.

Maher v. Roe

Forum: United States Supreme Court.

Case Citation: Maher v. Roe, 432 U.S. 464 (1977).

Date Argued: January 11, 1977.

Date of Decision: June 20, 1977.

Opinion of Court: Powell, J., in which Burger, C. J., and Stewart, White, Rehnquist, and Stevens, JJ., joined.

Concurring Opinion: Burger, C. J.

Dissenting Opinion: Brennan, J., in which Marshall and Blackmun, JJ., joined.

Dissenting Opinion: Marshall, J.

Dissenting Opinion: Blackmun, J., in which Brennan and Marshall, JJ., joined.

Counsel for Appellant: Edmund C. Walsh, Assistant Attorney General of Connecticut argued; on the brief was Carl R. Ajello, Attorney General.

Counsel for Appellees: Lucy V. Katz argued; on the brief were Kathryn Emmett and Catherine Roraback.

Amicus Brief for Appellant: William F. Hyland, Attorney General, Stephen Skillman, Assistant Attorney General, and Erminie L. Conley, Deputy Attorney General for the State of New Jersey.

Amicus Brief for Appellees: Sylvia A. Law, Harriet F. Pilpel, and Eve W. Paul for the American Public Health Assn. et al.

Issue Presented: Whether the Equal Protection Clause of the Fourteenth Amendment prohibited Connecticut from excluding nontherapeutic abortions from its Medicaid program?

Case Holding: The Equal Protection Clause of the Fourteenth Amendment did not prohibit Connecticut from excluding nontherapeutic abortions from its Medicaid program.

Background facts of case: A regulation of the Connecticut Welfare Department limited state Medicaid benefits to abortions that were determined to be medically necessary by the patient's attending physician. The appellees, two indigent women who were unable to obtain a physician certificate of medical necessity for abortions, filed a lawsuit in a federal district court in Connecticut against the appellant, a state agency official. The appellees challenged the regulation as violative of their constitutional rights, including the Fourteenth Amendment's guarantees of due process and equal protection. The district court held that the Equal Protection Clause prohibited the exclusion of nontherapeutic abortions from a state welfare program that generally subsidizes the medical expenses incident to pregnancy and childbirth. The Supreme Court granted certiorari to consider the matter.

Majority opinion by Justice Powell: Justice Powell held that the Equal Protection Clause was not violated by the regulation. He wrote as follows:

> This case involves no discrimination against a suspect class. An indigent woman desiring an abortion does not come within the limited category of disadvantaged classes so recognized by our cases. Nor does the fact that the impact of the regulation falls upon those who cannot pay lead to a different conclusion. In a sense, every denial of welfare to an indigent creates a wealth classification as compared to nonindigents who are able to pay for the desired goods or services. But this Court has never held that financial need alone identifies a suspect class for purposes of equal protection analysis. Accordingly, the central question in this case is whether the regulation impinges upon a fundamental right explicitly or implicitly protected by the Constitution....
>
> The Connecticut regulation before us is different in kind from the laws invalidated in our previous abortion decisions. The Connecticut regulation places no obstacles — absolute or otherwise — in the pregnant woman's path to an abortion. An indigent woman who desires an abortion suffers no disadvantage as a consequence of Connecticut's decision to fund childbirth; she continues as before to be dependent on private sources for the service she desires. The State may have made childbirth a more attractive alternative, thereby influencing the woman's decision, but it has imposed no restriction on access to abortions that was not already there. The indigency that may make it difficult — and in some cases, perhaps, impossible — for some women to have abortions is neither created nor in any way affected by the Connecticut regulation. We conclude that the Connecticut regulation does not impinge upon the fundamental right recognized in Roe v. Wade....
>
> The question remains whether Connecticut's regulation can be sustained under the less demanding test of rationality that applies in the absence of a suspect classification or the impingement of a fundamental right. This test requires that the distinction drawn between childbirth and nontherapeutic abortion by the regulation be rationally related to a constitutionally permissible purpose....
>
> Roe itself explicitly acknowledged the State's strong interest in protecting the potential life of the fetus. That interest exists throughout the pregnancy, growing in substantiality as the woman approaches term. Because the pregnant woman carries a potential human being, she cannot be isolated in her privacy. Her privacy is no longer sole and any right of privacy she possesses must be measured accordingly. The State unquestionably has a strong and legitimate interest in encouraging normal childbirth, an interest honored over the centuries. Nor can there be any question that the Connecticut regulation rationally furthers that interest. The medical costs associated with childbirth are substantial, and have increased significantly in recent years. As recognized by the District Court in this case, such costs are significantly greater than those normally associated with elective abortions during the first trimester. The subsidizing of costs incident to childbirth is a rational means of encouraging childbirth....
>
> The decision whether to expend state funds for nontherapeutic abortion is fraught with judgments of policy and value over which opinions are sharply divided. Our conclusion that the Connecticut regulation is constitutional is not based on a weighing of its wisdom or social desirability, for this Court does not strike down state laws because they may be unwise, improvident, or out of harmony with a particular school of thought. Indeed, when an issue involves policy choices as sensitive as those implicated by public funding of nontherapeutic abortions, the appropriate forum for their resolution in a democracy is the legislature. We

should not forget that legislatures are ultimate guardians of the liberties and welfare of the people in quite as great a degree as the courts.

Disposition of case: The judgment of the district court was reversed.

Concurring opinion by Chief Justice Burger: The Chief Justice wrote a brief opinion concurring in the majority decision. He wrote as follows:

> I join the Court's opinion. Like the Court, I do not read any decision of this Court as requiring a State to finance a nontherapeutic abortion. The Court's holdings in Roe v. Wade and Doe v. Bolton simply require that a State not create an absolute barrier to a woman's decision to have an abortion. These precedents do not suggest that the State is constitutionally required to assist her in procuring it.
>
> From time to time, every state legislature determines that, as a matter of sound public policy, the government ought to provide certain health and social services to its citizens. Encouragement of childbirth and child care is not a novel undertaking in this regard. Various governments, both in this country and in others, have made such a determination for centuries. In recent times, they have similarly provided educational services. The decision to provide any one of these services—or not to provide them —is not required by the Federal Constitution. Nor does the providing of a particular service require, as a matter of federal constitutional law, the provision of another.
>
> Here, the State of Connecticut has determined that it will finance certain childbirth expenses. That legislative determination places no state-created barrier to a woman's choice to procure an abortion, and it does not require the State to provide it. Accordingly, I concur in the judgment.

Dissenting opinion by Justice Brennan: Justice Brennan disagreed with the majority decision. He argued his position as follows:

> ... [A] distressing insensitivity to the plight of impoverished pregnant women is inherent in the Court's analysis. The stark reality for too many, not just some, indigent pregnant women is that indigency makes access to competent licensed physicians not merely difficult but impossible. As a practical matter, many indigent women will feel they have no choice but to carry their pregnancies to term because the State will pay for the associated medical services, even though they would have chosen to have abortions if the State had also provided funds for that procedure, or indeed if the State had provided funds for neither procedure. This disparity in funding by the State clearly operates to coerce indigent pregnant women to bear children they would not otherwise choose to have, and just as clearly, this coercion can only operate upon the poor, who are uniquely the victims of this form of financial pressure....
>
> The Court's premise is that only an equal protection claim is presented here. Claims of interference with enjoyment of fundamental rights have, however, occupied a rather protean position in our constitutional jurisprudence. Whether or not the Court's analysis may reasonably proceed under the Equal Protection Clause, the Court plainly errs in ignoring, as it does, the unanswerable argument of appellees, and the holding of the District Court, that the regulation unconstitutionally impinges upon their claim of privacy derived from the Due Process Clause....
>
> Until today, I had not thought the nature of the fundamental right established in Roe v. Wade was open to question, let alone susceptible of the interpretation advanced by the Court. The fact that the Connecticut scheme may not operate as an absolute bar preventing all indigent women from having abortions is not critical. What is critical is that the State has inhibited their fundamental right to make that choice free from state interference.

Dissenting opinion by Justice Marshall: Justice Marshall referenced to his dissenting opinion in *Beal v. Doe*, as the basis for his dissent.

Dissenting opinion by Justice Blackmun: Justice Blackman referenced to his dissenting opinion in *Beal v. Doe*, as the basis for his dissent. *See also* **Beal v. Doe; Hyde Amendment**

Maine

(1) OVERVIEW

The state of Maine enacted its first criminal abortion statute in 1840. The statute underwent several amendments prior to the 1973 decision by the United States Supreme Court in *Roe v. Wade*, which legalized abortion in the nation. Maine has taken affirmative steps to respond to *Roe* and its progeny. Maine has addressed numerous abortion issues by statute that include general abortion guidelines, informed consent, abortion by minors, use of facilities and people, ban on fetal sale or experiments, fetal death report, injury to pregnant woman, and ban on clinic obstructions.

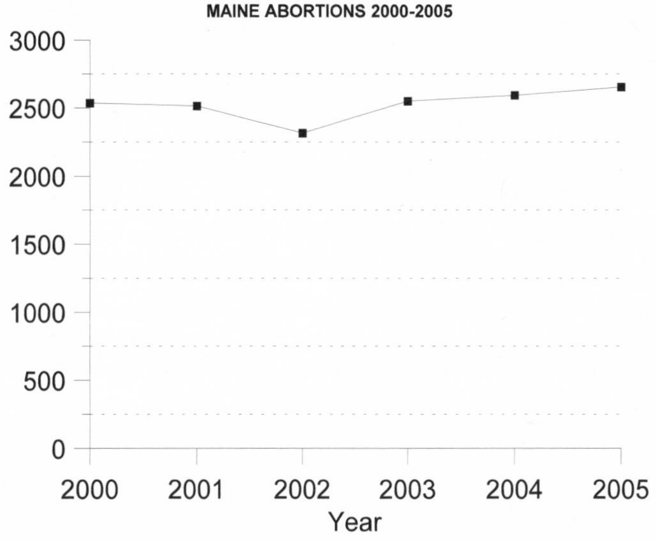

Source: **Maine Department for Disease Control and Prevention.**

Maine Abortion by Weeks of Gestation 2000–2005

	Year						
Weeks of Gestation	*2000*	*2001*	*2002*	*2003*	*2004*	*2005*	*Total*
<9	1,554	1,616	1,495	1,668	1,699	1,807	9,839
9	428	405	372	353	361	288	2,207
10	237	218	203	229	208	204	1,299
11	149	122	114	119	135	137	776
12	130	89	71	95	96	107	588
13	13	33	29	41	49	74	239
14	2	4	5	6	6	5	28
15	1	4	3	0	0	3	11
16	2	1	1	5	2	1	12
17	3	0	1	4	3	0	11
18	1	3	2	2	4	9	21
19	3	2	2	5	6	9	27
≥20	3	4	5	16	13	8	49
Not known	10	14	12	7	11	1	55

Source: **Maine Department for Disease Control and Prevention.**

(2) GENERAL ABORTION GUIDELINES

Maine has provided an affirmative statement that abortion is permitted prior to fetal viability. The state allows post-viability abortion only to save the life or health of the woman. Maine also limits the performance of abortion to physicians. The state criminalizes killing a fetus that is born alive during an abortion attempt. The statutes addressing the matters are set out below.

Maine Code Ti. 22, § 1598. Abortion

1. It is the public policy of the State that the State not restrict a woman's exercise of her private decision to terminate a pregnancy before viability except as provided in section 1597-A. After viability an abortion may be performed only when it is necessary to preserve the life or health of the mother. It is also the public policy of the State that all abortions may be performed only by a physician.

2. As used in this section, unless the context otherwise indicates, the following terms shall have the following meanings.

A. "Abortion" means the intentional interruption of a pregnancy by the application of external agents, whether chemical or physical or by the ingestion of chemical agents with an intention other than to produce a live birth or to remove a dead fetus.

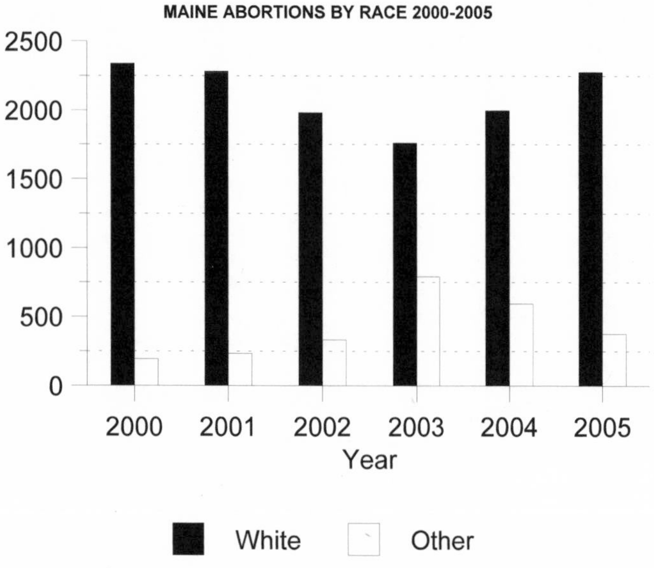

Source: Maine Department for Disease Control and Prevention.

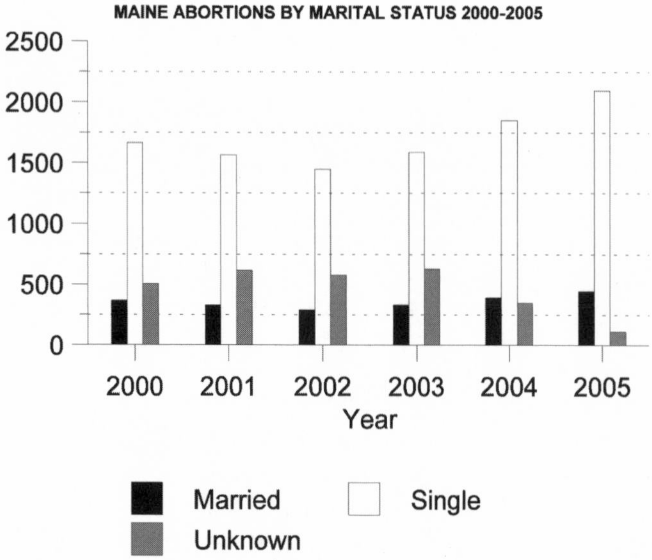

Source: Maine Department for Disease Control and Prevention.

Maine Abortion by Age Group 2000–2005
Age Group (yrs)

Year	*≤14*	*15-19*	*20-24*	*25-29*	*30-34*	*35-39*	*40-44*	*≥45*	*Unknown*
2000	11	571	773	515	338	241	66	1	20
2001	8	544	834	494	302	226	83	6	18
2002	7	483	811	436	297	179	64	4	34
2003	9	473	919	535	330	194	62	4	24
2004	8	506	867	564	318	229	74	8	19
2005	12	510	863	569	329	201	85	6	78
Total	55	3,087	5,067	3,113	1,914	1,270	434	29	193

Source: Maine Department for Disease Control and Prevention.

Maine Prior Abortion by Female 2000–2005
Prior Abortion

Year	*None*	*1*	*2*	*≥3*	*Not known*
2000	1,296	1,050	105	39	46
2001	1,662	639	159	55	0
2002	1,532	583	145	51	4
2003	1,609	658	201	81	1
2004	1,539	694	258	101	1
2005	1,764	621	186	82	0
Total	9,402	4,245	1,054	409	52

Source: Maine Department for Disease Control and Prevention.

B. "Viability" means the state of fetal development when the life of the fetus may be continued indefinitely outside the womb by natural or artificial life-supportive systems.

3. Persons who may perform abortions:

A. Only a person licensed under Title 32, chapter 36 or chapter 48, to practice medicine in Maine as a medical or osteopathic physician, may perform an abortion on another person.

B. Any person not so licensed who knowingly performs an abortion on another person or any person who knowingly assists a nonlicensed person to perform an abortion on another person is guilty of a Class C crime.

4. A person who performs an abortion after viability is guilty of a Class D crime if:

A. He knowingly disregarded the viability of the fetus; and

B. He knew that the abortion was not necessary for the preservation of the life or health of the mother.

Maine Code T. 22, § 1594. Failure to preserve life of live born person

Whenever an abortion procedure results in a live birth, failure to take all reasonable steps, in keeping with good medical practice, to preserve the life and health of the live born person shall subject the responsible party or parties to Maine law governing homicide, manslaughter and civil liability for wrongful death and medical malpractice.

Maine Code Ti. 22, § 1595. Live born and live birth defined

"Live born" and "live birth," as used in this chapter, shall mean a product of conception after complete expulsion or extraction from its mother, irrespective of the duration of pregnancy, which breathes or shows any other evidence of life such as beating of the heart, pulsation of the umbilical cord or definite movement of voluntary muscles, whether or not the umbilical cord has been cut or the placenta is attached. Each product of such a birth is considered live born and fully recognized as a human person under Maine law.

(3) INFORMED CONSENT

Prior to an abortion Maine requires that a woman be fully informed of the procedure to be used, the risks involved and alternatives to abortion. A woman must give written consent to the abortion. The statute addressing the matter is set out below.

Maine Code Ti. 22, § 1599-A. Consent to abortion

1. A physician may not perform an abortion unless, prior to the performance, the attending physician certifies in writing that the woman gave her informed written consent, freely and without coercion.

2. To ensure that the consent for an abortion is truly informed consent, the attending physician shall inform the woman, in a manner that in the physician's professional judgment is not misleading and that will be understood by the patient, of at least the following:

A. According to the physician's best judgment she is pregnant;

B. The number of weeks elapsed from the probable time of the conception;

C. The particular risks associated with her own pregnancy and the abortion technique to be performed; and

D. At the woman's request, alternatives to abortion such as childbirth and adoption and information concerning public and private agencies that will provide the woman with economic and other assistance to carry the fetus to term, including, if the woman so requests, a list of these agencies and the services available from each.

(4) ABORTION BY MINORS

Under the laws of Maine no physician may perform an abortion upon an unemancipated minor unless he/she first obtains the written consent of one parent, guardian or adult family member of the minor. The state also requires that a minor receive extensive counseling and information prior to an abortion, that informs the minor of the procedure to be used, the risks involved and alternatives to abortion.

In compliance with federal constitutional law, Maine has provided a judicial waiver procedure for an unemancipated minor to obtain an abortion without consent from a parent, guardian or adult family member. The minor may petition a trial court for a waiver of the consent requirement. A minor has a right to an attorney at the proceeding and if she cannot afford one, the court must appoint her an attorney. If a minor chooses, she may represent herself. The required consent from a parent, guardian or adult family member may be waived if the court finds either (1) that the minor is mature and well-informed enough to make the abortion decision on her own, or (2) that performance of the abortion would be in the best interest of the minor. An expedited appeal is available to any minor to whom the court denies a waiver of consent. The statute addressing the matters is set out below.

Maine Code Ti. 22, § 1597-A.
Parental consent and judicial bypass

1. As used in this section, unless the context otherwise indicates, the following terms have the following meanings.

A. "Abortion" means the intentional interruption of a pregnancy by the application of external agents, whether chemical or physical, or the ingestion of chemical agents with an intention other than to produce a live birth or to remove a dead fetus.

B. "Counselor" means a person who is: (1) A psychiatrist; (2) A psychologist licensed under Title 32, chapter 56; (3) A social worker licensed under Title 32, chapter 83; (4) An ordained member of the clergy; (5) A physician's assistant registered by the Board of Licensure in Medicine, Title 32, chapter 48; (6) A nurse practitioner registered by the Board of Licensure in Medicine, Title 32, chapter 48; (7) A certified guidance counselor; (8) A registered professional nurse licensed under Title 32, chapter 31; or (9) A practical nurse licensed under Title 32, chapter 31.

C. "Minor" means a person who is less than 18 years of age.

2. Except as otherwise provided by law, no person may knowingly perform an abortion upon a pregnant minor unless:

A. The attending physician has received and will make part of the medical record the informed written consent of the minor and one parent, guardian or adult family member;

B. The attending physician has secured the informed written consent of the minor as prescribed in subsection 3 and the minor, under all the surrounding circumstances, is mentally and physically competent to give consent;

C. The minor has received the information and counseling required under subsection 4, has secured written verification of receiving the information and counseling and the attending physician has received and will make part of the medical record the informed written consent of the minor and the written verification of receiving information and counseling required under subsection 4; or

D. The Probate Court or District Court issues an order under subsection 6 on petition of the minor or the next friend of the minor for purposes of filing a petition for the minor, granting:

(1) To the minor majority rights for the sole purpose of consenting to the abortion and the attending physician has received the informed written consent of the minor; or

(2) To the minor consent to the abortion, when the court has given its informed written consent and the minor is having the abortion willingly, in compliance with subsection 7.

3. No physician may perform an abortion upon a minor unless, prior to performing the abortion, the attending physician received the informed written consent of the minor.

A. To ensure that the consent for an abortion is informed consent, the attending physician shall:

(1) Inform the minor in a manner which, in the physician's professional judgment, is not misleading and which will be understood by the patient, of at least the following:

(a) According to the physician's best judgment the minor is pregnant;

(b) The number of weeks of duration of the pregnancy; and

(c) The particular risks associated with the minor's pregnancy, the abortion technique that may be performed and the risks involved for both;

(2) Provide the information and counseling described in subsection 4 or refer the minor to a counselor who will provide the information and counseling described in subsection 4; and

(3) Determines whether the minor is, under all the surrounding circumstances, mentally and physically competent to give consent.

B. No recovery may be allowed against any physician upon the grounds that the abortion was rendered without the informed consent of the minor when:

(1) The physician, in obtaining the minor's consent, acted in accordance with the standards of practice among members of the same health care profession with similar training and experience situated in the same or similar communities; or

(2) The physician has received and acted in good faith on the informed written consent to the abortion given by the minor to a counselor.

4. The provision of information and counseling by any physician or counselor for any pregnant minor for decision making regarding pregnancy shall be in accordance with this subsection.

A. Any physician or counselor providing pregnancy information and counseling under this subsection shall, in a manner that will be understood by the minor:

(1) Explain that the information being given to the minor is being given objectively and is not intended to coerce, persuade or induce the minor to choose either to have an abortion or to carry the pregnancy to term;

(2) Explain that the minor may withdraw a decision to have an abortion at any time before the abortion is performed or may reconsider a decision not to have an abortion at any time within

the time period during which an abortion may legally be performed;

(3) Clearly and fully explore with the minor the alternative choices available for managing the pregnancy, including:

(a) Carrying the pregnancy to term and keeping the child;

(b) Carrying the pregnancy to term and placing the child with a relative or with another family through foster care or adoption;

(c) The elements of prenatal and postnatal care; and

(d) Having an abortion;

(4) Explain that public and private agencies are available to provide birth control information and that a list of these agencies and the services available from each will be provided if the minor requests;

(5) Discuss the possibility of involving the minor's parents, guardian or other adult family members in the minor's decision making concerning the pregnancy and explore whether the minor believes that involvement would be in the minor's best interests; and

(6) Provide adequate opportunity for the minor to ask any questions concerning the pregnancy, abortion, child care and adoption, and provide the information the minor seeks or, if the person cannot provide the information, indicate where the minor can receive the information.

B. After the person provides the information and counseling to a minor as required by this subsection, that person shall have the minor sign and date a form stating that:

(1) The minor has received information on prenatal care and alternatives to abortion and that there are agencies that will provide assistance;

(2) The minor has received an explanation that the minor may withdraw an abortion decision or reconsider a decision to carry a pregnancy to term;

(3) The alternatives available for managing the pregnancy have been clearly and fully explored with the minor;

(4) The minor has received an explanation about agencies available to provide birth control information;

(5) The minor has discussed with the person providing the information and counseling the possibility of involving the minor's parents, guardian or other adult family members in the minor's decision making about the pregnancy;

(6) The reasons for not involving the minor's parents, guardian or other adult family members are put in writing on the form by the minor or the person providing the information and counseling; and

(7) The minor has been given an adequate opportunity to ask questions. The person providing the information and counseling shall also sign and date the form, and include that person's address and telephone number. The person shall keep a copy for that person's files and shall give the form to the minor or, if the minor requests and if the person providing the information is not the attending physician, transmit the form to the minor's attending physician.

5. An informed consent which is evidenced in writing containing information and statements provided in subsection 4 and which is signed by the minor shall be presumed to be a valid informed consent. This presumption may be subject to rebuttal only upon proof that the informed consent was obtained through fraud, deception or misrepresentation of material fact.

6. The court may issue an order for the purpose of consenting to the abortion by the minor under the following circumstances and procedures.

A. The minor or next friend of the minor for the purposes of filing a petition may make an application to the Probate Court or District Court which shall assist the minor or next friend in preparing the petition. The minor or the next friend of the minor shall file a petition setting forth:

(1) The initials of the minor;

(2) The age of the minor;

(3) That the minor has been fully informed of the risks and consequences of the abortion;

(4) That the minor is of sound mind and has sufficient intellectual capacity to consent to the abortion;

(5) That, if the court does not grant the minor majority rights for the purpose of consent to the abortion, the court should find that the abortion is in the best interest of the minor and give judicial consent to the abortion;

(7) That, if the minor does not have private counsel, that the court may appoint counsel. The minor or the next friend shall sign the petition.

B. The petition is a confidential record and the court files on the petition shall be impounded.

C. A hearing on the merits of the petition shall be held as soon as possible within 5 days of the filing of the petition. If any party is unable to afford counsel, the court shall appoint counsel at least 24 hours before the time of the hearing. At the hearing, the court shall hear evidence relating to:

(1) The emotional development, maturity, intellect and understanding of the minor;

(2) The nature, possible consequences and alternatives to the abortion; and

(3) Any other evidence that the court may find useful in determining whether the minor should be granted majority rights for the purpose of consenting to the abortion or whether the abortion is in the best interest of the minor. The hearing on the petition shall be held as soon as possible within 5 days of the filing of the petition. The court shall conduct the hearing in private with only the minor, interested parties as determined by the court and necessary court officers or personnel present. The record of the hearing is not a public record.

D. In the decree, the court shall for good cause:

(1) Grant the petition for majority rights for the sole purpose of consenting to the abortion;

(2) Find the abortion to be in the best interest of the minor and give judicial consent to the abortion, setting forth the grounds for the finding; or

(3) Deny the petition only if the court finds that the minor is not mature enough to make her own decision and that the abortion is not in her best interest.

E. If the petition is allowed, the informed consent of the minor, pursuant to a court grant of majority rights or the judicial consent, shall bar an action by the parent or guardian of the minor on the grounds of battery of the minor by those performing the abortion. The immunity granted shall only extend to the performance of the abortion and any necessary accompanying services which are performed in a competent manner.

F. The minor may appeal an order issued in accordance with this section to the Superior Court. The notice of appeal shall be filed within 24 hours from the date of issuance of the order. Any record on appeal shall be completed and the appeal shall be perfected within 5 days from the filing of notice to appeal. The Supreme Judicial Court shall, by court rule, provide for expedited appellate review of cases appealed under this section.

7. No abortion may be performed on any minor against her will, except that an abortion may be performed against the will of a minor pursuant to a court order described in subsection 6 that the abortion is necessary to preserve the life of the minor.

8. The following penalties apply to violations of this section.

A. A person may not knowingly perform or aid in the performance of an abortion in violation of this section. A person who violates this paragraph commits a Class D crime.

B. An attending physician or counselor may not knowingly fail to perform any action required by this section. A person who violates this paragraph commits a civil violation for which a fine of not more than $1,000 may be adjudged for each violation.

9. In the event that any portion of this section is held invalid, it is the intent of the Legislature that this entire section shall be invalid.

(5) USE OF FACILITIES AND PEOPLE

Under the laws of Maine medical facilities are not required to allow abortions at their facilities. The employees and physicians at medical facilities that do allow abortions are permitted to refuse to take part in abortions. The state bans discrimination against medical professionals who refuse to participate in abortions. The statutes addressing the matters are set out below.

Maine Code Ti. 22, § 1591.
Right to refuse to participate in abortion

No physician, nurse or other person who refuses to perform or assist in the performance of an abortion, and no hospital or health care facility that refuses to permit the performance of an abortion upon its premises, shall be liable to any person, firm, association or corporation for damages allegedly arising from the refusal, nor shall such refusal constitute a basis for any civil liability to any physician, nurse or other person, hospital or health care facility nor a basis for any disciplinary or other recriminatory action against them or any of them by the State or any person. No physician, nurse or other person, who refuses to perform or assist in the performance of an abortion, shall, because of that refusal, be dismissed, suspended, demoted or otherwise prejudiced or damaged by a hospital, health care facility, firm, association, professional association, corporation or educational institution with which he or she is affiliated or requests to be affiliated or by which he or she is employed, nor shall such refusal constitute grounds for loss of any privileges or immunities to which such physician, nurse or other person would otherwise be entitled nor shall submission to an abortion or the granting of consent therefor be a condition precedent to the receipt of any public benefits.

Maine Code Ti. 22, § 1592. Discrimination for refusal

No person, hospital, health care facility, firm, association, corporation or educational institution, directly or indirectly, by himself or another, shall discriminate against any physician, nurse or other person by refusing or withholding employment from or denying admittance, when such physician, nurse or other person refuses to perform, or assist in the performance of an abortion, nor shall such refusal constitute grounds for loss of any privileges or immunities to which such physician, nurse or other person would otherwise be entitled.

(6) BAN ON FETAL SALE OR EXPERIMENTS

Maine provides criminal penalties for anyone who traffics in or experiments with fetal remains. The statute addressing the matter is set out below.

Maine Code Ti. 22, § 1593. Trafficking in fetal remains

1. A person may not use, transfer, distribute or give away a live human fetus, whether intrauterine or extrauterine, or any product of conception considered live born, for scientific experimentation or for any form of experimentation.

2. A person may not consent to violating subsection 1 or aid or assist another in violating subsection 1.

3. A person who violates this section commits a Class C crime. Violation of this section is a strict liability crime as defined in Title 17-A, section 34, subsection 4-A.

(7) FETAL DEATH REPORT

Under the laws of Maine all abortions must be reported to the proper authorities. The statute addressing the matter is set out below.

Maine Code Ti. 22, § 1596. Abortion and miscarriage data

1. Definitions. As used in this section, unless the context otherwise indicates, the following terms have the following meanings.

A. "Abortion" means the intentional interruption of a pregnancy by the application of external agents, whether chemical or physical, or the ingestion of chemical agents with an intention other than to produce a live birth or to remove a dead fetus, regardless of the length of gestation.

B. "Miscarriage" means an interruption of a pregnancy other than as provided in paragraph A of a fetus of less than 20 weeks gestation.

2. Abortion reports. A report of each abortion performed shall be made to the Department of Health and Human Services on forms prescribed by the department. These report forms shall not identify the patient by name or otherwise and shall contain only the information requested on the United States Standard Report of Induced Termination of Pregnancy, published by the National Center for Health Statistics, dated January 1978, or any more recent revision of a standard report form.

The form containing that information and data shall be prepared and signed by the attending physician and transmitted to the department not later than 10 days following the end of the month in which the abortion is performed.

A physician who reports data on an abortion pursuant to this section shall be immune from any criminal liability for that abortion under section 1598.

3. Miscarriage reports. A report of each miscarriage shall be made by the physician in attendance at or after the occurrence of the miscarriage to the Department of Health and Human Services on forms prescribed by the department. These report forms shall contain all of the applicable information required on the certificate of fetal death in current use.

The report form shall be prepared and signed by the attending physician and transmitted to the department not later than 10 days following the end of the month in which the miscarriage occurs.

The identity of any patient or physician reporting pursuant to this section is confidential and the department shall take the steps which are necessary to insure the confidentiality of the identity of patients or physicians reporting pursuant to this section.

(8) INJURY TO PREGNANT WOMAN

Under the laws of Maine it is a criminal offense to cause injury to a woman who is pregnant. The statute addressing the matter is set out below.

Maine Code Ti. 17-A, § 208-C.
Elevated aggravated assault on pregnant person

1. A person is guilty of elevated aggravated assault on a pregnant person if that person intentionally or knowingly causes serious bodily injury to a person the person knows or has reason to know is pregnant. For the purposes of this subsection, "serious bodily injury" includes bodily injury that results in the termination of a pregnancy. This subsection does not apply to acts committed by:

A. Any person relating to an abortion for which the consent of the pregnant person, or a person authorized by law to act on her behalf, has been obtained or for which such consent is implied by law; or

B. Any person for any medical treatment of the pregnant person or the fetus.

2. Elevated aggravated assault on a pregnant person is a Class A crime.

(8) BAN ON CLINIC OBSTRUCTIONS

Maine prohibits pro-life activities that disrupt abortion facilities or causes harassment of abortion providers. The statute addressing the matter is set out below.

Maine Code Ti. 15, § 4684-B.
Unlawful health facility activities

1. As used in this section, unless the context otherwise indicates, the following terms have the following meanings.

A. "Building" means any structure having a roof or a partial roof supported by columns or walls that is used or intended to be used for shelter or enclosure of persons or objects regardless of the materials of which it is constructed.

B. "Health service" means any medical, surgical, laboratory, testing or counseling service relating to the human body.

C. "Physical obstruction" means rendering impassable ingress to or egress from a building or rendering passage to or from a building unreasonably difficult or hazardous.

2. It is a violation of this section for any person, whether or not acting under color of law, to intentionally interfere or attempt to intentionally interfere with the exercise or enjoyment by any other person of rights secured by the United States Constitution or the laws of the United States or of rights secured by the Constitution of Maine or laws of the State by any of the following conduct:

A. Engaging in the physical obstruction of a building;

B. Making or causing repeated telephone calls to a person or a building, whether or not conversation ensues, with the intent to impede access to a person's or building's telephone lines or otherwise disrupt a person's or building's activities;

C. Activating a device or exposing a substance that releases noxious and offensive odors within a building; or

D. After having been ordered by a law enforcement officer to cease such noise, intentionally making noise that can be heard within a building and with the further intent either:

(1) To jeopardize the health of persons receiving health services within the building; or

(2) To interfere with the safe and effective delivery of those services within the building.

Maine Right to Life Committee

Maine Right to Life Committee (MRLC) is a pro-life organization that believes in the sanctity and worth of all human life. The executive director of MRLC is Teresa Tumidajski. MRLC identifies, educates and mobilizes the pro-life population of Maine. The organization engages in many pro-life activities that include putting on educational programs; publishing a newsletter called "Life For Me"; providing speakers to schools, churches, pro-life and civic groups throughout the state; publishing and promoting a variety of educational materials; providing consultant services to schools and churches; providing education services that show people how they can be effective as citizen lobbyists, voters and members of political parties; and providing support to pro-life candidates for federal and state office. *See also* **Pro-Life Organizations**

Male Condom *see* **Condoms**

Male Reproductive System

The male reproductive system is designed to facilitate the ejaculation of sperm into the body of a female for the purpose of procreation. This process occurs through sexual intercourse. The male system may be viewed into two parts: external organs and internal organs.

(1) External Organs

The primary male external reproductive organs include the penis and scrotum.

Penis. The male penis is a cylindrical organ that facilitates the outward passage of urine and semen. The penis is made up of three columns of tissue (two dorsal corpora cavernosa and one corpus spongiosum) that are bound together by connective tissue (tunica albugenia) and covered by a thin layer of skin. The blood supply of the penis is provided through an artery that branches into nutrient arteries and helicine arteries. The nutrient arteries supply the blood that brings nutrients to the tissues of the penis. The helicine arteries provide the supply of blood to the erectile tissues. The frame of the penis consists of three main parts: root, body and glans penis. The root is attached to the abdominal wall. The body is the middle portion of the penis. The glans penis refers to the cone-shaped end of the penis. The opening of the urethra is at the tip of the glans penis. The base of the glans penis is referred to as the corona. In males that are not circumcised, the prepuce (foreskin) extends from the corona to cover the glans penis.

The penis becomes rigid and erect during sexual activity. This enables the penetration of the female vagina during sexual intercourse. An erection comes about as a result of nerve impulses from the autonomic nervous system that dilate the arteries of the penis. This dramatically increases the blood flow to the penis and causes it to expand in length and diameter. Sperm will be ejaculated when vaginal friction on the glans penis sends signals to the brain and spinal cord. Muscle contractions in the penis will force semen into the urethra and propel the semen out of the penis. When ejaculation takes place arteries constrict and veins relax. This will reduce blood inflow and the penis will return to its normal size.

Scrotum. The scrotum is a protective pouch that contains the testicles and part of the spermatic cord. It is attached at the base of the penis. The scrotum is divided internally into two halves by a membrane, with each half containing a testicle. It has an outer layer of thin and wrinkled skin. The scrotum functions as a climate-control system for the testicles, which need to be three to five degrees below body temperature to allow normal sperm development. Muscle fibers that line the scrotum wall are called cremaster. These muscles relax or contract to allow the testicles to hang farther from the body to cool or to be pulled closer to the body for warmth or protection.

(2) Internal Organs

The primary male internal reproductive organs include the testicles, epididymis, vas deferens, seminal vesicles, ejaculatory ducts, urethra, prostate gland, bulbourethral glands and semen.

Testicles. The testicles (testes) are the primary male reproductive organs. They are oval shaped glands the size of large olives, and are suspended inside the scrotum by a spermatic cord. Each testicle is surrounded by a special sac called the processus vaginalis and is enclosed by fibrous connective tissue (tunica albuginea). Normally the left testicle will hang a little lower than the right testicle.

The testicles produce sperm cells and testosterone (male sex hormones). Each testicle is organized into two separate compartments: the seminiferous tubules and the interstitial area. The seminiferous tubules produce sperm cells and the interstitial area produce testosterone.

Epididymis. The epididymis is a thread-like tube that is connected to the ducts within the testicles. They are contained in the scrotum. The epididymis secrete a hormone, glycogen, that helps sustain immature sperm cells and promotes their maturation. Sperm cells become mobile in the epididymis before leaving to enter the vas deferens.

Vas Deferens. The vas deferens are a pair of small cord-like tubes that connect the epididymis and ejaculatory ducts. They are contained in the scrotum. It serves as another storage site for sperm and also transports sperm from the epididymis to the ejaculatory ducts.

Seminal vesicles. The seminal vesicles are two pouches that are connected to the vas deferens. They secrete a slightly alkaline fluid that contains a variety of nutrients, such as fructose, that provides the sperm cells an energy source. At the point of ejaculation, the contents of the seminal vesicles empty into the ejaculatory ducts and increase the volume of fluid that is released by the vas deferens.

Ejaculatory ducts. Ejaculatory ducts form from the convergence of the vas deferens and the seminal vesicles. They open into the urethra to convey sperm cells.

Urethra. The urethra is a small tubular passageway for fluid. It runs through the prostate and the penis. The urethra is an important organ for both the urinary and reproductive systems. Its role in the reproductive system is to transport seminal fluid through the penis and into the female vagina. The urethra is also part of the urinary tract that transports urine from the bladder.

Prostate gland. The prostate gland is made of smooth muscle and glandular tissue. It is usually the size of a walnut, but enlarges with age. The prostate gland lies just under the bladder in the pelvis, and surrounds the middle portion of the urethra. It secretes an alkaline fluid that nourishes sperm, keeps the sperm mobile and protects it from the acid secretions of the female vagina. This fluid is discharged into the urethra as part of the ejaculation during sexual intercourse.

Bulbourethral glands. Bulbourethral glands (also called Cowper's glands), are two small structures about the size of peas that are located below the prostate gland. They are enclosed by fibers. The glands secrete a fluid that is released in response to sexual stimulation. The fluid provides some lubrication to the end of the penis in preparation for sexual intercourse.

Semen. Semen consists of sperm and fluids from the seminal vesicles, prostate and bulbourethral glands. It is ejaculated during sexual intercourse. The semen contains millions of sperm cells, but only one is needed to fertilize an egg. *See also* **Female Reproductive System**

Male Sterilization

Male sterilization (vasectomy) is considered an extreme form of birth control. This condition involves cutting and tying the tubes (vas deferens) that carry sperm out of the body. The procedure permanently prevents sperm from being ejaculated (in rare instances the procedure may be done so that it is reversible). *See also* **Contraception; Hysterectomy; Tubal Ligation**

Manual Vacuum Aspiration *see* **Mini Vac Aspiration**

MARAL Pro-Choice Michigan

MARAL Pro-Choice Michigan (MARAL) was founded in 1979, as a statewide organization that utilizes the political process to assure that women have the right to make personal decisions regarding the full range of reproductive choices, including preventing unintended pregnancies, bearing healthy children, and choosing legal abortion. The organization is devoted solely to political activism and advocacy on behalf of reproductive rights. MARAL is active in developing policies and strategies that: (1) ensure that all women have the constitutionally protected right to choose and obtain a safe and legal abortion; (2) ensure that women, men and teenagers have access to quality sexuality education and voluntary contraceptive care in order to prevent unintended pregnancy; (3) enable women and families who choose to have children to have healthy pregnancies and healthy children; and (4) ensure that the rights and conditions necessary to exercise these rights are available to everyone without regard to race, ethnicity, color, religion, age, gender, degree of physical ability, national origin, sexual orientation, marital status, political affiliation, economic means or educational status. MARAL actively supports pro-choice candidates for elective office. This activity includes publishing a voter guide, candidate recruitment and training, and financial support. *See also* **Pro-Choice Organizations**

March for Life

March for Life is an annual pro-life rally in Washington, D.C. The rally was started on January 22, 1974. It has been held on January 22 of every subsequent year to draw attention to the January 22, 1973, decision of the United States Supreme Court in *Roe v. Wade*, which legalized abortion in the nation.

In order to maintain the annual rally in an organized manner, March for Life was formed into an organization. The organization is led by its president Nellie Gray. As an organization March for Life advocates the adoption of a human life amendment, to the federal constitution, that would require society provide protection for the life of each human being in existence at conception. *See also* **Pro-Life Organizations**

March for Women's Lives *see* **National Organization for Women**

Marfan's Syndrome

Marfan's syndrome is an inherited (or spontaneous new mutation) condition that affects the skeletal system, cardiovascular system, eyes, and to a limited extent the central nervous system. Approximately 200,000 people in the United States have the disorder. Some of the more common symptoms of the disorder include a tall, lanky frame with long arms, chest abnormalities, long and narrow face, and spider-fingers. Common eye problems include nearsightedness and dislocation of the lens of the eye. The most significant disorder caused by the syndrome are cardiovascular abnormalities, which can result in death. The disorder is also known to cause a sudden collapse of a lung. Most problems associated with the disorder can be treated if diagnosed early. There is no way to prevent the disorder from occurring. *See also* **Birth Defects and Abortion**

Marital Status and Abortion *see* **Abortion**

Marshall, Thurgood

Thurgood Marshall (1908–1993) served as an associate justice of the United States Supreme Court from 1967 to 1991. While on the Supreme Court Justice Marshall was known as a liberal interpreter of the Constitution, with respect to individual liberties and rights.

Justice Marshall was born in Baltimore, Maryland. He obtained an undergraduate degree from Lincoln University and a law degree from Howard University School of Law in 1933. As an attorney he took up the cause of civil rights and comprised an impressive record of legal victories that helped dismantle racial segregation in the United States. Justice Marshall was appointed as an appellate judge for the Second Circuit Court of Appeals in 1961. In 1965 he was appointed Solicitor General of the United States. President Lyndon B. Johnson appointed Justice Marshall as the first African-American on the Supreme Court in 1967.

Distribution of the Abortion Voting Pattern of Justice Marshall Based Upon Opinions Filed by the Supreme Court

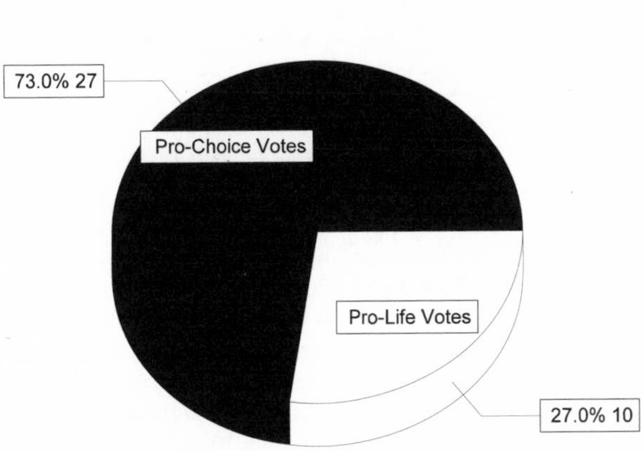

During Justice Marshall's tenure on the Supreme Court he issued a significant number of abortion related opinions. The written opinions and opinions simply voted on by Justice Marshall, indicate that he was in favor of using the constitution to expand abortion rights for women.

(1) Unanimous opinions voted with only. In *Bellotti v. Baird I* Justice Marshall voted with a unanimous opinion, which held that the federal district court had to certify appropriate questions to the supreme judicial court of Massachusetts, concerning the interpretation of that state's parental consent abortion statute for minors, before ruling on its constitutionality. In *Withrow v. Larkin* Justice Marshall joined a unanimous opinion, which held that constitutional due process was not violated by the mere fact that a Wisconsin medical examining board had the authority to both, investigate and adjudicate, allegations against a physician that included, among other things, permitting a nonphysician to perform an abortion.

(2) Majority opinions written. Justice Marshall wrote the majority opinion in *Bolger v. Youngs Drug Products Corp.*, which held that a provision of the Comstock Act, 39 U.S.C. § 3001(e)(2), that prohibited mailing unsolicited advertisements for contraceptives violated the Free Speech Clause of the First Amendment.

(3) Majority opinions voted with only. In *Automobile Workers v. Johnson Controls, Inc.* Justice Marshall voted with the majority opinion, which held that Title VII of the Civil Rights Act forbids sex-specific fetal-protection policies by an employer, that exclude a fertile female employee from certain jobs because of the employer's concern for the health of the fetus the woman might conceive. In *Federal Election Commission v. Massachusetts Citizens for Life, Inc.* Justice Marshall voted with the majority opinion, which held that federal law that prohibited the appellee from using its treasury funds to promote pro-life political candidates violated the Free Speech Clause of the First Amendment. Justice Marshall joined the majority decision in *Thornburgh v. American College of Obstetricians and Gynecologists*, which invalidated provisions in Pennsylvania's abortion statute that provided for maternal informed consent, abortion alternative printed information, abortion reporting requirements, determination of fetal viability, degree of care required in post-viability abortions, and a second-physician requirement. In *Diamond v. Charles*, Justice Marshall joined the majority opinion, which held that a citizen did not have standing to appeal a decision invalidating parts of Illinois' abortion statute that (1) imposed criminal penalties for violating a prescribed standard of care that had to be exercised by a physician in performing an abortion of a viable fetus, and of a possibly viable fetus; and (2) imposed criminal penalties for physicians who failed to provide patients with information about the type of abortifacient used.

Justice Marshall voted with the majority opinion in *City of Akron v. Akron Center for Reproductive Health, Inc.*, which invalidated an abortion ordinance that provided requirements for parental consent, informed consent, waiting period, hospitalization and disposal of fetal remains. Justice Marshall joined the majority opinion in *Simopoulos v. Virginia*, which upheld a Virginia statute requiring second trimester abortions be performed at hospitals, because under the statute an adequately equipped clinic could, upon proper application, obtain an outpatient hospital license that permitted the performance of second-trimester abortions. In *Colautti v. Franklin* Justice Marshall joined the majority opinion, which held that the constitution was violated by a vague and ambiguous provision in Pennsylvania's abortion statute that subjected a physician who performed an abortion to potential criminal liability, if he/she failed to utilize a statutorily prescribed technique when the fetus was viable or when there was sufficient reason to believe that the fetus may be viable.

In *Carey v. Population Services International* Justice Marshall voted with the majority opinion, which held that the constitution prohibited enforcement of a New York statute that made it a crime (1) for any person to sell or distribute any contraceptive of any kind to a minor under the age of 16 years; (2) for anyone other than a licensed pharmacist to distribute contraceptives to persons 16 or over; and (3) for anyone, including licensed pharmacists, to advertise or display contraceptives. Justice Marshall voted the majority opinion in *Planned Parenthood of Missouri v. Danforth*, which held that the constitution was not violated by provisions in Missouri's abortion statute involving the definition of fetal viability, woman's written consent, and record keeping and reporting requirements; but that the constitution prohibited the requirements concerning spousal consent, parental consent for minor, banning saline amniocentesis abortions, and physician's standard of care. Justice Marshall joined the majority opinion in *Anders v. Floyd*, which held that a federal district court erred in enjoining enforcement of a South Carolina statute that imposed criminal punishment for performing an abortion on a viable fetus.

In *Connecticut v. Menillo* Justice Marshall joined the majority per curiam opinion, which held that the constitution was not violated by criminal abortion statutes that prohibit nonphysicians from attempting or performing abortions at any stage of a pregnancy. Justice Marshall joined the majority opinion in *Bigelow v. Virginia*, which held that the Free Speech and Free Press Clauses of the First Amendment were violated by a Virginia penal statute that prohibited selling or circulating any publication that encouraged or promoted abortions. In *Weinberger v. Hynson, Westcott & Dunning* Justice Marshall joined the majority opinion, which held that the Food and Drug Administration could not deny a drug manufacturer a hearing to obtain marketing approval for a drug called Lutrexin, which provided treatment for premature labor and threatened and habitual abortion. In *Roe v. Wade* Justice Marshall joined the majority opinion, which held that the liberty component of the Due Process Clause of the Fourteenth Amendment prohibited states from criminalizing or preventing elective first trimester abortions. Justice Marshall voted with the majority opinion in *Doe v. Bolton*, which held that the Due Process Clause of the Fourteenth Amendment was violated by provisions in Georgia's -abortion statutes that required (1) abortions take place in accredited hospitals, (2) that an abortion be approved by a hospital abortion committee, (3) that the need for an abortion be confirmed by two independent physicians, and (4) that a woman seeking an abortion be a resident of Georgia. Justice Marshall voted with the majority opinion in *Eisenstadt v. Baird*, which held that the Equal Protection Clause of the Fourteenth Amendment was violated by a Massachusetts statute that made it a crime to give away a drug, medicine, instrument, or article for the prevention of conception except in the case of (1) a physician prescribing it for a married person, or (2) a pharmacist furnishing it to a married person presenting a physician's prescription.

(4) Plurality opinions voted with only. Justice Marshall joined the plurality opinion that announced the judgment of the Supreme Court in *Singleton v. Wulff*, which held that the Eighth Circuit court of appeals had jurisdiction to determine whether abortion providers had standing to challenge a provision in Missouri's abortion statute that limited Medicaid payment for abortions, but it did not have jurisdiction to rule that the provision violated the constitution because the district court did not address the issue.

(5) Concurring opinions voted with only. Justice Marshall concurred in the majority judgment in *Bellotti v. Baird II*, which held that Massachusetts' abortion statute for minors violated the constitution in light of an interpretation given by the state's highest court, that required parental notice of a judicial bypass proceeding invoked by a minor, and permitted a judge to deny an abortion even though the minor proved she had enough maturity to make an independent decision.

(6) Dissenting opinions written. Justice Marshall issued a dissenting statement in *United States Catholic Conference v. Abortion Rights*

Mobilization, which allowed the appellants to challenge having to turn over documents in a lawsuit seeking to strip them of their tax exempt status because of their active political abortion work. In *H. L. v. Matheson* Justice Marshall wrote an opinion dissenting from the majority opinion, which held that the constitution was not violated by Utah's requirement that the parents of a minor be notified, if possible, prior to performing an abortion. He believed the parental notification requirement violated the constitution. Justice Marshall wrote an opinion dissenting from the majority decision in *Harris v. McRae*, which held that Medicaid funding restrictions for abortion by the Hyde Amendment, did not violate the Due Process Clause nor the equal protection component of the Fifth Amendment. He believed the Hyde Amendment violated the constitution.

Justice Marshall wrote an opinion dissenting from the majority opinion in *Beal v. Doe*, which held that Pennsylvania's refusal to extend Medicaid coverage to nontherapeutic abortions was not invalid nor inconsistent with Title XIX of the Social Security Act. He believed Title XIX required funding for all abortions. Justice Marshall wrote an opinion dissenting from the majority decision in *Burns v. Alcala*, which held that states receiving federal financial aid under the program of Aid to Families with Dependent Children, were not required to offer welfare benefits to pregnant women for their unborn children. He believed states were required to provide aid to pregnant women for their unborn children.

(7) Dissenting opinions voted with only. Justice Marshall cast a dissenting vote in *Rust v. Sullivan*, which upheld federal regulations that prohibited pro-abortion counseling, referral, and advocacy by health care providers. In *Ohio v. Akron Center for Reproductive Health* Justice Marshall voted to dissent from the majority decision, which upheld the constitutionality of Ohio's abortion statute notice and judicial bypass requirements for pregnant female minors. In *Frisby v. Schultz* Justice Marshall voted to dissent from the majority decision, which upheld the constitutional validity of a town ordinance that was created to prevent pro-life picketing at the residence of an abortion doctor. He believed the ordinance was too broad in scope. In *Williams v. Zbaraz* Justice Marshall dissented from the majority opinion, which held that in light of the requirements of the Hyde Amendment, the Equal Protection Clause of the Fourteenth Amendment was not violated by an Illinois statute that prohibited state Medicaid payment for abortions, except when necessary to save the life of the pregnant woman. He believed the statute violated the constitution.

In *Maher v. Roe* Justice Marshall dissented from the majority opinion, which held that the Equal Protection Clause of the Fourteenth Amendment did not prohibit Connecticut from excluding nontherapeutic abortions from its Medicaid program. He believed the Equal Protection Clause required funding all abortions. Justice Marshall dissented from the per curiam opinion in *Poelker v. Doe*, which held that the Equal Protection Clause of the Fourteenth Amendment was not violated by a policy of the city of St. Louis, Missouri that denied publicly funded abortions to indigent women at city hospitals, except when a woman's health or life was in danger. He believed the city's policy violated the constitution. Justice Marshall dissented from the majority decision in *Geduldig v. Aiello*, which held that the Equal Protection Clause of the Fourteenth Amendment did not require a private sector employee disability insurance program, operated by the state of California, provide coverage for employee disabilities associated with normal pregnancies. He believed the Equal Protection Clause was violated.

(8) Concurring and dissenting opinions written. Justice Marshall wrote a concurring and dissenting opinion in *Hodgson v. Minnesota*, which upheld the constitutionality of Minnesota's requirement that a pregnant female minor could not obtain an abortion until at least 48 hours after both of her parents had been notified, except when (1) the attending physician certified that an immediate abortion was necessary to prevent the minor's death; (2) the minor declared that she was a victim of parental abuse or neglect; or (3) a court of competent jurisdiction ordered the abortion to proceed without notice upon proof that the minor was mature and capable of giving informed consent or that an abortion without notice to both parents would be in the minor's best interest. Justice Marshall dissented from the Court's determination that, although the two-parent notification requirement was invalid, the judicial bypass option cured the defect.

(9) Concurring and dissenting opinions voted with only. Justice Marshall voted to concur and dissent in *Webster v. Reproductive Health Services*, which upheld Missouri's prohibition on the use of public facilities or employees to perform abortions and a requirement that physicians conduct viability tests prior to performing abortions. He concurred only in the majority's decision that a prohibition on public funding of abortion counseling was rendered moot and would not be analyzed. In *Planned Parenthood Assn. v. Ashcroft* Justice Marshall concurred and dissented from the majority/plurality opinion, which held that the constitution was violated by Missouri's requirement that second trimester abortions take place in a hospital; but that the constitution was not violated by the state's requirement that a pathology report for each abortion be performed, that a second physician be present during abortions performed after viability, and parental or judicial consent for abortion by minors. Justice Marshall believed that all of the provisions of the statute violated the constitution. Justice Marshall voted to concur and dissent from the majority decision in *United States v. Vuitch*, which held that the criminal abortion statute of the District of Columbia, which only permitted therapeutic abortions, was not constitutionally vague insofar as there was no ambiguity in its use of the word health and it did not shift to the defendant the burden of proving innocence. He believed the statute was constitutionally valid, but that the Court did not have jurisdiction to hear the case.

Maryland

(1) OVERVIEW

The state of Maryland enacted its first criminal abortion statute on March 20, 1867. The statute underwent several amendments prior to the 1973 decision by the United States Supreme Court in *Roe v. Wade*, which legalized abortion in the nation. Maryland has taken affirmative steps to respond to *Roe* and its progeny. Maryland has addressed several abortion issues by statute that include general abortion guidelines, abortion by minors, use of facilities and people, injury to pregnant woman, ban human cloning, and a ban on clinic obstructions.

(2) GENERAL ABORTION GUIDELINES

Maryland has expressly recognized the right of a woman to an abortion before viability. Under the state's laws a post-viability abortion may occur to save the life or health of the woman, or when the fetus has a serious congenital defect. Maryland requires all abortions be performed by a physician. The statutes addressing the issues are set out below.

Maryland Code Health Gen. § 20-207. Definition of physician

In Part II of this subtitle, the word "physician" means any person, including a doctor of osteopathy, licensed to practice medicine in the State of Maryland in compliance with the provisions of Title 14 of the Health Occupations Article.

Maryland Code Health Gen. § 20-208. Requirement of license

An abortion must be performed by a licensed physician.

Maryland Code Health Gen. § 20-209. Abortion rights

(a) In this section, "viable" means that stage when, in the best medical judgment of the attending physician based on the particular facts of

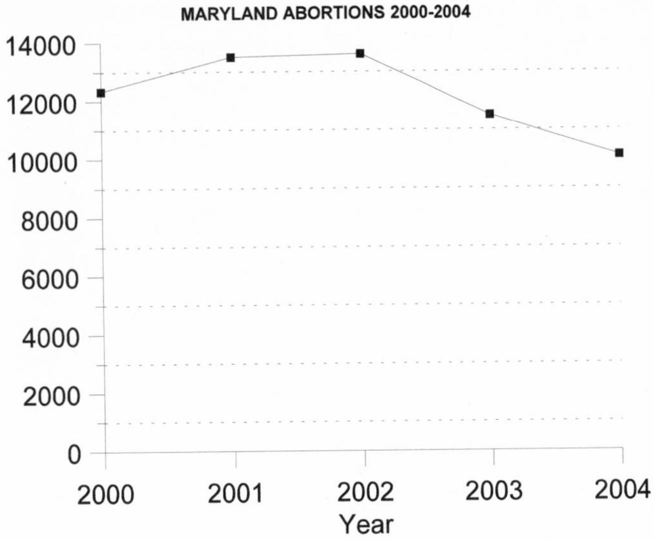

Source: National Center for Health Statistics.

Maryland Abortion by Age Group 2000–2004

	Age Group (yrs)						
Year	*<15*	*15–19*	*20–24*	*25–29*	*30–34*	*35–39*	*≥40*
2000	90	1,976	3,651	2,758	1,749	1,016	276
2001	96	2,170	4,358	2,918	1,910	968	281
2002	65	1,859	3,887	2,664	1,892	1,014	264
2003	31	1,399	2,912	2,244	1,645	819	271
2004	43	1,285	2,903	2,117	1,446	757	263
Total	325	8,689	17,711	12,701	8,642	4,574	1,355

Source: National Center for Health Statistics.

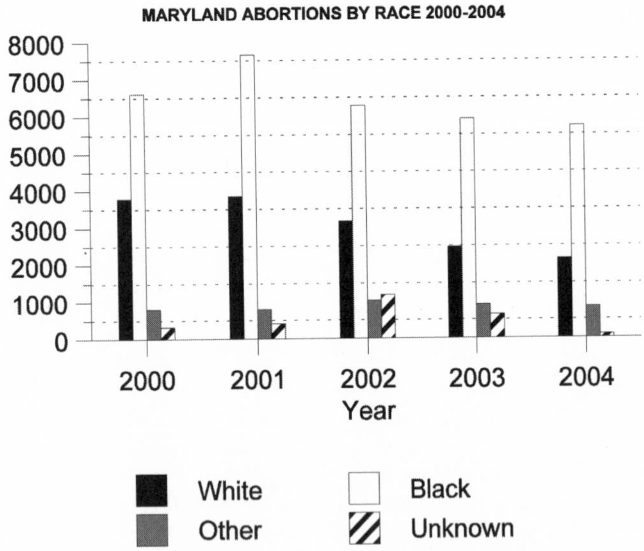

Source: National Center for Health Statistics.

the case before the physician, there is a reasonable likelihood of the fetus's sustained survival outside the womb.

(b) Except as otherwise provided in this subtitle, the State may not interfere with the decision of a woman to terminate a pregnancy:

(1) Before the fetus is viable; or

(2) At any time during the woman's pregnancy, if:

(i) The termination procedure is necessary to protect the life or health of the woman; or

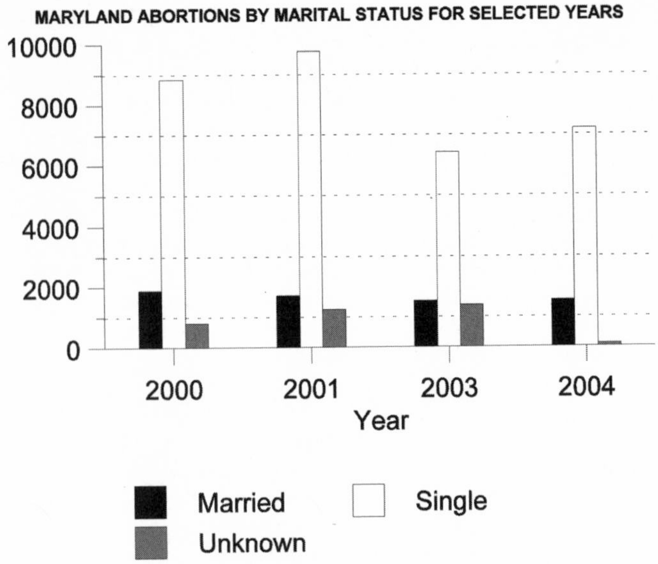

Source: National Center for Health Statistics.

Maryland Prior Abortion by Female 2000–2004

	Prior Abortion			
Year	*None*	*1*	*2*	*≥3*
2000	3,008	4,056	2,531	1,921
2001	3,638	4,384	2,602	2,077
2002	3,316	4,112	2,310	1,907
2003	2,760	3,022	1,864	1,675
2004	2,479	2,894	1,767	1,674
Total	15,201	18,468	11,074	9,254

Source: National Center for Health Statistics.

(ii) The fetus is affected by genetic defect or serious deformity or abnormality.

(c) The Department may adopt regulations that:

(1) Are both necessary and the least intrusive method to protect the life or health of the woman; and

(2) Are not inconsistent with established medical practice.

(d) Liability.— The physician is not liable for civil damages or subject to a criminal penalty for a decision to perform an abortion under this section made in good faith and in the physician's best medical judgment in accordance with accepted standards of medical practice.

(3) ABORTION BY MINORS

Under the laws of Maryland no physician may perform an abortion upon an unemancipated minor unless he/she first notifies a parent or the legal guardian of the minor. The notice requirement may be waived if the physician performing the abortion finds either (1) that the minor is mature and well-informed enough to make the abortion decision on her own, or (2) that performance of the abortion would be in the best interest of the minor. The statute addressing the matters is set out below.

Maryland Code Health Gen. § 20-103
Notice and physician bypass

(a) Except as provided in subsections (b) and (c) of this section, a physician may not perform an abortion on an unmarried minor unless the physician first gives notice to a parent or guardian of the minor.

(b) The physician may perform the abortion without notice to a parent or guardian if:

(1) The minor does not live with a parent or guardian; and

(2) A reasonable effort to give notice to a parent or guardian is unsuccessful.

(c)(1) The physician may perform the abortion, without notice to a parent or guardian of a minor if, in the professional judgment of the physician:

(i) Notice to the parent or guardian may lead to physical or emotional abuse of the minor;

(ii) The minor is mature and capable of giving informed consent to an abortion; or

(iii) Notification would not be in the best interest of the minor.

(2) The physician is not liable for civil damages or subject to a criminal penalty for a decision under this subsection not to give notice.

(d) The postal receipt that shows an article of mail was sent by certified mail, return receipt requested, bearing a postmark from the United States Postal Service, to the last known address of a parent or guardian and that is attached to a copy of the notice letter that was sent in that article of mail shall be conclusive evidence of notice or a reasonable effort to give notice, as the case may be.

(e) A physician may not provide notice to a parent or guardian if the minor decides not to have the abortion.

(4) USE OF FACILITIES AND PEOPLE

Under the laws of Maryland hospitals are not required to allow abortions at their facilities. The employees and physicians at hospitals that do allow abortions are permitted to refuse to take part in abortions. These issues were addressed in *County Executive of Prince George's County v. Doe*, 436 A.2d 459 (Md. 1981) and *St. Agnes Hosp. of City of Baltimore, Inc. v. Riddick*, 748 F.Supp. 319 (D.Md. 1990). The statute addressing the matters is set out below.

Maryland Code Health Gen. § 20-214.
Refusal to participate in abortion

(a) (1) A person may not be required to perform or participate in, or refer to any source for, any medical procedure that results in artificial insemination, sterilization, or termination of pregnancy.

(2) The refusal of a person to perform or participate in, or refer to a source for, these medical procedures may not be a basis for:

(i) Civil liability to another person; or

(ii) Disciplinary or other recriminatory action against the person.

(b)(1) A licensed hospital, hospital director, or hospital governing board may not be required:

(i) To permit, within the hospital, the performance of any medical procedure that results in artificial insemination, sterilization, or termination of pregnancy; or

(ii) To refer to any source for these medical procedures.

(2) The refusal to permit or to refer to a source for these procedures may not be grounds for:

(i) Civil liability to another person; or

(ii) Disciplinary or other recriminatory action against the person by this State or any person.

(c)(1) The refusal of an individual to submit to or give consent for an abortion or sterilization may not be grounds for loss of any privileges or immunities to which the individual otherwise would be entitled.

(2) Submitting to or granting consent for an abortion or sterilization may not be a condition precedent to the receipt of any public benefits.

(d) Notwithstanding any other provision of this section, a health care provider, a licensed hospital, a hospital director, or a hospital governing board is not immune from civil damages, if available at law, or from disciplinary or other recriminatory action, if the failure to refer a patient to a source for any medical procedure that results in sterilization or termination of pregnancy would reasonably be determined as:

(1) The cause of death or serious physical injury or serious long-lasting injury to the patient; and

(2) Otherwise contrary to the standards of medical care.

(5) INJURY TO PREGNANT WOMAN

Maryland makes it a criminal offense to injure a pregnant woman and thereby cause the death of a fetus. The statute addressing the matter is set out below.

Maryland Code Crim. Law § 2-103. Viable fetuses

(a) For purposes of a prosecution under this title, "viable" has the meaning stated in § 20-209 of the Health — General Article.

(b) Except as provided in subsections (d) through (f) of this section, a prosecution may be instituted for murder or manslaughter of a viable fetus.

(c) A person prosecuted for murder or manslaughter as provided in subsection (b) of this section must have:

(1) intended to cause the death of the viable fetus;

(2) intended to cause serious physical injury to the viable fetus; or

(3) wantonly or recklessly disregarded the likelihood that the person's actions would cause the death of or serious physical injury to the viable fetus.

(d) Nothing in this section applies to or infringes on a woman's right to terminate a pregnancy as stated in § 20-209 of the Health — General Article.

(e) Nothing in this section subjects a physician or other licensed medical professional to liability for fetal death that occurs in the course of administering lawful medical care.

(f) Nothing in this section applies to an act or failure to act of a pregnant woman with regard to her own fetus.

(g) Nothing in this section shall be construed to confer personhood or any rights on the fetus.

(h) The commission of first degree murder of a viable fetus under this section, in conjunction with the commission of another first degree murder arising out of the same incident, does not constitute an aggravating circumstance subjecting a defendant to the death penalty under § 2-303(g)(ix) of this title.

(6) BAN HUMAN CLONING

Maryland permits stem cell research, but prohibits human cloning. The statutes addressing the matters are set out below.

Maryland Code Art. 83A, § 5-2B-02. Research standards

(a) A person who conducts State-funded stem cell research shall conduct the research in a manner that considers the ethical and medical implications of the research.

(b) A person who conducts State-funded stem cell research may not engage in any research that intentionally and directly leads to human cloning.

Maryland Code Art. 83A, § 5-2B-13. Prohibited acts

(a) A person may not conduct or attempt to conduct human cloning.

(b) A person who violates this section is guilty of a felony and on conviction is subject to imprisonment not exceeding 10 years or a fine not exceeding $200,000 or both.

(7) BAN ON CLINIC OBSTRUCTIONS

Maryland has provided a penal statute to prohibit anti-abortion activities at medical clinics. The statute is primarily concerned with picketing conduct. The statute addressing the matter is set out below.

Maryland Crim. Law § 10-204.
Interference with access to medical facility

(a)(1) In this section the following words have the meanings indicated.

(2)(i) "Medical facility" means:

1. a facility as defined in § 10-101 of the Health — General Article; or

2. a health care facility as defined in § 19-114 of the Health — General Article.

(ii) "Medical facility" includes an agency, clinic, or office operated under the direction of the local health officer or under the regulatory authority of the Department of Health and Mental Hygiene.

(b)(1) This section does not apply to:

(i) the chief executive officer of the medical facility;

(ii) a designee of the chief executive officer of the medical facility;

(iii) an agent of the medical facility; or

(iv) a law enforcement officer.

(2) This section does not prohibit:

(i) speech; or

(ii) picketing in connection with a labor dispute as defined in § 4-301 of the Labor and Employment Article.

(c) A person may not intentionally act, alone or with others, to prevent another from entering or exiting a medical facility by physically:

(1) detaining the other; or

(2) obstructing, impeding, or hindering the other's passage.

(d) A person who violates this section is guilty of a misdemeanor and on conviction is subject to imprisonment not exceeding 90 days or a fine not exceeding $1,000 or both.

Mask of Pregnancy

Mask of pregnancy (melasma or chloasma) refers to a skin condition that is associated with pregnancy. The condition usually results in a patchy brownish discoloration of the skin. This condition will normally disappear after delivery.

Massachusetts

(1) OVERVIEW

The state of Massachusetts enacted its first criminal abortion statute on January 31, 1845. The statute underwent several amendments prior to the 1973 decision by the United States Supreme Court in *Roe v. Wade*, which legalized abortion in the nation. In spite of the decision in *Roe*, Massachusetts has not repealed its pre–*Roe* criminal abortion statutes. However, the statutes are constitutionally infirm.

Massachusetts has taken affirmative steps to respond to *Roe* and its progeny. Massachusetts has addressed numerous abortion issues by statute that include general abortion guidelines, informed consent and minors, use of facilities and people, ban on fetal experiments, ban on cloning, injury to pregnant woman, and a ban on anti-abortion activities.

(2) PRE-ROE ABORTION BAN

As previously indicated, Massachusetts has not repealed its pre–*Roe* criminal abortion laws. Under those laws the state criminalized performance of abortions, advertising abortion services, selling abortion instruments, and concealing the death of a fetus. In a 1972 abortion related case, *Eisenstadt v. Baird*, the United States Supreme Court held that the Equal Protection Clause of the Fourteenth Amendment was violated by a Massachusetts statute that made it a crime to give away a drug, medicine, instrument, or article for the prevention of conception.

Massachusetts Code Ti. 272, § 19. Procuring miscarriage

Whoever, with intent to procure the miscarriage of a woman, unlawfully administers to her, or advises or prescribes for her, or causes any poison, drug, medicine or other noxious thing to be taken by her or, with the like intent, unlawfully uses any instrument or other means whatever, or, with like intent, aids or assists therein, shall, if she dies in consequence thereof, be punished by imprisonment in the state prison for not less than five nor more than twenty years; and, if she does not die in consequence thereof, by imprisonment in the state prison for not more than seven years and by a fine of not more than two thousand dollars.

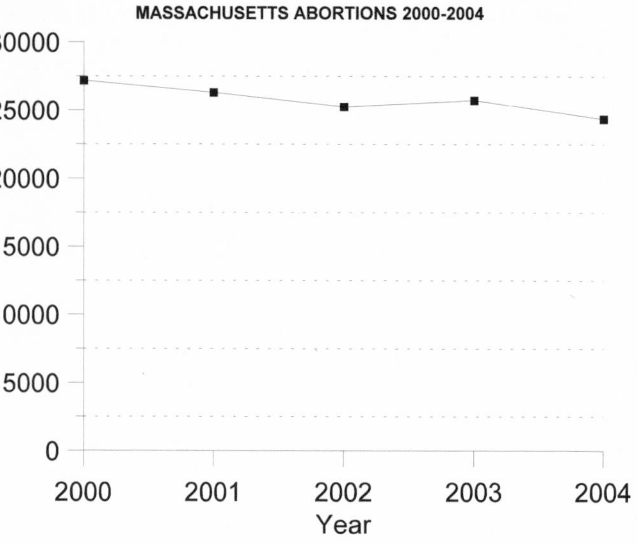

Source: National Center for Health Statistics.

Massachusetts Abortion by Age Group 2000-2004

Year	Age Group (yrs) <15	15–19	20–24	25–29	30–34	35–39	≥40	Unknown
2000	103	4,560	7,859	5,821	2,869	2,541	1,017	1,410
2001	78	3,735	8,163	5,676	3,926	2,479	1,037	1,199
2002	82	3,758	8,171	5,745	3,893	2,493	1,035	72
2003	101	4,454	7,986	5,630	3,960	2,558	1,004	48
2004	97	3,966	7,890	5,419	3,557	2,348	915	174
Total	461	20,473	40,069	28,291	18,205	12,419	5,008	2,903

Source: National Center for Health Statistics.

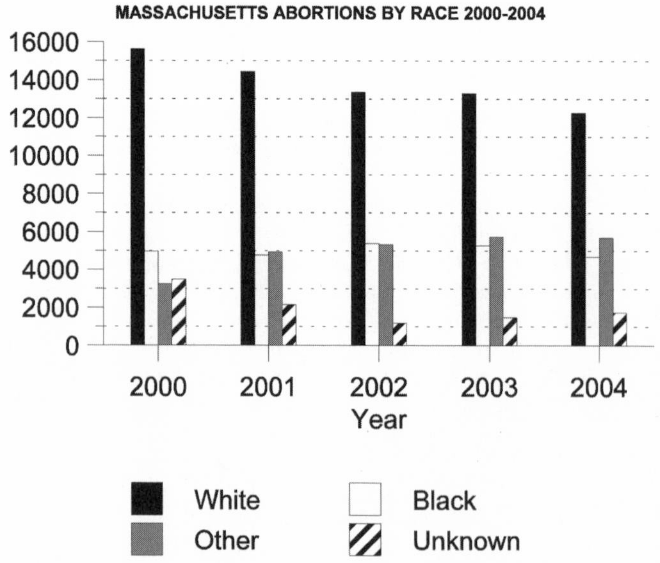

Source: National Center for Health Statistics.

Massachusetts Code Ti. 272, § 20.
Advertising relative to miscarriage

Except as provided in section twenty-one A, whoever knowingly advertises, prints, publishes, distributes or circulates, or knowingly causes to be

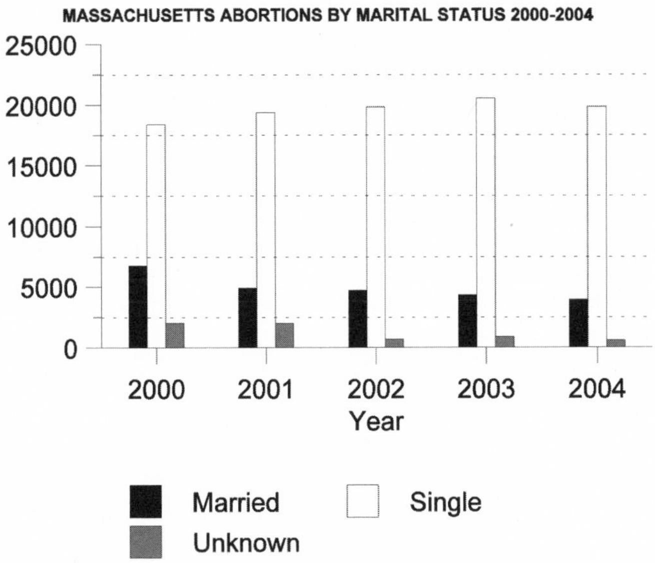

Source: National Center for Health Statistics.

Massachusetts Prior Abortion for Selected Years

Prior Abortion

Year	*None*	*1*	*2*	*≥3*	*Not known*
2000	12,447	6,306	3,014	1,927	3,486
2002	12,506	6,333	2,898	1,940	1,572
2003	12,353	6,618	3,123	2,194	1,453
2004	11,765	6,168	2,903	2,161	1,369
Total	49,071	25,425	11,938	8,222	7,880

Source: National Center for Health Statistics.

advertised, printed, published, distributed or circulated, any pamphlet, printed paper, book, newspaper, notice, advertisement or reference containing words or language giving or conveying any notice, hint or reference to any person, or to the name of any person, real or fictitious, from whom, or to any place, house, shop or office where any poison, drug, mixture, preparation, medicine or noxious thing, or any instrument or means whatever, or any advice, direction, information or knowledge may be obtained for the purpose of causing or procuring the miscarriage of a woman pregnant with child or of preventing, or which is represented as intended to prevent, pregnancy shall be punished by imprisonment in the state prison for not more than three years or in jail for not more than two and one half years or by a fine of not more than one thousand dollars.

Massachusetts Code Ti. 272, § 21. Abortion instruments

Except as provided in section twenty-one A, whoever sells, lends, gives away, exhibits, or offers to sell, lend or give away an instrument or other article intended to be used for self-abuse, or any drug, medicine, instrument or article whatever for the prevention of conception or for causing unlawful abortion, or advertises the same, or writes, prints, or causes to be written or printed a card, circular, book, pamphlet, advertisement or notice of any kind stating when, where, how, of whom or by what means such article can be purchased or obtained, or manufactures or makes any such article shall be punished by imprisonment in the state prison for not more than five years or in jail or the house of correction for not more than two and one half years or by a fine of not less than one hundred nor more than one thousand dollars.

Massachusetts Code Ti. 272, § 22.
Concealment of death of child born out of wedlock

A parent who conceals the death of the issue of such parent, which if born alive would be a child born out of wedlock, so that it cannot be ascertained whether it was born alive or, if born alive, whether it was murdered, shall be punished by a fine of not more than one hundred dollars or by imprisonment for not more than one year.

(3) GENERAL ABORTION GUIDELINES

Massachusetts has provided statutes that set out broad statements for performing abortions when a woman is less than 24 months pregnant, or more than 24 months pregnant. The statutes contain language that is constitutionally unenforceable, to the extent they interfere with a woman's right to freely have an abortion before fetal viability. The state has specific reporting requirements for post-viability abortions. The general abortion statutes are set out below.

Massachusetts Code Ti. 112, § 12K. Definitions

As used in section twelve L to section twelve U, inclusive, the following words shall have the following meanings:—

Abortion, the knowing destruction of the life of an unborn child or the intentional expulsion or removal of an unborn child from the womb other than for the principal purpose of producing a live birth or removing a dead fetus.

Hospital, a hospital as defined in section fifty-two of chapter one hundred and eleven of the General Laws, and duly licensed under the provisions of section fifty-one of chapter one hundred and eleven of the General Laws.

Physician, an individual lawfully authorized to practice medicine within the commonwealth.

Pregnancy, the condition of a mother carrying an unborn child.

Unborn child, the individual human life in existence and developing from implantation of the embryo in the uterus until birth.

Massachusetts Code Ti. 112, § 12L. Abortion for less than 24 weeks

If a pregnancy has existed for less than twenty-four weeks no abortion may be performed except by a physician and only if, in the best medical judgment of a physician, the abortion is necessary under all attendant circumstances.

Massachusetts Code Ti. 112, § 12M. Abortion for 24 weeks or more

If a pregnancy has existed for twenty-four weeks or more, no abortion may be performed except by a physician and only if it is necessary to save the life of the mother, or if a continuation of her pregnancy will impose on her a substantial risk of grave impairment of her physical or mental health.

Massachusetts Code Ti. 112, § 12N. Punishment

Any person who violates the provisions of sections twelve L or twelve M shall be punished by imprisonment for not less than one year nor more than five years. Conduct which violates the provisions of this act, which also violates any other criminal laws of the commonwealth, may be punished either under the provisions of sections 12K to 12U, inclusive, or under such other applicable criminal laws.

Massachusetts Code Ti. 112, § 12O.
Abortion performed pursuant to § 12M

If an abortion is performed pursuant to section twelve M, no abortion procedure which is designed to destroy the life of the unborn child or injure the unborn child in its mother's womb may be used unless, in the physician's best medical judgment, all other available procedures would create a greater risk of death or serious bodily harm to the mother either at the time of the abortion, or subsequently as the result of a future pregnancy, than the one being used.

Massachusetts Code Ti. 112, § 12P.
Abortion performed pursuant to § 12M

If an abortion is performed pursuant to section twelve M, the physician performing the abortion shall take all reasonable steps, both during and subsequent to the abortion, in keeping with good medical practice, consistent with the procedure being used, to preserve the life and health of the aborted child. Such steps shall include the presence of life-supporting equipment, as defined by the department of public health, in the room where the abortion is to be performed.

Massachusetts Code Ti. 112, § 12Q. Emergency exception

Except in an emergency requiring immediate action, no abortion may be performed under sections twelve L or twelve M unless the written informed consent of the proper person or persons has been delivered to the physician performing the abortion as set forth in section twelve S; and if the abortion is during or after the thirteenth week of pregnancy, it is performed in a hospital duly authorized to provide facilities for general surgery.

Except in an emergency requiring immediate action, no abortion may be performed under section twelve M unless performed in a hospital duly authorized to provide facilities for obstetrical services.

Massachusetts Code Ti. 112, § 12R.
Written statement of reasons for abortion

If the physician performing the abortion is not the physician who made the medical judgment required by section twelve M, before performing the abortion he shall obtain from the physician making such judgment a written statement setting forth the exception contained in section twelve M that in his best medical judgment permits the abortion and the specified reasons why the abortion qualifies under that exception. Prior to the performance of an abortion, the physician shall make a positive determination of pregnancy, test for blood type and Rh type, test for Rho(D) sensitization on each patient found to be Rho(D) negative by use of an antiglobulin (Coombs) test performed by a blood bank operated by a licensed hospital, or by a laboratory, and offer Rho(D) immune globulin (Human) to each Rho(D) negative patient with a negative sensitization test at the time of any abortion. The physician performing the abortion shall retain this written statement as an attachment to the file copy of his report required by this section. Within thirty days after the performance of an abortion, the physician performing such abortion shall file with the commissioner of public health on a form prescribed by him the following information to the best of his knowledge: the date and place of the abortion; if he was the physician making the medical judgment required by section twelve M, the exception contained in said section that in his best medical judgment permitted the abortion and the specific reasons why the abortion qualified under that exception; if he is not the physician who made such medical judgment, the name and address of the physician from whom he received the written statement required by this section and the exception contained in said section twelve M that permitted the abortion and a verbatim recitation of the specific reasons why the abortion qualified under either exception as set forth in the written statement he received from such physician; the age of the mother; the method used to perform the abortion; whether the mother survived the abortion; the details of any morbidity observed in the mother; the gestational age of the child; the weight and crown-rump length of the child if determinable; whether the unborn child was alive when removed or expelled from the mother and if so, the steps taken to preserve its life; and the length of time the child lived after removal or expulsion from the mother. The physician performing the abortion shall retain in his files for seven years after the abortion a copy of the report to which he should attach or otherwise add the name of the mother. The original of the report filed with the commissioner shall not contain the name of the mother and shall be maintained by the commissioner as a public record. The commissioner shall prepare from these reports such statistical tables with respect to maternal health, abortion procedures, the unborn child and viability as he deems useful and shall make an annual report thereof to the general court. Nothing in this section shall be construed to limit the authority of the department of public health to require reports pursuant to sections twenty-four A and twenty-five A of chapter one hundred and eleven.

Massachusetts Code Ti. 112, § 12T. Violations

Any person who commits an act in violation of sections twelve O or twelve P shall be punished by a fine of not less than five hundred dollars nor more than two thousand dollars, or by imprisonment of not less than three months nor more than five years, or by both said fine and imprisonment. Conduct which violates sections twelve O or twelve P which also violates any other criminal laws of the commonwealth, may be punished either under this section or under such other applicable criminal laws. Any person who willfully violates the provisions of section twelve Q or twelve R shall be punished by a fine of not less than one hundred dollars nor more than two thousand dollars.

(4) INFORMED CONSENT AND MINORS

Under the laws of Massachusetts a single statute sets out guidelines for informed consent abortions and circumstances for a minor obtaining an abortion. Prior to a physician performing an abortion, Massachusetts requires that a woman be fully informed of the procedure to be used, the risks involved and alternatives to abortion. An abortion may not take place until 24 hours after a woman has given her written consent to an abortion.

Under the laws of Massachusetts no physician may perform an abortion upon an unemancipated minor unless he/she first obtains the written consent of the minor's parent or guardian. The state's supreme judicial court held in *Planned Parenthood League v. Attorney General*, 677 N.E.2d 101 (Mass. 1997) that the requirement of notification to both parents, as opposed to just one parent, was invalid.

In compliance with federal constitutional law, Massachusetts has provided a judicial waiver procedure for an unemancipated minor to obtain an abortion without parental or guardian consent. If an unemancipated minor elects not to seek, or cannot for any reason obtain consent from her parents or legal guardian, the minor may petition a trial court for a waiver of the consent requirement. A minor has a right to an attorney at the proceeding and if she cannot afford one, the court must appoint her an attorney. If a minor chooses, she may represent herself. The required parental or guardian consent may be waived if the court finds either (1) that the minor is mature and well-informed enough to make the abortion decision on her own, or (2) that performance of the abortion would be in the best interest of the minor.

The provision concerning minors has been before the United States Supreme Court. In *Bellotti v. Baird I* the Supreme Court held that a federal district court had to certify appropriate questions to the supreme judicial court of Massachusetts, concerning the interpretation of that state's parental consent abortion statute for minors, before ruling on its constitutionality. In *Bellotti v. Baird II* the Supreme Court held that Massachusetts' abortion statute for minors violated the constitution in light of an interpretation given by the state's highest court, that required parental notice of a judicial bypass proceeding invoked by a minor, and permitted a judge to deny an abortion even though the minor proved she had enough maturity to make an independent decision. The state also has a statute permitting the attorney general, or other interested person, to seek a court order stopping an abortion when proper consent was not obtained. The statutes addressing the matters are set out below.

Massachusetts Code Ti. 112, § 12S. Informed consent and minors

No physician may perform an abortion upon a pregnant woman without first obtaining her written informed consent. The commissioner of public health shall prescribe a form for physicians to use in obtaining such consent. This form shall be written in a manner designed to permit a person unfamiliar with medical terminology to understand its purpose and content, and shall include the following information: a description of the stage of development of the unborn child; the type of procedure which the physician intends to use to perform the abortion; and the possible complications associated with the use of the procedure and with the performance of the abortion itself; the availability of alternatives to abortion; and a statement that, under the law of the commonwealth, a person's refusal to undergo an abortion does not constitute grounds for the denial of public assistance. A pregnant woman seeking an abortion shall sign the consent form described above at least twenty-four hours in advance of the time for which the abortion is scheduled, except in an emergency requiring immediate action. She shall then return it to the physician performing the abortion who shall maintain it in his files and destroy it seven years after the date upon which the abortion is performed.

The said consent form and any other forms, transcript of evidence, or written findings and conclusions of a court, shall be confidential and may not be released to any person except by the pregnant woman's written informed consent or by a proper judicial order, other than to the pregnant woman herself, to whom such documents relate, the operating physician, or any person whose consent is required pursuant to this section, or under the law. If a pregnant woman is less than eighteen years of age and has not married, a physician shall not perform an abortion upon her unless he first obtains both the consent of the pregnant woman and that of her parents, except as hereinafter provided. In deciding whether to grant such consent, a pregnant woman's parents shall consider only their child's best interests. If one of the pregnant woman's parents has died or is unavailable to the physician within a reasonable time and in a reasonable manner, consent of the remaining parent shall be sufficient. If both parents have died or are otherwise unavailable to the physician within a reasonable time and in a reasonable manner, consent of the pregnant woman's guardian or guardians shall be sufficient. If the pregnant woman's parents are divorced, consent of the parent having custody shall be sufficient. If a pregnant woman less than eighteen years of age has not married and if one or both of her parents or guardians refuse to consent to the performance of an abortion, or if she elects not to seek the consent of one or both of her parents or guardians, a judge of the superior court department of the trial court shall, upon petition, or motion, and after an appropriate hearing, authorize a physician to perform the abortion if said judge determines that the pregnant woman is mature and capable of giving informed consent to the proposed abortion or, if said judge determines that she is not mature, that the performance of an abortion upon her would be in her best interests. A pregnant woman less than eighteen years of age may participate in proceedings in the superior court department of the trial court on her own behalf, and the court may appoint a guardian ad litem for her. The court shall, however, advise her that she has a right to court appointed counsel, and shall, upon her request, provide her with such counsel. Proceedings in the superior court department of the trial court under this section shall be confidential and shall be given such precedence over other pending matters that the court may reach a decision promptly and without delay so as to serve the best interests of the pregnant woman. A judge of the superior court department of the trial court who conducts proceedings under this section shall make in writing specific factual findings and legal conclusions supporting his decision and shall order a record of the evidence to be maintained including his own findings and conclusions.

Nothing in this section is intended to abolish or limit any common law rights of persons other than those whose rights it governs for the purpose of any civil action or any action for injunctive relief under section twelve U.

Massachusetts Code Ti. 112, § 12U.
Enjoining performance of abortion

The attorney general or any person whose consent is required either pursuant to section twelve S or under common law, may petition the superior court for an order enjoining the performance of any abortion that may be performed contrary to the provisions of sections twelve L to twelve T, inclusive.

(5) USE OF FACILITIES AND PEOPLE

Under the laws of Massachusetts hospitals are not required to allow abortions at their facilities. The employees and physicians at hospitals that do allow abortions are permitted to refuse to take part in abortions. It was held by a federal court in *Doe v. Hale Hospital*, 500 F.2d 144 (1st Cir. 1974) that a Massachusetts public medical facility may not forbid elective abortions so long as it offers medically indistinguishable procedures. The statutes addressing the issues are set out below.

Massachusetts Code Ti. 112, § 12I.
Refusal to participate in abortion

A physician or any other person who is a member of or associated with the medical staff of a hospital or other health facility or any employee of a hospital or other health facility in which an abortion ... procedure is scheduled and who shall state in writing an objection to such abortion ... procedure on moral or religious grounds, shall not be required to participate in the medical procedures which result in such abortion ..., and the refusal of any such person to participate therein shall not form the basis for any claim of damages on account of such refusal or for any disciplinary or recriminatory action against such person. The refusal of any person who has made application to a medical, premedical, nursing, social work, or psychology program in the commonwealth to agree to counsel, suggest, recommend, assist, or in any way participate in the performance of an abortion ... contrary to his religious beliefs or moral convictions shall not form the basis for any discriminatory action against such person. Conscientious objection to abortion shall not be grounds for dismissal, suspension, demotion, failure to promote, discrimination in hiring, withholding of pay or refusal to grant financial assistance under any state aided project, or used in any way to the detriment of the individual in any hospital, clinic, medical, premedical, nursing, social work, or psychology school or state aided program or institution which is supported in whole or in part by the commonwealth.

Massachusetts Code Ti. 272, § 21B. Medical facilities

No privately controlled hospital or other health facility shall be required to admit any patient for the purpose of performing an abortion, performing any sterilization procedure, or receiving contraceptive devices or information.

No privately controlled hospital or other privately controlled health facility shall be required to permit any patient to have an abortion, or any sterilization procedure performed in said hospital or other health facility, or to furnish contraceptive devices or information to such patient, nor shall such a hospital or other health facility be required to furnish any family planning services within or through said hospital or other health facility or to make referrals to any other hospital or health facility for such services when said services or referrals are contrary to the religious or moral principles of said hospital or said health facility as expressed in its charter, by-laws or code of ethics, or vote of its governing body.

Any such hospital or other health facility exercising the rights granted in this section shall not on account of the exercise thereof, be disciplined or discriminated against in any manner or suffer any adverse determination by any person, firm, corporation, or other entity, including but in no way limited to any political subdivision, board, commission, department, authority, or agency of the commonwealth.

(6) BAN ON FETAL EXPERIMENTS

Massachusetts has generally banned fetal experiments. The state permits experiments on a dead fetus if the woman involved consents. Massachusetts also prohibits the sale of fetal remains. The statute addressing the matter is set out below.

Massachusetts Code Ti. 112, § 12J. Fetal experiments

(a) I. No person shall use any live human fetus whether before or after expulsion from its mother's womb, for scientific, laboratory, research or

other kind of experimentation. This section shall not prohibit procedures incident to the study of a human fetus while it is in its mother's womb, provided that in the best medical judgment of the physician, made at the time of the study, said procedures do not substantially jeopardize the life or health of the fetus, and provided said fetus is not the subject of a planned abortion. In any criminal proceeding a fetus shall be conclusively presumed not to be the subject of a planned abortion if the mother signed a written statement at the time of the study, that she was not planning an abortion.

This section shall not prohibit or regulate diagnostic or remedial procedures the purpose of which is to determine the life or health of the fetus involved or to preserve the life or health of the fetus involved or the mother involved.

A fetus is a live fetus for purposes of this section when, in the best medical judgment of a physician, it shows evidence of life as determined by the same medical standards as are used in determining evidence of life in a spontaneously aborted fetus at approximately the same stage of gestational development.

For the purposes of this section, "fetus" shall include a neonate and an embryo, but shall exclude a pre-implantation embryo or parthenote as defined in section 2 of chapter 111L and obtained in accordance with said chapter 111L.

(a) II. No experimentation may knowingly be performed upon a dead fetus unless the consent of the mother has first been obtained, provided, however, that such consent shall not be required in the case of a routine pathological study. In any criminal proceeding, consent shall be conclusively presumed to have been granted for the purposes of this section by a written statement, signed by the mother who is at least eighteen years of age, to the effect that she consents to the use of her fetus for scientific, laboratory, research or other kind of experimentation or study; such written consent shall constitute lawful authorization for the transfer of the dead fetus.

(a) III. No person shall perform or offer to perform an abortion where part or all of the consideration for said performance is that the fetal remains may be used for experimentation or other kind of research or study.

(a) IV. No person shall knowingly sell, transfer, distribute or give away any fetus for a use which is in violation of the provisions of this section. For purposes of this section, the word "fetus" shall include also an embryo or neonate, but shall exclude a pre-implantation embryo or parthenote as defined in section 2 of chapter 111L and obtained in accordance with said chapter 111L.

(a) V. Except as hereafter provided, whoever violates the provisions of this section shall be punished by imprisonment in a jail or house of correction for not less than one year nor more than two and one-half years or by imprisonment in the state prison for not more than five years and by the imposition of a fine of up to ten thousand dollars.

(a) VI. In any criminal action under this subsection (a), it shall be a complete defense that at the time of its performance the subject procedure had received the written approval of a duly appointed Institutional Review Board provided that such Board sets forth in its written approval that the procedure does not violate the provisions of this subsection (a) and sets forth therein a reasonable basis for such conclusion and provided that there was not outstanding, at any time that the subject procedure was being performed, a judgment of a court entered pursuant to the provisions of subsection (b), that the subject procedure violates the provisions of this subsection (a). The written approval shall contain a detailed description of the procedure by attachment of a protocol or other writing or otherwise and shall be maintained as a permanent record by such Board or by the hospital or other institution for which the Board acts.

A copy of the written approval, together with any attached protocol or other writing, shall be filed with the office of the attorney general. Such copy shall be available for public inspection at reasonable times. No member of an Institutional Review Board voting not to approve a procedure, or not present at such a vote, shall be criminally or civilly liable for such approval by the Institutional Review Board or for the performance of the procedure by others. No member of such a Board voting to approve a procedure shall be criminally or civilly liable for such approval by him or the performance of the procedure by others if, based on the written approval and the basis thereof referred to above, such a member acts on a good faith belief that the procedure does not violate the provisions of this section.

(a) VII. Where there is outstanding such a judgment that the subject procedure violates the provisions of this subsection (a), it shall not constitute a defense that the person performing said procedure did not receive notice, or otherwise know, of that judgment; provided, however, that until the attorney general files a copy of the judgment prohibiting a procedure with the Commissioner of Public Health as provided in subsection (b) VII it shall constitute a defense that the person performing the subject procedure did not have notice of the judgment and that he had obtained the approval of the Institutional Review Board for the subject procedure as provided in subsection (a) VI.

(b) I. Whenever a procedure has been approved by a duly appointed Institutional Review Board which the attorney general has reasonable grounds to believe is prohibited under the provisions of subsection (a), he shall file a complaint in the Superior Court sitting in a county where the procedure is performed seeking a determination of whether said procedure violates the provisions of this statute. The complaint shall describe the procedure and the reason or reasons why there are reasonable grounds to believe that the said procedure is in violation of the provisions of this statute. The complaint shall name as defendants those persons within his jurisdiction whom the attorney general reasonably believes have performed, are performing, or are about to perform, the described procedure and those institutions within his jurisdiction in which said procedure has been performed, is being performed, or is about to be performed; such defendants shall be served with a copy of the complaint and a summons in accordance with the provisions of Rule 4 of the Massachusetts Rules of Civil Procedure. Upon the filing of the complaint, notice thereof shall be given by the attorney general, by certified or registered mail, to the Commissioner of Public Health, who in turn shall give the same notice to those institutions in the Commonwealth who, in the judgment of said Commissioner, may be affected by a judgment in the action, and in any event to all of the licensed medical schools in the Commonwealth.

(b) II. Any person or institution which has performed, is performing, or is about to perform, a procedure, may file a complaint in the Superior Court seeking a determination of whether said procedure violates the provision of this statute. Said determination may be sought irrespective of whether said procedure has been approved by an institutional review board. The complaint, which shall have attached thereto a copy of any protocol relative to said procedure, shall describe the procedure and state the reason or reasons which cause the plaintiff to seek the judicial determination. The complaint shall name the attorney general as defendant in the action and he shall be served with a copy of the complaint, including the attached protocol, if any, and the summons in accordance with the provisions of Rule 4 of the Massachusetts Rules of Civil Procedure. Service shall be made by delivery to the office of said attorney general; or by mailing by certified or registered mail to said office. Upon receipt of service, notice shall be given by the attorney general, by certified or registered mail, to the Commissioner of Public Health who in turn shall give notice to those institutions who in the judgment of said commissioner may be affected by a judgment in the action, and in any event to all of the licensed medical schools in the Commonwealth.

(b) III. Any person or institution desiring to intervene in the action may file a motion to intervene with the court in which the action is pending within ten days from the mailing of such notice, except that the court, for good cause shown, may allow said motion after the ten-day period. A copy of the motion to intervene shall also be served upon the attorney general

and upon the persons or institutions initiating the action or against whom the action has been initiated. The motion shall be signed and certified under oath by the applicant and shall state the grounds therefore showing that the applicant claims an interest in the issue of the lawfulness of the subject procedure in that he has performed said procedure, or that he is performing said procedure, or that he is about to perform said procedure, and that the disposition of the action may impair or impede his ability to perform or continue to perform said procedure. Upon a determination by the court that the applicant has satisfied the requirement of this section, the court shall allow the applicant to intervene in the action.

(b) IV. After service of the complaint upon an original party, such party shall serve and file an answer within twenty days unless otherwise directed by order of the court. The answer shall state whether, in the opinion of the pleader, the subject procedure is prohibited by the provisions of this statute and the reason or reasons for such opinion. An intervenor may serve and file a pleading in support of either the complaint or answer within ten days from receipt of notice of the granting of the motion to intervene. Unless the court otherwise orders, no response to the pleading of an intervenor is required.

(b) V. Any party may move for summary judgment, in accordance with Rule 56 of the Massachusetts Rules of Civil Procedure, or for judgment on the pleadings in accordance with Rule 12(c) of the Massachusetts Rules of Civil Procedure. If, on a motion for judgment on the pleadings, matters outside the pleadings are presented to and not excluded by the court, the motion shall be treated as one for summary judgment, and all parties shall be given reasonable opportunity to present all material made pertinent to such a motion.

(b) VI. Any trial on the merits shall be without a jury. The court shall find the facts specially and shall set forth in writing separately its findings of facts and conclusions of law thereon and shall enter judgment accordingly. Such judgment may be appealed to the Supreme Judicial Court. Until reversed, however, by the Supreme Judicial Court, such judgment shall constitute an in rem judgment, binding within the Commonwealth of Massachusetts, that the subject procedure is prohibited or is not prohibited by the provisions of this statute.

(b) VII. Upon the entry of a judgment that a procedure is prohibited by the provisions of this statute, the attorney general shall promptly give notice by publication in a newspaper of general circulation in each of the counties of the Commonwealth and by sending notification by registered or certified mail to each licensed hospital and medical school in the Commonwealth; such notice shall contain a description of the prohibited medical procedure and shall state that the performance of such procedure constitutes a crime punishable under the provisions of this statute. A copy of all judgments and accompanying opinions permitting or prohibiting a procedure shall be filed by the attorney general with the Commissioner of Public Health. The Commissioner of Public Health shall maintain a permanent file of such judgments and opinions for public inspection.

(b) VIII. Any action brought under this statute to determine whether a procedure is prohibited by the provisions of this statute and any appeal of a judgment that a procedure is or is not prohibited by the provisions of this statute shall be advanced for a prompt and speedy disposition consistent, however, with a reasonable opportunity being afforded to the parties to properly prepare the case.

(b) IX. If any section, subsection, paragraph, sentence or clause of this statute is held to be unconstitutional, such holding shall not affect the remaining portions of this statute.

(7) BAN ON CLONING

Massachusetts prohibits human cloning and trafficking in human tissue for research purposes. The statute addressing the matter is set out below.

Massachusetts Code Ti. 111L, § 8.
Human reproductive cloning prohibited

(a) Human reproductive cloning is hereby prohibited. No person shall knowingly attempt, engage in, or assist in human reproductive cloning. No person shall knowingly purchase, sell, transfer or otherwise obtain human embryonic, gametic or cadaveric tissue for the purpose of human reproductive cloning.

(b) No person shall knowingly create an embryo by the method of fertilization with the sole intent of donating the embryo for research. Nothing in this section shall prohibit the creation of a pre-implantation embryo by somatic cell nuclear transfer, parthenogenesis or other asexual means for research purposes.

(c) No person shall knowingly and for valuable consideration purchase, sell, transfer or otherwise obtain human embryos, gametes or cadaveric tissue for research purposes. Nothing in this section shall prohibit a person from banking or donating their gametes for personal future use, or from donating their gametes to another person or from donating their gametes for research. Nothing in this chapter shall prohibit or regulate the use of in vitro fertilization for reproductive purposes.

(d) A person who is found to have knowingly violated subsection (a) shall be punished by imprisonment in a jail or house of correction for not less than 5 years nor more than 10 years or by imprisonment in the state prison for not more than 10 years or by a fine of not more than $1,000,000. In addition to such penalty, and at the discretion of the court, a person who is found to have knowingly violated this section and derives a personal financial profit from such violation may be ordered to pay all or part of any such profits to the commonwealth as damages.

(e) A person who is found to have knowingly violated subsection (b) or subsection (c) shall be punished by imprisonment in a jail or house of correction for not less than 1 year nor more than 2 years or by imprisonment in the state prison for not more than 5 years or by a fine of not more than $100,000.

(8) INJURY TO PREGNANT WOMAN

Massachusetts makes it a criminal offense to injure a woman while she is pregnant. The statute addressing the matter is set out below.

Massachusetts Code Ti. 265, § 13A(b).
Assault or assault and battery

Whoever commits an assault or an assault and battery:

(i) upon another and by such assault and battery causes serious bodily injury;

(ii) upon another who is pregnant at the time of such assault and battery, knowing or having reason to know that the person is pregnant; or

(iii) upon another who he knows has an outstanding temporary or permanent vacate, restraining or no contact order or judgment issued pursuant to section 18, section 34B or 34C of chapter 208, section 32 of chapter 209, section 3, 4 or 5 of chapter 209A, or section 15 or 20 of chapter 209C, in effect against him at the time of such assault or assault and battery; shall be punished by imprisonment in the state prison for not more than 5 years or in the house of correction for not more than 2½ years, or by a fine of not more than $5,000, or by both such fine and imprisonment.

(9) BAN ON ANTI-ABORTION ACTIVITIES

Massachusetts has responded to anti-abortion activities by enacting statutes that ban blockades of abortion facilities and interference with persons obtaining abortion services. The statutes are set out below.

Massachusetts Code Ti. 266, § 120E.
Obstructing medical facilities

As used in this section, the following words shall have the following meanings: "Medical facility," any medical office, medical clinic, medical laboratory, or hospital. "Notice," (i) receipt of or awareness of the con-

tents of a court order prohibiting blocking of a medical facility; (ii) oral request by an authorized representative of a medical facility, or law enforcement official to refrain from obstructing access to a medical facility; or (iii) written posted notice outside the entrance to a medical facility to refrain from obstructing access to a medical facility.

Whoever knowingly obstructs entry to or departure from any medical facility or who enters or remains in any medical facility so as to impede the provision of medical services, after notice to refrain from such obstruction or interference, shall be punished for the first offense by a fine of not more than one thousand dollars or not more than six months in jail or a house of correction or both, and for each subsequent violation of this section by a fine of not less than five hundred dollars and not more than five thousand dollars or not more than two and one-half years in jail or a house of correction or both. These penalties shall be in addition to any penalties imposed for violation of a court order.

A person who knowingly obstructs entry to or departure from such medical facility or who enters or remains in such facility so as to impede the provision of medical services after notice to refrain from such obstruction or interference, may be arrested by a sheriff, deputy sheriff, constable, or police officer.

Any medical facility whose rights to provide services under the provisions of this section have been violated or which has reason to believe that any person or entity is about to engage in conduct proscribed herein may commence a civil action for injunctive and other equitable relief, including the award of compensatory and exemplary damages. Said civil action shall be instituted either in superior court for the county in which the conduct complained of occurred, or in the superior court for the county in which any person or entity complained of resides or has a principal place of business. An aggrieved facility which prevails in an action authorized by this paragraph, in addition to other damages, shall be entitled to an award of the costs of the litigation and reasonable attorney's fees in an amount to be fixed by the court.

Nothing herein shall be construed to interfere with any rights provided by chapter one hundred and fifty A or by the federal Labor-Management Act of 1947 or other rights to engage in peaceful picketing which does not obstruct entry or departure.

Massachusetts Code Ti. 266, § 120E 1/2.
Reproductive health care facilities

(a) For the purposes of this section, "reproductive health care facility" means a place, other than within a hospital, where abortions are offered or performed.

(b) No person shall knowingly approach another person or occupied motor vehicle within six feet of such person or vehicle, unless such other person or occupant of the vehicle consents, for the purpose of passing a leaflet or handbill to, displaying a sign to, or engaging in oral protest, education or counseling with such other person in the public way or sidewalk area within a radius of 18 feet from any entrance door or driveway to a reproductive health care facility or within the area within a rectangle not greater than six feet in width created by extending the outside boundaries of any entrance door or driveway to a reproductive health care facility at a right angle and in straight lines to the point where such lines intersect the sideline of the street in front of such entrance door or driveway. This subsection shall not apply to the following:

(1) persons entering or leaving such facility;

(2) employees or agents of such facility acting within the scope of their employment;

(3) law enforcement, ambulance, firefighting, construction, utilities, public works and other municipal agents acting within the scope of their employment; and

(4) persons using the public sidewalk or street right-of-way adjacent to such facility solely for the purpose of reaching a destination other than such facility.

(c) The provisions of subsection (b) shall only take effect during a facility's business hours and if the area contained within the radius and rectangle described in said subsection (b) is clearly marked and posted.

(d) Whoever knowingly violates this section shall be punished, for the first offense, by a fine of not more than $500 or not more than three months in a jail or house of correction, or by both such fine and imprisonment, and for each subsequent offense, by a fine of not less than $500 and not more than $5,000 or not more than two and one-half years in a jail or house of correction, or both such fine and imprisonment. A person who knowingly violates this section may be arrested without a warrant by a sheriff, deputy sheriff or police officer if that sheriff, deputy sheriff, or police officer observes that person violating this section.

(e) Any person who knowingly obstructs, detains, hinders, impedes or blocks another person's entry to or exit from a reproductive health care facility shall be punished, for the first offense, by a fine of not more than $500 or not more than three months in a jail or house of correction, or by both such fine and imprisonment, and for each subsequent offense, by a fine of not less than $500 nor more than $5,000 or not more than two and one-half years in a jail or house of correction, or by both such fine and imprisonment. A person who knowingly violates this provision may be arrested without a warrant by a sheriff, deputy sheriff or police officer.

(f) A reproductive health care facility or a person whose rights to provide or obtain reproductive health care services have been violated or interfered with by a violation of this section or any person whose rights to express their views, assemble or pray near a reproductive health care facility have been violated or interfered with may commence a civil action for equitable relief. The civil action shall be commenced either in the superior court for the county in which the conduct complained of occurred, or in the superior court for the county in which any person or entity complained of resides or has a principal place of business.

Massachusetts Citizens for Life

Massachusetts Citizens for Life (MCL) is a pro-life organization that was founded in 1973. The president of MCL is Dr. Mildred F. Jefferson. MCL is the largest pro-life organization in the state of Massachusetts. The president of MCL is Ray Neary. The organization engages in educational, legislative, political, and charitable activities designed to ban abortion. *See also* **Pro-Life Organizations**

Maternal Deaths During Abortion *see* **Complications During and After Abortion**

Maternal Mirror Syndrome

Maternal mirror syndrome is a condition in which fetal distress or sickness appears to trigger a parallel illness in the expectant mother.

Maternal Serum Screening *see* **Obstetric Triple Screen**

Mazurek v. Armstrong

Forum: United States Supreme Court.

Case Citation: Mazurek v. Armstrong, 520 U.S. 968 (1997).

Date Argued: Did not argue.

Date of Decision: June 16, 1997.

Opinion of Court: Per Curiam.

Dissenting Opinion: Stevens, J., in which Ginsburg and Breyer, JJ., joined.

Counsel for Appellant: Not reported.

Counsel for Appellee: Not reported.

Amicus Brief for Appellant: Not reported.

Amicus Brief for Appellee: Not reported.

Issue Presented: Whether Montana's requirement that abortions be performed only by physicians was constitutionally valid?

Case Holding: Montana's requirement that abortions be performed only by physicians was constitutionally valid.

Background facts of case: Several physicians filed a lawsuit in a federal district court, seeking to prevent enforcement of a Montana statute that limited performance of abortions to physicians. The district court denied relief. On appeal, an appellate court reversed and remanded the case to determine whether the statute imposed an undue burden on a woman's right to an abortion. The United States Supreme Court granted certiorari to address the issue.

Majority opinion delivered Per Curiam: It was determined in the per curiam opinion that the court of appeals committed error in finding that the physicians had a fair chance of success on the merits. The per curiam opinion relied upon the decision in *Planned Parenthood of Southeastern Pennsylvania v. Casey* to find that Montana could limit the performance of abortions to physicians.

Disposition of case: The judgment of the appellate court was reversed.

Dissenting opinion by Justice Stevens: Justice Stevens dissented from the majority opinion. He argued that Montana's statute was created specifically to prevent the only nonphysician abortionist in the state from practicing her trade. He further argued that there was no medical necessity for preventing first trimester abortions from being performed by qualified nonphysicians.

See also **Physician Abortion Requirements**

Meconium

Meconium refers to a fetus' waste and first bowel movement. It is usually a dark green, sticky substance that is composed of amniotic fluid, mucus, lanugo, bile and discarded cells. The fetus' first bowel movement may occur before or during labor. Discharge of meconium within the uterus before birth can be a sign of fetal distress. *See also* **Meconium Aspiration Syndrome**

Meconium Aspiration Syndrome

Meconium (the feces of a fetus) aspiration syndrome involves a neonate inhaling meconium during labor and delivery. If the meconium mixture is inhaled into the lungs, it can cause a partial or complete blockage of the airway passage. This condition is a leading cause of severe illness (including brain damage) and death in newborns. The syndrome occurs in about 10 percent of births. Approximately one third of the infants with the condition will require some type of assisted breathing. The condition can be immediately treated by inserting a tube (endotracheal tube) into the trachea and suctioning out the meconium. This tube may also be used to help a fetus breathe after the meconium has been removed. *See also* **Meconium**

Medicaid Funding for Abortion *see* **Hyde Amendment**

Medical Abortion *see* **Methods of Abortion**

Medical Emergency Abortion

A medical emergency abortion is one in which it has been determined by one or more physicians, that a female's health or life is threatened by carrying a fetus to term. This type of abortion may arise in two contexts: post-viability abortion for an adult woman and an abortion for a female minor. The United States Supreme Court has ruled that states cannot deny a post-viability abortion to a woman, if it is medically determined that her health or life is endangered in bringing the pregnancy to term. States also cannot deny a female minor the right to an abortion, even though the child did not comply with parental notice or judicial bypass regulations, if it is medically determined that the child's health or life is endangered in bringing the pregnancy to term. *See also* **Planned Parenthood of Southeastern Pennsylvania v. Casey**

Medical Students for Choice

Medical Students for Choice (MSC) is a national college organization that was founded in 1993, by medical students who were concerned about the shortage of abortionists, the lack of abortion education in medical schools, and escalating violence against abortion providers. MSC represents more than 6,000 medical students and residents in the United States and Canada. The organization is dedicated to ensuring that women receive comprehensive reproductive health care, including abortion. To this end, MSC works with other national groups to encourage medical schools and residency programs to add training in abortion. *See also* **Pro-Choice Organizations**

Menarche

Menarche is the onset of menstruation and other physical and mental changes associated with puberty in females. This process signals a female's readiness for childbearing. It normally begins between the ages of ten and seventeen. *See also* **Dysmenorrhea; Menopause; Menstrual Cycle; Premenstrual Syndrome**

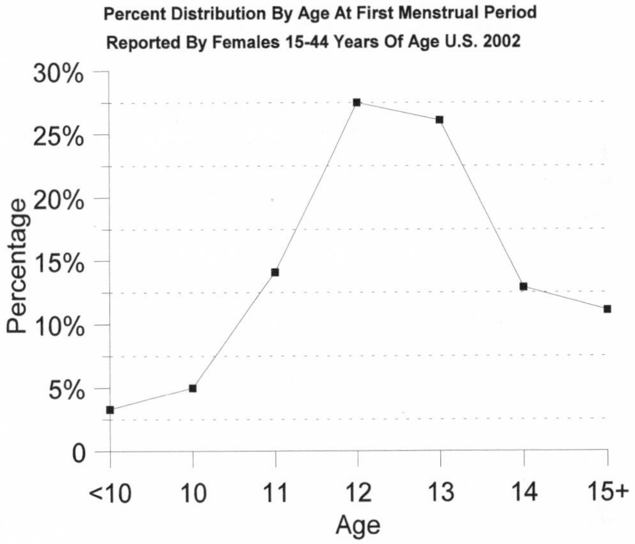

Source: National Center for Health Statistics.

Menopause

Menopause refers to the last menstrual flow of a woman's life and the physical and emotional changes that accompany it. For most women menopause begins between the ages of forty and sixty, and takes place over a period that ranges from 6 months to 3 years. During this episode ovaries stop releasing eggs, ovarian production of estrogen and other hormones decrease and menstruation eventually ceases. *See also* **Menarche; Menstrual Cycle**

Menses *see* **Menstrual Cycle**

Menstrual Age *see* **Gestational Age**

Menstrual Cycle

The menstrual cycle is a process that prepares the uterus for pregnancy. This process begins at puberty and occurs about every 28 days (it may vary in length from 26 to 35 days). It will continue, unless interrupted by pregnancy, until a woman reaches menopause. Bleeding (also called period, menstruation or menses) during the cycle ranges from two to eight days. The menstrual cycle can be divided into three phases: follicular phase, ovulatory phase, and luteal phase.

Follicular phase. The follicular phase starts from the first day of menstruation and continues to ovulation (covering about 13 or 14 days). During the first few days of the follicular phase the uterine lining built up in the previous cycle is cleared away in the form of blood and tissue. The pituitary gland, located in the brain, will then begin releasing what are called follicle stimulating hormone (FSH) and luteinizing hormone (LH). The role of FSH is to stimulate the growth of numerous follicles in the ovary (around 10 to 20), as well as the release of estrogen from the ovary. The estrogen will cause the lining of the uterus (endometrium) to thicken. Usually only one of the numerous follicles will mature and release the egg contained within it. LH is discharged in a sudden burst near the mid-cycle (13th or 14th day) and stimulates the release of the egg from the mature follicle.

Ovulatory phase. The ovulatory phase starts when the egg (ovum) is released from the mature follicle. This process is termed ovulation, due to the increased presence of the hormone LH. Ovulation generally occurs during the 16 to 32 hours following follicle exposure to increased LH. When the follicle ruptures it releases the egg into the fallopian tube. The egg is then swept into the fallopian tube by the fimbria (fringe-like extensions) and moved along towards the uterus, hoping to get fertilized along the way by a sperm. The egg is only fertilizable for about 36 hours. If fertilization does not occur, the egg will disintegrate.

Luteal phase. The luteal phase is the period following ovulation. It will last until the beginning of the next menstrual period. During this phase the follicle that ruptured and released the egg, closes and becomes a corpus luteum. The corpus luteum secretes progesterone and estrogen hormones. Both hormones act to prepare the lining of the uterus for the implantation of a fertilized egg. However, if fertilization and implantation do not occur, the corpus luteum will begin to degenerate and the levels of progesterone and estrogen will decline. This regression will result in the disintegration of the lining of the uterus and menstrual bleeding will follow. Should fertilization and implantation occur, the corpus luteum will be stimulated by human chorionic gonadotropin to continue its production of estrogen and progesterone to maintain the pregnancy. *See also* **Dysmenorrhea; Luteal Phase Defect; Menarche; Menopause; Premenstrual Syndrome**

Mercury and Pregnancy

Mercury is a metal that is found in various forms. It is present naturally in the environment, but its levels are increased by activities such as the burning of coal by power plants. Some of the most common ways in which people are exposed to mercury include breathing contaminated air and eating contaminated fish. Pregnant women who are exposed to high levels of mercury are at risk of having birth complications. Mercury can cross the placenta and cause severe birth defects to a fetus. *See also* **Lead and Pregnancy**

Metachromatic Leukodystrophy

Metachromatic leukodystrophy is an inherited disease involving the absence of an enzyme (arylsulfatase A) and increased storage of sulfatide. This disease causes decreased muscle tone, the loss of the ability to walk, blindness, seizures, and partial paralysis. No treatment for the disorder exists. Death usually occurs before the age of 10. *See also* **Birth Defects and Abortion**

Methods of Abortion Used for Selected States U.S. 2000–2004

Abortion Method	Year *2000*	*2001*	*2002*	*2003*	*2004*	*Total*
Surgical	585,921	546,427	578,126	567,161	656,853	2,934,488
Instillation	1,669	1,125	1,794	2,463	764	7,815
Medical	6,229	16,183	32,216	48,262	68,099	170,989
Other	2930	3,780	8,924	6,113	8,232	29,979

Source: **National Center for Health Statistics.**

Methods of Abortion

Legal abortion may be performed by using medical or surgical abortion methods. A medical abortion offers more privacy than a surgical abortion, because it may be done in the home. Additionally, medical abortions present far less risk of complications than surgical abortions.

Medical abortion. A medical abortion terminates a pregnancy through medications. Medical abortion is performed by using the drug mifepristone or methotrexate for termination of early pregnancies (less than 49 days pregnant). Medical abortion allows a woman to avoid the risks associated with surgery and anesthesia and it may be done in the privacy of the home. The procedure involved with medical abortion can take anywhere from a few days to several weeks. Medical abortion is generally irreversible once the mifepristone or methotrexate is taken. The success rate of medical abortions is about 90 to 95 percent. When a medical abortion does not work, a surgical abortion procedure must be performed.

Surgical abortion. Surgical abortion ends a pregnancy by emptying the uterus with special instruments. The most commonly used surgical abortion techniques are: the dilation and curettage procedure and the dilation and evacuation procedure. Surgical abortion is almost 100 percent successful.

Other abortion methods. Additional methods of abortion that are commonly used for late term pregnancies include instillation methods, dilation and extraction, mini vac aspiration; machine vacuum

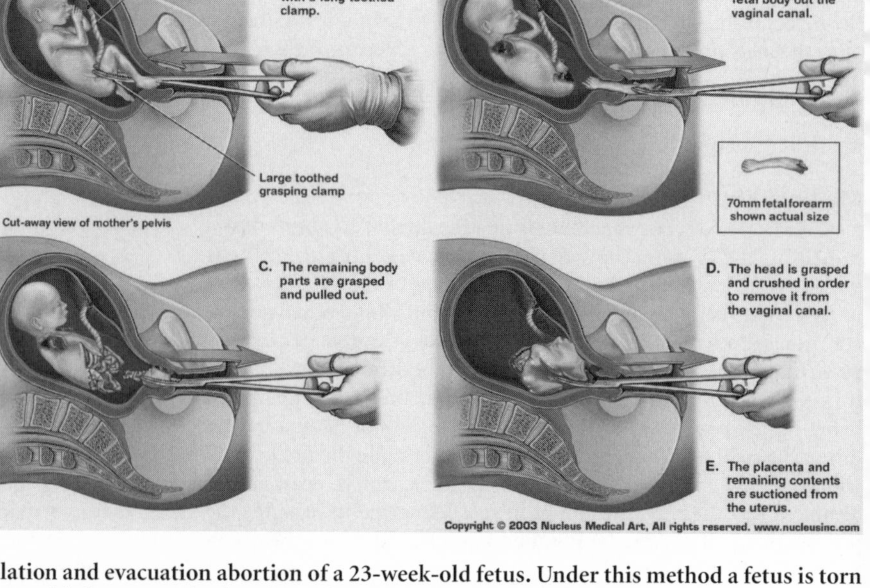

Dilation and evacuation abortion of a 23-week-old fetus. Under this method a fetus is torn apart with forceps and taken from the womb (illustration copyright © 2008 Nucleus Medical Art, all rights reserved, www.nucleusinc.com).

aspiration, hysterectomy, and hysterotomy. *See also* **Dilation and Curettage; Dilation and Evacuation; Dilation and Extraction; Hysterectomy Abortion; Hysterotomy Abortion; Instillation Methods; Machine Vacuum Aspiration; Methotrexate Induced Abortion; Mifepristone Induced Abortion; Mini Vac Aspiration**

Methotrexate Induced Abortion

Methotrexate is an alternative method for ending an early pregnancy (1–8 weeks) without surgery or anesthesia. This method of treatment has been in use since 1982. It is used to treat early ectopic (tubal) pregnancies, which are pregnancies that implant outside the uterus. Methotrexate stops rapidly growing embryonic and placental cells of early pregnancy from growing. It prevents cells from using vitamin folic acid and attacks the fast growing cells of the trophoblast as well, the tissue surrounding the embryo that eventually gives rise to the placenta.

Methotrexate is given by injection in a single dose calculated by a formula using the woman's height and weight. A woman must also take a second medication called misoprostol, a prostaglandin. The misoprostol causes the uterus to contract and cervix to dilate, causing the expulsion of the pregnancy from the body.

Methotrexate is administered through injection while a woman is at a clinical provider's facility. After receiving the injection the woman is given four misoprostol tablets to take home with instructions to insert them vaginally 5–7 days later. The misoprostol tablets will usually produce cramping and vaginal bleeding 2–4 hours after insertion. In most cases the pregnancy will be aborted within 24 hours of the insertion. The woman must return to the clinical provider one week after the vaginal insertion for a sonogram. Should the visit reveal that the abortion was not complete, additional misoprostol tablets or surgical abortion will be provided. If a pregnancy were to continue after the procedure, the fetus would most likely show deformities. Side effects from the methotrexate procedure are usually mild and occur for only a short duration. The side effects might include nausea, diarrhea, abdominal cramping pain, bleeding, vomiting, headache, hot flashes, dizziness, sleeplessness or sores in the mouth. *See also* **Methods of Abortion**

Mexico City Policy

On June 17, 1984 the administration of President Ronald Reagan announced what has been called the Mexico City Policy (also called the Gag Rule). This policy requires non-governmental organizations to agree as a condition of their receipt of federal funds that such organizations would neither perform nor actively promote abortion as a method of family planning in other nations. The policy received its name as a result of its announcement at a United Nations International Conference on Population in Mexico City, Mexico. The United States delegate, James L. Buckley, announced the policy at the conference. The policy was set forth, in relevant part, as follows:

The United Nations Declaration of the Rights of the Child calls for legal protection for children before birth as well as after birth. In keeping with this obligation, the United States does not consider abortion an acceptable element of family planning programs and will no longer contribute to those of which it is a part. Accordingly, when dealing with nations which support abortion with funds not provided by the United States Government, the United States will contribute to such nations through segregated accounts which cannot be used for abortion. Moreover, the United States will no longer contribute to separate nongovernmental organizations which perform or actively promote abortion as a method of family planning in other nations. With regard to the United Nations Fund for Population Activities [UNFPA], the U.S. will insist that no part of its contribution be used for abortion. The U.S. will also call for concrete assurances that the UNFPA is not engaged in, or does not provide funding for, abortion or coercive family planning programs; if such assurances are not forthcoming, the U.S. will redirect the amount of its contribution to other, non–UNFPA, family planning programs.

The policy was unsuccessfully challenged in the case of *DKT Memorial Fund Ltd. v. Agency for Int'l Dev.*, 887 F.2d 275 (D.C. Cir. 1989). The policy remained enforce from its inception until it was repealed by President Bill Clinton two days after he entered office in 1993. The policy was reinstated by President George Bush on January 22, 2001. The text of President Bush's Memorandum reinstating the policy is set out below.

The Mexico City Policy announced by President Reagan in 1984 required nongovernmental organizations to agree as a condition of their receipt of Federal funds that such organizations would neither perform nor actively promote abortion as a method of family planning in other nations. This policy was in effect until it was rescinded on January 22, 1993.

It is my conviction that taxpayer funds should not be used to pay for abortions or advocate or actively promote abortion, either here or abroad. It is therefore my belief that the Mexico City Policy should be restored. Accordingly, I hereby rescind the "Memorandum for the Acting Administrator of the Agency for International Development, Subject: AID Family Planning Grants/Mexico City Policy," dated January 22, 1993, and I direct the Administrator of the United States Agency for International Development to reinstate in full all of the requirements of the Mexico City Policy in effect on January 19, 1993.

See also **Helms Amendment; Public Resources for Abortions; United States Agency for International Development**

Michigan

(1) OVERVIEW

The state of Michigan enacted its first criminal abortion statute in 1846. The statute underwent several amendments prior to the 1973 decision by the United States Supreme Court in *Roe v. Wade*, which legalized abortion in the nation. In spite of the decision in *Roe*, Michigan has not repealed its pre–*Roe* criminal abortion laws. However, the laws are constitutionally infirm.

Michigan has taken affirmative steps to respond to *Roe* and its progeny. The state has addressed numerous abortion issues by statute that include legal definition of birth, born alive infant, informed consent, partial-birth abortion, abortion by minors, use of facilities and people, public funds for abortion, fetal or embryo experiments, ban human cloning, injury to pregnant woman, fetal death report, prohibit teaching students about abortion, and anti-abortion activities.

(2) PRE-ROE ABORTION BAN

As previously indicated, Michigan has not repealed its pre–*Roe* criminal abortion statutes. The laws remain on the books even though they were expressly found invalid in *People v. Bricker*, 208 N.W.2d 172 (Mich. 1973) and *Larkin v. Cahalan*, 208 N.W.2d 176 (Mich. 1973). However, the appellate court in *People v. Higuera*, 625 N.W.2d 444 (Mich.App. 2001) held that the statutes may be enforced to penalize post-viability abortions. Michigan also criminalized abortion advertising and the sale of abortion devices. The statutes are set out below.

Michigan Code § 750.14. Procuring miscarriage

Any person who shall wilfully administer to any pregnant woman any medicine, drug, substance or thing whatever, or shall employ any instrument or other means whatever, with intent thereby to procure the miscarriage of any such woman, unless the same shall have been necessary to preserve the life of such woman, shall be guilty of a felony, and in case the death of such pregnant woman be thereby produced, the offense shall be deemed manslaughter.

In any prosecution under this section, it shall not be necessary for the prosecution to prove that no such necessity existed.

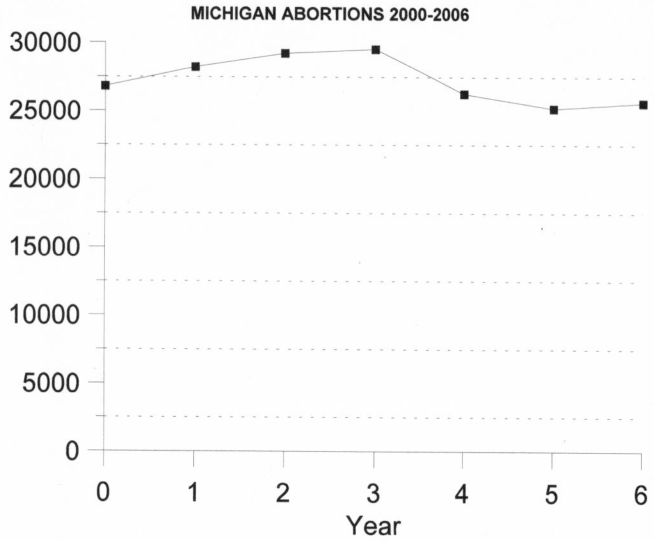

Source: Michigan Department of Community Health.

Michigan Residents Abortion by Age Group 2000-2006

	Age Group (yrs)			
Year	<20	20–24	25–29	≥30
2000	4,992	8,305	6,098	6,484
2001	5,033	9,064	6,201	6,760
2002	4,932	9,409	6,463	7,306
2003	5,033	9,379	6,574	7,456
2004	4,642	8,098	5,823	6,855
2005	4,575	7,986	5,520	6,396
2006	4,582	8,044	5,719	6,543
Total	33,789	60,285	42,398	47,800

Source: Michigan Department of Community Health.

Michigan Abortion by Weeks of Gestation 2000-2004

Weeks of Gestation	Year					Total
	2000	2001	2002	2003	2004	
≤8	15,673	17,301	18,129	18,345	16,771	86,219
9-10	5,155	5,207	5,180	5,177	4,324	25,043
11-12	2,175	2,447	2,492	2,699	2,115	11,928
13-15	1,787	1,799	1,986	1,990	1,872	9,434
16-20	1,228	896	947	841	772	4,684
≥21	275	202	199	244	195	1,115
Not known	514	368	304	244	220	1,650

Source: National Center for Health Statistics.

Michigan Code § 750.323. Death from medicine or instrument

Any person who shall administer to any woman pregnant with a quick child any medicine, drug or substance whatever, or shall use or employ any instrument or other means, with intent thereby to destroy such child, unless the same shall have been necessary to preserve the life of such mother, shall, in case the death of such child or of such mother be thereby produced, be guilty of manslaughter.

In any prosecution under this section, it shall not be necessary for the prosecution to prove that no such necessity existed.

Michigan Code § 750.15.
Advertising or selling abortion products

Any person who shall in any manner, except as hereinafter provided, advertise, publish, sell or publicly expose for sale any pills, powder, drugs or combination of drugs, designed expressly for the use of females for the purpose of procuring an abortion, shall be guilty of a misdemeanor.

Source: Michigan Department of Community Health.

Source: National Center for Health Statistics.

Michigan Prior Abortion by Female 2000–2004

	Prior Abortion				
Year	None	1	2	≥3	Not known
2000	13,794	6,988	3,475	2,503	47
2001	14,804	7,501	3,440	2,475	0
2002	14,861	7,610	3,829	2,931	0
2003	15,281	7,616	3,741	2,902	0
2004	13,679	6,757	3,255	2,574	4
Total	72,419	36,472	17,740	13,385	51

Source: National Center for Health Statistics.

Any drug or medicine known to be designed and expressly prepared for producing an abortion, shall only be sold upon the written prescription of an established practicing physician of the city, village, or township in which the sale is made; and the druggist or dealer selling the same shall, in a book provided for that purpose, register the name of the purchaser,

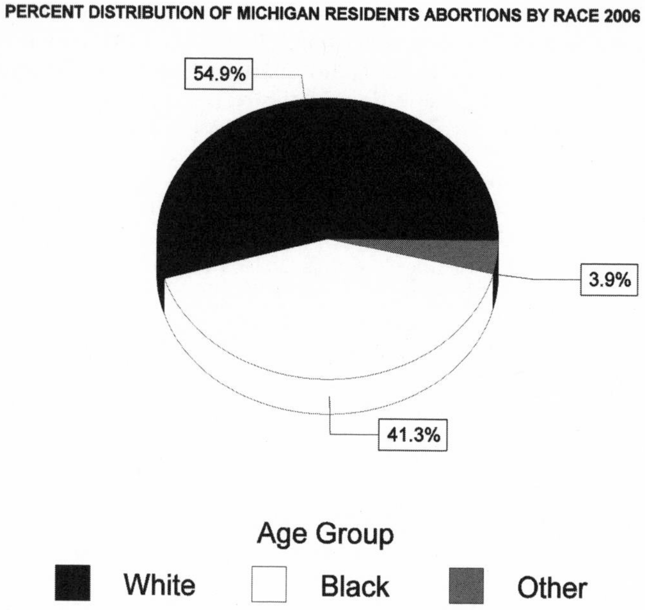

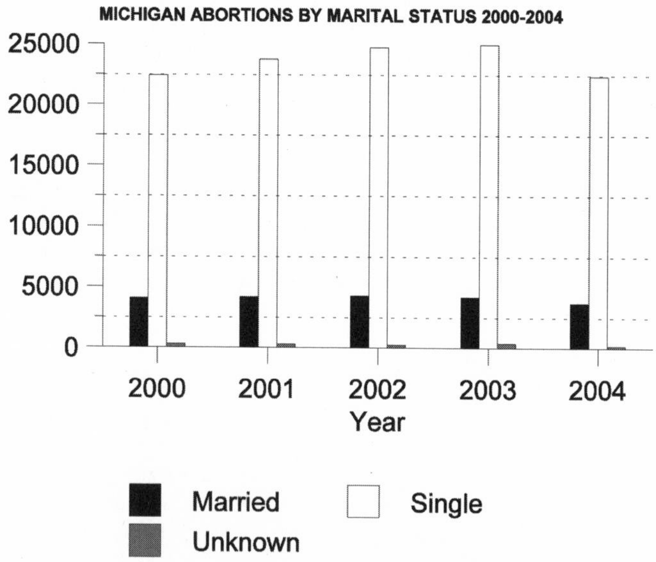

the date of the sale, the kind and quantity of the medicine sold, and the name and residence of the physician prescribing the same.

Michigan Code § 750.34.
Advertisements relating to treatment of sexual diseases

A person who advertises in his or her own name or in the name of another person, firm or pretended firm, association, or corporation or pretended corporation, in a newspaper, pamphlet, circular, periodical, or other written or printed paper, or the owner, publisher, or manager of a newspaper or periodical who permits to be published or inserted in a newspaper or periodical owned or controlled by him or her, an advertisement of the treating or curing of venereal diseases, the restoration of "lost manhood" or "lost vitality or vigor," or advertises in any manner that he or she is a specialist in diseases of the sexual organs, or diseases caused by sexual vice or masturbation, or in any diseases of like cause, or shall advertise in any manner any medicine, drug, compound, appliance, or any means whatever whereby sexual diseases of men or women may be cured or relieved, or miscarriage or abortion produced, is guilty of a misdemeanor punishable by imprisonment for not more than 1 year or a fine of not more than $1, 000.00.

Michigan Code § 750.40. Publication of cures

The publication or sale within this state of any circular, pamphlet or book containing recipes or prescriptions in indecent or obscene language for the cure of chronic female complaints or private diseases, or recipes or prescriptions for drops, pills, tinctures, or other compounds designed to prevent conception, or tending to produce miscarriage or abortion is hereby prohibited; and for each copy thereof, so published and sold, containing such prohibited recipes or prescriptions, the publisher and seller shall each be guilty of a misdemeanor.

(3) Legal Definition of Birth

Michigan enacted a series of statutes which define legal birth in such a manner as to have the effect of banning pre-viability abortion procedures. The statutes were declared unconstitutional in *Northland Family Planning Clinic, Inc. v. Cox*, 487 F.3d 323 (6th Cir. 2007). The statutes are set out below.

Michigan Code § 333.1081. Short title

This act shall be known and may be cited as the "legal birth definition act."

Michigan Code § 333.1082. Legislative findings

The following findings are hereby made:

(a) That in Roe v Wade the United States supreme court declared that an unborn child is not a person as understood and protected by the constitution, but any born child is a legal person with full constitutional and legal rights.

(b) That in Roe v Wade the United States supreme court made no effort to define birth or place any restrictions on the states in defining when a human being is considered born for legal purposes.

(c) That, when any portion of a human being has been vaginally delivered outside his or her mother's body, that portion of the body can only be described as born and the state has a rational basis for defining that human being as born and as a legal person.

(d) That the state has a compelling interest in protecting the life of a born person.

Michigan Code § 333.1083. Legal status of perinate

(1) A perinate shall be considered a legally born person for all purposes under the law.

(2) A physician or an individual performing an act, task, or function under the delegatory authority of a physician is immune from criminal, civil, or administrative liability for performing any procedure that results in injury or death of a perinate while completing the delivery of the perinate under any of the following circumstances:

(a) If the perinate is being expelled from the mother's body as a result of a spontaneous abortion.

(b) If in that physician's reasonable medical judgment and in compliance with the applicable standard of practice and care, the procedure was necessary in either of the following circumstances:

(i) To save the life of the mother and every reasonable effort was made to preserve the life of both the mother and the perinate.

(ii) To avert an imminent threat to the physical health of the mother, and any harm to the perinate was incidental to treating the mother and not a known or intended result of the procedure performed.

Michigan Code § 333.1084. Effect of act on existing legal rights

Nothing in this act shall abrogate any existing right, privilege, or protection under criminal or civil law that applies to an embryo or fetus.

Michigan Code § 333.1085. Definitions

As used in this act:

(a) "Anatomical part" means any portion of the anatomy of a human being that has not been severed from the body, but not including the umbilical cord or placenta.

(b) "Imminent threat to the physical health" means a physical condition that if left untreated would result in substantial and irreversible impairment of a major bodily function.

(c) "Live" means demonstrating 1 or more of the following biological functions:

(i) A detectable heartbeat.

(ii) Evidence of breathing.

(iii) Evidence of spontaneous movement.

(iv) Umbilical cord pulsation.

(d) "Perinate" means a live human being at any point after which any anatomical part of the human being is known to have passed beyond the plane of the vaginal introitus until the point of complete expulsion or extraction from the mother's body.

(e) "Physician" means an individual licensed by the state to engage in the practice of medicine or osteopathic medicine and surgery under article 15 of the public health code, 1978 PA 368, MCL 333.16101 to 333.18838.

(4) Born Alive Infant

Michigan provides by statutes for the preservation of an infant born after a failed abortion. The statutes addressing the matter are set out below.

Michigan Code § 333.1071. Title and definitions

(1) This act shall be known and may be cited as the "born alive infant protection act."

(2) As used in this act:

(a) "Abortion" means that term as defined in section 17015 of the public health code, 1978 PA 368, MCL 333.17015.

(b) "Live birth" means the complete expulsion or extraction of a product of conception from its mother, regardless of the duration of the pregnancy, that after expulsion or extraction, whether or not the umbilical cord has been cut or the placenta is attached, shows any evidence of life, including, but not limited to, 1 or more of the following:

(i) Breathing.

(ii) A heartbeat.

(iii) Umbilical cord pulsation.

(iv) Definite movement of voluntary muscles.

Michigan Code § 333.1072. Legislative findings

The legislature finds all of the following:

(a) The state has a paramount interest in protecting all individuals.

(b) If an abortion results in the live birth of a newborn, the newborn is a legal person for all purposes under the law.

(c) A woman's right to terminate pregnancy ends when the pregnancy is terminated. It is not an infringement on a woman's right to terminate her pregnancy for the state to assert its interest in protecting a newborn whose live birth occurs as the result of an abortion.

Michigan Code § 333.1073. Abortion resulting in live birth

(1) If an abortion results in a live birth and, after being informed of the newborn's live birth, the newborn's mother expresses a desire not to assume custody and responsibility for the newborn, by refusing to authorize all necessary life sustaining medical treatment for the newborn or releasing the newborn for adoption, the newborn shall be considered a newborn who has been surrendered to an emergency service provider under the safe delivery of newborns law, chapter XII of the probate code of 1939, 1939 PA 288, MCL 712.1 to 712.20. The procedures of the safe delivery of newborns law, chapter XII of the probate code of 1939, 1939 PA 288, MCL 712.1 to 712.20, shall be followed in regard to the custody and care of the newborn.

(2) If an abortion performed in a hospital setting results in a live birth, the physician attending the abortion shall provide immediate medical care to the newborn, inform the mother of the live birth, and request transfer of the newborn to a resident, on-duty, or emergency room physician who shall provide medical care to the newborn. If an abortion performed in other than a hospital setting results in a live birth, a physician attending the abortion shall provide immediate medical care to the newborn and call 9-1-1 for an emergency transfer of the newborn to a hospital that shall provide medical care to the newborn.

(3) A live birth described in this act shall be reported as required in section 2822 of the public health code, 1978 PA 368, MCL 333.2822.

(4) If a newborn is considered a newborn who has been surrendered to an emergency service provider under the safe delivery of newborns law, chapter XII of the probate code of 1939, 1939 PA 288, MCL 712.1 to 712.20, as provided in subsection (1), the identity of the newborn's mother and father becomes confidential and shall not be revealed, either orally or in writing.

(5) The attending physician who transfers care of a live newborn under this section to another physician or a 9-1-1 emergency responder shall transmit to the mother of the newborn any information provided to the attending physician by the emergency service provider who received custody of the newborn under the safe delivery of newborns law, chapter XII of the probate code of 1939, 1939 PA 288, MCL 712.1 to 712.20, as provided in section 3 of the safe delivery of newborns law, chapter XII of the probate code of 1939, 1939 PA 288, MCL 712.3.

Michigan Code § 333.2822.
Individuals required to report live births

(1) The following individuals shall report a live birth that occurs in this state:

(a) If a live birth occurs in an institution or enroute to an institution, the individual in charge of the institution or his or her designated representative shall obtain the personal data, prepare the certificate of birth, secure the signatures required by the certificate of birth, and file the certificate of birth with the local registrar or as otherwise directed by the state registrar within 5 days after the birth. The physician or other individual in attendance shall provide the medical information required by the certificate of birth and certify to the facts of birth not later than 72 hours after the birth. If the physician or other individual does not certify to the facts of birth within 72 hours, the individual in charge of the institution or his or her authorized representative shall complete and certify the facts of birth.

(b) If a live birth occurs outside an institution, the record shall be prepared, certified, and filed with the local registrar by 1 of the following individuals in the following order of priority:

(i) The physician in attendance at or immediately after the live birth.

(ii) Any other individual in attendance at or immediately after the live birth.

(iii) The father, the mother, or, in the absence of the father and the inability of the mother, the individual in charge of the premises where the live birth occurs.

(c) If a live birth occurs during an attempted abortion and the mother of the newborn has expressed a desire not to assume custody and responsibility for the newborn by refusing to authorize necessary life-sustaining medical treatment, the live birth shall be reported as follows:

(i) If the attempted abortion took place in an institution, the live birth shall be reported in the same manner as provided in subdivision (a), except that the parents shall be listed as "unknown" and the newborn shall be listed as "Baby Doe."

(ii) If the attempted abortion took place outside an institution, the live birth shall be reported in the same manner as provided in subdivision (b), except that the parents shall be listed as "unknown" and the newborn shall be listed as "Baby Doe."

(2) As used in this section, "abortion" means that term as defined in section 17015.

Michigan Code § 750.135.
Exposing with intent to injure or abandon

(1) Except as provided in subsection (3), a father or mother of a child under the age of 6 years, or another individual, who exposes the child in any street, field, house, or other place, with intent to injure or wholly to abandon the child, is guilty of a felony, punishable by imprisonment for not more than 10 years.

(2) Except for a situation involving actual or suspected child abuse or child neglect, it is an affirmative defense to a prosecution under subsection (1) that the child was not more than 72 hours old and was surrendered to an emergency service provider under chapter XII of the probate code of 1939, 1939 PA 288, MCL 712.1 to 712.20. A criminal investigation shall not be initiated solely on the basis of a newborn being surrendered to an emergency service provider under chapter XII of the probate code of 1939, 1939 PA 288, MCL 712.1 to 712.20.

(3) Subsection (1) does not apply to a mother of a newborn who is surrendered under the born alive infant protection act. Subsection (1) applies to an attending physician who delivers a live newborn as a result of an attempted abortion and fails to comply with the requirements of the born alive infant protection act.

Michigan Code § 712.3. Surrender of newborn child

(1) If a parent surrenders a child who may be a newborn to an emergency service provider, the emergency service provider shall comply with the requirements of this section under the assumption that the child is a newborn. The emergency service provider shall, without a court order, immediately accept the newborn, taking the newborn into temporary protective custody. The emergency service provider shall make a reasonable effort to do all of the following:

(a) Take action necessary to protect the physical health and safety of the newborn.

(b) Inform the parent that by surrendering the newborn, the parent is releasing the newborn to a child placing agency to be placed for adoption.

(c) Inform the parent that the parent has 28 days to petition the court to regain custody of the newborn.

(d) Provide the parent with written material approved by or produced by the department that includes, but is not limited to, all of the following statements:

(i) By surrendering the newborn, the parent is releasing the newborn to a child placing agency to be placed for adoption.

(ii) The parent has 28 days after surrendering the newborn to petition the court to regain custody of the newborn.

(iii) After the 28-day period to petition for custody elapses, there will be a hearing to determine and terminate parental rights.

(iv) There will be public notice of this hearing, and the notice will not contain the parent's name.

(v) The parent will not receive personal notice of this hearing.

(vi) Information the parent provides to an emergency service provider will not be made public.

(vii) A parent can contact the safe delivery line established under section 20 of this chapter for more information.

(2) After providing a parent with the information described in subsection (1), an emergency service provider shall make a reasonable attempt to do all of the following:

(a) Encourage the parent to provide any relevant family or medical information.

(b) Provide the parent with the pamphlet produced under section 20 of this chapter and inform the parent that he or she can receive counseling or medical attention.

(c) Inform the parent that information that he or she provides will not be made public.

(d) Ask the parent to identify himself or herself.

(e) Inform the parent that in order to place the newborn for adoption the state is required to make a reasonable attempt to identify the other parent, and then ask the parent to identify the other parent.

(f) Inform the parent that the child placing agency that takes temporary protective custody of the newborn can provide confidential services to the parent.

(g) Inform the parent that the parent may sign a release for the newborn that may be used at the parental rights termination hearing under this chapter.

(3) A newborn whose birth is described in the born alive infant protection act, 2002 PA 687, MCL 333.1071 to 333.1073, and who is in a hospital setting or transferred to a hospital under section 3(1) of the born alive infant protection act, 2002 PA 687, MCL 333.1073, is a newborn surrendered as provided in this chapter. An emergency service provider who has received a newborn under the born alive infant protection act, 2002 PA 687, MCL 333.1071 to 333.1073, shall do all of the following:

(a) Comply with the requirements of subsections (1) and (2) to obtain information from or supply information to the surrendering parent by requesting the information from or supplying the information to the attending physician who delivered the newborn.

(b) Make no attempt to directly contact the parent or parents of the newborn.

(c) Provide humane comfort care if the newborn is determined to have no chance of survival due to gestational immaturity in light of available neonatal medical treatment or other condition incompatible with life.

(5) INFORMED CONSENT

Prior to an abortion Michigan requires that a woman be fully informed of the procedure to be used, the risks involved and alternatives to abortion. An abortion may not take place until 24 hours after a woman has given her written consent to an abortion. The statutes addressing the matters are set out below.

Michigan Code § 333.17014. Legislative intent

The legislature recognizes that under federal constitutional law, a state is permitted to enact persuasive measures that favor childbirth over abortion, even if those measures do not further a health interest. Sections 17015 and 17515 are nevertheless designed to provide objective, truthful information, and are not intended to be persuasive. The legislature finds that the enactment of sections 17015 and 17515 is essential for all of the following reasons:

(a) The knowledgeable exercise of a woman's decision to have an abortion depends on the extent to which the woman receives sufficient information to make an informed choice regarding abortion.

(b) The decision to obtain an abortion is an important and often stressful one, and it is in the state's interest that the decision be made with full knowledge of its nature and consequences.

(c) Enactment of sections 17015 and 17515 is necessary to ensure that, before an abortion, a woman is provided information regarding her available alternatives, and to ensure that a woman gives her voluntary and informed consent to an abortion.

(d) The receipt of accurate information about abortion and its alternatives is essential to the physical and psychological well-being of a woman considering an abortion.

(e) Because many abortions in this state are performed in clinics devoted solely to providing abortions, women who seek abortions at these clinics normally do not have a prior patient-physician relationship with the physician performing the abortion nor do these women continue a patient-physician relationship with the physician after the abortion. In many instances, the woman's only actual contact with the physician performing the abortion occurs simultaneously with the abortion procedure, with little opportunity to receive counsel concerning her decision. Consequently, certain safeguards are necessary to protect a woman's opportunity to select the option best suited to her particular situation.

(f) This state has an interest in protecting women and, subject to United States constitutional limitations and supreme court decisions, this state has an interest in protecting the fetus.

(g) Providing a woman with factual, medical, and biological information about the fetus she is carrying is essential to safeguard the state's interests described in subdivision (f). The dissemination of the information set forth in sections 17015 and 17515 is necessary due to the irreversible nature of the act of abortion and the often stressful circumstances under which the abortion decision is made.

(h) Because abortion services are marketed like many other commercial enterprises, and nearly all abortion providers advertise some free services, including pregnancy tests and counseling, the legislature finds that consumer protection should be extended to women contemplating an abortion decision by delaying any financial transactions until after a 24-hour waiting period. Furthermore, since the legislature and abortion providers have determined that a woman's right to give informed consent to an abortion can be protected by means other than the patient having to travel to the abortion facility during the 24-hour waiting period, the legislature finds that abortion providers do not have a legitimate claim of necessity in obtaining payments during the 24-hour waiting period.

(i) The safeguards that will best protect a woman seeking advice concerning abortion include the following:

(i) Private, individual counseling, including dissemination of certain information, as the woman's individual circumstances dictate, that affect her decision of whether to choose an abortion.

(ii) A 24-hour waiting period between a woman's receipt of that information provided to assist her in making an informed decision, and the actual performance of an abortion, if she elects to undergo an abortion. A 24-hour waiting period affords a woman, in light of the information provided by the physician or a qualified person assisting the physician, an opportunity to reflect on her decision and to seek counsel of family and friends in making her decision.

(j) The safeguards identified in subdivision (i) advance a woman's interests in the exercise of her discretion to choose or not to choose an abortion, and are justified by the objectives and interests of this state to protect the health of a pregnant woman and, subject to United

States constitutional limitations and supreme court decisions, to protect the fetus.

Michigan § 333.17015. Informed consent

(1) Subject to subsection (10), a physician shall not perform an abortion otherwise permitted by law without the patient's informed written consent, given freely and without coercion.

(2) For purposes of this section:

(a) "Abortion" means the intentional use of an instrument, drug, or other substance or device to terminate a woman's pregnancy for a purpose other than to increase the probability of a live birth, to preserve the life or health of the child after live birth, or to remove a dead fetus. Abortion does not include the use or prescription of a drug or device intended as a contraceptive.

(b) "Fetus" means an individual organism of the species homo sapiens in utero.

(c) "Local health department representative" means a person, who meets 1 or more of the licensing requirements listed in subdivision (f) and who is employed by, or under contract to provide services on behalf of, a local health department.

(d) "Medical emergency" means that condition which, on the basis of the physician's good faith clinical judgment, so complicates the medical condition of a pregnant woman as to necessitate the immediate abortion of her pregnancy to avert her death or for which a delay will create serious risk of substantial and irreversible impairment of a major bodily function.

(e) "Medical service" means the provision of a treatment, procedure, medication, examination, diagnostic test, assessment, or counseling, including, but not limited to, a pregnancy test, ultrasound, pelvic examination, or an abortion.

(f) "Qualified person assisting the physician" means another physician or a physician's assistant licensed under this part or part 175, a fully licensed or limited licensed psychologist licensed under part 182, a professional counselor licensed under part 181, a registered professional nurse or a licensed practical nurse licensed under part 172, or a social worker licensed under part 185.

(g) "Probable gestational age of the fetus" means the gestational age of the fetus at the time an abortion is planned to be performed.

(h) "Provide the patient with a physical copy" means confirming that the patient accessed the internet website described in subsection (5) and received a printed valid confirmation form from the website and including that form in the patient's medical record or giving a patient a copy of a required document by 1 or more of the following means:

(i) In person.

(ii) By registered mail, return receipt requested.

(iii) By parcel delivery service that requires the recipient to provide a signature in order to receive delivery of a parcel.

(iv) By facsimile transmission.

(3) Subject to subsection (10), a physician or a qualified person assisting the physician shall do all of the following not less than 24 hours before that physician performs an abortion upon a patient who is a pregnant woman:

(a) Confirm that, according to the best medical judgment of a physician, the patient is pregnant, and determine the probable gestational age of the fetus.

(b) Orally describe, in language designed to be understood by the patient, taking into account her age, level of maturity, and intellectual capability, each of the following:

(i) The probable gestational age of the fetus she is carrying.

(ii) Information about what to do and whom to contact should medical complications arise from the abortion.

(iii) Information about how to obtain pregnancy prevention information through the department of community health.

(c) Provide the patient with a physical copy of the written summary described in subsection (11)(b) that corresponds to the procedure the patient will undergo and is provided by the department of community health. If the procedure has not been recognized by the department, but is otherwise allowed under Michigan law, and the department has not provided a written summary for that procedure, the physician shall develop and provide a written summary that describes the procedure, any known risks or complications of the procedure, and risks associated with live birth and meets the requirements of subsection (11)(b)(iii) through (vii).

(d) Provide the patient with a physical copy of a medically accurate depiction, illustration, or photograph and description of a fetus supplied by the department of community health pursuant to subsection (11)(a) at the gestational age nearest the probable gestational age of the patient's fetus.

(e) Provide the patient with a physical copy of the prenatal care and parenting information pamphlet distributed by the department of community health under section 9161.

(4) The requirements of subsection (3) may be fulfilled by the physician or a qualified person assisting the physician at a location other than the health facility where the abortion is to be performed. The requirement of subsection (3)(a) that a patient's pregnancy be confirmed may be fulfilled by a local health department under subsection (18). The requirements of subsection (3) cannot be fulfilled by the patient accessing an internet website other than the internet website described in subsection (5) that is maintained through the department.

(5) The requirements of subsection (3)(c) through (e) may be fulfilled by a patient accessing the internet website maintained and operated through the department and receiving a printed, valid confirmation form from the website that the patient has reviewed the information required in subsection (3)(c) through (e) at least 24 hours before an abortion being performed on the patient. The website shall not require any information be supplied by the patient. The department shall not track, compile, or otherwise keep a record of information that would identify a patient who accesses this website. The patient shall supply the valid confirmation form to the physician or qualified person assisting the physician to be included in the patient's medical record to comply with this subsection.

(6) Subject to subsection (10), before obtaining the patient's signature on the acknowledgment and consent form, a physician personally and in the presence of the patient shall do all of the following:

(a) Provide the patient with the physician's name and inform the patient of her right to withhold or withdraw her consent to the abortion at any time before performance of the abortion.

(b) Orally describe, in language designed to be understood by the patient, taking into account her age, level of maturity, and intellectual capability, each of the following:

(i) The specific risk, if any, to the patient of the complications that have been associated with the procedure the patient will undergo, based on the patient's particular medical condition and history as determined by the physician.

(ii) The specific risk of complications, if any, to the patient if she chooses to continue the pregnancy based on the patient's particular medical condition and history as determined by a physician.

(7) To protect a patient's privacy, the information set forth in subsection (3) and subsection (6) shall not be disclosed to the patient in the presence of another patient.

(8) If at any time prior to the performance of an abortion, a patient undergoes an ultrasound examination, or a physician determines that ultrasound imaging will be used during the course of a patient's abortion, the physician or qualified person assisting the physician shall provide the patient with the opportunity to view or decline to view an active ultrasound image of the fetus, and offer to provide the patient with a physi-

cal picture of the ultrasound image of the fetus prior to the performance of the abortion. Before performing an abortion on a patient who is a pregnant woman, a physician or a qualified person assisting the physician shall do all of the following:

(a) Obtain the patient's signature on the acknowledgment and consent form described in subsection (11)(c) confirming that she has received the information required under subsection (3).

(b) Provide the patient with a physical copy of the signed acknowledgment and consent form described in subsection (11)(c).

(c) Retain a copy of the signed acknowledgment and consent form described in subsection (11)(c) and, if applicable, a copy of the pregnancy certification form completed under subsection (18)(b), in the patient's medical record.

(9) This subsection does not prohibit notifying the patient that payment for medical services will be required or that collection of payment in full for all medical services provided or planned may be demanded after the 24-hour period described in this subsection has expired. A physician or an agent of the physician shall not collect payment, in whole or in part, for a medical service provided to or planned for a patient before the expiration of 24 hours from the time the patient has done either or both of the following, except in the case of a physician or an agent of a physician receiving capitated payments or under a salary arrangement for providing those medical services:

(a) Inquired about obtaining an abortion after her pregnancy is confirmed and she has received from that physician or a qualified person assisting the physician the information required under subsection (3)(c) and (d).

(b) Scheduled an abortion to be performed by that physician.

(10) If the attending physician, utilizing his or her experience, judgment, and professional competence, determines that a medical emergency exists and necessitates performance of an abortion before the requirements of subsections (1), (3), and (6) can be met, the physician is exempt from the requirements of subsections (1), (3), and (6), may perform the abortion, and shall maintain a written record identifying with specificity the medical factors upon which the determination of the medical emergency is based.

(11) The department of community health shall do each of the following:

(a) Produce medically accurate depictions, illustrations, or photographs of the development of a human fetus that indicate by scale the actual size of the fetus at 2-week intervals from the fourth week through the twenty-eighth week of gestation. Each depiction, illustration, or photograph shall be accompanied by a printed description, in nontechnical English, Arabic, and Spanish, of the probable anatomical and physiological characteristics of the fetus at that particular state of gestational development.

(b) Subject to subdivision (g), develop, draft, and print, in nontechnical English, Arabic, and Spanish, written standardized summaries, based upon the various medical procedures used to abort pregnancies, that do each of the following:

(i) Describe, individually and on separate documents, those medical procedures used to perform abortions in this state that are recognized by the department.

(ii) Identify the physical complications that have been associated with each procedure described in subparagraph (i) and with live birth, as determined by the department. In identifying these complications, the department shall consider the annual statistical report required under section 2835(6), and shall consider studies concerning complications that have been published in a peer review medical journal, with particular attention paid to the design of the study, and shall consult with the federal centers for disease control, the American college of obstetricians and gynecologists, the Michigan state medical society, or any other source that the department determines appropriate for the purpose.

(iii) State that as the result of an abortion, some women may experience depression, feelings of guilt, sleep disturbance, loss of interest in work or sex, or anger, and that if these symptoms occur and are intense or persistent, professional help is recommended.

(iv) State that not all of the complications listed in subparagraph (ii) may pertain to that particular patient and refer the patient to her physician for more personalized information.

(v) Identify services available through public agencies to assist the patient during her pregnancy and after the birth of her child, should she choose to give birth and maintain custody of her child.

(vi) Identify services available through public agencies to assist the patient in placing her child in an adoptive or foster home, should she choose to give birth but not maintain custody of her child.

(vii) Identify services available through public agencies to assist the patient and provide counseling should she experience subsequent adverse psychological effects from the abortion.

(c) Develop, draft, and print, in nontechnical English, Arabic, and Spanish, an acknowledgment and consent form that includes only the following language above a signature line for the patient:

"I, __________, hereby authorize Dr. __________("the physician") and any assistant designated by the physician to perform upon me the following operation(s) or procedure(s):

____

(Name of operation(s) or procedure(s))

____

I understand that I am approximately __________ weeks pregnant. I consent to an abortion procedure to terminate my pregnancy. I understand that I have the right to withdraw my consent to the abortion procedure at any time prior to performance of that procedure. I acknowledge that at least 24 hours before the scheduled abortion I have received a physical copy of each of the following:

(a) A medically accurate depiction, illustration, or photograph of a fetus at the probable gestational age of the fetus I am carrying.

(b) A written description of the medical procedure that will be used to perform the abortion.

(c) A prenatal care and parenting information pamphlet. If any of the above listed documents were transmitted by facsimile, I certify that the documents were clear and legible. I acknowledge that the physician who will perform the abortion has orally described all of the following to me:

(i) The specific risk to me, if any, of the complications that have been associated with the procedure I am scheduled to undergo.

(ii) The specific risk to me, if any, of the complications if I choose to continue the pregnancy.

I acknowledge that I have received all of the following information:

(d) Information about what to do and whom to contact in the event that complications arise from the abortion.

(e) Information pertaining to available pregnancy related services.

I have been given an opportunity to ask questions about the operation(s) or procedure(s). I certify that I have not been required to make any payments for an abortion or any medical service before the expiration of 24 hours after I received the written materials listed in paragraphs (a), (b), and (c) above, or 24 hours after the time and date listed on the confirmation form if paragraphs (a), (b), and (c) were viewed from the state of Michigan internet website.."

(d) Make available to physicians through the Michigan board of medicine and the Michigan board of osteopathic medicine and surgery, and any person upon request the copies of medically accurate depictions, illustrations, or photographs described in subdivision (a), the standardized written summaries described in subdivision (b), the

acknowledgment and consent form described in subdivision (c), the prenatal care and parenting information pamphlet described in section 9161, and the pregnancy certification form described in subdivision (f).

(e) The department shall not develop written summaries for abortion procedures under subdivision (b) that utilize medication that has not been approved by the United States food and drug administration for use in performing an abortion.

(f) Develop, draft, and print a certification form to be signed by a local health department representative at the time and place a patient has a pregnancy confirmed, as requested by the patient, verifying the date and time the pregnancy is confirmed.

(g) Develop and maintain an internet website that allows a patient considering an abortion to review the information required in subsection (3)(c) through (e). After the patient reviews the required information, the department shall assure that a confirmation form can be printed by the patient from the internet website that will verify the time and date the information was reviewed. A confirmation form printed under this subdivision becomes invalid 14 days after the date and time printed on the confirmation form.

(h) Include on the informed consent website developed under subdivision (g) a list of health care providers, facilities, and clinics that offer to perform ultrasounds free of charge. The list shall be organized geographically and shall include the name, address, and telephone number of each health care provider, facility, and clinic.

(12) A physician's duty to inform the patient under this section does not require disclosure of information beyond what a reasonably well-qualified physician licensed under this article would possess.

(13) A written consent form meeting the requirements set forth in this section and signed by the patient is presumed valid. The presumption created by this subsection may be rebutted by evidence that establishes, by a preponderance of the evidence, that consent was obtained through fraud, negligence, deception, misrepresentation, coercion, or duress.

(14) A completed certification form described in subsection (11)(f) that is signed by a local health department representative is presumed valid. The presumption created by this subsection may be rebutted by evidence that establishes, by a preponderance of the evidence, that the physician who relied upon the certification had actual knowledge that the certificate contained a false or misleading statement or signature.

(15) This section does not create a right to abortion.

(16) Notwithstanding any other provision of this section, a person shall not perform an abortion that is prohibited by law.

(17) If any portion of this act or the application of this act to any person or circumstances is found invalid by a court, that invalidity does not affect the remaining portions or applications of the act that can be given effect without the invalid portion or application, if those remaining portions are not determined by the court to be inoperable.

(18) Upon a patient's request, each local health department shall:

(a) Provide a pregnancy test for that patient to confirm the pregnancy as required under subsection (3)(a) and determine the probable gestational stage of the fetus. The local health department need not comply with this subdivision if the requirements of subsection (3)(a) have already been met.

(b) If a pregnancy is confirmed, ensure that the patient is provided with a completed pregnancy certification form described in subsection (11)(f) at the time the information is provided.

(19) The identity and address of a patient who is provided information or who consents to an abortion pursuant to this section is confidential and is subject to disclosure only with the consent of the patient or by judicial process.

(20) A local health department with a file containing the identity and address of a patient described in subsection (19) who has been assisted by the local health department under this section shall do both of the following:

(a) Only release the identity and address of the patient to a physician or qualified person assisting the physician in order to verify the receipt of the information required under this section.

(b) Destroy the information containing the identity and address of the patient within 30 days after assisting the patient under this section.

Michigan Code § 333.17515. Physician compliance required

A physician, before performing an abortion on a patient, shall comply with section 17015.

(6) PARTIAL-BIRTH ABORTION

Michigan criminalizes partial-birth abortions. One of the state's three statutes addressing the matter, infant protection act, was found unconstitutional in *WomanCare of Southfield, P.C. v. Granholm*, 143 F.Supp.2d 849 (E.D.Mich. 2001). The decision in *WomanCare* invalidated the statute based upon the United States Supreme Court decision in *Stenberg v. Carhart*, which invalidated a Nebraska statute that prohibited partial-birth abortions. However, subsequent to *Stenberg*, the United States Supreme Court approved of a federal partial-birth abortion ban statute in *Gonzales v. Carhart*. The Michigan statutes are set out below.

Michigan Code § 750.90g. Infant protection act

(1) This section shall be known and may be cited as the "infant protection act."

(2) The legislature finds all of the following:

(a) That the constitution and laws of this nation and this state hold that a live infant completely expelled from his or her mother's body is recognized as a person with constitutional and legal rights and protection.

(b) That a live infant partially outside his or her mother is neither a fetus nor potential life, but is a person.

(c) That the United States supreme court decisions defining a right to terminate pregnancy do not extend to the killing of a live infant that has begun to emerge from his or her mother's body.

(d) That the state has a compelling interest in protecting the life of a live infant by determining that a live infant is a person deserving of legal protection at any point after any part of the live infant exists outside of the mother's body.

(3) Except as provided in subsections (4) and (5), a person who intentionally performs a procedure or takes any action upon a live infant with the intent to cause the death of the live infant is guilty of a felony punishable by imprisonment for life or any term of years or a fine of not more than $50,000.00, or both.

(4) It is not a violation of subsection (3) if a physician takes measures at any point after a live infant is partially outside of the mother's body, that in the physician's reasonable medical judgment are necessary to save the life of the mother and if every reasonable precaution is also taken to save the live infant's life.

(5) Subsection (3) does not apply to an action taken by the mother. However, this subsection does not exempt the mother from any other provision of law.

(6) As used in this section:

(a) "Live infant" means a human fetus at any point after any part of the fetus is known to exist outside of the mother's body and has 1 or more of the following: (i) A detectable heartbeat. (ii) Evidence of spontaneous movement. (iii) Evidence of breathing.

(b) "Outside of the mother's body" means beyond the outer abdominal wall or beyond the plane of the vaginal introitus.

(c) "Part of the fetus" means any portion of the body of a human fetus that has not been severed from the fetus, but not including the umbilical cord or placenta.

(d) "Physician" means an individual licensed to engage in the

practice of allopathic medicine or the practice of osteopathic medicine and surgery under article 15 of the public health code.

Michigan Code § 333.17016. Partial-birth abortions

(1) Except as otherwise provided in subsection (2), a physician or an individual performing an act, task, or function under the delegatory authority of a physician shall not perform a partial-birth abortion, even if the abortion is otherwise permitted by law.

(2) A physician or an individual described in subsection (1) may perform a partial-birth abortion if the physician or other individual reasonably believes that performing the partial-birth abortion is necessary to save the life of a pregnant woman whose life is endangered by a physical disorder, physical illness, or physical injury and that no other medical procedure will accomplish that purpose.

(3) This section does not create a right to abortion.

(4) Notwithstanding any other provision of this section, a person shall not perform an abortion that is prohibited by law.

(5) As used in this section:

(a) "Abortion" means the intentional use of an instrument, drug, or other substance or device to terminate a woman's pregnancy for a purpose other than to increase the probability of a live birth, to preserve the life or health of the child after live birth, or to remove a dead fetus. Abortion does not include a procedure to complete a spontaneous abortion or the use or prescription of a drug or device intended as a contraceptive.

(b) "Fetus" means an individual organism of the species homo sapiens at any time before complete delivery from a pregnant woman.

(c) "Partial-birth abortion" means an abortion in which the physician or individual acting under the delegatory authority of the physician performing the abortion partially vaginally delivers a living fetus before killing the fetus and completing the delivery.

Michigan Code § 333.17516. Partial-birth abortions

(1) Except as otherwise provided in subsection (2), a physician or an individual performing an act, task, or function under the delegatory authority of a physician shall not perform a partial-birth abortion, even if the abortion is otherwise permitted by law.

(2) A physician or an individual described in subsection (1) may perform a partial-birth abortion if the physician or other individual reasonably believes that performing the partial-birth abortion is necessary to save the life of a pregnant woman whose life is endangered by a physical disorder, physical illness, or physical injury and that no other medical procedure will accomplish that purpose.

(3) This section does not create a right to abortion.

(4) Notwithstanding any other provision of this section, a person shall not perform an abortion that is prohibited by law.

(5) As used in this section:

(a) "Abortion" means the intentional use of an instrument, drug, or other substance or device to terminate a woman's pregnancy for a purpose other than to increase the probability of a live birth, to preserve the life or health of the child after live birth, or to remove a dead fetus. Abortion does not include a procedure to complete a spontaneous abortion or the use or prescription of a drug or device intended as a contraceptive.

(b) "Fetus" means an individual organism of the species homo sapiens at any time before complete delivery from a pregnant woman.

(c) "Partial-birth abortion" means an abortion in which the physician or individual acting under the delegatory authority of the physician performing the abortion partially vaginally delivers a living fetus before killing the fetus and completing the delivery.

(7) ABORTION BY MINORS

Under the laws of Michigan no physician may perform an abortion upon an unemancipated minor unless he/she first obtains the written consent of either parent or the legal guardian of the minor. In compliance with federal constitutional law, Michigan has provided a judicial waiver procedure for an unemancipated minor to obtain an abortion without parental or guardian consent. If an unemancipated minor elects not to seek, or cannot for any reason obtain consent from either of her parents or legal guardian, the minor may petition a trial court for a waiver of the consent requirement. A minor has a right to an attorney at the proceeding and if she cannot afford one, the court must appoint her an attorney. If a minor chooses, she may represent herself. The required parental or guardian consent may be waived if the court finds either (1) that the minor is mature and well-informed enough to make the abortion decision on her own, or (2) that performance of the abortion would be in the best interest of the minor. An expedited appeal is available to any minor to whom the court denies a waiver of consent. The statutes addressing the matters are set out below.

Michigan Code § 722.901. Short title

This act shall be known and may be cited as "the parental rights restoration act."

Michigan Code § 722.902. Definitions

As used in this act:

(a) "Abortion" means the intentional use of an instrument, drug, or other substance or device to terminate a woman's pregnancy for a purpose other than to increase the probability of a live birth, to preserve the life or health of the child after live birth, or to remove a dead fetus. Abortion does not include the use or prescription of a drug or device intended as a contraceptive.

(b) "Medical emergency" means that condition which, on the basis of a physician's good faith clinical judgment, so complicates the medical condition of a pregnant woman as to necessitate an immediate abortion of that woman's pregnancy to avert her death, or for which a delay in performing an abortion will create serious risk of substantial and irreversible impairment of a major bodily function.

(c) "Minor" means a person under the age of 18 years who is not emancipated pursuant to section 4 of Act No. 293 of the Public Acts of 1968, being section 722.4 of the Michigan Compiled Laws.

(d) "Next friend" means a person who is not 1 of the following:

(i) A physician who performs abortions.

(ii) A person who is employed by, or receives financial consideration from, a physician who performs abortions or an organization that provides abortions or abortion counseling and referral services.

(iii) A person who serves as a board member or volunteer to an organization that provides abortions or abortion counseling and referral services.

Michigan Code § 722.903. Parental consent

(1) Except as otherwise provided in this act, a person shall not perform an abortion on a minor without first obtaining the written consent of the minor and 1 of the parents or the legal guardian of the minor.

(2) If a parent or the legal guardian is not available or refuses to give his or her consent, or if the minor elects not to seek consent of a parent or the legal guardian, the minor may petition the probate court pursuant to section 4 for a waiver of the parental consent requirement of this section.

Michigan Code § 722.904. Judicial Bypass

(1) The probate court has jurisdiction of proceedings related to a minor's petition for a waiver of parental consent.

(2) Proceedings held pursuant to this act shall be completed with confidentiality and sufficient expedition to provide an effective opportunity for the minor to provide self-consent to an abortion, in accordance with all of the following:

(a) The probate court shall, upon its first contact with a minor

seeking a waiver of parental consent under this act, provide the minor with notice of the minor's right to all of the following:

(i) Confidentiality of the proceedings, including the right to use initials in the petition.

(ii) Court appointment of an attorney or guardian ad litem.

(iii) Assistance with preparing and filing the petition.

(b) A minor may file a petition for waiver of parental consent in the probate court of the county in which the minor resides. For purposes of this act, the county in which the minor resides means the county in which the minor's residence is located or the county in which the minor is found.

(c) Upon request of the minor, the probate court shall provide the minor with assistance in preparing and filing the petition for waiver of parental consent.

(d) A minor may file a petition for waiver of parental consent under this act on her own behalf or through a next friend. The minor may use initials or some other means of assuring confidentiality in the petition.

(e) Upon request of the minor, the probate court shall appoint an attorney or guardian ad litem within 24 hours to represent the minor in proceedings under this section.

(f) A minor is not required to pay a fee for proceedings under this section.

(g) A hearing on a petition for waiver of parental consent under this act shall be held within 72 hours, excluding Sundays and holidays, after the petition is filed and shall be closed to the public. All records of proceedings related to the petition for waiver of parental consent under this act are confidential.

(h) The probate court that hears the petition for waiver of parental consent shall issue and make a part of the confidential record its specific findings of fact and conclusions of law in support of its ruling either on the record or in a written opinion.

(i) A written order granting or denying a petition for waiver of parental consent filed pursuant to this act shall be issued within 48 hours, excluding Sundays and holidays, after the hearing on the petition is held.

(3) The probate court shall grant a waiver of parental consent if it finds either of the following:

(a) The minor is sufficiently mature and well-enough informed to make the decision regarding abortion independently of her parents or legal guardian.

(b) The waiver would be in the best interests of the minor.

(4) A minor who is denied a waiver under this section may appeal the probate court's decision to the court of appeals. Appeal proceedings shall be expedited and confidential. The notice of appeal shall be filed within 24 hours of the issuance of the order denying the petition. The appeal shall be perfected within 72 hours, excluding Sundays and holidays, from the filing of the notice of appeal.

(5) The confidentiality requirements of this section do not prevent the probate court from reporting suspected child abuse under section 4 of the child protection law, Act No. 238 of the Public Acts of 1975, being section 722.624 of the Michigan Compiled Laws.

(6) If a minor who is seeking a waiver of parental consent reveals to the probate court that she is the victim of sexual abuse, and that her pregnancy is, or may be, the result of sexual abuse, the probate court shall immediately do all of the following:

(a) Report the suspected sexual abuse to the department of social services or a law enforcement agency pursuant to the child protection law, Act No. 238 of the Public Acts of 1975, being sections 722.621 to 722.636 of the Michigan Compiled Laws.

(b) Inform the minor that there are laws designed to protect her, including all of the following provisions of chapter XIIA of the probate code, Act No. 288 of the Public Acts of 1939, being sections 712A.1 to 712A.28 of the Michigan Compiled Laws:

(i) That a law enforcement officer may without court order take the minor into temporary protective custody if, after investigation, the officer has reasonable grounds to conclude that the minor's health, safety, or welfare would be endangered by leaving her in the custody of her parent or legal guardian.

(ii) That the juvenile division of the probate court may, upon learning of the suspected sexual abuse, immediately hold a preliminary inquiry to determine whether a petition for court jurisdiction should be filed or whether other action should be taken.

(iii) That the juvenile court shall appoint an attorney to represent the minor in protective proceedings.

(iv) That after a petition has been filed, the juvenile court may order that the minor be placed with someone other than her parent or legal guardian pending trial or further court order if such placement is necessary to avoid substantial risk to the minor's life, physical health, or mental well-being.

(7) As used in this section, "child abuse" and "sexual abuse" mean those terms as defined in section 2 of the child protection law, Act No. 238 of the Public Acts of 1975, being section 722.622 of the Michigan Compiled Laws.

Michigan Code § 722.905. Medical emergency abortion

The requirements of [§ 722.903] do not apply to an abortion performed pursuant to a medical emergency.

Michigan Code § 722.906. Applicability to nonresidents

The requirements of this act apply regardless of whether the minor is a resident of this state.

Michigan Code § 722.907. Violation of act

(1) A person who intentionally performs an abortion in violation of this act is guilty of a misdemeanor.

(2) A person's failure to obtain either parental consent pursuant to this act or a copy of a waiver granted under section 4 before performing an abortion on a minor is prima facie evidence in appropriate civil actions of his or her failure to obtain informed consent to perform the abortion or of his or her interference with family relations. A court shall not construe the law of this state to preclude exemplary damages in a civil action related to violations of this act.

Michigan Code § 722.908. Right to abortion not created

(1) This act does not create a right to an abortion.

(2) Notwithstanding any other provision of this act, a person shall not perform an abortion that is prohibited by law.

(8) USE OF FACILITIES AND PEOPLE

Under the laws of Michigan hospitals are not required to allow abortions at their facilities. The employees and physicians at hospitals that do allow abortions are permitted to refuse to take part in abortions. The statutes addressing the matters are set out below.

Michigan Code § 333.20181.
Refusal of facility to participate in abortion

A hospital, clinic, institution, teaching institution, or other health facility is not required to admit a patient for the purpose of performing an abortion. A hospital, clinic, institution, teaching institution, or other health facility or a physician, member, or associate of the staff, or other person connected therewith, may refuse to perform, participate in, or allow to be performed on its premises an abortion. The refusal shall be with immunity from any civil or criminal liability or penalty.

Michigan Code § 333.20182.
Refusal of personnel to participate in abortion

A physician, or other individual who is a member of or associated with a hospital, clinic, institution, teaching institution, or other health facility, or a nurse, medical student, student nurse, or other employee of a hospital, clinic, institution, teaching institution, or other health facility in which an abortion is performed, who states an objection to abortion on professional, ethical, moral, or religious grounds, is not required to participate in the medical procedures which will result in abortion. The refusal by the individual to participate does not create a liability for damages on account of the refusal or for any disciplinary or discriminatory action by the patient, hospital, clinic, institution, teaching institution, or other health facility against the individual.

Michigan Code § 333.20183. Refusal to give advice

(1) A physician who informs a patient that he or she refuses to give advice concerning, or participate in, an abortion is not liable to the hospital, clinic, institution, teaching institution, health facility, or patient for the refusal.

(2) A civil action for negligence or malpractice or a disciplinary or discriminatory action may not be maintained against a person refusing to give advice as to, or participating in, an abortion based on the refusal.

Michigan Code § 333.20184.
Discrimination against abortion participant

A hospital, clinic, institution, teaching institution, or other health facility which refuses to allow abortions to be performed on its premises shall not deny staff privileges or employment to an individual for the sole reason that the individual previously participated in, or expressed a willingness to participate in, a termination of pregnancy. A hospital, clinic, institution, teaching institution, or other health facility shall not discriminate against its staff members or other employees for the sole reason that the staff members or employees have participated in, or have expressed a willingness to participate in, a termination of pregnancy.

(9) PUBLIC FUNDS FOR ABORTION

Michigan has enacted a number of statutes limiting or prohibiting the use of public funds to pay for abortions. One such statute, which banned the use of public funds for abortions by welfare recipients, was held invalid in *Planned Parenthood Affiliates v. Engler*, 73 F.3d 634 (6th Cir. 1996), to the extent that it conflicted with the federal requirement of having an abortion funding exception for pregnancies caused by rape or incest. The statutes are set out below.

Michigan Code § 400.109d. Legislative findings

(1) The legislature finds that the use of Medicaid funds for elective abortions has been clearly rejected by the people of Michigan through Act No. 59 of the Public Acts of 1987 [§ 400.109a], initiated by the citizens under the rights of the people reserved in the Michigan constitution, approved by a majority of this legislature, affirmed by the citizens at large through a statewide referendum, and sustained by the Michigan supreme court.

(2) In light of evidence that abortion providers, in conjunction with third party payors, may have devised and implemented plans for reimbursing services in violation of the intent of Act No. 59 of the Public Acts of 1987, the legislature finds the enactment of section 109e a necessary clarification of, and enforcement mechanism for, Act No. 59 of the Public Acts of 1987.

(3) The legislature finds that any practice of separating or unbundling services directly related to the performance of an abortion for the purposes of seeking Medicaid reimbursement, with those funds thereby subsidizing in whole or in part the cost of performing an abortion, is an inappropriate use of taxpayer funds in light of Act No. 59 of the Public Acts of 1987.

(4) Recognizing that certain services related to performing an abortion can also be part of legitimate and routine obstetric care, section 109e should not be construed to affect diagnostic testing or other nonabortion procedures. Only physicians who actually perform abortions, and particularly those who perform abortions but do not provide prenatal care or obstetric services, should view themselves as potentially affected by section 109e. Unacceptable requests for reimbursement include those services which would not have been performed, but for the preparation and performance of a planned or requested abortion.

Michigan Code § 400.109a. Abortion funding prohibition

Notwithstanding any other provision of this act, an abortion shall not be a service provided with public funds to a recipient of welfare benefits, whether through a program of medical assistance, general assistance, or categorical assistance or through any other type of public aid or assistance program, unless the abortion is necessary to save the life of the mother. It is the policy of this state to prohibit the appropriation of public funds for the purpose of providing an abortion to a person who receives welfare benefits unless the abortion is necessary to save the life of the mother.

Michigan Code § 400.109e. Seeking reimbursement for abortions

(1) As used in this section:

(a) "Abortion" means the intentional use of an instrument, drug, or other substance or device to terminate a woman's pregnancy for a purpose other than to increase the probability of a live birth, to preserve the life or health of the child after live birth, or to remove a dead fetus. Abortion does not include the use or prescription of a drug or device intended as a contraceptive.

(b) "Health care professional" means an individual licensed or registered under article 15 of the public health code, Act No. 368 of the Public Acts of 1978, being sections 333.16101 to 333.18838 of the Michigan Compiled Laws.

(c) "Health facility or agency" means a health facility or agency licensed under article 17 of Act No. 368 of the Public Acts of 1978, being sections 333.20101 to 333.22260 of the Michigan Compiled Laws.

(2) A health care professional or a health facility or agency shall not seek or accept reimbursement for the performance of an abortion knowing that public funds will be or have been used in whole or in part for the reimbursement in violation of section 109a of Act No. 280 of the Public Acts of 1939, being section 400.109a of the Michigan Compiled Laws, as added by Act No. 59 of the Public Acts of 1987.

(3) A person who violates this section is liable for a civil fine of up to $10,000.00 per violation. The department of community health shall investigate an alleged violation of this section and the attorney general, in cooperation with the department of community health, may bring an action to enforce this section.

(4) Nothing in this section restricts the right of a health care professional to discuss abortion or abortion services with a patient who is pregnant.

(5) This section does not create a right to an abortion.

(6) Notwithstanding any other provision of this section, a person shall not perform an abortion that is prohibited by law.

Michigan Code § 333.1091. Priorities in allocation of funds

(1) Except as otherwise provided in this section, it is the policy of this state for the department of community health to give priority under this subsection in the allocation of funds through grants or contracts for educational and other programs and services administered by the department of community health and primarily pertaining to family planning or reproductive health services, or both. This subsection applies to grants or contracts awarded to a qualified entity that does not engage in 1 or more of the following activities:

(a) Performing elective abortions or allowing the performance of elective abortions within a facility owned or operated by the qualified entity.

(b) Referring a pregnant woman to an abortion provider for an elective abortion.

(c) Adopting or maintaining a policy in writing that elective abor-

tion is considered part of a continuum of family planning or reproductive health services, or both.

(2) If each of the entities applying for a grant or contract described in subsection (1) engages in 1 or more of the activities listed in subsection (1)(a) to (c), the department of community health shall give priority to those entities that engage in the least number of activities listed in subsection (1)(a) to (c).

(3) Subsection (1) does not apply if the only applying entity for a grant or contract described in subsection (1) engages in 1 or more of the activities listed in subsection (1)(a) to (c).

(4) Subsection (1) does not apply to grants or contracts awarded by the department of community health other than family planning and pregnancy prevention awards under subpart a of part 59 of title 42 of the Code of Federal Regulations or state appropriated family planning or pregnancy prevention funds.

(5) In applying the priority established in subsection (1), the department of community health shall not take into consideration an activity listed in subsection (1)(a) to (c) if participating in that activity is required under federal law as a qualification for receiving federal funding.

(6) If an entity applying for a contract or grant described in subsection (1) is affiliated with another entity that engages in 1 or more of the activities listed in subsection (1)(a) to (c), the applying entity shall, for purposes of awarding a grant or contract under subsection (1), be considered independent of the affiliated entity if all of the following conditions are met:

(a) The physical properties and equipment of the applying entity are separate and not shared with the affiliated entity.

(b) The financial records of the applying entity and affiliated entity demonstrate that the affiliated entity receives no funds from the applying entity.

(c) The paid personnel of the applying entity do not perform any function or duty on behalf of the affiliated entity while on the physical property of the applying entity or during the hours the personnel are being paid by the applying entity.

(7) The department of community health shall award grants and contracts to qualified entities under this act to ensure that family planning services are adequately available and distributed in a manner that is reflective of the geographic and population diversity of this state. A qualified entity that is awarded a grant or contract must also be capable of serving the patient census reflected in the contract or grant for which the qualified entity is applying.

(8) As used in this act:

(a) "Affiliated" means the sharing between entities of 1 or more of the following:

(i) A common name or other identifier.

(ii) Members of a governing board.

(iii) A director.

(iv) Paid personnel.

(b) "Elective abortion" means the performance of a procedure involving the intentional use of an instrument, drug, or other substance or device to terminate a woman's pregnancy for a purpose other than to increase the probability of a live birth, to preserve the life or health of the child after live birth, or to remove a dead fetus. Elective abortion does not include either of the following:

(i) The use or prescription of a drug or device intended as a contraceptive.

(ii) The intentional use of an instrument, drug, or other substance or device by a physician to terminate a woman's pregnancy if the woman's physical condition, in the physician's reasonable medical judgment, necessitates the termination of the woman's pregnancy to avert her death.

(c) "Entity" means a local agency, organization, or corporation or a subdivision, contractee, subcontractee, or grant recipient of a local agency, organization, or corporation.

(d) "Qualified entity" means an entity reviewed and determined by the department of community health to be technically and logistically capable of providing the quality and quantity of services required within a cost range considered appropriate by the department.

(10) FETAL OR EMBRYO EXPERIMENTS

Michigan has provided several statutes banning fetal and embryo experiments in certain circumstances. The state permits such experiments when the woman involved gives consent. Michigan also bans the sale of a fetus or embryo. The statutes addressing the matters are set out below.

Michigan Code § 333.2685. Research on live fetus or embryo

(1) A person shall not use a live human embryo, fetus, or neonate for nontherapeutic research if, in the best judgment of the person conducting the research, based upon the available knowledge or information at the approximate time of the research, the research substantially jeopardizes the life or health of the embryo, fetus, or neonate. Nontherapeutic research shall not in any case be performed on an embryo or fetus known by the person conducting the research to be the subject of a planned abortion being performed for any purpose other than to protect the life of the mother.

(2) For purposes of subsection (1) the embryo or fetus shall be conclusively presumed not to be the subject of a planned abortion if the mother signed a written statement at the time of the research, that she was not planning an abortion.

Michigan Code § 333.2686. Procedures not prohibited

Sections 2685 to 2691 shall not prohibit or regulate diagnostic, assessment, or treatment procedures, the purpose of which is to determine the life or status or improve the health of the embryo, fetus, or neonate involved or the mother involved.

Michigan Code § 333.2687.
Determination of live embryo or fetus

An embryo, fetus, or neonate is a live embryo, fetus, or neonate for purposes of sections 2685 to 2691 if, in the best medical judgment of a physician, it shows evidence of life as determined by the same medical standards as are used in determining evidence of life in a spontaneously aborted embryo or fetus at approximately the same stage of gestational development.

Michigan Code § 333.2688.
Consent to research upon fetus or embryo

(1) Research may not knowingly be performed upon a dead embryo, fetus, or neonate unless the consent of the mother has first been obtained. Consent shall not be required in the case of a routine pathological study.

(2) For purposes of this section, consent shall be conclusively presumed to have been granted by a written statement, signed by the mother that she consents to the use of her dead embryo, fetus, or neonate for research.

(3) Written consent shall constitute lawful authorization for the transfer of the dead embryo, fetus, or neonate to medical research facilities.

(4) Research being performed upon a dead embryo, fetus, or neonate shall be conducted in accordance with the same standards applicable to research conducted pursuant to part 101.

Michigan Code § 333.2689.
Abortion as consideration for research

A person shall not perform or offer to perform an abortion where part or all of the consideration for the performance is that the embryo, or fetus, whether alive or dead, may be used for research or study.

Michigan Code § 333.2690. Sale of fetus or embryo

A person shall not knowingly sell, transfer, distribute, or give away an embryo, fetus, or neonate for a use which is in violation of sections 2685 to 2689.

Michigan Code § 333.2691. Penalty

A person who violates sections 2685 to 2690 is guilty of a felony, punishable by imprisonment for not more than 5 years.

Michigan Code § 333.2692. Nontherapeutic research defined

As used in sections 2685 to 2691, "nontherapeutic research" means scientific or laboratory research, or other kind of experimentation or investigation not designed to improve the health of the research subject.

(11) BAN HUMAN CLONING

Michigan has enacted a series of statutes that ban human cloning and prohibits the use of public funding for the same. The statutes are set out below.

Michigan Code § 333.16274. Human cloning banned

(1) A licensee or registrant shall not engage in or attempt to engage in human cloning.

(2) Subsection (1) does not prohibit scientific research or cell-based therapies not specifically prohibited by that subsection.

(3) A licensee or registrant who violates subsection (1) is subject to the administrative penalties prescribed in sections 16221 and 16226 and to the civil penalty prescribed in section 16275.

(4) This section does not give a person a private right of action.

(5) As used in this section:

(a) "Human cloning" means the use of human somatic cell nuclear transfer technology to produce a human embryo.

(b) "Human embryo" means a human egg cell with a full genetic composition capable of differentiating and maturing into a complete human being.

(c) "Human somatic cell" means a cell of a developing or fully developed human being that is not and will not become a sperm or egg cell.

(d) "Human somatic cell nuclear transfer" means transferring the nucleus of a human somatic cell into an egg cell from which the nucleus has been removed or rendered inert.

Michigan Code § 333.16275. Prohibition and penalty

(1) A licensee or registrant or other individual shall not engage in or attempt to engage in human cloning.

(2) Subsection (1) does not prohibit scientific research or cell-based therapies not specifically prohibited by that subsection.

(3) A licensee or registrant or other individual who violates subsection (1) is subject to a civil penalty of $10,000,000.00. A fine collected under this subsection shall be distributed in the same manner as penal fines are distributed in this state.

(4) This section does not give a person a private right of action.

(5) As used in this section, "human cloning" means that term as defined in section 16274.

Michigan Code § 750.430a. Human cloning by individual

(1) An individual shall not intentionally engage in or attempt to engage in human cloning.

(2) Subsection (1) does not prohibit scientific research or cell-based therapies not specifically prohibited by that subsection.

(3) An individual who violates subsection (1) is guilty of a felony punishable by imprisonment for not more than 10 years or a fine of not more than $10,000,000.00, or both.

(4) As used in this section, "human cloning" means that term as defined in section 16274 of the public health code, 1978 PA 368, MCL 333.16274.

Michigan Code § 333.20197. Human cloning by facility

(1) A health facility or agency shall not allow a licensee or registrant under article 15 or any other individual to engage in or attempt to engage in human cloning in a facility owned or operated by the health facility or agency.

(2) Subsection (1) does not prohibit a health facility or agency from allowing a licensee or registrant under article 15 or any other individual from engaging in scientific research or cell-based therapies not specifically prohibited by that subsection.

(3) A health facility or agency that violates subsection (1) is subject to the administrative penalties prescribed in section 20165(4).

(4) This section does not give a person a private right of action.

(5) As used in this section, "human cloning" means that term as defined in section 16274.

Michigan Code § 333.26401. Short title

This act shall be known and may be cited as "the human cloning funding prohibition act."

Michigan Code § 333.26402. Definition

As used in this act, "human cloning" means that term as defined in section 16274 of the public health code, 1978 PA 368, MCL 333.16274.

Michigan Code § 333.26403. Prohibition of use of state funds

A person shall not, use state funds to engage in or attempt to engage in human cloning.

Michigan Code § 333.26404.
Scientific research or cell-based therapies

Section 3 does not prohibit the use of state funds for scientific research or cell-based therapies not specifically prohibited by that section.

Michigan Code § 333.26405. Private right of action

This act does not give a person a private right of action.

Michigan Code § 333.26406. Violations

A person who violates section 3 is subject to a civil fine of $10,000,000.00. A civil fine imposed under this section shall be distributed in the same manner in which penal fines are distributed in this state.

(12) INJURY TO PREGNANT WOMAN

Michigan has enacted several statutes designed to protect a fetus. The state allows a civil action against anyone for wrongfully or negligently causing death to a fetus or embryo. The state has statutes that impose criminal punishment for intentional or grossly negligent conduct that kills a fetus or embryo. In addition, specific criminal statutes exists for killing a fetus or embryo while driving a motor vehicle. The state has also created a manslaughter offense for wilfully killing a fetus. The statutes are set out below.

Michigan Code § 600.2922a. Wrongful or negligent act

(1) A person who commits a wrongful or negligent act against a pregnant individual is liable for damages if the act results in a miscarriage or stillbirth by that individual, or physical injury to or the death of the embryo or fetus.

(2) This section does not apply to any of the following:

(a) An act committed by the pregnant individual.

(b) A medical procedure performed by a physician or other licensed health professional within the scope of his or her practice and with the pregnant individual's consent or the consent of an individual who may lawfully provide consent on her behalf or without consent as necessitated by a medical emergency.

(c) The lawful dispensation, administration, or prescription of medication.

(3) This section does not prohibit a civil action under any other applicable law.

(4) As used in this section, "physician or other licensed health professional" means a person licensed under article 15 of the public health code, 1978 PA 368, MCL 333.16101 to 333.18838.

Michigan Code § 750.90a. Intentional conduct

If a person intentionally commits conduct proscribed under sections 81 to 89 against a pregnant individual, the person is guilty of a felony pun-

ishable by imprisonment for life or any term of years if all of the following apply:

(a) The person intended to cause a miscarriage or stillbirth by that individual or death or great bodily harm to the embryo or fetus, or acted in wanton or willful disregard of the likelihood that the natural tendency of the person's conduct is to cause a miscarriage or stillbirth or death or great bodily harm to the embryo or fetus.

(b) The person's conduct resulted in a miscarriage or stillbirth by that individual or death to the embryo or fetus.

Michigan Code § 750.90b. Intentional conduct

A person who intentionally commits conduct proscribed under sections 81 to 89 against a pregnant individual is guilty of a crime as follows:

(a) If the conduct results in a miscarriage or stillbirth by that individual, or death to the embryo or fetus, a felony punishable by imprisonment for not more than 15 years or a fine of not more than $7,500.00, or both.

(b) If the conduct results in great bodily harm to the embryo or fetus, a felony punishable by imprisonment for not more than 10 years or a fine of not more than $5,000.00, or both.

(c) If the conduct results in serious or aggravated physical injury to the embryo or fetus, a misdemeanor punishable by imprisonment for not more than 1 year or a fine of not more than $1,000.00, or both.

(d) If the conduct results in physical injury to the embryo or fetus, a misdemeanor punishable by imprisonment for not more than 93 days or a fine of not more than $500.00, or both.

Michigan Code § 750.90c. Grossly negligent conduct

A person who commits a grossly negligent act against a pregnant individual is guilty of a crime as follows:

(a) If the act results in a miscarriage or stillbirth by that individual or death to the embryo or fetus, a felony punishable by imprisonment for not more than 15 years or a fine of not more than $7,500.00, or both.

(b) If the act results in great bodily harm to the embryo or fetus, a felony punishable by imprisonment for not more than 5 years or a fine of not more than $2,500.00, or both.

(c) If the act results in serious or aggravated physical injury to the embryo or fetus, a misdemeanor punishable by imprisonment for not more than 6 months or a fine of not more than $500.00, or both.

(d) If the act results in physical injury to the embryo or fetus, a misdemeanor punishable by imprisonment for not more than 93 days or a fine of not more than $500.00, or both.

Michigan Code § 750.90d. Vehicular accident

A person who engages in conduct proscribed under section 625(1) or (3) of the Michigan vehicle code, 1949 PA 300, MCL 257.625, that involves an accident with a pregnant individual is guilty of a felony punishable as follows:

(a) If the person's conduct causes a miscarriage or stillbirth by that individual or death to the embryo or fetus, imprisonment for not more than 15 years or a fine of not less than $2,500.00 or more than $10,000.00, or both.

(b) If the person's conduct causes great bodily harm or serious or aggravated injury to the embryo or fetus, imprisonment for not more than 5 years or a fine of not less than $1,000.00 or more than $5,000.00, or both.

Michigan Code § 750.90e. Careless or reckless operation of vehicle

If a person operates a motor vehicle in a careless or reckless manner, but not willfully or wantonly, that is the proximate cause of an accident involving a pregnant individual and the accident results in a miscarriage or stillbirth by that individual or death to the embryo or fetus, the person is guilty of a misdemeanor punishable by imprisonment for not more than 2 years or a fine of not more than $2,000.00, or both.

Michigan Code § 750.90f. Application of §§ 750.90a to 750.90e

(1) Sections 90a to 90e do not apply to any of the following:

(a) An act committed by the pregnant individual.

(b) A medical procedure performed by a physician or other licensed medical professional within the scope of his or her practice and with the pregnant individual's consent or the consent of an individual who may lawfully provide consent on her behalf or without consent as necessitated by a medical emergency.

(c) The lawful dispensation, administration, or prescription of medication.

(2) This section does not prohibit a prosecution under any other applicable law.

(3) As used in this section, "physician or other licensed medical professional" means a person licensed under article 15 of the public health code, 1978 PA 368, MCL 333.16101 to 333.18838.

Michigan Code § 750.322. Wilful killing of unborn quick child

The wilful killing of an unborn quick child by any injury to the mother of such child, which would be murder if it resulted in the death of such mother, shall be deemed manslaughter.

(13) FETAL DEATH REPORT

Michigan requires all abortions be reported to the proper authorities. It is also required that funeral directors make specific reports when an abortion fails and an infant is born alive, but subsequently dies. The state also requires specific reporting be made if a woman develops complications or dies while having an abortion. The statutes addressing the matters are set out below.

Michigan Code § 333.2835. Abortion reports

(1) As used in this section and section 2837:

(a) "Abortion" means that term as defined in section 17015.

(b) "Physical complication" means a physical condition occurring during or after an abortion that, under generally accepted standards of medical practice, requires medical attention. Physical complication includes, but is not limited to, infection, hemorrhage, cervical laceration, or perforation of the uterus.

(2) A physician who performs an abortion shall report the performance of that procedure to the department on forms prescribed and provided by the department. A physician shall transmit a report required under this subsection to the director within 7 days after the performance of the abortion.

(3) Each report of an abortion required under subsection (2) shall contain only the following information and no other information:

(a) The age of the woman at the time of the abortion.

(b) The marital status of the woman at the time of the abortion.

(c) The race of the woman.

(d) The city or township, county, and state in which the woman resided at the time of the abortion.

(e) The location and type of facility in which the abortion was performed.

(f) The source of referral to the physician performing the abortion.

(g) The number of previous pregnancies carried to term.

(h) The number of previous pregnancies ending in spontaneous abortion.

(i) The number of previous pregnancies terminated by abortion.

(j) The method used before the abortion to confirm the pregnancy, the period of gestation in weeks of the present pregnancy, and the first day of the last menstrual period.

(k) The method used to perform the abortion.

(l) The weight of the embryo or fetus, if determinable.

(m) Whether the fetus showed evidence of life when separated, expelled, or removed from the woman.

(n) The date of performance of the abortion.

(o) The method and source of payment for the abortion.

(p) A physical complication or death resulting from the abortion and observed by the physician or reported to the physician or his or her agent before the report required under subsection (2) is transmitted to the director.

(q) The physician's signature and his or her state license number.

(4) The report required under subsection (2) shall not contain the name of the woman, common identifiers such as her social security number or motor vehicle operator's license number or other information or identifiers that would make it possible to identify in any manner or under any circumstances an individual who has obtained or seeks to obtain an abortion. A state agency shall not compare data in an electronic or other information system file with data in another electronic or other information system that would result in identifying in any manner or under any circumstances an individual obtaining or seeking to obtain an abortion. Statistical information that may reveal the identity of a woman obtaining or seeking to obtain an abortion shall not be maintained.

(5) The department shall destroy each individual report required by this section and each copy of the report after retaining the report for 5 years after the date the report is received.

(6) The department shall make available annually in aggregate a statistical report summarizing the information submitted in each individual report required by this section. The department shall specifically summarize aggregate data regarding all of the following in the annual statistical report:

(a) The period of gestation in 4-week intervals from 5 weeks through 28 weeks.

(b) Abortions performed on women aged 17 and under.

(c) Physical complications reported under subsection (3)(o) and section 2837.

(7) The reports required under this section are statistical reports to be used only for medical and health purposes and shall not be incorporated into the permanent official records of the system of vital statistics.

(8) The department or an employee of the department shall not disclose to a person or entity outside the department the reports or the contents of the reports required by this section in a manner or fashion so as to permit the person or entity to whom the report is disclosed to identify in any way the person who is the subject of the report.

(9) A person who discloses confidential identifying information in violation of this section, section 2834(6), or section 2837 is guilty of a felony punishable by imprisonment for not more than 3 years, or a fine of not more than $5,000.00, or both.

Michigan Code § 333.2843. Funeral director of death

(1) A funeral director who first assumes custody of a dead body, either personally or through his or her authorized agent, shall report the death. For purposes of this subsection, "dead body" includes, but is not limited to, the body of an infant who survived an attempted abortion as described in the born alive infant protection act and who later died. The funeral director or the authorized agent shall obtain the necessary personal data from the next of kin or the best qualified individual or source available and shall obtain medical certification as follows:

(a) If the death occurred outside an institution, the medical certification portion of the death record shall be completed and certified not later than 48 hours after death by the attending physician; or in the absence of the attending physician, by a physician acting as the attending physician's authorized representative; or in the absence of an authorized representative, by the county medical examiner; or in the absence of the county medical examiner, by the county health officer or the deputy county medical examiner. If the death occurred in an institution, the medical certification shall be completed and signed not later than 48 hours after death by the attending physician; or in the absence of the attending physician, by a physician acting as the attending physician's authorized representative; or in the absence of an authorized representative, by the chief medical officer of the institution in which death occurred, after reviewing pertinent records and making other investigation as considered necessary, or by a pathologist.

(b) A physician, as described in subdivision (a), who for himself or herself or as an agent or employee of another individual neglects or refuses to certify a death record properly presented to him or her for certification by a funeral director or who refuses or neglects to furnish information in his or her possession, is guilty of a misdemeanor punishable by imprisonment for not more than 60 days, or a fine of not less than $25.00 nor more than $100.00, or both.

(2) The medical certification shall be provided not later than 48 hours after the death by the physician, as described in subsection (1)(a).

(3) A death record shall be certified by a funeral director licensed under article 18 of the occupational code, 1980 PA 299, MCL 339.1801 to 339.1812, and shall be filed with the local registrar of the district where the death occurred not later than 72 hours after the death.

(4) Except as otherwise provided in this subsection, the death of an infant who was born alive following an attempted abortion and was surrendered to an emergency service provider under the safe delivery of newborns law, sections 1 to 20 of chapter XII of the probate code of 1939, 1939 PA 288, MCL 712.1 to 712.20, and then died shall be reported in the same manner as for any death. However, the deceased infant shall be listed as "Baby Doe" and no information that would directly identify the deceased infant or the deceased infant's parents shall be reported, including, but not limited to, the following information:

(a) The name of the mother or father.

(b) The address of the mother or father.

(c) The name of the informant.

(d) The address of the informant.

Michigan Code § 333.2837.
Physical complication or deaths due to abortions

(1) A physician shall file a written report with the department regarding each patient who comes under the physician's professional care and who suffers a physical complication or death that is a primary, secondary, or tertiary result of an abortion.

(2) The department shall summarize aggregate data from the reports required under subsection (1) for purposes of inclusion into the annual statistical report on abortion required under section 2835.

(3) The department shall destroy each individual report required by this section and each copy of the report after retaining the report for 5 years after the date the report is received.

(4) The department shall develop and distribute a standardized form for the report required under subsection (1). The department shall not include on the standardized reporting form the name or address of the patient who is the subject of the report or any other information that could reasonably be expected to identify the patient who is the subject of the report. The department shall include on the standardized form a statement specifying the time period within which a report must be transmitted under section 2835(2).

(14) PROHIBIT TEACHING STUDENTS ABOUT ABORTION

Michigan authorizes public schools to provide education on family planning, but prohibits teaching on abortion as a family planning method. The state withholds funding from schools that dispense contraceptive devices or make abortion referrals. The statutes addressing the matters are set out below.

Michigan Code § 380.1506.
Reproductive health instruction program

(1) A program of instruction in reproductive health shall be supervised by a registered physician, a registered nurse, or other person certified

by the state board as qualified. Upon the written request of a pupil or the pupil's parent or guardian, a pupil shall be excused, without penalty or loss of academic credit, from attending classes in which the subject of reproductive health is under discussion.

(2) As used in subsection (1) and sections 1507 and 1508, "reproductive health" means that state of an individual's well-being which involves the reproductive system and its physiological, psychological, and endocrinological functions.

Michigan Code § 380.1507. Sex education instruction

(1) The board of a school district may engage qualified instructors and provide facilities and equipment for instruction in sex education, including family planning, human sexuality, and the emotional, physical, psychological, hygienic, economic, and social aspects of family life. Instruction may also include the subjects of reproductive health and the recognition, prevention, and treatment of sexually transmitted disease. Subject to subsection (7) and section 1507b, the instruction described in this subsection shall stress that abstinence from sex is a responsible and effective method of preventing unplanned or out-of-wedlock pregnancy and sexually transmitted disease and is a positive lifestyle for unmarried young people.

(2) The class described in subsection (1) shall be elective and not a requirement for graduation.

(3) A pupil shall not be enrolled in a class in which the subjects of family planning or reproductive health are discussed unless the pupil's parent or guardian is notified in advance of the course and the content of the course, is given a prior opportunity to review the materials to be used in the course and is notified in advance of his or her right to have the pupil excused from the class. The state board shall determine the form and content of the notice required in this subsection.

(4) Upon the written request of a pupil or the pupil's parent or legal guardian, a pupil shall be excused, without penalty or loss of academic credit, from attending a class described in subsection (1).

(5) A school district that provides a class as permitted by subsection (1) shall offer the instruction by teachers qualified to teach health education. A school district shall not offer this instruction unless a sex education advisory board is established by the board of the school district. The board of a school district shall determine terms of service for the sex education advisory board, the number of members to serve on the advisory board, and a membership selection process that reasonably reflects the school district population, and shall appoint 2 co-chairs for the advisory board, at least 1 of whom is a parent of a child attending a school operated by the school district. At least ½ of the members of the sex education advisory board shall be parents who have a child attending a school operated by the school district, and a majority of these parent members shall be individuals who are not employed by a school district. The board of a school district shall include pupils of the school district, educators, local clergy, and community health professionals on the sex education advisory board. Written or electronic notice of a sex education advisory board meeting shall be sent to each member at least 2 weeks before the date of the meeting. The advisory board shall do all of the following:

(a) Establish program goals and objectives for pupil knowledge and skills that are likely to reduce the rates of sex, pregnancy, and sexually transmitted diseases. This subdivision does not prohibit a school district from establishing additional program goals and objectives that are not contrary to this section, section 1169, or section 1507b.

(b) Review the materials and methods of instruction used and make recommendations to the board of the school district for implementation. The advisory board shall take into consideration the school district's needs, demographics, and trends, including, but not limited to, teenage pregnancy rates, sexually transmitted disease rates, and incidents of student sexual violence and harassment.

(c) At least once every 2 years, evaluate, measure, and report the attainment of program goals and objectives established under subdivision (a). The board of a school district shall make the resulting report available to parents in the school district.

(6) Before adopting any revisions in the materials or methods used in instruction under this section, including, but not limited to, revisions to provide for the teaching of abstinence from sex as a method of preventing unplanned or out-of-wedlock pregnancy and sexually transmitted disease, the board of a school district shall hold at least 2 public hearings on the proposed revisions. The hearings shall be held at least 1 week apart and public notice of the hearings shall be given in the manner required under section 1201 for board meetings. A public hearing held pursuant to this section may be held in conjunction with a public hearing held pursuant to section 1169.

(7) A person shall not dispense or otherwise distribute in a public school or on public school property a family planning drug or device.

(8) As used in this section, "family planning" means the use of a range of methods of fertility regulation to help individuals or couples avoid unplanned pregnancies; bring about wanted births; regulate the intervals between pregnancies; and plan the time at which births occur in relation to the age of parents. It may include the study of fetology. It may include marital and genetic information. Clinical abortion shall not be considered a method of family planning, nor shall abortion be taught as a method of reproductive health.

(9) As used in this section and sections 1506 and 1507a:

(a) "Class" means an instructional period of limited duration within a course of instruction and includes an assembly or small group presentation.

(b) "Course" means a series of classes linked by a common subject matter.

Michigan Code § 380.1507a. Enrollment of pupil in class

If a parent or legal guardian of a pupil files with the public school in which the pupil is enrolled a continuing written notice that the pupil is to be excused from a class described in section 1507, the pupil shall not be enrolled in a class described in section 1507 unless the parent or legal guardian submits a written authorization for that enrollment.

Michigan Code § 380.1507b.
Particular requirements for sex education instruction

(1) Instruction under section 1507 in sex education and instruction under section 1169 on human immunodeficiency virus infection and acquired immunodeficiency syndrome shall emphasize that abstinence from sex is a positive lifestyle for unmarried young people because abstinence is the only protection that is 100% effective against unplanned pregnancy, sexually transmitted disease, and sexually transmitted human immunodeficiency virus infection and acquired immunodeficiency syndrome.

(2) Material and instruction in the sex education curriculum under section 1507 that discusses sex shall be age-appropriate, shall not be medically inaccurate, and shall do at least all of the following:

(a) Discuss the benefits of abstaining from sex until marriage and the benefits of ceasing sex if a pupil is sexually active.

(b) Include a discussion of the possible emotional, economic, and legal consequences of sex.

(c) Stress that unplanned pregnancy and sexually transmitted diseases are serious possibilities of sex that are not fully preventable except by abstinence.

(d) Advise pupils of the laws pertaining to their responsibility as parents to children born in and out of wedlock.

(e) Ensure that pupils are not taught in a way that condones the violation of the laws of this state pertaining to sexual activity, including, but not limited to, sections 158, 335a, 338, 338a, 338b, and 520b to 520e of the Michigan penal code, 1931 PA 328, MCL 750.158, 750.335a, 750.338, 750.338a, 750.338b, and 750.520b to 750.520e.

(f) Teach pupils how to say "no" to sexual advances and that it is wrong to take advantage of, harass, or exploit another person sexually.

(g) Teach refusal skills and encourage pupils to resist pressure to engage in risky behavior.

(h) Teach that the pupil has the power to control personal behavior. Pupils shall be taught to base their actions on reasoning, self-discipline, a sense of responsibility, self-control, and ethical considerations such as respect for self and others.

(i) Provide instruction on healthy dating relationships and on how to set limits and recognize a dangerous environment.

(j) Provide information for pupils about how young parents can learn more about adoption services and about the provisions of the safe delivery of newborns law, chapter XII of the probate code of 1939, 1939 PA 288, MCL 712.1 to 712.20.

(k) Include information clearly informing pupils that having sex or sexual contact with an individual under the age of 16 is a crime punishable by imprisonment and that 1 of the other results of being convicted of this crime is to be listed on the sex offender registry on the internet for up to 25 years.

(3) This section does not prohibit a public school from offering sex education with behavioral risk reduction strategies, as defined by law, that are not 100% effective against unplanned pregnancy, sexually transmitted disease, and sexually transmitted human immunodeficiency virus infection and acquired immunodeficiency syndrome.

Michigan Code § 388.1766.
Dispensing family planning drug or abortion referral

A district in which a school official, member of a board, or other person dispenses or otherwise distributes a family planning drug or device in a public school in violation of section 1507 of the revised school code, being section 380.1507 of the Michigan Compiled Laws, dispenses prescriptions for any family planning drug, or makes referrals for abortions shall forfeit 5% of its total state aid appropriation.

(15) ANTI-ABORTION ACTIVITIES

Michigan has a statute that generally prohibits anti-abortion conduct at medical facilities that may be considered terrorizing, frightening, intimidating, threatening, harassing, or molesting. The statute addressing the issue is set out below.

Michigan Code § 333.20198. Unlawful anti-abortion conduct

(1) Subject to subsection (3), an individual shall not enter upon the premises of a health facility or agency that is an inpatient facility, an outpatient facility, or a residential facility for the purpose of engaging in an activity that would cause a reasonable person to feel terrorized, frightened, intimidated, threatened, harassed, or molested and that actually causes a health facility or agency employee, patient, resident, or visitor to feel terrorized, frightened, intimidated, threatened, harassed, or molested. This subsection does not prohibit constitutionally protected activity or conduct that serves a legitimate purpose.

(2) An individual who violates subsection (1) is guilty of a misdemeanor, punishable by imprisonment for not more than 1 year or a fine of not less than $1,000.00 or more than $10,000.00, or both.

(3) Subsections (1) and (2) do not apply to a nursing home covered under sections 21763(5) and 21799c(1)(c).

Michigan Christians for Life

Michigan Christians for Life (MCL) is a pro-life organization that was established by Rev. Art Mirek. MCL promotes the idea that a knowledge of Jesus Christ is the remedy for stopping abortion. It was created to offer Christians the opportunity to unite together, in prayer, for the success of pro-life efforts throughout the world. MCL produces Christian pro-life materials that are made available to members free of charge. *See also* **Pro-Life Organizations**

Michigan Pro-Choice Network

The Michigan Pro-Choice Network (MPCN) was established in 1989. After undergoing mergers with other local groups, MPCN operates primarily as a pro-choice political group. MPCN has assembled lists of pro-choice voters from all of its member organizations resulting in a data base of 55,000 pro-choice voters across the state. The organization utilizes its political power to support pro-choice candidates for office. *See also* **Pro-Choice Organizations**

Microcephaly

Microcephaly is a congenital disorder in which the skull does not develop to a normal head size. Symptoms of this disorder include impaired speech and motor function, hyperactivity, convulsions, and mental retardation. No effective treatment exists for the disease. It leaves many of its victims as quadriplegics. *See also* **Birth Defects and Abortion**

Midwife

A midwife is a person who has training in the delivery of uncomplicated, low risk births. In colonial America and the early history of the United States, midwives played a large role in childbirth and the diseases of children. In time, however, there role was diminished by advancements in the medical profession. The modern concept of midwifery dates back to 1925, when Mary Breckenridge developed the Frontier Nursing Service in Kentucky. This program was designed to provide low income pregnant women in the Appalachian mountains with a modest degree of professional midwife care in delivering birth. From its humble beginnings in Kentucky, midwifery went on to become an established professional institution in the nation.

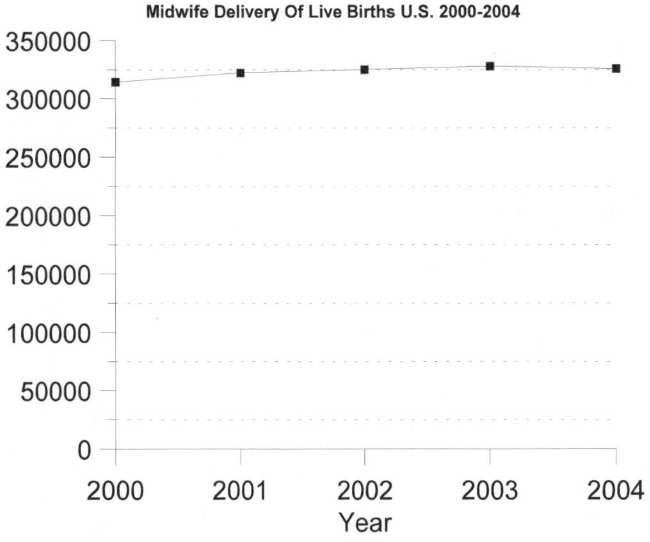

Source: **National Center for Health Statistics.**

In order to become a midwife today, a person must be a registered nurse, receive specific training in performing low risk deliveries, and pass a national certification examination. A midwife is generally not authorized to perform an abortion or a caesarean section. If unexpected complications arise with a delivery, a midwife must immediately call upon a physician to intervene. Midwives work in hospitals, birthing centers and private outpatient practices. *See also* **Doula; Physician Abortion Requirements**

Mifeprex *see* **Mifepristone Induced Abortion**

Mifepristone Induced Abortion

Mifepristone (trade name Mifeprex and also known as RU-486) is a drug used to induce an abortion. The pill was first marketed by the French pharmaceutical firm Roussel-Uclaf. It was first approved for use in France in 1988. Mifepristone blocks receptors of progesterone, which is needed for the establishment and maintenance of pregnancy. When used together with another drug called misoprostol, Mifepristone terminates pregnancy by causing early pregnancy to detach from the uterine wall. With Mifepristone the risk of complication from surgical abortion such as uterine injury, perforation, infection, and anesthesia complications are eliminated.

The use of the drug was resisted in the United States primarily because an incomplete miscarriage occurred in about 5 percent of the women who used it. Mifepristone was finally approved by the Food and Drug Administration (FDA) on September 28, 2000. Under the terms of the FDA's approval, mifepristone must be distributed to physicians who can accurately determine the duration of a woman's pregnancy and detect an ectopic (or tubal) pregnancy. The drug is manufactured by Danco Laboratories.

Mifepristone may only be used in the United States for the termination of early pregnancy, which the FDA has defined as 49 days or less, counting from the beginning of the last menstrual period. Pursuant to the treatment regimen approved by the FDA, an authorized clinical provider administers to a woman 600 milligrams of mifepristone (three 200 milligram pills) by mouth. Two days later, the woman must return to the provider and be administered 400 micrograms (two 200-microgram pills) of misoprostol, a prostaglandin. The misoprostol induces uterine contractions and causes the cervix to dilate, which helps the mifepristone to expel the pregnancy through the vagina. Most women experience bleeding and the passage of the pregnancy within four hours of receiving the misoprostol. After taking the misoprostol a woman must return for a follow-up visit to the clinical provider approximately 14 days after taking mifepristone to determine whether the pregnancy has been terminated.

Side effects of mifepristone may include mild nausea, vomiting, and diarrhea that last up to one day. The mifepristone treatment causes cramping and bleeding. Typically, bleeding and spotting last for between 9 and 16 days. (Bleeding can become too heavy and may require a surgical procedure to stop it.) These symptoms usually mean that the treatment is working. However, sometimes women may get cramping and bleeding and still be pregnant. For this reason, it is required that women make the scheduled follow-up appointments. *See also* **Benten, Leona; Methods of Abortion**

Military and Abortion

Since 1979 the federal government has forbidden the use of public funds for abortions for military personnel or their dependents, except in cases of life endangerment of the pregnant woman. In 1988 abortions were banned at all United States military facilities, so as to preclude the use of private payment for abortions at such facilities. In 1993 President Bill Clinton issued an executive order that allowed women to use their own money to pay for abortions in military hospitals overseas. However, in December of 1995 Congress reinstated the ban. Despite many attempts to remove the ban, it remains in place today.

10 U.S.C.A. § 1093. Military performance of abortions

(a) Funds available to the Department of Defense may not be used to perform abortions except where the life of the mother would be endangered if the fetus were carried to term.

(b) No medical treatment facility or other facility of the Department of Defense may be used to perform an abortion except where the life of the mother would be endangered if the fetus were carried to term or in a case in which the pregnancy is the result of an act of rape or incest.

See also **Public Resources for Abortions**

Mini-Pill *see* **Birth Control Pill**

Mini Vac Aspiration

Mini vac aspiration is an abortion procedure (also called manual vacuum aspiration). This procedure utilizes non-electric suction provided by a hand-held syringe to evacuate the uterine contents. This procedure involves insertion of a clear plastic tube into the uterus. The tube is attached to a suction device. The fetus and placenta are vacuumed out. When the tube has been removed, an instrument called a curette may be used to scrape the walls of the uterus to be sure it has been completely emptied of the pregnancy. Side effects of the procedure may include blood clots in the uterus, heavy bleeding, damaged cervix, perforation of the wall of the uterus, pelvic infection, incomplete abortion, or anesthesia-related complications. The procedure generally takes about ten minutes. Two major advantages of this procedure are less discomfort due to less cervical dilation and the absence of suction noise. This procedure has been proven effective for early pregnancies under 7 weeks gestation. *See also* **Machine Vacuum Aspiration; Methods of Abortion**

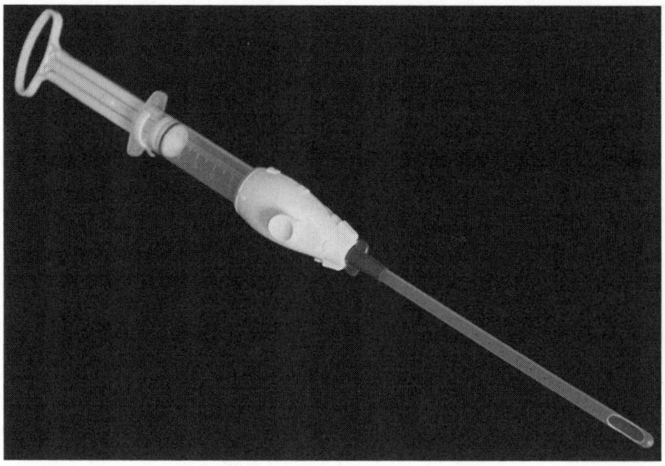

This handheld syringe is used to perform the mini vac aspiration (also called manual vacuum aspiration) abortion procedure. The syringe is inserted into the uterus and the fetus is vacuumed or suctioned out (Grantham Collection, all rights reserved).

Minnesota

(1) OVERVIEW

The state of Minnesota enacted its first criminal abortion statute in 1851. The statute underwent several amendments prior to the 1973 decision by the United States Supreme Court in *Roe v. Wade*, which legalized abortion in the nation. Although the state no longer has its pre–Roe abortion ban statute, it still retains pre–Roe abortion related statutes

Minnesota has taken affirmative steps to respond to *Roe* and its progeny. Minnesota has addressed numerous abortion issues by statute that include general abortion guidelines, abortion by minors, use of facilities and people, experiment or sale of fetus, wrongful life action, crime against fetus, ban on anti-abortion activity, fetal death report, abortion alternative programs, informed consent, sexual assault, and public funds for abortion.

(2) PRE-ROE ABORTION RELATED STATUTES

Minnesota retains certain pre–Roe abortion related statutes that are invalid insofar as they impinge upon a woman's right to a pre-viability abortion, and the right to have information concerning abor-

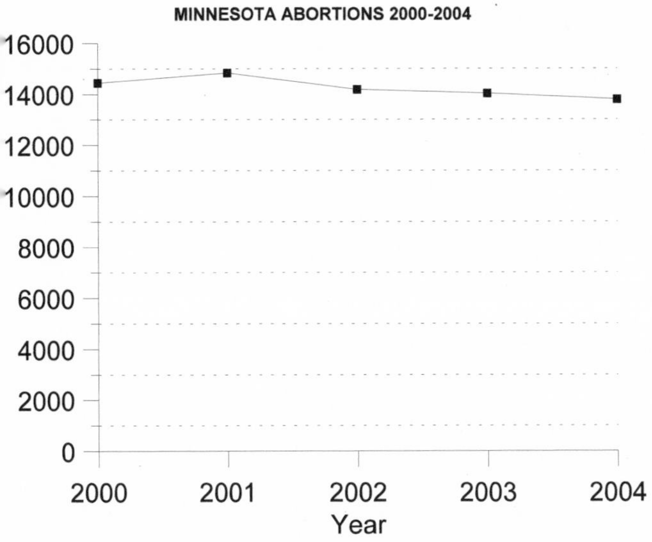

Source: Minnesota Department of Health.

Minnesota Abortion by Age Group 2000–2004

Age Group (yrs)

Year	*<15*	*15–17*	*18–19*	*20–24*	*25–29*	*30–34*	*35–39*	*≥40*	*Unknown*
2000	69	757	1,629	4,791	3,233	2,118	1,280	550	23
2001	63	775	1,675	5,052	3,251	2,181	1,342	491	3
2002	62	704	1,488	4,860	3,101	2,227	1,243	501	0
2003	47	726	1,353	4,858	3,219	2,085	1,277	458	1
2004	53	665	1,362	4,895	3,164	1,938	1,243	468	0
Total	294	3,627	7,507	24,456	15,968	10,549	6,385	2,468	27

Source: Minnesota Department of Health.

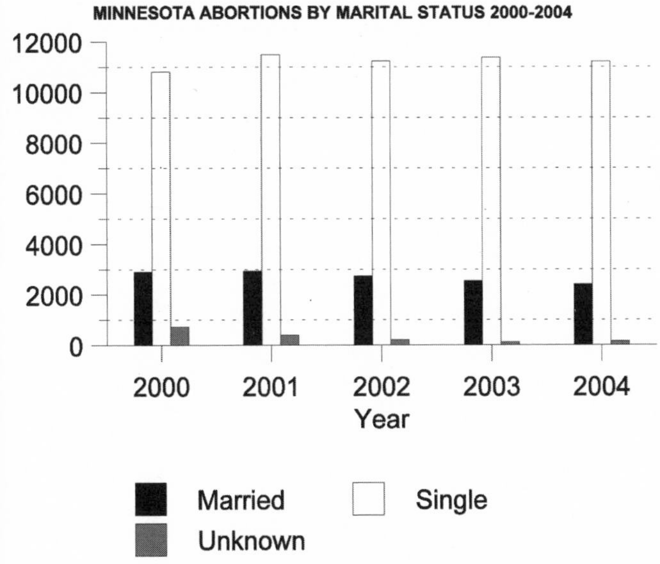

Source: Minnesota Department of Health.

tion. In fact, one of the statutes concerning abortion advertisements was expressly found invalid in *Meadowbrook Women's Clinic v. Minnesota*, 557 F.Supp. 1172 (D.Minn. 1983). The statutes in question include laws that prohibit the sale of drugs to cause an abortion, as well as distribution of articles or information regarding abortion, including advertisement. The statutes are set out below.

Minnesota Code § 617.20. Sale of product to cause abortion

Whoever shall manufacture, give, or sell an instrument, drug, or medicine, or any other substance, with intent that the same may be unlawfully used in producing the miscarriage of a woman, shall be guilty of a felony.

Minnesota Code § 617.25. Articles and information

Every person who shall sell, lend, or give away, or in any manner exhibit, or offer to sell, lend, or give away, or have in possession with intent to sell, lend, give away, or advertise or offer for sale, loan, or distribution, any instrument or article, or any drug or medicine for causing unlawful abortion; or shall write or print, or cause to be written or printed, a card, circular, pamphlet, advertisement, or notice of any kind, or shall give oral information, stating when, where, how, or whom, or by what means such article or medicine can be obtained or who manufactures it, shall be guilty of a gross misdemeanor and punished by imprisonment in the county jail for not more than one year or by a fine of not more than $3,000 or by both.

Minnesota Code § 617.251. Sale of contraceptives

Instruments, articles, drugs or medicines for the prevention of conception or disease may be sold, offered for sale, distributed or dispensed only by persons or organizations recognized as dealing primarily with health or welfare. Anyone convicted of violation of this section shall be guilty of a gross misdemeanor and punished by imprisonment not to exceed one year or by a fine of not more than $3,000 or both.

Minnesota Code § 617.26. Mailing abortion materials

Every person who shall deposit or cause to be deposited in any post office in the state, or place in charge of any express company or other common carrier or person for transportation, any of the articles or things specified in section ... 617.25, or any circular, book, pamphlet, advertisement or notice relating thereto, with the intent of having the same conveyed by mail, express, or in any other manner; or who shall knowingly or willfully receive the same with intent to carry or convey it, or shall knowingly carry or convey the same by express, or in any other manner except by United States mail, shall be guilty of a misdemeanor. The provisions of

Minnesota Abortion by Education Level of Female 2000–2004

Education Level Completed

Year	*≤8*	*9–11*	*12*	*≥13*	*Unknown*
2000	308	1,647	4,756	5,011	2,728
2001	315	1,669	5,257	4,777	2,815
2002	312	1,536	4,679	3,882	3,777
2003	245	1,491	4,312	3,025	4,951
2004	260	1,360	4,237	3,325	4,606
Total	1,440	7,703	23,241	20,020	18,877

Source: Minnesota Department of Health.

Minnesota Abortion by Weeks of Gestation 2000–2004

Year

Weeks of Gestation	*2000*	*2001*	*2002*	*2003*	*2004*	*Total*
≤8	8,695	9,008	9,071	9,082	8,670	44,526
9–10	2,663	2,601	2,397	2,165	2,253	12,079
11–12	1,529	1,627	1,301	1,323	1,313	7,093
13–15	783	773	702	669	793	3,720
16–20	668	685	601	660	692	3,306
21–24	104	123	109	121	66	523
25–30	8	8	4	3	0	23
≥31	0	0	1	0	1	2
Not known	0	8	0	1	0	9

Source: Minnesota Department of Health.

this section and section 617.25 shall not be construed to apply to an article or instrument used by physicians lawfully practicing, or by their direction or prescription, for the cure or prevention of disease.

Minnesota Code § 617.28.
Certain medical advertisements

1. Any person who shall advertise, in the person's own name or in the name of another person, firm or pretended firm, association, corporation or pretended corporation, in any newspaper, pamphlet, circular, or other written or printed paper, or the owner, publisher, or manager of any newspaper or periodical who shall permit to be inserted or published in any newspaper or periodical owned or controlled by the owner, publisher, or manager, ... any medicine, drug compound, appliance or any means whatever whereby it is claimed ... miscarriage or abortion [is] produced, shall be guilty of a gross misdemeanor and shall be punished by a fine of not less than $50 nor more than $3,000 or by imprisonment in the county jail for not more than six months.

2. Any person publishing, distributing, or causing to be distributed or circulated, any of the advertising matter hereinabove prohibited, shall be guilty of a misdemeanor and punished as prescribed in subdivision 1.

(3) GENERAL ABORTION GUIDELINES

Under the general abortion statute of Minnesota it is required that a woman be fully informed about the abortion procedure and possible consequences. Abortions performed after the first trimester must occur in a hospital or abortion facility. The state prohibits post-viability abortion except when necessary to preserve the life or health of the pregnant woman. A federal court upheld general abortion guidelines, in large part, in *Hodgson v. Lawson*, 542 F.2d 1350 (8th Cir. 1976). The decision in *Hodgson* disapproved of language in the statutes which referred to conduct occurring when a fetus was "potentially" viable. The statutes are set out below.

Minnesota Code § 145.411. Definitions

1. As used in sections 145.411 to 145.416, the terms defined in this section have the meanings given to them.

2. "Viable" means able to live outside the womb even though artificial aid may be required. During the second half of its gestation period a fetus shall be considered potentially "viable."

3. "Hospital" means an institution licensed by the state commissioner of health; adequately and properly staffed and equipped; providing services, facilities and beds for the reception and care of one or more nonrelated persons for a continuous period longer than 24 hours for diagnosis, treatment or care of illness, injury or pregnancy; and regularly providing clinical laboratory services, diagnostic x-ray services and treatment facilities for surgery, obstetrical care or other definitive medical treatment of similar extent. "Hospital" shall not include diagnostic or treatment centers, physicians' offices or clinics, or other facilities for the foster care of children licensed by the commissioner of human services.

4. "Abortion facility" means those places properly recognized and licensed by the state commissioner of health under lawful rules promulgated by the commissioner for the performance of abortions.

5. "Abortion" includes an act, procedure or use of any instrument, medicine or drug which is supplied or prescribed for or administered to a pregnant woman which results in the termination of pregnancy.

6. "Commissioner" means the commissioner of health.

Minnesota Code § 145.412. Abortion

1. It shall be unlawful to willfully perform an abortion unless the abortion is performed:

(1) by a physician licensed to practice medicine pursuant to chapter 147, or a physician in training under the supervision of a licensed physician;

Minnesota Prior Abortion by Female 2000–2004

		Prior Abortion								
Year	*None*	*1*	*2*	*3*	*4*	*5*	*6*	*7*	*≥8*	*Unknown*
2000	8,448	3,669	1,403	552	184	88	38	25	41	2
2001	8,809	3,705	1,370	547	215	85	40	26	35	1
2002	8,411	3,509	1,349	502	220	105	38	19	33	0
2003	7,952	3,641	1,412	574	225	107	55	29	28	1
2004	7,839	3,499	1,410	564	245	116	55	28	30	2
Total	41,459	18,023	6,944	2,739	1,089	501	226	127	167	6

Source: Minnesota Department of Health.

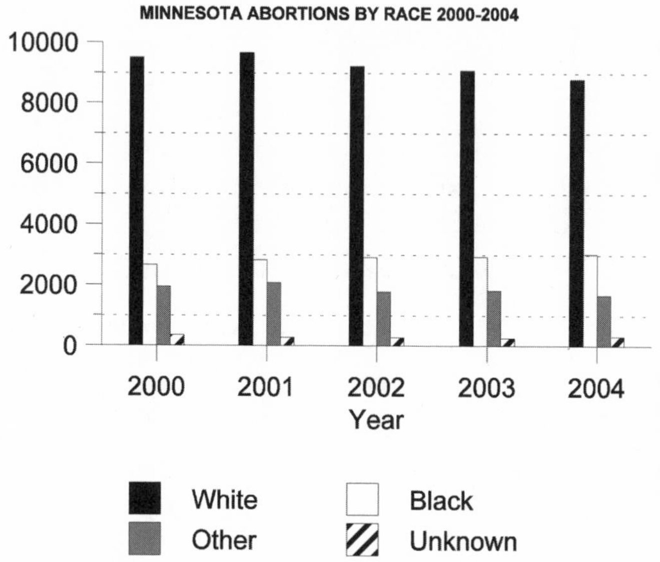

Source: National Center for Health Statistics.

(2) in a hospital or abortion facility if the abortion is performed after the first trimester;

(3) in a manner consistent with the lawful rules promulgated by the state commissioner of health; and

(4) with the consent of the woman submitting to the abortion after a full explanation of the procedure and effect of the abortion.

2. It shall be unlawful to perform an abortion upon a woman who is unconscious except if the woman has been rendered unconscious for the purpose of having an abortion or if the abortion is necessary to save the life of the woman.

3. It shall be unlawful to perform an abortion when the fetus is potentially viable unless:

(1) the abortion is performed in a hospital;

(2) the attending physician certifies in writing that in the physician's best medical judgment the abortion is necessary to preserve the life or health of the pregnant woman; and

(3) to the extent consistent with sound medical practice the abortion is performed under circumstances which will reasonably assure the live birth and survival of the fetus.

4. A person who performs an abortion in violation of this section is guilty of a felony.

Minnesota Code § 145.415. Live fetus after abortion

1. A potentially viable fetus which is live born following an attempted abortion shall be fully recognized as a human person under the law.

2. If an abortion of a potentially viable fetus results in a live birth, the responsible medical personnel shall take all reasonable measures, in keeping with good medical practice, to preserve the life and health of the live born person.

3. (1) Unless the abortion is performed to save the life of the woman or child, or, (2) unless one or both of the parents of the unborn child agrees within 30 days of the birth to accept the parental rights and responsibilities for the child if it survives the abortion, whenever an abortion of a potentially viable fetus results in a live birth, the child shall be an abandoned ward of the state and the parents shall have no parental rights or obligations as if the parental rights had been terminated pursuant to section 260C.301. The child shall be provided for pursuant to chapter 256J.

Minnesota Code § 145.423. Live births

1. A live child born as a result of an abortion shall be fully recognized as a human person, and accorded immediate protection under the law. All reasonable measures consistent with good medical practice, including the compilation of appropriate medical records, shall be taken to preserve the life and health of the child.

2. When an abortion is performed after the twentieth week of pregnancy, a physician, other than the physician performing the abortion, shall be immediately accessible to take all reasonable measures consistent with good medical practice, including the compilation of appropriate medical records, to preserve the life and health of any live birth that is the result of the abortion.

3. If a child described in subdivision 1 dies after birth, the body shall be disposed of in accordance with the provisions of section 145.1621.

Minnesota Code § 145.416.
Licensing and regulating abortion facilities

The state commissioner of health shall license and promulgate rules for facilities as defined in section 145.411, subdivision 4, which are organized for purposes of delivering abortion services.

(4) ABORTION BY MINORS

Under the laws of Minnesota no physician may perform an abortion upon an unemancipated minor, until 48 hours after he/she notifies the parents or the legal guardian of the minor. If the minor was the victim of sexual abuse, neglect, or physical abuse in the home, then notification is not required.

In compliance with federal constitutional law, Minnesota has provided a judicial waiver procedure for an unemancipated minor to obtain an abortion without parental or guardian notification. A minor may petition a trial court for a waiver of the notice requirement. A minor has a right to an attorney at the proceeding and if she cannot afford one, the court must appoint her an attorney. If a minor chooses, she may represent herself. The required parental or guardian notice may be waived if the court finds either (1) that the minor is mature and well-informed enough to make the abortion decision on her own, or (2) that performance of the abortion would be in the best interest of the minor. An expedited appeal is available to any minor to whom the court denies a waiver of consent.

In *Hodgson v. Minnesota* the United States Supreme Court upheld the constitutionality of Minnesota's requirement that a pregnant minor cannot obtain an abortion until at least 48 hours after both of her parents had been notified, and the judicial bypass exception to the notification requirement. The statute addressing the matters is set out below.

Minnesota Code § 144.343.
Notice, waiting period, and judicial bypass

1. Any minor may give effective consent for medical, mental and other health services to determine the presence of or to treat pregnancy and conditions associated therewith, venereal disease, alcohol and other drug abuse, and the consent of no other person is required.

2. Notwithstanding the provisions of section 13.02, subdivision 8, no abortion operation shall be performed upon an unemancipated minor or upon a woman for whom a guardian has been appointed pursuant to sections 525.5-101 to 525.5-102 because of a finding of incapacity, until at least 48 hours after written notice of the pending operation has been delivered in the manner specified in subdivisions 2 to 4.

(a) The notice shall be addressed to the parent at the usual place of abode of the parent and delivered personally to the parent by the physician or an agent.

(b) In lieu of the delivery required by clause (a), notice shall be made by certified mail addressed to the parent at the usual place of abode of the parent with return receipt requested and restricted delivery to the addressee which means postal employee can only deliver the mail to the authorized addressee. Time of delivery shall be deemed to occur at 12 o'clock noon on the next day on which regular mail delivery takes place, subsequent to mailing.

3. For purposes of this section, "parent" means both parents of the pregnant woman if they are both living, one parent of the pregnant woman if only one is living or if the second one cannot be located through reasonably diligent effort, or the guardian or conservator if the pregnant woman has one.

For purposes of this section, "abortion" means the use of any means to terminate the pregnancy of a woman known to be pregnant with knowledge that the termination with those means will, with reasonable likelihood, cause the death of the fetus and "fetus" means any individual human organism from fertilization until birth.

4. No notice shall be required under this section if:

(a) The attending physician certifies in the pregnant woman's medical record that the abortion is necessary to prevent the woman's death and there is insufficient time to provide the required notice; or

(b) The abortion is authorized in writing by the person or persons who are entitled to notice; or

(c) The pregnant minor woman declares that she is a victim of sexual abuse, neglect, or physical abuse as defined in section 626.556. Notice of that declaration shall be made to the proper authorities as provided in section 626.556, subdivision 3.

5. Performance of an abortion in violation of this section shall be a misdemeanor and shall be grounds for a civil action by a person wrongfully denied notification. A person shall not be held liable under this section if the person establishes by written evidence that the person relied upon evidence sufficient to convince a careful and prudent person that the representations of the pregnant woman regarding information necessary to comply with this section are bona fide and true, or if the person has attempted with reasonable diligence to deliver notice, but has been unable to do so.

6. If subdivision 2 of this law is ever temporarily or permanently restrained or enjoined by judicial order, subdivision 2 shall be enforced as though the following paragraph were incorporated as paragraph (c) of that subdivision; provided, however, that if such temporary or permanent restraining order or injunction is ever stayed or dissolved, or otherwise ceases to have effect, subdivision 2 shall have full force and effect, without being modified by the addition of the following substitute paragraph which shall have no force or effect until or unless an injunction or restraining order is again in effect.

(c)(i) If such a pregnant woman elects not to allow the notification of one or both of her parents or guardian or conservator, any judge of a court of competent jurisdiction shall, upon petition, or motion, and after an appropriate hearing, authorize a physician to perform the abortion if said judge determines that the pregnant woman is mature and capable of giving informed consent to the proposed abortion. If said judge determines that the pregnant woman is not mature, or if the pregnant woman does not claim to be mature, the judge shall determine whether the performance of an abortion upon her without notification of her parents, guardian, or conservator would be in her best interests and shall authorize a physician to perform the abortion without such notification if said judge concludes that the pregnant woman's best interests would be served thereby.

(ii) Such a pregnant woman may participate in proceedings in the court on her own behalf, and the court may appoint a guardian ad litem for her. The court shall, however, advise her that she has a right to court appointed counsel, and shall, upon her request, provide her with such counsel.

(iii) Proceedings in the court under this section shall be confidential and shall be given such precedence over other pending matters so that the court may reach a decision promptly and without delay so as to serve the best interests of the pregnant woman. A judge of the court who conducts proceedings under this section shall make in writing specific factual findings and legal conclusions supporting the decision and shall order a record of the evidence to be maintained including the judge's own findings and conclusions.

(iv) An expedited confidential appeal shall be available to any such pregnant woman for whom the court denies an order authorizing an abortion without notification. An order authorizing an abortion without notification shall not be subject to appeal. No filing fees shall be required of any such pregnant woman at either the trial or the appellate level. Access to the trial court for the purposes of such a petition or motion, and access to the appellate courts for purposes of making an appeal from denial of the same, shall be afforded such a pregnant woman 24 hours a day, seven days a week.

7. If any provision, word, phrase or clause of this section or the application thereof to any person or circumstance shall be held invalid, such invalidity shall not affect the provisions, words, phrases, clauses or application of this section which can be given effect without the invalid provision, word, phrase, clause, or application, and to this end the provisions, words, phrases, and clauses of this section are declared to be severable.

(5) USE OF FACILITIES AND PEOPLE

Under the laws of Minnesota hospitals are not required to allow abortions at their facilities. The employees and physicians at hospitals that do allow abortions are permitted to refuse to take part in abortions. In *Hodgson v. Lawson*, 542 F.2d 1350 (8th Cir. 1976) a federal court held that the refusal to participate laws could not be applied to public facilities. The state also provides that health plans are not required to offer coverage for abortions. The statutes addressing the matters are set out below.

Minnesota Code § 145.414. Refusal to participate

(a) No person and no hospital or institution shall be coerced, held liable or discriminated against in any manner because of a refusal to perform, accommodate, assist or submit to an abortion for any reason.

(b) It is the policy of the state of Minnesota that no health plan company as defined under section 62Q.01, subdivision 4, or health care cooperative as defined under section 62R.04, subdivision 2, shall be required to provide or provide coverage for an abortion. No provision of this chapter; of chapter 62A, 62C, 62D, 62H, 62L, 62M, 62N, 62R, 64B, or of any other chapter; of Minnesota Rules; or of Laws 1995, chapter 234, shall be construed as requiring a health plan company as defined under section 62Q.01, subdivision 4, or a health care cooperative as defined under section 62R.04, subdivision 2, to provide or provide coverage for an abortion.

(c) This section supersedes any provision of Laws 1995, chapter 234, or any act enacted prior to enactment of Laws 1995, chapter 234, that in any way limits or is inconsistent with this section. No provision of any act enacted subsequent to Laws 1995, chapter 234 shall be construed as in any way limiting or being inconsistent with this section, unless the act amends this section or expressly provides that it is intended to limit or be inconsistent with this section.

Minnesota Code § 145.42. Nonliability for refusal to perform

1. No physician, nurse, or other person who refuses to perform or assist in the performance of an abortion, and no hospital that refuses to permit the performance of an abortion upon its premises, shall be liable to any person for damages allegedly arising from the refusal.

2. No physician, nurse, or other person who refuses to perform or assist in the performance of an abortion shall, because of that refusal, be dismissed, suspended, demoted, or otherwise prejudiced or damaged by a hospital with which the person is affiliated or by which the person is employed.

Minnesota Code § 62A.041. Maternity benefits

1. Each group policy of accident and health insurance and each group health maintenance contract shall provide the same coverage for maternity benefits to unmarried women and minor female dependents that it provides to married women including the wives of employees choosing dependent family coverage. If an unmarried insured or an unmarried enrollee is a parent of a dependent child, each group policy and each group contract shall provide the same coverage for that child as that provided for the child of a married employee choosing dependent family coverage if the insured or the enrollee elects dependent family coverage.

Each individual policy of accident and health insurance and each individual health maintenance contract shall provide the same coverage for maternity benefits to unmarried women and minor female dependents as that provided for married women. If an unmarried insured or an unmarried enrollee is a parent of a dependent child, each individual policy and each individual contract shall also provide the same coverage for that child as that provided for the child of a married insured or a married enrollee choosing dependent family coverage if the insured or the enrollee elects dependent family coverage.

2. Each group policy of accident and health insurance, except for policies which only provide coverage for specified diseases, or each group subscriber contract of accident and health insurance or health maintenance contract, issued or renewed after August 1, 1987, shall include maternity benefits in the same manner as any other illness covered under the policy or contract.

3. For the purposes of this section, the term "maternity benefits" shall not include elective, induced abortion whether performed in a hospital, other abortion facility, or the office of a physician.

This section applies to policies and contracts issued, delivered, or renewed after August 1, 1985, that cover Minnesota residents.

(6) EXPERIMENT OR SALE OF FETUS

Minnesota prohibits trafficking in living fetuses. The state permits such trafficking in nonliving fetal remains. The statutes addressing the matter are set out below.

Minnesota Code § 145.421. Definitions

1. As used in this section and section 145.422, the terms defined in this section shall have the meanings given them.

2. "Human conceptus" means any human organism, conceived either in the human body or produced in an artificial environment other than the human body, from fertilization through the first 265 days thereafter.

3. "Living," as defined for the sole purpose of this section and section 145.422, means the presence of evidence of life, such as movement, heart or respiratory activity, the presence of electroencephalographic or electrocardiographic activity.

Minnesota Code § 145.422. Experimentation or sale

1. Whoever uses or permits the use of a living human conceptus for any type of scientific, laboratory research or other experimentation except to protect the life or health of the conceptus, or except as herein provided, shall be guilty of a gross misdemeanor.

2. The use of a living human conceptus for research or experimentation which verifiable scientific evidence has shown to be harmless to the conceptus shall be permitted.

3. Whoever buys or sells a living human conceptus or nonrenewable organ of the body is guilty of a gross misdemeanor. Nothing in this subdivision prohibits (1) the buying and selling of a cell culture line or lines taken from a nonliving human conceptus; (2) payments for reasonable expenses associated with the removal, storage, and transportation of a human organ, including payments made to or on behalf of a living organ donor for actual expenses such as medical costs, lost income, or travel expenses that are incurred as a direct result of the donation of the nonrenewable organ; or (3) financial assistance payments provided under insurance and Medicare reimbursement programs.

(7) WRONGFUL LIFE ACTION

Minnesota has taken an affirmative step to prevent wrongful life litigation, by prohibiting claims for negligent failure to abort a pregnancy. The law was upheld as valid in *Hickman v. Group Health Plan, Inc.*, 396 N.W.2d 10 (Minn. 1986). The statute addressing the matter is set out below.

Minnesota Code § 145.424. Prohibition of tort actions

1. No person shall maintain a cause of action or receive an award of damages on behalf of that person based on the claim that but for the negligent conduct of another, the person would have been aborted.

2. No person shall maintain a cause of action or receive an award of damages on the claim that but for the negligent conduct of another, a child would have been aborted.

3. Nothing in this section shall be construed to preclude a cause of action for intentional or negligent malpractice or any other action arising in tort based on the failure of a contraceptive method or sterilization procedure or on a claim that, but for the negligent conduct of another, tests or treatment would have been provided or would have been provided properly which would have made possible the prevention, cure, or amelioration of any disease, defect, deficiency, or disability; provided, however, that abortion shall not have been deemed to prevent, cure, or ameliorate any disease, defect, deficiency, or disability. The failure or refusal of any person to perform or have an abortion shall not be a defense in any action, nor shall that failure or refusal be considered in awarding damages or in imposing a penalty in any action.

(8) CRIME AGAINST FETUS

Minnesota has created several statutes imposing criminal penalties on anyone who injures or causes the death of a fetus, except in the case of lawful abortions. The statutes are set out below.

Minnesota Code § 609.266. Definitions

The definitions in this subdivision apply to sections 609.21, subdivision 1a, paragraphs (a) and (b), and 609.2661 to 609.2691:

(a) "Unborn child" means the unborn offspring of a human being conceived, but not yet born.

(b) "Whoever" does not include the pregnant woman.

Minnesota Code § 609.2661.
Murder of an unborn child in the first degree

Whoever does any of the following is guilty of murder of an unborn child in the first degree and must be sentenced to imprisonment for life:

(1) causes the death of an unborn child with premeditation and with intent to effect the death of the unborn child or of another;

(2) causes the death of an unborn child while committing or attempting to commit criminal sexual conduct in the first or second degree with force or violence, either upon or affecting the mother of the unborn child or another; or

(3) causes the death of an unborn child with intent to effect the death of the unborn child or another while committing or attempting to commit burglary, aggravated robbery, kidnapping, arson in the first or second degree, tampering with a witness in the first degree, or escape from custody.

Minnesota Code § 609.2662.
Murder of an unborn child in the second degree

Whoever does either of the following is guilty of murder of an unborn child in the second degree and may be sentenced to imprisonment for not more than 40 years:

(1) causes the death of an unborn child with intent to effect the death of that unborn child or another, but without premeditation; or

(2) causes the death of an unborn child, without intent to effect the death of any unborn child or person, while committing or attempting to commit a felony offense other than criminal sexual conduct in the first or second degree with force or violence.

Minnesota Code § 609.2663.
Murder of an unborn child in the third degree

Whoever, without intent to effect the death of any unborn child or person, causes the death of an unborn child by perpetrating an act eminently dangerous to others and evincing a depraved mind, without regard for human or fetal life, is guilty of murder of an unborn child in the third degree and may be sentenced to imprisonment for not more than 25 years.

Minnesota Code § 609.2664.
Manslaughter of an unborn child in the first degree

Whoever does any of the following is guilty of manslaughter of an unborn child in the first degree and may be sentenced to imprisonment for not more than 15 years or to payment of a fine of not more than $30,000, or both:

(1) intentionally causes the death of an unborn child in the heat of passion provoked by such words or acts of another as would provoke a person of ordinary self-control under like circumstances;

(2) causes the death of an unborn child in committing or attempting to commit a misdemeanor or gross misdemeanor offense with such force or violence that death of or great bodily harm to any person or unborn child was reasonably foreseeable, and murder of an unborn child in the first or second degree was not committed thereby; or

(3) intentionally causes the death of an unborn child because the actor is coerced by threats made by someone other than the actor's coconspirator and which cause the actor to reasonably believe that the act performed by the actor is the only means of preventing imminent death to the actor or another.

Minnesota Code § 609.2665.
Manslaughter of an unborn child in the second degree

A person who causes the death of an unborn child by any of the following means is guilty of manslaughter of an unborn child in the second degree and may be sentenced to imprisonment for not more than ten years or to payment of a fine of not more than $20,000, or both:

(1) by the actor's culpable negligence whereby the actor creates an unreasonable risk and consciously takes chances of causing death or great bodily harm to an unborn child or a person;

(2) by shooting the mother of the unborn child with a firearm or other dangerous weapon as a result of negligently believing her to be a deer or other animal;

(3) by setting a spring gun, pit fall, deadfall, snare, or other like dangerous weapon or device; or

(4) by negligently or intentionally permitting any animal, known by the person to have vicious propensities or to have caused great or substantial bodily harm in the past, to run uncontrolled off the owner's premises, or negligently failing to keep it properly confined.

If proven by a preponderance of the evidence, it shall be an affirmative defense to criminal liability under clause (4) that the mother of the unborn child provoked the animal to cause the unborn child's death.

Minnesota Code § 609.267.
Assault of an unborn child in the first degree

Whoever assaults a pregnant woman and inflicts great bodily harm on an unborn child who is subsequently born alive may be sentenced to imprisonment for not more than 15 years or to payment of a fine of not more than $30,000, or both.

Minnesota Code § 609.2671.
Assault of an unborn child in the second degree

Whoever assaults a pregnant woman and inflicts substantial bodily harm on an unborn child who is subsequently born alive may be sentenced to imprisonment for not more than five years or to payment of a fine of not more than $10,000, or both.

As used in this section, "substantial bodily harm" includes the birth of the unborn child prior to 37 weeks gestation if the child weighs 2,500 grams or less at the time of birth. "Substantial bodily harm" does not include the inducement of the unborn child's birth when done for bona fide medical purposes.

Minnesota Code § 609.2672.
Assault of an unborn child in the third degree

Whoever does any of the following commits an assault of an unborn child in the third degree and is guilty of a misdemeanor:

(1) commits an act with intent to cause fear in a pregnant woman of immediate bodily harm or death to the unborn child; or

(2) intentionally inflicts or attempts to inflict bodily harm on an unborn child who is subsequently born alive.

Minnesota Code § 609.268.
Injury or death of an unborn child in commission of crime

1. Whoever, in the commission of a felony or in a violation of section 609.224, 609.2242, 609.23, 609.231, 609.2325, or 609.233, causes the death of an unborn child is guilty of a felony and may be sentenced to imprisonment for not more than 15 years or to payment of a fine not more than $30,000, or both. As used in this subdivision, "felony" does not include a violation of sections 609.185 to 609.21, 609.221 to 609.2231, or 609.2661 to 609.2665.

2. Whoever, in the commission of a felony or in a violation of section 609.23, 609.231, 609.2325 or 609.233, causes great or substantial bodily harm to an unborn child who is subsequently born alive, is guilty of a felony and may be sentenced to imprisonment for not more than ten years or to payment of a fine of not more than $20,000, or both. As used in this subdivision, "felony" does not include a violation of sections 609.21, 609.221 to 609.2231, or 609.267 to 609.2672.

Minnesota Code § 609.21.
Criminal vehicular homicide and injury (abridged)

1. A person is guilty of criminal vehicular homicide or operation and may be sentenced as provided in subdivision 1a, if the person causes injury to or the death of another as a result of operating a motor vehicle:

(1) in a grossly negligent manner;

(2) in a negligent manner while under the influence of:

(i) alcohol;

(ii) a controlled substance; or

(iii) any combination of those elements;

(3) while having an alcohol concentration of 0.08 or more;

(4) while having an alcohol concentration of 0.08 or more, as measured within two hours of the time of driving;

(5) in a negligent manner while knowingly under the influence of a hazardous substance;

(6) in a negligent manner while any amount of a controlled substance listed in schedule I or II, or its metabolite, other than marijuana or tetrahydrocannabinols, is present in the person's body;

(7) where the driver who causes the accident leaves the scene of the accident in violation of section 169.09, subdivision 1 or 6; or

(8) where the driver had actual knowledge that a peace officer had previously issued a citation or warning that the motor vehicle was defectively maintained, the driver had actual knowledge that remedial action was not taken, the driver had reason to know that the defect created a present danger to others, and the injury or death was caused by the defective maintenance.

1a. (a) A person who violates subdivision 1 and causes the death of a human being not constituting murder or manslaughter or the death of an unborn child may be sentenced to imprisonment for not more than ten years or to payment of a fine of not more than $20,000, or both.

(b) A person who violates subdivision 1 and causes great bodily harm to another not constituting attempted murder or assault or great bodily harm to an unborn child who is subsequently born alive may be sentenced to imprisonment for not more than five years or to payment of a fine of not more than $10,000, or both.

(c) A person who violates subdivision 1 and causes substantial bodily harm to another may be sentenced to imprisonment for not more than three years or to payment of a fine of not more than $10,000, or both.

(d) A person who violates subdivision 1 and causes bodily harm to another may be sentenced to imprisonment for not more than one year or to payment of a fine of not more than $3,000, or both.

1b. A prosecution for or a conviction of a crime under this section relating to causing death or injury to an unborn child is not a bar to conviction of or punishment for any other crime committed by the defendant as part of the same conduct.

(9) BAN ON ANTI-ABORTION ACTIVITY

Minnesota prohibits conduct that obstructs passage to and from a health care facility. The state allows a monetary civil suit to be filed against anyone in engaging in such conduct. The statute addressing the matter is set out below.

Minnesota Code § 609.7495.
Interference with access to health care

1. For the purposes of this section, the following terms have the meanings given them.

(a) "Facility" means any of the following:

(1) a hospital or other health institution licensed under sections 144.50 to 144.56;

(2) a medical facility as defined in section 144.561;

(3) an agency, clinic, or office operated under the direction of or under contract with the commissioner of health or a community health board, as defined in section 145A.02;

(4) a facility providing counseling regarding options for medical services or recovery from an addiction;

(5) a facility providing emergency shelter services for battered women, as defined in section 611A.31, subdivision 3, or a facility providing transitional housing for battered women and their children;

(6) a facility as defined in section 626.556, subdivision 2, paragraph (f);

(7) a facility as defined in section 626.5572, subdivision 6, where the services described in that paragraph are provided;

(8) a place to or from which ambulance service, as defined in section 144E.001, is provided or sought to be provided; and

(9) a hospice provider licensed under section 144A.753.

(b) "Aggrieved party" means a person whose access to or egress from a facility is obstructed in violation of subdivision 2, or the facility.

2. A person is guilty of a gross misdemeanor who intentionally and physically obstructs any individual's access to or egress from a facility.

3. Nothing in this section shall be construed to impair the right of any individual or group to engage in speech protected by the United States Constitution, the Minnesota Constitution, or federal or state law, including but not limited to peaceful and lawful handbilling and picketing.

4. (a) A party who is aggrieved by an act prohibited by this section, or by an attempt or conspiracy to commit an act prohibited by this section, may bring an action for damages, injunctive or declaratory relief, as appropriate, in district court against any person or entity who has violated or has conspired to violate this section.

(b) A party who prevails in a civil action under this subdivision is entitled to recover from the violator damages, costs, attorney fees, and other relief as determined by the court. In addition to all other damages, the court may award to the aggrieved party a civil penalty of up to $1,000 for each violation. If the aggrieved party is a facility and the political subdivision where the violation occurred incurred law enforcement or prosecution expenses in connection with the same violation, the court shall award any civil penalty it imposes to the political subdivision instead of to the facility.

(c) The remedies provided by this subdivision are in addition to any other legal or equitable remedies the aggrieved party may have and are not intended to diminish or substitute for those remedies or to be exclusive.

(10) FETAL DEATH REPORT

Minnesota requires that all abortions and abortion complications be reported to the proper authorities. The state also specifically requires reporting the death of a woman caused by an abortion. The statutes addressing the matters are set out below.

Minnesota Code § 145.413.
Reporting woman's death from abortion

1. Repealed by Laws 2003, c. 14, art. 2, § 2.

2. Death of woman. If any woman who has had an abortion dies from any cause within 30 days of the abortion or from any cause potentially related to the abortion within 90 days of the abortion, that fact shall be reported to the state commissioner of health.

3. Penalty. A physician who performs an abortion and who fails to comply with subdivision 1 and transmit the required information to the state commissioner of health within 30 days after the abortion is guilty of a misdemeanor.

Minnesota Code § 145.4131. Reporting abortion data

1. (a) Within 90 days of July 1, 1998, the commissioner shall prepare a reporting form for use by physicians or facilities performing abortions. A copy of this section shall be attached to the form. A physician or facility performing an abortion shall obtain a form from the commissioner.

(b) The form shall require the following information:

(1) the number of abortions performed by the physician in the previous calendar year, reported by month;

(2) the method used for each abortion;

(3) the approximate gestational age expressed in one of the following increments:

(i) less than nine weeks;
(ii) nine to ten weeks;
(iii) 11 to 12 weeks;
(iv) 13 to 15 weeks;
(v) 16 to 20 weeks;
(vi) 21 to 24 weeks;
(vii) 25 to 30 weeks;
(viii) 31 to 36 weeks; or
(ix) 37 weeks to term;

(4) the age of the woman at the time the abortion was performed;

(5) the specific reason for the abortion, including, but not limited to, the following:

(i) the pregnancy was a result of rape;
(ii) the pregnancy was a result of incest;
(iii) economic reasons;
(iv) the woman does not want children at this time;
(v) the woman's emotional health is at stake;
(vi) the woman's physical health is at stake;
(vii) the woman will suffer substantial and irreversible impairment of a major bodily function if the pregnancy continues;
(viii) the pregnancy resulted in fetal anomalies; or
(ix) unknown or the woman refused to answer;

(6) the number of prior induced abortions;

(7) the number of prior spontaneous abortions;

(8) whether the abortion was paid for by:

(i) private coverage;
(ii) public assistance health coverage; or
(iii) self-pay;

(9) whether coverage was under:

(i) a fee-for-service plan;
(ii) a capitated private plan; or
(iii) other;

(10) complications, if any, for each abortion and for the aftermath of each abortion. Space for a description of any complications shall be available on the form; and

(11) the medical specialty of the physician performing the abortion.

2. A physician performing an abortion or a facility at which an abortion is performed shall complete and submit the form to the commissioner no later than April 1 for abortions performed in the previous calendar year. The annual report to the commissioner shall include the methods used to dispose of fetal tissue and remains.

3. Nothing in this section shall be construed to preclude the voluntary or required submission of other reports or forms regarding abortions.

Minnesota Code § 145.4132.
Reporting abortion complication data

1. (a) Within 90 days of July 1, 1998, the commissioner shall prepare an abortion complication reporting form for all physicians licensed and practicing in the state. A copy of this section shall be attached to the form.

(b) The Board of Medical Practice shall ensure that the abortion complication reporting form is distributed:

(1) to all physicians licensed to practice in the state, within 120 days after July 1, 1998, and by December 1 of each subsequent year; and

(2) to a physician who is newly licensed to practice in the state, at the same time as official notification to the physician that the physician is so licensed.

2. A physician licensed and practicing in the state who knowingly encounters an illness or injury that, in the physician's medical judgment, is related to an induced abortion or the facility where the illness or injury is encountered shall complete and submit an abortion complication reporting form to the commissioner.

3. A physician or facility required to submit an abortion complication reporting form to the commissioner shall do so as soon as practicable after the encounter with the abortion-related illness or injury.

4. Nothing in this section shall be construed to preclude the voluntary or required submission of other reports or forms regarding abortion complications.

Minnesota Code § 145.4133.
Reporting out-of-state abortions

The commissioner of human services shall report to the commissioner by April 1 each year the following information regarding abortions paid for with state funds and performed out of state in the previous calendar year:

(1) the total number of abortions performed out of state and partially or fully paid for with state funds through the medical assistance, general assistance medical care, or MinnesotaCare program, or any other program;

(2) the total amount of state funds used to pay for the abortions and expenses incidental to the abortions; and

(3) the gestational age at the time of abortion.

Minnesota Code § 145.4134. Commissioner's public report

(a) By July 1 of each year, except for 1998 and 1999 information, the commissioner shall issue a public report providing statistics for the previous calendar year compiled from the data submitted under sections 145.4131 to 145.4133 and sections 145.4241 to 145.4249. For 1998 and 1999 information, the report shall be issued October 1, 2000. Each report shall provide the statistics for all previous calendar years, adjusted to reflect any additional information from late or corrected reports. The commissioner shall ensure that none of the information included in the public reports can reasonably lead to identification of an individual having performed or having had an abortion. All data included on the forms under sections 145.4131 to 145.4133 and sections 145.4241 to 145.4249 must be included in the public report, except that the commissioner shall maintain as confidential, data which alone or in combination may constitute information from which an individual having performed or having had an abortion may be identified using epidemiologic principles. The commissioner shall submit the report to the senate Health and Family Security Committee and the house Health and Human Services Committee.

(b) The commissioner may, by rules adopted under chapter 14, alter the submission dates established under sections 145.4131 to 145.4133 for administrative convenience, fiscal savings, or other valid reason, provided that physicians or facilities and the commissioner of human services submit the required information once each year and the commissioner issues a report once each year.

Minnesota Code § 145.4135. Penalties

(a) If the commissioner finds that a physician or facility has failed to submit the required form under section 145.4131 within 60 days following the due date, the commissioner shall notify the physician or facility that the form is late. A physician or facility who fails to submit the required form under section 145.4131 within 30 days following notification from the commissioner that a report is late is subject to a late fee of $500 for each 30-day period, or portion thereof, that the form is overdue. If a physician or facility required to report under this section does not submit a report, or submits only an incomplete report, more than one year following the due date, the commissioner may take action to fine the physician or facility or may bring an action to require that the physician or facility be directed by a court of competent jurisdiction to submit a complete report within a period stated by court order or be subject to sanctions for civil contempt. Notwithstanding section 13.39 to the contrary, action taken by the commissioner to enforce the provision of this section shall be treated as private if the data related to this action, alone or in combination, may constitute information from which an individual having performed or having had an abortion may be identified using epidemiologic principles.

(b) If the commissioner fails to issue the public report required under section 145.4134 or fails in any way to enforce this section, a group of 100 or more citizens of the state may seek an injunction in a court of competent jurisdiction against the commissioner requiring that a complete report be issued within a period stated by court order or requiring that enforcement action be taken.

(c) A physician or facility reporting in good faith and exercising due care shall have immunity from civil, criminal, or administrative liability that might otherwise result from reporting. A physician who knowingly or recklessly submits a false report under this section is guilty of a misdemeanor.

(d) The commissioner may take reasonable steps to ensure compliance with sections 145.4131 to 145.4133 and to verify data provided, including but not limited to, inspection of places where abortions are performed in accordance with chapter 14.

(e) The commissioner shall develop recommendations on appropriate penalties and methods of enforcement for physicians or facilities who fail to submit the report required under section 145.4132, submit an incomplete report, or submit a late report. The commissioner shall also assess the effectiveness of the enforcement methods and penalties provided in paragraph (a) and shall recommend appropriate changes, if any. These recommendations shall be reported to the chairs of the senate Health and Family Security Committee and the house Health and Human Services Committee by November 15, 1998.

Minnesota Code § 145.4136. Severability

If any one or more provision, section, subdivision, sentence, clause, phrase, or word in sections 145.4131 to 145.4135, or the application thereof to any person or circumstance is found to be unconstitutional, the same is hereby declared to be severable and the balance of sections 145.4131 to 145.4135 shall remain effective notwithstanding such unconstitutionality. The legislature hereby declares that it would have passed sections 145.4131 to 145.4135, and each provision, section, subdivision, sentence, clause, phrase, or word thereof, irrespective of the fact that any one or more provision, section, subdivision, sentence, clause, phrase, or word be declared unconstitutional.

(11) ABORTION ALTERNATIVE PROGRAMS

Minnesota provides by statute for funding programs that provide abortion alternative services. The statutes addressing the matter are set out below.

Minnesota Code § 145.4235. Positive abortion alternatives

1. For purposes of this section, the following terms have the meanings given:

(1) "abortion" means the use of any means to terminate the pregnancy of a woman known to be pregnant with knowledge that the termination with those means will, with reasonable likelihood, cause the death of the unborn child. For purposes of this section, abortion does not include an abortion necessary to prevent the death of the mother;

(2) "nondirective counseling" means providing clients with:

(i) a list of health care providers and social service providers that provide prenatal care, childbirth care, infant care, foster care, adoption services, alternatives to abortion, or abortion services; and

(ii) nondirective, nonmarketing information regarding such providers; and

(3) "unborn child" means a member of the species Homo sapiens from fertilization until birth.

2. (a) The commissioner shall award grants to eligible applicants under paragraph (c) for the reasonable expenses of alternatives to abortion programs to support, encourage, and assist women in carrying their pregnancies to term and caring for their babies after birth by providing information on, referral to, and assistance with securing necessary services that enable women to carry their pregnancies to term and care for their babies after birth. Necessary services must include, but are not limited to:

(1) medical care;

(2) nutritional services;

(3) housing assistance;

(4) adoption services;

(5) education and employment assistance, including services that support the continuation and completion of high school;

(6) child care assistance; and

(7) parenting education and support services.

An applicant may not provide or assist a woman to obtain adoption services from a provider of adoption services that is not licensed.

(b) In addition to providing information and referral under paragraph (a), an eligible program may provide one or more of the necessary services under paragraph (a) that assists women in carrying their pregnancies to term. To avoid duplication of efforts, grantees may refer to other public or private programs, rather than provide the care directly, if a woman meets eligibility criteria for the other programs.

(c) To be eligible for a grant, an agency or organization must:

(1) be a private, nonprofit organization;

(2) demonstrate that the program is conducted under appropriate supervision;

(3) not charge women for services provided under the program;

(4) provide each pregnant woman counseled with accurate information on the developmental characteristics of babies and of unborn children, including offering the printed information described in section 145.4243;

(5) ensure that its alternatives-to-abortion program's purpose is to assist and encourage women in carrying their pregnancies to term and to maximize their potentials thereafter;

(6) ensure that none of the money provided is used to encourage or affirmatively counsel a woman to have an abortion not necessary to prevent her death, to provide her an abortion, or to directly refer her to an abortion provider for an abortion. The agency or organization may provide nondirective counseling; and

(7) have had the alternatives to abortion program in existence for at least one year as of July 1, 2005; or incorporated an alternative to abortion program that has been in existence for at least one year as of July 1, 2005.

(d) The provisions, words, phrases, and clauses of paragraph (c) are inseverable from this subdivision, and if any provision, word, phrase, or clause of paragraph (c) or its application to any person or circumstance is held invalid, the invalidity applies to all of this subdivision.

(e) An organization that provides abortions, promotes abortions, or directly refers to an abortion provider for an abortion is ineligible to receive a grant under this program. An affiliate of an organization that provides abortions, promotes abortions, or directly refers to an abortion provider for an abortion is ineligible to receive a grant under this section unless the organizations are separately incorporated and independent from each other. To be independent, the organizations may not share any of the following:

(1) the same or a similar name;

(2) medical facilities or nonmedical facilities, including but not limited to, business offices, treatment rooms, consultation rooms, examination rooms, and waiting rooms;

(3) expenses;

(4) employee wages or salaries; or

(5) equipment or supplies, including but not limited to, computers, telephone systems, telecommunications equipment, and office supplies.

(f) An organization that receives a grant under this section and that is affiliated with an organization that provides abortion services must maintain financial records that demonstrate strict compliance with this subdivision and that demonstrate that its independent affiliate that provides abortion services receives no direct or indirect economic or marketing benefit from the grant under this section.

(g) The commissioner shall approve any information provided by a grantee on the health risks associated with abortions to ensure that the information is medically accurate.

3. (a) Any program receiving a grant under this section must have a privacy policy and procedures in place to ensure that the name, address, telephone number, or any other information that might identify any woman seeking the services of the program is not made public or shared with any other agency or organization without the written consent of the woman. All communications between the program and the woman must remain confidential. For purposes of any medical care provided by the program, including, but not limited to, pregnancy tests or ultrasonic scanning, the program must adhere to the requirements in sections 144.291 to 144.298 that apply to providers before releasing any information relating to the medical care provided.

(b) Notwithstanding paragraph (a), the commissioner has access to any information necessary to monitor and review a grantee's program as required under subdivision 4.

4. The commissioner shall make grants under subdivision 2 beginning no later than July 1, 2006. In awarding grants, the commissioner shall consider the program's demonstrated capacity in providing services to assist a pregnant woman in carrying her pregnancy to term. The commissioner shall monitor and review the programs of each grantee to ensure that the grantee carefully adheres to the purposes and requirements of subdivision 2 and shall cease funding a grantee that fails to do so.

5. Except as provided in subdivision 2, paragraph (d), if any provision, word, phrase, or clause of this section or its application to any person or circumstance is held invalid, such invalidity shall not affect the provisions, words, phrases, clauses, or applications of this section that can be given effect without the invalid provision, word, phrase, clause, or application and to this end, the provisions, words, phrases, and clauses of this section are severable.

6. The Minnesota Supreme Court has original jurisdiction over an action challenging the constitutionality of this section and shall expedite the resolution of the action.

Minnesota Code § 145.925. Family planning grants

1. The commissioner of health may make special grants to cities, counties, groups of cities or counties, or nonprofit corporations to provide prepregnancy family planning services.

1a. "Family planning services" means counseling by trained personnel regarding family planning; distribution of information relating to family planning, referral to licensed physicians or local health agencies for consultation, examination, medical treatment, genetic counseling, and prescriptions for the purpose of family planning; and the distribution of family planning products, such as charts, thermometers, drugs, medical preparations, and contraceptive devices. For purposes of sections 145A.01 to 145A.14, family planning shall mean voluntary action by individuals to prevent or aid conception but does not include the performance, or make referrals for encouragement of voluntary termination of pregnancy.

2. The commissioner shall not make special grants pursuant to this section to any nonprofit corporation which performs abortions. No state funds shall be used under contract from a grantee to any nonprofit corporation which performs abortions. This provision shall not apply to hospitals licensed pursuant to sections 144.50 to 144.56, or health maintenance organizations certified pursuant to chapter 62D.

3. No funds provided by grants made pursuant to this section shall be used to support any family planning services for any unemancipated minor in any elementary or secondary school building.

4. Except as provided in sections 144.341 and 144.342, any person employed to provide family planning services who is paid in whole or in part from funds provided under this section who advises an abortion or sterilization to any unemancipated minor shall, following such a recommendation, so notify the parent or guardian of the reasons for such an action.

5. The commissioner of health shall promulgate rules for approval of plans and budgets of prospective grant recipients, for the submission of annual financial and statistical reports, and the maintenance of statements of source and application of funds by grant recipients. The commissioner of health may not require that any home rule charter or statutory city or county apply for or receive grants under this subdivision as a condition for the receipt of any state or federal funds unrelated to family planning services.

6. The request of any person for family planning services or the refusal to accept any service shall in no way affect the right of the person to receive public assistance, public health services, or any other public service. Nothing in this section shall abridge the right of the individual to make decisions concerning family planning, nor shall any individual be required to state a reason for refusing any offer of family planning services.

Any employee of the agencies engaged in the administration of the provisions of this section may refuse to accept the duty of offering family planning services to the extent that the duty is contrary to personal beliefs. A refusal shall not be grounds for dismissal, suspension, demotion, or any other discrimination in employment. The directors or supervisors of the agencies shall reassign the duties of employees in order to carry out the provisions of this section.

All information gathered by any agency, entity, or individual conducting programs in family planning is private data on individuals within the meaning of section 13.02, subdivision 12.

7. A grant recipient shall inform any person requesting counseling on family planning methods or procedures of:

(1) Any methods or procedures which may be followed, including identification of any which are experimental or any which may pose a health hazard to the person;

(2) A description of any attendant discomforts or risks which might reasonably be expected;

(3) A fair explanation of the likely results, should a method fail;

(4) A description of any benefits which might reasonably be expected of any method;

(5) A disclosure of appropriate alternative methods or procedures;

(6) An offer to answer any inquiries concerning methods of procedures; and

(7) An instruction that the person is free either to decline commencement of any method or procedure or to withdraw consent to a method or procedure at any reasonable time.

8. Any person who receives compensation for services under any program receiving financial assistance under this section, who coerces or endeavors to coerce any person to undergo an abortion or sterilization procedure by threatening the person with the loss of or disqualification for the receipt of any benefit or service under a program receiving state or federal financial assistance shall be guilty of a misdemeanor.

9. Notwithstanding any rules to the contrary, including rules proposed in the State Register on April 1, 1991, the commissioner, in allocating grant funds for family planning special projects, shall not limit the total amount of funds that can be allocated to an organization. The commissioner shall allocate to an organization receiving grant funds on July 1, 1997, at least the same amount of grant funds for the 1998 to 1999 grant cycle as the organization received for the 1996 to 1997 grant cycle, provided the organization submits an application that meets grant funding criteria. This subdivision does not affect any procedure established in rule for allocating special project money to the different regions. The commissioner shall revise the rules for family planning special project grants so that they conform to the requirements of this subdivision. In adopting these revisions, the commissioner is not subject to the rulemaking provisions of chapter 14, but is bound by section 14.386, paragraph (a), clauses (1) and (3). Section 14.386, paragraph (b), does not apply to these rules.

(12) INFORMED CONSENT

The laws of Minnesota set out guidelines for informed consent abortions. Prior to a physician performing an abortion, Minnesota requires that a woman be fully informed of the procedure to be used, the risks involved and alternatives to abortion. An abortion may not take place until 24 hours after a woman has given her written consent to an abortion. The state permits a civil lawsuit for failure to comply with the informed consent laws. The statutes are set out below.

Minnesota Code § 145.4241. Definitions

1. As used in sections 145.4241 to 145.4249, the following terms have the meaning given them.

2. "Abortion" means the use or prescription of any instrument, medicine, drug, or any other substance or device to intentionally terminate the pregnancy of a female known to be pregnant, with an intention other than to increase the probability of a live birth, to preserve the life or health of the child after live birth, or to remove a dead fetus.

3. "Attempt to perform an abortion" means an act, or an omission of a statutorily required act, that, under the circumstances as the actor believes them to be, constitutes a substantial step in a course of conduct planned to culminate in the performance of an abortion in Minnesota in violation of sections 145.4241 to 145.4249.

3a. "Fetal anomaly incompatible with life" means a fetal anomaly diagnosed before birth that will with reasonable certainty result in death of the unborn child within three months. Fetal anomaly incompatible with life does not include conditions which can be treated.

4. "Medical emergency" means any condition that, on the basis of the physician's good faith clinical judgment, so complicates the medical condition of a pregnant female as to necessitate the immediate abortion of her pregnancy to avert her death or for which a delay will create serious risk of substantial and irreversible impairment of a major bodily function.

4a. (a) "Perinatal hospice" means comprehensive support to the female and her family that includes support from the time of diagnosis through the time of birth and death of the infant and through the postpartum period. Supportive care may include maternal-fetal medical specialists, obstetricians, neonatologists, anesthesia specialists, clergy, social workers, and specialty nurses.

(b) The availability of perinatal hospice provides an alternative to families for whom elective pregnancy termination is not chosen.

5. "Physician" means a person licensed as a physician or osteopath under chapter 147.

6. "Probable gestational age of the unborn child" means what will, in the judgment of the physician, with reasonable probability, be the gestational age of the unborn child at the time the abortion is planned to be performed.

7. "Stable Internet Web site" means a Web site that, to the extent reasonably practicable, is safeguarded from having its content altered other than by the commissioner of health.

8. "Unborn child" means a member of the species Homo sapiens from fertilization until birth.

Minnesota Code § 145.4242. Informed consent

(a) No abortion shall be performed in this state except with the voluntary and informed consent of the female upon whom the abortion is to be performed. Except in the case of a medical emergency or if the fetus has an anomaly incompatible with life, and the female has declined perinatal hospice care, consent to an abortion is voluntary and informed only if:

(1) the female is told the following, by telephone or in person, by the physician who is to perform the abortion or by a referring physician, at least 24 hours before the abortion:

(i) the particular medical risks associated with the particular abortion procedure to be employed including, when medically accurate, the risks of infection, hemorrhage, breast cancer, danger to subsequent pregnancies, and infertility;

(ii) the probable gestational age of the unborn child at the time the abortion is to be performed;

(iii) the medical risks associated with carrying her child to term; and

(iv) for abortions after 20 weeks gestational, whether or not an anesthetic or analgesic would eliminate or alleviate organic pain to the unborn child caused by the particular method of abortion to be employed and the particular medical benefits and risks associated with the particular anesthetic or analgesic.

The information required by this clause may be provided by telephone without conducting a physical examination or tests of the patient, in which case the information required to be provided may be based on facts supplied to the physician by the female and whatever other relevant information is reasonably available to the physician. It may not be provided by a tape recording, but must be provided during a consultation in which the physician is able to ask questions of the female and the female is able to ask questions of the physician. If a physical examination, tests, or the availability of other information to the physician subsequently indicate, in the medical judgment of the physician, a revision of the information previously supplied to the patient, that revised information may be communicated to the patient at any time prior to the performance of the abortion. Nothing in this section may be construed to preclude provision of required information in a language understood by the patient through a translator;

(2) the female is informed, by telephone or in person, by the physician who is to perform the abortion, by a referring physician, or by an agent of either physician at least 24 hours before the abortion:

(i) that medical assistance benefits may be available for prenatal care, childbirth, and neonatal care;

(ii) that the father is liable to assist in the support of her child, even in instances when the father has offered to pay for the abortion; and

(iii) that she has the right to review the printed materials described in section 145.4243, that these materials are available on a state-sponsored Web site, and what the Web site address is. The physician or the physician's agent shall orally inform the female that the materials have been provided by the state of Minnesota and that they describe the unborn child, list agencies that offer alternatives to abortion, and contain information on fetal pain. If the female chooses to view the materials other than on the Web site, they shall either be given to her at least 24 hours before the abortion or mailed to her at least 72 hours before the abortion by certified mail, restricted delivery to addressee, which means the postal employee can only deliver the mail to the addressee.

The information required by this clause may be provided by a tape recording if provision is made to record or otherwise register specifically whether the female does or does not choose to have the printed materials given or mailed to her;

(3) the female certifies in writing, prior to the abortion, that the information described in clauses (1) and (2) has been furnished to her and that she has been informed of her opportunity to review the information referred to in clause (2), subclause (iii); and

(4) prior to the performance of the abortion, the physician who is to perform the abortion or the physician's agent obtains a copy of the written certification prescribed by clause (3) and retains it on file with the female's medical record for at least three years following the date of receipt.

(b) Prior to administering the anesthetic or analgesic as described in paragraph (a), clause (1), item (iv), the physician must disclose to the woman any additional cost of the procedure for the administration of the anesthetic or analgesic. If the woman consents to the administration of the anesthetic or analgesic, the physician shall administer the anesthetic or analgesic or arrange to have the anesthetic or analgesic administered.

(c) A female seeking an abortion of her unborn child diagnosed with fetal anomaly incompatible with life must be informed of available perinatal hospice services and offered this care as an alternative to abortion. If perinatal hospice services are declined, voluntary and informed consent by the female seeking an abortion is given if the female receives the information required in paragraphs (a), clause (1), and (b). The female must comply with the requirements in paragraph (a), clauses (3) and (4).

Minnesota Code § 145.4243. Printed information

(a) Within 90 days after July 1, 2003, the commissioner of health shall cause to be published, in English and in each language that is the primary language of two percent or more of the state's population, and shall cause to be available on the state Web site provided for under section 145.4244 the following printed materials in such a way as to ensure that the information is easily comprehensible:

(1) geographically indexed materials designed to inform the female of public and private agencies and services available to assist a female through pregnancy, upon childbirth, and while the child is dependent, including adoption agencies, which shall include a comprehensive list of the agencies available, a description of the services they offer, and a description of the manner, including telephone numbers, in which they might be contacted or, at the option of the commissioner of health, printed materials including a toll-free, 24-hours-a-day telephone number that may be called to obtain, orally or by a tape recorded message tailored to a zip code entered by the caller, such a list and description of agencies in the locality of the caller and of the services they offer;

(2) materials designed to inform the female of the probable anatomical and physiological characteristics of the unborn child at two-week gestational increments from the time when a female can be known to be pregnant to full term, including any relevant information on the possibility of the unborn child's survival and pictures or drawings representing the development of unborn children at two-week gestational increments, provided that any such pictures or drawings must contain the dimensions of the fetus and must be realistic and appropriate for the stage of pregnancy depicted. The materials shall be objective, nonjudgmental, and designed to convey only accurate scientific information about the unborn child at the various gestational ages. The material shall also contain objective information describing the methods of abortion procedures commonly employed, the medical risks commonly associated with each procedure, the possible detrimental psychological effects of abortion, and the medical risks commonly associated with carrying a child to term; and

(3) materials with the following information concerning an unborn child of 20 weeks gestational age and at two weeks gestational increments thereafter in such a way as to ensure that the information is easily comprehensible:

(i) the development of the nervous system of the unborn child;

(ii) fetal responsiveness to adverse stimuli and other indications of capacity to experience organic pain; and

(iii) the impact on fetal organic pain of each of the methods of abortion procedures commonly employed at this stage of pregnancy.

The material under this clause shall be objective, nonjudgmental, and designed to convey only accurate scientific information.

(b) The materials referred to in this section must be printed in a typeface large enough to be clearly legible. The Web site provided for under section 145.4244 shall be maintained at a minimum resolution of 70 DPI (dots per inch). All pictures appearing on the Web site shall be a minimum of 200x300 pixels. All letters on the Web site shall be a minimum of 11-point font. All information and pictures shall be accessible with an industry standard browser, requiring no additional plug-ins. The mate-

rials required under this section must be available at no cost from the commissioner of health upon request and in appropriate number to any person, facility, or hospital.

Minnesota Code § 145.4244. Internet Web site

The commissioner of health shall develop and maintain a stable Internet Web site to provide the information described under section 145.4243. No information regarding who uses the Web site shall be collected or maintained. The commissioner of health shall monitor the Web site on a weekly basis to prevent and correct tampering.

Minnesota Code § 145.4245.
Procedure in case of medical emergency

When a medical emergency compels the performance of an abortion, the physician shall inform the female, prior to the abortion if possible, of the medical indications supporting the physician's judgment that an abortion is necessary to avert her death or that a 24-hour delay will create serious risk of substantial and irreversible impairment of a major bodily function.

Minnesota Code § 145.4246. Reporting requirements

1. Within 90 days after July 1, 2003, the commissioner of health shall prepare a reporting form for physicians containing a reprint of sections 145.4241 to 145.4249 and listing:

(1) the number of females to whom the physician provided the information described in section 145.4242, clause (1); of that number, the number provided by telephone and the number provided in person; and of each of those numbers, the number provided in the capacity of a referring physician and the number provided in the capacity of a physician who is to perform the abortion;

(2) the number of females to whom the physician or an agent of the physician provided the information described in section 145.4242, clause (2); of that number, the number provided by telephone and the number provided in person; of each of those numbers, the number provided in the capacity of a referring physician and the number provided in the capacity of a physician who is to perform the abortion; and of each of those numbers, the number provided by the physician and the number provided by an agent of the physician;

(3) the number of females who availed themselves of the opportunity to obtain a copy of the printed information described in section 145.4243 other than on the Web site and the number who did not; and of each of those numbers, the number who, to the best of the reporting physician's information and belief, went on to obtain the abortion; and

(4) the number of abortions performed by the physician in which information otherwise required to be provided at least 24 hours before the abortion was not so provided because an immediate abortion was necessary to avert the female's death and the number of abortions in which such information was not so provided because a delay would create serious risk of substantial and irreversible impairment of a major bodily function.

2. The commissioner of health shall ensure that copies of the reporting forms described in subdivision 1 are provided:

(1) by December 1, 2003, and by December 1 of each subsequent year thereafter to all physicians licensed to practice in this state; and

(2) to each physician who subsequently becomes newly licensed to practice in this state, at the same time as official notification to that physician that the physician is so licensed.

3. By April 1, 2005, and by April 1 of each subsequent year thereafter, each physician who provided, or whose agent provided, information to one or more females in accordance with section 145.4242 during the previous calendar year shall submit to the commissioner of health a copy of the form described in subdivision 1 with the requested data entered accurately and completely.

4. Nothing in this section shall be construed to preclude the voluntary or required submission of other reports or forms regarding abortions.

5. Reports that are not submitted by the end of a grace period of 30 days following the due date shall be subject to a late fee of $500 for each additional 30-day period or portion of a 30-day period they are overdue. Any physician required to report according to this section who has not submitted a report, or has submitted only an incomplete report, more than one year following the due date, may, in an action brought by the commissioner of health, be directed by a court of competent jurisdiction to submit a complete report within a period stated by court order or be subject to sanctions for civil contempt.

6. By July 1, 2005, and by July 1 of each subsequent year thereafter, the commissioner of health shall issue a public report providing statistics for the previous calendar year compiled from all of the reports covering that year submitted according to this section for each of the items listed in subdivision 1. Each report shall also provide the statistics for all previous calendar years, adjusted to reflect any additional information from late or corrected reports. The commissioner of health shall take care to ensure that none of the information included in the public reports could reasonably lead to the identification of any individual providing or provided information according to section 145.4242.

7. The commissioner of health may consolidate the forms or reports described in this section with other forms or reports to achieve administrative convenience or fiscal savings or to reduce the burden of reporting requirements.

Minnesota Code § 145.4247. Remedies

1. Any person upon whom an abortion has been performed without complying with sections 145.4241 to 145.4249 may maintain an action against the person who performed the abortion in knowing or reckless violation of sections 145.4241 to 145.4249 for actual and punitive damages. Any person upon whom an abortion has been attempted without complying with sections 145.4241 to 145.4249 may maintain an action against the person who attempted to perform the abortion in knowing or reckless violation of sections 145.4241 to 145.4249 for actual and punitive damages. No civil liability may be assessed for failure to comply with section 145.4242, clause (2), item (iii), or that portion of section 145.4242, clause (2), requiring written certification that the female has been informed of her opportunity to review the information referred to in section 145.4242, clause (2), item (iii), unless the commissioner of health has made the printed materials or Web site address available at the time the physician or the physician's agent is required to inform the female of her right to review them.

2. If the commissioner of health fails to issue the public report required under section 145.4246, subdivision 6, or fails in any way to enforce Laws 2003, chapter 14, any group of ten or more citizens of this state may seek an injunction in a court of competent jurisdiction against the commissioner of health requiring that a complete report be issued within a period stated by court order. Failure to abide by such an injunction shall subject the commissioner to sanctions for civil contempt.

3. If judgment is rendered in favor of the plaintiff in any action described in this section, the court shall also render judgment for reasonable attorney fees in favor of the plaintiff against the defendant. If judgment is rendered in favor of the defendant and the court finds that the plaintiff's suit was frivolous and brought in bad faith, the court shall also render judgment for reasonable attorney fees in favor of the defendant against the plaintiff.

4. In every civil action brought under sections 145.4241 to 145.4249, the court shall rule whether the anonymity of any female upon whom an abortion has been performed or attempted shall be preserved from public disclosure if she does not give her consent to such disclosure. The court, upon motion or sua sponte, shall make such a ruling and, upon determining that her anonymity should be preserved, shall issue orders to the parties, witnesses, and counsel and shall direct the sealing of the record and exclusion of individuals from courtrooms or hearing rooms to the extent necessary to safeguard her identity from public disclosure. Each order must be accompanied by specific written findings explaining why the anonymity of the female should be preserved from public disclosure, why the order is essential to that end, how the order is narrowly tailored to serve that interest, and why no reasonable, less restrictive alternative exists. In the absence of written consent of the female upon whom an abortion has been performed or attempted, anyone, other than a public official, who brings an action under subdivision 1, shall do so under a pseudonym. This section may not be construed to conceal the identity of the plaintiff or of witnesses from the defendant.

Minnesota Code § 145.4248. Severability

If any one or more provision, section, subsection, sentence, clause, phrase, or word of sections 145.4241 to 145.4249 or the application thereof to any person or circumstance is found to be unconstitutional, the same is hereby declared to be severable and the balance of sections 145.4241 to 145.4249 shall remain effective notwithstanding such unconstitutionality. The legislature hereby declares that it would have passed sections 145.4241 to 145.4249, and each provision, section, subsection, sentence, clause, phrase, or word thereof, irrespective of the fact that any one or more provision, section, subsection, sentence, clause, phrase, or word be declared unconstitutional.

Minnesota Code § 145.4249. Supreme Court jurisdiction

The Minnesota Supreme Court has original jurisdiction over an action challenging the constitutionality of sections 145.4241 to 145.4249 and shall expedite the resolution of the action.

(13) SEXUAL ASSAULT

Minnesota requires that all sexual assault victims be informed of and, if requested, provided with emergency contraceptives. The statutes addressing the matter are set out below.

Minnesota Code § 145.4711. Definitions

1. For purposes of sections 145.4711 to 145.4713, the following definitions apply.

2. "Commissioner" means the commissioner of health.

3. "Emergency care to sexual assault victims" means medical examinations, procedures, and services provided at a hospital to a sexual assault victim following an alleged sexual assault.

4. "Emergency contraception" means a drug, drug regimen, or device approved by the federal Food and Drug Administration to prevent pregnancy when administered after sexual contact, including prescription and over-the-counter hormonal emergency contraception and intrauterine devices.

5. "Sexual assault" means criminal sexual conduct in the first degree under section 609.342, criminal sexual conduct in the second degree under section 609.343, criminal sexual conduct in the third degree under section 609.344, criminal sexual conduct in the fourth degree under section 609.345, or incest under section 609.365.

6. "Sexual assault victim" means a woman or man who alleges, or is alleged to have been, sexually assaulted and who presents at a hospital as a patient.

Minnesota Code § 145.4712.
Emergency care to sexual assault victims

1. (a) It shall be the standard of care for all hospitals that provide emergency care to, at a minimum:

(1) provide each female sexual assault victim with medically and factually accurate and unbiased written and oral information about emergency contraception from the American College of Obstetricians and Gynecologists and distributed to all hospitals by the Department of Health;

(2) orally inform each female sexual assault victim of the option of being provided with emergency contraception at the hospital; and

(3) immediately provide emergency contraception to each sexual assault victim who requests it provided it is not medically contraindicated and is ordered by a legal prescriber. Emergency contraception shall be administered in accordance with current medical protocols regarding timing and dosage necessary to complete the treatment.

(b) A hospital may administer a pregnancy test. If the pregnancy test is positive, the hospital does not have to comply with the provisions in paragraph (a).

2. It shall be the standard of care for all hospitals that provide emergency care to, at a minimum:

(1) provide each sexual assault victim with factually accurate and unbiased written and oral medical information about prophylactic antibiotics for treatment of sexually transmitted diseases;

(2) orally inform each sexual assault victim of the option of being provided prophylactic antibiotics for treatment of sexually transmitted diseases at the hospital; and

(3) immediately provide prophylactic antibiotics for treatment of sexually transmitted diseases to each sexual assault victim who requests it, provided it is not medically contraindicated and is ordered by a legal prescriber.

Minnesota Code § 145.4713. Complaints

The commissioner shall accept and investigate complaints regarding hospital compliance with section 145.4712. The commissioner shall periodically determine whether hospitals are in compliance with section 145.4712. Failure to comply with section 145.4712 may be grounds for the suspension or revocation of a hospital's license under section 144.55, subdivision 6.

(14) PUBLIC FUNDS FOR ABORTION

Minnesota has several statutes that prohibit public funds from being used to pay for elective abortions. The statutes banning such use were held invalid in *Women of State of Minn. v. Gomez*, 542 N.W.2d 17 Minn. 1995). The state also has a statute prohibiting public funds in a specific health program from being used for elective abortions, except in limited circumstances. The statutes are set out below.

Minnesota Code § 256B.40. Subsidy for abortions prohibited

No medical assistance funds of this state or any agency, county, municipality or any other subdivision thereof and no federal funds passing through the state treasury or the state agency shall be authorized or paid pursuant to this chapter to any person or entity for or in connection with any abortion that is not eligible for funding pursuant to sections 256B.02, subdivision 8, and 256B.0625.

Minnesota Code § 261.28. Subsidy for abortions prohibited

No funds of this state or any subdivision thereof administered under this chapter shall be authorized for or in connection with any abortion that is not eligible for funding pursuant to sections 256B.02, subdivision 8, and 256B.0625.

Minnesota Code § 393.07(11) Local social service agencies

In keeping with the public policy of Minnesota to give preference to childbirth over abortion, Minnesota local social services agencies shall not provide any medical assistance grant or reimbursement for any abortion not eligible for funding pursuant to sections 256B.02, subdivision 8, and 256B.0625.

Minnesota Code § 256L.03. Covered health services (abridged)

1. "Covered health services" means the health services reimbursed under chapter 256B, with the exception of inpatient hospital services, special education services, private duty nursing services, adult dental care services other than services covered under section 256B.0625, subdivision 9, orthodontic services, nonemergency medical transportation services, personal care assistant and case management services, nursing home or intermediate care facilities services, inpatient mental health services, and chemical dependency services.

No public funds shall be used for coverage of abortion under MinnesotaCare except where the life of the female would be endangered or substantial and irreversible impairment of a major bodily function would result if the fetus were carried to term; or where the pregnancy is the result of rape or incest.

Covered health services shall be expanded as provided in this section.

1a. Beginning January 1, 1999, children and pregnant women are eligible for coverage of all services that are eligible for reimbursement under the medical assistance program according to chapter 256B, except that abortion services under MinnesotaCare shall be limited as provided under subdivision 1. Pregnant women and children are exempt from the provisions of subdivision 5, regarding co-payments. Pregnant women and children who are lawfully residing in the United States but who are not "qualified noncitizens" under title IV of the Personal Responsibility and Work Opportunity Reconciliation Act of 1996, Public Law 104-193, Statutes at Large, volume 110, page 2105, are eligible for coverage of all services provided under the medical assistance program according to chapter 256B.

Minnesota Citizens Concerned for Life

Minnesota Citizens Concerned for Life (MCCL) is a pro-life organization that was founded in 1968, for the purpose of preventing the state from modifying its ban on abortion. The president of MCCL is Scott Fischbach. MCCL has subsequently fought to overturn legalization of abortion by the United States Supreme Court. MCCL is the largest pro-life organization in the state of Minnesota. The organization engages in activities to educate the public on issues relating to pregnancy and abortion. *See also* **Pro-Life Organizations**

Scott Fischbach is president of Minnesota Citizens Concerned for Life, a pro-life organization founded in 1968 (Scott Fischbach).

Minors and Abortion

The majority of states provide special statutes concerning the right of a pregnant female minor to have an abortion. A female minor is generally defined as being under 18 years of age and unemancipated by marriage. The United States Supreme Court has held that states may impose a requirement that pregnant female minors obtain consent from a one or both parents, or lawful guardian, before being permitted to have an abortion; provided that when such a requirement is imposed, the state must also provide for judicial bypass. Judicial bypass refers to authorization to have an abortion by an order of a court.

Case law. In *Hodgson v. Minnesota* the Supreme Court upheld the constitutionality of Minnesota's 48 hour waiting period for an abortion by minors. In *City of Akron v. Akron Center for Reproductive Health, Inc.* the Supreme Court invalidated a parental notice, consent

Pregnancy Outcome for Teenagers 15–19 for Selected Years U.S.

	Year				
Pregnancy Outcome	*1990*	*1995*	*2000*	*2002*	*Total*
Live birth	522,000	500,000	469,000	425,000	1,916,000
Induced abortion	351,000	263,000	235,000	215,000	1,064,000
Spontaneous abortion	145,000	140,000	129,000	117,000	531,000

Source: **National Center for Health Statistics.**

State Statutory Restrictions on Abortion for Minors

State	*Parental consent*	*Parental notice*	*Waiting period*	*Judicial bypass*	*Health exception*	*Lawsuit for violation*
Ala.	X			X	X	X
Alaska	X			X	X	X
Ariz.	X			X	X	
Ark.	X			X	X	
Cal.	X			X		
Colo.		X	48 hours	X	X	X
Conn.						
Del.		X	24 hours	X	X	X
D.C.						
Fla.		X	48 hours	X	X	
Ga.		X	24 hours	X	X	X
Haw.						
Idaho	X			X	X	
Ill.		X	48 hours	X	X	
Ind.	X			X	X	
Iowa		X	48 hours	X	X	
Kan.		X		X	X	
Ky.	X			X	X	X
La.	X			X	X	
Maine	X			X	X	
Md.		X			X	
Mass.	X			X		
Mich.	X			X	X	X
Minn.		X	48 hours	X	X	
Miss.	X			X	X	
Mo.	X			X	X	X
Mont.		X	48 hours	X	X	X
Neb.		X	48 hours	X	X	X
Nev.		X		X	X	
N.H.						
N.J.		X	48 hours	X	X	X
N.M.						
N.Y.						
N.C.	X			X		
N.D.	X		24 hours	X	X	X
*Ohio	X			X	X	X
Okla.	X		48 hours	X	X	X
Ore.						
Penn.	X			X	X	X
R.I.	X			X	X	
S.C.	X			X	X	X
S.D.		X	48 hours	X	X	
Tenn.	X			X	X	X
Tex.		X	48 hours	X	X	
Utah	X	X	24 hours	X	X	
Vt.						
Va.	X	X	24 hours	X	X	
Wash.						
W.Va.		X	24 hours	X	X	
Wis.	X			X	X	X
Wyo.	X		48 hours	X	X	

***Ohio has a notice and 24 hour waiting requirement if its consent requirement is ever found invalid.**

and judicial bypass ordinance for pregnant female minors. However, the Supreme Court subsequently reversed its position on this issue. In *Ohio v. Akron Center for Reproductive Health* and *Planned Parenthood Assn. v. Ashcroft*, the Supreme Court upheld the constitutionality of parental notice, consent and judicial bypass requirements for pregnant female minors. In *H. L. v. Matheson* the Supreme Court held that the constitution was not violated by Utah's requirement that the parents of a minor be notified, if possible, prior to performing an abortion. The Utah statute was distinguished because it did not require parental consent. The Supreme Court invalidated a provision in Missouri's statute, in *Planned Parenthood of Missouri v. Danforth*, that required parental consent, but did not provide for judicial bypass.

In *Bellotti v. Baird II* the Supreme Court held that Massachusetts' abortion statute for minors violated the constitution in light of an interpretation given by the state's highest court, that required parental notice of a judicial bypass proceeding invoked by a minor, and permitted a judge to deny an abortion even though the minor proved she had enough maturity to make an independent decision. The Supreme Court held in *Lambert v. Wicklund* that the constitution was not violated by a provision in Montana's abortion statute that allowed a court to waive the parental notice requirement for minors, if notification was not in minor's best interest.

In *Ayotte v. Planned Parenthood of Northern New England* abortion providers filed a lawsuit in a federal district court seeking to prohibit enforcement of New Hampshire's parental notification statute. The plaintiffs alleged that the statute was unconstitutional, because it failed to permit a physician to promptly provide an abortion to a minor whose health may be at risk by a delay in complying with the notification requirement. The district court agreed and declared the statute unconstitutional in its entirety. The United States Supreme Court agreed that the statute was invalid in part, but did not believe that it should have been struck down in its entirety. The Supreme Court vacated the decision and remanded the case for a less drastic remedy to be imposed. *See also* **Ayotte v. Planned Parenthood of Northern New England; Bellotti v. Baird II; City of Akron v. Akron Center for Reproductive Health, Inc.; H. L. v. Matheson; Hodgson v. Minnesota; Lambert v. Wicklund; Ohio v. Akron Center for Reproductive Health; Planned Parenthood Assn. v. Ashcroft; Planned Parenthood of Southeastern Pennsylvania v. Casey**

Miscarriage

A miscarriage (also called spontaneous abortion) refers to a pregnancy loss that occurs prior to 20 weeks of gestation. Most miscarriages, roughly 80 percent, occur during the first 13 weeks of pregnancy. It is estimated that up to 50 percent of all fertilized eggs die and are aborted spontaneously, usually before the woman knows she is pregnant. Among known pregnancies, the rate of spontaneous abortion is approximately 15 percent. After a spontaneous abortion the dead tissue is usually discarded naturally from the uterus over a period of days. Although the causes of all miscarriages are not fully known, there are some known factors associated with this: fetal chromosomal abnormalities (caused by a defective egg or sperm cell), problems with the uterus or cervix, infections, immune system problems, alcohol, cigarettes, and caffeine.

Miscarriage is viewed in several stages or types that include: threatened abortion, inevitable abortion, incomplete abortion, missed abortion, complete abortion and habitual abortion.

Threatened abortion. A threatened abortion is a condition of pregnancy, occurring before the 20th week of gestation, that indicates a miscarriage may occur. Symptoms of the condition involve some vaginal bleeding, with or without abdominal cramping. Approximately 20 percent of pregnant women have this experience. However, in most instances the pregnancies go on to term with or without treatment. A miscarriage occurs in less than 30 percent of the women who experience vaginal bleeding during pregnancy. Treatment for the condition may include recommending abstaining from intercourse until symptoms resolve and mild sedatives such as flurazepam may be prescribed.

Inevitable abortion. An inevitable abortion occurs when a woman experiences cramping and bleeding that will not stop, or there is a rupture of the membranes accompanied by pain and dilation of the cervix. When these conditions are present, spontaneous expulsion of the fetal and placental material will occur.

Incomplete abortion. An incomplete abortion is a condition in which a portion of the fetal or placental material is retained within the uterus after a spontaneous abortion. The usual symptoms of this condition include vaginal bleeding and lower abdominal cramping. Usually an incomplete abortion will require surgical intervention to remove the remaining material from the uterus, and to prevent prolonged bleeding or infection.

Missed abortion. A missed abortion involves an intrauterine death of a fetus that is not followed by the natural expulsion of the fetus. When this occurs, frequently labor must be induced to remove the dead fetus and other tissue.

Complete abortion. A complete abortion refers to a spontaneous abortion wherein the uterus does not contain the fetus or placental tissues.

Habitual abortion. Habitual abortion refers to the spontaneous loss (miscarriage) of 3 or more consecutive pregnancies. Up to 5 percent of couples have two consecutive miscarriages and about 1 percent of couples have three consecutive miscarriages. Habitual abortion is viewed as a form of infertility. Couples who have had two or more miscarriages have about a 5 percent chance that one member of the couple has a chromosome defect that is contributing to the miscarriages. *See also* **Abortion; Blighted Ovum; High-Risk Pregnancy; Luteal Phase Defect; Stillbirth**

Misoprostol *see* **Methotrexate Induced Abortion; Mifepristone Induced Abortion**

Missed Abortion *see* **Miscarriage**

Missionaries to the Preborn

Missionaries to the Preborn is a pro-life organization that was founded in 1990 in Milwaukee, Wisconsin by Rev. Matt Trewhella. Rev. Trewhella is also Pastor of Mercy Seat Christian Church. He was born August 19, 1960 in Detroit, Michigan, and educated at the Valley Forge Christian College. Rev. Trewhella has spent 14 months in jails across the country for protesting non-violently against abortion. He founded the Missionaries to the Preborn as a vehicle to express opposition to abortion in Milwaukee. Since the mission began, six of the eight abortion clinics in Milwaukee closed down. *See also* **Pro-Life Organizations**

Mississippi

(1) OVERVIEW

The state of Mississippi enacted its first criminal abortion statute on February 15, 1839. The statute underwent several amendments prior to the 1973 decision by the United States Supreme Court in *Roe v. Wade*, which legalized abortion in the nation. In spite of the decision in *Roe*, Mississippi has not repealed its pre–*Roe* criminal abortion laws. However, the laws are constitutionally infirm.

Mississippi has taken affirmative steps to respond to *Roe* and its progeny. The state has addressed numerous abortion issues by statute that include general abortion guidelines, informed consent, partial-birth abortion, abortion by minors, injury to a pregnant woman, abortion complication reports, use of public funds, providing contraceptives, abortion facilities, and Choose Life license plates.

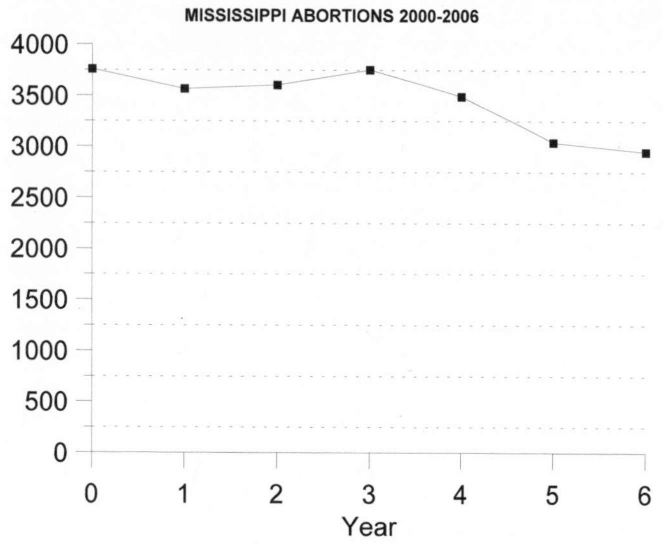

Source: Mississippi Department of Health.

Mississippi Abortion by Age Group 2000–2006

Year	Age Group (yrs) <15	15–19	20–24	25–29	30–34	35–39	≥40	Unknown
2000	49	756	1,400	811	407	245	83	7
2001	38	633	1,326	839	426	224	76	4
2002	35	645	1,313	811	447	244	104	6
2003	42	648	1,474	822	478	205	77	7
2004	46	577	1,370	781	440	196	76	7
2005	35	469	1,144	760	397	162	69	4
2006	17	450	1,115	735	381	192	57	2
Total	262	4,178	9,142	5,559	2,976	1,468	542	37

Source: Mississippi Department of Health.

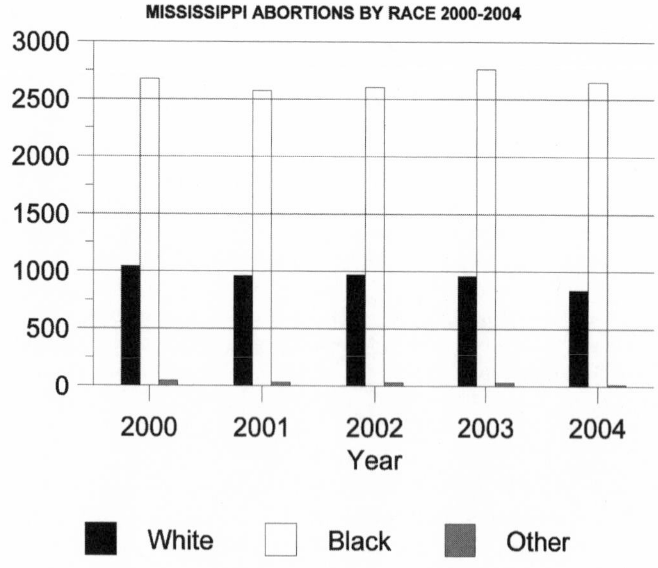

Source: National Center for Health Statistics.

(2) PRE-ROE ABORTION BAN

As previously indicated, Mississippi has not repealed its pre–*Roe* criminal abortion laws. The laws remain on the books even though several provisions in the laws were invalidated in *Spears v. State*, 278 So.2d 443 (Miss. 1973). Under those laws, abortion was criminalized if it was not performed to preserve the life or the pregnancy resulted from rape. The state also imposed criminal sanctions against anyone who distributed any drug, medicine, or device that cased an unlawful abortion. The statutes are set out below.

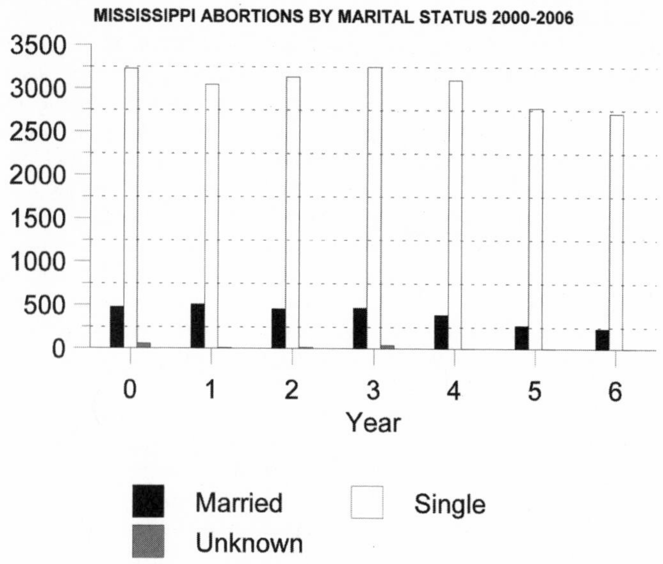

Source: Mississippi Department of Health.

Mississippi Abortion by Education Level of Female 2000–2006

Year	Education Level Completed <7	7–9	10–11	12	≥13	Unknown
2000	27	172	400	1,022	2,026	111
2001	20	125	337	1,112	1,916	56
2002	8	123	353	1,086	1,972	63
2003	25	140	362	1,052	2,115	57
2004	8	106	310	1,089	1,919	61
2005	2	76	233	1,060	1,634	36
2006	5	64	246	990	1,631	13
Total	95	806	2,241	7,411	13,213	397

Source: Mississippi Department of Health.

Mississippi Prior Abortion by Female 2000–2006

Year	Prior Abortion None	1	2	≥3	Not known
2000	2,594	865	231	62	6
2001	2,301	961	233	69	2
2002	2,361	899	272	72	1
2003	2,483	912	269	87	2
2004	2,201	912	301	79	0
2005	1,951	800	233	57	0
2006	1,854	806	228	60	1
Total	15,745	6,155	1,767	486	12

Source: Mississippi Department of Health.

Mississippi Code § 97-3-3. Criminal abortion

(1) Any person wilfully and knowingly causing, by means of any instrument, medicine, drug or other means whatever, any woman pregnant with child to abort or miscarry, or attempts to procure or produce an abortion or miscarriage shall be guilty of a felony unless the same were done by a duly licensed, practicing physician:

(a) Where necessary for the preservation of the mother's life;

(b) Where pregnancy was caused by rape.

Said person shall, upon conviction, be imprisoned in the State Penitentiary not less than one (1) year nor more than ten (10) years; pro-

Mississippi Abortion by Weeks of Gestation 2000–2006

Weeks of Gestation	Year 2000	2001	2002	2003	2004	2005	2006	Total
<9	1,951	1,805	1,844	2,005	1,772	1,443	1,542	12,362
9–10	837	792	760	819	805	587	585	5,185
11–12	533	501	501	491	416	274	236	2,952
13–15	356	321	292	298	262	182	67	1,778
16–20	44	48	37	21	49	21	15	235
≥21	7	8	2	1	2	2	1	23
Not known	30	91	169	118	187	532	503	1,630

Source: Mississippi Department of Health.

vided, however, if the death of the mother results therefrom, the person procuring, causing or attempting to procure or cause the illegal abortion or miscarriage shall be guilty of murder.

(2) No act prohibited in subsection (1) of this section shall be considered exempt under the provisions of subparagraph (a) thereof unless performed upon the prior advice in writing, of two (2) reputable licensed physicians.

(3) The license of any physician or nurse shall be automatically revoked upon conviction under the provisions of this section.

(4) Nothing in this section shall be construed as conflicting with § 41-41-73.

Mississippi Code § 97-3-5. Helping to obtain abortion

A person who sells, lends, gives away, or in any manner exhibits, or offers to sell, lend, or give away, or has in his possession with intent to sell, lend, or give away, or advertises or offers for sale, loan or distribution any instrument or article, or any drug or medicine, for causing unlawful abortion; or who writes or prints, or causes to be written or printed, a card, circular, pamphlet, advertisement, or notice of any kind, or gives information orally, stating when, where, how, of whom, or by what means such article or medicine can be purchased or obtained, or who manufactures any such article or medicine, is guilty of a misdemeanor, and, on conviction, shall be punished by fine not less than twenty-five dollars ($25.00) nor more than two hundred dollars ($200.00), and by imprisonment in the county jail not exceeding three (3) months.

(3) GENERAL ABORTION GUIDELINES

Mississippi has enacted general abortion guidelines that include a requirement that an ultrasound be taken before an abortion may occur. The state has also enacted a statute which criminalizes abortion in the event the United States Supreme Court overturns *Roe v. Wade*. The statutes are set out below.

Mississippi Code § 41-41-31. Definitions

The following words and phrases shall have the meanings ascribed in this section unless the context clearly indicates otherwise:

(a) "Abortion" means the use or prescription of any instrument, medicine, drug or any other substance or device to terminate the pregnancy of a woman known to be pregnant with an intention other than to increase the probability of a live birth, to preserve the life or health of the child after live birth or to remove a dead fetus.

(b) "Medical emergency" means that condition which, on the basis of the physician's best clinical judgment, so complicates a pregnancy as to necessitate an immediate abortion to avert the death of the mother or for which a twenty-four-hour delay will create grave peril of immediate and irreversible loss of major bodily function.

(c) "Probable gestational age of the unborn child" means what, in the judgment of the attending physician, will with reasonable probability be the gestational age of the unborn child at the time the abortion is planned to be performed.

Mississippi Code § 41-41-32. [unofficial citation]
Abortion definition if Roe v. Wade *overturned*

(1) As used in this section, the term "abortion" means the use or prescription of any instrument, medicine, drug or any other substance or device to terminate the pregnancy of a woman known to be pregnant with an intention other than to increase the probability of a live birth, to preserve the life or health of the child after live birth or to remove a dead fetus.

(2) No abortion shall be performed or induced in the State of Mississippi, except in the case where necessary for the preservation of the mother's life or where the pregnancy was caused by rape.

(3) For the purposes of this act, rape shall be an exception to the prohibition for an abortion only if a formal charge of rape has been filed with an appropriate law enforcement official.

(4) Any person, except the pregnant woman, who purposefully, knowingly or recklessly performs or attempts to perform or induce an abortion in the State of Mississippi, except in the case where necessary for the preservation of the mother's life or where the pregnancy was caused by rape, upon conviction, shall be punished by imprisonment in the custody of the Department of Corrections for not less than one (1) year nor more than ten (10) years.

Mississippi Code § 41-41-34.
Abortion pre-procedure requirements

(1) Before the performance of an abortion, as defined in Section 2 of this act, the physician who is to perform the abortion, or a qualified person assisting the physician, shall:

(a) Perform fetal ultrasound imaging and auscultation of fetal heart tone services on the patient undergoing the abortion;

(b) Offer to provide the patient with an opportunity to view the active ultrasound image of the unborn child and hear the heartbeat of the unborn child if the heartbeat is audible;

(c) Offer to provide the patient with a physical picture of the ultrasound image of the unborn child;

(d) Obtain the patient's signature on a certification form stating that the patient has been given the opportunity to view the active ultrasound image and hear the heartbeat of the unborn child if the heartbeat is audible, and that she has been offered a physical picture of the ultrasound image; and

(e) Retain a copy of the signed certification form in the patient's medical record.

(2) The State Department of Health shall enforce the requirements of this section.

(3) An ultrasound image must be of a quality consistent with standard medical practice in the community, shall contain the dimensions of the unborn child and shall accurately portray the presence of external members and internal organs, if present or viewable, of the unborn child.

Mississippi Code § 41-41-36. [unofficial citation]
Constitutionality of abortion prohibition

At such time as the Attorney General of Mississippi determines that the United States Supreme Court has overruled the decision of Roe v. Wade, *410 U.S. 113 (1973), and that as a result, it is reasonably probable that Section 2 of this act would be upheld by the court as constitutional, the Attorney General shall publish his determination of that fact in the administrative bulletin published by the Secretary of State as provided in Section 25-43-2.101, Mississippi Code of 1972.*

Mississippi Code § 41-41-37. Emergency abortion

When a medical emergency compels the performance or induction of an abortion, the physician shall inform the woman, before the abortion if possible, of the medical indications supporting his judgment that an abortion is necessary to avert her death or for which a twenty-four-hour delay will create grave peril of immediate and irreversible loss of major bodily function.

Mississippi Code § 41-41-38. [unofficial citation] Severability

(1) If any provision of this act is found to be unconstitutional, the provision is severable; and the other provisions of this act remain effective, except as provided in other sections of this act.

(2) Nothing in this act may be construed to repeal, by implication or otherwise, any provision not explicitly repealed.

(3) If any provision of this act is ever declared unconstitutional or its enforcement temporarily or permanently restricted or enjoined by judicial order, the provisions of Sections 41-41-31 through 41-41-91, Mississippi Code of 1972, shall be enforced. However, if such temporary or permanent restraining order or injunction is subsequently stayed or dissolved or such declaration vacated or any similar court order otherwise ceases to have effect, all provisions of this act that are not declared unconstitutional or whose enforcement is not restrained shall have full force and effect.

(4) Nothing in the provisions of Sections 41-41-31 through 41-41-91, Mississippi Code of 1972, shall be construed to permit any action that is prohibited by Senate Bill No. 2391, 2007 Regular Session, and to the extent that any provision of Sections 41-41-31 through 41-41-91, Mississippi Code of 1972, would be so construed, then the provisions of Senate Bill No. 2391, 2007 Regular Session, shall take precedence.

Mississippi Code § 41-41-39. Penalties for violations

Anyone who purposefully, knowingly or recklessly performs or attempts to perform or induce an abortion without complying with Sections 41-41-31 through 41-41-37 shall, upon conviction, be guilty of a misdemeanor and shall be punished by a fine of One Thousand Dollars ($1,000.00), by imprisonment in the county jail for a period of time not to exceed six (6) months or both such fine and imprisonment.

(4) INFORMED CONSENT

Prior to an abortion Mississippi requires that a woman be fully informed of the procedure to be used, the risks involved and alternatives to abortion. An abortion may not take place until 24 hours after a woman has given her written consent to an abortion. The statutes addressing the matters are set out below.

Mississippi Code § 41-41-33. Consent and waiting period

(1) No abortion shall be performed or induced except with the voluntary and informed consent of the woman upon whom the abortion is to be performed or induced. Except in the case of a medical emergency, consent to an abortion is voluntary and informed if and only if:

(a) The woman is told the following by the physician who is to perform or induce the abortion or by the referring physician, orally and in person, at least twenty-four (24) hours before the abortion:

(i) The name of the physician who will perform or induce the abortion;

(ii) The particular medical risks associated with the particular abortion procedure to be employed including, when medically accurate, the risks of infection, hemorrhage and breast cancer, and the danger to subsequent pregnancies and infertility;

(iii) The probable gestational age of the unborn child at the time the abortion is to be performed or induced; and

(iv) The medical risks associated with carrying her child to term.

(b) The woman is informed, by the physician or his agent, orally and in person, at least twenty-four (24) hours before the abortion:

(i) That medical assistance benefits may be available for prenatal care, childbirth and neonatal care;

(ii) That the father is liable to assist in the support of her child, even in instances in which the father has offered to pay for the abortion;

(iii) That there are available services provided by public and private agencies which provide pregnancy prevention counseling and medical referrals for obtaining pregnancy prevention medications or devices; and

(iv) That she has the right to review the printed materials described in Section 41-41-35(1)(a), (b) and (c). The physician or his agent shall orally inform the woman that those materials have been provided by the State of Mississippi and that they describe the unborn child and list agencies that offer alternatives to abortion. If the woman chooses to view those materials, copies of them shall be furnished to her. The physician or his agent may disassociate himself or themselves from those materials, and may comment or refrain from comment on them as he chooses. The physician or his agent shall provide the woman with the printed materials described in Section 41-41-35(1)(d).

(c) The woman certifies in writing before the abortion that the information described in paragraphs (a) and (b) of this section has been furnished to her, and that she has been informed of her opportunity to review the information referred to in subparagraph (iv) of paragraph (b) of this section.

(d) Before the abortion is performed or induced, the physician who is to perform or induce the abortion receives a copy of the written certification prescribed by this section.

(2) The State Department of Health shall enforce the provisions of Sections 41-41-31 through 41-41-39 at abortion facilities, as defined in Section 41-75-1.

Mississippi Code § 41-41-35. Duty to publish materials

(1) The State Department of Health shall cause to be published in English within sixty (60) days after the effective date of this act, the following easily comprehensible printed materials:

(a) Geographically indexed materials designed to inform the woman of public and private agencies and services available to assist a woman through pregnancy, upon childbirth and while the child is dependent, including adoption agencies, which shall include a comprehensive list of the agencies available, a description of the services they offer and a description of the manner, including telephone numbers, in which they might be contacted, or, at the option of the Department of Health, printed materials including a toll-free, twenty-four-hour-a-day telephone number which may be called to obtain, orally, such a list and description of agencies in the locality of the caller and of the services they offer.

(b) Materials designed to inform the woman of the probable anatomical and physiological characteristics of the unborn child at two-week gestational increments from the time when a woman can be known to be pregnant to full term, including any relevant information on the possibility of the unborn child's survival. The materials shall include color pictures representing the development of the child at two-week gestational increments. These pictures must contain the dimensions of the unborn child and must be realistic. The materials shall be objective, nonjudgmental and designed to convey only accurate scientific information about the unborn child at the various gestational ages.

(c) Materials that include the information described in subparagraphs (ii) and (iv) of paragraph (1)(a) of Section 41-41-33 and in subparagraphs (i), (ii) and (iii) of paragraph (1)(b) of Section 41-41-33.

(d) Materials designed to inform the woman of pregnancy prevention methods for females and males, which materials shall describe each method in detail and include pictures or diagrams that illustrate the proper usage of each method.

(2) The materials shall be printed in a typeface large enough to be clearly legible.

(3) The materials required under this section shall be available at no cost from the Department of Health upon request and in appropriate number to any person, facility or hospital.

(4) The Department of Health shall review the printed materials required by subsection (1) of this section on an annual basis in order to determine if any changes are needed to be made to the contents of the materials, and shall promulgate any rules and regulations necessary for considering and making such changes.

(5) PARTIAL-BIRTH ABORTION

Mississippi criminalizes partial-birth abortions. Until it is definitively determined by a court, Mississippi's partial-birth abortion statute may be invalid under the United States Supreme Court decision *in Stenberg v. Carhart*, which invalidated Nebraska's ban on partial-birth abortion. On the other hand, Mississippi's partial-birth abortion statute, as currently written, may be valid under the United States Supreme Court decision in *Gonzales v. Carhart*, which approved of a federal statute that bans partial-birth abortion.

In addition to purporting to ban partial-birth abortions, Mississippi has provided a civil cause of action for a married man whose spouse obtains a partial-birth abortion. In the case of a minor, the maternal grandparents of the fetus may file a civil lawsuit. The text of Mississippi's partial-birth abortion laws is set out below.

Mississippi Code § 41-41-71. Short title

Sections 41-41-71 through 41-41-73 may be cited as the Partial-Birth Abortion Ban Act.

Mississippi Code § 41-41-73. Partial-birth abortion offense

(1) Any physician who knowingly performs a partial-birth abortion and thereby kills a human fetus shall be guilty of a felony and, upon conviction thereof, shall be fined not more than Twenty-five Thousand Dollars ($25,000.00) or imprisoned in the State Penitentiary for not more than two (2) years, or both. This subsection shall not apply to a partial-birth abortion that is necessary to save the life of a mother whose life is endangered by a physical disorder, illness, or injury if no other medical procedure would suffice for that purpose.

(2)(a) As used in this section, "partial-birth abortion" means an abortion in which the person performing the abortion partially vaginally delivers a living fetus before killing the fetus and completing the delivery.

(b) As used in this section, "physician" means a doctor of medicine or osteopathy legally authorized to practice medicine and surgery by the State of Mississippi. However, any individual who is not a physician but who nevertheless directly performs a partial-birth abortion shall be subject to the provisions of this section.

(3)(a) The husband of a mother at the time she receives a partial-birth abortion procedure, and if the mother has not attained the age of eighteen (18) years at the time of the abortion, the mother's parents may in a civil action obtain appropriate relief, unless the pregnancy resulted from the plaintiff's criminal conduct or the plaintiff consented to the abortion.

(b) Such relief shall include:

(i) Money damages for all injuries, psychological and physical, occasioned by the violation of this section; and

(ii) Statutory damages equal to three (3) times the cost of the partial-birth abortion.

(4) A woman upon whom a partial-birth abortion is performed may not be prosecuted under this section for a conspiracy to violate this section.

(6) ABORTION BY MINORS

Under the laws of Mississippi no physician may perform an abortion upon an unemancipated minor unless he/she first obtains the written consent of both parents or the legal guardian of the minor. If a minor's pregnancy was caused by sexual intercourse with her natural father, adoptive father or stepfather, then written consent of the minor's mother is sufficient.

In compliance with federal constitutional law, Mississippi has provided a judicial waiver procedure for an unemancipated minor to obtain an abortion without parental or guardian consent. The minor may petition a trial court for a waiver of the consent requirement. A minor has a right to an attorney at the proceeding and if she cannot afford one, the court must appoint her an attorney. If a minor chooses, she may represent herself. The required parental or guardian consent may be waived if the court finds either (1) that the minor is mature and well-informed enough to make the abortion decision on her own, or (2) that performance of the abortion would be in the best interest of the minor. An expedited appeal is available to any minor to whom the court denies a waiver of consent. Mississippi's abortion laws for minors were upheld in *Barnes v. Mississippi*, 992 F.2d 1335 (5th Cir. 1993) and *Pro-Choice Mississippi v. Fordice*, 716 So.2d 645 (Miss. 1998). The statutes addressing the matters are set out below.

Mississippi Code § 41-41-51. Definitions

For purposes of Sections 41-41-51 through 41-41-63, the following definitions shall apply:

(a) "Minor" means any person under the age of eighteen (18) years;

(b) "Emancipated minor" means any minor who is or has been married or has by court order or otherwise been freed from the care, custody and control of her parents;

(c) "Abortion" means the use of any instrument, medicine, drug or any other substance or device with intent to terminate the pregnancy of a woman known to be pregnant, with intent other than to increase the probability of a live birth, to preserve the life or health of the child after live birth, or to remove a dead fetus.

Mississippi Code § 41-41-53. Parental consent

(1) Except as otherwise provided in subsections (2) and (3) of this section, no person shall perform an abortion upon an unemancipated minor unless he or his agent first obtains the written consent of both parents or the legal guardian of the minor.

(2)(a) If the minor's parents are divorced or otherwise unmarried and living separate and apart, then the written consent of the parent with primary custody, care and control of such minor shall be sufficient.

(b) If the minor's parents are married and one (1) parent is not available to the person performing the abortion in a reasonable time and manner, then the written consent of the parent who is available shall be sufficient.

(c) If the minor's pregnancy was caused by sexual intercourse with the minor's natural father, adoptive father or stepfather, then the written consent of the minor's mother shall be sufficient.

(3) A minor who elects not to seek or does not obtain consent from her parents or legal guardian under this section may petition, on her own behalf or by next friend, the chancery court in the county in which the minor resides or in the county in which the abortion is to be performed for a waiver of the consent requirement of this section pursuant to the procedures of Section 41-41-55.

Mississippi Code § 41-41-55. Judicial Bypass

(1) The requirements and procedures under Sections 41-41-51 through 41-41-63 shall apply and are available to minors whether or not they are residents of this state.

(2) The minor may participate in proceedings in the court on her own behalf. The court shall advise her that she has a right to court-appointed counsel and shall provide her with such counsel upon her request or if she is not already adequately represented.

(3) Court proceedings under this section shall be confidential and anonymous and shall be given such precedence over other pending matters as is necessary to insure that the court may reach a decision promptly, but in no case shall the court fail to rule within seventy-two (72) hours of the time the application is filed. If for any reason the court fails to rule

within seventy-two (72) hours of the time the application is filed, the minor may proceed as if the consent requirement of Section 41-41-53 has been waived.

(4) Consent shall be waived if the court finds by clear and convincing evidence either:

(a) That the minor is mature and well-informed enough to make the abortion decision on her own; or

(b) That performance of the abortion would be in the best interests of the minor.

(5) A court that conducts proceedings under this section shall issue written and specific factual findings and legal conclusions supporting its decision and shall order that a confidential record of the evidence be maintained.

(6) An expedited confidential and anonymous appeal shall be available to any minor to whom the court denies a waiver of consent. The Mississippi Supreme Court shall issue promptly such rules and regulations as are necessary to insure that proceedings under Sections 41-41-51 through 41-41-63 are handled in an expeditious, confidential and anonymous manner.

(7) No filing fees shall be required of any minor who avails herself of the procedures provided by this section.

Mississippi Code § 41-41-57. Emergencies

Sections 41-41-51 through 41-41-63 shall not apply when, in the best clinical judgment of the physician on the facts of the case before him, a medical emergency exists that so complicates the pregnancy as to require an immediate abortion. A physician who does not comply with Sections 41-41-53 and 41-41-55 by reason of this exception shall state in the medical record of the abortion the medical indications on which his judgment was based.

Mississippi Code § 41-41-59.
Violation as unprofessional conduct

If a physician performs an abortion in violation of the provisions of Sections 41-41-51 through 41-41-63 or fails to conform to any requirement of Sections 41-41-51 through 41-41-63, then his action shall be prima facie evidence of unprofessional conduct, subjecting him to action by the State Board of Medical Licensure.

Mississippi Code § 41-41-61. Confidentiality

(1) Records and information involving court proceedings conducted pursuant to Section 41-41-55 shall be confidential and shall not be disclosed other than to the minor, her attorney and necessary court personnel. Nothing in this subsection shall prohibit the keeping of statistical records and information as long as the anonymity of the minor is in no way compromised.

(2) Any person who shall disclose any records or information made confidential pursuant to subsection (1) of this section shall be guilty of a misdemeanor and upon conviction punished by a fine of not more than One Thousand Dollars ($1,000.00) or imprisonment in the county jail for not more than one (1) year, or both.

Mississippi Code § 41-41-63. Severability

If any provision, word, phrase or clause of Sections 41-41-51 through 41-41-63 or the application thereof to any person or circumstance shall be held invalid, such invalidity shall not affect the provisions, words, phrases, clauses or application of Sections 41-41-51 through 41-41-63 which can be given effect without the invalid provision, word, phrase, clause or application, and to this end the provisions, words, phrases and clauses of Sections 41-41-51 through 41-41-63 are declared to be severable.

(7) INJURY TO A PREGNANT WOMAN

Mississippi has created several offenses for an injury to a pregnant woman that causes death or harm to the fetus or embryo. In addition, the state criminalizes conduct that causes the death of a fetus born alive during a failed abortion. The statutes are set out below.

Mississippi Code § 97-3-37. Harming pregnant woman

(1) For purposes of the offenses enumerated in this subsection (1), the term "human being" includes an unborn child at every stage of gestation from conception until live birth and the term "unborn child" means a member of the species homo sapiens, at any stage of development, who is carried in the womb:

(a) Section 97-3-7, simple and aggravated assault and domestic violence;

(b) Section 97-3-15, justifiable homicide;

(c) Section 97-3-17, excusable homicide;

(d) Section 97-3-19, capital murder;

(e) Section 97-3-27, homicide while committing a felony;

(f) Section 97-3-29, homicide while committing a misdemeanor;

(g) Section 97-3-33, killing a trespasser unnecessarily;

(h) Section 97-3-35, killing without malice in the heat of passion;

(i) Section 97-3-45, homicide by means of a dangerous animal;

(j) Section 97-3-47, all other homicides;

(k) Section 97-3-61, poisoning with intent to kill or injure.

(2) A person who intentionally injures a pregnant woman is guilty of a crime as follows:

(a) If the conduct results in a miscarriage or stillbirth by that individual, a felony punishable by imprisonment for not more than twenty (20) years or a fine of not more than Seven Thousand Five Hundred Dollars ($7,500.00), or both.

(b) If the conduct results in great bodily harm to the embryo or fetus, a felony punishable by imprisonment for not more than twenty (20) years or a fine of not more than Five Thousand Dollars ($5,000.00), or both.

(c) If the conduct results in serious or aggravated physical injury to the embryo or fetus, a misdemeanor punishable by imprisonment for not more than one (1) year or a fine of not more than One Thousand Dollars ($1,000.00), or both.

(d) If the conduct results in physical injury to the embryo or fetus, a misdemeanor punishable by imprisonment for not more than ninety (90) days or a fine of not more than Five Hundred Dollars ($500.00), or both.

(3) The provisions of this section shall not apply to any legal medical procedure performed by a licensed physician or other licensed medical professional, including legal abortions, when done at the request of a mother of an unborn child or the mother's legal guardian, or to the lawful dispensing or administration of lawfully prescribed medication.

Mississippi Code § 97-3-4.
Allowing child delivered in failed abortion to die

(1) It shall be unlawful for any physician performing an abortion that results in the delivery of a living child to intentionally allow or cause the child to die.

(2) If the child is viable, such child shall be immediately provided appropriate medical care and comfort care necessary to sustain life. If the child is not viable, such child shall be provided comfort care. The provision of this section shall include, but not be limited to, a child born with physical or mental handicapping conditions which, in the opinion of the parent, the physician or other persons, diminishes the quality of the child's life, a child born alive during the course of an attempted abortion and a child not wanted by the parent.

(3) As used in this section the term "child" includes every infant member of the species homo sapiens who is born alive at any stage of development.

(4) Any person who violates this section shall be guilty of a felony and, upon conviction, be imprisoned for not less than one (1) year nor more than ten (10) years in the State Penitentiary and fined not more than Fifty Thousand Dollars ($50,000.00) but not less than Twenty-five Thousand Dollars ($25,000.00).

(8) ABORTION COMPLICATION REPORTS

Mississippi requires that all treatment for abortion complications be reported to the proper authorities. The statutes addressing the matter are set out below.

Mississippi Code § 41-41-75. Short title

Sections 41-41-75 through 41-41-80 shall be known and may be cited as the Abortion Complication Reporting Act.

Mississippi Code § 41-41-76. Definitions

As used in Sections 41-41-75 through 41-41-80:

(a) "Abortion" has the meaning as defined in Section 41-41-31.

(b) "Medical treatment" means, but is not limited to, hospitalization, laboratory tests, surgery or prescription of drugs.

(c) "Department" means the State Department of Health.

Mississippi Code § 41-41-77. Reporting

(1) A physician shall file a written report with the State Department of Health regarding each patient who comes under the physician's professional care and requires medical treatment or suffers death that the attending physician has a reasonable basis to believe is a primary, secondary, or tertiary result of an induced abortion.

(2) These reports shall be submitted within thirty (30) days of the discharge or death of the patient treated for the complication.

(3) The department shall summarize aggregate data from the reports required under this section for purposes of inclusion into the annual Vital Statistics Report.

(4) The department shall develop and distribute or make available online in a downloadable format a standardized form for the report required under this section.

(5) The department shall communicate this reporting requirement to all medical professional organizations, licensed physicians, hospitals, emergency rooms, abortion facilities, Department of Health clinics and ambulatory surgical facilities operating in the state.

(6) The department shall destroy each individual report required by this section and each copy of the report after retaining the report for five (5) years after the date the report is received.

(7) The report required under this section shall not contain the name of the woman, common identifiers such as her social security number or motor vehicle operator's license number or other information or identifiers that would make it possible to identify in any manner or under any circumstances an individual who has obtained or seeks to obtain an abortion. A state agency shall not compare data in an electronic or other information system file with data in another electronic or other information system that would result in identifying in any manner or under any circumstances an individual obtaining or seeking to obtain an abortion. Statistical information that may reveal the identity of a woman obtaining or seeking to obtain an abortion shall not be maintained.

(8) The department or an employee of the department shall not disclose to a person or entity outside the department the reports or the contents of the reports required under this section in a manner or fashion as to permit the person or entity to whom the report is disclosed to identify in any way the person who is the subject of the report.

(9) Disclosure of confidential identifying information in violation of this section shall constitute a felony which, upon conviction, shall be punished by imprisonment in the State Penitentiary for not more than three (3) years, or a fine of not more than Five Thousand Dollars ($5,000.00), or both.

Mississippi Code § 41-41-78. Contents of report

(1) Each report of medical treatment following abortion required under Section 41-41-77 shall contain the following information:

(a) The age and race of the patient;

(b) The characteristics of the patient, including residency status, county of residence, marital status, education, number of previous pregnancies, number of stillbirths, number of living children and number of previous abortions;

(c) The date the abortion was performed and the method used if known;

(d) The type of facility where the abortion was performed;

(e) The condition of the patient that led to treatment, including, but not limited to, pelvic infection, hemorrhage, damage to pelvic organs, renal failure, metabolic disorder, shock, embolism, coma or death.

(f) The amount billed to cover the treatment of the complication, including whether the treatment was billed to Medicaid, insurance, private pay or other method. This should include charges for physician, hospital, emergency room, prescription or other drugs, laboratory tests and any other costs for the treatment rendered.

(g) The charges are to be coded with IDC-9 classification numbers in such a way as to distinguish treatment following induced abortions from treatments following ectopic or molar pregnancies.

(2) Nothing in Sections 41-41-75 through 41-41-80 shall be construed as an instruction to discontinue collecting data currently being collected.

Mississippi Code § 41-41-79. Penalties

Willful violation of the provisions of Sections 41-41-75 through 41-41-80 shall constitute a misdemeanor and shall be punishable as provided for by law, except that disclosure of confidential identifying information shall constitute a felony as provided in subsection (9) of Section 41-41-77. No physician or hospital, its officers, employees or medical and nursing personnel practicing in the hospital shall be civilly liable for violation of the provisions of Sections 41-41-75 through 41-41-80, except to the extent of liability for actual damages in a civil action for willful or reckless and wanton acts or omissions constituting that violation. However, that liability shall be subject to any immunities or limitations of liability or damages provided by law.

Mississippi Code § 41-41-80. Severability

The provisions of Sections 41-41-75 through 41-41-80 are declared to be severable, and if any provision, word, phrase, or clause of Sections 41-41-75 through 41-41-80 or the application thereof to any person is held invalid, the invalidity shall not affect the validity of the remaining portions of Section 41-41-75 through 41-41-80.

(9) USE OF PUBLIC FUNDS

Mississippi prohibits the use of public funds for abortion, except in limited circumstances. The statute addressing the matter is set out below.

Mississippi Code § 41-41-91. Use of public funds for abortion

Notwithstanding any other provision of law to the contrary, no public funds that are made available to any institution, board, commission, department, agency, official, or employee of the State of Mississippi, or of any local political subdivision of the state, whether those funds are made available by the government of the United States, the State of Mississippi, or a local governmental subdivision, or from any other public source, shall be used in any way for, to assist in, or to provide facilities for abortion, except:

(a) When the abortion is medically necessary to prevent the death of the mother; or

(b) When the abortion is being sought to terminate a pregnancy resulting from an alleged act of rape or incest; or

(c) When there is a fetal malformation that is incompatible with the baby being born alive.

(10) PROVIDING CONTRACEPTIVES

Mississippi provides funding to family planning agencies for the purpose of making contraceptives available. The statutes addressing the matter are set out below.

Mississippi Code § 41-42-1. Short title

This chapter shall be known and may be cited as the "Family Planning Law of 1972."

Mississippi Code § 41-42-3. Definitions

For the purposes of this chapter and as used herein:

(a) "Board" means the Mississippi State Board of Health;

(b) "Physician" means any doctor of medicine duly licensed to practice his profession in Mississippi or the state in which he resides and lawfully practicing his profession;

(c) "Contraceptive procedures" means any medically accepted procedure designed to prevent conception;

(d) "Contraceptive supplies" means those medically approved items designed to prevent conception through chemical, mechanical, or other means.

Mississippi Code § 41-42-5. Functions of state board

The state board of health is authorized to receive and disburse such funds as may become available to it for family planning programs to any organization, public or private, engaged in providing contraceptive procedures, supplies, and information. Any family planning program administered by the board may be developed in consultation and coordination with other family planning agencies in this state.

The board is hereby authorized to adopt and promulgate rules and regulations to implement the provisions of this chapter.

The board may provide for the dissemination of medically acceptable contraceptive information and supplies by duly authorized persons in state and county health and welfare departments and in medical facilities at institutions of higher learning.

Mississippi Code § 41-42-7. Contraceptives to minors

Contraceptive supplies and information may be furnished by physicians to any minor who is a parent, or who is married, or who has the consent of his or her parent or legal guardian, or who has been referred for such service by another physician, a clergyman, a family planning clinic, a school or institution of higher learning, or any agency or instrumentality of this state or any subdivision thereof.

(11) ABORTION FACILITIES

Mississippi provides by statute for the operation and maintenance of abortion facilities. The statutes addressing the matters are set out below.

Mississippi Code § 41-75-1. Definitions

For the purpose of this chapter:

(a) "Ambulatory surgical facility" means a publicly or privately owned institution that is primarily organized, constructed, renovated or otherwise established for the purpose of providing elective surgical treatment of "outpatients" whose recovery, under normal and routine circumstances, will not require "inpatient" care. The facility defined in this paragraph does not include the offices of private physicians or dentists, whether practicing individually or in groups, but does include organizations or facilities primarily engaged in that outpatient surgery, whether using the name "ambulatory surgical facility" or a similar or different name. That organization or facility, if in any manner considered to be operated or owned by a hospital or a hospital holding, leasing or management company, either for profit or not for profit, is required to comply with all licensing agency ambulatory surgical licensure standards governing a "hospital affiliated" facility as adopted under Section 41-9-1 et seq., provided that the organization or facility does not intend to seek federal certification as an ambulatory surgical facility as provided for at 42 CFR, Parts 405 and 416. If the organization or facility is to be operated or owned by a hospital or a hospital holding, leasing or management company and intends to seek federal certification as an ambulatory facility, then the facility is considered to be "freestanding" and must comply with all licensing agency ambulatory surgical licensure standards governing a "freestanding" facility.

If the organization or facility is to be owned or operated by an entity or person other than a hospital or hospital holding, leasing or management company, then the organization or facility must comply with all licensing agency ambulatory surgical facility standards governing a "freestanding" facility.

(b) "Hospital affiliated" ambulatory surgical facility means a separate and distinct organized unit of a hospital or a building owned, leased, rented or utilized by a hospital and located in the same county in which the hospital is located, for the primary purpose of performing ambulatory surgery procedures. The facility is not required to be separately licensed under this chapter and may operate under the hospital's license in compliance with all applicable requirements of Section 41-9-1 et seq.

(c) "Freestanding" ambulatory surgical facility means a separate and distinct facility or a separate and distinct organized unit of a hospital owned, leased, rented or utilized by a hospital or other persons for the primary purpose of performing ambulatory surgery procedures. The facility must be separately licensed as defined in this section and must comply with all licensing standards promulgated by the licensing agency under this chapter regarding a "freestanding" ambulatory surgical facility. Further, the facility must be a separate, identifiable entity and must be physically, administratively and financially independent and distinct from other operations of any other health facility, and shall maintain a separate organized medical and administrative staff. Furthermore, once licensed as a "freestanding" ambulatory surgical facility, the facility shall not become a component of any other health facility without securing a certificate of need to do that.

(d) "Ambulatory surgery" means surgical procedures that are more complex than office procedures performed under local anesthesia, but less complex than major procedures requiring prolonged postoperative monitoring and hospital care to ensure safe recovery and desirable results. General anesthesia is used in most cases. The patient must arrive at the facility and expect to be discharged on the same day. Ambulatory surgery shall only be performed by physicians or dentists licensed to practice in the State of Mississippi.

(e) "Abortion" means the use or prescription of any instrument, medicine, drug or any other substances or device to terminate the pregnancy of a woman known to be pregnant with an intention other than to increase the probability of a live birth, to preserve the life or health of the child after live birth or to remove a dead fetus. Abortion procedures after the first trimester shall only be performed at a Level I abortion facility or an ambulatory surgical facility or hospital licensed to perform that service.

(f) "Abortion facility" means a facility operating substantially for the purpose of performing abortions and is a separate identifiable legal entity from any other health care facility. Abortions shall only be performed by physicians licensed to practice in the State of Mississippi. The term "abortion facility" includes physicians' offices that are used substantially for the purpose of performing abortions. An abortion facility operates substantially for the purpose of performing abortions if any of the following conditions are met:

(i) The abortion facility is a provider for performing ten (10) or more abortion procedures per calendar month during any month of a calendar year, or one hundred (100) or more in a calendar year.

(ii) The abortion facility, if operating less than twenty (20) days per calendar month, is a provider for performing ten (10) or more abortion procedures, or performing a number of abortion procedures that would be equivalent to ten (10) procedures per

month, if the facility were operating twenty (20) or more days per calendar month, in any month of a calendar year.

(iii) The abortion facility holds itself out to the public as an abortion provider by advertising by any public means, such as newspaper, telephone directory, magazine or electronic media, that it performs abortions.

(iv) The facility applies to the licensing agency for licensure as an abortion facility.

(g) "Licensing agency" means the State Department of Health.

(h) "Operating" an abortion facility means that the facility is open for any period of time during a day and has on site at the facility or on call a physician licensed to practice in the State of Mississippi available to provide abortions.

An abortion facility may apply to be licensed as a Level I facility or a Level II facility by the licensing agency. Level II abortion facilities shall be required to meet minimum standards for abortion facilities as established by the licensing agency. Level I abortion facilities shall be required to meet minimum standards for abortion facilities and minimum standards for ambulatory surgical facilities as established by the licensing agency.

Any abortion facility that begins operation after June 30, 1996, shall not be located within fifteen hundred (1500) feet from the property on which any church, school or kindergarten is located. An abortion facility shall not be in violation of this paragraph if it is in compliance with this paragraph on the date it begins operation and the property on which a church, school or kindergarten is located is later within fifteen hundred (1500) feet from the facility.

Mississippi Code § 41-75-3. Statement of purpose

The purpose of this chapter is to protect and promote the public welfare by providing for the development, establishment and enforcement of certain standards in the maintenance and operation of ambulatory surgical facilities and abortion facilities which will ensure safe, sanitary, and reasonably adequate care of individuals in such facilities.

Mississippi Code § 41-75-5. Requirement of license

No person as defined in Section 41-7-173, of the Mississippi Code of 1972, acting severally or jointly with any other person, shall establish, conduct, operate or maintain an ambulatory surgical facility or an abortion facility in this state without a license under this chapter.

Mississippi Code § 41-75-7. Application and fee

An application for a license shall be made to the licensing agency upon forms provided by it and shall contain such information as the licensing agency reasonably requires, which may include affirmative evidence of ability to comply with such reasonable standards, rules and regulations as are lawfully prescribed hereunder. Each application for a license shall be accompanied by a license fee of Three Thousand Dollars ($3,000.00), which shall be paid to the licensing agency.

Mississippi Code § 41-75-9. Terms of license

Upon receipt of an application for license and the license fee, the licensing agency shall issue a license if the applicant and the institutional facilities meet the requirements established under this chapter and the requirements of Section 41-7-173 et seq. where determined by the licensing agency to be applicable. A license, unless suspended or revoked, shall be renewable annually upon payment of a renewal fee of Three Thousand Dollars ($3,000.00), which shall be paid to the licensing agency, and upon filing by the licensee and approval by the licensing agency of an annual report upon such uniform dates and containing such information in such form as the licensing agency requires. Each license shall be issued only for the premises and person or persons named in the application and shall not be transferable or assignable. Licenses shall be posted in a conspicuous place on the licensed premises.

Mississippi Code § 41-75-11.
License denial or discipline procedures

The licensing agency after notice and opportunity for a hearing to the applicant or licensee is authorized to deny, suspend or revoke a license in any case in which it finds that there has been a substantial failure to comply with the requirements established under this chapter. Such notice shall be effected by registered mail, or by personal service setting forth the particular reasons for the proposed action and fixing a date not less than thirty (30) days from the date of such mailing or such service, at which time the applicant or licensee shall be given an opportunity for a prompt and fair hearing. On the basis of any such hearing, or upon default of the applicant or licensee, the licensing agency shall make a determination specifying its findings of fact and conclusions of law. A copy of such determination shall be sent by registered mail or served personally upon the applicant or licensee. The decision revoking, suspending or denying the license or application shall become final thirty (30) days after it is so mailed or served, unless the applicant or licensee, within such thirty (30) day period, appeals the decision to the chancery court in the county in which such facility is located in the manner prescribed in section 43-11-23, Mississippi Code of 1972. The procedure governing hearings authorized by this section shall be in accordance with rules promulgated by the licensing agency. A full and complete record shall be kept of all proceedings, and all testimony shall be recorded but need not be transcribed unless the decision is appealed pursuant to section 43-11-23, Mississippi Code of 1972. Witnesses may be subpoenaed by either party. Compensation shall be allowed to witnesses as in cases in the chancery court. Each party shall pay the expense of his own witnesses. The cost of the record shall be paid by the licensing agency provided any other party desiring a copy of the transcript shall pay therefor the reasonable cost of preparing the same.

Mississippi Code § 41-75-13. Rules and regulations

The licensing agency shall adopt, amend, promulgate and enforce rules, regulations and standards, including classifications, with respect to ambulatory surgical facilities and abortion facilities licensed, or which may be licensed, to further the accomplishment of the purpose of this chapter in protecting and promoting the health, safety and welfare of the public by ensuring adequate care of individuals receiving services from such facilities. The licensing agency also shall adopt, amend, promulgate and enforce rules, regulations and standards with respect to the enforcement of the informed consent requirements of Sections 41-41-31 through 41-41-39 at abortion facilities. Such rules, regulations and standards shall be adopted and promulgated by the licensing agency in accordance with the provisions of Section 25-43-1 et seq., and shall be recorded and indexed in a book to be maintained by the licensing agency in its main office in the State of Mississippi, entitled "Rules and Regulations for Operation of Ambulatory Surgical Facilities and Abortion Facilities." The book shall be open and available to all ambulatory surgical facilities and abortion facilities and the public during regular business hours.

Mississippi Code § 41-75-15. Existing facilities

Any ambulatory surgical facility which is in operation at the time of promulgation of any applicable rules or regulations or minimum standards under this chapter shall be given a reasonable time, under the particular circumstances not to exceed one (1) year from the date such are duly adopted, within which to comply with such rules and regulations and minimum standards.

Mississippi Code § 41-75-16.
Six month maximum abortion facilities

Any abortion facility which is in operation at the time of promulgation of any applicable rules or regulations or minimum standards under this chapter shall be given a reasonable time, under the particular circumstances not to exceed six (6) months from the date such are duly adopted, within which to comply with such rules and regulations and minimum standards.

Mississippi Code § 41-75-17.
Inspection and investigation authority

The licensing agency shall make or cause to be made such inspections and investigations as it deems necessary.

Mississippi Code § 41-75-18.
Monthly reports by abortion facilities

Each abortion facility shall report monthly to the State Department of Health such information as may be required by the department in its rules and regulations for each abortion performed by such facility.

Mississippi Code § 41-75-19. Confidentiality

Information received by the licensing agency through filed reports, inspection, or as otherwise authorized under this chapter, shall not be disclosed publicly in such manner as to identify individuals, except in a proceeding involving the questions of licensure.

Mississippi Code § 41-75-21. Annual report

The licensing agency shall prepare and publish an annual report of its activities and operations under this chapter. Copies of such publications shall be available in the office of the licensing agency and in the office of the Secretary of State, in compliance with Sections 25-43-7 and 25-43-11, Mississippi Code of 1972. A reasonable number of such publication(s) shall be available in the office of the licensing agency to be furnished to persons requesting, for a nominal fee.

Mississippi Code § 41-75-23. Appeal procedure

Any applicant or licensee aggrieved by the decision of the licensing agency after a hearing, may within thirty (30) days after the mailing or serving of notice of the decision as provided in Section 43-11-11, Mississippi Code of 1972, file a notice of appeal to the chancery court of the First Judicial District of Hinds County or in the chancery court of the county in which the institution is located or proposed to be located. Such appeal shall state briefly the nature of the proceedings before the licensing agency and shall specify the order complained of. Any person or entity whose rights may be materially affected by the action of the licensing agency may appear and become a party, or the court may, upon motion, order that any such person or entity be joined as a necessary party. Upon filing of the appeal, the clerk of the chancery court shall serve notice on the licensing agency, whereupon the licensing agency shall, within sixty (60) days or such additional time as the court may allow from the service of such notice, certify with the court a copy of the record and decision, including the transcript of the hearings on which the decision is based. No new or additional evidence shall be introduced in court; the case shall be determined upon the record certified to the court. The court may sustain or dismiss the appeal, modify or vacate the order complained of in whole or in part, as the case may be; but in case the order is wholly or partly vacated, the court may also, in its discretion, remand the matter to the licensing agency for such further proceedings, not inconsistent with the court's order, as, in the opinion of the court, justice may require. The order may not be vacated or set aside, either in whole or in part, except for errors of law, unless the court finds that the order of the licensing agency is not supported by substantial evidence, is contrary to the manifest weight of the evidence, is in excess of the statutory authority or jurisdiction of the licensing agency or violates any vested constitutional rights of any party involved in the appeal. Pending final disposition of the matter, the status quo of the applicant or licensee shall be preserved, except as the court otherwise orders in the public interest. Rules with respect to court costs in other cases in chancery shall apply equally to cases hereunder. Appeals in accordance with law may be had to the Supreme Court of the State of Mississippi from any final judgment of the chancery court.

Mississippi Code § 41-75-25. Penalties for violations

Any person or persons or other entity or entities establishing, managing or operating an ambulatory surgical facility or conducting the business of an ambulatory surgical facility without the required license, or which otherwise violate any of the provisions of this chapter of the "Mississippi Health Care Commission Law of 1979," as amended, or the rules, regulations or standards promulgated in furtherance of any law in which the commission has authority therefor shall be subject to the penalties and sanctions of section 41-7-209, Mississippi Code of 1972.

Mississippi Code § 41-75-26.
Enforcement against abortion facilities

(1) Any person or persons or other entity or entities establishing, managing or operating an abortion facility or conducting the business of an abortion facility without the required license, or which otherwise violate any provision of this chapter regarding abortion facilities or the rules, regulations and standards promulgated in furtherance thereof shall be subject to revocation of the license of the abortion facility or nonlicensure of the abortion facility. In addition, any violation of any provision of this chapter regarding abortion facilities or of the rules, regulations and standards promulgated in furtherance thereof by intent, fraud, deceit, unlawful design, willful and/or deliberate misrepresentation, or by careless, negligent or incautious disregard for such statutes or rules, regulations and standards, either by persons acting individually or in concert with others, shall constitute a misdemeanor and shall be punishable by a fine not to exceed One Thousand Dollars ($1,000.00) for each such offense. Each day of continuing violation shall be considered a separate offense. The venue for prosecution of any such violation shall be in any county of the state wherein any such violation, or portion thereof, occurred.

(2) The Attorney General, upon certification by the executive director of the licensing agency, shall seek injunctive relief in a court of proper jurisdiction to prevent violations of the provisions of this chapter regarding abortion facilities or the rules, regulations and standards promulgated in furtherance thereof in cases where other administrative penalties and legal sanctions imposed have failed to prevent or cause a discontinuance of any such violation.

Mississippi Code § 41-75-29.
Abortion facilities provision for emergency

(1) If unforeseen complications arise prior to or during an abortion facility procedure, the patient shall be transferred to the nearest hospital.

(2) Each abortion facility shall make arrangements with a local ambulance service, duly licensed by the State of Mississippi, for the transport of emergency patients to a hospital and provide documentation to the department of proof of such arrangements.

(12) CHOOSE LIFE LICENSE PLATE

Mississippi authorizes the sale of "Choose Life" license plates for motor vehicles. The statute addressing the matter is set out below.

Mississippi Code § 27-19-56.70. Choose Life license plate

(1) Any owner of a motor vehicle who is a resident of this state, upon payment of the road and bridge privilege taxes, ad valorem taxes and registration fees as prescribed by law for private carriers of passengers, pickup trucks and other noncommercial motor vehicles, and upon payment of an additional fee in the amount provided in subsection (4) of this section, shall be issued a distinctive license tag for each motor vehicle registered in his name, which shall be produced in such color and design as the State Tax Commission, with the advice of the Choose Life Advisory Committee, may prescribe. The words "Choose Life" shall be centered at the bottom of the license tag. The State Tax Commission shall prescribe such letters or numbers, or both, as may be necessary to distinguish each license tag.

(2) Application for the distinctive license tags authorized by this sec-

tion shall be made to the county tax collector on forms prescribed by the State Tax Commission. The application and the additional fee imposed under subsection (4) of this section, less Two Dollars ($2.00) to be retained by the tax collector, shall be remitted to the State Tax Commission on a monthly basis as prescribed by the commission. The portion of the additional fee retained by the tax collector shall be deposited into the county general fund.

(3) Beginning with any registration year commencing on or after July 1, 2002, any person applying for a distinctive license tag under this section shall pay an additional fee in the amount of Thirty Dollars ($30.00) for each distinctive license tag applied for under this section, which shall be in addition to all other taxes and fees. The additional fee paid shall be for a period of time to run concurrent with the vehicle's established license tag year. The additional fee is due and payable at the time the original application is made for a distinctive license tag under this section and thereafter annually at the time of renewal registration as long as the owner retains the distinctive license tag. If the owner does not wish to retain the distinctive license tag, he must surrender it to the local county tax collector.

(4) The State Tax Commission shall deposit all fees into the State Treasury on the day collected. At the end of each month, the State Tax Commission shall certify the total fees collected under this section to the State Treasurer who shall distribute such collections as follows:

(a) Twenty-four Dollars ($24.00) of each additional fee collected on distinctive license tags issued pursuant to this section shall be disbursed to the Choose Life Advisory Committee to be used as provided for in subsection (5) of this section.

(b) One Dollar ($1.00) of each additional fee collected on distinctive license tags issued pursuant to this section shall be deposited into the Mississippi Fire Fighter's Memorial Burn Center Fund created pursuant to Section 7-9-70.

(c) Two Dollars ($2.00) of each additional fee collected on distinctive license tags issued pursuant to this section shall be deposited to the credit of the State Highway Fund to be expended solely for the repair, maintenance, construction or reconstruction of highways.

(d) One Dollar ($1.00) of each additional fee collected on distinctive license tags issued pursuant to this section shall be deposited to the credit of the special fund created in Section 27-19-44.2.

(5) Funds disbursed to the Choose Life Advisory Committee under this section may be used for any purpose other than for administrative expenses, legal expenses, capital expenditures, attempting to influence any legislation or any political campaign on behalf or in opposition to any candidate for public office.

(6) A regular license tag must be properly displayed as required by law until replaced by a distinctive license tag under this section. The regular license tag must be surrendered to the tax collector upon issuance of the distinctive license tag under this section. The tax collector shall issue up to two (2) month and year license decals for each distinctive license tag issued under this section, which will expire the same month and year as the license tag.

(7) In the case of loss or theft of a distinctive license tag issued under this section, the owner may make application and affidavit for a replacement distinctive license tag as provided by Section 27-19-37. The fee for a replacement distinctive license tag shall be Ten Dollars ($10.00). The tax collector receiving such application and affidavit shall be entitled to retain and deposit into the county general fund five percent (5%) of the fee for such replacement license tag and the remainder shall be distributed in the same manner as funds from the sale of regular distinctive license tags issued under this section.

Missouri

(1) OVERVIEW

The state of Missouri enacted its first criminal abortion statute on February 12, 1825. The statute underwent several amendments prior to the 1973 decision by the United States Supreme Court in *Roe v. Wade*, which legalized abortion in the nation. Missouri has taken affirmative steps to respond to *Roe* and its progeny. The state has addressed numerous abortion issues by statute that include general abortion guidelines, informed consent, viability testing, post-viability abortion, partial-birth abortion, abortion by minors, use of facilities and people, public funds, employees and facilities, fetal experiments and cloning, wrongful life action, fetal death report, abortion alternative programs, and insurance policies.

(2) GENERAL ABORTION GUIDELINES

Missouri has several statutory general abortion guidelines. The state requires that abortions be performed by physicians and that abortions after the first trimester be performed in a hospital. However, in *Planned Parenthood Assn. v. Ashcroft* the United States Supreme Court held that the constitution was violated by Missouri's requirement that second trimester abortions take place in a hospital. The state also requires physicians performing abortions maintain medical malpractice insurance. The general abortion statutes are set out below.

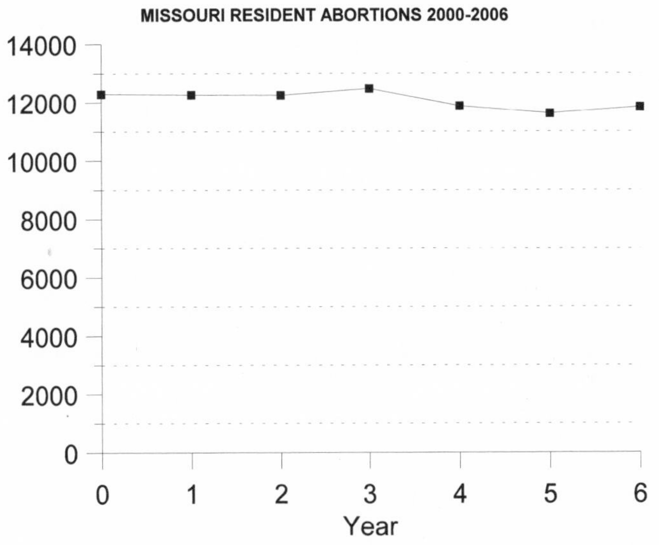

Source: Missouri Department of Health and Senior Services.

Missouri Code § 1.205. Life begins at conception

1. The general assembly of this state finds that:

(1) The life of each human being begins at conception;

(2) Unborn children have protectable interests in life, health, and well-being;

(3) The natural parents of unborn children have protectable interests in the life, health, and well-being of their unborn child.

2. Effective January 1, 1988, the laws of this state shall be interpreted and construed to acknowledge on behalf of the unborn child at every stage of development, all the rights, privileges, and immunities available to other persons, citizens, and residents of this state, subject only to the Constitution of the United States, and decisional interpretations thereof by the United States Supreme Court and specific provisions to the contrary in the statutes and constitution of this state.

3. As used in this section, the term "unborn children" or "unborn child" shall include all unborn child or children or the offspring of human be-

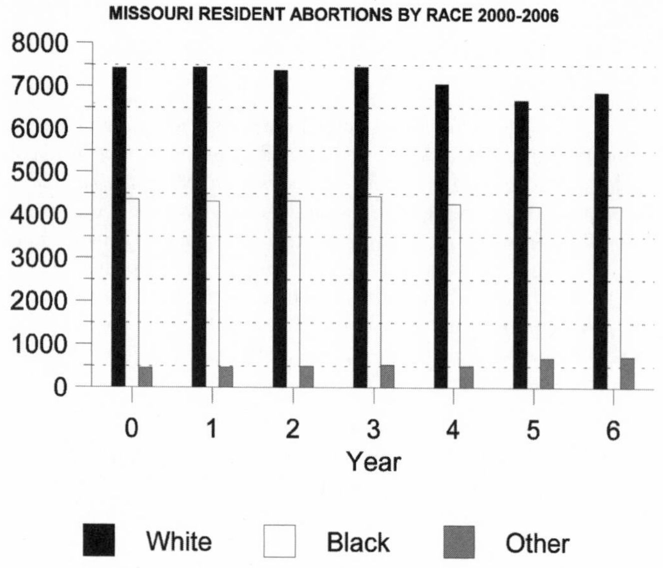

Source: Missouri Department of Health and Senior Services.

Missouri Resident Abortion by Weeks of Gestation 2000–2006

	Year							
Weeks of Gestation	*2000*	*2001*	*2002*	*2003*	*2004*	*2005*	*2006*	*Total*
<9	7,115	7,329	7,348	7,552	7,332	7,015	7,298	50,989
9–10	2,339	2,331	2,225	2,299	2,194	2,027	2,019	15,434
11–12	1,584	1,498	1,454	1,484	1,232	1,450	1,284	9,986
13–14	526	474	515	512	480	498	537	3,542
15–16	265	234	267	250	274	284	279	1,853
17–20	341	279	308	263	250	246	298	1,985
≥21	87	82	104	77	84	82	110	626
Not known	35	39	29	39	25	17	8	192

Source: Missouri Department of Health and Senior Services.

Missouri Resident Abortion By Age Group 2000-2006

	Age Group (yrs)							
Year	*<15*	*15–19*	*20–24*	*25–29*	*30–34*	*35–39*	*≥40*	*Unknown*
2000	87	2,151	3,970	2,877	1,741	1,080	381	5
2001	83	2,048	4,185	2,687	1,814	1,062	385	2
2002	88	2,086	4,094	2,738	1,827	1,062	353	2
2003	83	1,983	4,297	2,828	1,841	1,047	394	3
2004	85	1,941	3,993	2,783	1,737	954	377	1
2005	75	1,850	3,937	2,689	1,658	1,016	394	0
2006	73	1,950	3,997	2,828	1,639	993	351	2
Total	574	14,009	28,473	19,430	12,257	7,214	2,635	15

Source: Missouri Department of Health and Senior Services.

ings from the moment of conception until birth at every stage of biological development.

4. Nothing in this section shall be interpreted as creating a cause of action against a woman for indirectly harming her unborn child by failing to properly care for herself or by failing to follow any particular program of prenatal care.

Missouri Code § 188.010. Intent of general assembly

It is the intention of the general assembly of the state of Missouri to grant the right to life to all humans, born and unborn, and to regulate abortion to the full extent permitted by the Constitution of the United States, decisions of the United States Supreme Court, and federal statutes.

Missouri Code § 188.015. Definitions

As used in this chapter, the following terms mean:

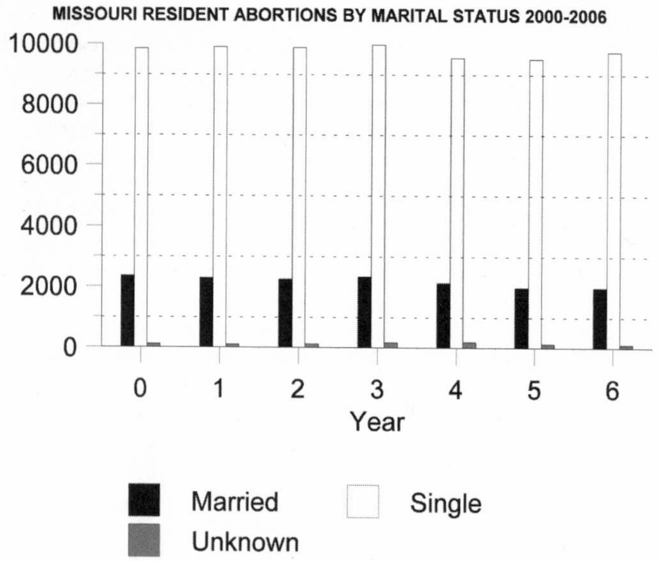

Source: Missouri Department of Health and Senior Services.

Missouri Resident Abortion by Education Level of Female 2000–2006

	Education Level Completed				
Year	*<9*	*9–11*	*12*	*≥13*	*Unknown*
2000	216	1,946	5,124	4,802	204
2001	228	1,960	5,255	4,576	247
2002	233	1,882	5,441	4,462	232
2003	268	1,846	5,619	4,503	240
2004	241	1,827	5,408	4,308	87
2005	231	1,694	5,468	4,091	135
2006	235	1,802	5,466	4,125	205
Total	1,652	12,957	37,781	30,867	1,350

Source: Missouri Department of Health and Senior Services.

(1) "Abortion," the intentional destruction of the life of an embryo or fetus in his or her mother's womb or the intentional termination of the pregnancy of a mother with an intention other than to increase the probability of a live birth or to remove a dead or dying unborn child;

(2) "Abortion facility," a clinic, physician's office, or any other place or facility in which abortions are performed or induced other than a hospital;

(3) "Conception," the fertilization of the ovum of a female by a sperm of a male;

(4) "Department," the department of health and senior services;

(5) "Gestational age," length of pregnancy as measured from the first day of the woman's last menstrual period;

(6) "Medical emergency," a condition which, on the basis of a

Missouri Resident Prior Abortion by Female 2000–2006

	Prior Abortion							
Year	*None*	*1*	*2*	*3*	*4*	*5*	*≥6*	*Not known*
2000	6,995	3,420	1,212	428	139	50	43	5
2001	6,981	3,313	1,275	440	159	56	40	2
2002	6,950	3,322	1,323	413	143	51	44	4
2003	7,071	3,372	1,293	470	162	59	44	5
2004	6,893	3,087	1,207	417	155	67	44	1
2005	6,591	3,025	1,292	451	153	60	44	3
2006	6,899	2,963	1,252	440	154	59	62	4
Total	48,380	22,502	8,854	3,059	1,065	402	321	24

Source: Missouri Department of Health and Senior Services.

physician's good faith clinical judgment, so complicates the medical condition of a pregnant woman as to necessitate the immediate abortion of her pregnancy to avert the death of the pregnant woman or for which a delay will create a serious risk of substantial and irreversible impairment of a major bodily function of the pregnant woman;

(7) "Physician," any person licensed to practice medicine in this state by the state board of registration of the healing arts;

(8) "Unborn child," the offspring of human beings from the moment of conception until birth and at every stage of its biological development, including the human conceptus, zygote, morula, blastocyst, embryo, and fetus;

(9) "Viability," that stage of fetal development when the life of the unborn child may be continued indefinitely outside the womb by natural or artificial life-supportive systems.

Missouri Code § 188.020. Physician required to perform

No person shall perform or induce an abortion except a physician.

Missouri Code § 188.025. Hospital required

Every abortion performed at sixteen weeks gestational age or later shall be performed in a hospital.

Missouri Code § 188.043.
Medical malpractice insurance required

1. No person shall perform or induce a surgical or medical abortion unless such person has proof of medical malpractice insurance with coverage amounts of at least five hundred thousand dollars.

2. For the purpose of this section, "medical malpractice insurance" means insurance coverage against the legal liability of the insured and against loss, damage, or expense incident to a claim arising out of the death or injury of any person as a result of the negligence or malpractice in rendering professional service by any health care provider.

3. No abortion facility or hospital shall employ or engage the services of a person to perform one or more abortions if the person does not have proof of medical malpractice insurance pursuant to this section, except the abortion facility or hospital may provide medical malpractice insurance for the services of persons employed or engaged by such facility or hospital.

4. Notwithstanding the provisions of section 334.100, RSMo, failure of a person to maintain the medical malpractice insurance required by this section shall be an additional ground for sanctioning of a person's license, certificate, or permit.

Missouri Code § 188.065. Revocation of license

Any practitioner of medicine, surgery, or nursing, or other health personnel who shall willfully and knowingly do or assist any action made unlawful by sections 188.010 to 188.085 shall be subject to having his license, application for license, or authority to practice his profession as a physician, surgeon, or nurse in the state of Missouri rejected or revoked by the appropriate state licensing board.

Missouri Code § 188.075. Violation of statutes

1. Any person who contrary to the provisions of sections 188. 010 to 188.085 knowingly performs, induces, or aids in the performance or inducing of any abortion or knowingly fails to perform any action required by sections 188.010 to 188.085 shall be guilty of a class A misdemeanor, unless a different penalty is provided for in state law, and, upon conviction, shall be punished as provided by law.

2. It shall be an affirmative defense for any person alleged to have violated any provision of this chapter that the person performed an action or did not perform an action because of a medical emergency. This affirmative defense shall be available in criminal, civil, and administrative actions or proceedings. The defendant shall have the burden of persuasion that the defense is more probably true than not.

Missouri Code § 188.080.
Abortion performed by person other than a physician

Any person who is not a physician who performs or induces or attempts to perform or induce an abortion on another is guilty of a class B felony, and, upon conviction, shall be punished as provided by law. Any physician performing or inducing an abortion who does not have clinical privileges at a hospital which offers obstetrical or gynecological care located within thirty miles of the location at which the abortion is performed or induced shall be guilty of a class A misdemeanor, and, upon conviction shall be punished as provided by law.

Missouri Code § 188.085. Statutes not to be deemed exclusive

Nothing in sections 188.010 to 188.085 shall be construed to exempt any person, firm, or corporation from civil liability for medical malpractice for negligent acts or certification under sections 188.010 to 188.085.

(3) INFORMED CONSENT

Prior to an abortion Missouri requires that a woman be fully informed of the procedure to be used, the risks involved and alternatives to abortion. It is required that a woman confirm in writing that she was given the information set out by statute. In *Planned Parenthood of Missouri v. Danforth* the United States Supreme Court held that the constitution was not violated by Missouri's written consent requirements. The informed consent statutes are set out below.

Missouri Code § 188.027. Consent, written and informed

No abortion shall be performed except with the prior, informed and written consent freely given of the pregnant woman.

Missouri Code § 188.039. Consent

1. For purposes of this section, "medical emergency" means a condition which, on the basis of the physician's good faith clinical judgment, so complicates the medical condition of a pregnant woman as to necessitate the immediate abortion of her pregnancy to avert her death or for which a delay will create a serious risk of substantial and irreversible impairment of a major bodily function.

2. Except in the case of medical emergency, no person shall perform or induce an abortion unless at least twenty-four hours prior thereto a treating physician has conferred with the patient and discussed with her the indicators and contraindicators, and risk factors including any physical, psychological, or situational factors for the proposed procedure and the use of medications, including but not limited to mifepristone, in light of her medical history and medical condition. For an abortion performed or an abortion induced by a drug or drugs, such conference shall take place at least twenty-four hours prior to the writing or communication of the first prescription for such drug or drugs in connection with inducing an abortion. Only one such conference shall be required for each abortion.

3. The patient shall be evaluated by a treating physician during the conference for indicators and contraindicators, risk factors including any physical, psychological, or situational factors which would predispose the patient to or increase the risk of experiencing one or more adverse physical, emotional, or other health reactions to the proposed procedure or drug or drugs in either the short or long term as compared with women who do not possess such risk factors.

4. At the end of the conference, and if the woman chooses to proceed with the abortion, a treating physician shall sign and shall cause the patient to sign a written statement that the woman gave her informed consent freely and without coercion after the physician had discussed with her the indicators and contraindicators, and risk factors, including any physical, psychological, or situational factors. All such executed statements shall be maintained as part of the patient's medical file, subject to the confidentiality laws and rules of this state.

5. The director of the department of health and senior services shall disseminate a model form that physicians may use as the written statement required by this section, but any lack or unavailability of such a model form shall not affect the duties of the physician set forth in subsections 2 to 4 of this section.

(4) VIABILITY TESTING

It is required by Missouri that a woman who is more than 19 weeks pregnant must, before obtaining an abortion, undergo testing for fetal viability. In *Webster v. Reproductive Health Services* the United States Supreme Court upheld Missouri's requirement that physicians conduct viability tests prior to performing abortions. The statute s set out below.

Missouri Code § 188.029. Viability determination

Before a physician performs an abortion on a woman he has reason to believe is carrying an unborn child of twenty or more weeks gestational age, the physician shall first determine if the unborn child is viable by using and exercising that degree of care, skill, and proficiency commonly exercised by the ordinarily skillful, careful, and prudent physician engaged in similar practice under the same or similar conditions. In making this determination of viability, the physician shall perform or cause to be performed such medical examinations and tests as are necessary to make a finding of the gestational age, weight, and lung maturity of the unborn child and shall enter such findings and determination of viability in the medical record of the mother.

(5) POST-VIABILITY ABORTION

Missouri has enacted a statute that prohibits post-viability abortions, except to save the life or health of the woman. A second physician is required to be present during a post-viability abortion. In *Planned Parenthood Assn. v. Ashcroft* the United States Supreme Court held that the constitution was not violated by the state's requirement that a second physician be present during abortions performed after viability. The statutes addressing the matter are set out below.

Missouri Code § 188.030. Abortion of viable unborn child

1. No abortion of a viable unborn child shall be performed unless necessary to preserve the life or health of the woman. Before a physician may perform an abortion upon a pregnant woman after such time as her unborn child has become viable, such physician shall first certify in writing that the abortion is necessary to preserve the life or health of the woman and shall further certify in writing the medical indications for such abortion and the probable health consequences.

2. Any physician who performs an abortion upon a woman carrying a viable unborn child shall utilize the available method or technique of abortion most likely to preserve the life and health of the unborn child. In cases where the method or technique of abortion which would most likely preserve the life and health of the unborn child would present a greater risk to the life and health of the woman than another available method or technique, the physician may utilize such other method or technique. In all cases where the physician performs an abortion upon a viable unborn child, the physician shall certify in writing the available method or techniques considered and the reasons for choosing the method or technique employed.

3. An abortion of a viable unborn child shall be performed or induced only when there is in attendance a physician other than the physician performing or inducing the abortion who shall take control of and provide immediate medical care for a child born as a result of the abortion. During the performance of the abortion, the physician performing it, and subsequent to the abortion, the physician required by this section to be in attendance, shall take all reasonable steps in keeping with good medical practice, consistent with the procedure used, to preserve the life and health of the viable unborn child; provided that it does not pose an increased risk to the life or health of the woman.

Missouri Code § 188.035. Death of child aborted alive

Whoever, with intent to do so, shall take the life of a child aborted alive, shall be guilty of murder of the second degree.

(6) PARTIAL-BIRTH ABORTION

Missouri criminalizes partial-birth abortions. In *Reproductive Health Services of Planned Parenthood of St. Louis Region, Inc. v. Nixon*, 429 F.3d 803 (8th Cir. 2005) a federal court of appeals found the ban on partial-birth abortions unconstitutional, in light of the United States Supreme Court decision in *Stenberg v. Carhart*, which invalidated a Nebraska statute that prohibited partial-birth abortions. However, the court of appeals decision was vacated by the United States Supreme Court in a memorandum opinion, *Nixon v. Reproductive Health Services of Planned Parenthood of St. Louis Region, Inc.*, 127 S.Ct. 2120 (2007). The Supreme Court remanded the case to the court of appeals for reconsideration of the decision in light of its 2007 decision in *Gonzales v. Carhart*, which approved of a federal statute that bans partial-birth abortion. The text of Missouri's partial-birth abortion statute is set out below.

Missouri Code § 565.300. Partial-birth abortion offense

1. This section shall be known and may be cited as the "Infant's Protection Act."

2. As used in this section, and only in this section, the following terms shall mean:

(1) "Born," complete separation of an intact child from the mother regardless of whether the umbilical cord is cut or the placenta detached;

(2) "Living infant," a human child, born or partially born, who is alive, as determined in accordance with the usual and customary standards of medical practice and is not dead as determined pursuant to section 194.005, RSMo, relating to the determination of the occurrence of death, and has not attained the age of thirty days post birth;

(3) "Partially born," partial separation of a child from the mother with the child's head intact with the torso. If vaginally delivered, a child is partially separated from the mother when the head in a cephalic presentation, or any part of the torso above the navel in a breech presentation, is outside the mother's external cervical os. If delivered abdominally, a child is partially separated from the mother when the child's head in a cephalic presentation, or any part of the torso above the navel in a breech presentation, is outside the mother's external abdominal wall.

3. A person is guilty of the crime of infanticide if such person causes the death of a living infant with the purpose to cause said death by an overt act performed when the infant is partially born or born.

4. The crime of infanticide shall be a class A felony.

5. A physician using procedures consistent with the usual and customary standards of medical practice to save the life of the mother during pregnancy or birth or to save the life of any unborn or partially born child of the same pregnancy shall not be criminally responsible under this section. In no event shall the mother be criminally responsible pursuant to this section for the acts of the physician if the physician is not held criminally responsible pursuant to this section.

6. This section shall not apply to any person who performs or attempts to perform a legal abortion if the act that causes the death is performed prior to the child being partially born, even though the death of the child occurs as a result of the abortion after the child is partially born.

7. Only that person who performs the overt act required under subsection 3 of this section shall be culpable under this section, unless a person, with the purpose of committing infanticide, does any act which is a substantial step towards the commission of the offense which results in the death of the living infant. A "substantial step" is conduct which is strongly corroborative of the firmness of the actor's purpose to complete the commission of the offense.

8. Nothing in this section shall be interpreted to exclude the defenses otherwise available to any person under the law including defenses provided pursuant to chapters 562 and 563, RSMo.

(7) ABORTION BY MINORS

Under the laws of Missouri no physician may perform an abortion upon an unemancipated minor unless he/she first obtains the written consent of either parent or the legal guardian of the minor. In compliance with federal constitutional law, Missouri has provided a judicial waiver procedure for an unemancipated minor to obtain an abortion without parental or guardian consent. The minor may petition a trial court for a waiver of the consent requirement. A minor has a right to an attorney at the proceeding and if she cannot afford one, the court must appoint her an attorney. If a minor chooses, she may represent herself. The required parental or guardian consent may be waived if the court finds either (1) that the minor is mature and well-informed enough to make the abortion decision on her own, or (2) that performance of the abortion would be in the best interest of the minor. An expedited appeal is available to any minor to whom the court denies a waiver of consent. In *Planned Parenthood Assn. v. Ashcroft* the United States Supreme Court held that the constitution was not violated by the state's requirement of parental or judicial consent for abortion by minors. The statutes addressing the issues are set out below.

Missouri Code § 188.028. Parental consent and judicial bypass

1. No person shall knowingly perform an abortion upon a pregnant woman under the age of eighteen years unless:

(1) The attending physician has secured the informed written consent of the minor and one parent or guardian; or

(2) The minor is emancipated and the attending physician has received the informed written consent of the minor; or

(3) The minor has been granted the right to self-consent to the abortion by court order pursuant to subsection 2 of this section, and the attending physician has received the informed written consent of the minor; or

(4) The minor has been granted consent to the abortion by court order, and the court has given its informed written consent in accordance with subsection 2 of this section, and the minor is having the abortion willingly, in compliance with subsection 3 of this section.

2. The right of a minor to self-consent to an abortion under subdivision (3) of subsection 1 of this section or court consent under subdivision (4) of subsection 1 of this section may be granted by a court pursuant to the following procedures:

(1) The minor or next friend shall make an application to the juvenile court which shall assist the minor or next friend in preparing the petition and notices required pursuant to this section. The minor or the next friend of the minor shall thereafter file a petition setting forth the initials of the minor; the age of the minor; the names and addresses of each parent, guardian, or, if the minor's parents are deceased and no guardian has been appointed, any other person standing in loco parentis of the minor; that the minor has been fully informed of the risks and consequences of the abortion; that the minor is of sound mind and has sufficient intellectual capacity to consent to the abortion; that, if the court does not grant the minor majority rights for the purpose of consent to the abortion, the court should find that the abortion is in the best interest of the minor and give judicial consent to the abortion; that the court should appoint a guardian ad litem of the child; and if the minor does not have private counsel, that the court should appoint counsel. The petition shall be signed by the minor or the next friend;

(2) A hearing on the merits of the petition, to be held on the record, shall be held as soon as possible within five days of the filing of the petition. If any party is unable to afford counsel, the court shall appoint counsel at least twenty-four hours before the time of the hearing. At the hearing, the court shall hear evidence relating to the emotional development, maturity, intellect and understanding of the minor; the nature, possible consequences, and alternatives to the abortion; and any other evidence that the court may find useful in determining whether the minor should be granted majority rights for the purpose of consenting to the abortion or whether the abortion is in the best interests of the minor;

(3) In the decree, the court shall for good cause:

(a) Grant the petition for majority rights for the purpose of consenting to the abortion; or

(b) Find the abortion to be in the best interests of the minor and give judicial consent to the abortion, setting forth the grounds for so finding; or

(c) Deny the petition, setting forth the grounds on which the petition is denied;

(4) If the petition is allowed, the informed consent of the minor, pursuant to a court grant of majority rights, or the judicial consent, shall bar an action by the parents or guardian of the minor on the grounds of battery of the minor by those performing the abortion. The immunity granted shall only extend to the performance of the abortion in accordance herewith and any necessary accompanying services which are performed in a competent manner. The costs of the action shall be borne by the parties;

(5) An appeal from an order issued under the provisions of this section may be taken to the court of appeals of this state by the minor or by a parent or guardian of the minor. The notice of intent to appeal shall be given within twenty-four hours from the date of issuance of the order. The record on appeal shall be completed and the appeal shall be perfected within five days from the filing of notice to appeal. Because time may be of the essence regarding the performance of the abortion, the supreme court of this state shall, by court rule, provide for expedited appellate review of cases appealed under this section.

3. If a minor desires an abortion, then she shall be orally informed of and, if possible, sign the written consent required by section 188.039 in the same manner as an adult person. No abortion shall be performed on any minor against her will, except that an abortion may be performed against the will of a minor pursuant to a court order described in subdivision (4) of subsection 1 of this section that the abortion is necessary to preserve the life of the minor.

Missouri Code § 188.031. Next friend defined

For purposes of section 188.028, the term "next friend" shall not include another minor child, or any entity or person in an individual or representative capacity that has a financial interest or potential gain from the proposed abortion, or any employee of or volunteer for such entity or person.

Missouri Code § 188.250.
Assisting minor to obtain abortion without required consent

1. No person shall intentionally cause, aid, or assist a minor to obtain an abortion without the consent or consents required by section 188.028.

2. A person who violates subsection 1 of this section shall be civilly liable to the minor and to the person or persons required to give the consent or consents under section 188.028. A court may award damages to the person or persons adversely affected by a violation of subsection 1 of this section, including compensation for emotional injury without the need for personal presence at the act or event, and the court may further award attorneys' fees, litigation costs, and punitive damages. Any adult who engages in or consents to another person engaging in a sex act with a minor in violation of the provisions of chapter 566, 567, 568, or 573, RSMo, which results in the minor's pregnancy shall not be awarded damages under this section.

3. It shall not be a defense to a claim brought under this section that the abortion was performed or induced pursuant to consent to the abortion given in a manner that is otherwise lawful in the state or place where the abortion was performed or induced.

4. An unemancipated minor does not have capacity to consent to any action in violation of this section or section 188.028.

5. A court may enjoin conduct that would be in violation of this section upon petition by the attorney general, a prosecuting or circuit attorney, or any person adversely affected or who reasonably may be adversely affected by such conduct, upon a showing that such conduct:

(1) Is reasonably anticipated to occur in the future; or

(2) Has occurred in the past, whether with the same minor or others, and that it is not unreasonable to expect that such conduct will be repeated.

(8) USE OF FACILITIES AND PEOPLE

Under the laws of Missouri hospitals are not required to allow abortions at their facilities. The employees and physicians at hospitals that do allow abortions are permitted to refuse to take part in abortions. The state also has statutes which prohibit discrimination by public and private employers against employees who refuse to take part in abortions. The statutes are set out below.

Missouri Code § 197.032. Hospitals and medical personnel

1. No physician or surgeon, registered nurse, practical nurse, midwife or hospital, public or private, shall be required to treat or admit for treatment any woman for the purpose of abortion if such treatment or admission for treatment is contrary to the established policy of, or the moral, ethical or religious beliefs of, such physician, surgeon, registered nurse, midwife, practical nurse or hospital. No cause of action shall accrue against any such physician, surgeon, registered nurse, midwife, practical nurse or hospital on account of such refusal to treat or admit for treatment any woman for abortion purposes.

2. No person or institution shall be denied or discriminated against in the reception of any public benefit, assistance or privilege whatsoever or in any employment, public or private, on the grounds that they refuse to undergo an abortion, to advise, consent to, assist in or perform an abortion.

3. Any person who shall deny or discriminate against another for refusal to perform or participate in an abortion shall be liable to the party injured in an action at law, suit in equity or other redress.

Missouri Code § 188.100. Definitions

Unless the language or context clearly indicates a different meaning is intended, the following words or phrases for the purposes of sections 188.100 to 188.120 shall mean:

(1) "Employer," the state, or any political or civil subdivision thereof, or any person employing two or more persons within the state, and any person acting as an agent of the employer;

(2) "Participate in abortion," to perform, assist in, refer for, promote, procure, or counsel a woman to have an abortion not necessary to save the life of the mother; or to undergo an abortion;

(3) "Person" includes one or more individuals, partnerships, associations, organizations, corporations, legal representatives, trustees, trustees in bankruptcy, receivers, or other organized groups of persons.

Missouri Code § 188.105. Discrimination by employer

1. It shall be unlawful:

(1) For an employer:

(a) To fail or refuse to hire or to discharge any individual, or otherwise to discriminate against any individual with respect to his or her compensation, terms, conditions, or privileges of employment, because of such individual's refusal to participate in abortion;

(b) To limit, segregate, or classify his, her, or its employees or applicants for employment in any way which would deprive or tend to deprive any individual of employment opportunities or otherwise adversely affect his or her status as an employee, because of such individual's refusal to participate in abortion;

(c) To discharge, expel, or otherwise discriminate against any person because he or she has opposed any practices forbidden under sections 188.100 to 188.120 or because he or she has filed a complaint, testified, or assisted in any legal proceeding under sections 188.100 to 188.120;

(2) For any person, whether an employer or employee, or not, to aid, abet, incite, compel, or coerce the doing of any of the acts forbidden under sections 188.100 to 188.120, or to attempt to do so.

2. Notwithstanding any other provision of sections 188.100 to 188.120, the acts proscribed in subsection 1 of this section shall not be unlawful if there can be demonstrated an inability to reasonably accommodate an individual's refusal to participate in abortion without undue hardship on the conduct of that particular business or enterprise, or in those certain instances where participation in abortion is a bona fide occupational qualification reasonably necessary to the normal operation of that particular business or enterprise.

3. Nothing contained in sections 188.100 to 188.120 shall be interpreted to require any employer to grant preferential treatment to any individual because of such individual's refusal to participate in abortion.

Missouri Code § 188.110.
Discrimination by colleges, universities and hospitals

1. No public or private college, university or hospital shall discriminate against any person for refusal to participate in abortion.

2. No applicant, student, teacher, or employee of any school shall be required to pay any fees that would in whole or in part fund an abortion for any other applicant, student, teacher, or employee of that school, if the individual required to pay the fee gives written notice to the proper school authorities that it would be in violation of his or her conscience or beliefs to pay for or fund abortions. The school may require the individual to pay that part of the fees not funding abortions, if the school makes reasonable precautions and gives reasonable assurance that the fees that are paid are segregated from any fund for the payment of abortions.

Missouri Code § 188.115. Severability clause

If any provision of sections 188.100 to 188.120 is found by a court of competent jurisdiction to be invalid or unconstitutional as applied to a specific person or class of persons, the provisions of sections 188.100 to 188.120 shall remain in full force and effect as to every other person or class of persons who is otherwise covered under these sections.

Missouri Code § 188.120.
Cause of action for violation of discrimination laws

Any individual injured by any person, association, corporation, or entity by reason of any action prohibited by sections 188.100 to 188.120, as now or hereafter amended, may commence a civil cause of action against the person, association, corporation, or entity who caused the injury, and shall recover treble damages, including pain and suffering, sustained by such individual, the costs of the suit and reasonable attorney's fees.

(9) PUBLIC FUNDS, EMPLOYEES AND FACILITIES

Missouri prohibits the use of public funds to pay for abortions, except to save the life of the woman. The state also prohibits the use of public employees and public facilities to assist in performing an abortion that is not necessary to save the life of a woman. In *Webster v. Reproductive Health Services* the United States Supreme Court upheld Missouri's prohibition on the use of public facilities or employees to perform abortions. The statutes addressing the matter are set out below.

Missouri Code § 188.200. Definitions

As used in sections 188.200 to 188.220, the following terms mean:

(1) "Public employee," any person employed by this state or any agency or political subdivision thereof;

(2) "Public facility," any public institution, public facility, public equipment, or any physical asset owned, leased, or controlled by this state or any agency or political subdivisions thereof;

(3) "Public funds," any funds received or controlled by this state or any agency or political subdivision thereof, including, but not limited to, funds derived from federal, state or local taxes, gifts or grants from any source, public or private, federal grants or payments, or intergovernmental transfers.

Missouri Code § 188.205. Public funds

It shall be unlawful for any public funds to be expended for the purpose of performing or assisting an abortion, not necessary to save the life of the mother, or for the purpose of encouraging or counseling a woman to have an abortion not necessary to save her life.

Missouri Code § 188.210. Public employees

It shall be unlawful for any public employee within the scope of his employment to perform or assist an abortion, not necessary to save the life of the mother. It shall be unlawful for a doctor, nurse or other health care personnel, a social worker, a counselor or persons of similar occupation who is a public employee within the scope of his public employment to encourage or counsel a woman to have an abortion not necessary to save her life.

Missouri Code § 188.215. Public facilities

It shall be unlawful for any public facility to be used for the purpose of performing or assisting an abortion not necessary to save the life of the mother or for the purpose of encouraging or counseling a woman to have an abortion not necessary to save her life.

Missouri Code § 188.220. Taxpayer standing to bring suit

Any taxpayer of this state or its political subdivisions shall have standing to bring suit in a circuit court of proper venue to enforce the provisions of sections 188.200 to 188.215.

Missouri Code § 188.230.
Persons authorized to perform abortions

Nothing in this act is intended to authorize anyone other than a physician to perform an abortion.

Missouri Code § 208.655. Abortion counseling prohibited

No funds used to pay for insurance or for services pursuant to sections 208.631 to 208.657 may be expended to encourage, counsel or refer for abortion unless the abortion is done to save the life of the mother or if the unborn child is the result of rape or incest. No funds may be paid pursuant to sections 208.631 to 208.657 to any person or organization that performs abortions or counsels or refers for abortion unless the abortion is done to save the life of the mother or if the unborn child is the result of rape or incest.

Missouri Code § 208.152. Medicaid services (abridged)

1. MO HealthNet payments shall be made on behalf of those eligible needy persons as defined in section 208.151 who are unable to provide for it in whole or in part, with any payments to be made on the basis of the reasonable cost of the care or reasonable charge for the services as defined and determined by the MO HealthNet division, unless otherwise hereinafter provided, for the following:

(11) Family planning as defined by federal rules and regulations; provided, however, that such family planning services shall not include abortions unless such abortions are certified in writing by a physician to the MO HealthNet agency that, in his professional judgment, the life of the mother would be endangered if the fetus were carried to term.

(10) FETAL EXPERIMENTS AND CLONING

Missouri has enacted several statutes that prohibit fetal experiments. The state has also created a statute that prohibits the use of public funds for human cloning. The statutes are set out below.

Missouri Code § 188.037. Experimentation on aborted live fetus

No person shall use any fetus or child aborted alive for any type of scientific, research, laboratory or other kind of experimentation either prior to or subsequent to any abortion procedure except as necessary to protect or preserve the life and health of such fetus or child aborted alive.

Missouri Code § 188.036. Prohibited fetal experiments

1. No physician shall perform an abortion on a woman if the physician knows that the woman conceived the unborn child for the purpose of providing fetal organs or tissue for medical transplantation to herself or another, and the physician knows that the woman intends to procure the abortion to utilize those organs or tissue for such use for herself or another.

2. No person shall utilize the fetal organs or tissue resulting from an abortion for medical transplantation, if the person knows that the abortion was procured for the purpose of utilizing those organs or tissue for such use.

3. No person shall offer any inducement, monetary or otherwise, to a woman or a prospective father of an unborn child for the purpose of conceiving an unborn child for the medical, scientific, experimental or therapeutic use of the fetal organs or tissue.

4. No person shall offer any inducement, monetary or otherwise, to the mother or father of an unborn child for the purpose of procuring an abortion for the medical, scientific, experimental or therapeutic use of the fetal organs or tissue.

5. No person shall knowingly offer or receive any valuable consideration for the fetal organs or tissue resulting from an abortion, provided that nothing in this subsection shall prohibit payment for burial or other final disposition of the fetal remains, or payment for a pathological examination, autopsy or postmortem examination of the fetal remains.

6. If any provision in this section or the application thereof to any person, circumstance or period of gestation is held invalid, such invalidity shall not affect the provisions or applications which can be given effect without the invalid provision or application, and to this end the provisions of this section are declared severable.

Missouri Code § 1.217. Cloning

No state funds shall be used for research with respect to the cloning of a human person. For purposes of this section, the term "cloning" means the replication of a human person by taking a cell with genetic material and cultivating such cell through the egg, embryo, fetal and newborn stages of development into a new human person.

Missouri Code § 196.1127. Limitations on use of public funds

1. The moneys appropriated to the life sciences research board pursuant to sections 196.1100 to 196.1124 shall be subject to the provisions of this section.

2. As used in this section, the following terms shall mean:

(1) "Abortion services" include performing, inducing, or assisting with abortions, as defined in section 188.015, RSMo, or encouraging patients to have abortions, referring patients for abortions not necessary to save the life of the mother, or development of drugs, chemicals, or devices intended to be used to induce an abortion;

(2) "Child," a human being recognized as a minor pursuant to the laws of this state, including if in vivo, an unborn child as defined in section 188.015, RSMo, and if in vitro, a human being at any of the stages of biological development of an unborn child from conception or inception onward;

(3) "Conception," the same meaning as such term is defined in section 188.015, RSMo;

(4) "Facilities and administrative costs," those costs that are incurred for common or joint objectives and therefore cannot be identified readily and specifically with a particular research project or any other institutional activity;

(5) "Human cloning," the creation of a human being by any means other than by the fertilization of an oocyte of a human female by a sperm of a human male;

(6) "Prohibited human research," research in a research project in which there is the taking or utilization of the organs, tissues, or cellular material of:

(a) A deceased child, unless consent is given by the parents in a manner provided in sections 194.210 to 194.290, RSMo, relating to anatomical gifts, and neither parent caused the death of such child or consented to another person causing the death of such child;

(b) A living child, when the intended or likely result of such taking or utilization is to kill or cause harm to the health, safety, or welfare of such child, or when the purpose is to target such child for possible destruction in the future;

(7) "Public funds," include:

(a) Any moneys received or controlled by the State of Missouri or any official, department, division, agency, or political subdivision thereof, including but not limited to moneys derived from federal, state, or local taxes, gifts, or grants from any source, settlements of any claims or causes of action, public or private, bond proceeds, federal grants or payments, or intergovernmental transfers;

(b) Any moneys received or controlled by an official, department, division, or agency of state government or any political subdivision thereof, or to any person or entity pursuant to appropriation by the general assembly or governing body of any political subdivision of this state;

(8) "Research project," research proposed to be funded by an award of public funds conducted under the auspices of the entity or entities that applied for and received such award, regardless of whether the research is funded in whole or in part by such award. Such research shall include basic research, including the discovery of new knowledge; translational research, including translational knowledge in a usable form; and clinical research, including but not limited to health research in human development and aging, cancer, endocrine, cardiovascular, neurological, pulmonary, and infectious disease.

3. Public funds shall not be expended, paid, or granted to or on behalf of an existing or proposed research project that involves abortion services, human cloning, or prohibited human research. A research project that receives an award of public funds shall not share costs with another research project, person, or entity not eligible to receive public funds pursuant to this subsection; provided that a research project that receives an award of public funds may pay a pro rata share of facilities and administrative costs determined in the award of public funds according to standards that ensure that public funds do not in any way subsidize facilities and administrative costs of other research projects, persons, or entities not eligible to receive public funds pursuant to this subsection. The application for an award of public funds shall set forth the proposed rates of pro rata cost reimbursement and shall provide supporting data and rationale for such rates. All applicants for and recipients of awards of public funds shall comply with the cost accounting principles set forth in Part 9905 of Title 48 of the Code of Federal Regulations, or successor regulations, in connection with the application for and administration of the research project. All moneys derived from an award of public funds shall be expended only by checks, drafts, or electronic transfers using a separate accounting process maintained for each research project. No moneys derived from an award of public funds shall be used to cover costs for any other research project or to any other person or entity. No moneys derived from an award of public funds shall be passed through to any other research project, person, or entity unless included in the original application for the award of public funds or in subsequent amendments or requests to use separate contractors. A research project that receives an award of public funds shall maintain financial records that demonstrate strict compliance with this subsection. Any audit conducted pursuant to any grant or contract awarding public funds shall also certify whether there is compliance with this subsection and shall note any noncompliance as a material audit finding.

4. The provisions of this section shall inure to the benefit of all residents of this state. Any taxpayer of this state or any political subdivision of this state shall have standing to bring suit against the State of Missouri or any official, department, division, agency, or political subdivision of this state, and any recipient of public funds who or which is in violation of this subsection in any circuit court with jurisdiction to enforce the provisions of this section.

5. This section shall not be construed to permit or make lawful any conduct that is otherwise unlawful pursuant to the laws of this state.

6. Any provision of this section is not severable from any appropriation subject to this section or any application declared by any court to be subject to this section. If any provision of this section is found to be invalid or unconstitutional, any appropriation subject to this section or any appropriation declared by any court to be subject to this section shall be void, invalid, and unenforceable.

(11) WRONGFUL LIFE ACTION

Missouri has taken an affirmative step to prevent wrongful life litigation, by prohibiting claims for negligent failure to abort a pregnancy. The statute addressing the matter is set out below.

Missouri Code § 188.130. Prohibition of tort actions

1. No person shall maintain a cause of action or receive an award of damages on behalf of himself or herself based on the claim that but for the negligent conduct of another, he or she would have been aborted.

2. No person shall maintain a cause of action or receive an award of damages based on the claim that but for the negligent conduct of another, a child would have been aborted.

(12) FETAL DEATH REPORT

Missouri requires that all abortions be reported to the proper authorities. The statutes addressing the matter are set out below.

Missouri Code § 188.047. Tissue sample authorized

A representative sample of tissue removed at the time of abortion shall be submitted to a board eligible or certified pathologist, who shall file a copy of the tissue report with the state department of health and senior services, and who shall provide a copy of the report to the abortion facility or hospital in which the abortion was performed or induced and the pathologist's report shall be made a part of the patient's permanent record.

Missouri Code § 188.052. Physician's report on abortion

1. An individual abortion report for each abortion performed or induced upon a woman shall be completed by her attending physician.

2. An individual complication report for any post-abortion care performed upon a woman shall be completed by the physician providing such post-abortion care. This report shall include:

(1) The date of the abortion;

(2) The name and address of the abortion facility or hospital where the abortion was performed;

(3) The nature of the abortion complication diagnosed or treated.

3. All abortion reports shall be signed by the attending physician, and submitted to the state department of health and senior services within forty-five days from the date of the abortion. All complication reports shall be signed by the physician providing the post-abortion care and submitted to the department of health and senior services within forty-five days from the date of the post-abortion care.

4. A copy of the abortion report shall be made a part of the medical record of the patient of the facility or hospital in which the abortion was performed.

5. The state department of health and senior services shall be responsible for collecting all abortion reports and complication reports and collating and evaluating all data gathered therefrom and shall annually publish a statistical report based on such data from abortions performed in the previous calendar year.

Missouri Code § 188.055. Forms

1. Every abortion facility, hospital, and physician shall be supplied with forms by the department of health and senior services for use in regards to the consents and reports required by sections 188.010 to 188.085. A purpose and function of such consents and reports shall be the preservation of maternal health and life by adding to the sum of medical knowledge through the compilation of relevant maternal health and life data and to monitor all abortions performed to assure that they are done only under and in accordance with the provisions of the law.

2. All information obtained by physician, hospital, or abortion facility from a patient for the purpose of preparing reports to the department of health and senior services under sections 188.010 to 188.085 or reports received by the division of health shall be confidential and shall be used only for statistical purposes. Such records, however, may be inspected and health data acquired by local, state, or national public health officers.

Missouri Code § 188.060. Records to be retained for seven years

All medical records, reports, and other documents required to be kept under sections 188.010 to 188.085 shall be maintained in the permanent files of the abortion facility or hospital in which the abortion was performed for a period of seven years.

Missouri Code § 188.023. Statutory rape victims

Any licensed health care professional who delivers a baby or performs an abortion, who has prima facie evidence that a patient has been the victim of statutory rape in the first degree or statutory rape in the second degree, or if the patient is under the age of eighteen, that he or she has been a victim of sexual abuse, including forcible rape, sexual assault, or incest, shall be required to report such offenses in the same manner as provided for by section 210.115, RSMo.

Missouri Code § 188.070. Breach of confidentiality prohibited

Any physician or other person who fails to maintain the confidentiality of any records or reports required under sections 188.010 to 188.085 is guilty of a misdemeanor and, upon conviction, shall be punished as provided by law.

(13) ABORTION ALTERNATIVE PROGRAMS

Missouri provides public funding for programs offering alternatives to abortion services. The statutes addressing the matter are set out below.

Missouri Code § 188.325.
Alternatives to abortion services program

1. There is hereby established the "Missouri Alternatives to Abortion Services Program" which shall be administered by a state agency or agencies, as designated by appropriations to such or each agency. The alternatives to abortion services program shall consist of services or counseling to pregnant women and continuing for one year after birth to assist women in carrying their unborn children to term instead of having abortions, and to assist women in caring for their dependent children or placing their children for adoption.

2. Services provided under the alternatives to abortion program shall include, but not be limited to the following:

(1) Prenatal care;
(2) Medical and mental health care;
(3) Parenting skills;
(4) Drug and alcohol testing and treatment;
(5) Child care, and newborn and infant care;
(6) Housing and utilities;
(7) Educational services;
(8) Food, clothing, and supplies relating to pregnancy, newborn care, and parenting;
(9) Adoption assistance;
(10) Job training and placement;
(11) Establishing and promoting responsible paternity;
(12) Ultrasound services;
(13) Case management;
(14) Domestic abuse protection; and
(15) Transportation.

3. Actual provision and delivery of services and counseling shall be dependent on client needs and not otherwise prioritized by the agency or agencies administering the program. Services and counseling shall be available only during pregnancy and continuing for one year after birth, and shall exclude any family planning services. The agency or agencies administering the program may contract with other public or private agencies or entities to provide the services or counseling on behalf of the agency or agencies administering the program. Such other public or private agencies or entities may provide additional services or counseling, or services or counseling for more than one year after birth, that are not funded under the alternatives to abortion services program, as long as such services or counseling are not inconsistent with the provisions of this section. Contractors for the alternatives to abortion services program may also be contractors for the alternatives to abortion public awareness program established in section 188.335.

4. The agency or agencies administering the program shall to the greatest extent possible supplement and match moneys appropriated for the alternatives to abortion services program with federal and other public moneys and with private moneys. The agency or agencies administering the program shall prioritize such additional federal, other public, and private moneys so that they are used preferentially for the alternatives to abortion services program and the alternatives to abortion public awareness program.

5. The alternatives to abortion services program and the moneys expended under this section shall not be used to perform or induce, assist in the performing or inducing of or refer for abortions. Moneys expended under this section shall not be granted to organizations or affiliates of organizations that perform or induce, assist in the performing or inducing of or refer for abortions.

Missouri Code § 188.335.
Alternatives to abortion public awareness program

1. There is hereby established the "Missouri Alternatives to Abortion Public Awareness Program" which shall be administered by a state agency or agencies, as designated by appropriations to such or each agency.

2. The purpose of the alternatives to abortion public awareness program is to help pregnant women at risk for having abortions to be made aware of the alternatives to abortion agencies located and alternatives to abortion services available to them in their local communities. The alternatives to abortion public awareness program shall include the development and promotion of a web site which provides a geographically indexed list of alternatives to abortion agencies as well as contractors for the alternatives to abortion services program established in section 188.325. As used in this section, "alternatives to abortion agencies" means agencies exempt from income taxation pursuant to the United States Internal Revenue Code that offer alternatives to abortion services as defined within section 188.325, including but not limited to maternity homes, pregnancy resource centers, and agencies commonly known and referred to as crisis pregnancy centers. The alternatives to abortion public awareness program may also include but need not be limited to the use of television, radio, outdoor advertising, newspapers, magazines, and other print media, and the Internet to provide information on these alternatives to abortion agencies and services. The state agency or agencies administering the alternatives to abortion public awareness program are encouraged to give first preference to contracting with private agencies or entities, which are exempt from income taxation pursuant to the United States Internal Revenue Code, to conduct the alternatives to abortion public awareness program. Contractors for the alternatives to abortion public awareness program may also be contractors for the alternatives to abortion services program established in section 188.325.

3. The agency or agencies administering the program shall to the greatest extent possible supplement and match moneys appropriated for the alternatives to abortion public awareness program with federal and other public moneys and with private moneys. The agency or agencies administering the program shall prioritize such additional federal, other public, and private moneys so that they are used preferentially for the alternatives to abortion public awareness program and the alternatives to abortion services program.

4. The alternatives to abortion public awareness program and the moneys expended under this section shall not be used to perform or induce, assist in the performing or inducing of or refer for abortions. Moneys expended under this section shall not be granted to organizations or affiliates of organizations that perform or induce, assist in the performing or inducing of or refer for abortions.

(14) INSURANCE POLICIES

Missouri prohibits insurance policies from being issued that cover elective abortions, unless the policies carry a separate premium for such services. The statutes addressing the matter are set out below.

Missouri Code § 376.805.
Additional premium for elective abortion

1. No health insurance contracts, plans, or policies delivered or issued for delivery in the state shall provide coverage for elective abortions except by an optional rider for which there must be paid an additional premium. For purposes of this section, an "elective abortion" means an abortion for any reason other than a spontaneous abortion or to prevent the death of the female upon whom the abortion is performed.

2. This section shall be applicable to all contracts, plans or policies of:

(1) All health insurers subject to this chapter; and

(2) All nonprofit hospital, medical, surgical, dental, and health service corporations subject to chapter 354, RSMo; and

(3) All health maintenance organizations.

3. This section shall be applicable only to contracts, plans or policies written, issued, renewed or revised, after September 28, 1983. For the purposes of this subsection, if new premiums are charged for a contract, plan or policy, it shall be determined to be a new contract, plan or policy.

Missouri Code § 376.1199. Health benefit plans (abridged)

1. Each health carrier or health benefit plan that offers or issues health benefit plans providing obstetrical/gynecological benefits and pharmaceutical coverage, which are delivered, issued for delivery, continued or renewed in this state on or after January 1, 2002, shall:

(1) Notwithstanding the provisions of subsection 4 of section 354.618, RSMo, provide enrollees with direct access to the services of a participating obstetrician, participating gynecologist or participating obstetrician/gynecologist of her choice within the provider network for covered services. The services covered by this subdivision shall be limited to those services defined by the published recommendations of the accreditation council for graduate medical education for training an obstetrician, gynecologist or obstetrician/gynecologist including but not limited to diagnosis, treatment and referral for such services. A health carrier shall not impose additional co-payments coinsurance or deductibles upon any enrollee who seeks or receives health care services pursuant to this subdivision, unless similar additional co-payments, coinsurance or deductibles are imposed for other types of health care services received within the provider network. Nothing in this subsection shall be construed to require a health carrier to perform, induce, pay for, reimburse, guarantee, arrange, provide any resources for or refer a patient for an abortion, as defined in section 188.015, RSMo, other than a spontaneous abortion or to prevent the death of the female upon whom the abortion is performed or to supersede or conflict with section 376.805.

Missouri Right to Life

Missouri Right to Life (MRL) is a pro-life organization headed by its executive director Patricia Skain. MRL believes that all persons have a fundamental, unalienable, natural right to life regardless of biological development or health function. The organization engages in activities that include educating the public on abortion, promoting right to life legislation, and supporting positive alternatives to abortion. *See also* **Pro-Life Organizations**

MIT Pro-Life

MIT Pro-Life is a student-run pro-life organization on the campus of MIT. The organization is devoted to fostering respect for human life from the moment of conception, and to promoting support for the pro-life position. The group's pro-life efforts are mainly educational and campus-oriented. It seeks to be a resource for MIT students to examine in depth the social, medical, and legal aspects of the pro-life response to abortion. The group has sponsored debates, speakers, information booths on campus, joint events with other collegiate pro-life groups, fund-raising rose sales (the rose is the international pro-life symbol), participation in the annual national pro-life March for Life in Washington, D.C., and volunteer work for pregnancy help centers. *See also* **Pro-Life Organizations**

Mobilization for Women's Lives

Mobilization for Women's Lives was a nationwide event staged on November 12, 1989 by over 1,000 pro-choice organizations. The event took place to reaffirm the commitment to legalized abortion by pro-choice advocates. It was estimated that over two million pro-choice advocates participated in the event in cities across the nation.

Mobius Syndrome

Mobius syndrome is a genetic disorder involving the absence or inadequate development of certain cranial nerves. The nerves affected control eye movements and facial expression. Symptoms associated with the disorder include lack of facial expression, eye sensitivity, motor delays, hearing and speech problems, physical deformities and mental retardation. Treatment for the disorder may include feeding tubes, surgery, and physical and speech therapy. *See also* **Birth Defects and Abortion**

Molar Pregnancy *see* **Gestational Trophoblastic Tumors**

Molluscum Contagiosum

Molluscum contagiosum is a sexually transmitted disease that causes lesions on the genitals, lower abdomen, buttocks, or inner thighs. In people with healthy immune systems, the virus usually disappears spontaneously over a period of months to years. However, the lesions may be extensive in people with AIDS or other conditions that affect the immune system. The disease itself cannot be killed. Individual lesions may be removed surgically, by scraping, freezing, or through needle electrosurgery. Surgical removal of individual lesions may result in scarring. Medications may be helpful in removal of lesions. Using latex condoms during sexual intercourse may prevent transmission of the disease. *See also* **Sexually Transmitted Diseases**

Mongolism *see* **Down Syndrome**

Monoamnionic Twin Gestation

Monoamnionic twin gestation is a condition involving twin fetuses sharing the same amniotic sac. This condition occurs in about 2 percent of all twin pregnancies. The likelihood of survival in this situation is approximately 50 percent. The major concern posed by this condition is that, because there is no membrane separating the fetuses, they are at risk for cord entanglement and death due to cessation of blood flow caused by the cord entanglement. Most pregnancies are believed to be lost due to cord entanglement. Additionally, the pregnancy may be lost or compromised if one of the fetuses dies, because this could lead to death or severe damage of the second fetus. *See also* **Fetal Transfusion Syndrome; Monochorionic Twin Gestation; Multifetal Pregnancy Reduction; Multiple Gestation; Twin Reversed Arterial Perfusion; Vanishing Twin Syndrome**

Monochorionic Twin Gestation

Monochorionic twin gestation is a condition involving twin fetuses sharing a unified placenta. This condition results in one of the fetuses being severely malformed and at a high risk of not surviving. The unhealthy fetus may compromise the life of both fetuses in two primary ways: causing an accumulation of amniotic fluid that leads to miscarriage; or the spontaneous death of the unhealthy fetus may result in death or brain damage to the other fetus. The overall survival rate of both fetuses is low, but with medical intervention to abort the unhealthy fetus, the healthy fetus has a higher survival rate. *See also* **Fetal Transfusion Syndrome; Monoamnionic Twin Gestation; Multifetal Pregnancy Reduction; Multiple Gestation; Twin Reversed Arterial Perfusion; Vanishing Twin Syndrome**

Montana

(1) OVERVIEW

The state of Montana enacted its first criminal abortion statute in 1864. The statute underwent several amendments prior to the 1973 decision by the United States Supreme Court in *Roe v. Wade*, which legalized abortion in the nation. Montana has taken affirmative steps to respond to *Roe* and its progeny. The state has addressed numerous abortion issues by statute that include general abortion guidelines, informed consent, partial-birth abortion, abortion by minors, use of facilities and people, and fetal death report.

(2) GENERAL ABORTION GUIDELINES

Under Montana's general abortion statutes the legislature has made clear that abortion is permitted only to the extent that the United States Supreme Court allows the same. Montana has enacted a penal statute that prohibits post-viability abortions, except to save the life or health of the woman. A post-viability abortion must be found necessary by two physicians, other than the physician performing the abortion. The state also requires that an abortion be performed by a physician. The physician only requirement was upheld by the United States Supreme Court in *Mazurek v. Armstrong*. The statutes are set out below.

Montana Code § 50-20-101. Short title

This part may be cited as the "Montana Abortion Control Act."

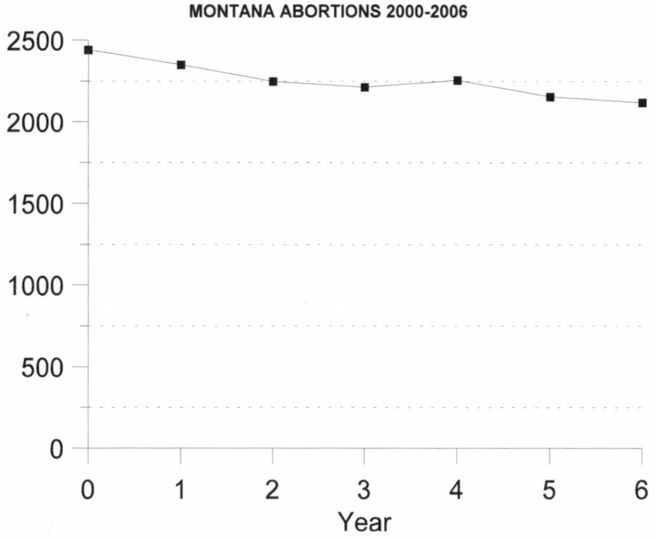

Source: Montana Department of Public Health and Human Services.

Montana Prior Abortion by Female 2000–2006

	Prior Abortion					
Year	*None*	*1*	*2*	*3*	*≥4*	*Not known*
2000	1,403	699	223	77	37	2
2001	1,499	578	178	61	34	0
2002	1,439	559	170	50	29	1
2003	1,431	543	168	48	23	0
2004	1,407	566	181	66	36	0
2005	1,293	571	193	67	29	2
2006	782	908	299	85	45	0
Total	9,254	4,424	1,412	454	233	5

Source: Montana Department of Public Health and Human Services.

Montana Abortion by Age Group 2000–2006

	Age Group (yrs)								
Year	*<15*	*15–17*	*18–19*	*20–24*	*25–29*	*30–34*	*35–39*	*≥40*	*Unknown*
2000	17	219	334	839	442	291	209	89	1
2001	13	196	330	794	410	286	220	93	8
2002	16	200	294	747	413	302	185	91	0
2003	9	180	284	742	471	255	179	89	4
2004	9	178	265	786	483	250	183	101	1
2005	7	206	261	737	412	289	170	72	1
2006	13	148	252	773	453	234	158	87	1
Total	84	1,327	2,020	5,418	3,084	1,907	1,304	622	16

Source: Montana Department of Public Health and Human Services.

Montana Abortion by Weeks of Gestation 2000–2006

	Year							
Weeks of Gestation	*2000*	*2001*	*2002*	*2003*	*2004*	*2005*	*2006*	*Total*
≤9	1,501	1,518	1,438	1,439	1,416	1,358	1,415	10,085
10–11	368	358	365	337	368	361	329	2,486
12–13	239	217	205	184	202	189	192	1,428
14–15	129	113	107	99	86	99	88	721
16–17	59	44	52	48	60	62	45	370
18–19	59	48	57	57	73	46	34	374
≥20	61	43	17	42	51	39	14	267
Not known	25	9	7	7	0	1	2	51

Source: Montana Department of Public Health and Human Services.

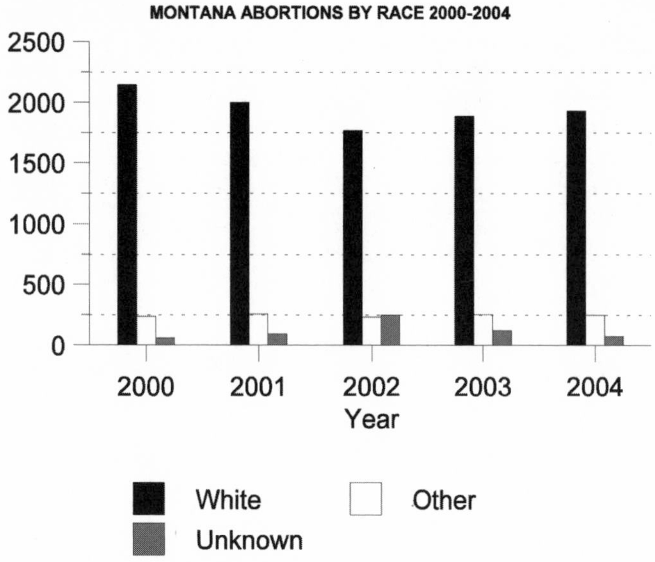

Source: National Center for Health Statistics.

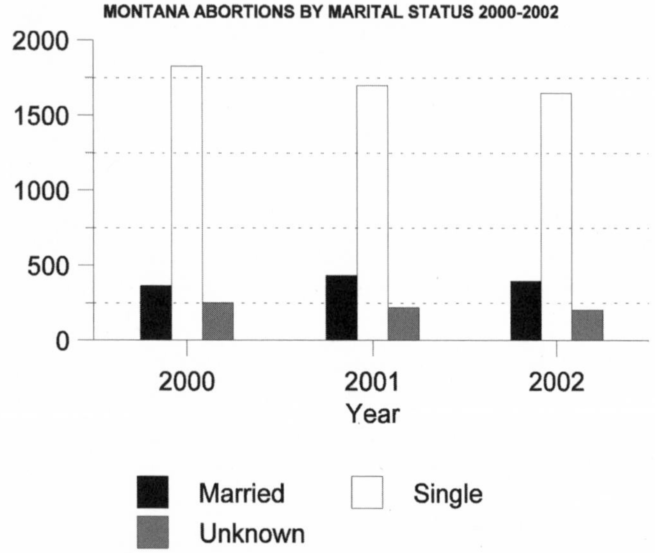

Source: National Center for Health Statistics.

Montana Code § 50-20-102. Statement of purpose

(1) The legislature reaffirms the tradition of the state of Montana to protect every human life, whether unborn or aged, healthy or sick. In keeping with this tradition and in the spirit of our constitution, we reaffirm the intent to extend the protection of the laws of Montana in favor of all human life. It is the policy of the state to preserve and protect the lives of all human beings and to provide protection for the viable human life. The protection afforded to a person by Montana's constitutional right of privacy is not absolute, but may be infringed upon by a compelling state interest. The legislature finds that a compelling state interest exists in the protection of viable life.

(2) The legislature finds, with respect to 50-20-401, that:

(a) the United States supreme court has determined that states have a legitimate interest in protecting both a woman's health and the potentiality of human life and that each interest grows and reaches a compelling point at various stages of a woman's approach to the full term of a pregnancy;

(b) the court has also determined that subsequent to viability, the state in promoting its interest in the potentiality of human life may, if it chooses, regulate and even proscribe abortion except when necessary, in appropriate medical judgment, for the preservation of the life or health of the woman;

(c) the holdings referred to in subsections (2)(a) and (2)(b) apply to unborn persons in order to extend to unborn persons the inalienable right to defend their lives and liberties;

(d) absent clear proof that an abortion is necessary to save the life of the woman, the abortion of a viable person is an infringement of that person's rights; and

(e) the state has a duty to protect innocent life and that duty has grown to a compelling point with respect to partial-birth abortion.

Montana Code § 50-20-103. Legislative intent

It is the intent of the legislature to restrict abortion to the extent permissible under decisions of appropriate courts or paramount legislation.

Montana Code § 50-20-104. Definitions

As used in this chapter, the following definitions apply:

(1) "Abortion" means the use or prescription of any instrument, medicine, drug, or other substance or device to intentionally terminate the pregnancy of a woman known to be pregnant, with an intention other than to increase the probability of a live birth, to preserve the life or health of the child after live birth, or to remove a dead fetus.

(2) "Attempted abortion" or "attempted" means an act or an omission of a statutorily required act that, under the circumstances as the actor believes them to be, constitutes a substantial step in a course of conduct planned to culminate in the performance of an abortion in violation of this chapter.

(3) "Department" means the department of public health and human services provided for in 2-15-2201.

(4) "Facility" means a hospital, health care facility, physician's office, or other place in which an abortion is performed.

(5) "Informed consent" means voluntary consent to an abortion by the woman upon whom the abortion is to be performed only after full disclosure to the woman by:

(a) the physician who is to perform the abortion of the following information:

(i) the particular medical risks associated with the particular abortion procedure to be employed, including, when medically accurate, the risks of infection, hemorrhage, breast cancer, danger to subsequent pregnancies, and infertility;

(ii) the probable gestational age of the unborn child at the time the abortion is to be performed; and

(iii) the medical risks of carrying the child to term;

(b) the physician or an agent of the physician:

(i) that medical assistance benefits may be available for prenatal care, childbirth, and neonatal care;

(ii) that the father is liable to assist in the support of the child, even in instances in which the father has offered to pay for the abortion; and

(iii) that the woman has the right to review the printed materials described in 50-20-304; and

(c) the physician or the agent that the printed materials described in 50-20-304 have been provided by the department and that the materials describe the unborn child and list agencies that offer alternatives to abortion.

(6) "Viability" means the ability of a fetus to live outside the mother's womb, albeit with artificial aid.

Montana Code § 50-20-105. Duties of department

(1) The department shall make regulations to provide for the humane disposition of dead infants or fetuses.

(2) The department shall make regulations for a comprehensive sys-

tem of reporting of maternal deaths and complications within the state resulting directly or indirectly from abortion, subject to the provisions of 50-20-110(5).

(3) The department shall report to the attorney general any apparent violation of this chapter.

Montana Code § 50-20-108.
Protection of premature infants born alive

(1) A person commits an offense, as defined in 45-5-102 through 45-5-104, if he purposely, knowingly, or negligently causes the death of a premature infant born alive, if such infant is viable.

(2) Whenever a premature infant which is the subject of abortion is born alive and is viable, it becomes a dependent and neglected child subject to the provisions of state law, unless:

(a) the termination of the pregnancy is necessary to preserve the life of the mother; or

(b) the mother and her spouse or either of them have agreed in writing in advance of the abortion or within 72 hours thereafter to accept the parental rights and responsibilities of the premature infant if it survives the abortion procedure.

(3) No person may use any premature infant born alive for any type of scientific research or other kind of experimentation except as necessary to protect or preserve the life and health of such premature infant born alive.

(4) Violation of subsection (3) of this section is a felony.

Montana Code § 50-20-109. Post-viability abortion

(1) Except as provided in 50-20-401, an abortion may not be performed within the state of Montana:

(a) except by a licensed physician or physician assistant;

(b) after viability of the fetus, except as provided in subsection (2).

(2) An abortion under subsection (1)(b) may be performed only to preserve the life or health of the mother and only if:

(a) the judgment of the physician who is to perform the abortion is first certified in writing by the physician, setting forth in detail the facts relied upon in making the judgment; and

(b) two other licensed physicians have first examined the patient and concurred in writing with the judgment. The certification and concurrence in this subsection (2)(b) are not required if a licensed physician certifies that the abortion is necessary to preserve the life of the mother.

(3) The timing and procedure used in performing an abortion under subsection (1)(b) must be such that the viability of the fetus is not intentionally or negligently endangered, as the term "negligently" is defined in 45-2-101. The fetus may be intentionally endangered or destroyed only if necessary to preserve the life or health of the mother.

(4) For purposes of this section, "health" means the prevention of a risk of substantial and irreversible impairment of a major bodily function.

(5) The supervision agreement of a physician assistant may provide for performing abortions.

(6) Violation of subsections (1) through (3) is a felony.

Montana Code § 50-20-112. Penalties

(1) A person convicted of deliberate, mitigated, or negligent homicide under this chapter is subject to the penalties prescribed by 45-5-102 through 45-5-104.

(2) A person convicted of a felony other than deliberate, mitigated, or negligent homicide under this chapter is subject to a fine not to exceed $1,000, imprisonment in the state prison for a term not to exceed 5 years, or both.

(3) A person convicted of a misdemeanor under this chapter is subject to a fine not to exceed $500, imprisonment in the county jail for a term not to exceed 6 months, or both.

(4) (a) A penalty may not be imposed against the woman upon whom the abortion is performed or attempted to be performed.

(b) A penalty may not be imposed for failure to comply with the provision of 50-20-106 that requires a written certification that the woman has been informed of the opportunity to review the information referred to in 50-20-304 if the department has not made the written materials available at the time that the physician or the physician's agent is required to inform the woman of the right to review the materials.

(3) INFORMED CONSENT

Prior to an abortion Montana requires that a woman be fully informed of the procedure to be used, the risks involved and alternatives to abortion. An abortion may not take place until 24 hours after a woman has been provided with the statutorily required information. The informed consent requirements may be dispensed with for medical emergencies. The statutes addressing the matters are set out below.

Montana Code § 50-20-106. Consent and waiting period

(1) An abortion may not be performed without the informed consent of the woman upon whom the abortion is to be performed. The informed consent must be received at least 24 hours prior to the abortion and certified prior to or at the time of the abortion.

(2) Informed consent must be certified by a written statement in a form prescribed by the department and signed by the physician and the woman upon whom the abortion is to be performed in which the physician certifies that the physician has made the full disclosure provided in 50-20-104(5) and in which the woman upon whom the abortion is to be performed acknowledges that the disclosures have been made to the woman and that the woman voluntarily consents to the abortion.

(3) If a woman chooses to review the written materials described in 50-20-304, the materials must be provided to her at least 24 hours before the abortion or be mailed to the woman by certified mail, with delivery restricted to the addressee, at least 72 hours before the abortion.

(4) The information required in 50-20-104(5)(a) may be provided by telephone without conducting a physical examination or tests of the patient. The information may be based on facts supplied to the physician by the woman and other relevant information that is reasonably available to the physician. The information may not be provided by a tape recording but must be provided during a consultation in which the physician is able to ask questions of the woman and the woman is able to ask questions of the physician. If a physical examination, tests, or the availability of other information subsequently indicates, in the medical judgment of the physician, a revision of information previously provided to the patient, the revised information may be communicated to the patient at any time prior to the performance of the abortion.

(5) The information required in 50-20-104(5)(b) may be provided by a tape recording if provision is made to record or otherwise register specifically whether the woman does or does not choose to review the printed materials.

(6) The informed consent or consent provided for in this section is not required if a licensed physician certifies that the abortion is necessary because of a medical emergency as defined in 50-20-303.

(7) An executive officer, administrative agency, or public employee of the state or of any local governmental body may not issue any order requiring an abortion or coerce any woman to have an abortion. A person may not coerce any woman to have an abortion.

(8) Violation of subsections (1) through (7) is a misdemeanor.

Montana Code § 50-20-301. Short title

This part may be cited as the "Woman's Right-to-Know Act."

Montana Code § 50-20-302. Legislative purpose and findings

(1) The legislature finds that:

(a) it is essential to the psychological and physical well-being of a

woman who is considering an abortion that the woman receive complete and accurate information on alternatives;

(b) the knowledgeable exercise of a woman's decision to have an abortion depends on the extent to which the woman receives sufficient information to make an informed choice between the alternatives of giving birth and having an abortion;

(c) in most instances, the only contact with a physician that a woman who has an abortion has occurs simultaneously with the abortion procedure, with little opportunity to receive counseling concerning the decision;

(d) the decision to abort is an important and often stressful one, and it is desirable and imperative that it be made with full knowledge of its nature and consequences;

(e) the medical, emotional, and psychological consequences of an abortion are serious and can be lasting;

(f) some abortion facilities or providers offer only limited or impersonal counseling opportunities; and

(g) some abortion facilities or providers hire untrained and unprofessional counselors whose primary goal is to sell abortion services.

(2) Based on the findings in subsection (1), it is the purpose of this part to:

(a) ensure that every woman who is considering an abortion receive complete information on alternatives and that every woman submitting to an abortion do so only after giving informed consent to the abortion procedure;

(b) protect unborn children from a woman's uninformed decision to have an abortion; and

(c) reduce the risk that a woman may elect an abortion, only to discover later, with devastating psychological consequences, that the decision was not fully informed.

Montana Code § 50-20-303. Definitions

As used in this part, unless the context requires otherwise, the following definitions apply:

(1) "Medical emergency" means a condition that, on the basis of the physician's good faith clinical judgment, so complicates the medical condition of a pregnant woman as to necessitate the immediate abortion of the woman's pregnancy to avert the woman's death or for which a delay will create serious risk of substantial and irreversible impairment of a major bodily function.

(2) "Physician" means a person licensed to practice medicine under Title 37, chapter 3.

(3) "Pregnant" or "pregnancy" means that female reproductive condition of having an unborn child in the woman's body.

(4) "Unborn child" means the offspring of human beings from conception until birth.

Montana Code § 50-20-304. Publication of materials

(1) The department shall publish and annually update easily comprehensible printed, unbiased materials that are geographically indexed and designed to inform women of public and private agencies and services available to assist a woman through pregnancy, during childbirth, and while a woman's child is dependent. The materials must:

(a) include adoption agencies;

(b) include a comprehensive list of the agencies, a description of the services offered, and the telephone numbers and addresses of the agencies;

(c) inform a woman about medical assistance benefits for prenatal care, childbirth, neonatal care, and child support obligations of a father of a child.

(2) The department shall ensure that the materials described in this section are comprehensive and do not directly or indirectly promote, exclude, or discourage the use of any agency or service. The materials must include a toll-free, 24-hour telephone number that may be called to orally obtain a list and description of agencies in the locality of the caller and of the services offered by the agencies.

(3) The materials must state that:

(a) it is unlawful for any individual to coerce a woman to undergo or not to undergo an abortion;

(b) a physician who performs an abortion on a woman without the woman's informed consent may be liable to the woman for damages in a civil action; and

(c) the law allows adoptive parents to pay the costs of prenatal care, childbirth, and neonatal care.

(4) The materials must inform the pregnant woman of the probable anatomical and physiological characteristics of the unborn child at 2-week gestational increments from fertilization to full term, including pictures or drawings representing the development of unborn children at 2-week gestational increments. The pictures or drawings must contain the dimensions of the unborn child and must be realistic. The materials must include any relevant information on the possibility of the unborn child's survival at each stage depicted. The materials must be objective, nonjudgmental, and designed to convey only accurate scientific information about the unborn child at the various gestational ages. The materials must contain objective information describing the methods of abortion procedures commonly employed, the medical risks commonly associated with each procedure, the possible detrimental psychological effects of abortion, the possible detrimental psychological effects of adoption, and the medical risks associated with carrying a child to term.

(5) The materials must be printed in a clearly legible typeface.

(6) The materials required to be produced under this section must be provided at no cost upon request and must be provided in appropriate quantities to any person, facility, or hospital.

Montana Code § 50-20-305. Emergency

When a medical emergency compels the performance of an abortion, the physician shall inform the woman, before the abortion if possible, of the medical indications supporting the physician's judgment that an abortion is necessary to avert the woman's death or that a 24-hour delay will create serious risk of substantial and irreversible impairment of a major bodily function.

Montana Code § 50-20-306. Physician reporting requirements

(1) Within 90 days after July 1, 1995, the department shall prepare a reporting form to be used by physicians that contains a reprint of this chapter and on which the physician shall list:

(a) the number of women to whom the physician provided the information described in 50-20-104(5)(a), including:

(i) the number of women provided the information by telephone and the number to whom it was provided in person; and

(ii) the number of women in each group referred to in subsection (1)(a)(i) to whom the physician provided the information in the capacity of a referring physician and the number to whom it was provided in the capacity of a physician who is to perform the abortion;

(b) the number of women to whom the physician or an agent of the physician provided the information described in 50-20-104(5)(b), including:

(i) the number of women to whom the physician provided the information by telephone and the number to whom it was provided in person;

(ii) the number of women in each group referred to in subsection (1)(b)(i) to whom the physician provided the information in the capacity of a referring physician and the number to whom it was provided in the capacity of a physician who is to perform the abortion; and

(iii) the number of women in each group referred to in subsection (1)(b)(ii) to whom information was provided by the physi-

cian and the number to whom it was provided by an agent of the physician;

(c) the number of women who availed themselves of the opportunity to obtain a copy of the printed information described in 50-20-304 and the number who did not;

(d) of each of the numbers described in subsections (1)(a) through (1)(c), the number who, to the best of the reporting physician's information and belief, obtained an abortion; and

(e) the number of abortions that were performed by the physician but in which information otherwise required to be provided at least 24 hours before the abortion was not provided because:

(i) an immediate abortion was necessary to avert the woman's death; or

(ii) a delay would create serious risk of substantial and irreversible impairment of a major bodily function.

(2) The department shall ensure that copies of the reporting forms described in subsection (1) are provided:

(a) by 120 days after July 1, 1995, to all physicians licensed in this state;

(b) to each physician licensed to practice after July 1, 1995, at the time of licensure;

(c) by December 1 of each succeeding year, to all physicians licensed to practice in this state.

(3) By February 28 of each year, each physician or the physician's agent who provided information to one or more women in accordance with 50-20-106 shall submit a copy of the reporting form described in subsection (1) to the department with the requested data entered accurately and completely.

(4) Reports that are not submitted by March 31 are subject to a penalty of $500 for each 30-day period that the reports are overdue. A physician who is required to report but who, more than 1 year after the due date, has not submitted a report or who has submitted an incomplete report may, in an action brought by the department, be directed by a district court to submit a complete report within a period stated in the court order or be subject to sanctions for civil contempt.

(5) By June 30 of each year, the department shall issue a public report providing statistics for the previous calendar year submitted in accordance with this section for each of the items listed in subsection (1). Each report must provide the statistics for all previous calendar years, adjusted to reflect information from late or corrected reports. The department shall ensure that none of the information included in the public reports could reasonably lead to the identification of an individual who was provided information in accordance with 50-20-106. The department shall design the reporting process to ensure that confidentiality regarding the physician or the physician's agent is maintained in the department records.

(6) The department may, by rule, alter the dates established by subsection (2)(c), (3), or (5) or consolidate the forms or reports described in this section with other forms or reports to achieve administrative convenience, achieve fiscal savings, or reduce the burden of reporting requirements. However, reporting forms must be sent to all licensed physicians at least once a year, and the report described in subsection (5) must be issued at least once a year.

Montana Code § 50-20-307. Civil remedies

(1) A person who performs an abortion in knowing or reckless violation of this chapter may be liable for actual and punitive damages in an action brought by the woman upon whom an abortion was performed or, if the woman is under 18 years of age or is physically or mentally incapacitated for purposes of being able to decide whether to bring and pursue an action, then, on the woman's behalf, by either:

(a) the father of the unborn child who was the subject of the abortion; or

(b) the grandparent of an unborn child who was the subject of the abortion.

(2) A person who attempts to perform an abortion in knowing or reckless violation of this chapter may be liable for actual and punitive damages in an action brought by the woman upon whom an abortion was attempted.

(3) If the department fails to issue the public report required in 50-20-306, a group of 10 or more citizens may seek an injunction, in a court of competent jurisdiction, against the director of the department to require that a complete report be issued within a period established by court order. Failure to comply with an injunction subjects the director to sanctions for civil contempt.

(4) If judgment is rendered in favor of the plaintiff in any action described in this section, the court shall award reasonable attorney fees in favor of the plaintiff against the defendant.

(5) An abortion or attempted abortion performed in violation of this chapter is the basis for a professional disciplinary action under 37-1-316.

Montana Code § 50-20-308.
Protection of privacy in court proceedings

In a civil or criminal proceeding under this chapter, the court shall determine whether the anonymity of a woman upon whom an abortion has been performed or attempted must be preserved from public disclosure, unless the woman waives anonymity. The court shall make a ruling and, upon determining that the woman's anonymity should be preserved, shall issue orders to the parties, witnesses, and counsel and shall direct the sealing of the record and the exclusion of individuals from the proceedings to the extent necessary to safeguard the woman's identity from public disclosure. Each order must be accompanied by specific written findings explaining why the anonymity of the woman should be preserved, why the order is necessary, how the order is tailored to protect the woman's privacy, and why no less restrictive alternative exists. In the absence of written consent of the woman upon whom an abortion has been performed or attempted, a person other than a public official who brings an action under 50-20-307(1) shall do so under a pseudonym.

(4) PARTIAL-BIRTH ABORTION

Montana prohibits partial-birth abortions and imposes severe criminal sanctions on anyone performing the procedure. Under Montana's statute a partial-birth abortion may be performed if necessary to save the life of a woman. Until it is definitively determined by a court, Montana's partial-birth abortion statute may be invalid under the United States Supreme Court decision *in Stenberg v. Carhart*, which invalidated Nebraska's ban on partial-birth abortion. On the other hand, Montana's partial-birth abortion statute, as currently written, may be valid under the United States Supreme Court decision in *Gonzales v. Carhart*, which approved of a federal statute that bans partial-birth abortion. The text of Montana's partial-birth abortion statute is set out below.

Montana Code § 50-20-401. Partial-birth abortion offense

(1) Except as provided in this section, a person commits an offense if the person purposely, knowingly, or negligently causes a partial-birth abortion.

(2) Subsection (1) does not apply to:

(a) a partial-birth abortion caused to save the life of a woman because the woman's life is endangered by a physical disorder, illness, or injury, including a life-endangering condition caused by or arising from the pregnancy itself, if no other medical procedure would save the life of the woman; or

(b) the woman upon whom a partial-birth abortion is performed.

(3) As used in this section, the following definitions apply:

(a) "Knowingly" has the meaning provided in 45-2-101.

(b) "Negligently" has the meaning provided in 45-2-101.

(c) (i) "Partial-birth abortion" means an abortion in which the person performing the abortion partially vaginally delivers a living human fetus before killing the fetus and completing the delivery.

(ii) A procedure that constitutes a partial-birth abortion is one in which the following steps occur:

(A) the living fetus is removed intact from the uterus until only the head remains in the uterus;

(B) all or a part of the intracranial contents of the fetus are evacuated;

(C) the head of the fetus is compressed; and

(D) following fetal demise, the fetus is removed from the birth canal.

(d) "Purposely" has the meaning provided in 45-2-101.

(4) A person committing the offense provided for in subsection (1) is guilty of a felony and shall be punished by:

(a) a fine of not more than $50,000;

(b) imprisonment in a correctional facility for a term of not less than 5 years and not more than 10 years; or

(c) both fine and imprisonment as provided in subsections (4)(a) and (4)(b); and

(d) permanent revocation of the license of the physician performing the partial-birth abortion. The provisions of 37-1-203 and 37-1-205 do not apply to a physician whose license is revoked pursuant to this section.

(5) ABORTION BY MINORS

Under the laws of Montana no physician may perform an abortion upon an unemancipated minor, until 48 hours after notice of the operation has been given to either parent of the minor or legal guardian. In compliance with federal constitutional law, Montana has provided a judicial waiver procedure for an unemancipated minor to obtain an abortion without parental notice. The minor may petition a trial court for a waiver of the notice requirement. A minor has a right to an attorney at the proceeding and if she cannot afford one, the court must appoint her an attorney. If a minor chooses, she may represent herself. The required parental notice may be waived if the court finds either (1) that the minor is mature and well-informed enough to make the abortion decision on her own, (2) that notification was not in the best interest of the minor, or (3) that there was evidence of physical, sexual, or emotional abuse of the minor by one or both parents, a guardian, or a custodian. An expedited appeal is available to any minor to whom the court denies a waiver of notice. The United States Supreme Court held in *Lambert v. Wicklund* that the constitution was not violated by the provision in Montana's abortion statute that allowed a court to waive the parental notice requirement for minors, if notification was not in minor's best interest. The statutes addressing the issues are set out below.

Montana Code § 50-20-201. Short title

This part may be cited as the "Parental Notice of Abortion Act."

Montana Code § 50-20-202. Legislative purpose and findings

(1) The legislature finds that:

(a) immature minors often lack the ability to make fully informed choices that take into account both immediate and long-range consequences;

(b) the medical, emotional, and psychological consequences of abortion are sometimes serious and can be lasting, particularly when the patient is immature;

(c) the capacity to become pregnant and the capacity for mature judgment concerning the wisdom of an abortion are not necessarily related;

(d) parents ordinarily possess information essential to a physician in the exercise of the physician's best medical judgment concerning the minor;

(e) parents who are aware that their minor daughter has had an abortion may better ensure that the daughter receives adequate medical care after the abortion; and

(f) parental consultation is usually desirable and in the best interests of the minor.

(2) The purpose of this part is to further the important and compelling state interests of:

(a) protecting minors against their own immaturity;

(b) fostering family unity and preserving the family as a viable social unit;

(c) protecting the constitutional rights of parents to rear children who are members of their household; and

(d) reducing teenage pregnancy and unnecessary abortion.

Montana Code § 50-20-203. Definitions

As used in this part, unless the context requires otherwise, the following definitions apply:

(1) "Actual notice" means the giving of notice directly in person or by telephone.

(2) "Coercion" means restraining or dominating the choice of a minor female by force, threat of force, or deprivation of food and shelter.

(3) "Emancipated minor" means a person under 18 years of age who is or has been married or who has been granted an order of limited emancipation by a court as provided in 41-3-438.

(4) "Incompetent person" means a person who is an incapacitated person or a protected person who has had a guardian appointed pursuant to Title 72, chapter 5.

(5) "Medical emergency" means a condition that, on the basis of the physician's good faith clinical judgment, so complicates the medical condition of a pregnant woman as to necessitate the immediate abortion of the woman's pregnancy to avert the woman's death or a condition for which a delay in treatment will create serious risk of substantial and irreversible impairment of a major bodily function.

(6) "Minor" means a female under 18 years of age who is not an emancipated minor.

(7) "Physical abuse" means any physical injury intentionally inflicted by a parent or legal guardian on a child.

(8) "Physician" means a person licensed to practice medicine under Title 37, chapter 3.

(9) "Sexual abuse" has the meaning given in 41-3-102.

Montana Code § 50-20-204. Parental notice and waiting period

A physician may not perform an abortion upon a minor or an incompetent person unless the physician has given at least 48 hours actual notice to one parent or to the legal guardian of the pregnant minor or incompetent person of the physician's intention to perform the abortion. The actual notice may be given by a referring physician. The physician who performs the abortion must receive the written statement of the referring physician certifying that the referring physician has given actual notice. If actual notice is not possible after a reasonable effort, the physician or the physician's agent shall give alternate notice as provided in 50-20-205.

Montana Code § 50-20-205. Alternative notice

In lieu of the actual notice required by 50-20-204, notice may be made by certified mail addressed to the parent at the usual place of residence of the parent with return receipt requested and delivery restricted to the addressee, which means a postal employee may deliver the mail only to the authorized addressee. Time of delivery is considered to occur at noon on the next day on which regular mail delivery takes place after mailing.

Montana Code § 50-20-208. Exceptions

Notice is not required under 50-20-204 or 50-20-205 if:

(1) the attending physician certifies in the patient's medical record

that a medical emergency exists and there is insufficient time to provide notice;

(2) notice is waived, in writing, by the person entitled to notice; or

(3) notice is waived under 50-20-212.

Montana Code § 50-20-209. Coercion prohibited

A parent, a guardian, or any other person may not coerce a minor to have an abortion. If a minor is denied financial support by the minor's parents, guardian, or custodian because of the minor's refusal to have an abortion, the minor must be considered an emancipated minor for the purposes of eligibility for public assistance benefits. The public assistance benefits may not be used to obtain an abortion.

Montana Code § 50-20-211. Reports

A monthly report indicating the number of notices issued under this part and the number of times in which exceptions were made to the notice requirement under 50-20-208, as well as the type of exceptions, must be filed with the department of public health and human services on forms prescribed by the department. Patient names and other identifying information may not be used on the forms. The department shall prepare and make available to the public on an annual basis a compilation of the data reported.

Montana Code § 50-20-212. Judicial bypass

(1) The requirements and procedures under this section are available to minors and incompetent persons whether or not they are residents of this state.

(2)(a) The minor or incompetent person may petition the youth court for a waiver of the notice requirement and may participate in the proceedings on the person's own behalf. The petition must include a statement that the petitioner is pregnant and is not emancipated. The court may appoint a guardian ad litem for the petitioner. A guardian ad litem is required to maintain the confidentiality of the proceedings. The youth court shall advise the petitioner of the right to assigned counsel and shall order the office of state public defender, provided for in 47-1-201, to assign counsel upon request.

(b) If the petition filed under subsection (2)(a) alleges abuse as a basis for waiver of notice, the youth court shall treat the petition as a report under 41-3-202. The provisions of Title 41, chapter 3, part 2, apply to an investigation conducted pursuant to this subsection.

(3) Proceedings under this section are confidential and must ensure the anonymity of the petitioner. All proceedings under this section must be sealed. The petitioner may file the petition using a pseudonym or using the petitioner's initials. All documents related to the petition are confidential and are not available to the public. The proceedings on the petition must be given preference over other pending matters to the extent necessary to ensure that the court reaches a prompt decision. The court shall issue written findings of fact and conclusions of law and rule within 48 hours of the time that the petition is filed unless the time is extended at the request of the petitioner. If the court fails to rule within 48 hours and the time is not extended, the petition is granted and the notice requirement is waived.

(4) If the court finds by clear and convincing evidence that the petitioner is sufficiently mature to decide whether to have an abortion, the court shall issue an order authorizing the minor to consent to the performance or inducement of an abortion without the notification of a parent or guardian.

(5) The court shall issue an order authorizing the petitioner to consent to an abortion without the notification of a parent or guardian if the court finds, by clear and convincing evidence, that:

(a) there is evidence of a pattern of physical, sexual, or emotional abuse of the petitioner by one or both parents, a guardian, or a custodian; or

(b) the notification of a parent or guardian is not in the best interests of the petitioner.

(6) If the court does not make a finding specified in subsection (4) or (5), the court shall dismiss the petition.

(7) A court that conducts proceedings under this section shall issue written and specific findings of fact and conclusions of law supporting its decision and shall order that a confidential record of the evidence, findings, and conclusions be maintained.

(8) The supreme court may adopt rules providing an expedited confidential appeal by a petitioner if the youth court denies a petition. An order authorizing an abortion without notice is not subject to appeal.

(9) Filing fees may not be required of a pregnant minor who petitions a court for a waiver of parental notification or appeals a denial of a petition.

Montana Code § 50-20-215. Criminal and civil penalties

(1) A person convicted of performing an abortion in violation of 50-20-204 or 50-20-205 shall be fined an amount not to exceed $500 or be imprisoned in the county jail for a term not to exceed 6 months, or both.

(2) Failure to provide the notice required under 50-20-204 or 50-20-205 is prima facie evidence in an appropriate civil action for a violation of a professional obligation. The evidence does not apply to issues other than failure to notify the parents or guardian. A civil action may be based on a claim that the failure to notify was the result of a violation of the appropriate legal standard of care. Failure to provide notice is presumed to be actual malice pursuant to the provisions of 27-1-221. This part does not limit the common-law rights of parents.

(3) A person who coerces a minor to have an abortion is guilty of a misdemeanor and upon conviction shall be fined an amount not to exceed $1,000 or be imprisoned in the county jail for a term not to exceed 1 year, or both. On a second or subsequent conviction, the person shall be fined an amount not less than $500 and not more than $50,000 and be imprisoned in the state prison for a term not less than 10 days and not more than 5 years, or both.

(4) A person not authorized to receive notice under 50-20-205 who signs a notice of waiver as provided in 50-20-208(2) is guilty of a misdemeanor.

(6) USE OF FACILITIES AND PEOPLE

Under the laws of Montana private medical facilities are not required to allow abortions at their premises. The employees and physicians at medical facilities that do allow abortions are permitted to refuse to take part in abortions. The statute addressing the matter is set out below.

Montana Code § 50-20-111.
Right to refuse participation in abortion

(1) No private hospital or health care facility shall be required contrary to the religious or moral tenets or the stated religious beliefs or moral convictions of its staff or governing board to admit any person for the purpose of abortion or to permit the use of its facilities for such purpose. Such refusal shall not give rise to liability of such hospital or health care facility or any personnel or agent or governing board thereof to any person for damages allegedly arising from such refusal or be the basis for any discriminatory, disciplinary, or other recriminatory action against such hospital or health care facility or any personnel, agent, or governing board thereof.

(2) All persons shall have the right to refuse to advise concerning, perform, assist, or participate in abortion because of religious beliefs or moral convictions. If requested by any hospital or health care facility or person desiring an abortion, such refusal shall be in writing signed by the person refusing, but may refer generally to the grounds of "religious beliefs and moral convictions." The refusal of any person to advise concerning, perform, assist, or participate in abortion shall not be a consideration in respect of staff privileges of any hospital or health care facility or a basis for any discriminatory, disciplinary, or other recriminatory action against

such person, nor shall such person be liable to any person for damages allegedly arising from refusal.

(3) It shall be unlawful to interfere or attempt to interfere with the right of refusal authorized by this section. The person injured thereby shall be entitled to injunctive relief, when appropriate, and shall further be entitled to monetary damages for injuries suffered.

(4) Such refusal by any hospital or health care facility or person shall not be grounds for loss of any privileges or immunities to which the granting of consent may otherwise be a condition precedent or for the loss of any public benefits.

(5) As used in this section, the term "person" includes one or more individuals, partnerships, associations, and corporations.

(7) FETAL DEATH REPORT

Montana requires that all abortions be reported to the proper authorities. The statute addressing the matter is set out below.

Montana Code § 50-20-110.
Reporting of practice of abortion

(1) Every facility in which an abortion is performed within the state shall keep on file upon a form prescribed by the department a statement dated and certified by the physician who performed the abortion setting forth such information with respect to the abortion as the department by regulation shall require, including but not limited to information on prior pregnancies, the medical procedure employed to administer the abortion, the gestational age of the fetus, the vital signs of the fetus after abortion, if any, and if after viability, the medical procedures employed to protect and preserve the life and health of the fetus.

(2) The physician performing an abortion shall cause such pathology studies to be made in connection therewith as the department shall require by regulation, and the facility shall keep the reports thereof on file.

(3) In connection with an abortion, the facility shall keep on file the original of each of the documents required by this chapter relating to informed consent, consent to abortion, certification of necessity of abortion to preserve the life or health of the mother, and certification of necessity of abortion to preserve the life of the mother.

(4) Such facility shall, within 30 days after the abortion, file with the department a report upon a form prescribed by the department and certified by the custodian of the records or physician in charge of such facility setting forth all of the information required in subsections (1), (2), and (3) of this section, except such information as would identify any individual involved with the abortion. The report shall exclude copies of any documents required to be filed by subsection (3) of this section, but shall certify that such documents were duly executed and are on file.

(5) All reports and documents required by this chapter shall be treated with the confidentiality afforded to medical records, subject to such disclosure as is permitted by law. Statistical data not identifying any individual involved in an abortion shall be made public by the department annually, and the report required by subsection (4) of this section to be filed with the department shall be available for public inspection except insofar as it identifies any individual involved in an abortion. Names and identities of persons submitting to abortion shall remain confidential among medical and medical support personnel directly involved in the abortion and among persons working in the facility where the abortion was performed whose duties include billing the patient or submitting claims to an insurance company, keeping facility records, or processing abortion data required by state law.

(6) Violation of this section is a misdemeanor and is punishable as provided in 46-18-212.

Moody, Rev. Howard *see* **Clergy Consultation Service on Abortion**

Moral Majority

The Moral Majority was a pro-life organization started in 1979 by Rev. Jerry Falwell (1933–2007). In addition to opposing abortion, the organization opposed the feminist backed Equal Rights Amendment and gay and lesbian rights. Through Rev. Falwell the organization also lobbied nationally and locally for the use of prayer and the teaching of creationism in public schools. The Moral Majority disbanded on August 31, 1989. *See also* **Pro-Life Organizations**

Morning After Pill

The Morning After Pill (MAP) is taken to prevent pregnancy when unprotected sex occurs. MAP does not have to be taken the "morning after" unprotected sex, but must be taken within 72 hours of the intercourse. There are two types of MAP contraceptives. One type uses hormones that are the same type and dose as hormones used in some kinds of ordinary birth control pills. These hormones are called estrogen and progestin. The other type of emergency contraceptive pill contains only the hormone called progestin. It is more effective than the first type. MAP does not cause a spontaneous abortion (miscarriage) and is not considered an abortion pill. Depending on the time of the woman's menstrual cycle when MAP is taken, the hormones in the pills may prevent the release of the egg from the ovary, prevent the fertilization of an egg or prevent the fertilized egg from implanting on the wall of the uterus. The usual side effects from MAP include nausea and vomiting. In some cases side effects may involve blood clots in the legs or lungs, stroke, heart attack, liver damage, liver tumor, gall bladder disease, or high blood pressure. *See also* **Contraception**

Morning Sickness

Morning sickness is a condition of nausea and vomiting that many pregnant women experience upon arising in the morning. The disorder is not considered threatening to a woman or her fetus. *See also* **Hyperemesis Gravidarum**

Morula *see* **Fetal Development**

Mucus Plug

Mucus plug is thick mucus that fills the cervical canal during pregnancy to help secure the fetus in the uterus. The mucus will be discharged near or during labor. *See also* **Incompetent Cervix**

Multifetal Pregnancy Reduction

Multifetal pregnancy reduction (MFPR) involves aborting one or more, but not all, fetuses (or embryos) in a multiple gestation pregnancy that has three or more fetuses. MFPR is used to reduce the number of fetuses in an effort to increase the likelihood that the pregnancy will continue, thereby reducing risks of complications to the mother and remaining fetuses. When MFPR is found necessary the number of fetuses is often reduced to two, though in rare instances they may be reduced to one. MFPR is rarely used when there are triplets or twins, because triplets and twins generally do not cause health risks to each other or the mother.

MFPR is most successful when performed early in the pregnancy; therefore it is normally performed between 9 and 12 weeks gestation (it has been performed as late as 24 weeks gestation). The procedure is performed by inserting a needle, guided by ultrasound, through either the abdomen or vagina and injecting potassium chloride into the heart of one or more fetuses thereby causing cardiac arrest. The incidence of miscarriage of the remaining fetuses is about 5 percent. Premature labor occurs in about 75 percent of MFPR abortions. *See also* **Fetal Transfusion Syndrome; Monoamnionic Twin Gestation; Monochorionic Twin Gestation; Multiple Gestation; Twin Reversed Arterial Perfusion; Vanishing Twin Syndrome**

Multiple Births *see* **Fetal Transfusion Syndrome; Monoamnionic Twin Gestation; Monochorionic Twin Gestation; Multifetal Pregnancy Reduction; Multiple Gestation; Twin Reversed Arterial Perfusion; Vanishing Twin Syndrome**

Multiple Gestation

Multiple gestation involves a pregnancy in which two or more fetuses are present in the uterus. This condition occurs in approximately 2 percent of all pregnancies. The average length of pregnancy is less for multiple gestations than single gestations. For a single gestation the average length of pregnancy is 39 weeks; for twins it is 35 weeks; for triplets it is 33 weeks; for quadruplets it is 29 weeks. Many risks are associated with multiple gestations. Risks to the fetuses include an increased chance of miscarriage, birth defects, premature birth, and mental or physical problems. The risks to the woman include premature labor, high blood pressure, diabetes, and vaginal or uterine hemorrhage. *See also* **Fetal Transfusion Syndrome; Monoamnionic Twin Gestation; Monochorionic Twin Gestation; Multifetal Pregnancy Reduction; Twin Reversed Arterial Perfusion; Vanishing Twin Syndrome**

Number of Multiple Births U.S. 2000–2005

Year	*Twins*	*Triplets*	*Quadruplets*	*Quintuplets and higher*
2000	118,916	6,742	506	77
2001	121,246	6,885	501	85
2002	125,134	6,898	434	69
2003	128,665	7,110	468	85
2004	132,219	6,750	439	86
2005	133,122	6,208	418	68
Total	759,302	40,593	2,766	470

Source: **National Center for Health Statistics.**

Muscular Dystrophy

Muscular dystrophy involves a group of genetic diseases that are characterized by increasing weakness and degeneration of skeletal muscles. Some forms of the disorder appear during childhood, while other forms may not appear until adulthood. There are at least nine forms of the disease: myotonic muscular dystrophy, Duchenne muscular dystrophy, Becker muscular dystrophy, limb-girdle muscular dystrophy, facioscapulohumeral muscular dystrophy, congenital muscular dystrophy, oculopharyngeal muscular dystrophy, distal muscular dystrophy and Emery-Dreifuss muscular dystrophy. Duchenne muscular dystrophy is the most common form of the disease that affects children. Myotonic muscular dystrophy is the most common form of the disease affecting adults. Symptoms for the disorder varies with its specific form. Some complications associated with the disorder in general include: muscle weakness, mental retardation, skeletal deformities, scoliosis, and death. There is no known cure for the various forms of the disease. Treatment is provided to control the symptoms of the disorder. *See also* **Birth Defects and Abortion**

Mutagens and Pregnancy

Mutagens are chemical or physical agents (natural or human-made) that can alter the structure or sequence of DNA (deoxyribonucleic acid). Examples of mutagens include: nitric acid, methyl methanesulfonate, bromouracil, aminopurine, acridine orange, proflavin, ethidium bromide, arsenic and ionizing radiation. High dose exposures to mutagens have occurred through nuclear explosions, cancer radiation and chemotherapy.

Mutagens can affect pregnancy in one of two ways. First, a woman who inherited DNA that was altered by mutagens has a risk of having a child with severe birth defects, or having habitual spontaneous abortions. Second, a pregnant woman who is exposed to mutagens during pregnancy has a risk of having a spontaneous abortion or her fetus could sustain severe birth defects, cancer and malformations. In many instances pregnant women who must undergo radiation or chemotherapy treatment for cancer, are advised to have an induced abortion. *See also* **X-rays and Pregnancy**

N

NARAL Pro-Choice America

NARAL Pro-Choice America (formerly National Abortion and Reproductive Rights Action League) is a Washington, D.C., based pro-choice organization that was founded in 1969, and is headed by its president, Nancy Keenan. The organization is dedicated to defending and securing a woman's freedom to choose, and advocating for policies and programs that enable women and men to make responsible and informed decisions about sexuality, contraception, pregnancy, childbirth and abortion. NARAL performs in-depth research and legal work, publishes substantive policy reports, mounts public education campaigns, and provides leadership training for pro-choice grassroots activists across the nation. It also maintains a political action committee that supports pro-choice candidates for political office. NARAL has filed amicus briefs in numerous abortion cases including decisions by the United States Supreme Court in *Ayotte v. Planned Parenthood of Northern New England*, *Gonzales v. Carhart*, *Scheidler v. National Organization for Women, Inc. (I)*, and *Scheidler v. National Organization for Women, Inc. (II)*. *See also* **Nathanson, Bernard; Pro-Choice Organizations**

NARAL Pro-Choice California

NARAL Pro-Choice California (PCC) is a pro-choice organization headquartered in San Francisco, California. The director of the organization is Amy Everitt. The mission of PCC is to develop and sustain a constituency that uses the political process to guarantee every woman the right to make personal decisions regarding the full range of reproductive choices, including preventing unintended pregnancy, bearing healthy children, and choosing legal abortion. The organization works on both the state and national levels to protect and defend a woman's right to choose. PCC also works to (1) educate voters about reproductive rights in California; (2) provide resources and information for voters who want to support pro-choice legislation; and (3) elect pro-choice legislators. *See also* **Pro-Choice Organizations**

NARAL Pro-Choice Maryland

NARAL Pro-Choice Maryland (PCM) is a pro-choice organization headquartered in Silver Spring, Maryland. The executive director PCM is Ariana Brannigan Kelly. PCM works to develop and sustain a constituency that works to guarantee every woman the right to make personal decisions regarding the full range of reproductive choices, including preventing unintended pregnancy, bearing healthy children, and choosing safe, legal abortion. PCM also sponsors the NARAL Pro-Choice Maryland Fund and the NARAL Pro-Choice Maryland Political Action Committee. The organization is engaged in work that includes providing comprehensive sexuality education, advocating for access to emergency contraception and statewide family planning services, and identifying and electing pro-choice candidates. *See also* **Pro-Choice Organizations**

Nathanson, Bernard

Bernard Nathanson was born in New York City on July 31, 1926. He obtained a pre-medical degree from Cornell University in 1945, and a medical degree from McGill University Medical College in 1949. As an obstetrician-gynecologist, Nathanson believed women should be allowed the choice of having an abortion. This belief led him to co-found the National Association for the Repeal of Abortion Laws (now called NARAL Pro-Choice America) in 1969.

Nathanson's pro-abortion work was instrumental in causing New York to legalize abortion in 1970, and in bringing national pressure that led to the 1973 decision by the United States Supreme Court finding abortion prohibition laws violated the federal constitution. His work as an abortionist included being the founder and director of what was once the largest abortion facility in the world, New York City's Center for Reproductive and Sexual Health. Nathanson publicly proclaimed that he was responsible for over 75,000 abortions.

Nathanson walked away from his abortion world in 1979 and became a pro-life advocate. He attributed his changed position to advancements in medical science, like the ultrasound, which permitted examination of a fetus while alive in the womb. The advancements in medical science forced him to conclude that a fetus was a human being. *See also* **NARAL Pro-Choice America**

National Abortion and Reproductive Rights Action League *see* **NARAL Pro-Choice America**

National Abortion Federation

The National Abortion Federation (NAF) was created in 1977 to be the policy coordinating organization for abortion providers in the United States (and Canada). The president of NAF is Vicki Saporta. Abortion providers associated with NAF include over 360 clinics, women's health centers, and Planned Parenthood facilities. NAF is also associated with private physicians, nationally and internationally recognized researchers, clinicians, and educators at major universities and teaching hospitals. The abortion providers affiliated with NAF render services for more than half of the women who choose abortion each year in the United States.

Vicki Saporta is the president of National Abortion Federation, a pro-choice organization created in 1977 to be the policy coordinating organization for abortion providers in the United States (Vicki Saporta).

The stated mission of NAF is to keep abortion safe, legal, and accessible in the United States. To carry out this mission NAF has set standards for quality abortion care through protocols, clinical policy guidelines, quality improvement programs, and accredited continuing medical education programs. It has also been committed to educating the public and lawmakers about abortion practices.

NAF has published a textbook, *A Clinician's Guide to Medical and Surgical Abortion* (1999), with over 50 nationally and internationally recognized contributors. It is the only textbook in existence that covers both surgical and medical abortion. NAF's educational resources also include works such as *Clinical Training Curriculum in Abortion Practice, Principals of Abortion Care: A Curriculum for Physician Assistants and Advanced Practice Nurses*, and *2000 Clinical Policy Guidelines*. Other services provided by NAF include direct assistance to abortion providers with field support, advocacy with law enforcement agencies, comprehensive statistics, and documentation on clinic violence and disruption. *See also* **Pro-Choice Organizations**

National Association for the Repeal of Abortion Laws *see* **Nathanson, Bernard**

National Association of Pro-Life Nurses

The National Association of Pro-Life Nurses (NAPLN) was created by nurses from around the country to promote respect for human life from conception to natural death. Under its leader and president Susan Meyers, RN, NAPLN established the following agenda: (1) to provide moral support for pro-life nurses; (2) to provide financial help for nurses involved in legal matters that are a result of their pro-life stance; (3) to provide copies of court briefs that have been written involving pro-life issues; (4) to educate its membership through the newsletter Pulse-line and the NAPLN website; and (5) to support political activism as it relates to protecting life. *See also* **Pro-Life Organizations**

Father James E. Goode founded the National Black Catholic Apostolate for Life as a pro-life organization in 1997 (James E. Goode).

National Black Catholic Apostolate for Life

National Black Catholic Apostolate for Life (NBCAL) is a pro-life organization that was founded in Manhattan, New York in 1997, by Father James E. Goode. The stated mission of NBCAL is that of being a ministry committed to pray, proclaim, and stand boldly for an end to abortion, all acts of violence and evil, and all injustice that destroys the sacredness of life. The organization is supported by all the major National Black Catholic organizations in the United States. Events for which NBCAL takes part in include March for Life, Mass for Life and the Black Catholic Rosary Across America for Life. *See also* **Pro-Life Organizations**

National Black Women's Health Project

National Black Women's Health Project (NBWHP) is a Washington, D.C., based health advocacy organization that was founded in 1981 by Byllye Avery. The president of NBWHP is Eleanor Hinton Hoytt. The organization's stated purpose is to improve the health status of African American women through health education, services and advocacy. NBWHP believes in and advocates for a woman's right to reproductive choice. The organization maintains a Reproductive Health and Rights program that works to assure safe and equitable reproductive health care for all women. The organization provides technical assistance and support to local groups on health and reproductive rights. *See also* **Pro-Choice Organizations**

National Coalition for Life and Peace

The National Coalition for Life and Peace (NCLP) was founded by Steven Ertelt as an ad hoc group of pro-life organizations formed for the purpose to ending abortion violence. NCLP has worked through the Internet to promote the pro-life movement's historical condemnation of abortion related violence. Pro-life persons and groups affiliated with NCLP are asked to sign a pledge which states: "As a pro-life person I affirm, with all alacrity and fervor, my unequivocal opposition to and condemnation of violence as a means to end the travesty of abortion. In my actions in support of life I will remain positive and peaceful and only engage in legal activities to protect unborn children and their mothers." *See also* **Pro-Life Organizations**

National Coalition of Abortion Providers

The National Coalition of Abortion Providers (NCAP) was created in 1990, by several abortion providers who felt they needed a lobbyist in Washington, D.C., who would be able to effectively communicate the need to preserve the right to abortion, and be familiar with the specific needs of independent abortion providers. NCAP represents the political interests of over 150 independent abortion providers throughout the United States. In addition to being a pro-choice lobbying organization, NCAP also works on behalf of its members to obtain low cost medical supplies, malpractice insurance, communication services, and pathology services. *See also* **Pro-Choice Organizations**

National Council of Jewish Women

The National Council of Jewish Women (NCJW) was founded in 1893 by social activist Hannah Greenebaum Solomon. The president of NCJW is Phyllis Snyder. The organization has a long history in promoting reproductive rights that dates back to the early 20th century. NCJW is dedicated to carrying out a reproductive rights campaign to educate and mobilize its membership and the larger Jewish community to advocate for a judiciary that will protect a woman's right to choose. The organization has been in the forefront in opposing appointed government officials who are against the basic reproductive rights of women. *See also* **Pro-Choice Organizations**

National Day of Appreciation for Abortion Providers

The National Day of Appreciation for Abortion Providers (Day of Appreciation) was initiated in 1996, by the pro-choice organization Refuse & Resist. The Day of Appreciation is an annual event that was implemented in order to create a positive climate for abortion providers across the country. Initially the Day of Appreciation was held on April 27. However, organizers subsequently decided to hold the event on the 10th of March of every year, to commemorate the murder of the first abortion provider, Dr. David Gunn, on March 10, 1993. The Day of Appreciation is not celebrated in one location. Abortion providers hold celebrations in large and small cities throughout the nation. *See also* **Pro-Choice Organizations; Refuse & Resist**

National Federation of Officers for Life

The National Federation of Officers for Life is a New York based pro-life organization that was founded in 1990 by its director Sgt. Ruben "Radar" Rodriguez. The membership of the organization consists of pro-life city police, county constables, corrections officers, court officers, sheriffs, deputies, state troopers and federal agents. The organization provides abortion education training through its Life-Force program. *See also* **Pro-Life Organizations**

National Institute of Family and Life Advocates

National Institute of Family and Life Advocates (NIFLA) is a Virginia based pro-life public interest law firm founded in 1993 by Thomas A. Glessner. NIFLA provides legal counsel and training for pregnancy help centers. It represents more than 1,050 pregnancy help centers in all 50 states. NIFLA has developed and implemented legal guidelines for pregnancy help centers to enable them to convert their operations into licensed medical clinics. *See also* **Pregnancy Help Centers; Pro-Life Organizations**

National Network of Abortion Funds

The National Network of Abortion Funds (NNAF) is an organization that was created in 1993, for the purpose of providing direct financial aid in the form of loans and/or grants to low-income women and girls seeking to terminate an unwanted pregnancy. NNAF also makes funds available for other needs such as pregnancy testing, ultrasound, contraception, child care, transportation and lodging, as well as information and referrals. The organization is committed to providing support for the creation of new abortion funds in unserved areas; exploring new ways to meet the immediate funding needs of women; and advocating on the national level on issues of access to abortion, reproductive freedom and health care. NNAF believes that the right to choose abortion is meaningless without access to abortion services; restrictions on abortion access and funding are discriminatory because they especially burden poor women; abortion is a component of basic health care, which is a right that should be guaranteed to all through an expanded Medicaid program or another universal national health care plan.

NNAF launched a Campaign for Access and Reproductive Equity (CARE) in 1999. The CARE program is a multi-issue, grassroots, public education effort to increase awareness of federal and state legislation impacting the reproductive health of low-income women. Its overall objective is to improve access to reproductive health services for women, while opposing prohibitive or restrictive state and federal legislation. *See also* **Pro-Choice Organizations**

National Organization for Women

The National Organization for Women (NOW) was founded in 1966 and is the largest organization of feminist activists in the United States. The president of NOW is Kim Gandy. NOW has 500,000 contributing members and 550 chapters in all 50 states and the District of Columbia. In 1967 NOW became the first national organization to call for the legalization of abortion and for the repeal of all anti-abortion laws. In 1994 NOW won a pivotal United States Supreme Court victory in the case of *National Organization for Women, Inc. v. Scheidler*. That decision affirmed NOW's right to use federal racketeering laws against anti-abortion extremists. NOW's abortion advocacy also includes lobbying against restrictions on Medicaid funding, parental involvement, elimination of abortion from federal government and military health insurance coverage and abortion procedure bans. The organization regularly sponsored a national abortion event called "March for Women's Lives," that attracted hundreds of thousands of pro-choice advocates to the nation's capital. *See also* **National Organization for Women, Inc. v. Scheidler; Pro-Choice Organizations**

National Organization for Women, Inc., v. Scheidler

Forum: United States Supreme Court.

Case Citation: National Organization for Women, Inc. v. Scheidler, 510 U.S. 249 (1994).

Date Argued: December 8, 1993.

Date of Decision: January 24, 1994.

Opinion of Court: Rehnquist, C.J., unanimous.

Concurring Opinion: Souter, J., in which Kennedy, J., joined.

Dissenting Opinion: None.

Counsel for Appellants: Fay Clayton.

Counsel for Appellees: G. Robert Blakey.

Amicus Brief for Appellants: None.

Amicus Brief for Appellees: None.

Issue Presented: Whether RICO required proof that either the racketeering enterprise or the predicate acts of racketeering were motivated by an economic purpose?

Case Holding: RICO does not require an economic motive.

Background facts of case: The appellants, National Organization For Women, Inc., Delaware Women's Health Organization, Inc., and Summit Women's Health Organization, Inc., filed a federal lawsuit in Illinois against the appellees, Joseph Scheidler, John Patrick Ryan, Randall A. Terry, Andrew Scholberg, Conrad Wojnar, Timothy Murphy, Monica Migliorino, Pro-Life Action Network, VitalMed Laboratories, Inc., Pro-Life Action League, Inc., Pro-Life Direct Action League, Inc., Operation Rescue, and Project Life. The appellants alleged that the appellees were members of a nationwide conspiracy to shut down abortion clinics through a pattern of racketeering activity, in violation of the Racketeer Influenced and Corrupt Organizations (RICO) chapter of the Organized Crime Control Act of 1970 (18 U.S.C. §§ 1961–1968), the Hobbs Act (18 U.S.C. § 1951), the Travel Act (18 U.S.C. § 1952) and various state law extortion crimes. It was further alleged that the appellees conspired to use threatened or actual force, violence, or fear to induce clinic employees, doctors, and patients to give up their jobs, their right to practice medicine, and their right to obtain clinic services; that the conspiracy injured the clinics' business and property interests; and that the appellees are a racketeering enterprise. The federal district court dismissed the case on the grounds that the appellants failed to state a cause of action, because they did not allege a profit-generating purpose in the appellees' activity or enterprise. The Seventh Circuit court of appeals affirmed the dismissal, after agreeing with the district court that there was an economic motive requirement implicit in the "enterprise" element of a RICO cause of action. The Supreme Court granted certiorari to consider the matter.

Unanimous opinion by Chief Justice Rehnquist: The Chief Justice initially examined the relevant section of the RICO statute, 18 U.S.C § 1962(c). It was said that Section 1962(c) makes it unlawful "for any person employed by or associated with any enterprise engaged in, or the activities of which affect, interstate or foreign commerce, to conduct or participate, directly or indirectly, in the conduct of such enterprise's affairs through a pattern of racketeering activity or collection of unlawful debt." The Chief Justice also noted that under Rico " was defined to "includ[e] any individual, partnership, corporation, association, or other legal entity, and any union or group of individuals associated in fact although not a legal entity." After this examination, the opinion held that "[n]owhere in ... RICO ... is there any indication that an economic motive is required...." The Chief Justice concluded:

> We therefore hold that [appellants] may maintain this action if [appellees] conducted the enterprise through a pattern of racketeering activity. The questions of whether the [appellees] committed the requisite predicate acts, and whether the commission of these acts fell into a pattern, are not before us. We hold only that RICO contains no economic motive requirement.

Disposition of case: The judgment of the court of appeals was reversed.

Concurring opinion by Justice Souter: Justice Souter concurred in the judgment of the Court. He wrote separately to express the following points:

> I join the Court's opinion and write separately to explain why the First Amendment does not require reading an economic motive requirement into the RICO, and to stress that the Court's opinion does not bar First Amendment challenges to RICO's application in particular cases....
>
> Even if the meaning of RICO were open to debate, ... it would not follow that the statute ought to be read to include an economic motive requirement, since such a requirement would correspond only poorly to free speech concerns.... [A]n economic motive requirement would protect too much with respect to First Amendment interests, since it would keep RICO from reaching ideological entities whose members commit acts of violence we need not fear chilling....
>
> This is not the place to catalog the speech issues that could arise in a RICO action against a protest group, and I express no view on the possibility of a First Amendment claim by the [appellees] in this case. But I think it prudent to notice that RICO actions could deter protected advocacy, and to caution courts applying RICO to bear in mind the First Amendment interests that could be at stake.

Note: Subsequent to the opinion in this case, two other appeals were granted in the case by the Supreme Court. *See also* **Hobbs Act; RICO; Scheidler v. National Organization for Women, Inc. (I); Scheidler v. National Organization for Women, Inc. (II); Travel Act**

National Organization of Episcopalians for Life

The National Organization of Episcopalians for Life (NOEL) is a pro-life organization. The organization was created to strengthen pro-life and pro-family ministries in the church and culture, emphasizing the guidance, strength and grace that it believes God provides through Jesus Christ. NOEL publishes educational resources and materials to provide information, support and guidance to clergy and laity for pro-life and pro-family ministries. The organization provides counseling services and support for pregnant women, teenagers and post-abortion women. NOEL also seeks to influence the Episcopal Church of the United States of America by introducing pro-life and pro-family resolutions at the churches General Conventions. *See also* **Pro-Life Organizations**

National Partnership for Women & Families

The National Partnership for Women & Families (NPWF) was founded in 1971, under the former name Women's Legal Defense Fund. The organization has its headquarters in Washington, D.C. The president of NPWF is Debra L. Ness. NPWF utilizes public education and advocacy to promote fairness in the workplace, quality health care, and policies that help women and men meet the dual demands of work and family. Since its founding, NPWF has actively supported women's freedom of choice, and has worked diligently to increase access to comprehensive, affordable reproductive health care services. NPWF has engaged in pro-choice battles that involved preserving funding for abortion services in the Medicaid program; allowing women serving overseas in the United States military to have access to privately paid abortion services in United States military health care facilities; fighting proposals that would have prevented teenagers from obtaining family planning services from federally funded clinics without parental consent; and lobbying for the enactment of the Freedom of Access to Clinic Entrances Act. *See also* **Pro-Choice Organizations**

National Right to Life Committee

The National Right to Life Committee (NRLC) is a Washington, D.C., based pro-life organization that was founded on May 14, 1973. NRLC was formed in response to the 1973 decision by the United States Supreme Court in *Roe v. Wade*, that legalized abortion in the nation. Headed by its president, Wanda Franz, NRLC is the largest pro-life organization in the United States. It has over 3,000 chapters in all 50 states. NRLC has focused upon changing public policy toward abortion. In doing so, it pursues a strategy of lobbying for the enactment of pro-life laws throughout the nation. NRLC has also engaged in educational formats to bring the public's attention to the need for limiting the right of abortion. Beginning on January 22, 1974, NRLC has sponsored an annual March for Life rally in the nation's capital. The date of the rally is the anniversary of the *Roe v. Wade* decision. *See also* **Pro-Life Organizations**

National Women's Health Organization

The National Women's Health Organization (NWHO) was founded in 1976 for the purpose of providing safe and compassionate abortion care to women. NWHO is headquartered in Raleigh, North Carolina. The president of NWHO is Susan Hill. Since its inception, NWHO has provided abortion services to over 600,000 women and low cost reproductive services to another 600,000 women. NWHO has eight clinics in the United States: Raleigh, North Carolina; Fargo, North Dakota; Jackson, Mississippi; Milwaukee, Wisconsin; Ft. Wayne, Indiana; Orlando, Florida; Columbus, Georgia; and Wilmington, Delaware. The organization also supplies physicians to other facilities as well as their own, on an emergency basis. *See also* **Pro-Choice Organizations**

National Women's Law Center

National Women's Law Center (NWLC) is a Washington, D.C., based organization that was created in 1972, to advance and protect the legal rights of women. NWLC focuses on major policy areas of importance to women and their families including education, employment and health. The organization has a long history of commitment to fighting for the rights of women to have abortions. Major initiatives by NWLC in the area of women's health care include: the development and production of the first women's health report card (an advocacy tool designed to change the paradigm for setting national priorities to address women's health); national advocacy efforts to protect and improve family planning and reproductive health services; and the development of legal theories and strategies to address mergers between health care providers that restrict reproductive choice. *See also* **Pro-Choice Organizations**

Native American Women and Abortion Funding

The federal government provides funding for Native American health care at many facilities located on lands reserved for them. Since 1988 appropriation legislation for such funds has prohibited use of the funds to perform abortions, as well as prohibited use of the facilities for abortions that are paid for with private funds. Only three exceptions to the prohibitions are allowed: therapeutic abortions, pregnancies resulting from rape, or pregnancies resulting from incest.

25 U.S.C.A. § 1676.

Funds appropriated for Native American Health Service

Any limitation on the use of funds contained in an Act providing appropriations for the Department of Health and Human Services for a period with respect to the performance of abortions shall apply for that period with respect to the performance of abortions using funds contained in an Act providing appropriations for the Indian Health Service.

See also **Public Resources for Abortions**

Native American Women's Health Education Resource Center

Native American Women's Health Education Resource Center was founded in 1988, in Lake Andes, South Dakota. The founder and executive director of the Center is Charon Asetoyer. The Center was the first resource facility located on a land reserve in the United States. The Center provides a variety of health services that also includes reproductive health services. Some of the stated principles the Center operates under include: (1) the right to knowledge and education for all family members, concerning sexuality and reproduction that is age, culture, and gender appropriate; (2) the right to all reproductive alternatives and the right to choose the size of families; (3) the right to access safe, free or affordable abortions, regardless of age, with confidentiality and free pre- and post-counseling; (4) the right to active involvement in the development and implementation of policies concerning reproductive issues, to include, but not limited to, pharmaceuticals and technology; (5) the right to include domestic violence, sexual assault and AIDS as reproductive rights issues; and (6) the right to stop coerced sterilization. *See also* **Pro-Choice Organizations**

Natural Childbirth Methods

Modern hospital birthing is being increasingly challenged by alternative birthing methods. The alternatives seek to make the birthing process a nonmedicated and nonsurgical process, i.e., a natural process. All of the natural birthing methods seek to place the pregnant woman in control of the delivery. Some of the new alternatives can take place in a hospital setting or birthing clinic, while others do not. In some cases health care providers may be present, while in others, no health care provider is immediately present. Some of the natural birthing methods include: Lamaze method, Leboyer method, Bradley method, waterbirth method, homebirth and hypnobirthing.

Lamaze method. The Lamaze method was started Dr. Fernand Lamaze, a French obstetrician. This method involves training the pregnant woman in relaxation methods, massage techniques, breathing exercises, and pushing during contractions. The husband/partner of the woman plays an active role in the birthing process as a coach and comforter.

Leboyer method. The Leboyer method was developed by a French obstetrician, Frederick Leboyer. This method focuses on both the mother and neonate. The central theme of this method is delivery without trauma. This technique does not allow the newborn to be held upside down and slapped, nor does it permit placement of silver nitrate in the neonate's eyes. After delivery the child is placed on the mother's stomach for bonding and immersed in water to relax. The use of soft lighting in the delivery room is required.

Bradley method. The Bradley method of childbirth was developed by Dr. Robert Bradley in the 1940s. This method emphasizes natural delivery, but does not rule out the use of medications in some instances. The central feature of this method is a series of classes that the pregnant woman and her husband/partner attend, in order to learn about proper nutrition, pain management, relaxation and the different things to expect during the birthing process.

Waterbirth method. The waterbirth method is a relatively new technique that relies upon water as the tranquilizer for pain during delivery. This method can be done at home and at hospitals that offer the service. The waterbirth method requires the pregnant women to immerse her body in a tub or pool of water during delivery. The neonate is delivered underwater. This method emphasizes the interaction of the water on the woman's body to reduce the intensity of birthing pains.

Homebirth. The basic idea behind homebirth is to allow delivery without drugs and in the familiar setting of the home. Homebirth advocates believe pregnancy and childbirth are normal processes, not emergencies requiring medical intervention. This method places sole responsibility for the delivery on the pregnant woman and her husband/partner. In some instances a midwife or physician may be present.

Hypnobirthing. Hypnobirthing is a method of childbirth that involves placing the pregnant woman in touch with her birthing muscles. This method requires a pregnant woman take courses that are designed help her focus internally and learn to be completely relaxed during the birthing process. *See also* **Childbirth and Labor**

Natural Family Planning Methods

Natural family planning (NFP) (also called fertility awareness) is the phrase used for methods of birth control that involve monitoring aspects of a woman's body. The NFP pregnancy preventive methods require abstaining from having sexual intercourse during the fertile days of a woman's menstrual cycle. The effectiveness of NFP depends on a woman's accuracy in recording information about her menstrual cycle and calculating safe or unsafe days for sexual intercourse.

During a woman's monthly menstrual cycle there are only a few days when she is potentially fertile. In a typical menstrual cycle, a woman will have several days of bleeding, followed by a few infertile days, which are then followed by several days in which fertile cervical fluid is produced, then ovulation. Roughly two weeks after ovulation the menstrual cycle terminates and bleeding for the next cycle begins. The point in the menstrual cycle when safe sex may occur is when no fertile cervical fluid is being produced. When fertile cervical fluid is not being produced ejaculated sperm quickly die and pregnancy is highly unlikely.

NFP methods assist in determining when a woman is not fertile during her menstrual cycle. There are several indicators of fertility which can provide an understanding of a woman's fertility patterns. The primary indicators are: basal body temperature, cervical changes, production of cervical mucus, and dried saliva. By observing any of these three indicators a woman may determine when she is fertile. There are four types of NFP methods that may be used in charting the indicators of fertility: basal body temperature method, Billings (or ovulation) method, symptothermal method, rhythm (or calendar) method, and the Ovu-Tec method.

Basal body temperature method. The basal body temperature method attempts to pin point the time of the month when ovulation is taking place. This method requires a woman to monitor her waking body temperature. When accurately done such monitoring may confirm ovulation. After ovulation occurs a woman's waking body temperature rises slightly and remains so until her next period. The shift in body temperature aids in identifying the start of the infertile phase. A woman may monitor her temperature orally, through her vagina or rectum.

Billings (or ovulation) method. The Billings (or ovulation) method derives its name from its developers, Drs. John and Evelyn Billings. This method requires monitoring the cervical mucus or fluid at the vaginal opening. During a woman's menstrual cycle changes take place in the mucus produced by the cells lining her cervical canal. Cervical mucus becomes clear and watery at its most fertile stage. Fertile mucus maintains the life of sperm and allows it to pass freely through the cervix. During a woman's post-ovulatory phase the slippery sensation of cervical mucus is lost. This symptom reflects the presence of progesterone, which thickens the mucus and forms a plug at the cervix that acts as a barrier to sperm. Cervical mucus can be determined by sensation, appearance and by testing with the finger-tip. The Billings method allows intercourse from the end of bleeding up to the time that sperm-sustaining fertile mucus appears.

Symptothermal method. The symptothermal method is a hybrid of other NFP methods. That is, the symptothermal method involves monitoring basal body temperature, cervical mucus, and changes in the cervix. Changes in the cervix take place over an interval of about ten days during the menstrual cycle. As ovulation approaches, the cervix begins to rise higher in the vagina. During the infertile phases of the cycle, the cervix is low in the vagina. A woman can detect changes in the cervix by feeling gently with a fingertip. The changes in the level of the cervix are subtle and gradual. However, by also monitoring the basal body temperature and cervical mucus, changes in the cervix can be confirmed.

Rhythm (or calendar) method. The rhythm (or calendar) method is the least reliable and recommended NFP method. It requires a woman to mathematically calculate her fertile days based upon her longest and shortest menstrual cycles. The primary problem presented by this method is knowing the exact time of the month when a woman is receptive to pregnancy. For illustrative purposes, assume that the typical woman's menstrual cycle is 28 days. Between day 1 and day 28 an egg will be released from the woman's ovaries and enter the uterus through the fallopian tubes. (Should sperm be present when the egg passes through the fallopian tubes, pregnancy may result.) The egg is usually released on day 14 of the cycle. Consequently, sexual intercourse should be avoided from about the 9th day to the 18th day of the cycle.

Ovu-Tec method. A seldom recognized or recommended NFP method is the Ovu-Tec method. This method is based upon a theory that hormonal changes during a woman's menstrual cycle have a direct effect on dried or crystallized saliva patterns. The Ovu-Tec method requires using a microscope to observe samples of dried saliva. During a woman's fertile phase the dried saliva will have a distinct shape; but during the infertile phase the dried saliva will have a shapeless structure. *See also* **Contraception; Lactational Amenorrhea Method**

Natural Killer Cells *see* **Alloimmune Factors**

Nebraska

(1) OVERVIEW

The state of Nebraska enacted its first criminal abortion statute in 1858. The statute underwent several amendments prior to the 1973 decision by the United States Supreme Court in *Roe v. Wade*, which legalized abortion in the nation. Nebraska has taken affirmative steps to respond to *Roe* and its progeny. The state has addressed numerous abortion issues by statute that include general abortion requirements, informed consent, partial-birth abortion, abortion by minors, use of facilities and people, fetal death report, fetal sale and experiments, fetal homicide and assault, and health insurance.

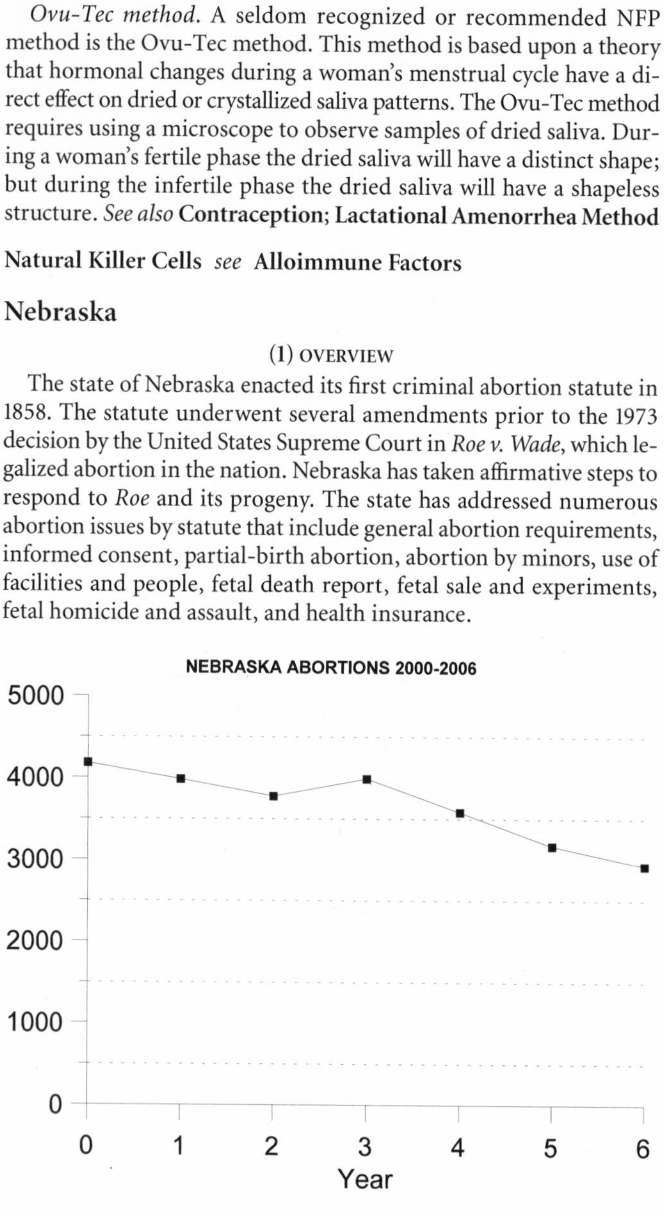

Source: **Nebraska Department of Health and Human Services.**

(2) GENERAL ABORTION REQUIREMENTS

Under its general abortion statutes Nebraska prohibits post-viability abortions, except to save the life or health of the woman. The state limits abortions to being performed by physicians only. The general abortion statutes are set out below.

Nebraska Code § 28-325. Declaration of purpose

The Legislature hereby finds and declares:

(1) That the following provisions were motivated by the legislative intrusion of the United States Supreme Court by virtue of its decision removing the protection afforded the unborn. Sections 28-325 to 28-345 are

Nebraska Abortion by Age Group 2000–2006

Year	<15	15–19	20–24	25–29	30–34	35–39	≥40
	Age Group (yrs)						
2000	26	864	1,381	885	546	351	125
2001	19	808	1,360	844	510	316	125
2002	23	688	1,319	804	524	298	119
2003	24	695	1,417	869	518	345	122
2004	17	613	1,239	792	482	301	140
2005	17	532	1,105	706	427	279	107
2006	12	448	991	716	423	241	96
Total	138	4,648	8,812	5,616	3,430	2,131	834

Source: **National Center for Health Statistics/Nebraska Department of Health and Human Services.**

Nebraska Prior Abortion by Female 2000–2006

Year	None	1	2	≥3
	Prior Abortion			
2000	2,846	855	300	177
2001	2,771	809	256	146
2002	2,621	762	237	155
2003	2,806	788	248	148
2004	2,450	722	263	149
2005	2,019	754	219	181
2006	1,869	696	240	122
Total	17,382	5,386	1,763	1,078

Source: **National Center for Health Statistics/Nebraska Department of Health and Human Services.**

in no way to be construed as legislatively encouraging abortions at any stage of unborn human development, but are rather an expression of the will of the people of the State of Nebraska and the members of the Legislature to provide protection for the life of the unborn child whenever possible;

(2) That the members of the Legislature expressly deplore the destruction of the unborn human lives which has and will occur in Nebraska as a consequence of the United States Supreme Court's decision on abortion of January 22, 1973;

(3) That it is in the interest of the people of the State of Nebraska that every precaution be taken to insure the protection of every viable unborn child being aborted, and every precaution be taken to provide life-supportive procedures to insure the unborn child its continued life after its abortion;

(4) That currently this state is prevented from providing adequate legal remedies to protect the life, health, and welfare of pregnant women and unborn human life; and

(5) That it is in the interest of the people of the State of Nebraska to maintain accurate statistical data to aid in providing proper maternal health regulations and education.

Nebraska Code § 28-326. Definitions

For purposes of sections 28-325 to 28-345, unless the context otherwise requires:

(1) Abortion means the use or prescription of any instrument, medicine, drug, or other substance or device intentionally to terminate the pregnancy of a woman known to be pregnant with an intention other than to increase the probability of a live birth, to preserve the life or health of the child after live birth, or to remove a dead unborn child, and which causes the premature termination of the pregnancy;

(2) Hospital means those institutions licensed by the Department of Health and Human Services Regulation and Licensure pursuant to the Health Care Facility Licensure Act;

(3) Physician means any person licensed to practice medicine in this state as provided in sections 71-102 to 71-110;

(4) Pregnant means that condition of a woman who has unborn human life within her as the result of conception;

(5) Conception means the fecundation of the ovum by the spermatozoa;

(6) Viability means that stage of human development when the unborn child is potentially able to live more than merely momentarily outside the womb of the mother by natural or artificial means;

(7) Emergency situation means that condition which, on the basis of the physician's good faith clinical judgment, so complicates the medical condition of a pregnant woman as to necessitate the immediate abortion of her pregnancy to avert her death or for which a delay will create serious risk of substantial impairment of a major bodily function;

(8) Probable gestational age of the unborn child means what will with reasonable probability, in the judgment of the physician, be the gestational age of the unborn child at the time the abortion is planned to be performed; and

(9) Partial-birth abortion means an abortion procedure in which the person performing the abortion partially delivers vaginally a living unborn child before killing the unborn child and completing the delivery. For purposes of this subdivision, the term partially delivers vaginally a living unborn child before killing the unborn child means deliberately and intentionally delivering into the vagina a living unborn child, or a substantial portion thereof, for the purpose of performing a procedure that the person performing such procedure knows will kill the unborn child and does kill the unborn child.

Nebraska Code § 28-329. Post-viability ban

No abortion shall be performed after the time at which, in the sound medical judgment of the attending physician, the unborn child clearly appears to have reached viability, except when necessary to preserve the life or health of the mother.

Nebraska Code § 28-330. Protection of viable fetus

In any abortion performed pursuant to section 28-329, all reasonable precautions, in accord with the sound medical judgment of the attending physician and compatible with preserving the life or health of the mother, shall be taken to insure the protection of the viable, unborn child.

Nebraska Code § 28-331. Care and treatment of child aborted

When as the result of an abortion a child is, in the sound medical judgment of the attending physician, born alive, then all reasonable steps, in accordance with the sound medical judgment of the attending physician, shall be employed to preserve the life of the child. For purposes of this section, born alive shall mean the complete expulsion or extraction of the child from the mother irrespective of the duration of the pregnancy and after such expulsion or extraction such child breathes or shows any other evidence of life such as beating of the heart, pulsation of the umbilical cord, or definite movement of voluntary muscles whether or not the umbilical cord has been cut or the placenta is attached.

Nebraska Code § 28-332. Violation

The intentional and knowing violation of section 28-329, 28-330, or 28-331 is a Class IV felony.

Nebraska Code § 28-335. Abortion by licensed physician

The performing of an abortion by any person other than a licensed physician is a Class IV felony.

Nebraska Code § 28-336.
Abortion by standard medical procedures

The performing of an abortion by using anything other than accepted medical procedures is a Class IV felony.

(3) INFORMED CONSENT

Prior to an abortion Nebraska requires that a woman be fully informed of the procedure to be used, the risks involved and alternatives to abortion. An abortion may not take place until 24 hours after a woman has given her written consent to an abortion. The statutes addressing the matters are set out below.

Nebraska Code § 28-327. Consent and waiting period

No abortion shall be performed except with the voluntary and informed consent of the woman upon whom the abortion is to be performed. Except in the case of an emergency situation, consent to an abortion is voluntary and informed only if:

(1) The woman is told the following by the physician who is to perform the abortion, by the referring physician, or by a licensed physician assistant or registered nurse who is an agent of either, at least twenty-four hours before the abortion:

(a) The particular medical risks associated with the particular abortion procedure to be employed including, when medically accurate, the risks of infection, hemorrhage, and danger to subsequent pregnancies and infertility;

(b) The probable gestational age of the unborn child at the time the abortion is to be performed; and

(c) The medical risks associated with carrying her child to term.

The person providing the information specified in this subdivision to the person upon whom the abortion is to be performed shall be deemed qualified to so advise and provide such information only if, at a minimum, he or she has had training in each of the following subjects: Sexual and reproductive health; abortion technology; contraceptive technology; short-term counseling skills; community resources and referral; and informed consent. The physician or the physician's agent may provide this information by telephone without conducting a physical examination or tests of the patient, in which case the information required to be supplied may be based on facts supplied by the patient and whatever other relevant information is reasonably available to the physician or the physician's agent;

(2) The woman is informed by telephone or in person, by the physician who is to perform the abortion, by the referring physician, or by an agent of either, at least twenty-four hours before the abortion:

(a) The name of the physician who will perform the abortion;

(b) That medical assistance benefits may be available for prenatal care, childbirth, and neonatal care;

(c) That the father is liable to assist in the support of her child, even in instances in which the father has offered to pay for the abortion; and

(d) That she has the right to review the printed materials described in section 28-327.01. The physician or his or her agent shall orally inform the woman that the materials have been provided by the Department of Health and Human Services and that they describe the unborn child and list agencies which offer alternatives to abortion. If the woman chooses to review the materials, they shall either be given to her at least twenty-four hours before the abortion or mailed to her at least seventy-two hours before the abortion by certified mail, restricted delivery to addressee, which means the postal employee can only deliver the mail to the addressee. The physician and his or her agent may disassociate themselves from the materials and may comment or refrain from commenting on them as they choose;

(3) The woman certifies in writing, prior to the abortion, that the information described in subdivisions (1) and (2)(a), (b), and (c) of this section has been furnished her and that she has been informed of her right to review the information referred to in subdivision (2)(d) of this section; and

(4) Prior to the performance of the abortion, the physician who is to perform the abortion or his or her agent receives a copy of the written certification prescribed by subdivision (3) of this section.

Nebraska Code § 28-327.01. Printed materials

(1) The Department of Health and Human Services shall cause to be published, within sixty days after September 9, 1993, the following easily comprehensible printed materials:

(a) Geographically indexed materials designed to inform the woman of public and private agencies and services available to assist a woman through pregnancy, upon childbirth, and while the child is dependent, including adoption agencies and agencies and services for prevention of unintended pregnancies, which materials shall include a comprehensive list of the agencies available, a description of the services they offer, and a description of the manner, including telephone numbers and addresses in which such agencies may be contacted or printed materials including a toll-free, twenty-four-hour-a-day telephone number which may be called to orally obtain such a list and description of agencies in the locality of the caller and of the services they offer; and

(b) Materials designed to inform the woman of the probable anatomical and physiological characteristics of the unborn child at two-week gestational increments from the time when a woman can be known to be pregnant to full term, including pictures or drawings representing the development of unborn children at the two-week gestational increments, and any relevant information on the possibility of the unborn child's survival. Any such pictures or drawings shall contain the dimensions of the unborn child and shall be realistic and appropriate for the stage of pregnancy depicted. The materials shall be objective, nonjudgmental, and designed to convey only accurate scientific information about the unborn child at the various gestational ages. The materials shall also contain objective information describing the methods of abortion procedures commonly employed, the medical risks commonly associated with each such procedure, the possible detrimental psychological effects of abortion, the medical risks commonly associated with abortion, and the medical risks commonly associated with carrying a child to term.

(2) The materials shall be printed in a typeface large enough to be clearly legible.

(3) The materials required under this section shall be available from the department upon the request by any person, facility, or hospital for an amount equal to the cost incurred by the department to publish the materials.

Nebraska Code § 28-327.02. Emergency situation

When an emergency situation compels the performance of an abortion, the physician shall inform the woman, prior to the abortion if possible, of the medical indications supporting his or her judgment that an abortion is necessary to avert her death or to avert substantial impairment of a major bodily function.

Nebraska Code § 28-327.03. Civil liability limitation

No civil liability for failure to comply with subdivision (2)(d) of section 28-327 or that portion of subdivision (3) of such section requiring a written certification that the woman has been informed of her right to review the information referred to in subdivision (2)(d) of such section may be imposed unless the Department of Health and Human Services has published and made available the printed materials at the time the physician or his or her agent is required to inform the woman of her right to review them.

Nebraska Code § 28-327.04. Civil cause of action

Any person upon whom an abortion has been performed or attempted in violation of section 28-327 or the parent or guardian of a minor upon whom an abortion has been performed or attempted in violation of such section shall have a right to maintain a civil cause of action against the person who performed the abortion or attempted to perform the abortion. A violation of such section shall be prima facie evidence of professional negligence. The written certification prescribed by subdivision (3) of section 28-327 signed by the person upon whom an abortion has been performed or attempted shall constitute and create a rebuttable presumption of full compliance with all provisions of section 28-327 in favor of the physician who performed or attempted to perform the abortion, the re-

ferring physician, or the agent of either. The written certification shall be admissible as evidence in the cause of action for professional negligence or in any criminal action. If judgment is rendered in favor of the plaintiff in any such action, the court shall also render judgment for a reasonable attorney's fee in favor of the plaintiff against the defendant.

Nebraska Code § 28-327.05. Civil action anonymity of woman

In every civil action brought pursuant to section 28-327.04, the court shall rule whether the anonymity of any woman upon whom an abortion is performed or attempted shall be preserved from public disclosure if she does not give her consent to such disclosure. The court, upon motion by a party or on its own motion, shall make such a ruling and, upon determining that her anonymity should be preserved, shall issue orders to the parties, witnesses, and counsel and shall direct the sealing of the record and exclusion of individuals from courtrooms or hearing rooms to the extent necessary to safeguard her identity from public disclosure. Each such order shall be accompanied by specific written findings explaining why the anonymity of the woman should be preserved from public disclosure, why the order is essential to that end, how the order is narrowly tailored to serve that interest, and why no reasonable less restrictive alternative exists. In the absence of written consent of the woman upon whom an abortion has been performed or attempted, anyone given standing under section 28-327.04 who brings a civil action under such section shall do so under a pseudonym. This section may not be construed to conceal the identity of the plaintiff or of witnesses from the defendant.

(4) PARTIAL-BIRTH ABORTION

Nebraska enacted a penal statute that prohibited partial-birth abortions. However, the ban was found unconstitutional by the United States Supreme Court in *Stenberg v. Carhart*. The state has not repealed the statute, though it is no longer enforceable. Under the statute partial-birth abortions were permitted when necessary to save the life of the woman. The statute is set out below.

Nebraska Code § 28-328. Partial-birth abortion offense

(1) No partial-birth abortion shall be performed in this state, unless such procedure is necessary to save the life of the mother whose life is endangered by a physical disorder, physical illness, or physical injury, including a life-endangering physical condition caused by or arising from the pregnancy itself.

(2) The intentional and knowing performance of an unlawful partial-birth abortion in violation of subsection (1) of this section is a Class III felony.

(3) No woman upon whom an unlawful partial-birth abortion is performed shall be prosecuted under this section or for conspiracy to violate this section.

(4) The intentional and knowing performance of an unlawful partial-birth abortion shall result in the automatic suspension and revocation of an attending physician's license to practice medicine in Nebraska by the Director of Regulation and Licensure pursuant to sections 71-147 to 71-161.20.

Upon the filing of criminal charges under this section by the Attorney General or a county attorney, the Attorney General shall also file a petition to suspend and revoke the attending physician's license to practice medicine pursuant to section 71-150. A hearing on such administrative petition shall be set in accordance with section 71-153. At such hearing, the attending physician shall have the opportunity to present evidence that the physician's conduct was necessary to save the life of a mother whose life was endangered by a physical disorder, physical illness, or physical injury, including a life-endangering physical condition caused by or arising from the pregnancy itself. A defendant against whom criminal charges are brought under this section may bring a motion to delay the beginning of the trial until after the entry of an order by the Director of Regulation and Licensure pursuant to section 71-155. The findings of the Director of Regulation and Licensure as to whether the attending physician's conduct was necessary to save the life of a mother whose life was endangered by a physical disorder, physical illness, or physical injury, including a life-endangering physical condition caused by or arising from the pregnancy itself, shall be admissible in the criminal proceedings brought pursuant to this section.

(5) ABORTION BY MINORS

Under the laws of Nebraska no physician may perform an abortion upon an unemancipated minor, until 48 hours after notice of the operation has been given to either parent of the minor. In compliance with federal constitutional law, Nebraska has provided a judicial waiver procedure for an unemancipated minor to obtain an abortion without parental notice. The minor may petition a trial court for a waiver of the notice requirement. A minor has a right to an attorney at the proceeding and if she cannot afford one, the court must appoint her an attorney. If a minor chooses, she may represent herself. The required parental notice may be waived if the court finds either (1) that the minor is mature and well-informed enough to make the abortion decision on her own, or (2) that performance of the abortion would be in the best interest of the minor. An expedited appeal is available to any minor to whom the court denies a waiver of notice. The statutes addressing the issues are set out below.

Nebraska Code § 71-6901. Definitions

For purposes of sections 71-6901 to 71-6908:

(1) Abortion shall mean an act, procedure, device, or prescription administered to a woman known by the person so administering to be pregnant and administered with the intent and result of producing the premature expulsion, removal, or termination of the human life within the womb of the pregnant woman, except that in cases in which the unborn child's viability is threatened by continuation of the pregnancy, early delivery after viability shall not be construed as an abortion;

(2) Facsimile copy shall mean a copy generated by a system that encodes a document or photograph into electrical signals, transmits those signals over telecommunications lines, and then reconstructs the signals to create an exact duplicate of the original document at the receiving end;

(3) Parent shall mean one parent or guardian of the pregnant woman selected by the pregnant woman. The attending physician shall certify in writing in the pregnant woman's medical record the parent or guardian selected by the woman;

(4) Physician or attending physician shall mean the physician intending to perform the abortion; and

(5) Pregnant woman shall mean an unemancipated woman under eighteen years of age who is pregnant or a pregnant woman for whom a guardian has been appointed pursuant to sections 30-2620 to 30-2629 because of a finding of incapacity, disability, or incompetency.

Nebraska Code § 71-6902. Parental notice

(1) No abortion shall be performed upon a pregnant woman until at least forty-eight hours after written notice of the pending abortion has been delivered in the manner specified in subsection (2) or (3) of this section.

(2) The notice shall be addressed to the parent at his or her usual place of residence and shall be delivered personally to the parent by the physician or an agent.

(3) In lieu of the delivery required by subsection (2) of this section, notice shall be made by registered or certified mail addressed to the parent at his or her usual place of residence with return receipt requested and restricted delivery to the addressee, which means the postal employee can only deliver mail to the authorized addressee. Time of delivery shall be deemed to occur at twelve o'clock noon on the next day on which regular mail delivery takes place subsequent to the mailing.

Nebraska Code § 71-6903. Judicial bypass

(1) If a pregnant woman elects not to notify her parent, a judge of a district court, separate juvenile court, or county court sitting as a juvenile court shall, upon petition or motion and after an appropriate hearing, authorize a physician to perform the abortion if the court determines that the pregnant woman is mature and capable of giving informed consent to the proposed abortion. If the court determines that the pregnant woman is not mature or if the pregnant woman does not claim to be mature, the court shall determine whether the performance of an abortion upon her without notification of her parent would be in her best interests and shall authorize a physician to perform the abortion without such notification if the court concludes that the best interests of the pregnant woman would be served thereby.

(2) A facsimile copy of the petition or motion may be transmitted directly to the court for filing. If a facsimile copy is filed in lieu of the original document, the party filing the facsimile copy shall retain the original document for production to the court if requested to do so.

(3) A court shall not be required to have a facsimile machine nor shall the court be required to transmit orders or other material to attorneys or parties via facsimile transmission.

(4) An action for waiver of notification shall be commenced by the filing of a petition or motion personally, by mail, or by facsimile on a form provided by the State Court Administrator. The State Court Administrator shall develop the petition form and accompanying instructions on the procedure for petitioning the court for a waiver of notification, including the name, address, telephone number, and facsimile number of each court in the state. A sufficient number of petition forms and instructions shall be made available in each courthouse in such place that members of the general public may obtain a form and instructions without requesting such form and instructions from the clerk of the court or other court personnel. The clerk of the court shall, upon request, assist in completing and filing the petition for waiver of notification.

(5) Proceedings in court pursuant to this section shall be confidential. Proceedings shall be held in camera. Only the pregnant woman, the pregnant woman's guardian ad litem, the pregnant woman's attorney, and a person whose presence is specifically requested by the pregnant woman, the pregnant woman's guardian ad litem, or the pregnant woman's attorney may attend the hearing on the petition. All testimony, all documents, all other evidence presented to the court, the petition and any order entered, and all records of any nature and kind relating to the matter shall be sealed by the clerk of the court and shall not be open to any person except upon order of the court for good cause shown. A separate docket for the purposes of this section shall be maintained by the clerk of the court and shall likewise be sealed and not opened to inspection by any person except upon order of the court for good cause shown.

(6) A pregnant woman who is subject to this section may participate in the court proceedings on her own behalf, and the court may appoint a guardian ad litem for her. The court shall advise the pregnant woman that she has a right to court-appointed counsel and shall, upon her request, provide her with such counsel. Such counsel shall receive a fee to be fixed by the court and to be paid out of the treasury of the county in which the proceeding was held.

(7) Proceedings in court pursuant to this section shall be given such precedence over other pending matters so that the court may reach a decision promptly and without delay to serve the best interests of the pregnant woman. In no case shall the court fail to rule within seven calendar days from the time the petition is filed. If the court fails to rule within the required time period, the pregnant woman may file an application for a writ of mandamus with the Supreme Court. If cause for a writ of mandamus exists, the writ shall issue within three days. If the judge issues a ruling adverse to the pregnant woman, the judge shall issue written findings of fact and conclusions of law.

(8) The court shall issue a written order which shall be provided immediately to the pregnant woman, the pregnant woman's guardian ad litem, the pregnant woman's attorney, or any other person designated by the pregnant woman to receive the order.

Nebraska Code § 71-6904. Appeal procedure

(1) An appeal to the Supreme Court shall be available to any pregnant woman for whom a court denies an order authorizing an abortion without notification. An order authorizing an abortion without notification shall not be subject to appeal.

(2) An adverse ruling by the court may be appealed to the Supreme Court.

(3) A pregnant woman may file a notice of appeal of any final order to the Supreme Court. The State Court Administrator shall develop the form for notice of appeal and accompanying instructions on the procedure for an appeal. A sufficient number of forms for notice of appeal and instructions shall be made available in each courthouse in such place that members of the general public can obtain a form and instructions without requesting such form and instructions from the clerk of the court or other court personnel.

(4) The clerk of the court shall cause the court transcript and bill of exceptions to be filed with the Supreme Court within four business days, but in no event later than seven calendar days, from the date of the filing of the notice of appeal.

(5) In all appeals under this section the pregnant woman shall have the right of a confidential and expedited appeal and the right to counsel at the appellate level if not already represented. Such counsel shall be appointed by the court and shall receive a fee to be fixed by the court and to be paid out of the treasury of the county in which the proceeding was held. The pregnant woman shall not be required to appear.

(6) The Supreme Court shall hear the appeal de novo on the record and issue a written decision which shall be provided immediately to the pregnant woman, the pregnant woman's guardian ad litem, the pregnant woman's attorney, or any other person designated by the pregnant woman to receive the order.

(7) The Supreme Court shall rule within seven calendar days from the time of the docketing of the appeal in the Supreme Court.

(8) The Supreme Court shall adopt and promulgate rules to ensure that proceedings under this section are handled in a confidential and expeditious manner.

Nebraska Code § 71-6905. Court fees or costs

No filing fees or costs shall be required of any pregnant woman at either the trial or appellate level for any proceedings pursuant to sections 71-6901 to 71-6908.

Nebraska Code § 71-6906. When notice not required

Notification shall not be required pursuant to sections 71-6901 to 71-6908 if any of the following conditions exist:

(1) The attending physician certifies in writing in the pregnant woman's medical record that continuation of the pregnancy provides an immediate threat and grave risk to the life or health of the pregnant woman and there is insufficient time to provide the required notification;

(2) The abortion is authorized in writing by the person who is entitled to notification; or

(3) The pregnant woman declares that she is a victim of abuse as defined in section 28-351, sexual abuse as defined in section 28-367, or child abuse or neglect as defined in section 28-710. Notice of such a declaration shall be made to the proper authorities as provided in sections 28-372 and 28-711. If such a declaration is made, the attending physician or his or her agent shall inform the pregnant woman of his or her duty to notify the proper authorities as provided in sections 28-372 and 28-711.

Nebraska Code § 71-6907. Violation by physician

(1) Any physician or attending physician who knowingly and intentionally performs an abortion in violation of sections 71-6901 to 71-6906 shall be guilty of a Class III misdemeanor.

(2) Performance of an abortion in violation of such sections shall be grounds for a civil action by a person wrongfully denied notification.

(3) A person shall be immune from liability under such sections (a) if he or she establishes by written evidence that he or she relied upon evidence sufficient to convince a careful and prudent person that the representations of the pregnant woman regarding information necessary to comply with such sections are bona fide and true, (b) if the person has attempted with reasonable diligence to deliver notification as required by section 71-6902 but has been unable to do so, or (c) if the person has performed an abortion authorized by a court order issued pursuant to section 71-6903 or 71-6904.

Nebraska Code § 71-6908. Family or foster family abuse

The Legislature recognizes and hereby declares that some teenage pregnancies are a direct or indirect result of family or foster family abuse, neglect, or sexual assault. The Legislature further recognizes that the actions of abuse, neglect, or sexual assault are crimes regardless of whether they are committed by strangers, acquaintances, or family members. The Legislature further recognizes the need for a parent or guardian notification bypass system as set out in section 71-6903 due to the number of unhealthy family environments in which some pregnant women reside. The Legislature encourages county attorneys to prosecute persons accused of committing acts of abuse, incest, neglect, or sexual assault pursuant to sections 28-319, 28-319.01, 28-320, 28-320.01, 28-703, and 28-707 even if the alleged crime is committed by a biological or adoptive parent, foster parent, or other biological, adoptive, or foster family member.

Nebraska Code § 28-706.
Criminal nonsupport for failing to pay for abortion (abridged)

(1) Any person who intentionally fails, refuses, or neglects to provide proper support which he or she knows or reasonably should know he or she is legally obliged to provide to a spouse, minor child, minor stepchild, or other dependent commits criminal nonsupport.

(2) A parent or guardian who refuses to pay hospital costs, medical costs, or any other costs arising out of or in connection with an abortion procedure performed on a minor child or minor stepchild does not commit criminal nonsupport if:

(a) Such parent or guardian was not consulted prior to the abortion procedure; or

(b) After consultation, such parent or guardian refused to grant consent for such procedure, and the abortion procedure was not necessary to preserve the minor child or stepchild from an imminent peril that substantially endangered her life or health.

(6) USE OF FACILITIES AND PEOPLE

Under the laws of Nebraska medical facilities are not required to allow abortions. The employees and physicians at medical facilities that do allow abortions are permitted to refuse to take part in abortions. The statutes addressing the matters are set out below.

Nebraska Code § 28-337. Hospitals, clinics, institutions

No hospital, clinic, institution, or other facility in this state shall be required to admit any patient for the purpose of performing an abortion nor required to allow the performance of an abortion therein, but the hospital, clinic, institution, or other facility shall inform the patient of its policy not to participate in abortion procedures. No cause of action shall arise against any hospital, clinic, institution, or other facility for refusing to perform or allow an abortion.

Nebraska Code § 28-338.
No person required to perform an abortion

No person shall be required to perform or participate in any abortion, and the refusal of any person to participate in an abortion shall not be a basis for civil liability to any person. No hospital, governing board, or any other person, firm, association, or group shall terminate the employment or alter the position of, prevent or impair the practice or occupation of, or impose any other sanction or otherwise discriminate against any person who refuses to participate in an abortion.

Nebraska Code § 28-339. Violation

Any violation of section 28-338 is a Class II misdemeanor.

Nebraska Code § 28-340. Civil lawsuit

Any person whose employment or position has been in any way altered, impaired, or terminated in violation of sections 28-325 to 28-345 may sue in the district court for all consequential damages, lost wages, reasonable attorney's fees incurred, and the cost of litigation.

Nebraska Code § 28-341. Injunctive relief

Any person whose employment or position has in any way been altered, impaired, or terminated because of his refusal to participate in an abortion shall have the right to injunctive relief, including temporary relief, pending trial upon showing of an emergency, in the district court, in accordance with the statutes, rules, and practices applicable in other similar cases.

(7) FETAL DEATH REPORT

Nebraska requires that all abortions be reported to the proper authorities. The statutes addressing the matter are set out below.

Nebraska Code § 28-343. Abortion reporting form

The Department of Health and Human Services Finance and Support shall prescribe an abortion reporting form which shall be used for the reporting of every abortion performed in this state. Such form shall include the following items:

(1) The age of the pregnant woman;

(2) The location of the facility where the abortion was performed;

(3) The type of procedure performed;

(4) Complications, if any;

(5) The name of the attending physician;

(6) The pregnant woman's obstetrical history regarding previous pregnancies, abortions, and live births;

(7) The stated reason or reasons for which the abortion was requested;

(8) The state of the pregnant woman's legal residence;

(9) The length and weight of the aborted child, when measurable;

(10) Whether an emergency situation caused the physician to waive any of the requirements of section 28-327; and

(11) Such other information as may be prescribed in accordance with section 71-602.

The completed form shall be signed by the attending physician and sent to the department within fifteen days after each reporting month. The completed form shall be an original, typed or written legibly in durable ink, and shall not be deemed complete unless the omission of any item of information required shall have been disclosed or satisfactorily accounted for. Carbon copies shall not be acceptable. The abortion reporting form shall not include the name of the person upon whom the abortion was performed. The abortion reporting form shall be confidential and shall not be revealed except upon the order of a court of competent jurisdiction in a civil or criminal proceeding.

Nebraska Code § 28-344. Violation

Violation of section 28-343 is a Class II misdemeanor.

Nebraska Code § 28-345. Retaining reporting information

The Department of Health and Human Services Finance and Support shall prepare and keep on permanent file compilations of the information submitted on the abortion reporting forms pursuant to such rules and regulations as established by the Department of Health and Human Services Finance and Support, which compilations shall be a matter of public record. Under no circumstances shall the compilations of information include the name of any attending physician or identify in any respect facilities where abortions are performed. The Department of Health and Human Services Finance and Support, in order to maintain and keep such compilations current, shall file with such reports any new or amended information.

(8) FETAL SALE AND EXPERIMENTS

Nebraska prohibits the sale of a fetus for experimentations. The statutes addressing the matter are set out below.

Nebraska Code § 28-342. Experimenting on viable fetus

The knowing, willful, or intentional sale, transfer, distribution, or giving away of any live or viable aborted child for any form of experimentation is a Class III felony. The knowing, willful, or intentional consenting to, aiding, or abetting of any such sale, transfer, distribution, or other unlawful disposition of an aborted child is a Class III felony. This section shall not prohibit or regulate diagnostic or remedial procedures the purpose of which is to preserve the life or health of the aborted child or the mother.

Nebraska Code § 28-346. Experimentation

No person shall knowingly, intentionally, or willfully use any premature infant aborted alive for any type of scientific, research, laboratory, or other kind of experimentation except as necessary to protect or preserve the life or health of such premature infant aborted alive. Violation of this section is a Class IV felony.

(9) FETAL HOMICIDE AND ASSAULT

Nebraska has created criminal fetal homicide and assault laws for death or injury caused to a fetus that was not the result of a lawful abortion. The statutes addressing the matter are set out below.

Nebraska Code § 28-388. Unborn child homicide act

Sections 28-388 to 28-394 shall be known and may be cited as the Homicide of the Unborn Child Act.

Nebraska Code § 28-389. Definitions

For purposes of the Homicide of the Unborn Child Act, unless the context otherwise requires:

(1) Premeditation means a design formed to do something before it is done; and

(2) Unborn child means an individual member of the species Homo sapiens, at any stage of development in utero, who was alive at the time of the homicidal act and died as a result thereof whether before, during, or after birth.

Nebraska Code § 28-390. Applicability of sections

Sections 28-391 to 28-394 do not apply to an act or conduct causing or contributing to the death of an unborn child when the act or conduct is:

(1) Committed or engaged in by the mother of the unborn child;

(2) Any medical procedure performed with the consent of the mother; or

(3) Dispensing a drug or device in accordance with law or administering a drug or device prescribed in accordance with law.

Nebraska Code § 28-391. Murder in the first degree

(1) A person commits murder of an unborn child in the first degree if he or she in committing an act or engaging in conduct that causes the death of an unborn child, intends, with deliberate and premeditated malice, to kill the unborn child or the mother of the unborn child with knowledge of the pregnancy.

(2) Murder of an unborn child in the first degree is a Class IA felony.

Nebraska Code § 28-392. Murder in the second degree

(1) A person commits murder of an unborn child in the second degree if he or she, in committing an act or engaging in conduct that causes the death of an unborn child, intends, but without premeditation, to kill the unborn child or another.

(2) Murder of an unborn child in the second degree is a Class IB felony.

Nebraska Code § 28-393. Manslaughter

(1) A person commits manslaughter of an unborn child if he or she (a) kills an unborn child without malice upon a sudden quarrel with any person or (b) causes the death of an unborn child unintentionally while in the perpetration of or attempt to perpetrate any criminal assault, any sexual assault, arson, robbery, kidnapping, intentional child abuse, hijacking of any public or private means of transportation, or burglary.

(2) Manslaughter of an unborn child is a Class III felony.

Nebraska Code § 28-394. Motor vehicle homicide

(1) A person who causes the death of an unborn child unintentionally while engaged in the operation of a motor vehicle in violation of the law of the State of Nebraska or in violation of any city or village ordinance commits motor vehicle homicide of an unborn child.

(2) Except as provided in subsection (3) of this section, motor vehicle homicide of an unborn child is a Class I misdemeanor.

(3)(a) If the proximate cause of the death of an unborn child is the operation of a motor vehicle in violation of section 60-6,213 or 60-6,214, motor vehicle homicide of an unborn child is a Class IV felony.

(b) Except as provided in subdivision (3)(c) of this section, if the proximate cause of the death of an unborn child is the operation of a motor vehicle in violation of section 60-6,196 or 60-6,197.06, motor vehicle homicide of an unborn child is a Class IV felony and the court shall, as part of the judgment of conviction, order the person not to drive any motor vehicle for any purpose for a period of at least sixty days and not more than fifteen years after the date ordered by the court and shall order that the operator's license of such person be revoked for the same period. The revocation shall not run concurrently with any jail term imposed.

(c) If the proximate cause of the death of an unborn child is the operation of a motor vehicle in violation of section 60-6,196 or 60-6,197.06 and the defendant has a prior conviction for a violation of section 60-6,196 or a city or village ordinance enacted in conformance with section 60-6,196, motor vehicle homicide of an unborn child is a Class III felony and the court shall, as part of the judgment of conviction, order the person not to drive any motor vehicle for any purpose for a period of at least sixty days and not more than fifteen years after the date ordered by the court and shall order that the operator's license of such person be revoked for the same period. The revocation shall not run concurrently with any jail term imposed.

Nebraska Code § 28-395. Unborn child assault act

Sections 28-395 to 28-3,101 shall be known and may be cited as the Assault of an Unborn Child Act.

Nebraska Code § 28-396. Definition

For purposes of the Assault of an Unborn Child Act, unborn child means an individual member of the species Homo sapiens at any stage of development in utero.

Nebraska Code § 28-397. Assault in the first degree

(1) A person commits the offense of assault of an unborn child in the first degree if he or she, during the commission of any criminal assault on

a pregnant woman, intentionally or knowingly causes serious bodily injury to her unborn child.

(2) Assault of an unborn child in the first degree is a Class III felony.

Nebraska Code § 28-398. Assault in the second degree

(1) A person commits the offense of assault of an unborn child in the second degree if he or she, during the commission of any criminal assault on a pregnant woman, recklessly causes serious bodily injury to her unborn child with a dangerous instrument.

(2) Assault of an unborn child in the second degree is a Class IIIA felony.

Nebraska Code § 28-399. Assault in the third degree

(1) A person commits the offense of assault of an unborn child in the third degree if he or she, during the commission of any criminal assault on a pregnant woman, recklessly causes serious bodily injury to her unborn child.

(2) Assault of an unborn child in the third degree is a Class I misdemeanor.

Nebraska Code § 28-3,100. Applicability of act

The Assault of an Unborn Child Act does not apply to:

(1) Any act or conduct that is committed or engaged in by the mother of the unborn child;

(2) Any medical procedure performed with the consent of the mother; or

(3) Dispensing a drug or device in accordance with law or administering a drug or device prescribed in accordance with law.

Nebraska Code § 28-3,101. Prosecution of separate acts

Assault on a pregnant woman and assault on her unborn child shall be considered as separate acts or conduct for purposes of prosecution.

(10) HEALTH INSURANCE

Nebraska prohibits the use of public funds to cover health insurance plans that cover abortions. The state does not require employers to provide abortion benefits. The statutes addressing the matters are set out below.

Nebraska Code § 44-1615.01. Public employees abortion coverage

No group insurance contract or health maintenance agreement providing hospitalization, medical, surgical, accident, sickness, or other health coverage paid for in whole or in part with public funds shall include coverage for abortion, as defined in section 28-326. This section shall not apply to coverage for an abortion which is verified in writing by the attending physician as necessary to prevent the death of the woman or to coverage for medical complications arising from an abortion. This section shall not prohibit the insurer from offering individual employees special coverage for abortion if the costs for such coverage are borne solely by the employee.

Nebraska Code § 48-1111(2). Terms of employment (abridged)

Women affected by pregnancy, childbirth, or related medical conditions shall be treated the same for all employment-related purposes, including receipt of employee benefits, as other persons not so affected but similar in their ability or inability to work, and nothing in this section shall be interpreted to provide otherwise.

This section shall not require an employer to provide employee benefits for abortion except when medical complications have arisen from an abortion.

Nothing in this section shall preclude an employer from providing employee benefits for abortion under fringe benefit programs or otherwise affect bargaining agreements in regard to abortion.

Nebraska Right to Life

Nebraska Right to Life (NRL) is a pro-life organization that was founded in 1973, and is headed by its executive director Julie Schmit-Albin. NRL seeks to restore legal protection to preborn human life. The organization engages in activities that include a unified statewide educational and legislative effort to end abortion, and serving as a clearinghouse of information for its local chapters, its individual members, the media, and the public. *See also* **Pro-Life Organizations**

Negron, Guadalupe

Guadalupe Negron was 33 years old and pregnant in 1993. She decided to have an abortion on July 9 of that year. Negron went to a Queens, New York, abortion clinic run by Dr. David Benjamin. Dr. Benjamin performed the abortion and Negron was taken to a recovery room. While in the recovery room Negron developed complications and died. It was later learned that Dr. Benjamin lacerated Negron's cervix and uterus, resulting in massive bleeding and a heart attack. Dr. Benjamin was later charged with second degree murder. A jury convicted him of the charge in 1995. During the sentencing hearing, Judge Robert Hanophy expressed his displeasure over Dr. Benjamin's conduct in Negron's death by stating: "Not one thing went right during this proceeding. I don't think you can find a better case for depraved-indifference murder. He chased a dollar and didn't care about his patient." Judge Hanophy then went on to impose upon Dr. Benjamin the maximum sentence allowed, 25 years to life in prison. *See also* **Complications During and After Abortion**

Neonatal Death *see* **Perinatal Mortality**

Neural Tube Defects *see* **Anencephaly; Birth Defects and Abortion; Encephaloceles; Folic Acid and Pregnancy; Spina Bifida**

Neurofibromatoses

Neurofibromatoses are genetic disorders of the nervous system. The disorders are classified as neurofibromatosis-1 and neurofibromatosis-2.

Neurofibromatosis-1. Neurofibromatosis-1 (NF1) is the more common type of the neurofibromatoses. NF1 is an inherited disorder that is characterized by formation of tumors in the skin, cranial nerves and spinal root nerves. Some of the common symptoms of the disorder include: impairment of intellectual function, convulsions, ringing ears, deafness, dizziness and blindness. Although NF1 causes mild mental impairment, it is considered to be a leading cause of retardation in the United States. Some problems associated with the disorder may be treated, such as removal of tumors.

Neurofibromatosis-2. Neurofibromatosis-2 (NF2) is an inherited disorder that is similar to NF1. NF2 affects about 1 in 40,000 persons. The disorder is characterized by bilateral tumors on the cranial nerve. The tumors cause progressive hearing loss. In some cases the disorder can cause life-threatening damage. Surgery is an option for removing the tumors. *See also* **Birth Defects and Abortion**

Nevada

(1) OVERVIEW

The state of Nevada enacted its first criminal abortion statute on November 26, 1861. The statute underwent several amendments prior to the 1973 decision by the United States Supreme Court in *Roe v. Wade*, which legalized abortion in the nation. In spite of the decision in *Roe*, Nevada has not repealed its pre-*Roe* criminal abortion statute.

Nevada has taken affirmative steps to respond to *Roe* and its progeny. The state has addressed numerous abortion issues by statute that include general abortion guidelines, informed consent, abortion by minors, use of facilities and people, commercial use of fetus or embryo, fetal death report, anti-abortion conduct, and injury to pregnant woman.

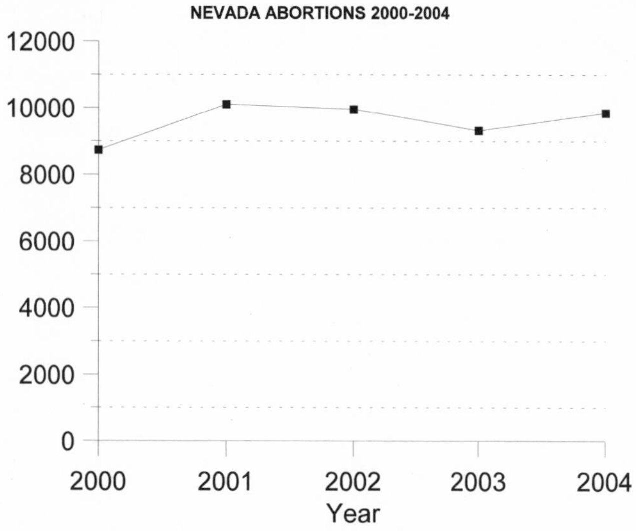

Source: Nevada Department of Health and Human Services.

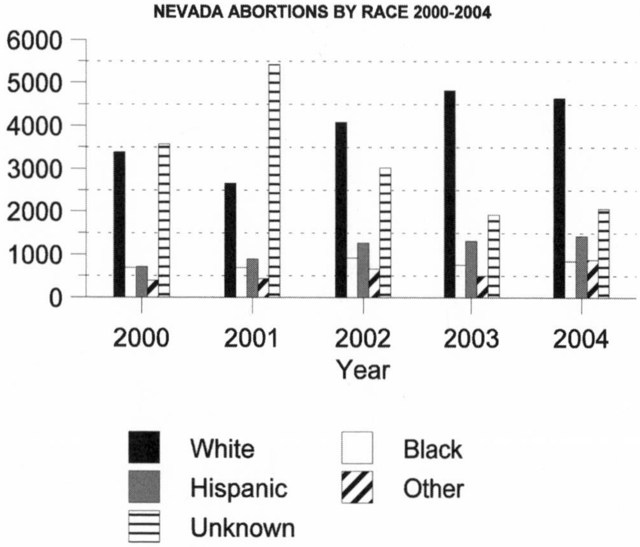

Source: Nevada Department of Health and Human Services.

(2) PRE-ROE ABORTION BAN

As previously indicated, Nevada has not repealed its pre-*Roe* abortion laws. However, the state has modified some of those laws so as to be incompliance with *Roe*. However, those laws still criminalize the sale and advertisement of abortifacients. The statutes are set out below.

Nevada Code § 201.120. Abortion definition

A person who:

1. Prescribes, supplies or administers to a woman, whether pregnant or not, or advises or causes her to take any medicine, drug or substance; or

2. Uses or causes to be used, any instrument or other means, to terminate a pregnancy, unless done pursuant to the provisions of NRS 442.250, or by a woman upon herself upon the advice of a physician acting pursuant to the provisions of NRS 442.250, is guilty of abortion which is a category B felony and shall be punished by imprisonment in the state prison for a minimum term of not less than 1 year and a maximum term of not more than 10 years, and may be further punished by a fine of not more than $10,000.

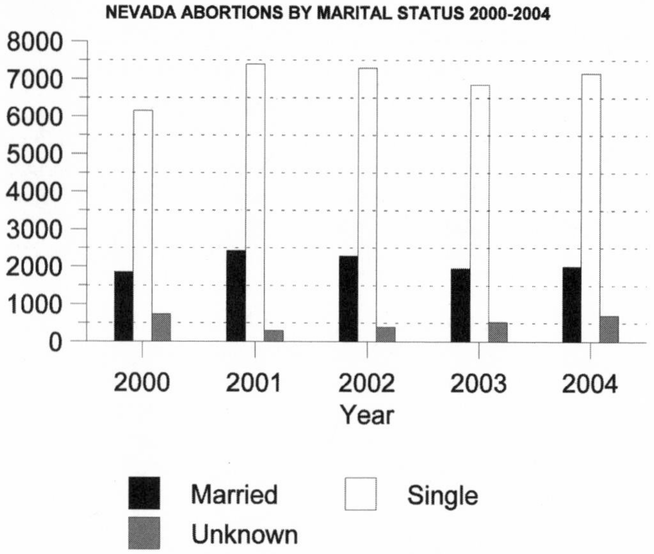

Source: Nevada Department of Health and Human Services.

Nevada Prior Abortion by Female 2000–2004

	Prior Abortion							
Year	*None*	*1*	*2*	*3*	*4*	*5*	*≥6*	*Not known*
2000	4,078	2,242	973	329	144	77	63	92
2001	5,072	2,444	1,004	411	159	77	78	81
2002	4,740	2,411	1,034	392	157	54	62	343
2003	4,606	2,236	970	418	149	57	64	195
2004	4,687	2,449	1,071	442	153	61	59	222
Total	23,183	11,782	5,052	1992	762	326	326	933

Source: Nevada Department of Health and Human Services.

Nevada Abortion by Weeks of Gestation 2000–2004

	Year					
Weeks of Gestation	*2000*	*2001*	*2002*	*2003*	*2004*	*Total*
≤8	4,461	5,306	5,282	4,979	4,535	24,563
9–11	1,690	2,022	2,173	2,168	2,080	10,133
12–14	535	689	692	795	749	3,460
15–17	117	187	201	199	245	949
18–20	58	85	67	53	93	356
≥21	9	14	34	12	15	84
Not known	157	211	205	157	1,130	1,860

Source: Nevada Department of Health and Human Services.

Nevada Abortion by Age Group 2000–2004

	Age Group (yrs)								
Year	*<15*	*15–17*	*18–19*	*20–24*	*25–29*	*30–34*	*35–39*	*≥40*	*Unknown*
2000	43	557	838	2,383	1,829	1,164	750	219	215
2001	47	598	1,055	2,725	2,082	1,420	877	265	257
2002	24	580	878	2,616	2,011	1,494	865	314	411
2003	32	505	867	2,602	1,855	1,379	818	252	385
2004	42	508	942	2,758	1,955	1,455	806	284	394
Total	188	2,748	4,580	13,084	9,732	6,912	4,116	1,334	1,662

Source: Nevada Department of Health and Human Services.

Nevada Code § 201.130. Selling drugs to produce miscarriage

Every person who shall manufacture, sell or give away any instrument, drug, medicine or other substance, knowing or intending that the same may be unlawfully used in procuring the miscarriage of a woman, shall be guilty of a gross misdemeanor.

Nevada Code § 201.140. Evidence

In any prosecution for abortion, attempting abortion, or selling drugs unlawfully, no person shall be excused from testifying as a witness on the ground that his testimony would tend to incriminate him, but such testimony shall not be used against him in any criminal prosecution except for perjury in giving such testimony.

Nevada Code § 201.150. Concealing birth

Every person who shall endeavor to conceal the birth of a child by any disposition of its dead body, whether the child died before or after its birth, shall be guilty of a gross misdemeanor.

Nevada Code § 175.301. Testimony

Upon a trial for procuring or attempting to procure an abortion, or aiding or assisting therein, the defendant must not be convicted upon the testimony of the person upon or with whom the offense has allegedly been committed, unless:

1. The testimony of that person is corroborated by other evidence; or

2. The person giving the testimony is, and was at the time the crime is alleged to have taken place, a police officer or deputy sheriff who was performing his duties as such.

Nevada Code § 202.200.
Advertising goods and services to produce miscarriage

1. It shall be unlawful for any person:

(a) To advertise or publish, or cause to be advertised or published in a newspaper, pamphlet, handbill, book or otherwise, any medicine, nostrum, drug, substance, instrument or device to produce the miscarriage or premature delivery of a woman pregnant with child, or which purports to be, or is represented to be, productive of such miscarriage or premature delivery; or

(b) To advertise in any manner his or her services, aid, assistance or advice, or the services, assistance or advice of any other person, in the procurement of such miscarriage or premature delivery.

2. Every person who shall violate the provisions of subsection 1 shall be guilty of a gross misdemeanor.

Nevada Code § 202.210.
Publishing advertisement containing prohibited matter

The proprietor or proprietors and the manager or managers of any newspaper, periodical or other printed sheet published or printed within this state, which shall contain any advertisement prohibited by NRS 202.200, shall, for each publication of such advertisement, be guilty of a misdemeanor.

Nevada Code § 202.220.
Circulation of publications containing prohibited matter

Every person who shall knowingly sell, distribute, give away, or in any manner dispose of or exhibit to another person any newspaper, pamphlet, book, periodical, handbill, printed slip or writing, or cause the same to be so sold, distributed, disposed of, or exhibited, containing any advertisement prohibited in NRS 202.200, or containing any description or notice of, or reference to, or information concerning, or direction how or where to procure any medicine, drug, nostrum, substance, device, instrument or service, the advertisement of which is prohibited or declared to be unlawful, shall be guilty of a misdemeanor.

(3) GENERAL ABORTION GUIDELINES

Under the laws of Nevada an abortion is expressly permitted during the first 24 weeks. The state prohibits abortion after 24 weeks, unless necessary to preserve the life or health of the woman. Nevada provides criminal punishment for a woman who unlawfully aborts a fetus after the 24th week of pregnancy. The general abortion statutes are set out below.

Nevada Code § 442.240. Abortion defined

As used in NRS 442.250 to 442.270, inclusive, unless the context requires otherwise, "abortion" means the termination of a human pregnancy with an intention other than to produce the birth of an infant capable of sustained survival by natural or artificial supportive systems or to remove a dead fetus.

Nevada Code § 442.250. Conditions for abortions

1. No abortion may be performed in this state unless the abortion is performed:

(a) By a physician licensed to practice in this state or by a physician in the employ of the government of the United States who:

(1) Exercises his best clinical judgment in the light of all attendant circumstances including the accepted professional standards of medical practice in determining whether to perform an abortion; and

(2) Performs the abortion in a manner consistent with accepted medical practices and procedures in the community.

(b) Within 24 weeks after the commencement of the pregnancy.

(c) After the 24th week of pregnancy only if the physician has reasonable cause to believe that an abortion currently is necessary to preserve the life or health of the pregnant woman.

2. All abortions performed after the 24th week of pregnancy or performed when, in the judgment of the attending physician, there is a reasonable likelihood of the sustained survival of the fetus outside of the womb by natural or artificial supportive systems must be performed in a hospital licensed under chapter 449 of NRS.

3. Before performing an abortion pursuant to subsection 2, the attending physician shall enter in the permanent records of the patient the facts on which he based his best clinical judgment that there is a substantial risk that continuance of the pregnancy would endanger the life of the patient or would gravely impair the physical or mental health of the patient.

Nevada Code § 442.256. Records

A physician who performs an abortion shall maintain a record of it for at least 5 years after it is performed. The record must contain:

1. The written consent of the woman;

2. A statement of the information which was provided to the woman pursuant to NRS 442.253; and

3. A description of efforts to give any notice required by NRS 442.255.

Nevada Code § 442.257. Criminal penalty

Any person who violates any provision of NRS 442.252 to 442.256, inclusive, is guilty of a misdemeanor.

Nevada Code § 442.270.
Failure to preserve life of infant born as result of attempted abortion

Whenever an abortion results in the birth of an infant capable of sustained survival by natural or artificial supportive systems, the failure to take all reasonable steps, in keeping with good medical practice, to preserve the life and health of the infant subjects the person performing the abortion to the laws of this state governing criminal liability and civil liability for wrongful death and medical malpractice.

Nevada Code § 200.220. Unlawfully terminating pregnancy

A woman who takes or uses, or submits to the use of, any drug, medicine or substance, or any instrument or other means, with the intent to terminate her pregnancy after the 24th week of pregnancy, unless the same is performed upon herself upon the advice of a physician acting pursuant to the provisions of NRS 442.250, and thereby causes the death of the child of the pregnancy, commits manslaughter and shall be punished for a category B felony by imprisonment in the state prison for a minimum term of not less than 1 year and a maximum term of not more *than 10 years, and may be further punished by a fine of not more than $10,000.*

(4) INFORMED CONSENT

Prior to an abortion Nevada requires that a woman be fully informed of the procedure to be used, the risks involved and post-abortion care. The informed consent statutes are set out below.

Nevada Code § 442.252. Physician to certify informed consent

No physician may perform an abortion in this state unless, before he performs it, he certifies in writing that the woman gave her informed written consent, freely and without coercion. The physician shall further certify in writing the pregnant woman's marital status and age based upon proof of age offered by her.

Nevada Code § 442.253. Requirements for consent

1. The attending physician or a person meeting the qualifications established by regulations adopted by the health division shall accurately and in a manner which is reasonably likely to be understood by the pregnant woman:

(a) Explain that, in his professional judgment, she is pregnant and a copy of her pregnancy test is available to her.

(b) Inform her of the number of weeks which have elapsed from the probable time of conception.

(c) Explain the physical and emotional implications of having the abortion.

(d) Describe the medical procedure to be used, its consequences and the proper procedures for her care after the abortion.

2. The attending physician shall verify that all material facts and information, which in his professional judgment are necessary to allow the woman to give her informed consent, have been provided to her and that her consent is informed.

3. If the woman does not understand English, the form indicating consent must be written in a language understood by her, or the attending physician shall certify on the form that the information required to be given has been presented in such a manner as to be understandable by her. If an interpreter is used, the interpreter must be named and reference to this use must be made on the form for consent.

(5) ABORTION BY MINORS

Under the laws of Nevada no physician may perform an abortion upon an unemancipated minor unless he/she first notifies either parent or the legal guardian of the minor. Nevada provides a unique initial alternative to notification. The state permits a minor to seek an "interview" with a judge to obtain judicial approval of an abortion without notification to a parent or guardian. Under the procedure a judge may authorize an abortion without such notification if the judge finds that (1) that the minor is mature and well-informed enough to make the abortion decision on her own, (2) that performance of the abortion would be in the best interest of the minor, or (3) the minor is financially independent or emancipated. If the judge refuses to authorize an abortion after the interview, the minor may file a formal petition with the court seeking judicial bypass. A minor has a right to an attorney at the proceeding and if she cannot afford one, the court must appoint her an attorney. If a minor chooses, she may represent herself. The required parental or guardian notice may be waived if the court finds "good cause" for waiver. The formal judicial bypass procedure was found inadequate by a federal court in *Glick v. McKay*, 937 F.2d 434 (9th Cir. 1991). The statutes are set out below.

Nevada Code § 442.255. Notice and judicial interview

1. Unless in the judgment of the attending physician an abortion is immediately necessary to preserve the patient's life or health or an abortion is authorized pursuant to subsection 2 or NRS 442.2555, a physician shall not knowingly perform or induce an abortion upon an unmarried and unemancipated woman who is under the age of 18 years unless a custodial parent or guardian of the woman is personally notified before the abortion. If the custodial parent or guardian cannot be so notified after a reasonable effort, the physician shall delay performing the abortion until he has notified the parent or guardian by certified mail at his last known address.

2. An unmarried or unemancipated woman who is under the age of 18 years may request a district court to issue an order authorizing an abortion. If so requested, the court shall interview the woman at the earliest practicable time, which must be not more than 2 judicial days after the request is made. If the court determines, from any information provided by the woman and any other evidence that the court may require, that:

(a) She is mature enough to make an intelligent and informed decision concerning the abortion;

(b) She is financially independent or is emancipated; or

(c) The notice required by subsection 1 would be detrimental to her best interests, the court shall issue an order within 1 judicial day after the interview authorizing a physician to perform the abortion in accordance with the provisions of NRS 442.240 to 442.270, inclusive.

3. If the court does not find sufficient grounds to authorize a physician to perform the abortion, it shall enter an order to that effect within 1 judicial day after the interview. If the court does not enter an order either authorizing or denying the performance of the abortion within 1 judicial day after the interview, authorization shall be deemed to have been granted.

4. The court shall take the necessary steps to ensure that the interview and any other proceedings held pursuant to this subsection or NRS 442.2555 are confidential. The rules of civil procedure do not apply to any action taken pursuant to this subsection.

Nevada Code § 442.2555. Judicial hearing

1. If the order is denied pursuant to NRS 442.255, the court shall, upon request by the minor if it appears that she is unable to employ counsel, appoint an attorney to represent her in the preparation of a petition, a hearing on the merits of the petition, and on an appeal, if necessary. The compensation and expenses of the attorney are a charge against the county as provided in the following schedule:

(a) For consultation, research and other time reasonably spent on the matter, except court appearances, $20 per hour.

(b) For court appearances, $30 per hour.

2. The petition must set forth the initials of the minor, the age of the minor, the estimated number of weeks elapsed from the probable time of conception, and whether maturity, emancipation, notification detrimental to the minor's best interests or a combination thereof are relied upon in avoidance of the notification required by NRS 442.255. The petition must be initialed by the minor.

3. A hearing on the merits of the petition, on the record, must be held as soon as possible and within 5 judicial days after the filing of the petition. At the hearing the court shall hear evidence relating to:

(a) The minor's emotional development, maturity, intellect and understanding;

(b) The minor's degree of financial independence and degree of emancipation from parental authority;

(c) The minor's best interests relative to parental involvement in the decision whether to undergo an abortion; and

(d) Any other evidence that the court may find useful in determining whether the minor is entitled to avoid parental notification.

4. In the decree, the court shall, for good cause:

(a) Grant the petition, and give judicial authorization to permit a physician to perform an abortion without the notification required in NRS 442.255; or

(b) Deny the petition, setting forth the grounds on which the petition is denied.

5. An appeal from an order issued under subsection 4 may be taken to the supreme court, which shall suspend the Nevada Rules of Appellate Procedure pursuant to N.R.A.P. 2 to provide for an expedited appeal. The notice of intent to appeal must be given within 1 judicial day after the issuance of the order. The record on appeal must be perfected within 5 judicial days after the filing of the notice of appeal and transmitted to the supreme court. The court, shall, by court order or rule, provide for a confidential and expedited appellate review of cases appealed under this section.

Nevada Code § 442.268. Civil immunity

If an abortion is judicially authorized and the provisions of NRS 442.240 to 442.270, inclusive, are complied with, an action by the parents or guardian of the minor against persons performing the abortion is barred. This civil immunity extends to the performance of the abortion and any necessary accompanying services which are performed in a competent manner. The costs of the action, if brought, must be borne by the parties respectively.

(6) USE OF FACILITIES AND PEOPLE

Under the laws of Nevada medical facilities are not required to allow abortions. The employees and physicians at medical facilities that do allow abortions are permitted to refuse to take part in abortions. The statutes addressing the matter are set out below.

Nevada Code § 449.191. Medical facility

1. A hospital or other medical facility licensed under the provisions of this chapter which is not operated by the state or a local government or an agency of either is not required to permit the use of its facilities for the induction or performance of an abortion, except in a medical emergency.

2. Such refusal does not give rise to a cause of action in favor of any person.

Nevada Code § 632.475. Medical personnel

1. An employer shall not require a registered nurse, a licensed practical nurse, a nursing assistant or any other person employed to furnish direct personal health service to a patient to participate directly in the induction or performance of an abortion if the employee has filed a written statement with the employer indicating a moral, ethical or religious basis for refusal to participate in the abortion.

2. If the statement provided for in subsection 1 is filed with the employer, the employer shall not penalize or discipline the employee for declining to participate directly in the induction or performance of an abortion.

3. The provisions of subsections 1 and 2 do not apply to medical emergency situations.

4. Any person violating the provisions of this section is guilty of a misdemeanor.

(7) COMMERCIAL USE OF FETUS OR EMBRYO

Nevada provides criminal punishment for commercially trafficking in the remains of an aborted fetus or embryo. The statute addressing the matter is set out below.

Nevada Code § 451.015.
Commercial use of aborted embryo or fetus

Any person who uses, or makes available for the use of another, the remains of an aborted embryo or fetus for any commercial purpose shall be fined not less than $250 nor more than $5,000.

(8) FETAL DEATH REPORT

Nevada requires that all abortions be reported to the proper authorities. The statutes addressing the matter are set out below.

Nevada Code § 442.260.
Regulations for performance and reporting of abortions

1. The health division shall adopt and enforce regulations governing the conditions under and the methods by which abortions may be performed, the reasonable minimum qualifications of a person authorized to provide the information required in NRS 442.253, as well as all other aspects pertaining to the performance of abortions pursuant to NRS 442.250.

2. The health division shall adopt and enforce regulations for a system for reporting abortions. This system must be designed to preserve confidentiality of information on the identity of women upon whom abortions are performed. The health division may require that the following items be reported for each abortion:

(a) The date of the abortion;

(b) The place of the abortion including the city, county and state;

(c) The type of facility;

(d) The usual residence of the woman, including the city, county and state;

(e) Her age;

(f) Her ethnic group or race;

(g) Her marital status;

(h) The number of previous live births;

(i) The number of previous induced abortions;

(j) The duration of her pregnancy, as measured from first day of last normal menses to date of abortion, and as estimated by uterine size prior to performance of the abortion;

(k) The type of abortion procedure; and

(l) If a woman has had a previously induced abortion, the information in paragraphs (a) to (k), inclusive, or as much thereof as can be reasonably obtained, for each previous abortion.

3. The health division may adopt regulations to permit studies of individual cases of abortion, but these studies must not be permitted unless:

(a) Absolute assurance is provided that confidentiality of information on the persons involved will be preserved;

(b) Informed consent of each person involved in the study is obtained in writing;

(c) The study is conducted according to established standards and ethics; and

(d) The study is related to problems of health and has scientific merit with regard to both design and the importance of the problems to be solved.

Nevada Code § 442.265. Hospital report

Each hospital shall submit a monthly report to the state registrar of vital statistics which contains the following information:

1. The number of patients admitted for hospital care for a complication which resulted from an abortion;

2. The nature of the complication by its diagnostic name; and

3. The type of abortion.

(9) ANTI-ABORTION CONDUCT

Nevada has responded to violent anti-abortion activities by criminalizing conduct that interferes with a woman's access to a medical facility. The state also prohibits unlawful conduct against employees of medical facilities. The statute addressing the issues is set out below.

Nevada Code § 449.760. Anti-abortion conduct

1. Except as otherwise provided in this section, a person shall not intentionally prevent another person from entering or exiting the office of a physician, a health facility, a nonprofit health facility, a public health center, a medical facility or a facility for the dependent by physically:

(a) Detaining the other person; or

(b) Obstructing, impeding or hindering the other person's movement.

2. The provisions of subsection 1 are inapplicable to:

(a) An officer, employee or agent of the physician, health facility, nonprofit health facility, public health center, medical facility or facility for the dependent; or

(b) *A peace officer as defined in NRS 169.125, while acting within the course and scope of his duties or employment.*

3. The provisions of subsection 1 do not prohibit a person from maintaining a picket during a strike or work stoppage in compliance with the provisions of NRS 614.160, or from engaging in any constitutionally protected exercise of free speech.

4. A person who violates the provisions of subsection 1 is guilty of a misdemeanor and shall be punished by a fine of not more than $1,000, or by imprisonment in the county jail for not more than 3 months, or by both fine and imprisonment.

5. As used in this section, the terms "health facility," "nonprofit health facility" and "public health center" have the meanings ascribed to them in NRS 449.260.

(10) INJURY TO PREGNANT WOMAN

Nevada imposes criminal sanctions against anyone who unlawfully injures a pregnant woman and causes the death of the woman's fetus. The statute addressing the issue is set out below.

Nevada Code § 200.210. Injury to pregnant woman

A person who willfully kills an unborn quick child, by any injury committed upon the mother of the child, commits manslaughter and shall be punished for a category B felony by imprisonment in the state prison for a minimum term of not less than 1 year and a maximum term of not more than 10 years, and may be further punished by a fine of not more than $10,000.

New Hampshire

The state of New Hampshire enacted its first criminal abortion statute on January 4, 1849. The statute underwent several amendments prior to the 1973 decision by the United States Supreme Court in *Roe v. Wade*, which legalized abortion in the nation. In 1997 the state repealed its abortion laws. In 2003 New Hampshire enacted a statute requiring parental notification before a minor could have an abortion. The statute was found unconstitutional in its entirety by a federal court because it did not contain an exception when a minor's health was at risk. However, the case was appealed to the United States Supreme Court in *Ayotte v. Planned Parenthood of Northern New England*. The Supreme Court vacated the decision and remanded the case for a determination of whether the statute could be found constitutional, by simply prohibiting enforcement of the statute when a minor's health was at risk. In 2007, a year after the decision in *Ayotte*, the New Hampshire legislature repealed its parental notification statute. The only relevant abortion related statutes that exists in the state concern dispensing emergency contraception and injury to a pregnant woman. The statutes addressing the matters are set out below.

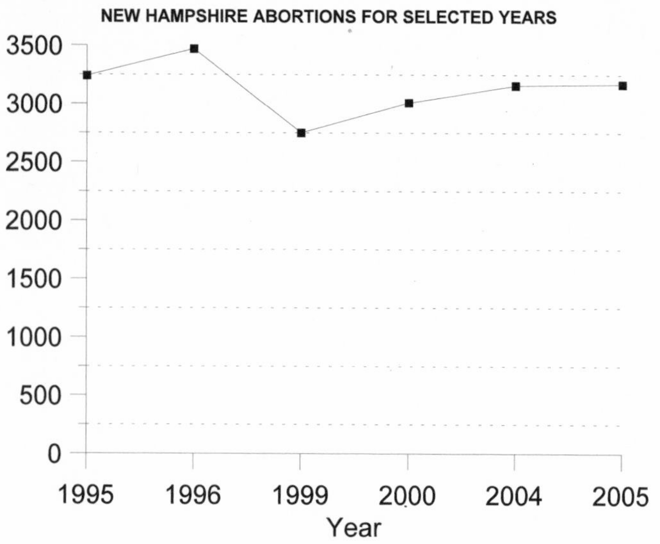

Source: **Guttmacher Institute.**

New Hampshire Code § 318:47-e.
Dispensing emergency contraception

I. In this section, "emergency contraception" means an elevated dose of hormones used to prevent pregnancy.

II. A pharmacist may initiate emergency contraception drug therapy in accordance with standardized procedures or protocols developed by the board, adopted pursuant to RSA 541-A, and an authorized prescriber who is acting within his or her scope of practice.

III. Prior to performing any procedure authorized under this section, a pharmacist shall successfully complete emergency contraception drug therapy education and training in accordance with continuing education requirements established by the board. A pharmacist who has had sufficient recent education and training in emergency contraception may be exempted from the requirements of this section.

IV. For each emergency contraception drug therapy initiated pursuant to this section, the pharmacist shall provide each recipient of the emergency contraceptive drugs with a standardized fact sheet that includes, but is not limited to: the indications for the use of the drug, the appropriate method for using the drug, information on the importance of follow-up health care, and health care referral information. The board shall develop this fact sheet in consultation with the commissioner of the department of health and human services, the American College of Obstetricians and Gynecologists, and other relevant health care organizations.

V. Nothing in the section shall affect the requirements of existing law relating to maintaining the confidentiality of medical records.

VI. Nothing in this section shall limit the manner in which emergency contraception can be dispensed.

New Hampshire Code § 631:2 Second degree assault

I. A person is guilty of a class B felony if he:

(a) Knowingly or recklessly causes serious bodily injury to another; or

(b) Recklessly causes bodily injury to another by means of a deadly weapon, except that if the deadly weapon is a firearm, he shall be sentenced in accordance with RSA 651:2, II-g; or

(c) Recklessly causes bodily injury to another under circumstances manifesting extreme indifference to the value of human life; or

(d) Purposely or knowingly causes bodily injury to a child under 13 years of age; or

(e) Recklessly or negligently causes injury to another resulting in miscarriage or stillbirth.

II. In this section:

(a) "Miscarriage" means the interruption of the normal development of the fetus other than by a live birth and not an induced abortion, resulting in the complete expulsion or extraction of a fetus; and

(b) "Stillbirth" means the death of a fetus prior to complete expulsion or extraction and not an induced abortion.

New Jersey

(1) OVERVIEW

The state of New Jersey enacted its first criminal abortion statute on March 1, 1849. The statute underwent several amendments prior to the 1973 decision by the United States Supreme Court in *Roe v. Wade*, which legalized abortion in the nation. New Jersey has taken affirmative steps to respond to *Roe* and its progeny. The state has addressed a few abortion issues by statute that include partial-birth abortion, abortion by minors, public funds for abortion, blood testing, use of facilities and people, and ban human cloning.

(2) PARTIAL-BIRTH ABORTION

New Jersey prohibits partial-birth abortions, except when necessary to save the life of the woman. However, the ban is infirm as a result of the United States Supreme Court decision in *Stenberg v. Carhart*, which invalidated a Nebraska statute that prohibited partial-birth abortions. In addition, a federal court specifically ruled in *Planned Parenthood of Central New Jersey v. Farmer*, 220 F.3d 127 (3d Cir. 2000), that the state's partial-birth abortion ban was unconstitutional. It should be noted, however, that the United States Supreme Court decision in *Gonzales v. Carhart* approved of a federal statute that bans partial-birth abortion. New Jersey's statutes are set out below.

New Jersey Code § 2A:65A-5. Short title

This act shall be known and may be cited as the "Partial-Birth Abortion Ban Act of 1997."

New Jersey Code § 2A:65A-6. Acts prohibited and definitions

a. No physician licensed in this State, other licensed health care professional authorized to perform abortions in this State, or ambulatory care facility licensed in this State shall perform a partial-birth abortion and thereby kill a human fetus.

b. The provisions of subsection a. of this section shall not apply to a partial-birth abortion that is necessary to save the life of the mother whose life is endangered by a physical disorder, illness or injury.

c. A physician or other health care professional licensed pursuant to Title 45 of the Revised Statutes who knowingly performs a partial-birth abortion in violation of this act shall be subject to immediate revocation of his professional license by the appropriate licensing board and subject to a penalty of $25,000 for each incident.

d. An ambulatory health care facility licensed pursuant to P.L.1971, c. 136 (C.26:2H-1 et seq.) in which a partial-birth abortion is performed in violation of this act shall be subject to immediate revocation of its license by the Department of Health and Senior Services.

e. As used in this act, "partial-birth abortion" means an abortion in which the person performing the abortion partially vaginally delivers a living human fetus before killing the fetus and completing the delivery.

f. As used in subsection e. of this section "vaginally delivers a living human fetus before killing the fetus" means deliberately and intentionally delivering into the vagina a living fetus, or a substantial portion thereof, for the purpose of performing a procedure the physician or other health care professional knows will kill the fetus, and the subsequent killing of the human fetus.

New Jersey Code § 2A:65A-7.
Civil and criminal immunity for patient

A woman upon whom a partial-birth abortion is performed shall be immune from civil or criminal liability for a violation of the provisions of this act.

(3) ABORTION BY MINORS

Under the laws of New Jersey no physician may perform an abortion upon an unemancipated minor, until 48 hours after notice of the operation has been given to either parent of the minor. In compliance with federal constitutional law, New Jersey has provided a judicial waiver procedure for an unemancipated minor to obtain an abortion without parental notice. The minor may petition a trial court for a waiver of the notice requirement. A minor has a right to an attorney at the proceeding and if she cannot afford one, the court must appoint her an attorney. If a minor chooses, she may represent herself. The required parental notice may be waived if the court finds either (1) that the minor is mature and well-informed enough to make the abortion decision on her own, (2) the minor is a victim of physical, sexual or emotional abuse by her parent, or (3) that notification would not be in the best interest of the minor. An expedited appeal is available to any minor to whom the court denies a waiver of notice. In *Planned Parenthood of Cent. New Jersey v. Farmer*, 762 A.2d 620 (N.J. 2000) it was held that the abortion statutes for minors violated the state's constitutional equal protection clause because the statutes conditioned a minor's right to obtain an abortion on parental notification, unless judicial waiver was obtained, but imposed no corresponding limitation on a minor who sought medical and surgical care otherwise related to her pregnancy. The statutes are set out below.

New Jersey Code § 9:17A-1.1. Short title

Sections 2 through 13 of this act shall be known and may be cited as the "Parental Notification for Abortion Act."

New Jersey Code § 9:17A-1.2. Legislative findings

The Legislature finds that there exist compelling and important State interests in protecting minors against their own immaturity, in fostering the family structure and preserving it as a viable social unit, and in protecting the rights of parents to rear their children.

The Legislature further finds that minors often lack the ability to make fully informed choices that take into account both immediate and long-range consequences of their actions; that the medical, emotional, and psychological consequences of abortion are serious and of indeterminate duration, particularly when the patient is a minor; that parents ordinarily possess information essential to a physician's exercise of his best medical judgment concerning their child; and that parents who are aware that their minor daughter has had an abortion may better insure that the minor receives adequate medical attention after her abortion. The Legislature further finds that parental consultation regarding abortion is desirable and in the best interests of the minor.

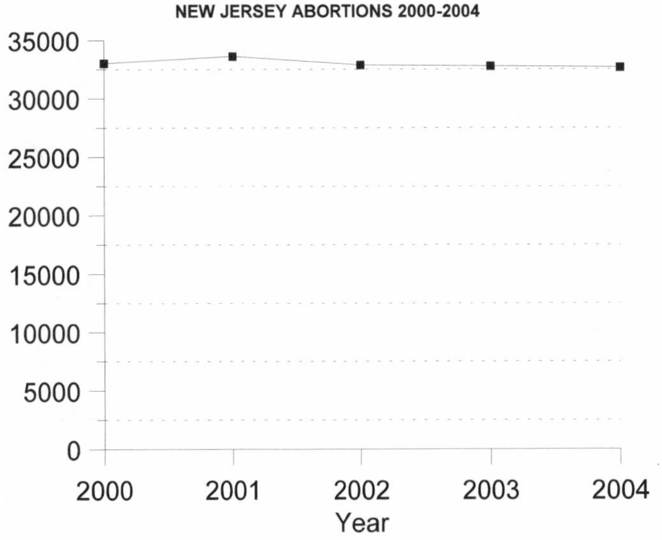

Source: New Jersey Department of Health and Senior Services.

New Jersey Abortion by Age Group 2000–2004

Age Group (yrs)

Year	*<15*	*15–17*	*18–19*	*20–24*	*25–29*	*30–34*	*35–39*	*≥40*	*Unknown*
2000	195	2,354	3,725	10,650	7,503	4,791	2,719	940	149
2001	242	2,375	3,603	11,090	7,613	4,836	2,794	966	87
2002	181	2,266	3,428	10,957	7,383	4,773	2,846	984	36
2003	186	2,335	3,407	10,649	7,537	4,738	2,801	1,078	31
2004	167	2,125	3,297	10,388	7,768	4,838	2,904	1,120	35
Total	971	11,455	17,460	53,734	37,804	23,976	14,064	5,088	338

Source: New Jersey Department of Health and Senior Services.

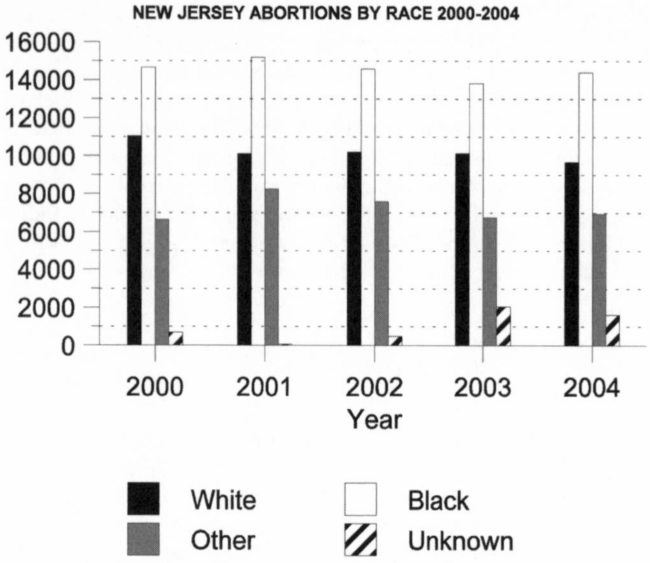

Source: New Jersey Department of Health and Senior Services.

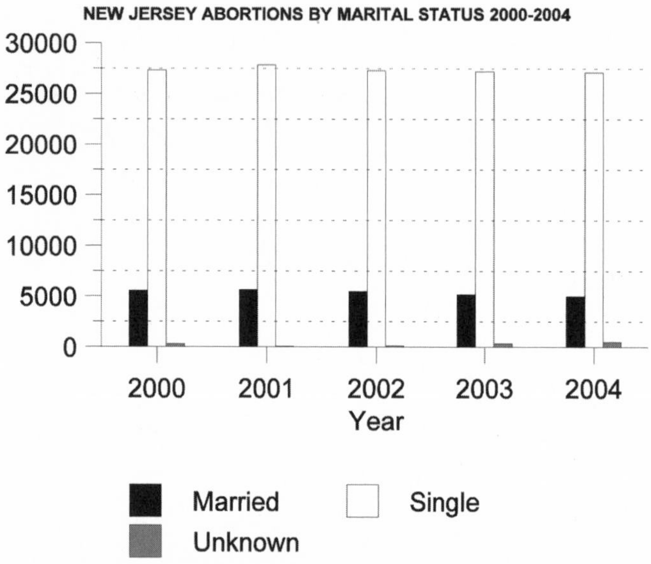

Source: New Jersey Department of Health and Senior Services.

New Jersey Prior Abortion by Female 2000–2004

Prior Abortion

Year	*None*	*1*	*2*	*≥3*	*Not known*
2000	17,126	8,054	3,817	2,823	1,206
2001	21,629	6,501	3,034	2,338	104
2002	22,005	5,595	2,840	2,308	106
2003	20,876	6,194	3,188	2,384	110
2004	19,692	6,275	3,613	2,763	299
Total	101,328	32,619	16,492	12,616	1,825

Source: New Jersey Department of Health and Senior Services.

New Jersey Abortion by Weeks of Gestation 2000–2004

	Year					
Weeks of Gestation	*2000*	*2001*	*2002*	*2003*	*2004*	*Total*
≤6	7,781	7,789	7,956	8,262	8,777	40,565
7	4,577	4,872	5,055	5,224	5,243	24,971
8	5,791	5,678	5,270	5,179	5,105	27,023
9	2,839	3,205	3,232	3,189	2,989	15,454
10	3,009	2,935	2,464	2,227	2,140	12,775
11	1,061	1,272	1,231	1,114	1,056	5,734
12	1,128	1,064	943	978	958	5,071
13	1,781	1,829	1,644	1,722	1,744	8,720
14	674	721	575	644	678	3,292
15	686	721	668	826	671	3,572
16	892	840	776	679	696	3,883
17	592	595	523	573	498	2,781
18	496	461	449	468	521	2,395
19	377	328	332	339	284	1,660
20	431	397	360	443	397	2,028
≥21	647	760	793	874	872	3,946
Not known	264	139	583	21	13	1,020

Source: New Jersey Department of Health and Senior Services.

It is, therefore, the intent of the Legislature to further the interests stated above by enacting this parental notice provision.

New Jersey Code § 9:17A-1.3. Definitions

As used in this act:

"Abortion" means the use of any means to terminate the pregnancy of a female known to be pregnant with knowledge that the termination with those means will, with reasonable likelihood, cause the death of the fetus.

"Medical emergency" means a condition which, on the basis of the physician's good faith clinical judgment, so complicates the medical condition of a pregnant unemancipated minor as to necessitate the immediate abortion of her pregnancy to avert her death or for which a delay will create serious risk of substantial and irreversible impairment of a major bodily function.

"Parent" means a parent with care and control of the unemancipated minor, unless the parent has no custodial rights; or if there is no parent with care and control, then the foster parent or the guardian of the unemancipated minor; or a person standing in loco parentis to the unemancipated minor.

"Person standing in loco parentis" means (1) that the biological or adoptive parent consented to and fostered, the person's formation and establishment of a parent-like relationship with the minor; (2) that the person and the minor live together in the same household; (3) that the person assumed obligations of parenthood by taking significant responsibility for the minor's care, education and development, including contributing towards the minor's support, without expectation of financial compensation; and (4) that the person has been in a parental role for a length of time sufficient to have established with the minor a bonded, dependent relationship parental in nature.

"Unemancipated minor" means a female under the age of 18 years who is unmarried and is not currently serving active duty in one of the military services of the United States of America or a female for whom a guardian has been appointed pursuant to N.J.S.3B:12-25 because of a finding of incompetency. For the purposes of this act, pregnancy does not emancipate a female under the age of 18 years.

New Jersey Code § 9:17A-1.4. Notice and waiting period

a. Notwithstanding any other provision of law to the contrary, an abortion shall not be performed upon an unemancipated minor until at least 48 hours after written notice of the pending operation has been delivered in the manner specified in this act.

b. The notice shall be addressed to the parent at the parent's last known address and delivered personally to the parent by the physician.

c. In lieu of the personal delivery required in subsection b. of this section, notice may be made by certified mail addressed to the parent at the parent's last known address with return receipt requested and restricted delivery to the addressee, which means a postal employee may only deliver the mail to the authorized addressee. At the same time that notice is mailed by certified mail, it shall also be sent by first class mail to the parent at the parent's last known address. The 48 hour period for notice sent under the provisions of this subsection shall begin at noon on the next day on which regular mail delivery takes place following the day on which the mailings are posted.

New Jersey Code § 9:17A-1.5. When notice not required

Notice of a pending abortion shall not be required under this act if the parent who is entitled to notice has set forth in a notarized writing that notice was received.

New Jersey Code § 9:17A-1.6. Medical emergency

Notice of a pending abortion shall not be required under this act if the attending physician certifies in the unemancipated minor's medical records that the abortion is necessary due to a medical emergency.

New Jersey Code § 9:17A-1.7. Judicial bypass

a. A minor may, by petition or motion, seek a waiver of parental notification from a judge of the Superior Court. The petition or motion shall include a statement that the minor is pregnant and is not emancipated.

b. The minor may participate in proceedings in the court on her own behalf, and the court may appoint a guardian ad litem for her. The court shall, however, advise her that she has a right to court appointed counsel, and shall, upon her request, provide her with such counsel.

c. Proceedings in the court under this section shall be confidential and insure the anonymity of the minor and shall be given such precedence over other pending matters so that the court may reach a decision promptly and without delay so as to serve the best interests of the minor. A judge of the Superior Court who conducts proceedings under this section shall make written factual findings and legal conclusions within 48 hours of the time that the petition or motion is filed unless the time is extended at the request of the unemancipated minor. If the court fails to rule within 48 hours and the time is not extended, the petition is granted and the notice requirement shall be waived. The judge shall order a record of the evidence to be maintained including the judge's written factual findings and legal conclusions supporting the decision.

d. (1) If the judge finds, by clear and convincing evidence, that the unemancipated minor is sufficiently mature to decide whether to have an abortion, the judge shall authorize a waiver of notification.

(2) If the judge finds, by clear and convincing evidence, that there is evidence of a pattern of physical, sexual or emotional abuse of the minor by the parent, guardian or legal custodian, the judge shall authorize a waiver of notification. Notice of a determination made under this paragraph shall be made to the Division of Youth and Family Services.

(3) If the judge finds, by clear and convincing evidence, that the notification of the parent is not in the best interests of the minor, the judge shall authorize a waiver of notification.

e. If the judge does not make a finding specified in subsection d. of this section, the judge shall dismiss the petition or motion and notice shall be given as provided for in section 5 of this act.

f. An expedited confidential appeal shall be available to a minor for whom the court denies an order waiving notification. No filing fees shall be required of any minor at either the trial or the appellate level. Access to the trial court for the purposes of such a petition or motion, and access to the appellate courts for purposes of making an appeal from denial of the same, shall be afforded such a minor on an emergent basis in accordance with the Rules of Court.

New Jersey Code § 9:17A-1.8. Information letter

The Department of Health and Senior Services shall prepare a fact sheet for distribution to unemancipated pregnant minors who are seeking abortion services.

a. The fact sheet shall be written in terms generally understood by a teenager and shall explain the parental notification requirements of this act, including, but not limited to:

(1) that a minor may, by petition or motion, seek a waiver of parental notification from a judge of the Superior Court;

(2) that a minor may participate in proceedings in the court on her own behalf, that the court may appoint a guardian ad litem for her and that the minor has a right to court appointed counsel, which shall be provided to her by the court upon her request; and

(3) the procedure established by the court for petitioning or making a motion before the court.

b. The department shall distribute the fact sheet, at no charge, to ambulatory care facilities and hospitals licensed pursuant to P.L.1971, c. 136 (C.26:2H-1 et seq.), public and private agencies and physicians' offices that provide family planning services and prenatal care.

c. The physician who is responsible for providing notification to an unemancipated minor's parent pursuant to this act, or his designee, shall provide the unemancipated minor with a copy of the fact sheet at the time the minor initially requests abortion services from the physician.

New Jersey Code § 9:17A-1.9. Legally entitled benefits

Nothing in this act shall be interpreted to deny a pregnant unemancipated minor who is under the age of 18 any benefits to which she would otherwise be entitled pursuant to law.

New Jersey Code § 9:17A-1.10. Penalties

Any person who performs an abortion in violation of this act shall be subject to a civil penalty of not less than $1,000 and not more than $5,000 and shall be liable in a civil action by a parent wrongfully denied notification. A person shall not be liable under this act if the person establishes by written evidence that the person relied upon evidence sufficient to convince a careful and prudent person that the representations of the unemancipated minor regarding information necessary to comply with this section are bona fide and true, or if the person has attempted with reasonable diligence to deliver notice, but has been unable to do so.

New Jersey Code § 9:17A-1.11. Rules and regulations

The Commissioner of the Department of Health and Senior Services, in consultation with the Department of Law and Public Safety, shall promulgate rules and regulations pursuant to the "Administrative Procedure Act," P.L.1968, c. 410 (C.52:14B-1 et seq.), concerning procedures for physicians to follow in effectuating the notice required pursuant to the provisions of P.L.1999, c. 145 (C.9:17A-1 et al.).

New Jersey Code § 9:17A-1.12. Severability

If any provision of this act or the application thereof to any person or circumstance is held invalid, the invalidity shall not affect other provisions or applications of the sections which can be given effect without the invalid provision or application, and to this end the provisions of this act are severable.

(4) PUBLIC FUNDS FOR ABORTION

New Jersey provides a statute that prohibits the use of public funds to perform an abortion, except when necessary to preserve a woman's life. The statute was found invalid in *Right to Choose v. Byrne*, 450 A.2d 925 (N.J. 1982), to the extent that the statute would not allow payment for all medically necessary abortions. The statute is set out below.

New Jersey Code § 30:4D-6.1. Public funds

No payments for medical assistance shall be made under the act hereby supplemented for the termination of a woman's pregnancy for any reason except where it is medically indicated to be necessary to preserve the woman's life. In any case where a pregnancy is so terminated, the act shall be performed in a hospital and the physician performing the act shall submit in writing a report to the division stating in detail his reasons for finding it necessary to terminate the pregnancy.

(5) BLOOD TESTING

New Jersey requires that a woman provide a blood sample before or shortly thereafter an abortion. The statute addressing the matter is set out below.

New Jersey Code § 26:2-143.
Blood specimen at time of abortion

Every licensed physician or other licensed health professional engaged in the prenatal care of a pregnant woman or attending the woman at the time of delivery, miscarriage or abortion shall obtain or cause to be obtained a blood specimen of the woman prior to delivery or abortion or within 24 hours after delivery, miscarriage or abortion.

(6) USE OF FACILITIES AND PEOPLE

Under the laws of New Jersey hospitals are not required to allow abortions at their facilities. The employees and physicians at hospitals that do allow abortions are permitted to refuse to take part in abortions. The statutes addressing the matter are set out below.

New Jersey Code § 2A:65A-1. Requirement of person

No person shall be required to perform or assist in the performance of an abortion or sterilization.

New Jersey Code § 2A:65A-2. Hospital refusal

No hospital or other health care facility shall be required to provide abortion or sterilization services or procedures.

New Jersey Code § 2A:65A-3. Refusal to perform

The refusal to perform, assist in the performance of, or provide abortion services or sterilization procedures shall not constitute grounds for civil or criminal liability, disciplinary action or discriminatory treatment.

(7) BAN HUMAN CLONING

New Jersey has made it a criminal offense to clone a human being. The statute addressing the matter is set out below.

New Jersey Code § 2C:11A-1. Human cloning

A person who knowingly engages or assists, directly or indirectly, in the cloning of a human being is guilty of a crime of the first degree.

As used in this section, "cloning of a human being" means the replication of a human individual by cultivating a cell with genetic material through the egg, embryo, fetal and newborn stages into a new human individual.

New Jersey Right to Life

New Jersey Right to Life (NJRL) is a pro-life organization that was established in 1972. NJRL is the largest and oldest pro-life organization in the state of New Jersey. The organization's president is Traude Barbiero. NJRL has established a working education program designed to inform the public about abortion, and a political action program that supports pro-life issues and political candidates. *See also* **Pro-Life Organizations**

New Mexico

(1) OVERVIEW

The state of New Mexico enacted its first criminal abortion statute on February 15, 1854. The statute underwent several amendments prior to the 1973 decision by the United States Supreme Court in *Roe v. Wade*, which legalized abortion in the nation. In spite of the decision in *Roe*, New Mexico has not repealed its pre-*Roe* criminal abortion laws. However, the laws are constitutionally infirm.

New Mexico has taken affirmative steps to respond to *Roe* and its progeny. The state has addressed a few abortion issues by statute that include partial-birth abortion; use of facilities and people; research on a fetus, pregnant woman or live-born infant; injury to a pregnant woman; and fetal death report.

(2) PRE-ROE ABORTION BAN

As previously indicated, New Mexico has not repealed its pre-*Roe* criminal abortion statutes. The statutes were specifically found unconstitutional in *State v. Strance*, 506 P.2d 1217 (N.M.Ct.App. 1973). Under the now unconstitutional laws, abortion was criminalized if it was not performed to preserve the life or health of the woman, to prevent the birth of a child with grave physical or mental defect, or the pregnancy resulted from rape or incest. The state required that a special hospital board approve of an abortion. There was also a requirement that a minor obtain the consent of a parent. The latter requirement is invalid because it does not provide for judicial bypass. The statutes are set out below.

New Mexico Code § 30-5-1. Abortion definitions

A. "pregnancy" means the implantation of an embryo in the uterus;

B. "accredited hospital" means one licensed by the health and social services department;

C. "justified medical termination" means the intentional ending of the pregnancy of a woman at the request of said woman or if said woman is under the age of eighteen years, then at the request of said woman and her then living parent or guardian, by a physician licensed by the state of New Mexico using acceptable medical procedures in an accredited hospital upon written certification by the members of a special hospital board that:

(1) the continuation of the pregnancy, in their opinion, is likely to result in the death of the woman or the grave impairment of the physical or mental health of the woman; or

(2) the child probably will have a grave physical or mental defect; or

(3) the pregnancy resulted from rape, as defined in Sections 40A-9-2 through 40A-9-4 NMSA 1953. Under this paragraph, to justify a medical termination of the pregnancy, the woman must present to the special hospital board an affidavit that she has been raped and that the rape has been or will be reported to an appropriate law enforcement official; or

(4) the pregnancy resulted from incest;

D. "special hospital board" means a committee of two licensed physicians or their appointed alternates who are members of the medical staff at the accredited hospital where the proposed justified medical termination would be performed, and who meet for the purpose of determining the question of medical justification in an individual case, and maintain a written record of the proceedings and deliberations of such board.

New Mexico Code § 30-5-3. Criminal abortion

Criminal abortion consists of administering to any pregnant woman any medicine, drug or other substance, or using any method or means whereby an untimely termination of her pregnancy is produced, or attempted to be produced, with the intent to destroy the fetus, and the termination is not a justified medical termination.

Whoever commits criminal abortion is guilty of a fourth degree felony. Whoever commits criminal abortion which results in the death of the woman is guilty of a second degree felony.

(3) PARTIAL-BIRTH ABORTION

New Mexico prohibits partial-birth abortions, except to preserve the life or health of the woman. Until it is definitively determined by a

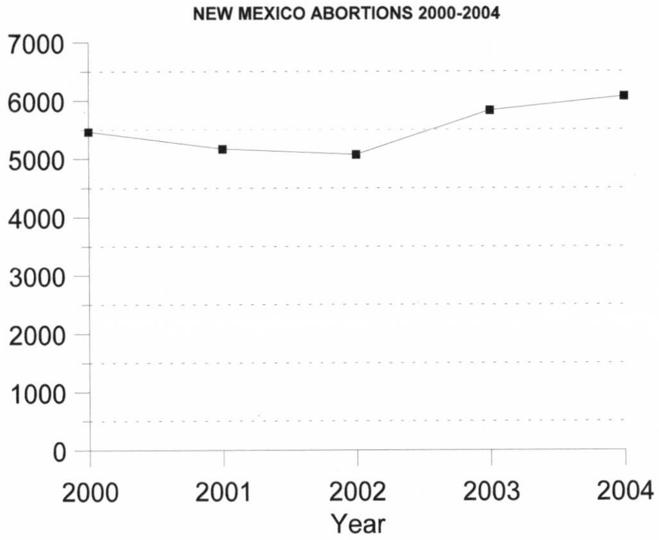

Source: **National Center for Health Statistics.**

New Mexico Abortion by Age Group 2000–2004

	Age Group (yrs)							
Year	*<15*	*15–19*	*20–24*	*25–29*	*30–34*	*35–39*	*≥40*	*Unknown*
2000	39	1,230	1,741	1,189	650	421	171	24
2001	29	1,089	1,752	1,029	659	394	172	42
2002	37	1,061	1,695	1,022	651	373	175	55
2003	35	1,247	1,991	1,205	791	394	151	78
2004	35	1,276	2,176	1,223	709	406	181	64
Total	175	5,903	9,355	5,668	3,460	1,988	850	263

Source: **National Center for Health Statistics.**

New Mexico Abortion by Weeks of Gestation 2000–2004

	Year					
Weeks of Gestation	*2000*	*2001*	*2002*	*2003*	*2004*	*Total*
≤8	3,019	2,835	3,044	3,613	3,648	16,159
9–10	1,109	1,022	807	901	884	4,723
11–12	577	528	512	529	565	2,711
13–15	426	402	308	353	355	1,844
16–20	258	289	297	325	373	1,542
≥21	41	44	59	63	117	324
Not known	35	46	42	48	128	299

Source: **National Center for Health Statistics.**

court, New Mexico's partial-birth abortion laws may be invalid under the United States Supreme Court decision *in Stenberg v. Carhart*, which invalidated Nebraska's ban on partial-birth abortion. On the other hand, New Mexico's partial-birth abortion laws, as currently written, may be valid under the United States Supreme Court decision in *Gonzales v. Carhart*, which approved of a federal statute that bans partial-birth abortion. In addition to purporting to ban partial-birth abortions, New Mexico has provided a civil cause of action for the biological father of the aborted fetus. In the case of a minor, the maternal grandparents of the fetus may file a civil lawsuit. The state also allows a cause of action by the pregnant woman, if she did not consent to a partial-birth abortion. The statutes addressing the issues are set out below.

New Mexico Code § 30-5A-1. Short title

This act may be cited as the "Partial-Birth Abortion Ban Act."

New Mexico Code § 30-5A-2. Definitions

As used in the Partial-Birth Abortion Ban Act:

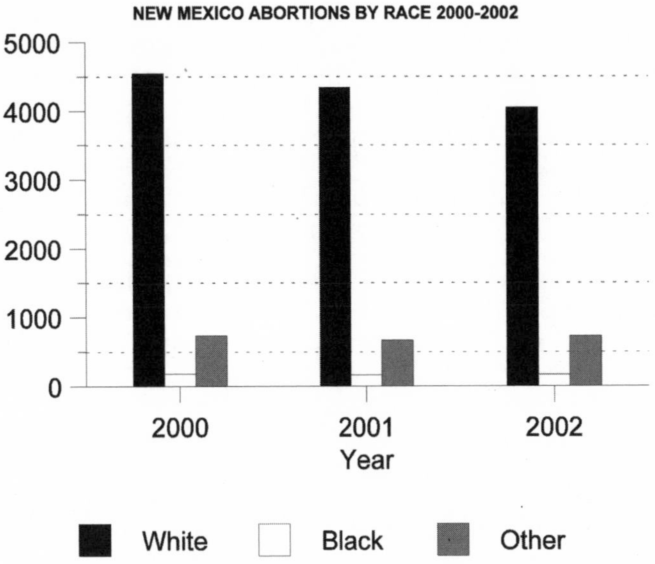

Source: **National Center for Health Statistics.**

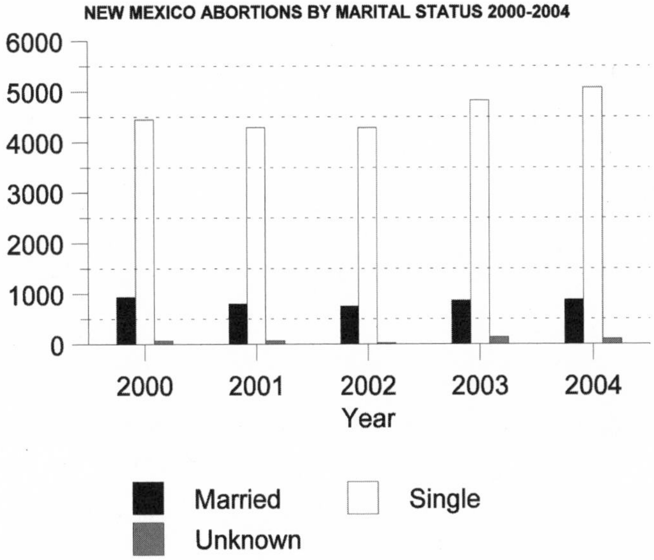

Source: **National Center for Health Statistics.**

New Mexico Prior Abortion by Female 2000–2002

	Prior Abortion				
Year	*None*	*1*	*2*	*≥3*	*Not known*
2000	3,586	1,150	355	182	192
2001	3,635	1,059	299	157	16
2002	3,130	1,000	328	162	449
Total	10,351	3,209	982	501	657

Source: **National Center for Health Statistics.**

A. "abortion" means the intentional termination of the pregnancy of a female by a person who knows the female is pregnant;

B. "fetus" means the biological offspring of human parents;

C. "partial-birth abortion" means a procedure in which any person, including a physician or other health care professional, intentionally extracts an independently viable fetus from the uterus into the vagina and mechanically extracts the cranial contents of the fetus in order to induce death; and

D. "physician" means a person licensed to practice in the state as a licensed physician pursuant to the Medical Practice Act or an osteopathic physician licensed pursuant to Chapter 61, Article 10 NMSA 1978.

New Mexico Code § 30-5A-3. Partial-birth abortion ban

No person shall perform a partial-birth abortion except a physician who has determined that in his opinion the partial-birth abortion is necessary to save the life of a pregnant female or prevent great bodily harm to a pregnant female:

A. because her life is endangered or she is at risk of great bodily harm due to a physical disorder, illness or injury, including a condition caused by or arising from the pregnancy; and

B. no other medical procedure would suffice for the purpose of saving her life or preventing great bodily harm to her.

New Mexico Code § 30-5A-4. Civil remedies

A. Except as provided in Subsection B of this section, the following persons may bring a civil action to obtain relief pursuant to this section against a person who has violated the provisions of Section 3 of the Partial-Birth Abortion Ban Act:

(1) the person on whom a partial-birth abortion was performed;

(2) the biological father of the fetus that was the subject of the partial-birth abortion; and

(3) the parents of the person on whom the partial-birth abortion was performed if that person had not reached the age of majority at the time of the abortion.

B. The persons named as having a right of action in Subsection A of this section are barred from bringing a civil action pursuant to this section if:

(1) the pregnancy of the person on whom the partial-birth abortion was performed resulted from criminal conduct of the person seeking to bring the action; or

(2) the partial-birth abortion was consented to by the person seeking to bring the action.

C. A person authorized to bring a civil action pursuant to this section may recover compensatory damages for loss caused by violation of Section 3 of the Partial-Birth Abortion Ban Act.

New Mexico Code § 30-5A-5. Criminal penalty

A. Except as provided in Subsections B, C, D and E of this section, a person who violates Section 3 of the Partial-Birth Abortion Ban Act is guilty of a fourth degree felony and shall be sentenced pursuant to Section 31-18-15 NMSA 1978.

B. The provisions of the Partial-Birth Abortion Ban Act shall apply only to the exact procedure specified in that act.

C. The provisions of the Partial-Birth Abortion Ban Act are not intended to criminalize any other method of terminating a woman's pregnancy.

D. The provisions of the Partial-Birth Abortion Ban Act are not intended to subject a woman, upon whom the procedure specified in that act is performed, to criminal culpability as an accomplice, aider, abettor, solicitor or conspirator.

E. The provisions of the Partial-Birth Abortion Ban Act are not intended to subject any person to criminal culpability pursuant to laws governing attempt, solicitation or conspiracy to commit a crime.

(4) USE OF FACILITIES AND PEOPLE

New Mexico retained its pre–*Roe* statute that provided hospitals were not required to allow abortions at their facilities. The employees and physicians at hospitals that do allow abortions are permitted to refuse to take part in abortions. The statute addressing the matters is set out below.

New Mexico Code § 30-5-2. Right to refuse abortion

This article does not require a hospital to admit any patient for the purposes of performing an abortion, nor is any hospital required to create a special hospital board. A person who is a member of, or associated with, the staff of a hospital, or any employee of a hospital, in which a justified medical termination has been authorized and who objects to the justified medical termination on moral or religious grounds shall not be required to participate in medical procedures which will result in the termination of pregnancy, and the refusal of any such person to participate shall not form the basis of any disciplinary or other recriminatory action against such person.

(5) RESEARCH ON A FETUS, PREGNANT WOMAN OR LIVE-BORN INFANT

Under the laws of New Mexico research on a fetus, pregnant woman or live-born infant is permitted, with the proper consent, for limited purposes. The state limits such research to meet the health needs of the particular fetus, pregnant woman or live-born infant that is the subject of the research. The statutes addressing the matters are set out below.

New Mexico Code § 24-9A-1. Definitions

As used in the Maternal, Fetal and Infant Experimentation Act:

A. "viability" means that stage of fetal development when the unborn child is potentially able to live outside the mother's womb, albeit with artificial aid;

B. "conception" means the fertilization of the ovum of a human female by the sperm of a human male;

C. "health" means physical or mental health;

D. "clinical research" means any biomedical or behavioral research involving human subjects, including the unborn, conducted according to a formal procedure. The term is to be construed liberally to embrace research concerning all physiological processes in human beings and includes research involving human in vitro fertilization, but shall not include diagnostic testing, treatment, therapy or related procedures conducted by formal protocols deemed necessary for the care of the particular patient upon whom such activity is performed and shall not include human in vitro fertilization performed to treat infertility; provided that this procedure shall include provisions to ensure that each living fertilized ovum, zygote or embryo is implanted in a human female recipient, and no physician may stipulate that a woman must abort in the event the pregnancy should produce a child with a disability. Provided that emergency medical procedures necessary to preserve the life or health of the mother or the fetus shall not be considered to be clinical research;

E. "subject at risk," "subject" or "at risk" means any person who may be exposed to the likelihood of injury, including physical or psychological injury, as a consequence of participation as a subject in:

(1) any research, development or related activity that departs from the application of those established and accepted methods deemed necessary to meet the person's needs;

(2) controlled research studies necessary to establish accepted methods designed to meet the person's needs; or

(3) research activity that poses a significant risk to the subject;

F. "significant risk" means an activity that is likely to cause disfigurement or loss or impairment of the function of any member or organ;

G. "fetus" means the product of conception from the time of conception until the expulsion or extraction of the fetus or the opening of the uterine cavity, but shall not include the placenta, extraembryonic membranes, umbilical cord, extraembryonic fluids and their resident cell types and cultured cells;

H. "live-born infant" means an offspring of a person that exhibits heartbeat, spontaneous respiratory activity, spontaneous movement of voluntary muscles or pulsation of the umbilical cord if still attached to the infant ex utero; provided the Maternal, Fetal and Infant Experimentation Act does not apply to a fetus or infant absent the characteristics set forth in this subsection;

I. "infant" means an offspring of a human being from the time it is born until the end of its first chronological year;

J. "born" means the time the head or any other part of the body of the fetus emerges from the vagina or the time the uterine cavity is opened during a caesarean section or hysterotomy; and

K. "in vitro fertilization" means any fertilization of human ova that occurs outside the body of a female, either through admixture of donor human sperm and ova or by any other means.

New Mexico Code § 24-9A-2. Pregnant woman

A. No woman, known to be pregnant according to generally accepted medical standards, shall be involved as a subject in any clinical research activity unless:

(1) the purpose of the activity is to meet the health needs of the mother or the fetus and the fetus will be placed at risk only to the minimum extent necessary to meet such needs; or

(2) there is no significant risk to the fetus.

B. An activity permitted under Subsection A of this section may be conducted only if the mother is legally competent and has given her informed consent after having been fully informed regarding possible impact on the fetus.

New Mexico Code § 24-9A-3. Fetus

A. No fetus shall be involved as a subject in any clinical research activity unless the purpose of the activity is to meet the health needs of the particular fetus and the fetus will be placed at risk only to the minimum extent necessary to meet such needs or no significant risk to the fetus is imposed by the research activity.

B. An activity permitted under Subsection A of this section shall be conducted only if the mother is legally competent and has given her informed consent.

New Mexico Code § 24-9A-4. Live-born infant

A. No live-born infant shall be involved as a subject in any clinical research activity unless the purpose of the activity is to meet the health needs of that particular infant, and the infant will be placed at risk only to the minimum extent necessary to meet such needs or no significant risk to such infant is imposed by the research activity.

B. An activity permitted under Subsection A of this section shall be conducted only if:

(1) the nature of the investigation is such that adults or mentally competent persons would not be suitable subjects; and

(2) the mother or father or the infant's legal guardian is mentally competent and has given his or her informed consent.

New Mexico Code § 24-9A-5 Research activity

A. No clinical research activity involving fetuses, live-born infants or pregnant women shall be conducted unless:

(1) appropriate studies on animals and nonpregnant human beings have been completed;

(2) anyone engaged in conducting the research activity will have no part in:

(a) any decisions as to the timing, method and procedures used to terminate the pregnancy; and

(b) determining the viability of the fetus at the termination of the pregnancy; and

(3) no procedural changes which may cause significant risk to the fetus or the pregnant woman will be introduced into the procedure for terminating the pregnancy solely in the interest of the research activity.

B. No inducements, monetary or otherwise, shall be offered to any woman to terminate her pregnancy for the purpose of subjecting her fetus or live-born infant to clinical research activity.

C. No consent to involve a pregnant woman, fetus or infant as a subject in clinical research activity shall be valid unless the pregnant woman or the parent or guardian of the infant has been fully informed of the following:

(1) a fair explanation of the procedures to be followed and their purposes, including identification of any procedures which are experimental;

(2) a description of any attendant discomforts and risks reasonably to be expected;

(3) a description of any benefits reasonably to be expected;

(4) a disclosure of any appropriate alternative procedures that might be advantageous for the subject;

(5) an offer to answer any inquiries concerning the procedure; and

(6) an instruction that the person who gave the consent is free to withdraw his consent and to discontinue participation in the project or activity at any time without prejudice to the subject.

New Mexico Code § 24-9A-6. Penalty

Whoever knowingly and willfully violates the provisions of Section 2, 3 or 4 of this act shall be deemed guilty of a misdemeanor, and upon conviction shall be punished by imprisonment in the county jail for a definite term of less than one year, or to the payment of a fine of not more than one thousand dollars ($1,000), or to both imprisonment and fine in the discretion of the judge.

(6) INJURY TO A PREGNANT WOMAN

New Mexico criminalizes the death of a fetus caused by injury to a pregnant woman, by a person engaged in the commission of a felony or while driving a motor vehicle under the influence of drugs or alcohol. The statutes addressing the matters are set out below.

New Mexico Code § 30-3-7. Injury during felony

A. Injury to [a] pregnant woman consists of a person other than the woman injuring a pregnant woman in the commission of a felony causing her to suffer a miscarriage or stillbirth as a result of that injury.

B. As used in this section:

(1) "miscarriage" means the interruption of the normal development of the fetus, other than by a live birth and which is not an induced abortion, resulting in the complete expulsion or extraction from a pregnant woman of a product of human conception; and

(2) "stillbirth" means the death of a fetus prior to the complete expulsion or extraction from its mother, irrespective of the duration of pregnancy and which is not an induced abortion; and death is manifested by the fact that after the expulsion or extraction the fetus does not breathe spontaneously or show any other evidence of life such as heart beat, pulsation of the umbilical cord or definite movement of voluntary muscles.

C. Whoever commits injury to [a] pregnant woman is guilty of a third degree felony and shall be sentenced pursuant to the provisions of Section 31-18-15 NMSA 1978.

New Mexico Code § 66-8-101.1 Injury by vehicle

A. Injury to pregnant woman by vehicle is injury to a pregnant woman by a person other than the woman in the unlawful operation of a motor vehicle causing her to suffer a miscarriage or stillbirth as a result of that injury.

B. As used in this section:

(1) "miscarriage" means the interruption of the normal development of the fetus, other than by a live birth and which is not an induced abortion, resulting in the complete expulsion or extraction from a pregnant woman of a product of human conception; and

(2) "stillbirth" means the death of a fetus prior to the complete expulsion or extraction from its mother, irrespective of the duration

of pregnancy and which is not an induced abortion; and death is manifested by the fact that after the expulsion or extraction the fetus does not breathe spontaneously or show any other evidence of life such as heartbeat, pulsation of the umbilical cord or definite movement of voluntary muscles.

C. Any person who commits injury to pregnant woman by vehicle while under the influence of intoxicating liquor or while under the influence of any drug or while violating Section 66-8-113 NMSA 1978 is guilty of a third degree felony and shall be sentenced pursuant to the provisions of Section 31-18-15 NMSA 1978, provided that violation of speeding laws as set forth in the Motor Vehicle Code shall not per se be a basis for violation of Section 66-8-113 NMSA 1978.

(7) FETAL DEATH REPORT

New Mexico requires that all abortions be reported to the proper authorities. The statute addressing the matter is set out below.

New Mexico Code § 24-14-18. Report of induced abortions

A. Each induced abortion which occurs in this state shall be reported to the state registrar within five days by the person in charge of the institution in which the induced abortion was performed. If the induced abortion was performed outside an institution, the attending physician shall prepare and file the report.

B. The reports required under this section are statistical reports to be used only for medical and health purposes and shall not be incorporated into the permanent official records of the system of vital statistics. The report shall not include the name or address of the patient involved in the abortion. The department shall not release the name or address of the physician involved in the abortion. A schedule for the disposition of these reports shall be provided for by regulation.

New Mexico Religious Coalition for Reproductive Choice

The New Mexico Religious Coalition for Reproductive Choice is a pro-choice religious organization headquartered in Albuquerque, New Mexico. The organization promotes the following principles; (1) that all persons desiring to be parents should have the right and opportunity to do so; (2) that all persons have a right to privacy; (3) that no person should ever be forced or coerced into contraception, sterilization, or abortion; (4) that caring communities have a responsibility to ensure that all young people have access to medically accurate, comprehensive sex education; (5) that all people should have access to all reproductive and sexual health information and services, including birthing options, contraception, sterilization and abortion; and (6) that all persons should be able to live a life free from violence, including physical and sexual violence, which prevents them from controlling their sexual and reproductive lives. The organization sponsors a clinic escort program called "Peaceful Presence," which provides drivers to take patients to their appointments, and home stay hosts. *See also* **Pro-Choice Organizations**

New York

(1) OVERVIEW

The state of New York enacted its first criminal abortion statute on December 10, 1828. Shortly before the 1973 decision by the United States Supreme Court in *Roe v. Wade*, which legalized abortion in the nation, New York had amended its criminal abortion statute to permit abortions. New York has addressed several abortion issues by statute that include general abortion guidelines, right to refuse participation in abortion, injury to a pregnant woman, and anti-abortion activity.

(2) GENERAL ABORTION GUIDELINES

Under the laws of New York abortion is prohibited after the 24th week of pregnancy, unless performed to save the woman's life. New York recognizes self-abortion, but the state also provides criminal punishment for a woman unlawfully performing self-abortion. New York requires abortions after the first trimester be performed in a hospital. However, this requirement is unconstitutional because the United States Supreme Court has determined that second trimester abortions cannot be restricted exclusively to hospitals. The state also mandates that a second physician be present whenever an abortion occurs after the 20th week of pregnancy. New York imposes limits who may have access to information about abortion referral services. The statutes addressing the matters are set out below.

New York Penal Code § 125.05. Definitions

The following definitions are applicable to this article:

1. "Person," when referring to the victim of a homicide, means a human being who has been born and is alive.

2. "Abortional act" means an act committed upon or with respect to a female, whether by another person or by the female herself, whether she is pregnant or not, whether directly upon her body or by the administering, taking or prescription of drugs or in any other manner, with intent to cause a miscarriage of such female.

3. "Justifiable abortional act." An abortional act is justifiable when committed upon a female with her consent by a duly licensed physician acting (a) under a reasonable belief that such is necessary to preserve her life, or, (b) within twenty-four weeks from the commencement of her pregnancy. A pregnant female's commission of an abortional act upon herself is justifiable when she acts upon the advice of a duly licensed physician (1) that such act is necessary to preserve her life, or, (2) within twenty-four weeks from the commencement of her pregnancy. The submission by a female to an abortional act is justifiable when she believes that it is being committed by a duly licensed physician, acting under a reasonable belief that such act is necessary to preserve her life, or, within twenty-four weeks from the commencement of her pregnancy.

New York Penal Code § 125.45. Abortion in the first degree

A person is guilty of abortion in the first degree when he commits upon a female pregnant for more than twenty-four weeks an abortional act which causes the miscarriage of such female, unless such abortional act is justifiable pursuant to subdivision three of section 125.05. Abortion in the first degree is a class D felony.

New York Penal Code § 125.40. Abortion in the second degree

A person is guilty of abortion in the second degree when he commits an abortional act upon a female, unless such abortional act is justifiable pursuant to subdivision three of section 125.05. Abortion in the second degree is a class E felony.

New York Penal Code § 125.55. Self-abortion in the first degree

A female is guilty of self-abortion in the first degree when, being pregnant for more than twenty-four weeks, she commits or submits to an abortional act upon herself which causes her miscarriage, unless such abortional act is justifiable pursuant to subdivision three of section 125.05. Self-abortion in the first degree is a class A misdemeanor.

New York Penal Code § 125.50. Self-abortion in the second degree

A female is guilty of self-abortion in the second degree when, being pregnant, she commits or submits to an abortional act upon herself, unless such abortional act is justifiable pursuant to subdivision three of section 125.05. Self-abortion in the second degree is a class B misdemeanor.

New York Penal Code § 125.60. Issuing abortion articles

A person is guilty of issuing abortional articles when he manufactures, sells or delivers any instrument, article, medicine, drug or substance with intent that the same be used in unlawfully procuring the miscarriage of a female.

Issuing abortional articles is a class B misdemeanor.

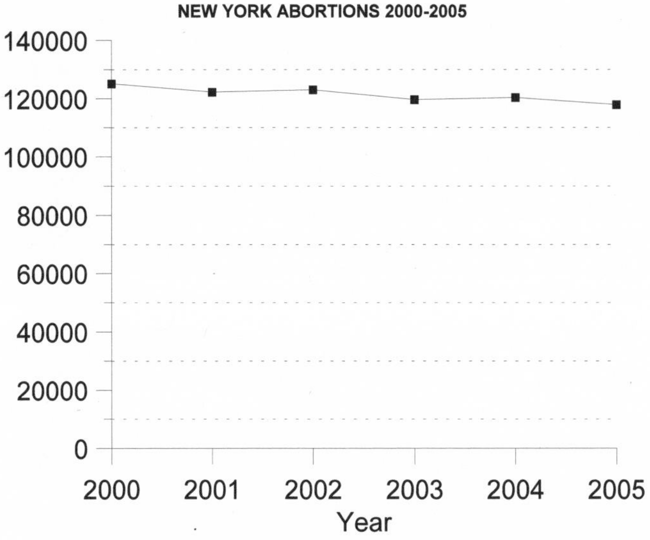

Source: New York State Department of Health.

New York Abortion by Age Group 2000–2005
Age Group (yrs)

Year	*<15*	*15–17*	*18–19*	*20–24*	*25–29*	*30–34*	*35–39*	*≥40*	*Unknown*
2000	793	9,079	13,299	37,684	28,602	19,872	11,789	3,800	228
2001	744	8,681	13,046	37,137	27,521	19,491	11,439	3,822	390
2002	714	8,679	12,680	37,647	27,977	19,445	11,527	4,013	366
2003	710	8,344	12,464	36,670	27,392	18,520	11,218	4,012	355
2004	741	8,499	12,612	37,000	27,978	18,136	11,094	4,044	297
2005	700	8,543	12,337	35,826	27,489	17,542	10,953	4,199	355
Total	4,402	51,825	76,438	221,964	166,959	113,006	68,020	23,890	1,991

Source: New York State Department of Health.

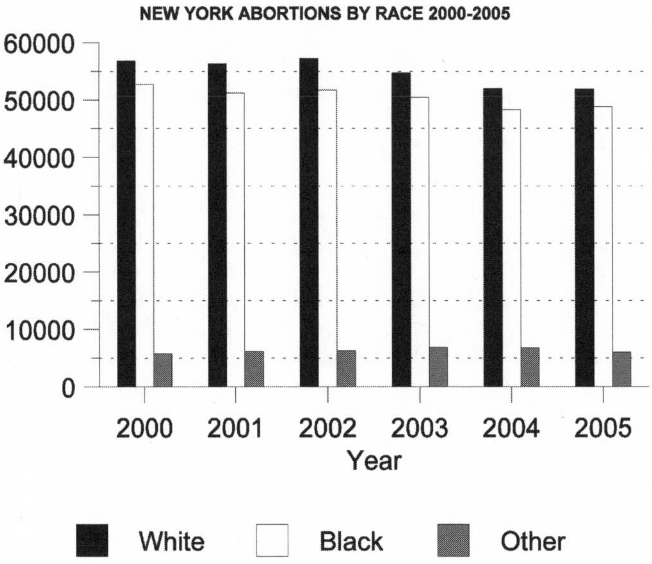

Source: New York State Department of Health.

New York Pub. Health Code § 4164.
Hospital and second physician

1. When an abortion is to be performed after the twelfth week of pregnancy it shall be performed only in a hospital and only on an in-patient basis. When an abortion is to be performed after the twentieth week of pregnancy, a physician other than the physician performing the abor-

New York Abortion by Weeks of Gestation 2000–2005
Year

Weeks of Gestation	*2000*	*2001*	*2002*	*2003*	*2004*	*2005*	*Total*
<9	66,263	66,082	68,122	65,441	66,718	65,692	398,318
9–10	23,434	22,583	22,134	21,525	21,288	20,507	131,471
11–12	11,942	11,339	10,802	10,838	10,676	10,141	65,738
13–15	7,005	6,543	6,553	6,509	6,388	6,268	39,266
16–19	4,384	4,135	4,217	4,167	3,975	4,126	25,004
≥20	2,035	2,353	2,286	2,385	2,013	2,431	13,503

Source: New York State Department of Health.

tion shall be in attendance to take control of and to provide immediate medical care for any live birth that is the result of the abortion. The commissioner of health is authorized to promulgate rules and regulations to insure the health and safety of the mother and the viable child, in such instances.

2. Such child shall be accorded immediate legal protection under the laws of the state of New York, including but not limited to applicable provisions of the social services law, article five of the civil rights law and the penal law.

3. The medical records of all life-sustaining efforts put forth for such a live aborted birth, their failure or success, shall be kept by attending physician. All other vital statistics requirements in the public health law shall be complied with in regard to such aborted child.

4. In the event of the subsequent death of the aborted child, the disposal of the dead body shall be in accordance with the requirements of this chapter.

New York Exec. Code § 291(3). Infant born alive

The opportunity to obtain medical treatment of an infant prematurely born alive in the course of an abortion shall be the same as the rights of an infant born spontaneously.

New York Gen. Bus. Code § 394-e.
Report on request for abortion services

1. It shall be unlawful for any person, firm or corporation doing business in this state to furnish a report of a referral for abortional services or a report of an inquiry or request therefor, to any person or government agency unless such person, firm or corporation has reasonable grounds to believe that the person or government agency requesting the report is (a) a law enforcement agency, or (b) the state department of health or the department of health of the city of New York, or (c) authorized in writing by the subject of such report, or (d) unless such person, firm or corporation shall have been ordered to furnish such report by a duly constituted court having jurisdiction to issue such an order. Every request for such a report shall be in writing and identify the name and address of the requestor. A request by a law enforcement agency shall include a sworn statement that the agency is requesting the report solely for law enforcement purposes.

New York Prior Abortion by Female 2000–2005
Prior Abortion

Year	*None*	*1*	*2*	*3*	*4*	*≥5*
2000	55,009	29,494	17,330	8,173	3,835	3,717
2001	52,106	29,941	17,541	8,394	3,963	3,897
2002	53,824	30,397	17,448	8,363	3,956	3,846
2003	52,368	29,954	17,090	8,298	3,772	3,717
2004	53,042	29,439	17,011	8,108	3,854	3,904
2005	52,798	28,799	16,090	7,868	3,692	3,690
Total	319,147	178,024	102,510	49,204	23,072	22,771

Source: New York State Department of Health.

2. A person may bring a civil action for damages or to restrain a person, firm or corporation from violating this act or both and, in such case, if it is found that such person, firm or corporation has wilfully violated this act the violator shall, in addition to any liability for actual damages as may be shown, be liable for exemplary damages of not less than one hundred dollars and not more than ten thousand dollars for each violation together with costs and reasonable attorney's fees and disbursements incurred by the person bringing the action.

3. Except as provided in this section, no person, firm or corporation shall be entitled to claim any privilege, absolute or qualified as a defense in any civil action brought by a person aggrieved by the publication or dissemination of information relating to referral for abortional services or an inquiry or request therefor.

4. Any person who requests or obtains a report of a referral for abortional services or an inquiry or request therefor from any person, firm or corporation under false pretenses or furnishes a report to any person except in accordance with this section shall be guilty of a class A misdemeanor.

(3) RIGHT TO REFUSE PARTICIPATION IN ABORTION

New York permits medical personnel to refuse to take part in abortions. The state also prohibits retaliation against a person who refuses to assist in abortions. The statute addressing the matter is set out below.

New York Civ. Rts. Code § 79-i. Refusing to perform abortion

1. When the performing of an abortion on a human being or assisting thereat is contrary to the conscience or religious beliefs of any person, he may refuse to perform or assist in such abortion by filing a prior written refusal setting forth the reasons therefor with the appropriate and responsible hospital, person, firm, corporation or association, and no such hospital, person, firm, corporation or association shall discriminate against the person so refusing to act. A violation of the provisions of this section shall constitute a misdemeanor.

2. No civil action for negligence or malpractice shall be maintained against a person so refusing to act based on such refusal.

(4) INJURY TO A PREGNANT WOMAN

Under the laws of New York it is a criminal offense to injure a pregnant woman and cause the death of a fetus more then twenty-fours weeks old. The statute addressing the matter is set out below.

New York Penal Code § 125.00. Homicide defined

Homicide means conduct which causes the death of ... an unborn child with which a female has been pregnant for more than twenty-four weeks under circumstances constituting murder, manslaughter in the first degree, manslaughter in the second degree, criminally negligent homicide, abortion in the first degree or self-abortion in the first degree.

(5) ANTI-ABORTION ACTIVITY

New York has responded to intimidating and violent anti-abortion activity by imposing criminal punishment specifically for such conduct. The statutes addressing the matter are set out below.

New York Penal Code § 240.70.
Interference in the second degree (abridged)

1. A person is guilty of criminal interference with health services ... in the second degree when:

(a) by force or threat of force or by physical obstruction, he or she intentionally injures, intimidates or interferes with, or attempts to injure, intimidate or interfere with, another person because such other person was or is obtaining or providing reproductive health services; or

(b) by force or threat of force or by physical obstruction, he or she intentionally injures, intimidates or interferes with, or attempts to injure, intimidate or interfere with, another person in order to discourage such other person or any other person or persons from obtaining or providing reproductive health services; or

(c) omitted; or

(d) he or she intentionally damages the property of a health care facility, or attempts to do so, because such facility provides reproductive health services....

2. A parent or legal guardian of a minor shall not be subject to prosecution for conduct otherwise prohibited by paragraph (a) or (b) of subdivision one of this section which is directed exclusively at such minor.

3. For purposes of this section:

(a) the term "health care facility" means a hospital, clinic, physician's office or other facility that provides reproductive health services, and includes the building or structure in which the facility is located;

(b) the term "interferes with" means to restrict a person's freedom of movement;

(c) the term "intimidates" means to place a person in reasonable apprehension of physical injury to himself or herself or to another person;

(d) the term "physical obstruction" means rendering impassable ingress to or egress from a facility that provides reproductive health services ... or rendering passage to or from such a facility ... unreasonably difficult or hazardous; and

(e) the term "reproductive health services" means health care services provided in a hospital, clinic, physician's office or other facility and includes medical, surgical, counseling or referral services relating to the human reproductive system, including services relating to pregnancy or the termination of a pregnancy.

Criminal interference with health care services ... in the second degree is a class A misdemeanor.

New York Penal Code § 240.71. Interference in the first degree

A person is guilty of criminal interference with health care services ... in the first degree when he or she commits the crime of criminal interference with health care services ... in the second degree and has been previously convicted of the crime of criminal interference with health care services ... in the first or second degree.

Criminal interference with health care services ... in the first degree is a class E felony.

New York Civ. Rts. Code § 79-m. Injunction

Whenever the attorney general or district attorney of the county where the affected health care facility or place of religious worship is located has reasonable cause to believe that any person or group of persons is being, has been, or may be injured by conduct constituting a violation of section 240.70 or 240.71 of the penal law, the attorney general or district attorney may bring an action in the name of the people of the state of New York to permanently enjoin such violation. In such action preliminary and temporary relief may be granted under article sixty-three of the civil practice law and rules.

New York State Right to Life Committee

New York State Right to Life Committee is a pro-life organization that was founded in 1972. The organization's mission is to engage in pro-life educational and charitable projects that include: (1) providing information upon which the general public may make an informed decision about the various topics of fetal development, abortion, and alternatives to abortion; (2) advocating the right to life for reborn human beings; and (3) promoting legal, political, social and cultural reforms designed to insure the right to life reborn human beings. *See also* **Pro-Life Organizations**

Nichols, Thomas Low

Thomas Low Nichols (1821–1861) was born in New Hampshire and educated at New York University, where he received a medical degree in 1850. Nichols and his wife, Mary Gove Nichols, were outspoken advocates of a woman's right to choose whether to have an abortion. Together they founded Memnonia Institute, in Yellow Springs, Ohio. The Institute acted as center for discussions and the development of social, sexual and spiritual reform. A central feature of the Institute was the belief in free and open sexual expression. In this regard, Nichols wrote an influential book setting out his ideas, *Esoteric Anthropology: A Comprehensive and Confidential Treatise on the Most Intimate Relations of Men and Women* (1853). The book was considered the most concise and open discussion of sexuality during its time, as well as being the leading work on contraceptive use and the defense of a woman's right to choose whether to have an abortion.

Niemann-Pick Disease

Niemann-Pick disease is a congenital disorder involving accumulation of harmful quantities of a fatty substance in the spleen, liver, lungs, bone marrow and brain. The disease can cause brain damage that kills before a child is 18 months old. Symptoms that occur in those who survive infancy include pulmonary difficulties, inability to look up and down, difficulty in walking and swallowing, and progressive loss of vision and hearing. Some treatments for symptoms of the disease include bone marrow transplant, enzyme replacement, low-cholesterol dietary regimen, and supplemental oxygen. *See also* **Birth Defects and Abortion**

Noise and Fetal Development

No study has shown a relationship between noise and an injury to or spontaneous abortion of a fetus. However, it has been recommended that pregnant women not expose the fetus to extremely loud and unusual noise.

Non-Immune Hydrops Fetalis

Non-immune hydrops fetalis is a condition involving the formation of excess fluid in two or more vascular sites. This condition causes vascular damage and heart failure. It is responsible for 3 percent of all stillbirths and neonate deaths. *See also* **Stillbirth**

Nonoxynol-9 *see* **Spermicides**

Nonphysicians and Abortion *see* **Criminal Abortions**

Nonsurgical Abortion *see* **Methods of Abortion**

Noonan Syndrome

Noonan syndrome is a disorder of unknown etiology that causes webbing of the neck, changes in the sternum, facial abnormalities, mild mental retardation, hearing loss and congenital heart disease. Treatment for the disorder focuses on the problems that occur. *See also* **Birth Defects and Abortion**

Norplant

Norplant is a female birth control method that can last for up to about 5 years. To use Norplant requires a surgical incision on the inside of a woman's arm, above the elbow. Once the incision is made, 6 small sticks (Norplants) containing a hormone (progestin) are implanted. The incision is then closed. The sticks slowly release the progestin into the blood stream to prevent pregnancies. After 5 years the sticks have to be removed (they can be removed before that if a woman chooses) and replaced. Side effects from Norplant include: sticks falling out or breaking, infections, headaches, acne, weight gain or loss, sore breasts, bloating, cysts on the ovaries, rashes, hair loss or facial hair growth, nervousness, depression, dizziness, and changes in menstrual cycle (many days in a row of spotting or bleeding, spotting between periods, and no bleeding at all). *See also* **Contraception**

North Carolina

(1) OVERVIEW

The state of North Carolina enacted its first criminal abortion statute on March 12, 1881. The statute underwent several amendments prior to the 1973 decision by the United States Supreme Court in *Roe v. Wade*, which legalized abortion in the nation. The state has not repealed its pre-*Roe* criminal abortion laws. However, the laws are constitutionally infirm.

North Carolina has taken affirmative steps to respond to *Roe* and its progeny. The state has addressed several abortion issues by statute that include general abortion guidelines, use of facilities and people, fetal death report, abortion by minors, injury to a pregnant woman, and banning anti-abortion activity.

(2) PRE-ROE ABORTION BAN

As previously indicated, North Carolina has not repealed its pre-*Roe* laws that banned abortion. The statutes are set out below.

North Carolina Code § 14-44.
Using drugs or instruments to destroy unborn child

If any person shall willfully administer to any woman, either pregnant or quick with child, or prescribe for any such woman, or advise or procure any such woman to take any medicine, drug or other substance whatever, or shall use or employ any instrument or other means with intent thereby to destroy such child, he shall be punished as a Class H felon.

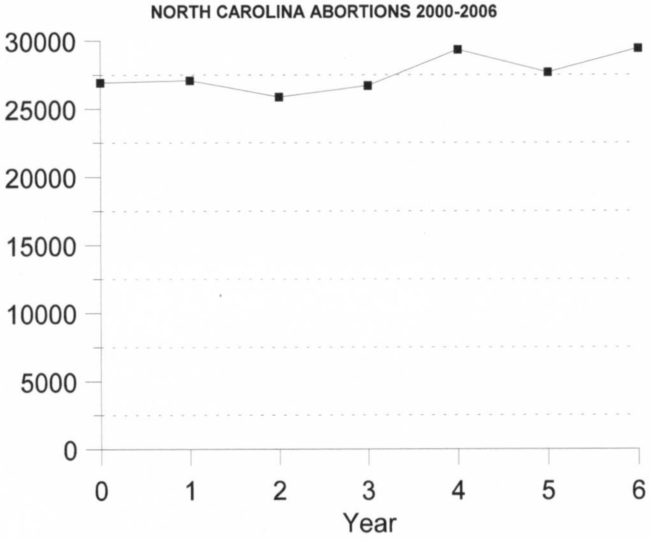

Source: North Carolina Department of Health and Human Services.

North Carolina Abortion by Age Group 2000–2006

	Age Group (yrs)						
Year	*<15*	*15–19*	*20–24*	*25–29*	*30–34*	*≥35*	*Unknown*
2000	209	4,455	8,996	6,210	3,555	2,508	1,009
2001	181	4,474	8,968	6,129	3,716	2,814	814
2002	174	4,105	8,465	5,883	3,785	2,597	874
2003	179	4,106	8,967	6,125	4,013	2,672	646
2004	185	4,479	9,762	6,853	4,483	2,916	659
2005	205	4,234	8,954	6,521	4,035	2,985	740
2006	146	4,395	9,600	6931	4,163	3,227	968
Total	1,279	30,248	63,712	44,652	27,750	19,719	5,710

Source: **North Carolina Department of Health and Human Services.**

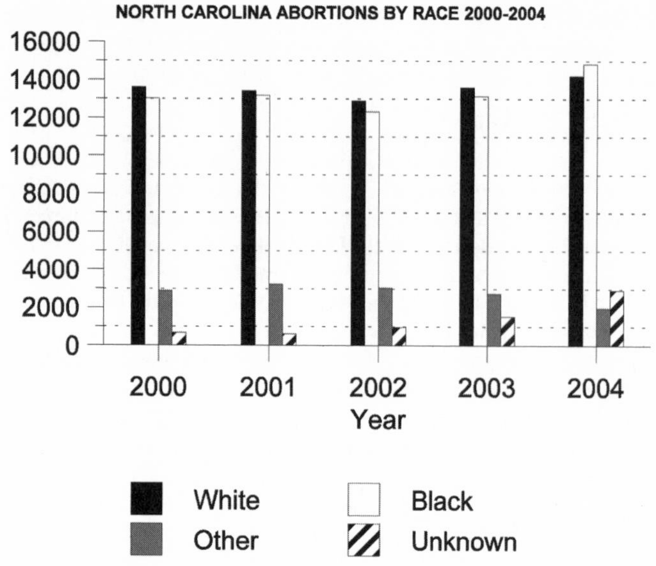

Source: National Center for Health Statistics.

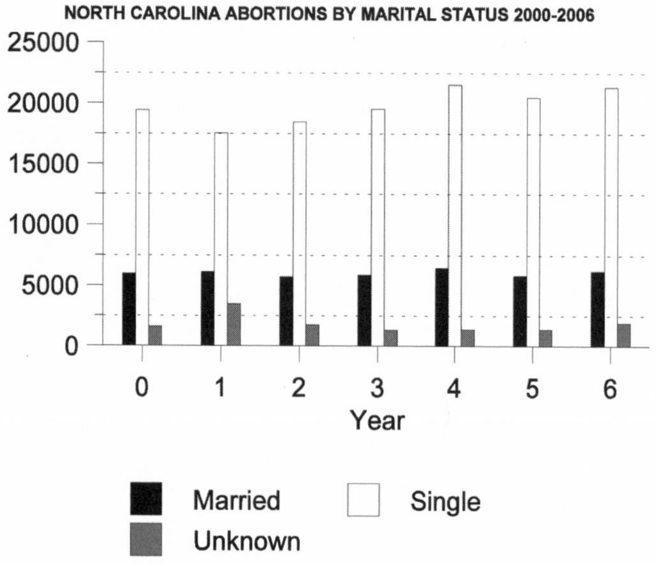

Source: North Carolina Department of Health and Human Services.

North Carolina Abortion by Education Level of Female 2000–2006

Education Level Completed

Year	*<9*	*9–11*	*12*	*≥13*	*Unknown*
2000	685	3,440	8,884	10,850	3,083
2001	690	3,033	8,443	10,205	4,725
2002	790	3,309	8,302	10,674	2,808
2003	846	3,273	9,245	10,515	2,829
2004	1063	3,662	9,742	11,865	3,005
2005	918	3,425	8,797	11,637	2,897
2006	911	3,537	9,583	12,324	3,075
Total	5,903	23,679	62,996	78,070	22,422

Source: North Carolina Department of Health and Human Services.

North Carolina Code § 14-45.
Producing miscarriage or injury to pregnant woman

If any person shall administer to any pregnant woman, or prescribe for any such woman, or advise and procure such woman to take any medicine, drug or anything whatsoever, with intent thereby to procure the miscarriage of such woman, or to injure or destroy such woman, or shall use any instrument or application for any of the above purposes, he shall be punished as a Class I felon.

(3) GENERAL ABORTION GUIDELINES

North Carolina expressly authorizes elective abortions during the first 20 weeks of pregnancy. After the 20th week the state permits abortion only to save the life or health of the woman. The state makes it a crime to conceal the birth and death of a fetus. The statutes addressing the matters are set out below.

North Carolina Code § 14-45.1.
When abortion lawful (abridged)

(a) Notwithstanding any of the provisions of G.S. 14-44 and 14-45, it shall not be unlawful, during the first 20 weeks of a woman's pregnancy, to advise, procure, or cause a miscarriage or abortion when the procedure is performed by a physician licensed to practice medicine in North Carolina in a hospital or clinic certified by the Department of Health and Human Services to be a suitable facility for the performance of abortions.

(b) Notwithstanding any of the provisions of G.S. 14-44 and 14-45, it shall not be unlawful, after the twentieth week of a woman's pregnancy, to advise, procure or cause a miscarriage or abortion when the procedure is performed by a physician licensed to practice medicine in North Carolina in a hospital licensed by the Department of Health and Human Services, if there is substantial risk that continuance of the pregnancy would threaten the life or gravely impair the health of the woman.

North Carolina Code § 14-46. Concealing birth of child

If any person shall, by secretly burying or otherwise disposing of the dead body of a newborn child, endeavor to conceal the birth of such child, such person shall be punished as a Class I felon. Any person aiding, counseling or abetting any other person in concealing the birth of a child in violation of this statute shall be guilty of a Class 1 misdemeanor.

(4) USE OF FACILITIES AND PEOPLE

Under the laws of North Carolina medical facilities are not required to permit abortions on their premises. The state allows physicians to refuse to take part in abortions. The state also charges a specific annual fee to facilities performing abortions. The statutes addressing the issues are set out below.

North Carolina Code § 14-45.1(e) & (f). Right to refuse

Nothing in this section shall require a physician licensed to practice medicine in North Carolina or any nurse who shall state an objection to abortion on moral, ethical, or religious grounds, to perform or participate in medical procedures which result in an abortion. The refusal of such physician to perform or participate in these medical procedures shall not be a basis for damages for such refusal, or for any disciplinary or any other recriminatory action against such physician.

Nothing in this section shall require a hospital or other health care institution to perform an abortion or to provide abortion services.

North Carolina Code § 131E-269. Authorization to charge fee

The Department of Health and Human Services shall charge each hospital or clinic certified by the Department as a facility suitable for the performance of abortions, as authorized under G.S. 14-45.1, a nonrefundable annual certification fee in the amount of seven hundred dollars ($700.00).

(5) FETAL DEATH REPORT

North Carolina requires that abortions be reported to the proper authorities. The state also provides by statute for the disposition of aborted fetuses. The statutes addressing the matters are set out below.

North Carolina Prior Abortion by Female 2000–2006

Year	Prior Abortion None	1	2	≥3	Not known
2000	13,950	5,930	2,122	1,031	3,909
2001	12,583	6,410	2,251	1,077	4,775
2002	12,503	5,451	1,991	1,021	4,917
2003	13,084	6,320	2,430	1,140	3,734
2004	14,738	7,223	2,747	1,394	3,235
2005	13,775	6,522	2,378	1,261	3,738
2006	14,753	6,736	2,519	1,289	4,133
Total	95,386	44,592	16,438	8,213	28,441

Source: **North Carolina Department of Health and Human Services.**

North Carolina Abortion by Weeks of Gestation 2000–2006

Weeks of Gestation	Year 2000	2001	2002	2003	2004	2005	2006	Total
<9	14,851	14,495	14,950	15,882	17,582	15,699	17,132	110,591
9–12	7,294	7,808	6,257	6,197	6,982	6,034	6,669	47,241
13–15	1,916	1,645	1,638	1,690	1,938	1,588	1,626	12,041
16–20	784	759	736	787	934	721	765	5,486
≥21	235	121	141	175	144	117	27	960
Not known	1,817	2,268	2,161	1,977	1,757	3,515	3,211	16,706

Source: **North Carolina Department of Health and Human Services.**

North Carolina Code § 14-45.1(c)

The Department of Health and Human Services shall prescribe and collect on an annual basis, from hospitals or clinics where abortions are performed, such representative samplings of statistical summary reports concerning the medical and demographic characteristics of the abortions provided for in this section as it shall deem to be in the public interest. Hospitals or clinics where abortions are performed shall be responsible for providing these statistical summary reports to the Department of Health and Human Services. The reports shall be for statistical purposes only and the confidentiality of the patient relationship shall be protected.

North Carolina Code § 130A-131.10.
Disposition of remains of pregnancies

(a) The Commission for Health Services shall adopt rules to ensure that all facilities authorized to terminate pregnancies, and all medical or research laboratories or facilities to which the remains of terminated pregnancies are sent by facilities authorized to terminate pregnancies, shall dispose of the remains in a manner limited to burial, cremation, or, except as prohibited by subsection (b) of this section, approved hospital type of incineration.

(b) A hospital or other medical facility or a medical or research laboratory or facility shall dispose of the remains of a recognizable fetus only by burial or cremation. The Commission shall adopt rules to implement this subsection.

(c) A hospital or other medical facility is relieved from the obligation to dispose of the remains in accordance with subsections (a) and (b) of this section if it sends the remains to a medical or research laboratory or facility.

(d) This section does not impose liability on a permitted medical waste treatment facility for a hospital's or other medical facility's violation of this section nor does it impose any additional duty on the treatment facility to inspect waste received from the hospital or medical facility to determine compliance with this section.

(6) ABORTION BY MINORS

Under the laws of North Carolina no physician may perform an abortion upon an unemancipated minor unless he/she first obtains the written consent of either parent or the legal guardian of the minor. In compliance with federal constitutional law, North Carolina has provided a judicial waiver procedure for an unemancipated minor to obtain an abortion without parental or guardian consent. If an unemancipated minor elects not to seek, or cannot for any reason obtain consent from either of her parents or legal guardian, the minor may petition a trial court for a waiver of the consent requirement. A minor has a right to an attorney at the proceeding and if she cannot afford one, the court must appoint her an attorney. If a minor chooses, she may represent herself. The required parental or guardian consent may be waived if the court finds either (1) that the minor is mature and well-informed enough to make the abortion decision on her own, or (2) that it would be in the minor's best interests that parental consent not be required, or (3) that the minor is a victim of rape or incest. An expedited appeal is available to any minor to whom the court denies a waiver of consent. North Carolina's abortion laws for minors were expressly upheld in *Manning v. Hunt*, 119 F.3d 254 (4th Cir. 1997). The statutes are set out below.

North Carolina Code § 90-21.6. Definitions

For the purposes of Part 2 only of this Article, unless the context clearly requires otherwise:

(1) "Unemancipated minor" or "minor" means any person under the age of 18 who has not been married or has not been emancipated pursuant to Article 35 of Chapter 7B of the General Statutes.

(2) "Abortion" means the use or prescription of any instrument, medicine, drug, or any other substance or device with intent to terminate the pregnancy of a woman known to be pregnant, for reasons other than to save the life or preserve the health of an unborn child, to remove a dead unborn child, or to deliver an unborn child prematurely, by accepted medical procedures in order to preserve the health of both the mother and the unborn child.

North Carolina Code § 90-21.7. Parental consent

(a) No physician licensed to practice medicine in North Carolina shall perform an abortion upon an unemancipated minor unless the physician or agent thereof or another physician or agent thereof first obtains the written consent of the minor and of:

(1) A parent with custody of the minor; or

(2) The legal guardian or legal custodian of the minor; or

(3) A parent with whom the minor is living; or

(4) A grandparent with whom the minor has been living for at least six months immediately preceding the date of the minor's written consent.

(b) The pregnant minor may petition, on her own behalf or by guardian ad litem, the district court judge assigned to the juvenile proceedings in the district court where the minor resides or where she is physically present for a waiver of the parental consent requirement if:

(1) None of the persons from whom consent must be obtained pursuant to this section is available to the physician performing the abortion or the physician's agent or the referring physician or the agent thereof within a reasonable time or manner; or

(2) All of the persons from whom consent must be obtained pursuant to this section refuse to consent to the performance of an abortion; or

(3) The minor elects not to seek consent of the person from whom consent is required.

North Carolina Code § 90-21.8. Judicial bypass

(a)The requirements and procedures under Part 2 of this Article are available and apply to unemancipated minors seeking treatment in this State.

(b) The court shall ensure that the minor or her guardian ad litem is given assistance in preparing and filing the petition and shall ensure that the minor's identity is kept confidential.

(c) The minor may participate in proceedings in the court on her own

behalf or through a guardian ad litem. The court shall advise her that she has a right to appointed counsel, and counsel shall be provided upon her request in accordance with rules adopted by the Office of Indigent Defense Services.

(d) Court proceedings under this section shall be confidential and shall be given precedence over other pending matters necessary to ensure that the court may reach a decision promptly. In no case shall the court fail to rule within seven days of the time of filing the application. This time limitation may be extended at the request of the minor. At the hearing, the court shall hear evidence relating to the emotional development, maturity, intellect, and understanding of the minor; the nature, possible consequences, and alternatives to the abortion; and any other evidence that the court may find useful in determining whether the parental consent requirement shall be waived.

(e) The parental consent requirement shall be waived if the court finds:

(1) That the minor is mature and well-informed enough to make the abortion decision on her own; or

(2) That it would be in the minor's best interests that parental consent not be required; or

(3) That the minor is a victim of rape or of felonious incest under G.S. 14-178.

(f) The court shall make written findings of fact and conclusions of law supporting its decision and shall order that a confidential record of the evidence be maintained. If the court finds that the minor has been a victim of incest, whether felonious or misdemeanor, it shall advise the Director of the Department of Social Services of its findings for further action pursuant to Article 3 of Chapter 7B of the General Statutes.

(g) If the female petitioner so requests in her petition, no summons or other notice may be served upon the parents, guardian, or custodian of the minor female.

(h) The minor may appeal an order issued in accordance with this section. The appeal shall be a de novo hearing in superior court. The notice of appeal shall be filed within 24 hours from the date of issuance of the district court order. The de novo hearing may be held out of district and out of session and shall be held as soon as possible within seven days of the filing of the notice of appeal. The record of the de novo hearing is a confidential record and shall not be open for general public inspection. The Chief Justice of the North Carolina Supreme Court shall adopt rules necessary to implement this subsection.

(i) No court costs shall be required of any minor who avails herself of the procedures provided by this section.

North Carolina Code § 90-21.9. Medical emergency exception

The requirements of parental consent prescribed by G.S. 90-21.7(a) shall not apply when, in the best medical judgment of the physician based on the facts of the case before the physician, a medical emergency exists that so complicates the pregnancy as to require an immediate abortion, or when the conditions prescribed by G.S. 90-21.1(4) are met.

North Carolina Code § 90-21.10. Penalty

Any person who intentionally performs an abortion with knowledge that, or with reckless disregard as to whether, the person upon whom the abortion is to be performed is an unemancipated minor, and who intentionally or knowingly fails to conform to any requirement of Part 2 of this Article shall be guilty of a Class 1 misdemeanor.

(7) INJURY TO A PREGNANT WOMAN

North Carolina provides criminal penalties for an injury to a pregnant woman that results in the death of the woman's fetus. The state specifically targets injuries received during the course of a felony offense, or during an incident of domestic violence. The statute addressing the matter is set out below.

North Carolina Code § 14-18.2. Injury to pregnant woman

(a) Definitions.— The following definitions shall apply in this section:

(1) Miscarriage.— The interruption of the normal development of the fetus, other than by a live birth, and which is not an induced abortion permitted under G.S. 14-45.1, resulting in the complete expulsion or extraction from a pregnant woman of the fetus.

(2) Stillbirth.— The death of a fetus prior to the complete expulsion or extraction from a woman irrespective of the duration of pregnancy and which is not an induced abortion permitted under G.S. 14-45.1.

(b) A person who in the commission of a felony causes injury to a woman, knowing the woman to be pregnant, which injury results in a miscarriage or stillbirth by the woman is guilty of a felony that is one class higher than the felony committed.

(c) A person who in the commission of a misdemeanor that is an act of domestic violence as defined in Chapter 50B of the General Statutes causes injury to a woman, knowing the woman to be pregnant, which results in miscarriage or stillbirth by the woman is guilty of a misdemeanor that is one class higher than the misdemeanor committed. If the offense was a Class A1 misdemeanor, the defendant is guilty of a Class I felony.

(d) This section shall not apply to acts committed by a pregnant woman which result in a miscarriage or stillbirth by the woman.

(8) BANNING ANTI-ABORTION ACTIVITY

North Carolina has responded to violent anti-abortion conduct by providing criminal penalties for unlawful conduct aimed at preventing abortions. The state protects pregnant women, their supporters, and abortion providers. A federal court upheld the constitutionality of the state's ban on anti-abortion conduct in *Hoffman v. Hunt*, 126 F.3d 575 (4th Cir. 1997). The statute addressing the matter is set out below.

North Carolina Code § 14-277.4.
Obstruction of health care facilities

(a) No person shall obstruct or block another person's access to or egress from a health care facility or from the common areas of the real property upon which the facility is located in a manner that deprives or delays the person from obtaining or providing health care services in the facility.

(b) No person shall injure or threaten to injure a person who is or has been:

(1) Obtaining health care services;

(2) Lawfully aiding another to obtain health care services; or

(3) Providing health care services.

(c) A violation of subsection (a) or (b) of this section is a Class 2 misdemeanor. A second conviction for a violation of either subsection (a) or (b) of this section within three years of the first shall be punishable as a Class 1 misdemeanor. A third or subsequent conviction for a violation of either subsection (a) or (b) of this section within three years of the second or most recent conviction shall be punishable as a Class I felony.

(d) Any person aggrieved under this section may seek injunctive relief in a court of competent jurisdiction to prevent threatened or further violations of this section. Any violation of an injunction obtained pursuant to this section constitutes criminal contempt and shall be punishable by a term of imprisonment of not less than 30 days and no more than 12 months.

(e) This section shall not prohibit any person from engaging in lawful speech or picketing which does not impede or deny another person's access to health care services or to a health care facility or interfere with the delivery of health care services within a health care facility.

(f) "Health care facility" as used in this section means any hospital, clinic, or other facility that is licensed to administer medical treatment or the primary function of which is to provide medical treatment in this State.—

(g) "Health care services" as used in this section means services provided in a health care facility.

(h) Persons subject to the prohibitions in subsection (a) of this section do not include owners, officers, agents, or employees of the health care

facility or law enforcement officers acting to protect real or personal property.

North Carolina Right to Life

North Carolina Right to Life (NCRL) is a pro-life organization that was formed in 1973. NCRL advocates public policy and legislation on both the federal and state levels to protect all human life threatened by abortion. The organization has a political action committee that supports pro-life political candidates. NCRL has also established an educational program that seeks to inform the public about the dangers of abortion and alternatives to abortion. The educational program provides the free distribution of literature, brochures, bumper stickers, lapel pins, and posters. The program also utilizes newspaper, television and radio advertisements. *See also* **Pro-Life Organizations**

North Dakota

(1) OVERVIEW

The state of North Dakota enacted its first criminal abortion statute on February 17, 1877. The statute underwent several amendments prior to the 1973 decision by the United States Supreme Court in *Roe v. Wade*, which legalized abortion in the nation. North Dakota has taken affirmative steps to respond to *Roe* and its progeny. The state has addressed several abortion issues by statute that include general abortion guidelines, informed consent, partial-birth abortion, abortion by minors, public funds for abortion, use of facilities and people, fetal death report, fetal experiments, wrongful life action, health insurance contracts, injury to a pregnant woman, and ban human cloning.

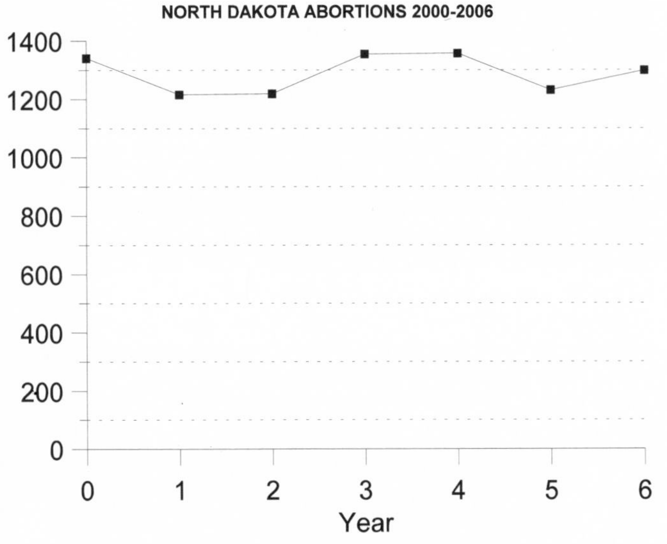

Source: **North Dakota Department of Health.**

(2) GENERAL ABORTION GUIDELINES

In 2007, North Dakota enacted a statute which, in effect, criminalizes abortion if not performed to save the life of the woman, or the pregnancy resulted from rape of a minor or incest. This statute represents an attempt to restore the state's pre–*Roe* position on abortion. Under the current decisions of the United States Supreme Court the 2007 statute is unconstitutional. Notwithstanding the 2007 statute, under the laws of North Dakota an abortion after the first trimester must occur at a hospital. However, the United States Supreme Court has held that states cannot limit the performance of pre-viability abortions to hospitals. North Dakota permits post-viability abortions only when necessary to preserve the life of the woman or when there is a substantial risk of grave impairment of the woman's physical or mental health. The state also requires two physicians concur in the opinion of the treating physician, that a post-viability abortion is necessary. The general abortion statutes are set out below.

North Dakota Abortion by Age Group 2000–2006

	Age Group (yrs)						
Year	*<15*	*15–19*	*20–24*	*25–29*	*30–34*	*35–39*	*≥40*
2000	7	290	440	274	162	128	40
2001	4	285	451	217	129	96	34
2002	5	261	469	222	132	90	40
2003	12	269	528	286	142	88	29
2004	4	271	512	289	167	86	28
2005	2	255	447	262	137	90	38
2006	5	224	497	303	139	101	29
Total	39	1,855	3,344	1,853	1,008	679	238

Source: **North Dakota Department of Health.**

North Dakota Abortion by Education Level of Female 2000–2006

	Education Level Completed			
Year	*<12*	*12*	*≥13*	*Unknown*
2000	191	560	583	7
2001	204	390	621	1
2002	188	368	650	13
2003	218	413	715	8
2004	233	419	698	7
2005	186	377	663	5
2006	185	363	634	15
Total	1,405	2,890	4,564	56

Source: **North Dakota Department of Health.**

North Dakota Prior Abortion by Female 2000–2006

	Prior Abortion					
Year	*None*	*1*	*2*	*3*	*≥4*	*Not known*
2000	593	322	265	109	51	1
2001	874	248	68	18	8	0
2002	876	247	61	23	10	2
2003	917	304	92	31	10	0
2004	963	269	90	26	9	0
2005	835	271	82	26	17	0
2006	893	268	87	38	12	0
Total	5,951	1,929	745	271	117	3

Source: **North Dakota Department of Health.**

North Dakota Code § 12.1-31-12. Abortion ban

1. As used in this section:

a. "Abortion" means the use or prescription of any substance, device, instrument, medicine, or drug to intentionally terminate the pregnancy of an individual known to be pregnant. The term does not include an act made with the intent to increase the probability of a live birth; preserve the life or health of a child after live birth; or remove a dead, unborn child who died as a result of a spontaneous miscarriage, an accidental trauma, or a criminal assault upon the pregnant female or her unborn child.

b. "Physician" means an individual licensed to practice medicine under chapter 43-17.

c. "Professional judgment" means a medical judgment that would be made by a reasonably prudent physician who is knowledgeable about the case and the treatment possibilities with respect to the medical conditions involved.

2. It is a class C felony for a person, other than the pregnant female upon whom the abortion was performed, to perform an abortion.

3. The following are affirmative defenses under this section:

a. That the abortion was necessary in professional judgment and was intended to prevent the death of the pregnant female.

b. That the abortion was to terminate a pregnancy that resulted from gross sexual imposition, sexual imposition, sexual abuse of a ward, or incest, as those offenses are defined in chapter 12.1-20.

c. That the individual was acting within the scope of that individual's regulated profession and under the direction of or at the direction of a physician.

North Dakota Code § 14-02.1-01. Purpose

The purpose of this chapter is to protect unborn human life and maternal health within present constitutional limits. It reaffirms the tradition of the state of North Dakota to protect every human life whether unborn or aged, healthy or sick.

North Dakota Code § 14-02.1-02. Definitions

As used in this chapter:

1. "Abortion" means the termination of human pregnancy with an intention other than to produce a live birth or to remove a dead embryo or fetus.

2. "Abortion facility" means a clinic, ambulatory surgical center, physician's office, or any other place or facility in which abortions are performed, other than a hospital.

3. "Hospital" means an institution licensed by the state department of health under chapter 23-16 and any hospital operated by the United States or this state.

4. "Infant born alive" or "live born child" means a born child which exhibits either heartbeat, spontaneous respiratory activity, spontaneous movement of voluntary muscles or pulsation of the umbilical cord if still attached to the child.

5. Omitted.

6. "Licensed physician" means a person who is licensed to practice medicine or osteopathy under chapter 43-17 or a physician practicing in the armed services of the United States or in the employ of the United States.

7. "Medical emergency" means that condition which, on the basis of the physician's best clinical judgment, so complicates a pregnancy as to necessitate an immediate abortion to avert the death of the mother or for which a twenty-four-hour delay will create grave peril of immediate and irreversible loss of major bodily function.

8. "Probable gestational age of the unborn child" means what, in the judgment of the attending physician, will with reasonable probability be the gestational age of the unborn child at the time the abortion is planned to be performed.

9. "Viable" means the ability of a fetus to live outside the mother's womb, albeit with artificial aid.

North Dakota Code § 14-02.1-04. Limitations on abortions

1. No abortion may be done by any person other than a licensed physician using medical standards applicable to all other surgical procedures.

2. After the first twelve weeks of pregnancy but prior to the time at which the fetus may reasonably be expected to have reached viability, no abortion may be performed in any facility other than a licensed hospital.

3. After the point in pregnancy where the fetus may reasonably be expected to have reached viability, no abortion may be performed except in a hospital, and then only if in the medical judgment of the physician the abortion is necessary to preserve the life of the woman or if in the physician's medical judgment the continuation of her pregnancy will impose on her a substantial risk of grave impairment of her physical or mental health.

An abortion under this subsection may only be performed if the

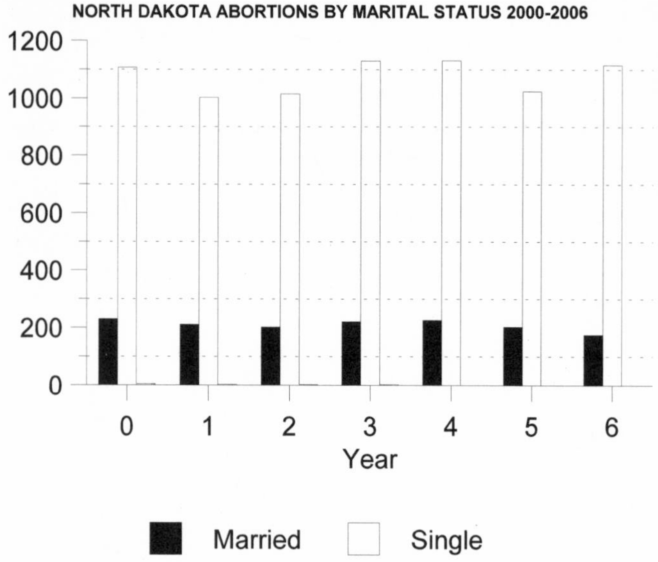

Source: North Dakota Department of Health.

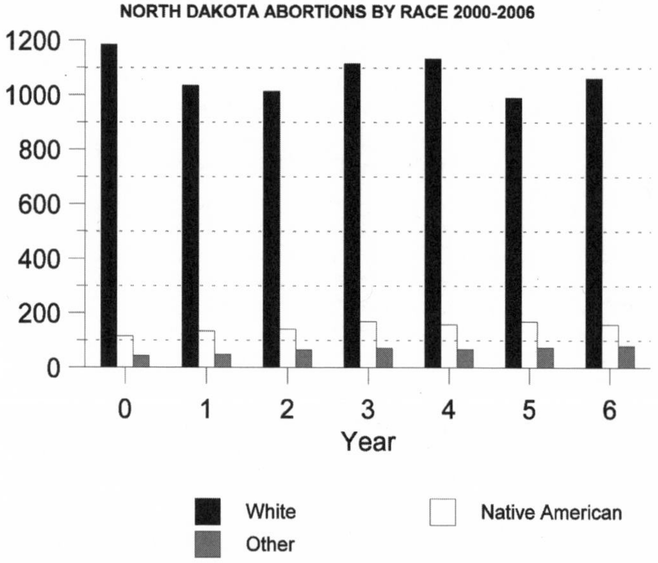

Source: North Dakota Department of Health.

North Dakota Abortion By Weeks Of Gestation 2000-2006

	Year							
Weeks of Gestation	*2000*	*2001*	*2002*	*2003*	*2004*	*2005*	*2006*	*Total*
<6	74	15	26	28	36	24	13	216
6	185	182	124	159	149	160	115	1,074
7	365	386	269	269	274	281	298	2,142
8	186	145	198	241	246	245	292	1,553
9	142	90	147	147	161	127	174	988
10	87	86	120	135	129	126	131	814
11	95	97	102	139	140	107	108	788
12	69	83	103	90	96	65	84	590
13	80	55	66	68	59	47	42	417
14	21	34	36	38	39	26	23	217
15	28	23	19	28	21	16	14	149
≥16	8	20	8	12	7	7	4	66
Not known	1	0	1	0	0	0	0	2

Source: North Dakota Department of Health.

above mentioned medical judgment of the physician who is to perform the abortion is first certified by the physician in writing, setting forth in detail the facts upon which the physician relies in making this judgment and if this judgment has been concurred in by two other licensed physicians who have examined the patient. The foregoing certification and concurrence is not required in the case of an emergency where the abortion is necessary to preserve the life of the patient.

4. Any licensed physician who performs an abortion without complying with the provisions of this section is guilty of a class A misdemeanor.

5. It is a class B felony for any person, other than a physician licensed under chapter 43-17, to perform an abortion in this state.

North Dakota Code § 14-02.1-05.
Preserving life of a viable child

An abortion of a viable child may be performed only when there is in attendance a physician other than the physician performing the abortion who shall take control and provide immediate medical care for the viable child born as a result of the abortion. The physician performing it, and subsequent to the abortion, the physician required by this section to be in attendance, shall take all reasonable steps in keeping with good medical practice, consistent with the procedure used, to preserve the life and health of the unborn child. Failure to do so is a class C felony.

North Dakota Code § 14-02.1-08. Viable fetus penalty

1. A person is guilty of a class C felony if the person knowingly, or negligently, causes the death of a viable fetus born alive.

2. Whenever a fetus which is the subject of abortion is born alive and is viable, it becomes an abandoned and deprived child, unless:

a. The termination of the pregnancy is necessary to preserve the life of the mother; or

b. The mother and her spouse, or either of them, have agreed in writing in advance of the abortion, or within seventy-two hours thereafter, to accept the parental rights and responsibilities for the fetus if it survives the abortion procedure.

North Dakota Code § 14-02.1-11. General penalty

A person violating any provision of this chapter for which another penalty is not specifically prescribed is guilty of a class A misdemeanor. Any person willfully violating a rule or regulation promulgated under this chapter is guilty of an infraction.

North Dakota Code § 14-02.1-03.2.
Civil damages for abortions without informed consent

Any person upon whom an abortion has been performed without informed consent as required by sections 14-02.1-02, 14-02.1-02.1, subsection 1 of section 14-02.1-03, 14-02.1-03.2, and 14-02.1-03.3 may maintain an action against the person who performed the abortion for ten thousand dollars in punitive damages and treble whatever actual damages the plaintiff may have sustained. Any person upon whom an abortion has been attempted without complying with sections 14-02.1-02, 14-02.1-02.1, subsection 1 of section 14-02.1-03, 14-02.1-03.2, and 14-02.1-03.3 may maintain an action against the person who attempted to perform the abortion for five thousand dollars in punitive damages and treble whatever actual damages the plaintiff may have sustained.

North Dakota Code § 14-02.1-03.3. Civil lawsuit privacy

In every proceeding or action brought under section 14-02.1-03.2, the court shall rule whether the anonymity of any woman upon whom an abortion is performed or attempted should be preserved from public disclosure if she does not give her consent to such disclosure. The court, upon motion or sua sponte, shall make such a ruling and, upon determining that her anonymity should be preserved, shall issue orders to the parties, witnesses, and counsel, and shall direct the sealing of the record and exclusion of individuals from courtrooms or hearing rooms, to the extent necessary to safeguard her identity from public disclosure. Each such order must be accompanied by specific written findings explaining why the anonymity of the woman should be preserved from public disclosure, why the order is essential to that end, how the order is narrowly tailored to serve that interest, and why no reasonable less restrictive alternative exists. This section may not be construed to conceal the identity of the plaintiff or of witnesses from the defendant.

(3) INFORMED CONSENT

Prior to an abortion North Dakota requires that a woman be fully informed of the procedure to be used, the risks involved and alternatives to abortion. The information required to be given to a woman must occur 24 hours before the abortion takes place. North Dakota requires spousal consent before a post-viability abortion may be performed. However, the United States Supreme Court held in *Planned Parenthood of Missouri v. Danforth*, that states may not require the consent of a spouse in order for a married woman to have an abortion. Although the decision in *Danforth* did not involve post-viability abortions, the opinion nevertheless probably invalidates North Dakota's spousal consent requirement. The statutes addressing the issues are set out below.

North Dakota Code § 14-02.1-03.
Consent required (abridged)

1. No physician shall perform an abortion unless prior to such performance the physician certified in writing that the woman gave her informed consent as defined and provided in section 14-02.1-02 and shall certify in writing the pregnant woman's marital status and age based upon proof of age offered by her.... None of the requirements of this subsection apply in the case of a medical emergency, except that when a medical emergency compels the performance of an abortion, the physician shall inform the woman, prior to the abortion if possible, of the medical indications supporting the physician's judgment that an abortion is necessary to avert her death or for which a twenty-four-hour delay will create grave peril of immediate and irreversible loss of major bodily function, and shall certify those indications in writing.

2. Subsequent to the period of pregnancy when the fetus may reasonably be expected to have reached viability, no abortion, other than an abortion necessary to preserve her life, or because the continuation of her pregnancy will impose on her a substantial risk of grave impairment of her physical or mental health, may be performed upon any woman in the absence of:

a. The written consent of her husband unless her husband is voluntarily separated from her[.]

3. No executive officer, administrative agency, or public employee of the state of North Dakota or any local governmental body has power to issue any order requiring an abortion, nor shall any such officer or entity coerce any woman to have an abortion, nor shall any other person coerce any woman to have an abortion.

North Dakota Code § 14-02.1-02(5).
Consent defined and waiting period

"Informed consent" means voluntary consent to abortion by the woman upon whom the abortion is to be performed provided that:

a. The woman is told the following by the physician who is to perform the abortion, by the referring physician, or by the physician's agent, at least twenty-four hours before the abortion:

(1) The name of the physician who will perform the abortion;

(2) The particular medical risks associated with the particular abortion procedure to be employed including, when medically accurate, the risks of infection, hemorrhage, danger to subsequent pregnancies, and infertility;

(3) The probable gestational age of the unborn child at the time the abortion is to be performed; and

(4) The medical risks associated with carrying her child to term.

b. The woman is informed, by the physician or the physician's agent, at least twenty-four hours before the abortion:

(1) That medical assistance benefits may be available for prenatal care, childbirth, and neonatal care;

(2) That the father is liable to assist in the support of her child, even in instances in which the father has offered to pay for the abortion; and

(3) That she has the right to review the printed materials described in section 14-02.1-02.1. The physician or the physician's agent shall orally inform the woman the materials have been provided by the state of North Dakota and that they describe the unborn child and list agencies that offer alternatives to abortion. If the woman chooses to view the materials, copies of them must be furnished to her. The physician and the physician's agent may disassociate themselves from the materials and may comment or refrain from comment on them, as they choose.

c. The woman certifies in writing, prior to the abortion, that the information described in subdivisions a and b has been furnished to her and that she has been informed of her opportunity to review the information referred to in paragraph 3 of subdivision b.

d. Prior to the performance of the abortion, the physician who is to perform or induce the abortion or the physician's agent receives a copy of the written certification prescribed by subdivision c.

North Dakota Code § 14-02.1-02.1.
Printed information

1. The state department of health shall publish in English, and in every other language that the department determines is the primary language of a significant number of state residents, the following easily comprehensible printed materials:

a. Geographically indexed materials designed to inform the woman of public and private agencies and services available to assist a woman through pregnancy, upon childbirth, and while the child is dependent, including adoption agencies. The materials must include a comprehensive list of the agencies available, a description of the services they offer and a description of the manner, including telephone numbers, in which they might be contacted, or, at the option of the department, printed materials including a toll-free, twenty-four-hour-a-day telephone number that may be called to obtain, orally, such a list and description of agencies in the locality of the caller and of the services they offer.

b. Materials, published in a booklet format, designed to inform the woman of the probable anatomical and physiological characteristics of the fetus at two-week gestational increments from the time when a woman can be known to be pregnant to full term, including any relevant information on the possibility of the survival of the fetus and pictures representing the development of a fetus at two-week gestational increments. The majority of the pictures included in the booklet must be full color photograph-style images and the pictures must contain the dimensions of the fetus and must be realistic and appropriate for the stage of pregnancy depicted. The materials must be objective, nonjudgmental, and designed to convey only accurate scientific information about the fetus at the various gestational ages. The materials required under this subsection must be reviewed, updated, and reprinted as needed.

2. The materials required under subsection 1 must be available at no cost from the state department of health upon request and in appropriate number to any person, facility, or hospital, and, except for copyrighted material, must be available on the department's internet web site. The department may make the copyrighted material available on its internet web site if the department pays the copyright royalties.

(4) PARTIAL-BIRTH ABORTION

North Dakota criminalizes partial-birth abortions, except when necessary to save the life of a woman. Until it is definitively determined by a court, North Dakota's partial-birth abortion statute may be invalid under the United States Supreme Court decision *in Stenberg v. Carhart*, which invalidated Nebraska's ban on partial-birth abortion. On the other hand, North Dakota's partial-birth abortion statute, as currently written, may be valid under the United States Supreme Court decision in *Gonzales v. Carhart*, which approved of a federal statute that bans partial-birth abortion. The North Dakota partial-birth abortion statutes are set out below.

North Dakota Code § 14-02.6-01. Definitions

As used in this chapter:

1. "Partially born" means the living intact fetus's body, with the entire head attached, is delivered so that any of the following has occurred:

a. The living intact fetus's entire head, in the case of a cephalic presentation, or any portion of the living intact fetus's torso above the navel, in the case of a breech presentation, is delivered past the mother's vaginal opening; or

b. The living intact fetus's entire head, in the case of a cephalic presentation, or any portion of the living intact fetus's torso above the navel, in the case of a breech presentation, is delivered outside the mother's abdominal wall.

2. "Sharp curettage or suction curettage abortion" means an abortion in which the developing child and products of conception are evacuated from the uterus with a sharp curettage or through a suction cannula with an attached vacuum apparatus.

North Dakota Code § 14-02.6-02.
Partial-birth abortion ban

1. Any person who intentionally causes the death of a living intact fetus while that living intact fetus is partially born is guilty of a class AA felony. A mother whose living intact fetus dies while partially born may not be prosecuted for a violation of this chapter or for conspiracy to violate this chapter.

2. This chapter does not apply to a sharp curettage or suction curettage abortion or to any offense committed under chapter 12.1-17.1 or chapter 14-02.1.

North Dakota Code § 14-02.6-03.
Exception for life of mother

Section 14-02.6-02 does not prohibit a physician from taking measures that in the physician's medical judgment are necessary to save the life of a mother whose life is endangered by a physical disorder, illness, or injury, if:

1. Every reasonable precaution is also taken, in this case, to save the child's life; and

2. The physician first certifies in writing, setting forth in detail the facts upon which the physician relies in making this judgment. This certification is not required in the case of an emergency and the procedure is necessary to preserve the life of the mother.

(5) ABORTION BY MINORS

Under the laws of North Dakota no physician may perform a pre-viability abortion upon an unemancipated minor unless he/she first obtains the written consent of both parents or the legal guardian of the minor twenty four hours before performing the abortion. In compliance with federal constitutional law, North Dakota has provided a judicial waiver procedure for an unemancipated minor to obtain an abortion without parental or guardian consent. The minor may petition a juvenile court for a waiver of the consent requirement. The required parental or guardian consent may be waived if the court finds either (1) that the minor is mature and well-informed enough to make the abortion decision on her own, or (2) that performance of the abortion would be in the best interest of the minor. An expedited appeal is available to any minor to whom the court denies a waiver of consent.

North Dakota also has a separate statute for post-viability abortions by minors. Under this law a physician must receive the consent of one parent or the legal guardian of the minor, before performing a post-viability abortion. The statutes are set out below.

North Dakota Code § 14-02.1-03.
Consent generally (abridged)

1. ... Prior to the period of pregnancy when the fetus may reasonably be expected to have reached viability, no abortion shall be performed upon an unemancipated minor unless the attending physician certifies in writing that each of the parents of the minor requesting the abortion has been provided by the physician in person with the information provided for in section 14-02.1-02 at least twenty-four hours prior to the minor's consent to the performance of abortion or unless the attending physician certifies in writing that the physician has caused materials of section 14-02.1-02 to be posted by certified mail to each of the parents of the minor separately to the last-known addresses at least forty-eight hours prior to the minor's consent to the performance of abortion. When a parent of the minor has died or rights and interests of such parent have been legally terminated, this subsection shall apply to the sole remaining parent. When both parents have died or the rights and interests of both parents have been legally terminated, this subsection shall apply to the guardian or other person standing in loco parentis. Notification by the attending physician is not required if the minor elects not to allow the notification of one or both parents or her guardian and the abortion is authorized by the juvenile court in accordance with section 14-02.1-03.1. None of the requirements of this subsection apply in the case of a medical emergency, except that when a medical emergency compels the performance of an abortion, the physician shall inform the woman, prior to the abortion if possible, of the medical indications supporting the physician's judgment that an abortion is necessary to avert her death or for which a twenty-four-hour delay will create grave peril of immediate and irreversible loss of major bodily function, and shall certify those indications in writing.

2. Subsequent to the period of pregnancy when the fetus may reasonably be expected to have reached viability, no abortion, other than an abortion necessary to preserve her life, or because the continuation of her pregnancy will impose on her a substantial risk of grave impairment of her physical or mental health, may be performed upon any woman in the absence of:

a. Omitted.

b. The written consent of a parent, if living, or the custodian or legal guardian of the woman, if the woman is unmarried and under eighteen years of age.

3. No executive officer, administrative agency, or public employee of the state of North Dakota or any local governmental body has power to issue any order requiring an abortion, nor shall any such officer or entity coerce any woman to have an abortion, nor shall any other person coerce any woman to have an abortion.

North Dakota Code § 14-02.1-03.1.
Parental consent and judicial bypass

The legislative assembly intends to encourage unmarried pregnant minors to seek the advice and counsel of their parents when faced with the difficult decision of whether or not to bear a child, to foster parental involvement in the making of that decision when parental involvement is in the best interests of the minor and to do so in a manner that does not unduly burden the right to seek an abortion.

1. No person may knowingly perform an abortion upon a pregnant woman under the age of eighteen years unless:

a. The attending physician has secured the written consent of the minor woman and both parents, if living, or the surviving parent if one parent is deceased, or the custodial parent if the parents are separated or divorced, or the legal guardian or guardians if the minor is subject to guardianship;

b. The minor woman is married and the attending physician has secured her informed written consent; or

c. The abortion has been authorized by the juvenile court in accordance with the provisions of this section.

2. Any pregnant woman under the age of eighteen or next friend is entitled to apply to the juvenile court for authorization to obtain an abortion without parental consent. Proceedings on such application must be conducted in the juvenile court of the county of the minor's residence before a juvenile judge or referee, if authorized by the juvenile court judge in accordance with the provisions of chapter 27-05, except that the parental notification requirements of chapter 27-20 are not applicable to proceedings under this section. All applications in accordance with this section must be heard by a juvenile judge or referee within forty-eight hours, excluding Saturdays and Sundays, of receipt of the application. The purpose of the hearing before the juvenile judge or referee must be to determine:

a. Whether or not the minor is sufficiently mature and well informed with regard to the nature, effects, and possible consequences of both having an abortion and bearing her child to be able to choose intelligently among the alternatives.

b. If the minor is not sufficiently mature and well informed to choose intelligently among the alternatives without the advice and counsel of her parents or guardian, whether or not it would be in the best interests of the minor to notify her parents or guardian of the proceedings and call in the parents or guardian to advise and counsel the minor and aid the court in making its determination and to assist the minor in making her decision.

c. If the minor is not sufficiently mature and well informed to choose intelligently among the alternatives and it is found not to be in the best interests of the minor to notify and call in her parents or guardian for advice and counsel, whether an abortion or some other alternative would be in the best interests of the minor.

3. All proceedings in connection with this section must be kept confidential and the identity of the minor must be protected in accordance with provisions relating to all juvenile court proceedings.

4. The court shall keep a stenographic or mechanically recorded record of the proceedings which must be maintained on record for forty-eight hours following the proceedings. If no appeal is taken from an order of the court pursuant to the proceedings, the record of the proceedings must be sealed as soon as practicable following such forty-eight-hour period.

5. Following the hearing and the court's inquiry of the minor, the court shall issue one of the following orders:

a. If the minor is sufficiently mature and well informed concerning the alternatives and without the need for further information, advice, or counseling, the court shall issue an order authorizing a competent physician to perform the abortion procedure on the minor.

b. If the minor is not sufficiently mature and well informed, the court may:

(1) Issue an order to provide the minor with any necessary information to assist her in her decision if the minor is mature enough to make the decision but not well informed enough to do so.

(2) Issue an order to notify the minor's parents or guardian of the pendency of the proceedings and calling for

their attendance at a reconvening of the hearing in order to advise and counsel the minor and assist the court in making its determination if the court finds that to do so would be in the best interests of the minor.

(3) Issue an order authorizing an abortion by a competent physician if the court has determined that it would not be in the best interests of the minor to call in her parents or guardian but has found that it would be in the minor's best interests to authorize the abortion.

6. The minor or next friend may appeal the determination of the juvenile court directly to the state supreme court. In the event of such an appeal, any and all orders of the juvenile court must be automatically stayed pending determination of the issues on appeal. Any appeal taken pursuant to this section by anyone other than the minor or next friend must be taken within forty-eight hours of the determination of the juvenile court by the filing of written notice with the juvenile court and a written application in the supreme court. Failure to file notice and application within the prescribed time results in a forfeiture of the right to appeal and render the juvenile court order or orders effective for all intents and purposes.

7. Upon receipt of written notice of appeal, the juvenile court shall immediately cause to be transmitted to the supreme court the record of proceedings had in the juvenile court.

8. An application for appeal pursuant to this section must be treated as an expedited appeal by the supreme court and must be set down for hearing within four days of receipt of the application, excluding Saturdays and Sundays.

9. The hearing, inquiry, and determination of the supreme court must be limited to a determination of the sufficiency of the inquiry and information considered by the juvenile court and whether or not the order or orders of the juvenile court accord with the information considered with respect to the maturity and information available to the minor and the best interests of the minor as determined by the juvenile court. The determination of the juvenile court may not be overturned unless found to be clearly erroneous.

10. After hearing the matter the supreme court shall issue its decision within twenty-four hours.

11. Within forty-eight hours of the hearing by the supreme court, the record of the juvenile court must be returned to the juvenile court and the juvenile court shall seal it at the earliest practicable time.

12. Nothing in this section may be construed to prevent the immediate performance of an abortion on an unmarried minor woman in an emergency where such action is necessary to preserve her life and no physician may be prevented from acting in good faith in such circumstances or made to suffer any sanction thereby other than those applicable in the normal course of events to the general review of emergency and nonemergency medical procedures.

13. Nothing in this section may be construed to alter the effects of any other section of this chapter or to expand the rights of any minor to obtain an abortion beyond the limits to such rights recognized under the Constitution of the United States or under other provisions of this code.

(6) PUBLIC FUNDS FOR ABORTION

North Dakota prohibits the use of public funds to pay for abortions, except for an abortion that is necessary to save the life of a woman. The state also prohibits the use of public funds by agencies that perform or refer persons for abortions. The state allows public funds to be used by agencies that provide alternatives to abortion. The statutes addressing the matter are set out below.

North Dakota Code § 14-02.3-01. Use of public funds

Between normal childbirth and abortion, it is the policy of the state of North Dakota that normal childbirth is to be given preference, encouragement, and support by law and by state action, it being in the best interests of the well-being and common good of North Dakota citizens.

No funds of this state or any agency, county, municipality, or any other subdivision thereof and no federal funds passing through the state treasury or a state agency may be used to pay for the performance, or for promoting the performance, of an abortion unless the abortion is necessary to prevent the death of the woman.

North Dakota Code § 14-02.3-02.
Use of public funds for family planning

No funds of this state or any agency, county, municipality, or any other subdivision thereof and no federal funds passing through the state treasury or a state agency may be used as family planning funds by any person or public or private agency which performs, refers, or encourages abortion.

North Dakota Code § 50-06-26.
Alternatives to abortion services programs

The department of human services shall disburse funds available through title IV-A of the Social Security Act [42 U.S.C. 601 et seq.] to nongovernmental entities that provide alternatives-to-abortion services and expend funds to inform the public about this program. The services must be outcome-based with positive outcome-based results. For purposes of this section, "alternatives-to-abortion services" are those services that promote childbirth instead of abortion by providing information, counseling, and support services that assist pregnant women or women who believe they may be pregnant to choose childbirth and to make informed decisions regarding the choice of adoption or parenting with respect to their children.

(7) USE OF FACILITIES AND PEOPLE

Under the laws of North Dakota hospitals are not required to allow abortions at their facilities. The employees and physicians at hospitals that do allow abortions are permitted to refuse to take part in abortions. North Dakota also prohibits the performance of abortions at state or local government hospitals, except for an abortion deemed necessary to save the life of a woman. The state prohibits school personnel from referring a student to an abortionist. The statutes addressing the matters are set out below.

North Dakota Code § 23-16-14. Participation in abortion

No hospital, physician, nurse, hospital employee, nor any other person is under any duty, by law or contract, nor may such hospital or person in any circumstances be required to participate in the performance of an abortion, if such hospital or person objects to such abortion. No such person or institution may be discriminated against because he or they so object.

North Dakota Code § 14-02.3-04.
Abortion in government hospitals

No person may authorize or perform an abortion in a hospital owned, maintained, or operated within the state by the state or any of its agencies or by any political subdivision of the state, unless the abortion is necessary to prevent the death of the woman.

North Dakota Code § 15.1-19-06. Abortion referrals

No person while acting in an official capacity as an employee or agent of a school district may refer a student to another person, agency, or entity for the purpose of obtaining an abortion. This provision does not extend to private communications between the employee or agent and a child of the employee or agent.

(8) FETAL DEATH REPORT

North Dakota requires that all abortions be reported to the proper authorities. The statutes addressing the matter are set out below.

North Dakota Code § 14-02.1-07.
Reporting of practice of abortion

1. Records:

a. All abortion facilities and hospitals in which abortions are performed shall keep records, including admission and discharge notes, histories, results of tests and examinations, nurses' worksheets, social service records, and progress notes, and shall further keep a copy of all written certifications provided for in this chapter as well as a copy of the constructive notice forms, consent forms, court orders, abortion reports, and complication reports. Records must be maintained in the permanent files of the hospital or abortion facility for a period of not less than seven years.

b. The medical records of abortion facilities and hospitals in which abortions are performed and all information contained therein must remain confidential and may be used by the state department of health only for gathering statistical data and ensuring compliance with the provisions of this chapter.

2. Reporting:

a. An individual abortion report for each abortion performed upon a woman must be completed by her attending physician. The report must be confidential and may not contain the name of the woman. This reporting must include the data called for in the United States standard report of induced termination of pregnancy as recommended by the national center for health statistics.

b. All abortion reports must be signed by the attending physician and submitted to the state department of health within thirty days from the date of the abortion. All complication reports must be signed by the physician providing the post-abortion care and submitted to the state department of health within thirty days from the date of the post-abortion care.

c. A copy of the abortion report must be made a part of the medical record of the patient at the facility or hospital in which the abortion was performed. In cases when post-abortion complications are discovered, diagnosed, or treated by physicians not associated with the facility or hospital where the abortion was performed, the state department of health shall forward a copy of the report to that facility or hospital to be made a part of the patient's permanent record.

d. The state department of health is responsible for collecting all abortion reports and complication reports and collating and evaluating all data gathered therefrom and shall annually publish a statistical report based on data from abortions performed in the previous calendar year.

e. The state department of health shall report to the attorney general any apparent violation of this chapter.

North Dakota Code § 14-02.1-07.1. Forms

The state department of health shall make available to physicians, hospitals, and all abortion facilities the forms required by this chapter.

North Dakota Code § 14-02.1-10.
Concealing stillbirth or death of infant

It is a class A misdemeanor for a person to conceal the stillbirth of a fetus or to fail to report to a physician or to the county coroner the death of an infant under two years of age.

(9) FETAL EXPERIMENTS

North Dakota has separate statutes that prohibit experiments on live and dead fetuses. Both statutes provide limited circumstances for allowing such experiments. The state also requires fetuses be disposed of humanely. The statutes are set out below.

North Dakota Code § 14-02.2-01.
Live fetal experimentation

1. A person may not use any live human fetus, whether before or after expulsion from its mother's womb, for scientific, laboratory, research, or other kind of experimentation. This section does not prohibit procedures incident to the study of a human fetus while it is in its mother's womb, provided that in the best medical judgment of the physician, made at the time of the study, the procedures do not substantially jeopardize the life or health of the fetus, and provided the fetus is not the subject of a planned abortion. In any criminal proceeding the fetus is conclusively presumed not to be the subject of a planned abortion if the mother signed a written statement at the time of the study, that the mother was not planning an abortion.

2. A person may not use a fetus or newborn child, or any tissue or organ thereof, resulting from an induced abortion in animal or human research, experimentation, or study, or for animal or human transplantation.

3. This section does not prohibit or regulate diagnostic or remedial procedures, the purpose of which is to determine the life or health of the fetus involved or to preserve the life or health of the fetus involved, or of the mother involved.

4. A fetus is a live fetus for the purposes of this section when, in the best medical judgment of a physician, it shows evidence of life as determined by the same medical standards as are used in determining evidence of life in a spontaneously aborted fetus at approximately the same stage of gestational development.

5. Any person violating this section is guilty of a class A felony.

North Dakota Code § 14-02.2-02.
Experimentation on dead fetus

1. An experimentation may not knowingly be performed upon a dead fetus resulting from an occurrence other than an induced abortion unless the consent of the mother has first been obtained; provided, however, that the consent is not required in the case of a routine pathological study. In any criminal proceeding, consent is conclusively presumed to have been granted for the purposes of this section by a written statement, signed by the mother who is at least eighteen years of age, to the effect that she consents to the use of her fetus for scientific, laboratory, research, or other kind of experimentation or study. Such written consent constitutes lawful authorization for the transfer of the dead fetus.

2. A person may not use a fetus or fetal organs or tissue resulting from an induced abortion in animal or human research, experimentation, or study, or for animal or human transplantation except for diagnostic or remedial procedures, the purpose of which is to determine the life or health of the fetus or to preserve the life or health of the fetus or mother, or pathological study.

3. A person may not perform or offer to perform an abortion where part or all of the consideration for the abortion is that the fetal organs or tissue may be used for animal or human transplantation, experimentation, or research or study.

4. A person may not knowingly sell, transfer, distribute, give away, accept, use, or attempt to use any fetus or fetal organs or tissue for a use that is in violation of this section. For purposes of this section, the word "fetus" includes also an embryo or neonate.

5. Violation of this section by any person is a class C felony.

North Dakota Code § 14-02.1-09.
Humane disposal of nonviable fetus

The licensed physician performing the abortion, if performed outside of a hospital, must see to it that the fetus is disposed of in a humane fashion under regulations established by the state department of health. A licensed hospital in which an abortion is performed must dispose of a dead fetus in a humane fashion in compliance with regulations promulgated by the state department of health.

(10) WRONGFUL LIFE ACTION

North Dakota has taken an affirmative step to prevent wrongful life litigation, by prohibiting claims for negligent failure to abort a pregnancy. The statute addressing the issue is set out below.

North Dakota Code § 32-03-43.
Wrongful life action prohibited

No person may maintain a claim for relief or receive an award for damages on that person's own behalf based on the claim that, but for the act or omission of another, that person would have been aborted. As used in this section "abortion" means the termination of human pregnancy with an intention other than to produce a live birth or to remove a dead embryo or fetus.

(11) HEALTH INSURANCE CONTRACTS

North Dakota prohibits issuance of health insurance contracts to cover abortions, unless a specific premium is charged. The statute addressing the matter is set out below.

North Dakota Code § 14-02.3-03.
Health insurance policies

No health insurance contracts, plans, or policies delivered or issued for delivery in this state may provide coverage for abortions except by an optional rider for which there must be paid an additional premium. Provided, however, that this section does not apply to the performance of an abortion necessary to prevent the death of the woman.

(12) INJURY TO A PREGNANT WOMAN

North Dakota has created a series of statutes that impose criminal penalties for injury or death to a fetus that did not result from a lawful abortion. The statutes are set out below.

North Dakota Code § 12.1-17.1-01. Definitions

As used in this chapter:

1. "Abortion" means the termination of human pregnancy with an intention other than to produce a live birth or to remove a dead embryo or fetus.

2. "Person" does not include the pregnant woman.

3. "Unborn child" means the conceived but not yet born offspring of a human being, which, but for the action of the actor would beyond a reasonable doubt have subsequently been born alive.

North Dakota Code § 12.1-17.1-02.
Murder of an unborn child

1. A person is guilty of murder of an unborn child, a class AA felony, if the person:

a. Intentionally or knowingly causes the death of an unborn child;

b. Causes the death of an unborn child under circumstances manifesting extreme indifference to the value of the life of the unborn child or the pregnant woman; or

c. Acting either alone or with one or more other persons, commits or attempts to commit treason, robbery, burglary, kidnapping, felonious restraint, arson, gross sexual imposition, or escape and, in the course of and in furtherance of such crime or of immediate flight therefrom, the person, or another participant, if any, causes the death of an unborn child; except that in any prosecution under this subsection in which the defendant was not the only participant in the underlying crime, it is an affirmative defense that the defendant:

(1) Did not commit the homicidal act or in any way solicit, command, induce, procure, counsel, or aid the commission thereof;

(2) Was not armed with a firearm, destructive device, dangerous weapon, or other weapon that under the circumstances indicated a readiness to inflict serious bodily injury;

(3) Reasonably believed that no other participant was armed with such a weapon; and

(4) Reasonably believed that no other participant intended to engage in conduct likely to result in death or serious bodily injury.

Subdivisions a and b are inapplicable in the circumstances covered by subsection 2.

2. A person is guilty of murder of an unborn child, a class A felony, if the person causes the death of an unborn child under circumstances which would be class AA murder, except that the person causes the death of the unborn child under the influence of extreme emotional disturbance for which there is reasonable excuse. The reasonableness of the excuse must be determined from the viewpoint of a person in the person's situation under the circumstances as the person believes them to be. An extreme emotional disturbance is excusable, within the meaning of this subsection only, if it is occasioned by substantial provocation or a serious event or situation for which the offender was not culpably responsible.

North Dakota Code § 12.1-17.1-03.
Manslaughter of an unborn child

A person is guilty of manslaughter of an unborn child, a class B felony, if the person recklessly causes the death of an unborn child.

North Dakota Code § 12.1-17.1-04.
Negligent homicide of an unborn child

A person is guilty of negligent homicide of an unborn child, a class C felony, if the person negligently causes the death of an unborn child.

North Dakota Code § 12.1-17.1-05.
Aggravated assault of an unborn child

A person is guilty of assault of an unborn child, a class C felony, if that person willfully assaults a pregnant woman and inflicts serious bodily injury on an unborn child.

North Dakota Code § 12.1-17.1-06.
Assault of an unborn child

A person is guilty of assault of an unborn child, a class A misdemeanor, if the person willfully assaults a pregnant woman and inflicts bodily injury on an unborn child.

North Dakota Code § 12.1-17.1-07. Exception

This chapter does not apply to acts or omissions that cause the death or injury of an unborn child if those acts or omissions are committed during an abortion performed by or under the supervision of a licensed physician to which the pregnant woman has consented, nor does it apply to acts or omissions that are committed pursuant to usual and customary standards of medical practice during diagnostic or therapeutic treatment performed by or under the supervision of a licensed physician.

(13) BAN HUMAN CLONING

North Dakota prohibits experiments designed to facilitate human cloning. The statutes addressing the matter are set out below.

North Dakota Code § 12.1-39-01. Definitions

As used in this chapter, unless the context otherwise requires:

1. "Fetus" means a living organism of the species homo sapiens from eight weeks' development until complete expulsion or extraction from a woman's body, or until removal from an artificial womb or other similar environment designed to nurture the development of such organism.

2. "Human cloning" means human asexual reproduction, accomplished by introducing the genetic material of a human somatic cell into a fertilized or unfertilized oocyte, the nucleus of which has been or will be removed or inactivated, to produce a living organism with a human or predominantly human genetic constitution.

3. "Human embryo" means a living organism of the species homo sapiens from the single-celled state to eight weeks' development.

4. "Human somatic cell" means a cell having a complete set of chromosomes obtained from a living or deceased human organism of the species homo sapiens at any stage of development.

5. "Oocyte" means a human female germ cell, also known as an egg.

North Dakota Code § 12.1-39-02. Human cloning

1. A person may not intentionally or knowingly:

a. Perform or attempt to perform human cloning;

b. Participate in performing or attempting to perform human cloning;

c. Transfer or receive the product of a human cloning for any purpose; or

d. Transfer or receive, in whole or in part, any oocyte, human embryo, human fetus, or human somatic cell, for the purpose of human cloning.

2. Nothing in subsection 1 restricts areas of scientific research not specifically prohibited, including in vitro fertilization, the administration of fertility-enhancing drugs, or research in the use of nuclear transfer or other cloning techniques to produce molecules, deoxyribonucleic acid, tissues, organs, plants, animals other than humans, or cells other than human embryos.

3. A person who violates subdivision a or b of subsection 1 is guilty of a class C felony. A person who violates subdivision c or d of subsection 1 is guilty of a class A misdemeanor.

Notre Dame Right to Life

Notre Dame Right to Life (NDRL) is a student-run pro-life organization on the campus of Notre Dame University. The purpose of the organization is to promote the sanctity of all human life from conception to natural death. The group carries out its stated purpose through prayer, education, and service. NDRL has established a service called Project MOM. Through this program NDRL collects donations and items (e.g., toys and baby clothing) that are distributed to specific pregnancy help centers for the benefit of pregnant women in need. *See also* **Pro-Life Organizations**

Nuremberg Files

Nuremberg Files was the name given to a World Wide Web page that was used to track people who were considered enemies of the anti-abortion movement. Names that appeared on the Web site included doctors, clinic workers, members of Congress, United States Supreme Court justices, and others. Visitors to the site were asked to collect personal information on the individuals listed, such as photos, home addresses, names of family members, and license plate numbers. *See also* **Abortion Violence, Property Destruction and Demonstrations**

O

Obstetric Cholestasis

Obstetric cholestasis is a liver disease that only occurs during pregnancy. The usual symptom of the disease for the mother is itching on the arms, legs, hands and feet. This condition completely disappears a few weeks before birth and does not pose any long term health problems for the mother. However, the disease may prove fatal to the infant. It is believed that the condition causes excessive bile salts in the mother's blood, and that this excess sets off a biochemical reaction in the baby that can result in stillbirth. The condition can be detected by a blood test, and medications exist to treat the condition. *See also* **Miscarriage; Stillbirth**

Obstetric Triple Screen

The obstetric triple screen involves three techniques for measuring a pregnant woman's blood to determine the potential for the fetus to have Down's syndrome, neural tube defects or other congenital problems.

Alpha-fetoprotein screening. Alpha-fetoprotein (AFP) is produced in the liver of a fetus. AFP is usually found in amniotic fluid as a result of fetal urination and in the woman's blood due to the passage across the placenta. The levels of AFP may be increased or decreased when there are certain developmental defects in the fetus. A woman's blood is tested to determine the level of AFP.

Estriol screening. Estriol is an estrogen produced by the placenta and enters a woman's blood system. The level of estriol produced is an indicator of a possible fetal defect. A woman's blood is tested to determine the level of estriol and the potential for fetal defect.

Human chorionic gonadotropin screening. Human chorionic gonadotropin (HCG) is a hormone produced by the placenta that finds its way into a woman's blood. The level of HCG produced may indicate the potential for a fetal defect. A woman's blood is tested to determine the level of HCG produced by the fetus. *See also* **Amniocentesis; Chorionic Villus Sampling; Ultrasound**

Obstetrician

An obstetrician is a physician who diagnoses and manages of all conditions occurring during pregnancy, including labor and delivery. *See also* **Gynecologist; Perinatologist; Physician Abortion Requirements**

O'Connor, Sandra Day

Sandra Day O'Connor was appointed an associate justice of the United States Supreme Court in 1981. While on the Supreme Court Justice O'Connor has displayed a moderate to conservative philosophy in her interpretation of the Constitution.

Justice O'Connor was born in El Paso, Texas on March 26, 1930. She graduated from Stanford University in 1950 and received her law degree from Stanford Law School in 1952. Her legal career included being a prosecutor, trial judge and appellate judge on the Arizona Court of Appeals. In 1981 President Ronald Reagan appointed Justice O'Connor as the first female associate justice on the Supreme Court. On January 31, 2006, Justice O'Connor retired from the Supreme Court.

During Justice O'Connor's tenure on the Supreme Court she has issued a significant number of abortion related opinions. The written opinions and opinions simply voted on by Justice O'Connor, indicate that she is hesitant in using the constitution to expand abortion rights for women.

(1) Unanimous opinions written. Justice O'Connor wrote a unanimous opinion in *Ayotte v. Planned Parenthood of Northern New England*, which held that the absence of a health exception in New Hampshire's parental notification abortion statute did not require the entire statute be invalidated.

(2) Unanimous opinions voted with only. In *Dalton v. Little Rock Family Planning Services*, Justice O'Connor voted with a unanimous Court in holding that an amendment to Arkansas' constitution which limited Medicaid payment only to therapeutic abortions, was invalid to the extent that Medicaid funds had to be made available for incest or rape pregnancies, but was valid for any purely state funded program. Justice O'Connor voted with a unanimous Supreme Court in *National Organization for Women, Inc. v. Scheidler*, which held that a group of pro-choice organizations could maintain a

RICO civil lawsuit against several anti-abortion individuals and groups.

(3) Majority opinions written. In *Planned Parenthood of Southeastern Pennsylvania v. Casey*, Justice O'Connor wrote a joint majority/plurality opinion with Justices Kennedy and Souter. The opinion held that the constitution was not violated by provisions in Pennsylvania's abortion statute that provided for: medical emergency abortion; 24 hour waiting period for abortion; parental notice and judicial bypass for abortion by a minor; and certain abortion facility reporting requirements. The decision found two provisions in the abortion statute unconstitutional: spousal notification before obtaining an abortion, and a requirement that a woman inform the abortion provider the reason for not notifying her spouse. In *Frisby v. Schultz* Justice O'Connor wrote the majority opinion, which upheld the constitutional validity of a town ordinance that was created to prevent pro-life picketing at the residence of an abortion doctor.

(4) Majority opinions voted with only. Justice O'Connor voted with the majority in *Ferguson v. City of Charleston*, in holding that patient consent or a search warrant was needed in order for a government hospital to turn over to the police drug test results that showed a woman used illegal drugs during her pregnancy. In *Hill v. Colorado* Justice O'Connor voted with the majority in upholding a Colorado statute that made it unlawful for any person within 100 feet of an abortion facility's entrance, to knowingly approach within 8 feet of another person, without that person's consent, in order to pass a leaflet, handbill, display a sign, engage in oral protest, education, or counseling with that person. Justice O'Connor voted with the majority in *Schenck v. Pro Choice Network of Western New York*, which held that a federal trial court's injunction provisions imposing fixed buffer zone limitations on abortion protesters were constitutional, but the provisions imposing floating buffer zone limitations violated the First Amendment. Justice O'Connor joined the majority opinion in *Scheidler v. National Organization for Women, Inc. (I)*, which held that evidence did not support finding that pro-life advocates violated the Hobbs Act, Travel Act and state law extortion crimes, for the purpose of awarding damages and granting an injunction against them under RICO. Justice O'Connor joined the majority opinion in *Mazurek v. Armstrong*, which held that Montana's requirement that abortions be performed only by physicians was constitutionally valid.

In *Lambert v. Wicklund* Justice O'Connor voted with the majority in holding that the constitution was not violated by a provision in Montana's abortion statute that allowed a court to waive the parental notice requirement for minors, if notification was not in minor's best interest. Justice O'Connor voted with the majority in *Leavitt v. Jane L.*, which held that the invalidity of Utah's statute regulating pregnancies 20 weeks old or less, may be severed so as to preserve that portion of the abortion statute that regulated pregnancies of more than 20 weeks. In *Madsen v. Women's Health Clinic, Inc.*, Justice O'Connor voted with the majority opinion, which upheld parts of an injunction that restricted noise by anti-abortionists at a clinic and imposed a 36 foot buffer zone around the clinic entrances and driveway. However, *Madsen* ruled that the Free Speech Clause was violated by a 36 foot buffer zone as applied to the private property to the north and west of the clinic, a restriction on the use of images observable by clinic patients, a 300 foot no approach zone around the clinic, and a 300 foot buffer zone around the residences, because these restrictions swept more broadly than necessary to accomplish the permissible goals of the injunction.

Distribution of the Abortion Voting Pattern of Justice O'Connor Based Upon Opinions Filed by the Supreme Court

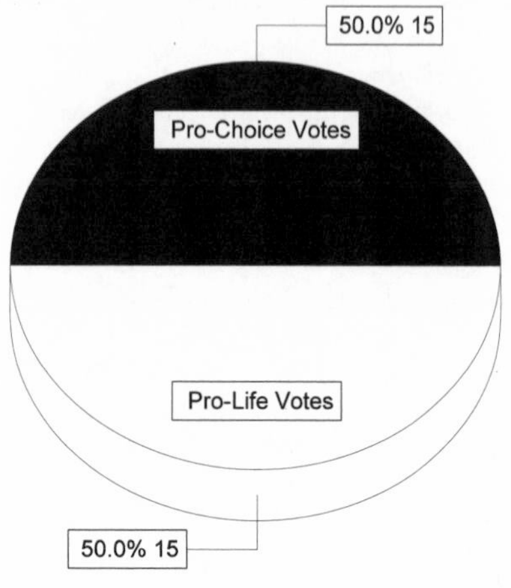

In *Daubert v. Merrell Dow Pharmaceuticals, Inc.*, a case involving children born with severe birth defects, Justice O'Connor voted with the majority in holding that the *Frye* rule on admissibility of expert testimony did not survive the enactment of the Federal Rules of Evidence. In *Automobile Workers v. Johnson Controls, Inc.* Justice O'Connor voted with the majority opinion, which held that Title VII of the Civil Rights Act forbids sex-specific fetal-protection policies by an employer, that exclude a fertile female employee from certain jobs because of the employer's concern for the health of the fetus the woman might conceive. In *Ohio v. Akron Center for Reproductive Health* Justice O'Connor voted with the majority opinion, which upheld the constitutionality of Ohio's abortion statute notice and judicial bypass requirements for pregnant female minors. Justice O'Connor voted with the majority opinion in *United States Catholic Conference v. Abortion Rights Mobilization*, which allowed the appellants to challenge having to turn over documents in a lawsuit seeking to strip them of their tax exempt status because of their active political abortion work. Justice O'Connor voted with the majority opinion in *Federal Election Commission v. Beaumont*, which held that the Federal Election Campaign Act's prohibition on corporate expenditures and contributions directly to candidates in federal elections, applies to a nonprofit pro-life organization.

(5) Concurring opinions written. In *Stenberg v. Carhart*, Justice O'Connor wrote a concurring opinion that agreed with the majority's decision to find Nebraska's statute banning partial-birth abortion unconstitutional. Justice O'Connor wrote a concurring opinion in *Hodgson v. Minnesota*, which upheld the constitutionality of Minnesota's requirement that a pregnant female minor could not obtain an abortion until at least 48 hours after both of her parents had been notified, except when (1) the attending physician certified that an immediate abortion was necessary to prevent the minor's death; (2) the minor declared that she was a victim of parental abuse or neglect; or (3) a court of competent jurisdiction ordered the abortion to proceed without notice upon proof that the minor was mature and capable of giving informed consent or that an abortion without notice to both parents would be in the minor's best interest.

Justice O'Connor wrote a concurring opinion in *Webster v. Reproductive Health Services*, which upheld Missouri's prohibition on the use of public facilities or employees to perform abortions and a requirement that physicians conduct viability tests prior to performing abortions. In *Federal Election Commission v. Massachusetts Citizens for Life, Inc.* Justice O'Connor wrote an opinion concurring with the majority decision, which held that federal law that prohibited the appellee from using its treasury funds to promote pro-life political candidates violated the Free Speech Clause of the First Amendment. In *Diamond v. Charles*, Justice O'Connor wrote an opinion concurring in the judgment of the Supreme Court, which held that a citizen did not have standing to appeal a decision invalidating parts of Illinois' abortion statute that (1) imposed criminal penalties for violating a prescribed standard of care that had to be exercised by a physician in performing an abortion of a viable fetus, and of a possibly viable fetus; and (2) imposed criminal penalties for physicians who failed to provide patients with information about the type of abortifacient used. Justice O'Connor wrote an opinion concurring with the majority decision in *Simopoulos v. Virginia*, which upheld a Virginia statute requiring second trimester abortions be performed at hospitals, because under the statute an adequately equipped clinic could, upon proper application, obtain an outpatient hospital license that permitted the performance of second-trimester abortions.

(6) Concurring opinions voted with only. Justice O'Connor concurred with the majority opinion in *Bolger v. Youngs Drug Products Corp.*, which held that a provision of the Comstock Act, 39 U.S.C. § 3001(e)(2), that prohibited mailing unsolicited advertisements for contraceptives violated the Free Speech Clause of the First Amendment.

(7) Dissenting opinions written. Justice O'Connor wrote a dissenting opinion in *Bray v. Alexandria Clinic*, which held that the Civil Rights Act of 1871, 42 U.S.C. § 1985(3), did not provide a cause of action against persons obstructing access to abortion clinics. She argued that the statute could be used by abortionists. Justice O'Connor wrote a dissenting opinion in *Rust v. Sullivan*, which upheld federal regulations that prohibited pro-abortion counseling, referral, and advocacy by health care providers. Justice O'Connor wrote a dissenting opinion in *Thornburgh v. American College of Obstetricians and Gynecologists*, which invalidated provisions in Pennsylvania's abortion statute that provided for maternal informed consent, abortion alternative printed information, abortion reporting requirements, determination of fetal viability, degree of care required in post-viability abortions, and a second-physician requirement. Justice O'Connor wrote an opinion dissenting from the majority opinion in *City of Akron v. Akron Center for Reproductive Health, Inc.*, which invalidated an abortion ordinance that provided requirements for parental consent, informed consent, waiting period, hospitalization and disposal of fetal remains.

(8) Concurring and dissenting opinions written. In *Planned Parenthood Assn. v. Ashcroft* Justice O'Connor wrote an opinion concurring and dissenting from the majority/plurality opinion, which held that the constitution was violated by Missouri's requirement that second trimester abortions take place in a hospital; but that the constitution was not violated by the state's requirement that a pathology report for each abortion be performed, that a second physician be present during abortions performed after viability, and parental or judicial consent for abortion by minors. Justice O'Connor believed that all of the provisions of the statute were constitutional.

Octoxynol-9 *see* **Spermicides**

Ohio

(1) Overview

The state of Ohio enacted its first criminal abortion statute on February 17, 1834. The statute underwent several amendments prior to the 1973 decision by the United States Supreme Court in *Roe v. Wade*, which legalized abortion in the nation. Ohio has taken affirmative steps to respond to *Roe* and its progeny. The state has addressed several abortion issues by statute that include general abortion guidelines, informed consent, abortion by minors, partial-birth abortion, use of facilities and people, use of public funds, fetal experiments, use of mifepristone, wrongful life action, fetal death report, injury to a pregnant woman, and choose life license plate.

(2) General Abortion Guidelines

Ohio prohibits post-viability abortions, except to preserve the life or health of the woman. A physician, other than the woman's treating physician, must agree that an exception exists for allowing a post-viability abortion. It is required by Ohio that a woman who is more than 22 weeks pregnant must, before obtaining an abortion, undergo testing for fetal viability. A federal court determined in *Women's Medical Professional Corp. v. Voinovich*, 130 F.3d 187 (6th Cir. 1997), that the state's viability testing requirement was unconstitutional. The general abortion statutes are set out below.

Ohio Code § 9.041.
Policy regarding childbirth

It is the public policy of the state of Ohio to prefer childbirth over abortion to the extent that is constitutionally permissible.

Ohio Code § 2701.15.
Court may not order an abortion

No person shall be ordered by a court to submit to an abortion.

Ohio Code § 5101.55.
Public agency may not force abortion (abridged)

(A) No person shall be ordered by a public agency or any person to submit to an abortion.

(B) The refusal of any person to submit to an abortion or to give consent therefor shall not result in the loss of public assistance benefits or any other rights or privileges.

Ohio Code § 3701.341.
Rules relating to abortions

(A) The public health council, pursuant to Chapter 119. and consistent with section 2317.56 of the Revised Code, shall adopt rules relating to abortions and the following subjects:

(1) Post-abortion procedures to protect the health of the pregnant woman;
(2) Pathological reports;
(3) Humane disposition of the product of human conception;
(4) Counseling.

(B) The director of health shall implement the rules and shall apply to the court of common pleas for temporary or permanent injunctions restraining a violation or threatened violation of the rules. This action is an additional remedy not dependent on the adequacy of the remedy at law.

Ohio Code § 2919.11. Abortion defined

As used in the Revised Code, "abortion" means the purposeful termination of a human pregnancy by any person, including the pregnant

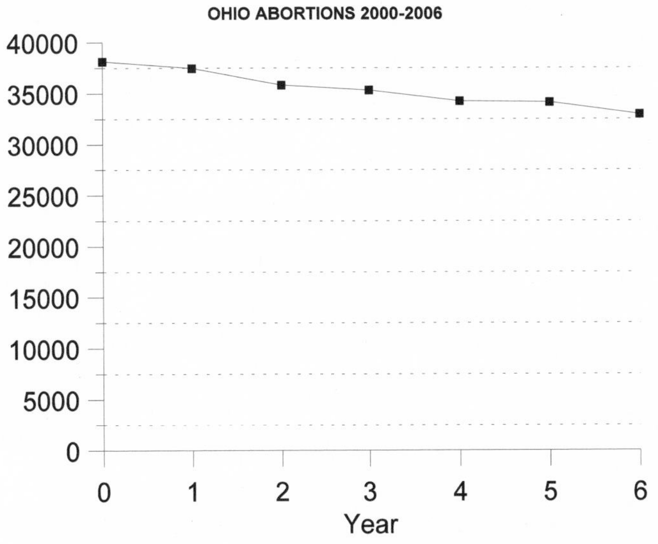

Source: **Ohio Department of Health.**

woman herself, with an intention other than to produce a live birth or to remove a dead fetus or embryo. Abortion is the practice of medicine or surgery for the purposes of section 4731.41 of the Revised Code.

Ohio Code § 2919.13. Abortion manslaughter

(A) No person shall purposely take the life of a child born by attempted abortion who is alive when removed from the uterus of the pregnant woman.

(B) No person who performs an abortion shall fail to take the measures required by the exercise of medical judgment in light of the attending circumstances to preserve the life of a child who is alive when removed from the uterus of the pregnant woman.

(C) Whoever violates this section is guilty of abortion manslaughter, a felony of the first degree.

Ohio Abortion by Age Group 2000–2006

	Age Group (yrs)								
Year	*<15*	*15–19*	*20–24*	*25–29*	*30–34*	*35–39*	*40–44*	*≥45*	*Unknown*
2000	314	6,860	13,029	8,885	5,073	2,957	948	53	21
2001	286	6,485	12,710	8,531	5,299	2,956	1,064	114	19
2002	277	6,098	12,370	7,984	5,205	2,775	906	61	154
2003	292	6,014	12,441	7,836	4,980	2,660	938	55	103
2004	253	5,911	11,772	7,655	4,875	2,589	910	68	209
2005	240	5,817	11,502	7,968	4,687	2,708	874	73	259
2006	292	5,603	11,123	7,720	4,333	2,741	845	53	226
Total	1,954	42,788	84,947	56,579	34,452	19,386	6,485	477	991

Source: Ohio Department of Health.

Ohio Abortion by Education Level of Female 2000–2006

	Education Level Completed			
Year	*<9*	*9–12*	*≥13*	*Unknown*
2000	612	24,281	12,823	424
2001	797	23,834	12,593	240
2002	755	22,742	11,893	440
2003	756	22,359	11,924	280
2004	675	21,222	11,763	582
2005	653	20,911	11,810	754
2006	662	20,515	11,064	695
Total	4,910	155,864	83,870	3,415

Source: Ohio Department of Health.

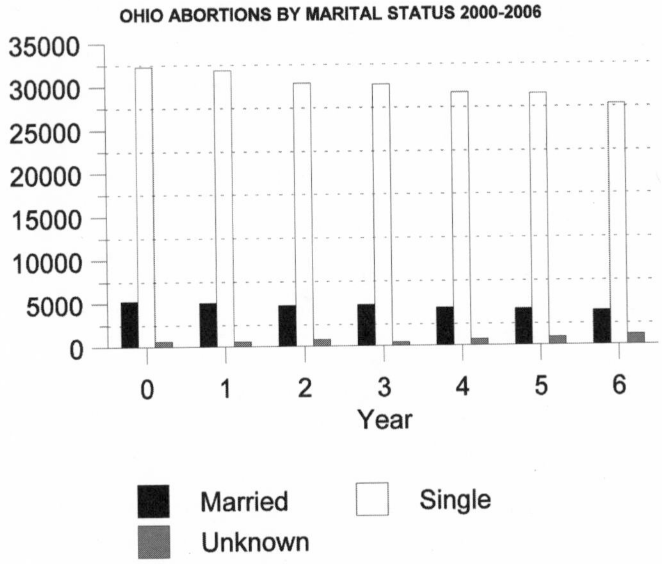

Source: Ohio Department of Health.

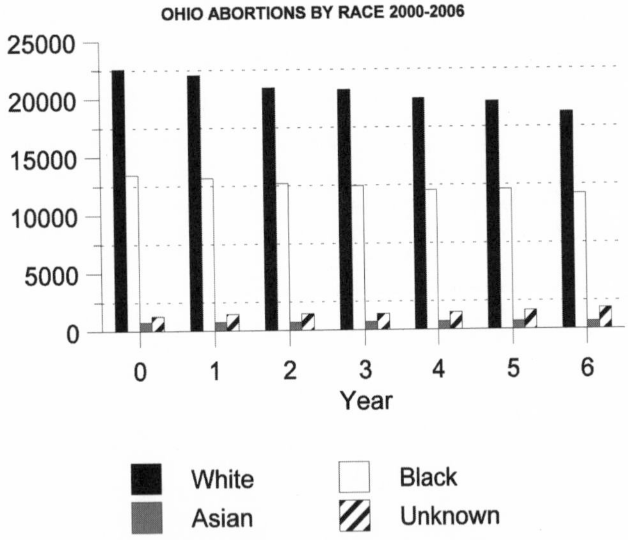

Source: Ohio Department of Health.

Ohio Resident Prior Abortion by Female 2001–2006

	Prior Abortion						
Year	*None*	*1*	*2*	*3*	*4*	*≥5*	*Not known*
2001	13,260	9,179	3,563	1,330	510	455	5,877
2002	14,335	8,481	3,535	1,328	548	439	4,021
2003	11,827	8,363	3,398	1,281	555	470	6,286
2004	11,737	8,271	3,337	1,279	487	372	5,908
2005	11,824	8,125	3,538	1,301	522	388	5,512
2006	14,733	7,963	3,352	1,243	454	372	2,692
Total	77,716	50,382	20,723	7,762	3,076	2,496	30,296

Source: Ohio Department of Health.

Ohio Code § 2919.16. Definitions

As used in sections 2919.16 to 2919.18 of the Revised Code:

(A) "Fertilization" means the fusion of a human spermatozoon with a human ovum.

(B) "Gestational age" means the age of an unborn human as calculated from the first day of the last menstrual period of a pregnant woman.

(C) "Health care facility" means a hospital, clinic, ambulatory surgical treatment center, other center, medical school, office of a physician, infirmary, dispensary, medical training institution, or other institution or location in or at which medical care, treatment, or diagnosis is provided to a person.

(D) "Hospital" has the same meanings as in sections 2108.01, 3701.01, and 5122.01 of the Revised Code.

Ohio Abortion by Weeks of Gestation 2000–2006

	Year							
Weeks of Gestation	*2000*	*2001*	*2002*	*2003*	*2004*	*2005*	*2006*	*Total*
<9	20,161	20,432	19,755	19,610	19,933	19,549	17,955	137,395
9–12	12,293	11,350	10,820	10,570	9,489	9,547	9,862	73,931
13–19	4,772	4,738	4,271	4,133	3,944	4,006	3,963	29,827
≥20	906	921	929	961	731	793	694	5,935

Source: Ohio Department of Health.

(E) "Live birth" has the same meaning as in division (A) of section 3705.01 of the Revised Code.

(F) "Medical emergency" means a condition that a pregnant woman's physician determines, in good faith and in the exercise of reasonable medical judgment, so complicates the woman's pregnancy as to necessitate the immediate performance or inducement of an abortion in order to prevent the death of the pregnant woman or to avoid a serious risk of the substantial and irreversible impairment of a major bodily function of the pregnant woman that delay in the performance or inducement of the abortion would create.

(G) "Physician" has the same meaning as in section 2305.113 of the Revised Code.

(H) "Pregnant" means the human female reproductive condition, that commences with fertilization, of having a developing fetus.

(I) "Premature infant" means a human whose live birth occurs prior to thirty-eight weeks of gestational age.

(J) "Serious risk of the substantial and irreversible impairment of a major bodily function" means any medically diagnosed condition that so complicates the pregnancy of the woman as to directly or indirectly cause the substantial and irreversible impairment of a major bodily function, including, but not limited to, the following conditions:

(1) Pre-eclampsia;

(2) Inevitable abortion;

(3) Prematurely ruptured membrane;

(4) Diabetes;

(5) Multiple sclerosis.

(K) "Unborn human" means an individual organism of the species homo sapiens from fertilization until live birth.

(L) "Viable" means the stage of development of a human fetus at which in the determination of a physician, based on the particular facts of a woman's pregnancy that are known to the physician and in light of medical technology and information reasonably available to the physician, there is a realistic possibility of the maintaining and nourishing of a life outside of the womb with or without temporary artificial life-sustaining support.

Ohio Code § 2919.17.
Terminating a human pregnancy after viability

(A) No person shall purposely perform or induce or attempt to perform or induce an abortion upon a pregnant woman if the unborn human is viable, unless either of the following applies:

(1) The abortion is performed or induced or attempted to be performed or induced by a physician, and that physician determines, in good faith and in the exercise of reasonable medical judgment, that the abortion is necessary to prevent the death of the pregnant woman or a serious risk of the substantial and irreversible impairment of a major bodily function of the pregnant woman.

(2) The abortion is performed or induced or attempted to be performed or induced by a physician and that physician determines, in good faith and in the exercise of reasonable medical judgment, after making a determination relative to the viability of the unborn human in conformity with division (a) of section 2919.18 of the Revised Code, that the unborn human is not viable.

(B)(1) Except as provided in division (B)(2) of this section, no physician shall purposely perform or induce or attempt to perform or induce an abortion upon a pregnant woman when the unborn human is viable and when the physician has determined, in good faith and in the exercise of reasonable medical judgment, that the abortion is necessary to prevent the death of the pregnant woman or a serious risk of the substantial and irreversible impairment of a major bodily function of the pregnant woman, unless each of the following conditions is satisfied:

(a) The physician who performs or induces or attempts to perform or induce the abortion certifies in writing that that physician has determined, in good faith and in the exercise of reasonable medical judgment, that the abortion is necessary to prevent the death of the pregnant woman or a serious risk of the substantial and irreversible impairment of a major bodily function of the pregnant woman.

(b) The determination of the physician who performs or induces or attempts to perform or induce the abortion that is described in division (B)(1)(a) of this section is concurred in by at least one other physician who certifies in writing that the concurring physician has determined, in good faith, in the exercise of reasonable medical judgment, and following a review of the available medical records of and any available tests results pertaining to the pregnant woman, that the abortion is necessary to prevent the death of the pregnant woman or a serious risk of the substantial and irreversible impairment of a major bodily function of the pregnant woman.

(c) The abortion is performed or induced or attempted to be performed or induced in a health care facility that has or has access to appropriate neonatal services for premature infants.

(d) The physician who performs or induces or attempts to perform or induce the abortion terminates or attempts to terminate the pregnancy in the manner that provides the best opportunity for the unborn human to survive, unless that physician determines, in good faith and in the exercise of reasonable medical judgment, that the termination of the pregnancy in that manner poses a significantly greater risk of the death of the pregnant woman or a serious risk of the substantial and irreversible impairment of a major bodily function of the pregnant woman than would other available methods of abortion.

(e) The physician who performs or induces or attempts to perform or induce the abortion has arranged for the attendance in the same room in which the abortion is to be performed or induced or attempted to be performed or induced of at least one other physician who is to take control of, provide immediate medical care for, and take all reasonable steps necessary to preserve the life and health of the unborn human immediately upon the unborn human's complete expulsion or extraction from the pregnant woman.

(2) Division (B)(1) of this section does not prohibit the performance or inducement or an attempted performance or inducement of an abortion without prior satisfaction of each of the conditions described in divisions (B)(1)(a) to (e) of this section if the physician who performs or induces or attempts to perform or induce the abortion determines, in good faith and in the exercise of reasonable medical judgment, that a medical emergency exists that prevents compliance with one or more of those conditions.

(C) For purposes of this section, it shall be rebuttably presumed that an unborn child of at least twenty-four weeks of gestational age is viable.

(D) Whoever violates this section is guilty of terminating or attempting to terminate a human pregnancy after viability, a felony of the fourth degree.

(E) A pregnant woman upon whom an abortion is performed or induced or attempted to be performed or induced in violation of division (A) or (B) of this section is not guilty of an attempt to commit, complicity in the commission of, or conspiracy in the commission of a violation of either of those divisions.

Ohio Code § 2919.18 Viability testing

(A)(1) Except as provided in division (A)(3) of this section, no physician shall perform or induce or attempt to perform or induce an abor-

tion upon a pregnant woman after the beginning of her twenty-second week of pregnancy unless, prior to the performance or inducement of the abortion or the attempt to perform or induce the abortion, the physician determines, in good faith and in the exercise of reasonable medical judgment, that the unborn human is not viable, and the physician makes that determination after performing a medical examination of the pregnant woman and after performing or causing the performing of gestational age, weight, lung maturity, or other tests of the unborn human that a reasonable physician making a determination as to whether an unborn human is or is not viable would perform or cause to be performed.

(2) Except as provided in division (A)(3) of this section, no physician shall perform or induce or attempt to perform or induce an abortion upon a pregnant woman after the beginning of her twenty-second week of pregnancy without first entering the determination described in division (A)(1) of this section and the associated findings of the medical examination and tests described in that division in the medical record of the pregnant woman.

(3) Divisions (A)(1) and (2) of this section do not prohibit a physician from performing or inducing or attempting to perform or induce an abortion upon a pregnant woman after the beginning of her twenty-second week of pregnancy without making the determination described in division (A)(1) of this section or without making the entry described in division (A)(2) of this section if a medical emergency exists.

(B) Whoever violates this section is guilty of failure to perform viability testing, a misdemeanor of the fourth degree.

Ohio Code § 2307.52.
Lawsuit for terminating pregnancy after viability

(A) As used in this section:

(1) "Frivolous conduct" has the same meaning as in section 2323.51 of the Revised Code.

(2) "Viable" has the same meaning as in section 2919.16 of the Revised Code.

(B)(1) A woman upon whom an abortion is purposely performed or induced or attempted to be performed or induced in violation of division (A) of section 2919.17 of the Revised Code has and may commence a civil action for compensatory damages, punitive or exemplary damages if authorized by section 2315.21 of the Revised Code, and court costs and reasonable attorney's fees against the person who purposely performed or induced or attempted to perform or induce the abortion in violation of division (A) of section 2919.17 of the Revised Code.

(2) A woman upon whom an abortion is purposely performed or induced or attempted to be performed or induced in violation of division (B) of section 2919.17 of the Revised Code has and may commence a civil action for compensatory damages, punitive or exemplary damages if authorized by section 2315.21 of the Revised Code, and court costs and reasonable attorney's fees against the person who purposely performed or induced or attempted to perform or induce the abortion in violation of division (B) of section 2919.17 of the Revised Code.

(C) If a judgment is rendered in favor of the defendant in a civil action commenced pursuant to division (B)(1) or (2) of this section and the court finds, upon the filing of a motion under section 2323.51 of the Revised Code, that the commencement of the civil action constitutes frivolous conduct and that the defendant was adversely affected by the frivolous conduct, the court shall award in accordance with section 2323.51 of the Revised Code reasonable attorney's fees to the defendant.

Ohio Code § 2305.11(B).
Time limitations for bringing abortion actions

A civil action for unlawful abortion pursuant to section 2919.12 of the Revised Code, a civil action authorized by division (H) of section 2317.56 of the Revised Code, a civil action pursuant to division (B)(1) or (2) of section 2307.51 of the Revised Code [repealed] for performing a dilation and extraction procedure or attempting to perform a dilation and extraction procedure in violation of section 2919.15 of the Revised Code, and a civil action pursuant to division (B)(1) or (2) of section 2307.52 of the Revised Code for terminating or attempting to terminate a human pregnancy after viability in violation of division (A) or (B) of section 2919.17 of the Revised Code shall be commenced within one year after the performance or inducement of the abortion, within one year after the attempt to perform or induce the abortion in violation of division (A) or (B) of section 2919.17 of the Revised Code, within one year after the performance of the dilation and extraction procedure, or, in the case of a civil action pursuant to division (B)(2) of section 2307.51 of the Revised Code, within one year after the attempt to perform the dilation and extraction procedure.

(3) INFORMED CONSENT

Prior to an abortion Ohio requires that a woman be fully informed of the procedure to be used, the risks involved and alternatives to abortion. An abortion may not take place until 24 hours after a woman has been fully informed of statutorily required information. The informed consent laws were upheld in *Cincinnati Women's Services, Inc. v. Taft*, 468 F.3d 361 (6th Cir. 2006). The statutes addressing the matter are set out below.

Ohio Code § 2317.56. Consent and waiting period

(A) As used in this section:

(1) "Medical emergency" means a condition of a pregnant woman that, in the reasonable judgment of the physician who is attending the woman, creates an immediate threat of serious risk to the life or physical health of the woman from the continuation of the pregnancy necessitating the immediate performance or inducement of an abortion.

(2) "Medical necessity" means a medical condition of a pregnant woman that, in the reasonable judgment of the physician who is attending the woman, so complicates the pregnancy that it necessitates the immediate performance or inducement of an abortion.

(3) "Probable gestational age of the embryo or fetus" means the gestational age that, in the judgment of a physician, is, with reasonable probability, the gestational age of the embryo or fetus at the time that the physician informs a pregnant woman pursuant to division (B)(1)(b) of this section.

(B) Except when there is a medical emergency or medical necessity, an abortion shall be performed or induced only if all of the following conditions are satisfied:

(1) At least twenty-four hours prior to the performance or inducement of the abortion, a physician meets with the pregnant woman in person in an individual, private setting and gives her an adequate opportunity to ask questions about the abortion that will be performed or induced. At this meeting, the physician shall inform the pregnant woman, verbally or, if she is hearing impaired, by other means of communication, of all of the following:

(a) The nature and purpose of the particular abortion procedure to be used and the medical risks associated with that procedure;

(b) The probable gestational age of the embryo or fetus;

(c) The medical risks associated with the pregnant woman carrying the pregnancy to term.

The meeting need not occur at the facility where the abortion is to be performed or induced, and the physician involved in the meeting need not be affiliated with that facility or with the physician who is scheduled to perform or induce the abortion.

(2) At least twenty-four hours prior to the performance or inducement of the abortion, one or more physicians or one or more agents

of one or more physicians do each of the following in person, by telephone, by certified mail, return receipt requested, or by regular mail evidenced by a certificate of mailing:

(a) Inform the pregnant woman of the name of the physician who is scheduled to perform or induce the abortion;

(b) Give the pregnant woman copies of the published materials described in division (C) of this section;

(c) Inform the pregnant woman that the materials given pursuant to division (B)(2)(b) of this section are provided by the state and that they describe the embryo or fetus and list agencies that offer alternatives to abortion. The pregnant woman may choose to examine or not to examine the materials. A physician or an agent of a physician may choose to be disassociated from the materials and may choose to comment or not comment on the materials.

(3) Prior to the performance or inducement of the abortion, the pregnant woman signs a form consenting to the abortion and certifies both of the following on that form:

(a) She has received the information and materials described in divisions (B)(1) and (2) of this section, and her questions about the abortion that will be performed or induced have been answered in a satisfactory manner.

(b) She consents to the particular abortion voluntarily, knowingly, intelligently, and without coercion by any person, and she is not under the influence of any drug of abuse or alcohol.

(4) Prior to the performance or inducement of the abortion, the physician who is scheduled to perform or induce the abortion or the physician's agent receives a copy of the pregnant woman's signed form on which she consents to the abortion and that includes the certification required by division (B)(3) of this section.

(C) The department of health shall cause to be published in English and in Spanish, in a typeface large enough to be clearly legible, and in an easily comprehensible format, the following materials:

(1) Materials that inform the pregnant woman about family planning information, of publicly funded agencies that are available to assist in family planning, and of public and private agencies and services that are available to assist her through the pregnancy, upon childbirth, and while the child is dependent, including, but not limited to, adoption agencies. The materials shall be geographically indexed; include a comprehensive list of the available agencies, a description of the services offered by the agencies, and the telephone numbers and addresses of the agencies; and inform the pregnant woman about available medical assistance benefits for prenatal care, childbirth, and neonatal care and about the support obligations of the father of a child who is born alive. The department shall ensure that the materials described in division (C)(1) of this section are comprehensive and do not directly or indirectly promote, exclude, or discourage the use of any agency or service described in this division.

(2) Materials that inform the pregnant woman of the probable anatomical and physiological characteristics of the zygote, blastocyte, embryo, or fetus at two-week gestational increments for the first sixteen weeks of pregnancy and at four-week gestational increments from the seventeenth week of pregnancy to full term, including any relevant information regarding the time at which the fetus possibly would be viable. The department shall cause these materials to be published only after it consults with the Ohio state medical association and the Ohio section of the American college of obstetricians and gynecologists relative to the probable anatomical and physiological characteristics of a zygote, blastocyte, embryo, or fetus at the various gestational increments. The materials shall use language that is understandable by the average person who is not medically trained, shall be objective and nonjudgmental, and shall include only accurate scientific information about the zygote, blastocyte, embryo, or fetus at the various gestational increments. If the materials use a pictorial, photographic, or other depiction to provide information regarding the zygote, blastocyte, embryo, or fetus, the materials shall include, in a conspicuous manner, a scale or other explanation that is understandable by the average person and that can be used to determine the actual size of the zygote, blastocyte, embryo, or fetus at a particular gestational increment as contrasted with the depicted size of the zygote, blastocyte, embryo, or fetus at that gestational increment.

(D) Upon the submission of a request to the department of health by any person, hospital, physician, or medical facility for one or more copies of the materials published in accordance with division (C) of this section, the department shall make the requested number of copies of the materials available to the person, hospital, physician, or medical facility that requested the copies.

(E) If a medical emergency or medical necessity compels the performance or inducement of an abortion, the physician who will perform or induce the abortion, prior to its performance or inducement if possible, shall inform the pregnant woman of the medical indications supporting the physician's judgment that an immediate abortion is necessary. Any physician who performs or induces an abortion without the prior satisfaction of the conditions specified in division (B) of this section because of a medical emergency or medical necessity shall enter the reasons for the conclusion that a medical emergency or medical necessity exists in the medical record of the pregnant woman.

(F) If the conditions specified in division (B) of this section are satisfied, consent to an abortion shall be presumed to be valid and effective.

(G) The performance or inducement of an abortion without the prior satisfaction of the conditions specified in division (B) of this section does not constitute, and shall not be construed as constituting, a violation of division (A) of section 2919.12 of the Revised Code. The failure of a physician to satisfy the conditions of division (B) of this section prior to performing or inducing an abortion upon a pregnant woman may be the basis of both of the following:

(1) A civil action for compensatory and exemplary damages as described in division (H) of this section;

(2) Disciplinary action under section 4731.22 of the Revised Code.

(H)(1) Subject to divisions (H)(2) and (3) of this section, any physician who performs or induces an abortion with actual knowledge that the conditions specified in division (B) of this section have not been satisfied or with a heedless indifference as to whether those conditions have been satisfied is liable in compensatory and exemplary damages in a civil action to any person, or the representative of the estate of any person, who sustains injury, death, or loss to person or property as a result of the failure to satisfy those conditions. In the civil action, the court additionally may enter any injunctive or other equitable relief that it considers appropriate.

(2) The following shall be affirmative defenses in a civil action authorized by division (H)(1) of this section:

(a) The physician performed or induced the abortion under the circumstances described in division (E) of this section.

(b) The physician made a good faith effort to satisfy the conditions specified in division (B) of this section.

(c) The physician or an agent of the physician requested copies of the materials published in accordance with division (C) of this section from the department of health, but the physician was not able to give a pregnant woman copies of the materials pursuant to division (B)(2) of this section and to obtain a certification as described in divisions (B)(3) and (4) of this section because the department failed to make the requested number of copies available to the physician or agent in accordance with division (D) of this section.

(3) An employer or other principal is not liable in damages in a civil action authorized by division (H)(1) of this section on the basis of the doctrine of respondeat superior unless either of the following applies:

(a) The employer or other principal had actual knowledge or, by the exercise of reasonable diligence, should have known that an employee or agent performed or induced an abortion with actual knowledge that the conditions specified in division (B) of this section had not been satisfied or with a heedless indifference as to whether those conditions had been satisfied.

(b) The employer or other principal negligently failed to secure the compliance of an employee or agent with division (B) of this section.

(4) Notwithstanding division (E) of section 2919.12 of the Revised Code, the civil action authorized by division (H)(1) of this section shall be the exclusive civil remedy for persons, or the representatives of estates of persons, who allegedly sustain injury, death, or loss to person or property as a result of a failure to satisfy the conditions specified in division (B) of this section.

(I) The department of job and family services shall prepare and conduct a public information program to inform women of all available governmental programs and agencies that provide services or assistance for family planning, prenatal care, child care, or alternatives to abortion.

Ohio Code § 2317.54. Health care facility liability precluded

No hospital, home health agency, ambulatory surgical facility, or provider of a hospice care program shall be held liable for a physician's failure to obtain an informed consent from the physician's patient prior to a surgical or medical procedure or course of procedures, unless the physician is an employee of the hospital, home health agency, ambulatory surgical facility, or provider of a hospice care program.

Written consent to a surgical or medical procedure or course of procedures shall, to the extent that it fulfills all the requirements in divisions (A), (B), and (C) of this section, be presumed to be valid and effective, in the absence of proof by a preponderance of the evidence that the person who sought such consent was not acting in good faith, or that the execution of the consent was induced by fraudulent misrepresentation of material facts, or that the person executing the consent was not able to communicate effectively in spoken and written English or any other language in which the consent is written. Except as herein provided, no evidence shall be admissible to impeach, modify, or limit the authorization for performance of the procedure or procedures set forth in such written consent.

(A) The consent sets forth in general terms the nature and purpose of the procedure or procedures, and what the procedures are expected to accomplish, together with the reasonably known risks, and, except in emergency situations, sets forth the names of the physicians who shall perform the intended surgical procedures.

(B) The person making the consent acknowledges that such disclosure of information has been made and that all questions asked about the procedure or procedures have been answered in a satisfactory manner.

(C) The consent is signed by the patient for whom the procedure is to be performed, or, if the patient for any reason including, but not limited to, competence, infancy, or the fact that, at the latest time that the consent is needed, the patient is under the influence of alcohol, hallucinogens, or drugs, lacks legal capacity to consent, by a person who has legal authority to consent on behalf of such patient in such circumstances.

Any use of a consent form that fulfills the requirements stated in divisions (A), (B), and (C) of this section has no effect on the common law rights and liabilities, including the right of a physician to obtain the oral or implied consent of a patient to a medical procedure, that may exist as between physicians and patients on July 28, 1975.

As used in this section the term "hospital" has the same meaning as in section 2305.113 of the Revised Code; "home health agency" has the same meaning as in section 5101.61 of the Revised Code; "ambulatory surgical facility" has the meaning as in division (A of section 3702.30 of the Revised Code; and "hospice care program" has the same meaning as in section 3712.01 of the Revised Code. The provisions of this division apply to hospitals, doctors of medicine, doctors of osteopathic medicine, and doctors of podiatric medicine.

(4) ABORTION BY MINORS

Ohio has enacted two alternative abortion statutes for minors. One statute requires consent and the other requires notice. The state has determined that if the consent statute is invalidated, then the notice statute would be used. Under the consent statute no physician may perform an abortion upon an unemancipated minor without the consent of parent or guardian. Under the notice statute an abortion on a minor may not occur until 24 hours after notice of the abortion has been given to either parent of the minor or a legal guardian. In compliance with federal constitutional law, Ohio has provided a judicial waiver procedure for an unemancipated minor to obtain an abortion without parental consent or notice. If an unemancipated minor elects not to obtain consent or provide notice to a parent or guardian, the minor may petition a trial court for a waiver of the consent or notice requirement. Pursuant to the judicial bypass procedure under the consent statute a court may appoint an attorney for the minor. In a proceeding under the consent judicial bypass procedure a court may permit the minor not to have to obtain the consent of a parent or guardian if the court (1) finds that the minor is sufficiently mature and well enough informed to decide intelligently whether to have an abortion, or (2) finds that the abortion is in the best interests of the minor. The consent and judicial bypass statute was upheld in *Cincinnati Women's Services, Inc. v. Taft*, 468 F.3d 361 (6th Cir. 2006). Under the notice and judicial bypass statutes a minor has a right to an attorney at a judicial bypass proceeding and if she cannot afford one, the court must appoint her an attorney. If a minor chooses, she may represent herself. The required parental notice may be waived if the court finds either (1) that the minor is mature and well-informed enough to make the abortion decision on her own, (2) that notification of the abortion would not be in the best interest of the minor, or (3) that the minor is a victim of physical, sexual, or emotional abuse by one or both of her parents, or legal guardian. In *Ohio v. Akron Center for Reproductive Health* the United States Supreme Court upheld the constitutionality of Ohio's notice and judicial bypass statutes. The statutes are set out below.

Ohio Code § 2919.12. Notice

(A) No person shall perform or induce an abortion without the informed consent of the pregnant woman.

(B)(1)(a) No person shall knowingly perform or induce an abortion upon a woman who is pregnant, unmarried, under eighteen years of age, and unemancipated unless at least one of the following applies:

(i) Subject to division (B)(2) of this section, the person has given at least twenty-four hours actual notice, in person or by telephone, to one of the woman's parents, her guardian, or her custodian as to the intention to perform or induce the abortion, provided that if the woman has requested, in accordance with division (B)(1)(b) of this section, that notice be given to a specified brother or sister of the woman who is twenty-one years of age or older or to a specified stepparent or grandparent of the woman instead of to one of her parents, her

guardian, or her custodian, and if the person is notified by a juvenile court that affidavits of the type described in that division have been filed with that court, the twenty-four hours actual notice described in this division as to the intention to perform or induce the abortion shall be given, in person or by telephone, to the specified brother, sister, stepparent, or grandparent instead of to the parent, guardian, or custodian;

(ii) One of the woman's parents, her guardian, or her custodian has consented in writing to the performance or inducement of the abortion;

(iii) A juvenile court pursuant to section 2151.85 of the Revised Code issues an order authorizing the woman to consent to the abortion without notification of one of her parents, her guardian, or her custodian;

(iv) A juvenile court or a court of appeals, by its inaction, constructively has authorized the woman to consent to the abortion without notification of one of her parents, her guardian, or her custodian under division (B)(1) of section 2151.85 or division (A) of section 2505.073 of the Revised Code.

(b) If a woman who is pregnant, unmarried, under eighteen years of age, and unemancipated desires notification as to a person's intention to perform or induce an abortion on the woman to be given to a specified brother or sister of the woman who is twenty-one years of age or older or to a specified stepparent or grandparent of the woman instead of to one of her parents, her guardian, or her custodian, the person who intends to perform or induce the abortion shall notify the specified brother, sister, stepparent, or grandparent instead of the parent, guardian, or custodian for purposes of division (B)(1)(a)(i) of this section if all of the following apply:

(i) The woman has requested the person to provide the notification to the specified brother, sister, stepparent, or grandparent, clearly has identified the specified brother, sister, stepparent, or grandparent and her relation to that person, and, if the specified relative is a brother or sister, has indicated the age of the brother or sister;

(ii) The woman has executed an affidavit stating that she is in fear of physical, sexual, or severe emotional abuse from the parent, guardian, or custodian who otherwise would be notified under division (B)(1)(a)(i) of this section, and that the fear is based on a pattern of physical, sexual, or severe emotional abuse of her exhibited by that parent, guardian, or custodian, has filed the affidavit with the juvenile court of the county in which the woman has a residence or legal settlement, the juvenile court of any county that borders to any extent the county in which she has a residence or legal settlement, or the juvenile court of the county in which the hospital, clinic, or other facility in which the abortion would be performed or induced is located, and has given the court written notice of the name and address of the person who intends to perform or induce the abortion;

(iii) The specified brother, sister, stepparent, or grandparent has executed an affidavit stating that the woman has reason to fear physical, sexual, or severe emotional abuse from the parent, guardian, or custodian who otherwise would be notified under division (B)(1)(a)(i) of this section, based on a pattern of physical, sexual, or severe emotional abuse of her by that parent, guardian, or custodian, and the woman or the specified brother, sister, stepparent, or grandparent has filed the affidavit with the juvenile court in which the affidavit described in division (B)(1)(b)(ii) of this section was filed;

(iv) The juvenile court in which the affidavits described in divisions (B)(1)(b)(ii) and (iii) of this section were filed has notified the person that both of those affidavits have been filed with the court.

(c) If an affidavit of the type described in division (B)(1)(b)(ii) of this section and an affidavit of the type described in division (B)(1)(b)(iii) of this section are filed with a juvenile court and the court has been provided with written notice of the name and address of the person who intends to perform or induce an abortion upon the woman to whom the affidavits pertain, the court promptly shall notify the person who intends to perform or induce the abortion that the affidavits have been filed. If possible, the notice to the person shall be given in person or by telephone.

(2) If division (B)(1)(a)(ii), (iii), or (iv) of this section does not apply, and if no parent, guardian, or custodian can be reached for purposes of division (B)(1)(a)(i) of this section after a reasonable effort, or if notification is to be given to a specified brother, sister, stepparent, or grandparent under that division and the specified brother, sister, stepparent, or grandparent cannot be reached for purposes of that division after a reasonable effort, no person shall perform or induce such an abortion without giving at least forty-eight hours constructive notice to one of the woman's parents, her guardian, or her custodian, by both certified and ordinary mail sent to the last known address of the parent, guardian, or custodian, or if notification for purposes of division (B)(1)(a)(i) of this section is to be given to a specified brother, sister, stepparent, or grandparent, without giving at least forty-eight hours constructive notice to that specified brother, sister, stepparent, or grandparent by both certified and ordinary mail sent to the last known address of that specified brother, sister, stepparent, or grandparent. The forty-eight-hour period under this division begins when the certified mail notice is mailed. If a parent, guardian, or custodian of the woman, or if notification under division (B)(1)(a)(i) of this section is to be given to a specified brother, sister, stepparent, or grandparent, the specified brother, sister, stepparent, or grandparent, is not reached within the forty-eight-hour period, the abortion may proceed even if the certified mail notice is not received.

(3) If a parent, guardian, custodian, or specified brother, sister, stepparent, or grandparent who has been notified in accordance with division (B)(1) or (2) of this section clearly and unequivocally expresses that he or she does not wish to consult with a pregnant woman prior to her abortion, then the abortion may proceed without any further waiting period.

(4) For purposes of prosecutions for a violation of division (B)(1) or (2) of this section, it shall be a rebuttable presumption that a woman who is unmarried and under eighteen years of age is unemancipated.

(C)(1) It is an affirmative defense to a charge under division (B)(1) or (2) of this section that the pregnant woman provided the person who performed or induced the abortion with false, misleading, or incorrect information about her age, marital status, or emancipation, about the age of a brother or sister to whom she requested notice be given as a specified relative instead of to one of her parents, her guardian, or her custodian, or about the last known address of either of her parents, her guardian, her custodian, or a specified brother, sister, stepparent, or grandparent to whom she requested notice be given and the person who performed or induced the abortion did not otherwise have reasonable cause to believe the pregnant woman was under eighteen years of age, unmarried, or unemancipated, to believe that the age of a brother or sister to whom she requested notice be given as a specified relative instead of to one of her parents, her guardian, or her custodian was not twenty-one years of age, or to believe that the last known address of either of her parents, her guardian, her custodian, or a specified brother, sister, steppar-

ent, or grandparent to whom she requested notice be given was incorrect.

(2) It is an affirmative defense to a charge under this section that compliance with the requirements of this section was not possible because an immediate threat of serious risk to the life or physical health of the pregnant woman from the continuation of her pregnancy created an emergency necessitating the immediate performance or inducement of an abortion.

(D) Whoever violates this section is guilty of unlawful abortion. A violation of division (A) of this section is a misdemeanor of the first degree on the first offense and a felony of the fourth degree on each subsequent offense. A violation of division (B) of this section is a misdemeanor of the first degree on a first offense and a felony of the fifth degree on each subsequent offense.

(E) Whoever violates this section is liable to the pregnant woman and her parents, guardian, or custodian for civil compensatory and exemplary damages.

(F) As used in this section "unemancipated" means that a woman who is unmarried and under eighteen years of age has not entered the armed services of the United States, has not become employed and self-subsisting, or has not otherwise become independent from the care and control of her parent, guardian, or custodian.

Ohio Code § 2151.85. Judicial bypass for notice requirement

(A) A woman who is pregnant, unmarried, under eighteen years of age, and unemancipated and who wishes to have an abortion without the notification of her parents, guardian, or custodian may file a complaint in the juvenile court of the county in which she has a residence or legal settlement, in the juvenile court of any county that borders to any extent the county in which she has a residence or legal settlement, or in the juvenile court of the county in which the hospital, clinic, or other facility in which the abortion would be performed or induced is located, requesting the issuance of an order authorizing her to consent to the performance or inducement of an abortion without the notification of her parents, guardian, or custodian.

The complaint shall be made under oath and shall include all of the following:

(1) A statement that the complainant is pregnant;

(2) A statement that the complainant is unmarried, under eighteen years of age, and unemancipated;

(3) A statement that the complainant wishes to have an abortion without the notification of her parents, guardian, or custodian;

(4) An allegation of either or both of the following:

(a) That the complainant is sufficiently mature and well enough informed to intelligently decide whether to have an abortion without the notification of her parents, guardian, or custodian;

(b) That one or both of her parents, her guardian, or her custodian was engaged in a pattern of physical, sexual, or emotional abuse against her, or that the notification of her parents, guardian, or custodian otherwise is not in her best interest.

(5) A statement as to whether the complainant has retained an attorney and, if she has retained an attorney, the name, address, and telephone number of her attorney.

(B)(1) The court shall fix a time for a hearing on any complaint filed pursuant to division (A) of this section and shall keep a record of all testimony and other oral proceedings in the action. The court shall hear and determine the action and shall not refer any portion of it to a referee. The hearing shall be held at the earliest possible time, but not later than the fifth business day after the day that the complaint is filed. The court shall enter judgment on the complaint immediately after the hearing is concluded. If the hearing required by this division is not held by the fifth business day after the complaint is filed, the failure to hold the hearing shall be considered to be a constructive order of the court authorizing the complainant to consent to the performance or inducement of an abortion without the notification of her parent, guardian, or custodian, and the complainant and any other person may rely on the constructive order to the same extent as if the court actually had issued an order under this section authorizing the complainant to consent to the performance or inducement of an abortion without such notification.

(2) The court shall appoint a guardian ad litem to protect the interests of the complainant at the hearing that is held pursuant to this section. If the complainant has not retained an attorney, the court shall appoint an attorney to represent her. If the guardian ad litem is an attorney admitted to the practice of law in this state, the court also may appoint him to serve as the complainant's attorney.

(C)(1) If the complainant makes only the allegation set forth in division (A)(4)(a) of this section and if the court finds, by clear and convincing evidence, that the complainant is sufficiently mature and well enough informed to decide intelligently whether to have an abortion, the court shall issue an order authorizing the complainant to consent to the performance or inducement of an abortion without the notification of her parents, guardian, or custodian. If the court does not make the finding specified in this division, it shall dismiss the complaint.

(2) If the complainant makes only the allegation set forth in division (A)(4)(b) of this section and if the court finds, by clear and convincing evidence, that there is evidence of a pattern of physical, sexual, or emotional abuse of the complainant by one or both of her parents, her guardian, or her custodian, or that the notification of the parents, guardian, or custodian of the complainant otherwise is not in the best interest of the complainant, the court shall issue an order authorizing the complainant to consent to the performance or inducement of an abortion without the notification of her parents, guardian, or custodian. If the court does not make the finding specified in this division, it shall dismiss the complaint.

(3) If the complainant makes both of the allegations set forth in divisions (A)(4)(a) and (b) of this section, the court shall proceed as follows:

(a) The court first shall determine whether it can make the finding specified in division (C)(1) of this section and, if so, shall issue an order pursuant to that division. If the court issues such an order, it shall not proceed pursuant to division (C)(3)(b) of this section. If the court does not make the finding specified in division (C)(1) of this section, it shall proceed pursuant to division (C)(3)(b) of this section.

(b) If the court pursuant to division (C)(3)(a) of this section does not make the finding specified in division (C)(1) of this section, it shall proceed to determine whether it can make the finding specified in division (C)(2) of this section and, if so, shall issue an order pursuant to that division. If the court does not make the finding specified in division (C)(2) of this section, it shall dismiss the complaint.

(D) The court shall not notify the parents, guardian, or custodian of the complainant that she is pregnant or that she wants to have an abortion.

(E) If the court dismisses the complaint, it immediately shall notify the complainant that she has a right to appeal under section 2505.073 of the Revised Code.

(F) Each hearing under this section shall be conducted in a manner that will preserve the anonymity of the complainant. The complaint and all other papers and records that pertain to an action commenced under this section shall be kept confidential and are not public records under section 149.43 of the Revised Code.

(G) The clerk of the supreme court shall prescribe complaint and notice of appeal forms that shall be used by a complainant filing a complaint under this section and by an appellant filing an appeal under section 2505.073 of the Revised Code. The clerk of each juvenile court shall

furnish blank copies of the forms, without charge, to any person who requests them.

(H) No filing fee shall be required of, and no court costs shall be assessed against, a complainant filing a complaint under this section or an appellant filing an appeal under section 2505.073 of the Revised Code.

(I) As used in this section, "unemancipated" means that a woman who is unmarried and under eighteen years of age has not entered the armed services of the United States, has not become employed and self-subsisting, or has not otherwise become independent from the care and control of her parent, guardian, or custodian.

Ohio Code § 2505.073.
Appeal of dismissal of complaint for abortion

(A) A complainant whose complaint under section 2151.85 of the Revised Code is dismissed by a juvenile court, may appeal in accordance with this section. Within four days after a notice of appeal is filed in an action arising under that section, the clerk of the juvenile court shall deliver a copy of the notice of appeal and the record on appeal to the clerk of the court of appeals named in the notice. Upon receipt of the notice and record, the clerk of the court of appeals shall place the appeal on the docket of the court.

The appellant shall file her brief within four days after the appeal is docketed. Unless the appellant waives the right to oral argument, the court of appeals shall hear oral argument within five days after the appeal is docketed. The court of appeals shall enter judgment in the appeal immediately after the oral argument or, if oral argument has been waived, within five days after the appeal is docketed.

No filing fee shall be required of, and no court costs shall be assessed against, an appellant who appeals under this section.

Upon motion of the appellant and for good cause shown, the court of appeals may shorten or extend any of the maximum times set forth in this division. However, in any case, if judgment is not entered within five days after the appeal is docketed, the failure to enter the judgment shall be considered to be a constructive order of the court authorizing the appellant to consent to the performance or inducement of an abortion without the notification of her parent, guardian, or custodian, and the appellant and any other person may rely on the constructive order to the same extent as if the court actually had entered a judgment under this section authorizing the appellant to consent to the performance or inducement of an abortion without such notification.

In the interest of justice, the court of appeals, in an appeal in accordance with this section, shall liberally modify or dispense with the formal requirements that normally apply as to the contents and form of an appellant's brief.

(B) All proceedings under division (A) of this section shall be conducted in a manner that will preserve the anonymity of the appellant on appeal. All papers and records that pertain to an appeal under this section shall be kept confidential and are not public records under section 149.43 of the Revised Code.

Ohio Code § 2919.121. Consent and judicial bypass

(A) For the purpose of this section, a minor shall be considered "emancipated" if the minor has married, entered the armed services of the United States, become employed and self-subsisting, or has otherwise become independent from the care and control of her parent, guardian, or custodian.

(B) No person shall knowingly perform or induce an abortion upon a pregnant minor unless one of the following is the case:

(1) The attending physician has secured the informed written consent of the minor and one parent, guardian, or custodian;

(2) The minor is emancipated and the attending physician has received her written informed consent;

(3) The minor has been authorized to consent to the abortion by a court order issued pursuant to division (C) of this section, and the attending physician has received her informed written consent;

(4) The court has given its consent in accordance with division (C) of this section and the minor is having the abortion willingly.

(C) The right of a minor to consent to an abortion under division (B)(3) of this section or judicial consent to obtain an abortion under division (B)(4) of this section may be granted by a court order pursuant to the following procedures:

(1) The minor or next friend shall make an application to the juvenile court of the county in which the minor has a residence or legal settlement, the juvenile court of any county that borders the county in which she has a residence or legal settlement, or the juvenile court of the county in which the facility in which the abortion would be performed or induced is located. The juvenile court shall assist the minor or next friend in preparing the petition and notices required by this section. The minor or next friend shall thereafter file a petition setting forth all of the following: the initials of the minor; her age; the names and addresses of each parent, guardian, custodian, or, if the minor's parents are deceased and no guardian has been appointed, any other person standing in loco parentis of the minor; that the minor has been fully informed of the risks and consequences of the abortion; that the minor is of sound mind and has sufficient intellectual capacity to consent to the abortion; that the minor has not previously filed a petition under this section concerning the same pregnancy that was denied on the merits; that, if the court does not authorize the minor to consent to the abortion, the court should find that the abortion is in the best interests of the minor and give judicial consent to the abortion; that the court should appoint a guardian ad litem; and if the minor does not have private counsel, that the court should appoint counsel. The petition shall be signed by the minor or the next friend.

(2) A hearing on the merits shall be held on the record as soon as possible within five days of filing the petition. If the minor has not retained counsel, the court shall appoint counsel at least twenty-four hours prior to the hearing. The court shall appoint a guardian ad litem to protect the interests of the minor at the hearing. If the guardian ad litem is an attorney admitted to the practice of law in this state, the court may appoint the guardian ad litem to serve as the minor's counsel. At the hearing, the court shall hear evidence relating to the emotional development, maturity, intellect, and understanding of the minor; the nature, possible consequences, and alternatives to the abortion; and any other evidence that the court may find useful in determining whether the minor should be granted the right to consent to the abortion or whether the abortion is in the best interests of the minor. If the minor or her counsel fail to appear for a scheduled hearing, jurisdiction shall remain with the judge who would have presided at the hearing.

(3) If the court finds that the minor is sufficiently mature and well enough informed to decide intelligently whether to have an abortion, the court shall grant the petition and permit the minor to consent to the abortion.

If the court finds that the abortion is in the best interests of the minor, the court shall give judicial consent to the abortion, setting forth the grounds for its finding.

If the court does not make either of the findings specified in division (C)(3) of this section, the court shall deny the petition, setting forth the grounds on which the petition is denied.

The court shall issue its order not later than twenty-four hours after the end of the hearing.

(4) No juvenile court shall have jurisdiction to rehear a petition concerning the same pregnancy once a juvenile court has granted or denied the petition.

(5) If the petition is granted, the informed consent of the minor, pursuant to a court order authorizing the minor to consent to the abortion, or judicial consent to the abortion, shall bar an action by the parents, guardian, or custodian of the minor for battery of the minor against any person performing or inducing the abortion. The immunity granted shall only extend to the performance or inducement of the abortion in accordance with this section and to any accompanying services that are performed in a competent manner.

(6) An appeal from an order issued under this section may be taken to the court of appeals by the minor. The record on appeal shall be completed and the appeal perfected within four days from the filing of the notice of appeal. Because the abortion may need to be performed in a timely manner, the supreme court shall, by rule, provide for expedited appellate review of cases appealed under this section.

(7) All proceedings under this section shall be conducted in a confidential manner and shall be given such precedence over other pending matters as will ensure that the court will reach a decision promptly and without delay.

The petition and all other papers and records that pertain to an action commenced under this section shall be kept confidential and are not public records under section 149.43 of the Revised Code.

(8) No filing fee shall be required of or court costs assessed against a person filing a petition under this section or appealing an order issued under this section.

(D) It is an affirmative defense to any civil, criminal, or professional disciplinary claim brought under this section that compliance with the requirements of this section was not possible because an immediate threat of serious risk to the life or physical health of the minor from the continuation of her pregnancy created an emergency necessitating the immediate performance or inducement of an abortion.

(E) Whoever violates division (B) of this section is guilty of unlawful abortion, a misdemeanor of the first degree. If the offender previously has been convicted of or pleaded guilty to a violation of this section, unlawful abortion is a felony of the fourth degree.

(F) Whoever violates division (B) of this section is liable to the pregnant minor and her parents, guardian, or custodian for civil, compensatory, and exemplary damages.

Ohio Code § 2919.122.
Compliance with consent statutes as complete defense

Section 2919.121 of the Revised Code applies in lieu of division (B) of section 2919.12 of the Revised Code whenever its operation is not enjoined. If section 2919.121 of the Revised Code is enjoined, division (B) of section 2919.12 of the Revised Code applies.

If a person complies with the requirements of division (B) of section 2919.12 of the Revised Code under the good faith belief that the application or enforcement of section 2919.121 of the Revised Code is subject to a restraining order or injunction, good faith compliance shall constitute a complete defense to any civil, criminal, or professional disciplinary action brought under section 2919.121 of the Revised Code.

If a person complies with the requirements of section 2919.121 of the Revised Code under the good faith belief that it is not subject to a restraining order or injunction, good faith compliance shall constitute a complete defense to any criminal, civil, or professional disciplinary action for failure to comply with the requirements of division (B) of section 2919.12 of the Revised Code.

(5) PARTIAL-BIRTH ABORTION

Ohio prohibits partial-birth abortions, except to preserve the life or health of the woman. The statute was upheld on constitutional grounds in *Women's Medical Professional Corp. v. Taft*, 353 F.3d 436 (6th Cir. 2003). Ohio has provided a civil cause of action for the mother and father of a fetus that was the victim of partial-birth abortion. In the case of a minor, the maternal grandparents of the fetus may file a civil lawsuit. The statutes are set out below.

Ohio Code § 2919.151. Partial-birth abortion

(A) As used in this section:

(1) "Dilation and evacuation procedure of abortion" does not include the dilation and extraction procedure of abortion.

(2) "From the body of the mother" means that the portion of the fetus' body in question is beyond the mother's vaginal introitus in a vaginal delivery.

(3) "Partial birth procedure" means the medical procedure that includes all of the following elements in sequence:

(a) Intentional dilation of the cervix of a pregnant woman, usually over a sequence of days;

(b) In a breech presentation, intentional extraction of at least the lower torso to the navel, but not the entire body, of an intact fetus from the body of the mother, or in a cephalic presentation, intentional extraction of at least the complete head, but not the entire body, of an intact fetus from the body of the mother;

(c) Intentional partial evacuation of the intracranial contents of the fetus, which procedure the person performing the procedure knows will cause the death of the fetus, intentional compression of the head of the fetus, which procedure the person performing the procedure knows will cause the death of the fetus, or performance of another intentional act that the person performing the procedure knows will cause the death of the fetus;

(d) Completion of the vaginal delivery of the fetus.

(4) "Partially born" means that the portion of the body of an intact fetus described in division (A)(3)(b) of this section has been intentionally extracted from the body of the mother.

(5) "Serious risk of the substantial and irreversible impairment of a major bodily function" means any medically diagnosed condition that so complicates the pregnancy of the woman as to directly or indirectly cause the substantial and irreversible impairment of a major bodily function.

(6) "Viable" has the same meaning as in section 2901.01 of the Revised Code.

(B) When the fetus that is the subject of the procedure is viable, no person shall knowingly perform a partial birth procedure on a pregnant woman when the procedure is not necessary, in reasonable medical judgment, to preserve the life or health of the mother as a result of the mother's life or health being endangered by a serious risk of the substantial and irreversible impairment of a major bodily function.

(C) When the fetus that is the subject of the procedure is not viable, no person shall knowingly perform a partial birth procedure on a pregnant woman when the procedure is not necessary, in reasonable medical judgment, to preserve the life or health of the mother as a result of the mother's life or health being endangered by a serious risk of the substantial and irreversible impairment of a major bodily function.

(D) Whoever violates division (B) or (C) of this section is guilty of partial birth feticide, a felony of the second degree.

(E) A pregnant woman upon whom a partial birth procedure is performed in violation of division (B) or (C) of this section is not guilty of committing, attempting to commit, complicity in the commission of, or conspiracy in the commission of a violation of those divisions.

(F) This section does not prohibit the suction curettage procedure of abortion, the suction aspiration procedure of abortion, or the dilation and evacuation procedure of abortion.

(G) This section does not apply to any person who performs or attempts to perform a legal abortion if the act that causes the death of the fetus is performed prior to the fetus being partially born even though the death of the fetus occurs after it is partially born.

Ohio Code § 2307.53(B).
Civil action for partial-birth abortion

(A) As used in this section:

(1) "Frivolous conduct" has the same meaning as in section 2323.51 of the Revised Code.

(2) "Partial birth procedure" has the same meaning as in section 2919.151 of the Revised Code.

(B) A woman upon whom a partial birth procedure is performed in violation of division (B) or (C) of section 2919.151 of the Revised Code, the father of the child if the child was not conceived by rape, or the parent of the woman if the woman is not eighteen years of age or older at the time of the violation has and may commence a civil action for compensatory damages, punitive or exemplary damages if authorized by section 2315.21 of the Revised Code, and court costs and reasonable attorney's fees against the person who committed the violation.

(C) If a judgment is rendered in favor of the defendant in a civil action commenced pursuant to division (B) of this section and the court finds, upon the filing of a motion under section 2323.51 of the Revised Code, that the commencement of the civil action constitutes frivolous conduct and that the defendant was adversely affected by the frivolous conduct, the court shall award in accordance with section 2323.51 of the Revised Code reasonable attorney's fees to the defendant.

Ohio Code § 2307.46. Confidentiality

(A) In any civil action based on or related to any injury, death, or loss to person or property suffered as a result of the performance or inducement of an abortion or suffered as a result of an attempt to perform or induce an abortion, the woman upon whom the abortion was allegedly performed, induced, or attempted, at the time of the filing of the complaint in the civil action, may file a motion with the court requesting that her identity only be revealed to the defendant and to the court and that in all other respects the civil action be conducted in a manner that maintains her confidentiality. The motion shall set forth the reasons for the requested confidentiality. Prior to service of the complaint, the court shall conduct an ex parte hearing in a timely manner to determine whether sufficient cause exists to require that the confidentiality of the movant be maintained in the civil action. The decision of the court on the motion is final and is not subject to appeal.

(B) The supreme court shall prescribe rules to implement division (A) of this section.

Ohio Code § 2305.114.
Limitation of action for partial-birth abortion

A civil action pursuant to section 2307.53 of the Revised Code for partial birth feticide shall be commenced within one year after the commission of that offense.

(6) USE OF FACILITIES AND PEOPLE

Under the laws of Ohio hospitals are not required to allow abortions at their facilities. The employees and physicians at hospitals that do allow abortions are permitted to refuse to take part in abortions. The statute addressing the matter is set out below.

Ohio Code § 4731.91. Right to refuse abortion

(A) No private hospital, private hospital director, or governing board of a private hospital is required to permit an abortion.

(B) No public hospital, public hospital director, or governing board of a public hospital is required to permit an abortion.

(C) Refusal to permit an abortion is not grounds for civil liability nor a basis for disciplinary or other recriminatory action.

(D) No person is required to perform or participate in medical procedures which result in abortion, and refusal to perform or participate in the medical procedures is not grounds for civil liability nor a basis for disciplinary or other recriminatory action.

(E) Whoever violates division (D) of this section is liable in civil damages.

(7) USE OF PUBLIC FUNDS

Ohio prohibits the use of public funds to pay for abortions, except abortions that are necessary to save the life or health of the woman, or where the pregnancy resulted from rape or incest. The state also prohibits government employment health plans from providing coverage for abortions, unless an employee pays premiums directly for such coverage. The statutes addressing the matter are set out below.

Ohio Code § 5101.55(C) Public funds

State or local public funds shall not be used to subsidize an abortion, except as provided in section 5101.56 of the Revised Code.

Ohio Code § 5101.56.
Limitation of public funds to subsidize abortion

(A) As used in this section, "physician" means a person who holds a valid certificate to practice medicine and surgery or osteopathic medicine and surgery issued under Chapter 4731. of the Revised Code.

(B) Unless required by the United States Constitution or by federal statute, regulation, or decisions of federal courts, state or local funds may not be used for payment or reimbursement for abortion services unless the certification required by division (C) of this section is made and one of the following circumstances exists:

(1) The woman suffers from a physical disorder, physical injury, or physical illness, including a life-endangering physical condition caused by or arising from the pregnancy, that would, as certified by a physician, place the woman in danger of death unless an abortion is performed.

(2) The pregnancy was the result of an act of rape and the patient, the patient's legal guardian, or the person who made the report to the law enforcement agency, certifies in writing that prior to the performance of the abortion a report was filed with a law enforcement agency having the requisite jurisdiction, unless the patient was physically unable to comply with the reporting requirement and that fact is certified by the physician performing the abortion.

(3) The pregnancy was the result of an act of incest and the patient, the patient's legal guardian, or the person who made the report certifies in writing that prior to the performance of the abortion a report was filed with either a law enforcement agency having the requisite jurisdiction, or, in the case of a minor, with a county children services agency established under Chapter 5153. of the Revised Code, unless the patient was physically unable to comply with the reporting requirement and that fact is certified by the physician performing the abortion.

(C)(1) Before payment of or reimbursement for an abortion can be made with state or local funds, the physician performing the abortion shall certify that one of the three circumstances in division (B) of this section has occurred. The certification shall be made on a form created by the Ohio department of job and family services known as the "Abortion Certification Form." The physician's signature shall be in the physician's own handwriting. The certification shall list the name and address of the patient. The certification form shall be attached to the billing invoice.

(2) The certification shall be as follows:

I certify that, on the basis of my professional judgment, this service was necessary because:

(a) The woman suffers from a physical disorder, physical injury, or physical illness, including a life-endangering physical condition caused by or arising from the pregnancy itself, that would place the woman in danger of death unless an abortion was performed;

(b) The pregnancy was the result of an act of rape and the patient, the patient's legal guardian, or the person who made the report to the law enforcement agency certified in writing that prior to the performance of the abortion a report was filed with a law enforcement agency having the requisite jurisdiction;

(c) The pregnancy was the result of an act of incest and the patient, the patient's legal guardian, or the person who made the report certified in writing that prior to the performance of the abortion a report was filed with either a law enforcement agency having the requisite jurisdiction or, in the case of a minor, with a county children services agency established under Chapter 5153. of the Revised Code;

(d) The pregnancy was the result of an act of rape and in my professional opinion the recipient was physically unable to comply with the reporting requirement; or

(e) The pregnancy was a result of an act of incest and in my professional opinion the recipient was physically unable to comply with the reporting requirement.

(D) Payment or reimbursement for abortion services shall not be made with state or local funds for associated services such as anesthesia, laboratory tests, or hospital services if the abortion service itself cannot be paid or reimbursed with state or local funds. All abortion services for which a physician is seeking reimbursement or payment for the purposes of this division shall be submitted on a hard-copy billing invoice.

(E) Documentation that supports the certification made by a physician shall be maintained by the physician in the recipient's medical record. When the physician certifies that circumstances described in division (C)(2)(b) or (c) of this section are the case, a copy of the statement signed by the patient, the patient's legal guardian, or the person who made the report shall be maintained in the patient's medical record.

(F) Nothing in this section denies reimbursement for drugs or devices to prevent implantation of the fertilized ovum, or for medical procedures for the termination of an ectopic pregnancy. This section does not apply to treatments for incomplete, missed, or septic abortions.

(G) If enforcement of this section will adversely affect eligibility of the state or a political subdivision of the state for participation in a federal program, this section shall be enforced to the extent permissible without preventing participation in that federal program.

Ohio Code § 124.85. State funded health insurance

(A) As used in this section:

(1) "Nontherapeutic abortion" means an abortion that is performed or induced when the life of the mother would not be endangered if the fetus were carried to term or when the pregnancy of the mother was not the result of rape or incest reported to a law enforcement agency.

(2) "Policy, contract, or plan" means a policy, contract, or plan of one or more insurance companies, medical care corporations, health care corporations, health maintenance organizations, preferred provider organizations, or other entities that provides health, medical, hospital, or surgical coverage, benefits, or services to elected or appointed officers or employees of the state, including a plan that is associated with a self-insurance program and a policy, contract, or plan that implements a collective bargaining agreement.

(3) "State" has the same meaning as in section 2744.01 of the Revised Code.

(B) Subject to division (C) of this section, but notwithstanding other provisions of the Revised Code that conflict with the prohibition specified in this division, funds of the state shall not be expended directly or indirectly to pay the costs, premiums, or charges associated with a policy, contract, or plan if the policy, contract, or plan provides coverage, benefits, or services related to a nontherapeutic abortion.

(C) Division (B) of this section does not preclude the state from expending funds to pay the costs, premiums, or charges associated with a policy, contract, or plan that includes a rider or other provision offered on an individual basis under which an elected or appointed official or employee who accepts the offer of the rider or provision may obtain coverage of a nontherapeutic abortion through the policy, contract, or plan if the individual pays for all of the costs, premiums, or charges associated with the rider or provision, including all administrative expenses related to the rider or provision and any claim made for a nontherapeutic abortion.

(D) In addition to the laws specified in division (A) of section 4117.10 of the Revised Code that prevail over conflicting provisions of agreements between employee organizations and public employers, divisions (B) and (C) of this section shall prevail over conflicting provisions of that nature.

(8) FETAL EXPERIMENTS

Under the laws of Ohio the use of fetal remains for experiments is prohibited. The statute addressing the issue is set out below.

Ohio Code § 2919.14. Fetal experiments

(A) No person shall experiment upon or sell the product of human conception which is aborted. Experiment does not include autopsies pursuant to sections 313.13 and 2108.50 of the Revised Code.

(B) Whoever violates this section is guilty of abortion trafficking, a misdemeanor of the first degree.

(9) USE OF MIFEPRISTONE

Ohio has enacted a statute banning the distribution of the abortion drug mifepristone (or RU-486) by nonphysicians. However, the statute was held unconstitutional in *Planned Parenthood Cincinnati Region v. Taft*, 459 F.Supp.2d 626 (S.D.Ohio 2006). The statute is set out below.

Ohio Code § 2919.123. Provision or use of RU-486

(A) No person shall knowingly give, sell, dispense, administer, otherwise provide, or prescribe RU-486 (mifepristone) to another for the purpose of inducing an abortion in any person or enabling the other person to induce an abortion in any person, unless the person who gives, sells, dispenses, administers, or otherwise provides or prescribes the RU-486 (mifepristone) is a physician, the physician satisfies all the criteria established by federal law that a physician must satisfy in order to provide RU-486 (mifepristone) for inducing abortions, and the physician provides the RU-486 (mifepristone) to the other person for the purpose of inducing an abortion in accordance with all provisions of federal law that govern the use of RU-486 (mifepristone) for inducing abortions. A person who gives, sells, dispenses, administers, otherwise provides, or prescribes RU-486 (mifepristone) to another as described in division (A) of this section shall not be prosecuted based on a violation of the criteria contained in this division unless the person knows that the person is not a physician, that the person did not satisfy all the specified criteria established by federal law, or that the person did not provide the RU-486 (mifepristone) in accordance with the specified provisions of federal law, whichever is applicable.

(B) No physician who provides RU-486 (mifepristone) to another for the purpose of inducing an abortion as authorized under division (A) of this section shall knowingly fail to comply with the applicable requirements of any federal law that pertain to follow-up examinations or care for persons to whom or for whom RU-486 (mifepristone) is provided for the purpose of inducing an abortion.

(C)(1) If a physician provides RU-486 (mifepristone) to another for the purpose of inducing an abortion as authorized under division (A) of this section and if the physician knows that the person who uses the RU-486 (mifepristone) for the purpose of inducing an abortion experiences during or after the use an incomplete abortion, severe bleeding, or an adverse reaction to the RU-486 (mifepristone) or is hospitalized, receives a transfusion, or experiences any other serious event, the physician promptly

must provide a written report of the incomplete abortion, severe bleeding, adverse reaction, hospitalization, transfusion, or serious event to the state medical board. The board shall compile and retain all reports it receives under this division. Except as otherwise provided in this division, all reports the board receives under this division are public records open to inspection under section 149.43 of the Revised Code. In no case shall the board release to any person the name or any other personal identifying information regarding a person who uses RU-486 (mifepristone) for the purpose of inducing an abortion and who is the subject of a report the board receives under this division.

(2) No physician who provides RU-486 (mifepristone) to another for the purpose of inducing an abortion as authorized under division (A) of this section shall knowingly fail to file a report required under division (C)(1) of this section.

(D) Division (A) of this section does not apply to any of the following:

(1) A pregnant woman who obtains or possesses RU-486 (mifepristone) for the purpose of inducing an abortion to terminate her own pregnancy;

(2) The legal transport of RU-486 (mifepristone) by any person or entity and the legal delivery of the RU-486 (mifepristone) by any person to the recipient, provided that this division does not apply regarding any conduct related to the RU-486 (mifepristone) other than its transport and delivery to the recipient;

(3) The distribution, provision, or sale of RU-486 (mifepristone) by any legal manufacturer or distributor of RU-486 (mifepristone), provided the manufacturer or distributor made a good faith effort to comply with any applicable requirements of federal law regarding the distribution, provision, or sale.

(E) Whoever violates this section is guilty of unlawful distribution of an abortion-inducing drug, a felony of the fourth degree. If the offender previously has been convicted of or pleaded guilty to a violation of this section or of section 2919.12, 2919.121, 2919.13, 2919.14, 2919.151, 2919.17, or 2919.18 of the Revised Code, unlawful distribution of an abortion-inducing drug is a felony of the third degree.

If the offender is a professionally licensed person, in addition to any other sanction imposed by law for the offense, the offender is subject to sanctioning as provided by law by the regulatory or licensing board or agency that has the administrative authority to suspend or revoke the offender's professional license, including the sanctioning provided in section 4731.22 of the Revised Code for offenders who have a certificate to practice or certificate of registration issued under that chapter.

(F) As used in this section:

(1) "Federal law" means any law, rule, or regulation of the United States or any drug approval letter of the food and drug administration of the United States that governs or regulates the use of RU-486 (mifepristone) for the purpose of inducing abortions.

(2) "Personal identifying information" has the same meaning as in section 2913.49 of the Revised Code.

(3) "Physician" has the same meaning as in section 2305.113 of the Revised Code.

(4) "Professionally licensed person" has the same meaning as in section 2925.01 of the Revised Code.

(10) WRONGFUL LIFE ACTION

Ohio has taken affirmative steps to prevent wrongful life lawsuits, by prohibiting claims for failure to abort a pregnancy. The statute addressing the issue is set out below.

Ohio Code § 2305.116.
No cause of action for nonperformance of abortion

(A) No person has a civil action or may receive an award of damages in a civil action, and no other person shall be liable in a civil action, upon a medical claim that because of an act or omission by the other person the person was not aborted.

(B) No person has a civil action or may receive an award of damages in a civil action, and no other person shall be liable in a civil action, upon a medical claim that because of an act or omission by the other person a child was not aborted.

(C) Nothing in this section shall preclude a person from bringing a civil action or from receiving an award of damages in a medical claim based upon an intentional or willful misrepresentation or omission of information related to medical diagnosis, care, or treatment.

(D) As used in this section, "medical claim" has the same meaning as in section 2305.113 of the Revised Code.

(11) FETAL DEATH REPORT

Ohio requires that all abortions be reported to the proper authorities. The statute addressing the matter is set out below.

Ohio Code § 3701.79. Collection of abortion data

(A) As used in this section:

(1) "Abortion" has the same meaning as in section 2919.11 of the Revised Code.

(2) "Abortion report" means a form completed pursuant to division (C) of this section.

(3) "Ambulatory surgical facility" has the same meaning as in section 3702.30 of the Revised Code.

(4) "Department" means the department of health.

(5) "Hospital" means any building, structure, institution, or place devoted primarily to the maintenance and operation of facilities for the diagnosis, treatment, and medical or surgical care for three or more unrelated individuals suffering from illness, disease, injury, or deformity, and regularly making available at least clinical laboratory services, diagnostic x-ray services, treatment facilities for surgery or obstetrical care, or other definitive medical treatment. "Hospital" does not include a "home" as defined in section 3721.01 of the Revised Code.

(6) "Physician's office" means an office or portion of an office that is used to provide medical or surgical services to the physician's patients. "Physician's office" does not mean an ambulatory surgical facility, a hospital, or a hospital emergency department.

(7) "Postabortion care" means care given after the uterus has been evacuated by abortion.

(B) The department shall be responsible for collecting and collating abortion data reported to the department as required by this section.

(C) The attending physician shall complete an individual abortion report for each abortion the physician performs upon a woman. The report shall be confidential and shall not contain the woman's name. The report shall include, but is not limited to, all of the following, insofar as the patient makes the data available that is not within the physician's knowledge:

(1) Patient number;

(2) The name and address of the facility in which the abortion was performed, and whether the facility is a hospital, ambulatory surgical facility, physician's office, or other facility;

(3) The date of the abortion;

(4) All of the following regarding the woman on whom the abortion was performed:

(a) Zip code of residence;

(b) Age;

(c) Race;

(d) Marital status;

(e) Number of previous pregnancies;

(f) Years of education;

(g) Number of living children;

(h) Number of previously induced abortions;

(i) Date of last induced abortion;

(j) Date of last live birth;

(k) Method of contraception at the time of conception;
(l) Date of the first day of the last menstrual period;
(m) Medical condition at the time of the abortion;
(n) Rh-type;
(o) The number of weeks of gestation at the time of the abortion.

(5) The type of abortion procedure performed;
(6) Complications by type;
(7) Type of procedure performed after the abortion;
(8) Type of family planning recommended;
(9) Type of additional counseling given;
(10) Signature of attending physician.

(D) The physician who completed the abortion report under division (C) of this section shall submit the abortion report to the department within fifteen days after the woman is discharged.

(E) The appropriate vital records report or certificate shall be made out after the twentieth week of gestation.

(F) A copy of the abortion report shall be made part of the medical record of the patient of the facility in which the abortion was performed.

(G) Each hospital shall file monthly and annual reports listing the total number of women who have undergone a post-twelve-week-gestation abortion and received postabortion care. The annual report shall be filed following the conclusion of the state's fiscal year. Each report shall be filed within thirty days after the end of the applicable reporting period.

(H) Each case in which a physician treats a post abortion complication shall be reported on a postabortion complication form. The report shall be made upon a form prescribed by the department, shall be signed by the attending physician, and shall be confidential.

(I)(1) Not later than the first day of October of each year, the department shall issue an annual report of the abortion data reported to the department for the previous calendar year as required by this section. The annual report shall include at least the following information:

(a) The total number of induced abortions;
(b) The number of abortions performed on Ohio and out-of-state residents;
(c) The number of abortions performed, sorted by each of the following:

(i) The age of the woman on whom the abortion was performed, using the following categories: under fifteen years of age, fifteen to nineteen years of age, twenty to twenty-four years of age, twenty-five to twenty-nine years of age, thirty to thirty-four years of age, thirty-five to thirty-nine years of age, forty to forty-four years of age, forty-five years of age or older;
(ii) The race and Hispanic ethnicity of the woman on whom the abortion was performed;
(iii) The education level of the woman on whom the abortion was performed, using the following categories or their equivalents: less than ninth grade, ninth through twelfth grade, one or more years of college;
(iv) The marital status of the woman on whom the abortion was performed;
(v) The number of living children of the woman on whom the abortion was performed, using the following categories: none, one, or two or more;
(vi) The number of weeks of gestation of the woman at the time the abortion was performed, using the following categories: less than nine weeks, nine to twelve weeks, thirteen to nineteen weeks, or twenty weeks or more;
(vii) The county in which the abortion was performed;
(viii) The type of abortion procedure performed;
(ix) The number of abortions previously performed on the woman on whom the abortion was performed;
(x) The type of facility in which the abortion was performed;
(xi) For Ohio residents, the county of residence of the woman on whom the abortion was performed.

(2) The report also shall indicate the number and type of the abortion complications reported to the department either on the abortion report required under division (C) of this section or the postabortion complication report required under division (H) of this section.

(3) In addition to the annual report required under division (I)(1) of this section, the department shall make available, on request, the number of abortions performed by zip code of residence.

(J) The director of health shall implement this section and shall apply to the court of common pleas for temporary or permanent injunctions restraining a violation or threatened violation of its requirements. This action is an additional remedy not dependent on the adequacy of the remedy at law.

(12) INJURY TO A PREGNANT WOMAN

Ohio has enacted numerous statutes that impose criminal penalties on anyone who injures or causes the death of a fetus, other than by a lawful abortion. The statutes are set out below.

Ohio Code § 2903.01. Aggravated murder (abridged)

(A) No person shall purposely, and with prior calculation and design, cause the death of another or the unlawful termination of another's pregnancy.

(B) No person shall purposely cause the death of another or the unlawful termination of another's pregnancy while committing or attempting to commit, or while fleeing immediately after committing or attempting to commit, kidnapping, rape, aggravated arson, arson, aggravated robbery, robbery, aggravated burglary, burglary, terrorism, or escape.

(C) Omitted.

(D) Omitted.

(E) Omitted.

(F) Whoever violates this section is guilty of aggravated murder, and shall be punished as provided in section 2929.02 of the Revised Code.

Ohio Code § 2903.02. Murder

(A) No person shall purposely cause the death of another or the unlawful termination of another's pregnancy.

(B) No person shall cause the death of another as a proximate result of the offender's committing or attempting to commit an offense of violence that is a felony of the first or second degree and that is not a violation of section 2903.03 or 2903.04 of the Revised Code.

(C) Division (B) of this section does not apply to an offense that becomes a felony of the first or second degree only if the offender previously has been convicted of that offense or another specified offense.

(D) Whoever violates this section is guilty of murder, and shall be punished as provided in section 2929.02 of the Revised Code.

Ohio Code § 2903.03. Voluntary manslaughter

(A) No person, while under the influence of sudden passion or in a sudden fit of rage, either of which is brought on by serious provocation occasioned by the victim that is reasonably sufficient to incite the person into using deadly force, shall knowingly cause the death of another or the unlawful termination of another's pregnancy.

(B) Whoever violates this section is guilty of voluntary manslaughter, a felony of the first degree.

Ohio Code § 2903.04. Involuntary manslaughter

(A) No person shall cause the death of another or the unlawful termination of another's pregnancy as a proximate result of the offender's committing or attempting to commit a felony.

(B) No person shall cause the death of another or the unlawful termination of another's pregnancy as a proximate result of the offender's com-

mitting or attempting to commit a misdemeanor of any degree, a regulatory offense, or a minor misdemeanor other than a violation of any section contained in Title XLV of the Revised Code that is a minor misdemeanor and other than a violation of an ordinance of a municipal corporation that, regardless of the penalty set by ordinance for the violation, is substantially equivalent to any section contained in Title XLV of the Revised Code that is a minor misdemeanor.

(C) Whoever violates this section is guilty of involuntary manslaughter. Violation of division (A) of this section is a felony of the first degree. Violation of division (B) of this section is a felony of the third degree.

(D) If an offender is convicted of or pleads guilty to a violation of division (A) or (B) of this section and if the felony, misdemeanor, or regulatory offense that the offender committed or attempted to commit, that proximately resulted in the death of the other person or the unlawful termination of another's pregnancy, and that is the basis of the offender's violation of division (A) or (B) of this section was a violation of division (A) or (B) of section 4511.19 of the Revised Code or of a substantially equivalent municipal ordinance or included, as an element of that felony, misdemeanor, or regulatory offense, the offender's operation or participation in the operation of a snowmobile, locomotive, watercraft, or aircraft while the offender was under the influence of alcohol, a drug of abuse, or alcohol and a drug of abuse, both of the following apply:

(1) The court shall impose a class one suspension of the offender's driver's or commercial driver's license or permit or nonresident operating privilege as specified in division (A)(1) of section 4510.02 of the Revised Code.

(2) The court shall impose a mandatory prison term for the violation of division (A) or (B) of this section from the range of prison terms authorized for the level of the offense under section 2929.14 of the Revised Code.

Ohio Code § 2903.041. Reckless homicide

(A) No person shall recklessly cause the death of another or the unlawful termination of another's pregnancy.

(B) Whoever violates this section is guilty of reckless homicide, a felony of the third degree.

Ohio Code § 2903.05. Negligent homicide

(A) No person shall negligently cause the death of another or the unlawful termination of another's pregnancy by means of a deadly weapon or dangerous ordnance as defined in section 2923.11 of the Revised Code.

(B) Whoever violates this section is guilty of negligent homicide, a misdemeanor of the first degree.

Ohio Code § 2903.06.
Aggravated vehicular homicide (abridged)

(A) No person, while operating or participating in the operation of a motor vehicle, motorcycle, snowmobile, locomotive, watercraft, or aircraft, shall cause the death of another or the unlawful termination of another's pregnancy in any of the following ways:

(1)(a) As the proximate result of committing a violation of division (A) of section 4511.19 of the Revised Code or of a substantially equivalent municipal ordinance;

(b) As the proximate result of committing a violation of division (A) of section 1547.11 of the Revised Code or of a substantially equivalent municipal ordinance;

(c) As the proximate result of committing a violation of division (A)(3) of section 4561.15 of the Revised Code or of a substantially equivalent municipal ordinance.

(2) In one of the following ways:

(a) Recklessly;

(b) As the proximate result of committing, while operating or participating in the operation of a motor vehicle or motorcycle in a construction zone, a reckless operation offense, provided that this division applies only if the person whose death is caused or whose pregnancy is unlawfully terminated is in the construction zone at the time of the offender's commission of the reckless operation offense in the construction zone and does not apply as described in division (F) of this section.

(3) In one of the following ways:

(a) Negligently;

(b) As the proximate result of committing, while operating or participating in the operation of a motor vehicle or motorcycle in a construction zone, a speeding offense, provided that this division applies only if the person whose death is caused or whose pregnancy is unlawfully terminated is in the construction zone at the time of the offender's commission of the speeding offense in the construction zone and does not apply as described in division (F) of this section.

(4) As the proximate result of committing a violation of any provision of any section contained in Title XLV of the Revised Code that is a minor misdemeanor or of a municipal ordinance that, regardless of the penalty set by ordinance for the violation, is substantially equivalent to any provision of any section contained in Title XLV of the Revised Code that is a minor misdemeanor....

[B] Aggravated vehicular homicide committed in violation of division (A)(1) of this section is a felony of the first degree....

[C] Except as otherwise provided in this division, aggravated vehicular homicide committed in violation of division (A)(2) of this section is a felony of the third degree.

[D] Whoever violates division (A)(3) of this section is guilty of vehicular homicide. Except as otherwise provided in this division, vehicular homicide is a misdemeanor of the first degree....

[E] Whoever violates division (A)(4) of this section is guilty of vehicular manslaughter. Except as otherwise provided in this division, vehicular manslaughter is a misdemeanor of the second degree.

Ohio Code § 2903.08.
Aggravated vehicular assault (abridged)

(A) No person, while operating or participating in the operation of a motor vehicle, motorcycle, snowmobile, locomotive, watercraft, or aircraft, shall cause serious physical harm to another person or another's unborn in any of the following ways:

(1)(a) As the proximate result of committing a violation of division (A) of section 4511.19 of the Revised Code or of a substantially equivalent municipal ordinance;

(b) As the proximate result of committing a violation of division (A) of section 1547.11 of the Revised Code or of a substantially equivalent municipal ordinance;

(c) As the proximate result of committing a violation of division (A)(3) of section 4561.15 of the Revised Code or of a substantially equivalent municipal ordinance.

(2) In one of the following ways:

(a) As the proximate result of committing, while operating or participating in the operation of a motor vehicle or motorcycle in a construction zone, a reckless operation offense, provided that this division applies only if the person to whom the serious physical harm is caused or to whose unborn the serious physical harm is caused is in the construction zone at the time of the offender's commission of the reckless operation offense in the construction zone and does not apply as described in division (E) of this section;

(b) Recklessly.

(3) As the proximate result of committing, while operating or participating in the operation of a motor vehicle or motorcycle in a construction zone, a speeding offense, provided that this division applies only if the person to whom the serious physical harm is caused or to

whose unborn the serious physical harm is caused is in the construction zone at the time of the offender's commission of the speeding offense in the construction zone and does not apply as described in division (E) of this section.

(B)(1) Whoever violates division (A)(1) of this section is guilty of aggravated vehicular assault....

(C)(1) Whoever violates division (A)(2) or (3) of this section is guilty of vehicular assault...

Ohio Code § 2903.11. Felonious assault (abridged)

(A) No person shall knowingly do either of the following:

(1) Cause serious physical harm to another or to another's unborn;

(2) Cause or attempt to cause physical harm to another or to another's unborn by means of a deadly weapon or dangerous ordnance.

(B) Omitted.

(C) Omitted.

(D)(1) Whoever violates this section is guilty of felonious assault, a felony of the second degree....

(2) In addition to any other sanctions imposed pursuant to division (D)(1) of this section for felonious assault committed in violation of division (A)(2) of this section, if the deadly weapon used in the commission of the violation is a motor vehicle, the court shall impose upon the offender a class two suspension of the offender's driver's license, commercial driver's license, temporary instruction permit, probationary license, or nonresident operating privilege as specified in division (A)(2) of section 4510.02 of the Revised Code.

Ohio Code § 2903.12.
Aggravated assault (abridged)

(A) No person, while under the influence of sudden passion or in a sudden fit of rage, either of which is brought on by serious provocation occasioned by the victim that is reasonably sufficient to incite the person into using deadly force, shall knowingly:

(1) Cause serious physical harm to another or to another's unborn;

(2) Cause or attempt to cause physical harm to another or to another's unborn by means of a deadly weapon or dangerous ordnance, as defined in section 2923.11 of the Revised Code.

(B) Whoever violates this section is guilty of aggravated assault, a felony of the fourth degree.

2903.13. Assault (abridged)

(A) No person shall knowingly cause or attempt to cause physical harm to another or to another's unborn.

(B) No person shall recklessly cause serious physical harm to another or to another's unborn.

(C) Whoever violates this section is guilty of assault. Except as otherwise provided in division (C)(1), (2), (3), (4), or (5) of this section, assault is a misdemeanor of the first degree.

Ohio Code § 2903.14. Negligent assault

(A) No person shall negligently, by means of a deadly weapon or dangerous ordnance as defined in section 2923.11 of the Revised Code, cause physical harm to another or to another's unborn.

(B) Whoever violates this section is guilty of negligent assault, a misdemeanor of the third degree.

Ohio Code § 2903.21. Aggravated menacing

(A) No person shall knowingly cause another to believe that the offender will cause serious physical harm to the person or property of the other person, the other person's unborn, or a member of the other person's immediate family.

(B) Whoever violates this section is guilty of aggravated menacing. Except as otherwise provided in this division, aggravated menacing is a misdemeanor of the first degree. If the victim of the offense is an officer or employee of a public children services agency or a private child placing agency and the offense relates to the officer's or employee's performance or anticipated performance of official responsibilities or duties, aggravated menacing is a felony of the fifth degree or, if the offender previously has been convicted of or pleaded guilty to an offense of violence, the victim of that prior offense was an officer or employee of a public children services agency or private child placing agency, and that prior offense related to the officer's or employee's performance or anticipated performance of official responsibilities or duties, a felony of the fourth degree.

Ohio Code § 2903.22. Menacing

(A) No person shall knowingly cause another to believe that the offender will cause physical harm to the person or property of the other person, the other person's unborn, or a member of the other person's immediate family.

(B) Whoever violates this section is guilty of menacing. Except as otherwise provided in this division, menacing is a misdemeanor of the fourth degree. If the victim of the offense is an officer or employee of a public children services agency or a private child placing agency and the offense relates to the officer's or employee's performance or anticipated performance of official responsibilities or duties, menacing is a misdemeanor of the first degree or, if the offender previously has been convicted of or pleaded guilty to an offense of violence, the victim of that prior offense was an officer or employee of a public children services agency or private child placing agency, and that prior offense related to the officer's or employee's performance or anticipated performance of official responsibilities or duties, a felony of the fourth degree.

(13) CHOOSE LIFE LICENSE PLATE

Ohio authorizes the issuance of Choose Life license plates. The statutes addressing the matter are set out below.

Ohio Code § 4503.91.
Application for choose life license plates

(A) The owner or lessee of any passenger car, noncommercial motor vehicle, recreational vehicle, or other vehicle of a class approved by the registrar of motor vehicles may apply to the registrar for the registration of the vehicle and issuance of "choose life" license plates. The application for "choose life" license plates may be combined with a request for a special reserved license plate under section 4503.40 or 4503.42 of the Revised Code. Upon receipt of the completed application and compliance with divisions (B) and (C) of this section, the registrar shall issue to the applicant the appropriate vehicle registration and a set of "choose life" license plates with a validation sticker or a validation sticker alone when required by section 4503.191 of the Revised Code.

In addition to the letters and numbers ordinarily inscribed on license plates, "choose life" license plates shall be inscribed with the words "choose life" and a marking designed by "choose life, inc.," a private, nonprofit corporation incorporated in the state of Florida. The registrar shall review the design and approve it if the design is feasible. If the design is not feasible, the registrar shall notify "choose life, inc.," and the organization may resubmit designs until a feasible one is approved. "Choose life" license plates shall bear county identification stickers that identify the county of registration by name or number.

(B) "Choose life" license plates and a validation sticker, or a validation sticker alone, shall be issued upon receipt of a contribution as provided in division (C) of this section and upon payment of the regular license tax prescribed in section 4503.04 of the Revised Code, any applicable motor vehicle tax levied under Chapter 4504. of the Revised Code, any applicable additional fee prescribed by section 4503.40 or 4503.42 of the Revised Code, a fee of ten dollars for the purpose of compensating the bureau of motor vehicles for additional services required in the issuing of

"choose life" license plates, and compliance with all other applicable laws relating to the registration of motor vehicles.

(C)(1) For each application for registration and registration renewal received under this section, the registrar shall collect a contribution of twenty dollars. The registrar shall transmit this contribution to the treasurer of state for deposit in the "choose life" fund created in section 3701.65 of the Revised Code.

(2) The registrar shall deposit the additional fee of ten dollars specified in division (B) of this section for the purpose of compensating the bureau for the additional services required in issuing "choose life" license plates in the state bureau of motor vehicles fund created in section 4501.25 of the Revised Code.

Ohio Code § 3701.65. Choose life fund

(A) There is hereby created in the state treasury the "choose life" fund. The fund shall consist of the contributions that are paid to the registrar of motor vehicles by applicants who voluntarily elect to obtain " choose life " license plates pursuant to section 4503.91 of the Revised Code and any money returned to the fund under division (E)(1)(d) of this section. All investment earnings of the fund shall be credited to the fund.

(B)(1) At least annually, the director of health shall distribute the money in the fund to any private, nonprofit organization that is eligible to receive funds under this section and that applies for funding under division (C) of this section.

(2) The director shall distribute the funds based on the county in which the organization applying for funding is located and in proportion to the number of " choose life " license plates issued during the preceding year to vehicles registered in each county. The director shall distribute funds allocated for a county to one or more eligible organizations located in contiguous counties if no eligible organization located within the county applies for funding. Within each county, eligible organizations that apply for funding shall share equally in the funds available for distribution to organizations located within that county.

(C) Any organization seeking funds under this section annually shall apply for distribution of the funds based on the county in which the organization is located. An organization may apply for funding in a contiguous county if it demonstrates that it provides services for pregnant women residing in that contiguous county. The director shall develop an application form and may determine the schedule and procedures that an organization shall follow when annually applying for funds. The application shall inform the applicant of the conditions for receiving and using funds under division (E) of this section. The application shall require evidence that the organization meets all of the following requirements:

(1) Is a private, nonprofit organization;

(2) Is committed to counseling pregnant women about the option of adoption;

(3) Provides services within the state to pregnant women who are planning to place their children for adoption, including counseling and meeting the material needs of the women;

(4) Does not charge women for any services received;

(5) Is not involved or associated with any abortion activities, including counseling for or referrals to abortion clinics, providing medical abortion-related procedures, or pro-abortion advertising;

(6) Does not discriminate in its provision of any services on the basis of race, religion, color, age, marital status, national origin, handicap, gender, or age.

(D) The director shall not distribute funds to an organization that does not provide verifiable evidence of the requirements specified in the application under division (C) of this section and shall not provide additional funds to any organization that fails to comply with division (E) of this section in regard to its previous receipt of funds under this section.

(E)(1) An organization receiving funds under this section shall do all of the following:

(a) Use not more than sixty per cent of the funds distributed to it for the material needs of pregnant women who are planning to place their children for adoption or for infants awaiting placement with adoptive parents, including clothing, housing, medical care, food, utilities, and transportation;

(b) Use not more than forty per cent of the funds distributed to it for counseling, training, or advertising;

(c) Not use any of the funds distributed to it for administrative expenses, legal expenses, or capital expenditures;

(d) Annually return to the fund created under division (A) of this section any unused money that exceeds ten per cent of the money distributed to the organization.

(2) The organization annually shall submit to the director an audited financial statement verifying its compliance with division (E)(1) of this section.

(F) The director, in accordance with Chapter 119. of the Revised Code, shall adopt rules to implement this section.

It is not the intent of the general assembly that the department create a new position within the department to implement and administer this section. It is the intent of the general assembly that the implementation and administration of this section be accomplished by existing department personnel.

Ohio Right to Life

Ohio Right to Life is a pro-life organization. It was founded to promote and defend the rights of all human beings from the time of fertilization until natural death by eliminating abortion. The organization engages in activities that include: (1) offering educational programs on fetal development, abortion, abortion alternatives, the pro-life movement, and current topics in bio-ethics to churches, schools, colleges, and community groups; (2) providing pro-life educational materials such as books, videos, pamphlets, and articles for use at churches, schools, fairs, and other public forums; (3) developing and maintaining a grassroots network of Ohioans who advocate for life issues with their elected state and federal representatives; (4) supporting appropriate legislation that helps protect the right to life of all human beings; (5) sponsoring pro-life statewide media campaigns—including billboard, radio, print, and television ads; and (6) publishing a bi-monthly newsletter to educate memberships about current pro-life initiatives. *See also* **Pro-Life Organizations**

Ohio v. Akron Center for Reproductive Health

Forum: United States Supreme Court.

Case Citation: Ohio v. Akron Center for Reproductive Health, 497 U.S. 502 (1990).

Date Argued: November 29, 1989.

Date of Decision: June 25, 1990.

Opinion of Court: Kennedy, J., in which Rehnquist, C.J., and White, Stevens, O'Connor, and Scalia, JJ.

Concurring Opinion: Scalia, J.

Concurring Opinion: Stevens, J.

Dissenting Opinion: Blackmun, J., in which Brennan and Marshall, JJ., joined.

Counsel for Appellant: Rita S. Eppler, Assistant Attorney General of Ohio, argued; on the brief were Anthony J. Celebrezze, Jr., Attorney General, and Thomas J. O'Connell and Suzanne E. Mohr, Assistant Attorneys General.

Counsel for Appellees: Linda R. Sogg argued; on the brief were Dara Klassel, Roger Evans, Barbara E. Otten, and Eve W. Paul.

Amicus Brief for Appellant: American Family Association, Inc., by Peggy M. Coleman; for the Association of American Physicians and

Surgeons by Ann-Louise Lohr, Paige Comstock Cunningham, and Kent Masterson Brown; for Concerned Women for America by Jordan W. Lorence, Cimron Campbell, and Wendell R. Bird; for the Knights of Columbus by Brendan V. Sullivan, Jr., Kevin J. Hasson, and Carl A. Anderson; for the United States Catholic Conference by Mark E. Chopko; and for Representative Jerome S. Luebbers et al. by Patrick J. Perotti.

Amicus Brief for Appellees: 274 Organizations in Support of Roe v. Wade by Kathleen M. Sullivan, Susan R. Estrich, Barbara Jordan, and Estelle H. Rogers; for the American College of Obstetricians and Gynecologists et al. by Carter G. Phillips, Elizabeth H. Esty, Ann E. Allen, Stephan E. Lawton, Laurie R. Rockett, and Joel I. Klein; and for the American Psychological Association et al. by Donald N. Bersoff.

Issue Presented: Whether the federal constitution was violated by Ohio's notice and judicial bypass requirements for pregnant female minors?

Case Holding: Ohio's notice and judicial bypass requirements for pregnant female minors did not infringe upon the constitution.

Background facts of case: The state of Ohio enacted an abortion statute pertaining to pregnant female minors that included provisions which made it a crime for a physician or other person to perform an abortion on an unemancipated female minor unless, inter alia, the physician provides timely notice to one of the minor's parents or a juvenile court issued an order authorizing the minor to consent to an abortion. The statute also allowed the physician to give constructive notice if actual notice to the parent proved impossible after a reasonable effort. To obtain the judicial bypass of the notice requirement, the minor had to present clear and convincing proof that she had sufficient maturity and information to make the abortion decision herself, that one of her parents had engaged in a pattern of physical, emotional, or sexual abuse against her, or that notice is not in her best interests. The statute also required the minor to file a judicial bypass complaint in the juvenile court on prescribed forms; required the court to appoint a guardian ad litem and an attorney for the minor if she had not retained counsel; mandated expedited bypass hearings and decisions in the juvenile court and expedited review by a court of appeals; provided constructive authorization for the minor to consent to the abortion if either court failed to act in a timely fashion; and specified that both courts must maintain the minor's anonymity and the confidentiality of all papers.

In March of 1986 the appellees, abortion providers and others, brought a facial challenge to the constitutionality of the statute in a federal district court in Ohio. The district court issued a permanent injunction preventing the state of Ohio from enforcing the statute. The Sixth Circuit court of appeals affirmed. The Supreme Court granted certiorari to consider the case.

Majority opinion by Justice Kennedy: Justice Kennedy found that Ohio's abortion provisions for minors passed constitutional muster. The opinion initially addressed the judicial bypass provision of the statute based upon criteria established in a prior decision of the Court:

> The principal opinion in *Bellotti v. Baird* stated four criteria that a bypass procedure in a consent statute must satisfy. Appellees contend that the bypass procedure does not satisfy these criteria. We disagree. First, the *Bellotti* principal opinion indicated that the procedure must allow the minor to show that she possesses the maturity and information to make her abortion decision, in consultation with her physician, without regard to her parents' wishes.... In the case now before us, we have no difficulty concluding that [the statute] allows a minor to show maturity in conformity with the principal opinion in *Bellotti*. The statute permits the minor to show that she is sufficiently mature and well enough informed to decide intelligently whether to have an abortion.
>
> Second, the *Bellotti* principal opinion indicated that the procedure must allow the minor to show that, even if she cannot make the abortion decision by herself, "the desired abortion would be in her best interests. We believe that [the statute] satisfies the *Bellotti* language as quoted. The statute requires the juvenile court to authorize the minor's consent where the court determines that the abortion is in the minor's best interest and in cases where the minor has shown a pattern of physical, sexual, or emotional abuse.
>
> Third, the *Bellotti* principal opinion indicated that the procedure must insure the minor's anonymity. [The statute] satisfies this standard. [It] the juvenile court shall not notify the parents, guardian, or custodian of the complainant that she is pregnant or that she wants to have an abortion....
>
> Fourth, the *Bellotti* plurality indicated that courts must conduct a bypass procedure with expedition to allow the minor an effective opportunity to obtain the abortion. [The statute] require the trial court to make its decision within five business days after the minor files her complaint; requires the court of appeals to docket an appeal within four days after the minor files a notice of appeal; and requires the court of appeals to render a decision within five days after docketing the appeal.
>
> The District Court and the Court of Appeals ... calculated ... that the procedure could take up to 22 calendar days, because the minor could file at a time during the year in which the 14 business days needed for the bypass procedure would encompass three Saturdays, three Sundays, and two legal holidays. Appellees maintain, on the basis of an affidavit included in the record, that a 3-week delay could increase by a substantial measure both the costs and the medical risks of an abortion. They conclude, as did those courts, that [the statute] does not satisfy the *Bellotti* principal opinion's expedition requirement.
>
> ... The Court of Appeals should not have invalidated the Ohio statute on a facial challenge based upon a worst-case analysis that may never occur. Moreover, under our precedents, the mere possibility that the procedure may require up to 22 days in a rare case is plainly insufficient to invalidate the statute on its face.

After determining that the statute satisfied the requirements of Bellotti, Justice Kennedy turned to other criteria that the appellees suggested the Court should consider. The other factors were rejected as follows:

> Appellees ask us, in effect, to extend the criteria used by some members of the Court in *Bellotti* and the cases following it by imposing three additional requirements on bypass procedures. First, they challenge the constructive authorization provisions in [the statute], which enable a minor to obtain an abortion without notifying one of her parents if either the juvenile court or the court of appeals fails to act within the prescribed time limits. They speculate that the absence of an affirmative order when a court fails to process the minor's complaint will deter the physician from acting.
>
> We discern no constitutional defect in the statute. Absent a demonstrated pattern of abuse or defiance, a State may expect that its judges will follow mandated procedural requirements. There is no showing that the time limitations imposed by [the statute] will be ignored. With an abundance of caution, and concern for the minor's interests, Ohio added the constructive authorization provision in [the statute] to ensure expedition of the bypass procedures even if these time limits are not met....
>
> Second, appellees ask us to rule that a bypass procedure cannot require a minor to prove maturity or best interests by a standard of clear and convincing evidence. They maintain that, when a State seeks to deprive an individual of liberty interests, it must take upon itself the risk of error. [The statute] violates this standard, in their opinion, not only by placing the burden of proof

upon the minor, but also by imposing a heightened standard of proof.

This contention lacks merit. A State does not have to bear the burden of proof on the issues of maturity or best interests. The principal opinion in *Bellotti* indicates that a State may require the minor to prove these facts in a bypass procedure. A State, moreover, may require a heightened standard of proof when, as here, the bypass procedure contemplates an ex parte proceeding at which no one opposes the minor's testimony. We find the clear and convincing standard used in [the statute] acceptable....

Third, appellees contend that the pleading requirements in [the statute] create a trap for the unwary. The minor, under the statutory scheme and the requirements prescribed by the Ohio Supreme Court, must choose among three pleading forms. The first alleges only maturity and the second alleges only best interests. She may not attempt to prove both maturity and best interests unless she chooses the third form, which alleges both of these facts. Appellees contend that the complications imposed by this scheme deny a minor the opportunity, required by the principal opinion in *Bellotti*, to prove either maturity or best interests or both.

Even on the assumption that the pleading scheme could produce some initial confusion because few minors would have counsel when pleading, the simple and straightforward procedure does not deprive the minor of an opportunity to prove her case. It seems unlikely that the Ohio courts will treat a minor's choice of complaint form without due care and understanding for her unrepresented status. In addition, we note that the minor does not make a binding election by the initial choice of pleading form. The minor, under [the statute], receives appointed counsel after filing the complaint and may move for leave to amend the pleadings.

Disposition of case: The statute was constitutionally valid and the judgment of the court of appeals was reversed.

Concurring opinion by Justice Scalia: Justice Scalia wrote a terse concurring opinion that provided the following:

> I join the opinion of the Court, because I agree that the Ohio statute neither deprives minors of procedural due process nor contradicts our holdings regarding the constitutional right to abortion. I continue to believe, however, ... that the Constitution contains no right to abortion. It is not to be found in the longstanding traditions of our society, nor can it be logically deduced from the text of the Constitution — not, that is, without volunteering a judicial answer to the nonjusticiable question of when human life begins. Leaving this matter to the political process is not only legally correct, it is pragmatically so.... The Court should end its disruptive intrusion into this field as soon as possible.

Concurring opinion by Justice Stevens: Justice Stevens agreed with the majority that the statute was facially sound. He wrote:

> There is some tension between the statutory requirement that the treating physician notify the minor's parent and our [prior decision] that a State may not require the attending physician to personally counsel an abortion patient. One cannot overlook the possibility that this provision was motivated more by a legislative interest in placing obstacles in the woman's path to an abortion, than by a genuine interest in fostering informed decisionmaking. I agree with the Court, however, that the Ohio statute requires only that the physician take "reasonable steps" to notify a minor's parent, and that such notification may contribute to the decisionmaking process. Accordingly, I am unable to conclude that this provision is unconstitutional on its face.

Dissenting opinion by Justice Blackmun: Justice Blackmun disagreed with the majority decision. He believed that the statute was unconstitutional in its entirety. Justice Blackmun wrote:

> The State of Ohio has acted with particular insensitivity in enacting the statute the Court today upholds. Rather than create a judicial bypass system that reflects the sensitivity necessary when dealing with a minor making this deeply intimate decision, Ohio has created a tortuous maze. Moreover, the State has failed utterly to show that it has any significant state interest in deliberately placing its pattern of obstacles in the path of the pregnant minor seeking to exercise her constitutional right to terminate a pregnancy. The challenged provisions of the Ohio statute are merely poorly disguised elements of discouragement for the abortion decision....
>
> I would affirm the judgments below on the grounds of the several constitutional defects identified by the District Court and the Court of Appeals. The pleading requirements, the so-called and fragile guarantee of anonymity, the insufficiency of the expedited procedures, the constructive authorization provision, and the clear and convincing evidence requirement, singly and collectively, cross the limit of constitutional acceptance.

Oklahoma

(1) OVERVIEW

The state of Oklahoma enacted its first criminal abortion statute in 1890. The statute underwent several amendments prior to the 1973 decision by the United States Supreme Court in *Roe v. Wade*, which legalized abortion in the nation. In spite of the decision in *Roe*, Oklahoma has not repealed its pre–*Roe* criminal abortion laws. However, the laws are constitutionally infirm.

Oklahoma has taken affirmative steps to respond to *Roe* and its progeny. The state has addressed several abortion issues by statute that include general abortion guidelines, fetal pain awareness, informed consent, abortion by minors, partial-birth abortion, use of facilities and people, fetal experiments, injury to a pregnant woman, fetal death report, abortion alternative programs, use of public funds, and health insurance.

(2) PRE-ROE ABORTION BAN

As previously indicated, Oklahoma has not repealed its pre–*Roe* criminal abortion laws. Under the now unconstitutional statutes, abortion was criminalized if it was not performed to preserve the life of the woman. Oklahoma imposed criminal punishment upon the abortioner and the woman who had an abortion. These laws were specifically held invalid in *Jobe v. State*, 509 P.2d 481 (Okla.Crim.App. 1973) and *Henrie v. Derryberry*, 358 F.Supp. 719 (N.D.Okla. 1973). The statutes are set out below.

Oklahoma Code Ti. 21, § 714.
Procuring destruction of unborn child

Every person who administers to any woman pregnant with a quick child, or who prescribes for such woman, or advises or procures any such woman to take any medicine, drug or substance whatever, or who uses or employs any instrument or other means with intent thereby to destroy such child, unless the same shall have been necessary to preserve the life of such mother, is guilty in case the death of the child or of the mother is thereby produced, of manslaughter in the first degree.

Oklahoma Code Ti. 21, § 861.
Procuring an abortion

Every person who administers to any woman, or who prescribes for any woman, or advises or procures any woman to take any medicine, drug or substance, or uses or employs any instrument, or other means whatever, with intent thereby to procure the miscarriage of such woman, unless the same is necessary to preserve her life, shall be guilty of a felony punishable by imprisonment in the State Penitentiary for not less than two (2) years nor more than five (5) years.

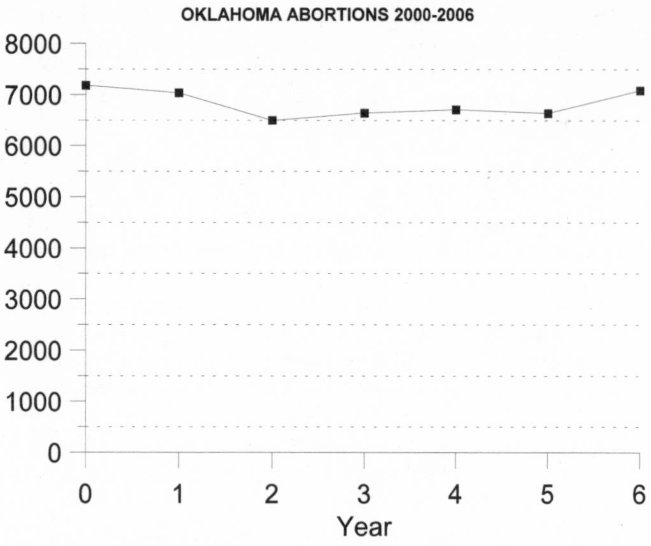

Source: Oklahoma Department of Health.

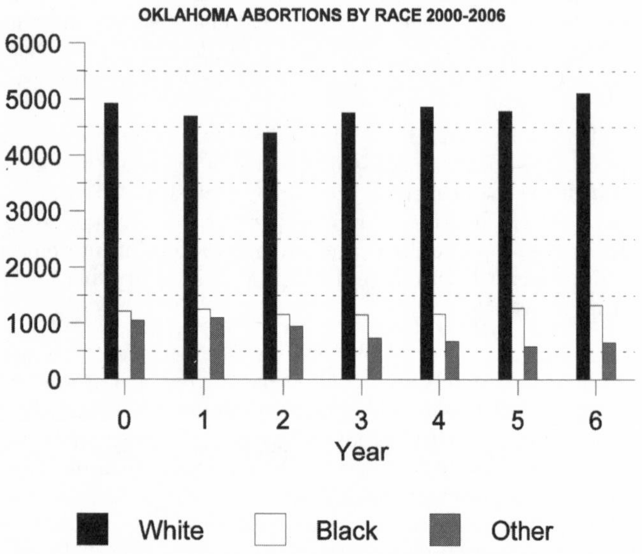

Source: Oklahoma Department of Health.

Oklahoma Code Ti. 21, § 862.
Submitting to abortion

Every woman who solicits of any person any medicine, drug, or substance whatever, and takes the same, or who submits to any operation, or to the use of any means whatever, with intent thereby to procure a miscarriage, unless the same is necessary to preserve her life, is punishable by imprisonment in the county jail not exceeding one year, or by fine not exceeding One Thousand Dollars ($1,000.00), or by both.

Oklahoma Code Ti. 21, § 863.
Concealing stillbirth or death of child

Every woman who endeavors either by herself or by the aid of others to conceal the stillbirth of an issue of her body, which if born alive would be a bastard, or the death of any such issue under the age of two (2) years, is punishable by imprisonment in the county jail not exceeding one (1) year, or by a fine not exceeding One Thousand Dollars ($1,000.00), or both.

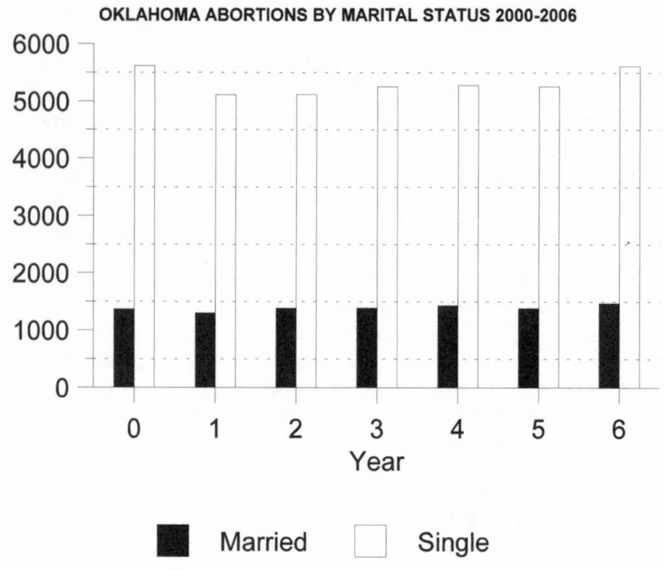

Source: Oklahoma Department of Health.

Oklahoma Abortion by Age Group 2000–2006
Age Group (yrs)

Year	*<15*	*15–19*	*20–24*	*25–29*	*30–34*	*35–39*	*≥40*	*Unknown*
2000	38	1,487	2,463	1,573	813	572	175	61
2001	49	1,317	2,436	1,541	964	505	196	38
2002	40	1,149	2,260	1,394	895	506	200	56
2003	52	1,242	2,325	1,451	932	450	192	0
2004	47	1,151	2,345	1,476	970	533	183	7
2005	34	1,099	2,312	1,524	930	523	181	38
2006	39	1,109	2,550	1,603	937	587	201	62
Total	299	8,554	16,691	10,562	6,441	3,676	1,328	262

Source: Oklahoma Department of Health.

Oklahoma Abortion by Education Level of Female 2002–2006
Education Level Completed

Year	*<9*	*9–12 (no diploma)*	*12*	*≥13*	*Unknown*
2002	179	997	2,697	2,627	0
2003	148	998	2,749	2,749	0
2004	118	981	2,817	2,795	1
2005	121	948	2,664	2,907	1
2006	135	956	2,923	3,074	0
Total	701	4,880	13,850	14,152	2

Source: Oklahoma Department of Health.

Oklahoma Prior Abortion by Female 2000–2006
Prior Abortion

Year	*None*	*1*	*2*	*≥3*
2000	4,606	1,746	515	266
2001	4,450	1,686	546	257
2002	4,022	1,655	529	294
2003	4,432	1,544	447	221
2004	4,276	1,655	510	271
2005	4,300	1,606	494	241
2006	4,496	1,796	507	289
Total	30,582	11,688	3,548	1,839

Source: Oklahoma Department of Health.

Oklahoma Abortion by Weeks of Gestation 2000–2006

Weeks of Gestation	Year 2000	2001	2002	2003	2004	2005	2006	Total
<9	3,698	3,682	3,982	4,011	4,102	4,273	4,366	28,114
9-10	1,601	1,528	1,301	1,341	1,253	1,137	1,343	9,504
11-12	1,198	1,134	660	691	698	613	648	5,642
13-15	370	399	365	396	376	390	454	2,750
16-20	217	207	180	198	268	220	262	1,552
≥21	30	14	12	7	14	8	13	98
Not known	68	73	0	0	1	0	2	144

Source: **Oklahoma Department of Health.**

(3) GENERAL ABORTION GUIDELINES

Oklahoma requires abortions be performed by physicians only. The state requires abortions after the first trimester be performed at a hospital. However, the hospital requirement is constitutionally invalid prior to fetal viability. Oklahoma has enacted a penal statute that prohibits post-viability abortions, except to save the life of the woman or to prevent the woman from having a severe health problem if the child was carried to term. A post-viability abortion must be certified as necessary and a physician, other than the one performing the abortion, must be present during the abortion.

Oklahoma Code Ti. 63, § 1-730. Definitions

As used in this article:

1. "Abortion" means the use or prescription of any instrument, medicine, drug, or any other substance or device intentionally to terminate the pregnancy of a female known to be pregnant with an intention other than to increase the probability of a live birth, to preserve the life or health of the child after live birth, to remove an ectopic pregnancy, or to remove a dead unborn child who died as the result of a spontaneous miscarriage, accidental trauma, or a criminal assault on the pregnant female or her unborn child;

2. "Unborn child" means the unborn offspring of human beings from the moment of conception, through pregnancy, and until live birth including the human conceptus, zygote, morula, blastocyst, embryo and fetus;

3. "Viable" means potentially able to live outside of the womb of the mother upon premature birth, whether resulting from natural causes or an abortion;

4. "Conception" means the fertilization of the ovum of a female individual by the sperm of a male individual;

5. "Health" means physical or mental health;

6. "Department" means the State Department of Health;

7. "Inducing an abortion" means the administration by any person, including the pregnant woman, of any substance designed or intended to cause an expulsion of the unborn child, effecting an abortion as defined above; and

8. Nothing contained herein shall be construed in any manner to include any birth control device or medication or sterilization procedure.

Oklahoma Code Ti. 63, § 1-731. Who may perform abortion

A. No person shall perform or induce an abortion upon a pregnant woman unless that person is a physician licensed to practice medicine in the State of Oklahoma. Any person violating this section shall be guilty of a felony punishable by imprisonment for not less than one (1) year nor more than three (3) years in the State Penitentiary.

B. No person shall perform or induce an abortion upon a pregnant woman subsequent to the end of the first trimester of her pregnancy, unless such abortion is performed or induced in a general hospital.

Oklahoma Code Ti. 63, § 1-732. Post-viability abortion

A. No person shall perform or induce an abortion upon a pregnant woman after such time as her unborn child has become viable unless such abortion is necessary to prevent the death of the pregnant woman or to prevent impairment to her health.

B. An unborn child shall be presumed to be viable if more than twenty-four (24) weeks have elapsed since the probable beginning of the last menstrual period of the pregnant woman, based upon either information provided by her or by an examination by her attending physician. If it is the judgment of the attending physician that a particular unborn child is not viable where the presumption of viability exists as to that particular unborn child, then he shall certify in writing the precise medical criteria upon which he has determined that the particular unborn child is not viable before an abortion may be performed or induced.

C. No abortion of a viable unborn child shall be performed or induced except after written certification by the attending physician that in his best medical judgment the abortion is necessary to prevent the death of the pregnant woman or to prevent an impairment to her health. The physician shall further certify in writing the medical indications for such abortion and the probable health consequences if the abortion is not performed or induced.

D. The physician who shall perform or induce an abortion upon a pregnant woman after such time as her unborn child has become viable shall utilize the available method or technique of abortion most likely to preserve the life and health of the unborn child, unless he shall first certify in writing that in his best medical judgment such method or technique shall present a significantly greater danger to the life or health of the pregnant woman than another available method or technique.

E. An abortion of a viable unborn child shall be performed or induced only when there is in attendance a physician other than the physician performing or inducing the abortion who shall take control of and provide immediate medical care for the child. During the performance or inducing of the abortion, the physician performing it, and subsequent to it, the physician required by this section to be in attendance, shall take all reasonable steps in keeping with good medical practice, consistent with the procedure used, to preserve the life and health of the child, in the same manner as if the child had been born naturally or spontaneously. The requirement of the attendance of a second physician may be waived when in the best judgment of the attending physician a medical emergency exists and further delay would result in a serious threat to the life or physical health of the pregnant woman. Provided that, under such emergency circumstances and waiver, the attending physician shall have the duty to take all reasonable steps to preserve the life and health of the child before, during and after the abortion procedure, unless such steps shall, in the best medical judgment of the physician, present a significantly greater danger to the life or health of the pregnant woman.

F. Any person violating subsection A of this section shall be guilty of homicide.

Oklahoma Code Ti. 63, § 1-733. Self-induced abortions

No woman shall perform or induce an abortion upon herself, except under the supervision of a duly licensed physician. Any physician who supervises a woman in performing or inducing an abortion upon herself shall fulfill all the requirements of this article which apply to a physician performing or inducing an abortion.

Oklahoma Code Ti. 63, § 1-734. Live-born fetus

A. No person shall purposely take the life of a child born as a result of an abortion or attempted abortion which is alive when partially or totally removed from the uterus of the pregnant woman.

B. No person shall purposely take the life of a viable child who is alive while inside the uterus of the pregnant woman and may be removed alive therefrom without creating any significant danger to her life or health.

C. Any person who performs, induces, or participates in the performance or inducing of an abortion shall take all reasonable measures to preserve the life of a child who is alive when partially or totally removed from the uterus of the pregnant woman, so long as the measures do not create any significant danger to her life or health.

D. Any person violating this section shall be guilty of homicide.

Oklahoma Code Ti. 63, § 1-736.
Advertising of counseling to pregnant women

No hospital in which abortions are performed or induced shall advertise or hold itself out as also providing counseling to pregnant women, unless:

1. The counseling is done by a licensed physician, a licensed registered nurse or by a person holding at least a bachelor's degree from an accredited college or university in psychology or some similarly appropriate field;

2. The counseling includes factual information, including explicit discussion of the development of the unborn child; and

3. The counseling includes a thorough discussion of the alternatives to abortion and the availability of agencies and services to assist her if she chooses not to have an abortion.

Oklahoma Code Ti. 63, § 1-737.
Hospitals which may perform abortions

An abortion otherwise permitted by law shall be performed only in a hospital, as defined in this article, which meets standards set by the Department. The Department shall develop and promulgate reasonable standards relating to abortions.

(4) FETAL PAIN AWARENESS

Oklahoma has enacted statutes that require a physician inform a woman about fetal pain. Under the statutes a woman must be told whether an anesthetic would eliminate organic pain to the fetus. The statutes are set out below.

Oklahoma Code Ti. 63, § 1-738.6. Short title

This act shall be known and may be cited as the "Unborn Child Pain Awareness/Prevention Act."

Oklahoma Code Ti. 63, § 1-738.7. Definitions

As used in the Unborn Child Pain Awareness/Prevention Act:

1. "Abortion" means the use or prescription of any instrument, medicine, drug, or any other substance or device intentionally to terminate the pregnancy of a female known to be pregnant with an intention other than to increase the probability of a live birth, to preserve the life or health of the child after live birth, to remove an ectopic pregnancy, or to remove a dead fetus who dies as the result of a spontaneous miscarriage, accidental trauma or a criminal assault on the pregnant female or her unborn child;

2. "Attempt to perform an abortion" means an act, or an omission of a statutorily required act that, under the circumstances as the actor believes them to be, constitutes a substantial step in a course of conduct planned to culminate in the performance of an abortion in Oklahoma in violation of the Unborn Child Pain Awareness/Prevention Act;

3. "Unborn child" means a member of the species homo sapiens from fertilization until birth;

4. "Medical emergency" means the existence of any physical condition, not including any emotional, psychological, or mental condition, which a reasonably prudent physician, with knowledge of the case and treatment possibilities with respect to the medical conditions involved, would determine necessitates the immediate abortion of the pregnancy of the female to avert her death or to avert substantial and irreversible impairment of a major bodily function arising from continued pregnancy;

5. "Physician" means a person licensed to practice medicine in this state pursuant to Sections 495 and 633 of Title 59 of the Oklahoma Statutes; and

6. "Probable gestational age" means the gestational age of the unborn child at the time the abortion is planned to be performed, as determined by the physician using reasonable probability.

Oklahoma Code Ti. 63, § 1-738.8. Review of materials

A. Except in the case of a medical emergency, at least twenty-four (24) hours prior to an abortion being performed on an unborn child whose probable gestational age is twenty (20) weeks or more, the physician performing the abortion or the agent of the physician shall inform the pregnant female, by telephone or in person, of the right to review the printed materials described in Section 10 of this act, that these materials are available on a state-sponsored web site, and the web address of that web site. The physician or the agent of the physician shall orally inform the female that the materials have been provided by the State of Oklahoma and that the materials contain information on pain and the unborn child. If the female chooses to view the materials other than on the web site, the materials shall either be given to the female at least twenty-four (24) hours before the abortion, or mailed to the female at least seventy-two (72) hours before the abortion by certified mail, restricted delivery to the addressee. The information required by this subsection may be provided by a tape recording if provision is made to record or otherwise register specifically whether the female does or does not choose to receive the printed materials given or mailed.

B. The female shall certify in writing, prior to the abortion, that the information described in subsection A of this section has been furnished to the female and that the female has been informed of the opportunity to review the printed materials described in Section 10 of this act. Prior to the performance of the abortion, the physician who is to perform the abortion or the agent of the physician shall obtain a copy of the written certification and retain the copy on file with the medical record of the female for at least three (3) years following the date of receipt.

Oklahoma Code Ti. 63, § 1-738.9.
Use of anesthetic to alleviate pain

Except in the case of a medical emergency, before an abortion is performed on an unborn child who is twenty (20) weeks gestational age or more, the physician performing the abortion or the agent of the physician shall inform the female if an anesthetic or analgesic would eliminate or alleviate organic pain to the unborn child caused by the particular method of abortion to be employed and inform the female of the particular medical risks associated with the particular anesthetic or analgesic. With the consent of the female, the physician shall administer the anesthetic or analgesic.

Oklahoma Code Ti. 63, § 1-738.10. Publication of materials

A. Within ninety (90) days after the Unborn Child Pain Awareness/Prevention Act becomes law, the State Board of Medical Licensure and Supervision shall cause to be published, in English and in each language which is the primary language of two percent (2%) or more of the population of the state, and shall cause to be available on the state web site provided for in Section 11 of this act, printed materials with the following statement concerning unborn children of twenty (20) weeks gestational age: "By twenty (20) weeks gestation, the unborn child has the physical structures necessary to experience pain. There is evidence that by twenty (20) weeks gestation unborn children seek to evade certain stimuli in a manner which in an infant or an adult would be interpreted to be a response to pain. Anesthesia is routinely administered to unborn children who are twenty (20) weeks gestational age or older who undergo prenatal surgery."

The materials shall be objective, nonjudgmental and designed to con-

vey only accurate scientific information about the human fetus at the various gestational ages.

B. The materials referred to in subsection A of this section shall be printed in a typeface large enough to be clearly legible. The web site provided for in Section 11 of this act shall be maintained at a minimum resolution of 70 DPI (dots per inch). All pictures appearing on this web site shall be a minimum of 200x300 pixels. All letters on the web site shall be a minimum of 11 point font. All information and pictures shall be accessible with an industry standard browser requiring no additional plug-ins.

C. The materials required under this section shall be available at no cost from the State Board of Medical Licensure and Supervision upon request and in appropriate number to any person, facility, or hospital.

Oklahoma Code Ti. 63, § 1-738.11.
Web site, development and maintenance

The State Board of Medical Licensure and Supervision shall develop and maintain a stable Internet web site to provide the information described under Section 10 of this act. No information regarding who uses the web site shall be collected or maintained. The State Board of Medical Licensure and Supervision shall monitor the web site on a daily basis to prevent and correct tampering.

Oklahoma Code Ti. 63, § 1-738.12. Medical emergency

When a medical emergency compels the performance of an abortion, the physician shall inform the female, prior to the abortion if possible, of the medical indications supporting the judgment of the physician that an abortion is necessary to avert the death of the female or that a twenty-four-hour delay will create serious risk of substantial and irreversible impairment of a major bodily function.

Oklahoma Code Ti. 63, § 1-738.13. Reporting forms

A. Within ninety (90) days after the Unborn Child Pain Awareness/Prevention Act becomes law, the State Department of Health shall prepare a reporting form for physicians containing a reprint of the Unborn Child Pain Awareness/Prevention Act and listing:

1. The number of females to whom the physician or an agent of the physician provided the information described in subsection A of Section 8 of this act; of that number, the number provided by telephone and the number provided in person; and of each of those numbers, the number provided in the capacity of a referring physician and the number provided in the capacity of a physician who is to perform the abortion or agent of such a physician;

2. The number of females who availed themselves of the opportunity to obtain a copy of the printed information described in Section 10 of this act other than on the web site, and the number who did not; and of each of those numbers, the number who, to the best of the information and belief of the reporting physician, went on to obtain the abortion; and

3. The number of abortions performed by the physician in which information otherwise required to be provided at least twenty-four (24) hours before the abortion was not so provided because an immediate abortion was necessary to avert the death of the female, and the number of abortions in which such information was not so provided because a delay would create serious risk of substantial and irreversible impairment of a major bodily function.

B. The Department shall ensure that copies of the reporting forms described in subsection A of this section are provided:

1. Within one hundred twenty days (120) days after the Unborn Child Pain Awareness/Prevention Act becomes law, to all physicians licensed to practice in this state;

2. To each physician who subsequently becomes newly licensed to practice in this state, at the same time as official notification to that physician that the physician is so licensed; and

3. By December 1 of each year, other than the calendar year in which forms are distributed in accordance with paragraph 1 of this subsection, to all physicians licensed to practice in this state.

C. By February 28 of each year following a calendar year in any part of which the Unborn Child Pain Awareness/Prevention Act was in effect, each physician who provided, or whose agent provided, information to one or more females in accordance with Section 8 of this act during the previous calendar year shall submit to the Department a copy of the form described in subsection A of this section, with the requested data entered accurately and completely.

D. Reports that are not submitted by the end of a grace period of thirty (30) days following the due date shall be subject to a late fee of Five Hundred Dollars ($500.00) for each additional thirty-day period or portion of a thirty-day period the reports are overdue. Any physician required to report in accordance with this section who has not submitted a report, or has submitted only an incomplete report, more than one (1) year following the due date may, in an action brought by the State Board of Medical Licensure and Supervision, be directed by a court of competent jurisdiction to submit a complete report within a period stated by court order or be subject to sanctions for civil contempt.

E. By June 30 of each year, the Department shall issue a public report providing statistics for the previous calendar year compiled from all of the reports covering that year submitted in accordance with this section for each of the items listed in subsection A of this section. Each such report shall also provide the statistics for all previous calendar years, adjusted to reflect any additional information from late or corrected reports. The Department shall take care to ensure that none of the information included in the public reports could reasonably lead to the identification of any individual providing or provided information in accordance with subsection A or B of Section 8 of this act.

F. The Department, by rule promulgated in accordance with the Administrative Procedures Act, may alter the dates established by paragraph 3 of subsection B, subsection C, or subsection E of this section or consolidate the forms or reports described in this section with other forms or reports to achieve administrative convenience or fiscal savings or to reduce the burden of reporting requirements, so long as reporting forms are sent to all licensed physicians in the state at least once every year and the report described in subsection E of this section is issued at least once every year.

Oklahoma Code Ti. 63, § 1-738.14. Violation of Act

Any person who knowingly or recklessly performs or attempts to perform an abortion in violation of the Unborn Child Pain Awareness/Prevention Act shall be guilty of a felony. Any physician who knowingly or recklessly submits a false report under subsection C of Section 13 of this act shall be guilty of a misdemeanor. No penalty may be assessed against the female upon whom the abortion is performed or attempted to be performed. No penalty or civil liability may be assessed for failure to comply with Section 8 of this act requiring a written certification that the female has been informed of the opportunity to review the information referred to in Section 8 of this act unless the State Department of Health has made the printed materials available at the time the physician or the agent of the physician is required to inform the female of the right to review the materials.

Oklahoma Code Ti. 63, § 1-738.15. Failure to comply with Act

A. Any person upon whom an abortion has been performed without the Unborn Child Pain Awareness/Prevention Act having been complied with, the father of the unborn child who was the subject of such an abortion, or the grandparent of such an unborn child may maintain an action against the person who performed the abortion in knowing or reckless violation of the Unborn Child Pain Awareness/Prevention Act for actual and punitive damages. Any person upon whom an abortion has been attempted without the Unborn Child Pain Awareness/Prevention Act having been complied with may maintain an action against the person *who attempted to perform the abortion in knowing or reckless violation of the Unborn Child Pain Awareness/Prevention Act for actual and punitive damages.*

B. If the Department fails to issue the public report required by the Statistical Reporting of Abortion Act of Oklahoma, an action pursuant to Title 12 of the Oklahoma Statutes may be initiated.

Oklahoma Code Ti. 63, § 1-738.16. Civil or criminal actions

In every civil or criminal proceeding or action brought under the Unborn Child Pain Awareness/Prevention Act, the court shall rule whether the anonymity of any female upon whom an abortion has been performed or attempted shall be preserved from public disclosure if the female does not give her consent to such disclosure. The court, upon motion or sua sponte, shall make such a ruling and, upon determining that the anonymity of the female should be preserved, shall issue orders to the parties, witnesses, and counsel and shall direct the sealing of the record and exclusion of individuals from courtrooms or hearing rooms to the extent necessary to safeguard the identity of the female from public disclosure. Each such order shall be accompanied by specific written findings explaining why the anonymity of the female should be preserved from public disclosure, why the order is essential to that end, how the order is narrowly tailored to serve that interest, and why no reasonable less restrictive alternative exists. In the absence of written consent of the female upon whom an abortion has been performed or attempted, anyone, other than a public official, who brings an action under subsection A of Section 15 of this act shall do so under a pseudonym. This section may not be construed to conceal the identity of the plaintiff or of witnesses from the defendant.

Oklahoma Code Ti. 63, § 1-738.17. Severability of provisions

If any one or more provision, section, subsection, sentence, clause, phrase or word of the Unborn Child Pain Awareness/Prevention Act or the application thereof to any person or circumstance is found to be unconstitutional, the same is hereby declared to be severable and the balance of the Unborn Child Pain Awareness/Prevention Act shall remain effective notwithstanding such unconstitutionality. The Legislature hereby declares that it would have passed the Unborn Child Pain Awareness/Prevention Act, and each provision, section, subsection, sentence, clause, phrase or word thereof, irrespective of the fact that any one or more provision, section, subsection, sentence, clause, phrase, or word be declared unconstitutional.

Oklahoma Code Ti. 63, § 1-739. Records

All hospitals shall keep records, including admission and discharge notes, histories, results of tests and examinations, nurses worksheets, social service records and progress notes of patients. All abortion facilities and hospitals in which abortions are performed shall also keep certifications of medical necessity, certifications of nonviability, certifications of nonavailability, abortion reports and complication reports as required in this act. Such records shall be maintained in the permanent files of the hospital for a period of not less than seven (7) years.

(5) Informed Consent

Prior to an abortion Oklahoma requires that a woman be fully informed of the procedure to be used, the risks involved and alternatives to abortion. An abortion may not take place until 24 hours after a woman has been fully informed of statutorily required information. The statutes addressing the matter are set out below.

Oklahoma Code Ti. 63, § 1-738.1. Definitions

As used in Sections 1-738.1 through 1-738.5 of this title:

1. "Abortion" means the term as is defined in Section 1-730 of this title;

2. "Attempt to perform an abortion" means an act, or an omission of a statutorily required act, that, under the circumstances as the actor believes them to be, constitutes a substantial step in a course of conduct planned to culminate in the performance of an abortion in this state in violation of this act;

3. "Board" means the State Board of Medical Licensure and Supervision;

4. "Medical emergency" means the existence of any physical condition, not including any emotional, psychological, or mental condition, which a reasonably prudent physician, with knowledge of the case and treatment possibilities with respect to the medical conditions involved, would determine necessitates the immediate abortion of the pregnancy of the female to avert her death or to avert substantial and irreversible impairment of a major bodily function arising from continued pregnancy;

5. "Physician" means a person licensed to practice medicine in this state pursuant to Sections 495 and 633 of Title 59 of the Oklahoma Statutes;

6. "Probable gestational age of the unborn child" means what, in the judgment of the physician, will with reasonable probability be the gestational age of the unborn child at the time the abortion is planned to be performed;

7. "Stable Internet web site" means a web site that, to the extent reasonably practicable, is safeguarded from having its content altered other than by the State Board of Medical Licensure and Supervision; and

8. "Unborn child" means the term as is defined in Section 1-730 of this title.

Oklahoma Code Ti. 63, § 1-738.2.
Voluntary and informed consent

A. No abortion shall be performed in this state except with the voluntary and informed consent of the woman upon whom the abortion is to be performed.

B. Except in the case of a medical emergency, consent to an abortion is voluntary and informed if and only if:

1. a. not less than twenty-four (24) hours prior to the performance of the abortion, the woman is told the following, by telephone or in person, by the physician who is to perform the abortion, or by a referring physician, or by an agent of either physician:

(1) the name of the physician who will perform the abortion,

(2) the medical risks associated with the particular abortion procedure to be employed,

(3) the probable gestational age of the unborn child at the time the abortion is to be performed,

(4) the medical risks associated with carrying her child to term, and

(5) that ultrasound imaging and heart tone monitoring that enable the pregnant woman to view her unborn child or listen to the heartbeat of the unborn child are available to the pregnant woman. The physician or agent of the physician shall inform the pregnant woman that the web site and printed materials described in Section 1-738.3 of this title, contain phone numbers and addresses for facilities that offer such services at no cost,

b. the information required by this paragraph may be provided by telephone without conducting a physical examination or tests of the woman. If the information is supplied by telephone, the information shall be based on facts supplied to the physician,

c. the information required by this paragraph shall not be provided by a tape recording, but shall be provided during a consultation in which the physician is able to ask questions of the woman and the woman is able to ask questions of the physician,

d. if a physical examination, tests, or other new information subsequently indicates, in the medical judgment of the physician, the need for a revision of the information previously supplied to the woman, that revised information may be communicated to the woman at any time prior to the performance of the abortion, and

e. nothing in subparagraph a of this paragraph may be construed to preclude provision of the required information in a language understood by the woman through a translator;

2. Not less than twenty-four (24) hours prior to the abortion, the woman is informed, by telephone or in person, by the physician who is to perform the abortion, by a referring physician, or by an agent of either physician:

a. that medical assistance benefits may be available for prenatal care, childbirth, and neonatal care,

b. that the father is liable to assist in the support of her child, even in instances in which the father has offered to pay for the abortion,

c. that:

(1) she has the option to review the printed materials described in Section 1-738.3 of this title,

(2) those materials have been provided by the State Board of Medical Licensure and Supervision, and

(3) they describe the unborn child and list agencies that offer alternatives to abortion, and

d. (1) if the woman chooses to exercise her option to view the materials in a printed form, they shall be mailed to her, by a method chosen by the woman, or

(2) if the woman chooses to exercise her option to view the materials via the Internet, the woman shall be informed at least twenty-four (24) hours before the abortion of the specific address of the Internet web site where the material can be accessed.

The information required by this paragraph may be provided by a tape recording if provision is made to record or otherwise register specifically whether the woman does or does not choose to review the printed materials;

3. The woman certifies in writing, prior to the abortion, that she has been told the information described in subparagraph a of paragraph 1 of this subsection and in subparagraphs a, b and c of paragraph 2 of this subsection and that she has been informed of her option to review or reject the printed information described in Section 1-738.3 of this title; and

4. Prior to the abortion, the physician who is to perform the abortion or the agent of the physician receives a copy of the written certification prescribed by paragraph 3 of this subsection.

C. The State Board of Medical Licensure and Supervision and the State Board of Osteopathic Examiners shall promulgate rules to ensure that physicians who perform abortions and referring physicians or agents of either physician comply with all the requirements of this section.

D. Before the abortion procedure is performed, the physician shall confirm with the patient that she has received information regarding:

1. The medical risks associated with the particular abortion procedure to be employed;

2. The probable gestational age of the unborn child at the time the abortion is to be performed; and

3. The medical risks associated with carrying the unborn child to term.

Oklahoma Code Ti. 63, § 1-738.3.
Print and online information

A. Within one hundred twenty (120) days of the effective date of this act, the State Board of Medical Licensure and Supervision shall cause to be published, in English and in Spanish, and shall update on an annual basis, the following printed materials in such a way as to ensure that the information is easily comprehensible:

1. a. geographically indexed materials designed to inform the woman of public and private agencies, including adoption agencies and services that are available to assist a woman through pregnancy, upon childbirth, and while the child is dependent, including:

(1) a comprehensive list of the agencies available,

(2) a description of the services they offer, including which agencies offer, at no cost to the pregnant woman, ultrasound imaging that enables a pregnant woman to view the unborn child or heart tone monitoring that enables the pregnant woman to listen to the heartbeat of the unborn child, and

(3) a description of the manner, including telephone numbers, in which they might be contacted, or

b. at the option of the Board a toll-free, twenty-four-hour-a-day telephone number which may be called to obtain, in a mechanical, automated, or auditory format, a list and description of agencies in the locality of the caller and of the services they offer; and

2. a. materials designed to inform the woman of the probable anatomical and physiological characteristics of the unborn child at two-week gestational increments from the time when a woman can be known to be pregnant to full term, including:

(1) any relevant information on the possibility of the survival of the unborn child, and

(2) pictures or drawings representing the development of unborn children at two-week gestational increments, provided that the pictures or drawings shall describe the dimensions of the unborn child and shall be realistic and appropriate for the stage of pregnancy depicted,

b. the materials shall be objective, nonjudgmental, and designed to convey only accurate scientific information about the unborn child at the various gestational ages, and

c. the material shall also contain objective information describing:

(1) the methods of abortion procedures commonly employed,

(2) the medical risks commonly associated with each of those procedures,

(3) the possible detrimental psychological effects of abortion and of carrying a child to term, and

(4) the medical risks commonly associated with carrying a child to term.

B. 1. The materials referred to in subsection A of this section shall be printed in a typeface large enough to be clearly legible.

2. The materials required under this section shall be available at no cost from the State Board of Medical Licensure and Supervision and shall be distributed upon request in appropriate numbers to any person, facility, or hospital.

C. 1. The Board shall provide on its stable Internet web site the information described under subsection A of this section.

2. The web site provided for in this subsection shall be maintained at a minimum resolution of 72 PPI.

Oklahoma Code Ti. 63, § 1-738.3a. Form tracking

A. By February 1, 2008, the State Department of Health shall prepare and make available on its stable Internet web site the form described in subsection B of this section. A copy of this act shall be posted on the web site. Physicians performing abortions shall complete and electronically submit the required forms to the Department no later than April 1 for the previous calendar year. Nothing in the report shall contain the name, address, or any other identifying information of any patient.

B. The form for physicians shall contain a listing for the following information:

1. The number of females to whom the physician, or an agent of the physician, provided the information described in Section 1-738.2 of Title 63 of the Oklahoma Statutes; of that number, the number provided the information by telephone and the number provided the information in person; and of each of those numbers, the number provided the information in the capacity of a referring physician and the number provided the information in the capacity of a physician who is to perform the abortion; and of each of those numbers, the number provided the information by the physician and the number provided the information by an agent of the physician;

2. The number of females who availed themselves of the opportunity to obtain a copy of the printed information described in Section 1-738.3 of Title 63 of the Oklahoma Statutes other than on the web site, and the number who did not; and of each of those numbers, the number who, to the best of the information and belief of the reporting physician, went on to obtain the abortion; and

3. The number of abortions performed by the physician in which information otherwise required to be provided at least twenty-four (24) hours before the abortion was not so provided because an immediate abortion was necessary to avert the death of the female, and the number of abortions in which the information was not so provided because a delay would cause substantial and irreversible impairment of a major bodily function.

C. The State Department of Health shall ensure that the reporting forms described in subsection B of this section are posted, on its stable Internet web site, within one hundred twenty (120) days after the effective date of this act. The State Department of Health shall notify the following of the requirements of this act:

1. By March 1, 2008, all physicians licensed to practice in this state;

2. Each physician who subsequently becomes newly licensed to practice in this state, at the same time as official notification to that physician that the physician is so licensed; and

3. By December 1 of each year, other than the calendar year in which forms are first made available to all physicians licensed to practice in this state.

D. By February 28 of each year following a calendar year in any part of which this section was in effect, each physician who provided, or whose agent provided, information to one or more females in accordance with Section 1-738.2 of Title 63 of the Oklahoma Statutes during the previous calendar year shall electronically submit to the State Department of Health the form described in subsection B of this section, with the requested data entered accurately and completely.

E. Reports that are not electronically submitted by the end of a grace period of thirty (30) days following the due date shall be subject to a late fee of Five Hundred Dollars ($500.00) for each additional thirty-day period or portion of a thirty-day period the reports are overdue. Any physician required to report in accordance with this section who has not completed and electronically submitted a report, or has electronically submitted only an incomplete report, more than one (1) year following the due date, may, in an action brought by the State Department of Health, be directed by a court of competent jurisdiction to electronically submit a complete report within a period stated by court order or be subject to sanctions for civil contempt.

F. By June 30 of each year, the State Department of Health shall prepare and make available on its stable Internet web site a public report providing statistics for the previous calendar year compiled from all items listed in subsection B of this section. Each report shall also provide statistics for all previous calendar years, adjusted to reflect any additional information from late or corrected reports. The State Department of Health shall take care to ensure that none of the information included in the public reports could reasonably lead to the identification of any individual providing or provided information in accordance with subsection B of this section.

G. The State Department of Health may promulgate rules in accordance with the Administrative Procedures Act to alter the dates established by this section or consolidate the form or report described in this section with other forms or reports to achieve administrative convenience, fiscal savings or to reduce the burden of reporting requirements, as long as reporting forms are made available, on its stable Internet web site to all licensed physicians in the state, and the report described in this section is issued at least once every year.

Oklahoma Code Ti. 63, § 1-738.4. Medical emergency

When a medical emergency compels the performance of an abortion, the physician shall inform the female, prior to the abortion if possible, of the medical indications supporting the physician's judgment that an abortion is necessary to avert her death or that a delay will create serious risk of substantial and irreversible impairment of a major bodily function.

Oklahoma Code Ti. 63, § 1-738.5.
Disciplinary action

A. Any physician who knowingly or recklessly performs or attempts to perform an abortion in violation of the provisions of this act shall be subject to disciplinary action by the State Board of Medical Licensure and Supervision or the State Board of Osteopathic Examiners.

B. No penalty may be assessed against the woman upon whom the abortion is performed or attempted to be performed.

C. No penalty or civil liability may be assessed for failure to comply with Section 1-738.2 of this title unless the State Board of Medical Licensure and Supervision has made the printed materials available at the time the physician or the agent of the physician is required to inform the woman of her right to review them.

D. Any person who knowingly or recklessly performs or attempts to perform an abortion in violation of this act shall be guilty of a felony.

(6) ABORTION BY MINORS

Under the laws of Oklahoma no physician may perform an abortion upon an unemancipated minor, unless the physician first obtains the written consent of a parent or the legal guardian of the minor 48 hours before performing the abortion. In compliance with federal constitutional law, Oklahoma has provided a judicial waiver procedure for an unemancipated minor to obtain an abortion without parental or guardian consent. The minor may petition a court for a waiver of the consent requirement. The required parental or guardian consent may be waived if the court finds either (1) that the minor is mature and well-informed enough to make the abortion decision on her own, or (2) that performance of the abortion would be in the best interest of the minor. An expedited appeal is available to any minor to whom the court denies a waiver of consent. The statutes addressing the issues are set out below.

Oklahoma Code Ti. 63, § 1-740.
Abortion without parental consent

Any person who performs an abortion on a minor without parental consent or knowledge shall be liable for the cost of any subsequent medical treatment such minor might require because of the abortion.

Oklahoma Code Ti. 63, § 1-740.1. Definitions

As used in Sections 1-740.1 through 1-740.5 of this title:

1. "Abortion" means the term as is defined in Section 1-730 of this title;

2. "Medical emergency" means the existence of any physical condition, not including any emotional, psychological, or mental condition, which a reasonably prudent physician, with knowledge of the case and treatment possibilities with respect to the medical conditions involved, would determine necessitates the immediate abortion of the pregnancy of the minor in order to avert her death or to avert substantial and irreversible impairment of a major bodily function arising from continued pregnancy, and there is insufficient time to provide the required notice and obtain the written informed consent of one parent;

3. "Parent" means one parent of the pregnant unemancipated minor or guardian if the pregnant unemancipated minor has one; and

4. "Unemancipated minor" means any person less than eighteen (18) years of age who is not or has not been married or who is under the care, custody and control of the person's parent or parents, guardian or juvenile court of competent jurisdiction.

Oklahoma Code Ti. 63, § 1-740.2.
Notification and consent of parent

A. Except in the case of a medical emergency, a physician may not perform an abortion on a pregnant female unless the physician has:

1. Obtained proof of age demonstrating that the female is not a minor;

2. Obtained proof that the female, although a minor, is emancipated; or

3. Complied with Section 1-740.3 of this title.

B. No abortion shall be performed upon an unemancipated minor or upon a female for whom a guardian has been appointed pursuant to Section 1-113 of Title 30 of the Oklahoma Statutes because of a finding of incompetency, except in a medical emergency or where a judicial waiver was obtained pursuant to Section 1-740.3 of this title, until at least forty-eight (48) hours after written notice of the pending abortion has been delivered in the manner specified in this subsection and the attending physician has secured proof of identification and the written informed consent of one parent.

1. The notice and request for written informed consent of one parent shall be addressed to the parent at the usual place of abode of the parent and delivered personally to the parent by the physician or an agent.

2. In lieu of the delivery required by paragraph 1 of this subsection, the notice and request for written informed consent of one parent shall be made by certified mail addressed to the parent at the usual place of abode of the parent with return-receipt requested and restricted delivery to the addressee, which means a postal employee can only deliver the mail to the authorized addressee. Time of delivery shall be deemed to occur at 12 noon on the next day on which regular mail delivery takes place, subsequent to mailing. The information concerning the address of the parent shall be that which a reasonable and prudent person, under similar circumstances, would have relied upon as sufficient evidence that the parent resides at that address.

3. a. The parent entitled to notice and consent shall provide to the physician a copy of proof of identification, and shall certify in a signed, dated, and notarized statement that he or she has been notified and consents to the abortion. The signed, dated, and notarized statement shall include: "I certify that I, (insert name of parent), am the parent of (insert name of minor daughter) and give consent for (insert name of physician) to perform an abortion on my daughter. I understand that any person who knowingly makes a fraudulent statement in this regard commits a felony."

b. The physician shall keep a copy of the proof of identification of the parent and the certified statement in the medical file of the minor for five (5) years past the majority of the minor, but in no event less than seven (7) years.

c. A physician receiving parental consent under this section shall execute for inclusion in the medical record of the minor an affidavit stating: "I, (insert name of physician), certify that according to my best information and belief, a reasonable person under similar circumstances would rely on the information presented by both the minor and her parent as sufficient evidence of identity."

C. No notice or request for written informed consent of one parent shall be required under this section if one of the following conditions is met:

1. The attending physician certifies in the medical records of the pregnant unemancipated minor that a medical emergency exists; provided, however, that the attending physician or an agent shall, within twenty-four (24) hours after completion of the abortion, notify one of the parents of the minor in the manner provided in Section 1-740.2 of this title that an emergency abortion was performed on the minor and of the circumstances that warranted invocation of this paragraph; or

2. The unemancipated minor declares that she is the victim of sexual abuse, as defined in Section 7102 of Title 10 of the Oklahoma Statutes and the attending physician has notified local law enforcement or the Department of Human Services about the alleged sexual abuse.

D. 1. Unless the unemancipated minor gives notice of her intent to seek a judicial waiver pursuant to Section 1-740.3 of this title, the attending physician, or the agent of the physician, shall verbally inform the parent of the minor within twenty-four (24) hours after the performance of a medical emergency abortion or an abortion that was performed to prevent her death that an abortion was performed on the unemancipated minor. The attending physician, or the agent of the attending physician, shall also inform the parent of the basis for the certification of the physician required under paragraph 1 or 2 of subsection C of this section. The attending physician, or the agent of the attending physician, shall also send a written notice of the performed abortion via the United States Post Office to the last-known address of the parent, restricted delivery, return receipt requested. The information concerning the address of the parent shall be that which a reasonable and prudent person, under similar circumstances, would have relied upon as sufficient evidence that the parent resides at that address.

2. If the unemancipated minor gives notice to the attending physician, or an agent of the physician, of her intent to seek a judicial waiver pursuant to Section 1-740.3 of this title, the physician, or an agent of the physician, shall file a notice with any judge of a court of competent jurisdiction that the minor has given such notice and shall provide the information the physician, or the agent of the physician, would have been required to provide the parent under paragraph 1 of this subsection if the unemancipated minor had not given notice of her intent to seek a judicial waiver. The court shall expeditiously schedule a conference with notice to the minor and the physician. If the minor is able to participate in the proceedings, the court shall advise the minor that she has the right to court-appointed counsel and shall, upon her request, provide the minor with such counsel. If the minor is unable to participate, the court shall appoint counsel on behalf of the minor. After an appropriate hearing, the court, taking into account the medical condition of the minor, shall set a deadline by which the minor must file a petition or motion pursuant to Section 1-740.3 of this title. The court may subsequently extend the deadline in light of the medical condition of the minor or other equitable considerations. If the minor does not file a petition or motion by the deadline, either in that court or in another court of competent jurisdiction with a copy filed in that court, the court shall direct that the court clerk provide the notice to a parent.

E. The State Board of Health shall adopt the forms necessary for physicians to obtain the certifications required by this section.

Oklahoma Code Ti. 63, § 1-740.3. Judicial bypass

A. If a pregnant unemancipated minor elects not to allow the notification and request for written informed consent of her parent, any judge of a court of competent jurisdiction shall, upon petition or motion, and after an appropriate hearing, authorize a physician to perform the abortion if the judge determines, by clear and convincing evidence, that the pregnant unemancipated minor is mature and capable of giving informed consent to the proposed abortion. If the judge determines that the pregnant unemancipated minor is not mature, or if the pregnant unemancipated minor does not claim to be mature, the judge shall determine, by clear and convincing evidence, whether the performance of an abortion upon her without notification and written informed consent of her parent would be in her best interest and shall authorize a physician to perform the abortion without notification and written informed consent if the judge concludes that the best interests of the pregnant unemancipated minor would be served thereby.

B. If the unemancipated minor, upon whom a medical emergency abortion or an abortion to prevent her death was performed, elects not to allow the notification of her parent, any judge of a court of competent jurisdiction shall, upon petition or motion and after an appropriate hearing, authorize the waiving of the required notice of the performed abortion if the judge determines, by clear and convincing evidence, that the unemancipated minor is mature and capable of determining whether notification should be given, or that the waiver would be in the best interest of the unemancipated minor.

C. A pregnant unemancipated minor may participate in proceedings in the court on her own behalf, and the court may appoint a guardian ad litem for her. The court shall advise the pregnant unemancipated minor that she has a right to court-appointed counsel and, upon her request, shall provide her with counsel.

D. Proceedings in the court under this section shall be confidential and shall be given precedence over other pending matters so that the court may reach a decision promptly and without delay so as to serve the best interests of the pregnant unemancipated minor. A judge of the court who conducts proceedings under this section shall make, in writing, specific factual findings and legal conclusions supporting the decision and shall order a record of the evidence to be maintained, including the findings and conclusions of the court.

E. An expedited confidential appeal shall be available to any pregnant unemancipated minor for whom the court denies an order authorizing an abortion without notification and written informed consent of one parent. An order authorizing an abortion without notification and written informed consent of one parent shall not be subject to appeal. No filing fees shall be required of any pregnant unemancipated minor at either the trial or the appellate level. Access to the trial court for the purpose of a petition or motion, and access to the appellate courts for the purpose of making an appeal from the denial of same, shall be afforded a pregnant unemancipated minor twenty-four (24) hours a day, seven (7) days a week.

Oklahoma Code Ti. 63, § 1-740.4.
Criminal and civil liability

Performance of an abortion in knowing or reckless violation of Sections 1-740.1 through 1-740.5 of this title shall be a misdemeanor and shall be grounds for actual and punitive damages in a civil action by a person wrongfully denied notification and request for written informed consent. A person shall not be held liable under this act if the person establishes by written evidence that the person relied upon evidence sufficient to convince a careful and prudent person that the representations of the pregnant unemancipated minor regarding information necessary to comply with this section are bona fide and true, or if the person has attempted with reasonable diligence to deliver the notice and request for written informed consent, but has been unable to do so.

Oklahoma Code Ti. 63, § 1-740.4a. Report of procedure

A. Any physician performing an abortion upon an unemancipated minor shall complete and electronically transmit to the State Department of Health a report of the procedure within thirty (30) days after having performed the abortion. Within ninety (90) days after this act becomes law, the State Department of Health shall prepare and make available on its stable Internet web site the reporting forms for this purpose to all physicians required to be licensed in this state and health facilities licensed in accordance with Section 1-702 of Title 63 of the Oklahoma Statutes. The reporting form regarding the minor receiving the abortion shall include, but not be limited to:

1. Age;
2. Educational level;
3. Number of previous pregnancies;
4. Number of previous live births;
5. Number of previous abortions;
6. Complications, if any, of the abortion being reported;
7. The city and county in which the abortion was performed;
8. Whether a parent gave consent to the physician, or an agent of the physician, pursuant to Section 1-740.2 of Title 63 of the Oklahoma Statutes; or
9. Whether the physician performed the abortion without first obtaining the consent of the parent of the minor as described in Section 1-740.2 of Title 63 of the Oklahoma Statutes; if so:
a. whether the minor was emancipated,
b. whether the abortion was performed because of a medical emergency,
c. whether the abortion was performed to prevent the death of the minor,
d. whether the parent was notified after the performance of a medical emergency abortion, and
e. whether the parent was notified after the performance of an abortion to prevent the death of the minor;
10. Whether a judicial waiver was obtained after the performance of a medical emergency abortion; and
11. Whether a judicial waiver was obtained after the performance of an abortion to prevent the death of the minor.

B. The State Department of Health shall ensure that the reporting forms described in this section, together with a reprint of this act, are posted on its stable Internet web site, within one hundred twenty (120) days after the effective date of this act. The State Department of Health shall notify:

1. Each physician who subsequently becomes newly licensed to practice in this state, simultaneously with the receipt of official notification to that physician that the physician is so licensed, of the requirements of this act; and
2. By December 1 of every year, other than the calendar year in which forms are made available in accordance with subsection A of this section, all physicians licensed to practice in this state.

C. By February 28 of each year following a calendar year in any part of which this act was in effect, each physician, or agent of a physician, who obtained the consent described in Section 1-740.2 of Title 63 of the Oklahoma Statutes, and any physician who knowingly performed an abortion upon a pregnant minor or upon a female for whom a guardian or conservator had been appointed pursuant to applicable federal law or as provided by Section 1-113 of Title 30 of the Oklahoma Statutes because of incompetency during the previous calendar year shall complete and electronically submit to the State Department of Health the form described in subsection A of this section, with the requested data entered accurately and completely. Any such report shall not contain the name, address, or other information by which the minor receiving the abortion may be identified.

D. Reports that are not submitted by the end of a grace period of thirty (30) days following the due date shall be subject to a late fee of Five Hundred Dollars ($500.00) for each additional thirty-day period or portion of a thirty-day period the reports are overdue. Any physician required to report in accordance with this section who has not electronically submitted a report, or has electronically submitted only an incomplete report, more than one (1) year following the due date, may, in an action brought by the State Department of Health, be directed by a court of competent *jurisdiction to submit a complete report within a period stated by court order or be subject to sanctions for civil contempt.*

E. By June 30 of each year, the State Department of Health shall post, on its stable Internet web site, a public report providing statistics for the previous calendar year compiled from all of the reports covering that year submitted in accordance with this section for each of the items listed in subsection A of this section. The report shall also include statistics giving the total number of petitions or motions filed under Section 1-740.3 of Title 63 of the Oklahoma Statutes and of that number:

1. The number in which the court appointed a guardian ad litem;

2. The number in which the court appointed counsel;

3. The number in which the judge issued an order authorizing an abortion without notification; and

4. The number in which the judge denied such an order, and of this:

a. the number of denials from which an appeal was filed,

b. the number of the appeals that resulted in the denial being affirmed, and

c. the number of appeals that resulted in reversals of the denials.

Each report shall also provide the statistics for all previous calendar years for which the public statistical report was required to be issued, adjusted to reflect any additional information from late or corrected reports. The State Department of Health shall take care to ensure that none of the information included in the public reports could reasonably lead to the identification of any individual female.

F. The State Department of Health may promulgate rules in accordance with the Administrative Procedures Act to alter the dates established by this section or consolidate the forms or reports to achieve administrative convenience, fiscal savings, or to reduce the burden of reporting requirements, as long as reporting forms are made available on its web site, to all licensed physicians in the state at least once every year and the report described in subsection E of this section is posted at least once every year.

G. If the State Department of Health fails to post the public report required by subsection E of this section, an action may be initiated pursuant to Title 12 of the Oklahoma Statutes.

H. If judgment is rendered in favor of the plaintiff in any action described in this section, the court shall also render judgment for a reasonable attorney fee in favor of the plaintiff against the defendant. If judgment is rendered in favor of the defendant and the court finds that the plaintiff's suit was frivolous and brought in bad faith, the court shall also render judgment for a reasonable attorney fee in favor of the defendant against the plaintiff.

Oklahoma Code Ti. 63, § 1-740.4b. Unlawful acts

A. A person who knowingly or recklessly uses a false governmental record or makes a fraudulent representation or statement in order to obtain an abortion for a minor in violation of this act commits a felony.

B. A physician who intentionally or knowingly performs an abortion on a pregnant unemancipated minor in violation of this act commits a felony.

C. 1. It is a defense to prosecution under subsection B of this section if the person falsely representing himself or herself as the parent or guardian of the minor displayed an apparently valid governmental record of identification such that a reasonable person, under similar circumstances, would have relied on the representation.

2. The defense does not apply if the physician, or agent of the physician, failed to use due diligence in determining the age of the minor or the identity of the person represented as the parent or guardian of the minor.

D. An unemancipated minor, or the parent of the minor, upon whom an abortion has been performed, or attempted to be performed, without complying with this act may maintain a cause of action against the person who performed, or attempted to perform, the abortion.

E. It is not a defense to a claim brought pursuant to this section that the minor gave informed and voluntary consent.

F. An unemancipated minor does not have the capacity to consent to any action that violates this act.

Oklahoma Code Ti. 63, § 1-740.5. Severability

If any one or more provision, section, subsection, sentence, clause, phrase or word of this act or the application thereof to any person or circumstance is found to be unconstitutional, the same is hereby declared to be severable and the balance shall remain effective notwithstanding such unconstitutionality. The Legislature hereby declares that it would have passed each provision, section, subsection, sentence, clause, phrase or word thereof, irrespective of the fact that any one or more provision, section, subsection, sentence, clause, phrase or word be declared unconstitutional.

Oklahoma Code Ti. 63, § 1-740.6. Enjoinder of act

If any court of law enjoins, suspends, or delays the implementation of the provisions of this act, the provisions of Sections 1-730, 1-738.1, 1-738.7, 1-740.1, 1-740.2 and 1-740.3 of Title 63 of the Oklahoma Statutes, as of December 31, 2006, are effective during the injunction, suspension, or delayed implementation.

(7) PARTIAL-BIRTH ABORTION

Oklahoma criminalizes performance of partial-birth abortions, unless necessary to save the life of a mother. Until it is definitively determined by a court, Oklahoma's partial-birth abortion statute may be invalid under the United States Supreme Court decision *in Stenberg v. Carhart*, which invalidated Nebraska's ban on partial-birth abortion. On the other hand, Oklahoma's partial-birth abortion statute, as currently written, may be valid under the United States Supreme Court decision in *Gonzales v. Carhart*, which approved of a federal statute that bans partial-birth abortion. In addition to purporting to ban partial-birth abortions, Oklahoma has provided a civil cause of action for a married man whose spouse obtains a partial-birth abortion. In the case of a minor, the maternal grandparents of the fetus may file a civil lawsuit. The text of the partial-birth abortion statute is set out below.

Oklahoma Code Ti. 21, § 684. Partial-birth abortion ban

A. Any physician who knowingly performs a partial-birth abortion and thereby kills a human fetus shall be fined Ten Thousand Dollars ($10,000.00), or imprisoned in the State Penitentiary for a period of not more than two (2) years, or by both such fine and imprisonment. This subsection shall not apply to a partial-birth abortion that is necessary to save the life of a mother whose life is endangered by a physical disorder, illness or injury.

B. Definitions. As used in this section:

1. "Partial-birth abortion" means an abortion in which the person performing the abortion partially vaginally delivers a living fetus before killing the fetus and completing the delivery.

2. "Physician" means a doctor of medicine or osteopathy legally authorized to practice medicine and surgery by the state, or any other individual legally authorized by the state to perform abortions; provided, however, that any individual who is not a physician or not otherwise legally authorized by the state to perform abortions, but who nevertheless directly performs a partial-birth abortion, shall be subject to the provisions of this section.

3. "Vaginally delivers a living fetus before killing the fetus" means deliberately and intentionally delivers into the vagina a living fetus or a substantial portion thereof, for the purpose of performing a procedure the physician knows will kill the fetus, and kills the fetus.

C. Civil Action:

1. The father, if married to the mother at the time she receives a partial-birth abortion procedure, and if the mother has not attained the age of eighteen (18) years at the time of the abortion, the mater-

nal grandparents of the fetus, may in a civil action obtain appropriate relief, unless the pregnancy resulted from the plaintiff's criminal conduct or the plaintiff consented to the abortion.

2. Such relief shall include money damages for all injuries, psychological and physical, occasioned by the violation of this section, and statutory damages equal to three times the cost of the partial-birth abortion.

D. Review by State Board of Medical Licensure and Supervision:

1. A defendant accused of an offense under this section may seek a hearing before the State Board of Medical Licensure and Supervision on whether the physician's conduct was necessary to save the life of the mother whose life was endangered by a physical disorder, illness or injury.

2. The findings on that issue are admissible at the trial of the defendant. Upon a motion of the defendant, the court shall delay the beginning of the trial for not more than thirty (30) days to permit such a hearing to take place.

E. A woman upon whom a partial-birth abortion is performed may not be prosecuted under this section or for a conspiracy to violate this section.

(8) USE OF FACILITIES AND PEOPLE

Under the laws of Oklahoma private hospitals are not required to allow abortions at their facilities. The employees and physicians at hospitals that do allow abortions are permitted to refuse to take part in abortions. The state also provides that genetic counselors do not have to advise patients about abortion as an option. The statutes addressing the matter are set out below.

Oklahoma Code Ti. 63, § 1-741.
Refusal to perform abortions

A. No private hospital, hospital director or governing board of a private hospital in Oklahoma, is required to permit abortions to be performed or induced in such hospital. Refusal to permit an abortion, in accordance with a standard policy, is not grounds for civil liability nor a basis for disciplinary or other recriminatory action.

B. No person may be required to perform, induce or participate in medical procedures which result in an abortion which are in preparation for an abortion or which involve aftercare of an abortion patient, except when the aftercare involves emergency medical procedures which are necessary to protect the life of the patient, and refusal to perform or participate in such medical procedures is not grounds for civil liability nor a basis for disciplinary or other recriminatory action.

C. The rights and immunities granted by this section shall not include medical procedures in which a woman is in the process of the spontaneous, inevitable abortion of an unborn child, the death of the child is imminent, and the procedures are necessary to prevent the death of the mother.

Oklahoma Code Ti. 63, § 1-741.1(A).
State employee or agency

It shall be unlawful for any person employed by this state or any agency or political subdivision thereof, within the scope of the person's employment, to perform or assist an abortion not necessary to save the life of the mother except when the pregnancy resulted from an act of forcible rape which was reported to the proper law enforcement authorities or when the pregnancy resulted from an act of incest committed against a minor and the perpetrator has been reported to the proper law enforcement authorities. It shall be unlawful for any public institution, public facility, public equipment, or other physical asset owned, leased or controlled by this state or any agency or political subdivisions thereof to be used for the purpose of performing or assisting an abortion not necessary to save the life of the mother except when the pregnancy resulted from an act of forcible rape which was reported to the proper law enforcement authorities or when the pregnancy resulted from an act of incest committed against a minor and the perpetrator has been reported to the proper law enforcement authorities. This subsection shall not be construed to prohibit use by private entities of public utilities or the services of firefighters or police.

Oklahoma Code Ti. 63, § 1-568(A). Genetic counselors

Nothing in the Genetic Counseling Licensure Act may be construed to require any genetic counselor or other person to mention, discuss, suggest, propose, recommend, or refer for, abortion, or to agree or indicate a willingness to do so, nor shall licensing of any genetic counselor be contingent upon acceptance of abortion as a treatment option for any genetic or other prenatal disease, anomaly, or disability.

(9) FETAL EXPERIMENTS

Oklahoma prohibits the sale of fetal remains and fetal experiments, unless an experiment is deemed therapeutic to the unborn child. The statute addressing the matter is set out below.

Oklahoma Code Ti. 63, § 1-735. Fetal experiments

A. No person shall sell a child, an unborn child or the remains of a child or an unborn child resulting from an abortion. No person shall experiment upon a child or an unborn child resulting from an abortion or which is intended to be aborted unless the experimentation is therapeutic to the child or unborn child.

B. No person shall experiment upon the remains of a child or an unborn child resulting from an abortion. The term "experiment" does not include autopsies performed according to law.

(10) INJURY TO A PREGNANT WOMAN

Oklahoma provides criminal statutes to punish conduct causing an injury or death to a fetus, that does not involve a lawful abortion. For the purposes of its homicide statutes, murder and manslaughter, the state defines a human being as including a fetus. The statutes are set out below.

Oklahoma Code Ti. 21, § 691. Homicide defined

A. Homicide is the killing of one human being by another.

B. As used in this section, "human being" includes an unborn child, as defined in Section 1-730 of Title 63 of the Oklahoma Statutes.

C. Homicide shall not include:

1. Acts which cause the death of an unborn child if those acts were committed during a legal abortion to which the pregnant woman consented; or

2. Acts which are committed pursuant to the usual and customary standards of medical practice during diagnostic testing or therapeutic treatment.

D. Under no circumstances shall the mother of the unborn child be prosecuted for causing the death of the unborn child unless the mother has committed a crime that caused the death of the unborn child.

Oklahoma Code Ti. 21, § 652.
Using firearm with intent to kill

A. Every person who intentionally and wrongfully shoots another with or discharges any kind of firearm, with intent to kill any person, including an unborn child as defined in Section 1-730 of Title 63 of the Oklahoma Statutes, shall upon conviction be guilty of a felony punishable by imprisonment in the State Penitentiary not exceeding life.

B. Every person who uses any vehicle to facilitate the intentional discharge of any kind of firearm, crossbow or other weapon in conscious disregard for the safety of any other person or persons, including an unborn child as defined in Section 1-730 of Title 63 of the Oklahoma Statutes, shall upon conviction be guilty of a felony punishable by imprisonment in the custody of the Department of Corrections for a term not less than two (2) years nor exceeding life.

C. Any person who commits any assault and battery upon another, in-

cluding an unborn child as defined in Section 1-730 of Title 63 of the Oklahoma Statutes, by means of any deadly weapon, or by such other means or force as is likely to produce death, or in any manner attempts to kill another, including an unborn child as defined in Section 1-730 of Title 63 of the Oklahoma Statutes, or in resisting the execution of any legal process, shall upon conviction be guilty of a felony punishable by imprisonment in the State Penitentiary not exceeding life.

D. The provisions of this section shall not apply to:

1. Acts which cause the death of an unborn child if those acts were committed during a legal abortion to which the pregnant woman consented; or

2. Acts which are committed pursuant to usual and customary standards of medical practice during diagnostic testing or therapeutic treatment.

E. Under no circumstances shall the mother of the unborn child be prosecuted for causing the death of the unborn child unless the mother has committed a crime that caused the death of the unborn child.

Oklahoma Code Ti. 21, § 723.
Offender's knowledge of victim's pregnancy

Any offense committed pursuant to the provisions of Sections 652 and 713 of Title 21 [repealed] of the Oklahoma Statutes does not require proof that the person engaging in the conduct had knowledge or should have had knowledge that the victim of the underlying offense was pregnant or that the offender intended to cause the death or bodily injury to the unborn child.

(11) FETAL DEATH REPORT

Oklahoma requires that all abortions be reported to the proper authorities. The statute addressing the matter is set out below.

Oklahoma Code Ti. 63, § 1-738. Form to be completed

A. The Department shall adopt a form which shall be completed by each attending physician who performs or induces an abortion which shall include all medical facts pertinent to the procedure and which shall allow the woman and her physician to volunteer other personal facts for statistical public health purposes. This abortion report shall also contain the following information about any consent form required by law:

1. Was the consent form signed?

2. Who signed the consent form? The patient, her parents, guardian, or a court?

3. If the consent is waived, what are the reasons? Forcible rape, incest or a medical necessity to save the life of the mother?

The Department shall be responsible for collecting all abortion reports and complication reports and collating and evaluating all data gathered therefrom.

B. The Department shall make available to all licensed physicians abortion report forms and complication report forms.

C. The report shall be confidential and shall not contain the name of the woman.

(12) ABORTION ALTERNATIVE PROGRAMS

Oklahoma makes available governmental funding for agencies that provide abortion alternatives services. The statutes addressing the matter are set out below.

Oklahoma Code Ti. 63, § 1-740.11.
Entities providing alternatives to abortion services

A. Before July 1, 2007, the State Department of Health shall establish and implement a program to facilitate funding to nongovernmental entities that provide alternatives-to-abortion services. The services must be outcome-based with positive outcome-based results.

B. During the 2006 interim, the State Department of Health shall make annual reports to the Speaker of the House of Representatives and the President Pro Tempore of the Senate regarding the status of the alternatives-to-abortion services funding, the first of which must be made by December 1, 2006.

C. The Department may contract with nongovernmental health care and special service organizations to provide services offered under the program. The services must be outcome-based with positive outcome-based results. The Department may not contract with a provider of adoption services not licensed by the state.

D. The State Department of Health shall promulgate rules necessary to implement the provisions of this act.

E. As used in this section, "alternatives-to-abortion services" means those services that promote childbirth instead of abortion by providing information, counseling, and support services that assist pregnant women or women who believe they may be pregnant to choose childbirth and to make informed decisions regarding the choice of adoption or parenting with respect to their children.

The information, counseling and services provided under this program may include, but are not limited to:

1. Medical care;

2. Nutritional services;

3. Housing assistance;

4. Adoption services;

5. Educational and employment assistance, including services that support the continuation and completion of high school;

6. Child care assistance; and

7. Parenting education and support services.

Oklahoma Code Ti. 63, § 1-740.12.
Alternatives to abortion fund

There is hereby created in the State Treasury a revolving fund for the State Department of Health to be designated the "Alternatives-to-Abortion Services Revolving Fund." The fund shall be a continuing fund, not subject to fiscal year limitations, and shall consist of all monies deposited to the credit of the fund by law. All monies accruing to the credit of the fund are hereby appropriated and may be budgeted and expended by the State Department of Health as provided in subsection A of Section 21 of this act. The fund shall not be available to any organization or affiliate of an organization which provides or promotes abortions or directly refers for abortion; provided, however, any nondirective counseling relating to the pregnancy shall not disqualify an organization from receiving these funds. Expenditures from the fund shall be made upon warrants issued by the State Treasurer against claims filed as prescribed by law with the Director of State Finance for approval and payment.

(13) USE OF PUBLIC FUNDS

Oklahoma prohibits the use of public funds to encourage abortion. The statute addressing the matter is set out below.

Oklahoma Code Ti. 63, § 1-741.1(B). Use of public funds

It shall be unlawful for any funds received or controlled by this state or any agency or political subdivision thereof, including, but not limited to, funds derived from federal, state or local taxes, gifts or grants, federal grants or payments, or intergovernmental transfers, to be used to encourage a woman to have an abortion not necessary to save her life, except to the extent required for continued participation in a federal program. Nothing in this subsection shall be construed to prohibit a physician from discussing options with a patient through nondirective counseling.

(4) HEALTH INSURANCE

Oklahoma prohibits health insurance policies from covering elective abortions, unless an additional premium is charged. The statute addressing the matter is set out below.

Oklahoma Code Ti. 63, § 1-741.2.
Limitation of insurance coverage

A. For purposes of this section, an "elective abortion" means an abortion for any reason other than a spontaneous miscarriage or to prevent the death of the female upon whom the abortion is performed or when the pregnancy resulted from an act of forcible rape which was reported to the proper law enforcement authorities or when the pregnancy resulted from an act of incest committed against a minor and the perpetrator has been reported to the proper law enforcement authorities. No health insurance contracts, plans, or policies delivered or issued for delivery in this state shall provide coverage for elective abortions except by an optional rider for which there shall be paid an additional premium.

B. This section shall be applicable to all contracts, plans, or policies of:

1. All nonprofit hospital, medical, surgical, dental, and health service corporations;

2. All health insurers subject to the laws of this state; and

3. All health maintenance organizations.

C. This section shall be applicable only to contracts, plans, or policies written, issued, renewed, or revised after November 1, 2007. For the purposes of this subsection, if new premiums are charged for a contract, plan, or policy, it shall be determined to be a new contract, plan, or policy.

Operation Rescue

Operation Rescue is a pro-life organization that was founded in Buffalo, New York in 1987 by Randall Terry (b.1959). Terry is considered the father of anti-abortion civil disobedience and militancy. In 1988 Operation Rescue launched a highly publicized blockade of Atlanta abortion clinics during the Democratic National Convention in Atlanta. After the Atlanta uprising, Operation Rescue went on to spearhead hundreds of mass blockades, in such places as Los Angeles, San Diego, Buffalo, New York City, Houston, Milwaukee, Philadelphia and Cleveland. The high point of the organization's national influence came in 1991, with a 46-day rally in Wichita, Kansas. The rally was attended by 25,000 supporters, and resulted in over 3,000 arrests. After the Wichita rally Terry lost control of Operation Rescue and the organization withered into virtual obscurity. The downfall of the organization was due in large part to civil law suits that were brought against it. After Terry left the organization to join the militia affiliated United States Taxpayers Party, Operation Rescue was eventually taken over in 1998 by its president, Troy Newman. Mr. Newman relocated the organization to Wichita, Kansas. *See also* **Pro-Life Organizations**

Oregon

(1) OVERVIEW

The state of Oregon enacted its first criminal abortion statute in 1854. The statute underwent several amendments prior to the 1973 decision by the United States Supreme Court in *Roe v. Wade*, which legalized abortion in the nation. In response to the decision in *Roe*, Oregon has repealed its abortion laws generally. Oregon has addressed only a few post-*Roe* abortion issues by statute that include refusal to have abortion, fetal death report, anti-abortion activities and the use of facilities and people.

(2) REFUSAL TO HAVE ABORTION

Oregon provides that no person refusing to consent to an abortion may suffer the loss of any benefit, because of such refusal. The statute addressing the matter is set out below.

Oregon Code § 435.435. Refusal to consent to termination

The refusal of any person to consent to a termination of pregnancy or to submit thereto shall not be grounds for loss of any privilege or immunity to which the person is otherwise entitled nor shall consent to or submission to a termination of pregnancy be imposed as a condition to the receipt of any public benefits.

(3) FETAL DEATH REPORT

Oregon requires that all abortions be reported to the proper authorities. The statute addressing the issue is set out below.

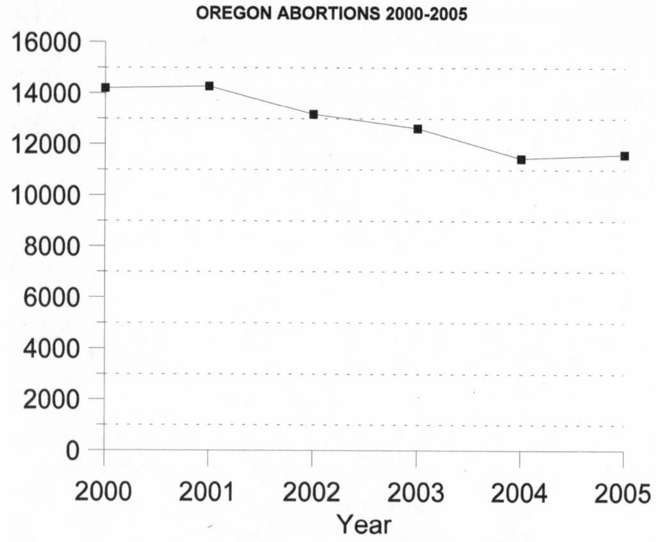

Source: Oregon Department of Human Services.

Oregon Abortion by Age Group 2000–2005
Age Group (yrs)

Year	*<15*	*15–19*	*20–24*	*25–29*	*30–34*	*35–39*	*≥40*	*Unknown*
2000	69	2,753	4,638	3,118	1,983	1,179	434	20
2001	64	2,622	4,922	3,064	2,024	1,158	403	15
2002	46	2,242	4,462	2,914	1,971	1,098	434	5
2003	52	2,154	4,398	2,690	1,829	1,077	399	23
2004	51	1,906	3,913	2,576	1,628	985	372	12
2005	48	1,899	3,759	2,672	1,686	1,061	499	28
Total	330	13,576	26,092	17,034	11,121	6,558	2,541	103

Source: Oregon Department of Human Services.

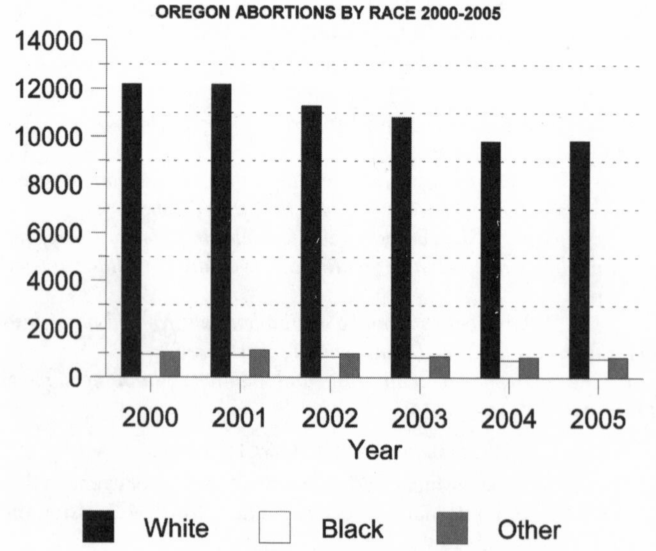

Source: Oregon Department of Human Services.

Oregon Code § 435.496. Abortion report

(1) Each induced termination of pregnancy which occurs in this state, regardless of the length of gestation, shall be reported to the Center for Health Statistics within 30 days by the person in charge of the institution in which the induced termination of pregnancy was performed. If the induced termination of pregnancy was performed outside an institution, the attending physician shall prepare and file the report.

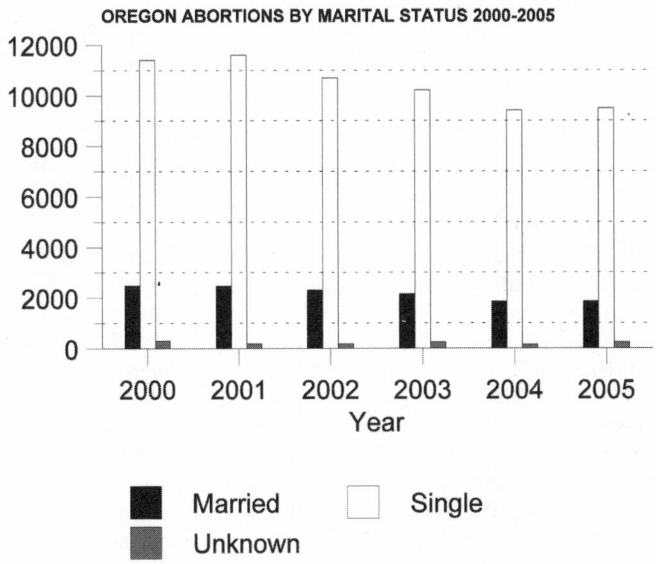

Source: **Oregon Department of Human Services.**

Oregon Abortion by Weeks of Gestation 2000–2005

	Year						
Weeks of Gestation	*2000*	*2001*	*2002*	*2003*	*2004*	*2005*	*Total*
<9	8,542	8,557	8,248	7,922	7,346	7,505	48,120
9–12	3,750	3,887	3,143	2,953	2,596	2,646	18,975
13–16	991	932	930	859	779	772	5,263
17–20	560	529	507	519	425	406	2,946
21–22	196	172	190	172	144	147	1,021
≥23	85	124	92	120	90	80	591
Not known	70	71	62	77	63	46	389

Source: **Oregon Department of Human Services.**

Oregon Prior Abortion by Female 2000–2004

	Prior Abortion				
Year	*None*	*1*	*2*	*≥3*	*Not known*
2000	8,089	3,635	1,466	955	49
2001	8,030	3,733	1,480	982	47
2002	7,239	3,543	1,402	954	34
2003	6,884	3,322	1,445	915	56
2004	6,360	2,963	1,238	852	30
Total	36,602	17,196	7,031	4,658	216

Source: **National Center for Health Statistics.**

(2) If the person who is required to file the report under subsection (1) of this section has knowledge that the person who underwent the induced termination of pregnancy also underwent a follow-up visit or had follow-up contact with a health care provider, the person shall include the fact of the follow-up visit or contact, and whether any complications were noted, in the report. If the person filing the report is not personally aware of the follow-up visit or contact but was informed of the visit or contact, the person shall include the source of that information in the report.

(3) Reports submitted under this section shall not disclose the names or identities of the parents.

(4) ANTI-ABORTION ACTIVITIES

Oregon makes it a criminal offense to engage in anti-abortion conduct that damages or obstructs abortion services. The statute addressing the issue is set out below.

Oregon Code § 164.365. Criminal mischief (abridged)

(1) A person commits the crime of criminal mischief in the first degree who, with intent to damage property, and having no right to do so nor reasonable ground to believe that the person has such right:

(a) Damages or destroys property of another:

(A) In an amount exceeding $750;

(B) By means of an explosive;

(C) Omitted;

(D) Omitted;

(E) Which is the property of a ... medical facility used in direct service to the public;

(F) By intentionally interfering with, obstructing or adulterating in any manner the service of a ... medical facility; or

(b) Intentionally uses, manipulates, arranges or rearranges the property of a ... medical facility used in direct service to the public so as to interfere with its efficiency.

(5) USE OF FACILITIES AND PEOPLE

Oregon permits private hospitals to adopt policies denying abortion services. However, the state prohibits governmental hospitals from refusing to perform abortion services. The employees and physicians at hospitals that do allow abortions are permitted to refuse to take part in abortions. The statutes addressing the matter are set out below.

Oregon Code § 435.475. Refusal by hospital

(1) Except as provided in subsection (3) of this section, no hospital is required to admit any patient for the purpose of terminating a pregnancy. No hospital is liable for its failure or refusal to participate in such termination if the hospital has adopted a policy not to admit patients for the purposes of terminating pregnancies. However, the hospital must notify the person seeking admission to the hospital of its policy.

(2) All hospitals that have not adopted a policy not to admit patients seeking termination of a pregnancy shall admit patients seeking such termination in the same manner and subject to the same conditions as imposed on any other patient seeking admission to the hospital.

(3) No hospital operated by this state or by a political subdivision in this state is authorized to adopt a policy of excluding or denying admission to any person seeking termination of a pregnancy.

Oregon Code § 435.485. Medical personnel

(1) No physician is required to give advice with respect to or participate in any termination of a pregnancy if the refusal to do so is based on an election not to give such advice or to participate in such terminations and the physician so advises the patient.

(2) No hospital employee or member of the hospital medical staff is required to participate in any termination of a pregnancy if the employee or staff member notifies the hospital of the election not to participate in such terminations.

Oregon Right to Life

Oregon Right to Life (ORL) is a pro-life organization. The executive director of ORL is Gayle Atteberry. ORL is the oldest and largest pro-life organization in Oregon. The group maintains a political action committee that supports

Gayle Atteberry is the executive director of Oregon Right to Life, the oldest and largest pro-life organization in Oregon (Gayle Atteberry).

pro-life candidates for state and federal office. It also has an educational program that offers speakers, seminars, teaching tools, and pro-life literature. *See also* **Pro-Life Organizations**

Organic Solvents and Pregnancy

Organic solvents, such as benzene, xylene, aliphatic and aromatic hydrocarbons, phenols, trichloroethylene, vinyl chloride, acetone and methyl ethyl ketone, are found in many household and industrial products. Studies have shown that these solvents can be dangerous to women who are pregnant. Exposure to high levels of organic solvents can cause spontaneous abortion, fetal malformations, central nervous system and cardiovascular malformations. *See also* **Fetal Solvent Syndrome**

Ortho Evra *see* **Patch Contraceptive**

Osteogenesis Imperfecta

Osteogenesis imperfecta is a congenital disorder involving abnormal fragility of the bones. This disease is classified into four types: type I (good life expectancy) type II (lethal), type III (decreased life expectancy), and type IV (good life expectancy). The disorder can cause multiple fractures which result in shortened arms and legs. The skull may be affected and can cause brain damage. Skull damage may result in stillbirth or an infant may die shortly after birth. Infants that survive may have permanent deformity of the extremities. Treatment for the disorder involves repairing fractures. No specific treatment exists for the underlying disease. *See* **Birth Defects and Abortion**

Ovarian Cancer

Ovarian cancer is a disease that develops from a thin layer of cells (epithelium) which cover a woman's ovaries. The disease is the fourth most common cause of cancer related death in women. About 1 in 70 women eventually develop ovarian cancer. The disease primarily affects post-menopausal women, but it is common in younger women. The disease is the second most frequent gynecologic cancer complicating pregnancy.

In those instances that a woman with ovarian cancer is pregnant, problems could rise for the fetus. The fact of pregnancy generally has no adverse effect on ovarian cancer, and ovarian cancer has no effect on the pregnancy. However, if certain cancer treatment methods are used during pregnancy, it may become necessary to have a therapeutic abortion, or the fetus could be exposed to birth defects. There are three main types of treatments for ovarian cancer: surgery, chemotherapy and radiation therapy: *See also* **Cancer and Pregnancy**; **Therapeutic Abortion**

Ovarian Cryopreservation *see* **Cryopreservation**

Ovarian Pregnancy *see* **Ectopic Pregnancy**

Ovary *see* **Female Reproductive System**

Ovulation *see* **Menstrual Cycle**

Ovulation Method *see* **Natural Family Planning Methods**

Ovum *see* **Menstrual Cycle**

Ovu-Tec Method *see* **Natural Family Planning Methods**

P

Parental Consent for Minor *see* **Minors and Abortion**

Partial-Birth Abortion

Partial-birth abortion is a late term abortion that is typically performed when the life of the mother is at risk, or the fetus is determined to have severe abnormalities. This type of abortion is done using the dilation and extraction procedure. In 2000 the United States Supreme Court issued an opinion in the case of *Stenberg v. Carhart*, which held Nebraska's statute banning partial-birth abortion was unconstitutional. Subsequently, in 2007 the Supreme Court decided the case of *Gonzales v. Carhart*, in which it upheld a federal statute that banned partial-birth abortion. A majority of states have passed legislation banning partial-birth abortion. Additionally, a minority of states have statutes with allow the father or maternal grandparents of a fetus to file a civil lawsuit against an abortion provider who terminates a pregnancy through partial-birth abortion. *See also* **Dilation and Extraction; Gonzales v. Carhart; Methods of Abortion; Partial-Birth Abortion Ban Act; Stenberg v. Carhart**

Partial-Birth Abortion Ban Act

In 2003 Congress passed into law the Partial-Birth Abortion Ban Act (Act). The Act was in response to a decision by the United States Supreme Court in *Stenberg v. Carhart*, which found a statute by Nebraska that banned partial-birth abortion to be unconstitutional. The constitutionality of the Act was challenged in two federal courts and found unconstitutional, primarily because of the decision in *Stenberg*. Both cases were appealed to the Supreme Court. The Supreme Court consolidated the cases and issued an opinion styled *Gonzales v. Carhart*, in which it held that the Act was facially constitutional. The Supreme Court distinguished the case of *Stenberg* from *Gonzales* on the grounds that the Act provided a detailed description of the procedure that was being banned, which was not done in the Nebraska statute. The text of the Act is set out below.

18 U.S.C.A. § 1531
Partial-Birth Abortion Ban Act

(a) Any physician who, in or affecting interstate or foreign commerce, knowingly performs a partial-birth abortion and thereby kills a human fetus shall be fined under this title or imprisoned not more than 2 years, or both. This subsection does not apply to a partial-birth abortion that is necessary to save the life of a mother whose life is endangered by a physical disorder, physical illness, or physical injury, including a life-endangering physical condition caused by or arising from the pregnancy itself. This subsection takes effect 1 day after the enactment.

(b) As used in this section—

(1) the term "partial-birth abortion" means an abortion in which the person performing the abortion—

(A) deliberately and intentionally vaginally delivers a living fetus until, in the case of a head-first presentation, the entire fetal head is outside the body of the mother, or, in the case of breech presentation, any part of the fetal trunk past the navel is outside the body of the mother, for the purpose of performing an overt act that the person knows will kill the partially delivered living fetus; and

(B) performs the overt act, other than completion of delivery, that kills the partially delivered living fetus; and

(2) the term "physician" means a doctor of medicine or osteopathy legally authorized to practice medicine and surgery by the State in which the doctor performs such activity, or any other individual

State Statutory Restrictions on Partial-Birth Abortion

State	*Prohibit*	*Life exception*	*Health exception*	*Lawsuit for violation*
Ala.	X	X		X
Alaska	X	X		
Ariz.	X	X		X
Ark.	X	X		
Cal.				
Colo.				
Conn.				
Del.				
D.C.				
Fla.	X	X		X
Ga.	X	X		X
Haw.				
Idaho	X	X		X
Ill.	X	X		X
Ind.	X	X		
Iowa	X	X		X
Kan.	X	X	X	
Ky.	X			
La.	X	X		X
Maine				
Md.				
Mass.				
Mich.	X	X		
Minn.				
Miss.	X	X		X
Mo.	X	X		
Mont.	X	X		
Neb.	X	X		
Nev.				
N.H.				
N.J.	X	X		
N.M.	X	X	X	X
N.Y.				
N.C.				
N.D.	X	X		
Ohio	X	X	X	X
Okla.	X	X		X
Ore.				
Penn.				
R.I.	X	X		X
S.C.	X	X		X
S.D.	X	X		X
Tenn.	X	X		
Tex.				
Utah	X	X		X
Vt.				
Va.	X	X		
Wash.				
W.Va.	X	X		
Wis.	X	X		X
Wyo.				

legally authorized by the State to perform abortions: Provided, however, That any individual who is not a physician or not otherwise legally authorized by the State to perform abortions, but who nevertheless directly performs a partial-birth abortion, shall be subject to the provisions of this section.

(c)(1) The father, if married to the mother at the time she receives a partial-birth abortion procedure, and if the mother has not attained the age of 18 years at the time of the abortion, the maternal grandparents of the fetus, may in a civil action obtain appropriate relief, unless the pregnancy resulted from the plaintiff's criminal conduct or the plaintiff consented to the abortion.

(2) Such relief shall include—

(A) money damages for all injuries, psychological and physical, occasioned by the violation of this section; and

(B) statutory damages equal to three times the cost of the partial-birth abortion.

(d)(1) A defendant accused of an offense under this section may seek a hearing before the State Medical Board on whether the physician's conduct was necessary to save the life of the mother whose life was endangered by a physical disorder, physical illness, or physical injury, including a life-endangering physical condition caused by or arising from the pregnancy itself.

(2) The findings on that issue are admissible on that issue at the trial of the defendant. Upon a motion of the defendant, the court shall delay the beginning of the trial for not more than 30 days to permit such a hearing to take place.

(e) A woman upon whom a partial-birth abortion is performed may not be prosecuted under this section, for a conspiracy to violate this section, or for an offense under section 2, 3, or 4 of this title based on a violation of this section.

See also **Born Alive Infants Protection Act; Dilation and Extraction; Gonzales v. Carhart; Methods of Abortion; Partial-Birth Abortion; Stenberg v. Carhart**

Patau Syndrome *see* **Trisomy 13**

Patch Contraceptive

The patch contraceptive (also called ortho evra) was submitted to the Food and Drug Administration (FDA) for marketing approval in December of 2000. The patch was submitted to the FDA by R.W. Johnson Pharmaceutical Research Institute. On November 20, 2001 the FDA announced its approval of the patch. The patch is composed of estrogen and progestin, hormones that aid in preventing pregnancy. Several studies have suggested that the patch may be as effective as birth control pills. To utilize the patch a woman must wear it on her body (e.g., abdomen or buttocks) for three consecutive weeks. That is, one patch every seven days. A patch is not required for the fourth week. At the end of the fourth week, a woman must repeat the three consecutive week cycle. The risks of using the patch are similar to the risks of using birth control pills, including an increased risk of blood clots, heart attack, and stroke. *See also* **Contraception**

Patent Ductus Arteriosus *see* **Congenital Heart Defect**

Pathfinder International

Pathfinder International (formerly Pathfinder Fund) was founded in 1957, by Dr. Clarence Gamble. Pathfinder is headquartered in Watertown, Massachusetts. The president of Pathfinder is Daniel E. Pellegrom. The organization was created to advocate the use of contraception by women in the United States and other countries. Pathfinder supports family planning and reproductive health initiatives in 37 countries. The organization believes that reproductive health is a basic human right and advocates sound reproductive health policies in the United States and abroad. *See also* **Gamble, Clarence; Pro-Choice Organizations**

Daniel E. Pellegrom is president of Pathfinder International, an organization created in 1957 for the purpose of advocating the use of contraception by women in the United States and other countries (Daniel E. Pellegrom).

Peace Corps Volunteers and Abortion Funding

The Peace Corps was established initially on March 1, 1961,

by an executive order of President John F. Kennedy. Congressional authorization for the agency was made September 22, 1961. There are more than 7,300 Peace Corps volunteers serving in 75 countries, working to bring clean water to communities, teaching children, and helping to start small businesses. Since 1979 Congressional appropriations legislation for the agency has prohibited the use of funds to provide abortion services for volunteers under all circumstances, including therapeutic abortions. Approximately 61 percent of the Peace Corps' volunteers are women. *See also* **Public Resources for Abortions**

Pelizaeus-Merzbacher Disease

Pelizaeus-Merzbacher disease is a congenital disorder involving an abnormal protein (proteolipid) in the fatty covering (myelin sheath) which insulates nerve fibers in the brain. Symptoms of the disease include convulsions, skeletal deformation, involuntary movements, speech impairment, seizures and deterioration of mental functions. Treatment for this disorder include medications for seizures and movement disorders. *See also* **Birth Defects and Abortion**

Pelvic Exam

A pelvic exam involves an invasive examination of the vagina, cervix, uterus, ovaries and fallopian tubes. This examination is done as a visual check for infections, tubal pregnancy or ovarian cysts. Usually a pap smear (taking swab of vaginal tissue to test for cancer) will be done during a pelvic exam.

Pelvic Floor Relaxation

Pelvic floor relaxation is a condition involving the dropping of the muscular wall that holds the abdominal contents above the vagina. Nearly all women who have delivered one or more babies vaginally will have some degree of pelvic floor relaxation. The condition causes sexual dissatisfaction after childbirth, urinary incontinence, and uterine prolapse. Stretching, tearing or loosening of the muscular attachments of the pelvic floor causes these symptoms.

Pelvic Inflammatory Disease

Pelvic inflammatory disease (PID) is a general phrase that is used to refer to an infection of the fallopian tubes and of other internal reproductive organs in women. Although many different organisms may cause PID, most cases are associated with the sexually transmitted diseases gonorrhea and chlamydia. PID can damage the fallopian tubes and tissues in and near the uterus and ovaries. Untreated PID may cause infertility, ectopic pregnancy, abscess formation, and chronic pelvic pain. In the United States more than 1 million women experience an episode of PID every year. The disease causes more than 100,000 women to become infertile each year. More than 150 women die every year from this infection.

PID symptoms range from none to severe. Women who do have symptoms of PID most commonly have lower abdominal pain, fever, unusual vaginal discharge that may have a foul odor, painful intercourse, painful urination, and irregular menstrual bleeding. PID can be cured with antibiotics. Prompt antibiotic treatment can prevent severe damage to pelvic organs, but antibiotic treatment does not reverse any damage that has already occurred to the reproductive organs. Women can protect themselves from PID by taking measures to prevent sexually transmitted diseases. *See also* **Chlamydia; Gonorrhea; Sexually Transmitted Diseases**

Penis *see* **Male Reproductive System**

Pennsylvania

(1) OVERVIEW

The state of Pennsylvania enacted its first criminal abortion statute on March 31, 1860. The statute underwent several amendments prior to the 1973 decision by the United States Supreme Court in *Roe v. Wade*, which legalized abortion in the nation. Pennsylvania has taken affirmative steps to respond to *Roe* and its progeny. The state has addressed several abortion issues by statute that include general abortion guidelines; informed consent and spousal notice; abortion by minors; fetal death report; facilities, people, public funds, and health insurance; family planning providers; fetal experimentation; injury to a pregnant woman; and wrongful birth or life action.

(2) GENERAL ABORTION GUIDELINES

Under the laws of Pennsylvania an abortion may only be performed when a physician determines that the abortion is necessary. This limitation is invalid to the extent that it impedes a woman's right to have a pre-viability abortion. The state has also prohibited an abortion that is sought only because of the sex of the fetus.

It is required by Pennsylvania that before an abortion is performed, a physician must determine the probable gestational age of the fetus. Pennsylvania prohibits an abortion after 23 weeks of pregnancy, unless it is necessary to prevent either the death of the pregnant woman or the substantial and irreversible impairment of a major bodily function of the woman. The state requires that, in addition to the treating

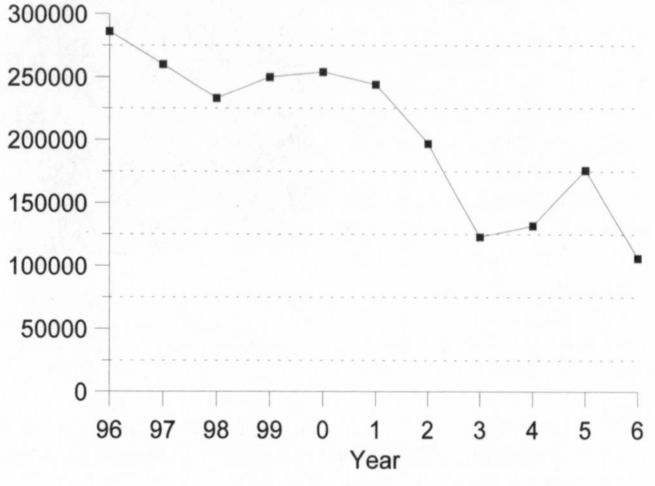

Source: National Disease and Therapeutic Index.

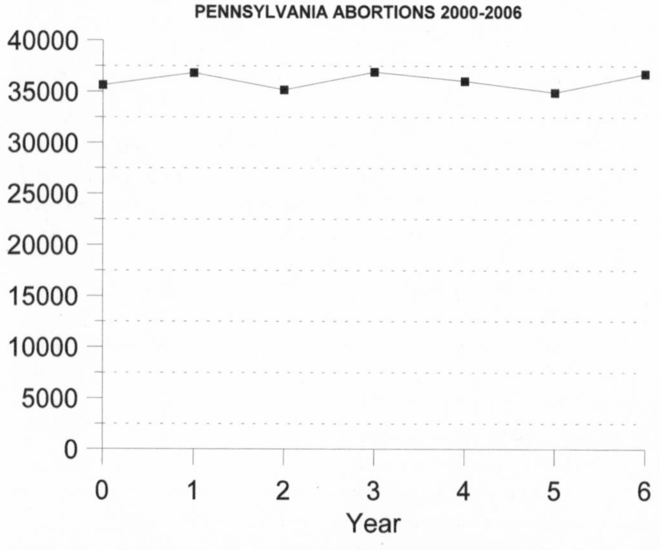

Source: Pennsylvania Department of Health.

physician, a second physician must concur in finding that an abortion is necessary under the law. Such an abortion must take place in a hospital, and a second physician must be present when it occurs. The general abortion statutes are set out below.

Pennsylvania Code Ti. 18, § 3201. Short title of chapter

This chapter shall be known and may be cited as the "Abortion Control Act."

Pennsylvania Code Ti. 18, § 3202. Legislative intent

(a) It is the intention of the General Assembly of the Commonwealth of Pennsylvania to protect hereby the life and health of the woman subject to abortion and to protect the life and health of the child subject to abortion. It is the further intention of the General Assembly to foster the development of standards of professional conduct in a critical area of medical practice, to provide for development of statistical data and to protect the right of the minor woman voluntarily to decide to submit to abortion or to carry her child to term. The General Assembly finds as fact that the rights and interests furthered by this chapter are not secure in the context in which abortion is presently performed.

(b) Reliable and convincing evidence has compelled the General Assembly to conclude and the General Assembly does hereby solemnly declare and find that:

(1) Many women now seek or are encouraged to undergo abortions without full knowledge of the development of the unborn child or of alternatives to abortion.

(2) The gestational age at which viability of an unborn child occurs has been lowering substantially and steadily as advances in neonatal medical care continue to be made.

(3) A significant number of late-term abortions result in live births, or in delivery of children who could survive if measures were taken to bring about breathing. Some physicians have been allowing these children to die or have been failing to induce breathing.

(4) Because the Commonwealth places a supreme value upon protecting human life, it is necessary that those physicians which it permits to practice medicine be held to precise standards of care in cases where their actions do or may result in the death of an unborn child.

(5) A reasonable waiting period, as contained in this chapter, is critical to the assurance that a woman elect to undergo an abortion procedure only after having the fullest opportunity to give her informed consent thereto.

(c) In every relevant civil or criminal proceeding in which it is possible to do so without violating the Federal Constitution, the common and statutory law of Pennsylvania shall be construed so as to extend to the unborn the equal protection of the laws and to further the public policy of this commonwealth encouraging childbirth over abortion.

(d) It is the further public policy of the Commonwealth of Pennsylvania to respect and protect the right of conscience of all persons who refuse to obtain, receive, subsidize, accept or provide abortions including those persons who are engaged in the delivery of medical services and medical care whether acting individually, corporately or in association with other persons; and to prohibit all forms of discrimination, disqualification, coercion, disability or imposition of liability or financial burden upon such persons or entities by reason of their refusing to act contrary to their conscience or conscientious convictions in refusing to obtain, receive, subsidize, accept or provide abortions.

Pennsylvania Code Ti. 18, § 3203. Definitions

The following words and phrases when used in this chapter shall have, unless the context clearly indicates otherwise, the meanings given to them in this section:

"Abortion." The use of any means to terminate the clinically diagnosable pregnancy of a woman with knowledge that the termination by those means will, with reasonable likelihood, cause the death of the unborn child except that, for the purposes of this chapter, abortion shall not mean the use of an intrauterine device or birth control pill to inhibit or prevent ovulation, fertilization or the implantation of a fertilized ovum within the uterus.

"Born alive." When used with regard to a human being, means that the human being was completely expelled or extracted from her or his mother and after such separation breathed or showed evidence of any of the following: beating of the heart, pulsation of the umbilical cord, definite movement of voluntary muscles or any brain-wave activity.

"Complication." Includes but is not limited to hemorrhage, infection, uterine perforation, cervical laceration and retained products. The department may further define complication.

"Conscience." A sincerely held set of moral convictions arising

Pennsylvania Abortion by Age Group 2000–2006

	Age Group (yrs)								
Year	*<15*	*15–19*	*20–24*	*25–29*	*30–34*	*35–39*	*40–44*	*≥45*	*Unknown*
2000	304	6,505	11,643	7,800	5,196	3,063	1,064	55	0
2001	285	6,463	12,212	8,156	5,467	3,192	977	67	1
2002	269	5,919	11,720	7,769	5,192	3,119	1,102	76	1
2003	269	6,245	12,276	8,062	5,545	3,336	1,090	85	0
2004	245	6,042	12,058	8,044	5,208	3,243	1,122	68	0
2005	226	5,760	11,714	7,903	5,028	3,105	1,098	74	1
2006	207	6,208	12,454	8,401	5,052	3,205	1,112	84	8
Total	1,805	43,142	84,077	56,135	36,688	22,263	7,565	509	11

Source: **Pennsylvania Department of Health.**

Pennsylvania Resident Abortion by Weeks of Gestation 2000–2006

	Year							
Weeks of Gestation	*2000*	*2001*	*2002*	*2003*	*2004*	*2005*	*2006*	*Total*
<9	18,528	20,031	19,049	20,722	20,152	19,632	20,479	138,593
9–10	7,452	7,400	7,087	6,959	6,747	6,574	6,990	49,209
11–12	3,710	3,602	3,593	3,735	3,618	3,506	3,579	25,343
13–14	1,880	1,766	1,693	1,904	1,904	1,777	1,966	12,890
15–17	1,157	1,182	1,219	1,118	1,293	1,272	1,339	8,580
18–20	781	732	630	560	589	550	618	4,460
21–23	393	312	232	217	214	156	221	1,745
≥24	0	0	0	0	0	1	0	1

Source: **Pennsylvania Department of Health.**

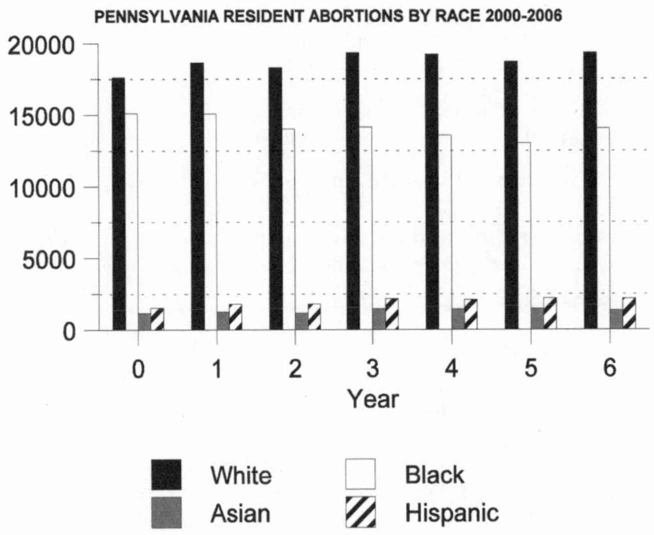

Source: **Pennsylvania Department of Health.**

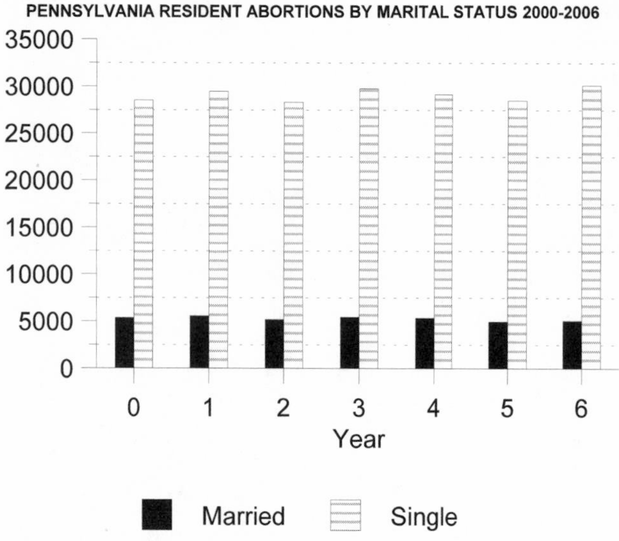

Source: National Center for Health Statistics.

Pennsylvania Prior Abortion by Female 2000–2004
Prior Abortion

Year	None	1	2	≥3	Not known
2000	19,693	9,396	3,984	2,538	19
2001	20,257	9,890	4,135	2,533	5
2002	19,326	9,314	4,025	2,497	5
2003	20,377	9,643	4,222	2,661	5
2004	19,382	9,916	4,074	2,654	4
Total	99,035	48,159	20,440	12,883	38

Source: National Center for Health Statistics.

from belief in and relation to a deity or which, though not so derived, obtains from a place in the life of its possessor parallel to that filled by a deity among adherents to religious faiths.

"Department." The Department of Health of the Commonwealth of Pennsylvania.

"Facility" or "medical facility." Any public or private hospital, clinic, center, medical school, medical training institution, health care facility, physician's office, infirmary, dispensary, ambulatory surgical treatment center or other institution or location wherein medical care is provided to any person.

"Fertilization" and "conception." Each term shall mean the fusion of a human spermatozoon with a human ovum.

"First trimester." The first 12 weeks of gestation.

"Gestational age." The age of the unborn child as calculated from the first day of the last menstrual period of the pregnant woman.

"Hospital." An institution licensed pursuant to the provisions of the law of this Commonwealth.

"In vitro fertilization." The purposeful fertilization of a human ovum outside the body of a living human female.

"Medical emergency." That condition which, on the basis of the physician's good faith clinical judgment, so complicates the medical condition of a pregnant woman as to necessitate the immediate abortion of her pregnancy to avert her death or for which a delay will create serious risk of substantial and irreversible impairment of major bodily function.

"Medical personnel." Any nurse, nurse's aide, medical school student, professional or any other person who furnishes, or assists in the furnishing of, medical care.

"Physician." Any person licensed to practice medicine in this Commonwealth. The term includes medical doctors and doctors of osteopathy.

"Pregnancy" and "pregnant." Each term shall mean that female reproductive condition of having a developing fetus in the body and commences with fertilization.

"Probable gestational age of the unborn child." What, in the judgment of the attending physician, will with reasonable probability be the gestational age of the unborn child at the time the abortion is planned to be performed.

"Unborn child" and "fetus." Each term shall mean an individual organism of the species homo sapiens from fertilization until live birth.

"Viability." That stage of fetal development when, in the judgment of the physician based on the particular facts of the case before him and in light of the most advanced medical technology and information available to him, there is a reasonable likelihood of sustained survival of the unborn child outside the body of his or her mother, with or without artificial support.

Pennsylvania Code Ti. 18, § 3204. Necessary abortion

(a) No abortion shall be performed except by a physician after either:

(1) He determines that, in his best clinical judgment, the abortion is necessary; or

(2) He receives what he reasonably believes to be a written statement signed by another physician, hereinafter called the "referring physician," certifying that in this referring physician's best clinical judgment the abortion is necessary.

(b) Except in a medical emergency where there is insufficient time before the abortion is performed, the woman upon whom the abortion is to be performed shall have a private medical consultation either with the physician who is to perform the abortion or with the referring physician. The consultation will be in a place, at a time and of a duration reasonably sufficient to enable the physician to determine whether, based on his best clinical judgment, the abortion is necessary.

(c) In determining in accordance with subsection (a) or (b) whether an abortion is necessary, a physician's best clinical judgment may be exercised in the light of all factors (physical, emotional, psychological, familial and the woman's age) relevant to the well-being of the woman. No abortion which is sought solely because of the sex of the unborn child shall be deemed a necessary abortion.

(d) Any person who intentionally, knowingly or recklessly violates the provisions of this section commits a felony of the third degree, and any physician who violates the provisions of this section is guilty of "unprofessional conduct" and his license for the practice of medicine and surgery shall be subject to suspension or revocation in accordance with procedures provided under the act of October 5, 1978 (P.L. 1109, No. 261), known as the Osteopathic Medical Practice Act, the act of December 20, 1985 (P.L. 457, No. 112), known as the Medical Practice Act of 1985, or their successor acts.

Pennsylvania Code Ti. 18, § 3210.
Determination of gestational age

(a) Except in the case of a medical emergency which prevents compliance with this section, no abortion shall be performed or induced unless the referring physician or the physician performing or inducing it has first made a determination of the probable gestational age of the unborn child. In making such determination, the physician shall make such inquiries of the patient and perform or cause to be performed such medical examinations and tests as a prudent physician would consider necessary to make or perform in making an accurate diagnosis with respect to gestational age. The physician who performs or induces the abortion shall report the type of inquiries made and the type of examinations and tests utilized to determine the gestational age of the unborn child and the basis for the diagnosis with respect to gestational age on forms provided by the department.

(b) Failure of any physician to conform to any requirement of this section constitutes "unprofessional conduct" within the meaning of the act of October 5, 1978 (P.L. 1109, No. 261), known as the Osteopathic Medical Practice Act, the act of December 20, 1985 (P.L. 457, No. 112), known as the Medical Practice Act of 1985, or their successor acts. Upon a finding by the State Board of Medicine or the State Board of Osteopathic Medicine that any physician has failed to conform to any requirement of this section, the board shall not fail to suspend that physician's license for a period of at least three months. Intentional, knowing or reckless falsification of any report required under this section is a misdemeanor of the third degree.

Pennsylvania Code Ti. 18, § 3211. Post-viability abortion

(a) Except as provided in subsection (b), no person shall perform or induce an abortion upon another person when the gestational age of the unborn child is 24 or more weeks.

(b)(1) It shall not be a violation of subsection (a) if an abortion is performed by a physician and that physician reasonably believes that it is necessary to prevent either the death of the pregnant woman or the substantial and irreversible impairment of a major bodily function of the woman. No abortion shall be deemed authorized under this paragraph if performed on the basis of a claim or a diagnosis that the woman will engage in conduct which would result in her death or in substantial and irreversible impairment of a major bodily function.

(2) It shall not be a violation of subsection (a) if the abortion is performed by a physician and that physician reasonably believes, after making a determination of the gestational age of the unborn child in compliance with section 3210 (relating to determination of gestational age), that the unborn child is less than 24 weeks gestational age.

(c) Except in the case of a medical emergency which, in the reasonable medical judgment of the physician performing the abortion, prevents compliance with a particular requirement of this subsection, no abortion which is authorized under subsection (b)(1) shall be performed unless each of the following conditions is met:

(1) The physician performing the abortion certifies in writing that, based upon his medical examination of the pregnant woman and his medical judgment, the abortion is necessary to prevent either the death of the pregnant woman or the substantial and irreversible impairment of a major bodily function of the woman.

(2) Such physician's judgment with respect to the necessity for the abortion has been concurred in by one other licensed physician who certifies in writing that, based upon his or her separate personal medical examination of the pregnant woman and his or her medical judgment, the abortion is necessary to prevent either the death of the pregnant woman or the substantial and irreversible impairment of a major bodily function of the woman.

(3) The abortion is performed in a hospital.

(4) The physician terminates the pregnancy in a manner which provides the best opportunity for the unborn child to survive, unless the physician determines, in his or her good faith medical judgment, that termination of the pregnancy in that manner poses a significantly greater risk either of the death of the pregnant woman or the substantial and irreversible impairment of a major bodily function of the woman than would other available methods.

(5) The physician performing the abortion arranges for the attendance, in the same room in which the abortion is to be completed, of a second physician who shall take control of the child immediately after complete extraction from the mother and shall provide immediate medical care for the child, taking all reasonable steps necessary to preserve the child's life and health.

(d) Any person who violates subsection (a) commits a felony of the third degree. Any person who violates subsection (c) commits a misdemeanor of the second degree for the first offense and a misdemeanor of the first degree for subsequent offenses.

Pennsylvania Code Ti. 18, § 3208.1. Contraceptions

The Commonwealth shall not interfere with the use of medically appropriate methods of contraception or the manner in which medically appropriate methods of contraception are provided.

Pennsylvania Code Ti. 18, § 3217. Civil penalties

Any physician who knowingly violates any of the provisions of section 3204 (relating to medical consultation and judgment) or 3205 (relating to informed consent) shall, in addition to any other penalty prescribed in this chapter, be civilly liable to his patient for any damages caused thereby and, in addition, shall be liable to his patient for punitive damages in the amount of $5,000, and the court shall award a prevailing plaintiff a reasonable attorney fee as part of costs.

Pennsylvania Code Ti. 18, § 3218. Criminal penalties

(a) Notwithstanding any other provision of this chapter, no criminal penalty shall apply to a woman who violates any provision of this chapter solely in order to perform or induce or attempt to perform or induce an abortion upon herself. Nor shall any woman who undergoes an abortion be found guilty of having committed an offense, liability for which is defined under section 306 (relating to liability for conduct of another; complicity) or Chapter 9 (relating to inchoate crimes), by reason of having undergone such abortion.

(b) A person commits a misdemeanor of the second degree if, with intent to mislead a public servant in performing his official function under this chapter, such person:

(1) makes any written false statement which he does not believe to be true; or

(2) submits or invites reliance on any writing which he knows to be forged, altered or otherwise lacking in authenticity.

(c) A person commits a misdemeanor of the third degree if such person makes a written false statement which such person does not believe to be true on a statement submitted as required under this chapter, bearing notice to the effect that false statements made therein are punishable.

(d) Section 4902(c) through (f) (relating to perjury) apply to subsections (b) and (c).

Pennsylvania Code Ti. 18, § 3219. Board of Medicine

(a) It shall be the duty of the State Board of Medicine and the State Board of Osteopathic Medicine to vigorously enforce those provisions of this chapter, violation of which constitutes "unprofessional conduct" within the meaning of the act of October 5, 1978 (P.L.1109, No.261), known as the Osteopathic Medical Practice Act, the act of December 20, 1985 (P.L.457, No.112), known as the Medical Practice Act of 1985, or their successor acts. Each board shall have the power to conduct, and its responsibilities shall include, systematic review of all reports filed under this chapter.

(b) Except as otherwise herein provided, upon a finding of "unprofessional conduct" under the provisions of this chapter, the board shall, for the first such offense, prescribe such penalties as it deems appropriate; for the second such offense, suspend the license of the physician for at least 90 days; and, for the third such offense, revoke the license of the physician.

(c) The board shall prepare and submit an annual report of its enforcement efforts under this chapter to the General Assembly, which shall contain the following items:

(1) number of violations investigated, by section of this chapter;

(2) number of physicians complained against;

(3) number of physicians investigated;

(4) penalties imposed; and

(5) such other information as any committee of the General Assembly shall require.

Such reports shall be available for public inspection and copying.

Pennsylvania Code Ti. 18, § 3220. Construction

(a) The provisions of section 503(3) of the act of June 29, 1953 (P.L. 304, No. 66), known as the "Vital Statistics Law of 1953," shall not be construed to require referral to the coroner of cases of abortions performed in compliance with this chapter.

(b) Apart from the provisions of subsection (a) and section 3214 (relating to reporting) nothing in this chapter shall have the effect of modifying or repealing any part of the "Vital Statistics Law of 1953" or section 5.2 of the act of October 27, 1955 (P.L. 744, No. 222), known as the "Pennsylvania Human Relations Act."

(c) When any provision of this chapter requires the furnishing or obtaining of a nonnotarized statement or verification, the furnishing or acceptance of a notarized statement or verification shall not be deemed a violation of that provision.

(3) INFORMED CONSENT AND SPOUSAL NOTICE

Prior to an abortion Pennsylvania requires that a woman be fully informed of the procedure to be used, the risks involved and alternatives to abortion. An abortion may not take place until 24 hours after a woman has been provided with statutorily required information. The United States Supreme Court held in *Planned Parenthood of Southeastern Pennsylvania v. Casey* that the constitution was not violated by provisions in Pennsylvania's abortion statute that provided for a 24 hour waiting period for an abortion. The state also has a statute that requires a married woman notify her husband of her decision to have an abortion, prior to the abortion taking place. If the woman does not provide such notification, she must explain in writing to a physician the reason why notification was not given. The United States Supreme Court held in *Planned Parenthood of Southeastern Pennsylvania v. Casey* that the constitution was violated by Pennsylvania's requirement of spousal notification before obtaining an abortion, and the requirement that a woman inform the abortion provider the reason for not notifying her spouse. The statutes are set out below.

Pennsylvania Code Ti. 18, § 3205. Consent and waiting period

(a) No abortion shall be performed or induced except with the voluntary and informed consent of the woman upon whom the abortion is to be performed or induced. Except in the case of a medical emergency, consent to an abortion is voluntary and informed if and only if:

(1) At least 24 hours prior to the abortion, the physician who is to perform the abortion or the referring physician has orally informed the woman of:

(i) The nature of the proposed procedure or treatment and of those risks and alternatives to the procedure or treatment that a reasonable patient would consider material to the decision of whether or not to undergo the abortion.

(ii) The probable gestational age of the unborn child at the time the abortion is to be performed.

(iii) The medical risks associated with carrying her child to term.

(2) At least 24 hours prior to the abortion, the physician who is to perform the abortion or the referring physician, or a qualified physician assistant, health care practitioner, technician or social worker to whom the responsibility has been delegated by either physician, has informed the pregnant woman that:

(i) The department publishes printed materials which describe the unborn child and list agencies which offer alternatives to abortion and that she has a right to review the printed materials and that a copy will be provided to her free of charge if she chooses to review it.

(ii) Medical assistance benefits may be available for prenatal care, childbirth and neonatal care, and that more detailed information on the availability of such assistance is contained in the printed materials published by the department.

(iii) The father of the unborn child is liable to assist in the support of her child, even in instances where he has offered to pay for the abortion. In the case of rape, this information may be omitted.

(3) A copy of the printed materials has been provided to the pregnant woman if she chooses to view these materials.

(4) The pregnant woman certifies in writing, prior to the abortion, that the information required to be provided under paragraphs (1), (2) and (3) has been provided.

(b) Where a medical emergency compels the performance of an abortion, the physician shall inform the woman, prior to the abortion if possible, of the medical indications supporting his judgment that an abortion is necessary to avert her death or to avert substantial and irreversible impairment of major bodily function.

(c) Any physician who violates the provisions of this section is guilty of "unprofessional conduct" and his license for the practice of medicine and surgery shall be subject to suspension or revocation in accordance with procedures provided under the act of October 5, 1978 (P.L. 1109, No. 261), known as the Osteopathic Medical Practice Act, the act of December 20, 1985 (P.L. 457, No. 112), known as the Medical Practice Act of 1985, or their successor acts. Any physician who performs or induces an abortion without first obtaining the certification required by subsection (a)(4) or with knowledge or reason to know that the informed consent of the woman has not been obtained shall for the first offense be guilty of a summary offense and for each subsequent offense be guilty of a misdemeanor of the third degree. No physician shall be guilty of violating this section for failure to furnish the information required by subsection (a) if he or she can demonstrate, by a preponderance of the evidence, that he or she reasonably believed that furnishing the information would have resulted in a severely adverse effect on the physical or mental health of the patient.

(d) Any physician who complies with the provisions of this section may not be held civilly liable to his patient for failure to obtain informed consent to the abortion within the meaning of that term as defined by the act of October 15, 1975 (P.L.390, No.111), known as the Health Care Services Malpractice Act.

Pennsylvania Code Ti. 18, § 3209. Spousal notice

(a) In order to further the Commonwealth's interest in promoting the integrity of the marital relationship and to protect a spouse's interests in having children within marriage and in protecting the prenatal life of that spouse's child, no physician shall perform an abortion on a married woman, except as provided in subsections (b) and (c), unless he or she has received a signed statement, which need not be notarized, from the woman upon whom the abortion is to be performed, that she has notified her spouse that she is about to undergo an abortion. The statement shall bear a notice that any false statement made therein is punishable by law.

(b) The statement certifying that the notice required by subsection (a) has been given need not be furnished where the woman provides the physician a signed statement certifying at least one of the following:

(1) Her spouse is not the father of the child.

(2) Her spouse, after diligent effort, could not be located.

(3) The pregnancy is a result of spousal sexual assault as described in section 3128 (relating to spousal sexual assault), which has been reported to a law enforcement agency having the requisite jurisdiction.

(4) The woman has reason to believe that the furnishing of notice to her spouse is likely to result in the infliction of bodily injury upon her by her spouse or by another individual.

Such statement need not be notarized, but shall bear a notice that any false statements made therein are punishable by law.

(c) The requirements of subsection (a) shall not apply in case of a medical emergency.

(d) The department shall cause to be published forms which may be

utilized for purposes of providing the signed statements required by subsections (a) and (b). The department shall distribute an adequate supply of such forms to all abortion facilities in this Commonwealth.

(e) Any physician who violates the provisions of this section is guilty of "unprofessional conduct," and his or her license for the practice of medicine and surgery shall be subject to suspension or revocation in accordance with procedures provided under the act of October 5, 1978 (P.L. 1109, No. 261), known as the Osteopathic Medical Practice Act, the act of December 20, 1985 (P.L. 457, No. 112), known as the Medical Practice Act of 1985, or their successor acts. In addition, any physician who knowingly violates the provisions of this section shall be civilly liable to the spouse who is the father of the aborted child for any damages caused thereby and for punitive damages in the amount of $5,000, and the court shall award a prevailing plaintiff a reasonable attorney fee as part of costs.

Pennsylvania Code Ti. 18, § 3208. Printed information

(a) The department shall cause to be published in English, Spanish and Vietnamese, within 60 days after this chapter becomes law, and shall update on an annual basis, the following easily comprehensible printed materials:

(1) Geographically indexed materials designed to inform the woman of public and private agencies and services available to assist a woman through pregnancy, upon childbirth and while the child is dependent, including adoption agencies, which shall include a comprehensive list of the agencies available, a description of the services they offer and a description of the manner, including telephone numbers, in which they might be contacted, or, at the option of the department, printed materials including a toll-free, 24-hour a day telephone number which may be called to obtain, orally, such a list and description of agencies in the locality of the caller and of the services they offer.

The materials shall provide information on the availability of medical assistance benefits for prenatal care, childbirth and neonatal care, and state that it is unlawful for any individual to coerce a woman to undergo abortion, that any physician who performs an abortion upon a woman without obtaining her informed consent or without according her a private medical consultation may be liable to her for damages in a civil action at law, that the father of a child is liable to assist in the support of that child, even in instances where the father has offered to pay for an abortion and that the law permits adoptive parents to pay costs of prenatal care, childbirth and neonatal care.

(2) Materials designed to inform the woman of the probable anatomical and physiological characteristics of the unborn child at two-week gestational increments from fertilization to full term, including pictures representing the development of unborn children at two-week gestational increments, and any relevant information on the possibility of the unborn child's survival; provided that any such pictures or drawings must contain the dimensions of the fetus and must be realistic and appropriate for the woman's stage of pregnancy. The materials shall be objective, nonjudgmental and designed to convey only accurate scientific information about the unborn child at the various gestational ages. The material shall also contain objective information describing the methods of abortion procedures commonly employed, the medical risks commonly associated with each such procedure, the possible detrimental psychological effects of abortion and the medical risks commonly associated with each such procedure and the medical risks commonly associated with carrying a child to term.

(b) The materials shall be printed in a typeface large enough to be clearly legible.

(c) The materials required under this section shall be available at no cost from the department upon request and in appropriate number to any person, facility or hospital.

Pennsylvania Code Ti. 18, § 3212. Live-born fetus

(a) The law of this Commonwealth shall not be construed to imply that any human being born alive in the course of or as a result of an abortion or pregnancy termination, no matter what may be that human being's chance of survival, is not a person under the Constitution and laws of this Commonwealth.

(b) All physicians and licensed medical personnel attending a child who is born alive during the course of an abortion or premature delivery, or after being carried to term, shall provide such child that type and degree of care and treatment which, in the good faith judgment of the physician, is commonly and customarily provided to any other person under similar conditions and circumstances. Any individual who intentionally, knowingly or recklessly violates the provisions of this subsection commits a felony of the third degree.

(c) Whenever the physician or any other person is prevented by lack of parental or guardian consent from fulfilling his obligations under subsection (b), he shall nonetheless fulfill said obligations and immediately notify the juvenile court of the facts of the case. The juvenile court shall immediately institute an inquiry and, if it finds that the lack of parental or guardian consent is preventing treatment required under subsection (b), it shall immediately grant injunctive relief to require such treatment.

Pennsylvania Code Ti. 18, § 3213. Prohibited acts

(a) Except in the case of a pregnancy which is not yet clinically diagnosable, any person who intends to perform or induce abortion shall, before accepting payment therefor, make or obtain a determination that the woman is pregnant. Any person who intentionally or knowingly accepts such a payment without first making or obtaining such a determination commits a misdemeanor of the second degree. Any person who makes such a determination erroneously either knowing that it is erroneous or with reckless disregard or negligence as to whether it is erroneous, and who either:

(1) Thereupon or thereafter intentionally relies upon that determination in soliciting or obtaining any such payment; or

(2) intentionally conveys that determination to any person or persons with knowledge that, or with reckless disregard as to whether, that determination will be relied upon in any solicitation or obtaining of any such payment;

commits a misdemeanor of the second degree.

(b) The payment or receipt of a referral fee in connection with the performance of an abortion is a misdemeanor of the first degree. For purposes of this section, "referral fee" means the transfer of anything of value between a physician who performs an abortion or an operator or employee of a clinic at which an abortion is performed and the person who advised the woman receiving the abortion to use the services of that physician or clinic.

(c) The department shall issue regulations to assure that prior to the performance of any abortion, including abortions performed in the first trimester of pregnancy, the maternal Rh status shall be determined and that anti–Rh sensitization prophylaxis shall be provided to each patient at risk of sensitization unless the patient refuses to accept the treatment. Except when there exists a medical emergency or, in the judgment of the physician, there exists no possibility of Rh sensitization, the intentional, knowing, or reckless failure to conform to the regulations issued pursuant to this subsection constitutes "unprofessional conduct" and his license for the practice of medicine and surgery shall be subject to suspension or revocation in accordance with procedures provided under the act of October 5, 1978 (P.L. 1109, No. 261), known as the Osteopathic Medical Practice Act, the act of December 20, 1985 (P.L. 457, No. 112), known as the Medical Practice Act of 1985, or their successor acts.

(d) Except for a facility devoted exclusively to the performance of abortions, no medical personnel or medical facility, nor any employee, agent or student thereof, shall be required against his or its conscience to aid,

abet or facilitate performance or an abortion or dispensing of an abortifacient and failure or refusal to do so shall not be a basis for any civil, criminal, administrative or disciplinary action, penalty or proceeding, nor may it be the basis for refusing to hire or admit anyone. Nothing herein shall be construed to limit the provisions of the act of October 27, 1955 (P.L. 744, No. 222), known as the "Pennsylvania Human Relations Act." Any person who knowingly violates the provisions of this subsection shall be civilly liable to the person thereby injured and, in addition, shall be liable to that person for punitive damages in the amount of $5,000.

(e) All persons conducting, or experimenting in, in vitro fertilization shall file quarterly reports with the department, which shall be available for public inspection and copying, containing the following information:

(1) Names of all persons conducting or assisting in the fertilization or experimentation process.

(2) Locations where the fertilization or experimentation is conducted.

(3) Name and address of any person, facility, agency or organization sponsoring the fertilization or experimentation except that names of any persons who are donors or recipients of sperm or eggs shall not be disclosed.

(4) Number of eggs fertilized.

(5) Number of fertilized eggs destroyed or discarded.

(6) Number of women implanted with a fertilized egg.

Any person required under this subsection to file a report, keep records or supply information, who willfully fails to file such report, keep records or supply such information or who submits a false report shall be assessed a fine by the department in the amount of $50 for each day in which that person is in violation hereof.

(f) (1) Except for a facility devoted exclusively to the performance of abortions, every facility performing abortions shall prominently post a notice, not less than eight and one-half inches by eleven inches in size, entitled "Right of Conscience," for the exclusive purpose of informing medical personnel, employees, agents and students of such facilities of their rights under subsection (d) and under section 5.2 of the Pennsylvania Human Relations Act. The facility shall post the notice required by this subsection in a location or locations where notices to employees, medical personnel and students are normally posted or, if notices are not normally posted, in a location or locations where the notice required by this subsection is likely to be seen by medical personnel, employees or students of the facility. The department shall prescribe a model notice which may be used by any facility, and any facility which utilizes the model notice or substantially similar language shall be deemed in compliance with this subsection.

(2) The department shall have the authority to assess a civil penalty of up to $5,000 against any facility for each violation of this subsection, giving due consideration to the appropriateness of the penalty with respect to the size of the facility, the gravity of the violation, the good faith of the facility and the history of previous violations. Civil penalties due under this subsection shall be paid to the department for deposit in the State Treasury and may be collected by the department in the appropriate court of common pleas. The department shall send a copy of its model notice to every facility which files a report under section 3207(b) (relating to abortion facilities). Failure to receive a notice shall not be a defense to any civil action brought pursuant to this subsection.

(4) ABORTION BY MINORS

Under the laws of Pennsylvania no physician may perform an abortion upon an unemancipated minor unless he/she first obtains the consent of either parent of the minor, or guardian. If a minor's pregnancy was caused by sexual intercourse with her natural father, then consent of the abortion by the minor's mother is sufficient.

In compliance with federal constitutional law, Pennsylvania has provided a judicial waiver procedure for an unemancipated minor to obtain an abortion without parental or guardian consent. The minor may petition a trial court for a waiver of the consent requirement. A minor has a right to an attorney at the proceeding and if she cannot afford one, the court must appoint her an attorney. If a minor chooses, she may represent herself. The required parental or guardian consent may be waived if the court finds either (1) that the minor is mature and well-informed enough to make the abortion decision on her own, or (2) that performance of the abortion would be in the best interest of the minor. An expedited appeal is available to any minor to whom the court denies a waiver of consent. The United States Supreme Court held in *Planned Parenthood of Southeastern Pennsylvania v. Casey* that the constitution was not violated by provisions in Pennsylvania's abortion statute that provided for parental or guardian consent and judicial bypass for an abortion by a minor. The statute addressing the issues is set out below.

Pennsylvania Code Ti. 18, § 3206.
Parental consent and judicial bypass

(a) Except in the case of a medical emergency, or except as provided in this section, if a pregnant woman is less than 18 years of age and not emancipated, or if she has been adjudged an incapacitated person under 20 Pa.C.S. § 5511 (relating to petition and hearing; independent evaluation), a physician shall not perform an abortion upon her unless, in the case of a woman who is less than 18 years of age, he first obtains the informed consent both of the pregnant woman and of one of her parents; or, in the case of a woman who is an incapacitated person, he first obtains the informed consent of her guardian. In deciding whether to grant such consent, a pregnant woman's parent or guardian shall consider only their child's or ward's best interests. In the case of a pregnancy that is the result of incest where the father is a party to the incestuous act, the pregnant woman need only obtain the consent of her mother.

(b) If both parents have died or are otherwise unavailable to the physician within a reasonable time and in a reasonable manner, consent of the pregnant woman's guardian or guardians shall be sufficient. If the pregnant woman's parents are divorced, consent of the parent having custody shall be sufficient. If neither any parent nor a legal guardian is available to the physician within a reasonable time and in a reasonable manner, consent of any adult person standing in loco parentis shall be sufficient.

(c) If both of the parents or guardians of the pregnant woman refuse to consent to the performance of an abortion or if she elects not to seek the consent of either of her parents or of her guardian, the court of common pleas of the judicial district in which the applicant resides or in which the abortion is sought shall, upon petition or motion, after an appropriate hearing, authorize a physician to perform the abortion if the court determines that the pregnant woman is mature and capable of giving informed consent to the proposed abortion, and has, in fact, given such consent.

(d) If the court determines that the pregnant woman is not mature and capable of giving informed consent or if the pregnant woman does not claim to be mature and capable of giving informed consent, the court shall determine whether the performance of an abortion upon her would be in her best interests. If the court determines that the performance of an abortion would be in the best interests of the woman, it shall authorize a physician to perform the abortion.

(e) The pregnant woman may participate in proceedings in the court on her own behalf and the court may appoint a guardian ad litem to assist her. The court shall, however, advise her that she has a right to court appointed counsel, and shall provide her with such counsel unless she wishes to appear with private counsel or has knowingly and intelligently waived representation by counsel.

(f)(1) Court proceedings under this section shall be confidential and

shall be given such precedence over other pending matters as will ensure that the court may reach a decision promptly and without delay in order to serve the best interests of the pregnant woman. In no case shall the court of common pleas fail to rule within three business days of the date of application. A court of common pleas which conducts proceedings under this section shall make in writing specific factual findings and legal conclusions supporting its decision and shall, upon the initial filing of the minor's petition for judicial authorization of an abortion, order a sealed record of the petition, pleadings, submissions, transcripts, exhibits, orders, evidence and any other written material to be maintained which shall include its own findings and conclusions.

(2) The application to the court of common pleas shall be accompanied by a non-notarized verification stating that the information therein is true and correct to the best of the applicant's knowledge, and the application shall set forth the following facts:

(i) The initials of the pregnant woman.

(ii) The age of the pregnant woman.

(iii) The names and addresses of each parent, guardian or, if the minor's parents are deceased and no guardian has been appointed, any other person standing in loco parentis to the minor.

(iv) That the pregnant woman has been fully informed of the risks and consequences of the abortion.

(v) Whether the pregnant woman is of sound mind and has sufficient intellectual capacity to consent to the abortion.

(vi) A prayer for relief asking the court to either grant the pregnant woman full capacity for the purpose of personal consent to the abortion, or to give judicial consent to the abortion under subsection (d) based upon a finding that the abortion is in the best interest of the pregnant woman.

(vii) That the pregnant woman is aware that any false statements made in the application are punishable by law.

(viii) The signature of the pregnant woman. Where necessary to serve the interest of justice, the orphans' court division, or, in Philadelphia, the family court division, shall refer the pregnant woman to the appropriate personnel for assistance in preparing the application.

(3) The name of the pregnant woman shall not be entered on any docket which is subject to public inspection. All persons shall be excluded from hearings under this section except the applicant and such other persons whose presence is specifically requested by the applicant or her guardian.

(4) At the hearing, the court shall hear evidence relating to the emotional development, maturity, intellect and understanding of the pregnant woman, the fact and duration of her pregnancy, the nature, possible consequences and alternatives to the abortion and any other evidence that the court may find useful in determining whether the pregnant woman should be granted full capacity for the purpose of consenting to the abortion or whether the abortion is in the best interest of the pregnant woman. The court shall also notify the pregnant woman at the hearing that it must rule on her application within three business days of the date of its filing and that, should the court fail to rule in favor of her application within the allotted time, she has the right to appeal to the Superior Court.

(g) Except in a medical emergency, no parent, guardian or other person standing in loco parentis shall coerce a minor or incapacitated woman to undergo an abortion. Any minor or incapacitated woman who is threatened with such coercion may apply to a court of common pleas for relief. The court shall provide the minor or incapacitated woman with counsel, give the matter expedited consideration and grant such relief as may be necessary to prevent such coercion. Should a minor be denied the financial support of her parents by reason of her refusal to undergo abortion, she shall be considered emancipated for purposes of eligibility for assistance benefits.

(h) No filing fees shall be required of any woman availing herself of the procedures provided by this section. An expedited confidential appeal shall be available to any pregnant woman whom the court fails to grant an order authorizing an abortion within the time specified in this section. Any court to which an appeal is taken under this section shall give prompt and confidential attention thereto and shall rule thereon within five business days of the filing of the appeal. The Supreme Court of Pennsylvania may issue such rules as may further assure that the process provided in this section is conducted in such a manner as will ensure confidentiality and sufficient precedence over other pending matters to ensure promptness of disposition.

(i) Any person who performs an abortion upon a woman who is an unemancipated minor or incapacitated person to whom this section applies either with knowledge that she is a minor or incapacitated person to whom this section applies, or with reckless disregard or negligence as to whether she is a minor or incapacitated person to whom this section applies, and who intentionally, knowingly or recklessly fails to conform to any requirement of this section is guilty of "unprofessional conduct" and his license for the practice of medicine and surgery shall be suspended in accordance with procedures provided under the act of October 5, 1978 (P.L. 1109, No. 261), known as the Osteopathic Medical Practice Act, the act of December 20, 1985 (P.L. 457, No. 112), known as the Medical Practice Act of 1985, or their successor acts, for a period of at least three months. Failure to comply with the requirements of this section is prima facie evidence of failure to obtain informed consent and of interference with family relations in appropriate civil actions. The law of this Commonwealth shall not be construed to preclude the award of exemplary damages or damages for emotional distress even if unaccompanied by physical complications in any appropriate civil action relevant to violations of this section. Nothing in this section shall be construed to limit the common law rights of parents.

(5) FETAL DEATH REPORT

Under the laws of Pennsylvania all abortions and abortion complications must be reported to the proper authorities. The statute addressing the matter is set out below.

Pennsylvania Code Ti. 18, § 3214. Reporting

(a) For the purpose of promotion of maternal health and life by adding to the sum of medical and public health knowledge through the compilation of relevant data, and to promote the Commonwealth's interest in protection of the unborn child, a report of each abortion performed shall be made to the department on forms prescribed by it. The report forms shall not identify the individual patient by name and shall include the following information:

(1) Identification of the physician who performed the abortion, the concurring physician as required by section 3211(c)(2) (relating to abortion on unborn child of 24 or more weeks gestational age), the second physician as required by section 3211(c)(5) and the facility where the abortion was performed and of the referring physician, agency or service, if any.

(2) The county and state in which the woman resides.

(3) The woman's age.

(4) The number of prior pregnancies and prior abortions of the woman.

(5) The gestational age of the unborn child at the time of the abortion.

(6) The type of procedure performed or prescribed and the date of the abortion.

(7) Pre-existing medical conditions of the woman which would complicate pregnancy, if any, and, if known, any medical complication which resulted from the abortion itself.

(8) The basis for the medical judgment of the physician who performed the abortion that the abortion was necessary to prevent ei-

ther the death of the pregnant woman or the substantial and irreversible impairment of a major bodily function of the woman, where an abortion has been performed pursuant to section 3211(b)(1).

(9) The weight of the aborted child for any abortion performed pursuant to section 3211(b)(1).

(10) Basis for any medical judgment that a medical emergency existed which excused the physician from compliance with any provision of this chapter.

(11) The information required to be reported under section 3210(a) (relating to determination of gestational age).

(12) Whether the abortion was performed upon a married woman and, if so, whether notice to her spouse was given. If no notice to her spouse was given, the report shall also indicate the reason for failure to provide notice.

(b) The reports shall be completed by the hospital or other licensed facility, signed by the physician who performed the abortion and transmitted to the department within 15 days after each reporting month.

(c) When there is an abortion performed during the first trimester of pregnancy, the tissue that is removed shall be subjected to a gross or microscopic examination, as needed, by the physician or a qualified person designated by the physician to determine if a pregnancy existed and was terminated. If the examination indicates no fetal remains, that information shall immediately be made known to the physician and sent to the department within 15 days of the analysis. When there is an abortion performed after the first trimester of pregnancy where the physician has certified the unborn child is not viable, the dead unborn child and all tissue removed at the time of the abortion shall be submitted for tissue analysis to a board eligible or certified pathologist. If the report reveals evidence of viability or live birth, the pathologist shall report such findings to the department within 15 days and a copy of the report shall also be sent to the physician performing the abortion. Intentional, knowing, reckless or negligent failure of the physician to submit such an unborn child or such tissue remains to such a pathologist for such a purpose, or intentional, knowing or reckless failure of the pathologist to report any evidence of live birth or viability to the department in the manner and within the time prescribed is a misdemeanor of the third degree.

(d) The department shall prescribe a form on which pathologists may report any evidence of absence of pregnancy, live birth or viability.

(e) (1) The department shall prepare a comprehensive annual statistical report for the General Assembly based upon the data gathered under subsections (a) and (h). Such report shall not lead to the disclosure of the identity of any person filing a report or about whom a report is filed, and shall be available for public inspection and copying.

(2) Reports filed pursuant to subsection (a) or (h) shall not be deemed public records within the meaning of that term as defined by the act of June 21, 1957 (P.L. 390, No. 212), referred to as the Right-to-Know Law, and shall remain confidential, except that disclosure may be made to law enforcement officials upon an order of a court of common pleas after application showing good cause therefor. The court may condition disclosure of the information upon any appropriate safeguards it may impose.

(3) Original copies of all reports filed under subsections (a), (f) and (h) shall be available to the State Board of Medicine and the State Board of Osteopathic Medicine for use in the performance of their official duties.

(4) Any person who willfully discloses any information obtained from reports filed pursuant to subsection (a) or (h), other than that disclosure authorized under paragraph (1), (2) or (3) hereof or as otherwise authorized by law, shall commit a misdemeanor of the third degree.

(f) Every facility in which an abortion is performed within this Commonwealth during any quarter year shall file with the department a report showing the total number of abortions performed within the hospital or other facility during that quarter year. This report shall also show the total abortions performed in each trimester of pregnancy. Any report shall be available for public inspection and copying only if the facility receives State-appropriated funds within the 12-calendar-month period immediately preceding the filing of the report. These reports shall be submitted on a form prescribed by the department which will enable a facility to indicate whether or not it is receiving State-appropriated funds. If the facility indicates on the form that it is not receiving State-appropriated funds, the department shall regard its report as confidential unless it receives other evidence which causes it to conclude that the facility receives State-appropriated funds.

(g) After 30 days' public notice, the department shall henceforth require that all reports of maternal deaths occurring within the Commonwealth arising from pregnancy, childbirth or intentional abortion in every case state the cause of death, the duration of the woman's pregnancy when her death occurred and whether or not the woman was under the care of a physician during her pregnancy prior to her death and shall issue such regulations as are necessary to assure that such information is reported, conducting its own investigation if necessary in order to ascertain such data. A woman shall be deemed to have been under the care of a physician prior to her death for the purpose of this chapter when she had either been examined or treated by a physician, not including any examination or treatment in connection with emergency care for complications of her pregnancy or complications of her abortion, preceding the woman's death at any time which is both 21 or more days after the time she became pregnant and within 60 days prior to her death. Known incidents of maternal mortality of nonresident women arising from induced abortion performed in this Commonwealth shall be included as incidents of maternal mortality arising from induced abortions. Incidents of maternal morality arising from continued pregnancy or childbirth and occurring after induced abortion has been attempted but not completed, including deaths occurring after induced abortion has been attempted but not completed as a result of ectopic pregnancy, shall be included as incidents of maternal morality arising from induced abortion. The department shall annually compile a statistical report for the General Assembly based upon the data gathered under this subsection, and all such statistical reports shall be available for public inspection and copying.

(h) Every physician who is called upon to provide medical care or treatment to a woman who is in need of medical care because of a complication or complications resulting, in the good faith judgment of the physician, from having undergone an abortion or attempted abortion shall prepare a report thereof and file the report with the department within 30 days of the date of his first examination of the woman, which report shall be on forms prescribed by the department, which forms shall contain the following information, as received, and such other information except the name of the patient as the department may from time to time require:

(1) Age of patient.

(2) Number of pregnancies patient may have had prior to the abortion.

(3) Number and type of abortions patient may have had prior to this abortion.

(4) Name and address of the facility where the abortion was performed.

(5) Gestational age of the unborn child at the time of the abortion, if known.

(6) Type of abortion performed, if known.

(7) Nature of complication or complications.

(8) Medical treatment given.

(9) The nature and extent, if known, of any permanent condition caused by the complication.

(i) (1) Any person required under this section to file a report, keep any

records or supply any information, who willfully fails to file such report, keep such records or supply such information at the time or times required by law or regulation is guilty of "unprofessional conduct" and his license for the practice of medicine and surgery shall be subject to suspension or revocation in accordance with procedures provided under the act of October 5, 1978 (P.L. 1109, No. 261), known as the Osteopathic Medical Practice Act, the act of December 20, 1985 (P.L. 457, No. 112), known as the Medical Practice Act of 1985, or their successor acts.

(2) Any person who willfully delivers or discloses to the department any report, record or information known by him to be false commits a misdemeanor of the first degree.

(3) In addition to the above penalties, any person, organization or facility who willfully violates any of the provisions of this section requiring reporting shall upon conviction thereof:

(i) For the first time, have its license suspended for a period of six months.

(ii) For the second time, have its license suspended for a period of one year.

(iii) For the third time, have its license revoked.

(6) FACILITIES, PEOPLE, PUBLIC FUNDS, AND HEALTH INSURANCE

Under the laws of Pennsylvania government medical facilities are not permitted to perform abortions, except to save the life of a woman or when the pregnancy resulted from rape or incest. The state also permits private medical facilities to refuse to perform abortions. Physicians and other medical personnel are not required to participate in abortions, even though the facility employing them performs abortions. The state prohibits health insurance policies from providing coverage for abortions. Pennsylvania prohibits the use of public funds to perform abortions, except to save a woman's life or when the pregnancy resulted from rape or incest. The United States Supreme Court held in *Beal v. Doe* that Pennsylvania's refusal to extend Medicaid coverage to nontherapeutic abortions was not invalid nor inconsistent with federal law. The state has a specific statute requiring regulations be created for facilities performing abortions. In addition the state requires abortion facilities that perform 100 or more abortions annually establish a patient safety program. The statutes addressing the issues are set out below.

Pennsylvania Code Ti. 18, § 3215.
Public facilities, officials, funds

(a) No hospital, clinic or other health facility owned or operated by the Commonwealth, a county, a city or other governmental entity (except the government of the United States, another state or a foreign nation) shall:

(1) Provide, induce, perform or permit its facilities to be used for the provision, inducement or performance of any abortion except where necessary to avert the death of the woman or where necessary to terminate pregnancies initiated by acts of rape or incest if reported in accordance with requirements set forth in subsection (c).

(2) Lease or sell or permit the subleasing of its facilities or property to any physician or health facility for use in the provision, inducement or performance of abortion, except abortion necessary to avert the death of the woman or to terminate pregnancies initiated by acts of rape or incest if reported in accordance with requirements set forth in subsection (c).

(3) Enter into any contract with any physician or health facility under the terms of which such physician or health facility agrees to provide, induce or perform abortions, except abortion necessary to avert the death of the woman or to terminate pregnancies initiated by acts of rape or incest if reported in accordance with requirements set forth in subsection (c).

(b) Nothing in subsection (a) shall be construed to preclude any hospital, clinic or other health facility from providing treatment for post-abortion complications.

(c) No Commonwealth funds and no Federal funds which are appropriated by the Commonwealth shall be expended by any State or local government agency for the performance of abortion, except:

(1) When abortion is necessary to avert the death of the mother on certification by a physician. When such physician will perform the abortion or has a pecuniary or proprietary interest in the abortion there shall be a separate certification from a physician who has no such interest.

(2) When abortion is performed in the case of pregnancy caused by rape which, prior to the performance of the abortion, has been reported, together with the identity of the offender, if known, to a law enforcement agency having the requisite jurisdiction and has been personally reported by the victim.

(3) When abortion is performed in the case of pregnancy caused by incest which, prior to the performance of the abortion, has been personally reported by the victim to a law enforcement agency having the requisite jurisdiction, or, in the case of a minor, to the county child protective service agency and the other party to the incestuous act has been named in such report.

(d) No health plan for employees, funded with any Commonwealth funds, shall include coverage for abortion, except under the same conditions and requirements as provided in subsection (c). The prohibition contained herein shall not apply to health plans for which abortion coverage has been expressly bargained for in any collective bargaining agreement presently in effect, but shall be construed to preclude such coverage with respect to any future agreement.

(e) All insurers who make available health care and disability insurance policies in this Commonwealth shall make available such policies which contain an express exclusion of coverage for abortion services not necessary to avert the death of the woman or to terminate pregnancies caused by rape or incest.

(f) Except in the case of a medical emergency, no court, judge, executive officer, administrative agency or public employee of the Commonwealth or of any local governmental body shall have power to issue any order requiring an abortion without the express voluntary consent of the woman upon whom the abortion is to be performed or shall coerce any person to have an abortion.

(g) No court, judge, executive officer, administrative agency or public employee of the Commonwealth or of any local governmental body shall withhold, reduce or suspend or threaten to withhold, reduce or suspend any benefits to which a person would otherwise be entitled on the ground that such person chooses not to have an abortion.

(h) Whoever orders an abortion in violation of subsection (f) or withholds, reduces or suspends any benefits or threatens to withhold, reduce or suspend any benefits in violation of subsection (g) commits a misdemeanor of the first degree.

(i) No Federal or State funds which are appropriated by the Commonwealth for the provision of legal services by private agencies, and no public funds generated by collection of interest on lawyer's trust accounts, as authorized by statute previously or subsequently enacted, may be used, directly or indirectly, to:

(1) Advocate the freedom to choose abortion or the prohibition of abortion.

(2) Provide legal assistance with respect to any proceeding or litigation which seeks to procure or prevent any abortion or to procure or prevent public funding for any abortion.

(3) Provide legal assistance with respect to any proceeding or litigation which seeks to compel or prevent the performance or assistance in the performance of any abortion, or the provision of facilities for the performance of any abortion.

Nothing in this subsection shall be construed to require or prevent the expenditure of funds pursuant to a court order awarding fees for attorney's services under the Civil Rights Attorney's Fees Awards Act of 1976

(Public law 94-559, 90 Stat. 2641), nor shall this subsection be construed to prevent the use of public funds to provide court appointed counsel in any proceeding authorized under section 3206 (relating to parental consent).

(j) No Commonwealth agency shall make any payment from Federal or State funds appropriated by the Commonwealth for the performance of any abortion pursuant to subsection (c)(2) or (3) unless the Commonwealth agency first:

(1) receives from the physician or facility seeking payment a statement signed by the physician performing the abortion stating that, prior to performing the abortion, he obtained a non-notarized, signed statement from the pregnant woman stating that she was a victim of rape or incest, as the case may be, and that she reported the crime, including the identity of the offender, if known, to a law enforcement agency having the requisite jurisdiction or, in the case of incest where a pregnant minor is the victim, to the county child protective service agency and stating the name of the law enforcement agency or child protective service agency to which the report was made and the date such report was made;

(2) receives from the physician or facility seeking payment, the signed statement of the pregnant woman which is described in paragraph (1). The statement shall bear the notice that any false statements made therein are punishable by law and shall state that the pregnant woman is aware that false reports to law enforcement authorities are punishable by law; and

(3) verifies with the law enforcement agency or child protective service agency named in the statement of the pregnant woman whether a report of rape or incest was filed with the agency in accordance with the statement.

The Commonwealth agency shall report any evidence of false statements, of false reports to law enforcement authorities or of fraud in the procurement or attempted procurement of any payment from Federal or State funds appropriated by the Commonwealth pursuant to this section to the district attorney of appropriate jurisdiction and, where appropriate, to the Attorney General.

Pennsylvania Code Ti. 43, § 955.2. Abortion immunity

(a) No hospital or other health care facility shall be required to, or held liable for refusal to, perform or permit the performance of abortion or sterilization contrary to its stated ethical policy. No physician, nurse, staff member or employee of a hospital or other health care facility, who shall state in writing to such hospital or health care facility an objection to performing, participating in, or cooperating in, abortion or sterilization on moral, religious or professional grounds, shall be required to, or held liable for refusal to, perform, participate in, or cooperate in such abortion or sterilization.

(b) It shall be an unlawful discriminatory practice:

(1) For any person to impose penalties or take disciplinary action against, or to deny or limit public funds, licenses, certifications, degrees, or other approvals or documents of qualification to, any hospital or other health care facility, refusal of such hospital or health care facility to perform or permit to be performed, participate in, or cooperate in, abortion or sterilization by reason of objection thereto on moral, religious or professional grounds, or because of any statement or other manifestation of attitude by such hospital or health care facility with respect to abortion or sterilization.

(2) For any person to impose penalties or take disciplinary action against, or to deny or limit public funds, licenses, certifications, degrees, or other approvals or documents of qualification to any physician, nurse or staff member or employee of any hospital or health care facility, due to the willingness or refusal of such physician, nurse or staff member or employee to perform or participate in abortion or sterilization by reason of objection thereto on moral, religious or professional grounds, or because of any statement or other manifestation of attitude by such physician, nurse or staff member or employee with respect to abortion or sterilization.

(3) For any public or private agency, institution or person, including a medical, nursing or other school, to deny admission to, impose any burdens in terms of conditions of employment upon, or otherwise discriminate against any applicant for admission thereto or any physician, nurse, staff member, student or employee thereof, on account of the willingness or refusal of such applicant, physician, nurse, staff member, student or employee to perform or participate in, abortion or sterilization by reason of objection thereto on moral, religious or professional grounds, or because of any statement or other manifestation of attitude by such person with respect to abortion or sterilization: Provided, however, That this subsection shall not apply to any health care facility operated exclusively for the performance of abortion or sterilization or directly related procedures or to a separate clinic of a health care facility for the performance of abortion or sterilization or directly related procedures.

Pennsylvania Code Ti. 62, § 453.
Expenditure of public funds

Since it is the public policy of the Commonwealth to favor childbirth over abortion, no Commonwealth funds and no Federal funds which are appropriated by the Commonwealth shall be expended by any State or local government agency for the performance of abortion: Provided, That nothing in this act shall be construed to deny the use of funds where a physician has certified in writing that the life of the mother would be endangered if the fetus were carried to full term or except for such medical procedures necessary for the victims of rape or incest when such rape or incest has been reported promptly to a law enforcement agency or public health service. Nothing contained in this section shall be interpreted to restrict or limit in any way, appropriations, made by the Commonwealth or a local governmental agency to hospitals for their maintenance and operation, or, for reimbursement to hospitals for services rendered which are not for the performance of abortions.

Pennsylvania Code Ti. 18, § 3207.
Abortion facility regulations

(a) The department shall have power to make rules and regulations pursuant to this chapter, with respect to performance of abortions and with respect to facilities in which abortions are performed, so as to protect the health and safety of woman having abortions and of premature infants aborted alive. These rules and regulations shall include, but not be limited to, procedures, staff, equipment and laboratory testing requirements for all facilities offering abortion services.

(b) Within 30 days after the effective date of this chapter, every facility at which abortions are performed shall file, and update immediately upon any change, a report with the department, containing the following information:

(1) Name and address of the facility.

(2) Name and address of any parent, subsidiary or affiliated organizations, corporations or associations.

(3) Name and address of any parent, subsidiary or affiliated organizations, corporations or associations having contemporaneous commonality of ownership, beneficial interest, directorship or officership with any other facility.

The information contained in those reports which are filed pursuant to this subsection by facilities which receive State appropriated funds during the 12-calendar-month period immediately preceding a request to inspect or copy such reports shall be deemed public information. Reports filed by facilities which do not receive State appropriated funds shall only be available to law enforcement officials, the State Board of Medicine and the State Board of Osteopathic Medicine for use in the performance of their official duties. Any facility failing to comply with the pro-

visions of this subsection shall be assessed by the department a fine of $500 for each day it is in violation hereof.

Pennsylvania Code Ti. 40, § 1303.315.
Abortion facility safety plan

(a) This section shall apply to abortion facilities.

(b) An abortion facility that performs 100 or more abortions after the effective date of this act during the calendar year in which this section takes effect shall be subject to the provisions of this chapter at the beginning of the immediately following calendar year and during each subsequent calendar year unless the facility gives the department written notice that it will not be performing 100 or more abortions during such following calendar year and does not perform 100 or more abortions during that calendar year.

(c) In the calendar years following the effective date of this act, this chapter shall apply to an abortion facility not subject to subsection (b) on the day following the performance of its 100th abortion and for the remainder of that calendar year and during each subsequent calendar year unless the facility gives the department written notice that it will not be performing 100 or more abortions during such following calendar year and does not perform 100 or more abortions during that calendar year.

(d) An abortion facility shall submit its patient safety plan under section 307(c) within 60 days following the application of this chapter to the facility.

(e) An abortion facility shall begin reporting serious events, incidents and infrastructure failures consistent with the requirements of section 313 upon the submission of its patient safety plan to the department.

(f) Nothing in this chapter shall be construed to limit the provisions of 18 Pa.C.S. Ch. 32 (relating to abortion) or any regulation adopted under 18 Pa.C.S. Ch. 32.

(7) FAMILY PLANNING PROVIDERS

Under the laws of Pennsylvania public funding is provided for family planning agencies that offer diagnosis, treatment, tests, drugs, supplies, counseling and other contraceptive services which are provided to individuals to prevent pregnancy. The state restricts the disbursement of public funds to family planning agencies that also provide for abortion. The statutes addressing the matter are set out below.

Pennsylvania Code Ti. 72, § 1701-D. Scope

This article relates to family planning funding limitations.

Pennsylvania Code Ti. 72, § 1702-D. Definitions

The following words and phrases when used in this article shall have the meanings given to them in this section unless the context clearly indicates otherwise:

"Abortion." As defined in 18 Pa.C.S. § 3203 (relating to definitions).

"Abortion-related activities." Activities that consist of any of the following:

(1) Performing or directly assisting in abortions.

(2) Referring a pregnant woman to an abortion provider for an abortion.

(3) Counseling that advocates for or promotes abortion, including counseling that advocates abortion as an option for dealing with an unwanted pregnancy.

"Family planning appropriation." Moneys appropriated by the General Assembly from Commonwealth revenue sources and Federal revenue sources for the purpose of funding family planning services or a combination of family planning services and other programs. In the case of a general appropriation or any other appropriation containing more than one line item, the term "family planning appropriation" shall only refer to those line items that may be expended for family planning services.

"Family planning services." Diagnosis, treatment, tests, drugs, supplies, counseling and other contraceptive services which are provided to an individual of childbearing age to enable that individual to prevent pregnancy. The term does not include abortion-related activities.

"Family planning services provider." A person that receives a grant or other payment or reimbursement from the Department of Public Welfare or the Department of Health, as appropriate, from a family planning appropriation for the purpose of providing family planning services, including, but not limited to, any appropriation for women's medical services, family planning service programs authorized under Medicaid and any programs funded through a Social Services Block Grant or a Temporary Assistance for Needy Families Block Grant.

"Person." Includes a corporation, partnership, limited liability company, business trust, other association, government entity, estate, trust, foundation or natural person.

"Project." A group or set of family planning services or a combination of family planning services and other services which are funded in whole or in part from a family planning appropriation and which are furnished pursuant to a grant, contract or other agreement between a family planning services provider and the Department of Public Welfare or the Department of Health, as appropriate, or furnished by a subcontractor of such provider pursuant to such grant, contract or other agreement.

"Subcontractor." A person who furnishes family planning services directly to individuals pursuant to a grant, contract or other agreement between that person and a family planning services provider or other entity that contracts with such provider for the purpose of providing family planning services, if family planning services furnished to such individuals are funded from a family planning appropriation.

"Women's medical services." A line item appropriation for a program that expressly authorizes the expenditure of funds for women's medical services and contraceptives.

Pennsylvania Code Ti. 72, § 1703-D.
Ban use of funds for abortion related activities

Except as provided in section 1705-D, no family planning services provider or subcontractor shall expend any funds received from a family planning services appropriation on abortion-related activities.

Pennsylvania Code Ti. 72, § 1704-D.
Duties of family planning services providers

(a) Each family planning services provider and subcontractor shall keep a project physically and financially separate from abortion-related activities conducted by that family planning services provider or subcontractor.

(b) The restrictions and conditions specified in this article shall be made a part of every grant, contract or other agreement between the Department of Public Welfare or the Department of Health, as appropriate, and each family planning services provider and every grant, contract or other agreement between a family planning services provider and a subcontractor.

(c) A family planning services provider who also performs abortion-related activities shall obtain an annual independent audit of its facilities to assure compliance with the physical and financial separation requirements of this article. The audit shall be conducted in accordance with standards prescribed by the Department of Public Welfare or the Department of Health, as appropriate, and shall be submitted to the department no later than January 30 of each year. Further evidence of such physical and financial separation shall be supplied through such documentation as the Department of Public Welfare or the Department of Health, as appropriate, shall request. The Department of Public Welfare or the Department of Health, as appropriate, shall make the audits required by this subsection available for public inspection and copying.

Pennsylvania Code Ti. 72, § 1705-D. Exclusions

(a) This article does not apply to any of the following:

(1) A licensed hospital.

(2) A family planning services provider who is a natural person, who is licensed to provide medical services in this Commonwealth and whose only public funding is through a medical assistance appropriation.

(b) No abortion, abortion counseling or abortion referral directly related thereto shall be deemed to fall within the definition of an abortion-related activity if:

(1) on the basis of the physician's good faith clinical judgment, the abortion is necessary to prevent the death of the mother or to prevent the serious risk of substantial and irreversible impairment of a major bodily function; or

(2) the abortion is performed in the case of a pregnancy caused by rape or incest.

(c) The requirements of this article shall not apply to a family planning services provider or subcontractor that receives Federal funds pursuant to Title X of the Public Health Service Act (58 Stat. 682, 42 U.S.C. § 201 et seq.) to the extent that:

(1) the family planning services provider or subcontractor performs only those nondirective abortion counseling and referral services required under Title X; and

(2) failure to perform those services will result in the withholding of Federal funds.

Pennsylvania Code Ti. 72, § 1706-D.
Reports to General Assembly

No later than March 30 of each year, the Department of Public Welfare and the Department of Health shall submit a report to the chairman and minority chairman of the Appropriations Committee of the Senate, to the chairman and minority chairman of the Appropriations Committee of the House of Representatives, to the chairman and minority chairman of the Public Health and Welfare Committee of the Senate and to the chairman and minority chairman of the Health and Human Services Committee of the House of Representatives regarding the audits obtained pursuant to section 1704-D(c), including the number and findings of such audits, the adequacy of the documentation submitted and any recommendations to revise the verification process.

Pennsylvania Code Ti. 72, § 1707-D. Construction

Nothing in this article shall be construed to:

(1) Repeal or otherwise restrict any provision of 18 Pa.C.S. Ch. 32 (relating to abortion).

(2) Prohibit the use of appropriations for which funding is permitted under 18 Pa.C.S. § 3215(c) (relating to publicly owned facilities; public officials and public funds) if funding for abortions is otherwise permitted under that appropriation and for any counseling or referral directly related thereto.

(3) Preclude, in addition to any remedy or penalty prescribed in this article, the exercise of any other civil or criminal remedy or penalty that is applicable to a failure to comply with this article.

Pennsylvania Code Ti. 72, § 1708-D. Expiration

This article shall expire immediately upon enactment of legislation which expressly imposes additional substantive programmatic or fiscal restrictions on the funding or delivery of any State-funded family planning services or on the funding or delivery of any family planning services authorized under section 1115 of the Social Security Act (49 Stat. 620, 42 U.S.C. § 1315).

(8) FETAL EXPERIMENTATION

Pennsylvania prohibits experiments on a live fetus, except when necessary to save the life of the fetus. The state also prohibits experiments on the remains of an aborted fetus, without consent of the woman involved. The statute addressing the matter is set out below.

Pennsylvania Code Ti. 18, § 3216. Fetal experimentation

(a) Any person who knowingly performs any type of nontherapeutic experimentation or nontherapeutic medical procedure (except an abortion as defined in this chapter) upon any unborn child, or upon any child born alive during the course of an abortion, commits a felony of the third degree. "Nontherapeutic" means that which is not intended to preserve the life or health of the child upon whom it is performed.

(b) The following standards govern the procurement and use of any fetal tissue or organ which is used in animal or human transplantation, research or experimentation:

(1) No fetal tissue or organs may be procured or used without the written consent of the mother. No consideration of any kind for such consent may be offered or given. Further, if the tissue or organs are being derived from abortion, such consent shall be valid only if obtained after the decision to abort has been made.

(2) No person who provides the information required by section 3205 (relating to informed consent) shall employ the possibility of the use of aborted fetal tissue or organs as an inducement to a pregnant woman to undergo abortion except that payment for reasonable expenses occasioned by the actual retrieval, storage, preparation and transportation of the tissues is permitted.

(3) No remuneration, compensation or other consideration may be paid to any person or organization in connection with the procurement of fetal tissue or organs.

(4) All persons who participate in the procurement, use or transplantation of fetal tissue or organs, including the recipients of such tissue or organs, shall be informed as to whether the particular tissue or organ involved was procured as a result of either: (i) stillbirth; (ii) miscarriage; (iii) ectopic pregnancy; (iv) abortion; or (v) any other means.

(5) No person who consents to the procurement or use of any fetal tissue or organ may designate the recipient of that tissue or organ, nor shall any other person or organization act to fulfill that designation.

(6) The department may assess a civil penalty upon any person who procures, sells or uses any fetal tissue or organs in violation of this section or the regulations issued thereunder. Such civil penalties may not exceed $5,000 for each separate violation. In assessing such penalties, the department shall give due consideration to the gravity of the violation, the good faith of the violator and the history of previous violations. Civil penalties due under this paragraph shall be paid to the department for deposit in the State Treasury and may be enforced by the department in the Commonwealth Court.

(c) Nothing in this section shall be construed to condone or prohibit the performance of diagnostic tests while the unborn child is in utero or the performance of pathological examinations on an aborted child. Nor shall anything in this section be construed to condone or prohibit the performance of in vitro fertilization and accompanying embryo transfer.

(9) INJURY TO A PREGNANT WOMAN

Pennsylvania has established separate criminal laws for the death or injury of a fetus, other than a lawful abortion. The statutes addressing the matter are set out below.

Pennsylvania Code Ti. 18, § 2601. Short title of chapter

This chapter shall be known and may be cited as the Crimes Against the Unborn Child Act.

Pennsylvania Code Ti. 18, § 2602. Definitions

The following words and phrases when used in this chapter shall have the meanings given to them in this section unless the context clearly indicates otherwise:

"Abortion." As defined in section 3203 (relating to definitions).

"Intentional killing." Killing by means of poison, or by lying in wait, or by any other kind of willful, deliberate and premeditated killing.

"Murder." As used in this chapter, the term includes the same element of malice which is required to prove murder under Chapter 25 (relating to criminal homicide).

"Perpetration of a felony." As defined in section 2502(d) (relating to murder).

"Principal." As defined in section 2502(d) (relating to murder).

"Serious bodily injury." Bodily injury which creates a substantial risk of death or which causes serious, permanent disfigurement or protracted loss or impairment of the function of any bodily member or organ.

"Serious provocation." As defined in section 2301 (relating to definitions).

"Unborn child." As defined in section 3203 (relating to definitions).

Pennsylvania Code Ti. 18, § 2603.
Criminal homicide of unborn child

(a) An individual commits criminal homicide of an unborn child if the individual intentionally, knowingly, recklessly or negligently causes the death of an unborn child in violation of section 2604 (relating to murder of unborn child) or 2605 (relating to voluntary manslaughter of unborn child).

(b) Criminal homicide of an unborn child shall be classified as murder of an unborn child or voluntary manslaughter of an unborn child.

Pennsylvania Code Ti. 18, § 2604. Murder of unborn child

(a) First degree murder of unborn child.

(1) A criminal homicide of an unborn child constitutes first degree murder of an unborn child when it is committed by an intentional killing.

(2) The penalty for first degree murder of an unborn child shall be imposed in accordance with section 1102(a)(2) (relating to sentence for murder and murder of an unborn child).

(b) Second degree murder of unborn child.

(1) A criminal homicide of an unborn child constitutes second degree murder of an unborn child when it is committed while the defendant was engaged as a principal or an accomplice in the perpetration of a felony.

(2) The penalty for second degree murder of an unborn child shall be the same as for murder of the second degree.

(c) Third degree murder of unborn child.

(1) All other kinds of murder of an unborn child shall be third degree murder of an unborn child.

(2) The penalty for third degree murder of an unborn child is the same as the penalty for murder of the third degree.

Pennsylvania Code Ti. 18, § 2605.
Voluntary manslaughter of unborn child

(a) A person who kills an unborn child without lawful justification commits voluntary manslaughter of an unborn child if at the time of the killing he is acting under a sudden and intense passion resulting from serious provocation by:

(1) the mother of the unborn child whom the actor endeavors to kill, but he negligently or accidentally causes the death of the unborn child; or

(2) another whom the actor endeavors to kill, but he negligently or accidentally causes the death of the unborn child.

(b) A person who intentionally or knowingly kills an unborn child commits voluntary manslaughter of an unborn child if at the time of the killing he believes the circumstances to be such that, if they existed, would justify the killing under Chapter 5 (relating to general principles of justification) but his belief is unreasonable.

(c) The penalty for voluntary manslaughter of an unborn child shall be the same as the penalty for voluntary manslaughter.

Pennsylvania Code Ti. 18, § 2606.
Aggravated assault of unborn child

(a) A person commits aggravated assault of an unborn child if he attempts to cause serious bodily injury to the unborn child or causes such injury intentionally, knowingly or recklessly under circumstances manifesting extreme indifference to the life of the unborn child.

(b) Aggravated assault of an unborn child is a felony of the first degree.

Pennsylvania Code Ti. 18, § 2607. Culpability

In any criminal prosecution pursuant to this chapter, the provisions of Chapter 3 (relating to culpability) shall apply except that:

(1) The term "different person" as used in section 303(b) and (c) (relating to causal relationship between conduct and result) shall also include an unborn child.

(2) The term "victim" as used in section 311 (relating to consent) shall not include the mother of the unborn child.

Pennsylvania Code Ti. 18, § 2608. Nonliability and defenses

(a) Nothing in this chapter shall impose criminal liability:

(1) For acts committed during any abortion or attempted abortion, whether lawful or unlawful, in which the pregnant woman cooperated or consented.

(2) For the consensual or good faith performance of medical practice, including medical procedures, diagnostic testing or therapeutic treatment, the use of an intrauterine device or birth control pill to inhibit or prevent ovulation, fertilization or the implantation of a fertilized ovum within the uterus.

(3) Upon the pregnant woman in regard to crimes against her unborn child.

(b) In any prosecution pursuant to this chapter, it shall be a defense that:

(1) The use of force that caused death or serious bodily injury to the unborn child would have been justified pursuant to Chapter 5 (relating to general principles of justification) if it caused death or serious bodily injury to the mother.

(2) Death or serious bodily injury to the unborn child was caused by the use of force which would have been justified pursuant to Chapter 5 if the same level of force was used upon or toward the mother.

Pennsylvania Code Ti. 18, § 2609. Construction

The provisions of this chapter shall not be construed to prohibit the prosecution of an offender under any other provision of law.

Pennsylvania Code Ti. 18, § 1102.
Sentence for murder of an unborn child

(a) (1) A person who has been convicted of a murder of the first degree shall be sentenced to death or to a term of life imprisonment in accordance with 42 Pa.C.S. § 9711 (relating to sentencing procedure for murder of the first degree).

(2) The sentence for a person who has been convicted of first degree murder of an unborn child shall be the same as the sentence for murder of the first degree, except that the death penalty shall not be imposed. This paragraph shall not affect the determination of an aggravating circumstance under 42 Pa.C.S. § 9711(d)(17) for the killing of a pregnant woman.

(b) A person who has been convicted of murder of the second degree or of second degree murder of an unborn child shall be sentenced to a term of life imprisonment.

(c) Notwithstanding section 1103(1) (relating to sentence of imprisonment for felony), a person who has been convicted of attempt, solicita-

tion or conspiracy to commit murder or murder of an unborn child where serious bodily injury results may be sentenced to a term of imprisonment which shall be fixed by the court at not more than 40 years. Where serious bodily injury does not result, the person may be sentenced to a term of imprisonment which shall be fixed by the court at not more than 20 years.

(d) Notwithstanding section 1103, a person who has been convicted of murder of the third degree or of third degree murder of an unborn child shall be sentenced to a term which shall be fixed by the court at not more than 40 years.

Pennsylvania Code Ti. 18, § 108. Prosecution time limitations

(a) Except as set forth in subsection (b), a prosecution for any offense under this title must be commenced within the period, if any, limited by Chapter 55 of Title 42 (relating to limitation of time).

(b) Offenses against unborn child.

(1) A prosecution for criminal homicide of an unborn child may be commenced at any time.

(2) A prosecution for an offense under section 2606 (relating to aggravated assault of unborn child) must be commenced within five years after it is committed.

Pennsylvania Code Ti. 42, § 6144.
Dying declarations in case of abortion

(a) The antemortem statements of any woman, who shall die in consequence of any criminal acts producing or intended to produce a miscarriage of such woman, as to the cause of her injuries shall be competent evidence on the trial of any person charged with the commission of such injuries, with like effect and under like limitations as apply to dying declarations in prosecutions for felonious homicide.

(b) Before such statement shall be submitted to the jury as evidence the Commonwealth shall, by competent and satisfactory evidence, prove that such woman was of sound mind at the time such ante mortem statements were made.

(10) WRONGFUL BIRTH OR LIFE ACTION

Under the laws of Pennsylvania no one may file a civil lawsuit seeking damages on a claim of wrongful birth or life. The statute addressing the matter is set out below.

Pennsylvania Code Ti. 42, § 8305.
Wrongful birth and wrongful life

(a) There shall be no cause of action or award of damages on behalf of any person based on a claim that, but for an act or omission of the defendant, a person once conceived would not or should not have been born. Nothing contained in this subsection shall be construed to prohibit any cause of action or award of damages for the wrongful death of a woman, or on account of physical injury suffered by a woman or a child, as a result of an attempted abortion. Nothing contained in this subsection shall be construed to provide a defense against any proceeding charging a health care practitioner with intentional misrepresentation under the act of October 5, 1978 (P.L. 1109, No. 261), known as the Osteopathic Medical Practice Act, the act of December 20, 1985 (P.L. 457, No. 112), known as the Medical Practice Act of 1985, or any other act regulating the professional practices of health care practitioners.

(b) There shall be no cause of action on behalf of any person based on a claim of that person that, but for an act or omission of the defendant, the person would not have been conceived or, once conceived, would or should have been aborted.

(c) A person shall be deemed to be conceived at the moment of fertilization.

Pennsylvania Pro-Life Federation

Pennsylvania Pro-Life Federation (PPLF) is a pro-life organization headquartered in Harrisburg, Pennsylvania. The executive director of PPLF is Michael Ciccocioppo. PPLF is committed to promoting the dignity and value of human life from conception to natural death, and to restoring legal protection for the unborn. The organization seeks legal protection and societal respect for the right of every child to live, and promote viable alternatives to abortion, such as adoption and assisted parenting. Some of the work done by PPLF includes: (1) successfully lobbying for passage of the state's Abortion Control Act, which provides women with information about the development of their baby and alternatives to abortion before having an abortion, and requires parental consent for a minor's decision to abort; (2) successfully lobbying the state legislature for the nation's first public funding of abortion alternatives; (3) successfully lobbying Congress for a partial-birth abortion ban. PPLF publishes a quarterly newsletter called "LifeLines." *See also*, **Pro-Life Organizations**

People Concerned for the Unborn Child

People Concerned for the Unborn Child (PCUC) is a Pittsburgh, Pennsylvania pro-life organization that was founded in 1969. The president of PCUC is Marlene Wohleber. The mission of PCUC is to speak for and act in defense of all innocent human life threatened by abortion. PCUC takes the position that (1) the unborn child is a human being entitled to the same rights as all other Americans; (2) abstinence is the only successful solution to the teenage pregnancy problem; and (3) food and water are basic human needs that should never be withheld. PCUC is opposed to (1) abortion on demand; (2) abortion as the "solution" to a rape/incest pregnancy; (3) experiments or processes in which the fetal material used are those which came from an elective abortion; (4) in-vitro fertilization; (5) non-profit organizations that advocate abortion as the cure for a particular genetic defect; and (6) any form of birth control that is an abortifacient such as "the pill," the IUD, RU-486, and Norplant. *See also* **Pro-Life Organizations**

Percutaneous Umbilical Blood Sampling

Percutaneous umbilical blood sampling (PUBS) involves the insertion of a needle through a woman's abdomen (as is done with amniocentesis), to obtain a blood sample from a fetal vein in the umbilical cord. PUBS allows for faster testing than amniocentesis extraction. The procedure is usually done to obtain fetal blood for rapid chromosome analysis or to evaluate the fetus for a risk of a number of blood disorders, such as anemia. PUBS also can detect fetal antibodies to such illnesses as toxoplasmosis and rubella. The procedure carries a high risk of infection and spontaneous abortion. *See also* **Amniocentesis**

Perinatal

Perinatal refers to the time period after the 28th week of gestation. It ends the first week after birth. *See also* **Postnatal; Prenatal**

Perinatal Care *see* **Prenatal Care**

Perinatal Mortality *see* **High-Risk Pregnancy**

Perinatologist

A perinatologist is a physician who specializes in treating pregnant women, particularly when the woman or fetus is at a high risk for complications. *See also* **Gynecologist**; **Obstetrician**

Period *see* **Menstrual Cycle**

Persistent Ectopic Pregnancy *see* **Ectopic Pregnancy**

Pharmacists for Life International

Pharmacists for Life International (PLI) is an Ohio based pro-life organization. Through its president, Karen Brauer, PLI represents almost 1500 pharmacists, and hundreds of lay supporters in the United States, Canada and worldwide. PLI's mission is to make pharmacy a life-saving profession. As part of this commitment, PLI is actively involved in educating pharmacists and other health professionals on the consequences of abortion. PLI also provides educational services for the general public and pregnancy help centers. *See also* **Pro-Life Organizations**

Physician Abortion Requirements

All jurisdictions provide, either by statute or regulation, that elective abortions must be performed by a physician. Kentucky and New York authorize self-abortion by statute (performed using medically prescribed abortifacients). States also provide diverse legislation to regulate the conduct of physicians performing abortions. The United States Supreme Court has been called upon on numerous occasions to determine the constitutionality specific laws regulating the conduct of physicians who perform abortions.

In *Mazurek v. Armstrong* the Supreme Court indicated that Montana's requirement that abortions be performed only by physicians was constitutionally valid. In *Planned Parenthood Assn. v. Ashcroft* the Supreme Court held that the constitution was not violated by a requirement that a second physician be present during abortions performed after viability. However, in *Thornburgh v. American College of Obstetricians and Gynecologists*, a case that was eventually overruled, the Supreme Court invalidated a provision of an abortion statute that required a second physician be present during an abortion performed when fetal viability was possible. It was held in *Doe v. Bolton* that states could not require, in addition to the treating physician, that two independent physicians approve of an abortion.

It was held by the Supreme Court in *Planned Parenthood of Southeastern Pennsylvania v. Casey* that a state may require that only physicians be allowed to inform a woman of her abortion rights prior to performing an abortion. The Supreme Court approved a statute in *Hodgson v. Minnesota* that required an attending physician certify that an immediate abortion was necessary to prevent a minor's death, when parental consent could not be obtained. In *Webster v. Reproductive Health Services* the Supreme Court approved of a statute requiring physicians conduct viability tests prior to performing abortions. In *Rust v. Sullivan* the Supreme Court upheld federal regulations that prohibited pro-abortion counseling, referral, and advocacy by health care providers.

In *Colautti v. Franklin* it was held by the Supreme Court that the constitution was violated by a vague and ambiguous provision in Pennsylvania's abortion statute that subjected a physician who performed an abortion to potential criminal liability, if he/she failed to utilize a statutorily prescribed technique when the fetus was viable or when there was sufficient reason to believe that the fetus may be viable. A similar provision was struck down in *Planned Parenthood of Missouri v. Danforth*. The decision in *Danforth* upheld the imposition of basic reporting requirements on physicians.

In *Withrow v. Larkin* the Supreme Court held that constitutional due process was not violated by the mere fact that a Wisconsin medical examining board had the authority to both, investigate and adjudicate, allegations against a physician that included, among other things, permitting a nonphysician to perform an abortion. In *State of Missouri ex rel. Hurwitz v. North* the Supreme Court held that the constitution was not violated when a physician was prevented from issuing subpoenas to have witnesses attend a hearing to revoke his medical license for performing an unlawful abortion, because the applicable rules required taking depositions of witnesses who would not voluntarily attend the hearing. *See also* **Colautti v. Franklin; Doe v. Bolton; Gynecologist; Hodgson v. Minnesota; Hospital/Clinic Abortion Requirements; Mazurek v. Armstrong; Obstetrician; Planned Parenthood Assn. v. Ashcroft; Planned Parenthood of Missouri v. Danforth;** *Planned Parenthood of Southeastern Pennsylvania v. Casey*; **Rust v. Sullivan; State of Missouri ex rel. Hurwitz v. North; Thornburgh v. American College of Obstetricians and Gynecologists; Webster v. Reproductive Health Services; Withrow v. Larkin**

Physicians for Reproductive Choice and Health

Physicians for Reproductive Choice and Health (PRCH) is a pro-choice organization that was founded in 1992. The executive director of PRCH is Jodi Magee. PRCH was started by a group of physicians who were concerned about medical clinics being barricaded by anti-choice organizations; the decrease in the number of physicians performing abortions; the targeting of physicians for violent attacks; and the impediments to bringing safe and effective medical abortion technology into the American market. PRCH believes that qualified physicians have an ethical, moral and public health responsibility to support and provide comprehensive reproductive care. Its mission is to enable concerned physicians to take a more active and visible role in support of universal reproductive health. PRCH is committed to ensuring that all people have the knowledge, access to quality services, and freedom of choice to make their own reproductive health decisions. The organization has set out five statements of principle which guide its programs and activities: (1) physicians should be educated in the full range of reproductive health care; (2) physicians should advocate the expansion of research and knowledge of human reproduction and health care; (3) physicians have an ethical obligation to support choice and access to reproductive health care for all women and men; (4) physicians should be supported in providing access to the full range of reproductive health care; and (5) physicians should take a pro-active role in discussions of human sexuality and in preventing unintended pregnancy. *See also* **Pro-Choice Organizations**

Picketing *see* **Abortion Violence, Property Destruction and Demonstrations**

PKU

PKU (phenylketonuria) is an inherited disorder that is characterized by a missing enzyme (phenylalanine hydroxylase). The missing enzyme prevents one of the eight essential amino acids, found in protein-containing foods, from being used in a normal fashion. This results in the development of compounds that are toxic to the central nervous system which can cause brain damage and mental retardation. The disorder can be easily detected by a blood test and is treatable. However, if treatment is started 3 years after birth, or if there is no treatment, brain damage is inevitable. PKU occurs about once out of 16,000 births in the United States. *See also* **Birth Defects and Abortion**

Placenta

The placenta (also called afterbirth) is an organ that develops in the uterus during pregnancy. It allows for the passage of oxygen, water, and nutrients from the woman; as well as expulsion of waste that will be processed and excreted by the mother. The placenta is connected to the uterus at one end and the umbilical cord at the other end. It is fully developed by the third month of pregnancy. It is extremely sensitive, in that almost all drugs, alcohol, and many other substances that may cause birth defects, can pass freely through it. *See also* **Umbilical Cord**

Placenta Abruptio

Placenta abruptio involves the separation of the placenta from its uterine implantation cite before delivery of the fetus. The condition occurs in the latter half of pregnancy and may be partial or complete. Factors that may cause placenta abruptio include: injury to the mother, premature rupture of membranes, maternal age (over 40 years), illegal drug use and alcohol.

When complete separation of the placenta occurs bleeding is extensive and requires replacement of the lost blood by transfusion. In cases of complete placenta abruptio the fetus will die unless delivered immediately. Placenta abruptio is a leading cause of fetal death in the third trimester. The incidence of placenta abruptio is approximately 1 out of 89 deliveries. However, the severe form occurs only in about 1 out of 750 deliveries. *See also* **Placenta; Placenta Previa**

Placenta Accreta

Placenta accreta refers to an abnormally deep implantation of the placenta into the uterus. This condition very often prevents the normal placental separation from the uterus after deliver. When the condition arises the healthcare provider must manually extract the placenta. *See also* **Placenta**

Placenta Previa

Placenta previa is a condition that involves the placenta being implanted in the lower part of the uterus and obstructing the cervical opening to the vagina. There are three types of placenta previa: total, partial, and marginal. Placenta previa may be caused by a scarred lining of the uterus, a large placenta, an abnormal uterus, or abnormal formation of the placenta. The incidence of placenta previa is about 1 out of 200 births.

About 20 percent of women with placenta previa will have contractions with bleeding (antepartum hemorrhage). Depending upon the specific position of the placenta, a caesarean section delivery may be necessary. The condition exposes the fetus to a risk of premature birth, intrauterine growth retardation, and death. The fetal death rate from placenta previa is about 15 percent to 20 percent. *See also* **Placenta; Placenta Abruptio**

Placental Failure

The placenta provides the fetus with oxygen and nutrients and gets rid of carbon dioxide and other wastes. By the third month of gestation it normally releases progesterone and other hormones that are necessary to maintain the pregnancy. If the placenta fails to produce progesterone, placental failure is said to occur. This condition will usually terminate the pregnancy. *See also* **Miscarriage**

Placental Insufficiency

Placental insufficiency refers to a reduction in the placental functions. This condition may be caused by placental separation or obstructions. It can cause spontaneous abortion or severe fetal injury, including intrauterine growth retardation. *See also* **Placenta Abruptio**

Planned Parenthood Assn. v. Ashcroft

Forum: United States Supreme Court.

Case Citation: Planned Parenthood Assn. v. Ashcroft, 462 U.S. 476 (1983).

Date Argued: November 30, 1982.

Date of Decision: June 15, 1983.

Opinion of Court: Powell, J., in which Burger, C. J., and Brennan, Marshall, Blackmun, and Stevens, JJ., joined in part, and White, Rehnquist, and O'Connor, JJ., joined in part.

Concurring and Dissenting Opinion: Blackmun, J., in which Brennan, Marshall, and Stevens, JJ., joined.

Concurring and Dissenting Opinion: O'Connor, J., in which White and Rehnquist, JJ., joined.

Counsel for Appellants: Frank Susman argued and filed brief.

Counsel for Appellees: John Ashcroft, Attorney General of Missouri, pro se, argued; on the brief was Michael L. Boicourt, Assistant Attorney General.

Amicus Brief for Appellants and Appellees: Dennis J. Horan, Victor G. Rosenblum, Patrick A. Trueman, and Thomas J. Marzen for Americans United for Life; Sylvia A. Law, Nadine Taub, and Ellen J. Winner for the Committee for Abortion Rights and Against Sterilization Abuse et al.; James Bopp, Jr., for the National Right to Life Committee, Inc.; Solicitor General Lee, Assistant Attorney General McGrath, and Deputy Solicitor General Geller for the United States; by Alan Ernest for the Legal Defense Fund for Unborn Children; by Judith Levin for the National Abortion Federation; by Phyllis N. Segal, Judith I. Avner, and Jemera Rone for the National Organization for Women; by Eve W. Paul and Dara Klassel for the Planned Parenthood Federation of America, Inc., et al.; by Nancy Reardan for Women Lawyers of Sacramento et al.; and by Susan Frelich Appleton and Paul Brest for Professor Richard L. Abel et al.

Issue Presented: Whether the constitution was violated by requirements in Missouri's abortion statute (1) that second trimester abortions be performed in a hospital; (2) that a pathology report for each abortion be performed; (3) that a second physician be present during abortions performed after viability; and (4) that minors secure parental or judicial consent for abortions?

Case Holding: The constitution was violated by Missouri's requirement that second trimester abortions take place in a hospital. The constitution was not violated by the state's requirement that a pathology report for each abortion be performed, that a second physician be present during abortions performed after viability, and parental or judicial consent for abortion by minors.

Background facts of case: The abortion statute of the state of Missouri contained provisions requiring (1) that second trimester abortions be performed in a hospital; (2) that a pathology report for each abortion performed; (3) the presence of a second physician during abortions performed after viability; and (4) that minors secure parental or judicial consent for abortions. The appellants, abortion providers, filed a complaint in a federal district court in Missouri challenging constitutionality of the provisions. The appellees, state officials, were named as defendants. The district court invalidated all of the provisions except the pathology requirement. The Eighth Circuit court of appeals reversed the district court's judgment with respect parental or judicial consent for minors, and the pathology requirement. The court of appeals affirmed the remainder of the district court's judgment. Both parties appealed to the Supreme Court. The Supreme Court granted certiorari for both appeals. (Although both parties were technically designated as appellants and appellees, they are not given the dual designations here.)

Majority/plurality opinion by Justice Powell: Justice Powell held that the constitution was violated by Missouri's requirement that second trimester abortions take place in a hospital. The opinion found that the constitution was not violated by the state's requirement that a pathology report for each abortion be performed, that a second physician be present during abortions performed after viability, and parental or judicial consent for abortion by minors. Justice Powell addressed each matter as follows:

> In City of Akron v. Akron Center for Reproductive Health, Inc., we invalidated a city ordinance requiring physicians to perform all second-trimester abortions at general or special hospitals accredited by the Joint Commission on Accreditation of Hospitals or by the American Osteopathic Association. Missouri's hospitalization requirements are similar to those enacted by Akron, as all second-trimester abortions must be performed in general, acute-care facilities. For the reasons stated in City of Akron, we held that such a requirement unreasonably infringes upon a woman's constitutional right to obtain an abortion. For the same reasons, we affirm the Court of Appeals' judgment that [Missouri's hospitalization requirement] is unconstitutional....

The statutory provision at issue in this case requires the attendance of a second physician at the abortion of a viable fetus....

The first physician's primary concern will be the life and health of the woman. Many third-trimester abortions in Missouri will be emergency operations, as the State permits these late abortions only when they are necessary to preserve the life or the health of the woman. It is not unreasonable for the State to assume that during the operation the first physician's attention and skills will be directed to preserving the woman's health, and not to protecting the actual life of those fetuses who survive the abortion procedure. Viable fetuses will be in immediate and grave danger because of their premature birth. A second physician, in situations where Missouri permits third-trimester abortions, may be of assistance to the woman's physician in preserving the health and life of the child.

By giving immediate medical attention to a fetus that is delivered alive, the second physician will assure that the State's interests are protected more fully than the first physician alone would be able to do. And given the compelling interest that the State has in preserving life, we cannot say that the Missouri requirement of a second physician in those unusual circumstances where Missouri permits a third-trimester abortion is unconstitutional. Preserving the life of a viable fetus that is aborted may not often be possible, but the State legitimately may choose to provide safeguards for the comparatively few instances of live birth that occur. We believe the second-physician requirement reasonably furthers the State's compelling interest in protecting the lives of viable fetuses, and we reverse the judgment of the Court of Appeals holding that [provision] is unconstitutional....

On its face and in effect, [the pathology requirement] is reasonably related to generally accepted medical standards and "furthers important health-related state concerns. As the Court of Appeals recognized, pathology examinations are clearly useful and even necessary in some cases, because abnormalities in the tissue may warn of serious, possibly fatal disorders. As a rule, it is accepted medical practice to submit all tissue to the examination of a pathologist. This is particularly important following abortion, because questions remain as to the long-range complications and their effect on subsequent pregnancies. Recorded pathology reports, in concert with abortion complication reports, provide a statistical basis for studying those complications....

In weighing the balance between protection of a woman's health and the comparatively small additional cost of a pathologist's examination, we cannot say that the Constitution requires that a State subordinate its interest in health to minimize to this extent the cost of abortions. Even in the early weeks of pregnancy, certain regulations that have no significant impact on the woman's exercise of her right to decide to have an abortion may be permissible where justified by important state health objectives. We think the cost of a tissue examination does not significantly burden a pregnant woman's abortion decision.... Accordingly, we reverse the judgment of the Court of Appeals on this issue....

On its face, [the parental or judicial consent provision for minors] authorizes Juvenile Courts to choose among any of the alternatives outlined in the section. The Court of Appeals concluded that a denial of the petition permitted in [the provision] would initially require the court to find that the minor was not emancipated and was not mature enough to make her own decision and that an abortion was not in her best interests. [Appellants] contend that this interpretation is unreasonable. We do not agree.

Where fairly possible, courts should construe a statute to avoid a danger of unconstitutionality. The Court of Appeals was aware, if the statute provides discretion to deny permission to a minor for any good cause, that arguably it would violate the principles that this Court has set forth. It recognized, however, that before exercising any option, the Juvenile Court must receive evidence on the emotional development, maturity, intellect and understanding of the minor. The court then reached the logical conclusion that findings and the ultimate denial of the petition must be supported by a showing of good cause. The Court of Appeals reasonably found that a court could not deny a petition for good cause unless it first found — after having received the required evidence — that the minor was not mature enough to make her own decision. We conclude that the Court of Appeals correctly interpreted the statute and that [the provision], as interpreted, avoids any constitutional infirmities.

Disposition of case: The judgment of the court of appeals was affirmed in part and reversed in part.

Concurring and dissenting opinion by Justice Blackmun: Justice Blackmun agreed with the Court that the hospitalization requirement was unconstitutional. He dissented from the Court's holding that the other provisions past constitutional muster. Justice Blackmun wrote in dissent as follows:

> Missouri's requirement of a pathologist's report is not justified by important health objectives. Although pathology examinations may be useful and even necessary in some cases, Missouri requires more than a pathology examination and a pathology report; it demands that the examination be performed and the report prepared by a board eligible or certified pathologist rather than by the attending physician.... [T]his requirement of a report by a pathologist is not in accord with generally accepted medical standards. The routine and accepted medical practice is for the attending physician to perform a gross (visual) examination of any tissue removed during an abortion. Only if the physician detects abnormalities is there a need to send a tissue sample to a pathologist....
>
> On the record before us, I must conclude that the State has not met its burden of demonstrating that the pathologist requirement furthers important health-related State concerns. There has been no showing that tissue examinations by a pathologist do more to protect health than examinations by a nonpathologist physician. Missouri does not require pathologists' reports for any other surgical procedures performed in clinics, or for minor surgery performed in hospitals. Moreover, I cannot agree ... that Missouri's pathologist requirement has no significant impact on a woman's exercise of her right to an abortion. It is undisputed that this requirement may increase the cost of a first-trimester abortion by as much as $40. Although this increase may seem insignificant from the Court's comfortable perspective, I cannot say that it is equally insignificant to every woman seeking an abortion. For the woman on welfare or the unemployed teenager, this additional cost may well put the price of an abortion beyond reach....
>
> The second-physician requirement is upheld in these cases on the basis that it reasonably furthers the State's compelling interest in protecting the lives of viable fetuses. While I agree that a second physician indeed may aid in preserving the life of a fetus born alive, this type of aid is possible only when the abortion method used is one that may result in a live birth. Although Missouri ordinarily requires a physician performing a postviability abortion to use the abortion method most likely to preserve fetal life, this restriction does not apply when this method would present a greater risk to the life and health of the woman....
>
> [The majority] apparently believes that the State's interest in preserving potential life justifies the State in requiring a second physician at all postviability abortions because some methods other than D&E may result in live births. But this fact cannot justify requiring a second physician to attend an abortion at which the chance of a live birth is nonexistent. The choice of method presumably will be made in advance, and any need for a second physician disappears when the woman's health requires that the choice be D&E. Because the statute is not tailored to protect the State's legitimate interests, I would hold it invalid....

Until today, the Court has never upheld a requirement of a consent substitute, either parental or judicial. In Planned Parenthood of Central Missouri v. Danforth, the Court invalidated a parental-consent requirement on the ground that the State does not have the constitutional authority to give a third party an absolute, and possibly arbitrary, veto over the decision of the physician and his patient to terminate the patient's pregnancy, regardless of the reason for withholding the consent. In Bellotti v. Baird, eight Justices agreed that a Massachusetts statute permitting a judicial veto of a mature minor's decision to have an abortion was unconstitutional....

Because [Missouri's statute] permits a parental or judicial veto of a minor's decision to obtain an abortion, I would hold it unconstitutional.

Concurring and dissenting opinion by Justice O'Connor: Justice O'Connor concurred in all of the Court's opinion, except the decision regarding hospitalization. She wrote as follows, regarding the latter issue: "... I believe that the second-trimester hospitalization requirement imposed ... does not impose an undue burden on the limited right to undergo an abortion. Assuming, arguendo, that the requirement was an undue burden, it would nevertheless reasonably relate to the preservation and protection of maternal health. I therefore dissent from the Court's judgment that the requirement is unconstitutional."

Planned Parenthood Federation of America

The origins of Planned Parenthood Federation of America (PPFA) date back to 1916, when Margaret Sanger founded the nation's first birth control clinic in Brooklyn, New York. Sanger went on to establish the Birth Control Clinical Research Bureau and the American Birth Control League. These organizations would eventually merge to become PPFA.

The president of PPFA is Cecile Richards. PPFA is the world's largest and oldest voluntary family planning organization, as well as the world's leading abortion advocacy institution. The guiding philosophy of PPFA is that every individual has a fundamental right to decide when or whether to have a child, and that every child born should be wanted and loved. It believes in the fundamental right of each individual to manage his or her fertility, regardless of the individual's income, marital status, race, ethnicity, sexual orientation, age, national origin, or residence.

The stated mission of PPFA is: to provide comprehensive reproductive and complementary health care services in settings which preserve and protect the essential privacy and rights of each individual; to advocate public policies which guarantee these rights and ensure access to such services; to provide educational programs which enhance understanding of individual and societal implications of human sexuality; to promote research and the advancement of technology in reproductive health care and encourage understanding of their inherent bioethical, behavioral, and social implications.

It is the policy of PPFA to ensure that women have the right to seek and obtain medically safe, legal abortions under dignified conditions and at reasonable cost. PPFA also believes that public funds should be made available to subsidize the cost of abortion services for those who choose abortion but cannot afford it. PPFA provides access to high quality, confidential abortion services directly through its affiliates' medical facilities and/or indirectly through referral to other competent medical facilities in the community. The organization believes that adolescents should have access to information about human sexuality and to reproductive health care services. It opposes any limitation or restriction on the access of adolescents to confidential reproductive health services, including contraception and abortion. PPFA also supports a range of activities designed to reduce adolescent pregnancy and childbearing, such as expanded sexuality education, increased service accessibility, enhanced public awareness, behavioral research, and the development of contraceptive methods specially suited to adolescents.

PPFA is committed to advancing the understanding of the interrelationship between population growth and the quality of human life. It believes that voluntary family planning programs and sound population policies contribute to the process of socioeconomic development and to family health. Therefore, PPFA is committed to providing education in the communities it serves, to enable people to understand the scope of world population growth and its impact on the economic, political, social, and physical environment of the world. To this end, PPFA supports voluntary sterilization as a medically accepted means of permanent contraception. It believes that all providers of sterilization services should exercise special diligence in assuring that the sterilization of socially disadvantaged, economically disadvantaged, or mentally handicapped individuals is, in fact, voluntary. PPFA takes the position that public funds should be made available to subsidize the cost of voluntary sterilization services for those who choose the procedure but cannot afford it. *See also* **Pro-Choice Organizations; Sanger, Margaret**

Planned Parenthood of Missouri v. Danforth

Forum: United States Supreme Court.

Case Citation: Planned Parenthood of Missouri v. Danforth, 428 U.S. 52 (1976).

Date Argued: March 23, 1976.

Date of Decision: July 1, 1976.

Opinion of Court: Blackmun, J., in which Brennan, Stewart, Marshall, and Powell, JJ., joined.

Concurring Opinion: Stewart, J., in which Powell, J., joined.

Concurring and Dissenting Opinion: White, J., in which Burger, C. J., and Rehnquist, J., joined.

Concurring and Dissenting Opinion: Stevens, J.

Counsel for Appellants: Frank Susman argued; on the brief was Judith Mears.

Counsel for Appellees: John C. Danforth, Attorney General of Missouri, argued; on the brief were D. Brook Bartlett, First Assistant Attorney General, and Karen M. Iverson and Christopher R. Brewster, Assistant Attorneys General.

Amicus Brief for Appellants and Appellees: Rhonda Copelon and Nancy Stearns for the Center for Constitutional Rights et al.; Eugene Krasicky, George E. Reed, and Patrick F. Geary for the United States Catholic Conference; Harriet F. Pilpel for Planned Parenthood Federation of America, Inc., et al.; John J. Donnelly for Lawyers for Life, Inc., et al.; and by Jerome M. McLaughlin for Missouri Nurses for Life.

Issue Presented: Whether the constitution was violated by provisions in Missouri's abortion statute involving the definition of fetal viability, woman's written consent, record keeping and reporting requirements, spousal consent, parental consent for minor, prohibiting saline amniocentesis abortions, and physician's standard of care?

Case Holding: The constitution was not violated by provisions in Missouri's abortion statute involving the definition of fetal viability, woman's written consent, and record keeping and reporting requirements; but the constitution prohibited the requirements concerning spousal consent, parental consent for minor, banning saline amniocentesis abortions, and physician's standard of care.

Background facts of case: The appellants, abortion providers, filed a lawsuit in a federal district court in Missouri challenging several provisions of that state's abortion statute. The appellees, government officials, were named as defendants. The provisions challenged included: (1) the definition of "viability" to mean that stage of fetal development when the life of the unborn child may be continued indefinitely outside the womb by natural or artificial support; (2) a requirement that a woman must consent in writing to the abortion; (3) a requirement of the written consent of the spouse of a woman seeking an abortion unless a licensed physician certifies that the abortion is necessary to preserve the mother's life; (4) a requirement of written parental consent for a minor to have an abortion; (5) a requirement that the physician exercise professional care to preserve the fetus' life and health, (6) prohibiting after the first 12 weeks of pregnancy the abortion procedure of saline amniocentesis; and (7) prescribing reporting and record keeping requirements for health facilities and physicians performing abortions.

The district court upheld all of the provisions, except the professional care requirement. Both parties appealed to the United States Supreme Court. The Supreme Court granted certiorari for both appeals. (Although both parties were technically designated as appellants and appellees, they are not given the dual designations here.)

Majority opinion by Justice Blackmun: Justice Blackmun found that the constitution was not violated by Missouri's provisions regarding the definition of viability, a woman's written consent, and the record keeping and reporting requirements. However, he determined that the constitution did not permit the requirements concerning spouse's consent, parental consent for minor, banning saline amniocentesis abortions, and the physician's standard of care. Justice Blackmun addressed each issue as follows:

> The definition of viability.... [T]he Act defines "viability" as "that stage of fetal development when the life of the unborn child may be continued indefinitely outside the womb by natural or artificial life-supportive systems." Appellants claim that this definition violates and conflicts with the discussion of viability in our opinion in Roe v. Wade. In particular, appellants object to the failure of the definition to contain any reference to a gestational time period, to its failure to incorporate and reflect the three stages of pregnancy, to the presence of the word "indefinitely," and to the extra burden of regulation imposed. It is suggested that the definition expands the Court's definition of viability, as expressed in Roe, and amounts to a legislative determination of what is properly a matter for medical judgment. It is said that the mere possibility of momentary survival is not the medical standard of viability....
>
> We agree with the District Court and conclude that the definition of viability in the Act does not conflict with what was said and held in Roe. In fact, we believe that [it] ... reflects an attempt on the part of the Missouri General Assembly to comply with our observations and discussion in Roe relating to viability.... [W]e recognized in Roe that viability was a matter of medical judgment, skill, and technical ability, and we preserved the flexibility of the term....
>
> In any event, we agree with the District Court that it is not the proper function of the legislature or the courts to place viability, which essentially is a medical concept, at a specific point in the gestation period. The time when viability is achieved may vary with each pregnancy, and the determination of whether a particular fetus is viable is, and must be, a matter for the judgment of the responsible attending physician. The definition of viability in [the Act] merely reflects this fact....
>
> The woman's consent. Under ... the Act, a woman, prior to submitting to an abortion during the first 12 weeks of pregnancy, must certify in writing her consent to the procedure and that her consent is informed and freely given and is not the result of coercion. Appellants argue that this requirement is violative of Roe v. Wade, by imposing an extra layer and burden of regulation on the abortion decision....
>
> We do not disagree with the result reached by the District Court.... It is true that ... the State may not restrict the decision of the patient and her physician regarding abortion during the first stage of pregnancy.... The decision to abort, indeed, is an important, and often a stressful one, and it is desirable and imperative that it be made with full knowledge of its nature and consequences. The woman is the one primarily concerned, and her awareness of the decision and its significance may be assured, constitutionally, by the State to the extent of requiring her prior written consent.
>
> We could not say that a requirement imposed by the State that a prior written consent for any surgery would be unconstitutional. As a consequence, we see no constitutional defect in requiring it only for some types of surgery as, for example, an intracardiac procedure, or where the surgical risk is elevated above a specified mortality level, or, for that matter, for abortions.
>
> The spouse's consent. [The Act] requires the prior written consent of the spouse of the woman seeking an abortion during the first 12 weeks of pregnancy, unless the abortion is certified by a licensed physician to be necessary in order to preserve the life of the mother....
>
> In Roe ... we specifically reserved decision on the question whether a requirement for consent by the father of the fetus, by the spouse, or by the parents, or a parent, of an unmarried minor, may be constitutionally imposed. We now hold that the State may not constitutionally require the consent of the spouse, ... as a condition for abortion during the first 12 weeks of pregnancy.... [T]he State cannot delegate to a spouse a veto power which the state itself is absolutely and totally prohibited from exercising during the first trimester of pregnancy. Clearly, since the State cannot regulate or proscribe abortion during the first stage, when the physician and his patient make that decision, the State cannot delegate authority to any particular person, even the spouse, to prevent abortion during that same period....
>
> We recognize, of course, that when a woman, with the approval of her physician but without the approval of her husband, decides to terminate her pregnancy, it could be said that she is acting unilaterally. The obvious fact is that when the wife and the husband disagree on this decision, the view of only one of the two marriage partners can prevail. Inasmuch as it is the woman who physically bears the child and who is the more directly and immediately affected by the pregnancy, as between the two, the balance weighs in her favor....
>
> Parental Consent. [The Act] requires, with respect to the first 12 weeks of pregnancy, where the woman is unmarried and under the age of 18 years, the written consent of a parent or person in loco parentis unless, again, the abortion is certified by a licensed physician as necessary in order to preserve the life of the mother. It is to be observed that only one parent need consent....
>
> We agree with appellants ... that the State may not impose a blanket provision ... requiring the consent of a parent or person in loco parentis as a condition for abortion of an unmarried minor during the first 12 weeks of her pregnancy. Just as with the requirement of consent from the spouse, so here, the State does not have the constitutional authority to give a third party an absolute, and possibly arbitrary, veto over the decision of the physician and his patient to terminate the patient's pregnancy, regardless of the reason for withholding the consent.
>
> We emphasize that our holding that [the parental consent provision] is invalid does not suggest that every minor, regardless of age or maturity, may give effective consent for termination of her pregnancy. The fault with [provision] is that it imposes a special-consent provision, exercisable by a person other than the woman and her physician, as a prerequisite to a minor's termination of her pregnancy and does so without a sufficient justification for the restriction....
>
> Saline amniocentesis.... [T]he statute prohibits the use of saline amniocentesis, as a method or technique of abortion, after the first 12 weeks of pregnancy.... Appellants challenge this provision on

the ground that it operates to preclude virtually all abortions after the first trimester....

We feel that the [district court], in reaching its conclusion, failed to appreciate and to consider several significant facts. First, it did not recognize the prevalence, as the record conclusively demonstrates, of the use of saline amniocentesis as an accepted medical procedure in this country; the procedure ... is employed in a substantial majority (the testimony from both sides ranges from 68 percent to 80 percent) of all post-first-trimester abortions. Second, it failed to recognize that at the time of trial, there were severe limitations on the availability of the prostaglandin technique, which, although promising, was used only on an experimental basis until less than two years before. And appellees offered no evidence that prostaglandin abortions were available in Missouri. Third, the statute's reference to the insertion of a saline or other fluid appears to include within its proscription the intra-amniotic injection of prostaglandin itself and other methods that may be developed in the future and that may prove highly effective and completely safe. Finally, the [district court] did not consider the anomaly inherent in [the provision] when it proscribes the use of saline but does not prohibit techniques that are many times more likely to result in maternal death.

These unappreciated or overlooked factors place the State's decision to bar use of the saline method in a completely different light. The State ... would prohibit the use of a method which the record shows is the one most commonly used nationally by physicians after the first trimester and which is safer, with respect to maternal mortality, than even continuation of the pregnancy until normal childbirth. Moreover, as a practical matter, it forces a woman and her physician to terminate her pregnancy by methods more dangerous to her health than the method outlawed.

As so viewed, particularly in the light of the present unavailability — as demonstrated by the record — of the prostaglandin technique, the outright legislative proscription of saline fails as a reasonable regulation for the protection of maternal health. It comes into focus, instead, as an unreasonable or arbitrary regulation designed to inhibit, and having the effect of inhibiting, the vast majority of abortions after the first 12 weeks. As such, it does not withstand constitutional challenge.

Record keeping.... [T]he Act impose[s] record keeping requirements for health facilities and physicians concerned with abortions irrespective of the pregnancy stage. Under [it], each such facility and physician is to be supplied with forms "the purpose and function of which shall be the preservation of maternal health and life by adding to the sum of medical knowledge through the compilation of relevant maternal health and life data and to monitor all abortions performed to assure that they are done only under and in accordance with the provisions of the law." The statute states that the information on the forms "shall be confidential and shall be used only for statistical purposes." The "records, however, may be inspected and health data acquired by local, state, or national public health officers." Under [the statute] the records are to be kept for seven years in the permanent files of the health facility where the abortion was performed....

Record keeping and reporting requirements that are reasonably directed to the preservation of maternal health and that properly respect a patient's confidentiality and privacy are permissible. This surely is so for the period after the first stage of pregnancy, for then the State may enact substantive as well as record keeping regulations that are reasonable means of protecting maternal health. As to the first stage, one may argue forcefully, as the appellants do, that the State should not be able to impose any record keeping requirements that significantly differ from those imposed with respect to other, and comparable, medical or surgical procedures. We conclude, however, that the provisions of [the statute], while perhaps approaching impermissible limits, are not constitutionally offensive in themselves. Record keeping of this kind, if not abused or overdone, can be useful to the State's interest in protecting the health of its female citizens, and may be a resource that is relevant to decisions involving medical experience and judgment. The added requirements for confidentiality, with the sole exception for public health officers, and for retention for seven years, a period not unreasonable in length, assist and persuade us in our determination of the constitutional limits. As so regarded, we see no legally significant impact or consequence on the abortion decision or on the physician-patient relationship....

Standard of care.... ... [The Act] requires the physician to exercise the prescribed skill, care, and diligence to preserve the life and health of the fetus. It does not specify that such care need be taken only after the stage of viability has been reached. As the provision now reads, it impermissibly requires the physician to preserve the life and health of the fetus, whatever the stage of pregnancy....

Disposition of case: The judgment of the district court was affirmed in part and reversed in part.

Concurring opinion by Justice Stewart: Justice Stewart agreed with the Court's decision. He wrote separately to emphasize a few points, as follows:

> With respect to the state law's requirement of parental consent, I think it clear that its primary constitutional deficiency lies in its imposition of an absolute limitation on the minor's right to obtain an abortion. The Court's opinion today in Bellotti v. Baird, suggests that a materially different constitutional issue would be presented under a provision requiring parental consent or consultation in most cases but providing for prompt (i) judicial resolution of any disagreement between the parent and the minor, or (ii) judicial determination that the minor is mature enough to give an informed consent without parental concurrence or that abortion in any event is in the minor's best interest. Such a provision would not impose parental approval as an absolute condition upon the minor's right but would assure in most instances consultation between the parent and child.

Concurring and dissenting opinion by Justice White: Justice White concurred in that part of the Court's decision which upheld the constitutionality of the provisions addressing the definition of viability, a woman's written consent, and the record keeping and reporting requirements. He dissented from the remainder of the decision. He wrote as follows:

> In Roe v. Wade this Court recognized a right to an abortion free from state prohibition. The task of policing this limitation on state police power is and will be a difficult and continuing venture in substantive due process. However, even accepting Roe v. Wade, there is nothing in the opinion in that case and nothing articulated in the Court's opinion in this case which justifies the invalidation of four provisions of [the statute]. Accordingly, I dissent, in part....

Concurring and dissenting opinion by Justice Stevens: Justice Stevens concurred in all of the Court's opinion, except with respect to the issue of parental consent for minors. He stated his position on the issue as follows:

> In my opinion, however, the parental-consent requirement is consistent with the holding in Roe v. Wade. The State's interest in the welfare of its young citizens justifies a variety of protective measures. Because he may not foresee the consequences of his decision, a minor may not make an enforceable bargain. He may not lawfully work or travel where he pleases, or even attend exhibitions of constitutionally protected adult motion pictures. Persons below a certain age may not marry without parental consent. Indeed, such consent is essential even when the young woman is already pregnant. The State's interest in protecting a young per-

son from harm justifies the imposition of restraints on his or her freedom even though comparable restraints on adults would be constitutionally impermissible. Therefore, the holding in Roe v. Wade that the abortion decision is entitled to constitutional protection merely emphasizes the importance of the decision; it does not lead to the conclusion that the state legislature has no power to enact legislation for the purpose of protecting a young pregnant woman from the consequences of an incorrect decision....

The Court assumes that parental consent is an appropriate requirement if the minor is not capable of understanding the procedure and of appreciating its consequences and those of available alternatives. This assumption is, of course, correct and consistent with the predicate which underlies all state legislation seeking to protect minors from the consequences of decisions they are not yet prepared to make. In all such situations chronological age has been the basis for imposition of a restraint on the minor's freedom of choice even though it is perfectly obvious that such a yardstick is imprecise and perhaps even unjust in particular cases. The Court seems to assume that the capacity to conceive a child and the judgment of the physician are the only constitutionally permissible yardsticks for determining whether a young woman can independently make the abortion decision. I doubt the accuracy of the Court's empirical judgment. Even if it were correct, however, as a matter of constitutional law I think a State has power to conclude otherwise and to select a chronological age as its standard.

In short, the State's interest in the welfare of its young citizens is sufficient, in my judgment, to support the parental-consent requirement.

Planned Parenthood of Southeastern Pennsylvania v. Casey

Forum: United States Supreme Court.

Case Citation: Planned Parenthood of Southeastern Pennsylvania v. Casey, 505 U.S. 833 (1992).

Date Argued: April 22, 1992.

Date of Decision: June 29, 1992.

Joint Opinion of Court: O'Connor, Kennedy, and Souter, JJ., in which Blackmun and Stevens, JJ., joined in part.

Concurring and Dissenting Opinion: Stevens, J.

Concurring and Dissenting Opinion: Blackmun, J.

Concurring and Dissenting Opinion: Rehnquist, C.J., in which White, Scalia, and Thomas, JJ., joined.

Concurring and Dissenting Opinion: Scalia, J., in which Rehnquist, C.J., and White and Thomas, JJ., joined.

Counsel for Appellants: Kathryn Kolbert argued; on the brief were Janet Benshoof, Lynn M. Paltrow, Rachael N. Pine, Steven R. Shapiro, John A. Powell, Linda J. Wharton, and Carol E. Tracy.

Counsel for Appellees: Ernest D. Preate, Jr., Attorney General of Pennsylvania, argued; on the brief were John G. Knorr III, Chief Deputy Attorney General, and Kate L. Mershimer, Senior Deputy Attorney General.

Amicus Brief for United States in Support of Appellees: Solicitor General Starr argued; on the brief were Assistant Attorney General Gerson, Paul J. Larkin, Jr., Thomas G. Hungar, and Alfred R. Mollin.

Amicus Briefs for Appellants and Appellees: Robert Abrams, Attorney General of New York, Jerry Boone, Solicitor General, Mary Ellen Burns, Chief Assistant Attorney General, and Sanford M. Cohen, Donna I. Dennis, Marjorie Fujiki, and Shelley B. Mayer, Assistant Attorneys General, and John McKernan, Governor of Maine, and Michael E. Carpenter, Attorney General, Richard Blumenthal, Attorney General of Connecticut, Charles M. Oberly III, Attorney General of Delaware, Warren Price III, Attorney General of Hawaii, Roland W. Burris, Attorney General of Illinois, Bonnie J. Campbell, Attorney General of Iowa, J. Joseph Curran, Jr., Attorney General of Maryland, Scott Harshbarger, Attorney General of Massachusetts, Frankie Sue Del Papa, Attorney General of Nevada, Robert J. Del Tufo, Attorney General of New Jersey, Tom Udall, Attorney General of New Mexico, Lacy H. Thornburg, Attorney General of North Carolina, James E. O'Neil, Attorney General of Rhode Island, Dan Morales, Attorney General of Texas, Jeffrey L. Amestoy, Attorney General of Vermont, and John Payton, Corporation Counsel of District of Columbia; for the State of Utah by R. Paul Van Dam, Attorney General, and Mary Anne Q. Wood, Special Assistant Attorney General; for the city of New York et al. by O. Peter Sherwood, Conrad Harper, Janice Goodman, Leonard J. Koerner, Lorna Bade Goodman, Gail Rubin, and Julie Mertus; for 178 Organizations by Pamela S. Karlan and Sarah Weddington; for Agudath Israel of America by David Zwiebel; for the Alan Guttmacher Institute et al. by Colleen K. Connell and Dorothy B. Zimbrakos; for the American Academy of Medical Ethics by Joseph W. Dellapenna; for the American Association of Prolife Obstetricians and Gynecologists et al. by William Bentley Ball, Philip J. Murren, and Maura K. Quinlan; for the American College of Obstetricians and Gynecologists et al. by Carter G. Phillips, Ann E. Allen, Laurie R. Rockett, Joel I. Klein, Nadine Taub, and Sarah C. Carey; for the American Psychological Association by David W. Ogden; for Texas Black Americans for Life by Lawrence J. Joyce and Craig H. Greenwood; for Catholics United for Life et al. by Thomas Patrick Monaghan, Jay Alan Sekulow, Walter M. Weber, Thomas A. Glessner, Charles E. Rice, and Michael J. Laird; for the Elliot Institute for Social Sciences Research by Stephen R. Kaufmann; for Feminists for Life of America et al. by Keith A. Fournier, John G. Stepanovich, Christine Smith Torre, Theodore H. Amshoff, Jr., and Mary Dice Grenen; for Focus on the Family et al. by Stephen H. Galebach, Gregory J. Granitto, Stephen W. Reed, David L. Llewellyn, Jr., Benjamin W. Bull, and Leonard J. Pranschke; for the Knights of Columbus by Carl A. Anderson; for Life Issues Institute by James Bopp, Jr., and Richard E. Coleson; for the NAACP Legal Defense and Educational Fund, Inc., et al. by Julius L. Chambers, Ronald L. Ellis, and Alice L. Brown; for the National Legal Foundation by Robert K. Skolrood; for National Right to Life, Inc., by Messrs. Bopp and Coleson, Robert A. Destro, and A. Eric Johnston; for the Pennsylvania Coalition Against Domestic Violence et al. by Phyllis Gelman; for the Rutherford Institute et al. by Thomas W. Strahan, John W. Whitehead, Mr. Johnston, Stephen E. Hurst, Joseph Secola, Thomas S. Neuberger, J. Brian Heller, Amy Dougherty, Stanley R. Jones, David Melton, Robert R. Melnick, William Bonner, W. Charles Bundren, and James Knicely; for the Southern Center for Law & Ethics by Tony G. Miller; for the United States Catholic Conference et al. by Mark E. Chopko, Phillip H. Harris, Michael K. Whitehead, and Forest D. Montgomery; for University Faculty for Life by Clarke D. Forsythe and Victor G. Rosenblum; for Certain American State Legislators by Paul Benjamin Linton; for 19 Arizona Legislators by Ronald D. Maines; for Representative Henry J. Hyde et al. by Albert P. Blaustein and Kevin J. Todd; for Representative Don Edwards et al. by Walter Dellinger and Lloyd N. Cutler; and for 250 American Historians by Sylvia A. Law.

Issue Presented: Whether the federal constitution was violated by provisions in Pennsylvania's abortion statute, which required that: a woman seeking an abortion give her informed consent prior to the abortion procedure, which included being provided with certain information at least 24 hours before the abortion was performed; a female minor seeking an abortion obtain the consent of one of her parents, or obtain judicial authorization if the minor does not wish to or cannot obtain a parent's consent; a married woman seeking an abortion must sign a statement indicating that she has notified her husband of her intended abortion; in the event of a medical emergency the latter three requirements were exempted; and facilities providing abortion services had to comply with certain reporting requirements?

Case Holding: The provisions in Pennsylvania's abortion statute which did not violate the constitution included: the medical emergency provision, the 24 hour waiting period and attending requirements thereto, the parental notice and judicial bypass provision, and all but one of the abortion facility reporting requirements. The provisions of the statute that did violate the constitution included: spousal notification before obtaining an abortion, and a requirement that a woman inform the abortion provider the reason for not notifying her spouse.

Background facts of case: The appellants, several abortion providers, filed a lawsuit in a federal district court challenging the constitutionality of a number of provisions in the abortion statute of the state of Pennsylvania. The lawsuit named several state officials, appellees herein, as defendants. The provisions challenged included: (1) a requirement that a woman seeking an abortion give her informed consent prior to the abortion procedure, which includes being provided with certain information at least 24 hours before the abortion is performed; (2) that a female minor seeking an abortion obtain the consent of one of her parents, or obtain judicial authorization if the minor does not wish to or cannot obtain a parent's consent; (3) a married woman seeking an abortion must sign a statement indicating that she has notified her husband of her intended abortion; (4) exemption from the above three requirements in the event of a medical emergency; and (5) imposition of certain reporting requirements on facilities that provide abortion services.

The district court entered a permanent injunction against appellees' enforcement of the challenged provisions. The Third Circuit court of appeals affirmed in part and reversed in part. The appellate court found all of the provisions were constitutionally valid, except for the husband notification requirement. Both the appellants and appellees appealed to the Supreme Court. The Supreme Court granted certiorari for both appeals. (Although both parties were technically designated as appellants and appellees, they are not given the dual designations here.)

Joint majority/plurality opinion by Justices O'Connor, Kennedy, and Souter: The joint opinion noted initially that the "liberty" provision of the Due Process Clause of the Fourteenth Amendment provides protection of a woman's decision to terminate her pregnancy. The opinion then set out the following five principles that would be used in reaching a decision on the merits of the case:

> (a) To protect the central right recognized by Roe v. Wade while at the same time accommodating the State's profound interest in potential life, we will employ the undue burden analysis.... An undue burden exists, and therefore a provision of law is invalid, if its purpose or effect is to place a substantial obstacle in the path of a woman seeking an abortion before the fetus attains viability.
>
> (b) We reject the rigid trimester framework of Roe v. Wade. To promote the State's profound interest in potential life, throughout pregnancy, the State may take measures to ensure that the woman's choice is informed, and measures designed to advance this interest will not be invalidated as long as their purpose is to persuade the woman to choose childbirth over abortion. These measures must not be an undue burden on the right.
>
> (c) As with any medical procedure, the State may enact regulations to further the health or safety of a woman seeking an abortion. Unnecessary health regulations that have the purpose or effect of presenting a substantial obstacle to a woman seeking an abortion impose an undue burden on the right.
>
> (d) Our adoption of the undue burden analysis does not disturb the central holding of Roe v. Wade, and we reaffirm that holding. Regardless of whether exceptions are made for particular circumstances, a State may not prohibit any woman from making the ultimate decision to terminate her pregnancy before viability.
>
> (e) We also reaffirm Roe's holding that, subsequent to viability, the State, in promoting its interest in the potentiality of human life, may, if it chooses, regulate, and even proscribe, abortion except where it is necessary, in appropriate medical judgment, for the preservation of the life or health of the mother.

The joint opinion then addressed the medical emergency provision of appellees' abortion statute. The medical emergency allowed an abortion to be performed without complying with certain requirements. The statute defined medical emergency as: "[t]hat condition which, on the basis of the physician's good faith clinical judgment, so complicates the medical condition of a pregnant woman as to necessitate the immediate abortion of her pregnancy to avert her death or for which a delay will create serious risk of substantial and irreversible impairment of a major bodily function." After discussing the provision at length, the joint opinion concluded that the medical emergency provision passed constitutional muster because it "imposes no undue burden on a woman's abortion right."

The three Justices then turned to the informed consent requirement. This provision required that at least 24 hours before performing an abortion, a physician must inform the woman of the nature of the procedure, the health risks of the abortion and of childbirth, and the probable gestational age of the unborn child. Also, the physician or a qualified nonphysician must inform the woman of the availability of printed materials published by the State describing the fetus and providing information about medical assistance for childbirth, information about child support from the father, and a list of agencies which provide adoption and other services as alternatives to abortion. The woman must also certify in writing that she was informed of the availability of the printed materials and was provided with them if she wanted. The joint opinion for these requirements did not violate the constitution. The opinion addressed the matters as follows:

> To the extent City of Akron v. Akron Center for Reproductive Health, Inc. and Thornburgh v. American College of Obstetricians and Gynecologists find a constitutional violation when the government requires, as it does here, the giving of truthful, nonmisleading information about the nature of the procedure, the attendant health risks and those of childbirth, and the probable gestational age of the fetus, those cases go too far, are inconsistent with Roe's acknowledgment of an important interest in potential life, and are overruled.... If the information the State requires to be made available to the woman is truthful and not misleading, the requirement may be permissible.
>
> We also see no reason why the State may not require doctors to inform a woman seeking an abortion of the availability of materials relating to the consequences to the fetus, even when those consequences have no direct relation to her health.... In short, requiring that the woman be informed of the availability of information relating to fetal development and the assistance available should she decide to carry the pregnancy to full term is a reasonable measure to ensure an informed choice, one which might cause the woman to choose childbirth over abortion. This requirement cannot be considered a substantial obstacle to obtaining an abortion, and, it follows, there is no undue burden....
>
> Our analysis of Pennsylvania's 24-hour waiting period between the provision of the information deemed necessary to informed consent and the performance of an abortion under the undue burden standard requires us to reconsider the premise behind the decision in Akron invalidating a parallel requirement. In Akron we said: Nor are we convinced that the State's legitimate concern that the woman's decision be informed is reasonably served by requiring a 24-hour delay as a matter of course. We consider that conclusion to be wrong.... In theory, at least, the waiting period is a reasonable measure to implement the State's

interest in protecting the life of the unborn, a measure that does not amount to an undue burden....

The three Justices next confronted the provision of the statute which required notification to a spouse, before an abortion could take place. The joint opinion found this provision unconstitutional, as follows:

> ... In well-functioning marriages, spouses discuss important intimate decisions such as whether to bear a child. But there are millions of women in this country who are the victims of regular physical and psychological abuse at the hands of their husbands. Should these women become pregnant, they may have very good reasons for not wishing to inform their husbands of their decision to obtain an abortion. Many may have justifiable fears of physical abuse, but may be no less fearful of the consequences of reporting prior abuse to the Commonwealth of Pennsylvania.... Many may fear devastating forms of psychological abuse from their husbands, including verbal harassment, threats of future violence, the destruction of possessions, physical confinement to the home, the withdrawal of financial support, or the disclosure of the abortion to family and friends. These methods of psychological abuse may act as even more of a deterrent to notification than the possibility of physical violence....
>
> The spousal notification requirement is thus likely to prevent a significant number of women from obtaining an abortion. It does not merely make abortions a little more difficult or expensive to obtain; for many women, it will impose a substantial obstacle. We must not blind ourselves to the fact that the significant number of women who fear for their safety and the safety of their children are likely to be deterred from procuring an abortion as surely as if the Commonwealth had outlawed abortion in all cases....
>
> [The provision] embodies a view of marriage consonant with the common law status of married women, but repugnant to our present understanding of marriage and of the nature of the rights secured by the Constitution. Women do not lose their constitutionally protected liberty when they marry. The Constitution protects all individuals, male or female, married or unmarried, from the abuse of governmental power, even where that power is employed for the supposed benefit of a member of the individual's family. These considerations confirm our conclusion that [the provision] is invalid.

The joint opinion focused next on the parental notification and judicial bypass provision of the statute. The three Justices found this provision passed constitutional muster as follows:

> ... Except in a medical emergency, an unemancipated young woman under 18 may not obtain an abortion unless she and one of her parents (or guardian) provides informed consent.... If neither a parent nor a guardian provides consent, a court may authorize the performance of an abortion upon a determination that the young woman is mature and capable of giving informed consent and has, in fact, given her informed consent, or that an abortion would be in her best interests.
>
> Our cases establish, and we reaffirm today, that a State may require a minor seeking an abortion to obtain the consent of a parent or guardian, provided that there is an adequate judicial bypass procedure. Under these precedents, in our view, the one-parent consent requirement and judicial bypass procedure are constitutional.

The three Justices addressed the last issue concerning reporting requirements of abortion facilities. This provision was found constitutional except for a requirement that a woman give reasons for not notifying her spouse. The joint opinion examined the matter as follows:

> Under the recordkeeping and reporting requirements of the statute, every facility which performs abortions is required to file a report stating its name and address as well as the name and address of any related entity, such as a controlling or subsidiary organization. In the case of state-funded institutions, the information becomes public.
>
> For each abortion performed, a report must be filed identifying: the physician (and the second physician where required); the facility; the referring physician or agency; the woman's age; the number of prior pregnancies and prior abortions she has had; gestational age; the type of abortion procedure; the date of the abortion; whether there were any preexisting medical conditions which would complicate pregnancy; medical complications with the abortion; where applicable, the basis for the determination that the abortion was medically necessary; the weight of the aborted fetus; and whether the woman was married, and if so, whether notice was provided or the basis for the failure to give notice. Every abortion facility must also file quarterly reports showing the number of abortions performed broken down by trimester. In all events, the identity of each woman who has had an abortion remains confidential.
>
> ... We think that ... all the provisions at issue here except that relating to spousal notice are constitutional. Although they do not relate to the State's interest in informing the woman's choice, they do relate to health. The collection of information with respect to actual patients is a vital element of medical research, and so it cannot be said that the requirements serve no purpose other than to make abortions more difficult. Nor do we find that the requirements impose a substantial obstacle to a woman's choice. At most, they might increase the cost of some abortions by a slight amount. While at some point increased cost could become a substantial obstacle, there is no such showing on the record before us.
>
> ... [T]he reporting provision requires the reporting of, among other things, a married woman's reason for failure to provide notice to her husband. This provision in effect requires women, as a condition of obtaining an abortion, to provide the Commonwealth with the precise information we have already recognized that many women have pressing reasons not to reveal. Like the spousal notice requirement itself, this provision places an undue burden on a woman's choice, and must be invalidated for that reason.

Disposition of case: The judgment of the Third Circuit was affirmed in part and reversed in part, and the case was remanded.

Concurring and dissenting opinion by Justice Stevens: Justice Stevens concurred in the decision to invalidate two aspects of Pennsylvania's statute. However, he dissented from the decision to uphold the validity of the remaining provisions. He wrote succinctly:

> My disagreement with the joint opinion begins with its understanding of the trimester framework established in Roe. Contrary to the suggestion of the joint opinion, it is not a "contradiction" to recognize that the State may have a legitimate interest in potential human life and, at the same time, to conclude that that interest does not justify the regulation of abortion before viability (although other interests, such as maternal health, may). The fact that the State's interest is legitimate does not tell us when, if ever, that interest outweighs the pregnant woman's interest in personal liberty. It is appropriate, therefore, to consider more carefully the nature of the interests at stake.

Concurring and dissenting opinion by Justice Blackmun: Justice Blackmun agreed with the decision of the joint opinion to invalidate two provisions in the statute. He dissented from the opinion insofar as it upheld the remaining provisions. Justice Blackmun wrote:

> In sum, Roe's requirement of strict scrutiny as implemented through a trimester framework should not be disturbed. No other approach has gained a majority, and no other is more protective of the woman's fundamental right. Lastly, no other approach properly accommodates the woman's constitutional right with the State's legitimate interests.

Application of the strict scrutiny standard results in the invalidation of all the challenged provisions. Indeed, as this Court has invalidated virtually identical provisions in prior cases, stare decisis requires that we again strike them down.

Concurring and dissenting opinion by Chief Justice Rehnquist: The Chief Justice concurred in the decision to uphold the majority of the provisions in the statute. He dissented from the decision to invalidate two of the provisions. The Chief Justice wrote:

> The joint opinion, following its newly minted variation on stare decisis, retains the outer shell of Roe v. Wade, but beats a wholesale retreat from the substance of that case. We believe that Roe was wrongly decided, and that it can and should be overruled consistently with our traditional approach to stare decisis in constitutional cases. We would adopt the approach of the plurality in Webster v. Reproductive Health Services, and uphold the challenged provisions of the Pennsylvania statute in their entirety....
>
> For the reasons stated, we therefore would hold that each of the challenged provisions of the Pennsylvania statute is consistent with the Constitution. It bears emphasis that our conclusion in this regard does not carry with it any necessary approval of these regulations. Our task is, as always, to decide only whether the challenged provisions of a law comport with the United States Constitution. If, as we believe, these do, their wisdom as a matter of public policy is for the people of Pennsylvania to decide.

Concurring and dissenting opinion by Justice Scalia: Justice Scalia concurred in the decision to uphold the majority of the provisions in the statute. He dissented from the decision to invalidate two of the provisions. Justice Scalia wrote:

> ... The issue is whether [abortion] is a liberty protected by the Constitution of the United States. I am sure it is not. I reach that conclusion not because of anything so exalted as my views concerning the concept of existence, of meaning, of the universe, and of the mystery of human life. Rather, I reach it for the same reason I reach the conclusion that bigamy is not constitutionally protected — because of two simple facts: (1) the Constitution says absolutely nothing about it, and (2) the longstanding traditions of American society have permitted it to be legally proscribed.

Note: The decision in the case was significant because of the modification it made to the decision in *Roe v. Wade*. The joint opinion opened the door for states to regulate pre-viability pregnancies, so long as such regulations did not impose an undue burden on a woman's right to have a pre-viability abortion. *See also* **Roe v. Wade**

Poe v. Ullman

Forum: United States Supreme Court.

Case Citation: Poe v. Ullman, 367 U.S. 497 (1961).

Date Argued: March 1–2, 1961.

Date of Decision: June 19, 1961.

Opinion of Court: Frankfurter, J., in which Warren, C.J., and Clark and Whittaker, JJ., joined.

Concurring Opinion: Brennan, J.

Dissenting Opinion: Douglas, J.

Dissenting Opinion: Harlan, J.

Dissenting Statement: Stewart, J.

Dissenting Statement: Black, J.

Counsel for Appellants: Fowler V. Harper argued and filed a brief.

Counsel for Appellee: Raymond J. Cannon, Assistant Attorney General of Connecticut, argued; on the brief was Albert L. Coles, Attorney General.

Amicus Brief for Appellants: Harriet Pilpel, Morris L. Ernst and Nancy F. Wechsler for Planned Parenthood Federation of America, Inc.; by Whitney North Seymour for Dr. Willard Allen et al., and by Osmond K. Fraenkel and Rowland Watts for the American Civil Liberties Union et al.

Amicus Brief for Appellee: None

Issue Presented: Whether the constitution was violated by a Connecticut statute that made it a crime to give married persons contraceptive information and devices?

Case Holding: The appellants did not have standing to challenge the constitutionality of a Connecticut statute, that made it a crime to give married persons contraceptive information and devices.

Background facts of case: A Connecticut statute made it a crime for any person to use any drug or article to prevent conception. The appellants, two married woman and a physician, filed separate lawsuits in a state trial court seeking to have the statute declared unconstitutional. The lawsuits were consolidated for disposition. The trial court dismissed the cases on the grounds that the appellants did not present a triable issue, because the state's highest court found the statute valid in 1940. The appellate courts in the state affirmed the dismissal. The United States Supreme Court agreed to hear the cases.

Plurality opinion by Justice Frankfurter: Justice Frankfurter announced the judgment of the Court to dismiss the cases, because none of the appellants had been prosecuted for violating the statute. The plurality opinion provided the following justification:

> The Connecticut law prohibiting the use of contraceptives has been on the State's books since 1879. During the more than three-quarters of a century since its enactment, a prosecution for its violation seems never to have been initiated, save in State v. Nelson, 126 Conn. 412, 11 A. 2d 856 (1940). The circumstances of that case, decided in 1940, only prove the abstract character of what is before us.... The unreality of these law suits is illumined by another circumstance. We were advised by counsel for appellants that contraceptives are commonly and notoriously sold in Connecticut drug stores. Yet no prosecutions are recorded; and certainly such ubiquitous, open, public sales would more quickly invite the attention of enforcement officials than the conduct in which the present appellants wish to engage — the giving of private medical advice by a doctor to his individual patients, and their private use of the devices prescribed. The undeviating policy of nullification by Connecticut of its anti-contraceptive laws throughout all the long years that they have been on the statute books bespeaks more than prosecutorial paralysis....
>
> Insofar as appellants seek to justify the exercise of our declaratory power by the threat of prosecution, facts which they can no more negative by complaint and demurrer than they could by stipulation preclude our determining their appeals on the merits. It is clear that the mere existence of a state penal statute would constitute insufficient grounds to support a federal court's adjudication of its constitutionality in proceedings brought against the State's prosecuting officials if real threat of enforcement is wanting. If the prosecutor expressly agrees not to prosecute, a suit against him for declaratory and injunctive relief is not such an adversary case as will be reviewed here. Eighty years of Connecticut history demonstrate a similar, albeit tacit agreement. The fact that Connecticut has not chosen to press the enforcement of this statute deprives these controversies of the immediacy which is an indispensable condition of constitutional adjudication. This Court cannot be umpire to debates concerning harmless, empty shadows. To find it necessary to pass on these statutes now, in order to protect appellants from the hazards of prosecution. would be to close our eyes to reality....
>
> Justiciability is of course not a legal concept with a fixed content or susceptible of scientific verification. Its utilization is the resultant of many subtle pressures, including the appropriateness of the issues for decision by this Court and the actual hardship to the litigants of denying them the relief sought. Both these factors justify withholding adjudication of the constitutional issue

raised under the circumstances and in the manner in which they are now before the Court.

Disposition of case: Appeal dismissed.

Concurring opinion by Justice Brennan: Justice Brennan agreed with the Court's judgment. He gave the following brief comments:

> I agree that this appeal must be dismissed for failure to present a real and substantial controversy which unequivocally calls for adjudication of the rights claimed in advance of any attempt by the State to curtail them by criminal prosecution. I am not convinced, on this skimpy record, that these appellants as individuals are truly caught in an inescapable dilemma. The true controversy in this case is over the opening of birth-control clinics on a large scale; it is that which the State has prevented in the past, not the use of contraceptives by isolated and individual married couples. It will be time enough to decide the constitutional questions urged upon us when, if ever, that real controversy flares up again. Until it does, or until the State makes a definite and concrete threat to enforce these laws against individual married couples— a threat which it has never made in the past except under the provocation of litigation — this Court may not be compelled to exercise its most delicate power of constitutional adjudication.

Dissenting opinion by Justice Douglas: Justice Douglas dissented from the Court's decision. He believed the case presented a justiciable issue and that the Court should have struck down the statute. Justice Douglas wrote the following:

> These cases are dismissed because a majority of the members of this Court conclude, for varying reasons, that this controversy does not present a justiciable question. That conclusion is too transparent to require an extended reply. The device of the declaratory judgment is an honored one. Its use in the federal system is restricted to cases or controversies within the meaning of Article III. The question must be appropriate for judicial determination, not hypothetical, abstract, academic or moot. It must touch the legal relations of parties having adverse legal interests. It must be real and substantial and admit of specific relief through a decree of a conclusive character. The fact that damages are not awarded or an injunction does not issue, the fact that there are no allegations of irreparable injury are irrelevant....
>
> I dissent from a dismissal of these cases and our refusal to strike down this law.

Dissenting opinion by Justice Harlan: Justice Harlan believed the Court should have decided the case on its merits and that the statute should have been found unconstitutional. He wrote as follows:

> I am compelled, with all respect, to dissent from the dismissal of these appeals. In my view the course which the Court has taken does violence to established concepts of justiciability, and unjustifiably leaves these appellants under the threat of unconstitutional prosecution....
>
> ... In my view of these cases a present determination of the Constitutional issues is the only course which will advance justice, and I can find no sound reason born of considerations as to the possible inadequacy or ineffectiveness of the judgment that might be rendered which justifies the Court's contrary disposition. While ordinarily I would not deem it appropriate to deal, in dissent, with Constitutional issues which the Court has not reached, I shall do so here because such issues, as I see things, are entangled with the Court's conclusion as to the nonjusticiability of these appeals....
>
> I consider that this Connecticut legislation, as construed to apply to these appellants, violates the Fourteenth Amendment. I believe that a statute making it a criminal offense for married couples to use contraceptives is an intolerable and unjustifiable invasion of privacy in the conduct of the most intimate concerns of an individual's personal life. I reach this conclusion, even though I find it difficult and unnecessary at this juncture to accept appellants' other argument that the judgment of policy behind the statute, so applied, is so arbitrary and unreasonable as to render the enactment invalid for that reason alone....

Dissenting statement by Justice Stewart: Justice Stewart gave a statement indicating he dissented from the dismissal of the case.

Dissenting statement by Justice Black: Justice Black gave a statement indicating he dissented from the dismissal of the case.

Note: The statute in the case was eventually brought before the Court again in *Griswold v. Connecticut*, wherein the Court found the statute unconstitutional. *See* **Griswold v. Connecticut**

Poelker v. Doe

Forum: United States Supreme Court.

Case Citation: Poelker v. Doe, 432 U.S. 519 (1977).

Date Argued: January 11, 1977.

Date of Decision: June 20, 1977.

Opinion of Court: Per Curiam.

Concurring Opinion: None.

Dissenting Opinion: Brennan, J., in which Marshall and Blackmun, JJ., joined.

Dissenting Opinion: Marshall, J.

Dissenting Opinion: Blackmun, J., in which Brennan and Marshall, JJ., joined.

Counsel for Appellants: Eugene P. Freeman argued; on the brief was Jack L. Koehr.

Counsel for Appellee: Frank Susman argued and filed a brief.

Amicus Brief for Appellants: Dennis J. Horan, Dolores V. Horan, and Victor G. Rosenblum for Americans United for Life, Inc.; by Jerome M. McLaughlin for Missouri Doctors for Life; and by Robert E. Ratermann for James R. Butler et al.

Amicus Brief for Appellee: Leo Pfeffer for the American Jewish Congress et al.; and by Sylvia A. Law, Harriet F. Pilpel, and Eve W. Paul for the American Public Health Assn. et al.

Issue Presented: Whether the Equal Protection Clause of the Fourteenth Amendment was violated by a policy of the city of St. Louis, Missouri to deny publicly funded abortions to indigent women at city hospitals, except when there was a threat of grave injury or death to the mother?

Case Holding: The Equal Protection Clause of the Fourteenth Amendment was not violated by a policy of the city of St. Louis, Missouri that denied publicly funded abortions to indigent women at city hospitals, except when a woman's health or life was in danger.

Background facts of case: The appellee, Jane Doe, was an indigent woman who had been denied an elective abortion at a hospital maintained by the city of St. Louis, Missouri. The denial was based upon a policy directive issued by the city's mayor, that precluded municipal funding of abortions for indigent women, except when a woman's health or life was in danger. The appellee filed a law suit in a federal district court in Missouri, challenging the constitutionality of the policy. The appellants, city officials, were named as defendants. The district court denied relief. However, the Eighth Circuit court of appeals reversed. The appeals court held that the city's abortion policy violated the Equal Protection Clause of the Fourteenth Amendment. The Supreme Court granted certiorari to consider the issue.

Majority opinion delivered Per Curiam: The per curiam opinion held that under the Court's decision in *Maher v. Roe*, decided in the same Term of Court, the Equal Protection Clause was not violated by the city's policy. The issue was addressed in the per curiam opinion as follows:

> We agree that the constitutional question presented here is identical in principle with that presented by a State's refusal to provide Medicaid benefits for abortions while providing them for

> childbirth. This was the issue before us in Maher v. Roe. For the reasons set forth in our opinion in that case, we find no constitutional violation by the city of St. Louis in electing, as a policy choice, to provide publicly financed hospital services for childbirth without providing corresponding services for nontherapeutic abortions.
>
> In the decision of the Court of Appeals and in the briefs supporting that decision, emphasis is placed on Mayor Poelker's personal opposition to abortion, characterized as "a wanton, callous disregard" for the constitutional rights of indigent women. Although the Mayor's personal position on abortion is irrelevant to our decision, we note that he is an elected official responsible to the people of St. Louis. His policy of denying city funds for abortions such as that desired by Doe is subject to public debate and approval or disapproval at the polls. We merely hold, for the reasons stated in Maher, that the Constitution does not forbid a State or city, pursuant to democratic processes, from expressing a preference for normal childbirth as St. Louis has done.

Disposition of case: The judgment of the court of appeals was reversed.

Dissenting opinion by Justice Brennan: Justice Brennan referenced to his dissenting opinion in *Maher v. Roe*, as the basis of his dissent. He went on, however, to make the following observations:

> ... Here the fundamental right of a woman freely to choose to terminate her pregnancy has been infringed by the city of St. Louis through a deliberate policy based on opposition to elective abortions on moral grounds by city officials. While it may still be possible for some indigent women to obtain abortions in clinics or private hospitals, it is clear that the city policy is a significant, and in some cases insurmountable, obstacle to indigent pregnant women who cannot pay for abortions in those private facilities. Nor is the closing of St. Louis' public hospitals an isolated instance with little practical significance. The importance of today's decision is greatly magnified by the fact that during 1975 and the first quarter of 1976 only about 18 percent of all public hospitals in the country provided abortion services, and in 10 States there were no public hospitals providing such services.
>
> A number of difficulties lie beneath the surface of the Court's holding. Public hospitals that do not permit the performance of elective abortions will frequently have physicians on their staffs who would willingly perform them. This may operate in some communities significantly to reduce the number of physicians who are both willing and able to perform abortions in a hospital setting. It is not a complete answer that many abortions may safely be performed in clinics, for some physicians will not be affiliated with those clinics, and some abortions may pose unacceptable risks if performed outside a hospital. Indeed, such an answer would be ironic, for if the result is to force some abortions to be performed in a clinic that properly should be performed in a hospital, the city policy will have operated to increase rather than reduce health risks associated with abortions....
>
> The Court's holding will also pose difficulties in small communities where the public hospital is the only nearby health care facility. If such a public hospital is closed to abortions, any woman — rich or poor — will be seriously inconvenienced; and for some women — particularly poor women — the unavailability of abortions in the public hospital will be an insuperable obstacle. Indeed, a recent survey suggests that the decision in this case will be felt most strongly in rural areas, where the public hospital will in all likelihood be closed to elective abortions, and where there will not be sufficient demand to support a separate abortion clinic.
>
> Because the city policy constitutes coercion of women to bear children which they do not wish to bear, Roe v. Wade and the cases following it require that the city show a compelling state interest that justifies this infringement upon the fundamental right to choose to have an abortion. Expressing a preference for normal childbirth does not satisfy that standard. Roe explicitly held that during the first trimester no state interest in regulating abortions was compelling, and that during the second trimester the State's interest was compelling only insofar as it protected maternal health. Under Roe, the State's important and legitimate interest in potential life — which I take to be another way of referring to a State's preference for normal childbirth — becomes compelling only at the end of the second trimester. Thus it is clear that St. Louis' policy preference is insufficient to justify its infringement on the right of women to choose to have abortions during the first two trimesters of pregnancy without interference by the State on the ground of moral opposition to abortions. St. Louis' policy therefore unduly burdens the right to seek an abortion.

Dissenting opinion by Justice Marshall: Justice Marshall referenced to his dissenting opinion in *Beal v. Doe*, as the basis for his dissent.

Dissenting opinion by Justice Blackmun: Justice Blackmun referenced to his dissenting opinion in *Beal v. Doe*, as the basis for his dissent. *See also* **Beal v. Doe; Maher v. Roe**

Political Research Associates

Political Research Associates (PRA) is a think-tank organization that was founded in 1981, by Jean Hardisty. PRA was created to develop and disseminate strategies to combat conservative encroachments on basic civil liberties. The organization devised a widely adopted plan for pro-choice advocates called Defending Reproductive Rights. This plan offers a comprehensive look at the attack on reproductive freedoms by pro-life advocates, and offers strategies for fighting such attacks. *See also* **Pro-Choice Organizations**

Polycystic Kidney Disease *see* **Genital and Urinary Tract Birth Defects**

Polycystic Ovarian Syndrome and Pregnancy

Polycystic ovarian syndrome (also called Stein-Leventhal syndrome) is an endocrine (hormonal) disorder that afflicts about 10 percent of all women. The disorder involves the failure of the body to respond properly to insulin that is produced in the pancreas. This problem causes the pancreas to pump out excessive insulin. Increased levels of insulin cause the ovaries to produce excessive amounts of the male hormone testosterone. The testosterone in turn may prevent the ovaries from releasing an egg each month. High testosterone levels in women may cause acne, male-pattern baldness, excess hair growth, obesity, diabetes and hypertension. Treatment for the disorder includes medications and dietary plans. The disease is one of the leading causes of infertility in women. Roughly 44 percent of all pregnant women with the disorder have a first trimester spontaneous abortion. *See also* **Anovulation; Miscarriage**

Polyhydramnios

Polyhydramnios is a condition involving the amniotic fluid that surrounds and cushions a fetus throughout development. The condition arises when a fetus fails to swallow and absorb amniotic fluid in excess of normal amounts. This may occur as a result of gastrointestinal obstruction, neurological problems, or a variety of other causes. If the condition is severe it will cause stillbirth. *See also* **Stillbirth**

Population Council

The Population Council is an organization that was established in 1952 by John D. Rockefeller III. The Council was started for the purpose of researching and studying problems associated with the world's population. The information gathered from population research is used to help change reproductive health and population growth. The research conducted by the Council consists of three types: biomedical, social science, and public health. The Council engages in research involving demographic studies, sexually transmitted diseases, reproductive physiology, and the development of new contraceptives. The Council's headquarters is in New York City. The president of the Council is Peter J. Donaldson.

From its inception, the Council has been criticized as being an organization whose sole purpose was to control the reproductive habits of poor people. This criticism was based on the theory that poor people demand greater help from governments, which translates into higher taxes for the wealthy. For the most part, the Council's work has been focused on populations outside the United States. *See also* **Pro-Choice Organizations**

Porencephaly

Porencephaly is a congenital disorder involving cysts or cavities in a cerebral hemisphere. Symptoms of the disorder include paralysis, low muscle tone, seizures, speech impairment and mental retardation. Treatment for the disorder may include physical therapy and medication for seizures. The disease can be fatal. *See also* **Birth Defects and Abortion**

Post-Abortion Syndrome

Post-abortion syndrome (PAS) is associated with and is a form of post traumatic stress syndrome. PAS comes about when a woman has an abortion and the event is too stressful and traumatic for her to cope with. A PAS victim is unable to simply resume her life where it left off after the abortion. Instead, she may experience a variety of reactions that are destructive to her. Some of the symptoms of PAS include: depression, thoughts of suicide, sudden and uncontrollable crying, reduced motivation, sleeplessness, loss of appetite, sexual disturbances, re-experiencing the abortion, and alcohol and drug abuse. Counseling is available for victims of PAS. *See also* **Complications During and After Abortion; Postpartum Depression**

Postnatal

Postnatal (also puerperium or postpartum) is the period of time immediately after delivery and continues for about six weeks. *See also* **Perinatal; Postnatal**

Postpartum Depression

Postpartum depression (PPD) is a condition that affects about 30 percent of all women after the birth of a child. PPD can develop immediately after birth or up to four weeks afterward. It may last anywhere from a few weeks to a year. Some of the symptoms of PPD include insomnia, anxiety, headaches, chest pain, loss of appetite, lack of bonding with infant and violence toward the infant. *See also* **Post-Abortion Syndrome**

Prevalence of Three Levels of Self-Reported Postpartum Depression 2000

	None %	*Low to Moderate %*	*Severe %*
Age (years)			
<20	34.0	57.1	8.9
20–24	37.5	52.4	10.0
25–34	43.2	51.0	5.8
35+	47.0	47.6	5.3
Race			
White	41.1	52.3	6.6
Black	42.2	48.3	9.5
Other	39.2	52.1	8.7
Education			
<12 years	39.0	50.7	10.3
12 years	39.2	52.7	8.0
≥13 years	43.3	51.3	5.4

Source: **Centers for Disease Control and Prevention.**

Post-Term Pregnancy

A normal term pregnancy has a duration of 38 to 42 weeks. Post-term pregnancy occurs when a child is delivered during a gestation period of more than 42 weeks. Roughly 4 percent of all babies are born at 42 weeks or later. About two-thirds of all post-term pregnancies are due to incorrect dates. Most post-term babies are delivered healthy. However, risks are involved with post-term pregnancies.

Post-term pregnancy exposes a women to an increased risk of vaginal birth trauma due to a large baby. Caesarean delivery is twice as likely to be used because of the size of the baby. Women are also at an increased risk for infection and wound complications. There are also risks for the newborn. Amniotic fluid volume may decrease and the fetus may stop gaining weight, or could lose weight. Birth injury may occur because of the baby's size. The baby is also more likely to have a bowel movement, called meconium, which it may inhale into its lungs where it could cause pneumonia. *See also* **Gestational Age; Pre-Term Pregnancy**

Post-Viability Abortion *see* **Criminal Abortions**

Powell, Lewis F., Jr.

Lewis F. Powell, Jr. (1907–1998) served as an associate justice of the United States Supreme Court from 1972 to 1987. While on the Supreme Court Justice Powell was known as a moderate conservative interpreter of the Constitution.

Justice Powell was born in Suffolk, Virginia. He was educated at Washington and Lee University where he received a bachelor's degree in 1929 and a law degree in 1931. Justice Powell also received a graduate degree from Harvard Law School in 1932. He led a relatively obscure and nonpolitical life as a practicing attorney until President Richard M. Nixon appointed him to the Supreme Court in 1972.

During Justice Powell's tenure on the Supreme Court he issued a number of abortion related opinions. The written opinions and opinions simply voted on by Justice Powell, indicate that he was not in favor of using the constitution to expand abortion rights for women.

Distribution of the Abortion Voting Pattern of Justice Powell Based Upon Opinions Filed by the Supreme Court

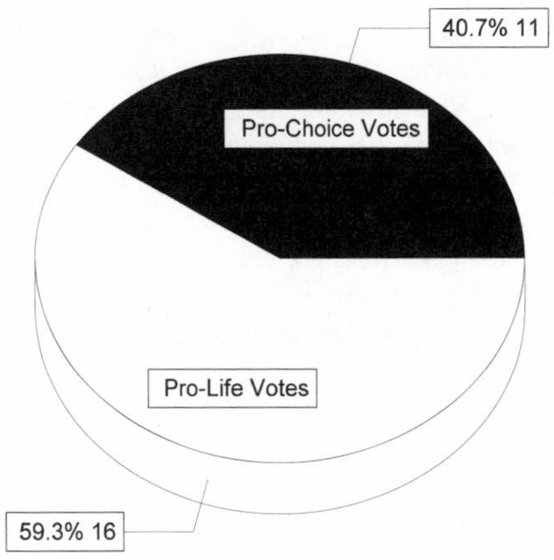

(1) *Unanimous opinions voted with only*. In *Bellotti v. Baird I* Justice Powell voted with a unanimous opinion, which held that the federal district court had to certify appropriate questions to the supreme judicial court of Massachusetts, concerning the interpretation of that

state's parental consent abortion statute for minors, before ruling on its constitutionality. In *Withrow v. Larkin* Justice Powell joined a unanimous opinion, which held that constitutional due process was not violated by the mere fact that a Wisconsin medical examining board had the authority to both, investigate and adjudicate, allegations against a physician that included, among other things, permitting a nonphysician to perform an abortion.

(2) Majority opinions written. Justice Powell wrote the majority opinion in *City of Akron v. Akron Center for Reproductive Health, Inc.*, which invalidated an abortion ordinance that provided requirements for parental consent, informed consent, waiting period, hospitalization and disposal of fetal remains. In *Planned Parenthood Assn. v. Ashcroft* Justice Powell wrote the majority/plurality opinion, which held that the constitution was violated by Missouri's requirement that second trimester abortions take place in a hospital; but that the constitution was not violated by the state's requirement that a pathology report for each abortion be performed, that a second physician be present during abortions performed after viability, and parental or judicial consent for abortion by minors. Justice Powell wrote the majority opinion in *Simopoulos v. Virginia*, which upheld a Virginia statute requiring second trimester abortions be performed at hospitals, because under the statute an adequately equipped clinic could, upon proper application, obtain an outpatient hospital license that permitted the performance of second-trimester abortions.

Justice Powell wrote the majority opinion in *Beal v. Doe*, which held that Pennsylvania's refusal to extend Medicaid coverage to nontherapeutic abortions was not invalid nor inconsistent with Title XIX of the Social Security Act. In *Maher v. Roe* Justice Powell wrote the majority opinion, which held that the Equal Protection Clause of the Fourteenth Amendment did not prohibit Connecticut from excluding nontherapeutic abortions from its Medicaid program. Justice Powell wrote the majority opinion in *Burns v. Alcala*, which held that states receiving federal financial aid under the program of Aid to Families with Dependent Children, were not required to offer welfare benefits to pregnant women for their unborn children.

(3) Majority opinions voted with only. In *Federal Election Commission v. Massachusetts Citizens for Life, Inc.* Justice Powell voted with the majority opinion, which held that federal law that prohibited the appellee from using its treasury funds to promote pro-life political candidates violated the Free Speech Clause of the First Amendment. Justice Powell joined the majority decision in *Thornburgh v. American College of Obstetricians and Gynecologists*, which invalidated provisions in Pennsylvania's abortion statute that provided for maternal informed consent, abortion alternative printed information, abortion reporting requirements, determination of fetal viability, degree of care required in post-viability abortions, and a second-physician requirement. In *Diamond v. Charles*, Justice Powell joined the majority opinion, which held that a citizen did not have standing to appeal a decision invalidating parts of Illinois' abortion statute that (1) imposed criminal penalties for violating a prescribed standard of care that had to be exercised by a physician in performing an abortion of a viable fetus, and of a possibly viable fetus; and (2) imposed criminal penalties for physicians who failed to provide patients with information about the type of abortifacient used. Justice Powell voted with the majority opinion in *Bolger v. Youngs Drug Products Corp.*, which held that a provision of the Comstock Act, 39 U.S.C. § 3001(e)(2), that prohibited mailing unsolicited advertisements for contraceptives violated the Free Speech Clause of the First Amendment.

Justice Powell joined the majority opinion in *Harris v. McRae*, which held that Medicaid funding restrictions for abortion by the Hyde Amendment, did not violate the Due Process Clause nor the equal protection component of the Fifth Amendment. In *Williams v. Zbaraz* Justice Powell voted with the majority opinion, which held that in light of the requirements of the Hyde Amendment, the Equal Protection Clause of the Fourteenth Amendment was not violated by an Illinois statute that prohibited state Medicaid payment for abortions, except when necessary to save the life of the pregnant woman. In *Colautti v. Franklin* Justice Powell joined the majority opinion, which held that the constitution was violated by a vague and ambiguous provision in Pennsylvania's abortion statute that subjected a physician who performed an abortion to potential criminal liability, if he/she failed to utilize a statutorily prescribed technique when the fetus was viable or when there was sufficient reason to believe that the fetus may be viable. Justice Powell joined the per curiam opinion in *Poelker v. Doe*, which held that the Equal Protection Clause of the Fourteenth Amendment was not violated by a policy of the city of St. Louis, Missouri that denied publicly funded abortions to indigent women at city hospitals, except when a woman's health or life was in danger.

In *Connecticut v. Menillo* Justice Powell joined the majority per curiam opinion, which held that the constitution was not violated by criminal abortion statutes that prohibit nonphysicians from attempting or performing abortions at any stage of a pregnancy. Justice Powell joined the majority opinion in *Bigelow v. Virginia*, which held that the Free Speech and Free Press Clauses of the First Amendment were violated by a Virginia penal statute that prohibited selling or circulating any publication that encouraged or promoted abortions. Justice Powell voted with the majority opinion in *Geduldig v. Aiello*, which held that the Equal Protection Clause of the Fourteenth Amendment did not require a private sector employee disability insurance program, operated by the state of California, provide coverage for employee disabilities associated with normal pregnancies. Justice Powell joined the majority opinion in *Anders v. Floyd*, which held that a federal district court erred in enjoining enforcement of a South Carolina statute that imposed criminal punishment for performing an abortion on a viable fetus.

In *Roe v. Wade* Justice Powell joined the majority opinion, which held that the liberty component of the Due Process Clause of the Fourteenth Amendment prohibited states from criminalizing or preventing elective first trimester abortions. Justice Powell voted with the majority opinion in *Doe v. Bolton*, which held that the Due Process Clause of the Fourteenth Amendment was violated by provisions in Georgia's abortion statutes that required (1) abortions take place in accredited hospitals, (2) that an abortion be approved by a hospital abortion committee, (3) that the need for an abortion be confirmed by two independent physicians, and (4) that a woman seeking an abortion be a resident of Georgia.

(4) Plurality opinions written. Justice Powell wrote a plurality opinion and announced the judgment of the Court in *Bellotti v. Baird II*, which held that Massachusetts' abortion statute for minors violated the constitution in light of an interpretation given by the state's highest court, that required parental notice of a judicial bypass proceeding invoked by a minor, and permitted a judge to deny an abortion even though the minor proved she had enough maturity to make an independent decision.

(5) Concurring opinions written. In *H. L. v. Matheson* Justice Powell wrote an opinion concurring in the majority decision, which held that the constitution was not violated by Utah's requirement that the parents of a minor be notified, if possible, prior to performing an abortion. In *Carey v. Population Services International* Justice Powell wrote an opinion concurring with the majority decision, which held that the constitution prohibited enforcement of a New York statute that made it a crime (1) for any person to sell or distribute any contraceptive of any kind to a minor under the age of 16 years; (2) for anyone other than a licensed pharmacist to distribute contraceptives to persons 16 or over; and (3) for anyone, including licensed pharmacists, to advertise or display contraceptives. In *Weinberger v. Hynson,*

Westcott & Dunning Justice Powell wrote an opinion concurring in the majority decision, which held that the Food and Drug Administration could not deny a drug manufacturer a hearing to obtain marketing approval for a drug called Lutrexin, which provided treatment for premature labor and threatened and habitual abortion.

(6) Concurring opinions voted with only. Justice Powell concurred in the majority decision in *Planned Parenthood of Missouri v. Danforth,* which held that the constitution was not violated by provisions in Missouri's abortion statute involving the definition of fetal viability, woman's written consent, and recordkeeping and reporting requirements; but that the constitution prohibited the requirements concerning spousal consent, parental consent for minor, banning saline amniocentesis abortions, and physician's standard of care.

(7) Concurring and dissenting opinions written. Justice Powell wrote an opinion concurring and dissenting in *Singleton v. Wulff,* which held that the Eighth Circuit court of appeals had jurisdiction to determine whether abortion providers had standing to challenge a provision in Missouri's abortion statute that limited Medicaid payment for abortions, but it did not have jurisdiction to rule that the provision violated the constitution because the district court did not address the issue. He dissented from language in the plurality opinion that indicated the abortion providers could assert on remand, in addition to their own rights, the constitutional rights of their patients who would be eligible for Medicaid assistance in obtaining elective abortions.

Power of Choice Project

Power of Choice Project is a pro-choice organization that was formed in 2003, in Menlo Park, California. The Project is composed of a group of concerned citizens who share the same goal of educating the public and activating supporters of reproductive freedom through film. The Project has released a film called "Motherhood by Choice, Not Chance," which is reported to have been aired by television stations in 15 states. *See also* **Pro-Choice Organizations**

Preclinical Pregnancy *see* **Chemical Pregnancy**

Preeclampsia

Preeclampsia is a condition affecting a pregnant woman that involves swelling of the hands and face, high blood pressure, nausea, vomiting, abdominal pain, and protein in the urine. The exact cause of this condition is not known, although several theories have been offered (e.g., genetic, dietary, vascular and autoimmune factors). The condition occurs in about 5 percent of all pregnancies. Treatment for this disorder depends upon the stage of development of the fetus. Research has shown that prolonging pregnancies when preeclampsia arises may result in complications for the mother, as well as infant death. Ordinarily bed rest is suggested until the fetus has a high probability of surviving outside the womb. In situations where the condition is serious and the fetus is beyond 28 weeks of gestation, delivery is usually recommended. In some instances preeclampsia may develop into eclampsia, the occurrence of seizures. The condition also increases the risk for placenta abruptio. *See also* **Eclampsia; Placenta Abruptio**

Pregnancy

Pregnancy is a condition in a female that arises after the union of an egg and sperm in her fallopian tubes. The duration of pregnancy is about 280 days. Symptoms of pregnancy include cessation of menses, nausea, breast enlargement, and progressive enlargement of the abdomen. *See also* **Fetal Development; Gestational Age**

Pregnancy Discrimination Act

Under the Pregnancy Discrimination Act of 1978, 42 U.S.C.A. 2000e(k), Congress explicitly prohibited employment discrimination due to pregnancy. The Pregnancy Discrimination Act provides in relevant part:

> *... [W]omen affected by pregnancy, childbirth, or related medical conditions shall be treated the same for all employment-related purposes, including receipt of benefits under fringe benefit programs, as other persons not so affected but similar in their ability or inability to work, and nothing in section 2000e-2(h) of this title shall be interpreted to permit otherwise. This subsection shall not require an employer to pay for health insurance benefits for abortion, except where the life of the mother would be endangered if the fetus were carried to term, or except where medical complications have arisen from an abortion: Provided, That nothing herein shall preclude an employer from providing abortion benefits or otherwise affect bargaining agreements in regard to abortion.*

In *Automobile Workers v. Johnson Controls, Inc.* the United States Supreme Court held that the Pregnancy Discrimination Act forbids sex-specific fetal-protection policies by an employer, that exclude a fertile female employee from certain jobs because of the employer's concern for the health of the fetus the woman might conceive. *See also* **Automobile Workers v. Johnson Controls, Inc.; Title VII of the Civil Rights Act**

Pregnancy Help Centers

Pregnancy help centers are primarily pro-life facilities that provide assistance and viable alternatives to abortion for women in crisis pregnancies. Some of the services provided by pregnancy help centers include pregnancy testing, counseling on the emotional and psychological consequences of abortion, adoption guidance and financial assistance. Many centers also provide post-abortion counseling and support. There are over three thousand pregnancy help centers nationwide. *See also* **Care Net; National Institute of Family and Life Advocates**

Pregnancy Test

A pregnancy test is a blood or urine analysis that determines the level of the human chorionic gonadotropin hormone in a woman's body. An elevated level of this hormone is chemical evidence of a pregnancy. *See also* **Amenorrhea; Chadwick's Sign; Hegar's Sign**

Pregnancy Ultrasound *see* **Ultrasound**

Premature Birth *see* **Pre-Term Pregnancy**

Premature Labor

Premature labor occurs when a woman has contractions after the 20th week of gestation, but before the start of the 37th week of gestation. These contractions are usually irregular and brief, and are deemed false labor (Braxton Hicks contractions). However, in some instances premature labor may start because of some problem that could result in the birth of a premature baby. Premature labor is the greatest cause of perinatal death in the United States.

Most causes of premature labor are unknown. Some contributing factors include: smoking, drug abuse, poor diet, infections, illness (such as high blood pressure, kidney disease, or diabetes), multiple gestation (such as twins or triplets). There are medications that may be taken, such as tocolytic agents, to treat premature labor and permit pregnancy to proceed to term. *See also* **Pre-Term Pregnancy**

Premenstrual Syndrome

Premenstrual syndrome (PMS) refers to the various physical and emotional symptoms that occur during the second half of a female's menstrual cycle (after ovulation). The symptoms may include headaches, mood shifts, breast tenderness, bloating, edema, weight fluctuation, backache and anxiety. There are medications for PMS that include analgesics, diuretics and sedatives. *See also* **Dysmenorrhea; Menarche; Menstrual Cycle**

Prenatal

Prenatal refers to the time period between conception and birth. *See also* **Perinatal; Postnatal**

Prenatal Care

Prenatal care involves ongoing medical evaluation of a women and her fetus before birth. With prenatal care an expectant mother can obtain useful information about proper nutrition, as well as learn of any health problems she may have that could negatively impact the fetus or herself. Some of the usual tests that may be performed on the mother include: testing for gonorrhea, HIV, chlamydia, syphilis, hepatitis B, rubella, blood type and Rh testing, Pap smear, urine culture testing. Health care providers can also obtain helpful information about the development of a fetus by studying images and cells of the fetus. Some of the diagnostic methods employed include amniocentesis, chorionic villus sampling and ultrasound.

Part of prenatal care includes screening to determine if a woman has an increased chance of bearing an abnormal child. Approximately 250 birth defects can be diagnosed in an unborn fetus, most of which cannot be treated or cured. Various tests can be conducted to make a birth defect determination. For example, the level of alpha-fetoprotein (a protein produced by the fetus) can be measured in the woman's blood. If the level is high, the woman may be carrying a fetus with a neural tube defect (e.g., spina bifida). If the level is low, the fetus may have chromosomal abnormalities, such as Down syndrome. Timely information regarding the chances of a fetus having a birth defect permits the opportunity to decide whether to take the fetus to term or have an abortion. *See also* **Birth Defects and Abortion; Sexually Transmitted Diseases**

Prenatal Injuries *see* **Trauma and Pregnancy**

Presbyterians Pro-Life

Presbyterians Pro-Life (PPL) is a religious base pro-life organization. The executive director of PPL is Marie Bowen. PPL is not part of the structure of the Presbyterian Church (U.S.A.), though it is made up of members and pastors of the Presbyterian Church (U.S.A.). PPL is committed to strengthening the bonds of family love and nurture, and to protecting all human life from conception to natural death. The organization offers a variety of written resources to the broader Christian community to help Christians approach matters of life and sexuality from the perspective of biblical faith. Some of the work done by PPL includes: (1) equipping and informing local Presbyterians about abortion and other life issues through study groups and workshops; (2) sponsoring meetings to educate and help build the pro-life constituency in the denomination; (3) encourage Presbyterians to support and become involved in ministries that provide alternatives to abortion, and follow-up for women who have had abortions and regret their decision; (4) support churches that become Resource Centers for Alternatives to Abortion; (5) encourage local churches to take a pro-life position on abortion; (6) develop initiatives for change in the denomination's position on abortion; and (7) support and encourage biblical sexuality, particularly in instructional materials for children and youth. *See also* **Pro-Life Organizations**

Presentation and Position of the Fetus

The presentation and position of a fetus affect how the fetus will pass through the vagina for delivery. An incorrect presentation or positioning of the fetus can require greater time for delivery and pose more difficulties in obtaining a safe delivery for both the fetus and woman.

(1) Presentation. Presentation refers to how the fetus is situated in the uterus. The part of the fetus that is closest to the cervix is called the presenting part. There are a few different types of presentation.

(i) *Vertex or cephalic presentation.* This is the most common and safest birth presentation. It is where the crown of the fetus' head is the presenting part.

(ii) *Transverse lie or shoulder presentation.* This presentation always requires a caesarean section for delivery. It involves a shoulder as the presenting part.

(iii) *Breech presentation.* A breech presentation occurs when the fetus' buttocks is the presenting part. About 4 percent of all deliveries involve breech presentation. This presentation often involves a longer labor, because the buttocks does not as easily open the cervix. Caesarean section is the most common method for delivery in breech presentation.

There are several types of breech presentations, which include: complete breech (legs crossed); frank breech (legs straight up); footing breech (one or both feet presenting); incomplete breech (one or both legs pointing down); and knee breech (knee presents before the foot).

(2) Position. The position of the fetus refers to the direction that the fetus is facing. Usually the fetus' position is anterior, with the back of the head touching the abdomen wall. Occasionally a fetus will be in a posterior position, with the back of the head against the spine. *See also* **Caesarean Section; Childbirth and Labor**

Pre-Term Pregnancy

Pre-term pregnancy (premature birth) occurs when a child is delivered during a gestation period of less than thirty-eight weeks. Premature delivery usually poses very little risk to the mother, but generally does pose a risk to the infant. A pre-term baby is likely to require assistance with breathing, eating and keeping warm; is more likely to die within a year; and may have serious health problems and disabilities related to incomplete development. Pre-term infants may suffer from respiratory distress, brain hemorrhage, abnormal blood conditions, congenital defects, or underdeveloped internal organs. These conditions may result in death in some babies. Pre-term births account for roughly 75 percent of newborn deaths that are not associated with birth defects.

About 40 percent of all pre-term births occur for unknown reasons. Some of the known reasons include: preeclampsia, separation of

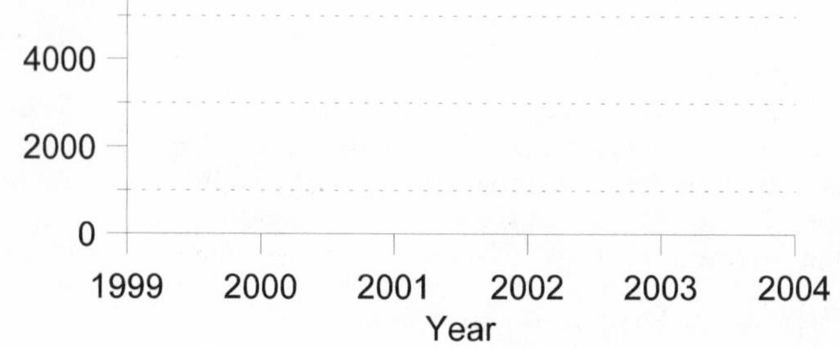

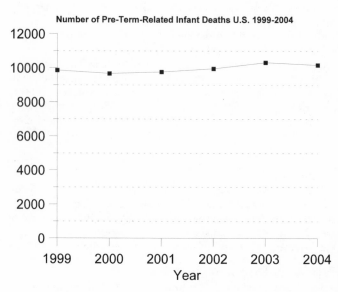

Source: **Centers for Disease Control and Prevention.**

the placenta from the uterine wall, premature rupture of the infant's sac, kidney infection, diabetes, heart disease, excess amniotic fluid, and uterine infection.

In many instances it may be possible to prevent a pre-term birth by knowing the warning signs of premature labor, and seeking immediate care if these warning signs should occur. Some of the warning signs of pre-term birth include: (1) uterine contractions that happen every ten minutes or more often; (2) menstrual-like cramps in lower abdomen; (3) backache felt below the waistline; (4) pelvic pressure that feels like the fetus is pushing down; (5) abdominal cramping; and (6) changes in vaginal discharge. *See also* **Gestational Age; Post-Term Pregnancy; Premature Labor; Prior Abortion and Future Pregnancy**

Priests for Life

Priests for Life is a Catholic pro-life organization that was formed in 1991 by Father Lee Kaylor, a priest of the Archdiocese of San Francisco. Father Frank Pavone of the New York Archdiocese is the national director of the organization. The organization was formed in order to encourage priests to preach and teach on the sanctity of life. The mission statement of Priests for Life identifies three ways in which its overall goal may be achieved. First, networking of priests to exchange ideas, resources and experiences concerning effective pro-life ministry. Second, assisting priests who may be hesitant about addressing the abortion issue. This is accomplished by means of literature, tapes, seminars and direct personal assistance. The third aspect of the mission statement is to help priests to relate to pro-life organizations, and vice versa. *See also* **Pro-Life Organizations**

Prior Abortion and Future Pregnancy

In a study published in 2007, researchers reported that the odds of a pregnant woman having a low birthweight infant or giving birth prematurely was directly related to the number of prior abortions she had experienced. The study suggested that a woman having one, two, or three prior abortions was almost three, five, and nine times as likely to give birth to a low birthweight infant. Further, the study revealed that a woman who had one or two abortions was 67% more likely to have a premature birth; while a woman who had three or more abortions was three times as likely to have a premature birth. *See also* **Low Birthweight; Pre-Term Pregnancy**

Prison *see* **Incarcerated Pregnant Women**

Pro-Choice

Pro-choice is a term of art used to refer to individuals and organizations that favor or support the legal right of females to choose whether or not to continue a pregnancy to term. *See also* **Pro-Choice Organizations**

Pro-Choice Network of Western New York

Pro-Choice Network of Western New York was created in 1988, in Buffalo, New York in response to a pro-life blockade that closed a local women's clinic for two days. The organization believes that reproductive choices should not be denied by the government or through violence, intimidation and misinformation. In keeping with this belief, the organization is dedicated to keeping the choice for abortion and all other reproductive rights safe, legal and accessible for every woman. The organization makes available an escort service to abortion clinics. *See also* **Pro-Choice Organizations**

Pro-Choice Organizations

There are two basic types of pro-choice organizations in the United States: groups created specifically to advance reproductive rights, and groups that make advancement of reproductive rights an aspect of their overall larger purpose. The history of pro-choice activity dates back to the 19th century and involved advocating the use of contraceptives. This initial beginning involved individuals and not organizations.

Pro-choice organizational activity began in earnest with the work of Margaret Sanger, when she founded Planned Parenthood Federation of America in 1916. Organizational activities by the early pro-choice groups were confined to promoting the use of contraceptives, which had been banned by the federal government and states. Pro-choice organizational activities supporting legalization of abortion did not become meaningful until the 1960s. By the time the United States Supreme Court permitted abortion in the nation in 1973, pro-choice abortion organizations were already firmly rooted in several states that had allowed abortions under limited circumstances in the late 1960s. After 1973 hundreds of pro-choice organizations formed around the country to promote and protect women's right to abortion. In addition, thousands of organizations that promoted other social causes appended the right of abortion as an issue to protect.

Pro-choice advocates believe that women and pregnant teenagers should be allowed to have abortions prior to fetal viability without requiring any stated reason. Most pro-choice advocates agree that once fetal viability is present, abortion should be restricted to situations like incest, rape, saving the mothers life or severe fetal birth defects. Pro-choice advocates also take the position that abortion should be funded by governments to aid the poor, and should be made a part of employment health care insurance plans. *See also* **Abortion Access Project; Abortion Clinics OnLine; ACCESS; Alliance for Reproductive Justice; American Association of University Women; American Civil Liberties Union; American Medical Women's Association; Association of Reproductive Health Professionals; Brooklyn Pro-Choice Network; Catholics for a Free Choice; Center for Reproductive Rights; Choice USA; Civil Liberties and Public Policy Program; Clergy Consultation Service on Abortion; EMILY's List; Feminist Majority Foundation; Family Planning Advocates of New York State; Feminist Women's Health Center; Guttmacher Institute; Indiana Religious Coalition for Reproductive Choice; Juneau Pro-Choice Coalition; Kentucky Religious Coalition for Reproductive Choice; K.U. Pro-Choice Coalition; League of Women Voters of the United States; Life and Liberty for Women; MARAL Pro-Choice Michigan; Medical Students for Choice; Michigan Pro-Choice Network; NARAL Pro-Choice America; NARAL Pro-Choice California; NARAL Pro-Choice Maryland; National Abortion Federation; National Black Women's Health Project; National Coalition of Abortion Providers; National Council of Jewish Women; National Network of Abortion Funds; National Organization for Women; National Partnership for Women & Families; National Women's Health Organization; National Women's Law Center; Native American Women's Health Education Resource Center; New Mexico Religious Coalition for Reproductive Choice; Pathfinder International; Physicians for Reproductive Choice and Health; Planned Parenthood Federation of America; Political Research Associates; Population Council; Power of Choice Project; Pro-Choice Network of Western New York; Pro-Choice Public Education Project; ProChoice Resource Center; ProKanDo; Refuse & Resist; Religious Coalition for Reproductive Choice; Republican Majority for Choice; Unitarian Universalist Association; Voters for Choice; Westchester Coalition for Legal Abortion; WISH List**

Pro-Choice Public Education Project

The Pro-Choice Public Education Project is a collaborative program governed by national pro-choice organizations dedicated to building the next generation of pro-choice leaders and supporters. The Project is aimed at (1) message development and evaluation; (2) media placement; and (3) grassroots outreach to young women. The work carried out by the project includes conducting public opinion research on 16- to 25-year-old young women and using the results of this research to craft innovative messages and strategies to educate women about threats to reproductive rights. The Project also creates advertising to raise young women's public awareness of reproductive rights. *See also* **Pro-Choice Organizations**

ProChoice Resource Center

The ProChoice Resource Center (PCRC) was established in 1991, as an organization designed to provide pro-choice groups with strategies for promoting reproductive freedom and other basic liberties. Headquartered in Port Chester, New York, PCRC provides a variety of resources to grassroots pro-choice groups, such as: training to educate and organize supporters, fundraising, media relations, coalition-building, organizational development, and effective use of technology. *See also* **Pro-Choice Organizations**

Progestasert *see* **Intrauterine Contraceptive Devices**

Progesterone

Progesterone is a female sex hormone that is produced by the ovaries and placenta. This hormone prepares the lining of the uterus (endometrium) for implantation of a fertilized egg and helps maintain the pregnancy. Insufficient levels of progesterone will increase the risk of miscarriage. *See also* **Estrogens; Placental Failure**

ProKanDo

ProKanDo is a Kansas based pro-choice state political action committee that was founded in 2002. The chief executive officer of the organization is Julie Burkhart. ProKanDo supports the freedom of women to make their own choices about fertility, with the support of their physicians, without coercion or fear of prosecution by the government or any individual. The organization was created for the purpose of helping elect pro-choice candidates to all levels of state office. During the state legislative session, ProKanDo lobbies the legislature to support of bills that protect the reproductive rights of women, as well as lobbying to defeat any harmful legislation that would potentially turn back the clock on women's rights. *See also* **Pro-Choice Organizations**

Pro-Life

Pro-life is a term of art used to refer to individuals and organizations that oppose the legal right of females to choose whether or not to continue a pregnancy to term. *See also* **Pro-Life Organizations**

Pro-Life Action League

Pro-Life Action League (PLAL) is a Chicago based anti-abortion organization that was founded in 1980, by Joseph M. Scheidler. PLAL was formed for the purpose of saving lives through direct action. The direct action approach used by PLAL is described in a book, *CLOSED: 99 Ways to Stop Abortion*, written by Scheidler. Activities engaged in by the organization includes sidewalk counseling of women and picketing at abortion clinics. PLAL credits itself with having closed eight abortion clinics in Chicago, and nearly a hundred across the country. The organization conducts seminars, conferences and lectures before student groups, as well as help other anti-abortion activists organize programs and provide direct action training. *See also* **Pro-Life Organizations**

Joseph M. Scheidler, the author of *CLOSED: 99 Ways to Stop Abortion*, founded the Pro-Life Action League in 1980 (Eric Scheidler).

Pro-Life Alliance of Gays and Lesbians

The Pro-Life Alliance of Gays and Lesbians (PLAGL) was founded in 1990 by local groups in Washington D.C., and Minneapolis. The president of PLAGL is Cecilia Brown. PLAGAL seeks to encourage gays and lesbians to participate in the pro-life movement. It has regional groups throughout the country that present educational forums and support programs that serve pregnant women and their children. *See also* **Pro-Life Organizations**

Pro-Life Organizations

Pro-life organizations have their origin in the late 1960s, after a few states began to modify their abortion laws so as to permit abortion under narrow and limited circumstances. One of the first of such organizations was the Minnesota Citizens Concerned for Life, which was founded in 1968.

The real push and perceived need for pro-life organizations began after the United States Supreme Court legalized abortion throughout the nation in 1973, with its decision in *Roe v. Wade*. The *Roe* opinion gave birth to thousands of pro-life organizations all across the nation.

Most pro-life advocates seek the same objective: to ban abortion in the nation under all conditions. A few pro-life advocates would permit abortion if it was necessary to save the life of the mother. Pro-life advocates believe that life begins at conception, i.e., when fertilization of the egg and sperm occurs. Because of this belief, pro-life advocates have sought an amendment to the federal constitution that would recognize and protect human life at conception.

During the early years of the pro-life movement organizations voiced their objections to the *Roe* decision in relatively peaceful ways, such as candlelight vigils, prayers, letter writing campaigns to government officials and peaceful marches. The situation changed drastically in 1987 with the emergence of the militant pro-life organization Operation Rescue and its founder Randall Terry. Terry launched militant and massive abortion clinic blockades, sit-ins and picketing in numerous states. In time, hundreds of pro-life organizations began to mimic Terry's strategy all across the nation. Terry's call for direct confrontation with pro-choice advocates started a waive of arson and bombing attacks on abortion facilities throughout the nation. As a result of this new and intimidating strategy, abortion clinics began to shut down and abortion providers became security conscious.

The need for heightened security at abortion clinics became unquestionably necessary after the March 10, 1993 murder in Florida of Dr. David Gunn, an abortionist, by militant pro-life advocate Michael Griffin. By the end of 1998, militant pro-life advocates had murdered 6 pro-choice victims.

Arson, bombings, murders and physical assaults by militant pro-life advocates led to the enactment of federal and local laws designed to exact heavy criminal sanctions for pro-life conduct that threatened pro-choice advocates. Along with such laws, there came sweeping condemnations of violence by the vast majority of pro-life organizations. However, the few extremists among pro-life organizations did not go away. The militant pro-life faction turned to the Internet as a vehicle for inciting murder and other atrocities, by posting names and personal information on abortionists that were considered necessary casualties in the undeclared war against abortionists. *See also* **40 Days for Life; Advocates for Life Ministries; American Coalition of Life Activists; American Life League; Americans United for Life; Baptists for Life; Berkeley Students for Life; California Pro-Life Council; Catholic Campaign for America; Children of the Rosary; Christian Coalition of America; Christians and Jews for Life; Colorado Right to Life; Concerned Women for America; Duke Students for Life; Eagle**

Forum; Elliot Institute; Family Research Council; Feminists for Life; Florida Right to Life; Focus on the Family; Georgetown University Right to Life; Helpers of God's Precious Infants; Human Life International; Human Life of Washington; Illinois Federation for Right to Life; Illinois State University Collegians for Life; Indiana Right to Life; International Life Services; Iowa Right to Life Committee; Ivy League Coalition for Life; Jews for Life; Kentucky Right to Life Association; LEARN Northeast; Libertarians for Life; Life and Liberty Ministries; Life Dynamics; Life Education Fund of Colorado; Life Enterprises Unlimited; Lutherans for Life; Maine Right to Life Committee; Massachusetts Citizens for Life; Michigan Christians for Life; Minnesota Citizens Concerned for Life; Missionaries to the Preborn; Missouri Right to Life; MIT Pro-Life; National Association of Pro-Life Nurses; National Black Catholic Apostolate for Life; National Coalition for Life and Peace; National Federation of Officers for Life; National Institute of Family and Life Advocates; National Organization of Episcopalians for Life; National Right to Life Committee; Nebraska Right to Life; New Jersey Right to Life; New York State Right to Life Committee; North Carolina Right to Life; Notre Dame Right to Life; Ohio Right to Life; Operation Rescue; Oregon Right to Life; Pennsylvania Pro-Life Federation; People Concerned for the Unborn Child; Pharmacists for Life International; Presbyterians Pro-Life; Priests for Life; Pro-Life Action League; Pro-Life Alliance of Gays and Lesbians; Pro-Life Wisconsin; Purdue Students for Life; Republican National Coalition for Life; Right to Life of Michigan; St. Thomas Students for Human Life; Secretariat for Pro-Life Activities; Stanford Students for Life; Tennessee Right to Life; Texas Right to Life; Vanderbilt Students for Life; Vermont Right to Life Committee; Virginia Society for Human Life; Volunteers for Life; West Virginians for Life; William & Mary Alternatives to Abortion; Xavier University Students for Life

Pro-Life Wisconsin

Pro-Life Wisconsin (PLW) is a pro-life educational and legislative organization that was founded in 1992, and is headquartered in Brookfield, Wisconsin. The director of PLW is Peggy Hamill. PLW was founded for the purpose of restoring and protecting the inalienable right to life for all citizens, whether born or preborn, young, old, disabled or terminally ill. The organization takes the position that the right to life exists at the moment of fertilization and extends until natural death, and that this fact was handed down by God and articulated in the Declaration of Independence. PLW opposes all abortions, euthanasia, assisted suicide and infanticide. PLW represents over 30,000 families across the state of Wisconsin. The organization provides pro-life educational resources to the public, monitors state legislation and has established the "Sharon Schumer Memorial Scholarship" for college-bound students. *See also* **Pro-Life Organizations**

Prosecuting Women for Having Abortion *see* **Criminal Abortions**

Prostaglandin

Prostaglandin is a fatty-acid derivative that is found in almost all tissues in the human body. It is also produced as a drug in a gel or tablet form, that is used to induce labor for delivery or abortion. The usual form of the drug is prostaglandin E2 (known as prostin, dinoprostone, or prepidil) and prostaglandin E1 (known as cytotec or misoprostol). *See also* **Induced Labor; Instillation Methods; Methotrexate Induced Abortion; Mifepristone Induced Abortion**

Proteinuria

Proteinuria is a condition involving protein in the urine. This condition is often considered a warning sign of preeclampsia. If protein is found in the urine of a pregnant woman very early in pregnancy, there is an increased risk of complications such as premature birth. *See also* **Preeclampsia**

Public Health Service Act *see* **Title X of the Public Health Service Act**

Public Resources for Abortions

Immediately following legalization of abortion in the 1973 decision by the United States Supreme Court in *Roe v. Wade*, federal and state public resources (money and facilities) were made available for all legal abortions. The use of public resources was short lived, however, in the wake of subsequent federal and state legislation.

Under federal legislation states cannot allocate federal monies they receive for the purpose of performing abortions, unless it is a therapeutic abortion or the pregnancy resulted from rape or incest. As a consequence of federal restrictions on the use of federal money, the majority of states reacted by passing legislation that prohibited the use of state money and facilities for abortions, except for pregnancies that resulted from rape or incest, or for therapeutic abortions. In 1989 the United States Supreme Court ruled in *Webster v. Reproductive Health Services*, that a Missouri statute which prohibited public employees

States with Statutes That Prohibit the Use of Public Funds for Abortion

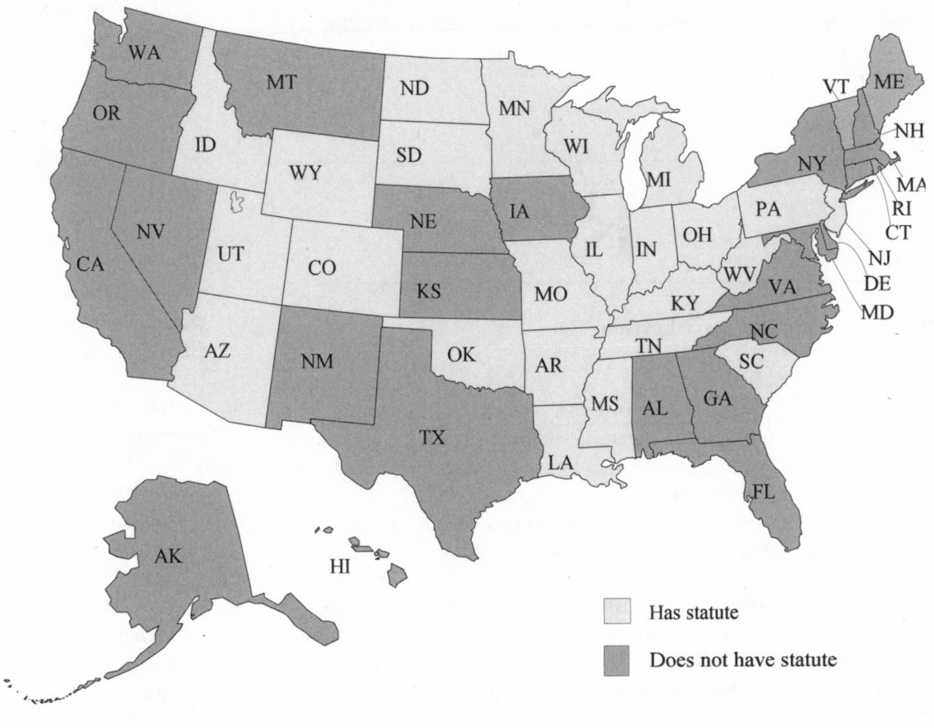

District of Columbia does not have statute.

from performing abortions and banned the use of public facilities for non-therapeutic abortion services, did not violate the federal constitution.

In addition to the restrictions the federal government imposes on states with respect to spending federal funds, federal legislation also prohibits the use of federal funds and facilities for abortions by its employees, including the military, unless it is a therapeutic abortion or a pregnancy that resulted from rape or incest. *See also* **Federal Employees and Abortion; Federal Female Prisoners and Abortion; Helms Amendment; Hyde Amendment; Insurance Coverage for Abortion; Mexico City Policy; Military and Abortion; Native American Women and Abortion Funding; Peace Corps Volunteers and Abortion Funding; Title X of the Public Health Service Act; United States Agency for International Development; Webster v. Reproductive Health Services**

Pulmonary Stenosis *see* **Congenital Heart Defect**

Purdue Students for Life

Purdue Students for Life is a pro-life student-run organization on the campus of Purdue University. The organization's mission is to protect human life from conception to natural death. Activities engaged in by the group include bringing pro-life speakers to the campus, supporting local organizations that aid women in crisis pregnancies, and erecting a Cemetery of the Innocents to commemorate fetal deaths. *See also* **Pro-Life Organizations**

Q

Quickening

Quickening refers to fetal movement felt by a woman. The movement may resemble the feeling of gas bubbles or a light tapping. Quickening is usually discerned around the 20th week of gestation, although it may be recognized by some women several weeks earlier. *See also* **Abortion**

R

Race and Abortion *see* **Abortion**

Red Rose Symbol

Pro-life advocates use the red rose as a symbol to unite around. The red rose has been given the meaning of short life and martyrdom, which is equated with the idea that a fetus is a person who died after a short life. Pro-life advocates annually launch a "Say It with Roses Campaign," and send red roses to government officials as a form of protest. *See also* **Pro-Life Organizations**

Refusal to Perform Abortion

In 1973 Congress passed legislation to prohibit compelling a health care provider (person or facility) to participate in abortions, as well as prohibiting discrimination against health care providers that refuse to participate in abortions. The legislation is based upon refusal of a health care provider to take part in abortions because of religious beliefs or moral convictions. In response to the federal statute, a majority of states enacted laws that permit health care providers to refuse to take part in abortions. In addition, Congress has also passed legislation that prohibits discrimination against institutions that do not provide abortion training to physicians; as well as legislation that does not prohibit or require educational institutions that receive federal funds provide expenditures for abortion services. The federal statutes addressing the issues are set out below.

42 U.S.C.A. § 300a-7.
Right to Refuse to Participate in abortion

(a) Omitted

(b) The receipt of any grant, contract, loan, or loan guarantee under the Public Health Service Act, the Community Mental Health Centers Act, or the Developmental Disabilities Services and Facilities Construction Act by any individual or entity does not authorize any court or any public official or other public authority to require

(1) such individual to perform or assist in the performance of any ... abortion if his performance or assistance in the performance of such ... abortion would be contrary to his religious beliefs or moral convictions; or

(2) such entity to

(A) make its facilities available for the performance of any ... abortion if the performance of such ... abortion in such facilities is prohibited by the entity on the basis of religious beliefs or moral convictions, or

(B) provide any personnel for the performance or assistance in the performance of any ... abortion if the performance or assistance in the performance of such ... abortion by such personnel would be contrary to the religious beliefs or moral convictions of such personnel.

(c)(1) No entity which receives a grant, contract, loan, or loan guarantee under the Public Health Service Act, the Community Mental Health Centers Act, or the Developmental Disabilities Services and Facilities Construction Act after June 18, 1973, may

(A) discriminate in the employment, promotion, or termination of employment of any physician or other health care personnel, or

(B) discriminate in the extension of staff or other privileges to any physician or other health care personnel, because he performed or assisted in the performance of a lawful ... abortion, because he refused to perform or assist in the performance of such ... abortion on the grounds that his performance or assistance in the performance of the ... abortion would be contrary to his religious beliefs or moral convictions, or because of his religious beliefs or moral convictions respecting ... abortions.

(2) No entity which receives after July 12, 1974, a grant or contract for biomedical or behavioral research under any program administered by the Secretary of Health and Human Services may

(A) discriminate in the employment, promotion, or termination of employment of any physician or other health care personnel, or

(B) discriminate in the extension of staff or other privileges to any physician or other health care personnel, because he performed or assisted in the performance of any lawful health service or research activity, because he refused to perform or assist in the performance of any such service or activity on the grounds that his performance or assistance in the performance of such service or activity would be contrary to his religious beliefs or moral convictions, or because of his religious beliefs or moral convictions respecting any such service or activity.

(d) No individual shall be required to perform or assist in the performance of any part of a health service program or research activity

funded in whole or in part under a program administered by the Secretary of Health and Human Services if his performance or assistance in the performance of such part of such program or activity would be contrary to his religious beliefs or moral convictions.

(e) No entity which receives, after September 29, 1979, any grant, contract, loan, loan guarantee, or interest subsidy under the Public Health Service Act, the Community Mental Health Centers Act, or the Developmental Disabilities Assistance and Bill of Rights Act may deny admission or otherwise discriminate against any applicant (including applicants for internships and residencies) for training or study because of the applicant's reluctance, or willingness, to counsel, suggest, recommend, assist, or in any way participate in the performance of abortions ... contrary to or consistent with the applicant's religious beliefs or moral convictions.

STATES WITH STATUTES THAT PERMIT MEDICAL FACILITIES AND PERSONNEL TO REFUSE TO PARTICIPATE IN ABORTIONS

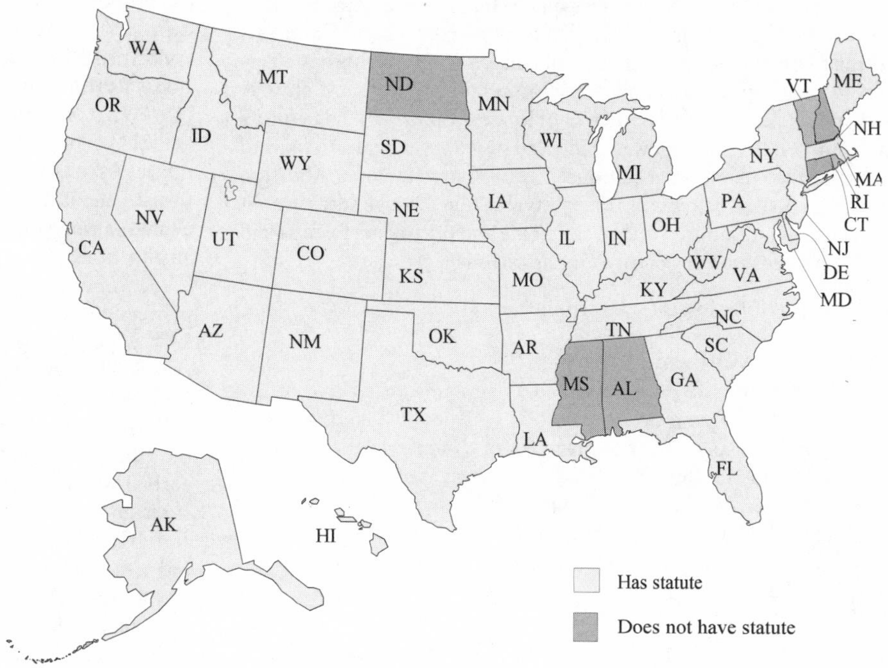

*District of Columbia does not have statute.

42 U.S.C.A. § 238n.
Abortion discrimination
regarding training physicians

(a) In general

The Federal Government, and any State or local government that receives Federal financial assistance, may not subject any health care entity to discrimination on the basis that—

(1) the entity refuses to undergo training in the performance of induced abortions, to require or provide such training, to perform such abortions, or to provide referrals for such training or such abortions;

(2) the entity refuses to make arrangements for any of the activities specified in paragraph (1); or

(3) the entity attends (or attended) a post-graduate physician training program, or any other program of training in the health professions, that does not (or did not) perform induced abortions or require, provide or refer for training in the performance of induced abortions, or make arrangements for the provision of such training.

(b) Accreditation of postgraduate physician training programs

(1) In general

In determining whether to grant a legal status to a health care entity (including a license or certificate), or to provide such entity with financial assistance, services or other benefits, the Federal Government, or any State or local government that receives Federal financial assistance, shall deem accredited any postgraduate physician training program that would be accredited but for the accrediting agency's reliance upon an accreditation standards that requires an entity to perform an induced abortion or require, provide, or refer for training in the performance of induced abortions, or make arrangements for such training, regardless of whether such standard provides exceptions or exemptions. The government involved shall formulate such regulations or other mechanisms, or enter into such agreements with accrediting agencies, as are necessary to comply with this subsection.

(2) Rules of construction

(A) In general

With respect to subclauses (I) and (II) of section 292d(a)(2)(B)(i) of this title (relating to a program of insured loans for training in the health professions), the requirements in such subclauses regarding accredited internship or residency programs are subject to paragraph (1) of this subsection.

(B) Exceptions

This section shall not—

(i) prevent any health care entity from voluntarily electing to be trained, to train, or to arrange for training in the performance of, to perform, or to make referrals for induced abortions; or

(ii) prevent an accrediting agency or a Federal, State or local government from establishing standards of medical competency applicable only to those individuals who have voluntarily elected to perform abortions.

(c) Definitions

For purposes of this section:

(1) The term "financial assistance," with respect to a government program, includes governmental payments provided as reimbursement for carrying out health-related activities.

(2) The term "health care entity" includes an individual physician, a postgraduate physician training program, and a participant in a program of training in the health professions.

(3) The term "postgraduate physician training program" includes a residency training program.

20 U.S.C.A. § 1688. Neutrality with respect to abortion

Nothing in this chapter shall be construed to require or prohibit any person, or public or private entity, to provide or pay for any benefit or service, including the use of facilities, related to an abortion. Nothing in this section shall be construed to permit a penalty to be imposed on any person or individual because such person or individual is seeking or has received any benefit or service related to a legal abortion.

See also **Title X of the Public Health Service Act**

Refuse & Resist

Refuse & Resist is an organization that was formed in 1987 by artists, lawyers and activists. The organization was formed in response to a perceived shift in governmental policy toward repression of nonconformist political, social and cultural behavior. The group has chapters in many large and small cities throughout the nation. Refuse & Resist has taken a position in favor of legalized abortion. The group's commitment to abortion was evidenced in 1996 when it initiated and organized the first annual National Day of Appreciation for Abortion Providers. Refuse & Resist also supports abortion through speaking out in schools, communities and in the media and organizing forums and meetings. *See also* **Pro-Choice Organizations**

Regulating Abortion *see* **Abortion**

Rehnquist, William Hubbs

William Hubbs Rehnquist served as an associate justice of the United States Supreme Court from 1971 to 1986. In 1986 he was appointed chief justice of the Supreme Court. While on the Supreme Court Chief Justice Rehnquist has been known as an ultra conservative in his interpretation of the Constitution.

Chief Justice Rehnquist was born on October 1, 1924, in Milwaukee, Wisconsin. In 1952 he graduated from Stanford University Law School. In 1953 he began the private practice of law. In 1969 he took a position as an attorney with the Department of Justice. President Richard M. Nixon appointed Chief Justice Rehnquist to the United States Supreme Court as an associate justice in 1971. President Ronald Reagan elevated him to the position of Chief Justice of the Supreme Court in 1986. Chief Justice Rehnquist died while in office on September 3, 2005.

During Chief Justice Rehnquist's tenure on the Supreme Court he has issued a significant number of abortion related opinions (both as chief justice and associate justice). The written opinions and opinions simply voted on by him, indicate that he is not in favor of using the constitution to expand abortion rights for women.

(1) Unanimous opinions written. Chief Justice Rehnquist wrote the opinion for a unanimous Supreme Court in *National Organization for Women, Inc. v. Scheidler*, which held that a group of pro-choice organizations could maintain a RICO civil lawsuit against several anti-abortion individuals and groups.

(2) Unanimous opinions voted with only. In *Dalton v. Little Rock Family Planning Services*, Chief Justice Rehnquist voted with a unanimous Court in holding that an amendment to Arkansas' constitution which limited Medicaid payment only to therapeutic abortions, was invalid to the extent that Medicaid funds had to be made available for incest or rape pregnancies, but was valid for any purely state funded program. In *Bellotti v. Baird I* Justice Rehnquist voted with a unanimous opinion, which held that the federal district court had to certify appropriate questions to the supreme judicial court of Massachusetts, concerning the interpretation of that state's parental consent abortion statute for minors, before ruling on its constitutionality. In *Withrow v. Larkin* Justice Rehnquist joined a unanimous opinion, which held that constitutional due process was not violated by the mere fact that a Wisconsin medical examining board had the authority to both, investigate and adjudicate, allegations against a physician that included, among other things, permitting a nonphysician to perform an abortion.

(3) Majority opinions written. Chief Justice Rehnquist wrote the majority opinion in *Schenck v. Pro Choice Network of Western New York*, which held that a federal trial court's injunction provisions imposing fixed buffer zone limitations on abortion protesters were constitutional, but the provisions imposing floating buffer zone limitations violated the First Amendment. In *Madsen v. Women's Health Clinic, Inc.* Chief Justice Rehnquist wrote the majority opinion, which upheld parts of an injunction that restricted noise by anti-abortionists at a clinic and imposed a 36 foot buffer zone around the clinic entrances and driveway. However, *Madsen* ruled that the Free Speech Clause was violated by a 36 foot buffer zone as applied to the private property to the north and west of the clinic, a restriction on the use of images observable by clinic patients, a 300 foot no approach zone around the clinic, and a 300 foot buffer zone around the residences, because these restrictions swept more broadly than necessary to accomplish the permissible goals of the injunction. Chief Justice Rehnquist wrote the majority opinion in *Rust v. Sullivan*, which upheld federal regulations that prohibited pro-abortion counseling, referral, and advocacy by health care providers. Chief Justice Rehnquist wrote the majority opinion in *Scheidler v. National Organization for Women, Inc. (I)*, which held that evidence did not support finding that pro-life advocates violated the Hobbs Act, Travel Act and state law extortion crimes, for the purpose of awarding damages and granting an injunction against them under RICO.

(4) Majority opinions voted with only. Chief Justice Rehnquist voted with the majority in *Leavitt v. Jane L.*, which held that the invalidity of Utah's statute regulating pregnancies 20 weeks old or less, may be severed so as to preserve that portion of the abortion statute that regulated pregnancies of more than 20 weeks. In *Lambert v. Wicklund* Chief Justice Rehnquist voted with the majority in holding that the constitution was not violated by a provision in Montana's abortion statute that allowed a court to waive the parental notice requirement for minors, if notification was not in minor's best interest. Chief Justice Rehnquist joined the majority opinion in *Mazurek v. Armstrong*, which held that Montana's requirement that abortions be performed only by physicians was constitutionally valid. In *Hill v. Colorado* Chief Justice Rehnquist voted with the majority in upholding a Colorado statute that made it unlawful for any person within 100 feet of an abortion facility's entrance, to knowingly approach within 8 feet of another person, without that person's consent, in order to pass a leaflet, handbill, display a sign, engage in oral protest, education, or counseling with that person.

Chief Justice Rehnquist voted with the majority opinion in *Bray v. Alexandria Clinic*, which held that the Civil Rights Act of 1871, 42 U.S.C. § 1985(3), did not provide a cause of action against persons obstructing access to abortion clinics. In *Ohio v. Akron Center for Reproductive Health* Chief Justice Rehnquist voted with the majority opinion, which upheld the constitutionality of Ohio's abortion statute notice and judicial bypass requirements for pregnant female minors. In *Frisby v. Schultz* Chief Justice Rehnquist voted with the majority opinion, which upheld the constitutional validity of a town ordinance

Distribution of the Abortion Voting Pattern of Justice/Chief Justice Rehnquist Based Upon Opinions Filed by the Supreme Court

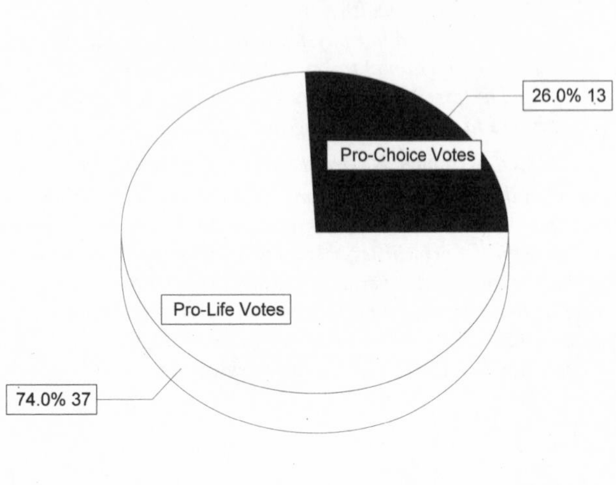

that was created to prevent pro-life picketing at the residence of an abortion doctor. Chief Justice Rehnquist voted with the majority opinion in *United States Catholic Conference v. Abortion Rights Mobilization*, which allowed the appellants to challenge having to turn over documents in a lawsuit seeking to strip them of their tax exempt status because of their active political abortion work.

In *Diamond v. Charles*, Justice Rehnquist joined the judgment of the Court, which held that a citizen did not have standing to appeal a decision invalidating parts of Illinois' abortion statute that (1) imposed criminal penalties for violating a prescribed standard of care that had to be exercised by a physician in performing an abortion of a viable fetus, and of a possibly viable fetus; and (2) imposed criminal penalties for physicians who failed to provide patients with information about the type of abortifacient used. In *H. L. v. Matheson* Justice Rehnquist joined the majority opinion, which held that the constitution was not violated by Utah's requirement that the parents of a minor be notified, if possible, prior to performing an abortion. Justice Rehnquist joined the majority opinion in *Harris v. McRae*, which held that Medicaid funding restrictions for abortion by the Hyde Amendment, did not violate the Due Process Clause nor the equal protection component of the Fifth Amendment. In *Williams v. Zbaraz* Justice Rehnquist voted with the majority opinion, which held that in light of the requirements of the Hyde Amendment, the Equal Protection Clause of the Fourteenth Amendment was not violated by an Illinois statute that prohibited state Medicaid payment for abortions, except when necessary to save the life of the pregnant woman.

Justice Rehnquist joined the majority opinion in *Beal v. Doe*, which held that Pennsylvania's refusal to extend Medicaid coverage to nontherapeutic abortions was not invalid nor inconsistent with Title XIX of the Social Security Act. In *Maher v. Roe* Justice Rehnquist joined the majority opinion, which held that the Equal Protection Clause of the Fourteenth Amendment did not prohibit Connecticut from excluding nontherapeutic abortions from its Medicaid program. Justice Rehnquist joined the per curiam opinion in *Poelker v. Doe*, which held that the Equal Protection Clause of the Fourteenth Amendment was not violated by a policy of the city of St. Louis, Missouri that denied publicly funded abortions to indigent women at city hospitals, except when a woman's health or life was in danger. In *Connecticut v. Menillo* Justice Rehnquist joined the majority per curiam opinion, which held that the constitution was not violated by criminal abortion statutes that prohibit nonphysicians from attempting or performing abortions at any stage of a pregnancy. Justice Rehnquist joined the majority opinion in *Anders v. Floyd*, which held that a federal district court erred in enjoining enforcement of a South Carolina statute that imposed criminal punishment for performing an abortion on a viable fetus.

Justice Rehnquist voted with the majority opinion in *Burns v. Alcala*, which held that states receiving federal financial aid under the program of Aid to Families with Dependent Children, were not required to offer welfare benefits to pregnant women for their unborn children. Justice Rehnquist voted with the majority opinion in *Geduldig v. Aiello*, which held that the Equal Protection Clause of the Fourteenth Amendment did not require a private sector employee disability insurance program, operated by the state of California, provide coverage for employee disabilities associated with normal pregnancies. In *Weinberger v. Hynson, Westcott & Dunning* Justice Rehnquist joined the majority opinion, which held that the Food and Drug Administration could not deny a drug manufacturer a hearing to obtain marketing approval for a drug called Lutrexin, which provided treatment for premature labor and threatened and habitual abortion. Chief Justice Rehnquist voted with the majority in *Federal Election Commission v. Beaumont*, which held that the Federal Election Campaign Act's prohibition on corporate expenditures and contributions directly to candidates in federal elections, applies to a nonprofit pro-life organization.

(5) Plurality opinions written. Chief Justice Rehnquist wrote a majority/plurality opinion in *Webster v. Reproductive Health Services*, which upheld Missouri's prohibition on the use of public facilities or employees to perform abortions and a requirement that physicians conduct viability tests prior to performing abortions.

(6) Concurring opinions written. Justice Rehnquist wrote a concurring opinion in *Bolger v. Youngs Drug Products Corp.*, which held that a provision of the Comstock Act, 39 U.S.C. § 3001(e)(2), that prohibited mailing unsolicited advertisements for contraceptives violated the Free Speech Clause of the First Amendment. Justice Rehnquist wrote an opinion concurring in the majority judgment in *Bellotti v. Baird II*, which held that Massachusetts' abortion statute for minors violated the constitution in light of an interpretation given by the state's highest court, that required parental notice of a judicial bypass proceeding invoked by a minor, and permitted a judge to deny an abortion even though the minor proved she had enough maturity to make an independent decision.

(7) Concurring opinions voted with only. In *Automobile Workers v. Johnson Controls, Inc.* Chief Justice Rehnquist voted to concur in the majority opinion, which held that Title VII of the Civil Rights Act forbids sex-specific fetal-protection policies by an employer, that exclude a fertile female employee from certain jobs because of the employer's concern for the health of the fetus the woman might conceive. Justice Rehnquist voted to concur with the majority opinion in *Simopoulos v. Virginia*, which upheld a Virginia statute requiring second trimester abortions be performed at hospitals, because under the statute an adequately equipped clinic could, upon proper application, obtain an outpatient hospital license that permitted the performance of second-trimester abortions.

(8) Dissenting opinions written. Chief Justice Rehnquist dissented in the case of *Ferguson v. City of Charleston*, which held that patient consent or a search warrant was needed in order for a government hospital to turn over to the police drug test results that showed a woman used illegal drugs during her pregnancy. In *Stenberg v. Carhart*, Chief Justice Rehnquist wrote a dissenting opinion opposing the majority's decision to find Nebraska's statute banning partial-birth abortion unconstitutional.

In *Carey v. Population Services International* Justice Rehnquist wrote an opinion dissenting from the majority decision, which held that the constitution prohibited enforcement of a New York statute that made it a crime (1) for any person to sell or distribute any contraceptive of any kind to a minor under the age of 16 years; (2) for anyone other than a licensed pharmacist to distribute contraceptives to persons 16 or over; and (3) for anyone, including licensed pharmacists, to advertise or display contraceptives. He believed the statute passed constitutional muster. Justice Rehnquist wrote an opinion dissenting from the majority decision in *Bigelow v. Virginia*, which held that the Free Speech and Free Press Clauses of the First Amendment were violated by a Virginia penal statute that prohibited selling or circulating any publication that encouraged or promoted abortions. He believed the statute passed constitutional muster.

In *Roe v. Wade* Justice Rehnquist wrote an opinion dissenting from the majority decision, which held that the liberty component of the Due Process Clause of the Fourteenth Amendment prohibited states from criminalizing or preventing elective first trimester abortions. He did not believe that the constitution prohibited states from criminalizing abortion. Justice Rehnquist wrote an opinion dissenting from the majority decision in *Doe v. Bolton*, which held that the Due Process Clause of the Fourteenth Amendment was violated by provisions in Georgia's abortion statutes that required (1) abortions take place in accredited hospitals, (2) that an abortion be approved by a hospital abortion committee, (3) that the need for an abortion be confirmed by two independent physicians, and (4) that a woman seeking an abortion be a resident of Georgia. He believed the provisions passed constitutional muster.

(9) Dissenting opinions voted with only. Justice Rehnquist voted to dissent in *Thornburgh v. American College of Obstetricians and Gynecologists,* which invalidated provisions in Pennsylvania's abortion statute that provided for maternal informed consent, abortion alternative printed information, abortion reporting requirements, determination of fetal viability, degree of care required in post-via--bility abortions, and a second-physician requirement. Justice Rehnquist dissented from the majority opinion in *City of Akron v. Akron Center for Reproductive Health, Inc.*, which invalidated an abortion ordinance that provided requirements for parental consent, informed consent, waiting period, hospitalization and disposal of fetal remains.

In *Colautti v. Franklin* Justice Rehnquist dissented from the majority decision, which held that the constitution was violated by a vague and ambiguous provision in Pennsylvania's abortion statute that subjected a physician who performed an abortion to potential criminal liability, if he/she failed to utilize a statutorily prescribed technique when the fetus was viable or when there was sufficient reason to believe that the fetus may be viable. He believed the provision was constitutionally valid.

(10) Concurring and dissenting opinions written. In *Daubert v. Merrell Dow Pharmaceuticals, Inc.*, a case involving children born with severe birth defects, Chief Justice Rehnquist wrote a concurring and dissenting opinion. He agreed with the majority that the *Frye* rule on admissibility of expert testimony did not survive the enactment of the Federal Rules of Evidence, but disagreed with discussion in the opinion that went beyond the narrow issue of admissibility of expert testimony. In *Planned Parenthood of Southeastern Pennsylvania v. Casey,* Chief Justice Rehnquist wrote a concurring and dissenting opinion. He concurred in the majority's decision that the constitution was not violated by provisions in Pennsylvania's abortion statute that provided for: medical emergency abortion; 24 hour waiting period for abortion; parental notice and judicial bypass for abortion by a minor; and certain abortion facility reporting requirements. He dissented from the majority's decision that found two provisions in the abortion statute unconstitutional: spousal notification before obtaining an abortion, and a requirement that a woman inform the abortion provider the reason for not notifying her spouse.

In *Federal Election Commission v. Massachusetts Citizens for Life, Inc.* Chief Justice Rehnquist wrote an opinion concurring and dissenting from the majority decision, which held that federal law that prohibited the appellee from using its treasury funds to promote pro-life political candidates violated the Free Speech Clause of the First Amendment. Chief Justice Rehnquist agreed with the majority that the law applied to the appellee, but dissented from the decision to find the law unconstitutional.

(11) Concurring and dissenting opinions voted with only. Chief Justice Rehnquist voted to concur and dissent in *Hodgson v. Minnesota,* which upheld the constitutionality of Minnesota's requirement that a pregnant female minor could not obtain an abortion until at least 48 hours after both of her parents had been notified, except when (1) the attending physician certified that an immediate abortion was necessary to prevent the minor's death; (2) the minor declared that she was a victim of parental abuse or neglect; or (3) a court of competent jurisdiction ordered the abortion to proceed without notice upon proof that the minor was mature and capable of giving informed consent or that an abortion without notice to both parents would be in the minor's best interest. Chief Justice Rehnquist dissented from the Court's determination that the two-parent notification requirement was invalid, but concurred in the determination that the judicial bypass option cured the defect.

In *Planned Parenthood Assn. v. Ashcroft* Justice Rehnquist concurred and dissented from the majority/plurality opinion, which held that the constitution was violated by Missouri's requirement that second trimester abortions take place in a hospital; but that the constitution was not violated by the state's requirement that a pathology report for each abortion be performed, that a second physician be present during abortions performed after viability, and parental or judicial consent for abortion by minors. Justice Rehnquist believed that all of the provisions of the statute were constitutional.

Justice Rehnquist voted to concur and dissent from the majority decision in *Planned Parenthood of Missouri v. Danforth,* which held that the constitution was not violated by provisions in Missouri's abortion statute involving the definition of fetal viability, woman's written consent, and record keeping and reporting requirements; but that the constitution prohibited the requirements concerning spousal consent, parental consent for minor, banning saline amniocentesis abortions, and physician's standard of care. Justice Rehnquist believed that all of the provisions of the statute were constitutionally valid.

Justice Rehnquist voted to concur and dissent in *Singleton v. Wulff,* which held that the Eighth Circuit court of appeals had jurisdiction to determine whether abortion providers had standing to challenge a provision in Missouri's abortion statute that limited Medicaid payment for abortions, but it did not have jurisdiction to rule that the provision violated the constitution because the district court did not address the issue. He dissented from language in the plurality opinion that indicated the abortion providers could assert on remand, in addition to their own rights, the constitutional rights of their patients who would be eligible for Medicaid assistance in obtaining elective abortions.

Religion and Abortion

In a 1998 national survey of Protestant and Jewish clergy over 80 percent supported a woman's right to a safe and legal abortion. This finding is consistent with research which has shown that non–Catholic religious leaders played a critical role in helping to bring about the climate in the United States that led to legalization of abortion throughout the nation in 1973. Much of the early history of religious leaders who were tolerant with abortion is lost, because that history represented individual acts of guidance to women in need during a period when abortion was illegal. A rich and active history of the acts of religious leaders who were tolerant toward abortion began in the 1960s. It was in 1967 that 26 religious leaders in New York decided to organize for the purpose of steering pregnant women to safe places for abortions. The religious leaders called their organization Clergy Consultation Service on Abortion. Shortly after this organization was started, religious leaders across the nation began to collectively assist women who sought abortions.

The Unitarian Universalist Association publicly supported a woman's right to choose in 1963 and has maintained its position. The Protestant denominations maintained a consistent pro-choice position since 1970. During the 1992 General Conference of The United Methodist Church, an overwhelming majority of religious leaders affirmed a woman's right to choose. In 1993, the General Assembly of the Presbyterian Church (USA) reaffirmed its support for legal abortion. The General Convention of the Episcopal Church adopted a resolution in 1994 that expressed opposition to any laws that would abridge the right of a woman to reach an informed decision about the termination of pregnancy. While there is no uniformity in Judaism on elective abortions, therapeutic abortion has historically been mandatory in Judaism. The United Synagogue of Conservative Judaism has strongly supported abortion. The Central Conference of

American Rabbis, as well as the Union of American Hebrew Congregations have formally supported a woman's right to choose. Orthodox women must consult their rabbis on the question of abortion.

Catholicism and abortion. The Catholic Church has had an inconsistent history with abortion. St. Augustine (A.D. 354–430) set out principles which sanctioned abortion up to 80 days for a female fetus and up to 40 days for a male fetus. In the 13th century, Pope Innocent III wrote that abortion was not a homicide prior to "quickening." In 1588 Pope Sixtus prohibited all abortions. However, in 1591 Pope Gregory XIV rescinded the anti-abortion edict by Pope Sixtus. The position of Pope Gregory XIV held firm in the Catholic Church until 1869, when Pope Pius IX prohibited all abortions. The position taken by Pope Pius IX is the official position of the Catholic Church today.

While the Catholic Church prohibits abortion under all circumstances, the majority of Catholic laity in the United States disagree with that position. Studies have shown that Catholic women have abortions at the same rate as women in the population as a whole. In a national survey, 82 percent of Catholic laity indicated that abortion should be legal, at least in some situations. *See also* **40 Days for Life; Advocates for Life Ministries; Baptists for Life; Catholic Campaign for America; Catholics for a Free Choice; Children of the Rosary; Christian Coalition of America; Christians and Jews for Life; Clergy Consultation Service on Abortion; Encyclical Evangelium Vitae; Encyclical Humanae Vitae; Helpers of God's Precious Infants; Indiana Religious Coalition for Reproductive Choice; Jews for Life; Kentucky Religious Coalition for Reproductive Choice; LEARN Northeast; Life and Liberty Ministries; Lutherans for Life; Michigan Christians for Life; Missionaries to the Preborn; National Black Catholic Apostolate for Life; National Organization of Episcopalians for Life; New Mexico Religious Coalition for Reproductive Choice; Presbyterians Pro-Life; Priests for Life; Religious Coalition for Reproductive Choice; Secretariat for Pro-Life Activities; Unitarian Universalist Association**

Religious Coalition for Reproductive Choice

The Religious Coalition for Reproductive Choice (RCRC) was founded in 1973, in response to efforts to overturn the United States Supreme Court decision legalizing abortion in *Roe v. Wade.* RCRC is headquartered in Washington, D.C. The president of RCRC is Reverend Carlton W. Veazey. RCRC is comprised of more than 40 national religious organizations and 22 state affiliates. Some of the religious institutions include the Episcopal Church, Presbyterian Church (USA), United Church of Christ, United Methodist Church, Unitarian Universalist Association, and the Conservative, Humanist, Reconstructionist, and Reform movements of Judaism.

The Rev. Carlton W. Veazey is president of Religious Coalition for Reproductive Choice, an organization founded in 1973 in response to efforts to overturn the United States Supreme Court decision legalizing abortion in *Roe v. Wade* (Carlton W. Veazey).

RCRC is united in a commitment to preserve reproductive choice as an element of religious liberty. The organization maintains high respect for the value of potential human life, but remains committed to women as responsible, moral decision makers. RCRC opposes any attempt to enact secular laws that impose restrictions on reproductive choice. It provides educational materials in support of full reproductive health care, including comprehensive sexuality education, family planning, contraception, teen pregnancy prevention, and abortion. RCRC also seeks to articulate various religious foundations of pro-choice views; provide opportunities for religious people to examine and articulate their own pro-choice positions; increase the visibility and voice of religious pro-choice people through exposure in denominational and other religious media; and generate public responses to anti-choice activities and violence conducted in the name of religion. *See also* **Pro-Choice Organizations; Religion and Abortion**

Renaerts, Ximena

Ximena Renaerts' mother, Nadine Bourne, traveled to an abortion clinic in Bellingham, Washington on December 12, 1985 to abort her. When her mother returned home in Vancouver, Canada, she became ill and went to a hospital on December 16. While at the hospital medical personnel removed what they thought were the remains of a successful abortion. However, the fetus that was expelled on December 17 was alive. After some hesitation, the fetus was treated and Renaerts' life was saved. The abortion attempt and delayed medical care left Renaerts with severe mental and physical disabilities. Renaerts was eventually adopted. *See also* **Survivors of Abortion**

Renal Agenesis *see* **Genital and Urinary Tract Birth Defects**

Reporting Requirements *see* **Hospital/Clinic Abortion Requirements; Physician Abortion Requirements**

Reproductive Freedom Project *see* **American Civil Liberties Union**

Republican Majority for Choice

Republican Majority for Choice (RMC) is a Washington, D.C., based organization of Republican men and women who support the protection of reproductive rights, including the full range of reproductive options. The executive director of RMC is Kellie Rose Ferguson. RMC believes that personal and medical decisions are best made between a woman, her doctor and her family and not the government. The organization is actively working with moderate and conservative members of Congress to promote measures that all Republicans can support, such as positive family planning initiatives, instead of pushing irresponsible laws that actually worsen social problems. RMC has expressed concern with the direction of the Republican Party in advocating a social agenda that is both intrusive and alienating. *See also* **Pro-Choice Organizations**

Republican National Coalition for Life

The Republican National Coalition for Life (RNCL) is an Illinois based pro-life organization that was founded in 1990 by Phyllis Schlafly. The executive director of RNCL is Colleen Parro. RNCL was created specifically for the purpose of continuing a pro-life plank in the national Republican Party platform. The organization is active at Republican Party conventions and primaries, and supports delegates to the Republican National Convention who take strong pro-life positions. *See also* **Pro-Life Organizations**

Residency Requirements

In *Doe v. Bolton* the United States Supreme Court struck down a Georgia statute, which had restricted the performance of abortions to residents of the state. *Doe* reasoned that to allow such a restriction would mean that a state could limit to its own residents, the general medical care available within its borders. *See also* **Doe v. Bolton**

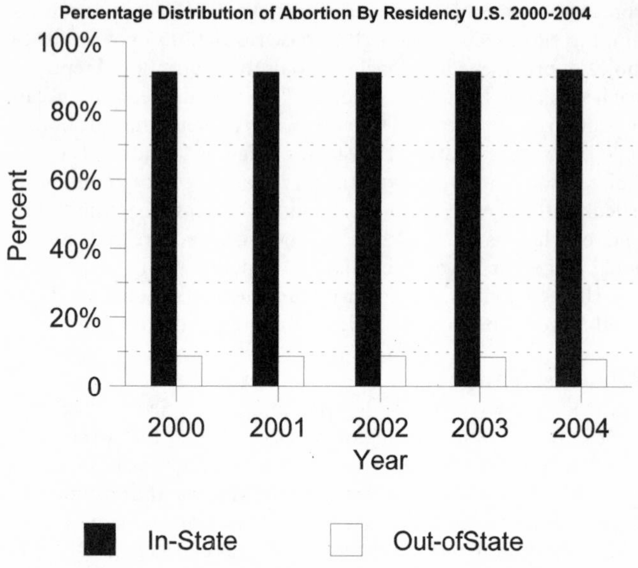

Source: **National Center for Health Statistics.**

Respiratory Distress Syndrome

Respiratory distress syndrome is a condition that usually occurs in premature babies. The syndrome is associated with the lack of a chemical that normally appears in mature lungs (pulmonary surfactant). The absence of the chemical causes a collapse of air sacs and an inability to exchange oxygen and carbon dioxide within the lungs. In some instances long-term complications will develop, such as mental retardation, blindness, and hemorrhage into the lungs or brain. The disease, if severe, will kill. Medical treatment can correct some of the problems associated with the disease. Adequate prenatal care may also help reduce the risk of a child getting the disease. *See also* **Birth Defects and Abortion**

Retained Placenta

Retained placenta refers to a placenta that remained in the womb after birth. Usually a placenta will separate and be expelled from the womb about 30 minutes after delivery. However, when a placenta is retained in the womb and cannot be removed by tugging on the umbilical cord, it must be forced out by manual extraction. *See also* **Placenta**

Retroverted Uterus

A retroverted uterus (also called tipped) refers to a uterus that is tilted toward the bladder or the small of the back. In most women, the uterus is tilted upward and forward. A retroverted uterus occurs in about 20 percent of women. It is usually congenital, but may occur because of labor while giving birth, or a disease or infection. A retroverted uterus usually does not cause any complications in achieving a pregnancy or in carrying a fetus to term. The condition can make it more difficult for monitoring fetal heart tones early in pregnancy. *See also* **Bicornuate Uterus**

Rh Incompatibility

Rh incompatibility occurs when there is a difference in the Rh blood type of the mother (Rh negative) and that of the fetus (Rh positive). This condition can result in anti–Rh positive antibodies forming in the mother's system. The anti–Rh positive antibodies move through the placenta into the fetus and destroy the fetus' red blood cells. In its mildest form, Rh incompatibility may cause the infant to become yellow (jaundiced). In its severest form, Rh incompatibility cause massive fetal red blood cell destruction, which can result in fetal heart failure, total body swelling, respiratory distress and circulatory collapse. This condition often results in death of the infant shortly before or after delivery. Rh incompatibility is almost completely preventable through the use of medications. Proper prenatal care may detect Rh incompatibility and prevent its occurrence. There are about 4,000 infants born each year in the United States with the Rh disease. *See also* **Birth Defects and Abortion**

Rhode Island

(1) OVERVIEW

The state of Rhode Island enacted its first criminal abortion statute in 1896. The statute underwent several amendments prior to the 1973 decision by the United States Supreme Court in *Roe v. Wade*, which legalized abortion in the nation. Rhode Island has taken affirmative steps to respond to *Roe* and its progeny. Abortion is expressly addressed in the state's constitution and the state has addressed several abortion issues by statute that include post-viability abortion ban, informed consent and spousal notice, partial-birth abortion, abortion by minors, right to refuse participation, fetal experimentation and cloning, and health insurance.

(2) STATE CONSTITUTION

Under the equal protection and due process provisions of the Rhode Island's constitution, it is expressly provided that the constitution does not grant a right to abortion or funding. The constitutional provision is set out below.

Rhode Island Const. Art. 1, § 2. No right to abortion granted

All free governments are instituted for the protection, safety, and happiness of the people. All laws, therefore, should be made for the good of

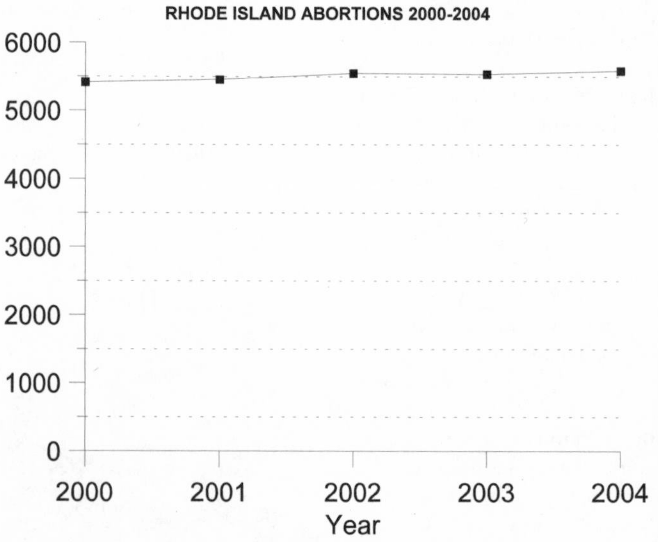

Source: **National Center for Health Statistics.**

Rhode Island Abortion by Age Group 2000–2004

				Age Group (yrs)				
Year	*<15*	*15–19*	*20–24*	*25–29*	*30–34*	*35–39*	*≥40*	*Unknown*
2000	30	939	1,821	1,132	821	470	200	0
2001	26	943	1,935	1,117	796	461	178	0
2002	30	945	1,963	1,182	781	483	163	3
2003	23	966	1,904	1,207	769	488	180	1
2004	25	974	1,838	1,231	773	481	162	103
Total	134	4,767	9,461	5,869	3,940	2,383	883	107

Source: **National Center for Health Statistics.**

Rhode Island Abortion by Weeks of Gestation 2000–2004

Weeks of Gestation	2000	2001	2002	2003	2004	Total
<9	3,596	3,520	3,661	3,701	3,839	18,317
9–10	881	967	895	867	759	4,369
11–12	447	472	397	356	398	2,070
13–15	296	321	356	383	311	1,667
16–20	175	161	219	206	169	930
≥21	8	11	8	12	5	44
Not known	11	3	14	13	106	147

Source: **National Center for Health Statistics.**

Rhode Island Prior Abortion by Female 2000–2004

Year	None	1	2	≥3	Not known
2000	3,047	1,442	530	371	23
2001	2,977	1,468	589	386	35
2002	3,001	1,450	660	416	23
2003	2,966	1,507	609	428	28
2004	2,936	1,506	649	417	79
Total	14,927	7,373	3,037	2,018	188

Source: **National Center for Health Statistics.**

the whole; and the burdens of the state ought to be fairly distributed among its citizens. No person shall be deprived of life, liberty or property without due process of law, nor shall any person be denied equal protection of the laws. No otherwise qualified person shall, solely by reason of race, gender or handicap be subject to discrimination by the state, its agents or any person or entity doing business with the state. Nothing in this section shall be construed to grant or secure any right relating to abortion or the funding thereof.

(3) POST-VIABILITY ABORTION BAN

Rhode Island prohibits post-viability abortion, unless it is necessary to preserve the life of the woman. The state also makes it a crime to destroy any fetus born alive during an attempted abortion. The statutes addressing the matter are set out below.

Rhode Island Code § 11-23-5. Post-viability abortion

(a) The willful killing of an unborn quick child by any injury to the mother of the child, which would be murder if it resulted in the death of the mother; the administration to any woman pregnant with a quick child of any medication, drug, or substance or the use of any instrument or device or other means, with intent to destroy the child, unless it is necessary to preserve the life of the mother; in the event of the death of the child; shall be deemed manslaughter.

(b) In any prosecution under this section, it shall not be necessary for the prosecution to prove that any necessity existed.

(c) For the purposes of this section, "quick child" means an unborn child whose heart is beating, who is experiencing electronically-measurable brain waves, who is discernibly moving, and who is so far developed and matured as to be capable of surviving the trauma of birth with the aid of usual medical care and facilities available in this state.

Rhode Island Code § 11-9-18.
Care of babies born alive during attempted abortions

Any physician, nurse, or other licensed medical person who knowingly and intentionally fails to provide reasonable medical care and treatment to an infant born alive in the course of an abortion shall be guilty of a felony and upon conviction shall be fined not exceeding five thousand dollars ($5,000), or imprisoned not exceeding five (5) years, or both. Any physician, nurse, or other licensed medical person who knowingly and intentionally fails to provide reasonable medical care and treatment to an infant born alive in the course of an abortion, and, as a result of that failure, the infant dies, shall be guilty of the crime of manslaughter.

(4) INFORMED CONSENT AND SPOUSAL NOTICE

Prior to an abortion Rhode Island requires that a woman be fully informed of the procedure to be used, the risks involved and alternatives to abortion. A woman must provide written consent to an abortion after receiving the statutorily required information. Rhode Island requires an abortion provider notify the husband of a woman seeking an abortion, prior to performing the procedure. However, the United States Supreme Court found spousal notice requirements unconstitutional in *Planned Parenthood of Southeastern Pennsylvania v. Casey*. In addition, Rhode Island's spousal notice requirement was specifically invalidated in *Planned Parenthood of Rhode Island v. Board of Medical Review*, 598 F.Supp. 625 (D.R.I. 1984). The statutes addressing the issues are set out below.

Rhode Island Code § 23-4.7-1. Abortion defined

"Abortion" for the purpose of this chapter means administering to a woman, known to be pregnant, any medicine, drug, substance, or thing whatever, or the employment upon her of any instrument or means whatever, with intent to terminate a pregnancy. The term shall not include the administering of any medicine, drug, substance, or thing or the employment of any instrument or means for the purpose of completing an incomplete, spontaneous miscarriage.

Rhode Island Code § 23-4.7-2. Consent required

In order to insure that a woman's consent to abortion is truly informed consent, an abortion shall be performed only after the woman has given her consent, in writing, in a form satisfying the provisions of § 23-4.7-5.

Rhode Island Code § 23-4.7-3. Required disclosures

(a) Either the physician who is to perform the abortion or his or her authorized agent or another physician or his or her authorized agent shall:

(1) Inform the woman that she is pregnant and inform her of the estimated gestational age of the fetus at the time of such disclosure.

(2) Explain to the woman the medical nature of an abortion, including the probable gestational age of the fetus at the time the abortion is to be performed.

(3) Explain to the woman the medical or surgical procedure to be employed to perform the abortion.

(4) Explain to the woman all known material medical risks associated with the particular abortion procedure to be employed. In the event a physician or his or her authorized agent determines that the disclosure of a known material risk should not be made, that risk need not be disclosed, provided the medical basis for the nondisclosure is certified in writing in the patient's medical record.

(b) In addition, a physician or his or her authorized agent may inform the woman of any other material facts or opinions or otherwise state anything with respect to the disclosures required herein which, in the exercise of his or her best medical judgment, is reasonably necessary to enable the woman to give her informed consent to the proposed abortion, with full knowledge of its nature and consequences.

Rhode Island Code § 23-4.7-4. Medical emergency

Where there is an emergency requiring immediate action, the requirements of this chapter may be waived. The woman's attending physician shall certify in writing in the patient's medical record that an emergency exists and the medical basis for his or her opinion.

Rhode Island Code § 23-4.7-5. Consent form

(a) The woman's written consent required by § 23-4.7-2 shall be on a form provided by the physician or facility and containing:

(1) The disclosures required by § 23-4.7-3; and

(2) The woman's acknowledgment that either the physician who is to perform the abortion or his or her authorized agent or another physician or his or her authorized agent has provided her with the information required by § 23-4.7-3.

(b)(1) The form shall in addition include the following statement: "If you decide to carry your pregnancy to term but not to keep the child, you may be able to place the child with either a relative, or with another family through foster care or adoption."

(2) The person making the disclosures required under § 23-4.7-3 shall not be required to state anything with respect to the contents of subdivision (1) of this subsection.

(c) In cases where the woman does not understand English, either the consent form shall be written in a language understood by her, or the person informing her shall certify on the consent form that in his or her opinion, the information required to be given by § 23-4.7-3 has been given in a manner as to be understandable by her; if an interpreter is used, the interpreter shall be named and reference to that use shall be made on the consent form.

(d) A copy of the form shall be made available to the woman upon her request.

Rhode Island Code § 23-4.7-7. Liability of physician

Any physician who knowingly violates the requirements of this chapter shall be deemed to have engaged in "unprofessional conduct" for the purposes of § 5-37-5.1. The willful failure to provide the woman with the substance of the information pursuant to the requirements of § 23-4.7-3 shall be prima facie evidence of failure to obtain informed consent in an action at law or in equity.

Rhode Island Code § 23-4.7-8. Severability

If any section or provision of this chapter or the application of any section or provision is held invalid, that invalidity shall not affect other sections, provisions, or applications, and to this end the sections and provisions of this chapter are declared severable.

Rhode Island Code § 23-4.8-1. Declaration of purpose

The purpose of this chapter is to promote the state's interest in furthering the integrity of the institutions of marriage and the family.

Rhode Island Code § 23-4.8-2. Spousal notice requirements

If a married woman consents to an abortion, as such consent is required by chapter 4.7 of this title, the physician who is to perform the abortion or his or her authorized agent shall, if reasonably possible, notify the husband of that woman of the proposed abortion before it is performed.

Rhode Island Code § 23-4.8-3. Exceptions to spousal notice

The requirements of § 23-4.8-2 shall not apply if:

(1) The woman having the abortion furnishes to the physician who is to perform the abortion or the physician's authorized agent prior to the abortion being performed a written statement that she has given notice to her husband of the proposed abortion; or a written statement that the fetus was not fathered by her husband; or

(2) The woman or her husband are living separate and apart; or either spouse has filed a petition or complaint for divorce in a court of competent jurisdiction; or

(3) The physician who is to perform the abortion or his or her authorized agent receives the written affirmation of the husband that he has been notified of the proposed abortion; or

(4) There is an emergency requiring immediate action. In the case of an emergency, the woman's attending physician shall certify in writing on the patient's medical record that an emergency exists and the medical basis for his or her opinion.

Rhode Island Code § 23-4.8-4. Penalties

In the event a physician performs an abortion, as defined by chapter 4.7 of this title, upon a woman who he or she knows is married and the physician knowingly and intentionally violates the requirements of this chapter, he or she shall be guilty of "unprofessional conduct" for the purposes of § 5-37-5.1.

Rhode Island Code § 23-4.8-5. Severability

If any section or provision of this chapter or the application of any section or provision is held invalid, that invalidity shall not affect other sections, provisions or applications, and to this end the sections and provisions of this chapter are declared severable.

(5) PARTIAL-BIRTH ABORTION

Rhode Island prohibits partial-birth abortions. However, the ban was held unconstitutional in *Rhode Island Medical Soc. v. Whitehouse*, 239 F.3d 104 (1st Cir. 2001). In addition to purporting to ban partial-birth abortions, Rhode Island has provided a civil cause of action for the father and maternal grandparents of a fetus destroyed using partial-birth abortion. The statutes addressing the matter are set out below.

Rhode Island Code § 23-4.12-1.
Partial-birth abortion definitions

(a) For purposes of this chapter, "partial birth abortion" means an abortion in which the person performing the abortion vaginally delivers a living human fetus before killing the infant and completing the delivery.

(b) For purposes of this chapter, the terms "fetus" and "infant" are used interchangeably to refer to the biological offspring of human parents.

(c) As used in this section, the term "vaginally delivers a living fetus before killing the infant" means deliberately and intentionally delivers into the vagina a living fetus, or a substantial portion thereof, for the purpose of performing a procedure the person performing the abortion knows will kill the infant, and kills the infant.

Rhode Island Code § 23-4.12-2. Partial-birth abortion ban

No person shall knowingly perform a partial birth abortion.

Rhode Island Code § 23-4.12-3. Life of the mother exception

Section 23-4.12-2 shall not apply to a partial birth abortion that is necessary to save the life of a mother because her life is endangered by a physical disorder, physical illness, or physical injury, including a life-endangering condition caused by or arising from the pregnancy itself; provided, that no other medical procedure would suffice for that purpose.

Rhode Island Code § 23-4.12-4. Civil remedies

(a) The woman upon whom a partial birth abortion has been performed in violation of § 23-4.12-2, the father of the fetus or infant, and the maternal grandparents of the fetus or infant, and the maternal grandparents of the fetus or infant if the mother has not attained the age of eighteen (18) years at the time of the abortion, may obtain appropriate relief in a civil action, unless the pregnancy resulted from the plaintiff's criminal conduct or the plaintiff consented to the abortion.

(b) Such relief shall include:

(1 Money damages for all injuries, psychological and physical occasioned by the violation of this chapter; and

(2) Statutory damages equal to three (3) times the cost of the partial birth abortion.

(c) If judgment is rendered in favor of the plaintiff in an action described in this section, the court shall also render judgment for a reasonable attorney's fee in favor of the plaintiff against the defendant. If the judgment is rendered in favor of the defendant and the court finds that the plaintiff's suit was frivolous and brought in bad faith, the court shall also render judgment for a reasonable attorney's fee in favor of the defendant against the plaintiff.

Rhode Island Code § 23-4.12-5. Penalty

(a) Performance of a partial birth abortion deliberately and intentionally is a violation of this chapter and shall be a felony.

(b) A woman upon whom a partial birth abortion is performed may not be prosecuted under this chapter for violating this chapter, or any provision of this chapter, or for conspiracy to violate this chapter or any provision of this chapter.

Rhode Island Code § 23-4.12-6. Severability

(a) If any one (1) or more provisions, clauses, phrases, or words of § 23-4.12-3 or the application of that section to any person or circumstance is found to be unconstitutional, it is hereby declared to be inseverable.

(b) If any one (1) or more provisions, sections, subsections, sentences, clauses, phrases or words of the remaining sections or the application of them to any person or circumstance is found to be unconstitutional, they are hereby declared to be severable and the balance of the chapter shall remain effective notwithstanding the unconstitutionality. The legislature declares that it would have passed this chapter, and each provision, section, subsection, sentence, clause, phrase, or words, with the exception of § 23-4.12-3, irrespective of the fact that any one (1) or more provisions, sections, subsections, sentences, clauses, phrases, or words be declared unconstitutional.

(6) ABORTION BY MINORS

Under the laws of Rhode Island no physician may perform an abortion upon an unemancipated minor unless he/she first obtains the consent of either parent or guardian of the minor. In compliance with federal constitutional law, Rhode Island has provided a judicial waiver procedure for an unemancipated minor to obtain an abortion without parental or guardian consent. If an unemancipated minor elects not to seek, or cannot for any reason obtain consent from either of her parents or guardian, the minor may petition a trial court for a waiver of the consent requirement. The required parental consent may be waived if the court finds either (1) that the minor is mature and well-informed enough to make the abortion decision on her own, or (2) that performance of the abortion would be in the best interest of the minor. The statute addressing the matter is set out below.

Rhode Island Code § 23-4.7-6.
Parental consent and judicial bypass

Except in the case of a minor who has been found by a court of competent jurisdiction to be emancipated, if a pregnant woman is less than eighteen (18) years of age and has not married, an abortion shall not be performed upon her unless both the consent of the pregnant woman and that of at least one of her parents is obtained, except as provided in this section. In deciding whether to grant such consent, a pregnant woman's parents shall consider only their child's best interests. If both parents have died or are otherwise unavailable to the physician within a reasonable time and in a reasonable manner, consent of the pregnant woman's legal guardian or one of her guardians shall be sufficient. If a pregnant woman less than eighteen (18) years of age has not married and if neither of her parents or guardians agree to consent to the performance of an abortion, or if she elects not to seek the consent of either of her parents or guardians, a judge of the family court shall, upon petition, or motion, and after an appropriate hearing, authorize a physician to perform the abortion, if the judge determines that the pregnant woman is mature and capable of giving informed consent to the proposed abortion or if the judge determines that she is not mature, but that the performance of an abortion upon her would be in her best interests. A pregnant woman less than eighteen (18) years of age may participate in proceedings in the family court on her own behalf, and she shall be represented in her proceeding by a guardian ad litem. Proceedings in the family court under this section shall be confidential and shall be given such precedence over other pending matters that the court may reach a decision promptly and without delay so as to serve the best interests of the pregnant woman. A judge of the family court who conducts proceedings under this section shall make in writing specific factual findings and legal conclusions supporting his or her decision and shall order a record of the evidence to be maintained including his or her own findings and conclusions.

(7) RIGHT TO REFUSE PARTICIPATION

Rhode Island permits medical personnel to refuse to take part in abortions on religious or moral grounds. The state prohibits retaliation against any medical person who refused to participate in an abortion. The statute addressing the matter is set out below.

Rhode Island Code § 23-17-11. Right not to participate

A physician or any other person who is a member of or associated with the medical staff of a health care facility or any employee of a health care facility in which an abortion or any sterilization procedure is scheduled, and who shall state in writing an objection to the abortion or sterilization procedure on moral or religious grounds, shall not be required to participate in the medical procedures which result in the abortion or sterilization, and the refusal of the person to participate in the medical procedures shall not form the basis for any claim of damages on account of the refusal or for any disciplinary or recriminatory action against the person.

(8) FETAL EXPERIMENTATION AND CLONING

Rhode Island has banned live fetal experimentation, unless it is done to preserve the life of a fetus. The state prohibits experiments on a dead fetus, unless the woman involved consents thereto. A statute has also been enacted by Rhode Island that bans cloning of human beings. The statutes addressing the matters are set out below.

Rhode Island Code § 11-54-1. Fetal experimentation

(a) No person shall use any live human fetus, whether before or after expulsion from its mother's womb, for scientific, laboratory research, or other kind of experimentation. This section shall not prohibit procedures incident to the study of a human fetus while it is in its mother's womb, provided that in the best medical judgment of the physician, made at the time of the study, the procedures do not substantially jeopardize the life or health of the fetus, and provided the fetus is not the subject of a planned abortion. In any criminal proceeding the fetus shall be conclusively presumed not to be the subject of a planned abortion if the mother signed a written statement at the time of the study that she was not planning an abortion.

(b) This section shall not prohibit or regulate diagnostic or remedial procedures, the purpose of which is to determine or to preserve the life or health of the fetus involved or the mother involved.

(c) A fetus is a live fetus for purposes of this section when, in the best medical judgment of a physician, it shows evidence of life as determined by the same medical standards as are used in determining evidence of life in a spontaneously aborted fetus at approximately the same stage of gestational development.

(d) No experimentation may knowingly be performed upon a dead fetus unless the consent of its mother has first been obtained, provided, that such consent shall not be required in the case of a routine pathological study. In any criminal proceeding, consent shall be conclusively presumed to have been granted for the purposes of this section by a written statement, signed by the mother, who is at least eighteen (18) years of age, to the effect that she consents to the use of her fetus for scientific, laboratory, research, or other kind of experimentation or study; that written consent shall constitute lawful authorization for the transfer of the dead fetus.

(e) No person shall perform or offer to perform an abortion where part or all of the consideration for the performance is that the fetal remains may be used for experimentation or other kinds of research or study.

(f) No person shall knowingly sell, transfer, distribute, or give away

any fetus for a use which is in violation of the provisions of this section. For purposes of this section, the word "fetus" includes an embryo or neonate.

Rhode Island Code § 11-54-2. Penalties

Any person who performs any of the acts prohibited by this chapter shall be guilty of a felony and shall be punished by a fine of at least one thousand dollars ($1,000) or shall be imprisoned for a period of at least one year, or both.

Rhode Island Code § 23-16.4-1.
Declaration of intent and purpose

Whereas, recent medical and technological advances have had tremendous benefit to patients, and society as a whole, and biomedical research for the purpose of scientific investigation of disease or cure of a disease or illness should be preserved and protected and not be impeded by regulations involving the cloning of an entire human being; and

Whereas, molecular biology, involving human cells, genes, tissues, and organs, has been used to meet medical needs globally for twenty (20) years, and has proved a powerful tool in the search for cures, leading to effective medicines to treat cystic fibrosis, diabetes, heart attack, stroke, hemophilia, and HIV/AIDS;

The purpose of this legislation is to place a ban on the creation of a human being through division of a blastocyst, zygote, or embryo or somatic cell nuclear transfer, and to protect the citizens of the state from potential abuse deriving from cloning technologies. This ban is not intended to apply to the cloning of human cells, genes, tissues, or organs that would not result in the replication of an entire human being. Nor is this ban intended to apply to in vitro fertilization, the administration of fertility enhancing drugs, or other medical procedures used to assist a woman in becoming or remaining pregnant, so long as that procedure is not specifically intended to result in the gestation or birth of a child who is genetically identical to another conceptus, embryo, fetus, or human being, living or dead.

Rhode Island Code § 23-16.4-2. Cloning of human beings

(a) No person or entity shall utilize somatic cell nuclear transfer for the purpose of initiating or attempting to initiate a human pregnancy nor shall any person create genetically identical human beings by dividing a blastocyst, zygote, or embryo.

(b) Definitions

(1) "Nucleus" means the cell structure that houses the chromosomes, and thus the genes;

(2) "Oocyte" means the female germ cell, the egg;

(3) "Somatic cell" means any cell of a conceptus, embryo, fetus, child, or adult not biologically determined to become a germ cell; and

(4) "Somatic cell nuclear transfer" means transferring the nucleus of a human somatic cell into an oocyte from which the nucleus has been removed.

(c) Protected research and practices

(1) Nothing in this section shall be construed to restrict areas of biomedical, microbiological, and agricultural research or practices not expressly prohibited in this section, including research or practices that involve the use of:

(i) Somatic cell nuclear transfer or other cloning technologies to clone molecules, DNA, cells, and tissues;

(ii) Mitochondrial, cytoplasmic, or gene therapy; or

(iii) Somatic cell nuclear transfer techniques to create animals.

(2) Nothing in this section shall be construed to prohibit:

(i) In vitro fertilization, the administration of fertility-enhancing drugs, or other medical procedures used to assist a woman in becoming or remaining pregnant, so long as that pregnancy is not specifically intended to result in the production of a child who is genetically identical to another human being, living or dead;

(ii) Any activity or procedure that results, directly or indirectly in two or more natural identical twins.

Rhode Island Code § 23-16.4-3. Penalties

(a) For violations of § 23-16.4-1 the director of the Department of Health may, after appropriate notice and opportunity for hearing, by order, levy administrative penalties as follows:

(1) If the violator is a corporation, firm, clinic, hospital, laboratory, or research facility, by a civil penalty of not more than one million dollars ($1,000,000), or the applicable amount under subdivision (a)(3), whichever is greater.

(2) If the violator is an individual or an employee of the firm, clinic, hospital, laboratory, or research facility acting without the authorization of the firm, clinic, hospital, or research facility, by a civil penalty of not more than two hundred fifty thousand dollars ($250,000) or the applicable amount under subdivision (a)(3), whichever is greater.

(3) If any violator derives pecuniary gain from a violation of this section, the violator may be assessed a civil penalty of not more than an amount equal to the amount of the gross gain multiplied by two (2).

(b) The administrative penalties provided in this section shall be paid to the general fund.

(c) Nothing in this chapter shall be construed to give any person a private right of action.

Rhode Island Code § 23-16.4-4. Sunset clause

The prohibition in § 23-16.4-2 shall expire on July 7, 2010.

(9) HEALTH INSURANCE

Rhode Island prohibits private health insurance plans from providing coverage for abortion, unless a specific premium is paid for such coverage. The state also prohibits government health insurance plans from providing coverage for abortions. In addition, Rhode Island prohibits health coverage for non–F.D.A. approved contraceptive drugs and devices requiring a prescription. The statutes addressing the matter are set out below.

Rhode Island Code § 27-18-28.
Private health insurance contracts

(a) No health insurance contract, plan, or policy, delivered or issued for delivery in the state, shall provide coverage for induced abortions, except where the life of the mother would be endangered if the fetus were carried to term or where the pregnancy resulted from rape or incest, and except by an optional rider for which there must be paid an additional premium. This section shall be applicable to all contracts, plans, or policies of:

(1) All health insurers subject to this title;

(2) All group and blanket health insurers subject to this title;

(3) All nonprofit hospital, medical, surgical, dental, and health service corporations; and

(4) All health maintenance organizations;

(5) Any provision of medical, hospital, surgical, and funeral benefits, and of coverage against accidental death or injury, when the benefits or coverage are incidental to or part of other insurance authorized by the statutes of this state.

(b) Nothing contained in this section shall be construed to pertain to insurance coverage for complications as the result of an abortion.

Rhode Island Code § 36-12-2.1.
Government health insurance benefits

(a) The state of Rhode Island or any city or town shall not include in any health insurance contracts, plans, or policies covering employees,

any provision which shall provide coverage for induced abortions (except where the life of the mother would be endangered if the fetus were carried to term, or where the pregnancy resulted from rape or incest). This section shall be applicable to all contracts, plans or policies of:

(1) All health insurers subject to title 27;

(2) All group and blanket health insurers subject to title 27;

(3) All nonprofit hospital, medical, surgical, dental, and health service corporations;

(4) All health maintenance organizations; and

(5) Any provision of medical, hospital, surgical, and funeral benefits and of coverage against accidental death or injury when the benefits or coverage are incidental to or part of other insurance authorized by the statutes of this state.

(b) Provided, however, that the provisions of this section shall not apply to benefits provided under existing collective bargaining agreements entered into prior to June 30, 1982.

(c) Nothing contained herein shall be construed to pertain to insurance coverage for complications as the result of an abortion.

Rhode Island Code § 27-18-57.
F.D.A. approved contraceptive drugs and devices

(a) Every individual or group health insurance contract, plan, or policy that provides prescription coverage and is delivered, issued for delivery, or renewed in this state shall provide coverage for F.D.A. approved contraceptive drugs and devices requiring a prescription. Provided, that nothing in this subsection shall be deemed to mandate or require coverage for the prescription drug RU 486.

(b) Notwithstanding any other provision of this section, any insurance company may issue to a religious employer an individual or group health insurance contract, plan, or policy that excludes coverage for prescription contraceptive methods which are contrary to the religious employer's bona fide religious tenets.

(c) As used in this section, "religious employer" means an employer that is a "church or a qualified church-controlled organization" as defined in 26 U.S.C. § 3121.

(d) This section does not apply to insurance coverage providing benefits for: (1) hospital confinement indemnity; (2) disability income; (3) accident only; (4) long term care; (5) Medicare supplement; (6) limited benefit health; (7) specified diseased indemnity; (8) sickness of bodily injury or death by accident or both; and (9) other limited benefit policies.

(e) Every religious employer that invokes the exemption provided under this section shall provide written notice to prospective enrollees prior to enrollment with the plan, listing the contraceptive health care services the employer refuses to cover for religious reasons.

Rhythm Method *see* **Natural Family Planning Methods**

RICO

Congress enacted the Racketeer Influenced and Corrupt Organizations (RICO) statute to combat organized drug trafficking and other notorious organized criminal activities. RICO has both criminal and civil liability remedies. The prohibited conduct under RICO is provided by the following provision:

18 U.S.C.A. § 1962 Prohibited activities

(a) It shall be unlawful for any person who has received any income derived, directly or indirectly, from a pattern of racketeering activity or through collection of an unlawful debt in which such person has participated as a principal within the meaning of section 2, title 18, United States Code, to use or invest, directly or indirectly, any part of such income, or the proceeds of such income, in acquisition of any interest in, or the establishment or operation of, any enterprise which is engaged in, or the activities of which affect, interstate or foreign commerce. A purchase of securities on the open market for purposes of investment, and without the intention of controlling or participating in the control of the issuer, or of assisting another to do so, shall not be unlawful under this subsection if the securities of the issuer held by the purchaser, the members of his immediate family, and his or their accomplices in any pattern or racketeering activity or the collection of an unlawful debt after such purchase do not amount in the aggregate to one percent of the outstanding securities of any one class, and do not confer, either in law or in fact, the power to elect one or more directors of the issuer.

(b) It shall be unlawful for any person through a pattern of racketeering activity or through collection of an unlawful debt to acquire or maintain, directly or indirectly, any interest in or control of any enterprise which is engaged in, or the activities of which affect, interstate or foreign commerce.

(c) It shall be unlawful for any person employed by or associated with any enterprise engaged in, or the activities of which affect, interstate or foreign commerce, to conduct or participate, directly or indirectly, in the conduct of such enterprise's affairs through a pattern of racketeering activity or collection of unlawful debt.

(d) It shall be unlawful for any person to conspire to violate any of the provisions of subsection (a), (b), or (c) of this section.

In *National Organization for Women, Inc. v. Scheidler*, the United States Supreme Court held that a group of pro-choice organizations could maintain a RICO civil lawsuit against several anti-abortion individuals and groups. The lawsuit was initially dismissed by lower federal courts, on the grounds that RICO could not be used to combat militant anti-abortion activities. The Supreme Court disagreed with the lower courts and sent the case back for trial. On remand of the case a jury found in favor of the pro-choice organizations. However, the Supreme Court reversed the judgment in the opinion styled *Scheidler v. National Organization for Women, Inc. (I). See also* **National Organization for Women, Inc. v. Scheidler; Scheidler v. National Organization for Women, Inc. (I)**

Right to Life of Michigan

Right to Life of Michigan (RLM) is a pro-life organization that is headed by its president Barbara Listing. RLM believes that each human being, from the time of fertilization to natural death, has an immeasurable dignity and unalienable right to life. The organization works to educate people on identified pro-life issues, to motivate them to action, to encourage community support for programs that foster respect for human life and to promote pro-life candidates and legislation. *See also* **Pro-Life Organizations**

Riley-Day Syndrome

Riley-Day syndrome is an inherited disease that affects the sensory and autonomic function in many organ systems. This disorder causes feeding problems, vomiting and sweating spells, breath-holding spells that produce unconsciousness, insensitivity to pain, deficient temperature regulation and seizures. Treatment for the disease may include anticonvulsant therapy for seizures and antiemetics to control vomiting. The disease is fatal and most children die in childhood. *See also* **Birth Defects and Abortion**

Roberts, John G., Jr.

John G. Roberts, Jr. was nominated by President George W. Bush to fill an associate justice vacancy on the United States Supreme Court in July of 2005. However, while the nomination was pending confirmation by the United States Senate, the chief justice of the Supreme Court died on September 3, 2005. Consequently, President Bush withdrew Roberts' nomination for associate justice and, on September 6, 2005, Roberts was nominated to be chief justice of the Supreme Court. After swift confirmation proceedings, Roberts took his seat as chief justice on September 29, 2005. Chief Justice Roberts came to the

Chief Justice Roberts came to the Supreme Court with a reputation of supporting the views of pro-life abortion advocates (collection, Supreme Court Historical Society, photograph by Steve Petteway, Supreme Court).

Supreme Court with a reputation of having a conservative judicial philosophy.

Chief Justice Roberts was born in Buffalo, New York, on January 27, 1955. He received an undergraduate degree from Harvard College in 1976, and a law degree from Harvard Law School in 1979. After leaving law school Chief Justice Roberts served briefly as a law clerk for the United States Court of Appeals for the Second Circuit and the United States Supreme Court. From 1981 to 1993 Chief Justice Roberts served as an attorney for several federal agencies. Between the period 1993 to 2003 Chief Justice Roberts maintained a private law practice in Washington, D.C. In 2003 he was appointed to the United States Court of Appeals for the District of Columbia Circuit, where he served until his appointment to the Supreme Court.

During the Chief Justice's tenure on the Supreme Court he has voted in a few abortion related cases. Thus far his voting pattern indicates that he is not in favor of using the constitution to expand abortion rights for women.

(1) Plurality opinions written. Chief Justice Roberts wrote a plurality opinion in *Federal Election Commission v. Wisconsin Right to Life, Inc.*, which held that the electioneering communications provisions of a federal statute violated a pro-life organization's First Amendment right to broadcast political issue oriented advertisements shortly before primary and general elections.

(2) Unanimous opinions voted with only. Chief Justice Roberts voted with a unanimous Court in *Scheidler v. National Organization for Women, Inc. (II)*, which held pro-choice advocates could not sue pro-life advocates under the Hobbs Act for allegations of physical violence that did not involve extortion. Chief Justice Roberts joined a unanimous opinion in *Ayotte v. Planned Parenthood of Northern New England*, which held that the absence of a health exception in New Hampshire's parental notification abortion statute did not require the entire statute be invalidated.

(3) Majority opinions voted with only. Chief Justice Roberts voted with the majority opinion in *Gonzales v. Carhart*, which held that the Partial-Birth Abortion Ban Act of 2003 was not facially unconstitutional, because it outlined the abortion procedure that was banned, and the Act did not have to provide an exception for the health of a woman.

Rodriquez, Ana Rosa

Ana Rosa Rodriquez survived an attempt to abort her, and was born in 1991 in New York City. Ana's mother, Rosa Rodriquez, was seven months pregnant when she went to the abortion clinic of Dr. Abu Hayat in October of 1991. Dr. Hayat began performing the abortion, but stopped when complications arose and told the mother to return the next day to complete expulsion of the fetus. During this first attempt, Dr. Hayat ripped off the right arm of the fetus. The mother did not return for a second attempt. Instead, she went to a local hospital where, five hours after the abortion attempt, she gave birth to Ana, who had a missing right arm. Dr. Hayat was prosecuted for attempting an unlawful third trimester abortion. He was eventually convicted of assault and illegal abortion. *See also* **Survivors of Abortion**

Roe v. Wade

Forum: United States Supreme Court.
Case Citation: Roe v. Wade, 410 U.S. 113 (1973).
Date Argued: December 13, 1971; reargued October 11, 1972.
Date of Decision: January 22, 1973.
Opinion of Court: Blackmun, J., in which Burger, C. J., and Douglas, Brennan, Stewart, Marshall, and Powell, JJ., joined.
Concurring Opinion: Burger, C. J.
Concurring Opinion: Douglas, J.
Concurring Opinion: Stewart, J.
Dissenting Opinion: White, J., in which Rehnquist, J., joined.
Dissenting Opinion: Rehnquist, J.
Counsel for Appellant: Sarah Weddington argued; on the brief were Roy Lucas, Fred Bruner, Roy L. Merrill, Jr., and Norman Dorsen.
Counsel for Appellee: Robert C. Flowers and Jay Floyd, Assistant Attorneys General of Texas, argued; on the brief were Crawford C. Martin, Attorney General, Nola White, First Assistant Attorney General, Alfred Walker, Executive Assistant Attorney General, Henry Wade, and John B. Tolle.
Amicus Brief for Appellant and Appellee: Gary K. Nelson, Attorney General of Arizona, Robert K. Killian, Attorney General of Connecticut, Ed W. Hancock, Attorney General of Kentucky, Clarence A. H. Meyer, Attorney General of Nebraska, and Vernon B. Romney, Attorney General of Utah; by Joseph P. Witherspoon, Jr., for the Association of Texas Diocesan Attorneys; by Charles E. Rice for Americans United for Life; by Eugene J. McMahon for Women for the Unborn et al.; by Carol Ryan for the American College of Obstetricians and Gynecologists et al.; by Dennis J. Horan, Jerome A. Frazel, Jr., Thomas M. Crisham, and Dolores V. Horan for Certain Physicians, Professors and Fellows of the American College of Obstetrics and Gynecology; by Harriet F. Pilpel, Nancy F. Wechsler, and Frederic S. Nathan for Planned Parenthood Federation of America, Inc., et al.; by Alan F. Charles for the National Legal Program on Health Problems of the Poor et al.; by Marttie L. Thompson for State Communities Aid Assn.; by Alfred L. Scanlan, Martin J. Flynn, and Robert M. Byrn for the National Right to Life Committee; by Helen L. Buttenwieser for the American Ethical Union et al.; by Norma G. Zarky for the American

Association of University Women et al.; by Nancy Stearns for New Women Lawyers et al.; by the California Committee to Legalize Abortion et al.; and by Robert E. Dunne for Robert L. Sassone.

Issue Presented: Whether the Due Process Clause of the Fourteenth Amendment was violated by the criminal abortion statutes of Texas, which prohibited all abortions except to save the life of a pregnant woman?

Case Holding: The liberty component of the Due Process Clause of the Fourteenth Amendment prohibited states from criminalizing or preventing elective first trimester abortions.

Background facts of case: The abortion statutes of Texas made it a crime to procure an abortion, except with respect to an abortion procured by medical advice for the purpose of saving the life of the mother. In 1970 the appellant, Jane Roe, was a single and pregnant resident of Texas who desired an elective abortion. In March of that year the appellant filed a lawsuit in a federal district court in Texas, challenging the constitutionality of that state's criminal abortion statutes. While the suit was pending, James Hubert Hallford, a licensed physician, sought and was granted leave to intervene in the appellant's case as a plaintiff. Dr. Hallford alleged that he had been arrested previously for violations of the Texas criminal abortion statutes and that two such prosecutions were pending against him. Additionally, a separate lawsuit was filed in the federal district court by John and Mary Doe, a married couple. The Does alleged that, because of health reasons to Mrs. Doe, she did not wish to have a child and that in the event she became pregnant, she wanted to have an abortion and not face criminal prosecution. The two lawsuits were consolidated and heard together. The district court held that appellant and Dr. Hallford had standing to sue and presented justiciable controversies, but that the Does had failed to allege facts sufficient to state a present controversy and did not have standing. The district court therefore dismissed the Does' complaint. It was further determined that, although the criminal abortion statutes of Texas were unconstitutional, the court would not issue an injunction prohibiting enforcement of the statutes. The Supreme Court granted certiorari to consider the matter.

Majority opinion by Justice Blackmun: Justice Blackmun held in the first part of the opinion that the district court was correct in dismissing the Does' complaint. The opinion also found that the district court was wrong in not dismissing Dr. Hallford from the case. Justice Blackmun indicated that Dr. Hallford's only remedy would be an appeal from his criminal cases. The opinion then turned to the merits of the appellant's case. Justice Blackmun held that Texas' criminal abortion statutes were unconstitutional and enforceable. The opinion addressed the issue as follows:

> The principal thrust of appellant's attack on the Texas statutes is that they improperly invade a right, said to be possessed by the pregnant woman, to choose to terminate her pregnancy. Appellant would discover this right in the concept of personal "liberty" embodied in the Fourteenth Amendment's Due Process Clause....
>
> The Constitution does not explicitly mention any right of privacy. In a line of decisions, however, ... the Court has recognized that a right of personal privacy, or a guarantee of certain areas or zones of privacy, does exist under the Constitution....
>
> This right of privacy, whether it be founded in the Fourteenth Amendment's concept of personal liberty and restrictions upon state action, as we feel it is, or, as the District Court determined, in the Ninth Amendment's reservation of rights to the people, is broad enough to encompass a woman's decision whether or not to terminate her pregnancy. The detriment that the State would impose upon the pregnant woman by denying this choice altogether is apparent. Specific and direct harm medically diagnosable even in early pregnancy may be involved. Maternity, or additional offspring, may force upon the woman a distressful life and future. Psychological harm may be imminent. Mental and physical health may be taxed by child care. There is also the distress, for all concerned, associated with the unwanted child, and there is the problem of bringing a child into a family already unable, psychologically and otherwise, to care for it. In other cases, as in this one, the additional difficulties and continuing stigma of unwed motherhood may be involved. All these are factors the woman and her responsible physician necessarily will consider in consultation.
>
> On the basis of elements such as these, appellant and some amici argue that the woman's right is absolute and that she is entitled to terminate her pregnancy at whatever time, in whatever way, and for whatever reason she alone chooses. With this we do not agree. Appellant's arguments that Texas either has no valid interest at all in regulating the abortion decision, or no interest strong enough to support any limitation upon the woman's sole determination, are unpersuasive. The Court's decisions recognizing a right of privacy also acknowledge that some state regulation in areas protected by that right is appropriate.... [A] State may properly assert important interests in safeguarding health, in maintaining medical standards, and in protecting potential life. At some point in pregnancy, these respective interests become sufficiently compelling to sustain regulation of the factors that govern the abortion decision. The privacy right involved, therefore, cannot be said to be absolute. In fact, it is not clear to us that the claim asserted by some amici that one has an unlimited right to do with one's body as one pleases bears a close relationship to the right of privacy previously articulated in the Court's decisions. The Court has refused to recognize an unlimited right of this kind in the past.
>
> We, therefore, conclude that the right of personal privacy includes the abortion decision, but that this right is not unqualified and must be considered against important state interests in regulation....
>
> With respect to the State's important and legitimate interest in the health of the mother, the compelling point, in the light of present medical knowledge, is at approximately the end of the first trimester. This is so because of the now-established medical fact ... that until the end of the first trimester mortality in abortion may be less than mortality in normal childbirth. It follows that, from and after this point, a State may regulate the abortion procedure to the extent that the regulation reasonably relates to the preservation and protection of maternal health. Examples of permissible state regulation in this area are requirements as to the qualifications of the person who is to perform the abortion; as to the licensure of that person; as to the facility in which the procedure is to be performed, that is, whether it must be a hospital or may be a clinic or some other place of less-than-hospital status; as to the licensing of the facility; and the like.
>
> This means, on the other hand, that, for the period of pregnancy prior to this compelling point, the attending physician, in consultation with his patient, is free to determine, without regulation by the State, that, in his medical judgment, the patient pregnancy should be terminated. If that decision is reached, the judgment may be effectuated by an abortion free of interference by the State.
>
> With respect to the State's important and legitimate interest in potential life, the compelling point is at viability. This is so because the fetus then presumably has the capability of meaningful life outside the mother's womb. State regulation protective of fetal life after viability thus has both logical and biological justifications. If the State is interested in protecting fetal life after viability, it may go so far as to proscribe abortion during that period, except when it is necessary to preserve the life or health of the mother.
>
> Measured against these standards ..., the Texas Penal Code, in restricting legal abortions to those procured or attempted by medical advice for the purpose of saving the life of the mother,

sweeps too broadly. The statute makes no distinction between abortions performed early in pregnancy and those performed later, and it limits to a single reason, saving the mother's life, the legal justification for the procedure. The statute, therefore, cannot survive the constitutional attack made upon it here....

To summarize and to repeat:

1. A state criminal abortion statute of the current Texas type, that excepts from criminality only a life-saving procedure on behalf of the mother, without regard to pregnancy stage and without recognition of the other interests involved, is violative of the Due Process Clause of the Fourteenth Amendment.

(a) For the stage prior to approximately the end of the first trimester, the abortion decision and its effectuation must be left to the medical judgment of the pregnant woman's attending physician.

(b) For the stage subsequent to approximately the end of the first trimester, the State, in promoting its interest in the health of the mother, may, if it chooses, regulate the abortion procedure in ways that are reasonably related to maternal health.

(c) For the stage subsequent to viability, the State in promoting its interest in the potentiality of human life may, if it chooses, regulate, and even proscribe, abortion except where it is necessary, in appropriate medical judgment, for the preservation of the life or health of the mother.

2. The State may define the term "physician," to mean only a physician currently licensed by the State, and may proscribe any abortion by a person who is not a physician as so defined.

Disposition of case: The judgment of the district court was affirmed in part and reversed in part.

Concurring opinion by Chief Justice Burger: The Chief Justice referenced to his concurring opinion in *Doe v. Bolton*, as the basis for his concurrence.

Concurring opinion by Justice Douglas: Justice Douglas referenced to his concurring opinion in *Doe v. Bolton*, as the basis for his concurrence.

Concurring opinion by Justice Stewart: Justice Stewart made the following observations in his concurring opinion:

> Several decisions of this Court make clear that freedom of personal choice in matters of marriage and family life is one of the liberties protected by the Due Process Clause of the Fourteenth Amendment. As recently as last Term, in Eisenstadt v. Baird, we recognized the right of the individual, married or single, to be free from unwarranted governmental intrusion into matters so fundamentally affecting a person as the decision whether to bear or beget a child. That right necessarily includes the right of a woman to decide whether or not to terminate her pregnancy....
>
> Clearly, therefore, the Court today is correct in holding that the right asserted by Jane Roe is embraced within the personal liberty protected by the Due Process Clause of the Fourteenth Amendment.
>
> It is evident that the Texas abortion statute infringes that right directly. Indeed, it is difficult to imagine a more complete abridgment of a constitutional freedom than that worked by the inflexible criminal statute now in force in Texas. The question then becomes whether the state interests advanced to justify this abridgment can survive the particularly careful scrutiny that the Fourteenth Amendment here requires.
>
> The asserted state interests are protection of the health and safety of the pregnant woman, and protection of the potential future human life within her. These are legitimate objectives, amply sufficient to permit a State to regulate abortions as it does other surgical procedures, and perhaps sufficient to permit a State to regulate abortions more stringently or even to prohibit them in the late stages of pregnancy. But such legislation is not before us, and I think the Court today has thoroughly demonstrated that these state interests cannot constitutionally support the broad abridgment of personal liberty worked by the existing Texas law. Accordingly, I join the Court's opinion holding that that law is invalid under the Due Process Clause of the Fourteenth Amendment.

Dissenting opinion by Justice White: Justice White referenced to his dissenting opinion in *Doe v. Bolton*, as the basis for his dissent.

Dissenting opinion by Justice Rehnquist: Justice Rehnquist disagreed with some of the facts in the majority opinion and the legal conclusion reached. He wrote as follows:

> The Court's opinion decides that a State may impose virtually no restriction on the performance of abortions during the first trimester of pregnancy. Our previous decisions indicate that a necessary predicate for such an opinion is a plaintiff who was in her first trimester of pregnancy at some time during the pendency of her law-suit. While a party may vindicate his own constitutional rights, he may not seek vindication for the rights of others. The Court's statement of facts in this case makes clear, however, that the record in no way indicates the presence of such a plaintiff. We know only that plaintiff Roe at the time of filing her complaint was a pregnant woman; for aught that appears in this record, she may have been in her last trimester of pregnancy as of the date the complaint was filed.
>
> Nothing in the Court's opinion indicates that Texas might not constitutionally apply its proscription of abortion as written to a woman in that stage of pregnancy. Nonetheless, the Court uses her complaint against the Texas statute as a fulcrum for deciding that States may impose virtually no restrictions on medical abortions performed during the first trimester of pregnancy. In deciding such a hypothetical lawsuit, the Court departs from the longstanding admonition that it should never formulate a rule of constitutional law broader than is required by the precise facts to which it is to be applied.
>
> Even if there were a plaintiff in this case capable of litigating the issue which the Court decides, I would reach a conclusion opposite to that reached by the Court. I have difficulty in concluding, as the Court does, that the right of privacy is involved in this case. Texas, by the statute here challenged, bars the performance of a medical abortion by a licensed physician on a plaintiff such as Roe. A transaction resulting in an operation such as this is not private in the ordinary usage of that word. Nor is the privacy that the Court finds here even a distant relative of the freedom from searches and seizures protected by the Fourth Amendment to the Constitution, which the Court has referred to as embodying a right to privacy.
>
> If the Court means by the term "privacy" no more than that the claim of a person to be free from unwanted state regulation of consensual transactions may be a form of liberty protected by the Fourteenth Amendment, there is no doubt that similar claims have been upheld in our earlier decisions on the basis of that liberty.... But that liberty is not guaranteed absolutely against deprivation, only against deprivation without due process of law. The test traditionally applied in the area of social and economic legislation is whether or not a law such as that challenged has a rational relation to a valid state objective. The Due Process Clause of the Fourteenth Amendment undoubtedly does place a limit, albeit a broad one, on legislative power to enact laws such as this. If the Texas statute were to prohibit an abortion even where the mother's life is in jeopardy, I have little doubt that such a statute would lack a rational relation to a valid state objective.... But the Court's sweeping invalidation of any restrictions on abortion during the first trimester is impossible to justify under that standard, and the conscious weighing of competing factors that the Court's opinion apparently substitutes for the established test is far more appropriate to a legislative judgment than to a judicial one....
>
> Even if one were to agree that the case that the Court decides

were here, and that the enunciation of the substantive constitutional law in the Court's opinion were proper, the actual disposition of the case by the Court is still difficult to justify. The Texas statute is struck down in toto, even though the Court apparently concedes that at later periods of pregnancy Texas might impose these selfsame statutory limitations on abortion. My understanding of past practice is that a statute found to be invalid as applied to a particular plaintiff, but not unconstitutional as a whole, is not simply struck down but is, instead, declared unconstitutional as applied to the fact situation before the Court.

Note: The decision in the case changed the landscape of abortion in the nation. Pursuant to the decision, states could not prohibit first trimester abortions. In subsequent decisions, the Supreme Court would abandon the trimester standard and prohibit states from criminalizing or preventing abortions prior to fetal viability. *See also* **Doe v. Bolton; McCorvey, Norma; Planned Parenthood of Southeastern Pennsylvania v. Casey**

RU-486 *see* **Mifepristone Induced Abortion**

RU-486 Patient Health and Safety Protection Act

The RU-486 Health and Safety Protection Act was a bill that was sponsored by pro-life members of Congress beginning in 2000. This bill was intended to create additional restrictions for doctors wishing to provide the abortion drug mifepristone. Among its provisions, the bill required that a doctor be able to provide surgical intervention her/himself, in cases where the mifepristone abortion failed; to have admitting privileges at a hospital within an hour's drive of the physician's office; and required the doctor to be certified for ultrasound dating of the pregnancy and detection of ectopic pregnancy. This bill was criticized as an effort to impede the use of mifepristone, by limiting its use to physicians who could meet all of the requirements specified in the bill. The text of the bill introduced in Congress in 2001 is set out below.

Section 1. Title

This Act may be cited as the "RU-486 Patient Health and Safety Protection Act."

Section 2. Restrictions regarding prescribing of certain abortion drug

With respect to the application that was submitted under section 505(b) of the Federal Food, Drug, and Cosmetic Act for the drug mifepristone (commonly referred to as RU-486, to be marketed as MIFEPREX), and that was approved on September 28, 2000, the Secretary of Health and Human Services, acting through the Commissioner of Food and Drugs, shall promptly modify the conditions of the approval of such drug to establish the additional restriction that the drug may not be prescribed by any person other than a licensed physician who meets the following requirements:

(1) The physician is qualified to handle complications resulting from an incomplete abortion or ectopic pregnancy.

(2) The physician has been trained to perform surgical abortions and has met all applicable legal requirements to perform such abortions.

(3) The physician is certified for ultrasound dating of pregnancy and detecting ectopic pregnancy.

(4) The physician has completed a program regarding the prescribing of such drug that uses a curriculum approved by the Secretary.

(5) The physician has admitting privileges at a hospital to which the physician can travel in one hour or less, determined on the basis of starting at the principal medical office of the physician and traveling to the hospital, using the transportation means normally used by the physician to travel to the hospital, and under the average conditions of travel for the physician.

See also **Mifepristone Induced Abortion**

Rubella *see* **Congenital Rubella Syndrome**

Rudolph, Eric Robert

Eric Robert Rudolph (b.1966) was a carpenter from Murphy, North Carolina, and a militant anti-abortionist who was charged by the Federal Bureau of Investigation with a series of bombing attacks. Rudolph was charged with the fatal bombing at a Birmingham, Alabama, abortion clinic on January 29, 1998, that killed Robert Sanderson, a Birmingham police officer working at the clinic as a security guard, and severely injured Emily Lyons, a clinic nurse. He was also charged with the double bombings at the Sandy Springs Professional Building in north Atlanta on January 16, 1997; the double bombings at The Otherside Lounge in Atlanta on February 21, 1997; and the July 27, 1996, bombing at Atlanta's Centennial Olympic Park that killed Alice Hawthorne and injured 100 others. A $1 million reward was posted for Rudolph's capture by the Federal Bureau of Investigation.

Rudolph was eventually captured in North Carolina in May of 2003. In 2005 Rudolph agreed to plead guilty to various charges and, on July 18, 2005, he was sentenced to several terms of life imprisonment. Rudolph is serving his time in federal prison. *See also* **Abortion Violence, Property Destruction and Demonstrations**

Ruptured Ectopic Pregnancy *see* **Ectopic Pregnancy**

Rust v. Sullivan

Forum: United States Supreme Court.

Case Citation: Rust v. Sullivan, 500 U.S. 173 (1991).

Date Argued: October 30, 1990.

Date of Decision: May 23, 1991.

Opinion of Court: Rehnquist, C.J., in which White, Kennedy, Scalia, and Souter, JJ., joined.

Concurring Opinion: None.

Dissenting Opinion: Blackmun, J., in which Marshall, O'Connor, and Stevens, JJ., joined.

Dissenting Opinion: Stevens, J.

Dissenting Opinion: O'Connor, J.

Counsel for Appellants: Laurence H. Tribe argued; on the brief were Kathleen M. Sullivan, Rachael N. Pine, Janet Benshoof, Lynn Paltrow, Kathryn Kolbert, Steven R. Shapiro, Norman Siegel, Arthur Eisenberg, Roger K. Evans, Laurie R. Rockett, Peter J. Rubin, Robert Abrams, O. Peter Sherwood, Suzanne M. Lynn, Sanford M. Cohen, Victor A. Kovner, Leonard J. Koerner, Lorna Bade Goodman, Gail Rubin, and Hillary Weisman.

Counsel for Appellee: Solicitor General Starr argued; on the brief were Assistant Attorney General Gerson, Deputy Solicitor General Roberts, Jeffrey P. Minear, Anthony J. Steinmeyer, Lowell V. Sturgill, Jr., and Joel Mangel.

Amicus Brief for Appellants: Commonwealth of Massachusetts et al. by David D. Cole, James M. Shannon, Attorney General of Massachusetts, and Ruth A. Bourquin, Assistant Attorney General; for Anthony J. Celebrezze, Jr., Attorney General of Ohio, et al. by Mr. Celebrezze, pro se, Suzanne E. Mohr and Jack W. Decker, Assistant Attorneys General, and Rita S. Eppler, Douglas B. Baily, Attorney General of Alaska, John K. Van de Kamp, Attorney General of California, Clarine Nardi Riddle, Attorney General of Connecticut, Charles M. Oberly III, Attorney General of Delaware, Herbert O. Reid, Sr., Corporation Counsel for the District of Columbia, James E. Tierney, Attorney General of Maine, Hubert H. Humphrey III, Attorney General of Minnesota, Robert M. Spire, Attorney General of Nebraska, Robert J. Del Tufo, Attorney General of New Jersey, Dave Frohnmayer, Attorney General of Oregon, Jim Mattox, Attorney General of Texas, Jeffrey L. Amestoy, Attorney General of Vermont, and Mary Sue Terry, Attorney General of Virginia; for the American College of Obstetricians and Gynecologists et al. by Carter G. Phillips, Ann E. Allen, Kirk B. Johnson, Laurie R. Rockett, Joel I. Klein, and Jack R. Bierig; for the American Library Association et al. by Bruce J. Ennis, Jr., and David W. Ogden; for the American Public Health Association et al. by Larry M. Lavinsky, Charles S. Sims, Michele M. Ovesey, and Nadine Taub; for the Association of the Bar of the City of New York by Conrad K. Harper, Janice Goodman, and Diane S. Wilner; for the NAACP Legal Defense and Educational Fund, Inc., et al. by Julius LeVonne Chambers and Charles Stephen Ralston; for the National Association of Women Lawyers et al. by James F. Fitzpatrick, L. Hope O'Keeffe, and Walter Dellinger; for the Planned Parenthood Federation of America et al. by Dara Klassel, Eve W. Paul, and Barbara E. Otten; for Twenty-Two Biomedical Ethicists by Michael E. Fine and Douglas W. Smith; and for Representative Patricia Schroeder et al. by David M. Becker.

Amicus Brief for Appellee: American Academy of Medical Ethics by Carolyn B. Kuhl; for the Association of American Physicians and Surgeons by Clarke D. Forsythe and Kent Masterson Brown; for Feminists for Life of America et al. by Edward R. Grant; for the Knights of Columbus by Carl A. Anderson; for the Rutherford Institute et al. by Wm. Charles Bundren, John W. Whitehead, A. Eric Johnston, David E. Morris, Stephen E. Hurst, Joseph P. Secola, Thomas S. Neuberger, J. Brian Heller, Thomas W. Strahan, William Bonner, Larry Crain, and James Knicely; for the United States Catholic Conference by Mark E. Chopko and Phillip H. Harris; and for Senator Gordon J. Humphrey et al. by James Bopp, Jr., and Richard E. Coleson.

Issue Presented: Whether new federal regulations, that prohibited pro-abortion counseling, referral, and advocacy by health care providers, were authorized by statute and had the effect of infringing upon constitutionally protected rights?

Case Holding: The new federal regulations that prohibited certain pro-abortion conduct by health care providers were validly created and did not violate the constitution.

Background facts of case: In 1988 the Secretary of the Department of Health and Human Services, appellee, promulgated new regulations for operating Title X of the Public Health Service Act (42 U.S.C. § 300-300a-6), which provides federal funding for family planning services. The new regulations imposed three primary restrictions on abortion as conditions for receiving federal funds under Title X. First, the regulations specified that a Title X project may not provide counseling concerning the use of abortion as a method of family planning or provide referral for abortion as a method of family planning. Second, the regulations broadly prohibited a Title X project from engaging in activities that encourage, promote or advocate abortion as a method of family planning. Third, the regulations required that Title X projects be organized so that they were physically and financially separate from prohibited abortion activities.

The new regulations were challenged in two separate lawsuits that were filed in a federal district court by the appellants, Title X grantees and doctors who supervise Title X funds. The lawsuits were consolidated. The appellants sought declaratory and injunctive relief to prevent implementation of the regulations, on the grounds that the regulations were not authorized by statute and that they violated the First and Fifth Amendment. The district court rejected the claims and granted summary judgment dismissal to the appellee. The Second Circuit court of appeals affirmed. The Supreme Court granted certiorari to consider the matter.

Majority opinion by Chief Justice Rehnquist: The Chief Justice rejected the claims made by the appellants. The majority opinion held that, although the enabling statute did not specifically provide authority to promulgate the new regulations, the appellee had discretion to create them. It was also said that the new regulations did not offend the constitution. The Chief Justice addressed the constitutional arguments as follows:

> [Appellants] contend that the regulations violate the First Amendment by impermissibly discriminating based on viewpoint because they prohibit all discussion about abortion as a lawful option — including counseling, referral, and the provision of neutral and accurate information about ending a pregnancy — while compelling the clinic or counselor to provide information that promotes continuing a pregnancy to term. They assert that the regulations violate the free speech rights of private health care organizations that receive Title X funds, of their staff, and of their patients by impermissibly imposing viewpoint-discriminatory conditions on government subsidies, and thus penalize speech funded with non–Title X monies....
>
> It could be argued by analogy that traditional relationships such as that between doctor and patient should enjoy protection under the First Amendment from government regulation, even when subsidized by the Government. We need not resolve that question here, however, because the Title X program regulations do not significantly impinge upon the doctor-patient relationship. Nothing in them requires a doctor to represent as his own, any opinion that he does not in fact hold. Nor is the doctor-patient relationship established by the Title X program sufficiently all-encompassing so as to justify an expectation on the part of the patient of comprehensive medical advice. The program does not provide post-conception medical care, and therefore a doctor's silence with regard to abortion cannot reasonably be thought to mislead a client into thinking that the doctor does not consider abortion an appropriate option for her. The doctor is always free to make clear that advice regarding abortion is simply beyond the scope of the program. In these circumstances, the general rule that the Government may choose not to subsidize speech applies with full force....
>
> We turn now to [appellants'] argument that the regulations violate a woman's Fifth Amendment right to choose whether to terminate her pregnancy.... The Government has no constitutional duty to subsidize an activity merely because the activity is constitutionally protected, and may validly choose to fund childbirth over abortion and implement that judgment by the allocation of public funds for medical services relating to childbirth, but not to those relating to abortion. The Government has no affirmative duty to commit any resources to facilitating abortions, and its decision to fund childbirth but not abortion places no governmental obstacle in the path of a woman who chooses to terminate her pregnancy, but rather, by means of unequal subsidization of abortion and other medical services, encourages alternative activity deemed in the public interest.
>
> That the regulations do not impermissibly burden a woman's Fifth Amendment rights.... Congress' refusal to fund abortion counseling and advocacy leaves a pregnant woman with the same choices as if the Government had chosen not to fund family planning services at all. The difficulty that a woman encounters when a Title X project does not provide abortion counseling or referral leaves her in no different position than she would have been if the Government had not enacted Title X.

Disposition of case: The judgment of the court of appeals was affirmed.

Dissenting opinion by Justice Blackmun: Justice Blackmun disagreed with the majority opinion. He believed the new regulations violated the constitution. Justice Blackmun wrote as follows:

> Casting aside established principles of statutory construction and administrative jurisprudence, the majority in these cases today unnecessarily passes upon important questions of constitutional law. In so doing, the Court, for the first time, upholds viewpoint-based suppression of speech solely because it is imposed on those dependent upon the Government for economic support. Under essentially the same rationale, the majority upholds direct regulation of dialogue between a pregnant woman and her physician

when that regulation has both the purpose and the effect of manipulating her decision as to the continuance of her pregnancy. I conclude that the Secretary's regulation of referral, advocacy, and counseling activities exceeds his statutory authority, and also that the Regulations violate the First and Fifth Amendments of our Constitution. Accordingly, I dissent, and would reverse the divided-vote judgment of the Court of Appeals.

Dissenting opinion by Justice Stevens: Justice Stevens dissented from the majority opinion. He argued that no authority existed for creating the new regulations. Justice Stevens addressed the issue as follows:

> The entirely new approach adopted by the Secretary in 1988 was not, in my view, authorized by the statute. The new regulations did not merely reflect a change in a policy determination that the Secretary had been authorized by Congress to make. Rather, they represented an assumption of policymaking responsibility that Congress had not delegated to the Secretary. In a society that abhors censorship and in which policymakers have traditionally placed the highest value on the freedom to communicate, it is unrealistic to conclude that statutory authority to regulate conduct implicitly authorized the Executive to regulate speech.
>
> Because I am convinced that the 1970 Act did not authorize the Secretary to censor the speech of grant recipients or their employees, I would hold the challenged regulations invalid and reverse the judgment of the Court of Appeals.

Dissenting opinion by Justice O'Connor: Justice O'Connor dissented from the decision of the majority. She did not believe that the enabling statute gave authorization to create the new regulations. Justice O'Connor stated her position as follows:

> This Court acts at the limits of its power when it invalidates a law on constitutional grounds. In recognition of our place in the constitutional scheme, we must act with great gravity and delicacy when telling a coordinate branch that its actions are absolutely prohibited absent constitutional amendment. In this case, we need only tell the Secretary that his regulations are not a reasonable interpretation of the statute; we need not tell Congress that it cannot pass such legislation. If we rule solely on statutory grounds, Congress retains the power to force the constitutional question by legislating more explicitly. It may instead choose to do nothing. That decision should be left to Congress; we should not tell Congress what it cannot do before it has chosen to do it. It is enough in this case to conclude that neither the language nor the history of [the statute] compels the Secretary's interpretation, and that the interpretation raises serious First Amendment concerns. On this basis alone, I would reverse the judgment of the Court of Appeals and invalidate the challenged regulations.

S

Saia, Alexandria

Alexandria Saia was born after a failed abortion attempt by her mother, Nicole Saia. Nicole went to a clinic in mid–2000, in Gainesville, Florida to have the abortion. Nicole was injected with a chemical, methotrexate, that was supposed to destroy the fetus. She was also given suppositories that she had to take five days later to induce contractions that would expel the dead fetus. However, two days after being injected with the methotrexate, Nicole changed her mind and did not want to abort her baby. She went to Citrus Memorial Hospital and consulted Dr. Steven Roth. Dr. Roth informed Nicole that the fetus was still alive and that he would provide her with a drug, leucovorin, that might destroy the methotrexate before it destroyed the fetus. Nicole took the drug and on April 5, 2001, she gave live birth to Alexandria. *See also* **Survivors of Abortion**

St. Thomas Students for Human Life

St. Thomas Students for Human Life is a student-run pro-life organization on the campus of the University of St. Thomas, in St. Paul, Minnesota. The organization advocates respect for the sanctity of human life and opposes the intentional killing of innocent human beings through abortion. The group considers abortion to be equivalent to murder, and contrary to natural law. Its members seek to combat abortion through a program that consists of educating students and the University of St. Thomas community at large, using rational arguments against abortion. The organization also works to promote legislation securing the right to life from conception to natural death, assisting in offering realistic alternatives to abortion, and coordinating services and resources with other right-to-life organizations. *See also* **Pro-Life Organizations**

Saline Amniocentesis *see* **Instillation Methods**

Salvi, John C., III

In 1994 John C. Salvi III was a 22-year-old mentally disturbed New Hampshire hairdresser and militant anti-abortionist. During the summer of 1994 Salvi and other anti-abortionists conducted demonstrations at abortion clinics in Brookline, Massachusetts. On December 30, 1994, Salvi returned to Brookline, alone, but armed with a .22-caliber Sturm Ruger semiautomatic rifle and 1,000 hollow-tip bullets. Salvi entered a Planned Parenthood Federation of America clinic in Brookline, pulled out the rifle and opened fire. He killed a receptionist, 25-year-old Shannon Lowney, and wounded three other people in the clinic's waiting room. Salvi fled the scene and drove about two miles to the Preterm Health Services clinic and opened fire once again. He killed another receptionist, 38-year-old Lee Ann Nichols, and wounded two others. Salvi then escaped and drove to an abortion clinic in Norfolk, Virginia. He fired 23 shots into the clinic building.

Salvi was apprehended in Virginia and extradited to Massachusetts. On March 18, 1996, a jury convicted Salvi of two counts of murder and five counts of armed assault with intent to murder. The trial judge imposed two life imprisonment sentences for the murders, and a term of years for the attempted murder convictions. On November 29, 1996, Salvi was found dead under his cell bed with a plastic garbage bag tied around his head, a gag in his mouth, and his hands bound with shoelaces. His death was ruled suicide by asphyxiation. *See also* **Abortion Violence, Property Destruction and Demonstrations**

Sanford, Edward T.

Edward T. Sanford (1865–1930) served as an associate justice of the United States Supreme Court from 1923 to 1930. While on the Supreme Court Justice Sanford was considered a moderate in his interpretation of the Constitution.

Justice Sanford was born in Knoxville, Tennessee. His higher education began at the University of Tennessee and culminated with a law degree from Harvard Law School in 1889. Justice Sanford's early legal career was spent in private practice and as an assistant U.S. attorney general. In 1908 President Theodore Roosevelt nominated Justice Sanford for a position as a federal district court judge in Tennessee. He remained at that position until 1923 when President Warren Harding nominated him to the Supreme Court.

During Justice Sanford's tenure on the Supreme Court he was involved in only one abortion related opinion. Justice Sanford voted with a unanimous opinion in *State of Missouri ex rel. Hurwitz v. North*, which held that the constitution was not violated when a physician was prevented from issuing subpoenas to have witnesses attend a hearing to revoke his medical license for performing an unlawful abortion, because the applicable rules required taking depositions of witnesses who would not voluntarily attend the hearing.

Sanger, Margaret

Margaret Sanger (1883–1966) was a pioneer in the birth control movement in the United States. Born in Corning, New York, Sanger studied abroad in England where she developed moral and philosophical concerns toward poor women who gave birth to children they could neither feed, clothe nor educate. Upon returning to the United States, Sanger launched a life long campaign to educate poor women on the use of birth control methods. In 1915 she was indicted for distributing birth control information through the mails. Undaunted by the indictment, Sanger opened the first birth control clinic in the United States in 1916, in Brooklyn, New York. The clinic was soon closed and Sanger was prosecuted and sentenced to 30 days in jail for operating it. Sanger went on to establish the Birth Control Clinical Research Bureau and the American Birth Control League. These organizations eventually merged and became known as Planned Parenthood Federation of America. Sanger authored numerous works on family planning including, *Woman and the New Race* (1920) and *Happiness in Marriage* (1926). *See also* **Planned Parenthood Federation of America**

Margaret Sanger was a pioneer in the birth control movement. She opened the first birth control clinic in the United States in 1916, in Brooklyn, New York (Library of Congress).

Santoro, Geraldine

Geraldine "Gerri" Santoro (1935–1964) became a national symbol of the evils associated with "backroom" unlawful abortions. In 1964 Santoro, who was estranged from her husband, was living in Connecticut with her two daughters. Santoro entered into a relationship with a man named Clyde Dixon. Santoro became pregnant as a result of the relationship. When she was about six months pregnant, Santoro and Dixon concocted a plan to have Dixon perform an abortion. On June 8, 1964 they rented a room in a hotel in Norwich, Connecticut. While in the room Dixon attempted to perform the abortion. However, something went wrong and Dixon fled the hotel leaving Santoro on the floor to die. Santoro's nude and dead body was found lying on the floor the next day by a hotel maid. The police took pictures of the body. Dixon was apprehended by the police a few days after Santoro's death. He was prosecuted for manslaughter and received a one year prison sentence.

In 1973 one of the photographs taken by the police of Santoro's nude body, was published in *Ms.* Magazine without any identification of who the dead woman was. Santoro's sister, Leona Gordon, saw the picture and identified the body as that of Santoro. The life and death of Santoro was eventually made into a movie, called *Leona's Sister Gerri*, by filmmaker Jane Gillooly. The photo of Santoro published by Ms. Magazine eventually became a symbol for pro-choice advocates. *See also* **Complications During and After Abortion**

Sarcoma of the Uterus

Sarcoma of the uterus is a rare disease in which malignant cancer cells grow in the muscles of the uterus. The disease usually occurs in middle aged and elderly women, although it may affect younger women as well. Risk factors for the disease includes having previous pelvic radiation therapy.

In the rare instance that a woman with sarcoma of the uterus is pregnant, problems could rise for the fetus. The fact of pregnancy generally has no adverse effect on sarcoma of the uterus, and sarcoma of the uterus has no effect on the pregnancy. However, if certain cancer treatment methods are used during pregnancy, it may become necessary to have a therapeutic abortion, or the fetus could be exposed to birth defects. Four kinds of treatment are used in combating the disease: surgery, radiation therapy, chemotherapy and hormone therapy. *See also* **Cancer and Pregnancy; Therapeutic Abortion**

Scalia, Antonin

Antonin Scalia was appointed to serve as an associate justice of the United States Supreme Court in 1986. While on the Supreme Court Justice Scalia has displayed an ultra conservative interpretation of the Constitution.

Justice Scalia was born in Trenton, New Jersey, on March 11, 1936. He attended Georgetown University and received a law degree from Harvard Law School in 1960. Justice Scalia taught administrative law at the University of Chicago before being appointed as an appellate judge on the Court of Appeals for the District of Columbia. In 1986 President Ronald Reagan appointed Justice Scalia to the Supreme Court.

During Justice Scalia's tenure on the Supreme Court he has issued a number of abortion related opinions. The written opinions and opinions simply voted on by Justice Scalia, indicate that he is not in favor of using the constitution to expand abortion rights for women.

(1) Unanimous opinions voted with only. Justice Scalia voted with a unanimous Court in *Scheidler v. National Organization for Women, Inc. (II)*, which held pro-choice advocates could not sue pro-life advocates under the Hobbs Act for allegations of physical violence that did not involve extortion. In *Dalton v. Little Rock Family Planning Services*, Justice Scalia voted with a unanimous Court in holding that an amendment to Arkansas' constitution which limited Medicaid payment only to therapeutic abortions, was invalid to the extent that Medicaid funds had to be made available for incest or rape pregnancies, but was valid for any purely state funded program. Justice Scalia voted with a unanimous Court in *National Organization for Women, Inc. v. Scheidler*, which held that a group of pro-choice organizations could maintain a RICO civil lawsuit against several anti-abortion individuals and groups. Justice Scalia joined a unanimous opinion in *Ayotte v. Planned Parenthood of Northern New England*, which held that the absence of a health exception in New Hampshire's parental notification abortion statute did not require the entire statute be invalidated.

Distribution of the Abortion Voting Pattern of Justice Scalia Based Upon Opinions Filed by the Supreme Court

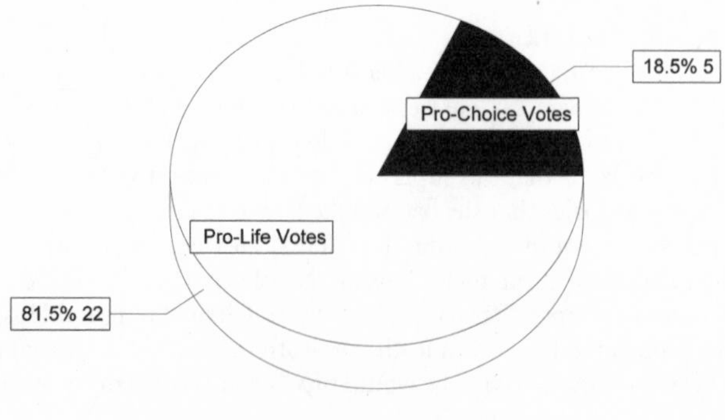

(2) Majority opinions written. Justice Scalia wrote the majority opinion in *Bray v. Alexandria Clinic*, which held that the Civil Rights Act of 1871, 42 U.S.C. § 1985(3), did not provide a cause of action against persons obstructing access to abortion clinics.

(3) Majority opinions voted with only. In *Lambert v. Wicklund* Justice Scalia voted with the majority in holding that the constitution was not violated by a provision in Montana's abortion statute that allowed a court to waive the parental notice requirement for minors, if notification was not in minor's best interest. Justice Scalia voted with the majority in *Leavitt v. Jane L.*, which held that the invalidity of Utah's statute regulating pregnancies 20 weeks old or less, may be severed so as to preserve that portion of the abortion statute that regulated pregnancies of more than 20 weeks. In *Daubert v. Merrell Dow Pharmaceuticals, Inc.*, a case involving children born with severe birth defects, Justice Scalia voted with the majority in holding that the *Frye* rule on admissibility of expert testimony did not survive the enactment of the Federal Rules of Evidence. Justice Scalia voted with the majority in *Rust v. Sullivan*, which upheld federal regulations that prohibited pro-abortion counseling, referral, and advocacy by health care providers. Justice Scalia joined the majority opinion in *Mazurek v. Armstrong*, which held that Montana's requirement that abortions be performed only by physicians was constitutionally valid.

In *Frisby v. Schultz* Justice Scalia voted with the majority opinion, which upheld the constitutional validity of a town ordinance that was created to prevent pro-life picketing at the residence of an abortion doctor. Justice Scalia voted with the majority opinion in *United States Catholic Conference v. Abortion Rights Mobilization*, which allowed the appellants to challenge having to turn over documents in a lawsuit seeking to strip them of their tax exempt status because of their active political abortion work. In *Federal Election Commission v. Massachusetts Citizens for Life, Inc.* Justice Scalia voted with the majority opinion, which held that federal law that prohibited the appellee from using its treasury funds to promote pro-life political candidates violated the Free Speech Clause of the First Amendment. Justice Scalia joined the majority opinion in *Scheidler v. National Organization for Women, Inc. (I)*, which held that evidence did not support finding that pro-life advocates violated the Hobbs Act, Travel Act and state law extortion crimes, for the purpose of awarding damages and granting an injunction against them under RICO.

(4) Concurring opinions written. In *Automobile Workers v. Johnson Controls, Inc.* Justice Scalia wrote an opinion concurring with the majority opinion, which held that Title VII of the Civil Rights Act forbids sex-specific fetal-protection policies by an employer, that exclude a fertile female employee from certain jobs because of the employer's concern for the health of the fetus the woman might conceive. In *Ohio v. Akron Center for Reproductive Health* Justice Scalia wrote an opinion concurring with the majority decision, which upheld the constitutionality of Ohio's abortion statute notice and judicial bypass requirements for pregnant female minors. Justice Scalia wrote a concurring opinion in *Webster v. Reproductive Health Services*, which upheld Missouri's prohibition on the use of public facilities or employees to perform abortions and a requirement that physicians conduct viability tests prior to performing abortions. Justice Scalia wrote a concurring opinion in *Federal Election Commission v. Wisconsin Right to Life, Inc.*, which held that the electioneering communications provisions of a federal statute violated a pro-life organization's First Amendment right to broadcast political issue oriented advertisements shortly before primary and general elections.

(5) Concurring opinions voted with only. Justice Scalia joined the concurring opinion in *Gonzales v. Carhart*, which held that the Partial-Birth Abortion Ban Act of 2003 was not facially unconstitutional, because it outlined the abortion procedure that was banned, and the Act did not have to provide an exception for the health of a woman.

Justice Scalia's voting pattern favors the views of pro-life advocates (collection, Supreme Court Historical Society, photograph by Mollie Isaacs, F2 Photographic Studios).

(6) Dissenting opinions written. Justice Scalia wrote a dissenting opinion in *Ferguson v. City of Charleston* where he argued that patient consent or a search warrant was not needed, in order for a government hospital to turn over to the police drug test results that showed a woman used illegal drugs during her pregnancy. In *Stenberg v. Carhart*, Justice Scalia wrote a dissenting opinion opposing the majority's decision to find Nebraska's statute banning partial-birth abortion unconstitutional. In *Hill v. Colorado* Justice Scalia wrote a dissenting opinion in which he disagreed with the majority decision to uphold a Colorado statute that made it unlawful for any person within 100 feet of an abortion facility's entrance, to knowingly approach within 8 feet of another person, without that person's consent, in order to pass a leaflet, handbill, display a sign, engage in oral protest, education, or counseling with that person.

(7) Dissenting opinions voted with only. Justice Scalia joined the dissenting opinion in *Federal Election Commission v. Beaumont*, which held that the Federal Election Campaign Act's prohibition on corporate expenditures and contributions directly to candidates in federal elections, applies to a nonprofit pro-life organization.

(8) Concurring and dissenting opinions written. Justice Scalia wrote a concurring and dissenting opinion in *Schenck v. Pro Choice Network of Western New York*, which held that a federal trial court's injunction provisions imposing fixed buffer zone limitations on abortion protesters were constitutional, but the provisions imposing floating buffer zone limitations violated the First Amendment. Justice Scalia believed

that the fixed buffer zone limitations were invalid also. In *Madsen v. Women's Health Clinic, Inc.*, Justice Scalia wrote a concurring and dissenting opinion. The decision in *Madsen* upheld parts of an injunction that restricted noise by anti-abortionists at a clinic and imposed a 36 foot buffer zone around the clinic entrances and driveway. Justice Scalia dissented from that part of the decision. However, *Madsen* ruled that the Free Speech Clause was violated by a 36 foot buffer zone as applied to the private property to the north and west of the clinic, a restriction on the use of images observable by clinic patients, a 300 foot no approach zone around the clinic, and a 300 foot buffer zone around the residences, because these restrictions swept more broadly than necessary to accomplish the permissible goals of the injunction. Justice Scalia concurred with the majority's decision finding some provisions in the injunction violated the Free Speech Clause.

In *Planned Parenthood of Southeastern Pennsylvania v. Casey*, Justice Scalia wrote a concurring and dissenting opinion. He concurred in the majority's decision that the constitution was not violated by provisions in Pennsylvania's abortion statute that provided for: medical emergency abortion; 24 hour waiting period for abortion; parental notice and judicial bypass for abortion by a minor; and certain abortion facility reporting requirements. He dissented from the majority's decision that found two provisions in the abortion statute unconstitutional: spousal notification before obtaining an abortion, and a requirement that a woman inform the abortion provider the reason for not notifying her spouse.

Justice Scalia wrote a concurring and dissenting opinion in *Hodgson v. Minnesota*, which upheld the constitutionality of Minnesota's requirement that a pregnant female minor could not obtain an abortion until at least 48 hours after both of her parents had been notified, except when (1) the attending physician certified that an immediate abortion was necessary to prevent the minor's death; (2) the minor declared that she was a victim of parental abuse or neglect; or (3) a court of competent jurisdiction ordered the abortion to proceed without notice upon proof that the minor was mature and capable of giving informed consent or that an abortion without notice to both parents would be in the minor's best interest. Justice Scalia dissented from the Court's determination that the two-parent notification requirement was invalid, but concurred in the determination that the judicial bypass option cured the defect.

Scheidler v. National Organization for Women, Inc. (I)

Forum: United States Supreme Court.

Case Citation: Scheidler v. National Organization for Women, Inc., 537 U.S. 393 (2003).

Date Argued: December 2, 2002.

Date of Decision: February 26, 2003.

Opinion of Court: Rehnquist, C.J., in which O'Connor, Scalia, Kennedy, Souter, Thomas, Ginsburg, and Breyer, JJ., joined.

Concurring Opinion: Ginsburg, J., in which Breyer, J., joined.

Dissenting Opinion: Stevens, J.

Counsel for Appellants: Roy T. Englert, Jr., argued; on the brief were Walter M. Weber, Larry L. Crain, David A. Cortman, Robert W. Ash, Thomas P. Monaghan, Charles E. Rice, Jay Alan Sekulow, Colby M. May, Stuart J. Roth, James M. Henderson, Sr., Vincent P. McCarthy, Thomas Brejcha, Deborah Fischer Thomas, D. Colette Wilson, Alan Untereiner, Arnon D. Siegel, Kathryn S. Zecca, and Sherri Lynn Wolson.

Counsel for Appellees: Fay Clayton argued; on the brief were A. Stephen Hut, Jr., David W. Ogden, Terry A. Maroney, Kimberly A. Parker, Rachel A. Shachter, Kerry A. Miller, Susan Valentine, Joyce A. Pollack, and Lowell E. Sachnoff.

Amicus Brief for Appellants: Life Legal Defense Foundation; Americans United for Life; Center for Individual Rights; National Association of Criminal Defense Lawyers; New York Council of Defense Lawyers; People for the Ethical Treatment of Animals, Inc.; Rutherford Institute; Seamless Garment Network; Feminists for Life of America; The Fund for Animals; Not Dead Yet; Sojourners; Witnesses for Reconciliation; Wendell Berry, Abe Bonowitz, Bernard Broussard, Carol Crossed, Will Davis Campbell, Ruth Enero, Nat Hentoff, Kathy Kelly, Rachel MacNair, Michele Pflaum, Mary S. Rider, Martin Sheen, and Howard Zinn; the states of Alabama, Nebraska, North Dakota and South Dakota, and the Commonwealth of the Northern Mariana Islands; Center for Individual Rights; Liberty Counsel; Catholics for Life; Concerned Women for America; Catholic Conference of Illinois; Francis Cardinal George; Joseph L. Imesch; Wilton D. Gregory; George J. Lucas; and Steven Rohlfs.

Amicus Brief for Appellees: Feminist Majority Foundation; Planned Parenthood Federation of America, Inc.; Center for Reproductive Law & Policy; Medical Students for Choice; National Abortion Federation; Physicians for Reproductive Choice and Health; Voters for Choice; Former Federal Prosecutors and Women in Federal Law Enforcement, Inc.; Motorola Credit Corporation; Religious Coalition for Reproductive Choice; the states of California, New York, Connecticut, Maryland, Massachusetts, Montana, Nevada, Washington and West Virginia; Lawyers' Committee for Civil Rights Under Law; NARAL Foundation/NARAL; American Association of University Women; Asian American Legal Defense and Education Fund; Center for Disability and Elder Law; Chicago Foundation for Women; Human Rights Campaign; National Center for Lesbian Rights; National Council of Negro Women, Inc.; National Gay and Lesbian Task Force; National Partnership for Women & Families; National Women's Law Center; Northwest Women's Law Center; Now Legal Defense and Education Fund; People for the American Way Foundation; Rainbow Push Coalition, Inc.; Southern Poverty Law Center; Women Employed, Women's Law Project; and Emily Lyons.

Issue Presented: Whether the evidence supported finding that pro-life advocates violated the Hobbs Act, Travel Act and state law extortion crimes, for the purpose of awarding damages and granting an injunction against them under RICO?

Case Holding: The evidence did not support finding that pro-life advocates violated the Hobbs Act, Travel Act and state law extortion crimes, for the purpose of awarding damages and granting an injunction against them under RICO.

Background facts of case: The appellees, National Organization For Women, Inc., Delaware Women's Health Organization, Inc., and Summit Women's Health Organization, Inc., filed a federal lawsuit in Illinois against the appellants, Joseph Scheidler, John Patrick Ryan, Randall A. Terry, Andrew Scholberg, Conrad Wojnar, Timothy Murphy, Monica Migliorino, Pro-Life Action Network, VitalMed Laboratories, Inc., Pro-Life Action League, Inc., Pro-Life Direct Action League, Inc., Operation Rescue, and Project Life. The appellees alleged that the appellants were members of a nationwide conspiracy to shut down abortion clinics through a pattern of racketeering activity, in violation of the Racketeer Influenced and Corrupt Organizations (RICO) chapter of the Organized Crime Control Act of 1970 (18 U.S.C. §§ 1961–1968), the Hobbs Act (18 U.S.C. § 1951), the Travel Act (18 U.S.C. § 1952) and various state law extortion crimes. It was further alleged that the appellants conspired to use threatened or actual force, violence, or fear to induce clinic employees, doctors, and patients to give up their jobs, their right to practice medicine, and their right to obtain clinic services; that the conspiracy injured the clinics' business and property interests; and that the appellants are a racketeering enterprise. The federal district court dismissed the case on the grounds that the appellees failed to state a cause of action, because they did not allege a profit-generating purpose in the appellants' activity or enterprise.

The Seventh Circuit court of appeals affirmed the dismissal, after agreeing with the district court that there was an economic motive requirement implicit in the "enterprise" element of a RICO cause of action. The Supreme Court granted certiorari to consider the matter. The Supreme Court reversed the dismissal on the grounds that RICO did not require an economic motive.

After the case was remanded to the district court a jury trial was held. The jury found in favor of the appellees. The district thereafter entered judgment on jury verdict awarding damages to appellees and a permanent, nationwide injunction restricting protest activities of the appellants. The court of appeals affirmed. The Supreme Court granted certiorari to consider the case.

Majority opinion by Chief Justice Rehnquist: The Chief Justice found that the evidence failed to establish that there was a violation of the Hobbs Act, Travel Act, RICO or state law extortion crimes. The opinion addressed the issues as follows:

> There is no dispute in these cases that [appellants] interfered with, disrupted, and in some instances completely deprived [appellees] of their ability to exercise their property rights. Likewise, [appellants'] counsel readily acknowledged at oral argument that aspects of his clients' conduct were criminal. But even when their acts of interference and disruption achieved their ultimate goal of "shutting down" a clinic that performed abortions, such acts did not constitute extortion because [appellants] did not "obtain" [appellees'] property. [Appellants] may have deprived or sought to deprive [appellees] of their alleged property right of exclusive control of their business assets, but they did not acquire any such property. [Appellants] neither pursued nor received "something of value from" [appellees] that they could exercise, transfer, or sell. To conclude that such actions constituted extortion would effectively discard the statutory requirement that property must be obtained from another, replacing it instead with the notion that merely interfering with or depriving someone of property is sufficient to constitute extortion.
>
> Eliminating the requirement that property must be obtained to constitute extortion would not only conflict with the express requirement of the Hobbs Act, it would also eliminate the recognized distinction between extortion and the separate crime of coercion — a distinction that is implicated in these cases. The crime of coercion, which more accurately describes the nature of [appellants'] actions, involves the use of force or threat of force to restrict another's freedom of action....
>
> Because we find that [appellants] did not obtain or attempt to obtain property from [appellees], we conclude that there was no basis upon which to find that they committed extortion under the Hobbs Act....
>
> Because [appellants] did not obtain or attempt to obtain [appellees'] property, both the state extortion claims and the claim of attempting or conspiring to commit state extortion were fatally flawed. The 23 violations of the Travel Act and 23 acts of attempting to violate the Travel Act also fail. These acts were committed in furtherance of allegedly extortionate conduct. But we have already determined that [appellants] did not commit or attempt to commit extortion.
>
> Because all of the predicate acts supporting the jury's finding of a RICO violation must be reversed, the judgment that [appellants] RICO must also be reversed. Without an underlying RICO violation, the injunction issued by the District Court must necessarily be vacated.

Disposition of case: The judgment of the appellate court was reversed.

Concurring opinion by Justice Ginsburg: Justice Ginsburg joined the majority opinion and judgment. She wrote a terse concurring opinion in which she indicated that RICO should not be interpreted so broadly as to allow the type of action brought in the case.

Dissenting opinion by Justice Stevens: Justice Stevens dissented from the majority judgment. He took the position that a Hobbs Act violation was established. Justice Stevens wrote as follows:

> The term "extortion" as defined in the Hobbs Act refers to "the obtaining of property from another." The Court's murky opinion seems to hold that this phrase covers nothing more than the acquisition of tangible property. No other federal court has ever construed this statute so narrowly.
>
> For decades federal judges have uniformly given the term "property" an expansive construction that encompasses the intangible right to exercise exclusive control over the lawful use of business assets. The right to serve customers or to solicit new business is thus a protected property right. The use of violence or threats of violence to persuade the owner of a business to surrender control of such an intangible right is an appropriation of control embraced by the term "obtaining." That is the commonsense reading of the statute that other federal judges have consistently and wisely embraced in numerous cases that the Court does not discuss or even cite. Recognizing this settled definition of property, as I believe one must, the conclusion that [appellants] obtained this property from [appellees] is amply supported by the evidence in the record.

See also **Hobbs Act; National Organization for Women, Inc. v. Scheidler; RICO; Scheidler v. National Organization for Women, Inc. (II); Travel Act**

Scheidler v. National Organization for Women, Inc. (II)

Forum: United States Supreme Court.

Case Citation: Scheidler v. National Organization for Women, Inc., 547 U.S. 9 (2006).

Date Argued: November 30, 2005.

Date of Decision: February 28, 2006.

Opinion of Court: Breyer, J., unanimous; Alito, J., did not participate.

Concurring Opinion: None.

Dissenting Opinion: None.

Counsel for Appellants: Alan Untereiner argued; on the brief were Thomas Brejcha, Deborah Fischer, Christopher Henning, Thomas More, D. Coletre Wilson, Roy T. Englert, Jr., Kathryn S. Zecca, Noah Messing Robbins, Thomas P. Monaghan, John P. Tuskey, Laura B. Hernandez, Shannon D. Woodruff, Larry L. Crain, Robert W. Ash, Jay Alan Sekulow, Walter M. Weber, Stuart J. Roth, Vincent P. McCarthy, and Ann-Louise Lohr.

Counsel for Appellees: Erwin Chemerinsky argued; on the brief were Paul Hoffman, Laurie Levenson, Catherine Fisk, Fay Clayton, Adam Hirsch, Lowell E. Sachnoff, Jack L. Block, and Frank Susman.

Amicus Brief for Appellants: American Federation of Labor and Congress of Industrial Organizations; the States of Alabama, Colorado, Delaware, Kansas, Michigan, Ohio, South Dakota, Texas, and Utah; Consistent Life, Catholic-Labor Network, Citizens United for Alternatives to the Death Penalty, the Conference of Major Superiors of Men, Interfaith Worker Justice, The Leadership Conference of Women Religious, People for the Ethical Treatment of Animals, Sojourners, Daniel Berrigan, Will Davis Campbell, Carol Crossed, Thomas Gumbleton, Kathy Kelly, Rachel MacNair, Helen Prejean, Martin Sheen, Howard Zinn, Stephen Zunes; Concerned Women for America; Life Legal Defense Foundation; and Americans United for Life.

Amicus Brief for Appellees: NARAL Pro-Choice America, American Association of University Women, Americans for Democratic Action, Inc., Black Women's Health Imperative, Center for Reproductive Rights, Center for Women Policy Studies, Hadassah, WZOA, Inc., Legal Momentum, National Asian Pacific American Women's Forum,

National Center for Lesbian Rights, National Council of Jewish Women, Inc., National Health Law Program, National Latina Institute for Reproductive Health, National Partnership for Women & Families, National Women's Law Center, Women Employed, Women's Law Project and Woodhull Freedom Foundation; Lawyers' Committee for Civil Rights Under Law and the National Association for the Advancement of Colored People; Feminist Majority Foundation, Planned Parenthood Federation of America, Inc., Medical Students for Choice, National Abortion Federation, National Coalition of Abortion Providers, and Physicians for Reproductive Choice and Health; 47 Members of the United States Congress; Abner J. Mikva and William A. Norris; Religious Coalition for Reproductive Choice; and Emily Lyons.

Issue Presented: Whether pro-choice advocates can sue pro-life advocates under the Hobbs Act for allegations of violence that did not involve extortion?

Case Holding: Pro-choice advocates could not sue pro-life advocates under the Hobbs Act for allegations of physical violence that did not involve extortion.

Background facts of case: The appellees, National Organization For Women, Inc., Delaware Women's Health Organization, Inc., and Summit Women's Health Organization, Inc., filed a federal lawsuit in Illinois against the appellants, Joseph Scheidler, John Patrick Ryan, Randall A. Terry, Andrew Scholberg, Conrad Wojnar, Timothy Murphy, Monica Migliorino, Pro-Life Action Network, VitalMed Laboratories, Inc., Pro-Life Action League, Inc., Pro-Life Direct Action League, Inc., Operation Rescue, and Project Life. The appellees alleged that the appellants were members of a nationwide conspiracy to shut down abortion clinics through a pattern of racketeering activity, in violation of the Racketeer Influenced and Corrupt Organizations (RICO) chapter of the Organized Crime Control Act of 1970 (18 U.S.C. §§ 1961–1968), the Hobbs Act (18 U.S.C. § 1951), the Travel Act (18 U.S.C. § 1952) and various state law extortion crimes. It was further alleged that the appellants conspired to use threatened or actual force, violence, or fear to induce clinic employees, doctors, and patients to give up their jobs, their right to practice medicine, and their right to obtain clinic services; that the conspiracy injured the clinics' business and property interests; and that the appellants are a racketeering enterprise. The federal district court dismissed the case on the grounds that the appellees failed to state a cause of action, because they did not allege a profit-generating purpose in the appellants' activity or enterprise. The Seventh Circuit court of appeals affirmed the dismissal, after agreeing with the district court that there was an economic motive requirement implicit in the "enterprise" element of a RICO cause of action. The Supreme Court granted certiorari to consider the matter. The Supreme Court reversed the dismissal on the grounds that RICO did not require an economic motive.

After the case was remanded to the district court a jury trial was held. The jury found in favor of the appellees. The district thereafter entered judgment on jury verdict awarding damages to appellees and a permanent, nationwide injunction restricting protest activities of the appellants. The court of appeals affirmed. The Supreme Court granted certiorari to consider the case. The Supreme Court reversed the jury verdict and injunction, on the grounds that the extortion conduct alleged against the appellants was not actionable under the Hobbs Act. The case was remanded to the court of appeals. While the case was pending before the court of appeals, the appellees argued that the jury verdict and injunction should be reinstated, because their lawsuit involved allegations of violence that were independent of extortion. The court of appeals decided to remand the case to the district court to consider the new argument. However, the Supreme Court granted certiorari to decide whether the court of appeals erred in its remand instructions.

Unanimous opinion by Justice Breyer: Justice Breyer wrote a unanimous opinion finding that the Hobbs Act did not allow the appellees to sue the appellants on a theory of violent conduct that did not involve violence. The opinion addressed the matter as follows:

> We first set forth the Hobbs Act's text. The relevant statutory section imposes criminal liability on
>
> > "[w]hoever in any way or degree obstructs, delays, or affects commerce or the movement of any article or commodity in commerce, by robbery or extortion or attempts or conspires so to do, or commits or threatens physical violence to any person or property *in furtherance of a plan or purpose to do anything in violation of this section* ...."
>
> The question, as we have said, concerns the meaning of the phrase that modifies the term "physical violence," namely, the words "in furtherance of a plan or purpose to do anything in violation of this section." Do those words refer to violence (1) that furthers a plan or purpose to "affec[t] commerce ... by robbery or extortion," or to violence (2) that furthers a plan or purpose simply to "affec[t] commerce"? We believe the former, more restrictive, reading of the text — the reading that ties the violence to robbery or extortion — is correct.
>
> For one thing, the language of the statute makes the more restrictive reading the more natural one. The text that precedes the physical violence clause does not forbid *obstructing, delaying, or affecting commerce* (or the movement of any article or commodity in commerce); rather, it forbids *obstructing, delaying, or affecting commerce "by robbery or extortion."* (emphasis added). This language means that behavior that obstructs, delays, or affects commerce is a "violation" of the statute only if that behavior also involves robbery or extortion (or related attempts or conspiracies). Consequently, the reference in the physical violence clause to actions or threats of violence "in furtherance of a plan or purpose *to do anything in violation of this section*" (emphasis added) would seem to mean acts or threats of violence in furtherance of a plan or purpose *to engage in robbery or extortion,* for that is the only kind of behavior that the section otherwise makes a violation....
>
> We conclude that Congress did not intend to create a freestanding physical violence offense in the Hobbs Act. It did intend to forbid acts or threats of physical violence in furtherance of a plan or purpose to engage in what the statute refers to as robbery or extortion (and related attempts or conspiracies).

Disposition of case: The judgment of the appellate court was reversed.

See also **Hobbs Act; National Organization for Women, Inc. v. Scheidler; RICO; Scheidler v. National Organization for Women, Inc. (I); Travel Act**

Schenck v. Pro Choice Network of Western New York

Forum: United States Supreme Court.

Case Citation: Schenck v. Pro Choice Network of Western New York, 519 U.S. 357 (1997).

Date Argued: October 16, 1996.

Date of Decision: February 19, 1997.

Opinion of Court: Rehnquist, C. J., unanimous with respect to some parts of opinion.

Concurring and Dissenting Opinion: Scalia, J., in which Kennedy and Thomas, JJ., joined.

Concurring and Dissenting Opinion: Breyer, J.

Counsel for Appellants: Not Reported.

Counsel for Appellees: Not Reported.

Amicus Brief for Appellants: Not Reported.

Amicus Brief for Appellees: Not Reported.

Issue Presented: Whether an injunction that places restrictions on demonstrations outside abortion clinics violates the First Amendment?

Case Holding: The injunction provisions imposing fixed buffer zone limitations were constitutional, but the provisions imposing floating buffer zone limitations violated the First Amendment.

Background facts of case: On September 24, 1990 the appellees, abortion providers, filed a complaint in a federal district court in New York against fifty individuals and three organizations. The complaint alleged that the defendants had consistently engaged in illegal blockades and other illegal conduct at abortion facilities operated by the appellees. The unlawful conduct included numerous large scale blockades in which protesters marched, stood, knelt, sat, or lay in clinic parking lot driveways and doorways, blocking or hindering cars from entering the lots, and patients and clinic employees from entering the clinics. In addition, smaller groups of protesters consistently attempted to stop or disrupt clinic operations by, among other things, milling around clinic doorways and driveway entrances, trespassing onto clinic parking lots, crowding around cars, and surrounding, crowding, jostling, grabbing, pushing, shoving, and yelling and spitting at women entering the clinics and their escorts. The local police were unable to respond effectively to the protests. The district court issued a preliminary injunction in February 1992. The injunction provided as follows:

> Defendants, the officers, directors, agents, and representatives of defendants, and all other persons whomsoever, known or unknown, acting in their behalf or in concert with them, and receiving actual or constructive notice of this Order, are:
>
> 1. Enjoined and restrained in any manner or by any means from:
>
> (a) trespassing on, sitting in, blocking, impeding, or obstructing access to, ingress into or egress from any facility, including, but not limited to, the parking lots, parking lot entrances, driveways, and driveway entrances, at which abortions are performed in the Western District of New York;
>
> (b) demonstrating within fifteen feet from either side or edge of, or in front of, doorways or doorway entrances, parking lot entrances, driveways and driveway entrances of such facilities, or within fifteen feet of any person or vehicle seeking access to or leaving such facilities, except that the form of demonstrating known as sidewalk counseling by no more than two persons as specified in paragraph (c) shall be allowed;
>
> (c) physically abusing, grabbing, touching, pushing, shoving, or crowding persons entering or leaving, working at or using any services at any facility at which abortions are performed; provided, however, that sidewalk counseling consisting of a conversation of a non threatening nature by not more than two people with each person or group of persons they are seeking to counsel shall not be prohibited. Also provided that no one is required to accept or listen to sidewalk counseling, and that if anyone or any group of persons who is sought to be counseled wants to not have counseling, wants to leave, or walk away, they shall have the absolute right to do that, and in such event all persons seeking to counsel that person or group of persons shall cease and desist from such counseling, and shall thereafter be governed by the provisions of paragraph (b) pertaining to not demonstrating within fifteen feet of persons seeking access to or leaving a facility. In addition, it is further provided that this right to sidewalk counseling as defined herein shall not limit the right of the Police Department to maintain public order or such reasonably necessary rules and regulations as they decide are necessary at each particular demonstration site;
>
> (d) using any mechanical loudspeaker or sound amplification device or making any excessively loud sound which injures, disturbs, or endangers the health or safety of any patient or employee of a health care facility at which abortions are performed, nor shall any person make such sounds which interfere with the rights of anyone not in violation of this Order;
>
> (e) attempting, or inducing, directing, aiding, or abetting in any manner, others to take any of the actions described in paragraphs (a) through (d) above.

Two of the defendants, appellants Paul Schenck and Dwight Saunders, appealed to the Court of Appeals for the Second Circuit. The appellate court affirmed the district court. The United States Supreme Court granted certiorari to consider the matter.

Majority opinion by Chief Justice Rehnquist: The Chief Justice determined that the injunction was valid in imposing fixed buffer zone limitations on protestors, but the provisions of the injunction that imposed floating buffer zone limitations violated the First Amendment. The opinion addressed the issues as follows:

> We strike down the floating buffer zones around people entering and leaving the clinics because they burden more speech than is necessary to serve the relevant governmental interests. The floating buffer zones prevent defendants—except for two sidewalk counselors, while they are tolerated by the targeted individual—from communicating a message from a normal conversational distance or handing leaflets to people entering or leaving the clinics who are walking on the public sidewalks. This is a broad prohibition, both because of the type of speech that is restricted and the nature of the location. Leafletting and commenting on matters of public concern are classic forms of speech that lie at the heart of the First Amendment, and speech in public areas is at its most protected on public sidewalks, a prototypical example of a traditional public forum. On the other hand, we have before us a record that shows physically abusive conduct, harassment of the police that hampered law enforcement, and the tendency of even peaceful conversations to devolve into aggressive and sometimes violent conduct. In some situations, a record of abusive conduct makes a prohibition on classic speech in limited parts of a public sidewalk permissible. We need not decide whether the governmental interests involved would ever justify some sort of zone of separation between individuals entering the clinics and protesters, measured by the distance between the two. We hold here that because this broad prohibition on speech floats, it cannot be sustained on this record....
>
> We likewise strike down the floating buffer zones around vehicles. Nothing in the record or the District Court's opinion contradicts the commonsense notion that a more limited injunction—which keeps protesters away from driveways and parking lot entrances (as the fixed buffer zones do) and off the streets, for instance—would be sufficient to ensure that drivers are not confused about how to enter the clinic and are able to gain access to its driveways and parking lots safely and easily. In contrast, the 15 foot floating buffer zones would restrict the speech of those who simply line the sidewalk or curb in an effort to chant, shout, or hold signs peacefully. We therefore conclude that the floating buffer zones around vehicles burden more speech than necessary to serve the relevant governmental interests.
>
> We uphold the fixed buffer zones around the doorways, driveways, and driveway entrances. These buffer zones are necessary to ensure that people and vehicles trying to enter or exit the clinic property or clinic parking lots can do so. ...[T]he record shows that protesters purposefully or effectively blocked or hindered people from entering and exiting the clinic doorways, from driving up to and away from clinic entrances, and from driving in and out of clinic parking lots. Based on this conduct ... the District Court was entitled to conclude that the only way to ensure access was to move back the demonstrations away from the driveways and parking lot entrances. Similarly, sidewalk counselors ... followed and crowded people right up to the doorways of the clinics (and sometimes beyond) and then tended to stay in the doorways, shouting at the individuals who had managed to get inside. In addition, as the District Court found, defendants' harassment of the local police made it far from certain that the police would be

able to quickly and effectively counteract protesters who blocked doorways or threatened the safety of entering patients and employees. Based on this conduct, the District Court was entitled to conclude that protesters who were allowed close to the entrances would continue right up to the entrance, and that the only way to ensure access was to move all protesters away from the doorways. Although one might quibble about whether 15 feet is too great or too small a distance if the goal is to ensure access, we defer to the District Court's reasonable assessment of the number of feet necessary to keep the entrances clear.

Disposition of case: Affirmed in part, reversed in part, and remanded.

Concurring and dissenting opinion by Justice Scalia: Justice Scalia concurred with the Supreme Court's decision to reverse the floating buffer zone provisions of the injunction, but dissented from the decision to affirm the fixed buffer zone provisions. He wrote as follows:

> Today's opinion makes a destructive inroad upon First Amendment law in holding that the validity of an injunction against speech is to be determined by an appellate court on the basis of what the issuing court might reasonably have found as to necessity, rather than on the basis of what it in fact found. And it makes a destructive inroad upon the separation of powers in holding that an injunction may contain measures justified by the public interest apart from remediation of the legal wrong that is the subject of the complaint. Insofar as the first point is concerned, the Court might properly have upheld the fixed buffer zone without the cease and desist provision, since the District Court evidently did conclude (with proper factual support, in my view) that limiting the protesters to two was necessary to prevent repetition of the obstruction of access that had occurred in the past. But even that more limited injunction would be invalidated by the second point: the fact that no cause of action related to obstruction of access was properly found to support the injunction. Accordingly, I dissent from the Court's judgment upholding the fixed buffer zone, and would reverse the decision of the Court of Appeals in its entirety.

Concurring and dissenting opinion by Justice Breyer: Justice Breyer concurred in the Supreme Court's decision to affirm the fixed buffer zone provisions of the injunction, but dissented from the decision to reverse the floating buffer zone provisions. He stated his position as follows:

> I recognize that the District Court, interpreting or reinterpreting the key language, might find that it creates some kind of bubble that floats.... But even then, the constitutional validity of its interpretation would depend upon the specific interpretation that the court then gave and the potentially justifying facts. Some bubbles that "float" in time or space would seem to raise no constitutional difficulty. For example, a 15 foot buffer zone that is "fixed" in place around a doorway but that is activated only when a clinic patient is present can be said to "float" in time or, to a small degree, in space. Another example of a possibly constitutional "floating" bubble would be one that protects a patient who alights from a vehicle at the curbside in front of the Buffalo GYN Women services clinic and must cross the two foot stretch of sidewalk that is outside the 15 foot fixed buffer. Other bubbles, such as a bubble that follows a clinic patient to a grocery store three miles away, apparently are of no interest to anyone in this case. A floating bubble that follows a patient who is walking along the sidewalk just in front of a clinic, but outside the 15 foot fixed zone, could raise a constitutional problem. But the constitutional validity of that kind of bubble should depend upon the particular clinic and the particular circumstances to which the District Court would point in justification. The Court of Appeals wisely recognized that these matters should be left in the first instance to the consideration of the District Court....
>
> In sum, ordinary principles of judicial administration would permit the District Court to deal with the [appellants'] current objection. These principles counsel against this Court's now offering its own interpretation of the injunction — an interpretation that is not obvious from the language and that has never been considered by the District Court. I do not see how the Court's review of the key language, in the absence of special need and in violation of those principles, can make the lower courts' difficult, ongoing, circumstance specific task any easier. To the contrary, district judges cannot assure in advance, without the benefit of argument by the parties, that the language of complex, fact based injunctions is free of every ambiguity that later interpretation or misinterpretation finds possible. And I see no special need here for the Court to make an apparently general statement about the law of "floating bubbles," which later developments may show to have been unnecessary or unwise. Hence, I would affirm the judgment of the Court of Appeals in its entirety.

See also **Buffer Zones at Abortion Facilities**

Scrotum *see* **Male Reproductive System**

Second Trimester Abortion *see* **Abortion**

Secretariat for Pro-Life Activities

Secretariat for Pro-Life Activities is a pro-life program sponsored by the National Conference of Catholic Bishops. The executive director of the program is Tom Grenchik. The program's mission is to act to protect all human life, including the unborn. The guiding doctrine for the program is *The Gospel of Life*, Pope John Paul II's 1995 encyclical letter on the inestimable value and inviolability of human life. The Secretariat conducts ongoing information and education efforts, within the Church and in the public, to deepen respect for the sanctity of human life. The Secretariat also publishes liturgical suggestions and three newsletters, as well as a biweekly syndicated column for Catholic newspapers. It also designs and helps implement major pro-life programs in the Church, including the annual Respect Life Program and the Diocesan Development Program for Natural Family Planning. The Secretariat also interacts with national groups and various agencies of the federal government on pertinent issues. *See also* **Pro-Life Organizations**

Section 1983

Section 1983 of the Civil Rights Act of 1871 was enacted by Congress to prohibit State officials from creating and enforcing laws that violated an individual's rights, privileges, or immunities that were guaranteed by federal law. The statute is set out below.

42 U.S.C.A. § 1983.
Civil action for deprivation of rights

Every person who, under color of any statute, ordinance, regulation, custom, or usage, of any State or Territory or the District of Columbia, subjects, or causes to be subjected, any citizen of the United States or other person within the jurisdiction thereof to the deprivation of any rights, privileges, or immunities secured by the Constitution and laws, shall be liable to the party injured in an action at law, suit in equity, or other proper proceeding for redress, except that in any action brought against a judicial officer for an act or omission taken in such officer's judicial capacity, injunctive relief shall not be granted unless a declaratory decree was violated or declaratory relief was unavailable. For the purposes of this section, any Act of Congress applicable exclusively to the District of Columbia shall be considered to be a statute of the District of Columbia.

In *Ayotte v. Planned Parenthood of Northern New England* abortion providers filed a lawsuit under § 1983, in a federal district court seeking to prohibit enforcement of New Hampshire's Parental Notification Prior to Abortion Act of 2003 (Act). The plaintiffs alleged that the Act was unconstitutional because, among other things, it failed to permit a physician to promptly provide an abortion to a minor whose health may be at risk by a delay in complying with the notification requirement. The district court agreed with the plaintiffs and declared the Act unconstitutional in its entirety. An appellate court affirmed the decision. The United States Supreme Court agreed that the Act was invalid in part, but did not believe that it should have been struck down in its entirety. The Supreme Court vacated the decision and remanded the case for a less drastic remedy to be imposed. *See also* **Ayotte v. Planned Parenthood of Northern New England**

Section 1985(3) and Anti-Abortion Protests

Section 1985(3) of the Civil Rights Act of 1871 was enacted by Congress to provide a civil remedy for unlawful racial discrimination by two or more people. The statute reads as follows:

42 U.S.C.A. § 1985(3).
Depriving persons of rights or privileges

If two or more persons in any State or Territory conspire or go in disguise on the highway or on the premises of another, for the purpose of depriving, either directly or indirectly, any person or class of persons of the equal protection of the laws, or of equal privileges and immunities under the laws; or for the purpose of preventing or hindering the constituted authorities of any State or Territory from giving or securing to all persons within such State or Territory the equal protection of the laws; or if two or more persons conspire to prevent by force, intimidation, or threat, any citizen who is lawfully entitled to vote, from giving his support or advocacy in a legal manner, toward or in favor of the election of any lawfully qualified person as an elector for President or Vice President, or as a Member of Congress of the United States; or to injure any citizen in person or property on account of such support or advocacy; in any case of conspiracy set forth in this section, if one or more persons engaged therein do, or cause to be done, any act in furtherance of the object of such conspiracy, whereby another is injured in his person or property, or deprived of having and exercising any right or privilege of a citizen of the United States, the party so injured or deprived may have an action for the recovery of damages occasioned by such injury or deprivation, against any one or more of the conspirators.

In *Bray v. Alexandria Women's Health Clinic* abortion providers brought a civil lawsuit under § 1985(3) against militant anti-abortionists. A federal district court and court of appeals held that the statute could be used against abortion protestors. However, the United States Supreme Court disagreed and held that § 1985(3) was not intended, nor could it be used to seek redress against abortion protestors. *See also* **Bray v. Alexandria Women's Health Clinic**

Self-Induced Abortion *see* **Abortion**

Semen *see* **Male Reproductive System**

Septic Abortion

A septic abortion is an abortion that is complicated by an infection of the uterus before, during or after an abortion. There are two major factors that contribute to the development of septic abortion. First, retained products of conception from an abortion may cause septic abortion. Second, introduction of infection into the uterus from normal vaginal flora and sexually transmitted bacteria may cause septic abortion. Pelvic inflammatory disease is the most common complication of septic abortion.

Prior to the legalization of abortion in the United States septic abortions were often associated with induced abortions performed by untrained persons using nonsterile techniques. Since the legalization of abortion the incidence of septic abortion has fallen dramatically. The decrease in septic abortions also contributed to the decline in maternal deaths caused by septic abortions. *See also* **Abortion; Pelvic Inflammatory Disease**

Sexual Intercourse During Pregnancy

No study has shown that normal sexual intercourse during pregnancy will cause injury to or spontaneous abortion of a fetus. Research has shown that women are less receptive to sexual intercourse while pregnant.

Sexually Transmitted Diseases

Sexually transmitted diseases (STDs) (also known as sexually transmitted infections) are illnesses that are easily spread through sexual or intimate physical contact. The United States has the highest rates of STDs in the industrialized world. More than 65 million people in the country are currently living with an incurable sexually transmitted disease. In addition, an estimated 15.3 million new cases of STDs occur each year.

STDs are traced to bacteria, viruses, protozoa, or parasites. There are over 20 known STDs. Some of the most common include chlamydia, genital herpes, gonorrhea, hepatitis B, syphilis, and HIV/AIDS. These diseases may be deceptive. A person might have an STD without noticing any symptoms or signs. Symptoms may not appear for several weeks or months after sexual contact. If untreated, many STDs cause serious health problems that include infertility, impotency, immune deficiency, mental retardation, and death.

The consequences posed by STDs are increased for women who are pregnant. Among the additional consequences women may suffer from STDs while pregnant are: early onset of labor, premature rupture of the membranes surrounding the baby in the uterus, and uterine infection after delivery. STDs can be transmitted from a pregnant woman to the fetus or newborn before, during, or after birth. Some STDs (like HIV or syphilis) infect the fetus during its development. Other diseases (like gonorrhea or chlamydia) are transmitted from the mother to the newborn as the infant passes through the birth canal. Additionally, HIV may infect an infant as a result of breast-feeding.

Some of the effects of STDs on babies include: stillbirth, brain damage, pneumonia, blindness, deafness, low birthweight, meningitis, chronic liver disease, and cirrhosis. Some of these consequences may be apparent at birth, while others may not be detected until months or even years later.

Some STDs, like chlamydia, gonorrhea, and syphilis may be treated and cured with antibiotics during pregnancy. Others, like genital herpes and HIV, cannot be cured, but may be treated with antiviral med-

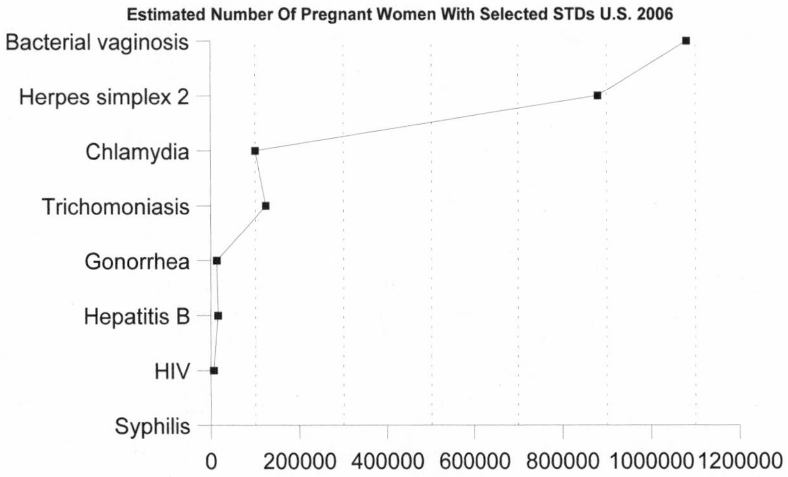

Source: **Centers for Disease Control and Prevention.**

Reported Cases of Selected Sexually Transmitted Diseases U.S. 2000–2005
Sexually Transmitted Disease

Year	*Syphilis*	*Chlamydia*	*Gonorrhea*	*Chancroid*
2000	31,618	709,452	363,136	78
2001	32,283	783,242	361,705	38
2002	32,918	834,555	351,852	48
2003	34,289	877,478	335,104	54
2004	33,419	929,462	330,132	30
2005	33,278	976,445	339,593	17
Total	197,805	5,110,634	2,081,522	265

Source: **Centers for Disease Control and Prevention.**

ications to reduce symptoms in the pregnant woman. *See also* **Chancroid; Chlamydia; CMV; Genital Herpes; Genital HPV; Gonorrhea; Hepatitis B Virus; HIV/AIDS; Molluscum Contagiosum; Syphilis; Vaginitis**

Shannon, Rachelle Ranae

Rachelle Ranae (aka Shelley) Shannon (b.1956) had a long history of violent anti-abortion activities prior to her imprisonment for the attempted murder of Dr. George Tiller at his clinic in Wichita, Kansas, on August 19, 1993. Shannon shot Dr. Tiller in both arms. She received an eleven year prison sentence for shooting Dr. Tiller. While Shannon was in prison authorities learned that she was also responsible for committing numerous violent attacks in Oregon, Nevada and California, including six clinic arson attacks and two butyric acid attacks. Shannon pleaded guilty to 10 charges and was sentenced to 20 years in prison on September 8, 1995. In exchange for her guilty plea, authorities dropped 20 additional charges. *See also* **Abortion Violence, Property Destruction and Demonstrations**

Sharp Curettage *see* **Dilation and Curettage**

Sickle Cell Anemia

Sickle cell anemia is an inherited disease in which the red blood cells take on an abnormal crescent shape. This condition causes the red blood cells to function improperly and break down. Symptoms of this disease usually do not occur until after 4 months of age, even it is inherited and present at birth. The disease can cause attacks of pain, damage to the kidneys, lungs, bone, liver, central nervous system and possibly early death. The incidence of the disease in the United States is about eight out of 100,000 people. Sickle cell anemia is more common among African Americans.

The disease can only occur when the mother and father of a child carry the sickle cell trait. There is no known cure for the disease. Medications and treatments are available to address some of the symptoms of the disease. Prenatal diagnosis of sickle cell anemia is possible. *See also* **Birth Defects and Abortion**

Simopoulos v. Virginia

Forum: United States Supreme Court.

Case Citation: Simopoulos v. Virginia, 462 U.S. 506 (1983).

Date Argued: November 30, 1982.

Date of Decision: June 15, 1983.

Opinion of Court: Powell, J., in which Burger, C. J., and Brennan, Marshall, and Blackmun, JJ., joined; and White, Rehnquist, and O'-Connor, JJ., joined in part.

Concurring Opinion: O'Connor, J., in which White and Rehnquist, JJ., joined.

Dissenting Opinion: Stevens, J.

Counsel for Appellant: Roy Lucas argued; on the brief was William P. Marshall.

Counsel for Appellee: William G. Broaddus, Chief Deputy Attorney General of Virginia, argued; on the brief were Gerald L. Baliles, Attorney General, and Thomas D. Bagwell and Julia Krebs-Markrich, Assistant Attorneys General.

Amicus Brief for Appellant: Sylvia A. Law, Nadine Taub, and Ellen J. Winner for the Committee for Abortion Rights and Against Sterilization Abuse et al.

Amicus Brief for Appellee: Dennis J. Horan, Victor G. Rosenblum, Patrick A. Trueman, and Thomas J. Marzen for Americans United for Life.

Issue Presented: Whether Virginia's mandatory hospitalization requirement for performing second trimester abortions was constitutional?

Case Holding: Virginia's statute requiring second trimester abortions be performed at hospitals was constitutional, because under the statute an adequately equipped clinic could, upon proper application, obtain an outpatient hospital license that permitted the performance of second-trimester abortions.

Background facts of case: The appellant, an obstetrician-gynecologist, was convicted by the state of Virginia for violating its statutory provision that made it unlawful to perform an abortion during the second trimester of pregnancy outside of a licensed hospital. The evidence at the trial established that in November of 1979, the appellant performed a second-trimester abortion at his unlicensed clinic on an unmarried minor by an injection of saline solution. Within 48 hours after receiving the saline injection, the minor went to a motel where she expelled the fetus. The appellant was eventually arrested and convicted for performing the abortion at an unauthorized facility. The Virginia supreme court affirmed appellant's conviction. The United States Supreme Court granted certiorari to consider the constitutionality of the state's mandatory requirement that second trimester abortions be performed at hospitals.

Majority opinion by Justice Powell: Justice Powell upheld the hospitalization abortion statute, on the grounds that the statute permitted second trimester abortions at licensed clinics. He addressed the matter as follows:

> ... [T]he Virginia statutes and regulations do not require that second-trimester abortions be performed exclusively in full-service hospitals. Under Virginia's hospitalization requirement, outpatient surgical hospitals may qualify for licensing as "hospitals" in which second-trimester abortions lawfully may be performed....
>
> Given the plain language of the Virginia regulations and the history of their adoption, we see no reason to doubt that an adequately equipped clinic could, upon proper application, obtain an outpatient hospital license permitting the performance of second-trimester abortions. We conclude that Virginia's requirement that second-trimester abortions be performed in licensed clinics is not an unreasonable means of furthering the State's compelling interest in protecting the woman's own health and safety. As we emphasized in Roe v. Wade, the State has a legitimate interest in seeing to it that abortion, like any other medical procedure, is performed under circumstances that insure maximum safety for the patient.... Virginia's statute and regulations do not require that the patient be hospitalized as an inpatient or that the abortion be performed in a full-service, acute-care hospital. Rather, the State's requirement that second-trimester abortions be performed in licensed clinics appears to comport with accepted medical practice, and leaves the method and timing of the abortion precisely where they belong — with the physician and the patient.

Disposition of case: The judgment of the Virginia supreme court was affirmed.

Concurring opinion by Justice O'Connor: Justice O'Connor concurred in the Court's decision and wrote the following brief comment:

> I concur in the judgment of the Court insofar as it affirms the conviction.... I do not agree that the constitutional validity of the Virginia mandatory hospitalization requirement is contingent in any way on the trimester in which it is imposed. Rather, I believe that the requirement in this case is not an undue burden on the decision to undergo an abortion.

Dissenting opinion by Justice Stevens: Justice Stevens dissented from the Court's decision. He argued that the Court should have reversed the conviction and remanded the case for the Virginia supreme court to determine whether the hospital abortion statute permitted clinics to qualify for performing second trimester abortions. Justice Stevens wrote as follows:

> ... [T]he Court may well be correct in its interpretation of the Virginia statute. The word "hospital" in [the statute] could incorporate by reference any institution licensed in accord[ingly]. It is not this Court's role, however, to interpret state law. We should not rest our decision on an interpretation of state law that was not endorsed by the court whose judgment we are reviewing. The Virginia Supreme Court's opinion was written on the assumption that the Commonwealth could constitutionally require all second-trimester abortions to be performed in a full-service, acute-care hospital.... The proper disposition of this appeal is therefore to vacate the judgment of the Supreme Court of Virginia and to remand the case to that court to reconsider its holding[.]

Singleton v. Wulff

Forum: United States Supreme Court.

Case Citation: Singleton v. Wulff, 428 U.S. 106 (1976).

Date Argued: March 23, 1976.

Date of Decision: July 1, 1976.

Opinion of Court: Blackmun, J., in which Brennan, White, and Marshall, JJ., joined.

Concurring Opinion: Stevens, J.

Concurring and Dissenting Opinion: Powell, J., in which Burger, C. J., and Stewart and Rehnquist, JJ., joined.

Counsel for Appellant: Michael L. Boicourt, Assistant Attorney General of Missouri, argued; on the brief was John C. Danforth, Attorney General.

Counsel for Appellees: Frank Susman argued and filed a brief.

Amicus Brief for Appellant: None.

Amicus Brief for Appellees: None.

Issue Presented: Whether the Eighth Circuit court of appeals had jurisdiction to determine if abortion providers had standing to challenge a provision in Missouri's abortion statute that limited Medicaid payment for abortions, and to rule that the provision violated the constitution?

Case Holding: The Eighth Circuit court of appeals had jurisdiction to determine whether abortion providers had standing to challenge a provision in Missouri's abortion statute that limited Medicaid payment for abortions, but it did not have jurisdiction to rule that the provision violated the constitution because the district court did not address the issue.

Background facts of case: The appellees, two abortion providers, filed a lawsuit in a federal district court in Missouri challenging a provision in the state's abortion statute that limited Medicaid payment for abortions to those that were medically necessary. The district court dismissed the complaint on the grounds that the appellees did not have standing to bring the lawsuit. The Eighth Circuit court of appeals reversed. The appellate court determined that the appellees had standing, and went on to find the Medicaid limitation violated the Equal Protection Clause of the Fourteenth Amendment. The appellant, a state official, appealed. The Supreme Court granted certiorari to consider the issue.

Plurality opinion by Justice Blackmun: Justice Blackmun found that the appellees had standing to bring the lawsuit, but determined that the court of appeals should have remanded the case for the district court to make a ruling on the merits of the lawsuit. He wrote as follows:

> It is the general rule, of course, that a federal appellate court does not consider an issue not passed upon below. In Hormel v. Helvering, 312 U.S. 552 (1941), the Court explained that this is "essential in order that parties may have the opportunity to offer all the evidence they believe relevant to the issues ... [and] in order that litigants may not be surprised on appeal by final decision there of issues upon which they have had no opportunity to introduce evidence." We have no idea what evidence, if any, [appellant] would, or could, offer in defense of this statute, but this is only because [appellant] has had no opportunity to proffer such evidence. Moreover, even assuming that there is no such evidence, [appellant] should have the opportunity to present whatever legal arguments he may have in defense of the statute. We think he was justified in not presenting those arguments to the Court of Appeals, and in assuming, rather, that he would at least be allowed to answer the complaint, should the Court of Appeals reinstate it.
>
> The matter of what questions may be taken up and resolved for the first time on appeal is one left primarily to the discretion of the courts of appeals, to be exercised on the facts of individual cases. We announce no general rule. Certainly there are circumstances in which a federal appellate court is justified in resolving an issue not passed on below, as where the proper resolution is beyond any doubt, or where injustice might otherwise result. Suffice it to say that this is not such a case. The issue resolved by the Court of Appeals has never been passed upon in any decision of this Court. This being so, injustice was more likely to be caused than avoided by deciding the issue without [appellant's] having had an opportunity to be heard.

Disposition of case: The judgment of the court of appeals was affirmed in part and reversed in part, and the case was remanded.

Concurring opinion by Justice Stevens: Justice Stevens wrote a terse opinion concurring in the judgment of the Court.

Concurring and dissenting opinion by Justice Powell: Justice Powell agreed with the Court that the appellees had standing and that the case should be reversed on the issue of the constitutionality of the Medicaid provision. He dissented from language in the opinion that indicated the appellees "may assert, in addition to their own rights, the constitutional rights of their patients who would be eligible for Medicaid assistance in obtaining elective abortions but for the exclusion of such abortions in [the statute].

Slepian, Dr. Bernard *see* **Kopp, James Charles**

Smith, Jacqueline

In 1955 Jacqueline Smith was a 20-year-old aspiring fashion designer who left her home in Pennsylvania, to pursue a career in New York. Shortly after arriving in New York Smith met Thomas G. Daniels and started a romantic relationship with him. Smith became pregnant and told Daniels in December of 1955. The two decided on an abortion. Daniels made arrangements for the abortion to be performed at the home of an abortionist named Leobaldo Pejan.

During the abortion complications arose and Smith died. Pejan and Daniels panicked. The two decided to cut up Smith's body and dispose of it in garbage cans. Smith's father contacted the police and reported her missing after he visited her apartment but could not find her. An investigation was launched that quickly led the police to charge Pejan and Daniels with criminal homicide. Pejan eventually entered a plea of guilty and agreed to testify against Daniels. Pejan received a prison sentence of 7½ years. Daniels was convicted and sentenced to 8 years in prison. *See also* **Complications During and After Abortion**

Smith, Sarah

Sarah Smith's mother, Betty Smith, attempted to abort her at a clinic in Los Angeles in November of 1970. During the abortion procedure a male fetus was expelled. However, the abortionist failed to realize that a second fetus, Sarah, was lodged in the womb. Several weeks after the abortion, Sarah's mother realized she was still pregnant. A second abortion attempt was not made and Sarah was allowed to be born alive. The first abortion attempt, however, left Sarah with bilateral, congenital dislocated hips and other physical handicaps. *See also* **Survivors of Abortion**

Smoking and Pregnancy

Research studies have determined that cigarette smoking during pregnancy increases the risk of endangering the health of babies. One of the biggest risks caused by smoking is giving birth to low birthweight babies. In a 1998 report it was estimated that 12 percent of infants born to smoking mothers in the United States were low birthweight babies. Low birthweight infants are susceptible to many health problems, including mental retardation and death. Other complications for infants associated with smoking during pregnancy include: increased risk of preterm delivery; ectopic pregnancy; miscarriage; stillbirth; placental complications; sudden infant death syndrome; asthma; and learning and behavioral problems. *See also* **Birth Defects and Abortion; Drug Use and Pregnancy; Fetal Alcohol Syndrome**

Sonogram *see* **Ultrasound**

Souter, David H.

David H. Souter was appointed as an associate justice of the United States Supreme Court in 1990. While on the Supreme Court Justice Souter has displayed a moderate judicial philosophy in his interpretation of the Constitution.

Justice Souter was born in Melrose, Massachusetts on September 17, 1939. He graduated from Harvard University in 1961. His educational training included studying law at Harvard Law School and Oxford University. In addition to serving on the supreme court of New Hampshire, Justice Souter was appointed in 1990 as an appellate judge for the First Circuit Court of Appeals. A few months after his federal bench appoint, President George Bush appointed Justice Souter to the Supreme Court.

During Justice Souter's tenure on the Supreme Court he has issued a number of abortion related opinions. The written opinions and opinions simply voted on by Justice Souter, indicate that he is in favor of using the constitution to expand abortion rights for women.

Justice Souter's voting pattern favors the views of pro-choice advocates (collection, Supreme Court Historical Society, photograph by Joseph H. Bailey, National Geographic Society).

Distribution of the Abortion Voting Pattern of Justice Souter Based Upon Opinions Filed by the Supreme Court

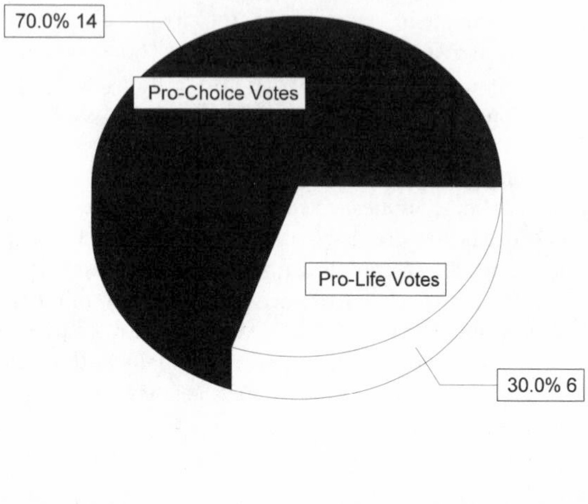

(1) Unanimous opinions voted with only. In *Dalton v. Little Rock Family Planning Services*, Justice Souter voted with a unanimous Court in holding that an amendment to Arkansas' constitution which limited Medicaid payment only to therapeutic abortions, was invalid to the extent that Medicaid funds had to be made available for incest or rape pregnancies, but was valid for any purely state funded program. Justice Souter voted with a unanimous Court in *Scheidler v. National Organization for Women, Inc. (II)*, which held pro-choice advocates could not sue pro-life advocates under the Hobbs Act for allegations of physical violence that did not involve extortion. Justice Souter joined a unanimous opinion in *Ayotte v. Planned Parenthood of Northern New England*, which held that the absence of a health exception in New Hampshire's parental notification abortion statute did not require the entire statute be invalidated.

(2) Majority opinions written. In *Planned Parenthood of Southeastern Pennsylvania v. Casey*, Justice Souter wrote a joint majority/plurality opinion with Justices Kennedy and O'Connor. The opinion held that the constitution was not violated by provisions in Pennsylvania's abortion statute that provided for: medical emergency abortion; 24 hour waiting period for abortion; parental notice and judicial bypass for abortion by a minor; and certain abortion facility reporting requirements. The decision found two provisions in the abortion statute unconstitutional: spousal notification before obtaining an abortion, and

a requirement that a woman inform the abortion provider the reason for not notifying her spouse. Justice Souter wrote the majority opinion in *Federal Election Commission v. Beaumont*, which held that the Federal Election Campaign Act's prohibition on corporate expenditures and contributions directly to candidates in federal elections, applies to a nonprofit pro-life organization.

(3) Majority opinions voted with only. Justice Souter voted with the majority in *Ferguson v. City of Charleston*, in holding that patient consent or a search warrant was needed in order for a government hospital to turn over to the police drug test results that showed a woman used illegal drugs during her pregnancy. In *Stenberg v. Carhart*, Justice Souter voted with the majority's decision to find Nebraska's statute banning partial-birth abortion unconstitutional. Justice Souter voted with the majority in *Schenck v. Pro Choice Network of Western New York*, which held that a federal trial court's injunction provisions imposing fixed buffer zone limitations on abortion protesters were constitutional, but the provisions imposing floating buffer zone limitations violated the First Amendment.

In *Lambert v. Wicklund* Justice Souter voted with the majority in holding that the constitution was not violated by a provision in Montana's abortion statute that allowed a court to waive the parental notice requirement for minors, if notification was not in minor's best interest. Justice Souter joined the majority opinion in *Mazurek v. Armstrong*, which held that Montana's requirement that abortions be performed only by physicians was constitutionally valid. In *Daubert v. Merrell Dow Pharmaceuticals, Inc.*, a case involving children born with severe birth defects, Justice Souter voted with the majority in holding that the *Frye* rule on admissibility of expert testimony did not survive the enactment of the Federal Rules of Evidence.

Justice Souter voted with the majority in *Rust v. Sullivan*, which upheld federal regulations that prohibited pro-abortion counseling, referral, and advocacy by health care providers. In *Automobile Workers v. Johnson Controls, Inc.* In *Scheidler v. National Organization for Women, Inc. (I)* Justice Souter joined the majority opinion, which held that evidence did not support finding that pro-life advocates violated the Hobbs Act, Travel Act and state law extortion crimes, for the purpose of awarding damages and granting an injunction against them under RICO. Justice Souter voted with the majority opinion, which held that Title VII of the Civil Rights Act forbids sex-specific fetal-protection policies by an employer, that exclude a fertile female employee from certain jobs because of the employer's concern for the health of the fetus the woman might conceive.

(4) Concurring opinions written. In *Hill v. Colorado* Justice Souter wrote a concurring opinion that agreed with the majority's decision to uphold a Colorado statute that made it unlawful for any person within 100 feet of an abortion facility's entrance, to knowingly approach within 8 feet of another person, without that person's consent, in order to pass a leaflet, handbill, display a sign, engage in oral protest, education, or counseling with that person. In *Madsen v. Women's Health Clinic, Inc.*, Justice Souter wrote a concurring opinion agreeing with the majority to uphold parts of an injunction that restricted noise by anti-abortionists at a clinic and imposed a 36 foot buffer zone around the clinic entrances and driveway. However, *Madsen* ruled that the Free Speech Clause was violated by a 36 foot buffer zone as applied to the private property to the north and west of the clinic, a restriction on the use of images observable by clinic patients, a 300 foot no approach zone around the clinic, and a 300 foot buffer zone around the residences, because these restrictions swept more broadly than necessary to accomplish the permissible goals of the injunction.

Justice Souter wrote a concurring opinion in *National Organization for Women, Inc. v. Scheidler*, which held that a group of pro-choice organizations could maintain a RICO civil lawsuit against several anti-abortion individuals and groups.

(5) Dissenting opinions written. Justice Souter wrote a dissenting opinion in *Federal Election Commission v. Wisconsin Right to Life, Inc.*, which held that the electioneering communications provisions of a federal statute violated a pro-life organization's First Amendment right to broadcast political issue oriented advertisements shortly before primary and general elections.

(6) Dissenting opinions voted with only. Justice Souter joined the dissenting opinion in *Leavitt v. Jane L.*, which held that the invalidity of Utah's statute regulating pregnancies 20 weeks old or less, may be severed so as to preserve that portion of the abortion statute that regulated pregnancies of more than 20 weeks. Justice Souter joined the dissenting opinion in *Gonzales v. Carhart*, which held that the Partial-Birth Abortion Ban Act of 2003 was not facially unconstitutional, because it outlined the abortion procedure that was banned, and the Act did not have to provide an exception for the health of a woman.

(7) Concurring and dissenting opinions written. Justice Souter wrote a concurring and dissenting opinion in *Bray v. Alexandria Clinic*, which held that the Civil Rights Act of 1871, 42 U.S.C. § 1985(3), did not provide a cause of action against persons obstructing access to abortion clinics. He agreed with the majority to remand the case for further consideration, but Justice Souter disagreed with the majority's position that no cause of action could be maintained under the statute.

South Carolina

(1) OVERVIEW

The state of South Carolina enacted its first criminal abortion statute on March 24, 1883. The statute underwent several amendments prior to the 1973 decision by the United States Supreme Court in *Roe v. Wade*, which legalized abortion in the nation. South Carolina has taken affirmative steps to respond to *Roe* and its progeny. The state has addressed several abortion issues by statute that include general abortion guidelines, informed consent, abortion by minors, partial-birth abortion, use of facilities and people, public funds for abortion, fetal death report, abortion facility requirements, injury to a pregnant woman, and choose life license plate.

(2) GENERAL ABORTION GUIDELINES

South Carolina acknowledges by statute a woman's right to an unimpeded abortion during the first and second trimesters. However, the state imposes several unconstitutional restrictions upon a third trimester abortion. South Carolina provides that a married woman must obtain the consent of her husband, before having a third trimester abortion. However, the United States Supreme Court found spousal notice requirements unconstitutional in *Planned Parenthood of Southeastern Pennsylvania v. Casey*. South Carolina also provides that third trimester abortions are not permitted unless necessary to save a woman's life or health. In *Whitner v. State*, 492 S.E.2d 777 (S.C. 1997) the South Carolina Supreme Court ruled that a viable fetus was a child within the meaning of the criminal child abuse laws of the state. Therefore, a pregnant woman could be criminally prosecuted for ingesting cocaine during her third trimester of pregnancy and causing the baby to be born with cocaine derivatives in its system. The general abortion statutes are set out below.

South Carolina Code § 44-41-10. Definitions

As used in this chapter:

(a) "Abortion" means the use of an instrument, medicine, drug, or other substance or device with intent to terminate the pregnancy of a woman known to be pregnant for reasons other than to increase the probability of a live birth, to preserve the life or health of the child after live birth, or to remove a dead fetus.

(b) "Physician" means a person licensed to practice medicine in this State.

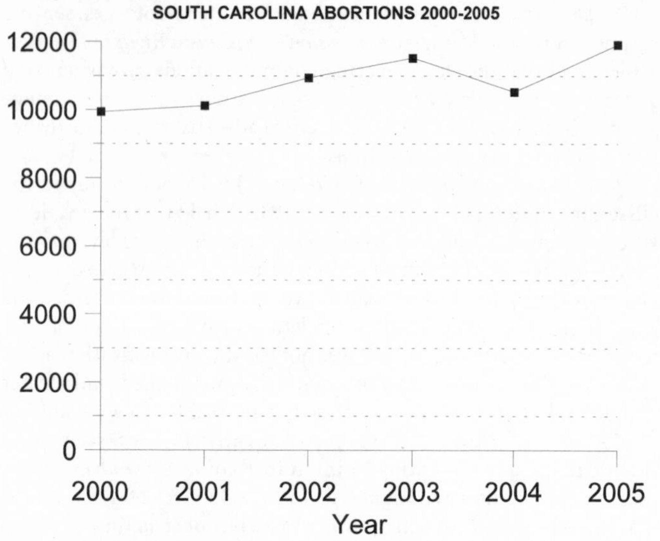

Source: South Carolina Department of Health and Environmental Control.

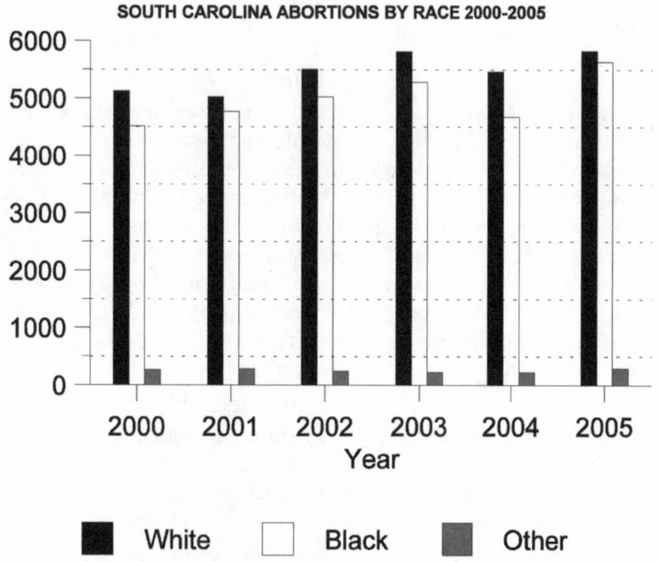

Source: South Carolina Department of Health and Environmental Control.

(c) "Department" means the South Carolina Department of Health and Environmental Control.

(d) "Hospital" means those institutions licensed for hospital operation by the department in accordance with Article 3, Chapter 7 of this title and which have also been certified by the department to be suitable facilities for the performance of abortions.

(e) "Clinic" shall mean any facility other than a hospital as defined in subsection (d) which has been licensed by the Department, and which has also been certified by the Department to be suitable for the performance of abortions.

(f) "Pregnancy" means the condition of a woman carrying a fetus or embryo within her body as the result of conception.

(g) "Conception" means the fecundation of the ovum by the spermatozoa.

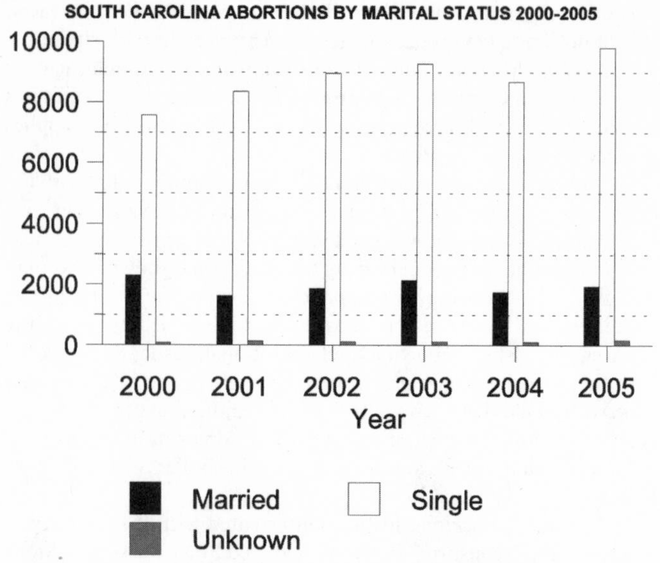

Source: South Carolina Department of Health and Environmental Control.

South Carolina Abortion by Education Level of Female 2000–2005
Education Level Completed

Year	*<12*	*12*	*≥13*	*Unknown*
2000	1,558	4,283	3,898	207
2001	1,491	4,406	4,022	205
2002	1,623	4,247	4,812	265
2003	1,829	4,749	4,707	242
2004	1,609	4,405	4,279	241
2005	1,759	5,033	4,792	335
Total	9,869	27,123	26,510	1,495

Source: South Carolina Department of Health and Environmental Control.

(h) "Consent" means a signed and witnessed voluntary agreement to the performance of an abortion.

(i) "First trimester of pregnancy" means the first twelve weeks of pregnancy commencing with conception rather than computed on the basis of the menstrual cycle.

(j) "Second trimester of pregnancy" means that portion of a pregnancy following the twelfth week and extending through the twenty-fourth week of gestation.

(k) "Third trimester of pregnancy" means that portion of a pregnancy beginning with the twenty-fifth week of gestation.

(l) "Viability" means that stage of human development when the fetus is potentially able to live outside of the mother's womb with or without the aid of artificial life support systems. For the purposes of

South Carolina Abortion by Age Group 2000–2005
Age Group (yrs)

Year	*<15*	*15–17*	*18–19*	*20–24*	*25–29*	*30–34*	*35–44*	*≥45*	*Unknown*
2000	75	786	1,199	3,350	2,271	1,251	964	12	38
2001	74	720	1,139	3,405	2,240	1,382	1,057	15	91
2002	70	760	1,134	3,740	2,570	1,511	1,048	9	105
2003	97	759	1,194	3,981	2,686	1,621	1,109	16	64
2004	72	670	1,139	3,630	2,357	1,539	1,067	12	48
2005	86	723	1,236	3,992	2,813	1,755	1,187	18	109
Total	474	4,418	7,041	22,098	14,937	9,059	6,432	82	455

Source: South Carolina Department of Health and Environmental Control.

this chapter, a legal presumption is hereby created that viability occurs no sooner than the twenty-fourth week of pregnancy.

(m) "Minor" means a female under the age of seventeen.

(n) "Emancipated minor" means a minor who is or has been married or has by court order been freed from the care, custody, and control of her parents.

(o) "In loco parentis" means any person over the age of eighteen who has placed himself or herself in the position of a lawful parent by assuming obligations which are incidental to the parental relationship and has so served for a period of sixty days.

South Carolina Code § 44-41-20. Abortions

Abortion shall be a criminal act except when performed under the following circumstances:

(a) During the first trimester of pregnancy the abortion is performed with the pregnant woman's consent by her attending physician pursuant to his professional medical judgment.

(b) During the second trimester of pregnancy the abortion is performed with the pregnant woman's consent by her attending physician in a hospital or clinic certified by the Department.

(c) During the third trimester of pregnancy, the abortion is performed with the pregnant woman's consent, and if married and living with her husband the consent of her husband, in a certified hospital, and only if the attending physician and one additional consulting physician, who shall not be related to or engaged in private practice with the attending physician, certify in writing to the hospital in which the abortion is to be performed that the abortion is necessary based upon their best medical judgment to preserve the life or health of the woman. In the event that the preservation of the woman's mental health is certified as the reason for the abortion, an additional certification shall be required from a consulting psychiatrist who shall not be related to or engaged in private practice with the attending physician. All facts and reasons supporting such certification shall be set forth by the attending physician in writing and attached to such certificate.

South Carolina Code § 44-41-30.
Persons from whom consent is required

(A) Consent is required before the performance of an abortion from the pregnant woman in every case and in the case of a minor, it must be obtained pursuant to the provisions of Section 44-41-31.

(B) In the case of a woman who is under adjudication of mental incompetency by a court of competent jurisdiction, consent must be obtained from her spouse or a legal guardian if she is married; if she is not married, from one parent or a legal guardian.

(C) Notwithstanding the consent required in subsections (A) and (B) consent must be waived if:

(1) a physician determines that a medical emergency exists involving the life of or grave physical injury to the pregnant woman; or

(2) the pregnancy is the result of incest.

(D) In cases of incest the physician performing the abortion shall report the alleged incest to the local county department of social services or to a law enforcement agency in the county where the child resides or is found. Failure to report is a violation punishable under the child abuse laws of this State.

(E) Nothing in this section permits a physician to perform an abortion without first obtaining the consent of the pregnant woman if she is capable of giving consent.

South Carolina Code § 44-41-80.
Performing unlawful abortion

(a) Any person, except as permitted by this chapter, who provides, supplies, prescribes or administers any drug, medicine, prescription or substance to any woman or uses or employs any device, instrument or other means upon any woman, with the intent to produce an abortion shall be deemed guilty of a felony and, upon conviction, shall be punished by imprisonment for a term of not less than two nor more than five years or fined not more than five thousand dollars, or both. Provided, that the provisions of this item shall not apply to any woman upon whom an abortion has been attempted or performed.

(b) Except as otherwise permitted by this chapter, any woman who solicits of any person or otherwise procures any drug, medicine, prescription or substance and administers it to herself or who submits to any operation or procedure or who uses or employs any device or instrument or other means with intent to produce an abortion, unless it is necessary to preserve her life, shall be deemed guilty of a misdemeanor and, upon conviction, shall be punished by imprisonment for a term of not more than two years or fined not more than one thousand dollars, or both.

(c) Any woman upon whom an abortion has been performed or attempted in violation of the provisions of this chapter may be compelled to testify in any criminal prosecution initiated pursuant to subsection (a) of this section; provided, however, that such testimony shall not be admissible in any civil or criminal action against such woman and she shall be forever immune from any prosecution for having solicited or otherwise procured the performance of the abortion or the attempted performance of the abortion upon her.

(3) INFORMED CONSENT

Prior to an abortion South Carolina requires that a woman be fully informed of the procedure to be used, the risks involved and alternatives to abortion. An abortion may not take place until at least one hour after a woman acknowledges receipt of statutorily required information. The statutes addressing the matter are set out below.

South Carolina Code § 44-41-310. Short title

This article may be cited as the "Woman's Right to Know Act."

South Carolina Code § 44-41-320. Definitions

As used in this article:

(1) "Medical emergency" means that condition which, on the basis of the physician's good faith judgment, so complicates a pregnancy as to necessitate an immediate abortion to avert the risk of her death or for which a delay will create serious risk of substantial and irreversible impairment of major bodily function.

(2) "Probable gestational age of the embryo or fetus" means what, in the judgment of the attending physician based upon the attending physician's examination and the woman's medical history, is with reasonable probability the gestational age of the embryo or fetus at the time the abortion is planned to be performed.

South Carolina Code § 44-41-330.
Consent and waiting period

(A) Except in the case of a medical emergency and in addition to any other consent required by the laws of this State, no abortion may be performed or induced unless the following conditions have been satisfied:

(1) The woman must be informed by the physician who is to perform the abortion or by an allied health professional working in conjunction with the physician of the procedure to be involved and by the physician who is to perform the abortion of the probable gestational age of the embryo or fetus at the time the abortion is to be performed.

(2) The woman must be presented by the physician who is to perform the abortion or by an allied health professional working in conjunction with the physician a written form containing the following statement: "You have the right to review printed materials prepared by the State of South Carolina which describe fetal development, list agencies which offer alternatives to abortion, and describe medical assistance benefits which may be available for prenatal care, childbirth, and neonatal care." This form must be signed and dated by both the physician who is to perform the procedure and the pregnant woman upon whom the procedure is to be performed.

(3) The woman must certify in writing, before the abortion, that the information described in item (1) of this subsection has been furnished her, and that she has been informed of her opportunity to review the information referred to in item (2) of this subsection.

(4) Before performing the abortion, the physician who is to perform or induce the abortion must determine that the written certification prescribed by item (3) of this subsection or the certification required by subsection (D) has been signed. This subsection does not apply in the case where an abortion is performed pursuant to a court order.

(B) Nothing herein limits the information provided by the physician who is to perform the abortion or allied health professional to the person upon whom the abortion procedure is to be performed.

(C) No abortion may be performed sooner than one hour after the woman receives the written materials and certifies this fact to the physician or the physician's agent.

(D) If the clinic or other facility where the abortion is to be performed or induced mails the printed materials described in Section 44-41-340 to the woman upon whom the abortion is to be performed or induced or if the woman obtains the information at the county health department and if the woman verifies in writing, before the abortion, that the printed materials were received by her more than one hour before the abortion is scheduled to be performed or induced, that the information described in item (A)(1) has been provided to her, and that she has been informed of her opportunity to review the information referred to in item (A)(2), then the waiting period required pursuant to subsection (C) does not apply.

(E) In the event the person upon whom the abortion is to be performed or induced is an unemancipated minor, as defined in Section 44-41-10, the information described in Section 44-41-330(A)(1) and (2) must be furnished and offered respectively to a parent of the minor, a legal guardian of the minor, a grandparent of the minor, or any person who has been standing in loco parentis to the minor for a period of not less than sixty days. The parent, legal guardian, grandparent, or person who has been standing in loco parentis, as appropriate, must make the certification required by Section 44-41-330(A)(3). In the event the person upon whom the abortion is to be performed is under adjudication of mental incompetency by a court of competent jurisdiction, the information must be furnished and offered respectively to her spouse or a legal guardian if she is married; if she is not married, from one parent or a legal guardian. The spouse, legal guardian, or parent, as appropriate, must make the certification required by Section 44-41-330(A)(3). This subsection does not apply in the case of an abortion performed pursuant to a court order.

(F) A clinic or other facility must maintain, for three years after the abortion is performed or induced, the woman's written verification that the information was so provided and the printed materials were so offered. In the case of an unemancipated minor or mentally incompetent person, the clinic or other facility is required to maintain a copy of the court order or the medical records and written consent for three years after the procedure is performed.

(G) This section does not apply if a clinic or other facility where abortions are performed or induced does not have, through no fault of the clinic or facility and if the clinic or facility can demonstrate through written evidence the unavailability of the materials described in Section 44-41-340.

South Carolina Code § 44-41-340. Publication of materials

(A) The South Carolina Department of Health and Environmental Control shall cause to be published the following printed materials:

(1) geographically indexed materials designed to inform the woman of public and private agencies and services available to assist a woman through pregnancy, upon childbirth, and while the child is dependent, including adoption agencies, which include a comprehensive list of the agencies available, a description of the services they offer, and a description of the manner, including telephone numbers, in which they may be contacted;

(2) materials designed to inform the woman of the probable anatomical and physiological characteristics of the embryo or fetus at two-week gestational increments from the time when a woman can be known to be pregnant to full term. Any photograph, drawing or other depiction must state in bold letters, which are easily legible, stating the magnification of the photograph, drawing or depiction if it is not the actual size of the embryo or fetus at the age indicated. The materials must be objective, nonjudgmental, and designed to convey only accurate scientific information about the embryo or fetus at the various gestational ages;

(3) materials designed to inform the woman of the principal types of abortion procedures and the major risks associated with each procedure, as well as the major risks associated with carrying a fetus to full-term;

(4) materials designed to inform the woman that medical assistance benefits may be available for prenatal care, childbirth, and neonatal care by providing the names, addresses, and phone numbers of appropriate agencies that provide or have information available on these benefits;

(5) materials designed to inform the woman of the mechanisms available for obtaining child support payments.

(B) The materials must be easily comprehendible and must be printed in a typeface large enough to be clearly legible.

(C) The materials required under this section must be available from the South Carolina Department of Health and Environmental Control upon request and in appropriate number to any person, facility, or hospital.

South Carolina Code § 44-41-350. Penalties

A physician who performs an abortion when the physician knows or should know that the provisions of this article have not been complied with before the abortion is guilty of a misdemeanor and, upon conviction:

(1) for a first or second offense, must be fined not more than one thousand dollars. No term of imprisonment may be imposed for a first or second offense.

(2) for a third or subsequent offense, must be imprisoned not more than three years or fined not more than five thousand dollars, or both.

§ 44-41-360.
Preservation of anonymity of woman having abortion

In every proceeding or action brought under this article, the court shall rule whether the anonymity of any woman upon whom an abortion is performed or attempted shall be preserved from public disclosure if she does not give her consent to such a disclosure. The court, upon motion of any person or upon its own motion, shall make such a ruling and, upon determining that her anonymity be preserved, shall issue orders to the parties, witnesses, and counsel, and shall direct the sealing of the record and exclusion of individuals from courtrooms or hearing rooms to the extent necessary to safeguard her identity from public disclosure. Each order under this section must be accompanied by specific written findings explaining why the anonymity of the woman should be preserved from public disclosure, why the order is essential to that end, how the order is narrowly tailored to serve that interest, and why no reasonable, less restrictive alternative exists. This section may not be construed to conceal the identity of the plaintiff or of the prosecutrix or of witnesses from the defendant or to abridge or deny the defendant's ability to conduct discovery under applicable rules of court or the defendant's right to a trial by jury or to cross examination.

South Carolina Code § 44-41-370. Applicability of article

This article applies only to facilities in which any second trimester or five or more first trimester abortions are performed in a month.

South Carolina Code § 44-41-380.
Severability of provisions of article

If any provision, word, phrase, or clause of Article 3, Chapter 41, Title 44 of the 1976 Code as added by this act [1995 Act No. 1], or the application thereof to any person or circumstance is held invalid, such invalidity shall not affect the provisions, words, phrases, clauses, or applications of Article 3, Chapter 41, Title 44 which can be given effect without the invalid provision, word, phrase, clause, or application, and, to this end, the provisions, words, phrases, and clauses of Article 3, Chapter 41, Title 44 are declared to be severable.

(4) ABORTION BY MINORS

Under the laws of South Carolina no physician may perform an abortion upon an unemancipated minor unless he/she first obtains the written consent of either parent or the legal guardian of the minor. In compliance with federal constitutional law, South Carolina has provided a judicial waiver procedure for an unemancipated minor to obtain an abortion without parental or guardian consent. The minor may petition a trial court for a waiver of the consent requirement. A minor has a right to an attorney at the proceeding and if she cannot afford one, the court must appoint her an attorney. If a minor chooses, she may represent herself. The required parental or guardian consent may be waived if the court finds either (1) that the minor is mature and well-informed enough to make the abortion decision on her own, or (2) that performance of the abortion would be in the best interest of the minor. A minor may appeal an adverse decision by a trial judge. The statutes addressing the issues are set out below.

South Carolina Code § 44-41-31. Consent requirement

(A) No person may perform an abortion upon a minor unless consent is obtained in accordance with one of the following provisions:

(1) the attending physician or his agent or the referring physician or his agent has secured the informed written consent, signed and witnessed, of the pregnant minor and:

(a) one parent of the minor; or

(b) a legal guardian of the minor; or

(c) a grandparent of the minor; or

(d) any person who has been standing in loco parentis to the minor for a period not less than sixty days;

(2) the minor is emancipated and the attending physician or his agent has received the informed signed written consent of the minor; or

(3) the attending physician or his agent has obtained the informed signed written consent of the minor and has received the order of the court obtained by the minor pursuant to this chapter.

(B) If a parent or legal guardian refuses to give the informed written consent for the minor's abortion and there has been a judicial finding of refusal of consent, and the minor has a child or children as a result of that pregnancy, the duty imposed by law of supporting the child or children extends to the minor and jointly and severally to the refusing parent or legal guardian and the natural father until the minor reaches the age of eighteen years or is emancipated.

(C) Any person standing in loco parentis and who consents to the abortion of the minor as permitted in subsection (A)(1) of this section shall sign an affidavit indicating the nature and length of his or her relationship with the minor. The affidavit must state the penalties for wilfully or knowingly making a false representation. Anyone who knowingly or wilfully makes a false representation in the affidavit shall be guilty of a misdemeanor and, upon conviction, must be fined not more than three thousand dollars or imprisoned for not more than one year.

South Carolina Code § 44-41-32. Petitioning court

Every minor has the right to petition the court for an order granting her the right to obtain an abortion without the consent required in Section 44-41-31(1). In seeking this relief the following procedures apply:

(1) The minor may prepare and file a petition in either the circuit or family court. The petition may be filed in the name of Jane Doe to protect the anonymity of the minor.

(2) The Adoption and Birth Parent Services Division of the Department of Social Services, upon request of the minor, must provide assistance to the minor in preparing and filing the petition. Preparation and filing of the petition must be completed within forty-eight hours after the request. The Department of Social Services shall promulgate regulations establishing the procedures to be followed in providing this assistance.

(3) Upon the filing of the petition, the court shall appoint a guardian ad litem for the minor, taking into consideration the preference of the minor. The minor may participate in court proceedings on her own behalf, but the court shall advise her that she has a right to court-appointed counsel and shall provide her with counsel upon her request.

(4) All proceedings pursuant to this section must be given precedence over other matters pending before the court.

(5) The court shall hold a hearing and rule on the merits of the petition within seventy-two hours of the filing of the petition. This time may be extended upon the request of the minor. The court shall consider the emotional development, maturity, intellect, and understanding of the minor; the nature and possible consequences of the abortion and of the alternatives to the abortion; and other evidence that the court may find useful in determining whether the minor should be granted the right on her own behalf to consent to the abortion or whether the abortion is in the best interest of the minor.

South Carolina Code § 44-41-33. Judicial decision

(A) The court shall enter a written order stating findings of fact and conclusions of law in support of its decision to:

(1) grant the minor the right on her own behalf to consent to the abortion if the court finds that the minor is mature and well-informed enough to make the abortion decision on her own;

(2) grant consent for the abortion if the court finds that the performance of the abortion would be in the minor's best interest; or

(3) deny the petition if the court finds that the minor is immature and that performance of the abortion would not be in the minor's best interest. If the father of the child born after the denial of the petition is identified by adjudication, he shall share in the expenses of the delivery and rearing of the child as determined by the court. Orders issued under this item shall specify that the minor shall have the right to counseling services, appropriate prenatal care, delivery, neonatal, and post-natal care, the cost of which may be paid by the State. Additionally, the State shall have subrogation rights against the father for payments made by the State on behalf of the child.

(B) The court shall immediately issue a written order to the minor, her guardian ad litem, attorney, or other person designated by the minor to receive notice on her behalf.

South Carolina Code § 44-41-34. Appeal

(A) A minor has the right to appeal to the Supreme Court a decision rendered pursuant to Section 44-41-33. She is entitled to an anonymous and expeditious appellate review which takes precedence over other matters pending before the court.

(B) A minor who declares she has insufficient funds to pursue the procedures provided in this section or in Section 44-41-32 must not be required to pay the costs associated with these procedures.

(C) The notice of intent to appeal must be filed with the court issuing the order described in Section 44-41-33 within seventy-two hours from the date the order is received. The record on appeal must be completed and the appeal must be perfected within ten days from the filing of the notice of intent to appeal. These filing requirements are not considered jurisdictional and may be extended by the Supreme Court upon request of the minor for good cause shown.

(D) All hearings conducted under Sections 44-41-32 and 44-41-34 must be closed to the public. All records related to these sections and Section 44-41-33 are not open to public examination and must be sealed by the court.

(E) The Supreme Court shall adopt rules governing the administration of the courts or practice and procedure before such courts necessary to carry out the provisions of Sections 44-41-32, 44-41-33, and 44-41-34.

South Carolina Code § 44-41-35.
Failure to obtain required consent

Failure to obtain required consent constitutes prima facie evidence of interference with family relations in appropriate civil actions. The law of this State does not preclude the award of exemplary damages in an appropriate civil action relevant to violations concerning a minor. Nothing in this chapter may be construed to limit the common law rights of parents.

South Carolina Code § 44-41-36.
Penalty for failing to conform with requirements

(A) A person who intentionally performs an abortion with knowledge that, or with reckless disregard as to whether, the person upon whom the abortion is to be performed is an unemancipated minor, and who intentionally or knowingly fails to conform to any requirement in Sections 44-41-10 through 44-41-36 is guilty of a misdemeanor and, upon conviction, must be fined not less than two thousand dollars nor more than ten thousand dollars or imprisoned for not more than three years, or both. No part of the minimum fine may be suspended. For conviction of a third or subsequent offense, the sentence must be imprisonment for not less than sixty days nor more than three years, none of which may be suspended.

(B) A physician or any person employed or connected with a physician, hospital, or health care facility performing abortions who acts in good faith is justified in relying on the representations of the unemancipated minor or of any other person providing the information required under this chapter. A physician or other person who furnishes professional services related to an act authorized or required by this chapter and who relies upon the information furnished pursuant to this chapter may not be held to have violated any criminal law or to be civilly liable for the reliance, provided that the physician or other person acted in good faith.

South Carolina Code § 44-41-37. Disclosure requirements

A physician or other professional person or agency counseling or discussing with a minor the question of her obtaining an abortion shall fully inform her of the procedures she must follow under law to obtain an abortion without the consent required in Section 44-41-31(1).

The Adoption and Birth Parent Services Division of the Department of Social Services shall develop and distribute brochures to health and education professionals for use in counseling pregnant minors. This brochure shall include the following:

(1) how to access her local health department for prenatal care;

(2) how to access her local Adoption and Birth Parent Services Division of the Department of Social Services or any private not for profit adoption service;

(3) the parental consent requirement as outlined in this bill;

(4) the judicial by-pass procedure as referred in Sections 44-41-32, 44-41-33, and 44-41-34; and

(5) how to access her local mental health center for counseling services.

(5) PARTIAL-BIRTH ABORTION

South Carolina criminalizes partial-birth abortions, unless performed to save the life of the woman. Until it is definitively determined by a court, South Carolina's partial-birth abortion statute may be invalid under the United States Supreme Court decision *in Stenberg v. Carhart*, which invalidated Nebraska's ban on partial-birth abortion. On the other hand, South Carolina's partial-birth abortion statute, as currently written, may be valid under the United States Supreme Court decision in *Gonzales v. Carhart*, which approved of a federal statute that bans partial-birth abortion. In addition to purporting to ban partial-birth abortions, South Carolina has provided a civil cause of action for a married man whose spouse obtains a partial-birth abortion. In the case of a minor, the maternal grandparents of the fetus may file a civil lawsuit. The partial-birth abortion statute is set out below.

South Carolina Code § 44-41-85. Partial-birth abortion ban

(A) A physician who knowingly performs a partial-birth abortion and thereby kills a human fetus is guilty of a felony and, upon conviction, must be fined not less than five thousand dollars or imprisoned for not less than five years, or both. This section shall not apply to a partial-birth abortion that is necessary to save the life of a mother whose life is endangered by a physical disorder, a physical illness, or a physical injury if no other medical procedure would suffice for that purpose.

(B) As used in this section:

(1) the term "partial-birth abortion" means an abortion in which the person performing the abortion partially vaginally delivers a living fetus before killing the fetus and completing the delivery.

(2) the term "physician" means a physician, surgeon, or osteopath authorized to practice medicine in this State and licensed pursuant to Chapter 47 of Title 40. However, an individual who is not a physician, but who directly and knowingly performs a partial-birth abortion is also subject to the provisions of this section.

(C)(1) The father, if married to the mother at the time she receives a partial-birth abortion, and if the mother has not attained the age of eighteen years at the time of the abortion, the maternal grandparents of the fetus have a cause of action against the physician or other person unlawfully performing a partial-birth abortion and may obtain appropriate relief, unless the pregnancy resulted from the plaintiff's criminal conduct or the plaintiff consented to the abortion.

(2) Such relief includes, but is not limited to:

(a) actual damages which shall be trebled;

(b) punitive damages for all injuries, psychological and physical, occasioned by the violation of this section; and

(c) reasonable costs and attorney's fees.

(D) A woman upon whom a partial-birth abortion is performed may not be prosecuted for a violation of this section, for a conspiracy to violate this section, or for any other offense which is based on a violation of this section.

(6) USE OF FACILITIES AND PEOPLE

Under the laws of South Carolina hospitals and clinics are not required to allow abortions at their facilities. The employees and physicians at hospitals and clinics that do allow abortions are permitted to refuse to take part in abortions. The statutes addressing the matter are set out below.

South Carolina Code § 44-41-40. Medical facilities

No private or nongovernmental hospital or clinic shall be required to admit any patient for the purpose of terminating a pregnancy, nor shall such institutions be required to permit their facilities to be utilized for the performance of abortions. No cause of action shall arise against any such hospital or clinic for refusal to perform or to allow the performance of an abortion if the institution has adopted a policy not to admit patients for the purpose of terminating pregnancies; provided, that no hospital or clinic shall refuse an emergency admittance.

South Carolina Code § 44-41-50. Medical employees

(a) No physician, nurse, technician or other employee of a hospital, clinic or physician shall be required to recommend, perform or assist in the performance of an abortion if he advises the hospital, clinic or employing physician in writing that he objects to performing, assisting or oth-

erwise participating in such procedures. Such notice will suffice without specification of the reason therefor.

(b) No physician, nurse, technician or other person who refuses to perform or assist in the performance of an abortion shall be liable to any person for damages allegedly arising from such refusal.

(c) No physician, nurse, technician or other person who refuses to perform or assist in the performance of an abortion shall because of that refusal be dismissed, suspended, demoted, or otherwise disciplined or discriminated against by the hospital or clinic with which he is affiliated or by which he is employed. A civil action for damages or reinstatement of employment, or both, may be prosecuted by any person whose employment or affiliation with a hospital or clinic has been altered or terminated in violation of this chapter.

(d) Any physician who performs an abortion shall also provide, for proper compensation, necessary aftercare for his patient unless released by the patient in writing. The extent of aftercare required shall be that care customarily provided by physicians in such cases in accordance with accepted medical practice.

(7) PUBLIC FUNDS FOR ABORTION

South Carolina prohibits the use of public funds for abortions, except under conditions allowed by federal Medicaid legislation (to save a woman's life or health, or pregnancy involving rape or incest). The statute addressing the matter is set out below.

South Carolina Code § 1-1-1035. Public funds

No state funds or Medicaid funds shall be expended to perform abortions, except for those abortions authorized by federal law under the Medicaid program.

(8) FETAL DEATH REPORT

South Carolina requires that all abortions be reported to the proper authorities. The statute addressing the issue is set out below.

South Carolina Code § 44-41-60. Abortions reported

Any abortion performed in this State must be reported by the performing physician on the standard form for reporting abortions to the state registrar, Department of Health and Environmental Control, within seven days after the abortion is performed. The names of the patient and physician may not be reported on the form or otherwise disclosed to the state registrar. The form must indicate from whom consent was obtained or circumstances waiving consent.

(9) ABORTION FACILITY REQUIREMENTS

South Carolina regulates facilities that perform abortions. The statutes addressing the issue are set out below.

South Carolina Code § 44-41-70.
Promulgation of rules and regulations

(a) The department shall promulgate and enforce regulations for the certification of hospitals as defined in Section 44-41-10(d) as suitable facilities for the performance of abortions.

(b) The department shall promulgate and enforce regulations for the licensing and certification of facilities other than hospitals as defined in Section 44-41-10(d) wherein abortions are to be performed as provided for in Section 44-41-20(a) and (b).

South Carolina Code § 44-41-75.
Licensing of certain abortion facilities

(A) A facility in which any second trimester or five or more first trimester abortions are performed in a month must be licensed by the department to operate as an abortion clinic and must comply with the provisions of Article 3.

(B) The department shall promulgate regulations concerning sanitation, housekeeping, maintenance, staff qualifications, emergency equipment and procedures to provide emergency care, medical records and reports, laboratory, procedure and recovery rooms, physical plant, quality assurance, infection control, and information on and access to patient follow-up care necessary to carry out the purposes of this section.

(10) INJURY TO A PREGNANT WOMAN

South Carolina provides criminal penalties for an injury to a pregnant woman, that results in injury or death to her fetus. The statute addressing the matter is set out below.

South Carolina Code § 16-3-1083. Death or injury to fetus

(A)(1) A person who commits a violent crime, as defined in Section 16-1-60, that causes the death of, or bodily injury to, a child who is in utero at the time that the violent crime was committed, is guilty of a separate offense under this section.

(2)(a) Except as otherwise provided in this subsection, the punishment for a separate offense, as provided for in subsection (A)(1), is the same as the punishment provided for that criminal offense had the death or bodily injury occurred to the unborn child's mother.

(b) Prosecution of an offense under this section does not require proof that:

(i) the person committing the violent offense had knowledge or should have had knowledge that the victim of the underlying offense was pregnant; or

(ii) the defendant intended to cause the death of, or bodily injury to, the unborn child.

(c) If the person engaging in the violent offense intentionally killed or attempted to kill the unborn child, that person must, instead of being punished under subsection (A)(2)(a), be punished for murder or attempted murder.

(d) Notwithstanding any provision of this section or any other provision of law, the death penalty must not be imposed for an offense prosecuted under this section.

(B) Nothing in this section may be construed to permit the prosecution under this section:

(1) of a person for conduct relating to an abortion for which the consent of the pregnant woman, or a person authorized by law to act on her behalf, has been obtained or for which such consent is implied by law;

(2) of a person for any medical treatment of the pregnant woman or her unborn child; or

(3) of a woman with respect to her unborn child.

(C) As used in this section, the term "unborn child" means a child in utero, and the term "child in utero" or " child who is in utero" means a member of the species homo sapiens, at any state of development, who is carried in the womb.

(D) Nothing in this section shall be construed to broaden or restrict any other rights currently existing for the child who is in utero.

(11) CHOOSE LIFE LICENSE PLATE

South Carolina authorizes the issuance of Choose Life license plates. The statute addressing the issue is set out below.

South Carolina Code § 56-3-8910.
"Choose Life" special license plates

(A) The Department of Motor Vehicles shall issue special motor vehicle license plates to owners of private passenger carrying motor vehicles or light pickups having an empty weight of seven thousand pounds or less and a gross weight of nine thousand pounds or less registered in their names which shall have imprinted on the plate the words "Choose Life." The fee for this special license plate is seventy dollars every two years in addition to the regular motor vehicle license fee set forth in Article 5. This special license plate must be of the same size and general design of regular motor vehicle license plates. The special license plates must be issued or revalidated for a biennial period which expires twenty-four months from the month they are issued.

(B) The fees collected pursuant to this section, after the costs to pro-

duce and administer the distribution of this special license plate, must be deposited in a special account, separate and apart from the general fund, designated for use by the Department of Social Services to be used to support local crisis pregnancy programs. Local private nonprofit tax exempt organizations offering crisis pregnancy services may apply for grants from this fund to further their tax exempt purposes. Grants must be awarded not more than once a year, and an applicant must receive as a grant an amount of the total revenues in the fund multiplied by the percentage that the applicant's case load in the preceding calendar year was of the total case load of all applicants in that year. Grants may not be awarded to any agency, institution, or organization that provides, promotes, or refers for abortion.

(C) Before the Department of Motor Vehicles produces and distributes a special license plate pursuant to this section, it must receive four hundred prepaid applications for the special license plate or a deposit of four thousand dollars from the individual or organization seeking issuance of the license plate. If a deposit of four thousand dollars is made by an individual or organization pursuant to this section, the department must refund the four thousand dollars once an equivalent amount of license plate fees is collected for that organization's license plate. If the equivalent amount is not collected within four years of the first issuance of the license plate, the department shall retain the deposit.

(D) If the department receives less than three hundred biennial applications and renewals for the " Choose Life " special license plate, it may not produce additional special license plates in that series. However, the department shall continue to issue special license plates of that series until the existing inventory is exhausted.

South Dakota

(1) OVERVIEW

The state of South Dakota enacted its first criminal abortion statute in 1877. The statute underwent several amendments prior to the 1973 decision by the United States Supreme Court in *Roe v. Wade*, which legalized abortion in the nation. South Dakota has taken affirmative steps to respond to *Roe* and its progeny. The state has addressed several abortion issues by statute that include general abortion guidelines, informed consent, abortion by minors, partial-birth abortion, public funds and abortion, use of facilities and people, fetal and embryo experiments, injury to a pregnant woman, wrongful birth action, fetal death report, abortion facilities, abortion litigation fund, and human cloning.

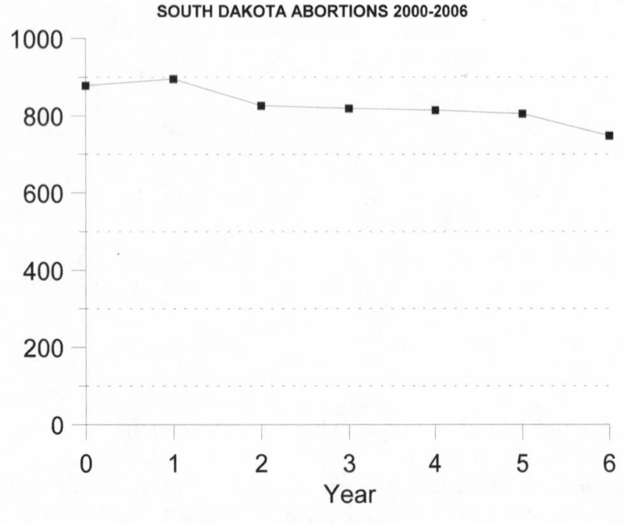

Source: National Center for Health Statistics/South Dakota Department of Health.

South Dakota Abortion by Age Group 2000–2004

Year	*<15*	*15–19*	*20–24*	*25–29*	*30–34*	*35–39*	*≥40*
	Age Group (yrs)						
2000	4	185	294	182	123	65	25
2001	4	190	294	190	120	67	30
2002	11	160	266	175	110	82	22
2003	7	162	286	162	105	79	18
2004	2	148	286	164	111	80	23
Total	28	845	1,426	873	569	373	118

Source: National Center for Health Statistics.

South Dakota Abortion by Weeks of Gestation 2000–2004

Weeks of Gestation	Year *2000*	*2001*	*2002*	*2003*	*2004*	*Total*
<9	484	447	368	402	400	2,101
9–10	235	257	290	260	259	1,301
11–12	121	152	130	127	120	650
13–15	23	28	28	33	21	133
16–20	4	6	4	4	0	18
≥21	0	5	4	1	7	17
Not known	11	0	2	2	0	15

Source: National Center for Health Statistics.

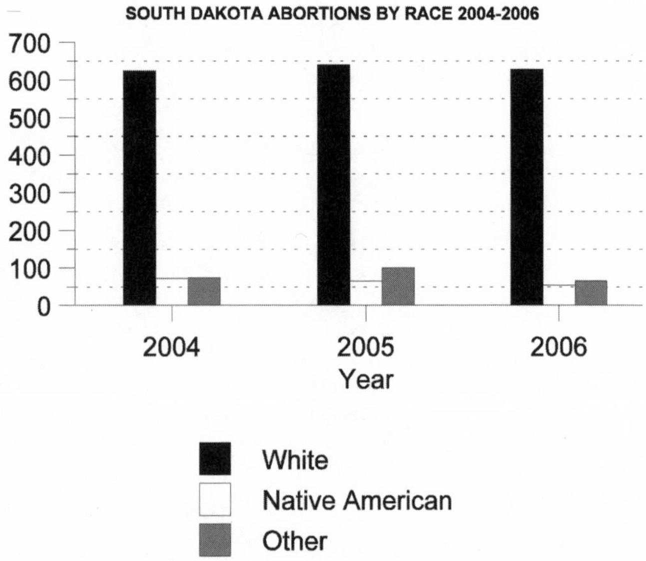

Source: South Dakota Department of Health.

(2) GENERAL ABORTION GUIDELINES

South Dakota expressly permits an abortion through the 24th week of pregnancy. The state generally requires an abortion after the 12th week be performed in a hospital. However, the United States Supreme Court has held that states cannot prevent second trimester abortions from being performed in authorized clinics. The state prohibits third trimester abortions, unless performed to save the life or health of the woman. In 2005 South Dakota enacted a statute that bans all abortions, if the United States Supreme Court ever renders a decision giving states authority to prohibit abortions at all stages. The general abortion statutes are set out below.

South Dakota Code § 34-23A-1. Definition of terms

Terms as used in this chapter mean:

(1) "Abortion," the use of any means to intentionally terminate the pregnancy of a woman known to be pregnant with knowledge that the termination with those means will, with reasonable likelihood, cause the death of the fetus;

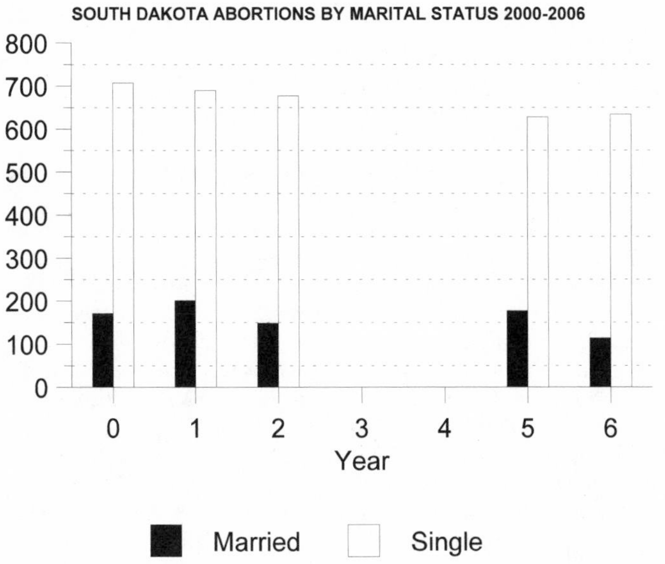

Source: **National Center for Health Statistics/South Dakota Department of Health.**

South Dakota Prior Abortion by Female 2000–2004

Prior Abortion

Year	*None*	*1*	*2*	*≥3*	*Not known*
2000	627	189	38	22	2
2001	682	145	49	19	0
2002	749	60	12	5	0
2003	639	117	45	18	0
2004	618	144	38	14	0
Total	3,315	655	182	78	2

Source: **National Center for Health Statistics.**

South Dakota Abortion by Education Level of Female 2004–2006

Education Level Completed

Year	*<12*	*12*	*≥13*	*Unknown*
2004	114	275	396	29
2005	127	267	407	4
2006	109	228	411	0
Total	350	770	1,214	33

Source: **South Dakota Department of Health.**

(1A) "Abortion facility," a place where abortions are performed;

(1B) "Department," the South Dakota Department of Health;

(2) "Fetus," the biological offspring, including the implanted embryo or unborn child, of human parents;

(3) "Fertilization," that point in time when a male human sperm penetrates the zona pellucida of a female human ovum;

(4) "Human being," an individual living member of the species of Homo sapiens, including the unborn human being during the entire embryonic and fetal ages from fertilization to full gestation;

(5) "Medical emergency," any condition which, on the basis of the physician's good faith clinical judgment, so complicates the medical condition of a pregnant woman as to necessitate the immediate abortion of her pregnancy to avert her death or for which a delay will create serious risk of substantial and irreversible impairment of a major bodily function;

(6) "Parent," one parent or guardian of the pregnant minor or the guardian or conservator of the pregnant woman;

(7) "Physician," a person licensed under the provisions of chapter 36-4 or a physician practicing medicine or osteopathy in the employ of the government of the United States or of this state;

(8) "Probable gestational age of the unborn child," what, in the judgment of the physician, will with reasonable probability be the gestational age of the unborn child at the time the abortion is planned to be performed.

South Dakota Code § 34-23A-1.1.
Attempt to perform abortion defined

For the purposes of this chapter, an attempt to perform an abortion is an act or omission that, under the circumstances as the actor believes them to be, constitutes a substantial step in a course of conduct planned to culminate in the performance of an abortion in South Dakota.

South Dakota Code § 34-23A-1.2. Legislative findings

The Legislature finds that all abortions, whether surgically or chemically induced, terminate the life of a whole, separate, unique, living human being.

South Dakota Code § 34-23A-1.3.
Pregnant woman and unborn child

The Legislature finds that there is an existing relationship between a pregnant woman and her unborn child during the entire period of gestation.

South Dakota Code § 34-23A-2.
Abortion lawful only under specified conditions

An abortion may be performed in this state only if it is performed in compliance with § 34-23A-3, 34-23A-4, or 34-23A-5.

South Dakota Code § 34-23A-2.1. Medical emergency

If a medical emergency compels the performance of an abortion, the physician shall inform the female, prior to the abortion if possible, of the medical indications supporting his judgment that an abortion is necessary to avert her death or that a delay will create serious risk of substantial and irreversible impairment of a major bodily function.

South Dakota Code § 34-23A-3.
Abortion during first twelve weeks

An abortion may be performed by a physician during the first twelve weeks of pregnancy. The abortion decision and its effectuation must be left to the medical judgment of the pregnant woman's attending physician during the first twelve weeks of pregnancy.

South Dakota Code § 34-23A-4.
Abortion during second twelve weeks

An abortion may be performed following the twelfth week of pregnancy and through the twenty-fourth week of pregnancy by a physician only in a hospital licensed under the provisions of chapter 34-12 or in a hospital operated by the United States, this state, or any department, agency or political subdivision of either or in the case of hospital facilities not being available, in the licensed physician's medical clinic or office of practice subject to the requirements of § 34-23A-6.

South Dakota Code § 34-23A-5.
Abortion after twenty-four weeks

An abortion may be performed following the twenty-fourth week of pregnancy by a physician only in a hospital authorized under § 34-23A-4 and only if there is appropriate and reasonable medical judgment that performance of an abortion is necessary to preserve the life or health of the mother.

South Dakota Code § 34-23A-6.
Blood supply and testing facilities

Any abortion performed under the provisions of § 34-23A-4 or 34-23A-5 shall be performed only in a facility which has a blood bank or a sufficient supply of blood immediately available and such facilities shall provide for Rhesus factor (Rh) testing and Rho-gam, Gammulin or any other product of equivalency inoculations shall be required for women undergoing abortion who have the Rh-negative factor.

South Dakota Code § 34-23A-10.2. Penalty

A physician who, knowingly or in reckless disregard, violates § 34-23A-2.1, 34-23A-7, or 34-23A-10.1 is guilty of a Class 2 misdemeanor. The court in which a conviction of a violation of § 34-23A-2.1, 34-23A-7, or 34-23A-10.1 occurs shall report such conviction to the Board of Medical and Osteopathic Examiners.

No penalty may be assessed against the female upon whom the abortion is performed or attempted to be performed. No criminal penalty or civil liability for failure to comply with subsection 34-23A-10.1(2)(c) or that portion of subsection 34-23A-10.1(3) requiring a written certification that the woman has been informed of her opportunity to review the information referred to in subsection 34-23A-10.1(2)(c) may be assessed unless the department of health has made the printed materials available at the time the physician or the physician's agent is required to inform the female of her right to review them.

South Dakota Code § 22-17-5.
Unauthorized abortion as felony

Any person who performs, procures or advises an abortion other than authorized by chapter 34-23A is guilty of a Class 6 felony.

South Dakota Code § 34-23A-16.
Birth certificate for live birth resulting from abortion

Whenever an abortion procedure results in a live birth, a birth certificate shall be issued certifying the birth of said live born person even though said live person may thereafter die in a short time. In the event death does ensue after a short time, a death certificate shall be issued; both the birth and death certificates shall be issued pursuant to law and rules and regulations of the State Department of Health.

South Dakota Code § 34-23A-16.1.
Right to life of babies born alive

All persons born alive, whether in the course of an abortion procedure or not, shall have the same rights to medical treatment and other necessary health care.

South Dakota Code § 34-23A-18.
Abortion as evidence to terminate parental rights

Whenever a person is born alive in the course of an abortion procedure, the facts and circumstances involving the birth and the abortion procedure shall be considered relevant and material evidence in any proceeding under chapters 26-7A, 26-8A, 26-8B, and 26-8C for termination of parental rights or adjudication of dependency or neglect; and the Department of Social Services may commence such proceeding as it deems applicable under that chapter.

South Dakota Code § 34-23A-22.
Cause of action for certain abortions

If any person performs an abortion willfully, wantonly, or maliciously in disregard to § 34-23A-2.1, 34-23A-7, or 34-23A-10.1, the person upon whom such an abortion has been performed, and the parent of a minor child upon whom such an abortion was performed, or any of them, may maintain an action against the person who performed the abortion not to exceed ten thousand dollars in punitive damages. Any person upon whom such an abortion has been attempted may maintain an action against the person who attempted to perform the abortion not to exceed five thousand dollars in punitive damages.

If judgment is rendered in favor of the plaintiff in any such action, the court shall also render judgment for a reasonable attorney's fee in favor of the plaintiff against the defendant. If judgment is rendered in favor of the defendant and the court finds that the plaintiff's suit was frivolous or brought in bad faith, the court shall also render judgment for a reasonable attorney's fee in favor of the defendant against the plaintiff.

South Dakota Code § 34-23A-23.
Anonymity of female plaintiff

In every civil or criminal proceeding or action brought pursuant to this chapter, the court shall rule whether the anonymity of any female upon whom an abortion is performed or attempted shall be preserved from public disclosure if she does not give her consent to such disclosure. The court, upon motion or sua sponte, shall make such a ruling and, upon determining that her anonymity should be preserved, shall issue orders to the parties, witnesses, and counsel, and shall direct the sealing of the record and exclusion of individuals from courtrooms or hearing rooms, to the extent necessary to safeguard her identity from public disclosure. Each such order shall be accompanied by specific written findings explaining why the anonymity of the female should be preserved from public disclosure, why the order is essential to that end, how the order is narrowly tailored to serve that interest, and why no reasonable less restrictive alternative exists. In the absence of written consent of the female upon whom an abortion has been performed or attempted, anyone, other than a public official, who brings an action pursuant to this chapter shall do so under a pseudonym. This section may not be construed to conceal the identity of the plaintiff or of witnesses from the defendant.

South Dakota Code § 22-17-5.1.
Act of 2005 prohibiting abortions

Any person who administers to any pregnant female or who prescribes or procures for any pregnant female any medicine, drug, or substance or uses or employs any instrument or other means with intent thereby to procure an abortion, unless there is appropriate and reasonable medical judgment that performance of an abortion is necessary to preserve the life of the pregnant female, is guilty of a Class 6 felony.

(3) INFORMED CONSENT

Prior to an abortion South Dakota requires that a woman be fully informed of the procedure to be used, the risks involved and alternatives to abortion. An abortion may not take place until 24 hours after a woman has given all of the statutorily required information. The statutes are set out below.

South Dakota Code § 34-23A-1.4.
Risks to life and health of pregnant woman

The Legislature finds that procedures terminating the life of an unborn child impose risks to the life and health of the pregnant woman. The Legislature further finds that a woman seeking to terminate the life of her unborn child may be subject to pressures which can cause an emotional crisis, undue reliance on the advice of others, clouded judgment, and a willingness to violate conscience to avoid those pressures. The Legislature therefore finds that great care should be taken to provide a woman seeking to terminate the life of her unborn child and her own constitutionally protected interest in her relationship with her child with complete and accurate information and adequate time to understand and consider that information in order to make a fully informed and voluntary consent to the termination of either or both.

South Dakota Code § 34-23A-1.5.
Special protection of rights of pregnant women

The Legislature finds that pregnant women contemplating the termination of their right to their relationship with their unborn children, including women contemplating such termination by an abortion procedure, are faced with making a profound decision most often under stress and pressures from circumstances and from other persons, and that there exists a need for special protection of the rights of such pregnant women, and that the State of South Dakota has a compelling interest in providing such protection.

South Dakota Code § 34-23A-1.6.
Standard of practice requiring informed consent

The Legislature finds that, through the common law, the courts of the State of South Dakota have imposed a standard of practice in the health care profession that, except in exceptional circumstances, requires physicians and other health care practitioners to provide patients with such facts about the nature of any proposed course of treatment, the risks of the proposed course of treatment, the alternatives to the proposed course, including any risks that would be applicable to any alternatives, as a reasonable patient would consider significant to the decision of whether to undergo the proposed course of treatment.

South Dakota Code § 34-23A-10.1.
Consent and waiting period

No abortion may be performed unless the physician first obtains a voluntary and informed written consent of the pregnant woman upon whom the physician intends to perform the abortion, unless the physician determines that obtaining an informed consent is impossible due to a medical emergency and further determines that delaying in performing the procedure until an informed consent can be obtained from the pregnant woman or her next of kin in accordance with chapter 34-12C is impossible due to the medical emergency, which determinations shall then be documented in the medical records of the patient. A consent to an abortion is not voluntary and informed, unless, in addition to any other information that must be disclosed under the common law doctrine, the physician provides that pregnant woman with the following information:

(1) A statement in writing providing the following information:

(a) The name of the physician who will perform the abortion;

(b) That the abortion will terminate the life of a whole, separate, unique, living human being;

(c) That the pregnant woman has an existing relationship with that unborn human being and that the relationship enjoys protection under the United States Constitution and under the laws of South Dakota;

(d) That by having an abortion, her existing relationship and her existing constitutional rights with regards to that relationship will be terminated;

(e) A description of all known medical risks of the procedure and statistically significant risk factors to which the pregnant woman would be subjected, including:

(i) Depression and related psychological distress;

(ii) Increased risk of suicide ideation and suicide;

(iii) A statement setting forth an accurate rate of deaths due to abortions, including all deaths in which the abortion procedure was a substantial contributing factor;

(iv) All other known medical risks to the physical health of the woman, including the risk of infection, hemorrhage, danger to subsequent pregnancies, and infertility;

(f) The probable gestational age of the unborn child at the time the abortion is to be performed, and a scientifically accurate statement describing the development of the unborn child at that age; and

(g) The statistically significant medical risks associated with carrying her child to term compared to undergoing an induced abortion.

The disclosures set forth above shall be provided to the pregnant woman in writing and in person no later than two hours before the procedure is to be performed. The physician shall ensure that the pregnant woman signs each page of the written disclosure with the certification that she has read and understands all of the disclosures, prior to the patient signing a consent for the procedure. If the pregnant woman asks for a clarification or explanation of any particular disclosure, or asks any other question about a matter of significance to her, the explanation or answer shall be made in writing and be given to the pregnant woman before signing a consent for the procedure and shall be made part of the permanent medical record of the patient;

(2) A statement by telephone or in person, by the physician who is to perform the abortion, or by the referring physician, or by an agent of both, at least twenty-four hours before the abortion, providing the following information:

(a) That medical assistance benefits may be available for prenatal care, childbirth, and neonatal care;

(b) That the father of the unborn child is legally responsible to provide financial support for her child following birth, and that this legal obligation of the father exists in all instances, even in instances in which the father has offered to pay for the abortion;

(c) The name, address, and telephone number of a pregnancy help center in reasonable proximity of the abortion facility where the abortion will be performed; and

(d) That she has a right to review all of the material and information described in § 34-23A-1, §§ 34-23A-1.2 to 34-23A-1.7, inclusive, § 34-23A-10.1, and § 34-23A-10.3, as well as the printed materials described in § 34-23A-10.3, and the website described in § 34-23A-10.4. The physician or the physician's agent shall inform the pregnant woman, orally or in writing, that the materials have been provided by the State of South Dakota at no charge to the pregnant woman. If the pregnant woman indicates, at any time, that she wants to review any of the materials described, such disclosures shall be either given to her at least twenty-four hours before the abortion or mailed to her at least seventy-two hours before the abortion by certified mail, restricted delivery to addressee, which means the postal employee can only deliver the mail to the addressee;

Prior to the pregnant woman signing a consent to the abortion, she shall sign a written statement that indicates that the requirements of this section have been complied with. Prior to the performance of the abortion, the physician who is to perform the abortion shall receive a copy of the written disclosure documents required by this section, and shall certify in writing that all of the information described in those subdivisions has been provided to the pregnant woman, that the physician is, to the best of his or her ability, satisfied that the pregnant woman has read the materials which are required to be disclosed, and that the physician believes she understands the information imparted.

South Dakota Code § 34-23A-10.3.
Publication of educational materials

The health department shall publish, in culturally sensitive languages, within one hundred eighty days after July 1, 2005, the following printed materials in such a way as to ensure that the information is easily comprehensible:

(1) Materials designed to inform the pregnant woman of all the disclosures enumerated in § 34-23A-10.1;

(2) Materials designed to inform the pregnant woman of public and private agencies and services available to assist a pregnant woman through pregnancy, upon childbirth and while the child is dependent, including adoption agencies, which shall include a list of the agencies available and a description of the services they offer; and

(3) Materials designed to inform the pregnant woman of the probable anatomical and physiological characteristics of the unborn child at two-week gestational increments from the time when a pregnant woman can be known to be pregnant to full term, including any relevant information on the possibility of the unborn child's survival and pictures or drawings representing the development of unborn

children at two-week gestational increments. Such pictures or drawings shall contain the dimensions of the fetus and shall be realistic and appropriate for the stage of pregnancy depicted. The materials shall be objective, nonjudgmental, and designed to convey only accurate scientific information about the unborn child at the various gestational ages.

The materials shall be printed in a typeface large enough to be clearly legible and shall be available at no cost from the Department of Health upon request and in appropriate number to any person, facility or hospital.

South Dakota Code § 34-23A-10.4. Multi-media website

The Department of Health shall, by January 1, 2004, develop and maintain a multi-media website that contains web pages covering each of the following topics:

(1) Embryonic and fetal development at various gestational stages;

(a) Anatomical and physiological characteristics; and

(b) Survival possibilities of the unborn child;

(2) Abortion methods commonly used for each trimester of pregnancy;

(3) Statistically significant abortion method risks, including infection, hemorrhage, danger to subsequent pregnancies, and infertility;

(4) Important pre-abortion procedures;

(a) Confirmation of pregnancy via sonogram; and

(b) Counseling and discussion of medical history to detect possible abortion risks;

(5) Post-abortion psychological and emotional complications;

(6) Parental notification as required by 34-23A-7;

(7) Assistance, benefits, and services:

(a) Names and contact information of public and private agencies; and

(b) Types and availability of public medical benefits and services;

(8) Responsibility of the father of the unborn child;

(9) Statistically significant pregnancy risks;

(10) Adoption options:

(a) Names and contact information of public and private agencies; and

(b) Description of services.

The state shall collect and maintain web statistics regarding the website developed and maintained pursuant to this section. However, no personal information may be collected.

South Dakota Code § 34-23A-1.7.
Medical malpractice informed consent claims

The South Dakota common law cause of action for medical malpractice informed consent claims based upon the reasonable patient standard is reaffirmed and is hereby expressly declared to apply to all abortion procedures. The duty of a physician to disclose all facts about the nature of the procedure, the risks of the procedure, and the alternatives to the procedure that a reasonable patient would consider significant to her decision of whether to undergo or forego the procedure applies to all abortions. Nothing in § 34-23A-1, §§ 34-23A-1.2 to 34-23A-1.7, inclusive, § 34-23A-10.1, and § 34-23A-10.3 may be construed to render any of the requirements otherwise imposed by common law inapplicable to abortion procedures or diminish the nature or the extent of those requirements. The disclosure requirements expressly set forth in § 34-23A-1, §§ 34-23A-1.2 to 34-23A-1.7, inclusive, § 34-23A-10.1, and § 34-23A-10.3 are an express clarification of, and are in addition to, those common law disclosure requirements.

South Dakota Code § 34-23A-37. Information collection form

The Department of Health shall prepare a reporting form for physicians which shall provide for the collection of the following information:

(1) The number of females to whom the physician provided the information described in subdivision 34-23A-10.1(1); of that number, the number provided by telephone and the number provided in person; and of each of those numbers, the number provided in the capacity of a referring physician and the number provided in the capacity of a physician who is to perform the abortion;

(2) The number of females to whom the physician provided the information described in subdivision 34-23A-10.1(2); of that number, the number provided by telephone and the number provided in person; of each of those numbers, the number provided in the capacity of a referring physician and the number provided in the capacity of a physician who is to perform the abortion; and of each of those numbers, the number provided by the physician and the number provided by an agent of the physician;

(3) The number of females who availed themselves of the opportunity to obtain a copy of the printed information described in § 34-23A-10.3, and the number who did not; and of each of those numbers, the number who, to the best of the reporting physician's information and belief, went on to obtain the abortion;

(4) The number of abortions performed by the physician in which information otherwise required to be provided at least twenty-four hours before the abortion was not provided because an immediate abortion was necessary to avert the female's death, and the number of abortions in which such information was not so provided because a delay would create serious risk of substantial and irreversible impairment of a major bodily function;

(5) The name of hospital or physician office;

(6) The date of report by month, day, and year; and

(7) A unique patient number that can be used to link the report to medical report for inspection, clarification, and correction purposes but that cannot, of itself, reasonably lead to the identification of any person obtaining an abortion.

South Dakota Code § 34-23A-38.
Submission of information collection form

By February twenty-eighth of each year, each physician who provided, or whose agent provided, information to one or more females in accordance with § 34-23A-10.1 during the previous calendar year shall submit to the Department of Health a copy of the physicians' information report form described in § 34-23A-37 with the requested data entered accurately and completely.

(4) ABORTION BY MINORS

Under the laws of South Dakota no physician may perform an abortion upon an unemancipated minor unless he/she first notifies a parent or guardian of the minor 48 hours prior to the abortion. In compliance with federal constitutional law, South Dakota has provided a judicial waiver procedure for an unemancipated minor to obtain an abortion without parental or guardian notice. The minor may petition a trial court for a waiver of the notice requirement. A minor has a right to an attorney at the proceeding and if she cannot afford one, the court must appoint her an attorney. If a minor chooses, she may represent herself. The required notice may be waived if the court finds either (1) that the minor is mature and well-informed enough to make the abortion decision on her own, or (2) that performance of the abortion would be in the best interest of the minor. An expedited appeal is available to any minor to whom the court denies a waiver of notice. The statutes addressing the matter are set out below.

South Dakota Code § 34-23A-7. Notice and judicial bypass

No abortion may be performed upon an unemancipated minor or upon a female for whom a guardian has been appointed because of a finding of incompetency, until at least forty-eight hours after written notice of the pending operation has been delivered in the manner specified in this section. The notice shall be addressed to the parent at the usual place of abode of the parent and delivered personally to the parent by the physician or an agent. In lieu of such delivery, notice may be made by certified mail addressed to the parent at the usual place of abode of the parent with return receipt requested and restricted delivery to the addressee, which means a postal employee can only deliver the mail to the authorized addressee. If notice is made by certified mail, the time of delivery shall be deemed to occur at twelve noon on the next day on which regular mail delivery takes place, subsequent to mailing.

No notice is required under this section if:

(1) The attending physician certifies in the pregnant unemancipated minor's medical record that, on the basis of the physician's good faith clinical judgment, a medical emergency exists and there is insufficient time to provide the required notice. Unless the unemancipated minor gives notice of her intent to seek a judicial waiver, a good faith effort shall be made by the attending physician or the physician's agent to verbally inform the parent within twenty-four hours after the performance of the emergency abortion, that an emergency abortion was performed on the unemancipated minor and shall also be sent a written notice, in the manner described in this section, of the performed emergency abortion. If the unemancipated minor, upon whom an emergency abortion was performed, elects not to allow the notification of her parent, any judge of a circuit court shall, upon petition, or motion, and after an appropriate hearing, authorize the waiving of the required notice of the performed abortion if the judge determines, by clear and convincing evidence that the unemancipated minor is mature and capable of determining whether notification should be given, or that the waiver would be in the unemancipated minor's best interest; or

(2) The person who is entitled to notice certifies in writing that the person has been notified. The certification is valid only if the signature has been notarized. If the person does not provide a notarized signature, the person shall be sent a written notice as described in this section. No abortion as described in this section may be performed until at least forty-eight hours after written notice of the pending operation has been delivered in the manner specified in this section; or

(3) A pregnant female elects not to allow the notification of her parent, in which case, any judge of a circuit court shall, upon petition, or motion, and after an appropriate hearing, authorize a physician to perform the abortion if the judge determines, by clear and convincing evidence, that the pregnant female is mature and capable of giving informed consent to the proposed abortion. If the judge determines that the pregnant female is not mature, or if she does not claim to be mature, the judge shall determine, by clear and convincing evidence, whether the performance of an abortion upon her without notification of her parent would be in her best interests and shall authorize a physician to perform the abortion without such notification if the judge concludes that her best interests would be served thereby.

South Dakota Code § 34-23A-7.1.
Right to counsel and appeal

In any proceeding pursuant to subdivision 34-23A-7(1) or 34-23A-7(3), the pregnant female may participate in proceedings in the court on her own behalf, and the court may appoint a guardian ad litem for her. The court shall, however, advise her that she has a right to court-appointed counsel and shall, upon her request, provide her with such counsel. Proceedings in the court under subdivision 34-23A-7(1) or 34-23A-7(3) shall be confidential and shall be given such precedence over other pending matters so that the court may reach a decision promptly and without delay so as to serve the best interests of the pregnant female. A judge of the court who conducts proceedings under subdivision 34-23A-7(1) or 34-23A-7(3) shall make in writing specific factual findings and legal conclusions supporting the decision and shall order a record of the evidence to be maintained including the judge's own findings and conclusions.

An expedited confidential appeal shall be available to any such pregnant female for whom the court denies an order authorizing an abortion without notification. An order authorizing an abortion without notification is not subject to appeal. No filing fees are required of any such pregnant female at either the trial or the appellate level. Access to the trial court for the purposes of such a petition or motion, and access to the appellate courts for purposes of making an appeal from denial of the same, shall be afforded such a pregnant female twenty-four hours a day, seven days a week. Notwithstanding any other provision of law, all pleadings, papers, and other documents filed pursuant to this section are confidential, are not public records, and are not open for inspection by any member of the public for any purpose.

South Dakota Code § 34-23A-39.
Reporting form for use of notice

The Department of Health shall prepare a reporting form for physicians which shall provide for the collection of the following information:

(1) The number of females or parents whom the physician or agent of the physician provided the notice described in § 34-23A-7; and of each of those numbers, the number of females who, to the best of the reporting physician's information and belief, went on to obtain the abortion;

(2) The number of females upon whom the physician performed an abortion without providing to the parent of the minor the notice described in § 34-23A-7; of that number, the number who were emancipated minors, and the numbers from whom each of the exceptions to § 34-23A-7 were applicable;

(3) The number of abortions performed upon a female by the physician after receiving judicial authorization to do so without parental notice;

(4) The same information described in subdivisions (1) through (3) of this section with respect to females for whom a guardian or conservator has been appointed pursuant to statutes on guardianship or conservatorship because of finding of incompetency;

(5) The name of hospital or physician office;

(6) The date of report by month, day, and year; and

(7) A unique patient number that can be used to link the report to medical report for inspection, clarification, and correction purposes but that cannot, of itself, reasonably lead to the identification of any person obtaining an abortion.

South Dakota Code § 34-23A-40.
Submission of reporting form

By February twenty-eighth of each year, each physician who provided, or whose agent provided, the notice described in § 34-23A-7, and any physician who knowingly performed an abortion upon a female or upon a female for whom a guardian or conservator had been appointed because of a finding of incompetency during the previous calendar year shall submit to the Department of Health a copy of the physicians' information report form described in § 34-23A-39 with the requested data entered accurately and completely.

(5) PARTIAL-BIRTH ABORTION

South Dakota prohibits partial-birth abortions, unless necessary to save the life of the woman. Until it is definitively determined by a court, South Dakota's partial-birth abortion statute may be invalid under the United States Supreme Court decision *in Stenberg v. Carhart*, which invalidated Nebraska's ban on partial-birth abortion. On the other hand, South Dakota's partial-birth abortion statute, as currently written, may be valid under the United States Supreme Court decision in *Gonzales v. Carhart*, which approved of a federal statute that bans partial-birth abortion. In addition to purporting to ban partial-birth abortions, South Dakota has provided a civil cause of action for the father of a fetus destroyed by partial-birth abortion. In the case of a minor, the maternal grandparents of the fetus may file a civil lawsuit. The statutes addressing the matter are set out below.

South Dakota Code § 34-23A-32.
Partial-birth abortion defined

For the purposes of §§ 34-23A-27 to 34-23A-33, inclusive, a partial-birth abortion is any abortion in which the person who performs the abortion causes a living human fetus to be partially vaginally delivered before killing the infant and completing the delivery.

South Dakota Code § 34-23A-33. Fetus and infant defined

For the purposes of §§ 34-23A-27 to 34-23A-33, inclusive, the term, fetus, and the term, infant, are used interchangeably to refer to the biological offspring of human parents.

South Dakota Code § 34-23A-27. Partial-birth abortion ban

No person may perform a partial-birth abortion which results in the death of a human fetus or infant. A violation of this section is a Class 6 felony.

South Dakota Code § 34-23A-28. Exception

The provisions of §§ 34-23A-27 to 34-23A-33, inclusive, do not apply to any partial-birth abortion that is necessary to save the life of the mother because her life is endangered by a physical disorder, illness, or injury, including a life-endangering condition caused by or arising from the pregnancy itself, if no other medical procedure would suffice for that purpose.

South Dakota Code § 34-23A-29. Civil action

In the case of the death of a human fetus or infant as the result of a partial-birth abortion, the father of the human fetus or infant and, if the mother has not attained the age of eighteen years at the time of the partial-birth abortion, the maternal grandparents of the human fetus or infant may file a civil action to obtain appropriate relief, unless the plaintiff consented to the partial-birth abortion or unless the plaintiff's criminal conduct caused the pregnancy.

South Dakota Code § 34-23A-30.
Money damages in partial-birth abortion

Civil relief pursuant to § 34-23A-29 includes money damages for all injuries, psychological or physical, that are proximately caused by a partial-birth abortion in violation of § 34-23A-27. Any plaintiff with standing to sue pursuant to § 34-23A-29 who has paid for the costs of a partial-birth abortion may recover treble the costs in damages.

South Dakota Code § 34-23A-31. Prosecution of woman

No woman upon whom a partial-birth abortion is performed may be prosecuted under the provisions of §§ 34-23A-27 to 34-23A-33, inclusive, for conspiracy to violate § 34-23A-27.

(6) PUBLIC FUNDS AND ABORTION

South Dakota prohibits the use of public funds to pay for an abortion, except when the procedure is necessary to save the life of the woman. The statutes addressing the matter are set out below.

South Dakota Code § 28-6-4.5. Public funds

No funds of the state of South Dakota or any agency, county, municipality or any other political subdivision thereof and no federal funds passing through the state treasury or any agency of the state of South Dakota, county, municipality or any other political subdivision thereof, shall be authorized or paid to or on behalf of any person or entity for or in connection with any abortion that is not necessary for the preservation of the life of the person upon whom the abortion is performed.

South Dakota Code § 25-10-21. Domestic abuse funds

No funds authorized or awarded under the provisions of §§ 25-10-15 to 25-10-21, inclusive, shall be used to promote or pay, directly or indirectly, for the elective termination of a pregnancy, sterilization, or control of birth by medication or device.

(7) USE OF FACILITIES AND PEOPLE

Under the laws of South Dakota social workers may but are not required to give advise regarding abortions. The state does not requires pharmacists to dispense drugs for abortions. Hospitals in the state are not required to allow abortions at their facilities. The employees and physicians at facilities that do allow abortions are permitted to refuse to take part in abortions. The statutes addressing the matters are set out below.

South Dakota Code § 34-23A-11.
Counselor or social worker

No counselor, social worker, or anyone else who may be in such a position where the abortion question may appear as a part of their workday routine, shall be liable to any person for damages allegedly arising from advising or helping to arrange for or for refusal to arrange or encourage abortion, and there shall be no retaliation from any agency or institution with which such person may be affiliated or by which he may be employed.

South Dakota Code § 34-23A-12.
No liability for refusal to perform abortion

No physician, nurse, or other person who refuses to perform or assist in the performance of an abortion shall be liable to any person for damages arising from that refusal.

South Dakota Code § 36-11-70.
Refusal to dispense medication

No pharmacist may be required to dispense medication if there is reason to believe that the medication would be used to:

(1) Cause an abortion; or

(2) Destroy an unborn child as defined in subdivision 22-1-2(50A); or

(3) Cause the death of any person by means of an assisted suicide, euthanasia, or mercy killing.

No such refusal to dispense medication pursuant to this section may be the basis for any claim for damages against the pharmacist or the pharmacy of the pharmacist or the basis for any disciplinary, recriminatory, or discriminatory action against the pharmacist.

South Dakota Code § 34-23A-13. Medical personnel

No physician, nurse or other person who performs or refuses to perform or assist in the performance of an abortion shall, because of that performance or refusal, be dismissed, suspended, demoted, or otherwise prejudiced or damaged by a hospital or other medical facility with which he is affiliated or by which he is employed.

South Dakota Code § 34-23A-14. Hospitals

No hospital licensed pursuant to the provisions of chapter 34-12 is required to admit any patient for the purpose of terminating a pregnancy pursuant to the provisions of this chapter. No hospital is liable for its failure or refusal to participate in such termination if the hospital has adopted a policy not to admit patients for the purpose of terminating pregnancies as provided in this chapter.

(8) FETAL AND EMBRYO EXPERIMENTS

South Dakota prohibits experimentation on an aborted fetus. The state also prohibits selling or experimenting on embryos. The state provides by statutes for the disposition of aborted fetuses. The statutes addressing the matter are set out below.

South Dakota Code § 34-23A-17. Fetal experiments

An unborn or newborn child who has been subject to an induced abortion other than an abortion necessary to prevent the death of the mother or any tissue or organ thereof may not be used in animal or human re-

search or for animal or human transplantation. This section may not be construed to preclude any therapy intended to directly benefit the unborn or newborn child who has been subject to the abortion. This section does not prohibit the use for human transplantation of an unborn child or any tissue or organ thereof if removed in the course of removal of an ectopic or a molar pregnancy.

South Dakota Code § 34-14-16. Research on embryo

No person may knowingly conduct nontherapeutic research that destroys a human embryo. A violation of this section is a Class 1 misdemeanor.

South Dakota Code § 34-14-17. Selling embryo

No person may knowingly conduct nontherapeutic research that subjects a human embryo to substantial risk of injury or death. No person may sell or transfer a human embryo with the knowledge that the embryo will be subjected to nontherapeutic research. A violation of this section is a Class 1 misdemeanor.

South Dakota Code § 34-25-32.3.
Disposition of remains of embryo or fetus

Remains of a human embryo or fetus resulting from an abortion or miscarriage, induced or occurring accidentally or spontaneously at a hospital, clinic, or medical facility shall be disposed of in the manner provided by §§ 34-25-32.3 to 34-25-32.7, inclusive.

South Dakota Code § 34-25-32.4.
Disposal of aborted fetuses

Any hospital, clinic, or medical facility in which abortions are induced or occur spontaneously or accidentally or any laboratory to which the remains of human embryos or fetuses are delivered shall arrange for the disposal of the remains by cremation, interment by burial, or by incineration in a medical waste incinerator approved by the Department of Environment and Natural Resources. If incineration is used, the remains of the human embryo or fetus shall be incinerated separately from other medical waste. The hospital, clinic, medical facility, or laboratory may perform any laboratory tests necessary for the health of the woman or her future offspring, or for the purposes of a criminal investigation, or for determination of parentage prior to disposing of the remains.

South Dakota Code § 34-25-32.5.
Failure to comply as public nuisance

Any failure to comply with the provisions of §§ 34-25-32.3 to 34-25-32.7, inclusive, constitutes a public nuisance. Any person, firm, or corporation failing to comply with the provisions of §§ 34-25-32.3 to 34-25-32.7, inclusive, is guilty of a Class 1 misdemeanor.

South Dakota Code § 34-25-32.6. Religious service

No religious service or ceremony is required as part of the disposition of the remains of a human embryo or fetus. The hospital, clinic, or medical facility shall discuss or disclose the method of disposition with the woman who had the miscarriage.

South Dakota Code § 34-25-32.7. Fetal donation

Tissue and organ donation may occur in cases of spontaneous abortions if the consent of the mother is obtained.

(9) INJURY TO A PREGNANT WOMAN

South Dakota has created the crime of feticide or fetal homicide, for wrongful conduct that injures a pregnant woman and causes the death of the fetus. The state also has a penal statute for intentionally killing a fetus. The statutes are set out below.

South Dakota Code § 22-16-1.1 Fetal homicide

Homicide is fetal homicide if the person knew, or reasonably should have known, that a woman bearing an unborn child was pregnant and caused the death of the unborn child without lawful justification and if the person:

(1) Intended to cause the death of or do serious bodily injury to the pregnant woman or the unborn child; or

(2) Knew that the acts taken would cause death or serious bodily injury to the pregnant woman or her unborn child; or

(3) If perpetrated without any design to effect death by a person engaged in the commission of any felony.

Fetal homicide is a Class B felony.

This section does not apply to acts which cause the death of an unborn child if those acts were committed during any abortion, lawful or unlawful, to which the pregnant woman consented.

South Dakota Code § 22-17-6. Intentional killing of fetus

Any person who intentionally kills a human fetus by causing an injury to its mother, which is not authorized by chapter 34-23A, is guilty of a Class 4 felony.

South Dakota Code § 21-5-1. Liability for wrongful death

Whenever the death or injury of a person, including an unborn child, shall be caused by a wrongful act, neglect, or default, and the act, neglect, or default is such as would have entitled the party injured to maintain an action and recover damages in respect thereto, if death had not ensued, then and in every such case, the corporation which, or the person who, would have been liable, if death had not ensued, or the personal representative of the estate of such person as such personal representative, shall be liable, to an action for damages, notwithstanding the death of the person injured, and although the death shall have been caused under such circumstances as amount in law to a felony; and when the action is against such personal representative, the damages recovered shall be a valid claim against the estate of such deceased person. However, an action under this section involving an unborn child shall be for the exclusive benefit of the mother or the lawfully married parents of the unborn child.

(10) WRONGFUL BIRTH ACTION

South Dakota has taken an affirmative step to prevent wrongful birth litigation, by prohibiting claims for negligent failure to abort a pregnancy. The statutes addressing the matter are set out below.

South Dakota Code § 21-55-1.
Wrongful birth action prohibited

There shall be no cause of action or award of damages on behalf of any person based on the claim of that person that, but for the conduct of another, he would not have been conceived or, once conceived, would not have been permitted to have been born alive. The term "conception," as used in this section, means the fertilization of a human ovum by a human sperm, which occurs when the sperm has penetrated the cell membrane of the ovum.

South Dakota Code § 21-55-2.
Action for birth of another prohibited

There shall be no cause of action or award of damages on behalf of any person based on the claim that, but for the conduct of another, a person would not have been permitted to have been born alive.

South Dakota Code § 21-55-3. Limits on evidence

The failure or the refusal of any person to prevent the live birth of a person may not be considered in awarding damages or in imposing a penalty in any action. The failure or the refusal of any person to prevent the live birth of a person is not a defense in any action.

South Dakota Code § 21-55-4. Limited effect of chapter

The provisions of this chapter do not prohibit a cause of action or the awarding of damages, except as specifically provided in this chapter, by or on behalf of any person based on the claim that a person is liable for injury caused by such person's willful acts or caused by such person's want of ordinary care or skill.

(11) FETAL DEATH REPORT

Under the laws of South Dakota all abortions must be reported to the proper authorities. The statutes addressing the issue are set out below.

South Dakota Code § 34-23A-19. Reports required

Any facility or physician performing abortions in this state shall report to the state department of health as follows:

(1) Total number of abortions performed;

(2) Method of abortion used in each abortion performed;

(3) Complete pathology reports giving period of gestation of fetuses, presence of abnormality, and measurements of fetuses, if the facility where the abortion is performed is so equipped to complete such reports;

(4) Numbers of maternal deaths due directly or indirectly to abortions;

(5) Reports of all follow-up, including short- and long-term complications in the female due to abortion;

(6) Other information required by the regulations issued by the department pursuant to this section.

No report made under this section shall include the name of any female receiving an abortion.

The Department of Health may promulgate rules pursuant to chapter 1-26 to provide for the reporting of such information concerning abortion as will enable the department to provide complete reporting to the centers for disease control of the public health services in the United States Department of Health and Human Services of all abortion-related data the centers for disease control recommend be reported to them by states.

South Dakota Code § 34-23A-34. Physician's reporting form

The Department of Health shall prepare a reporting form for physicians which shall provide for the collection of the following information:

(1) The month, day, and year of the induced abortion;

(2) The method of abortion used for each induced abortion;

(3) The approximate gestational age, in weeks, of the unborn child involved in the abortion;

(4) The age of the mother at the time of the abortion and, if the mother was younger than sixteen years of age at the time the child was conceived, the age of the father, if known;

(5) The specific reason for the induced abortion, including the following:

(a) The pregnancy was a result of rape;

(b) The pregnancy was a result of incest;

(c) The mother could not afford the child;

(d) The mother did not desire to have the child;

(e) The mother's emotional health was at risk;

(f) The mother would suffer substantial and irreversible impairment of a major bodily function if the pregnancy continued;

(g) Other, which shall be specified;

(6) Whether the induced abortion was paid for by:

(a) Private insurance;

(b) Public health plan;

(c) Other, which shall be specified;

(7) Whether coverage was under:

(a) A-fee-for-service insurance company;

(b) A managed care company; or

(c) Other, which shall be specified;

(8) A description of the complications, if any, for each abortion and for the aftermath of each abortion;

(9) The fee collected for performing or treating the abortion;

(10) The type of anesthetic, if any, used for each induced abortion;

(11) The method used to dispose of fetal tissue and remains;

(12) The specialty area of the physician;

(13) Whether the physician performing the induced abortion has been subject to license revocation or suspension or other professional sanction;

(14) The number of previous abortions the mother has had;

(15) The number of previous live births of the mother, including both living and deceased;

(16) The date last normal menses began for the mother;

(17) The name of physician performing the induced abortion;

(18) The name of hospital or physician office where the induced abortion was performed;

(19) A unique patient number that can be used to link the report to medical report for inspection, clarification, and correction purposes but that cannot, of itself, reasonably lead to the identification of any person obtaining an abortion; and

(20) Certain demographic information including:

(a) State, county, and city of occurrence of abortion;

(b) State, county, and city of residence of mother;

(c) Marital status of mother;

(d) Education status of mother;

(e) Race and hispanic origin of mother; and

(21) Certain Rhesus factor (Rh) information including:

(a) Whether the mother received the Rh test;

(b) Whether the mother tested positive for the Rh-negative factor;

(c) Whether the mother received a Rho(D) immune globulin injection.

South Dakota Code § 34-23A-35.
Submission of physician's information report

By January fifteenth of each year, each physician who performed or treated an induced abortion during the previous calendar year or the physician's agent, shall submit to the department a copy of the physicians' information report described in § 34-23A-34 with the requested data entered accurately and completely.

South Dakota Code § 34-23A-36. Annual public report

The department shall issue a public report annually providing the same detailed information required by the reporting forms required by §§ 34-23A-34 to 34-23A-45, inclusive. The public report shall cover the entire previous calendar year and shall be compiled from the data in all the reporting forms required by §§ 34-23A-34 to 34-23A-45, inclusive, and submitted to the department in accordance with §§ 34-23A-34 to 34-23A-45, inclusive. Each public report shall also provide such detailed information for all previous calendar years, adjusted to reflect any additional information from late or corrected reports. The department shall take care to ensure that none of the information included in the public reports may reasonably lead to identification of any physician who performed or treated an abortion or any mother who has had an abortion.

South Dakota Code § 34-23A-41.
Penalty for failure to submit reporting form

Any physician who fails to submit any report required by §§ 34-23A-34 to 34-23A-45, inclusive, within a grace period of thirty days following the due date is subject to a late fee of five hundred dollars for each additional thirty-day period, or portion of a thirty-day period, that each report is overdue. Any physician who has not submitted a report, or has submitted only an incomplete report, more than one year following the due date, is also subject to a civil action brought by the department. A court of competent jurisdiction may direct the physician to submit a complete report within a period stated by court order or be subject to sanctions for civil contempt.

South Dakota Code § 34-23A-42. Misdemeanor

Any person who knowingly or recklessly fails to submit any report required by §§ 34-23A-34 to 34-23A-45, inclusive, or submits false infor-

mation under §§ 34-23A-34 to 34-23A-45, inclusive, is guilty of a Class 2 misdemeanor.

South Dakota Code § 34-23A-43.
Department to ensure compliance

The department shall ensure compliance with §§ 34-23A-34 to 34-23A-45, inclusive, and shall verify the data provided by periodic inspection of places where induced abortions are performed.

South Dakota Code § 34-23A-44.
Department to ensure anonymity

No report made under §§ 34-23A-34 to 34-23A-45, inclusive, may include the name of any female having an abortion. The Department of Health shall take care to ensure that none of the information included in any report required by §§ 34-23A-34 to 34-23A-45, inclusive, including printed records, computerized records, or stored information of any type, can reasonably lead to the identification of any person obtaining an abortion. Except in the case of a mother who was younger than the age of sixteen at the time her child was conceived, any information collected by or under the direction of a physician or psychotherapist for the purpose of completing a report required by §§ 34-23A-34 to 34-23A-45, inclusive, is privileged as a confidential communication under § 19-13-7. In the case of a mother who was younger than the age of sixteen at the time the child was conceived, the privilege of confidentiality set forth in § 19-13-7 may not be claimed in any judicial proceeding involving § 22-22-1.

South Dakota Code § 34-23A-45.
"Induced abortion" defined

For purposes of §§ 34-23A-34 to 34-23A-45, inclusive, only, the term, induced abortion, means the use of any means to intentionally terminate the pregnancy of a female known to be pregnant with knowledge that the termination with those means will, with reasonable likelihood, cause the death of the embryo or fetus.

South Dakota Code § 34-23A-25.
Analyses of pregnancy outcomes

The department may collect data from health providers and medical facilities for purposes of performing analyses of pregnancy outcomes to determine the number, or if that is not possible, the best available estimate of the number, of each of the following:

(1) Ectopic pregnancies;
(2) Stillbirths;
(3) Live births;
(4) Molar pregnancies;
(5) Spontaneous abortions;
(6) Induced abortions; and
(7) Any other pregnancy-related classifications the department deems useful.

(12) ABORTION FACILITIES

South Dakota has established statutory requirements for facilities that perform abortions. The statutes are set out below.

South Dakota Code § 34-23A-46. Licensing of abortion facilities

Except as provided by § 34-23A-47, no person may establish or operate an abortion facility in this state without an appropriate license issued under §§ 34-23A-46 to 34-23A-51, inclusive. Each abortion facility shall have a separate license. No abortion facility license is transferrable or assignable.

South Dakota Code § 34-23A-47.
Exceptions to abortion facility license requirement

The following facilities need not be licensed under §§ 34-23A-46 to 34-23A-51, inclusive:

(1) A health care facility licensed pursuant to chapter 34-12; or
(2) The office of a physician licensed pursuant to chapter 36-4 unless the office is used for performing abortions.

South Dakota Code § 34-23A-48.
Application for abortion facility license

An applicant for an abortion facility license shall submit an application to the department on a form prescribed by the department. The application shall be accompanied by a nonrefundable license fee in an amount set by the department by rules promulgated pursuant to chapter 1-26. The license fee may not exceed two thousand dollars. The application shall contain evidence that there are one or more physicians on the staff of the facility who are licensed by the State Board of Medical and Osteopathic Examiners. The department shall issue a license if, after inspection and investigation, it finds that the applicant and the abortion facility meet the requirements of §§ 34-23A-46 to 34-23A-51, inclusive, and the standards promulgated in rules adopted pursuant to §§ 34-23A-46 to 34-23A-51, inclusive. As a condition for renewal of a license, the licensee shall submit to the department the annual license renewal fee set by rules promulgated pursuant to chapter 1-26.

South Dakota Code § 34-23A-49. Compliance inspections

The department may inspect an abortion facility at reasonable times as necessary to ensure compliance with §§ 34-23A-46 to 34-23A-51, inclusive. The department shall inspect an abortion facility before renewing the facility's license.

South Dakota Code § 34-23A-50. Fees

Any fees collected under §§ 34-23A-46 to 34-23A-51, inclusive, shall be deposited in the abortion facility licensing fund and are continuously appropriated to administer and enforce §§ 34-23A-46 to 34-23A-51, inclusive.

South Dakota Code § 34-23A-51. Promulgation of rules

The department shall adopt rules pursuant to chapter 1-26 for the issuance, renewal, denial, suspension, and revocation of a license to operate an abortion facility. The department shall adopt, by rules promulgated pursuant to chapter 1-26, minimum standards to protect the health and safety of a patient of an abortion facility. The rules shall establish minimum standards regarding:

(1) Facility safety and sanitation;
(2) Qualifications and supervision of professional and nonprofessional personnel;
(3) Emergency equipment and procedures to provide emergency care;
(4) Medical records and reports;
(5) Procedure and recovery rooms;
(6) Infection control;
(7) Medication control;
(8) Quality assurance;
(9) Facility and laboratory equipment requirements, sanitation, testing, and maintenance;
(10) Information on and access to patient follow-up care; and
(11) Patient screening, assessment, and monitoring.

(13) ABORTION LITIGATION FUND

South Dakota has established a special fund to cover the costs of litigation involved with its abortion statutes. The statute addressing the matter is set out below.

South Dakota Code § 1-14-3.1.
Extraordinary litigation fund

There is established in the state treasury the extraordinary litigation fund. The fund shall be maintained separately and administered by the Bureau of Administration. The fund may be used for plaintiff attorney fee awards, retention of outside counsel, settlement costs, or other litigation expenses not otherwise eligible to be paid under § 3-22-1. Unexpended money and any interest that may be credited to the fund shall remain in the fund. The extraordinary litigation fund, including any subfunds created within it, is hereby continuously appropriated and shall be budgeted through the informational budget process. The creation and funding of this fund does not constitute a waiver of the state's sovereign immunity.

The life protection subfund is established within the extraordinary litigation fund. The subfund shall be used to cover the litigation costs, including expert witness fees and attorney fees awarded under 42 U.S.C. § 1988 or other applicable statutes, associated with defending South Dakota statutes that regulate or proscribe abortion or contraception. In addition to moneys that the Legislature may appropriate to the subfund, the commissioner of the Bureau of Administration may accept private contributions for the subfund's purposes and deposit those moneys in the subfund. The life protection litigation subfund shall retain the interest income derived from the moneys credited to the subfund in accordance with §§ 4-5-30 and 4-5-30.1.

(14) HUMAN CLONING

Under the laws of South Dakota human cloning is prohibited. The statutes addressing the matter are set out below.

South Dakota Code § 34-14-26. Definition of terms

Terms used in §§ 34-14-26 to 34-14-28, inclusive, mean:

(1) "Human cloning," human asexual reproduction accomplished by introducing the nuclear material of a human somatic cell into a fertilized or unfertilized oocyte whose nucleus has been removed or inactivated to produce a living organism, at any stage of development, with a human or predominantly human genetic constitution;

(2) "Human somatic cell," a diploid cell, having a complete set of chromosomes, obtained or derived from a living or deceased human body at any stage of development;

(3) "Nuclear transplantation," transferring the nucleus of a human somatic cell into an oocyte from which the nucleus or all chromosomes have been or will be removed or rendered inert;

(4) "Nucleus," the cell structure that houses the chromosomes, and thus the genes;

(5) "Oocyte," the female germ cell, the egg.

South Dakota Code § 34-14-27. Human cloning as felony

No person or entity, public or private, may:

(1) Perform or attempt to perform human cloning;

(2) Participate in an attempt to perform human cloning;

(3) Transfer or receive the product of human cloning; or

(4) Transfer or receive, in whole or in part, any oocyte, embryo, fetus, or human somatic cell, for the purpose of human cloning.

Any person that knowingly or recklessly violates this section is guilty of a Class 6 felony. Any person or entity that violates this section and derives a pecuniary gain from such violation is subject to a civil penalty of two thousand dollars or twice the amount of gross gain, or any intermediate amount at the discretion of the court.

South Dakota Code § 34-14-28. Scientific research

Nothing in §§ 34-14-26 to 34-14-28, inclusive, restricts areas of scientific research not specifically prohibited by §§ 34-14-26 to 34-14-28, inclusive, including research in the use of nuclear transfer or other cloning techniques to produce molecules, deoxyribonucleic acid, cells other than human embryos, tissues, organs, plants, or animals other than humans.

Speculum

Speculum is a metal instrument used for dilating or opening the vagina for examination or surgical operation. *See also* **Forceps Delivery; Vacuum Extractor**

Spencer, Dr. Robert Douglas

Dr. Robert Douglas Spencer (1889–1969) practiced general medicine for over fifty years in the small coal-mining town of Ashland, Pennsylvania. Although much of Dr. Spencer's practice was devoted to responding to routine injuries and illnesses of the people in his community, he had a special practice that was known by many throughout the nation. Beginning in 1925 and lasting until his death, Dr. Spencer performed over 100,000 illegal abortions. His abortion work resulted in three arrests, blackmail, censure by the American Medical Association, and a reputation as King of the Abortionists.

Sperm *see* **Female Reproductive System; Male Reproductive System**

Sperm Bank *see* **Cryopreservation**

Spermatozoon

A spermatozoon is a mature male germ cell. It is the generative element of the semen that fertilizes the ovum. *See also* **Male Reproductive System**

Spermicides

Spermicides are chemical agents that may prevent pregnancy. Spermicides form a chemical barrier that either kills sperm or makes them inactive and thus unable to pass through the cervix to the egg. The primary ingredient in spermicides is a chemical called nonoxynol-9 (a few products use octoxynol-9). Spermicides have been found to prevent certain sexually transmitted diseases such as gonorrhea, genital herpes, trichomonas and syphilis. It was once thought that spermicides (specifically nonoxynol-9) could prevent HIV; however, studies reported in 2000 indicated that spermicides were not an effective means of HIV prevention.

Spermicides can be delivered through foam, cream, jelly, film, suppositories, tablets or sponge. They may be used alone or with other contraceptive devices like a diaphragm. Spermicides have been known to cause allergy, irritation, and an increased risk of painful urinary tract infections in women. Most spermicides can be purchased over-the-counter at drugstores or supermarkets.

Foams. Spermicidal foam is produced in a small container. To apply the foam the container should first be shaken well. Next, the foam should be placed on an applicator. Once on the applicator, the foam is inserted through the vagina to the tip of the cervix. The foam works immediately and continues to provide protection for up to an hour after it is inserted.

Creams and jellies. Spermicidal cream and jelly are produced in tubes. The cream or jelly is squeezed onto an applicator. The applicator is then placed in the vagina and the cream or jelly is deposited near the tip of the cervix. The cream and jelly work immediately. If the cream or jelly is used alone protection is provided for an hour. If either is used with a diaphragm, the protection lasts for up to 6 hours.

Film. Spermicidal film (also called vaginal contraceptive film) is composed of a sheet of film that is about 2 inches by 2 inches. The film is packaged in a pouch. To use the film it must be removed from the pouch and folded in half. The folded film is then inserted in the vagina until it reaches the cervix. The film will begin to dissolve once inserted. Protection begins about 15 minutes after insertion. Protection lasts for about an hour.

Suppositories and tablets. Spermicidal suppositories and tablets are individually packaged. After removing a suppository or tablet from its wrapping, insert the suppository or tablet in the vagina as close to the cervix as possible. A suppository or tablet takes 10 to 30 minutes to be effective. The protection lasts up to an hour after insertion.

Sponge. The spermicidal sponge (trade name "Today Sponge") was invented by Dr. Bruce Vorhauer and was placed on the market in the United States in 1983. The sponge was pulled from the market in 1995 by its manufacturer, Whitehall-Robins Health care, after an inspection by the Food and Drug Administration found water contamination at a manufacturing plant. The manufacturer cited extraordinary costs in meeting federal standards as the reason for pulling the sponge from the market. In 1999 a New Jersey based manufacturer, Allendale Pharmaceuticals Inc., announced that it would reintroduce the sponge to the market in the United States.

The sponge is made of polyurethane foam that absorbs semen and destroys it. To use the sponge it must first be moistened with water and squeezed until suds appears. Next, it should be inserted into the vagina and placed near the cervix. The sponge has a dimple on one side which should face the cervix. It should be left in at least six hours after sexual intercourse. However, the sponge provides protection for up to 24 hours. *See also* **Contraception**

Spina Bifida

Spina bifida is the most common disease of a group of birth defects that are called neural tube defects. The disease involves the failure of the backbone and spinal canal to close before birth. This condition causes the spinal cord and the covering membranes to protrude out of the child's back. The cause of the disease is unknown, although it is among the most common severe birth defects in the United States. There are three forms of spina bifida: meningocele, occulta, and myelomeningocele.

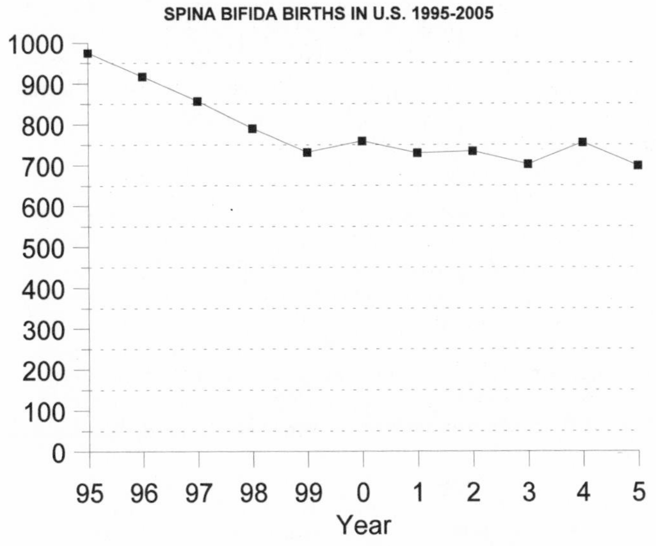

Source: **Centers for Disease Control and Prevention.**

Meningocele. Meningocele is the rarest form of spina bifida. With this disease a cyst pokes through the open part of the spine. The cyst can be removed through surgery. Most children with this condition develop normally.

Occulta. Occulta is a symptomless form of the disease that involves a small gap in one of the vertebrae of the spine. This condition normally causes no problem for its victims, and usually requires no treatment.

Myelomeningocele. Myelomeningocele is the most severe form of spina bifida. Most children with this condition have a tethered spinal cord (the spinal cord does not slide up and down with movement as it should). This condition usually requires surgery within 48 hours after birth. Immediate surgery is required to prevent additional nerve damage from infection or trauma. In spite of surgery, however, some degree of leg paralysis and bladder and bowel control problems remain. Roughly 90 percent of children with the condition develop fluid on the brain (hydrocephalus). Without treatment for this fluid buildup, mental retardation and other neurological damage may result. Other complications associated with the condition include obesity, gut and urinary tract disorders, and learning disabilities. *See also* **Anencephaly; Birth Defects and Abortion; Encephaloceles; Folic Acid and Pregnancy**

Spitz, Donald *see* **Army of God**

Spontaneous Abortion *see* **Miscarriage**

Stanford Students for Life

Stanford Students for Life is a pro-life student-run organization on the campus of Stanford University. The organization is active in providing pro-life services to the university community. Some of the activities the organization takes part in include bringing pro-life speakers to the campus, holding candlelight vigils to remember the victims of abortion, providing educational information on sexual development for teenagers and college students, which includes alternatives to abortion, and the consequences of abortion. *See also* **Pro-Life Organizations**

State of Missouri ex rel. Hurwitz v. North

Forum: United States Supreme Court.

Case Citation: State of Missouri ex rel. Hurwitz v. North, 271 U.S. 40 (1926).

Date Argued: March 12, 1926.

Date of Decision: April 12, 1926.

Opinion of Court: Stone, J.

Concurring Opinion: None.

Dissenting Opinion: None.

Counsel for Appellant: I. V. McPherson argued and filed a brief.

Counsel for Appellee: North T. Gentry argued; on the brief were J. Henry Caruthers and Jesse W. Barrett.

Amicus Brief for Appellant: None

Amicus Brief for Appellee: None.

Issue Presented: Whether the constitution was violated because a physician was not allowed to subpoena witnesses to attend a hearing to revoke his medical license for performing an unlawful abortion?

Case Holding: The constitution was not violated when a physician was prevented from issuing subpoenas to have witnesses attend a hearing to revoke his medical license for performing an unlawful abortion, because the applicable rules required taking depositions of witnesses who would not voluntarily attend the hearing.

Background facts of case: The appellant, a physician, had his medical license revoked by the state medical board of health of Missouri. The appellant's medical license was revoked as a result of performing an unlawful abortion. The proceedings before the medical board were reviewed and affirmed by a state trial court. On appeal to the Missouri supreme court the judgment was also affirmed. The state's highest court rejected the appellant's contention that he was denied constitutional due process of law, because he was not permitted to subpoena witnesses to testify before the medical board. The United States Supreme Court agreed to hear the appeal.

Unanimous opinion by Justice Stone: Justice Stone ruled that the appellant was not denied due process of law during the administrative revocation proceedings. He wrote as follows:

> It has been so often pointed out in the opinions of this court that the Fourteenth Amendment is concerned with the substance and not with the forms of procedure as to make unnecessary any extended discussion of the question here presented. The due process clause does not guarantee to a citizen of a state any particular form or method of state procedure. Its requirements are satisfied if he has reasonable notice, and reasonable opportunity to be heard and to present his claim or defense; due regard being had to the nature of the proceedings and the character of the rights which may be affected by it.

The procedure authorized by the Missouri statute, as it was applied by the board, satisfied these requirements. The notice prescribed was reasonable. The testimony of all witnesses who appeared before the board was taken and recorded, including that of the [appellant]. Although the statute did not authorize the board to issue subpoenas, the [appellant] was authorized, as the state court held, to take the depositions of witnesses who did not voluntarily appear. Officers who take depositions are authorized to compel witnesses to attend and give testimony. The depositions, when taken, may be read at the hearing before the board. The procedure prescribed and followed here gave ample opportunity to [appellant] to make a defense to the charges preferred, and there was no denial of due process.

Disposition of case: The judgment of the Missouri supreme court was affirmed.

Stenberg v. Carhart

Forum: United States Supreme Court.

Case Citation: Stenberg v. Carhart, 530 U.S. 914 (2000).

Date Argued: April 25, 2000.

Date of Decision: June 28, 2000.

Opinion of Court: Breyer, J., in which Stevens, O'Connor, Souter, and Ginsburg, JJ., joined.

Concurring Opinion: Stevens, J., in which Ginsburg, J., joined.

Concurring Opinion: O'Connor, J.

Concurring Opinion: Ginsburg, J., in which Stevens, J., joined.

Dissenting Opinion: Rehnquist, C. J.

Dissenting Opinion: Scalia, J.,

Dissenting Opinion: Kennedy, J., in which Rehnquist, C. J., joined.

Dissenting Opinion: Thomas, J., in which Rehnquist, C. J., and Scalia, J., joined.

Counsel for Appellant: Not Reported.

Counsel for Appellee: Not Reported.

Amicus Brief for Appellant: Not Reported.

Amicus Brief for Appellee: Not Reported.

Issue Presented: Whether Nebraska's statute, making criminal the performance of a partial-birth abortion, violated the federal constitution?

Case Holding: Nebraska's statute criminalizing the performance of partial-birth abortions violated the federal constitution because the law lacked any exception for the preservation of the health of the mother, and imposed an undue burden on a woman's ability to choose a D & E abortion, thereby unduly burdening the right to choose abortion itself.

Background facts of case: The Appellee, Dr. Leroy Carhart, was a Nebraska physician who performed abortions. He filed a lawsuit in a federal district court seeking a declaration that the Nebraska' statute banning partial-birth abortion violated the federal constitution, and asking for an injunction forbidding its enforcement. After a trial, the district court held the statute unconstitutional. On appeal by the state of Nebraska, the Eighth Circuit affirmed the decision of the district court. The Supreme Court granted certiorari to consider the matter.

Majority opinion by Justice Breyer. Justice Breyer set out three principles of law that guided the disposition of the case. First, it was said that before viability a pregnant woman has a right to choose to terminate her pregnancy. Second, a law designed to further a state's interest in fetal life which imposed an undue burden on the woman's decision to choose abortion before fetal viability is unconstitutional. An undue burden referred to a state regulation that had the purpose or effect of placing a substantial obstacle in the path of a woman seeking an abortion of a nonviable fetus. Third, subsequent to viability, the state in promoting its interest in the potentiality of human life may, if it chooses, regulate, and even proscribe, abortion except where it is necessary, in appropriate medical judgment, for the preservation of the life or health of the mother.

The opinion next set out the applicable Nebraska law that banned partial-birth abortion, which read as follows:

> No partial birth abortion shall be performed in this state, unless such procedure is necessary to save the life of the mother whose life is endangered by a physical disorder, physical illness, or physical injury, including a life-endangering physical condition caused by or arising from the pregnancy itself.

Partial birth means an abortion procedure in which the person performing the abortion partially delivers vaginally a living unborn child before killing the unborn child and completing the delivery.

Partially delivers vaginally a living unborn child before killing the unborn child means deliberately and intentionally delivering into the vagina a living unborn child, or a substantial portion thereof, for the purpose of performing a procedure that the person performing such procedure knows will kill the unborn child and does kill the unborn child.

Justice Breyer found that the above Nebraska law violated the Supreme Court's decision in *Planned Parenthood of Southeastern Pennsylvania v. Casey*. It was said that while the statute attempted to ban an abortion procedure called D & X (used to perform partial-birth abortions), it also had the effect of banning another procedure known as D & E. The opinion also concluded that the law lacked any exception for the preservation of the health of the mother and it imposed an undue burden on a woman's ability to choose a D & E abortion, thereby unduly burdening the right to choose abortion itself. It was said that Nebraska's law impermissibly applied to both pre- and post-viability. Justice Breyer wrote:

> Even if the statute's basic aim is to ban D & X, its language makes clear that it also covers a much broader category of procedures. The language does not track the medical differences between D & E and D & X — though it would have been a simple matter, for example, to provide an exception for the performance of D & E and other abortion procedures. Nor does the statute anywhere suggest that its application turns on whether a portion of the fetus' body is drawn into the vagina as part of a process to extract an intact fetus after collapsing the head as opposed to a process that would dismember the fetus. Thus, the dissenters' argument that the law was generally intended to bar D & X can be both correct and irrelevant. The relevant question is not whether the legislature wanted to ban D & X it is whether the law was intended to apply only to D & X. The plain language covers both procedures. Both procedures can involve the introduction of a "substantial portion" of a still living fetus, through the cervix, into the vagina....

In finding Nebraska's statute overbroad and violative of the Supreme Court's prior decisions on regulating abortion, Justice Breyer concluded:

> In sum, Nebraska has not convinced us that a health exception is never necessary to preserve the health of women. Rather, a statute that altogether forbids D & X creates a significant health risk. The statute consequently must contain a health exception. This is not to say ... that a State is prohibited from proscribing an abortion procedure whenever a particular physician deems the procedure preferable. By no means must a State grant physicians unfettered discretion in their selection of abortion methods. But where substantial medical authority supports the proposition that banning a particular abortion procedure could endanger women's health, *Casey* requires the statute to include a health exception when the procedure is necessary, in appropriate medical judgment, for the preservation of the life or health of the mother. Requiring such an exception in this case is no departure from *Casey*, but simply a straightforward application of its holding.

Disposition of case: The judgment of the Eighth Circuit was affirmed.

Concurring opinion by Justice Stevens: Justice Stevens agreed with the position stated in the majority opinion. He wrote separately to make the following point clear:

> Although much ink is spilled today describing the gruesome nature of late-term abortion procedures, that rhetoric does not provide me a reason to believe that the procedure Nebraska here claims it seeks to ban is more brutal, more gruesome, or less respectful of "potential life" than the equally gruesome procedure Nebraska claims it still allows.... [D]uring the past 27 years, the central holding of *Roe v. Wade* has been endorsed by all but 4 of the 17 Justices who have addressed the issue. That holding — that the word "liberty" in the Fourteenth Amendment includes a woman's right to make this difficult and extremely personal decision — makes it impossible for me to understand how a State has any legitimate interest in requiring a doctor to follow any procedure other than the one that he or she reasonably believes will best protect the woman in her exercise of this constitutional liberty. But one need not even approach this view today to conclude that Nebraska's law must fall. For the notion that either of these two equally gruesome procedures performed at this late stage of gestation is more akin to infanticide than the other, or that the State furthers any legitimate interest by banning one but not the other, is simply irrational.

Concurring opinion by Justice O'Connor. Justice O'Connor agreed with the majority opinion, but wrote separately to indicate her belief that a carefully crafted statute banning partial-birth abortion would pass constitutional muster. She wrote as follows:

> If Nebraska's statute limited its application to the D & X procedure and included an exception for the life and health of the mother, the question presented would be quite different than the one we face today. As we held in *Casey*, an abortion regulation constitutes an undue burden if it "has the purpose or effect of placing a substantial obstacle in the path of a woman seeking an abortion of a nonviable fetus." If there were adequate alternative methods for a woman safely to obtain an abortion before viability, it is unlikely that prohibiting the D & X procedure alone would amount in practical terms to a substantial obstacle to a woman seeking an abortion. Thus, a ban on partial-birth abortion that only proscribed the D&X method of abortion and that included an exception to preserve the life and health of the mother would be constitutional in my view.
>
> Nebraska's statute, however, does not meet these criteria. It contains no exception for when the procedure, in appropriate medical judgment, is necessary to preserve the health of the mother; and it proscribes not only the D & X procedure but also the D & E procedure, the most commonly used method for previability second trimester abortions, thus making it an undue burden on a woman's right to terminate her pregnancy. For these reasons, I agree with the Court that Nebraska's law is unconstitutional.

Concurring opinion by Justice Ginsburg. Justice Ginsburg joined the majority opinion, but wrote separately to express her view that the ban on partial-birth abortion was nothing more than an attempt by pro-life advocates to dilute a woman's right to an abortion. She wrote as follows:

> I write separately only to stress that amidst all the emotional uproar caused by an abortion case, we should not lose sight of the character of Nebraska's partial birth abortion law. As the Court observes, this law does not save any fetus from destruction, for it targets only a method of performing abortion. Nor does the statute seek to protect the lives or health of pregnant women. Moreover, the most common method of performing previability second trimester abortions is no less distressing or susceptible to gruesome description. Seventh Circuit Chief Judge Posner correspondingly observed, regarding similar bans in Wisconsin and Illinois, that the law prohibits the D & X procedure "not because the procedure kills the fetus, not because it risks worse complications for the woman than alternative procedures would do, not because it is a crueler or more painful or more disgusting method of terminating a pregnancy." *Hope Clinic* v. *Ryan*, 195 F. 3d 857, 881 (7th Cir. 1999) (dissenting opinion). Rather, Chief Judge Posner commented, the law prohibits the procedure because the State legislators seek to chip away at the private choice shielded by *Roe* v. *Wade*, even as modified by *Casey*.

Dissenting opinion by Chief Justice Rehnquist: The Chief Justice wrote a terse one paragraph dissent stating that he believed the decision in *Casey* was decided wrong, and that he further joined the dissenting opinions by Justices Kennedy and Thomas.

Dissenting opinion by Justice Scalia: Justice Scalia wrote in his dissent that he believed the decision in *Casey* should be overruled and that Nebraska's statute was constitutional. It was said in the dissent:

> ... The method of killing a human child — one cannot even accurately say an entirely unborn human child — proscribed by this statute is so horrible that the most clinical description of it evokes a shudder of revulsion. And the Court must know (as most state legislatures banning this procedure have concluded) that demanding a health exception — which requires the abortionist to assure himself that, in his expert medical judgment, this method is, in the case at hand, marginally safer than others (how can one prove the contrary beyond a reasonable doubt?) — is to give live-birth abortion free rein. The notion that the Constitution of the United States, designed, among other things, "to establish Justice, insure domestic Tranquility, ... and secure the Blessings of Liberty to ourselves and our Posterity," prohibits the States from simply banning this visibly brutal means of eliminating our half-born posterity is quite simply absurd.

Dissenting opinion by Justice Kennedy: Justice Kennedy believed that Nebraska's statute was constitutional and that the majority opinion misunderstood the facts at issue. He wrote as follows:

> The Court's failure to accord any weight to Nebraska's interest in prohibiting partial-birth abortion is erroneous and undermines its discussion and holding. The Court's approach in this regard is revealed by its description of the abortion methods at issue, which the Court is correct to describe as clinically cold or callous. The majority views the procedures from the perspective of the abortionist, rather than from the perspective of a society shocked when confronted with a new method of ending human life....
>
> ...Nebraska seeks only to ban the D & X. In light of the description of the D & X procedure, it should go without saying that Nebraska's ban on partial-birth abortion furthers purposes States are entitled to pursue. Dr. Carhart nevertheless maintains the State has no legitimate interest in forbidding the D & X. As he interprets the controlling cases in this Court, the only two interests the State may advance through regulation of abortion are in the health of the woman who is considering the procedure and in the life of the fetus she carries. The Court, as I read its opinion, accedes to his views, misunderstanding *Casey* and the authorities it confirmed.
>
> The holding of *Casey*, allowing a woman to elect abortion in defined circumstances, is not in question here. Nebraska, however, was entitled to conclude that its ban, while advancing important interests regarding the sanctity of life, deprived no woman of a safe abortion and therefore did not impose a substantial obstacle on the rights of any woman....
>
> Ignoring substantial medical and ethical opinion, the Court substitutes its own judgment for the judgment of Nebraska and some 30 other States and sweeps the law away. The Court's hold-

ing stems from misunderstanding the record, misinterpretation of *Casey*, outright refusal to respect the law of a State, and statutory construction in conflict with settled rules. The decision nullifies a law expressing the will of the people of Nebraska that medical procedures must be governed by moral principles having their foundation in the intrinsic value of human life, including life of the unborn. Through their law the people of Nebraska were forthright in confronting an issue of immense moral consequence. The State chose to forbid a procedure many decent and civilized people find so abhorrent as to be among the most serious of crimes against human life, while the State still protected the woman's autonomous right of choice as reaffirmed in *Casey*.

Dissenting opinion of Justice Thomas: Justice Thomas wrote in his dissent that he did not believe Nebraska's statute banned the D & E procedure. He also believed that the majority opinion applied in correct principles in reaching the decision to find the statute unconstitutional. Justice Thomas wrote as follows:

> To reach its decision, the majority must take a series of indefensible steps. The majority must first disregard the principles that this Court follows in every context but abortion: We interpret statutes according to their plain meaning and we do not strike down statutes susceptible of a narrowing construction. The majority also must disregard the very constitutional standard it purports to employ, and then displace the considered judgment of the people of Nebraska and 29 other States. The majority's decision is lamentable, because of the result the majority reaches, the illogical steps the majority takes to reach it, and because it portends a return to an era I had thought we had at last abandoned.
>
> Nebraska, along with 29 other States, has attempted to ban the partial birth abortion procedure. Although the Nebraska statute purports to prohibit only partial birth abortion, a phrase which is commonly used ... to refer to the breech extraction version of intact D & E, the majority concludes that this statute could also be read in some future case to prohibit ordinary D & E.... According to the majority, such an application would pose a substantial obstacle to some women seeking abortions and, therefore, the statute is unconstitutional. The majority errs with its very first step. I think it is clear that the Nebraska statute does not prohibit the D & E procedure.
>
> We were reassured repeatedly in *Casey* that not all regulations of abortion are unwarranted and that the States may express profound respect for fetal life. Under *Casey*, the regulation before us today should easily pass constitutional muster. But the Court's abortion jurisprudence is a particularly virulent strain of constitutional exegesis. And so today we are told that 30 States are prohibited from banning one rarely used form of abortion that they believe to border on infanticide. It is clear that the Constitution does not compel this result.

Note: Subsequent to the decision in this case the Supreme Court decided the case of *Gonzales v. Carhart*, upheld the validity of a federal statute that banned partial-birth abortion. The decision in Gonzales upheld the statute on the grounds that it was more narrower than the Nebraska statute and provided details of the procedure that was being banned. *See also* **Dilation and Extraction; Gonzales v. Carhart; Partial-Birth Abortion; Partial-Birth Abortion Ban Act;**

Stevens, John Paul

John Paul Stevens was appointed as an associate justice of the United States Supreme Court in 1975. While on the Supreme Court Justice Stevens has displayed a judicial philosophy that straddles between moderate and liberal.

Justice Stevens was born in Chicago, Illinois, on April 20, 1920. He was a 1941 graduate of Chicago University. In 1947 he received a law degree from Northwestern University School of Law. Justice Stevens developed a successful law practice before being nominated in 1970 as an appellate judge on the Seventh Circuit Court of Appeals. In 1975 President Gerald Ford appointed Justice Stevens to the Supreme Court.

Distribution of the Abortion Voting Pattern of Justice Stevens Based Upon Opinions Filed by the Supreme Court

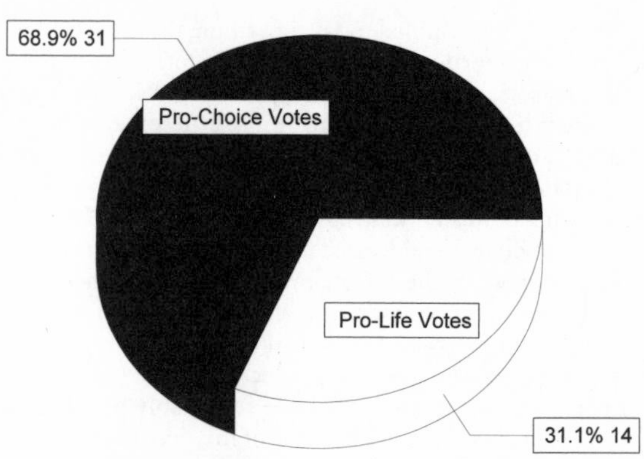

During Justice Stevens' tenure on the Supreme Court he has issued a number of abortion related opinions. The written opinions and

Justice Stevens' voting pattern favors the views of pro-choice advocates (collection, Supreme Court Historical Society, photograph by Joseph H. Bailey, National Geographic Society).

opinions simply voted on by Justice Stevens, indicate that he is in favor of using the constitution to expand abortion rights for women.

(1) Unanimous opinions voted with only. In *Dalton v. Little Rock Family Planning Services*, Justice Stevens voted with a unanimous Court in holding that an amendment to Arkansas' constitution which limited Medicaid payment only to therapeutic abortions, was invalid to the extent that Medicaid funds had to be made available for incest or rape pregnancies, but was valid for any purely state funded program. Justice Stevens voted with a unanimous Court in *National Organization for Women, Inc. v. Scheidler*, which held that a group of pro-choice organizations could maintain a RICO civil lawsuit against several anti-abortion individuals and groups. In *Bellotti v. Baird I* Justice Stevens voted with a unanimous opinion, which held that the federal district court had to certify appropriate questions to the supreme judicial court of Massachusetts, concerning the interpretation of that state's parental consent abortion statute for minors, before ruling on its constitutionality. Justice Stevens voted with a unanimous Court in *Scheidler v. National Organization for Women, Inc. (II)*, which held pro-choice advocates could not sue pro-life advocates under the Hobbs Act for allegations of physical violence that did not involve extortion. Justice Stevens joined a unanimous opinion in *Ayotte v. Planned Parenthood of Northern New England*, which held that the absence of a health exception in New Hampshire's parental notification abortion statute did not require the entire statute be invalidated.

(2) Majority opinions written. Justice Stevens wrote the majority opinion in *Ferguson v. City of Charleston* which held that patient consent or a search warrant was needed, in order for a government hospital to turn over to the police drug test results that showed a woman used illegal drugs during her pregnancy. In *Hill v. Colorado* Justice Stevens wrote the majority opinion upholding a Colorado statute that made it unlawful for any person within 100 feet of an abortion facility's entrance, to knowingly approach within 8 feet of another person, without that person's consent, in order to pass a leaflet, handbill, display a sign, engage in oral protest, education, or counseling with that person.

Justice Stevens wrote the majority opinion and a dissenting opinion in *Hodgson v. Minnesota*, which upheld the constitutionality of Minnesota's requirement that a pregnant female minor could not obtain an abortion until at least 48 hours after both of her parents had been notified, except when (1) the attending physician certified that an immediate abortion was necessary to prevent the minor's death; (2) the minor declared that she was a victim of parental abuse or neglect; or (3) a court of competent jurisdiction ordered the abortion to proceed without notice upon proof that the minor was mature and capable of giving informed consent or that an abortion without notice to both parents would be in the minor's best interest. Justice Stevens dissented from the Court's determination that, although the two-parent notification requirement was invalid, the judicial bypass option cured the defect.

(3) Majority opinions voted with only. Justice Stevens voted with the majority in *Schenck v. Pro Choice Network of Western New York*, which held that a federal trial court's injunction provisions imposing fixed buffer zone limitations on abortion protesters were constitutional, but the provisions imposing floating buffer zone limitations violated the First Amendment. In *Automobile Workers v. Johnson Controls, Inc.* Justice Stevens voted with the majority opinion, which held that Title VII of the Civil Rights Act forbids sex-specific fetal-protection policies by an employer, that exclude a fertile female employee from certain jobs because of the employer's concern for the health of the fetus the woman might conceive. Justice Stevens voted with the majority opinion in *United States Catholic Conference v. Abortion Rights Mobilization*, which allowed the appellants to challenge having to turn over documents in a lawsuit seeking to strip them of their tax exempt status because of their active political abortion work. Justice Stevens joined the majority opinion in *Federal Election Commission v. Beaumont*, which held that the Federal Election Campaign Act's prohibition on corporate expenditures and contributions directly to candidates in federal elections, applies to a nonprofit pro-life organization.

Justice Stevens voted with the majority opinion in *City of Akron v. Akron Center for Reproductive Health, Inc.*, which invalidated an abortion ordinance that provided requirements for parental consent, informed consent, waiting period, hospitalization and disposal of fetal remains. In *Colautti v. Franklin* Justice Stevens joined the majority opinion, which held that the constitution was violated by a vague and ambiguous provision in Pennsylvania's abortion statute that subjected a physician who performed an abortion to potential criminal liability, if he/she failed to utilize a statutorily prescribed technique when the fetus was viable or when there was sufficient reason to believe that the fetus may be viable. Justice Stevens joined the majority opinion in *Beal v. Doe*, which held that Pennsylvania's refusal to extend Medicaid coverage to nontherapeutic abortions was not invalid nor inconsistent with Title XIX of the Social Security Act. In *Maher v. Roe* Justice Stevens joined the majority opinion, which held that the Equal Protection Clause of the Fourteenth Amendment did not prohibit Connecticut from excluding nontherapeutic abortions from its Medicaid program. Justice Stevens joined the per curiam opinion in *Poelker v. Doe*, which held that the Equal Protection Clause of the Fourteenth Amendment was not violated by a policy of the city of St. Louis, Missouri that denied publicly funded abortions to indigent women at city hospitals, except when a woman's health or life was in danger. Justice Stevens joined the majority opinion in *Anders v. Floyd*, which held that a federal district court erred in enjoining enforcement of a South Carolina statute that imposed criminal punishment for performing an abortion on a viable fetus.

(4) Concurring opinions written. In *Stenberg v. Carhart*, Justice Stevens wrote a concurring opinion that agreed with the majority's decision to find Nebraska's statute banning partial-birth abortion unconstitutional. In *Lambert v. Wicklund* Justice Stevens wrote an opinion concurring in the majority decision that held the constitution was not violated by a provision in Montana's abortion statute that allowed a court to waive the parental notice requirement for minors, if notification was not in minor's best interest.

In *Ohio v. Akron Center for Reproductive Health* Justice Stevens wrote an opinion concurring with the majority decision, which upheld the constitutionality of Ohio's abortion statute notice and judicial bypass requirements for pregnant female minors. Justice Stevens wrote a concurring opinion in *Thornburgh v. American College of Obstetricians and Gynecologists*, which invalidated provisions in Pennsylvania's abortion statute that provided for maternal informed consent, abortion alternative printed information, abortion reporting requirements, determination of fetal viability, degree of care required in post-viability abortions, and a second-physician requirement. Justice Stevens wrote a concurring opinion in *Bolger v. Youngs Drug Products Corp.*, which held that a provision of the Comstock Act, 39 U.S.C. § 3001(e)(2), that prohibited mailing unsolicited advertisements for contraceptives violated the Free Speech Clause of the First Amendment.

In *H. L. v. Matheson* Justice Stevens wrote an opinion concurring in the majority decision, which held that the constitution was not violated by Utah's requirement that the parents of a minor be notified, if possible, prior to performing an abortion. Justice Stevens wrote an opinion concurring in the majority judgment in *Bellotti v. Baird II*, which held that Massachusetts' abortion statute for minors violated the constitution in light of an interpretation given by the state's highest court, that required parental notice of a judicial bypass proceeding invoked by a minor, and permitted a judge to deny an abortion even though the minor proved she had enough maturity to make an independent decision. In *Carey v. Population Services International* Justice Stevens wrote an opinion concurring with the majority decision, which held that the constitution prohibited enforcement of a New York statute that made it a crime (1) for any person to sell or distribute any contraceptive of any kind to a minor under the age of 16 years; (2) for anyone other than a licensed pharmacist to distribute contraceptives to persons 16 or over; and (3) for anyone, including licensed pharmacists, to advertise or display contraceptives.

Justice Stevens wrote an opinion concurring in the judgment of the Supreme Court in *Singleton v. Wulff*, which held that the Eighth Circuit court of appeals had jurisdiction to determine whether abortion providers had standing to challenge a provision in Missouri's abortion statute that limited Medicaid payment for abortions, but it did not have jurisdiction to rule that the provision violated the constitution because the district court did not address the issue.

(5) Dissenting opinions written. Justice Stevens wrote a dissenting opinion in *Leavitt v. Jane L.*, which held that the invalidity of Utah's statute regulating pregnancies 20 weeks old or less, may be severed so as to preserve that portion of the abortion statute that regulated pregnancies of more than 20 weeks. Justice Stevens wrote a dissenting opinion in *Bray v. Alexandria Clinic*, which held that the Civil Rights Act of 1871, 42 U.S.C. § 1985(3), did not provide a cause of action against persons obstructing access to abortion clinics. He argued that the statute could be used by abortionists. Justice Stevens wrote a dissenting opinion in *Rust v. Sullivan*, which upheld federal regulations that prohibited pro-abortion counseling, referral, and advocacy by health care providers. Justice Stevens wrote a dissenting opinion in *Mazurek v. Armstrong*, which held that Montana's requirement that abortions be performed only by physicians was constitutionally valid.

In *Frisby v. Schultz* Justice Stevens wrote an opinion dissenting from the majority decision, which upheld the constitutional validity of a town ordinance that was created to prevent pro-life picketing at the residence of an abortion doctor. He believed the ordinance was too broad in scope. Justice Stevens wrote an opinion dissenting from the majority opinion in *Simopoulos v. Virginia*, which upheld a Virginia statute requiring second trimester abortions be performed at hospitals, because under the statute an adequately equipped clinic could, upon proper application, obtain an outpatient hospital license that permitted the performance of second-trimester abortions. Justice Stevens believed the Virginia supreme court should have been allowed to determine whether the statute permitted second trimester abortions at licensed clinics.

Justice Stevens wrote an opinion dissenting from the majority decision in *Harris v. McRae*, which held that Medicaid funding restrictions for abortion by the Hyde Amendment, did not violate the Due Process Clause nor the equal protection component of the Fifth Amendment. He believed the Hyde Amendment violated the constitution. In *Scheidler v. National Organization for Women, Inc. (I)* Justice Stevens dissented from the majority's holding that evidence did not support finding that pro-life advocates violated the Hobbs Act, Travel Act and state law extortion crimes, for the purpose of awarding damages and granting an injunction against them under RICO.

(6) Dissenting opinions voted with only. In *Williams v. Zbaraz* Justice Stevens dissented from the majority opinion, which held that in light of the requirements of the Hyde Amendment, the Equal Protection Clause of the Fourteenth Amendment was not violated by an Illinois statute that prohibited state Medicaid payment for abortions, except when necessary to save the life of the pregnant woman. He believed the statute violated the constitution. Justice Stevens joined the dissenting opinion in *Federal Election Commission v. Wisconsin Right to Life, Inc.*, which held that the electioneering communications provisions of a federal statute violated a pro-life organization's First Amendment right to broadcast political issue oriented advertisements shortly before primary and general elections. Justice Stevens joined the dissenting opinion in *Gonzales v. Carhart*, which held that the Partial-Birth Abortion Ban Act of 2003 was not facially unconstitutional, because it outlined the abortion procedure that was banned, and the Act did not have to provide an exception for the health of a woman.

(7) Concurring and dissenting opinions written. In *Madsen v. Women's Health Clinic, Inc.*, Justice Stevens wrote a concurring and dissenting opinion. The decision in *Madsen* upheld parts of an injunction that restricted noise by anti-abortionists at a clinic and imposed a 36 foot buffer zone around the clinic entrances and driveway. Justice Stevens concurred in that part of the decision. However, *Madsen* ruled that the Free Speech Clause was violated by a 36 foot buffer zone as applied to the private property to the north and west of the clinic, a restriction on the use of images observable by clinic patients, a 300 foot no approach zone around the clinic, and a 300 foot buffer zone around the residences, because these restrictions swept more broadly than necessary to accomplish the permissible goals of the injunction. Justice Stevens dissented from the majority decision to invalidate the 300 foot no approach zone restriction.

In *Planned Parenthood of Southeastern Pennsylvania v. Casey*, Justice Stevens wrote a concurring and dissenting opinion. He dissented from the majority's decision that the constitution was not violated by provisions in Pennsylvania's abortion statute that provided for: medical emergency abortion; 24 hour waiting period for abortion; parental notice and judicial bypass for abortion by a minor; and certain abortion facility reporting requirements. He concurred in the majority's decision that found two provisions in the abortion statute unconstitutional: spousal notification before obtaining an abortion, and a requirement that a woman inform the abortion provider the reason for not notifying her spouse.

Justice Stevens wrote a concurring and dissenting opinion in *Webster v. Reproductive Health Services*, which upheld Missouri's prohibition on the use of public facilities or employees to perform abortions and a requirement that physicians conduct viability tests prior to performing abortions. He concurred only in the majority's decision that a prohibition on public funding of abortion counseling was rendered moot and would not be analyzed. Justice Stevens wrote an opinion concurring and dissenting from the majority decision in *Planned Parenthood of Missouri v. Danforth*, which held that the constitution was not violated by provisions in Missouri's abortion statute involving the definition of fetal viability, woman's written consent, and record keeping and reporting requirements; but that the constitution prohibited the requirements concerning spousal consent, parental consent for minor, banning saline amniocentesis abortions, and physician's standard of care. Justice Stevens believed that the parental consent for minors was constitutionally valid.

(8) Concurring and dissenting opinions voted with only. In *Daubert v. Merrell Dow Pharmaceuticals, Inc.*, a case involving children born with severe birth defects, Justice Stevens voted to concur and dissent. He agreed with the majority that the *Frye* rule on admissibility of expert testimony did not survive the enactment of the Federal Rules of Evidence, but disagreed with discussion in the opinion that went beyond the narrow issue of admissibility of expert testimony. In *Federal Election Commission v. Massachusetts Citizens for Life, Inc.* Justice Stevens voted to concur and dissent from the majority decision, which held that federal law that prohibited the appellee from using its treasury funds to promote pro-life political candidates violated the Free Speech Clause of the First Amendment. Justice Stevens agreed with the majority that the law applied to the appellee, but dissented from the decision to find the law unconstitutional.

In *Planned Parenthood Assn. v. Ashcroft* Justice Stevens concurred and dissented from the majority/plurality opinion, which held that the constitution was violated by Missouri's requirement that second trimester abortions take place in a hospital; but that the constitution was not violated by the state's requirement that a pathology report for each abortion be performed, that a second physician be present during abortions performed after viability, and parental or judicial consent for abortion by minors. Justice Stevens believed that all of the provisions of the statute violated the constitution.

Stewart, Potter

Potter Stewart (1915–1985) served as an associate justice of the United States Supreme Court from 1958 to 1981. While on the Supreme Court Justice Stewart was known as a moderate interpreter of the Constitution.

Justice Stewart was born in Jackson, Michigan. He received educational training at University School, Yale and Cambridge. He obtained a law degree from Yale Law School in 1941. In 1954 Justice Stewart was appointed as an appellate judge to the Sixth Circuit Court of Appeals. President Dwight Eisenhower appointed Justice Stewart to the Supreme Court in 1958.

During Justice Stewart's tenure on the Supreme Court he issued a number of abortion related opinions. The written opinions and opinions simply voted on by Justice Stewart, indicate that he was not in favor of using the constitution to expand abortion rights for women.

(1) Unanimous opinions voted with only. In *Bellotti v. Baird I* Justice Stewart voted with a unanimous opinion, which held that the federal district court had to certify appropriate questions to the supreme judicial court of Massachusetts, concerning the interpretation of that state's parental consent abortion statute for minors, before ruling on its constitutionality. In *Withrow v. Larkin* Justice Stewart joined a unanimous opinion, which held that constitutional due process was not violated by the mere fact that a Wisconsin medical examining board had the authority to both, investigate and adjudicate, allegations against a physician that included, among other things, permitting a nonphysician to perform an abortion.

(2) Majority opinions written. Justice Stewart wrote the majority opinion in *Harris v. McRae*, which held that Medicaid funding restrictions for abortion by the Hyde Amendment, did not violate the Due Process Clause nor the equal protection component of the Fifth Amendment. In *Williams v. Zbaraz* Justice Stewart wrote the majority opinion, which held that in light of the requirements of the Hyde Amendment, the Equal Protection Clause of the Fourteenth Amendment was not violated by an Illinois statute that prohibited state Medicaid payment for abortions, except when necessary to save the life of the pregnant woman. Justice Stewart wrote the majority opinion in *Geduldig v. Aiello*, which held that the Equal Protection Clause of the Fourteenth Amendment did not require a private sector employee disability insurance program, operated by the state of California, provide coverage for employee disabilities associated with normal pregnancies.

Distribution of the Abortion Voting Pattern of Justice Stewart Based Upon Opinions Filed by the Supreme Court

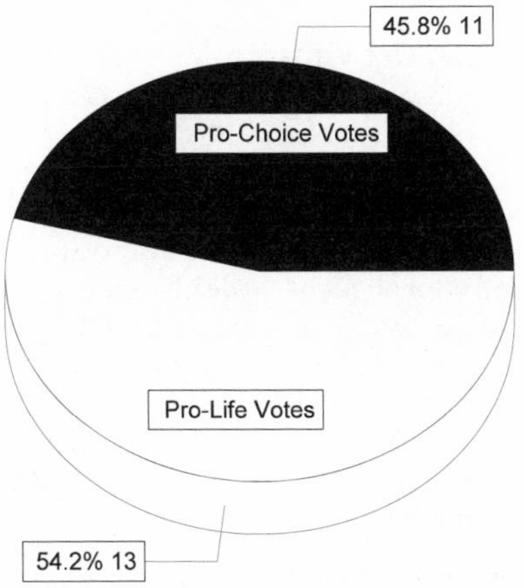

(3) Majority opinions voted with only. Justice Stewart joined the majority judgment in *Bellotti v. Baird II*, which held that Massachusetts' abortion statute for minors violated the constitution in light of an interpretation given by the state's highest court, that required parental notice of a judicial bypass proceeding invoked by a minor, and permitted a judge to deny an abortion even though the minor proved she had enough maturity to make an independent decision. In *Colautti v. Franklin* Justice Stewart joined the majority opinion, which held that the constitution was violated by a vague and ambiguous provision in Pennsylvania's abortion statute that subjected a physician who performed an abortion to potential criminal liability, if he/she failed to utilize a statutorily prescribed technique when the fetus was viable or when there was sufficient reason to believe that the fetus may be viable. Justice Stewart joined the majority opinion in *Beal v. Doe*, which held that Pennsylvania's refusal to extend Medicaid coverage to nontherapeutic abortions was not invalid nor inconsistent with Title XIX of the Social Security Act.

In *Maher v. Roe* Justice Stewart joined the majority opinion, which held that the Equal Protection Clause of the Fourteenth Amendment did not prohibit Connecticut from excluding nontherapeutic abortions from its Medicaid program. Justice Stewart joined the per curiam opinion in *Poelker v. Doe*, which held that the Equal Protection Clause of the Fourteenth Amendment was not violated by a policy of the city of St. Louis, Missouri that denied publicly funded abortions to indigent women at city hospitals, except when a woman's health or life was in danger. In *Carey v. Population Services International* Justice Stewart voted with the majority opinion, which held that the constitution prohibited enforcement of a New York statute that made it a crime (1) for any person to sell or distribute any contraceptive of any kind to a minor under the age of 16 years; (2) for anyone other than a licensed pharmacist to distribute contraceptives to persons 16 or over; and (3) for anyone, including licensed pharmacists, to advertise or display contraceptives.

In *Connecticut v. Menillo* Justice Stewart joined the majority per curiam opinion, which held that the constitution was not violated by criminal abortion statutes that prohibit nonphysicians from attempting or performing abortions at any stage of a pregnancy. Justice Stewart joined the majority opinion in *Bigelow v. Virginia*, which held that the Free Speech and Free Press Clauses of the First Amendment were violated by a Virginia penal statute that prohibited selling or circulating any publication that encouraged or promoted abortions. Justice Stewart voted with the majority opinion in *Burns v. Alcala*, which held that states receiving federal financial aid under the program of Aid to Families with Dependent Children, were not required to offer welfare benefits to pregnant women for their unborn children.

Justice Stewart voted with the majority opinion in *Doe v. Bolton*, which held that the Due Process Clause of the Fourteenth Amendment was violated by provisions in Georgia's abortion statutes that required (1) abortions take place in accredited hospitals, (2) that an abortion be approved by a hospital abortion committee, (3) that the need for an abortion be confirmed by two independent physicians, and (4) that a woman seeking an abortion be a resident of Georgia. Justice Stewart voted with the majority opinion in *Eisenstadt v. Baird*, which held that the Equal Protection Clause of the Fourteenth Amendment was violated by a Massachusetts statute that made it a crime to give away a drug, medicine, instrument, or article for the prevention of conception except in the case of (1) a physician prescribing it for a married person, or (2) a pharmacist furnishing it to a married person presenting a physician's prescription.

(4) Concurring opinions written. Justice Stewart wrote an opinion concurring in the majority decision in *Planned Parenthood of Missouri v. Danforth*, which held that the constitution was not violated by provisions in Missouri's abortion statute involving the definition of fetal viability, woman's written consent, and recordkeeping and reporting requirements; but that the constitution prohibited the requirements concerning spousal consent, parental consent for minor, banning saline amniocentesis abortions, and physician's standard of care. In *Roe v. Wade* Justice Stewart wrote an opinion concurring in the majority decision, which held that the liberty component of the Due Process Clause of the Fourteenth Amendment prohibited states from criminalizing or preventing elective first trimester abortions.

(5) Concurring opinions voted with only. In *H. L. v. Matheson* Justice Stewart concurred in the majority opinion, which held that the constitution was not violated by Utah's requirement that the parents of a minor be notified, if possible, prior to performing an abortion.

(6) Dissenting opinions written. In *Griswold v. Connecticut* Justice Stewart wrote an opinion dissenting from the majority decision, which held that the right of privacy found in the constitution prohibited enforcement of a Connecticut statute that made it a crime to give married persons contraceptive information and devices. He did not believe the statute violated the constitution. Justice Stewart issued a statement dissenting from the majority decision in *Poe v. Ullman*, which held that the appellants did not have standing to challenge the constitutionality of a Connecticut statute, that made it a crime to give married persons contraceptive information and devices. He believed the appellants had standing.

(7) Dissenting without opinion. Justice Stewart dissented without issuing an opinion in *Anders v. Floyd*, which held that a federal district court erred in enjoining enforcement of a South Carolina statute that imposed criminal punishment for performing an abortion on a viable fetus.

(8) Concurring and dissenting opinions written. Justice Stewart wrote an opinion concurring and dissenting from the majority decision in *United States v. Vuitch*, which held that the criminal abortion statute of the District of Columbia, which only permitted therapeutic abortions, was not constitutionally vague insofar as there was no ambiguity in its use of the word health and it did not shift to the defendant the burden of proving innocence. He believed the statute was constitutionally invalid.

(9) Concurring and dissenting opinions voted with only. Justice Stewart voted to concur and dissent in *Singleton v. Wulff*, which held that the Eighth Circuit court of appeals had jurisdiction to determine whether abortion providers had standing to challenge a provision in Missouri's abortion statute that limited Medicaid payment for abortions, but it did not have jurisdiction to rule that the provision violated the constitution because the district court did not address the issue. He dissented from language in the plurality opinion that indicated the abortion providers could assert on remand, in addition to their own rights, the constitutional rights of their patients who would be eligible for Medicaid assistance in obtaining elective abortions.

Stillbirth

Stillbirth refers to a fetal death that occurs 20 weeks or more after gestation. This condition occurs in about one out of every 200 pregnancies. The most common known causes for stillbirth include placental problems, birth defects, maternal illness, fetal growth restriction, and infections. *See also* **Abortion**; **High-Risk Pregnancy**; **Miscarriage**

Stone, Harlan F.

Harlan F. Stone (1872–1946) served as an associate justice of the United States Supreme Court from 1925 to 1941. He also served as chief justice of the Supreme Court from 1941 to 1946. While on the Supreme Court Stone's judicial philosophy floated between moderate and liberal in his interpretation of the Constitution.

Stone was born in Chesterfield, New Hampshire. He received an undergraduate degree from Amherst College in 1894 and a law degree from Columbia Law School in 1898. In addition to being a successful attorney, he served as dean of Columbia Law School and as United States Attorney General. In 1925 President Calvin Coolidge nominated Stone to the Supreme Court. In 1941 President Franklin D. Roosevelt nominated Stone as chief justice.

While on the Supreme Court Stone wrote only one abortion related opinion. As Justice Stone he wrote a unanimous opinion in *State of Missouri ex rel. Hurwitz v. North*, which held that the constitution was not violated when a physician was prevented from issuing subpoenas to have witnesses attend a hearing to revoke his medical license for performing an unlawful abortion, because the applicable rules required taking depositions of witnesses who would not voluntarily attend the hearing.

Storer, Horatio R.

Horatio R. Storer (1830–1922) was a physician and the guiding force behind the American Medical Association's opposition to abortion during the 19th century. Storer was born in Boston. He received medical training at Harvard, where his father taught as a professor of Obstetrics and Medical Jurisprudence. Storer went on to specialize in gynecology and abdominal surgery.

In 1857 Storer launched a movement to criminalize abortion throughout the nation. He was motivated in part, by concerns his father expressed to him regarding the adverse effects abortions had on the health of women. Storer enlisted the services of the American Medical Association to help him abolish abortion in the nation. He created and was made chairman of the AMA's Committee on Criminal Abortion. The Committee was formed with seven of the most prominent physicians in the nation. In 1859 the Committee issued a report outlining the dangers associated with abortion and a plan to end the practice. Storer and his Committee were ultimately successful in bringing to the forefront a national awareness of how dangerous abortion was to women. This new awareness was instrumental in prompting states to follow Storer's lead and enact laws prohibiting abortion. The laws Storer brought into being remained largely intact until 1973, when the United States Supreme Court found those laws violated the federal constitution.

Substance Abuse and Pregnancy *see* **Drug Use and Pregnancy**

Suction Curettage *see* **Machine Vacuum Aspiration**

Sudden Infant Death Syndrome

Sudden infant death syndrome (SIDS), also called crib death, is a phrase used to describe the sudden death of an infant (1 to 12 months old) under unexplained circumstances. SIDS is attached to a death after all known and possible causes have been ruled out through autopsy, criminal investigation, and medical history. Between 1983 and 1992 SIDS accounted for about 6,000 deaths annually. Since that period SIDS deaths have steadily declined. In 1998 there were approximately 2,500 SIDS death. Some theories that have developed to explain SIDS include: infant stress, birth defect, breathing problems, heart problems, and failure to develop. Some research studies have suggested that breast feeding may decrease the risk of SIDS. *See also* **Birth Defects and Abortion**

Surgical Abortion *see* **Methods of Abortion**

Surrogacy

Surrogacy involves a woman becoming contractually pregnant with a child for another woman. This option for having a child is most often done when a woman is infertile, unable to carry a child because of abnormalities in her uterus, or if she has had a hysterectomy. A surrogate mother usually conceives after being artificially inseminated with a man's sperm. Once the child is born, the surrogate mother gives the baby to the couple and terminates her parental rights. The woman unable to become pregnant can then apply to legally adopt the baby.

With the use of certain artificial reproductive methods it is possible for a surrogate mother to carry a baby that is completely the biological child of the infertile couple (e.g., using an embryo conceived through in vitro fertilization)

Surrogate arrangements are typically set up through agencies, although private arrangements exist. In either situation, the infertile couple will usually pay the surrogate mother's expenses.

Two well known legal cases have highlighted the negative side of surrogacy. In the first case, a childless New Jersey couple, William and Elizabeth Stern, arranged to have Mary Beth Whitehead (a married mother of two) act as a surrogate mother using Mr. Stern's sperm. A fee of $10,000 was promised to Mrs. Whitehead. On March 27, 1986, Mrs. Whitehead gave birth to a child, Baby M. The child was turned over to the Sterns by Mrs. Whitehead. However, Mrs. Whitehead returned later and pleaded with the Sterns to let her keep Baby M. for a short time. The Sterns agreed and Mrs. Whitehead took the child.

A week after Mrs. Whitehead took Baby M., she informed the Sterns that she had decided to keep the child. The Sterns obtained a court order to regain custody of Baby M., but before the police could execute the order, Mrs. Whitehead fled with the child to Florida. It was not until July of 1986 that Florida police were able to locate Baby M. and turn the child over to the Sterns.

A long court battle took place in New Jersey over the custody of Baby M. On March 31, 1987, Judge Harvey R. Sorkow ruled that the surrogacy contract was valid and enforceable. Mrs. Stern was thereafter allowed to legally adopt the child. The trial court's decision was appealed to the New Jersey Supreme Court. In the case of *In the Matter of Baby M.*, 537 A.2d 1227 (N.J. 1988) the New Jersey Supreme Court issued an opinion reversing the trial court's decision. The New Jersey high court held that a surrogacy contract which provides money for the surrogate mother was invalid and unenforceable. Therefore, the adoption of Baby M by Mrs. Stern was improper, and Mrs. Whitehead remained the child's legal mother.

The New Jersey high court held further that the best interests of Baby M. required that the child remain with her father, Mr. Stern and his wife. Mrs. Whitehead, as Baby M's legal and natural mother, was given visitation rights to Baby M.

The second surrogacy case to gain national attention involved a California couple, John and Luanne Buzzanca. On August 25, 1994, the couple arranged to have a surrogate mother give birth to a child for them using donated egg and sperm. A month before the child was born, Mr. Buzzanca filed for a divorce on March 30, 1995. Subsequently the child, Jaycee, was born and turned over to Mrs. Buzzanca. During the divorce proceeding the trial judge held that Mr. Buzzanca did not adopt the child, therefore he did not have to pay child support.

The trial court's ruling was reversed by the California Court of Appeal for the Fourth Appellate District, in *In re Marriage of Buzzanca*, 61 Cal.App.4th 1410 (1998). The appellate court held that parental relationships may be established when intended parents initiate and consent to medical procedures, even when there is no biological relationship between them and the child. Therefore, Mr. Buzzanca was the legal father of the child. *See also* **Cryopreservation; Assisted Reproductive Technology**

Survivors of Abortion

No accurate estimate is known of the number of children who were born, even though their mothers attempted to have them aborted. It is known that in many instances, abortion survivors suffer physical and/or mental impairments. In some instances an aborting mother will keep the child, while in other instances the child is placed up for adoption. *See also* **Brown, Sarah; Jessen, Gianna; Renaerts, Ximena; Rodriquez, Ana Rosa; Saia, Alexandria; Smith, Sarah; Wrongful Birth Lawsuits**

Sutherland, George

George Sutherland (1862–1942) served as an associate justice of the United States Supreme Court from 1922 to 1938. While on the Supreme Court Justice Sutherland was known as a conservative interpreter of the Constitution.

Justice Sutherland was born in Buckinghamshire, England. His family immigrated to the United States during his adolescent years and settled in Utah. He was a graduate of Brigham Young University in 1881, and thereafter studied law at the University of Michigan Law School. His career included serving in the Utah legislature, the United States House of Representatives and the United States Senate. In 1922 President Warren G. Harding appointed Justice Sutherland to the Supreme Court.

Justice Sutherland was involved in only abortion related opinion while on the Supreme Court. Justice Sutherland voted with a unanimous opinion In *State of Missouri ex rel. Hurwitz v. North*, which held that the constitution was not violated when a physician was prevented from issuing subpoenas to have witnesses attend a hearing to revoke his medical license for performing an unlawful abortion, because the applicable rules required taking depositions of witnesses who would not voluntarily attend the hearing.

Symptothermal Method *see* **Natural Family Planning Methods**

Syphilis

Syphilis is a sexually transmitted disease that is caused by a bacterium called *Treponema pallidum*. The disease can be contracted through the skin or mucous membranes of the genital area, the mouth, or the anus of a sexual partner. It may also pass through broken skin on other parts of the body. The initial infection produces an ulcer at the site of the infection. The disease will then move throughout the body and damage many organs over time. The actual course of the

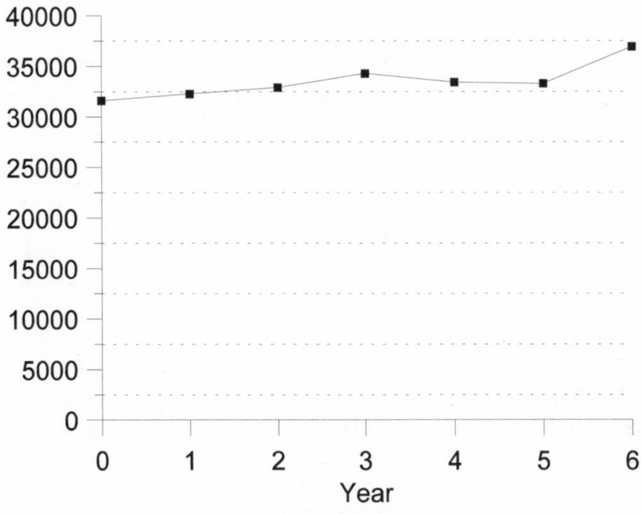

Source: **Centers for Disease Control and Prevention.**

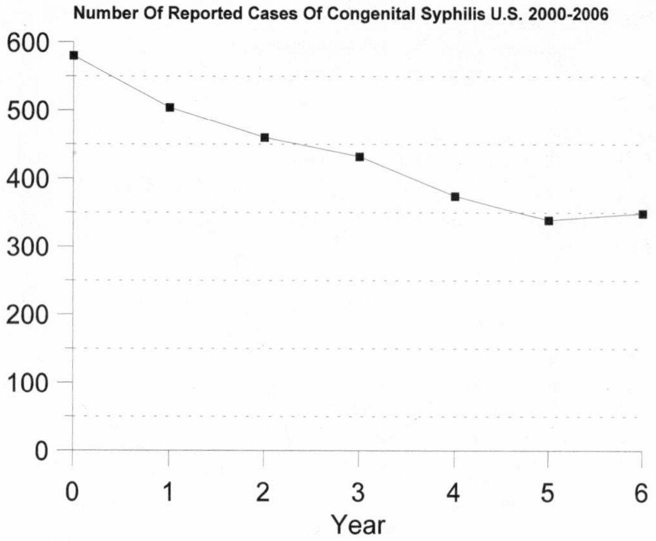

Source: **Centers for Disease Control and Prevention.**

disease is described in three stages— primary, secondary, and late (tertiary). The first two stages usually last one to two years. A person with the disease who has not been treated may infect others during the first two stages. The disease is not contagious during its late stage, but it can cause heart abnormalities, mental disorders, blindness, neurologic problems, and death. In 2006 there were 36,935 reported cases of syphilis in the United States.

A pregnant woman who has syphilis can pass the infection to her unborn child. As a result, the child may be born with mental and physical problems. About 25 percent of such pregnancies result in stillborn or neonatal death. There were 349 cases of congenital syphilis in newborns in 2006.

Syphilis usually is treated with penicillin. A single dose of penicillin will cure a person who has had syphilis for less than a year. Larger doses are needed to cure someone who has had it for longer than a year. Other antibiotics can be used for patients allergic to penicillin. A person usually can no longer transmit syphilis 24 hours after beginning treatment. The use of latex condoms during sexual intercourse may prevent the spread of syphilis. *See also* **Sexually Transmitted Diseases**

Systemic Lupus Erythematosus *see* **Lupus**

T

Taft, William Howard

William Howard Taft (1857–1930) served as chief justice of the United States Supreme Court from 1921 to 1930. While on the Supreme Court Chief Justice Taft was known as a moderate interpreter of the Constitution.

Chief Justice Taft was born in Cincinnati, Ohio. He was educated at Yale University and received a law degree from Cincinnati Law School in 1880. His career included being a trial court judge in Ohio, an appellate court judge for the Sixth Circuit Court of Appeals, United States Solicitor General and President of the United States. In 1921 President Warren G. Harding nominated him as chief justice for the Supreme Court.

Chief Justice Taft was involved in only one abortion related opinion while on the Supreme Court. Chief Justice Taft voted with a unanimous opinion in *State of Missouri ex rel. Hurwitz v. North*, which held that the constitution was not violated when a physician was prevented from issuing subpoenas to have witnesses attend a hearing to revoke his medical license for performing an unlawful abortion, because the applicable rules required taking depositions of witnesses who would not voluntarily attend the hearing.

Talipes Equinovarus *see* **Clubfoot**

Tamoxifen

Tamoxifen (brand name Nolvadex) is a drug that is used primarily to treat breast cancer in women. It may also be used to treat other kinds of cancer. The drug has been heavily criticized because of its potential side effects on women and fetuses. Tamoxifen has been said to cause miscarriages, still births and birth defects. Other side effects associated with the drug include uterine cancer, heart problems, hot flashes, nausea, vaginal bleeding, vaginal discharge, skin rash, increase in calcium in the body, swelling of the limbs, loss of appetite, leg cramps, and hair thinning. *See also* **Bendectin; DES**

Tariff Act

The Tariff Act of 1930 was a Congressional legislation designed to prohibit importing certain items into the United States. Among the items banned under the Act was drugs used for causing an unlawful abortion. The relevant portions of the text of Act are set out below.

19 U.S.C.A. § 1305. Importation prohibited

(a) All persons are prohibited from importing into the United States from any foreign country any ... drug or medicine or any article whatever for causing unlawful abortion.... No such articles whether imported separately or contained in packages with other goods entitled to entry, shall be admitted to entry; and all such articles and, unless it appears to the satisfaction of the appropriate customs officer that the ... prohibited articles contained in the package were inclosed therein without the knowledge or consent of the importer, owner, agent, or consignee, the entire contents of the package in which such articles are contained, shall be subject to seizure and forfeiture as hereinafter provided: Provided, That the drugs hereinbefore mentioned, when imported in bulk and not put up for any of the purposes hereinbefore specified, are excepted from the operation of this subdivision....

(b) Upon the appearance of any such ... matter at any customs office, the same shall be seized and held by the appropriate customs officer to await the judgment of the district court as hereinafter provided; and no protest shall be taken to the United States Court of International Trade from the decision of such customs officer. Upon the seizure of such ... or matter, such customs officer shall transmit information thereof to the United States attorney of the district in which is situated either—

(1) the office at which such seizure took place; or

(2) the place to which such ... matter is addressed;

and the United States attorney shall institute proceedings in the district court for the forfeiture, confiscation, and destruction of the ... matter seized. Upon the adjudication that such ... matter thus seized is of the character the entry of which is by this section prohibited, it shall be ordered destroyed and shall be destroyed. Upon adjudication that such ... matter thus seized is not of the character the entry of which is by this section prohibited, it shall not be excluded from entry under the provisions of this section.

In any such proceeding any party in interest may upon demand have the facts at issue determined by a jury and any party may have an appeal or the right of review as in the case of ordinary actions or suits.

See also **Comstock Act**

Tay-Sachs Disease

Tay-Sachs disease is an inherited disorder involving a deficiency of an enzyme necessary for breaking down certain fatty substances in brain and nerve cells. This condition gradually destroys brain and nerve cells, until the central nervous system stops working. Infants born with the disease appear healthy at birth. However, within 4 to 6 months affected children gradually become blind and paralyzed. Death will usually occur around age 5. There is no cure for the disease, nor any treatment to prevent the disease from running its course. Prenatal tests can diagnose the disease before birth. This disease is most prevalent in east European Jewish families. *See also* **Birth Defects and Abortion**

Telemetry Monitor

A telemetry monitor is a device that permits monitoring of a fetus' heart. This device does not require connecting wires to the woman and a monitoring machine. When the device is placed on the woman, it transmits radio waves of the fetus' heart to a monitor at a nurse's station. *See also* **Fetal Monitoring**

Tennessee

(1) OVERVIEW

The state of Tennessee enacted its first criminal abortion statute on March 26, 1883. The statute underwent several amendments prior to the 1973 decision by the United States Supreme Court in *Roe v. Wade*, which legalized abortion in the nation. Tennessee has taken affirmative steps to respond to *Roe* and its progeny. The state has addressed several abortion issues by statute that include general abortion guidelines, informed consent, abortion by minors, partial-birth abortion, use of facilities and people, experimentation and sale of fetus, fetal death report, injury to a pregnant woman, use of state funds, and Choose Life license plate.

(2) GENERAL ABORTION GUIDELINES

Tennessee expressly provides for pre-viability abortion. The state requires abortions after the first trimester be performed at a hospital. However, this restriction was found invalid in *Planned Parenthood of Middle Tennessee v. Sundquist*, 38 S.W.3d 1 (Tenn. 2000). The state prohibits post-viability abortion, except to save the life or health of the woman. Tennessee prohibits abortions for nonresidents. The residency requirement is invalid, however, as a result of the United States

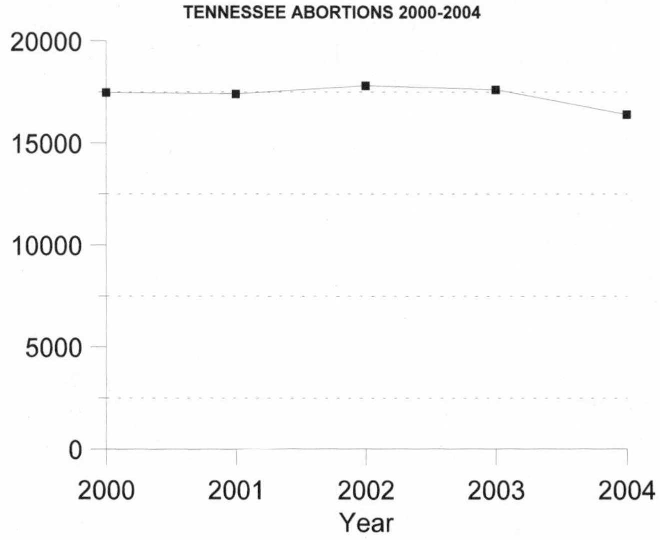

Source: National Center for Health Statistics.

Tennessee Abortion by Age Group 2000–2004

Year	Age Group (yrs) <15	15–19	20–24	25–29	30–34	35–39	≥40	Unknown
2000	118	3,063	6,171	4,180	2,258	1,307	368	14
2001	131	2,994	6,114	4,109	2,334	1,283	420	20
2002	139	2,827	6,308	4,203	2,548	1,308	432	42
2003	173	2,740	6,199	4,151	2,598	1,294	405	50
2004	119	2,538	5,633	3,995	2,433	1,212	425	45
Total	680	14,162	30,425	20,638	12,171	6,404	2,050	171

Source: National Center for Health Statistics.

Tennessee Abortion by Weeks of Gestation 2000–2004

Weeks of Gestation	Year 2000	2001	2002	2003	2004	Total
<9	10,656	10,981	11,551	11,508	10,652	55,348
9–10	3,721	3,409	3,023	2,966	2,823	15,942
11–12	2,272	2,262	2,387	2,219	2,142	11,282
13–15	744	644	642	679	594	3,303
16–20	37	60	89	91	65	342
≥21	24	17	10	12	21	84
Not known	25	32	105	135	103	400

Source: National Center for Health Statistics.

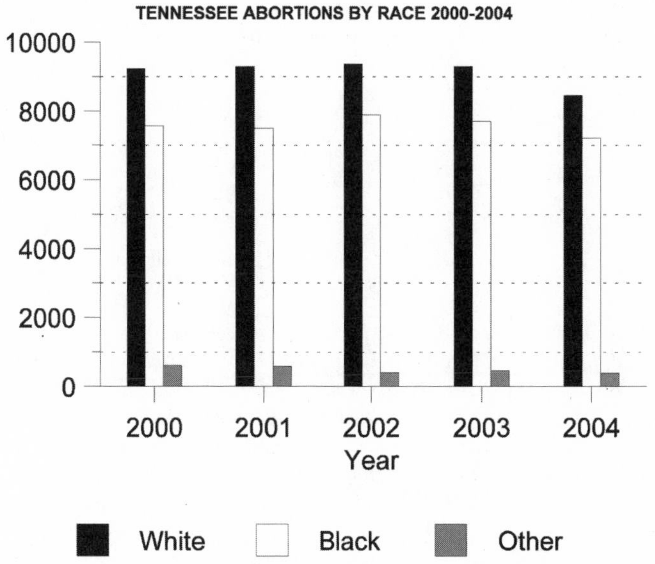

Source: National Center for Health Statistics.

Supreme Court decision in *Doe v. Bolton*, which struck down a Georgia statute that limited abortions to residents. The state imposes an affirmative duty on medical professionals to provide appropriate care to a child born alive during an attempted abortion. The general abortion statutes are set out below.

Tennessee Code § 39-15-201. Abortion guidelines

(a) For the purpose of this section:

(1) "Abortion" means the administration to any woman pregnant with child, whether the child be quick or not, of any medicine, drug, or substance whatever, or the use or employment of any instrument, or other means whatever, with the intent to destroy the child, thereby destroying the child before the child's birth; and

(2) "Attempt to procure a miscarriage" means the administration of any substance with the intention to procure the miscarriage of a woman or the use or employment of any instrument or other means with such intent.

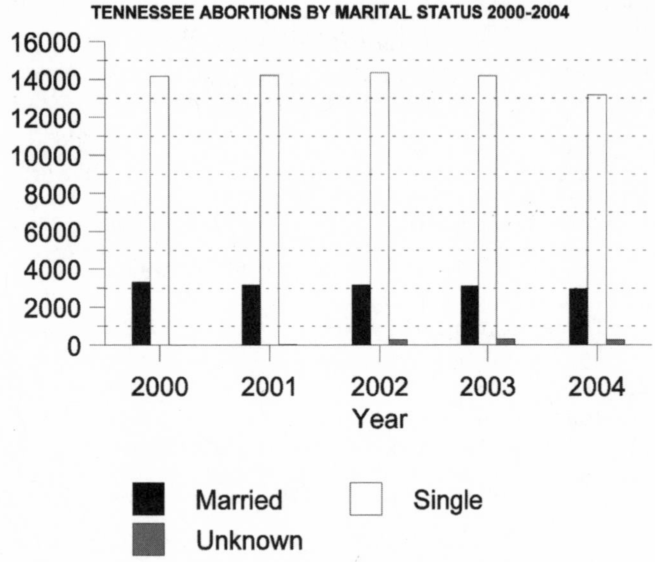

Source: National Center for Health Statistics.

Tennessee Prior Abortion by Female
2000–2004
Prior Abortion

Year	*None*	*1*	*2*	*≥3*	*Not known*
2000	9,222	4,748	2,154	1,332	23
2001	9,203	4,688	2,058	1,431	25
2002	9,207	4,760	2,211	1,546	83
2003	8,916	4,767	2,203	1,620	104
2004	8,492	4,328	2,022	1,445	113
Total	45,040	23,291	10,648	7,374	348

Source: National Center for Health Statistics.

(b)(1) Every person who performs an abortion commits the crime of criminal abortion, unless such abortion is performed in compliance with the requirements of subsection (c). Criminal abortion is a Class C felony.

(2) Every person who attempts to procure a miscarriage commits the crime of attempt to procure criminal miscarriage, unless the attempt to procure a miscarriage is performed in compliance with the requirements of subsection (c). Attempt to procure a criminal miscarriage is a Class E felony.

(3) Every person who compels, coerces, or exercises duress in any form with regard to any other person in order to obtain or procure an abortion on any female commits a misdemeanor. A violation of this section is a Class A misdemeanor.

(c) No person is guilty of a criminal abortion or an attempt to procure criminal miscarriage when an abortion or an attempt to procure a miscarriage is performed under the following circumstances:

(1) During the first three (3) months of pregnancy, if the abortion or attempt to procure a miscarriage is performed with the pregnant woman's consent and pursuant to the medical judgment of the pregnant woman's attending physician who is licensed or certified under title 63, chapter 6 or 9;

(2) After three (3) months, but before viability of the fetus, if the abortion or attempt to procure a miscarriage is performed with the pregnant woman's consent and in a hospital as defined in § 68-11-201, licensed by the state department of health, or a hospital operated by the state of Tennessee or a branch of the federal government, by the pregnant woman's attending physician, who is licensed or certified under title 63, chapter 6 or 9, pursuant to the attending physician's medical judgment; or

(3) During viability of the fetus, if the abortion or attempt to procure a miscarriage is performed with the pregnant woman's consent and by the pregnant woman's attending physician, who is licensed or certified under title 63, chapter 6 or 9; and, if all the circumstances and provisions required for a lawful abortion or lawful attempt to procure a miscarriage during the period set out in subdivision (c)(2) are adhered to; and if, prior to the abortion or attempt to procure a miscarriage the physician has certified in writing to the hospital in which the abortion or attempt to procure a miscarriage is to be performed, that in the physician's best medical judgment, after proper examination, review of history, and such consultation as may be required by either the rules and regulations of the board for licensing health care facilities promulgated pursuant to § 68-11-209, or the administration of the hospital involved, or both, the abortion or attempt to procure a miscarriage is necessary to preserve the life or health of the mother, and shall have filed a copy of the certificate with the district attorney general of the judicial district wherein the abortion or attempt to procure a miscarriage is to be performed.

(d) No abortion shall be performed on any pregnant woman unless such woman first produces evidence satisfactory to the physician performing the abortion that she is a bona fide resident of Tennessee. Evidence to support such claim of residence shall be noted in the records kept by the physician and, if the abortion is performed in a hospital, in the records kept by the hospital. A violation of this subsection is punished as provided by subdivision (b)(1).

Tennessee Code § 39-15-206.
Infant born alive during abortion

(a) The rights to medical treatment of an infant prematurely born alive in the course of an abortion are the same as the rights of an infant of similar medical status prematurely born spontaneously. Any person who performs or induces an abortion of an infant shall exercise that degree of professional skill, care, and diligence in accordance with good medical practice necessary to preserve the life and health of an infant prematurely born alive in the course of an abortion, except that if it can be determined, through amniocentesis or medical observation, that the fetus is severely malformed, the use of extraneous life support measures need not be attempted.

(b) Any person who violates this section commits a Class E felony.

(c) No cause of action for wrongful death shall be brought which arises out of the death of a fetus or infant during the course of a lawful abortion, whether the fetus or infant is quick or not, so long as the abortion is performed in accordance with the provisions of this part; however, once an infant is born alive, any person in attendance shall be civilly responsible for providing all reasonable and necessary care reasonable under the circumstances in the general vicinity in which the person in attendance practices.

Tennessee Code § 39-15-207.
Custody of infant born alive during abortion

An infant prematurely born alive in the course of a voluntary abortion is declared abandoned for purposes of custody only, and the department of children's services shall care for the infant as provided in § 34-1-103.

(3) INFORMED CONSENT

Tennessee requires that a woman be fully informed of the procedure to be used, the risks involved and alternatives to abortion. An abortion may not take place until two days after a woman has been given the required statutory information. Many of the requirements of the informed consent statute were found invalid in *Planned Parenthood of Middle Tennessee v. Sundquist*, 38 S.W.3d 1 (Tenn. 2000). The statute is set out below.

Tennessee Code § 39-15-202. Consent and waiting period

(a) An abortion otherwise permitted by law shall be performed or induced only with the informed written consent of the pregnant woman, given freely and without coercion. Such consent shall be treated as confidential.

(b) In order to ensure that a consent for an abortion is truly informed consent, an abortion shall be performed or induced upon a pregnant woman only after she has been orally informed by her attending physician of the following facts and has signed a consent form acknowledging that she has been informed as follows:

(1) That according to the best judgment of her attending physician she is pregnant;

(2) The number of weeks elapsed from the probable time of the conception of her unborn child, based upon the information provided by her as to the time of her last menstrual period or after a history, physical examination, and appropriate laboratory tests;

(3) That if more than twenty-four (24) weeks have elapsed from the time of conception, her child may be viable, that is, capable of surviving outside of the womb, and that if such child is prematurely born alive in the course of an abortion her attending physician has a legal obligation to take steps to preserve the life and health of the child;

(4) That abortion in a considerable number of cases constitutes a major surgical procedure;

(5) That numerous public and private agencies and services are available to assist her during her pregnancy and after the birth of her child, if she chooses not to have the abortion, whether she wishes to keep her child or place the child for adoption, and that her physician will provide her with a list of such agencies and the services available if she so requests; or

(6) Numerous benefits and risks are attendant either to continued pregnancy and childbirth or to abortion depending upon the circumstances in which the patient might find herself. The physician shall explain these benefits and risks to the best of such physician's ability and knowledge of the circumstances involved.

(c) At the same time the attending physician provides the information required by subsection (b), such physician shall inform the pregnant woman of the particular risks associated with her pregnancy and childbirth and the abortion or child delivery technique to be employed, including providing her with at least a general description of the medical instructions to be followed subsequent to the abortion or childbirth in order to ensure her safe recovery.

(d)(1) There shall be a two-day waiting period after the physician provides the required information, excluding the day on which such information was given. On the third day following the day such information was given, the patient may return to the physician and sign a consent form.

(2) A violation of this subsection by a physician is a Class E felony.

(3) This subsection shall not apply when the attending physician, utilizing experience, judgment or professional competence, determines that a two-day waiting period or any waiting period would endanger the life of the pregnant woman. Such determination made by the attending physician shall be in writing and shall state the physician's medical reasons upon which the physician bases the opinion that the waiting period would endanger the life of the pregnant woman. This provision shall not relieve the attending physician of the duty to the pregnant woman to inform her of the facts under subsection (b).

(e) The attending physician performing or inducing the abortion shall provide the pregnant woman with a duplicate copy of the consent form signed by her.

(f) "The physician" or "the attending physician," as used in this section, means any licensed physician on the service treating the pregnant woman.

(g) The provisions of this section shall not apply in those situations where an abortion is certified by a licensed physician as necessary to preserve the life of the pregnant woman.

(4) ABORTION BY MINORS

Under the laws of Tennessee no physician may perform an abortion upon an unemancipated minor unless he/she first obtains the written consent of either parent or the legal guardian of the minor. In compliance with federal constitutional law, Tennessee has provided a judicial waiver procedure for an unemancipated minor to obtain an abortion without parental or guardian consent. The minor may petition a trial court for a waiver of the consent requirement. A minor has a right to an attorney at the proceeding and if she cannot afford one, the court must appoint her an attorney. If a minor chooses, she may represent herself. The required parental or guardian consent may be waived if the court finds either (1) that the minor is mature and well-informed enough to make the abortion decision on her own, or (2) that performance of the abortion would be in the best interest of the minor. An expedited appeal is available to any minor to whom the court denies a waiver of consent. The state also has a statute which imposes specific reporting requirements on a physician performing an abortion on a minor who is less than 13 years of age and was the victim of rape. The statutes are set out below.

Tennessee Code § 37-10-301. Legislative intent

(a) It is the intent of the general assembly in enacting this parental consent provision to further the important and compelling state interests of:

(1) Protecting minors against their own immaturity;

(2) Fostering the family structure and preserving it as a viable social unit; and

(3) Protecting the rights of parents to rear children who are members of their household.

(b) The general assembly finds as fact that:

(1) Immature minors often lack the ability to make fully informed choices that take into account of both immediate and long-range consequences;

(2) The medical, emotional, and psychological consequences of abortion are serious and can be lasting, particularly when the patient is immature;

(3) The capacity to become pregnant and the capacity for mature judgment concerning the wisdom of an abortion are not necessarily related;

(4) Parents ordinarily possess information essential to a physician's exercise of the physician's best medical judgment concerning the child; and

(5) Parents who are aware that their minor daughter has had an abortion may better ensure that their daughter receives adequate medical attention after the abortion.

(c) The general assembly further finds that parental consultation is usually desirable and in the best interests of the minor.

Tennessee Code § 37-10-302. Definitions

As used in this part, unless the context otherwise requires:

(1) "Abortion" means the use of any instrument, medicine, drug, or any other substance or device with intent to terminate the pregnancy of a woman known to be pregnant with intent other than to increase the probability of a live birth, to preserve the life or health of the child after live birth, or to remove a dead fetus;

(2) "Emancipated minor" means any minor who is or has been married or has by court order or otherwise been freed from the care, custody and control of the minor's parents; and

(3) "Minor" means any person under eighteen (18) years of age.

Tennessee Code § 37-10-303. Parental consent

(a)(1) No person shall perform an abortion on an unemancipated minor unless such person or such person's agent first obtains the written

consent of one (1) parent or the legal guardian of the minor. The consent shall be signed. The person shall obtain some written documentation, other than the written consent itself, that purports to establish the relationship of the parent or guardian to the minor and the documentation, along with the signed consent, shall be retained by the person for a period of at least one (1) year. Failure of the person performing the abortion to obtain or retain the documentation and consent is a Class B misdemeanor, punishable only by a fine, unless the failure of the person performing the abortion to retain the required documentation was due to a bona fide, imminent medical emergency to the minor, in which case there is no violation.

(2) A person commits a Class A misdemeanor who impersonates the parent or legal guardian of an unemancipated minor for the purpose of circumventing the requirements of subdivision (a)(1).

(b) If neither a parent nor a legal guardian is available to the person performing the abortion or such person's agent, or the party from whom consent must be obtained pursuant to this section refuses to consent to the performance of an abortion, or the minor elects not to seek consent of the parent or legal guardian whose consent is required, then the minor may petition, on the minor's own behalf, or by next friend, the juvenile court of any county of this state for a waiver of the consent requirement of this section, pursuant to the procedures of § 37-10-304.

(c) If a criminal charge of incest is pending against a parent of such minor pursuant to § 39-15-302, the written consent of such parent, as provided for in subdivision (a)(1), is not required.

Tennessee Code § 37-10-304. Judicial bypass

(a) The requirements and procedures under this part are available and apply to minors, whether or not they are residents of this state.

(b) The court shall ensure that the minor's identity is kept anonymous. The minor shall be allowed to proceed under a pseudonym and shall be allowed to sign all documents, including the petition, by that pseudonym. In any proceedings involving the use of a pseudonym by the minor, the court shall require one (1) copy of the petition to be filed, under seal, that contains the true name of the minor. This copy of the petition shall be kept in a separate file, under seal, and shall not be available for inspection by anyone, except as provided in subsection (h).

(c)(1) The minor may participate in proceedings in the court on the minor's own behalf or through a next friend. The court shall advise the minor that the minor has a right to court-appointed counsel and shall provide the minor with such counsel upon the minor's request. The state shall further provide a court-appointed advocate in each judicial district to give information regarding the legal process to the minor and to coordinate with the court-appointed counsel. Such court-appointed advocates shall be compensated from funds appropriated for the reimbursement of court-appointed counsel.

(2) The department of children's services shall assign from existing staff at least one (1) court advocate in each judicial district to provide minors with information regarding requirements and procedures established by the provisions of this part, to assist in coordination of the activities of court-appointed counsel, to attend legal proceedings with the minor or the minor's next friend, and to make available written material concerning the provisions and applications of this part. The advocate shall be trained in the juvenile court procedures, in the procedures established by this part, and in counseling minors. The department shall provide a toll-free telephone number for minors to use in order to obtain the telephone number and address of a court advocate. The department shall further provide and distribute a written brochure or information sheet that summarizes the provisions and applications of this part and that contains the toll-free telephone number as well as the names, addresses, and telephone numbers of the court advocates in each judicial district.

(d) Court proceedings under this section shall be given such precedence over other pending matters as is necessary to ensure that the court may reach a decision promptly, but in no case shall the court fail to rule within forty-eight (48) hours of the time of application; provided, that the forty-eight-hour limitation may be extended at the request of the minor. If, for any reason except the request of the minor, the court shall not have ruled within forty-eight (48) hours, the minor may deem the petition denied and immediately appeal the denial as provided in subsection (g). This provision is not deemed to restrict or forbid any other remedy now existing or hereafter enacted in such a situation.

(e) The consent requirement shall be waived if the court finds either that:

(1) The minor is mature and well-informed enough to make the abortion decision on the minor's own; or

(2) The performance of the abortion would be in the minor's best interests.

(f) A court that conducts proceedings under this section shall issue written and specific factual findings and legal conclusions supporting its decision and shall order that a confidential record of the evidence be maintained.

(g) An expedited, anonymous appeal shall be available to any minor. The appeal shall be de novo to the circuit court for the county in which the juvenile court is located. The appeal may be heard by the circuit court judge sitting in another county if necessary to meet the time limitations of this section. A notice of appeal shall be filed within twenty-four (24) hours of the decision by the juvenile court, but may be filed at any time, if the juvenile court has not ruled within forty-eight (48) hours of the filing of the petition. The record from the juvenile court must be received in the circuit court and the appeal docketed there within five (5) calendar days of the filing of the notice of appeal. The appeal shall be heard and a decision rendered by the circuit court within five (5) calendar days from when the case is docketed in the circuit court. For the purpose of expediting the appellate procedure under this section, the time requirements of this section may be reduced by the Tennessee supreme court pursuant to its rulemaking authority in order to ensure an expedited appeal. The decision of the circuit court shall be appealable to the Tennessee supreme court in an anonymous and expedited manner as provided by the rules of the Tennessee supreme court. Jurisdiction under this section will remain in the Tennessee supreme court, notwithstanding the provision of any other statute or rule to the contrary.

(h) All court files, documents, exhibits, and all other records lodged in or subject to the control of the court shall be kept confidential and under seal. Statistical summaries of these proceedings may be compiled for such reporting purposes as the supreme court may by rule require or allow. However, no information shall be released for these purposes that would tend to identify any minor who has made use of this procedure.

(i) The supreme court is respectfully requested to promulgate any rules necessary to ensure that proceedings under this part are handled in an expeditious and anonymous manner, including any amendments to the Tennessee Rules of Appellate Procedure, Tennessee Rules of Civil Procedure and Tennessee Rules of Juvenile Procedure.

(j) No fees shall be required of any minor who makes use of the procedures provided by this section.

Tennessee Code § 37-10-305. Emergencies

The requirements of § 37-10-303 shall not apply when, in the best medical judgment of the physician based on the facts of the case before the physician, a medical emergency exists that so complicates the pregnancy as to require an immediate abortion.

Tennessee Code § 37-10-306. Crimes and offenses

Any person who intentionally performs an abortion with knowledge that, or with reckless disregard as to whether the person upon whom the abortion is to be performed is an unemancipated minor, and who intentionally or knowingly fails to conform to any requirement of this part, commits a Class A misdemeanor.

Tennessee Code § 37-10-307. Common law rights of parents

Failure to obtain consent pursuant to the requirements of this part is prima facie evidence of failure to obtain informed consent and of interference with family relations in appropriate civil actions. The law of this state shall not be construed to preclude the award of exemplary damages in any appropriate civil action relevant to violations of this part. Nothing in this part shall be construed to limit the common law rights of parents.

Tennessee Code § 37-10-308. Unconstitutionality of part

If any one (1) or more provision, section, subsection, sentence, clause, phrase or word of this part or the application thereof to any person or circumstance is found to be unconstitutional, the same is declared to be severable and the balance of this part shall remain effective notwithstanding the unconstitutionality. The legislature declares that it would have passed this part, and each provision, section, subsection, sentence, clause, phrase or word thereof, irrespective of the fact that any one (1) or more provision, section, subsection, sentence, clause, phrase or word be declared unconstitutional.

Tennessee Code § 39-15-210. Child rape protection act

(a) This section shall be known and may be cited as the "Child Rape Protection Act of 2006."

(b) When a physician has reasonable cause to report the sexual abuse of a minor pursuant to § 37-1-605, because the physician has been requested to perform an abortion on a minor who is less than thirteen (13) years of age, the physician shall, at the time of the report, also notify the official to whom the report is made of the date and time of the scheduled abortion and that a sample of the embryonic or fetal tissue extracted during the abortion will be preserved and available to be turned over to the appropriate law enforcement officer conducting the investigation into the rape of the minor.

(c)(1) In the transmission of the embryonic or fetal tissue sample to the appropriate law enforcement officer, in order to protect the identity and privacy of the minor, all identifying information concerning the minor shall be treated as confidential and shall not be released to anyone other than the investigating and prosecuting authorities directly involved in the case of the particular minor.

(2) Where the minor has obtained a judicial waiver of the parental notification requirements pursuant to Title 37, Chapter 10, Part 13, confidentiality shall be maintained as provided in that part.

(d) It is an offense for a physician licensed or certified under Title 63, Chapter 6 or 9, or other person to knowingly fail to comply with the provisions of this section or any rule or regulation adopted pursuant to this section.

(1) A first violation of this section is a civil penalty to be assessed by the provider's health related board of not less than five hundred dollars ($500);

(2) A second violation of this section is a civil penalty to be assessed by the provider's health related board of not less than one thousand dollars ($1,000); and

(3) A third or subsequent violation of this section is a Class A misdemeanor.

(e) If the person performing the abortion is a physician licensed or certified under Title 63, Chapter 6 or 9, the violation constitutes unprofessional conduct. The conduct subjects the physician, in addition to the penalties set out in subsection (d), to disciplinary action.

(5) PARTIAL-BIRTH ABORTION

Tennessee criminalizes performance of partial-birth abortions, unless done to save the life of the woman. Until it is definitively determined by a court, Tennessee's partial-birth abortion statute may be invalid under the United States Supreme Court decision *in Stenberg v. Carhart*, which invalidated Nebraska's ban on partial-birth abortion. On the other hand, Tennessee's partial-birth abortion statute, as currently written, may be valid under the United States Supreme Court decision in *Gonzales v. Carhart*, which approved of a federal statute that bans partial-birth abortion. The text of the partial-birth abortion statute is set out below.

Tennessee Code § 39-15-209. Partial-birth abortion ban

(a) For purposes of this section, unless the context otherwise requires:

(1) "Partial-birth abortion" means an abortion in which the person performing the abortion partially vaginally delivers a living fetus before killing the fetus and completing the delivery; and

(2) "Vaginally delivers a living fetus before killing the fetus" means deliberately and intentionally delivers into the vagina a living fetus, or a substantial portion thereof, for the purpose of performing a procedure the physician knows will kill the fetus, and kills the fetus.

(b) No person shall knowingly perform a partial-birth abortion.

(c) Subsection (b) shall not apply to a partial-birth abortion that is necessary to save the life of the mother whose life is endangered by a physical disorder, illness or injury.

(d)(1) A defendant accused of an offense under this section may seek a hearing before the state medical board which licenses the physician, on whether the physician's conduct was necessary to save the life of the mother whose life was endangered by a physical disorder, illness or injury.

(2) The findings on that issue are admissible on that issue at the trial of the defendant. Upon a motion of the defendant, the court shall delay the beginning of the trial for not more than thirty (30) days to permit such a hearing to take place.

(e)(1) Performance of a partial-birth abortion in knowing or reckless violation of this section shall be a Class C felony.

(2) A woman upon whom a partial-birth abortion is performed may not be prosecuted under this section for violating this section or any of its provisions, or for conspiracy to violate this section or any of its provisions.

(6) USE OF FACILITIES AND PEOPLE

Tennessee permits hospitals, physicians, and other medical personnel to refuse to participate in performing abortions. The state also provides that hospitals do not have to admit a woman for an abortion. Tennessee further prohibits public school nurses from making abortion referrals. The statutes addressing the matter are set out below.

Tennessee Code § 39-15-204. Right to refuse abortions

No physician shall be required to perform an abortion and no person shall be required to participate in the performance of an abortion. No hospital shall be required to permit abortions to be performed therein.

Tennessee Code § 39-15-205. Hospital refusing patients

No section of this part shall be construed to force a hospital to accept a patient for an abortion.

Tennessee Code § 68-1-1205. Public school nurses

Each employee of the [public school nurse] program, including each intern resident employed pursuant to § 68-1-1203(c), shall at all times remain in compliance with, and shall fully abide by, all applicable federal, state and local statutes, rules, regulations, ordinances and policies pertaining to abortion. Furthermore, each employee of the program, including each intern or resident employed pursuant to § 68-1-1203(c), shall at all times remain in compliance with and shall fully abide by all applicable federal, state and local statutes, rules, regulations, ordinances and policies pertaining to birth control devices and contraceptives. While present on the property or premises of any local education agency or while otherwise engaged in the activities of the program, no such employee shall at any time make abortion referrals or otherwise advocate or encourage abortion nor prescribe any form of birth control device or contraceptive. It shall be the policy of the program, and of each employee engaged in the activities of the program, including each intern or resident employed pursuant to § 68-1-1203(c), to vigorously encourage and urge students to abstain from entering into any sexual relationship or activity.

(7) EXPERIMENTATION AND SALE OF FETUS

Experimentation or research on an aborted fetus is prohibited by Tennessee, unless consented to by the woman who aborted the fetus. The state prohibits trafficking in fetuses. The statute addressing the matter is set out below.

Tennessee Code § 39-15-208. Experimentation and sale

(a) It is unlawful for any person, agency, corporation, partnership or association to engage in medical experiments, research, or the taking of photographs upon an aborted fetus without the prior knowledge and consent of the mother.

(b) No person, agency, corporation, partnership or association shall offer money or anything of value for an aborted fetus; nor shall any person, agency, corporation, partnership or association accept any money or anything of value for an aborted fetus.

(c) It is the express intent of the general assembly that nothing in the provisions of this section shall be construed to grant to a fetus any legal right not possessed by such fetus prior to July 1, 1979.

(d) A violation of this section is punishable as a Class E felony.

(8) FETAL DEATH REPORT

Tennessee requires that all abortions be reported to the proper authorities. The statutes addressing the issue are set out below.

Tennessee Code § 39-15-203. Records and reports

A physician performing an abortion shall keep a record of each operation and shall make a report to the commissioner of health with respect thereto at the time and in the form as the commissioner may reasonably prescribe. Each record and report shall be confidential in nature and shall be inaccessible to the public.

Tennessee Code § 68-3-505. Abortions reports

(a) Each induced termination of pregnancy that occurs in this state shall be reported to the office of vital records within ten (10) days after the procedure by the person in charge of the institution in which the induced termination of pregnancy was performed. If the induced termination of pregnancy was performed outside an institution, the attending physician shall prepare and file the report.

(b) The individual undergoing the induced termination of pregnancy shall not be identified by name on the report, though some means of identification shall be used to provide retrieval of further information if necessary.

(9) INJURY TO A PREGNANT WOMAN

Tennessee has several statutes that make it a criminal offense to injure a pregnant woman and thereby injure or cause the death of a fetus. The statutes are set out below.

Tennessee Code § 39-13-107. Definition of assault victim

(a) For purposes of this part, "another," "individual," "individuals," and "another person" include a viable fetus of a human being, when any such term refers to the victim of any act made criminal by the provisions of this part.

(b) Nothing in this section shall be construed to amend the provisions of § 39-15-201, or §§ 39-15-203–39-15-205 and 39-15-207.

(c) It is the legislative intent that this section shall in no way affect abortion, which is legal in Tennessee. This section shall in no way apply to acts that are committed pursuant to usual and customary standards of medical practice during diagnostic or therapeutic treatment.

Tennessee Code § 39-13-101. Assault

(a) A person commits assault who:

(1) Intentionally, knowingly or recklessly causes bodily injury to another [including a viable fetus];

(2) Intentionally or knowingly causes another to reasonably fear imminent bodily injury; or

(3) Intentionally or knowingly causes physical contact with another and a reasonable person would regard the contact as extremely offensive or provocative.

(b)(1) Assault is a Class A misdemeanor unless the offense is committed under subdivision (a)(3), in which event assault is a Class B misdemeanor.

(2) Omitted.

Tennessee Code § 39-13-102. Aggravated assault

(a) A person commits aggravated assault who:

(1) Intentionally or knowingly commits an assault as defined in § 39-13-101 and:

(A) Causes serious bodily injury to another [including a viable fetus]; or

(B) Uses or displays a deadly weapon; or

(2) Recklessly commits an assault as defined in § 39-13-101(a)(1), and:

(A) Causes serious bodily injury to another [including a viable fetus]; or

(B) Uses or displays a deadly weapon.

(b) Omitted.

(c) A person commits aggravated assault who, after having been enjoined or restrained by an order, diversion or probation agreement of a court of competent jurisdiction from in any way causing or attempting to cause bodily injury or in any way committing or attempting to commit an assault against an individual or individuals, intentionally or knowingly attempts to cause or causes bodily injury or commits or attempts to commit an assault against the individual or individuals [including a viable fetus].

(d)(1) Aggravated assault under subdivision (a)(1) or subsection (b) or (c) is a Class C felony. Aggravated assault under subdivision (a)(2) is a Class D felony.

(2) Omitted.

Tennessee Code § 39-13-103. Reckless endangerment

(a) A person commits an offense who recklessly engages in conduct that places or may place another person [including a viable fetus] in imminent danger of death or serious bodily injury.

(b) Reckless endangerment is a Class A misdemeanor; however, reckless endangerment committed with a deadly weapon is a Class E felony.

Tennessee Code § 39-13-106. Vehicular assault

(a) A person commits vehicular assault who, as the proximate result of the person's intoxication as set forth in § 55-10-401, recklessly causes serious bodily injury to another person [including a viable fetus] by the operation of a motor vehicle. For the purposes of this section, "intoxication" includes alcohol intoxication as defined by § 55-10-408, drug intoxication, or both.

(b) A violation of this section is a Class D felony.

(c) Omitted.

Tennessee Code § 39-13-214. Definition of homicide victim

(a) For purposes of this part, "another" and "another person" include a viable fetus of a human being, when any such term refers to the victim of any act made criminal by the provisions of this part.

(b) Nothing in this section shall be construed to amend the provisions of § 39-15-201, or §§ 39-15-203–39-15-205 and 39-15-207.

(c) It is the legislative intent that this section shall in no way affect abortion, which is legal in Tennessee. This section shall in no way apply to acts that are committed pursuant to usual and customary standards of medical practice during diagnostic or therapeutic treatment.

Tennessee Code § 39-13-202. First degree murder

(a) First degree murder is:

(1) A premeditated and intentional killing of another [including a viable fetus];

(2) A killing of another [including a viable fetus] committed in the perpetration of or attempt to perpetrate any first degree murder, act of terrorism, arson, rape, robbery, burglary, theft, kidnapping, aggravated child abuse, aggravated child neglect, rape of a child, aggravated rape of a child or aircraft piracy; or

(3) A killing of another [including a viable fetus] committed as the result of the unlawful throwing, placing or discharging of a destructive device or bomb.

(b) No culpable mental state is required for conviction under subdivision (a)(2) or (a)(3), except the intent to commit the enumerated offenses or acts in those subdivisions.

(c) A person convicted of first degree murder shall be punished by:

(1) Death;

(2) Imprisonment for life without possibility of parole; or

(3) Imprisonment for life.

(d) Omitted.

Tennessee Code § 39-13-210. Second degree murder

(a) Second degree murder is:

(1) A knowing killing of another [including a viable fetus]; or

(2) A killing of another [including a viable fetus] that results from the unlawful distribution of any Schedule I or Schedule II drug, when the drug is the proximate cause of the death of the user.

(b) Omitted.

(c) Second degree murder is a Class A felony.

Tennessee Code § 39-13-211. Voluntary manslaughter

(a) Voluntary manslaughter is the intentional or knowing killing of another [including a viable fetus] in a state of passion produced by adequate provocation sufficient to lead a reasonable person to act in an irrational manner.

(b) Voluntary manslaughter is a Class C felony.

Tennessee Code § 39-13-212. Criminally negligent homicide

(a) Criminally negligent conduct that results in death constitutes criminally negligent homicide.

(b) Criminally negligent homicide is a Class E felony.

Tennessee Code § 39-13-213. Vehicular homicide

(a) Vehicular homicide is the reckless killing of another [including a viable fetus] by the operation of an automobile, airplane, motorboat or other motor vehicle, as the proximate result of:

(1) Conduct creating a substantial risk of death or serious bodily injury to a person [including a viable fetus];

(2) The driver's intoxication, as set forth in § 55-10-401. For the purposes of this section, "intoxication" includes alcohol intoxication as defined by § 55-10-408, drug intoxication, or both; or

(3) As the proximate result of conduct constituting the offense of drag racing as prohibited by Title 55, Chapter 10, Part 5.

(b)(1) Vehicular homicide under subsection (a)(1) or (a)(3) is a Class C felony.

(2) Vehicular homicide under subsection (a)(2) is a Class B felony.

(c) Omitted.

(10) USE OF STATE FUNDS

Except for limited circumstances, Tennessee prohibits the use of state funds for elective abortions. The statute addressing the matter is set out below.

Tennessee Code § 9-4-5116. State funding of abortions

No state funds shall be expended to perform abortions. The limitations established in this section shall not apply to an abortion if:

(1) The pregnancy is the result of an act of rape or incest; or

(2) In the case where a woman suffers from a physical disorder, physical injury, or physical illness, including a life-endangering physical condition caused by or arising from the pregnancy itself, that would, as certified by a physician, place the woman in danger of death unless the abortion is performed.

(11) CHOOSE LIFE LICENSE PLATE

Tennessee authorizes the issuance of Choose Life license plates for motor vehicles. The law permitting the use of such license plates was approved of in *American Civil Liberties Union of Tennessee v. Bredesen*, 441 F.3d 370 (6th Cir. 2006). The statute addressing the issue is set out below.

Tennessee Code § 55-4-306. Choose life license plate

(a) An owner or lessee of a motor vehicle who is a resident of this state, upon complying with state motor vehicle laws relating to registration and licensing of motor vehicles and paying the regular fee applicable to the motor vehicle and the fee provided for in § 55-4-203, shall be issued a Choose Life new specialty earmarked license plate for a motor vehicle authorized by § 55-4-210(c).

(b) The new specialty earmarked license plates provided for in this section shall contain an appropriate logo and design. Such plates shall be designed in consultation with a representative of New Life Resources.

(c) The funds produced from the sale of Choose Life new specialty earmarked license plates shall be allocated to New Life Resources in accordance with the provisions of § 55-4-215. Such funds shall be used exclusively for counseling and financial assistance, including food, clothing, and medical assistance for pregnant women in Tennessee.

(d)(1) Funds produced by the sale of license plates pursuant to this section shall also comply with the provisions of this subsection (d).

(2) Omitted.

(3) New Life Resources is a 501(c)(3) nonprofit organization incorporated in 1995 to provide resources for women and families facing difficult or unexpected pregnancies. "Choose Life" Plate proceeds will be used to coordinate statewide awareness campaigns, a toll-free helpline and to reimburse social service providers who prepare adoptions throughout the state for services and programs targeting at-risk women and families.

(4) Disbursement of funds shall begin within forty-five (45) days of receiving the first plate proceeds. As the number of plates sold increases, additional funding will be used to increase each line item above.

(5) As a 501(c)(3), New Life Resources may not use any funds for the purposes of lobbying, promoting legislation or the election or defeat of any political candidate.

(6)(A) The nonprofit agencies identified in this subdivision (d)(6)(B) shall maintain a partnership with New Life Resources for purposes of providing adoption social services at no cost to Tennessee's at-risk women and families.

(B) Omitted.

Tennessee Right to Life

Tennessee Right to Life is a pro-life organization. The organization is dedicated to protecting preborn human life. Work engaged in by the organization includes education through the presentation of detailed and factual information about fetal development, fetal experimentation, fetal pain, abortion, and alternatives to abortion; organizing and identifying the pro-life population of the state of Tennessee into an effective force; and advocating for a Human Life Amendment to the federal constitution. *See also* **Pro-Life Organizations**

Teratogen

Teratogen is the term used for any medication, chemical, infectious disease, or environmental agent that may interfere with fetal development and cause the loss of a pregnancy, a birth defect or a pregnancy complication. Examples of teratogen include radiation, cigarettes, alcohol, infections, certain drugs and poisons. *See also* **Birth Defects and Abortion**

Terry, Randall *see* **Operation Rescue**

Testicles *see* **Male Reproductive System**

Tetralogy of Fallot

Tetralogy of Fallot is a congenital disease involving the heart. It consists of 4 defects that result in inadequate oxygen in blood. Due to a decreased blood flow to the lungs the disease causes a bluish-purple coloration to the skin (cyanosis), shortness of breath, difficulty in feeding, failure to gain weight, slow growth and clubbing of fingers The disease affects approximately 50 out of 100,000 infants in the United States. There is no known prevention for the condition. The problem usually can be corrected through surgery to repair the heart. If surgery is not performed, death will usually occur to the victim when he or she is around 20 years of age. *See also* **Birth Defects and Abortion**

Texas

(1) OVERVIEW

The state of Texas enacted its first criminal abortion statute on February 9, 1854. The statute underwent several amendments prior to being found unconstitutional in 1973 by the United States Supreme Court in *Roe v. Wade*. The invalidation of Texas' abortion statute in *Roe* legalized abortion in the nation. Although *Roe* invalidated Texas' abortion laws, the state still maintains one of those laws on its books. Subsequent to the *Roe* decision has addressed a few abortion issues by statute that include general abortion guidelines, informed consent, abortion by minors, use of facilities and people, abortion facility requirements, termination of parental rights, health insurance, and sale of fetal tissue.

(2) PRE-ROE ABORTION STATUTE

As previously indicated, Texas still has one of its pre–*Roe* abortion statutes on the books. Under the statute the state makes it a crime to kill a fetus that is in the process of being delivered. The statute is set out below.

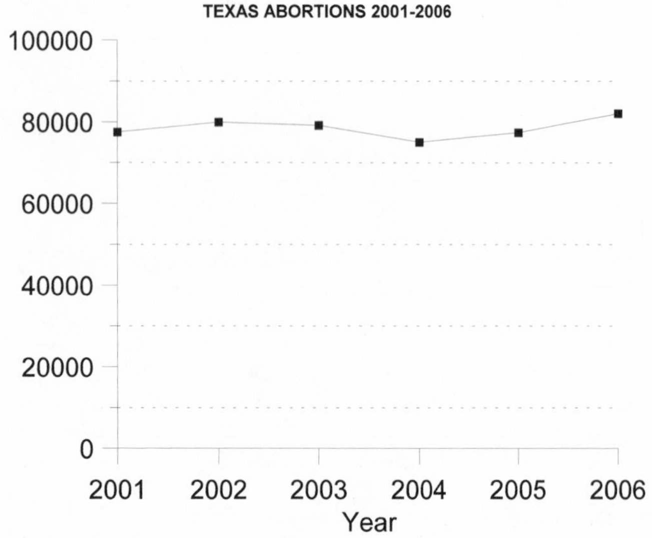

Source: **Texas Department of State Health Services.**

Texas Abortion by Age Group 2001–2006

	Year						
Age Group	*2001*	*2002*	*2003*	*2004*	*2005*	*2006*	*Total*
≤11	3	5	2	3	0	3	16
12–13	85	73	38	48	46	44	334
14–15	741	744	740	586	636	675	4,122
16–17	2,744	2,677	2,789	2,513	2,521	2,625	15,869
18–19	7,448	7,301	7,080	6,657	6,627	6,906	42,019
20–24	25,808	25,705	26,619	24,847	25,371	27,070	155,420
25–29	17,615	17,324	18,129	17,709	18,943	20,245	109,965
30–34	10,909	11,145	11,561	11,078	11,341	11,911	67,945
35–39	5,853	5,847	5,899	6,021	6,470	6,952	37,042
≥40	2,238	2,330	2,558	2,415	2,441	2,598	14,580
Unknown	657	3,127	604	564	3	12	4,967

Source: **Texas Department of State Health Services.**

Texas Abortion by Race 2001–2006

	Race						
Year	*Asian*	*Hispanic*	*White*	*Black*	*Nat. Amer.*	*Other*	*Unknown*
2001	3,121	27,102	26,081	15,590	112	900	1,595
2002	2,773	28,183	26,240	16,458	100	622	1,902
2003	2,971	27,502	26,843	16,249	99	597	1,758
2004	2,962	26,341	25,020	16,436	78	349	1,255
2005	2,953	26,657	25,827	17,503	100	262	1,097
2006	3,041	28,558	26,925	18,554	204	1,362	397
Total	17,821	164,343	156,936	100,790	693	4,092	8,004

Source: **Texas Department of State Health Services.**

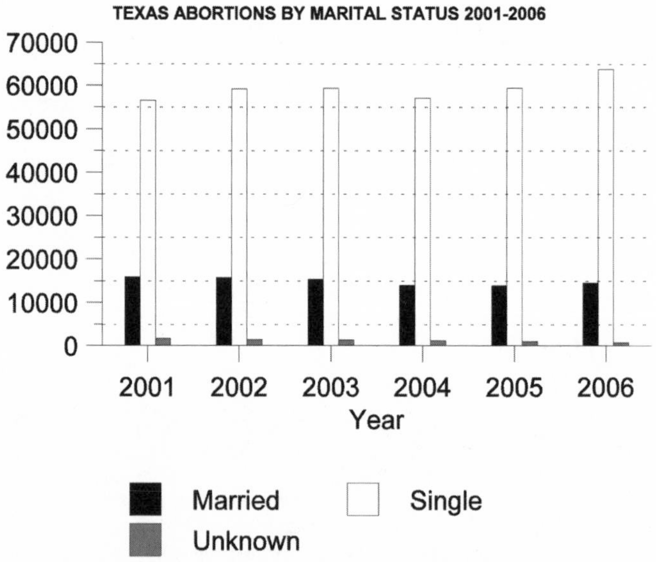

Source: **Texas Department of State Health Services.**

Texas Civ. St. Art. 4512.5. Destroying unborn child

Whoever shall during parturition of the mother destroy the vitality or life in a child in a state of being born and before actual birth, which child would otherwise have been born alive, shall be confined in the penitentiary for life or for not less than five years.

(3) GENERAL ABORTION GUIDELINES

Texas prohibits post-viability abortion unless it is necessary to prevent death or serious physical or mental harm to the woman. The state also permits post-viability abortion if the fetus has a severe defect. Texas requires abortions be performed by a physician. The statutes addressing the matters are set out below.

Texas Abortion by Weeks of Gestation 2001–2006

Weeks of Gestation	Year *2000*	*2001*	*2002*	*2003*	*2004*	*2005*	*2006*	*Total*
<9	45,211	47,177	47,422	49,409	52,218	55,928	297,365	
9–10	13,413	12,852	12,701	11,257	10,679	10,965	71,867	
11–12	6,760	6,992	6,917	5,699	5,496	5,550	37,414	
13–14	3,611	3,536	3,609	3,336	3,187	3,492	20,771	
15–16	2,019	2,073	2,000	1,774	1,667	1,748	11,281	
17–20	1,818	2,163	2,016	226	712	810	7,745	
21–25	646	769	779	159	400	534	3,287	
≥26	58	43	45	13	32	10	201	
Not known	565	673	530	568	8	4	2,348	

Source: **Texas Department of State Health Services.**

Texas Prior Abortion by Female 2001–2006

Year	Prior Abortion *None*	*1*	*2*	*3*	*4*	*≥5*	*Not known*
2001	43,174	20,234	6,918	2,216	769	574	216
2002	44,172	20,322	7,513	2,415	849	684	323
2003	43,718	20,341	7,456	2,523	831	659	491
2004	40,544	20,020	7,576	2,609	916	593	183
2005	41,764	20,556	7,850	2,670	894	628	37
2006	45,530	21,255	7,885	2,664	928	702	77
Total	258,902	122,728	45,198	15,097	5,187	3,840	1,327

Source: **Texas Department of State Health Services.**

Texas Health & Safety Code § 170.001. Definitions

In this chapter:

(1) "Abortion" means an act involving the use of an instrument, medicine, drug, or other substance or device developed to terminate the pregnancy of a woman if the act is done with an intention other than to:

(A) increase the probability of a live birth of the unborn child of the woman;

(B) preserve the life or health of the child; or

(C) remove a dead fetus.

(2) "Physician" means an individual licensed to practice medicine in this state.

(3) "Viable" means the stage of fetal development when, in the medical judgment of the attending physician based on the particular facts of the case, an unborn child possesses the capacity to live outside its mother's womb after its premature birth from any cause. The term does not include a fetus whose biparietal diameter is less than 60 millimeters.

Texas Health & Safety Code § 170.002.
Post-viability abortion ban

(a) Except as provided by Subsection (b), a person may not intentionally or knowingly perform an abortion on a woman who is pregnant with a viable unborn child during the third trimester of the pregnancy.

(b) Subsection (a) does not prohibit a person from performing an abortion if at the time of the abortion the person is a physician and concludes in good faith according to the physician's best medical judgment that:

(1) the fetus is not a viable fetus and the pregnancy is not in the third trimester;

(2) the abortion is necessary to prevent the death or a substantial risk of serious impairment to the physical or mental health of the woman; or

(3) the fetus has a severe and irreversible abnormality, identified by reliable diagnostic procedures.

(c) A physician who performs an abortion that, according to the physician's best medical judgment at the time of the abortion, is to abort a viable unborn child during the third trimester of the pregnancy shall certify in writing to the department, on a form prescribed by the department, the medical indications supporting the physician's judgment that the abortion was authorized by Subsection (b)(2) or (3). The certification must be made not later than the 30th day after the date the abortion was performed.

Texas Health & Safety Code § 171.003. Physician only

An abortion may be performed only by a physician licensed to practice medicine in this state.

Texas Health & Safety Code § 171.004.
Abortion after 16 weeks

An abortion of a fetus age 16 weeks or more may be performed only at an ambulatory surgical center or hospital licensed to perform the abortion.

(4) INFORMED CONSENT

Texas requires that a woman be fully informed of the procedure to be used, the risks involved and alternatives to abortion. An abortion may not take place until 24 hours after a woman has been given the required statutory information. The statutes addressing the matters are set out below.

Texas Health & Safety Code § 171.001. Short title

This chapter may be called the Woman's Right to Know Act.

Texas Health & Safety Code § 171.002. Definition

In this chapter, "abortion" means the use of any means to terminate the pregnancy of a female known by the attending physician to be pregnant with the intention that the termination of the pregnancy by those means will, with reasonable likelihood, cause the death of the fetus.

Texas Health & Safety Code § 171.011.
Informed consent required

A person may not perform an abortion without the voluntary and informed consent of the woman on whom the abortion is to be performed.

Texas Health & Safety Code § 171. 012.
Consent and waiting period

(a) Except in the case of a medical emergency, consent to an abortion is voluntary and informed only if:

(1) the physician who is to perform the abortion or the referring physician informs the woman on whom the abortion is to be performed of:

(A) the name of the physician who will perform the abortion;

(B) the particular medical risks associated with the particular abortion procedure to be employed, including, when medically accurate:

(i) the risks of infection and hemorrhage;

(ii) the potential danger to a subsequent pregnancy and of infertility; and

(iii) the possibility of increased risk of breast cancer following an induced abortion and the natural protective effect of a completed pregnancy in avoiding breast cancer;

(C) the probable gestational age of the unborn child at the time the abortion is to be performed; and

(D) the medical risks associated with carrying the child to term;

(2) the physician who is to perform the abortion or the physician's agent informs the woman that:

(A) medical assistance benefits may be available for prenatal care, childbirth, and neonatal care;

(B) the father is liable for assistance in the support of the child without regard to whether the father has offered to pay for the abortion;

(C) public and private agencies provide pregnancy prevention counseling and medical referrals for obtaining pregnancy prevention medications or devices, including emergency contraception for victims of rape or incest; and

(D) the woman has the right to review the printed materials described by Section 171.014, that those materials have been provided by the Texas Department of Health and are accessible on an Internet website sponsored by the department, and that the materials describe the unborn child and list agencies that offer alternatives to abortion;

(3) the woman certifies in writing before the abortion is performed that the information described by Subdivisions (1) and (2) has been provided to her and that she has been informed of her opportunity to review the information described by Section 171.014; and

(4) before the abortion is performed, the physician who is to perform the abortion receives a copy of the written certification required by Subdivision (3).

(b) The information required to be provided under Subsections (a)(1) and (2) must be provided:

(1) orally by telephone or in person; and

(2) at least 24 hours before the abortion is to be performed.

(c) When providing the information under Subsection (a)(2)(D), the physician or the physician's agent must provide the woman with the address of the Internet website on which the printed materials described by Section 171.014 may be viewed as required by Section 171.014(e).

(d) The information provided to the woman under Subsection (a)(2)(B) must include, based on information available from the Office of the Attorney General and the United States Department of Health and Human Services Office of Child Support Enforcement for the three-year period preceding the publication of the information, information regarding the statistical likelihood of collecting child support.

(e) The department is not required to republish informational materials described by Subsection (a)(2)(B) because of a change in information described by Subsection (d) unless the statistical information in the materials changes by five percent or more.

Texas Health & Safety Code § 171.013.
Distribution of materials

(a) If the woman chooses to view the materials described by Section 171.014, the physician or the physician's agent shall furnish copies of the materials to her at least 24 hours before the abortion is to be performed. A physician or the physician's agent may furnish the materials to the woman by mail if the materials are mailed, restricted delivery to addressee, at least 72 hours before the abortion is to be performed.

(b) A physician or the physician's agent is not required to furnish copies of the materials if the woman provides the physician with a written statement that she chooses to view the materials on the Internet website sponsored by the department.

(c) The physician and the physician's agent may disassociate themselves from the materials and may choose to comment on the materials or to refrain from commenting.

Texas Health & Safety Code § 171.014.
Informational materials

(a) The department shall publish informational materials that include:

(1) the information required to be provided under Sections 171.012 (a)(1)(B) and (D) and (a)(2)(A), (B), and (C); and

(2) the materials required by Sections 171.015 and 171.016.

(b) The materials shall be published in:

(1) English and Spanish;

(2) an easily comprehensible form; and

(3) a typeface large enough to be clearly legible.

(c) The materials shall be available at no cost from the department on request. The department shall provide appropriate quantities of the materials to any person.

(d) The department shall annually review the materials to determine if changes to the contents of the materials are necessary. The department shall adopt rules necessary for considering and making changes to the materials.

(e) The department shall develop and maintain an Internet website to display the information required to be published under this section. In developing and maintaining the website the department shall, to the extent reasonably practicable, safeguard the website against alterations by anyone other than the department and shall monitor the website each day to prevent and correct tampering. The department shall ensure that the website does not collect or maintain information regarding access to the website.

(f) In addition to any other organization or entity, the department shall use the American College of Obstetricians and Gynecologists as the resource in developing information required to be provided under Sections 171.012(a)(1)(B) and (D), Sections 171.012(a)(2)(A), (B), and (C), and Section 171.016, and in maintaining the department's Internet website.

Texas Health & Safety Code § 171.015.
Public and private agency information

The informational materials must include either:

(1) geographically indexed materials designed to inform the woman of public and private agencies and services that:

(A) are available to assist a woman through pregnancy, childbirth, and the child's dependency, including:

(i) a comprehensive list of adoption agencies;

(ii) a description of the services the adoption agencies offer; and

(iii) a description of the manner, including telephone numbers, in which an adoption agency may be contacted;

(B) do not provide abortions or abortion-related services or make referrals to abortion providers; and

(C) are not affiliated with organizations that provide abortions or abortion-related services or make referrals to abortion providers; or

(2) a toll-free, 24-hour telephone number that may be called to obtain an oral list and description of agencies described by Subdivision (1) that are located near the caller and of the services the agencies offer.

Texas Health & Safety Code § 171.016.
Information on unborn child

(a) The informational materials must include materials designed to inform the woman of the probable anatomical and physiological characteristics of the unborn child at two-week gestational increments from the time when a woman can be known to be pregnant to full term, including any relevant information on the possibility of the unborn child's survival.

(b) The materials must include color pictures representing the development of the child at two-week gestational increments. The pictures must contain the dimensions of the unborn child and must be realistic.

(c) The materials provided under this section must be objective and nonjudgmental and be designed to convey only accurate scientific information about the unborn child at the various gestational ages.

Texas Health & Safety Code § 171.017.
Periods run concurrently

If the woman is an unemancipated minor subject to Chapter 33, Family Code, the 24-hour periods established under Sections 171.012(b) and 171.013(a) may run concurrently with the period during which actual or constructive notice is provided under Section 33.002, Family Code.

Texas Health & Safety Code § 171.018. Offense

A physician who intentionally performs an abortion on a woman in violation of this subchapter commits an offense. An offense under this section is a misdemeanor punishable by a fine not to exceed $10,000. In this section, "intentionally" has the meaning assigned by Section 6.03(a), Penal Code.

(5) ABORTION BY MINORS

Under the laws of Texas no physician may perform an abortion upon an unemancipated minor, until 48 hours after notice of the operation has been given to either parent or a legal guardian of the minor. In compliance with federal constitutional law, Texas has provided a judicial waiver procedure for an unemancipated minor to obtain an abortion without parental or guardian notice. The minor may petition a trial court for a waiver of the notice requirement. A minor has a right to an attorney at the proceeding and if she cannot afford one, the court must appoint her an attorney. If a minor chooses, she may represent herself. The required parental or guardian notice may be waived if the court finds either (1) that the minor is mature and well-informed enough to make the abortion decision on her own, (2) that notification would not be in the best interest of the minor, or (3) that notification may lead to physical, sexual, or emotional abuse of the minor. An expedited appeal is available to any minor to whom the court denies a waiver of notice. The statutes are set out below.

Texas Family Code § 33.001. Definitions

In this chapter:

(1) "Abortion" means the use of any means to terminate the pregnancy of a female known by the attending physician to be pregnant, with the intention that the termination of the pregnancy by those means will with reasonable likelihood cause the death of the fetus. This definition, as applied in this chapter, applies only to an unemancipated minor known by the attending physician to be pregnant and may not be construed to limit a minor's access to contraceptives.

(2) "Fetus" means an individual human organism from fertilization until birth.

(3) "Guardian" means a court-appointed guardian of the person of the minor.

(4) "Physician" means an individual licensed to practice medicine in this state.

(5) "Unemancipated minor" includes a minor who:

(A) is unmarried; and

(B) has not had the disabilities of minority removed under Chapter 31.

Texas Family Code § 33.002. Notice and waiting period

(a) A physician may not perform an abortion on a pregnant unemancipated minor unless:

(1) the physician performing the abortion gives at least 48 hours actual notice, in person or by telephone, of the physician's intent to perform the abortion to:

(A) a parent of the minor, if the minor has no managing conservator or guardian; or

(B) a court-appointed managing conservator or guardian;

(2) the judge of a court having probate jurisdiction, the judge of a county court at law, the judge of a district court, including a family district court, or a court of appellate jurisdiction issues an order authorizing the minor to consent to the abortion as provided by Section 33.003 or 33.004;

(3) a probate court, county court at law, district court, including a family district court, or court of appeals, by its inaction, constructively authorizes the minor to consent to the abortion as provided by Section 33.003 or 33.004; or

(4) the physician performing the abortion:

(A) concludes that on the basis of the physician's good faith clinical judgment, a condition exists that complicates the medical condition of the pregnant minor and necessitates the immediate abortion of her pregnancy to avert her death or to avoid a serious risk of substantial and irreversible impairment of a major bodily function; and

(B) certifies in writing to the Texas Department of Health and in the patient's medical record the medical indications supporting the physician's judgment that the circumstances described by Paragraph (A) exist.

(b) If a person to whom notice may be given under Subsection (a)(1) cannot be notified after a reasonable effort, a physician may perform an abortion if the physician gives 48 hours constructive notice, by certified mail, restricted delivery, sent to the last known address, to the person to whom notice may be given under Subsection (a)(1). The period under this subsection begins when the notice is mailed. If the person required to be notified is not notified within the 48-hour period, the abortion may proceed even if the notice by mail is not received.

(c) The requirement that 48 hours actual notice be provided under this section may be waived by an affidavit of:

(1) a parent of the minor, if the minor has no managing conservator or guardian; or

(2) a court-appointed managing conservator or guardian.

(d) A physician may execute for inclusion in the minor's medical record an affidavit stating that, according to the best information and belief of the physician, notice or constructive notice has been provided as required by this section. Execution of an affidavit under this subsection creates a presumption that the requirements of this section have been satisfied.

(e) The Texas Department of Health shall prepare a form to be used for making the certification required by Subsection (a)(4).

(f) A certification required by Subsection (a)(4) is confidential and privileged and is not subject to disclosure under Chapter 552, Government Code, or to discovery, subpoena, or other legal process. Personal or identifying information about the minor, including her name, address, or social security number, may not be included in a certification under Subsection (a)(4). The physician must keep the medical records on the minor in compliance with the rules adopted by the Texas State Board of Medical Examiners under Section 153.003, Occupations Code.

(g) A physician who intentionally performs an abortion on a pregnant unemancipated minor in violation of this section commits an offense. An offense under this subsection is punishable by a fine not to exceed $10,000. In this subsection, "intentionally" has the meaning assigned by Section 6.03(a), Penal Code.

(h) It is a defense to prosecution under this section that the minor falsely represented her age or identity to the physician to be at least 18 years of age by displaying an apparently valid governmental record of identification such that a reasonable person under similar circumstances would have relied on the representation. The defense does not apply if the physician is shown to have had independent knowledge of the minor's actual age or identity or failed to use due diligence in determining the minor's age or identity. In this subsection, "defense" has the meaning and application assigned by Section 2.03, Penal Code.

(i) In relation to the trial of an offense under this section in which the conduct charged involves a conclusion made by the physician under Subsection (a)(4), the defendant may seek a hearing before the Texas State Board of Medical Examiners on whether the physician's conduct was necessary to avert the death of the minor or to avoid a serious risk of substantial and irreversible impairment of a major bodily function. The findings of the Texas State Board of Medical Examiners under this subsection are admissible on that issue in the trial of the defendant. Notwithstanding any other reason for a continuance provided under the Code of Criminal Procedure or other law, on motion of the defendant, the court

shall delay the beginning of the trial for not more than 30 days to permit a hearing under this subsection to take place.

Texas Family Code § 33.003. Judicial bypass

(a) A pregnant minor who wishes to have an abortion without notification to one of her parents, her managing conservator, or her guardian may file an application for a court order authorizing the minor to consent to the performance of an abortion without notification to either of her parents or a managing conservator or guardian.

(b) The application may be filed in any county court at law, court having probate jurisdiction, or district court, including a family district court, in this state.

(c) The application must be made under oath and include:

(1) a statement that the minor is pregnant;

(2) a statement that the minor is unmarried, is under 18 years of age, and has not had her disabilities removed under Chapter 31;

(3) a statement that the minor wishes to have an abortion without the notification of either of her parents or a managing conservator or guardian; and

(4) a statement as to whether the minor has retained an attorney and, if she has retained an attorney, the name, address, and telephone number of her attorney.

(d) The clerk of the court shall deliver a courtesy copy of the application made under this section to the judge who is to hear the application.

(e) The court shall appoint a guardian ad litem for the minor. If the minor has not retained an attorney, the court shall appoint an attorney to represent the minor. If the guardian ad litem is an attorney admitted to the practice of law in this state, the court may appoint the guardian ad litem to serve as the minor's attorney.

(f) The court may appoint to serve as guardian ad litem:

(1) a person who may consent to treatment for the minor under Sections 32.001(a)(1)-(3);

(2) a psychiatrist or an individual licensed or certified as a psychologist under Chapter 501, Occupations Code;

(3) an appropriate employee of the Department of Protective and Regulatory Services;

(4) a member of the clergy; or

(5) another appropriate person selected by the court.

(g) The court shall fix a time for a hearing on an application filed under Subsection (a) and shall keep a record of all testimony and other oral proceedings in the action. The court shall enter judgment on the application immediately after the hearing is concluded.

(h) The court shall rule on an application submitted under this section and shall issue written findings of fact and conclusions of law not later than 5 p.m. on the second business day after the date the application is filed with the court. On request by the minor, the court shall grant an extension of the period specified by this subsection. If a request for an extension is made, the court shall rule on an application and shall issue written findings of fact and conclusions of law not later than 5 p.m. on the second business day after the date the minor states she is ready to proceed to hearing. If the court fails to rule on the application and issue written findings of fact and conclusions of law within the period specified by this subsection, the application is deemed to be granted and the physician may perform the abortion as if the court had issued an order authorizing the minor to consent to the performance of the abortion without notification under Section 33.002. Proceedings under this section shall be given precedence over other pending matters to the extent necessary to assure that the court reaches a decision promptly.

(i) The court shall determine by a preponderance of the evidence whether the minor is mature and sufficiently well informed to make the decision to have an abortion performed without notification to either of her parents or a managing conservator or guardian, whether notification would not be in the best interest of the minor, or whether notification may lead to physical, sexual, or emotional abuse of the minor. If the court finds that the minor is mature and sufficiently well informed, that notification would not be in the minor's best interest, or that notification may lead to physical, sexual, or emotional abuse of the minor, the court shall enter an order authorizing the minor to consent to the performance of the abortion without notification to either of her parents or a managing conservator or guardian and shall execute the required forms.

(j) If the court finds that the minor does not meet the requirements of Subsection (i), the court may not authorize the minor to consent to an abortion without the notification authorized under Section 33.002(a)(1).

(k) The court may not notify a parent, managing conservator, or guardian that the minor is pregnant or that the minor wants to have an abortion. The court proceedings shall be conducted in a manner that protects the anonymity of the minor. The application and all other court documents pertaining to the proceedings are confidential and privileged and are not subject to disclosure under Chapter 552, Government Code, or to discovery, subpoena, or other legal process. The minor may file the application using a pseudonym or using only her initials.

(l) An order of the court issued under this section is confidential and privileged and is not subject to disclosure under Chapter 552, Government Code, or discovery, subpoena, or other legal process. The order may not be released to any person but the pregnant minor, the pregnant minor's guardian ad litem, the pregnant minor's attorney, another person designated to receive the order by the minor, or a governmental agency or attorney in a criminal or administrative action seeking to assert or protect the interest of the minor. The supreme court may adopt rules to permit confidential docketing of an application under this section.

(m) The clerk of the supreme court shall prescribe the application form to be used by the minor filing an application under this section.

(n) A filing fee is not required of and court costs may not be assessed against a minor filing an application under this section.

Texas Family Code § 33.004. Appeal

(a) A minor whose application under Section 33.003 is denied may appeal to the court of appeals having jurisdiction over civil matters in the county in which the application was filed. On receipt of a notice of appeal, the clerk of the court that denied the application shall deliver a copy of the notice of appeal and record on appeal to the clerk of the court of appeals. On receipt of the notice and record, the clerk of the court of appeals shall place the appeal on the docket of the court.

(b) The court of appeals shall rule on an appeal under this section not later than 5 p.m. on the second business day after the date the notice of appeal is filed with the court that denied the application. On request by the minor, the court shall grant an extension of the period specified by this subsection. If a request for an extension is made, the court shall rule on the appeal not later than 5 p.m. on the second business day after the date the minor states she is ready to proceed. If the court of appeals fails to rule on the appeal within the period specified by this subsection, the appeal is deemed to be granted and the physician may perform the abortion as if the court had issued an order authorizing the minor to consent to the performance of the abortion without notification under Section 33.002. Proceedings under this section shall be given precedence over other pending matters to the extent necessary to assure that the court reaches a decision promptly.

(c) A ruling of the court of appeals issued under this section is confidential and privileged and is not subject to disclosure under Chapter 552, Government Code, or discovery, subpoena, or other legal process. The ruling may not be released to any person but the pregnant minor, the pregnant minor's guardian ad litem, the pregnant minor's attorney, another person designated to receive the ruling by the minor, or a governmental agency or attorney in a criminal or administrative action seeking to assert or protect the interest of the minor. The supreme court may adopt rules to permit confidential docketing of an appeal under this section.

(d) The clerk of the supreme court shall prescribe the notice of appeal form to be used by the minor appealing a judgment under this section.

(e) A filing fee is not required of and court costs may not be assessed against a minor filing an appeal under this section.

(f) An expedited confidential appeal shall be available to any pregnant minor to whom a court of appeals denies an order authorizing the minor to consent to the performance of an abortion without notification to either of her parents or a managing conservator or guardian.

Texas Family Code § 33.005. Affidavit of physician

(a) A physician may execute for inclusion in the minor's medical record an affidavit stating that, after reasonable inquiry, it is the belief of the physician that:

(1) the minor has made an application or filed a notice of an appeal with a court under this chapter;

(2) the deadline for court action imposed by this chapter has passed; and

(3) the physician has been notified that the court has not denied the application or appeal.

(b) A physician who in good faith has executed an affidavit under Subsection (a) may rely on the affidavit and may perform the abortion as if the court had issued an order granting the application or appeal.

Texas Family Code § 33.006. Guardian ad litem immunity

A guardian ad litem appointed under this chapter and acting in the course and scope of the appointment is not liable for damages arising from an act or omission of the guardian ad litem committed in good faith. The immunity granted by this section does not apply if the conduct of the guardian ad litem is committed in a manner described by Sections 107.003(b)(1)-(4).

Texas Family Code § 33.007. Costs

(a) A court acting under Section 33.003 or 33.004 may issue an order requiring the state to pay:

(1) the cost of any attorney ad litem and any guardian ad litem appointed for the minor;

(2) notwithstanding Sections 33.003(n) and 33.004(e), the costs of court associated with the application or appeal; and

(3) any court reporter's fees incurred.

(b) An order issued under Subsection (a) must be directed to the comptroller, who shall pay the amount ordered from funds appropriated to the Texas Department of Health.

Texas Family Code § 33.008. Duty to report abuse of a minor

(a) A physician who has reason to believe that a minor has been or may be physically or sexually abused by a person responsible for the minor's care, custody, or welfare, as that term is defined by Section 261.001, shall immediately report the suspected abuse to the Department of Protective and Regulatory Services and shall refer the minor to the department for services or intervention that may be in the best interest of the minor.

(b) The Department of Protective and Regulatory Services shall investigate suspected abuse reported under this section and, if appropriate, shall assist the minor in making an application with a court under Section 33.003.

Texas Family Code § 33.009.
Other reports of sexual abuse of a minor

A court or the guardian ad litem or attorney ad litem for the minor shall report conduct reasonably believed to violate Section 21.02, 22.011, 22.021, or 25.02, Penal Code, based on information obtained during a confidential court proceeding held under this chapter to:

(1) any local or state law enforcement agency;

(2) the Department of Family and Protective Services, if the alleged conduct involves a person responsible for the care, custody, or welfare of the child;

(3) the state agency that operates, licenses, certifies, or registers the facility in which the alleged conduct occurred, if the alleged conduct occurred in a facility operated, licensed, certified, or registered by a state agency; or

(4) an appropriate agency designated by the court.

Texas Family Code § 33.010. Confidentiality

Notwithstanding any other law, information obtained by the Department of Family and Protective Services or another entity under Section 33.008 or 33.009 is confidential except to the extent necessary to prove a violation of Section 21.02, 22. 011, 22.021, or 25.02, Penal Code.

Texas Family Code § 33.011.
Information relating to judicial bypass

The Texas Department of Health shall produce and distribute informational materials that explain the rights of a minor under this chapter. The materials must explain the procedures established by Sections 33.003 and 33.004 and must be made available in English and in Spanish. The material provided by the department shall also provide information relating to alternatives to abortion and health risks associated with abortion.

(6) USE OF FACILITIES AND PEOPLE

Under the laws of Texas private hospitals are not required to allow abortions at their facilities, unless the pregnant woman's life is endanger. The employees and physicians at medical facilities that do allow abortions are permitted to refuse to take part in abortions. The statutes addressing the matter are set out below.

Texas Occupations Code § 103.001. Medical personnel

A physician, nurse, staff member, or employee of a hospital or other health care facility who objects to directly or indirectly performing or participating in an abortion procedure may not be required to directly or indirectly perform or participate in the procedure.

Texas Occupations Code § 103.002. Discrimination prohibited

(a) A hospital or health care facility may not discriminate against a physician, nurse, staff member, or employee, or an applicant for one of those positions, who refuses to perform or participate in an abortion procedure.

(b) A hospital or health care facility may not discriminate against a physician, nurse, staff member, or employee because of the person's willingness to participate in an abortion procedure at another facility.

(c) An educational institution may not discriminate against an applicant for admission or employment as a student, intern, or resident because of the applicant's attitude concerning abortion.

Texas Occupations Code § 103.003. Remedies

A person whose rights under this chapter are violated may sue a hospital, health care facility, or educational institution in district court in the county where the hospital, facility, or institution is located for:

(1) an injunction against any further violation;

(2) appropriate affirmative relief, including admission or reinstatement of employment with back pay plus 10 percent interest; and

(3) any other relief necessary to ensure compliance with this chapter.

Texas Occupations Code § 103.004. Medical facilities

A private hospital or private health care facility is not required to make its facilities available for the performance of an abortion unless a physician determines that the life of the mother is immediately endangered.

(7) ABORTION FACILITY REQUIREMENTS

Texas has established detailed requirements for the operation of abortion facilities. The statutes addressing the matter are set out below.

Texas Health & Safety Code § 245.001. Short title

This chapter may be cited as the Texas Abortion Facility Reporting and Licensing Act.

Texas Health & Safety Code § 245.002. Definitions

In this chapter:

(1) "Abortion" means an act or procedure performed after pregnancy has been medically verified and with the intent to cause the termination of a pregnancy other than for the purpose of either the birth of a live fetus or removing a dead fetus. The term does not include birth control devices or oral contraceptives.

(2) "Abortion facility" means a place where abortions are performed.

(3) "Board" means the Texas Board of Health.

(4) "Department" means the Texas Department of Health.

(5) "Patient" means a female on whom an abortion is performed, but does not include a fetus.

(6) "Person" means an individual, firm, partnership, corporation, or association.

Texas Health & Safety Code § 245.003. License required

(a) Except as provided by Section 245.004, a person may not establish or operate an abortion facility in this state without an appropriate license issued under this chapter.

(b) Each abortion facility must have a separate license.

(c) A license is not transferable or assignable.

Texas Health & Safety Code § 245.004. Exemptions

(a) The following facilities need not be licensed under this chapter:

(1) a hospital licensed under Chapter 241 (Texas Hospital Licensing Law);

(2) the office of a physician licensed under Subtitle B, Title 3, Occupations Code, unless the office is used substantially for the purpose of performing abortions; or

(3) an ambulatory surgical center licensed under Chapter 243.

(b) For purposes of this section, a facility is used substantially for the purpose of performing abortions if the facility:

(1) is a provider for performing:

(A) at least 10 abortion procedures during any month; or

(B) at least 100 abortion procedures in a year;

(2) operates less than 20 days in a month and the facility, in any month, is a provider for performing a number of abortion procedures that would be equivalent to at least 10 procedures in a month if the facility were operating at least 20 days in a month;

(3) holds itself out to the public as an abortion provider by advertising by any public means, including advertising placed in a newspaper, telephone directory, magazine, or electronic medium, that the facility performs abortions; or

(4) applies for an abortion facility license.

(c) For purposes of this section, an abortion facility is operating if the facility is open for any period of time during a day and has on site at the facility or on call a physician available to perform abortions.

Texas Health & Safety Code § 245.005. License application

(a) An applicant for an abortion facility license must submit an application to the department on a form prescribed by the department.

(b) Each application must be accompanied by a nonrefundable license fee in an amount set by the board.

(c) The application must contain evidence that there are one or more physicians on the staff of the facility who are licensed by the Texas State Board of Medical Examiners.

(d) The department shall issue a license if, after inspection and investigation, it finds that the applicant and the abortion facility meet the requirements of this chapter and the standards adopted under this chapter.

(e) As a condition for renewal of a license, the licensee must submit to the department the annual license renewal fee and an annual report, including the report required under Section 245.011.

(f) Information regarding the licensing status of an abortion facility is an open record for the purposes of Chapter 552, Government Code, and shall be made available by the department on request.

Texas Health & Safety Code § 245.006. Inspections

(a) The department may inspect an abortion facility at reasonable times as necessary to ensure compliance with this chapter.

(b) The department shall inspect an abortion facility before renewing the facility's license under Section 245.005(e).

Texas Health & Safety Code § 245.007. Fees

The board shall set fees imposed by this chapter in amounts reasonable and necessary to defray the cost of administering this chapter and Chapter 171.

Texas Health & Safety Code § 245.008.
Abortion facility licensing fund

All fees collected under this chapter shall be deposited in the state treasury to the credit of the abortion facility licensing fund and may be appropriated to the department only to administer and enforce this chapter.

Texas Health & Safety Code § 245.009. Adoption of rules

The board shall adopt rules necessary to implement this chapter, including requirements for the issuance, renewal, denial, suspension, and revocation of a license to operate an abortion facility.

Texas Health & Safety Code § 245.010. Minimum standards

(a) The rules must contain minimum standards to protect the health and safety of a patient of an abortion facility and must contain provisions requiring compliance with the requirements of Subchapter B, Chapter 171.

(b) Only a physician as defined by Subtitle B, Title 3, Occupations Code, may perform an abortion.

(c) The standards may not be more stringent than Medicare certification standards, if any, for:

(1) qualifications for professional and nonprofessional personnel;

(2) supervision of professional and nonprofessional personnel;

(3) medical treatment and medical services provided by an abortion facility and the coordination of treatment and services, including quality assurance;

(4) sanitary and hygienic conditions within an abortion facility;

(5) the equipment essential to the health and welfare of the patients;

(6) clinical records kept by an abortion facility; and

(7) management, ownership, and control of the facility.

(d) This section does not authorize the board to:

(1) establish the qualifications of a licensed practitioner; or

(2) permit a person to provide health care services who is not authorized to provide those services under other laws of this state.

Texas Health & Safety Code § 245.0105. Identifying number

(a) The department shall assign to each abortion facility a unique license number that may not change during the period the facility is operating in this state.

(b) An abortion facility shall include the unique license number assigned to the facility by the department in any abortion advertisement directly relating to the provision of abortion services at the facility.

(c) In this section, "abortion advertisement" means:

(1) any communication that advertises the availability of abortion services at an abortion facility and that is disseminated through a public medium, including an advertisement in a newspaper or other publication or an advertisement on television, radio, or any other electronic medium; or

(2) any commercial use of the name of the facility as a provider of

abortion services, including the use of the name in a directory, listing, or pamphlet.

Texas Health & Safety Code § 245.011.
Reporting requirements

(a) Each abortion facility must submit an annual report to the department on each abortion that is performed at the abortion facility. The report must be submitted on a form provided by the department.

(b) The report may not identify by any means the physician performing the abortion or the patient.

(c) The report must include:

(1) whether the abortion facility at which the abortion is performed is licensed under this chapter;

(2) the patient's year of birth, race, marital status, and state and county of residence;

(3) the type of abortion procedure;

(4) the date the abortion was performed;

(5) whether the patient survived the abortion, and if the patient did not survive, the cause of death;

(6) the period of gestation based on the best medical judgment of the attending physician at the time of the procedure;

(7) the date, if known, of the patient's last menstrual cycle;

(8) the number of previous live births of the patient; and

(9) the number of previous induced abortions of the patient.

(d) Except as provided by Section 245.023, all information and records held by the department under this chapter are confidential and are not open records for the purposes of Chapter 552, Government Code. That information may not be released or made public on subpoena or otherwise, except that release may be made:

(1) for statistical purposes, but only if a person, patient, or abortion facility is not identified;

(2) with the consent of each person, patient, and abortion facility identified in the information released;

(3) to medical personnel, appropriate state agencies, or county and district courts to enforce this chapter; or

(4) to appropriate state licensing boards to enforce state licensing laws.

(e) A person commits an offense if the person violates this section. An offense under this subsection is a Class A misdemeanor.

Texas Health & Safety Code § 245.012.
Denial or suspension of license

(a) The department may deny, suspend, or revoke a license for a violation of this chapter or a rule adopted under this chapter.

(b) The denial, suspension, or revocation of a license by the department and the appeal from that action are governed by the procedures for a contested case hearing under Chapter 2001, Government Code.

(c) The department may immediately suspend or revoke a license when the health and safety of persons are threatened. If the department issues an order of immediate suspension or revocation, the department shall immediately give the chief executive officer of the abortion facility adequate notice of the action and the procedure governing appeal of the action. A person whose license is suspended or revoked under this subsection is entitled to a hearing not later than the 14th day after the effective date of the suspension or revocation.

(d) If the department finds that an abortion facility is in repeated noncompliance with this chapter or rules adopted under this chapter but that the noncompliance does not in any way involve the health and safety of the public or an individual, the department may schedule the facility for probation rather than suspending or revoking the facility's license. The department shall provide notice to the facility of the probation and of the items of noncompliance not later than the 10th day before the date the probation period begins. The department shall designate a period of not less than 30 days during which the facility will remain under probation. During the probation period, the facility must correct the items that were in noncompliance and report the corrections to the department for approval.

(e) The department may suspend or revoke the license of an abortion facility that does not correct items that were in noncompliance or that does not comply with this chapter or the rules adopted under this chapter within the applicable probation period.

Texas Health & Safety Code § 245.013. Injunction

(a) The department may petition a district court for a temporary restraining order to restrain a continuing violation of the standards or licensing requirements provided under this chapter if the department finds that the violation creates an immediate threat to the health and safety of the patients of an abortion facility.

(b) A district court, on petition of the department and on a finding by the court that a person is violating the standards or licensing requirements provided under this chapter, may by injunction:

(1) prohibit a person from continuing a violation of the standards or licensing requirements provided under this chapter;

(2) restrain or prevent the establishment or operation of an abortion facility without a license issued under this chapter; or

(3) grant any other injunctive relief warranted by the facts.

(c) The attorney general may institute and conduct a suit authorized by this section at the request of the department.

(d) Venue for a suit brought under this section is in the county in which the abortion facility is located or in Travis County.

Texas Health & Safety Code § 245.014. Criminal penalty

(a) A person commits an offense if the person violates Section 245.003(a).

(b) An offense under this section is a Class A misdemeanor.

(c) Each day of a continuing violation constitutes a separate offense.

Texas Health & Safety Code § 245.015. Civil penalty

(a) A person who knowingly violates this chapter or who knowingly fails to comply with a rule adopted under this chapter is liable for a civil penalty of not less than $100 or more than $500 for each violation if the department determines the violation threatens the health and safety of a patient.

(b) Each day of a continuing violation constitutes a separate ground for recovery.

Texas Health & Safety Code § 245.016.
Abortion to prevent death or impairment

This chapter does not remove the responsibility or limit the ability of a physician to perform an abortion in an unlicensed abortion facility if, at the commencement of the abortion, the physician reasonably believes that the abortion is necessary to prevent the death of the patient or to prevent serious impairment of the patient's physical health.

Texas Health & Safety Code § 245.017. Administrative penalty

(a) The department may assess an administrative penalty against a person who violates this chapter or a rule adopted under this chapter.

(b) The penalty may not exceed $1,000 for each violation. Each day of a continuing violation constitutes a separate violation.

(c) In determining the amount of an administrative penalty assessed under this section, the department shall consider:

(1) the seriousness of the violation;

(2) the history of previous violations;

(3) the amount necessary to deter future violations;

(4) efforts made to correct the violation; and

(5) any other matters that justice may require.

(d) All proceedings for the assessment of an administrative penalty under this chapter are subject to Chapter 2001, Government Code.

Texas Health & Safety Code § 245.018.
Report recommending penalty

(a) If, after investigation of a possible violation and the facts surrounding that possible violation, the department determines that a violation has occurred, the department shall give written notice of the violation to the person alleged to have committed the violation. The notice shall include:

(1) a brief summary of the alleged violation;

(2) a statement of the amount of the proposed penalty, based on the factors listed in Section 245.017(c); and

(3) a statement of the person's right to a hearing on the occurrence of the violation, the amount of the penalty, or both the occurrence of the violation and the amount of the penalty.

(b) Not later than the 20th day after the date the notice is received, the person notified may accept the determination of the department made under this section, including the recommended penalty, or make a written request for a hearing on that determination.

(c) If the person notified of the violation accepts the determination of the department, the commissioner of public health or the commissioner's designee shall issue an order approving the determination and ordering the person to pay the recommended penalty.

Texas Health & Safety Code § 245.019. Hearing

(a) If the person requests a hearing, the commissioner of public health or the commissioner's designee shall:

(1) set a hearing;

(2) give written notice of the hearing to the person; and

(3) designate a hearings examiner to conduct the hearing.

(b) The hearings examiner shall make findings of fact and conclusions of law and shall promptly issue to the commissioner a proposal for decision as to the occurrence of the violation and a recommendation as to the amount of the proposed penalty, if a penalty is determined to be warranted.

(c) Based on the findings of fact and conclusions of law and the recommendations of the hearings examiner, the commissioner by order may find that a violation has occurred and may assess a penalty or may find that no violation has occurred.

Texas Health & Safety Code § 245.020.
Notice and payment of penalty

(a) The commissioner of public health or the commissioner's designee shall give notice of the commissioner's order under Section 245.019(c) to the person alleged to have committed the violation. The notice must include:

(1) separate statements of the findings of fact and conclusions of law;

(2) the amount of any penalty assessed; and

(3) a statement of the right of the person to judicial review of the commissioner's order.

(b) Not later than the 30th day after the date the decision is final as provided by Chapter 2001, Government Code, the person shall:

(1) pay the penalty in full;

(2) pay the amount of the penalty and file a petition for judicial review contesting the occurrence of the violation, the amount of the penalty, or both the occurrence of the violation and the amount of the penalty; or

(3) without paying the amount of the penalty, file a petition for judicial review contesting the occurrence of the violation, the amount of the penalty, or both the occurrence of the violation and the amount of the penalty.

(c) Within the 30-day period, a person who acts under Subsection (b)(3) may:

(1) stay enforcement of the penalty by:

(A) paying the amount of the penalty to the court for placement in an escrow account; or

(B) giving to the court a supersedeas bond that is approved by the court for the amount of the penalty and that is effective until all judicial review of the commissioner's order is final; or

(2) request the court to stay enforcement of the penalty by:

(A) filing with the court a sworn affidavit of the person stating that the person is financially unable to pay the amount of the penalty and is financially unable to give the supersedeas bond; and

(B) giving a copy of the affidavit to the department by certified mail.

(d) If the department receives a copy of an affidavit under Subsection (c)(2), the department may file with the court, within five days after the date the copy is received, a contest to the affidavit. The court shall hold a hearing on the facts alleged in the affidavit as soon as practicable and shall stay the enforcement of the penalty on finding that the alleged facts are true. The person who files an affidavit has the burden of proving that the person is financially unable to pay the amount of the penalty and to give a supersedeas bond.

(e) If the person does not pay the amount of the penalty and the enforcement of the penalty is not stayed, the department may refer the matter to the attorney general for collection of the amount of the penalty.

(f) Judicial review of the order of the commissioner of public health:

(1) is instituted by filing a petition as provided by Subchapter G, Chapter 2001, Government Code; and

(2) is under the substantial evidence rule.

(g) If the court sustains the occurrence of the violation, the court may uphold or reduce the amount of the penalty and order the person to pay the full or reduced amount of the penalty. If the court does not sustain the occurrence of the violation, the court shall order that no penalty is owed.

(h) When the judgment of the court becomes final, the court shall proceed under this subsection. If the person paid the amount of the penalty and if that amount is reduced or is not upheld by the court, the court shall order that the appropriate amount plus accrued interest be remitted to the person. The rate of the interest is the rate charged on loans to depository institutions by the New York Federal Reserve Bank, and the interest shall be paid for the period beginning on the date the penalty was paid and ending on the date the penalty is remitted. If the person gave a supersedeas bond and if the amount of the penalty is not upheld by the court, the court shall order the release of the bond. If the person gave a supersedeas bond and if the amount of the penalty is reduced, the court shall order the release of the bond after the person pays the amount.

Texas Health & Safety Code § 245.021.
Penalty deposited in state treasury

A civil or administrative penalty collected under this chapter shall be deposited in the state treasury to the credit of the general revenue fund.

Texas Health & Safety Code § 245.022. Recovery of costs

(a) The department may assess reasonable expenses and costs against a person in an administrative hearing if, as a result of the hearing, the person's license is denied, suspended, or revoked or if administrative penalties are assessed against the person. The person shall pay expenses and costs assessed under this subsection not later than the 30th day after the date a board order requiring the payment of expenses and costs is final. The department may refer the matter to the attorney general for collection of the expenses and costs.

(b) If the attorney general brings an action against a person under Section 245.013 or 245.015 or an action to enforce an administrative penalty assessed under Section 245.017 and an injunction is granted against the person or the person is found liable for a civil or administrative penalty, the attorney general may recover, on behalf of the attorney general and the department, reasonable expenses and costs.

(c) For purposes of this section, "reasonable expenses and costs" include expenses incurred by the department and the attorney general in the investigation, initiation, or prosecution of an action, including rea-

sonable investigative costs, attorney's fees, witness fees, and deposition expenses.

Texas Health & Safety Code § 245.023. Public information

(a) The department on request shall make the following information available to the public:

(1) the status of the license of any abortion facility;

(2) the date of the last inspection of the facility, any violation discovered during that inspection that would pose a health risk to a patient at the facility, any challenge raised by the facility to the allegation that there was a violation, and any corrective action that is acceptable to the department and that is being undertaken by the facility with respect to the violation; and

(3) an administrative or civil penalty imposed against the facility or a physician who provides services at the facility, professional discipline imposed against a physician who provides services at the facility, and any criminal conviction of the facility or a physician who provides services at the facility that is relevant to services provided at the facility.

(b) Subsection (a) does not require the department to provide information that is not in the possession of the department. The Texas State Board of Medical Examiners shall provide to the department information in the possession of the board that the department is required to provide under Subsection (a).

(c) The department shall maintain a toll-free telephone number that a person may call to obtain the information described by Subsection (a).

(d) An abortion facility shall provide to a woman, at the time the woman initially consults the facility, a written statement indicating the number of the toll-free telephone line maintained under Subsection (c). The written statement must be available in English and Spanish and be in substantially the following form:

"(toll-free telephone number)

You have a right to access certain information concerning this abortion facility by using the toll-free telephone number listed above. If you make a call to the number, your identity will remain anonymous. The toll-free telephone line can provide you with the following information:

(1) Whether this abortion facility is licensed by the Texas Department of Health.

(2) The date of the last inspection of this facility by the Texas Department of Health and any violations of law or rules discovered during that inspection that may pose a health risk to you.

(3) Any relevant fine, penalty, or judgment rendered against this facility or a doctor who provides services at this facility."

(e) This section does not authorize the release of the name, address, or phone number of any employee or patient of an abortion facility or of a physician who provides services at an abortion facility.

(8) TERMINATION OF PARENTAL RIGHTS

Texas authorizes a state agency to take custody of a child born alive after an attempted abortion. The state also permits the termination of parental rights to a child born after an attempted abortion. The statutes addressing the matter are set out below.

Texas Family Code § 151.002. Rights of a child after abortion

(a) A living human child born alive after an abortion or premature birth is entitled to the same rights, powers, and privileges as are granted by the laws of this state to any other child born alive after the normal gestation period.

(b) In this code, "born alive" means the complete expulsion or extraction from its mother of a product of conception, irrespective of the duration of pregnancy, which, after such separation, breathes or shows any other evidence of life such as beating of the heart, pulsation of the umbilical cord, or definite movement of voluntary muscles, whether or not the umbilical cord has been cut or the placenta is attached. Each product of the birth is considered born alive.

Texas Family Code § 262.006.
Taking custody of child after abortion

(a) An authorized representative of the Department of Protective and Regulatory Services may assume the care, control, and custody of a child born alive as the result of an abortion as defined by Chapter 161.

(b) The department shall file a suit and request an emergency order under this chapter.

(c) A child for whom possession is assumed under this section need not be delivered to the court except on the order of the court.

Texas Family Code § 161.006.
Terminating parental rights after abortion

(a) A petition requesting termination of the parent-child relationship with respect to a parent who is not the petitioner may be granted if the child was born alive as the result of an abortion.

(b) In this code, "abortion" means an intentional expulsion of a human fetus from the body of a woman induced by any means for the purpose of causing the death of the fetus.

(c) The court or the jury may not terminate the parent-child relationship under this section with respect to a parent who:

(1) had no knowledge of the abortion; or

(2) participated in or consented to the abortion for the sole purpose of preventing the death of the mother.

(9) HEALTH INSURANCE

Under the laws of Texas employers are not prohibited from, nor required to provide employees health insurance benefits that cover abortion. The state also does not require health benefit plan insurers to provide reimbursement for abortions. The statutes addressing the issues are set out below.

Texas Labor Code § 21.107. Employer and abortion benefits

This chapter does not:

(1) require an employer to pay for health insurance benefits for abortion unless the life of the mother would be endangered if the fetus were carried to term;

(2) preclude an employer from providing abortion benefits; or

(3) affect a bargaining agreement relating to abortion.

Texas Insurance Code § 1454.052.
Reimbursement not required

This chapter does not require a health benefit plan issuer to provide reimbursement for an abortion, as defined by the Family Code, or for a service related to an abortion.

(10) SALE OF FETAL TISSUE

Texas prohibits the sale of fetal tissue and body parts. The statute addressing the matter is set out below.

Texas Penal Code § 48.02.
Purchase and sale of human organs

(a) "Human organ" means the human kidney, liver, heart, lung, pancreas, eye, bone, skin, fetal tissue, or any other human organ or tissue, but does not include hair or blood, blood components (including plasma), blood derivatives, or blood reagents.

(b) A person commits an offense if he or she knowingly or intentionally offers to buy, offers to sell, acquires, receives, sells, or otherwise transfers any human organ for valuable consideration.

(c) It is an exception to the application of this section that the valuable consideration is: (1) a fee paid to a physician or to other medical personnel for services rendered in the usual course of medical practice or a fee paid for hospital or other clinical services; (2) reimbursement of legal or medical expenses incurred for the benefit of the ultimate receiver of the

organ; or (3) reimbursement of expenses of travel, housing, and lost wages incurred by the donor of a human organ in connection with the donation of the organ.

(d) A violation of this section is a Class A misdemeanor.

Texas Right to Life

Texas Right to Life (TRL) is the oldest and largest pro-life organization in Texas. TRL is headquartered in Houston, Texas. The executive director of TRL is James J. Graham. The mission of TRL is to seek to articulate and protect the right to life of defenseless human beings, born and unborn, through legal and peaceful means. TRL believes that each human being, from the moment of fertilization until natural death, has an immeasurable dignity and inalienable right to life. The organization opposes abortion at any point of gestation, because it believes abortion destroys a living, growing human life. TRL takes the position that in the extremely rare case where a pregnancy threatens the life of the mother, and both lives cannot be saved, the life of the mother should be preserved until that day when technology will allow for both mother and unborn child to live. The organization engages in pro-life educational, legislative, political and grassroots activities. Some of the educational activities include (1) monitoring biotechnology assaults on innocent human life; (2) ministering to women and families facing unplanned pregnancies; (3) publishing a newsletter called the LifeLink; and (4) recommending and sponsoring college students for pro-life leadership training opportunities. *See also* **Pro-Life Organizations**

Thalidomide

Thalidomide is a sleep-inducing drug that was used by pregnant women in Europe in the late 1950s, as a treatment for morning sickness (as well as anxiety and insomnia). The drug was also marketed in Japan, Australia, and Canada. The Food and Drug Administration did not give approval for marketing the drug in the United States during this period. The drug was withdrawn from the international market in the early 1960s, after doctors learned that the drug caused birth defects. It was estimated that more than 10,000 babies around the globe were born with major deformities, including missing arms and legs, as a result of their mothers taking the drug while pregnant.

In 1998 the Food and Drug Administration issued approval for thalidomide to be marketed in the United States, for the treatment of certain complications associated with leprosy. Research is also being done to determine the viability of using thalidomide to treat AIDS, cancer, tuberculosis and a number of other diseases. The known side effects of thalidomide include: constipation, skin rash, severe headaches, nausea, depression and severe birth defects if taken during pregnancy. *See also* **Birth Defects and Abortion**

Therapeutic Abortion

Therapeutic abortion is an abortion that is performed in order to prevent death or serious injury to the pregnant woman. This type of abortion has generally always been permitted in the United States. It has been estimated that close to 9,000 therapeutic abortions were performed each year prior to legalization of abortion in the nation in 1973. Hospitals usually had therapeutic abortion committees that made the decision as to whether a woman's life or health was in danger by continuing a pregnancy.

Under modern laws many types of incidents could trigger the need for a therapeutic abortion, such as the need for aggressive cancer treatment for a pregnant women. The statutes in most states require affirmative proof from attending physicians that a therapeutic abortion is necessary, when a woman is carrying a viable fetus. *See also* **Abortion; Eugenic Abortion**

Third Trimester Abortion *see* **Abortion**

Thomas, Clarence

Clarence Thomas was appointed as an associate justice of the United States Supreme Court in 1991. While on the Supreme Court Thomas has revealed an ultra conservative philosophy in his interpretation of the Constitution.

Distribution of the Abortion Voting Pattern of Justice Thomas Based Upon Opinions Filed by the Supreme Court

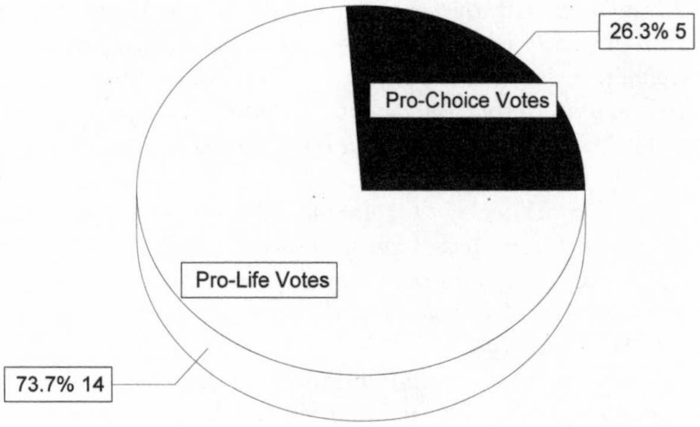

Justice Thomas was born in Pin Point, Georgia, on June 23, 1948. He was a graduate of Holy Cross College in 1971, and received a law degree from Yale University Law School in 1974. He rose quickly in his legal career and was appointed an appellate judge for the Court of Appeals of the District of Columbia in 1990. In 1991 President George Bush nominated Justice Thomas to the Supreme Court.

During Justice Thomas' tenure on the Supreme Court he has been involved with a number of abortion related opinions. The written opinions and opinions simply voted on by Justice Thomas, indicate that he is not in favor of using the constitution to expand abortion rights for women.

(1) Unanimous opinions voted with only. Justice Thomas voted with a unanimous Court in *Scheidler v. National Organization for Women, Inc. (II)*, which held pro-choice advocates could not sue pro-life advocates under the Hobbs Act for allegations of physical violence that did not involve extortion. In *Dalton v. Little Rock Family Planning Services*, Justice Thomas voted with a unanimous Court in holding that an amendment to Arkansas' constitution which limited Medicaid payment only to therapeutic abortions, was invalid to the extent that Medicaid funds had to be made available for incest or rape pregnancies, but was valid for any purely state funded program. Justice Thomas voted with a unanimous Court in *National Organization for Women, Inc. v. Scheidler*, which held that a group of pro-choice organizations could maintain a RICO civil lawsuit against several anti-abortion individuals and groups. Justice Thomas joined a unanimous opinion in *Ayotte v. Planned Parenthood of Northern New England*, which held that the absence of a health exception in New Hampshire's parental notification abortion statute did not require the entire statute be invalidated.

(2) Majority opinions voted with only. In *Lambert v. Wicklund* Justice Thomas voted with the majority in holding that the constitution was not violated by a provision in Montana's abortion statute that allowed a court to waive the parental notice requirement for minors, if notification was not in minor's best interest. Justice Thomas joined the majority opinion in *Mazurek v. Armstrong*, which held that Montana's requirement that abortions be performed only by physicians was con-

Justice Thomas' voting pattern favors the views of pro-life advocates (collection, Supreme Court Historical Society, photograph by Hugh Talman, Smithsonian Institution).

stitutionally valid. Justice Thomas voted with the majority in *Leavitt v. Jane L.*, which held that the invalidity of Utah's statute regulating pregnancies 20 weeks old or less, may be severed so as to preserve that portion of the abortion statute that regulated pregnancies of more than 20 weeks.

In *Daubert v. Merrell Dow Pharmaceuticals, Inc.*, a case involving children born with severe birth defects, Justice Thomas voted with the majority in holding that the *Frye* rule on admissibility of expert testimony did not survive the enactment of the Federal Rules of Evidence. Justice Thomas voted with the majority opinion in *Bray v. Alexandria Clinic*, which held that the Civil Rights Act of 1871, 42 U.S.C. § 1985(3), did not provide a cause of action against persons obstructing access to abortion clinics. Justice Thomas joined the majority opinion in *Scheidler v. National Organization for Women, Inc. (I)*, which held that evidence did not support finding that pro-life advocates violated the Hobbs Act, Travel Act and state law extortion crimes, for the purpose of awarding damages and granting an injunction against them under RICO.

(3) Dissenting opinions written. In *Stenberg v. Carhart*, Justice Thomas wrote a dissenting opinion opposing the majority's decision to find Nebraska's statute banning partial-birth abortion unconstitutional. Justice Thomas dissented from the majority opinion in *Federal Election Commission v. Beaumont*, which held that the Federal Election Campaign Act's prohibition on corporate expenditures and contributions directly to candidates in federal elections, applies to a nonprofit pro-life organization.

(4) Dissenting opinions voted with only. Justice Thomas dissented in the case of *Ferguson v. City of Charleston*, which held that patient consent or a search warrant was needed in order for a government hospital to turn over to the police drug test results that showed a woman used illegal drugs during her pregnancy. In *Hill v. Colorado* Justice Thomas cast a dissenting vote to the majority decision to uphold a Colorado statute that made it unlawful for any person within 100 feet of an abortion facility's entrance, to knowingly approach within 8 feet of another person, without that person's consent, in order to pass a leaflet, handbill, display a sign, engage in oral protest, education, or counseling with that person.

(5) Concurring opinions written. Justice Thomas wrote a concurring opinion in *Gonzales v. Carhart*, which held that the Partial-Birth Abortion Ban Act of 2003 was not facially unconstitutional, because it outlined the abortion procedure that was banned, and the Act did not have to provide an exception for the health of a woman.

(6) Concurring opinions voted with only. Justice Thomas joined a concurring opinion in *Federal Election Commission v. Wisconsin Right to Life, Inc.*, which held that the electioneering communications provisions of a federal statute violated a pro-life organization's First Amendment right to broadcast political issue oriented advertisements shortly before primary and general elections.

(7) Concurring and dissenting opinions voted with only. Justice Thomas voted to concur and dissent in *Schenck v. Pro Choice Network of Western New York*, which held that a federal trial court's injunction provisions imposing fixed buffer zone limitations on abortion protesters were constitutional, but the provisions imposing floating buffer zone limitations violated the First Amendment. Justice Thomas believed that the fixed buffer zone limitations were invalid also.

In *Madsen v. Women's Health Clinic, Inc.*, Justice Thomas voted to concur in part and dissent in part. The decision in *Madsen* upheld parts of an injunction that restricted noise by anti-abortionists at a clinic and imposed a 36 foot buffer zone around the clinic entrances and driveway. Justice Thomas voted to dissent from that part of the decision. However, *Madsen* ruled that the Free Speech Clause was violated by a 36 foot buffer zone as applied to the private property to the north and west of the clinic, a restriction on the use of images observable by clinic patients, a 300 foot no approach zone around the clinic, and a 300 foot buffer zone around the residences, because these restrictions swept more broadly than necessary to accomplish the permissible goals of the injunction. Justice Thomas voted to concur with the majority's decision finding some provisions in the injunction violated the Free Speech Clause.

In *Planned Parenthood of Southeastern Pennsylvania v. Casey*, Justice Thomas voted to concur and dissent. He concurred in the majority's decision that the constitution was not violated by provisions in Pennsylvania's abortion statute that provided for: medical emergency abortion; 24 hour waiting period for abortion; parental notice and judicial bypass for abortion by a minor; and certain abortion facility reporting requirements. He dissented from the majority's decision that found two provisions in the abortion statute unconstitutional: spousal notification before obtaining an abortion, and a requirement that a woman inform the abortion provider the reason for not notifying her spouse.

Thornburgh v. American College of Obstetricians and Gynecologists

Forum: United States Supreme Court.

Case Citation: Thornburgh v. American College of Obstetricians and Gynecologists, 476 U.S. 747 (1986).

Date Argued: November 5, 1985.

Date of Decision: June 11, 1986.

Opinion of Court: Blackmun, J., in which Brennan, Marshall, Powell, and Stevens, JJ., joined.

Concurring Opinion: Stevens, J.
Dissenting Opinion: Burger, C. J.
Dissenting Opinion: White, J., in which Rehnquist, J., joined.
Dissenting Opinion: O'Connor, J., in which Rehnquist, J., joined.
Counsel for Appellants: Andrew S. Gordon, Senior Deputy Attorney General of Pennsylvania, argued; on the brief were LeRoy S. Zimmerman, Attorney General, and Allen C. Warshaw, Chief Deputy Attorney General.
Counsel for Appellees: Kathryn Kolbert argued; on the brief was Thomas E. Zemaitis.
Amicus Brief for Appellants: United States by Acting Solicitor General Fried, Acting Assistant Attorney General Willard, Deputy Assistant Attorney General Kuhl, John F. Cordes, and John M. Rogers; for the National Right to Life Committee, Inc., by James Bopp, Jr.; for the United States Catholic Conference by Wilfred R. Caron and Mark E. Chopko; for Senator Gordon J. Humphrey et al. by Robert A. Destro and Basile J. Uddo; for Watson D. Bowes, Jr., et al. by Steven Frederick McDowell; and for John D. Lane et al. by John E. McKeever.
Amicus Brief for Appellees: Attorney General of New York by Robert Abrams, Attorney General, pro se, Robert Hermann, Solicitor General, Rosemarie Rhodes, Assistant Attorney General, and Lawrence S. Kahn, Sanford M. Cohen, and Martha J. Olson, Assistant Attorneys General; for the American Civil Liberties Union et al. by Nan D. Hunter, Janet Benshoof, and Suzanne M. Lynn; for the American Medical Association et al. by Benjamin W. Heineman, Jr., Carter G. Phillips, Newton N. Minow, Jack R. Bierig, Stephan E. Lawton, Joel I. Klein, Joseph A. Keyes, Jr., and Ann E. Allen; for the Center for Constitutional Rights et al. by Anne E. Simon, Nadine Taub, Rhonda Copelon, and Judith Levin; for the National Abortion Federation by David I. Shapiro, Sidney Dickstein, Kenneth M. Simon, and Amy G. Applegate; for the National Abortion Rights Action League et al. by Lynn I. Miller; for the National Family Planning and Reproductive Health Association, Inc., by Robert T. Crothers; for the National Organization for Women et al. by Diane E. Thompson; and for the Planned Parenthood Federation of America, Inc., et al. by Dara Klassel and Eve W. Paul.
Issue Presented: Whether the federal constitution was violated by provisions in Pennsylvania's abortion statute that provided for maternal informed consent, abortion alternative printed information, abortion reporting requirements, determination of fetal viability, degree of care required in post-viability abortions, and a second-physician requirement?
Case Holding: Each of the challenged provisions of Pennsylvania's abortion statute violated the federal constitution.
Background facts of case: The appellees, American College of Obstetricians and Gynecologists and others, filed a lawsuit in a federal district court in Pennsylvania attacking the constitutionality of the state's abortion statute. The appellants, state officials, were named as defendants. The district court granted a preliminary injunction, after finding only one provision in the statute was invalid. The Third Circuit court of appeals disagreed with the district court and held unconstitutional, the following six provisions of the statute: (1) a provision requiring a woman give her informed consent to an abortion, including that she be informed of the name of the physician who would perform the abortion, the particular medical risks of the abortion procedure to be used and of carrying her child to term, and the facts that there may be detrimental physical and psychological effects, medical assistance benefits that may be available for prenatal care, childbirth, and neonatal care, that the father is liable to assist in the child's support, and printed materials that describe the fetus and list agencies offering alternatives to abortion; (2) a provision that required such printed materials to include a statement that there are agencies willing to help the mother carry her child to term and to assist her after the child is born and a description of the probable anatomical and physiological characteristics of an unborn child at two-week gestational increments; (3) a provision that required the physician to report, among other things, identification of the performing and referring physicians, information as to the woman's residence, age, race, marital status, and number of prior pregnancies, and the basis for any judgment that a medical emergency existed or for any determination of nonviability, and the method of payment for the abortion, and that such reports would not be deemed public records but would be available for public inspection and copying in a form that would not lead to disclosure of the identity of any person filing a report; (4) a provision that required the physician, after the first trimester, to report the basis for his/her determination that a child is not viable; (5) a provision that required a physician performing a post-viability abortion to exercise the degree of care required to preserve the life and health of any unborn child intended to be born and to use the abortion technique that would provide the best opportunity for the unborn child to be aborted alive unless it would present a significantly greater medical risk to the pregnant woman's life or health; and (6) a provision that required that a second physician be present during an abortion performed when viability is possible, which physician is to take all reasonable steps necessary to preserve the child's life and health. The Supreme Court granted certiorari to consider the issues.
Majority opinion by Justice Blackmun: Justice Blackmun held that each of the challenged six provisions of the state's statute violated the constitution. He addressed the matters as follows:

> The printed materials required by [by the statute] seem to us to be nothing less than an outright attempt to wedge the Commonwealth's message discouraging abortion into the privacy of the informed-consent dialogue between the woman and her physician. The mandated description of fetal characteristics at 2-week intervals, no matter how objective, is plainly overinclusive. This is not medical information that is always relevant to the woman's decision, and it may serve only to confuse and punish her and to heighten her anxiety, contrary to accepted medical practice. Even the listing of agencies in the printed Pennsylvania form presents serious problems; it contains names of agencies that well may be out of step with the needs of the particular woman and thus places the physician in an awkward position and infringes upon his or her professional responsibilities. Forcing the physician or counselor to present the materials and the list to the woman makes him or her in effect an agent of the State in treating the woman and places his or her imprimatur upon both the materials and the list. All this is, or comes close to being, state medicine imposed upon the woman, not the professional medical guidance she seeks, and it officially structures—as it obviously was intended to do—the dialogue between the woman and her physician.
>
> The requirements of [the statute] that the woman be advised that medical assistance benefits may be available, and that the father is responsible for financial assistance in the support of the child similarly are poorly disguised elements of discouragement for the abortion decision. Much of this would be nonmedical information beyond the physician's area of expertise and, for many patients, would be irrelevant and inappropriate. For a patient with a life-threatening pregnancy, the information in its very rendition may be cruel as well as destructive of the physician-patient relationship. As any experienced social worker or other counselor knows, theoretical financial responsibility often does not equate with fulfillment. And a victim of rape should not have to hear gratuitous advice that an unidentified perpetrator is liable for support if she continues the pregnancy to term. Under the guise of informed consent, the [statute] requires the dissemination of information that is not relevant to such consent, and, thus, it advances no legitimate state interest.
>
> The requirements of [the statute] that the woman be informed

by the physician of detrimental physical and psychological effects and of all particular medical risks compound the problem of medical attendance, increase the patient's anxiety, and intrude upon the physician's exercise of proper professional judgment. This type of compelled information is the antithesis of informed consent. That the Commonwealth does not, and surely would not, compel similar disclosure of every possible peril of necessary surgery or of simple vaccination, reveals the anti-abortion character of the statute and its real purpose. Pennsylvania ... has gone far beyond merely describing the general subject matter relevant to informed consent. In addition, the Commonwealth would require the physician to recite its litany regardless of whether in his judgment the information is relevant to [the patient's] personal decision.... [The] informational requirements therefore are facially unconstitutional....

The scope of the information required and its availability to the public belie any assertions by the Commonwealth that it is advancing any legitimate interest.... [W]e [have] recognized that recordkeeping and reporting provisions that are reasonably directed to the preservation of maternal health and that properly respect a patient's confidentiality and privacy are permissible. But the reports required under the [statute] before us today go well beyond ... health-related interests.... Pennsylvania would require ... information as to method of payment, as to the woman's personal history, and as to the bases for medical judgments....

The required Pennsylvania reports ... while claimed not to be public, are available nonetheless to the public for copying. Moreover, there is no limitation on the use to which the Commonwealth or the public copiers may put them.... The decision to terminate a pregnancy is an intensely private one that must be protected in a way that assures anonymity....

A woman and her physician will necessarily be more reluctant to choose an abortion if there exists a possibility that her decision and her identity will become known publicly. Although the statute does not specifically require the reporting of the woman's name, the amount of information about her and the circumstances under which she had an abortion are so detailed that identification is likely. Identification is the obvious purpose of these extreme reporting requirements....

... Pennsylvania's reporting requirements raise the specter of public exposure and harassment of women who choose to exercise their personal, intensely private, right, with their physician, to end a pregnancy. Thus, they pose an unacceptable danger of deterring the exercise of that right, and must be invalidated....

The Court of Appeals ruled that [the statute] was unconstitutional because it required a trade-off between the woman's health and fetal survival, and failed to require that maternal health be the physician's paramount consideration.... [T]his Court [has] recognized the undesirability of any trade-off between the woman's health and additional percentage points of fetal survival.

Appellants do not take any real issue with this proposition. They argue instead, as did the District Court, that the statute's words "significantly greater medical risk" for the life or health of the woman do not mean some additional risk but only a meaningfully increased risk. That interpretation, said the District Court, renders the statute constitutional. The Court of Appeals disagreed, pointing out that such a reading is inconsistent with the statutory language and with the legislative intent reflected in that language.... We agree with the Court of Appeals and therefore find the statute to be facially invalid....

... [T]he Pennsylvania statute contains no express exception for an emergency situation ... and evinces no intent to protect a woman whose life may be at risk. [The statute] provides only a defense to criminal liability for a physician who concluded, in good faith, that a fetus was nonviable or that the abortion was necessary to preserve maternal life or health. It does not relate to the second-physician requirement and its words are not words of emergency.

It is clear that the Pennsylvania Legislature knows how to provide a medical-emergency exception when it chooses to do so.... We necessarily conclude that the legislature's failure to provide a medical-emergency exception ... was intentional. All the factors are here for chilling the performance of a late abortion, which, more than one performed at an earlier date, perhaps tends to be under emergency conditions....

Disposition of case: The judgment of the court of appeals was affirmed.

Concurring opinion by Justice Stevens: Justice Stevens agreed with the judgment of the Court. He wrote separately to challenge the position taken by the dissents and to make the following point:

> In the final analysis, the holding in Roe v. Wade presumes that it is far better to permit some individuals to make incorrect decisions than to deny all individuals the right to make decisions that have a profound effect upon their destiny. Arguably a very primitive society would have been protected from evil by a rule against eating apples; a majority familiar with Adam's experience might favor such a rule. But the lawmakers who placed a special premium on the protection of individual liberty have recognized that certain values are more important than the will of a transient majority.

Dissenting opinion by Chief Justice Burger: The Chief Justice dissented from the majority opinion. He believed the constitution was not violated by the state's abortion statute. The Chief Justice wrote as follows:

> ... [T]oday the Court astonishingly goes so far as to say that the State may not even require that a woman contemplating an abortion be provided with accurate medical information concerning the risks inherent in the medical procedure which she is about to undergo and the availability of state-funded alternatives if she elects not to run those risks. Can anyone doubt that the State could impose a similar requirement with respect to other medical procedures? Can anyone doubt that doctors routinely give similar information concerning risks in countless procedures having far less impact on life and health, both physical and emotional than an abortion, and risk a malpractice lawsuit if they fail to do so?
>
> Yet the Court concludes that the State cannot impose this simple information-dispensing requirement in the abortion context where the decision is fraught with serious physical, psychological, and moral concerns of the highest order. Can it possibly be that the Court is saying that the Constitution forbids the communication of such critical information to a woman? We have apparently already passed the point at which abortion is available merely on demand. If the statute at issue here is to be invalidated, the "demand" will not even have to be the result of an informed choice.

Dissenting opinion by Justice White: Justice White dissented from the majority decision. He couched his concerns through criticism of the decision in Roe v. Wade as follows:

> Today the Court carries forward the difficult and continuing venture in substantive due process that began with the decision in Roe v. Wade, and has led the Court further and further afield in the 13 years since that decision was handed down. I was in dissent in Roe v. Wade and am in dissent today....
>
> If the woman's liberty to choose an abortion is fundamental, then, it is not because any of our precedents (aside from Roe itself) command or justify that result; it can only be because protection for this unique choice is itself implicit in the concept of ordered liberty or, perhaps, deeply rooted in this Nation's history and tradition. It seems clear to me that it is neither. The

Court's opinion in Roe itself convincingly refutes the notion that the abortion liberty is deeply rooted in the history or tradition of our people, as does the continuing and deep division of the people themselves over the question of abortion. As for the notion that choice in the matter of abortion is implicit in the concept of ordered liberty, it seems apparent to me that a free, egalitarian, and democratic society does not presuppose any particular rule or set of rules with respect to abortion. And again, the fact that many men and women of good will and high commitment to constitutional government place themselves on both sides of the abortion controversy strengthens my own conviction that the values animating the Constitution do not compel recognition of the abortion liberty as fundamental. In so denominating that liberty, the Court engages not in constitutional interpretation, but in the unrestrained imposition of its own, extraconstitutional value preferences....

The governmental interest at issue is in protecting those who will be citizens if their lives are not ended in the womb. The substantiality of this interest is in no way dependent on the probability that the fetus may be capable of surviving outside the womb at any given point in its development, as the possibility of fetal survival is contingent on the state of medical practice and technology, factors that are in essence morally and constitutionally irrelevant. The State's interest is in the fetus as an entity in itself, and the character of this entity does not change at the point of viability under conventional medical wisdom. Accordingly, the State's interest, if compelling after viability, is equally compelling before viability....

The majority's opinion evinces no deference toward the State's legitimate policy. Rather, the majority makes it clear from the outset that it simply disapproves of any attempt by Pennsylvania to legislate in this area. The history of the state legislature's decade-long effort to pass a constitutional abortion statute is recounted as if it were evidence of some sinister conspiracy. In fact, of course, the legislature's past failure to predict the evolution of the right first recognized in Roe v. Wade is understandable and is in itself no ground for condemnation. Moreover, the legislature's willingness to pursue permissible policies through means that go to the limits allowed by existing precedents is no sign of mens rea. The majority, however, seems to find it necessary to respond by changing the rules to invalidate what before would have seemed permissible. The result is a decision that finds no justification in the Court's previous holdings, departs from sound principles of constitutional and statutory interpretation, and unduly limits the State's power to implement the legitimate (and in some circumstances compelling) policy of encouraging normal childbirth in preference to abortion....

Even if the Pennsylvania statute is properly interpreted as requiring a pregnant woman seeking abortion of a viable fetus to endure a method of abortion chosen to protect the health of the fetus despite the existence of an alternative that in some substantial degree is more protective of her own health, I am not convinced that the statute is unconstitutional....

The Court's ruling today that any tradeoff between the woman's health and fetal survival is impermissible is not only inconsistent with Roe's recognition of a compelling state interest in viable fetal life; it directly contradicts one of the essential holdings of Roe — that is, that the State may forbid all postviability abortions except when necessary to protect the life or health of the pregnant woman. As is evident, this holding itself involves a tradeoff between maternal health and protection of the fetus, for it plainly permits the State to forbid a postviability abortion even when such an abortion may be statistically safer than carrying the pregnancy to term, provided that the abortion is not medically necessary. The tradeoff contained in the Pennsylvania statute, even as interpreted by the majority, is no different in kind: the State has simply required that when an abortion of some kind is medically necessary, it shall be conducted so as to spare the fetus (to the greatest degree possible) unless a method less protective of the fetus is itself to some degree medically necessary for the woman. That this choice may involve the imposition of some risk on the woman undergoing the abortion should be no more troublesome than that a prohibition on nonnecessary postviability abortions may involve the imposition of some risk on women who are thereby forced to continue their pregnancies to term; yet for some reason, the Court concludes that whereas the tradeoffs it devises are compelled by the Constitution, the essentially indistinguishable tradeoff the State has attempted is foreclosed. This cannot be the law....

The decision today appears symptomatic of the Court's own insecurity over its handiwork in Roe v. Wade and the cases following that decision. Aware that in Roe it essentially created something out of nothing and that there are many in this country who hold that decision to be basically illegitimate, the Court responds defensively. Perceiving, in a statute implementing the State's legitimate policy of preferring childbirth to abortion, a threat to or criticism of the decision in Roe v. Wade, the majority indiscriminately strikes down statutory provisions that in no way contravene the right recognized in Roe. I do not share the warped point of view of the majority, nor can I follow the tortuous path the majority treads in proceeding to strike down the statute before us. I dissent.

Dissenting opinion by Justice O'Connor: Justice O'Connor disagreed with the position taken by the majority. She was convinced that the issues decided were not properly before the Court for resolution. Justice O'Connor wrote as follows:

This Court's abortion decisions have already worked a major distortion in the Court's constitutional jurisprudence. Today's decision goes further, and makes it painfully clear that no legal rule or doctrine is safe from ad hoc nullification by this Court when an occasion for its application arises in a case involving state regulation of abortion. The permissible scope of abortion regulation is not the only constitutional issue on which this Court is divided, but — except when it comes to abortion — the Court has generally refused to let such disagreements, however longstanding or deeply felt, prevent it from evenhandedly applying uncontroversial legal doctrines to cases that come before it. That the Court's unworkable scheme for constitutionalizing the regulation of abortion has had this institutionally debilitating effect should not be surprising, however, since the Court is not suited to the expansive role it has claimed for itself in the series of cases that began with Roe v. Wade.

The Court today holds that the Court of Appeals correctly invalidated the specified provisions of Pennsylvania's 1982 Abortion Control Act. In so doing, the Court prematurely decides serious constitutional questions on an inadequate record, in contravention of settled principles of constitutional adjudication and procedural fairness. The constitutionality of the challenged provisions was not properly before the Court of Appeals, and is not properly before this Court. There has been no trial on the merits, and appellants have had no opportunity to develop facts that might have a bearing on the constitutionality of the statute. The only question properly before the Court is whether or not a preliminary injunction should have been issued to restrain enforcement of the challenged provisions pending trial on the merits.... [It is clear] that no preliminary injunction should have issued....

In my view, today's decision makes bad constitutional law and bad procedural law. The undesired and uncomfortable straitjacket in this case, is not the one the Court purports to discover in Pennsylvania's statute; it is the one the Court has tailored for the 50 States. I respectfully dissent.

Note: The position taken by the dissenting opinions ultimately prevailed in subsequent decisions by the Court. Much of the majority opinion in this case was later overruled by the decision in *Planned Parenthood of Southeastern Pennsylvania v. Casey*. *See also* **Planned Parenthood of Southeastern Pennsylvania v. Casey**

Threatened Abortion *see* **Miscarriage**

Title VII of the Civil Rights Act

Title VII of the Civil Rights Act of 1964 prohibits discrimination in the employment sector. The following is specifically prohibited under Title VII:

42 U.S.C.A. § 2000e-2. Unlawful employment practices

(a) Employer practices

It shall be an unlawful employment practice for an employer—

(1) to fail or refuse to hire or to discharge any individual, or otherwise to discriminate against any individual with respect to his compensation, terms, conditions, or privileges of employment, because of such individual's race, color, religion, sex, or national origin; or

(2) to limit, segregate, or classify his employees or applicants for employment in any way which would deprive or tend to deprive any individual of employment opportunities or otherwise adversely affect his status as an employee, because of such individual's race, color, religion, sex, or national origin.

In *Automobile Workers v. Johnson Controls, Inc.* the United States Supreme Court held that Title VII forbids sex-specific fetal-protection policies by an employer, that exclude a fertile female employee from certain jobs because of the employer's concern for the health of the fetus the woman might conceive. *See also* **Automobile Workers v. Johnson Controls, Inc.; Pregnancy Discrimination Act**

Title X of the Public Health Service Act

Under Title X of the Public Health Service Act, 42 U.S.C.A. §§ 300-300a-6, Congress makes funds available to both public and private medical facilities for family planning services for low income women. The 1970 enabling legislation for Title X prohibited use of federal funds to perform abortions. In February 1988, the Department of Health and Human Services adopted regulations, which became known as the "Gag Rule" (this is different from the Mexico City Policy which is also called the Gag Rule). Under the Gag Rule family planning service providers receiving federal funds through Title X, were prohibited from providing their patients with information, counseling, or referrals concerning abortion. In addition, the Gag Rule required separation of any of a clinic's privately funded abortion related activities from its Title X project activities. In 1991 the Supreme Court held in *Rust v. Sullivan* that the Gag Rule was constitutional. However, on January 22, 1993, President Bill Clinton ordered the suspension of the Gag Rule on the grounds that it "endangers women's lives and health by preventing them from receiving complete and accurate medical information and interferes with the doctor-patient relationship by prohibiting information that medical professionals are otherwise ethically and legally required to provide to their patients." A regulation repealing the Gag Rule was published on July 3, 2000. *See also* **Public Resources for Abortions; Refusal to Perform Abortion; Rust v. Sullivan**

Today Sponge *see* **Spermicides**

TORCH Infections

TORCH infections refers to a group of disorders that can cause birth defects, spontaneous abortions or stillbirths. TORCH stands for toxoplasmosis, others, rubella, cytomegalovirus and herpes. *See also* **Congenital Rubella Syndrome; Genital Herpes; Toxoplasmosis**

Toxic Shock Syndrome

Toxic shock syndrome (TSS) is caused by a toxin produced by a bacteria (staphylococcus aureus). The bacteria is often present in the nose, skin or vagina and usually causes no problems. However, a wound or surgery may cause the bacteria to release life-threatening poisons into the body. TSS symptoms typically begin with sudden high fever, vomiting, and profuse watery diarrhea. The disease may progress to hypotensive shock within 48 hours. Respiratory distress or cardiac dysfunction may also be seen. The disease can lead to death, or the amputation of fingers, toes, or legs due to a loss of blood circulation during shock.

Although the TSS has been observed in children and men, an outbreak of the disease in women in the late 1970s sounded an alarm. Researchers quickly discovered that the disease was common in menstruating women using highly absorbent tampons. It was learned that tampon use can produce lesions and lacerations in the vagina wall that allow the bacteria to enter. Certain synthetic material used in tampons, such as polyacrylate rayon (no longer used), also contributed to the problem. Super-absorbent tampons were found to be quite dangerous, because they can expand greatly and attach to the vaginal wall. While removing the tampon layers of tissue could peel off, which increased the risk of bacterial infection.

The TSS outbreak peaked in 1980, when more than 800 menstrual-related cases were reported and 38 women died. Most of the incidents were connected to the use of a particular brand of highly absorbent tampons. That brand was removed from the market. In 1982, the Food and Drug Administration (FDA) issued a regulation requiring that tampon package labels advise women to use the lowest absorbency tampons compatible with their needs. By 1986, very high absorbency products were used by only 1 percent of women who used tampons. Effective March 1990, the FDA instituted standardized absorbency labeling of tampons. By 1997 there were only five cases of menstrual-related TSS reported and no deaths. TSS is treated with antibiotics. The manifestations of shock are treated by intravenous fluid and blood pressure support. It is generally recommended that women refrain from tampon use if they have suffered from TSS in the past.

Toxoplasmosis

Toxoplasmosis is an infection caused by a microscopic parasite (toxoplasma gondii). The parasite causing the illness may be found in raw or undercooked meat; unpasteurized dairy products (cow or goat's milk); and cat feces, cat litter, and soil that contains cat feces. An infection may be treated with antibiotics. However, the infection is dangerous if contracted by a woman while she is pregnant. The fetus of a women with the infection may sustain birth defects that include blindness, brain damage, jaundice, eye lesions, and neurological problems. Prenatal testing can inform an infected pregnant woman whether the fetus is also infected. If a woman contracts the illness during the early stages of pregnancy, she is at a risk of having a miscarriage. *See also* **Birth Defects and Abortion**

Transvaginal Ultrasound

A transvaginal ultrasound involves the insertion of an instrument (ultrasound transducer) directly into the vagina of a pregnant women. This procedure is used as an alternative to an ultrasound examination. The purpose of the procedure is to detect any pelvic masses, ectopic pregnancy, ovarian cysts or tumors, premature labor, and pelvic inflammatory disease. The instrument used in the procedure produces images that are seen on a video monitor. *See also* **Ultrasound**

Trauma and Pregnancy

Trauma during pregnancy refers to a blunt or penetrating injury to a woman's body, or severe shock. Trauma may arise from many causes, but the most frequent cause is automobile accidents. Roughly 7 percent of all pregnancies are complicated by trauma. It has become the leading cause of mortality in pregnant women. Maternal shock is the most common cause of fetal death. Trauma may also arise due to fetal injuries that result from mistakes attributed to the delivering physician or midwife. *See also* **Miscarriage; Stillbirth**

Travel Act

The Travel Act is a federal statute that was designed to prevent, among other things, individuals from using interstate travel for the purpose of engaging in unlawful conduct. Pro-choice advocates have attempted to use this statute to bring a civil lawsuit against pro-life advocates for their conduct in obstructing abortion providers. However, the United States Supreme Court has indicated that the statute cannot be used in such a manner. The Travel Act is set out below.

18 U.S.C.A. § 1952(a).
Interstate and foreign travel or transportation
in aid of racketeering enterprises

(a) Whoever travels in interstate or foreign commerce or uses the mail or any facility in interstate or foreign commerce, with intent to—

(1) distribute the proceeds of any unlawful activity; or

(2) commit any crime of violence to further any unlawful activity; or

(3) otherwise promote, manage, establish, carry on, or facilitate the promotion, management, establishment, or carrying on, of any unlawful activity,

and thereafter performs or attempts to perform—

(A) an act described in paragraph (1) or (3) shall be fined under this title, imprisoned not more than 5 years, or both; or

(B) an act described in paragraph (2) shall be fined under this title, imprisoned for not more than 20 years, or both, and if death results shall be imprisoned for any term of years or for life.

See also **National Organization for Women, Inc. v. Scheidler; Scheidler v. National Organization for Women, Inc. (I); Scheidler v. National Organization for Women, Inc. (II)**

Trichomoniasis *see* **Vaginitis**

Tricuspid Atresia *see* **Congenital Heart Defect**

Triple Screen Test *see* **Obstetric Triple Screen**

Trisomy 13

Trisomy 13 (also called Patau syndrome) is a congenital defect involving the presence of an extra number 13 chromosome. This condition occurs in about 1 out of every 20,000 live births. This disease has multiple abnormalities, many of which cause death. Some of the abnormalities include severe mental defects, seizures, heart disease, apnea, deafness, hernias, cleft lip and cleft palate, genital abnormalities and visual impairment. Nearly half of all affected infants will not survive beyond the first month, and roughly three quarters will die within six months. Trisomy 13 can be diagnosed prenatally. Usually life-sustaining procedures are not attempted for victims of the disorder. *See also* **Birth Defects and Abortion**

Trisomy 18

Trisomy 18 (also called Edwards syndrome) is a congenital defect involving the presence of an extra number 18 chromosome. This disease affects approximately 1 out of 8,000 live births. Female infants are affected more than twice as often as male infants. Trisomy 18 has multiple abnormalities, many of which result in death. Abnormalities associated with the disorder include low birthweight, mental retardation, malformed ears, small jaw, hand abnormalities, heart disease, and hernias. Few infants with trisomy 18 survive beyond more than a year. Prenatal diagnosis of trisomy 18 is possible. Life-sustaining measures are usually not recommended. *See also* **Birth Defects and Abortion**

Trisomy 21 *see* **Down Syndrome**

Tubal Abortion *see* **Ectopic Pregnancy**

Tubal Ligation

Tubal ligation is a surgical procedure designed to prevent pregnancy. The procedure involves an incision around the edge of the navel area and the insertion of a laparoscope, a long thin optical instrument. The laparoscope allows the physician to see the fallopian tubes in order to tie and cut or clamp them. Once the fallopian tubes are closed, sperm cannot reach the eggs and eggs cannot pass through the tubes. Therefore, the woman cannot become pregnant. Tubal ligation does not affect a woman's period. *See also* **Contraception; Hysterectomy; Male Sterilization**

Tubal Pregnancy *see* **Ectopic Pregnancy**

Tuberous Sclerosis

Tuberous sclerosis is a genetic disorder that can affect the brain, kidneys, heart, eyes, lungs, and other organs. Symptoms of the disorder include seizures, mental retardation, and skin and eye lesions. There is no cure for the disease, but treatment for some of the symptoms may include anticonvulsant therapy for seizures, drug therapy for behavioral problems, and surgery to remove tumors. *See also* **Birth Defects and Abortion**

Turner's Syndrome

Turner's syndrome is a genetic disorder found in females. It is caused by a missing X chromosome. The disorder retards sexual development and causes infertility. Other problems caused by the disorder include short stature, webbing of the skin of the neck, absence of menstruation, narrowing of the aorta, and eye and bone abnormalities. This disorder affects 1 out of 3,000 live births. Some treatment is available that includes growth hormone replacement and cardiac surgery to correct heart defects. *See also* **Birth Defects and Abortion**

Twin Reversed Arterial Perfusion

Twin reversed arterial perfusion (TRAP) involves multiple gestation where one fetus lacks a functioning cardiac system and receives blood from the normally developing twin fetus. Under this condition blood enters the abnormal twin through the umbilical artery (which usually carries blood away from the fetus back to the placenta) and exits through the umbilical vein, which normally carries blood from the placenta to the fetus. TRAP occurs in approximately 1 percent of twin pregnancies. This condition places a great demand on the normal fetus' heart and poses the risk of cardiac failure. Without medical intervention, the normally developing fetus will die in about 75 percent of the cases. Medical intervention usually will occur only if the normally developing fetus is free of any underlying congenital disorder. If medical intervention is made, surgery is performed to interrupt the blood circulation to the abnormally developing fetus. Due to the low oxygen content of the blood received by the abnormal fetus, a number of anomalies occur to it, such as: absence of the head, absent or rudimentary heart, and severe skin swelling. As a result of the severe nature of the anomalies, the abnormal fetus cannot survive. *See also* **Fetal Transfusion Syndrome; Monoamnionic Twin Gestation; Monochorionic Twin Gestation; Multifetal Pregnancy Reduction; Multiple Gestation; Vanishing Twin Syndrome**

Twin-Twin Transfusion Syndrome *see* **Fetal Transfusion Syndrome**

Twins *see* **Fetal Transfusion Syndrome; Monoamnionic Twin Gestation; Monochorionic Twin Gestation; Multifetal Pregnancy Reduction; Multiple Gestation; Twin Reversed Arterial Perfusion; Vanishing Twin Syndrome**

U

Ultrasound

Ultrasound is a diagnostic technique that utilizes sound waves to show a picture of a fetus in the womb. Scanning the womb using ultrasound involves bouncing sound waves off the developing fetus. The bouncing sound waves produce echoes which are converted into an image, called a sonogram, on a monitor. Approximately 70 percent of pregnant women in the United States have an ultrasound examination. Some of the most common reasons ultrasound is used include: confirm due date; evaluate fetal growth; identify potential miscarriage; diagnose possible birth defects; identify ectopic pregnancy; determine if there are multiple fetuses; isolate the cause any late-term bleeding; general monitoring of fetal development; and assist in selecting delivery method. *See also* **Amniocentesis; Chorionic Villus Sampling; Obstetric Triple Screen**

Umbilical Cord

The umbilical cord is the lifeline of the fetus. It is a vascular structure that allows the fetus to receive nutrients such as oxygen, glucose, and protein, and to dispose of waste. There are normally three vessels in the cord, two arteries and one vein. It is connected to the fetus' abdomen at one end and the woman's placenta at the other end. The cord is formed during the fifth week of gestation and connects the fetus' circulation with the woman's placenta. At birth it is about 2 feet long and 0.5 inches in diameter. After birth the cord is clamped and cut short leaving a stump that will eventually fall off and leave a navel indentation. *See also* **Placenta**

Umbilical Cord Blood Transplantation

Umbilical cord blood transplantation is an alternative to bone marrow transplantation for people with certain life-threatening cancers or blood disorders. Cord blood is the blood that remains in the umbilical cord following birth. Cord blood is a rich source of stem-cells, which are the building blocks of blood and the immune system. The stem-cells reproduce into red blood cells (which carry oxygen throughout the body), white blood cells (which fight infections), and platelets (which are necessary for clotting). The stem-cells in cord blood are missing in adult blood.

Cord blood stem-cells have the ability to treat the same diseases as bone marrow, but with significantly less rejection. Stem-cells from cord blood are being used as treatment for a variety of cancers and blood diseases.

Cord blood is collected for storage, with parental consent, after a baby is born and the umbilical cord has been clamped and cut. Specialized blood banks exist for storing cord blood. Cord blood banking is the process of collecting the blood from an umbilical cord immediately after delivery, and freezing it for long-term cryogenic storage. When a doctor has a patient who needs a transplant, cord blood banks are contacted to locate a match for the patient.

The first successful cord blood transplantation occurred in 1988 in France. The transplantation involved an American youth, six-year-old Matthew Farrow of Salisbury, North Carolina. Matthew suffered from Fanconi's anemia, a genetic blood disease that usually kills its victims by the age of 12. Matthew was unable to find a bone marrow donor. As matters turned out, his parents gave birth to a daughter who was a match for performing a bone marrow transplant. However, his parents were told of a new procedure involving cord blood transplantation that could be performed in France (cord blood transplants were not being performed in the United States at that time). Matthew's parents consented to allowing him to go to France, where Dr. Eliane Gluckman made history by performing the world's first successful cord blood transplantation on Matthew. Since Matthew's ground breaking transplantation, over 2000 cord blood transplantations have been performed world-wide. *See also* **Embryonic and Fetal Stem-Cell Research**

Umbilical Knot

Umbilical knot refers to the accidental formation of knots in the umbilical cord. This condition may cause spontaneous abortion or severe injury to the fetus, due to insufficient blood and nutrients going to the fetus. *See also* **Miscarriage**

Unborn Victims of Violence Act

The Unborn Victims of Violence Act was a bill that was sponsored by pro-life members of Congress beginning in the late 1990s. This legislation would have created penalties for anyone who caused injury or death to a fetus, while committing a federal crime. The bill was criticized because it failed to address the underlying problem of violence against women. Opponents of the bill argued that it emphasized the fetus over the woman, diverted attention away from violence against women, and failed to recognize that the best way to protect a fetus is to better protect women from violence. The bill was also argued against because it would set a legal precedent by establishing in law that an unborn child was an individual separate from a woman, and elevating its status above that of a woman. In 2004 Congress passed a version of the Unborn Victims of Violence Act (also called Laci and Conner's Law), and President George Bush signed the legislation into law on April 1, 2004. The Act covers both federal and military crimes against a fetus. The text of the federal and military components of the Act are set out below.

18 U.S.C.A. § 1841. Protection of unborn children

(a)(1) Whoever engages in conduct that violates any of the provisions of law listed in subsection (b) and thereby causes the death of, or bodily injury (as defined in section 1365) to, a child, who is in utero at the time the conduct takes place, is guilty of a separate offense under this section.

(2)(A) Except as otherwise provided in this paragraph, the punishment for that separate offense is the same as the punishment provided under Federal law for that conduct had that injury or death occurred to the unborn child's mother.

(B) An offense under this section does not require proof that—

(i) the person engaging in the conduct had knowledge or should have had knowledge that the victim of the underlying offense was pregnant; or

(ii) the defendant intended to cause the death of, or bodily injury to, the unborn child.

(C) If the person engaging in the conduct thereby intentionally kills or attempts to kill the unborn child, that person shall instead of being punished under subparagraph (A), be punished as provided under sections 1111, 1112, and 1113 of this title for intentionally killing or attempting to kill a human being.

(D) Notwithstanding any other provision of law, the death penalty shall not be imposed for an offense under this section.

(b) The provisions referred to in subsection (a) are the following:

(1) Sections 36, 37, 43, 111, 112, 113, 114, 115, 229, 242, 245, 247, 248, 351, 831, 844(d), (f), (h)(1), and (i), 924(j), 930, 1111, 1112, 1113,

1114, 1116, 1118, 1119, 1120, 1121, 1153(a), 1201(a), 1203, 1365(a), 1501, 1503, 1505, 1512, 1513, 1751, 1864, 1951, 1952 (a)(1)(B), (a) (2)(B), and (a)(3)(B), 1958, 1959, 1992, 2113, 2114, 2116, 2118, 2119, 2191, 2231, 2241(a), 2245, 2261, 2261A, 2280, 2281, 2332, 2332a, 2332b, 2340A, and 2441 of this title.

(2) Section 408(e) of the Controlled Substances Act of 1970 (21 U.S.C. 848(e)).

(3) Section 202 of the Atomic Energy Act of 1954 (42 U.S.C. 2283).

(c) Nothing in this section shall be construed to permit the prosecution—

(1) of any person for conduct relating to an abortion for which the consent of the pregnant woman, or a person authorized by law to act on her behalf, has been obtained or for which such consent is implied by law;

(2) of any person for any medical treatment of the pregnant woman or her unborn child; or

(3) of any woman with respect to her unborn child.

(d) As used in this section, the term "unborn child" means a child in utero, and the term "child in utero" or "child, who is in utero" means a member of the species homo sapiens, at any stage of development, who is carried in the womb.

10 U.S.C.A. § 919a.
Military law for death or injury of an unborn child

(a)(1) Any person subject to this chapter who engages in conduct that violates any of the provisions of law listed in subsection (b) and thereby causes the death of, or bodily injury (as defined in section 1365 of title 18) to, a child, who is in utero at the time the conduct takes place, is guilty of a separate offense under this section and shall, upon conviction, be punished by such punishment, other than death, as a court-martial may direct, which shall be consistent with the punishments prescribed by the President for that conduct had that injury or death occurred to the unborn child's mother.

(2) An offense under this section does not require proof that—

(i) the person engaging in the conduct had knowledge or should have had knowledge that the victim of the underlying offense was pregnant; or

(ii) the accused intended to cause the death of, or bodily injury to, the unborn child.

(3) If the person engaging in the conduct thereby intentionally kills or attempts to kill the unborn child, that person shall, instead of being punished under paragraph (1), be punished as provided under sections 880, 918, and 919(a) of this title (articles 80, 118, and 119(a)) for intentionally killing or attempting to kill a human being.

(4) Notwithstanding any other provision of law, the death penalty shall not be imposed for an offense under this section.

(b) The provisions referred to in subsection (a) are sections 918, 919(a), 919(b)(2), 920(a), 922, 924, 926, and 928 of this title (articles 118, 119(a), 119(b)(2), 120(a), 122, 124, 126, and 128).

(c) Nothing in this section shall be construed to permit the prosecution—

(1) of any person for conduct relating to an abortion for which the consent of the pregnant woman, or a person authorized by law to act on her behalf, has been obtained or for which such consent is implied by law;

(2) of any person for any medical treatment of the pregnant woman or her unborn child; or

(3) of any woman with respect to her unborn child.

(d) In this section, the term "unborn child" means a child in utero, and the term "child in utero" or "child, who is in utero" means a member of the species homo sapiens, at any stage of development, who is carried in the womb.

See also **Feticide; Injury to Pregnant Woman**

Unitarian Universalist Association

The Unitarian Universalist Association (UUA) is a religious organization that was formed in 1961, through the consolidation of two religious denominations: the Universalists (est.1793) and the Unitarians (est.1825). UUA represents the interests of more than one thousand congregations worldwide. The organization provides resources and offers consultations to local congregations, creates religious education curricula, spurs social action efforts, and produces pamphlets, devotional material, and a bimonthly journal, *The World*. Since 1962 the UUA has repeatedly addressed the issues of family planning and abortion rights through passage of public policy resolutions by its General Assemblies. In 1963 UUA passed a general resolution that supported enactment of a uniform statute making abortion legal under limited circumstances. In 1968 the organization passed a resolution supporting the legalization of abortion along the lines as announced in 1973 by United States Supreme Court decision in *Roe v. Wade*. Subsequent to the *Roe* decision, UUA has been vigilant in supporting efforts to expand abortion rights and fighting efforts to limit those rights. *See also* **Pro-Choice Organizations; Religion and Abortion**

United States Agency for International Development

The United States Agency for International Development (USAID) is the principal federal agency to extend assistance to countries recovering from disaster, trying to escape poverty, and engaging in democratic reforms. USAID is an independent federal government agency that receives overall foreign policy guidance from the Secretary of State. The agency works in six principal areas: economic growth and agricultural development; population, health and nutrition; environment; democracy and governance; education and training, and; humanitarian assistance. USAID provides assistance in four regions of the world: Sub-Saharan Africa, Asia and the Near East; Latin America and the Caribbean, and; Europe and Eurasia.

Since 1965 USAID sponsored a family planning program that has been involved in all major innovations in international family planning. The agency is recognized for its leadership in the field. USAID support for family planning has helped developing countries provide family planning services to more that 100 million couples, in 28 countries since 1965. Since 1973 USAID has been legally prohibited by the Helms Amendment from supporting or encouraging abortion as a method of family planning. Under the Mexico City Policy, USAID is forbidden from providing funding to non-governmental organizations that perform or actively promote abortion as a method of family planning in other nations. *See also* **Helms Amendment; Mexico City Policy; Public Resources for Abortions**

United States Catholic Conference v. Abortion Rights Mobilization

Forum: United States Supreme Court.

Case Citation: United States Catholic Conference v. Abortion Rights Mobilization, 487 U.S. 72 (1988).

Date Argued: April 18, 1988.

Date of Decision: June 20, 1988.

Opinion of Court: Kennedy, J., in which Rehnquist, C. J., and Brennan, White, Blackmun, Stevens, O'Connor, and Scalia, JJ., joined.

Concurring Opinion: None.

Dissenting Opinion: Marshall, J.

Counsel for Appellants: Kevin T. Baine argued; on the brief were Edward Bennett Williams, Charles H. Wilson, Richard S. Hoffman, Mark E. Chopko, and Phillip H. Harris.

Counsel for Appellees: Marshall Beil argued and filed a brief.

Counsel for United States: Alan I. Horowitz argued; on the brief were Solicitor General Fried, Assistant Attorney General Rose, Deputy

Solicitor General Wallace, Robert S. Pomerance, and Teresa E. McLaughlin.

Amicus Brief for Appellants: Christian Legal Society by Michael J. Woodruff and Samuel E. Ericsson; and for the National Council of Churches of Christ in the U.S.A. et al. by Edward McGlynn Gaffney, Jr., and Douglas Laycock.

Amicus Brief for Appellees: National Abortion Rights Action League et al. by Ellyn R. Weiss; and for the National Association of Laity by Cletus P. Lyman.

Issue Presented: Whether a nonparty to a lawsuit may challenge a subpoena on the grounds that the court issuing the subpoena lacked subject matter jurisdiction over the underlying case?

Case Holding: A nonparty to a lawsuit may challenge a subpoena by alleging that the court issuing the subpoena did not have subject matter jurisdiction over the underlying litigation.

Background facts of case: The appellants, the United States Catholic Conference and the National Conference of Catholic Bishops, were sued in a federal district court in New York, along with the United States Secretary of the Treasury and the Commissioner of Internal Revenue by the appellees, Abortion Rights Mobilization, Inc. and others. The appellees alleged that the appellants had violated the rules governing their tax exempt status, by engaging in a persistent and regular pattern of intervening in elections nationwide in favor of candidates who support their position on abortion and in opposition to candidates with opposing views. The appellants were dismissed from the lawsuit, but the federal defendants remained.

After the appellants were dismissed from the lawsuit, the appellees served subpoenas on them seeking extensive documentary evidence to support the lawsuit. The appellants refused to comply with the subpoenas, on the grounds that the district court lacked subject matter jurisdiction in the underlying suit. The district court held the appellants in contempt and assessed a fine of $50,000 against each appellant for each day of further noncompliance. The Second Circuit court of appeals affirmed. The Supreme Court granted certiorari to consider the matter.

Majority opinion by Justice Kennedy: Justice Kennedy held that the appellants alleged a valid defense, in claiming that the subpoenas were invalid because the district court lacked subject matter jurisdiction in the underlying case. The opinion resolved the issue as follows:

> We hold that [the appellants] can challenge the court's lack of subject-matter jurisdiction in defense of a civil contempt citation, notwithstanding the absence of a final judgment in the underlying action. Federal Rule of Civil Procedure 45 grants a district court the power to issue subpoenas as to witnesses and documents, but the subpoena power of a court cannot be more extensive than its jurisdiction. It follows that if a district court does not have subject-matter jurisdiction over the underlying action, and the process was not issued in aid of determining that jurisdiction, then the process is void and an order of civil contempt based on refusal to honor it must be reversed.... Therefore, [the appellants] may attack a civil contempt citation by asserting that the issuing court lacks jurisdiction over the case....
>
> Accordingly, on remand, the Court of Appeals must determine whether the District Court had subject-matter jurisdiction in the underlying action. If not, then the subpoenas duces tecum are void, and the civil contempt citation must be reversed in its entirety.

Disposition of case: The judgment of the court of appeals was reversed, and the case was remanded for further proceedings.

Dissenting opinion by Justice Marshall: Justice Marshall issued a terse dissenting statement as follows: "I respectfully dissent. I would affirm the judgment of the Court of Appeals for the Second Circuit for much the same reasons set forth in [that court's] opinion[.]"

United States Supreme Court Abortion Related Opinions

The United States Supreme Court has shaped the contours and content of abortion related laws in the nation through its opinions. A summary of each abortion related opinion issued by the Court is set out in reversed chronological order.

Distribution of the Abortion Opinions Issued by the Supreme Court 1926-2

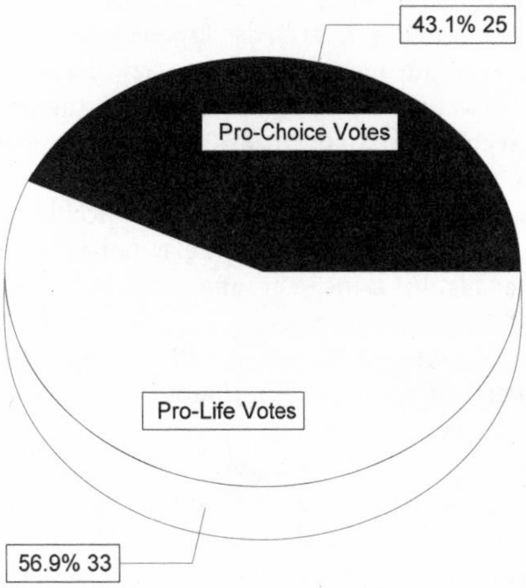

2007 opinions. In *Federal Election Commission v. Wisconsin Right to Life, Inc.*, it was held that the electioneering communications provisions of a federal statute violated a pro-life organization's First Amendment right to broadcast political issue oriented advertisements shortly before primary and general elections. In *Gonzales v. Carhart* it was held that the Partial-Birth Abortion Ban Act of 2003 was not facially unconstitutional, because it outlined the abortion procedure that was banned, and the Act did not have to provide an exception for the health of a woman.

2006 opinions. In *Ayotte v. Planned Parenthood of Northern New England* it was held that the absence of a health exception in New Hampshire's parental notification abortion statute did not require the entire statute be invalidated.

2003 opinions. In *Scheidler v. National Organization for Women, Inc. (I)* it was held that evidence did not support finding that pro-life advocates violated the Hobbs Act, Travel Act and state law extortion crimes, for the purpose of awarding damages and granting an injunction against them under RICO. In *Federal Election Commission v. Beaumont* it was held that the Federal Election Campaign Act's prohibition on corporate expenditures and contributions directly to candidates in federal elections, applies to a nonprofit pro-life organization.

2001 opinions. In *Ferguson v. City of Charleston* it was held that patient consent or a search warrant was needed, in order for a government hospital to turn over to the police drug test results that showed a woman used illegal drugs during her pregnancy.

2000 opinions. In *Stenberg v. Carhart* it was held that Nebraska's statute banning partial-birth abortion was unconstitutional. In *Hill v. Colorado* the Supreme Court upheld the constitutionality of a Colorado statute which made it unlawful for any person within 100 feet of an abortion facility's entrance, to knowingly approach within 8 feet of another person, without that person's consent, in order to pass a leaflet, handbill, display a sign, engage in oral protest, education, or counseling with that person.

1997 opinions. It was ruled in *Schenck v. Pro Choice Network of West-*

ern New York that a federal trial court's injunction provisions imposing fixed buffer zone limitations on abortion protesters were constitutional, but the provisions imposing floating buffer zone limitations violated the First Amendment. The Supreme Court held in *Lambert v. Wicklund* that the constitution was not violated by a provision in Montana's abortion statute that allowed a court to waive the parental notice requirement for minors, if notification was not in minor's best interest. In *Mazurek v. Armstrong* the Supreme Court indicated that Montana's requirement that abortions be performed only by physicians was constitutionally valid.

1996 opinions. In *Leavitt v. Jane L.*, the Supreme Court held that the invalidity of Utah's statute regulating pregnancies 20 weeks old or less, may be severed so as to preserve that portion of the abortion statute that regulated pregnancies of more than 20 weeks. The Supreme Court held in *Dalton v. Little Rock Family Planning Services* that an amendment to Arkansas' constitution which limited Medicaid payment only to therapeutic abortions, was invalid to the extent that Medicaid funds had to be made available for incest or rape pregnancies, but was valid for any purely state funded program.

1994 opinions. In *Madsen v. Women's Health Clinic, Inc.* the Supreme Court upheld parts of an injunction that restricted noise by anti-abortionists at a clinic and imposed a 36 foot buffer zone around the clinic entrances and driveway. However, *Madsen* ruled that the Free Speech Clause was violated by a 36 foot buffer zone as applied to the private property to the north and west of the clinic, a restriction on the use of images observable by clinic patients, a 300 foot no approach zone around the clinic, and a 300 foot buffer zone around the residences, because these restrictions swept more broadly than necessary to accomplish the permissible goals of the injunction. The Supreme Court ruled in *National Organization for Women, Inc. v. Scheidler* that a group of pro-choice organizations could maintain a RICO civil lawsuit against several anti-abortion individuals and groups.

1993 opinions. In *Daubert v. Merrell Dow Pharmaceuticals, Inc.*, a case involving children born with severe birth defects from their mothers' use of a morning sickness drug, the Supreme Court held that the *Frye* rule on admissibility of expert testimony did not survive the enactment of the Federal Rules of Evidence. The Supreme Court ruled in *Bray v. Alexandria Clinic* that the Civil Rights Act of 1871, 42 U.S.C. § 1985(3), did not provide a cause of action against persons obstructing access to abortion clinics.

1994 opinions. In *Planned Parenthood of Southeastern Pennsylvania v. Casey* it was held that the constitution was not violated by provisions in Pennsylvania's abortion statute that provided for: medical emergency abortion; 24 hour waiting period for abortion; parental notice and judicial bypass for abortion by a minor; and certain abortion facility reporting requirements. *Casey* found two provisions in the abortion statute unconstitutional: spousal notification before obtaining an abortion, and a requirement that a woman inform the abortion provider the reason for not notifying her spouse.

1991 opinions. In *Rust v. Sullivan* the Supreme Court upheld federal regulations that prohibited pro-abortion counseling, referral, and advocacy by health care providers. In *Automobile Workers v. Johnson Controls, Inc.* it was held that Title VII of the Civil Rights Act forbids sex-specific fetal-protection policies by an employer, that exclude a fertile female employee from certain jobs because of the employer's concern for the health of the fetus the woman might conceive.

1990 opinions. In *Hodgson v. Minnesota* the Supreme Court upheld the constitutionality of Minnesota's requirement that a pregnant female minor could not obtain an abortion until at least 48 hours after both of her parents had been notified, except when (1) the attending physician certified that an immediate abortion was necessary to prevent the minor's death; (2) the minor declared that she was a victim of parental abuse or neglect; or (3) a court of competent jurisdiction ordered the abortion to proceed without notice upon proof that the minor was mature and capable of giving informed consent or that an abortion without notice to both parents would be in the minor's best interest. In *Ohio v. Akron Center for Reproductive Health* the Supreme Court upheld the constitutionality of Ohio's abortion statute notice and judicial bypass requirements for pregnant female minors.

1989 opinions. The Supreme Court ruled in *Webster v. Reproductive Health Services* that the constitution was not violated by Missouri's prohibition on the use of public facilities or employees to perform abortions and a requirement that physicians conduct viability tests prior to performing abortions.

1988 opinions. In *Frisby v. Schultz* the Supreme Court upheld the constitutional validity of a town ordinance that was created to prevent pro-life picketing at the residence of an abortion doctor. It was ruled in *United States Catholic Conference v. Abortion Rights Mobilization* that the appellants, nonparties in an underlying action, could challenge having to turn over documents in a lawsuit seeking to strip them of their tax exempt status because of their active political abortion work.

1986 opinions. In *Federal Election Commission v. Massachusetts Citizens for Life, Inc.* it was held that federal law which prohibited the appellee from using its treasury funds to promote pro-life political candidates violated the Free Speech Clause of the First Amendment. The decision in *Thornburgh v. American College of Obstetricians and Gynecologists* invalidated provisions in Pennsylvania's abortion statute that provided for maternal informed consent, abortion alternative printed information, abortion reporting requirements, determination of fetal viability, degree of care required in post-viability abortions, and a second-physician requirement. In *Diamond v. Charles* it was held that a citizen did not have standing to appeal a decision invalidating parts of Illinois' abortion statute that (1) imposed criminal penalties for violating a prescribed standard of care that had to be exercised by a physician in performing an abortion of a viable fetus, and of a possibly viable fetus; and (2) imposed criminal penalties for physicians who failed to provide patients with information about the type of abortifacient used.

1983 opinions. The decision in *Bolger v. Youngs Drug Products Corp.* held that a provision of the Comstock Act, 39 U.S.C. § 3001(e)(2), that prohibited mailing unsolicited advertisements for contraceptives violated the Free Speech Clause of the First Amendment. In *City of Akron v. Akron Center for Reproductive Health, Inc.* the Supreme Court invalidated an abortion ordinance that provided requirements for parental consent, informed consent, waiting period, hospitalization and disposal of fetal remains. In *Planned Parenthood Assn. v. Ashcroft* it was held that the constitution was violated by Missouri's requirement that second trimester abortions take place in a hospital; but that the constitution was not violated by the state's requirement that a pathology report for each abortion be performed, that a second physician be present during abortions performed after viability, and parental or judicial consent for abortion by minors. The Supreme Court, in *Simopoulos v. Virginia*, upheld a Virginia statute requiring second trimester abortions be performed at hospitals, because under the statute an adequately equipped clinic could, upon proper application, obtain an outpatient hospital license that permitted the performance of second-trimester abortions.

1981 opinions. In *H. L. v. Matheson* the Supreme Court held that the constitution was not violated by Utah's requirement that the parents of a minor be notified, if possible, prior to performing an abortion.

1980 opinions. The Supreme Court ruled in *Harris v. McRae*, that the Medicaid funding restrictions for abortion by the Hyde Amendment, did not violate the Due Process Clause nor the equal protection component of the Fifth Amendment. In *Williams v. Zbaraz* the Supreme Court held that in light of the requirements of the Hyde Amendment, the Equal Protection Clause of the Fourteenth Amendment was not violated by an Illinois statute that prohibited state Medicaid payment for abortions, except when necessary to save the life of the pregnant woman.

1979 opinions. In *Bellotti v. Baird II* the Supreme Court held that Massachusetts' abortion statute for minors violated the constitution in light of an interpretation given by the state's highest court, that required parental notice of a judicial bypass proceeding invoked by a minor, and permitted a judge to deny an abortion even though the minor proved she had enough maturity to make an independent decision. In *Colautti v. Franklin* it was held by the Supreme Court that the constitution was violated by a vague and ambiguous provision in Pennsylvania's abortion statute that subjected a physician who performed an abortion to potential criminal liability, if he/she failed to utilize a statutorily prescribed technique when the fetus was viable or when there was sufficient reason to believe that the fetus may be viable. In *Anders v. Floyd* it was held that a federal district court erred in enjoining enforcement of a South Carolina statute that imposed criminal punishment for performing an abortion on a viable fetus.

1977 opinions. The Supreme Court held in *Beal v. Doe* that Pennsylvania's refusal to extend Medicaid coverage to nontherapeutic abortions was not invalid nor inconsistent with Title XIX of the Social Security Act. In *Maher v. Roe* the Supreme Court held that the Equal Protection Clause of the Fourteenth Amendment did not prohibit Connecticut from excluding nontherapeutic abortions from its Medicaid program. It was held *Poelker v. Doe* by the Supreme Court that the Equal Protection Clause of the Fourteenth Amendment was not violated by a policy of the city of St. Louis, Missouri that denied publicly funded abortions to indigent women at city hospitals, except when a woman's health or life was in danger. In *Carey v. Population Services International* the Supreme Court held that the constitution prohibited enforcement of a New York statute that made it a crime (1) for any person to sell or distribute any contraceptive of any kind to a minor under the age of 16 years; (2) for anyone other than a licensed pharmacist to distribute contraceptives to persons 16 or over; and (3) for anyone, including licensed pharmacists, to advertise or display contraceptives.

1976 opinions. In *Planned Parenthood of Missouri v. Danforth* the Supreme Court held that the constitution was not violated by provisions in Missouri's abortion statute involving the definition of fetal viability, woman's written consent, and record keeping and reporting requirements; but that the constitution prohibited the requirements concerning spousal consent, parental consent for minor, banning saline amniocentesis abortions, and physician's standard of care. The Supreme Court held in *Bellotti v. Baird I* that the federal district court had to certify appropriate questions to the supreme judicial court of Massachusetts, concerning the interpretation of that state's parental consent abortion statute for minors, before ruling on its constitutionality. In *Singleton v. Wulff* the Supreme Court held that the Eighth Circuit court of appeals had jurisdiction to determine whether abortion providers had standing to challenge a provision in Missouri's abortion statute that limited Medicaid payment for abortions, but it did not have jurisdiction to rule that the provision violated the constitution because the district court did not address the issue.

1975 opinions. In *Connecticut v. Menillo* the Supreme Court held that the constitution was not violated by criminal abortion statutes that prohibit nonphysicians from attempting or performing abortions at any stage of a pregnancy. The Supreme Court held in *Bigelow v. Virginia* that the Free Speech and Free Press Clauses of the First Amendment were violated by a Virginia penal statute that prohibited selling or circulating any publication that encouraged or promoted abortions. In *Withrow v. Larkin* the Supreme Court held that constitutional due process was not violated by the mere fact that a Wisconsin medical examining board had the authority to both, investigate and adjudicate, allegations against a physician that included, among other things, permitting a nonphysician to perform an abortion. The Supreme Court held in *Burns v. Alcala* that states receiving federal financial aid under the program of Aid to Families with Dependent Children, were not required to offer welfare benefits to pregnant women for their unborn children.

1974 opinions. In *Geduldig v. Aiello* the Supreme Court held that the Equal Protection Clause of the Fourteenth Amendment did not require a private sector employee disability insurance program, operated by the state of California, provide coverage for employee disabilities associated with normal pregnancies.

1973 opinions. In *Weinberger v. Hynson, Westcott & Dunning* the Supreme Court held that the Food and Drug Administration could not deny a drug manufacturer a hearing to obtain marketing approval for a drug called Lutrexin, which provided treatment for premature labor and threatened and habitual abortion. The Supreme Court held in *Roe v. Wade* that the liberty component of the Due Process Clause of the Fourteenth Amendment prohibited states from criminalizing or preventing elective first trimester abortions. In *Doe v. Bolton* the Supreme Court held that the Due Process Clause of the Fourteenth Amendment was violated by provisions in Georgia's abortion statutes that required (1) abortions take place in accredited hospitals, (2) that an abortion be approved by a hospital abortion committee, (3) that the need for an abortion be confirmed by two independent physicians, and (4) that a woman seeking an abortion be a resident of Georgia.

1972 opinions. In *Eisenstadt v. Baird* the Supreme Court held that the Equal Protection Clause of the Fourteenth Amendment was violated by a Massachusetts statute that made it a crime to give away a drug, medicine, instrument, or article for the prevention of conception except in the case of (1) a physician prescribing it for a married person, or (2) a pharmacist furnishing it to a married person presenting a physician's prescription.

1971 opinions. In *United States v. Vuitch* the Supreme Court held that the criminal abortion statute of the District of Columbia, which only permitted therapeutic abortions, was not constitutionally vague insofar as there was no ambiguity in its use of the word health and it did not shift to the defendant the burden of proving innocence.

1965 opinions. In *Griswold v. Connecticut* it was held by the Supreme Court that the right of privacy found in the constitution, prohibited enforcement of a Connecticut statute that made it a crime to give married persons contraceptive information and devices.

1961 opinions: The Supreme Court held in *Poe v. Ullman* that the appellants did not have standing to challenge the constitutionality of a Connecticut statute, that made it a crime to give married persons contraceptive information and devices.

1926 opinions. In *State of Missouri ex rel. Hurwitz v. North* the Supreme Court held that the constitution was not violated when a physician was prevented from issuing subpoenas to have witnesses attend a hearing to revoke his medical license for performing an unlawful abortion, because the applicable rules required taking depositions of witnesses who would not voluntarily attend the hearing.

United States v. Vuitch

Forum: United States Supreme Court.

Case Citation: United States v. Vuitch, 402 U.S. 62 (1971).

Date Argued: January 12, 1971.

Date of Decision: April 21, 1971.

Opinion of Court: Black, J., in which Burger, C. J., and Douglas, Harlan, Stewart, Blackmun, and White, JJ.

Concurring Opinion: White, J.

Concurring and Dissenting Opinion: Douglas, J.

Concurring and Dissenting Opinion: Harlan, J., in which Brennan, Marshall, and Blackmun, JJ., joined.

Concurring and Dissenting Opinion: Stewart, J.

Concurring and Dissenting Opinion: Blackmun, J.

Counsel for Appellant: Samuel Huntington argued; on the brief were Solicitor General Griswold, Assistant Attorney General Wilson, Jerome M. Feit, and Roger A. Pauley.

Counsel for Appellee: Joseph L. Nellis and Norman Dorsen argued; on the brief was Joseph Sitnick.

Amicus Brief for Appellant and Appellee: David W. Louisell for Dr. Bart Heffernan; by Alfred L. Scanlan, Thomas J. Ford, and Gary R. Alexander for Dr. William F. Colliton, Jr., et al.; by Robert E. Dunne for Robert L. Sassone; by Marilyn G. Rose for the National Legal Program on Health Problems of the Poor; by Sylvia S. Ellison for Human Rights for Women, Inc.; by Lola Boswell for the Joint Washington Office for Social Concern et al.; and by Ralph Temple, Melvin L. Wulf, and Norma G. Zarky for the American Civil Liberties Union et al.

Issue Presented: Whether the criminal abortion statute of the District of Columbia, which only permitted therapeutic abortions, shifted to the defendant the burden of proving innocence, and presented ambiguity in its use of the word health?

Case Holding: The criminal abortion statute of the District of Columbia, which only permitted therapeutic abortions, was not constitutionally vague insofar as there was no ambiguity in its use of the word health and it did not shift to the defendant the burden of proving innocence.

Background facts of case: Under the statute of the District of Columbia abortion was unlawful unless it was done to save a woman's life or health. The appellee, Milan Vuitch, was a physician who was indicted by the District of Columbia for producing and attempting to produce abortions in violation of law. Before the trial began, the district judge dismissed the indictments on the grounds that the District of Columbia's abortion law was unconstitutionally vague for two reasons: (1) the statute shifted to the appellee the burden of proving his innocence, and (2) the presence of ambiguity in the word health. The United States appealed to the Supreme Court.

Majority opinion by Justice Black: The first issued addressed by Justice Black concerned the jurisdiction of the Court to hear the appeal. Justice Black indicated that the Court could hear the appeal, even though an appeal was not taken to the court of appeals. He then turned to the merits of the case as found that the statute was not vague. Justice Black wrote as follows:

> The statute does not outlaw all abortions, but only those which are not performed under the direction of a competent, licensed physician, and those not necessary to preserve the mother's life or health. It is a general guide to the interpretation of criminal statutes that when an exception is incorporated in the enacting clause of a statute, the burden is on the prosecution to plead and prove that the defendant is not within the exception. When Congress passed the District of Columbia abortion law in 1901 and amended it in 1953, it expressly authorized physicians to perform such abortions as are necessary to preserve the mother's life or health. Because abortions were authorized only in more restrictive circumstances under previous D.C. law, the change must represent a judgment by Congress that it is desirable that women be able to obtain abortions needed for the preservation of their lives or health. It would be highly anomalous for a legislature to authorize abortions necessary for life or health and then to demand that a doctor, upon pain of one to ten years' imprisonment, bear the burden of proving that an abortion he performed fell within that category. Placing such a burden of proof on a doctor would be peculiarly inconsistent with society's notions of the responsibilities of the medical profession. Generally, doctors are encouraged by society's expectations, by the strictures of malpractice law and by their own professional standards to give their patients such treatment as is necessary to preserve their health. We are unable to believe that Congress intended that a physician be required to prove his innocence. We therefore hold that under [the statute] the burden is on the prosecution to plead and prove that an abortion was not necessary for the preservation of the mother's life or health.
>
> There remains the contention that the word "health" is so imprecise and has so uncertain a meaning that it fails to inform a defendant of the charge against him and therefore the statute offends the Due Process Clause of the Constitution. We hold that it does not. The trial court apparently felt that the term was vague because there is no indication whether it includes varying degrees of mental as well as physical health. It is true that the legislative history of the statute gives no guidance as to whether health refers to both a patient's mental and physical state.... [T]he general usage and modern understanding of the word "health," ... includes psychological as well as physical well-being. Indeed Webster's Dictionary, in accord with that common usage, properly defines health as the "[s]tate of being ... sound in body [or] mind." Viewed in this light, the term "health" presents no problem of vagueness. Indeed, whether a particular operation is necessary for a patient's physical or mental health is a judgment that physicians are obviously called upon to make routinely whenever surgery is considered.
>
> We therefore hold that properly construed the District of Columbia abortion law is not unconstitutionally vague, and that the trial court erred in dismissing the indictments on that ground.

Disposition of case: The judgment of the district court was reversed and the case remanded.

Concurring opinion by Justice White: Justice White agreed with the decision of the Court. He wrote separately to make the following points:

> I join the Court's opinion and judgment. As to the facial vagueness argument, I have these few additional words. This case comes to us unilluminated by facts or record. The District Court's holding that the District of Columbia statute is unconstitutionally vague on its face because it proscribes all abortions except those necessary for the preservation of the mother's life or health was a judgment that the average person could not understand which abortions were permitted and which were prohibited. But surely the statute puts everyone on adequate notice that the health of the mother, whatever that phrase means, is the governing standard. It should also be absolutely clear that a doctor is not free to perform an abortion on request without considering whether the patient's health requires it. No one of average intelligence could believe that under this statute abortions not dictated by health considerations are legal. Thus even if the "health" standard were unconstitutionally vague, which I agree is not the case, the statute is not void on its face since it reaches a class of cases in which the meaning of "health" is irrelevant and no possible vagueness problem could arise. We do not, of course, know whether this is one of those cases. Until we do facial vagueness claims must fail.

Concurring and dissenting opinion by Justice Douglas: Justice Douglas concurred in the Court's ruling that it had jurisdiction to hear the appeal. He dissented from the Court's decision finding the statute constitutionally valid. Justice Douglass wrote as follows:

> While I agree with ... the Court's opinion that we have jurisdiction over this appeal, I do not think the statute meets the requirements of procedural due process.
>
> The District of Columbia Code makes it a felony for a physician to perform an abortion unless the same were done as necessary for the preservation of the mother's life or health.
>
> I agree with the Court that a physician — within the limits of his own expertise — would be able to say that an abortion at a

particular time performed on a designated patient would or would not be necessary for the preservation of her life or health. That judgment, however, is highly subjective, dependent on the training and insight of the particular physician and his standard as to what is necessary for the preservation of the mother's life or health....

The subject of abortions—like cases involving obscenity—is one of the most inflammatory ones to reach the Court. People instantly take sides and the public, from whom juries are drawn, makes up its mind one way or the other before the case is even argued. The interests of the mother and the fetus are opposed. On which side should the State throw its weight? The issue is volatile; and it is resolved by the moral code which an individual has. That means that jurors may give it such meaning as they choose, while physicians are left to operate outside the law. Unless the statutory code of conduct is stable and in very narrow bounds, juries have a wide range and physicians have no reliable guide-posts. The words "necessary for the preservation of the motherlife or health" become free-wheeling concepts, too easily taking on meaning from the juror's predilections or religious prejudices.

I would affirm the dismissal of these indictments and leave to the experts the drafting of abortion laws that protect good-faith medical practitioners from the treacheries of the present law.

Concurring and dissenting opinion by Justice Harlan: Justice Harlan dissented from the Court's determination that it had jurisdiction to hear the appeal. However, he concurred with the Court's determination of the merits of the case.

Concurring and dissenting opinion by Justice Stewart: Justice Stewart agreed with the Court that it had jurisdiction to hear the appeal. He disagreed with the Court's decision to find that the statute was constitutionally valid. Justice Stewart wrote the following:

> I agree that we have jurisdiction of this appeal for the reasons stated in Part I of the Court's opinion.
>
> As to the merits of this controversy, I share at least some of the constitutional doubts about the abortion statute expressed by the District Court....
>
> The statute legalizes any abortion performed under the direction of a competent licensed practitioner of medicine if necessary for the preservation of the mother's life or health. Under the statute, therefore, the legal practice of medicine in the District of Columbia includes the performing of abortions. For the practice of medicine consists of doing those things which, in the judgment of a physician, are necessary to preserve a patient's life or health....
>
> It follows, I think, that when a physician has exercised his judgment in favor of performing an abortion, he has, by hypothesis, not violated the statute. To put it another way, I think the question of whether the performance of an abortion is necessary for the mother's life or health is entrusted under the statute exclusively to those licensed to practice medicine, without the overhanging risk of incurring criminal liability at the hands of a second-guessing lay jury. I would hold, therefore, that a competent licensed practitioner of medicine is wholly immune from being charged with the commission of a criminal offense under this law.

Concurring and Dissenting opinion by Justice Blackmun: Justice Blackmun dissented from the Court's decision to find that it had jurisdiction to hear the appeal. However, he concurred with the Court's determination of the merits of the case.

Urea *see* **Instillation Methods**

Ureaplasma

Ureaplasma is a bacteria found in the urinary tract. In women the bacteria can cause an inflammation of the uterine lining (endometrium) that results in a spontaneous abortion, due to implantation problems. It may also contribute to pelvic inflammatory disease in women. *See also* **Miscarriage; Pelvic Inflammatory Disease**

Utah

(1) OVERVIEW

The state of Utah enacted its first criminal abortion statute in 1876. The statute underwent several amendments prior to the 1973 decision by the United States Supreme Court in *Roe v. Wade*, which legalized abortion in the nation. Utah has taken affirmative steps to respond to *Roe* and its progeny. The state has addressed several abortion issues by statute that include general abortion guidelines, informed consent, abortion by minors, partial-birth and saline abortion, use of facilities and people, public funds and abortion, wrongful life action, selling or experimentation with fetus, fetal death report, abortion litigation fund, and injury to a pregnant woman.

(2) GENERAL ABORTION GUIDELINES

Under the laws of Utah the state permits an abortion before 21 weeks of pregnancy only when necessary to save the life or health of the

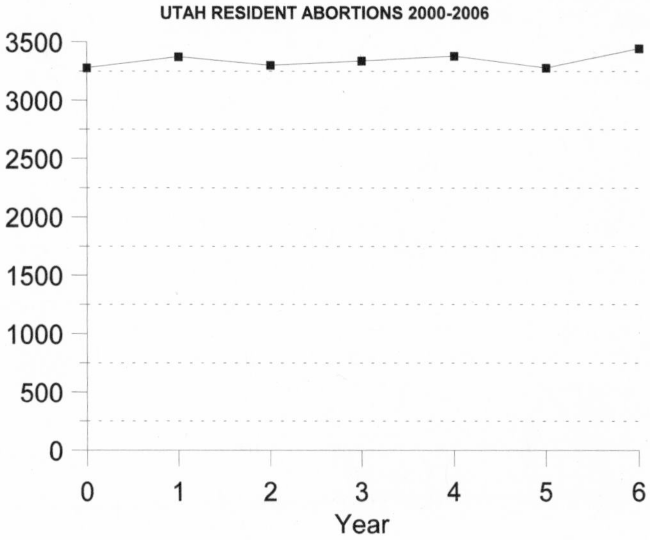

Source: Utah Department of Health.

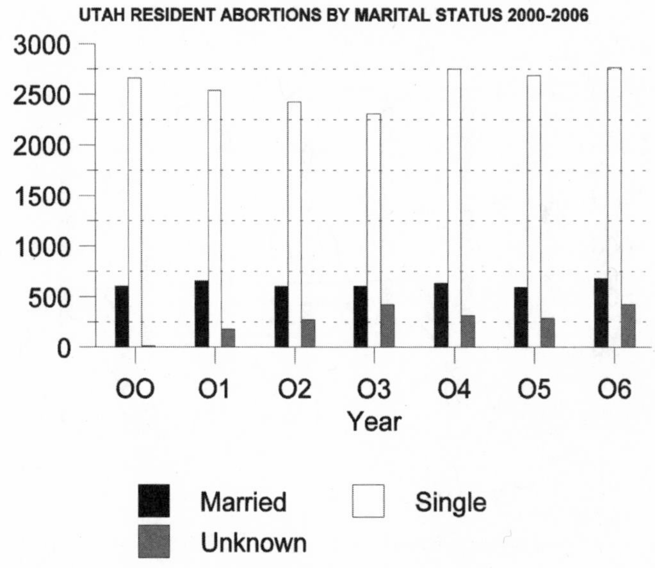

Source: Utah Department of Health.

Utah Resident Abortion by Age Group 2000–2006

	Age Group (yrs)							
Year	*<15*	*15–19*	*20–24*	*25–29*	*30–34*	*35–39*	*≥40*	*Unknown*
2000	24	576	1,169	719	433	254	91	13
2001	14	546	1,154	730	487	279	96	66
2002	12	504	1,147	772	458	274	99	34
2003	24	527	1,115	766	495	284	99	28
2004	10	507	1,187	755	495	284	107	34
2005	12	512	1,041	788	462	315	91	58
2006	10	554	1,118	844	484	289	95	50
Total	106	3,726	7,931	5,374	3,314	1,979	678	283

Source: Utah Department of Health.

Utah Resident Prior Abortion by Female 2000–2006

	Prior Abortion						
Year	*None*	*1*	*2*	*3*	*4*	*≥5*	*Not known*
2000	2,184	736	209	74	41	22	13
2001	2,253	693	227	70	24	13	92
2002	2,126	754	232	69	27	18	74
2003	2,225	689	221	68	21	11	103
2004	2,287	712	196	62	16	19	87
2005	2,104	756	239	61	22	13	84
2006	2,265	739	236	82	27	20	75
Total	15,444	5,079	1,560	486	178	116	528

Source: Utah Department of Health.

Utah Resident Abortion by Weeks of Gestation 2000–2006

	Year							
Weeks of Gestation	*2000*	*2001*	*2002*	*2003*	*2004*	*2005*	*2006*	*Total*
<5	74	117	51	79	59	72	98	550
5–6	983	984	819	829	803	770	956	6,144
7–8	1,089	1,162	1,163	1,264	1,348	1,312	1,263	8,601
9–10	680	592	604	541	566	492	507	3,982
11–12	215	255	260	237	220	241	219	1,647
13–14	113	108	203	179	172	192	197	1,164
15–20	121	118	161	191	192	182	182	1,147
≥21	0	0	0	2	6	6	13	27
Not known	4	36	39	16	13	12	9	129

Source: Utah Department of Health.

Utah Resident Abortion by Education Level of Female 2000–2006

	Education Level Completed			
Year	*<12*	*12*	*≥13*	*Unknown*
2000	511	1,572	1,146	50
2001	481	1,438	1,088	365
2002	501	1,219	1,136	444
2003	463	1,329	1,086	460
2004	437	1,468	1,105	369
2005	479	1,192	1,168	440
2006	378	1,249	1,108	709
Total	3,250	9,467	7,837	2,837

Source: Utah Department of Health.

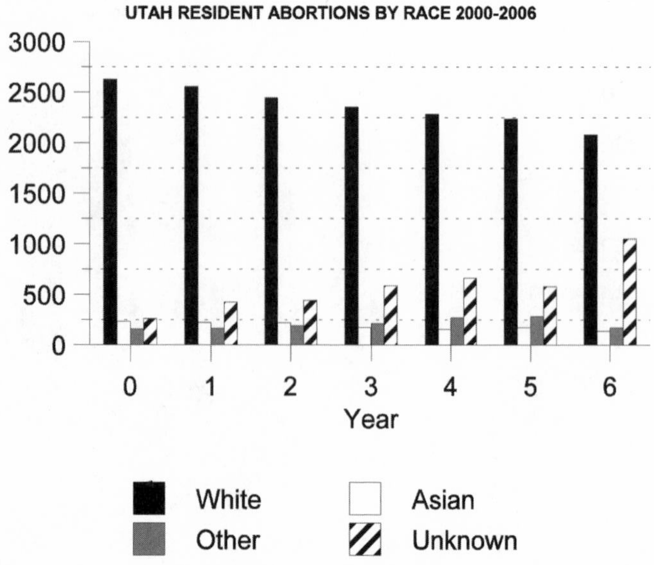

Source: Utah Department of Health.

woman, the pregnancy resulted from rape or incest, or the fetus had severe birth defects. A federal district court found this restriction unconstitutional in *Jane L. v. Bangerter*, 809 F.Supp. 865 (D.Utah 1992). An abortion after 20 weeks is permitted in order to save the life or health of the woman, or if the fetus suffered from severe birth defects. This restriction was found unconstitutional in *Jane L. v. Bangerter*, 102 F.3d 1112 (10th Cir. 1996). The statutes are set out below.

Utah Code § 76-7-301. Definitions

As used in this part:

(1) "Abortion" means the intentional termination or attempted termination of human pregnancy after implantation of a fertilized ovum, and includes any and all procedures undertaken to kill a live unborn child and includes all procedures undertaken to produce a miscarriage. "Abortion" does not include removal of a dead unborn child.

(2) "Medical emergency" means that condition which, on the basis of the physician's good faith clinical judgment, so threatens the life of a pregnant woman as to necessitate the immediate abortion of her pregnancy to avert her death, or for which a delay will create serious risk of substantial and irreversible impairment of major bodily function.

(3)(a) "Partial birth abortion" means an abortion in which the person performing the abortion:

(i) deliberately and intentionally vaginally delivers a living fetus until, in the case of a head first presentation, the entire fetal head is outside the body of the mother, or, in the case of breech presentation, any part of the fetal trunk past the navel is outside the body of the mother, for the purpose of performing an overt act that the person knows will kill the partially delivered living fetus; and

(ii) performs the overt act, other than completion of delivery, that kills the partially living fetus.

(b) "Partial birth abortion" does not include the dilation and evacuation procedure involving dismemberment prior to removal, the suction curettage procedure, or the suction aspiration procedure for abortion.

(4) "Physician" means a medical doctor licensed to practice medicine and surgery under Title 58, Chapter 67, Utah Medical Practice Act, a physician in the employment of the government of the United States who is similarly qualified, or an osteopathic physician licensed to practice osteopathic medicine under Title 58, Chapter 68, Utah Osteopathic Medical Practice Act.

(5) "Hospital" means a general hospital licensed by the Department of Health according to Title 26, Chapter 21, Health Care Facility Licensing and Inspection Act, and includes a clinic or other medical facility to the extent that such clinic or other medical facility provides equipment and personnel sufficient in quantity and quality to provide the same degree of safety to the pregnant woman and the unborn child as would be provided for the particular medical proce-

dures undertaken by a general hospital licensed by the Department of Health. It shall be the responsibility of the Department of Health to determine if such clinic or other medical facility so qualifies and to so certify.

Utah Code § 76-7-301.1. Findings and policies of legislature

(1) It is the finding and policy of the Legislature, reflecting and reasserting the provisions of Article I, Sections 1 and 7, Utah Constitution, which recognize that life founded on inherent and inalienable rights is entitled to protection of law and due process; and that unborn children have inherent and inalienable rights that are entitled to protection by the state of Utah pursuant to the provisions of the Utah Constitution.

(2) The state of Utah has a compelling interest in the protection of the lives of unborn children.

(3) It is the intent of the Legislature to protect and guarantee to unborn children their inherent and inalienable right to life as required by Article I, Sections 1 and 7, Utah Constitution.

(4) It is also the policy of the Legislature and of the state that, in connection with abortion, a woman's liberty interest, in limited circumstances, may outweigh the unborn child's right to protection. These limited circumstances arise when the abortion is necessary to save the pregnant woman's life or prevent grave damage to her medical health, and when pregnancy occurs as a result of rape or incest. It is further the finding and policy of the Legislature and of the state that a woman may terminate the pregnancy if the unborn child would be born with grave defects.

Utah Code § 76-7-302. Conditions for abortion

(1) An abortion may be performed in this state only by a physician licensed to practice medicine under Title 58, Chapter 67, Utah Medical Practice Act or an osteopathic physician licensed to practice medicine under Title 58, Chapter 68, Utah Osteopathic Medical Practice Act and, if performed 90 days or more after the commencement of the pregnancy as defined by competent medical practices, it shall be performed in a hospital.

(2) An abortion may be performed in this state only under the following circumstances:

(a) in the professional judgment of the pregnant woman's attending physician, the abortion is necessary to save the pregnant woman's life;

(b) the pregnancy is the result of rape or rape of a child, as defined by Sections 76-5-402 and 76-5-402.1, that was reported to a law enforcement agency prior to the abortion;

(c) the pregnancy is the result of incest, as defined by Subsection 76-5-406(10) or Section 76-7-102, and the incident was reported to a law enforcement agency prior to the abortion;

(d) in the professional judgment of the pregnant woman's attending physician, to prevent grave damage to the pregnant woman's medical health; or

(e) in the professional judgment of the pregnant woman's attending physician, to prevent the birth of a child that would be born with grave defects.

(3) After 20 weeks gestational age, measured from the date of conception, an abortion may be performed only for those purposes and circumstances described in Subsections (2)(a), (d), and (e).

(4) The name of a victim reported pursuant to Subsection (b) or (c) is confidential and may not be revealed by law enforcement or any other party except upon approval of the victim. This subsection does not effect or supersede parental notification requirements otherwise provided by law.

Utah Code § 76-7-303. Concurrence of physician

No abortion may be performed in this state without the concurrence of the attending physician, based on his best medical judgment.

Utah Code § 76-7-307.
Medical procedure required to save life of unborn child

If an abortion is performed when the unborn child is sufficiently developed to have any reasonable possibility of survival outside its mother's womb, the medical procedure used must be that which, in the best medical judgment of the physician will give the unborn child the best chance of survival. No medical procedure designed to kill or injure that unborn child may be used unless necessary, in the opinion of the woman's physician, to prevent grave damage to her medical health.

Utah Code § 76-7-308.
Medical skills required to preserve life of unborn child

Consistent with the purpose of saving the life of the woman or preventing grave damage to the woman's medical health, the physician performing the abortion must use all of his medical skills to attempt to promote, preserve and maintain the life of any unborn child sufficiently developed to have any reasonable possibility of survival outside of the mother's womb.

Utah Code § 76-7-312.
Intimidation or coercion to obtain abortion

No person shall intimidate or coerce in any way any person to obtain an abortion.

Utah Code § 76-7-314. Violations of abortion laws

(1)(a) Any person who intentionally performs an abortion other than as authorized by this part is guilty of a felony of the third degree.

(b)(i) Notwithstanding any other provision of law, a woman who seeks to have or obtains an abortion for herself is not criminally liable.

(ii) A woman upon whom a partial birth abortion is performed may not be prosecuted under Section 76-7-326 or 76-7-329 for a conspiracy to violate Section 76-7-326 or 76-7-329.

(2) A willful violation of Section 76-7-307, 76-7-308, 76-7-310, 76-7-310.5, 76-7-311, or 76-7-312 is a felony of the third degree.

(3) A violation of Section 76-7-326 or 76-7-329 is a felony of the third degree.

(4) A violation of any other provision of this part is a class A misdemeanor.

Utah Code § 76-7-315. Serious medical emergencies

When due to a serious medical emergency, time does not permit compliance with Section 76-7-302, 76-7-305, 76-7-305.5, or 76-7-310.5 the provisions of those sections do not apply.

Utah Code § 76-7-316. Civil actions not precluded

Nothing in this part shall preclude any person believing himself aggrieved by another under this part, from bringing any other action at common law or other statutory provision.

Utah Code § 76-7-317. Separability clause

If any one or more provision, section, subsection, sentence, clause, phrase or word of this part or the application thereof to any person or circumstance is found to be unconstitutional, the same is hereby declared to be severable and the balance of this part shall remain effective notwithstanding such unconstitutionality. The legislature hereby declares that it would have passed this part, and each provision, section, subsection, sentence, clause, phrase or word thereof, irrespective of the fact that any one or more provision, section, subsection, sentence, clause, phrase, or word be declared unconstitutional.

Utah Code § 76-7-317.2.
Finding of unconstitutionality — revival of old law

If Section 76-7-302 as amended by Senate Bill 23, 1991 Annual General Session, is ever held to be unconstitutional by the United States Supreme Court, Section 76-7-302, as enacted by Chapter 33, Laws of Utah 1974, is reenacted and immediately effective.

(3) INFORMED CONSENT

Prior to an abortion Utah requires that a woman be fully informed of the procedure to be used, the risks involved and alternatives to abortion. An abortion may not take place until 24 hours after a woman has been given the required statutory information. The statutes are set out below.

Utah Code § 76-7-305. Consent and waiting period

(1) No abortion may be performed unless a voluntary and informed written consent, consistent with Section 8.08 of the American Medical Association's Code of Medical Ethics, Current Opinions, and the provisions of this section is first obtained by the attending physician from the woman upon whom the abortion is to be performed.

(2) Except in the case of a medical emergency, consent to an abortion is voluntary and informed only if:

(a) at least 24 hours prior to the abortion, the physician who is to perform the abortion, the referring physician, a registered nurse, nurse practitioner, advanced practice registered nurse, certified nurse midwife, or physician's assistant, in a face-to-face consultation, orally informs the woman of:

(i) consistent with Subsection (3)(a), the nature of the proposed abortion procedure or treatment, specifically how that procedure will affect the fetus, and the risks and alternatives to an abortion procedure or treatment that any person would consider material to the decision of whether or not to undergo an abortion;

(ii) the probable gestational age and a description of the development of the unborn child at the time the abortion would be performed; and

(iii) the medical risks associated with carrying her child to term;

(b) at least 24 hours prior to the abortion the physician who is to perform the abortion, the referring physician, or, as specifically delegated by either of those physicians, a registered nurse, licensed practical nurse, certified nurse-midwife, advanced practice registered nurse, clinical laboratory technologist, psychologist, marriage and family therapist, clinical social worker, or certified social worker has orally, in a face-to-face consultation, informed the pregnant woman that:

(i) the Department of Health, in accordance with Section 76-7-305.5, publishes printed material and an informational video that:

(A) provides medically accurate information regarding all abortion procedures that may be used;

(B) describes the gestational stages of an unborn child; and

(C) includes information regarding public and private services and agencies available to assist her through pregnancy, at childbirth, and while the child is dependent, including private and agency adoption alternatives;

(ii) the printed material and a viewing of or a copy of the informational video shall be provided to her free of charge;

(iii) medical assistance benefits may be available for prenatal care, childbirth, and neonatal care, and that more detailed information on the availability of that assistance is contained in the printed materials and the informational video published by the Department of Health;

(iv) except as provided in Subsection (3)(b), the father of the unborn child is legally required to assist in the support of her child, even in instances where he has offered to pay for the abortion, and that the Office of Recovery Services within the Department of Human Services will assist her in collecting child support; and

(v) she has the right to view an ultrasound of the unborn child, at no expense to her, upon her request;

(c) the information required to be provided to the pregnant woman under Subsection (2)(a) is also provided by the physician who is to perform the abortion, in a face-to-face consultation, prior to performance of the abortion, unless the attending or referring physician is the individual who provides the information required under Subsection (2)(a);

(d) a copy of the printed materials published by the Department of Health has been provided to the pregnant woman;

(e) the informational video, published by the Department of Health, has been provided to the pregnant woman in accordance with Subsection (4); and

(f) the pregnant woman has certified in writing, prior to the abortion, that the information required to be provided under Subsections (2)(a) through (e) was provided, in accordance with the requirements of those subsections.

(3)(a) The alternatives required to be provided under Subsection (2)(a)(i) shall include:

(i) a description of adoption services, including private and agency adoption methods; and

(ii) a statement that it is legal for adoptive parents to financially assist in pregnancy and birth expenses.

(b) The information described in Subsection (2)(b)(iv) may be omitted from the information required to be provided to a pregnant woman under this section if the woman is pregnant as the result of rape.

(4) When the informational video described in Section 76-7-305.5 is provided to a pregnant woman, the person providing the information shall first request that the woman view the video at that time or at another specifically designated time and location. If the woman chooses not to do so, a copy of the video shall be provided to her.

(5) When a serious medical emergency compels the performance of an abortion, the physician shall inform the woman prior to the abortion, if possible, of the medical indications supporting the physician's judgment that an abortion is necessary.

(6) Any physician who violates the provisions of this section:

(a) is guilty of unprofessional conduct as defined in Section 58-67-102 or 58-68-102; and

(b) shall be subject to suspension or revocation of the physician's license for the practice of medicine and surgery in accordance with Sections 58-67-401 and 58-67-402, Utah Medical Practice Act, or Sections 58-68-401 and 58-68-402, Utah Osteopathic Medical Practice Act.

(7) A physician is not guilty of violating this section for failure to furnish any of the information described in Subsection (2), if:

(a) the physician can demonstrate by a preponderance of the evidence that the physician reasonably believed that furnishing the information would have resulted in a severely adverse effect on the physical or mental health of the pregnant woman;

(b) in the physician's professional judgment, the abortion was necessary to save the pregnant woman's life;

(c) the pregnancy was the result of rape or rape of a child, as defined in Sections 76-5-402 and 76-5-402.1;

(d) the pregnancy was the result of incest, as defined in Subsection 76-5-406(10) and Section 76-7-102;

(e) in his professional judgment the abortion was to prevent the birth of a child who would have been born with grave defects; or

(f) the pregnant woman was 14 years of age or younger.

(8) A physician who complies with the provisions of this section and Section 76-7-304.5 may not be held civilly liable to the physician's patient for failure to obtain informed consent under Section 78-14-5.

Utah Code § 76-7-305.5.
Printed materials and informational video

(1) In order to insure that a woman's consent to an abortion is truly an informed consent, the Department of Health shall publish printed ma-

terials and produce an informational video in accordance with the requirements of this section. The department and each local health department shall make those materials and a viewing of the video available at no cost to any person. The printed material and the informational video shall be comprehensible and contain all of the following:

(a) geographically indexed materials informing the woman of public and private services and agencies available to assist her, financially and otherwise, through pregnancy, at childbirth, and while the child is dependent, including services and supports available under Section 35A-3-308. Those materials shall contain a description of available adoption services, including a comprehensive list of the names, addresses, and telephone numbers of public and private agencies and private attorneys whose practice includes adoption, and explanations of possible available financial aid during the adoption process. The information regarding adoption services shall include the fact that private adoption is legal, and that the law permits adoptive parents to pay the costs of prenatal care, childbirth, and neonatal care. The printed information and video shall present adoption as a preferred and positive choice and alternative to abortion. The department may, at its option, include printed materials that describe the availability of a toll-free 24-hour telephone number that may be called in order to obtain, orally, the list and description of services, agencies, and adoption attorneys in the locality of the caller;

(b) truthful and nonmisleading descriptions of the probable anatomical and physiological characteristics of the unborn child at two-week gestational increments from fertilization to full term, accompanied by pictures or video segments representing the development of an unborn child at those gestational increments. The descriptions shall include information about brain and heart function and the presence of external members and internal organs during the applicable stages of development. Any pictures used shall contain the dimensions of the fetus and shall be realistic and appropriate for that woman's stage of pregnancy. The materials shall be designed to convey accurate scientific information about an unborn child at the various gestational ages, and to convey the state's preference for childbirth over abortion;

(c) truthful, nonmisleading descriptions of abortion procedures used in current medical practice at the various stages of growth of the unborn child, the medical risks commonly associated with each procedure, including those related to subsequent childbearing, the consequences of each procedure to the fetus at various stages of fetal development, the possible detrimental psychological effects of abortion, and the medical risks associated with carrying a child to term;

(d) any relevant information on the possibility of an unborn child's survival at the two-week gestational increments described in Subsection (1)(b);

(e) information on the availability of medical assistance benefits for prenatal care, childbirth, and neonatal care;

(f) a statement conveying that it is unlawful for any person to coerce a woman to undergo an abortion;

(g) a statement conveying that any physician who performs an abortion without obtaining the woman's informed consent or without according her a private medical consultation in accordance with the requirements of this section, may be liable to her for damages in a civil action at law;

(h) a statement conveying that the state prefers childbirth over abortion; and

(i) information regarding the legal responsibility of the father to assist in child support, even in instances where he has agreed to pay for an abortion, including a description of the services available through the Office of Recovery Services, within the Department of Human Services, to establish and collect that support.

(2)(a) The materials described in Subsection (1) shall be produced and printed in a way that conveys the state's preference for childbirth over abortion.

(b) The printed material described in Subsection (1) shall be printed in a typeface large enough to be clearly legible.

(3) Every facility in which abortions are performed shall immediately provide the printed informed consent materials and a viewing of or a copy of the informational video described in Subsection (1) to any patient or potential patient prior to the performance of an abortion, unless the patient's attending or referring physician certifies in writing that he reasonably believes that provision of the materials or video to that patient would result in a severely adverse effect on her physical or mental health.

(4) The Department of Health shall produce a standardized videotape that may be used statewide, containing all of the information described in Subsection (1), in accordance with the requirements of that subsection and Subsection (2). In preparing the video, the department may summarize and make reference to the printed comprehensive list of geographically indexed names and services described in Subsection (1)(a). The videotape shall, in addition to the information described in Subsection (1), show an ultrasound of the heart beat of an unborn child at three weeks gestational age, at six to eight weeks gestational age, and each month thereafter, until 14 weeks gestational age. That information shall be presented in a truthful, nonmisleading manner designed to convey accurate scientific information, the state's preference for childbirth over abortion, and the positive aspects of adoption.

(5) The Department of Health and local health departments shall provide ultrasounds in accordance with the provisions of Subsection 76-7-305(2)(b), at no expense to the pregnant woman.

(6) The Department of Health shall compile and report the following information annually, preserving physician and patient anonymity:

(a) the total amount of informed consent material described in Subsection (1) that was distributed;

(b) the number of women who obtained abortions in this state without receiving those materials;

(c) the number of statements signed by attending physicians certifying to his opinion regarding adverse effects on the patient under Subsection (3); and

(d) any other information pertaining to protecting the informed consent of women seeking abortions.

(4) ABORTION BY MINORS

Under the laws of Utah no physician may perform an abortion upon an unemancipated minor unless he/she first notifies either parent or the legal guardian 24 hours before the abortion, and obtains the written consent of either parent or the legal guardian of the minor. In compliance with federal constitutional law, Utah has provided a judicial waiver procedure for an unemancipated minor to obtain an abortion without parental or guardian consent. The minor may petition a trial court for a waiver of the consent requirement. The required parental or guardian consent may be waived if the court finds either (1) that the minor is mature and well-informed enough to make the abortion decision on her own, or (2) that performance of the abortion would be in the best interest of the minor. An appeal is available to any minor to whom the court denies a waiver of consent. The state also restricts the use of public funds to provide abortion services or contraceptives to a minor, unless prior consent has been given by a parent or guardian. The statutes addressing the matters are set out below.

Utah Code § 76-7-304. Notice to a parent or guardian

(1) As used in this section:

(a) "abuse" is as defined in Section 62A-4a-101; and

(b) "minor" means a person who is:

(i) under 18 years of age;

(ii) unmarried; and

(iii) not emancipated.

(2) To enable the physician to exercise the physician's best medical judgment, the physician shall consider all factors relevant to the well-being of the woman upon whom the abortion is to be performed including:

(a) her physical, emotional and psychological health and safety;

(b) her age; and

(c) her familial situation.

(3) Subject to Subsection (4), at least 24 hours before a physician performs an abortion on a minor, the physician shall notify a parent or guardian of the minor that the minor intends to have an abortion.

(4) A physician is not required to comply with Subsection (3) if:

(a) subject to Subsection (5)(a):

(i) a medical condition exists that, on the basis of the physician's good faith clinical judgment, so complicates the medical condition of a pregnant minor as to necessitate the abortion of her pregnancy to avert:

(A) the minor's death; or

(B) a serious risk of substantial and irreversible impairment of a major bodily function of the minor; and

(ii) there is not sufficient time to give the notice required under Subsection (3) before it is necessary to terminate the minor's pregnancy in order to avert the minor's death or impairment described in Subsection (4)(a)(i);

(b) subject to Subsection (5)(b):

(i) the physician complies with Subsection (6); and

(ii)(A) the minor is pregnant as a result of incest to which the parent or guardian was a party; or

(B) the parent or guardian has abused the minor; or

(c) subject to Subsection (5)(b), the parent or guardian has not assumed responsibility for the minor's care and upbringing.

(5)(a) If, for the reason described in Subsection (4)(a), a physician does not give the 24-hour notice described in Subsection (3), the physician shall give the required notice as early as possible before the abortion, unless it is necessary to perform the abortion immediately in order to avert the minor's death or impairment described in Subsection (4)(a)(i).

(b) If, for a reason described in Subsection (4)(b) or (c), a parent or guardian of a minor is not notified that the minor intends to have an abortion, the physician shall notify another parent or guardian of the minor, if the minor has another parent or guardian that is not exempt from notification under Subsection (4)(b) or (c).

(6) If, for a reason described in Subsection (4)(b)(ii)(A) or (B), a physician does not notify a parent or guardian of a minor that the minor intends to have an abortion, the physician shall report the incest or abuse to the Division of Child and Family Services within the Department of Human Services.

Utah Code § 76-7-304.5. Consent required

(1) As used in this section, "minor" is as defined in Subsection 76-7-304(1).

(2) In addition to the other requirements of this part, a physician may not perform an abortion on a minor unless:

(a) the physician obtains the informed written consent of a parent or guardian of the minor, consistent with Section 76-7-305;

(b) the minor is granted the right, by court order under Subsection (5)(b), to consent to the abortion without obtaining consent from a parent or guardian; or

(c)(i) a medical condition exists that, on the basis of the physician's good faith clinical judgment, so complicates the medical condition of a pregnant minor as to necessitate the abortion of her pregnancy to avert:

(A) the minor's death; or

(B) a serious risk of substantial and irreversible impairment of a major bodily function of the minor; and

(ii) there is not sufficient time to obtain the consent in the manner chosen by the minor under Subsection (3) before it is necessary to terminate the minor's pregnancy in order to avert the minor's death or impairment described in Subsection (2)(c)(i).

(3) A pregnant minor who wants to have an abortion may choose:

(a) to seek consent from a parent or guardian under Subsection (2)(a); or

(b) to seek a court order under Subsection (2)(b).

(4) If a pregnant minor fails to obtain the consent of a parent or guardian of the minor to the performance of an abortion, or if the minor chooses not to seek the consent of a parent or guardian, the minor may file a petition with the juvenile court to obtain a court order under Subsection (2)(b).

(5)(a) A hearing on a petition described in Subsection (4) shall be closed to the public.

(b) After considering the evidence presented at the hearing, the court shall order that the minor may obtain an abortion without the consent of a parent or guardian of the minor if the court finds by a preponderance of the evidence that:

(i) the minor:

(A) has given her informed consent to the abortion; and

(B) is mature and capable of giving informed consent to the abortion; or

(ii) an abortion would be in the minor's best interest.

(6) The Judicial Council shall make rules that:

(a) provide for the administration of the proceedings described in this section;

(b) provide for the appeal of a court's decision under this section;

(c) ensure the confidentiality of the proceedings described in this section and the records related to the proceedings; and

(d) establish procedures to expedite the hearing and appeal proceedings described in this section.

Utah Code § 76-7-321. Definitions

As used in Sections 76-7-321 through 76-7-325:

(1) "Abortion services" means any material, program, plan, or undertaking which seeks to promote abortion, encourages individuals to obtain an abortion, or provides abortions.

(2) "Contraceptive services" means any material, program, plan, or undertaking that is used for instruction on the use of birth control devices and substances, encourages individuals to use birth control methods, or provides birth control devices.

(3) "Funds" means any money, supply, material, building, or project provided by this state or its political subdivisions.

(4) "Minor" means any person under the age of 18 who is not otherwise emancipated, married, or a member of the armed forces of the United States.

Utah Code § 76-7-322.
Public funds for contraceptive or abortion services restricted

No funds of the state or its political subdivisions shall be used to provide contraceptive or abortion services to an unmarried minor without the prior written consent of the minor's parent or guardian.

Utah Code § 76-7-323.
Entities providing contraceptive or abortion services

No agency of the state or its political subdivisions shall approve any application for funds of the state or its political subdivisions to support, directly or indirectly, any organization or health care provider that provides contraceptive or abortion services to an unmarried minor without the prior written consent of the minor's parent or guardian. No institution shall be denied state or federal funds under relevant provisions of law on the ground that a person on its staff provides contraceptive or abortion services in that person's private practice outside of such institution.

Utah Code § 76-7-324. Penalty

Any agent of a state agency or political subdivision, acting alone or in concert with others, who violates Section 76-7-322, 76-7-323, or 76-7-331 is guilty of a class B misdemeanor.

Utah Code § 76-7-325. Notice to parent or guardian

(1) Any person before providing contraceptives to a minor shall notify, whenever possible, the minor's parents or guardian of the service requested to be provided to such minor. Contraceptives shall be defined as appliances (including but not limited to intrauterine devices), drugs, or medicinal preparations intended or having special utility for prevention of conception.

(2) Any person in violation of this section shall be guilty of a class C misdemeanor.

Utah Code § 62A-4a-408. Child abuse or neglect reports

(1) Reports made pursuant to this part shall be followed by a written report within 48 hours, if requested by the division. The division shall immediately forward a copy of that report to the statewide central register, on forms supplied by the register.

(2) If, in connection with an intended or completed abortion by a minor, a physician is required to make a report of incest or abuse of a minor, the report may not include information that would in any way disclose that the report was made in connection with:

(a) an abortion; or

(b) a consultation regarding an abortion.

(5) PARTIAL-BIRTH AND SALINE ABORTION

Utah prohibits partial-birth and saline induced abortions. The ban on saline abortion may be infirm as a result of the United States Supreme Court's decision in *Planned Parenthood of Missouri v. Danforth*, which struck down a Missouri statute that banned the use of saline abortion. Until it is definitively determined by a court, Utah's partial-birth abortion statute may be invalid under the United States Supreme Court decision *in Stenberg v. Carhart*, which invalidated Nebraska's ban on partial-birth abortion. On the other hand, Utah's partial-birth abortion statute, as currently written, may be valid under the United States Supreme Court decision in *Gonzales v. Carhart*, which approved of a federal statute that bans partial-birth abortion. The statutes are set out below.

Utah Code § 76-7-310.5. Saline abortion

(1) As used in this section, "saline abortion procedure" means performance of amniocentesis and injection of saline into the amniotic sac within the uterine cavity.

(2)(a) After viability has been determined in accordance with Subsection (2)(b), no person may knowingly perform a saline abortion procedure unless all other available abortion procedures would pose a risk to the life or the health of the pregnant woman.

(b) For purposes of this section determination of viability shall be made by the physician, based upon his own best clinical judgment. The physician shall determine whether, based on the particular facts of a woman's pregnancy that are known to him, and in light of medical technology and information reasonably available to him, there is a realistic possibility of maintaining and nourishing a life outside of the womb, with or without temporary, artificial life-sustaining support.

(3) Intentional, knowing, and willful violation of this section is a third degree felony.

Utah Code § 76-7-326. Partial-birth abortions

Any physician who knowingly performs a partial birth abortion and thereby kills a human fetus shall be fined or imprisoned, or both, as provided under this part. This section does not apply to a partial birth abortion that is necessary to save the life of a mother whose life is endangered by a physical disorder, physical illness, or physical injury, including a life endangering physical condition caused by or arising from the pregnancy itself.

Utah Code § 76-7-327.
Remedies for father or maternal grandparents

(1) The father, if married to the mother at the time she receives a partial birth abortion, and if the mother has not attained the age of 18 years at the time of the abortion, the maternal grandparents of the fetus, may in a civil action obtain appropriate relief, unless the pregnancy resulted from the plaintiff's criminal conduct or the plaintiff consented to the abortion.

(2) Such relief shall include:

(a) money damages for all injuries, psychological and physical, occasioned by the violation of Section 76-7-326 or 76-7-329; and

(b) statutory damages equal to three times the cost of the partial birth abortion.

Utah Code § 76-7-328.
Hearing to determine necessity of physician's conduct

(1) A physician accused of an offense under Section 76-7-326 may seek a hearing before the Physicians Licensing Board created in Section 58-67-201, or the Osteopathic Physician and Surgeon's Licensing Board created in Section 58-68-201 on whether the physician's conduct was necessary to save the life of the mother whose life was endangered by a physical disorder, physical illness, or physical injury, including a life endangering physical condition caused by or arising from the pregnancy itself.

(2) The findings on that issue are admissible on that issue at the trial of the physician. Upon a motion from the physician, the court shall delay the beginning of the trial for not more than 30 days to permit such a hearing to take place.

Utah Code § 76-7-329.
Person unauthorized to perform abortions

A person who is not legally authorized by the state to perform abortions, but who nevertheless directly performs a partial birth abortion, is subject to Sections 76-7-301, 76-7-314, 76-7-326, and 76-7-327.

Utah Code § 76-7-330.
Contingent continuance of prior law

(1) If the implementation of Section 76-7-326 enacted by this bill is stayed or otherwise ordered by a court of competent jurisdiction to not be implemented, beginning on the day on which the implementation of Section 76-7-326 is stayed or otherwise ordered not to be implemented the statutes listed in Subsection (2) shall:

(a) be given effect as if this bill did not amend those statutes; and

(b) remain in effect as if not amended by this bill until the day on which a court orders that Section 76-7-326 may be implemented.

(2) Subsection (1) applies to:

(a) Section 76-7-301;

(b) Section 76-7-310.5; and

(c) Section 76-7-314.

(3) Nothing in this section prevents the Legislature from amending, repealing, or taking any other action regarding the sections listed in Subsection (2) in this or a subsequent session.

(6) USE OF FACILITIES AND PEOPLE

Under the laws of Utah private hospitals are not required to allow abortions at their facilities. The employees and physicians at hospitals that do allow abortions are permitted to refuse to take part in abortions. The statute addressing the matter is set out below.

Utah Code § 76-7-306.
Right to refuse to participate in abortion

(1) A physician, or any other person who is a member of or associated with the staff of a hospital, or any employee of a hospital in which an abortion has been authorized, who states an objection to an abortion or the

practice of abortion in general on moral or religious grounds shall not be required to participate in the medical procedures which will result in the abortion, and the refusal of any person to participate shall not form the basis of any claim for damages on account of the refusal or for any disciplinary or recriminatory action against such person, nor shall any moral or religious scruples or objections to abortions be the grounds for any discrimination in hiring in this state.

(2) Nothing in this part shall require any private and/or denominational hospital to admit any patient for the purpose of performing an abortion.

(7) PUBLIC FUNDS AND ABORTION

Utah prohibits the use of Medicaid funds for abortion, unless an abortion is necessary to save the life of the woman. A federal court ruled in *Utah Women's Clinic, Inc. v. Graham*, 892 F.Supp. 1379 (D.Utah 1995) that the Medicaid limitation was invalid, insofar as it did not include coverage for pregnancies resulting from rape or incest. Under the state's own indigent medical care program funding for abortion is prohibited. The state also has a statute that prohibits the use of all public funds for abortions, except in limited situations. The statutes are set out below.

Utah Code § 26-18-4. Medicaid funds

(1) The department may develop standards and administer policies relating to eligibility under the Medicaid program as long as they are consistent with Subsection 26-18-3(6). An applicant receiving Medicaid assistance may be limited to particular types of care or services or to payment of part or all costs of care determined to be medically necessary.

(2) The department shall not provide any funds for medical, hospital, or other medical expenditures or medical services to otherwise eligible persons where the purpose of the assistance is to perform an abortion, unless the life of the mother would be endangered if an abortion were not performed.

(3) Any employee of the department who authorizes payment for an abortion contrary to the provisions of this section is guilty of a class B misdemeanor and subject to forfeiture of office.

(4) Any person or organization that, under the guise of other medical treatment, provides an abortion under auspices of the Medicaid program is guilty of a third degree felony and subject to forfeiture of license to practice medicine or authority to provide medical services and treatment.

Utah Code § 26-18-10. Utah medical assistance program

(1) The division shall develop a medical assistance program, which shall be known as the Utah Medical Assistance Program, for low income persons who are not eligible under the state plan for Medicaid under Title XIX of the Social Security Act or Medicare under Title XVIII of that act.

(2) Persons in the custody of prisons, jails, halfway houses, and other nonmedical government institutions are not eligible for services provided under this section.

(3) The department shall develop standards and administer policies relating to eligibility requirements, consistent with Subsection 26-18-3(6), for participation in the program, and for payment of medical claims for eligible persons.

(4) The program shall be a payor of last resort. Before assistance is rendered the division shall investigate the availability of the resources of the spouse, father, mother, and adult children of the person making application.

(5) The department shall determine what medically necessary care or services are covered under the program, including duration of care, and method of payment, which may be partial or in full.

(6) The department shall not provide public assistance for medical, hospital, or other medical expenditures or medical services to otherwise eligible persons where the purpose of the assistance is for the performance of an abortion, unless the life of the mother would be endangered if an abortion were not performed.

(7) The department may establish rules to carry out the provisions of this section.

Utah Code § 26-40-107. Utah children's health insurance act

Abortion is not a covered benefit, except as provided in 42 U.S.C. Sec. 1397ee.

Utah Code § 76-7-331. Public funding of abortion forbidden

(1) As used in this section, "damage to a major bodily function" refers only to injury or impairment of a physical nature and may not be interpreted to mean mental, psychological, or emotional harm, illness, or distress.

(2) Public funds of the state, its institutions, or its political subdivisions may not be used to pay or otherwise reimburse, either directly or indirectly, any person, agency, or facility for the performance of any induced abortion services unless:

(a) in the professional judgment of the pregnant woman's attending physician, the abortion is necessary to save the pregnant woman's life;

(b) the pregnancy is the result of rape or incest reported to law enforcement agencies, unless the woman was unable to report the crime for physical reasons or fear of retaliation; or

(c) in the professional judgment of the pregnant woman's attending physician, the abortion is necessary to prevent permanent, irreparable, and grave damage to a major bodily function of the pregnant woman provided that a caesarian procedure or other medical procedure that could also save the life of the child is not a viable option.

(3) Any officer or employee of the state who knowingly authorizes the use of funds prohibited by this section shall be dismissed from that person's office or position and the person's employment shall be immediately terminated.

(8) WRONGFUL BIRTH ACTION

Utah has taken an affirmative step to prevent wrongful life litigation, by prohibiting claims for negligent failure to abort a pregnancy. The statute addressing the matter is set out below.

Utah Code § 78-11-24. Wrongful life action

A cause of action shall not arise, and damages shall not be awarded, on behalf of any person, based on the claim that but for the act or omission of another, a person would not have been permitted to have been born alive but would have been aborted.

(9) SELLING OR EXPERIMENTATION WITH FETUS

Utah prohibits trafficking in living fetuses. The state also prohibits the use of live fetuses for experiments. The statutes addressing the matter are set out below.

Utah Code § 76-7-310 Experimentation upon fetus

Live unborn children may not be used for experimentation, but when advisable, in the best medical judgment of the physician, may be tested for genetic defects.

Utah Code § 76-7-311. Selling or buying fetus

Selling, buying, offering to sell and offering to buy unborn children is prohibited.

(10) FETAL DEATH REPORT

Utah requires that all abortions be reported to the proper authorities. The statutes addressing the matter are set out below.

Utah Code § 76-7-313. Physician's report

In order for the state Department of Health to maintain necessary statistical information and ensure enforcement of the provisions of this part, any physician performing an abortion must obtain and record in writing: the age of the pregnant woman; her marital status and county of residence; the number of previous abortions performed on her; the hospital or other facility where performed; the weight in grams of the unborn child aborted, if it is possible to ascertain; the pathological description of the unborn child; the given menstrual age of the unborn child; the measurements, if possible to ascertain; and the medical procedure used. This information, and a copy of the pathologist's report, as required in Section 76-7-309, together with an affidavit that the required consent was obtained pursuant to Section 76-7-305 and a certificate by the physician that the unborn child was or was not capable of survival outside of the mother's womb, must be filed by the physician with the state Department of Health within 10 days after the abortion. All information supplied to the state Department of Health shall be confidential and privileged pursuant to Title 26, Chapter 25.

Utah Code § 76-7-309. Pathologist's report

Any human tissue removed during an abortion shall be submitted to a pathologist who shall make a report, including, but not limited to whether there was a pregnancy, and if possible, whether the pregnancy was aborted by evacuating the uterus.

Utah Code § 26-2-23. Health care institutions

(1)(a) All administrators or other persons in charge of hospitals, nursing homes, or other institutions, public or private, to which persons resort for treatment of diseases, confinements, or are committed by law, shall record all the personal and statistical information about patients of their institutions as required in certificates prescribed by this chapter.

(b) This information shall be recorded for collection at the time of admission of the patients and shall be obtained from the patient, if possible, and if not, the information shall be secured in as complete a manner as possible from other persons acquainted with the facts.

(2) When a dead body or dead fetus is released or disposed of by an institution, the person in charge of the institution shall keep a record showing the name of the deceased, date of death, name and address of the person to whom the dead body or dead fetus is released, and date of removal from the institution. If final disposal is by the institution, the date, place, manner of disposition, and the name of the person authorizing disposition shall be recorded.

(3) Not later than the tenth day of each month, the administrator of each institution shall cause to be sent to the local registrar and the department a list of all births, deaths, fetal deaths, and induced abortions occurring in his institution during the preceding month. The lists shall be in the form prescribed by the state registrar.

(11) ABORTION LITIGATION FUND

Utah has established a special fund to be used in defense of challenges to its abortion laws. The statute addressing the matter is set out below.

Utah Code § 76-7-317.1. Abortion litigation trust account

(1)(a) There is created in the General Fund a restricted account known as the Abortion Litigation Trust Account. All money received by the state from private sources for litigation expenses connected with the defense of Senate Bill 23, passed in the 1991 Annual General Session, shall be deposited in that account.

(b) On behalf of the Abortion Litigation Trust Account, the Division of Finance may accept grants, gifts, bequests, or any money made available from any private sources to implement this section.

(2) Money shall be appropriated by the Legislature from the account to the Office of the Attorney General under Title 63, Chapter 38, Budgetary Procedures Act.

(3) The Abortion Litigation Trust Account may be used only for costs, expenses, and attorneys fees connected with the defense of the abortion law identified in Subsection (1).

(4) Any funds remaining in the abortion litigation trust account after final appellate procedures shall revert to the General Fund, to be first used to offset the monies expended by the state in connection with litigation regarding Senate Bill 23.

(12) INJURY TO A PREGNANT WOMAN

Utah imposes criminal penalties on anyone who injures a pregnant woman and thereby causes the death of a fetus. The statute addressing the matter is set out below.

Utah Code § 76-5-201. Criminal homicide

(1)(a) A person commits criminal homicide if he intentionally, knowingly, recklessly, with criminal negligence, or acting with a mental state otherwise specified in the statute defining the offense, causes the death of another human being, including an unborn child at any stage of its development.

(b) There shall be no cause of action for criminal homicide for the death of an unborn child caused by an abortion.

(2) Criminal homicide is aggravated murder, murder, manslaughter, child abuse homicide, homicide by assault, negligent homicide, or automobile homicide.

Uterine Fibroids

Uterine fibroids are benign tumors (called leiomyoma) that arise from the muscle tissue of the uterus. The tumors may grow into the uterine cavity and wall or protrude outside of the uterine wall. Roughly 25 percent of all woman over the age of 35 have uterine fibroids. Most uterine fibroids will not complicate a pregnancy. However, when the fibroids are very close to the lining of the uterus, they will interfere with the implantation of the embryo in the uterus and cause a spontaneous abortion. Additionally, the fibroids may block the vagina and require birth by caesarean section. In rare instances the fibroids may cause infertility. Medications or surgery can be used to remove the fibroids. *See also* **Miscarriage**

Uterine Rupture

Rupture or tearing of the wall of a woman's uterus while pregnant may occur suddenly during labor or delivery. Uterine rupture occurs in less than 1 percent of all pregnancies. This condition may occur because of an incomplete healing of a prior surgery, weak uterine muscles after several pregnancies, excessive use of labor inducing agents, or through the use of birthing instruments (e.g., forceps). Whatever the cause for a uterine rupture, the potential consequence is always the same: a life threatening condition for the fetus and woman. Studies show that if surgical teams respond quickly to uterine ruptures mothers and babies do well. An untimely response is usually fatal for the fetus and mother. This is because the longer it takes to respond to a uterine rupture, the more likely it is that the fetus will be pushed through the uterine wall and into the mother's abdominal cavity.

The frequency of a uterine rupture is greater for women who have had a prior caesarean section, than for women who never had the procedure. Women who space their pregnancies close together increase their risk of uterine rupture, if they attempt a vaginal birth after a prior caesarean delivery. Studies haves shown that if a woman had an interval of only 18 months or less between her caesarean and vaginal births, she has a threefold increased risk of uterine rupture compared to women who had longer intervals between deliveries.

Uterus *see* **Female Reproductive System**

V

Vacuum Aspiration *see* **Machine Vacuum Aspiration; Mini Vac Aspiration**

Vacuum Extractor

The vacuum extractor is a cap-like device that is attached to a fetus' head, when necessary, to help deliver a live birth. It enables traction to be applied to the fetal head in the birth canal by means of a suction cup that is attached to the scalp. The device is powered by an external vacuum source. With the suction cup fitting over part of the fetus' head, the attending physician can ease the fetus through the birth canal. The device is normally used when the fetus has an abnormal presentation or position in the womb. The vacuum extractor is smoother and less damaging to the woman's tissues than forceps. However, excessive suction may cause injury to the woman or fetus. *See also* **Forceps Delivery; Presentation and Position of the Fetus**

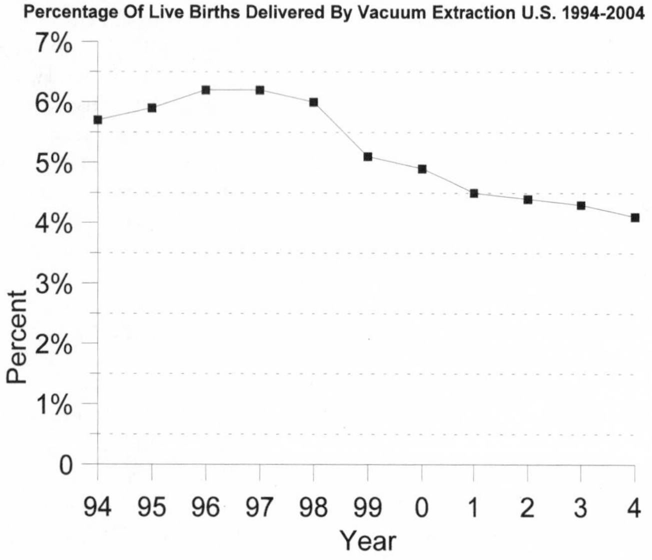

Source: **National Center for Health Statistics.**

Vagina *see* **Female Reproductive System**

Vaginal Birth

Vaginal birth refers to the delivery of a fetus through the birth canal, of which the vagina is a component. It is the normal method of birth when there are no complications, such as a breech presentation. The alternative method of birth that is used as a result of complications is a caesarean section. *See also* **Caesarean Section**

Vaginal Birth After Caesarean

For many years it was thought that vaginal birth could not occur, if there was a previous caesarean section birth. This is not necessarily so, if the caesarean section was performed low on the uterus. Usually the scar from a low cut is sufficiently strong to withstand labor and vaginal birth. However, vaginal birth after a caesarean is not advisable if the previous caesarean cut was made high up on the uterus. An attempted vaginal birth in this situation could cause uterine rupture during labor. Uterine rupture could pose severe consequences for the woman and the fetus. *See also* **Uterine Rupture**

Vaginal Bleeding During Pregnancy

Vaginal bleeding during pregnancy may be normal and harmless or it could be life threatening to the fetus or woman. Bleeding may arise at any time during a pregnancy. However, there are some common causes of bleeding associated with whether it occurs early or late in the pregnancy.

Early pregnancy vaginal bleeding. Several common potential reasons exist for vaginal bleeding during the early stages of a pregnancy. Those reasons include: cervical trauma due to injury or sex; initial implantation of the egg into the uterine wall; a tumor; a spontaneous abortion; or the pregnancy was an ectopic pregnancy.

Late pregnancy vaginal bleeding. There are three recurring reasons for late pregnancy vaginal bleeding. First, the bleeding may be a normal sign of labor as the cervix opens. Second, the bleeding may be due to the placenta detaching itself from the uterine wall before or during labor. This condition is dangerous and could be fatal to the woman and fetus because the bleeding is heavy. About 1 percent of all pregnancies present this situation. It may occur because of illegal drug use, abdominal trauma or high blood pressure. The third potential reason for late pregnancy vaginal bleeding is the abnormal placement of the placenta over the cervix, which blocks the birth canal. This situation can lead to heavy bleeding that poses potential fatal consequences to the fetus and woman.

Preventive measures. Preventing vaginal bleeding during pregnancy depends upon its cause. Early and continued prenatal care allows health care providers an opportunity to screen for risk factors that could cause bleeding.

Vaginal Cancer

Vaginal cancer is a disease in which malignant cancer cells are found in the tissues of the vagina. There are two types of vaginal cancer: squamous cell cancer and adenocarcinoma. Squamous carcinoma develops in women between the ages of 60 and 80; whereas adenocarcinoma is more often found in women between the ages of 12 and 30.

In the rare instance that a woman with vaginal cancer is pregnant, problems could rise for the fetus. The fact of pregnancy generally has no adverse effect on vaginal cancer, and vaginal cancer has no effect on the pregnancy. However, if certain cancer treatment methods are used during pregnancy, it may become necessary to have a therapeutic abortion, or the fetus could be exposed to birth defects. Treatments are available for vaginal cancer include surgery, radiation therapy and chemotherapy. *See also* **Cancer and Pregnancy; Therapeutic Abortion**

Vaginal Contraceptive Film *see* **Spermicides**

Vaginal Douching and the Risk of Ectopic Pregnancy

Vaginal douching has been linked to ectopic pregnancies. Studies have shown a link between the length of time a woman has douched and the risk of ectopic pregnancy. It has been observed that women who douched at least once a month for 5 years had a significant risk of ectopic pregnancy, as compared to women who never douched. While none of the studies are conclusive, researchers recommend women consult their doctors before deciding to begin or continue douching. *See also* **Ectopic Pregnancy**

Vaginal Fibronectin Screening

Vaginal fibronectin screening is a test for determining premature labor. Fibronectin is a protein found in connective tissues throughout the body. It is present in the placenta and in a woman's vaginal and cervical secretions in the first and early second trimesters. Vaginal and cervical secretions are tested to show alterations in fetal fibronectin levels. An increase in fetal fibronectin levels is an indication of possible premature labor. The testing is done by taking a swab, inserting it in the woman's vagina, and extracting secretions therefrom. *See also* **Premature Labor**

Vaginal Pouch *see* **Condoms**

Vaginal Ring *see* **Intrauterine Contraceptive Devices**

Vaginal Yeast Infection *see* **Vaginitis**

Vaginitis

Vaginitis is the term used to refer to any infection or inflammation of the vagina. The onset of vaginitis may be due to bacteria, yeast, viruses, irritations from chemicals in creams, sprays, or organisms that are passed between sexual partners. The three most common vaginal infections are bacterial vaginosis, trichomoniasis, and vaginal yeast infection.

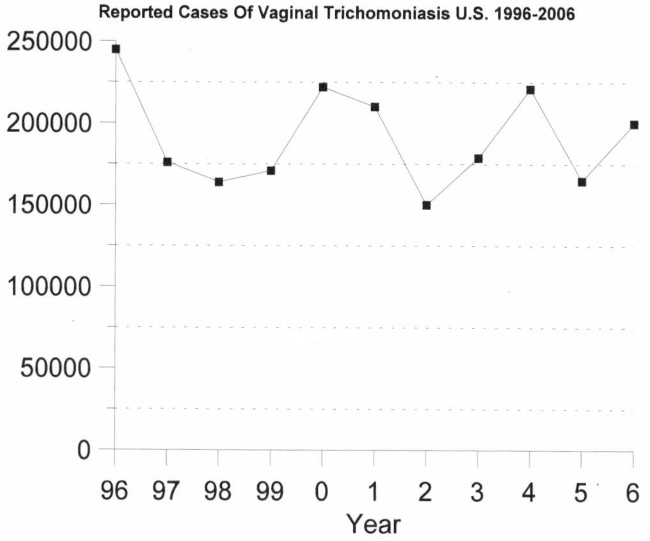

Source: **National Disease and Therapeutic Index.**

Bacterial vaginosis. Bacterial vaginosis (BV) affects about 800,000 pregnant women each year in the United States. BV is caused by an overgrowth of anaerobic bacteria (requiring no oxygen) and an organism called Gardnerella. It is also associated with unsafe sexual activity. Although nearly half of the women with clinical signs of BV report no symptoms, the primary known symptoms include abnormal odor, excessive vaginal discharge, and vaginal itching or burning are also sometimes present. BV has been linked to causing pelvic inflammatory disease, pregnancy complications, post-operative infections, premature delivery and low birthweight infants. BV can be treated with antibiotics (e.g., metronidazole or clindamycin).

Trichomoniasis. Trichomoniasis (Trich) is a vaginal infection in women (men may have the infection in the urethra) that is caused by a parasite (Trichomonas vaginalis).The infection is associated with unsafe sexual activity. Trich often occurs without any symptoms. When symptoms do surface they may include a heavy vaginal discharge, vaginal odor, painful urination, irritation and itching, and on rare occasions abdominal pain. Research has suggested that Trich is associated with an increased risk of transmission of HIV and may cause a woman to deliver a low birthweight or premature infant. Trich is treated with a drug called metronidazole.

Vaginal yeast infection. Vaginal yeast infection (also called candidiasis) is a common cause of vaginal irritation. Yeast are always present in the vagina in small numbers, and symptoms only appear with an overgrowth of yeast. Factors that are associated with this overgrowth include pregnancy, oral contraceptives, antibiotics, douches, perfumed feminine hygiene sprays, and wearing tight clothing or underwear. It is not known whether yeast can be transmitted sexually. It has been estimated that nearly 75 percent of all women experience at least one yeast infection during their lifetimes.

Common symptoms of yeast infection include vaginal itching, burning, and irritation, painful urination, uncomfortable intercourse, and minimal vaginal discharge. Yeast infection may be treated with antifungal vaginal medications in the form of creams, tablets, or suppositories. *See also* **Sexually Transmitted Diseases**

Vanderbilt Students for Life

Vanderbilt Students for Life (VSL) is a student-run pro-life organization on Vanderbilt campus. The group seeks to provide community education about abortion and the sanctity of human life from conception. VSL provides a forum for speakers and pro-life conferences. *See also* **Pro-Life Organizations**

Vanishing Twin Syndrome

Vanishing twin syndrome (VTS) involves the identification of multiple gestations in a uterus and the subsequent natural disappearance of one (or more) of the fetuses. With the use of ultrasound in early pregnancy, researchers have found that VTS occurs in about 30 percent of multiple gestations. VTS may occur as a result of complete re-absorption of one of the fetuses, formation of a compressed fetus (papyraceous), or transformation into a subtle abnormality on the placenta such as a cyst.

The timing of VTS affects the outcome of the viable twin and maternal complications. If VTS occurs during the first trimester, neither the remaining fetus nor the mother should be in danger. However, should VTS occur during the second half of pregnancy the remaining fetus may develop cerebral palsy or other defects, and the mother may have preterm labor, infection, hemorrhage, or obstruction of labor. *See also* **Fetal Transfusion Syndrome; Monoamnionic Twin Gestation; Monochorionic Twin Gestation; Multifetal Pregnancy Reduction; Multiple Gestation; Twin Reversed Arterial Perfusion**

Vasa Previa

Vasa previa is a rare condition in which the umbilical cord is the presenting part of an infant as he or she moves down the birth canal. This is a dangerous condition because the umbilical vessels can be pinched off or ruptured while being compressed between the infant and the walls of the birth canal. This situation is usually fatal for infants. *See also* **Miscarriage; Presentation and Position of the Fetus; Stillbirth**

Vasectomy *see* **Male Sterilization**

Venereal Diseases *see* **Sexually Transmitted Diseases**

Vermont

(1) OVERVIEW

The state of Vermont enacted its first criminal abortion statute on October 30, 1846. The statute underwent several amendments prior to the 1973 decision by the United States Supreme Court in *Roe v. Wade*, which legalized abortion in the nation. In spite of the decision in *Roe*, Vermont has not repealed its pre-*Roe* criminal abortion laws. However, those laws are constitutionally infirm.

Vermont has not taken any affirmative steps to respond to *Roe* and its progeny, by setting out constitutionally acceptable abortion guidelines. The state has, however, addressed the issue of a fetal death report.

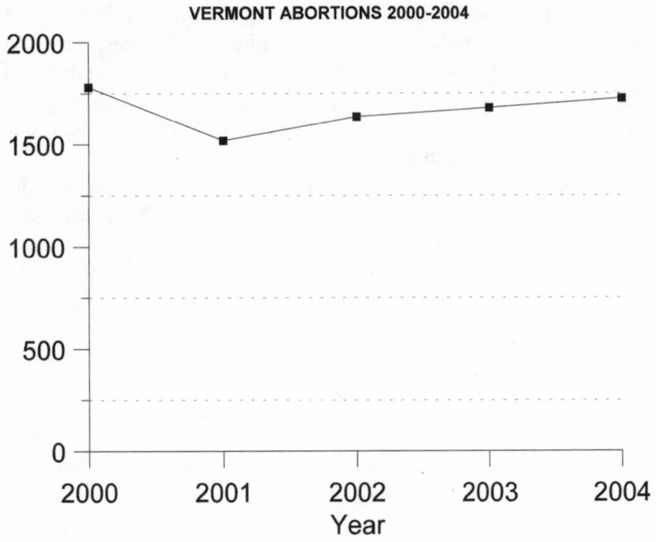

Source: National Center for Health Statistics.

Vermont Abortion by Age Group 2000–2004

Year	Age Group (yrs) <15	15–19	20–24	25–29	30–34	35–39	≥40	Unknown
2000	4	369	594	347	223	166	77	1
2001	6	323	532	280	179	138	60	1
2002	4	343	549	322	212	141	63	1
2003	6	324	601	310	198	137	101	2
2004	8	312	650	361	206	126	62	0
Total	28	1,671	2,926	1,620	1,018	708	363	5

Source: National Center for Health Statistics.

Vermont Abortion by Weeks of Gestation 2000–2004

Weeks of Gestation	Year 2000	2001	2002	2003	2004	Total
<9	1,131	966	1,108	1,126	1,182	5,513
9–10	412	332	296	319	268	1,627
11–12	161	136	135	117	156	705
13–15	71	83	86	106	99	445
16–20	5	1	7	10	12	35
≥21	1	0	1	2	8	12
Not known	0	1	2	0	0	3

Source: National Center for Health Statistics.

Vermont Abortion by Education Level of Female 2000–2004

Year	Education Level Completed <12	12	≥13	Unknown
2000	260	706	796	19
2001	222	570	708	13
2002	210	660	688	67
2003	236	699	708	53
2004	250	671	792	29
Total	1,178	3,306	3,692	181

Source: Vermont Department of Health.

(2) PRE-ROE ABORTION BAN

As previously indicated, Vermont has not repealed its pre-*Roe* criminal abortion laws. Under the now unconstitutional laws, abortion was criminalized if it was not performed to preserve the life of the woman. This restriction was held invalid in *Beecham v. Leahy*, 287

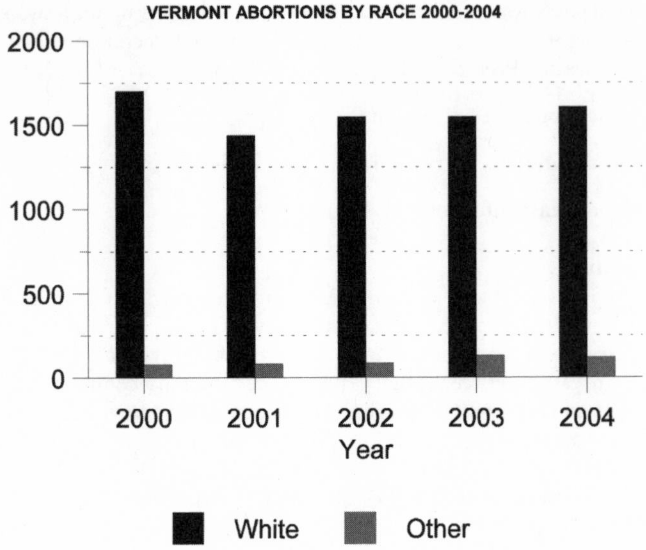

Source: National Center for Health Statistics.

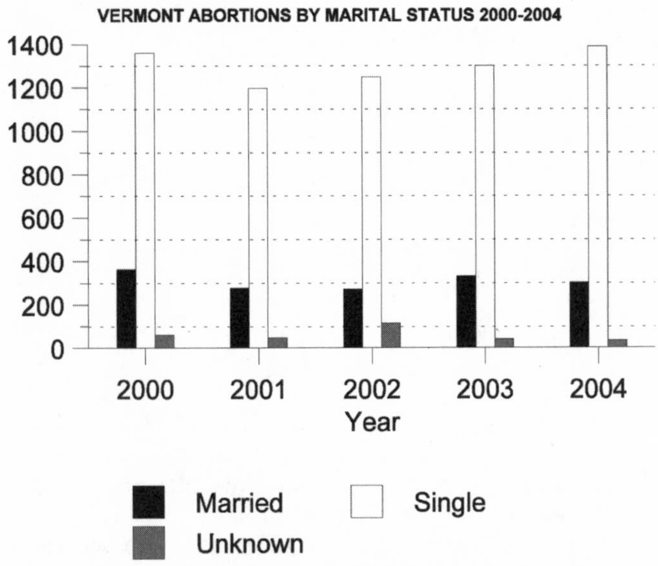

Source: National Center for Health Statistics.

Vermont Prior Abortion by Female 2000–2004

Year	Prior Abortion None	1	2	≥3	Not known
2000	1,123	424	142	90	2
2001	926	379	130	81	3
2002	976	432	142	84	1
2003	1,012	420	152	93	2
2004	1,012	435	175	103	0
Total	5,049	2,090	741	451	8

Source: National Center for Health Statistics.

A.2d 836 (Vt. 1972). The state also made it a crime to advertise abortion services. The statutes are set out below.

Vermont Code Ti. 13, § 101. Abortion prohibited

A person who wilfully administers, advises or causes to be administered anything to a woman pregnant, or supposed by such person to be pregnant, or employs or causes to be employed any means with intent to pro-

cure the miscarriage of such woman, or assists or counsels therein, unless the same is necessary to preserve her life, if the woman dies in consequence thereof, shall be imprisoned not more than twenty years nor less than five years. If the woman does not die in consequence thereof, such person shall be imprisoned not more than ten years nor less than three years. However, the woman whose miscarriage is caused or attempted shall not be liable to the penalties prescribed by this section.

Vermont Code Ti. 13, § 102. Dying declaration as evidence

In all prosecutions under the provisions of section 101 of this title, the dying declaration of the woman whose death is produced by any of the means set forth in such section may be admitted in evidence subject to the same restrictions as in cases of homicide.

Vermont Code Ti. 13, § 103. Joining with murder indictment

A person who is indicted for the murder of an infant child, or of a woman pregnant or supposed by such person to be pregnant, may be charged in the same indictment with the offenses under section 101 of this title, and may be found guilty of any charge in the indictment sustained by the proof, and judgment and sentence shall be awarded accordingly.

Vermont Code Ti. 13, § 104. Advertising for abortion

A person who knowingly causes to be made public by print, writing, words or language that give any information where anything, or any advice or information, may be obtained for the purpose of causing or procuring the miscarriage of a pregnant woman, shall be imprisoned not more than ten years nor less than three years. A person who sells or gives away anything for the purpose of producing such miscarriage shall be imprisoned not more than three years nor less than one year and fined not more than $500.00 nor less than $200.00, or both.

(3) FETAL DEATH REPORT

Vermont requires that all abortions be reported to the proper authorities. The statute addressing the matter is set out below.

Vermont Code Ti. 18, § 5222. Reports

(a) The following fetal deaths shall be reported by the hospital, physician, or funeral director directly to the commissioner within seven days after delivery on forms prescribed by the board:

(1) All fetal deaths of 20 or more weeks of gestation or, if gestational age is unknown, of 400 or more grams, 15 or more ounces, fetal weight shall be reported;

(2) All therapeutic or induced abortions, as legally authorized to be performed, of any length gestation or weight shall be reported;

(3) Spontaneous abortions and ectopic pregnancies of less than 20 weeks gestation are not required to be reported.

(b) The physician who treats a woman as a result of a miscarriage or abortion shall report the fetal death if it is not known to be previously reported under subsection (a) of this section. If there is evidence of violence or other unusual or suspicious circumstances, the medical examiner shall be immediately notified, and he shall complete at least the medical items on the report. If a funeral director is to be involved, the physician may delegate to the funeral director the responsibility for completing items other than those of a medical nature. Similarly, the physician may delegate the responsibility for completion of nonmedical items to appropriate personnel having access to records containing the information.

(c) If a fetal death occurs on a moving conveyance, the place of occurrence shall be given as the town or city where removal from the vehicle took place.

(d) Fetal death reports are for statistical purposes only and are not public records. They shall be destroyed after five years.

Vermont Right to Life Committee

Vermont Right to Life Committee (VRLC) is a pro-life organization that was founded in 1973. The executive director of VRLC is Mary Beerworth. VRLC is the oldest and largest pro-life group in the state of Vermont. The organization seeks to achieve universal recognition and respect for the sanctity of human life from conception through natural death. The group engages in peaceful, legal means to seek changes in public opinion, public policy, the law, and individual behavior toward abortion. It works with churches, schools, service organizations, and political groups at both the state and local level. The organization publishes a newspaper four times per year, hosts a daily radio program, sponsors a yearly educational conference featuring nationally recognized speakers, and publishes the "Life Pages," a compendium of prolife businesses, churches, and individuals who support the work of the organization. *See also* **Pro-Life Organizations**

Viability of Fetus *see* **Abortion**

Viability Testing

Viability testing refers to a medical procedure used to determine whether a fetus has reached the minimum stage of development to exist outside the mothers womb with or without artificial life support. An abortion may not be performed on a viable fetus, unless necessary to save the life or health of the mother. A minority of states require viability testing prior to the performance of an abortion at any stage of pregnancy. *See also* **Abortion; Criminal Abortion**

Virginia

(1) OVERVIEW

The state of Virginia enacted its first criminal abortion statute on March 14, 1848. The statute underwent several amendments prior to the 1973 decision by the United States Supreme Court in *Roe v. Wade*, which legalized abortion in the nation. Virginia has taken affirmative steps to respond to *Roe* and its progeny. The state has addressed several abortion issues by statute that include general abortion guidelines, informed consent, partial-birth abortion, abortion by minors, use of facilities and people, fetal death report, injury to a pregnant woman, and human cloning ban.

(2) GENERAL ABORTION GUIDELINES

Virginia expressly authorizes abortion during the first and second trimesters. The state requires second trimester abortions be performed at a hospital. The United States Supreme Court held in *Simopoulos v. Virginia* that Virginia's statute, requiring second trimester abortions be performed at hospitals, was valid because under the statute an ad-

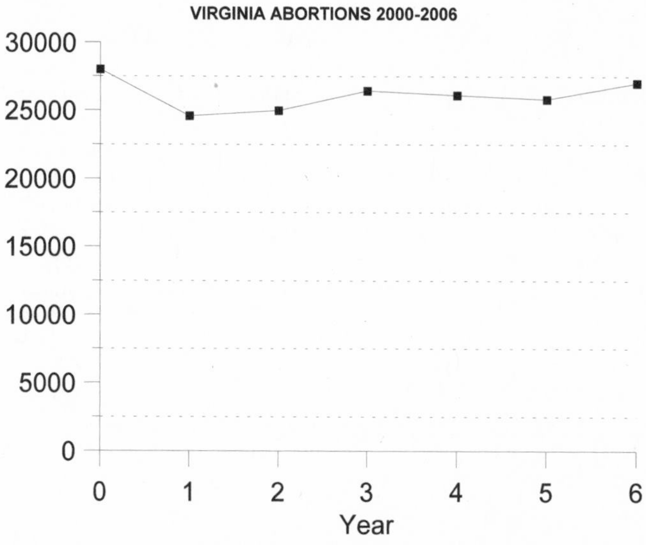

Source: **National Center for Health Statistics/Virginia Department of Health.**

Virginia Abortion by Weeks of Gestation 2000–2004

Weeks of Gestation	Year *2000*	*2001*	*2002*	*2003*	*2004*	*Total*
<9	18,354	16,964	17,661	17,962	17,562	88,503
9–10	5,700	4,524	4,295	4,722	4,628	23,869
11–12	2,882	2,148	2,046	2,454	2,681	12,211
13–15	676	557	577	512	741	3,063
16–20	243	210	231	232	248	1,164
≥21	64	67	57	76	78	342
Not known	80	116	125	479	179	979

Source: National Center for Health Statistics.

Virginia Abortion By Age Group 2000-2004

Year	Age Group (yrs) *<15*	*15–19*	*20–24*	*25–29*	*30–34*	*35–39*	*≥40*	*Unknown*
2000	153	4,435	9,092	6,508	4,190	2,557	846	218
2001	143	3,961	7,985	5,492	3,814	2,275	762	154
2002	129	3,760	8,368	5,718	3,814	2,258	797	148
2003	118	4,005	8,864	6,029	3,942	2,326	848	305
2004	128	3,810	8,910	6,037	3,887	2,204	934	207
Total	671	19,971	43,219	29,784	19,647	11,620	4,187	1,032

Source: National Center for Health Statistics.

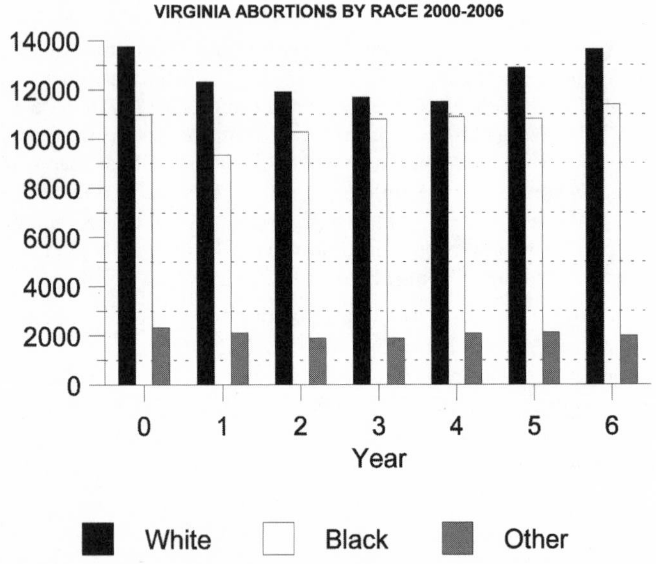

Source: **National Center for Health Statistics/Virginia Department of Health.**

equately equipped clinic could obtain an outpatient hospital license that permitted the performance of second trimester abortions. Virginia permits a third trimester abortion, but only if necessary to prevent the death of the woman or substantially and irremediably impair the mental or physical health of the woman. The statutes addressing the issues are set out below.

Virginia Code § 18.2-71. Producing abortion or miscarriage

Except as provided in other sections of this article, if any person administer to, or cause to be taken by a woman, any drug or other thing, or use means, with intent to destroy her unborn child, or to produce abortion or miscarriage, and thereby destroy such child, or produce such abortion or miscarriage, he shall be guilty of a Class 4 felony.

Virginia Code § 18.2-72. First trimester abortion

Notwithstanding any of the provisions of § 18.2-71, it shall be lawful for any physician licensed by the Board of Medicine to practice medi-

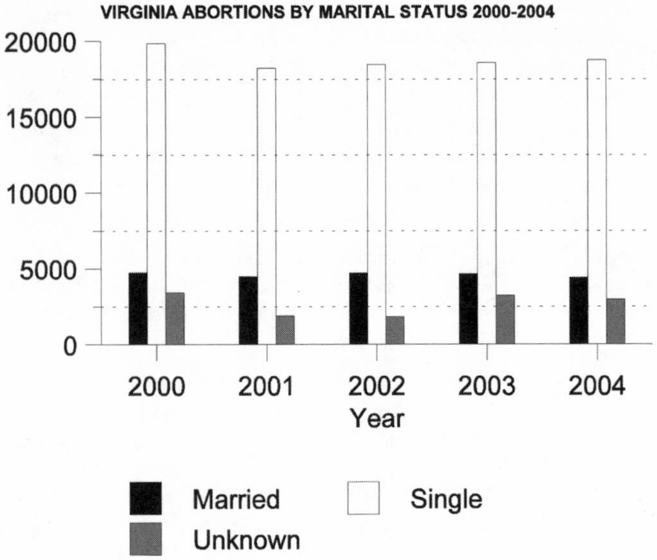

Source: National Center for Health Statistics.

Virginia Prior Abortion by Female 2000–2004

Year	Prior Abortion *None*	*1*	*2*	*≥3*	*Not known*
2000	12,886	8,025	2,943	1,396	2,749
2001	13,328	6,904	2,731	1,307	316
2002	13,470	7,109	2,763	1,332	318
2003	13,615	7,186	2,679	1,204	1,663
2004	14,084	7,159	2,831	1,320	723
Total	67,383	36,383	13,947	6,559	5,769

Source: National Center for Health Statistics.

cine and surgery, to terminate or attempt to terminate a human pregnancy or aid or assist in the termination of a human pregnancy by performing an abortion or causing a miscarriage on any woman during the first trimester of pregnancy.

Virginia Code § 18.2-73. Second trimester abortion

Notwithstanding any of the provisions of § 18.2-71 and in addition to the provisions of § 18.2-72, it shall be lawful for any physician licensed by the Board of Medicine to practice medicine and surgery, to terminate or attempt to terminate a human pregnancy or aid or assist in the termination of a human pregnancy by performing an abortion or causing a miscarriage on any woman during the second trimester of pregnancy and prior to the third trimester of pregnancy provided such procedure is performed in a hospital licensed by the State Department of Health or under the control of the State Board of Mental Health, Mental Retardation and Substance Abuse Services.

Virginia Code § 18.2-74. Third trimester abortion

Notwithstanding any of the provisions of § 18.2-71 and in addition to the provisions of §§ 18.2-72 and 18.2-73, it shall be lawful for any physician licensed by the Board of Medicine to practice medicine and surgery to terminate or attempt to terminate a human pregnancy or aid or assist in the termination of a human pregnancy by performing an abortion or causing a miscarriage on any woman in a stage of pregnancy subsequent to the second trimester provided the following conditions are met:

(a) Said operation is performed in a hospital licensed by the Virginia State Department of Health or under the control of the State Board of Mental Health, Mental Retardation and Substance Abuse Services.

(b) The physician and two consulting physicians certify and so

enter in the hospital record of the woman, that in their medical opinion, based upon their best clinical judgment, the continuation of the pregnancy is likely to result in the death of the woman or substantially and irremediably impair the mental or physical health of the woman.

(c) Measures for life support for the product of such abortion or miscarriage must be available and utilized if there is any clearly visible evidence of viability.

Virginia Code § 18.2-74.1.
Abortion necessary to save life of woman

In the event it is necessary for a licensed physician to terminate a human pregnancy or assist in the termination of a human pregnancy by performing an abortion or causing a miscarriage on any woman in order to save her life, in the opinion of the physician so performing the abortion or causing the miscarriage, §§ 18.2-71, 18.2-73 and 18.2-74 shall not be applicable.

Virginia Code § 18.2-76.1.
Encouraging or promoting abortion

If any person, by publication, lecture, advertisement, or by the sale or circulation of any publication, or through the use of a referral agency for profit, or in any other manner, encourage or promote the performing of an abortion or the inducing of a miscarriage in this Commonwealth which is prohibited under this article, he shall be guilty of a Class 3 misdemeanor.

Virginia Code § 32.1-92.2.
Funding abortion when fetus deformed

From the moneys appropriated to the Department from the general fund, the Board shall fund abortions for women who otherwise meet the financial eligibility criteria of the State Medical Assistance Plan in any case in which a physician who is trained and qualified to perform such tests certifies in writing, after appropriate tests have been performed, that he believes the fetus will be born with a gross and totally incapacitating physical deformity or with a gross and totally incapacitating mental deficiency.

Virginia Code § 32.1-92.1.
Funding abortion for rape or incest victim

From the moneys appropriated to the Department from the general fund, the Board shall fund abortions for women who otherwise meet the financial eligibility criteria of the State Medical Assistance Plan in any case in which a pregnancy occurs as a result of rape or incest and which is reported to a law-enforcement or public health agency.

(3) INFORMED CONSENT

Prior to an abortion Virginia requires that a woman be fully informed of the procedure to be used, the risks involved and alternatives to abortion. An abortion may not take place until 24 hours after a woman has been given the required statutory information. The statute addressing the matter is set out below.

Virginia Code § 18.2-76. Consent and waiting period

A. Before performing any abortion or inducing any miscarriage or terminating a pregnancy as provided in §§ 18.2-72, 18.2-73 or § 18.2-74, the physician shall obtain the informed written consent of the pregnant woman. However, if the woman has been adjudicated incapacitated by any court of competent jurisdiction or if the physician knows or has good reason to believe that such woman is incapacitated as adjudicated by a court of competent jurisdiction, then only after permission is given in writing by a parent, guardian, committee, or other person standing in loco parentis to the woman, may the physician perform the abortion or otherwise terminate the pregnancy.

B. For purposes of this section:

"Informed written consent" means the knowing and voluntary written consent to abortion by a pregnant woman of any age, without undue inducement or any element of force, fraud, deceit, duress, or other form of constraint or coercion by the physician who is to perform the abortion or his agent. The basic information to effect such consent, as required by this subsection, shall be provided by telephone or in person to the woman at least 24 hours before the abortion by the physician who is to perform the abortion, by a referring physician, or by a licensed professional or practical nurse working under the direct supervision of either the physician who is to perform the abortion or the referring physician; however, the information in subdivision 5 may be provided instead by a licensed health-care professional working under the direct supervision of either the physician who is to perform the abortion or the referring physician. This basic information shall include:

1. A full, reasonable and comprehensible medical explanation of the nature, benefits, and risks of and alternatives to the proposed procedures or protocols to be followed in her particular case;

2. An instruction that the woman may withdraw her consent at any time prior to the performance of the procedure;

3. An offer for the woman to speak with the physician who is to perform the abortion so that he may answer any questions that the woman may have and provide further information concerning the procedures and protocols;

4. A statement of the probable gestational age of the fetus at the time the abortion is to be performed; and

5. An offer to review the printed materials described in subsection D. If the woman chooses to review such materials, they shall be provided to her in a respectful and understandable manner, without prejudice and intended to give the woman the opportunity to make an informed choice and shall be provided to her at least 24 hours before the abortion or mailed to her at least 72 hours before the abortion by first-class mail or, if the woman requests, by certified mail, restricted delivery. This offer for the woman to review the material shall advise her of the following: (i) the Department of Health publishes printed materials that describe the unborn child and list agencies that offer alternatives to abortion; (ii) medical assistance benefits may be available for prenatal care, childbirth and neonatal care, and that more detailed information on the availability of such assistance is contained in the printed materials published by the Department; (iii) the father of the unborn child is liable to assist in the support of her child, even in instances where he has offered to pay for the abortion, that assistance in the collection of such support is available, and that more detailed information on the availability of such assistance is contained in the printed materials published by the Department; and (iv) she has the right to review the materials printed by the Department and that copies will be provided to her free of charge if she chooses to review them. Where the woman has advised that the pregnancy is the result of a rape, the information in clause (iii) above may be omitted.

The information required by this subsection may be provided by telephone without conducting a physical examination of or tests upon the woman, in which case the information required to be provided may be based on facts supplied by the woman and whatever other relevant information is reasonably available to the physician. If a physical examination, tests or the availability of other information to the physician or the nurse subsequently indicates, in the medical judgment of the physician or the nurse, a revision of the information previously supplied to the woman, that revised information may be communicated to the woman at any time prior to the performance of the abortion.

C. The physician need not obtain the informed written consent of the woman when the abortion is to be performed pursuant to a medical emergency. "Medical emergency" means any condition which, on the basis of the physician's good faith clinical judgment, so complicates the medical condition of a pregnant woman as to necessitate the immediate abortion of her pregnancy to avert her death or for which a delay will create a serious risk of substantial and irreversible impairment of a major bodily function.

D. On or before October 1, 2001, the Department of Health shall publish, in English and in each language which is the primary language of two percent or more of the population of the Commonwealth, the following printed materials in such a way as to ensure that the information is easily comprehensible:

1. Geographically indexed materials designed to inform the woman of public and private agencies and services available to assist a woman through pregnancy, upon childbirth and while the child is dependent, including, but not limited to, information on services relating to (i) adoption as a positive alternative, (ii) information relative to counseling services, benefits, financial assistance, medical care and contact persons or groups, (iii) paternity establishment and child support enforcement, (iv) child development, (v) child rearing and stress management, and (vi) pediatric and maternal health care. The materials shall include a comprehensive list of the names and telephone numbers of the agencies, or, at the option of the Department of Health, printed materials including a toll-free, 24-hour-a-day telephone number which may be called to obtain, orally, such a list and description of agencies in the locality of the caller and of the services they offer;

2. Materials designed to inform the woman of the probable anatomical and physiological characteristics of the human fetus at two-week gestational increments from the time when a woman can be known to be pregnant to full term, including any relevant information on the possibility of the fetus's survival and pictures or drawings representing the development of the human fetus at two-week gestational increments. Such pictures or drawings shall contain the dimensions of the fetus and shall be realistic and appropriate for the stage of pregnancy depicted. The materials shall be objective, non-judgmental and designed to convey only accurate scientific information about the human fetus at the various gestational ages; and

3. Materials containing objective information describing the methods of abortion procedures commonly employed, the medical risks commonly associated with each such procedure, the possible detrimental psychological effects of abortion, and the medical risks commonly associated with carrying a child to term.

The Department of Health shall make these materials available at each local health department and, upon request, to any person or entity, in reasonable numbers and without cost to the requesting party.

E. Any physician who fails to comply with the provisions of this section shall be subject to a $2,500 civil penalty.

(4) PARTIAL-BIRTH ABORTION

Virginia prohibits partial-birth abortions, except to save the life of the woman. A federal court of appeals held that Virginia's partial-birth abortion statute was invalid in *Richmond Medical Center for Women v. Hicks*, 409 F.3d 619 (4th Cir. 2005), as a result of the United States Supreme Court decision in *Stenberg v. Carhart*, which invalidated a Nebraska statute that prohibited partial-birth abortions. However, in a memorandum opinion, *Herring v. Richmond Medical Center for Women*, 127 S.Ct. 2094 (2007), the United States Supreme Court vacated the judgment of the court of appeals and remanded the case for further consideration in light of the Supreme Court's decision in *Gonzales v. Carhart*, which had upheld a federal statute that banned partial-birth abortion. The state statute is set out below.

Virginia Code § 18.2-71.1. Partial-birth abortion ban

A. Any person who knowingly performs partial birth infanticide and thereby kills a human infant is guilty of a Class 4 felony.

B. For the purposes of this section, "partial birth infanticide" means any deliberate act that (i) is intended to kill a human infant who has been born alive, but who has not been completely extracted or expelled from its mother, and that (ii) does kill such infant, regardless of whether death occurs before or after extraction or expulsion from its mother has been completed.

The term "partial birth infanticide" shall not under any circumstances be construed to include any of the following procedures: (i) the suction curettage abortion procedure, (ii) the suction aspiration abortion procedure, (iii) the dilation and evacuation abortion procedure involving dismemberment of the fetus prior to removal from the body of the mother, or (iv) completing delivery of a living human infant and severing the umbilical cord of any infant who has been completely delivered.

C. For the purposes of this section, "human infant who has been born alive" means a product of human conception that has been completely or substantially expelled or extracted from its mother, regardless of the duration of pregnancy, which after such expulsion or extraction breathes or shows any other evidence of life such as beating of the heart, pulsation of the umbilical cord, or definite movement of voluntary muscles, whether or not the umbilical cord has been cut or the placenta is attached.

D. For purposes of this section, "substantially expelled or extracted from its mother" means, in the case of a headfirst presentation, the infant's entire head is outside the body of the mother, or, in the case of breech presentation, any part of the infant's trunk past the navel is outside the body of the mother.

E. This section shall not prohibit the use by a physician of any procedure that, in reasonable medical judgment, is necessary to prevent the death of the mother, so long as the physician takes every medically reasonable step, consistent with such procedure, to preserve the life and health of the infant. A procedure shall not be deemed necessary to prevent the death of the mother if completing the delivery of the living infant would prevent the death of the mother.

F. The mother may not be prosecuted for any criminal offense based on the performance of any act or procedure by a physician in violation of this section.

(5) ABORTION BY MINORS

Under the laws of Virginia no physician may perform an abortion upon an unemancipated minor, without the consent of a parent or legal guardian, and until 24 hours after notice of the operation has been given to either parent of the minor or a legal guardian. In compliance with federal constitutional law, Virginia has provided a judicial waiver procedure for an unemancipated minor to obtain an abortion without parental or guardian notice. If an unemancipated minor elects not to provide notice, the minor may petition a trial court for a waiver of the notice requirement. A minor has a right to an attorney at the proceeding and if she cannot afford one, the court must appoint her an attorney. If a minor chooses, she may represent herself. The required parental notice may be waived if the court finds either (1) that the minor is mature and well-informed enough to make the abortion decision on her own, or (2) that performance of the abortion would be in the best interest of the minor. An expedited appeal is available to any minor to whom the court denies a waiver of notice. Parental notice or judicial authorization is not required if the minor declares that she is an abused or neglected child. The statute addressing the matters is set out below.

Virginia Code § 16.1-241(V). Notice and judicial bypass

[[E]ach juvenile and domestic relations district court shall have ... concurrent jurisdiction with the juvenile court or courts of the adjoining city or county, over all cases, matters and proceedings involving] [p]etitions filed by a juvenile seeking judicial authorization for a physician to perform an abortion if a minor elects not to seek consent of an authorized person.

After a hearing, a judge shall issue an order authorizing a physician to perform an abortion, without the consent of any authorized person, if he finds that (i) the minor is mature enough and well enough informed to make her abortion decision, in consultation with her physician, independent of the wishes of any authorized person, or (ii) the minor is not mature enough or well enough informed to make such decision, but the desired abortion would be in her best interest.

If the judge authorizes an abortion based on the best interests of the minor, such order shall expressly state that such authorization is subject to the physician or his agent giving notice of intent to perform the abortion; however, no such notice shall be required if the judge finds that such notice would not be in the best interest of the minor. In determining whether notice is in the best interest of the minor, the judge shall consider the totality of the circumstances; however, he shall find that notice is not in the best interest of the minor if he finds that (i) one or more authorized persons with whom the minor regularly and customarily resides is abusive or neglectful, and (ii) every other authorized person, if any, is either abusive or neglectful or has refused to accept responsibility as parent, legal guardian, custodian or person standing in loco parentis.

The minor may participate in the court proceedings on her own behalf, and the court may appoint a guardian ad litem for the minor. The court shall advise the minor that she has a right to counsel and shall, upon her request, appoint counsel for her.

Notwithstanding any other provision of law, the provisions of this subsection shall govern proceedings relating to consent for a minor's abortion. Court proceedings under this subsection and records of such proceedings shall be confidential. Such proceedings shall be given precedence over other pending matters so that the court may reach a decision promptly and without delay in order to serve the best interests of the minor. Court proceedings under this subsection shall be heard and decided as soon as practicable but in no event later than four days after the petition is filed.

An expedited confidential appeal to the circuit court shall be available to any minor for whom the court denies an order authorizing an abortion without consent or without notice. Any such appeal shall be heard and decided no later than five days after the appeal is filed. The time periods required by this subsection shall be subject to subsection B of § 1-210. An order authorizing an abortion without consent or without notice shall not be subject to appeal.

No filing fees shall be required of the minor at trial or upon appeal.

If either the original court or the circuit court fails to act within the time periods required by this subsection, the court before which the proceeding is pending shall immediately authorize a physician to perform the abortion without consent of or notice to an authorized person.

Nothing contained in this subsection shall be construed to authorize a physician to perform an abortion on a minor in circumstances or in a manner that would be unlawful if performed on an adult woman.

A physician shall not knowingly perform an abortion upon an unemancipated minor unless consent has been obtained or the minor delivers to the physician a court order entered pursuant to this section and the physician or his agent provides such notice as such order may require. However, neither consent nor judicial authorization nor notice shall be required if the minor declares that she is abused or neglected and the attending physician has reason to suspect that the minor may be an abused or neglected child as defined in § 63.2-100 and reports the suspected abuse or neglect in accordance with § 63.2-1509; or if there is a medical emergency, in which case the attending physician shall certify the facts justifying the exception in the minor's medical record.

For purposes of this subsection:

"Authorization" means the minor has delivered to the physician a notarized, written statement signed by an authorized person that the authorized person knows of the minor's intent to have an abortion and consents to such abortion being performed on the minor.

"Authorized person" means (i) a parent or duly appointed legal guardian or custodian of the minor or (ii) a person standing in loco parentis, including, but not limited to, a grandparent or adult sibling with whom the minor regularly and customarily resides and who has care and control of the minor. Any person who knows he is not an authorized person and who knowingly and willfully signs an authorization statement consenting to an abortion for a minor is guilty of a Class 3 misdemeanor.

"Consent" means that (i) the physician has given notice of intent to perform the abortion and has received authorization from an authorized person, or (ii) at least one authorized person is present with the minor seeking the abortion and provides written authorization to the physician, which shall be witnessed by the physician or an agent thereof. In either case, the written authorization shall be incorporated into the minor's medical record and maintained as a part thereof.

"Medical emergency" means any condition which, on the basis of the physician's good faith clinical judgment, so complicates the medical condition of the pregnant minor as to necessitate the immediate abortion of her pregnancy to avert her death or for which a delay will create a serious risk of substantial and irreversible impairment of a major bodily function.

"Notice of intent to perform the abortion" means that (i) the physician or his agent has given actual notice of his intention to perform such abortion to an authorized person, either in person or by telephone, at least 24 hours previous to the performance of the abortion; or (ii) the physician or his agent, after a reasonable effort to notify an authorized person, has mailed notice to an authorized person by certified mail, addressed to such person at his usual place of abode, with return receipt requested, at least 72 hours prior to the performance of the abortion.

"Perform an abortion" means to interrupt or terminate a pregnancy by any surgical or nonsurgical procedure or to induce a miscarriage as provided in § 18.2-72, 18.2-73, or 18.2-74.

"Unemancipated minor" means a minor who has not been emancipated by (i) entry into a valid marriage, even though the marriage may have been terminated by dissolution; (ii) active duty with any of the Armed Forces of the United States; (iii) willingly living separate and apart from his or her parents or guardian, with the consent or acquiescence of the parents or guardian; or (iv) entry of an order of emancipation pursuant to Article 15 (§ 16.1-331 et seq.) of this chapter.

(6) USE OF FACILITIES AND PEOPLE

Under the laws of Virginia hospitals are not required to allow abortions at their facilities. The employees and physicians at hospitals that do allow abortions are permitted to refuse to take part in abortions. The statute addressing the matter is set out below.

Virginia Code § 18.2-75. Right not to participate in abortion

Nothing in §§ 18.2-72, 18.2-73 or § 18.2-74 shall require a hospital or other medical facility or physician to admit any patient under the provisions hereof for the purpose of performing an abortion. In addition, any person who shall state in writing an objection to any abortion or all abortions on personal, ethical, moral or religious grounds shall not be required to participate in procedures which will result in such abortion, and the refusal of such person, hospital or other medical facility to participate therein shall not form the basis of any claim for damages on account of such refusal or for any disciplinary or recriminatory action against such person, nor shall any such person be denied employment because of such objection or refusal. The written objection shall remain in effect until such person shall revoke it in writing or terminate his association with the facility with which it is filed.

(7) FETAL DEATH REPORT

Virginia requires by statute that all abortions be reported to the proper authorities. The statute addressing the matter is set out below.

Virginia Code § 32.1-264. Reports of fetal deaths

A. A fetal death report for each fetal death which occurs in this Commonwealth shall be filed, on a form furnished by the State Registrar, with the registrar of the district in which the delivery occurred or the abortion was performed within three days after such delivery or abortion and shall be registered with such registrar if it has been completed and filed in accordance with this section; provided that:

1. If the place of fetal death is unknown, a fetal death report shall be filed in the registration district in which a dead fetus was found within three days after discovery of such fetus; and

2. If a fetal death occurs in a moving conveyance, a fetal death report shall be filed in the registration district in which the fetus was first removed from such conveyance.

B. The funeral director or person who first assumes custody of a dead fetus or, in the absence of a funeral director or such person, the hospital representative who first assumes custody of a fetus shall file the fetal death report; in the absence of such a person, the physician or other person in attendance at or after the delivery or abortion shall file the report of fetal death. The person completing the forms shall obtain the personal data from the next of kin or the best qualified person or source available, and he shall obtain the medical certification of cause of death from the person responsible for preparing the same as provided in this section. In the case of induced abortion, such forms shall not identify the patient by name.

C. The medical certification portion of the fetal death report shall be completed and signed within twenty-four hours after delivery or abortion by the physician in attendance at or after delivery or abortion except when inquiry or investigation by a medical examiner is required.

D. When a fetal death occurs without medical attendance upon the mother at or after the delivery or abortion or when inquiry or investigation by a medical examiner is required, the medical examiner shall investigate the cause of fetal death and shall complete and sign the medical certification portion of the fetal death report within twenty-four hours after being notified of a fetal death.

E. The reports required pursuant to this section are statistical reports to be used only for medical and health purposes and shall not be incorporated into the permanent official records of the system of vital records. A schedule for the disposition of these reports may be provided by regulation.

F. The physician or facility attending an individual who has delivered a dead fetus shall maintain a copy of the fetal death report for one year and, upon written request by the individual and payment of an appropriate fee, shall furnish the individual a copy of such report.

(8) INJURY TO A PREGNANT WOMAN

Virginia has a few criminal statutes that provide punishment for anyone who harms a pregnant woman and thereby cause the death of her fetus. The statutes are set out below.

Virginia Code § 18.2-32.2. Killing a fetus

A. Any person who unlawfully, willfully, deliberately, maliciously and with premeditation kills the fetus of another is guilty of a Class 2 felony.

B. Any person who unlawfully, willfully, deliberately and maliciously kills the fetus of another is guilty of a felony punishable by confinement in a state correctional facility for not less than five nor more than 40 years.

Virginia Code § 18.2-32.1. Murdering a pregnant woman

The willful and deliberate killing of a pregnant woman without premeditation by one who knows that the woman is pregnant and has the intent to cause the involuntary termination of the woman's pregnancy without a live birth shall be punished by a term of imprisonment of not less than ten years nor more than forty years.

Virginia Code § 18.2-51.2. Aggravated malicious wounding

A. If any person maliciously shoots, stabs, cuts or wounds any other person, or by any means causes bodily injury, with the intent to maim, disfigure, disable or kill, he shall be guilty of a Class 2 felony if the victim is thereby severely injured and is caused to suffer permanent and significant physical impairment.

B. If any person maliciously shoots, stabs, cuts or wounds any other woman who is pregnant, or by any other means causes bodily injury, with the intent to maim, disfigure, disable or kill the pregnant woman or to cause the involuntary termination of her pregnancy, he shall be guilty of a Class 2 felony if the victim is thereby severely injured and is caused to suffer permanent and significant physical impairment.

C. For purposes of this section, the involuntary termination of a woman's pregnancy shall be deemed a severe injury and a permanent and significant physical impairment.

(9) HUMAN CLONING BAN

Virginia prohibits the cloning of human life. The state provides for a civil penalty to be assessed against anyone taking part in human cloning. The statutes addressing the issue are set out below.

Virginia Code § 32.1-162.21. Definitions

As used in this chapter, unless the context clearly requires another meaning:

"Cloning" means the production of a precise genetic copy of a molecule, including deoxyribonucleic acid (DNA), or of chromosomes.

"Human cloning" means the creation of or attempt to create a human being by transferring the nucleus from a human cell from whatever source into an oocyte from which the nucleus has been removed.

"Nucleus" means the cell structure that houses the chromosomes and, thus, the genes.

"Oocyte" means the ovum or egg.

"Somatic cell" means a mature, diploid cell, i.e., a cell having a complete set of chromosomes.

"Somatic cell nuclear transfer" means transferring the nucleus of a somatic cell of an existing or deceased human into an oocyte from which the chromosomes are removed or rendered inert.

Virginia Code § 32.1-162.22. Human cloning prohibited

A. No person shall (i) perform human cloning or (ii) implant or attempt to implant the product of somatic cell nuclear transfer into a uterine environment so as to initiate a pregnancy or (iii) possess the product of human cloning or (iv) ship or receive the product of a somatic cell nuclear transfer in commerce for the purpose of implanting the product of somatic cell nuclear transfer into a uterine environment so as to initiate a pregnancy.

B. This section shall not be construed to restrict biomedical and agricultural research or practices unless expressly prohibited herein, including research or practices that involve the use of (i) somatic cell nuclear transfer or other cloning technologies to clone molecules, including DNA, cells, or tissues; (ii) gene therapy; or (iii) somatic cell nuclear transfer techniques to create animals other than humans.

C. In addition to any other penalty provided by law, any person violating the provisions of this section shall be liable for a civil penalty in an amount not to exceed $50,000 for each incident.

Virginia Society for Human Life

Virginia Society for Human Life (VSHL) is a pro-life organization that was founded in 1967, in response to efforts to modify the state's abortion ban. The president of VSHL is Olivia Gains. Through education and legislative activity, VSHL's purpose is to promote measures which will insure protection for all human life. VSHL pursues its goals through educational, legislative and political action. It makes available speakers, literature, videos and publishes a bi-monthly newsletter called "Lifesaver." *See also* **Pro-Life Organizations**

Volunteers for Life

Volunteers for Life (VFL) is a religious based pro-life organization that was founded in Los Angeles, California in 1997, by Sister Paula Vandegaer. The membership of VFL is composed of people who give one or more years of their life in full time volunteer service. VFL trains its members to: (1) run chastity and abstinence programs; (2) promote natural family planning; (3) combat the growing threat of euthanasia; (4) to work in school-based chastity programs; and (5) to become pro-life leaders in the community. VFL members are placed in pro-life agencies in Southern California. In addition, VFL has worked with other pro-life groups to start pro-life pregnancy service centers. *See also* **Pro-Life Organizations**

Von Hippel–Lindau Disease

Von Hippel–Lindau disease is a congenital multi-system disorder involving the abnormal growth of tumors in the brain, retina, adrenal glands, kidneys and pancreas. Symptoms of the disorder include headaches, vision problems, dizziness, high blood pressure, problems with balance and walking, and weakness of the limbs. Victims of the disorder are at a higher risk for certain types of cancer. Treatment usually involves surgery or irradiation to remove the tumors. If the disease is left untreated, it may result in blindness or brain damage. Death can occur due to complications caused by brain tumors or kidney cancer. *See also* **Birth Defects and Abortion**

Voters for Choice

Voters for Choice is an organization that was founded by Gloria Steinem. The organization was created to function as a political action committee that provides support for pro-choice political candidates, regardless of party affiliation. The organization is also active in encouraging people to register to vote, and to vote for pro-choice candidates. *See also* **Pro-Choice Organizations**

Vulva *see* **Female Reproductive System**

Vulva Cancer

Vulva cancer is a disease in which malignant cancer develops in the vulva (the outer part of a woman's vagina). This form of cancer usually afflicts elderly women in the United States, but can develop in women under 40.

In the rare instance that a woman with vulva cancer is pregnant, problems could rise for the fetus. The fact of pregnancy generally has no adverse effect on vulva cancer, and vulva cancer has no effect on the pregnancy. However, if certain cancer treatment methods are used during pregnancy, it may become necessary to have a therapeutic abortion, or the fetus could be exposed to birth defects. Three kinds of treatment are used for vulva cancer: surgery, radiation therapy and chemotherapy. *See also* **Cancer and Pregnancy; Therapeutic Abortion**

W

Waagner, Clayton Lee

Clayton Lee Waagner (b.1956) was arrested in 1999 in Illinois while driving a stolen vehicle and possessing several stolen handguns. At the time of his arrest Waagner stated that he had intended to shoot an abortion doctor. Waagner was prosecuted by the federal government after his arrest because he crossed state lines in a stolen car. In 2001, after being convicted of possession of a stolen car and handguns, Waagner escaped from jail before he received his sentence.

Waagner remained an escaped felon for about nine months. During that time Waagner traveled throughout the country committing petty crimes. Among the crimes committed by him was sending hundreds of letters to abortion clinics threatening them with exposure to anthrax. He also used the internet to post threats to abortion providers and clinic staff. Waagner was eventually arrested in Ohio by the United States Marshals on December 5, 2001.

After his capture Waagner was extradited to Illinois to be sentenced on the charges he was convicted of before his escape. In 2002, a federal judge sentenced Waagner to 30 years in prison. He was subsequently prosecuted on federal charges in Ohio, where he was convicted and sentenced to 19 years in prison. Thereafter, in 2003 Waagner was prosecuted in federal court in Pennsylvania for his anthrax letter threats. A federal grand jury indicted Waagner on 53 charges stemming from the anthrax letters. After a trial by jury Waagner was convicted on 51 of the counts of the indictment. He was sentenced to 19 years in a federal prison. *See also* **Abortion Violence, Property Destruction and Demonstrations**

Waiting Period for Abortion

The United States Supreme Court invalidated a 24 hour waiting period before obtaining an abortion in *City of Akron v. Akron Center for Reproductive Health, Inc.* However, subsequent to that decision the Supreme Court reversed its position on waiting period requirements. In *Planned Parenthood of Southeastern Pennsylvania v. Casey* the Supreme Court held that imposition of a 24 hour waiting period for an abortion by the state of Pennsylvania did not violate the federal constitution. In *Hodgson v. Minnesota* the Supreme Court upheld the constitutionality of Minnesota's 48 hour waiting period for an abortion by minors. A majority of jurisdictions have imposed a statutory waiting period before an abortion may occur for an adult. *See also* **City of Akron v. Akron Center for Reproductive Health, Inc.; Hodgson v. Minnesota; Informed Consent Before Abortion; Minors and Abortion; Planned Parenthood of Southeastern Pennsylvania v. Casey**

States with Statutory Informed Consent Waiting Period for Abortion

State	*48 hour wait*	*24 hour wait*	*Less than 24 hour wait*
Ala.		X	
Alaska			
Ariz.			
Ark.			
Cal.			
Colo.			
Conn.			
Del.		X	
D.C.			
Fla.			
Ga.		X	
Haw.			
Idaho		X	
Ill.			
Ind.			X
Iowa			
Kan.		X	
Ky.		X	
La.		X	
Maine			
Md.			
Mass.		X	
Mich.		X	
Minn.		X	
Miss.		X	
Mo.		X	

(continued on page 570)

State	*48 hour wait*	*24 hour wait*	*Less than 24 hour wait*
Mont.		X	
Neb.		X	
Nev.			
N.H.			
N.J.			
N.M.			
N.Y.			
N.C.			
N.D.		X	
Ohio		X	
Okla.		X	
Ore.			
Penn.		X	
R.I.			
S.C.			X
S.D.		X	
Tenn.	X		
Tex.		X	
Utah		X	
Vt.			
Va.		X	
Wash.			
W.Va.		X	
Wis.		X	
Wyo.			

Warren, Earl

Earl Warren (1891–1974) served as chief justice of the United States Supreme Court from 1953 to 1969. While on the Supreme Court Chief Justice Warren was known as an ultra liberal interpreter of the Constitution.

Chief Justice Warren was born in Los Angeles, California. He was educated at the University of California at Berkeley, where he received an undergraduate degree and law degree. He was admitted to the California bar in 1914. His career included being elected attorney general and Governor of California. In 1953 President Dwight D. Eisenhower nominated him for chief justice of the Supreme Court.

Chief Justice Warren was involved in only two abortion related opinions while on the Supreme Court. In *Griswold v. Connecticut* Chief Justice Warren concurred with the majority opinion, which held that the right of privacy found in the constitution prohibited enforcement of a Connecticut statute that made it a crime to give married persons contraceptive information and devices. Chief Justice Warren joined a plurality opinion in *Poe v. Ullman*, which held that the appellants did not have standing to challenge the constitutionality of a Connecticut statute, that made it a crime to give married persons contraceptive information and devices.

Washington

(1) OVERVIEW

The state of Washington enacted its first criminal abortion statute on April 28, 1854. Shortly before the 1973 decision by the United States Supreme Court in *Roe v. Wade*, which legalized abortion in the nation, Washington had repealed most of its criminal abortion laws. The state has retained one of it pre–*Roe* abortion statutes. Washington has taken affirmative steps to respond to *Roe* and its progeny. The state has addressed several abortion issues by statute that include general abortion guidelines, use of facilities and people, anti-abortion activity, public funds and abortion, and injury to a pregnant woman.

(2) PRE-ROE ABORTION STATUTE

Washington still retains its pre–*Roe* statute that prohibits the distribution of any item that may be used to perform an unlawful abortion. The statute is set out below.

Washington Code § 9.68.030. Abortion articles

Every person who shall expose for sale, loan or distribution, any instrument or article, or any drug or medicine, for causing unlawful abortion; or shall write, print, distribute or exhibit any card, circular, pamphlet, advertisement or notice of any kind, stating when, where, how or of whom such article or medicine can be obtained, shall be guilty of a misdemeanor.

(3) GENERAL ABORTION GUIDELINES

Washington expressly authorizes abortions prior to fetal viability. The state permits post-viability abortions when necessary to save the life or health of the woman. The state's general abortion guidelines are set out below.

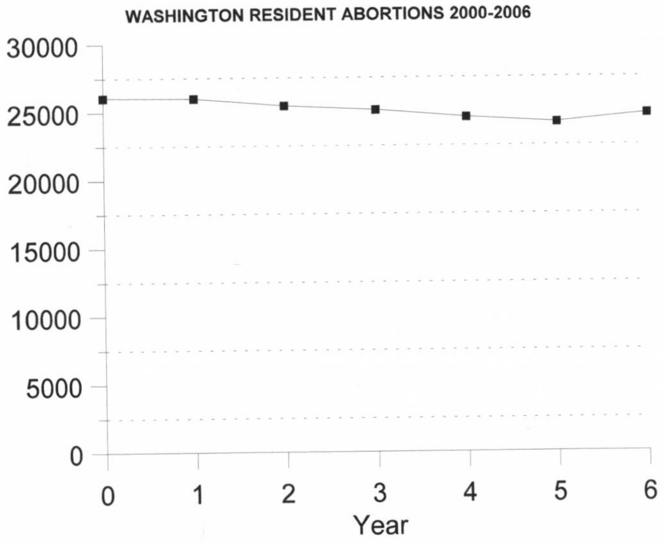

Source: **Washington State Department of Health.**

Washington Resident Abortion by Weeks of Gestation 2000–2006

	Year							
Weeks of Gestation	*2000*	*2001*	*2002*	*2003*	*2004*	*2005*	*2006*	*Total*
<5	137	165	318	314	282	355	264	1,835
5–8	14,908	15,639	15,779	15,407	14,881	14,682	14,899	106,195
9	2,873	2,546	2,432	2,371	2,296	2,266	2,382	17,166
10	2,019	1,932	1,721	1,753	1,691	1,669	1,753	12,538
11	1,639	1,534	1,289	1,407	1,283	1,294	1,366	9,812
12	1,035	1,004	893	913	915	896	1,034	6,690
13–15	1,750	1,556	1,463	1,425	1,519	1,386	1,426	10,525
16–19	1,053	945	885	940	1,024	986	1,060	6,893
≥20	603	601	533	530	586	574	548	3,975
Not known	46	76	133	46	91	54	58	504

Source: **Washington State Department of Health.**

Washington Resident Abortion by Age Group 2000–2006

	Age Group (yrs)								
Year	*<15*	*15–19*	*20–24*	*25–29*	*30–34*	*35–39*	*40–44*	*≥45*	*Unknown*
2000	122	5,180	8,213	5,641	3,821	2,230	774	62	20
2001	139	5,023	8,633	5,437	3,765	2,129	769	61	42
2002	121	4,821	8,489	5,260	3,666	2,183	793	82	31
2003	117	4,609	8,534	5,310	3,505	2,092	853	67	19
2004	130	4,414	8,250	5,343	3,432	2,080	823	67	29
2005	124	4,359	8,070	5,349	3,303	2,116	769	57	15
2006	86	4,450	8,214	5,720	3,191	2,258	752	92	27
Total	839	32,856	58,403	38,060	24,683	15,088	5,533	488	183

Source: **Washington State Department of Health.**

Washington Resident Prior Abortion by Female 2000–2006

Prior Abortion

Year	None	1	2	3	4	≥5	Not known
2000	14,001	6,892	2,930	1,237	470	424	109
2001	13,970	6,924	2,970	1,228	453	358	95
2002	13,377	6,928	3,070	1,132	475	384	80
2003	12,647	6,448	3,023	1,221	484	402	881
2004	12,732	6,497	3,040	1,317	526	399	57
2005	12,547	6,406	2,862	1,258	570	471	48
2006	13,121	6,474	2,933	1,222	546	469	25
Total	92,395	46,569	20,828	8,615	3,524	2,907	1,295

Source: **Washington State Department of Health.**

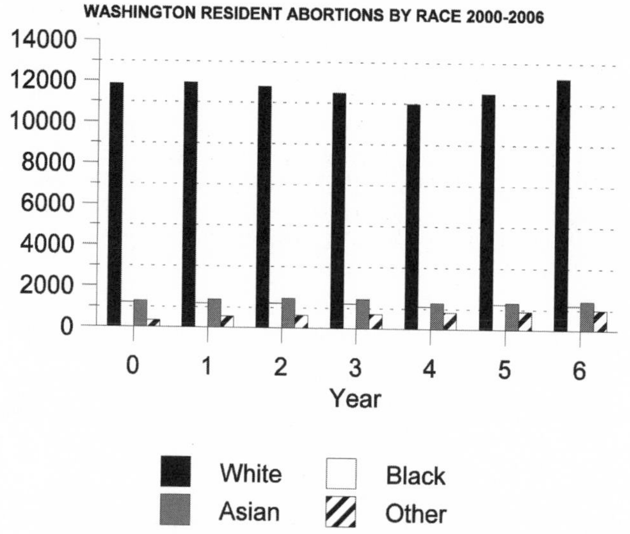

Source: **Washington State Department of Health.**

Washington Code § 9.02.902. Short title

RCW 9.02.100 through 9.02.170 and 9.02.900 through 9.02.902 shall be known and may be cited as the Reproductive Privacy Act.

Washington Code § 9.02.170. Definitions

For purposes of this chapter:

(1) "Viability" means the point in the pregnancy when, in the judgment of the physician on the particular facts of the case before such physician, there is a reasonable likelihood of the fetus's sustained survival outside the uterus without the application of extraordinary medical measures.

(2) "Abortion" means any medical treatment intended to induce the termination of a pregnancy except for the purpose of producing a live birth.

(3) "Pregnancy" means the reproductive process beginning with the implantation of an embryo.

(4) "Physician" means a physician licensed to practice under chapter 18.57 or 18.71 RCW in the state of Washington.

(5) "Health care provider" means a physician or a person acting under the general direction of a physician.

(6) "State" means the state of Washington and counties, cities, towns, municipal corporations, and quasi-municipal corporations in the state of Washington.

(7) "Private medical facility" means any medical facility that is not owned or operated by the state.

Washington Code § 9.02.100. Reproductive privacy

The sovereign people hereby declare that every individual possesses a fundamental right of privacy with respect to personal reproductive decisions.

Accordingly, it is the public policy of the state of Washington that:

(1) Every individual has the fundamental right to choose or refuse birth control;

(2) Every woman has the fundamental right to choose or refuse to have an abortion, except as specifically limited by RCW 9.02.100 through 9.02.170 and 9.02.900 through 9.02.902;

(3) Except as specifically permitted by RCW 9.02.100 through 9.02.170 and 9.02.900 through 9.02.902, the state shall not deny or interfere with a woman's fundamental right to choose or refuse to have an abortion; and

(4) The state shall not discriminate against the exercise of these rights in the regulation or provision of benefits, facilities, services, or information.

Washington Code § 9.02.110. Right to have abortion

The state may not deny or interfere with a woman's right to choose to have an abortion prior to viability of the fetus, or to protect her life or health.

A physician may terminate and a health care provider may assist a physician in terminating a pregnancy as permitted by this section.

Washington Code § 9.02.120. Unauthorized abortions

Unless authorized by RCW 9.02.110, any person who performs an abortion on another person shall be guilty of a class C felony punishable under chapter 9A.20 RCW.

Washington Code § 9.02.130. Defenses to prosecution

The good faith judgment of a physician as to viability of the fetus or as to the risk to life or health of a woman and the good faith judgment of a health care provider as to the duration of pregnancy shall be a defense in any proceeding in which a violation of this chapter is an issue.

Washington Code § 9.02.140. State regulation

Any regulation promulgated by the state relating to abortion shall be valid only if:

(1) The regulation is medically necessary to protect the life or health of the woman terminating her pregnancy,

(2) The regulation is consistent with established medical practice, and

(3) Of the available alternatives, the regulation imposes the least restrictions on the woman's right to have an abortion as defined by RCW 9.02.100 through 9.02.170 and 9.02.900 through 9.02.902.

Washington Code § 9.02.050. Concealing birth

Every person who shall endeavor to conceal the birth of a child by any disposition of its dead body, whether the child died before or after its birth, shall be guilty of a gross misdemeanor.

Washington Code § 9.02.900. Construction

RCW 9.02.100 through 9.02.170 and 9.02.900 through 9.02.902 shall not be construed to define the state's interest in the fetus for any purpose other than the specific provisions of RCW 9.02.100 through 9.02.170 and 9.02.900 through 9.02.902.

Washington Code § 9.02.901. Severability

If any provision of RCW 9.02.100 through 9.02.170 and 9.02.900 through 9.02.902 or its application to any person or circumstance is held invalid, the remainder of RCW 9.02.100 through 9.02.170 and 9.02.900 through 9.02.902 or the application of the provision to other persons or circumstances is not affected.

Washington Code § 18.71.240.
Right to medical treatment of infant born alive

The right of medical treatment of an infant born alive in the course of an abortion procedure shall be the same as the right of an infant born prematurely of equal gestational age.

(4) USE OF FACILITIES AND PEOPLE

Under the laws of Washington private hospitals are not required to allow abortions at their facilities. The employees and physicians at hospitals that do allow abortions are permitted to refuse to take part in abortions. The statute addressing the matter is set out below.

Washington Code § 9.02.150. Refusing to perform

No person or private medical facility may be required by law or contract in any circumstances to participate in the performance of an abortion if such person or private medical facility objects to so doing. No person may be discriminated against in employment or professional privileges because of the person's participation or refusal to participate in the termination of a pregnancy.

(5) ANTI-ABORTION ACTIVITY

Washington has take affirmative step to prevent violent anti-abortion conduct. The state criminalizes conduct that interferes with abortion facilities, providers or patients. The state also allows for civil remedies for unlawful interference with health care facilities. The statutes addressing the matter are set out below.

Washington Code § 9A.50.005. Finding

The legislature finds that seeking or obtaining health care is fundamental to public health and safety.

Washington Code § 9A.50.010. Definitions

Unless the context clearly requires otherwise, the definitions in this section apply throughout this chapter.

(1) "Health care facility" means a facility that provides health care services directly to patients, including but not limited to, a hospital, clinic, health care provider's office, health maintenance organization, diagnostic or treatment center, neuropsychiatric or mental health facility, hospice, or nursing home.

(2) "Health care provider" has the same meaning as defined in RCW 7.70.020 (1) and (2), and also means an officer, director, employee, or agent of a health care facility who sues or testifies regarding matters within the scope of his or her employment.

(3) "Aggrieved" means:

(a) A person, physically present at the health care facility when the prohibited actions occur, whose access is or is about to be obstructed or impeded;

(b) A person, physically present at the health care facility when the prohibited actions occur, whose care is or is about to be disrupted;

(c) The health care facility, its employees, or agents;

(d) The owner of the health care facility or the building or property upon which the health care facility is located.

Washington Code § 9A.50.020.
Interference with health care facility

It is unlawful for a person except as otherwise protected by state or federal law, alone or in concert with others, to willfully or recklessly interfere with access to or from a health care facility or willfully or recklessly disrupt the normal functioning of such facility by:

(1) Physically obstructing or impeding the free passage of a person seeking to enter or depart from the facility or from the common areas of the real property upon which the facility is located;

(2) Making noise that unreasonably disturbs the peace within the facility;

(3) Trespassing on the facility or the common areas of the real property upon which the facility is located;

(4) Telephoning the facility repeatedly, or knowingly permitting any telephone under his or her control to be used for such purpose; or

(5) Threatening to inflict injury on the owners, agents, patients, employees, or property of the facility or knowingly permitting any telephone under his or her control to be used for such purpose.

Washington Code § 9A.50.030. Penalty

A violation of RCW 9A.50.020 is a gross misdemeanor. A person convicted of violating RCW 9A.50.020 shall be punished as follows:

(1) For a first offense, a fine of not less than two hundred fifty dollars and a jail term of not less than twenty-four consecutive hours;

(2) For a second offense, a fine of not less than five hundred dollars and a jail term of not less than seven consecutive days; and

(3) For a third or subsequent offense, a fine of not less than one thousand dollars and a jail term of not less than thirty consecutive days.

Washington Code § 9A.50.040. Civil remedies

(1) A person or health care facility aggrieved by the actions prohibited by RCW 9A.50.020 may seek civil damages from those who committed the prohibited acts and those acting in concert with them. A plaintiff in an action brought under this chapter shall not recover more than his or her actual damages and additional sums authorized in RCW 9A.50.050. Once a plaintiff recovers his or her actual damages and any additional sums authorized under this chapter, additional damages shall not be recovered. A person does not have to be criminally convicted of violating RCW 9A.50.020 to be held civilly liable under this section. It is not necessary to prove actual damages to recover the additional sums authorized under RCW 9A.50.050, costs, and attorneys' fees. The prevailing party is entitled to recover costs and attorneys' fees.

(2) The superior courts of this state shall have authority to grant temporary, preliminary, and permanent injunctive relief to enjoin violations of this chapter.

In appropriate circumstances, any superior court having personal jurisdiction over one or more defendants may issue injunctive relief that shall have binding effect on the original defendants and persons acting in concert with the original defendants, in any county in the state.

Due to the nature of the harm involved, injunctive relief may be issued without bond in the discretion of the court, notwithstanding any other requirement imposed by statute.

The state and its political subdivisions shall cooperate in the enforcement of court injunctions that seek to protect against acts prohibited by this chapter.

Washington Code § 9A.50.050. Civil damages

In a civil action brought under this chapter, an individual plaintiff aggrieved by the actions prohibited by RCW 9A.50.020 may be entitled to recover up to five hundred dollars for each day that the actions occurred, or up to five thousand dollars for each day that the actions occurred if the plaintiff aggrieved by the actions prohibited under RCW 9A.50.020 is a health care facility.

Washington Code § 9A.50.060. Informational picketing

Nothing in RCW 9A.50.020 shall prohibit either lawful picketing or other publicity for the purpose of providing the public with information.

Washington Code § 9A.50.070.
Protection of health care patients and providers

A court having jurisdiction over a criminal or civil proceeding under this chapter shall take all steps reasonably necessary to safeguard the individual privacy and prevent harassment of a health care patient or health care provider who is a party or witness in a proceeding, including granting protective orders and orders in limine.

Washington Code § 9A.50.900. Construction

Nothing in this chapter shall be construed to limit the right to seek other available criminal or civil remedies. The remedies provided in this chapter are cumulative, not exclusive.

Washington Code § 9A.50.901. Severability

If any provision of this act or its application to any person or circumstance is held invalid, the remainder of the act or the application of the provision to other persons or circumstances is not affected.

(6) PUBLIC FUNDS AND ABORTION

Washington requires the use of state funds to pay for abortions, to the extent that such funds are used to pay for normal births. The statute addressing the matter is set out below.

Washington Code § 9.02.160. State funds

If the state provides, directly or by contract, maternity care benefits, services, or information to women through any program administered or funded in whole or in part by the state, the state shall also provide women otherwise eligible for any such program with substantially equivalent benefits, services, or information to permit them to voluntarily terminate their pregnancies.

(7) INJURY TO A PREGNANT WOMAN

Washington has criminal statutes that punish anyone who injures a pregnant woman, and thereby injures or causes the death of the woman's fetus. The statutes addressing the issue are set out below.

Washington Code § 9A.32.060.
Manslaughter in the first degree

(1) A person is guilty of manslaughter in the first degree when:
(a) Omitted.
(b) He intentionally and unlawfully kills an unborn quick child by inflicting any injury upon the mother of such child.
(2) Manslaughter in the first degree is a class A felony.

Washington Code § 9A.36.021. Assault in the second degree

(1) A person is guilty of assault in the second degree if he or she, under circumstances not amounting to assault in the first degree:
(a) Omitted.
(b) Intentionally and unlawfully causes substantial bodily harm to an unborn quick child by intentionally and unlawfully inflicting any injury upon the mother of such child; or
(c) Omitted.
(d) Omitted.
(e) Omitted.
(f) Omitted.
(g) Omitted.
(2)(a) Except as provided in (b) of this subsection, assault in the second degree is a class B felony.
(b) Omitted.

Waterbirth Method *see* **Natural Childbirth Methods**

Watson, Virginia Hopkins

Virginia Hopkins Watson was a world-class swimmer in the 1930s. She set a world record in the women's fifty-meter swimming race in 1938. Watson was also a member of the 1939 women's record-setting relay swimming team. In 1954, while living in California, she received a minor role in a movie with Johnny Weissmuller. She was, however, pregnant at the time she was given the part. Watson believed that her pregnancy would cause her to lose the role in the movie and end her planned movie career. Consequently, Watson decided to have an unlawful abortion. On December 3, 1954, Watson died from complications caused by the abortion. Her death was attributed to the development of peritonitis and pneumonia that was caused by the abortion. *See also* **Complications During and After Abortion**

Wattleton, Faye

Faye Wattleton (b.1943) was appointed as the first African American president of the Planned Parenthood Federation of America in 1978. Wattleton was born in St. Louis, Missouri. She received a nursing degree from Ohio State University in 1964 and a graduate degree from Columbia University in 1967. After completing her graduate studies, Wattleton settled in Ohio where she worked productively in prenatal health care services for a local county government agency. Her work in prenatal care lead to an appointment as executive director of the Dayton Planned Parenthood board. Wattleton's dedicated and innovative work as an executive director prompted her eventual appointment as national president of Planned Parenthood.

In her role as president of Planned Parenthood, Wattleton is credited with expanding the services provided by the organization in all areas of family planning, including contraception, infertility counseling, pregnancy testing, and prenatal care. Along the way to transforming the organization, Wattleton authored a book, *How to Talk with Your Child About Sexuality* (1986), and was the recipient of numerous humanitarian awards, including the Humanist of the Year Award. Wattleton left the organization in 1992 to host a daytime television show. *See also* **Planned Parenthood Federation of America**

Webster v. Reproductive Health Services

Forum: United States Supreme Court.

Case Citation: Webster v. Reproductive Health Services, 492 U.S. 490 (1989).

Date Argued: April 26, 1989.

Date of Decision: July 3, 1989.

Opinion of Court: Rehnquist, C. J., in which White, O'Connor, Scalia, and Kennedy, JJ., joined.

Concurring Opinion: O'Connor, J.

Concurring Opinion: Scalia, J.

Concurring and Dissenting Opinion: Blackmun, J., in which Brennan and Marshall, JJ., joined.

Concurring and Dissenting Opinion: Stevens, J.

Counsel for Appellants: William L. Webster, Attorney General of Missouri, argued; on the brief were Michael L. Boicourt and Jerry L. Short, Assistant Attorneys General.

Counsel for Appellees: Frank Susman argued; on the brief were Roger K. Evans, Dara Klassel, Barbara E. Otten, Thomas M. Blumenthal, and Janet Benshoof.

Amicus Brief for United States in Support of Appellants: Charles Fried argued; on the brief were Acting Solicitor General Bryson, Assistant Attorney General Bolton, Deputy Solicitor General Merrill, Roger Clegg, Steven R. Valentine, and Michael K. Kellogg.

Amicus Brief for Appellants: Alabama Lawyers for Unborn Children, Inc., by John J. Coleman III and Thomas E. Maxwell; for the American Association of Prolife Obstetricians and Gynecologists et al. by Dolores Horan and Paige Comstock Cunningham; for the American Family Association, Inc., by Peggy M. Coleman; for the American Life League, Inc., by Marion Edwyn Harrison and John S. Baker, Jr.; for the Catholic Health Association of the United States by J. Roger Edgar, David M. Harris, Kathleen M. Boozang, J. Stuart Showalter, and Peter E. Campbell; for the Catholic Lawyers Guild of the Archdiocese of Boston, Inc., by Calum B. Anderson and Leonard F. Zandrow, Jr.; for the Center for Judicial Studies et al. by Jules B. Gerard; for Covenant House et al. by Gregory A. Loken; for Focus On The Family et al. by H. Robert Showers; for the Holy Orthodox Church by James George Jatras; for the Knights of Columbus by Robert J. Cynkar and Brendan V. Sullivan, Jr.; for the Lutheran Church–Missouri Synod et al. by Philip E. Draheim; for the Missouri Catholic Conference by David M. Harris, J. Roger Edgar, Bernard C. Huger, Kathleen M. Boozang, and Louis C. DeFeo, Jr.; for the National Legal Foundation by Douglas W. Davis and Robert K. Skolrood; for Right to Life Advocates, Inc., by Richard W. Schmude and Rory R. Olsen; for the Rutherford Institute et al. by James J. Knicely, John W. Whitehead, Thomas W. Strahan, David E. Morris, William B. Hollberg, Amy Dougherty, Randall A. Pentiuk, William Bonner, Larry L. Crain, and W. Charles Bundren; for the Southern Center for Law and Ethics by Albert L. Jordan; for the Southwest Life and Law Center, Inc., by David Burnell

Smith; for the United States Catholic Conference by Mark E. Chopko and Phillip H. Harris; for 127 Members of the Missouri General Assembly by Timothy Belz, Lynn D. Wardle, and Richard G. Wilkins; and for James Joseph Lynch, Jr., by Mr. Lynch, pro se.

Amicus Brief for Appellees: American Civil Liberties Union et al. by Burt Neuborne, Janet Benshoof, Rachael N. Pine, and Lynn M. Paltrow; for the American Jewish Congress et al. by Martha L. Minow; for the American Library Association et al. by Bruce J. Ennis and Mark D. Schneider; for the American Medical Association et al. by Jack R. Bierig, Carter G. Phillips, Elizabeth H. Esty, Stephan E. Lawton, Ann E. Allen, Laurie R. Rockett, and Joel I. Klein; for the American Psychological Association by Donald N. Bersoff; for the American Public Health Association et al. by John H. Hall and Nadine Taub; for Americans for Democratic Action et al. by Marsha S. Berzon; for Americans United for Separation of Church and State by Lee Boothby, Robert W. Nixon, and Robert J. Lipshutz; for the Association of Reproductive Health Professionals et al. by Colleen K. Connell and Dorothy B. Zimbrakos; for Bioethicists for Privacy by George J. Annas; for Catholics for a Free Choice et al. by Patricia Hennessey; for the Center for Population Options et al. by John H. Henn and Thomas Asher; for the Committee on Civil Rights of the Bar of the City of New York et al. by Jonathan Lang, Diane S. Wilner, Arthur S. Leonard, Audrey S. Feinberg, and Janice Goodman; for 22 International Women's Health Organizations by Kathryn Kolbert; for the American Nurses' Association et al. by E. Calvin Golumbic; for the National Coalition Against Domestic Violence by David A. Strauss; for the National Family Planning and Reproductive Health Association by James L. Feldesman, Jeffrey K. Stith, and Thomas E. Zemaitis; for the National Association of Public Hospitals by Alan K. Parver and Phyllis E. Bernard; for Population-Environment Balance et al. by Dina R. Lassow; for 281 American Historians by Sylvia A. Law; and for 2,887 Women Who Have Had Abortions et al. by Sarah E. Burns.

Issue Presented: Whether the federal constitution was violated by amendments to Missouri's abortion statute that placed restrictions on a woman's right to an abortion?

Case Holding: The restrictions imposed by the amendments did not hinder a woman's right to an abortion.

Background facts of case: In 1986 the state of Missouri amended its abortion laws. Some of the changes included (1) a preamble that stated the legislature found that the life of each human being begins at conception, and that unborn children have protectable interests in life, health, and well-being; (2) a prohibition on the use of public employees and facilities to perform or assist abortions not necessary to save the mother's life; (3) a prohibition on the use of public funds, employees, or facilities for the purpose of encouraging or counseling a woman to have an abortion not necessary to save her life; and (4) a requirement that, prior to performing an abortion on any woman whom a physician has reason to believe is 20 or more weeks pregnant, the physician must ascertain whether the fetus is viable.

The appellees, five health professionals employed by the state and two nonprofit corporations, filed a class action in a federal district court in Missouri challenging the constitutionality of the amended statute. The appellants, state officials, were named as defendants. The district court declared the amended provisions unconstitutional and enjoined their enforcement. The Eighth Circuit court of appeals affirmed. The Supreme Court granted certiorari to consider the issues.

Majority/plurality opinion by Chief Justice Rehnquist: The Chief Justice held that the constitution was not violated by the statutory amendments involving the prohibition on the use of public facilities or employees to perform abortions and the requirement that physicians conduct viability tests prior to performing abortions. The opinion found that the issue concerning the preamble was premature and would not therefore be decided; and it was said that the prohibition on public funding of abortion counseling was rendered moot and would not be analyzed. The Chief Justice addressed each of the matters as follows:

> We think the extent to which the preamble's language might be used to interpret other state statutes or regulations is something that only the courts of Missouri can definitively decide.... It will be time enough for federal courts to address the meaning of the preamble should it be applied to restrict the activities of appellees in some concrete way. Until then, this Court is not empowered to decide abstract propositions, or to declare, for the government of future cases, principles or rules of law which cannot affect the result as to the thing in issue in the case before it. We therefore need not pass on the constitutionality of the Act's preamble....
>
> We think that ... the State's decision here to use public facilities and staff to encourage childbirth over abortion places no governmental obstacle in the path of a woman who chooses to terminate her pregnancy.... Missouri's refusal to allow public employees to perform abortions in public hospitals leaves a pregnant woman with the same choices as if the State had chosen not to operate any public hospitals at all. The challenged provisions only restrict a woman's ability to obtain an abortion to the extent that she chooses to use a physician affiliated with a public hospital....
>
> ... [T]he State need not commit any resources to facilitating abortions, even if it can turn a profit by doing so.... Thus we uphold the Act's restrictions on the use of public employees and facilities for the performance or assistance of nontherapeutic abortions....
>
> The Missouri Act contains [a] provision relating to encouraging or counseling a woman to have an abortion not necessary to save her life. The [Act] states that no public funds can be used for this purpose; that public employees cannot, within the scope of their employment, engage in such speech; and forbids such speech in public facilities....
>
> ... A majority of the Court agrees with appellees that the controversy over [latter provision] is now moot, because appellees' argument amounts to a decision to no longer seek a declaratory judgment that [provision] is unconstitutional and accompanying declarative relief. We accordingly direct the Court of Appeals to vacate the judgment of the District Court with instructions to dismiss the relevant part of the complaint....
>
> The viability-testing provision of the Missouri Act is concerned with promoting the State's interest in potential human life rather than in maternal health. [The provision] creates what is essentially a presumption of viability at 20 weeks, which the physician must rebut with tests indicating that the fetus is not viable prior to performing an abortion. It also directs the physician's determination as to viability by specifying consideration, if feasible, of gestational age, fetal weight, and lung capacity. The District Court found that the medical evidence is uncontradicted that a 20-week fetus is not viable, and that 23½ to 24 weeks gestation is the earliest point in pregnancy where a reasonable possibility of viability exists....
>
> The tests that [the provision] requires the physician to perform are designed to determine viability. The State here has chosen viability as the point at which its interest in potential human life must be safeguarded. It is true that the tests in question increase the expense of abortion, and regulate the discretion of the physician in determining the viability of the fetus. Since the tests will undoubtedly show in many cases that the fetus is not viable, the tests will have been performed for what were in fact second-trimester abortions. But we are satisfied that the requirement of these tests permissibly furthers the State's interest in protecting potential human life, and we therefore believe [the provision] to be constitutional.

Disposition of case: The judgment of the court of appeals was reversed.

Concurring opinion by Justice O'Connor: Justice O'Connor agreed with the disposition of the case. She wrote separately to underscore her commitment to retaining the abortion protections afforded by *Roe v. Wade*. She disapproved of language in the majority/plurality opinion that seemed to suggest a retreat from *Roe*.

Concurring opinion by Justice Scalia: Justice Scalia agreed with the Court's judgment. He wrote separately to point out that he did not believe the Court should be involved in deciding abortion issues.

Concurring and dissenting opinion by Justice Blackmun: Justice Blackmun concurred in the Court's decision to find the prohibition on public funding of abortion counseling was rendered moot and would not be analyzed. He dissented from the remainder of the Court's opinion. Justice Blackmun wrote:

> Today, Roe v. Wade and the fundamental constitutional right of women to decide whether to terminate a pregnancy, survive but are not secure. Although the Court extricates itself from this case without making a single, even incremental, change in the law of abortion, the plurality and Justice Scalia would overrule Roe (the first silently, the other explicitly) and would return to the States virtually unfettered authority to control the quintessentially intimate, personal, and life-directing decision whether to carry a fetus to term. Although today, no less than yesterday, the Constitution and the decisions of this Court prohibit a State from enacting laws that inhibit women from the meaningful exercise of that right, a plurality of this Court implicitly invites every state legislature to enact more and more restrictive abortion regulations in order to provoke more and more test cases, in the hope that sometime down the line the Court will return the law of procreative freedom to the severe limitations that generally prevailed in this country before January 22, 1973. Never in my memory has a plurality announced a judgment of this Court that so foments disregard for the law and for our standing decisions.
>
> Nor in my memory has a plurality gone about its business in such a deceptive fashion. At every level of its review, from its effort to read the real meaning out of the Missouri statute, to its intended evisceration of precedents and its deafening silence about the constitutional protections that it would jettison, the plurality obscures the portent of its analysis. With feigned restraint, the plurality announces that its analysis leaves Roe undisturbed, albeit modified and narrowed. But this disclaimer is totally meaningless. The plurality opinion is filled with winks, and nods, and knowing glances to those who would do away with Roe explicitly, but turns a stone face to anyone in search of what the plurality conceives as the scope of a woman's right under the Due Process Clause to terminate a pregnancy free from the coercive and brooding influence of the State. The simple truth is that Roe would not survive the plurality's analysis, and that the plurality provides no substitute for Roe's protective umbrella.
>
> I fear for the future. I fear for the liberty and equality of the millions of women who have lived and come of age in the 16 years since Roe was decided. I fear for the integrity of, and public esteem for, this Court.

Concurring and dissenting opinion by Justice Stevens: Justice Stevens agreed with the Court's decision to find the prohibition on public funding of abortion counseling was rendered moot and would not be analyzed. He dissented from the remainder of the Court's opinion. He was particularly disturbed that the Court did not find Missouri's abortion statute preamble violated the constitution.

Weddington, Sarah

Sarah Weddington was the attorney who successfully represented the plaintiff in the 1973 decision of the United States Supreme Court in *Roe v. Wade*, which legalized abortion in the nation. At the time of her landmark victory, Weddington was only 26 years old. She is thought to be the youngest woman to ever win a case in the Supreme Court.

Weddington received her law degree from the University of Texas School of Law in 1967. Subsequent to her victory in *Roe*, she received numerous honors and awards, including honorary doctorates from McMurry University, Hamilton College, Austin College and Southwestern University; named one of the "Outstanding Young American Leaders" by Time magazine; received the "Woman of the Future" award from Ladies Home Journal; and was selected as one of the ten "Outstanding Women in America." In 1972 Weddington was the first woman ever elected from Austin, Texas, to be a member of the Texas House of Representatives. She served as assistant to President Jimmy Carter from 1978 to 1981. *See also* **Roe v. Wade**

Weiler, Robert Francis, Jr.

In October of 2006, Robert Francis Weiler, Jr., (b.1980) pleaded guilty to federal charges of possessing a pipe bomb, being a felon in possession of a firearm and attempting to destroy or damage an abortion clinic. Weiler's arrest and prosecution began on June 7, 2006, when he telephoned and spoke with agents of the Bureau of Alcohol, Tobacco, Firearms and Explosives (ATF). At the time of the telephone conversation ATF agents were interviewing a friend of Weiler's regarding a tip involving a plot to blow up an abortion clinic. For reasons unknown, Weiler told the ATF agents that he was at a rest stop in Western Maryland and wanted to surrender. Weiler stated that he was in possession of a handgun and that he had constructed a pipe bomb that was concealed in a house located in Riverdale, Maryland. Weiler remained at the rest stop until local authorities arrived and arrested him. After his arrest Weiler informed the ATF agents that he had intended to blow up an abortion clinic in Greenbelt, Maryland, as well as shoot abortion doctors. ATF agents and local authorities discovered the bomb where Weiler indicated it was located. Subsequent to Weiler's guilty plea, he was sentenced on December 18, 2006 by a federal judge to five years in prison and three years of supervised release. *See also* **Abortion Violence, Property Destruction and Demonstrations**

Weinberger v. Hynson, Westcott & Dunning

Forum: United States Supreme Court.

Case Citation: Weinberger v. Hynson, Westcott & Dunning, 412 U.S. 609 (1973).

Date Argued: April 17, 1973.

Date of Decision: June 18, 1973.

Opinion of Court: Douglas, J., in which Burger, C. J., and White, Marshall, Blackmun, and Rehnquist, JJ., joined.

Concurring Opinion: Powell, J.

Dissenting Opinion: None.

Not Participating: Brennan and Stewart, JJ.

Counsel for Appellant: Deputy Solicitor General Friedman and Andrew L. Frey argued; on the brief were Solicitor General Griswold, Assistant Attorney General Kauper, Deputy Solicitor General Wallace, Robert B. Nicholson, Howard E. Shapiro, and Peter Barton Hutt.

Counsel for Appellee: Edward Brown Williams argued; on the brief was Jan Edward Williams.

Amicus Brief for Appellant and Appellee: Lloyd N. Cutler, Daniel Marcus, and William T. Lake for Pharmaceutical Manufacturers Assn.; by Bruce J. Terris, Joseph Onck, and Peter II. Schuck for American Public Health Assn. et al.; by Thomas D. Finney. Jr., Thomas Richard Spradlin, and Daniel F. O'Keefe, Jr., for the Proprietary Assn; by Alan II. Kaplan for E. R. Squibb & Sons, Inc.; and by Robert L. Wald, Selma M. Levine, Joel E. Hoffman, Philip Elman, and Philip J. Franks for USV Pharmaceutical Corp.

Issue Presented: Whether the Food and Drug Administration could deny a drug manufacturer a hearing to obtain marketing approval for a drug called Lutrexin, which provided treatment for premature labor and threatened and habitual abortion?

Case Holding: The Food and Drug Administration could not deny a drug manufacturer a hearing to obtain marketing approval for a drug called Lutrexin, which provided treatment for premature labor and threatened and habitual abortion.

Background facts of case: In 1962 Congress amended the Federal Food, Drug, and Cosmetic Act of 1938, so as to provide new standards and procedures for the approval of new drugs by the Food and Drug Administration (FDA). The appellee, Hynson, Westcott & Dunning, Inc., filed a drug application with FDA under the 1938 version of the Act. The appellee sought approval for a drug called Lutrexin, which provided treatment for premature labor and threatened and habitual abortion. FDA informed the appellee that its studies submitted with the application were not sufficient for a new drug under the new standards. The appellee argued that it was not subject to the new regulations and that Lutrexin was not a new drug. The appellee sought a hearing before the FDA on the matter. The FDA denied the request for a hearing. The appellee filed an appeal with a federal court of appeals. The court of appeals reversed, holding that while the drug in question was not exempt, the appellee was entitled to a hearing in a district court to determine whether Lutrexin was a new drug. The Supreme Court granted certiorari to consider the matter.

Majority opinion by Justice Douglas: Justice Douglas agreed with the court of appeals that the Lutrexin was not exempt from the 1962 amendments to the Act. However, he indicated that FDA and not a district court, had jurisdiction to determine whether Lutrexin was a new drug. Justice Douglas wrote as follows:

> To be sure, the Act requires FDA to give due notice and opportunity for hearing to the applicant.... FDA, however, by regulation, requires any applicant who desires a hearing to submit reasons why the application should not be withdrawn, together with a well-organized and full-factual analysis of the clinical and other investigational data he is prepared to prove in support of his opposition to the notice of opportunity for a hearing. When it clearly appears from the data in the application and from the reasons and factual analysis in the request for the hearing that there is no genuine and substantial issue of fact e. g., no adequate and well-controlled clinical investigations to support the claims of effectiveness, the [FDA] may deny a hearing and enter an order withdrawing the application based solely on these data. What the agency has said, then, is that it will not provide a formal hearing where it is apparent at the threshold that the applicant has not tendered any evidence which on its face meets the statutory standards as particularized by the regulations....
>
> ... Congress surely has great leeway in setting standards for releasing on the public, drugs which may well be miracles or, on the other hand, merely easy money-making schemes through use of fraudulent articles labeled in mysterious scientific dress. The standard of "well-controlled investigations" particularized by the regulations is a protective measure designed to ferret out those drugs for which there is no affirmative, reliable evidence of effectiveness. The drug manufacturers have full and precise notice of the evidence they must present ..., and under these circumstances we find FDA hearing regulations unexceptionable on any statutory or constitutional ground.
>
> Our conclusion that the summary judgment procedure of FDA is valid does not end the matter, for [the appellee] argues that its submission to FDA satisfied its threshold burden.... There is a contrariety of opinion within the Court concerning the adequacy of [appellee's] submission. Since a majority are of the view that the submission was sufficient to warrant a hearing, we affirm the Court of Appeals on that phase of the case.
>
> ... The Court of Appeals suggested that only a district court has authority to determine whether Lutrexin is a new drug. The [FDA] contends that [it] has authority to determine new drug status....
>
> It is clear to us that FDA has power to determine whether particular drugs require an approved [new drug application] in order to be sold to the public. FDA is indeed the administrative agency selected by Congress to administer the Act, and it cannot administer the Act intelligently and rationally unless it has authority to determine what drugs are new drugs ... and whether they are exempt from the efficacy requirements of the 1962 amendments by the grandfather clause....
>
> ... The heart of the new procedures designed by Congress is the grant of primary jurisdiction to FDA, the expert agency it created. FDA does not have the final say, for review may be had, not in a district court (except in a limited group of cases we will discuss), but in a court of appeals. FDA does not have unbridled discretion to do what it pleases. Its procedures must satisfy the rudiments of fair play. Judicial relief is available only after administrative remedies have been exhausted....
>
> The question then presented is whether FDA properly exercised its jurisdiction in this instance. As indicated above, [the appellee] in requesting an administrative hearing also asked FDA to decide that Lutrexin is not a new drug.... In addition, it asked that Lutrexin be grandfathered under ... the 1962 amendments. The Court of Appeals affirmed the [FDA] ruling that Lutrexin is not exempt [from the 1962 amendments]. It did not discuss [the] holding that Lutrexin currently is a new drug. Although we agree that the [FDA] properly ruled that Lutrexin [is not exempt from the 1962 amendments], we conclude that the [FDA] order with respect to Lutrexin's new drug status must be vacated....
>
> We accordingly have concluded that ... [FDA] was not justified in withdrawing [appellee's] new drug application without a prior hearing on whether [appellee] had submitted substantial evidence of Lutrexin's effectiveness. Consequently, any ruling as to Lutrexin's "new drug" status is premature and must await the outcome of this hearing.

Disposition of case: The judgment of the court of appeals was affirmed as modified.

Concurring opinion by Justice Powell: Justice Powell agreed with the Court's disposition of the case. He expressed reservations about some dicta in the opinion as follows:

> Insofar as the Court today sustains the holding below that [appellee's] submission to FDA raised a genuine and substantial issue of fact requiring a hearing on the ultimate issue of efficacy, I am in accord. [Appellee's] presentation in support of the efficacy of Lutrexin clearly justified a hearing as to whether the drug was supported by adequate and well-controlled investigations.... For this reason I concur in the result reached in this case. I cannot agree on this record, however, with any implications or conclusions in the Court's opinion to the effect that the regulations— as construed and applied by the [FDA] in this case — are either compatible with the statutory scheme or constitutional under the Due Process Clause. Such questions have not been squarely presented here and, in light of the Court's conclusion that [appellee] has complied with the regulations, their resolution is unnecessary to the Court's decision.

Werdnig-Hoffmann Disease

Werdnig-Hoffmann disease is a group of congenital diseases that cause progressive muscle degeneration and weakness. The disease has three forms. In type I, the most severe form, death results by the third year of a child's life. In type II, there is less severe muscle degeneration during early infancy and death may not occur. In type III, muscle degenerative symptoms may not appear until the second year of life, and death is not inevitable. Treatment for type II and III includes physiotherapy and the use of braces. *See also* **Birth Defects and Abortion**

West Virginia

(1) OVERVIEW

The state of West Virginia enacted its first criminal abortion statute in 1868. The statute underwent several amendments prior to the 1973 decision by the United States Supreme Court in *Roe v. Wade*, which legalized abortion in the nation. In spite of the decision in *Roe*, West Virginia has not repealed its pre–*Roe* criminal abortion statute. However, the statute is constitutionally infirm.

West Virginia has taken affirmative steps to respond to *Roe* and its progeny. The state has addressed several abortion issues by statute that include informed consent, abortion by minors, partial-birth abor-

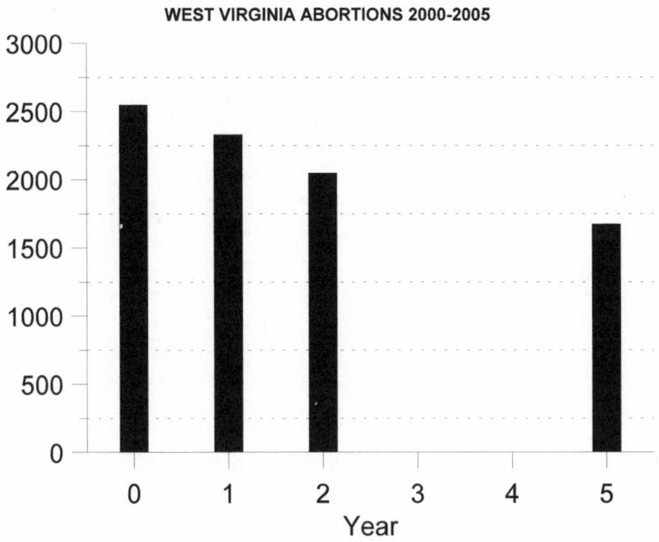

Source: National Center for Health Statistics/West Virginia Department of Health and Human Resources. Data was not compiled by any agency for 2003–04.

West Virginia Abortion by Age Group 2000–2005

	Age Group (yrs)							
Year	*<15*	*15–19*	*20–24*	*25–29*	*30–34*	*35–39*	*≥40*	*Unknown*
2000	21	511	905	530	346	190	45	1
2001	11	451	889	461	296	152	47	25
2002	9	359	780	464	245	128	46	18
2003	N/A	N/A	N/A	N/A	N/A	N/A	N/A	N/A
2004	N/A	N/A	N/A	N/A	N/A	N/A	N/A	N/A
2005	5	144	295	238	144	75	18	0
Total	46	1,465	2,869	1,693	1,031	545	156	44

Source: National Center for Health Statistics/West Virginia Department of Health and Human Resources.

West Virginia Abortion by Weeks of Gestation 2000–2005

	Year						
Weeks of Gestation	*2000*	*2001*	*2002*	*2003*	*2004*	*2005*	*Total*
<9	1,079	963	756	N/A	N/A	919	3,717
9–10	709	616	602	N/A	N/A	394	2,321
11–12	396	416	340	N/A	N/A	195	1,347
13–15	221	219	195	N/A	N/A	131	766
16–20	125	109	144	N/A	N/A	24	402
≥21	11	4	10	N/A	N/A	10	35
Not known	8	5	2	N/A	N/A	1	16

Source: National Center for Health Statistics/West Virginia Department of Health and Human Resources.

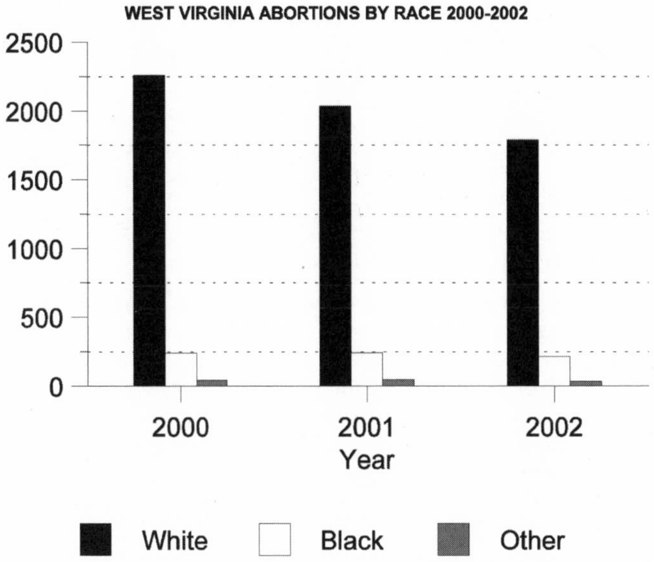

Source: National Center for Health Statistics.

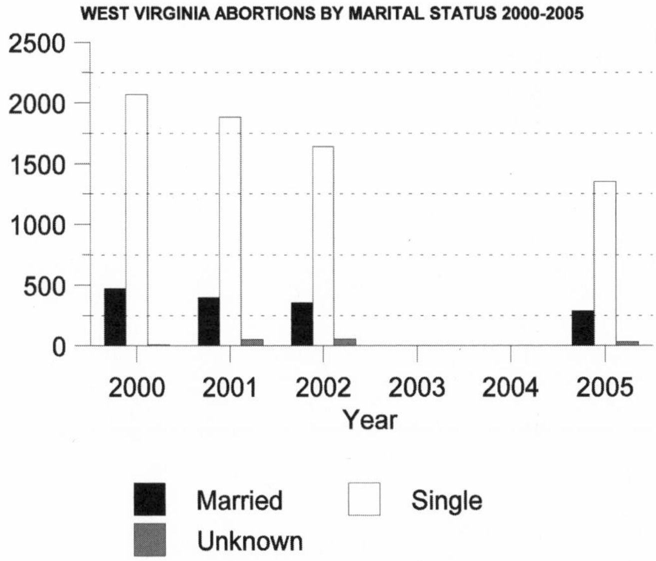

Source: National Center for Health Statistics/West Virginia Department of Health and Human Resources. Data was not compiled by any agency for 2003–04.

West Virginia Prior Abortion by Female 2000–2005

	Prior Abortion				
Year	*None*	*1*	*2*	*≥3*	*Not known*
2000	1,900	469	113	67	0
2001	1,762	427	89	54	0
2002	1,314	492	143	80	20
2003	N/A	N/A	N/A	N/A	N/A
2004	N/A	N/A	N/A	N/A	N/A
2005	1,142	370	110	52	0
Total	6,118	1,758	455	253	20

Source: National Center for Health Statistics/West Virginia Department of Health and Human Resources.

tion, medical personnel, public funds and abortion, injury to a pregnant woman, and fetal death report.

(2) PRE-ROE ABORTION BAN

As previously indicated, West Virginia has not repealed its pre–*Roe* criminal abortion statute. The statute was expressly declared unconstitutional in *Doe v. Charleston Area Medical Center, Inc.*, 529 F.2d 638 (4th Cir. 1975). Under the now unconstitutional statute, abortion was criminalized if it was not performed to preserve the life of the woman. The statute is set out below.

West Virginia Code § 61-2-8. Criminal abortion

Any person who shall administer to, or cause to be taken by, a woman, any drug or other thing, or use any means, with intent to destroy her unborn child, or to produce abortion or miscarriage, and shall thereby destroy such child, or produce such abortion or miscarriage, shall be guilty of a felony, and, upon conviction, shall be confined in the penitentiary not less than three nor more than ten years; and if such woman die by reason of such abortion performed upon her, such person shall be guilty of murder. No person, by reason of any act mentioned in this section, shall be punishable where such act is done in good faith, with the intention of saving the life of such woman or child.

(3) INFORMED CONSENT

Prior to an abortion West Virginia requires that a woman be fully informed of the procedure to be used, the risks involved and alternatives to abortion. An abortion may not take place until 24 hours after a woman has been given the required statutory information. The statutes addressing the matters are set out below.

West Virginia Code § 16-2I-1. Definitions

For the purposes of this article, the words or phrases defined in this section have these meanings ascribed to them.

(a) "Abortion" means the use or prescription of any instrument, medicine, drug or any other substance or device intentionally to terminate the pregnancy of a female known to be pregnant with an intention other than to increase the probability of a live birth, to preserve the life or health of the child after live birth or to remove a dead embryo or fetus.

(b) "Attempt to perform an abortion" means an act, or an omission of a statutorily required act, that, under the circumstances as the actor believes them to be, constitutes a substantial step in a course of conduct planned to culminate in the performance of an abortion in West Virginia in violation of this article.

(c) "Medical emergency" means any condition which, on the basis of a physician's good-faith clinical judgment, so complicates the medical condition of a pregnant female as to necessitate the immediate termination of her pregnancy to avert her death or for which a delay will create serious risk of substantial and irreversible impairment of a major bodily function.

(d) "Physician" means any medical or osteopathic doctor licensed to practice medicine in this state.

(e) "Probable gestational age of the embryo or fetus" means what, in the judgment of the physician, will with reasonable probability be the gestational age of the embryo or fetus at the time the abortion is planned to be performed.

(f) "Stable internet website" means a website that, to the extent reasonably practicable, is safeguarded from having its content altered other than by the department of health and human resources.

West Virginia Code § 16-2I-2. Informed consent

No abortion may be performed in this state except with the voluntary and informed consent of the female upon whom the abortion is to be performed. Except in the case of a medical emergency, consent to an abortion is voluntary and informed if, and only if:

(a) The female is told the following, by telephone or in person, by the physician or the licensed health care professional to whom the responsibility has been delegated by the physician who is to perform the abortion at least twenty-four hours before the abortion:

(1) The particular medical risks associated with the particular abortion procedure to be employed, including, when medically accurate, the risks of infection, hemorrhage, danger to subsequent pregnancies and infertility;

(2) The probable gestational age of the embryo or fetus at the time the abortion is to be performed; and

(3) The medical risks associated with carrying her child to term.

The information required by this subsection may be provided by telephone without conducting a physical examination or tests of the patient, in which case the information required to be provided may be based on facts supplied by the female to the physician or other licensed health care professional to whom the responsibility has been delegated by the physician and whatever other relevant information is reasonably available to the physician or other licensed health care professional to whom the responsibility has been delegated by the physician. It may not be provided by a tape recording, but must be provided during a consultation in which the physician or licensed health care professional to whom the responsibility has been delegated by the physician is able to ask questions of the female and the female is able to ask questions of the physician or the licensed health care professional to whom the responsibility has been delegated by the physician.

If a physical examination, tests or the availability of other information to the physician or other licensed health care professional to whom the responsibility has been delegated by the physician subsequently indicate, in the medical judgment of the physician or the licensed health care professional to whom the responsibility has been delegated by the physician, a revision of the information previously supplied to the patient, that revised information may be communicated to the patient at any time prior to the performance of the abortion procedure.

Nothing in this section may be construed to preclude provision of required information in a language understood by the patient through a translator.

(b) The female is informed, by telephone or in person, by the physician who is to perform the abortion, or by an agent of the physician, at least twenty-four hours before the abortion procedure:

(1) That medical assistance benefits may be available for prenatal care, childbirth and neonatal care through governmental or private entities;

(2) That the father, if his identity can be determined, is liable to assist in the support of her child based upon his ability to pay even in instances in which the father has offered to pay for the abortion; and

(3) That she has the right to review the printed materials described in section three of this article, that these materials are available on a state-sponsored website and the website address.

The physician or an agent of the physician shall orally inform the female that the materials have been provided by the state of West Virginia and that they describe the embryo or fetus and list agencies and entities which offer alternatives to abortion.

If the female chooses to view the materials other than on the website, then they shall either be provided to her at least twenty-four hours before the abortion or mailed to her at least seventy-two hours before the abortion by first class mail in an unmarked envelope.

The information required by this subsection may be provided by a tape recording if provision is made to record or otherwise register specifically whether the female does or does not choose to have the printed materials given or mailed to her.

(c) The female shall certify in writing, prior to the abortion, that the information described in subsections (a) and (b) of this section has been provided to her and that she has been informed of her opportunity to review the information referred to in subdivision (3), subsection (b) of this section.

(d) Prior to performing the abortion procedure, the physician who is to perform the abortion or the physician's agent shall obtain a copy of the executed certification required by the provisions of subsection (c) of this section.

West Virginia Code § 16-2I-3. Printed information

(a) Within ninety days of the effective date of this article, the secretary of the department of health and human resources shall cause to be published, in English and in each language which is the primary language of two percent or more of the state's population, as determined by the most recent decennial census performed by the U. S. census bureau, and shall cause to be available on the website provided for in section four of this article the following printed materials in such a way as to ensure that the information is easily comprehensible:

(1) Geographically indexed materials designed to inform the reader of public and private agencies and services available to assist a female through pregnancy, upon childbirth and while the child is dependent, including adoption agencies, which shall include a comprehensive list of the agencies available, a description of the services they offer and a description of the manner, including telephone numbers. At the option of the secretary of health and human resources, a 24-hour-a-day telephone number may be established with the number being published in such a way as to maximize public awareness of its existence which may be called to obtain a list and description of agencies in the locality of the caller and of the services they offer; and

(2) Materials designed to inform the female of the probable anatomical and physiological characteristics of the embryo or fetus at two-week gestational increments from the time when a female can be known to be pregnant to full term, including any relevant information on the possibility of the embryo or fetus's survival and pictures or drawings representing the development of an embryo or fetus at two-week gestational increments: Provided, That any such pictures or drawings must contain the dimensions of the embryo or fetus and must be realistic and appropriate for the stage of pregnancy depicted. The materials shall be objective, nonjudgmental and designed to convey only accurate scientific information about the embryo or fetus at the various gestational ages. The material shall also contain objective information describing the methods of abortion procedures commonly employed, the medical risks commonly associated with each procedure, the possible detrimental psychological effects of abortion and the medical risks commonly associated with carrying a child to term.

(b) The materials referred to in subsection (a) of this section shall be printed in a typeface large enough to be clearly legible. The website provided for in section four of this article shall be maintained at a minimum resolution of seventy dots per inch. All pictures appearing on the website shall be a minimum of 200 × 300 pixels. All letters on the website shall be a minimum of eleven-point font. All information and pictures shall be accessible with an industry standard browser requiring no additional plug-ins.

(c) The materials required under this section shall be available at no cost from the department of health and human resources upon request and in appropriate numbers to any person, facility or hospital.

West Virginia Code § 16-2I-4. Internet website

Within ninety days of the effective date of this article, the secretary of the department of health and human resources shall develop and maintain a stable internet website to provide the information required to be provided pursuant to the provisions of section three of this article. No information regarding persons visiting the website may be collected or maintained. The secretary of the department of health and human resources shall monitor the website on a daily basis to prevent and correct tampering.

West Virginia Code § 16-2I-5.
Procedure in case of medical emergency

When a medical emergency compels the performance of an abortion, the physician shall inform the female, prior to the abortion if possible, of the medical indications supporting the physician's judgment that an abortion is necessary to avert her death or that a 24-hour delay will create serious risk of substantial and irreversible impairment of a major bodily function.

West Virginia Code § 16-2I-6.
Protection of privacy in court proceedings

In every civil or criminal proceeding or action brought under this article, the court shall rule whether the anonymity of any female upon whom an abortion has been performed or attempted shall be preserved from public disclosure if she does not give her consent to such disclosure. The court, upon motion or sua sponte, shall make such a ruling and, upon determining that her anonymity should be preserved, shall issue orders to the parties, witnesses and counsel and shall direct the sealing of the record and exclusion of individuals from courtrooms or hearing rooms to the extent necessary to safeguard her identity from public disclosure. Each such order shall be accompanied by specific written findings explaining why the anonymity of the female should be preserved from public disclosure, why the order is essential to that end, how the order is narrowly tailored to serve that interest and why no reasonable, less restrictive alternative exists. In the absence of written consent of the female upon whom an abortion has been performed or attempted, anyone, other than a public official, who brings an action under section nine of this article shall do so under a pseudonym. This section may not be construed to conceal the identity of the plaintiff or of witnesses from the defendant.

West Virginia Code § 16-2I-7. Reporting requirements

(a) Within ninety days of the effective date of this article, the secretary of the department of health and human resources shall prepare a reporting form for physicians containing a reprint of this article and listing:

(1) The number of females to whom the information described in subsection (a), section two of this article was provided;

(2) The number of females to whom the physician or an agent of the physician provided the information described in subsection (b), section two of this article;

(3) The number of females who availed themselves of the opportunity to obtain a copy of the printed information described in section three of this article other than on the website;

(4) The number of abortions performed in cases involving medical emergency; and

(5) The number of abortions performed in cases not involving a medical emergency.

(b) The secretary of the department of health and human resources shall ensure that copies of the reporting forms described in subsection (a) of this section are provided:

(1) Within one hundred twenty days after the effective date of this article to all physicians licensed to practice in this state;

(2) To each physician who subsequently becomes newly licensed to practice in this state, at the same time as official notification to that physician that the physician is so licensed; and

(3) By the first day of December of each year, other than the calendar year in which forms are distributed in accordance with subdivision (1) of this subsection, to all physicians licensed to practice in this state.

(c) By the twenty-eighth day of February of each year following a calendar year in any part of which this act was in effect, each physician who provided, or whose agent provided, information to one or more females in accordance with section two of this article during the previous calendar year shall submit to the secretary of the department of health and human resources a copy of the form described in subsection (a) of this section with the requested data entered accurately and completely.

(d) Reports that are not submitted by the end of a grace period of thirty days following the due date are subject to a late fee of five hundred dollars for each additional thirty-day period or portion of a thirty-day period they are overdue. Any physician required to report in accordance with this section who has not submitted a report, or has submitted only an incomplete report, more than one year following the due date may, in an action brought by the secretary of the department of health and human resources, be directed by a court of competent jurisdiction to submit a complete report within a period stated by court order or be subject to sanctions for civil contempt.

(e) By the first day of August of each year, the secretary of the department of health and human resources shall issue a public report providing statistics for the previous calendar year compiled from all of the reports covering that year submitted in accordance with this section for each of the items listed in subsection (a) of this section. Each report shall also provide the statistics for all previous calendar years, adjusted to reflect any additional information from late or corrected reports. The secretary of the department of health and human resources shall prevent any of the information from being included in the public reports that could reasonably lead to the identification of any physician who performed or treated an abortion, or any female who has had an abortion, in accordance with subsection (a), (b) or (c) of this section. Any information that could reasonably lead to the identification of any physician who performed or treated an abortion, or any female who has had an abortion, in accordance with subsection (a), (b) or (c) of this section is exempt from disclosure under the freedom of information act, article one, chapter twenty-nine-b of this code.

(f) The secretary of the department of health and human resources may propose rules for legislative approval in accordance with the provisions of article three, chapter twenty-nine-a of this code which alter the dates established by subdivision (3), subsection (b) of this section or subsection (c) or (e) of this section or consolidate the forms or reports described in this section with other forms or reports to achieve administrative convenience or fiscal savings or to reduce the burden of reporting requirements, so long as reporting forms are sent to all licensed physicians in the state at least once every year and the report described in subsection (e) of this section is issued at least once every year.

West Virginia Code § 16-2I-8. Administrative remedies

(a) Any person or entity may make a complaint to the licensing board, if any, of a person whose conduct is regulated by the provisions of this article and may charge such person with a violation of this article.

(b) Any physician or agent thereof who willfully violates the provisions of this article is subject to sanctions by the licensing board governing his or her profession. For the first violation, the licensing board shall issue a written reprimand to the violator. For the second violation, the licensing board shall revoke the violator's license.

(c) No penalty or civil liability may be assessed for failure to comply with paragraph (3), subsection (b), section two of this article or that portion of subsection (c) of said section requiring a written certification that the female has been informed of her opportunity to review the information referred to in paragraph (3), of subsection (b) of said section unless the department of health and human resources has made the printed materials available at the time the physician or the licensed health care professional to whom the responsibility has been delegated by the physician is required to inform the female of her right to review them.

West Virginia Code § 16-2I-9. Civil remedies

Any person upon whom an abortion has been attempted or performed without section two of this article having been complied with may maintain an action against the person who attempted to perform or did perform the abortion with a knowing or consciously, subjectively and deliberately formed intention to violate this article for compensatory damages. If the person upon whom an abortion has been attempted or performed without section two of this article having been complied with is a minor, the legal guardian of the minor may maintain an action against the person who attempted to perform or did perform the abortion with a knowing or consciously, subjectively and deliberately formed intention to violate this article for compensatory damages.

West Virginia Code § 16-2I-10. Severability

If any one or more provision, section, subsection, sentence, clause, phrase or word of this article or the application thereof to any person or circumstance is found to be unconstitutional, the same is hereby declared to be severable and the balance of this article shall remain effective notwithstanding such unconstitutionality. The Legislature hereby declares that it would have passed this article, and each provision, section, subsection, sentence, clause, phrase or word thereof, irrespective of the fact that any one or more provision, section, subsection, sentence, clause, phrase or word be declared unconstitutional.

(4) ABORTION BY MINORS

Under the laws of West Virginia no physician may perform an abortion upon an unemancipated minor, until 24 hours after notice of the operation has been given to either parent of the minor or legal guardian. The state authorizes a waiver of the notice requirement if an independent physician, who is not performing the abortion, finds that the minor is mature enough to make the abortion decision or that notification would not be in the minor's best interest. Additionally, and in compliance with federal constitutional law, West Virginia has provided a judicial waiver procedure for an unemancipated minor to obtain an abortion without parental or guardian notice. If an unemancipated minor elects not to provide notice to either of her parents or guardian, the minor may petition a trial court for a waiver of the notice requirement. A minor has a right to an attorney at the proceeding and if she cannot afford one, the court must appoint her an attorney. If a minor chooses, she may represent herself. The required parental notice may be waived if the court finds either (1) that the minor is mature and well-informed enough to make the abortion decision on her own, or (2) that notification would not be in the best interest of the minor. An expedited appeal is available to any minor to whom the court denies a waiver of notice. The statutes addressing the issues are set out below.

West Virginia Code § 16-2F-1. Legislative findings and intent

The legislature finds that immature minors often lack the ability to make fully informed choices that take into account both immediate and long-range consequences of their actions; that the medical, emotional and psychological consequences of abortion are serious and of indeterminate duration, particularly when the patient is immature; that in its current abortion policy, as expressed in Bellotti v. Baird, 443 U.S. 622 (1979) and H. L. v. Matheson, 450 U.S. 398 (1981), the United States Supreme Court clearly relies on physicians' commitment to consider all factors, physical and otherwise, before performing abortions on minors; that parents ordinarily possess information essential to a physician's exercise of his best medical judgment concerning their child; and that parents who are aware that their minor daughter has had an abortion may better ensure that the minor receives adequate medical attention after her abortion. The legislature further finds that parental consultation regarding abortion is usually desirable and in the best interests of the minor.

The legislature further finds in accordance with the U.S. Supreme

Court's decision in Bellotti v. Baird, 443 U.S. 622 (1979), and H. L. v. Matheson, 450 U.S. 398 (1981), that there exists important and compelling state interests (i) in protecting minors against their own immaturity, (ii) in fostering the family structure and preserving it as a viable social unit, and (iii) in protecting the rights of parents to rear their own children in their own household.

It is, therefore, the intent of the legislature to further these interests by enacting this parental notice provision.

West Virginia Code § 16-2F-2. Definitions

For purposes of this article, unless the context in which used clearly requires otherwise:

(1) "Minor" means any person under the age of eighteen years who has not graduated from high school.

(2) "Unemancipated minor" means any minor who is neither married nor who has not been emancipated pursuant to applicable federal law or as provided by section twenty-seven, article seven, chapter forty-nine of this Code.

(3) "Actual notice" means the giving of notice directly, in person or by telephone.

(4) "Constructive notice" means the giving of notice by certified mail to the last known address of the parents or legal guardian, return receipt requested.

(5) "Abortion" means the use of any instrument, medicine, drug or any other substance or device with intent to terminate the pregnancy of a female known to be pregnant and with intent to cause the expulsion of a fetus other than by live birth: Provided, That nothing in this article shall be construed so as to prevent the prescription, sale or transfer of intrauterine contraceptive devices or other contraceptive devices or other generally medically accepted contraceptive devices, instruments, medicines or drugs for a female who is not known to be pregnant and for whom such contraceptive devices, instruments, medicines or drugs were prescribed by a physician solely for contraceptive purposes and not for the purpose of inducing or causing the termination of a known pregnancy.

West Virginia Code § 16-2F-3.
Notice and waiting period

(a) No physician may perform an abortion upon an unemancipated minor unless such physician has given or caused to be given at least twenty-four hours actual notice to one of the parents or to the legal guardian of the pregnant minor of his intention to perform the abortion, or, if the parent or guardian cannot be found and notified after a reasonable effort so to do, without first having given at least forty-eight hours constructive notice computed from the time of mailing to the parent or to the legal guardian of the minor: Provided, That prior to giving the notification required by this section, the physician shall advise the unemancipated minor of the right of petition to the circuit court for waiver of notification: Provided, however, That any such notification may be waived by a duly acknowledged writing signed by a parent or the guardian of the minor.

(b) Upon notification being given to any parent or to the legal guardian of such pregnant minor, the physician shall refer such pregnant minor to a counselor or caseworker of any church or school or of the department of human services or of any other comparable agency for the purpose of arranging or accompanying such pregnant minor in consultation with her parents. Such counselor shall thereafter be authorized to monitor the circumstances and the continued relationship of and between such minor and her parents.

(c) Parental notification required by subsection (a) of this section may be waived by a physician, other than the physician who is to perform the abortion, if such other physician finds that the minor is mature enough to make the abortion decision independently or that notification would not be in the minor's best interest: Provided, That such other physician shall not be associated professionally or financially with the physician proposing to perform the abortion.

West Virginia Code § 16-2F-4. Judicial bypass

(a) A minor who objects to such notice being given to her parent or legal guardian may petition for a waiver of such notice to the circuit court of the county in which the minor resides or in which the abortion is to be performed, or to the judge of either of such courts. Such minor may so petition and proceed in her own right or, at her option, by a next friend.

(b) Such petition need not be made in any specific form and shall be sufficient if it fairly sets forth the facts and circumstances of the matter, but shall contain the following information:

(i) The age of the petitioner and her educational level;

(ii) The county and state in which she resides; and

(iii) A brief statement of petitioner's reason or reasons for the desired waiver of notification of the parent or guardian of such minor petitioner.

No such petition shall be dismissed nor shall any hearing thereon be refused because of any defect in the form of the petition.

(c) Upon the effective date of this article or as soon thereafter as may be, the attorney general shall prepare suggested form petitions and accompanying instructions and shall make the same available to the several clerks of the circuit courts. Such clerks shall see that a sufficient number of such suggested form petitions and instructions are available in the clerk's office for the use of any person desiring to use the same for the purposes of this section.

(d) All proceedings held pursuant to this article shall be confidential and the court shall conduct all such proceedings in camera. The court shall inform the minor petitioner of her right to be represented by counsel and that if she is without the requisite funds to retain the services of an attorney, that the court will appoint an attorney to represent her interest in the matter. If the minor petitioner desires the services of an attorney, an attorney shall be appointed to represent such minor petitioner, if she advises the court under oath or affidavit that she is financially unable to retain counsel. Any attorney appointed to represent such minor petitioner shall be appointed and paid for his services pursuant to the provisions of article twenty-one [§§ 29-21-1 et seq.], chapter twenty-nine of this Code: Provided, That the pay to any such attorney pursuant to such appointment shall not exceed the sum of one hundred dollars.

(e) The court shall conduct a hearing upon the petition without delay, but in no event shall the delay exceed the next succeeding judicial day, and the court shall render its decision immediately upon its submission and, in any event, an order reflecting the findings of fact and conclusions of law reached by the court and its judgment shall be endorsed by the judge thereof not later than twenty-four hours following such submission and shall be forthwith entered of record by the clerk of the court....

(f) Notice as required by section three [§ 16-2F-3] of this article shall be ordered waived by the court if the court finds either:

(1) That the minor petitioner is mature and well informed sufficiently to make the decision to proceed with the abortion independently and without the notification or involvement of her parent or legal guardian, or

(2) That notification to the person or persons to whom such notification would otherwise be required would not be in the best interest of the minor petitioner.

(g) If or when the circuit court, or the judge thereof, shall refuse to order the waiver of the notification required by section three of this article, a copy of the petition and all orders entered in the matter and all other documents and papers submitted to the circuit court, may be presented to the supreme court of appeals, or to any justice thereof if such court then be in vacation, and such court or justice if deemed proper, may thereupon order the waiver of notification otherwise required by section three of this article. The supreme court of appeals or justice thereof

shall hear and decide the matter without delay and shall enter such orders as such court or justice may deem appropriate.

(h) If either the circuit court or the supreme court of appeals, or any judge or justice thereof if either of such courts be then in vacation, shall order a waiver of the notification required by section three of this article, any physician to whom a certified copy of said order shall be presented may proceed to perform the abortion to the same extent as if such physician were in compliance with the provisions of said section three and, notwithstanding the fact that no notification is given to either the parent or legal guardian of any such unemancipated minor, any such physician shall not be subject to the penalty provisions which may be prescribed by this article for such failure of notification.

(i) No filing fees may be required of any minor who avails herself of any of the procedures provided by this section.

West Virginia Code § 16-2F-5. Emergency exception

The notification requirements of section three of this article do not apply where there is an emergency need for an abortion to be performed if the continuation of the pregnancy constitutes an immediate threat and grave risk to the life or health of the pregnant minor and the attending physician so certifies in writing setting forth the nature of such threat or risk and the consequences which may be attendant to the continuation of the pregnancy. Such writing shall be maintained with the other medical records relating to such minor which are maintained by the physician and the facility at which such abortion is performed.

West Virginia Code § 16-2F-6.
Reporting requirements for physicians

Any physician performing an abortion upon an unemancipated minor shall provide the department of health a written report of the procedure within thirty days after having performed the abortion. The department of health shall provide reporting forms for this purpose to all physicians and public health facilities required to be licensed pursuant to article five-B of this chapter. The following information, in addition to any other information which may be required by the department of health, regarding the minor receiving the abortion shall be included in such reporting form:

(1) Age;
(2) Educational level;
(3) Previous pregnancies;
(4) Previous live births;
(5) Previous abortions;
(6) Complications, if any, of the abortion being reported;
(7) Reason for waiver of notification of the minor's parent or guardian, if such notice was waived; and
(8) The city and county in which the abortion was performed.

Any such report shall not contain the name, address or other information by which the minor receiving the abortion may be identified.

West Virginia Code § 16-2F-8. Penalties

Any person who knowingly performs an abortion upon an unemancipated minor in violation of this article or who knowingly fails to conform to any requirement of this article shall be guilty of a misdemeanor, and, upon conviction thereof, shall be fined not less than five hundred dollars nor more than one thousand dollars or imprisoned in the county jail not more than thirty days, or both fined and imprisoned.

West Virginia Code § 16-2F-9. Severability

The provisions of subsection (cc), section ten, article two, chapter two of this Code shall apply to the provisions of this article to the same extent as if said subsection were set forth in extenso herein.

(5) PARTIAL-BIRTH ABORTION

West Virginia criminalizes performance of partial-birth abortions, unless it is done to preserve the life of the woman. A federal court issued an order enjoining enforcement of the statute in *Daniel v. Underwood*, 102 F.Supp. 680 (S.D.W.Va. 2000), based upon the United States Supreme Court decision in *Stenberg v. Carhart*, which invalidated a Nebraska statute that prohibited partial-birth abortions. However, subsequent to *Stenberg* the Supreme Court decided the case of *Gonzales v. Carhart*, in which it approved of a federal statute that prohibited partial-birth abortion. The state statute is set out below.

West Virginia Code § 33-42-8. Partial-birth abortion ban

(a) Any person who knowingly performs a partial-birth abortion and thereby kills a human fetus is guilty of a felony and shall be fined not less than ten thousand dollars, nor more than fifty thousand dollars, or imprisoned not more than two years, or both fined and imprisoned. This section does not apply to a partial-birth abortion that is necessary to save the life of a mother when her life is endangered by a physical disorder, illness or injury.

(b) A physician charged pursuant to this section may seek a hearing before the West Virginia board of medicine on the issue of whether the physician's act was necessary to save the life of a mother pursuant to the provisions of subsection (a) of this section. The findings of the board of medicine are admissible on this issue at the trial of the physician. Upon a motion by the defendant, the court shall delay the beginning of trial for not more than thirty days to permit the board of medicine hearing to take place.

(c) No woman may be prosecuted under the provisions of this section for having a partial-birth abortion, nor may she be prosecuted for conspiring to violate the provisions of this section.

(6) MEDICAL PERSONNEL

West Virginia permits physicians and other medical personnel to refuse to take part in the performance of abortions. The statute addressing the matter is set out below.

West Virginia Code § 16-2F-7.
Right to refuse participation in abortion

Nothing in this article, nor in any order issued pursuant thereto, shall require that a physician perform an abortion or that any person be required to assist in the performance of an abortion if such physician or person, for any reason, medical or otherwise, does not wish to perform or assist in such abortion.

(7) PUBLIC FUNDS AND ABORTION

West Virginia prohibits the use of Medicaid funds to pay for abortions, except when necessary to save the life or health of the woman, or the fetus has a severe defect, or the pregnancy resulted from rape or incest. The highest court of West Virginia held in *Women's Health Center v. Panepinto*, 446 S.E.2d 658 (W.Va. 1993), that the Medicaid limitation violated the state constitution. The statute is set out below.

West Virginia Code § 9-2-11. Limitation on use of funds

(a) No funds from the Medicaid program accounts may be used to pay for the performance of an abortion by surgical or chemical means unless:

(1) On the basis of the physician's best clinical judgment, there is:

(i) A medical emergency that so complicates a pregnancy as to necessitate an immediate abortion to avert the death of the mother or for which a delay will create grave peril of irreversible loss of major bodily function or an equivalent injury to the mother: Provided, That an independent physician concurs with the physician's clinical judgment; or

(ii) Clear clinical medical evidence that the fetus has severe congenital defects or terminal disease or is not expected to be delivered; or

(2) The individual is a victim of incest or the individual is a victim of rape when the rape is reported to a law-enforcement agency.

(b) The Legislature intends that the state's Medicaid program not provide coverage for abortion on demand and that abortion services be provided only as expressly provided for in this section.

(8) INJURY TO A PREGNANT WOMAN

Under the laws of West Virginia an injury to a pregnant woman that causes the death or an injury to a fetus is a criminal offense. The statute addressing the matter is set out below.

West Virginia Code § 61-2-30.
Unborn child as victim of certain crimes

(a) This section may be known and cited as the Unborn Victims of Violence Act.

(b) For the purposes of this article, the following definitions shall apply: Provided, That these definitions only apply for purposes of prosecution of unlawful acts under this section and may not otherwise be used: (i) To create or to imply that a civil cause of action exists; or (ii) for purposes of argument in a civil cause of action, unless there has been a criminal conviction under this section.

(1) "Embryo" means the developing human in its early stages. The embryonic period commences at fertilization and continues to the end of the embryonic period and the beginning of the fetal period, which occurs eight weeks after fertilization or ten weeks after the onset of the last menstrual period.

(2) "Fetus" means a developing human that has ended the embryonic period and thereafter continues to develop and mature until termination of the pregnancy or birth.

(c) For purposes of enforcing the provisions of sections one [murder], four [manslaughter] and seven [attempt to kill] of this article, subsections (a) [malicious wounding] and (c) [battery], section nine of said article, sections ten [assault] and ten-b [malicious assault] of said article and subsection (a) [domestic battery], section twenty-eight of said article, a pregnant woman and the embryo or fetus she is carrying in the womb constitute separate and distinct victims.

(d) The provisions of this section do not apply to:

(1) Acts committed during a legal abortion to which the pregnant woman, or a person authorized by law to act on her behalf, consented or for which the consent is implied by law;

(2) Acts or omissions by medical or health care personnel during or as a result of medical or health-related treatment or services, including, but not limited to, medical care, abortion, diagnostic testing or fertility treatment;

(3) Acts or omissions by medical or health care personnel or scientific research personnel in performing lawful procedures involving embryos that are not in a stage of gestation in utero;

(4) Acts involving the use of force in lawful defense of self or another, but not an embryo or fetus; and

(5) Acts or omissions of a pregnant woman with respect to the embryo or fetus she is carrying.

(e) For purposes of the enforcement of the provisions of this section, a violation of the provisions of article two-i, chapter sixteen of this code shall not serve as a waiver of the protection afforded by the provisions of subdivision (1), subsection (d) of this section.

(f) A prosecution for or conviction under this section is not a bar to conviction of or punishment for any other crime committed by the defendant arising from the same incident.

(9) FETAL DEATH REPORT

West Virginia requires every abortion be reported to the proper authorities. The statute addressing the matter is set out below.

West Virginia Code § 16-5-22.
Reports of induced termination of pregnancy

(a) Each induced termination of pregnancy which occurs in this state, regardless of the length of gestation, shall be reported to the section of vital statistics no later than the tenth day of the month following the month the procedure was performed by the person in charge of the institution in which the induced termination of pregnancy was performed. If the induced termination of pregnancy was performed outside an institution, it shall be reported by the attending physician. The State Registrar shall prepare a form or provide a suitable electronic process for the transmission of the reports from the institution or physician to the section of vital statistics. Information to be collected shall include:

(1) The gestational age of the fetus;

(2) The state and county of residence of the woman;

(3) The age of the woman;

(4) The type of medical or surgical procedure performed;

(5) The method of payment for the procedure;

(6) Whether birth defects were known, and if so, what birth defects; and

(7) Related information as required by the commissioner, other applicable sections of this code, or by the legislative rule: Provided, That:

(A) No personal identifiers, including, but not limited to, name, street address, city, zip code, or social security number, will be collected; and

(B) Individual records may only be released for research purposes as approved by the State Registrar and may be released in a format designed to further protect the confidentiality of the woman as the State Registrar deems necessary.

(b) An analysis of the compiled information relating to induced terminations of pregnancy shall be included in the annual report of vital statistics.

West Virginians for Life

West Virginians for Life (WVL) is a pro-life organization headed by its president Shirley Stanton. The organization was formed to promote the protection of human life, from conception until natural death. To accomplish its goal, WVL works to educate the public through the presentation of information about fetal development, abortion, and alternatives to abortion.

WVL publishes a bi-monthly newspaper, *Life Matters*, to inform its members of current pro-life issues. It also makes available for the public pro-life books, videos, informational literature, speakers and slide presentations. Each year, WVL holds several events, including: the Pro-life Rally and Day at the Legislature, the Mother's Day Walk for Life, the annual WVL Convention, an Oratory Contest, WV Teens for Life Convention, and a Rally at the Capitol for teens. *See also* **Pro-Life Organizations**

Westchester Coalition for Legal Abortion

Westchester Coalition for Legal Abortion (WCLA) is a New York based pro-choice organization that was founded in 1972, after the New York legislature unsuccessfully attempted to repeal its 1970 legislation permitting abortion. WCLA was created as a political organization with the purpose of promoting and supporting pro-choice candidates for office. The organization is committed to making certain that abortion and contraception remain legal and accessible in New York, as well as working to assure that those who provide and receive abortions are physically safe from illegal actions by anti-abortion militants. *See also* **Pro-Choice Organizations**

White, Byron R.

Byron R. White (1917–2002) served as an associate justice of the United States Supreme Court from 1962 to 1993. While on the Supreme Court Justice White was known for a judicial philosophy that swayed between conservative and moderate.

Justice White was born in Fort Collins, Colorado. He graduated from the University of Colorado in 1938. He played professional foot-

Distribution of the Abortion Voting Pattern of Justice White Based Upon Opinions Filed by the Supreme Court

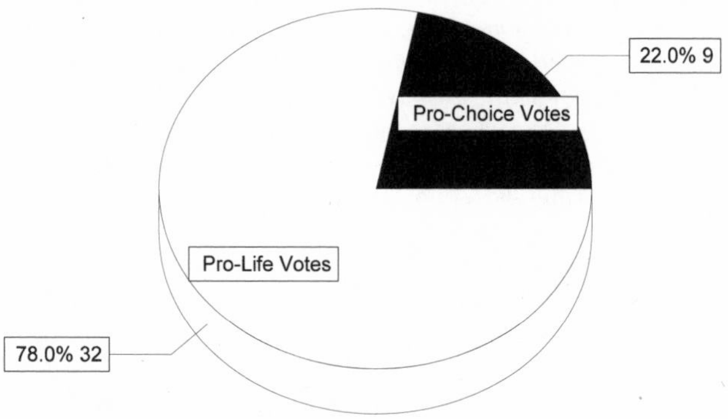

ball while studying law at Yale University Law School, where he received a law degree in 1946. In 1962 President John F. Kennedy appointed him to the Supreme Court.

Justice White retired from the Supreme Court in 1993. During Justice White's tenure on the Supreme Court he issued a significant number of abortion related opinions. The written opinions and opinions simply voted on by Justice White, indicate that he was not in favor of using the constitution to expand abortion rights for women.

(1) Unanimous opinions written. In *Withrow v. Larkin* Justice White wrote a unanimous opinion, which held that constitutional due process was not violated by the mere fact that a Wisconsin medical examining board had the authority to both, investigate and adjudicate, allegations against a physician that included, among other things, permitting a nonphysician to perform an abortion.

(2) Unanimous opinions voted with only. In *Bellotti v. Baird I* Justice White voted with a unanimous opinion, which held that the federal district court had to certify appropriate questions to the supreme judicial court of Massachusetts, concerning the interpretation of that state's parental consent abortion statute for minors, before ruling on its constitutionality.

(3) Majority opinions voted with only. Justice White voted with the majority in *Rust v. Sullivan*, which upheld federal regulations that prohibited pro-abortion counseling, referral, and advocacy by health care providers. Justice White voted with the majority opinion in *Bray v. Alexandria Clinic*, which held that the Civil Rights Act of 1871, 42 U.S.C. § 1985(3), did not provide a cause of action against persons obstructing access to abortion clinics. In *Ohio v. Akron Center for Reproductive Health* Justice White voted with the majority opinion, which upheld the constitutionality of Ohio's abortion statute notice and judicial bypass requirements for pregnant female minors. Justice White voted with the majority decision in *Webster v. Reproductive Health Services*, which upheld Missouri's prohibition on the use of public facilities or employees to perform abortions and a requirement that physicians conduct viability tests prior to performing abortions.

Justice White voted with the majority opinion in *United States Catholic Conference v. Abortion Rights Mobilization*, which allowed the appellants to challenge having to turn over documents in a lawsuit seeking to strip them of their tax exempt status because of their active political abortion work. Justice White voted with the majority opinion in *Bolger v. Youngs Drug Products Corp.*, which held that a provision of the Comstock Act, 39 U.S.C. § 3001(e)(2), that prohibited mailing unsolicited advertisements for contraceptives violated the Free Speech Clause of the First Amendment. In *Daubert v. Merrell Dow Pharmaceuticals, Inc.*, a case involving children born with severe birth defects, Justice White voted with the majority in holding that the *Frye* rule on admissibility of expert testimony did not survive the enactment of the Federal Rules of Evidence. Justice White joined the majority opinion in *Anders v. Floyd*, which held that a federal district court erred in enjoining enforcement of a South Carolina statute that imposed criminal punishment for performing an abortion on a viable fetus.

In *H. L. v. Matheson* Justice White joined the majority opinion, which held that the constitution was not violated by Utah's requirement that the parents of a minor be notified, if possible, prior to performing an abortion. In *Williams v. Zbaraz* Justice White voted with the majority opinion, which held that in light of the requirements of the Hyde Amendment, the Equal Protection Clause of the Fourteenth Amendment was not violated by an Illinois statute that prohibited state Medicaid payment for abortions, except when necessary to save the life of the pregnant woman. Justice White joined the majority opinion in *Beal v. Doe*, which held that Pennsylvania's refusal to extend Medicaid coverage to nontherapeutic abortions was not invalid nor inconsistent with Title XIX of the Social Security Act. In *Maher v. Roe* Justice White joined the majority opinion, which held that the Equal Protection Clause of the Fourteenth Amendment did not prohibit Connecticut from excluding nontherapeutic abortions from its Medicaid program.

Justice White joined the per curiam opinion in *Poelker v. Doe*, which held that the Equal Protection Clause of the Fourteenth Amendment was not violated by a policy of the city of St. Louis, Missouri that denied publicly funded abortions to indigent women at city hospitals, except when a woman's health or life was in danger. Justice White voted with the majority opinion in *Burns v. Alcala*, which held that states receiving federal financial aid under the program of Aid to Families with Dependent Children, were not required to offer welfare benefits to pregnant women for their unborn children. Justice White voted with the majority opinion in *Geduldig v. Aiello*, which held that the Equal Protection Clause of the Fourteenth Amendment did not require a private sector employee disability insurance program, operated by the state of California, provide coverage for employee disabilities associated with normal pregnancies. In *Weinberger v. Hynson, Westcott & Dunning* Justice White joined the majority opinion, which held that the Food and Drug Administration could not deny a drug manufacturer a hearing to obtain marketing approval for a drug called Lutrexin, which provided treatment for premature labor and threatened and habitual abortion.

(4) Plurality opinions voted with only. Justice White joined the plurality opinion that announced the judgment of the Supreme Court in *Singleton v. Wulff*, which held that the Eighth Circuit court of appeals had jurisdiction to determine whether abortion providers had standing to challenge a provision in Missouri's abortion statute that limited Medicaid payment for abortions, but it did not have jurisdiction to rule that the provision violated the constitution because the district court did not address the issue.

(5) Concurring opinions written. In *Automobile Workers v. Johnson Controls, Inc.* Justice White wrote an opinion concurring with the majority decision, which held that Title VII of the Civil Rights Act forbids sex-specific fetal-protection policies by an employer, that exclude a fertile female employee from certain jobs because of the employer's concern for the health of the fetus the woman might conceive. In *Frisby v. Schultz* Justice White wrote an opinion concurring with the majority decision, which upheld the constitutional validity of a town ordinance that was created to prevent pro-life picketing at the residence of an abortion doctor.

Justice White wrote an opinion concurring in the majority decision in *Harris v. McRae*, which held that Medicaid funding restrictions for abortion by the Hyde Amendment, did not violate the Due Process Clause nor the equal protection component of the Fifth

Amendment. In *Diamond v. Charles*, Justice White issued a statement concurring in the judgment of the Court, which held that a citizen did not have standing to appeal a decision invalidating parts of Illinois' abortion statute that (1) imposed criminal penalties for violating a prescribed standard of care that had to be exercised by a physician in performing an abortion of a viable fetus, and of a possibly viable fetus; and (2) imposed criminal penalties for physicians who failed to provide patients with information about the type of abortifacient used.

In *Carey v. Population Services International* Justice White wrote an opinion concurring with the majority decision, which held that the constitution prohibited enforcement of a New York statute that made it a crime (1) for any person to sell or distribute any contraceptive of any kind to a minor under the age of 16 years; (2) for anyone other than a licensed pharmacist to distribute contraceptives to persons 16 or over; and (3) for anyone, including licensed pharmacists, to advertise or display contraceptives. Justice White wrote an opinion concurring in the majority decision in *Eisenstadt v. Baird*, which held that the Equal Protection Clause of the Fourteenth Amendment was violated by a Massachusetts statute that made it a crime to give away a drug, medicine, instrument, or article for the prevention of conception except in the case of (1) a physician prescribing it for a married person, or (2) a pharmacist furnishing it to a married person presenting a physician's prescription. Justice White wrote an opinion concurring with the majority decision in *United States v. Vuitch*, which held that the criminal abortion statute of the District of Columbia, which only permitted therapeutic abortions, was not constitutionally vague insofar as there was no ambiguity in its use of the word health and it did not shift to the defendant the burden of proving innocence. In *Griswold v. Connecticut* Justice White wrote an opinion concurring with the majority decision, which held that the right of privacy found in the constitution prohibited enforcement of a Connecticut statute that made it a crime to give married persons contraceptive information and devices.

(6) Concurring opinions voted with only. Justice White voted to concur with the majority opinion in *Simopoulos v. Virginia*, which upheld a Virginia statute requiring second trimester abortions be performed at hospitals, because under the statute an adequately equipped clinic could, upon proper application, obtain an outpatient hospital license that permitted the performance of second-trimester abortions. In *Connecticut v. Menillo* Justice White concurred in the majority per curiam opinion, which held that the constitution was not violated by criminal abortion statutes that prohibit nonphysicians from attempting or performing abortions at any stage of a pregnancy.

(7) Dissenting opinions written. Justice White wrote a dissenting opinion in *Thornburgh v. American College of Obstetricians and Gynecologists*, which invalidated provisions in Pennsylvania's abortion statute that provided for maternal informed consent, abortion alternative printed information, abortion reporting requirements, determination of fetal viability, degree of care required in post-viability abortions, and a second-physician requirement. Justice White wrote an opinion dissenting from the majority judgment in *Bellotti v. Baird II*, which held that Massachusetts' abortion statute for minors violated the constitution in light of an interpretation given by the state's highest court, that required parental notice of a judicial bypass proceeding invoked by a minor, and permitted a judge to deny an abortion even though the minor proved she had enough maturity to make an independent decision. He believed the statute passed constitutional muster.

In *Colautti v. Franklin* Justice White wrote an opinion dissenting from the majority decision, which held that the constitution was violated by a vague and ambiguous provision in Pennsylvania's abortion statute that subjected a physician who performed an abortion to potential criminal liability, if he/she failed to utilize a statutorily prescribed technique when the fetus was viable or when there was sufficient reason to believe that the fetus may be viable. He believed the provision was constitutionally valid.

Justice White wrote an opinion dissenting from the majority decision in *Doe v. Bolton*, which held that the Due Process Clause of the Fourteenth Amendment was violated by provisions in Georgia's abortion statutes that required (1) abortions take place in accredited hospitals, (2) that an abortion be approved by a hospital abortion committee, (3) that the need for an abortion be confirmed by two independent physicians, and (4) that a woman seeking an abortion be a resident of Georgia. He believed the provisions passed constitutional muster.

(8) Dissenting opinions voted with only. Justice White dissented from the majority opinion in *City of Akron v. Akron Center for Reproductive Health, Inc.*, which invalidated an abortion ordinance that provided requirements for parental consent, informed consent, waiting period, hospitalization and disposal of fetal remains. Justice White dissented from the majority decision in *Bigelow v. Virginia*, which held that the Free Speech and Free Press Clauses of the First Amendment were violated by a Virginia penal statute that prohibited selling or circulating any publication that encouraged or promoted abortions. He believed the statute passed constitutional muster. In *Roe v. Wade* Justice White dissented from the majority opinion, which held that the liberty component of the Due Process Clause of the Fourteenth Amendment prohibited states from criminalizing or preventing elective first trimester abortions. He did not believe that the constitution prohibited states from criminalizing abortion.

(9) Concurring and dissenting opinions written. Justice White wrote an opinion concurring and dissenting from the majority decision in *Planned Parenthood of Missouri v. Danforth*, which held that the constitution was not violated by provisions in Missouri's abortion statute involving the definition of fetal viability, woman's written consent, and record keeping and reporting requirements; but that the constitution prohibited the requirements concerning spousal consent, parental consent for minor, banning saline amniocentesis abortions, and physician's standard of care. Justice White believed that all of the provisions of the statute were constitutionally valid.

(10) Concurring and dissenting opinions voted with only. In *Planned Parenthood of Southeastern Pennsylvania v. Casey*, Justice White voted to concur and dissent. He concurred in the majority's decision that the constitution was not violated by provisions in Pennsylvania's abortion statute that provided for: medical emergency abortion; 24 hour waiting period for abortion; parental notice and judicial bypass for abortion by a minor; and certain abortion facility reporting requirements. He dissented from the majority's decision that found two provisions in the abortion statute unconstitutional: spousal notification before obtaining an abortion, and a requirement that a woman inform the abortion provider the reason for not notifying her spouse.

Justice White voted to concur and dissent in *Hodgson v. Minnesota*, which upheld the constitutionality of Minnesota's requirement that a pregnant female minor could not obtain an abortion until at least 48 hours after both of her parents had been notified, except when (1) the attending physician certified that an immediate abortion was necessary to prevent the minor's death; (2) the minor declared that she was a victim of parental abuse or neglect; or (3) a court of competent jurisdiction ordered the abortion to proceed without notice upon proof that the minor was mature and capable of giving informed consent or that an abortion without notice to both parents would be in the minor's best interest. Justice White dissented from the Court's determination that the two-parent notification requirement was invalid, but concurred in the determination that the judicial bypass option cured the defect.

In *Federal Election Commission v. Massachusetts Citizens for Life,*

Inc. Justice White voted to concur and dissent from the majority decision, which held that federal law that prohibited the appellee from using its treasury funds to promote pro-life political candidates violated the Free Speech Clause of the First Amendment. Justice White agreed with the majority that the law applied to the appellee, but dissented from the decision to find the law unconstitutional. In *Planned Parenthood Assn. v. Ashcroft* Justice White concurred and dissented from the majority/plurality opinion, which held that the constitution was violated by Missouri's requirement that second trimester abortions take place in a hospital; but that the constitution was not violated by the state's requirement that a pathology report for each abortion be performed, that a second physician be present during abortions performed after viability, and parental or judicial consent for abortion by minors. Justice White believed that all of the provisions of the statute were constitutional.

Whittaker, Charles E.

Charles E. Whittaker (1901–1973) served as an associate justice of the United States Supreme Court from 1957 to 1962. While on the Supreme Court Justice Whittaker was known as a conservative interpreter of the Constitution.

Justice Whittaker was born in Troy, Kansas. He received a law degree from the University of Kansas City Law School in 1923. He maintained a successful law practice before being appointed a position as a federal district court judge in 1954. President Dwight D. Eisenhower appointed Justice Whittaker to the Supreme Court in 1957.

Justice Whittaker was involved in only one abortion related opinion while on the Supreme Court. Justice Whittaker joined a plurality opinion in *Poe v. Ullman*, which held that the appellants did not have standing to challenge the constitutionality of a Connecticut statute, that made it a crime to give married persons contraceptive information and devices.

William & Mary Alternatives to Abortion

William & Mary Alternatives to Abortion is a pro-life student-run organization that was founded in 1985, on the campus of the College of William & Mary. The organization focuses primarily on bringing positive alternatives to abortion to students at the college community. Its members work closely with community pregnancy help centers. The organization provides many pro-life services that include distributing pro-life literature, dorm talks, films, debates, maintaining an education website, fundraising for pregnancy help centers, and hosting speakers. *See also* **Pro-Life Organizations**

Williams v. Zbaraz

Forum: United States Supreme Court.

Case Citation: Williams v. Zbaraz, 448 U.S. 358 (1980).

Date Argued: April 21, 1980.

Date of Decision: June 30, 1980.

Opinion of Court: Stewart, J., in which Burger, C. J., and White, Powell, and Rehnquist, JJ., joined.

Concurring Opinion: None.

Dissenting Opinion: Brennan, J., in which Marshall and Blackmun, JJ., joined.

Dissenting Opinion: Marshall, J.

Dissenting Opinion: Blackmun, J.

Dissenting Opinion: Stevens, J.

Counsel for Appellants: Victor G. Rosenblum argued; on the brief were Dennis J. Horan, John D. Gorby, and Patrick A. Trueman. William A. Wenzel III, Special Assistant Attorney General of Illinois, argued; on the brief were William J. Scott, Attorney General, and James C. O'Connell and Ellen P. Brewin, Special Assistant Attorneys General. Solicitor General McCree argued; on the brief were Assistant Attorney General Daniel and Eloise E. Davies.

Counsel for Appellees: Robert W. Bennett argued; on the brief were Lois J. Lipton, David Goldberger, Aviva Futorian, Robert E. Lehrer, and James D. Weill.

Amicus Brief for Appellants: Robert B. Hansen, Attorney General, Paul M. Tinker, Assistant Attorney General, and Lynn D. Wardle for the State of Utah; by Bronson C. La Follette, Attorney General of Wisconsin, F. Joseph Sensenbrenner, Jr., Assistant Attorney General, and William J. Brown, Attorney General of Ohio, for the States of Wisconsin et al.; by George E. Reed and Patrick F. Geary for the United States Catholic Conference; by Daniel J. Popeo for the Washington Legal Foundation. John J. Degnan, Attorney General, Erminie L. Conley, Assistant Attorney General, and Andrea M. Silkowitz, Deputy Attorney General, for the State of New Jersey; James Bopp, Jr., and David D. Haynes for the National Right to Life Committee, Inc.

Amicus Brief for Appellees: Paul Bender, Thomas Harvey, and Roland Morris for Jane Roe et al.; and by Margo K. Rogers; Eve W. Paul for the Planned Parenthood Federation of America, Inc., et al.; Francis X. Bellotti, Attorney General of Massachusetts, Garrick F. Cole, Assistant Attorney General, John D. Ashcroft, Attorney General of Missouri, Paul L. Douglas, Attorney General of Nebraska, and William J. Brown, Attorney General of Ohio, for the Commonwealth of Massachusetts et al.; by Dorothy T. Lang for the Physicians National Housestaff Association et al.; and by Francis D. Morrissey for Certain Physicians, Professors and Fellows of the American College of Obstetrics and Gynecology.

Issue Presented: Whether the Equal Protection Clause of the Fourteenth Amendment was violated by an Illinois statute that prohibited state Medicaid payment for abortions except when necessary to save the life of the pregnant woman?

Case Holding: In light of the requirements of the Hyde Amendment, the Equal Protection Clause of the Fourteenth Amendment was not violated by an Illinois statute that prohibited state Medicaid payment for abortions, except when necessary to save the life of the pregnant woman.

Background facts of case: The appellees, abortion providers and a Jane Doe, filed a lawsuit in a federal district court in Illinois challenging the enforcement of a state statute that prohibited state medical assistance payments for all abortions except those necessary for the preservation of the life of the woman seeking such treatment. The state statute was promulgated as a result of the Hyde Amendment, which prohibited states from using federal Medicaid funds, paid through Title XIX of the Social Security Act, for abortions except in limited situations. The appellees named a state official as the defendant. Subsequently, the federal government and two citizens joined the suit as defendants. The district court ultimately held that the state statute and the Hyde Amendment were unconstitutional. The court enjoined enforcement of the state statute, but did not enjoin any action by the United States. An appeal to the United States Supreme Court was made by the state, federal government and the two intervening citizens. The Supreme Court granted certiorari and consolidated the appeals.

Majority opinion by Justice Stewart: Justice Stewart wrote a very brief opinion for the Court that set aside the district court's decision. He was brief because the issue presented was decided in another case, *Harris v. McRae*, during the same Term of Court. Justice Stewart wrote as follows:

> Disposition of the merits of these appeals does not require extended discussion. Insofar as we have ... concluded that the District Court lacked jurisdiction to declare the Hyde Amendment unconstitutional, that portion of its judgment must be vacated. The remaining questions concern the Illinois statute. The appellees argue that (1) Title XIX requires Illinois to provide coverage in its state Medicaid plan for all medically necessary abortions, whether or not the life of the pregnant woman is endan-

gered, and (2) the funding by Illinois of medically necessary services generally, but not of certain medically necessary abortions, violates the Equal Protection Clause of the Fourteenth Amendment. Both arguments are foreclosed by our decision today in Harris v. McRae. As to the appellees' statutory argument, we have concluded in McRae that a participating State is not obligated under Title XIX to pay for those medically necessary abortions for which federal reimbursement is unavailable under the Hyde Amendment. As to their constitutional argument, we have concluded in McRae that the Hyde Amendment does not violate the equal protection component of the Fifth Amendment by withholding public funding for certain medically necessary abortions, while providing funding for other medically necessary health services. It follows, for the same reasons, that the comparable funding restrictions in the Illinois statute do not violate the Equal Protection Clause of the Fourteenth Amendment.

Disposition of case: The judgment of the district court was vacated.

Dissenting opinion by Justice Brennan: Justice Brennan referenced to his dissenting opinion in *Harris v. McRae*, as the basis for his dissent.

Dissenting opinion by Justice Marshall: Justice Marshall referenced to his dissenting opinion in *Harris v. McRae*, as the basis for his dissent.

Dissenting opinion by Justice Blackmun: Justice Blackman referenced to his dissenting opinion in *Harris v. McRae*, as the basis for his dissent.

Dissenting opinion by Justice Stevens: Justice Stevens referenced to his dissenting opinion in *Harris v. McRae*, as the basis for his dissent. *See also* **Hyde Amendment**; **Harris v. McRae**

Wilson's Disease

Wilson's disease is a congenital disorder involving excessive amounts of copper buildup in the body being deposited in the liver, brain, kidneys, and the eyes. This condition causes a variety of effects including liver disease and damage to the central nervous system. Treatment for the disorder includes reduction in the amount of copper in the body and management of the symptoms of the disorder. Lifelong treatment is necessary to control the disorder. In some instances treatment is ineffective and the disorder may cause fatal effects. *See also* **Birth Defects and Abortion**

Wisconsin

(1) OVERVIEW

The state of Wisconsin enacted its first criminal abortion statute in 1849. The statute underwent several amendments prior to the 1973 decision by the United States Supreme Court in *Roe v. Wade*, which legalized abortion in the nation. In spite of the decision in *Roe*, Wisconsin has not repealed its pre–*Roe* criminal abortion statute. However, the statute is constitutionally infirm.

Wisconsin has taken affirmative steps to respond to *Roe* and its progeny. The state has addressed several abortion issues by statute that include post-viability abortion, informed consent, abortion by minors, partial-birth abortion, use of facilities and people, public funds and abortion, anti-abortion activity, injury to a pregnant woman, health insurance coverage, and fetal death report.

(2) PRE-ROE ABORTION BAN

As previously indicated, Wisconsin has not repealed its pre–*Roe* criminal abortion statute. However, the statute was found invalid in *Babbitz v. McCann*, 310 F.Supp. 293 (E.D.Wis. 1970), to the extent that it infringed upon a woman's right to abort a nonviable fetus. Under the statute abortion is criminalized if it was not performed to preserve the life of the woman. The statute punishes the abortionist and the pregnant woman. The statute is set out below.

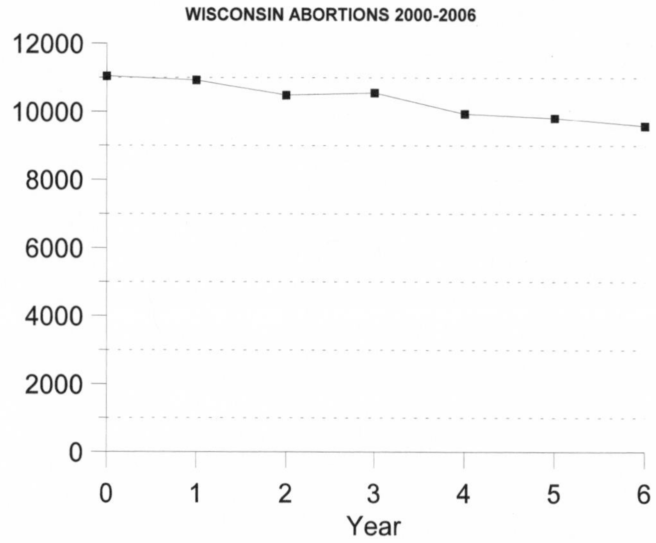

Source: Wisconsin Department of Health and Family Services.

Wisconsin Abortion by Age Group 2000–2006

Year	Age Group (yrs) <15	15–17	18–19	20–24	25–29	30–34	35–39	40–44	≥45
2000	76	743	1,389	3,615	2,457	1,464	976	300	20
2001	76	736	1,275	3,820	2,375	1,446	871	300	26
2002	81	646	1,223	3,548	2,310	1,449	878	329	25
2003	64	690	1,208	3,566	2,282	1,411	968	338	30
2004	56	621	1,094	3,474	2,157	1,362	868	285	26
2005	54	602	1,128	3,418	2,132	1,338	819	310	16
2006	48	564	1,100	3,237	2,233	1,310	789	276	23
Total	455	4,602	8,417	24,678	15,946	9,780	6,169	2,138	166

Source: Wisconsin Department of Health and Family Services.

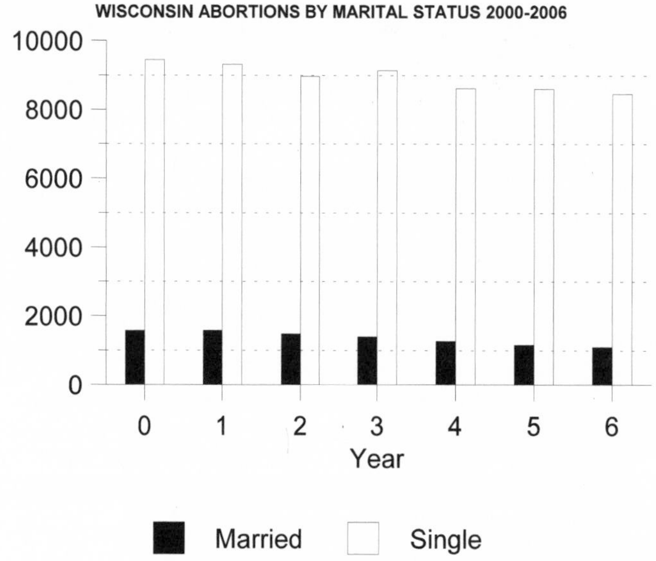

Source: Wisconsin Department of Health and Family Services.

Wisconsin Code § 940.04. Criminal abortion

(1) Any person, other than the mother, who intentionally destroys the life of an unborn child is guilty of a Class H felony.

(2) Any person, other than the mother, who does either of the following is guilty of a Class E felony:

(a) Intentionally destroys the life of an unborn quick child; or

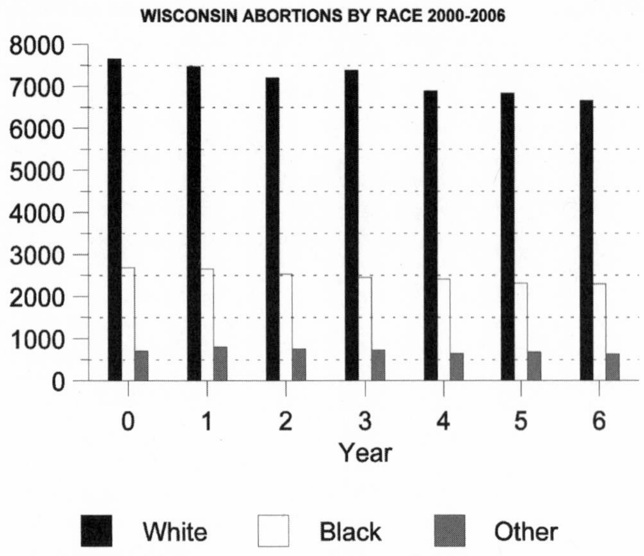

Source: Wisconsin Department of Health and Family Services.

Wisconsin Abortion by Education Level of Female 2000–2006
Education Level Completed

Year	*<9*	*9–11*	*12*	*≥13*	*Unknown*
2000	290	1,780	4,661	4,272	37
2001	281	1,750	4,762	4,132	0
2002	311	1,477	4,689	4,012	0
2003	216	1,500	4,858	3,983	0
2004	238	1,458	4,479	3,768	0
2005	214	1,361	4,618	3,624	0
2006	207	1,317	4,311	3,745	0
Total	1,757	10,643	32,378	27,536	37

Source: Wisconsin Department of Health and Family Services.

Wisconsin Abortion by Weeks of Gestation 2000–2006
Year

Weeks of Gestation	*2000*	*2001*	*2002*	*2003*	*2004*	*2005*	*2006*	*Total*
<9	5,788	6,032	5,939	6,042	5,582	5,308	4,958	39,649
9–10	2,318	2,109	2,040	1,885	1,790	1,828	1,883	13,853
11–12	1,310	1,260	1,128	1,162	1,150	1,171	1,173	8,354
13–15	821	767	694	724	717	783	839	5,345
16–20	595	550	487	534	520	508	530	3,724
≥21	208	207	201	210	184	219	197	1,426

Source: Wisconsin Department of Health and Family Services.

(b) Causes the death of the mother by an act done with intent to destroy the life of an unborn child. It is unnecessary to prove that the fetus was alive when the act so causing the mother's death was committed.

(3) Any pregnant woman who intentionally destroys the life of her unborn child or who consents to such destruction by another may be fined not more than $200 or imprisoned not more than 6 months or both.

(4) Any pregnant woman who intentionally destroys the life of her unborn quick child or who consents to such destruction by another is guilty of a Class I felony.

(5) This section does not apply to a therapeutic abortion which:

(a) Is performed by a physician; and

(b) Is necessary, or is advised by 2 other physicians as necessary, to save the life of the mother; and

(c) Unless an emergency prevents, is performed in a licensed maternity hospital.

(6) In this section "unborn child" means a human being from the time of conception until it is born alive.

(4) POST-VIABILITY ABORTION

Wisconsin has enacted a penal statute that prohibits post-viability abortions, except to save the life or health of the woman. A post-viability abortion must take place in a hospital. The statute is set out below.

Wisconsin Code § 940.15. Post-viability ban

(1) In this section, "viability" means that stage of fetal development when, in the medical judgment of the attending physician based on the particular facts of the case before him or her, there is a reasonable likelihood of sustained survival of the fetus outside the womb, with or without artificial support.

(2) Whoever intentionally performs an abortion after the fetus or unborn child reaches viability, as determined by reasonable medical judgment of the woman's attending physician, is guilty of a Class I felony.

(3) Subsection (2) does not apply if the abortion is necessary to preserve the life or health of the woman, as determined by reasonable medical judgment of the woman's attending physician.

(4) Any abortion performed under sub. (3) after viability of the fetus or unborn child, as determined by reasonable medical judgment of the woman's attending physician, shall be performed in a hospital on an inpatient basis.

(5) Whoever intentionally performs an abortion and who is not a physician is guilty of a Class I felony.

(6) Any physician who intentionally performs an abortion under sub. (3) shall use that method of abortion which, of those he or she knows to be available, is in his or her medical judgment most likely to preserve the life and health of the fetus or unborn child. Nothing in this subsection requires a physician performing an abortion to employ a method of abortion which, in his or her medical judgment based on the particular facts of the case before him or her, would increase the risk to the woman. Any physician violating this subsection is guilty of a Class I felony.

(7) Subsections (2) to (6) and s. 939.05, 939.30 or 939.31 do not apply to a woman who obtains an abortion that is in violation of this section or otherwise violates this section with respect to her unborn child or fetus.

(4) INFORMED CONSENT

Prior to an abortion Wisconsin requires that a woman be fully informed of the procedure to be used, the risks involved and alternatives to abortion. An abortion may not take place until 24 hours after a woman has been informed of the statutory requirements. The statutes addressing the matter are set out below.

Wisconsin Code § 253.10. Consent and waiting period

(1) (a) The legislature finds that:

1. Many women now seek or are encouraged to undergo elective abortions without full knowledge of the medical and psychological risks of abortion, development of the unborn child or of alternatives to abortion. An abortion decision is often made under stressful circumstances.

2. The knowledgeable exercise of a woman's decision to have an elective abortion depends on the extent to which the woman receives sufficient information to make a voluntary and informed choice between 2 alternatives of great consequence: carrying a child to birth or undergoing an abortion.

3. The U.S. supreme court has stated: "In attempting to ensure that a woman apprehend the full consequences of her decision, the State furthers the legitimate purpose of reducing the risk that a woman may elect an abortion, only to discover later, with devastating psychological consequences, that her decision was not fully informed." Planned Parenthood of Southeastern Pennsylvania v. Casey, 112 U.S. 2791, 2823 (1992).

4. It is essential to the psychological and physical well-being of a woman considering an elective abortion that she receive complete and accurate information on all options available to her in dealing with her pregnancy.

5. The vast majority of elective abortions in this state are performed in clinics that are devoted solely to providing abortions and family planning services. Women who seek elective abortions at these facilities normally do not have a prior patient-physician relationship with the physician who is to perform or induce the abortion, normally do not return to the facility for post-operative care and normally do not continue a patient-physician relationship with the physician who performed or induced the abortion. In most instances, the woman's only actual contact with the physician occurs simultaneously with the abortion procedure, with little opportunity to receive personal counseling by the physician concerning her decision. Because of this, certain safeguards are necessary to protect a woman's right to know.

6. A reasonable waiting period is critical to ensure that a woman has the fullest opportunity to give her voluntary and informed consent before she elects to undergo an abortion.

(b) It is the intent of the legislature in enacting this section to further the important and compelling state interests in all of the following:

1. Protecting the life and health of the woman subject to an elective abortion and, to the extent constitutionally permissible, the life of her unborn child.

2. Fostering the development of standards of professional conduct in the practice of abortion.

3. Ensuring that prior to the performance or inducement of an elective abortion, the woman considering an elective abortion receive personal counseling by the physician and be given a full range of information regarding her pregnancy, her unborn child, the abortion, the medical and psychological risks of abortion and available alternatives to the abortion.

4. Ensuring that a woman who decides to have an elective abortion gives her voluntary and informed consent to the abortion procedure.

(2) In this section:

(a) "Abortion" means the use of an instrument, medicine, drug or other substance or device with intent to terminate the pregnancy of a woman known to be pregnant or for whom there is reason to believe that she may be pregnant and with intent other than to increase the probability of a live birth, to preserve the life or health of the infant after live birth or to remove a dead fetus.

(b) "Agency" means a private nonprofit organization or a county department under s. 46.215, 46.22 or 46.23.

(c) "Disability" means a physical or mental impairment that substantially limits one or more major life activities, a record of having such an impairment or being regarded as having such an impairment. "Disability" includes any physical disability or developmental disability, as defined in s. 51.01(5)(a).

(d) "Medical emergency" means a condition, in a physician's reasonable medical judgment, that so complicates the medical condition of a pregnant woman as to necessitate the immediate abortion of her pregnancy to avert her death or for which a 24-hour delay in performance or inducement of an abortion will create serious risk of substantial and irreversible impairment of one or more of the woman's major bodily functions.

(e) "Probable gestational age of the unborn child" means the number of weeks that have elapsed from the probable time of fertilization of a woman's ovum, based on the information provided by the woman as to the time of her last menstrual period, her medical history, a physical examination performed by the physician who is to perform or induce the abortion or by any other qualified physician and any appropriate laboratory tests performed on her.

(f) "Qualified person assisting the physician" means a social worker certified under ch. 457, a registered nurse or a physician assistant to whom a physician who is to perform or induce an abortion has delegated the responsibility, as the physician's agent, for providing the information required under sub. (3)(c)2.

(g) "Qualified physician" means a physician who by training or experience is qualified to provide the information required under sub. (3)(c)1.

(h) "Viability" has the meaning given in s. 940.15(1).

(3)(a) An abortion may not be performed or induced unless the woman upon whom the abortion is to be performed or induced has and, if the woman is a minor and s. 48.375(4)(a)2. does not apply, the individual who also gives consent under s. 48.375(4)(a)1. have given voluntary and informed written consent under the requirements of this section.

(b) Consent under this section to an abortion is voluntary only if the consent is given freely and without coercion by any person.

(c) Except if a medical emergency exists, a woman's consent to an abortion is informed only if all of the following first take place:

1. Except as provided in sub. (3m), at least 24 hours before the abortion is to be performed or induced, the physician who is to perform or induce the abortion or any other qualified physician has, in person, orally informed the woman of all of the following:

a. Whether or not, according to the reasonable medical judgment of the physician, the woman is pregnant.

b. The probable gestational age of the unborn child at the time that the information is provided. The physician or other qualified physician shall also provide this information to the woman in writing at this time.

c. The particular medical risks, if any, associated with the woman's pregnancy.

d. The probable anatomical and physiological characteristics of the woman's unborn child at the time the information is given.

e. The details of the medical or surgical method that would be used in performing or inducing the abortion.

f. The medical risks associated with the particular abortion procedure that would be used, including the risks of infection, psychological trauma, hemorrhage, endometritis, perforated uterus, incomplete abortion, failed abortion, danger to subsequent pregnancies and infertility.

g. That fetal ultrasound imaging and auscultation of fetal heart tone services are available that enable a pregnant woman to view the image or hear the heartbeat of her unborn child. In so informing the woman and describing these services, the physician shall advise the woman as to how she may obtain these services if she desires to do so.

h. The recommended general medical instructions for the woman to follow after an abortion to enhance her safe recovery and the name and telephone number of a physician to call if complications arise after the abortion.

i. If, in the reasonable medical judgment of the physician, the woman's unborn child has reached viability, that the physician who is to perform or induce the abortion is required to take all steps necessary under s. 940.15 to preserve and maintain the life and health of the child.

j. Any other information that a reasonable patient would consider material and relevant to a decision of whether or not to carry a child to birth or to undergo an abortion.

k. That the woman may withdraw her consent to have an abortion at any time before the abortion is performed or induced.

l. That, except as provided in sub. (3m), the woman is not required to pay any amount for performance or inducement of the abortion until at least 24 hours have elapsed after the requirements of this paragraph are met.

2. Except as provided in sub. (3m), at least 24 hours before the abortion is to be performed or induced, the physician who is to perform or induce the abortion, a qualified person assisting the physician or another qualified physician has, in person, orally informed the woman of all of the following:

a. That benefits under the medical assistance program may be available for prenatal care, childbirth and neonatal care.

b. That the father of the unborn child is liable for assistance in the support of the woman's child, if born, even if the father has offered to pay for the abortion.

c. That the woman has a legal right to continue her pregnancy and to keep the child; to place the child in a foster home or treatment foster home for 6 months or to petition a court for placement of the child in a foster home, treatment foster home or group home or with a relative; or to place the child for adoption under a process that involves court approval both of the voluntary termination of parental rights and of the adoption.

d. That the woman has the right to receive and review the printed materials described in par. (d). The physician or qualified person assisting the physician shall physically give the materials to the woman and shall, in person, orally inform her that the materials are free of charge, have been provided by the state and describe the unborn child and list agencies that offer alternatives to abortion and shall provide her with the current updated copies of the printed materials free of charge.

e. If the woman has received a diagnosis of disability for her unborn child, that the printed materials described in par. (d) contain information on community-based services and financial assistance programs for children with disabilities and their families, information on support groups for people with disabilities and parents of children with disabilities and information on adoption of children with special needs.

f. If the woman asserts that her pregnancy is the result of sexual assault or incest, that the printed materials described in par. (d) contain information on counseling services and support groups for victims of sexual assault and incest and legal protections available to the woman and her child if she wishes to oppose establishment of paternity or to terminate the father's parental rights.

g. That the printed materials described in par. (d) contain information on the availability of public and private agencies and services to provide the woman with information on family planning, as defined in s. 253.07(1)(a), including natural family planning information.

3. The information that is required under subds. 1. and 2. is provided to the woman in an individual setting that protects her privacy, maintains the confidentiality of her decision and ensures that the information she receives focuses on her individual circumstances. This subdivision may not be construed to prevent the woman from having a family member, or any other person of her choice, present during her private counseling.

4. Whoever provides the information that is required under subd. 1. or 2., or both, provides adequate opportunity for the woman to ask questions, including questions concerning the pregnancy, her unborn child, abortion, foster care and adoption, and provides the information that is requested or indicates to the woman where she can obtain the information.

5. The woman certifies in writing on a form that the department shall provide, prior to performance or inducement of the abortion, that the information that is required under subds. 1. and 2. has been provided to her in the manner specified in subd. 3., that she has been offered the information described in par. (d) and that all of her questions, as specified under subd. 4., have been answered in a satisfactory manner. The physician who is to perform or induce the abortion or the qualified person assisting the physician shall write on the certification form the name of the physician who is to perform or induce the abortion. The woman shall indicate on the certification form who provided the information to her and when it was provided.

6. Prior to the performance or the inducement of the abortion, the physician who is to perform or induce the abortion or the qualified person assisting the physician receives the written certification that is required under subd. 5. The physician or qualified person assisting the physician shall place the certification in the woman's medical record and shall provide the woman with a copy of the certification.

7. If the woman considering an abortion is a minor, unless s. 48.375(4)(a) 2. applies, the requirements to provide information to the woman under subds. 1. to 6. apply also to require provision of the information to the individual whose consent is also required under s. 48.375(4)(a)1. If the woman considering an abortion is an individual adjudicated incompetent in this state, the requirements to provide information to the woman under subds. 1. to 6. apply to also require provision of the information to the person appointed as the woman's guardian.

(d) By the date that is 60 days after May 16, 1996, the department shall cause to be published in English, Spanish, and other languages spoken by a significant number of state residents, as determined by the department, materials that are in an easily comprehensible format and are printed in type of not less than 12-point size. The department shall distribute a reasonably adequate number of the materials to county departments as specified under s. 46.245 and upon request, shall annually review the materials for accuracy and shall exercise reasonable diligence in providing materials that are accurate and current. The materials shall be all of the following:

1. Geographically indexed materials that are designed to inform a woman about public and private agencies, including adoption agencies, and services that are available to provide information on family planning, as defined in s. 253.07(1)(a), including natural family planning information, to provide ultrasound imaging services, to assist her if she has received a diagnosis that her unborn child has a disability or if her pregnancy is the result of sexual assault or incest and to assist her through pregnancy, upon childbirth and while the child is dependent. The materials shall include a comprehensive list of the agencies available, a description of the services that they offer and a description of the manner in which they may be contacted, including telephone numbers and addresses, or, at the option of the department, the materials shall include a toll-free, 24-hour telephone number that may be called to obtain an oral listing of available agencies and services in the locality of the caller and a description of the services that the agencies offer and the manner in which they may be contacted. The materials shall provide information on the availability of governmentally funded programs that serve pregnant women and children. Services identified for the woman shall include medical assistance for pregnant women and children under s. 49.47(4)(am) and 49.471, the availability of family or medical leave under s. 103.10, the Wisconsin works program under ss. 49.141 to 49.161, child care services, child support laws and programs and the credit for expenses for household and dependent care and services nec-

essary for gainful employment under section 21 of the internal revenue code. The materials shall state that it is unlawful to perform an abortion for which consent has been coerced, that any physician who performs or induces an abortion without obtaining the woman's voluntary and informed consent is liable to her for damages in a civil action and is subject to a civil penalty, that the father of a child is liable for assistance in the support of the child, even in instances in which the father has offered to pay for an abortion, and that adoptive parents may pay the costs of prenatal care, childbirth and neonatal care. The materials shall include information, for a woman whose pregnancy is the result of sexual assault or incest, on legal protections available to the woman and her child if she wishes to oppose establishment of paternity or to terminate the father's parental rights. The materials shall state that fetal ultrasound imaging and auscultation of fetal heart tone services are obtainable by pregnant women who wish to use them and shall describe the services.

2. Materials, including photographs, pictures or drawings, that are designed to inform the woman of the probable anatomical and physiological characteristics of the unborn child at 2-week gestational increments for the first 16 weeks of her pregnancy and at 4-week gestational increments from the 17th week of the pregnancy to full term, including any relevant information regarding the time at which the unborn child could possibly be viable. The pictures or drawings must contain the dimensions of the unborn child and must be realistic and appropriate for the stage of pregnancy depicted. The materials shall be objective, nonjudgmental and designed to convey only accurate scientific information about the unborn child at the various gestational ages, including appearance, mobility, brain and heart activity and function, tactile sensitivity and the presence of internal organs and external members. The materials shall also contain objective, accurate information describing the methods of abortion procedures commonly employed, the medical and psychological risks commonly associated with each such procedure, including the risks of infection, psychological trauma, hemorrhage, endometritis, perforated uterus, incomplete abortion, failed abortion, danger to subsequent pregnancies and infertility, and the medical risks commonly associated with carrying a child to birth.

3. A certification form for use under par. (c)5. that lists, in a check-off format, all of the information required to be provided under that subdivision.

(e) A physician who intends to perform or induce an abortion or another qualified physician, who reasonably believes that he or she might have a patient for whom the information under par. (d) is required to be given, shall request a reasonably adequate number of the materials that are described under par. (d) from the department under par. (d) or from a county department as specified under s. 46.245.

(f) If a medical emergency exists, the physician who is to perform or induce the abortion necessitated by the medical emergency shall inform the woman, prior to the abortion if possible, of the medical indications supporting the physician's reasonable medical judgment that an immediate abortion is necessary to avert her death or that a 24-hour delay in performance or inducement of an abortion will create a serious risk of substantial and irreversible impairment of one or more of the woman's major bodily functions. If possible, the physician shall obtain the woman's written consent prior to the abortion. The physician shall certify these medical indications in writing and place the certification in the woman's medical record.

(g) Satisfaction of the conditions required under par. (c) creates a rebuttable presumption that the woman's consent and, if the woman is a minor and if s. 48.375(4)(a)2. does not apply, the consent of the individual who also gives consent under s. 48.375(4)(a)1. to an abortion is informed. The presumption of informed consent may be overcome by a preponderance of evidence that establishes that the consent was obtained through fraud, negligence, deception, misrepresentation or omission of a material fact. There is no presumption that consent to an abortion is voluntary.

(3m)(a) A woman seeking an abortion may waive the 24-hour period required under sub. (3)(c)1.(intro.) and L. and 2.(intro.) if all of the following are first done:

1. The woman alleges that the pregnancy is the result of sexual assault under s. 940.225(1), (2) or (3) and states that a report alleging the sexual assault has been made to law enforcement authorities.

2. Whoever provides the information that is required under sub. (3)(c)1. or 2., or both, confirms with law enforcement authorities that a report on behalf of the woman about the sexual assault has been made to law enforcement authorities, makes a notation to this effect and places the notation in the woman's medical record.

(b) The 24-hour period required under sub. (3)(c)1.(intro.) and L. and 2. (intro.) is reduced to at least 2 hours if all of the following are first done:

1. The woman alleges that the pregnancy is the result of incest under s. 948.06(1) or (1m) and states that a report alleging the incest has been made to law enforcement authorities.

2. Whoever provides the information that is required under sub. (3)(c)1. or 2., or both, confirms with law enforcement authorities that a report on behalf of the woman about the incest has been made to law enforcement authorities, makes a notation to this effect and places the notation in the woman's medical record.

(c) Upon receipt by the law enforcement authorities of a request for confirmation under par. (a)2. or (b)2., and after reasonable verification of the identity of the woman and her consent to release of the information, the law enforcement authorities shall confirm whether or not the report has been made. No record of a request or confirmation made under this paragraph may be disclosed by the law enforcement authorities.

(4) The department may maintain a toll-free telephone number that is available 24 hours each day, to provide the materials specified in sub. (3)(d)1.

(5) Any person who violates sub. (3) or (3m)(a)2. or (b)2. shall be required to forfeit not less than $1,000 nor more than $10,000.

(6)(a) A person who violates sub. (3) or (3m)(a)2. or (b)2. is liable to the woman on or for whom the abortion was performed or induced for damages arising out of the performance or inducement of the abortion, including damages for personal injury and emotional and psychological distress.

(b) A person who has been awarded damages under par. (a) shall, in addition to any damages awarded under par. (a), be entitled to not less than $1,000 nor more than $10,000 in punitive damages for a violation that satisfies a standard under s. 895.043(3).

(c) A conviction under sub. (5) is not a condition precedent to bringing an action, obtaining a judgment or collecting the judgment under this subsection.

(d) Notwithstanding s. 814.04(1), a person who recovers damages under par. (a) or (b) may also recover reasonable attorney fees incurred in connection with the action.

(e) A contract is not a defense to an action under this subsection.

(f) Nothing in this subsection limits the common law rights of a person that are not in conflict with sub. (3).

(7) No person is liable under sub. (5) or (6) or under s. 441.07(1)(f),448.02(3)(a) or 457.26(2)(gm) for failure under sub. (3)(c)2.d. to provide the printed materials described in sub. (3)(d) to a woman or for

failure under sub. (3)(c)2.d., e., f. or g. to describe the contents of the printed materials if the person has made a reasonably diligent effort to obtain the printed materials under sub. (3)(e) and s. 46.245 and the department and the county department under s. 46.215, 46.22 or 46.23 have not made the printed materials available at the time that the person is required to give them to the woman.

(8) Nothing in this section may be construed as creating or recognizing a right to abortion or as making lawful an abortion that is otherwise unlawful.

Wisconsin Code § 46.245.
Information for certain pregnant women

Upon request, a county department under s. 46.215, 46.22 OR 46.23 shall distribute the materials described under s. 253.10(3)(d), as prepared and distributed by the department. A physician who intends to perform or induce an abortion or another qualified physician, as defined in s. 253.10(2)(g), who reasonably believes that he or she might have a patient for whom the information under s. 253.10(3)(d) is required to be given, shall request a reasonably adequate number of the materials from the county department under this section or from the department under s. 253.10(3)(d). An individual may request a reasonably adequate number of the materials.

(5) ABORTION BY MINORS

Under the laws of Wisconsin no physician may perform an abortion upon an unemancipated minor unless he/she first obtains the written consent of either parent or the legal guardian of the minor. The state permits a physician to perform an abortion on a minor without the required consent, if the minor was a victim of sexual assault or incest, or the physician is informed by a mental health professional that the minor may commit suicide if her parents are informed.

In compliance with federal constitutional law, Wisconsin has provided a judicial waiver procedure for an unemancipated minor to obtain an abortion without parental or guardian consent. If an unemancipated minor elects not to seek, or cannot for any reason obtain consent from either of her parents or legal guardian, the minor may petition a trial court for a waiver of the consent requirement. A minor has a right to an attorney at the proceeding and if she cannot afford one, the court must appoint her an attorney. If a minor chooses, she may represent herself. The required parental or guardian consent may be waived if the court finds either (1) that the minor is mature and well-informed enough to make the abortion decision on her own, or (2) that performance of the abortion would be in the best interest of the minor. An expedited appeal is available to any minor to whom the court denies a waiver of consent. The state imposes criminal penalties and a civil cause of action against anyone violating its minor's abortion statute. The statutes addressing the matters are set out below.

Wisconsin Code § 48.375. Consent and judicial bypass

(1)(a) The legislature finds that:

1. Immature minors often lack the ability to make fully informed choices that take account of both immediate and long-range consequences.

2. The medical, emotional and psychological consequences of abortion and of childbirth are serious and can be lasting, particularly when the patient is immature.

3. The capacity to become pregnant and the capacity for mature judgment concerning the wisdom of bearing a child or of having an abortion are not necessarily related.

4. Parents ordinarily possess information essential to a physician's exercise of the physician's best medical judgment concerning a minor.

5. Parents who are aware that their minor is pregnant or has had an abortion may better ensure that she receives adequate medical attention during her pregnancy or after her abortion.

6. Parental knowledge of a minor's pregnancy and parental consent to an abortion are usually desirable and in the best interest of the minor.

(b) It is the intent of the legislature in enacting this section to further the purposes set forth in s. 48.01, and in particular to further the important and compelling state interests in:

1. Protecting minors against their own immaturity.

2. Fostering the family structure and preserving it as a viable social unit.

3. Protecting the rights of parents to rear minors who are members of their households.

(2) In this section:

(a) "Abortion" means the use of any instrument, medicine, drug or any other substance or device with intent to terminate the pregnancy of a minor after implantation of a fertilized human ovum and with intent other than to increase the probability of a live birth, to preserve the life or health of the infant after live birth or to remove a dead fetus.

(b) "Adult family member" means any of the following who is at least 25 years of age:

1. Grandparent.

2. Aunt.

3. Uncle.

4. Sister.

5. Brother.

(c) "Counselor" means a physician including a physician specializing in psychiatry, a licensed psychologist, as defined in s. 455.01(4), or an ordained member of the clergy. "Counselor" does not include any person who is employed by or otherwise affiliated with a reproductive health care facility, a family planning clinic or a family planning agency; any person affiliated with the performance of abortions, except abortions performed to save the life of the mother; or any person who may profit from giving advice to seek an abortion.

(d) Notwithstanding s. 48.02(2m), "court" means any circuit court within this state.

(e) "Emancipated minor" means a minor who is or has been married; a minor who has previously given birth; or a minor who has been freed from the care, custody and control of her parents, with little likelihood of returning to the care, custody and control prior to marriage or prior to reaching the age of majority.

(em) "Member of the clergy" has the meaning given in s. 765.002(1).

(g) "Physician" means a person licensed to practice medicine and surgery under ch. 448.

(h) "Referring physician" means a physician who refers a minor to another physician for the purpose of obtaining an abortion.

(3) This section applies whether or not the minor who initiates the proceeding is a resident of this state.

(4) (a) Except as provided in this section, no person may perform or induce an abortion on or for a minor who is not an emancipated minor unless the person is a physician and one of the following applies:

1. The person or the person's agent has, either directly or through a referring physician or his or her agent, received and made part of the minor's medical record, under the requirements of s. 253.10, the voluntary and informed written consent of the minor and the voluntary and informed written consent of one of her parents; or of the minor's guardian or legal custodian, if one has been appointed; or of an adult family member of the minor; or of one of the minor's foster parents or treatment foster parents, if the minor has been placed in a foster home or treatment foster home and the minor's parent has signed a waiver granting the de-

partment, a county department, the foster parent or the treatment foster parent the authority to consent to medical services or treatment on behalf of the minor.

2. The court has granted a petition under sub. (7).

(b) Paragraph (a) does not apply if the person who intends to perform or induce the abortion is a physician and any of the following occurs:

1. The person who intends to perform or induce the abortion believes, to the best of his or her medical judgment based on the facts of the case before him or her, that a medical emergency exists that complicates the pregnancy so as to require an immediate abortion.

1g. The minor provides the person who intends to perform or induce the abortion with a written statement, signed and dated by the minor, in which the minor swears that the pregnancy is the result of a sexual assault in violation of s. 940.225(1), (2) or (3) in which the minor did not indicate a freely given agreement to have sexual intercourse. The person who intends to perform or induce the abortion shall place the statement in the minor's medical record and report the sexual intercourse as required under s. 48.981(2) or (2m)(e). Any minor who makes a false statement under this subdivision, which the minor does not believe is true, is subject to a proceeding under s. 938.12 or 938.13(12), whichever is applicable, based on a violation of s. 946.32(2).

1m. A physician who specializes in psychiatry or a licensed psychologist, as defined in s. 455.01(4), states in writing that the physician or psychologist believes, to the best of his or her professional judgment based on the facts of the case before him or her, that the minor is likely to commit suicide rather than file a petition under s. 48.257 or approach her parent, or guardian or legal custodian, if one has been appointed, or an adult family member of the minor, or one of the minor's foster parents or treatment foster parents, if the minor has been placed in a foster home or treatment foster home and the minor's parent has signed a waiver granting the department, a county department, the foster parent or the treatment foster parent the authority to consent to medical services or treatment on behalf of the minor, for consent.

2. The minor provides the person who intends to perform or induce the abortion with a written statement, signed and dated by the minor, that the pregnancy is the result of sexual intercourse with a caregiver specified in s. 48.981(1)(am)1, 2, 3, 4 or 8. The person who intends to perform or induce the abortion shall place the statement in the minor's medical record. The person who intends to perform or induce the abortion shall report the sexual intercourse as required under s. 48.981(2m)(d)1.

3. The minor provides the person who intends to perform or induce the abortion with a written statement, signed and dated by the minor, that a parent who has legal custody of the minor, or the minor's guardian or legal custodian, if one has been appointed, or an adult family member of the minor, or a foster parent or treatment foster parent, if the minor has been placed in a foster home or treatment foster home and the minor's parent has signed a waiver granting the department, a county department, the foster parent or the treatment foster parent the authority to consent to medical services or treatment on behalf of the minor, has inflicted abuse on the minor. The person who intends to perform or induce the abortion shall place the statement in the minor's medical record. The person who intends to perform or induce the abortion shall report the abuse as required under s. 48.981(2).

(5) Any minor who is pregnant and who is seeking an abortion and any minor who has had an abortion may receive counseling from a counselor of her choice. A county department may refer the minor to a private counselor.

(6) Any pregnant minor who is seeking an abortion in this state, and any member of the clergy on the minor's behalf, may file a petition specified under s. 48.257 with any court for a waiver of the parental consent requirement under sub. (4)(a)1.

(7)(a) On the date that a petition under s. 48.257 is filed, or if it is impossible to do so on that day, on the next calendar day, the court shall hold an initial appearance in chambers at which the minor or the member of the clergy who filed the petition on behalf of the minor, if any, is present and shall do all of the following:

1. Appoint legal counsel under s. 48.23(1m)(cm) for the minor if the minor is not represented by counsel.

[2]. Set a time for a hearing on the petition that will enable the court to comply with the time limit specified in par. (d)1.

[3]. Notify the minor, the minor's counsel, if any, the member of the clergy who filed the petition on behalf of the minor, if any, and the minor's guardian ad litem, if any, of the time, date and place of the hearing.

(am) At the initial appearance under par. (a), the court may also, in its discretion, appoint a guardian ad litem under s. 48.235(1)(d).

(b) The court shall hold a confidential hearing on a petition that is filed by a minor. The hearing shall be held in chambers, unless a public fact-finding hearing is demanded by the minor through her counsel. At the hearing, the court shall consider the report of the guardian ad litem, if any, and hear evidence relating to all of the following:

1. The emotional development, maturity, intellect and understanding of the minor.

2. The understanding of the minor about the nature of, possible consequences of and alternatives to the intended abortion procedure.

3. Any other evidence that the court may find useful in making the determination under par. (c).

(bm) If a member of the clergy files a petition under s. 48.257 on behalf of a minor, the member of the clergy shall file with the petition an affidavit stating that the member of the clergy has met personally with the minor and has explored with the minor the alternative choices available to the minor for managing the pregnancy, including carrying the pregnancy to term and keeping the infant, carrying the pregnancy to term and placing the infant with a relative or with another family for adoption or having an abortion, and has discussed with the minor the possibility of involving one of the persons specified in sub. (4)(a)1 in the minor's decision making concerning the pregnancy and whether or not in the opinion of the minor that involvement would be in the minor's best interests. The court may make the determination under par. (c) on the basis of the ordained member of the clergy's affidavit or may, in its discretion, require the minor to attend an interview with the court in chambers before making that determination. Any information supplied by a minor to a member of the clergy in preparation of the petition under s. 48.257 or the affidavit under this paragraph shall be kept confidential and may only be disclosed to the court in connection with a proceeding under this subsection.

(c) The court shall grant the petition if the court finds that any of the following standards applies:

1. That the minor is mature and well-informed enough to make the abortion decision on her own.

2. That the performance or inducement of the abortion is in the minor's best interests.

(d) 1. The court shall make the determination under par. (c) and issue an order within 3 calendar days after the initial appearance unless the minor and her counsel, or the member of the clergy who filed the petition on behalf of the minor, if any, consent to an extension of the time period. The order shall be effective immediately. The court shall prepare and file with the clerk of court findings of fact, conclusions of law and a final order granting or denying the petition within

24 hours after making the determination and order. If the court grants the petition, the court shall immediately so notify the minor by personal service on her counsel, or the member of the clergy who filed the petition on behalf of the minor, if any, of a certified copy of the court's order granting the petition. If the court denies the petition, the court shall immediately so notify the minor by personal service on her counsel, or the member of the clergy who filed the petition on behalf of the minor, if any, of a copy of the court's order denying the petition and shall also notify the minor by her counsel, or the member of the clergy who filed the petition on behalf of the minor, if any, that she has a right to initiate an appeal under s. 809.105.

1m. Except as provided under s. 48.315(1)(b), (c), (f), and (h), if the court fails to comply with the time limits specified under subd. 1. without the prior consent of the minor and the minor' s counsel, if any, or the member of the clergy who filed the petition on behalf of the minor, if any, the minor and the minor's counsel, if any, or the member of the clergy, if any, shall select a temporary reserve judge, as defined in s. 753.075(1)(b), to make the determination under par. (c) and issue an order granting or denying the petition and the chief judge of the judicial administrative district in which the court is located shall assign the temporary reserve judge selected by the minor and the minor's counsel, if any, or the member of the clergy, if any, to make the determination and issue the order. A temporary reserve judge assigned under this subdivision to make a determination under par. (c) and issue an order granting or denying a petition shall make the determination and issue the order within 2 calendar days after the assignment, unless the minor and her counsel, if any, or the member of the clergy who filed the petition on behalf of the minor, if any, consent to an extension of that time period. The order shall be effective immediately. The court shall prepare and file with the clerk of court findings of fact, conclusions of law and a final order granting or denying the petition, and shall notify the minor of the court's order, as provided under subd. 1.

2. Counsel for the minor, or the member of the clergy who filed the petition on behalf of the minor, if any, shall immediately, upon notification under subd. 1 or 1m that the court has granted or denied the petition, notify the minor. If the court has granted the petition, counsel for the minor, or the member of the clergy who filed the petition on behalf of the minor, if any, shall hand deliver a certified copy of the court order to the person who intends to perform or induce the abortion. If with reasonable diligence the person who intends to perform or induce the abortion cannot be located for delivery, then counsel for the minor, or the member of the clergy who filed the petition on behalf of the minor, if any, shall leave a certified copy of the order with the person's agent at the person's principal place of business. If a clinic or medical facility is specified in the petition as the corporation, limited liability company, partnership or other unincorporated association that employs the person who intends to perform or induce the abortion, then counsel for the minor, or the member of the clergy who filed the petition on behalf of the minor, if any, shall hand deliver a certified copy of the order to an agent of the corporation, limited liability company, partnership or other unincorporated association at its principal place of business. There may be no service by mail or publication. The person or agent who receives the certified copy of the order under this subdivision shall place the copy in the minor's medical record.

(e) The identity of a minor who files or for whom is filed a petition under s. 48.257 and all records and other papers relating to a proceeding under this subsection shall be kept confidential except for use in a forfeiture action under s. 895.037(2), a civil action filed under s. 895.037(3) or a child abuse or neglect investigation under s. 48.981.

(f) No parent, or guardian or legal custodian, if one has been appointed, or foster parent or treatment foster parent, if the minor has been placed in a foster home or treatment foster home and the minor's parent has signed a waiver granting the department, a county department, the foster parent or the treatment foster parent the authority to consent to medical services or treatment on behalf of the minor, or adult family member, of any minor who is seeking a court determination under this subsection may attend, intervene or give evidence in any proceeding under this subsection.

(8) An appeal by a minor from an order of the trial court denying a petition under sub. (7) may be taken to the court of appeals as a matter of right under s. 808.03(1) and is governed by s. 809.105.

(9) If a minor who is contemplating an abortion requests assistance from a county department under s. 46.215, 46.22 or 46.23 in seeking the consent of the minor's parent, guardian or legal custodian, or in seeking the consent of an adult family member, for the contemplated abortion or in seeking a waiver from the circuit court, the county department shall provide assistance, including, if so requested, accompanying the minor as appropriate.

Wisconsin Code § 895.037. Penalties

(1) In this section:

(a) "Abortion" has the meaning given in s. 48.375(2)(a).

(c) "Emancipated minor" has the meaning given in s. 48.375 (2)(e).

(2)(a) Any person who, in violation of s. 48.375(4), intentionally performs or induces an abortion on or for a minor whom the person knows or has reason to know is not an emancipated minor may be required to forfeit not more than $10,000.

(b) Any person who intentionally violates s. 48.375(7)(e) or 809.105(12) may be required to forfeit not more than $10,000.

(3)(a) A person who intentionally violates s. 48.375(4) is liable to the minor on or for whom the abortion was performed or induced and to the minor's parent, guardian and legal custodian for damages arising out of the performance or inducement of the abortion including, but not limited to, damages for personal injury and emotional and psychological distress.

(b) If a person who has been awarded damages under par. (a) proves by clear and convincing evidence that the violation of s. 48.375(4) was willful, wanton or reckless, that person shall also be entitled to punitive damages.

(c) A conviction under sub. (2)(a) is not a condition precedent to bringing an action, obtaining a judgment or collecting that judgment under this subsection.

(d) A person who recovers damages under par. (a) or (b) may also recover reasonable attorney fees incurred in connection with the action, notwithstanding s. 814.04(1).

(e) A contract is not a defense to an action under this subsection.

(f) Nothing in this subsection limits the common law rights of parents, guardians, legal custodians and minors.

(4) The identity of a minor who is the subject of an action under this section and the identity of the minor's parents, guardian and legal custodian shall be kept confidential and may not be disclosed, except to the court, the parties, their counsel, witnesses and other persons approved by the court. All papers filed in and all records of a court relating to an action under this section shall identify the minor as "Jane Doe" and shall identify her parents, guardian and legal custodian by initials only. All hearings relating to an action under this section shall be held in chambers unless the minor demands a hearing in open court and her parents, guardian or legal custodian do not object. If a public hearing is not held, only the parties, their counsel, witnesses and other persons requested by the court, or requested by a party and approved by the court, may be present.

(6) PARTIAL-BIRTH ABORTION

Wisconsin prohibits partial-birth abortions, except when necessary to save the life of the woman. The ban was found unconstitutional in *Hope Clinic v. Ryan*, 249 F.3d 603 (7th Cir. 2001), based upon the United States Supreme Court decision in *Stenberg v. Carhart*, which invalidated a Nebraska statute that prohibited partial-birth abortions. However, subsequent to *Stenberg* the Supreme Court decided the case of *Gonzales v. Carhart*, in which it approved of a federal statute that prohibited partial-birth abortion. In addition to purporting to ban partial-birth abortions, Wisconsin has provides a civil cause of action for the father of a fetus destroyed through a partial-birth abortion procedure. In the case of a minor, the maternal grandparents of the fetus may file a civil lawsuit. The statutes are set out below.

Wisconsin Code § 940.16. Partial-birth abortion ban

(1) In this section:

(a) "Child" means a human being from the time of fertilization until it is completely delivered from a pregnant woman.

(b) "Partial-birth abortion" means an abortion in which a person partially vaginally delivers a living child, causes the death of the partially delivered child with the intent to kill the child, and then completes the delivery of the child.

(2) Except as provided in sub. (3), whoever intentionally performs a partial-birth abortion is guilty of a Class A felony.

(3) Subsection (2) does not apply if the partial-birth abortion is necessary to save the life of a woman whose life is endangered by a physical disorder, physical illness or physical injury, including a life-endangering physical disorder, physical illness or physical injury caused by or arising from the pregnancy itself, and if no other medical procedure would suffice for that purpose.

Wisconsin Code § 895.038.
Partial-birth abortions civil liability

(1) In this section:

(a) "Child" has the meaning given in s. 940.16 (1) (a).

(b) "Partial-birth abortion" has the meaning given in s. 940.16 (1) (b).

(2)(a) Except as provided in par. (b), any of the following persons has a claim for appropriate relief against a person who performs a partial-birth abortion:

1. If the person on whom a partial-birth abortion was performed was a minor, the parent of the minor.

2. The father of the child aborted by the partial-birth abortion.

(b) A person specified in par. (a) 1. or 2. does not have a claim under par. (a) if any of the following apply:

1. The person consented to performance of the partial-birth abortion.

2. The pregnancy of the woman on whom the partial-birth abortion was performed was the result of a sexual assault in violation of s. 940.225, 944.06, 948.02, 948.025, 948.06, 948.085, or 948.09 that was committed by the person.

(3) The relief available under sub. (2) shall include all of the following:

(a) If the abortion was performed in violation of s. 940.16, damages arising out of the performance of the partial-birth abortion, including damages for personal injury and emotional and psychological distress.

(b) Exemplary damages equal to 3 times the cost of the partial-birth abortion.

(4) Subsection (2) applies even if the mother of the child aborted by the partial-birth abortion consented to the performance of the partial-birth abortion.

(7) USE OF FACILITIES AND PEOPLE

Under the laws of Wisconsin hospitals are not required to allow abortions at their facilities. The employees and physicians at hospitals that do allow abortions are permitted to refuse to take part in abortions on moral or religious grounds. The statutes addressing the matter are set out below.

Wisconsin Code § 253.09. Refusal to take part in abortion

(1) No hospital shall be required to admit any patient or to allow the use of the hospital facilities for the purpose of performing a sterilization procedure or removing a human embryo or fetus. A physician or any other person who is a member of or associated with the staff of a hospital, or any employee of a hospital in which such a procedure has been authorized, who shall state in writing his or her objection to the performance of or providing assistance to such a procedure on moral or religious grounds shall not be required to participate in such medical procedure, and the refusal of any such person to participate therein shall not form the basis of any claim for damages on account of such refusal or for any disciplinary or recriminatory action against such person.

(2) No hospital or employee of any hospital shall be liable for any civil damages resulting from a refusal to perform sterilization procedures or remove a human embryo or fetus from a person, if such refusal is based on religious or moral precepts.

(3) No hospital, school or employer may discriminate against any person with regard to admission, hiring or firing, tenure, term, condition or privilege of employment, student status or staff status on the ground that the person refuses to recommend, aid or perform procedures for sterilization or the removal of a human embryo or fetus, if the refusal is based on religious or moral precepts.

(4) The receipt of any grant, contract, loan or loan guarantee under any state or federal law does not authorize any court or any public official or other public authority to require:

(a) Such individual to perform or assist in the performance of any sterilization procedure or removal of a human embryo or fetus if the individual's performance or assistance in the performance of such a procedure would be contrary to the individual's religious beliefs or moral convictions; or

(b) Such entity to:

1. Make its facilities available for the performance of any sterilization procedure or removal of a human embryo or fetus if the performance of such a procedure in such facilities is prohibited by the entity on the basis of religious beliefs or moral convictions; or

2. Provide any personnel for the performance or assistance in the performance of any sterilization procedure or assistance if the performance or assistance in the performance of such procedure or the removal of a human embryo or fetus by such personnel would be contrary to the religious beliefs or moral convictions of such personnel.

Wisconsin Code § 448.03(5)(a). Physician

No person licensed or certified under this subchapter shall be liable for any civil damages resulting from such person's refusal to perform sterilization procedures or to remove or aid in the removal of a human embryo or fetus from a person if such refusal is based on religious or moral precepts.

Wisconsin Code § 441.06(6). Registered nurse

No person licensed as a registered nurse under this section is liable for any civil damages resulting from his or her refusal to perform sterilization procedures or to remove or aid in the removal of a human embryo or fetus from a person, if the refusal is based on religious or moral precepts.

(8) PUBLIC FUNDS AND ABORTION

Wisconsin prohibits state and local funds from being given to agencies that perform or make abortion referrals. The state also prohibits the use of state and local public funds to pay for abortions, except to save the life or health of the woman, or if the pregnancy resulted from sexual assault or incest. The statutes addressing the matters are set out below.

Wisconsin Code § 20.9275.
Funding for abortion related activities

(1) In this section:

(a) "Abortion" has the meaning given in s. 253.10(2)(a).

(b) "Local governmental unit" means a city, village, town, county or long-term care district under s. 46.2895 or an agency or subdivision of a city, village, town or county.

(c) "Organization" means a nonprofit corporation, as defined in s. 66.0129(6)(b), or a public agency, as defined in s. 46.856(1)(b).

(d) Omitted.

(e) "Pregnancy program, project or service" means a program, project or service of an organization that provides services for pregnancy prevention, family planning, as defined in s. 253.07(1)(a), pregnancy testing, pregnancy counseling, prenatal care, pregnancy services and reproductive health care services that are related to pregnancy.

(f) "Program funds" means all of the following funds distributed or attributable to an organization for operation of a pregnancy program, project or service:

1. Funds specified under sub. (2)(intro.).

2. Income derived from a grant, subsidy or other funding specified under sub. (2)(intro.) or from a pregnancy program, project or service funded by a grant, subsidy or other funding specified under sub. (2)(intro.).

3. Funds that are matching funds to a grant, subsidy or other funding specified under sub. (2)(intro.).

(g) "State agency" means an office, department, agency, institution of higher education, association, society or other body in state government created or authorized to be created by the constitution or any law, which is entitled to expend moneys appropriated by law, including the legislature, the courts and an authority created in ch. 231 or 233.

(2) No state agency or local governmental unit may authorize payment of funds of this state, of any local governmental unit or, subject to sub. (3m), of federal funds passing through the state treasury as a grant, subsidy or other funding that wholly or partially or directly or indirectly involves pregnancy programs, projects or services, that is a grant, subsidy or other funding under s. 48.487, 48.545, 253.05, 253.07, 253.08 or 253.085 or 42 USC 701 to 710, if any of the following applies:

(a) The pregnancy program, project or service using the state, local or federal funds does any of the following:

1. Provides abortion services.

2. Promotes, encourages or counsels in favor of abortion services.

3. Makes abortion referrals either directly or through an intermediary in any instance other than when an abortion is directly and medically necessary to save the life of the pregnant woman.

(b) The pregnancy program, project or service is funded from any other source that requires, as a condition for receipt of the funds, that the pregnancy program, project or service perform any of the activities specified in par. (a)1. to 3.

(2m) Nothing in sub. (2) prohibits the providing of nondirective information explaining any of the following:

(a) Prenatal care and delivery.

(b) Infant care, foster care or adoption.

(c) Pregnancy termination.

(3) Subject to sub. (3m), no organization that receives funds specified under sub. (2)(intro.) may use program funds for an activity that is specified under sub. (2)(a)1. to 3.

(3m) The restriction under subs. (2) and (3) on the authorization of payment and the use of federal funds passing through the state treasury shall apply only to the extent that the application of the restriction does not result in the loss of any federal funds.

(4) If an organization that receives funds specified under sub. (2)(intro.) violates sub. (3), all of the following shall apply:

(a) The organization may not receive funds specified under sub. (2)(intro.) for 24 months after the date on which the state agency or local governmental unit last authorized payment or the date on which the organization, under a pregnancy program, project or service, last violated sub. (3), whichever is later.

(b) The grant, subsidy or other funding under which an organization, under a pregnancy program, project or service, has used funds in violation of sub. (3), is terminated; and the organization shall return to the state agency or local governmental unit all funds that have been paid to the organization under the grant, subsidy or other funding.

(5) If a state agency or local governmental unit authorizes payment in violation of sub. (2), the grant, subsidy or other funding under which the state agency or local governmental unit authorized payment in violation of sub. (2), is terminated; and the organization shall return to the state agency or local governmental unit funds that have been paid to the organization under the grant, subsidy or other funding.

Wisconsin Code § 20.927. Prohibit payment for abortion

(1g) In this section, "abortion" means the intentional destruction of the life of an unborn child, and "unborn child" means a human being from the time of conception until it is born alive.

(1m) Except as provided under subs. (2) and (3), no funds of this state or of any county, city, village, town or long-term care district under s. 46.2895 or of any subdivision or agency of this state or of any county, city, village or town and no federal funds passing through the state treasury shall be authorized for or paid to a physician or surgeon or a hospital, clinic or other medical facility for the performance of an abortion.

(2)(a) This section does not apply to the performance by a physician of an abortion which is directly and medically necessary to save the life of the woman or in a case of sexual assault or incest, provided that prior thereto the physician signs a certification which so states, and provided that, in the case of sexual assault or incest the crime has been reported to the law enforcement authorities. The certification shall be affixed to the claim form or invoice when submitted to any agency or fiscal intermediary of the state for payment, and shall specify and attest to the direct medical necessity of such abortion upon the best clinical judgment of the physician or attest to his or her belief that sexual assault or incest has occurred.

(b) This section does not apply to the performance by a physician of an abortion if, due to a medical condition existing prior to the abortion, the physician determines that the abortion is directly and medically necessary to prevent grave, long-lasting physical health damage to the woman, provided that prior thereto the physician signs a certification which so states. The certification shall be affixed to the claim form or invoice when submitted to any agency or fiscal intermediary of the state for payment, and shall specify and attest to the direct medical necessity of such abortion upon the best clinical judgment of the physician.

(3) This section does not apply to the authorization or payment of funds to a physician or surgeon or a hospital, clinic or medical facility for or in connection with the prescription of a drug or the insertion of a device to prevent the implantation of the fertilized ovum.

Wisconsin Code § 66.0601. Municipalities

(1)(a) Omitted.

(b) No city, village, town, long-term care district under s. 46.2895 or agency or subdivision of a city, village or town may authorize funds

for or pay to a physician or surgeon or a hospital, clinic or other medical facility for the performance of an abortion except those permitted under and which are performed in accordance with s. 20.927.

(c) No city, village, town, long-term care district under s. 46.2895 or agency or subdivision of a city, village or town may authorize payment of funds for a grant, subsidy or other funding involving a pregnancy program, project or service if s. 20.9275(2) applies to the pregnancy program, project or service.

(2) Omitted.

Wisconsin Code § 59.53(13).
Payments for abortions and abortion related activity restricted

(a) No county, or agency or subdivision of the county, may authorize funds for or pay to a physician or surgeon or a hospital, clinic or other medical facility for the performance of an abortion except those permitted under and which are performed in accordance with s. 20.927.

(b) No county or agency or subdivision of a county may authorize payment of funds for a grant, subsidy or other funding involving a pregnancy program, project or service if s. 20.9275(2) applies to the pregnancy program, project or service.

(9) ANTI-ABORTION ACTIVITY

Wisconsin has responded to violent anti-abortion conduct by enacting a specific statute that criminalizes disruptive conduct at abortion facilities. The statute addressing the matter is set out below.

Wisconsin Code § 943.145.
Criminal trespass to a medical facility

(1) In this section, "medical facility" means a hospital under s. 50.33(2) or a clinic or office that is used by a physician licensed under ch. 448 and that is subject to rules promulgated by the medical examining board for the clinic or office that are in effect on November 20, 1985.

(2) Whoever intentionally enters a medical facility without the consent of some person lawfully upon the premises, under circumstances tending to create or provoke a breach of the peace, is guilty of a Class B misdemeanor.

(3) This section does not prohibit any person from participating in lawful conduct in labor disputes under s. 103.53.

(10) INJURY TO A PREGNANT WOMAN

Wisconsin has enacted a number of statutes that criminalize conduct which causes the death or injury to a fetus. The statutes are set out below.

Wisconsin Code § 940.01. First-degree intentional homicide

(1) (a) Except as provided in sub. (2), whoever causes the death of another human being with intent to kill that person or another is guilty of a Class A felony.

(b) Except as provided in sub. (2), whoever causes the death of an unborn child with intent to kill that unborn child, kill the woman who is pregnant with that unborn child or kill another is guilty of a Class A felony.

(2) Omitted.

(3) Omitted.

Wisconsin Code § 940.02. First-degree reckless homicide

(1) Whoever recklessly causes the death of another human being under circumstances which show utter disregard for human life is guilty of a Class B felony.

(1m) Whoever recklessly causes the death of an unborn child under circumstances that show utter disregard for the life of that unborn child, the woman who is pregnant with that unborn child or another is guilty of a Class B felony.

(2) Omitted.

Wisconsin Code § 940.05. Second-degree intentional homicide

(1) Omitted.

(2) Omitted.

(2g) Whoever causes the death of an unborn child with intent to kill that unborn child, kill the woman who is pregnant with that unborn child or kill another is guilty of a Class B felony if:

(a) In prosecutions under s. 940.01, the state fails to prove beyond a reasonable doubt that the mitigating circumstances specified in s. 940.01 (2) did not exist as required by s. 940.01 (3); or

(b) The state concedes that it is unable to prove beyond a reasonable doubt that the mitigating circumstances specified in s. 940.01 (2) did not exist. By charging under this section, the state so concedes.

(2h) In prosecutions under sub. (2g), it is sufficient to allege and prove that the defendant caused the death of an unborn child with intent to kill that unborn child, kill the woman who is pregnant with that unborn child or kill another.

(3) Omitted.

Wisconsin Code § 940.06. Second-degree reckless homicide

(1) Whoever recklessly causes the death of another human being is guilty of a Class D felony.

(2) Whoever recklessly causes the death of an unborn child is guilty of a Class D felony.

Wisconsin Code § 940.08.
Homicide by negligent handling of dangerous weapon

(1) Whoever causes the death of another human being by the negligent operation or handling of a dangerous weapon, explosives or fire is guilty of a Class G felony.

(2) Whoever causes the death of an unborn child by the negligent operation or handling of a dangerous weapon, explosives or fire is guilty of a Class G felony.

Wisconsin Code § 940.09.
Homicide by intoxicated use of vehicle or firearm

(1) Any person who does any of the following may be penalized as provided in sub. (1c):

(a) Omitted.

(am) Omitted.

(b) Omitted.

(bm) Omitted.

(c) Causes the death of an unborn child by the operation or handling of a vehicle while under the influence of an intoxicant.

(cm) Causes the death of an unborn child by the operation or handling of a vehicle while the person has a detectable amount of a restricted controlled substance in his or her blood.

(d) Causes the death of an unborn child by the operation or handling of a vehicle while the person has a prohibited alcohol concentration, as defined in s. 340.01 (46m).

(e) Causes the death of an unborn child by the operation of a commercial motor vehicle while the person has an alcohol concentration of 0.04 or more but less than 0.08.

(1c)(a) Except as provided in par. (b), a person who violates sub. (1) is guilty of a Class D felony.

(b) Omitted.

(1d) Omitted.

(1g) Any person who does any of the following is guilty of a Class D felony:

(a) Omitted.

(am) Omitted.

(b) Omitted.

(c) Causes the death of an unborn child by the operation or handling of a firearm or airgun while under the influence of an intoxicant.

(cm) Causes the death of an unborn child by the operation or han-

dling of a firearm or airgun while the person has a detectable amount of a restricted controlled substance in his or her blood.

(d) Causes the death of an unborn child by the operation or handling of a firearm or airgun while the person has an alcohol concentration of 0.08 or more.

(1m) Omitted.

(2) Omitted.

(3) Omitted.

Wisconsin Code § 940.10.
Homicide by negligent operation of vehicle

(1) Whoever causes the death of another human being by the negligent operation or handling of a vehicle is guilty of a Class G felony.

(2) Whoever causes the death of an unborn child by the negligent operation or handling of a vehicle is guilty of a Class G felony.

Wisconsin Code § 940.13. Abortion exception

No fine or imprisonment may be imposed or enforced against and no prosecution may be brought against a woman who obtains an abortion or otherwise violates any provision of any abortion statute with respect to her unborn child or fetus, and s. 939.05, 939.30 or 939.31 does not apply to a woman who obtains an abortion or otherwise violates any provision of any abortion statute with respect to her unborn child or fetus.

Wisconsin Code § 940.195. Battery to an unborn child

(1) Whoever causes bodily harm to an unborn child by an act done with intent to cause bodily harm to that unborn child, to the woman who is pregnant with that unborn child or another is guilty of a Class A misdemeanor.

(2) Whoever causes substantial bodily harm to an unborn child by an act done with intent to cause bodily harm to that unborn child, to the woman who is pregnant with that unborn child or another is guilty of a Class I felony.

(4) Whoever causes great bodily harm to an unborn child by an act done with intent to cause bodily harm to that unborn child, to the woman who is pregnant with that unborn child or another is guilty of a Class H felony.

(5) Whoever causes great bodily harm to an unborn child by an act done with intent to cause great bodily harm to that unborn child, to the woman who is pregnant with that unborn child or another is guilty of a Class E felony.

(6) Whoever intentionally causes bodily harm to an unborn child by conduct that creates a substantial risk of great bodily harm is guilty of a Class H felony.

Wisconsin Code § 940.23. Reckless injury

(1)(a) Whoever recklessly causes great bodily harm to another human being under circumstances which show utter disregard for human life is guilty of a Class D felony.

(b) Whoever recklessly causes great bodily harm to an unborn child under circumstances that show utter disregard for the life of that unborn child, the woman who is pregnant with that unborn child or another is guilty of a Class D felony.

(2)(a) Whoever recklessly causes great bodily harm to another human being is guilty of a Class F felony.

(b) Whoever recklessly causes great bodily harm to an unborn child is guilty of a Class F felony.

Wisconsin Code § 940.24.
Injury by negligent handling of dangerous weapon

(1) Whoever causes bodily harm to another by the negligent operation or handling of a dangerous weapon, explosives or fire is guilty of a Class I felony.

(2) Whoever causes bodily harm to an unborn child by the negligent operation or handling of a dangerous weapon, explosives or fire is guilty of a Class I felony.

Wisconsin Code § 940.25.
Injury by intoxicated use of a vehicle

(1) Any person who does any of the following is guilty of a Class F felony:

(a) Omitted.

(am) Omitted.

(b) Omitted.

(bm) Omitted.

(c) Causes great bodily harm to an unborn child by the operation of a vehicle while under the influence of an intoxicant.

(cm) Causes great bodily harm to an unborn child by the operation of a vehicle while the person has a detectable amount of a restricted controlled substance in his or her blood.

(d) Causes great bodily harm to an unborn child by the operation of a vehicle while the person has a prohibited alcohol concentration, as defined in s. 340.01 (46m).

(e) Causes great bodily harm to an unborn child by the operation of a commercial motor vehicle while the person has an alcohol concentration of 0.04 or more but less than 0.08.

(1d) Omitted.

(1m) Omitted.

(2) Omitted.

(3) Omitted.

(11) HEALTH INSURANCE COVERAGE

Wisconsin prohibits employer health insurance plans from providing coverage for abortions, unless an additional premium is charged for such coverage. The statute addressing the matter is set out below.

Wisconsin Code § 40.98(5)(bm).
Private employer health care coverage

No health care coverage plan under the health care coverage program may provide coverage of a nontherapeutic abortion except by an optional rider or supplemental coverage provision that is offered and provided on an individual basis and for which an additional, separate premium or charge is paid by the individual to be covered under the rider or supplemental coverage provision. Only funds attributable to premiums or charges paid for coverage under the rider or supplemental coverage provision may be used for the payment of any claim, and related administrative expenses, that relates to a nontherapeutic abortion. Such funds may not be used for the payment of any claim or administrative expenses that relate to any other type of coverage provided by the insurer under the health care coverage plan. Nothing in this paragraph requires an insurer or an employer to offer or provide coverage of an abortion under a health care coverage plan under the health care coverage program.

(12) FETAL DEATH REPORT

Under the laws of Wisconsin all abortions must be reported to the proper authorities. The statute addressing the matter is set out below.

Wisconsin Code § 69.186. Induced abortion reporting

(1) On or before January 15 annually, each hospital, clinic or other facility in which an induced abortion is performed shall file with the department a report for each induced abortion performed in the hospital, clinic or other facility in the previous calendar year. Each report shall contain all of the following information with respect to each patient obtaining an induced abortion in the hospital, clinic or other facility:

(a) The state and, if this state, the county, of residence.

(b) Patient number.

(c) Race.

(d) Age.

(e) Marital status.

(f) Month and year in which the induced abortion was performed.

(g) Education.

(h) The number of weeks since the patient's last menstrual period.

(hm) Whether the abortion was a chemically induced abortion, a surgical abortion or a surgical abortion following a failed or incomplete chemical abortion.

(i) Complications, if any, resulting from performance of the induced abortion.

(j) If the patient is a minor, whether consent was provided under s. 48.375(4)(a)1. for the abortion and, if so, the relationship of the individual providing consent to the minor; or, if consent under s. 48.375(4)(a)1. was not provided, on which of the bases under s. 48.375(4)(a)2. or (b)1., 1g., 1m., 2. or 3. the abortion was performed.

(2) The department shall collect the information under sub. (1) in a manner which the department shall specify and which ensures the anonymity of a patient who receives an induced abortion, a health care provider who provides an induced abortion and a hospital, clinic or other facility in which an induced abortion is performed. The department shall publish annual demographic summaries of the information obtained under this section, except that the department may not disclose any information obtained under this section that reveals the identity of any patient, health care provider or hospital, clinic or other facility and shall ensure anonymity in all of the following ways:

(a) The department may use information concerning the patient number under sub. (1)(b) or concerning the identity of a specific reporting hospital, clinic or other facility for purposes of information collection only and may not reproduce or extrapolate this information for any purpose.

(b) The department shall immediately destroy all reports submitted under sub. (1) after information is extrapolated from the reports for use in publishing the annual demographic summary under this subsection.

Wisconsin Right to Life, Inc.

Wisconsin Right to Life, Inc. (WRTL) is a pro-life organization that is headquartered in Milwaukee, Wisconsin. The organization was founded for the purpose of making abortion, euthanasia, and infanticide unacceptable practices in the nation. WRTL played a significant role in getting the Wisconsin legislature to pass the state's Parental Consent Law and Women's Right to Know Act. In 2007 the organization won a case in the United States Supreme Court, *Federal Election Commission v. Wisconsin Right to Life, Inc.*, which permitted the organization to run issue oriented political advertisements prior to primary and general elections. *See also* **Federal Election Commission v. Wisconsin Right to Life, Inc.; Pro-Life Organizations**

WISH List

The WISH (Women In the Senate and House) List is a nationwide political organization that was founded in 1992. The president of WISH is Pat Giardina Carpenter. WISH was created for the purpose of raising funds for Republican pro-choice female candidates. Since its inception, WISH has directed more than $1.5 million in contributions to pro-choice Republican candidates for Congress, as well as candidates for governor and other statewide offices. *See also* **Pro-Choice Organizations**

Withrow v. Larkin

Forum: United States Supreme Court.

Case Citation: Withrow v. Larkin, 421 U.S. 35 (1975).

Date Argued: December 18, 1974.

Date of Decision: April 16, 1975.

Opinion of Court: White, J.

Concurring Opinion: None.

Dissenting Opinion: None.

Counsel for Appellants: Betty R. Brown, Solicitor General of Wisconsin, argued; on the brief were Robert W. Warren, Attorney General, and LeRoy L. Dalton, Assistant Attorney General.

Counsel for Appellee: Robert H. Friebert argued and filed a brief.

Amicus Brief for Appellant: None.

Amicus Brief for Appellee: None.

Issue Presented: Whether constitutional due process prohibited a Wisconsin medical examining board from both, investigating and adjudicating, allegations against a physician that included, among other things, permitting a nonphysician perform an abortion?

Case Holding: Constitutional due process was not violated by the mere fact that a Wisconsin medical examining board had the authority to both, investigate and adjudicate, allegations against a physician that included, among other things, permitting a nonphysician to perform an abortion.

Background facts of case: The statutes of Wisconsin prohibited various acts of professional misconduct by physicians and empowered a State Examining Board, the appellants, to warn and reprimand physicians, to temporarily suspend licenses, and to institute criminal action or action to revoke a license. The appellants instituted proceedings against the appellee, Dr. Duane Larkin, to determine, among other things, whether he permitted an unlicensed physician to perform abortions at his abortion clinic during the year 1972. The appellee subsequently filed a lawsuit in a federal district court in Wisconsin seeking injunctive relief and a temporary restraining order against the proceedings, on the grounds that the applicable statutes were unconstitutional and that appellants' acts with respect to appellee violated his constitutional rights. The district court ultimately entered a temporary restraining order and preliminary injunction prohibiting the appellants from proceeding further, on the grounds that the appellee would be denied due process of law by having the appellants both investigate and determine his guilt. The Supreme Court granted certiorari to consider the issue.

Unanimous opinion by Justice White: Justice White determined that the constitution was not violated by the fact that an administrative board had both investigative and adjudicative powers. He wrote as follows:

> The contention that the combination of investigative and adjudicative functions necessarily creates an unconstitutional risk of bias in administrative adjudication has a ... difficult burden of persuasion to carry. It must overcome a presumption of honesty and integrity in those serving as adjudicators; and it must convince that, under a realistic appraisal of psychological tendencies and human weakness, conferring investigative and adjudicative powers on the same individuals poses such a risk of actual bias or prejudgment that the practice must be forbidden if the guarantee of due process is to be adequately implemented....
>
> This Court has [previously] ruled that a hearing examiner who has recommended findings of fact after rejecting certain evidence as not being probative was not disqualified to preside at further hearings that were required when reviewing courts held that the evidence had been erroneously excluded....
>
> More recently we have sustained against due process objection a system in which a Social Security examiner has responsibility for developing the facts and making a decision as to disability claims, and observed that the challenge to this combination of functions assumes too much and would bring down too many procedures designed, and working well, for a governmental structure of great and growing complexity.
>
> That is not to say that there is nothing to the argument that those who have investigated should not then adjudicate. The issue is substantial, it is not new, and legislators and others concerned

with the operations of administrative agencies have given much attention to whether and to what extent distinctive administrative functions should be performed by the same persons. No single answer has been reached. Indeed, the growth, variety, and complexity of the administrative processes have made any one solution highly unlikely....

... When the Board instituted its investigative procedures, it stated only that it would investigate whether proscribed conduct had occurred. Later in noticing the adversary hearing, it asserted only that it would determine if violations had been committed which would warrant suspension of appellee's license. Without doubt, the Board then anticipated that the proceeding would eventuate in an adjudication of the issue; but there was no more evidence of bias or the risk of bias or prejudgment than inhered in the very fact that the Board had investigated and would now adjudicate. Of course, we should be alert to the possibilities of bias that may lurk in the way particular procedures actually work in practice. The processes utilized by the Board, however, do not in themselves contain an unacceptable risk of bias. The investigative proceeding had been closed to the public, but appellee and his counsel were permitted to be present throughout; counsel actually attended the hearings and knew the facts presented to the Board. No specific foundation has been presented for suspecting that the Board had been prejudiced by its investigation or would be disabled from hearing and deciding on the basis of the evidence to be presented at the contested hearing. The mere exposure to evidence presented in nonadversary investigative procedures is insufficient in itself to impugn the fairness of the Board members at a later adversary hearing. Without a showing to the contrary, state administrators are assumed to be men of conscience and intellectual discipline, capable of judging a particular controversy fairly on the basis of its own circumstances.

We are of the view, therefore, that the District Court was in error when it entered the restraining order against the Board's contested hearing and when it granted the preliminary injunction based on the untenable view that it would be unconstitutional for the Board to suspend appellee's license at its own contested hearing on charges evolving from its own investigation. The contested hearing should have been permitted to proceed.

Disposition of case: The judgment of the district court was reversed.

Wrongful Birth Lawsuits

A legal trend has begun whereby individuals who survived unsuccessful abortion attempts are suing abortionists to obtain monetary compensation for being born alive. This type of legal action is called a wrongful birth or life lawsuit. As a general matter a wrongful birth lawsuit is a claim that, but for an act or omission of the abortionist, a person once conceived would not or should not have been born. A few states have enacted statutes that prohibit such lawsuits.

In addition to wrongful birth lawsuits against abortion providers, there have been lawsuits brought against parents by their children, claiming they should not have been born. A minority of states, including Idaho, Indiana, Minnesota, Missouri, North Dakota, Ohio, Pennsylvania, South Dakota, and Utah, have responded to such lawsuits by statutorily prohibiting wrongful birth lawsuits. *See also* **Survivors of Abortion**

Wyoming

(1) OVERVIEW

The state of Wyoming enacted its first criminal abortion statute in 1869. The statute underwent several amendments prior to the 1973 decision by the United States Supreme Court in *Roe v. Wade*, which legalized abortion in the nation. Wyoming has taken affirmative steps to respond to *Roe* and its progeny. The state has addressed several abortion issues by statute that include general abortion guidelines,

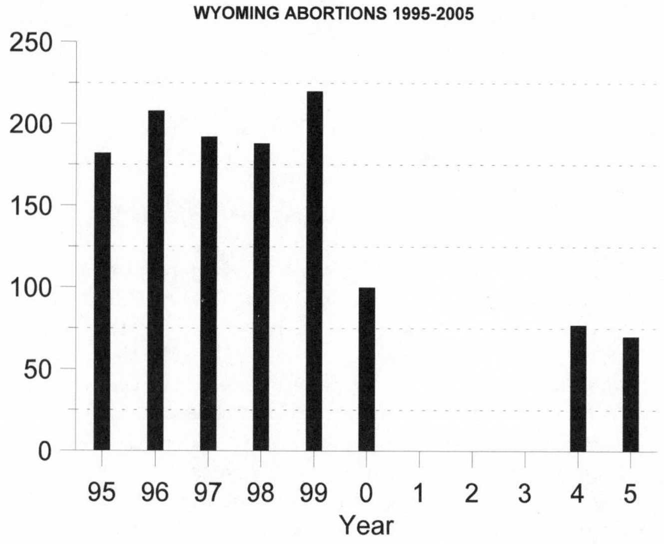

Source: **National Center for Health Statistics/Guttmacher Institute.**

abortion by minors, use of facilities and people, public funds and abortion, fetal experiments, fetal death reports, and injury to a pregnant woman.

(2) GENERAL ABORTION GUIDELINES

Wyoming prohibits post-viability abortion, except when necessary preserve the life or health of the woman. The state permits an abortion to be performed only by a physician. Wyoming also has retained a pre–*Roe* statute that bans advertisement of abortifacients. The general abortion statutes are set out below.

Wyoming Code § 35-6-101. Definitions

(a) As used in the act, unless the context otherwise requires:

(i) "Abortion" means an act, procedure, device or prescription administered to or prescribed for a pregnant woman by any person with knowledge of the pregnancy, including the pregnant woman herself, with the intent of producing the premature expulsion, removal or termination of a human embryo or fetus, except that in cases in which the viability of the embryo or fetus is threatened by continuation of the pregnancy, early delivery after viability by commonly accepted obstetrical practices shall not be construed as an abortion;

(ii) "Accepted medical procedures" means procedures of the type and performed in a manner and in a facility which is equipped with surgical, anaesthetic, resuscitation and laboratory equipment sufficient to meet the standards of medical care which physicians engaged in the same or similar lines of work in the community would ordinarily exercise and devote to the benefit of their patients;

(iii) "Conception" means the fecundation of the ovum by the spermatozoa;

(iv) "Hospital" means those institutions licensed by the state department of health as hospitals;

(v) "Physician" means any person licensed to practice medicine in this state;

(vi) "Pregnant" means that condition of a woman who has a human embryo or fetus within her as the result of conception;

(vii) "Viability" means that stage of human development when the embryo or fetus is able to live by natural or life-supportive systems outside the womb of the mother according to appropriate medical judgment;

(viii) "Woman" means any female person;

(ix) The singular where used herein includes the plural, the plural includes the singular, and the masculine includes the feminine or

neuter, when consistent with the intent of this act and when necessary to effect its purpose;

(x) "Minor" means a pregnant woman under the age of eighteen (18), but does not include any woman who:

(A) Is legally married;

(B) Is in active military service; or

(C) Has lived apart from her parents or guardian, has been financially independent and has managed her own affairs for at least six (6) months prior to a proposed abortion.

(xi) "Parents" means both parents of a minor if they are both living, or one (1) parent of the minor if only one (1) is living or if the second parent cannot be located through a reasonably diligent effort;

(xii) "This act" means W.S. 35-6-101 through 35-6-118.

Wyoming Code § 35-6-102. Post-viability abortion

An abortion shall not be performed after the embryo or fetus has reached viability except when necessary to preserve the woman from an imminent peril that substantially endangers her life or health, according to appropriate medical judgment.

Wyoming Code § 35-6-103. Viability not affected by abortion

A physician who performs an abortion procedure employed pursuant to W.S. 35-6-102 shall not intentionally terminate the viability of the unborn infant prior to, during or following the procedure.

Wyoming Code § 35-6-104.
Means of treatment for viable abortion

The commonly accepted means of care shall be employed in the treatment of any viable infant aborted alive with any chance of survival.

Wyoming Code § 35-6-110. Penalty

Any physician or other person who violates any provision of W.S. 35-6-102, 35-6-103 or 35-6-104 is guilty of a felony punishable by imprisonment in the penitentiary for not more than fourteen (14) years.

Wyoming Code § 35-6-111. Physician to perform abortion

Any person other than a licensed physician who performs an abortion is guilty of a felony punishable by imprisonment in the penitentiary for not less than one (1) year nor more than fourteen (14) years.

Wyoming Code § 35-6-112.
Penalty for not using commonly accepted medical procedures

Any person who performs or prescribes an abortion by using anything other than accepted medical procedures is guilty of a felony punishable by imprisonment in the penitentiary for not more than fourteen (14) years.

Wyoming Code § 35-6-116.
Advertising drug for procuring abortion or miscarriage

Whoever prints or publishes any advertisement of any drug or nostrum with intent to obtain utilization of such drug or nostrum for procuring abortion or miscarriage; or sells or gives away, or keeps for sale or gratuitous distribution, any newspaper, circular, pamphlet, or book containing such advertisement, or any account or description, of such drug or nostrum with intent to obtain utilization of such drugs or nostrum to procure abortion or miscarriage, shall be fined not more than one hundred dollars ($100.00), to which may be added imprisonment in the county jail for not more than six (6) months.

(3) ABORTION BY MINORS

Under the laws of Wyoming no physician may perform an abortion upon an unemancipated minor unless a parent or guardian of the minor is notified 48 hours before the abortion, and the parent or guardian provides written consent to the abortion. In compliance with federal constitutional law, Wyoming has provided a judicial waiver procedure for an unemancipated minor to obtain an abortion without parental or guardian notice and consent. The minor may petition a court for a waiver of the notice and consent requirement. A minor has a right to an attorney at the proceeding and if she cannot afford one, the court must appoint her an attorney. If a minor chooses, she may represent herself. The required parental or guardian notice and consent may be waived if the court finds either (1) that the minor is mature and well-informed enough to make the abortion decision on her own, or (2) that performance of the abortion would be in the best interest of the minor. An expedited appeal is available to any minor to whom the court denies a waiver of notice and consent. The statute addressing the matters is set out below.

Wyoming Code § 35-6-118. Consent and judicial bypass

(a) An abortion shall not be performed upon a minor unless at least one (1) of the minor's parents or her guardian are notified in writing at least forty-eight (48) hours before the abortion, and the attending physician has obtained the written consent of the minor and at least one (1) parent or guardian of the minor, unless:

(i) The minor, in a closed hearing, is granted the right to self-consent to an abortion by court order pursuant to subparagraph (b)(v)(B) of this section and the attending physician receives a certified copy of the court order and the written consent of the minor; or

(ii) The abortion is authorized by court order pursuant to subparagraph (b)(v)(C) of this section and the attending physician receives a certified copy of the court order.

(b) A juvenile court of jurisdiction may grant the right of a minor to self-consent to an abortion or may authorize an abortion upon a minor in accordance with the following procedure:

(i) The minor shall apply to the juvenile court for assistance either in person or through an adult of the minor's choice. The court shall assist the minor in preparing the petition and notices required under this subsection;

(ii) Notwithstanding W.S. 14-6-212, the minor or an adult of the minor's choice shall file a petition with the court, signed by the minor and setting forth:

(A) The initials of the minor and the minor's date of birth;

(B) The names and addresses, if known, of the minor's parents, guardian, custodian or, if the minor's parents are deceased and a guardian or custodian has not been appointed, any other person standing in loco parentis of the minor;

(C) That the minor has been informed by her treating physician of the risks and consequences of an abortion;

(D) That the minor is mature and wishes to have an abortion; and

(E) Facts indicating why an abortion is in the best interest of the minor.

(iii) The court may appoint a guardian ad litem of the minor and may appoint legal counsel for the minor;

(iv) Within five (5) days after the petition is filed under paragraph (ii) of this subsection, a hearing on the merits of the petition shall be held on the record. Any appointed counsel shall be appointed and notified by the court at least forty-eight (48) hours before the time set for hearing. At the hearing, the court shall hear evidence relating to:

(A) The maturity and understanding of the minor;

(B) The nature of the abortion, risks and consequences of the abortion, and alternatives to the abortion; and

(C) Whether an abortion is in the best interest of the minor.

(v) In its order, which shall be issued within twenty-four (24) hours of the hearing, the court shall enter findings of fact and conclusions of law, order the record of the hearing sealed and shall:

(A) Deny the petition, setting forth the grounds on which the petition is denied;

(B) Grant the minor the right to self-consent to the abortion based upon a finding by clear and convincing evidence that the minor is sufficiently mature and adequately informed to make her own decision, in consultation with her physician, independently of the wishes of her parents or guardian; or

(C) Authorize the abortion based upon a finding by clear and convincing evidence that the abortion is in the best interest of the minor.

(vi) Any order entered pursuant to paragraph (v) of this subsection may be appealed by a party to the supreme court in accordance with the Wyoming Rules of Appellate Procedure. Notwithstanding W.S. 14-6-233, the supreme court shall by rule provide for expedited appellate review of appeals under this paragraph.

(c) The provisions of this section shall not apply in an emergency medical situation when, to a reasonable degree of medical probability, the attending physician determines that an abortion is necessary to preserve the minor from an imminent peril that substantially endangers her life, and so certifies in the minor's medical record.

(d) The written notifications required under this section shall be delivered:

(i) Personally by the minor, attending physician or an agent; or

(ii) By certified mail addressed to the parent at the usual place of abode of the parent with return receipt requested and restricted delivery to the addressee.

(e) No parent, guardian or spouse shall require a minor to submit to an abortion against her wishes.

(f) Any physician or other person who knowingly performs an abortion on a minor in violation of W.S. 35-6-118 is guilty of a misdemeanor punishable by a fine of not more than one thousand dollars ($1,000.00), imprisonment for not more than one (1) year, or both.

(4) USE OF FACILITIES AND PEOPLE

Under the laws of Wyoming private medical facilities are not required to permit abortions at their premises. The employees and physicians at medical facilities that do allow abortions are permitted to refuse to take part in abortions. The statutes addressing the matter are set out below.

Wyoming Code § 35-6-105. Private medical facilities

No private hospital, clinic, institution or other private facility in this state is required to admit any patient for the purpose of performing an abortion nor to allow the performance of an abortion therein. The private hospital, clinic, institution or any other private facility shall inform any prospective patient seeking an abortion of its policy not to participate in abortion procedures. No cause of action shall arise against any private hospital, clinic, institution or any other private facility for refusing to perform or allow an abortion.

Wyoming Code § 35-6-106. Medical personnel

No person shall, in any way, be required to perform or participate in any abortion or in any act or thing which accomplishes or performs or assists in accomplishing or performing a human miscarriage, euthanasia or any other death of a human fetus or human embryo. The refusal of any person to do so is not a basis for civil liability to any person. No hospital, governing board or any other person, firm, association or group shall terminate the employment of, alter the position of, prevent or impair the practice or occupation of, or impose any other sanction or otherwise discriminate against any person who refuses to perform or participate in any abortion or in any act or thing which accomplishes, performs or assists in accomplishing or performing a human miscarriage, euthanasia or any other death of a human fetus or embryo.

Wyoming Code § 35-6-113. Penalty

Any person, firm, corporation, group or association who violates W.S. 35-6-106 is guilty of an offense punishable by a fine of not more than ten thousand dollars ($10,000.00).

Wyoming Code § 35-6-114. Right to civil action

Any person or persons injured by any action prohibited in W.S. 35-6-106 may by civil action obtain injunctive relief or damages.

(5) PUBLIC FUNDS AND ABORTION

Wyoming prohibits the use of state funds to pay for abortions, except to save the life of the woman, or if the pregnancy result from sexual assault or incest. The statute addressing the matter is set out below.

Wyoming Code § 35-6-117. Public funds

No funds appropriated by the legislature of the state of Wyoming shall be used to pay for abortions except when the pregnancy is the result of incest as defined by W.S. 6-4-402 or sexual assault as defined by W.S. 6-2-301 if the assault is reported to a law enforcement agency within five (5) days after the assault or within five (5) days after the time the victim is capable of reporting the assault, or when the life of the mother would be endangered if the unborn child was carried to full term.

(6) FETAL EXPERIMENTS

Wyoming has banned the sale of live or aborted fetuses for experiments. The state has created criminal punishments for violating its ban. The statute addressing the matter is set out below.

Wyoming Code § 35-6-115. Fetal experiments

Whoever sells, transfers, distributes or gives away any live or viable aborted child for any form of experimentation is guilty of a felony punishable by a fine of not less than ten thousand dollars ($10,000.00) and by imprisonment in the penitentiary for not less than one (1) year nor more than fourteen (14) years. Any person consenting, aiding or abetting such sale, transfer, distribution or other unlawful disposition of an aborted child is guilty of a felony punishable by a fine of not less than ten thousand dollars ($10,000.00) and by imprisonment in the penitentiary for not less than one (1) year nor more than fourteen (14) years or both, and shall also be subject to prosecution for violation of any other criminal statute.

(7) FETAL DEATH REPORTS

Wyoming requires by statute that all abortions be reported to the proper authorities. The state also provides for the disposition of fetuses. The statutes addressing the matter are set out below.

Wyoming Code § 35-6-107. Forms for reporting abortions

(a) The state office of vital records services shall establish an abortion reporting form which shall be used after May 27, 1977 for the reporting of every abortion performed or prescribed in this state. The form shall include the following items in addition to such other information as may be necessary to complete the form, but in no case shall information be required that would tend to disclose the identity of any individual participating in an abortion:

(i) The age of the pregnant woman;

(ii) The type of procedure performed or prescribed;

(iii) Complications, if any;

(iv) A summary of the pregnant woman's obstetrical history regarding previous pregnancies, abortions and live births;

(v) The length and weight of the aborted fetus or embryo, when measurable;

(vi) Type of facility where the abortion is performed (i.e., hospital, clinic, physician's office, or other).

(b) The form shall be completed by the attending physician and sent to the state health officer as defined in W.S. 9-2-103(e) within twenty (20) days after the abortion is performed.

Wyoming Code § 35-6-108. Compilations of abortions

The state office of vital records services shall prepare and after May 27, 1977 keep on file for seven (7) years compilations of the information submitted on the abortion reporting forms. The compilations shall be avail-

able only to a local, state or national public health official or a physician upon his written request. The state health officer, in order to maintain and keep such compilations current, shall file with the reports any new or amended information. The information submitted under W.S. 35-6-107 and compiled under this section shall not be stored in any computer.

Wyoming Code § 35-6-109.
Disposal of bodies and parts thereof

The state department of health may prescribe rules and regulations for the disposal of the bodies, tissues, organs and parts thereof of an unborn child, human fetus or human embryo which has been aborted.

(8) INJURY TO A PREGNANT WOMAN

Wyoming makes it a criminal offense to injure a woman who is pregnant. The statute addressing the matter is set out below.

Wyoming Code § 6-2-502. Aggravated assault and battery

(a) A person is guilty of aggravated assault and battery if he:

(i) Causes serious bodily injury to another intentionally, knowingly or recklessly under circumstances manifesting extreme indifference to the value of human life;

(ii) Attempts to cause, or intentionally or knowingly causes bodily injury to another with a deadly weapon;

(iii) Threatens to use a drawn deadly weapon on another unless reasonably necessary in defense of his person, property or abode or to prevent serious bodily injury to another; or

(iv) Intentionally, knowingly or recklessly causes bodily injury to a woman whom he knows is pregnant.

(b) Aggravated assault and battery is a felony punishable by imprisonment for not more than ten (10) years.

X

Xavier University Students for Life

Xavier University Students for Life (XUSL) is a pro-life student group at Xavier University in Cincinnati, Ohio. XUSL was established to defend and act as advocates for unborn children. It seeks the abolishment of abortion. XUSL engages in community education programs to put forth its ideas in opposition to abortion. *See also* **Pro-Life Organizations**

X-rays and Pregnancy

X-rays are a form of radiation that are used to make images of bones and organs. Measurements of x-rays are done in units called rads. A rad is the amount of energy that is exposed to the body. Pregnant women are at an increased risk of birth complications if they are exposed to 2–6 rads of x-rays (the exact rad exposure is debated by researchers). Studies have shown that high rad exposure may cause spontaneous abortion, fetal malformations, cancer (especially leukemia), brain damage, and mental and growth retardation. As a general rule, fetal exposure to x-rays should not exceed 0.5 rads. *See also* **Mutagens and Pregnancy**

Y

Youth and Abortion *see* **Minors and Abortion**

Z

Zellweger Syndrome

Zellweger syndrome is a congenital disorder involving the reduction or absence of certain cells (peroxisomes) of the liver, kidneys, and brain. The most common symptoms of the disorder include prenatal growth failure, unusual facial characteristics, mental retardation, an enlarged liver, high levels of iron and copper in the blood, and vision disturbances. There is no cure for this rare disease. Death usually occurs less than 6 months after the onset of the condition. *See also* **Birth Defects and Abortion**

Zygote *see* **Fetal Development**

Zygote Intrafallopian Transfer *see* **Assisted Reproductive Technology**

Bibliography

Andrusko, Dave. *To Rescue the Future: The Pro Life Movement in the 1980s*. Niagara Falls, NY: Life Cycle, 1987.

Andryszewski, Tricia. *Abortion: Rights, Options, and Choices*. Brookfield, CT: Millbrook, 1996.

Bachiochi, Erika. *The Cost of Choice: Women Evaluate the Impact of Abortion*. New York: Encounter, 2004.

Baird, Robert M., and Stuart E. Rosenbaum. *The Ethics of Abortion: Pro-Life vs. Pro-Choice*. Amherst, NY: Books, 2001.

Baird-Windle, Patricia, and Eleanor J. Bader. *Targets of Hatred: Anti-Abortion Terrorism*. New York: Palgrave Macmillan, 2001.

Beckman, Linda J., and S. Marie Harvey. *The New Civil War: The Psychology, Culture, and Politics of Abortion*. Washington, D.C.: American Psychological Association, 1998.

Beckwith, Francis J. *Defending Life: A Moral and Legal Case Against Abortion Choice*. New York: Cambridge University Press, 2007.

Bender, David, Bruno Leone, Katie De Koster and Scott Barbour. *The Abortion Controversy*. Chicago, IL: Greenhaven, 1994.

Bender, Karen. *Choice: True Stories of Birth, Contraception, Infertility, Adoption, Single Parenthood, and Abortion*. San Francisco, CA: MacAdam/Cage, 2007.

Berne, Emma Carlson. *Abortion: Introducing Issues with Opposing Viewpoints*. Chicago, IL: Greenhaven, 2007.

Bondeson, William B. *Abortion and the Status of the Fetus*. Dordrecht, Holland: D. Reidel, 1983.

Bowers, James R. *Pro-Choice and Anti-Abortion*. Westport, CT: Greenwood, 1997.

Bridgewater, Pamela D. *Breeding a Nation: Reproductive Slavery, the Thirteenth Amendment, and the Pursuit of Freedom*. Cambridge, MA: South End, 2008.

Brien, Joanna, and Ida Fairbairn. *Pregnancy and Abortion Counselling*. New York: Routledge, 1996.

Brodie, Janet Farrell. *Contraception and Abortion in Nineteenth-Century America*. Ithaca, NY: Cornell University Press, 1997.

Brown, Judie, *The Facts About Abortion*. Stafford, VA: American Life League, 1997.

Callahan, Sidney, and Daniel Callahan. *Abortion: Understanding Differences*. New York: Plenum, 1984.

Camasso, Michael. *Family Caps, Abortion and Women of Color: Research Connection and Political Rejection*. New York: Oxford University Press, 2007.

Candace, De Puy, and Dana Dovitch. *The Healing Choice: Your Guide to Emotional Recovery After an Abortion*. New York: Fireside, 1997.

Capo, Beth Widmaier. *Textual Contraception: Birth Control and Modern American Fiction*. Columbus: Ohio State University Press, 2007.

Caron, Simone M. *Who Chooses? American Reproductive History Since 1830*. Gainesville: University Press of Florida, 2008.

Chalker, Rebecca, Carol Downer and Suzann Gage. *A Woman's Book of Choices: Abortion, Menstrual Extraction, Ru-486*. New York: Seven Stories, 1996.

Chilton, Craig. *The Pro-Choice Victory Handbook: Strategies for Keeping Your Abortion Rights*. Evansdale, IA: Boiled Owl, 1992.

Condit, Celeste Michelle. *Decoding Abortion Rhetoric: Communicating Social Change*. Champaign: University of Illinois Press, 1994.

Critchlow, Donald T. *Intended Consequences: Birth Control, Abortion, and the Federal Government in Modern America*. New York: Oxford University Press, 1999.

Davis, Tom. *Sacred Work: Planned Parenthood and Its Clergy Alliances*. Piscataway, NJ: Rutgers University Press, 2006.

Day, Kristen. *Democrats for Life: Pro-Life Politics and the Silenced Majority*. Green Forest, AR: New Leaf, 2006.

Doan, Alesha. *Opposition and Intimidation: The Abortion Wars and Strategies of Political Harassment*. Ann Arbor: University of Michigan Press, 2007.

Dombrowski, Daniel A., and Robert Deltete. *A Brief, Liberal, Catholic Defense of Abortion*. Champaign: University of Illinois Press, 2006.

Durrett, Deanne. *The Abortion Conflict: A Pro/Con Issue*. Berkeley Heights, NJ: Enslow, 2000.

Dworkin, Ronald. *Life's Dominion: An Argument About Abortion, Euthanasia, and Individual Freedom*. New York: Vintage, 1994.

Dyer, Frederick N. *The Physicians' Crusade Against Abortion*. Sagamore Beach, MA: Science History, 2005.

Ehrenreich, Nancy. *The Reproductive Rights Reader: Law, Medicine, and the Construction of Motherhood*. New York: New York University Press, 2008.

Farmer, Ann. *By Their Fruits: Eugenics, Population Control, and the Abortion Campaign*. Washington, D.C.: Catholic University of America Press, 2008.

Farrell, Courtney. *The Abortion Debate*. Edina, MN: Abdo, 2008.

Faux, Marian. *Crusaders: Voices from the Abortion Front*. New York: Birch Lane, 1990.

Feinman, Clarice. *The Criminalization of a Woman's Body*. New York: Routledge, 1992.

Feldt, Gloria. *The War on Choice: The Right-Wing Attack on Women's Rights and How to Fight Back*. New York: Bantam Dell, 2007.

Fried, Marlene Gerber. *From Abortion to Reproductive Freedom: Transforming a Movement*. Cambridge, MA: South End, 1990.

Garrow, David J. *Liberty and Sexuality: The Right to Privacy and the Making of Roe v. Wade*. Berkeley: University of California Press, 1998.

Ginsburg, Faye D. *Contested Lives: The Abortion Debate in an American Community*. Berkeley: University of California Press, 1998.

Gordon, Linda. *The Moral Property of Women: A History of Birth Control Politics in America*. Champaign: University of Illinois Press, 2007.

Gorman, Michael J. *Abortion and the Early Church: Christian, Jewish and Pagan Attitudes in the Greco-Roman World*. Eugene, OR: Wipf & Stock, 1998.

Gorney, Cynthia. *Articles of Faith: A Frontline History of the Abortion Wars*. Clearwater, FL: Touchstone, 2000.

Grant, George. *Grand Illusions: The Legacy of Planned Parenthood.* Nashville, TN: Cumberland House, 2000.

Hadley, Janet. *Abortion: Between Freedom and Necessity.* Philadelphia, PA: Temple University Press, 1997.

Hoshiko, Sumi. *Our Choices: Women's Personal Decisions About Abortion.* New York: Harrington Park, 1993.

Hull, N.E.H., and Peter Charles Hoffer. *Roe v. Wade: The Abortion Rights Controversy in American History.* Lawrence: University Press of Kansas, 2001.

_____, Williamjames Hoffer and Peter Charles Hoffer. *The Abortion Rights Controversy in America: A Legal Reader.* Chapel Hill: University of North Carolina Press, 2004.

Ide, Arthur Frederick. *Abortion Handbook: The History, Legal Progress, Practice and Psychology of Abortion.* Las Colinas, TX: Liberal, 1988.

Jacob, Krista. *Abortion Under Attack: Women on the Challenges Facing Choice.* New York: Seal, 2006.

Judges, Donald P. *Hard Choices, Lost Voices: How the Abortion Conflict Has Divided America, Distorted Constitutional Rights, and Damaged the Courts.* Chicago, IL: Ivan R. Dee, 2007.

Kahlenborn, Chris. *Breast Cancer: Its Link to Abortion and the Birth Control Pill.* Dayton, OH: One More Soul, 2000.

Kamm, Frances Myrna. *Creation and Abortion: A Study in Moral and Legal Philosophy.* New York: Oxford University Press, 1992.

Kaplan, Laura. *The Story of Jane: The Legendary Underground Feminist Abortion Service.* Chicago: University of Chicago Press, 1997.

Kaufmann, K. *The Abortion Resource Handbook.* New York: Fireside, 1997.

King, Alveda C. *How Can the Dream Survive If We Murder the Children? Abortion Is Not a Civil Right!* Bloomington, Indiana: AuthorHouse, 2008.

Kirton, Isabella. *Spirit Child: Healing the Wound of Abortion.* Forres, Scotland: Findhorn, 1998.

Klimek, Daniel P. *Secrets of the High Court: On Political Culture, U.S. Constitutionalism, and the Foundations of the Abortion Industry.* Parker, CO: Outskirts, 2007.

Kluger-Bell, Kim. *Unspeakable Losses: Healing from Miscarriage, Abortion and Other Pregnancy Loss.* New York: HarperCollins, 2000.

Kopaczynski, Germain. *No Higher Court: Contemporary Feminism and the Right to Abortion.* Scranton, PA: University of Scranton Press, 2005.

Koukl, Gregory. *Precious Unborn Human Persons.* San Pedro, CA: Stand to Reason, 1999.

Kreeft, Peter. *The Unaborted Socrates: A Dramatic Debate on the Issues Surrounding Abortion.* Downers Grove, IL: Intervarsity, 1983.

Kulczycki, Andrzej. *The Abortion Debate in the World Arena.* New York: Routledge, 1999.

Lader, Lawrence, and Eleanor Smeal. *A Private Matter: Ru 486 and the Abortion Crisis.* Amherst, NY: Prometheus, 1995.

Lee, Ellie. *Abortion Law and Politics Today.* New York: Palgrave Macmillan, 1998.

Lee, Patrick. *Abortion and Unborn Human Life.* Washington, D.C.: Catholic University of America Press, 1996.

Lewis, Larry L. *Proclaiming the Pro-Life Message: Christian Leaders Address the Abortion Issue.* Garland, TX: Hannibal, 1997.

Maestri, William F. *Do Not Lose Hope: Healing the Wounded Heart of Women Who Have Had* Abortions. Staten Island, NY: Alba House, 2000.

Maguire, Daniel C. *Sacred Rights: The Case for Contraception and Abortion in World Religions.* New York, NY: Oxford University Press, 2003.

Masse, Sydna, and Joan Phillips. *Her Choice to Heal: Finding Spiritual and Emotional Peace after Abortion.* Colorado Springs, CO: Chariot Victor, 1998.

Mathewes-Green, Frederica. *Real Choices: Listening to Women, Looking for Alternatives to Abortion.* Ben Lomond, CA: Conciliar, 1997.

McBride, Dorothy. *Abortion in the United States: A Reference Handbook.* Santa Barbara, CA: ABC-CLIO, 2007.

McFarlane, Deborah R., and Kenneth J. Meier. *The Politics of Fertility Control: Family Planning & Abortion Policies in the American States.* New York: Chatham House, 2000.

Messer, Ellen, and Kathryn E. May. *Back Rooms: Voices from the Illegal Abortion Era.* Amherst, NY: Prometheus, 1994.

Michelman, Kate. *Protecting the Right to Choose.* New York: Plume, 2007.

Michels, Nancy. *Helping Women Recover from Abortion.* Grand Rapids, MI Bethany House, 1988.

Mohr, James C. *Abortion in America: The Origins and Evolution of National Policy, 1800–1900.* New York: Oxford University Press, 1979.

Moore, Michele C., and Caroline M. de Costa. *Just the Facts: Abortion A to Z.* Victoria, Canada: Trafford, 2007.

Nathanson, Bernard N. *The Hand of God: A Journey from Death to Life by the Abortion Doctor Who Changed His Mind.* Washington, D.C.: Regnery, 2001.

Needle, Rachel, and Lenore Walker. *Abortion Counseling: A Clinician's Guide to Psychology, Legislation, Politics, and Competency.* New York: Springer, 2007.

Nossiff, Rosemary. *Before Roe: Abortion Policy in the States.* Philadelphia, PA: Temple University Press, 2000.

Peterson, Virginia. *Abortion: A Serious Issue.* Farmington Hills, MI: Information Plus, 2000.

Piehl, Norah. *Abortion: Social Issues Firsthand.* Chicago, IL: Greenhaven, 2006.

Poppema, Suzanne T., and Mike Henderson. *Why I Am an Abortion Doctor.* Amherst, NY: Prometheus, 1996.

Powell, John. *Abortion: The Silent Holocaust.* Allen, TX: Thomas More, 1981.

Powers, Meghan. *American Social Movements: The Abortion Rights Movement.* Chicago, IL: Greenhaven, 2005.

Reagan, Leslie J. *When Abortion Was a Crime: Women, Medicine, and Law in the United States, 1867–1973.* Berkeley, California: University of California Press, 1998.

Reagan, Ronald. *Abortion and the Conscience of the Nation.* Sacramento, CA: New Regency, 2001.

Reardon, David C. *Making Abortion Rare: A Healing Strategy for a Divided Nation.* Kansas City, MO: Acorn, 1996.

Rein, Mei Ling. *Abortion 2000: An Eternal Social and Moral Issue.* Farmington Hills, MI: Information Plus, 2000.

Reiter, Jerry. *Live from the Gates of Hell: An Insider's Look at the Anti-Abortion Movement.* Amherst, NY: Prometheus, 2000.

Riddle, John M. *Eve's Herbs: A History of Contraception and Abortion in the West.* Cambridge, MA: Harvard University Press, 1999.

Rini, Suzanne M. *Beyond Abortion: A Chronicle of Fetal Experimentation.* Rockford, IL: TAN, 1993.

Risen, James, and Judy L. Thomas. *Wrath of Angels: The American Abortion War.* New York, NY: Basic, 1999.

Rodman, Hyman, Joy W. Bonar and Betty Sarvis. *The Abortion Question.* New York, NY: Columbia University Press, 1990.

Rose, Melody. *Abortion: A Documentary and Reference Guide.* Westport, CT: Greenwood, 2008.

_____. *Safe, Legal, and Unavailable? Abortion Politics in the United States.* Washington, D.C.: CQ, 2006.

Roth, Rachel. *Making Women Pay: The Hidden Costs of Fetal Rights.* Ithaca, NY: Cornell University Press, 1999.

Sachdev, Paul. *International Handbook on Abortion.* Westport, CT: Greenwood, 1988.

Saletan, William. *Bearing Right: How Conservatives Won the Abortion War.* Berkeley, CA: University of California Press, 2004.

Saltenberger, Ann. *Every Woman Has a Right to Know the Dangers of Legal Abortion.* Stafford, VA: American Life League, 1984.

Sanger, Alexander. *Beyond Choice: Reproductive Freedom in the 21st Century.* New York: Public Affairs, 2005.

Schoen, Johanna. *Choice and Coercion: Birth Control, Sterilization, and Abortion in Public Health and Welfare.* Chapel Hill: University of North Carolina Press, 2005.

Schroedel, Jean Reith. *Is the Fetus a Person? A Comparison of Policies Across the Fifty States.* Ithaca, NY: Cornell University Press, 2000.

Schwartz, Lewis M. *Arguing About Abortion.* Belmont, CA: Wadsworth, 1993.

Segers, Mary C., and Timothy A. Byrnes. *Abortion Politics in American States.* Armonk, NY: M.E. Sharpe, 1994.

Shapiro, Ian. *Abortion: The Supreme Court*

Decisions, 1965–2007. Indianapolis, IN: Hackett, 2008.

Shaver, Jessica, and Diana DePaul. *Gianna: Aborted ... and Lived to Tell About It.* Colorado Springs, CO: Focus on the Family, 1999.

Sheeran, Patrick J. *Women, Society, the State, and Abortion.* Westport, CT: Praeger, 1987.

Shrage, Laurie. *Abortion and Social Responsibility: Depolarizing the Debate.* New York: Oxford University Press, 2003.

Shullenberger, Bonnie, and Stanley Hauerwas. *A Time to Be Born.* Cambridge, MA: Cowley, 1996.

Silverstein, Helena. *Girls on the Stand: How Courts Fail Pregnant Minors.* New York: New York University Press, 2007.

Simon, Rita James. *Abortion.* Westport, CT: Praeger, 1998.

Solinger, Rickie. *Pregnancy and Power: A Short History of Reproductive Politics in America.* New York: New York University Press, 2005.

Staggenborg, Suzanne. *The Pro-Choice Movement: Organization and Activism in the Abortion Conflict.* New York: Oxford University Press, 1994.

Steffen, Lloyd. *Life/Choice: The Theory of Just Abortion.* Eugene, OR: Wipf & Stock, 2000.

Steinbock, Bonnie. *Life Before Birth: The Moral and Legal Status of Embryos and Fetuses.* New York: Oxford University Press, 1992.

Stotland, Nada Logan. *Abortion: Facts and Feelings: A Handbook for Women and the People Who Care About Them.* Arlington, VA: American Psychiatric, 1998.

Torr, James D. *Abortion: Opposing Viewpoints.* Chicago, IL: Greenhaven, 2005.

Tribe, Laurence H. *Abortion: The Clash of Absolutes.* New York: W.W. Norton, 1992.

Weddington, Sarah. *A Question of Choice.* New York: Penguin, 1993.

Wells, Jon. *Sniper: The True Story of Anti-Abortion Killer James Kopp.* Hoboken, NJ: Wiley, 2008.

Welton, K.B. *Abortion Is Not a Sin.* Dana Point, CA: Pandit, 1987.

Wetstein, Matthew E. *Abortion Rates in the United States: The Influence of Opinion and Policy.* Albany: State University of New York Press, 1996.

Williams, Wendy, and Ann Caldwell. *Empty Arms: More Than 60 Life-Giving Stories of Hope from the Devastation of Abortion.* Chattanooga, TN: AMG, 2005.

Wilt, Judith. *Abortion, Choice, and Contemporary Fiction: The Armageddon of the Maternal Instinct.* Chicago, IL: University of Chicago Press, 1990.

Index